Henry David Thoreau in 1854, from the Rowse Crayon in the Concord Public Library

THE JOURNAL OF
HENRY D. THOREAU

Edited by Bradford Torrey and Francis H. Allen

With a Foreword By Walter Harding
Secretary, The Thoreau Society

In Fourteen Volumes Bound as Two
Vols. VIII - XIV
(November, 1855 - 1861)

DOVER PUBLICATIONS, INC.
NEW YORK

This new Dover edition, first published in 1962, is an unabridged republication of the work first published by the Houghton Mifflin Company in 1906. The work originally appeared in fourteen volumes, and now appears in two volumes in this redesigned format.

This edition also contains a new Foreword, written especially for this Dover Edition by Walter Harding, Secretary, The Thoreau Society, and a photographic reproduction of one page of the manuscript journal.

Standard Book Number: 486-20313-1
Library of Congress Catalog Card Number: 63-3123

Manufactured in the United States of America

Dover Publications, Inc.
180 Varick Street
New York 14, N. Y.

CONTENTS

v

Contents

The Journal of Henry D. Thoreau

VOLUME VIII

(November, 1855 – August, 1856)

Baker Farm and Fair Haven Pond

CONTENTS

Vol. VIII

Vol. VIII

THE JOURNAL OF
HENRY DAVID THOREAU

VOLUME VIII

I

NOVEMBER, 1855 (ÆT. 38)

Nov. 1. *Thursday.* P. M. — Up Assabet, a-wooding.

After a rain-threatening morning it is a beautiful Indian-summer day, the most remarkable hitherto and equal to any of the kind. Yet we kept fires in the forenoon, the warmth not having got into the house. It is akin to sin to spend such a day in the house. The air is still and warm. This, too, is the *recovery* of the year, — as if the year, having nearly or quite accomplished its work, and abandoned all design, were in a more favorable and poetic mood, and thought rushed in to fill the vacuum. The river is perfectly smooth. Whole schools of *little* minnows leap from the surface at once with a silvery gleam. The wool-grass, with its drooping head and the slender withered leaves dangling about its stem, stands in little sheaves upon its tussocks, clean dry straw, and is thus reflected in the water. This is the November shore. The maples and swamp oaks and willows are for the most part bare, but some of

the oaks are partly clothed yet with withered ones [*sic*]. I see one white maple quite thick and green, and *some* black willows are thinly clad with *green* leaves, and many yellowish leaves are seen on the sallows rising above the bare button-bushes. Yet I see no painted tortoises out, and I think it is about a fortnight since I saw any.[1]

As I pushed up the river past Hildreth's, I saw the blue heron (probably of last Monday) arise from the shore and disappear with heavily-flapping wings around a bend in front; the greatest of the bitterns (*Ardeæ*), with heavily-undulating wings, low over the water, seen against the woods, just disappearing round a bend in front; with a great slate-colored expanse of wing, suited to the shadows of the stream, a tempered blue as of the sky and dark water commingled. This is the aspect under which the Musketaquid might be represented at this season: a long, smooth lake, reflecting the bare willows and button-bushes, the stubble, and the wool-grass on its tussock, a muskrat-cabin or two conspicuous on its margin amid the unsightly tops of pontederia, and a bittern disappearing on undulating wing around a bend.

The wood I get is pretty rotten. The under side of an oak which has lain for years on the miry bank is turned almost to mould, — in this I find ants, — while the upper is hard and dry. Or else it is stumps whose fangs have so rotted off that I can kick them over at last, but then I must shake out a half a peck or more of mould. I made out to get one great and heavy stump

[1] See forward, Nov. 11.

to the water twenty rods distant by ant-like turning it over and over laboriously. It sunk my craft low in the water. Others are boughs which in the winter fell or were dragged down by the ice, their tops in the water and their butts on shore. These I saw off where they dip into the water, though the saw pinches.

Returning in the twilight, I see a bat over the river.

Nov. 4. P. M. — To Hill by Assabet.

This forenoon the boys found a little black kitten about a third grown on the Island or Rock, but could not catch it. We supposed that some one had cast it in to drown it. This afternoon, as I was paddling by the Island, I saw what I thought a duck swimming down the river diagonally, to the south shore just below the grassy island, opposite the rock; then I thought it two ducks, then a muskrat. It passed out of sight round a bend. I landed and walked alongshore, and found that it was a kitten, which had just got ashore. It was quite wet excepting its back. It swam quite rapidly, the whole length of its back out, but was carried down about as fast by the stream. It had probably first crossed from the rock to the grassy island, and then from the lower end of this to the town side of the stream, on which side it may have been attracted by the noise of the town. It was rather weak and staggered as it ran, from starvation or cold, being wet, or both. A very pretty little black kitten.

It is a dark, almost rainy day. Though the river *appears* to have risen considerably, it is not more than nine or ten inches above the lowest summer level, as

I see by the bridge. Yet it brings along a little drift-wood. Whatever rails or boards have been left by the water's edge the river silently takes up and carries away. Much small stuff from the pail-factory.

The winter is approaching. The birds are almost all gone. The note of the *dee de de* sounds now more distinct, prophetic of winter, as I go amid the wild apples on Nawshawtuct. The autumnal dandelion sheltered by this apple-tree trunk is drooping and half closed and shows but half its yellow, this dark, late, wet day in the fall.

Gathered a bag of wild apples. A great part are decayed now on the ground. The snail slug is still eating them. Some have very fiery crimson spots or eyes on a very white ground.

Returned, and went up the main stream. Larches are now quite yellow, — in the midst of their fall.

The river-brink — at a little distance at least — is now all sere and rustling, except a few yellowed sallow leaves, though beyond in the meadows there is some fresh greenness, but cattle seem to stray wider for food than they did. They are turned into the meadows now, where is all the greenness. New fences are erected to take advantage of all the fall feed. But the rank herbage of the river's brink is more tender and has fallen before the frosts. Many new muskrat-houses have been erected this wet weather, and much gnawed root is floating. When I look away to the woods, the oaks have a dull, dark red now, without brightness. The willow-tops on causeways have a pale, bleached, silvery, or wool-grass-like look.

ing myself and others to the extent of my ability. But what is the use in trying to live simply, raising what you eat, making what you wear, building what you inhabit, burning what you cut or dig, when those to whom you are allied insanely want and will have a thousand other things which neither you nor they can raise and nobody else, perchance, will pay for? The fellow-man to whom you are yoked is a steer that is ever bolting right the other way.

I was suggesting once to a man who was wincing under some of the consequences of our loose and expensive way of living, "But you might raise all your own potatoes, etc., etc." We had often done it at our house and had some to sell. At which he demurring, I said, setting it high, "You could raise twenty bushels even." "But," said he, "I use thirty-five." "How large is your family?" "A wife and three infant children." This was the real family; I need not enumerate those who were hired to *help* eat the potatoes and waste them. So he had to hire a man to raise his potatoes.

Thus men invite the devil in at every angle and then prate about the garden of Eden and the fall of man.

I know many children to whom I would fain make a present on some one of their birthdays, but they are so far gone in the luxury of presents — have such perfect museums of costly ones — that it would absorb my entire earnings for a year to buy them something which would not be beneath their notice.

P. M. — To foot of Fair Haven Hill *via* Hubbard's Grove.

See some large flocks of *F. hyemalis*, which fly with a clear but faint chinking chirp, and from time to time you hear quite a strain, half warbled, from them. They rise in a body from the ground and fly to the trees as you approach. There are a few tree sparrows with them. These and one small soaring hawk are all the birds I see.

I have failed to find white pine seed this year, though I began to look for it a month ago. The cones were fallen and open. Look the first of September.

From my experience with wild apples I can understand that there may be a reason for a savage preferring many kinds of food which the civilized man rejects. The former has the palate of an outdoor man. It takes a savage or wild taste to appreciate a wild apple.[1] I remember two old maids to whose house I enjoyed carrying a purchaser to talk about buying their farm in the winter, because they offered us wild apples, though with an unnecessary apology for their wildness.

Nov. 5. I hate the present modes of living and getting a living. Farming and shopkeeping and working at a trade or profession are all odious to me. I should relish getting my living in a simple, primitive fashion. The life which society proposes to me to live is so artificial and complex — bolstered up on many weak supports, and sure to topple down at last — that no man surely can ever be inspired to live it, and only "old fogies" ever praise it. At best some think it their duty to live it. I believe in the infinite joy and satisfaction of help-

[1] [*Excursions*, p. 313; Riv. 385.]

I see the shepherd's-purse, hedge-mustard, and red clover, — November flowers. Crossing the Depot Field Brook, I observe the downy, fuzzy globular tops of the *Aster puniceus*. They are slightly tinged with yellow, compared with the hoary gray of the goldenrod. The distant willow-tops are yellowish like them in the right light.

At Hubbard's Crossing I see a large male hen-harrier skimming over the meadow, its deep slate somewhat sprinkled or mixed with black; perhaps young. It flaps a little and then sails straight forward, so low it must rise at every fence. But I perceive that it follows the windings of the meadow over many fences. I pass a great white pine stump, — half a cord in it and more, — turned up out of a meadow. I look upon it with interest, and wish I had it at my door, for there are many warm fires in that. You could have many thoughts and tell many stories while that was burning.

Walked through Potter's Swamp. That white birch fungus always presents its face to the ground, parallel with it. For here are some on an upright dead birch whose faces or planes are at right angles with the axis of the tree as usual, looking down; but others, attached to the top of the tree, which lies prostrate on the ground, have their planes parallel with the axis of the tree, as if looking round the birch. When the epidermis is cracked, apparently as they grew, they are watered handsomely with white streams an eighth of an inch wide above. They have remarkably thick necks. They protrude through a rent in the bark, carrying it along with their necks, a little way.

The brightness of the foliage generally ceased pretty exactly with October. The still bright leaves which I see as I walk along the river edge of this swamp are birches, clear yellow at top; high blueberry, some very bright scarlet red still; some sallows; *Viburnum nudum*, fresh dark red; alder sprouts, large *green* leaves. Swamp-pink buds now begin to show. The late growth of the pyrus is now checked by the frost. The bark of many frostweeds is now cracked or burst off, and curled backward in five or six strips for about an inch, leaving the woody part bare at, or an inch above, the ground, sometimes five or six inches above the ground. I *suspect* the frost is the dying breath of the weed congealed.

I am pleased to see that the lower and larger four or five leaves of the water andromeda on the edge of the meadow next the swamp are pretty commonly turned a dark scarlet now, just as they fall, confirming my old impression. I have not observed for some years.

A nest made very thick, of grass and stubble, and lined with finer grass and horsehair, as big as a kingbird's, on an alder, within eighteen inches of ground, close to the water, at Cardinal Shore. The alder had been broken down at that height by the ice, and the nest rested on the stub ends. I took a few dead leaves out and to my surprise found an egg, — *very pale* greenish-blue. Probably the *wood thrush*,[1] if not the olivaceous one, whose eggs I have not seen described. Not *quite* so big as a bluebird's. This egg popped and

[1] No.

burst suddenly, with a noise about as loud as popping corn, or like a pop-gun, while I held it in my hand in my chamber. It had been addled when new. I had another pop in the chamber some months ago. So you must blow them before you bring them into a warm room.[1]

I am puzzled with the lecheas. Are there not four kinds? First, there is the *L. major*, with broad leaves; and second, the *least*, with fine spreading branches and with *branched* shoots at base. Third, there is the very common one, intermediate in size, with large fruit and linear-lanceolate leaves, now commonly fallen. But I see, fourth (?), this afternoon, one fifteen inches high, half a dozen rods from Cardinal Shore, and stout, with leaves like the third, but fruit very small and *abundant* (there is apparently a little recent-growth opening of leaves at the extremities of it, some radical shoots on stem six inches from ground!); and fifth, close by, a slender one a foot high, with leaves elliptic pointed, one half inch by one sixth, and larger fruit than last, at top and generally. (May be a variety of *L. major?* It has some leaves like it.) It is perhaps the third kind which, when only three or four inches high now, has such dense linear leaves one half inch plus long, pine-tree-like and spreading branches just above radical shoots.[2]

I find that one of my old oak logs, which was lying on the damp bank of the river, half rotted through below, contained many great black ants gone into winter quarters in those great eaten cells of the rotten wood. Yet this would have been covered with water

[1] *Vide* Nov. 13.   [2] *Vide* July 30, 1856.

Vol. VIII

in the winter. Those with wings were three quarters of an inch or more long. They move but slowly when exposed. In one I set up for splitting in the yard, I find a clamshell, carried in by a muskrat.

Nov. 6. A mizzling rain from the east drives me home from my walk. The knawel in the sand on the railroad causeway grows in dense green tufts like the hudsonia, six or eight inches in diameter and one or two high. It is still in bloom. The gooseberry leaves at the end of the currant row, being wet, are a still more brilliant scarlet.

A great many rainy or mizzling days the last fortnight, yet not much rain.

Pennyroyal has a long time stood withered and dark, blackish brown, in the fields, yet scented.

I can hardly resist the inclination to collect driftwood, to collect a great load of various kinds, which will sink my boat low in the water, and paddle or sail slowly home with it. I love this labor so much that I would gladly collect it for some person of simple habits who might want it. Men ordinarily do not have the pleasure of sawing and splitting their wood even, for while they are buying it an Irishman stands by with his sawhorse on his back, and the next thing I see him in their yards — him and his understrapper — sawing for dear life and two shillings a cut. When I think, too, of the many decaying stumps and logs which the coming freshets will carry off perchance to sea. Rails and posts and bits of boards and boughs are carried far into the swamps.

Nov. 7. Another drizzling day, — as fine a mist as can *fall*.

P. M. — Up Assabet.

I see a painted tortoise swimming under water, and to my surprise another afterward out on a willow trunk this dark day. It is long since I have seen one of any species except the *insculpta*. They must have begun to keep below and go into winter quarters (?) about three weeks ago.[1]

Looking west over Wheeler's meadow, I see that there has been much gossamer on the grass, and it is now revealed by the dewy mist which has collected on it. Some green-briar leaves still left, a dull red or scarlet, others yellowish; also the silky cornel is conspicuously dull-red, and others yellowish-red. And the sallow on river's brink (not *cordata*), with a narrow leaf pointed at both ends, shows some clear chrome-yellow leaves atop. The white birches lose their lower leaves first, and now their tops show crescents or cones of bright-yellow (spiring flames) leaves, some of the topmost even *green* still. The black willows almost everywhere entirely bare, yet the color of their twigs gives them the aspect of the crisp brown weeds of the river's brink. How completely crisp and shrivelled the leaves and stems of the *Polygonum amphibium* var. *terrestre*, still standing above the water and grass! The river has risen a little more, the North Branch especially, and the pail-stuff which has drifted down it has been carried a few rods up the main stream above the junction. It rises and falls very suddenly, and I was

[1] Come out again. *Vide* Nov. 11.

surprised to see the other day a line of sawdust more than a foot above the water's edge, showing that it had risen to that height and suddenly fallen without my knowledge.

Opened a muskrat-house nearly two feet high, but there was no hollow to it. Apparently they do not form that part yet.

I find it good to be out this still, dark, mizzling afternoon; my walk or voyage is more suggestive and profitable than in bright weather. The view is contracted by the misty rain, the water is perfectly smooth, and the stillness is favorable to reflection. I am more open to impressions, more sensitive (not calloused or indurated by sun and wind), as if in a chamber still. My thoughts are concentrated; I am all compact. The solitude is real, too, for the weather keeps other men at home. This mist is like a roof and walls over and around, and I walk with a domestic feeling. The sound of a wagon going over an unseen bridge is louder than ever, and so of other sounds. I am *compelled* to look at near objects. All things have a soothing effect; the very clouds and mists brood over me. My power of observation and contemplation is much increased. My attention does not wander. The world and my life are simplified. What now of Europe and Asia?

Birds are pretty rare now. I hear a few tree sparrows in one place on the trees and bushes near the river, — a clear, chinking chirp and a half-strain, — a jay at a distance; and see a nuthatch flit with a ricochet flight across the river, and hear his *gnah* half uttered when he alights.

A gray squirrel — as day before yesterday — runs down a limb of an oak and hides behind the trunk and I lose him. A red one runs along the trees to scold at me, boldly or carelessly, with a chuckling, bird-like note and that other peculiar sound at intervals, between a purr and a grunt. He is more familiar than the gray and more noisy. What sound does the gray make?

Some of my driftwood is the burnt timbers of a mill, which the swollen river has gleaned for me.

Found in Wheeler's potato-field, which has been burned over to get rid of the weeds before digging, near the Hemlocks [1] by river, a little mouse dead. Whole length three inches (minus); tail hardly seven eighths of an inch, so short (less than half the body) I thought at first it had been bitten off by some animal. General color above, a rust of brown or tawny brown, with mouse-color seen through it; beneath, rather hoary mouse-color, but nowhere white; the fur dark-slate. Snout and head blunt, the latter large. Hind legs longest. Ears quite concealed in the fur. It answers to Emmons's *Arvicola hirsutus*, or meadow mouse, except that it is smaller. Is it a young one? Tips of incisors light-yellow.

Nov. 8. A quite warm and foggy morning. I can sit with my window open and no fire. Much warmer than this time last year. Though there is quite a fog over the river and doubtful weather behind, the reflection

[1] Hemlock cones all closed, but open partly next day in chamber, and *entirely* in a day or two.

of the wool-grass, etc., is quite distinct, the reflection from the fog or mist making the water light for a background.

Nov. 9. 7 A. M. — Grass white and stiff with frost. 9 A. M. — With Blake up Assabet. A clear and beautiful day after frost.

Looking over the meadow westward from Merrick's Pasture Shore, I see the alders beyond Dodd's, now quite bare and gray (maple-like) in the morning sun (the frost melted off, though I found a little *ice on* my boat-seat), — that true November sight, — ready to wear frost leaves and to transmit (so open) the tinkle of tree sparrows. How wild and refreshing to see these old black willows of the river-brink, unchanged from the first, which man has never cut for fuel or for timber! Only the muskrat, tortoises, blackbirds, bitterns, and swallows use them.

Two blackbirds fly over pretty near, with a chuck, — either red-wings or grackles, but *I see no red.* See a painted tortoise and a wood tortoise in different places *out on the bank* still!

Saw in the pool at the Hemlocks what I at first thought was a brighter leaf moved by the zephyr on the surface of the smooth dark water, but it was a splendid male summer duck, which allowed us to approach within seven or eight rods, sailing up close to the shore, and then rose and flew up the curving stream. We soon overhauled it again, and got a fair and long view of it. It was a splendid bird, a perfect floating gem, and Blake, who had never seen the like, was greatly surprised, not

knowing that so splendid a bird was found in this part of the world. There it was, constantly moving back and forth by invisible means and wheeling on the smooth surface, showing now its breast, now its side, now its rear. It had a large, rich, flowing, green burnished crest, — a most ample head-dress, — two crescents of dazzling white on the side of the head and the black neck, a pinkish(?)-red bill (with black tip) and similar irides, and a long white mark under and at wing point on sides; the side, as if the form of wing at this distance, light bronze or greenish brown; but, above all, its breast, when it turns into the right light, all aglow with splendid purple (?) or ruby (?) reflections, *like the throat of the hummingbird.* It might not appear so close at hand. This was the most surprising to me. What an ornament to a river to see that glowing gem floating in contact with its waters! As if the hummingbird should recline its ruby throat and its breast on the water. Like dipping a glowing coal in water! It so affected me.

It became excited, fluttered or flapped its wings with a slight whistling noise, and arose and flew two or three rods and alighted. It sailed close up to the edge of a rock, by which it lay pretty still, and finally sailed fast up one side of the river by the willows, etc., off the duck swamp beyond the spring, now and then turning and sailing back a foot or two, while we paddled up the opposite side a rod in the rear, for twenty or thirty rods. At length we went by it, and it flew back low a few rods to where we roused it. It never offered to dive. We came equally near it again on our return. Unless you are thus near, and have a glass, the splendor and beauty of its colors will not be discovered.

Found a good stone jug, small size, floating stopple up. I drew the stopple and smelled, as I expected, molasses and water, or something stronger (black-strap?), which it *had* contained. Probably some meadow-haymakers' jug left in the grass, which the recent rise of the river has floated off. It will do to put with the white pitcher I found and keep flowers in. Thus I get my furniture.

Yesterday I got a perfectly sound oak timber, eight inches square and twenty feet long, which had lodged on some rocks. It had probably been the sill of a building. As it was too heavy to lift aboard, I towed it. As I shall want some shelves to put my Oriental books on,[1] I shall begin to save boards now.

I deal so much with my fuel, — what with finding it, loading it, conveying it home, sawing and splitting it, — get so many values out of it, am warmed in so many ways by it, that the heat it will yield when in the stove is of a lower temperature and a lesser value in my eyes, — though when I feel it I am reminded of all my adventures. I just turned to put on a stick. I had my choice in the box of gray chestnut rail, black and brown snag of an oak stump, dead white pine top, gray and round, with stubs of limbs, or else old bridge plank, and chose the last. Yes, I lose sight of the ultimate uses of this wood and work, the immediate ones are so great, and yet most of mankind, those called

[1] [Cholmondeley's gift arrived Nov. 30. See p. 25 and *Familiar Letters*, p. 270; Riv. 319.]

most successful in obtaining the necessaries of life, — getting their living, — obtain none of this, except a mere vulgar and perhaps stupefying warmth. I feel disposed, to this extent, to do the getting a living and the living for any three or four of my neighbors who really want the fuel and will appreciate the act, now that I have supplied myself. There was a fat pine plank, heavy as lead, I gave to Aunt L. for kindling.

That duck was all jewels combined, showing different lustres as it turned on the unrippled element in various lights, now brilliant glossy green, now dusky violet, now a rich bronze, now the reflections that sleep in the ruby's grain.

I see floating, just above the Hemlocks, the large sliding door of a railroad car, burnt to a cinder on one side and lettered in large bright-yellow letters on the other, "Cheshire 1510." It may have been cast over at the railroad bridge.

I affect what would commonly be called a mean and miserable way of living. I thoroughly sympathize with all savages and gypsies in so far as they merely assert the original right of man to the productions of Nature and a place in her. The Irishman moves into the town, sets up a shanty on the railroad land, and then gleans the dead wood from the neighboring forest, which would never get to market. But the so-called owner forbids it and complains of him as a trespasser. The highest law gives a thing to him who can use it.

Nov. 11. P. M. — Up Assabet.
As long as the sun is out, it is warm and pleasant.

Vol. VIII

The water is smooth. I see the reflections, not only of the wool-grass, but the bare button-bush, with its brown balls beginning to crumble and show the lighter inside, and the brittle light-brown twigs of the black willow, and the coarse rustling sedge, now completely withered (and hear it pleasantly whispering), and the brown and yellowish sparganium blades curving over like well-tempered steel, and the gray cottony mikania.

The bricks of which the muskrat builds his house are little masses or wads of the dead weedy rubbish on the muddy bottom, which it probably takes up with its mouth. It consists of various kinds of weeds, now agglutinated together by the slime and dried confervæ threads, utricularia, hornwort, etc., — a streaming, tuft-like wad. The building of these cabins appears to be coincident with the commencement of their clam diet, for now their vegetable food, excepting roots, is cut off. I see many small collections of shells already left along the river's brink. Thither they resort with their clam to open and eat it. But if it is the edge of a meadow which is being overflowed, they must raise it and make a permanent dry stool there, for they cannot afford to swim far with each clam. I see where one has left half a peck of shells on perhaps the foundation of an old stool or a harder clod, which the water is just about to cover, and he has begun his stool by laying two or three *fresh* wads upon the shells, the foundation of his house. Thus their cabin is first apparently intended merely for a stool, and afterward, when it is large, is perforated as if it were the bank! There is no cabin for a long way above

the Hemlocks, where there is no low meadow bordering the stream.

The clamshells freshly opened are handsomest this month (or rather are most observable, before the ice and snow conceal them) and in the spring.

I am surprised to see quite a number of painted tortoises out on logs and stones and to hear the wood tortoise rustling down the bank. Frogs are rare and sluggish, as if going into winter quarters. A cricket also sounds rather rare and distinct.

At the Hemlocks I see a narrow reddish line of hemlock leaves and, half an inch below, a white line of sawdust, eight inches above the present surface, on the upright side of a rock, both mathematically level. This chronicles the hemlock fall, which I had not noticed, we have so few trees, and also the river's rise. The North Branch must have risen suddenly before the South, for I see much pail-stuff from the Fort Pond Brook, which has been carried eighteen rods up the latter stream above the Rock, or as far as it extends immediately due west there. By "pail-stuff" I mean the curved and grooved pieces which form the sides and the flat ones for the bottom and their trimmings.

High blueberry leaves still conspicuous bright scarlet; also duller and darker green-briar leaves hold on on the Island.

I hear gray squirrels coursing about on the dry leaves, pursuing one another, and now they come in sight, coursing from pine to pine on their winding way, on their unweariable legs, on their undulating and winding course. It is a motion intermediate between running and flying. I hear but a tree sparrow and a chick-adee this voyage.

Nov. 13. In mid-forenoon (10.45), seventy or eighty geese, in three harrows successively smaller, flying southwest — pretty well west — over the house. A completely overcast, occasionally drizzling forenoon. I at once heard their clangor and rushed to and opened the window. The three harrows were gradually formed into one great one before they were out of sight, the geese shifting their places without slacking their progress.

P. M. — To Cardinal Shore.

Going over Swamp Bridge Brook at 3 P. M., I saw in the pond by the roadside, a few rods before me, the sun shining bright, a mink swimming, the whole length of his back out. It was a rich brown fur, glowing internally as the sun fell on it, like some ladies' boas, not black, as it sometimes appears, especially on ice. It landed within three rods, showing its long, somewhat cat-like neck, and I observed was carrying something by its mouth, dragging it overland. At first I thought it a fish, maybe an eel, and when it had got half a dozen feet, I ran forward, and it dropped its prey and went into the wall. It was a muskrat, the head and part of the fore legs torn off and gone, but the rest still fresh and quite heavy, including hind legs and tail. It had probably killed this muskrat in the brook, eaten so much, and was dragging the remainder to its retreat in the wall.

Vol. VIII

I suppose the strain only needed to be relieved in one point for the whole to go off.

I was remarking to-day to Mr. Rice on the pleasantness of this November thus far, when he remarked that he remembered a similar season fifty-four years ago, and he remembered it because on the 13th of November that year he was engaged in *pulling turnips* and saw wild geese go over, when one came to tell him that his father was killed by a bridge giving way when his team was crossing it, and the team falling on him walking at its side.

P. M. — Up Assabet with Sophia.

A clear, bright, warm afternoon. A painted tortoise swimming under water and a wood tortoise out on the bank. The rain has raised the river an additional foot or more, and it is *creeping over the meadows.* My boat is two thirds full and hard to come at. The old weedy margin is covered and a new grassy one acquired. The current is stronger, though the surface is pretty smooth. Much small rubbish is drifting down and slowly turning in the eddies. The motion of my boat sends an undulation to the shore, which rustles the dry sedge half immersed there, as if a tortoise were tumbling through it. Leaves and sticks and billets of wood come floating down in middle of the full, still stream, turning round in the eddies, and I mistake them for ducks at first. See two red-wing blackbirds alight on a black willow.

Nov. 15. The river rising. I see a spearer's light to-night.

A fine clear afternoon after the misty morning and heavy rain of the night. Even after all this rain I see the streaming lines of gossamer from trees and fences. From Fair Haven Hill the air is clear and fine-grained, and now it is a perfect russet November landscape, — including the reddish brown of the oaks, excepting where the winter-rye fields and some low meadows show their green, the former quite bright, and also the evergreen patches of pines, edged in the northwest by the blue mountain ridges.

Got the wood thrush's (?) nest of November 5th. It is about five inches [in] diameter from outside to outside, and two and a half within. Outside of some weedy tufts (beneath), weed stems and stubble (some dry galium stems, small), and lined with a little fine grass and horsehair. I found the egg partly concealed by some dry alder leaves which had fallen into the nest.

Nov. 14. Minott hears geese to-day.

Heard to-day in my chamber, about 11 A. M., a singular sharp crackling sound by the window, which made me think of the snapping of an insect (with its wings, or striking something). It was produced by one of three *small* pitch pine cones which I gathered on the 7th, and which lay in the sun on the window-sill. I noticed a slight motion in the scales at the apex, when suddenly, with a louder crackling, it burst, or the scales separated, with a snapping sound on all sides of it. It was a general and sudden bursting or expanding of all the scales with a sharp crackling sound and motion of the whole cone, as by a force pent up within it.

Nov. 16. Minott speaks of the last fortnight as good weather to complete the harvesting, — corn, potatoes, turnips, carrots, etc. It seemed late for harvest, but some of the above crops were not gathered.

A part of to-day and yesterday I have been making shelves for my Oriental books, which I hear to-day are now on the Atlantic in the Canada.

Mr. Rice asked me to-night if I knew how hard a head a goat had. When he lived in Roxbury a man asked him to kill a goat for him. He accordingly struck the goat with a hatchet, hard enough, as he supposed, to dash his brains out, but the goat instantly, with a bleat, leaped on to a wall and ran twenty rods on the wall faster than they could on the ground after him, and he saw him as much as a month afterward none the worse for the blow.

He thinks that muskrats have always, even in the winter, a dry bed in the bank, as well as the wet place to eat in their cabins. Told me again the story of the muskrat which he saw *resting* under the ice, he himself lying flat and still upon the ice and the muskrat having a long way to go from the bank to his cabin. As soon as he stopped with his nose against the ice, a bubble issued from his mouth and flatted out to three inches in diameter against the ice, and he remained for half a minute with his mouth in it. Then drew it in, all but a little, and proceeded.

He spoke of the mud turtle resting on the "river-bush" (meaning the button-bush) in the spring, so near the top of the water that he could put his snout out when he pleased. Has taken them in April formerly, on Fast-Day.

I think that by the "swamp robin" he means the veery.

I see many more nests in the alders now than I suspected in the summer.

Nov. 17. Just after dark the first snow is falling, after a chilly afternoon with cold gray clouds, when my hands were uncomfortably cold.

It is interesting to me to talk with Rice, he lives so thoroughly and satisfactorily to himself. He has learned that rare art of living, the very elements of which most professors do not know. His life has been not a failure but a success. Seeing me going to sharpen some plane-irons, and hearing me complain of the want of tools, he said that I ought to have a chest of tools. But I said it was not worth the while. I should not use them enough to pay for them. "You would use them more, if you had them," said he. "When I came to do a piece of work I used to find commonly that I wanted a certain tool, and I made it a rule first always to make that tool. I have spent as much as $3000 thus on my tools." Comparatively speaking, his life is a success; not such a failure as most men's. He gets more out of any enterprise than his neighbors, for he helps himself more and hires less. Whatever pleasure there is in it he enjoys. By good sense and calculation he has become rich and has invested his property well, yet practices a fair and neat economy, dwells not in untidy luxury. It costs him less to live, and he gets more out of life, than others. To get his living, or keep it, is not a hasty or disagreeable toil. He works slowly but surely, en-

joying the sweet of it. He buys a piece of meadow at a profitable rate, works at it in pleasant weather, he and his son, when they are inclined, goes a-fishing or a-bee-hunting or a-rifle-shooting quite as often, and thus the meadow gets redeemed, and potatoes get planted, perchance, and he is very sure to have a good crop stored in his cellar in the fall, and some to sell. He always has the best of potatoes there. In the same spirit in which he and his son tackle up their Dobbin (he never keeps a fast horse) and go a-spearing or a-fishing through the ice, they also tackle up and go to their Sudbury farm to hoe or harvest a little, and when they return they bring home a load of stumps in their hay-rigging, which impeded their labors, but, perchance, supply them with their winter wood. All the woodchucks they shoot or trap in the bean-field are brought home also. And thus their life is a long sport and they know not what hard times are.

Rice says there are no bees worth hunting about here now. He has sometimes been to a large wood in the west part of Sudbury, and also to Nagog, yet there was little honey there.

Saw Goodwin this afternoon returning from the river with two minks, one trapped, the other shot, and half a dozen muskrats. Mink seem to be more commonly seen now, and the rising of the river begins to drive out the muskrats.

Labaume says that he wrote his journal of the Campaign in Russia each night, in the midst of incredible danger and suffering, with "a raven's quill, and a little gunpowder, mixed with some melted snow, in the

Vol. VIII

hollow of my hand," the quill cut and mended with "the knife with which I had carved my scanty morsel of horse-flesh." Such a statement promises well for the writer's qualifications to treat such a theme.

Nov. 18. About an inch of snow fell last night, but the ground was not at all frozen or prepared for it. A little greener grass and stubble here and there seems to burn its way through it this forenoon.

It clears up at noon, and at

2 P. M. I go to Fair Haven Hill *via* Hubbard's Grove.

As I sat in the house, I was struck with the brightness and heat of the sun reflected from this our first snow. There was an intenser light in the house, and I felt an uncommon heat from the sun's rays on my back. The air is very clear, and the sky heavenly, with a few floating downy clouds. I am prepared to hear sharp, screaming notes rending the air, from the winter birds. I do, in fact, hear many jays, and the tinkling, like rattling glass, from chickadees and tree sparrows. I do not detect any peculiar brightness whatever in the osiers on the Hubbard causeway; they are scarcely, if at all, brighter than the tops of the trees. Now first mark the stubble and numerous withered weeds rising above the snow. They have suddenly acquired a new character. Tansy still shows its yellow disks, but yarrow is particularly fresh and perfect, cold and chaste, with its pretty little dry-looking rounded white petals and green leaves. Its very color gives it a right to bloom above the snow, — as level as a snow-crust on the top

of the stubble. It looks like a virgin wearing a white ruff.

The snow is the great track-revealer. I come across the tracks of persons who, at a different hour from myself, have crossed, and perhaps often cross, some remote field on their errands, when I had not suspected a predecessor; and the track of the dog or staff are seen too. The cattle have tracked their whole pasture over, as if there had been a thousand. I have this silent but unerring evidence of any who have crossed the fields since last night. It is pleasant to see tracks leading towards the woods, — to be reminded that any have engagements there. Yet for the most part the snow is quite untrodden. Most fields have no track of man in them. I only see where a squirrel has leaped from the wall.

I now remark how the perfectly leafless alder thickets are much darker than the maples, now that the ground is whitened. The pasture directly under my face is white, but, seen aslant a few rods off, mostly russet. Gathered a bagful of fair apples on Fair Haven, showing their red cheeks above the snow.

I was so warmed in spirit in *getting* my wood that the heat it finally yielded when burnt was coldness in comparison. That first is a warmth which you cannot buy.

These apples which I get nowadays — russets and Baldwins — are the ripest of all, being acted on by the frost and partly left because they were slightly over-ripe for keeping. I come home with a heavy bagful and rob no one.

Instead of walking in the wood-market amid sharp-visaged teamsters, I float over dark reflecting waters in which I see mirrored the stumps on the bank, and am dazzled by the beauty of a summer duck. Though I should get no wood, I should get a beauty perhaps more valuable. The price of this my wood, however high, is the very thing which I delight to pay. What I obtain with the most labor — the most water-logged and heaviest wood which I fish up from the bottom and split and dry — warms the most. The greater, too, the distance from which I have conveyed it, the more I am warmed by it in my thought. All the intervening shores glow and are warmed by it as it passes, or as I repass them in my mind. And yet men will cut their wood with sorrow, and burn it with lucifer matches. This was where I drove my team afield, and, instead of the grey-fly,[1] I heard the wood tortoises even yet rustling through the sedge to the water, or the gray squirrel coursing from maple to maple.

One man thinks that he has a right to burn his thirty cords in a year because he can give a certain sum of money in exchange for them, but that another has no right to pick up the fagots which else nobody would burn. They who will remember only this kind of right do as if they stood under a shed and affirmed that they were under the unobscured heavens. The shed has its use, but what is it to the heavens above?[2]

So of the *warmth* which food, shelter, and clothing

---

[1] ["We drove a-field, and both together heard
  What time the grey-fly winds her sultry horn." — *Lycidas*.]
[2] [Channing, p. 90.]

afford, or might afford, if we used *economical stoves*. We might burn the smoke which now puts our eyes out. The pleasure, the warmth, is not so much in *having* as in a true and simple manner *getting* these necessaries.

Men prefer foolishly the gold to that of which it is the symbol, — simple, honest, independent labor. Can gold be said to buy food, if it does not buy an appetite for food? It is fouler and uglier to have too much than not to have enough.

Nov. 19. A cold, gray day, once spitting snow. Water froze in tubs enough to bear last night.

Minott had two cats on his knee. One given away without his knowledge a fortnight before had just found its way back. He says he would not kill a cat for twenty dollars, — no, not for fifty. Finally he told his women folks that he would not do it for five hundred, or any sum. He thought they loved life as well as we. Johnny Vose would n't do it. He used to carry down milk to a shop every day for a litter of kittens.

Speaking of geese, he says that Dr. Hurd told a tough story once. He said that when he went out to the well there came a flock of geese flying so low that they had to rise to clear the well-sweep. M. says that there used to be a great many more geese formerly; he used to hear a great many flocks in a day go "yelling" over. Brant, too, he used to see.

Told me of his fishing for pickerel once in the brook, when a mink leaped into the water toward his bait (a frog), but, seeing the end of his pole, he dived and

---

made off. Some years ago he saw a mink steal out of the brook, which, being disturbed, dropped a pout half grown which it had caught. This was in his rye, then five or six inches high. Presently it returned and carried the pout to the wall by the elm at R. W. E.'s bound. He followed, looked under a rock, and saw two young minks. He has taken the jackets off many a one, but they smell so rank it is unpleasant work.

Rice says that that brook which crosses the road just beyond his brother Israel's is called Cold Brook. It comes partly from Dunge Hole. When the river is rising it will flow up the brook a great way.

Rice told his turtle story the other night: "One day I was going through Boston market and I saw a huddle of men around something or other. I edged my way between them and saw that they had got a great mud turtle on a plank, and a butcher stood over him with a cleaver in his hand. 'Eh,' said I, 'what are you trying to do?' 'We are waiting for him to put out his head so that we may cut it off. Look out,' they said; 'don't come so near, or he'll bite you.' 'Look here,' said I, 'let me try. I guess I can make him put his head out.' 'Let him try. Let him try,' they said, with a laugh. So I stepped into the ring and stood astride of the turtle, while they looked on to see the sport. After looking at him a moment, I put down my hands and turned him over on to his back, whereupon he immediately ran out his head and pushed against the plank to turn himself back, but, as they were not ready to cut at once, or his neck was not in a good position, I seized his head in both hands and,

putting my feet against his breast-bone, drew his head out the full length of his neck and said, 'Now cut away. Only take care you don't cut my fingers.' They cut, and I threw the head down on the floor. As I walked away, some one said, 'I guess that fellow has seen mud turtles before to-day.'"

Nov. 20. Again I hear that sharp, crackling, snapping sound and, hastening to the window, find that another of the pitch pine cones gathered November 7th, lying in the sun, or which the sun has reached, has separated its scales very slightly at the apex. It is only discoverable on a close inspection, but while I look the whole cone opens its scales with a smart crackling and rocks and seems to bristle up, scattering the dry pitch on the surface. They all thus fairly loosen and open, though they do not at once spread wide open. It is almost like the disintegration of glass. As soon as the tension is relaxed in one part, it is relaxed in every part.

A cold day. The snow that fell November 17th in the evening is still seen on the ground.

Nov. 24. Geese went over on the 13th and 14th, on the 17th the first snow fell, and the 19th it began to be cold and blustering. That first slight snow has not yet gone off! and *very little* has been added. The last three or four days have been quite cold, the sidewalks a glare of ice and very little melting. To-day has been exceedingly blustering and disagreeable, as I found while surveying for Moore. The farmers now bring the apples they have engaged (and the cider); it is time to put them in the cellar, and the turnips. Ice has frozen pretty thick in the bottom of my boat.

Nov. 26. Bottom of boat covered with ice. The ice next the shore bore me and my boat.

Nov. 27. P. M. — By river to J. Farmer's.

He gave me the head of a gray rabbit which his boy had snared. This rabbit is white beneath, the whole length, reddish-brown on the sides, and the same spotted with black, above; the hairs coarse and homely, yet the fur beneath thick and slate-colored as usual. Well defended from the cold. Sides I might say *pale* brick-color, the brown part. The fur under the feet dirty-yellowish, as if stained by what it trod upon. He makes no use of their skins or fur. The skin is very tender. The tail, short and curled up, is white on the inside like that of the deer described by Loskiel, *q. v.*, Indian book.

He showed me the preserved skin of the heads of a double-headed calf, still-born, also the adjoining portion of the spine, where two short spinal columns, two or three inches long, merged in one. Only one body and other organs.

I told him I saw a mink. He said he would have given me $1.50 and perhaps something more for him. I hear that he gives $1.75, and sells them again at a profit. They are used to trim ladies' coats with, among other things. A mink skin which he showed me was a darker brown than the one I saw last (he says they

changed suddenly to darker *about* a fortnight since); and the tail was nearly all black.

He said that his grandfather, who could remember one hundred and twenty-five years before this, told him that they used to catch wolves in what is now Carter's pasture by the North River (east of Dodge's Brook) in this manner: They piled up logs, cob-house fashion, beginning with a large base, eight or ten feet square, and narrowing successively each tier, so as to make steps for the wolves to the top, say ten feet high. Then they put a dead sheep within. A wolf soon found it in the night, sat down outside and howled till he called his comrades to him, and then they ascended step by step and jumped down within; but when they had done they could not get out again. They always found one of the wolves dead, and supposed that he was punished for betraying the others into this trap.

A man in Brighton, whom he fully believes, told him that he built a bower near a dead horse and placed himself within to shoot crows. One crow took his station as sentinel on the top of the tree, and thirty or forty alighted upon the horse. He fired and killed seven or eight, but the rest, instead of minding him, immediately flew to their sentinel and pecked him to pieces before his eyes. Also Mr. Joseph Clark told him that, as he was going along the road, he cast a stick over the wall and hit some crows in a field, whereupon they flew directly at their sentinel on an apple tree and beat and buffeted him away to the woods as far as he could see.

There is little now to be heard along the river but

the sedge rustling on the brink. There is a little ice along most of the shore throughout the day.

Farmer told me that some one told him he found a pickerel washed up in the river, choked by a bream which it had endeavored to swallow.

Nov. 30. River skimmed over behind Dodd's and elsewhere. Got in my boat. River remained iced over all day.

This evening I received Cholmondeley's gift of Indian books, forty-four volumes in all, which came by the Canada, reaching Boston on the morning of the 24th. Left Liverpool the 10th.

Goodwin and Farmer think that a dog will not touch the dead body of a mink, it smells so strongly. The former, after skinning them, throws the carcass into a tree for the crows. He has got eleven this fall; shot two and trapped the rest.

On the 27th, when I made my last voyage for the season, I found a large sound pine log about four feet long floating, and brought it home. Off the larger end I sawed two wheels, about a foot in diameter and seven or eight inches thick, and I fitted to them an axle-tree made of a joist, which also I found in the river, and thus I had a convenient pair of wheels on which to get my boat up and roll it about. The assessors called me into their office this year and said they wished to get an inventory of my property; asked if I had any real estate. No. Any notes at interest or railroad shares? No. Any taxable property? None that I knew of. "I own a boat," I said; and one of

them thought that that might come under the head of a pleasure carriage, which is taxable. Now that I have wheels to it, it comes nearer to it. I was pleased to get my boat in by this means rather than on a borrowed wheelbarrow. It was fit that the river should furnish the material, and that in my last voyage on it, when the ice reminded me that it was time to put it in winter quarters.

I am waiting for colder weather to survey a swamp, now inaccessible on account of the water.

I asked Aunt L. to-night why *Scheeter* Potter was so called. She said, because his neighbors regarded him as so small a man that they said in jest that it was his business to make mosquitoes' bills. He was accused of catching his neighbor's hens in a trap and eating them. But he was crazy.

William Wheeler says that he went a-spearing on the 28th (night before Thanksgiving) and, besides pouts and pickerel, caught two great suckers. He had one of the last stuffed and baked for Thanksgiving, and made himself sick by eating too heartily of it.

II

DECEMBER, 1855

(ÆT. 38)

Dec. 3. Monday. A pleasant day. No snow yet (since that first whitening which lasted so long), nor do I see any ice to speak of.

Hear and see, of birds, only a tree sparrow in the willows on the Turnpike. Met Goodwin going out with his gun. He shot (evidently) some crossbills once in Roxbury. He sometimes gets a skunk drowned in his muskrat or mink traps, and so can get at their secretion without being disturbed by the scent. He, too, has heard that it is a sure cure for the phthisic.

The fields and woods seem now particularly empty and bare. No cattle in pasture; only here and there a man carting or spreading manure.

Every larger tree which I knew and admired is being gradually culled out and carried to mill. I see one or two more large oaks in E. Hubbard's wood lying high on stumps, waiting for snow to be removed. I miss them as surely and with the same feeling that I do the old inhabitants out of the village street. To me they were something more than timber; to their owner not so.

Dec. 4. Melvin says that he shot a sheldrake once in the act of swallowing a perch seven or eight inches

long He had got nothing to-day, for he forgot his caps.

A pleasant day and yet no snow nor ice. The younger osiers on Shattuck's row *do* shine.

Dec. 6. 10 P. M. — Hear geese going over.

Dec. 8. Saturday. Still no snow, — nor ice noticeable. I might have left my boat out till now. I have not worn gloves yet.

This afternoon I go to the woods down the railroad, seeking the society of some flock of little birds, or some squirrel, but in vain. I only hear the faint lisp of (probably) a tree sparrow. I go through empty halls, apparently unoccupied by bird or beast. Yet it is cheering to walk there while the sun is reflected from far through the aisles with a silvery light from the needles of the pine. The contrast of light or sunshine and shade, though the latter is now so thin, is food enough for me. Some scarlet oak leaves on the forest floor, when I stoop low, appear to have a little blood in them still. The shrivelled Solomon's-seal berries are conspicuously red amid the dry leaves. I visited the door of many a squirrel's burrow, and saw his nutshells and cone-scales and tracks in the sand, but a snow would reveal much more. Let a snow come and clothe the ground and trees, and I shall see the tracks of many inhabitants now unsuspected, and the very snow covering up the withered leaves will supply the place of the green ones which are gone. In a little busy flock of lisping birds, — chickadees or lesser redpolls, —

even in a nuthatch or downy woodpecker, there would have been a sweet society for me, but I did not find [it]. Yet I had the sun penetrating into the deep hollows through the aisles of the wood, and the silvery sheen of its reflection from masses of white pine needles.

Met Therien coming from Lincoln on the railroad. He says that he carried a cat from Jacob Baker's to Riordan's shanty in a bag in the night, but she ran home again. "Had they not a cat in the shanty?" I asked. "Yes," said he, "but she was run over by the cars and killed; they found her head on the track separated from her body, just below the pond." That cat of Baker's used to eat eggs and so he wished to get rid of her. He carried her in a bag to Waltham, but she came back.

Therien had several times seen where tortoises had been run over. They lie just under the rail, and put their heads out upon the rail to see what is coming, and so their heads are crushed. Also he has seen snakes cut in two. The men on the road told him that small birds were frequently run over.

Jacob Farmer brought me the head of a mink to-night and took tea here. He says that partridges sometimes fly against a house in the night, he thinks when started by a fox. His man found one in his barn this fall, which had come in in the night, and caught it before it could get out.

The mink has a delicate pard-like nose, cat-like. The long hairs are black or blackish, yet the general aspect is brown.

Farmer says he can call a male quail close to him

by imitating the note of the female, which is only a single faint whistle. He says if you take eggs out of a partridge's nest and put them back, you will find just as many cast out afterwards as you took out.

Dec. 9. A still, completely gray, overcast, chilly morning. At 8.30 a fine snow begins to fall, increasing very gradually, perfectly straight down, till in fifteen minutes the ground is white, the smooth places first, and thus the winter landscape is ushered in. And now it is falling thus all the land over, sifting down through the tree-tops in woods, and on the meadow and pastures, where the dry grass and weeds conceal it at first, and on the river and ponds, in which it is dissolved. But in a few minutes it turns to rain, and so the wintry landscape is postponed for the present.

Dec. 10. To Cambridge.

Dec. 11. P. M. — To Holden Swamp, Conantum.

For the first time I wear gloves, but I have not walked *early* this season.

I see no birds, but hear, methinks, one or two tree sparrows. No snow; scarcely any ice to be detected. It is only an aggravated November. I thread the tangle of the spruce swamp, admiring the leafets of the swamp pyrus which had put forth again, now frost-bitten, the great yellow buds of the swamp-pink, the round red buds of the high blueberry, and the fine sharp red ones of the panicled andromeda. Slowly I worm my way amid the snarl, the thicket of black alders and blueberry, etc.; see the forms, apparently, of rabbits at the foot of maples, and catbirds' nests now exposed in the leafless thicket.

Standing there, though in this *bare* November landscape, I am reminded of the incredible phenomenon of small birds in winter, — that ere long, amid the cold powdery snow, as it were a fruit of the season, will come twittering a flock of delicate crimson-tinged birds, lesser redpolls, to sport and feed on the seeds and buds now just ripe for them on the sunny side of a wood, shaking down the powdery snow there in their cheerful social feeding, as if it were high midsummer to them. These crimson aerial creatures have wings which would bear them quickly to the regions of summer, but here is all the summer they want. What a rich contrast! tropical colors, crimson breasts, on cold white snow! Such etherealness, such delicacy in their forms, such ripeness in their colors, in this stern and barren season! It is as surprising as if you were to find a brilliant crimson flower which flourished amid snows. They greet the chopper and the hunter in their furs. Their Maker gave them the last touch and launched them forth the day of the Great Snow. He made this bitter imprisoning cold before which man quails, but He made at the same time these warm and glowing creatures to twitter and be at home in it. He said not only, Let there be linnets in winter, but linnets of rich plumage and pleasing twitter, bearing summer in their natures. The snow will be three feet deep, the ice will be two feet thick, and last night, perchance, the mercury sank to thirty degrees below zero. All the fountains of nature

seem to be sealed up. The traveller is frozen on his way. But under the edge of yonder birch wood will be a little flock of crimson-breasted lesser redpolls, busily feeding on the seeds of the birch and shaking down the powdery snow! As if a flower were created to be now in bloom, a peach to be now first fully ripe on its stem. I am struck by the perfect confidence and success of nature. There is no question about the existence of these delicate creatures, their adaptedness to their circumstances. There is superadded superfluous paintings and adornments, a crystalline, jewel-like health and soundness, like the colors reflected from ice-crystals.

When some rare northern bird like the pine grosbeak is seen thus far south in the winter, he does not suggest poverty, but dazzles us with his beauty. There is in them a warmth akin to the warmth that melts the icicle. Think of these brilliant, warm-colored, and richly warbling birds, birds of paradise, dainty-footed, downy-clad, in the midst of a New England, a Canadian winter. The woods and fields, now somewhat solitary, being deserted by their more tender summer residents, are now frequented by these rich but delicately tinted and hardy northern immigrants of the air. Here is no imperfection to be suggested. The winter, with its snow and ice, is not an evil to be corrected. It is as it was designed and made to be, for the artist has had leisure to add beauty to use. My acquaintances, angels from the north. I had a vision thus prospectively of these birds as I stood in the swamps. I saw this familiar — too *familiar* — fact at a different angle, and

Vol. VIII

I was charmed and haunted by it. But I could only attain to be thrilled and enchanted, as by the sound of a strain of music dying away. I had seen into paradisaic regions, with their air and sky, and I was no longer wholly or merely a denizen of this vulgar earth. Yet had I hardly a foothold there. I was only sure that I was charmed, and no mistake. It is only necessary to behold thus the least fact or phenomenon, however familiar, from a point a hair's breadth aside from our habitual path or routine, to be overcome, enchanted by its beauty and significance. Only what we have touched and worn is trivial, — our scurf, repetition, tradition, conformity. To perceive freshly, with fresh senses, is to be inspired. Great winter itself looked like a precious gem, reflecting rainbow colors from one angle.

My body is all sentient. As I go here or there, I am tickled by this or that I come in contact with, as if I touched the wires of a battery. I can generally recall — have fresh in my mind — several scratches last received. These I continually recall to mind, reimpress, and harp upon. The age of miracles is each moment thus returned. Now it is wild apples, now river reflections, now a flock of lesser redpolls. In winter, too, resides immortal youth and perennial summer. Its head is not silvered; its cheek is not blanched but has a ruby tinge to it.

If any part of nature excites our pity, it is for ourselves we grieve, for there is eternal health and beauty. We get only transient and partial glimpses of the beauty of the world. Standing at the right angle, we are dazzled by the colors of the rainbow in colorless ice. From the

right point of view, every storm and every drop in it is a rainbow. Beauty and music are not mere traits and exceptions. They are the rule and character. It is the exception that we see and hear. Then I try to discover what it was in the vision that charmed and translated me. What if we could daguerreotype our thoughts and feelings! for I am surprised and enchanted often by some quality which I cannot detect. I have seen an attribute of another world and condition of things. It is a wonderful fact that I should be affected, and thus deeply and powerfully, more than by aught else in all my experience, — that this fruit should be borne in me, sprung from a seed finer than the spores of fungi, floated from other atmospheres! finer than the dust caught in the sails of vessels a thousand miles from land! Here the invisible seeds settle, and spring, and bear flowers and fruits of immortal beauty.

Dec. 13. This morning it is snowing, and the ground is whitened. The countless flakes, seen against the dark evergreens like a web that is woven in the air, impart a cheerful and busy aspect to nature. It is like a grain that is sown, or like leaves that have come to clothe the bare trees. Now, by 9 o'clock, it comes down in larger flakes, and I apprehend that it will soon stop. It does.

How pleasant a sense of preparedness for the winter, — plenty of wood in the shed and potatoes and apples, etc., in the cellar, and the house banked up! Now it will be a cheerful sight to see the snows descend and hear the blast howl.

Sanborn tells me that he was waked up a few nights ago in Boston, about midnight, by the sound of a flock of geese passing over the city, probably about the same night I heard them here. They go honking over cities where the arts flourish, waking the inhabitants; over State-houses and capitols, where legislatures sit; over harbors where fleets lie at anchor; mistaking the city, perhaps, for a swamp or the edge of a lake, about settling in it, not suspecting that greater geese than they have settled there.

Dec. 14. It began to snow again last evening, but soon ceased, and now it has turned out a fine winter morning, with half an inch of snow on the ground, the air full of mist, through which the smokes rise up perfectly straight; and the mist is frozen in minute leafets on the fences and trees and the needles of the pines, silvering them.

I stood by Bigelow the blacksmith's forge yesterday, and saw him repair an axe. He burned the handle out, then, with a chisel, cut off the red-hot edge even, there being some great gaps in it, and by hammering drew it out and shaped it anew, — all in a few minutes. It was interesting to see performed so simply and easily, by the aid of fire and a few rude tools, a work which would have surpassed the skill of a tribe of savages.

P. M. — To Pink Azalea Woods.

The warm sun has quite melted the thin snow on the south sides of the hills, but I go to see the tracks of animals that have been out on the north sides. First, getting over the wall under the walnut trees, on the south

brow of the hill, I see the broad tracks of squirrels, probably red, where they have ascended and descended the trees, and the empty shells of walnuts which they have gnawed left on the snow. The snow is so very shallow that the impression of their toes is the more distinctly seen. It imparts life to the landscape to see merely the squirrels' track in the snow at the base of the walnut tree. You almost realize a squirrel at every tree. The attractions of nature are thus condensed or multiplied. You see not merely bare trees and ground which you might suspect that a squirrel had left, but you have this unquestionable and significant evidence that a squirrel has been there since the snow fell, — as conclusive as if you had seen him.

A little further I heard the sound [of] a downy woodpecker tapping a pitch pine in a little grove, and saw him inclining to dodge behind the stem. He flitted from pine to pine before me. Frequently, when I pause to listen, I hear this sound in the orchards or streets. This was in one of these dense groves of young pitch pines.

Suddenly I heard the screwing mew and then the whir of a partridge on or beneath an old decaying apple tree which the pines had surrounded. There were several such, and another partridge burst away from one. They shoot off swift and steady, showing their dark-edged tails, almost like a cannon-ball. I saw one's track under an apple tree and where it had pecked a frozen-thawed apple.

Then I came upon a fox-track made last night, leading toward a farmhouse, — Wheeler's, where there

are many hens, — running over the side of the hill parallel with Wheeler's new wall. He was dainty in the choice of his ground, for I observed that for a mile he had adhered to a narrow cow-path, in which the snow lay level, for smoothness. Sometimes he had cantered, and struck the snow with his foot between his tracks. Little does the farmer think of the danger which threatens his hens.

In a little hollow I see the sere gray pennyroyal rising above the snow, which, snuffed, reminds me of garrets full of herbs.

Now I hear, half a mile off, the hollow sound of woodchopping, the work of short winter days begun, which is gradually laying bare and impoverishing our landscape. In two or three thicker woods which I have visited this season, I was driven away by this ominous sound.

Further over toward the river, I see the tracks of a deer mouse on a rock, which suddenly come to an end where apparently it had ascended a small pine by a twig which hung over it. Sometimes the mark of its tail was very distinct. Afterwards I saw in the pasture westward where many had run about in the night. In one place many had crossed the cow-path in which I was walking, in one trail, or the same one had come and gone many times. In the large hollows where rocks have been blasted, and on the sides of the river, I see irregular spaces of dark ice bare of snow, which was frozen after the snow ceased to fall. But this ice is rotten and mixed with snow. I am surprised to see the river frozen over for the most part with this thin and

rotten snow ice, and the drooping or bent alders are already frozen into this slush, giving to the stream a very wintry aspect. I see some squirrel-tracks about a hole in a stump.

At the azalea meadow or swamp, the red tops of the osiers, which are very dense and of a uniform height, are quite attractive, in the absence of color at this season. Any brighter and warmer color catches our eye at this season. I see an elm there whose bark is worn quite smooth and white and bare of lichens, showing exactly the height at which the ice stood last winter.

Looking more closely at the light snow there near the swamp, I found that it was sprinkled all over (as with pellets of cotton) with regular star-shaped cottony flakes with six points, about an eighth of an inch in diameter and on an average a half an inch apart. It snowed geometry.

How snug and warm a hemlock looks in the winter! That by the azalea looks thus: There is a tendency in the limbs to arrange themselves ray-wise about a point one third from the base to the top. What singular regularity in the outline of a tree!

I noticed this morning successive banks of frost on the windows, marked by their irregular waving edges, like the successive five, ten, and fifteen fathom lines which mark the depth of the shores on charts.

Thus by the snow I was made aware in this short

walk of the recent presence there of squirrels, a fox, and countless mice, whose trail I had crossed, but none of which I saw, or probably should have seen before the snow fell. Also I saw this afternoon the track of one sparrow, probably a tree sparrow, which had run among the weeds in the road.

Dec. 15. This morning it has begun to snow apparently in earnest. The air is quite thick and the view confined. It is quite still, yet some flakes come down from one side and some from another, crossing each other like woof and warp apparently, as they are falling in different eddies and currents of air. In the midst of it, I hear and see a few little chickadees prying about the twigs of the locusts in the graveyard. They have come into town with the snow. They now and then break forth into a short sweet strain, and then seem suddenly to check themselves, as if they had done it before they thought.

The boys have skated a little within two or three days, but it has not been thick enough to bear a man yet.

How like a bird of ill omen the crow behaves! Still holding its ground in our midst like a powwow that is not to be exterminated! Sometimes when I am going through the Deep Cut, I look up and see half a dozen black crows flitting silently across in front and ominously eying down; passing from one wood to another, yet as if their passage had reference to me.

The snow turned to rain, and this afternoon I walk

in it down the railroad and through the woods. The low grass and weeds, bent down with a myriad little crystalline drops, ready to be frozen perhaps, are very interesting, but wet my feet through very soon. A steady but gentle, warm rain.

Dec. 16. Steady, gentle, warm rain all the forenoon, and mist and mizzling in the afternoon, when I go round by Abel Hosmer's and back by the railroad.

The mist makes the near trees dark and noticeable, like pictures, and makes the houses more interesting, revealing but one at a time. The old apple trees are very important to this landscape, they have so much body and are so dark. It is very pleasing to distinguish the dim outline of the woods, more or less distant, through the mist, sometimes the merest film and suspicion of a wood. On one side it is the plump and rounded but soft masses of pitch pines, on another the brushy tops of maples, birches, etc. Going by Hosmer's, the very heaps of stones in the pasture are obvious as cairns in one of Ossian's landscapes.

Saw two red squirrels on the fence, one on each side of his house, particularly red along their backs and top of head and tail. They are remarkably tame. One sits twirling apparently a dried apple in his paws, with his tail curled close over his back as if to keep it warm, fitting its curve. How much smothered sunlight in their wholesome brown red this misty day! It is clear New England, *Nov-anglia*, like the red subsoil. It is springlike.

As we go over the bridge, admire the reflection of

the trees and houses from the smooth open water over the channel, where the ice has been dissolved by the rain.

Dec. 17. 9.30 A. M. — To Hill.

A remarkably fine, springlike morning. The earth all bare; the sun so bright and warm; the steam curling up from every fence and roof, and carried off at [an] angle by the slight northwesterly air. After those rainy days the air is apparently uncommonly clear, and hence (?) the sound of cock-crowing is so sweet, and I hear the sound of the sawmill even at the door, also the cawing of crows. There is a little ice, which makes it as yet good walking, in the roads. The peculiar brightness and sunniness may be partly owing to the sun being reflected through the cleansed air from the more than russet, the bleached, surface of the earth. Methinks every squirrel will be out now. This is the morning. Ere long the wind will rise and this season will be over. There will probably be some wrack in the afternoon sky.

Columella says you must be careful not to carry out seeds in your manure and so have *segetes herbidas* (weedy crops).

Dec. 18. Saw to-day a dark-colored spider of the *very largest* kind on ice, — the mill-pond at E. Wood's in Acton.

J. Farmer says that he once tried to kill a cat by taking her by the legs and striking her head against a stone, but she made off, and in a week was about again,

apparently as well as ever, and he did not meddle with her again.

Dec. 20. Still no snow, and, as usual, I wear no gloves.

P. M. — To Hubbard's skating meadow.

A few chickadees busily inspecting the buds at the willow-row ivy tree, for insects, with a short, clear *chink* from time to time, as if to warn me of their neighborhood.

Boys are now devoted to skating after school at night, far into evening, going without their suppers. It is pretty good on the meadows, which are somewhat overflown, and the sides of the river, but the greater part of it is open. I walk along the side of the river, on the ice beyond the Bath Place. Already there is dust on this smooth ice, on its countless facets, revealed by the sun. How warm the dull-red cranberry vine rises above the ice here and there! I stamped and shook the ice to detect the holes and weak places where that little brook comes in there. They were plainly revealed, for the water beneath, being agitated, proclaimed itself at every hole far and wide or for three or four rods. The edge of the ice toward the channel is either rubbed up or edged with a ridge of frozen foam.

I see *some* gossamer on the weeds above the ice. Also, in now hard, dark ice, the tracks apparently of a fox, made when it was saturated snow. So long his trail is revealed, but over the pastures no hound can now trace him. There has been much overflow about every tussock in the meadow, making that rough, opaque ice, like yeast. I mark the many preparations for another year which the farmer has made, — his late plowings, his muck-heaps in fields, perhaps of grass, which he intends to plow and cultivate, his ditches to carry off the winter's floods, etc. How placid, like silver or like steel in different lights, the surface of the still, living water between these borders of ice, reflecting the weeds and trees, and now the warm colors of the sunset sky! The ice is that portion of the flood which is congealed and laid up in our fields for a season.

Dec. 21. Going to the post-office at 9 A. M. this very pleasant morning, I hear and see tree sparrows on Wheildon's pines, and just beyond scare a downy woodpecker and a brown creeper in company, from near the base of a small elm within three feet of me. The former dashes off with a loud rippling of the wing, and the creeper flits across the street to the base of another small elm, whither I follow. At first he hides behind the base, but ere long works his way upward and comes in sight. He is a gray-brown, a low curve from point of beak to end of tail, resting flat against the tree.

P. M. — *Via* Hubbard's Grove and river to Fair Haven Pond. Return by Andromeda Ponds.

See only a jay (?) flying high over the fields, and chickadees. The last rarely seem to mind you, keeping busy at work, yet hop nearer and nearer. Hubbard's barren pasture under Fair Haven Hill, whose surface

is much broken, alternate sod and bare sand, is now tinged with the pale leather or cinnamon color of the second-sized pinweed, which thickly covers it.

I here take to the riverside. The broader places are frozen over, but I do not trust them yet. Fair Haven is entirely frozen over, probably some days. Already some eager fisherman has been here, this morning or yesterday, and I hear that a great pickerel was carried through the street. I see, close under the high bank on the east side, a distinct tinge of that red in the ice for a rod.

I remark the different pale colors to which the grasses have faded and bleached. Those coarse sedges amid the button-bushes are bleached particularly light. Some, more slender, in the Pleasant Meadow, is quite light with singular reddish or pinkish radical blades making a mat at the base. Some dense sedge or rushes in tufts in the Andromeda Ponds have a decided greenish tinge, *somewhat* like well-cured hay.

A few simple colors now prevail. Even the apples on the trees have assumed the brown color of the leaves.

I do not remember to have seen the Andromeda Ponds so low. The weedy and slimy bottom is for the most part exposed. The slime, somewhat clay-colored, is collected here and there into almost organic forms, — manna[?]-like, with a skin to it. I make a nosegay of the sphagnum, which must suffer from this unusual exposure. It is frozen stiff at the base. What rugged castellated forms it takes at the base of the

andromeda which springs from it! Some is green or yellowish-green, some bright-crimson, some brown, some quite white, with different shades of all these colors. Such are the temples and cheeks of these soft crags. What a primitive and swampy wilderness for the wild mice to run amidst! — the andromeda woods!

Walden is skimmed over, all but an acre, in my cove. It will probably be finished to-night.[1]

No doubt the healthiest man in the world is prevented from doing what he would like by sickness.

Dec. 22. Dull overcast morning, so warm that it has actually thawed in the night, and there is a wet space larger than the ice on the sidewalk. It draws forth crowing from cockerels, as spring does rills from glaciers.

P. M. — Warm rain and frost coming out and muddy walking.

In reading Columella I am frequently reminded, not only by the general tone, but even by the particular warnings and directions, of our agricultural journals and reports of farmers' clubs. Often what is last and most insisted on among us, was most insisted on by the Romans. As when he says it is better to cultivate a little land well than a great deal ill, and quotes the poet: —

> "... Laudato ingentia rura,
>   Exiguum colito."

"Modus ergo, qui in omnibus rebus, etiam parandis agris adhibebitur: tantum enim obtinendum est, quanto est opus, ut emisse videamur quo potiremur,

[1] No, it proved too warm.

non quo oneraremur ipsi, atque aliis fruendum eripe-remus, more praepotentium, qui possident fines gentium, quos ne circumire equis quidem valent, sed proculcandos pecudibus, et vastandos ac populandos feris derelinquunt, aut occupatos nexu civium, et ergastulis tenent." (Therefore, as in all things, so in buying land moderation will be used; for only so much is to be obtained as is necessary, to make it appear that we have bought what we can use, not what we may be burdened with, and hinder others from enjoying, like those overpowerful ones who possess the territory of nations, which they cannot go round even with horses, but leave to be trampled by herds, and to be laid waste and depopulated by wild beasts, or keep occupied by *nexu civium* [1] and prisons.)

This reminds me of those extensive tracts said to belong to the Peter Piper estate, running back a mile or more and absorbing several old farms, but almost wholly neglected and run out, which I often traverse and am better acquainted with than their so-called owners. Several times I have had to show such the nearest way out of their wood-lots.[2] Extensive wood-lots and cranberry meadows, perhaps, and a rambling old country house on one side, but you can't buy an acre of land for a house-lot. "Where wealth accumulates and men decay."

Dec. 23. P. M. — To Conantum-End.

[1] Confinement and compulsory labor on farms of fellow-citizens for debt.

[2] [*Excursions*, p. 185; Riv. 226.]

A very bright and pleasant day with remarkably soft wind from a little north of west. The frost has come out so in the rain of yesterday that I avoid the muddy plowed fields and keep on the grass ground, which shines with moisture. I think I do not remember such and so much pleasant, springlike weather as this and some other days of this month.

I admire those old root fences which have almost entirely disappeared from tidy fields, — white pine roots got out when the neighboring meadow was a swamp, — the monuments of many a revolution. These roots have not penetrated into the ground, but spread over the surface, and, having been cut off four or five feet from the stump, were hauled off and set up on their edges for a fence. The roots are not merely interwoven, but grown together into solid frames, full of loopholes like Gothic windows of various sizes and all shapes, triangular and oval and harp-like, and the slenderer parts are dry and resonant like harp-strings. They are rough and unapproachable, with a hundred snags and horns which bewilder and balk the calculation of the walker who would surmount them. The part of the trees above ground presents no such fantastic forms. Here is one seven paces, or more than a rod, long, six feet high in the middle, and yet only one foot thick, and two men could turn it up, and in this case the roots were six or nine inches thick at the extremities. The roots of pines growing in swamps grow thus in the form of solid frames or rackets, and those of different trees are interwoven with all so that they stand on a very broad foot and stand or fall together to some

extent before the blasts, as herds meet the assault of beasts of prey with serried front. You have thus only to dig into the swamp a little way to find your fence, — post, rails, and slats already solidly grown together and of material more durable than any timber. How pleasing a thought that a field should be fenced with the roots of the trees got out in clearing the land a century before! I regret them as mementoes of the primitive forest. The tops of the same trees made into fencing-stuff would have decayed generations ago. These roots are singularly unobnoxious to the effects of moisture.

The swamp is thus covered with a complete web of roots. Wild trees, such as are fitted to grow in the uncultivated swamps.

I detect the Irishman where the elms and maples on the causeway are cut off at the same height with the willows *to make pollards* of !

I sit on the hillside near the wall corner, in the further Conantum field, as I might in an Indian-summer day in November or October. These are the colors of the earth now: all land that has been some time cleared, except it is subject to the plow, is russet, the color of withered herbage and the ground finely commixed, a lighter straw-color where are rank grasses next water; sprout-lands, the pale leather-color of dry oak leaves; pine woods, green; deciduous woods (bare twigs and stems and withered leaves commingled), a brownish or reddish gray; maple swamps, smoke-color; land just cleared, dark brown and earthy; plowed land, dark brown or blackish; ice and water, slate-color or

blue; andromeda swamps, dull red and dark gray; rocks, gray.

At Lee's Cliff I notice these radical (?) leaves quite fresh: saxifrage, sorrel, polypody, mullein, columbine, veronica, thyme-leaved sandwort, spleenwort, strawberry, buttercup, radical johnswort, mouse-ear, radical pinweeds, cinquefoils, checkerberry, wintergreen, thistles, catnip, *Turritis stricta* especially fresh and bright. What is that fine very minute plant thickly covering the ground, like a young arenaria?

Think of the life of a kitten, ours for instance: last night her eyes set in a fit, doubtful if she will ever come out of it, and she is set away in a basket and submitted to the recuperative powers of nature; this morning running up the clothes-pole and erecting her back in frisky sport to every passer.

Dec. 25. 9 A. M. — Snow driving almost horizontally from the northeast and fast whitening the ground, and with it the first tree sparrows I have noticed in the yard. It turns partly to rain and hail at midday.

Dec. 26. After snow, rain, and hail yesterday and last night, we have this morning quite a glaze, there being at last an inch or two of crusted snow on the ground, the most we have had. The sun comes out at 9 A. M. and lights up the ice-incrusted trees, but it is pretty warm and the ice rapidly melts.

I go to Walden *via* the almshouse and up the railroad. Trees seen in the west against the dark cloud, the sun shining on them, are perfectly white as frostwork, and their outlines very perfectly and distinctly revealed,

great wisps that they are and ghosts of trees, with recurved twigs. The walls and fences are encased, and the fields bristle with a myriad of crystal spears. Already the wind is rising and a brattling is heard overhead in the street. The sun, shining down a gorge over the woods at Brister's Hill, reveals a wonderfully brilliant as well as seemingly solid and diversified region in the air. The ice is from an eighth to a quarter of an inch thick about the twigs and pine-needles, only half as thick commonly on one side. Their heads are bowed; their plumes and needles are stiff, as if preserved under glass for the inspection of posterity.

Thus is our now especially slow-footed river laid up not merely on the meadows, but on the twigs and leaves of the trees, on the needles of the pines. The pines thus weighed down are sharp-pointed at top and remind me of firs and even hemlocks, their drooping boughs being wrapped about them like the folds of a cloak or a shawl. The crust is already strewn with bits of the green needles which have been broken off. Frequently the whole top stands up bare, while the middle and lower branches are drooping and massed together, resting on one an-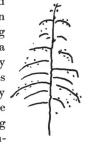other. But the low and spreading weeds in the fields and the wood-paths are the most interesting. Here are asters, savory-leaved, whose flat imbricated calyxes, three quarters of an inch over, are surmounted and inclosed in a perfectly transparent ice button, like a glass knob, through which you see the reflections of the brown calyx. These are very common. Each little blue-curls calyx has a spherical button like those brass ones on little boys' jackets, — little sprigs on them, — and the pennyroyal has still smaller spheres, more regularly arranged about its stem, chandelier-wise, and still smells through the ice. The finest grasses support the most wonderful burdens of ice and most branched on their minute threads. These weeds are spread and arched over into the snow again, — countless little arches a few inches high, each cased in ice, which you break with a tinkling crash at each step.

The scarlet fruit of the cockspur lichen, seen glowing through the more opaque whitish or snowy crust of a stump, is, on close inspection, the richest sight of all, for the scarlet is increased and multiplied by reflection through the bubbles and hemispherical surfaces of the crust, as if it covered some vermilion grain thickly strewn. And the brown cup lichens stand in their midst. The whole rough bark, too, is encased.

Already a squirrel has perforated the crust above the mouth of his burrow, here and there by the side of the path, and left some empty acorn shells on the snow. He has shovelled out this morning before the snow was frozen on his door-step.

Now, at 10 A. M., there blows a very strong wind from the northwest, and it grows cold apace.

Particularly are we attracted in the winter by greenness and signs of growth, as the green and white shoots of grass and weeds, pulled or floating on the water, and also by color, as cockspur lichens and crimson birds, etc.

Thorny bushes look more thorny than ever; each thorn is prolonged and exaggerated.

Some boys have come out to a wood-side hill to coast. It must be sport to them, lying on their stomachs, to hear their sled cronching the crystalled weeds when they have reached the more weedy pasture below.

4 P. M. — Up railroad.

Since the sun has risen higher and fairly triumphed over the clouds, the ice has glistened with all the prismatic hues. On the trees it is now considerably dissipated, but rather owing to the wind than the sun. The ice is chiefly on the upper and on the storm side of twigs, etc. The whole top of the pine forest, as seen miles off in the horizon, is of sharp points, the leading shoots with a few plumes, even more so than I have drawn on the last page but one.

It has grown cold, and the crust bears. The weeds and grasses, being so thickened by this coat of ice, appear much more numerous in the fields. It is surprising what a bristling crop they are. The sun is gone before five. Just before I looked for rainbow flocks in the west, but saw none, — only some small *pink-dun* (?) clouds. In the east still larger ones, which after sunset turned to pale slate.

In a true history or biography, of how little consequence those events of which so much is commonly made! For example, how difficult for a man to remember in what towns or houses he has lived, or when! Yet one of the first steps of his biographer will be to establish these facts, and he will thus give an undue importance to many of them. I find in my Journal that the most important events in my life, if recorded at all, are not dated.

Dec. 27. Recalled this evening, with the aid of Mother, the various houses (and towns) in which I have lived and some events of my life.

Born, July 12, 1817, in the

Minott House,	on the Virginia Road, where Father occupied Grandmother's thirds, carrying on the farm. The Catherines the other half of the house. Bob Catherines and John threw up the turkeys. Lived there about eight months. Si Merriam next neighbor. Uncle David died when I was six weeks old. I was baptized in old M. H. by Dr. Ripley, when I was three months, and did not cry.
The *Red House,*	where Grandmother lived, we the west side till October, 1818, hiring of Josiah Davis, agent for Woodwards. (There were Cousin Charles and Uncle C. more or less.) Accord-

	ing to day-book, Father hired of Proctor, October 16, 1818, and shop of *Spaulding, November 10, 1818.* Day-book first used by Grandfather, dated 1797. His part cut out and used by Father in Concord in 1808–9, and in Chelmsford, 1818–19–20–21.
Chelmsford,	till March, 1821. (Last charge in Chelmsford about middle of March, 1821.) Aunt Sarah taught me to walk there when fourteen months old. Lived next the meeting-house, where they kept the powder in the garret. Father kept shop and painted signs, etc.
Pope's House,	at South End in Boston, five or six (?) months, a ten-footer. Moved from Chelmsford through Concord, and may have tarried in Concord a little while. Day-book says, "Moved to Pinkney Street Sep 10th 1821 on Monday."
Whitwell's House,	Pinckney Street, Boston, to March, 1823 (?).
Brick House,	Concord, to spring of 1826.
Davis's House	(next to S. Hoar's) to May 7th, 1827.
Shattuck House (Hollis Hall, Cambridge)	(now William Monroe's) to spring of 1835. (Hollis, Cambridge, 1833.)
Aunt's House,	to spring of 1837. At Brownson's

(Hollis Hall and Canton)   while teaching in winter of 1835. Went to New York with Father, peddling, in 1836.

Parkman House, (Hollis, Cambridge)   to fall of 1844. Was graduated in 1837. Kept town school a fortnight in 1837 (?). Began the big Red Journal, October, 1837. Found first arrowheads, fall of 1837. Wrote a lecture (my first) on Society, March 14th, 1838, and read it before the Lyceum in the Masons' Hall, April 11th, 1838. Went to Maine for a school in May, 1838. Commenced school in the house in summer of 1838. Wrote an essay on Sound and Silence, December, 1838. Fall of 1839 up Merrimack to White Mountains. "Aulus Persius Flaccus," first printed paper of consequence, February 10th, 1840. The Red Journal of 546 pages ended, June, 1840. Journal of 396 pages ended January 31st, 1841. Went to

(R. W. E.'s)   R. W. E.'s in spring of 1841 and stayed there to summer of 1843.

(William Emerson's, Staten Island)   Went to Staten Island, June, 1843,[1] and returned in December, 1843, or to Thanksgiving. Made pencils in 1844.

[1] [It was really in May of that year that he went to Staten Island. See *Familiar Letters,* p. 68; Riv. 79, 80.]

maries (?) black, and some white appears when it flies. Most distinctive its small hooked bill (upper mandible). It makes no sound, but flits to the *top* of an oak further off. Probably a male.

Am surprised to find eight or ten acres of Walden still open, notwithstanding the cold of the 26th, 27th, and 28th and of to-day. It must be owing to the wind partly. If quite cold, it will probably freeze to-night.[1]

I find in the andromeda bushes in the Andromeda Ponds a great many nests apparently of the red-wing (?)[2] suspended after their fashion amid the twigs of the andromeda, each now filled with ice. I count twenty-one within fifteen rods of a centre, and have no doubt there are a hundred in that large swamp, for I only looked about the edge part way. It is remarkable that I do not remember to have seen flocks of these birds there. It is an admirable place for them, these swamps are so impassable and the andromeda so dense. It would seem that they steal away to breed here, are not noisy here as along the river.[3]

I never knew, or rather do not remember, the crust so strong [and] hard as it is now and has been for three days. You can skate over it as on ice in any direction. I see the tracks of skaters on all the roads, and they seem hardly to prefer the ice. Above Abiel Wheeler's, on the back road, the crust is not broken yet, though many sleds and sleighs have passed. The tracks of the skaters are as conspicuous [as] any there. But the snow is but two or three inches deep. Jonas Potter

[1] Not quite. Say the night of the 30th.
[2] Yes.   [3] *Vide* next page.

Texas House, (Walden) (R. W. E.'s)   to August 29th, 1850. At Walden, July, 1845, to fall of 1847, then at R. W. E.'s to fall of 1848, or while he was in Europe.

Yellow House,   reformed, till present.

Dec. 28. P. M. — Hollowell place and back near Hubbard's Bridge.

To-day and yesterday the boys have been skating on the crust in the streets, — it is so hard, the snow being very shallow. Considerable ice still clings to the rails and trees and especially weeds, though much attenuated. The birches were most bent — and are still — in hollows on the north sides of hills. Saw some rabbit's fur on the crust and some (apparently bird?) droppings, since the sleet fell, — a few pinches of fur the only trace of the murder. Was it a hawk's work? Crossed the river on the ice in front of Puffer's. What do the birds do when the seeds and bark are thus encased in ice?

Dec. 29. Down railroad to Andromeda Ponds.

I occasionally see a small snowflake in the air against the woods. It is quite cold, and a serious storm seems to be beginning. Just before reaching the Cut I see a shrike flying low beneath the level of the railroad, which rises and alights on the topmost twig of an elm within four or five rods. All ash or bluish-slate above down to middle of wings; dirty-white breast, and a broad black mark through eyes on side of head; pri-

Vol. VIII

tells me that [he] has known the crust on snow two feet deep to be as strong as this, so that he could drive his sled anywhere over the walls; so that he cut off the trees in Jenny's lot three feet from the ground, and cut again after the snow was melted.

When two men, Billings and Prichard, were dividing the stock of my father and Hurd, the former acting for Father, P. was rather tight for Hurd. They came to a cracked bowl, at which P. hesitated and asked, "Well, what shall we do with this?" B. took it in haste and broke it, and, presenting him one piece, said, "There, that is your half and this is ours."

A good time to walk in swamps, there being ice but no snow to speak of, — all crust. It is a good walk along the edge of the river, the wild side, amid the button-bushes and willows. The eupatorium stalks still stand there, with their brown hemispheres of little twigs, orreries.

The nests of last page are suspended very securely between eight or ten andromeda stems, about halfway up them; made of more or less coarse grass or sedge without, then about half an inch of *dense and fine, now frozen sphagnum,* then fine wild grass or sedge very regularly, and sometimes another layer of sphagnum and of fine grass above these, the whole an inch thick, the bottom commonly rounded. The outside grasses are well twisted about whatever andromeda stems stand at or near the river. I saw the traces of mice in some of them.

Dec. 30. The snow which began last night has continued to fall very silently but steadily, and now it is not far from a foot deep, much the most we have had yet; a dry, light, powdery snow. When I come down I see it in miniature drifts against the panes, alternately streaked dark and light as it is more or less dense. A remarkable, perfectly regular conical peak, a foot high, with concave sides, stands in the fireplace under the sink-room chimney. The pump has a regular conical Persian (?) cap, and every post about the house a similar one. It is quite light, but has not drifted. About 9 A. M. it ceases, and the sun comes out, and shines dazzlingly over the white surface. Every neighbor is shovelling out, and hear the sound of shovels scraping on door-steps. Winter now first fairly commenced, I feel.

The places which are slowest to freeze in our river are, first, *on account of warmth as well as motion,* where a brook comes in, and also probably where are springs in banks and under bridges; then, on account of shallowness and rapidity, at bends. I perceive that the cold respects the same places every winter. In the dark, or after a heavy snow, I know well where to cross the river most safely. Where the river is most like a lake, broad with a deep and muddy bottom, there it freezes first and thickest. The open water at a bend seems to be owing to the swiftness of the current, and this to the shallowness, and this to the sands taken out of the opposing bank and deposited there.

There was yesterday eight or ten acres of open water at the west end of Walden, where is depth and breadth combined.

What a *horrid* shaggy and stiff low wilderness were the Andromeda Ponds yesterday! What then must they have been on the 21st! As it was, it was as if I walked through a forest of glass (with a tough woody core) up to my middle. That dense tufted grass with a greenish tinge was still stiffly coated with ice, as well

as everything else, and my shoes were filled with the fragments, but here and there the crimson sphagnum blushed through the crust beneath. Think of that dense grass, a *horrid* stiff crop,

[Water Milkweed Pods. See page 72]   each stem as big as your finger, firm but brittle and about two feet high, and the countless birds' nests filled even with ice!

P. M. — Across river and over Hill.

The wind has been blowing and the snow drifting.

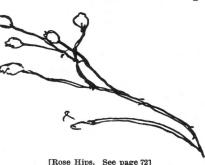

[Rose Hips. See page 72]

The paths are filled up again. The surface of the snow is coarsely waved and rough now, as if it caught at every straw and faced its windy foe again. It appears a coarser grain now. By the river are conspicuous the now empty and spread pods of the water milkweed, gray-brown without, silky-white within, — in some a seed or two left still; also the late rose corymbs of red hips; also the eupatorium drawn at venture four pages back, or more erect, thus, — some with brown fuzz and seeds still; the sium sometimes, with its very flat cymes; and that light-brown sedge or rush. Some black ash keys still hang on amid the black abortions (?).

For a few days I have noticed the snow sprinkled with alder and birch scales. I go now through the birch meadow southwest of the Rock. The high wind is scattering them over the snow there. See one downy (?) woodpecker and one or two chickadees. The track of a squirrel on the Island Neck. Tracks are altered by the depth of the snow. Looking up over the top of the hill now, The Meadow-Sweet southwest, at 3.30 P. M., I see a few mother-o'-pearl tints, and methinks the same or rainbow tints in the drifting snow there, against the bright light of the unseen sun. Only in such clear cold air as this have the small clouds in the west that fine evanishing edge. It requires a state of the air that quickly dissipates all

moisture. It must be rare in summer. In this rare atmosphere all cloud is quickly dissipated and mother-o'-pearl tinted as it passes away. The snow is too deep and soft yet for many tracks. No doubt the mice have been out beneath it.

Recrossing the river behind Dodd's, now at 4 P. M., the sun quite low, the open reach just below is quite green, a vitreous green, as if seen through a junk-bottle. Perhaps I never observed this phenomenon but when the sun was low.

He who would study birds' nests must look for them in November and in winter as well as in midsummer, for then the trees are bare and he can see them, and the swamps and streams are frozen and he can approach new kinds. He will often be surprised to find how many have haunted where he little suspected, and will receive many hints accordingly, which he can act upon in the summer. I am surprised to find many new ones (*i. e.* not new species) in groves which I had examined several times with particular care in the summer.

This was not a lodging snow, and the wind has already blown most of it off the trees, yet the long-limbed oak on the north of the hill still supports a ridge of its pure white as thick as its limbs. They lie parallel like the ulna and radius, and one is a bare white bone.

Beside the other weeds I might have shown the tall rough golden-rod, still conspicuous:—

Found, in the Wheeler meadow, south-west of the Island, a nest in the fork of an alder about eight feet from ground, partly saddled on, made apparently chiefly of fine grass and bark fibres, quite firm and very thick bottomed, and well bound without with various kind of lint. This is a little oval, three by three and a half inches within and seven eighths deep, with a very firm, smooth rim of fine grass and dark shreds, lined with the same and some lint. A few alder leaves dangle from the edge, and, what is remarkable, the outer edge *all around* is defiled, quite covered, with black and white caterpillar-like droppings of the young birds. It is broader and shallower than a yellowbird's and larger than a wood pewee's. Can it be a redstart's? I should think it too large.

Dec. 31. It is one of the mornings of *creation*, and the trees, shrubs, etc., etc., are covered with a fine leaf frost, as if they had their morning robes on, seen against the sun. There has been a mist in the night. Now, at 8.30 A. M., I see, collected over the low grounds behind Mr. Cheney's, a dense fog (over a foot of snow), which looks dusty like smoke by contrast with the snow. Though limited to perhaps twenty or thirty acres, it [is] as dense as any in August. This accounts for the frost on the twigs. It consists of minute leaves, the longest an eighth of an inch, all around the twigs, but longest commonly on one side, in one instance the southwest side.

Clearing out the paths, which the drifting snow had filled, I find already quite [a] crust, from the sun and the blowing making it compact; but it is soft in the woods.

9 A. M. — To Partridge Glade.

III

JANUARY, 1856

(ÆT. 38)

Jan. 1. Speaking of foxes, J. Farmer told me last evening that some time ago Sherman Barrett's folks heard a squealing, and, running up, saw a fox leap out of the pen with a sucking-pig in his mouth and escape with it. Farmer says they commonly take the dead lambs from the fields, though most dogs will not.

P. M. — To Walden.

Walden is covered with white snow ice six inches thick, for it froze while it was snowing, though commonly there is a thin dark beneath. This is now, therefore, bare, while the river, which was frozen before, is covered with snow. A very small patch of Walden, frozen since the snow, looks at a little distance exactly like open water by contrast with the snow ice, the trees being reflected in it, and indeed I am not certain but a *very small* part of this patch was water.

The track-repairers have shovelled four little paths by the sides of the rails, all the way from the depot to Walden. As I went by the engine- house, I saw great icicles four feet long hanging from the eastern eaves, like slender pointed spears, the last half blown aside by the wind: and still more. By the side of the Deep Cut are the tracks of probably tree sparrows about the weeds, and of partridges.

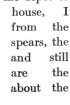

I see many partridge-tracks in the light snow, where they have sunk deep amid the shrub oaks; also gray rabbit and deer mice tracks, for the last ran over this soft surface last night. In a hollow in the glade, a gray rabbit's track, apparently, leading to and from a hole in the snow, which, following, and laying open, I found to extend curving about this pit, four feet through and under the snow, to a small hole in the earth, which apparently led down deep.

At ten the frost leaves are nearly all melted.

It is invariably the east track on the railroad causeway which has the least snow on it. Though it is nearly all blown off elsewhere on the causeway, Trillium Woods have prevented its being blown off opposite to them. The snow-plow yesterday cast the snow six feet one side the edge of the cars, and it fell thick and rich, evenly broken like well-plowed land. It lies like a rich tilth in the sun, with its glowing cottony-white ridges and its shadowy hollows.

Vol. VIII

On the ice at Walden are very beautiful great leaf crystals in great profusion. The ice is frequently thickly covered with them for many rods. They seem to be connected with the rosettes, — a running together of them. They look like a loose web of small white feathers springing from a tuft of down, for their shafts are lost in a tuft of fine snow like the down about the shaft of a feather, as if a feather bed had been shaken over the ice. They are, on a close examination, surprisingly perfect leaves, like ferns, only very broad for their length and commonly more on one side the midrib than the other. They are from an inch to an inch and a half long and three quarters wide, and slanted, where I look, from the southwest. They have, first, a very distinct midrib, though so thin that they cannot be taken up; then, distinct ribs branching from this, commonly opposite, and minute ribs springing again from these last, as in many ferns, the last run- ning to each crenation in the border. How much further they are subdi- vided, the naked eye can- not discern. They are so  thin and fragile that they melt under your breath while looking closely at them. A fisherman says they were much finer in the morning. In other places the ice is strewn with a different kind of frostwork in little patches, as if oats had been spilled, like fibres of asbestos rolled, a half or three quarters of an inch long and an eighth or more wide. Here and there patches of them a foot or two over. Like some boreal grain spilled.

Here are two fishermen, and one has preceded them. They have not had a bite, and know not why. It has been a clear winter day.

On the north shore, near the railroad, I see the tracks apparently of a white rabbit, afterward many tracks of gray rabbits, and where they had squatted under or rather by the side of an alder stem or the like, and left many balls in the pure snow. Many have run in one course. In the midst of them I see the track of a large rabbit, probably a white one, which was evidently on the full spring. Its tracks are four feet apart, and, unlike the others, which are on the surface even of this light snow, these break through deep, making a hole six inches over. Why was this one in such haste? I conclude to trace him back and find out. His bounds grow greater and greater as I go back, now six feet quite, and a few rods further are the tracks of a fox (*possibly* a dog, but I think not) exactly on the trail![1] A little further, where the rabbit was ascending a considerable slope, through this snow nearly a foot deep, the bounds measure full seven feet, leaving the snow untouched for that space between. It appeared that the fox had started the rabbit from a bank on which it was resting, near a young hemlock, and pursued it only a dozen rods up the hill, and then gave up the chase, — and well he might, methought.

Goodwin says that the white rabbit never burrows, but the gray regularly. Yet he once knew a white one to earth itself.

[1] All doubtful.

In a rabbit's track   the two fore feet are the furthest apart, thus :

This chase occurred probably in the night, either the last or night before, when there was not a man within a mile; but, treading on these very deep and distinct tracks, it was as if I had witnessed it, and in imagination I could see the sharp eyes of the crafty fox and the palpitating breast of the timorous rabbit, listening behind. We unwittingly traverse the scenery of what tragedies! Every square rod, perchance, was the scene of a life or death struggle last night. As you track the rabbit further off, its bounds becoming shorter and shorter, you follow also surely its changing moods from desperate terror till it walks calmly and reassured over the snow without breaking its very slight crust, — perchance till it gnaws some twig composedly, — and in the other direction you trace the retreating steps of the disappointed fox until he has forgotten this and scented some new game, maybe dreams of partridges or wild mice. Your own feelings are fluttered proportionably.[1]

Jan. 2. Probably the coldest morning yet, our thermometer 6° below zero at 8 A. M.; yet there was quite a mist in the air.[2] The neighbors say it was 10° below zero at 7 A. M.

P. M. — To Walden.

As for the fox and rabbit race described yesterday, I find that the rabbit was going *the other way*, and pos-

[1] *Vide* [below].
[2] This mist for several mornings after the first deep snow.

sibly the fox was a rabbit, for, tracing back the rabbit, I found that it had first been walking with alternate steps, fox-like.

There were many white rabbits' tracks in those woods, and many more of the gray rabbit, but the former broke through and made a deep track, except where there was a little crust on the south slope, while the latter made but a faint impression on the surface. The latter run very much in the same path, which is well trodden, and you would think you were in the midst of quite a settlement of them.

Crossing the railroad at the Heywood meadow, I saw some snow buntings rise from the side of the embankment, and with surging, rolling flight wing their way up through the cut. I walked through the westernmost Heywood swamp. There are the tracks of many rabbits, both gray and white, which have run about the edges of these swamps since this snow came, amid the alders and shrub oaks, and one white one has crossed it. The cat-tails rise high above the snow in the swamp, their brown heads bursting on one side into creamy (?) billows and wreaths, or partly bare. Also the rattlesnake grass is still gracefully drooping on every side, with the weight of its seeds, — a rich, wild grain. And other wild grasses and rushes rise above the snow. There is the wild-looking remnant of a white pine, quite dead, rising fifteen or twenty feet, which the woodpeckers have bored; and it is still clad with sulphur lichens and many dark-colored tufts of cetraria in the forks of its branches.

Returning, I saw, near the back road and railroad,

a small flock of eight snow buntings feeding on the seeds of the pigweed, picking them from the snow, — apparently flat on the snow, their legs so short, — and, when I approached, alighting on the rail fence. They were pretty black, with white wings and a brown crescent on their breasts. They have come with this deeper snow and colder weather.

Jan. 3. Snows again. About two inches have fallen in the night, but it turns to a fine mist. It was a damp snow.

P. M. — To Hill.

The snow turned to a fine mist or mizzling, through which I see a little blue in the snow, lurking in the ruts.

In the river meadows and on the (perhaps moist) sides of the hill, how common and conspicuous the brown spear-heads of the hardhack, above the snow, and looking black by contrast with it!

Just beyond the Assabet Spring I see where a squirrel, gray or red, dug through the snow last night in search of acorns. I know it was last night, for it was while the last snow was falling, and the tracks are partly filled by it; they are like this: This squirrel has burrowed to the   ground in many places within a few yards, probing the leaves for acorns in various directions, making a short burrow under the snow, sometimes passing under the snow a yard and coming out at another place; for, though it is somewhat hardened on the surface by the nightly freezing and the hail, it is still quite soft and light beneath next the earth, and a squirrel or mouse can burrow very fast indeed there. I am surprised to find how easily I can pass my hand through it there. In many places it has dropped the leaves, etc., about the mouth of the hole. (The whole snow about ten inches deep.) I see where it sat in a young oak and ate an acorn, dropping the shells on the snow beneath, for there is no track to the shells, but only to the base of the oak. How independently they live, not alarmed, though the snow be two feet deep!

Now, when all the fields and meadows are covered deep with snow, the warm-colored shoots of osiers, red and yellow, rising above it, remind me of flames.

It is astonishing how far a merely well-dressed and good-looking man may go without being challenged by any sentinel. What is called good society will bid high for such.

The man whom the State has raised to high office, like that of governor, for instance, from some, it may be, honest but less respected calling, cannot return to his former humble but profitable pursuits, his old customers will be so shy of him. His ex-honorableness-ship stands seriously in his way, whether he is a lawyer or a shopkeeper. He can't get ex-honorated. So he becomes a sort of State pauper, an object of charity on its hands, which the State is bound in honor to see through and provide still with offices of similar respectability, that he may not come to want. A man who has been President becomes the Ex-President, and can't travel or stay at home anywhere but men will persist in paying respect to his ex-ship. It is cruel

to remember his deeds so long. When his time is out, why can't they let the poor fellow go?

Jan. 4.[1] A clear, cold day.

P. M. — To Walden to examine the ice.

I think it is only such a day as this, when the fields on all sides are well clad with snow, over which the sun shines brightly, that you observe the blue shadows on the snow. I see a little of it to-day.

December 29th there were eight or ten acres of Walden still open. That evening it began to snow and snowed all night, and the remainder of the pond was frozen on that [and] the succeeding night. But on January 1st I was surprised to find all the visible ice snow ice, when I expected that only the eight or ten acres would be; but it appeared that the weight of the snow had sunk the ice already formed and then partly dissolved in the water, which rose above it and partly was frozen with it. The whole ice January 1st was about six inches thick, and I should have supposed that over the greater part of the pond there would be a clear ice about two inches thick on the lower side, yet, where I cut through near the shore, I distinguished two kinds of ice, the upper two and a half inches thick and evidently snow ice, the lower about four inches thick and clearer, yet not remarkably clear.

Some fishermen had, apparently by accident, left two of their lines there, which were frozen in. I could see their tracks leading from hole to hole, where they

[1] [The first page of the manuscript journal which begins here is headed "The Long, Snowy Winter."]

Vol. VIII

had run about day before yesterday, or before the snow, and their dog with them. And the snow was stained with tobacco-juice. They had had lines set in two or three distant coves. They had, apparently, taken no fish, for they had cut no well to put them in. I cut out the lines, the ice being about an inch thick around them, and pulled up a fine yellow pickerel which would weigh two pounds or more. At first I thought there was none, for he was tired of struggling, but soon I felt him. The hook had caught in the outside of his jaws, and the minnow hung entire by his side. It was very cold, and he struggled but a short time, not being able to bend and quirk his tail; in a few minutes became quite stiff as he lay on the snowy ice. The water in his eyes was frozen, so that he looked as if he had been dead a week. About fifteen minutes after, thinking of what I had heard about fishes coming to life again after being frozen, on being put into water, I thought I would try it. This one was to appearance as completely dead as if he had been frozen a week. I stood him up on his tail without bending it. I put him into the water again without removing the hook. The ice melted off, and its eyes looked bright again; and after a minute or two [I] was surprised by a sudden, convulsive quirk of the fish, and a minute or two later by another, and I saw that it would indeed revive, and drew it out again. Yet I do not believe that if it had been frozen solid through and through it would have revived, but only when it is superficially frozen.

This reminded me of the pickerel which I caught here under similar circumstances for Peter Hutchin-

son, and thrust my mittened hands in after. When I put this pickerel in again after half an hour, it did not revive, but I held it there only three or four minutes, not long enough to melt the ice which encased it.

Another man had passed since the last snow fell, and pulled up at least one of the lines. I knew it was to-day and not yesterday by the character of his track, for it was made since the stiff crust formed on this snow last night, a broad depression cracking the crust around; but yesterday it was comparatively soft and moist.

Aunt says that Mr. Hoar tells a story of Abel Davis to this purport: He had once caught a pickerel in the brook near his house and was overheard to say, "Why, who'd 'a' thought to find you here in Temple Brook. With a slice of pork you'll make Rhody" (or whatever the name of his wife was) "and I a good meal." He probably was not much of a fisherman, and could hardly contain himself for joy.

It is snapping cold this night (10 P. M.). I see the frost on the windows sparkle as I go through the passageway with a light.

Jan. 5. One of the coldest mornings. Thermometer −9°, say some.

P. M. — Up river to Hubbard's Bridge.

It has been trying to snow all day, but has not succeeded; as if it were too cold. Though it has been falling all day, there has not been enough to whiten the coat of the traveller. I come to the river, for here it is the best walking. The snow is not so deep over the ice. Near the middle, the superincumbent snow has so far been converted into a coarse snow ice that it will bear me, though occasionally I slump through intervening water to another ice below. Also, perhaps, the snow has been somewhat blown out of the river valley. At any rate, by walking where the ice was frozen last, or over the channel, I can get along quite comfortably, while it is hard travelling through this crusted snow in the fields. Generally, to be sure, the river is but a white snow-field, indistinguishable from the fields, but over the channel there is a thread, commonly, of yellowish porous-looking snow ice.

The hardhack above the snow has this form: 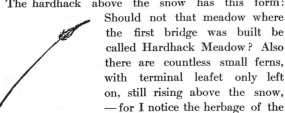 Should not that meadow where the first bridge was built be called Hardhack Meadow? Also there are countless small ferns, with terminal leaflet only left on, still rising above the snow, — for I notice the herbage of the riverside now, — thus, like the large ones in swamps: 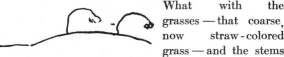 What with the grasses — that coarse, now straw-colored grass — and the stems of the button-bushes, the snow about the button-bushes forms often broad, — several rods broad, — low mounds, nearly burying the bushes, along which the tops of the button-bushes and that broad-bladed, now straw-colored grass still rise, with masses of thin, now black-looking balls, erect or

dangling. The black willows have here and there still a very few little curled and crispy leaves.

The river is last open, methinks, just below a bend,[1] as now at the Bath Place and at Clamshell Hill; and quite a novel sight is the dark water there. How little locomotive now look the boats whose painted sterns I just detect where they are half filled with ice and almost completely buried in snow, so neglected by their improvident owners, — some frozen in the ice, opening their seams, some drawn up on the bank. This is not merely improvidence; it is ingratitude.

Now and then I hear a sort of creaking twitter, maybe from a passing snow bunting. This is the weather for them. I am surprised that Nut Meadow Brook has overflowed its meadow and converted it into that coarse yellowish snow ice. Otherwise it had been a broad snow-field, concealing a little ice under it. There is a narrow thread of open water over its channel.

The thin snow now driving from the north and lodging on my coat consists of those beautiful star crystals, not cottony and chubby spokes, as on the 13th December, but thin and partly transparent crystals. They are about a tenth of an inch in diameter, perfect little wheels with six spokes without a tire, or rather with six perfect little leafets, fern-like, with a distinct straight and slender midrib, raying from the centre. On each side of each midrib there is a transparent thin blade with a crenate edge, thus: How full of the creative genius is the air in which these are generated! I should hardly admire more if real stars fell and

[1] *Vide* the 27th *inst.*

lodged on my coat. Nature is full of genius, full of the divinity; so that not a snowflake escapes its fashioning hand. Nothing is cheap and coarse, neither dewdrops nor snowflakes. Soon the storm increases, — it was already very severe to face, — and the snow comes finer, more white and powdery. Who knows but this is the original form of all snowflakes, but that when I observe these crystal stars falling around me they are but just generated in the low mist next the earth? I am nearer to the source of the snow, its primal, auroral, and golden hour or infancy, but commonly the flakes reach us travel-worn and agglomerated, comparatively without order or beauty, far down in their fall, like men in their advanced age.

As for the circumstances under which this phenomenon occurs, it is quite cold, and the driving storm is bitter to face,[1] though very little snow is falling. It comes almost horizontally from the north. Methinks this kind of snow never falls in any quantity.[2]

A divinity must have stirred within them before the crystals did thus shoot and set. Wheels of the storm-chariots. The same law that shapes the earth-star shapes the snow-star. As surely as the petals of a flower are fixed, each of these countless snow-stars comes whirling to earth, pronouncing thus, with emphasis, the number six. Order, κόσμος.[3]

On the Saskatchewan, when no man of science is there to behold, still down they come, and not the less

[1] *Vide* Mar. 19th.   [2] Yes, it does.
[3] This was the beginning of a storm which reached far and wide and elsewhere was more severe than here.

fulfill their destiny, perchance melt at once on the Indian's face. What a world we live in! where myriads of these little disks, so beautiful to the most prying eye, are whirled down on every traveller's coat, the observant and the unobservant, and on the restless squirrel's fur, and on the far-stretching fields and forests, the wooded dells, and the mountain-tops. Far, far away from the haunts of man, they roll down some little slope, fall over and come to their bearings, and melt or lose their beauty in the mass, ready anon to swell some little rill with their contribution, and so, at last, the universal ocean from which they came. There they lie, like the wreck of chariot-wheels after a battle in the skies. Meanwhile the meadow mouse shoves them aside in his gallery, the schoolboy casts them in his snowball, or the woodman's sled glides smoothly over them, these glorious spangles, the sweeping of heaven's floor. And they all sing, melting as they sing of the mysteries of the number six, — six, six, six. He takes up the water of the sea in his hand, leaving the salt; He disperses it in mist through the skies; He recollects and sprinkles it like grain in six-rayed snowy stars over the earth, there to lie till He dissolves its bonds again.[1]

Found on a young red maple near the water, in Hubbard's riverside grove, a nest, perhaps a size bigger than a summer yellowbird's, chiefly of bark shreds, bound and lined with lint and a little of something like dried hickory blossoms.[2]
A little feather, yellow at the extremity, attached to the

[1] [Channing, p. 112.]   [2] No.

outside. It was on a slanting twig or small branch about eighteen feet high, and I shook it down. The rim of fine shreds of grape-vine bark chiefly, the outer edge being covered with considerable of the droppings of the young birds. I thought it the same kind with that found December 30th *ult.* Can it be a redstart, or is [it] one of the vireos possibly? or a goldfinch? which would account for the yellow-tipped feather.

In the blueberry swamp near by, which was cut down by the ice, another, perhaps a little smaller, of very similar materials but more of the hickory (??) blossoms on the outside beneath, but this was in a nearly upright fork of a red maple about seven feet high. The little nest of June 26th, 1855, looks like the inside of one of these. Upon these two nests found to-day and on that of the 30th December, I find the same sort of dried catkin (apparently *not* hickory) connected with a little sort of brown bud, maybe birch or alder. This makes me suspect they may be all one kind, though the last was in an upright fork and had no droppings on it.

Jan. 6. High wind and howling and driving snowstorm all night, now much drifted. There is a great drift in the front entry and at the crack of every door and on the window-sills. Great drifts on the south of walls.

Clears up at noon, when no vehicle had passed the house.

Frank Morton has brought home, and I opened,

that pickerel of the 4th. It is frozen solid. Yellow spawn as big as a pin-head, with smaller between, enwraps its insides the whole length, half an inch thick. It must spawn very early then. I find in its gullet, or paunch, or maw (the long white bag), three young perch, one of them six inches long, and the tail of a fourth. Its belly was considerably puffed out. Two of the perch lay parallel, side by side, of course head downward, in its gullet (?). The upper and largest perch was so high that he was cut in two in the middle in cutting off the head. And yet it was caught in endeavoring to swallow another large minnow! This is what you may call voracity.

P. M. — To Drifting Cut.

The snow is now probably more than a foot deep on a level.

While I am making a path to the pump, I hear hurried *rippling* notes of birds, look up, and see quite a flock of snow buntings coming to alight amid the currant-tops in the yard. It is a sound almost as if made with their wings. What a pity our yard was made so tidy in the fall with rake and fire, and we have now no tall crop of weeds rising above this snow to invite these birds!

I am come forth to observe the drifts. They are, as usual, on the south side of the walls and fences and, judging from the direction of their ridges, the wind was due north. Behind Monroe's tight board fence it is a regularly swelled, unbroken bank, but behind the wall this side carved into countless scallops, perforations, scrolls, and copings. An open wall is, then,

the best place for a drift. Yet these are not remarkably rich. The snow was perhaps too dry. Perhaps six more inches on a level has fallen, or more. It has not lodged on the trees.

Now, at 4.15, the blue shadows are very distinct on the snow-banks.

On the north side of the Cut, above the crossing, the jutting edges of the drift are quite handsome upon the bank. The snow is raised twelve feet above the track, and it is all scalloped with projecting eaves or copings, like turtle-shells.

They project from three to five feet, and I can stand under them. They are in three or four great layers, one lapping over another like the coarse edge of a shell. Looking along it, they appear somewhat thus: —

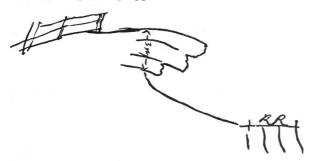

Often this coping has broken by its own weight, and great blocks have fallen down the bank, like smoothed

blocks of white marble. The exquisite purity of the snow and the gracefulness of its curves are remarkable.

Around some houses there is not a single track. Neither man, woman, nor child, dog nor cat nor fowl, has stirred out to-day. There has been no meeting. Yet this afternoon, since the storm, it has not been very bad travelling.

Jan. 7. At breakfast time the thermometer stood at −12°. Earlier it was probably much lower. Smith's was at −24° early this morning. The latches are white with frost at noon. They say there was yet more snow at Boston, two feet even.

They tell how I swung on a gown [?] on the stairway when I was at Chelmsford. The gown [?] gave way; I fell and fainted, and it took two pails of water to bring me to, for I was remarkable for holding my breath in those cases.

Mother tried to milk the cow which Father took on trial, but she kicked at her and spilt the milk. (They say a dog had bitten her teats.) Proctor laughed at her as a city girl, and then he tried, but the cow kicked him over, and he finished by beating her with his cowhide shoe. Captain Richardson milked her warily, standing up. Father came home, and thought he would "brustle right up to her," for she needed much to be milked, but suddenly she lifted her leg and "struck him fair and square right in the muns," knocked him flat, and broke the bridge of his nose, which shows it yet. He distinctly heard her hoof rattle on his nose. This "started the claret," and, without stanching the blood, he at once drove her home to the man he had her of. She ran at some young women by the way, who saved themselves by getting over the wall in haste.

Father complained of the powder in the meeting-house garret at town meeting, but it did not get moved while we lived there. Here he painted over his old signs for guide-boards, and got a fall when painting Hale's (?) factory. Here the bladder John was playing with burst on the hearth. The cow came into the entry after pumpkins. I cut my toe, and was knocked over by a hen with chickens, etc., etc.

Mother tells how, at the brick house, we each had a little garden a few feet square, and I came in one day, having found a potato just sprouted, which by her advice I planted in my garden. Ere long John came in with a potato which he had found and had it planted in his garden, — "Oh, mother, I have found a potato all sprouted. I mean to put it in my garden," etc. Even Helen is said to have found one. But next I came crying that somebody had got my potato, etc., etc., but it was restored to me as the youngest and original discoverer, if not inventor, of the potato, and it grew in *my* garden, and finally its crop was dug by myself and yielded a dinner for the family.

I was kicked down by a passing ox. Had a chicken given me by Lidy — Hannah — and peeped through the keyhole at it. Caught an eel with John. Went to bed with new boots on, and after with cap. "Rasselas" given me, etc., etc. Asked P. Wheeler, "Who owns all the land?" Asked Mother, having got the medal for geography, "Is Boston in Concord?" If I had gone to

more than twenty rods south of the nearest and only birch, and trace them north to it.

Jan. 8. P. M. — To Walden.

The snow is about a foot, or probably a little more, deep on a level, and considerably drifted, but on the pond it is not more than five inches deep on an average, being partly turned into snow ice by the sinking of the ice, and perhaps partly blown off.

Many catbird-nests about the pond. In apparently one I see a snake's slough interwoven. The leaves of red oak shrubs are still quite bloody-colored. All of the pitch pine cones that I see, but one, are open.[1] I see prying into the black fruit of the alder, along the pond-side, a single probably lesser redpoll (?). Yellowish breast and distinct white bar on wing.

Monroe is fishing there. As usual, a *great* pickerel had bitten and ran off, and was lost, he supposed, among the brush by the shore. He tells of an eel up the North Branch that weighed seven pounds; also that George Melvin, spearing one night, speared a large owl (probably cat owl) that sat near by.

For a couple of days the cars have been very much delayed by the snow, and it is now drifting somewhat. The fine dry snow is driving over the fields like steam, if you look toward the sun, giving a new form to the surface, spoiling the labor of the track-repairers, gradually burying the rails. The surface of the snow on the pond is finely scored in many places by the oak leaves which have been blown across it. They have furrowed deeper

[1] *Vide* 22d *inst.*

Miss Wheeler a little longer, should have received the chief prize book, "Henry Lord Mayor," etc., etc.

P. M. — Up river.

The snow is much deeper on the river than it was, — on an average, eight or nine inches. The cold weather has brought the crows, and for the first time this winter I hear them cawing amid the houses. I noticed yesterday, from three to six feet behind or northwest of a small elm, a curve in a drift answering to the tree, showing how large an eddy it had produced. The whole surface of the snow on fields and river is composed now of flat, rough little drifts, like the surface of some rough slaty rocks. Hardly anywhere is the ice visible now.

It is completely frozen at the Hubbard's Bath bend now, — a small strip of dark ice, thickly sprinkled with those rosettes of crystals, two or three inches in diameter, this surrounded by a broad border of yellowish spew. The water has oozed out from the thinnest part of the black ice, and I see a vapor curling up from it. There is also much vapor in the air, looking toward the woods. I go along the edge of the Hubbard Meadow woods, the north side, where the snow is gathered, light and up to my middle, shaking down birds' nests. Returning, just before sunset, the few little patches of ice look green as I go from the sun (which is in clouds). It is probably a constant phenomenon in cold weather when the ground is covered with snow and the sun is low, morning or evening, and you are looking from it.

I see birch scales (bird-like) on the snow on the river

than a mouse's track and might puzzle a citizen. They are more frisky than a squirrel. Many of the young oaks appear not to have lost any leaves yet. They are so full of them that they still sustain some masses of snow, as if there were birds' nests for a core. I see the great tracks of white rabbits that have run and frisked in the night along the pond-side.

Jan. 9. Clear, cold morning. Smith's thermometer — 16°; ours — 14° at breakfast time, — 6° at 9 A. M.

3 P. M. — To Beck Stow's.

The thermometer at + 2°. When I return at 4.30, it is at — 2°. Probably it has been below zero *far* the greater part of the day. I meet choppers, apparently coming home early on account of the cold. I wade through the swamp, where the snow lies light eighteen inches[1] deep on a level, a few leaves of andromedas, etc., peeping out. (I am a-birds'-nesting.) The mice have been out and run over it. I see one large bush of winter-berries still quite showy, though somewhat discolored by the cold. The rabbits have run in paths about the swamp. Go now anywhere in the swamp and fear no water. The fisherman whom I saw on Walden last night will find his lines well frozen in this morning.

In passing through the deep cut on the new Bedford road, [I saw] that a little sand, which was pretty coarse, almost gravel, had fallen from the bank, and was blown over the snow, here and there. The surface of the snow was diversified by those slight drifts, or perhaps cliffs, which are left a few inches high (like the fracture of

[1] Two feet. *Vide* Jan. 12th.

slate rocks), with a waved outline, and all the sand was

collected in waving lines just on the edge of these little drifts, in ridges, maybe an eighth of an inch high. This may help decide how those drifts (?) or cliffs (?) are formed.[1]

It has not been so cold throughout the day, before, this winter. I hear the boots of passing travellers squeak.

Jan. 10. The weather has considerably moderated; — 2° at breakfast time (it was — 8° at seven last evening); but this has been the coldest night probably. You lie with your feet or legs curled up, waiting for morning, the sheets shining with frost about your mouth. Water left by the stove is frozen thickly, and what you sprinkle in bathing falls on the floor ice. The house plants are all frozen and soon droop and turn black. I look out on the roof of a cottage covered a foot deep with snow, wondering how the poor children in its garret, with their few rags, contrive to keep their toes warm. I mark the white smoke from its chimney, whose contracted wreaths are soon dissipated in this stinging air, and think of the size of their wood-pile, and again I try to realize how they panted for a breath of cool air those sultry nights last summer. Realize it now if you can. Recall the hum of the mosquito.

[1] Yet when it blows and drifts again it presents a similar appearance.

great yellow and red forward-looking buds of the azalea, the plump red ones of the blueberry, and the fine sharp red ones of the panicled andromeda, sleeping along its stem, the speckled black alder, the rapid-growing dogwood, the pale-brown and cracked blueberry, etc. Even a little shining bud which lies sleeping behind its twig and dreaming of spring, perhaps half concealed by ice, is object enough. I feel myself upborne on the andromeda bushes beneath the snow, as on a springy basketwork, then down I go up to my middle in the deep but silent snow, which has no sympathy with my mishap. Beneath the level of this snow how many sweet berries will be hanging next August!

This freezing weather I see the pumps dressed in mats and old clothes or bundled up in straw. Fortunate he who has placed his cottage on the south side of some high hill or some dense wood, and not on the middle of the Great Fields, where there is no hill nor tree to shelter it. There the winds have full sweep, and such a day as yesterday the house is but a fence to stay the drifting snow. Such is the piercing wind, no man loiters between his house and barn. The road-track is soon obliterated, and the path which leads round to the back of the house, dug this morning, is filled up again, and you can no longer see the tracks of the master of the house, who only an hour ago took refuge in some half-subterranean apartment there. You know only by an occasional white wreath of smoke from his chimney, which is at once snapped up by the hungry air, that he sits warming his wits there within, studying the almanac to learn how long it is before spring. But his

It seems that the snow-storm of Saturday night was a remarkable one, reaching many hundred miles along the coast. It is said that some thousands passed the night in cars.

The kitchen windows were magnificent last night, with their frost sheaves, surpassing any cut or ground glass.

I love to wade and flounder through the swamp now,[1] these bitter cold days when the snow lies deep on the ground, and I need travel but little way from the town to get to a Nova Zembla solitude, — to wade through the swamps, all snowed up, untracked by man, into which the fine dry snow is still drifting till it is even with the tops of the water andromeda and halfway up the high blueberry bushes. I penetrate to islets inaccessible in summer, my feet slumping to the sphagnum far out of sight beneath, where the alder berry glows yet and the azalea buds, and perchance a single tree sparrow or a chickadee lisps by my side, where there are few tracks even of wild animals; perhaps only a mouse or two have burrowed up by the side of some twig, and hopped away in straight lines on the surface of the light, deep snow, as if too timid to delay, to another hole by the side of another bush; and a few rabbits have run in a path amid the blueberries and alders about the edge of the swamp. This is instead of a Polar Sea expedition and going after Franklin. There is but little life and but few objects, it is true. We are reduced to admire buds, even like the partridges, and bark, like the rabbits and mice, — the

[1] Remembering the walk of yesterday.

Vol. VIII

neighbor, who, only half a mile off, has placed his house in the shelter of a wood, is digging out of a drift his pile of roots and stumps, hauled from the swamp, at which he regularly dulls his axe and saw, reducing them to billets that will fit his stove. With comparative safety and even comfort he labors at this mine.

As for the other, the windows give no sign of inhabitants, for they are frosted over as if they were ground glass, and the curtains are down beside. The path is snowed up, and all tracks to and fro. No sound issues from within. It remains only to examine the chimney's nostrils. I look long and sharp at it, and fancy that I see some smoke against [the] sky there, but this [is] deceptive, for, as we are accustomed to walk up to an empty fireplace and imagine that we feel some heat from it, so I have convinced myself that I saw smoke issuing from the chimney of a house which had not been inhabited for twenty years. I had so vivid an idea of smoke curling up from a chimney's top that no painter could have matched my imagination. It was as if the spirits of the former inhabitants, revisiting their old haunts, were once more boiling a spiritual kettle below, — a small whitish-bluish cloud, almost instantly dissipated, as if the fire burned with a very clear flame, or else, the postmeridian hours having arrived, it were partially raked up, and the inhabitants were taking their siesta.

P. M. — Worked on flower-press.

Jan. 11. P. M. — To Walden.
Cold as the weather has been for some days, it [is]

melting a little on the south side of houses to-day for the first time for quite a number of days, though the 9th was the coldest day thus far, the thermometer hardly going above zero during the day. Yet whenever I have been to Walden, as January 4th, 8th, and to-day, I have found much water under the snow above the ice, though there is but about five inches, both snow and water, above the ice. January 4th was the coldest day that I have been there, and yet I slumped through the snow into water, which evidently was prevented from freezing at once by the snow. I think that you may find water on the ice thus at any time, however cold, and however soon it may freeze. Probably some of the overflow I noticed on the river a few days ago was owing to the weight of the snow, as there has been no thaw.

Observed that the smooth sumachs about the north side of the Wyman meadow had been visited by partridges and a great many of the still crimson berries were strewn on the snow.[1] There they had eaten them, perched on the twigs. Elsewhere they had tracked the snow from bush to bush, visiting almost every bush

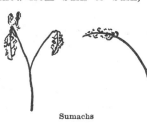

and leaving their traces. The mice, also, had run from the base of one sumach to that of another on all sides, though there was no entrance to the ground there. Probably they had climbed the

Sumachs

[1] The same next day on the other side the pond.

Mother reminds me that when we lived at the Parkman house she lost a ruff a yard and a half long and with an edging three yards long to it, which she had laid on the grass to whiten, and, looking for it, she saw a robin tugging at the tape string of a stay on the line. He would repeatedly get it in his mouth, fly off and be brought up when he got to the end of his tether. Miss Ward thereupon tore a fine linen handkerchief into strips and threw them out, and the robin carried them all off. She had no doubt that he took the ruff.

It is commonly said that fishes are long-lived on account of the equable temperature of their element. The temperature of the body of Walden may perhaps range from 85° — perhaps at bottom much less — down to 32°, or 53°, while that of the air ranges from 100° down to − 28°, or 128°, more than twice as much. Yet how large a portion of animal life becomes dormant or migrates in the winter! And on those that remain with us there is an increase of fur, and probably of down, corresponding to the increased cold. If there is no corresponding thickening of the integument or scales of fishes on the approach of winter, they would seem to enjoy no advantage over land animals. Beside their thick coats, most land animals seek some comparatively warm and sheltered place in which to sleep, but where do the fishes resort? They may sink to the bottom, but it is scarcely so warm there as at the bottom of a gray rabbit's or a fox's burrow. Yet the fish is a tender animal in respect to cold. Pull him out in the coldest weather, and he at once becomes encased in ice and as stiff as a stake, and a fox (?)

stems for berries. Most of the bunches now hang half broken off, by time, etc.[1]

The lespedeza, now a very pale brown, looks thus: —

The sunsets, I think, are now particularly interesting. The colors of the west seem more than usually warm, perhaps by contrast with this simple snow-clad earth over which we look and the clear cold sky, — a sober but extensive redness, almost every night passing into a dun. There is nothing to distract our attention from it.

Monroe, who left his lines in Walden on the 8th, cut them out to-day, but he got no fish, though all his bait were gone.

The *January Sunsets*.

To-day I burn the first stick of the wood which I bought and did not get from the river. What I have still left of the river wood, added to what of it I reserve for other uses, would last me a week longer.

Animals that live on such cheap food as buds and leaves and bark and wood, like partridges and rabbits and wild mice, never need apprehend a famine.

I have not done wondering at that voracity of the pickerel, — three fresh perch and part of another in its maw! If there are a thousand pickerel in the pond, and they eat but one meal a day, there go a thousand perch or shiners for you out of this small pond. One year would require 365,000! not distinguishing frogs. Can it be so? The fishermen tell me that when they catch the most, the fish are fullest.

[1] See Jan. 30th.

stands at his ease on the ice devouring him. Frogs, which, perchance, are equally tender, and must (?) come to the air occasionally, are therefore compelled [to] go into the mud and become dormant. They may be said to live there in a southern climate. Even the tough mud turtle possesses a southern constitution. He would snap in vain, and soon cease snapping, at the northwest wind when the thermometer is at 25° below zero. Wild mice and spiders and snow-fleas would be his superiors.

Jan. 12. Moderating, though at zero at 9 A. M.

P. M. — To Andromeda Swamps, measuring snow. It is a fortnight since we had about a foot of snowfall on two or three inches which was firmly crusted, and a week since about six inches fell upon the last, — I guess at these depths, — and we have had clear cold weather ever since. I carry a four-foot stick marked in inches, striking it down as far as it will go at every tenth step. First, beginning in the first field west of the railroad causeway, four to six rods from the railroad, and walking parallel with the railroad, — open fields north to south: —

[For table of measurements, see next page.]

		145	309			
	19	10	10	10	11	Then Trillium, a
	11	8	12	8	8	thick, chiefly pine
	14	9	11	8	10	wood, seventy-
	10	14	6	8	13	five years old.
	7	15	8	12	9	8 North to south.
	12	13	7	8	10	12
	9	22	9	12	13	8
	7	wall	10	14 fence)	10	11
apple	6	7	11	9	10	8
tree	7	6	9	7	wall	11
	9	7	11	10	20	11
	9	7	9	10	16	9
	10	7	422	10	598	8
	10	8	Then cross	7	73)728	9
	6	10	to east of	9	Average	10
	9	12	railroad,	14	say 10²	10
	145¹	9	six rods	9		7
		309	off, in	11		10
			Stow's	422		12
			meadow.	598		8
						9
						10
						11
					19)182 (say	
					9½	

Other things being equal, the snow should be deeper in woods than in open fields because the trunks of trees take up room there, but this may be more than balanced by what is dissipated on the branches.

¹ [A mistake in addition here. The column foots up 155.]

² Add 2 for ice at bottom to all the depths of snow to Feb. 12th, q. v.

Then sprout-land between railroad and Andromeda Pond, down-hill toward the west.

The first Andromeda Swamp from east to west. The snow in the swamp was within about three inches of the top of the *highest* andromeda bushes and was swelled about three or four inches higher there than between such. Foxes had sunk from one to four inches in it.

Wheeler's squirrel wood, west of railroad, measuring from south to north parallel with railroad. An average mixed pine and oak wood, not very level, say seventy-five years old.

15	24	12
11	16	9
20	20	10
17	26	12
17	29	10
13	26	10
14	16	12
16	19	12
15	27	8
17	27	9
15	24	11
17	21	7
12)187(say 15½ ¹	27	7
	22	12
	16	12
	17	8
	28	7
	33	12
	28	12
	30	19)192(say 10 ³
	20)476(say 23⅘ ²	

The result of 34 measures on Walden, eight or ten acres of which did not freeze till during the snow of a fortnight ago, gave 5⅙.

¹ 17½.   ² 25⅘.   ³ 12.

Vol. VIII

Probably there is less snow in the woods than in open land, though it may lie high and light.

In the swamp the dull-red leaves of the andromeda were just peeping out, the snow lying not quite level, but with gentle swells about the highest clumps of bushes.

Deep as the snow was, it was no harder but perhaps easier walking there than in summer. It would not much impede a mouse running about below.

Though the snow is only ten inches deep on a level, farmers affirm that it is two feet deep, confidently.

Jan. 13. Sunrise. — A heavy lodging snow, almost rain, has been falling — how long? — coming from the eastward. The weather comparatively warm, but windy. It will probably turn to rain. Say four or five inches deep. It sticks to the sides of the houses.

Took to pieces a pensile nest which I found the 11th on the south shore of Walden on an oak sapling (red or black), about fifteen feet from the ground. Though small, it measures three inches by three in the extreme, and was hung between two horizontal twigs or in a fork forming about a right angle, the third side being regularly rounded without any very stiff material. The twigs extended two or three inches beyond the nest. The bulk of it is composed of fine shreds or fibres, pretty long (say three to six inches), of apparently inner oak (?) bark, judging from some scraps of the epidermis adhering. It looks at first sight like sedge or grass. The bottom, which I accidentally broke off and disturbed the arrangement of, was composed of this

and white and pitch pine needles and little twigs about the same size and form, rough with little leaf-stalks or feet (probably hemlock (?) ¹), and also strips and curls of paper birch epidermis, and some hornet or other wasp nest used like the last. I mention the most abundant material first. Probably the needles and twigs were used on account of their curved form ² and elasticity, to give shape to the bottom. The sides, which were not so thick, were composed of bark shreds, paper birch, and hornet-nest (the two latter chiefly outside, probably to bind and conceal and keep out the wind), agglutinated together. But most pains was taken with the thin edge and for three quarters of an inch down, where, beside the bark-fibres, birch paper, and hornets' nest, some silky reddish-brown and also white fibre was used to bind all with, almost spun into threads and passed over the twigs and agglutinated to them, or over the bark edge. The shreds of birch paper were smaller there, and the hornets' nest looked as if it had been reduced to a pulp by the bird and spread very thinly here and there over all, mixed with the brown silk. This last looked like cow's hair, but as I found a piece of a small brown cocoon, though a little paler, I suspect it was from that. ³ The white may have been from a cocoon, or else vegetable silk. Probably a vireo's nest, maybe red-eye's.

In our workshops we pride ourselves on discovering a use for what had previously been regarded as waste, but how partial and accidental our economy compared

¹ Yes, they are.   ² Perhaps bent by the bird.

³ Some of the same on my red-eye's nest.

with Nature's. In Nature nothing is wasted. Every decayed leaf and twig and fibre is only the better fitted to serve in some other department, and all at last are gathered in her compost-heap. What a wonderful genius it is that leads the vireo to select the tough fibres of the inner bark, instead of the more brittle grasses, for its basket, the elastic pine-needles and the twigs, curved as they dried to give it form, and, as I suppose, the silk of cocoons, etc., etc., to bind it together with! I suspect that extensive use is made of these abandoned cocoons by the birds, and they, if anybody, know where to find them. There were at least seven materials used in constructing this nest, and the bird visited as many distinct localities many times, always with the purpose or design to find some particular one of these materials, as much as if it had said to itself, "Now I will go and get some old hornets' nest from one of those that I saw last fall down in the maple swamp — perhaps thrust my bill into them — or some silk from those cocoons I saw this morning."

It turned to rain before noon, four or five inches of very moist snow or sleet having fallen.

Jan. 14. Sunrise. — Snows again. I think that you can best tell from what side the storm came by observing on which side of the trees the snow is plastered.

The crows are flitting about the houses and alight upon the elms.

After snowing an inch or two it cleared up at night. Boys, etc., go about straddling the fences, on the crust.

Jan. 15. A fine, clear winter day.

P. M. — To Hemlocks on the crust, slumping in every now and then.

A bright day, not cold. I can comfortably walk without gloves, yet my shadow is a most celestial blue. This only requires a clear bright day and snow-clad earth, not great cold. I cross the river on the crust with some hesitation. The snow appears considerably deeper than the 12th, maybe four or five inches deeper, and the river is indicated by a mere depression in it.

In the street not only fences but trees are obviously shortened, as by a flood. You are sensible that you are walking at a level a foot or more above the usual one. Seeing the tracks where a leaf had blown along and then tacked and finally doubled and returned on its trail, I thought it must be the tracks of some creature new to me.

I find under the hemlocks, in and upon the snow, apparently brought down by the storm, an abundance of those little dead hemlock twigs described on the 13th. They are remarkably slender, and without stiffness like the fir (and I think spruce) twigs, and this gives the hemlock its peculiar grace. These are not yet curved much, and perhaps they got that form from being placed in the nest.

Jan. 16. 8 A. M. — Down railroad, measuring snow, having had one bright day since the last flake fell; but, as there was a crust which would bear yesterday

(as to-day), it cannot have settled much. The last storms have been easterly and northeasterly.

Why so much (five and one half inches) more now in the woods than on the 12th, as compared with open fields? Was the driving snow caught in a small wood, or did it settle less in the rain there, or since the snow on account of bushes?

I hear flying over (and see) a snow bunting, — a clear loud *tcheep* or *tcheop*, sometimes rapidly trilled or quavered, — calling its mates.

With this snow the fences are scarcely an obstruction to the traveller; he easily steps over them. Often they are buried. I suspect it is two and a half feet deep in Andromeda Swamps now. The snow is much deeper in yards, roads, and all small inclosures than in broad fields.

Jan. 17. Henry Shattuck tells me that the quails come almost every day and get some saba beans within two or three rods of his house, — some which he neglected to gather. Probably the deep snow drives them to it.

Jan. 18. J. B. Moore says that he has caught twenty pounds of pickerel in Walden in one winter, etc., and had had nearly as good luck five or six times the same winter there, not less than ten pounds at one time. Suppose, then, that he has caught fifty pickerel there in one winter, and all others the same winter a hundred and fifty, you have two hundred caught in one winter. I suspect there are as many as two thousand that will

weigh a pound. Five men caught three hundred and thirty-three pounds in a pond in Eastham in one day this winter, say the papers, — largest five and a half pounds.

Analyzed a nest which I found January 7th in an upright fork of a red maple sapling on the edge of Hubbard's Swamp Wood, north side, near river, about eight feet from the ground, the deep grooves made by the twigs on each side. It *may* be a yellowbird's.

Extreme breadth outside, three inches; inside, one and a half. Extreme height outside, three inches; inside, one and five eighths; sides, three quarters of an inch thick.

It is composed of seven principal materials. (I name the most abundant first; I mean most abundant when compressed.)

1. Small compact lengths of silvery pappus about seven eighths of an inch long, perhaps of erechthites, one half inch deep and nearly pure, a very warm bed, chiefly concealed, just beneath the lining inside.

2. Slender catkins, often with the buds and twig ends (of perhaps hazel), throughout the whole bottom and sides, making it thick but open and light, mixed with

(3) milkweed silk, *i. e.* fibres like flax, but white, being bleached, also in sides and rim, some of it almost threadlike, white with some of the dark epidermis. From the pods?[1]

4. Thin and narrow strips of grape-vine bark, chiefly in the rim and sides for three quarters of an inch down, and here and there throughout.

[1] No, I am about certain, from comparison, that it is the fibres of the bark of the stem. *Vide* 19th *inst.*

5. Wads of apparently brown fern wool, mixed with the last three.

6. Some finer pale-brown and thinner shreds of bark within the walls and bottom, apparently not grape. If this were added to the grape, these five materials would be not far from equally abundant.

7. Some very fine pale-brown wiry fibres for a lining, just above the pappus and somewhat mixed with it, perhaps for coolness, being springy.

Directly beneath the pappus were considerable other shreds of grape and the other bark, short and broken. In the rim and sides some cotton ravellings and some short shreds of fish-line or crow-fence. A red maple leaf within the bottom; a kernel of corn just under the lining of fibres (perhaps dropped by a crow or blackbird or jay or squirrel while the nest was building). A few short lengths of stubble or weed stems in the bottom and sides. A very little brown wool, like, apparently, that in the nest last described, which may be brown fern wool. The milkweed and fern wool conspicuous without the rim and about the twigs. I was most struck by that mass of pure pappus under the inside lining.

P. M. — To Walden to learn the temperature of the water.

The snow is so deep at present in the streets that it is very difficult turning out, and there are cradle-holes between this and the post-office. The sidewalks being blotted out, the street, like a woodman's path, looks like a hundred miles up country. I see where children

have for some days come to school across the fields on the crust from Abiel Wheeler's to the railroad crossing. I see their tracks in the slight snow upon the crust which fell the 14th. They save a great distance and enjoy the novelty.

This is a very mild, melting winter day, but clear and bright, yet I see the blue shadows on the snow at Walden. The snow lies very level there, about ten inches deep, and for the most part bears me as I go across with my hatchet. I think I never saw a more elysian blue than my shadow. I am turned into a tall blue Persian from my cap to my boots, such as no mortal dye can produce, with an amethystine hatchet in my hand. I am in raptures at my own shadow. What if the substance were of as ethereal a nature? Our very shadows are no longer black, but a celestial blue. This has nothing to do with cold, methinks, but the sun must not be too low.

I cleared a little space in the snow, which was nine to ten inches deep over the deepest part of the pond, and cut through the ice, which was about seven inches thick, only the first four inches, perhaps, snow ice, the other three clear. The moment I reached the water, it gushed up and overflowed the ice, driving me out this yard in the snow, where it stood at last two and a half inches deep above the ice.

The thermometer indicated $33\frac{1}{2}°$ at top and $34\frac{2}{3}°$ when drawn up rapidly from thirty feet beneath. So, *apparently,* it is not much warmer beneath.

Goodwin was fishing there. He says he once caught fifty pounds of pickerel here in two days; he thought

twenty-five or thirty fishes. Thought that there were many hundred caught here in a winter; that nearly all were females.

Observed some of those little hard galls on the high blueberry, pecked or eaten into by some bird (or *possibly* mouse), for the little white grubs which lie curled up in them. What entomologists the birds are! Most men do not suspect that there are grubs in them, and how secure the latter seem under these thick dry shells! Yet there is no secret but it is confided to some one.

Jan. 19. Another bright winter day.
P. M. — To river to get some water asclepias to see what birds' nests are made of.

The only open place in the river between Hunt's Bridge and the railroad bridge is a small space against Merrick's pasture just below the Rock.[1] As usual, just below a curve, in shallow water, with the added force of the Assabet.

The willow osiers of last year's growth on the pollards in Shattuck's row, Merrick's pasture, from four to seven feet long, are *perhaps* as bright as in the spring, the lower half yellow, the upper red, but they are a *little* shrivelled in the bark.

Measured again the great elm in front of Charles Davis's on the Boston road, which he is having cut down. The chopper, White, has taken off most of the limbs and just begun, tried his axe, on the foot of the

[1] Hubbard's Bridge and, I have no doubt, Lee's Bridge, as I learned in my walk the next day.

tree. He will probably fall it on Monday, or the 21st. At the smallest place between the ground and the limbs, seven feet from the ground, it is fifteen feet and two inches in circumference; at one foot from the ground on the lowest side, twenty-three feet and nine inches. White is to have ten dollars for taking off the necessary limbs and cutting it down merely, help being found him. He began on Wednesday. Davis and the neighbors were much alarmed by the creaking in the late storms, for fear it would fall on their roofs. It stands two or three feet into Davis's yard.

As I came home through the village at 8.15 P. M., by a bright moonlight, the moon nearly full and not more than 18° from the zenith, the wind northwest, but not strong, and the air pretty cold, I saw the melon-rind arrangement of the clouds on a larger scale and more distinct than ever before. There were eight or ten courses of clouds, so broad that with equal intervals of blue sky they occupied the whole width of the heavens, broad white cirro-stratus in perfectly regular curves from west to east across the whole sky. The four middle ones, occupying the greater part of the visible cope, were particularly distinct. They were all as regularly arranged as the lines on a melon, and with much straighter sides, as if cut with a knife. I hear that it attracted the attention of those who were abroad at 7 P. M., and now, at 9 P. M., it is scarcely less remarkable. On one side of the heavens, north or south, the intervals of blue look almost black by contrast. There is now, at nine, a strong wind from the northwest. Why do these bars extend east and west? Is it the influence of the sun, which set so long ago? or of the rotation of the earth? The bars which I notice so often, morning and evening, are apparently connected with the sun at those periods.

In Oliver N. Bacon's History of Natick, page 235, it is said that, of phænogamous plants, "upwards of 800 species were collected from Natick soil in three years' time, by a single individual." I suspect it was Bacon the surveyor. There is given a list of those which are rare in that vicinity. Among them are the following which I do not know to grow here: *Actæa rubra* (W.),[1] *Asclepias tuberosa,*[2] *Alopecurus pratensis,*[1] *Corallorhiza odontorhiza* (?) (Nutt.), *Drosera filiformis* (Nutt.), *Ledum latifolium,*[1] *Malaxis lilifolia* (W.) (what in Gray?), *Sagina procumbens.*[1] Among those rare there but common here are *Calla Virginica, Glecoma hederacea, Iris prismatica, Lycopus Virginicus, Mikania scandens, Prunus borealis, Rhodora Canadensis, Xyris aquatica, Zizania aquatica.* They, as well as we, have *Equisetum hyemale, Kalmia glauca, Liatris scariosa, Ulmus fulva, Linnæa borealis, Pyrola maculata,* etc., etc.

Bacon quotes White, who quotes Old Colony Memorial account of manners and customs, etc., of our ancestors.

Bacon says that the finest elm in Natick stands in front of Thomas F. Hammond's house, and was set out "about the year 1760." "The trunk, five feet from the ground, measures fifteen and a half feet." G. Emerson gives a different account, *q. v.*

[1] Found since.   [2] Probably here.

has used perhaps the strongest fibre which the fields afforded and which most civilized men have not detected.

Knocked down the bottom of that summer yellow-bird's nest made on the oak at the Island last summer. It is chiefly of fern wool and also, *apparently,* some sheep's wool (?), with a fine green moss (apparently that which grows on button-bushes) inmixed, and some milkweed fibre, and all very firmly agglutinated together. Some shreds of grape-vine bark about it. Do not know what portion of the whole nest it is.

Jan. 20. In my experience I have found nothing so truly impoverishing as what is called wealth, *i. e.* the command of greater means than you had before possessed, though comparatively few and slight still, for you thus inevitably acquire a more expensive habit of living, and even the very same necessaries and comforts cost you more than they once did. Instead of gaining, you have lost some independence, and if your income should be suddenly lessened, you would find yourself poor, though possessed of the same means which once made you rich. Within the last five years I have had the command of a little more money than in the previous five years, for I have sold some books and some lectures; yet I have not been a whit better fed or clothed or warmed or sheltered, not a whit richer, except that I have been less concerned about my living, but perhaps my life has been the less serious for it, and, to balance it, I feel now that there is a possibility of

Observed within the material of a robin's nest, this afternoon, a cherry-stone.

Gathered some dry water milkweed stems to compare with the materials of the bird's nest of the 18th. The bird used, I am almost certain, the fibres of the bark of the stem, — not the pods, — just beneath the epidermis; only the bird's is older and more fuzzy and finer, like worn twine or string. The fibres and bark have otherwise the same appearance under the microscope. I stripped off some bark about one sixteenth of an inch wide and six inches long and, separating ten or twelve fibres from the epidermis, rolled it in my fingers, making a thread about the ordinary size. This I could not break by direct pulling, and no man could. I doubt if a thread of flax or hemp of the same size could be made so strong. What an admirable material for the Indian's fish-line! I can easily get much longer fibres. I hold a piece of the dead weed in my hands, strip off a narrow shred of the bark before my neighbor's eyes and separate ten or twelve fibres as fine as a hair, roll them in my fingers, and offer him the thread to try its strength. He is surprised and mortified to find that he cannot break it. Probably both the Indian and the bird discovered for themselves this same (so to call it) wild hemp. The corresponding fibres of the mikania seem not so divisible, become not so fine and fuzzy; though somewhat similar, are not nearly so strong. I have a hang-bird's nest from the riverside, made almost entirely of this, in narrow shreds or strips with the epidermis on, wound round and round the twigs and woven into a basket. That is, this bird

failure. Who knows but I *may* come upon the town, if, as is likely, the public want no more of my books, or lectures (which last is already the case)? Before, I was much likelier to take the town upon my shoulders. That is, I have lost some of my independence on them, when they would say that I had gained an independence. If you wish to give a man a sense of poverty, give him a thousand dollars. The next hundred dollars he gets will not be worth more than ten that he used to get. Have pity on him; withhold your gifts.

P. M. — Up river to Hollowell place.

I see the blue between the cakes of snow cast out in making a path, in the triangular recesses, though it is pretty cold, but the sky is completely overcast.

It is now good walking on the river, for, though there has been no thaw since the snow came, a great part of it has been converted into snow ice by sinking the old ice beneath the water, and the crust of the rest is stronger than in the fields, because the snow is so shallow and has been so moist. The river is thus an advantage as a highway, not only in summer and when the ice is bare in the winter, but even when the snow lies very deep in the fields. It is invaluable to the walker, being now not only the most interesting, but, excepting the narrow and unpleasant track in the highways, the only practicable route. The snow never lies so deep over it as elsewhere, and, if deep, it sinks the ice and is soon converted into snow ice to a great extent, beside being blown out of the river valley. Neither is it drifted here. Here, where you cannot walk at all in the summer, is better walking than elsewhere in the winter. But what a different aspect the river's brim now from what it wears in summer! I do not this moment hear an insect hum, nor see a bird, nor a flower. That museum of animal and vegetable life, a meadow, is now reduced to a uniform level of white snow, with only half a dozen kinds of shrubs and weeds rising here and there above it.

Nut Meadow Brook is open in the river meadow, but not into the river. It is remarkable that the short strip in the middle below the Island (*vide* yesterday) should be the only open place between Hunt's Bridge and Hubbard's, at least, — probably as far as Lee's. The river has been frozen solidly ever since the 7th, and that small open strip of yesterday (about one rod wide and in middle) was probably not more than a day or two old. It is very rarely closed, I suspect, *in all places* more than two weeks at a time. Ere long it wears its way up to the light, and its blue artery again appears here and there. In one place close to the river, where the forget-me-not grows, that springy place under the bank just above the railroad bridge, the snow is quite melted and the bare ground and flattened weeds exposed for four or five feet.

Broke open a frozen nest of mud and stubble in a black willow, probably a robin's, in which were a snail (?) shell ⟲ and a skunk-cabbage seed (?). Were they ⟲ not left there by a mouse? Or could they ⟲ have been taken up with the mud? They were somewhat in the mud. A downy woodpecker without red on head the only bird seen in this walk [?]. I stand within twelve feet.

The arrangement of the clouds last night attracted attention in various parts of the town.

A probable kingbird's nest, on a small horizontal branch of a young swamp white oak, amid the twigs, about ten feet from ground. This tree is very scraggy; has numerous short twigs at various angles with the branches, making it unpleasant to climb and affording support to birds' nests. The nest is round, running to rather a sharp point on one side beneath. Extreme diameter outside, four and a half to five inches; within, three inches; depth within, two inches; without, four or more. The principal materials are ten, in the order of their abundance thus: —

1. Reddish and gray twigs, some a foot and more in length, which are cranberry vines, with now and then a leaf on, probably such as were torn up by the rakers. Some are as big round as a knitting-needle, and would be taken for a larger bush. These make the stiff mass of the outside above and rim.

2. Woody roots, rather coarser, intermixed from waterside shrubs. Probably some are from cranberry vines. These are mixed with the last and with the bottom.

3. Softer and rather smaller roots and root-fibres of herbaceous plants, mixed with the last and a little further inward, for the harshest are always most external.

4. (Still to confine myself to the order of abundance) withered flowers and short bits of the gray downy stems of the fragrant everlasting; these more or less compacted and apparently agglutinated from the mass of

Vol. VIII

the solid bottom, and more loose, with the stems run down to a point on one side the bottom.

5. What I think is the fibrous growth of a willow, moss-like with a wiry dark-colored hair-like stem (pos-

sibly it is a moss). This, with or without the tuft, is the lining, and lies contiguous in the sides and bottom.

6. What looks like brown decayed leaves and confervæ from the dried bottom of the riverside, mixed with the everlasting-tops internally in the solid bottom.

7. Some finer brown root-fibres, chiefly between the lining of No. 6 and hair and the coarser fibres of No. 3.

8. A dozen whitish cocoons, mixed with the everlasting-tops and dangling about the bottom peak externally; a few within the solid bottom. Also eight or ten very minute cocoons mixed with these, attached in a cluster to the top of an everlasting.

9. A few black much branched roots (?) (perhaps some utricularia from the dried bottom of river), mixed with Nos. 2 and 3.

10. Some horsehair, white and black, together with No. 5 forming the lining.

There are also, with the cocoons and everlasting-tops externally, one or two cotton-grass heads, one small white feather, and a little greenish-fuscous moss from the button-bush, and, in the bottom, a small shred of grape-vine bark.

Jan. 21. Four men, cutting at once, began to fell the big elm (*vide* 19th) at 10 A. M., went to dinner at 12, and got through at 2.30 P. M. They used a block and tackle with five falls, fastened to the base of a buttonwood, and drawn by a horse, to pull it over the right way; so it fell without harm down the road. One said he pulled twenty turns. I measured it at 3 P. M., just after the top had been cut off.

It was 15 feet to the first crotch. At 75 feet, the most upright and probably highest limb was cut off, and measured 27 inches in circumference. As near as I could tell from the twigs on the snow, and what the choppers said who had just removed the top, it was about 108 feet high. At 15 feet from the stump, it divided into two parts, about an equal size. One was decayed and broken in the fall, being undermost, the other (which also proved hollow) at its origin was $11\frac{4}{12}$ feet in circumference. (The whole tree directly beneath this crotch was $19\frac{3}{12}$ round.) This same limb branched again at $36\frac{8}{12}$ from the stump, and there measured, just beneath the crotch, $14\frac{10}{12}$ in circumference. At the ground the stump measured $8\frac{4}{12}$ one way, $8\frac{3}{12}$ another, $7\frac{1}{2}$ another. It was solid quite through at butt (excepting 3 inches in middle), though somewhat decayed within, and I could count pretty well 105 rings, to which add 10 more for the hollow and you have 115.[1]

There was a currant bush opposite the first crotch, in a large hole at that height, where probably a limb

---

[1] This is wrong. *Vide* 26th *inst*. I could not count the decayed part there well.

once broke off (making three there), and also a great many stones bigger than a hen's egg, probably cast in by the boys. There was also part of an old brick with some clay, thirty or forty years within the tree at the stump, completely overgrown and cut through by the axe. I judged that there were at least seven cords then in the road, supposing one main limb sound, and Davis thought that the pile in the yard, from the limbs taken off last week, contained four more. He said that there were some flying squirrels within and upon it when they were taking off the limbs. There was scarcely any hollowness to be discovered. It had grown very rapidly the first fifty years or so. You could see where there had once been deep clefts between different portions of the trunk at the stump, but the tree had afterward united and overgrown them, leaving some bark within the wood. In some places the trunk as it lay on the ground (though flatwise) was as high as a man's head.

This tree stood directly under the hill, which is some sixty feet high, the old burying hill continued, south of where the flagstaff was planted when the British marched into town. This tree must have been some fifty years old and quite sizable then. White, when taking off the limbs, said that he could see all over Sleepy Hollow, beyond the hill. There were several great wens on the trunk, a foot in diameter and nearly as much in height. The tree was so sound I think it might have lived fifty years longer; but Mrs. Davis said that she would not like to spend another such a week as the last before it was cut down. They heard

it creak in the storm. One of the great limbs which reached over the house was cracked. The two main limbs proved hollow.

Jan. 22. P. M. — To Walden.

The Walden road is nearly full of snow still, to the top of the wall on the north side, though there has been no snow falling since the 14th. The snow lies particularly solid. Looking toward the sun, the surface consists of great patches of shining crust and dry driving snow, giving it a *watered* appearance.

Miss Minott talks of cutting down the oaks about her house for fuel, because she cannot get her wood sledded home on account of the depth of the snow, though it lies all cut there. James, at R. W. E.'s, waters his cows at the door, because the brook is frozen.

If you wish to know whether a tree is hollow, or has a hole in it, ask the squirrels. They know as well as whether they have a home or not. Yet a man lives under it all his life without knowing, and the chopper must fairly cut it up before he can tell. If there is a cleft in it, he is pretty sure to find some nutshell or materials of a bird's nest left in it.

At Brister's Spring I see where a squirrel has been to the spring and also sat on a low alder limb and eaten a hazelnut. Where does he find a sound hazelnut now? Has them in a hollow tree.

See tracks of fishermen and pickerel. *Vide* forward.

At Walden, near my old residence, I find that since I was here on the 11th, apparently within a day or two, some gray or red squirrel or squirrels have been feeding

on the pitch pine cones extensively. The snow under one young pine is covered quite thick with the scales they have dropped while feeding overhead. I count the cores of thirty-four cones on the snow there, and that is not all. Under another pine there are more than twenty, and a well-worn track from this to a fence-post three rods distant, under which are the cores of eight cones and a corresponding amount of scales. The track is like a very small rabbit. They have gnawed off the cones which were perfectly closed. I see where one has taken one of a pair and left the other partly off. He had first sheared off the needles that were in the way, and then gnawed off the sides or cheeks of the twig to come at the stem of the cone, which as usual was cut by successive cuts

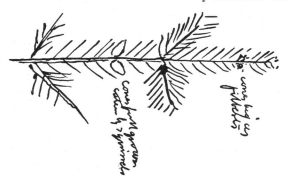

as with a knife, while bending it. One or two small, perhaps dead,[1] certainly unripe ones were taken off and left unopened. I find that many of those young

[1] Probably died last summer when little over a year old.

pines are now full of unopened cones, which apparently will be two years old next summer, and these the squirrel now eats. There are also some of them open, perhaps on the most thrifty twigs.

F. Morton hears to-day from Plymouth that three men have just caught in Sandy Pond, in Plymouth, about two hundred pounds of pickerel in two days.

Somebody has been fishing in the pond this morning, and the water in the holes is beginning to freeze. I see the track of a crow,[1] the toes as usual less spread

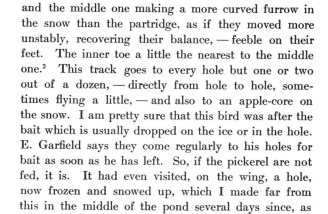

and the middle one making a more curved furrow in the snow than the partridge, as if they moved more unstably, recovering their balance, — feeble on their feet. The inner toe a little the nearest to the middle one.[2] This track goes to every hole but one or two out of a dozen, — directly from hole to hole, sometimes flying a little, — and also to an apple-core on the snow. I am pretty sure that this bird was after the bait which is usually dropped on the ice or in the hole. E. Garfield says they come regularly to his holes for bait as soon as he has left. So, if the pickerel are not fed, it is. It had even visited, on the wing, a hole, now frozen and snowed up, which I made far from this in the middle of the pond several days since, as I discovered by its droppings, the same kind that it had left about the first holes.

I was surprised, on breaking with my foot the ice in a pickerel-hole near the shore, evidently frozen only

[1] *Vide* 24th *inst.*   [2] *Vide* Feb. 1st.

last night, to see the water rise at once half an inch above it. Why should the ice be still sinking? Is it growing more solid and heavier?

Most were not aware of the size of the great elm till it was cut down. I surprised some a few days ago by saying that when its trunk should lie prostrate it would be higher than the head of the tallest man in the town, and that two such trunks could not stand in the chamber we were then in, which was fifteen feet across; that there would be ample room for a double bedstead on the trunk, nay, that the very dinner-table we were sitting at, with our whole party of seven, chairs and all, around it, might be set there. On the decayed part of the butt end there were curious fine black lines, giving it a geographical look, here and there, half a  dozen inches long, sometimes following the line of the rings; the boundary of a part which had reached a certain stage of decay. The force on the pulleys broke off more than a foot in width in the middle of the tree, much decayed.

I have attended the felling and, so to speak, the funeral of this old citizen of the town, — I who commonly do not attend funerals, — as it became me to do. I was the chief if not the only mourner there. I have taken the measure of his grandeur; have spoken a few words of eulogy at his grave, remembering the maxim *de mortuis nil nisi bonum* (in this case *magnum*). But there were only the choppers and the passers-by to hear me. Further the town was not represented;

the fathers of the town, the selectmen, the clergy were not there. But I have not known a fitter occasion for a sermon of late. Travellers whose journey was for a short time delayed by its prostrate body were forced to pay it some attention and respect, but the axe-boys had climbed upon it like ants, and commenced chipping at it before it had fairly ceased groaning. There was a man already bargaining for some part. How have the mighty fallen! Its history extends back over more than half the whole history of the town. Since its kindred could not conveniently attend, I attended. Methinks its fall marks an epoch in the history of the town. It has passed away together with the clergy of the old school and the stage-coach which used to rattle beneath it. Its virtue was that it steadily grew and expanded from year to year to the very last. How much of old Concord falls with it! The town clerk will not chronicle its fall. I will, for it is of greater moment to the town than that of many a human inhabitant would be. Instead of erecting a monument to it, we take all possible pains to obliterate its stump, the only monument of a tree which is commonly allowed to stand. Another link that bound us to the past is broken. How much of old Concord was cut away with it! A few such elms would alone constitute a township. They might claim to send a representative to the General Court to look after their interests, if a fit one could be found, a native American one in a true and worthy sense, with catholic principles. Our town has lost some of its venerableness. No longer will our eyes rest on its massive gray trunk, like a vast

Corinthian column by the wayside; no longer shall we walk in the shade of its lofty, spreading dome. It is as if you had laid the axe at the feet of some venerable Buckley or Ripley. You have laid the axe, you have made fast your tackle, to one of the king-posts of the town. I feel the whole building wracked by it. Is it not sacrilege to cut down the tree which has so long looked over Concord beneficently?

Supposing the first fifteen feet to average six feet in diameter, they would contain more than three cords and a foot of wood; but probably not more than three cords.

With what feelings should not the citizens hear that the biggest tree in the town has fallen! A traveller passed through the town and saw the inhabitants cutting it up without regret.

The tracks of the partridges by the sumachs, made before the 11th, are perhaps more prominent now than ever, for they have consolidated the snow under them so that as it settled it has left them *alto-relievo*. They look like broad chains extending straight far over the snow.

I brought home and examined some of the droppings of the crow mentioned [three] pages back. They were brown and dry, though partly frozen. After long study with a microscope, I discovered that they consisted of the seeds and skins and other indigestible parts of red cedar berries and some barberries (I detected the imbricated scale-like leaves of a berry stem and then the seeds and the now black skins of the cedar berries, but easily the large seeds of the barberries) and perhaps something more, and I knew whence it had probably come, *i. e.* from the cedar woods and

barberry bushes by Flint's Pond. These, then, make part of the food of crows in severe weather when the snow is deep, as at present.

Jan. 23. Brown is filling his ice-house. The *clear* ice is only from one and a half to four inches thick; all the rest, or nearly a foot, is snow ice, formed by the snow sinking the first under the water and freezing with the water. The same is the case at Walden. To get ice at all clear or transparent, you must scrape the snow off after each fall. Very little ice is formed by addition below, such a snowy winter as this.

There was a white birch scale yesterday on the snowed-up hole which I made in the very middle of Walden. I have no doubt they blow across the widest part of the pond.

When approaching the pond yesterday, through my bean-field, I saw where some fishermen had come away, and the tails of their string of pickerel had trailed on the deep snow where they sank in it. I afterward saw where they had been fishing that forenoon, the water just beginning to freeze, and also where some had fished the day before with red-finned minnows, which were frozen into an inch of ice; that these men had chewed tobacco and ate apples. All this I knew, though I saw neither man nor squirrel nor pickerel nor crow.

Measured, this afternoon, the snow in the same fields which I measured just a week ago, to see how it had settled. It has been uniformly fair weather of average winter coldness, without any thaw.[1] West of railroad

[1] Add 2 for ice at bottom. *Vide* Feb. 12th.

it averages $11\frac{1}{3}+$. (On the 16th it was $12\frac{1}{4}$.) East of railroad, 14 inches (16th, $15\frac{5}{8}$). Or average of both $12\frac{1}{3}+^1$ — say $12\frac{1}{2}$. It has settled, therefore, in open fields $1\frac{1}{10}$ inches, showing how very solid it is, as many have remarked. Not allowing for what of the light snow above the crust may have drifted against the railroad embankment (though I measured on both sides of it).[2] Trillium Woods, $13\frac{1}{4}+$;[3] 16th it was 17.[4] Has settled $3\frac{3}{4}$. It seems, then, that, as it lies light in the wood at first, it settles much faster there, so that, though it was nearly $3\frac{1}{2}$ inches the deepest there a week ago, it is less than 1 inch the deepest there now.

Jan. 24. A journal is a record of experiences and growth, not a preserve of things well done or said. I am occasionally reminded of a statement which I have made in conversation and immediately forgotten, which would read much better than what I put in my journal. It is a ripe, dry fruit of long-past experience which falls from me easily, without giving pain or pleasure. The charm of the journal must consist in a certain greenness, though freshness, and not in maturity. Here I cannot afford to be remembering what I said or did, my scurf cast off, but what I am and aspire to become.

Reading the hymns of the Rig Veda, translated by Wilson, which consist in a great measure of simple epithets addressed to the firmament, or the dawn, or

---

[1] $14\frac{1}{3}+$.
[2] The drifting of light surface snow *may* have produced nearly all the change.
[3] $15\frac{1}{4}+$.   [4] 19.

Keyes's land, near by (call it the Jones elm): 17 feet 6 inches, at two behind and one plus before; 15 feet 10 inches, at four; 15 feet 5 inches, at six; 16 feet at seven and a half, or spike on west side. At the smallest place between the ground and branches, this is a little bigger than the Davis elm, but it is not so big at or near the ground, nor is it so high to the branching, — about twelve feet, — nor are the branches so big, but it is much sounder, and its top broader, fuller, and handsomer. This has an uncommonly straight-sided and solid-looking trunk, measuring only two feet less at six feet from the ground than at two.

P. M. — Up Assabet.

Even the patches of shining snow-crust between those of dry white surface snow are slightly blue, like ice and water.

You may walk anywhere on the river now. Even the open space against Merrick's, below the Rock, has been closed again, and there is only six feet of water there now. I walk with a peculiar sense of freedom over the snow-covered ice, not fearing that I shall break through. I have not been able to find any tracks of muskrats this winter. I suspect that they very rarely venture out in winter with their wet coats.

I see squirrel-tracks about the hemlocks. They are much like rabbits, only the toes are very distinct. From this they pass into a semicircular figure sometimes. Some of the first are six inches from outside to outside lengthwise, with one to two feet of interval.

the winds, which mean more or less as the reader is more or less alert and imaginative, and seeing how widely the various translators have differed, they regarding not the poetry, but the history and philology, dealing with very concise Sanscrit, which must almost always be amplified to be understood, I am sometimes inclined to doubt if the translator has not made something out of nothing, — whether a real idea or sentiment has been thus transmitted to us from so primitive a period. I doubt if learned Germans might not thus edit pebbles from the seashore into hymns of the Rig Veda, and translators translate them accordingly, extracting the meaning which the sea has imparted to them in very primitive times. While the commentators and translators are disputing about the meaning of this word or that, I hear only the resounding of the ancient sea and put into it all the meaning I am possessed of, the deepest murmurs I can recall, for I do not the least care where I get my ideas, or what suggests them.

I knew that a crow had that day plucked the cedar berries and barberries by Flint's Pond and then flapped silently through the trackless air to Walden, where it dined on fisherman's bait, though there was no living creature to tell me.

Holbrook's elm measured to-day 11 feet 4 inches in circumference at six feet from ground, the size of one of the branches of the Davis elm (call it the Lee elm, for a Lee formerly lived there). Cheney's largest in front of Mr. Frost's, 12 feet 4 inches, at six feet; 16 feet 6 inches, at one foot. The great elm opposite

Are these the gray or red?

A great many hemlock cones have fallen on the snow and rolled down the hill.

Higher up, against the Wheeler Swamp, I see where many squirrels — perhaps red, for the tracks appear smaller — have fed on the alder cones on the twigs which are low or frozen into the ice, stripping them to the core just as they do the pine cones.

Here are the tracks of a crow, like those of the 22d, with a *long hind toe*, nearly two inches. The two feet are also nearly two inches apart. I see where the bird alighted, descending with an impetus and breaking through the slight crust, planting its feet side by side.

How different this partridge-track, with its slight hind toe, open and wide-spread toes on each side, both feet forming one straight line, exactly thus: —

(Five inches from centre to centre.) The middle toe alternately curved to the right and to the left, and what is apparently the outer toe in each case shorter than the inner one.

I see under a great many trees, black willow and swamp white oak, the bark scattered over the snow, some pieces six inches long, and above see the hole which a woodpecker has bored.

The snow is so deep along the sides of the river that I can now look into nests which I could hardly reach in the summer. I can hardly believe them the same. They have only an ice egg in them now. Thus we go

Frost-Crystals on Ice

Concord Elms

about, raised, generally speaking, more than a foot above the summer level. So much higher do we carry our heads in the winter. What a great odds such a little difference makes! When the snow raises us one foot higher than we have been accustomed to walk, we are surprised at our elevation! So we soar.

I do not find a foot of open water, even, on this North Branch, as far as I go, *i. e.* to J. Hosmer's lot. The river has been frozen unusually long and solidly. They have been sledding wood along the river for a quarter of a mile in front of Merriam's and past the mouth of Sam Barrett's Brook, where it is bare of snow, — hard, glare ice on which there is scarcely a trace of the sled or oxen. They have sledded home a large oak which was cut down on the bank. Yet this is one of the rockiest and swiftest parts of the stream. Where I have so often stemmed the swift current, dodging the rocks, with my paddle, there the heavy, slow-paced oxen, with their ponderous squeaking load, have plodded, while the teamster walked musing beside it.

That Wheeler swamp is a great place for squirrels. I observe many of their tracks along the riverside there. The nests are of leaves, and apparently of the gray species.

There is much of the water milkweed on the little island just above Dove Rock. It rises above the deep snow there.

It is remarkable how much the river has been tracked by dogs the week past, not accompanied by their masters. They hunt, perchance, in the night more than is supposed, for I very rarely see one alone by day.

The river is pretty low and has fallen within a month, for there has been no thaw. The ice has broken and settled around the rocks, which look as if they had burst up through it. Some maple limbs which were early frozen in have been broken and stripped down by this irresistible weight.

You see where the big dogs have slipped on one or two feet in their haste, sinking to the ice, but, having two more feet, it did not delay them.

I walk along the sides of the stream, admiring the rich mulberry catkins of the alders, which look almost edible. They attract us because they have so much of spring in them. The clear red osiers, too, along the riverside in front of Merriam's on Wheeler's side.

I have seen many a collection of stately elms which better deserved to be represented at the General Court than the manikins beneath, — than the barroom and victualling cellar and groceries they overshadowed. When I see their magnificent domes, miles away in the horizon, over intervening valleys and forests, they suggest a village, a community, there. But, after all, it is a secondary consideration whether there are human dwellings beneath them; these may have long since passed away. I find that into my idea of the village has entered more of the elm than of the human being. They are worth many a political borough. They constitute a borough. The poor human representative of his party sent out from beneath their shade will not suggest a tithe of the dignity, the true nobleness and comprehensiveness of view, the sturdiness and independence, and the serene beneficence that they do. They look from town-

Vol. VIII

ship to township. A fragment of their bark is worth the backs of all the politicians in the union. They are free-soilers in their own broad sense. They send their roots north and south and east and west into many a conservative's Kansas and Carolina, who does not suspect such underground railroads, — they improve the subsoil he has never disturbed, — and many times their length, if the support of their principles requires it. They battle with the tempests of a century. See what scars they bear, what limbs they lost before we were born! Yet they never adjourn; they steadily vote for their principles, and send their roots further and wider from the *same centre*. They die at their posts, and they leave a tough butt for the choppers to exercise themselves about, and a stump which serves for their monument. They attend no caucus, they make no compromise, they use no policy. Their one principle is growth. They combine a true radicalism with a true conservatism. Their radicalism is not cutting away of roots, but an infinite multiplication and extension of them under all surrounding institutions. They take a firmer hold on the earth that they may rise higher into the heavens. Their conservative heart-wood, in which no sap longer flows, does not impoverish their growth, but is a firm column to support it; and when their expanding trunks no longer require it, it utterly decays. Their conservatism is a dead but solid heart-wood, which is the pivot and firm column of support to all this growth, appropriating nothing to itself, but forever by its support assisting to extend the area of their radicalism. Half a century after they are dead

at the core, they are preserved by radical reforms. They do not, like men, from radicals turn conservative. Their conservative part dies out first; their radical and growing part survives. They acquire new States and Territories, while the old dominions decay, and become the habitation of bears and owls and coons.

Jan. 25. P. M. — Up river.

The hardest day to bear that we have had, for, beside being 5° at noon and at 4 P. M., there is a strong northwest wind. It is worse than when the thermometer was at zero all day. Pierce says it is the first day that he has not been able to work outdoors in the sun. The snow is now very dry and powdery, and, though so hard packed, drifts somewhat. The travellers I meet have red faces. Their ears covered. Pity those who have not thick mittens. No man could stand it to travel far toward this wind. It stiffens the whole face, and you feel a tingling sensation in your forehead. Much worse to bear than a still cold. I see no life abroad, no bird nor beast. What a stern, bleak, inhospitable aspect nature now wears! (I am off Clamshell Hill.) Where a few months since was a fertilizing river reflecting the sunset, and luxuriant meadows resounding with the hum of insects, is now a uniform crusted snow, with dry powdery snow drifting over it and confounding river and meadow. I make haste away, covering my ears, before I freeze there. The snow in the road has frozen dry, as dry as bran.

A closed pitch pine cone gathered January 22d opened last night in my chamber. If you would be convinced how differently armed the squirrel is naturally for dealing with pitch pine cones, just try to get one off with your teeth. He who extracts the seeds from a single closed cone with the aid of a knife will be constrained to confess that the squirrel earns his dinner. It is a rugged customer, and will make your fingers bleed. But the squirrel has the key to this conical and spiny chest of many apartments. He sits on a post, vibrating his tail, and twirls it as a plaything.

But so is a man commonly a locked-up chest to us, to open whom, unless we have the key of sympathy, will make our hearts bleed.

The elms, they adjourn not night nor day; they pair not off. They stand for magnificence; they take the brunt of the tempest; they attract the lightning that would smite our roofs, leaving only a few rotten members scattered over the highway. The one by Holbrook's is particularly regular and lofty for its girth, a perfect sheaf, but thin-leaved, apparently a slow grower. It bore a tavern sign for many a year. Call it the Bond (?) elm.

Jan. 26. When I took the ether my consciousness amounted to this: I put my finger on myself in order to keep the place, otherwise I should never have returned to this world.

They have cut and sawed off the butt of the great elm at nine and a half feet from the ground, and I counted the annual rings there with the greatest ease and accuracy. Indeed I never saw them so distinct on a large butt. The tree was quite sound there, not the

least hollow even at the pith. There were one hundred and twenty-seven rings. Supposing the tree to have been five years old when nine and a half feet high, then it was one hundred and thirty-two years old, or came up in the year 1724, just before Lovewell's Fight.

There were two centres, fourteen inches apart. The accompanying coarse sketch will give a *general* idea of it. There were thirteen distinct rings about each centre, before they united and one ring inclosed both. Then there was a piece of bark, — which may be rudely represented by the

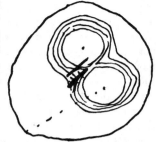

upper black mark, — say six or eight inches long. This was not overgrown but by the twenty-fourth ring. These two centres of growth corresponded in position to the two main branches six feet above, and I inferred that when the tree was about eighteen years old, the fork commenced at nine and a half feet from the ground, but as it increased in diameter, it united higher and higher up. I remember that the bark was considerably nearer one centre than the other. There was bark in several places completely overgrown and included on the extreme butt end where cut off, having apparently overgrown its own furrows.

Its diameter, where I counted the rings, was, one way, as near as I could measure in spite of the carf,

four feet and three inches; another, four feet and eight inches; and five feet. On the line by which I counted, which was the long way of the tree, it had grown in the first fifty years twenty inches, or two fifths of an inch a year; the last fifty, five and three quarters inches or about one ninth of an inch a year; and there was a space of about five inches between the two, or for the intermediate twenty-seven years. At this height, it had grown on an average annually nearly twenty-four one-hundredths of an inch from the centre on one side.

The white or sap wood averaged about two inches thick. The bark was from one to two inches thick, and

 in the last case I could count from twelve to fifteen distinct rings in it, as if it were regularly shed after that period.

The court-house elm measured, at six feet from the ground on the west side, twelve feet one and one half inches in circumference. The willow by the Jim Jones house, fourteen feet at about eighteen inches from ground; thirteen feet eight inches, at about six inches from ground; and it bulged out much larger above this.

P. M. — Walked down the river as far as the south bend behind Abner Buttrick's. I also know its condition as far as the Hubbard Bridge in the other direction. There is not a square foot open between these extremes, and, judging from what I know of the river beyond

these limits, I may safely say that it is not open (the main stream, I mean) anywhere in the town. (Of the North Branch above the Bath Place, the goose ground, say to the stone bridge, I cannot speak confidently.[1]) The same must have been the case yesterday, since it was colder. Probably the same has been true of the river, excepting the small space against Merrick's below the Rock (now closed), since January 7th, when it closed at the Hubbard Bath, or nearly three weeks, — a long time, methinks, for it to be frozen so solidly. A sleigh might safely be driven now from Carlisle Bridge to the Sudbury meadows on the river. Methinks it is a remarkably cold, as well as snowy, January, for we have had good sleighing ever since the 26th of December and no thaw.

Walked as far as Flint's Bridge with Abel Hunt, where I took to the river. I told him I had come to walk on the river as the best place, for the snow had drifted somewhat in the road, while it was converted into ice almost entirely on the river. "But," asked he, "are you not afraid that you will get in?" "Oh, no, it will bear a load of wood from one end to the other." "But then there may be some weak places." Yet he is some seventy years old and was born and bred immediately on its banks. Truly one half the world does not know how the other half lives.

Men have been talking now for a week at the post-office about the age of the great elm, as a matter inter-

[1] *Vide* 27th *inst.*

esting but impossible to be determined. The very choppers and travellers have stood upon its prostrate trunk and speculated upon its age, as if it were a profound mystery. I stooped and read its years to them (127 at nine and a half feet), but they heard me as the wind that once sighed through its branches. They still surmised that it might be two hundred years old, but they never stooped to read the inscription. Truly they love darkness rather than light. One said it was probably one hundred and fifty, for he had heard somebody say that for fifty years the elm grew, for fifty it stood still, and for fifty it was dying. (Wonder what portion of his career he stood still!) Truly all men are not men of science. They dwell within an integument of prejudice thicker than the bark of the cork-tree, but it is valuable chiefly to stop bottles with. Tied to their buoyant prejudices, they keep themselves afloat when honest swimmers sink.

Talking with Miss Mary Emerson this evening, she said, "It was not the fashion to be so original when I was young." She is readier to take my view — look through my eyes for the time — than any young person that I know in the town.

The white maple buds look large, with bursting downy scales as in spring.

I observe that the crust is strongest over meadows, though the snow is deep there and there is no ice nor water beneath, but in pastures and upland generally I break through. Probably there is more moisture to be frozen in the former places, and the snow is more compact.

Jan. 27. I have just sawed a wheel an inch and three quarters thick off the end of (apparently) a stick of red oak in my pile. I count twenty-nine rings, and about the same number of rings, or divisions of some kind, with more or less distinctness, in the bark, which is about a quarter of an inch thick. Is not the whole number of rings contained in the bark of all trees which have a bark externally smooth? This stick has two centres of growth, each a little one side of the middle. I trace one easily to a limb which was cut off close to the tree about three and a half inches above the lower side of the section. The two centres are one inch apart on the lower side, two inches and five eighths on the upper side. There are three complete circles to the main one on the lower side, and ten on the upper side, before they coalesce; hence it was seven years closing up through an inch and three quarters of height. There is a rough ridge, confined to the bark only and about a quarter of an inch high, extending from the

crotch diagonally down the tree, apparently to a point over the true centre of growth.

P. M. — Walked on the river from the old stone to Derby's Bridge. It is open a couple of rods under the stone bridge, but not a rod below it, and also for forty rods below the mouth of Loring's Brook, along the west side, probably because this is a mill-stream. The only other open places within the limits mentioned yesterday are in one or two places close under the bank, and concealed by it, where warm springs issue, the

river, after freezing, having shrunk and the ice settled a foot or eighteen inches there, so that you can see water over its edge.

The white maple at Derby's Bridge measures fifteen feet in circumference at ground, including apparently a very large sucker, and ten feet five inches, at four feet above the ground, not including sucker, there free.

The lodging snow of January 13th, just a fortnight ago, still adheres in deep and conspicuous ridges to large exposed trees, too stubborn to be shaken by the wind, showing from which side the storm came.

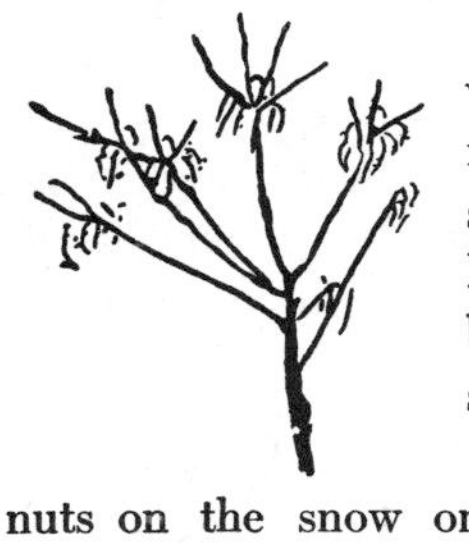

The fruit stems of the dogwood still hold on, and a little fruit. (Of course, the limbs should be smoother.) The outline much like a peach tree, but it is without the numerous small limbs or twigs.

Saw what I think were bass nuts on the snow on the river, at Derby's railroad bridge, probably from up-stream.

Jan. 28. Snowed all day, about two inches falling. They say it snowed about the same all yesterday in New York. Cleared up at night.

Jan. 29. P. M. — Measured the snow in the same places measured the 16th and 23d, having had, except yesterday, fair weather and no thaw.[1]

[1] Add 2 for ice at bottom. *Vide* Feb. 12th.

				Average of both sides.
West of railroad, average	$11\frac{1}{2}$ +	East of railroad,	17	$13\frac{3}{4}$ −
On the 23d it was	$11\frac{1}{3}$		14	$12\frac{1}{3}$ +
" " 16th " "	$12\frac{1}{4}$		$15\frac{5}{8}$	$13\frac{6}{10}$
Trillium Woods to-day	$14\frac{6}{10}$			
the 23d	$13\frac{1}{4}$ +			
16th	17			

As I measured oftener west than east of railroad, the snow is probably about fourteen on a level in open fields now, or *quite* as deep as at any time this winter. Yet it has apparently been settling a little the last six days. In the woods, apparently, it has also been settling, but it is not so deep there as on the 16th, because it settled rapidly soon after that date. It is deeper east of railroad, evidently because it lies behind it like a wall, though I measure from six to ten or twelve rods off on that side. Since the 13th there has been at no time less than one foot on a level in open fields.

It is interesting to see near the sources, even of small streams or brooks, which now flow through an open country, perhaps shrunken in their volume, the traces of ancient mills, which have devoured the primitive forest, the earthen dams and old sluiceways, and ditches and banks for obtaining a supply of water. These relics of a more primitive period are still frequent in our midst. Such, too, probably, has been the history of the most thickly settled and cleared countries of Europe. The saw-miller is neighbor and successor to the Indian.

It is observable that not only the moose and the wolf disappear before the civilized man, but even many species of insects, such as the black fly and the almost microscopic "no-see-em." How imperfect a notion have we commonly of what was the actual condition of the place where we dwell, three centuries ago!

For the most part the farmers have not been able to get into the woods for the last fortnight or more, on account of the snow, and some who had not got up their wood before are now put to their trumps, for though it may not be more than eighteen inches deep on a level in sprout-lands, the crust cuts the legs of the cattle, and the occasional drifts are impassable. Sometimes, with two yoke of oxen and a horse attached to the sled, the farmer attempts to break his way into his lot, one driving while another walks before with a shovel, treading and making a path for the horse, but they must take off the cattle at last and turn the sled with their hands.

Miss Minott has been obliged to have some of her locusts about the house cut down. She remembers when the whole top of the elm north of the road close to Dr. Heywood's broke off, — when she was a little girl. It must have been there before 1800.

Jan. 30. 8 A. M. — It has just begun to snow, — those little round dry pellets like shot.

George Minott says that he was standing with Bowers (?) and Joe Barrett near Dr. Heywood's barn in the September gale, and saw an elm, twice as big as that which broke off before his house, break off ten feet from the ground, — splinter all up, — and the

barn bent and gave so that he thought it was time to be moving. He saw stones "as big as that [air-tight] stove, blown right out of the wall." So, by bending to the blast, he made his way home. All the *small* buildings on the Walden road across the brook were blown back toward the brook. Minott lost the roof of his shed. The wind was southerly.

As I walked above the old stone bridge on the 27th, I saw where the river had recently been open under the wooded bank on the west side; and recent sawdust and shavings from the pail-factory, and also the ends of saplings and limbs of trees which had been bent down by the ice, were frozen in. In some places some water stood above the ice, and as I stood there, I saw and heard it gurgle up through a crevice and spread over the ice. This was the influence of Loring's Brook, far above.

Stopped snowing before noon, not having amounted to anything.

P. M. — Measured to see what difference there was in the depth of the snow in different adjacent fields as nearly as possible alike and similarly situated. Commenced fifteen or twenty rods east of the railroad and measured across Hubbard's (?), Stow's, and Collier's fields toward a point on the south side of the last, twenty-five rods east of Trillium Woods. These three fields were nearly level, somewhat meadowy, especially the second, and at least twenty-five rods from the nearest disturbing influence, such as the railroad embankment or a wood.

Vol. VIII

North	AB	BC	[CD]	Average of
A Wall and riders	22	20	21	all three,
	19	27	12	14 —.¹
Average 14⅝ Hub.'s (?)	14	12	13	
	13	9	8	
	13	9	14	
B Rail fence	17	8	11	
	13	10	15	
	10	10	14	
Average 12½ Stow's	21	9	10	
	13	8	14	
C Rail fence	13	15	15	
and ditch	12	11)137(12½	16	
	11		15	
	14		16	
Average 14 Collier's	12		10	
D Wall and riders	17		14	
	16)234(14⅝		21	
South			17)239(14	

The walls, no doubt, gave the first and third fields somewhat more snow. Yet I am inclined to think that in this trial the snow is shallower very nearly as the fields are more moist. It is three inches shallower here than nearer the railroad, where I measured yesterday, showing the effect of that bank very clearly, six to fifteen rods off, but the average is the same obtained yesterday for open fields east and west of railroad, and proves the truth of that measuring. The snow in the first field measured two inches more than that in the second!

The andromeda swamp gave 26½ +² (on the 12th it was 23⅘³). It has probably been more than 2½ feet, say on the 16th. The *Andromeda calyculata* is now quite covered, and I walk on the crust over an almost uninterrupted plain there; only a few blueberries and

¹ Add 2 for ice at bottom = 16 —. *Vide* Feb. 12th.
² +2 = 28½ +.   ³ +2 = 25⅘.

Andromeda paniculata rise above it. Near the last, I break through. It is so light beneath that the crust breaks there in great cakes under my feet, and immediately falls about a foot, making a great hole, so that once pushing my way through — for regularly stepping is out of the question in the weak places — makes a pretty good path.

In Wheeler's squirrel wood, which on the 12th gave 10 ¹ inches of snow now gives 15,² which is what I should have judged from the changes in Trillium Wood. They are affected alike.

The sprout-land just south of this wood gives as average of fourteen measurements 21 4/10,³ which I suspect is too much, it is so sheltered a place.

By the railroad against Walden I heard the lisping of a chickadee, and saw it on a sumach. It repeatedly hopped to a bunch of berries, took one, and, hopping

to a more horizontal twig, placed it under one foot and hammered at it with its bill. The snow was strewn with

¹ +2 = 12.   ² +2 = 17.   ³ +2 = 23 4/10.

the berries under its foot, but I could see no *shells* of the fruit. Perhaps it clears off the crimson only. Some of the bunches are very large and quite upright there still.

Again, I suspect that on meadows the snow is not so deep and has a firmer crust. In an ordinary storm the depth of the snow will be affected by a wood twenty or more rods distant, or as far as the wood is a fence.

The snow is so light in the swamps under the crust, amid the andromeda, that a cat could almost run there. There are but few tracks of mice, now the snow is so deep. They run underneath.

The drift about Lynch's house is like this: —

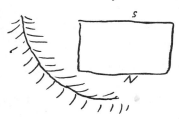

There is a strong wind this afternoon from northwest, and the snow of the 28th is driving like steam over the fields, drifting into the roads. On the railroad causeway it lies in perfectly straight and regular ridges a few feet apart, northwest and southeast. It is dry and scaly, like coarse bran. Now that there is so much snow, it slopes up to the tops of the walls on both sides.

What a difference between life in the city and in the country at present, — between walking in Washington Street, threading your way between countless sledges and travellers, over the discolored snow, and crossing Walden Pond, a spotless field of snow surrounded by woods, whose intensely blue shadows and your own

are the only objects. What a solemn silence reigns here!

Jan. 31. P. M. — Up North Branch.

There are a few inches of light snow on top of the little, hard and crusted, that I walked on here last, above the snow ice. The old tracks are blotted out, and new and fresher ones are to be discerned. It is a *tabula rasa.* These fresh falls of snow are like turning over a new leaf of Nature's *Album.* At first you detect no track of beast or bird, and Nature looks more than commonly silent and blank. You doubt if anything has been abroad, though the snow fell three days ago, but ere long the track of a squirrel is seen making to or from the base of a tree, or the hole where he dug for acorns, and the shells he dropped on the snow around that stump.

The wind of yesterday has shaken down countless oak leaves, which have been driven hurry-scurry over this smooth and delicate and unspotted surface, and now there is hardly a square foot which does not show some faint trace of them. They still spot the snow thickly in many places, though few can be traced to their lairs. More hemlock cones also have fallen and rolled down the bank. The fall of these withered leaves after each rude blast, so clean and dry that they do not soil the snow, is a phenomenon quite in harmony with the winter.

Perhaps the tracks of the mice are the most amusing of any, they take such various forms and, though small, are so distinct. Here is where one has come down the bank and hopped meanderingly across the river.

Vol. VIII

Or —⊶ —⊶ —⊶ —⊷ An inch and a quarter wide by five, six, or seven apart from centre to centre.

But what track is this, just under the bank?

It must be a bird, which at last struck the snow with its wings and took to flight. There were but four hops in all, and then it ended as above, though there was nothing near enough for it to hop upon from the snow. The form of the foot was somewhat like that of a squirrel, though only the outline was distinguished. The foot was about two inches long, and it was about two inches from outside of one foot to outside of the other. Sixteen inches from hop to hop, the rest in proportion. Looking narrowly, I saw where one wing struck the bank ten feet ahead, thus: ═══ as it passed. A quarter of a mile down-stream it occurred again, thus:

and near by still less of a track, but marks as if it had pecked in the snow. Could it be the track of a crow with its toes unusually close together? Or was it an owl?[1]

Some creature has been eating elm blossom-buds and dropping them over the snow.

[1] Probably a crow. *Vide* Feb. 1st. Hardly a doubt of it.

The tracks of the mice suggest extensive hopping in the night and going a-gadding. They commence and terminate in the most insignificant little holes by the side of a twig or tuft, and occasionally they give us the type of their tails very distinctly, even sidewise to the course on a bank-side, thus: —

Saw also the tracks, probably of a muskrat, for a few feet leading from hole to hole just under the bank.

FEBRUARY, 1856

(ÆT. 38)

Feb. 1. Our kitten Min, two-thirds grown, was playing with Sophia's broom this morning, as she was sweeping the parlor, when she suddenly went into a fit, dashed round the room, and, the door being opened, rushed up two flights of stairs and leaped from the attic window to the ice and snow by the side of the doorstep, — a descent of a little more than twenty feet, — passed round the house and was lost. But she made her appearance again about noon, at the window, quite well and sound in every joint, even playful and frisky.

P. M. — Up river.

What gives to the excrements of the fox that clay-color often, even at this season? Left on an eminence.

I scented a fox's trail this afternoon (and have done so several times before), where he crossed the river, just three rods distant. Looked sharp, and discovered where it had stopped by a prominence. Yet he could not have passed since last night, or twelve hours before, it being near the village. How widely they range these nights! I hear that Daniel Foster of Princeton had eleven turkeys taken from under his barn in one night last fall, probably by a fox. Two were found a week after, buried under some brush in a neighboring wood.

26th of December, — not less than a foot at any time since January 6th on a level in open fields, in swamps much more. Cars have been detained; the wood-lots for the most part inaccessible. The river has been closed up from end to end, with the exception of one or two insignificant openings on a few days. No bare ice. The crows have been remarkably bold, coming to eat the scraps cast out behind the houses. They alight in our yard. I think I have not noticed a tree sparrow during the month. Blue jays and chickadees also common in the village, more than usual. We have completely forgotten the summer. There has been no January thaw, though one prophesied it a fortnight ago because he saw snow-fleas. The ponds are yielding a good crop of ice. The eaves have scarcely run at all. It has been what is called "an old-fashioned winter."

Feb. 2. Snowed again last night, perhaps an inch, erasing the old tracks and giving us a blank page again, restoring the purity of nature. It may be even a trifle deeper now than hitherto.

Feb. 3. Analyzed the crow blackbird's nest from which I took an egg last summer, eight or ten feet up a white maple by river, opposite Island. Large, of an irregular form, appearing as if wedged in between a twig and two large contiguous trunks. From outside to outside it measures from six to eight inches; inside, four; depth, two; height, six. The foundation is a loose mass of coarse strips of grape-vine bark chiefly, some eighteen inches long by five eighths of an inch

The snow is somewhat banked toward the sides of the river, but shows darker-yellowish or icy in the middle. Lichens, blown from the black willows, lie here and there on the snow. Nut Meadow Brook open for some distance in the meadow. I was affected by the sight of some green polygonum leaves there. Some kind of minnow darted off. I see where a crow has walked along its side. In one place it hopped, and its feet were side by side, as in the track of yesterday, though a little more spread, the toes. I have but little doubt that yesterday's track was a crow's. The two inner toes are near together; the middle, more or less curved often.

I see a gray rabbit amid the young oaks in Hubbard's riverside grove, curled and shrunk up, squatting on the snow. I advance and begin to sketch it, when it plunges into a little hole in the snow by its side, the entrance to its burrow, three inches wide by a little more in length. The track of its foot is about one inch wide.

I see a pitch pine seed, blown thirty rods from J. Hosmer's little grove.

The Sheldon house in Deerfield, pulled down about eight years since, represented in *Gleason's Pictorial* for 1851 and in Barber, is in the style of the Hunt house, except that there is but one window on each side of the door. It and the meeting-house alone of those within the fort survived the assault of 1704, and the door through which a hole was cut and a woman shot is still preserved.

This has been a memorable January for snow and cold. It has been excellent sleighing ever since the

wide; also slender grass and weed stems, mikania stems, a few cellular river weeds, as rushes, sparganium, pipe-grass, and some soft, coarse, fibrous roots. The same coarse grape-vine bark and grass and weed stems, together with some harder, wiry stems, form the sides and rim, the bark being passed around the twig. The nest is lined with the finer grass and weed stems, etc. The solid part of the nest is of half-decayed vegetable matter and mud, full of fine fibrous roots and wound internally with grass stems, etc., and some grape bark, being an inch and a half thick at bottom. Pulled apart and lying loose, it makes a great mass of material. This, like similar nests, is now a great haunt for spiders.

P. M. — Up North Branch.

A strong northwest wind (and thermometer 11°), driving the surface snow like steam. About five inches of soft snow now on ice. See many seeds of the hemlock on the snow still, and cones which have freshly rolled down the bank.

Tracked some mice to a black willow by riverside, just above spring, against the open swamp; and about three feet high, in apparently an old woodpecker's hole, was probably the mouse-nest, a double handful, consisting, four ninths, of fine shreds of inner bark, perhaps willow or maple; three ninths, the greenish moss, apparently, of button-bush; two ninths, the gray-slate fur, apparently, of rabbits or mice. Half a dozen hog's bristles might have been brought by some bird to its nest there. These made a very warm and soft nest.

Got some kind of vireo's nest from a maple far up

the stream, a dozen feet high, pensile; within, almost wholly rather coarse grape-vine shreds; without, the same and bark, covered with the delicate white spider-nests (?), birch-bark shreds, and brown cocoon silk.

Returning, saw near the Island a shrike glide by, cold and blustering as it was, with a remarkably even and steady sail or gliding motion like a hawk, eight or ten feet above the ground, and alight in a tree, from which at the same instant a small bird, perhaps a creeper or nuthatch, flitted timidly away. The shrike was apparently in pursuit.

We go wading through snows now up the bleak river, in the face of the cutting northwest wind and driving snow-steam, turning now this ear, then that, to the wind, and our gloved hands in our bosoms or pockets. Our tracks are obliterated before we come back. How different this from sailing or paddling up the stream here in July, or poling amid the rocks! Yet still, in one square rod, where they have got out ice and a thin transparent ice has formed, I can see the pebbly bottom the same as in summer.

It is a cold and windy Sunday. The wind whistles round the northwest corner of the house and penetrates every crevice and consumes the wood in the stoves, — soon blows it all away. An armful goes but little way. Such a day makes a great hole in the wood-pile. [It] whisks round the corner of the house, in at a crevice, and flirts off with all the heat before we have begun to feel it.

Some of the low drifts but a few inches deep, made by the surface snow blowing, over the river especially,

are of a fine, pure snow, so densely packed that our feet make hardly any impression on them.

River still tight at Merrick's.

There comes a deep snow in midwinter, covering up the ordinary food of many birds and quadrupeds, but anon a high wind scatters the seeds of pines and hemlocks and birch and alder, etc., far and wide over the surface of the snow for them.

You may now observe plainly the habit of the rabbits to run in paths about the swamps.

Mr. Emerson, who returned last week from lecturing on the Mississippi, having been gone but a month, tells me that he saw boys skating on the Mississippi and on Lake Erie and on the Hudson, and has no doubt they are skating on Lake Superior; and probably at Boston he saw them skating on the Atlantic.

The inside of the gray squirrel, or leaf, nests is of leaves chewed or broken up finely. I see where one, by the snow lodging on it, has helped weigh down a birch.

In Barber's "Historical Collections,"[1] page 476, there is a letter by Cotton Mather, dated "Boston, 10th Dec. 1717," describing the great snow of the previous February, from which I quote: —

"On the twentieth of the last February there came on a snow, which being added unto what had covered the ground a few days before, made a thicker mantle for our mother than what was usual: And the storm with it was, for the following day, so violent as to make all communication between the neighbors everywhere to cease. People, for some hours, could not pass from

[1] [*The History and Antiquities of New England*, etc.]

Vol. VIII

one side of a street unto another. . . . On the 24th day of the month, comes Pelion upon Ossa: Another snow came on which almost buried the memory of the former, with a storm so famous that Heaven laid an interdict on the religious assemblies throughout the country, on this Lord's day, the like whereunto had never been seen before. The Indians near an hundred years old affirm that their fathers never told them of anything that equalled it. Vast numbers of cattle were destroyed in this calamity. Whereof some there were, of the stranger [stronger? mine] sort, were found standing dead on their legs, as if they had been alive many weeks after, when the snow melted away. And others had their eyes glazed over with ice at such a rate, that being not far from the sea, their mistake of their way drowned them there. One gentleman, on whose farms were now lost above 1100 sheep, which with other cattle, were interred (shall I say) or innived, in the snow, writes me word that there were two sheep very singularly circumstanced. For no less than eight and twenty days after the storm, the people pulling out the ruins of above an hundred sheep out of a snow bank which lay sixteen foot high, drifted over them, there was two found alive, which had been there all this time, and kept themselves alive by eating the wool of their dead companions. When they were taken out they shed their own fleeces, but soon got into good case again."

"A man had a couple of young hogs, which he gave over for dead, but on the 27th day after their burial, they made their way out of a snow-bank, at the bottom of which they had found a little tansy to feed upon."

"Hens were found alive after seven days; Turkeys were found alive after five and twenty days, buried in the snow, and at a distance from the ground, and altogether destitute of anything to feed them."

"The wild creatures of the woods, the out-goings of the evening, made their descent as well as they could in this time of scarcity for them towards the sea-side. A vast multitude of deer, for the same cause, taking the same course, and the deep snow spoiling them of their only defence, which is to run, they became such a prey to these devourers that it is thought not one in twenty escaped."

"It is incredible how much damage is done to the orchards, for the snow freezing to a crust, as high as the bows of the trees, anon split them to pieces. The cattle, also, walking on the crusted snow a dozen foot from the ground, so fed upon the trees as very much to damnify them." "Cottages were totally covered with the snow, and not the very tops of their chimneys to be seen." These "odd accidents," he says, "would afford a story. But there not being any relation to Philosophy in them, I forbear them." He little thought that his simple testimony to such facts as the above would be worth all the philosophy he might dream of.

Feb. 4. P. M. — To Walden.

I go to walk at 3 P. M., thermometer 18°. It has been about this (and 22°) at this hour for a week or two. All the light snow, some five inches above the crust, is adrift these days and driving over the fields like steam, or like the foam-streaks on a flooded meadow, from northwest to southeast. The surface of the fields is rough, like a lake agitated by the wind.

I see that the partridges feed quite extensively on the sumach berries, *e. g.* at my old house. They come to them after every snow, making fresh tracks, and have now stripped many bushes quite bare.

At Tanager Glade I see where the rabbits have gnawed the bark of the shrub oaks extensively, and the twigs, down to the size of a goose-quill, cutting them off as smoothly as a knife. They have also gnawed some young white oaks, black cherry, and apple. The shrub oaks look like hedges which have been trimmed or clipped.

I have often wondered how red cedars could have sprung up in some pastures which I knew to be miles distant from the nearest fruit-bearing cedar, but it now occurs to me that these and barberries, etc., may be planted by the crows, and probably other birds.

The oak leaves which have blown over the snow are collected in dense heaps on the still side of the bays at Walden, where I suspect they make warm beds for the rabbits to squat on.

Feb. 5. The weather is still clear, cold, and unrelenting. I have walked much on the river this winter, but, ever since it froze over, it has been on a snow-clad river, or pond. They have been river walks because the snow was shallowest there. Even the meadows, on account of the firmer crust, have been more passable than the uplands. In the afternoons I have walked off freely up or down the river, without impediment or fear,

Vol. VIII

looking for birds and birds' nests and the tracks of animals; and, as often as it was written over, a new snow came and presented a new blank page. If it were still after it, the tracks were beautifully distinct. If strong winds blew, the dry leaves, losing their holds, traversed and scored it in all directions. The sleighing would have been excellent all the month past if it had not been for the drifting of the surface snow into the track whenever the wind blew, but that crust on the old snow has prevented very deep drifts. I should [say] the average cold was about 8° at 8 A. M. and 18° or 20° at 3 P. M.

Feb. 6. P. M. — To Walden.

The down is just peeping out from some of the aspen buds. Cut a cake of ice out of the middle of Walden, within three rods of where I cut on the 18th of January. The snow was about an inch deep only, so fast has it been converted into snow ice. I was obliged to make a hole about four feet square in order to get out a cake, and with great care to approach the water evenly on all sides, so that I might have the less chopping to do after the water began to rush in, which would wet me through. It was surprising with what violence the water rushed in as soon as a hole was made, under the pressure of that body of ice. On the 18th of January the ice had been about seven inches thick here, about four being snow ice and about three water ice. It was now 19 inches thick, $11\frac{1}{2}$ — being snow ice and $7\frac{1}{2}$ + water ice. Supposing it an inch thick only here when the snow began to fall on it (for it be-

gan to fall almost immediately), it had increased since that time $6\frac{1}{2}$ + inches downward and $11\frac{1}{2}$ — upward. Since the 18th of January, when there was ten inches of snow on it, it had increased about $4\frac{1}{2}$ downward and about $7\frac{1}{2}$ upward. I was not prepared to find that *any* ice had formed on the under side since the 18th. The water ice was very crystalline. This ice was thicker than the snow has been in open fields any time this winter, yet this winter has been remarkable for the abundance of snow. I also cut through and measured in the Ice Heap Cove. The snow ice was $12\frac{1}{4}$, and the water ice about 6, but perhaps a little was broken off in cutting through the last. In all about $18\frac{1}{4}$ inches. I was not prepared to find it thickest in the middle. Earlier in the winter, or on the 18th January, it was thickest near the shore.

Goodwin says that he has caught two crows this winter in his traps set *in water* for mink, and baited with fish. The crows, probably put to it for food and looking along the very few open brooks, attracted by this bait, got their feet into the traps. He thinks that [what] I call muskrat-tracks are mink-tracks by the Rock, and that muskrat do not come out at all this weather. I saw a clamshell opened, and they say minks do not open them (?).

Feb. 7. Began to snow at 8 A. M.; turned to rain at noon, and cleared off, or rather ceased raining, at night, with some glaze on the trees. This the first thawing, though slight, since the 25th of December. During the rain the air was thick, the distant woods bluish,

and the single trees, etc., on the hill, under the dull, mist-covered sky, remarkably distinct and black.

Feb. 8. 9 A. M. — To Fair Haven Pond.

A clear and a pleasanter and warmer day than we have had for a long time. The snow begins (at noon) to soften somewhat in the road.

For two or three weeks, successive light and dry snows have fallen on the old crust and been drifting about on it leaving it at last three quarters bare and forming drifts against the fences, etc., or here and there low, slaty, fractured ones in mid-field, or pure white hard-packed ones. These drifts on the crust are commonly quite low and flat. But yesterday's snow turning to rain, which froze as it fell, there is now a glaze on the trees, giving them a hoary look, icicles like rakes' teeth on the rails, and a thin crust over all the snow. At this hour the crust sparkles with a myriad brilliant points or mirrors, one to every six inches, at least. This crust is cracked like ice into irregular figures a foot or two square. *Perhaps* the snow has settled considerably, for the track in the roads is the highest part. Some heard a loud cracking in the ground or ice last night.

I cut through, five or six rods from the east shore of Fair Haven, and find seven inches of snow, nine inches of snow ice and eight of water ice, — seventeen of both. The water rises to within half an inch of the top of the ice. Isaac Garfield has cut a dozen holes on the west side. The ice there averages nineteen inches in thickness. Half the holes are five or six rods from the shore, and the rest nine or ten, the water from three to seven feet deep. In some places more than half the whole depth is ice. The thinnest ice is 17 inches; the thickest, 20 + .[1] The inner row invariably the thickest. The water rises above the ice in some cases.

Edward and Isaac Garfield were fishing there, and Puffer came along, and afterward Lewis Miner with his gun. He cannot get near the partridges on account of the cracklings of the crust. I saw the last two approaching with my glass.

The fishermen agree in saying that the pickerel have generally been eating, and are full, when they bite. Puffer thinks they eat a good deal, but seldom. Some think it best to cut the holes the day before, because the noise frightens them; and the crackling of the crust to-day was thought to frighten them. E. Garfield says that his Uncle Daniel was once scaling a pickerel, when he pricked his finger against the horn of a pout which the pickerel had swallowed. He himself killed a pickerel with a paddle, in the act of swallowing a large perch. Puffer had taken a striped snake out of one.

They send to Lowell for their bait, and fishermen send thither from far and wide, so that there is not a sufficient supply for them. I. Garfield once caught an eel there with his pickerel bait, through the ice; also speared a trout that weighed three and a half pounds, he says, off Well Meadow.

E. Garfield says that he was just turning into the pond from up-stream when he heard a loud sound and

[1] In the middle of river, in front of our house, same day, it is 13¼ inches thick, only 5 of it snow ice, it having been late to freeze there, comparatively.

saw and caught those two great mud turtles. He let the boat drift down upon them. One had got the other by the neck, and their shells were thumping together and their tails sticking up. He caught one in each hand suddenly, and succeeded in getting them into the boat only by turning them over, since they resisted with their claws against the side; then stood on them turned over, paddled to nearest shore, pulled his boat up with his heel, and, taking a tail in each hand, walked backward through the meadow in water a foot deep, dragging them; then carried one a few rods, left him and returned for the other, and so on. One weighed forty-three and the other forty-seven pounds, together ninety. Puffer said that he never saw two together so heavy. I. Garfield said that he had seen one that weighed sixty-three pounds. All referred to the time when (about fifteen years ago; one said the year of the Bunker Hill Monument celebration) some forty were found dead on the meadows between there and Sudbury. It was about the end of March, and Puffer inferred that they had come out thus early from the river, and, the water going down, the ice had settled on them and killed them; but the Garfields thought that the ice, which tore up the meadows very much that year, exposed them and so they froze. I think the last most likely. Puffer searches for them in May under the cranberry vines with a spear, and calls one of the small kinds the "grass tortoise."

E. Garfield says that he saw the other day where a fox had caught in the snow three partridges and eaten two. He himself last winter caught two, on the hillside

south of Fair Haven, with his hands. They flew before him and dived into the snow, which was about a foot deep, going twice their length into it. He thrust his hand in and caught them. Puffer said that his companion one night speared a partridge on the alders on the south side the pond.

E. Garfield says there were many quails here last fall, but that they are suffering now. One night as he was spearing on Conant's cranberry meadow, just north the pond, his dog caught a sheldrake in the water by the shore. Some days ago he saw what he thought a hawk, as white as snow, fly over the pond, but it *may* have been a white owl (which last he never saw).[1] He sometimes sees a hen-hawk in the winter, but never a partridge or other small hawk at this season. Speaks again of that large speckled hawk he killed once, which some called a "Cape eagle." Had a hum-bird's nest behind their house last summer, and was amused to see the bird drive off other birds; would pursue a robin and alight on his back; let none come near. I. Garfield saw one's nest on a horizontal branch of a white pine near the Charles Miles house, about seven feet from ground. E. Garfield spoke of the wren's nest as not uncommon, hung in the grass of the meadows, and how swiftly and easily the bird would run through a winrow of hay.

Puffer saw a couple of foxes cross the pond a few days ago. The wheelwright in the Corner saw four at once, about the same time.

They think that most squirrel-tracks now are of

[1] Was it a gyrfalcon?

the gray ones; that they do not lay up anything. Their tracks are much larger than those of the red. Puffer says that five gray squirrels came out of one of their leafy nests in a middle-sized white pine, *after* it was cut down, behind the Harrington house the other day, and, a day or two after, three out of another. He says that they, too, use bark in making their nests, as well [as] leaves, — the inner bark of old chestnut rails, which looks like seaweed.

E. Garfield says the chip squirrels come out this month.

Puffer saw a star-nosed mole yesterday in the road. Its track was · ˍ • ˍ ˙ ˍ ˙· ˙ · ˍ ·ˍ·ˍ. dog-like.

Coming home at twelve, the ice is fast melting on the trees, and I see in the drops the colors of all the gems. The snow is soft, and the eaves begin to run as not for many weeks.

Thermometer at 3.30 P. M., 31°.

Puffer once found the nest of what he calls the deer mouse (probably jumping) in pile of wood at what is now R. Rice's place in Sudbury, and the old one carried off nine young clinging to her teats. These men do not chop now; they saw, because the snow is so deep and the crust cuts their legs.

Mr. Prichard tells me that he remembers a six weeks of more *uninterruptedly severe* cold than we have just [had], and that was in '31, ending the middle of January. The eaves on the south side of his house did not once run during that period, but they have run or dripped a trifle on several days during the past six weeks.

Puffer says that he and Daniel (?) Haynes set lines

once when there was good skating in all the bays, from the long causeway in Sudbury down to the railroad bridge, but caught only two or three perch.

Feb. 9. How much the northwest wind prevails in the winter! Almost all our storms come from that quarter, and the ridges of snow-drifts run that way. If the Indians placed their heaven in the southwest on account of the warmth of the southwest wind, they might have made a stern winter god of the northwest wind.

P. M. — Up Assabet.

3.30 P. M., thermometer 30°. This and yesterday comparatively warm weather. Half an inch of snow fell this forenoon, but now it has cleared up. I see a *few* squirrel-tracks, but no mice-tracks, for no night has intervened since the snow. It is only where the river washes a wooded bank that I see mice or even squirrel tracks; elsewhere only where dogs and foxes have traversed it. For example, there are no tracks on the side of the river against Hosmer's and Emerson's land, though many alders, etc., there, but many tracks *commonly* on the opposite wooded side. In the swamp west of Pigeon Rock, I see where the rabbits have bitten off the swamp white oak sprouts, where they have sprung up tender, looking like poplar, from stocks broken by the ice last winter.

I hear a phœbe note from a chickadee.

Saw a pensile nest eighteen feet high, within a lichen-clad red maple on the edge of the Assabet Spring or Pink Azalea Swamp. It looked very much like a bunch of the lichens dangling, and I was not sure it was not

till I climbed up to it. Without, it was chiefly the coarse greenish lichens of the maple, bound with coarse bits of bark and perhaps bleached milkweed bark (??) and brown cocoon silk, and within, a thin lining of pine-needles, hemlock twigs, and the like. Was it a yellow-throat vireo's? It was not shaped like the red-eye's, but, sidewise, thus: looking down upon it, thus: On a side twig to one of the limbs and about a foot from the end of the twig.

Feb. 10. Speaking about the weather and the fishing with E. and I. Garfield on the 8th, I was amused to hear these two young farmers suddenly disputing as to whether the moon (?), if that be it, was in the Feet or the Head or elsewhere. Though I know far more of astronomy than they, I should not know how at once to find out this nonsense in an almanac. Yet they talk very glibly about it, and go a-fishing accordingly. Again, in the evening of the same day, I overtook Mr. Prichard and observed that it was time for a thaw, but said he, "That does not look like it," pointing to the moon in the west. "You could hang a powder-horn upon that pretty well."

P. M. — To Walden.

Returning, I saw a fox on the railroad, at the crossing below the shanty site, eight or nine rods from me. He looked of a dirty yellow and lean. I did not notice the white tip to his tail. Seeing me, he pricked up his ears and at first ran up and along the east bank on the crust, then changed his mind and came down the steep

bank, crossed the railroad before me, and, gliding up the west bank, disappeared in the woods. He coursed, or glided, along easily, appearing not to lift his feet high, leaping over obstacles, with his tail extended straight behind. He leaped over the ridge of snow about two feet high and three wide between the tracks, very easily and gracefully.

I followed, examining his tracks. There was about a quarter of an inch of recent snow above the crust, but for the most part he broke in two or three inches. I slumped from one to three feet. His tracks when running, as I have described, were like this:—

being about two by five inches, as if he slid a little, no marks of toes being seen in that shallow snow; the greatest interval above, one foot. Soon after, thus:

The greatest interval sometimes four feet even. Sometimes the three tracks merged together where the crust broke:

When walking

at ease, before he saw me his tracks were more round and nearer together, — about two inches by two and a half, thus:—

Sometimes I thought his tail had scraped the snow.

He went off at an easy gliding pace such as he might

keep up for a long time, pretty direct after his first turning.

Feb. 11. P. M. — To Fair Haven Pond by river.

Israel Rice says that he does not know that he can remember a winter when we had as much snow as we have had this winter. Eb. Conant says as much, excepting the year when he was twenty-five, about 1803. It is now fairly thawing, the eaves running; and puddles stand in some places. The boys can make snowballs, and the horses begin to slump occasionally.

Saw a partridge by the riverside, opposite Fair Haven Hill, which at first I mistook for the top of a fence-post above the snow, amid some alders. I shouted and waved my hand four rods off, to see if it was one, but there was no motion, and I thought surely it must be a post. Nevertheless I resolved to investigate. Within three rods, I saw it to be indeed a partridge, to my surprise, standing perfectly still, with its head erect and neck stretched upward. It was as complete a deception as if it had designedly placed itself on the line of the fence and in the proper place for a post. It finally stepped off daintily with a teetering gait and head up, and took to wing.

I thought it would be a thawing day by the *sound*, the peculiar sound, of cock-crowing in the morning.

It will indicate what steady cold weather we have had to say that the lodging snow of January 13th, though it did not lodge remarkably, has not yet completely melted off the sturdy trunks of large trees.

Feb. 12. Thawed all day yesterday and rained somewhat last night; clearing off this morning. Heard the eaves drop all night. The thermometer at 8.30 A. M., 42°. The snow or crust and cold weather began December 26th, and not till February 7th was there any considerable relenting, when it rained a little; *i. e.* forty-three days of uninterrupted cold weather, and no serious thaw till the 11th, or yesterday. How different the sunlight over thawing snow from the same over dry, frozen snow! The former excites me strangely, and I experience a springlike melting in my thoughts. Water now stands above the ice and snow on the river.

I find, on shovelling away the snow, that there is about two inches of solid ice at the bottom, — that thin crusted snow of December 26th. These two inches must be added, then, to my measures of January 12th, 16th, 23d, 29th, and 30th. To-day I find it has settled since the 29th — owing, of course, mainly to the rain of the 7th and especially of last night — about two inches in open land and an inch and a half in Trillium Woods. Thus, west of railroad, $11\frac{1}{4}+2=12\frac{1}{4}$ [*sic*]; east of railroad, $13\frac{1}{5}+2=15\frac{1}{5}$; Trillium Woods, $13+2=15$; average, $12+2=14$. There has been scarcely any loss on the west side of the railroad, but $3\frac{3}{4}$ on the east side. It may be owing to the drifting since the 29th.

From January 6th to January 13th, not less than a foot of snow on a level in open land, and from January 13th to February 7th, not less than sixteen inches on a level at any one time in open land, and still there is

fourteen on a level.[1] That is, for twenty-five days the snow was sixteen inches deep in open land!!

Feb. 13. Grew cold again last night, with high wind. The wind began about midday. I think a high wind commonly follows rain or a thaw in winter. The thermometer at 8.30 A. M. is at zero. (At 1 P. M., 8° + .) This fall of 42° from 8.30 A. M. yesterday to the same time to-day has produced not a thin and smooth, but a very firm and thick, uneven crust, on which I go in any direction across the fields, stepping over the fences; yet there is some slosh at the bottom of the snow, above the icy foundation.

Now, no doubt, many sportsmen are out with their dogs, who have been imprisoned by the depth of the snow. In the woods where there are bushes beneath, you still slump more or less.

The crust is quite green with the needles of pitch pines, sometimes whole plumes which have recently fallen. Are these chiefly last year's needles brought down by the glaze, or those of the previous year which had not fallen before? I suspect they are chiefly the former, but *maybe* some of the latter.[2]

Feb. 14. Still colder this morning, — 7° at 8.30 A. M. P. M. — To Walden.

I find that a great many pine-needles, both white and pitch, of '54 still hold on, bristling around the twigs, especially if the tree has not grown much the last

[1] *Vide* forward, Mar. 19th.
[2] *Vide* Feb. 14th.

year. So those that strew the snow now are of both kinds.

I can now walk on the crust in every direction at the Andromeda Swamp; can run and stamp without danger of breaking through, raised quite above the andromeda (which is entirely concealed), more than two feet above the ground. But in the woods, and even in wood-paths, I slump at every other step.

In all the little valleys in the woods and sprout-lands, and on the southeast sides of hills, the oak leaves which have blown over the crust are gathered in dry and warm-looking beds, often five or six feet in diameter, about the base of the shrub oaks. So clean and crisply dry and warm above the cold, white crust, they are singularly inviting to my eye. No doubt they are of service to conceal and warm the rabbit and partridge and other beasts and birds. They fill every little hollow, and betray thus at a distance a man's tracks made a week ago, or a dog's many rods off on a hillside. If the snow were not crusted, they would not be gathered thus in troops.

I walk in the bare maple swamps and detect the minute pensile nests of some vireo high over my head, in the fork of some unattainable twig, where I never suspected them in summer, — a little basket cradle that rocked so high in the wind. And where is that young family now, while their cradle is filled with ice?

I was struck to-day by the size and continuousness of the natural willow hedge on the east side of the railroad causeway, at the foot of the embankment, next to the fence. Some twelve years ago, when that cause-

way was built through the meadows, there were no willows there or near there, but now, just at the foot of the sand-bank, where it meets the meadow, and on the line of the fence, quite a dense willow hedge has planted itself. I used to think that the seeds were brought with the sand from the Deep Cut in the woods, but there is no golden willow there; but now I think that the seeds have been blown hither from a distance, and lodged against the foot of the bank, just as the snow-drift accumulates there, for I see several ash trees among them, which have come from an ash ten rods east in the meadow, though none has sprung up elsewhere. There are also a few alders, elms, birch, poplars, and some elder. For years a willow might not have been persuaded to take root in that meadow; but run a barrier like this through it, and in a few years it is lined with them. They plant themselves here solely, and not in the open meadow, as exclusively as along the shores of a river. The sand-bank is a shore to them, and the meadow a lake. How impatient, how rampant, how precocious these osiers! They have hardly made two shoots from the sand in as many springs, when silvery catkins burst out along them, and anon golden blossoms and downy seeds, spreading their race with incredible rapidity. Thus they multiply and clan together. Thus they take advantage even of the railroad, which elsewhere disturbs and invades their domains. May I ever be in as good spirits as a willow! How tenacious of life! How withy! How soon it gets over its hurts! They never despair. Is there no moisture longer in nature which they can transmute into sap?

They are emblems of youth, joy, and everlasting life. Scarcely is their growth restrained by winter, but their silvery down peeps forth in the warmest days in January (?). The very trees and shrubs and weeds, if we consider their origin, have drifted thus like snow against the fences and hillsides. Their growth is protected and favored there. Soon the alders will take their places with them. This hedge is, of course, as straight as the railroad or its bounding fence.

Over this crust, alder and birch and pine seeds, etc., which in summer would have soon found a resting-place, are blown far and wide.

Feb. 16. P. M. — To Walden.

It has been trying to snow for two days. About one inch fell last night, but it clears up at noon, and sun comes out very warm and bright. Wild says it is the warmest day at 12 M. since the 22d of December, when the thermometer stood at 50°. To-day it is at 44. I hear the eaves running before I come out, and our thermometer at 2 P. M. is 38°. The sun is most pleasantly warm on my cheek; the melting snow shines in the ruts; the cocks crow more than usual in barns; my greatcoat is an incumbrance.

There is no down visible on the sallows when I descend the east side of the railroad, unless a scale has come off.

Where I measured the ice in the middle of Walden on the 6th I now measure again, or close by it, though without cutting out the cake. I find about $11\frac{1}{4}$ (probably about same as the 6th, when called $11\frac{1}{2}$ —) of

snow ice and $21\frac{1}{2}$ in all, leaving $10\frac{1}{4}$ clear ice, which would make the ice to have increased beneath through all this thickness and in spite of the thaws $2\frac{3}{4}$ — inches. Near the shore in one place it was twenty-two inches.

Feb. 17. Some three or four inches of snow fallen in the night and now blowing. At noon begins to snow again, as well as *blow*. Several more inches fall.

Feb. 18. Yesterday's snow drifting. No cars from above or below till 1 P. M.

Feb. 19. Measure snow again, on account of what fell on 17th. West of railroad, $15 + + 2$; east of railroad, $12\frac{1}{2} - + 2$; average of both, $14 + 2 = 16$; Trillium Wood, $18\frac{1}{2} + 2 = 20\frac{1}{2}$. The great body of the last snow appears to have settled under the east side of the railroad. There are five and one half inches more in the wood than on the 12th, and I think this is about the average of what fell on the 17th (night and day). Accordingly, the snow has been deeper since the 17th than before this winter. I think if the drifts could be fairly measured it might be found to be seventeen or eighteen inches deep on a level. This snow, you may say, is all drifted, for in the fields east of the railroad there is not so much as there was a week ago, while west there is about four inches more.

Feb. 20. P. M. — Up Assabet.

See a broad and distinct otter-trail, made last night or yesterday. It came out to the river through the low

woods north of Pinxter Swamp, making a very conspicuous trail, from seven to nine or ten inches wide and three or four deep, with sometimes singularly upright sides, as if a square timber had been drawn along, but commonly rounded. It made some short turns and zigzags; passed *under* limbs which were only five inches above the snow, not over them; had apparently slid down all banks and declivities, making a uniform broad hollow trail there without any mark of its feet. On reaching the river, it had come along under the bank, from time to time looking into the crevices where it might get under the ice there, sometimes ascending the bank and sliding back. On level ground its trail had this appearance:

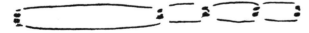

Commonly seven to nine or ten inches wide, and tracks of feet twenty to twenty-four apart; but sometimes there was no track of the feet for twenty-five feet, frequently for six; in the last case *swelled* in the outline, as above. Having come down as far as opposite the great white [*sic*] on the hill, it returned on its track and entered a hole under the ice at Assabet Spring, from which it has not issued.

Feb. '22. P. M. — To Assabet stone bridge and home on river.

It is a pleasant and warm afternoon, and the snow is melting. Yet the river is still perfectly closed (as it has been for many weeks), both against Merrick's

and in the Assabet, excepting directly under this upper stone bridge and probably at mouth of Loring's Brook. I am surprised that the warm weather within ten days has not caused the river to open at Merrick's, but it was too thick to be melted.

Now first, the snow melting and the ice beginning to soften, I see those slender grayish-winged insects creeping with closed wings over the snow-clad ice, — Perla (?). On all parts of the river. Have seen none before, this winter.[1] Just below this bridge begins an otter-track, several days old yet very distinct, which I trace half a mile down the river. In the snow less than an inch deep, on the ice, each foot makes a track three inches wide, apparently enlarged in melting, and the whole four appear thus: The clear interval, sixteen inches; the length occupied by the four feet, fourteen inches. It looks as if some one had dragged a round timber down the middle of the river a day or two since, which bounced as it went.

There is now a crack running down the middle of the river, and it is slightly elevated there, owing, probably, to the increasing temperature.

Feb. 23. 9 A. M. — To Fair Haven Pond, up river.

A still warmer day. The snow is so solid that it still bears me, though we have had several warm suns on

[1] From a third of an inch to an inch long; of various sizes, etc. And every warm day afterward. Have in fact four wings. *Vide* Mar. 22.

it. It is melting gradually under the sun. In the morning I make but little impression in it. As it melts, it acquires a rough but regularly waved surface. It is inspiriting to feel the increased heat of the sun reflected from the snow. There is a slight mist above the fields, through which the crowing of cocks sounds springlike.

I sit by a maple on a maple [*sic*]. It wears the same shaggy coat of lichens summer and winter.

At 2 P. M. the thermometer is 47°. Whenever it is near 40 there is a speedy softening of the snow.

I read in the papers that the ocean is frozen, — not to bear or walk on safely, — or has been lately, on the back side of Cape Cod; at the Highland Light, one mile out from the shore. A phenomenon which, it is said, the oldest have not witnessed before.

Feb. 24. Dr. Jarvis tells me that he thinks there was as much snow as this in '35, when he lived in the Parkman house and drove in his sleigh from November 23d to March 30th excepting one day.

Feb. 25. P. M. — To Walden and Fair Haven.

The only bare ground is the railroad track, where the snow was thin. The crust still bears, and [I] left the railroad at Andromeda Ponds and went through on crust to Fair Haven. Was surprised to see some little minnows only an inch long in an open place in Well Meadow Brook. As I stood there, saw that they had just felled my bee tree, the hemlock. The chopper even then stood at its foot. I went over and saw him cut into the cavity by my direction. He broke a piece out of

his axe as big as my nail against a hemlock knot in the meanwhile. There was no comb within. They have just been cutting wood at Bittern Cliff. The sweet syrup is out on the ends of the hickory logs there.

Gathered some facts from Henry Bond's "Genealogies of the Families of Watertown, etc."

My mother's mother was *Mary Jones*, only daughter of "Col. Elisha Jones, Esq., of Weston. A Boston newspaper, of Feb. 15, 1775, says 'On Monday last, died, in this town, in the sixty-sixth year of his age, Elisha Jones Esq., late of Weston, for many years a magistrate, Col. of a Regiment of Militia, and member of the General Assembly. In the many departments in which he acted, he eminently showed the man of principle, virtue,' &c. He married, Jan. 24, 1733–4, Mary Allen, and occupied his father's homestead." (Mary Allen was the daughter of Abel Allen, who was the son of Lewis Allen of Watertown Farms, who died 1707–8.)

The children of E. Jones and Mary Allen were (1) Nathan (2d son died in infancy), (3) Elisha, (4) Israel, (5) Daniel, (6) Elias, (7) Josiah, (8) Silas, (9) Mary (b. 1748), (10) Ephraim, (11) Simon (or Simeon), (12) Stephen, (13) Jonas, (14) Phillemore, (15) Charles.

Colonel Elisha Jones was born 1710, the son of *Captain Josiah Jones* (born, 1670, in Weston) and *Abigail Barnes*. Captain Josiah Jones was the son of *Josiah Jones* of Watertown Farms (born 1643) and *Lydia Treadway* (daughter of Nathaniel Treadway, who died in Watertown, 1689). Josiah Jones was son of *Lewis Jones*

(who appears to have moved from Roxbury to Watertown about 1650, and died 1684) and Anna (perhaps Stone? born in England). This Josiah Jones in 1666 bought "of John Stone and wife Sarah, of Wat[ertown], a farm of 124 acres on the N. side of Sud[bury] highway, about two miles from Sud[bury]."

Feb. 26. P. M. — To Hubbard's Close.

I see at bottom of the mill brook, below Emerson's, two dead frogs. The brook has part way yet a snowy bridge over it. Were they left by a mink, or killed by cold and ice? In Hubbard's maple swamp beyond, I see the snow under a dead maple, where a woodpecker has drilled a handsome round hole. Excepting the carrying it downward within, it is ready for a nest. May they not have a view to this use even now?

Feb. 27. Wednesday. P. M. — Up Assabet.

Am surprised to see how the ice lasts on the river. It but just begins to be open for a *foot or two* at Merrick's, and you see the motion of the stream. It has overflowed the ice for many rods a few feet in width. It has been tight even there (and of course everywhere else on the main stream, and on North Branch except at Loring's Brook and under stone bridge) since January 25th, and elsewhere on the main stream since January 7th, as it still is. That is, we may say that the river has been frozen solidly for seven weeks. On the 25th I saw a load of wood drawn by four horses up the middle of the river above Fair Haven Pond. On that day, the 25th, they were cutting the last of Baker's

wood-lot on the south side of Fair Haven. They cut the greater part of it last winter, and this was the wood they were hauling off.

I see many birch scales, freshly blown over the snow. They are falling all winter. What is that narrow, twisted, yellowish-brown scale which is seen on the snow all winter near woods?
Shaped like this:[1] —

Found, in the snow in E. Hosmer's meadow, a gray rabbit's hind leg, freshly left there, perhaps by a fox.

The papers are talking about the prospect of a war between England and America. Neither side sees how its country can avoid a long and fratricidal war without sacrificing its honor. Both nations are ready to take a desperate step, to forget the interests of civilization and Christianity and their commercial prosperity and fly at each other's throats. When I see an individual thus beside himself, thus desperate, ready to shoot or be shot, like a blackleg who has little to lose, no serene aims to accomplish, I think he is a candidate for bedlam. What asylum is there for nations to go to? Nations are thus ready to talk of wars and challenge one another,[2] because they are made up to such an extent of poor, low-spirited, despairing men, in whose eyes the chance of shooting somebody else without being shot themselves exceeds their actual good fortune. Who, in fact, will be the first to enlist but

[1] Probably pine stipule.

[2] Will it not be thought disreputable at length, as duelling between individuals now is?

the most desperate class, they who have lost all hope? And they may at last infect the rest.

Minott says that partridges will bud on black birches as on apple trees.

Feb. 28. P. M. — To Nut Meadow.

Mother says that the cat lay on her bread one night and caused it to rise finely all around her.

I go on the crust which we have had since the 13th, *i. e.* on the solid frozen snow, which settles very gradually in the sun, across the fields and brooks.

The very beginning of the river's breaking up appears to be the oozing of water through cracks in the thinnest places, and standing in shallow puddles there on the ice, which freeze solid at night. The river and brooks are quite shrunken. The brooks flow far under the hollow ice and snow-crust a foot thick, which here and there has fallen in, showing the shrunken stream far below. The surface of the snow melts into a regular waved form, like raised scales.

Miles is repairing the damage done at his new mill by the dam giving way. He is shovelling out the flume, which was half filled with sand, standing in the water. His sawmill, built of slabs, reminds me of a new country. He has lost a head of water equal to two feet by this accident. Yet he sets his mill agoing to show me how it works. What a smell as of gun-wash when he raised the gate! He calls it the sulphur from the pond. It must be the carburetted hydrogen gas from the bottom of the pond under the ice. It powerfully scents the whole mill. A powerful smelling-bottle. How pleasant are

Vol. VIII

the surroundings of a mill! Here are the logs (pail-stuff), already drawn to the door from a neighboring hill before the mill is in operation. The dammed-up meadow, the meadow [*sic*], the melted snow, and welling springs are the serf he compels to do his work. He is unruly as yet, has lately broken loose, filled up the flume, and flooded the fields below. He uses the dam of an old mill which stood here a hundred years ago, which now nobody knows anything about. The mill is built of slabs, of the worm-eaten sap-wood. The old dam had probably been undermined by muskrats. It would have been most prudent to have built a new one. Rude forces, rude men, and rude appliances.

Martial Miles, who is there, says that there are many trout in this brook. He sees them running down just before winter, and at that time Charles Snow once speared a great many, one weighing four pounds. He once came within four feet of an otter at 10 P. M., in the middle of the road, by the guide-board just north of this brook. Spoke of the one shot in a ditch at Donge Hole, as I had heard before; also of the three killed (shot) at Farrar's Swamp. The one who shot them told him that he attempted to kill them with a shovel, but that they would take it out of his hands as often as he attempted it.

Coombs came along with his dog and gun, on his way to shoot partridges, which will come out to bud this evening on certain young apple trees. He has got four or five for several nights in succession, and sees foxes there, running about on the crust. Francis Wheeler says he sold two young fox-skins to a tin ped-

dler to-day for a dollar. Coombs says they got a silver-gray fox in Lincoln this winter, and sold its skin for sixteen dollars! He says that he killed a sheldrake a month or six weeks ago in a small open place beneath the falls at the factory. This shows what hardy birds they are. Last summer he found a black duck's nest on one of the islands in Loring's Pond. He saw the duck hide in the grass, came up, and put his hand on a parcel of feathers and, raising a handful, was surprised to find the eggs under them.

How various are the talents of men! From the brook in which one lover of nature has never during all his lifetime detected anything larger than a minnow, another extracts a trout that weighs three pounds, or an otter four feet long. How much more game he will see who carries a gun, *i. e.* who goes to see it! Though you roam the woods all your days, you never will see by chance what he sees who goes on purpose to see it. One gets his living by shooting woodcocks; most never see one in their lives.

Coombs goes to shoot partridges this evening by a far-off wood-side, and M. Miles goes home to load up, for he is going to Boston with a load of wood to-night.

Our young maltese cat Min, which has been absent five cold nights, the ground covered deep with crusted snow, — her first absence, — and given up for dead, has at length returned at daylight, awakening the whole house with her mewing and afraid of the strange girl we have got in the meanwhile. She is a mere wrack of skin and bones, with a sharp nose and wiry tail. She is as one returned from the dead. There is as much

rejoicing as at the return of the prodigal son, and if we had a fatted calf we should kill it. Various are the conjectures as to her adventures, — whether she has had a fit, been shut up somewhere, or lost, torn in pieces by a certain terrier or frozen to death. In the meanwhile she is fed with the best that the house affords, minced meats and saucers of warmed milk, and, with the aid of unstinted sleep in all laps in succession, is fast picking up her crumbs. She has already found her old place under the stove, and is preparing to make a stew of her brains there.

That strong gun-wash scent from the mill-pond water was very encouraging. I who never partake of the sacrament make the more of it.

How simple the machinery of the mill! Miles has dammed a stream, raised a pond or head of water, and placed an old horizontal mill-wheel in position to receive a jet of water on its buckets, transferred the motion to a horizontal shaft and saw by a few cog-wheels and simple gearing, and, throwing a roof of slabs over all, at the outlet of the pond, you have a mill.

Returning on the crust, over Puffer's place, I saw a fine, plump hen hanging from an apple tree and a crow from another, probably poisoned to kill foxes with, — a hen which probably a fox had killed.

Stopped at Martial Miles's to taste his cider. Marvellously sweet and spirited without being bottled; alum and mustard put into the barrels.

A weight of water stored up in a meadow, applied to move a saw, which scratches its way through the trees placed before it. So simple is a sawmill.

A millwright comes and builds a dam across the foot of the meadow, and a mill-pond is created, in which, at length, fishes of various kinds are found; and muskrats and minks and otter frequent it. The pond is like a weight wound up.

Feb. 29. Minott told me this afternoon of his catching a pickerel in the Mill Brook once, — before the pond was drawn off, when the brook had four or five times as much water as now, — which weighed four pounds. Says they stayed in it all winter in those days. This was near his land up the brook. He once also caught there, when fishing for pickerel, a trout which weighed three and a half pounds. He fell within two feet of the water, but [he] succeeded in tossing him higher up. When cutting peat thereabouts, he saw a stinkpot turtle in the water eating a frog which it had just caught. Speaks of seeing a mink swimming along a little [*sic*] in his beech wood-lot, and from time to time running along the shore; part way up an alder and down again.

He loves to recall his hunting days and adventures, and I willingly listen to the stories he has told me half a dozen times already. One day he saw about twenty black ducks on Goose Pond, and stole down on them, thinking to get a shot, but it chanced that a stray dog scared them up before he was ready. He stood on the point of the neck of land between the ponds, and watched them as they flew high toward Flint's Pond. As he looked, he saw one separate from the flock when they had got half-way to Flint's Pond, or half a mile, and return straight toward Goose Pond again. He

thought he would await him, and give him a shot if he came near enough. As he flew pretty near and rather low, he fired, whereupon the duck rose right up high into the air, and he saw by his motions that he was wounded. Suddenly he dropped, by a slanting fall, into the point of a thick pine wood, and he heard him plainly strike the ground like a stone. He went there and searched for a long time, and was about giving it up, when at length he saw the duck standing, still alive and bleeding, by the side of a stump, and made out to kill him with a stick before he could reach the water.

He said he saw Emerson come home from lecturing the other day with his knitting-bag (lecture-bag) in his hand. He asked him if the lecturing business was as good as it used to be. Emerson said he did n't see but it was as good as ever; guessed the people would want lectures "as long as he or I lived."

Told again of the partridge hawk striking down a partridge which rose before him and flew across the run in the beech woods, — how suddenly he did it, — and he, hearing the fluttering of the partridge, came up and secured it, while the hawk kept out of gun-shot.

Vol. VIII

ago, five or six feet high and thickly, as if they were an irregular stake fence a rod out.

Going up the hill again, I slump in up to my middle.

At Flint's I find half a dozen fishing. The pond cracks a very little while I am there, say at half past ten. I think I never saw the ice so thick. It measures just two feet thick in shallow water, twenty rods from shore.

Goodwin says that somewhere where he lived they called cherry-birds "port-royals."

Haynes of Sudbury brought some axe-helves which he had been making to Smith's shop to sell to-day. Those made by hand are considered stronger than those which are turned, because their outline conforms to the grain. They told him they had not sold any of the last yet. "Well," said he, "you may depend on it you will. They 've got to come after them yet, for they have n't been able to get into the woods this winter on account of the snow, and they 'll have to do all their chopping this month."

I like to see the farmer whittling his own axe-helve, as I did E. Hosmer a white oak one on the 27th *ult.*

It is remarkable that though I have not been able to find any open place in the river almost all winter, except under the further stone bridge and at Loring's Brook, — this winter so remarkable for ice and snow, — Coombs should (as he says) have killed two sheldrakes at the falls by the factory, a place which I had forgotten, some four or six weeks ago. Singular that this hardy bird should have found this small opening, which I had forgotten, while the ice everywhere else

V

MARCH, 1856

(ÆT. 38)

March 1. 9 A. M. — To Flint's Pond *via* Walden, by railroad and the crust.

I hear the hens cackle as not before for many months. Are they not now beginning to lay?

The catkins of the willow by the causeway and of the aspens appear to have pushed out a little further than a month ago. I see the down of half a dozen on that willow by the causeway; on the aspens pretty generally. As I go through the cut it is still, warm, and more or less sunny, springlike (about 40° +), and the sand and reddish subsoil is bare for about a rod in width on the railroad. I hear several times the fine-drawn *phe-be* note of the chickadee, which I heard only once during the winter. Singular that I should hear this on the first spring day.

I see a pitch pine seed with its wing, far out on Walden.

Going down the hill to Goose Pond, I slump now and then. Those dense, dry beds of leaves are gathered especially about the leafy tops of young oaks, which are bent over and held down by the snow. They lie up particularly light and crisp. The birch stubs stand around Goose Pond, killed by the water a year or two

was from one to two feet thick, and the snow sixteen inches on a level. If there is a crack amid the rocks of some waterfall, this bright diver is sure to know it. Ask the sheldrake whether the rivers are completely sealed up.

March 2. Has snowed three or four inches — very damp snow — in the night; stops about 9 A. M. This will probably help carry off the old snow, so solid and deep.

P. M. — Walking up the river by Prichard's, was surprised to see, on the snow over the river, a great many seeds and scales of birches, though the snow had so recently fallen, there had been but little wind, and it was already spring. There was one seed or scale to a square foot, yet the nearest birches were, about fifteen of them, along the wall thirty rods east. As I advanced toward them, the seeds became thicker and thicker, till they quite discolored the snow half a dozen rods distant, while east of the birches there was not one. The birches appear not to have lost a quarter of their seeds yet. As I went home up the river, I saw some of the seeds forty rods off, and *perhaps*, in a more favorable direction, I might have found them much further. It suggested how unwearied Nature is, spreading her seeds. Even the spring does not find her unprovided with birch, aye, and alder and pine seed. A great proportion of the seed that was carried to a distance lodged in the hollow over the river, and when the river breaks up will be carried far away, to distant shores and meadows.

March 5. Snowed an inch or two in the night.
Went to Carlisle, surveying.

It is very hard turning out, there is so much snow in the road. Your horse springs and flounders in it. The snow in the wood-lot which I measured was about two feet on a level.

March 6. P. M. — Up Assabet.
The snow is softening. Methinks the lichens are a little greener for it. A thaw comes, and then the birches, which were gray on their white ground before, appear prettily clothed in green. I see various kinds of insects out on the snow now. On the rock this side the Leaning Hemlocks, is the track of an otter. He has left some scentless jelly-like substance an inch and a half in diameter there, yellowish beneath, maybe part of a fish, or clam (?), or himself. The leaves still hanging on some perhaps young swamp white oaks are remarkably fresh, almost ochre-colored brown.

See the snow discolored yellowish under a (probably) gray squirrel's nest high in a pitch pine, and acorn-shells about on it. Also a squirrel's track on the snow over Lee's Hill. The outside toe on the fore feet is nearly at right angles with the others. This also distinguishes it from a rabbit's track. It visits each apple tree, digs up frozen apples and sometimes filberts, and when it starts again, aims for an apple tree, though fifteen rods distant.

March 7. P. M. — Measured snow on account of snow which fell 2d and 4th. West of railroad, 16 + ;

The opening in the river at Merrick's is now increased to ten feet in width in some places.

I can hardly believe that hen-hawks may be beginning to build their nests now, yet their young were a fortnight old the last of April last year.

March 3. To Cambridge.

March 4. To Carlisle, surveying.
I had two friends. The one offered me friendship on such terms that I could not accept it, without a sense of degradation. He would not meet me on equal terms, but only be to some extent my patron. He would not come to see me, but was hurt if I did not visit him. He would not readily accept a favor, but would gladly confer one. He treated me with ceremony occasionally, though he could be simple and downright sometimes; and from time to time acted a part, treating me as if I were a distinguished stranger; was on stilts, using made words. Our relation was one long tragedy, yet I did not directly speak of it. I do not believe in complaint, nor in explanation. The whole is but too plain, alas, already. We grieve that we do not love each other, that we cannot confide in each other. I could not bring myself to speak, and so recognize an obstacle to our affection.

I had another friend, who, through a slight obtuseness, perchance, did not recognize a fact which the dignity of friendship would by no means allow me to descend so far as to speak of, and yet the inevitable effect of that ignorance was to hold us apart forever.

east of railroad, 16; average, say 16 + ; Trillium Wood, 21. Probably quite as deep as any time before, this year. There are still two or more inches of ice next the ground in open land.

I may say that there has not been less than sixteen inches of snow on a level in open land since January 13th. My stick entered the earth in some cases in the wood, as it has not done before. There has been some thawing under the snow.

March 9. Thermometer at 2 P. M. 15°, sixteen inches of snow on a level in open fields, hard and dry, ice in Flint's Pond two feet thick, and the aspect of the earth is that of the middle of January in a severe winter. Yet this is about the date that bluebirds arrive commonly. A pail of water froze nearly half an inch thick in my chamber, with fire raked up. The train which should have got down last night did not arrive till this afternoon (Sunday), having stuck in a drift.

March 10. Thermometer at 7 A. M. 6° below zero. Dr. Bartlett's, between 6.30 and 7 A. M., was at −13°; Smith's at −13° or −14°, at 6 A. M.

P. M. — Up river to Hubbard Bridge.
Thermometer + 9° at 3.30 P. M. (the same when I return at five). The snow hard and dry, squeaking under the feet; excellent sleighing. A biting northwest wind *compels* to cover the ears. It is one of the hardest days of the year to bear. Truly a memorable 10th of March. There is no opening yet in the main stream at Prichard's, Hubbard Bath, or the Clamshell, or probably any-

where but at Merrick's, and that a dozen rods long by ten feet; and it is tight and strong under the bridges. A bluebird would look as much out of place now as the 10th of January.

I suspect that in speaking of the springing of plants in previous years I have been inclined to make them start too early generally.

The ice on ponds is as solid as ever. There has been no softening of it. Now is a good time to begin to cut; only its great thickness would hinder you. The blue shadows on snow are as fine as ever. It is hard to believe the records of previous years.

I have not seen a tree sparrow, methinks, since January. Probably the woods have been so generally buried by the snow this winter that they have migrated further south. There has not been one in the yard the past winter, nor a redpoll. I saw perhaps one redpoll in the town; that is all. The pinched crows are feeding in the road to-day in front of the house and alighting on the elms, and blue jays also, as in the middle of the hardest winter, for such is this weather. The blue jays hop about in yards.

The past has been a winter of such unmitigated severity that I have not chanced to notice a snow-flea, which are so common in thawing days.

I go over the fields now in any direction, sinking but an inch or two to the old solid snow of the winter. In the road you are on a level with the fences, and often considerably higher, and sometimes, where it is a level causeway in summer, you climb up and coast down great swells of hard-frozen snow, much higher than

the fences. I may say that I have not had to climb a fence this winter, but have stepped over them on the snow.

Think of the art of printing, what miracles it has accomplished! Covered the very waste paper which flutters under our feet like leaves and is almost as cheap, a stuff now commonly put to the most trivial uses, with thought and poetry! The woodchopper reads the wisdom of ages recorded on the paper that holds his dinner, then lights his pipe with it. When we ask for a scrap of paper for the most trivial use, it may have the confessions of Augustine or the sonnets of Shakespeare, and we not observe it. The student kindles his fire, the editor packs his trunk, the sportsman loads his gun, the traveller wraps his dinner, the Irishman papers his shanty, the schoolboy peppers the plastering, the belle pins up her hair, with the printed thoughts of men. Surely he who can see so large a portion of earth's surface thus darkened with the record of human thought and experience, and feel no desire to learn to read it, is without curiosity. He who cannot read is worse than deaf and blind, is yet but half alive, is still-born.

Still there is little or no chopping, for it will not pay to shovel the snow away from the trees; unless they are quite large, and then you must work standing in it two feet deep. There is an eddy about the large trees beside, which produces a hollow in the snow about them, but it lies close up to the small ones on every side.

10 P. M. — Thermometer at zero.

I read, when last at Cambridge, in the Philadelphia

Vol. VIII

Philosophical Transactions, that, in the cold winter of 1780, many shellfish, frogs, insects, etc., as well as birds and plants, perished.

March 11. Thermometer at 7 A. M. 6°, yet, the fire going out, Sophia's plants are frozen again. Dr. Bartlett's was − 4°.

When it was proposed to me to go abroad, rub off some rust, and *better my condition* in a worldly sense, I fear lest my life will lose some of its homeliness. If these fields and streams and woods, the phenomena of nature here, and the simple occupations of the inhabitants should cease to interest and inspire me, no culture or wealth would atone for the loss. I fear the dissipation that travelling, going into society, even the best, the enjoyment of intellectual luxuries, imply. If Paris is much in your mind, if it is more and more to you, Concord is less and less, and yet it would be a wretched bargain to accept the proudest Paris in exchange for my native village. At best, Paris could only be a school in which to learn to live here, a stepping-stone to Concord, a school in which to fit for this university. I wish so to live ever as to derive my satisfactions and inspirations from the commonest events, every-day phenomena, so that what my senses hourly perceive, my daily walk, the conversation of my neighbors, may inspire me, and I may dream of no heaven but that which lies about me. A man may acquire a taste for wine or brandy, and so lose his love for water, but should we not pity him?

The sight of a marsh hawk in Concord meadows is

worth more to me than the entry of the allies into Paris. In this sense I am not ambitious. I do not wish my native soil to become exhausted and run out through neglect. Only that travelling is good which reveals to me the value of home and enables me to enjoy it better. That man is the richest whose pleasures are the cheapest.

It is strange that men are in such haste to get fame as teachers rather than knowledge as learners.

I hear that Goodwin found one of his traps frozen in this morning, where it has not frozen before this year.

P. M. — 3.30, thermometer 24°.

Cut a hole in the ice in the middle of Walden. It is just 24¼ inches thick, 11½ + being snow ice, 12¾ water ice; and there is between 3 and 4 inches of crusted snow above this. The water rises to within 2½ inches of the top of the ice, *i. e.* between a ninth and tenth of the whole thickness. The clear ice has therefore gained 2¾ inches beneath since the 16th of February. It has gone on freezing under 21½ inches of ice. Yet people very commonly say that it will not continue to freeze under half that thickness of snow and ice. It is a job to cut a hole now. Snow and ice together make a curtain twenty-eight inches thick now drawn over the pond. Such is the prospect of the fishes!

March 12. The last four cold days have closed the river again against Merrick's, and probably the few other small places which *may* have opened in the town, at the mouth of one or two brooks. I hear, from two sources, of portions of brooks, etc., being frozen over within two days, which had not frozen before this winter.

We had a colder day in the winter of '54 and '55 than in the last, yet the ice did not get to be so thick. It is *long-continued*, *steady* cold which produces thick ice. If the present cold should continue uninterrupted a thousand years would not the pond become solid?

Rufus Hosmer says he has known the ground here to be frozen four feet deep.

I never saw such solid mountains of snow in the roads. You travel along for many rods over excellent dry solid sleighing, where the road is perfectly level, not thinking but you are within a foot of the ground, then suddenly descend four or five feet and find, to your surprise, that you had been traversing the broad back of a drift.

The crow has been a common bird in our street and about our house the past winter.

One large limb of the great elm  at Davis's, sawed off, presented this outline: a perfect harp.

March 13. P. M. — To Flint's Pond.

Much warmer at last. On Flint's Pond I cut a hole and measured the ice twenty-two rods from the shore nearest to Walden, where the water was nine feet deep (measuring from its surface in the hole). The ice was twenty-six inches thick, thirteen and one half of it being snow ice, and the ice rose above the water two inches. This ice is as solid as at any time in the winter. Three inches of snow above. It was so much work to cut this hole with a dull axe that I did not try any other place

where it may have been thicker. Perhaps it was thicker in the middle, as in '47.[1]

March 14. *Friday.* Quite warm. Thermometer 46°. 3 P. M. — Up Assabet.

The ice formed the fore part of this week, as that at Merrick's noticed on the 12th, and heard of elsewhere in the Mill Brook, appears to have been chiefly snow ice, though no snow fell. It was apparently blown into the water during those extremely cold nights and assisted its freezing. So that it is a question whether the river would have closed again at Merrick's on the night of the 10th and 11th, notwithstanding the intense cold, if the snow had not been blown into it, — a question, I say, because the snow *was* blown into it.

I think it remarkable that, cold as it was, I should not have supposed from my sensations that it was nearly so cold as the thermometer indicated.

Tapped several white maples with my knife, but find no sap flowing; but, just above Pinxter Swamp, one red maple limb was moistened by sap trickling along the bark. Tapping this, I was surprised to find it flow freely. Where the sap had dried on the bark, shining and sticky, it tasted quite sweet. Yet Anthony Wright tells me that he attempted to trim some apple trees on the 11th, but was obliged to give up, it was so cold. They were frozen solid. This is the only one of eight or ten white and red maples that flows. I do not see why it should be.

As I return by the old Merrick Bath Place, on the

[1] Probably not, judging from Walden. *Vide* 19th.

river, — for I still travel everywhere on the middle of the river, — the setting sun falls on the osier row toward the road and attracts my attention. They certainly look brighter now and from this point than I have noticed them before this year, — greenish and yellowish below and reddish above, — and I fancy the sap fast flowing in their pores. Yet I think that on a close inspection I should find no change. Nevertheless, it is, on the whole, perhaps the most springlike sight I have seen.

March 15. Put a spout in the red maple of yesterday, and hung a pail beneath to catch the sap. Mr. Chase (of the Town School), who has lived a hundred miles distant in New Hampshire, speaks of the snow-fleas as a spring phenomenon, — probably because the winter is more uniformly cold there, — and says that they think it time to stop making maple-sugar when they observe them. They get into the sap by myriads and trouble them much.

March 16. 7 A. M. — The sap of that red maple has not begun to flow yet. The few spoonfuls in the pail and in the hole are frozen.

These few rather warmer days have made a little impression on the river. It shows a rough, snowy ice in many places, suggesting that there is a river beneath, the water having probably oozed up or the snow blown and melted off there. A rough, softening snowy ice, with some darker spots where you suspect weakness, though it is still thick enough.

2 P. M. — The red maple [sap] is now about an inch

deep in a quart pail, — nearly all caught since morning. It now flows at the rate of about six drops in a minute. Has probably flowed faster this forenoon. It is perfectly clear, like water. Going home, slipped on the ice, throwing the pail over my head to save myself, and spilt all but a pint. So it was lost on the ice of the river. When the river breaks up, it will go down the Concord into the Merrimack, and down the Merrimack into the sea, and there get salted as well as diluted, part being boiled into sugar. It suggests, at any rate, what various liquors, beside those containing salt, find their way to the sea, — the sap of how many kinds of trees!

There is, at any rate, such a phenomenon as the willows shining in the spring sun, however it is to be accounted for.

March 17. *Monday.* Snow going off very gradually under the sun alone. Going begins to be bad; horses slump; hard turning out. See where the cattle, which have stepped a few inches one side the sled-track, have slumped two feet or more, leaving great holes.

March 18. P. M. — Up river.

It is still quite tight at Hubbard's Bath Bend and at Clamshell, though I hesitate a little to cross at these places. There are dark spots in the soft, white ice, which will be soon worn through.

What a solid winter we have had! No thaw of any consequence; no bare ground since December 25th; but an unmelting mass of snow and ice, hostile to all greenness. Have not seen a green radical leaf even, as usual, all being covered up.

Nut Meadow Brook is open for a dozen rods from its mouth, and for a rod into the river. Higher up, it is still concealed by a snowy bridge two feet thick. I see the ripples made by some fishes, which were in the small opening at its mouth, making haste to hide themselves in the ice-covered river. This square rod and one or two others like it in the town are the only places where I could see this phenomenon now. Thus early they appear, ready to be the prey of the fish hawk. Within the brook I see quite a school of little minnows, an inch long, amid or over the bare dead stems of polygonums, and one or [two] little water-bugs (apple-seeds). The last also in the broad ditch on the Corner road, in Wheeler's meadow. Notwithstanding the backwardness of the season, all the town still under deep snow and ice, here they are, in the first open and smooth water, governed by the altitude of the sun.

I see many small furrows, freshly made, in the sand at the bottom of the brook, from half an inch to three quarters wide, which I suspect are made by some small shellfish already moving, perhaps *Paludina!* [1]

March 19. P. M. — To Walden.

Measured the snow again. West of railroad, 15; east of railroad, 11$\frac{4}{5}$; average, 13$\frac{2}{5}$; Trillium Woods, 16$\frac{3}{4}$. The last measurement was on the 7th, when it averaged about sixteen inches in the open land. This depth it must have preserved, owing to the remarkably cold weather, till the 13th at least. So it chances that the snow was constantly sixteen inches deep, at least,

[1] *Vide* 20th.

on a level in open land, from January 13th to March 13th. It is remarkable how rapidly it has settled on the east of the railroad as compared with the west since the 7th (or I may say rather the 13th). The whole average settling, in open land, since say the 13th, is a little less than three inches.

The thickness of the ice on Walden in the long cove on the south side, about five rods from shore, where the water is nineteen and a half feet deep, is just twenty-six inches, about one foot being snow ice. In the middle it was twenty-four and a quarter on the 11th. It is the same there now, and undoubtedly it was then twenty-six in the long cove. Probably got to be the thickest on this side. Since the warmer weather which began on the 13th, the snow, which was three or four inches deep, is about half melted on the ice, under the influence of the sun alone, and the ice is considerably softened within the last five days, thus *suddenly*, quite through, it being easier to cut and more moist, quite fine and white like snow in the hole, sticking together as damp snow when I shovel it out on my axe, the dust not at all hard, dry, and crystalline. Apparently, then, Walden is as thickly frozen about shore as Flint's.

While I am measuring, though it is quite warm, the air is filled with large, moist snowflakes, of the star form, which are rapidly concealing the very few bare spots on the railroad embankment. It is, indeed, a new snow-storm.

Another old red maple bleeds now, on the warm south edge of Trillium Wood. The first maple was old and in a warm position.

Vol. VIII

WHAT BEFELL AT MRS. BROOKS'S.

On the morning of the 17th, Mrs. Brooks's Irish girl Joan fell down the cellar stairs, and was found by her mistress lying at the bottom, apparently lifeless. Mrs. Brooks ran to the street-door for aid to get her up, and asked a Miss Farmer, who was passing, to call the blacksmith near by. The latter lady turned instantly, and, making haste across the road on this errand, fell flat in a puddle of melted snow, and came back to Mrs. Brooks's, bruised and dripping and asking for opodeldoc. Mrs. Brooks again ran to the door and called to George Bigelow to complete the unfinished errand. He ran nimbly about it and fell flat in another puddle near the former, but, his joints being limber, got along without opodeldoc and raised the blacksmith. He also notified James Burke, who was passing, and he, rushing in to render aid, fell off one side of the cellar stairs in the dark. They no sooner got the girl up-stairs than she came to and went raving, then had a fit.

Haste makes waste. It never rains but it pours. I have this from those who have heard Mrs. Brooks's story, seen the girl, the stairs, and the puddles.

No sooner is some opening made in the river, a square rod in area, where some brook or rill empties in, than the fishes apparently begin to seek it for light and warmth, and thus early, perchance, may become the prey of the fish hawk. They are seen to ripple the water, darting out as you approach.

I noticed on the 18th that springy spot on the shore just above the railroad bridge, by the ash, which for a month has been bare for two or three feet, now enlarged to eight or ten feet in diameter. And in a few other places on the meadowy shore, *e. g.* just above mouth of Nut Meadow, I see great dimples in the deep snow, eight or ten feet over, betraying springs. There the pads (*Nuphar*) and cress already spring, and shells are left by the rat. At the broad ditch on the Corner road, opposite Bear Garden, the snowy crust had slumped or fallen in here and there, and, where the bridge was perfect, I saw it quite two feet thick. In the smooth open water there, small water-bugs were gyrating singly, not enough to play the game.

I am surprised at the sudden change in the Walden ice within five days. In cutting a hole now, instead of hard, dry, transparent chips of ice, you make a fine white snow, very damp and adhering together, with but few chips in it. The ice has been affected throughout its twenty-six inches, though most, I should say, above. Hard to say exactly where the ice begins, under the two inches of snow.

March 20. It snowed three or four inches of damp snow last afternoon and night, now thickly adhering to the twigs and branches. Probably it will soon melt and help carry off the snow.

P. M. — To Trillium Wood and to Nut Meadow Brook to tap a maple, see paludina, and get elder and sumach spouts, slumping in the deep snow. It is now so softened that I slump at every third step. The sap of red maples in *low and warm* positions now generally flows, but not in high and exposed ones.

Where I saw those furrows in the sand in Nut Meadow Brook the other day, I now explore, and find within a square foot or two half a dozen of *Paludina decisa* with their feet out, within an inch of the surface, so I have scarcely a doubt that they made them. I suppose that they do not furrow the bottom thus under the ice, but as soon as the spring sun has thawed it, they come to the surface, — *perhaps* at night only, — where there is some little sand, and furrow it thus by their motions. Maybe it is the love season. *Perhaps* these make part of the food of the crows which visit this brook and whose tracks I now see on the edge, and have all winter. Probably they also pick up some dead frogs.

Father read in a paper to-day of seven hundred and forty-odd apple tree buds recently taken out of the crop of a partridge.

Last night's snow, which is melting very fast, is evidently helping to rot the ice very fast, in the absence of rain, by settling into it, as did the older snow, indeed. Maybe it will thaw the ground in the same way. Considering how solid and thick the river was a week ago, I am surprised to find how cautious I have grown about crossing it in many places now.

For two or three days I have heard the gobbling of turkeys, the first spring sound, after the chickadees and hens, that I think of. The river has just begun to open at Hubbard's Bend. It has been closed there since January 7th, *i. e.* ten weeks and a half.

Vol. VIII

other poison-dogwood has a very large pith, and I am not sure about the scent. The juice of the bark is not white.

March 21. George Brooks, of the North Quarter, tells me that he went a-fishing at Nagog Pond on the 18th and found the ice from thirty to thirty-seven inches thick (the greater part, or all but about a foot, snow ice), the snow having blown on to the ice there. He measured it with a rule and a hooked stick. (But at Walden, where I measured, there was no drifting of the snow.) It may have been no thicker at Nagog on an average. He says that both the gray squirrel and the red eat pine seed, but not in company. The former have been quite common about his house the past winter, and his neighbor caught two in his yard.

10 A. M. — To my red maple sugar camp. Found that, after a pint and a half had run from a single tube after 3 P. M. yesterday, it had frozen about half an inch thick, and this morning a quarter of a pint more had run. Between 10.30 and 11.30 A. M. this forenoon, I caught two and three quarters pints more, from six tubes, at the same tree, though it is completely overcast and threatening rain. Four and one half pints in all. This sap is an agreeable drink, like iced water (by chance), with a pleasant but slight sweetish taste. I boiled it down in the afternoon, and it made an ounce and a half of sugar, without any molasses, which appears to be the average amount yielded by the sugar maple in similar situations, *viz.* south edge of a wood, a tree partly decayed, two feet [in] diameter.

Set a pail before coming here to catch red maple sap, at Trillium Wood. I am now looking after elder and sumach for spouts. I find the latter best, for though the former has as large a pith (larger in proportion to its size), its wood commonly being less, it does not fill so large a hole, nor is it so strong. Yet there is some by A. Barrett's ditch more than two inches in diameter, very strong, but its pith small. The pith, etc., of the smooth smells to me like weak tobacco. What other shrubs have a large pith?[1] Got my smooth sumach on the south side of Nawshawtuct. I know of no shrubs hereabout except elders and the sumachs which have a suitable pith and wood for such a purpose. The pith of the smooth sumach is a light brown, like *yellow* snuff. The ring of old wood next to it is a decayed-looking greenish yellow; the sap-wood is white. When cut or broken, it has a singularly particolored and decayed look, there being often but a small proportion of sap-wood. A white sticky juice oozes out of the edge of the bark where cut, and soon turns yellow and hard in drops like pitch or hickory sap. This pith does not come out quite so entire and smooth as elder, being drier now at least. You can shove it past the axils of twigs. The old wood of the ivy is also yellow like this, but there is more and harder sap-wood and the pith is quite small. The pith of the poison sumach or dogwood is considerably smaller, but I think it has the same scent with the smooth. An-

[1] Only those plants which have a great growth the first year can have much pith, since apparently this does not increase afterward. *Vide* April 22d for mountain sumach.

It is worth the while to know that there is all this sugar in our woods, much of which might be obtained by using the refuse wood lying about, without damage to the proprietors, who use neither the sugar nor the wood.

I left home at ten and got back before twelve with two and three quarters pints of sap, in addition to the one and three quarters I found collected.

I put in saleratus and a little milk while boiling, the former to neutralize the acid, and the latter to collect the impurities in a skum. After boiling it till I burned it a little, and my small quantity would not flow when cool, but was as hard as half-done candy, I put it on again, and in a minute it was softened and turned to sugar.

While collecting sap, the little of yesterday's lodging snow that was left, dropping from the high pines in Trillium Wood and striking the brittle twigs in its descent, makes me think that the squirrels are running there.

I noticed that my fingers were purpled, evidently from the sap on my auger.

Had a dispute with Father about the *use* of my making this sugar when I knew it could be done and might have bought sugar cheaper at Holden's. He said it took me from my studies. I said I made it my study; I felt as if I had been to a university.

It dropped from each tube about as fast as my pulse beat, and, as there were three tubes directed to each vessel, it flowed at the rate of about one hundred and eighty drops in a minute into it. One maple, standing immediately north of a thick white pine, scarcely flowed at all, while a smaller, farther in the wood, ran pretty well. The south side of a tree bleeds first in spring. I hung my pails on the tubes or a nail. Had two tin pails and a pitcher. Had a three-quarters-inch auger. Made a dozen spouts, five or six inches long, hole as large as a pencil, smoothed with a pencil.

March 22. Saturday. P. M. — To white maples and up Assabet.

The ice of the river is very rapidly softening, still concealed by snow, the upper part becoming homogeneous with the melting snow above it. I *sometimes* slump into snow and *ice* six or eight inches, to the harder ice beneath.

I walk up the middle of the Assabet, and most of the way on middle of South Branch.

Many tracks of crows in snow along the edge of the open water against Merrick's at Island. They thus visit the edge of water — this and brooks — before any ground is exposed. Is it for small shellfish? The snow now no longer bears you. It has become very coarse-grained under the sun, and I hear it sink around me as I walk.

Part of the white maples now begin to flow, some perhaps two or three days. Probably in equally warm positions they would have begun to flow as early as those red ones which I have tapped. Their buds, and apparently some of the red ones, are visibly swollen. This probably follows directly on the flowing of the sap. In three instances I cut off a twig, and sap flowed

and dropped from the part attached to the tree, but in no case would any sap flow from the part cut off (I mean where I first had cut it), which appears to show that the sap is now *running up.*[1] I also cut a notch in a branch two inches in diameter, and the upper side of the cut remained dry, while sap flowed from the lower side, but in another instance both sides were wet at once and equally. The sap, then, is now generally flowing upward in red and white maples in *warm positions.* See it flowing from maple twigs which were gnawed off by rabbits in the winter.

The down of willow catkins in very warm places has in almost every case peeped out an eighth of an inch, generally over the whole willow.

On water standing above the ice under a white maple, are many of those *Perla* (?) insects, with four wings, drowned, though it is all ice and snow around the country over. Do not see any flying, nor before this.

The woodchoppers, who are cutting the wood at Assabet Spring, now at last go to their work up the middle of the river, but one got in yesterday, one leg the whole length. It is rotted through in many places behind Prichard's.

At the red maple which I first tapped, I see the sap still running and wetting the whole side of the tree. It has also oozed out from the twigs, especially those that are a little drooping, and run down a foot or two bathing them sometimes all around, both twigs and

[1] Yet the next day at Walden it flowed from *both parts*, though *considerably more* from the end attached to the tree. It will also drip from the upper carf of a woodchopper.

buds sometimes, or collected in drops on the under sides of the twigs and all evaporated to molasses, which is, for the most part, as black as blacking or ink, having probably caught the dust, etc., even over all this snow. Yet it is as sweet and thick as molasses, and the twigs and buds look as if blacked and polished. Black drops of this thick, sweet syrup spot the under sides of the twigs. No doubt the bees and other insects frequent the maples now. I thought I heard the hum of a bee, but perhaps it was a railroad whistle on the Lowell Railroad. It is as thick as molasses. See a fuzzy gnat on it. It is especially apt to collect about the bases of the twigs, where the stream is delayed. Where the sap is flowing, the red maple being cut, the inner bark turns crimson. I see many snow-fleas on the moist maple chips.

Saw a pigeon woodpecker under the swamp white oak in Merrick's pasture, where there is a small patch of bare ground. Probably Minott saw one in his dooryard in midwinter.

March 23. I spend a considerable portion of my time observing the habits of the wild animals, my brute neighbors. By their various movements and migrations they fetch the year about to me. Very significant are the flight of geese and the migration of suckers, etc., etc. But when I consider that the nobler animals have been exterminated here, — the cougar, panther, lynx, wolverene, wolf, bear, moose, deer, the beaver, the turkey, etc., etc., — I cannot but feel as if I lived in a tamed, and, as it were, emasculated country. Would

not the motions of those larger and wilder animals have been more significant still? Is it not a maimed and imperfect nature that I am conversant with? As if I were to study a tribe of Indians that had lost all its warriors. Do not the forest and the meadow now lack expression, now that I never see nor think of the moose with a lesser forest on his head in the one, nor of the beaver in the other? When I think what were the various sounds and notes, the migrations and works, and changes of fur and plumage which ushered in the spring and marked the other seasons of the year, I am reminded that this my life in nature, this particular round of natural phenomena which I call a year, is lamentably incomplete. I listen to [a] concert in which so many parts are wanting. The whole civilized country is to some extent turned into a city, and I am that citizen whom I pity. Many of those animal migrations and other phenomena by which the Indians marked the season are no longer to be observed. I seek acquaintance with Nature, — to know her moods and manners. Primitive Nature is the most interesting to me. I take infinite pains to know all the phenomena of the spring, for instance, thinking that I have here the entire poem, and then, to my chagrin, I hear that it is but an imperfect copy that I possess and have read, that my ancestors have torn out many of the first leaves and grandest passages, and mutilated it in many places. I should not like to think that some demigod had come before me and picked out some of the best of the stars. I wish to know an entire heaven and an entire earth. All the great trees and beasts, fishes and fowl are gone. The streams, perchance, are somewhat shrunk.

I see that a shopkeeper advertises among his perfumes for handkerchiefs "meadow flowers" and "new-mown hay."

P. M. — To Walden.

The sugar maple sap flows, and for aught I know is as early as the red.

I think I may say that the snow has been *not less than a foot deep on a level* in open land until to-day, since January 6th, about eleven weeks. It probably begins to be less about this date. The bare ground begins to appear where the snow is worn in the street. It has been steadily melting since March 13th, the thermometer rising daily to 40 and 45 at noon, but no rain.

The east side of the Deep Cut is nearly bare, as is the railroad itself, and, on the driest parts of the sandy slope, I go looking for *Cicindela*, — to see it run or fly amid the sere blackberry vines, — some life which the warmth of the dry sand under the spring sun has called forth; but I see none. I am reassured and reminded that I am the heir of eternal inheritances which are inalienable, when I feel the warmth reflected from this sunny bank, and see the yellow sand and the reddish subsoil, and hear some dried leaves rustle and the trickling of melting snow in some sluiceway. The eternity which I detect in Nature I predicate of myself also. How many springs I have had this same experience! I am encouraged, for I recognize this

Vol. VIII

steady persistency and recovery of Nature as a quality of myself.

The first places which I observe to be bare now, though the snow is generally so deep still, are the steep hillsides facing the south, as the side of the Cut (though it looks not south exactly) and the slope of Heywood's Peak toward the pond, also under some trees in a meadow (there is less snow there on account of eddy, and apparently the tree absorbs heat), or a ridge in the same place. Almost the whole of the steep hillside on the north of Walden is now bare and dry and warm, though fenced in with ice and snow. It has attracted partridges, four of which whir away on my approach. There the early sedge is exposed, and, looking closer, I observe that it has been sheared off close down, when green, far and wide, and the fallen withered tops are little handfuls of hay by their sides, which have been covered by the snow and sometimes look as if they had served as nests for the mice, — for their green droppings are left in them abundantly, — yet not such plain nests as in the grain-field last spring, — probably the *Mus leucopus*, — and the wintergreen and the sere pennyroyal still retain some fragrance.

As I was returning on the railroad, at the crossing beyond the shanty, hearing a rustling, I saw a striped squirrel amid the sedge on the bare east bank, twenty feet distant. After observing me a few moments, as I stood perfectly still between the rails, he ran straight up to within three feet of me, out of curiosity; then, after a moment's pause, and looking up to my face, turned back and finally crossed the railroad. All the

red was on his rump and hind quarters. When running he carried his tail erect, as he scratched up the snowy bank.

Now then the steep south hillsides begin to be bare, and the early sedge and sere, but still fragrant, pennyroyal and rustling leaves are exposed, and you see where the mice have sheared off the sedge and also made nests of its top during the winter. There, too, the partridges resort, and perhaps you hear the bark of a striped squirrel, and see him scratch toward his hole, rustling the leaves. For all the inhabitants of nature are attracted by this bare and dry spot, as well as you.

The muskrat-houses were certainly very few and small last summer, and the river has been remarkably low up to this time, while, the previous fall, they [were] very numerous and large, and in the succeeding winter the river rose remarkably high. So much for the muskrat sign. The bare ground just begins to appear in a few spots in the road in middle of the town.

March 24. Monday. Very pleasant day. Thermometer 48° at noon.

9 A. M. — Start to get two quarts of white maple sap and home at 11.30. One *F. hyemalis* in yard. Spend the forenoon on the river at the white maples. I hear a bluebird's warble and a song sparrow's chirp. So much partly for being out the whole forenoon. Bluebirds seen in all parts of the town to-day for first time, as I hear. The *F. hyemalis* has been seen two or three days. Cross the river behind Monroe's. Go everywhere on the North Branch — it is all solid — and

almost everywhere on the South Branch. The crust bears in the morning. The snow is so coarse-grained and hard that you can hardly get up a handful to wash your hands with, except the dirty surface. The early aspen buds down very conspicuous, half an inch long; yet I detect no flow of sap.

The white maple sap does not flow fast generally at first, — or 9 A. M., — not till about ten. Yet last year I paddled my boat to Fair Haven Pond on the 19th of March! Before noon I slump two feet in the snow.

You bore a little hole with your knife, and presently the wounded sap-wood begins to glisten with moisture, and anon a clear crystalline tear-like drop flows out and runs down the bark, or drops at once to the snow. This is the sap of which the far-famed maple-sugar is made. That's the sweet liquor which the Indians boiled a thousand years ago.

Cut a piece of *Rhus Toxicodendron* resting on rock at Egg Rock, five eighths of an inch in diameter, which had nineteen rings of annual growth. It is quite hard and stiff.

My sugar-making was spoiled by putting in much soda instead of saleratus by accident. I suspect it would have made more sugar than the red did. It proved only brittle black candy. This sap flowed just about as fast as that of the red maple.

It is said that a great deal of sap will run from the yellow birch.

The river begins to open generally at the bends for ten or twenty rods, and I see the dark ice alternating with dark water there, while the rest of the river is still covered with snow.

March 25. P. M. — To Walden.

The willow and aspen catkins have pushed out considerably since the 1st of February in warm places.

I have frequently seen the sap of maples flow in warm days in the winter, in warm localities. This was in twigs. Would it in the trunks of large trees? And if not, is not this an evidence that *this* sap did not come up from the roots?

The meadow east of the railroad causeway is bare in many spots, while that on the west is completely and deeply covered; yet a few weeks ago it was deepest on the east. I think of no reason for this, except that the causeway may keep off the cold northwest winds from the former meadow. For thirty rods distant there are no bare spots. Why is the eastern slope, now, as every spring, (almost completely) bare, long before the western? The road runs north and south, and the sun lies on the one side as long as on the other. Is it more favorable that the frozen snow be acted on by the warmed air before the sun reaches it than after it has left it? Another and second reason is probably that there is less snow on that side or on the west slope of a hill than on the eastern. Snow drifting from the northwest lodges under the west bank. So I observe to-day that the hills rising from the north and *west* (and this seems to give weight to the second reason urged above) sides of Walden are partially bare, while those on the south and east are deeply and completely covered with

snow. Mr. Bull tells me that his grapes grow faster and ripen sooner on the west than the east side of his house.

There have been few if any small migratory birds the past winter. I have not seen a tree sparrow, nuthatch, creeper, nor more than one redpoll since Christmas. They probably went further south.

I now slump from two to four inches into Walden, though there has been no rain since I can remember. I cannot cut through, on account of the water in the softened ice flowing into the hole. At last, in a drier place, I was not troubled with water, till I had cut about a foot, or through the snow ice, when two or three streams of water half an inch or more in diameter spurted up through holes in the disorganized, partly honeycombed clear ice; so I failed to get through. Probably the clear ice is thus riddled all over the pond, for this was a drier place than usual. Is it the effect of the melted snow and surface working down? or partly of water pressing up? The whole mass in the middle is about twenty-four inches thick, but I scrape away about two inches of the surface with my foot, leaving twenty-two inches. For about a rod from the shore, on the north and west sides (I did not examine the others), it is comparatively firm and dry, then for two rods you slump four inches or more, then, and generally, only about two. Is that belt the effect of reflection from the hills?

Hear the hurried and seemingly frightened notes of a robin and see it flying over the railroad lengthwise, and afterwards its *tut tut* at a distance. This and the

birds of yesterday have come, though the ground generally is covered deep with snow. They will not only stay with us through a storm, but come when there are but resting-places for them. It must be hard for them to get their living now.

The tallest water andromedas now rise six or eight inches above the snow in the swamp.

March 26. To Cambridge.

I hear that Humphrey Buttrick found a whole covey of quails dead.[1] At Philadelphia, a month or two since, they offered a reward for live ones, more than market price, to preserve them. We have heard of an unusual quantity of ice in the course of the Liverpool packets this winter. Perhaps the Pacific has been sunk by one, as we hear that some other vessels have been. Yet the papers say it has been warmer about Lake Superior than in Kansas and that the lake will break up earlier than usual.

They are just beginning to use wheels in Concord, but only in the middle of the town, where the snow is at length worn and melted down to bare ground in the middle of the road, from two to ten feet wide. Sleighs are far the most common, even here. In Cambridge there is no sleighing. For the most part, the *middle* of the road from Porter's to the College is bare and even *dusty* for twenty to thirty feet in width. The College Yard is one half bare. So, if they have had more snow than we, as some say, it has melted much faster.

[1] *He* tells me that his dog found *four* in the winter, and as other coveys are missing, thinks they have starved.

There is also less in the towns between us and Cambridge than in Concord. The snow lies longer on the low, level plain surrounded by hills in which Concord is situated. I am struck by the more wintry aspect — almost entirely uninterrupted snow-fields — on coming into Concord in the cars.

The Romans introduced husbandry into England, where but little was practiced before, and the English have introduced it into America. So we may well read the Roman authors for a history of this art as practiced by us.

I am sometimes affected by the consideration that a man may spend the whole of his life after boyhood in accomplishing a particular design; as if he were put to a special and petty use, without taking time to look around him and appreciate the phenomenon of his existence. If so many purposes are thus necessarily left unaccomplished, perhaps unthought of, we are reminded of the transient interest we have in *this life.* Our interest in our country, in the spread of liberty, etc., strong and, as it were, innate as it is, cannot be as transient as our present existence here. It cannot be that all those patriots who die in the midst of their career have no further connection with the career of their country.

March 27. Uncle Charles died this morning, about midnight, aged seventy-six.

The frost is now entirely out in some parts of the New Burying-Ground, the sexton tells me, — half-way up the hill which slopes to the south, unless it is bare of snow, he says. In our garden, where it chances to be bare, two or more rods from the house, I was able to dig through the slight frost. In another place near by I could not.

The river is now open in reaches of twenty or thirty rods, where the ice has disappeared by melting.

Elijah Wood, Senior, about seventy, tells me he does not remember that the river was ever frozen so long, nor that so much snow lay on the ground so long. People do not remember when there was so much old snow on the ground at this date.

March 28. Uncle Charles buried. He was born in February, 1780, the winter of the Great Snow, and he dies in the winter of another great snow, — a life bounded by great snows.

Cold, and the earth stiff again, after fifteen days of steady warm and, for the most part, sunny days (without rain), in which the snow and ice have rapidly melted.

Sam Barrett tells me that a boy caught a crow in his neighborhood the other day in a trap set for mink. Its leg was broken. He brought it home under his arm, and laid it down in a shop, thinking to keep it there alive. It looked up sidewise, as it lay seemingly helpless on the floor, but, the door being open, all at once, to their surprise, it lifted itself on its wings and flitted out and away without the least trouble. Many crows have been caught in mink-traps the past winter, they have been compelled to visit the few openings in brooks, etc., so much for food.

Barrett has suffered all winter for want of water.

I think to say to my friend, There is but one interval

between us. You are on one side of it, I on the other. You know as much about it as I, — how wide, how impassable it is. I will endeavor not to blame you. Do not blame me. There is nothing to be said about it. Recognize the truth, and pass over the intervals that are bridged.

Farewell, my friends, my path inclines to this side the mountain, yours to that. For a long time you have appeared further and further off to me. I see that you will at length disappear altogether. For a season my path seems lonely without you. The meadows are like barren ground. The memory of me is steadily passing away from you. My path grows narrower and steeper, and the night is approaching. Yet I have faith that, in the definite future, new suns will rise, and new plains expand before me, and I trust that I shall therein encounter pilgrims who bear that same virtue that I recognized in you, who will be that very virtue that was you. I accept the everlasting and salutary law, which was promulgated as much that spring that I first knew you, as this that I seem to lose you.

My former friends, I visit you as one walks amid the columns of a ruined temple. You belong to an era, a civilization and glory, long past. I recognize still your fair proportions, notwithstanding the convulsions which we have felt, and the weeds and jackals that have sprung up around. I come here to be reminded of the past, to read your inscriptions, the hieroglyphics, the sacred writings. We are no longer the representatives of our former selves.

Love is a thirst that is never slaked. Under the

coarsest rind, the sweetest meat. If you would read a friend aright, you must be able to read through something thicker and opaquer than horn. If you can read a friend, all languages will be easy to you. Enemies publish themselves. They declare war. The friend never declares his love.

March 29. Another cold day. Scarcely melts at all. Water skimmed over in chamber, with fire.

March 30. P. M. — To Walden and Fair Haven.

Still cold and blustering. I come out to see the sand and subsoil in the Deep Cut, as I would to see a spring flower, some redness in the cheek of Earth. These cold days have made the ice of Walden dry and pretty hard again at top. It is just twenty-four inches thick in the middle, about eleven inches of snow ice. It has lost but a trifle on the surface. The inside is quite moist, the clear ice very crystalline and leaky, letting the water up from below, so as to hinder my cutting. It seems to be more porous and brittle than the snow ice.

I go to Fair Haven *via* the Andromeda Swamps. The snow is a foot and more in depth there still. There is a little bare ground in and next to the swampy woods at the head of Well Meadow, where the springs and little black rills are flowing. I see already one blade, three or four inches long, of that purple or lake grass, lying flat on some water, between snow-clad banks, — the first leaf with a rich bloom on it. How silent are the footsteps of Spring! There, too, where there is a fraction of the meadow, two rods over, quite bare, under the

bank, in this warm recess at the head of the meadow, though the rest of the meadow is covered with snow a foot or more in depth, I am surprised to see the skunk-cabbage, with its great spear-heads open and ready to blossom (*i. e.* shed pollen in a day or two); and the *Caltha palustris* bud, which shows yellowish; and the golden saxifrage, green and abundant; also there are many fresh tender leaves of (apparently) the gold-thread[1] in open meadow there, all surrounded and hemmed in by snow, which [has] covered the ground since Christmas and stretches as far as you can see on every side; and there are as intense blue shadows on the snow as I ever saw. The spring advances in spite of snow and ice, and cold even. The ground under the snow has long since felt the influence of the spring sun, whose rays fall at a more favorable angle. The tufts or tussocks next the edge of the snow were crowned with dense phalanxes of stiff spears of the stiff triangularish sedge-grass, five inches high but quite yellow with a very slight greenness at the tip, showing that they pushed up through the snow, which melting, they had not yet acquired color. This is the greatest growth of any plant I have seen. I had not suspected *any*. I can just see a little greening on our bare and dry south bank. In warm recesses and clefts in meadows and rocks in the midst of ice and snow, nay, even under the snow, vegetation commences and steadily advances.

I find Fair Haven Pond and the river lifted up a foot or more, the result [of] the long, steady thaw in the sun. The water of the pond and river has run over the

[1] ? Probably not.

meadows, mixing with and partly covering the snow, making it somewhat difficult to get into the river on the east side. On the east side of the pond, the ice next the shore is still frozen to the bottom under water by one edge, while the other slants upward to meet the main body of the ice of the pond. This sort of canal on one or both sides of the river is from a rod to three or four rods wide. This is the most decided step toward breaking up as yet. But the pond and river are very solid yet. I walk over the pond and down on the middle of the river to the bridge, without seeing an opening.

Saw probably a hen-hawk (?) (saw the black tips to wings), sailing low over the low cliff next the river, looking probably for birds.[1] The south hillsides no sooner begin to be bare, and the striped squirrels and birds resort there, than the hawks come from southward to prey on them. I think that even the hen-hawk is here in winter only as the robin is.

For twenty-five rods the Corner road is impassable to horses, because of their slumping in the old snow; and a new path has been dug, which a fence shuts off the old. Thus they have served the roads on all sides the town.

March 31. P. M. — To Peter's *via* Winter Street [?].

I see the scarlet tops of white maples nearly a mile off, down the river, the lusty shoots of last year. Those of the red maple do not show thus.

I see many little holes in this old and solid snow where leaves have sunk down gradually and per-

[1] May have been a marsh hawk or harrier.

pendicularly, eleven or twelve inches, — the hole no larger at the top than at the bottom, nay, often partly closed at top by the drifting, and exactly the form and size of the leaf. It is as if the sun had driven this thin shield like a bullet thus deep into the solid snow. It is remarkable how deep the leaves settle into an old snow like this.

See a small ant running about over a piece of meadow turf. The celandine begins to be conspicuous, springing under Brown's fence.

VI

APRIL, 1856

(ÆT. 38)

April 1. P. M. — Down railroad, measuring snow, and to Fair Haven Hill.

West of railroad	East of railroad	Average		Trillium Wood
2	3	0	5½ inches	22
0	3	0		11
3	9	0		11
5	7	0		7
4	11	0		8
4	13	10		12
4	13	8		11
5	12	0		11
3	13	0		11
5	14	0		6
5	13	0		9
7	15	0		14
8	16	0		11
14	13	0		10
9	12	0		10
7	17	0		11
3	11	0		8
10	11	0		8
5	15	3		6
5	15	9		3
40)344(8½		6		20)200(10 inches
		0		
		1		
		20		
		24)57(2½		

It appears from the above how rapidly the snow has melted on the east side of the railroad causeway, though eight to twelve rods from it, being sheltered by it from the northwest wind.[1] It is for the most part bare ground there. Adhering to these localities, the average depth in open land is five and one half inches, but the east side of railroad is a peculiarly sheltered place and hence bare, while the earth generally is covered. It is probably about seven inches deep on a level generally in open land. It has melted at about the same rate west of railroad and in Trillium Woods since the 19th. It is a question whether it is better sleighing or wheeling now, taking all our roads together. At any rate we may say the sleighing lasted till April. In some places it still fills the roads level with the walls, and bears me up still in the middle of the day. It grows more and more solid, apparently freezing at night quite through. William Wheeler (of the Corner road) tells me that it was more solid this morning than any time in the winter, and he was surprised to find that it would bear his oxen where three or four feet deep behind his house. On some roads you walk in a path recently shovelled out, with upright walls of snow three or four feet high on each side and a foot of snow beneath you, for twenty or thirty rods; and this is old snow. We have had none since March 20th, and that was very moist and soon melted. The drifts on the east side of the depot, which have lain there a great part of the winter, still reach up to the top of the first pane of glass. But, generally speaking, we slump so much, especially

[1] *Vide* Apr. 11.

in the woods, except in the morning, and the snow is so deep, that we are confined to the roads or the river still. Choppers cannot work in the woods yet, and teams cannot get in for wood yet.

A new snow of this depth would soon go off, but this old snow is solid and icy and wastes very slowly. It seems to be gradually turning to ice. I observe that, while the snow has melted unevenly in waves and ridges, there is a transparent icy glaze about one sixteenth of an inch thick but as full of holes as a riddle, spread like gauze level over all, resting on the prominent parts of the snow, leaving hollows beneath from one inch to six or more inches in depth. I often see the spiders running underneath this. This is the surface, which has melted and formed an icy crust, and, being transparent, it has transmitted the heat to the snow beneath and has outlasted that. This crashes and rattles under your feet.

The bare places now are the steep south and west, or southwest, sides of hills and cliffs, and also next to woods and houses on the same sides, the bridges and brows of hills and slighter ridges and prominences in the fields, low open ground protected from the northwest wind, under trees, etc. I might have put the roads second.

Going by the path to the Springs, I find great beds of oak leaves, sometimes a foot thick, very dry and crisp and filling the path, or one side of it, in the woods for a quarter of a mile, inviting one to lie down. They have absorbed the heat and settled, like the single one seen yesterday, in mass a foot or more, making a path to

that depth. Yet when they are unusually thick they preserve the snow beneath and are found to cover an almost icy mound.

April 2. 8 a. m. — To Lee's Cliff *via* railroad, Andromeda Ponds, and Well Meadow.

I go early, while the crust is hard. I hear a few song sparrows tinkle on the alders by the railroad. They skulk and flit along below the level of the ground in the ice-filled ditches; and bluebirds warble over the Deep Cut. A foot or more of snow in Andromeda Ponds.

In the warm recess at the head of Well Meadow, which makes up on the northeast side of Fair Haven, I find many evidences of spring. Pushed up through the dead leaves, yet flattened by the snow and ice which has just melted here, behold! the skunk-cabbage has been in bloom, *i. e.* has shed pollen some time and been frost-bitten and decayed. All that now sheds pollen here has been frost-bitten. Others are ready to shed it in a day or two. I find no other flower nearly so forward as this. The cowslip appears to be coming next to it. Its buds are quite yellowish and half an inch, almost, in diameter. The alder scales do not even appear relaxed yet. This year, at least, the cabbage is the first flower; and perhaps it is always earlier than I have thought, if you seek it in a favorable place.[1] The springy soil in which it grows melts the snows early, and if, beside, it is under the south side of a hill in an open oozy alder swamp in a recess sheltered from cold winds like this, it *may commonly* be the first flower.[2]

[1] It *may* possibly be a little. *Vide* the 4th *inst.*   [2] Doubtful.

It will take you half a lifetime to find out where to look for the earliest flower. I have hitherto found my earliest at Clamshell, a much more exposed place.[1] Look for some narrow meadowy bay, running north into a hill and protected by the hill on the north and partly on the east and west. At the head of this meadow, where many springs ooze out from under the hill and saturate all the ground, dissolving the snow early in the spring, in the midst, or on the edge, of a narrow open alder swamp, there look for the earliest skunk-cabbage and cowslip, where some little black rills are seen to meander or heard to tinkle in the middle of the coldest winter. There appear the great spear-heads of the skunk-cabbage, yellow and red or uniform mahogany-color, ample hoods sheltering their purple spadixes. The plaited buds of the hellebore are four or five inches high. There are beds of fresh green moss in the midst of the shallow water. What is that coarse sedge-like grass, rather broadly triangularish, two inches high in the water? This and the cress have been eaten, probably by the rabbits, whose droppings are abundant. I see where they have gnawed and chipped off the willow osiers. Common grass is quite green.

Here, where I come for the earliest flowers, I might also come for the earliest birds. They seek the same warmth and vegetation. And so probably with quadrupeds, — rabbits, skunks, mice, etc. I hear now, as I stand over the first skunk-cabbage, the notes of the first red-wings,[2] like the squeaking of a sign, over amid the maples yonder. Robins are peeping and flitting

[1] *Vide* 4th.   [2] Or grackles?

about. Am surprised to hear one sing regularly their morning strain, seven or eight rods off, yet so low and smothered with its ventriloquism that you would say it was half a mile off. It seems to be wooing its mate, that sits within a foot of it.

There are many holes in the surface of the bare, springy ground amid the rills, made by the skunks or mice, and now their edges are bristling with feather-like frostwork, as if they were the breathing-holes or nostrils of the earth.

That grass which had grown five inches on the 30th is apparently the cut-grass of the meadows. The withered blades which are drooping about the tufts are two feet long. I break the solid snow-bank with my feet and raise its edge, and find the stiff but tender yellow shoots beneath it. They seem not to have pierced it, but are prostrate beneath it. They have actually grown beneath it, but not directly up into it to any extent; rather flattened out beneath it.

Cross Fair Haven Pond to Lee's Cliff. The crowfoot and saxifrage seem remarkably backward; no growth as yet. But the catnep has grown even six inches, and perfumes the hillside when bruised. The columbine, with its purple leaves, has grown five inches, and one is flower-budded, apparently nearer to flower than anything there. *Turritis stricta* very forward, four inches high.

It is evident that it depends on the character of the season whether this flower or that is the most forward; whether there is more or less snow or cold or rain, etc. I am tempted to stretch myself on the bare ground above the Cliff, to feel its warmth in my back, and smell the earth and the dry leaves. I see and hear flies and bees about. A large buff-edged butterfly flutters by along the edge of the Cliff, — *Vanessa antiopa.* Though so little of the earth is bared, this frail creature has been warmed to life again. Here is the broken shell of one of those large white snails (*Helix albolabris*) on the top of the Cliff. It is like a horn with ample mouth wound on itself. I am rejoiced to find anything so pretty. I cannot but think it nobler, as it is rarer, to appreciate some beauty than to feel much sympathy with misfortune. The Powers are kinder to me when they permit me to enjoy this beauty than if they were to express any amount of compassion for me. I could never excuse them that.

A woodchuck has been out under the Cliff, and patted the sand, cleared out the entrance to his burrow.

Muskrat-houses have been very scarce indeed the past winter. If they were not killed off, I cannot but think that their instinct foresaw that the river would not rise. The river has been at summer level through the winter up to April!

I returned down the middle of the river to near the Hubbard Bridge without seeing any opening.

Some of the earliest plants are now not started because covered with snow, as the stellaria and shepherd's-purse. Others, like the *Carex Pennsylvanica*, the crowfoot, saxifrage, callitriche, are either covered or recently uncovered. I think it must be partly owing to the want of rain, and not wholly to the snow, that the first three are so backward.

The white maples and hazels and, for the most part, the alders still stand in snow; yet those alders on the bare place by the skunk-cabbage, above named, appear to be no more forward! Maybe trees, rising so high, are more affected by cold winds than herbaceous plants.

April 3. When I awoke this morning I heard the almost forgotten sound of rain on the roof. I think there has not been any of any consequence since Christmas Day. Looking out, I see the air full of fog, and that the snow has gone off wonderfully during the night. The drifts have settled and the patches of bare ground extended themselves, and the river is fast spreading over the meadows. The pattering of the rain is a soothing, slumberous sound, which tempts me to lie late, yet there is more fog than rain. Here, then, at last, is the end of the sleighing, which began the 25th of December. Not including that date and to-day it has lasted ninety-nine days. I hear that young Demond of the Factory will have come into town one hundred times in his sleigh the past winter, if he comes to-day, having come probably only once in a day.

P. M. — To Hunt's Bridge.

It is surprising how the earth on bare south banks begins to show some greenness in its russet cheeks in this rain and fog, — a precious emerald-green tinge, almost like a green mildew, the growth of the night, — a *green* blush suffusing her cheek, heralded by twittering birds. This sight is no less interesting than the corresponding bloom and ripe blush of the fall. How encouraging to perceive again that faint tinge of green,

Vol. VIII

spreading amid the russet on earth's cheeks! I revive with Nature; her victory is mine. This is my jewelry. It rains very little, but a dense fog, fifteen or twenty feet high, rests on the earth all day, spiriting away the snow, — behind which the cockerels crow and a few birds sing or twitter. The osiers look bright and fresh in the rain and fog, like the grass. Close at hand they are seen to be beaded with drops from the fog. There seems to be a little life in the bark now, and it strips somewhat more freely than in winter. What a lusty growth have these yellow osiers! Six feet is common the last year, chiefly from the summit of the pollards, — but also from the sides of the trunk, — filling a quadrant densely with their yellow rays. The white maple buds on the south side of some trees have slightly opened, so that I can peep into their cavities and detect the stamens.[1] They will probably come next to the skunk-cabbage this year, if the cowslip does not. Yet the trees stand in the midst of the old snow.

I see small flocks of robins running on the bared portions of the meadow. Hear the sprayey tinkle of the song sparrow along the hedges. Hear also squeaking notes of an advancing flock of red-wings,[2] somewhere high in the sky. At length detect them high overhead, advancing northeast in loose array, with a broad extended front, competing with each other, winging their way to some northern meadow which they remember. The note of

[1] This happened in February (!), 1857.
[2] Or grackles; am uncertain which makes that squeak.

some is like the squeaking of many signs, while others accompany them with a steady dry *tchuck, tchuck.*

Hosmer is overhauling a vast heap of manure in the rear of his barn, turning the ice within it up to the light; yet he asks despairingly what life is for, and says he does not expect to stay here long. But I have just come from reading Columella, who describes the same kind of spring work, in that to him new spring of the world, with hope, and I suggest to be brave and hopeful with nature. Human life may be transitory and full of trouble, but the perennial mind, whose survey extends from that spring to this, from Columella to Hosmer, is superior to change. I will identify myself with that which did not die with Columella and will not die with Hosmer.[1]

Coming home along the causeway, a robin sings (though faintly) as in May. The road is a path, here and there shovelled through drifts which are considerably higher than a man's head on each side.

People are talking about my Uncle Charles. Minott tells how he heard Tilly Brown once asking him to show him a peculiar (inside?) lock in wrestling. "Now, don't hurt me, don't throw me hard." He struck his antagonist inside his knees with his feet, and so deprived him of his legs. Hosmer remembers his tricks in the barroom, shuffling cards, etc. He could do anything with cards, yet he did not gamble. He would toss up his hat, twirling it over and over, and catch it on his head invariably. Once wanted to live at Hosmer's, but the latter was afraid of him. "Can't we study up something?" he asked. H. asked him into the house

[1] [Channing, p. 88.]

and brought out apples and cider, and Charles talked. "You!" said he, "I burst the bully of Lowell" (or Haverhill?). He wanted to wrestle; would not be put off. "Well, we won't wrestle in the house." So they went out to the yard, and a crowd got round. "Come spread some straw here," said C. "I don't want to hurt him." He threw him at once. They tried again. He told them to spread more straw and he "burst" him.

He had a strong head and never got drunk; would drink gin sometimes, but not to excess. Did not use tobacco, except snuff out of another's box sometimes. Was very neat in his person. Was not profane, though vulgar.

Very few men take a wide survey; their knowledge is very limited and particular. I talked with an old man the other day about the snow, hoping he would give me some information about past winters. I said, "I guess you don't remember so much old snow on the ground at this season." He answered, "I never saw the snow so deep between my house and John's." It was n't a stone's throw.[1]

Uncle Charles used to say that he had n't a single tooth in his head. The fact was they were all double, and I have heard that he lost about all of them by the time he was twenty-one. Ever since I knew him he could swallow his nose.

The river is now generally and rapidly breaking up. It is surprising what progress has been made since yesterday. It is now generally open about the town. It has gradually worn and melted away at the bends,

[1] The same man in summer of '59 said he never saw the river so low!! Of what use to be old?

Vol. VIII

where it is shallow and swift, and now small pieces are breaking off around the edges and floating down these reaches. It is not generally floated off, but dissolved and melted where it is, for the open reaches gradually extend themselves till they meet, and there is no space or escape for floating ice in any quantity, until the ice is all gone from the channel. I think that what I have seen floating in former years is *commonly* such as had risen up afterward from the bottom of flooded meadows. Sometimes, however, you observe great masses of floating ice, consisting of that which is later to break up, the thicker and more lasting ice from broad bays or between bridges. There is now an open water passage on each side of the broad field of ice in the bay above the railroad. The water, which is rapidly rising, has overflowed the icy snow on the meadows, which is seen a couple of feet beneath it, for there is no true ice there. It is this rising of the water that breaks up the ice more than anything. The Mill Brook has risen much higher comparatively than the river.

April 4. P. M. -- To Clamshell, etc.
The alder scales south of the railroad, beyond the bridge, are loosened. This corresponds to the opening (not merely expansion showing the fuzziness) of the white maple buds.

There is still but little rain, but the fog of yesterday still rests on the earth. My neighbor says it is the frost coming out of the ground. This, perhaps, is not the best description of it. It is rather the moisture in this warm air, condensed by contact with the snow and ice

and frozen ground. Where the fields are bare I slump now three or four inches into the oozy surface, also on the bare brows of hills clad with cladonias. These are as full of water as a sponge. The muskrats, no doubt, are now being driven out of the banks. I hear, as I walk along the shore, the dull sound of guns — probably most of them fired at muskrats — borne along the river from different parts of the town; one every two or three minutes.

Already I hear of a small fire in the woods in Emerson's lot, set by the engine, the leaves that are bare are so dry.

I find many sound cabbages shedding their pollen under Clamshell Hill. They are even more forward *generally* here than at Well Meadow. Probably two or three only, now dead among the alders at the last place, were earlier. This is simply the earliest flower such a season as this, *i. e.* when the ground continues covered with snow till very late in the spring. For this plant occupies ground which is the earliest to be laid bare, those great dimples in the snow about a springy place in the meadow, five or ten feet over, where the sun and light have access to the earth a month before it is generally bare. In such localities, then, they will enjoy the advantage over most other plants, for they will not have to contend with abundance of snow, but only with the cold air, which may be no severer than usual. Cowslips and a few other plants sometimes enjoy the same advantage. Sometimes, *apparently*, the original, now outer, spathe has been frost-bitten and is decayed, and a fresh one is pushing up. I see some

of these in full bloom, though the opening to their tents is not more than half an inch wide. They are lapped like tent doors, effectually protected. Methinks most of these hoods open to the south. It is remarkable how completely the spadix is protected from the weather, first by the ample hood, whose walls are distant from it, next by the narrow tent-like doorway, admitting air and light and sun, generally I think on the south side, and also by its pointed top, curved downward protectingly over it. It looks like a monk in his crypt with powdered head. The sides of the doorway are lapped or folded, and one is considerably in advance of the other. It is contrived best to catch the vernal warmth and exclude the winter's cold. Notwithstanding all the snow the skunk-cabbage is earlier than last year, when it was also the earliest flower and blossomed on the 5th of April. It is, perhaps, owing to the long-continued warm weather from March 13th to 28th.

Yet it has been a hard winter for many plants, on dry, exposed hills. I am surprised to see the clover, cinquefoil, etc., etc., on the top of the bank at Clamshell completely withered and straw-colored, probably from the snow resting on it so long and incessantly. And plants that grow on high land are more backward than last year.

The ground no sooner begins to be bare to a considerable extent than I see a marsh hawk, or harrier.

The sap of the *white* birch at Clamshell begins to flow.

April 5. The April weather still continues. It looks repeatedly as if the sun would shine, and it rains five minutes after. I look out to see how much the river has risen. Last night there were a great many portions or islets visible, now they are engulfed, and it is a smooth expanse of water and icy snow. The water has been steadily deepening on Concord meadows all night, rising with a dimple about every stem and bush.

P. M. — To North River at Tarbell's.

Fair weather again. Saw half a dozen blackbirds, uttering that sign-like note, on the top of Cheney's elm, but noticed no red at this distance. Were they grackles? Hear after some red-wings sing *boby-lee*. Do these ever make the sign-like note? Is not theirs a fine shrill *whistle*?

The ice from the sides of the rivers has wheeled round in great cakes and lodged against each of the railroad bridges, *i. e.* over each stream. Near the town there is the firmest body of ice (in the river proper) above Hubbard's Bridge.

A warm and pleasant afternoon. The river not yet so high by four or five feet as last winter. Hear, on all sunny hillsides where the snow is melted, the chink-clicking notes of the *F. hyemalis* flitting before me. I am sitting on the dried grass on the south hillside behind Tarbell's house, on the way to Brown's. These birds know where there is a warm hillside as well as we. The warble of the bluebird is in the air. From Tarbell's bank we had looked over the bright moving flood of the Assabet with many maples standing in it, the purling and eddying stream, with a hundred rills of snow water trickling into it.

Further toward J. P. Brown's, saw two large ant-hills (red before, black abdomens), quite covered on all the sunny portion with ants, which appeared to have come forth quite recently and were removing obstructions from their portals. Probably the frost is quite out there. Their black abdomens glistened in the sun. Each was bringing up some rubbish from beneath. The outlines of one of these hills were a very regular cone; both were graceful curves.

Came out upon the high terrace behind Hosmer's, whence we overlooked the *bright-blue* flood alternating with fields of ice (we being on the same side with the sun). The first sight of the blue water in the spring is exhilarating.

Saw half a dozen white sheldrakes in the meadow, where Nut Meadow Brook was covered with the flood. There were two or three females with them. These ducks would all swim together first a little way to the right, then suddenly turn together and swim to the left, from time to time making the water fly in a white spray, apparently with a wing. Nearly half a mile off I could see their green crests in the sun. They were partly concealed by some floating pieces of ice and snow, which they resembled.

On the hill beyond Clamshell scared up two turtle doves.

It is that walking when we must pick the hardest and highest ground or ice, for we commonly sink several inches in the oozy surface.

April 6. 7 a. m. — To Willow [1] Bay.

The meadow has frozen over, skimmed over in the

[1] That is, Lily.

night. The ducks must have had a cold night of it. I thought [I] heard white-bellied swallows over the house before I arose.[1] The hedges resound with the song of the song sparrow. He sits high on a spray singing, while I stand near, but suddenly, becoming alarmed, drops down and skulks behind the bushes close to the ground, gradually removing far to one side. I am not certain but I have seen the grass-bird [2] as well as song sparrow this year, — on the 2d, — a sparrow with a light breast and less brown about the cheeks and head. The song sparrow I see now has a very brown breast. What a sly, skulking fellow! I have a glimpse of him skulking behind a stone or a bush next to the ground, or perhaps he drops into a ditch just before me, and when I run forward he is not to be seen in it, having flitted down it four or five rods to where it intersected with another, and then up that, all beneath the level of the surface, till he is in the rear of me.

Just beyond Wood's Bridge, I hear the pewee. With what confidence after the lapse of many months, I come out to this waterside, some warm and pleasant spring morning, and, listening, hear, from farther or nearer, through the still concave of the air, the note of the first pewee! If there is one within half a mile, it will be here, and I shall be sure to hear its simple notes from those trees, borne over the water. It is remarkable how large a mansion of the air you can explore with your ears in the still morning by the waterside.

[1] Probably, for they surely came next morning. They twitter over the house only in the morning at first.
[2] No, probably not, for it has no dark splashes on throat. *Vide* 7th.

I can dig in the garden now, where the snow is gone, and even under six inches of snow and ice I make out to get through the frost with a spade. The frost will all be out about as soon as last year, for the melting of the snow has been taking it out. It is remarkable how rapidly the ground dries, for where the frost is out the water does not stand, but is soaked up.

There has been no skating the last winter, the snow having covered the ice immediately after it formed and not melting, and the river not rising till April, when it was too warm to freeze thick enough.

As we sat yesterday under the warm, dry hillside, amid the *F. hyemalis* by Tarbell's, I noticed the first bluish haze — a small patch of it — over the true Nut Meadow, seen against the further blue pine forest over the near low yellow one. This was of course the subtle vapor which the warmth of the day raised from Nut Meadow. This, while a large part of the landscape was covered with snow, an affecting announcement of the approach of summer. The one wood seemed but an underwood on the edge of the other, yet all Nut Meadow's varied surface intervened, with its brook and its cranberries, its sweet-gale, alder, and willow, and this was its blue feather!

P. M. — To Hubbard's second grove, by river.

At Ivy Tree, hear the fine *tseep* of a sparrow, and detect the fox-colored sparrow on the lower twigs of the willows and from time to time scratching the ground beneath. It is quite tame, — a single one with its ashy head and mottled breast.

It is a still and warm, overcast afternoon, and I am

come to look for ducks on the smooth reflecting water which has suddenly surrounded the village, — water half covered with ice or icy snow. On the 2d it was a winter landscape, — a narrow river covered thick with ice for the most part, and only snow on the meadows. In three or four days the scene is changed to these vernal lakes, and the ground more than half bare. The reflecting water alternating with unreflecting ice.

Apparently song sparrows may have the dark splash on each side of the throat but be more or less brown on the breast and head. Some are quite light, some quite dark. Here is one of the light-breasted on the top of an apple tree, sings unweariedly at regular intervals something like *tchulp | chilt chilt, chilt chilt,* (faster and faster) *chilt chilt, chilt chilt | tuller tchay ter splay-ee.* The last, or third, bar I am not sure about. It flew too soon for me. I only remember that the last part was sprinkled on the air like drops from a rill, as if its strain were moulded by the spray it sat upon. Now see considerable flocks of robins hopping and running in the meadows; crows next the water-edge, on small isles in the meadow.

As I am going along the Corner road by the meadow mouse brook, hear and see, a quarter of a mile northwest, on those conspicuous white oaks near the river in Hubbard's second grove, the crows buffeting some intruder. The crows had betrayed to me some large bird of the hawk kind which they were buffeting. I suspected it before I looked carefully. I saw several crows on the oaks, and also what looked to my naked eye like a cluster of the palest and most withered oak

leaves with a black base about as big as a crow. Looking with my glass, I saw that it was a great bird. The crows sat about a rod off, higher up, while another crow was occasionally diving at him, and all were cawing. The great bird was just starting. It was chiefly a dirty white with great broad wings with black tips and black on other parts, giving it the appearance of dirty white, barred with black. I am not sure whether it was a white-headed eagle or a fish hawk. There appeared much more white than belongs to either, and more black than the fish hawk has. It rose and wheeled, flapping several times, till it got under way; then, with its rear to me, presenting the least surface, it moved off steadily in its orbit over the woods northwest, with the slightest possible undulation of its wings, — a noble planetary motion, like Saturn with its ring seen edgewise. It is so rare that we see a large body self-sustained in the air. While crows sat still and silent and confessed their lord. Through my glass I saw the outlines of this sphere against the sky, trembling with life and power as it skimmed the topmost twigs of the wood toward some more solitary oak amid the meadows. To my naked eye it showed only so much black as a crow in its talons might. Was it not the white-headed eagle in the state when it is called the sea eagle? Perhaps its neck-feathers were erected.

I went to the oaks. Heard there a nuthatch's faint vibrating *tut-tut,* somewhat even like croaking of frogs, as it made its way up the oak bark and turned head down to peck. Anon it answered its mate with a *gnah gnah.* Smelt a skunk on my return, at Hubbard's blue-

berry swamp, which some dogs that had been barking there for half an hour had probably worried, for I did not smell it when I went along first. I smelt this all the way thence home, the wind being southwest, and it was quite as perceptible in our yard as at the swamp. The family had already noticed it, and you might have supposed that there was a skunk in the yard, yet it was three quarters of a mile off, at least.

April 7. Monday. Launched my boat, through three rods of ice on the riverside, half of which froze last night. The meadow is skimmed over, but by midforenoon it is melted.

P. M. — Up river in boat.

The first boats I have seen are out to-day, after muskrats, etc. Saw one this morning breaking its way far through the meadow, in the ice that had formed in the night. How independent they look who have come forth for a day's excursion! Melvin is out, and Goodwin, and another boat still. They can just row through the thinnest of the ice. The first boat on the meadows is exciting as the first flower or swallow. It is seen stealing along in the sun under the meadow's edge. One breaks the ice before it with a paddle, while the other pushes or paddles, and it grates and wears against the bows.

We see Goodwin skinning the muskrats he killed this forenoon on bank at Lee's Hill, leaving their red and mutilated carcasses behind. He says he saw a few geese go over the Great Meadows on the 6th. The half of the meadows next the river, or more, is covered with

snow ice at the bottom, which from time to time rises up and floats off. These and more solid cakes from over the river clog the stream where it is least broken up, bridging it quite over. Great cakes rest against every bridge. We were but just able to get under the stone arches by lying flat and pressing our boat down, after breaking up a large cake of ice which had lodged against the upper side. Before we get to Clamshell, see Melvin ahead scare up two black ducks, which make a wide circuit to avoid both him and us. Sheldrakes pass also, with their heavy bodies. See the red and black bodies of more muskrats left on the bank at Clamshell, which the crows have already attacked. Their hind legs are *half-webbed,* the fore legs not at all. Their paunches are full apparently of chewed roots, yellowish and bluish. Goodwin says they are fatter than usual, perhaps because they have not been driven out of their holes heretofore. The open channel is now either over the river or on the upper side of the meadows next the woods and hills. Melvin floats slowly and quietly along the willows, watching for rats resting there, his white hound sitting still and grave in the prow, and every little while we hear his gun announcing the death of a rat or two. The dog looks on understandingly and makes no motion.

At the Hubbard Bridge, we hear the incessant note of the phœbe, — *pevet, pe-e-vet, pevee',* — its innocent, somewhat impatient call. Surprised to find the river not broken up just above this bridge and as far as we can see, probably through Fair Haven Pond. Probably in some places you can cross the river still on the ice.

Yet we make our way with some difficulty, through a very narrow channel over the meadow and drawing our boat over the ice on the river, as far as foot of Fair Haven. See clams, fresh-opened, and roots and leaf-buds left by rats on the edge of the ice, and see the rats there. By rocking our boat and using our paddles, we can make our way through the softened ice, six inches or more in thickness.

The tops of young white birches now have a red-pink color. Leave boat there.

See a yellow-spotted tortoise in a ditch; and a bay-wing sparrow. It has no dark splash on throat and has a light or gray head.

April 8. 1 P. M. — To boat at Cardinal Shore, and thence to Well Meadow and back to port.

Another very pleasant and warm day. The white-bellied swallows have paid us twittering visits the last three mornings. You must rush out quickly to see them, for they are at once gone again. Warm enough to do without greatcoat to-day and yesterday, though I carry it and put it on when I leave the boat.

Hear the crack of Goodwin's piece close by, just as I reach my boat. He has killed another rat. Asks if I am bound up-stream. "Yes, to Well Meadow." Says I can't get above the hay-path a quarter of a mile above on account of ice; if he could, he'd 'a' been at Well Meadow before now. But I think I will try, and he thinks if I succeed he will try it. By standing on oars, which sink several inches, and hauling over one cake of ice, I manage to break my way into an open canal

above, where I soon see three rats swimming. Goodwin says that he got twenty-four minks last winter, more than ever before in one season; trapped most, shot only two or three. From opposite Bittern Cliff, I pushed along, with more or less difficulty, to Well Meadow Brook. There was a water passage ten feet wide, where the river had risen beyond the edge of the ice, but not more than four or five feet was clear of the bushes and trees. By the side of Fair Haven Pond it was particularly narrow. I shoved the ice on the one hand and the bushes and trees on the other all the way. Nor was the passage much wider below, as far back as where I had taken my boat. For all this distance, the river *for the most part*, as well as all the pond, was an unbroken field of ice. I went winding my way and scraping between the maples. Half a dozen rods off on the ice, you would not have supposed that there was room for a boat there. In some places you could have got on to the ice from the shore without much difficulty. But all of Well Meadow was free of ice, and I paddled up to within a rod or two of where I found the cowslips so forward on the 2d. It is difficult pushing a boat over the meadows now, for even where the bottom is not covered with slippery snow ice which affords no hold to the paddle, the meadow is frozen and icy hard, for it thaws slowly under water. *This* meadow is completely open, because none of the snow ice has risen up. Sometimes you see a small piece that has been released come up suddenly, with such force as to lift it partly out of water, but, sinking again at once, it looks like a sheldrake which has dived at a distance.

Vol. VIII

There, in that slow, muddy brook near the head of Well Meadow, within a few rods of its source, where it winds amid the alders, which shelter the plants somewhat, while they are open enough now to admit the sun, I find two cowslips in full bloom, shedding pollen; and they may have opened two or three days ago; for I saw many conspicuous buds here on the 2d which now I do not see. Have they not been eaten off? Do we not often lose the earliest flowers thus? A little more, or if the river had risen as high as frequently, they would have been submerged. What an arctic voyage was this in which I find cowslips, the pond and river still frozen over for the most part as far down as Cardinal Shore!

Saw two marsh hawks this afternoon, circling low over the meadows along the water's edge. This shows that frogs must be out. Goodwin and Puffer both fired at one from William Wheeler's shore. They say they made him duck and disturbed his feathers some. The muskrats are now very fat. They are reddish-brown beneath and dark-brown above. I see not a duck in all this voyage. Perhaps they are moving forward this bright and warm day.

Was obliged to come down as far as Nut Meadow (being on the west side), before I could clear the ice, and, setting my sail, tack across the meadow for home, the wind northwesterly. The river is still higher than yesterday.

About 8.30 P. M., hear geese passing quite low over the river.

Found beneath the surface, on the sphagnum, near

the cowslips, a collection of little hard nuts with wrinkled shells, a little like nutmegs, perhaps bass nuts, collected after a freshet by mice! I noticed that the fibres of the alder roots in the same place were thickly [*sic*] with little yellow knubby fruit. Was not that clear light-brown snail in that sphagnum a different species from the common one in brooks? See a few cranberries and smell muskrats.

On the Fair Haven Cliff, crowfoot and saxifrage are very backward. That dense-growing moss on the rocks shows now a level surface of pretty crimson cups.

Noticed, returning, this afternoon, a muskrat sitting on the ice near a small hole in Willow Bay, so motionless and withal round and featureless, of so uniform a color, that half a dozen rods off I should not have detected him if not accustomed to observing them. Saw the same thing yesterday. It reminds me of the truth of the Indian's name for it, — "that sits in a round form on the ice." You would think it was a particularly round clod of meadow rising above the ice. But while you look, it concludes its meditations or perchance its meal, and deliberately takes itself off through a hole at its feet, and you see no more of it. I noticed five muskrats this afternoon without looking for them very carefully. Four were swimming in the usual manner, showing the vertical tail, and plunging with a half-somerset suddenly before my boat. While you are looking, these brown clods slide off the edge of the ice, and it is left bare. You would think that so large an animal, sitting right out upon the ice, would be sure to be seen or detected, but not so. A citizen might paddle within two rods and not suspect them. Most countrymen might paddle five miles along the river now and not see one muskrat, while a sportsman a quarter of a mile before or behind would be shooting one or more every five minutes. The other, left to himself, might not be able to guess what he was firing at.

The marsh hawks flew in their usual irregular low tacking, wheeling, and circling flight, leisurely flapping and beating, now rising, now falling, in conformity with the contour of the ground. The last I think I have seen on the same beat in former years. He and his race must be well acquainted with the Musketicook and its meadows. No sooner is the snow off than he is back to his old haunts, scouring that part of the meadows that is bare, while the rest is melting. If he returns from so far to these meadows, shall the sons of Concord be leaving them at this season for slight cause?

River had risen so since yesterday I could not get under the bridge, but was obliged to find a round stick and roll my boat over the road.

April 9. Wednesday. Another fine day.
7 A. M. — To Trillium Woods.

Air full of birds. The line I have measured west of railroad is now just bare of snow, though a broad and deep bank of it lies between that line and the railroad. East of railroad has been bare some time. The line in Trillium Woods is apparently just bare also. There is just about as much snow in these woods now as in the meadows and fields around generally; *i. e.*, it is confined to the coldest sides, as in them. There is not so

Vol. VIII

much as on the east side of Lee's Hill. It is toward the north and east sides of the wood. Hence, apparently, in a level wood of this character the snow lies no longer than in adjacent fields divided by fences, etc., or even without them.

The air is full of birds, and as I go down the causeway, I distinguish the seringo note. You have only to come forth each morning to be surely advertised of each newcomer into these broad meadows. Many a larger animal might be concealed, but a cunning ear detects the arrival of each new species of bird. These birds give evidence that they prefer the fields of New England to all other climes, deserting for them the warm and fertile south. Here is their paradise. It is here they express the most happiness by song and action. Though these spring mornings may often be frosty and rude, they are exactly tempered to their constitutions, and call forth the sweetest strains.

The yellow birch sap has flowed abundantly, probably before the white birch.

8 A. M. — By boat to V. palmata[1] Swamp for *white birch sap.*

Leave behind greatcoat. The waters have stolen higher still in the night around the village, bathing higher its fences and its dry withered grass stems with a dimple. See that broad, smooth vernal lake, like a painted lake. Not a breath disturbs it. The sun and warmth and smooth water and birds make it a carnival of Nature's. I am surprised when I perceive men

[1] Muhlenbergii.

going about their ordinary occupations. I presume that before ten o'clock at least all the villagers will have come down to the bank and looked over this bright and placid flood, — the child and the man, the housekeeper and the invalid, — even as the village beholds itself reflected in it. How much would be subtracted from the day if the water was taken away! This liquid transparency, of melted snows partially warmed, spread over the russet surface of the earth! It is certainly important that there be some priests, some worshippers of Nature. I do not imagine anything going on to-day away from and out of sight of the waterside.

Early aspen catkins have curved downward an inch, and began to shed pollen apparently yesterday. White maples also, the sunny sides of clusters and sunny sides of trees in favorable localities, shed pollen to-day.

I hear the note of a lark amid the other birds on the meadow. For two or three days, have heard delivered often and with greater emphasis the loud, clear, sweet *phebe* note of the chickadee, elicited by the warmth. Cut across Hosmer's meadow from Island to Black Oak Creek, where the river, still rising, is breaking over with a rush and a rippling. Paddled quite to the head of Pinxter Swamp, where were two black ducks amid the maples, which went off with a hoarse quacking, leaving a feather on the smooth dark water amid the fallen tree-tops and over the bottom of red leaves.

Set two sumach spouts in a large white birch in the southward swamp, and hung a tin pail to them, and set off to find a yellow birch. Wandering over that

high huckleberry pasture, I hear the sweet jingle of the *Fringilla juncorum.*

In a leafy pool in the low wood toward the river, hear a rustling, and see yellow-spot tortoises dropping off an islet, into the dark, stagnant water, and four or five more lying motionless on the dry leaves of the shore and of islets about. Their spots are not very conspicuous out of water, and in most danger. The warmth of the day has penetrated into these low, swampy woods on the northwest of the hill and awakened the tortoises from their winter sleep. These are the only kind of tortoise I have seen this year. Probably because the river did not rise earlier, and the brooks, and thaw them out. When I looked about, I saw the shining black backs of four or five still left, and when I threw snowballs at them, they would not move. Yet from time to time I walk four or five rods over deep snow-banks, slumping in on the north and east sides of hills and woods. Apparently they love to feel the sun on their shells.

As I walk in the woods where the dry leaves are just laid bare, I see the bright-red berries of the Solomon's-seal still here and there above the leaves, affording food, no doubt, for some creatures.

Not finding the birches, I returned to the first swamp and tapped two more white birches. They flow generally faster than the red or white maples when I tried them. I sit on a rock in the warm, sunny swamp, where the ground is bare, and wait for my vessels to be filled. It is perfectly warm and perhaps drier than ever here. The great butterflies, black with buff-edged wings, are fluttering about, and flies are buzzing over this rock. The spathes of the skunk-cabbage stand thickly amid the dead leaves, the only obvious sign of vegetable life. A few rods off I hear some sparrows busily scratching the floor of the swamp, uttering a faint *tseep tseep* and from time to time a sweet strain. It is probably the fox-colored sparrow. These always feed thus, I think, in woody swamps, a flock of them rapidly advancing, flying before one another, through the swamp. A robin peeping at a distance is mistaken for a hyla. A gun fired at a muskrat on the other side of the island towards the village sounds like planks thrown down from a scaffold, borne over the water. Meanwhile I hear the sap dropping into my pail. The birch sap flows thus copiously before there is any other sign of life in the tree, the buds not visibly swollen. Yet the aspen, though in bloom, shows no sap when I cut it, nor does the alder. Will their sap flow later? Probably this birch sap, like the maple, flows little if any at night. It is remarkable that this dead-looking trunk should observe such seasons, — that a stock should distinguish between day and night.

When I return to my boat, I see the snow-fleas like powder, in patches on the surface of the smooth water, amid the twigs and leaves. I had paddled far into the swamp amid the willows and maples. The flood has reached and upset, and is floating off the chopper's corded wood. Little did he think of this thief. It is quite hazy to-day. The red-wing's *o'gurgle-ee-e* is in singular harmony with the sound and impression of the lapsing stream or the smooth, swelling flood beneath his perch. He gives expression to the flood. The water

reaches far in amid the trees on which he sits, and they seem like a water-organ played on by the flood. The sound rises up through their pipes. There was no wind, and the water was perfectly smooth, — a Sabbath stillness till 11 A. M. We have had scarcely any wind for a month.

Now look out for fires in the woods, for the leaves are never so dry and ready to burn as now. The snow is no sooner gone, — nay, it may still cover the north and west sides of hills, — when a day or two's sun and wind will prepare the leaves to catch at the least spark. Indeed these are such leaves as have never yet been wet, as have blown about and collected in heaps on the snow, and they would burn there in midwinter, though the fire could not spread much.

If the ground were *covered* with snow, would any degree of warmth produce a *blue* haze like this?

But such a fire can only run up the south and southwest sides of hills at this season. It will stop at the summit and not advance forward far, nor descend at all toward the north and east.

P. M. — Up railroad. A very warm day.

The *Alnus incana*, especially by the railroad opposite the oaks, sheds pollen. At the first-named alder saw a striped snake, which probably I had scared into the water from the warm railroad bank, its head erect as it lay on the bottom and swaying back and forth with the waves, which were quite high, though considerably above it. I stood there five minutes at least, and probably it could remain there an indefinite period.

Vol. VIII

The wind has now risen, a warm, but pretty stormy southerly wind, and is breaking up those parts of the river which were yet closed. The great mass of ice at Willow Bay has drifted down against the railroad bridge. I see no ducks, and it is too windy for muskrat-shooters. In a leafy pond by railroad, which will soon dry up, I see large skater insects, where the snow is not all melted. The willow catkins there near the oaks show the red of their scales at the base of the catkins dimly through their down, — a warm crimson glow or blush. They are an inch long, others about as much advanced but rounded. They will perhaps blossom by day after to-morrow, and the hazels on the hillside beyond as soon at least, if not sooner. They are loose and begin to dangle. The stigmas already peep out, minute crimson stars, — Mars. The skaters are as forward to play on the first smooth and melted pool, as boys on the first piece of ice in the winter. It must be cold to their feet.

I go off a little to the right of the railroad, and sit on the edge of that sand-crater near the spring by the railroad. Sitting there on the warm bank, above the broad, shallow, crystalline pool, on the sand, amid russet banks of curled early sedge-grass, showing a little green at base, and dry leaves, I hear one hyla peep faintly several times. This is, then, a degree of warmth sufficient for the hyla. He is the first of his race to awaken to the new year and pierce the solitudes with his voice. He shall wear the medal for this year. You hear him, but you will never find him. He is somewhere down amid the withered sedge and alder bushes there

by the water's edge, but where? From that quarter his shrill blast sounded, but he is silent, and a kingdom will not buy it again.

The communications from the gods to us are still deep and sweet, indeed, but scanty and transient, — enough only to keep alive the memory of the past. I remarked how many old people died off on the approach of the present spring. It is said that when the sap begins to flow in the trees our diseases become more violent. It is now advancing toward summer apace, and we seem to be reserved to taste its sweetness, but to perform what great deeds? Do we detect the reason why we also did not die on the approach of spring?

I measured a white oak stump, just sawed off, by the railroad there, averaging just two feet in diameter with one hundred and forty-two rings; another, near by, an inch and a half broader, had but one hundred and five rings.

While I am looking at the hazel, I hear from the old locality, the edge of the great pines and oaks in the swamp by the railroad, the note of the pine warbler. It sounds far off and faint, but, coming out and sitting on the iron rail, I am surprised to see it within three or four rods, on the upper part of a white oak, where it is busily catching insects, hopping along toward the extremities of the limbs and looking off on all sides, twice darting off like a wood pewee, two rods, over the railroad, after an insect and returning to the oak, and from time to time uttering its simple, rapidly iterated, cool-sounding notes. When heard a little within the wood, as he hops to that side of the oak, they sound particularly cool and inspiring, like a part of the ever-green forest itself, the trickling of the sap. Its bright-yellow or golden throat and breast, etc., are conspicuous at this season, — a greenish yellow above, with two white bars on its bluish-brown wings. It sits often with loose-hung wings and forked tail.

Meanwhile a bluebird sits on the same oak, three rods off, pluming its wings. I hear faintly the warbling of one, apparently a quarter of a mile off, and [am] very slow to detect that it is even this one before me, which, in the intervals of pluming itself, is apparently practicing in an incredibly low voice.

The water on the meadows now, looking with the sun, is a far deeper and more exciting blue than the heavens.

The thermometer at 5 P. M. is 66° +, and it has probably been 70° or more; and the last two days have been nearly as warm.

This degree of heat, then, brings the *Fringilla juncorum* and pine warbler and awakes the hyla.

April 10. *Thursday.* Fast-Day. — Some fields are dried sufficiently for the games of ball with which this season is commonly ushered in. I associate this day, when I can remember it, with games of baseball played over behind the hills in the russet fields toward Sleepy Hollow, where the snow was just melted and dried up, and also with the uncertainty I always experienced whether the shops would be shut, whether we should have an ordinary dinner, an extraordinary one, or none at all, and whether there would be more than one service at

the meeting-house. This last uncertainty old folks share with me. This is a windy day, drying up the fields; the first we have had for a long time.

Therien describes to me the diagonal notch he used to cut in maples and birches (not having heard of boring) and the half-round spout, cut out of chestnut or other straight-grained wood with a half-round chisel, sharped and driven into a new-moon cut made by the same tool partly sidewise to the tree. This evidently injured the trees more than the auger. He says they used to boil the birch down to a syrup, and he thought that the black birch would run more than any tree.

P. M. — I set out to sail, the wind northwest, but it is so strong, and I so feeble, that I gave it up. The waves dashed over into the boat and with their sprinkling wet me half through in a few moments. Our meadow looks as angry now as it ever can. I reach my port, and go to Trillium Wood to get yellow birch sap.

The Deep Cut is full of dust. This wind, unlike yesterday's, has a decidedly cold vein in it. The ditch by Trillium Wood is strewn with yellowish hemlock leaves, which are still falling. In the still warmer and broader continuation of this ditch, south of the wood, in the southwest recess, I see three or four frogs jump in, some probably large *Rana palustris*, others quite small. They are in before I see them plainly, and bury themselves in the mud before I can distinguish them clearly. They were evidently sitting in the sun by that leafy ditch in that still and warm nook. Let them beware of marsh hawks. I saw also four yellow-spot tor-

toises paddling about under the leaves on the bottom there. Once they were all together. This ditch is commonly dry in the summer.

The yellow birch sap runs very fast. I set three spouts in a tree one foot in diameter, and hung on a quart pail; then went to look at the golden saxifrage in Hubbard's Close. When I came back, the pail was running over. This was about 3 P. M. Each spout dropped about as fast as my pulse, but when I left, at 4 P. M., it was not dropping so fast. The red maples here do not run at all now, nor did they yesterday. Yet one up the Assabet did yesterday. Apparently the early maples have ceased to run.

We may now say that the ground is bare, though we still see a few patches or banks of snow on the hillsides at a distance, especially on the northeast sides of hills. You see much more snow looking west than looking east. Thus does this remarkable winter disappear at last. Here and there its veteran snow-banks spot the russet landscapes. In the shade of walls and north hillsides and cool hollows in the woods, it is panting its life away. I look with more than usual respect, if not with regret, on its last dissolving traces.

Is not that a jungermannia which so adorns the golden epidermis of the yellow birch with its fine fingers?

I boil down about two quarts of this yellow birch sap to two teaspoonfuls of a smart-tasting syrup. I stopped there; else should have boiled it all away. A slightly medicinal taste, yet not disagreeable to me. It yields but little sugar, then.

April 11. 8.30 A. M. — To Tarbell's to get black and canoe birch sap.

Going up the railroad, I see a male and female rusty grackle alight on an oak near me, the latter apparently a flaxen brown, with a black tail. She looks like a different species of bird. Wilson had heard only a *tchuck* from the grackle, but this male, who was courting his mate, broke into incipient warbles, like a bubble burst as soon as it came to the surface, it was so aerated. Its air would not be fixed long enough.

Set two spouts in a canoe birch fifteen inches [in] diameter, and two in a black birch two feet plus in diameter. Saw a kingfisher on a tree over the water. Does not its arrival mark some new movement in its finny prey? He is the bright buoy that betrays it! And hear in the old place, the pitch pine grove on the bank by the river, the pleasant ringing note of the pine warbler. Its *a-che, vitter vitter, vitter vitter, vitter vitter, vitter vitter, vet* rings through the open pine grove very rapidly. I also heard it at the old place by the railroad, as I came along. It is remarkable that I have so often heard it first in these two localities, *i. e.* where the railroad skirts the north edge of a small swamp densely filled with tall old white pines and a few white oaks, and in a young grove composed wholly of pitch pines on the otherwise bare, very high and level bank of the Assabet. When the season is advanced enough, I am pretty sure to hear its ringing note in both those places.

The hazel sheds pollen to-day; some elsewhere possibly yesterday. The sallow up railroad will, if it is pleasant, to-morrow.[1]

[1] Not till 13th.

When I cut or break white pine twigs now, the turpentine exudes copiously from the bark, even from twigs broken off in the fall and now freshly broken, clear as water, or crystal. How early did it?

The canoe birch sap flowed rather the fastest. I have now got four kinds of birch sap. That of the white birch is a little tinged brown, apparently by the bark; the others are colorless as water. I am struck by the coolness of the sap, though the weather may be warm. Like wild apples, it must be tasted in the fields, and then it has a very slightly sweetish and acid taste, and cool as iced water. I do not think I could distinguish the different kinds of birch with my eyes shut. I drank some of the black birch wine with my dinner for the name of it; but, as a steady drink, it is only to be recommended to outdoor men and foresters. Now is apparently the very time to tap birches of all kinds. I saved a bottleful each of the white, canoe, and black birch sap (the yellow I boiled), and, in twenty-four hours, they had all three acquired a slight brown tinge but the white birch the most brown. They were at first colorless. On the whole, I have not observed so much difference in the amount of sap flowing from the six kinds of trees which I have tapped as I have observed between different trees of the same kind, depending on position and size, etc. This flowing of the sap under the dull rinds of the trees is a tide which few suspect.

Though the snow melted so much sooner on the east side of the railroad causeway than on the west, I notice that it still lies in a broad, deep bank on the east side

of Cheney's row of arbor-vitæ, while the ground is quite bare on the west. Whence this difference?

A few more hylas peep to-day, though it is not so warm as the 9th.

These warm pleasant days I see very few ducks about, though the river is high.

The current of the Assabet is so much swifter, and its channel so much steeper than that of the main stream, that, while a stranger frequently cannot tell which way the latter flows by his eye, you can perceive the declination of the channel of the former within a very short distance, even between one side of a tree and another. You perceive the waters heaped on the upper side of rocks and trees, and even twigs that trail in the stream.

Saw a pickerel washed up, with a wound near its tail, dead a week at least. Was it killed by a fish hawk? Its oil, when disturbed, smoothed the surface of the water with splendid colors. Thus close ever is the fair to the foul. The iridescent, oily surface. The same object is ugly or beautiful, according to the angle from which you view it. Here, also, in the river wreck is the never-failing teazle, telling of the factory above, and sawdust from the mill. The *teased* river! These I do not notice on the South Branch.

I hear of one field plowed and harrowed, — George Heywood's. Frost out there earlier than last year.

You thread your way amid the rustling oak leaves on some warm hillside sloping to the south, detecting no growth as yet, unless the flower-buds of the amelanchier are somewhat expanded, when, glancing along the dry stems, in the midst of all this dryness, you detect

Vol. VIII

the crimson stigmas of the hazel, like little stars peeping forth, and perchance a few catkins are dangling loosely in the zephyr and sprinkling their pollen on the dry leaves beneath.

You take your way along the edge of some swamp that has been cleared at the base of some south hillside, where there is sufficient light and air and warmth, but the cold northerly winds are fended off, and there behold the silvery catkins of the sallows, which have already crept along their lusty osiers, more than an inch in length, till they look like silvery wands, though some are more rounded, like bullets. The lower part of some catkins which have lost their bud-scales emit a tempered crimson blush through their down, from the small scales within. The catkins grow longer and larger as you advance into the warmest localities, till at last you discover one catkin in which the reddish anthers are beginning to push from one side near the end, and you know that a little yellow flame will have burst out there by to-morrow, if the day is fair.

I might [have] said on the 8th: Behold that little hemisphere of green in the black and sluggish brook, amid the open alders, sheltered under a russet tussock. It is the cowslips' forward green. Look narrowly, explore the warmest nooks; here are buds larger yet, showing more yellow, and yonder see two full-blown yellow disks, close to the water's edge. Methinks they dip into it when the frosty nights come. Have not these been mistaken for dandelions?

Or, on the 9th: This still warm morning paddle your boat into yonder smooth cove, close up under the

south edge of that wood which the April flood is bathing, and observe the great mulberry-like catkins of yonder aspen curving over and downward, some already an inch or more in length, like great reddish caterpillars covered thickly with down, forced out by heat, and already the sides and ends of some are loose and of a pale straw-color, shedding their pollen. These, for their forwardness, are indebted to the warmth of their position.

Now for the white maple the same day: Paddle under yonder graceful tree which marks where is the bank of the river, though now it stands in the midst of a flood a quarter of a mile from land; hold fast by one of its trailing twigs, for the stream runs swiftly here. See how the tree is covered with great globular clusters of buds. Are there no anthers nor stigmas to be seen? Look upward to the sunniest side. Steady! When the boat has ceased its swaying, do you not see two or three stamens glisten like spears advanced on the sunny side of a cluster? Depend on it, the bees will find it out before noon, far over the flood as it is.

Seek out some young and lusty-growing alder (as on the 9th), with clear, shining, and speckled bark, in the warmest possible position, perchance where the heat is reflected from some bank or hillside and the water bathes its foot. The scales of the catkins generally are loosened, but on the sunniest cheek of the clump, behold one or two far more considerably loosened, wholly or partially dangling and showing their golden insides. Give the most forward of these a chuck, and you will get a few grains of its yellow dust in your hand. Some will be in full bloom above, while their extremities are comparatively dead, as if struck with a palsy in the winter. Soon will come a rude wind and shake their pollen copiously over the water.

April 12. There is still a little snow ice on the north side of our house, two feet broad, a relic of the 25th of December. This is all there is on our premises.

According to Rees's Cyclopædia, the sap of the birches is fermentable in its natural state. Also, "Ratray, the learned Scot, affirms, that he has found by experiment, that the liquor which may be drawn from the birch tree in the springtime is equal to the whole weight of the tree, branches, roots, and all together."

I think on the whole that, of the particular trees which I tapped, the yellow and canoe birches flowed the fastest.

Hazy all day, with wind from the west, threatening rain. Haze gets to be very thick and perhaps smoky in the afternoon, concealing distinct forms of clouds, if there are any. Can it have anything to do with fires in woods west and southwest? Yet it is warm.

5 P. M. — Sail on the meadow.

There suddenly flits before me and alights on a small apple tree in Mackay's field, as I go to my boat, a splendid purple finch. Its glowing redness is revealed when it lifts its wings, as when the ashes is blown from a coal of fire. Just as the oriole displays its gold.

The river is going down and leaving the line of its wrack on the meadow. It was at its height when the snow *generally* was quite melted here, i. e. yesterday.

Vol. VIII

Rains considerably in the evening. Perhaps this will raise the river again.[1]

April 13. Sunday. 8 A. M. — Up railroad.

Cold, and froze in the night. The sallow will not open till some time to-day.

I hear a bay-wing on the railroad fence sing — the rhythm — somewhat like, *char char* (or *here here*), *che che, chip chip chip* (fast), *chitter chitter chitter chit* (very fast and jingling), *tchea tchea* (jinglingly). It has another strain, considerably different, but a second also sings the above. Two on different posts are steadily singing the same, as if contending with each other, notwithstanding the cold wind.

P. M. — To Walden and Fair Haven Ponds.

Still cold and windy.

The early gooseberry leaf-buds in garden have burst, — now like small green frilled horns. Also the amelanchier flower-buds are bursting.

As I go down the railroad causeway, I see a flock of eight or ten bay-wing sparrows flitting along the fence and alighting on an apple tree. There are many robins about also. Do they not incline more to fly in flocks a cold and windy day like this?

The snow ice is now all washed and melted off of Walden, down to the dark-green clear ice, which appears to be seven or eight inches thick and is quite hard still. At a little distance you would mistake it for water; further off still, as from Fair Haven Hill, it is blue as in

[1] No.

summer. You can still get on to it from the southerly side, but elsewhere there is a narrow canal, two or three to twelve feet wide, next the shore. It may last four or five days longer, even if the weather is warm.

As I go by the Andromeda Ponds, I hear the *tut tut* of a few croaking frogs, and at Well Meadow I hear once or twice a prolonged stertorous sound, as from river meadows a little later usually, which is undoubtedly made by a different frog from the first.

Fair Haven Pond, to my surprise, is completely open. It was so entirely frozen over on the 8th that I think the finishing stroke must have been given to it but by last night's rain. Say then apparently April 13th (?).

Return over the Shrub Oak Plain and the Cliff. Still no cowslips nor saxifrage. There were alders out at Well Meadow Head, as large bushes as any. Can they be *A. serrulata? Vide* leaves by and by.

Standing on the Cliffs, I see most snow when I look southwest; indeed scarcely a particle in any other direction, far or near, from which and from other observations, I infer that there is most snow now under the northeast sides of the hills, especially in ravines there.

At the entrance to the Boiling Spring wood, just beyond the orchard (of Hayden), the northeast angle of the wood, there is still a snow-drift as high as the wall, or three and a half feet deep, stretching quite across the road at that height, and the snow reaches six rods down the road. I doubt if there is as much in the road anywhere else in the town. It is quite impassable there still to a horse, as it has been all winter. This is the heel of the winter.

Scare up two turtle doves in the dry stubble in Wheeler's hill field by the railroad. I saw two together once before this year; probably they have paired.

April 14. Monday. A raw, overcast morning.

8 A. M. — Up Assabet.

See one striped squirrel chasing another round and round the Island, with a faint squeak from time to time and a rustling of the dry leaves. They run quite near to the water.

Hear the flicker's cackle on the old aspen, and his tapping sounds afar over the water. Their tapping resounds thus far, with this peculiar ring and distinctness, because it is a hollow tree they select to play on, as a drum or tambour. It is a hollow sound which rings distinct to a great distance, especially over water.

I still find small turtle's eggs on the surface entire, while looking for arrowheads by the Island.

See from my window a fish hawk flying high west of the house, cutting off the bend between Willow Bay and the meadow, in front of the house, between one vernal lake and another. He suddenly wheels and, straightening out his long narrow wings, makes one circle high above the last meadow, as if he had caught a glimpse of a fish beneath, and then continues his course down the river.

P. M. — Sail to Hill by Bedford line.

Wind southwest and pretty strong; sky overcast; weather cool. Start up a fish hawk from near the swamp white oaks southwest of the Island, undoubtedly the one of the morning. I now see that this is a much darker bird, both above and beneath, than that bird of the 6th. It flies quite low, surveying the water, in an undulating, buoyant manner, like a marsh hawk, or still more a nighthawk, with its long curved wings. He flies so low westward that I lose sight of him against the dark hillside and trees.

The river is going down rapidly, yet the Hunt's Bridge causeway is but just bare. The south side of Ponkawtasset looks much greener and more forward than any part of the town I have noticed. It is almost like another season there. They are already plowing there.

I steer down straight through the Great Meadows, with the wind almost directly aft, feeling it more and more the farther I advance into them. They make a noble lake now. The boat, tossed up by the rolling billows, keeps falling again on the waves with a chucking sound which is inspiriting. There go a couple of ducks, which probably I have started, now scaling far away on motionless pinions, with a slight descent in their low flight, toward some new cove. Anon I scare up two black ducks which make one circle around me, reconnoitring and rising higher and higher, then go down the river. Is it they that so commonly practice this manœuvre? Peter's is now far behind on a forgotten shore. The boat moored beneath his hill is no longer visible, and the red russet hill which is my goal rises before me. I moor my boat to a tree at the base of this hill.

The waves are breaking with violence on this shore,

as on a sea-beach, and here is the first painted tortoise just cast up by them and lying on his back amid the stones, in the most favorable position to display his bright-vermilion marks, as the waves still break over him. He makes no effort to turn himself back, probably being weary contending with the waves. A little further is another, also at the mercy of the waves, which greatly interfere with its staid and measured ways, its head helplessly wagging with every billow. Their scales are very clean and bright now. The only yellow I notice is about the head and *upper* part of the tail. The scales of the back are separated or bordered with a narrow greenish-yellow edging.

Looking back over the meadow from the top of this hill, I see it regularly *watered* with foam-streaks from five to ten feet apart, extending quite across it in the direction of the wind. Washed up against this shore, I see the first dead sucker. You see nowadays on every side, on the meadow bottom, the miserable carcasses of the musquash stripped of their pelts. I saw one plunge from beneath the monument. There is much lumber — fencing-stuff, etc. — to be gathered now by those inclined.

I see an elm-top at the Battle-Ground covered [with blackbirds] uttering their *squeaks* and split whistles, as if they had not got their voices yet, and a coarse, rasping *tchuck* or *char*, not in this case from a crow blackbird.

Again I see the fish hawk, near the old place. He alights on the ground where there is a ridge covered with bushes, surrounded by water, but I scare him

Vol. VIII

again, and he finally goes off northeast, flying high. He had apparently stayed about that place all day fishing.

April 15. 6.30 A. M. — To Hill.

It is warmer and quite still; somewhat cloudy in the east. The water quite smooth, — April smooth waters. I hear very distinctly Barrett's sawmill at my landing. The purple finch is singing on the elms about the house, together with the robins, whose strain its resembles, ending with a loud, shrill, ringing *chilt chilt chilt chilt*. I push across the meadow and ascend the hill. The white-bellied swallows are circling about and twittering above the apple trees and walnuts on the hillside. Not till I gain the hilltop do I hear the note of the *Fringilla juncorum* (huckleberry-bird) from the plains beyond. Returned again toward my boat, I hear the rich watery note of the martin, making haste over the edge of the flood. A warm morning, over smooth water, before the wind rises, is the time to hear it. Near the water are many recent skunk probings, as if a drove of pigs had passed along last night, death to many beetles and grubs. From amid the willows and alders along the wall there, I hear a bird sing, *a-chitter chitter chitter chitter chitter chitter, che che che che*, with increasing intensity and rapidity, and the yellow redpoll hops in sight. A grackle goes over (with two females), and I hear from him a sound like a watchman's rattle, — but little more musical.

What I think the *Alnus serrulata* (?) will shed pollen to-day on the edge of Catbird Meadow. Is that one at

Brister's Spring and at Depot Brook crossing? Also grows on the west edge of Trillium Wood.

Coming up from the riverside, I hear the harsh rasping *char-r char-r* of the crow blackbird, like a very coarsely vibrating metal, and, looking up, see three flying over.

Some of the early willow catkins have opened in my window. As they open, they curve backwards, exposing their breasts to the light.

By 9 A. M. the wind has risen, the water is ruffled, the sun seems more permanently obscured, and the character of the day is changed. It continues more or less cloudy and rain-threatening all day.

First salmon and shad at Haverhill to-day.

Ed. Emerson saw a toad in his garden to-day, and, coming home from his house at 11 P. M., a still and rather warm night, I am surprised to hear the first loud, clear, prolonged ring of a toad, when I am near Charles Davis's house. The same, or another, rings again on a different key. I hear not more than two, perhaps only one. I had only thought of them as commencing in the warmest part of some day, but it would seem that [they] may first be heard in the night. Or perhaps this one may have piped in the day and his voice been drowned by day's sounds. Yet I think that this night is warmer than the day has been. While all the hillside else, perhaps, is asleep, this toad has just awaked to a new year. It was a rather warm, moist night, the moon partially obscured by misty clouds, all the village asleep, only a few lights to be seen in some windows, when, as I passed along under the warm hillside, I heard a clear, shrill, prolonged ringing note from a toad, the first toad of the year, sufficiently countenanced by its Maker in the night and the solitude, and then again I hear it (before I am out of hearing, *i. e.* it is deadened by intervening buildings), on a little higher key. At the same time, I hear a part of the hovering note of my first snipe, circling over some distant meadow, a mere waif, and all is still again. A-lulling the watery meadows, fanning the air like a spirit over some far meadow's bay. And now for vernal sounds there is only the low sound of my feet on the Mill-Dam sidewalks.

April 16. I have not seen a tree sparrow, I think, since December.

5.30 A. M. — To Pinxter Swamp over Hill.

A little sunshine at the rising. I, standing by the river, see it first reflected from E. Wood's windows before I can see the sun. Standing there, I hear that same stertorous note of a frog or two as was heard the 13th, apparently from quite across all this flood, and which I have so often observed before. What kind is it? It seems to come from the edge of the meadow, which has been recently left bare. Apparently this low sound can be heard very far over the water. The robins sing with a will now. What a burst of melody! It gurgles out of all conduits now; they are choked with it. There is such a tide and rush of song as when a river is straightened between two rocky walls. It seems as if the morning's throat were not large enough to emit all this sound. The robin sings most before 6 o'clock now. I note

Vol. VIII

where some suddenly cease their song, making a quite remarkable vacuum.

As I walk along the bank of the Assabet, I hear the *yeep yeep yeep yeeep yeeep yeep*, or perhaps *peop*, of a fish hawk, repeated *quite fast*, but not so shrill and whistling as I think I have heard it, and directly I see his long curved wings undulating over Pinxter Swamp, now flooded.

From the hilltop I see bare ground appearing in ridges here and there in the Assabet meadow.

A grass-bird, with a sort of spot on its breast, sings, *here here hé, che che che, chit chit chit, t' chip chip chip chip chip.* The latter part especially fast. The *F. juncorum* says, *phe phe phe phe ph-ph-p-p-p-p-p-p-p-p-p,* faster and faster; flies as I advance, but is heard distinctly still further off.

A moist, misty, rain-threatening April day. About noon it *does* mizzle a little. The robin sings throughout it. It is rather raw, tooth-achy weather.

P. M. — Round Walden.

The *Stellaria media* is abundantly out. I did not look for it early, it was so snowy. It evidently blossomed as soon after the 2d of April — when I may say the [snow] began to go off in earnest — as possible. The shepherd's-purse, too, is well out, three or four inches high, and may have been some days at least.

Cheney's elm shows stamens on the warm side pretty numerously. Probably that at Lee's Cliff a little earlier.

Plowing and planting are now going on commonly. As I go down the railroad, I see two or three teams in

the fields. Frost appears to be out of most soil. I see a pine warbler, much less yellow than the last, searching about the needles of the pitch and white pine. Its note is somewhat shorter, — a very rapid and continuous trill or jingle which I remind myself of by *vetter vetter vetter vetter vet'*, emphasizing the last syllable.

Walden is still covered with ice, which [is] still darker green and more like water than before. A large tract in the middle is of a darker shade and particularly like water. Mr. Emerson told me yesterday that there was a large tract of water in the middle! This ice trembles like a batter for a rod around when I throw a stone on to it. One as big as my fist, thrown high, goes through. It appears to be three or four inches thick. It extends quite to the shore on the north side and is there met by snow.

The needles of the pines still show where they were pressed down by the great burden of snow last winter. I see a maple twig eaten off by a rabbit four and a quarter feet from the ground, showing how high the snow was there. Golden saxifrage at Hubbard's Close. Frogs sit round Callitriche Pool, where the tin is cast. We have waste places — pools and brooks, etc., — where to cast tin, iron, slag, crockery, etc. No doubt the Romans and Ninevites had such places. To what a perfect system this world is reduced! A place for everything and everything in its place!

April 17. Was awakened in the night by a thunder and lightning shower and hail-storm — the old familiar burst and rumble, as if it had been rumbling somewhere

else ever since I heard it last, and had not lost the knack. I heard a thousand hailstones strike and bounce on the roof at once. What a clattering! Yet it did not last long, and the hail took a breathing-space once or twice. I did not know at first but we should lose our windows, the blinds being away at the painters'. These sounds lull me into a deeper slumber than before. Hail-storms are milked out of the first summer-like warmth; they belong to lingering cool veins in the air, which thus burst and come down. The thunder, too, sounds like the final rending and breaking up of winter; thus precipitous is its edge. The first one is a skirmish between the cool rear-guard of winter and the warm and earnest vanguard of summer. Advancing summer strikes on the edge of winter, which does not drift fast enough away, and fire is elicited. Electricity is engendered by the early heats. I love to hear the voice of the first thunder as of the toad (though it returns irregularly like pigeons), far away in *his* moist meadow where he is warmed to life, and see the flash of his eye.

Hear a chip-bird high on an elm this morning, and probably that was one I heard on the 15th. You would not be apt to distinguish the note of the earliest. I still see quite a snow-bank from my window on the hillside at the northeast end of Clamshell, say a northeast exposure. This is on the surface, but the snow lies there in still greater quantity, in two hollows where sand has been dug for the meadow, on the hillside, though sloping to the southeast, where it is quite below the general surface. We have had scarcely any rain this spring, and the snow has been melting very gradually in the sun.

P. M. — Start for Conantum in boat, wind southwest. I can hide my oars and sail up there and come back another day. A moist muggy afternoon, rain-threatening, true April weather, after a particularly warm and pleasant forenoon. The meadows are still well covered, and I cut off the bends. The red-wing goes over with his *che-e-e che-e-e*, chatter, chatter, chatter. On Hubbard's great meadow I hear the sound of some fowl, perhaps a loon, rushing through the water, over by Dennis's Hill, and push for it. Meanwhile it grows more and more rain-threatening, — all the air moist and muggy, a great ill-defined cloud darkening all the west, — but I push on till I feel the first drops, knowing that the wind will take me back again. Now I hear ducks rise, and know by their hoarse quacking that they are black ones, and see two going off as if with one mind, along the edge of the wood.

Now comes the rain with a rush. In haste I put my boat about, raise my sail, and, cowering under my umbrella in the stern, with the steering oar in my hand, begin to move homeward. The rain soon fills up my sail, and it catches all the little wind. From under the umbrella I look out on the scene. The big drops pepper the watery plain, the *aequor*, on every side. It is not a hard, dry pattering, as on a roof, but a softer, liquid pattering, which makes the impression of a double wateriness. You do not observe the drops descending but where they strike, for there they batter and indent the surface deeply like buckshot, and they, or else other drops which they create, rebound or hop up an inch or two, and these last you see, and also when they

fall back broken into small shot and roll on the surface. Around each shot-mark are countless circling dimples, running into and breaking one another, and very often a bubble is formed by the force of the shot, which floats entire for half a minute. These big shot are battering the surface every three inches or thicker. I make haste to take down my sail at the bridges, but at the stone arches forgot my umbrella, which was unavoidably crushed in part. Even in the midst of this rain I am struck by the variegated surface of the water, different portions reflecting the light differently, giving what is called a watered appearance. Broad streams of light water stretch away between streams of dark, as if they were different kinds of water unwilling to mingle, though all are equally dimpled by the rain, and you detect no difference in their condition. As if Nature loved variety for its own sake. It is a true April shower, or rain, — I think the first. It rains so easy, — has a genius for it and infinite capacity for [it]. Many showers will not exhaust the moisture of April.

When I get home and look out the window, I am surprised to see how it has greened the grass. It springs up erect like a green flame in the ditches on each side the road, where we had not noticed it before. Grass is born. There is a quite distinct tinge of green on the hillside seen from my window now. I did not look for the very first.

I learn from the papers that an unusual number of fruit trees have been girdled by the mice under the deep snow of the past winter. Immense damage has been done to nurseries and orchards. I saw where a prostrate

maple in the Great Meadows had been gnawed nearly bare.

Our river was *generally* breaking up on the 3d of April, though some parts were frozen till the 12th.

I see by the papers that the ice had left Lake St. Peter (St. Lawrence) the 12th. Another paper (of the 11th) has heard that the St. Lawrence was open from Quebec to Three Rivers, or before the Hudson. The ice on Lake Champlain was broken up on the 12th. Fair Haven Pond was quite open the 13th. The ice moved down the Penobscot, and the river opened the 15th. Lake Ontario was free of ice the 16th. The Kennebec is expected to open this week. (To-day is Thursday.) There is still ice in Walden.[1]

April 18. P. M. — To Lee's Cliff by boat.

A strong northwest wind. The waves were highest off Hubbard's second grove, where they had acquired their greatest impetus and felt the full force of the wind. Their accumulated volume was less beyond on account of the turn in the river. The greatest undulation is at the leeward end of the longest broad reach in the direction of the wind. I was steering there diagonally across the black billows, my boat inclined so as almost to drink water. Scare up the same two black ducks (and twice again). The under sides of their wings show quite light and silvery as they rise in the light.

Red maple stamens in some places project considerably, and it will probably blossom to-morrow if it is pleasant.[2]

[1] Opens 18th.   [2] *Vide* 23d.

The farmer neglects his team to watch my sail. The slippery elm, with its round rusty woolly buds and pale-brown ashy twigs. That pretty, *now brown-stemmed* moss with green oval fruit. Common saxifrage and also early sedge I am surprised to find abundantly out — both — considering their backwardness April 2d. Both must have been out some, *i. e.* four or five, days half-way down the face of the ledge. Crowfoot, apparently two or three days. Antennaria at end of Cliff as you descend, say yesterday. *Turritis stricta.* Columbine, and already eaten by bees. Some with a hole in the side. It is worth the while to go there to smell the catnep. I always bring some home for the cat at this season.

See those great chocolate puffballs burst and diffusing their dust on the side of the hill. At the sandy place where I moored my boat, just this side this Cliff, the *Selaginella apus* is abundant, and on Conantum shore near elms thirty or forty rods below.

Left boat opposite Bittern Cliff.

Bear-berry grows by path from river, seven rods beyond last pine, south side, now strongly flower-budded. Observed a large mass of white lily root with the mud washed up, the woolly steel-blue root, with singular knobs for offshoots and long, large, succulent white roots from all sides, the leaf-buds yellow and lightly rolled up on each side. Small sallow next above *tristis*, three feet high, in path to Walden.

Walden is open entirely to-day for the first time,

owing to the rain of yesterday and evening. I have observed its breaking up of different years commencing in '45, and the average date has been April 4th.

This evening I hear the snipes *generally* and peeping of hylas from the door.

A small brown wasps' (?) nest (last year's, of course) hung to a barberry bush on edge of Lee's Cliff.

April 19. Was awakened in the night to a strain of music dying away, — passing travellers singing. My being was so expanded and infinitely and divinely related for a brief season that I saw how unexhausted, how almost wholly unimproved, was man's capacity for a divine life. When I remembered what a narrow and finite life I should anon awake to!

Though, with respect to our channels, our valleys, and the country we are fitted to drain, we are Amazons, we ordinarily live with dry channels.

The arbor-vitæ by riverside behind Monroe's appears to be just now fairly in blossom. I notice acorns sprouted. My birch wine now, after a week or more, has become pretty clear and colorless again, the brown part having settled and now coating the glass.

Helped Mr. Emerson set out in Sleepy Hollow two over-cup oaks, one beech, and two arbor-vitæs.

As dryness will open the pitch pine cone, so moisture closes it up again. I put one which had been open all winter into water, and in an hour or two it shut up nearly as tight as at first.

April 20. Rain, rain, rain, — a northeast storm. I

see that it is raising the river somewhat again. Some little islets which had appeared on the meadow northwest of Dodd's are now fast being submerged again.

April 22. It has rained two days and nights, and now the sun breaks out, but the wind is still easterly, and the storm probably is not over. In a few minutes the air is full of mizzling rain again.

8 A. M. — Go to my boat opposite Bittern Cliff.

Monroe's larches by river will apparently shed pollen soon. The staminate flowers look forward, but the pistillate scarcely show any red. There is snow still (of the winter) in the hollows where sand has been dug on the hillside east of Clamshell. Going through Hubbard's root-fence field, see a pigeon woodpecker on a fence-post. He shows his lighter back between his wings cassock-like and like the smaller woodpeckers. Joins his mate on a tree and utters the wooing note *o-week o-week*, etc.

The seringo also sits on a post, with a very distinct yellow line over the eye, and the *rhythm* of its strain is *ker chick* | *ker che* | *ker-char-r-r-r* | *chick*, the last two bars being the part chiefly heard. The huckleberry buds are much swollen. I see the tracks of some animal which has passed over Potter's sand, perhaps a skunk. They are quite distinct, the ground being smoothed and softened by rain. The tracks of all animals are much more distinct at such a time. By the path, and in the sandy field beyond, are many of those star-fingered puffballs. I think they must be those which are so white, like pigeons' eggs, in the fall, the thick, leathery rind

bursting into eight to eleven segments, like those of a boy's batting ball, and curving back. They are very pretty and remarkable now, sprinkled over the sand, smooth and plump on account of the rain. (I find some beyond at Mountain Sumach Knoll, smaller with a very thin rind and more turned back, a different species plainly.) The inside of the rind, which is uppermost, approaches a chocolate-color; the puffball is a rough dirty or brownish white; the dust which does not fly now at any rate is chocolate-colored. Seeing these thus open, I should know there had been wet weather.[1]

The mountain sumach berries have no redness now, though the smooth sumach berries have. Its twigs are slender and so have a small pith. Its heart-wood is not yellow, like the smooth and the dogwood, but green. Its bark is more gray than that of the smooth, which last, when wet, is slightly reddish. Its bark sap or juice is not yellow like that of the smooth, and is slower to harden.

Some hellebore leaves are opened in the Cliff Brook Swamp. My boat is half full of water. There are myriads of snow-fleas in the water amid the bushes, apparently washed out of the bark by the rain and rise of river.

I push up-stream to Lee's Cliff, behind Goodwin, who is after musquash. Many suckers and one perch have washed up on the Conantum shore, the wind being southeasterly. I do not detect any wound. Their eyes are white, — it would be worth while to see how long before this happens, — and they appear to have

[1] *Vide* two pages forward.

been dead some time; their fins are worn, and they are slimy. I cut open a sucker, and it looked rather yellow within. I also see sometimes their bladders washed up. They float on their backs. When cut open they sink, but the double bladder is uppermost and protruded as far as possible. Saw some pieces of a sucker recently dropped by some bird or beast, eight or ten rods from the shore. Much root and leaf-bud washed up. A gull. Very perfect and handsome clamshells, recently opened by the musquash, *i. e.* during the storm, lie on the meadow and the hillside just above water-mark. They are especially handsome because wet by the rain. I buy a male muskrat of Goodwin, just killed. He sometimes baits his mink-traps with muskrat; always with some animal food. The musquash does not eat this, though he sometimes treads on the trap and is caught. It rains hard and steadily again, and I sail before it. Now I see many more ducks than in all that fair weather, — sheldrakes, etc. A marsh hawk, in the midst of the rain, is skimming along the shore of the meadow, close to the ground, and, though not more than thirty rods off, I repeatedly lose sight of it, it is so nearly the color of the hillside beyond. It is looking for frogs. The small slate-colored hawk which I have called pigeon hawk darts away from a bushy island in the meadow.

The muskrat, which I bought for twelve cents, weighs three pounds, six ounces. Goodwin thought that some would weigh a half to three quarters of a pound more than this; I think a pound more. Thought this was a young one of last year, — judged by the tail,

— and that they hardly came to their growth in one year. Extreme length, twenty-three inches; length of *bare* tail, nine inches; breadth of tail, seven eighths of an inch; breadth of body, etc., as it lies, six and a half. An oval body, dark-brown above (black in some lights, the coarse wind hairs aft), reddish-brown beneath. Thus far the color of the hair. The fur within slate-color. Tail black; feet a delicate glossy dark slate (?), with white nails. The hind feet half webbed, and their sides and toes fringed thickly with stiff hair, apparently to catch water; ears (the head is wet and bruised), partly concealed in the fur, short and round; long black mustachial bristles; fore legs, quite short, more like hands; hind ones, about three inches without the line of the body's fur and hair. Tail, on the skin, is a little curved downwards.

The star fungi, as they dried in my chamber in the course of two or three hours, drew in the fingers. The different segments curled back tightly upon the central puff, the points being strongly curled downward into the middle dimple-wise. It requires wet weather, then, to expand and display them to advantage. They are hygrometers. Their coat seems to be composed of two thicknesses of different material and quality, and I should guess that the inside chocolate-colored had a great affinity for moisture and, being saturated with it, swelled, and so necessarily burst off and turned back, and perchance the outside dirty-white or pale-brown one expands with dryness.

A single male sheldrake rose from amid the alders against Holden Swamp Woods, as I was sailing down in

the rain, and flew with outstretched neck at right angles across my course, only four or five rods from me and a foot or two above the water, finally circling round into my rear.

Soon after I turned about in Fair Haven Pond, it began to rain hard. The wind was but little south of east and therefore not very favorable for my voyage. I raised my sail and, cowering under my umbrella in the stern, wearing the umbrella like a cap and holding the handle between my knees, I steered and paddled, almost perfectly sheltered from the heavy rain. Yet my legs and arms were a little exposed sometimes, in my endeavors to keep well to windward so as to double certain capes ahead. For the wind occasionally drove me on to the western shore. From time to time, from under my umbrella, I could see the ducks spinning away before me, like great bees. For when they are flying low directly from you, you see hardly anything but their vanishing dark bodies, while the rapidly moving wings or paddles, seen edgewise, are almost invisible. At length, when the river turned more easterly, I was obliged to take down my sail and paddle slowly in the face of the rain, for the most part not seeing my course, with the umbrella slanted before me. But though my progress was slow and laborious, and at length I began to get a little wet, I enjoyed the adventure because it combined to some extent the advantages of being at home in my chamber and abroad in the storm at the same time.

It is highly important to invent a dress which will enable us to be abroad with impunity in the severest

Vol. VIII

storms. We cannot be said to have fully invented clothing yet. In the meanwhile the rain-water collects in the boat, and you must sit with your feet curled up on a paddle, and you expose yourself in taking down your mast and raising it again at the bridges. These rain-storms — this is the third day of one — characterize the season, and belong rather to winter than to summer. Flowers delay their blossoming, birds tarry in their migrations, etc., etc. It is surprising how so many tender organizations of flowers and insects survive them uninjured.

The muskrat must do its swimming chiefly with its hind feet. They are similar in form and position to those of the sheldrake. Its broad oval and flattish body, too, must help keep it up.

Those star puffballs which had closed up in my chamber, put into water, opened again in a few hours.

What is that little bodkin-shaped bulb which I found washed up on the edge of the meadow, white with a few small greenish rounded leafets? [1]

On the 19th, when setting out one of those over-cup oaks in Sleepy Hollow, digging at the decayed stump of an apple tree, we disturbed, dug up, a toad, which probably had buried itself there last fall and had not yet come out.

April 23. P. M. — Up Assabet to white cedars.

The river risen again, on account of the rain of the

[1] *Ludwigia palustris.*

last three days, to nearly as high as on the 11th. I can just get over Hosmer's meadow. The red maple did not shed pollen on the 19th and could not on the 20th, 21st, or 22d, on account of rain; so this must be the first day, — the 23d, — though I see none quite so forward by the river. The wind is now westerly and pretty strong. No sap to be seen in the bass. The white birch sap flows yet from a stump cut last fall, and a few small bees, flies, etc., are attracted by it. Along the shore by Dove Rock I hear a faint *tseep* like a fox-colored sparrow, and, looking sharp, detect upon a maple a white-throated sparrow. It soon flies to the ground amid the birches two or three rods distant, a plump-looking bird and, with its bright white and yellow marks on the head distinctly separated from the slate-color, methinks the most brilliant of the sparrows. Those bright colors, however, are not commonly observed.

The white cedar swamp consists of hummocks, now surrounded by water, where you go jumping from one to another. The fans are now dotted with the minute reddish staminate flowers, ready to open. The skunk-cabbage leaf has expanded in one open place there; so it is at least as early as the hellebore of yesterday. Returning, when near the Dove Rock saw a musquash crossing in front. He dived without noise in the middle of the river, and I saw by a bubble or two where he was crossing my course, a few feet before my boat. He came up quietly amid the alders on my right, and lay still there with his head and back partly out. His back looked reddish-brown with a black grain inmixed.

I think that that white root washed up since the ice broke up, with a stout stem flat on one side and narrow green or yellowish leaf-bud rolled up from each side, with a figure in the middle, is the yellow lily, and probably I have seen no pontederia. The white lily root is thickly clothed with a slate-blue fur or felt, close-fitting, reflecting prismatic colors under the microscope, but generally the slate-color of the fur of most animals, and perhaps it is designed to serve a similar use, *viz.* for warmth and dryness. The end of the root is abruptly rounded and sends forth leaves, and along the sides of the root are attached oval bulb-like offshoots, one or two inches long, with very narrow necks, ready, apparently, to be separated soon from the parent stock.

Hear the yellow redpoll sing on the maples below Dove Rock, — a peculiar though not very interesting strain, or jingle.

A very handsome little beetle, deep, about a quarter of an inch long, with *pale*-golden wing-cases, artificially and handsomely marked with burnished dark-green marks and spots, one side answering to the other; front and beneath burnished dark-green; legs brown or cinnamon-color. It was on the side of my boat. Brought it home in a clam's shells tied up, — a good insect-box.

April 24. A rain-threatening April day. Sprinkles a little in the forenoon.

P. M. — To mayflower.

The yellow willow peels fairly, probably for several days. Its buds are bursting and showing a little green,

at end of railroad bridge. On Money-Diggers' Shore, much *large* yellow lily root washed up; that white root with white fibres and yellowish leaf-buds. I doubt if I have seen any pontederia this year. I find, on the southeast side of Lupine Hill, nearly four rods from the water and a dozen feet above its level, a young *Emys picta*, one and five eighths inches long and one and a half wide. I think it must have been hatched year before last. It was headed up-hill. Its rear above was already covered with some kind of green moss (?) or the like, which probably had adhered or grown to it in its winter quarters.

Warren Miles at his new mill tells me that he found a mud turtle of middling size in his brook there last Monday, or the 21st. I saw a wood tortoise there. He has noticed several dead trout, the young man says, and eels, about the shore of the pond, which had apparently died in the winter, washed up about his mill, some that would weigh a pound, and thought that they had been killed by that strong-scented stagnant water of his pond. They could not get down. Also they can't get above his mill *now*, in the spring. He says that at his mill near the factory, where he used a small undershot wheel, eighteen inches in diameter, for grinding lead, he was prevented from grinding at night by the eels stopping the wheel. It was in August, and they were going down-stream. They never ran till about dark, nor after daylight, but at that season one would get under the wheel every five minutes and stop it, and it had to be taken out. There was not width enough beneath the wheel, a small undershot one, *i. e.* between

the wheel and the apron, to allow an eel of ordinary size to pass, and they were washed in sidewise so as to shut this space up completely. They were never troubled by them when going up, which he thought was in April. At the factory they can sometimes catch a bushel in a night at the same time in the box of wire in which they wash wool. Said that they had a wheel at the paper-mills above which killed every eel that tried to go through.

A Garfield (I judge from his face) confirmed the story of sheldrakes killed in an open place in the river between the factory and Harrington's, just after the first great snow-storm (which must have been early in January), when the river was all frozen elsewhere. There were three, and they persisted in staying and fishing there. He killed one.

The epigæa on the upper edge of the bank shows a good deal of the pink, and may open in two or three days if it is pleasant. *Equisetum arvense*, by path beyond second brook, probably yesterday. As usual, am struck with the forwardness of the dark patch of slender rush at the cowslip place.

Returning, in the low wood just this side the first Second Division Brook, near the meadow, see a brown bird flit, and behold my hermit thrush, with one companion, flitting silently through the birches. I saw the fox-color on his tail-coverts, as well as the brown streaks on the breast. Both kept up a constant jerking of the tail as they sat on their perches.

This season of rain and superabundant moisture makes attractive many an unsightly hollow and recess.

I see some roadside lakes, where the grass and clover had already sprung, owing to previous rain or melted snow, now filled with perfectly transparent April rain-water, through which I see to their emerald bottoms, — paved with emerald. In the pasture beyond Nut Meadow Brook Crossing, the unsightly holes where rocks have been dug and blasted out are now converted into perfect jewels. They are filled with water of crystalline transparency, paved with the same emerald, with a few hardhacks and meadow-sweets standing in them, and jagged points of rock, and a few skaters gliding over them. Even these furnish goblets and vases of perfect purity to hold the dews and rains, and what more agreeable bottom can we look to than this which the earliest moisture and sun had tinged green? We do not object to see dry leaves and withered grass at the bottom of the goblet when we drink, if these manifestly do not affect the purity of the water. What wells can be more charming? If I see an early grasshopper drowning in one, it looks like a fate to be envied.[1] Here is no dark unexplored bottom, with its imagined monsters and mud, but perfect sincerity, setting off all that it reveals. Through this medium we admire even the decaying leaves and sticks at the bottom.

The brook had risen so, owing to Miles's running his mill, that I could not get over where I did going.

April wells, call them, vases clean as if enamelled.[2]

There is a slight sea-turn. I saw it like a smoke beyond Concord from Brown's high land, and felt the cool fresh east wind. Is it not common thus early?

The old caterpillar-nests which now lie on the ground

---

[1] [Channing, p. 100.]   [2] [*Ibid.*]

under wild cherry trees, and which the birds may use, are a quite light-colored cottony web, close and thick-matted, together with the dried excrement of caterpillars, etc., on the inside.

See a dog's-bane with two pods open and partially curved backward on each side, but a third not yet open. This soon opens and scatters its down and seeds in my chamber. The outside is a dull reddish or mahogany-

color, but the inside is a singularly *polished* very pale brown. The inner bark of this makes a strong twine like that of the milkweed, but there is not so much of it.

What is that now ancient and decayed fungus by the first mayflowers, — trumpet-shaped with a very broad mouth, the chief inner part green, the outer dark brown?

The earliest gooseberry leaf has spread a third of an inch or more.

Goodwin shot, about 6 P. M., and brought to me a cinereous coot (*Fulica Americana*) which was flying over the willows at Willow Bay, where the water now runs up.

It measures fourteen inches to end of tail; eighteen and one half to end of legs. Tail projects a half-inch beyond closed wings. Alar extent twenty-six inches. (These dimensions are somewhat stretched.) Above it is a bluish slate, passing into olive behind the wings, the primaries more brownish. Beneath, ash-color or pale slate. Head and neck, uniform deep black. Legs, clear green in front, passing into lead-color behind and on the lobes. Edging of wings, white; also the tips of the secondaries for one fourth of an inch, and a small space under the tail. Wings beneath, very light, almost silvery, slate. Vent, for a small space, black. Bill, bluish-white, with a chestnut bar near tip, and corresponding chestnut spot on each side of lower mandible and a somewhat diamond-shaped chestnut spot at base in front. No noticeable yellow on bill. Irides, reddish. No noticeable whitish spot beneath eyes; only bare lid. Legs and feet are very neat; talons very slender, curving, and sharp, the middle ones ½ inch + long. Lobes chiefly on the inner side of the toes. Legs bare half an inch above the joint. From its fresh and tender look I judge it to be a last year's bird. It is quite lousy.

According to Nuttall, they range from 55° north latitude to Florida and Jamaica and west to Oregon (?) and Mexico. Probably breed in every part of North

America, — even· in Fresh Pond, he would imply, — but their nests, eggs, and breeding-habits are yet unknown. Nocturnal, hiding by day. In Florida in the winter. Come to Fresh Pond in September. A pair there in April, and seen with young birds in June. When alarmed utter a "hoarse *kruk*." Called "flusterers" in Carolina, according to Lawson, because they fly trailing their legs or pattering with them over the water. Food: vegetables, also small shellfish, insects, gravel, etc. Leave the Northern States in November.

April 25. Minott tells me of David Wheeler of the Virginia Road, who used to keep an account of the comings and goings, etc., of animals. He was one of the few who knew [how] to set a trap for a fox so that he would get into it; scented it in a peculiar way, perhaps. Brought one home once on his shoulder, feigning death, which came to life suddenly in his entry and ran off with the trap.

Minott says that he could hardly raise cucumbers in his garden by the brook, the tortoises (painted, I judge, from his description) used to eat them so, both small and large, eating out the insides of the last. He sometimes found three or four there at once, and they lay all day hid among the vines.

Saw wasps about his dooryard.

P. M. — To Hill by boat.

Sweet-gale is out in some parts of the Island birch meadow, next the Indian field, probably several days, at least in some places. Larch not yet sheds pollen.

The toads have begun fairly to ring at noonday in

earnest. I rest awhile on my oars in this meadow amid the birches [?] to hear them. The wind is pretty strong and easterly. There are many, probably squatted about the edge of the falling water, in Merrick's pasture. (The river began to fall again, I think, day before yesterday.) It is a low, terrene sound, the undertone of the breeze. Now it sounds low and indefinitely far, now rises, as if by general consent, to a higher key, as if in another and nearer quarter, — a singular alternation. The now universal hard metallic ring of toads blended and partially drowned by the rippling wind. The voice of the toad, the herald of warmer weather.

The cinquefoil well out. I see two or three on the hemlock dry plain, — probably a day or two. I observe a male grackle with a brownish head and the small female on one tree, red-wings on another. Return over the top of the hill against the [wind]. The Great Meadows now, at 3.30 P. M., agitated by the strong easterly wind this clear day, when I look against the wind with the sun behind me, look particularly *dark* blue.

Aspen bark peels; how long?

I landed on Merrick's pasture near the rock, and when I stepped out of the boat and drew it up, a snipe flew up, and lit again seven or eight rods off. After trying in vain for several minutes to see it on the ground there, I advanced a step and, to my surprise, scared up two more, which had squatted on the bare meadow all the while within a rod, while I drew up my boat and made a good deal of noise. In short, I scared up twelve, one or two at a time, within a few rods, which were feeding on the edge of the meadow just laid bare, each rising with a sound like *squeak squeak*, hoarsely. That part of the meadow seemed all alive with them. It is almost impossible to see one on the meadow, they squat and run so low, and are so completely the color of the ground. They rise from within a rod, fly half a dozen rods, and then drop down on the bare open meadow before your eyes, where there seems not stubble enough to conceal [them], and are at once lost as completely as if they had sunk into the earth. I observed that some, when finally scared from this island, flew off rising quite high, one a few rods behind the other, in their peculiar zigzag manner, rambling about high over the meadow, making it uncertain where they would settle, till at length I lost sight of one and saw the other drop down almost perpendicularly into the meadow, as it appeared.

5 P. M. — Went to see Tommy Wheeler's bounds. Warren Miles had caught three more snapping turtles since yesterday, at his mill, one middling-sized one and two smaller. He said they could come down through his mill without hurt. Were they all bound down the brook to the river? [1] I brought home one of the small ones. It was seven and one eighth inches long. Put it in a firkin for the night, but it got out without upsetting it. It had four points on each side behind, and when I put it in the river I noticed half a dozen points or projections on as many of its rear plates, in keeping with the crest of its tail. It buried itself in the grassy bottom within a few feet of the shore. Moves off very flat on

[1] They all came down from the pond through the mill, and another one the 7th of May, *q. v.*

Vol. VIII

the bottom. These turtles have been disturbed or revealed by his operations.

Anne Karney, our neighbor, looking over her garden yesterday with my father, saw what she said was shamrock, which the Irish wear on their caps on St. Patrick's Day, the first she had ever seen in this country. My father pointed it out in his own garden to the Irishman who was working for him, and he was glad to see it, for he had had a dispute with another Irishman as to whether it grew in this country and now he could convince him, and he put it in his pocket. I saw it afterward and pronounced it common white clover, and, looking into Webster's Dictionary, I read, under Shamrock: "The Irish name for a three-leafed plant, the *Oxalis Acetosella*, or common wood-sorrel. It has been often supposed to be the *Trifolium repens*, white trefoil or white clover." This was very satisfactory, though perhaps Webster's last sentence should have been, The *Trifolium repens* has often been mistaken for it.

At evening see a spearer's light.

April 26. Worm-piles about the door-step this morning; how long?

The white cedar gathered the 23d does not shed pollen in house till to-day, and I doubt if it will in swamp before to-morrow.[1] Monroe's larch will, apparently, by day after to-morrow. The white birch at Clamshell, which I tapped long ago, still runs and is partly covered with a pink froth. Is not this the only birch which shows this colored froth, as its sap is the

[1] *Vide* 29th.

most tinged and most inclined to ferment? — a sort of mother which is left on the bark and in the hole.

Looked over hastily the first two hundred lines of Lucretius, but was struck only with the lines referring to Prometheus, whose *vivida vis animi*

" extra
Processit longe flammantia moenia mundi.

"But the custom of our ancestors also permitted these things on holidays: to pound wheat, cut torches, make candles, cultivate a hired vineyard, clear out and purge fish-ponds, ponds, and old ditches, mow grass ground a second time, spread dung, store up hay on scaffolds, gather the fruit of a hired olive yard, spread apples, pears, and figs, make cheese, bring home trees for the sake of planting on our shoulders or on a pack-mule, but not with one harnessed to a cart, nor to plant them when brought home, nor to open the ground, nor prune a tree, not even to attend to sowing seed, unless you have first sacrificed a puppy." [1]

This reminds me of my bringing home an apple tree on my shoulder one Sunday and meeting the stream of meeting-goers, who seemed greatly outraged; but they did not know whether I set it out or not that day, or but that I sacrificed a puppy if I did.

April 27. P. M. — Up Assabet.
I find none of Monroe's larch buds shedding pollen, but the anthers look crimson and yellow, and the female flowers are now fully expanded and very pretty, but small. I think it will first scatter pollen to-morrow.

[1] [Columella.]

Apparently a small bullfrog by riverside, though it looks somewhat like a *Rana fontinalis;* also two or three (apparently) *R. palustris* in that well of Monroe's, which have jumped in over the curb, perhaps. I see quite a number of tortoises out sunning, just on the edge of the Hosmer meadow, which is rapidly becoming bare. Their backs shine from afar in the sun. Also one *Emys insculpta* out higher up. From close by I hear a red-wing's clear, loud whistle, — not squeak (which I think may be confined to the grackle). It is like *pte'-a pte'-a*, or perhaps without the *p*.

The tapping of a woodpecker is made a more remarkable and emphatic sound by the hollowness of the trunk, the expanse of water which conducts the sound, and the morning hour at which I commonly hear it. I think that the pigeon woodpeckers must be building, they frequent the old aspen now so much.

At the Hemlocks I see a rock which has been moved since last fall seven or eight feet into the river, though the ground is but little descending. The rock is about five and a half feet by three by one. I see [a] rather large devil's-needle coursing over the low osiers in Pinxter Swamp. Is it not early for one? The white birch which I tapped in V. palmata Swamp still runs; and the holes are full of, and the base of the tree covered with, a singular sour-tasted, rather hard-crusted *white* (not pink) froth, and a great many of those flat beetles (?), lightning-bug-like, and flies, etc., are sucking it.

April 28. Surveying the Tommy Wheeler farm.[1]

[1] I believe it was this morning there was quite a fog.

Again, as so many times, I [am] reminded of the advantage to the poet, and philosopher, and naturalist, and whomsoever, of pursuing from time to time some other business than his chosen one, — seeing with the side of the eye. The poet will so get visions which no deliberate abandonment can secure. The philosopher is so forced to recognize principles which long study might not detect. And the naturalist even will stumble upon some new and unexpected flower or animal.

Mr. Newton, with whom I rode, thought that there was a peculiar kind of sugar maple which he called the white; knew of a few in the middle of Framingham and said that there was one on our Common.

How promising a simple, unpretending, quiet, somewhat reserved man, whether among generals or scholars or farmers! How rare an equanimity and serenity which are an encouragement to all observers! Some youthfulness, some manliness, some goodness. Like Tarbell, a man apparently made a deacon on account of some goodness, and not on account of some hypocrisy and badness as usual.

Is not the Hubbard Ditch plant the same I see in a Nut Meadow pool, and a remarkable evergreen? with much slime and many young snails on it?

I hear to-day frequently the *seezer seezer seezer* of the black and white creeper, or what I have referred to that, from J. P. Brown's wood bounding on Dugan.[1] It is not a note, nor a bird, to attract attention; only suggesting still warmer weather, — that the season has revolved so much further. See, but not yet hear, the familiar

[1] Can it be myrtle-birds?

chewink amid the dry leaves amid the underwood on the meadow's edge.

Many *Anemone nemorosa* in full bloom at the further end of Yellow Thistle Meadow, in that warm nook by the brook, some probably a day or two there. I think that they are thus early on account of Miles's dam having broken away and washed off all the snow for some distance there, in the latter part of the winter, long before it melted elsewhere. It is a warm corner under the south side of a wooded hill, where they are not often, if ever before, flooded.

As I was measuring along the Marlborough road, a fine little blue-slate butterfly fluttered over the chain. Even its feeble strength was required to fetch the year about. How daring, even rash, Nature appears, who sends out butterflies so early! Sardanapalus-like, she loves extremes and contrasts.[1]

I began to survey the meadow there early, before Miles's new mill had been running long this Monday morning and flooded it, but a great stream of water was already rushing down the brook, and it almost rose over our boots in the meadow before we had done.

Observing the young pitch pines by the road south of Loring's lot that was so heavily wooded, George Hubbard remarked that if they were cut down oaks would spring up, and sure enough, looking across the road to where Loring's white pines recently stood so densely, the ground was all covered with young oaks. *Mem.* — Let me look at the site of some thick pine woods which I remember, and see what has sprung up; *e. g.*

[1] [Channing, p. 104.]

Vol. VIII

the pitch pines on Thrush Alley and the white pines on Cliffs, also at Baker's chestnuts, and the chestnut lot on the Tim. Brooks farm.

This was a very pleasant or rather warm day, looking a little rainy, but on our return the wind changed to easterly, and I felt the cool, fresh sea-breeze.

This has been a remarkably pleasant, and I think warm, spring. We have not had the usual sprinklings of snow, having had so much in the winter, — none since [that] I can remember. There is none to come down out of the air.

April 29. Was awakened early this morning by thunder and some rain, — the second thunder-shower of the season, — but it proved a fair day. At mid-forenoon saw a fish hawk flying leisurely over the house northeasterly.

P. M. — To Cedar Swamp.

Monroe's larch staminate buds have now erected and separated their anthers, and they look *somewhat* withered, as if they had shed a part of their pollen. *If so,* they began yesterday.

It was quite warm when I first came out, but about 3 P. M. I felt a fresh easterly wind, and saw quite a mist in the distance produced by it, a sea-turn. There was the same phenomenon yesterday at the same hour, and on the 24th, later in the day. Yet to-day the air was not much cooled. Your first warning of it *may* be the seeing a thick mist on all the hills and in the horizon. The wind is southeast.

I see great devil's-needles whiz by, coupled.

Do not sail well till I reach Dove Rock, then glide swiftly up the stream. I move upward against the current with a moderate but fair wind, the waves somewhat larger, probably because the wind contends with the current. The sun is in my face, and the waves look particularly lively and sparkling. I can steer and write at the same time. They gurgle under my stern, in haste to fill the hollow which I have created. The waves seem to leap and roll like porpoises, with a slight surging sound when their crests break, and I feel an agreeable sense that I am swiftly gliding over and through them, bound on my own errands, while their motion is chiefly but an undulation, and an apparent one. It is pleasant, exhilarating, to feel the boat tossed up a little by them from time to time. Perhaps a wine-drinker would say it was like the effect of wine. It is flattering to a sense of power to make the wayward wind our horse and sit with our hand on the tiller. Sailing is much like flying, and from the birth of our race men have been charmed by it.

Near the little larch, scared a small dark-brown hawk from an apple tree, which flew off low to another apple tree beside Barrett's Pond. Just before he flew again I saw with my glass that his tail was barred with white. Must it not be a pigeon hawk then? He looked a dark slate as he sat, with tawny-white thighs and under head, — far off. He soon started a third time, and a crow seemed to be in chase of him. I think I have not described this white-barred hawk before, but for the black-barred *vide* May 8, 1854, and April 16, 1855.

The white cedar now sheds pollen abundantly.

Many flowers are effete, though many are not open. Probably it began as much as three days ago. I strike a twig, and its peculiar pinkish pollen fills the air. Sat on the knoll in the swamp, now laid bare. How pretty a red maple in bloom (they are now in prime), seen in the sun against a pine wood, like these little ones in the swamp against the neighboring wood, they are so light and ethereal, not a heavy mass of color impeding the passage of the light, and they are of so cheerful and lively a color.

The pine warbler is heard very much now at midday, when already most birds are quiet. It must be the female which has so much less yellow beneath. Do not the toads ring most on a windy day like this? I heard but few on the still 27th. A pigeon woodpecker alights on a dead cedar top near me. Its cackle, thus near, sounds like *eh eh eh eh eh*, etc., rapidly and emphatically repeated. Some birch sprouts in the swamp are leafed as much as any shrub or tree. Barn swallows and chimney, with white-bellied swallows, are flying together over the river. I thought before that I distinguished the twitter of the chimney swallow.

April 30. Surveying the Tommy Wheeler farm.

A fine morning. I hear the first brown thrasher singing within three or four rods of me on the shrubby hillside in front of the Hadley place. I think I had a glimpse of one darting down from a sapling-top into the bushes as I rode by the same place on the morning of the 28th. This, I think, is the very place to hear them early, a dry hillside sloping to the south, covered with young

wood and shrub oaks. I am the more attracted to that house as a dwelling-place. To live where you would hear the first brown thrasher! First, perchance, you have a glimpse of one's ferruginous long brown back, instantly lost amid the shrub oaks, and are uncertain if it was a thrasher, or one of the other thrushes; and your uncertainty lasts commonly a day or two, until its rich and varied strain is heard. Surveying seemed a noble employment which brought me within hearing of this bird. I was trying to get the exact course of a wall thickly beset with shrub oaks and birches, making an opening through them with axe and knife, while the hillside seemed to quiver or pulsate with the sudden melody. Again, it is with the side of the ear that you hear. The music or the beauty belong not to your work itself but some of its accompaniments. You would fain devote yourself to the melody, but you will hear more of it if you devote yourself to your work.

Cutting off the limbs of a young white pine in the way of my compass, I find that it strips freely. How long this?

By the time I have run through to the Harvard road, I hear the small pewee's *tche-vet'* repeatedly.

The Italian with his hand-organ stops to stare at my compass, just as the boys are curious about *his* machine. We have exchanged places.

As I go along the Assabet, a peetweet skims away from the shore. The canoe birch sap still flows. It is much like that of the white, and is now pink, white, and yellow on the bark.

Bluets out on the bank by Tarbell's spring brook, maybe a day or two.

This was a very warm as well as pleasant day, but at one o'clock there was the usual fresh easterly wind and sea-turn, and before night it grew quite cold for the season. The regularity of the recurrence of this phenomenon is remarkable. I have noticed [it], at least, on the 24th late in the day, the 28th and the 29th about 3 P. M., and to-day at 1 P. M. It has been the order. Early in the afternoon, or between one and four, the wind changes (I suppose, though I did not notice its direction in the forenoon), and a fresh cool wind from the sea produces a mist in the air.

About 3.30 P. M., when it was quite cloudy as well as raw, and I was measuring along the river just south of the bridge, I was surprised by the great number of swallows — white-bellied and barn swallows and perhaps republican — flying round and round, or skimming very low over the meadow, just laid bare, only a foot above the ground. Either from the shape of the hollow or their circling, they seemed to form a circular flock three or four rods in diameter and one swallow deep. There were two or three of these centres and some birds equally low over the river. It looked like rain, but did not rain that day or the next. Probably their insect food was flying at that height over the meadow at that time. There were a thousand or more of swallows, and I think that they had recently arrived together on their migration. Only this could account for there being so many together. We were measuring through one little circular meadow, and many of them were not driven off by our nearness. The noise of their wings and their twittering was quite loud.

VII

MAY, 1856

(ÆT. 38)

May 1. 6 P. M. — To Hill.

I judge that the larch blossomed when the anthers began to be loose and dry and yellow on their edges. Say then the 28th. The water on the meadows is rapidly going down. I am now confined to the river for the most part. The water begins to feel as warm or warmer than the air when cool.

The scrolls of the ferns clothed in wool at Sassafras Shore, five or six inches high. *Thalictrum anemonoides* well out, probably a day or two, same shore, by the apple trees. *Viola ovata* [1] on southwest side of hill, high up near pines. How pleasing that early purple grass in smooth water! Half a dozen long, straight purple blades of different lengths but about equal width, close together and exactly parallel, resting flat on the surface of the water. There is something agreeable in their parallelism and flatness.

From the hilltop I look over Wheeler's maple swamp. The maple-tops are now, I should say, a bright brick red. It is the red maple's reign now, as the peach and the apple will have theirs. Looking over the swamps a quarter of a mile distant, you see dimly defined cres-

[1] Edith Emerson, Apr. 29th.

cents of bright brick red above and amid a maze of ash-colored branches.

May 2. The *tea lee* of the yellow-rump warbler [1] in the street, at the end of a cool, rainy day.

May 3. Another cool, rainy day. A staminate balm-of-Gilead poplar by Peter's path. Many of the catkins fallen and effete in the rain, but many anthers still red and unopen. Probably began five or six days ago.

May 4. P. M. — To Cedar Swamp *via* Assabet.

Among others, I see republican swallows flying over river at Island. Again I see, as on the 30th of April, swallows flying low over Hosmer's meadow, over water, though comparatively few. About a foot above the water, about my boat, are many of those little fuzzy gnats, and I suspect that it is these they are attracted by. (On the 6th, our house being just painted, the paint is peppered with the *myriads* of the same insects which have stuck to it. They are of various sizes, though all small, and there are a few shad-flies also caught. They are particularly thick on the coping under the eaves, where they look as if they had been dusted on, and dense swarms of them are hovering within a foot. Paint a house now, and these are the insects you catch. I suspect it is these fuzzy gnats that the swallows of the 30th were catching.)

The river is gone down so much — though checked by the rain of the 2d and 3d — that I now observe the tortoises on the bottom, a sternothærus among them.

[1] White-throat sparrow.

Hear the something like *twe twe twe twe twé*, *ter té te twe twe* of the myrtle-bird, and see the bird on the swamp white oaks by Island.

The aspen there just begun to leaf; not quite the white maple. I observe that the river meadows, especially Hosmer's, are divided by two or more ridges and valleys (the latter alone now covered with water and so revealed), parallel with the river. The same phenomenon, but less remarkable, on the Wheeler meadow. Are they the traces of old river-banks, or where, in freshets, the current of the river meets the meadow current, and the sediment is deposited?

See a peetweet on Dove Rock, which just peeps out. As soon as the rocks begin to be bare the peetweet comes and is seen teetering on them and skimming away from me.

Having fastened my boat at the maple, met, on the bank just above, Luke Dodge, whom I met in a boat fishing up that way once or twice last summer and previous years. Was surprised to hear him say, "I am in my eighty-third year." He still looks pretty strong and has a voice like a nutmeg-grater. Within two or three years at most, I have seen him walking, with that remarkable gait. It is encouraging to know that a man may fish and paddle in this river in his eighty-third year. He says he is older than Winn, though not the oldest man in the town. Mr. Tolman is in his eighty-sixth year.

Went up Dodge's (an Englishman who once lived up it and no relation of the last-named) Brook and across Barrett's dam. In the Cedar Swamp *Andromeda caly-*

culata abundantly out; how long? *Viburnum nudum* leafing. *Smilacina trifolia* recently up; will apparently open in ten or twelve days.

At the dam, am amused with the various curves of jets of water which leak through at different heights. According to the pressure. For the most part a thin sheet was falling smoothly over the top and cutting short off some smaller jets from the first crack (or edge of the first plank), leaving them like white spikes seen through the water. The dam leaked in a hundred places between and under the planks, and there were as many jets of various size and curve. Reminds me of the tail-piece in Bewick, of landlord drawing beer (?) from two holes, and knowledge of artist shown.

Shad-flies on the water, schooner-like. Hear and see a goldfinch, on the ground.

May 6. To Clamshell by river.

Our earliest currant out. Oat spawn showing little pollywogs (?) in meadow water. The horse-chestnut and mountain-ash leafing. Knawel out at Clamshell; how long? Cerastium out there under the bank. That early white birch there has about done running sap. *Equisetum sylvaticum* a day or two on the ditch bank there.

May 7. Wednesday. Fresh easterly wind.
2 P. M. — To bear-berry on Major Heywood road.

In Deacon Hosmer's barn meadows, hear the *don't don't* of a bullfrog.

In the first hollow in the bank this side of Clam-

shell, where sand has been dug for the meadow, are a hundred or more bank swallows at 2 P. M. (I suspect I have seen them for some time) engaged in prospecting and digging their holes and circling about. It is a snug place for them, — though the upright portion of the bank is only four or five feet high, — a semicircular recess facing the southeast. Some are within scratching out the sand, — I see it cast out of the holes behind them, — others hanging on to the entrance of the holes, others on the flat sandy space beneath in front, and others circling about, a dozen rods off over the meadow. Theirs is a low, dry, grating twitter, or rather rattle, less metallic or musical than the *vite vite* and twittering notes of barn and white-bellied swallows. They are white-bellied, dark winged and tailed, with a crescent of white [*sic*] nearly around the lower part of the neck, and mouse-colored heads and backs. The upper and greater part of this bank is a coarse sliding gravel, and they build only in the perpendicular and sandy part (I sit and watch them within three or four rods) and close to the upper part of it. While I am looking, they all suddenly with one consent take to wing, and circle over the hillside and meadow, as if they chose to work at making their holes a little while at a time only. I find the holes on an average about a foot deep only as yet, some but a few inches.

In the meanwhile I hear, through this fresh, raw east wind, the *te-a-lea* of myrtle-birds [1] from the woods across the river.

The bear-berry will perhaps open to-morrow.[2]

[1] White-throat sparrows.   [2] It does.

I hear the evergreen-forest note close by; and hear and see many myrtle-birds, at the same time that I hear what I have called the black and white creeper's note. Have I ever confounded them?

Over the edge of Miles's mill-pond, now running off, a bumblebee goes humming over the dry brush. I think I saw one on the 5th also.

Miles began last night to let the water run off. The pond falls about three inches in twenty-four hours. The brook below is full of fishes, — suckers, pouts, eels, trouts, — endeavoring to get up, but his dam prevents. This morning his young man killed a number of pouts and eels and suckers with a shovel. Here he comes now, at 4 P. M., with a spear, and raises the gate and waits a few moments for the water, which was two or three feet deep just below the mill, to run off; and then I see a good-sized trout, four or five pouts, and several suckers, and one eel still making their way upward, though the water hardly covers their backs. They do not turn and go down the stream with the water which is thus suddenly and rapidly let off. Meanwhile this young man picks out half a dozen pouts, eels, and suckers with his spear. Twenty rods down the brook I saw many more suckers trying to make their way up. They found it difficult now to get over the bars where the water was very shallow, and were sometimes confined to the hollows between. I saw two or three in company trying to squeeze through a narrow passage under some alder boughs, which was blocked up by two spotted tortoises; and one large eel squirming directly over an indifferent wood turtle, concluding

to go down the stream, but it soon hid under a projecting bank. The pouts, etc., would suddenly bury themselves in the sand or mud and be lost. The fishes seemed unwilling to turn and go down the brook, and for the most part would come so near in the shallow water that they could easily be struck with the spear.

The water thus suddenly let off, there were many spotted and wood tortoises seen crawling about on the bottom. One little snapping (making the fifth of its species here), three and a half inches long, going down a few rods below the dam. This, like the larger ones, going down the brook. Where to? and why? He cannot be old enough to breed yet, and it is too early to be laying at the desert. This young snapping turtle was very strong-scented. Its tail appeared particularly long, as long as its shell, and very tapering, and very distinctly and sharply keeled. The first half-dozen of its dorsal serrations were very prominent and sharp, and its bill was very sharp also. It had four sharp points on each side of its shell behind, and I noticed that it swam better than other kinds of tortoises. Its head was as large as that of an ordinary wood tortoise. There were tracks of other turtles on the sandy bank.

The young man said that the eels came along as many as three in an hour in the night, and this morning there were a great many of them about the wheel. Last fall (this dam being made late in the fall), they found in the hollow under the wheel which they bailed out sixteen trout which weighed eight pounds. It is surprising how many fishes will run up and breed in such a little brook as this. The fishes generally would

conceal themselves in the mud under a projecting bank, or in some deep hole in the sand in mid-channel which communicated with the mud beneath.

One of those larger snapping turtles seized the one I had by the head and they braced and struggled awhile.

The miller now raises his gate and lets his pond run off. Do they not generally earlier?

For a week the road has been full of cattle going up country.

May 10. The third day of rain. The river has again gone over the meadows, which were almost bare.

P. M. — To Walden in rain.

R. Rice speaks of having seen myriads of eels formerly, going down the Charles River, young ones not longer than his hand, stopped behind a board at the dam. That once there, when repairing the dam, he saw, while standing on the bared bottom below it, a large eel come up close by it through hard gravel and he believed it had just come down the river and had penetrated through six feet in thickness of the same character, for the dam was carried down to that depth below the bottom of the river.

That the snapping turtle caught fish by lying buried in the mud with only his eyes out, was Rice's supposition.

Some Vaccinium Pennsylvanicum out in Cut woods; maybe a day, as it has rained steadily the last two days. It seems to bloom with or immediately after the bearberry.

I would gladly walk far in this stormy weather, for now I see and get near to large birds. Two quails

whir away from the old shanty stubble-field, and two turtle doves go off from an apple tree with their *clikit.* Also at Walden shore a pigeon hawk (or else sharpshinned), with deep-brown back, went off from close at hand.

I see there, just above the edge of the Pool in Hubbard's Wood Path, the *Viola blanda* passing into the *V. lanceolata,* which last also is now in bloom, probably earlier there than in wetter places. May have been as early as the *blanda.*

Where the pitch pines were cut some years ago on Thrush Alley, I now see birches, oaks, and pitch and white pines.

On the railroad causeway against Trillium Wood, I see an apparently native willow, a shrub, with greenish bark and conspicuous yellow catkins, now in full bloom, apparently a little earlier than the *Salix alba,* but its leafets or bracts much less advanced and conspicuous. Another on the Walden road. What is it? Mr. Prichard's Canada plum will open as soon as it is fair weather.[1]

May 11. Rains still.

I noticed the other day that the stump of the large oak at Clamshell Hill, cut down fifteen years ago or more, was quite rotten, while the trunk which lay by its side, having never been removed, was comparatively sound.

The Roman writers Columella and Palladius warn not to build in a low valley or by a marsh, and the same

[1] *Vide* 12th.

rule is observed here to-day. In the West the prudent settler avoids the banks of rivers, choosing high and open land. It suggests that man is not completely at one with Nature, or that she is not yet fitted to be his abode. Adam soon found that he must give a marsh a wide berth, — that he must not put his bower in or near a swamp in the new country, — else he would get the fever and ague or an intermittent fever. Either nature may be changed or man. Some animals, as frogs and musquash, are fitted to live in the marsh. Only a portion of the earth is habitable by man. Is the earth improving or deteriorating in this respect? Does it require to be improved by the hands of man, or is man to live more naturally and so more safely?

P. M. — To Cedar Swamp up Assabet.

There is at length a prospect of fair weather. It will clear up at evening this fourth day of the rain. The river is nearly as high as it has been this spring.

The *Salix alba* by my boat is out and beaten by the rain; perhaps three or four days in some places, but not on the 6th. It does not rain now, though completely overcast, but looks as if it would clear up before night.

There are many swallows circling low over the river behind Monroe's, — bank swallows, barn, republican, chimney, and white-bellied. These are all circling together a foot or two over the water, passing within ten or twelve feet of me in my boat. It is remarkable how social the different species of swallow are one with another. They recognize their affinity more than usual. On the prospect of fair weather after so long a storm,

the birds are more lively than ever. As I float through the Wheeler Indian field meadow, I see a veery hopping silent under the alders. The black and white creeper also is descending the oaks, etc., and uttering from time to time his *seeser seeser seeser*. What a rich, strong striped blue-black (?) and white bird, much like the myrtle-bird at a little distance, when the yellow of the latter is not seen. At a distance I hear the first yellow-bird.

The *Salix sericea* at Island rock is out, also the *S. cordata* off Prichard's, both apparently with *S. alba*. But I have not yet compared them (for date) *quite* accurately enough. I think I can pretty well distinguish the *sericea* by the grayness of the female catkins, twig and all, but am not sure I have seen the staminate. Neither am I sure that I see the staminate *S. cordata*. Those at Prichard's are apparently all female. There are many staminate ones now in full bloom in the Wheeler meadow, I suspect like that of the railroad causeway, male and female side by side, five rods north of *S. alba;* also male, west side below ring-post (*vide* May 10th), or they may be staminate plants of *S. cordata*, or some perhaps of *S. sericea*. *Vide* how many different kinds of leaves and mark them six weeks hence. *Vide* if those just off the north end of Holden Wood (Conantum) are all *S. cordata*, for there are many staminate ones like the last-named; also *vide* that one on the north side of the road and root fence beyond brook on Corner road (perhaps like the railroad one), male and female now a little past prime. All these willows blossom when the early willows, which bloom before leafing, are going to seed.

Vol. VIII

Large white maples are leafing.

I see, near the top of the bank at the further end of the first hemlocks, dirty-white fungi in nests, each about three quarters of an inch [in] diameter, without any thick rind which peels off. Each one is burst a little at top, and is full of dust of a yellowish rotten-stone color, which is perfectly dry and comes forth like a puff of smoke on being pinched, now after four days of rain, before the fair weather has come, and though each one is nearly half full of water. This dust certainly has but little affinity for moisture and might be of use in some cases.

I leave my boat in Hosmer's *pokelogan* and walk up the bank. A bluebird's nest and five eggs in a hollow apple tree three feet from ground near the old bank swallow pit, made with much stubble and dried grass. Can see the bird sitting from without.

There are a great many large flat black cockroach(?)-like beetles floating and paddling on the flood on the meadows, which have perhaps fallen in in the night (if not washed out of the grass); also a few of the thick dull reddish-brown ones.

May 12. A glorious day.

P. M. — Walked round by Dennis's and Hollowell place with Alcott.

It is suddenly very warm. A *washing* day, with a slight haze accompanying the strong, warm wind. I see, in the road beyond Luther Hosmer's, in different places, two bank swallows which were undoubtedly killed by the four days' northeast rain we have just had.

Puffer says he has seen two or three dead sparrows also. The sudden heat compels us to sit in the shade at the bars above Puffer's, whence we hear the first bobolink. How suddenly the birds arrive after the storm, — even yesterday before it was fairly over, — as if they had foreseen its end! How much life the note of the bobolink imparts to the meadow! I see a cultivated cherry in bloom, and Prichard's Canada plum will probably bloom to-morrow. The river is higher than yesterday, about the same as when highest before this spring, and goes no higher. Thus attains its height the day after the rain.

May 13. Hear a warbling vireo. Dandelions by roadside; probably several days in some places.

P. M. — Up river to Kalmia glauca Swamp.

In the swallows' holes behind Dennis's, I find two more dead bank swallows, and one on the sand beneath, and the feathers of two more which some creature has eaten. This makes at least seven dead bank swallows in consequence of the long, cold northeast rain. A male harrier, skimming low, had nearly reached this sandpit before he saw me and wheeled. Could it have been he that devoured the swallows?

These swallows were $10\frac{3}{4}+$ alar extent, $4\frac{3}{4}$ inches long; a wing $4\frac{3}{4}+$ by $1\frac{3}{4}+$. Above they were a light brown on their backs, wings blackish, beneath white, with a dark-brown band over the breast and again white throat and side of neck; bill small and black; reddish-brown legs, with long, sharp, slender claws. It chanced that each one of two I tried weighed between five and six sixteenths of an ounce, or between five and six drams avoirdupois. This seems to be the average weight, or say six drams because they have pined a little. A man who weighs one hundred and fifty pounds weighs sixty-four hundred times as much as one. The wing of one contains about seven square inches, the body about five, or whole bird nineteen. If a man were to be provided with wings, etc., in proportion to his weight, they would measure about 844 square feet, and one wing would cover 311 feet, or be about 33 feet long by 14 wide. This is to say nothing of his muscles.

The *Kalmia glauca* will not open for some days at least.

Mrs. Ripley told me last night that Hill said the toads rang till they died if their call was not answered or attended to.

At the swamp, hear the *yorrick* of Wilson's thrush; the tweezer-bird or *Sylvia Americana*. Also the oven-bird sings. Caterpillars' nests on an apple two inches [in] diameter. Downy amelanchier just out at Lupine Bank; elsewhere, *maybe*, a day or two.

Where my sap has dried on the white birch bark it has now turned a bright light red. What a variety of colors it assumes!

Potter has a remarkable field of mulleins, sown as thickly as if done with a machine (under Bear Garden Hill). I remarked them last year. William Wheeler thinks the seed lies in the ground an indefinite period ready to come up. I thought that it might have been introduced with his grain when it was sown lately. Wheeler says that many a pasture, if you plow it up

Vol. VIII

after it has been lying still ten years, will produce an abundant crop of wormwood, and its seeds must have lain in the ground. Why do not the chemists in their analyses of soils oftener mention the seeds of plants? Would not a careful analysis of old pasture sod settle the question?

I suspect that I can throw a little light on the fact that when a dense pine wood is cut down oaks, etc., may take its place. There were only pines, no other tree. They are cut off, and, after two years have elapsed, you see oaks, or perhaps a few other hard woods, springing up with scarcely a pine amid them, and you wonder how the acorns could have lain in the ground so long without decaying. There is a good example at Loring's lot. But if you look through a thick pine wood, even the exclusively pitch pine ones, you will detect many little oaks, birches, etc., sprung probably from seeds carried into the thicket by squirrels, etc., and blown thither, but which are overshadowed and choked by the pines. This planting under the shelter of the pines may be carried on annually, and the plants annually die, but when the pines are cleared off, the oaks, etc., having got just the start they want, and now secured favorable conditions, immediately spring up to trees. Scarcely enough allowance has been made for the agency of squirrels and birds in dispersing seeds.[1]

At the Kalmia Swamp, the parti-colored warbler, and was that *switter switter switter switter swit'* also by it?[2]

[1] [*Excursions*, pp. 188, 189; Riv. 231, 232.]

[2] Probably by this or the redstart, which last I distinguish on the 17th *inst*.

May 14. Air full of golden robins. Their loud clear note betrays them as soon as they arrive. Yesterday and to-day I see half a dozen tortoises on a rail, — their first appearance in numbers. Catbird amid shrub oaks. Female red-wing. Flood tells me he saw cherry-birds on the 12th of April in Monroe's garden.

May 15. A fog this morning. Our peach out.

P. M. — To beeches.

As I sat by the Riordan crossing, thought it was the tanager I heard? I think now, only because it is so early, that it *may* have been the yellow-throat vireo.[1]

See also, for a moment, in dry woods, a warbler with blue-slate head and apparently all yellow beneath for a minute, nothing else conspicuous; note slightly like *tseep, tseep, tseep, tseep, tsit sitter ra-re-ra*, the last fast, on maples, etc. Maybe I heard the same yesterday.[2]

Northern wild red cherry out, cut by railroad; maybe day or two elsewhere. At Heywood Spring I see a clumsy woodchuck, now, at 4 P. M., out feeding, gray or grizzly above, brown beneath. It runs, or waddles, to its hole two or three rods off, and as usual pauses, listening, at its entrance till I start again, then dives in.

Viola cucullata abundant now. Just on the brink of this Heywood Spring, I find what may be the *Stellaria borealis* (if it is not the *longifolia*, but it is not in cymes like that; only a single flower to each axil, now at

[1] No; it must have been a tanager, which I hear frequently the 19th.

[2] No doubt the *Sylvia Americana*, blue yellow-back or parti-colored warbler; heard before.

least), though Bigelow makes its calyx-divisions nerve-less. These are three-nerved, and one flower, at least, has five (!) styles. It has been out perhaps several days. Some of the flowers are without petals, others with those very deeply cleft or divided white petals. The others *may* have pollen.[1]

Strawberry well out; how long? On *Amelanchier Botryapium*, many narrow dark bronze-colored beetles (say three fourths inch long) coupled and at same time eating the flowers, calyx and all. Night-warbler. Hickory leafets not so large as beech. Beech leaves two inches long. Say it has leafed a day or two. White birch pollen. Beech not out yet.

Checker-berries very abundant on south side of Pine Hill, by pitch pine wood. Now is probably best time to gather them.

Cleared out the Beech Spring, which is a copious one. So I have done some service, though it was a wet and muddy job. Cleared out a spring while you have been to the wars. Now that warmer days make the traveller thirsty, this becomes an important work. This spring was filled and covered with a great mass of beech leaves, amid and beneath which, damp and wet as they were, were myriads of snow-fleas and also their white exuviæ; the latter often whitening a whole leaf, mixed with live ones. It looks as if for coolness and moisture — which the snow had afforded — they were compelled to take refuge here.

Cerasus pumila, south side Pine Hill, not yet by Cut woods. Perceive *some* of that delicious meadow fra-

[1] Two inches high; leaves rather broad. *Vide* the 21st.

grance coming over the railroad causeway. **Measured a chestnut stump cut last winter on Pine Hill; twenty-five inches in diameter and fifty-six rings.**

May 16. Rainy day.

May 17. Rain still or lowering.

P. M. — To my boat at Cardinal Shore, thence to Lee's Cliff.

Kingbird. The beech twigs I gathered the 15th show anthers to-day in chamber; so it probably blossoms to-day or to-morrow in woods. *Vaccinium vacillans* apparently a day or two at least. *Veronica serpyllifolia* abundant now on banks, erected. Maryland yellow-throat heard afar in meadows, as I go along the road towards Hubbard's Bridge. It is warm, but still overcast and sprinkling occasionally, near the end of the rain, and the birds are very lively. A goldfinch twitters over.

In the dry lupine bank pasture, about fifteen rods from the river, apparently travelling up the hill, I see a box tortoise, the first I have found in Concord.[1] Beside being longer (its upper shell five and one half by four and one fourth inches), it is much flatter and more oblong, less oval, than the one I found on Cape Cod last July. Especially it is conspicuously broader and flatter forward. The two rear marginal plates have a triangular sinus between them while the Cape Cod ones come to a point. The fifth and sixth marginal plates do not project by their edges beyond the

[1] *Vide* July 19.

shell. The yellow marks are much narrower, and more interrupted and like Oriental characters, than in the Cape Cod one. The sternum also is less oval, uniformly blackish-brown except a few slight bone- [?] or horn-colored blotches, while the Cape Cod one is light-yellow with a few brown blotches. The scales of the sternum in this are much less sharp-angled than in the Cape Cod one. The sternum more hollow or depressed.

The tail about three eighths of an inch long only, beyond the anus (?). The bill is very upright, somewhat like this: A beak like any Cæsar's. Fore with legs covered scales. orange-colored mostly Hind ones with a brown or bronze few orange spots. Beside the usual hiss, uttered in the evening as I was carrying it, a single, as it were involuntary, squeak much like a croaking frog. Iris, bright light red, or rather vermilion, remarkable. Head, brown above with yellow spots; orange beneath and neck.

The river is about a foot lower than on the 13th, notwithstanding yesterday's and to-day's rain.

At the Kalmia Swamp, see and hear the redstart, very lively and restless, flirting and spreading its reddish tail. The sylvias — *S. Americana* and redstart and summer yellowbird, etc. — are very lively there now after the rain, in the warm, moist air, amid the hoary bursting buds of maples, oaks, etc.

I stand close on the edge of the swamp, looking for

the kalmia. Nothing of its flower to be seen yet. The rhodora *there* will open in a day or two.

Meanwhile I hear a loud hum and see a splendid male hummingbird coming zigzag in long tacks, like a bee, but far swifter, along the edge of the swamp, in hot haste. He turns aside to taste the honey of the *Andromeda calyculata* (already visited by bees) within a rod of me. This golden-green gem. Its burnished back looks as if covered with green scales dusted with gold. It hovers, as it were stationary in the air, with an intense humming before each little flower-bell of the humble *Andromeda calyculata*, and inserts its long tongue in each, turning toward me that splendid ruby on its breast, that glowing ruby. Even this is coal-black in some lights! There, along with me in the deep, wild swamp, above the andromeda, amid the spruce. Its hum was heard afar at first, like that of a large bee, bringing a larger summer. This sight and sound would make me think I was in the tropics, — in Demerara or Maracaibo.[1]

Nemopanthes on that very swamp-edge. *Vaccinium corymbosum* (?) or the high blueberry.

Hear the first veery note and doubtless the *Muscicapa olivacea*. The *Sylvia Americana* (parti-colored warbler, etc.) is very numerous there, darting about amid the hoary buds of the maples and oaks, etc. It seems the most restless of all birds, blue more [or] less deep above, with yellow dust on the back, yellow breast, and white beneath (the male with bright-orange throat, and some with a rufous crescent on breast); wings and tail,

[1] Another on our cherry blossoms the next day. A long, slender black bill.

dark, black, with two white bars or marks, dark bill and legs.

At Lee's the *Turritis stricta* pods three inches long, and plant two and a half feet high by measure. Get some to press. *Myosotis stricta* above there, maybe several days. *Ranunculus bulbosus* a day or two at least. *Arenaria serpyllifolia*.

Mrs. Ripley showed me, from her son Gore in Minnesota, a few days ago, the first spring flower of the prairie there, a hairy-stemmed, slender-divisioned, and hairy-involucred, six-petalled blue flower, probably a species of hepatica. No leaves with it. Not described in Gray.[1]

Yellow columbine well out at Lee's, one rod from rock, one rod east of ash.

How plainly we are a part of nature! For we live like the animals around us. All day the cow is cropping the grass of yonder meadow, appropriating, as it were, a part of the solid earth into herself, except when she rests and chews the cud; and from time to time she wends her way to the river and fills her belly with that. Her food and drink are not scarce and precious, but the commonest elements of which nature is composed. The dry land in these latitudes, except in woods and deserts, is almost universally clothed with her food, and there are inland seas, ready mixed, of the wine that she loves. The Mississippi is her drink, the prairie grass her food.

The shrub oak and some other oak leafets, just expanding, now begin to be pretty.

Within the shell of my box turtle, in the cavity be-

[1] Yes. They say it is *Pulsatilla patens*.

tween its thighs and its body, were small dry leaves and seeds, showing where it laid. From these I should say it had come from amidst the alders.

May 18. Ed. Emerson says he saw at Medford yesterday many ground-birds' nests and eggs under apple trees.

R. W. E.'s black currant [1] (which the wild *Ribes floridum* is said to be much like), maybe a day.

R. W. E. says that Agassiz tells him he has had turtles six or seven years, which grew so little, compared with others of the same size killed at first, that he thinks they may live four or five hundred years.

P. M. — To Kalmia Swamp.

Go across fields from R. W. E.'s to my boat at Cardinal Shore. In A. Wheeler's stubble-field west of Deep Cut, a female (?) goldfinch on an oak, without any obvious black, is mewing incessantly, the note ending rather musically. When I get over the fence, a flock of twenty or more, male and female, rise from amid the stubble, and, alighting on the oaks, sing pleasantly all together, in a lively manner.

Going along the Spring Path, hear an oft-repeated *tchip tchar*, *tchip tchar*, etc., or *tchip tcharry* (this is a common note with birds) from a large bird on a treetop, a sort of flaxen olive. Made me think of a female rose-breasted grosbeak, though we thought the beak more slender.

On the surface of the water amid the maples, on the Holden Wood shore where I landed, I noticed some of

[1] Apparently it is American.

---

the most splendid iridescence or opalescence from some oily matter, where the water was smooth amid the maples, that I ever saw. It was where some sucker or other fish, perchance, had decayed. The colors are intense blue and crimson, with dull golden. The whole at first covering seven or eight inches, but broken by the ripples I have made into polygonal figures like the fragments of a most wonderfully painted mirror. These fragments drift and turn about, apparently, as stiffly on the surface as if they were as thick and strong as glass. The colors are in many places sharply defined in fine lines, making unaccountable figures, as if they were produced by a sudden crystallization. How much color or expression can reside in so thin a substance! With such accompaniments does a sucker die and mix his juices with the river. This beauty like the rainbow and sunset sky marks the spot where his body has mingled with the elements. A somewhat similar beauty reappears painted on the clam's shell. Even a dead sucker suggests a beauty and so a glory of its own. I leaned over the edge of my boat and admired it as much as ever I did a rainbow or sunset sky. The colors were not faint, but strong and fiery, if not angry.

Found a young turtle about two inches long of a flat roundish form, with scales as rough as usual, but a dull reddish or yellowish spot in middle of each scale, and edges beneath were also a pinkish red. Can it be a young yellow-spot?

I have not noticed a tree sparrow since December!

A *Sylvia Americana*, — parti-colored warbler, — in

---

the Holden Wood, sings *a, tshrea tshrea tshrea, tshre' tshritty tshrit'*.

One low *Kalmia glauca*, before any rhodora thereabouts. Several kalmias, no doubt, to-morrow. The rhodora there maybe to-morrow. Elsewhere I find it (on Hubbard's meadow) to-day.

The swamp is all alive with warblers about the hoary expanding buds of oaks, maples, etc., and amid the pine and spruce. They swarm like gnats now. They fill the air with their little *tshree tshree* sprayey notes. I see close by, hopping close up to the main stem of young white pines, what you would call a Maryland yellow-throat, but less chubby, yellow throat, beneath, and vent, and dark under tail, black side; but hear no note. Also another clear pure white beneath, and vent, and side-head; black above, finely marked with yellow; yellow bars on wings; and golden crown; black bill and legs; with a clear, sweet warble like *tche tche tche, tchut tchutter we*. Can this be a chestnut-sided warbler, and I not see the chestnut? [1] Hopping amid oak twigs? I think I hear a yellow-throated vireo. Hear a tree-toad.

Sailed back on Hubbard's redstart path, and there saw a mud turtle draw in his head, of which I saw the half, about eight rods off. Pushed to the spot, where the water was about a foot deep, and at length detected him spread out on the bottom, his monstrous head and tail and legs outspread, probably directly under where he had appeared. At first, I suspect, I mistook him for a rock, for he was thickly covered with a short green moss-like conferva (?), — a venerable object,

[1] It is. *Vide* 20th. Saw it also the 17th here.

---

a true son of the meadow, suggesting what vigor! what naturalness! Perchance to make the moss grow on your back without injuring your health! How many things can he sustain on his shell where the mosses grow? He looked like an antediluvian under that green, shaggy shell, tougher than the rock you mistake it for. No wonder the Indian reverenced him as a god. Think of the time when he was an infant. There is your native American, who was before Columbus, perchance. Grown, not gray, but green with the lapse of ages. Living with the life of the meadow. I took off my coat, stripped up my shirt-sleeve, and caught him by his great rough tail. He snapped at me and my paddle, striking his snout against the side of the boat till he made it bleed. Though I held him down with an oar for a lever and my foot on it, he would suddenly lift all together, or run out his head and knock the oar and my leg aside. He held up his head to me and, with his mouth wide open, hissed in his breathing like a locomotive for a quarter of an hour, and I could look straight down his monstrous gullet ten inches. The only way to hold him and paddle too was to turn him on his back, then, putting the end of a paddle under a seat, slant it over his sternum and press my foot on the other end. He was fourteen and one half inches long by twelve at the broadest places, and weighed twenty-five pounds and three ounces. The claws were an inch and a quarter long beyond the skin, and very stout. You had to exert yourself to turn him over on a plane surface, he held down so firmly with his claws, as if grown to it. He took my hand into his shell with his tail and took the skin off it. The sternum is broadest forward. This turtle was not roundish like the shell I have, but nearly an oblong square; nearly as long as that, but much less wide. The usual number of scallops behind.

I know of a young lady who, when riding, came across one in the road, which not wishing to run over, she got out and tried to drive it out of the way with her whip, but it "screamed" at and terrified her. A caravan could not make him budge under those circumstances.

E. Emerson finds half a dozen yellow violets. A hair-bird's nest building. I hear whip-poor-wills about R. W. E.'s.

May 19. Thick fog in the morning, which lasted late in the forenoon and left behind it rainy clouds for the afternoon.

P. M. — To Cedar Swamp.

Landed at Island Neck, and saw a small striped snake in the act of swallowing a *Rana palustris*, within three feet of the water. The snake, being frightened, released his hold, and the frog hopped off to the water. Hear and see a yellow-throated vireo, which methinks I have heard before. Going and coming, he is in the top of the same swamp white oak and singing indolently, *ullia — eelyee*, and sometimes varied to *eelyee*. The tanager is now heard plainly and frequently.

I see running along the water's edge on the Island Neck, amid the twigs, a new bird, slender and somewhat warbler-like, but plainly a *Turdus*, with a deep, dark chocolate-brown back (apparently uniformly), apparently cream-colored beneath, handsomely and abundantly

spotted with dark brown, vent white, light flesh-colored legs, yellowish or cream-colored line over eyes. Methinks it teetered or wagged its tail. Flew soon and was quite shy. I think it must have been the *Turdus aquaticus* from its dark chocolate-brown back and running along the water's edge. Feel pretty sure, yet that is said to have white (?) over eye. I lost it before I had examined fully. Quite a discovery. *Vide* golden-crowned thrush carefully.

Apple in bloom; some, no doubt, earlier. Night-hawk's squeak. Red-wing's nest made, and apparently a kingbird's (?), on black willow four feet above water.[1]

As I sail up the reach of the Assabet above Dove Rock with a fair wind, a traveller riding along the highway is watching my sail while he hums a tune. How inspiring and elysian it is to hear when the traveller or the laborer from a call to his horse or the murmur of ordinary conversation rises into song! It paints the landscape suddenly as no agriculture, no flowery crop that can be raised. It is at once another land, the abode of poetry. I am always thus affected when I hear in the fields any singing or instrumental music at the end of the day. It implies a different life and pursuits than the ordinary. As he looked at my sail, I listened to his singing. Perchance they were equally poetic, and we repaid each other. Why will not men oftener advertise me of musical thoughts? The singer is in the attitude of one inviting the muse, — aspiring.

The Maryland yellow-throat amid the alders sings now, *whit-we-chee whit-we-chee whit-we-chee whit-whit,*

[1] It is a robin's without mud.

the last two fast, or *whit* alone, or none. Wood pewee. Woolly aphides on alder.

The *Smilacina trifolia* will apparently bloom to-morrow or next day.[1]

Returning, stopped at Barrett's sawmill while it rained a little. Was also attracted by the music of his saw. He was sawing a white oak log; was about to saw a very ugly and knotty white oak log into drag plank, making an angle. Said that about as many logs were brought to his mill as ten years ago, — he did not perceive the difference, — but they were not so large, and perhaps they went further for them. I observed that he was not grinding. No, he said, it was the first day he had not had a grist, though he had plenty of water; probably because the farmers were busy planting. There [were] white oak, pine, maple, and walnut logs waiting to be sawed.

A bullfrog, sluggish, by my boat's place.

On the 13th I saw washed up to the edge of the meadow, this side of Clamshell, portions of one or two large bluish-white eggs, apparently a size larger than hens' eggs, which may have been laid last year by some wild fowl in the meadow.

If my friend would take a quarter part the pains to show me himself that he does to show me a piece of roast beef, I should feel myself irresistibly invited. He says, —

"Come and see
Roast beef and me."

I find the beef fat and well done, but him rare.

[1] In house, the 21st.

May 20. Fir-balsam (ours in grove) apparently two or three days, for it [is] almost entirely effete; cones white, one inch long nearly.

Was awaked and put into sounder sleep than ever early this morning by the distant crashing of thunder, and now, —

P. M. (to Beck Stow's), —

I hear it in mid-afternoon, muttering, crashing in the muggy air in mid-heaven, a little south of the village as I go through it, like the tumbling down of piles of boards, and get a few sprinkles in the sun. Nature has found her hoarse summer voice again, like the lowing of a cow let out to pasture. It is Nature's rutting season. Even as the birds sing tumultuously and glance by with fresh and brilliant plumage, so now is Nature's grandest voice heard, and her sharpest flashes seen. The air has resumed its voice, and the lightning, like a yellow spring flower, illumines the dark banks of the clouds. All the pregnant earth is bursting into life like a mildew, accompanied with noise and fire and tumult. Some œstrus stings her that she dashes headlong against the steeples and bellows hollowly, making the earth tremble. She comes dropping rain like a cow with overflowing udder. The winds drive her; the dry fields milk her. It is the familiar note of another warbler, just arrived, echoing amid the roofs.[1]

I see, on a locust in the locust [*sic*] burying-ground, the *Sylvia striata*, or black-poll warbler, busily picking about the locust buds and twigs. Black head and above, with olive (green) wings and two white bars; white all

[1] [Channing, p. 123.]

beneath, with a very distinct black line from throat to shoulders; flesh-colored legs; bill, dark above, light beneath. Hear no note. Saw it well.

At Moore's Swamp on Bedford road, myriads of pollywogs half an inch long darken or blacken the shore, chiefly head as yet. Bank swallows are very lively about the low sand-bank just beyond, in which are fifty holes.

I now see distinctly the chestnut-sided warbler (of the 18th and 17th), by Beck Stow's. It is very lively on the maples, birches, etc., over the edge [of] the swamp. Sings *eech eech eech | wichy wichy | tchea* or *itch itch itch | witty witty | tchea.* Yet this note I represented on the 18th by *tche tche tche | tchut tchutter we.*

The andromeda has apparently been out several days, but no buck-bean there yet, nor will for a day or two.[1]

See and hear a stake-driver in the swamp. It took one short pull at its pump and stopped. Two marsh hawks, male and female, flew about me a long time, screaming, the female largest, with ragged wings, as I stood on the neck of the peninsula. This induced me to climb four pines, but I tore my clothes, got pitched all over, and found only squirrel; yet they have, no doubt, a nest thereabouts.

Haynes the carpenter calls that large glaucous puff that grows on the *Andromeda paniculata,* swamp-apple; says he has eaten as much as three bushels (!) of them when he was a boy, and likes them. That is what he was raised on.

After I got him home, I observed a large leech on the upper shell of my great turtle. He stoutly resisted being

[1] *Vide* 21st.

The buck-bean in Everett's Pool abundantly out, say four or five days. It is earlier than at B. Stow's. *Myosotis laxa* by Turnpike, near Hosmer Spring, may have been out several days; two or three at least.

May 22. P. M. — To *Viola Muhlenbergii,* which is abundantly out; how long? A small pale-blue flower growing in dense bunches, but in spots a little drier than the *V. cucullata* and *blanda. Veronica peregrina,* apparently several days. A yellow butterfly over the middle of the flooded meadow. *Polygonatum pubescens* at rock. *Aralia nudicaulis,* apparently a day or two where heat is reflected from the rock on Island. Choke-cherry and cratægus there in a day or two. The *Cornus florida* does not bloom this year. Hemlock and creeping juniper, not quite yet. The red and cream-colored cone-shaped staminate buds of the black spruce will apparently shed pollen in one to three days? They are nearly half an inch long. I see beds or under this form: of anemones amid clumps of hazels, of a mass of their pretty leaves and flowers, five or six feet in diameter. I see a common *Vaccinium vacillans* (?), with a leaf much like that of the *V. Pennsylvanicum,* also the common *V. vacillans* with more rounded glaucous leaves.

I noticed a cobweb the other day, between the thole-pins of my boat, which was perfectly black with those little fuzzy gnats which fly at that height and take shelter from wind in boats and the like.

A little clammy hairy cerastium (?) (like a *Cerastium*

turned over, by sinking his claws into the ground; was aware that that was his weak side, and, when turned, would instantly run out his head and turn himself back. No wonder the Orientals rested the world on such a broad back. Such broad health and strength underlies Nature.

May 21. Wednesday. P. M. — To Saw Mill Brook. Chelidonium. *Rubus triflorus* abundantly out at the Saw Mill Brook; how long? A robin's nest without mud, on a young white oak in woods, with three eggs. Saw two splendid rose-breasted grosbeaks with females in the young wood in Emerson's lot. What strong-colored fellows, black, white, and fiery rose-red breasts! Strong-natured, too, with their stout bills. A clear, sweet singer, like a tanager but hoarse somewhat, and not shy. The redstarts are inquisitive and hop near. The *Polygonatum pubescens* there, in shade, almost out; perhaps elsewhere already.

At the trough near Turnpike, near Hosmer's Spring, the (perhaps) *Stellaria borealis* of the 15th. I am still in doubt whether it is a stellaria or cerastium. This is quite smooth, four to five inches high, spreading and forking, with a single flower each fork, on a long peduncle; square-stemmed, oblong-lanceolate leaves, slightly ciliate and connate: ten stamens, five long, five short. Aspect of a smooth cerastium, but this has four to seven styles, oftenest perhaps five, all apetalous, except one petal shorter than the calyx; leaves one-nerved, sepals three-nerved! The bare and small plants are reddish-stemmed. Can it be *Stellaria longipes?*

viscosum, slender and erect), about three inches high, will open in a day or two on the rock near the bass.[1]

May 23. P. M. — To Heywood Spring.

Sorrel well open on west side of railroad causeway against H. Wheeler's land. Noticed the earliest willow catkins turned to masses of cotton yesterday; also a little of the mouse-ear down begins to be loose. Hear often and distinctly, apparently from H. Wheeler's black spruce wood-lot, the *phe phee-ar* of the new muscicapa. Red-eye and wood thrush. Houstonias whiten the fields, and looked yesterday like snow, a sugaring of snow, on the side of Lee's Hill. Heard partridges drum yesterday and to-day. Observed the pads yesterday just begun to spread out on the surface with wrinkled edges and here and there a bullet-like bud; the red white lily pads still more rare as yet.

The stellaria at Heywood Spring must be the same with that near the E. Hosmer Spring, though the former has commonly fewer styles and rather slenderer leaves. It appears to be the *S. borealis,* though the leaves are *narrowly* lanceolate; has three to seven styles; a few petals (cleft almost to the bottom) or none; pods, some larger than the calyx [2] and apparently ten-ribbed; petals, now about the length of the sepals.[3]

After sunset on river.

A warm summer-like night. A bullfrog trumps once. A large devil's-needle goes by after sundown. The ring of toads is loud and incessant. It seems more prolonged

[1] *Vide* June 5th.   [2] At last twice as long.
[3] Keeps, and grows and blossoms, in a tumbler.

than it is. I think it not more than two seconds in each case. At the same time I hear a low, stertorous, dry, but hard-cored note from some frog in the meadows and along the riverside; often heard in past years but not accounted for. Is it a *Rana palustris?*

Dor-bugs hum in the yard, — and were heard against the windows some nights ago. The cat is springing into the air for them.

May 24. Pratt gave me the wing of a sparrow (?) hawk which he shot some months ago. He was coming from his house to his shop early in the morning when he saw this small hawk, which looked like a pigeon, fly past him over the Common with a sparrow in his clutches, and alight about six feet up the south button-wood in front of Tolman's. Having a small Maynard's revolver in his pocket, loaded with a ball size of a pea, he followed, and, standing twenty-two paces from the tree in the road, aimed and brought down both hawk and sparrow at a distance of about six rods, cutting off the wing of the former with the ball. This he confessed he could not do again if he should try a hundred times. It must be a sparrow hawk, according to Wilson and Nuttall, for the inner vanes of the primaries and secondaries are thickly spotted with brownish white.

Humphrey Buttrick says that he hears the note of the woodcock from the village in April and early in May (too late now); that there were some this year breeding or singing by the riverside in front of Abel Heywood's. He says that when you see one spring right up straight into the air, you may go to the spot, and he will surely

come down again after some minutes to within a few feet of the same spot and of you. Has known a partridge to fly at once from one to two miles after being wounded (tracked them by the blood) without alighting. Says he has caught as many as a dozen partridges in his hands. He lies right down on them, or where he knows them to be, then passes his hands back and forth under his body till he feels them. You must not lift your body at all or they will surely squeeze out, and when you feel one must be sure you get hold of their legs or head, and not feathers merely.

To-day is suddenly overpoweringly warm. Thermometer at 1 P. M., 94° in the shade! but in the afternoon it suddenly fell to 56, and it continued cold the next two days.

May 25. 10 A. M. — To Fair Haven Pond with Blake and Brown.

I found five arrowheads at Clamshell Hill. Saw, just before, on the flat meadow on the right, feeding on the edge of the meadow just left bare, along with the peetweets, a bird a size larger with an apparently light-brown back, a ring or crescent of black on its breast and side of neck, and a black patch including the eye. Can it be the *Charadrius semipalmatus?* or else *Wilsonius?* It looks like the latter in Wilson's larger plates. It reminded me of the piping plover, but was not so white; and of the killdeer, but was not so large.

Pyrus on side of Fair Haven Hill, yesterday at least. Huckleberry there, yesterday also at least. On the Cliffs, orobanche; *Veronica arvensis*, the little one on

the rocks there, well out. Also low blackberry on the rocks a day or two. Blackburnian warbler and rose-breasted grosbeak.

Lupines, apparently yesterday. Young phœbes in the Baker house. The bird flitted out as we entered. I reached to an old shelf and felt the warm but callow young. *Azalea nudiflora* in garden. Polygala, fringed, by path beyond Hubbard Grove; how long?

May 27. To Kalmia Swamp with Sanborn.

Fringilla melodia's nest in midst of swamp, with four eggs, made partly of usnea; two stories, *i. e.* upon an old nest, elevated one foot above the water; eggs with very dark blotches. Kalmia in prime, and rhodora. Apparently the oldest-blossomed kalmia the palest. Saw probably a deer mouse jumping off by the side of the swamp; short leaps of apparently ten inches. The pyrus (smooth-leaved) out apparently a day or two. See men fishing, one or two, and often perceived the meadow fragrance.

My three kinds of birch sap have now become more acid, especially the white and canoe birch. The black birch is milder and more agreeable. With sugar it is an agreeable drink. I prefer it to cream-o'-tartar water. This is the real birch wine.

May 28. Rainy.
To Painted-Cup Meadow.
Potentilla argentea, maybe several days. *Trifolium pratense.*

A seringo or yellow-browed (??) sparrow's nest about

ten or twelve rods southwest of house-leek rock, between two rocks which are several rods apart northwest and southeast; four eggs. The nest of coarse grass stubble, lined with fine grass, and is two thirds at least covered by a jutting sod. Egg, bluish-white ground, thickly blotched with brown, yet most like a small ground-bird's egg, rather broad at one end, pretty fresh.[1]

A cricket creaks. *Hypoxis erecta*, maybe a day or two. *Thalictrum dioicum* abundantly out, apparently in prime, male and female, some effete, perhaps a week, near wall in Painted-Cup Meadow, fifteen to eighteen inches high.

I think it was a mass of young *Thalictrum Cornuti* leaves which had that rank, dog-like scent.[2] Painted-cup pollen a good while ago. Saw, under an apple tree, nearly half a pint of some white grub with a light-reddish head, like a small potato-worm, one inch long, and part of a snake-skin, making the greater part of the fæces of some animal, — chiefly the grubs, — a formless soft mass. Skunk?

May 29. P. M. — Ride to Painted-Cup Meadow.

Two *Arethusa bulbosa* at Hubbard's Close apparently a day or two. Golden senecio there, a day or two, at least. White clover. *Ranunculus repens* (sepals not recurved and leaves a spotted look), apparently a day.

[1] July 2d, at Natural History Rooms, Boston, saw the egg of yellow-shouldered sparrow, light-colored with a ring of brown spots at large end; that of Savannah sparrow all mottled over with brown! ! *Vide* June 26.

[2] Yes; and this thalictrum is generally but a foot high now and expanding.

Geum rivale, well out. Common cratægus, apparently some days. *Juniperus communis*, a day or two at least, probably more.

To return to Painted-Cup Meadow, I do not perceive the rank odor of *Thalictrum Cornuti* expanding leaves to-day. How more than fugacious it is! Evidently this odor is emitted only at particular times. A cuckoo's note, loud and hollow, from a wood-side. Found a painted-cup with more yellow than usual in it, and at length Edith found one perfectly yellow. What a flowery place, a vale of Enna, is that meadow! Painted-cup, *Erigeron bellidifolius*, *Thalictrum dioicum*, *Viola Muhlenbergii*, fringed polygala, buck-bean, pedicularis, orobanche, etc., etc. Where you find a rare flower, expect to find more rare ones. Saw sanicle well flower-budded. Cherry-birds on the apple trees. Blue-eyed grass, probably to-morrow.

May 30. P. M. — To Linnæa Wood-lot.
Apparently this flower does not bloom there this year.[1]
The lady's-slipper in pitch pine wood-side near J. Hosmer's Desert, probably about the 27th. That desert, small as it now is (for it is partly reclaimed by using pine boughs as a salve), is scored with circles (like that of Provincetown) made by the dry *Polygonum articulatum* blown about. It is but a lesser Sahara, and I cannot see it without being reminded that, in some parts of the globe, sand prevails like an ocean. What are those black masses of fibrous roots mixed with smaller dark-gray, cone-like tubers, on the sand?

[1] Yes, it did later.

Vol. VIII

bloomed the 22d, are now entirely out of bloom on the hill. How short their flower lasts!
Ranunculus Purshii, probably earlier in some places, but water high. That little cerastium on the rock at the Island, noticed the 22d, which probably opened about that time, is now out of bloom. It is about three inches high and has long pods, more than twice the length of the calyx, which turn upward. I have seen no petals. It *seems* to be the *C. nutans* (?), from size, erectness, and form of pods and leaves. It has viscid hairs or with glands at end. The red oak is so forward, compared with the rest, that it is more difficult to get a sprig in flower small enough (its leaves) to press.

As I return in the dusk, *many* nighthawks, with their great spotted wings, are circling low over the river, as the swallows were when I went out. They skim within a rod of me. After dusk these greater swallows come forth, and circle and play about over the water like those lesser ones, or perhaps making a larger circuit, also uttering a louder note. It would not be safe for such great birds to fly so near and familiarly by day. It has been *very* cold for two or three days, and to-night a frost is feared. The telegraph says it snowed in Bangor to-day. The hickory leaves are blackened by blowing in the cold wind.

Return *via* Clamshell. Yellow clover abundantly out, though the heads are small yet. Are they quite open? *Comandra umbellata*, apparently a day or two.

Frank Harding caught five good-sized chivin this cold and windy day from the new stone bridge. The biggest one was quite red or coppery; the others but slightly, except the head. Is it a peculiarity of age?

May 31. P. M. — To Clintonia Swamp (Hubbard's) Grove.
A ground-bird's nest (*melodia* or *graminea?*), with six of those oblong narrow gray [eggs] speckled with much brown at end. When I looked again half an hour after, one egg was hatched. The bird would steal out through the grass when I came within a rod, and then, after running a rod or two, take to wing. Tied a string about a low pyrus a rod or so to right of entrance to Hubbard's Pyrus Swamp and two feet west of a pitch pine stump, and pressed a twig of it. Clintonia. *Nuphar advena* first noticed; may have been out some time in *some* places, but just out in river. Pink, common wild, maybe two or three days.[1]

Sundown. — To Hill and Island.
Have noticed within a week, from time to time, the water-line on the bushes along the shore — the water going down — unusually distinct, for while the exposed parts have leaved out, the lower are quite bare and black.
Hemlock and creeping juniper, where had not

[1] For they are very abundant at Heywood Peak on June 1st; some white.

VIII

JUNE, 1856

(ÆT. 38)

June 1. Horse-radish in yard, to-morrow.
Picked up an entire sternothærus shell yesterday, without scales. In the upper shell there appear to be six small segments of shell wholly dorsal, seventeen wholly lateral (nine in front), and twenty-two marginal, forty-five in all. The ribs, in this case spreading out and uniting to form a sharp and tight roof, suggest that ribs were the first rafters. So we turn our backs to the storm and shelter ourselves under this roof. The scales upon the shell answer to the shingles on the roof, breaking joints.

Saw the shell of another turtle, apparently a young painted turtle, one inch long, curiously wrinkled and turned up, like that found in Middleborough. This had been washed up on to meadow some weeks ago, apparently.

P. M. — To Walden.
Somewhat warmer at last, after several very cold, as well as windy and rainy, days. Was soothed and cheered by I knew not what at first, but soon detected the now more general creak of crickets. A striped yellow bug in fields. Most of the leaves of the *Polygonatum pubescens* which I gathered yesterday at Island had been eaten up by some creature.

A chewink's nest a rod and a half south of Walden

road, opposite Goose Pond path, under a young oak, covered by overarching dry sedge; four eggs, *pretty* fresh. I am pretty sure the bird uttered the unusual hoarse and distressed note while I was looking at them.

Linaria Canadensis on Emerson Cliff. Rock-rose, a day or two there. Whiteweed by railroad at pond to-morrow. Cotton-grass, several days before the 29th May. Heard a quail whistle May 30th. The late cratægus on hill, about May 31st.

June 2. Carum, i. e. caraway, in garden. Saw most hummingbirds when cherries were in bloom, — on them.

P. M. — With R. W. E. to Perez Blood's auction.

Telescope sold for fifty-five dollars; cost ninety-five plus ten. See Camilla on rye, undulating light and shade; not 19th of April.[1] Returned by bridle-road. *Myrica cerifera*, possibly yesterday. Very few buds shed pollen yet; more, probably, to-day. Leaves nearly an inch long, and shoot and all no more. English hawthorn will open apparently in two days.

Agassiz tells his class that the intestinal worms in the mouse are not developed except in the stomach of the cat.

5 P. M. — To *Azalea nudiflora*, which is in prime. *Ranunculus recurvatus* the same; how long? White maple keys conspicuous.

In the first volume of Brewster's "Life of Newton" I

[1] [Alluding to the tradition that on the day of the "Concord Fight" (April 19, 1775) grass and grain were already waving in the wind, the season being exceptionally early.]

read that with one of the early telescopes they could read the "Philosophical Transactions" at five hundred feet distance.

June 3. Tuesday. Surveying for John Hosmer beyond pail-factory.

Hosmer says that seedling white birches do not grow larger than your arm, but cut them down and they spring up again and grow larger.

While clearing a line through shrub oak, which put his eyes out, he asked, "What is shrub oak made for?" R. Hoar, I believe, bought that (formerly) pine lot of Loring's which is now coming up shrub oak. Hosmer says that he will not see any decent wood there as long as he lives. H. says he had a lot of pine in Sudbury, which being cut, shrub oak came up. He cut and burned and raised rye, and the next year (it being surrounded by pine woods on three sides) a dense growth of pine sprang up.

As I have said before, it seems to me that the squirrels, etc., disperse the acorns, etc., amid the pines, they being a covert for them to lurk in, and when the pines are cut the fuzzy shrub oaks, etc., have the start. If you cut the shrub oak soon, probably pines or birches, maples, or other trees which have light seeds will spring next, because squirrels, etc., will not be likely to carry acorns into open land. If the pine wood had been surrounded by white oak, probably that would have come up after the pine.[1]

While running a line in the woods, close to the water,

[1] [*Excursions*, p. 190; Riv. 233.]

on the southwest side of Loring's Pond, I observed a chickadee sitting quietly within a few feet. Suspecting a nest, I looked and found it in a small hollow maple stump which was about five inches in diameter and two feet high. I looked down about a foot and could just discern the eggs. Breaking off a little, I managed to get my hand in and took out some eggs. There were seven, making by their number an unusual figure as they lay in the nest, a sort of egg rosette, a circle around with one (or more) in the middle. In the meanwhile the bird sat silent, though rather restless, within three feet. The nest was very thick and warm, of average depth, and made of the bluish-slate rabbit's (?) fur. The eggs were a perfect oval, five eighths inch long, white with small reddish-brown or rusty spots, especially about larger end, partly developed. The bird sat on the remaining eggs next day. I called off the boy in another direction that he might not find it.

Plucked a white lily pad with rounded sinus and lobes in Loring's Pond, a variety.

Picked up a young wood tortoise, about an inch and a half long, but very orbicular. Its scales very distinct, and as usual very finely and distinctly sculptured, but there was no orange on it, only buff or leather-color on the sides beneath. So the one of similar rounded form and size and with distinct scales but faint yellow spots on back must have been a young spotted turtle, I think, after all.

June 4. Surveying for J. Hosmer.
Very warm.

While running a line on the west edge o. Loring's Pond, south of the brook, found, on a hummock in the open swamp, in the midst of bushes, at the foot of a pitch pine, a nest about ten inches over, made of dry sedge and moss. I think it must have been a duck's nest. This pond and its islets, half flooded and inaccessible, afford excellent places.

Anthony Wright says that he used to get slippery elm bark from a place southwest of Wetherbee's Mill, about ten rods south of the brook. He says there was once a house at head of hollow next beyond Clamshell. Pointed out the site of "Perch" Hosmer's house in the small field south of road this side of Cozzens's; all smooth now. Dr. Heywood worked over him a fortnight, while the perch was dissolving in his throat. He got little compassion generally, and the nickname "Perch" into the bargain. Think of going to sleep for fourteen nights with a perch, his fins set and his scales (!), dissolving in your throat!! What dreams! What waking thoughts! Also showed where one Shaw, whom he could just remember, used to live, in the low field north of Dennis's barn, and also another family in another house by him.

English hawthorn from Poplar Hill blossoms in house.

June 5. Thursday. P. M. — To Indian Ditch.
Achillea Millefolium. Black cherry, apparently yesterday. The *Muscicapa Cooperi* sings *pe pe pe'*, sitting on the top of a pine, and shows white rump (?), etc., unlike kingbird.

Return by J. Hosmer Desert.

Everywhere now in dry pitch pine woods stand the

red lady's-slippers over the red pine leaves on the forest floor, rejoicing in June, with their two broad curving green leaves, — some even in swamps. Uphold their rich, striped red, drooping sack. This while rye begins to wave richly in the fields.

A brown thrasher's nest with four eggs considerably developed, under a small white pine on the old north edge of the desert, lined with root-fibres. The bird utters its peculiar *tchuck* near by.

Pitch pine out, the first noticed on low land, *maybe* a day or two. Froth on pitch pine.

A blue jay's nest on a white pine, eight feet from ground, next to the stem, of twigs lined with root-fibres; three fresh eggs, dark dull greenish, with dusky spots equally distributed all over, in Hosmer (?) pines twenty-seven paces east of wall and fifty-seven from factory road by wall. Jay screams as usual. Sat till I got within ten feet at first.

A cuckoo's nest[1] with three light bluish-green eggs partly developed, short with rounded ends, nearly of a size; in the thicket up railroad this side high wood, in a black cherry that had been lopped three feet from ground, amid the thick sprouts; a nest of nearly average depth (?), of twigs lined with *green* leaves, pine-needles, etc., and edged with some dry, branchy weeds. The bird stole off silently at first. Five rods south of railroad.

I must call that cerastium of May 22d *C. nutans* (??), at least for the present, though I do not see grooves in stem. Oakes, in his catalogue in Thompson's "History

[1] *Vide* 10th.

of Vermont," says it is not found in New England out of that State. The pods of the common one also turn upward. It is about four flowered; no petals; pods, which have formed in tumbler, more than twice but not thrice as long as calyx, bent down nearly at right angles with peduncles and then *curving upward*. The common cerastium is in tufts, spreading, a darker green and much larger, hairy but not glutinous, pods but little longer than calyx (as yet) and upright.[1]

June 6. P. M. — To Andromeda Ponds.
Cold mizzling weather.

In the large circular hole or cellar at the turntable on the railroad, which they are repairing, I see a star-nosed mole endeavoring in vain to bury himself in the sandy and gravelly bottom. Some inhuman fellow has cut off his tail. It is blue-black with much fur, a very thick, plump animal, apparently some four inches long, but he occasionally shortens himself a third or more. Looks as fat as a fat hog. His fore feet are large and set sidewise or on their edges, and with these he shovels the earth aside, while his large, long, starred snout is feeling the way and breaking ground. I see deep indentations in his fur where his eyes are situated, and once I saw distinctly his eye open, a dull blue (?)-black bead, not so very small, and he very plainly noticed my movements two feet off. He was using his eye as plainly as any creature that I ever saw. Yet Emmons says it is a question whether their eyes are not merely rudimentary. I suppose this was the *Condylura*

[1] I afterward see these curving upward like the former!

macroura, since that is most common, but only an inch of its tail was left, and that was quite stout. I carried him along to plowed ground, where he buried himself in a minute or two.

Still see cherry-birds in flocks of five or six. A catbird-nest on shore of Andromeda and in shrub oak, three feet high, twigs and bark shreds lined with root-fibres; three eggs. Those nests in the andromeda are blackbird's. Many sound the alarm while I am wading through the swamp. Noticed one with three eggs.

That willow, male and female, opposite to Trillium Woods on the railroad, I find to be the *Salix rostrata*, or long-beaked willow, one of the *ochre-flowered* (I had remarked the peculiar yellow of its flowers) willows (*fulvæ*) of Barratt. It is now just beginning to open its long beaks. The *S. cordata* is another of the ochre-flowered ones.

How well suited the lining of a bird's nest, not only for the comfort of the young, but to keep the eggs from breaking! Fine elastic grass stems or root-fibres, pine-needles, or hair, or the like. These tender and brittle things which you can hardly carry in cotton lie there without harm.

J. Hosmer, who is prosecuting Warner for flowing his land, says that the trees are not only broken off when young by weight of ice, but, being rubbed and barked by it, become warty or bulge out there.

June 8. We have had six days either rain-threatening or rainy, the last two somewhat rainy or mizzling.
P. M. — To Cedar Swamp.

Pulled up a yellow lily root, four feet long and branching, two and a half inches [in] diameter and about same size at each end where it had broken off, tree-like. Broken off, it floats. Great white rootlets put out all along it.

I find no *Andromeda racemosa* in flower. It is dead at top and slightly leafed below. Was it the severe winter, or cutting off the protecting evergreens? It grows four or five rods from knoll near a sawed stump between two large red maple clumps. The three-leaved Solomon's-seal has almost entirely done, while the two-leaved is quite abundant. *Stellaria longifolia* opposite Barbarea Shore not yet out. It is obviously different from what I call *S. borealis*, much more tall (one foot high) and upright, with branches ascending (not spreading) (the other grows in a dense mass at Corner Spring); leaves longer and more linear, and not at all ciliate like the other; stem much sharper-angled, almost winged; flower-buds more long and slender; and grows in high grass and is later.

I observe in a mass of damp shavings and leaves and sand there, in the shade, a little prostrate willow just coming into flower, perhaps a black willow. Pulling it up, I find it to be a twig about sixteen inches long, two thirds buried in the damp mass. This was probably broken off by the ice, brought down, washed up, and buried like a layer there; and now, for two thirds its length, it has put out rootlets an inch or two long abundantly, and leaves and catkins from the part above ground. So vivacious is the willow, availing itself of every accident to spread along the river's bank. The ice that

Lady's-Slippers

Skunk-Cabbage

strips it only disperses it the more widely. It never says die. May I be as vivacious as a willow. Some species are so brittle at the base of the twigs that they break on the least touch, but they are as tough above as tender at base, and these twigs are only thus shed like seeds which float away and plant themselves in the first bank on which they lodge. I commonly litter my boat with a shower of these black willow twigs whenever I run into them.

A kingbird's nest on a black cherry, above Barbarea Shore, loosely constructed, with some long white rags dangling; one egg. At Cedar Swamp, saw the pe-pe catching flies like a wood pewee, darting from its perch on a dead cedar twig from time to time and returning to it. It appeared to have a black crown with some crest, yellowish (?) bill, gray-brown back, black tail, two faint whitish bars on wings, a dirty cream-white throat, and a gray or ash white breast and beneath, whitest in middle.

I had noticed when coming up the river two or three dead suckers, one with a remarkable redness about the anal fins; and this reminded me of the ephemeræ. It was the 2d of June, 1854, that I observed them in such numbers. When I returned to my boat, about five, the weather being mizzling enough to require an umbrella, with an easterly wind and dark for the hour, my boat being by chance at the same place where it was in '54, I noticed a great flight of ephemeræ over the water, though not so great as that. The greater part were flying down-stream against the wind, but if you watched one long enough you would see him suddenly turn at

length and fly swiftly back up the stream. They advanced against the wind faster than I floated along. They were not coupled nor coupling, — I only noticed two coupled, — but flew, most of them, with their bodies curved, thus: or more, and from time to time each one descended to the water and touched it, or rested on it a second or two, sometimes several minutes. They were generally able to rise, but very often before it arose, or not being able to rise, it was seized by a fish. While some are flying down they are met by others coming up. The water was dimpled with the leaping fish. They reach about ten or fifteen feet high over the water, and I also saw a stream of them about as thick over a narrow meadow a dozen rods from the water in the woods. The weather was evidently unfavorable, what with the wind and the rain, and they were more or less confined to the shore, hovering high over the bushes and trees, where the wind was strong over the river. I had not noticed any on leaves. At one place, against Dodge's Brook, where they were driven back by a strong head wind at a bend, more than usual were wrecked on the water and the fishes were leaping more numerously than elsewhere. The river was quite alive with them, and I had not thought there were so many in it, — great black heads and tails continually thrust up on all sides of my boat. You had only to keep your eye on a floating fly a minute to see some fishy monster rise and swallow it with more or less skill and plashing. Some skillfully seized their prey without

much plashing, rising in a low curve and just showing their backs; others rose up perpendicularly, half their length out of water, showing their black backs or white bellies or gleaming sides; others made a noisy rush at their prey and leaped entirely out of water, falling with a loud plash. You saw twenty black points at once. They seemed to be suckers; large fish, at any rate, and probably various kinds. What a sudden surfeit the fishes must have!

They are of various sizes, but generally their solid bodies about three quarters of an inch long or less, yellowish tinge, transparent, with rows of brown spots; wings gauze-like, with a few opaque brown spots.[1]

June 9. P. M. — To Corner Spring.

Without an umbrella, thinking the weather settled at last. There are some large cumuli with glowing downy cheeks floating about. Now I notice where an elm is in the shadow of a cloud, — the black elm-tops and shadows of June. It is a dark eyelash which suggests a flashing eye beneath. It suggests houses that lie under the shade, the repose and siesta of summer noons, the thunder-cloud, bathing, and all that belongs to summer. These veils are now spread here and there over the village. It suggests also the creak of crickets, a June sound now fairly begun, inducing contemplation and philosophic thoughts, — the sultry hum of insects.

A yellowbird's nest in a poplar on Hubbard's Bridge

[1] Three which I brought home were dead the next morning. A shad-fly on our window is rather smaller than the average of the former; has but two streamers and no dark spots on wings.

causeway; four fresh eggs; ten feet high, three rods beyond fence. *Veronica scutellata* (how long?) at Corner Spring. Compelled to squat under a bank and stand under a wood-pile through a shower.

6.30 P. M. — Up Assabet.

Again, about seven, the ephemeræ came out, in numbers as many as last night, now many of them coupled, even tripled; and the fishes leap as before.

A young robin abroad.

June 10. 8 A. M. — Getting lily pads opposite Badger's.

Already the pads are much eaten before they are grown, and underneath, on the under side of almost every one, are the eggs of various species of insect, some so minute as to escape detection at first, in close, flat, straight-sided nests.

The yellow lily and kalmiana are abundantly out. The under sides of the pads, their stems, and the *Ranunculus Purshii* and other water-plants are thickly covered and defiled with the sloughs, perhaps of those little fuzzy gnats (in their first state) which have so swarmed over the river. It is quite difficult to clean your specimens of them.

P. M. — To Dugan Desert.

Cornus alternifolia a day or two, up railroad; maybe longer elsewhere. *Spergularia rubra* by railroad, it having been dug up last year, and so delayed.

The cuckoo of June 5th has deserted her nest, and I

find the fragments of egg-shells in it; probably because I found it.

Oxalis freshly out; how long? Apparently but two or three days. I find *some* linnæa well out, after all, within a rod of the top of the hill, apparently two or three days. If it flowered more abundantly, probably it would be earlier. Chewink's nest with four young in the dry sprout-land of Loring's thick wood that was, under a completely overarching tuft of dry sedge grass. I hear the huckleberry-bird now add to its usual strain *a-tea tea tea tea tea.*

A painted tortoise laying her eggs ten feet from the wheel-track on the Marlborough road. She paused at first, but I sat down within two feet, and she soon resumed her work. Had excavated a hollow about five inches wide and six long in the moistened sand, and cautiously, with long intervals, she continued her work, resting always on the same spot her fore feet, and never looking round, her eye shut all but a narrow slit. Whenever I moved, perhaps to brush off a mosquito, she paused. A wagon approached, rumbling afar off, and then there was a pause, till it had passed and long, long after, a tedious, *naturlangsam* pause of the slow-blooded creature, a sacrifice of time such as those animals are up to which slumber half a year and live for centuries. It was twenty minutes before I discovered that she was not making the hole but filling it up slowly, having laid her eggs. She drew the moistened sand under herself, scraping it along from behind with both feet brought together, the claws turned inward. In the long pauses the ants troubled her (as mosquitoes me) by running

over her eyes, which made her snap or dart out her head suddenly, striking the shell. She did not dance on the sand, nor finish covering the hollow quite so carefully as the one observed last year. She went off suddenly (and quickly at first), with a slow but sure instinct through the wood toward the swamp.

The clustered blackberry of Dugan Desert not yet out, nor apparently for two or three days. Sweet viburnum apparently two or three days at most, by Warren Miles's, Nut Meadow Pond.

In a hollow apple tree, hole eighteen inches deep, young pigeon woodpeckers, large and well feathered. They utter their squeaking hiss whenever I cover the hole with my hand, apparently taking it for the approach of the mother. A strong, rank fetid smell issues from the hole.

Ripe strawberries, even in a meadow on sand thrown out of a ditch, hard at first to detect amid the red radical leaves.

The flower-buds of late there have now that rank smell. Lambkill out, at Clamshell. The *Cratægus Crus-Galli* is out of bloom. *Arenaria serpyllifolia* is out of bloom at Clamshell.[1]

Side-flowering sandwort abundantly out this side of Dugan Spring. Solanum well out, by Wood's Bridge.

June 11. P. M. — To Flint's Pond.

The locust in graveyard shows but few blossoms yet. It is very hot this afternoon, and that peculiar stillness of summer noons now reigns in the woods. I observe

[1] Abundant there June 20.

and appreciate the shade, as it were the shadow of each particular leaf on the ground. I think that this peculiar darkness of the shade, or of the foliage as seen between you and the sky, is not accounted for merely by saying that we have not yet got accustomed to clothed trees, but the leaves are rapidly acquiring a darker green, are more and more opaque, and, besides, the sky is lit with the intensest light. It reminds me of the thunder-cloud and the dark eyelash of summer. Great cumuli are slowly drifting in the intensely blue sky, with glowing white borders. The red-eye sings incessant, and the more indolent yellow-throat vireo, and the creeper, and perhaps the redstart? or else it is the parti-colored warbler.

I perceive that scent from the young sweet-fern shoots and withered blossoms which made the first settlers of Concord to faint on their journey.

Saw yesterday a *great* yellow butterfly with black marks.

See under an apple tree, at entrance of Goose Pond Path from Walden road, a great fungus with hollow white stem, eight or nine inches high, whose black funereal top has melted this morning, leaving a black centre with thin white scales on it. All the cistuses are shut now that I see, and also the veiny-leaved hieracium with one leaf on its stem, not long open. I notice no white lily pads near the bathing-rock in Flint's Pond. See a bream's nest two and a quarter feet [in] diameter, laboriously scooped out, and the surrounding bottom for a diameter of eight feet (!!) comparatively white and clean, while all beyond is mud and leaves, etc., and a very large green and cupreous bream with a

red spot on the operculum is poised over the centre, while half a dozen shiners are hovering about, apparently watching a chance to steal the spawn.

A partridge with young in the Saw Mill Brook path. Could hardly tell what kind of creature it was at first, it made such a noise and fluttering amid the weeds and bushes. Finally ran off with its body flat and wings somewhat spread.

Utricularia vulgaris very abundant in Everett's Pool. A beautiful grass-green snake about fifteen inches long, light beneath, with a yellow space under the eyes along the edge of the upper jaw.

The *Rubus triflorus* apparently out of bloom at Saw Mill, before the high blackberry has begun.

Rice tells me he found a turtle dove's nest on an apple tree near his farm in Sudbury two years ago, with white eggs; so thin a bottom you could see the eggs through.

June 12. P. M. — To Conantum on foot.

Sophia has sent me, in a letter from Worcester, part of an orchis in bloom, apparently *Platanthera Hookeri* (?), or smaller round-leafed orchis, from the Hermitage Wood, so called, northeast of the town; but the two leaves are elliptical. *Utricularia vulgaris* was abundantly out yesterday in Everett's Pool; how long? Sidesaddle-flower numerously out now. Apparently a small pewee nest on apple in Miles's meadow. Bird on, and not to be frightened off, though I throw sticks and climb the tree to near her.

June 13. *Friday.* To Worcester.

See the common iris in meadow in Acton. Brown shows me from his window the word "guano" written on the grass in a field near the hospital, say three quarters of a mile distant. It was one of the lions of Worcester last year, and I can now read some of the letters distinctly, so permanent are the effects of the guano. The letters may be two or more rods long, and the green is darker and more luxuriant. (On the side of a hill.)

June 14. Walk to Hermitage Woods with Sophia and aunts. *Uvularia perfoliata* very common there; now out of bloom. *Rhamnus cathartica*, common buckthorn, naturalized in those woods, now going out of bloom. It is diœcious, twelve feet high, north side. Maple-leaved viburnum out a day or more there apparently. Mallows abundantly out in street.

June 15. Mrs. Brown reads a letter from John Downs in Philadelphia to Mr. Brown, in which he remembers his early youth in Shrewsbury and the pout accompanied by her young. A Miss Martha Le Barron describes to me a phosphorescence on the beach at night in Narragansett Bay. They wrote their names with some minute creatures on the sand.

P. M. — To some woods southwest of Worcester.

The moist bass bark just stripped from a sapling swells very like a cucumber. All three of us were struck by it. A night-flowering cereus opens three or four times at a Mrs. Newton's while I am there. Once it opened at about 9 P. M., and closed and drooped and came to an end like a wet rag wrung out, at daylight. Transient

as my mushroom. Was about a foot in diameter, but an ordinary stem, like the turkey's feet. Diervilla well out.

June 16. Saw at the Natural History Rooms a shell labelled *Haliotis splendens*, apparently same with mine from Ricketson's son, with holes and green reflections.

To Purgatory in Sutton: by railroad to Wilkinsonville in the northeast corner of Sutton (thirty cents) and by buggy four or five miles to Purgatory in the south or southeast part of the town, some twelve miles from Worcester.

The stream rising from the bottom of it must empty into the Blackstone, perhaps through the Mumford River. Sutton is much wooded. The woman at the last house told [of] an animal seen in the neighborhood last year. Well, she " had no doubt that there had been a bad animal about." A Mr. Somebody, who could be relied on, between there and Sutton Centre, had been aroused by [a] noise early one morning, and, looking out, saw this animal near a wood-pile in his yard, as big as a good-sized dog. He soon made off, making nothing of the walls and fences, before he and his sons got their guns ready. They raised part of the town, a body of shoemakers, and surrounded a swamp into which it was supposed to have entered, but they did not dare to go into it. Also a strange large track was seen where it crossed the road.

Found at the very bottom of this Purgatory, where it was dark and damp, on the steep moss and fern covered side of a rock which had fallen into it, a wood thrush's

Vol. VIII

nest. Scarcely a doubt of the bird, though I saw not its breast fairly. Heard the note around, and the eggs (one of which I have) correspond. Nest of fine moss from the rock (hypnum?), and lined with pine-needles; three eggs, fresh.

Found in the Purgatory the panicled elder (*Sambucus pubens*), partly gone to ribbed seed, but some in flower, new to me; *Polygonum cilinode* (?), not yet in flower; moose-wood or striped maple; and also, close by above, *Actæa alba*, out of bloom; and a chestnut oak common. Cow-wheat numerously out. Heard around, from within the Purgatory, not only Wilson's thrush, but evergreen-forest note and tanager; and saw chip-squirrels within it.

June 17. Go to Blake's.
Indigo-bird on his trees.

A. M. — Ride with him and Brown and Sophia round a part of Quinsigamond Pond into Shrewsbury.

The southerly end of the pond covered for a great distance with pads of yellow and white lily. Measured one of the last: nine and seven eighths inches long by nine and six eighths, with sharp lobes, etc., and a reddish petiole. Small primrose well out; how long? The cedar swamp, source of Assabet, must be partly in Grafton, as well as Westboro near railroad, according to a farmer in Shrewsbury.

P. M. — Went to Rev. Horace James's reptiles (Orthodox).

He had, set up, a barred owl, without horns and a little less than the cat owl. Also a large lobe-footed bird

which I think must have been a large grebe, killed in Fitchburg. He distinguished the *Rana halecina* in the alcohol by more squarish (?) spots. Showed me the horned frog (?), (or toad?); also alive in bottle, with moss and water, the violet-colored salamander (*S. venenosa*) with yellow spots (five or six inches long), probably same I found in stump at Walden; and, in spirits, smaller, the *S. erythronota*, with a conspicuous red back. What looked like mine, or the common one in springs here, was *Triton niger*. I think he said Holbrook made the water ones tritons and land ones salamanders. Another small one, all red, with spots; another with a line of red spots on each side; and others. He finds a variety of *Emys guttata* with striated scales (mentioned by Holbrook and Storer). Saw a common box turtle shell with initials in sternum. One thought that whatever was cut in the scale was renewed in the new scale. Saw, in spirits, the *Heterodon platyrhinus* from Smithfield, R. I., flat-snouted, somewhat like a striped snake; and a very small brown snake. James gave me some of the spawn of a shellfish from a string of them a foot long.

At Natural History Rooms, a great cone from a southern pine and a monstrous nutshell from the East Indies (?); seed of the *Lodoicea Sechellarum*, Seychelles Islands.

June 18. Hale says the tiarella grows here, and showed it me pressed; also *Kalmia glauca* formerly, hobble-bush still, and yellow lady's-slipper near the Quarry.

June 19. Looked at a collection of the rarer plants made by Higginson and placed at the Natural History Rooms. Among which noticed : —

> *Ranunculus Purshii* varieties α and β, with no difference apparent, unless in upper leaves being more or less divided.
>
> *Ribes lacustre*, or swamp gooseberry, with a loose raceme such as I have not seen, from White Mountains.
>
> A *circæa*, or enchanter's-nightshade, with a very large raceme and with longer branchlets than I have seen, methinks.[1]
>
> *Calla palustris*, very different from the *Peltandra Virginica*.
>
> *Cerastium arvense*, with linear leaves, quite new to me.
>
> *Smilacina stellata*, from Dr. Harris, very different from the *racemosa*, being simple.
>
> *Ledum latifolium*, from White Mountains, rather broader-leafed than mine from Maine.
>
> *Barbarea sativa*, from Cambridge, apparently like my *B. vulgaris*.

Is the *Smilacina racemosa* with such long lower branchlets peculiar, there in Worcester? I saw several in woods.

On way to Concord see mountain laurel out in Lancaster. Had seen none out in Worcester.

June 20. *Friday*. A. M. — To Baker Farm with Ricketson.

[1] No, not longer.

peared, and came quite near, while I stood in the tree, keeping up an incessant loud and shrill scolding note, and also after I descended; not to be relieved.

Potentilla Norvegica; apparently petals blown away. Five young phœbes in a nest, apparently upon a swallow-nest, in Conant's old house, just ready to fly. *Rudbeckia hirta* budded.

June 21. P. M. — To Walden.

Much pine pollen is washed up on the northwest side of the pond. Must it not have come from pines at a distance? Very hot day, as was yesterday, — 98° at 2 P. M., 99° at 3, and 128° in sun. Nighthawks numerously squeak at 5 P. M. and boom. Saw them fly low and touch the water like swallows over Walden. Find a dozen of the hydropeltis out, apparently several days. My canoe birch wine smells and tastes like mead considerably. All my birch wines are now more acid and very good indeed with sugar. Am surprised to see it effervesce, all white with white sugar only, like a soda-water.

June 22. *Sunday*. P. M. — To Walden.

Ricketson says that they say at New Bedford that the song sparrow says, *Maids, maids, maids,* — *hang on your tea-kettle-ettle-ettle-ettle-ettle.*

R. W. E. imitates the wood thrush by *he willy willy* — *ha willy willy* — *O willy O.* The woods still resound with the note of my tweezer-bird, or *Sylvia Americana*.

June 23. To New Bedford with Ricketson.

A very hot day.

Two *Sternothærus odoratus* by heap in Sanborn's garden, one making a hole for its eggs, the rear of its shell partly covered. See a great many of these out to-day on ground and on willows.

Swamp-pink out apparently two or three days at Clamshell Ditch. Late thalictrum apparently a day or two there. Archangelica apparently two or three days.

A phœbe nest, second time, with four cream-white eggs. Got one. The second brood in the same nest. Saw a snap-turtle out in sun on tussock opposite Bittern Cliff. Probably the water was too warm for him. They had at Middlesex House, yesterday, snuff flavored with ground or pulverized black birch bark.

Walking under an apple tree in the little Baker Farm peach orchard, heard an incessant shrill musical twitter or peeping, as from young birds, over my head, and, looking up, saw a hole in an upright dead bough, some fifteen feet from ground. Climbed up and, finding that the shrill twitter came from it, guessed it to be the nest of a downy woodpecker, which proved to be the case, — for it reminded me of the hissing squeak or squeaking hiss of young pigeon woodpeckers, but this was more musical or bird-like.[1] The bough was about four and a half inches in diameter, and the hole perfectly circular, about an inch and a quarter in diameter. Apparently nests had been in holes above, now broken out, higher up. When I put my fingers in it, the young breathed their shrill twitter louder than ever. Anon the old ap-

[1] *Vide* July 19th.

In R.'s mowing, apparently lucerne, out some days. His son Walton showed me one of four perfectly white eggs taken from a hole in an apple tree eight feet from ground. I examined the hole. He had seen a bluebird there, and I saw a blue feather in it and apparently a bluebird's nest. Were not these the eggs of a downy woodpecker laid in a bluebird's nest? They were all gone now.

Bay-wings sang morning and evening about R.'s house, often sitting on a bean-pole and dropping down and running and singing on the bare ground amid the potatoes. Its note somewhat like *Come, here here, there there,* — *quick quick quick* (fast), — *or I 'm gone.*

Prinos lævigatus common and just begun to bloom behind R.'s house.

June 24. To Sassacowen Pond and to Long Pond.

Common yellow thistle abundant about R.'s; open a good while. Maryland yellow-throats very common in bushes behind his house; nest with young. American holly now in prime. The light-colored masses of mountain laurel were visible across Sassacowen. A kingbird's nest just completed in an apple tree.

Lunched by the spring on the Brady farm in Freetown, and there it occurred to me how to get clear water from a spring when the surface is covered with dust or insects. Thrust your dipper down deep in the middle of the spring and lift it up quickly straight and square. This will heap up the water in the middle so that the scum will run off.

We were surrounded by whiteweed. The week before

I had seen it equally abundant in Worcester (in many fields the flowers placed in one plane would more than cover the surface), and here as there each flower had a dark ring of small black insects on its disk. Think of the many dense white fields between here and there, aye and for a thousand miles around, and then calculate the amount of insect life of one obscure species!

Went off to Nelson's Island (now Briggs's) in Long Pond by a long, very narrow bar (fifty rods as I paced it), in some places the water over shoes and the sand commonly only three or four feet wide. This is a noble island, maybe of eight or ten acres, some thirty feet high and just enough wooded, with grass ground and grassy hollows. There was a beech wood at the west end, where R.'s son Walton found an arrowhead when they were here before, and the hemlocks resounded with the note of the tweezer-bird (*Sylvia Americana*). There were many ephemeræ half dead on the bushes. R. dreams of residing here.

June 25. An abundance of the handsome corncockle (*Lychnis*), apparently in prime, in midst of a rye-field, together with morning-glories by the Acushnet shore. Black-grass in bloom, partly done. A kind of rush (?) with terete leaves and a long spike of flowers, one to two feet high, *somewhat* like a loose plantain spike. It inclines to grow in circles a foot or more in diameter. Seaside plantain and rosemary, not long out. *Veronica arvensis* one foot high (!) on the shore there. *Spergularia rubra* var. *marina*.

P. M. — Called at Thomas A. Greene's in New

Bedford, said to be best acquainted with the botany of this vicinity (also acquainted with shells, and somewhat with geology). In answer to my question what were the rare or peculiar plants thereabouts, he looked over his botany deliberately and named the *Aletris farinosa*, or star-grass; the *Hydrocotyle vulgaris* (probably *interrupta* of Gray), which he thought was now gone; *Proserpinaca pectinacea*, at the shallow pond in Westport where I went last fall with Ricketson; *Panax trifolium*. That chenopodium-like plant on the salt-marsh shore, with hastate leaves, mealy under sides, is *Atriplex patula*, not yet out.

Brewer, in a communication to Audubon (as I read in his hundred(?)-dollar edition), makes two kinds of song sparrows, and says that Audubon has represented one, the most common about houses, with a spot in the centre of the breast, and Wilson the other, more universally spotted on the breast. The latter's nest will be two feet high in a bush and sometimes covered over and with an arched entrance and with six eggs (while the other has not more than five), larger and less pointed than the former's and apparently almost wholly rusty-brown. This builds further from houses.[1]

June 26.   Thursday.   In Loudon's "Encyclopædia of Agriculture" *far* (of the Romans) is translated Indian corn or *zea!*

According to Audubon's and Wilson's plates, the *Fringilla passerina* has a for the most part clear yellowish-white breast (*vide* May 28th), but the Savannah

[1] *Vide* June 23, 1860.

Vol. VIII

sparrow no conspicuous yellow on shoulder, a yellow brow, and white crown line. Rode to Sconticut Neck or Point in Fairhaven, five or six miles, and saw, apparently, the *F. Savanna* near their nests (my seringo note), restlessly flitting about me from rock to rock within a rod. Distinctly yellow-browed and spotted breast, not like plate of *passerina*. Audubon says that the eggs of the Savannah sparrow "are of a pale bluish color, softly mottled with purplish brown," and those of the yellow-winged sparrow are "of a dingy white, sprinkled with brown spots." The former is apparently my seringo's egg of May 28th. Is not Nuttall mistaken when he describes the notes of the Savannah sparrow in March in Georgia as "very long, piping, and elevated" and says that they sometimes have a note like a cricket? Audubon refers to the last note only.

Saw a farmer on the Neck with one of Palmer's patent wooden legs. He went but little lame and said that he did his own mowing and most of his ordinary farm work, though plowing in the present state of his limb, which had not yet healed, wrenched him some. He had lost a leg just below the knee, and was supported mainly on his thigh above the stump.

The older houses about New Bedford, as on this neck (and one a hundred years old is an old one), have commonly stone chimneys, which are agreeable to my eye and built with more taste than brick ordinarily, *i. e.* more elaborately. Yet they are now pulled down and brick substituted, or else concealed with a coat of mortar!

This neck, like the New Bedford country generally, is

very flat to my eye, even as far inland as Middleborough. When R. decided to take another road home from the latter place, because it was less hilly, I said I had not observed a hill in all our ride. I found on the rocky and rather desolate extremity of this point the common *Oxalis stricta* on the seashore, abundant, going to seed; apparently carrots (?) naturalized; atriplex not yet out; beach pea, still out and going to seed. An abundance of the small iris in the field near by. It was thick weather, after a drizzling forenoon, and we could just see across Buzzard's Bay from the point to Falmouth. Mattapoisett was the point next above on this side. I had been expecting to find the aletris about New Bedford, and when taking our luncheon on this neck what should I see rising above the luncheon-box, between me and R., but what I knew must be the *Aletris farinosa;* not yet out, but one near by would open apparently in two or three days.

I was struck by the number of quails thereabouts, and elsewhere in this vicinity. They keep up an incessant whistling these days, as also about R.'s house, within a stone's throw of it; and I several times saw them in the middle of the road in front of his house, in coveys, and on the road fence there. Also saw cowbirds in flocks on the road there. Around R.'s shanty was heard an incessant whistling of quails, and, morning and evening, the strain of the bay-wing, and some rather feeble purple finches, young males without the purple, dark-colored.

Talked with a farmer by name of Slocum, hoeing on the Neck, a rather dull and countrified fellow for our neighborhood, I should have said. Asked him, by chance, about getting to Cuttyhunk, if it was safe to cross the bay in a whale-boat. Yes, or "Ye-e-s," his boat was only some twelve feet long and went over two or three times a year. His relations lived there. Perhaps he understood navigating here. Well, he 'd been round the world considerably. "Have you been master of a whaler?" Yes; he 'd been to most all parts of the world.

Heard of, and sought out, the hut of Martha Simons, the only pure-blooded Indian left about New Bedford. She lives alone on the narrowest point of the Neck, near the shore, in sight of New Bedford. Her hut stands some twenty-five rods from the road on a small tract of Indian land, now wholly hers. It was formerly exchanged by a white man for some better land, then occupied by Indians, at Westport, which he wanted. So said a Quaker minister, her neighbor. The squaw was not at home when we first called. It was a little hut not so big as mine. *Vide* sketch by R., with the bay not far behind it. No garden; only some lettuce amid the thin grass in front, and a great white pile of clam and quahog shells one side. She ere long came in from the seaside, and we called again. We knocked and walked in, and she asked us to sit down. She had half an acre of the real tawny Indian face, broad with high cheek-bones, black eyes, and straight hair, originally black but now a little gray, parted in the middle. Her hands were several shades darker than her face. She had a peculiarly vacant expression, perhaps characteristic of the Indian, and answered our questions listlessly, without being interested or implicated, mostly in monosyllables, as if

hardly present there. To judge from her physiognomy, she might have been King Philip's own daughter. Yet she could not speak a word of Indian, and knew nothing of her race. Said she had lived with the whites, gone out to service to them when seven years old. Had lived part of her life at Squaw Betty's Neck, Assawampsett Pond. Did she know Sampson's? She 'd ought to; she 'd done work enough there. She said she was sixty years old, but was probably nearer seventy. She sat with her elbows on her knees and her face in her hands and that peculiar vacant stare, perhaps looking out the window between us, not repelling us in the least, but perfectly indifferent to our presence.

She was born on that spot. Her grandfather also lived on the same spot, though not in the same house. He was the last of her race who could speak Indian. She had heard him pray in Indian, but could only understand "Jesus Christ." Her only companion was a miserable tortoise-shell kitten which took no notice of us. She had a stone chimney, a small cooking-stove without fore legs, set up on bricks within it, and a bed covered with dirty bed-clothes. Said she hired out her field as pasture; better for her than to cultivate it. There were two young heifers in it. The question she answered with most interest was, "What do you call that plant?" and I reached her the aletris from my hat. She took it, looked at it a moment, and said, "That 's husk-root. It 's good to put into bitters for a weak stomach." The last year's light-colored and withered leaves surround the present green star like a husk. This must be the origin of the name. Its root

is described as intensely bitter. I ought to have had my hat full of plants.

A conceited old Quaker minister, her neighbor, told me with a sanctified air, "I think that the Indians were human beings; dost thee not think so?" He only convinced me of his doubt and narrowness.

June 27. P. M. — Went with R. and his boys in the Steamer Eagle's Wing, with a crowd and band of music, to the northeast end of Naushon, "Woods Hole," some fifteen miles from New Bedford; about two hours going. Talked with a Mr. Congdon, cashier of a bank and a vegetarian. Saw all the Elizabeth Isles, going and coming. They are mostly bare, except the east end of Naushon. This island is some seven miles long, by one to two wide. I had some two and a half hours there. I was surprised to find such a noble primitive wood, chiefly beech, such as the English poets celebrate, and oak (black oak, I think), large and spreading like pasture oaks with us, though in a wood. The ground under the beeches was covered with the withered leaves and peculiarly free from vegetation. On the edge of a swamp I saw great tupelos running up particularly tall, without lower branches, two or three feet in diameter, with a rough light-colored bark. Noticed a thorn, perhaps cockspur, with an undivided leaf, gooseberries, staghorn sumach, not in bloom. Most of the passengers expected to find strawberries. Saw a common wild grape-vine running over a beech, which was apparently flattened out by it, which vine measured, at six feet from ground, twenty-three inches in circumference. It was

large below, where it had already forked. At five feet from ground it divided into three great branches. It did not rise directly, but with a great half-spiral sweep or *anguish*. No sight could be more primeval. It was partly or chiefly dead. This was in the midst of the woods, by a path-side. Just beyond we started up two deer.

I suppose the white gull I saw and heard (somewhat like the sound of the small mackerel gull of the Cape) at Naushon was the *Sterna hirundo*, or great tern, with long forked tail. A Mr. Wall, artist, at New Bedford, told me of a high pine wood or swamp some miles down Naushon with "storks' nests" (!) in the pines. Were they blue herons?

Naushon is said to be part of the township of Chilmark, Martha's Vineyard, and to belong to Mr. Swain of New Bedford and Forbes of Boston; some say to Swain alone.

Walton Ricketson went down in a schooner the next day again, and found the pond near Swain's well stocked with pickerel, of which he caught many in a few hours.

Returning, I caught sight of Gay Head and its lighthouse with my glass, between Pasque and Nashawena. This lighthouse, according to Congdon, who says he measured it trigonometrically, is not more than one hundred and fifty feet above the sea. The passages between the islands are called "holes." Quick's is one. Cuttyhunk was very plain. Congdon said that he was there about thirty years ago, but could see no traces of Gosnold there, and does not believe there are any. Captain Slocum (of the day before), who has relations there, never saw any. Mr. Wall said that there was one old gentleman still alive, a Mr. Howland, who went on there with Belknap, who could tell all about it. The island is cultivated.

June 28. *Lamium amplexicaule* still out behind R.'s shanty. I picked up two arrowheads amid oyster and clam shells by a rock at the head of the creek opposite R.'s. One was of peculiar form, quite blunt and small, thus: of quartz, apparently to knock over small game without breaking the skin.

P. M. — I paddled up the Acushnet, about a mile above the paper-mill, as far as the ruined mill, in Walton's skiff with Arthur R. (Walton was named from I. Walton, the angler, and Arthur from Dana's hero in "Sun not set yet," etc.) I never saw such an abundance of peltandra as borders that sluggish and narrow stream, in bunches alternating with pickerel-weed; leaves of very various forms and sizes.

June 29. *Sunday.* P. M. — Bathed in the creek, which swarms with terrapins, as the boys called them. I find no account of them in Storer!! They put their heads out and floated about just like the *Emys picta*, and often approached and played (?) with each other. Some were apparently seven or eight inches long and of a yellowish color. A man by the riverside told us that he had two young ducks which he let out to seek their food along the riverside at low tide that morning. At length he noticed that one remained stationary amid the grass or salt weeds and something prevented its follow-

ing the other. He went to its rescue and found its foot shut tightly in a quahog's shell amid the grass which the tide had left. He took up all together, carried to his house, and his wife opened the shell with a knife, released the duck, and cooked the quahog.[1] Bathed again near Dogfish Bar. It was warm and dirty water, muddy bottom. I probably found an Indian's bone at Throgg's Point,[2] where their bodies have been dug up.

June 30. *Monday.* A. M. — To Middleborough ponds in the new town of Lakeville (some three years old). What a miserable name! It should have been Assawampsett or, perchance, Sanacus, if that was the name of the Christian Indian killed on the pond. By the roadside, Long Plain, North Fairhaven, observed a tupelo seven feet high with a rounded top, shaped like an umbrella, eight feet [in] diameter, spreading over the wall, and the main stem divided suddenly at two feet only below the top, where it was six inches in diameter!

On the right hand in the old orchard near the Quitticus Ponds, heard and at last saw my tweezer-bird, which is extremely restless, flitting from bough to bough and apple tree to apple tree. Its note like *ah, zre zre zre, zritter zritter zrit'*. *Sylvia Americana*, parti-colored warbler, with golden-green reflections on the back, two white bars on wings, all beneath white, large orange mark on breast, bordered broadly with lemon yellow, and yellow throat. These were making the woods ring

[1] [*Cape Cod*, p. 86; Riv. 100, 101.]
[2] [Coggeshall's Point (W. Ricketson).]

in Concord when I left and are very common hereabouts.

Saw a haymaker with his suspenders crossed before as well as behind. A valuable hint, which I think I shall improve upon, since I am much troubled by mine slipping off my shoulders.

Borrowed Roberts's boat, shaped like a pumpkin-seed, for we wished to paddle on Great Quitticus. We landed and lunched on Haskell's Island, which contains some twenty-five or thirty acres. Just beyond this was Reed's Island, which was formerly cultivated, the cattle being swum across, or taken over in a scow. A man praised the soil to me and said that rye enough had been raised on it to cover it six inches deep. At one end of Haskell's Island was apparently a piece of primitive wood, — beech, hemlock, etc. Under the first I found some low, dry brown plants, perhaps beech-drops and the like, two species, but saw none of this year. One who formerly owned Reed's Island said that a man once lived on Haskell's Island and had a hennery there. The tweezer-birds were lively in the hemlocks.

Rode on to the old Pond Meeting-house, whence there is a fine view of Assawampsett. It is probably the broadest lake in the State. Uriah (?) Sampson told me it was about eight or ten feet deep in the middle, but somewhat deeper about the sides. The main outlet of these ponds is northeast, by Taunton River, though there is some connection with the Mattapoisett River, and Assonet River drains the neighborhood of Long Pond on the west.

Two men spoke of loon's eggs on a rocky isle in

Little Quitticus. I saw the *Lobelia Dortmanna* in bloom in the last.

A southwest breeze springs up every afternoon at this season, comparatively cool and refreshing from the sea.

As we were returning, a Mr. Sampson was catching perch at the outlet from Long Pond, where it emptied into Assawampsett with a swift current. The surface of the rippling water there was all alive with yellow perch and white ones, whole schools showing their snouts or tails as they rose for the young alewives which *appeared* to be passing out of the brook. These, some of which I have in spirits, were about an inch and a half long. Sampson fished with these for bait, trailing or jerking it along the surface exactly as for pickerel, and the perch bit very fast. He showed me one white perch. It was a broader fish than the yellow, but much softer-scaled and generally preferred. He said they would not take the hook after a certain season. He swept out some young alewives (herring) with a stick on to the shore, and among them were young yellow perch also an inch and a half long, with the transverse bands perfectly distinct. I have some in spirit. The large ones were devouring these, no doubt, together with the alewives. Is not June the month when most of our freshwater fish are spawned?

IX

JULY, 1856

(ÆT. 38–39)

July 1. P. M. — Paddled on the Acushnet.
Passed through some schools of fishes which were rippling the surface about us in midstream. The back fins, very long and sharp, projected two or three inches above water. Walton said afterward that they were menhaden.[1]

July 2. Return to Concord.
Looked at the birds in the Natural History Rooms in Boston. Observed no white spots on the sparrow hawk's wing, or on the pigeon or sharp-shinned hawk's. Indeed they were so closed that I could not have seen them. Am uncertain to which my wing belongs. May I not have seen the white-crowned sparrow in company with the white-throated? They are much alike. Yet Wilson says they rarely associate. The hemlock and pine warbler are much alike. Is it possible I have confounded them?

July 3. P. M. — To Assabet River.
In the main stream, at the Rock, I am surprised to see flags and pads, laying the foundation of an islet in the middle, where I had thought it deep before. Apparently a hummock lifted by ice sunk there in the

[1] [*Cape Cod*, p. 120; Riv. 143.]

spring, and this may be the way in which many an island has been formed in the river.

I scare up one or two woodcocks in different places by the shore, where they are feeding, and in a meadow. They go off with a whistling flight. Can see where their bills have probed the mud.

See a sternothærus on a small stump two feet over water. I approach and take hold of it, but cannot easily remove it. It appears to be shrunk on, withering away and dying there. It barely moves its head and eyes slightly, and its flippers look very much shrunken, yet it tumbles off after I leave. Apparently a male. I notice afterward, on succeeding days, many of them resting thus sluggishly, and find that I can approach and handle them and leave them as I found them. They appear much more sluggish than the other kinds now, though they were active enough in the spring. The tortoises improve every rock, and willow slanting over the water, and every floating board and rail. You will see one on the summit of a black willow stump several feet high, and two or more part way up. Some tumble from a height of five or six feet into the water before you. Even the great snap-turtle puts his head out and climbs up a rock on the bank with the rest.

July 5. A. M. — To Loring's Pond.
Pink-colored yarrow. *Epilobium coloratum*, a day or more. Young partridges (with the old bird), as big as robins, make haste into the woods from off the railroad. Plucked some large luscious purple pyrus berries. Lactuca some days out.

Borrowed Witherell's boat and paddled over Loring's Pond. A kingbird's nest in fork of a button-bush five feet high on shore (not saddled on); three young just hatched and one egg.

Much of this pond is now very shallow and muddy and crowded with pads, etc. I can hardly push through them. Yet I can see no more white lily pads shaped as that appears to have been which I found here a few weeks since. Many pickerel dart away from amidst the pads, and in one place I see one or two great snap-turtles.

I notice two varieties (?), perhaps, of *Asclepias Cornuti* now out, one on the railroad meadow this side the Brooks Crossing, the other beyond the first mile-post above. The last has broader leaves and blunter and more decidedly mucronate, and pedicels and peduncles quite downy, the former little more than twice the length of the petals. The other has narrower and more pointed leaves, peduncles and pedicels but little downy comparatively, the latter more than three times the length of the petals and not so numerous as in the other. *Vide* their pods, if spiny, by and by.

The *Spergularia rubra* was not open in the morning when I passed up, at 8 or 9 A. M., but was opened when I returned at noon, but closed again at 5 P. M.

The notes of barn swallows, perhaps with their young, are particularly loud now and almost metallic, like that of a mackerel gull.

The large evening-primrose below the foot of our garden does not open till some time between 6.30 and 8 P. M. or sundown. It was not open when I went to

bathe, but freshly out in the cool of the evening at sundown, as if enjoying the serenity of the hour.

July 6. P. M. — To Assabet Bath.
Campanula aparinoides, roadside opposite centaurea, several days. Early low blueberries ripe.

Crossed the river at bath place. On the sandy bank opposite, saw a wood tortoise voraciously eating sorrel leaves, under my face. In A. Hosmer's ice-bared meadow south of Turnpike, hear the distressed or anxious *peet* of a peetweet, and see it hovering over its young, half grown, which runs beneath and suddenly hides securely in the grass when but few feet from me. White avens, evidently Bigelow's *Geum album* (which Gray makes only a variety of *G. Virginianum*), a good while, very rough and so much earlier than the *G. Virginianum* that only one flower remains. The heads have attained their full size, with twisted tails to the awns, while the other will not open for some days. I think Bigelow must be right. *Lysimachia lanceolata*, a day or two. *Rhus typhina* in our yard; how long? Did not see it out in New Bedford ten days ago. There is a young red mulberry in the lower hedge beneath the celtis.

G. Emerson says the sweet-briar was doubtless introduced, yet, according to Bancroft, Gosnold found it on the Elizabeth Isles.

July 7. I see a difference now between the alder leaves near Island and edge of meadow westward, on Hill; the former slightly downy beneath, the latter (apparently *Alnus serrulata*) green and smooth but yet *not pointed at base*. Do I not see a taller kind of wool-grass in that birch meadow east of Hill?

P. M. — To Gowing's Swamp.

The purple finch still sings over the street. The sagittaria, large form, is out, roadside, Moore's Swamp. The *Vaccinium Oxycoccus* is almost entirely out of bloom, and the berries are as big as small huckleberries [1] (while the *V. macrocarpon* is in full bloom, and no berries appear on it). It must therefore have begun about the 1st of June. Saw the *Kalmia glauca* by the small cranberry, betrayed by its two-edged twig. The snake-head arethusa is now abundant amid the cranberries there.

July 8. 3 P. M. — To Baker Farm by boat.
River down to lower side of long rock.

When I landed on Hosmer flat shore, started a large water adder, apparently running on the bank. It ran at once into the river and was lost under the pads. *Ranunculus reptans* is abundantly out at mouth of brook, Baker shore. Is that small sparganium there, now abundantly out, about eighteen inches high, with leaves narrow and convex below, concave above, the same species with the larger? Some in press.

Got the downy woodpecker's nest, some days empty. [2]

Find several large and coarse *Potentilla arguta*, two and a half feet high and more, at Bittern Cliff, nearly out of bloom. Flowers in crowded corymbs. They are *white*, not yellow, as Gray calls them. In the side-

[1] Or as the common cranberry on the 20th. [2] *Vide* 19th.

hill wood-lot (or spring wood-lot) behind, where the wood was cut last winter, poke-leaved milkweed (*Asclepias phytolaccoides*), apparently a day or two, and *Circæa alpina*, some days, a foot high with opaque leaves and *bracts* (in press). This I find to be the same with the small, also bracted, one at Corner Spring (whose leaves were perhaps more transparent when in shade, but which now grows larger in sun). [1]

Sophia saw this afternoon two great snap-turtles fighting near the new stone bridge, making a great commotion in the river and not regarding the spectators, she and another, and a teamster who stopped his team to observe them.

Sam Wheeler, who did not know there were snap-turtles here, says he saw opposite to his boarding-house, on the sidewalk, in New York, the other day, a green turtle which weighed seven hundred and twenty pounds, which in a short time dropped eggs enough to fill a vessel some feet in diameter. He partook of some of the soup made of it, and there were several eggs in it, which were luscious.

After Jules Gérard, the lion-killer, had hunted lions for some time, and run great risk of losing his life, though he struck the lions in the right place with several balls, the lions steadily advancing upon him even though they had got a death-wound, he discovered that it was not enough to be brave and take good aim, — that his balls, which were of lead, lacked penetration and were flattened against the lions' bones; and accordingly he sent to France and obtained balls which were pointed with

[1] *Vide* [p. 406] and also July 24.

Vol. VIII

steel and went through and through both shoulder-blades. So I should say that the weapons or balls which the Republican Party uses lacked penetration, and their foe steadily advances nevertheless, to tear them in pieces, with their well-aimed balls flattened on his forehead.

In Gérard's book I find, according to a Mohammedan tradition, "when the lion roars, he says, 'Ya rabbi, ma teçallot mi â la ed-dâbèome,' which signifies 'Seignior, deliver to my power the wicked only, and let the good go free.'"

July 10. Yesterday a heavy rain.
A. M. — To Laurel Glen.

Chenopodium album, by railroad. Succory a week or more, by railroad causeway. *Stachys aspera* well out two or three days, low ground. *Chimaphila umbellata*, some days. *Pyrola elliptica*, how long? *P. chlorantha* done, near part of Cut woods. *P. rotundifolia* (how long?), Cut woods hollow. *Galium triflorum* of Bigelow (?), prostrate, from one centre, Laurel Glen hillside; how long? But the branches are not three-flowered, but have three pedicels and one, two, or all of them (commonly but one) are subdivided into two. Also *G. circæzans* gone to seed. I have pressed apparently *Galium lanceolatum*. *Sericocarpus conyzoides*, Deep Cut path.

Asclepias obtusifolia, which was out well on the 5th, has a bloom, and the curved horns are *elevated* above the flower.

See and hear young barn swallows about.

5 P. M. — Up Assabet.

As I was bathing under the swamp white oaks at 6 P. M., heard a suppressed sound often repeated, like, perhaps, the working of beer through a bung-hole, which I already suspected to [be] produced by owls. I was uncertain whether it was far or near. Proceeding a dozen rods up-stream on the south side, toward where a catbird was incessantly me...ng, I found myself suddenly within a rod of a gray screech owl sitting on an alder bough with horns erect, turning its head from side to side and up and down, and peering at me in that same ludicrously solemn and complacent way that I had noticed in one in captivity. Another, more red, also horned, repeated the same warning sound, or apparently call to its young, about the same distance off, in another direction, on an alder. When they took to flight they made some noise with their wings. With their short tails and squat figures they looked very clumsy, all head and shoulders. Hearing a fluttering under the alders, I drew near and found a young owl, a third smaller than the old, all gray, without obvious horns, only four or five feet distant. It flitted along two rods, and I followed it. I saw at least two or more young. All this was close by that thick hemlock grove, and they perched on alders and an apple tree in the thicket there. These birds kept opening their eyes when I moved, as if to get clearer sight of me. The young were very quick to notice any motion of the old, and so betrayed their return by looking in that direction when they returned, though I had not heard it. Though they permitted me to come so near with so much noise, as if bereft of half their senses, they at [once] noticed the coming and going of the old birds, even when I did not. There were four or five owls in all. I have heard a somewhat similar note, further off and louder, in the night.

I find (July 14th) (and it has been out some days), at Muhlenbergii Brook, circæas which are distinctly branched and with *large* leaf-like bracts, some nearly two feet high. Yet they are evidently the same species that I have found before, and I think that there is but one hereabouts, say *C. alpina*, which, however, is poorly described by Gray and inadequately by Bigelow. It is from four or five (in shade) to, as here, about two feet high (in sun); is never pubescent, but quite smooth, round-stemmed, swelling at the joints, more or less branched, in large specimens sometimes very much so (*vide* pressed one), with bracts quite small and slender in small ones, and very large and leaf-like (two on a common axillary branch) in large plants; leaves opaque in open places, heart-shaped, *rather* slightly and distantly toothed, of the large specimens, at least, *not* shining.[1]

July 11. A. M. — To Tarbell Swamp Hill all day with W. E. C.

Landed at path end, Great Meadows. No haying there yet. In the now isolated ditches, etc., there [are] thousands of little pouts about one inch long, more or less. The water is muddy, and I see no old ones. They are rather difficult to catch (like minnows generally, but

[1] *Vide* 24th.

---

less so), but I got two and have them in spirit. I scare up several apparent snipes (?), which go off with a *crack*. They are rather heavy-looking, like woodcocks, but have gray breasts. Are probing the meadow. Quite numerous there. The *Ludwigia sphærocarpa*, which had been out apparently a week on the 6th of August, 1855, shows hardly a sign of a flower yet. So it will hardly open before August 1st. The grass on the islets in those pools is much flattened in many places by the turtles, which lie out sunning on it. They tumble in before me, and by the sound and marks of one I suspect it a snap-turtle. They are commonly *E. picta*.

Bathed and lunched under the oak at Tarbell's first shore. It is about as cool a place as you can find, where you get the southwest breeze from over the broad meadow, for it draws through the valley behind. While sitting there, saw, some twenty-five rods up-stream, amid the pads on the south side, where we had passed, several apparently young ducks, which soon disappeared again in the meadow-grass. Saw them hereabouts August 6th last year. They regularly breed hereabouts, and the broad meadow affords lurking-places. The meadow is so broad and level that you see shadows of clouds on it as on the sea. A great snap-turtle floated by us with his head out, in midstream, reconnoitring us. Rambled over the hill at angle. Allium out some time on the shore. I have only seen it here, methinks, and on the Assabet shores.

Hear now the *link* of bobolinks, and see quite a flock of red-wing blackbirds and young (?). The water milk-weed, or *Asclepias pulchra*.

July 12. P. M. — Down Turnpike to Red Lily Meadow.

Hear the plaintive note of young bluebirds, a reviving and gleaming of their blue ray. In Moore's meadow by Turnpike, see the vetch in purple patches weighing down the grass, as if a purple tinge were reflected there. White vervain. Smooth sumach, apparently yesterday. Rue is beginning now to whiten the meadows on all hands. The *Ranunculus aquatilis* appears to be about done, though it may have been submerged by the rain of yesterday. I see hardly one freshly open, and it [is] quite moist and lowering yet. By the myosotis ditch there, is an abundance of *Galium trifidum* (apparently *obtusum* or *latifolium*, in press). It is densely massed and quite prickly, with three corolla-lobes. As yet I think I have observed only two varieties of *G. trifidum*, smooth and rough. *Lactuca sanguinea*, some time, with dark-purple stem, widely branched. *Pycnanthemum muticum* and the narrow-leaved, not long.[1]

In the still wet road on the hill, just beyond Lincoln bound, a short-tailed shrew (*Sorex brevicaudus* of Say), dead after the rain. I have found them thus three or four times before. It is $4\frac{1}{2}$ inches long; tail 1 +; head and snout, 1 +. Roundish body. Lead-color above, somewhat lighter beneath, with a long snout, $\frac{3}{8}$ inch beyond lower jaw, incisors black, delicate light-colored (almost silvery) mustachial bristles, and also from lower lip; nose emarginate; nails long and slender, a purple bar across each; ears white and concealed in the fur; the nostrils plainly perforated, though Emmons says that in

[1] Several days at least.

---

the specimens of *Sorex* he had seen he could detect no perforations with a microscope. It has a peculiar but not *very* strong muskiness. There was an insect-wing in its mouth. Its numerous teeth distinct. Have I not commonly noticed them dead after rain? I am surprised to read in Emmons that it was first observed in Missouri, and that he has "not been able to meet with it" and doubts its existence in the State; retains it on the authority of former catalogues; says it nests on the surface and is familiar with water. In spirits.[1]

Red lilies in prime, single upright fiery flowers, their throats how splendidly and *variously* spotted, hardly two of quite the same hue and not two spotted alike, —leopard-spotted,—averaging a foot or more in height, amid the huckleberry and lambkill, etc., in the moist, meadowy pasture.

Apparently a bluebird's egg in a woodpecker's hole in an apple tree, second brood, just laid. In collection. Parsnip at Bent's orchard; how long? Also on July 5th, almost out. Agrimony well out. Chestnut in prime. See *Lysimachia quadrifolia* with from three to five (or six?) leaves in a whorl. *Iberis umbellata*, candytuft, roadside, Tuttle's, naturalized; how long? New plant.

July 13. P. M. — To Corner Spring.

Orchis lacera, apparently several days, lower part of spike, willow-row, Hubbard side, opposite Wheildon's land. See quite a large flock of chattering red-wings, the flight of first broods. Thimble-berries are now fairly ripe and abundant along walls, to be strung on herd's-

[1] Given to Agassiz for Baird. *Vide* Oct. 25, 1856.

grass, but not much flavor to them; honest and whole-some. See where the mowers have plucked them. Gather the large black and blackening ones. No drought has shrivelled them this year.

Heard yesterday a sharp and loud *ker-pheet*, I think from a surprised woodchuck, amid bushes, — the *siffleur*. Reminds me somewhat of a peetweet, and also of the squeak of a rabbit, but much louder and sharper. And all is still.

Hubbard's meadow — or I will call it early meadow — aster, some days, now rather slender and small-bushed. *Drosera longifolia* and also *rotundifolia*, some time. *Polygala sanguinea*, some time, Hubbard's Meadow Path; say meadow-paths and banks. Saw and heard two or three redstarts at Redstart Woods, where they probably have nests. Have noticed bright-red geranium and pyrus leaves a week or more.

In Hubbard's euphorbia pasture, cow blackbirds about cows. At first the cows were resting and ruminating in the shade, and no birds were seen. Then one after another got up and went to feeding, straggling into the midst of the field. With a chattering appeared a cowbird, and, with a long slanting flight, lit close to a cow's nose, within the shadow of it, and watched for insects, the cow still eating along and almost hitting it, taking no notice of it. Soon it is joined by two or three more birds.

An abundance of spurry in the half-grown oats adjoining, apparently some time out. Yellow lily, how long? Am surprised to see an *Aster lævis*, out a day or two, in road on sandy bank. Goldfinches twitter over. Hydrocotyle, some time.

July 14. P. M. — To Muhlenbergii Brook.

Anthony Wright found a lark's nest with fresh eggs on the 12th in E. Hubbard's meadow by ash tree, — two nests, probably one a second brood. *Nasturtium hispidum* (?), apparently three or four days. See and hear martins twittering *on the elms* by riverside. Bass out about two days at Island. There is a pyrus twenty feet high with small fruit at Assabet Spring.

Noli-me-tangere already *springs* at Muhlenbergii Brook, some days. Saw apparently my little ruby (?)-crested wren (?) on the weeds there. Senecio long gone to seed and dispersed. Canada thistle some time on Huckleberry Pasture-side beyond. Ceratophyllum with a dense whorl of twelve little oval red-dotted apparent flower-buds (?) in an axil.

While drinking at Assabet Spring in woods, noticed a cherry-stone on the bottom. A bird that came to drink must have brought it half a mile. So the tree gets planted!

July 15. P. M. — To Hubbard's Close and Walden.

Carrots by railroad, how long? I notice the froth concealing a grub, not only on trees and bushes, but on *Potentilla Norvegica*, *Lechea* (great-fruited), etc., etc., *Pycnanthemum muticum*, even *Lobelia inflata*, red clover, *Aster puniceus*.[1] This spots my clothes when going through bushes. Both small hypericums, *Canadense* and *mutilum*, apparently some days at least by Stow's ditch. Bobolinks are heard — their *link, link* — above and amid the tall rue which now whitens the

[1] Also Aug. 1st on sweet-gale and Roman wormwood.

Vol. VIII

meadows. Checkerberry, a day or two. *Spiranthes gracilis* well out, in dry, slender grass by roadside. I do not notice the krigia out in my afternoon walks, and so it is not known by many, but in the morning its disk is very commonly seen.

When I crossed the entrance to the pond meadow on a stick, a pout ran ashore and was lodged so that I caught it in the grass, apparently frightened. While I held it, I noticed another, very large one approach the shore very boldly within a few feet of me. Going in to bathe, I caught a pout on the bottom within a couple of rods of the shore. It seemed sick. Then, wading into the shallow entrance of the meadow, I saw a school of a thousand little pouts about three quarters of an inch long without any attending pout, and now have no doubt that the pout I had caught (but let go again) was tending them, and the large one was the father, apparently further off. The mother had perhaps gone into deep water to recruit after her air-bath. The young were pretty shy; kept in shallow water, and were taking pretty good care of themselves. If the water should suddenly fall, they might be caught in the meadow.

Ludwigia alternifolia not quite; in a day or two.

Amid the high grass or rushes by that meadow-side started a water adder. It was about three feet long, but large round in proportion, with about one hundred and forty abdominal plates and a long, slender tail. It was black above, with indistinct transverse brown bands. Under its head white; first half of belly white, with triangular or conical dark brown-red marks

on sides; the white gradually becomes more narrow and yellowish for the latter half of the abdomen, bordered by more numerous and still darker reddish marks, becoming confluent and alternating with silvery ones, giving a handsome regularly mottled or spotted look. The silvery thus across the belly: The barred part dark-reddish. Under the tail no reddish.

Corylus rostrata differs from common in the twig being smooth and not glandular-hairy. *Scutellaria galericulata*, some time. *Polygonum sagittatum*, almost.

That green *sponge* plant gathered yesterday is remarkably slow to dry; though it has been many hours exposed to the sun and wiped with many papers and has been a whole day exposed to the air, it is far from dry yet. It is more pungent and strong-scented than ever and sickens me to stay in the room with a little of it.

July 16. Sium out not long. I see many young shiners (?) [1] (they have the longitudinal bar), one to two and a half inches long, and young breams two or three inches long and quite broad. *Geum Virginianum*, apparently two or three days.

See several bullfrogs lying fully out on pads at 5 P. M. They trump well these nights.

It is remarkable how a copious rain, raising the river a little, flattens down the heart-leaf and other weeds at bathing-places.

[1] Probably minnows.

July 17. Found a great many insects in white lilies which opened in pan this forenoon, which had never opened before. What regular and handsome petals! regularly concave toward the inside, and calyx hooked at tip.

P. M. — To Water Dock Meadow and Linnæa Hillside.

Hear a new note from bank swallows when going over the Hosmer pastures, a sort of *screep screep*, shrill and like what I have referred to the barn swallow. They are probably out with young.

Ludwigia palustris and ilysanthes have been out apparently some time on the flat Hosmer shore or meadow, where the surface has been laid bare by the ice. There, too, the *Hypericum Sarothra* has pushed up abundantly. I see many young toads hopping about on that bared ground amid the thin weeds, not more than five eighths to three quarters of an inch long; also young frogs a little larger. Horse-mint out at Clamshell, apparently two or three days.

Bathed at Clamshell. See great schools of minnows, apparently shiners, hovering in the clear shallow next the shore. They seem to choose such places for security. They take pretty good care of themselves and are harder to catch with the hands than you expect, darting out of the way at last quite swiftly. Caught three, however, between my hands. They have brighter golden irides, all the abdomen conspicuously pale-golden, the back and half down the sides pale-brown, a broad, distinct black band along sides (which methinks marks the shiner), and comparatively transparent beneath behind vent. When the water is gone I am surprised to see how they

can skip or spring from side to side in my cup-shaped two hands for a long time. This to enable them to get off floating planks or pads on the shore when in fright they may have leaped on to them. But they are very tender, and the sun and air soon kill them. If there is any water in your hand they will pass out through the smallest crack between your fingers. They are about three quarters of an inch long generally, though of various sizes.

Half a dozen big bream come quite up to me, as I stand in the water. They are not easily scared in such a case.

The large skunk-cabbage fruit looks quite black now where the haymakers have passed. Stooping to drink at the Hosmer Spring, I saw a hundred caddis-cases, of light-colored pebbles, at the bottom, and a dozen or twenty crawled half-way up the side of the tub, apparently on their way out to become perfect insects.

Cows in their pasture, going to water or elsewhere, make a track four or five inches deep and frequently not more than ten inches wide.

The great water dock has been out some days at least. Its valves are quite small at first, but lower leaves *pointed*. I hear in the meadow there a faint incessant z-ing sound, as of small locusts in the meadow-grass. Under the oak in Brown's moraine pasture, by Water Dock Meadow, a great arum more than three feet high, like a tropical plant, in open land, with leafets more than a foot long. There is rich-weed there, apparently not quite out.

Going up the hillside, between J. P. Brown's and rough-cast house, am surprised to see great plump ripe low blackberries. How important their acid (as

well as currants) this warm weather! It is 5 P. M. The wood thrush begins to sing.

A very warm afternoon. Thermometer at 97° at the Hosmer Desert. I hear the early locust. I have come to collect birds' nests. The thrasher's is apparently made partly beneath the surface, some dirt making its sides. I find the nests by withered twigs and leaves broken off in the spring, but commonly nearly concealed by the recent growth. The jay's nest had been filled with white oak leaves. Not one could have been blown into it. On Linnæa Hill many thimble-berries and some raspberries.

Evening by river to Ed. Hosmer's. Hear at distance the hum of bees from the bass with its drooping flowers at the Island, a few minutes only before sunset. It sounds like the rumbling of a distant train of cars. Returning after ten, by moonlight, see the bullfrogs lying at full length on the pads where they trump.

July 18. P. M. — To Wheeler meadow to look at willows.

Again scare up a woodcock, apparently *seated* or sheltered in shadow of ferns in the meadow on the cool mud in the hot afternoon. *Rosa Carolina*, some time, at edge of Wheeler meadow near Island Neck.

You see almost everywhere on the muddy river bottom, rising toward the surface, first, the coarse multifid leaves of the *Ranunculus Purshii*, now much the worse for the wear; second, perhaps, in coarseness, the ceratophyllum, standing upright; third, perhaps, the *Bidens Beckii*, with its leafets at top; then the *Utricu-*

laria vulgaris, with its black or green bladders, and the two lesser utricularias in many places.

July 19. P. M. — Marlborough Road *via* railroad and Dugan wood-lot.

A box tortoise, killed a good while, on the railroad, at Dogwood Swamp; quite dry now. This the fourth I have ever found: first one, alive, in Truro; second one, dead, on shore of Long Pond, Lakeville; third one, alive, under Fair Haven Hill; and fourth, this. This appeared to have been run over, but both upper and under shells were broken into several pieces each, *in no case* on the line of the serrations or of the edges of the scales (proving that they are as strong one way as the other), but at various angles across them, which, I think, proves it to have been broken while the animal was alive or fresh and the shell not dry. I picked up only the after half or two thirds and one foot. The upper shell was at the widest place four and three eighths inches. It was broken irregularly across the back, from about the middle of the second lateral scale from the front on the left to the middle of the third lateral on the right, and was, at the angle of the marginal scales, about sixteen fortieths to seventeen fortieths of an inch thick, measured horizontally. The sides under the lateral scales and half the dorsal were from four to five fortieths of an inch thick. The thinnest part was about three eighths of an inch from middle of back on each side, directly between the spring of the sides [?], where it was but little more than two fortieths thick. So nature makes an arch. I have about half the sternum, the rear of it at one point reaching to the hinge. It is thickest vertically just at the side hinges, where it is one fourth thick; thinnest three eighths from this each side, where it is one eighth thick; and thence thickens to the middle of the sternum, where it [is] seven and a half fortieths thick. The upper shell in this case (*vide* May 17, 1856) is neither pointed nor notched behind, but quite straight. The sternum and the *lower* parts of the marginal scales are chiefly dark-brown. The marking above is sufficiently like that of the Cape Cod specimen, with a still greater proportion of yellow, now faded to a yellowish brown.

On Linnæa Hills, sarsaparilla berries. *Lobelia inflata*, perhaps several days; little white glands (?) on the edges of the leaves. On the under side of a *Lobelia spicata* leaf, a sort of *loose-spun* cocoon, about five eighths of an inch long, of golden-brown silk, beneath which silky mist a hundred young spiders swarm.

Examined painted tortoise eggs of June 10th. One of those great spider(?)-holes made there since then, close to the eggs. The eggs are large and rather pointed, methinks at the larger end. The young are half developed. Fleets of yellow butterflies on road. Small white rough-coated puffballs (?) in pastures. Appear not to have two coats like that of Potter's Path, *q. v.*

As I come by the apple tree on J. P. B.'s land, where I heard the young woodpeckers hiss a month or so ago, I now see that they have flown, for there is a cobweb over the hole.

Plucked a handful of gooseberries at J. P. B.'s bush, probably ripe some time. It is of fair size, red-purple

and greenish, and apparently like the first in garden, except it is not slightly bristly like that, nor has so much flavor and agreeable tartness. Also the stalk is not so prickly, but for the most part has one small prickle where ours has three stout ones. Our second gooseberry is more purple (or dark-purple with bloom) and the twig less prickly than the wild. Its flavor is insipid and in taste like the wild.

It is the *Hypericum ellipticum* and *Canadense* (linear-leaved) whose *red* pods are noticed now.

On the sand thrown out by the money-diggers, I found the first ripe blackberries thereabouts. The heat reflected from the sand had ripened them earlier than elsewhere. It did not at first occur to me what sand it was, nor that I was indebted to the money-diggers, or their Moll Pitcher who sent them hither, for these blackberries. I am probably the only one who has got any fruit out of that hole. It 's an ill wind that blows nobody any good. Looking up, I observed that they had dug another hole a rod higher up the hill last spring (for the blackberries had not yet spread over it), and had partly filled it up again. So the result of some idler's folly and some spiritualist's nonsense is that I get my blackberries a few days the earlier.

The downy woodpecker's nest which I got July 8th was in a dead and partly rotten upright apple bough four and three quarters inches [in] diameter. Hole *perfectly* elliptical (or oval) one and two sixteenths by one and five sixteenths inches; whole depth below it eight inches. It is excavated directly inward about three and a half inches, with a conical roof, also arching at back, with a

recess in one side on level with the hole, where the bird turns. Judging from an old hole in the same bough, directly above, it enlarges directly to a diameter of two and one fourth to two and one half inches, not in this case descending exactly in the middle of the bough, but leaving one side not a quarter of an inch thick. At the hole it is left one inch thick. At the nest it is about two and three eighths inches [in] diameter. I find nothing in the first but bits of rotten wood, remains of insects, etc., when I tip it up, — for I cannot see the bottom, — yet in the old one there is also quite a nest of fine stubble (?), bark shred (?), etc., mixed with the bits of rotten wood.

July 20. P. M. — Up Assabet.

Button-bush, apparently two or three days.

I suspect that those very variously formed leaves in and about woods which come to naught — like the sium in deep water — are of the nabalus.

Caught a middle-sized copper-colored devil's-needle (with darker spots on wings), sluggish, on a grass stem, with many dark-colored elliptical eggs packed closely to outside, under its breast.

July 21. P. M. — To A. Wheeler's grape meadow.

Mimulus, not long. *Hypericum corymbosum*, a day or two. Rusty cotton-grass, how long?

The small hypericums are open only in the forenoon. Pursley, also, in our garden opens *now* not till 8 A. M., and shuts up before 12 M.

The flat euphorbia is now in prime on the sandy path beyond Potter's Desert, five-finger fungus path.

Plucked a handful of huckleberries from one bush! The *Vaccinium vacillans* thick enough to go picking, and probably for a day or two in some places. Low blackberries thick enough to pick in some places, three or four days. Thimble-berries about the 12th, and *V. Pennsylvanicum* much longer.

These hot afternoons I go panting through the close sprout-lands and copses, as now from Cliff Brook to Wheeler meadow, and occasionally come to sandy places a few feet in diameter where the partridges have dusted themselves. Gérard, the lion-killer of Algiers, speaks of seeing similar spots when tracking or patiently waiting the lion there, and his truth in this particular is a confirmation of the rest of his story. But his pursuit dwarfs this fact and makes it seem trivial. Shall not my pursuit also contrast with the trivialness of the partridges' dusting? It is interesting to find that the same phenomena, however simple, occur in different parts of the globe. I have found an arrowhead or two in such places even. Far in warm, sandy woods in hot weather, when not a breath of air is stirring, I come upon these still sandier and warmer spots where the partridges have dusted themselves, now all still and deserted, and am not relieved, yet pleased to find that I have been preceded, by any creature.

Grapes ready to stew.

Mr. Russell writes me to-day that he visited the locality of the *Magnolia glauca* the 18th, on Cape Ann, and saw lingering still a few flowers and flower-buds. It is quite open and rising above the bushes.

The brook cress might be called river cress, for it is

very abundant rising above the surface in all the shallower parts of the river.

Verbena hastata, apparently several days.

Sonchus, some time.

This has been a peculiarly fine afternoon. When I looked about casually, was surprised at the fairness of the landscape. Though warm, it is clear and fresh, and the air imparts to all surfaces a peculiar fine glaucous color, full of light, without mistiness, like the under side of the *Salix lucida* (?) leaves at present. Not only the under sides of the leaves, but the very afternoon landscape, has become glaucous. Now, when the fashionable world goes to Saratoga, Nahant, and Newport, we frequent our oldest haunts with new love and reverence and sail into new ports with each fresh varnish of the air.

July 23. 9 A. M. — Up river for *Nuphar Kalmiana* with Russell.

Pasture thistle, not long. *Hypericum Sarothra*, not long, or perhaps some days. *Antennaria margaritacea. Scutellaria lateriflora*, apparently some days.

R. says that my five-finger fungus is the *Lycoperdon stellatum* and can be found now. I find it in some places. (It is different from the white rough-coated puffball now found.) It was exhibited lately in Boston as the "resurrection plant" (! !) to compete with the one imported from Palestine. That what I have called fresh-water sponge is such, *Spongea fluviatilis*, and, like the marine, is uncertain whether vegetable or animal. When burned it leaves a mass of white spicula which have been mistaken for infusoria! Thinks the dry brown last-year's

plant I brought from Haskell's Island, Lakeville, the *Epiphegus.* That the *Rubus Canadensis*, low blackberry, is not found far west of us. That there is described — he thinks in Hooker's English Flora — a certain massing up of a conferva similar to that of my eriocaulon balls. Has seen a Mexican species, allied to the potato, cultivated hereabouts, which became a weed, — would not become larger than a walnut. Speaks of the young pouts *with their bladders attached,* accompanied by the old. That the berries of the celtis are pleasant to taste, those of the sassafras abominable. Showed me the *Dulichium spathaceum*, leaves in three ranks, so common along river, now in bloom; also the *Carex lupulina* (?) or *retrorsa* (?), hop sedge, with the inflated perigynia. Said that those reddish clusters of buds on a rush or carex were enlarged by disease. That the two white cotton-grasses (*Eriophorum*) were probably but one species, taller and shorter; also the two wool-grasses Scirpus — Trichophorum [*sic*] were probably but one species, the tall and short. That there was an account of the lecheas by Tuckerman in *Silliman's Journal.*

P. M. — To Walden for hydropeltis.

A young sternothærus which R. picked up recently dead, on the shore of the pond, was one and one sixteenth inches long, — the upper shell, — probably therefore a last year's one, or not yet one year old. Very high and sharp back, but broader than old. No hook to upper bill.

That fern leaf on my coal (?) is probably the *Neuropteris* as figured in Richardson's Botany.

Saw at Hydropeltis Meadow a small bullfrog in the act of swallowing a young but pretty sizable apparently *Rana palustris*, such as now hop about, an inch and a half long. He took it down head foremost, and as the legs were slowly taken in, — stuffing himself, — for the legs were often straightened out, — I wondered what satisfaction it could be to the larger to have that cold slimy fellow, entire, lying head to tail within him! I sprang to make him disgorge, but it was too late to save him. Though I tossed the bullfrog out of the water, the *palustris* was entombed. So little while had he been in the light when he fell into that recess! Bathing in Walden, I find the water considerably colder at the bottom while I stand up to my chin, but the sandy bottom much warmer to my feet than the water. The heat passes *through* the water with[out] being absorbed by it much. The hydropeltis leaves so crowded they cannot lie flat, but their edges show (a good part [of] the under side) as if blown up by wind.

The water adder killed on the 15th and left hanging on a twig has decayed wonderfully. I perceive no odor, and it is already falling to pieces. I can see most of its ribs and through and through in many directions!! It is already mere skin and skeleton, as empty as [a] flute. I can count the bare ribs, and it [is] inoffensive to the smell.

See apparently young goldfinches about, very *freshly* bright golden and black.

The small potamogeton, *heterophyllus* (?) or *hybridus* (?), out some time. *Ludwigia alternifolia*, five or six days.

July 24. P. M. — To Flint's Pond.

Solidago stricta,[1] Ingraham Path, well out, some days. *Chimaphila maculata*, three flowers, apparently but few days, while the *umbellata* is quite done there. Leaves just shooting up. See those light-bordered dark spots on tall and other goldenrod leaves (fungi (?) says Russell). In the low Flint's Pond Path, beyond Britton's, the tall rough goldenrod makes a thicket higher than my head. Many hazelnut burs now look rough and reddish about the base. Tobacco-pipe much blackened, out a long time.

I find, at the shallow stone wharf shore, three balls in good condition, walking about half the length of that shore. Methinks it was about a week earlier than this that they were found last year. There is on the surface of the water, washed up and floating about, a good deal of the eriocaulon, loosened up, perhaps, by pouts or other creatures, and also some other *fine* weeds with it. Yet the eriocaulon has but just begun to bloom! So also the vallisneria has washed up some time in river. There is also a very fine rush (?) on the bottom there like hair. Is that a little submerged kind of utricularia or ranunculus on the sandy bottom in shallow water there, looking thin and dissolving from above, like a conferva? — like little regular green masses of conferva?

The red lilies are completely out of bloom now at Smith's meadow pasture, but the yellow ones are still very abundant in the meadows. The *Ranunculus Purshii* is now very hard to meet with. Saw one double

[1] *Arguta* var. *juncea.*

flower with sixteen petals (at least) in two rows. Time to get seeds of it. Hardhack well out, how long? The small purple fringed orchis, apparently three or four days at least. The fall has already come to skunk-cabbage and hellebore. Their yellow and black decaying leaves and stems now cover the floor of the swamps which they recently clothed in early green. The *Lobelia Dortmanna* still, but no full spikes. It is apparently the worse for the wear. The oldest stems of it are covered here and there with apparently the red ova of some insect. Some *Gnaphalium uliginosum* going to seed; how long?

July 25. Friday. A. M. — Up river to see hypericums out.

Lycopus Virginicus, with its runners, perhaps some days, in Hosmer Flat Meadow. Whorled utricularia very abundantly out, apparently in its prime. *Lysimachia ciliata* some days. The *Hieracium Canadense* grows by the road fence in Potter's hydrocotyle field, some seven or eight inches high, in dense tufts!

The haymakers getting in the hay from Hubbard's meadow tell me the cock says we are going to have a long spell of dry weather or else very wet. "Well, there's some difference between them," I answer; "how do you know it?" "I just heard a cock crow at noon, and that's a sure sign it will either be very dry or very wet."

The *Hypericum perforatum*, *corymbosum*, and *ellipticum* are not open this forenoon, but the *angulosum*, *Canadense*, *mutilum*, and *Sarothra* are partly curled up

(their petals) even by 9 A. M.; perhaps because it is very warm, for day before yesterday, methinks, I saw the *mutilum* and *Sarothra* open later.

The street is now strewn with bark under the buttonwood at the brick house. Has not the hot weather taken the bark off?

The air begins to be thick and almost smoky.

July 26. Saturday. 5 A. M. — Up Assabet.

The sun's disk is seen round and red for a long distance above the horizon, through the thick but cloudless atmosphere, threatening heat, — hot, dry weather.

At five the lilies had not opened, but began about 5.15 and were abundantly out at six.

Arranged the hypericums in bottles this morning and watched their opening.

The *H. angulosum* (?) has a pod one-celled (with three parietal placentæ), conical, oblong, acute, at length longer than the sepals, purple. (The *Canadense* has from three to five (!) placentæ and the *mutilum* three to four (!), as I find, notwithstanding Gray.) Styles three, short, distinct, and spreading; stamens twenty, more or less, obscurely clustered. Petals oblong. (Do not see the single lateral tooth mentioned by Eaton.) Corolla twelve to fourteen fortieths of an inch in diameter. It is strict, slender, ten to twenty inches high; stem sharply four-angled, like *Canadense*, and cyme as naked or more so. The large ones make a singularly *compact* (flat-topped) corymb, of many narrow pods at last. Leaves oblong-lanceolate or linear-lanceolate, commonly blunt, but often gradually tapering and acute,

broadest near the base and clasping, one to one and a half inches long by one eighth to three eighths wide, black-dotted beneath. Ground neither very dry nor very moist. It differs from *Canadense*, which it resembles, in being a larger plant every way, narrower in proportion to height, having more stamens, and in the form of its leaves.

Corolla of *mutilum* nine to eleven fortieths of an inch in diameter; *Canadense*, twelve to thirteen fortieths; *corymbosum* eighteen fortieths.

The *corymbosum* in chamber shut up at night. All but *Sarothra*, which *may* not be advanced enough, (I have no *elodea*), opened by 5 A. M., *corymbosum* and *angulosum* very fairly; but *mutilum*, *Canadense*, and *angulosum* curled and shut up by 9 A. M.!! The *corymbosum* shut up in afternoon. The *perforatum* and *ellipticum* alone were open all day. The four lesser ones are very shy to open and remain open very little while, this weather at least. I suspect that in the fields, also, they are open only very early or on cloudy days. *H. Canadense* and *mutilum* are often fifteen inches high.

The largest and most conspicuous purple pods are those of the *ellipticum*. Those of the *angulosum* and *Canadense* are smaller and more pointed; are also purple, and the *mutilum* perhaps duller purple and less conspicuous.

The pod of the *ellipticum*, when cut, smells like a bee. The united styles arm it like a beak or spine. This appears to be the most nearly out of bloom of all. I am surprised that Gray says it is somewhat four-angled. It is distinctly two-angled and round between.

The Hubbard aster may be the *A. Tradescanti*.[1]

The large potamogeton off Dodd's seems to be the *natans*, from size of nutlets, etc. Then there is the second, off Clamshell, a long time out.[2] And the third, *heterophyllus* (?), or what I have called *hybridus*, also long out.

Drank up the last of my birch wine. It is an exceedingly grateful drink now, especially the aromatic, mead-like, apparently checkerberry-flavored one, which on the whole I think must be the black birch. It is a surprisingly high-flavored drink, thus easily obtained, and considering that it had so little taste at first. Perhaps it would have continued to improve.

P. M. — To Poorhouse Pasture.

Nettle, some time. *Ambrosia botrys*, apparently a few days. *A. Radula*, ditch by pasture, several days apparently. *Lycopus sinuatus*, some time.

I see *young* larks fly pretty well before me.

Smaller bur-reed (*Sparganium Americanum*), judging from form of stigma (ovate and oblique), yet the leaves are almost entirely concave (!), Stow's ditch. Is this the same with that in river? How long?

It is very still and sultry this afternoon, at 6 P. M. even. I cannot even sit down in the pasture for want of air, but must keep up and moving, else I should suffocate. Thermometer ninety-seven and ninety-eight to-day. The pig pants and melts in his pen, and water must be cast on him.

---

[1] *Vide* Aug. 21, 1854.
[2] Observed yesterday. *Vide* Aug. 3d.

Vol. VIII

Agassiz says he has discovered that the haddock, *a deep-sea fish*, is viviparous.

July 27. *Lobelia cardinalis*, three or four days, with similar white glands (?) on edges of leaves as in *L. spicata*. Why is not this noticed? *Cornus sericea* about done.

As I was paddling by Dodge's Brook, a great devil's-needle lit on my paddle, between my hands. It was about three inches long and three and a half in spread of wings, without spots, black and yellow, with green eyes (?). It kept its place within a few inches of my eyes, while I was paddling some twenty-five rods against a strong wind, clinging closely. Perhaps it chose that place for coolness this hot day.

To-day, as yesterday, it is more comfortable to be walking or paddling at 2 and 3 P. M., when there is wind, but at five the wind goes down and it is very still and suffocating.

I afterward saw other *great* devil's-needles, the forward part of their bodies light-blue and very stout.

The *Stellaria longifolia* is out of bloom and drying up. *Vide* some of this date pressed.

At Bath Place, above, many yellow lily pads are left high and dry for a long time, in the zizania hollow, a foot or more above the dry sand, yet with very firm and healthy green leaves, almost the only ones not eaten by insects now.

This river is quite low. The yellow lilies stand up seven or eight inches above the water, and, opposite

to Merriam's, the rocks show their brown backs very thick (though some are concealed), like sheep and oxen lying down and chewing the cud in a meadow. I frequently run on to one — glad when it 's the smooth side — and am tilted up this way or that, or spin round as on a central pivot. They bear the red or blue paint from many a boat, and here their moss has been rubbed off.

Ceratophyllum is now apparently in bloom commonly, with its crimson-dotted involucre.

I am surprised to find kalmiana lilies scattered thinly all along the Assabet, a few *small*, commonly reddish pads in middle of river, but I see no flowers. It is their great bluish waved (some green) radical leaves which I had mistaken for those of the heart-leaf, the floating leaves being so small. These and vallisneria washed up some time. The radical leaves of the heart-leaf are very small and rather triangular.

I see, on a rock in midstream, a peetweet within a foot of a turtle, both eying me anxiously within two rods, but not minding each other.

Zizania scarce out some days at least.

July 28. At 1.30 a thunder-shower, which was much needed, the corn having rolled and trees suffered.

3.30 P. M. — To Climbing Fern.

Virgin's-bower, apparently two or three days. *Nabalus albus*, a day or two.

Sand cherry ripe. The fruit droops in umble-like clusters, two to four peduncles together, on each side the

axil of a branchlet or a leaf. Emerson and Gray call it dark-red. It is black when ripe. Emerson, Gray, and Bigelow speak of it as rare in this State! It is common enough here. I have seen it as abundant as anywhere on Weir (or Ware) Hill in Sudbury, Bigelow's own town.[1] Cherry three eighths of an inch [in] diameter, peduncle seven sixteenths long. Emerson calls it eatable! On Linnæa Hill. By factory road clearing, the small rough sunflower, two or three days. *Gerardia flava*, apparently several days. *Cicuta bulbosa*, several days. Richweed at Brown's oak, several days (since 16th; say 22d).

July 29. Rhexia. Probably would be earlier if not mowed down. What I have called *Hieracium Gronovii*, with three cauline leaves and without veins, has achenia like *H. venosum;* so I will give it up. Its radical leaves are very hairy beneath, especially along midrib. Another smart rain, with lightning.

Pratt gave me a chimney swallow's nest, which he says fell down Wesson's chimney with young in it two or three days ago. As it comes to me, it is in the form of the segment of the circumference of a sphere whose diameter is three and a half inches, the segment being two plus wide, one side, of course, longer than the other. It bears a little soot on the inner side. It may have been placed against a slanting part of the chimney, or perhaps some of the outer edge is broken off. It is composed wholly of stout twigs, one to two inches long, one sixteenth to one eighth inch [in] diameter, held quasi cob-

[1] Was it not choke-berry?

fashion, so as to form a sort of basketwork one third to one half inch thick, without any lining, at least in this, but very open to the air. These twigs, which are quite knubby, seem to be of the apple, elm, and the like, and are firmly fastened together by a very conspicuous whitish semi-transparent glue, which is laid on pretty copiously, sometimes extending continuously one inch. It reminds me of the edible nests of the Chinese swallow. Who knows but their edibleness is due to a similar glue secreted by the bird and used still more profusely in building its nests? The chimney swallow is said to break off the twigs as it flies.

Pratt says he one day walked out with Wesson, with their rifles, as far as Hunt's Bridge. Looking downstream, he saw a swallow sitting on a bush very far off, at which he took aim and fired with ball. He was surprised to see that he had touched the swallow, for it flew directly across the river toward Simon Brown's barn, always descending toward the earth or water, not being able to maintain itself; but what surprised him most was to see a second swallow come flying behind and repeatedly strike the other with all his force beneath, so as to toss him up as often as he approached the ground and enable him to continue his flight, and thus he continued to do till they were out of sight. Pratt said he resolved that he would never fire at a swallow again.

Looked at a Sharp's rifle, a Colt's revolver, a Maynard's, and a Thurber's revolver. The last fires fastest (by a steady pull), but not so smartly, and is not much esteemed.

July 30. P. M. — To *Rudbeckia laciniata via* Assabet.
Amaranthus hybridus and *albus*, both some days at least; first apparently longest.

This is a perfect dog-day. The atmosphere thick, mildewy, cloudy. It is difficult to dry anything. The sun is obscured, yet we expect no rain. Bad hay weather. The streams are raised by the showers of yesterday and day before, and I see the farmers turning their black-looking hay in the flooded meadows with a fork. The water is suddenly clear, as if clarified by the white of an egg or lime. I think it must be because the light is reflected downward from the overarching dog-day sky. It assists me very much as I go looking for the cerato-phyllum, potamogetons, etc. All the secrets of the river bottom are revealed. I look down into sunny depths which before were dark. The wonderful clearness of the water, enabling you to explore the river bottom and many of its secrets now, exactly as if the water had been clarified. This is our compensation for a heaven concealed. The air is close and still. Some days ago, before this weather, I saw haymakers at work dressed simply in a straw hat, boots, shirt, and pantaloons, the shirt worn like a frock over their pants. The laborer cannot endure the contact with his clothes.

I am struck with the splendid crimson-red under sides of the white lily pads where my boat has turned them, at my bath place near the Hemlocks. For these pads, *i. e.* the white ones, are but little eaten yet.

Rudbeckia laciniata, perhaps a week. When I have just rowed about the Island a green bittern crosses in my rear with heavy flapping flight, its legs dangling, not observing me. It looks deep slate-blue above, yellow legs, whitish streak along throat and breast, and slowly plows the air with its prominent breast-bone, like the stake-driver.

July 31. *Thursday.* P. M. — To Decodon Pond.
Erigeron Canadensis, some time. Alisma mostly gone to seed. Thoroughwort, several days. Penthorum, a good while. Trichostema has now for some time been springing up in the fields, giving out its aromatic scent when bruised, and I see one ready to open.

For a morning or two I have noticed dense crowds of little tender whitish parasol toadstools, one inch or more in diameter, and two inches high or more, with simple plaited wheels, about the pump platform; first fruit of this dog-day weather.

Measured a *Rudbeckia hirta* flower; more than three inches and three eighths in diameter.

As I am going across to Bear Garden Hill, I see much *white Polygala sanguinea* with the red in A. Wheeler's meadow (next to Potter's). Also much of the *Bartonia tenella*, which has been out some days at least, five rods from ditch, and three from Potter's fence.

Went through Potter's *Aster Radula* swamp this dog-day afternoon. As I make my way amid rank weeds still wet with the dew, the air filled with a decaying musty scent and the z-ing of small locusts, I hear the distant

Vol. VIII

sound of a flail, and thoughts of autumn occupy my mind, and the memory of past years. Some late rue leaves on a broken twig have turned all a uniform clear purple.

How thick the berries — low blackberries, *Vaccinium vacillans*, and huckleberries — on the side of Fair Haven Hill! The berries are large, for no drought has shrunk them. They are very abundant this year to compensate for the want of them the last. The children should grow rich if they can get eight cents a quart for black-berries, as they do.

Again I am attracted by the hoary, as it were misty morning light on the base of the upper leaves of the velvety *Pycnanthemum incanum*. It is the most interesting of this genus here. The smooth sumach is pretty generally crimson-berried on the Knoll, and its lower leaves are scarlet-tipped (though there are some blossoms yet), but the *Rhus copallina* there is not yet out. See dense fields of the great epilobium now in its prime, like soldiers in the meadow, resounding with the hum of bees. The butterflies are seen on the pearly everlasting, etc., etc. *Hieracium paniculatum* by *Gerardia quercifolia* path in woods under Cliffs, two or three days. Elodea two and a half feet high, how long? The flowers at 3 P. M. nearly shut, cloudy as it is. Yet the next day, later, I saw some open, I think.

Another short-tailed shrew dead in the wood-path. Near Well Meadow, hear the distant scream of a hawk, apparently anxious about her young, and soon a large apparent hen-hawk (?) comes and alights on the very top of the highest pine there, within gunshot, and utters

its angry scream. This a sound of the season when they probably are taking their first (?) flights.

See yellow Bethlehem-star still.

As I look out through the woods westward there, I see, sleeping and gleaming through the stagnant, misty, glaucous dog-day air, *i. e.* blue mist, the smooth silvery surface of Fair Haven Pond. There is a singular charm about it in this setting. The surface has a dull, gleaming polish on it, though draped in this glaucous mist.

The *Solidago gigantea* (?), three-ribbed, out a long time at Walden shore by railroad, more perfectly out than any solidago I have seen. I will call this *S. gigantea*, yet it has a yellowish-green stem, slightly pubescent above, and leaves slightly rough to touch *above*, rays small, about fifteen.[1]

Mine must be the *Aster Radula* (if any) of Gray, yet the scales of the involucre are not appressed, but *rather* sub-squamose, nor is it *rare*. Pursh describes it, or the *Radula*, as *white*-flowered, and mentions several closely allied species.

Waded through the northernmost Andromeda Pond. Decodon not nearly out *there*.

Did I not see some kind of sparrow about the shore, with yellow beneath?

Mountain cranberries apparently full grown, many at least.

[1] *Vide* Aug. 2d.

X

AUGUST, 1856

(ÆT. 39)

Aug. 1. To *Ludwigia sphærocarpa.*

Burdock, several days at least. Erechthites, apparently two or three days, by Peter's Path, end of Cemetery, the middle flowers first. Crotalaria in fine lechea field, how long? Still out, and some pods·fully grown. Liatris will apparently open in a day or two. *Diplopappus umbellatus* at Peter's wall. *Desmodium Canadense,* some time; several great stems five feet high, a little spreading.

Since July 30th, inclusive, we have had perfect dog-days without interruption. The earth has suddenly [become] invested with a thick musty mist. The sky has become a mere fungus. A thick blue musty veil of mist is drawn before the sun. The sun has not been visible, except for a moment or two once or twice a day, all this time, nor the stars by night. Moisture reigns. You cannot dry a napkin at the window, nor press flowers without their mildewing. You imbibe so much moisture from the atmosphere that you are not so thirsty, nor is bathing so grateful as a week ago. The burning heat is tempered, but as you lose sight of the sky and imbibe the musty, misty air, you exist as a vegetable, a fungus. Unfortunate those who have not got their hay. I see them wading in overflowed meadows and pitching

the black and mouldy swaths about in vain that they may dry. In the meanwhile, vegetation is becoming rank, vines of all kinds are rampant. Squashes and melons *are said* to grow a foot in a night. But weeds grow as fast. The corn unrolls. Berries abound and attain their full size. Once or twice in the day there is an imperfect gleam of yellow sunlight for a moment through some thinner part of the veil, reminding us that we have not seen the sun so long, but no blue sky is revealed. The earth is completely invested with cloud-like wreaths of vapor (yet fear no rain and need no veil), beneath which flies buzz hollowly and torment, and mosquitoes hum and sting as if they were born of such an air. The drooping spirits of mosquitoes revive, and they whet their stings anew. Legions of buzzing flies blacken the furniture. (For a week *at least* have heard that snapping sound under pads.[1]) We have a dense fog every night, which lifts itself but a short distance during the day. At sundown I see it curling up from the river and meadows. However, I love this moisture in its season. I believe it is good to breathe, wholesome as a vapor bath. Toadstools shoot up in the yards and paths.

The Great Meadows being a little wet, — hardly so much as usual, — I took off my shoes and went barefoot some two miles through the cut-grass, from Peter's to Sphærocarpa Pools and backward by river. Very little grass cut there yet. The cut-grass is bad for tender feet, and you must be careful not to let it draw through your hands, for it will cut like a fine saw.

[1] And of course a great while.

I was surprised to see dense beds of rhexia in full bloom there, apparently on hummocks a rod in diameter left by the ice, or in long ridges mixed with ferns and some *Lysimachia lanceolata*, arrowhead, etc. They make a splendid show, these brilliant rose-colored patches, especially in the neighborhood of Copan. It is about the richest color to be seen now. Yet few ever see them in this perfection, unless the haymaker who levels them, or the birds that fly over the meadow. Far in the broad wet meadows, on the hummocks and ridges, these bright beds of rhexia turn their faces to the heavens, seen only by the bitterns and other meadow birds that fly over. We, dwelling and walking on the dry upland, do not suspect their existence. How obvious and gay to those creatures that fly over the meadow! Seen only by birds and mowers. These gay standards otherwise unfurled in vain.

Snake-head arethusa still in the meadow there. *Ludwigia sphærocarpa* apparently a week out, a foot and a half to two feet high.

Aug. 2. P. M. — To Hill.

A green bittern comes, noiselessly flapping, with stealthy and inquisitive looking to this side the stream and then that, thirty feet above the water. This antediluvian bird, creature of the night, is a fit emblem of a dead stream like this Musketicook. This especially is the bird of the river. There is a sympathy between its sluggish flight and the sluggish flow of the stream, — its slowly lapsing flight, even like the rills of Musketicook and my own pulse sometimes.

Very common now are the few green emerald leafets of the *Bidens Beckii*, which will ere long yellow the shallow parts.

Acalypha, apparently not long. Dodder, not long (not out 27th of July at railroad bridge), say four or five days. A three-ribbed goldenrod by small apple, by wall at foot east side of Hill (*S. gigantea?* or one of the two preceding), not nearly out. It differs from *my gigantea* apparently only in the leaves being *perfectly smooth* above and the stem smooth and pink [?] glaucous (excepting a *little* pubescence near the top). Very tall. *Vide* it by and by.

The lower leaves of some catnep are now of that delicate lake or claret color. Some waxwork leaves have felt the heat and slight drought. Their green is spotted with yellow, distinct yellow and green; others a very delicate clear yellow; others faded quite white.

Aug. 3. *Sunday.* P. M. — To Lee's Cliff by river.

Landing at flat shore. The sium and sarothra apparently now in prime. The central umbel of the sium going or gone to seed. The whorled utricularia is open all day. The *Hypericum ellipticum* is apparently out of bloom, there at least.

At length from July 30th inclusive the cloud-like wreaths of mist of these dog-days lift somewhat, and the sun shines out more or less, a short time, at 3 P. M.

The sun coming out when I am off Clamshell, the abundant small dragon-flies of different colors, bright-blue and lighter, looped along the floating vallisneria, make a very lively and gay appearance. I fancy these bright loops adorn or set forth the river like triumphal arches for my procession, stretching from side to side. The floating vallisneria is very thick at the shallow bends. I see many of its narrow, erect, spoon-shaped tops.[1]

Cornus alternifolia berries ripe, as I go from Holden Swamp shore to Miles Swamp. They are in open cymes, dull-blue, somewhat depressed globular, tipped with the persistent styles, yet already, as usual, mostly fallen. But handsomer far are the pretty (bare) red peduncles and pedicels, like fairy fingers spread. They make a show at a distance of a dozen rods even. Something light and open about this tree, but a sort of witch's tree nevertheless.

The purple utricularia abundant, but I did not chance to notice it July 25th. At Bittern Cliff again lucky enough to find *Polygonum tenue*, apparently out but a short time, say one week at most. Have marked the spot by a stone from the wall; further north than formerly. *Selaginella rupestris* (?) shows yellow fruit now at Bittern Cliff. *Gerardia quercifolia*, three to four feet high, out there, apparently two or three days. Yet none of the leaves I have are twice pinnatifid. Pennyroyal there, apparently some days. *Diplopappus corni- folius*, some time. *Desmodium acuminatum* a long time out and also gone to seed. *Lespedeza hirta*, Blackberry Steep, how long? High blackberries beginning; a few ripe. Parietaria a foot high, some time, under the slippery elm.

What is that tall (four feet), long-bearded grass, now nearly ripe, under this end of Lee's Cliff?

[1] Probably pickerel-weed.

I see blackened haycocks on the meadows. Think what the farmer gets with his hay, — what his river-meadow hay consists of, — how much of fern and osier and sweetgale and *Polygonum hydropiperoides* and rhexia (I trust the cattle love the scent of it as well as I) and lysimachia, etc., etc., and rue, and sium and cicuta. In a meadow now being mown I see that the ferns and small osiers are as thick as the grass. If modern farmers do not collect elm and other leaves for their cattle, they do thus mow and cure the willows, etc., etc., to a considerable extent, so that they come to large bushes or trees only on the edge of the meadow.

Two small ducks (probably wood ducks) flying south. Already grown, and at least looking south!! It reminds me of the swift revolution of the seasons.

Our river is so sluggish and smooth that sometimes I can trace a boat that has passed half an hour before, by the bubbles on its surface, which have not burst. I have known thus which stream another party had gone up long before. A swift stream soon blots out such traces.

Cirsium lanceolatum at Lee's Cliff, apparently some days. Its leaves are long-pointed and a much darker green than those of the pasture thistle. On the under sides of its leaves I noticed very large ants attending peculiar large dark-colored aphides, for their milch cows.

The prevailing willow off Holden Swamp is *sericea*-like, but the leaf is narrow, more shining above, and merely glaucous beneath, longer-petioled, the serratures not so much bent toward the point. The twigs

not nearly so brittle at the base, but bringing away strings of bark. Stipules probably fallen or inconspicuous. Can it be *S. petiolaris?* and is it the same with that above Hemlocks, north side? Or is it *S. lucida?* [1] *Vide* in press.

Edge of grain-field next Bittern Cliff Wood, common spurge; and, with it, apparently the same, half ascendant and covered or spotted with a minute fungus.

Aug. 4. P. M. — Carried party a-berrying to Conantum in boat.

Lespedeza violacea, perhaps the largest-leafed variety, leaflets one inch by one third inch, petioled, well out on side of Blackberry Steep.

Scare up a young apparently summer duck, floating amid the pads, and the same again, coming within gunshot. I think it young because it is not very shy.

Have heard the alder *cricket* some days. The turning-point is reached.

Conantum hillside is now literally black with berries. What a profusion of this kind of food Nature provides, as if to compensate for the scarcity last year! Fortunate that these cows in their pasture do not love them, but pass them by. The blackberries are already softening, and of all kinds there are many, many more than any or all creatures can gather. They are literally five or six species deep. First, away down in the shade under all you find, still fresh, the great very light blue (*i. e.* with a very thick blue bloom) *Vaccinium Pennsylvanicum* in heavy clusters, that early ambrosial fruit,

[1] No.

delicate-flavored, thin-skinned, and cool, — Olympian fruit; then, next above, the still denser bunches and clusters of *V. vacillans*, of various varieties, firm and sweet, solid food; and, rising above these, large blue and also shining black huckleberries (*Gaylussacia resinosa*) of various flavors and qualities; and over all runs rampant the low blackberry (*Rubus Canadensis*), weighing down the thicket with its wreaths of black fruit. Also here and there the high blackberry, just beginning, towers over all. You go daintily wading through this thicket, picking, perchance, only the biggest of the blackberries — as big as your thumb — and clutching here and there a handful of huckleberries or blueberries, but never, perchance, suspecting the delicious cool blue-bloomed ones under all. This favorable moist weather has expanded some of the huckleberries to the size of bullets. Each patch, each bush, seems fuller and blacker than the last. Such a profusion, yet you see neither birds nor beasts eating them, unless ants and the huckleberry-bug! I carried my hands full of bushes to the boat, and, returning, the two ladies picked fully three pints from these alone, casting the bare bushes into the stream.

Aug. 5. A. M. — On river.
Mikania a day or two. *Polygonum amphibium* in water, slightly hairy, well out. *Polygonum orientale*, how long?

P. M. — To house-leek *via* Assabet Bath.
Trichostema, maybe several days in some places. Nightshade berries, how long?

When I crossed the new stone bridge a great water adder lay on it, full five feet long and nearly as big round as my arm. It turned and ran along, with a coarse grating rustle, to the end of the railing, and then dropped deliberately head foremost from the last abutment, full nine feet, to the gravelly ground, amid the osiers, making a loud sound when he struck; at once took to the water, and showed his head amid the pads. I also saw another similar one at House-leek Rock.

Centaurea well out, how long? *Aster dumosus*, apparently a day or two, with its large conspicuous flower-buds at the end of the branchlets and linear-spatulate involucral scales.

A[t] haunted house site, as at Bittern Cliff grain-field, I see much apparent *Euphorbia maculata* semi-erect in the grass. *Eupatorium pubescens*, by Pear Path.

I now find an abundance of the clustered rubus ripe. It is not large and has a clammy, subacid taste, but some are very sweet. Clusters generally drooping.

Now, at 4 P. M. this dog-day, cloudy weather, the *Hypericum mutilum* is abundantly open in the *Solidago lanceolata* path, sometimes fifteen inches high, while the *Canadense* and *angulatum* are shut. *S. lanceolata*, some days. *S. nemoralis*, two or three days.

Choke-cherries near House-leek Rock begin to be ripe, though still red. They are scarcely edible, but their beauty atones for it. See those handsome racemes of ten or twelve cherries each, dark glossy red, semi-transparent. You love them not the less because they are not quite palatable. Along fences or hedgerows.

To my surprise one house-leek (apparently *Semper-*

vivum tectorum of Dewey) has shot up twenty-two inches high and is apparently nearly out,[1] though the petals are erect, not spread. The stem is clothed with the same thick leaves, only smaller and lessening upward and forming a column about one and a half inches in diameter (with the leaves). The top is a broad raceme (?), about eight inches wide and two thirds as long, of eleven long, spreading, and recurved branches, lined with flowers on the upper side only. These consist of twelve to thirteen lanceolate calyx-segments and as many still longer dull-purple petals and about twenty pistils within and short stamens around them. It is a strange but rather stately cactus-like plant. The children call the pretty clusters of radical leaves hen and chickens. In this case the radical leaves are withered, and a fusi-form root sustains the flower. This one is not on the bare rock, but lower amid the huckleberry bushes.

At the Assabet stone bridge, apparently freshly in flower, — though it may have been out nearly as long as the *androsæmifolium*, — apparently the *Apocynum cannabinum* var. *hypericifolium* (?). The tallest is four feet high. The flowers very small (hardly more than an eighth of an inch in diameter), the segments of the corolla not revolute but nearly erect. There are twenty to thirty flowers at end of a branch. The divisions of the calyx are longer than in the common, long ovate. Yet it differs from Gray's *hypericifolium* in having flowers rose-streaked within like the common, the cymes *not* shorter than the leaves, and the tube of the corolla rather longer than the divisions of the calyx. The leaves

[1] In house the 10th; say then Aug. 10.

are hardly more downy or heart-shaped below than the common. *Hypericifolium* is a separate species in Pursh and some others. And the branches are less ascending than the common, making an angle of about 62° with the stem (the four lower), while three of the lower of a common one make an angle of 44°.

Aug. 6. Copious and continuous rain in the night, deluging, soaking rain, with thunder and lightning, beating down the crops; and this morning it is cooler and clearer and windier.

P. M. — To Walden.

The wind, or motion of the air, makes it much cooler on the railroad causeway or hills, but in the woods it is as close and melting as before. *Solidago altissima*, a small specimen, a day or two. *Apios tuberosa*, some days. *Rubus hispidus* ripe. Middle umbels of the bristly aralia ripe. *Desmodium nudiflorum*, some time out at Peak. It is sometimes three feet high! Holly berries ripe. Clethra, how long? Some anychia shows green seed. *Desmodium rotundifolium*, some days at least. *Cynoglossum Morisoni* mostly gone to seed, roadside, at grape-vine just beyond my bean-field. Some is five feet high. *Aster macrophyllus*, apparently two or three days, at hillside, under beaked hazel. *Eupatorium purpureum* at Stow's Pool, apparently several days, but more common there the tall hollow one, *whorled to top*, also out. Hear a nuthatch. *Hieracium scabrum*.

Artificial, denaturalized persons cannot handle nature without being poisoned. If city-bred girls visit

their country cousins, — go a-berrying with them, — they are sure to return covered with blueberry bumps at least. They exhaust all the lotions of the country apothecary for a week after. Unnamable poisons infect the air, as if they were pursued by imps. I have known those who forbade their children going into the woods at all.

Aug. 7. Hemp, perhaps a week.

Heard this forenoon what I thought at first to be children playing on pumpkin stems in the next yard, but it turned out to be the new steam-whistle music, what they call the Calliope (!) in the next town. It sounded still more like the pumpkin stem near at hand, only a good deal louder. Again I mistook it for an instrument in the house or at the door, when it was a quarter of a mile off, from habit locating it by its loudness. At Acton, six miles off, it sounded like some new seraphim in the next house with the blinds closed. All the milkmen and their horses stood still to hear it. The horses stood it remarkably well. It was not so musical as the ordinary whistle.

P. M. — With a berry party, ride to Conantum.

At Blackberry Steep, apparently an early broad-leafed variety of *Desmodium paniculatum*, two or three days. This and similar plants are common there and may almost name the place. The *D. rotundifolium* is there abundant; also, beside, *Lespedeza hirta* and *capitata*, the elliptic-oblong *L. violacea* and the *angustata*, as also at Heywood Peak. All these plants seem to love a dry open hillside, a steep one. Are rarely upright, but spreading, wand-like. *Aster patens,* a day or more. Inula, some time. Mulgedium, perhaps a fortnight. *Eupatorium sessilifolium,* apparently about August 5th. I suspect that I see but one species of smooth-stemmed grape as yet.

I must contrast the *Galium circæzans* and *pilosum* (?) more carefully. *Vide* if the first ever has purple flowers. The only difference, perhaps, that I yet notice is that the leaves of the latter are scarcely three-nerved and are more rounded or obovate, and it is a later plant.

I see that common gall on goldenrods now on an *S. cæsia.*

The river has been raised by the rain, and water stands still in low grass ground. The leaves in low land, as of the mulgedium, are white with mildew, owing [to] the continued dampness of dog-days. One mulgedium at Corner Spring is at least ten feet high and hollow all the way.

Those who have weak eyes complain of the darkness of the late dog-days.

Aug. 8. Rain, lightning, and thunder all day long in torrents. The ground was already saturated on the night of the 5th, and now it fills all gutters and low grounds. No sooner has one thunder-shower swept over and the sky begun to light up a little, than another darkens the west. We were told that lightning cleared the air and so cleared itself, but now we lose our faith in that theory, for we have thunder[-shower] after thunder-shower and lightning is become a drug. Na-

ture finds it just as easy to lighten the last time as at first, and we cannot believe that the air was so very impure.

3.30 P. M. — When I came forth, thinking to empty my boat and go a-meditating along the river, — for the full ditches and drenched grass forbade other routes, except the highway, — and this is one advantage of a boat, — I learned to my chagrin that Father's pig was gone. He had leaped out of the pen some time since his breakfast, but his dinner was untouched. Here was an ugly duty not to be shirked, — a wild shoat that weighed but ninety to be tracked, caught, and penned, — an afternoon's work, at least (if I were lucky enough to accomplish it so soon), prepared for me, quite different from what I had anticipated. I felt chagrined, it is true, but I could not ignore the fact nor shirk the duty that lay so near to me. Do the duty that lies nearest to thee. I proposed to Father to sell the pig as he was running (somewhere) to a neighbor who had talked of buying him, making a considerable reduction. But my suggestion was not acted on, and the responsibilities of the case all devolved on me, for I could run faster than Father. Father looked to me, and I ceased to look to the river. Well, let us see if we can track him. Yes, this is the corner where he got out, making a step of his trough. Thanks to the rain, his tracks are quite distinct. Here he went along the edge of the garden over the water and muskmelons, then through the beans and potatoes, and even along the front-yard walk I detect the print of his divided hoof, his two sharp toes (*ungulæ*). It 's a wonder we

did not see him. And here he passed out under the gate, across the road, — how naked he must have felt! — into a grassy ditch, and whither next? Is it of any use to go hunting him up unless you have devised some mode of catching him when you have found? Of what avail to know where he has been, even where he is? He was so shy the little while we had him, of course he will never come back; he cannot be tempted by a swill-pail. Who knows how many miles off he is! Perhaps he has taken the back track and gone to Brighton, or Ohio! At most, probably we shall only have the satisfaction of glimpsing the nimble beast at a distance, from time to time, as he trots swiftly through the green meadows and corn-fields. But, now I speak, what is that I see pacing deliberately up the middle of the street forty rods off? It is *he*. As if to tantalize, to tempt us to waste our afternoon without further hesitation, he thus offers himself. He roots a foot or two and then lies down on his belly in the middle of the street. But think not to catch him a-napping. He has his eyes about, and his ears too. He has already been chased. He gives that wagon a wide berth, and now, seeing me, he turns and trots back down the street. He turns into a front yard. Now if I can only close that gate upon him ninety-nine hundredths of the work is done, but ah! he hears me coming afar off, he foresees the danger, and, with swinish cunning and speed, he scampers out. My neighbor in the street tries to head him; he jumps to this side the road, then to that, before him; but the third time the pig was there first and went by. "Whose is it?" he shouts. "It 's ours." He bolts into that neighbor's

yard and so across his premises. He has been twice there before, it seems; he knows the road; see what work he has made in his flower-garden! He must be fond of bulbs. Our neighbor picks up one tall flower with its bulb attached, holds it out at arm's length. He is excited about the pig; it is a subject he is interested in. But where is [he] gone now? The last glimpse I had of him was as he went through the cow-yard; here are his tracks again in this corn-field, but they are lost in the grass. We lose him; we beat the bushes in vain; he may be far away. But hark! I heard a grunt. Nevertheless for half an hour I do not see him that grunted. At last I find fresh tracks along the river, and again lose them. Each neighbor whose garden I traverse tells me some anecdote of losing pigs, or the attempt to drive them, by which I am not encouraged. Once more he crosses our first neighbor's garden and is said to be in the road. But I am not there yet; it is a good way off. At length my eyes rest on him again, after three quarters of an hour's separation. There he trots with the whole road to himself, and now again drops on his belly in a puddle. Now he starts again, seeing me twenty rods [off], deliberates, considers which way I want him to go, and goes the other. There was some chance of driving him along the sidewalk, or letting him go rather, till he slipped under our gate again, but of what avail would that be? How corner and catch him who keeps twenty rods off? He never lets the open side of the triangle be less than half a dozen rods wide. There was one place where a narrower street turned off at right angles with the main one, just this side our yard, but I could not drive him past that. Twice he ran up the narrow street, for he knew I did not wish it, but though the main street was broad and open and no traveller in sight, when I tried to drive him past this opening he invariably turned his piggish head toward me, dodged from side to side, and finally ran up the narrow street or down the main one, as if there were a high barrier erected before him. But really he is no more obstinate than I. I cannot but respect his tactics and his independence. He will be he, and I may be I. He is not unreasonable because he thwarts me, but only the more reasonable. He has a strong will. He stands upon his idea. There is a wall across the path not where a man bars the way, but where he is resolved not to travel. Is he not superior to man therein? Once more he glides down the narrow street, deliberates at a corner, chooses wisely for him, and disappears through an openwork fence eastward. He has gone to fresh gardens and pastures new. Other neighbors stand in the doorways but half sympathizing, only observing, "Ugly thing to catch." "You have a job on your hands." I lose sight of him, but hear that he is far ahead in a large field. And there we try to let him alone a while, giving him a wide berth.

At this stage an Irishman was engaged to assist. "I can catch him," says he, with Buonapartean confidence. He thinks him a family Irish pig. His wife is with him, bareheaded, and his little flibbertigibbet of a boy, seven years old. "Here, Johnny, do you run right off there " (at the broadest possible angle with his own course). "Oh, but he can't do anything." "Oh, but I only want him to tell me where he is, — to keep

sight of him." Michael soon discovers that he is not an Irish pig, and his wife and Johnny's occupation are soon gone. Ten minutes afterward I am patiently tracking him step by step through a corn-field, a near-sighted man helping me, and then into garden after garden far eastward, and finally into the highway, at the grave-yard; but hear and see nothing. One suggests a dog to track him. Father is meanwhile selling him to the blacksmith, who also is trying to get sight of him. After fifteen minutes since he disappeared eastward, I hear that he has been to the river twice far on [?] the north, through the first neighbor's premises. I wend that way. He crosses the street far ahead, Michael behind; he dodges up an avenue. I stand in the gap there, Michael at the other end, and now he tries to corner him. But it is a vain hope to corner him in a yard. I see a carriage-manufactory door open. "Let him go in there, Flannery." For once the pig and I are of one mind; he bolts in, and the door is closed. Now for a rope. It is a large barn, crowded with carriages. The rope is at length obtained; the windows are barred with carriages lest he bolt through. He is resting quietly on his belly in the further corner, thinking unutterable things.

Now the course recommences within narrower limits. Bump, bump, bump he goes, against wheels and shafts. We get no hold yet. He is all ear and eye. Small boys are sent under the carriages to drive him out. He froths at the mouth and deters them. At length he is stuck for an instant between the spokes of a wheel, and I am securely attached to his hind leg. He squeals deafen-

ingly, and is silent. The rope is attached to a hind leg. The door is opened, and the *driving* commences. Roll an egg as well. You may drag him, but you cannot drive him. But he is in the road, and now another thunder-shower greets us. I leave Michael with the rope in one hand and a switch in the other and go home. He seems to be gaining a little westward. But, after long delay, I look out and find that he makes but doubtful progress. A boy is made to face him with a stick, and it is only when the pig springs at him savagely that progress is made homeward. He will be killed before he is driven home. I get a wheelbarrow and go to the rescue. Michael is alarmed. The pig is rabid, snaps at him. We drag him across the barrow, hold him down, and so, at last, get him home.

If a wild shoat like this gets loose, first track him if you can, or otherwise discover where he is. Do not scare him more than you can help. Think of some yard or building or other inclosure that will hold him and, by showing your forces — yet as if uninterested parties — fifteen or twenty rods off, let him of his own accord enter it. Then slightly shut the gate. Now corner and tie him and put him into a cart or barrow.

All progress in driving at last was made by facing and endeavoring to switch him from home. He rushed upon you and made a few feet in the desired direction. When I approached with the barrow he advanced to meet it with determination.

So I get home at dark, wet through and supperless, covered with mud and wheel-grease, without any rare flowers.

To the eyes of men there is something tragic in death. We hear of the death of any member of the human family with something more than regret, — not without a slight shudder and feeling of commiseration. The churchyard is a *grave* place.

Aug. 9. Saturday. Notwithstanding the very copious rain, with lightning, on the night of August 5th and the deluge which fell yesterday, raising the river still higher, it rained again and again with very vivid lightning, more copiously than ever, last night, and without long intervals all this day. Few, if any, can remember such a succession of thunder-storms merged into one long thunder-storm, lasting almost continuously (the storm does) two nights and two days. We are surprised to see that it can lighten just as vividly, thunder just as loud, rain just as copiously at last as at first.

P. M. — Up Assabet.

The river is raised about two feet! My boat is nearly even full, though under the willows. The water stands nearly a foot over the highest part of the large flat rock by Island. There is more current. The pads are drowned; hardly one to be seen afloat; the utmost length of their tethers does not permit them to come within a foot or ten inches of the surface. They lay smoothly on the top before, with considerable spare coil beneath; now they strain in vain toward the surface. All the *Bidens Beckii* is drowned too, and will be delayed, if not exterminated for this year. The water is cool to the bather after so much rain.

The notes of the wood pewee and warbling vireo are more prominent of late, and of the goldfinch twittering over. Does the last always utter his twitter when ascending? These are already feeding on the thistle seeds.

Again I am surprised to see the *Apocynum cannabinum* close to the rock at the Island, several plants, apparently not more than ten days out; say July 25th, including the ones I saw before. The flowers of this are white, with divisions of the corolla erect or nearly so, corolla not one eighth of an inch wide, calyx-segments lanceolate, pointed, *as long as* the tube of the corolla. I now notice that *all* the branches are about equally upright, and hence the upper ones are much more upright than the upper ones of the *A. androsæmifolium*. The plant is inclined to be taller and narrower than that, perhaps because it grows by water. The leaves are more oblong or lanceolate and pointed, the downiness and petioles about the same with that of the common; in this case, none heart-shaped. The one found the 5th was between this and the common, a rose-streaked one, in fact colored like the common; this, a *white* one with still longer calyx-segments and no heart-shaped leaves. This is rather smooth. Say, then, for that of the 5th and this, they are varieties of the *A. cannabinum*.[1]

[1] At Astor Library, New York, Nov. 8th, 1856, in Richardson's *Flora Boreali*, etc., the leaves of *Apocynum cannabinum* in the plate are an inch or more beyond the flowers, and not hearted! Of the *A. hypericifolium*, the lower leaves are decidedly hearted, and the flowers are about terminal.

I scare up a couple of wood ducks separately, undoubtedly birds bred and dispersed about here. The rise of the river attracts them.

What I have called *Aster corymbosus* out a day, above Hemlocks. It has eight to twelve white rays, smaller than those of the *macrophyllus*, and a dull-red stem commonly. It differs from Gray's *corymbosus* in the achenia being apparently *not* slender, not opening in July, and there being no need of distinguishing it from *A. macrophyllus*; from his *cordifolius* in the rays *not* being numerous, nor the panicled heads very numerous (sometimes pretty numerous), and the rays not pale-blue. Perhaps I must call it *A. cordifolius*, yet the lower and principal petioles are naked (Gray makes them so commonly!), not at all winged, though the upper are. Found one individual at Miles Swamp whose lower petioles were winged. Its petioles (the lower) are only sometimes winged here. The flowers of *A. macrophyllus* are white with a very slight bluish tinge, in a coarse flat-topped corymb. Flowers nine to ten eighths of an inch in diameter. *A. cordifolius* flowers six eighths of an inch [in] diameter.

Aug. 10. Sunday. The weather is fair and clear at last. The dog-days over at present, which have lasted since July 30th.

P. M. — To Fair Haven Hill and Walden.

Fragrant everlasting, maybe some days.

Rhus copallina not yet for two or three days. The *Pycnanthemum incanum*, the handsomest of the pycnanthemums, grows also at the west end [of] the Knoll

with the *R. copallina*. All the upper leaves are equally hoary there in the light. The corymbs are an inch across, and the flowers large and very prettily purple-spotted. They are swarming with great wasps of different kinds, and bees.

Hear the wood thrush still.

I go across lots like a hunting dog. With what tireless energy and abandonment they dash through the brush and up the sides of hills! I meet two white foxhounds, led by an old red one. How full of it they are! How their tails work! They are not tied to paths; they burst forth from the thickest shrub oak lot, and immediately dive into another as the fox did.

There are more varieties of blackberries between the low and the high than I take notice of. *Vide* that kind in the Well Meadow Field.

The fine (early sedge?) grass in the frosty hollows about Walden (where no bushes have sprung up) looks like an unkempt head.

Vernonia, how long?

The river has been rising all day. It is between two and a half and three feet higher than ten days ago. Even the white umbels of the sium are drowned, except here and there where they stand over the water. It is within nine and a half inches of the top of Hoar's wall at 6 P. M. The meadows have quite a springlike look, yet the grass conceals the extent of the flood. It appears chiefly where it is mown. Yet a quarter part as much rain would have raised the river more in the spring, so much of it was soaked up by the thirsty earth.

Aug. 11. This morning the river is an inch and a half higher, or within eight inches of the top of Hoar's wall.

The other evening, returning down the river, I think I detected the convexity of the earth within a short distance. I saw the western landscape and horizon, reflected in the water fifty rods behind me, all lit up with the reflected sky, though it was a narrow [?] picture. A stroke of my oar and the dark intervening water was interposed like a dark, opaque wall. Moving my head a few inches up or down produced the same effect; *i. e.*, by raising my head three inches I could partially oversee the plane of the water at that point, which was otherwise concealed by the slightest convexity.

P. M. — Walk to Conantum with Mr. Bradford. He gives me a sprig of *Cassia Marilandica*, wild senna, found by Minot Pratt just below Leighton's by the roadside. How long? P. thought it in prime August 10th.[1] *Aster puniceus* a day or more. A new sunflower at Wheeler's Bank, this side Corner Spring, which I will call the *tall* rough sunflower; opened say August 1st (?). (I saw it out the 7th.) It does not correspond exactly to any described. Stem three to six feet high, branched at top, purple with a bloom, roughish, especially the peduncles. Leaves opposite, except a few small ones amid the branches, thick, ovate or ovate-lanceolate, taper-pointed, three-nerved, obscurely and remotely toothed, rough above, smooth and whitish below, abruptly contracted into margined petioles. Scales of the involucre lanceolate, taper-pointed, subequal, exceeding the disk,

[1] *Vide* 16th [*Journal*, vol. ix, p. 4].

ciliate; rays eight or nine, one and a half or more inches long, chaff black. Edge of meadow.

Measured a mulgedium, eight feet three inches long and hollow all the way. Some boy had fixed an archangelica stem so as to conduct the water at the spring close by. Elder-berries in a day or two. I see some *Hypericum angulosum* turned a delicate clear purple. *Polygonum dumetorum* at Bittern Cliff, one flower gone to seed (!); say day or two.

7 P. M. — The river has risen about two inches today, and is now within six inches of the top of Hoar's wall.

Aug. 12. 11 A. M. — To Hill.

The *Hypericum mutilum* is well out at this hour. The river is now at a standstill, some three feet above its usual level. The pickerel-weed is all covered, and lilies, and much of the button-bush and mikania. It is as great an accident as can befall these flowers.

It is novel to behold this great, full tide in which you perceive some current by the eddies, in which no snarl of weeds is seen. So different from that Potamogeton River, where you caught a crab at every stroke of the oar, and farmers drove their hay-carts across. Instead of watery gleaming fields of potamogetons in which the boatman was entangled, and drifting vallisneria on which the dragon-flies alighted, I see a deep full river on which vessels may float, and I feel at a distance from *terra firma* when on its bosom.

P. M. — To Moore's Swamp.

Gerardia purpurea, two or three days. The mulgedium in that swamp is very abundant and a very stately plant, so erect and soldier-like, in large companies, rising above all else, with its very regular long, sharp, elliptic head and bluish-white flowers.

Again I examine that very strict solidago, which perhaps I must call wand-stemmed. Perhaps it is only a swamp variety of *S. stricta*, yet the leaves are thicker and darker(?)-green, and the upper commonly broader, often elliptic, pointed, less recurved and not wavy. Stem and head is *now* commonly much more strict and branches more erect, and racemes less one-sided, but in larger and maturer ones they are at length recurving and forming a pyramid like *S. stricta*. Rays are fewer and broader, five or six; stem reddish, with apparently more branchlets or leafets in axils.[1]

Am surprised to see still a third species or variety of helianthus (which may have opened near August 1st, say only a week). Only the first flowers out. At edge of the last clearing south of spring. I cannot identify it. It has very short but not margined petioles; leaves narrower than yesterday's, and rough beneath as well as above. The outer scales of involucre a little the longest; but I think this of little importance, for the involucre of the *H. divaricatus* is very variable, hardly two alike; rays about ten. In some respects it is most like *H. strumosus*, but not downy beneath.[2]

[1] *Vide* Aug. 30th.

[2] It has decidedly thick leaves, unlike that of Aug. 29, and flowers two and a half or more inches in diameter.

The bruised leaves of these helianthuses are rather fragrant.

It is thick, smoky, dog-day weather again. Bradford speaks of the dog's-tooth violet as a plant which disappears early.

The *Aster patens* is very handsome by the side of Moore's Swamp on the bank, — large flowers, more or less purplish or violet, each commonly (four or five) at the end of a long peduncle, three to six inches long, at right angles with the stem, giving it an open look. Snake-head, or chelone. On the edge of the ditch opposite the spring, *Epilobium coloratum*, and also what I must call *E. palustre* of Willdenow and Pursh and Eaton. It is smooth or smoothish, leaves somewhat toothed or subdenticulate, peduncle one inch long, flowers white.

The most interesting domes I behold are not those of Oriental temples and palaces, but of the toadstools. On this knoll in the swamp they are little pyramids of Cheops or Cholula, which also stand on the plain, very delicately shaded off. They have burst their brown tunics as they expanded, leaving only a clear-brown apex, and on every side these swelling roofs or domes are patched and shingled with the fragments, delicately shaded off thus into every tint of brown to the edge. As if this creation of a night would thus imitate the weather-stains of centuries. Toads' temples. So charming is gradation![1]

Gerardia pedicularia, how long?

What a wilderness of weeds is Moore's Swamp now!

[1] [Channing, p. 290.]

Tall rough goldenrods, erechthites, poke, *Aster Radula*, dogwood, etc., etc. It looks as if the potatoes which grew there would be poisonous.

An arrowhead in Peter's Path. How many times I have found an arrowhead by that path, as if that had been an Indian trail! Perchance it was, for some of the paths we travel are much older than we think, especially some which the colored race in our midst still use, for they are nearest to the Indian trails. The Emerson children say that *Aralia nudicaulis* berries are good to eat.

The leaves of *Sericocarpus conyzoides* are fragrant when bruised. Black cherries ripe.

Labor Lost. — For one of this generation to talk with a man of the old school. You might have done a solid work the meanwhile with a contemporary. I thought of this when I saw Neighbor B., the worthy man! and thought of my interviews with him. If I could only get the parish clerk to read what I have to say to him!

Saw the primrose open at sundown. The corolla burst part way open and unfolded rapidly; the sepals flew back with a smart spring. In a minute or two the corolla was opened flat and seemed to rejoice in the cool, serene light and air.

Lespedeza capitata, not long.

The sarothra — as well as small hypericums generally — has a lemon scent.

The late rains have tried the roofs severely. Tenants have complained to their landlords, and now I see carpenters setting up their staging and preparing to shingle on various sides.

Aug. 13. P. M. — To Conantum.

Beck says of the small circæa (*C. alpina*), "Many botanists consider this a mere variety of the preceding." I am not sure but it is more deeply toothed than the large.[1] Its leaves are of the same color with those of the large at Bittern Cliff, but more decidedly toothed; *q. v.* Why does it not grow larger at Corner Spring?

The root of the *Polygala verticillata* also has the checkerberry odor.

In Bittern Cliff Woods that (apparently) very oblong elliptical leafed *Lespedeza violacea* (?), growing very loose and open on a few long petioles, one foot high by four or five inches wide. Is this because it grows in woods? It is not in bloom.

Is there not now a prevalence of aromatic herbs in prime? — The polygala roots, blue-curls, wormwood, pennyroyal, *Solidago odora*, rough sunflowers, horse-mint, etc., etc. Does not the season require this tonic?

I stripped off a shred of Indian hemp bark and could not break it. It is as strong as anything of the kind I know.

Aug. 14. P. M. — To Flint's Pond *via* Saw Mill Brook.

Aster Tradescanti, apparently a day or two. Hypopitys, just beyond the last large (two-stemmed) chestnut at Saw Mill Brook, about done. Apparently a fungus-like plant. It erects itself in seed. Gymnadenia nearer the brook, how long? Is that slender erect shrub near oak stump at Saw Mill *Cornus circinata*?[2]

[1] It is as far as I observe.   [2] *Viburnum nudum.*

Solidago odora abundantly out.

The low wood-paths are strewn with toadstools now, and I begin to perceive their musty scent, — great *tumbae*, or, as R. W. E. says, *tuguria*, — *crowding* one another by the path-side when there was not a fellow in sight; great towers that have fallen and made the plain shake; ponderous wheels that have lost their fellows, broken their axles, abandoned by the toady or swampy teamsters. Some whose eaves have been nibbled apparently by turtles. Ricketson says he saw a turtle eating a toadstool once. Some great dull-yellow towers, — towers of strength, to judge from their mighty columns, — like the South African honey-birds' (?) nests.

The recent heavy rains have caused many leaves to fall, especially chestnut. They already spot the ground, rapidly yellowing and very handsomely spotted. I never weary of their colors. I see those eye-spots on the low hickory leaves also. All the Flint's Pond wood-paths are strewn with these gay-spotted chestnut leaves, and the changing sarsaparilla leaves begin to yellow the forest floor.

Sedum Telephium, some time. Flowering blackberry[1] still. A short elliptic-leaved *Lespedeza violacea*, loose and open in Veery Nest Path, at Flint's Pond. In press.

On roadside heap at Emerson's, a portulaca with leaves one inch wide and seven petals (!) instead of five.

Meet a little boy with six young blind mice in his

[1] Raspberry?

Vol. VIII

hat, which Horatio Watts has given [him]. He did not find them till he came to fork over and turn the hay. There were six of these little brown blind meadow mice (I suppose *Arvicola hirsutus?*), with short tails and blunt muzzles and great heads, looking like little bull-dogs. The nest was open on the surface amid the roots of the grass; of dried grass, like a bird's, three and a half inches [in] diameter, with a gallery or two leading from it. Watts said these were the kind that clung to the mother! But why did they not? Sometimes find nine of them.

Aug. 15. *Friday.* P. M. — To Minot Pratt's.

Pratt is collecting his parsnip seed. This the second or third cutting. It takes three cuttings, the central umbellets ripening first. It takes a sharp knife not to shake out the seeds, and, as it is, enough to seed ten times the ground is lost. Almost every one is poisoned, says P., by this work. The skin comes off the back of the hand, making tanned hands look white-spotted. This from handling the parsnip in its second year only. Great rank poisonous-looking and really poisonous parsnips gone to seed. It is not quite time to cut the carrot seed.

END OF VOLUME VIII

The Journal of Henry D. Thoreau

VOLUME IX

(August, 1856 — August, 1857)

Hubbard's Bridge and Water-lilies

CONTENTS

Vol. IX

THE JOURNAL OF
HENRY DAVID THOREAU

VOLUME IX

I

AUGUST, 1856 (ÆT. 39)

Aug. 16. 8 A. M. — To Cassia Field.

Chenopodium hybridum, a tall rank weed, five feet at least, dark-green, with a heavy (poisonous?) odor compared to that of stramonium; great maple(?)-shaped leaves. How deadly this peculiar heavy odor! *Diplopappus linariifolius,* apparently several days.

Ambrosia pollen now begins to yellow my clothes.

Cynoglossum officinale, a long time, mostly gone to seed, at Bull's Path and north roadside below Leppleman's. Its great radical leaves made me think of smooth mullein. The flower has a very peculiar, rather sickening odor; Sophia thought like a warm apple pie just from the oven (I did not perceive this). A pretty flower, however. I thoughtlessly put a handful of the nutlets into my pocket with my handkerchief. But it took me a long time to pick them out [of] my handkerchief when I got home, and I pulled out many threads in the process.

At roadside opposite Leighton's, just this side his

barn, *Monarda fistulosa,* wild bergamot, nearly done, with terminal whorls and fragrance mixed of balm and summer savory.[1] The petioles are not ciliated like those on Strawberry Hill road.

Am surprised to find the cassia so obvious and abundant. Can see it yellowing the field twenty-five rods off, from top of hill. It is perhaps the prevailing shrub over several acres of moist rocky meadow pasture on the brook; grows in bunches, three to five feet high (from the ground this year), in the neighborhood of alders, hardhack, elecampane, etc. The lower flowers are turning white and going to seed, — pods already three inches long, — a few upper not yet opened. It resounds with the hum of bumblebees. It is branched above, some of the half-naked (of leaves) racemes twenty inches long by five or six wide. Leaves alternate, of six or eight pairs of leafets and often an odd one at base, locust-like. Looked as if they had shut up in the night. Mrs. Pratt says they do.[2] E. Hoar says she has known it here since she was a child.

The cynoglossum by roadside opposite, and, by side of tan-yard, the apparently true *Mentha viridis,* or spearmint, growing very rankly in a dense bed, some four feet high, spikes rather dense, one to one and a half inches long, stem often reddish, leaves nearly sessile. Say August 1st at least.

Some elecampane with the cassia is six feet high, and blades of lower leaves twenty inches by seven or nine.

[1] Apparently the same kind in Loring's yard.
[2] I observe it myself.

What a variety of old garden herbs — mints, etc. — are naturalized along an old settled road, like this to Boston which the British travelled! And then there is the site, apparently, of an old garden by the tanyard, where the spearmint grows so rankly. I am intoxicated with the fragrance. Though I find only one new plant (the cassia), yet old acquaintances grow so rankly, and the spearmint intoxicates me so, that I am bewildered, as it were by a variety of new things. An infinite novelty. All the roadside is the site of an old garden where fragrant herbs have become naturalized, — hounds-tongue, bergamot, spearmint, elecampane, etc. I see even the tiger lily, with its bulbs, growing by the roadside far from houses (near Leighton's graveyard). I think I have found many new plants, and am surprised when I can reckon but one. A little distance from my ordinary walk and a little variety in the growth or luxuriance will produce this illusion. By the discovery of one new plant all bounds seem to be infinitely removed.

Amphicarpæa some time; pods seven eighths of an inch long. *Mimulus ringens* four feet high, and chelone six feet high!

Am frequently surprised to find how imperfectly water-plants are known. Even good shore botanists are out of their element on the water. I would suggest to young botanists to get not only a botany-box but a boat, and know the water-plants not so much from the shore as from the water side.

White morning-glory up the Assabet. I find the dog's-bane (*Apocynum androsæmifolium*) bark not nearly so strong as that of the *A. cannabinum. Amaranthus hypochondriacus*, how long?

Minott says that the meadow-grass will be good for nothing after the late overflow, when it goes down. The water has *steamed* the grass. I see the rue all turned yellow by it prematurely. Bathing at Merrick's old place, am surprised to find how swift the current. Raise the river two feet above summer level and let it be running off, and you can hardly swim against it. It has fallen about fifteen inches from the height.

My plants in press are in a sad condition; mildew has invaded them during the late damp weather, even those that were nearly dry. I find more and other plants than I counted on. Very bad weather of late for pressing plants. Give me the dry heat of July. Even growing leaves out of doors are spotted with fungi now, much more than mine in press.

Aug. 17. P. M. — Walked with Minot Pratt behind his house.

Hypericum Canadense well out at 2 P. M. *Ludwigia alternifolia* still with red or scarlet calyx-lobes to the seed, roadside this side H. Shattuck's. *Aster miser* some time, turned purple. *A. longifolius* not long. *Hieracium Canadense*. Pratt describes finding one or two small yellowish plants on the edge of his field under the hill, like a polygala, but twice as large, stiff, and points of the flowers turned down [?]; leaf clover-like, three-foliate. Russell had suggested genista. He has in his garden the mountain fringe (*Adlumia cirrhosa*), which grows in Maine and he thought in

the western part of this State. Also wood geranium (*G. dissectum* (Big.)) from Fitzwilliam, though Gray seems to think that the *Carolinianum* has been mistaken for it. *Rhus copallina* already going to seed by the wall, apparently on what was W. E. C.'s ground. Saw again the red huckleberry and the white hardhack. I think this the lay of the land:—

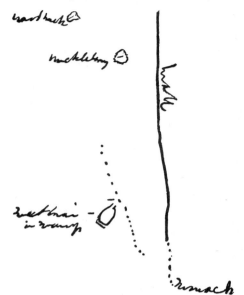

The red huckleberry is as easily distinguished in the green state as when ripe. It is then red with a white cheek, often slightly pear-shaped, semitransparent with a lustre, very finely and indistinctly white-dotted. I do

not perceive any very marked peculiarity in the bush, unless that the recent twigs are red. The last year's a peculiar ochreous color and the red buds in the axils larger. It might be called *Gaylussacia resinosa* var. *erythrocarpa*.

Aug. 18. P. M. — To Beck Stow's.

Now, perhaps, get thoroughwort. The lecheas in the Great Fields are now turning red, especially the fine one.

As I go along the hillsides in sprout-lands, amid the *Solidago stricta*, looking for the blackberries left after the rain, the sun warm as ever, but the air cool nevertheless, I hear the *steady* (not intermittent) shrilling of apparently the alder cricket, clear, loud, and autumnal, a season sound. Hear it, but see it not. It reminds me of past autumns and the lapse of time, suggests a pleasing, thoughtful melancholy, like the sound of the flail. Such preparation, such an outfit has our life, and so little brought to pass!

Hear a *faint*-warbling bird amid birches and pines. Clear-yellow throat and breast, greenish-yellow head, conspicuous white bar on wings, white beneath, forked tail, bluish legs. Can it be pine warbler? The note, *thus faint*, is not like it.

See black and white creeper.

Yellow Bethlehem-star yet, and indigo.

Saw yesterday and some days before a monster aphis some five eighths of an inch long on a huckleberry leaf. I mistook it, as before, for a sort of loose-spun cocoon. It was obovate, indistinctly ribbed, of

long, loose, white, streaming down, but being touched it recoiled and, taken off the leaf, rolled itself into a ball. The father of all the aphides. *Œnothera pumila* still.

Aug. 19. P. M. — To Fair Haven Hill.

Dog-day weather as for clouds, but less smoky than before the rains of ten days ago. I see *Hypericum Canadense* and *mutilum* abundantly open at 3 P. M. Apparently they did not bear the dry, hot weather of July so well. They are apparently now in prime, but the *Sarothra* is not open at this hour. The *perforatum* is quite scarce now, and apparently the *corymbosum;* the *ellipticum* quite done. The small hypericums have a peculiar smart, somewhat lemon-like fragrance, but bee-like.

The dangle-berries in Hubbard's Grove have a peculiar, not very pleasant, flavor and a tough skin. I see white buds on swamp-pink, just formed, also green checkerberries about grown.

In the radula swamp the sweet scent of clethra;[1] some peculiarly bright orange toadstools with a wavy edge. Now for spotted aralia leaves, brown pupils with yellow iris amid the green.

The whorled polygala is a plant almost universally dispersed but inconspicuous.

I spent my afternoon among the desmodiums and lespedezas, sociably. The further end of Fair Haven Hill-side is a great place for them.

All the lespedezas are apparently more open and

[1] Which lasts ten days at least.

delicate in the woods, and of a darker green, especially the violet ones. When not too much crowded, their leaves are very pretty and perfect.

Ivy berries dry and apparently ripe on the rocks (*Toxicodendron*).

Low blueberries, though some are a very little wilted, are very sweet and good as well as abundant. Huckleberries getting to be suspected. What countless varieties of low blackberries! Here, in this open pine grove, I pluck some large fresh and very sweet ones when they are mostly gone without. So they are continued a little longer to us.

Lobelia spicata still.

The wind rises and the pasture thistle down is blown about.

Lespedezas and desmodiums are now generally in prime. The latter are an especially interesting family, with commonly such delicate, spreading panicles, the plants themselves in their distribution so scattered and inobvious, and the open and spreading panicle of commonly verdigris-green flowers (in drying) make them to be unobserved when you are near them. The panicle of flowers often as large or larger than all the rest of the plant, with their peculiar chain-like seedpods, rhomboidal or semiorbicular, or with concave backs. They love dry hillsides. They are not so abundant, after all, but I feel an agreeable surprise as often as I come across a new locality for desmodiums. Rarely find one kind without one or two more species near, their great spreading panicles, yet delicate, open, and airy, occupying the August air. Like raking masts

with countless guys slanted far over the neighboring plants.

Some of these desmodiums, the *paniculatum*, *Marilandicum*, *nudiflorum*, *rigidum*, and *Dillenii*, are so fine and inobvious that a careless observer would look through their thin flowery panicles without observing any flower at all. The flowery beds of *D. Marilandicum* reveal themselves to me like a blue-green mist or gauze veil spread on the grass. I find them abundant in some places where I am sure there were none last year. They are outsiders, few and far between, further removed from man's walks than most plants, considering that there is such a variety of them. A dry, thin family of many species, nowhere abundant, yet widely dispersed, looking out from dry hillsides and exercising their dry wit on the race of man. The lespedezas and *D. Canadense*, more stiff and wand-like, nearer to man and his paths. The *D. rigidum*, *Dillenii*, etc., etc., more spreading and open, thin and fleeting and dispersed like the aborigines. They occupy the same dry soil, too.

When huckleberries are getting stale on dry hillsides, amid the huckleberry bushes and in sprout-lands and by paths you may observe them. The broad meshes of their panicles rarely catch the eye. There is something witch-like about them; though so rare and remote, yet evidently, from those bur-like pods, expecting to come in contact with some travelling man or beast without their knowledge, to be transported to new hillsides; lying in wait, as it were, to catch by the hem of the berry-pickers' garments and so get a lift to new

quarters. They occupy a great deal of room, but are the less obvious for it. They put their chains about you, and they cling like savage children to their mother's back or breast. They escape your observation, as it were under bare poles. You only notice as far up as their green sails are set, perchance, or to the crosstrees, not the tall, tapering, raking spars, whence are looped the life-lines and halyards. Or it is like that slanting mast and rigging in navy-yards where masts are inserted.

Aug. 20. Rain all night and to-day, making it a little chilly. Though I sit with open window, I should think it uncomfortably cool with it closed. Some must have a little fire.

Aug. 21. Rains still all day, and wind rises, and shakes off much fruit and beats down the corn.

The prevailing solidagos now are, 1st, *stricta* (the upland [1] and also meadow one which I seem to have called *puberula*);[2] 2d, the three-ribbed, of apparently several varieties, which I have called *arguta* or *gigantea* (apparently truly the last); 3d, *altissima*, though commonly only a part of its panicles; 4th, *nemoralis*, just beginning generally to bloom. Then there is the *odora*, 5th, out some time, but not common; and, 6th, the *bicolor*, just begun in some places.

The commonest asters now are, 1st, the *Radula*; 2d, *dumosus*; 3d, *patens*; 4th, say *puniceus*; 5th, *cordifolius*; 6th, *macrophyllus*; (these two a good while);

[1] That is, *arguta* var. *juncea*.   [2] That is, true *stricta*.

7th, say *Tradescanti;* 8th, *miser;* 9th, *longifolius;* (these three quite rare yet); 10th, probably *acuminatus*, some time (not seen); 11th, *undulatus;* 12th, *lœvis;* (these two scarcely to be seen yet).

N. B. Water so high I have not seen early meadow aster lately.

Aug. 22. Fair weather at last.

P. M. — Up Assabet.

Owing to the rain of the 8th and before, two days and two nights, the river rose to within six inches of the top of Hoar's wall. It had fallen about one half, when the rain began again on the night of the 20th, and again continued about two nights and two days, though so much did not fall as before; but, the river being high, it is now rising fast. The Assabet is apparently at its height, and rushing very swiftly past the Hemlocks, where it is narrow and choked with rocks, I can hardly row against it there. I see much hay floating, and two or three cocks, quite black, carried round and round in a great eddy by the side of the stream, which will ere long be released and continue their voyage down-stream. The water is backing up the main stream so that there is no current whatever in that, as far up as my boat's place, at least. When I rest on my oars the boat will not after any waiting drift down-stream. It is within three inches of the top of Hoar's wall at 7 P. M.

I notice three or four clumps of white maples, at the swamp up the Assabet, which have turned as red (dull red) as ever they do, fairly put on their autumnal hue. But we have had no dry weather and no frost, and this is apparently a premature ripening of the leaves. The water stands around and affects them as it does the weeds and grass, — steams them too. They, as it were, take these for the fall rains, the latter rain, accept their fates, and put on the suitable dress. This shows how little frost has to do with such changes, except as a ripener of the leaves. The trees are so ready for this change that only a copious rain and rise of the waters as in the fall produces the same effect. Also some red maples on hillsides have a crisped look for the same reason, actually ripening and drying without turning and without drought or frost.

I find that much of the faint warbling I hear nowadays is from apparently *the young* Maryland yellow-throats, as it were practicing against another spring, — half-finished strains. They are also more inquisitive and bold than usual, hopping quite near.

The creak of the mole cricket is heard along the shore.

Aug. 23. P. M. — To Walden.

I see a bed of *Antennaria margaritacea*, now in its prime, by the railroad, and very handsome. It has fallen outward on all sides ray-wise, and rests on the ground, forming [a] perfectly regular circle, four feet in diameter and fifteen inches high, with a dark ash-colored centre, twenty inches in diameter, composed of the stems, then a wide circumference, one foot or more broad, of dense pearly masses of flowers covered

with bees and butterflies. This is as regular as a wheel. So fair and pure and abundant.

Elder-berries, now looking purple, are weighing down the bushes along fences by their abundance. White goldenrod, not long commonly. Decodon getting stale at Second Andromeda Pond. Often the end has rooted itself, and the whole forms a loop four feet long and twenty or more inches high in the middle, with numerous branches, making it rather troublesome to wade through. Where the stems bend down and rest on the water, they swell to several times their usual size and acquire that thick, soft bark, and put forth numerous roots; not the extreme point, but a space just short of it, while that starts up again.

On R. W. E.'s hillside by railroad, burnt over by the engine in the spring, the erechthites has shot up abundantly, very tall and straight, some six or seven feet high.

Those singular crowded and wrinkled dry galls, red and cream-color mingled, on white oak shrubs, with their grubs in them.

On the west side of Emerson's Cliff, I notice many *Gerardia pedicularia* out. A bee is hovering about

one bush. The flowers are not yet open, and if they were, perhaps he could not enter. He proceeds at once, head downwards, to the base of the tube, extracts the sweet there, and departs. Examining, I find that every flower has a small hole pierced through the tube, commonly through calyx and all, opposite the nectary. This does not hinder its opening. The Rape of the Flower! The bee knew where the sweet lay, and was unscrupulous in his mode of obtaining it. A certain violence tolerated by nature.

Now for high blackberries, though the low are gone. At the Lincoln bound hollow, Walden, there is a dense bed of the *Rubus hispidus*, matting the ground seven or eight inches deep, and full of the small black fruit, now in its prime. It is especially abundant where the vines lie over a stump. Has a peculiar, hardly agreeable acid.

On this *Lespedeza Stuvei*, a green locust an inch and three quarters long.

The scent of decaying fungi in woods is quite offensive now in many places, like carrion even. I see many red ones eaten more or less in the paths, nibbled out on the edges.

7 P. M. — The river has risen four inches since last night and now is one inch above the wall, and there is a little current there. Probably, then, the Assabet has begun to fall, — if this has not risen higher than that.

J. Farmer says that he found that the gummed twig of a chimney swallow's nest, though it burned when held in a flame, went out immediately when taken out

of it, and he thinks it owing to a peculiarity in the gum, rendering the twig partly fire-proof, so that they cannot be ignited by the sparks in a chimney. I suggested that these swallows had originally built in hollow trees, but it would be interesting to ascertain whether they constructed their nests in the same way and of the same material then.

Aug. 24. 3 P. M. — Up river to Clamshell.

Polygonum tenue abundant and in bloom, on side of Money-Diggers' Hill, especially at south base, near apple tree. The choke-cherry by fence beyond spring, being dead ripe and a little wilted, is at length tolerable eating, much better than I ever tasted, but the stones are much in the way.

I was surprised to hear Peter Flood mention it as an objection to a certain peat meadow that he would have to dry the peat on the adjacent upland. But he explained that peat dried thus was apt to crumble, and so was not so good as that dried gradually and all alike on damper ground; so an apparent disadvantage is a real advantage, according to this.

It rained a little last night, and the river at 3 P. M. is at the same height as last night. It is not remembered when it was so high at this season. I have not seen a white lily nor a yellow one in the river for a fortnight. The river meadows probably will not be mown this year. I can hardly get under the stone bridge without striking my boat. Cardinal-flowers, etc., etc., are drowned before they are fairly in bloom.

River at same height as yesterday.

Aug. 25. P. M. — To Hill by boat.

Silvery cinquefoil now begins to show itself commonly again. Perhaps it is owing to the rain, springlike, which we have in August.

I paddle directly across the meadow, the river is so high, and land east of the elm on the third or fourth row of potatoes. The water makes more show on the meadows than yesterday, though hardly so high, because the grass is more flatted down. I easily make my way amid the thin spires. Almost every stem which rises above the surface has a grasshopper or caterpillar upon it. Some have seven or eight grasshoppers, clinging to their masts, one close and directly above another, like shipwrecked sailors, now the third or fourth day exposed. Whither shall they jump? It is a quarter of a mile to shore, and countless sharks lie in wait for them. They are so thick that they are like a crop which the grass bears; some stems are bent down by their weight. This flood affects other inhabitants of these fields than men; not only the owners of the grass, but its inhabitants much more. It drives them to their upper stories, — to take refuge in the rigging. Many that have taken an imprudent leap are seen struggling in the water. How much life is drowned out that inhabits about the roots of the meadow-grass! How many a family, perchance, of short-tailed meadow mice has had to scamper or swim!

The river-meadow cranberries are covered deep. I can count them as they lie in dense beds a foot under water, so distinct and white, or just beginning to have a red cheek. They will probably be spoiled, and this

crop will fail. Potatoes, too, in the low land on which water has stood so long, will rot.

The farmers commonly say that the spring floods, being of cold water, do not injure the grass like later ones when the water is warm, but I suspect it is not so much owing to the warmth of the water as to the age and condition of the grass and whatever else is exposed to them. They say that if you let the water rise and stand some time over the roots of trees in warm weather it will kill them. This, then, may be the value of these occasional freshets in August: they steam and kill the shrubs and trees which had crept into the river meadows, and so keep them open perpetually, which, perchance, the spring floods alone might not do. It is commonly supposed that our river meadows were much drier than now originally, or when the town was settled. They were probably drier before the dam was built at Billerica, but if they were much or at all drier than now originally, I ask what prevented their being converted into maple swamps? Maples, alders, birches, etc., are creeping into them quite fast on many sides at present. If they had been so dry as is supposed they would not have been open meadows. It seems to be true that high water in midsummer, when perchance the trees and shrubs are in a more tender state, kills them. It "steams" them, as it does the grass; and maybe the river thus asserts its rights, and possibly it would still to great extent, though the meadows should be considerably raised. Yet, I ask, why do maples, alders, etc., at present border the stream, though they do not spring up to any

Vol. IX

extent in the open meadow? Is it because the immediate bank is commonly more firm as well as higher (their seeds also are more liable to be caught there), and where it is low they are protected by willows and button-bushes, which can bear the flood? Not even willows and button-bushes prevail in the Great Meadows, — though many of the former, at least, spring up there, — except on the most elevated parts or hummocks. The reason for this cannot be solely in the fact that the water stands over them there a part of the year, because they are still more exposed to the water in many places on the shore of the river where yet they thrive. Is it then owing to the soft character of the ground in the meadow and the ice tearing up the meadow so extensively? On the immediate bank of the river that kind of sod and soil is not commonly formed which the ice lifts up. Why is the black willow so strictly confined to the bank of the river? What is the use, in Nature's economy, of these occasional floods in August? Is it not partly to preserve the meadows open?

Mr. Rice says that the brook just beyond his brother Israel's in Sudbury rises and runs out before the river, and then you will see the river running up the brook as fast as the brook ran down before.

Apparently half the pads are now afloat, notwithstanding the depth of the water, but they are almost all white lily pads, the others being eaten and decayed. They have apparently lengthened their stems somewhat. They generally lie with more or less coil, prepared for a rise of the water, and perhaps the length

of that coil shows pretty accurately to how great a rise they are ordinarily subject at this season.

I was suggesting yesterday, as I have often before, that the town should provide a stone monument to be placed in the river, so as to be surrounded by water at its lowest stage, and a dozen feet high, so as to rise above it at its highest stage; on this feet and inches to be permanently marked; and it be made some one's duty to record each high or low stage of the water. Now, when we have a remarkable freshet, we cannot tell surely whether it is higher than the one thirty or sixty years ago or not. It would be not merely interesting, but often practically valuable, to know this. Reuben Rice was telling me to-night that the great freshet of two or three years ago came, according to his brother Israel, within two inches of one that occurred about forty years ago. I asked how he knew. He said that the former one took place early (February?), and the surface froze so that boys skated on it, and the ice marked a particular apple tree, girdled it, so that it is seen to this day. But we wish to speak more confidently than this allows. It is important when building a causeway, or a bridge, or a house even, in some situations, to know exactly how high the river has ever risen. It would need to be a very large stone or pile of stones, which the ice could not move or break. Perhaps one corner of a bridge abutment would do.

Rice killed a woodchuck to-day that was shearing off his beans. He was very fat.

I cross the meadows in the face of a thunder-storm

rising very dark in the north. There were several boats out, but their crews soon retreated homeward before the approaching storm. It came on rapidly, with vivid lightning striking the northern earth and heavy thunder following. Just before, and in the shadow of, the cloud, I saw, advancing majestically with wide circles over the meadowy flood, a fish hawk and, apparently, a black eagle (maybe a young white-head). The first, with slender curved wings and silvery breast, four or five hundred feet high, watching the water while he circled slowly southwesterly. What a vision that could detect a fish at that distance! The latter, with broad black wings and broad tail, thus: hovered only about one hundred feet high; evidently a different species, and what else but an eagle? They soon disappeared southwest, cutting off a bend. The thunder-shower passed off to the southeast.

Aug. 26. Tuesday. More wind and quite cold this morning, but very bright and sparkling, autumn-like air, reminding of frosts to be apprehended,[1] also tempting abroad to adventure. The fall cricket — or is it alder locust? —sings the praises of the day.

So about 9 A. M. up river to Fair Haven Pond.

The flooded meadow, where the grasshoppers cling to the grass so thickly, is alive with swallows skimming just over the surface amid the grass-tops and *apparently* snapping up insects there. Are they catch-

[1] We see no effects of frost yet in garden, but hear a rumor of a little somewhere. First muskmelon gathered.

ing the grasshoppers as they cling to bare poles? (I see the swallows equally thick there at 5 P. M. when I return also.) River slowly falling. The most conspicuous weed rising above the water is the wool-grass, with its great, rich, seedy heads, which rise from a few inches to a foot above at present, as I push over the uncut meadows. I see many white lilies fairly and freshly in bloom after all this flood, though it looks like a resurrection. The wind is northwest, apparently by west, and I sail before it and under Hubbard's Bridge. The red maples of Potter's Swamp show a dull-purple blush and sometimes a low scarlet bough, the effect evidently of the rain ripening them.

Rice told me about their crossing the causeway from Wayland to Sudbury some sixty years ago in a freshet which he could just remember, in a half-hogshead tub, used for scalding pigs, having nailed some boards on the bottom to keep it from upsetting. It was too deep for a team.

We begin to apprehend frosts before the melons are ripe!

A blue heron sails away from a pine at Holden Swamp shore and alights on the meadow above. Again he flies, and alights on the hard Conantum side, where at length I detect him standing far away stake-like (his body concealed), eying me and depending on his stronger vision.

The desmodium flowers are pure purple, rose-purple in the morning when quite fresh, excepting the two green spots. The *D. rotundifolium* also has the two green (or in its case greenish) spots on its very large

flower. These desmodiums are so fine and inobvious that it is difficult to detect them. I go through a grove in vain, but when I get away, find my coat covered with their pods. They found me, though I did not them. The round-leafed desmodium has sometimes seven pods and large flowers still fresh.

The *Lespedeza Stuvei* is very abundant on Blackberry Steep, two and a half to three feet high. It has a looser top and less dense spikes than the *hirta.* It gives a pink hue to the hillside. The *L. violacea* is smaller and much more violet, the *hirta* more white. *Galium pilosum* still common; and *Desmodium acuminatum* still by rock on Blackberry Steep. This to be added to the desmodiums of this place.

As I stand there, a young male goldfinch darts away with a twitter from a spear thistle top close to my side, and, alighting near, makes frequent returns as near to me and the thistle as it dares pass, not yet knowing man well enough to fear him.

I rest and take my lunch on Lee's Cliff, looking toward Baker Farm. What is a New England landscape this sunny August day? A weather-painted house and barn, with an orchard by its side, in midst of a sandy field surrounded by green woods, with a small blue lake on one side. A sympathy between the color of the weather-painted house and that of the lake and sky. I speak not of a country road between its fences, for this house lies off one, nor do I commonly approach them from this side. The weather-painted house. This is the New England color, homely but fit as that of a toadstool. What matter though this one has not

been inhabited for thirty years? Methinks I hear the crow of a cock come up from its barn-yard.

I think I hear the pine warbler's note in the woods behind me. Hear a plain *phebe* note from a chickadee. Bluets still. Epilobium down flies abundantly on hillsides. I gather a bundle of pennyroyal; it grows largest and rankest high and close under these rocks, amid the loose stones. I tie my bundle with the purple bark of the poke-weed.

Sailed across to Bee Tree Hill. This hillside, laid bare two years ago and partly last winter, is almost covered with the *Aster macrophyllus*, now in its prime. It grows large and rank, two feet high. On one I count seventeen central flowers withered, one hundred and thirty in bloom, and half as many buds. As I looked down from the hilltop over the sprout-land, its rounded grayish tops amid the bushes I mistook for gray, lichen-clad rocks, such was its profusion and harmony with the scenery, like hoary rocky hilltops amid bushes. There were acres of it, densely planted. Also erechthites as abundant and rank in many places there as if it had been burnt over! So it does not necessarily imply fire. I thought I was looking down on gray, lichen-clad rocky summits on which a few bushes thinly grew. These rocks were asters, single ones a foot over, many prostrate, and making a gray impression. Many leaves of shrubs are crisp and withered and fallen there, though as yet no drought nor frost. Nothing but rain can have done it.

Aspen leaves are blackened. Stonecrop still. Another monster aphis on a huckleberry leaf. *Galium triflorum* still. See a great many young oaks and shrub oaks stripped by caterpillars of different kinds now.

Last Friday (the 22d) afternoon (when I was away), Father's pig got out again and took to the riverside. The next day he was heard from, but not found. That night he was seen on an island in the meadow, in the midst of the flood, but thereafter for some time no account of him. J. Farmer advised to go to Ai Hale, just over the Carlisle line. He has got a dog which, if you put him on the track of the pig not more than four hours' old, will pursue and catch him and hold him by the ear without hurting him till you come up. That's the best way. Ten men cannot stop him in the road, but he will go by them. It was generally conceded that the right kind of dog was all that was wanted, like Ai Hale's, one that would hold him by the ear, but not uselessly maim him. One or two said, "If I only had such a one's dog, I'd catch him for so much."

Neighbors sympathized as much as in them lay. It was the town talk; the meetings were held at Wolcott & Holden's. Every man told of his losses and disappointments in this line. One had heard of his pig last up in Westford, but never saw him again; another had only caught his pig by his running against a post so hard as to stun himself for a few moments. It was thought this one must have been born in the woods, for he would run and leap like a wolf. Some advised not to build so very high, but lay the upper board flat over the pen, for then, when he caught by his fore feet, his body would swing under to no purpose. One said you would not catch him to buy

a pig out of a drove. Our pig ran as if he *still* had the devil in him. It was generally conceded that a good dog was the desideratum. But thereupon Lawrence, the harness-maker, came forward and told his experience. He once helped hunt a pig in the next town. He weighed two hundred; had been out some time (though not in '75), but they learned where he resorted; but they got a capital dog of the right kind. They had the dog tied lest he should scare the pig too soon. They crawled along very carefully near to the hollow where the pig was till they could hear him. They knew that if he should hear them and he was wide awake, he would dash off with a grunt, and that would be the last of him, but what more could they do? They consulted in a whisper and concluded to let the dog go. They did so, and directly heard an awful yelp; rushed up; the pig was gone, and there lay the dog torn all to pieces! At this there was a universal *haw! haw!* and the reputation of dogs fell, and the chance of catching the pig seemed less.

Two dollars reward was offered to him who would catch and return him without maiming him. At length, the 26th, he was heard from. He was caught and tied in north part of the town. Took to a swamp, as they say they are inclined. He was chased two hours with a spaniel dog, which never faced him, nor touched him, but, as the man said, "tuckered him out," kept him on the go and showed where he was. When at a distance the pig stopped and faced the dog until the pursuers came up. He was brought home the 27th, all his legs tied, and put into his new pen. It was a very deep one.

Vol. IX

It might have been made deeper, but Father did not wish to build a wall, and the man who caught him and got his two dollars for it thought it ought to hold any decent pig. Father said he didn't wish to keep him in a well.

Aug. 27. P. M. — To Clintonia Swamp and Cardinal Ditch.

Unusually cold last night.

Goodyera pubescens, rattlesnake-plantain, is apparently a *little* past its prime. It is very abundant on Clintonia Swamp hillside, quite erect, with its white spike eight to ten inches high on the sloping hillside, the lower half or more turning brown, but the beautifully reticulated leaves which pave the moist shady hillside about its base are the chief attraction. These oval leaves, perfectly smooth like velvet to the touch, about one inch long, have a broad white midrib and four to six longitudinal white veins, very prettily and thickly connected by other conspicuous white veins transversely and irregularly, all on a dark rich green ground. Is it not the prettiest leaf that paves the forest floor? As a cultivated exotic it would attract great attention for its leaf. Many of the leaves are eaten. Is it by partridges? It is a leaf of firm texture, not apt to be partially eaten by insects or decayed, and does not soon wilt. So unsoiled and undecayed. It might be imitated on carpets and rugs. Some old withered stems of last year still stand.

On dry, open hillsides and fields the *Spiranthes gracilis* is very common of late, rising tall and slender,

with its spiral of white flowers like a screw-thread at top; sometimes fifteen inches high.

There are, close by the former, the peculiar large dark blue indigo clintonia berries of irregular form and dark-spotted, in umbels of four or five on very brittle stems which break with a snap and on erectish stemlets or pedicels.

See no fringed gentian yet. *Veronica serpyllifolia* again by Brister's Spring. Krigia yesterday at Lee's Cliff, apparently again, though it may be uninterruptedly. Tobacco-pipe still. The rhexia greets me in bright patches on meadow banks. *Ludwigia alternifolia* still. It is abundant in Cardinal Ditch, twenty rods from road. *Bidens frondosa*, how long? *Hypericum Canadense* and *mutilum* now pretty generally open at 4 P. M., thus late in the season, it being more moist and cooler.

The cardinals in this ditch make a splendid show now, though they would have been much fresher and finer a week ago. They nearly fill the ditch for thirty-five rods perfectly straight, about three feet high. I count at random ten in one square foot, and as they are two feet wide by thirty-five rods, there are four or five thousand at least, and maybe more. They look like slender plumes of soldiers advancing in a dense troop, and a few white (or rather pale-pink) ones are mingled with the scarlet. That is the most splendid show of cardinal-flowers I ever saw. They are mostly gone to seed, *i. e.* the greater part of the spike.

Mimulus there still common.

Near the clintonia berries, I found the *Polygonatum*

pubescens berries on its handsome leafy stem recurved over the hillside, generally two slaty-blue (but dark-green beneath the bloom) berries on an axillary peduncle three quarters of an inch long, hanging straight down; eight or nine such peduncles, dividing to two short pedicels at end; the berries successively smaller from below upwards, from three eighths of an inch [in] diameter to hardly more than one eighth.

There are many wild-looking berries about now. The *Viburnum Lentago* begin to show their handsome red cheeks, rather elliptic-shaped and mucronated, one cheek clear red with a purplish bloom, the other pale green, *now*. Among the handsomest of berries, one half inch long by three eighths by two eighths, being somewhat flattish. Then there are the *Viburnum dentatum* berries, in flattish cymes, dull lead-colored berries, depressed globular, three sixteenths of an inch in diameter, with a mucronation, hard, seedy, dryish, and unpalatable.

The large depressed globular hips of the moss rose begin to turn scarlet in low ground.

Aug. 28. First watermelon.

P. M. — To tortoise eggs, Marlborough road.

Potentilla Norvegica again. I go over linnæa sprout-lands. The panicled cornel berries are whitening, but already mostly fallen. As usual the leaves of this shrub, though it is so wet, are rolled like corn, showing the paler under sides. At this season it would seem that rain, frost, and drought all produce similar effects. Now the black cherries in sprout-lands are in their

prime, and the black choke-berries just after huckleberries and blueberries. They are both very abundant this year. The branches droop with cherries. Those on some trees are very superior to others. The bushes are weighed down with choke-berries, which no creature appears to gather. This crop is as abundant as the huckleberries have been. They have a sweet and pleasant taste enough, but leave a mass of dry pulp in the mouth., But it is worth the while to see their profusion, if only to know what nature can do. Huckleberries are about given up, low blueberries more or less shrivelled, low blackberries done, high blackberries still to be had. *Viburnum nudum* berries are beginning; I already see a few shrivelled purple ones amid the light green. Poke berries also begun.

A goldfinch twitters away from every thistle now, and soon returns to it when I am past. I see the ground strewn with the thistle-down they have scattered on every side.

At Tarbell's andromeda swamp. A probable *Bidens connata* or small *chrysanthemoides*.

I open the painted tortoise nest of June 10th, and find a young turtle partly out of his shell. He is roundish and the sternum clear uniform pink. The marks on the sides are pink. The upper shell is fifteen sixteenths of an inch plus by thirteen sixteenths. He is already wonderfully strong and precocious. Though those eyes never saw the light before, he watches me very warily, even at a distance. With what vigor he crawls out of the hole I have made, over opposing weeds! He struggles in my fingers with great strength;

has none of the tenderness of infancy. His whole snout is convex, and curved like a beak. Having attained the surface, he pauses and warily watches me. In the meanwhile another has put his head out of his shell, but I bury the latter up and leave them.

Meanwhile a striped squirrel sits on the wall across the road under a pine, eying me, with his cheek-pouches stuffed with nuts and puffed out ludicrously, as if he had the mumps, while the wall is strewn with the dry brown husks of hazelnuts he has stripped. A bird, perhaps a thrasher, in the pine close above him is hopping restlessly and scolding at him.

June, July, and August, the tortoise eggs are hatching a few inches beneath the surface in sandy fields. You tell of active labors, of works of art, and wars the past summer; meanwhile the tortoise eggs underlie this turmoil. What events have transpired on the lit and airy surface three inches above them! Sumner knocked down; Kansas living an age of suspense. Think what is a summer to them! How many worthy men have died and had their funeral sermons preached since I saw the mother turtle bury her eggs here! They contained an undeveloped liquid then, they are now turtles. June, July, and August, — the livelong summer, — what are they with their heats and fevers but sufficient to hatch a tortoise in. Be not in haste; mind your private affairs. Consider the turtle. A whole summer — June, July, and August — is not too good nor too much to hatch a turtle in. Perchance you have worried yourself, despaired of the world, meditated the end of life, and all things seemed rushing to de-

struction; but nature has steadily and serenely advanced with a turtle's pace. The young turtle spends its infancy within its shell. It gets experience and learns the ways of the world through that wall. While it rests warily on the edge of its hole, rash schemes are undertaken by men and fail. Has not the tortoise also learned the true value of time? You go to India and back, and the turtle eggs in your field are still unhatched. French empires rise or fall, but the turtle is developed only so fast. What's a summer? Time for a turtle's eggs to hatch. So is the turtle developed, fitted to endure, for he outlives twenty French dynasties. One turtle knows several Napoleons. They have seen no berries, had no cares, yet has not the great world existed for them as much as for you?

Euphorbia hypericifolia, how long? It has pretty little white and also rose-colored petals, or, as they are now called, involucre. Stands six inches high, regularly curving, with large leaves prettily arranged at an angle with both a horizontal and perpendicular line. See the great oval masses of scarlet berries of the arum now in the meadows. Trillium fruit, long time.

The river being thus high, for ten days or more I have seen little parcels of shells left by the muskrats. So they eat them thus early. Peppermint, how long? May be earlier than I have thought, for the mowers clip it.

The bright china-colored blue berries of the *Cornus sericea* begin to show themselves along the river, amid their red-brown leaves, — the *kinnikinnic* of the Indians.

Aug. 29. Heavy rain in the night and this forenoon.
P. M. — To J. Farmer's by river.

The *Helianthus decapetalus*, apparently a variety, with eight petals, about three feet high, leaves petioled, but not wing-petioled, and broader-leaved than that of August 12th, quite ovate with a tapering point, with ciliate petioles, thin but quite rough beneath and above, stem purple and smoothish, Hosmer's bank, opposite Azalea Swamp. Fragrant everlasting in prime and very abundant, whitening Carter's pasture. Ribwort still. An apparent white vervain with bluish flowers, as blue as bluets even or more so, roadside beyond Farmer's barn.

Aug. 30. Rain again in the night, as well as most of yesterday, raising the river a second time. They say there has not been such a year as this for more than half a century, — for winter cold, summer heat, and rain.

P. M. — To Vaccinium Oxycoccus Swamp.
Fair weather, clear and rather cool.

Pratt shows me at his shop a bottle filled with alcohol and camphor. The alcohol is clear and the camphor beautifully crystallized at the bottom for nearly an inch in depth, in the form of small feathers, like a hoar frost. He has read that this is as good a barometer as any. It stands quite still, and has not been unstoppled for a year; yet some days the alcohol will be quite clear, and even no camphor will be seen, and again it will be quite full of fine feathery particles, or it will be partly clear, as to-day.

Bidens connata abundant at Moore's Swamp, how long? The aspect of some of what I have called the swamp *Solidago stricta* there at present makes me doubt if it be not more than a variety, the leaves are so broad, smooth (*i. e.* uncurled or wrinkled), and thick, and some cauline ones so large, almost *speciosa*-like, to say nothing of size of rays.

The *Aster puniceus* is hardly yet in prime; its great umbel-shaped tops not yet fully out. Its leaves are pretty generally whitened with mildew and unsightly. Even the chelone, where prostrate, has put forth roots from its stem, near the top.

The sarothra is now apparently in prime on the Great Fields, and comes near being open now, at 3 P. M. Bruised, it has the fragrance of sorrel and lemon, rather pungent or stinging, like a bee. *Hypericum corymbosum* lingers still, with *perforatum*.

I have come out this afternoon a-cranberrying, chiefly to gather some of the small cranberry, *Vaccinium Oxycoccus*, which Emerson says is the common cranberry of the north of Europe. This was a small object, yet not to be postponed, on account of imminent frosts, *i. e.*, if I would know this year the flavor of the European cranberry as compared with our larger kind. I thought I should like to have a dish of this sauce on the table at Thanksgiving of my own gathering. I could hardly make up my mind to come this way, it seemed so poor an object to spend the afternoon on. I kept foreseeing a lame conclusion, — how I should cross the Great Fields, look into Beck Stow's, and then retrace my steps no richer than

before. In fact, I expected little of this walk, yet it did pass through the side of my mind that somehow, on this very account (my small expectation), it would turn out well, as also the advantage of having some purpose, however small, to be accomplished, — of letting your deliberate wisdom and foresight in the house to some extent direct and control your steps. If you would really take a position outside the street and daily life of men, you must have deliberately planned your course, you must have business which is not your neighbors' business, which they cannot understand. For only absorbing employment prevails, succeeds, takes up space, occupies territory, determines the future of individuals and states, drives Kansas out of your head, and actually and permanently occupies the only desirable and free Kansas against all border ruffians. The attitude of resistance is one of weakness, inasmuch as it only faces an enemy; it has its back to all that is truly attractive. You shall have your affairs, I will have mine. You will spend this afternoon in setting up your neighbor's stove, and be paid for it; I will spend it in gathering the few berries of the *Vaccinium Oxycoccus* which Nature produces here, before it is too late, and *be paid for it also* after another fashion. I have always reaped unexpected and incalculable advantages from carrying out at last, however tardily, any little enterprise which my genius suggested to me long ago as a thing to be done, — some step to be taken, however slight, out of the usual course.

How many schools I have thought of which I might

go to but did not go to! expecting foolishly that some greater advantage or schooling would come to me! It is these comparatively cheap and private expeditions that substantiate our existence and batten our lives, as, where a vine touches the earth in its undulating course, it puts forth roots and thickens its stock. Our employment generally is tinkering, mending the old worn-out teapot of society. Our stock in trade is solder. Better for me, says my genius, to go cranberrying this afternoon for the *Vaccinium Oxycoccus* in Gowing's Swamp, to get but a pocketful and learn its peculiar flavor, aye, and the flavor of Gowing's Swamp and of *life* in New England, than to go consul to Liverpool and get I don't know how many thousand dollars for it, with no such flavor. Many of our days should be spent, not in vain expectations and lying on our oars, but in carrying out deliberately and faithfully the hundred little purposes which every man's genius must have suggested to him. Let not your life be wholly without an object, though it be only to ascertain the flavor of a cranberry, for it will not be only the quality of an insignificant berry that you will have tasted, but the flavor of your life to that extent, and it will be such a sauce as no wealth can buy.

Both a conscious and an unconscious life are good. Neither is good exclusively, for both have the same source. The wisely conscious life springs out of an unconscious suggestion. I have found my account in travelling in having prepared beforehand a list of questions which I would get answered, not trusting to my interest at the moment, and can then travel with the most profit. Indeed, it is by obeying the suggestions of a higher light within you that you escape from yourself and, in the transit, as it were see with the unworn sides of your eye, travel totally new paths. What is that pretended life that does not take up a claim, that does not occupy ground, that cannot build a causeway to its objects, that sits on a bank looking over a bog, singing its desires?

However, it was not with such blasting expectations as these that I entered the swamp. I saw bags of cranberries, just gathered and tied up, on the banks of Beck Stow's Swamp. They must have been raked out of the water, now so high, before they should rot. I left my shoes and stockings on the bank far off and waded barelegged through rigid andromeda and other bushes a long way, to the soft open sphagnous centre of the swamp.

I found these cunning little cranberries lying high and dry on the firm uneven tops of the sphagnum, — their weak vine considerably on one side, — sparsely scattered about the drier edges of the swamp, or sometimes more thickly occupying some little valley a foot or two over, between two mountains of sphagnum. They were of two varieties, judging from the fruit. The one, apparently the ripest, colored most like the common cranberry but more scarlet, i. e. yellowish-green, blotched or checked with dark scarlet-red, commonly pear-shaped; the other, also pear-shaped, or more bulged out in the middle, thickly and finely dark-spotted or peppered on yellowish-green or straw-

Vol. IX

colored or pearly ground, — almost exactly like the smilacina and convallaria berries now, except that they are a little larger and not so spherical, — and with a tinge of purple. A singular difference. They both lay very snug in the moss, often the whole of the long (an inch and a half or more) peduncle buried, their vines very inobvious, projecting only one to three inches, so that it was not easy to tell what vine they belonged to, and you were obliged to open the moss carefully with your fingers to ascertain it; while the common large cranberry there, with its stiff erect vine, was commonly lifted above the sphagnum. The grayish speckled variety was particularly novel and pretty, though not easy to detect. It lay here and there snugly sunk in the sphagnum, whose drier parts it exactly resembled in color, just like some kind of swamp sparrows' eggs in their nest. I was obliged with my finger carefully to trace the slender pedicel through the moss to its vine, when I would pluck the whole together. Like jewels worn on, or set in, these sphagnous breasts of the swamp, — swamp pearls, call them. One or two to a vine and, on an average, three eighths of an inch in diameter. They are so remote from their vines, on their long thread-like peduncles, that they remind you the more forcibly of eggs, and in May I might mistake them for such. These plants are almost parasitic, resting wholly on the sphagnum, in water instead of air. The sphagnum is a living soil for it. It rests on and amid this, on an acre of sponges. They are evidently earlier than the common. A few are quite soft and red-purple.

I waded quite round the swamp for an hour, my bare feet in the cold water beneath, and it was a relief to place them on the warmer surface of the sphagnum. I filled one pocket with each variety, but sometimes, being confused, crossed hands and put them into the wrong pocket.

I enjoyed this cranberrying very much, notwithstanding the wet and cold, and the swamp seemed to be yielding its crop to me alone, for there are none else to pluck it or to value it. I told the proprietor once that they grew here, but he, learning that they were not abundant enough to be gathered for the market, has probably never thought of them since. I am the only person in the township who regards them or knows of them, and I do not regard them in the light of their pecuniary value. I have no doubt I felt richer wading there with my two pockets full, treading on wonders at every step, than any farmer going to market with a hundred bushels which he has raked, or hired to be raked. I got further and further away from the town every moment, and my good genius seemed [to] have smiled on me, leading me hither, and then the sun suddenly came out clear and bright, but it did not warm my feet. I would gladly share my gains, take one, or twenty, into partnership and get this swamp with them, but I do not know an individual whom this berry cheers and nourishes as it does me. When I exhibit it to them I perceive that they take but a momentary interest in it and commonly dismiss it from their thoughts with the consideration that it cannot be profitably cultivated. You could not get a pint at one haul of a rake, and Slocum would not give

you much for them. But I love it the better partly for that reason even. I fill a basket with them and keep it several days by my side. If anybody else — any farmer, at least — should spend an hour thus wading about here in this secluded swamp, barelegged, intent on the sphagnum, filling his pocket only, with no rake in his hand and no bag or bushel on the bank, he would be pronounced insane and have a guardian put over him; but if he'll spend his time skimming and watering his milk and selling his small potatoes for large ones, or generally in skinning flints, he will probably be made guardian of somebody else. I have not garnered any rye or oats, but I gathered the wild vine of the Assabet.[1]

As I waded there I came across an ant-like heap, and, breaking it open with my hand, found it to my surprise to be an ant-hill in the sphagnum, full of ants with their young or ova. It consisted of particles of sphagnum like sawdust, was a foot and a half in diameter, and my feet sunk to water all around it! The ants were small and of a uniform pale sorrel-color.

I noticed also a few small peculiar-looking huckleberries hanging on bushes amid the sphagnum, and, tasting, perceived that they were hispid, a new kind to me. *Gaylussacia dumosa* var. *hirtella* (perhaps just after *resinosa*), though Gray refers it to a "*sandy* low soil" and says nothing of the hispid fruit. It grows from one to two feet high, the leaves minutely resinous-dotted — are not others? — and mucronate, the racemes long, with leaf-like bracts now turned conspicu-

[1] *Vide* [3] pages forward.

ously red. Has a small black hairy or hispid berry, shining but insipid and inedible, with a tough, hairy skin left in the mouth; has very prominent calyx-lobes.

I seemed to have reached a new world, so wild a place that the very huckleberries grew hairy and were inedible. I feel as if I were in Rupert's Land, and a slight cool but agreeable shudder comes over me, as if equally far away from human society. What's the need of visiting far-off mountains and bogs, if a half-hour's walk will carry me into such wildness and novelty? But why should not as wild plants grow here as in Berkshire, as in Labrador? Is Nature so easily tamed? Is she not as primitive and vigorous here as anywhere? How does this particular acre of secluded, unfrequented, useless (?) quaking bog differ from an acre in Labrador? Has any white man ever settled on it? Does any now frequent it? Not even the Indian comes here now. I see that there are some square rods within twenty miles of Boston just as wild and primitive and unfrequented as a square rod in Labrador, as unaltered by man. Here grows the hairy huckleberry as it did in Squaw Sachem's day and a thousand years before, and concerns me perchance more than it did her. I have no doubt that for a moment I experience exactly the same sensations as if I were alone in a bog in Rupert's Land, and it saves me the trouble of going there; for what in any case makes the difference between being here and being there but many such little differences of flavor and roughness put together? Rupert's Land is recognized as much by one sense as another. I felt a shock, a thrill, an agree-

able surprise in one instant, for, no doubt, all the possible inferences were at once drawn, with a rush, in my mind, — I could be in Rupert's Land and supping at home within the hour! This beat the railroad. I recovered from my surprise without danger to my sanity, and permanently annexed Rupert's Land. That wild hairy huckleberry, inedible as it was, was equal to a domain secured to me and reaching to the South Sea. That was an unexpected harvest. I hope you have gathered as much, neighbor, from your corn and potato fields. I have got in my huckleberries. I shall be ready for Thanksgiving. It is in vain to dream of a wildness distant from ourselves. There is none such. It is the bog in our brain and bowels, the primitive vigor of Nature in us, that inspires that dream. I shall never find in the wilds of Labrador any greater wildness than in some recess in Concord, *i. e.* than I import into it. A little more manhood or virtue will make the surface of the globe anywhere thrillingly novel and wild. That alone will provide and pay the fiddler; it will convert the district road into an untrodden cranberry bog, for it restores all things to their original primitive flourishing and promising state.

A cold white horizon sky in the north, forerunner of the fall of the year. I go to bed and dream of cranberry-pickers far in the cold north. With windows partly closed, with continent concentrated thoughts, I dream. I get my new experiences still, not at the opera listening to the Swedish Nightingale, but at Beck Stow's Swamp listening to the native wood thrush.

Vol. IX

Wading in the cold swamp braces me. I was invigorated, though I tasted not a berry. The frost will soon come and smite them on the surface of the sphagnum.

Consider how remote and novel that swamp. Beneath it is a quaking bed of sphagnum, and in it grow *Andromeda Polifolia, Kalmia glauca,* menyanthes (or buck-bean), *Gaylussacia dumosa, Vaccinium Oxycoccus,* — plants which scarcely a citizen of Concord ever sees. It would be as novel to them to stand there as in a conservatory, or in Greenland.

Better it is to go a-cranberrying than to go a-huckleberrying. For that is cold and bracing, leading your thoughts beyond the earth, and you do not surfeit on crude or terrene berries. It feeds your spirit, now in the season of white twilights, when frosts are apprehended, when edible berries are mostly gone.

Those small gray sparrow-egg cranberries lay so prettily in the recesses of the sphagnum, I could wade for hours in the cold water gazing at them, with a swarm of mosquitoes hovering about my bare legs, — but at each step the friendly sphagnum in which I sank protected my legs like a buckler, — not a crevice by which my foes could enter.

I see that all is not garden and cultivated field and crops, that there are square rods in Middlesex County as purely primitive and wild as they were a thousand years ago, which have escaped the plow and the axe and the scythe and the cranberry-rake, little oases of wildness in the desert of our civilization, wild as a square rod on the moon, supposing it to be uninhabited. I believe almost in the personality of such

planetary matter, feel something akin to reverence for it, can even worship it as terrene, titanic matter extant in my day. We are so different we admire each other, we healthily attract one another. I love it as a maiden. These spots are meteoric, aerolitic, and such matter has in all ages been worshipped. Aye, when we are lifted out of the slime and film of our habitual life, we see the whole globe to be an aerolite, and reverence it as such, and make pilgrimages to it, far off as it is. How happens it that we reverence the stones which fall from another planet, and not the stones which belong to this, — another globe, not this, — heaven, and not earth? Are not the stones in Hodge's wall as good as the aerolite at Mecca? Is not our broad back-door-stone as good as any corner-stone in heaven?

It would imply the regeneration of mankind, if they were to become elevated enough to truly worship stocks and stones. It is the sentiment of fear and slavery and habit which makes a heathenish idolatry. Such idolaters abound in all countries, and heathen cross the seas to reform heathen, dead to bury the dead, and all go down to the pit together. If I could, I would worship the parings of my nails. If he who makes two blades of grass grow where one grew before is a benefactor, he who discovers two gods where there was only known the one (and such a one!) before is a still greater benefactor. I would fain improve every opportunity to wonder and worship, as a sunflower welcomes the light.[1] The more thrilling, wonderful, divine

[1] [Channing, p. 89.]

objects I behold in a day, the more expanded and immortal I become. If a stone appeals to me and elevates me, tells me how many miles I have come, how many remain to travel, — and the more, the better, — reveals the future to me in some measure, it is a matter of private rejoicing. If it did the same service to all, it might well be a matter of public rejoicing.

Aug. 31. Sunday. P. M. — To Hubbard Bath Swamp by boat.

There sits one by the shore who wishes to go with me, but I cannot think of it. I must be fancy-free. There is no such mote in the sky as a man who is not perfectly transparent to you, — who has any opacity. I would rather attend to him earnestly for half an hour, on shore or elsewhere, and then dismiss him. He thinks I could merely take him into my boat and then not mind him. He does not realize that I should by the same act take him into my mind, where there is no room for him, and my bark would surely founder in such a voyage as I was contemplating. I know very well that I should never reach that expansion of the river I have in my mind, with him aboard with his broad terrene qualities. He would sink my bark (not to another sea) and never know it. I could better carry a heaped load of meadow mud and sit on the thole-pins. There would be more room for me, and I should reach that expansion of the river nevertheless.

I could better afford to take him into bed with me, for then I might, perhaps, abandon him in my dreams.

Vol. IX

Ah! you are a heavy fellow, but I am well disposed. If you could go without going, then you might go. There's the captain's stateroom, empty to be sure, and you say you could go in the steerage. I know very well that only your baggage would be dropped in the steerage, while you would settle right down into that other snug recess. Why, I am *going*, not staying. I have come on purpose to sail, to paddle away from such as you, and you have waylaid me at the shore. You have chosen to make your assault at the moment of embarkation. Why, if I thought you were steadily gazing after me a mile off, I could not endure it. It is because I trust that I shall ere long depart from your thoughts, and so you from mine, that I am encouraged to set sail at all. I make haste to put several meanders and some hills between us. This Company is obliged to make a distinction between dead freight and passengers. I will take almost any amount of freight for you cheerfully, — anything, my dear sir, but yourself.

Some are so inconsiderate as to ask to walk or sail with me regularly every day — I have known such — and think that, because there will be six inches or a foot between our bodies, we shall not interfere! These things are settled by fate. The good ship sails when she is ready. For freight or passage apply to —?? Ask my friend where. What is getting into a man's carriage when it is full, compared with putting your foot in his mouth and popping right into his mind without considering whether it is occupied or not? If I remember aright, it was only on condition *that you were*

asked, that you were to go with a man one mile or twain.[1] Suppose a man asks, not you to go with him, but to go with you! Often, I would rather undertake to shoulder a barrel of pork and carry it a mile than take into my company a man. It would not be so heavy a weight upon my mind. I could put it down and only feel my *back* ache for it.

The birches on Wheeler's meadow have begun to yellow, apparently owing to the water. The *Cornus sericea*, with its berries just turning, is generally a dull purple now, the first conspicuous change, methinks, along the river; half sunk in water.

Captain Hubbard is out inspecting his river meadow and his cranberries. Says he never saw the water so high at this season before. I am surprised that the river is not more than two inches higher than yesterday, or than the day before, notwithstanding the last copious rain; but Hubbard says he has heard that they have just lowered their dam a foot at Billerica. He sees that the water has fallen a little in his meadow. It leaves a scum on the grass and gives it a smell and taste, which makes the cattle reject it. He gets into my boat, and we obtain some cranberries from beneath the water. Some of them are softened and spoiled. H. thinks it depends on the warmth of the water how much they are injured. This is what calls the farmer out now, — to inspect his cranberries or his grass. He talks with his neighbor about it at church.

I am frequently amused when I come across the proprietor in my walks, and he asks me if I am not

[1] [Channing, pp. 119, 120.]

lost. I commonly approach his territory by the river, or some other back way, and rarely meet with him. The other day Conant observed to me, "Well, you have to come out once in a while to take a survey." He thinks that I do not visit his neighborhood more than once in a year, but I go there about once a week, and formerly much oftener; perhaps as often as he.

H. says he has found coal at the bottom of his meadow under the mud, three feet deep.

The *Viburnum nudum* berries are now in prime, a handsome rose-purple. I brought home a bunch of fifty-three berries, all of this color, and the next morning thirty were turned dark purple. In this state they are soft and just edible, having somewhat of a cherry flavor, not a large stone.

A painted tortoise shedding its scales.

Coral Fungus

Bateman's Pond

II

SEPTEMBER, 1856

(ÆT. 39)

Sept. 1. P. M. — With R. W. E. to Saw Mill and *Solidago odora.*

He has just had four of his fir trees next his house cut, they shaded his windows so. They were set out by Coolidge, E. thinks twenty-eight years ago. The largest has thirty-seven annual rings at the base and measures at one foot from the ground forty-six and a half inches in circumference; has made, on an average, about half an inch of wood in every direction.

There is no *Bidens cernua*, if that is it, by the Turnpike. It was apparently killed by the recent high water. *Solidago latifolia* not out quite.

We go admiring the pure and delicate tints of fungi on the surface of the damp swamp there, following up along the north side of the brook past the right of the old camp. There are many very beautiful lemon-yellow ones of various forms, some shaped like buttons, some becoming finely scalloped on the edge, some club-shaped and hollow, of the most delicate and rare but decided tints, contrasting well with the decaying leaves about them. There are others also pure white, others a wholesome red, others brown, and some even a light indigo-blue above and beneath and throughout. When colors come to be taught in the schools, as they should

be, both the prism (or the rainbow) and these fungi should be used by way of illustration, and if the pupil does not learn colors, he may learn fungi, which perhaps is better. You almost envy the wood frogs and toads that hop amid such gems, — some pure and bright enough for a breastpin. Out of every crevice between the dead leaves oozes some vehicle of color, the unspent wealth of the year, which Nature is now casting forth, as if it were only to empty herself.

Cohush berries appear now to be in their prime, and arum berries, and red choke-berries, which last further up in this swamp, with their peculiar glossy red and squarish form, are really very handsome. A few medeola berries ripe. The very dense clusters of the smilacina berries, finely purple-dotted on a pearly ground, are very interesting; also the smaller and similar clusters of the two-leaved convallaria. Many of the last and a few of the first are already turned red, clear semilucent red. They have a pleasant sweetish taste.

Cistus flowers well out again in the old camp path, now nearly all grown up. I notice that the birches have sprung up in close, straight rows in the old ruts there.

I think it stands about thus with asters and goldenrods now : —

The early meadow aster is either quite withered or much the worse for the wear, partly on account of the freshet.
Diplopappus cornifolius, not seen of late.
D. umbellatus, perhaps in prime or approaching it, but not much seen.
A. patens, apparently now in prime and the most abundant of the larger asters.

Vol. IX

A. macrophyllus, probably past prime.
A. acuminatus, not seen at all.
A. Radula, rather past prime.
A. dumosus, very common, most so of the small white, and in prime.
D. linariifolius, hardly noticed.
A. undulatus, hardly one seen yet open, a late aster.
A. corymbosus, in prime, or maybe past.
A. lævis, just beginning.[1]
A. Tradescanti, got to be pretty common, but not yet in prime.
A. puniceus, hardly yet in prime.[2]
A. longifolius, hardly one seen yet.
A. multiflorus, not one seen yet.[3]
Solidago stricta, still very abundant, though probably a little past prime.
S. gigantea, say in prime.
S. nemoralis, not quite in prime, but very abundant.
S. altissima, perhaps in prime.
S. odora, in prime, or maybe a little past.
S. puberula, just beginning, rare in any case.
S. bicolor, not quite in prime, but common.
S. lanceolata, in prime, or past.[4]
S. latifolia, not yet at all.
S. cæsia, just begun.
S. speciosa, not at all yet.

Sept. 2. P. M. — To Painted-Cup Meadow.

Clear bright days of late, with a peculiar sheen on the leaves, — light reflected from the surface of each one, for they are grown and worn and washed smooth at last, no infantile downiness on them. This, say ever since August 26th, and we have had no true dog-day

[1] Can this be the same open July 13th? [2] *Vide* Sept. 5.
[3] (Oct. 8th) *A. miser* (omitted). If I mistake not it began to be common about Sept. 1st.
[4] *Vide* Sept. 5.

weather since the copious rains began, or three or four weeks. A sheeny light reflected from the burnished leaves as so many polished shields, and a steady creak from the locusts these days. Frank Harding has caught a dog-day locust which lit on the bottom of my boat, in which he was sitting, and z-ed there. When you hear him you have got to the end of the alphabet and may imagine the &. It has a mark somewhat like a small writing *w* on the top of its thorax.

A few pigeons were seen a fortnight ago. I have noticed none in all walks, but G. Minott, whose mind runs on them so much, but whose age and infirmities confine him to his wood-shed on the hillside, saw a small flock a fortnight ago. I rarely pass at any season of the year but he asks if I have seen any pigeons. One man's mind running on pigeons, [he] will sit thus in the midst of a village, many of whose inhabitants never see nor dream of a pigeon except in the pot, and where even naturalists do not observe [them], and he, looking out with expectation and faith from morning till night, will surely see them.

I think we may detect that some sort of preparation and faint expectation preceded every discovery we have made. We blunder into no discovery but it will appear that we have prayed and disciplined ourselves for it. Some years ago I sought for Indian hemp (*Apocynum cannabinum*) hereabouts in vain, and concluded that it did not grow here. A month or two ago I read again, as many times before, that its blossoms were very small, scarcely a third as large as those of the common species, and for some unaccountable reason this distinction kept recurring to me, and I regarded the size of the flowers I saw, though I did not believe that it grew here; and in a day or two my eyes fell on [it], aye, in three different places, and different varieties of it. Also, a short time ago, I was satisfied that there was but one kind of sunflower (*divaricatus*) indigenous here. Hearing that one had found another kind, it occurred to me that I had seen a taller one than usual lately, but not so distinctly did I remember this as to name it to him or even fully remember it myself. (I rather remembered it afterward.) But within that hour my genius conducted me to where I had seen the tall plants, and it was the other man's new kind. The next day I found a third kind, miles from there, and, a few days after, a fourth in another direction.

It commonly chances that I make my most interesting botanical discoveries when I [am] in a thrilled and expectant mood, perhaps wading in some remote swamp where I have just found something novel and feel more than usually remote from the town. Or some rare plant which for some reason has occupied a strangely prominent place in my thoughts for some time will present itself. My expectation ripens to discovery. I am prepared for strange things.

My father asked John Legross if he took an interest in politics and did his duty to his country at this crisis. He said he did. He went into the wood-shed and read the newspaper Sundays. Such is the dawn of the literary taste, the first seed of literature that is planted

any such preferences. Perchance the ocean seemed wilder to them than the woods. As if there were primarily and essentially any more wildness in a western acre than an eastern one!

The *S. lucida* makes about the eleventh willow that I have distinguished. (When I find a new and rare plant in Concord I seem to think it has but just sprung up here, — that it is, and not I am, the newcomer, — while it has grown here for ages before I was born.) It transports me in imagination to the Saskatchewan. It grows alike on the bank of the Concord and of the Mackenzie River, proving them a kindred soil. I see their broad and glossy leaves reflecting the autumn light this moment all along those rivers. Through this leaf I communicate with the Indians who roam the boundless Northwest. It tastes the same nutriment in sand of the Assabet and its water as in that of the Saskatchewan and Jasper Lake, suggesting that a short time ago the shores of this river were as wild as the shores of those.

We are dwelling amid these wild plants still, we are eating the huckleberries which lately only the Indian ate and dried, we are raising and eating his wild and nutritive maize, and if we have imported wheat, it is but our wild rice, which we annually gather with grateful awe, like Chippewas. Potatoes are our groundnuts.

Spiranthes cernua, apparently some days at least, though not yet generally; a cool, late flower, growing with fringed gentian. I cannot yet even find the leaves of the latter — at the house-leek brook. I had come

in the new country. His grandson may be the author of a Bhagvat-Geeta.

I see bright-yellow blossoms on perfectly crimson *Hypericum angulosum* in the *S. lanceolata* path. By the Indian hemp at the stone bridge, am surprised to see the *Salix lucida*, a small tree with very marked and handsome leaves, on the sand, water's edge, at the great eddy. The branches of an inch in diameter are smooth and ash-colored, maple-like; the recent shoots stout and yellowish-green, very brittle at base. The leaves are the largest of any willow I have seen, ovate-oblong or ovate-lanceolate, with a long, narrow, tapering point (cuspidate), some on vigorous shoots, two and a half by seven inches wide in the blade, glandular-serrate, with pedicellate glands at the rounded base, thick, smooth, and glossy above, smooth and green beneath, with broad crescent-shaped, glandular-toothed stipules at base of petioles, five eighths to one inch long. According to Emerson, "Sir W. J. Hooker says it is one of the most generally diffused of all the willows in British North America."

Captain Hubbard said on Sunday that he had plowed up an Indian gouge, but how little impression that had made on him compared with the rotting of his cranberries or the loss of meadow-grass! It seemed to me that it made an inadequate impression compared with many trivial events. Suppose he had plowed up five dollars!

The botanist refers you, for wild [*sic*] and we presume wild plants, further inland or westward to so many miles from Boston, as if Nature or the Indians had

to the Assabet, but could not wade the river, it was so deep and swift. The very meadow, poke-logan, was a quarter of a mile long and as deep as the river before. So I had come round over the bridge.

In Painted-Cup Meadow the ferns are yellowing, imbrowned, and crisped, as if touched by frost (?), yet it may be owing to the rains. It is evident that, at this season, excessive rain will ripen and kill the leaves as much as a drought does earlier. I think our strawberries recently set out have died, partly in consequence. Perhaps they need some dryness as well as warmth at this season. Plainly dog-days and rain have had the most to do as yet with the changing and falling of the leaves. So trees by water change earliest, sassafrases at Cardinal Shore, for example, while those on hill are not turned red at all. These ferns I see, with here and there a single maple bough turned scarlet, — this quite rare.

Some of the small early blueberry bushes are a clear red (*Vaccinium Pennsylvanicum*), and the lingering clusters of blueberries contrast strangely with the red leaves of the *V. vacillans*. Smooth sumachs show quite red on dry, warm hillsides.

While I am plucking the almost spicy blueberries amid the crimson leaves there on the springy slope, the cows gather toward the outlet of their pastures and low for the herdsman, reminding me that the day is drawing to a close.

Centaurea will apparently be entirely done in a week.

How deceptive these maps of western rivers! Methought they were scattered according to the fancy of the map-maker, — were dry channels at best, — but it turns out that the Missouri at Nebraska City is three times as wide as the Mississippi at Burlington, and Grasshopper Creek, perhaps, will turn out to be as big as the Thames or Hudson.

There was an old gentleman here to-day who lived in Concord when he was young and remembers how Dr. Ripley talked to him and other little boys from the pulpit, as they came into church with their hands full of lilies, saying that those lilies looked so fresh that they must have been gathered that morning! Therefore they must have committed the sin of bathing this morning! Why, this is as sacred a river as the Ganges, sir.

I feel this difference between great poetry and small: that in the one, the sense outruns and overflows the words; in the other, the words the sense.

Sept. 3. P. M. — To Hubbard's Swamp for *Viburnum nudum* berries.

The river smooth, though full, with the autumn sheen on it, as on the leaves. I see painted tortoises with their entire backs covered with perfectly fresh clean black scales, such as no rubbing nor varnishing can produce, contrasting advantageously with brown and muddy ones. One little one floats past on a drifting pad which he partly sinks.

I find one sassafras berry, dark-blue in its crimson cup, club-shaped. It is chiefly stone, and its taste is like that of *tar* (!), methinks, far from palatable.

So many plants, the indigenous and the bewildering variety of exotics, you see in conservatories and nurserymen's catalogues, or read of in English books, and the Royal Society did not make one of them, and knows no more about them than you! All truly indigenous and wild on this earth. I know of no mark that betrays an introduced plant, as none but the gardener can tell what flower has strayed from its parterre; but where the seed will germinate and the plant spring and grow, there it is at home.

Weeds are uncultivated herbaceous plants which do not bear handsome flowers.

Polygala sanguinea is now as abundant, at least, as at any time, and perhaps more conspicuous in the meadows where I look for fringed gentian.

Gathered four or five quarts of *Viburnum nudum* berries, now in their prime, attracted more by the beauty of the cymes than the flavor of the fruit. The berries, which are of various sizes and forms, — elliptical, oblong, or globular, — are in different stages of maturity on the same cyme, and so of different colors, — green or white, rose-colored, and dark purple or black, — i. e. three or four very distinct and marked colors, side by side. If gathered when rose-colored, they soon turn dark purple and are soft and edible, though before bitter. They add a new and variegated wildness to the swampy sprout-lands. Remarkable for passing through so many stages of color before they arrive at maturity. A singular and pleasing contrast, also, do the different kinds of viburnum and cornel berries present when compared with each other.

Vol. IX

The white berries of the panicled cornel, soon and apparently prematurely dropping from its pretty fingers, are very bitter. So also are those of the *C. sericea*.

One carrion-flower berry is turning blue in its dense spherical cluster. Castile-soap galls are crowding the more legitimate acorn on the shrub oak.

Sept. 4. P. M. — To Miles Swamp, Conantum.

What are those small yellow birds with two white bars on wings, about the oak at Hubbard's Grove? *Aralia racemosa* berries just ripe, at tall helianthus by bass [?] beyond William Wheeler's; not edible. Indian hemp out of bloom. Butterflies in road a day or two. The crackling flight of grasshoppers. The grass also is all alive with them, and they trouble me by getting into my shoes, which are loose, and obliging me to empty them occasionally. Measured an archangelica stem (now of course dry) in Corner Spring Swamp, eight feet eight inches high, and seven and a quarter inches in circumference at ground. It is a somewhat zigzag stem with few joints and a broad umbelliferous top, so that it makes a great show. One of those plants that have their fall early. There are many splendid scarlet arum berries there now in prime,[1] forming a dense ovate head on a short peduncle; the individual berries of various sizes, between pear and mitre and club form, flattened against each other on a singular (now purple and white) core, which is hollow. What rank and venomous luxuriance in this swamp sprout-land! *Viola pedata* again. I see where squirrels have

[1] And last ten days more at least.

eaten green sweet viburnum berries on the wall, together with hazelnuts. The former, gathered red, turn dark purple and shrivelled, like raisins, in the house, and are edible, but chiefly seed. The fever-bush is conspicuously flower-budded. Even its spicy leaves have been cut by the tailor bee, and circular pieces taken out. He was, perhaps, attracted by its smoothness and soundness. Large puffballs, sometime.

Sept. 5. Friday. To Brattleboro, Vt.

Will not the prime of goldenrods and asters be just before the first severe frosts?

As I ride along in the cars, I think that the ferns, etc., are browned and crisped more than usual at this season, on account of the very wet weather.

Found on reaching Fitchburg that there was an interval of three and a half hours between this and the Brattleboro train, and so walked on, on the track, with shouldered valise. Had observed that the Nashua River in Shirley was about one mile west of Groton Junction, if I should ever want to walk there. Observed by railroad, in Fitchburg, low slippery elm shrubs with great, rough, one-sided leaves.

Solidago lanceolata past prime, a good deal. *Aster puniceus* in prime. About one mile from West Fitchburg depot, westward, I saw the panicled elder berries on the railroad but just beginning to redden, though it is said to ripen long before this. As I was walking through Westminster, I remembered that G. B. Emerson says that he saw a handsome clump of the *Salix lucida* on an island in Meeting-House Pond in this town, and, looking round, I saw a shrub of it by the rail-road, about one mile west of West Fitchburg depot, and several times afterward within a mile or two. Also in the brook behind Mr. Alcott's house in Walpole, N. H.

Took the cars again in Westminster. The scenery began to be mountainous and interesting in Royalston and Athol, but was more so in Erving. In North-field first observed fields of broom-corn very common, *Sorghum saccharatum*, taller than corn. Alcott says they bend down the heads before they gather them, to fit them for brooms. Hereabouts women and children are already picking hops in the fields, in the shade of large white sheets, like sails.

Sept. 6. At Brattleboro.

Mr. Charles C. (?) Frost showed me a printed list of the flowers of B., furnished by him to a newspaper in B. some years since. He says he finds *Aster simplex* and *A. ptarmicoïdes* there (according to Oakes the latter is not found in New England out of Vermont), the latter now covered by the high water of the river; also *A. concinnus*, of Wood, perhaps (not in Gray) (*vide* specimen pressed); also *Solidago patula* and *serótina*, as well as *Canadensis* and *gigantea*. Also finds, he says, *Helianthus giganteus* (Oakes gives only *H. divaricatus* and *decapetalus* to Vermont), with quite small flowers, bank of river, behind town-house; and *decapetalus* and *strumosus*. Speaks of the fragrance of the dicksonia fern and the sensitiveness of the sensitive fern. If you take a tender plant by the stem, the warmth of your hand will cause the leaves to curl.

Thought my great dish-cover fungus a *Coprolus* (?) (so called from growing in dung?).

Read in Thompson's History of Vermont, which contains very good natural history, including a catalogue of the Plants of Vermont made by Oakes and, in the last edition, additional ones found by Frost.

A. M. — Walked down the railroad about a mile, returning partly by river-bank.

The depot is on the site of "Thunderbolt's" house. He was a Scotch highwayman. Called himself Dr. Wilson (?) when here. The prevailing polygonum in B. was a new one to me, *P. Pennsylvanicum*, but not roughish on the veins, apparently in prime, with the aspect of *P. Persicaria*, sometimes spreading and stretching four feet along a hillside, but commonly in rather low ground, roadsides. For the first time distinguish the *Aster cordifolius*, a prevailing one in B. and but just beginning to flower; like an *A. undulatus* with narrow-winged petioles and sharp-toothed leaves; amid bushes and edges of woods, sometimes four feet high, panicled.

I see the flowering raspberry still in bloom. This plant is quite common here. The fruit, now ripe, is red and quite agreeable, but not abundant. *Desmodium Canadense* still. Maple-leaved viburnum very abundant here, a prevailing shrub. Berries apparently now in prime, or a little earlier than this, ovoid, dull blue-black. Pluck some rose leaves by Connecticut (*vide* press), with now smooth, somewhat pear-shaped hips; not a sweet-briar. Also *Cornus circinata* berries, very light blue or bluish-white.

Cirsium discolor, roadside below depot, apparently in prime, much like *lanceolatum*, but smaller leaves, whitish beneath and inner scales unarmed.

Frost said that Dr. Kane left B. the morning of the day I arrived, and had given him a list of arctic plants brought home by him, which he showed me, — pages from his Report, in press.

The *Solidago Canadensis* very common, apparently in prime; also perfectly smooth ones with glaucous stems like some of ours. I am in doubt whether the last, or any that we have in Concord, is the *S. serotina* or *gigantea*. Frost says he distinguishes both, but Oakes does not give the *S. serotina* to Vermont. I should say *he* had but one kind, which varied from leaves rough above and on the veins beneath, and stems smooth below and pubescent above, to leaves quite smooth on both sides and stems very smooth and glaucous; rays also vary very much in size. Or are these only varieties of the *Canadensis* ??

I find small grapes a third of an inch in diameter, many ripe, on the bank of the Connecticut, — pleasantly acid. Clusters three to four or five inches long. The leaves are sharply toothed and green on both sides. Is it the *Vitis cordifolia?*[1] I see also a vine with leaves rusty-downy beneath and not conspicuously toothed, with equally small now green grapes, apparently like ours. Is not this *V. æstivalis?* Of the latter the berries are said to be pleasant, and ripe in October.[2]

[1] Apparently it is, but berries already ripe.
[2] *Vide* Oct. 27, 1856.

Eupatorium ageratoides, white snake-root, in rather low ground or on banks along riverside, apparently in prime. Apparently *Helianthus decapetalus*, or cut-toothed helianthus, the teeth much larger than with us. *Solidago arguta* very common, apparently in prime, with sharp-toothed, more or less elliptic leaves and slender terminal drooping racemes; size of *S. stricta*.

Sept. 7. Sunday.[1] At Brattleboro, Vt. A. M. — Climbed the hill behind Mr. Addison Brown's.

The leaves of the *Tiarella cordifolia* very abundant in the woods, but hardly sharp-lobed. Also observed the leaves of the *Hepatica triloba*. Was that *Sium lineare* in the pool on the hilltop? Oakes allows only *S. latifolium* to grow in Vermont. The seeds are apparently ribbed like ours. (*Vide* press.) Found the lemna mantling that pool. Mrs. Brown has found it in flower there. Flowering dogwood on hill.

P. M. — Up the bank of the Connecticut to West River, up that to a brook, and up that nearly to hospital.

The Connecticut, though unusually high (several feet more than usual), looks low, there being four or five or six rods of bare gravel on each side, and the bushes and weeds covered with clayey soil from a freshet. Not a boat to be seen on it. The Concord is worth a hundred of it for my purposes. It looks narrow as well as shallow. No doubt it is dwarfed by

[1] [The manuscript volume which begins with this date has on its first page, "The cold winter and warm February."]

the mountain rising directly from it in front, which, as usual, looking nearer than it is, makes the opposite shore seem nearer.

The *Solidago Canadensis*, and the smooth three ribbed one, and *nemoralis*, etc., the helianthus (apparently *decapetalus*), and *Aster* or *Diplopappus linariifolius*, *Vitis cordifolius* (?) (now beginning to be ripe) are quite common along the bank. On a bank-side on West River, *Urtica Canadensis*, apparently in prime and going to seed, the same that Mr. Whitlow once recommended as a substitute for hemp. Near by the phryma, or lopseed, with still a few small rose-white flowers. I at first thought it a circæa. Plenty of harebells thereabouts, and, by the brook, *Polygonum Virginianum*, three feet high, mostly gone to seed. Apparently *Cornus stolonifera* (?) by brook (*vide* press), with the *sericea*. *Aster macrophyllus* much past prime.

Sept. 8. Brattleboro. — Rains.

Frost gives me an aster which he thinks *A. concinnus* of Wood; grows in woods and yet longer leaved.

P. M. — Clearing up. I went a-botanizing by the Coldwater Path, for the most part along a steep wooded hillside on Whetstone Brook and through its interval.

In the last heavy rain, two or three weeks since, there was a remarkable freshet on this brook, such as has not been known before, the bridge and road carried away, the bed of the stream laid bare, a new channel being made, the interval covered with sand and gravel, and trees (buttonwood, etc.) brought

down; several acres thus buried. Frost escaped from his house on a raft. I observed a stream of large bare white rocks four or five rods wide, which at first I thought had been washed down, but it seems this was the former bed of the stream, it having worn a new channel further east.

Witch-hazel out, maybe a day or two, in some places, but the Browns do not think the fringed gentian out yet.

There for the first time I see growing indigenously the *Dirca palustris*, leather-wood, the largest on the low interval by the brook. I notice a bush there seven feet high. In its form it is somewhat like a quince bush, though less spreading, its leaves broad, like entire sassafras leaves; now beginning to turn yellow. It has a remarkably strong thick bark and soft white wood which bends like lead (Gray says it is brittle!), the different layers separating at the end. I cut a good-sized switch, which was singularly tough and flexible, just like a cowhide, and would answer the purpose of one admirably. The color of the bark is a very pale brown. I was much interested in this shrub, since it was the Indian's rope. Frost said that the farmers of Vermont used it to tie up their fences with. Certainly there can be no wood equal to it as a withe. He says it is still strong when dry. I should think it would be worth the while for the farmers to cultivate for this purpose. How often in the woods and fields we want a string or rope and cannot find one. This is the plant which Nature has made for this purpose. The Browns gave me some of the flowers, which ap-

Vol. IX

pear very early in spring. Gray says that in northern New England it is called *wicopy*. Potter, in History of Manchester, says Indians sewed canoes with it. Beck says, "The bark has a sweetish taste, and when chewed excites a burning sensation in the fauces," and, according to Emerson, the bark of this family, "taken into the stomach causes heat and vomiting, or purging." According to the latter, cordage has been made from the bark of this family, also paper. Emerson says of this plant in particular, "The fresh bark produces a sensation of heat in the stomach, and at last brings on vomiting. . . . It has such strength that a man cannot pull apart so much as covers a branch of half or a third of an inch in diameter. It is used by millers and others for thongs." Indian cordage. I feel as if I had discovered a more indigenous plant than usual, it was so peculiarly useful to the aborigines.

On that wooded hillside, I find small-flowered asters, *A. miser*-like, hairy, but very long linear leaves; possibly the var. *hirsuta* of *A. miser* (Oakes gives of *A. miser*, only the var. *hirsuticaulis* to Vermont) or else a neighboring species, for they seem distinct. (*Vide* press.) There is the hobble-bush with its berries and large roundish leaves, now beginning to turn a deep dull crimson red. Also mountain maples, with sharp-lobed leaves and downy beneath, the young plants numerous. The *Ribes cynosbati*, or prickly gooseberry, with its bur-like fruit, dry and still hanging here and there. Also the ground-hemlock, with its beautiful fruit, like a red waxen cup with a purple (?)

fruit in it. By the edge of a ditch, where it had been overwhelmed and buried with mud by the later freshet, the *Solidago Muhlenbergii* in its prime. (*Vide* press.) Near by, on the bank of the ditch, leaves of coltsfoot. I had cut across the interval, but, taking to the Coldwater Path again near its southeast end, I found, at an angle in it near the canal, beech-drops under a beech, not yet out, and the *Equisetum scirpoides*, also radical leaves, very broad, perhaps of a sedge, some much longer. (*Vide* press.)

Gathered flowering raspberries in all my walks and found them a pleasant berry, large, but never abundant. In a wet place on the interval the *Veronica Americana*, according to Frost (*beccabunga* of some), not in bloom. Along this path observed the *Nabalus altissimus*, flowers in a long panicle of axillary and terminal branches, small-flowered, now in prime. Leaves apparently of *Oxalis Acetosella*. Large roundish radical leaves on the moist wooded hillside, which the Browns thought of the round-leaved violet. Low, flat-topped, very rough hairy, apparently *Aster acuminatus*. *Erigeron annuus*, broad, thin, toothed leaves. Also another, perhaps hirsute *A. miser*, with toothed leaves.

I hear that two thousand dollars' worth of huckleberries have been sold by the town of Ashby this season.

Also gathered on this walk the *Polypodium Dryopteris* and *Polystichum acrostichoides* and a short heavy-odored (like stramonium) plant with aspect of lilac, not in bloom. (*Vide* press.)

Sept. 9. Tuesday. 8 A. M. — Ascend the Chesterfield Mountain with Miss Frances and Miss Mary Brown.

The Connecticut is about twenty rods wide between Brattleboro and Hinsdale. This mountain, according to Frost, 1064 feet high. It is the most remarkable feature here. The village of Brattleboro is peculiar for the nearness of the primitive wood and the mountain. Within three rods of Brown's house was excellent botanical ground on the side of a primitive wooded hillside, and still better along the Coldwater Path. But, above all, this everlasting mountain is forever lowering over the village, shortening the day and wearing a misty cap each morning. You look up to its top at a steep angle from the village streets. A great part belongs to the Insane Asylum. This town will be convicted of folly if they ever permit this mountain to be laid bare. Francis [*sic*] B. says its Indian name is Wantastiquet, from the name of West River above. Very abundant about B. the *Gerardia tenuifolia*, in prime, which I at first mistook for the *purpurea*. The latter I did not see. High up the mountain the *Aster macrophyllus* as well as *corymbosus*. The (apparently) *Platanthera orbiculata* (?) leaves, round and flat on ground (*vide* press); another by it with larger and more oblong leaves. Pine-sap. A tuft of five-divided leaves, fifteen or eighteen inches high, slightly fern-like (*vide* press). *Galium circœzans* var. *lanceolatum*. Top of the mountain covered with wood. Saw Ascutney, between forty and fifty miles up the river, but not Monadnock on account of woods.

P. M. — To and up a brook north of Brown's house.

A large alternate cornel, four or five inches in diameter, a dark-gray stem. The kidney-shaped leaves of the *Asarum Canadense* common there. *Panax quinquefolium*, with peculiar flat scarlet fruit in a little umbel. *Clinopodium vulgare*, or basil, apparently flatted down by a freshet, rather past prime; and spearmint in brook just above. Close behind Brown's, *Liparis liliifolia*, or tway-blade, leaves and bulb.

A very interesting sight from the top of the mountain was that of the cars so nearly under you, apparently creeping along, you could see so much of their course.

The epigæa was very abundant on the hill behind Brown's and elsewhere in B. The *Populus monilifera* grows on West River, but I did not see it. The *Erigeron Philadelphicus* I saw pressed, with innumerable fine rays. Scouring-rush was common along the Coldwater Path and elsewhere.

The most interesting sight I saw in Brattleboro was the skin and skull of a panther (*Felis concolor*) (cougar, catamount, painter, American lion, puma), which was killed, according to a written notice attached, on the 15th of June by the Saranac Club of Brattleboro, six young men, on a fishing and hunting excursion. This paper described it as eight feet in extreme length and weighing one hundred and ten pounds. The Brattleboro newspaper says its body was "4 feet 11 inches in length, and the tail 2 feet 9 inches; the animal weighed 108 pounds." I was surprised at its great size and apparent strength. It gave one a new idea of our American forests and the vigor of nature here. It

was evident that it could level a platoon of men with a stroke of its paw. I was particularly impressed by the size of its limbs, the size of its canine teeth, and its great white claws. I do not see but this affords a sufficient foundation for the stories of the lion heard and its skins seen near Boston by the first settlers. This creature was very catlike, though the tail was not tapering, but as large at the extremity as anywhere, yet not tufted like the lion's. It had a long neck, a long thin body, like a lean cat. Its fore feet were about six inches long by four or five wide, as set up.

I talked with the man who shot him, a Mr. Kellogg, a lawyer. They were fishing on one of the Saranac Lakes, their guide being the Harvey Moody whom Hammond describes, when they heard the noise of some creature threshing about amid the bushes on the hillside. The guide suspected that it was a panther which had caught a deer. He reconnoitred and found that it was a panther which had got one fore paw (the left) in one of his great double-spring, long teethed or hooked bear-traps. He had several of these traps set (without bait) in the neighborhood. It fell to Kellogg's lot to advance with the guide and shoot him. They approached within six or seven rods, saw that the panther was held firmly, and fired just as he raised his head to look at them. The ball entered just above his nose, pierced his brain, and killed him at once. The guide got the bounty of twenty-five dollars, but the game fell to his employers. A slice had been sheared off one side of each ear to secure this with. It was a male. The guide thought it an old

one, but Kellogg said that, as they were returning with it, the inhabitants regarded it as common; they only kicked it aside in the road, remarking that [it] was a large one.

I talked also with the Mr. Chamberlin who set it up. He showed me how sharp the edges of the broad grinders were just behind the canine teeth. They were zigzag, thus: and shut over the under, scraping close like shears and, as he proved, would cut off a straw clean. This animal looked very thin as set up, and probably in some states of his body would have weighed much more. Kellogg said that, freshly killed, the body *showed the nerves* much more than as set up. The color, etc., agreed very well with the account in Thompson's History of Vermont, except that there was, now at least, no yellow about the mouth or chin, but whitish. It was, in the main, the universal color of this family, or a little browner. According to Thompson, it is brownred on the back, reddish-gray on the sides, whitish or light-ash on the belly; tail like the back above, except its extremity, which is brownish-black, not tufted; chin, upper lip, and inside of ears, yellowish-white. Hairs on back, short, brownish tipped with red; on the belly, longer, lighter, tipped with white; hairs of face like back with whitish hairs intermingled. Canines conical, claws pearly-white. Length, nose to tail, four feet eight inches; tail, two feet six inches; top of head to point of nose, ten inches; width across forehead, eight inches. Length of fore legs, one foot two inches; hind, one foot four inches. Weight usually about one hundred pounds. The largest he ever knew was seven feet in extreme length and weighed one hundred and eighteen pounds. One had been known to leap up a precipice fifteen feet high with a calf in his mouth. *Vide* Lawson, Hunter, and Jefferson in Book of Facts. Hunter when near the Rocky Mountains says, "So much were they to be apprehended . . . that no one ever ventured to go out alone, even on the most trifling occasion." He makes two kinds.

Emmons makes the extreme length of one of the largest cougars nine feet four inches, and the greatest length of the canine tooth of the upper jaw from the gum nine tenths of an inch. I think that the teeth of the one I saw were much larger. Says it is cowardly and "rarely if ever attacks man;" that a hunter met five in St. Lawrence County, N. Y., and, with his dog and gun only, killed three that day and the other two the next. Yet he will follow a man's track a great distance. Scream at evening heard for miles. Thinks about 45° its northern range.[1]

Sept. 10. 10.30 A. M. — Took the cars to Bellows Falls, through Dummerston, Putney, and Westminster.

Looked at the falls and rocks. River higher than usual at this season, yet could cross all but about twenty feet on the rocks. Some pot-holes of this form: real pot-holes, but commonly several curves commingled, thus: or the whole more rounded. Found, spreading prostrate on the rocks amid the

[1] *Vide* forward, Oct. 4th and 25th.

pot-holes, apparently a small willow,[1] with shining dark-red stems and smooth, spatulate, rather obtuse serrate leaves. (*Vide* press.) I read that salmon passed these falls but not shad. When the water is lowest, it is contracted to sixteen feet here, and Peters's, an old history of Connecticut, says it was so condensed that you could not thrust a crowbar into it. It did me good to read his wholesale hearty statements, — strong, living, human speech, so much better than the emasculated modern histories, like Bancroft's and the rest, cursed with a style.[2] I would rather read such histories, though every sentence were a falsehood, than our dull emasculated reports which bear the name of histories. The former, having a human breath and interest behind them, are nearer to nature and to truth, after all. The historian is required to feel a human interest in his subject and to so express it. President Dwight, speaking of the origin of those pot-holes, says, "The river now is often fuller than it probably ever was before the country above was cleared of its forests: the snows in open ground melting much more suddenly, and forming much greater freshets, than in forested ground." (Vol. ii, page 92.)

Ascended the Fall Mountain with a heavy valise on my back, against the advice of the toll-man. But when I got up so soon and easily I was amused to remember his anxiety. It is seven hundred and fifty feet high, according to Gazetteer. Saw great red oaks on this hill, particularly tall, straight, and bare of limbs,

[1] *Prunus depressa.*
[2] [Channing, p. 272. C. puts "Prescott's" for "Bancroft's."]

for a great distance, amid the woods. Here, as at Brattleboro, a fine view of the country immediately beneath you; but these views lack breadth, a distant horizon. There is a complete view of the falls from this height.

Saw a pair of middle-sized black hawks hovering about this cliff, with some white spots, with peculiar shrill snapping notes like a gull, a new kind to me.

Descending the steep south end of this hill, I saw an apparent *Corydalis glauca*, mostly withered, three feet or more, and more than usually broad and stout in proportion. (*Vide* press.) My shoes were very smooth, and I got many falls descending, battering my valise. By the railroad below, the *Solanum nigrum*, with white flowers but yet green fruit.

Just after crossing Cold River, bathed in the Connecticut, evidently not far from site of the old Kilbourn fort. Clay-muddy shore. Near the site of the old Bellows Fort, saw completely purple *Polygala verticillata* abundant in road.

Rode the last mile into Walpole with a lumberer, who said that when he commenced operations at Bellows Falls he thought that there was not more than one hundred thousand there, but they had already got out four millions. He imported some of those masts I had seen go through Concord from Canada West. They were rafted along Lake Erie (a Mr. Dorr of Buffalo afterward told me that he did this part with steamers, merely running an inch chain through the butt of each log and fastening the ends to a boom, which surrounded the whole, leaving the small ends to play) and in small rafts by canal to Albany, and

thence by railroad *via* Rutland to Portland, for the navy; and it cost only one third more to get them from Canada West than from Bellows Falls. Remembering the difficulty in old times of loading one of these sticks in New Hampshire for the King's Navy, this seemed the greatest triumph of the railroad.

In Walpole, the *Chenopodium Botrys*.

Sept. 11. P. M. — Walked over what Alcott calls Farm Hill, east of his house.

Erigeron annuus, four feet high, by roadside; also *Ranunculus Pennsylvanicus*, or bristly crowfoot, still in bloom. *Vide* press. A fine view of the Connecticut valley from the hilltop, and of Ascutney Mountain, but not of Monadnock. Descended a steep side of the hill by a cow-path, made with great judgment regularly zigzag, thus: well worn and deep. Visited the grave-yard and the Colonel Benjamin Bellows, founder's, gravestone and more recent monument.

In the evening read an interesting pamphlet account of the Bellows family of Walpole, prepared by Dr. Bellows of New York, on occasion of the family gathering and erection of the monument. A large part of the inhabitants of Walpole are descendants of Colonel B. Bellows. The writer quotes from a paper in "the Cheshire *Gazette* of April 28, 1826," "understood to be prepared by our respected townsman, Dr. Morse," Dr. B. saying first, "A Mrs. Watson of Germantown, Pennsylvania, was alive in 1826, who resided in Wal pole in 1762, then only 8 years old," but she had a remarkable memory. He then quotes Morse, who states that her father came and built a house in Walpole in 1762. "The roof of the house was covered with bark, and the gable ends remained open some time, which enabled them to hear the barking of foxes, the howling of wolves, and the cries of the panther, while sitting before the fire. The latter resembled the voice of a woman in distress, and [seemed][1] intended to decoy people into the woods, where the salutations of these roving gentry were apt to prove troublesome, unless prevented by the presence of fire-arms." According to this woman (and Morse), "a shad was taken near the falls which had a rattlesnake's head in its stomach."

Dr. B. states that there is a tradition that the founder, Colonel B., once killed, on Fall Mountain, two bears and a very large panther, which last alarmed him considerably. According to Morse and the woman, "a large portion of pin money was derived from the sale of golden thread, ginseng, and snakeroot, which were procured from their [the ladies'][2] own hands." This should probably be "lands," or the preposition, "by."

In Alcott's yard, sprung up from his bird's seed, hemp, like common except fragrant.[3]

These are the plants I obtained on this excursion: —

> Panicled elder *berries*, Fitchburg.
> *Aster concinnus* (?), Frost, Brattleboro.

[1] [This word is probably supplied by Thoreau.]
[2] [Thoreau's brackets.]   [3] So is ours.

Vol. IX

> *Asarum Canadense*, leaves.
> *Panax quinquefolium*, in fruit.
> *Clinopodium vulgare*.
> *Liparis liliifolia*, not in flower.
> Red-stemmed willow at Bellows Falls.
> *Solanum nigrum*, Walpole.
> Purple *Polygala verticillata*, Walpole.
> *Ranunculus Pennsylvanicus*, Walpole.
> *Cannabis*, a fragrant kind, Walpole.

Also these were given me, pressed by the Browns: —

> *Dentaria diphylla*.
> *Viburnum lantanoides*, in flower.
> *Trillium erectum*.
> *Epigæa* (fairer than ours).
> *Sanguinaria Canadensis*.
> *Erythronium Americanum*.
> *Arabis lævigata*.
> *Viola rostrata*.
> *Panax trifolium*.
> *Pulsatilla patens*, leaves.
> *Tussilago Farfara*, without leaves.
> *A. Ribes*.
> *Hepatica triloba*.
> *H. acutiloba*, leaves (flowers same?).
> *Mitella diphylla*.

Sept. 12. Return to Concord.

Sept. 13. Saturday. At Concord. — After all, I am struck by the greater luxuriance of the same species of plants here than up-country, though our soil is considered leaner. Also I think that no view I have had of the Connecticut Valley, at Brattleboro or Walpole, is equal to that of the Concord from Nawshaw-

> *Solidago Canadensis.*
> *A. cordifolius.*
> *Urtica gracilis* (?).
> Pear-hipped rose.
> *Vitis cordifolia.*
> *Eupatorium ageratoides.*
> *Helianthus decapetalus.*
> *Solidago arguta.*
> *A. tenuifolius* (?), Frost.
> *Hepatica triloba*, leaves.
> *Tiarella cordifolia*, leaves and dried stem.
> *Sium lineare* (?).
> *Urtica Canadensis.*
> *Phryma Leptostachya.*
> *Campanula rotundifolia.*
> *Polygonum Virginianum.*
> *Cornus stolonifera* (?).
> *Dirca palustris*, leaves.
> *A. miser* var. *hirsuta* (?).
> *Viburnum lantanoides*, leaves.
> *Acer spicatum*, leaves.
> *Ribes cynosbati*, in fruit.
> *Taxus Canadensis*, in fruit.
> *Solidago Muhlenbergii.*
> *Tussilago Farfara*, leaves.
> *Epiphegus Americana.*
> *Equisetum scirpoides.*
> *Veronica Americana*, not in flower.
> *Nabalus altissimus.*
> *Oxalis Acetosella*, leaves.
> *Viola rotundifolia* (??), radical leaves.
> *Erigeron annuus.*
> *Polypodium Dryopteris*, in fruit.
> Heavy scented plant.
> *Gerardia tenuifolia.*
> *Platanthera orbiculata* (?), out of bloom.
> Tufted and divided leaves on mountain.
> *Aster, longifolius*-like, on Island.

tuct. Here is a more interesting horizon, more variety and richness. Our river is much the most fertile in every sense. Up there it is nothing but river-valley and hills. Here there is so much more that we have forgotten that we live in a valley.

8 A. M. — Up Assabet.

Gathered quite a parcel of grapes, quite ripe. Difficult to break off the large bunches without some dropping off. Yet the best are more admirable for fragrance than for flavor. Depositing them in the bows of the boat, they filled all the air with their fragrance, as we rowed along against the wind, as if we were rowing through an endless vineyard in its maturity.

The *Aster Tradescanti* now sugars the banks densely, since I left, a week ago. Nature improves this her last opportunity to empty her lap of flowers.

Ascended the hill. The barberries are abundant there, and already handsomely red, though not much more than half turned. Was surprised at the profusion of autumnal dandelions in their prime on *the top of the hill*, about the oaks. Never saw them thicker in a meadow. A cool, spring-suggesting yellow. They reserve their force till this season, though they begin so early. Cool to the eye, as the creak of the cricket to the ear.

The *Viburnum Lentago*, which I left not half turned red when I went up-country a week ago, are now quite black-purple and shrivelled like raisins on my table, and sweet to taste, though chiefly seed.

Sept. 14. P. M. — To Hubbard's Close and Cardinal Ditch.

Now for the *Aster Tradescanti* along low roads, like the Turnpike, swarming with butterflies and bees. Some of them are pink. How ever unexpected are these later flowers! You thought that Nature had about wound up her affairs. You had seen what she could do this year, and had not noticed a few weeds by the roadside, or mistook them for the remains of summer flowers now hastening to their fall; you thought you knew every twig and leaf by the roadside, and nothing more was to be looked for there; and now, to your surprise, these ditches are crowded with millions of little stars. They suddenly spring up and face you, with their legions on each side the way, as if they had lain in ambuscade there. The flowering of the ditches. Call them travellers' thoughts, numerous though small, worth a penny at least, which, sown in spring and summer, in the fall spring up unobserved at first, successively dusted and washed, mingled with nettles and beggar-ticks as a highway harvest. A starry meteoric shower, a milky way, in the flowery kingdom in whose aisles we travel. Let the traveller bethink himself, elevate and expand his thoughts somewhat, that his successors may oftener hereafter be cheered by the sight of an *Aster Novæ-Angliæ* or *spectabilis* here and there, to remind him that a poet or philosopher has passed this way. The gardener with all his assiduity does not raise such a variety, nor so many successive crops on the same space, as Nature in the very roadside ditches. There they have stood, begrimed

with dust and the wash of the road so long, and made acquaintance with passing sheep and cattle and swine, gathering a trivial experience, and now at last the fall rains have come to wash off some of that dust, and even they exhibit these dense flowery panicles as the result of all that experience, as pure for an hour as if they grew by some wild brook-side. Successor to Mayweed & Co. Is not mayweed, by the way, the flower furthest advanced into the road rut or mid-channel, like the kalmiana lily in the river? The mid-channel, where the stream of travel flows deep and strong, unless it is far up the stream toward its fountainhead, no flower invades. Mayweed! what a misnomer! Call it *rut-weed* rather.

Goodyera pubescens apparently just done. Fringed gentian well out (and some withered or frost-bitten?), say a week, though there was none to be seen here August 27th. I see the fruit and flowers of *Polygonum Careyi* affected with smut like corn.

Sept. 15. *Monday.* Sophia says, bringing company into my sanctum, by way of apology, that I regard the dust on my furniture like the bloom on fruits, not to be swept off. Which reminds me that the bloom on fruits and stems is the only dust which settles on Nature's furniture.

P. M. — To Hubbard's Swamp.

Aster longifolius and *puniceus* and *Spiranthes cernua* in prime. Early *Solidago stricta* [1] done, but some putting out again in the axils, while dead at top,

¹ That is, *arguta.*

Vol. IX

maybe owing to the rains. Meadow-sweet lingers yet!

What I must call *Bidens cernua*, like a small *chrysanthemoides*, is *bristly hairy, somewhat* connate and apparently regularly toothed. The hypericums generally appear to be now about done. I see none.

Sept. 16. P. M. — To Harris's Mill, Acton, with Father.

Aster lævis apparently in prime; very handsome its long, slanting, broad-topped wands by the roadside, even in dry soil, its rays longer and richer purple than usual. See a flock of pigeons dash by. From a stout breast they taper straightly and slenderly to the tail. They have been catching them a while.

William Monroe is said to have been the first who raised teasels about here. He was very sly about it, and fearful lest he should have competitors. At length he lent his wagon to a neighbor, who discovered some teasel seed on the bottom, which he carefully saved and planted, and so competed with Monroe.

Sept. 18. P. M. — By boat to Conantum, barberrying.

Diplopappus linariifolius in prime. River gone down more than I expected after the great rise, to within some eighteen inches of low-water mark, but on account of freshet I have seen no *Bidens Beckii* nor *chrysanthemoides* nor *Polygonum amphibium* var. *aquaticum* in it, nor elsewhere the myriophyllums this year. The witch-hazel at Conantum just begun here and there; some may have been out two or three days. It is apparently

later with us than the fringed gentian, which I have supposed was out by September 7th. Yet I saw the witch-hazel out in Brattleboro September 8th, then apparently for a day or two, while the Browns *thought* the gentian was not out. It is still a question, perhaps, though unquestionably the gentian is now far more generally out here than the hazel. Lespedezas, *violacea, hirta, Stuvei,* etc., — at Blackberry Steep, done. *Solidago cæsia* in prime at Bittern Cliff Wood.

The barberries are not fairly turned, but I gather them that I may not be anticipated, — a peck of large ones. I strip off a whole row of racemes at one sweep, bending the prickles and getting as few leaves as possible, so getting a handful at once. The racemes appear unusually long this season, and the berries large, though not so thick as I have seen them. I consider myself a dextrous barberry-picker, as if I had been born in the Barberry States. A pair of gloves would be convenient, for, with all my knack, it will be some days before I get all the prickles out of my fingers. I get a full peck from about three bushes.

Scared up the same flock of four apparent summer ducks, which, what with myself, a belated (in season) haymaker, and a fisherman above, have hardly a resting-place left. The fisherman takes it for granted that I am after ducks or fishes, surely.

I see no traces of frost yet along the river. See no pontederia fall, for they are covered with water. The *Cornus sericea* is most changed and drooping. Smilacina berries of both kinds now commonly ripe, but not so edible as at first, methinks.

Sept. 19. Am surprised to find the *Polygonum Pennsylvanicum* abundant, by the roadside near the bank. First saw it the other day at Brattleboro. This makes, as I reckon, twenty polygonums that I know, all but *cilinode* and *Virginianum* in Concord. Is not this a late kind? It grows larger than the *Persicaria*. Observed an *Aster undulatus* behind oak at foot of hill on Assabet, with lower leaves not heart-shaped, but thus:

Gathered just half a bushel of barberries on hill in less than two hours, or three pecks to-day and yesterday in less than three hours. It is singular that I have so few, if any, competitors. I have the pleasure also of bringing them home in my boat. They will be more valuable this year, since apples and cranberries are scarce. These barberries are more than the apple crop to me, for we shall have them on the table daily all winter, while the two barrels of apples which we lay up will not amount to so much.

Also, what is the pear crop to the huckleberry crop? They make a great ado about their pears, those who get any, but how many families raise or buy a barrel of pears all told? The pear crop is insignificant compared with the huckleberry crop. The one does not concern me, the other does. I do not taste more than six pears annually, and I suspect the majority fare worse than I, but nature heaps the table with berries for six weeks or more. Indeed the apple crop is not so important as the huckleberry crop. Probably the apples consumed in this town do not amount to more than one barrel a family, but what is this to a month

Vol. IX

or more of huckleberrying for every man, woman, and child, and the birds into the bargain? They are not unprofitable in a pecuniary sense. I hear that some of the inhabitants of Ashby have sold two thousand dollars' worth the past season.

Sept. 20. Melvin says that there are many teal about the river now.

Rain in afternoon. Rain again in the night, hard.

Sept. 21. P. M. — To Cliffs.

Asclepias Cornuti discounting. The seeded parachutes which I release soon come to earth, but probably if they waited for a stronger wind to release them they would be carried far. *Solidago nemoralis* mostly done. *Aster undulatus* in prime, in the dry woods just beyond Hayden's, large slanting, pyramidal panicles of some lilac-tinged, others quite white, flowers, size of *Diplopappus linariifolius*. *Solidago altissima* past prime. Prinos berries. I hear of late faint *chewink* notes in the shrubbery, as if they were meditating their strains in a subdued tone against another year. *A. dumosus* past prime.

Am surprised to see on top of Cliffs, where Wheeler burned in the spring and had cut rye, by a large rock, some very large perfectly fresh *Corydalis glauca*, still well in bloom as well as gone to seed, two and a half feet high and five eighths of an inch thick at base. There are also many large tufts of its glaucous leaves on the black burnt ground which have not come to flower, amid the rye stubble. The bumblebees are

sucking its flowers. Beside the young oak and the sprouts, poke-weed, erechthites, and this corydalis even are common there. How far is this due to the fire, aside from the clearing? Was not the fireweed seed sown by the wind last fall, blown into the woods, where there was a lull which caused it to settle? Perhaps it is fitted to escape or resist fire. The wind which the fire creates may, perchance, lift it again out of harm's way.

The *Asclepias, ob-tusifolia* is turned yellow. I see its often per-fectly upright slender pod five inches long, thus:[1] On top of Cliff, behind the big stump, a yellow white goldenrod, var. *con-color*, which Gray refers to Pennsylvania, ap-parently with the common. That is a great place for white gold-enrod, now in its prime and swarming with honey-bees.

Scare up turtle doves in the stubble. Uva-ursi berries quite ripe. Find, for first time in Concord, *Solanum nigrum*, berries apparently just ripe, by a rock northwest of corydalis. Thus I have within a week found in Concord two of the new plants I found up-country. Such is the advantage of going abroad, — to enable [you] to detect your own plants. I detected them first abroad, because there I was *looking for* the *strange*.

It is a warm and very hazy day, with wreaths of mist in horizon.

[1] It soon bursts in my chamber and shows its beautiful straw-colored lining. A fairy-like casket, shaped like a canoe, with its closely packed imbricated brown seeds, with their yet compressed silvery parachutes like finest unsoiled silk in the right position *above* them, ready to be wafted some dry and breezy day to their destined places.

Saw, in the cow-killer on railroad, a small mountain-ash naturalized!

Sept. 22. A rainy day. Tried some pennyroyal tea, but found it too medicinal for my taste. Yet I collect these herbs, biding the time when their use shall be discovered.

Sept. 23. Rainy day.

Sept. 24. P. M. — To Saw Mill Brook.

Not a sign of an artichoke flower yet below Moore's! May they not be earlier elsewhere?

At brook, cohush and arum berries still fresh, and *Viburnum acerifolium* berries. Apparently *Asplenium Thelypteroides*, a large fern, its under side covered with linear fruit.

Methinks it stands thus with goldenrods and asters now: —

Early   *S. stricta*, done some time.
Swamp   "   "   *probably* past prime.
My *S. gigantea* (?), *probably* done.
S. nemoralis, about done.
S. altissima, much past prime.
S. odora, not seen but *probably* done.
S. puberula, say in good condition, or in **prime**.
S. bicolor and var. *concolor*, in prime.
S. lanceolata, say done.
S. latifolia, in prime.
S. cæsia, in prime.
S. speciosa (none the 15th).[1]
Early meadow aster, say done long time.

[1] Not quite out the 26th of September.

Diplopappus cornifolius, not seen of late.

D. umbellatus, still abundant.

A. patens, some still fresh but not common.

A. macrophyllus, not observed of late.

A. acuminatus, not observed at all in C.

A. Radula, probably about done, not seen of late.

A. dumosus, considerably past prime.

D. linariifolius, in prime, abundant.

A. undulatus, in prime, abundant.

A. corymbosus, still fresh though probably past prime.

A. lævis, probably still in prime.

A. Tradescanti, in prime.

A. puniceus, still in prime (??).

A. longifolius, in prime.

A. multiflorus, in prime.[1]

Sept. 25. The river has risen again *considerably* (this I believe the fourth time), owing to the late copious rains. This before the farmers have succeeded in their *late* attempt to get their meadow-hay after all.

It had not got down before this last rain but to within some eighteen inches, at least, of the usual level in September.

P. M. — To Harrington road.

A golden-crowned thrush runs off, a few feet at a time, on hillside on Harrington road, as if she had a nest still! The haws of the common [thorn] are now very good eating and handsome. Some of the *Cratægus Crus-Galli* on the old fence line between Tarbell and T. Wheeler beyond brook are smaller, stale, and not good at all. The urtica just beyond Widow Hosmer's barn *appears* the same with that I called *U. gracilis* (?) in Brattleboro.

[1] Oct. 8. *A. miser* (omitted), say still in prime or very common.

Sept. 27. The bluebird family revisit their box and warble as in spring.

P. M. — To Clamshell by boat.

Solidago speciosa not quite out!! *Viburnum nudum* berries are soon gone. I noticed none to speak of in Hubbard's Swamp, September 15th. Start up a snipe in the meadow. Bathed at Hubbard's Bath, but found the water very cold. Bathing about over.

It is a very fine afternoon to be on the water, somewhat Indian-summer-like. I do not know what constitutes the peculiarity and charm of this weather; the broad water so smooth, notwithstanding the slight wind, as if, owing to some oiliness, the wind slid over without ruffling it. There is a slight coolness in the air, yet the sun is occasionally very warm. I am tempted to say that the air is singularly clear, yet I see it is quite hazy. Perhaps it is that transparency it is said to possess when full of moisture and before or after rain. Through this I see the colors of trees and shrubs beginning to put on their October dress, and the creak of the mole cricket sounds late along the shore.

The *Aster multiflorus* may easily be confounded with the *A. Tradescanti*. Like it, it whitens the roadside in some places. It has purplish disks, but a less straggling top than the *Tradescanti*.

Sept. 28. P. M. — To old mill-site behind Ponkawtasset.

Poke berries in the sprout-land east of the red huckleberry still fresh and abundant, perhaps a little past prime. I never saw so many. The plants stand

Vol. IX

close together, and their drooping racemes three to five inches long, of black or purplish-black berries (ending in red and less [an indecipherable word]), almost crowd one another, hanging around the bright-purple, now for the most part bare, stems. I hear some birds about, but see none feeding on the berries. I could soon gather bushels there.

The arum berries are still fresh and abundant, perhaps in their prime. A large cluster is two and a half inches long by two wide and rather flattish. One, which has ripened prematurely, the stalk being withered and drooping, resembles a very short thick ear of scarlet corn. *This* might well enough be called snake-corn. These singular vermilion-colored berries, about a hundred of them, surmount a purple bag on a peduncle six or eight inches long. It is one of the most remarkable and dazzling, if not the handsomest, fruits we have. These were by violet wood-sorrel wall. How many fruits are scarlet now! — barberries, prinos, etc.

A flock of vireo-like, somewhat yellowish birds, very neat, white beneath and olive above, in garden.

Sept. 29. P. M. — To Grape Cliff.

The pea-vine fruit is partly ripe, little black-dotted beans, about three in a pod.

I can hardly clamber along the grape cliff now without getting my clothes covered with desmodium ticks, — there especially the *rotundifolium* and *paniculatum*. Though you were running for your life, they would have time to catch and cling to your clothes, — often

the whole row of pods of the *D. paniculatum*, like a piece of a saw blade with three teeth. You pause at a convenient place and spend a long time picking them off, which it took so short a time to attach. They will even cling to your hand as you go by. They cling like babes to the mother's breast, by instinct. Instead of being caught and detained ourselves by birdlime, we are compelled to catch these seeds and carry them with us. These almost invisible nets, as it were, are spread for us, and whole coveys of desmodium and bidens seeds and burs steal transportation out of us. I have found myself often covered, as it were with an imbricated scaly coat of the brown desmodium seeds or a bristling *chevaux-de-frise* of beggar-ticks, and had to spend a quarter of an hour or more picking them off at some convenient place; and so they got just what they wanted, deposited in another place. How surely the desmodium, growing on some rough cliffside, or the bidens, on the edge of a pool, prophesy the coming of the traveller, brute or human, that will transport their seeds on his coat!

I am late for grapes; most have fallen. The fruit of what I have called *Vitis æstivalis* has partly fallen. It is dark-purple, about seven sixteenths of an inch in diameter, very acid and commonly hard. Stem and petiole smooth and purplish, but leaf not smooth or green beneath. Should not this be called frost grape, rather than the earlier one I ate at Brattleboro? Grapes are singularly various for a wild fruit, like many cultivated ones.

Dr. Reynolds told me the other day of a Canada

lynx (?) killed in Andover, in a swamp, some years ago, when he was teaching school in Tewksbury; thought to be one of a pair, the other being killed or seen in Derry. Its large track was seen in the snow in Tewksbury and traced to Andover and back. They saw where it had leaped thirty feet! and where it devoured rabbits. Was on a tree when shot. Skin stuffed somewhere.[1]

Sept. 30. Cattle-Show. An overcast, mizzling, and rainy day.

Minott tells of a General Hull, who lived somewhere in this county, who, he remembers, called out the whole division once or twice to a muster. He sold the army under him to the English in the last war, — though General Miller of Lincoln besought [him] to let him lead them, — and never was happy after it, had no peace of mind. It was said that his life was in danger here in consequence of his treason. Once, at a muster in front of the Hayden house, when there was a sham fight, and an Indian party took a circuit round a piece of wood, some put green grapes into their guns, and he, hearing one whistle by his head, thought some one wished to shoot him and ordered them to disperse, — dismissed them.

Speaking of the meadow-hay which is lost this year, Minott said that the little they had got since the last flood before this was good for nothing, would only poison the cattle, being covered with the dried slime and filth of the freshet. When you mowed it there

[1] *Vide* September, 1860.

Vol. IX

III

OCTOBER, 1856

(ÆT. 39)

Oct. 1. Very heavy rain in the night; cooler now. P. M. — To Walden.

Examined an *Asclepias Cornuti* pod, already opening by the wall. As they dry, the pods crack and open by the seam along the convex or outer side of the pods, revealing the seeds, with their silky parachutes, closely packed in an imbricated manner, already right side up to the number, in one instance, of one hundred and thirty-four (as I counted) and again two hundred and seventy. As they lie they resemble somewhat a round plump fish with the silk ends exposed at the tail. Children call them fishes. The silk is divided once or twice by their raised partitions of the spongy core around which they are arranged. At the top of some more open and drier, is already a little cloud of loosened seeds and down, two or three inches in diameter, held by the converging tips of the down like meridians, just ready to float away when the wind rises.

It is cooler and windier, and I wear two thin coats.

I do not perceive the poetic and dramatic capabilities of an anecdote or story which is told me, its significance, till some time afterwards. One of the qualities of a pregnant fact is that it does not surprise us, and we only perceive afterward how interesting it is, and

arose a great dust. He spoke of this grass, thus left over winter to next year, as "old fog." Said that Clark (Daniel or Brooks) asked him the other day what made so many young alders and birches and willows spring up in the river meadows of late years; it did n't use to be so forty or fifty years ago; and he told him that in old times, when they were accustomed to take something strong to drink, they did n't stand for such shrubs but mowed all clear as they went, but now, not feeling so much energy for want of the stimulant, when they came to a bush, though no bigger than a pipe-stem, they mowed all round it and left it standing.

then must know all the particulars. We do not enjoy poetry fully unless we know it to be poetry.

Oct. 2. P. M. — To Cliffs *via* Hubbard's meadow.

Succory still, with its cool blue, here and there, and *Hieracium Canadense* still quite fresh, with its very pretty broad strap-shaped rays, broadest at the end, alternately long and short, with five very regular sharp teeth in the end of each. The scarlet leaves and stem of the rhexia, some time out of flower, makes almost as bright a patch in the meadow now as the flowers did, with its bristly leaves. Its seed-vessels are perfect little cream-pitchers of graceful form. The mountain sumach now a dark scarlet quite generally.

The prinos berries are in their prime, seven sixteenths of an inch in diameter. They are scarlet, somewhat lighter than the arum berries. They are now very fresh and bright, and what adds to their effect is the perfect freshness and greenness of the leaves amid which they are seen. *Gerardia purpurea* still. Brakes in Hubbard's Swamp Wood are withered, quite dry. *Solidago speciosa* completely out, though not a flower was out September 27th, or five days ago; say three or four days.

The river is still higher, owing to the rain of September 30th, partly covering the meadows; yet they are endeavoring to rake cranberries. After all, I perceive that *in some places* the greatest injury done by the water to these berries has probably been that it prevented their ripening, but generally it has been by softening them. They carry them home, spread, and dry them, and pick out the spoilt ones. One gets only fifty bushels where he would have had two hundred. *Eupatorium purpureum* is generally done. Now and then I see a *Hypericum Canadense* flower still. The leaves, etc., of this and the *angulosum* are turned crimson.

I am amused to see four little Irish boys only five or six years old getting a horse in a pasture, for their father apparently, who is at work in a neighboring field. They have all in a row got hold of a very long halter and are leading him. All wish to have a hand in it. It is surprising that he obeys such small specimens of humanity, but he seems to be very docile, a real family horse. At length, by dint of pulling and shouting, they get him into a run down a hill, and though he moves very deliberately, scarcely faster than a walk, all but the one at the end of the line soon cut and run to right and left, without having looked behind, expecting him to be upon them. They haul up at last at the bars, which are down, and then the family puppy, a brown pointer (?), about two-thirds grown, comes bounding to join them and assist. He is as youthful and about as knowing as any of them. The horse marches gravely behind, obeying the faint tug at the halter, or honestly stands still from time to time, as if not aware that they are pulling at all, though they are all together straining every nerve to start him. It is interesting to behold this faithful beast, the oldest and wisest of the company, thus implicitly obeying the lead of the youngest and weakest.

The second lechea radical shoots are one inch long. *Solidago bicolor* considerably past prime. Corydalis still fresh.

Saw apparently two phœbes on the tops of the dry mulleins. Why so rarely seen for so many months?

Oct. 3. The white pines are now getting to be pretty generally parti-colored, the lower yellowing needles ready to fall. The sumachs are generally crimson (darker than scarlet), and young trees and bushes by the water and meadows are generally beginning to glow red and yellow. Especially the hillsides about Walden begin to wear these autumnal tints in the cooler air. These lit leaves, this glowing, bright-tinted shrubbery, is in singular harmony with the dry, stony shore of this cool and deep well.

The frost keeps off remarkably. I have seen none, though I hear that there was some two or three mornings ago.

I detect the crotalaria behind the Wyman site, by hearing the now rattling seeds in its pods as I go through the grass, like the trinkets about an Indian's leggins, or a rattlesnake.

Oct. 4. *Helianthus tuberosus*, apparently several days, in Reynolds's yard (the butcher's).

P. M. — Down river.

Wind from northeast. Some water milkweed flying. Its pods small, slender, straight, and pointed perfectly upright; seeds large with much wing. The hibiscus gone to seed, and pods opened showing the

seed, opposite Ostrya Island [1] or Rock below Battle-Ground.

In an article on the alligator in *Harper's Magazine* for December, 1854, it is said that mosquitoes "surround its head in clouds; and we have heard the negroes assert that the reptile opened its mouth until its interior was fully lined, and suddenly closing it up, would swallow the accumulated marauders, and then set its huge jaws as a trap for more." This reminds me of the swarms of mosquitoes about frogs and, I think, turtles.

In another article, of May, 1855, on "The Lion and his Kind," the animals are placed in this order: the domestic cat, wildcat, the ocelot or tiger-cat of Peru and Mexico, the caracal of Asia and Africa, the lynx of North America, the chetah of India and Africa, the ounce of India (perhaps a rough variety of the leopard), the leopard, the jaguar, the cougar, the tiger, the lion. "The Cougar is the American lion — at least it bears a closer resemblance to that noble brute than any other of the feline family, for it is destitute of the stripes of the tiger, the spots of the leopard, and the rosettes of the jaguar; but when full-grown possesses a tawny-red color, almost uniform over the whole body, and hence the inference that it is like the lion." "Cougar is a corruption of the Mexican name." Ranges between Paraguay and the Great Lakes of North America. "In form it is less attractive than the generality of its species, there being an apparent want of symmetry; for it is observable that

[1] Burr's Island.

its back is hollow, its legs short and thick, and its tail does not gracefully taper; yet nature has invested the cougar with other qualities as a compensation, the most remarkable of which is an apparent power to render itself quite invisible; for so cunningly tinged is its fur, that it perfectly mingles with the bark of trees — in fact, with all subdued tints — and stretched upon a limb, or even extended upon the floor of its dimly lighted cage, you must prepare your eye by considerable mental resolution to be assured of its positive presence." Its flesh is eaten by some. Mrs. Jane Swisshelm kept one which grew to be nine feet long, and, according to her, in this writer's words, "If in exceeding good-humor he would purr; but if he wished to intimidate, he would raise his back, erect his hair, and spit like a cat. In the twilight of the evening the animal was accustomed to pace back and forth to the full extent of his limits, ever and anon uttering a short, piercing shriek, which made the valley reverberate for half a mile or more in every direction. Mrs. Swisshelm says these sounds were the shrillest, and at the same time the most mournful she ever heard. They might, perhaps, be likened to the scream of a woman in an agony of terror." He once sprang at her, but was brought up by his chain. When preparing to spring, his eyes were "green and blazing, and the tip of his tail moving from side to side." This paper describes "a full-grown royal tiger, measuring four feet seven inches from the nose to the insertion of the tail. . . . Unlike the miserable wretches we see in our menageries, etc." The Brattleboro paper makes the panther four feet eleven inches, so measured!!

I hear that a Captain Hurd, of Wayland or Sudbury, estimates the loss of river meadow-hay this season in those two towns on account of the freshet at twelve hundred tons.

Oct. 5. Sunday.   P. M. — To Hill and over the pastures westward.

Sally Cummings and Mike Murray are out on the Hill collecting apples and nuts. Do they not rather belong to such children of nature than to those who have merely bought them with their money? There are few apples for them this year, however, and it is too early for walnuts (too late for hazelnuts). The grapes are generally gone, and their vines partly bare and yellowed, though without frost. I amuse myself on the hilltop with pulling to pieces and letting fly the now withered and dry pasture thistle tops. They have a much coarser pappus than the milkweeds. I am surprised, amid these perfectly withered and bleached thistles, to see one just freshly in flower. The autumnal dandelion is now comparatively scarce there. In the huckleberry pasture, by the fence of old barn boards, I notice many little pale-brown dome-shaped (puckered to a centre beneath) puffballs, which emit their dust. When you pinch them, a smoke-like brown dust (snuff-colored) issues from the orifice at their top, just like smoke from a chimney. It is so fine and light that it rises into the air and is wafted away like smoke. They

Vol. IX

are low Oriental domes or mosques. Sometimes crowded together in nests, like a collection of humble cottages on the moor, in the coal-pit or Numidian style; for there is suggested some humble hearth beneath, from which this smoke comes up, as it were the homes of slugs and crickets. They please me not a little by their resemblance to rude dome-shaped, turf-built cottages on the plain, wherein some humble but everlasting life is lived. Amid the low and withering grass or the stubble there they are gathered, and their smoke ascends between the legs of the herds and the traveller. I imagine a hearth and pot, and some snug but humble family passing its Sunday evening beneath each one. Some, when you press them harder, emit clear water — the relics of rain or dew — along with the dust, which last, however, has no affinity for it, but is quite dry-and smoke-like. I locate there at once all that is simple and admirable in human life. There is no virtue which their roofs exclude. I imagine with what contentment and faith I could come home to them at evening.[1] I see some not yet ripe, still entire and rounded at top. When I break them open, they are found to be quite soggy, of a stringy white consistency, almost cream-like, riper and yellowish at top, where they will burst by and by. Many have holes eaten into them. On one I find a slug feeding, with a little hole beneath him,[2] and a cricket has

[1] [Channing, p. 101.]
[2] This was a different species, the white pigeon-egg, with that rough, crystalled surface.

eaten out the whole inside of another in which he is housed. This before they are turned to dust. Large chocolate-colored ones have long since burst and are spread out wide like a shallow dish.

Crickets are seen now moving slowly about in the paths, often with their heads only concealed in a burrow, as if looking out for winter quarters. I saw, on my return, a dozen crickets of various sizes gathered on an apple paring which I had dropped in the path when I came along.

The sweet-briar rose hips are very handsome now, but these hips do not deserve to be coupled with haws as articles of food, even in extremities. They are very dry, hard, seedy, and unpalatable. I see some fresh-grown callitriche in some clear well-filled leafy pools which are commonly dry at this season. The singular long pointed reddish bulbs in the axils of the *Lysimachia stricta* are one of the signs of the season, cool and late.

It is well to find your employment and amusement in simple and homely things. These wear best and yield most. I think I would rather watch the motions of these cows in their pasture for a day, which I now see all headed one way and slowly advancing, — watch them and project their course carefully on a chart, and report all their behavior faithfully, — than wander to Europe or Asia and watch other motions there; for it is only ourselves that we report in either case, and perchance we shall report a more restless and worthless self in the latter case than in the first.

Oct. 6. I notice the effects of some frost this morning in garden. Some pumpkin vines drooping and black.

P. M. — Carried Sophia and Aunt up the Assabet.

The reflections of the bright-tinted maples very perfect. The common notes of the chickadee, so rarely heard for a long time, and also one *phebe* strain from it,[1] amid the Leaning Hemlocks, remind me of pleasant winter days, when they are more commonly seen. The jay's shrill note is more distinct of late about the edges of the woods, when so many birds have left us. Were suddenly driven home by a slight thunder-shower!

Oct. 8. P. M. — To Smith Chestnut Grove by Turnpike, and Saw Mill.

At length I discover some white pine cones, a few, on Emerson Heater Piece trees. They are all open, and the seeds, all the sound ones but one, gone. So September is the time to gather them. The tip of each scale is covered with fresh flowing pitch.

The trees and weeds by the Turnpike are all alive this pleasant afternoon with twittering sparrows, Emerson's buckthorn hedge especially, and Watts's weeds adjoining. I observe white-throated sparrows, song sparrows, I think some *Fringilla juncorum*, etc. (*maybe* tree sparrows ???). They are all together and keep up a faint warbling, apparently the white-throats and tree sparrows, — if the last are there. A song sparrow utters a full strain.

[1] This again the 8th. It is an anticipation of spring.

Asters and goldenrods are now scarce; no longer that crowd along the low roadsides.

The following is the condition of the asters and goldenrods, judging from my observations on this walk alone. I will only refer to those which were not done September 24th. I speak of their general condition, though a very few specimens here and there may present a different appearance.

Swamp *stricta*, done, some hoary.

S. nemoralis, done, many hoary, though a *very few* flowers linger.

S. altissima, done, many hoary,

S. puberula, not seen.

S. bicolor and variety, probably done (not seen out).

S. latifolia, far gone.

S. cæsia, much the worse for the wear, but freshest of any seen.

S. speciosa, not seen (it was in prime Oct. 2d).

Diplopappus cornifolius, not seen, probably done.

D. umbellatus, not seen, probably done.[1]

A. patens, apparently done.

A. macrophyllus, not seen.

A. acuminatus, not seen.

A. dumosus, probably done.

D. linariifolius, apparently nearly done.

A. undulatus, *comparatively* fresh.

A. corymbosus, looks fresh !

A. lævis, not noticed, probably done (?) *generally*.

A. Tradescanti, a few still.

A. puniceus, hardly seen, probably nearly done.

A. longifolius, a few still.

A. multiflorus, none observed.

A. miser, a very few left.

Of solidagos, I judge that only the last three named, and perhaps *puberula* and *S. bicolor* in some places,

[1] Certainly done the 14th.

are common still; and, of asters, only *corymbosus*, *undulatus*, *Tradescanti*, and *longifolius* (know not of *multiflorus*) are common.

The *Bidens cernuum* is quite common and fresh yet in Everett's meadow by Turnpike. A few chestnut burs are open, and have been some days, before they could have felt frost, showing that they would open without it, but a stone will not jar them down, nor a club thrown into the tree yet. I get half a pocketful out of slightly gaping burs at the expense of many prickles in my fingers. The squirrels have cut off some burs. I see the marks of their teeth. Find many checker-berries on Smith's hill beyond the chestnut grove, which appear to be just ripe, a lighter pink color, with two little white checks on the stem side, the marks of what I suppose are the two outer calyx-leaves. Near by, a short fertile fern with large shelly capsules, perhaps a botrychium.[1] A great deal, a great part, of the dicksonia fern at Saw Mill is now whitened or whitening. I see, as I go through the hollow behind Britton's shanty, the already hoary tops of many *S. nemoralis* and also the yellowish spheres of the *Hieracium scabrum* amid the scarlet (or crimson) sumach and reddened comptonia. So fast the winter advances. I notice a large toad amid the dead leaves in the woods at *Chimaphila maculata*, colored like the leaves, a much darker brown than usual, proving that they resemble the ground they occupy.

Meet Nealy, short and thick, in the woodland path, with his great silent mastiff by his side and his double-

[1] Yes, small botrychium. *Vide* 19th *inst.*

barrelled gun in his palm, all dangerously cocked. He is eager for partridges, but only guilty of killing a jay, I judge, from his report. Once or twice I hear the report of his fowling-piece. I heard partridges *drum* the 3d instant. Observed in the woods a very large, perhaps owl pellet, or possibly fox stercus, of gray fur and small bones and the jaw of a rodent, apparently a wild mouse.

The hickory leaves are among the handsomest now, varying from green through yellow, more or less broadly green-striped on the principal veins, to pure yellow, at first almost lemon-yellow, at last browner and crisped. This mingling of yellow and green on the same leaf, the green next the veins where the life is most persistent, is very pleasing.

Sophia brings home two or three clusters of very large freshly ripe thimble-berries, with some unripe, a second crop, apparently owing to the abundance of rain for the last six weeks.

Oct. 10. These are the finest days in the year, Indian summer. This afternoon it was 80°, between three and four, and at 6.30 this evening my chamber is oppressively sultry, and the thermometer on the north side of the house is at 64°. I lie with window wide open under *a single sheet* most of the night. But I anticipate. The *phebe* note of the chickadee is now often heard in the yards, and the very Indian summer itself is a similar renewal of the year, with the faint warbling of birds and second blossoming of flowers. Going to E. Hosmer's by boat, saw quite a flock of

wild ducks in front of his house, close by the bridge. While moving the fence to-day, dug up a large reddish, mummy-like chrysalid or nymph.[1]

Oct 11. P. M. — To Cliffs.

The Indian summer continues. Solidagos now generally show woolly heads along the fences and brooks.

E. Hosmer said yesterday that his father remembered when there was but one store in Concord, and that the little office attached to Dr. Heywood's house, kept by Beatton. I remember the old shutters with names of groceries on them.[2] Perhaps, then, Jones was the only shopkeeper in *his* day. I was speaking of it to Farrar, the blacksmith, to-day, and he said, yes, he had heard his father speak of Beatton as "the most honestest man that ever was." When a child was sent to his store and he could not make change within half a penny he would stick a row of pins in the child's sleeve, enough to make all square. He said he had only a keg of molasses and a bladder of snuff when he began. Farrar thought that the spirit manufactured a century ago was not so adulterated and poisonous as that now made. He could remember when delirium tremens was very rare. There was Luke Dodge; he could remember him a drunkard for more than forty years, yet he was now between eighty and ninety.

Farrar gave me a wing and foot of a hawk which he shot about three weeks ago as he was sitting on a woodpile by the railroad, against R. W. E.'s lot. He called

[1] That is, of the sphinx moth.

[2] No, it probably was not there.

it a partridge hawk; said he was about as big as a partridge and his back of a similar color, and had not a white rump. This foot has a sharp shin [1] and stout claws, but the wing is much larger than that of the *Falco fuscus* (or sharp-shinned hawk), being, with the shoulder attached, sixteen inches long, which would make the alar extent some thirty-three inches, which is the size of the *F. Pennsylvanicus.* This wing corresponds in its markings very exactly with the description of that, and I must so consider it. Peabody does not describe any such bird, and Nuttall describes it as very rare, — apparently he has not seen one, — and says that Wilson had seen only two.

Bay-wing sparrows numerous. In the woods I hear the note of the jay, a metallic, *clanging* sound, sometimes a mew. Refer any strange note to him. The scent of decaying leaves after the wet fall is a very agreeable fragrance on all sides in the woods now, like a garret full of herbs. In the path, as I go up the hill beyond the springs, on the edge of Stow's sprout-land, I find a little snake which somebody has killed with his heel. It is apparently *Coluber amœnus*, the red snake. Brown above, light-red beneath, about eight inches long, but the end of its tail is gone (only three quarters of an inch of it left). I count some one hundred and twenty-seven plates. It is a conspicuous light red beneath, then a bluish-gray line along the sides, and above this brown with a line of lighter or yellowish brown down the middle of the back.

The sprout-land and stubble behind the Cliffs are

[1] I had reference to the sharp angle of the *rear* edge of the shin.

Vol. IX

pigeon-egg fungus (one was noticed in report of October 5th) are puffballs. The outer thick white coat peels off first. I see it so now, but not in segments like the *stellata.*

A pasture thistle with many fresh flowers and bees on it.

Oct. 12. It is interesting to see how some of the few flowers which still linger are frequented by bees and other insects. Their resources begin to fail and they are improving their last chance. I have noticed them of late, especially on white goldenrod and pasture thistles, etc.; and to-day, on a small watermelon cut open ten days ago, in the garden, I see half a dozen honeybees, many more flies, some wasps, a grasshopper, and a *large* handsome butterfly, with dark snuff-colored wings and a stripe of blue eyes on them. The restless bees keep buzzing toward the butterfly, but it keeps them off by opening and shutting its wings, but does not much mind the other insects. I did not suspect such a congregation in the desolate garden.

Wasps for some time looking about for winter quarters.

Oct. 14. A sudden change in the weather after remarkably warm and pleasant weather. Rained in the night, and finger-cold to-day. Your hands instinctively find their way to your pockets. Leaves are fast falling, and they are already past their brightness, perhaps earlier than usual [1] on account of wet.

[1] No.

all alive with restless flocks of sparrows of various species. I distinguish *F. hyemalis*, song sparrow, apparently *F. juncorum* or maybe tree sparrows,[1] and chip-birds (?). They are continually flitting past and surging upward, two or more in pursuit of each other, in the air, where they break like waves, and pass along with a faint cheep. On the least alarm many will rise from a juniper bush on to a shrub oak above it, and, when all is quiet, return into the juniper, perhaps for its berries. It is often hard to detect them as they sit on the young trees, now beginning to be bare, for they are very nearly the color of the bark and are very cunning to hide behind the leaves. There are apparently two other kinds, one like purple finches, another more like large Savannah sparrows.

The shrub oak plain is now in the perfection of its coloring, the red of young oaks with the green of spiring birches intermixed. A rich rug.

It is perfect Indian summer, a thick haze forming wreaths in the near horizon. The sun is almost shorn of its rays now at mid-afternoon, and there is only a sheeny reflection from the river.

The patches of huckleberries on Conantum are now red. Here on the Cliffs are fresh poke flowers and small snapdragon and corydalis. The white goldenrod is still common here, and covered with bees. *Hieracium venosum* still. I see pretty dense spreading radical leaves about the pinweeds, apparently recent.

A cuckoo is heard.

I find that the rough, white, crystalled-surfaced

[1] Probably not.

P. M. — To Hubbard's Close.

Huckleberries perfectly plump and fresh on the often bare bushes (always (else) red-leaved). The bare gray twigs begin to show, the leaves fast falling. The maples are nearly bare. The leaves of red maples, still bright, strew the ground, often crimson-spotted on a yellow ground, just like some apples.[1] Pineneedles, just fallen, now make a thick carpet.

Going to Laurel Glen in the hollow beyond Deep Cut Woods, I see now withered erechthites and epilobium standing thick on the bare hillside, where the hemlocks were cut, exposing the earth, though no fire has been there. They seem to require only that the earth shall be laid bare for them.

In Laurel Glen, an aspen sprout which has grown seven to eight feet high, its lower and larger leaves, already fallen and blackened (a dark slate), about. One green and perfect leaf measures ten inches in length and nine broad, heart-shaped. Others, less perfect, are half an inch or more larger each way.

Any flowers seen now may be called late ones. I see perfectly fresh succory, not to speak of yarrow, a *Viola ovata*, some *Polygala sanguinea*, autumnal dandelion, tansy, etc., etc.

Oct. 15. P. M. — Up Assabet.

A smart frost, which even injured plants in house. Ground stiffened in morning; ice seen.

River lower than for some months. Banks begin to wear almost a Novemberish aspect. The black willow

[*Excursions*, p. 265; Riv. 325.]

almost completely bare; many quite so. It loses its leaves about same time with the maples. The large ferns are now rapidly losing their leaves except the terminal tuft. Other species about the edges of swamps were turned suddenly dark cinnamon-color by the frost of yesterday. The water is very calm and full of reflections. Large fleets of maple and other leaves are floating on its surface as I go up the Assabet, leaves which apparently came down in a shower with yesterday morning's frost. Every motion of the turtles is betrayed by their rustling now.[1] Mikania is all whitish woolly now. Yet many tortoises are still out in the sun. An abundance of checkerberries by the hemlock at V. Muhlenbergii Brook. A remarkable year for berries. Even this, too, is abundant like the rest. They are tender and more palatable than ever now. I find a little pile of them, maybe fifteen or twenty, on the moss with each a little indentation or two on it, made apparently by some bird or beast. The chickadees are hopping near on the hemlock above. They resume their winter ways before the winter comes. A great part of the hemlock seeds fallen.

Oct. 16. Ground all white with frost.

P. M. — To chestnuts, down Turnpike.

I notice these flowers on the way by the roadside, which survive the frost, *i. e.* a few of them: hedge-mustard, mayweed, tall crowfoot, autumnal dandelion, yarrow, some *Aster Tradescanti*, and some red clover.[2]

---

[1] [*Excursions*, pp. 266, 267; Riv. 327.]

[2] Catnep. Tansy next day, and a very few meagre *S. cæsia* and

Polygonum orientale was finished by yesterday's frost. There was plenty of the front-rank polygonum freshly open along river on the 13th. Perhaps the frosts have nipped it.

I saw a farmer busily collecting his pumpkins on the 14th, — Abel Brooks, — rambling over his corn-fields and bringing the pumpkins out to the sides on the path, on the side of the field, where he can load them. The ground was so stiff on the 15th, in the morning, that some could not dig potatoes. Bent is now making haste to gather his apples. I. Wright, too, is collecting some choice barrels of golden russets. Many times he turns it over before he leaves out a specked one. A poor story if the farmer cannot get rich, for everything he has is salable, even every load of mud on his farm.

At the Everett meadow a large flock of mewing and lisping goldfinches, with but little yellow, pass over the Turnpike.

Many chestnut burs are now open, yet a stone will not jar down many nuts yet. Burs which were quite green on the 8th are now all brown and dry, and the prickles come off in your hand when you touch them, yet the nuts do not readily drop out. Many nuts have fallen within two or three days, but many squirrels have been busily picking them up.

Found amid the sphagnum on the dry bank on the south side of the Turnpike, just below Everett's meadow, a rare and remarkable fungus, such as I have heard of but never seen before. The whole height six and

---

A. undulatus, and, on the 19th, snapdragon, *Ranunculus bulbosus,* shepherd's-purse, and chickweed, of course.

three quarters inches, two thirds of it being buried in the sphagnum. It may be divided into three parts, pileus, stem, and base, — or scrotum, for it is a perfect phallus. One of those fungi named *impudicus*, I think.[1] In all respects a most disgusting object, yet very suggestive. It is hollow from top to bottom, the form of the hollow answering to that of the outside. The color of the outside white excepting the pileus, which is olive-colored and somewhat coarsely corrugated, with an oblong mouth at tip about one eighth of an inch long, or, measuring the white lips, half an inch. This cap is thin and white within, about one and three eighths inches high by one and a half wide. The stem (bare portion) is three inches long (tapering more rapidly than in the drawing), horizontally viewed of an oval form. Longest diameter at base one and a half inches, at top (on edge of pileus) fifteen sixteenths of an inch. Short diameters in both cases about two thirds as much. It is a delicate white cylinder of a finely honeycombed and crispy material about three sixteenths of an inch thick, or more, the whole very straight and regular. The base, or scrotum, is of an irregular bag form, about one inch by two in the extremes, consisting of a thick trembling gelatinous mass surrounding the bottom of the stem and covered with a tough white skin of a darker tint than the stem. The whole plant rather frail and trembling. There was at first a very thin delicate white collar (or *volva?*) about the base of the stem above the scrotum.

---

[1] This is very similar to if not the same with that represented in Loudon's *Encyclopædia* and called "*Phallus impudicus*, Stinking Morel, very fetid."

It was as offensive to the eye as to the scent, the cap rapidly melting and defiling what it touched with a fetid, olivaceous, semiliquid matter. In an hour or two the plant scented the whole house wherever placed, so that it could not be endured. I was afraid to sleep in my chamber where it had lain until the room had been well ventilated. It smelled like a dead rat in the ceiling, in all the ceilings of the house. Pray, what was Nature thinking of when she made this? She almost puts herself on a level with those who draw in privies. The cap had at first a smooth and almost dry surface, of a sort of olive slate-color, but the next day this colored surface all melted out, leaving deep corrugations or gills — rather honeycomb-like cells — with a white bottom.

Oct. 17. Noticed some of the fungus called spunk, very large, on the large white oak in Love Lane, eight or nine feet from the ground on the east side, on a protuberance where a limb was formerly cut off. It is now green and moist, of a yellowish color, composed of several flakes one above the other; the length of the shelf, or chord of the arc, twenty-one inches; depth from the tree, or width of shelf, about one foot.

Frost has now within three or four days turned almost all flowers to woolly heads, — their November aspect. Fuzzy, woolly heads now reign along all hedgerows and over many broad fields.

Some trees, as small hickories, appear to have dropped their leaves instantaneously, as at a signal, as a soldier grounds arms. The ground under such reflects a blaze of light from now crisped yellow leaves.[1] Down they have come on all sides, as if touched by fairy fingers. Boys are raking leaves in the street, if only for the pleasure of dealing with such clean, crisp substances.[2] Countless leafy skiffs are floating on pools and lakes and rivers and in the swamps and meadows, often concealing the water quite from foot and eye. Each leaf, still crisply curled up on its edges, makes as yet a tight boat like the Indian's hide one, but ere long it will become relaxed and flatted out and sink to the bottom, *i. e.* if it is driven out to sea, but most are drifted toward the shore, which is converted into one long, crowded haven where the water is concealed, and they settle close to land.[3]

Many fringed gentians quite fresh yet, though most are faded and withered. I suspect that their very early and sudden fading and withering has nothing, or little, to do with frost after all, for why should so many fresh ones succeed still? My pressed ones have all faded in like manner!!

It would be too late to look for bees now at Wyman's; the flowers are too far gone.

I go down the path through Charles Bartlett's land. The young white oak leaves are now generally withered in and on the sides of the hollows there, also the black scrub, while the red and black oaks are still commonly red and so far alive.

As I stood looking at Emerson's bound under the

[1] [*Excursions*, p. 264; Riv. 324.]
[2] [*Excursions*, p. 266; Riv. 326.]
[3] [See *Excursions*, pp. 266–268; Riv. 326–328.]

Vol. IX

than two good nuts, very often only one, the middle one, both sides of which will then be convex, each way bulging out into a thin abortive mere reminiscence of a nut, all shell, beyond it. It is a rich sight, that of a large chestnut tree with a dome-shaped top, where the yellowing leaves have become thin, — for most now strew the ground evenly as a carpet throughout the chestnut woods and so save some seed, — all richly rough with great brown burs, which are opened into several segments so as to show the wholesome-colored nuts peeping forth, ready to fall on the slightest jar. The individual nuts are very interesting, of various forms, according to the season and the number in a bur. The base of each where it was joined to the bur is marked with an irregular dark figure on a light ground, oblong or crescent-shaped commonly, like a spider or other insect with a dozen legs, while the upper or small end tapers into a little white, woolly spire crowned with a star, and the whole upper slopes of the nuts are covered with the same hoary wool, which reminds you of the frosts on whose advent they peep forth. Each nut stretches forth a little starry hand at the end of a slender arm — and by this, when mature, you may pull it out without fear of prickles. Within this thick prickly bur the nuts are about as safe until they are quite mature, as a porcupine behind its spines. Yet I see where the squirrels have gnawed through many closed burs and left the pieces on the stumps.

The late goldenrod (*S. latifolia*) is all gone, on account of frost.

railroad embankment, I heard a smart *tche-day-day-day* close to my ear, and, looking up, saw four of these birds, which had come to scrape acquaintance with me, hopping amid the alders within three and four feet of me. I had heard them further off at first, and they had followed me along the hedge. They *day-day*'d and lisped their faint notes alternately, and then, as if to make me think they had some other errand than to peer at me, they pecked the dead twigs with their bills — the little top-heavy, black-crowned, volatile fellows.

Oct. 18. Rain all night and half this day.

P. M. — A-chestnutting down Turnpike and across to Britton's, thinking that the rain now added to the frosts would relax the burs which were open and let the nuts drop.

The sugar maples are now in their glory, all aglow with yellow, red, and green. They are remarkable for the contrast they afford of deep blushing red on one half and green on the other.[1]

The chestnuts are not so ready to fall as I expected. Perhaps the burs require to be dried now after the rain. In a day or two they will nearly all come down. They are a pretty fruit, thus compactly stowed away in this bristly chest, — three is the regular number, and there is no room to spare, — the two outside nuts having each one convex side without and a flat side within; the middle nut has two flat sides. Sometimes there are several more nuts in a bur, but this year the burs are small, and there are not commonly more

[1] [*Excursions*, p. 271; Riv. 332.]

Men commonly exaggerate the theme. Some themes they think are significant and others insignificant. I feel that my life is very homely, my pleasures very cheap. Joy and sorrow, success and failure, grandeur and meanness, and indeed most words in the English language do not mean for me what they do for my neighbors. I see that my neighbors look with compassion on me, that they think it is a mean and unfortunate destiny which makes me to walk in these fields and woods so much and sail on this river alone. But so long as I find here the only real elysium, I cannot hesitate in my choice. My work is writing, and I do not hesitate, though I know that no subject is too trivial for me, tried by ordinary standards; for, ye fools, the theme is nothing, the life is everything. All that interests the reader is the depth and intensity of the life excited. We touch our subject but by a point which has no breadth, but the pyramid of our experience, or our interest in it, rests on us by a broader or narrower base. That is, man is all in all, Nature nothing, but as she draws him out and reflects him. Give me simple, cheap, and homely themes.[1]

I forgot to say that there are sometimes two meats within one chestnut shell, divided transversely, and each covered by its separate brown-ribbed skin.[2]

I still see a yellow butterfly occasionally zigzagging by the roadside.

What a strong medicinal but rich scent now after the

[1] [Channing, p. 83.]
[2] As if Nature had smuggled the seed of one more tree into this chest.

rain, from decaying weeds, perhaps ferns, by the roadside! The rain, falling on the fresh dried herbs and filling the ditches into which they drooped, has converted them into tea.[1]

Apple leaves are now pretty generally brown and crisp.

I see where the chestnut trees have been sadly bruised by the large stones cast against them in previous years and which still lie around.

That was an interesting sight described on the 12th, the winged insects of various kinds gathered on the last fragment of a watermelon in the garden, to taste the last sweets of the year. In midsummer they are dispersed and not observed, but now, as in the spring, they are congregated about the little sweet that is left.

Minott told me one of his hunting stories yesterday, how he saw a very large hen-hawk come sailing from over the hill, just this side of where Moore lives now. He did n't expect to reach her, but he knew that he had a plaguy smart little piece, — it was a kind of half-stocked one (he always speaks of the gun he used on a particular occasion as if it were a new one, describing it minutely, though he never had more than three, perhaps not more than two, in his life, I suspect), — so he thought he 'd give her a try, and, faith, she pitched down into the little meadow on the north side the road there, and when he came up she bristled up to him so that he was obliged to give her another charge.

[1] [*Excursions*, p. 268; Riv. 329.]

Oct. 19. P. M. — To Conantum.

The fall, now and for some weeks, is the time for flocks of sparrows of various kinds flitting from bush to bush and tree to tree — and both bushes and trees are thinly leaved or bare — and from one seared meadow to another. They are mingled together, and their notes, even, being faint, are, as well as their colors and motions, much alike. The sparrow youth are on the wing. They are still further concealed by their resemblance in color to the gray twigs and stems, which are now beginning to be bare. I have not noticed any kind of blackbird for a long time.

The most prominent of the few lingering solidagos which I have noticed since the 8th is the *S. cæsia*, though that is very scarce indeed now, hardly survives at all. Of the asters which I have noticed since that date, the *A. undulatus* is, perhaps, the only one of which you can find a respectable specimen. I see one so fresh that there is a bumblebee on it. Of lingering flowers which I have noticed during the last three or four days (*vide* list under 16th), not including fringed gentian and witch-hazel, the freshest, and at same time commonest, is the yarrow.

I noticed, two or three days ago, after one of those frosty mornings, half an hour before sunset of a clear and pleasant day, a swarm, — were they not of winter gnats? — between me and the sun like so many motes, seven or eight feet from the ground, by the side of a young cherry tree in the yard. The swarm was some three feet in diameter and seemed to have been revealed by the level rays of the sun. Each insect was acting

Vol. IX

its part in a ceaseless dance, rising and falling a few inches while the swarm kept its place. Is not this a forerunner of winter?

I go across Hubbard's land and find that I must go round the corners of two or three new winter-rye fields, which show very green by contrast with the seared grass. I sit on the old Conantum door-step, where the wind rattles the loose clapboards above my head, though for the most part only the horizontal rows of wrought nails are left to show where the clapboards have been. It is affecting to behold a peach and apple orchard just come to maturity by the side of this house, which was planted since this house was an uninhabited ruin, as if the first step would have been to pull down the house.

See quite a flock of myrtle-birds, — which I might carelessly have mistaken for slate-colored snowbirds, — flitting about on the rocky hillside under Conantum Cliff. They show about three white or light-colored spots when they fly, *commonly* no bright yellow, though some are pretty bright. They perch on the side of the dead mulleins, on rocks, on the ground, and directly dart off, apparently in pursuit of some insect. I hear no note from them. They are thus near or on the ground, then, not as in spring.

Both the white and black ash are quite bare, and some of the elms there. The bass has lost, apparently, more than half its leaves.

The *Botrychium lunarioides*, now shedding its pale whitish dust when struck by the foot, but apparently *generally* a little past its maturity, is quite common

in the pasture near the wall where I sat to watch the eagle. At first you notice only the stipe, four to seven or eight inches high, like a narrow hand partly closed, for the small (now dull-purplish) frond unites with it below the surface.

Walking through the reddened huckleberry bushes, whose leaves are fast falling, I notice the birds' nests already filling with withered leaves.

Witch-hazel is in prime, or probably a little past, though some buds are not yet open. Their leaves are all gone. They form large clumps on the hillside there, even thirty to fifty stems from one to two or three inches in diameter and the highest twelve feet high, falling over on every side. The now imbrowned ferns around indicate the moist soil which they like.

I have often noticed the inquisitiveness of birds, as the other day of a sparrow, whose motions I should not have supposed to have any reference to me, if I had not watched it from first to last. I stood on the edge of a pine and birch wood. It flitted from seven or eight rods distant to a pine within a rod of me, where it hopped about stealthily and chirped awhile, then flew as many rods the other side and hopped about there a spell, then back to the pine again, as near me as it dared, and again to its first position, very restless all the while. Generally I should have supposed that there was more than one bird, or that it was altogether accidental, — that the chipping of this sparrow eight or ten rods [away] had no reference to me, — for I could see nothing peculiar about it. But when I brought my glass to bear on it, I found that it was almost steadily eying me and was all alive with excitement.

Pokeweed has been killed by the severe frosts of the last three or four days.

 The *Asclepias Cornuti* pods are now apparently in the midst of discounting. They point at various angles with the stem like a flourish. The pretty brown fishes have loosened and lifted their scales somewhat, are bristling a little. Or, further advanced, the outer part of the down of the upper seeds is blown loose, while  they are still retained by the ends of the middle portion in loops attached to the core. These white tufts, ready to burst and take to flight on the least jar, show afar as big as your fist. There they dangle and flutter, till they are quite dry and the wind rises. Others again are open and empty, except of the brown core, and you see what a delicate smooth white (slightly cream-colored) lining this casket has.

The hypericums — the whole plant — have now generally been killed by the frost. A large pasture thistle bud close to the ground amid its leaves, as in spring.

Among the dirty woolly heads of plants now gone to seed, I notice for the first time the peculiar matted, woolly top of the tall anemone, rising above some red-leaved huckleberries. I am surprised to see to what length and breadth one of these little compact conical heads has puffed out. Here are five which have flown

Vol. IX

---

and matted together into a mass four or five inches long, perpendicularly, by two wide, full of seeds with their wool.

I return by the west side of Lee's Cliff hill, and sit on a rounded rock there, covered with fresh-fallen pine-needles, amid the woods, whence I see Wachusett. How little unevenness and elevation is required for Nature's effects! An elevation one thousand or fifteen hundred feet above the plain is seen from all eminences and level open plains, as from over the opening made by a pond, within thirty miles. Nature is not obliged to lift her mountains very high in the horizon, after all, to make them visible and interesting.

The rich sunny yellow of the old pitch pine needles, just ready to fall, contrasting with the new and unmixed masses above, makes a very pleasing impression, as I look down into the hollows this side of Lee's Cliff.

I noticed the small woodpecker several days ago.

Oct. 20. P. M. — To Hill, to look for ground squirrel nests.

The river-banks have now assumed almost their November aspect. The button-bushes are nearly bare. The water is smooth, the sun warm, and the reflections particularly fine and distinct; but there are reflected now, for the most part, only gray twigs and a few sere and curled brown leaves, wool-grass, etc. Land at Hemlocks, in the eddy there, where the white bits of sawdust keep boiling up and down and whirling round as in a pot.

Amid the young pitch pines in the pasture behind I notice, as elsewhere of late, a great many brownish-yellow (and some pink) election-cake fungi, eaten by crickets; about three inches in diameter. Some of those spread chocolate-colored ones have many grubs in them, though dry and dusty. Think I heard the very faint *gnah* of a nuthatch. Thus, of late, when the season is declining, many birds have departed, and our thoughts are turned towards winter (began to have a fire, more or less, say ten days or a fortnight ago), we hear the jay again more frequently, and the chickadees are more numerous and lively and familiar and utter their *phebe* note, and the nuthatch is heard again, and the small woodpecker seen amid the bare twigs.

Owing to the great height of the river, there has been no *Bidens Beckii* nor *Polygonum amphibium* to my knowledge this year, nor have I found any myriophyllum.

I dig into two or three squirrel-holes under a black oak, and in a rotten stump trace them a foot or more and lose them, or else they come to an end? Though I saw a squirrel enter the ground, I dug and lost it. They are apparently very busy now laying up their stores. I see a gray one making haste with waving tail across the field from the nut trees to the woods.

Looking up the side of the hill toward the sun, I see a little gossamer on the sweet-fern, etc.; and, from my boat, little flocks of white gossamer occasionally, three quarters of an inch long, in the air or caught on twigs, as if where a spider had hauled in his line. I

---

think that all spiders can walk on water, for when, last summer, I knocked one off my boat by chance, he ran swiftly back to the boat and climbed up, as if more to avoid the fishes than the water. This would account for those long lines stretched low over the water from one grass stem to another. I see one of them now five or six feet long and only three or four inches above the surface, and it is remarkable that there is no perceptible sag to it, weak as the line must be. The pinweeds are now bare, and their stem and fruit turned a dark brown. The thorns on the hill are all bare.

There are fewer turtles, now and for some time, out sunning. A very little *Solidago nemoralis* in one place from the axil.

I hear from my chamber the note of myrtle-birds [1] mingled with sparrows, in the yard, especially in the morning, quite like a clear, *sweet* squeaking wheelbarrow.

Oct. 21. A *very* warm Indian-summer day, too warm for a thick coat. It is remarkably hazy, too, but when I open the door I smell smoke, which may in part account for it. After being out awhile I do not perceive the smoke, only on first opening the door. It is so thick a blue haze that, when, going along in Thrush Alley Path, I look through the trees into Abel Brooks's deep hollow, I cannot see across it to the woods beyond, though it is only a stone's throw. Like a deep blue lake at first glance.

Had a chat with Minott, sitting on a log by his

[1] White-throat sparrow.

door. He says he began to carry a gun when he was fifteen or sixteen years old; afterward he owned three at one time, one training-piece and two fowling-pieces. He lived at James Baker's seven years; not till after he was of age. He used to range all over that neighborhood, away down into Lexington, and knew every stone and stump; used to go chestnutting about Flint's Pond, and a-fishing there, too. The fish and fowl were ten times as plenty as they are now. Why, he has been along the ridges (the moraines toward Ditch Pond) when, the ducks rising up on each side, the sky was black with them. His training-piece was an old king's-arm, taken from the British some time, he supposed. It was a capital piece, even for shot, and thoroughly made, made upon honor every part of it. There are no such guns made in this country. The lock was strong and smart, so that when you snapped it, it filled the pan chock-full of fire, and he could burn a single kernel of powder in it. But it took a good deal of powder to load it. He kept its brass mountings burnished so bright that you could see your face in them. He had also owned a French piece. Once, too, he had a little English cocking-piece, i. e. fowling-piece. It had the word "London" on the barrel close to the lock. It was a plaguy smart piece, bell-muzzled, and would carry ball well. He could knock over a robin with it eight rods off with ball or a slug. He had a rifle once. What did they use rifles for? Oh, for turkey-shooting.

Once, one Rice, who lived in Lincoln where Hayden does now. made a turkey-shooting, and he went to it

with his English fowling-piece. He saw many on the road going to it. Saw Dakin [and] Jonas Minott (Captain Minott's son, who spent quite a fortune on shooting), one offering to take another down to the shooting for a mug of flip. They asked him what he was going to do with that little thing. You paid fourpence a shot at a live turkey only twenty rods off. Those who had rifles were not allowed to rest. Amos Baker was there (who was at Concord Fight). The turkey was a large white one. Minott rammed down his slug and, getting down behind a fence, rested on it while the rest laughed at him. He told Amos to look sharp and tell him where his ball struck, and fired. Amos said the ball struck just above the turkey. Others were firing in the meanwhile. Minott loaded and tried once more, and this time his ball cut off the turkey's neck, and it was his; worth a dollar, at least. You only had to draw blood to get the turkey. Another, a black one, was set up, and this time his ball struck the ground just this side the turkey, then scaled up and passed right through its body, lodging under the skin on the opposite side, and he cut it out.

Rice made his money chiefly by his liquor, etc. Some set up the turkeys they had gained; others "hustled" for liquor or for a supper; i. e., they would take sides and then, putting seven coppers in a hat, shake them up well and empty them, and the party that got the fewest heads after three casts paid for the supper.

M. says that, in all the time he lived at Baker's, in fact in all his life, he never went to market.

Told me how they used to carry on, on Concord Common formerly, on great days. Once, when they were shaking dice there in the evening for money, round a table with twenty-five or thirty dollars in cash upon it, some rogue fastened a rope to one leg of the table, and so at a distance suddenly started off with the table, at the same time upsetting and extinguishing the light. This made a great outcry. They ran up crying, "Mister, I'll help you pick up your money," but they put the half into their own pockets.

Father told me about his father the other night, — that he remembers his father used to breakfast before the family at one time, on account of his business, and he with him. His father used to eat the under crusts of biscuits, and he the upper. His father died in 1801, aged forty-seven. When the war came on, he was apprentice or journeyman to a cooper who employed many hands. He called them together, and told them that on account of the war his business was ruined and he had no more work for them. So, my father thinks, his father went privateering. Yet he remembers his telling him of his being employed digging at some defenses, when a cannon-ball came and sprinkled the sand all over them.

After the war he went into business as a merchant, commencing with a single hogshead of sugar. His shop was on Long Wharf. He was a short man, a little taller than my father, stout and very strong for his size. Levi Melchier [?], a powerful man, who was his clerk or tender, used to tell my father that he did not believe he was so strong a man as his father was.

He would never give in to him in handling a hogshead of molasses, — setting it on its head, or the like.

Minott, too, sings the praises of Beatton, the storekeeper, though of course he does not remember him. He was a Scotchman and a peddler, and the most honest man that is mentioned in Concord history. You might send a child to the store, and if there was a fraction still due the child after making change, he would give him a needle or a large pin.

Oct. 24. Friday. 12 м. — Set out for Eagleswood, Perth Amboy, N. J.

Spent the afternoon in Worcester.

By cars in evening to Allyn's Point and Steamer Commonwealth to New York.

Oct. 25. Saw, at Barnum's Museum, the stuffed skin of a cougar that was found floating dead in the Hudson many years ago. The stuffed jaguar there looks rather the largest. Had seen a clergyman in Worcester the previous afternoon (at Higginson's) who told me of one killed near the head of the Delaware, in New York State, by an acquaintance of his. His dog had treed it or found it on a tree on a mountainside, and the hunter first saw it as he came up from below, stretched out on a limb and looking intently at him, ready to spring. He fired and wounded it, but, as usual, it sprang as soon as struck, in the direction it was pointing. It struck seventy feet down the mountain from the tree, or a hundred feet distant, tearing off the sleeve of the hunter's very thick and stout coat, as it passed, and marking his arm from shoulder to hand. It took to a tree, and again, and this time approaching it from above, he shot it. The specimens I have seen were long-bodied. Looked into De Kay's Report at the Astor Library. He describes one, the largest "of which we have any account," killed in Lake Fourth, Herkimer County. "It had a total length of 11 feet 3 inches." He says that Vanderdonk speaks of lions and their skins, only the latter seen by Christians, meaning panthers. According to D., haunts ledges of rocks called "panther ledges." There is no well-authenticated account of their having attacked a man, and it is not well established that the northern and southern species are the same.[1]

De Kay describes the *Sorex Dekayi*, "nearly allied to *brevicaudus*, but is larger and more robust in its form." From Massachusetts to Virginia. "Cheek teeth $\frac{18}{10}$," instead of $\frac{18}{10}$ in *S. brevicaudus*. The color resembles the fur of the star-nosed mole. Length of head and body, 4.8 inches; tail, .8; to end of hairs, .9. He never met with *S. brevicaudus* in New York. Is not this my sorex of July 12th, 1856? Or is mine possibly the *Sorex Fosteri*, whose cheek teeth are $\frac{18}{10}$; and total length, 4; tail, 1.5.

Arrived at Eagleswood, Perth Amboy, Saturday, 5 p. m., October 25th.[2]

[1] Apparently a panther was killed after this, this fall in Rhode Island.

[2] [Concerning this visit, its object, and the interesting people with whom it made Thoreau acquainted, see *Familiar Letters*, pp. 283 286–291; Riv. 333–341.]

Vol. IX

is not good for much. They would be more edible if it were not for the numerous large seeds, and when you have rejected them there is little but skin left. Yet I was surprised that the fruit was not more generally gathered.

The sassafras was common.

Saw and heard a katydid about the 1st of November.

Oct. 27. Monday. Began to survey along the shore and through the woods. One of the largest and commonest trees, the tulip, in the moist ravines; its dried tulip-shaped relic of a flower, the broad flat stamens still remaining. Noticed a medicinal odor, somewhat like fever-bush, in the bark of twigs. It is said to be a valuable tonic.

The liquidambar or sweet-gum trees, very common and large, oak-like. The corky bark on young trees and twigs was raised into two ears, so as to form a channel, which would conduct the rain down the branches to the main stem, I should say. The fruit was a coarse, rigid, spherical bur, an inch or more in diameter, which opened and dropped much fine seed in my trunk.

Black walnut and bayberry were pretty common, though I noticed no berries on the last.

Oct. 26. Sunday. An abundance of a viburnum, making thickets in dry woods and ravines and set out about houses, now full of edible fruit like that of *V. nudum*, and also of leaves. At first I was inclined to call it *V. nudum*, but beside that it bears an abundance of berries still, long after the *V. nudum* berries have fallen with us (and they hold on for three or four weeks afterward at least), it grows generally in dry woods and ravines and uplands; the leaf is quite thin, now reddened, of various forms; and the bush is quite thorny (!), in the woods making almost impenetrable thickets in many places, like a thorn bush, and gave me much trouble to cut through in surveying, as did the cat-briar. I think it must be the *V. prunifolium*, or black haw. It is quite ornamental, with its abundance of purple fruit, which tastes much like dates. I think I have never seen it in Concord, and perhaps Emerson and others confounded it with *V. nudum*. It is thorny like a wild apple, but of course much more slender. The privet was a very common shrub, with its black berries.

Flowers almost entirely done. See apparently the seaside goldenrod, lingering still by the Raritan River, and a new aster.

The persimmon (*Diospyros Virginiana*) quite common. Saw some trees quite full of fruit. There was a little left on the trees when I left, November 24th, but I should think it was in its prime about the end of the first week of November, *i. e.*, what would readily shake off. Before, it was commonly puckery. In any case it furs the mouth just like the choke-cherry. It

IV

NOVEMBER, 1856

(ÆT. 39)

Nov. 2. Sunday. Took a walk two miles west of Eagleswood. The *Quercus palustris*, or pin oak, very common there, much like the scarlet oak. Name said to be derived from the dead stub ends of branches on the trunk beneath, like pins or treenails. Its acorns subglobose, and marked with meridional lines. A mile and a half west of Spring's, a new oak, with narrow and entire willow-like leaves, apparently *Q. imbricaria*, laurel or shingle oak, or perhaps Michaux's *Q. cinerea*, which may be a variety of it. According to Michaux's plates, I see that the leaves of the *Q. Phellos*, or willow oak, are about two and three quarters by one third plus inches, of the laurel oak three and a half by seven eighths. *His* upland willow oak (*Q. cinerea*) leaf is about three by three quarters and less tapering at base.

The *Cornus florida* was exceedingly common and large there. Conspicuous with its scarlet berries, fed on by robins. The leaves were turned a brown scarlet or orange red.

About the 10th of November, I first noticed long bunches of very small dark-purple or black grapes fallen on the dry leaves in the ravine east of Spring's house. Quite a large mass of clusters remained hanging on the leafless vine, thirty feet overhead there, till I left, on the 24th November. These grapes were much shrivelled, but they had a very agreeably spicy acid taste, evidently not acquired till after the frosts. I thought them quite a discovery and ate many from day to day, swallowing the skins and stones, and recommended them to Spring. He said that they were very much like a certain French grape, which he had eaten in France. It is a true frost grape, but apparently answers to *Vitis æstivalis* (?). *Vide* fruit and leaves. One I opened has only two seeds, while *one* of the early ones at Brattleboro has four, but one of the late ones of Brattleboro has only two, which also I have called *V. æstivalis*.

Was interested by Pierce's Perpetual Calendar on a round stick (sometimes on a pencil-case), by which you tell the day of the week, etc., for any date.

Visited the principal antique bookstore, in Fulton Street, upstairs, west of Broadway; also Tunison's antique bookstore, 138 Fulton Street.

May be worth while to get Oswald's Etymological Dictionary and, if possible, Smith's (smaller) (abridged) Dictionary of Antiquities. He is the author of the Latin Dictionary.

I suspect it is the *Quercus montana*, var. *monticola* of *Prinus*, so common at Eagleswood, with its large acorns now sprouted. Indeed, almost every acorn of white and chestnut oaks was sprouted.

Noticed plenty of *Chimaphila maculata* in the great ravine.

Saw more rabbits and wild mice there than here.

Game is protected. The boys said the wild rabbits played with the tame ones in the yard.

The prevailing trees there are red cedar, tulip, white oak, pin oak, chestnut oak, etc., gum-tree, pitch pine, and, of smaller trees, the *Cornus florida*. There was no white pine and but two or three small white birches.

The wire fence was something new, and the tongue used by an Irishwoman to wipe a cinder out of her son's eye. The four feet of flame issuing from one chimney of the State of Maine steamer after we passed her (the sun just set), not yellow and fiery but white like a lit cloud, or her smoke reflecting the departing day.

A clayey soil at Eagleswood, making very bad walking even after a frosty night only. Clay mixed with the red sandstone sand. When I washed my hands, though but little soiled, the water was colored red.

Am glad to get back to New England, the dry, sandy, wholesome land, land of scrub oaks and birches and white pines, now in her russet dress, reminding me of her flaxen-headed children.

Saw some very large true hornbeams.

The pastures, etc., at Eagleswood were densely overrun with wild carrots, the commonest weed and a great pest.

When I got back to New England the grass seemed bleached a shade or two more flaxen, more completely withered.

Nov. 25. Tuesday. Get home again this morning.

Vol. IX

Nov. 27. P. M. — Take a turn down the river. A painted tortoise sinking to the bottom, and apparently tree sparrows along the shore.

Nov. 28. P. M. — To chestnut wood by Turnpike, to see if I could find my comb, probably lost out of my pocket when I climbed and shook a chestnut tree more than a month ago.

Unexpectedly find many chestnuts in the burs which have fallen some time ago. Many are spoiled, but the rest, being thus moistened, are softer and sweeter than a month ago, very agreeable to my palate. The burs from some cause having fallen without dropping their nuts.

As I stood looking down the hill over Emerson's young wood-lot there, perhaps at 3.30 P. M., the sunlight reflected from the many ascending twigs of bare young chestnuts and birches, very dense and ascendant with a marked parallelism, they reminded me of the lines of gossamer at this season, being almost exactly similar to the eye. It is a true November phenomenon.

Nov. 29. Begins to snow this morning and snows slowly and interruptedly with a little fine hail all day till it is several inches deep. This the first snow I have seen, but they say the ground was whitened for a short time some weeks ago.

It has been a remarkably pleasant November, warmer and pleasanter than last year.

Nov. 30. Sunday. P. M. — To Cliffs *via* Hubbard's Grove.

Several inches of snow, but a rather soft and mild air still. Now see the empty chalices of the blue-curls and the rich brown-fruited pinweed above the crust. (The very cat was full of spirits this morning, rushing about and frisking on the snow-crust, which bore her alone. When I came home from New Jersey the other day, was struck with the sudden growth and stateliness of our cat Min, — his cheeks puffed out like a regular grimalkin. I suspect it is a new coat of fur against the winter chiefly. The cat is a third bigger than a month ago, like a patriarch wrapped in furs; and a mouse a day, I hear, is nothing to him now.) This as I go through the Depot Field, where the stub ends of corn-stalks rise above the snow. I find half a dozen russets, touched and discolored within by frost, still hanging on Wheeler's tree by the wall.

I see the fine, thin, yellowish stipule of the pine leaves now, on the snow by Hubbard's Grove and where some creature has eaten the resinous terminal pitch pine buds.[1] In Hubbard's bank wall field, beyond the brook, see the tracks of many sparrows that have run from weed to weed, as if a chain had dropped there. Not an apple is left in the orchard on Fair Haven Hill; not a track there of walker. Now all plants are withered and blanched, except perhaps some *Vaccinium vacillans* red leaves which sprang up in the burning last spring. Here and there a squirrel or a rabbit has hastily crossed the path.

Minott told me on Friday of an oldish man and woman who had brought to a muster here once a great

[1] *Vide* spring of '59.

leg of bacon boiled, to turn a penny with. The skin, as thick as sole-leather, was flayed and turned back, displaying the tempting flesh. A tall, raw-boned, omnivorous heron of a Yankee came along and bargained with the woman, who was awaiting a customer, for as much of that as he could eat. He ate and ate and ate, making a surprising hole, greatly to the amusement of the lookers-on, till the woman in her despair, unfaithful to her engagement, appealed to the police to drive him off.

Sophia, describing the first slight whitening of snow a few weeks ago, said that when she awoke she noticed a certain bluish-white reflection on the wall and, looking out, saw the ground whitened with snow.

My first sight of snow this year I got as I was surveying about the 5th of November in a great wooded gully making up from the Raritan River, in Perth Amboy, N. J. It was a few fine flakes in the chilly air, which very few who were out noticed at all.

That country was remarkable for its gullies, commonly well wooded, with a stream at the bottom. One was called Souman's [?] Gully, the only good name for any feature of the landscape thereabouts, yet the inhabitants objected especially to this word "gully."

That is a great place for oysters, and the inhabitants of Amboy are said to be very generally well off in consequence. All are allowed to gather oysters on the flats at low tide, and at such times I saw thirty or forty wading about with baskets and picking them up, the indigenous ones. Off the mouth of the Raritan, I saw about seventy-five boats one morning busily taking up

the oysters which they had laid down, — their usual morning's work.

I used to get my clothes covered with beggar-ticks in the fields there, and burs, small and large.

Minot Pratt tells me that he watched the fringed gentian this year, and it lasted till the first week in November.

V

DECEMBER, 1856

(ÆT. 39)

Dec. 1. P. M. — By path around Walden.

With this little snow of the 29th *ult.* there is yet pretty good sledding, for it lies solid.

I see the old pale-faced farmer out again on his sled now for the five-thousandth time,[1] — Cyrus Hubbard, a man of a certain New England probity and worth, immortal and natural, like a natural product, like the sweetness of a nut, like the toughness of hickory. He, too, is a redeemer for me. How superior actually to the faith he professes! He is not an office-seeker. What an institution, what a revelation is a man! We are wont foolishly to think that the creed which a man professes is more significant than the fact he is. It matters not how hard the conditions seemed, how mean the world, for a man is a prevalent force and a new law himself. He is a system whose law is to be observed. The old farmer condescends to countenance still this nature and order of things. It is a great encouragement that an honest man makes this world his abode. He rides on the sled drawn by oxen, world-wise, yet comparatively so young, as if they had seen scores of winters. The farmer spoke to me, I can swear, clean, cold, moderate as the snow.

[1] [Channing, p. 108.]

He does not melt the snow where he treads. Yet what a faint impression that encounter may make on me after all! Moderate, natural, true, as if he were made of earth, stone, wood, snow.[1] I thus meet in this universe kindred of mine, composed of these elements. I see men like frogs; their peeping I partially understand.

I go by Hayden's and take A. Wheeler's wood-path to railroad.

Slate-colored snowbirds flit before me in the path, feeding on the seeds on the snow, the countless little brown seeds that begin to be scattered over the snow, so much the more obvious to bird and beast. A hundred kinds of indigenous grain are harvested now, broadcast upon the surface of the snow. Thus at a critical season these seeds are shaken down on to a clean white napkin, unmixed with dirt and rubbish, and off this the little pensioners pick them. Their clean table is thus spread a few inches or feet above the ground. Will wonder become extinct in me? Shall I become insensible as a fungus?

A ridge of earth, with the red cockscomb lichen on it, peeps out still at the rut's edge. The dear wholesome color of shrub oak leaves, so clean and firm, not decaying, but which have put on a kind of immortality, not wrinkled and thin like the white oak leaves, but full-veined and plump, as nearer earth. Well-tanned leather on the one side, sun-tanned, color of colors, color of the cow and the deer, silver-downy beneath, turned toward the late bleached and russet fields.

[1] [Channing, pp. 68, 69.]

What are acanthus leaves and the rest to this? Emblem of my winter condition. I love and could embrace the shrub oak with its scanty garment of leaves rising above the snow, lowly whispering to me, akin to winter thoughts, and sunsets, and to all virtue. Covert which the hare and the partridge seek, and I too seek. What cousin of mine is the shrub oak? How can any man suffer long? For a sense of want is a prayer, and all prayers are answered. Rigid as iron, clean as the atmosphere, hardy as virtue, innocent and sweet as a maiden is the shrub oak. In proportion as I know and love it, I am natural and sound as a partridge. I felt a positive yearning toward one bush this afternoon. There was a match found for me at last. I fell in love with a shrub oak.[1] Tenacious of its leaves, which shrivel not but retain a certain wintry life in them, firm shields, painted in fast colors a rich brown. The deer mouse, too, knows the shrub oak and has its hole in the snow by the shrub oak's stem.

Now, too, I remark in many places ridges and fields of fine russet or straw-colored grass rising above the snow, and beds of empty straw-colored heads of everlasting and ragged-looking Roman wormwood.

The blue-curls' chalices stand empty, and waiting evidently to be filled with ice.

I see great thimble-berry bushes rising above the snow, with still a rich, rank bloom on them, as in July. Hypæthral mildew, elysian fungus! To see the bloom on a thimble-berry stem lasting into midwinter! What a salve that would make, collected and boxed![2]

[1] [Channing, p. 102.]   [2] [Channing, pp. 112, 113.]

No, I am a stranger in your towns. I am not at home at French's, or Lovejoy's, or Savery's. I can winter more to my mind amid the shrub oaks. I have made arrangements to stay with them.

The shrub oak, lowly, loving the earth and spreading over it, tough, thick-leaved; leaves firm and sound in winter and rustling like leather shields; leaves fair and wholesome to the eye, clean and smooth to the touch. Tough to support the snow, not broken down by it. Well-nigh useless to man. A sturdy phalanx, hard to break through. Product of New England's surface. Bearing many striped acorns.[1]

I have seen more chestnuts in the streets of New York than anywhere else this year, large and plump ones, roasting in the street, roasting and popping on the steps of banks and exchanges. Was surprised to see that the citizens made as much of the nuts of the wild-wood as the squirrels. Not only the country boys, all New York goes a-nutting. Chestnuts for cabmen and newsboys, for not only are squirrels to be fed.

Well named *shrub oak*. Low, robust, hardy, indigenous. Well known to the striped squirrel and the partridge and rabbit. The squirrel nibbles its nuts sitting upon an old stump of its larger cousins. What is Peruvian bark to your bark? How many rents I owe to you! how many eyes put out! how many bleeding fingers! How many shrub oak patches I have been through, stooping, winding my way, bending the twigs aside, guiding myself by the sun, over hills and valleys and plains, resting in clear grassy spaces! I love to go

[1] [Channing, p. 102.]

through a patch of shrub oak in a bee-line, where you tear your clothes and put your eyes out.[1]

Dec. 2. P. M. — Got in my boat, which before I had got out and turned up on the bank. It made me sweat to wheel it home through the snow, I am so unused to the work of late.

Then walked up the railroad. The clear straw-colored grass and some weeds contrasting with the snow it rises above. Saw little in this walk. Saw Melvin's lank bluish-white black-spotted hound, and Melvin with his gun near, going home at eve. He follows hunting, praise be to him, as regularly in our tame fields as the farmers follow farming. Persistent Genius! How I respect him and thank him for him! [*sic*] I trust the Lord will provide us with another Melvin when he is gone. How good in him to follow his own bent, and not continue at the Sabbath-school all his days! What a wealth he thus becomes in the neighborhood! Few know how to take the census. I thank my stars for Melvin. I think of him with gratitude when I am going to sleep, grateful that he exists, — that Melvin who is such a trial to his mother. Yet he is agreeable to me as a tinge of russet on the hillside. I would fain give thanks morning and evening for my blessings. Awkward, gawky, loose-hung, dragging his legs after him. He is my contemporary and neighbor. He is one tribe, I am another, and we are not at war.

I saw but little in my walk. Saw no bird, only a crow's track in the snow.

[1] [Channing, pp. 102, 103.]

How quickly men come out on to the highways with their sleds and improve the first snow! The farmer has begun to play with his sled as early as any of the boys. See him already with mittens on and thick boots well greased — been soaking in grease all summer, perhaps — and fur cap and red comforter about his throat, though it is not yet cold, walking beside his team with contented thoughts. This drama every day in the streets! This is the theatre I go to. There he goes with his venture behind him, and often he gets aboard for a change.

As for the sensuality in Whitman's "Leaves of Grass," I do not so much wish that it was not written, as that men and women were so pure that they could read it without harm.

Dec. 3. About as much more snow as fell on the 29th November has fallen in the night upon that, so stilly that we were not aware of it till we looked out. It has not even lodged on the window-sashes, and I am first convinced it has fallen by seeing the old tracks in the road covered and the roofs uniformly white. It is now somewhat misty, or perhaps a fine rain beginning.

Fewer weeds now rise above the snow. Pinweed (or sarothra) is quite concealed. It is a uniform white napkin in many fields. But not yet are the Great Meadows fairly whitened. There, as I look sideways at them, I see still the stretching acres of straw-colored brown grass and weeds. The pastures are uniformly white, but the meadows are that rich, wild brown straw-color, or only white in ridges where there is less grass, reminding of the fall, and of water beneath.

The steam of the locomotive stretches low over the earth, enveloping the cars.

The sight of the sedgy meadows that are not yet snowed up while the cultivated fields and pastures are a uniform white, — fenny places which are longer enabled to resist the aggressions of winter! It takes a deep snow to blot out the traces of summer there, for the grass did not get cut this year.

Mizzles and rains all day, making sloshy walking which sends us all to the shoemaker's. Bought me a pair of cowhide boots, to be prepared for winter walks. The shoemaker praised them because they were made a year ago. I feel like an armed man now. The man who has bought his boots feels like him who has got in his winter's wood. There they stand beside me in the chamber, expectant, dreaming of far woods and wood-paths, of frost-bound or sloshy roads, or of being bound with skate-straps and clogged with ice-dust.

For years my appetite was so strong that I fed — I browsed — on the pine forest's edge seen against the winter horizon. How cheap my diet still! Dry sand that has fallen in railroad cuts and slid on the snow beneath is a condiment to my walk. I ranged about like a gray moose, looking at the spiring tops of the trees, and fed my imagination on them, — far-away, ideal trees not disturbed by the axe of the wood-cutter, nearer and nearer fringes and eyelashes of my eye. Where was the sap, the fruit, the value of the forest for me, but in that line where it was relieved against the sky?

Vol. IX

That was my wood-lot; that was my lot in the woods. The silvery needles of the pine straining the light.

A man killed at the fatal Lincoln Bridge died in the village the other night. The only words he uttered while he lingered in his delirium were "All right," probably the last which he had uttered before he was struck, — brave, prophetic words to go out of the world with! good as "I still live," but on no razors.[1]

How I love the simple, reserved countrymen, my neighbors, who mind their own business and let me alone, who never waylaid nor shot at me, to my knowledge, when I crossed their fields, though each one has a gun in his house! For nearly twoscore years I have known, at a distance, these long-suffering men, whom I never spoke to, who never spoke to me, and now feel a certain tenderness for them, as if this long probation were but the prelude to an eternal friendship. What a long trial we have withstood, and how much more admirable we are to each other, perchance, than if we had been bedfellows! I am not only grateful because Veias, and Homer, and Christ, and Shakespeare have lived, but I am grateful for Minott, and Rice, and Melvin, and Goodwin, and Puffer even. I see Melvin all alone filling his sphere, in russet suit, which no other could fill or suggest. He takes up as much room in nature as the most famous.

Six weeks ago I noticed the advent of chickadees and their winter habits. As you walk along a wood-side, a restless little flock of them, whose notes you hear at

[1] [Daniel Webster's last words were at one time etched on razors made by Wade & Butcher of Sheffield.]

a distance, will seem to say, "Oh, there he goes! Let's pay our respects to him." And they will flit after and close to you, and naïvely peck at the nearest twig to you, as if they were minding their own business all the while without any reference to you.

Dec. 4. Ceased raining and mizzling last evening, and cleared off, with a high northwest wind, which shook the house, coming in fitful gusts, but only they who slept on the west sides of houses knew of it.

7.30 A. M. — Take a run down the riverside.

Scare up a few sparrows, which take shelter in Keyes's arbor-vitæ row. The snow has now settled, owing to the rain, and presents no longer a level surface, but a succession of little hills and hollows, as if the whole earth had been a potato or corn field, and there is a slight crust to it.

Dark waves are chasing each other across the river from northwest to southeast and breaking the edge of the snow ice which has formed for half a rod in width along the edge, and the fragments of broken ice, what arctic voyagers call "brash," carry forward the undulation.

I am pleased to see from afar the highest water-mark of a spring freshet on Cheney's boat-house, a level light-colored mark about an inch wide running the whole length of the building, now several years old, where probably a thin ice chafed it.

2 P. M. — By Clamshell and back over Hubbard's Bridge.

I notice that the swallow-holes in the bank behind Dennis's, which is partly washed away, are flat-elliptical, three times or more as wide horizontally as they are deep vertically, or about three inches by one.

Saw and heard cheep faintly one little tree sparrow, the neat chestnut crowned and winged and white-barred bird, perched on a large and solitary white birch. So clean and tough, made to withstand the winter. This color reminds me of the upper side of the shrub oak leaf. I love the few homely colors of Nature at this season, — her strong wholesome browns, her sober and primeval grays, her celestial blue, her vivacious green, her pure, cold, snowy white.[1] An *F. hyemalis* also.

In the sprout-land by the road, in the woods this side of C. Miles's, much gray goldenrod is mixed with the shrub oak. It reminds me of the color of the rabbits which run there. Thus Nature feeds her children chiefly with color. I have no doubt that it is an important relief to the eyes which have long rested on snow, to rest on brown oak leaves and the bark of trees. We want the greatest variety within the smallest compass, and yet without glaring diversity, and we have it in the colors of the withered oak leaves. The white, so curled and shrivelled and *pale;* the black (?), more flat and glossy and darker brown; the red, much like the black, but *perhaps* less dark, and less deeply cut. The scarlet still occasionally retains some blood in its veins.

Smooth white reaches of ice, as long as the river,

[1] [Channing, p. 98.]

on each side are threatening to bridge over its dark-blue artery any night. They remind me of a trap that is set for it, which the frost will spring. Each day at present, the wriggling river nibbles off the edges of the trap which have advanced in the night. It is a close contest between day and night, heat and cold.

Already you see the tracks of sleds leading by unusual routes, where will be seen no trace of them in summer, into far fields and woods, crowding aside and pressing down the snow to where some heavy log or stone has thought itself secure, and the spreading tracks also of the heavy, slow-paced oxen, of the well-shod farmer, who turns out his feet. Ere long, when the cold is stronger, these tracks will lead the walker deep into remote swamps impassable in summer. All the earth is a highway then.

I see where the pretty brown bird-like birch scales and winged seeds have been blown into the numerous hollows of the thin crusted snow. So bountiful a table is spread for the birds. For how many thousand miles this grain is scattered over the earth, under the feet of all walkers, in Boxboro and Cambridge alike! and rarely an eye distinguishes it.

Sophia says that just before I came home Min caught a mouse and was playing with it in the yard. It had got away from her once or twice, and she had caught it again; and now it was stealing off again, as she lay complacently watching it with her paws tucked under her, when her friend Riordan's stout but solitary cock stepped up inquisitively, looked down at it with one eye, turning his head, then picked it up by the tail and

gave it two or three whacks on the ground, and giving it a dexterous toss into the air, caught it in its open mouth, and it went head foremost and alive down his capacious throat in the twinkling of an eye, never again to be seen in this world, Min, all the while, with paws comfortably tucked under her, looking on unconcerned. What matters it one mouse more or less to her? The cock walked off amid the currant bushes, stretched his neck up, and gulped once or twice, and the deed was accomplished, and then he crowed lustily in celebration of the exploit. It might be set down among the *gesta* (if not *digesta*) *Gallorum.* There were several human witnesses. It is a question whether Min ever understood where that mouse went to. Min sits composedly sentinel, with paws tucked under her, a good part of her days at present, by some ridiculous little hole, the possible entryway of a mouse. She has a habit of stretching or sharpening her claws on all smooth hair-bottomed chairs and sofas, greatly to my mother's vexation.

He who abstains from visiting another for magnanimous reasons enjoys better society alone.

I for one am not bound to flatter men. That is not exactly the value of me.

How many thousand acres are there now of pitchered blue-curls and ragged wormwood rising above the shallow snow? The granary of the birds. They were not observed against the dark ground, but the first snow comes and reveals them. Then I come to fields in which the fragrant everlasting, straw-colored and almost odorless, and the dark taller St. John's-wort prevail.

Vol. IX

When I bought my boots yesterday, Hastings ran over his usual rigmarole. Had he any stout old-fashioned cowhide boots? Yes, he thought he could suit me. "There 's something that 'll turn water about as well as anything. Billings had a pair just like them the other [day], and he said they kept his feet as dry as a bone. But what 's more than that, they were made above a year ago upon honor. They are just the thing, you may depend on it. I had an eye to you when I was making them." "But they are too soft and thin for me. I want them to be thick and stand out from my foot." "Well, there is another pair, maybe a little thicker. I 'll tell you what it is, these were made of dry hide." Both were warranted single leather and not split. I took the last. But after wearing them round this cold day I found that the little snow which rested on them and melted wet the upper leather through like paper and wet my feet, and I told H. of it, that he might have an offset to Billings's experience. "Well, you can't expect a new pair of boots to turn water at first. I tell the farmers that the time to buy boots is at midsummer, or when they are hoeing their potatoes, and the pores have a chance to get filled with dirt."

It is remarkably good sleighing to-day, considering the little snow and the rain of yesterday, but it is slippery and hobbly for walkers.

My first botany, as I remember, was Bigelow's "Plants of Boston and Vicinity," which I began to use about twenty years ago, looking chiefly for the popular names and the short references to the localities of plants, even without any regard to the plant. I also learned the

names of many, but without using any system, and forgot them soon. I was not inclined to pluck flowers; preferred to leave them where they were, liked them best there. I was never in the least interested in plants in the house. But from year to year we look at Nature with new eyes. About half a dozen years ago I found myself again attending to plants with more method, looking out the name of each one and remembering it. I began to bring them home in my hat, a straw one with a scaffold lining to it, which I called my botany-box. I never used any other, and when some whom I visited were evidently surprised at its dilapidated look, as I deposited it on their front entry table, I assured them it was not so much my hat as my botany-box. I remember gazing with interest at the swamps about those days and wondering if I could ever attain to such familiarity with plants that I should know the species of every twig and leaf in them, that I should be acquainted with every plant (excepting grasses and cryptogamous ones), summer and winter, that I saw. Though I knew most of the flowers, and there were not in any particular swamp more than half a dozen shrubs that I did not know, yet these made it seem like a maze to me, of a thousand strange species, and I even thought of commencing at one end and looking it faithfully and laboriously through till I knew it all. I little thought that in a year or two I should have attained to that knowledge without all that labor. Still I never studied botany, and do not to-day systematically, the most natural system is still so artificial. I wanted to know my neighbors, if possible, — to get a little nearer to them.

I soon found myself observing when plants first blossomed and leafed, and I followed it up early and late, far and near, several years in succession, running to different sides of the town and into the neighboring towns, often between twenty and thirty miles in a day. I often visited a particular plant four or five miles distant, half a dozen times within a fortnight, that I might know exactly when it opened, beside attending to a great many others in different directions and some of them equally distant, at the same time. At the same time I had an eye for birds and whatever else might offer.

Dec. 5. Clear, cold winter weather. What a contrast between this week and last, when I talked of setting out apple trees!

P. M. — Walked over the Hill.

The Indians have at length got a regular load of wood. It is odd to see a pile of good oak wood beside their thin cotton tents in the snow, the wood-pile which is to be burnt within is so much more substantial than the house. Yet they do not appear to mind the cold, though one side the tent is partly open, and all are flapping in the wind, and there is a sick child in one. The children play in the snow in front, as before more substantial houses.

The river is well skimmed over in most places, though it will not bear, — wherever there is least current, as in broad places, or where there is least wind, as by the bridges. The ice trap was sprung last night.

As I walk along the side of the Hill, a pair of nut-

hatches flit by toward a walnut, flying low in midcourse and then ascending to the tree. I hear one's faint *tut tut* or *gnah gnah* — no doubt heard a good way by its mate now flown into the next tree — as it is ascending the trunk or branch of a walnut in a zigzag manner, hitching along, prying into the crevices of the bark; and now it has found a savory morsel, which it pauses to devour, then flits to a new bough. It is a chubby bird, white, slate-color, and black.

It is a perfectly cloudless and simple winter sky. A white moon, half full, in the pale or dull blue heaven and a whiteness like the reflection of the snow, extending up from the horizon all around a quarter the way up to the zenith. I can imagine that I see it shooting up like an aurora. This at 4 P. M. About the sun it is only whiter than elsewhere, or there is only the faintest possible tinge of yellow there.

There are a great many walnuts on the trees, seen black against the sky, and the wind has scattered many over the snow-crust. It would be easier gathering them now than ever.

The johnswort and the larger pinweed are conspicuous above the snow. Some fine straw-colored grasses, as delicate as the down on a young man's cheek, still rise above this crusted snow, and even a recess is melted around them, so gently has it been deposited.

The sun goes down and leaves not a blush in the sky.

This morning I saw Riordan's cock thrust out the window on to the snow to seek his sustenance, and now, as I go by at night, he is waiting on the front door-step to be let in.

My themes shall not be far-fetched. I will tell of homely every-day phenomena and adventures. Friends! Society! It seems to me that I have an abundance of it, there is so much that I rejoice and sympathize with, and men, too, that I never speak to but only know and think of. What you call bareness and poverty is to me simplicity. God could not be unkind to me if he should try. I love the winter, with its imprisonment and its cold, for it compels the prisoner to try new fields and resources. I love to have the river closed up for a season and a pause put to my boating, to be obliged to get my boat in. I shall launch it again in the spring with so much more pleasure. This is an advantage in point of abstinence and moderation compared with the seaside boating, where the boat ever lies on the shore. I love best to have each thing in its season only, and enjoy doing without it at all other times. It is the greatest of all advantages to enjoy no advantage at all. I find it invariably true, the poorer I am, the richer I am. What you consider my disadvantage, I consider my advantage. While you are pleased to get knowledge and culture in many ways, I am delighted to think that I am getting rid of them. I have never got over my surprise that I should have been born into the most estimable place in all the world, and in the very nick of time, too.[1]

[1] [Channing, p. 89.]

Dec. 6. Saturday. 2 P. M. — To Hubbard's Bridge and Holden Swamp and up river on ice to F. Pond Crossing, just below pond; back on east side of river.

Skating is fairly begun. The river is generally frozen over, though it will bear quite across in very few places. Much of the ice in the middle is dark and thin, having been formed last night, and when you stamp you see the water trembling in spots here and there.

I can walk through the spruce swamp now dry-shod, amid the water andromeda and *Kalmia glauca.* I feel an affection for the rich brown fruit of the panicled andromeda growing about the swamp, hard, dry, inedible, suitable to the season. The dense panicles of the berries are of a handsome form, made to endure, lasting often over two seasons, only becoming darker and gray.

How handsome every one of these leaves that are blown about the snow-crust or lie neglected beneath, soon to turn to mould! Not merely a matted mass of fibres like a sheet of paper, but a perfect organism and system in itself, so that no mortal has ever yet discerned or explored its beauty.

Against this swamp I take to the riverside where the ice will bear. White snow ice it is, but pretty smooth, but it is quite glare close to the shore and wherever the water overflowed yesterday. On the meadows, where this overflow was so deep that it did not freeze solid, it cracks from time to time with a threatening squeak. I see here and there very faint tracks of muskrats or minks, made when it was soft and sloshy, leading from the springy shore to the then open middle, — the faintest possible vestiges, which are only seen in a favorable light.

Just this side of Bittern Cliff, I see a very remarkable track of an otter, made undoubtedly December 3d, when this snow ice was mere slosh. It had come up through a hole (now black ice) by the stem of a button-bush, and, apparently, pushed its way through the slosh, as through snow on land, leaving a track eight inches wide, more or less, with the now frozen snow shoved up two inches high on each side, i. e. two inches above the general level. Where the ice was firmer are seen only the tracks of its feet. It had crossed the open middle (now thin black ice) and continued its singular trail to the opposite shore, as if a narrow sled had been drawn bottom upward.

At Bittern Cliff I saw where they had been playing, sliding, or fishing, apparently to-day, on the snow-covered rocks, on which, for a rod upward and as much in width, the snow was trodden and worn quite smooth, as if twenty had trodden and slid there for several hours. Their droppings are a mass of fishes' scales and bones, — loose, scaly black masses. At this point the black ice approached within three or four feet of the rock, and there was an open space just there, a foot or two across, which appeared to have been kept open by them. I continued along up that side and crossed on white ice just below the pond. The river was all tracked up with otters, from Bittern Cliff upward. Sometimes one had trailed his tail, apparently edgewise, making a mark like the tail of a deer mouse;

sometimes they were moving fast, and there was an interval of five feet between the tracks. I saw one place where there was a zigzag piece of black ice two rods long and one foot wide in the midst of the white, which I was surprised to find had been made by an otter pushing his way through the slosh. He had left fishes' scales, etc., at the end. These very conspicuous tracks generally commenced and terminated at some button-bush or willow, where a black ice now masked the hole of that date. It is surprising that our hunters know no more about them.

I see also what I take to be rabbit's tracks made in that slosh, shaped like a horse's track, only rather longer and larger. They had set out to cross the river, but, coming to open water, turned back.

Each pinweed, etc., has melted a little hollow or rough cave in the snow, in which the lower part at least snugly hides. They are never more interesting than now on Lechea Plain, since they are perfectly relieved, brown on white.

Far the greater part of the shrub oak leaves are fallen.

When I speak of the otter to our oldest village doctor, who should be *ex officio* our naturalist, he is greatly surprised, not knowing that such an animal is found in these parts, and I have to remind him that the Pilgrims sent home many otter skins in the first vessels that returned, together with beaver, mink, and black fox skins, and 1156 pounds of otter skins in the years 1631–36, which brought fourteen or fifteen shillings

Vol. IX

a pound, also 12,530 pounds of beaver skin. *Vide* Bradford's History.

Though so many oak leaves hang on all winter, you will be surprised on going into the woods at any time, only a short time after a fall of snow, to see how many have lately fallen on it and are driven about over it, so that you would think there could be none left till spring.

Where I crossed the river on the roughish white ice, there were coarse ripple-marks two or three feet apart and convex to the south or up-stream, extending quite

across, and many spots of black ice a foot wide, more or less in the midst of the white, where probably was water yesterday. The water, apparently, had been blown southerly on to the ice already formed, and hence the ripple-marks.

In many places the otters appeared to have gone floundering along in the sloshy ice and water.

On all sides, in swamps and about their edges and in the woods, the bare shrubs are sprinkled with buds, more or less noticeable and pretty, their little gemmæ or gems, their most vital and attractive parts now, almost all the greenness and color left, greens and salads for the birds and rabbits. Our eyes go searching along the stems for what is most vivacious and characteristic, the concentrated summer gone into winter quarters. For we are hunters pursuing the summer on snow-shoes and skates, all winter long. There is really but one season in our hearts.

What variety the pinweeds, clear brown seedy plants, give to the fields, which are yet but shallowly covered with snow! You were not aware before how extensive these grain-fields. Not till the snow comes are the beauty and variety and richness of vegetation ever fully revealed. Some plants are now seen more simply and distinctly and to advantage. The pinweeds, etc., have been for the most part confounded with the russet or brown earth beneath them, being seen against a background of the same color, but now, being seen against a pure white background, they are as distinct as if held up to the sky.

Some plants seen, then, in their prime or perfection, when supporting an icy burden in their empty chalices.

Dec. 7. Sunday. P. M. — Take my first skate to Fair Haven Pond.

It takes my feet a few moments to get used to the skates. I see the track of one skater who has preceded me this morning. This is the first skating. I keep mostly to the smooth ice about a rod wide next the shore commonly, where there was an overflow a day or two ago. There is not the slightest overflow to-day, and yet it is warm (thermometer at 25 at 4.30 P. M.). It must be that the river is falling. Now I go shaking over hobbly places, now shoot over a bridge of ice only a foot wide between the water and the shore at a bend, — Hubbard Bath, — always so at first there. Now I suddenly see the trembling surface of water where I thought were black spots of ice only around me. The river is rather low, so that I cannot keep the river above the Clamshell Bend. I am confined to a very narrow edging of ice in the meadow, gliding with unexpected ease through withered sedge, but slipping sometimes on a twig; again taking to the snow to reach the next ice, but this rests my feet; straddling the bare black willows, winding between the button-bushes, and following narrow threadings of ice amid the sedge, which bring me out to clear fields unexpectedly. Occasionally I am obliged to take a few strokes over black and thin-looking ice, where the neighboring bank is springy, and am slow to acquire confidence in it, but, returning, how bold I am! Where the meadow seemed only sedge and snow, I find a complete ice connection.

At Cardinal Shore, as usual, there is a great crescent of hobbly ice, where, two or three days ago, the north-

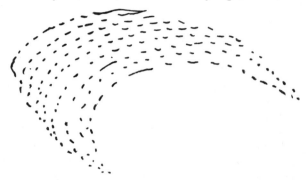

west wind drove the waves back up-stream and broke up the edge of the ice. This crescent is eight or ten rods wide and twice as many long, and consists of cakes of ice from a few inches to half a dozen feet in

diameter, with each a raised edge all around, where apparently the floating sludge has been caught and accumulated. (Occasionally the raised edge is six inches high!) This is mottled black and white, and is not yet safe. It is like skating over so many rails, or the edges of saws. Now I glide over a field of white air-cells close to the surface, with coverings no thicker than egg-shells, cutting through with a sharp crackling sound. There are many of those singular spider-shaped dark places amid the white ice, where the surface water has run through some days ago.

As I enter on Fair Haven Pond, I see already three pickerel-fishers retreating from it, drawing a sled through the Baker Farm, and see where they have been fishing, by the shining chips of ice about the holes. Others were here even yesterday, as it appears. The pond must have been frozen by the 4th at least. Some fisherman or other is ready with his reels and bait as soon as the ice will bear, whether it be Saturday or Sunday. Theirs, too, is a sort of devotion, though it be called hard names by the preacher, who perhaps could not endure the cold and wet any day. Perhaps he dines off their pickerel on Monday at the hotel. The ice appears to be but three or four inches thick.

That grand old poem called Winter is round again without any connivance of mine. As I sit under Lee's Cliff, where the snow is melted, amid sere pennyroyal and frost-bitten catnep, I look over my shoulder upon an arctic scene. I see with surprise the pond a dumb white surface of ice speckled with snow, just as so many winters before, where so lately were lapsing waves or

smooth reflecting water. I see the holes which the pickerel-fisher has made, and I see him, too, retreating over the hills, drawing his sled behind him. The water is already skimmed over again there. I hear, too, the familiar belching voice of the pond. It seemed as if winter had come without any interval since midsummer, and I was prepared to see it flit away by the time I again looked over my shoulder. It was as if I had dreamed it. But I see that the farmers have had time to gather their harvests as usual, and the seasons have revolved as slowly as in the first autumn of my life. The winters come now as fast as snowflakes. It is wonderful that old men do not lose their reckoning. It was summer, and now again it is winter. Nature loves this rhyme so well that she never tires of repeating it. So sweet and wholesome is the winter, so simple and moderate, so satisfactory and perfect, that her children will never weary of it. What a poem! an epic in blank verse, enriched with a million tinkling rhymes. It is solid beauty. It has been subjected to the vicissitudes of millions of years of the gods, and not a single superfluous ornament remains. The severest and coldest of the immortal critics have shot their arrows at and pruned it till it cannot be amended.[1]

The swamp white oak leaves are like the shrub oak in having two colors above and beneath. They are considerably curled, so as to show their silvery lining, though firm. Hardy and handsome, with a fair silver winter lining.

Am pleased to see the holes where men have dug for

[1] [Channing, p. 111.]

money, since they remind me that some are dreaming still like children, though of impracticable things, — dreaming of finding money, and trying to put their dream in practice. It proves that men live Arabian nights and days still. I would [rather] they should have even that kind of faith than none at all. If any silly or abominable or superstitious practice ever prevailed among any savage race, just that may be repeated in the most civilized society to-day.

You will see full-grown woods where the oaks and pines or birches are separated by right lines, growing in squares or other rectilinear figures, because different lots were cut at different times.

Dec. 8. Thermometer at 8 A. M. 8° above zero. Probably the coldest day yet.

Bradford, in his "History of the Plymouth Plantation," remembering the condition of the Pilgrims on their arrival in Cape Cod Bay the 11th of November, 1620, O. S. (page 79): "Which way soever they turned their eyes (save upward to the heavens) they could have little solace or content in respect of any outward objects. For summer being done, all things stand upon them with a weather-beaten face; and the whole country, full of woods and thickets, represented a wild and savage hue." Such was a New England November in 1620 to Bradford's eyes, and such, no doubt, it would be to his eyes in the country still. However, it required no little courage to found a colony here at that season of the year.

The earliest mention of anything like a glaze in New

England that I remember is in Bradford's "History of the Plymouth Plantation," page 83, where he describes the second expedition with the shallop from Cape Cod Harbor in search of a settlement, the 6th of December, O. S. "The weather was very cold, and it froze so hard as the spray of the sea lighting on their coats, they were as if they had been glazed." Bradford was one of the ten principal ones. That same night they reached the bottom of the Bay and saw the Indians cutting up a blackfish. Nature has not changed one iota.

Dec. 9. P. M. — Railroad to Lincoln Bridge and back by road.

There is scarcely a particle of ice in Walden yet, and that close to the edge, apparently, on the west and northwest sides. Yet Fair Haven was so solidly frozen on the 6th that there was fishing on it, and yesterday I met Goodwin bringing a fine lot of pickerel from Flint's, which was frozen at least four inches thick. This is, no doubt, owing solely to the greater depth of Walden.

As I stand on the railroad against Heywood's meadow, the sun now getting low in the west, the leaves of the young oaks in Emerson's sprout-land on the side of the hill make a very agreeable thick, rug-like stuff for the eye to rest on. The white oak leaves are a very pale brown, but the scarlet oaks are quite red now in the sun. Near at hand they are conspicuously ruddy in any light, the scarlet oaks. (Those black oaks which I examine near at hand afterward are a pure, somewhat yellowish brown.) This slight difference of shading makes a very pleasing variety on this densely covered

hillside, like a rich embroidered stuff. One species does not stand by itself, but they are dispersed and intimately mingled. These oak leaves have more distinct characters now at this distance than in summer. It is as if a rich rug, with stuff six or eight feet deep, had been dropped over this hill, opening the stuff on the brow, dyed of various shades of enduring brown, the wholesome and strong color which Nature loves; and here and there the now dark green of a pine is seen. When the wind rises, the leaves rustle their content.

The sunlight reveals no redness in the white oak leaves. The bright colors of autumn are transient; these browns are permanent. These are not so much withered leaves, for they have a wintry life in them still, and the tanned or bronzed color of assured health. They are a sort of epidermis or bark, not at once thrown off, serving, perhaps, to protect the trees as well as the quadrupeds and birds.

Coming through the Walden woods, I see already great heaps of oak leaves collected in certain places on the snow-crust by the roadside, where an eddy deposited them. It suggests that a certain law has attended their movements, which appeared so lawless, even as with the iron filings under the influence of music. The greater part that have fallen are deposited in clear and crispy heaps in particular places. They are beds which invite the traveller to repose on them, even in this wintry weather.

From a little east of Wyman's I look over the pond westward. The sun is near setting, away beyond Fair Haven. A bewitching stillness reigns through all the

Vol. IX

woodland and over the snow-clad landscape. Indeed, the winter day in the woods or fields has commonly the stillness of twilight. The pond is perfectly smooth and full of light. I hear only the strokes of a lingering woodchopper at a distance, and the melodious hooting of an owl, which is as common and marked a sound as the axe or the locomotive whistle. Yet where does the ubiquitous hooter sit, and who sees him? In whose wood-lot is he to be found? Few eyes have rested on him hooting; few on him silent on his perch even. Yet cut away the woods never so much year after year, though the chopper has not seen him and only a grove or two is left, still his aboriginal voice is heard indefinitely far and sweet, mingled oft, in strange harmony, with the newly invented din of trade, like a sentence of Allegri sounded in our streets, — hooting from invisible perch at his foes the woodchoppers, who are invading his domains. As the earth only a few inches beneath the surface is undisturbed and what it was anciently, so are heard still some primeval sounds in the air. Some of my townsmen I never see, and of a great proportion I do not hear the voices in a year, though they live within my horizon; but every week almost I hear the loud voice of the hooting owl, though I do not see the bird more than once in ten years.

I perceive that more or other things are seen in the reflection than in the substance. As I look now over the pond westward, I see in substance the now bare outline of Fair Haven Hill a mile beyond, but in the reflection I see not this, only the tops of some pines, which stand close to the shore but are invisible against

the dark hill beyond, and these are indefinitely prolonged into points of shadow.

The sun is set, and over the valley, which looks like an outlet of Walden toward Fair Haven, I see a burnished bar of cloud stretched low and level, as if it were the bar over that passageway to Elysium, the last column in the train of the sun.

When I get as far as my bean-field, the reflected white in the winter horizon of this perfectly cloudless sky is being condensed at the horizon's edge, and its hue deepening into a dun golden, against which the tops of the trees — pines and elms — are seen with beautiful distinctness, and a slight blush begins to suffuse the eastern horizon, and so the picture of the day is done and set in a gilded frame.

Such is a winter eve. Now for a merry fire, some old poet's pages, or else serene philosophy, or even a healthy book of travels, to last far into the night, eked out perhaps with the walnuts which we gathered in November.

The worker who would accomplish much these short days must shear a dusky slice off both ends of the night. The chopper must work as long as he can see, often returning home by moonlight, and set out for the woods again by candle-light.

In many parts of the river the ice has been formed with remarkably coarse crystallization, the surface being starred with great raised rays as thick as your thumb and several feet long, as it were the beginning of a bony system, as if under the action of a strong wind which rippled the water while it was freezing. All covered with these rounded plaits. Soon, where there is much current, even in pretty cold weather, the ice is worn thin during the day, and when you are following the tracks of one who has preceded you by half a dozen hours over the black ice, you are surprised by seeing the trembling water reveal itself at numerous holes otherwise not noticeable close about you.

The northwest wind, meeting the current in an exposed place, produces that hobbly ice which I described at Cardinal Shore day before yesterday. This is the case in this place every year, and no doubt this same phenomenon occurred annually at this point on this river a thousand years before America was discovered. This regularity and permanence make these phenomena more interesting to me.

Dec. 10. A fine, clear, cold winter morning, with a small leaf frost on trees, etc. The thermometer at 7.15 and at 7.30 3°. Going to the post-office at the former hour, I notice those level bars, as it were, of frozen mist against the Walden wood. When I return, the sun is rising and the smokes from the chimneys, which slant from northwest to southeast, though it seems quite still, blush like sunset clouds.

It is remarkable how suggestive the slightest drawing as a memento of things seen. For a few years past I have been accustomed to make a rude sketch in my journal of plants, ice, and various natural phenomena, and though the fullest accompanying description may

fail to recall my experience, these rude outline drawings do not fail to carry me back to that time and scene. It is as if I saw the same thing again, and I may again attempt to describe it in words if I choose.

Yesterday I walked under the murderous Lincoln Bridge, where at least ten men have been swept dead from the cars within as many years. I looked to see if their heads had indented the bridge, if there were sturdy blows given as well as received, and if their brains lay about. But I could see neither the one nor the other. The bridge is quite uninjured, even, and straight, not even the paint worn off or discolored. The ground is clean, the snow spotless, and the place looks as innocent as a bank whereon the wild thyme grows. It does its work in an artistic manner. We have another bridge of exactly the same character on the other side of the town, which has killed one, at least, to my knowledge. Surely the approaches to our town are well guarded. These are our modern Dragons of Wantley. Boucaniers of the Fitchburg Railroad, they lie in wait at the narrow passes and decimate the employees. The Company has signed a bond to give up one employee at this pass annually. The Vermont mother commits her son to their charge, and when she asks for him, again the Directors say: "I am not your son's keeper. Go look beneath the ribs of the Lincoln Bridge." It is a monster which would not have minded Perseus with his Medusa's head. If he could be held back only four feet from where he now crouches, all travellers might pass in safety and laugh him to scorn. This would require but a little resolution in our legis-

lature, but it is preferred to pay tribute still. I felt a curiosity to see this famous bridge, naturally far greater than my curiosity to see the gallows on which Smith was hung, which was burned in the old court-house, for the exploits of this bridge are ten times as memorable. Here they are killed without priest, and the bridge, unlike the gallows, is a fixture. Besides, the gallows bears an ill name, and I think deservedly. No doubt it has hung many an innocent man, but this Lincoln Bridge, long as it has been in our midst and busy as it has been, no legislature, nobody, indeed, has ever seriously complained of, unless it was some bereaved mother, who was naturally prejudiced against it. To my surprise, I found no difficulty in getting a sight of it. It stands right out in broad daylight in the midst of the fields. No sentinels, no spiked fence, no crowd about it, and you have to pay no fee for looking at it. It is perfectly simple and easy to construct, and does its work silently. The days of the gallows are numbered. The next time this county has a Smith to dispose of, they have only to hire him out to the Fitchburg Railroad Company. Let the priest accompany him to the freight-train, pray with him, and take leave of him there. Another advantage I have hinted at, an advantage to the morals of the community, that, strange as it may seem, no crowd ever assembles at this spot; there are no morbidly curious persons, no hardened reprobates, no masculine women, no anatomists there.

Does it not make life more serious? I feel as if these were stirring times, as good as the days of the Crusaders, the Northmen, or the Boucaniers.

Gathered this afternoon quite a parcel of walnuts on the hill. It has not been better picking this season there. They lie on the snow, or rather sunk an inch or two into it. And some trees hang quite full.[1] See the squirrel-tracks leading straight from tree to tree.

It has been a warm, clear, glorious winter day, the air full of that peculiar vapor. How short the afternoons! I hardly get out a couple of miles before the sun is setting. The nights are light on account of the snow, and, there being a moon, there is no distinct interval between the day and night. I see the sun set from the side of Nawshawtuct, and make haste to the post-office with the red sky over my shoulder. When the mail is distributed and I come forth into the street on my return, the apparently full moon has fairly commenced her reign, and I go home by her light.

Bradford, in his "History of the Plymouth Plantation," written between 1630 and 1650, uses, on page 235, the word "kilter," speaking of guns being out of kilter, proving that this is an old word; yet it is not in my dictionaries.

Dec. 11. Minott tells me that his and his sister's wood-lot together contains about ten acres and has, with a very slight exception at one time, supplied all their fuel for thirty years, and he thinks would constantly continue to do so. They keep one fire all the time, and two some of the time, and burn about eight cords in a year. He knows his wood-lot and what grows

[1] So, too, the shagbarks hang on the trees on the Souhegan, where they have not been gathered.

in it as well as an ordinary farmer does his corn-field, for he has cut his own wood till within two or three years; knows the history of every stump on it and the age of every sapling; knows how many beech trees and black birches there are there, as another knows his pear or cherry trees. He complains that the choppers make a very long carf nowadays, doing most of the cutting on one side, to avoid changing hands so much. It is more economical, as well as more poetical, to have a wood-lot and cut and get out your own wood from year to year than to buy it at your door. Minott may say to his trees: "Submit to my axe. I cut your father on this very spot." How many sweet passages there must have been in his life there, chopping all alone in the short winter days! How many rabbits, partridges, foxes he saw! A rill runs through the lot, where he quenched his thirst, and several times he has laid it bare. At last rheumatism has made him a prisoner, and he is compelled to let a stranger, a vandal, it may be, go into his lot with an axe. It is fit that he should be buried there.

Dec. 12. Wonderful, wonderful is our life and that of our companions! That there should be such a thing as a brute animal, not human! and that it should attain to a sort of society with our race! Think of cats, for instance. They are neither Chinese nor Tartars. They do not go to school, nor read the Testament; yet how near they come to doing so! how much they are like us who do so! What sort of philosophers are we, who know absolutely nothing of the origin and des-

tiny of cats? At length, without having solved any of these problems, we fatten and kill and eat some of our cousins!

As soon as the snow came, I naturally began to observe that portion of the plants that was left above the snow, not only the weeds but the withered leaves, which before had been confounded with the russet earth. Yesterday afternoon, after a misty forenoon, it began to rain by degrees, and in the course of the night more than half the snow has disappeared, revealing the ground here and there; and already the brown weeds and leaves attract me less.

This morning it is fair again.

P. M. — To Saw Mill Brook and back by Red Choke-berry Path and Walden.

Large oaks in thick woods have not so many leaves on them as in pastures, methinks (?). At the wall between Saw Mill Brook Falls and Red Choke-berry Path, I see where a great many chestnut burs have been recently chewed up fine by the squirrels, to come at the nuts. The wall for half a dozen rods and the snow are covered with them. You can see where they have dug the burs out of the snow, and then sat on a rock or the wall and gnawed them in pieces. I, too, dig many burs out of the snow with my foot, and though many of *these* nuts are softened and discolored they have a peculiarly sweet and agreeable taste.

Yesterday morning I noticed that several people were having their pigs killed, not foreseeing the thaw. Such warm weather as this the animal heat will hardly get out before night. I saw Peter, the dexterous pig-butcher,

Vol. IX

busy in two or three places, and in the afternoon I saw him with washed hands and knives in sheath and his leather overalls drawn off, going to his solitary house on the edge of the Great Fields, carrying in the rain a piece of the pork he had slaughtered, with a string put through it. Often he carries home the head, which is less prized, taking his pay thus in kind, and these supplies do not come amiss to his outcast family.

I saw Lynch's dog stealthily feeding at a half of his master's pig, which lay dressed on a wheelbarrow at the door. A little yellow-brown dog, with fore feet braced on the ice and outstretched neck, he eagerly browsed along the edge of the meat, half a foot to right and left, with incessant short and rapid snatches, which brought it away as readily as if it had been pudding. He evidently knew very well that he was stealing, but made the most of his time. The little brown dog weighed a pound or two more afterward than before.

Where is the great natural-historian? Is he a butcher, or the patron of butchers? As well look for a great anthropologist among cannibals, New-Zealanders.

Dec. 13. P. M. — To Hill and round by J. Hosmer woodland and Lee house.

I see some of those great andromeda puffs still hanging on the twigs behind Assabet Spring, black and shrivelled bags. The river is generally open again. The snow is mostly gone. In many places it is washed away down to the channels made by the mice, branching galleries. I go through the lot where Wheeler's Irishmen cut last winter. Though they changed hands, they did not

cut twice in a place, and the stump, instead of having a smooth surface, is roughly hacked.

There is a fine healthy and handsome scarlet oak between Muhlenbergii Brook and the Assabet River watering-place, in the open land. It is about thirty-five feet high and spreads twenty-five, perfectly regular. It is very full of leaves, excepting a crescent of bare twigs at the summit about three feet wide in the middle. The leaves have a little redness in them.

There is a dense growth of young birches from the seed in the sprout-land lot just beyond on the riverside, now apparently two or three years old, and they have a peculiar pink tint seen in the mass.

Dec. 14. This morning it begins to snow, and the ground is whitened again, but in an hour or two it turns to rain, and rains all the rest of the day. At night clears up, and in the night a strong and gusty northwest wind blows, which, by morning, —

Dec. 15, has dried up almost all the water in the road. It still blows hard at 2 P. M., but it is not cold.

3 P. M. — To Walden.

The high northwest wind of this morning, with what of cold we have, has made *some* of those peculiar rake-toothed icicles on the dead twigs, etc., about the edge of the pond at the east end. To produce this pheno-menon is required only open water, a high wind, and sufficiently cold weather to freeze the spray. I observe B——'s boat left out at the pond, as last winter. When I see that a man neglects his boat thus, I do not wonder that he fails in his business. It is not only shiftlessness or unthrift, but a sort of filthiness to let things go to wrack and ruin thus.

I still recall to mind that characteristic winter eve of December 9th; the cold, dry, and wholesome diet my mind and senses necessarily fed on,—oak leaves, bleached and withered weeds that rose above the snow, the now dark green of the pines, and perchance the faint metallic chip of a single tree sparrow; the hushed stillness of the wood at sundown, aye, all the winter day; the short boreal twilight; the smooth serenity and the reflections of the pond, still alone free from ice; the melodious hooting of the owl, heard at the same time with the yet more distant whistle of a locomotive, more aboriginal, and perchance more enduring here than that, heard above the voices of all the wise men of Concord, as if they were not (how little he is Anglicized!); the last strokes of the woodchopper, who presently bends his steps homeward; the gilded bar of cloud across the apparent outlet of the pond, conducting my thoughts into the eternal west; the deepening horizon glow; and the hasty walk homeward to enjoy the long winter evening. The hooting of the owl! That is a sound which my red predecessors heard here more than a thousand years ago. It rings far and wide, occupying the spaces rightfully,—grand, primeval, aboriginal sound. There is no whisper in it of the Buckleys, the Flints, the Hosmers who recently squatted here, nor of the first parish, nor of Concord Fight, nor of the last town meeting.

Mrs. Moody very properly calls eating nuts "a mouse-

like employment." It is quite too absorbing; you can't read at the same time, as when you are eating an apple.

Dec. 17. P. M. — Cold, with a piercing northwest wind and bare ground still. The river, which was raised by the rain of the 14th and ran partly over the meadows, is frozen over again, and I go along the edge of the meadow under Clamshell and back by Hubbard's Bridge.

At Clamshell, to my surprise, scare up either a woodcock or a snipe. I think the former, for I plainly saw considerable red on the breast, also a light stripe along the neck. It was feeding alone, close to the edge of the hill, where it is springy and still soft, almost the only place of this character in the neighborhood, and though I started it three times, it each time flew but little way, round to the hillside again, perhaps the same spot it had left a moment before, as if unwilling to leave this unfrozen and comparatively warm locality. It was a great surprise this bitter cold day, when so many springs were frozen up, to see this hardy bird loitering still. Once alighted, you could not see it till it arose again.

In Saw Mill Brook, as I crossed it, I saw the tail disappearing of some muskrat or other animal, flapping in the cold water, where all was ice around. A flock of a dozen or more tree sparrows flitting through the edge of the birches, etc., by the meadow front of Puffer's. They make excursions into the open meadow and, as I approach, take refuge in the brush. I hear their faint *cheep,* a very feeble evidence of their existence, and also a pretty little suppressed warbling from them.

To-day, though so cold, there is much of the frozen overflow, a broad border of it, along the meadow, a discolored yellowish and soft ice (it probably ran out yesterday or last night), the river still rising a little.

The wind is so cold and strong that the Indians that are encamped in three wigwams of cloth in the railroad wood-yard have all moved into two and closed them up tight.

That feeble *cheep* of the tree sparrow, like the tinkling of an icicle, or the chafing of two hard shrub oak twigs, is probably a call to their mates, by which they keep together. These birds, when perched, look larger than usual this cold and windy day; they are puffed up for warmth, have added a porch to their doors.

It is pretty poor picking out of doors to-day. There's but little comfort to be found. You go stumping over bare frozen ground, sometimes clothed with curly yellowish withered grass like the back of half-starved cattle late in the fall, now beating this ear, now that, to keep them warm. It is comparatively summer-like under the south side of woods and hills.

When I returned from the South the other day, I was greeted by withered shrub oak leaves which I had not seen there. It was the most homely and agreeable object that met me. I found that I had no such friend as the shrub oak hereabouts. A farmer once asked me what shrub oaks were made for, not knowing any use they served. But I can tell him that they do me good. They are my parish ministers, regularly settled. They never did any man harm that I know.

Yesterday afternoon I was running a line through the

woods. How many days have I spent thus, sighting my way in direct lines through dense woods, through cat-briar and viburnum in New Jersey, through shrub oak in New England, requiring my axeman to shear off twigs and bushes and dead limbs and masses of withered leaves that obstruct the view, and then set up a freshly barked stake exactly on the line; looking at these barked stakes from far and near as if I loved them; not knowing where I shall come out; my duty then and there perhaps merely to locate a straight line between two points.

Now you have the foliage of summer painted in brown. Go through the shrub oaks. All growth has ceased; no greenness meets the eye, except what there may be in the bark of this shrub. The green leaves are all turned to brown, quite dry and sapless. The little buds are sleeping at the base of the slender shrunken petioles. Who observed when they passed from green to brown? I do not remember the transition; it was very gradual. But these leaves still have a kind of life in them. They are exceedingly beautiful in their withered state. If they hang on, it is like the perseverance of the saints. Their colors are as wholesome, their forms as perfect, as ever. Now that the crowd and bustle of summer is passed, I have leisure to admire them. Their figures never weary my eye. Look at the few broad scallops in their sides. When was that pattern first cut? With what a free stroke the curve was struck! With how little, yet just enough, variety in their forms! Look at the fine bristles which arm each pointed lobe, as perfect now as when the wild bee hummed about them, or the chewink scratched beneath them. What pleasing and harmonious colors within and without, above and below! The smooth, delicately brown-tanned upper surface, acorn-color, the very pale (some silvery or ashy) ribbed under side. How poetically, how like saints or innocent and beneficent beings, they give up the ghost! How spiritual! Though they have lost their sap, they have not given up the ghost. Rarely touched by worm or insect, they are as fair as ever. These are the forms of some: —

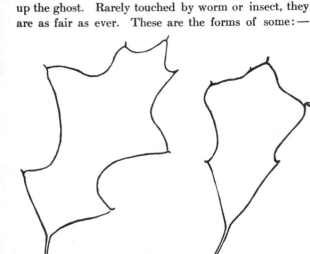

When was it ordained that this leaf should turn brown in the fall?

Dec. 18. 12 M. Start for Amherst, N. H.

A very cold day. Thermometer at 8 A. M. — 8° (and

I hear of others very much lower at an earlier hour), — 2° at 11.45.

I find the first snow enough to whiten the ground beyond Littleton, and it deepens all the way to Amherst. The steam of the engine hugs the earth very close. Is it because it [is] a very clear, cold day?

The last half the route from Groton Junction to Nashua is along the Nashua River mostly. This river looks less interesting than the Concord. It appears even more open, *i. e.* less wooded (?). At any rate the banks are more uniform, and I notice none of our meadows on it. At Nashua, hire a horse and sleigh, and ride to Amherst, eleven miles, against a strong northwest wind, this bitter cold afternoon. When I get to South Merrimack, about 3.15 P. M., they tell me the thermometer is — 3°. While the driving hand is getting benumbed, I am trying to warm the other against my body under the buffalo. Warm myself there in the shop of a tub and pail maker, who does his work by hand, splitting out the staves with a curved knife and smoothing them with curved shaves. His hoops are white ash, shaved thin. After entering Amherst territory, near the Souhegan, notice many shagbark trees, which they tell me the owners value as they do a good apple tree, getting a dozen bushels of shelled nuts sometimes from a tree. I see the nuts on some still.

At my lecture, the audience attended to me closely, and I was satisfied; that is all I ask or expect generally. Not one spoke to me afterward, nor needed they. I have no doubt that they liked it, in the main, though few of them would have dared say so, provided they were

conscious of it. Generally, if I can only get the ears of an audience, I do not care whether they say they like my lecture or not. I think I know as well as they can tell. At any rate, it is none of my business, and it would be impertinent for me to inquire. The stupidity of most of these country towns, not to include the cities, is in its innocence infantile. Lectured in basement (vestry) of the orthodox church, and I trust helped to undermine it.

I was told to stop at the U. S. Hotel, but an old inhabitant had never heard of it and could not tell me where to find it, but I found the letters on a sign without help. It was the ordinary unpretending (?) desolate-looking country tavern. The landlord apologized to me because there was to be a ball there that night which would keep me awake, and it did. He and others there, horrible to relate, were in the habit of blowing their noses with their fingers and wiping them on their boots! Champney's U. S. Hotel was an ordinary team tavern, and the letters U. S., properly enough, not very conspicuous on the sign.

A paper called the *Farmer's Cabinet* is published there. It has reached its fifty-fifth volume. I rode back to Nashua in the morning of —

Dec. 19. Knew the road by some yellow birch trees in a swamp and some rails set on end around a white oak in a pasture. These it seems were the objects I had noticed. In Nashua observed, as I thought, some elms in the distance which had been whitewashed. It turned out that they were covered from top to bottom, on one

side, with the frozen vapor from a fall on the canal. Walked a little way along the bank of the Merrimack, which was frozen over, and was agreeably reminded of my voyage up it. The night previous, in Amherst, I had been awaked by the loud cracking of the ground, which shook the house like the explosion of a powdermill. In the morning there was to be seen a long crack across the road in front. I saw several of these here in Nashua, and ran a bit of stubble into them but in no place more than five inches. This is a sound peculiar to the coldest nights. Observed that the Nashua in Pepperell was frozen to the very edge of the fall, and even further in some places.

Got home at 1.30 P. M.

P. M. — To Walden.

Walden froze completely over last night. This is very sudden, for on the evening of the 15th there was not a particle of ice in it. In just three days, then, it has been completely frozen over, and the ice is now from two and a half to three inches thick, a transparent green ice, through which I see the bottom where it is seven or eight feet deep. I detect its thickness by looking at the cracks, which are already very numerous, but, having been made at different stages of the ice, they indicate very various thicknesses. Often one only an inch deep crosses at right angles another two and a half inches deep, the last having been recently made and indicating the real thickness of the ice. I advance confidently toward the middle, keeping within a few feet of some distinct crack two inches or more deep, but when that fails me and I see only cracks an inch or an inch and a half deep, or none at all, I walk with great caution and timidity, though the ice may be as thick as ever, but I have no longer the means of determining its thickness. The ice is so transparent that it is too much like walking on water by faith.

The portion of the pond which was last frozen is a thinner and darker ice stretching about across the middle from southeast to northwest, *i. e.* from the shoulder of the Deep Cove to nearly midway between the bar and Ice-Fort Cove Cape. Close to the northwest end of this, there is a small and narrow place twenty feet long east and west, which is still so thin that a small stone makes a hole. The water, judging from my map, may[be] seventy or seventy-five feet deep there. It looks as if that had been the warmest place in the surface of the pond and therefore the last to yield to the frost king. Into this, or into the thinner ice at this point, there empties, as it were, a narrow meandering creek from near the western shore, which was nearly as late to freeze as any part. All this, I think, I have noticed in previous years. About the edge of all this more recent and darker ice, the thicker ice is white with a feathery frost, which seems to have been produced by the very fine spray, or rather the vapor, blown from the yet unfrozen surface on to the ice by the strong and cold wind. Here is where, so to speak, its last *animal heat* escaped, the dying breath of the pond frozen on its lips. It had the same origin with the frost about the mouth of a hole in the ground whence warm vapors had escaped. The fluid, timid pond was

encircled within an ever-narrowing circle by the icy grasp of winter, and this is a trace of the last vaporous breath that curled along its trembling surface. Here the chilled pond gave up the ghost.

As I stand here, I hear the hooting of my old acquaintance the owl in Wheeler's Wood. Do I not oftenest hear it just before sundown? This sound, heard near at hand, is more simply animal and guttural, without resonance or reverberation, but, heard here from out the depths of the wood, it sounds peculiarly hollow and drum-like, as if it struck on a tense skin drawn around, the tympanum of the wood, through which all we denizens of nature hear. Thus it comes to us an accredited and universal or melodious sound; is more than the voice of the owl, the voice of the wood as well. The owl only touches the stops, or rather wakes the reverberations. For all Nature is a musical instrument on which her creatures play, celebrating their joy or grief unconsciously often. It sounds now, *hoo | hoo hoo* (very fast) | *hoo-rer | hoo.*

Withered leaves! this is our frugal winter diet, instead of the juicy salads of spring and summer. I think I could write a lecture on "Dry Leaves," carrying a specimen of each kind that hangs on in the winter into the lecture-room as the heads of my discourse. They have long hung to some extent in vain, and have not found their poet yet. The pine has been sung, but not, to my knowledge, the shrub oak. Most think it is useless. How glad I am that it serves no vulgar use! It is never seen on the woodman's cart. The citizen who has just bought a sprout-land on which shrub oaks alone come

up only curses it. But it serves a higher use than they know. Shrub oak! how true its name! Think first what a family it belongs to. The oak, the king of trees, is its own brother, only of ampler dimensions. The oaks, so famous for grandeur and picturesqueness, so prized for strength by the builder, for knees or for beams; and this is the oak of smaller size, the Esquimau of oaks, the shrub oak! The oaken shrub! I value it first for the noble family it belongs to. It is not like brittle sumach or venomous dogwood, which you must beware how you touch, but wholesome to the touch, though rough; not producing any festering sores, only honest scratches and rents.

Dr. Kane says in his "Arctic Explorations," page 21, that at Fiskernaes in Greenland "the springs, which well through the mosses, frequently remain unfrozen throughout the year."

Dec. 20. Rain more or less all day.

Dec. 21. Sunday. Think what a pitiful kind of life ours is, eating our kindred animals! and in some places one another! Some of us (the Esquimaux), half whose life is spent in the dark, wholly dependent on one or two animals not many degrees removed from themselves for food, clothing, and fuel, and partly for shelter; making their sledges "of small fragments of porous bones [of whale],[1] admirably knit together by thongs of hide" (Kane's last book, vol. i, page 205), thus getting about, sliding about, on the bones of our cousins.

[1] [Supplied by Thoreau.]

Where Kane wintered in the Advance in 1853–54, on the coast of Greenland, about $78\frac{1}{2}°$ north latitude, or further north than any navigator had been excepting Parry at Spitzbergen, he meets with Esquimaux, and "the fleam-shaped tips of their lances were of unmistakable steel." "The metal was obtained in traffic from the more southern tribes." Such is trade.

P. M. — To Walden.

The pond is open again *in the middle*, owing to the rain of yesterday. I go across to the cliffs by way of the Andromeda Ponds.

How interesting and wholesome their color now! A broad level thick stuff, without a crevice in it, composed of the dull brown-red andromeda. Is it not the most uniform and deepest red that covers a large surface now? No withered oak leaves are nearly as red at present. In a broad hollow amid the hills, you have this perfectly level red stuff, marked here and there only with gray streaks or patches of bare high blueberry bushes, etc., and all surrounded by a light border of straw-colored sedge, etc.

Even the little red buds of the *Vaccinium Pennsylvanicum* and *vacillans* on the now bare and dry-looking stems attract me as I go through the open glades between the first Andromeda Pond and the Well Meadow Field. Many twigs of the *Vaccinium vacillans* appear to have been nibbled off, and some of its *buds have unfolded*, apparently in the fall. I observe sage willows with many leaves on them still.

Apparently the red oak retains much fewer leaves than the white, scarlet, and black. I notice the petioles of both the black and red twisted in that peculiar way. The red oak leaves look thinner and flatter, and therefore perhaps show the lobes more, than those of the black. The white oak leaves are the palest and most shrivelled, the lightest, perhaps a shade of buff, but they are of various shades, some pretty dark with a salmon tinge. The swamp white oak leaves (which I am surprised to find Gray makes a variety (*discolor*) of the *Quercus Prinus*) are very much like the shrub oak, but more curled. These two are the best preserved, though they do not hang on so well as the white and scarlet. Both remarkable for their thick, leathery, sound leaves, uninjured by insects, and their very light downy under sides. The black oak leaves are the darkest brown, with clear or deep yellowish-brown under sides, obovate in outline. The scarlet oak leaves, which are very numerous still, are of a ruddy color, having much blood in their cheeks. They are all winter the reddest on the hillsides. They still spread their ruddy fingers to the breeze. After the shrub and swamp white, they are perhaps the best preserved of any I describe. The red oak leaves are a little lighter brown than the black oak, less yellowish beneath. Their lobes, methinks, are narrower and straighter-sided. They are the color of their own acorns.

Dec. 22. To Boston and Cambridge.

Dec. 23. Some savage tribes must share the experience of the lower animals in their relation to man. With what thoughts must the Esquimau manufacture

his knife from the rusty hoop of a cask drifted to his shores, not a natural but an artificial product, the work of man's hands, the waste of the commerce of a superior race, whom perchance he never saw!

The cracking of the ground is a phenomenon of the coldest nights. After being awaked by the loud cracks the night of the 18th at Amherst (a man told me in the morning that he had seen a crack running across the plain (I saw it), almost broad enough to put his hand into; this was an exaggeration; it was not a quarter of an inch wide), I saw a great many the same forenoon running across the road in Nashua, every few rods, and also by our house in Concord the same day when I got home. So it seems the ground was cracking all the country over, partly, no doubt, because there was so little snow, or none (none at Concord).

If the writer would interest readers, he must report so much life, using a certain satisfaction always as a *point d'appui*. However mean and limited, it must be a genuine and contented life that he speaks out of. They must have the essence or oil of himself, tried out of the fat of his experience and joy.[1]

P. M. — Surveying for Cyrus Jarvis.

Snows more or less all day, making an inch or two.

Dec. 24. More snow in the night and to-day, making nine or ten inches.

P. M. — To Walden and Baker Farm with Ricketson, it still snowing a little.

Turned off from railroad and went through Wheeler,

[1] [Channing, p. 97.]

or Owl, Wood. The snow is very light, so that sleighs cut through it, and there is but little sleighing. It is very handsome now on the trees by the main path in Wheeler Wood; also on the weeds and twigs that rise  above the snow, resting on them just like down, light towers of down with the bare extremity of the twig peeping out above. We push through the light dust, throwing it before our legs as a husbandman grain which he is sowing. It is only in still paths in the woods that it rests on the trees much. Am surprised to find Walden still open in the middle. When I push aside the snow with my feet, the ice appears quite black by contrast. There is considerable snow on the edge of the pine woods where I used to live. It rests on the successive tiers of boughs, perhaps weighing them down, so that the trees are opened into great flakes from top to bottom. The snow collects and is piled up in little columns like down about every twig and stem, and this is only seen in perfection, complete to the last flake, while it is snowing, as now.

Returned across the pond and went across to Baker Farm.

Noticed, at east end of westernmost Andromeda Pond, the slender spikes of lycopus with half a dozen

distant little spherical dark-brown whorls of pungently fragrant or spicy seeds, somewhat nutmeg-like, or even

like flagroot (?), when bruised. I am not sure that the seeds of any other mint are thus fragrant now. It scents your handkerchief or pocketbook finely when the crumbled whorls are sprinkled over them.

It was very pleasant walking thus before the storm was over, in the soft, subdued light. We are also more domesticated in nature when our vision is confined to near and familiar objects. Did not see a track of any animal till returning near the Well Meadow Field, where many foxes (?), one of whom I had a glimpse of, had been coursing back and forth in the path and near it for three quarters of a mile. They had made quite a path.

I do not take snuff. In my winter walks, I stoop and bruise between my thumb and finger the dry whorls of the lycopus, or water horehound, just rising above the snow, stripping them off, and smell that. That is as near as I come to the Spice Islands. That is my smelling-bottle, my ointment.[1]

Dec. 25. P. M. — To Lee's Cliff.

A strong wind from the northwest is gathering the snow into picturesque drifts behind the walls. As usual they resemble shells more than anything, sometimes prows of vessels, also the folds of a white napkin or counterpane dropped over a bonneted head. There are no such picturesque snow-drifts as are formed behind loose and open stone walls. Already yesterday it had drifted so much, *i. e.* so much ground was bare, that there were as many carts as sleighs in the streets.

[1] [*Daniel Ricketson and his Friends*, pp. 348–350.]

Just beyond Hubbard's Bridge, on Conant's Brook Meadow, I am surprised to find a tract of ice, some thirty by seven or eight rods, blown quite bare. It shows how unstable the snow is.

Sanborn got some white spruce and some usnea for Christmas in the swamp. I thought the last would be the most interesting and *weird*.

On the north sides of the walls we go over boots and get them full, then let ourselves down into the shell-work on the south side; so beyond the brows of hills.

At Lee's Cliff I pushed aside the snow with my foot and got some fresh green catnip for Min.

I see the numerous tracks there, too, of foxes, or else hares, that have been running about in the light snow.

Called at the Conantum House. It grieves me to see these interesting relics, this and the house at the Baker Farm, going to complete ruin.

Met William Wheeler's shaggy gray terrier, or Indian dog, going home. He got out of the road into the field and went round to avoid us.

Take long walks in stormy weather or through deep snows in the fields and woods, if you would keep your spirits up. Deal with brute nature. Be cold and hungry and weary.

Dec. 27. Saturday. Walden is still open in one place of considerable extent, just off the east cape of long southern bay.

Dec. 28. Sunday. Am surprised to see the *F. hyemalis* here.

Vol. IX

or lifting its gills from time to time, gasping its life away.

I thrive best on solitude. If I have had a companion only one day in a week, unless it were one or two I could name, I find that the value of the week to me has been seriously affected. It dissipates my days, and often it takes me another week to get over it. As the Esquimaux of Smith's Strait in North Greenland laughed when Kane warned them of their utter extermination, cut off as they were by ice on all sides from their race, unless they attempted in season to cross the glacier southward, so do I laugh when you tell me of the danger of impoverishing myself by isolation. It is here that the walrus and the seal, and the white bear, and the eider ducks and auks on which I batten, most abound.

Dec. 29. The snow is softened yet more, and it thaws somewhat. The cockerels crow, and we are reminded of spring.

P. M. — To Warren Miles's mill.

We must go out and re-ally ourselves to Nature every day. We must make root, send out some little fibre at least, even every winter day. I am sensible that I am imbibing health when I open my mouth to the wind. Staying in the house breeds a sort of insanity always. Every house is in this sense a hospital. A night and a forenoon is as much confinement to those wards as I can stand. I am aware that I recover some sanity which I had lost almost the instant that I come abroad.

Do not the *F. hyemalis*, lingering yet, and the *numerous* tree sparrows foretell an open winter?

Walden completely frozen over again last night. Goodwin & Co. are fishing there to-day. Ice about four inches thick, occasionally sunk by the snow beneath the water. They have had but poor luck. One middling-sized pickerel and one large yellow perch only, since 9 or 10 A. M. It is now nearly sundown. The perch is very full of spawn. How handsome, with its broad dark transverse bars, sharp narrow triangles, broadest on the back!

The men are standing or sitting about a smoky fire of damp dead wood, near by the spot where many a fisherman has sat before, and I draw near, hoping to hear a fish story. One says that Louis Menan, the French Canadian who lives in Lincoln, fed his ducks on the fresh-water clams which he got at Fair Haven Pond. He saw him open the shells, and the ducks snapped them up out of the shells very fast.

I observe that some shrub oak leaves have but little silveriness beneath, as if they were a variety, the color of the under approaching that of the upper surface somewhat.

Since the snow of the 23d, the days seem considerably lengthened, owing to the increased light after sundown.

The fishermen sit by their damp fire of rotten pine wood, so wet and chilly that even smoke in their eyes is a kind of comfort. There they sit, ever and anon scanning their reels to see if any have fallen, and, if not catching many fish, still getting what they went for, though they may not be aware of it, *i. e.* a wilder experience than the town affords.

There lies a pickerel or perch on the ice, waving a fin

The fields behind Dennis's have but little snow on them; the weeds rising above it imbrown them. It is collected in deep banks on the southeast slopes of the hills, — the wind having been northwest, — and there no weeds rise above it.

By Nut Meadow Brook, just beyond Brown's fence crossing, I see a hornets' nest about seven inches in diameter on a thorn bush, only eighteen inches from the ground. Do they ever return to the same nests?

White oaks standing in open ground will commonly have more leaves now than black or red oaks of the same size, also standing exposed.

Miles is sawing pail-stuff. Thus the full streams and ponds supply the farmer with winter work. I see two trout four or five inches long in his brook a few rods below the mill. The water is quite low, he having shut it off. Rich copper-brown fish darting up and down the fast-shoaling stream.

When I return by Clamshell Hill, the sun has set, and the cloudy sky is reflected in a short and narrow open reach at the bend there. The water and reflected sky are a dull, dark green, but not the real sky.

Dec. 30. Surveying the W—— farm.

Parker, the Shaker that was, my assistant, says that the first year he came to live with W——, he worked on the farm, and that when he was digging potatoes on that jog (of about an acre) next to the site of the old Lee house, he found snakes' eggs in many hills, perhaps half a dozen together, he thinks as many as seventy in all. He did not perceive that they were united as he hoed them out, but may have separated them. When he broke the eggs, the young snakes, two or three inches long, wriggled out and about.

Had the experience of losing a pin and then hunting for it a long time in vain.

What an evidence it is, after all, of civilization, or of a capacity for improvement, that savages like our Indians, who in their protracted wars stealthily slay men, women, and children without mercy, with delight, who delight to burn, torture, and devour one another, proving themselves more inhuman in these respects even than beasts, — what a wonderful evidence it is, I say, of their capacity for improvement that even they can enter into the most formal compact or treaty of peace, burying the hatchet, etc., etc., and treating with each other with as much consideration as the most enlightened states. You would say that they had a genius for diplomacy as well as for war. Consider that Iroquois, torturing his captive, roasting him before a slow fire, biting off the fingers of him alive, and finally eating the heart of him dead, betraying not the slightest evidence of humanity; and now behold him in the council-chamber, where he meets the representatives of the hostile nation to treat of peace, conducting with such perfect dignity and decorum, betraying such a sense of justness. These savages are equal to us civilized men in their treaties, and, I fear, not essentially worse in their wars.

Jan. 1. I observe a shelf of ice — what arctic voyagers call the ice-belt or ice-foot (which they see on a very great scale sledging upon it) — adhering to the walls and banks at various heights, the river having fallen nearly two feet since it first froze. It is often two or three feet wide and now six inches thick.

Am still surveying the W—— or Lee farm. W—— cleared out and left this faithful servant like a cat in some corner of this great house, but without enough to buy him a pair of boots, I hear. Parker was once a Shaker at Canterbury. He is now Captain E——'s right-hand man. He found him in the house. P. does the chores. Complains that, as they dine at fashionable hours, he does n't get enough to support him when he goes home at noon from helping me. When he sees how much dead wood there is on the farm, he says they ought to have a "gundalo," meaning a large, square kind of boat, to cart it off with.

E——, having lent W—— money, was obliged to take the farm to save himself, but he is nearly blind, and is anxious to get rid of it. Says that the buildings are either new or in excellent repair. He understands that in W——'s day they mixed paint by the hogshead. Parker

has told him of logs cut two years ago which lie rotting in the swamp, and he is having them hauled out and to mill.

Jan. 2. To-day I see Parker is out with horse and cart, collecting dead wood at the Rock and drawing it home over the meadow. I saw the English servant-girl with one of the children flat on the ice hard at work on the river cutting a hole with a hatchet, but, as the ice was thick and the water gushed up too soon for her, I saw that she would fail and directed her to an open place. She was nearly beat out. The hole, she said, was to drown a cat in; probably one which the W——s left behind as they did Parker. E—— is resolved on a general clearing-up.

It is singular that the nuthatch and the creeper should be so rare, they are so regular.

Jan. 3. Snows all day, falling level, without wind, a moist and heavy snow. Snowed part of the night also. But to my surprise a high wind arose in the night and that and the cold so dried the snow that —

(*Jan. 4*) this morning it is a good deal drifted. It did not freeze together, or crust, as you might have expected. You would not suppose it had been moist when it fell. About eight inches have fallen, yet there is very little on the river. It blows off, unless where water has oozed out at the sides or elsewhere, and the rough, flowing, scaly mass is frozen into a kind of batter, like mortar, or bread that has spewed out in

the oven. Deep and drifted as the snow is, I found, when I returned from my walk, some dry burs of the burdock adhering to the lining of my coat. Even in the middle of winter, aye, in middle of the Great Snow, Nature does not forget these her vegetable economies.

It does look sometimes as if the world were on its last legs. How many there are whose principal employment it is nowadays to eat their meals and go to the post-office!

After spending four or five days surveying and drawing a plan incessantly, I especially feel the necessity of putting myself in communication with nature again, to recover my tone, to withdraw out of the wearying and unprofitable world of affairs. The things I have been doing have but a fleeting and accidental importance, however much men are immersed in them, and yield very little valuable fruit. I would fain have been wading through the woods and fields and conversing with the sane snow. Having waded in the very shallowest stream of time, I would now bathe my temples in eternity. I wish again to participate in the serenity of nature, to share the happiness of the river and the woods. I thus from time to time break off my connection with eternal truths and go with the shallow stream of human affairs, grinding at the mill of the Philistines; but when my task is done, with never-failing confidence I devote myself to the infinite again. It would be sweet to deal with men more, I can imagine, but where dwell they? Not in the fields which I traverse.

Jan. 5. A cold, cutting northwest wind.

Jan. 6. Still colder and perhaps windier. The river is now for the most part covered with snow again, which has blown from the meadows and been held by the water which has oozed out. I slump through snow into that water for twenty rods together, which is not frozen though the thermometer says − 8°. I think that the bright-yellow wood of the barberry, which I have occasion to break in my surveying, is the most interesting and remarkable for its color of any. When I get home after that slumping walk on the river, I find that the slush has balled and frozen on my boots two or three inches thick, and can only be thawed off by the fire, it is so solid.

I frequently have occasion in surveying to note the position or bearing of the edge of a wood, which I describe as edge of wood. In such a way apparently the name Edgewood originated.

Beatton, the old Scotch storekeeper, used to say of one Deacon (Joe?) Brown, a grandfather of the milkman, who used to dine at his house on Sundays and praise his wife's dinners but yet prevented her being admitted to the church, that his was like a " coo's (cow's) tongue, rough one side and smooth the other."

A man asked me the other night whether such and such persons were not as happy as anybody, being conscious, as I perceived, of much unhappiness himself and not aspiring to much more than an animal content. "Why!" said I, speaking to his condition, "the stones are happy, Concord River is happy, and I am happy too. When I took up a fragment of a walnut-shell

this morning, I saw by its very grain and composition, its form and color, etc., that it was made for happiness. The most brutish and inanimate objects that are made suggest an everlasting and thorough satisfaction; they are the homes of content. Wood, earth, mould, etc., exist for joy. Do you think that Concord River would have continued to flow these millions of years by Clamshell Hill and round Hunt's Island, if it had not been happy, — if it had been miserable in its channel, tired of existence, and cursing its maker and the hour that it sprang?"

Though there is an extremely cold, cutting northwest wind, against which I see many travellers turning their backs, and so advancing, I hear and see an unusual number of merry little tree sparrows about the few weeds that are to be seen. They look very chipper, flitting restlessly about and jerking their long tails.

Jan. 7. P. M. — To Walden down railroad and return over Cliffs.

I should not be ashamed to have a shrub oak for my coat-of-arms.

It is bitter cold, with a cutting northwest wind. The pond is now a plain snow-field, but there are no tracks of fishers on it. It is too cold for them. The surface of the snow there is finely waved and grained, giving it a sort of slaty fracture, the appearance which hard, dry *blown* snow assumes. All animate things are reduced to their lowest terms. This is the fifth day of cold, blowing weather. All tracks are concealed in an hour or two. Some have to make their paths two or three times

over in a day. The fisherman is not here, for his lines would freeze in.

I go through the woods toward the Cliffs along the side of the Well Meadow Field.

There is nothing so sanative, so poetic, as a walk in the woods and fields even now, when I meet none abroad for pleasure. Nothing so inspires me and excites such serene and profitable thought. The objects are elevating. In the street and in society I am almost invariably cheap and dissipated, my life is unspeakably mean. No amount of gold or respectability would in the least redeem it, — dining with the Governor or a member of Congress!! But alone in distant woods or fields, in unpretending sprout-lands or pastures tracked by rabbits, even in a bleak and, to most, cheerless day, like this, when a villager would be thinking of his inn, I come to myself, I once more feel myself grandly related, and that cold and solitude are friends of mine. I suppose that this value, in my case, is equivalent to what others get by churchgoing and prayer. I come to my solitary woodland walk as the homesick go home. I thus dispose of the superfluous and see things as they are, grand and beautiful. I have told many that I walk every day about half the daylight, but I think they do not believe it. I wish to get the Concord, the Massachusetts, the America, out of my head and be sane a part of every day. If there are missionaries for the heathen, why not send them to me? I wish to know something; I wish to be made better. I wish to forget, a considerable part of every day, all mean, narrow, trivial men (and this requires usually to forego and forget

all personal relations so long), and therefore I come out to these solitudes, where the problem of existence is simplified. I get away a mile or two from the town into the stillness and solitude of nature, with rocks, trees, weeds, snow about me. I enter some glade in the woods, perchance, where a few weeds and dry leaves alone lift themselves above the surface of the snow, and it is as if I had come to an open window. I see out and around myself. Our *skylights* are thus far away from the ordinary resorts of men. I am not satisfied with ordinary windows. I must have a true *skylight*. My true sky light is on the outside of the village. I am not thus expanded, recreated, enlightened, when I meet a company of men. It chances that the sociable, the town and county, or the farmers' club does not prove a skylight to me. I do not invariably find myself translated under those circumstances. They bore me. The man I meet with is not often so instructive as the silence he breaks. This stillness, solitude, wildness of nature is a kind of thoroughwort, or boneset, to my intellect. This is what I go out to seek. It is as if I always met in those places some grand, serene, immortal, infinitely encouraging, though invisible, companion, and walked with him. There at last my nerves are steadied, my senses and my mind do their office. I am aware that most of my neighbors would think it a hardship to be compelled to linger here one hour, especially this bleak day, and yet I receive this sweet and ineffable compensation for it. It is the most agreeable thing I do. Truly, my coins are uncurrent with them.

I love and celebrate nature, even in detail, merely

because I love the scenery of these interviews and translations. I love to remember every creature that was at this *club*. I thus get off a certain social scurf and scaliness. I do not consider the other animals brutes in the common sense. I am attracted toward them undoubtedly because I never heard any nonsense from them. I have not convicted them of folly, or vanity, or pomposity, or stupidity, in dealing with me. Their vices, at any rate, do not interfere with me. My fairies invariably take to flight when a man appears upon the scene. In a caucus, a meeting-house, a lyceum, a club-room, there is nothing like it in my experience. But away out of the town, on Brown's scrub oak lot, which was sold the other day for six dollars an acre, I have company such as England cannot buy, nor afford. This society is what I live, what I survey, for. I subscribe generously to *this* — all that I have and am.

There, in that Well Meadow Field, perhaps, I feel in my element again, as when a fish is put back into the water. I wash off all my chagrins. All things go smoothly as the axle of the universe. I can remember that when I was very young I used to have a dream night after night, over and over again, which might have been named Rough and Smooth. All existence, all satisfaction and dissatisfaction, all event was symbolized in this way. Now I seemed to be lying and tossing, perchance, on a horrible, a fatal rough surface, which must soon, indeed, put an end to my existence, though even in the dream I knew it to be the symbol merely of my misery; and then again, suddenly, I was lying on a delicious smooth surface, as of a summer sea,

as of gossamer or down or softest plush, and life was such a luxury to live. My waking experience *always* has been and is such an alternate Rough and Smooth. In other words it is Insanity and Sanity.

Might I aspire to praise the moderate nymph Nature! I must be like her, moderate.[1]

This snow which fell last Saturday so moist and heavy is now surprisingly dry and light and powdery. In the wood-path between the Well Meadow Field and the Cliff, it is all scored with the tracks of leaves that have scurried over it. Some might not suspect the cause of these fine and delicate traces, for the cause is no longer obvious. Here and there is but a leaf or two to be seen in the snow-covered path. The myriads which scampered here are now at rest perhaps far on one side. I have listened to the whispering of the dry leaves so long that whatever meaning it has for my ears, I think that I must have heard it.

On the top of the Cliff I am again exposed to the cutting wind. It has blown the hilltops almost bare, and the snow is packed in hard drifts, in long ridges or coarse folds, behind the walls there. Fine, dry snow, thus blown, will become hard enough to bear. Especially the flat rocks are bared, the snow having nothing to hold by.

Going down path to the spring, I see where some fox (apparently) has passed down it, and though the rest of the broad path is else perfectly unspotted white, each track of the fox has proved a trap which has caught from three or four to eight or ten leaves each, snugly packed; and thus it is reprinted.

[1] [Channing, p. 113.]

Vol. IX

Jan. 8. I find by hanging Smith's thermometer on the same nail with ours that it stands 5° below ours.

It was 18° at 3 P. M. by ours when I went out to walk. I picked up on the bare ice of the river, opposite the oak in Shattuck's land, on a small space blown bare of snow, a fuzzy caterpillar, black at the two ends and red-brown in the middle, rolled into a ball or close ring, like a woodchuck. I pressed it hard between my fingers and found it frozen. I put it into my hat, and when I took it out in the evening, it soon began to stir and at length crawled about, but a portion of it was not quite flexible. It took some time for it to thaw. This is the fifth cold day, and it must have been frozen so long. It was more than an inch long.

Miss Minott tells me that she does not think her brother George has ever been to Boston more than once (though she tells me he says he has been twice),[1] and certainly not since 1812. He was born in the Casey house, *i. e.* the same in which C. lived, the second of three that stood beyond the old black house beyond Moore's. Casey was a Guinea negro. Casey used to weep in his latter days when he thought of his wife and two children in Africa from whom he was kidnapped. Minott went only to the East Quarter schools. The house he now lives in is about sixty years old, was moved from beside Casey's to where it now stands before it was roofed. Minott says he has lived where he now does as much as sixty years. He has not been up in town for three years, on account of his rheumatism. Does nothing whatever in the house but read the news-

[1] *He* since tells me *once*.

papers and few old books they have, the Almanac especially, and hold the cats, and very little indeed out of the house. Is just able to saw and split the wood.

Jan. 11. Began snowing yesterday afternoon, and it is still snowing this forenoon.

Mother remembers the Cold Friday very well. She lived in the house where I was born. The people in the kitchen — Jack Garrison, Esther, and a Hardy girl — drew up close to the fire, but the dishes which the Hardy girl was washing froze as fast as she washed them, close to the fire. They managed to keep warm in the parlor by their great fires.

The other day a man came " just to get me to run a line in the woods." This is the usual request. " Do you know where one end of it is ? " I asked. (It was the Stratton lot.) " No," said he, " I don't know either end; that is what I want to find." " Do you know either of the next sides of the lot ? " Thinking a moment, he answered, " No." " Well, do you know any one side of the whole lot, or any corner ? " After a little hesitation he said that he did not. Here, then, was a wood-lot of half a dozen acres, well enough described in a deed dated 1777, courses and distances given, but he could not tell exactly in what part of the universe any particular part of it was, but he expected me to find out. This was what he understood by " running." On the strength of this deed he had forbidden a man to chop wood somewhere.

Frequently, when my employer does not know where his land lies, and has put into my hands an ancient and tattered piece of paper called his deed, which throws no light at all on the question, he turns away, saying, "I want you to make it all right. Give me all that belongs to me."

In the deed of the Stratton wood-lot, dated 1777, there is no mention [of] any building on [it] to be conveyed, so that probably there was only a cellar-hole there then, eighty years ago, as now. For so long, at least, it has been a mere dent in the earth there, to which, from time to time, dead horses or hogs were drawn from the village and cast in. These are our Ninevehs and Babylons. I approach such a cellar-hole as Layard the scene of his labors, and I do not fail to find there relics as interesting to me as his winged bulls.

For some years past I have partially offered myself as a lecturer; have been advertised as such several years. Yet I have had but two or three invitations to lecture in a year, and some years none at all. I congratulate myself on having been permitted to stay at home thus, I am so much richer for it. I do not see what I should have got of much value, but money, by going about, but I do see what I should have lost. It seems to me that I have a longer and more liberal lease of life thus. I cannot afford to be telling my experience, especially to those who perhaps will take no interest in it. I wish to be getting experience. You might as well recommend to a bear to leave his hollow tree and run about all winter scratching at all the hollow trees in the woods. He would be leaner in the spring than if he had stayed at home and sucked his claws. As for the lecture-goers, it is none

Vol. IX

rather. But I have tried them. I have sat down with a dozen of them together in a club, and instantly — they did not inspire me. One or another abused our ears with many words and a few thoughts which were not theirs. There was very little genuine goodness apparent. We are such hollow pretenders. I lost my time.

But out there! Who shall criticise that companion? It is like the hone to the knife. I bathe in that climate and am cleansed of all social impurities. I become a witness with unprejudiced senses to the order of the universe. *There* is nothing petty or impertinent, none to say, "See what a great man I am!" *There* chiefly, and not in the society of the wits, am I cognizant of wit. Shall I prefer a part, an infinitely small fraction, to the whole? There I get my underpinnings laid and repaired, cemented, levelled. There is my country club. We dine at the sign of the Shrub Oak, the New Albion House.[1]

I demand of my companion some evidence that he has travelled further than the sources of the Nile, that he has seen something, that he has been *out of town, out of the house*. Not that he can tell a good story, but that he can keep a good silence. Has he attended to a silence more significant than any story? Did he ever get out of the road which all men and fools travel? You call yourself a great traveller, perhaps, but can you get beyond the influence of a certain class of ideas?

I expect the time when there will be founded hospitals for the founders of hospitals.

[1] [Channing, p. 113.]

of their business what I think. I perceive that most make a great account of their relations, more or less personal and direct, to many men, coming before them as lecturers, writers, or public men. But all this is impertinent and unprofitable to me. I never yet recognized, nor was recognized by, a crowd of men. I was never assured of their existence, nor they of mine.

There was wit and even poetry in the negro's answer to the man who tried to persuade him that the slaves would not be obliged to work in heaven. "Oh, you g' way, Massa. I know better. If dere's no work for cullud folks up dar, dey'll *make* some fur 'em, and if dere's nuffin better to do, dey'll make 'em *shub de clouds along*. You can't fool this chile, Massa."

I was describing the other day my success in solitary and distant woodland walking outside the town. I do not go there to get my dinner, but to get that sustenance which dinners only preserve me to enjoy, without which dinners are a vain repetition. But how little men can help me in this! only by having a kindred experience. Of what use to tell them of my happiness? Thus, if ever we have anything important to say, it might be introduced with the remark: "It is nothing to you, in particular. It is none of your business, I know." *That* is what might be called going into *good society*. I never chanced to meet with any man so cheering and elevating and encouraging, so infinitely suggestive, as the stillness and solitude of the Well Meadow Field.

Men even think me odd and perverse because I do not prefer their society to this nymph or wood-god

Jan. 13. I hear one thrumming a guitar below stairs. It reminds me of moments that I have lived. What a comment on our life is the least strain of music! It lifts me up above all the dust and mire of the universe. I soar or hover with clean skirts over the field of my life. It is ever life within life, in concentric spheres. The field wherein I toil or rust at any time is at the same time the field for such different kinds of life! The farmer's boy or hired man has an instinct which tells him as much indistinctly, and hence his dreams and his restlessness; hence, even, it is that he wants money to realize his dreams with. The identical field where I am leading my humdrum life, let but a strain of music be heard there, is seen to be the field of some unrecorded crusade or tournament the thought of which excites in us an ecstasy of joy. The way in which I am affected by this faint thrumming advertises me that there is still some health and immortality in the springs of me. What an elixir is this sound! I, who but lately came and went and lived under *a dish cover*, live now under the heavens. It releases me; it bursts my bonds. Almost all, perhaps all, our life is, speaking comparatively, a stereotyped despair; *i. e.*, we never at any time realize the full grandeur of our destiny. We forever and ever and habitually underrate our fate. Talk of infidels! Why, all of the race of man, except in the rarest moments when they are lifted above themselves by an ecstasy, are infidels. With the very best disposition, what does my belief amount to? This poor, timid, unenlightened, thick-skinned creature, what *can* it believe? I am, of course, hopelessly ignorant and unbelieving until some divinity stirs within me. Ninety-nine one-hundredths of our lives we are mere hedgers and ditchers, but from time to time we meet with reminders of our destiny.

We hear the kindred vibrations, music! and we put out our dormant feelers unto the limits of the universe. We attain to a wisdom that passeth understanding. The stable continents undulate. The hard and fixed becomes fluid.

> "Unless above himself he can
> Erect himself, how poor a thing is man!"

When I *hear* music I fear no danger, I am invulnerable, I see no foe. I am related to the earliest times and to the latest.[1]

There are infinite degrees of life, from that which is next to sleep and death, to that which is forever awake and immortal. We must not confound man with man. We cannot conceive of a greater difference than between the life of one man and that of another. I am constrained to believe that the mass of men are never so lifted above themselves that their destiny is seen to be transcendently beautiful and grand.

P. M. — On the river to Bittern Rock.

The river is now completely concealed by snow. I come this way partly because it is the best walking here, the snow not so deep. The only wild life I notice is a crow on a distant oak. The snow is drifted and much deeper about the button-bushes, etc. It is surprising

[1] [Channing, p. 332.]

what an effect a thin barrier of bushes has on it, causing it to lodge there until often a very large drift is formed more or less abrupt on the south. Woolgrass still rises above the snow along the sides.

In a very few places, for half a dozen feet the snow is blown off, revealing the dark transparent ice, in which I see numerous great white cleavages, which show its generous thickness, a foot at least. They cross each other at various angles and are frequently curved vertically, reflecting rainbow tints from within. Small triangles only a foot or two over are seen to be completely cracked around at the point of convulsion, yet it is as firm there as anywhere. I am proud of the strength of my floor, and love to jump and stamp there and bear my whole weight on it. As transparent as glass, yet you might found a house on it. Then there are little feathery flake-like twisted cleavages, which extend not more than an inch into it.

I see no tracks but of mice, and apparently of foxes, which have visited every muskrat-house and then turned short away.

Am surprised to see, returning, how much it has drifted in the Corner road. It has overflowed from the northern fields and lodged behind the north wall, forming drifts as high as the wall, which extend from one third to two thirds across the road for two long reaches, driving the traveller into the neighboring field, having

Vol. IX

taken down the fence. It must be pleasant to ride along in the narrow path against the untouched and spotless edge of the drift, which curves over sharp like the visor of a cap. Sometimes this edge is bent down till it is almost vertical, yet a foot or two wide and only a few inches thick.

Jan. 14. P. M. — Up Assabet on ice.

I go slumping four or five inches in the snow on the river, and often into water above the ice, breaking through a slight crust under the snow, which has formed in the night. Each cold day this concealed overflow, mixing with the snow beneath, is converted into ice, and so raises it, makes the surface snow shallower, and improves the walking; but unless it is quite cold, this snow and water is apt to get a slight crust only, through which you sink.

I notice, on the black willows and also on the alders and white maples overhanging the stream, numerous dirty-white cocoons, about an inch long, attached by their sides to the base of the recent twigs and disguised by dry leaves curled about them, — a sort of fruit which these trees bear now. The leaves are not attached to the twigs, but artfully arranged about and fastened to the cocoons. Almost every little cluster of leaves contains a cocoon, apparently of one species. So that often when you would think that the trees were retaining their leaves, it is not the trees but the caterpillars that have retained them. I do not see a cluster of leaves on a maple, unless on a dead twig, but it conceals a cocoon. Yet I cannot find one alive; they are all crumbled

within. The black willows retain very few of their narrow curled leaves here and there, like the terminal leaflet of a fern (the alders and maples scarcely any ever), yet these few are just enough to withdraw attention from those which surround the cocoons. What kind of understanding was there between the mind that determined that these leaves should hang on during the winter, and that of the worm that fastened a few of these leaves to its cocoon in order to disguise it?[1] I thus walk along the edge of the trees and bushes which overhang the stream, gathering the cocoons, which probably were thought to be doubly secure here. These cocoons, of course, were attached before the leaves had fallen. Almost every one is already empty, or contains only the relics of a nymph. It has been attacked and devoured by some foe. These numerous cocoons attached to the twigs overhanging the stream in the still and biting winter day suggest a certain fertility in the river borders, — impart a kind of life to them, — and so are company to me. There is so much more life than is suspected in the most solitary and dreariest scene. They are as much as the lisping of a chickadee.

Hemlock seeds are scattered over the snow. The birch (white) catkins appear to lose their seeds first at the base, though that may be the uppermost. They are blown or shaken off, leaving a bare threadlike core.

Mr. Wild tells me that while he lived on Nantucket he never observed the thermometer lower than 2° above zero.

[1] [Channing, p. 122.]

Jan. 15. P. M. — To Fair Haven Pond and across to railroad.

As I passed the south shed at the depot, observed what I thought a tree sparrow on the wood in the shed, a mere roof open at the side, under which several men were at that time employed sawing wood with a horse-power. Looking closer, I saw, to my surprise, that it must be a song sparrow, it having the usual marks on its breast and no bright-chestnut crown. The snow is nine or ten inches deep, and it appeared to have taken refuge in this shed, where was much bare ground exposed by removing the wood. When I advanced, instead of flying away, it concealed itself in the wood, just as it often dodges behind a wall.[1]

What is there in music that it should so stir our deeps? We are all ordinarily in a state of desperation; such is our life; ofttimes it drives us to suicide. To how many, perhaps to most, life is barely tolerable, and if it were not for the fear of death or of dying, what a multitude would immediately commit suicide! But let us hear a strain of music, we are at once advertised of a life which no man had told us of, which no preacher preaches. Suppose I try to describe faithfully the prospect which a strain of music exhibits to me. The field of my life becomes a boundless plain, glorious to tread, with no death nor disappointment at the end of it. All meanness and trivialness disappear. I become adequate to any deed. No particulars survive this expansion; persons do not survive it. In the light of this strain there is no thou nor I. We are actually lifted above ourselves.

[1] *Vide* Jan. 22d.

The tracks of the mice near the head of Well Meadow were particularly interesting. There was a level surface of pure snow there, unbroken by bushes or grass, about four rods across, and here were nine tracks of mice running across it from the bushes on this side to those on the other, the tracks quite near together but repeatedly crossing each other at very acute angles, but each particular course was generally quite direct. The snow was so light that only one distinct track was made by all four of the feet, five or six inches apart, but the tail left a very distinct mark. A single track, thus stretching away almost straight, sometimes half a dozen rods, over unspotted snow, is very handsome, like a chain of a new pattern; and then they suggest an airy lightness in the body that impressed them. Though there may have been but one or two here, the tracks suggesting quite a little company that had gone gadding over to their neighbors under the opposite bush. Such is the delicacy of the impression on the surface of the lightest snow, where other creatures sink, and night, too, being the season when these tracks are made, they remind me of a fairy revel. It is almost as good as if the actors were here. I can easily imagine all the rest. Hopping is expressed by the tracks themselves. Yet I should like much to see by broad daylight a company of these revellers hopping over the snow. There is a still life in America that is little observed or dreamed of. Here were possible auditors and critics which the lecturer at the Lyceum last night did not think of. How snug they are somewhere under the snow now, not to be thought of, if it were not for these pretty tracks! And for a week, or

fortnight even, of pretty still weather the tracks will remain, to tell of the nocturnal adventures of a tiny mouse who was not beneath the notice of the Lord. So it was so many thousands of years before Gutenberg invented printing with *his* types, and so it will be so many thousands of years after his types are forgotten, perchance. The deer mouse will be printing on the snow of Well Meadow to be read by a new race of men.

Cold as the weather is and has been, almost all the brook is open in the meadow there, an artery of black water in the midst of the snow, and there are many sink-holes, where the water is exposed at the bottom of a dimple in the snow. Indeed, in some places these little black spots are distributed very thickly, the snow in swells covering the intervening tussocks.

Jan. 16. P. M. — Up Assabet.

This morning was one of the coldest. It improves the walking on the river, freezing the overflow beneath the snow. As I pass the Island (Egg Rock), I notice the ice-foot adhering to the rock about two feet above the surface of the ice generally. The ice there for a few feet in width slants up to it, and, owing to this, the snow is blown off it. This edging of ice revealed is peculiarly green by contrast with the snow, methinks. So, too, where the ice, settling, has rested on a rock which has burst it and now holds it high above the surrounding level. The same phenomena, no doubt, on a much larger scale occur at the north.

I observe that the holes which I bored in the white maples last spring were nearly grown over last summer,

commonly to within a quarter or an eighth of an inch, but in one or two instances, in very thriftily growing trees, they were entirely closed.

When I was surveying Shattuck's Merrick's pasture fields the other day, McManus, who was helping me, said that they would be worth a hundred or two hundred dollars more if it were not for the willow-rows which bound and separate them, for you could not plow parallel with them within five rods on account of the roots, you must plow at right angles with them. Yet it is not many years since they were set out, as I remember. However, there should be a great amount of root to account for their wonderful vivaciousness, making seven or eight feet in a year when trimmed.

Jan. 18. A very cold day. Thermometer at 7.30 A. M., $-14°$ (Smith's hanging on same nail $-20°$); at 1.15 P. M., $-3°$; 2.15 P. M., $-4°$; 3.45 P. M., 0°. It is cloudy and no sun all day, and considerable wind also. There was no Sabbath-school on account of the cold; could not warm the room.

We sometimes think that the inferior animals act foolishly, but are there any greater fools than mankind? Consider how so many, perhaps most, races — Chinese, Japanese, Arabs, Mussulmans generally, Russians — treat the traveller; what fears and prejudices he has to contend with. So many millions believing that he has come [to] do them some harm. Let a traveller set out to go round the world, visiting every race, and he shall meet with such treatment at their hands that he will be obliged to pronounce them incorrigible fools. Even in

Virginia a naturalist who was seen crawling through a meadow catching frogs, etc., was seized and carried before the authorities.

Three little pigs were frozen to death in an Irishman's pen last night at the Green Store.

Began to snow in the evening, the thermometer at zero.

Jan. 19. A snow-storm with very high wind all last night and to-day. Though not much snow falls (perhaps seven or eight inches), it is exceedingly drifted, so that the first train gets down about noon and none gets up till about 6 P. M.! There is no vehicle passing the house before 2 P. M.! A fine dry snow, intolerable to face.

Jan. 20. There probably is not more than twelve to fifteen inches of snow on a level, yet the drifts are very large. Neither milkman nor butcher got here yesterday, and to-day the milkman came with oxen, partly through the fields. Though the snow is nowhere deep in the middle of the main street, the drifts are very large, especially on the north side, so that, as you look down the street, it appears as uneven as a rolling prairie.

Heard, in the Dennis swamp by the railroad this afternoon, the peculiar goldfinch-like mew — also like some canaries — of, I think, the lesser redpoll (?). Saw several. Heard the same a week or more ago.

I hear that Boston Harbor froze over on the 18th, down to Fort Independence. The river has been frozen everywhere except at the very few swiftest places since

about December 18th, and *everywhere* since about January 1st.

At R. W. E.'s this evening, at about 6 P. M., I was called out to see Eddy's cave in the snow. It was a hole about two and a half feet wide and six feet long, into a drift, a little winding, and he had got a lamp at the inner extremity. I observed, as I approached in a course at right angles with the length of the cave, that the mouth of the cave was lit as if the light were close to it, so that I did not suspect its depth. Indeed, the light of this lamp was remarkably reflected and distributed. The snowy walls were one universal reflector with countless facets. I think that one lamp would light sufficiently a hall built of this material. The snow about the mouth of the cave within had the yellow color of the flame to one approaching, as if the lamp were close to it. We afterward buried the lamp in a little crypt in this snow-drift and walled it in, and found that its light was visible, even in this *twilight*, through fifteen inches' thickness of snow. The snow was all aglow with it. If it had been darker, probably it would have been visible through a much greater thickness. But, what was most surprising to me, when Eddy crawled into the extremity of his cave and shouted at the top of his voice, it sounded ridiculously faint, as if he were a quarter of a mile off, and at first I could not believe that he spoke loud, but we all of us crawled in by turns, and though our heads were only six feet from those outside, our loudest shouting only amused and surprised them. Apparently the porous snow drank up all the sound. The voice was, in fact, muffled by the surrounding snow walls, and

I saw that we might lie in that hole screaming for assistance in vain, while travellers were passing along twenty feet distant. It had the effect of ventriloquism. So you only need make a snow house in your yard and pass an hour in it, to realize a good deal of Esquimau life.

Jan. 21. P. M. — Up river to W. Wheeler's Bridge and back by road.

The roads are perhaps more blocked up than last winter, yet with hardly more than half as much snow. The river is now so concealed that a common eye would not suspect its existence. It is drifted on it exactly as on the meadow, *i. e.* successive low drifts with a bluff head toward the wind.

It is remarkable how many tracks of foxes you will see quite near the village, where they have been in the night, and yet a regular walker will not glimpse one oftener than once in eight or ten years.

The overflow, under the snow, is generally at the bends, where the river is narrower and swifter.

I noticed that several species of birds lingered late this year. The *F. hyemalis,* and then there was that woodcock, and song sparrow! What does it mean?

As I flounder along the Corner road against the root fence, a very large flock of snow buntings alight with a wheeling flight amid the weeds rising above the snow in Potter's heater piece, — a hundred or two of them. They run restlessly amid the weeds, so that I can hardly get sight of them through my glass; then suddenly all arise and fly only two or three rods, alighting within

three rods of me. (They keep up a constant twittering.) It was as if they were any instant ready for a longer flight, but their leader had not so ordered it. Suddenly away they sweep again, and I see them alight in a distant field where the weeds rise above the snow, but in a few minutes they have left that also and gone further north. Beside their *rippling* note, they have a vibratory twitter, and from the loiterers you hear quite a tender peep, as they fly after the vanishing flock.

What independent creatures! They go seeking their food from north to south. If New Hampshire and Maine are covered deeply with snow, they scale down to Massachusetts for their breakfasts. Not liking the grain in this field, away they dash to another distant one, attracted by the weeds rising above the snow. Who can guess in what field, by what river or mountain they breakfasted this morning. They did not seem to regard me so near, but as they went off, their wave actually broke over me as a rock. They have the pleasure of society at their feasts, a hundred dining at once, busily talking while eating, remembering what occurred at Grinnell Land. As they flew past me they presented a pretty appearance, somewhat like broad bars of white alternating with bars of black.

Jan. 22. Snows all day, clearing up at night, — a remarkably fine and dry snow, which, looking out, you might suspect to be blowing snow merely. Yet thus it snows all day, driving almost horizontally, but it does not amount to much.

P. M. — To Walden.

I never knew it to make such a business of snowing and bring so little to pass. The air is filled, so that you cannot see far against it, *i. e.* looking north-north-west, yet but an inch or two falls all day. There is some drifting, however.

You wonder how the tree sparrows can seek their food on the railroad causeway, flying in the face of such a fine, cold, driving snow-storm. Within the woods it is comparatively still. In the woods by Abel Brooks's rye hollow I hear a faint note, and see undoubtedly a brown creeper inspecting the branches of the oaks. It has white and black bars on the head, uttering from time to time a fine, wiry, *screeping tse, tse,* or *tse, tse, tse.*

Minott tells me that Sam Barrett told him once when he went to mill that a song sparrow took up its quarters in his grist-mill and stayed there all winter. When it did not help itself he used to feed it with meal, for he was glad of its company; so, what with the dashing water and the crumbs of meal, it must have fared well.

I asked M. about the Cold Friday. He said, "It was plaguy cold; it stung like a wasp." He remembers seeing them toss up water in a shoemaker's shop, usually a very warm place, and when it struck the floor it was frozen and rattled like so many shot. Old John Nutting used to say, "When it is cold it is a sign it's going to be warm," and "When it's warm it's a sign it's going to be cold."

Jan. 23. The coldest day that I remember recording, clear and bright, but very high wind, blowing the snow. Ink froze. Had to break the ice in my pail with a ham-

mer. Thermometer at 6.45 A. M., − 18°; at 10.30, − 14° (Smith's, − 20°; Wilds', − 7°, the last being in a more sheltered place); at 12.45, − 9°; at 4 P. M., − 5½°; at 7.30 P. M., − 8°. I may safely say that − 5° has been the highest temperature to-day by our thermometer.

Walking this afternoon, I notice that the face inclines to stiffen, and the hands and feet get cold soon. On first coming out in very cold weather, I find that I breathe fast, though without walking faster or exerting myself any more than usual.

Jan. 24. Thermometer about 6.30 A. M. in the bulb !! but Smith's on the same nail, − 30°; Wilds', early, − 16°; Emerson's, the same; at 9.15 A. M., ours, − 18°; Smith's, − 22°; which would indicate that ours would have stood at − 26° at 6.30, if the thermometer had been long enough. At 11.30 A. M. ours was − 1°, at 4 P. M., + 12°. So the cold spell that began the evening of the 22d ended to-day noon.[1]

Jan. 25. Still another very cold morning. Smith's thermometer over ours at − 29°, ours in bulb; but about seven, ours was at − 18° and Smith's at − 24; ours therefore at first about − 23°.

P. M. — To Bittern Rock on river.

The road beyond Hubbard's Bridge has been closed by snow for two or three weeks; only the walls show that there has been a road there. Travellers take to the fields.

I see the track of a fox or dog across the meadow,

[1] No. *Vide* below.

made some time ago. Each track is now a pure white snowball rising three inches above the surrounding surface, and this has formed a lee behind which a narrow drift has formed, extending a foot or two south-easterly.

Jan. 26. Another cold morning. None looked early, but about eight it was − 14°.

A. M. — At Cambridge and Boston.

Saw Boston Harbor frozen over (for some time). Reminded me of, I think, Parry's Winter Harbor, with vessels frozen in. Saw thousands on the ice, a stream of men reaching down to Fort Independence, where they were cutting a channel toward the city. Ice said to reach fourteen miles. Snow untracked on many decks.[1]

At 10 P. M., + 14°.

Jan. 27. Thawing a little at last. Thermometer 35°.

The most poetic and truest account of objects is generally by those who first observe them, or the discoverers of them, whether a sharper perception and curiosity in them led to the discovery or the greater novelty more inspired their report. Accordingly I love most to read the accounts of a country, its natural productions and curiosities, by those who first settled it, and also the earliest, though often unscientific, writers on natural science.

Hear the unusual sound of pattering rain this afternoon, though it is not yet in earnest. Thermometer

[1] Ice did not finally go out till about Feb. 15th.

to-day commonly at 38°. Wood in the stove is slow to burn; often goes out with this dull atmosphere. But it is less needed.

10 P. M. — Hear music below. It washes the dust off my life and everything I look at.

Was struck to-day with the admirable simplicity of Pratt. He told me not only of the discovery of the tower of Babel, which, from the measures given, he had calculated could not stand between the roads at the Mill Pond, but of the skeleton of a man twenty feet long. Also of an eyestone which he has, bought of Betty Nutting, about as big as half a pea. Just lay it in your eye, bind up your eye with a handkerchief, and go to bed. It will not pain you, but you will feel it moving about, and when it has gathered all the dirt in the eye to itself, it will always come out, and you will probably find it in the handkerchief. It is a little thing and you must look sharp for it. He often lends his.

Jan. 28. Am again surprised to see a song sparrow sitting for hours on our wood-pile in the yard, in the midst of snow in the yard. It is unwilling to move. People go to the pump, and the cat and dog walk round the wood-pile without starting it. I examine it at my leisure through a glass. Remarkable that the coldest of all winters these summer birds should remain. Perhaps it is no more comfortable this season further south, where they are accustomed to abide. In the afternoon this sparrow joined a flock of tree sparrows on the bare ground west of the house. It was amusing to see the tree sparrows wash themselves, standing in the puddles and tossing the water over themselves. Minott says they wade in to where it is an inch deep and then "splutter splutter," throwing the water over them. They have had no opportunity to wash for a month, perhaps, there having been no thaw. The song sparrow did not *go off* with them.

P. M. — To Walden.

Notice many heaps of leaves on snow on the hillside southwest of the pond, *as usual*. Probably the rain and thaw have brought down some of them.

Jan. 31. Snows fast, turning to rain at last.

VII

FEBRUARY, 1857

(ÆT. 39)

Feb. 1. 3 P. M. — Down railroad.

Thermometer at 42°. Warm as it is, I see a large flock of snow buntings on the railroad causeway. Their wings are white above next the body, but black or dark beyond and on the back. This produces that regular black and white effect when they fly past you.

A laborer on the railroad tells me it is Candlemas Day (February 2d) to-morrow and the winter half out. "Half your wood and half your hay," etc., etc.; and, as that day is, so will be the rest of the winter.

Feb. 2. The snow-crust on all hills and knolls is now marked by the streams of water that have flowed down it, like a coarsely combed head; *i. e.*, the unbroken crust is in alternate ridges and furrows from the tops of the hills to the bottoms.

Feb. 3. To Fitchburg to lecture.

Observed that the Nashua at the bridge beyond Groton Junction was open for twenty rods, as the Concord is not anywhere in Concord. This must be owing to the greater swiftness of the former.

Though the snow was not deep, I noticed that an unbroken snow-crust stretched around Fitchburg, and

Vol. IX

its several thousand inhabitants had been confined so long to the narrow streets, some of them a track only six feet wide. Hardly one individual had anywhere departed from this narrow walk and struck out into the surrounding fields and hills. If I had had my cowhide boots, I should not have confined myself to those narrow limits, but have climbed some of the hills. It is surprising to go into a New England town in midwinter and find its five thousand inhabitants all living thus on the limits, confined at most to their narrow moose-yard in the snow. Scarcely here and there has a citizen stepped aside one foot to let a sled pass. And almost as circumscribed is their summer life, going only from house to shop and back to house again. If, Indian-like, one examined the dew or bended grass, he would be surprised to discover how little trodden or frequented the surrounding fields were, to discover perhaps large tracts wholly untrodden, which await, as it were, for some caravan to assemble before any will traverse them. It is as if some vigilance committee had given notice that if any should transgress those narrow limits he should be outlawed and his blood should be upon his own head. You don't see where the inhabitants get sufficient exercise, unless they swing dumb-bells down cellar. Let a slight snow come and cover the earth, and the tracks of men will show how little the woods and fields are frequented.

I was pleased to see several loads entirely of beech wood in the street at Fitchburg. It had a peculiarly *green*, solid, sappy look, coasting down the hills into Fitchburg.

Feb. 4. Met Theodore Parker in the cars, who told me that he had recently found in Lake Michigan a single ball, five inches in diameter, like those I presented to the Natural History Society, though he did not observe the eriocaulon. It was late in the season.

Yet along that sled-track (*vide* the 3d) they will have their schools and lyceums and churches, like the snow-heaps crowded up by the furrow, and consider themselves liberally educated, notwithstanding their narrow views and range. And the bare track that leads to the next town and seaboard, only six inches' breadth of iron rails! and a one-eighth-inch wire in the air!

I sometimes hear a prominent but dull-witted worthy man say, or hear that he has said, rarely, that if it were not for his firm belief in "an overruling power," or a "perfect Being," etc., etc. But such poverty-stricken expressions only convince me of his habitual doubt and that he is surprised into a transient belief. Such a man's expression of faith, moving solemnly in the traditional furrow, and casting out all free-thinking and living souls with the rusty mould-board of his compassion or contempt, thinking that he has Moses and all the prophets in his wake, discourages and saddens me as an expression of his narrow and barren want of faith. I see that the infidels and skeptics have formed themselves into churches and weekly gather together at the ringing of a bell.

Sometimes when, in conversation or a lecture, I have been grasping at, or even standing and reclining upon, the serene and everlasting truths that underlie and support our vacillating life, I have seen my auditors standing on their *terra firma*, the quaking earth, crowded together on their Lisbon Quay, and compassionately or timidly watching my motions as if they were the antics of a rope-dancer or mountebank pretending to walk on air; or here and there one creeping out upon an overhanging but cracking bough, unwilling to drop to the adamantine floor beneath, or perchance even venturing out a step or two, as if it were a dangerous kittly-bender, timorously sounding as he goes. So the other day, as I stood on Walden, drinking at a puddle on the ice, which was probably two feet thick, and thinking how lucky I was that I had not got to cut through all that thickness, I was amused to see an Irish laborer on the railroad, who had come down to drink, timidly tiptoeing toward me in his cowhide boots, lifting them nearly two feet at each step and fairly trembling with fear, as if the ice were already bending beneath his ponderous body and he were about to be engulfed. "Why, my man," I called out to him, "this ice will bear a loaded train, half a dozen locomotives side by side, a whole herd of oxen," suggesting whatever would be a weighty argument with him. And so at last he fairly straightened up and quenched his thirst. It was very ludicrous to me, who was thinking, by chance, what a labor it would be to get at the water with an axe there and that I was lucky to find some on the surface.

So, when I have been resting and quenching my thirst on the eternal plains of truth, where rests the base of those beautiful columns that sustain the heavens, I have been amused to see a traveller who had long

confined himself to the quaking shore, which was all covered with the traces of the deluge, come timidly tiptoeing toward me, trembling in every limb.

I see the crowd of materialists gathered together on their Lisbon Quay for safety, thinking it a *terra firma*.

Though the farmer has been all winter teaming wood along the river, the timid citizen that buys it, but who has not stepped out of the road, thinks it all kittly-benders there and warns his boys not to go near it.

Minott says that Dr. Heywood used to have a crazy hen (and he, too, has had one). She went about by herself uttering a peevish *craw craw*, and did not lay. One day he was going along on the narrow peninsula of Goose Pond looking for ducks, away in Walden Woods a mile and a half from Heywood's, when he met this very hen, which passed close by him, uttering as usual a faint *craw craw*. He knew her perfectly well, and says that he was never so surprised at anything in his life. How she had escaped the foxes and hawks was more than he knew.

Told a story about one Josh Piper, a harelipped man, who lived down east awhile, whose wife would not let him occupy her bed; but he used to catch ducks there in a net on the shore as they do pigeons, and so got feathers enough to fill the bed, and therefore thought he had a right to lie on it.

Feb. 5. Mizzling rain.

Feb. 6. 9 A. M. — Down railroad to see the *glaze*, the first we have had this year, but not a very good one.

It is about a fifth or a sixth of an inch thick on the northeast sides of twigs, etc., not transparent, but of an opaque white, granular character. The woods, especially wooded hillsides half a mile or more distant, have a rich, hoary, frosted look, still and stiff, yet it is not so thick but that the green of the pines and the yellow of the willow bark and the leather-color of oak leaves show through it. These colors are pleasantly toned down. The pines transmit a subdued green, — some pitch pines a livelier grass green, — deepest in the recesses, and a delicate buff (?) tinge is seen through the frosty veil of the willow. The birches, owing to the color of their trunks, are the most completely hoary. The elms, perhaps, are the most distinctly frosted, revealing their whole outlines like ghosts of trees, even a mile off, when seen against a dark hillside. The ground is encased in a thin *black* glaze (where it chances to be bare) and the iron rails and the telegraph wire. Insignificant weeds and stubble along the railroad causeway and elsewhere are now made very conspicuous, both by their increased size and bristling stiffness and their whiteness. Each wiry grass stem is become a stiff wand. The wind that begins to rise does not stir them; you only hear a fine crackling sound when it blows hardest. Behind each withered vegetable plant stands a stout ice plant, overlapping and concealing it. Stem answers to stem, and fruit to fruit. The heads of tansy are converted into confectionery somewhat like sugared almonds and regularly roughened (like orange-peel), and those of evening-primrose, and mullein, and hardhack, and lespedeza bear a still

coarser kind. The wild carrot's bird's-nest umbel, now contracted above, is converted into almost a perfect hollow sphere, composed of contiguous thickened meridional ribs, which remind me of the fingers of a starfish (or five-finger). Each plant preserves its character, though exaggerated. Pigweed and Roman wormwood are ragged as ever on a larger scale, and the butterweed as stiffly upright. Tall goldenrod still more recurved. You naturally avoid running against the plant which you did not notice before. Standing on the southeast side, I see the fine dark cores which the stems make. On the opposite side, only the pure white ice plant is seen.

When I reach the woods I am surprised to find that the twigs, etc., are bristling with fine spiculæ, which stand on a thin glaze. I do not remember to have seen them previous winters. They are from one quarter to five eighths of an inch long by one twenty-fifth to one fiftieth of an inch wide at base and quite sharp, commonly on the storm side of the twig only and pointing in all directions horizontally and even vertically within an arc of 90°, but sometimes on opposite sides of the twig. They answer exactly to prickles or spines, especially to those of the locust. I observe them on the locust itself by chance, an icy spine at right angles on a vegetable one, making such a branch as is seen on some species. There are often ten or twelve within an inch along the twigs, but they are most like thorns when fewer. All the twigs and weeds and leaves, even the pine-needles, are armed with them. The pine-needles especially, beside their hoary glaze, are bristling with countless fine spiculæ, which appear to point in almost all directions. It is also interesting to meet with them by accident on the edges of oak leaves, answering exactly to the vegetable spines there (though they are commonly at right angles with the plane of the leaf and often almost as thick as a comb), and on pine cones, suggesting that there should be something in that soil especially favorable to promote the growth of spines. As far as I observed, these spines were chiefly confined to the woods, — at least I had not noticed them on the causeway, — as if a fog might have collected in the former place but not in the last. They were, then, built in the mist, by a more delicate accretion. Thus it seems that not leaves only but other forms of vegetation are imitated by frost.

Already the white pine plumes were drooping, but the pitch pines stood stiffly erect. I was again struck by the deep open cup at the extremity of the latter, formed by the needles standing out very regularly around the red-brown buds at the bottom. It is very warm, and by ten o'clock this ice is rapidly falling from the trees and covering the ground like hail; and before noon all that jewelry was dissolved.

Rice tells me that there was a lark on his place in Sudbury about the 1st of January.

One who has seen them tells me that a covey of thirteen quails daily visits Hayden's yard and barn, where he feeds them and can almost put his hands on them.

Thermometer at noon 52°.

Winckelmann says in his "History of Ancient Art,"

vol. i, page 95: "I am now past forty, and therefore at an age when one can no longer sport freely with life. I perceive, also, that a certain delicate spirit begins to evaporate, with which I raised myself, by powerful soarings, to the contemplation of the beautiful."

Feb. 7. Another warm day, the snow fast going off.

I am surprised to see over Walden Pond, which is covered with puddles, that seething or shimmering in the air which is observed over the fields in a warm day in summer, close over the ice for several feet in height, notwithstanding that the sky is completely overcast. The thermometer was at 52½° when I came out at 3 p. m. The water on the ice is for the most part several inches deep, and trees reflected in it appear as when seen through a mist or smoke, apparently owing to the color of the ice. It is so warm that I am obliged to take off my greatcoat and carry it on my arm. Now the hollows are full of those greenish pods.

As I was coming through the woods from Walden to Hayden's, I heard a loud or tumultuous warbling or twittering of birds coming on in the air, much like a flock of red-wings in the spring, and even expected to see them at first, but when they came in sight and passed over my head I saw that they were probably redpolls. They fly rather slowly.

Hayden the elder tells me that the quails have come to his yard every day for almost a month and are just as tame as chickens. They come about his wood-shed, he supposes to pick up the worms that have dropped out of the wood, and when it storms hard gather together

in the corner of the shed. He walks within, say, three or four feet of them without disturbing them. They come out of the woods by the graveyard, and sometimes they go down toward the river. They will be about his yard the greater part of the day; were there yesterday, though it was so warm, but now probably they can get food enough elsewhere. They go just the same to Poland's, across the road. About ten years ago there was a bevy of fifteen that used to come from the same woods, and one day, they being in the barn and scared by the cat, four ran into the hay and died there. The former do not go to the houses further from the woods. Thus it seems in severe winters the quails venture out of the woods and join the poultry of the farmer's yard, if it be near the edge of the wood. It is remarkable that this bird, which thus half domesticates itself, should not be found wholly domesticated before this.

Several men I have talked with froze their ears a fortnight ago yesterday, the cold Friday; one who had never frozen his ears before.

Many of the roads about the town, which for long distances have been completely closed by the snow for more than a month, are just beginning to be open. The sleighs, etc., which have all this time gone round through the fields, are now trying to make their way through in some places. I do not [know] when they have been so much obstructed.

Feb. 8. Debauched and worn-out senses require the violent vibrations of an instrument to excite them, but *sound* and still youthful senses, not enervated by

luxury, hear music in the wind and rain and running water. One would think from reading the critics that music was intermittent as a spring in the desert, dependent on some Paganini or Mozart, or heard only when the Pierians or Euterpeans drive through the villages; but music is perpetual, and only hearing is intermittent. I hear it in the softened air of these warm February days which have broken the back of the winter.

For two nights past it has not frozen, but a thick mist has overhung the earth, and you awake to the unusual and agreeable sight of water in the streets. Several strata of snow have been washed away from the drifts, down to that black one formed when dust was blowing from plowed fields.

Riordan's solitary cock, standing on such an icy snow-heap, feels the influence of the softened air, and the steam from patches of bare ground here and there, and has found his voice again. The warm air has thawed the music in his throat, and he crows lustily and unweariedly, his voice rising to the last. Yesterday morning our feline Thomas, also feeling the springlike influence, stole away along the fences and walls, which raise him above the water, and only returned this morning reeking with wet. Having got his breakfast, he already stands on his hind legs, looking wishfully through the window, and, the door being opened a little, he is at once off again in spite of the rain.

Again and again I congratulate myself on my socalled poverty. I was almost disappointed yesterday to find thirty dollars in my desk which I did not know that I possessed, though now I should be sorry to lose it. The week that I go away to lecture, however much I may get for it, is unspeakably cheapened. The preceding and succeeding days are a mere sloping down and up from it.

In the society of many men, or in the midst of what is called success, I find my life of no account, and my spirits rapidly fall. I would rather be the barrenest pasture lying fallow than cursed with the compliments of kings, than be the sulphurous and accursed desert where Babylon once stood. But when I have only a rustling oak leaf, or the faint metallic cheep of a tree sparrow, for variety in my winter walk, my life becomes continent and sweet as the kernel of a nut. I would rather hear a single shrub oak leaf at the end of a wintry glade rustle of its own accord at my approach, than receive a shipload of stars and garters from the strange kings and peoples of the earth.

By poverty, *i. e.* simplicity of life and fewness of incidents, I am solidified and crystallized, as a vapor or liquid by cold. It is a singular concentration of strength and energy and flavor. Chastity is perpetual acquaintance with the All. My diffuse and vaporous life becomes as the frost leaves and spiculæ radiant as gems on the weeds and stubble in a winter morning. You think that I am impoverishing myself by withdrawing from men, but in my solitude I have woven for myself a silken web or *chrysalis*, and, nymph-like, shall ere long burst forth a more perfect creature, fitted for a higher society. By simplicity, commonly called poverty, my life is concentrated and so becomes organ-

ized, or a κόσμος, which before was inorganic and lumpish.

The otter must roam about a great deal, for I rarely see fresh tracks in the same neighborhood a second time the same winter, though the old tracks may be apparent all the winter through. I should not wonder if one went up and down the whole length of the river.

Hayden senior (sixty-eight years old) tells me that he has been at work regularly with his team almost every day this winter, in spite of snow and cold. Even that cold Friday, about a fortnight ago, he did not go to a fire from early morning till night. As the thermometer, even at 12.45 P. M., was at −9°, with a very violent wind from the northwest, this was as bad as an ordinary arctic day. He was hauling logs to a mill, and persevered in making his paths through the drifts, he alone breaking the road. However, he froze his ears that Friday. Says he never knew it so cold as the past month. He has a fine elm directly behind his house, divided into many limbs near the ground. It is a question which is the most valuable, this tree or the house. In hot summer days it shades the whole house. He is going to build a shed around it, inclosing the main portion of the trunk.

P. M. — To Hubbard Bath.

Another very warm day, I should think warmer than the last. The sun is from time to time promising to show itself through the mist, but does not. A thick steam is everywhere rising from the earth and snow,

and apparently this makes the clouds which conceal the sun, the air being so much warmer than the earth. The snow is gone off very rapidly in the night, and much of the earth is bare, and the ground partially thawed. It is exciting to walk over the moist, bare pastures, though slumping four or five inches, and see the green mosses again. This vapor from the earth is so thick that I can hardly see a quarter of a mile, and ever and anon it condenses to rain-drops, which are felt on my face. The river has risen, and the water is pretty well over the meadows. If this weather holds a day or two longer, the river will break up generally.

I see one of those great ash-colored puffballs with a tinge of purple, open like a cup, four inches in diameter. The upper surface is (as it were bleached) quite hoary. Though it is but just brought to light from beneath the deep snow, and the last two days have been misty or rainy without sun, it is just as dry and dusty as ever, and the drops of water rest on it, at first undetected, being coated with its dust, looking like unground pearls. I brought it home and held it in a basin of water. To my surprise, when held under water it looked like a mass of silver or melted lead, it was so coated with air, and when I suffered it to rise, — for it had to be kept down by force, — instead of being heavy like a sponge which has soaked water, it was as light as a feather, and its surface perfectly dry, and when touched it gave out its dust the same as ever. It was impossible to wet. It seems to be encased in a silvery coat of air which is water-tight. The water did not penetrate into it at all, and running off as you lifted it up, it was just as dry as

before, and on the least jar floating in dust above your head.

The ground is so bare that I gathered a few Indian relics.

And now another friendship is ended. I do not know what has made my friend doubt me, but I know that in love there is no mistake, and that every estrangement is well founded. But my destiny is not narrowed, but if possible the broader for it. The heavens withdraw and arch themselves higher. I am sensible not only of a moral, but even a grand physical pain, such as gods may feel, about my head and breast, a certain ache and fullness. This rending of a tie, it is not my work nor thine. It is no accident that we mind; it is only the awards of fate that are affecting. I know of no æons, or periods, no life and death, but these meetings and separations. My life is like a stream that is suddenly dammed and has no outlet; but it rises the higher up the hills that shut it in, and will become a deep and silent lake. Certainly there is no event comparable for grandeur with the eternal separation — if we may conceive it so — from a being that we have known. I become in a degree sensible of the meaning of finite and infinite. What a grand significance the word "never" acquires! With one with whom we have walked on high ground we cannot deal on any lower ground ever after. We have tried for so many years to put each other to this immortal use, and have failed. Undoubtedly our good genii have mutually found the material unsuitable. We have hitherto paid each other the highest possible compliment; we have recognized each other constantly as divine, have afforded each other that opportunity to live that no other wealth or kindness can afford. And now, for some reason inappreciable by us, it has become necessary for us to withhold this mutual aid. Perchance there is none beside who knows us for a god, and none whom we know for such. Each man and woman is a veritable god or goddess, but to the mass of their fellows disguised. There is only one in each case who sees through the disguise. That one who does not stand so near to any man as to see the divinity in him is truly alone. I am perfectly sad at parting from you. I could better have the earth taken away from under my feet, than the thought of you from my mind. One while I think that some great injury has been done, with which you are implicated, again that you are no party to it. I fear that there may be incessant tragedies, that one may treat his fellow as a god but receive somewhat less regard from him. I now almost for the first time *fear* this. Yet I believe that in the long run there is no such inequality.

Here we are in the backwoods of America repeating Hebrew prayers and psalms in which occur such words as *amen* and *selah*, the meaning of some of which we do not quite understand, reminding me of Moslem prayers in which, it seems, the same or similar words are used. How Mormon-like!

Feb. 10. The thaw which began on the 4th lasted through the 8th.

When I surveyed Shattuck's Merrick's pasture fields, about January 10th, I was the more pleased with the

task because of the three willow-rows about them. One, trimmed a year before, had grown about seven feet, a dense hedge of bright-yellow osiers. But MacManus, who was helping me, said that he thought the land would be worth two hundred dollars more if the willows were out of the way, they so filled the ground with their roots. He had found that you could not plow within five rods [*sic*] of them, unless at right angles with the rows. Hayden, senior, tells me that when he lived with Abel Moore, Moore's son Henry one day set out a row of willow boughs for a hedge, but the father, who had just been eradicating an old willow-row at great labor and expense, asked Hayden who had done that and finally offered him a dollar if he would destroy them, which he agreed to do. So each morning, as he went to and from his work, he used to pull some of them up a little way, and if there were many roots formed he rubbed them off on a rock. And when, at the breakfast-table, Henry expressed wonder that his willows did not grow any better, being set in a rich soil, the father would look at Hayden and laugh.

Burton, the traveller, quotes an Arab saying, "Voyaging is a victory," which he refers to the feeling of independence on overcoming the difficulties and dangers of the desert. But I think that commonly voyaging is a defeat, a rout, to which the traveller is compelled by want of valor. The traveller's peculiar *valor* is commonly a bill of exchange. He is at home anywhere but where he was born and bred. Petitioning some Sir Joseph Banks or other representative of a Geographical

Society to avail himself of his restlessness, and, if not receiving a favorable answer, necessarily going off somewhere next morning. It is a prevalent disease, which attacks Americans especially, both men and women, the opposite to nostalgia. Yet it does not differ much from nostalgia. I read the story of one voyageress round the world, who, it seemed to me, having started, had no other object but to get home again, only she took the longest way round. Snatching at a fact or two in behalf of science as he goes, just as a panther in his leap will take off a man's sleeve and land twenty feet beyond him when travelling down-hill, being fitted out by some Sir Joseph Banks.

It seems that in Arabia, as well as in New England, they have the art of springing a prayer upon you. The Madani or inhabitants of El Medinah are, according to Burton, notwithstanding an assumed austerity and ceremoniousness, not easily matched in volubility and personal abuse. "When a man is opposed to more than his match in disputing or bargaining, . . . he interrupts the adversary with a 'Sall' ala Mohammed,' — bless the Prophet. Every good Moslem is obliged to obey such requisition by responding, 'Allahumma salli alayh,' — O Allah bless him! But the Madani curtails the phrase to 'A'n,' supposing it to be an equivalent, and proceeds in his loquacity. Then perhaps the baffled opponent will shout out 'Wahhid,' *i. e.* 'Attest the unity of the Deity;' when, instead of employing the usual religious phrases to assert that dogma, he will briefly ejaculate, 'Al,' and hurry on with the course of conversation." (Page 283.)

Feb. 11. *Wednesday.* The meadows, flooded by the thaw of the last half of last week and Sunday, are now frozen hard enough to bear, and it is excellent skating.

Near the other swamp white oak on Shattuck's piece I found another caterpillar on the ice. From its position I thought it *possible* that it had been washed from its winter quarters by the freshet, and so left on top of the ice. It was not frozen in, and may have been blown from the oak. It was of a different species from that of January 8th, about one and one tenth inches long, with but little fuzziness, black with three longitudinal buff stripes, the two lateral quite pale, and a black head; the foremost feet black, the others lighter-colored. It was frozen quite stiffly, as many tested, being curled up like the other, and I did not dare to bend it hard for fear of breaking it, even after I took it out in the house. But being placed on the mantelpiece it soon became relaxed, and in fifteen minutes began to crawl.

Feb. 12. 7.30 A. M. — The caterpillar, which I placed last night on the snow beneath the thermometer, is frozen stiff again, this time not being curled up, the temperature being −6° now. Yet, being placed on the mantelpiece, it thaws and begins to crawl in five or ten minutes, before the rear half of its body is limber. Perhaps they were revived last week, when the thermometer stood at 52 and 53.

To Worcester.

I observe that the Nashua in Lancaster has already

fallen about three feet, as appears by the ice on the trees, walls, banks, etc., though the main stream of the Concord has not begun to fall at all. (It is hardly fallen perceptibly when I return on the 14th. Am not sure it has.) The former is apparently mostly open, the latter all closed.

When I skated on the 11th I saw several pretty large open spaces on the meadow, notwithstanding that the boys had begun to skate on the meadow the 10th and it had been steadily growing colder, and the ice was on the 11th from two and a half to three inches thick generally. These open spaces were evidently owing to the strong wind of the night before, and which was then blowing, but I neglected to observe what peculiarity there was in the locality. Perhaps it was very shallow with an uneven bottom.

Feb. 14. Higginson told me yesterday of a large tract near Fayal and near Pico (Mountain), covered with the reindeer (?) (as I suggested and he assented) lichens, very remarkable and desolate, extending for miles, the effect of an earthquake, which will in course of time be again clothed with a larger vegetation. Described at length remarkable force of the wind on the summit of Pico. Told of a person in West Newbury, who told him that he once saw the moon rising out of the sea from his house in that place, and on the moonlight in his room the distinct shadow of a vessel which was somewhere on the sea between him and the moon!!

It is a fine, somewhat springlike day. The ice is

Vol. IX

of Henry Woodies in 1654 is mentioned. Under date 1666, Shattuck finds in the South Quarter, among the names of the town at that time, "Henry Woodhouse 1 [lot] 360 [acres]," etc.

When I returned from Worcester yesterday morning, I found that the Lee house, of which six weeks ago I made an accurate plan, had been completely burned up the evening before, *i. e.* the 13th, while I was lecturing in Worcester. (It took fire and came near being destroyed in the night of the previous December 18th, early in morning. I was the first to get there *from town*.) In the course of the forenoon of yesterday I walked up to the site of the house, whither many people were flocking, on foot and in carriages. There was nothing of the house left but the chimneys and cellar walls. The eastern chimney had fallen in the night. On my way I met Abel Hunt, to whom I observed that it was perhaps the oldest house in town. "No," said he, "they saw the date on it during the fire, — 1707." When I arrived I inquired where the date had been seen, and read it for myself on the chimney, but there was too much smouldering fire to permit of my approaching it nearly.

I was interested in the old elm near the southeast corner of the house, which I found had been a mere shell a few years since, now filled up with brick. Flood, who has lived there, told me that Wheeler asked his advice with regard to that tree, — whether he could do better than lay the axe at its root. F. told him that he had seen an ash in the old country which was in the same condition, and is a tenderer tree than an "elum,"

softening so that skates begin to cut in, and numerous caterpillars are now *crawling* about on the ice and snow, the thermometer in the shade north of house standing 42°. So it appears that they must often thaw in the course of the winter, and find nothing to eat.

Feb. 15. About the 1st of January, when I was surveying the Lee farm, Captain Elwell, the proprietor, asked me how old I thought the house was.

I looked into Shattuck's History and found that, according to him, "*Henry Woodhouse*, or Woodis, as his name was sometimes written, came to Concord from London, about 1650, freeman 1656. His farm, estimated at three hundred and fifty acres, lay between the two rivers, and descended to his son-in-law, Joseph Lee, whose posterity successively held it for more than one hundred years. . . . He d[ied] June 16, 1701." (*Vide* page 389.)

Shattuck says that the principal sachem of our Indians, Tahattawan, lived "near Nahshawtuck hill." Shattuck (page 28) says that the celebrated Waban originally lived in Concord, and he describes Squaw Sachem and John Tahattawan, son of Tahattawan, as Musketaquid Indians. In 1684 "Mantatukwet, a Christian Indian of Natick, aged 70 years or thereabouts," according to the Register at Cambridge, deposed "that about 50 years since he lived within the bounds of that place which is now called Concord, at the foot of an hill, named Nahshawtuck, now in the possession of Mr. Henry Woodis," etc. (page 7). A vote

preserved by being filled up, and with masonry, and then cemented over. So, soon after, the mason was set to work upon it under his directions, Flood having scraped out all the rotten wood first with a hoe. The cavity was full three feet wide and eight or ten high commencing at the ground. The mason had covered the bricks and rounded off with mortar, which he had scored with his trowel so that [one] did not observe but it was bark. It seemed an admirable plan, and not only improved the appearance but the strength and durability of the tree.

This morning (the 15th), it having rained in the night, and thinking the fire would be mostly out, I made haste to the ruins of the Lee house to read that inscription. By laying down boards on the bricks and cinders, which were quite too hot to tread on and covered a smothered fire, I was able to reach the chimney. The inscription was on the east side of the east chimney (which had fallen), at the bottom, in a cupboard on the west side of the late parlor, which was on a level with the ground on the east and with the cellar on the extreme west and the cellar kitchen on the north. There was a narrow lower (milk) cellar south and southeast of it, and an equally lower and narrower cellar east of it, under the parlor. This side of the chimney was perhaps fifteen feet from the east side of the house and as far from the north side. The inscription was in a slight recess in the chimney three feet four inches wide and a little more in height up and down, as far as I could see into the pile of bricks, thus : —

It appeared to have been made by the finger or a stick, in the mortar when fresh, which had been spread an inch to an inch and a quarter thick over the bricks, and, where it was too dry and hard, to have been pecked with the point of a trowel. The first three words and the " 16 " were perfectly plain, the " 5 " was tolerably plain, though some took it for a three, but I could *feel* it yet more distinctly. The mortar was partly knocked off the rest, apparently by this fire, but the top of some capital letter like a " C," and the letters " netty " were about as plain as represented, and the rest looked like " Henry " (Woodhouse?) or " l (t?) kinry " (?) the " y " (?) at end being crowded for want of room next the side. These last two words *quite* uncertain. The surface of

this recess was slightly swelling or bulging, somewhat like the outside of an oven, and above it the chimney was sloped and rounded off to the narrower shaft of it. The letters were from two and one half to three inches long and one eighth to one half inch deep.

This chimney, as well as the more recent westerly one, had been built chiefly with clay mortar, and I brought away a brick, of a soft kind, eight and seven eighths inches—some nine—long, four and one fourth plus wide, varying one fourth, and two and one half thick, though there were some much smaller near it, probably not so old. The clay (for mortar) was about as hard as mortar on it. The mortar in which the inscription was made contained considerable straw (?) and some *lumps* of clay, now crumbling like sand, with the lime and sand. The outside was white, but the interior ash-colored.

I discovered that the mortar of the inscription was not so old as the chimney, for the bricks beneath it, over which it was spread, were covered with soot, uniformly to the height of seven or eight feet, and the mortar fell off with an eighth of an inch thickness of this soot adhering to it, as if the recess had been a fireplace mortared over.

I have just been reading the account of Dr. Ball's sufferings on the White Mountains. Of course, I do not wonder that he was lost. I should say: Never undertake to ascend a mountain or thread a wilderness where there is any danger of being lost, without taking thick clothing, partly india-rubber, if not a tent or material for one; the best map to be had and a compass;

Vol. IX

salt pork and hard-bread and salt; fish-hooks and lines; a good jack-knife, at least, if not a hatchet, and perhaps a gun; matches in a vial stopped water-tight; some strings and paper. Do not take a dozen steps which you could not with tolerable accuracy protract on a chart. I never do otherwise. Indeed, you must have been living all your life in some such methodical and assured fashion, though in the midst of cities, else you will be lost in spite of all this preparation.

HOW TO CATCH A PIG

If it is a wild shoat, do not let him get scared; shut up the dogs and keep mischievous boys and men out of the way. Think of some suitable inclosure in the neighborhood, no matter if it be a pretty large field, if it chances to be tightly fenced; and with the aid of another prudent person give the pig all possible opportunities to enter it. Do not go very near him nor appear to be driving him, only let him avoid you, persuade him to prefer that inclosure. If the case is desperate and it is necessary, you may make him think that you wish him to [go] anywhere else but into that field, and he will be pretty sure to go there. Having got him into that inclosure and put up the fence, you can contract it at your leisure. When you have him in your hands, if he is obstinate, do not try to drive him with a rope round one leg. Spare the neighbors' ears and your pig's feelings, and put him into a cart or wheelbarrow.

The brick above described appears to be of the same size with those of Governor Craddock's house in Med-

ford, said to have been built in 1634 and measured by Brooks. (*Vide* Book of Facts.)

It is remarkable that though Elwell, the last occupant of this house, never has seen this inscription, it being in this obscure nook in the cellar, the inscriber's purpose is served, for now nothing stands but the other chimney and the foundation of this, and the inscription is completely exposed to the daylight and to the sun, and far more legible even a rod or two off than it could have been when made. There it is, staring all visitors in the face, on that clear space of mortar just lifted above the mouldering ruins of the chimney around it. Yesterday you could not get within a rod of it, but distinctly read it over the furnace of hot bricks and coals.

I brought away a brick and a large flake of the mortar with letters on it, but it crumbled in my hands, and I was reminded of the crumbling of some of the slabs of Nineveh in the hands of Layard as soon as brought to light, and felt a similar grief because I could not transport it entire to a more convenient place than that scorching pile, or even lay the crumbling mass down, without losing forever the outlines and the significance of those yet undeciphered words. But I laid it down, of necessity, and that was the end of it. There was our sole Nineveh slab, perhaps the oldest *engraving* in Concord.[1]

Webster prided himself on being the first *farmer* in the south parish of Marshfield, but if he was the first they must have been a sorry set, for his farming was a complete failure. It cost a great deal more than it

[1] No; some gravestones are undoubtedly older.

came to. He used other people's capital, and was insolvent when he died, so that his friends and relatives found it difficult to retain the place, if indeed they have not sold it. How much cheaper it would have been for the town or county to have maintained him in the almshouse than as a farmer at large! How many must have bled annually to manure his broad potato-fields, who without inconvenience could have contributed sufficient to maintain him in the almshouse!

Feb. 16. 8 A. M. — To Lee house site again.

It was a rough-cast house when I first knew it. The fire still glowing among the bricks in the cellar. Richard Barrett says he remembers the inscription and the date 1650, but not the rest distinctly. I find that this recess was not in the cellar, but on the west side of the parlor, which was on the same level with the upper cellar at the west end of the house. It was on the back side of a cupboard (in that parlor), which was a few inches deep at the bottom and sloped back to a foot perhaps at top, or on the brick jog three inches at bottom and five and a half at top, and had shelves. The sitting-room of late was on the same level, the west side of this chimney.

The old part of the chimney, judging from the clay and the size of the brick, was seven feet wide east and west and about ten north and south. There was the back side of an old oven visible on the south side (late the front of the house) under the stairs (that had been), which had been filled up with the large bricks in clay.

The chimney above and behind the oven and this recess had been filled in with great stones, many much bigger than one's head, packed in clay mixed with the coarsest meadow-hay. Sometimes there were masses of pure clay and hay a foot in diameter. There was a very great proportion of the hay, consisting of cut-grass, three-sided carex, ferns, and still stouter woody stems, apparently a piece of corn-husk one inch wide and several long. And impressions in the clay of various plants, — grasses, ferns, etc., — exactly like those in coal in character. These are perhaps the oldest pressed plants in Concord. I have a mass eight or nine inches in diameter which is apparently one third vegetable. About these stones there is generally only the width (four and one quarter inches) of one brick, so that the chimney was a mere shell.

Though the inscription was in a coarse mortar mixed with straw, the sooty bricks over which it was spread were laid in a better mortar, without straw, and yet the mass of the bricks directly above this recess, in the chimney, were all laid in *clay.* Perhaps they had used plastering *there* instead of clay because it was a fireplace. A thin coating of whiter and finer mortar or plastering without straw had been spread over the sloping and rounded chimney above the recess and on each side and below it, and this covered many small bricks mingled with the large ones, and though this looked more modern, the straw-mixed mortar of the inscription overlapped at the top about a foot, proving the coarser mortar the more recent.

The inscription, then, was made after the chimney

was built, when some alteration was made, and a small brick had come to be used. Yet so long ago that straw was mixed with the mortar.

If that recess was an old fireplace, then, apparently, the first house fronted east, for the oven was on the south side.

A boy who was at the fire said to me, "This was the chimney in which the cat was burned up; she ran into a stove, and we heard her cries in the midst of the fire." Parker says there was no cat; she was drowned.

According to Shattuck, Johnson, having the period from 1645 to 1650 in view, says of Concord that it *had* been more populous. "The number of families at present are about 50. Their buildings are conveniently placed, chiefly in one straite street under a sunny banke in a low level," etc. (History, page 18.)

According to Shattuck (page 14), Governor Winthrop "selected (judiciously, I think) a lot in Concord [apparently in 1638],[1] which 'he intended to build upon,' near where Captain Humphrey Hunt now lives."

I was contending some time ago that our meadows must have been wetter once than they now are, else the trees would have got up there more. I see that Shattuck says under 1654 (page 33), "The meadows were somewhat drier, and ceased to be a subject of frequent complaint."

According to Wood's "New England's Prospect," the first settlers of Concord for meat bought "venison or rockoons" of the Indians. The latter must have been common then. The wolves robbed them of their swine.

[1] [Brackets in original journal.]

A wonderfully warm day (the third one); about 2 P. M., thermometer in shade 58.

I perceive that some, commonly talented, persons are enveloped and confined by a certain crust of manners, which, though it may sometimes be a fair and transparent enamel, yet only repels and saddens the beholder, since by its rigidity it seems to repress all further expansion. They are viewed as at a distance, or like an insect under a tumbler. They have, as it were, prematurely hardened both seed and shell, and this has severely taxed, if not put a period to, the life of the plant. This is to stand upon your dignity.

Genius has evanescent boundaries, like an altar from which incense rises.

The former are, after all, but hardened sinners in a mild sense. The pearl is a hardened sinner. Manners get to be human parchment, in which sensible books are often bound and honorable titles engrossed, though they may be very stiff and dry.

Feb. 17. Thermometer at 1 P. M., 60°.

The river is fairly breaking up, and men are out with guns after muskrats, and even boats. Some are apprehending loss of fruit from this warm weather. It is as open as the 3d of April last year, at least.

P. M. — To the old Hunt house.

The bricks of the old chimney which has the date on it vary from eight to eight and one half inches in length, but the oldest in the chimney in the rear part are nine to nine and one fourth long by four and one fourth plus wide and two and one fourth to two and one half thick. This the size also of the bricks in clay behind the boarding of the house. There is straw in the clay and also in the lime used as plastering in both these chimneys. That on the first has a singular blue color. This house is about forty-nine feet on the front by twenty. The middle of door about twenty-five and a half feet from east end. House from fourteen to fifteen feet high. There was a door at the west end within Abel Hunt's remembrance; you can see where. The rear part has a wholly oak frame, while the front is pine. But I doubt if it is older, because the boards on the main part are feather-edged even within this part, as if they had once been on the outside. E. Hosmer says that his father said that Dr. Lee told him that he put on the whole upper, *i. e.* third, story of the Lee house. Says his old house where Everett lives was dated 1736.

Feb. 18. Another remarkably warm and pleasant day. The nights of late nearly as warm as the day. When I step out into the yard I hear that earliest spring note from some bird, perhaps a pigeon woodpecker (or can it be a nuthatch, whose ordinary note I hear?), the rapid *whar whar, whar whar, whar whar,* which I have so often heard before any other note.[1]

The snow is nearly all gone, and it is so warm and springlike that I walk over to the hill, listening for spring birds. The roads are beginning to be settled. I step excited over the moist mossy ground, dotted with the green stars of thistles, crowfoot, etc., the outsides of which are withered.

[1] *Vide* Mar. 18th.

Amid the pitch pines by the hemlocks I am surprised to find a great mildew on the ground, three or four feet long by two and a half wide and one fourth to one inch thick, investing the pine-needles and grass stubble and fallen hemlock twigs, like a thick cobweb or veil, through which the ground, etc., is seen dimly. It has a regular vegetable or lichen-like border, creeping outward from a centre, and is more cottony and fibrous there. Like the ground generally thereabouts, it has an inspiring sweet, musty scent when I stoop close to it. I was surprised to find how sweet the whole ground smelled when I lay flat and applied my nose to it; more so than any cow; as it were the promise of the perfect man and new springs to eternity. The mildew apparently occupied the place where a mass of snow ice rested yesterday (it was not yet wholly gone on one side). It was the snow-bank's footprint, or rather its *plantain.* One of the first growths of the new year, surely. Further in the pines there was more of it wherever the snow had but just disappeared, a great many square rods of it all put together. But also there was, very similar to it, yet only a thin veil, the apparent gossamer of spring and fall, close to the edge of the melting snow, and I saw a spider or two. This had only the thickness of a cobweb and was covered with dew, yet was rather hard to distinguish from the mildew. Thin cobwebs were very widely dispersed in the meadows where the snow had just melted.[1]

I *thought* at one time that I heard a bluebird. Hear a fly buzz amid some willows.

[1] *Vide* next page [below]. *Vide* Mar. 4, 1860.

Vol. IX

Thermometer at 1 P. M., 65.

Sophia says that Mrs. Brooks's spiræas have started considerably!

I hear that geese went over Cambridge last night.

I sit all this day and evening without a fire, and some even have windows open.

P. M. — To Hubbard's Bath.

The frost out of the ground and the ways settled in many places. I see much more of that gossamer (?) of the morning, — still regarding the large mildew as different. It abounds in all low grounds where there is a firm pasture sod, where a snow-bank has just melted or on the edge of one that is fast disappearing. I observe some remarkable ones on Hubbard's land just below the mountain sumachs. They are thin webs over the grass just laid bare close to the snow commonly and over the icy edge of the snow. They are not under the snow. I thought at first it had been formed on the surface of the snow and when it melted rested lightly on the stubble beneath, but I could detect none extending more than three or four inches over the icy edge of the snow, though every stubble half exposed amid the snow even was the source or *point d'appui* of some. Sometimes, to my surprise, it was an extremely thin, but close-woven (?), perhaps air-tight veil, of the same color but still thinner than the thinnest tissue paper or membrane, in patches one to three feet in diameter, resting lightly on the stubble, which supports it in the form of little tents. This is now dry and very brittle, yet I can get up pieces an inch across. It suggests even a scum on the edge of the melting snow, which has

at last dried and hardened into a web. Here is one which, as commonly, springs from three or four inches within the melted snow, partly resting close and flat upon it, and extends thence several feet from its edge over the stubble. None of these have the thickness of mildew, and for cobwebs I see but two or three spiders about and cannot believe that they can have done all this in one night, nor do they make a close web. It lies lightly upon the stubble and the edge of the snow, as if it had settled in the night from the atmosphere. Can it be a scum formed on the melting snow, caught at last on the stubble like the pap of paper taken up in a sieve? Further off on every side I see the same now fretted away, like a coarse and worn-out sieve, where it was perfect perhaps yesterday.

Thus it lasts all day, conspicuous many rods off. I think there must be a square mile of this, at least, in Concord. It is after a very warm, muggy, but fair night, the last snow going off and the thermometer at 50°. Thinnest, frailest, gossamer veils dropped from above on the stubble, as if the fairies had dropped their veils or handkerchiefs after a midnight revel, rejoicing at the melting of the snow.

What can it be? Is it animal or vegetable? I suspect it is allied to mould; or is it a scum? or have the spiders anything to do with it? It suggests even a nebulous vegetable matter in the air, which, under these circumstances, in a muggy night, is condensed into this primitive vegetable form. Is it a sort of *flowing* of the earth, a waste fertility anticipating the more regular growths of spring?

Has not some slightly glutinous substance been deposited from the atmosphere on the snow, which is thus collected into a thin sort of paper, even like the brown-paper conferva? Is it a species of conferva?

I am excited by this wonderful air and go listening for the note of the bluebird or other comer. The very grain of the air seems to have undergone a change and is ready to split into the form of the bluebird's warble. Methinks if it were visible, or I could cast up some fine dust which would betray it, it would take a corresponding shape. The bluebird does not come till the air consents and his wedge will enter easily. The air over these fields is a foundry full of moulds for casting bluebirds' warbles.[1] Any sound uttered now would take that form, not of the harsh, vibrating, rending scream of the jay, but a softer, flowing, curling warble, like a purling stream or the lobes of flowing sand and clay. Here is the soft air and the moist expectant apple trees, but not yet the bluebird. They do not quite attain to song.

What a poem is this of spring, so often repeated! I am thrilled when I hear it spoken of, — as the *spring* of such a year, that fytte of the glorious epic.

Picked up a mouse-nest in the stubble at Hubbard's mountain sumachs, left bare by the melting snow. It is about five inches wide and three or four high, with one, if not two, small round indistinct entrances on the side, not very obvious till you thrust your finger through them and press aside the fine grass that closes them, ready to yield to the pressure of the mouse's body. It

[1] [Channing, pp. 78, 79.]

Vol. IX

is made very firmly and round, far more so than an oven-bird's nest, of the rye and grass stubble which was at hand under the snow, gnawed off to convenient lengths. A very snug and warm nest, where several might have lain very cosily under the snow in the hardest winter. Near by were collected many large green droppings of the usual form, as if for cleanliness, several feet off. Many galleries were visible close to the ground, in the withered grass under the snow. Is it not the nest of a different mouse from the *Mus leucopus* of the woods?

Mr. Prichard says that when he first came to Concord wood was $2.50 per cord. Father says that good wood was $3.00 per cord, and he can remember the longest; white pine, $2.00; maple, sixteen shillings.

When I approached the bank of a ditch this afternoon, I saw a frog diving to the bottom. The warmer water had already awaked him, and perhaps he had been sitting on the bank.

The above-described gossamer often has small roundish spots on it, two or three inches in diameter, which are whiter and much thicker, even like the silvery scales under which some kinds of insects lurk, somewhat. I see none of this over sand or in the road, as I suppose would be the case if it were a mere scum on the snow, or a deposition from the atmosphere. Must it not be of the nature of mildew? It is as if it were a thin and tender membrane that envelops the infant earth in earliest spring, at once rent and dissipated.

Feb. 19. Cloudy and somewhat rainy, the thermometer at last fallen to thirty-two and thirty-three degrees.

I have often noticed that the surface of the snow was rippled or waved like water. The dust from plowed ground collects on the ridges which bound these waves, and there it becomes very conspicuous as the snow melts, the ridges standing out more and more, for the dirt apparently protects the snow from the sun. Why do water and snow take just this form?

Some willow catkins have crept a quarter of an inch from under their scales and look very red, probably on account of the warm weather.

A man cannot be said to succeed in this life who does not satisfy one friend.

An old man, one of my neighbors, is so demented that he put both legs into one leg of his pantaloons the other morning!

Mr. Cheney tells me that Goodwin brought him a partridge to sell in the midst of the late severe weather. C. said it was a pity to kill it, it must find it hard to get a living. "I guess she did n't find it any harder than I do," answered G.

It would be pleasant to recall to mind the different styles of boats that have been used on this river from the first, beginning with the bark canoe and the dugout, or log canoe, or pirogue. Then, perhaps, some simple log canoe, or such a boat as now prevails, which probably has its prototype on English rivers, — call it dory, skiff, or what-not, — made as soon as boards were sawed here; the smaller, punt-like ones for one man; the round-bottomed boats from below, and the

half-round or lapstreaked, sometimes with sails; the great canal-boats; and the hay-boats of the Sudbury meadows; and lastly what the boys call "shell-boats," introduced last year, in imitation of the Esquimau kayack.

At evening it begins to snow, and —

(*Feb.* 20) this morning the ground is once more covered about one inch deep.

Minott says that the house he now lives in was framed and set up by Captain Isaac Hoar just beyond the old house by Moore's, this side the one he was born in, his mother's (?) house (whose well is that buried by Alcott on the sidewalk), and there the frame stood several years, Hoar having gone off, he thinks, to Westminster. (M. helped a man take down its chimney when he was a boy; it was very old, laid in clay.) He was quite a lad and used to climb up on the frame and, with a teaspoon, take the eggs of the house wren out of the mortise-holes. At last his grandfather, Dr. Abel Prescott, "an eminent physitian," bought it and moved it to where it now stands, and died in [it] in 1805, aged eighty-eight (born 1717). Said he died exactly where I sat, and the bed stood so and so, north and south from the clock. This Dr. Prescott had once probably lived with his nephew Willoughby Prescott, where Loring's is. After, when married, lived in the old rough-cast house near the poorhouse where Minott's mother was born. It was Dr. Abel P.'s son Abel (Minott's uncle) who rode into Concord before the British. Minott's father was rich, and died early in the army, Aunt says.

Minott always sits in the corner behind the door, close to the stove, with commonly the cat by his side, often in his lap. Often he sits with his hat on. He says that Frank Buttrick (who for a great many years worked at carpentering for John Richardson, and was working for him when he died) told him that Richardson called him when he was at the point of death and told him that he need not stop working on account of his death, but he might come in to the prayer if he wished to. R. is spoken of as a strong and resolute man.

I wish that there was in every town, in some place accessible to the traveller, instead [of] or beside the common directories, etc., a list of the worthies of the town, *i. e.* of those who are *worth* seeing.

Miss Minott has several old pieces of furniture that belonged to her grandfather Prescott, one a desk made for him and marked 1760. She said the looking-glass was held oldest furniture, she thought. It has the name John scratched on the middle by a madcap named John Bulkley from college, who had got so far with a diamond before he was stopped.

Beverley, after describing the various kinds of fowl that frequented the shores of Virginia, "not to mention beavers, otters, musk rats, minxes," etc., etc., says, "Although the inner lands want these benefits (which, however, no pond or plash is without)," etc. I admire the offhand way of describing the superfluous fertility of the land and water.

What is the relation between a bird and the ear that appreciates its melody, to whom, perchance, it is more

charming and significant than to any else? Certainly they are intimately related, and the one was made for the other. It is a natural fact. If I were to discover that a certain kind of stone by the pond-shore was affected, say partially disintegrated, by a particular natural sound, as of a bird or insect, I see that one could not be completely described without describing the other. I am that rock by the pond-side.

What is hope, what is expectation, but a seed-time whose harvest cannot fail, an irresistible expedition of the mind, at length to be victorious?

Feb. 21. The puffball is used by doctors to stop bleeding. Has not this property to do with its power of repelling moisture? Some have now almost entirely lost their dust, leaving a dry almost woolly substance. Am surprised to see this afternoon a boy collecting red maple sap from some trees behind George Hubbard's. It runs freely. The earliest sap I made to flow last year was March 14th. It must be owing to the warm weather we have had.

The river for some days has been open and its sap visibly flowing, like the maple.

Feb. 22. P. M. — To Dugan Desert.
The Tommy Wheeler house, like the Hunt house, has the sills projecting inside. Its bricks are about the same size with those of the Lee chimney; they are eight and three quarters to nine inches long by four and a half, but not in clay. A part at least of the back side has bricks on their edges in clay, as at the Hunt house, and there

are bricks in clay flat on the plate, close under roof at the eaves. I think that by the size of the bricks you cannot tell the age of an *old* house within fifty years.

Feb. 23. P. M. — See two yellow-spotted tortoises in the ditch south of Trillium Wood. You saunter expectant in the mild air along the soft edge of a ditch filled with melted snow and paved with leaves, in some sheltered place, yet perhaps with some ice at one end still, and are thrilled to see stirring amid the leaves at the bottom, sluggishly burying themselves from your sight again, these brilliantly spotted creatures. There are commonly two, at least. The tortoise is stirring in the ditches again. In your latest spring they still look incredibly strange when first seen, and not like cohabitants and contemporaries of yours.

I say in my thought to my neighbor, who was once my friend, "It is of no use to speak the truth to you, you will not hear it. What, then, shall I say to you?" At the instant that I seem to be saying farewell forever to one who has been my friend, I find myself unexpectedly near to him, and it is our very nearness and dearness to each other that gives depth and significance to that forever. Thus I am a helpless prisoner, and these chains I have no skill to break. While I think I have broken one link, I have been forging another.

I have not yet known a friendship to cease, I think. I fear I have experienced its decaying. Morning, noon, and night, I suffer a physical pain, an aching of the breast which unfits me for my tasks. It is perhaps most intense at evening. With respect to Friendship I feel

like a wreck that is driving before the gale, with a crew suffering from hunger and thirst, not knowing what shore, if any, they may reach, so long have I *breasted* the conflicting waves of this sentiment, my seams open, my timbers laid bare. I float on Friendship's sea simply because my specific gravity is less than its, but no longer that stanch and graceful vessel that careered so buoyantly over it. My planks and timbers are scattered. At most I hope to make a sort of raft of Friendship, on which, with a few of our treasures, we may float to some firm land.

That aching of the breast, the grandest pain that man endures, which no ether can assuage.

You cheat me, you keep me at a distance with your manners. I know of no other dishonesty, no other devil. Why this doubleness, these compliments? They are the worst of lies. A lie is not worse between traders than a compliment between friends. I would not, I cannot speak. I will let you *feel* my thought, my feeling.

Friends! they are united for good and for evil. They can delight each other as none other can. They can distress each other as none other can. Lying on lower levels is but a trivial offense compared with civility and compliments on the level of Friendship.

I visit my friend for joy, not for disturbance. If my coming hinders him in the least conceivable degree, I will exert myself to the utmost to stay away, I will get the Titans to help me stand aloof, I will labor night and day to construct a rampart between us. If my coming casts but the shadow of a shadow before it, I will retreat swifter than the wind and more untrackable. I will be gone irrevocably, if possible, before he fears that I am coming.

If the teeth ache they can be pulled. If the heart aches, what then? Shall we pluck it out?

Must friends then expect the fate of those Oriental twins, — that one shall at last bear about the corpse of the other, by that same ligature that bound him to a living companion?

Look before you leap. Let the isthmus be cut through, unless sea meets sea at exactly the same level, unless a perfect understanding and equilibrium has been established from the beginning around Cape Horn and the unnamed northern cape. What a tumult! It is Atlantic and Atlantic, or it is Atlantic and Pacific.

What mean these turtles, these coins of the muddy mint issued in early spring? The bright spots on their backs are vain unless I behold them. The spots *seem* brighter than ever when first beheld in the spring, as does the bark of the willow.

I have seen signs of the spring. I have seen a frog swiftly sinking in a pool, or where he dimpled the surface as he leapt in. I have seen the brilliant spotted tortoises stirring at the bottom of ditches. I have seen the clear sap trickling from the red maple.

Feb. 24. A fine spring morning. The ground is almost completely bare again. There has been a frost in the night. Now, at 8.30, it is melted and wets my feet like a dew. The water on the meadow this still, bright morning is smooth as in April. I am surprised to hear the strain of a song sparrow from the riverside, and as

Vol. IX

I cross from the causeway to the hill, thinking of the bluebird, I that instant hear one's note from deep in the softened air. It is already 40°, and by noon is between 50° and 60°. As the day advances I hear more bluebirds and see their azure flakes settling on the fence-posts. Their short, rich, crispy warble curls through the air. Its grain now lies parallel to the curve of the bluebird's warble, like boards of the same lot. It *seems* to be one of those early springs of which we have heard but have never experienced. Perhaps they are fabulous. I have seen the probings of skunks for a week or more. I now see where one has pawed out the worm-dust or other chankings from a hole in base of a walnut and torn open the fungi, etc., there, exploring for grubs or insects. They are very busy these nights.

If I should make the least concession, my friend would spurn me. I am obeying his law as well as my own.

Where is the actual friend you love? Ask from what hill the rainbow's arch springs! It adorns and crowns the earth.

Our friends are our kindred, of our species. There are very few of our species on the globe.

Between me and my friend what unfathomable distance! All mankind, like motes [?] and insects, are between us.

If my friend says in his mind, I will *never* see you again, I translate it of necessity into *ever*. That is its definition in Love's lexicon.

Those whom we can love, we can hate; to others we are indifferent.

P. M. — To Walden.

The railroad in the Deep Cut is dry as in spring, almost dusty. The best of the sand foliage is already gone. I walk without a greatcoat. A chickadee with its winter lisp flits over, and I think it is time to hear its *phebe* note, and that instant it pipes it forth. Walden is still covered with thick ice, though melted a foot from the shore.

The French (in the Jesuit Relations) say *fil de l'eau* for that part of the current of a river in which any floating thing would be carried, generally about equidistant from the two banks. It is a convenient expression, for which I think we have no equivalent.[1]

Get my boat out the cellar.

Feb. 25. I hear of lilac buds expanding, but have not looked at them. I go through the woods behind the Kettle place. The leaves rustle and look all dry on the ground in the woods, as if quite ready to burn. The flies buzz out of doors. Though I left my outside coat at home, this single thick one is too much. I go across the Great Fields to Peter's, but can see no ducks on the meadows. I suspect they have not come yet, in spite of the openness. The fragrant everlasting has retained its fragrance all winter. That mildew, or gossamer-like scum, of the 18th is still visible here and there. It is like very thin and frail isinglass. Goodwin says he saw a robin this morning. The thermometer is at 65° at noon.

---

[1] [Thoreau afterward used an English equivalent, "thread of the river." See *postea*. The term is given in the dictionaries, but may be more recent than Thoreau's time.]

Feb. 26. Cold and windy. The river fast going down. Paint the bottom of my boat.

What an accursed land, methinks unfit for the habitation of man, where the wild animals are monkeys!

I saw Mrs. Brooks's spiræas to-day grown half an inch (!!), whose starting I heard of on the 18th.[1]

Feb. 27. Before I opened the window this cold morning, I heard the peep of a robin, that sound so often heard in cheerless or else rainy weather, so often heard first borne on the cutting March wind or through sleet or rain, as if its coming were premature.

P. M. — To the Hill.

The river has skimmed over again in many places. I see many crows on the hillside, with their sentinel on a tree. They are picking the cow-dung scattered about, apparently for the worms, etc., it contains. They have done this in so many places that it looks as if the farmer had been at work with his maul. They must save him some trouble thus.[2] I see cinders two or three inches in diameter, apparently burnt clapboards, on the bank of the North River, which came from the burning Lee house! Yet it was quite a damp night, after rain in the afternoon, and rather still. They are all curled by the heat, so that you can tell which side was first exposed to it. The grain is more distinct than ever. Nature so abhors a straight line that she curls each cinder as she launches it on the fiery whirlwind. All the *light*ness and ethereal spirit of the wood is gone.

---

[1] *Vide* Mar. 4th.
[2] Notice the like extensively early in March, 1860.

and this black earthy residuum alone returned. The russet hillside is spotted with them. They suggest some affinity with the cawing crows.

I see some of those large purplish chocolate-colored puffballs. They grow in dry pastures. They are in various states. I do not understand their changes.[1] Some are quite pulverulent, and emitting a cloud of dust at every touch. Others present a firm, very light ash-colored surface above, in a shallow saucer, with a narrow, wrinkled, crenate border, and beneath this firm skin is a perfectly dry spongy mass, less ashy, more reddish than the last, and fibrous, with very little dust in it but many small ribbed grubs. The surface often looks as if it had been pecked by birds in search of these grubs. Sometimes there is, above the white skin of the saucer, considerable pulverulent substance, as if in the other case this had been dissipated. Sometimes two large ones are joined at the root. Was there any portion (now dissipated) above this light-colored skin? Did the portion beneath the skin originally contain more dust, which has escaped? Or will it yet come to dust?

Are not fungi the best hygrometers?

Feb. 28. Nearly two inches of snow in the night.
P. M. — To Lee's Cliff.

I see the track, apparently of a muskrat (?), — about five inches wide with very sharp and distinct trail of tail, — on the snow and thin ice over the little rill in

[1] See both these and *Lycoperdon stellatum* when ground is laid bare in spring, as about Mar. 1, 1860 (no account).

the Miles meadow. It was following up this rill, often not more than thrice as wide as itself, and sometimes its precise locality concealed under ice and snow, yet he kept exactly above it on the snow through all its windings, where it was open occasionally taking to the water and sometimes swimming under the ice a rod or two. It is interesting to see how every little rill like this will be haunted by muskrats or minks. Does the mink ever leave a track of its tail?

At the Cliff, the tower-mustard, early crowfoot, and perhaps buttercup appear to have started of late. It takes several years' faithful search to learn where to look for the earliest flowers.

It is a singular infatuation that leads men to become clergymen in regular, or even irregular, standing. I pray to be introduced to new men, at whom I may stop short and taste their peculiar sweetness. But in the clergyman of the most liberal sort I see no perfectly independent human nucleus, but I seem to see some indistinct scheme hovering about, to which he has lent himself, to which he belongs. It is a very fine cobweb in the lower stratum of the air, which stronger wings do not even discover. Whatever he may say, he does not know that one day is as good as another. Whatever he may say, he does not know that a man's creed can never be written, that there are no particular expressions of belief that deserve to be prominent. He dreams of a certain sphere to be filled by him, something less in diameter than a great circle, maybe not greater than a hogshead. All the staves are got out, and his sphere is already hooped. What's the use of talking to

him? When you spoke of sphere-music he thought only of a thumping on his cask. If he does n't know something that nobody else does, that nobody told him, then he's a telltale. What great interval is there between him who is caught in Africa and made a plantation slave of in the South, and him who is caught in New England and made a Unitarian minister of? In course of time they will abolish the one form of servitude, and, not long after, the other. I do not see the necessity for a man's getting into a hogshead and so narrowing his sphere, nor for his putting his head into a halter. Here's a man who can't butter his own bread, and he has just combined with a thousand like him to make a dipped toast for all eternity![1]

Nearly one third the channel is open in Fair Haven Pond. The snow lies on the ice in large but very shallow drifts, shaped, methinks, much like the holes in ice, broad crescents (apparently) convex to the northwest.

[1] [Channing, p. 90.]

VIII

MARCH, 1857

(ÆT. 39)

March 2. At Cambridge. Very gusty day. An inch or two of snow falls, — all day about it, — and strangely blown away.

March 3. P. M. —To Fair Haven Hill.
3 P. M., 24° in shade. The red maple sap, which I first noticed the 21st of February, is now frozen up in the auger-holes and thence down the trunk to the ground, except in one place where the hole was made in the south side of the tree, where it is melted and is flowing a little. Generally, then, when the thermometer is thus low, say below freezing-point, it does not thaw in the auger-holes. There is no expanding of buds of any kind, nor early birds, to be seen. Nature was thus premature — anticipated her own revolutions — with respect to the sap of trees, the buds (spiræa at least), and birds. The warm spell ended with February 26th.

The crust of yesterday's snow has been converted by the sun and wind into flakes of thin ice from two or three inches to a foot in diameter, scattered like a mackerel sky over the pastures, as if all the snow had been blown out from beneath. Much of this thin ice is partly opaque and has a glutinous look even, reminding me of frozen glue. Probably it has much dust mixed with it.

I go along below the north end of the Cliffs. The rocks in the usual place are buttressed with icy columns, for water in almost imperceptible quantity is trickling down the rocks. It is interesting to see how the dry black or ash-colored umbilicaria, which get a little moisture when the snow melts and trickles down along a seam or shallow channel of the rock, become relaxed and turn olive-green and enjoy their spring, while a few inches on each side of this gutter or depression in the face of the rock they are dry and crisp as ever. Perhaps the greater part of this puny rill is drunk up by the herbage on its brink.

These are among the consequences of the slight robin snow of yesterday. It is already mostly dissipated, but where a heap still lingers, the sun on the warm face of this cliff leads down a puny trickling rill, moistening the gutters on the steep face of the rocks where patches of umbilicaria lichens grow, of rank growth, but now thirsty and dry as bones and hornets' nests, dry as shells, which crackle under your feet. The more fortunate of these, which stand by the moistened seams or gutters of the rock, luxuriate in the grateful moisture — as in their spring. Their rigid nerves relax, they unbend and droop like limber infancy, and from dry ash and leather-color turn a lively olive-green. You can trace the course of this trickling stream over the rock through such a patch of lichens by the olive-green of the lichens alone.

Here and there, too, the same moisture refreshes and

Vol. IX

brightens up the scarlet crowns of some little cockscomb lichen, and when the rill reaches the perpendicular face of the cliff, its constant drip at night builds great organ-pipes of a ringed structure, which run together, buttressing the rock.

Skating yesterday and to-day.

March 5. P. M. — To Hill.

See the tracks of a woodchuck in the sand-heap about the mouth of his hole, where he has cleared out his entry. The red ground under a large pitch pine is strewn with scales of the ashy-brown bark over a diameter of ten or twelve feet, where some woodpecker has searched and hammered about the stem.

I scare up six male sheldrakes, with their black heads, in the Assabet, — the first ducks I have seen. Methought I heard a slight frog-like croak from them before.

The sap of the buttonwood flows; how long? The lilac buds cannot have swollen any since the 25th of February, on account of the cold. On examining, they look as if they had felt the influence of the previous heat a little. There are narrow light-green spaces laid bare along the edges of the brown scales, as if they had expanded so much.

This and the last four or five days very gusty. Most of the warmth of the fire is carried off by the draught, which consumes the wood very fast, faster than a much colder but still day in winter. My kindlings spend very fast now, for I do not commonly keep fire at night.

Thomas Morton in his "New English Canaan" has this epitaph on an infant that died apparently as soon as born, without being baptized: —

"Underneath this heap of stones
Lieth a parcel of small bones,
What hope at last can such imps have,
That from the womb go to the grave?"

Winckelmann in his "History of Ancient Art," vol. ii, page 27, says of Beauty, "I have meditated long upon it, but my meditations commenced too late, and in the brightest glow of mature life its essential has remained dark to me; I can speak of it, therefore, only feebly and spiritlessly." — Lodge's translation.

March 8. P. M. — To Hill.

When I cut a white pine twig the crystalline sap instantly exudes. How long has it been thus?

Get a glimpse of a hawk, the first of the season. The tree sparrows sing a little on this still sheltered and sunny side of the hill, but not elsewhere. A partridge goes off from amid the pitch pines. It lifts each wing so high above its back and flaps so low, and withal so rapidly, that they present the appearance of a broad wheel, almost a revolving sphere, as it whirs off like a cannon-ball shot from a gun.

Minott told me again the reason why the bushes were coming in so fast in the river meadows. Now that the mower takes nothing stronger than molasses and water, he darsn't meddle with anything bigger than a pipe-stem.

March 11. I see and talk with Rice, sawing off the ends of clapboards which he has planed, to make them square, for an addition to his house. He has got a fire in his shop, and plays at house-building there. His life is poetic. He does the work himself. He combines several qualities and talents rarely combined. Though he owns houses in the city, whose repair he attends to, finds tenants for them, and collects the rent, he also has his Sudbury farm and bean-fields. Though he lived in a city, he would still be natural and related to primitive nature around him. Though he owned all Beacon Street, you might find that his mittens were made of the skin of a woodchuck that had ravaged his bean-field, which he had cured. I noticed a woodchuck's skin tacked up to the inside of his shop. He said it had fatted on his beans, and William had killed [it] and expected to get another to make a pair of mittens of, one not being quite large enough. It was excellent for mittens. You could hardly wear it out.

Spoke of the cuckoo, which was afraid of the birds, was easily beaten; would dive right into the middle of a poplar, then come out on to some bare twig and look round for a nest to rob of young or eggs. Had noticed a pigeon woodpecker go repeatedly in a straight line from his nest in an apple tree to a distant brook-side in a meadow, dive down there, and in a few minutes return.

March 12. P. M. — To Hill.

Observe the waxwork twining about the smooth sumach. It winds against the sun. It is at first loose about the stem, but this ere long expands to and overgrows it. Observed the track of a squirrel in the snow under one of the apple trees on the southeast side of the Hill, and, looking up, saw a red squirrel with a nut or piece of frozen apple (?) in his mouth, within six feet, sitting in a constrained position partly *crosswise* on a limb over my head, perfectly still, and looking not at me, but off into the air, evidently expecting to escape my attention by this trick. I stood and watched and chirruped to him about five minutes so near, and yet he did not at once turn his head to look at me or move a foot or wink. The only motion was that of his tail curled over his back in the wind. At length he did change his attitude a little and look at me a moment. Evidently this is a trick they often practice. If I had been farther off he might have scolded at me.

Snowed again last night, as it has done once or twice before within ten days without my recording it, — robin snows, which last but a day or two.

March 13. Thermometer this morning, about 7 A. M., 2°, and the same yesterday. This month has been windy and cold, a succession of snows one or two inches deep, soon going off, the spring birds all driven off. It is in strong contrast with the last month.

Captain E. P. Dorr of Buffalo tells me that there is a rise and fall daily of the lakes about two or three inches, not accounted for. A difference between the lakes and sea is that when there is no wind the former are quite smooth, no swell. Otherwise he thought that no one could tell whether he was on the lakes or the

ocean. Described the diver's descending one hundred and sixty-eight feet to a sunken steamer and getting up the safe after she had been sunk three years. Described the breeding of the capelin at Labrador, a small fish about as big as a sardine. They crowd along the shore in such numbers that he had seen a cartload crowded quite on to the shore high and dry by those in the rear.

Elliott, the botanist, says (page 184) that the *Lechea villosa* (*major* of Michaux), "if kept from running to seed, would probably form a very neat edging for the beds of a flower garden; the foliage of the radical branches is very handsome during the winter, and the size of the plant is well suited to such a purpose."

Rhus Toxicodendron (page 363): "The juice which exudes on plucking the leaf-stalks from the stem of the *R. radicans* is a good indelible dye for marking linen or cotton."

Of the *Drosera rotundifolia* (page 375), "This fluid never appears to fall from the hairs, but is secreted nearly in proportion to its evaporation, and the secretion is supposed to be greatest in dry clear weather;" hence called sundew.

Howitt, in his "Boy's Adventures in Australia," says, "People here thought they had discovered large numbers of the graves of the blacks, lying lengthways, as amongst the whites, but these have turned out to be a natural phenomenon, and called Dead Men's Graves." The natives generally bury — when they do not burn — in a sitting posture. Is the country cold enough to allow these mounds to have been made by the ice?

Vol. IX

March 14. A warmer day at last. It has been steadily cold and windy, with repeated light snows, since February 26th came in. This afternoon is comparatively warm, and the few signs of spring are more reliable.

I go down the bank of the river in the Great Meadows. Many of those small, slender insects, with long, narrow wings (some apparently of same species without), are crawling about in the sun on the snow and bark of trees, etc.

The maples, apple trees, etc., have been barked by the ice, and show light-colored bands one or two feet from the ground about their trunks. I find on examination that in these cases the bark has not been worn off by the floating ice rubbing against them, as happens when they are directly on the edge of the stream, for this light and barked surface occurs often when the trunk is surrounded by a hedge of sprouts or of other twigs only six inches distant, which show no marks of attrition; and the inner or true bark of the tree is not injured, only the thick epidermis or scaly outer bark has been detached, though that may have been very firmly attached to the trunk. The ice has evidently frozen to this, and when the water fell, has taken it off with itself; but the smaller twigs appear to have been [*sic*] and recovered again. Tough outer scales, which you could not possibly detach nor begin to detach with your hands, will be taken off quite clean, leaving exposed the yellowish surface of the inner bark.

I see that some white maple buds apparently opened a little in that warm spell before the 26th of February, for such have now a minute orifice at the apex, through which you can even see the anthers.

March 15. P. M. — To Hubbard's Close and Walden.

I see in the ditches in Hubbard's Close the fine green tips of spires of grass just rising above the surface of the water in one place, as if unwilling to trust itself to the frosty air. Favored by the warmth of the water and sheltered by the banks of the ditch, it has advanced thus far. But generally I see only the flaccid and floating frost-bitten tops of grass which apparently started that warm spell in February. The surface of the ditches is spotted with these pale and withered frost-bitten bladelets. It was the first green blush, as it were, — nay, it is purple or lake often, and a true blush, — of spring, of that *Indian spring* we had in February. An early dawn and premature blush of spring, at which I was not present. To be present at the instant when the springing grass at the bottoms of ditches lifts its spear above the surface and bathes in the spring air! Many a first faint crop mantling the pools thus early is mown down by the frost before the village suspects that vegetation has reawakened.

The trout darts away in the puny brook there so swiftly in a zigzag course that commonly I only see the ripple that he makes, in proportion, in this brook only a foot wide, like that made by a steamer in a canal. Or if I catch a glimpse of him before he buries himself in the mud, it is only a dark film without distinct outline. By his zigzag course he bewilders the eye, and avoids capture perhaps.

As usual at this date and earlier, there are a few square rods of green grass tufts at Brister's springs, like a green fire under the pines and alders, and in one place an apparent growth of golden saxifrage.

At Heywood's Peak, I start partridges from the perfectly bare hillside. Such the spots they frequent at this season. I cross one of the bays of Walden, and might the middle.

By Thrush Alley, where they have been cutting more wood this winter, I see one of those beetles made of an oak excrescence, such as I have heard of, left by the chopper. The whole is a little over four feet long. The head nine or ten inches and the handle about three and a half feet, but all one piece. It was apparently of a young tree, or perhaps a limb, about four inches in diameter with a regular excrescence about it still, eight or nine inches in diameter. This head had been smoothed or trimmed and made more regular by the axe, cut off rather square at the end, and the lower part cut down to a handle of convenient size. And thus the chopper had made in a few moments in the woods a really efficient implement, with his axe only, out of some of the very wood he wished to split. A natural beetle. There was no danger that the handle would come off or the head crack. It needed no ringing. And thus he saved the head of his axe. We are singularly pleased and contented when a mere excrescence is thus converted into a convenient implement. Who was it, what satyr, that invented this rustic beetle? It was shaped:

An indispensable piece of woodcraft.

March 16. To Cambridge and Boston.

March 17. These days, beginning with the 14th, more springlike. Last night it rained a little, carrying off nearly all the little snow that remained, but this morning it is fair, and I hear the note of the woodpecker on the elms (that early note) and the bluebird again. Launch my boat.

No mortal is alert enough to be present at the first dawn of the spring, but he will presently discover some evidence that vegetation had awaked some days at least before. Early as I have looked this year, perhaps the first unquestionable growth of an indigenous plant detected was the fine tips of grass blades which the frost had killed, floating pale and flaccid, though still attached to their stems, spotting the pools like a slight fall or flurry of dull-colored snowflakes. After a few mild and sunny days, even in February, the grass in still muddy pools or ditches sheltered by the surrounding banks, which reflect the heat upon it, ventures to lift the points of its green phalanx into the mild and flattering atmosphere, advances rapidly from the saffron even to the rosy tints of morning. But the following night comes the frost, which, with rude and ruthless hand, sweeps the surface of the pool, and the advancing morning pales into the dim light of earliest dawn. I thus detect the first approach of spring by finding here and there its scouts and vanguard which have been slain by the rear-guard of retreating winter.

It is only some very early still, warm, and pleasant morning in February or March that I notice that wood-

pecker-like *whar-whar-whar-whar-whar-whar*, earliest spring sound.[1]

March 18. 9 A. M. — Up Assabet.
A still and warm but overcast morning, threatening rain. I now again hear the song sparrow's tinkle along the riverside, probably to be heard for a day or two, and a robin, which also has been heard a day or two. The ground is almost completely bare, and but little ice forms at night along the riverside.

I meet Goodwin paddling up the still, dark river on his first voyage to Fair Haven for the season, looking for muskrats and from time to time picking driftwood — logs and boards, etc. — out of the water and laying it up to dry on the bank, to eke out his wood-pile with. He says that the frost is not out so that he can lay wall, and so he thought he ['d] go and see what there was at Fair Haven. Says that when you hear a woodpecker's *rat-tat-tat-tat-tat* on a dead tree it is a sign of rain. While Emerson sits writing [in] his study this still, overcast, moist day, Goodwin is paddling up the still, dark river. Emerson burns twenty-five cords of wood and fourteen (?) tons of coal; Goodwin perhaps a cord and a half, much of which he picks out of the river. He says he 'd rather have a boat leak some for fishing. I hear the report of his gun from time to time for an hour, heralding the death of a muskrat and reverberating far down the river.

Goodwin had just seen Melvin disappearing up the North River, and I turn up thither after him. The

ice-belt still clings to the bank on each side, a foot or more above the water, and is now fringed with icicles of various lengths, only an inch or two apart, where it is melting by day and dripping into the river. Being distinctly reflected, you think you see two, two feet apart, the water-line not being seen.

I land and walk half-way up the hill. A red squirrel runs nimbly before me along the wall, his tail in the air at a right angle with his body; leaps into a walnut and winds up his clock.

The reindeer lichens on the pitch pine plain are moist and flaccid. I hear the faint fine notes of apparent nuthatches coursing up the pitch pines, a pair of them, one answering to the other, as it were like a vibrating watch-spring. Then, at a distance, that *whar-whar-whar-whar-whar-whar*, which after all I suspect may be the note of the nuthatch and not a woodpecker. And now from far southward coming on through the air, the chattering of blackbirds, — probably red-wings, for I hear an imperfect *conqueree*. Also I hear the *chill-lill* or *tchit-a-tchit* of the slate-colored sparrow, and see it.

On the pitch pine plain, nearly the whole of a small turtle's egg, by the side of its excavated nest.

Save with my boat the dead top of (apparently) a pine, divested of its bark and bleached. Before the bark fell off it was curiously etched by worms in variously curved lines and half-circles, often with regular short recurving branches, thus:

Père Buteux, going on commission to the Attikamègues in 1651, describes a fall away up there, where a river falls into a sort of trough or cradle a hundred paces long. "In this cradle the river boils (*bouillonne*) in such a fashion, that if you cast a stick (*baston*) into it, it remains some time without appearing, then all at once it elevates itself (*il s'élève en haut*) to the height of two pikes, at forty or fifty paces from the place where you cast it in."

It is to be observed that in the old deed of the Hunt farm, written in 1701, though the whole, consisting of something more than one hundred and fifty acres, is minutely described in thirteen different pieces, no part is described as woodland or wood-lot, only one piece as *partly unimproved*. This shows how little account was made of wood. Mr. Nathan Brooks reminds me that not till recently, *i. e.* not till within forty years, have wood-lots begun to be taxed for anything like their full value.

March 19. Heavy rain in the night and to-day, *i. e.* A. M. This, as usual, rapidly settles the ways, for, taking the frost out, the water that stood on the surface is soaked up, so that it is even drier and better walking before this heavy rain is over than it was yesterday before it began. It is April weather. I observed yesterday a dead shiner by the riverside, and to-day the first sucker.

March 20. Dine with Agassiz at R. W. E.'s. He thinks that the suckers die of asphyxia, having very large air-bladders and being in the habit of coming to the surface for air. But then, he is thinking of a

different phenomenon from the one I speak of, which last is confined to the very earliest spring or winter. He says that the *Emys picta* does not copulate till seven years old, and then does not lay till four years after copulation, or when eleven years old. The *Cistuda Blandingii* (which he has heard of in Massachusetts only at Lancaster) copulates at eight or nine years of age. He says this is not a *Cistuda* but an *Emys*. He has eggs of the *serpentina* from which the young did not come forth till the next spring. He thinks that the Esquimau dog is the only indigenous one in the United States. He had not observed the silvery appearance and the dryness of the lycoperdon fungus in water which I showed. He had broken caterpillars and found the crystals of ice in them, but had not thawed them. When I began to tell him of my experiment on a frozen fish, he said that Pallas had shown that fishes were frozen and thawed again, but I affirmed the contrary, and then Agassiz agreed with me. Says Aristotle describes the care the pouts take of their young. I told him of Tanner's account of it, the only one I had seen.

The river over the meadows again, nearly as high as in February, on account of rain of the 19th.

March 24. P. M. — Paddle up Assabet.
The water is fast going down. See a small water-bug. It is pretty still and warm. As I round the Island rock, a striped squirrel that was out [on] the steep polypody rock scampered up with a chuckle. On looking close, I see the crimson white maple stigmas [1] here

[1] *Vide* 27th.

and there, and some early alder catkins are relaxed and extended and almost shed pollen. I see many of those narrow four-winged insects (perla?) of the ice now fluttering on the water like ephemeræ. They have two pairs of wings indistinctly spotted dark and light.

Humphrey Buttrick says he saw two or three fish hawks down the river by Carlisle Bridge yesterday; also shot three black ducks and two green-winged teal, — though the latter had no green on their wings, it was rather the color of his boat, but Wesson assured him that so they looked in the spring. Buttrick had a double-barrelled gun with him, which he said he bought of a broker in Boston for five dollars! Thought it had cost eighteen dollars. He had read Frank Forester and believed him, and accordingly sent to New York and got one of Mullin's guns for sixty dollars. It was the poorest gun he ever had. He sold it for forty. As for cheap or old-fashioned guns bursting, there was Melvin; he had used his long enough, and it had not burst yet. He had given thirty-five dollars for it, say thirty years ago. Had had but one, or no other since.

If you are describing any occurrence, or a man, make two or more distinct reports at different times. Though you may think you have said all, you will to-morrow remember a whole new class of facts which perhaps interested most of all at the time, but did not present themselves to be reported. If we have recently met and talked with a man, and would report our experience, we commonly make a very partial report at first, failing to seize the most significant, picturesque, and dramatic points; we describe only what we have had time to

digest and dispose of in our minds, without being conscious that there were other things really more novel and interesting to us, which will not fail to recur to us and impress us suitably at last. How little that occurs to us in any way are we prepared at once to appreciate! We discriminate at first only a few features, and we need to reconsider our experience from many points of view and in various moods, to preserve the whole fruit of it.

Melvin's — and Minott's still more — is such a gun as Frank Forester says he would not fire for a hundred dollars, and yet Melvin has grown gray with using it; *i. e.*, he thinks that it would not be safe to fire a two-barrelled gun offered *new* for less than fifty dollars.

March 26. P. M. — To Walden and Fair Haven.
Though there has been quite a number of light snows, we have had no sleighing fairly since about February 14th. Walden is already on the point of breaking up. In the shallow bays it is melted six or eight rods out, and the ice looks dark and soft.

As I go through the woods by Andromeda Ponds, though it is rather cool and windy in exposed places, I hear a faint, stertorous croak from a frog in the open swamp; at first one faint note only, which I could not be sure that I had heard, but, after listening long, one or two more suddenly croaked in confirmation of my faith, and all was silent again. When first in the spring, as you walk over the rustling leaves amid bare and ragged bushes, you hear this at first faint, hard, dry, and short sound, it hardly sounds like the note of an

animal. It may have been heard some days.[1] I lay
down on the fine, dry sedge in the sun, in the deep and
sheltered hollow a little further on, and when I had
lain there ten or fifteen minutes, I heard one fine, faint
peep from over the windy ridge between the hollow in
which I lay and the swamp, which at first I referred to
a bird, and looked round at the bushes which crowned
the brim of this hollow to find it, but ere long a regularly but faintly repeated *phe-phe-phe-phe* revealed the
Hylodes Pickeringii. It was like the light reflected
from the mountain-ridges within the shaded portions
of the moon, — forerunner and herald of the spring.

At Well Meadow Head, am surprised to find the
skunk-cabbage in flower, though the flower is very
little exposed yet, and some still earlier have been
killed by frost. Some of those cabbage buds are
curved and short like the beak of a bird. The buds of
the cowslip are very yellow, and the plant is not observed a rod off, it lies so low and close to the surface
of the water in the meadow. It may bloom and wither
there several times before villagers discover or suspect
it. The chrysosplenium is very conspicuous and pretty
now. This can afford to be forward, it lies so flat and
unexposed.

Fair Haven is open; may have been open several
days; there is only a little ice on the southeast shore.
I sit on the high eastern bank. Almost every cistus
stem has had its bark burst off and left hanging rag-
gedly for an inch or more next the ground by the crystals

[1] The next day at 2.30 P. M., or about the same time, and about
the same weather, our thermometer is at 48°.

Vol. IX

It is surprising always to see this on dry plains or banks
where there is so little evidence of life beside.

Farrar spoke of horses driven "tantrum."

You take your walk some pretty cold and windy, but
sunny March day, through rustling woods, perhaps, glad
to take shelter in the hollows or on the south side
of the hills or woods. When ensconced in some sunny
and sheltered hollow, with some just melted pool at
its bottom, as you recline on the fine withered sedge,
in which the mice have had their galleries, leaving
it pierced with countless holes, and are, perchance,
dreaming of spring there, a single dry, hard croak, like
a grating twig, comes up from the pool. Such is the
earliest voice of the pools, where there is a small smooth
surface of melted ice bathing the bare button-bushes or
water andromeda or tufts of sedge; such is the earliest
voice of the liquid pools, hard and dry and grating.
Unless you watch long and closely, not a ripple nor a
bubble will be seen, and a marsh hawk will have to
look sharp to find one. The notes of the croaking frog
and the hylodes are not only contemporary with, but
analogous to, the blossoms of the skunk-cabbage and
white maple.

Are not March and November *gray* months?

Men will hardly believe me when I tell them of the
thickness of snow and ice at this time last year.

March 27. There is no snow now visible from my
window except on the heel of a bank in the swallow-
hole behind Dennis's. A sunny day, but rather cold
air.

which formed round it in the fall and winter, but some
have escaped.

As I come out of the Spring Woods I see Abiel
Wheeler planting peas and covering them up on his
warm sandy hillside, in the hollow next the woods. It
is a novel sight, that of the farmer distributing manure
with a shovel in the fields and planting again. The
earth looks warm and genial again. The sight of the
earliest planting with carts in the field so lately occupied with snow is suggestive of the genialness of Nature.
I could almost lie down in the furrow and be warmed
into her life and growth.

Stopped at Farrar's little stithy. He is making two
nuts to mend a mop with, and when at length he has
forged and filed them and cut the thread, he remarks
that it is a puttering job and worth a good deal more
than he can charge. He has sickness in the house, a
daughter in consumption, which he says is a flattering
disease, up one day and down the next. Seeing a
monstrous horseshoe nailed against his shop inside,
with a little one within it, I asked what that was for.
He said that he made the big one when he was an
apprentice (of three months' standing) for a sign, and
he picked up the little one the other day in the road and
put it within it for the contrast. But he thought that
the big one was hardly too big for one of the fore feet
of the horse Columbus, which he had seen.

The first croaking frogs, the hyla, the white maple
blossoms, the skunk-cabbage, and the alder's catkins
are observed about the same time.

I saw one hazel catkin much elongated and relaxed

8.30 A. M. — Up Assabet in boat.

At last I push myself gently through the smooth and
sunny water, sheltered by the Island woods and hill,
where I listen for birds, etc. There I may expect to
hear a woodpecker tapping the rotten aspen tree. There
I pause to hear the faint voice of some early bird amid
the twigs of the still wood-side. You are pretty sure to
hear a woodpecker early in the morning over these still
waters. But now chiefly there comes borne on the
breeze the tinkle of the song sparrow along the riverside, and I push out into wind and current. Leave the
boat and run down to the white maples by the bridge.
The white maple is well out with its pale [?] stamens
on the southward boughs, and probably began about the
24th. That would be about fifteen days earlier than
last year.

I find a very regular elliptical rolled stone in the
freshly (last fall) plowed low ground there, evidently
brought from some pond or seaside. It is about seven
inches long. The Indians prized such a stone, and
have found many of them where they haunted. Commonly one or both ends will be worn, showing that they
have used it as a pestle or hammer.

As I go up the Assabet, I see two *Emys insculpta*
on the bank in the sun, and one *picta.* They are all
rather sluggish, and I can paddle up and take them
up.

Found on the edge of Dodge's Brook, about midway
in the cedar field, what I did not hesitate to regard as an
Emys insculpta, but thickly spotted with rusty-yellowish
spots on the scales above, and the back was singularly

depressed. Was it a variety? It looked like a very old turtle, though not unusually large; the shell worn pretty smooth beneath. I could count more than thirty striæ above. When it dropped into the brook, I saw that the rusty-yellow spots served admirably to conceal it, for while the shell was bronze-colored (for a ground-work), the rusty-yellow spots were the color of the sandy and pebbly bottom of the brook. It was very differently shaped from the shell I have, and Storer does not mention yellow spots. Heard a lark in that meadow. Twitters over it on quivering wing and awakes the slumbering life of the meadow. The turtle and frog peep stealthily out and see the first lark go over.

Farmer was plowing a level pasture, unplowed for fourteen years, but in some places the frost was not quite out. Farmer says that he heard geese go over two or three nights ago.

I would fain make two reports in my Journal, first the incidents and observations of to-day; and by to-morrow I review the same and record what was omitted before, which will often be the most significant and poetic part. I do not know at first what it is that charms me. The men and things of to-day are wont to lie fairer and truer in to-morrow's memory.

I saw quail-tracks some two months ago, much like smaller partridge-tracks.

Farmer describes a singular track in the snow the past winter from near his house to Annursnack. Traced it in all five or six miles to a hemlock on the west side, and there he lost it. It travelled like a mink; made a track with all its four feet together, about as big as that of a horse's foot, eighteen inches apart more or less. Wondered if it was a pine marten.

Men talk to me about society as if I had none and they had some, as if it were only to be got by going to the sociable or to Boston.

Compliments and flattery oftenest excite my contempt by the pretension they imply, for who is he that assumes to flatter me? To compliment often implies an assumption of superiority in the complimenter. It is, in fact, a subtle detraction.

Pickerel begin to dart in shallows.

March 28. 8.30 A. M. — Up river to Fair Haven by boat.

A pleasant morning; the song of the earliest birds, *i. e.* tree sparrows, (now decidedly) and song sparrows and bluebirds, in the air. A red-wing's gurgle from a willow.

The *Emys picta*, now pretty numerous, when young and fresh, with smooth black scales without moss or other imperfection, unworn, and with claws perfectly sharp, is very handsome. When the scales are of this clear, though dull, black, the six middle ones, counting from side to side, are edged forward with broad dull greenish-yellow borders, the others with a narrow whitish border, and the singular vermilion and yellow marks of the marginal scales extend often on to the lateral scales. The concentric lines of growth are indistinguishable. The fore and hind legs and tail are slashed or streaked horizontally with broad clear vermilion and also a fine yellow line or two, answering to

Vol. IX

those on the hinge scales continued, showing the tenant to be one with the house he occupies. He who painted the tortoise thus, what were his designs? Beneath it is a clear buff.

At Lee's Cliff and this side, I see half a dozen buff-edged butterflies (*Vanessa Antiopa*) and pick up three dead or dying, two together, the edges of their wings gone. Several are fluttering over the dry rock débris under the cliff, in whose crevices probably they have wintered. Two of the three I pick up are not dead, though they will not fly. Verily their day is a short one. What has checked their frail life? Within, the buff edge is black with bright sky-blue spots, and the main part within is a purplish brown. Those little oblong spots on the black ground are light as you look directly down on them, but from one side they vary through violet to a crystalline rose-purple.

I can remember now some thirty years — after a fashion — of life in Concord, and every spring there are many dead suckers floating belly upward on the meadows. This phenomenon of dead suckers is as constant as the phenomenon of living ones; nay, as a phenomenon it is far more apparent.

Farmer thinks pickerel may have been frozen through half a day and yet come to. Instances pickerel he caught a very cold day on Bateman's Pond, which he brought home frozen and put in a pail of water in his cellar and after found them alive. A Mr. Parkhurst of Carlisle assures him that though minnows put into a half-hogshead of water will die in forty-eight hours unless you change the water, if you put with it a piece of granite a foot square they will live all winter, and that he keeps his minnows in this way.

A pleasing sight this of the earlier painted tortoises which are seen along the edge of the flooded meadows, often three or four suddenly dimpling the smooth surface of a ditch, which had been sunning on a tussock, sluggish moving flakes of clear black. Soon they rise again and put their heads out warily, looking about and showing the yellow stripes on their necks. They seem to feel the very jar of the ground as you approach. They rest with their shells at an angle in the water, their heads out and their feet outstretched, or partly bury themselves in the grassy bottom. Often hindered by the bushes, between which their shells are caught. Poking their heads through, they are impeded by their shells. The very earliest I see moving along the bottom on the meadows, but soon after they begin to lie out in the sun on the banks and tussocks as I have mentioned.

The *Emys guttata* is found in brooks and ditches. I passed three to-day, lying cunningly quite motionless, with heads and feet drawn in, on the bank of a little grassy ditch, close to a stump, in the sun, on the russet flattened grass, like snails, or rather scales, under which some insects might lurk, with their high-arched backs. When out of water they are the less exposed to observation by their shells drying and their spots being dimmed.

Do I ever see a yellow-spot turtle in the river? Do I ever see a wood tortoise in the South Branch?

There is consolation in the fact that a particular evil, which perhaps we suffer, is of a venerable antiquity, for it proves its necessity and that it is part of the *order*, not disorder, of the universe. When I realize that the mortality of suckers in the spring is as old a phenomenon, perchance, as the race of suckers itself, I contemplate it with serenity and joy even, as one of the signs of spring. Thus they have fallen on fate. And so, many a fisherman is not seen on the shore who the last spring did not fail here.

Flood tells me to-day that he finds no frost to trouble him in Monroe's garden. He can put his spade or fork in anywhere.

Chestnut, evidently because it is packed as in a little *chest*.

The maple sap has been flowing well for two or three weeks.

When I witness the first plowing and planting, I acquire a long-lost confidence in the earth, — that it will nourish the seed that is committed to its bosom. I am surprised to be reminded that there is warmth in it. We have not only warmer skies, then, but a warmer earth. The frost is out of it, and we may safely commit these seeds to it in some places. Yesterday I walked with Farmer beside his team and saw one furrow turned quite round his field. What noble work is plowing, with the broad and solid earth for material, the ox for fellow-laborer, and the simple but efficient plow for tool! Work that is not done in any shop, in a cramped position, work that tells, that concerns all men, which the sun shines and the rain falls on, and the birds sing over! You turn over the whole vegetable mould, expose how many grubs, and put a new aspect on the face of the

Vol. IX

earth. It comes pretty near to making a world. Redeeming a swamp does, at any rate. A good plowman is a *terrae filius*. The plowman, we all know, whistles as he drives his team afield.

The broad buff edge of the *Vanessa Antiopa's* wings harmonizes with the russet ground it flutters over, and as it stands concealed in the winter, with its wings folded above its back, in a cleft in the rocks, the gray-brown under side of its wings prevents its being distinguished from the rocks themselves.

Often I can give the truest and most interesting account of any adventure I have had after years have elapsed, for then I am not confused, only the most significant facts surviving in my memory. Indeed, all that continues to interest me after such a lapse of time is sure to be pertinent, and I may safely record all that I remember.

Farmer tells me that his bees are killing one another nowadays,[1] *i. e.* as he supposes: and he is probably right; the workers are killing the drones.

March 29. P. M. — To Walden and river.

Walden open, say to-day, though there is still a little ice in the deep southern bay and a very narrow edging along the southern shore.

Cross through the woods to my boat under Fair Haven Hill. How empty and silent the woods now, before leaves have put forth or thrushes and warblers are come! Deserted halls, floored with dry leaves, where scarcely an insect stirs as yet.

[1] Probably a mistake.

Taking an average of eight winters, it appears that Walden is frozen about ninety-eight days in the year.

When I have put my boat in its harbor, I hear that sign-squeaking blackbird, and, looking up, see half a dozen on the top of the elm at the foot of Whiting's lot. They are not red-wings, and by their size they make me think of crow blackbirds, yet on the whole I think them grackles (?).[1] *Possibly* those I heard on the 18th were the same?? Does the red-wing ever make a noise like a rusty sign?

March 31. A very pleasant day. Spent a part of it in the garden preparing to set out fruit trees. It is agreeable once more to put a spade into the warm mould. The victory is ours at last, for we remain and take possession of the field. In this climate, in which we do not commonly bury our dead in the winter on account of the frozen ground, and find ourselves exposed on a hard bleak crust, the coming out of the frost and the first turning up of the soil with a spade or plow is an event of importance.

P. M. — To Hill.

As I rise the east side of the Hill, I hear the distant faint peep of hylodes and the *tut tut* of croaking frogs from the west of the Hill. How gradually and imperceptibly the peep of the hylodes mingles with and swells the volume of sound which makes the voice of awakening nature! If you do not listen carefully for its first note, you probably will not hear it, and, not having heard that, your ears become used to the sound,

[1] *Vide* Apr. 1st.

so that you will hardly notice it at last, however loud and universal. I hear it now faintly from through and over the bare gray twigs and the sheeny needles of an oak and pine wood and from over the russet fields beyond, and it is so intimately mingled with the murmur or roar of the wind as to be well-nigh inseparable from it. It leaves such a lasting trace on the ear's memory that often I think I hear their peeping when I do not. It is a singularly emphatic and ear-piercing proclamation of animal life, when with a very few and slight exceptions vegetation is yet dormant. The dry croaking and *tut tut* of the frogs (a sound which ducks seem to imitate, a kind of *quacking*, — and they are both of the water!) is plainly enough down there in some pool in the woods, but the shrill peeping of the hylodes locates itself nowhere in particular, but seems to take its rise at an indefinite distance over wood and hill and pasture, from clefts or hollows in the March wind. It is a wind-born sound.[1]

To-day both croakers and peepers are pretty numerously heard, and I hear one *faint stertorous* (bullfrog-like??) sound on the river meadow.

What an important part to us the little peeping hylodes acts, filling all our ears with sound in the spring afternoons and evenings, while the existence of the otter, our largest wild animal, is not betrayed to any of our senses (or at least not to more than one in a thousand)!

The voice of the peepers is not so much of the earth earthy as of the air airy. It rises at once on the wind

[1] This must be the *Rana halecina*. *Vide* Apr. 3d, 1858.

and is at home there, and we are incapable of tracing it further back.

The earliest gooseberry in the garden begins to show a little green near at hand.

An Irishman is digging a ditch for a foundation wall to a new shop where James Adams's shop stood. He tells me that he dug up three cannon-balls just in the rear of the shop lying within a foot of each other and about eighteen inches beneath the surface. I saw one of them, which was about three and a half inches in diameter and somewhat eaten with rust on one side. These were probably thrown into the pond by the British on the 19th of April, 1775. Shattuck says that five hundred pounds of balls were thrown into the pond and wells. These may have been dropped out the back window.

The tortoises now quite commonly lie out sunning on the sedge or the bank. As you float gently down the stream, you hear a slight rustling and, looking up, see the dark shining back of a *picta* sliding off some little bed of straw-colored coarse sedge which is upheld by the button-bushes or willows above the surrounding water. They are very wary and, as I go up the Assabet, will come rolling and sliding down a rod or two, though they appear to have but just climbed up to that height.

IX

APRIL, 1857

(ÆT. 39)

April 1. 8 A. M. — Up Assabet.

See an *Emys guttata* sunning on the bank. I had forgotten whether I ever saw it in this river. Hear a phœbe, and this morning the tree sparrows sing very sweetly about Keyes's arbor-vitæ and Cheney's pines and apple trees. Crow blackbirds. I think it must have been these I saw the 29th of March. Checker-berries very fair and abundant now near Muhlenbergii Brook, contrasting with the red-brown leaves. They are not commonly touched by the frost. I see children picking spring cranberries in the meadows. It is a true April evening, feeling and looking as if it would [rain], and already I hear a robin or two singing their evening song.

April 2. Go to New Bedford.

A great change in the weather. I set out apple trees yesterday, but in the night it was very cold, with snow, which is now several inches deep. On the sidewalk in Cambridge I see a toad, which apparently hopped out from under a fence last evening, frozen quite hard in a sitting posture. Carried it into Boston in my pocket, but could not thaw it into life.

The other day as I came to the front of the house I

caught sight of a genuine wayfaring man, an oldish countryman, with a frock and a bundle strapped to his back, who was speaking to the butcher, just then driving off in his cart. He was a gaunt man with a flashing eye, as if half crazy with travel, and was complaining, "You see it shakes me so, I would rather travel the common road." I supposed that he referred to the railroad, which the butcher had recommended for shortness. I was touched with compassion on observing the butcher's apparent indifference, as, jumping to his seat, he drove away before the traveller had finished his sentence, and the latter fell at once into the regular wayfarer's gait, bending under his pack and holding the middle of the road with a teetering gait.

On my way to New Bedford, see within a couple of rods of the railroad, in some country town, a boy's box trap set for some muskrat or mink by the side of a little pond. The lid was raised, and I could see the bait on its point.

A black snake was seen yesterday in the Quaker burying-ground here.

April 3. In Ricketson's shanty. R. has seen white-bellied swallows more than a week. I walk down the side of the river and see Walton's ice-boat left on the bank.

Hear R. describing to Alcott his bachelor uncle James Thornton. When he awakes in the morning he lights the fire in his stove (all prepared) with a match on the end of a stick, without getting up. When he gets up he first attends to his ablutions, being personally

very clean, cuts off a head of tobacco to clean his teeth with, eats a hearty breakfast, sometimes, it was said, even buttering his sausages. Then he goes to a relative's store and reads the *Tribune* till dinner, sitting in a corner with his back to those who enter. Goes to his boarding-house and dines, eats an apple or two, and then in the afternoon frequently goes about the solution of some mathematical problem (having once been a schoolmaster), which often employs him a week.[1]

April 4. Saturday. Walk down the shore of the river. A Dutchman pushes out in his skiff after qua-hogs. He also took his eel-spear, thinking to try for eels if he could not get quahogs, for, owing to the late cold weather, they might still be buried in the mud. I saw him raking up the quahogs on the flats at high (?) tide, in two or three feet of water. He used a sort of coarse, long-pronged hoe. Keeps anchoring on the flats and searches for a clam on the bottom with his eye, then rakes it up and picks it off his rake.

Am not sure what kind of large gulls I see there, some more white, some darker, methinks, than the herring gull.

R. tells me that he found dead in his piazza the south side of his house, the 23d of last January, the snow being very deep and the thermometer − 12° at sunrise, a warbler, which he sent to Brewer. I read Brewer's note to him, in which he said that he took it to be the *Sylvicola coronata* and would give it to the Natural

___

[1] [*Daniel Ricketson and his Friends*, p. 350.]

History Society, thinking it remarkable that it was found at that time. B. says that he discovered "for the first time its nest in the heart of Nova Scotia near Parrsboro mountains [I think last season].[1] It was the only *new* egg of that trip. Yet I felt well repaid, for 'no other white man had ever before seen that egg to know it,' as Audubon says of another species."

Caught a croaking frog in some smooth water in the railroad gutter. Above it was a uniform (perhaps olive?) brown, without green, and a yellowish line along the edge of the lower jaws. It was, methinks, larger than a common *Rana palustris*. Near by was its spawn, in very handsome spherical masses of transparent jelly, two and a half to three inches in diameter, suspended near the surface of some weed, as goldenrod or aster, and consisting of globules about a third of an inch in diameter, with a black or dark centre as big as a large shot. Only these black centres were visible at a little distance in the water, and so much the more surprising and interesting is the translucent jelly when you lift it to the light. It even suggested the addition of cream and sugar, for the table. Yet this pool must have been frozen over last night! What frog can it be?[2]

April 5. Sunday. Arthur R. has been decking a new Vineyard boat which he has bought, and making a curb about the open part.

P. M. — Walked round by the ruins of the factory. See in many places the withered leaves of the aletris in

---

[1] [The brackets are Thoreau's.]
[2] *Vide* Apr. 4th, 1857. *R. sylvatica.*

rather low ground, about the still standing withered stems. It was well called husk-root by the squaw.

Arthur says that he just counted, at 9.30 p. m., twenty toads that had hopped out from under the wall on to the sidewalk near the house. This, then, is apparently the way with the toads. They very early hop out from under walls on to sidewalks in the warmer nights, long before they are heard to ring, and are often frozen and then crushed there. Probably single ones ring earlier than I supposed. I hear the croaking frogs at 9.30 p. m., also the *speed speed* over R.'s meadow, which I once referred to the snipe, but R. says is the woodcock, whose other strain he has already heard.

April 6. P. M. — To New Bedford Library.

Mr. Ingraham, the librarian, says that he once saw frog-spawn in New Bedford the 4th of March. Take out Emmons's Report on the insects injurious to vegetation in New York. See a plate of the *Colias Philodice*, or common sulphur-yellow butterfly, male and female of different tinge. *Areoda lanigera* is apparently the common yellow dor-bug. Arthur has *Tabanus*, the great horse-fly. Emmons says of *Scutelleridæ:* "The disagreeable smelling bugs that frequent berry bushes and strawberry vines belong here. . . . Of this family the genus Pentatoma is one of the most common and feeds upon the juice of plants. Sometimes it has only to pass over a fruit, to impart to it its offensive odor." The one represented looks like the huckleberry one.

April 7. Tuesday. Went to walk in the woods. When I had got half a mile or more away in the woods alone, and was sitting on a rock, was surprised to be joined by R.'s large Newfoundland dog Ranger, who had smelled me out and so tracked me. Would that I could add his woodcraft to my own! He would trot along before me as far as the winding wood-path allowed me to see him, and then, with the shortest possible glance over his shoulder, ascertain if I was following. At a fork in the road he would pause, look back at me, and deliberate which course I would take.

At sundown I went out to gather bayberries to make tallow of. Holding a basket beneath, I rubbed them off into it between my hands, and so got about a quart, to which were added enough to make about three pints. They are interesting little gray berries clustered close about the short bare twigs, just below the last year's growth. The berries have little prominences, like those of an orange, encased with tallow, the tallow also filling the interstices, down to the nut.

They require a great deal of boiling to get out all the tallow. The outmost case soon melted off, but the inmost part I did not get even after many hours of boiling. The oily part rose to the top, making it look like a savory black broth, which smelled just like balm or other herb tea. I got about a quarter of a pound by weight from these say three pints of berries, and more yet remained. Boil a great while, let it cool, then skim off the tallow from the surface; melt again and strain it. What I got was more yellow than what I have seen in the shops. A small portion cooled in the form

of small corns (nuggets I called them when I picked them out from amid the berries), flat hemispherical, of a very pure lemon yellow, and these needed no straining. The berries were left black and massed together by the remaining tallow.[1]

Cat-briar (*Smilax*) they call here "the devil's wrapping yarn." I see several emperor moth cocoons, with small eggs on the back, apparently of the ichneumon-fly, that has destroyed the nymph.

April 8. I discovered one convenient use the bayberries served, — that if you got your hands pitched in pine woods, you had only to rub a parcel of these berries between your hands to start the pitch off. Arthur said the shoemakers at the Head of the River used the tallow to rub the soles of their shoes with to make them shine. I gathered a quart in about twenty minutes with my hands. You might gather them much faster with a suitable rake and a large shallow basket, or if one were clearing a field he could cut the bushes and thresh them in a heap.

April 9. Thursday. A. M. — To the cove south of the town.

See them haul two seines. They caught chiefly alewives, from sixty to a hundred at a haul, seine twelve to fifteen feet wide. There were also caught with the alewives, skates, two or three "drums" (like flatfish, only the mouth twisted the other way and not good), flatfish, smelts, sculpins, five-fingers, and a lobster with

---

[1] [*Cape Cod*, p. 103; Riv. 121, 122.]

red claws. This was what the seine would catch in making a large circuit. It seemed to be pretty hard work hauling it in, employing two or three men or boys at each end. A fisherman said that they caught the first alewife the 28th of March there.

Picked up many handsome scallop shells beyond the ice-houses, with wormy-shaped parasites on them.

April 10. *Friday.* Rain.

D. R.'s shanty is about half a dozen rods southwest of his house (which may be forty rods from the road), nearly between his house and barn; is twelve by fourteen feet, with seven-feet posts, with common pent-roof. In building it, he directed the carpenter to use Western boards and timber, though some Eastern studs (spruce?) were inserted. He had already occupied a smaller shanty at "Woodlee" about a mile south. The roof is shingled and the sides made of matched boards and painted a light clay-color with chocolate(?)-colored blinds. Within, it is not plastered and is open to the roof, showing the timbers and rafters and rough boards and cross-timbers overhead as if ready for plastering. The door is at the east end with a small window on each side of it; a similar window on each side the building, and one at the west end, the latter looking down the garden walk. In front of the last window is a small box stove with a funnel rising to a level with the plate, and there inserted in a small brick chimney which rests on planks. On the south side the room, against the stove, is a rude settle with a coarse cushion and pillow; on the opposite side, a large low

desk, with some book-shelves above it; on the same side, by the window, a small table covered with books; and in the northeast corner, behind the door, an old-fashioned secretary, its pigeonholes stuffed with papers. On the opposite side as you enter, is place for fuel, which the boy leaves each morning, a place to hang greatcoats. There were two small pieces of carpet on the floor, and Ricketson or one of his guests swept out the shanty each morning. There was a small kitchen clock hanging in the southwest corner and a map of Bristol County behind the settle.

The west and northwest side is well-nigh covered with slips of paper, on which are written some sentence or paragraph from R.'s favorite books. I noticed, among the most characteristic, Dibdin's "Tom Tackle," a translation of Anacreon's "Cicada," lines celebrating tobacco, Milton's "How charming is divine philosophy," etc., "Inveni requiem: Spes et Fortuna valete. Nil mihi vobiscum est: ludite nunc alios" (is it Petrarch?) (this is also over the door), "Mors aequo pulsat," etc., some lines of his own in memory of A. J. Downing, "Not to be in a hurry," over the desk, and many other quotations celebrating retirement, country life, simplicity, humanity, sincerity, etc., etc., from Cowper and other English poets, and similar extracts from newspapers. There were also two or three advertisements, — one of a cattle-show exhibition, another warning not to kill birds contrary to law (he being one of the subscribers ready to enforce the act), advertisement of a steamboat on Lake Winnepiseogee, etc., cards of his business friends. The size of different

brains from *Hall's Journal of Health,* and "Take the world easy." A sheet of blotted blotting-paper tacked up, and of Chinese character from a tea-chest. Also a few small pictures and pencil sketches, the latter commonly caricatures of his visitors or friends, as "The Trojan" (Channing) and "Van Best." I take the more notice of these particulars because his peculiarities are so commonly unaffected. He has long been accustomed to put these scraps on his walls and has a basketful somewhere, saved from the old shanty. Though there were some quotations which had no right there, I found all his peculiarities faithfully expressed, — his humanity, his fear of death, love of retirement, simplicity, etc.

The more characteristic books were Bordley's "Husbandry," Drake's "Indians," Barber's "Historical Collections," Zimmermann on Solitude, Bigelow's "Plants of Boston, etc.," Farmer's "Register of the First Settlers of New England," Marshall's "Gardening," Nicol's "Gardener," John Woolman, "The Modern Horse Doctor," Downing's "Fruits, etc.," "The Farmer's Library," "Walden," Dymond's Essays, Job Scott's Journal, Morton's Memorial, Bailey's Dictionary, Downing's "Landscape Gardening, etc.," "The Task," Nuttall's Ornithology, Morse's Gazetteer, "The Domestic Practice of Hydropathy," "John Buncle," Dwight's Travels, Virgil, Young's "Night Thoughts," "History of Plymouth," and other "*Shanty Books.*"

There was an old gun, hardly safe to fire, said to be loaded with an inextractable charge, and also an old sword over the door, also a tin sign "D. Ricketson's

Office" (he having set up for a lawyer once) and a small crumpled horn there. I counted more than twenty rustic canes scattered about, a dozen or fifteen pipes of various patterns, mostly the common, two spy-glasses, an open paper of tobacco, an Indian's jaw dug up, a stuffed blue jay and pine grosbeak, and a rude Indian stone hatchet, etc., etc. There was a box with fifteen or twenty knives, mostly very large and old-fashioned jack-knives, kept for curiosity, occasionally given away to a boy or friend. A large book full of pencil sketches to be inspected by whomsoever, containing countless sketches of his friends and acquaintances and himself and of wayfaring men whom he had met, Quakers, etc., etc., and now and then a vessel under full sail or an old-fashioned house, sketched on a peculiar pea-green paper. A pail of water stands behind the door, with a peculiar tin cup for drinking made in France.[1]

April 11. *Saturday.* 8 P. M. — Went to the Head of the River to see them catch smelts. The water there is fresh when the tide is out. They use nets five or six feet square, stretched from the ends of crossed semicircular hoops, at the ends of poles about twelve feet long. The net bags down when raised. There were twenty or thirty fishermen standing close together, half on each side of the narrow river, each managing one of these nets, while a good part of the village appeared to be collected on the bridge. The tide was then coming in, but the best time is when it is going out. A fisher-

[1] [*Daniel Ricketson and his Friends,* pp. 350–354.]

man told me that the smelt run up in the night only. These fishers stood just below a two-arched bridge. The tide was coming up between the arches, while the fresh water which the smelt preferred was running down next the shore on each side. The smelt were ascending in these streams of fresh water on each side. The shore for half a dozen rods on each side was lined with fishers, each wielding a single net. This man told me that the smelt had been running up about one month and were now about done. The herring had been seen for a fortnight. They will run this month and all the next. The former leave off when the latter begin. Shad have not been caught yet. They come after herring. Eels, too, are occasionally caught now, going up from the deeper river below. These fishes spawn in the little pond just above the bridge. They let the net rest on the bottom and every two or three minutes lift it up. They get thirty or many more smelt sometimes at one lift and catch other fish in the same way, even bass, sea perch, pickerel, eels, and sometimes a trout. The shad make a ripple like a harrow, and you know when to raise the net. The villagers were talking across the stream, calling each other by their Christian names. Even mothers mingled with the fishermen, looking for their children. It suggested how much we had lost out of Concord River without realizing it. This is the critical season of a river, when it is fullest of life, its flowering season, the wavelets or ripples on its surface answering to the scales of the fishes beneath.

I saw the herring on sticks at the doors of many shops in New Bedford.

Vol. IX

I saw the myrtle-bird here about a week ago.

If salmon, shad, and alewives were pressing up our river now, as formerly they were, a good part of the villagers would thus, no doubt, be drawn to the brink at this season. Many inhabitants of the neighborhood of the ponds in Lakeville, Freetown, Fairhaven, etc., have petitioned the legislature for permission to connect Little Quitticus Pond with the Acushnet River by digging, so that the herring can come up into it. The very fishes in countless schools are driven out of a river by the *improvements* of the civilized man, as the pigeon and other fowls out of the air. I can hardly imagine a greater change than this produced by the influence of man in nature. Our Concord River is a dead stream in more senses than we had supposed. In what sense now does the spring ever come to the river, when the sun is not reflected from the scales of a single salmon, shad, or alewife? No doubt there is *some* compensation for this loss, but I do not at this moment see clearly what it is. That river which the aboriginal and indigenous fishes have not deserted is a more primitive and interesting river to me. It is as if some vital quality were to be lost out of a man's blood and it were to circulate more lifelessly through his veins. We are reduced to a few migrating (?) suckers, perchance.

April 12. *Sunday.* I think I hear the bay-wing here.

April 13. *Monday.* To Middleborough ponds. There was no boat on Little Quitticus; so we could

not explore it. Set out to walk round it, but, the water being high, — higher than anciently even, on account of dams, — we had to go round a swamp at the south end, about Joe's Rocks, and R. gave it up. I went to Long Pond and waited for him. Saw a strange turtle, much like a small snapping turtle or very large *Sternothærus odoratus*, crawling slowly along the bottom next the shore. Poked it ashore with a stick. It had a peculiarly square snout, two hinges to the sternum and both parts movable. Was very sluggish; would not snap nor bite. Looked old, being mossy above on the edge, and the scales greenish and eaten beneath. The flesh slate-colored.[1]

[1] [The following (written on the back of a lottery circular!) is pasted into the Journal:]

The Freetown Turtle compared with Storer's *Sternothærus*.

Answers to the generic description, except perhaps that the posterior valve of the sternum is movable.

Compared with the *S. odoratus.*

There is no peculiar scent to it. The upper shell is flattened on the dorsal ridge for the width of the dorsal plates and is not carinated there. (I find one as flat, and others are not carinated.) Color out of water a dirty brown. The marginal plates are a little narrower.

The sternum (as well as that of my *S. odoratus*) is apparently composed of 11 instead of 9 plates, the anterior portion being composed of 5 instead of 3 plates. The posterior portion is distinctly movable, much more than the *odoratus*, and it is quite rounded on the sides.

Irides not distinct. It appears as if blind. No yellow lines whatever on the head or neck. Jaws not dark-brown, but bluish-slate, as is the skin generally.

My two *S. odoratus* are 3⅜ inches long by 2½ wide and 1½ inches high, being highest behind. The Freetown turtle is 4 inches long by 2¾ and 1⅝ high, being highest forward. It has much green moss (?) on the rear and marginal plates, and the scales of the sternum are

I saw that it was new and wished to bring it away, but had no paper to wrap it in. So I peeled a white birch, getting a piece of bark about ten inches long. I noticed that the birch sap was flowing. This bark at once curled back so as to present its yellow side outward. I rolled it about the turtle and folded the ends back and tied it round with a strip of birch bark, making a very nice and airy box for the creature, which would not be injured by moisture, far better than any paper, and so I brought it home to Concord at last. As my coat hung in R.'s shanty, over a barrel of paper, the morning that I came away the turtle made a little noise, scratching the birch bark in my pocket. R. observed, "There is a mouse in that barrel. What would you do about it?" "Oh, let him alone," said I, "he'll get out directly." "They often get among my papers," he added. "I guess I'd better set the barrel outdoors." I did not explain, and perhaps he experimented on the barrel after my departure.[1]

As I sat on the shore there, waiting for R., I saw many mosquitoes flying low over the water close to the sandy shore.

greenish and worn or carious. It is quite sluggish. Otherwise it apparently answers to Storer's *S. odoratus.*

Get a sternothærus May 13th within ¼ inch as long and about as flat above. *Vide* July 20th, 1857.

[1] [*Daniel Ricketson and his Friends*, pp. 354, 355. The editors insert the following note: —

"This might appear like a practical joke, but we are inclined to think it was out of consideration for Father's sensitiveness regarding all dumb animals that Mr. Thoreau kept him 'in the dark' as to his specimen, fearing he might be disturbed."]

The turtle when I first saw him was slowly and tremblingly pacing along the bottom, rather toward the shore, with its large head far out on its outstretched neck. From its *size* and general color and aspect, I did not doubt at first that it was a snapping turtle, notwithstanding the season.

April 14. Tuesday. Rains all day.

April 15. Wednesday. Leave New Bedford.

I had been surprised to find the season more backward, *i. e.* the vegetation, in New Bedford than in Concord. I could find no alder and willow and hazel catkins and no caltha and saxifrage so forward as in Concord. The ground was a uniform russet when I left, but when I had come twenty miles it was visibly greener, and the greenness steadily increased all the way to Boston. Coming to Boston, and also to Concord, was like coming from early spring to early summer. It was as if a fortnight at least had elapsed. Yet New Bedford is much warmer in the winter. Why is it more backward than Concord? The country is very flat and exposed to southerly winds from the sea, which, to my surprise, were raw and chilly. Also the soil is wet and cold, unlike our warm sandy soil, which is dry the day after a rainstorm. Perhaps, as the ground is more bare in the winter, vegetation suffers more after all. One told me that there was more cloudy weather than here. It seemed to me that there was a deficiency of warm hollows and sheltered places behind hills and woods, which abound with us. On such cliffs as they have facing the south, vege-

tation was much more backward than in like positions with us, apparently owing to sea-turns and chilly south winds.

April 16. At Concord.

Get birch sap, — two bottles yellow birch and five of black birch, — now running freely, though not before I left Concord. Meanwhile I hear the note of the pine warbler. Last night was very cold, and some ditches are frozen this morning. This is Fast-Day. I think if you should tap all the trees in a large birch swamp, you would make a stream large enough to turn a mill.

About a month ago, at the post-office, Abel Brooks, who is pretty deaf, sidling up to me, observed in a loud voice which all could hear, "Let me see, your society is pretty large, ain't it?" "Oh, yes, large enough," said I, not knowing what he meant. "There's Stewart belongs to it, and Collier, he's one of them, and Emerson, and my boarder" (Pulsifer), "and Channing, I believe, I think he goes there." "You mean the *walkers;* don't you?" "Ye-es, I call you the Society. All go to the woods; don't you?" "Do you miss any of your wood?" I asked. "No, I hain't worried any yet. I believe you're a pretty clever set, as good as the average," etc., etc.

Telling Sanborn of this, he said that, when he first came to town and boarded at Holbrook's, he asked H. how many religious societies there were in town. H. said that there were three, — the Unitarian, the Orthodox, and the Walden Pond Society. I asked Sanborn

with which Holbrook classed himself. He said he believes that he put himself with the last.

April 17. Rain. It rains about every other day now for a fortnight past.

April 18. P. M. — To Conantum.

Hear the huckleberry-bird, also the seringo. The beaked hazel, if that is one just below the little pine at Blackberry Steep, is considerably later than the common, for I cannot get a whole twig fully out, though the common is too far gone to gather there. The catkins, too, are shorter.

April 20. Arbor-vitæ apparently in full bloom.

April 21. Tuesday. Mr. Loomis writes me that he saw two barn swallows in Cambridge April 1st! I have the *Corema Conradii* from Plymouth, in bloom.

It snows hard all day. If it did not melt so fast, would be a foot deep. As it is, is about three inches on a level.

April 22. Wednesday. Fair again.
To Great Sudbury Meadow by boat.

The river higher than before and rising. C. and I sail rapidly before a strong northerly wind, — no need of rowing upward, only of steering, — cutting off great bends by crossing the meadows. We have to roll our boat over the road at the stone bridge, Hubbard's causeway, (to save the wind), and at Pole Brook (to save

distance). It is worth the while to hear the surging of the waves and their gurgling under the stern, and to feel the great billows toss us, with their foaming yellowish crests. The world is not aware what an extensive navigation is now possible on our overflowed fresh meadows. It is more interesting and fuller of life than the sea bays and permanent ponds. A dozen gulls are circling over Fair Haven Pond, some very white beneath, with very long, narrow-pointed, black-tipped wings, almost regular semicircles like the new moon. As they circle beneath a white scud in this bright air, they are almost invisible against it, they are so nearly the same color. What glorious fliers! But few birds are seen; only a crow or two teetering along the water's edge looking for its food, with its large, clumsy head, and on unusually long legs, as if stretched, or its pants pulled up to keep it from the wet, and now flapping off with some large morsel in its bill; or robins in the same place; or perhaps the sweet song of the tree sparrows from the alders by the shore, or of a song sparrow or blackbird. The phœbe is scarcely heard. Not a duck do we see! All the shores have the aspect of winter, covered several inches deep with snow, and we see the shadows on the snow as in winter; but it is strange to see the green grass burning up through in warmer nooks under the walls.

We pause or lay to from time to time, in some warm, smooth lee, under the southwest side of a wood or hill, as at Hubbard's Second Grove and opposite Weir Hill, pushing through saturated snow like ice on the surface of the water. There we lie awhile amid the bare alders, maples, and willows, in the sun, see the expanded sweet-gale and early willows and the budding swamp pyrus looking up drowned from beneath. As we lie in a broad field of meadow wrack, — floating cranberry leaves and finely bruised meadow-hay, — a wild medley. Countless spiders are hastening over the water. We pass a dozen boats sunk at their moorings, at least at one end, being moored too low.

Near Tall's Island, rescued a little pale or yellowish brown snake that was coiled round a willow half a dozen rods from the shore and was apparently chilled by the cold. Was it not Storer's "little brown snake?" It had a flat body. Frank Smith lives in a shanty on the hill near by.

At the Cliff Brook I see the skunk-cabbage leaves not yet unrolled, with their points gnawed off. Some very fresh brown fungi on an alder, tender and just formed one above another, flat side up, while those on the birch are white and flat side down. They soon dry white and hard. This melting snow makes a great crop of fungi.

Turritis stricta, nearly out (in two or three days).

Observed the peculiar dark lines on a birch (*Betula* 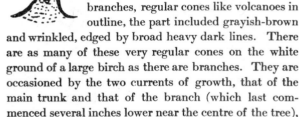 *populifolia*) at the insertion of the branches, regular cones like volcanoes in outline, the part included grayish-brown and wrinkled, edged by broad heavy dark lines. There are as many of these very regular cones on the white ground of a large birch as there are branches. They are occasioned by the two currents of growth, that of the main trunk and that of the branch (which last commenced several inches lower near the centre of the tree),

meeting and being rucked or turned up at the line of contact like a surge, exposing the edges of the inner bark there, decayed and dark, while the bark within the lines approaches the darker color of the limb. The larger were six or seven inches high by as much in width at the bottom. You observe the same manner of growth in other trees. That portion of the bark below the limb obeys the influence of the limb and endeavors to circle about it, but soon encounters the growth of the main stem. There are interesting figures on the stem of a large white birch, arranged spirally about it.

The river has risen several inches since morning, so that we push over Hubbard Bridge causeway, where we stuck in the morning.

April 23. I saw at Ricketson's a young woman, Miss Kate Brady, twenty years old, her father an Irishman, a worthless fellow, her mother a smart Yankee. The daughter formerly did sewing, but now keeps school for a livelihood. She was born at the Brady house, I think in Freetown, where she lived till twelve years old and helped her father in the field. There she rode horse to plow and was knocked off the horse by apple tree boughs, kept sheep, caught fish, etc., etc. I never heard a girl or woman express so strong a love for nature. She purposes to return to that lonely ruin, and dwell there alone, since her mother and sister will not accompany her; says that she knows all about farming and keeping sheep and spinning and weaving, though it would puzzle her to shingle the old house. There she thinks she can "live free." I was pleased to hear

of her plans, because they were quite cheerful and original, not professedly reformatory, but growing out of her love for "Squire's Brook and the Middleborough ponds." A strong love for outward nature is singularly rare among both men and women. The scenery immediately about her homestead is quite ordinary, yet she appreciates and can use that part of the universe as no other being can. Her own sex, so tamely bred, only jeer at her for entertaining such an idea, but she has a strong head and a love for good reading, which may carry her through. I would by no means discourage, nor yet particularly encourage her, for I would have her so strong as to succeed in spite of all ordinary discouragements.

It is very rare that I hear one express a strong and imperishable attachment to a particular scenery, or to the whole of nature, — I mean such as will control their whole lives and characters. Such seem to have a true home in nature, a hearth in the fields and woods, whatever tenement may be burned. The soil and climate is warm to them. They alone are naturalized, but most are tender and callow creatures that wear a house as their outmost shell and must get their lives insured when they step abroad from it. They are lathed and plastered in from all natural influences, and their delicate lives are a long battle with the dyspepsia. The others are fairly rooted in the soil, and are the noblest plant it bears, more hardy and natural than sorrel. The dead earth seems animated at the prospect of their coming, as if proud to be trodden on by them. It recognizes its lord. Children of the Golden Age. Hospitals and almshouses are not their destiny. When I

hear of such an attachment in a reasonable, a divine, creature to a particular portion of the earth, it seems as if then first the earth succeeded and rejoiced, as if it had been made and existed only for such a use. These various soils and reaches which the farmer plods over, which the traveller glances at and the geologist dryly describes, then first flower and bear their fruit. Does he chiefly own the land who coldly uses it and gets corn and potatoes out of it, or he who loves it and gets inspiration from it? How rarely a man's love for nature becomes a ruling principle with him, like a youth's affection for a maiden, but more enduring! All nature is my bride. That nature which to one is a stark and ghastly solitude is a sweet, tender, and genial society to another.

They told me at New Bedford that one of their whalers came in the other day with a black man aboard whom they had picked up swimming in the broad Atlantic, without anything to support him, but nobody could understand his language or tell where he came from. He was in good condition and well-behaved. My respect for my race rose several degrees when I heard this, and I thought they had found the true merman at last. "What became of him?" I inquired. "I believe they sent him to the State Almshouse," was the reply. Could anything have been more ridiculous? That he should be beholden to Massachusetts for his support who floated free where Massachusetts with her State Almshouse could not have supported herself for a moment. They should have dined him, then accompanied him to the nearest cape and bidden him good-by.

The State would do well to appoint an intelligent standing committee on such curious [sic], in behalf of philologists, naturalists, and so forth, to see that the proper disposition is made of such visitors.

April 24. Sail to Ball's Hill.

The water is at its height, higher than before this year. I see a few shad-flies on its surface. Scudding over the Great Meadows, I see the now red crescents of the red maples in their prime round about, above the gray stems. The willow osiers require to be seen endwise the rows, to get an intense color. The clouds are handsome this afternoon: on the north, some dark, windy clouds, with rain falling thus beneath: —

but it is chiefly wind; southward, those summer clouds in numerous isles, light above and dark-barred beneath. Now the sun comes out and shines on the pine hill west of Ball's Hill, lighting up the light-green pitch pines and the sand and russet-brown lichen-clad hill. That is a very New England landscape. Buttrick's yellow farmhouse near by is in harmony with it. The little fuzzy gnats are about. I see a vertical circular cobweb, more than a foot in diameter, nearly filled with them, and this revealed the existence of the swarms that had filled the air on all sides. If it had been as

many yards wide as it was inches, it would probably have been just as full.

Saw on a small oak slanting over water in a swamp, in the midst of a mass of cat-briar, about ten feet from the ground, a very large nest, of that hypnum (?) moss, in the form of an inverted cone, one foot across above and about eight inches deep, with a hole in the side very thick and warm; probably a mouse-nest, for there were mouse droppings within.

April 25. Saturday. P. M. — Down Turnpike to Smith's Hill and return by Goose Pond.

Saw a large old hollow log with the upper side [gone], which [made] me doubt if it was not a trough open at the ends, and suggested that the first trough was perhaps such a hollow log with one side split off and the ends closed.

It is cool and windy this afternoon. Some sleet falls, but as we sit on the east side of Smith's chestnut grove, the wood, though so open and leafless, makes a perfect lee for us, apparently by breaking the force of the wind. A dense but bare grove of slender chestnut trunks a dozen rods wide is a perfect protection against this violent wind, and makes a perfectly calm lee.

I find that I can very easily make a convenient box of the birch bark, at this season at least, when the sap is running, to carry a moss or other thing in safely. I have only to make three cuts and strip off a piece from a clear space some ten inches long, and then, rolling it up wrong side outward, as it naturally curls backward

Vol. IX

as soon as taken off (the dry side shrinking, the moist swelling) and so keeps its place, I bend or fold the ends back on it, as if it were paper, and so close them, and, if I please, tie it round with a string of the same bark. This is resilient or elastic, and stands out from a plant, and also is not injured by moisture like paper. When the incision is made now, the crystalline drops of sap follow the knife down the tree. This box dries yellow or straw-colored, with large clouds of green derived from the inner bark. The inner bark of the *Betula populifolia* just laid bare is green with a yellow tinge; that of the *B. papyracea* is buff. The undermost layer of the outer bark of the last, next to the inner bark, is straw-colored and exceedingly thin and delicate, and smoother to the lips than any artificial tissue.

Bluets numerous and fully out at the Smith hillside between trough and Saw Mill Brook Falls.

Got to-day unquestionable *Salix humilis* in the Britton hollow, north of his shanty, but all there that I saw (and elsewhere as yet) [are] pistillate. It is apparently now in prime, and apparently the next to bloom after the various larger and earlier ones, all which I must call as yet *S. discolor*. This *S. humilis* is small-catkined and loves a dry soil.

A correspondent of the *Tribune* of April 24th, 1857, who signs "Lyndeborough, N. H., April 15, 1857. J. Herrick," says that he taps his sugar maples four feet from the ground so that cattle may not disturb the buckets, and that the sap will run as freely from the topmost branch as from a root. "Any one may learn this fact from the red squirrel, who, by the way, is a

famous sugar maker, and knows when to tap a tree and where to do it. He performs his tapping in the highest perpendicular limbs or twigs, and leaves the sun and wind to do the evaporating, and in due season and pleasant weather you will see him come round and with great gusto gather his sirup into his stomach."

The dense, green, rounded beds of mosses in springs and old water-troughs are very handsome now, — intensely cold green cushions.

Again we had, this afternoon at 2 o'clock, those wild, scudding wind-clouds in the north, spitting cold rain or sleet, with the curved lines of falling rain beneath. The wind is so strong that the thin drops fall on you in the sunshine when the cloud has drifted far to one side. The air is peculiarly clear, the light intense, and when the sun shines slanting under the dark scud, the willows, etc., rising above the dark flooded meadows, are lit with a fine straw-colored light like the spirits of trees.

I see winkle fungi comparatively fresh, whose green and reddish-brown and pale-buff circles above turn to light and dark slate and white, and so finally fade all to white. The beds of fine mosses on bare yellow mouldy soil are now in fruit and very warmly red in the sun when seen a little from one side.

No pages in my Journal are so suggestive as those which contain a rude sketch.

Suppose we were to drink only the yellow birch sap and mix its bark with our bread, would not its yellow curls sprout from our foreheads, and our breath and persons exhale its sweet aroma? What sappy vigor there would be in our limbs! What sense we should have to explore the swamps with!

April 26. Riordan's cock follows close after me while spading in the garden, and hens commonly follow the gardener and plowman, just as cowbirds the cattle in a pasture.

I turn up now in the garden those large leather-colored nymphs.

P. M. — Up Assabet to White Cedar Swamp.

See on the water over the meadow, north of the boat's place, twenty rods from the nearest shore and twice as much from the opposite shore, a very large striped snake swimming. It swims with great ease, and lifts its head a foot above the water, darting its tongue at us. A snake thus met with on the water appears far more monstrous, not to say awful and venomous, than on the land. It is always something startling and memorable to meet with a serpent in the midst of a broad water, careering over it. But why had this one taken to the water? Is it possible that snakes ever hibernate in meadows which are subject to be overflown? This one when we approached swam toward the boat, apparently to rest on it, and when I put out my paddle, at once coiled itself partly around it and allowed itself to be taken on board. It did not hang down from the paddle like a dead snake, but stiffened and curved its body in a loose coil about it.

This snake was two feet and eleven inches long; the tail alone, seven and a quarter. There [were] one hundred and forty-five large abdominal plates, besides the

three smaller under the head, and sixty-five pairs of caudal scales. The central stripe on the back was not bright-yellow, as Storer describes, but a pale brown or clay-color; only the more indistinct lateral stripes were a greenish yellow, the *broad* dark-brown stripes being between; beneath greenish. Beneath the tail in centre, a dark, somewhat greenish line.

This snake was killed about 2 P. M.; *i. e.*, the head was perfectly killed then; yet the posterior half of the body was apparently quite alive and would curl strongly around the hand at 7 P. M. It had been hanging on a tree in the meanwhile.

I have the same objection to killing a snake that I have to the killing of any other animal, yet the most humane man that I know never omits to kill one.

I see a great many beetles, etc., floating and struggling on the flood.

We sit on the shore at Wheeler's fence, opposite Merriam's. At this season still we go seeking the sunniest, most sheltered, and warmest place. C. says this is the warmest place he has been in this year. We are in this like snakes that lie out on banks. In sunny and sheltered nooks we are in our best estate. There our thoughts flow and we flourish most. By and by we shall seek the shadiest and coolest place. How well adapted we are to our climate! In the winter we sit by fires in the house; in spring and fall, in sunny and sheltered nooks; in the summer, in shady and cool groves, or over water where the breeze circulates. Thus the average temperature of the year just suits us. Generally, whether in summer or winter. we are not sensible either of heat or cold.

A great part of our troubles are literally domestic or originate in the house and from living indoors. I could write an essay to be entitled "Out of Doors," — undertake a crusade against houses. What a different thing Christianity preached to the house-bred and to a party who lived out of doors! Also a sermon is needed on economy of fuel. What right has my neighbor to burn ten cords of wood, when I burn only one? Thus robbing our half-naked town of this precious covering. Is he so much colder than I? It is expensive to maintain him in our midst. If some earn the salt of their porridge, are we certain that they earn the fuel of their kitchen and parlor? One man makes a little of the driftwood of the river or of the dead and refuse (unmarketable!) [wood] of the forest suffice, and Nature rejoices in him. Another, Herod-like, requires ten cords of the best of young white oak or hickory, and he is commonly esteemed a virtuous man. He who burns the most wood on his hearth is the least warmed by the sight of it growing. Leave the trim wood-lots to widows and orphan girls. Let men tread gently through nature. Let us religiously burn stumps and worship in groves, while Christian vandals lay waste the forest temples to build miles of meeting-houses and horse-sheds and feed their box stoves.

The white cedar is apparently just out. The higher up the tree, the earlier. Towed home an oak log some eighteen feet long and more than a foot through, with a birch withe around it and another birch fastened to that.

Father says he saw a boy with a snapping turtle yesterday.

April 27. I hear the prolonged *che che che che che*, etc., of the chip-bird this morning as I go down the street. It is a true April morning with east wind, the sky overcast with wet-looking clouds, and already some drops have fallen. It will surely rain to-day, but when it will begin in earnest and how long it will last, none can tell. The gardener makes haste to get in his peas, getting his son to drop them. He who requires fair weather puts off his enterprises and resumes them in his mind many times in the forenoon, as the clouds fall lower and sprinkle the fields, or lift higher and show light streaks. He goes half a mile and is overtaken by thick sprinkling drops, falling faster and faster. He pauses and says to himself, this may be merely a shower, which will soon be over, or it may come to a steady rain and last all day. He goes a few steps further, thinking over the condition of a wet man, and then returns. Again it holds up and he regrets that he had not persevered; but the next hour it is stiller and darker, with mist beneath the investing cloud, and then commences a gentle, deliberate rain, which will probably last all day. So he puts on patience and the house.

I dig up those reddish-brown dor-bugs in the garden. They stir a little.

Ricketson frequents his shanty by day and evening as much as his house, but does not sleep there, partly on account of his fear of lightning, which he cannot overcome. His timidity in this respect amounts to an idiosyncrasy. I was awaked there in a thunder-storm at midnight by Ricketson rushing about the house, calling to his sons to come down out of the attic where they slept and bolting in to leave a light in my room. His fear of death is equally singular. The thought of it troubles him more perhaps than anything else. He says that he knows nothing about another life, he would like to stay here always. He does not know what to think of the Creator that made the lightning and established death.

April 28. A. M. — Surveying for Willard Farrar by Walden.

While standing by my compass over the supposed town bound beyond Wyman's, Farrar having just gone along northeast on the town line, I saw with the side of my eye some black creature crossing the road, reminding me of a black cat two thirds grown. Turning, I saw it plainly for half a minute. It crossed to my side about twenty-five feet off, apparently not observing me, and disappeared in the woods. It was perfectly black, for aught I could see (not brown), some eighteen or twenty inches or more in length from tip to tip, and I first thought of a large black weasel, then of a large black squirrel, then wondered if it could be a pine marten. I now try to think it a mink; yet it appeared *larger* and with a *shorter* body. It had a straight, low, bushy tail about two inches thick, short legs, and carried its tail and legs about on the same level. It was nearly, if not quite, as large as a muskrat. Has the mink such a tail?

Looking for an "old   pine stump" mentioned in a deed and digging into a hillock with our hands to discover it, we turned up, amid the reddish virgin mould, — quite turned to soil, — a large body

of short, chunked, yellowish ants, say five twelfths (?) of an inch long, with their white larvæ (?). I perceived at more than a foot distant a very strong penetrating scent, yet agreeable and very spicy. It reminded me at first of the cherry pectoral; but it was not that; it was very strong lemon-peel. The "Library of Entertaining Knowledge" says that the odor of the wood ant will suffocate a frog dropped among them. Are not these the American "wood ant"?

Icy cold northwest wind, and snow whitening the mountains.

April 29. Purple finch sings on R. W. E.'s trees.
P. M. — To Dugan Desert.

At Tarbell's watering-place, see a dandelion, its conspicuous bright-yellow disk in the midst of a green space on the moist bank. It is thus I commonly meet with the earliest dandelion set in the midst of some liquid green patch. It seems a sudden and decided progress in the season. On the pitch pines beyond John Hosmer's, I see old cones within two feet of the ground on the trunk, — sometimes a circle of them around it, — which must have been formed on the young tree some fifteen years ago. Sweet-fern at entrance of Ministerial Swamp. A partridge there drums incessantly. C. says it makes his heart beat with it, or he feels it in his breast.

I find that that clayey-looking soil on which the bæomyces grows is a very thin crust on common sand only.

I have seen that pretty little hair-cap moss (*Pogo-*

natum brevicaule? [1]) for a fortnight out at least; like little pine trees; the staminate pretty, cup-shaped and shorter.

A steel-blue-black flattish beetle, which, handled, imparted a very disagreeable carrion-like scent to fingers.

Miles's Pond is running off. The sweet-gale, willows, etc., which have been submerged and put back, begin to show themselves and are trying to catch up with their fellows.

I am surprised to see how some blackberry pastures and other fields are filling up with pines, trees which I thought the cows had almost killed two or three years ago; so that what was then a pasture is now a young wood-lot. A little snow still lies in the road in one place, the relic of the snow of the 21st.

April 30. *Thursday.* A. M. — Surveying for Farrar and Heywood by Walden.

Hear a kingfisher at Goose Pond. Hear again the same bird heard at Conantum April 18th, which I think must be the ruby-crowned wren. As we stood looking for a bound by the edge of Goose Pond, a pretty large hawk alighted on an oak close by us. It probably has a nest near by and was concerned for its young.

The larch plucked yesterday sheds pollen to-day in house, probably to-day abroad. Balm-of-Gilead plucked yesterday, *not yet* (nor on May 1st) in house.

       [1] No.

X

MAY, 1857

(ÆT. 39)

May 1. *Friday.* 2 P. M. — First notice the ring of the toad, as I am crossing the Common in front of the meeting-house. There is a cool and breezy south wind, and the ring of the first toad leaks into the general stream of sound, unnoticed by most, as the mill-brook empties into the river and the voyager cannot tell if he is above or below its mouth. The bell was ringing for town meeting, and every one heard it, but none heard this older and more universal bell, rung by more native Americans all the land over. It is a sound from amid the waves of the aerial sea, that breaks on our ears with the surf of the air, a sound that is almost breathed with the wind, taken into the lungs instead of being heard by the ears. It comes from far over or through the troughs of the aerial sea, like a petrel, and who can guess by what pool the singer sits? whether behind the meeting-house horse-sheds, or from over the burying-ground hill, or from the riverside? A new reign has commenced. Bufo the First has ascended to his throne, the surface of the earth, led into office by the south wind. Bufo the Double-chinned inflates his throat. Attend to his message. Take off your greatcoats, swains! and prepare for the summer campaign. Hop a few paces further toward your goals. The measures

I shall advocate are warmth, moisture, and low-flying insects.

White-throated sparrow in shrub oaks by Walden road. Is that moss with little green pendulous fruit on reddish stems *Bryum pyriforme?* Apparently a skunk has picked up what I took to be the dead shrew in the Goose Pond Path. How they ransack the paths these nights! The ground is spotted with their probings. Plucked the *Arum triphyllum,* three inches high, with its acrid corm (solid bulb), from the edge of Saw Mill Brook.

It is foolish for a man to accumulate material wealth chiefly, houses and land. Our stock in life, our real estate, is that amount of thought which we have had, which we have thought out. The ground we have thus created is forever pasturage for our thoughts. I fall back on to visions which I have had. What else adds to my possessions and makes me rich in all lands? If you have ever done any work with these finest tools, the imagination and fancy and reason, it is a new creation, independent on the world, and a possession forever. You have laid up something against a rainy day. You have to that extent cleared the wilderness.

Is a house but a gall on the face of the earth, a nidus which some insect has provided for its young?

May 2. Saturday. Building a fence between us and Mrs. Richardson. In digging the holes I find the roots of small apple trees, seven or eight feet distant and four or more inches in diameter, two feet underground, and as big as my little finger. This is two or three feet

beyond any branches. They reach at least twice as far as the branches. The branches get trimmed, the roots do not.

May 3. Sunday. A remarkably warm and pleasant morning.

A. M. — To Battle-Ground by river.

I heard the ring of toads at 6 A. M. The flood on the meadows, still high, is quite smooth, and many are out this still and suddenly very warm morning, pushing about in boats. Now, thinks many a one, is the time to paddle or push gently far up or down the river, along the still, warm meadow's edge, and perhaps we may see some large turtles, or muskrats, or otter, or rare fish or fowl. It will be a grand forenoon for a cruise, to explore these meadow shores and inundated maple swamps which we have never explored. Now we shall be recompensed for the week's confinement to shop or garden. We will spend our Sabbath exploring these smooth warm vernal waters. Up or down shall we go? To Fair Haven Bay and the Sudbury meadows, or to Ball's Hill and Carlisle Bridge? Along the meadow's edge, lined with willow and alders and maples, under the catkins of the early willow, and brushing those of the sweet-gale with our prow, where the sloping pasture and the plowed ground, submerged, are fast drinking up the flood. What fair isles, what remote coast shall we explore? What San Salvador or Bay of All Saints arrive at? All are tempted forth, like flies, into the sun. All isles seem fortunate and blessed to-day; all capes are of Good Hope. The same sun and calm that tempts

the turtles out tempts the voyagers. It is an opportunity to explore their own natures, to float along their own shores. The woodpecker cackles and the crow blackbird utters his jarring chatter from the oaks and maples. All well men and women who are not restrained by superstitious custom come abroad this morning by land or water, and such as have boats launch them and put forth in search of adventure. Others, less free or, it may be, less fortunate, take their station on bridges, watching the rush of water through them and the motions of the departing voyagers, and listening to the notes of blackbirds from over the smooth water. They see a swimming snake, or a muskrat dive, — airing and sunning themselves there until the first bell rings.

Up and down the town, men and boys that are under subjection are polishing their shoes and brushing their go-to-meeting clothes. I, a descendant of Northmen who worshipped Thor, spend my time worshipping neither Thor nor Christ; a descendant of Northmen who sacrificed men and horses, sacrifice neither men nor horses. I care not for Thor nor for the Jews. I sympathize not to-day with those who go to church in newest clothes and sit quietly in straight-backed pews. I sympathize rather with the boy who has none to look after him, who borrows a boat and paddle and in common clothes sets out to explore these temporary vernal lakes. I meet such a boy paddling along under a sunny bank, with bare feet and his pants rolled up above his knees, ready to leap into the water at a moment's warning. Better for him to read "Robinson Crusoe" than Baxter's "Saints' Rest."

I hear the soft, purring, stertorous croak of frogs on the meadow.[1]

The pine warbler is perhaps the commonest bird heard now from the wood-sides. It seems left [to] it almost alone to fill their empty aisles.

The above boy had caught a snapping turtle, the third he had got this year. The first he said he got the fore part of April. He also had caught a bullfrog sitting on the shore just now.

Thermometer from 1 to 2 P. M., at 78°. Neighbors come forth to view the expanding buds in their gardens.

I see where some fish, probably a pickerel, darted away from high on the meadows, toward the river, and swims so high that it makes a long ripple for twenty rods.

3 P. M. — To Cliffs.

In the pool which dries up in Jonathan Wheeler's orchard, I see toads, or maybe frogs, spread out on the surface, uttering a short, loud, peculiar croak, not like that of the early croaking frog, nor the smooth, purring, stertorous one of this morning, but a coarse belching croak, at a little distance like *quor* and *quar*, being on various keys, but nearer like *ow-oo-uk* though one syllable or *ar-r-r*. Thus they lie, perhaps within a foot or two and facing each other, and alternately throwing their heads back, *i. e.* upward, swelling their *white* throats and uttering this abominable noise.[2] Then one rushes upon the other, leaps upon him. They struggle

[1] Probably *Rana palustris. Vide* May 1st, 1858.
[2] [Spade-foot toads, it seems likely.]

and roll over and sink for a moment, and presently they show their heads again a foot or two apart. There are a dozen or more, with very prominent eyes, with bright golden irides.

In another pool, in Warren's meadow, I hear the ring of toads and the peep of hylodes, and, taking off my stockings and shoes, at length stand in their midst. There are a hundred toads close around me, copulating or preparing to. These look at a little distance precisely like the last, but no one utters that peculiar rough, belching croak, only their common musical ring, and occasionally a short, fainter, interrupted, quivering note, as of alarm. They are continually swimming to and leaping upon each other. I see many large reddish-brown ones, probably females, with small grayish ones lying flat on their backs, the fore feet clasped around them. These commonly lie flat on the bottom, often as if dead, but from time [to time] the under one rises with its load to the surface, puts its nose out and then sinks again. The single ones leap upon these double ones and roll them over in vain like the rest. It is the single ones that ring and are so active. They make great gray, yellowish, greenish, or whitish bubbles (different specimens being thus various), as big as their heads. One that rings within a foot of me seems to make the earth vibrate, and I feel it and am thrilled to my very spine, it is so terrene a sound. It reminds me of many a summer night on the river. A bubbling ring, which is continuous about a minute, and then its bag must be inflated again. When I move suddenly, it is the single ones chiefly that con-

ceal themselves. The others are not so easily disturbed. You would hardly believe that toads could be so excited and active. When that nearest ringer sounded, the very sod by my feet (whose spires rose above water) seemed to tremble, and the earth itself, and I was thrilled to my spine and vibrated to it. They like a rest for their toes when they ring. It is a sound as crowded with protuberant bubbles as the rind of an orange. A clear, ringing note with a bubbling trill. It takes complete possession of you, for you vibrate to it, and can hear nothing else.

At length, too, a hylodes or two were heard close about me, but not one was seen. The nearest seemed to have his residence in my ear alone. It took such possession of my ear that I was unable to appreciate the source whence it came.

It is so warm, mosquitoes alight on my hands and face.

As I approach the entrance to the spring path, I hear some chickadees *phe-be*-ing. One sings *phe-e — be' be — be' be*, just as if another struck in immediately after the usual strain.

Salix tristis is out to-day at least, perhaps yesterday, by what I may call S. *tristis* Path. *Viola ovata* is *pretty* common there.

Above the Cliffs, scare up a pair of turtle doves from the stubble, which go off with their shrill rattling whistle. *Corydalis glauca* is five inches high. The pistillate *Equisetum arvense* shows itself.

To-day we sit without fire.

Emerson says that Brewer tells him my "night warbler" is probably the Nashville warbler.

Vol. IX

May 4. Rain. The barber tells me that the masons of New York tell him that they would prefer human hair to that of cattle to mix with their plastering.

Balm-of-Gilead pollen in house to-day; outdoors, say to-morrow, if fair.

Minott tells me of one Matthias Bowers, a native of Chelmsford and cousin of C. Bowers, a very active fellow, who used to sleep with him and when he found the door locked would climb over the roof and come in at the dormer-window. One Sunday, when they were repairing the old Unitarian church and there was a staging just above the belfry, he climbed up the lightning-rod and put his arm round the ball at the top of the spire and swung his hat there. He then threw it down and the crown was knocked out. Minott saw him do it, and Deacon White ordered him to come down. M. also told of a crazy fellow who got into the belfry of the Lincoln church with an axe and began to cut the spire down, but was stopped after he had done considerable damage.

When M. lived at Baker's, B. had a dog Lion, famous for chasing squirrels. The gray squirrels were numerous and used to run over the house sometimes. It was an old-fashioned house, slanting to one story behind, with a ladder from the roof to the ground. One day a gray squirrel ran over the house, and Lion, dashing after him up the ladder, went completely over the house and fell off the front side before he could stop, putting out one of his toes. But the squirrel did not put out any of his toes.

Wyman told Minott that he used to see *black snakes*

crossing Walden and would wait till they came ashore and then kill them. One day he saw a bull on the northerly side swim across to get at some cows on the south.

It has rained all day, and I see in the footpath across the Common, where water flows or has flown, a great many worms, apparently drowned. Did they not come out in unusual numbers last night because it was so warm, and so get overtaken by the rain? But how account for the worms said to be found in tubs of water?

Perhaps the most generally interesting event at present is a perfectly warm and pleasant day. It affects the greatest number, the well out of doors and the sick in chambers. No wonder the weather is the universal theme of conversation.

A warm rain; and the ring of the toads is heard all through it.

May 5. Tuesday. Building fence east of house.

Hear the *tull-lull* of a myrtle-bird [1] (very commonly heard for three or four days after). Have dug up in the garden this season half a dozen of those great leather-colored pupæ (with the tongue-case bent round to breast like a long urn-handle) of the sphinx moth. First potato-worm. Staminate *Salix rostrata*, possibly yesterday.

May 6. Wednesday. A beautiful and warm day. I go to build an arbor for R. W. E. The thrasher has been heard this morning. While at work I hear the bobolink and, methinks, peetweet along the brook

[1] White-throat sparrow.

(surely see it on the 9th). Sugar maple by Dr. Barrett's, possibly to-day.

May 7. A second fine day.
Small pewee and, methinks, golden robin (?).

May 8. A third fine day.
The sugar maple at Barrett's is now in full bloom. I finish the arbor to-night. This has been the third of these remarkably warm and beautiful [days]. I have worked all the while in my shirt-sleeves. Summer has suddenly come upon us, and the birds all together. Some boys have bathed in the river.

Walk to first stone bridge at sunset. *Salix alba,* possibly the 6th. It is a glorious evening. I scent the expanding willow leaves (for there are very few blossoms yet) fifteen rods off. Already hear the cheerful, sprightly note of the yellowbird amid them. It is perfectly warm and still, and the green grass reminds me of June. The air is full of the fragrance of willow leaves. The high water stretches smooth around. I hear the sound of Barrett's sawmill with singular distinctness. The ring of toads, the note of the yellowbird, the rich warble of the red-wing, the thrasher on the hillside, the robin's evening song, the woodpecker tapping some dead tree across the water; and I see countless little fuzzy gnats in the air, and dust over the road, between me and the departed sun. Perhaps the evenings of the 6th and 7th were as pleasant. But such an evening makes a crisis in the year. I must make haste home and go out on the water.

sence of eight years, not in a shining suit of black, with polished boots and a beaver or silk hat, as if on a furlough from human duties generally, — a mere clotheshorse, — but clad in an honest clay-colored suit and a snug every-day cap. It showed unusual manhood. Most returning sons come home dressed for the occasion. The birds and beasts are not afraid of me now. A mink came within twenty feet of me the other day as soon as my companion had left me, and if I had had my gray sack on as well as my corduroys, it would perhaps have come quite up to me. Even farmers' boys, returning to their native town, though not unfamiliar with homely and dirty clothes, make their appearance on this new stage in a go-to-meeting suit.

May 9. Another *fine* day.
6 A. M. — On water.
Maryland yellow-throat. Aspen leaves one inch over. Hear stake-driver. Black and white creeper's *fine* note. *Er-te-ter-twee,* or evergreen-forest note. Golden-crowned thrush note. Kingbird.

P. M. To Gilson's Mill, Littleton.
George Brooks points to an old house of which one half the roof only has been shingled, etc., etc., and says he guessed it to be a widow's dower from this, and on inquiry found it so.
Went to Gilson's tumble-down mill and house. He appeared, licking his chaps after dinner, in a mealy coat, and suddenly asked in the midst of a sentence, with a shrug of his shoulders, "Is n't there something painted

I paddle to the Wheeler meadow east of hill after sundown. From amid the alders, etc., I hear the mew of the catbird and the *yorrick* of Wilson's thrush. One bullfrog's faint *er-er-roonk* from a distance. (Perhaps the *Amphibia,* better than any creatures, celebrate the changes of temperature.) One *dump* note. It grows dark around. The full moon rises, and I paddle by its light. It is an evening for the soft-snoring, *purring* frogs (which I suspect to be *Rana palustris*). I get within a few feet of them as they sit along the edge of the river and meadow, but cannot see them. Their croak is very fine or rapid, and has a soft, purring sound at a little distance. I see them paddling in the water like toads.

Within a week I have had made a pair of corduroy pants, which cost when done $1.60. They are of that peculiar clay-color, reflecting the light from portions of their surface. They have this advantage, that, beside being very strong, they will look about as well three months hence as now, — or as ill, some would say. Most of my friends are disturbed by my wearing them. I can get four or five pairs for what one ordinary pair would cost in Boston, and each of the former will last two or three times as long under the same circumstances. The tailor said that the stuff was not made in this country; that it was worn by the Irish at home, and now they would not look at it, but others would not wear it, durable and cheap as it is, because it is worn by the Irish. Moreover, I like the color on other accounts. Anything but black clothes. I was pleased the other day to see a son of Concord return after an ab-

on my back?" There were some marks in red chalk they used to chalk the bags with, and he said he thought he had felt his son at the mill chalking his back. He feared he was making an exhibition before strangers.

The boy speared fishes, chiefly suckers, pouts, etc. A fire in a hand-crate carried along the bank of the brook (Stony Brook). He had lately speared a sucker weighing five and a quarter pounds, which he sold; went back and forth some twenty-five rods and found the suckers less shy at last than at first. Saw otter there. I saw many perch at the foot of the falls. He said that they and trout could get up five or six feet over the rocks there into the pond, it being a much broken fall.

May 10. Cultivated cherry out.
P. M. — Up river.
Salix Babylonica behind Dodd's, how long? Say with *S. alba.* I observe that the fertile flowers of many plants are more late than the barren ones, as the sweetgale (whose fertile are now in prime), the sweet-fern, etc.

See twenty or thirty tortoises on one stump by stone bridge and more still within a rod along the bank of E. Wood's ditch. Now the *Emys picta* lie out in great numbers, this suddenly warm weather, and when you go along the road within a few rods they tumble in. The banks of some ditches look almost as if paved with them.

I went looking for snapping turtles over the meadow south of railroad. Now I see one large head like a brown stake projecting three or four inches above the water four rods off, but it is slowly withdrawn, and I paddle up and catch the fellow lying still in the dead grass there. Soon after I paddle within ten feet of one whose eyes like knobs appear on the side of the stake, and touch him with my paddle.

This side Clamshell, strawberries and cinquefoil are abundant. *Equisetum sylvaticum.*

There is a strong wind, against which I push and paddle. But now at last I do not go seeking the warm, sunny, and sheltered coves; the strong wind is enlivening and agreeable. It is a *washing* day. I love the wind at last.

Before night a sudden shower with some thunder and lightning; the first.

May 11. Warbling vireo and chewink. A very cold northwest wind. I hear they had a snow-storm yesterday in Vermont.

May 12. How rarely I meet with a man who can be free, even in thought! We live according to rule. Some men are bedridden; all, world-ridden. I take my neighbor, an intellectual man, out into the woods and invite him to take a new and absolute view of things, to empty clean out of his thoughts all institutions of men and start again; but he can't do it, he sticks to his traditions and his crotchets. He thinks that governments, colleges, newspapers, etc., are from everlasting to everlasting.

The *Salix cordata* var. *Torreyana* is distinguished by its naked ovaries more or less red-brown, with flesh-colored stigmas, with a distinct slender woolly rachis

and conspicuous stalks, giving the ament a loose and open appearance.

When I consider how many species of willow have been planted along the railroad causeway within ten years, of which no one knows the history, and not one in Concord beside myself can tell the name of one, so that it is quite a discovery to identify a single one in a year, and yet within this period the seeds of all these kinds have been conveyed from some other locality to this, I am reminded how much is going on that man wots not of.

While dropping beans in the garden at Texas just after sundown (May 13th), I hear from across the fields the note of the bay-wing, *Come here here there there quick quick quick or I'm gone* (which I have no doubt sits on some fence-post or rail there), and it instantly translates me from the sphere of my work and repairs all the world that we jointly inhabit. It reminds me of so many country afternoons and evenings when this bird's strain was heard far over the fields, as I pursued it from field to field. The spirit of its earth-song, of its serene and true philosophy, was breathed into me, and I saw the world as through a glass, as it lies eternally. Some of its aboriginal contentment, even of its domestic felicity, possessed me. What he suggests is permanently true. As the bay-wing sang many a thousand years ago, so sang he to-night. In the beginning God heard his song and pronounced it good, and hence it has endured. It reminded me of many a summer sunset, of many miles of gray rails, of many a rambling pasture, of the farmhouse far in the fields,

its milk-pans and well-sweep, and the cows coming home from pasture.

I would thus from time to time take advice of the birds, correct my human views by listening to their volucral (?). He is a brother poet, this small gray bird (or bard), whose muse inspires mine. His lay is an idyl or pastoral, older and sweeter than any that is classic. He sits on some gray perch like himself, on a stake, perchance, in the midst of the field, and you can hardly see him against the plowed ground. You advance step by step as the twilight deepens, and lo! he is gone, and in vain you strain your eyes to see whither, but anon his tinkling strain is heard from some other quarter. One with the rocks and with us.

Methinks I hear these sounds, have these reminiscences, only when well employed, at any rate only when I have no reason to be ashamed of my employment. I am often aware of a certain compensation of this kind for doing something from a sense of duty, even unconsciously. Our past experience is a never-failing capital which can never be alienated, of which each kindred future event reminds us. If you would have the song of the sparrow inspire you a thousand years hence, let your life be in harmony with its strain to-day.

I ordinarily plod along a sort of whitewashed prison entry, subject to some indifferent or even grovelling mood. I do not distinctly realize my destiny. I have turned down my light to the merest glimmer and am doing some task which I have set myself. I take incredibly narrow views, live on the limits, and have no

recollection of absolute truth. Mushroom institutions hedge me in. But suddenly, in some fortunate moment, the voice of eternal wisdom reaches me, even in the strain of the sparrow, and liberates me, whets and clarifies my senses, makes me a competent witness.[1]

The second amelanchier out, in garden. Some fir balsams, as Cheney's. Is not ours in the grove, with the chip-bird's nest in it, the *Abies Fraseri?* Its cones are short. I hear of, and also find, a ground-bird's (song sparrow's) nest with five eggs.

P. M. — To Miles Swamp, Conantum.

I hear a yorrick, apparently anxious, near me, utter from time to time a sharp grating *char-r-r*, like a fine watchman's rattle. As usual, I have not heard them sing yet. A night-warbler, plainly light beneath. It always flies to a new perch immediately after its song. Hear the *screep* of the parti-colored warbler.

Veronica serpyllifolia is abundantly out at Corner Spring. As I go along the hillside toward Miles Swamp, I mistake the very light gray cliff-sides east of the river at Bittern Cliff for amelanchier in bloom.

The brother of Edward Garfield (after dandelions!) tells me that two years ago, when he was cutting wood at Bittern Cliff in the winter, he saw something dark squatting on the ice, which he took to be a mink, and taking a stake he went to inspect it. It turned out to be a bird, a new kind of duck, with a long, slender, pointed bill (he thought red). It moved off backwards, hissing at him, and he threw his stake about a rod and partly

[1] [Channing, p. 93.]

broke its neck, then killed it. It was very lean and the river was nowhere open. He sent it to Waltham and sold it for twenty-five cents.

Black ash, maybe a day.

Vaccinium Pennsylvanicum. I see a whitish cocoon on a small carpinus. It is artfully made where there is a short crook in the main stem, so as to just fill the hollow and make an even surface, the stick forming one side.

May 13. Work in garden. I see a toad only an inch and a quarter long; so they must be several years growing.

P. M. — To Leaning Hemlocks.

A large bunch of oat spawn in meadow water. Scare up a black duck and apparently two summer ducks. Canoe birch, how long? Sternothærus.

May 14. P. M. — To Assabet Bath and stone bridge.

I hear two thrashers plainly singing in emulation of each other.

At the temporary brush fence pond, now going down, amid the sprout-land and birches, I see, within a dozen rods along its shore, one to three rods from edge, thirteen wood tortoises on the grass, at 4 P. M. this cloudy afternoon. This is apparently a favorite resort for them, — a shallow open pool of half an acre, which dries up entirely a few weeks later, in dryish, mossy ground in an open birch wood, etc., etc. They take refuge in the water and crawl out over the mossy ground. They lie

about in various positions, very conspicuous there, at every rod or two. They are of various forms and colors: some almost regularly oval or elliptical, even pointed behind, others very broad behind, more or less flaring and turned up on the edge; some a dull lead-color and almost smooth, others brown with dull-yellowish marks. I see one with a large dent three eighths of an inch deep and nearly two inches long in the middle of its back, where it was once partially crushed. Hardly one has a perfect shell. The males (?), with concave sternums; the females, even or convex. They have their reddish-orange legs stretched out often, listlessly, when you approach, draw in their heads with a hiss when you take them up, commonly taking a bit of stubble with them.

See a pair of marsh hawks, the smaller and lighter-colored male, with black tips to wings, and the large brown female, sailing low over J. Hosmer's sprout-land and screaming, apparently looking for frogs or the like. Or have they not a nest near? They hover very near me. The female, now so near, sails very grandly, with the outer wing turned or tilted up when it circles, and the bars on its tail when it turns, etc., reminding me of a great brown moth. Sometimes alone; and when it approaches its mate it utters a low, grating note like *cur-r-r*. Suddenly the female holds straight toward me, descending gradually. Steadily she comes on, without swerving, until only two rods off, then wheels.

I find an old bog-hoe left amid the birches in the low ground, the handle nearly rotted off. In the low birch

land north of the pear tree the old corn-hills are very plain still, and now each hill is a dry moss-bed, of various species of cladonia. What a complete change from a dusty corn-hill!

Abel Hosmer tells me that he has collected and sown white pine seed, and that he has found them in the crop of pigeons. (?)

Salix lucida at bridge; maybe staminate earlier. Herb-of-St.-Barbara, how long?

May 15. Black currant at R. W. E.'s.

Abel Hosmer thought that the *Salix alba* roots might reach half a dozen rods into his field as big as your finger. Thought that they made the grass grow as much as the locust; only they made it rough plowing by throwing the plow out.

May 16. P. M. — To Hill for pines.

The meadows are now mostly bare, the grass showing itself above the water that is left, and an unusual number of swallows are flying low over it. A yellow lily out, and, on the hill, a red cedar, maybe a day.

May 17. P. M. — Round Walden.

Gold-thread is abundantly out at Trillium Woods. The yellow birch catkins, now fully out or a little past prime, are very handsome now, numerous clusters of rich golden catkins hanging straight down at a height from the ground on the end of the pendulous branches, amid the *just* expanding leaf-buds. It is like some great chandelier hung high over the underwood. So,

too, with the canoe birch. Such black as I see is not quite so forward yet. The canoe, yellow, and black birches are among the handsomest trees when in bloom. The bunches of numerous rich golden catkins, hanging straight down on all sides and trembling in the breeze, contrast agreeably with the graceful attitude of the tree, commonly more or less inclined, the leaves not being enough expanded to conceal them in the least. They should be seen against evergreens on a hillside, — something so light and airy, so graceful. What nymphs are they?

What was that peculiar spawn on a submerged alder stem seen the 13th? It looked like a fresh light-colored fungus, flattish and circular, a third of an inch over, and waving in the water, but, taken out, hung down longer. In the midst of this jelly were minute eggs.

I just notice the fertile sweet-fern bloom on *tall* plants,[1] where the sterile catkins are falling off above it. Most plants have none.

Two cocoons of apparently the *Attacus Promethea* on a small black birch, the silk wound round the leaf-stalk.

May 18. P. M. — To Bateman's Pond *via* Yellow Birch Swamp with Pratt.

Pratt says he saw the first rhodora and cultivated pear out yesterday. Many are now setting out pines and other evergreens, transplanting some wildness into the neighborhood of their houses. I do not know of

[1] And others.

a white pine that has been set out twenty-five years in the town. It is a new fashion. Judging from the flowering of such of the plants as I notice, this is a backward season. There is a very grand and picturesque old yellow birch in the old cellar northwest the yellow birch swamp. Though this stands out in open land, it does not shed its pollen yet, and its catkins are not much more than half elongated, but it is very beautiful as it is, with its dark-yellowish tassels variegated with brown. Yet in the swamp westerly the yellow birches are in full bloom, and many catkins strew the ground. They are four or five inches long when in bloom. They *begin* to shed their pollen at the base of the catkin, as, I think, other birches do.

In the yellow birch and ash swamp west of big yellow birch, I hear the fine note of cherry-birds, much like that of young partridges, and see them on the ash trees. *Viola Muhlenbergii* abundantly out, how long? The fever-bush in this swamp is very generally killed, at least the upper part, so that it has not blossomed. This is especially the case in the swamp; on higher ground, though exposed, it is in better condition. It appears to have been killed in the spring, for you see the unexpanded flower-buds quite conspicuous. Pratt shows me the fringed gentian stems by a swamp northeast of Bateman's Pond, but we find no traces of a new plant, and I think it must be annual there. The violet woodsorrel is apparently later than the *Oxalis stricta*, not now so forward, lower, and darker green, only a few of the leaves showing that purplish mark. Hear the pepe, how long? In woods close behind Easterbrook's

place, whence it probably strayed, several Canada plums now in bloom, showing the pink. Interesting to see a wild apple tree in the old cellar there, though with a forward caterpillar's nest on it. Call it *Malus cellaris*, that grows in an old cellar-hole.[1] Pedicularis, some time. The blossom-buds of the *Cornus florida* have been killed when an eighth of an inch in diameter, and are black within and fall on the least touch or jar; all over the town. There is a large tree on the further side the ravine near Bateman's Pond and another by some beeches on the rocky hillside a quarter of a mile northeast. In the swampy meadow north of this Pratt says he finds the calla. The *Rubus triflorus* is well out there on the hummocks. The white ash is not yet out in most favorable places. The red huckleberry looks more forward — blossom-buds more swollen — than those of common there. Some high blueberry. Pratt has found perfectly white *Viola pedata* behind Easterbrook place, and cultivated them, but now lost them. Says he saw two "black" snakes intertwined (copulating?) yesterday.

May 19. A. M. — Surveying D. Shattuck's woodlot beyond Peter's.

See myriads of minute pollywogs, recently hatched, in the water of Moore's Swamp on Bedford road. Digging again to find a stake in woods, came across a nest or colony of wood ants, yellowish or sand-color, a third of an inch long, with their white grubs, now squirming, still larger, and emitting that same pungent

[1] [*Excursions*, p. 316; Riv. 388.]

Vol. IX

spicy odor, perhaps too pungent to be compared with lemon-peel. This is the second time I have found them in this way this spring (*vide* April 28th). Is not the pungent scent emitted by wasps quite similar?

I see the ferns all blackened on the hillside next the meadow, by the frost within a night or two.

That ant scent is not at all sickening, but tonic, and reminds me of a bitter flavor like that of peachmeats.

May 20. Began to rain the latter part of yesterday, and rains all day against all desire and expectation, raising the river and, in low land, rotting the seed. Gardeners wish that their land had not been planted nor plowed. Postpone your journey till the May storm is over.

It has been confidently asserted and believed that if the cold in the winter exceeded a certain degree it surely killed the peach blossoms. Last winter we had greater cold than has ever been generally observed here, and yet it is a remarkable spring for peach blossoms; thus once for all disproving that assertion. Everything in the shape of a peach tree blossoms this season, even a mutilated shrub on the railroad causeway, sprung from a stone which some passenger cast out. Nevertheless the lowest limbs, which were covered by the drifts, have blossomed much the earliest and fullest, as usual, and this *after-blow* is quite unexpected. Peach trees are revealed along fences where they were quite unobserved before.

The expression in Sophocles' Œdipus at Colonos,

"White Colonos," said to refer to the silvery soil, reminded me at first of the tracts now whitened by the pyrus blossoms, which may be mistaken for hoary rocks. *Vide* this description of Colonos. Have all the Canada plums that striking pink color at the base of the blossoms at last?

I find that the corydalis sprig which I brought home five days ago keeps fresh and blossoms remarkably well in water, — its delicate bright flesh-colored or pink flowers and glaucous leaves!

How suddenly, after all, pines seem to shoot up and fill the pastures! I wonder that the farmers do not earlier encourage their growth. To-day, perchance, as I go through some run-out pasture, I observe many young white pines dotting the field, where last year I had noticed only blackberry vines; but I see that many are already destroyed or injured by the cows which have dived into them to scratch their heads or for sport (such is their habit; they break off the leading shoot and bend down the others of different evergreens), or perchance where the farmer has been mowing them down, and I think the owner would rather have a pasture here than a wood-lot. A year or two later, as I pass through the same field, I am surprised to find myself in a flourishing young wood-lot, from which the cows are now carefully fenced out, though there are many open spaces, and I perceive how much further advanced it would have been if the farmer had been more provident and had begun to abet nature a few years earlier. It is surprising by what leaps — two or three feet in a season — the pines stretch toward the sky, affording shelter also to various hardwoods which plant themselves in their midst.

I do not know a white pine in the town which has been set out twenty-five years.

May 21. Rains still, more or less, all day. But it is an ill wind that blows nobody any good; this weather is good for cuttings and transplanted trees.

P. M. — To Hill.

Sassafras (fertile) will apparently bloom to-morrow. These, too, — the young trees, — have been killed the past winter, like the fever-bush.

There is, leaning over the Assabet at the Grape Bower, an amelanchier variety *Botryapium* about five inches in diameter and some twenty-eight feet long, a light and graceful tree. The leaves of this are, as usual, nearly smooth and quite brown, of a delicate tint (purplish?). At the spring just beyond, is another amelanchier, and other small ones are not uncommon, differing from the last, not in the form of its petals and leaves, but the latter are green, or very slightly streaked with purplish. It seems to be a common variety of the variety *Botryapium* and quite downy, though not so downy as those of the *oblongifolia*. The bark of these trees is much like that of a maple.

I find checkerberries still fresh and abundant. Last year was a remarkable one for them. They lurk under the low leaves, scarcely to be detected, often, as you are standing up, almost below the level of the ground, dark-scarlet berries, some of them half an inch in diameter, broad pear-shaped, of a pale or hoary pink color be-

neath. The peduncle curves downward between two leaves. There they lurk under the glossy, dark-green, brown-spotted leaves, close to the ground. They make a very handsome nosegay.

I saw yesterday a parrot exceedingly frightened in its cage at a window. It rushed to the bars and struggled to get out. A piece of board had been thrown from the window above to the ground, which probably the parrot's instinct had mistaken for a hawk. Their eyes are very open to danger from above.

The staminate buds of the black spruce are quite a bright red.

May 22. After two or three days more of rainy weather, it is fair and warm at last. Thermometer seventy-odd degrees above zero. When the May storm is over, then the summer is fairly begun.

9 A. M. — I go up the Assabet in boat to stone bridge.

Is it not summer when we do not go seeking sunny and sheltered places, but also love the wind and shade?

As I stand on the sand-bank below the Assabet stone bridge and look up through the arch, the river makes a pretty picture. It is perfectly smooth above the bridge and appears two or three feet higher (it is probably half as much) than below and rushes to its fall very regularly thus, the bridge partially damming the stream: the smoothness extends part way under the bridge in the middle, the turbulent water rushing down each side.

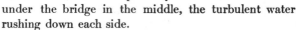

May 23. P. M. — To Holden Swamp by boat.

River still high *generally* over the meadows. Can sail across the Hubbard meadow. Off Staples wood-lot, hear the *ah tche tche chit-i-vet* of the redstart.

Tortoises out again abundantly. Each particularly warm and sunny day brings them out on to every floating rail and stump. I count a dozen within three or four feet on a rail. It is a tortoise day. I hear one regular bullfrog trump, and as I approach the edge of the Holden Swamp, the tree-toads. Hear the pe-pe there, and the redstarts, and the chestnut-sided warbler. It appears striped slate and black above, white beneath, yellow-crowned with black side-head, two yellow bars on wing, white side-head below the black, black bill, and long chestnut streak on side. Its song lively and rather long, about as the summer yellowbird, but not in two bars; *tse tse tse | te tsah tsah tsah | te sah yer se* is the rhythm. *Kalmia glauca* yesterday. Rhodora, on shore there, a little before it. Nemopanthes, a day or two.

This is the time and place to hear the new-arriving warblers, the first fine days after the May storm. When the leaves generally are just fairly expanding, and the deciduous trees are hoary with them, — a silvery hoariness, — then, about the edges of the swamps in the woods, these birds are flitting about in the tree-tops like gnats, catching the insects about the expanding leaf-buds.

I wade in the swamp for the kalmia, amid the water andromeda and the sphagnum, scratching my legs with the first and sinking deep in the last. The water is now gratefully cool to my legs, so far from being poisoned

in the strong water of the swamp. It is a sort of baptism for which I had waited.

At Miles Swamp, the carpinus sterile catkins, apparently a day or two, but I see no fertile ones, unless that is one (pressed) at the southeast edge of swamp near grafted apple, and its catkins are effete! Hear the first veery strain. The small twigs of the carpinus are singularly tough, as I find when I try to break off the flowers. They bend without breaking. Sand cherry at Lupine Bank, possibly a day. Sassafras, a day or two. Fringed polygala, I hear of.

The first goldfinch twitters over, and at evening I hear the *spark* of a nighthawk.

May 24. A. M. — To Hill.

White ash, apparently yesterday, at Grape Shore but not at Conantum. What a singular appearance for some weeks its great masses of dark-purple anthers have made, fruit-like on the trees!

A very warm morning. Now the birds sing more than ever, methinks, now, when the leaves are fairly expanding, the first really warm summer days. The water on the meadows is perfectly smooth nearly all the day. At 3 P. M. the thermometer is at 88°. It soon gets to be quite hazy. Apple out. Heard one speak to-day of his sense of awe at the thought of God, and suggested to him that awe was the cause of the potato-rot.[1] The same speaker dwelt on the sufferings of life, but my advice was to go about one's business, suggesting that no ecstasy was ever interrupted, nor its

[1] [Channing, p. 89.]

fruit blasted. As for completeness and roundness, to
be sure, we are each like one of the laciniæ of a lichen,
a torn fragment, but not the less cheerfully we expand
in a moist day and assume unexpected colors. We want
no completeness but intensity of life. Hear the first
cricket as I go through a warm hollow, bringing round
the summer with his everlasting strain.[1]

May 25. P. M. — With Ricketson to my boat under
Fair Haven Hill.

In Hubbard's Grove, hear the shrill chattering of
downy woodpeckers, very like the red squirrel's *tche
tche.* Thermometer at 87° at 2.30 P. M. It is interesting
to hear the bobolinks from the meadow sprinkle their
lively strain along amid the tree-tops as they fly over
the wood above our heads. It resounds in a novel manner through the aisles of the wood, and at the end that
fine buzzing, wiry note. The black spruce of Holden's,
apparently yesterday, but not the 23d. What a glorious
crimson fire as you look up to the sunlight through the
thin edges of the scales of its cones! So intensely glowing in their cool green beds! while their purplish sterile
blossoms shed pollen on you. Took up four young
spruce and brought them home in the boat.

After all, I seem to have distinguished only one spruce,
and that the black, judging by the cones, — perhaps the
dark and light varieties of it, for the last is said to be
very like the white spruce. The white spruce cones are
cylindrical and have an entire firm edge to the scales,
and the needles are longer.

[1] [*Daniel Ricketson and his Friends,* pp. 355, 356.]

Some of the earliest willows about warm edges of
woods are gone to seed and downy.

P. M. — To Saw Mill Brook.

It is very hazy after a sultry morning, but the wind is
getting east and cool. The oaks are in the gray, or a
little more, and the silvery leafets of the deciduous trees
invest the woods like a permanent mist. At the same
season with this haze of buds comes also the kindred
haziness of the air.

I see the common small reddish butterflies.

Very interesting now are the red tents of expanding
oak leaves, as you go through sprout-lands, — the crimson velvet of the black oak and the more pinkish white
oak. The salmon and pinkish-red canopies or umbrellas
of the white oak are particularly interesting. The very
sudden expansion of the great hickory buds, umbrella-
wise. Now, at last, all leaves dare unfold, and twigs
begin *to shoot.*

As I am going down the footpath from Britton's
camp to the spring, I start a pair of nighthawks (they
had the white on the wing) from amid the dry leaves
at the base of a bush, a bunch of sprouts, and away
they flitted in zigzag noiseless flight a few rods through
the sprout-land, dexterously avoiding the twigs, uttering a faint hollow *what,* as if made by merely closing
the bill, and one alighted flat on a stump.

On those carpinus trees which have fertile flowers,
the sterile are effete and drop off.

The red choke-berry not in bloom, while the black
is, for a day or more at least.

Roadside near Britton's camp, see a grosbeak, ap-

Though the river is thus high, we bathe at Cardinal Shore and find the water unexpectedly warm and
the air also delicious. Thus we are baptized into nature.

May 26. Pink azalea in garden. Mountain-ash a
day; also horse-chestnut the same. Beach plum well
out, several days at least. Wood pewee, and Minott
heard a loon go laughing over this morning.

The vireo days have fairly begun. They are now
heard amid the elm-tops. Thin coats and straw hats
are worn.

I have noticed that notional nervous invalids, who
report to the community the exact condition of their
heads and stomachs every morning, as if they alone
were blessed or cursed with these parts; who are old
betties and quiddles, if men; who can't eat their breakfasts when they are ready, but play with their spoons,
and hanker after an ice-cream at irregular hours; who
go more than half-way to meet any invalidity, and go
to bed to be sick on the slightest occasion, in the
middle of the brightest forenoon, — improve the least
opportunity to be sick; — I observe that such are self-
indulgent persons, without any regular and absorbing
employment. They are nice, discriminating, experienced
in all that relates to bodily sensations. They come to
you stroking their wens, manipulating their ulcers, and
expect you to do the same for them. Their religion
and humanity stick. They spend the day manipulating
their bodies and doing no work; can never get their
nails clean.

Vol. IX

parently female of the rose-breasted, quite tame, as
usual, brown above, with black head and a white
streak over the eye, a less distinct one beneath it, two
faint bars on wings, dirty-white bill, white breast,
dark spotted or streaked, and from time [to time] utters
a very sharp *chirp* of alarm or interrogation as it peers
through the twigs at me.

A lady's-slipper. At Cliffs, no doubt, before. At
Abel Brooks's (or Black Snake, or Red Cherry, or
Rye) Hollow, hear the wood thrush.

In Thrush Alley, see one of those large ant-hills,
recently begun, the grass and moss partly covered with
sand over a circle two feet in diameter, with holes two
to five inches apart, and the dry sand is dark-spotted
with the fresh damp sand about each hole.

My mother was telling to-night of the sounds which
she used to hear summer nights when she was young and
lived on the Virginia Road, — the lowing of cows, or
cackling of geese, or the beating of a drum as far off as
Hildreth's, but above all Joe Merriam whistling to his
team, for he was an admirable whistler. Says she used
to get up at midnight and go and sit on the door-step
when all in the house were asleep, and she could hear
nothing in the world but the ticking of the clock in the
house behind her.

May 27. P. M. — To Hill.

I hear the sound of fife and drum the other side of
the village, and am reminded that it is May Training.
Some thirty young men are marching in the streets in
two straight sections, with each a very heavy and warm

cap for the season on his head and a bright red stripe down the legs of his pantaloons, and at their head march two with white stripes down their pants, one beating a drum, the other blowing a fife. I see them all standing in a row by the side of the street in front of their captain's residence, with a dozen or more ragged boys looking on, but presently they all remove to the opposite side, as it were with one consent, not being satisfied with their former position, which probably had its disadvantages. Thus they march and strut the better part of the day, going into the tavern two or three times, to abandon themselves to unconstrained positions out of sight, and at night they may be seen going home singly with swelling breasts.

When I first saw them as I was ascending the Hill, they were going along the road to the Battle-Ground far away under the hill, a fifer and a drummer to keep each other company and spell one another. Ever and anon the drum sounded more hollowly loud and distinct, as if they had just emerged from a subterranean passage, though it was only from behind some barn, and following close behind I could see two platoons of awful black beavers, rising just above the wall, where the warriors were stirring up the dust of Winter Street, passing Ex-Captain Abel Heywood's house, probably with trailed arms. There might have been some jockey in their way, spending his elegant leisure teaching his horse to stand fire, or trying to run down an orphan boy. I also hear, borne down the river from time to time, regular reports of small arms from Sudbury or Wayland, where they are probably firing by platoons.

Celtis occidentalis, perhaps yesterday. How the staminate flowers drop off, even before opening! I perceived that rare meadow fragrance on the 25th. Is it not the sweet-scented vernal grass? [1] I see what I have called such, now very common. The earliest thorn on hill, a day or more. Hemlock, apparently a day or two. Some butternut catkins; the leaves have been touched by frost. This is blossom week, beginning last Sunday (the 24th). At evening, the first bat.

May 28. Rain again in the night, and this forenoon, more or less. In some places the ground is strewn with apple blossoms, quite concealing it, as white and thick as if a snow-storm had occurred.

May 29. P. M. — To Lee's Cliff.

A fine-grained air, June-like, after a cloudy, rain-threatening or rainy morning. Sufficient [*sic*] with a still, clear air in which the hum of insects is heard, and the sunniness contrasts with the shadows of the freshly expanded foliage, like the glances of an eye from under the dark eyelashes of June. The grass is not yet dry. The birds sing more lively than ever now after the rain, though it is only 2 P. M.

On the Corner road I overtake a short, thick-set young man dressed in thick blue clothes, with a large basket of scions, etc., on his arm, who has just come from Newton in the cars and is going to graft for Lafayette Garfield, thus late. He does not think much of the Baldwin, and still less of the Porter. The last is too

[1] Think not, but perceive that in any case.

sour! and, above all, does not bear well!! Has set more scions of Williams' Favorite than of any other, and thinks much of Seaver's apple, a sweeting, etc. Verily, it is all *de gustibus*. Having occasion to speak of his father, who had been unfortunate, he said, "We boys (his sons) clubbed together and bought the old fellow a farm" just before he died. He had a very broad, round face, and short front teeth half buried in the gums, for he exposed the whole of his gums when he opened his mouth.

I think I have noticed that coarse-natured farmers' boys, etc., have not a sufficiently fine and delicate taste to appreciate a high-flavored apple. It is commonly too acid for them, and they prefer some tame, sweet thing, fit only for baking, as a pumpkin sweeting.

Men derive very various nutriment from the same nature, their common habitat, like plants. Some derive, as it were directly from the soil, a brawny body, and their cheeks bulge out like pumpkin sweetings. They seem more thoroughly naturalized here, and the elements are kinder to them. They have more of the wind and rain and meadow muck in their composition. They flourish in the swampy soil like vegetables and do not fear toothache or neuralgia. Some grow like a pumpkin pine, at least. They fish and hunt and get the meadow-hay. Compared with ordinary men, they grow like a Rohan potato beside a Lady's-Finger. Their system has great power of assimilation. The soil is native to them. As different elements go to the composition of two human bodies as the thoughts that occupy their brains are different. How much more readily one na-

ture assimilates to beef and potatoes and makes itself a brawny body of them, than another!

We sat and talked a spell at the Corner Spring. What is the new warbler I see and hear frequently now, with apparently a black head, white side-head, brown back, forked tail, and light legs?

The sun came out an hour or more ago, rapidly drying the foliage, and for the first time this year I noticed the little shades produced by the foliage which had expanded in the rain, and long narrow dark lines of shade along the hedges or willow-rows. It was like the first bright flashings of an eye from under dark eyelashes after shedding warm tears.

Now I see a great dark low-arching cloud in the northwest already dropping rain there and steadily sweeping southeast, as I go over the first Conantum Hill from the spring. But I trust that its southwest end will drift too far north to strike me. The rest of the sky is quite serene, sprinkled here and there with bright downy, glowing summer clouds. The grass was not yet dried before this angry summer-shower cloud appeared. I go on, uncertain whether it is broad or thin and whether its heel will strike me or not.

How universal that strawberry-like fragrance of the fir-balsam cone and wilted twig! My meadow fragrance (also perceived on hillsides) reminds me of it. Methinks that the fragrance of the strawberry may stand for a large class of odors, as the terebinthine odors of firs and arbor-vitæ and cedar (as the harp stands for music). There is a certain sting to it, as to them.

Black shrub oaks well out. *Oxalis stricta.*

The *Veronica serpyllifolia*, now erect, is commonly found in moist depressions or hollows in the pastures, where perchance a rock has formerly been taken out and the grass is somewhat thicker and deeper green; also in the grassy ruts of old, rarely used cart-paths.

Red and black oaks are out at Lee's Cliff, well out, and already there are crimson spots on the red oak leaves. Also the fine red *mammillæ* galls stud the black cherry leaves. Galls begin with the very unfolding of the leaves. The *Polygonatum pubescens* out there. Some, nay most, *Turritis stricta* quite out of bloom.

Fair Haven Lake now, at 4.30 P. M., is perfectly smooth, reflecting the darker and glowing June clouds as it has not before. Fishes incessantly dimple it here and there, and I see afar, approaching steadily but diagonally toward the shore of the island, some creature on its surface, maybe a snake, — but my glass shows it to be a muskrat, leaving two long harrow-like ripples behind. Soon after, I see another, quite across the pond on the Baker Farm side, and even distinguish that to be a muskrat. The fishes, methinks, are busily breeding now. These things I see as I sit on the top of Lee's Cliff, looking into the light and dark eye of the lake. The heel of that summer-shower cloud, seen through the trees in the west, has extended further south and looks more threatening than ever. As I stand on the rocks, examining the blossoms of some forward black oaks which close overhang it, I think I hear the sound of flies against my hat. No, it is scattered raindrops, though the sky is perfectly clear above me, and the cloud from which they come is yet far on

one side. I see through the tree-tops the thin vanguard of the storm scaling the celestial ramparts, like eager light infantry, or cavalry with spears advanced. But from the west a great, still, ash-colored cloud comes on. The drops fall thicker, and I seek a shelter under the Cliffs. I stand under a large projecting portion of the Cliff, where there is ample space above and around, and I can move about as perfectly protected as under a shed. To be sure, fragments of rock look as if they would fall, but I see no marks of recent ruin about me.

Soon I hear the low all-pervading hum of an approaching hummingbird circling above the rock, which afterward I mistake several times for the gruff voices of men approaching, unlike as these sounds are in some respects, and I perceive the resemblance even when I know better. Now I am sure it is a hummingbird, and now that it is two farmers approaching. But presently the hum becomes more sharp and thrilling, and the little fellow suddenly perches on an ash twig within a rod of me, and plumes himself while the rain is fairly beginning. He is quite out of proportion to the size of his perch. It does not acknowledge his weight.

I sit at my ease and look out from under my lichen-clad rocky roof, half-way up the Cliff, under freshly leafing ash and hickory trees on to the pond, while the rain is falling faster and faster, and I am rather glad of the rain, which affords me this experience. The rain has compelled me to find the cosiest and most homelike part of all the Cliff. The surface of the pond, though the rain dimples it all alike and I perceive no

wind, is still divided into irregular darker and lighter spaces, with distinct boundaries, as it were *watered* all over. Even now that it rains very hard and the surface is all darkened, the boundaries of those spaces are not quite obliterated. The countless drops seem to spring again from its surface like stalagmites.

A mosquito, sole living inhabitant of this antrum, settles on my hand. I find here sheltered with me a sweet-briar growing in a cleft of the rock above my head, where perhaps some bird or squirrel planted it. Mulleins beneath. *Galium Aparine*, just begun to bloom, growing next the rock; and, in the earth-filled clefts, columbines, some of whose cornucopias strew the ground. *Ranunculus bulbosus* in bloom; saxifrage; and various ferns, as spleenwort, etc. Some of these plants are never rained on. I perceive the buttery-like scent of barberry bloom from over the rock, and now and for some days the bunches of effete white ash anthers strew the ground.

It lights up a little, and the drops fall thinly again, and the birds begin to sing, but now I see a new shower coming up from the southwest, and the wind seems to have changed somewhat. Already I had heard the low mutterings of its thunder — for this is a thunder-shower — in the midst of the last. It seems to have shifted its quarters merely to attack me on a more exposed side of my castle. Two foes appear where I had expected none. But who can calculate the tactics of the storm? It is a first regular summer thunder-shower, preceded by a rush of wind, and I begin to doubt if my quarters will prove a sufficient shelter. I am fairly

besieged and know not when I shall escape. I hear the still roar of the rushing storm at a distance, though no trees are seen to wave. And now the forked flashes descending to the earth succeed rapidly to the hollow roars above, and down comes the deluging rain. I hear the alarmed notes of birds flying to a shelter. The air at length is cool and chilly, the atmosphere is darkened, and I have forgotten the smooth pond and its reflections. The rock feels cold to my body, as if it were a different season of the year. I almost repent of having lingered here; think how far I should have got if I had started homeward. But then what a condition I should have been in! Who knows but the lightning will strike this cliff and topple the rocks down on me? The crashing thunder sounds like the overhauling of lumber on heaven's loft. And now, at last, after an hour of steady confinement, the clouds grow thin again, and the birds begin to sing. They make haste to conclude the day with their regular evening songs (before the rain is fairly over) according to the program. The pepe on some pine tree top was heard almost in the midst of the storm. One or two bullfrogs trump. They care not how wet it is. Again I hear the still rushing, all-pervading roar of the withdrawing storm, when it is at least half a mile off, wholly beyond the pond, though no trees are seen to wave. It is simply the sound of the countless drops falling on the leaves and the ground. You were not aware what a sound the rain made. Several times I attempt to leave my shelter, but return to it. My first stepping abroad seems but a signal for the rain to commence again. Not till after an hour and a half do I escape. After all, my feet and legs are drenched by the wet grass.[1]

Those great hickory buds, how much they contained! You see now the large reddish scales turned back at the base of the new twigs. Suddenly the buds burst, and those large pinnate leaves stretched forth in various directions.

I see and hear the cuckoo. The *Salix nigra,* apparently several days, at Corner Bridge.

Many of the black spruce have the terminal twigs dead. They are a slow-growing tree. It is encouraging to see thrifty-growing white pines by their side, which have added three feet to their height the last year.

With all this opportunity, this comedy and tragedy, how near all men come to doing nothing! It is strange that they did not make us more intense and emphatic, that they do not goad us into some action. Generally, with all our desires and restlessness, we are no more likely to embark in any enterprise than a tree is to walk to a more favorable locality. The seaboard swarms with adventurous and rowdy fellows, but how unaccountably they train and are held in check! They are as likely to be policemen as anything. It exhausts their wits and energy merely to get their living, and they can do no more. The Americans are very busy and adventurous sailors, but all in somebody's employ, — as hired men. I have not heard of one setting out in his own bark, if only to run down our own coast on a voyage of adventure or observation, on his own account.

[1] *Vide* forward [next date].

Vol. IX

to the light! How suddenly Nature spreads her umbrellas! How little delay in expanding leaves! They seem to expand before our eyes, like the wings of moths just fallen from the cocoon.

Buttercups thickly spot the churchyard.

Perhaps I could write meditations under a rock in a shower.

When first I had sheltered myself under the rock, I began at once to look out on the pond with new eyes, as from my house. I was at Lee's Cliff as I had never been there before, had taken up my residence there, as it were. Ordinarily we make haste away from all opportunities to be where we have instinctively endeavored to get. When the storm was over where I was, and only a few thin drops were falling around me, I plainly saw the rear of the rain withdrawing over the Lincoln woods south of the pond, and, above all, heard the grand rushing sound made by the rain falling on the freshly green forest, a very different sound when thus heard at a distance from what it is when we are in the midst of it. In the latter case we are soothed by a gentle pattering and do not suspect the noise which a rainstorm makes. This Cliff thus became my house. I inhabited it. When, at length, it cleared up, it was unexpectedly early and light, and even the sun came out and shone warm on my back as I went home. Large puddles occupied the cart-paths and rose above the grass in the fields.

In the midst of the shower, though it was not raining very hard, a black and white creeper came and inspected the limbs of a tree before my rock, in his usual

May 30. P. M. — To chestnut oaks.

I think that there are many chestnut-sided warblers this season. They are pretty tame. One sits within six feet of me, though not still. He is much painted up.

Blue-stemmed goldenrod is already a foot high. I see the geranium and two-leaved Solomon's-seal out, the last abundant. The red pyrus by the path, not yet, but probably the same elsewhere.

The young black oak leafets are dark red or reddish, thick and downy; the scarlet oak also are somewhat reddish, thick and downy, or thin and green and little downy, like red oak, but rather more deeply cut; the red oak broad, thin, green and not downy; the white pink-red. Was it not a whip-poor-will I scared up at the base of a bush in the woods to-day, that went off with a clumsy flight?

By the path near the northeast shore of Flint's Pond, just before reaching the wall by the brook, I see what I take to be an uncommonly large *Uvularia sessilifolia* flower, but, looking again, am surprised to find it the *Uvularia perfoliata,* which I have not found hereabouts before. It is a taller and much more erect plant than the other, with a larger flower, methinks. It is considerably past its prime and probably began with the other.

Chestnut oak not yet in bloom, though the black and scarlet are well out in ordinary places. Its young leaves have a reddish-brown tinge. All the large trees are cut down. The white oak is not out.

It is remarkable that many beach and chestnut oak leaves, which so recently expanded, have already attained their full size! How they launch themselves forth

zigzag, prying way, head downward often, and when it thundered loudest, heeded it not. Birds appear to be but little incommoded by the rain. Yet they do not often sing in it.

The blue sky is never more celestial to our eyes than when it is first seen here and there between the clouds at the end of a storm, — a sign of speedy fair weather. I saw clear blue patches for twenty minutes or more in the southwest before I could leave my covert, for still I saw successive fine showers falling between me and the thick glaucous white pine beneath.

I think that such a projection as this, or a cave, is the only effectual protection that nature affords us against the storm.

I sang "Tom Bowling" there in the midst of the rain, and the dampness seemed to be favorable to my voice.[1] There was a slight rainbow on my way home. Met Conant riding home, who had been caught in town and detained, though he had an umbrella. Already a spider or other insect had drawn together the just expanded leaves of a hickory before my door with its web within them, making a close tent. This twig extended under my rocky roof and was quite dry. Probably a portion of the Cliff, being undermined by rain, had anciently fallen out and left this rocky roof above.

May 31. P. M. — To Gowing's Swamp and to *Pinus resinosa.*

In the ditches in Moore's Swamp on the new Bedford

[1] [This was Thoreau's favorite song. See Sanborn, pp. 268, 269, 272, especially the quotation from Mr. Ricketson.]

road, the myriads of pollywogs, now three quarters of an inch long, crowding close to the edge, make a continuous black edging to the pool a foot wide. I see where thousands have been left high and dry and are now trodden into the sand, yet preserving their forms, spotting it with black. The water looks too full of yellowish sediment to support them. That central meadow and pool in Gowing's Swamp is its very navel, *omphalos*, where the umbilical cord was cut that bound it to creation's womb. Methinks every swamp tends to have or suggests such an interior tender spot. The sphagnous crust that surrounds the pool is pliant and quaking, like the skin or muscles of the abdomen; you seem to be slumping into the very bowels of the swamp. Some seem to have been here to collect sphagnum, either for wells, or to wrap plants in. There grow the white spruce and the larch. The spruce cones, though now erect, at length turn down. The sterile flowers on lower twigs around stand up now three quarters of an inch long, open and reddish-brown. *Andromeda Polifolia*, much past its prime. I detect no hairy huckleberry. The *Vaccinium Oxycoccus* is almost in bloom! and has grown three inches; is much in advance of the common.

The *Pinus resinosa* not yet out; will be apparently with the *rigida*. It has no fertile flowers or cones. The sterile flower-buds are dark-purple, while those of the *rigida there* are light-green. The largest tree is about ten inches in diameter. It is distinguished, at a distance even, by its lighter-colored and smoother or flatter bark. It is also very straight and perpendicular, with its

branches in regular whorls, and its needles are very long.

Rhodora now in its prime.

I see in open land a hollow circle of *Lycopodium dendroideum*, ten feet in diameter; some of the inner portion is dead. This too, then, like the flowering fern, grows or spreads in circles. Also the cinnamon fern grows in circles.

See an ants' nest, just begun, which covers the grass with sand for more than ten feet in one direction and seven in the other and is thickly pierced with holes.

bloom is much whiter at a little distance than that of an apple tree, which has a blue tinge (or, earlier, rosaceous). This thorn has pink anthers, seen close at hand. The leaves are very evenly distributed amid the bloom. I see a swamp white [oak] fully and abundantly out, apparently a day or two; so the chestnut oak (which begins to shed pollen in house June 2d; its young reddish leaves resemble the young *Q. Chinquapin*, and its bloom, and apparently it opens with it in similar places) may be put apparently with the white oak. But it grows in a rather late place.

P. arbutifolia var. *erythrocarpa* in house; perhaps a day or two earlier in some places.

A red-wing's nest, four eggs, low in a tuft of sedge in an open meadow. What Champollion can translate the hieroglyphics on these eggs? It is always writing of the same character, though much diversified. While the bird picks up the material and lays the egg, who determines the style of the marking? When you approach, away dashes the dark mother, betraying her nest, and then chatters her anxiety from a neighboring bush, where she is soon joined by the red-shouldered male, who comes scolding over your head, chattering and uttering a sharp *phe phee-e*.

I hear the note of a bobolink concealed in the top of an apple tree behind me. Though this bird's full strain is ordinarily somewhat trivial, this one appears to be meditating a strain as yet unheard in meadow or orchard. *Paulo majora canamus.* He is just touching the strings of his theorbo, his glassichord, his water organ, and one or two notes globe themselves and fall

XI

JUNE, 1857

(ÆT. 39)

June 1. P. M. — To Hill.

The weather has been less reliable for a few weeks past than at any other season of the year. Though fair in the forenoon, it may rain in the afternoon, and the continuance of the showers surpasses all expectation. After several days of rain a fair day may succeed, and you close your eyes at night on a starlit sky, but you awake unexpectedly to a steady rain in the morning.

The morus at the Lee house is apparently the same with that at Howe's and Pratt's, and the berries are now three quarters of an inch long. I see no staminate blossoms. It must have been out several days. It is undoubtedly the *Morus rubra*, our only native one, for the *nigra* has lobed leaves and is a smaller tree, rare, and not quite hardy enough to do well in New England, they say.[1]

The second thorn on Hill will evidently open tomorrow. It is altogether smooth while the first has downy peduncles, and its sepals are about entire while those of the first are cut-fringed. That largest and earliest thorn is now in full bloom, and I notice that its

[1] I read in Michaux, June 12, that the sexes of the *rubra* are *usually* separate, and that the fruit of the black is three or four times as large as this.

in liquid bubbles from his teeming throat.[1] It is as if he touched his harp within a vase of liquid melody, and when he lifted it out, the notes fell like bubbles from the trembling strings. Methinks they are the most *liquidly* sweet and melodious sounds I ever heard. They are refreshing to my ear as the first distant tinkling and gurgling of a rill to a thirsty man. Oh, never advance farther in your art, never let us hear your full strain, sir. But away he launches, and the meadow is all bespattered with melody. His notes fall with the apple blossoms, in the orchard. The very divinest part of his strain dropping from his overflowing breast *singultim*, in globes of melody. It is the foretaste of such strains as never fell on mortal ears, to hear which we should rush to our doors and contribute all that we possess and are. Or it seemed as if in that vase full of melody some notes sphered themselves, and from time to time bubbled up to the surface and were with difficulty repressed.

June 2. Sterile buttonwood, not yet *generally*, but some apparently several days at least.

It was a portion of the natural surface of the earth itself which jutted out and became my roof the other day. How fit that Nature should thus shelter her own children! The first drops were dimpling the pond even as the fishes had done.

The grass is flaming up through the shallow water on the meadows.

It is very warm till 3 P. M., and then a washing breeze

[1] [Channing, p. 96.]

Vol. IX

arises, and before night probably distant thundershowers have cooled the air, for after dark we see the flashes called heat lightning in the north, and hear the distant thunder. Geraniums bring thunder.

That bobolink's song affected me as if one were endeavoring to keep down globes of melody within a vase full of liquid, but some bubbled up irrepressible, — kept thrusting them down with a stick, but they slipped and came up one side.

A young sparrow already flies.

Drove this afternoon to Painted-Cup Meadow.

A tanager yesterday.

June 3. P. M. — To White Cedar Swamp.

Salix lucida out of bloom, but *S. nigra* still in bloom. I see a large branch of *S. lucida*, which has been broken off probably by the ice in the winter and come down from far up-stream and lodged, butt downward, amid some bushes, where it has put forth pink fibres from the butt end in the water, and is growing vigorously, though not rooted in the bottom. It is thus detained by a clump of bushes at high water, where it begins to sprout and send its pink fibres down to the mud, and finally the water, getting down to the summer level, leaves it rooted in the bank.

The first cratægus on Hill is in many instances done, while the second is not fairly or generally in bloom yet. The pitch pine at Hemlocks is in bloom. The sterile flowers are yellowish, while those of the *P. resinosa* are dark-purple. As usual, when I jar them the pollen rises in a little cloud about the pistillate flowers and the

tops of the twigs, there being a little wind. The bass at the Island will not bloom this year.[1] The racemed andromeda (*Leucothoë*) has been partly killed, — the extremities of the twigs, — so that its racemes are imperfect, the lower parts only green. It is not quite out; probably is later for this injury.

The ground of the cedar swamp, where it has been burnt over and sprouts, etc., have sprung up again, is covered with the *Marchantia polymorpha*. Now shows its starlike or umbrella-shaped fertile flowers and its shield-shaped sterile ones. It is a very rank and wild-looking vegetation, forming the cuticle of the swamp's foundation.

I feel the suckers' nests with my paddle, but do not see them on account of the depth of the river. Many small devil's-needles, like shad-flies, in bushes.

Early potatoes are being hoed. The gardener is killing the piper grass.

I have several friends and acquaintances who are very good companions in the house or for an afternoon walk, but whom I cannot make up my mind to make a longer excursion with; for I discover, all at once, that they are too gentlemanly in manners, dress, and all their habits. I see in my mind's eye that they wear black coats, considerable starched linen, glossy hats and shoes, and it is out of the question. It is a great disadvantage for a traveller to be a gentleman of this kind; he is so ill-treated, only a prey to landlords. It would be too much of a circumstance to enter a strange town or house with such a companion. You could not

[1] ?

travel incognito; you might get into the papers. You should travel as a common man. If such a one were to set out to make a walking-journey, he would betray himself at every step. Every one would see that he was trying an experiment, as plainly as they see that a lame man is lame by his limping. The natives would bow to him, other gentlemen would invite him to ride, conductors would warn him that this was the second-class car, and many would take him for a clergyman; and so he would be continually pestered and balked and run upon. You would not see the natives at all. Instead of going in quietly at the back door and sitting by the kitchen fire, you would be shown into a cold parlor, there to confront a fireboard, and excite a commotion in a whole family. The women would scatter at your approach, and their husbands and sons would go right up to hunt up their black coats, — for they all have them; they are as cheap as dirt. You would go trailing your limbs along the highways, mere bait for corpulent innholders, as a pickerel's [sic] leg is trolled along a stream, and your part of the profits would be the frog's. No, you must be a common man, or at least travel as one, and then nobody will know that you are there or have been there. I would not undertake a simple pedestrian excursion with one of these, because to enter a village, or a hotel, or a private house, with such a one, would be too great a circumstance, would create too great a stir. You could only go half as far with the same means, for the price of board and lodgings would rise everywhere; so much you have to pay for wearing that kind of coat. Not that the difference is in

the coat at all, for the character of the scurf is determined by that of the true liber beneath. Innkeepers,
stablers, conductors, clergymen, know a true wayfaring
man at first sight and let him alone. It is of no use
to shove your gaiter shoes a mile further than usual.
Sometimes it is mere shiftlessness or want of originality,
— the clothes wear them; sometimes it is egotism, that
cannot afford to be treated like a common man, — they
wear the clothes. They wish to be at least fully appreciated by every stage-driver and schoolboy. They
would like well enough to see a new place, perhaps,
but then they would like to be regarded as important
public personages. They would consider it a misfortune if their names were left out of the published list
of passengers because they came in the steerage, — an
obscurity from which they might never emerge.

June 4. P. M. — To Bare Hill.

The early potentilla is now erect in the June grass.
Salix tristis is going to seed, showing some cotton; also
some *S. rostrata.* I am surprised to see some kind of
fish dart away in Collier's veronica ditch, for it about
dries up and has no outlet.

I observed yesterday, the first time this year, the lint
on the smooth surface of the Assabet at the Hemlocks,
giving the water a stagnant look. It is an agreeable
phenomenon to me, as connected with the season and
suggesting warm weather. I suppose it to be the down
from the new leaves which so rapidly become smooth.
There *may be* a *little* pitch pine pollen with it now.
The current is hardly enough to make a clear streak

in it here and there. The stagnant-looking surface,
where the water slowly circles round in that great eddy,
has the appearance of having been dusted over. This
lint now covers my clothes as I go through the sprout-
lands, but it gets off remarkably before long. Each
under side of a leaf you strike leaves the mark of its lint
on your clothes, but it is clean dirt and soon wears
off.

One thing that chiefly distinguishes this season from
three weeks ago is that fine serene undertone or earth-
song as we go by sunny banks and hillsides, the creak
of crickets, which affects our thoughts so favorably,
imparting its own serenity. It is time now to bring our
philosophy out of doors. Our thoughts pillow themselves unconsciously in the troughs of this serene, rippling sea of sound. Now first we begin to be peripatetics.
No longer our ears come in contact with the bold
echoing earth, but everywhere recline on the spring
cushion of a cricket's chirp. These rills that ripple
from every hillside become at length a universal sea of
sound, nourishing our ears when we are most unconscious.

In that first apple tree at Wyman's an apparent
hairy woodpecker's nest (from the size of the bird),
about ten feet from ground. The bird darts away with
a shrill, loud chirping of alarm, incessantly repeated,
long before I get there, and keeps it up as long as I
stay in the neighborhood. The young keep up an incessant fine, breathing peep which can be heard across
the road and is much increased when they hear you
approach the hole, they evidently expecting the old bird.

Vol. IX

I perceive no offensive odor. I saw the bird fly out of
this hole, May 1st, and probably the eggs were laid
about that time. *Vide* it next year.

In the high pasture behind Jacob Baker's, soon after
coming out of the wood, I scare up a bay-wing. She
runs several rods close to the ground through the thin
grass, and then lurks behind tussocks, etc. The nest
has four eggs, dull pinkish-white with brown spots;
nest low in ground, of stubble lined with white horsehair.

Carya glabra, apparently a day at least.

Oldenlandia on Bare Hill, along above wall opposite
the oak, a rod or more off and westerly. Apparently
several days at least, but it appears not to do well. It
has a dry, tufted look, somewhat like young savory-
leaved aster, on the bare rocky hill and in the clear
spaces between the huckleberry bushes. Reminds me
of a heath. Does not blossom so full as once I saw it.
Arethusa. Crimson fungus (?) on black birch leaves, as
if bespattered with blood.

*June 5. P. M. — To Gowing's Swamp and Poplar
Hill.*

The shad-flies were very abundant probably last evening about the house, for this morning they are seen
filling and making black every cobweb on the side of
the house, blinds, etc. All freshly painted surfaces are
covered with them. The surface of pools and ditches
also is remarkably thick with them. The living ones are
on the bushes which I pluck, far from any water.

I find one *Vaccinium Oxycoccus* open. The petals

are not white like the common, but pink like the bud.
That low reedy sedge about the edge of the central
pool in the swamp is just out of bloom and shows the
seeds.[1]

I see a great many tortoises in that pool, showing
their heads and backs above water and pursuing each
other about the pool. It is evidently their copulating-
season. Their shells are yellow-spotted, and their
throats are of a reddish yellow (?). Are they the *Emys
guttata?*[2] It is a wonder how they made their way to
this water through so many twiggy bushes and over
so many tussocks. How should they know of such a
wild water? To this wild water, then, the tortoises which
inhabit the swamps resort in their breeding-season, and
are there undisturbed. You would think it almost the
labor of a lifetime for a tortoise to make its way from
the surrounding shrubbery to this water, and how do
they know that there is water here?

The larch cones are still very beautiful against the
light, but some cones, I perceive, are merely green. Some
apparent beach plum (?) almost completely out of bloom,
ten to twelve feet high, along the wall behind Adolphus
Clark's. This is the largest I know of. Lambkill. The
mocker-nuts on Mrs. Ripley's hill apparently a day or
more. Some red maples are much more fertile than
others. Their keys are now very conspicuous. But
such trees have comparatively few leaves and have
grown but little as yet.

[1] Scheuchzeria.
[2] Probably, for I have found two on the sphagnum close by it
since. *Vide* 1860, May or June.

At evening, paddle up Assabet. There are many ephemeræ in the air; but it is cool, and their great flight is not yet. Pincushion gall on oak.

I am interested in each contemporary plant in my vicinity, and have attained to a certain acquaintance with the larger ones. They are cohabitants with me of this part of the planet, and they bear familiar names. Yet how essentially wild they are! as wild, really, as those strange fossil plants whose impressions I see on my coal. Yet I can imagine that some race gathered those too with as much admiration, and knew them as intimately as I do these, that even they served for a language of the sentiments. Stigmariæ stood for a human sentiment in that race's flower language. Chickweed, or a pine tree, is but little less wild. I assume to be acquainted with these, but what ages between me and the tree whose shade I enjoy! It is as if it stood substantially in a remote geological period.

June 6. 8 A. M. — To Lee's Cliff by river.

Salix pedicellaris off Holden's has been out of bloom several days at least. So it is earlier to begin and to end than *our S. lucida.*

This is June, the month of grass and leaves. The deciduous trees are investing the evergreens and revealing how dark they are. Already the aspens are trembling again, and a new summer is offered me. I feel a little fluttered in my thoughts, as if I might be too late. Each season is but an infinitesimal point. It no sooner comes than it is gone. It has no duration. It simply gives a tone and hue to my thought. Each annual

Vol. IX

phenomenon is a reminiscence and prompting. Our thoughts and sentiments answer to the revolutions of the seasons, as two cog-wheels fit into each other. We are conversant with only one point of contact at a time, from which we receive a prompting and impulse and instantly pass to a new season or point of contact. A year is made up of a certain series and number of sensations and thoughts which have their language in nature. Now I am ice, now I am sorrel. Each experience reduces itself to a mood of the mind. I see a man grafting, for instance. What this imports chiefly is not apples to the owner or bread to the grafter, but a certain mood or train of thought to my mind. That is what this grafting is to me. Whether it is anything at all, even apples or bread, to anybody else, I cannot swear, for it would be worse than swearing *through glass.* For I only see those other facts as through a glass darkly.

Cratægus Crus-Galli, maybe a day. Early iris. *Viburnum Lentago,* a day or more. Krigias, with their somewhat orange yellow, spot the dry hills all the forenoon and are very common, but as they are closed in the afternoon, they are but rarely noticed by walkers. The long mocker-nut on Conantum not yet out, and the second, or round, one will be yet later. Its catkins are more grayish.

I see many great devil's-needles in an open wood, — and for a day or two, — stationary on twigs, etc., standing out more or less horizontally like thorns, holding by their legs and heads (?). They do not incline to move when touched, and their eyes look whitish and

opaque, as if they were blind. They were evidently just escaped from the slough. I often see the slough on plants and, I think, the pupa in the water, as at Callitriche Pool.

As I sit on Lee's Cliff, I see a pe-pe on the topmost dead branch of a hickory eight or ten rods off. Regularly, at short intervals, it utters its monotonous note like *till-till-till,* or *pe-pe-pe.* Looking round for its prey and occasionally changing its perch, it every now and then darts off (phœbe-like), even five or six rods, toward the earth to catch an insect, and then returns to its favorite perch. If I lose it for a moment, I soon see it settling on the dead twigs again and hear its *till, till, till.* It appears through the glass mouse-colored above and head (which is perhaps darker), white throat, and narrow white beneath, with no white on tail.

There is a thorn now in its prime, *i. e.* near the beaked hazel, Conantum, with leaves more wedge-shaped at base than the *Cratægus coccinea;* apparently a variety of it, between that and *Crus-Galli.* (In press.)

A kingbird's nest, with two of its large handsome eggs, very loosely set over the fork of a horizontal willow by river, with dried everlasting of last year, as usual, just below Garfield's boat. Another in black willow south of long cove (east side, north of Hubbard's Grove) and another north of said cove. A brown thrasher's nest, with two eggs, on ground, near lower lentago wall and toward Bittern Cliff. The *Ranunculus Purshii* is in some places abundantly out now and quite showy. It must be our largest ranunculus (flower).

June 7. Sunday. P. M. — To river and Ponkawtasset with M. Pratt.

Now I notice many bubbles left on the water in my wake, as if it were more sluggish or had more viscidity than earlier. Far behind me they rest without bursting. Pratt has got the *Calla palustris,* in prime, — some was withering, so it may have been out ten days,[1] — from the bog near Bateman's Pond; also *Oxalis violacea,* which he says began about last Sunday, or May 31st, larger and handsomer than the yellow, though it blossoms but sparingly. Red huckleberry about same time. It is sticky like the black. His geranium from Fitzwilliam is well in bloom. It seems to be herbrobert, but without any offensive odor ! (?)

A small elm in front of Pratt's which he says three years ago had flowers in flat cymes, like a cornel ! ![2] I have pressed some leaves.

At the cross-wall below N. Hunt's, some way from road, the red cohush, one plant only in flower, the rest going to seed. Probably, therefore, with the white. It has slender pedicels and petals shorter than the white. Garlic grows there, not yet out. *Rubus triflorus* still in bloom there.

At the base of some hellebore, in a tuft a little from under the east edge of an apple tree, below violet woodsorrel, a nest well made outside of leaves, then grass, lined with fine grass, very deep and narrow, with thick sides, with four small somewhat cream-colored eggs with small brown and some black spots chiefly toward

[1] Or more, for it is past prime the 9th.
[2] He must be mistaken.

larger end. The bird, which flew off quickly, made me think of a wren and of a Maryland yellow-throat, though I saw no yellow.[1]

June 8. P. M. — To Saw Mill Brook.

White actæa done there. There are two good-sized black walnuts at Cyrus Smith's, by wall, out apparently a day. When I split the twigs they seemed hollowed by a worm or disease, the pith being (as is said of the butternut also) in plates. The fertile flower is probably not obvious yet. That of the butternut is now very distinct with its crimson stigmas.

Mother was saying to-day that she bought no new clothes for John until he went away into a store, but made them of his father's old clothes, which made me say that country boys could get enough cloth for their clothes by robbing the scarecrows. So little it need cost to live.

June 9. A large fog. *Celastrus scandens*, maybe a day. Triosteum, apparently several days (not at all June 1st).

Both kinds of sap, yellow birch and black, are now, in some bottles, quite aromatic and alike; but this year, methinks, it has a more *swampy* taste and musty, and most of the bottles are merely sour.

P. M. — To Violet Sorrel and Calla Swamp.

A peetweet's nest near wall by Shattuck's barn,

[1] It was a Maryland yellow-throat. Egg fresh. She is very shy and will not return to nest while you wait, but keeps up a very faint chip in the bushes or grass at some distance.

Merrick's pasture, at base of a dock; four eggs just on the point of being hatched. A regular nest of weak stubble set in ground.

In the sprout-land beyond the red huckleberry, an indigo-bird, which *chips* about me as if it had a nest there. This is a splendid and marked bird, high-colored as is the tanager, looking strange in this latitude. Glowing indigo. It flits from top of one bush to another, chirping as if anxious. Wilson says it sings, not like most other birds in the morning and evening chiefly, but also in the middle of the day. In this I notice it is like the tanager, the other fiery-plumaged bird. They seem to love the heat. It probably had its nest in one of those bushes.

The calla is generally past prime and going to seed.

I had said to Pratt, "It will be worth the while to look for other rare plants in Calla Swamp, for I have observed that where one rare plant grows there will commonly be others." Carrying out this design, this afternoon, I had not taken three steps into the swamp barelegged before I found the *Naumbergia thyrsiflora* in sphagnum and water, which I had not seen growing before. (Channing brought one to me from Hubbard's Great Meadow once.) It is hardly beginning yet. (In prime June 24th. *Vide* June 24th.)

The water in this Calla Swamp feels cold to my feet, and perhaps this is a peculiarity of it; on the north side a hill.

When I was at the yellow-throat's nest (as above) I heard that very loud sharp *pheet pheet* of a woodchuck (?) or rabbit which I have often heard before.

Vol. IX

The hellebore was very much eaten off about the wall whence it proceeded. It was kept up from time to time while I stayed.

June 10. At R. W. E.'s a viburnum, apparently *nudum* var. *cassinoides* (?) (*pyrifolium* Pursh), four or five days at least. (*Vide* in press.) It agrees with Bigelow's account, except that the leaves are decidedly serrate and the calyx-segments not acute. Has but a very slight tendency to thorns!! Twigs of this year red. The cymes are nearly sessile; petioles, etc., *very little* rusty-dotted. Compare it with *prunifolium*, and see fruit. It stands in a row with E.'s pear trees and has been mistaken for one, which, when not in flower, it very much resembles. Probably came from Watson's with them. (On the 13th I see apparently the same at Watson's, Plymouth, which he calls, and imported as, *V. prunifolium!*)

P. M. — To White Cedar Swamp.

A wood tortoise making a hole for her eggs just like a picta's hole. The *Leucothoë racemosa*, not yet generally out, but a little (it being mostly killed) a day or two.

In Julius Smith's yard, a striped snake (so called) was running about this forenoon, and in the afternoon it was found to have shed its slough, leaving it halfway out a hole, which probably it used to confine it in. It was about in its new skin. Many creatures — devil's-needles, etc., etc. — cast their sloughs now. Can't I?

Farmer tells me to-day that he has seen a regular barn swallow with forked tail about his barn, which was *black*,

---

not rufous; also of an owl's nest in a pine, the young probably two or three weeks old. *Vide* June 24th.

June 12. Friday. 8.30 A. M. — Set out for CAPE COD.

EGGS. —

At Natural History Rooms. —

The egg found on ground in R. W. E.'s garden some weeks since cannot be the bobolink's, for that is about as big as a bay-wing's but more slender, dusky-white, with numerous brown and black blotches. The egg of the *Turdus solitarius* is lettered "*Swamp Robin.*" Is this what they so call at New Bedford? The wood thrush's is a slender egg, a little longer than a catbird's and uniform greenish-blue. The yellow-shouldered sparrow's egg is size of Maryland yellow-throat's, white with brown spots, sometimes in a ring at the larger end. The Savannah sparrow's is about the same size, dirty-white with thick brown blotches. I find that the egg Farmer gave me for the "chicklisee's" is enough like the yellow-throat's to be it. Can he be thinking of the note, *whittichee?* Or is it the yellow-shouldered sparrow's egg? The egg of the hermit thrush[1] is about as big as that of Wilson's thrush, but darker green.

Some edible swallows' (?) nests, on a stick, side by side, shallow and small and shaped like oyster-shells, light-colored, but yet placed somewhat like the chimney swallows'.

Among the frogs in alcohol I notice the *Scaphiopus solitarius*, Cambridge!!

[1] Which variety?

Michaux says that mocker-nuts are of various sizes and forms, some round, some oblong. So I have found them. He also says that "the red-flowering maple [*Acer rubrum*][1] is the earliest tree whose bloom announces the return of Spring." This is a mistake, the white maple being much earlier.

I have not found the white spruce yet.

P. M. — At Watson's, Plymouth.

W. has several varieties of the English hawthorn (*oxyacantha*), pink and rose-colored, double and single, and very handsome now.

His English oak is almost entirely out of bloom, though I got some flowers. The biggest, which was set out in '49, is about thirty feet high, and, as I measured, just twenty inches in circumference at four inches from the ground. A very rapid growth.

I obtained there specimens of the plum-leaved willow, come well ditto, — because it comes on fast, — and *Salix rosmarinifolia*. Only some lingering bloom with the last.

He has the foreign *Betula alba* (much like our *populifolia*), its bark loosened up like our *papyracea*, but not so white; and what was sent him for *populifolia*, much like our *red birch*, the bark much like that of *alba* loosened up, but more reddish, the limbs red, leaves like a balm-of-Gilead somewhat, large (*vide* press). The *papyracea* leaves are unusually wedge-shaped at base, methinks.

The moosewood is chiefly fruiting, but some still

[1] [The brackets are Thoreau's.]

in bloom. *Cornus sanguinea*, in its prime. Its bark is *bright-red* and greenish. That of *C. sericea* (not well named) is dark-purplish. The Oriental is later to bloom than ours or else smaller-fruited.

The American mountain-ash not yet out (Cheney's in Concord, a day or two, June 25th). Nuttall says its leaves are at last very smooth. I have hitherto observed the *Pyrus aucuparia*, or European, at Prichard's, Whiting's, etc.

W. has the *Cratægus prunifolius*, with its thorns (*vide* herbarium); *Castanea vesca*, Spanish chestnut, of which ours is made a variety merely; *Populus monilifera*, as he calls it, and another very like it.

Bayberry well out. *Senecio vulgaris* a common weed, apparently in prime. Honkenya and beach pea well out on Plymouth beach.

W. has a very flourishing and large white maple of his setting, and they stand in Plymouth streets also, very pretty.

June 13. I see large mosses on the beach, crimson and lighter, already spread on the sand. See children going a-flagging and returning with large bundles, for the sake of the inmost tender blade. They go miles for them here.

June 14. Sunday. 7 A. M. — To Clark's Island.

B. M. Watson tells me that he learns from pretty good authority that Webster once saw the sea-serpent. It seems it was first seen, in the bay between Manomet and Plymouth Beach, by a perfectly relia-

ble witness (many years ago), who was accustomed to look out on the sea with his glass every morning the first thing as regularly as he ate his breakfast. One morning he saw this monster, with a head somewhat like a horse's raised some six feet above the water, and his body the size of a cask trailing behind. He was careering over the bay, chasing the mackerel, which ran ashore in their fright and were washed up and died in great numbers. The story is that Webster had appointed to meet some Plymouth gentlemen at Manomet and spend the day fishing with them. After the fishing was [over], he set out to return to Duxbury in his sailboat with Peterson, as he had come, and on the way they saw the sea-serpent, which answered to the common account of this creature. It passed directly across their bows only six or seven rods off and then disappeared. On the sail homeward, Webster having had time to reflect on what had occurred, at length said to Peterson, "For God's sake, never say a word about this to any one, for if it should be known that I have seen the sea-serpent, I should never hear the last of it, but wherever I went should have to tell the story to every one I met." So it has not leaked out till now.

Watson tells me (and Ed. Watson confirms it, his father having probably been of the party) that many years ago a party of Plymouth gentlemen rode round by the shore to the Gurnet and there had a high time. When they set out to return they left one of their number, a General Winslow, asleep, and as they rode along homeward, amused themselves with conjecturing what

he would think when he waked up and found himself alone. When at length he awoke, he comprehended his situation at once, and, being somewhat excited by the wine he had drunk, he mounted his horse and rode along the shore to Saquish Head in the opposite direction. From here to the end of Plymouth Beach is about a mile and a quarter, but, it being low tide, he waded his horse as far as the beacon north of the channel, at the entrance to Plymouth Harbor, about three quarters of a mile, and then boldly swam him across to the end of Plymouth Beach, about half a mile further, notwithstanding a strong current, and, having landed safely, he whipped up and soon reached the town, having come only about eight miles, and had ample time to warm and dry himself at the tavern before his companions, who had at least twenty miles to ride about through Marshfield and Duxbury. And when they found him sitting by the tavern fire, they at first thought it was his ghost.

Mr. Ed. Watson's brother (half?), the one who used to live in his schooner, told me that he saw (I suppose not long before) a stream of what they call "kelp flies," supposed to be generated by the rotting kelp, flying along just under the bank, on the shore in Duxbury, some ten feet wide by six deep and of indefinite length, — for he did not know how long they would be passing, — and flying as close as they could conveniently. Ed. Watson had no doubt of it. They also have what they call menhaden flies. This was an offset to my account of the ephemeræ.

Mr. Albert Watson's sons are engaged in lobster-catching. One will get two hundred in a day. I was surprised to hear that their lobster-traps 🪤🪤 were made in Vermont, costing something over a dollar apiece, — much timber, — but it seems they can be made cheaper there and sent down by railroad. They use sculpins, perch, etc., etc., for bait, catching it in a circular net with an iron rim. There were a couple of quarts of pine plugs or wedges in a boat, with which to plug the claws of the lobsters to prevent their fighting and tearing each other's claws off in the cars. There are large crates of latticework, six or eight feet square, sunk to a level with the water, in which they keep them fresh. They get three cents apiece for them, not boiled.

Saw them swim three horses across from Saquish Head to the island, a quarter of a mile or more. One rows a small boat while a man holds the bridle. At first the horses swam faster than the man could row, but soon they were somewhat drawn after the boat. They have sometimes driven a whole drove of cattle over at once.

Saw an abundance of horseshoe crabs on the Saquish shore, generally coupled, the rearmost or male (if that is he with two club feet) always the smaller. Often there were three or even four in a string, all moving about close to the shore, which apparently they affect. The pigs get a little nutriment out of them.

Looking from the island, the water is a light green over a shoal.

In a little red cedar grove, of young trees surrounding an old trunk, the only indigenous wood on the island, some three rods by two, and fifteen feet high,

I counted thirty-five crow blackbirds' nests, sometimes two or three near together in a tree, the young fluttering about and some dead beneath. The old in numbers were meanwhile coarsely chattering over our heads. The nests appeared to be made partly of the grassy seaweed.

E. Watson says that he saw a hen catch and devour a mouse, rather young, that was running across his barn floor.

In the shade of the orchard there, amid seaweed, a variety of whiteweed with more entire leaves, etc., and apparently without rays. Is it the Connecticut variety, with short rays?

Mr. Watson describes a sea turtle, as big as a mud turtle, found on the shore once. It had a large dent in its back, in which you [could] lay your hand, — a wound.

Evening. — At B. M. Watson's again. Hear a *new song*, very sweet and clear from what at first sounded like a golden robin, then a purple finch. It was not the first.

B. M. Watson speaks of an old lady named Cotton, now alive and over ninety, who is the Plymouth oracle. He says that his father-in-law Russell (whom I saw and who told me this once) knew a Cobb, who had seen Peregrine White.

Watson had a colt born about ten or eleven the last evening. I went out to see it early this morning, as it lay in the cold pasture. It got up alarmed and trotted about on its long large legs, and even nibbled a little grass, and behaved altogether as if it had been an in-

habitant of this planet for some years at least. They are as precocious as young partridges. It ran about most of the day in the pasture with its mother. Watson was surprised to see it so much larger than the night before. Probably they expand at once on coming to the light and air, like a butterfly that has just come out of its chrysalis.

June 15. Monday. A. M. — Walked to James Spooner's farm in a valley amid the woods; also to a swamp where white cedars once grew, not far behind the town, and now full of their buried trunks, though I hear of no tradition of trees there. In digging mud there recently, hog's bristles were found three or four feet deep. Watson told me of such places in Plymouth as "Small Gains" and "Shall I go naked?"

2 P. M. — Ride to Manomet with Watson and wife, through Manomet Ponds village, about eight miles. At the mouth of Eel River, the marsh vetchling (*Lathyrus palustris*), apparently in prime, some done. The curve of the shore on the east of Plymouth Beach is said to resemble the Bay of Naples. Manomet was quite a hill, over which the road ran in the woods. We struck the shore near Holmes's Hotel about half a mile north of Manomet Point.

There I shouldered my pack and took leave of my friends, — who thought it a dreary place to leave me, — and my journey along the shore was begun. Following the rocky shore round the point, I went considerably round without knowing it. Found there many of

the small shells that R. W. E. brought from Pigeon Cove. Having got round the point, I found a smooth sandy shore with pretty high sand-banks, like the back side of the Cape (though less). The vegetation on the top of the bank, too, was similar. I could see scattered small houses on the road a little inland. The *Hudsonia tomentosa* was apparently in prime there. Passed a few fishers' boats on the s , with a long rope and anchor carried high up, and one or two places where they land wood. Some three miles below Manomet, there appeared another blunt cape in front, which I avoided by going inland, falling into a small road near the coast, on which were two or three houses. Within a mile I crossed the stream or brook laid down on the map, by a rail, in low woods, leaving a wooded hill between me and the shore, then went along the edge of a swamp. It was pleasant walking thus at 5 P. M. by solitary sandy paths, through commonly low dry woods of oak or pine, through glistening oak woods (their fresh leaves in the June air), where the yellow-throat (or black-throat?[1]) was heard and the wood thrush sang, and, as I passed a swamp, a bittern boomed. As I stood quite near, I heard distinctly two or three dry, hard sucks, as if the bird were drawing up water from the swamp, and then the sounds usually heard, as if ejecting it. From time to time passed a yellow-spot or a painted turtle in the path, for now is their laying-season. One of the former was laying. We had before been obliged to stop our horse for fear of running over one in the rut. Now is the time that they are killed in

[1] [That is, black-throated bunting. See June 16.]

the ruts all the country over. They are caught in them, the clumsy fellows, as in a trap. Now the tortoises are met with in sandy woods and, delaying, are run over in the ruts.

One old man directed me on my way through the "plewed" land. Was amused at the simple and obliging but evidently despairing way in which a man at the last house endeavored to direct me further on my way by cart-paths through the woods, he evidently not having any faith that I could keep the route, but, getting the general course by compass, I did.

Having left Ship's Pond and Centre Hill Pond and a cedar swamp on my left, I at length reached one Harlow's, to whom I was recommended, but his neighbors said that "he lived *alone* like a beast" there ten years. I put up at Samuel Ellis's, just beyond the Salt Pond near by, having walked six or seven miles from Manomet through a singularly out-of-the-way region, of which you wonder if it is ever represented in the legislature.

Mrs. Ellis agreed to take me in, though they had already supped and she was unusually tired, it being washing-day. They were accustomed to put up peddlers from time to time, and had some pies just baked for such an emergency. At first took me for a peddler and asked what I carried in my bag. I was interested in a young peddler who soon after arrived and put up with his horse and cart, a simple and well-behaved boy of sixteen or seventeen only, peddling cutlery, who said that he started from Conway in this State. In answer to my question how he liked ped-

Vol. IX

dling, he said that he liked it on some accounts, it enabled him to see the world. I thought him an unusually good specimen of Young America. He found cutlery not good wares for that region; could do better where he came from, and was on his way to Boston for dry goods. Arranged to pay for his keeping partly in kind.

I saw menhaden skipping in the pond as I came along, it being connected with the sea.

Ellis, an oldish man, said that lobsters were plentier than they used to be, that one sometimes got three hundred and upward in a day, and he thought the reason was that they spawned in the cars and so the young were protected from fishes that prey on them. He told me of a man whom he had known, who once leaped upon a blackfish that had run or been driven ashore at the head of Buzzard's Bay, where they are very rare, in order to dispatch him, and as he was making a hole in the side of his head, he looked up and found himself a quarter of a mile from land, not having noticed any motion. The fish blowed blood with such force that it cut like a knife, and he saw his shirt-sleeve which appeared as if riddled with shot. He managed with his knife to head him toward shore again, and there landed. Told of finding a mud turtle so large that he walked with him standing on his back, though the turtle did not fairly stand up. He had killed a deer close by his house within two or three years. Hunters were then after it. Hearing the noise, he rushed into his house, seized his gun and fired hastily and carelessly, so as to mortally wound his dog (as well as the deer),

which he "would not have taken five dollars for!!" and had to dispatch at last. His wife and child also were nearly within range.

Speaking of the cold of last winter, he said he had no glass, but he knew it was extremely cold by seeing so great a fog on the sea in the morning as never before, which lasted unusually long. Said they fished on a shoal lying northeast, where there were seventeen fathoms of water, but when there was a fog on it, the fishes were gone, and he reckoned that the cold struck through.

Ellis told of a Boston man who thought he could catch some large trout in his brook with his fine tackling, but, as E. foretold, it broke, and the man offered five dollars apiece for the trout delivered in Boston, whether fresh or not. E. caught them soon after and sent them to Boston by water, but they, being spoiled by delay, were never delivered.

I heard him praying after I went to bed, and at breakfast the next morning —

(*June* 16) he gave thanks that we "of all the pale-faces were preserved alive." He was probably a Methodist. But the worst of it is that these evidences of "religion" are no evidence to the traveller of hospitality or generosity. Though he hears the sound of family prayer and sees sanctified faces and a greasy Bible or prayer-book, he feels not the less that he is in the hands of the Philistines, and perceives not the less the greasy and musty scent of a household whose single purpose is to scrape more pennies together, when it has already

more than enough for *its uses*, and it is to be preserved and abetted in this enterprise that they pray. What's the use of ushering the day with prayer, if it is thus consecrated to turning a few more pennies merely? All genuine goodness is original and as free from cant and tradition as the air. It is heathen in its liberality and independence on tradition. The accepted or established church is in alliance with the graveyards.

7 A. M. — I go along the sandy road through a region of small hills about half a mile from the sea, between slight gray fences, either post and rail, or slanting rails, ————✕✕✕✕✕———— a foot apart, resting on ————— two crossed stakes, the rails of unequal length, looking agreeably loose and irregular.

Within half a mile I come to the house of an Indian, a gray one-storied cottage, and there were two or three more beyond. They were just *beginning to build a meeting-house to-day!* Mrs. Ellis had told me that they were worthy people, especially such a family, that were members of the church, and the others were decent people, though they were not "professors of religion," — as if they were consequently less trustworthy. Ellis thought that if they should get angry with you they wouldn't make anything of taking your life. He had seen it in their eyes. The usual suspicion. I asked the way of an Indian whom I met in the road, a respectable-looking young man not darker than a sunburnt white man, with black eyes and the usual straight black hair of his race. He was apparently of mixed race, however. When I observed to him that he was one of the aboriginal stock, he answered, "I suppose so." We could see even to Sandwich Meeting-house as we stood in the road, and he showed me where to turn up from the shore to go to Scusset.

I turned off to the seashore at his house, going down through shrubbery enlivened by the strain of the yellow-throat (or black-throat bunting?). The seringo and bay-wing were also very common near the sea to-day and yesterday.

The shore between Manomet and Sandwich has in it two or three rocky capes, which interrupt the view along it, but are not very obvious on the map, between which are successive curving sandy beaches, Bays of Naples of the approved pattern. Swallows have their nests in the high bank from time to time, as at Cape Cod. Crows are seen lazily flapping away from the shore on your approach. Even a robin was seeking its food there.

The piping plover, as it runs half invisible on the sand before you, utters a shrill peep on an elevated key (different birds on different keys), as if to indicate its locality from time to time to its kind, or it utters a succession of short notes as it flies low over the sand or water. Ever and anon stands still tremblingly, or teeteringly, wagtail-like, turning this way and that.

Now and then a rock or two occurs on the sandy shore left by the undermining of the bank, even as on our Assabet, and I used one to-day (as yesterday) in my bathing.

From time to time, summer and winter and far inland, I call to mind that peculiar prolonged cry of the

upland plover on the bare heaths of Truro in July, heard from sea to sea, though you cannot guess how far the bird may be, as if it were a characteristic sound of the Cape.

In a genuine Cape Cod road you see simple dents in the sand, but cannot tell by what kind of foot they were made, the sand is so light and flowing.

The whole length of the Cape the beach-flea is skipping and the plover piping.

Where I turned up to go to Scusset village I saw some handsome patches of *Hudsonia tomentosa* (not yet had seen the *ericoides*), its fine bright-yellow flowers open chiefly about the edges of the hemispherical mounds.

About 11 A. M. take the cars from Scusset to Sandwich. See in the marshes by the railroad the *Potentilla anserina*, now apparently in prime, like a buttercup.

Stopped on the northwest edge of Yarmouth and inquired of the ticket-master the way to Friends Village in the southeast part of the town. He never heard of it. A stage-driver said it was five miles, and both directed me first northerly a quarter of a mile to the main street and then down that easterly some two miles before I turned off; and when I declared it must be nearer to go across lots, the driver said he would rather go round than get over the fences. Thus it is commonly; the landlords and stage-drivers are bent on making you walk the whole length of their main street first, wherever you are going. They know no road but such as is fit for a coach and four. I looked despairingly at this straggling village whose street I must run the gantlet

Vol. IX

of, — so much time and distance lost. Nevertheless, I turned off earlier than they directed, and found that, as usual, I might have taken a shorter route across the fields and avoided the town altogether.

With my chart and compass I can generally find a shorter way than the inhabitants can tell me. I stop at a depot a little one side of a village and ask the way to some place I am bound to. The landlords and stage-drivers would fain persuade me to go first down on to the main street and follow that a piece; and when I show them a shorter way on the map, which leaves their village on one side, they shrug their shoulders, and say they would rather go round than get over the fences. I have found the compass and chart safer guides than the inhabitants, though the latter universally abuse the maps. I do not love to go through a village street any more than a cottage yard. I feel that I am there only by sufferance; but I love to go by the villages by my own road, seeing them from one side, as I do theoretically. When I go through a village, my legs ache at the prospect of the hard gravelled walk. I go by the tavern with its porch full of gazers, and meet a miss taking a walk or the doctor in his sulky, and for half an hour I feel as strange as if I were in a town in China; but soon I am at home in the wide world again, and my feet rebound from the yielding turf.

I followed a retired road across the Cape diagonally some five miles to Friends Village, the southeast part of the town, on Bass River, over at first bare upland with pine plantations, gradually at last rising a low but very broad and flat-backed hill (German's?) in the

woods. The pine and oak woods were quite extensive, but the trees small. See the *Hudsonia ericoides*, with a *peduncle*. The road ran directly through woods the last half the way.

Passed Long Pond just before reaching Friends Village. Passed through the latter and crossed Bass River by a toll-bridge, and so on through Crowell Village, Grand Cove, to Isaiah Baker's in West Harwich, some eight miles from Yarmouth Depot.

Just after crossing Bass River, plucked a plant in the marsh by the roadside like (if not) mullein pink. At Swan Pond River in Dennis, where they were just completing a new bridge, plucked the *Potentilla Anserina*, now apparently in prime, with a handsome leaf, silvery beneath, in the marsh.

From near Long Pond, Friends Village, thus far, and also the two miles further that I walked due east the next day, or for five miles at least, it was a continuous street, without a distinct village, the houses but a few rods apart all the way on each side. A sandy road, small houses, with small pine and oak wood close bordering the road, making the soil appear more fertile than in reality it is. As in Canada along the St. Lawrence, you never got out of the village, only came to a meeting-house now and then. And they told me there was another similar street parallel with this further north. But all this street had a peculiarly Sabbath-day appearance, for there was scarcely an inhabitant to be seen, and they were commonly women or young children, for the greater part of the able-bodied men were gone to sea, as usual. This makes them very quiet towns. Baker said that half or three quarters of the men were gone.

This afternoon it mizzled a little. At the supper-table there was a youngish man who, looking very serious, at length observed to me, "Your countenance is very familiar to me, sir." "Where do you think you have seen me?" I asked. "It seems to me that I have been *consigned to you*," said he. This was said with such a serious tone and look that the suspicion crossed my mind that he meant spiritually, but I soon remembered where I was and the employment of the inhabitants.

Herring River was near by, and Baker sent a little boy to set an eel-pot for eels for breakfast. We had some of the herring for supper. He said that the eels went *down* the river in the spring, and *up* in the fall! That last winter many were found in holes under the ice (where passers broke through), left dry by the tide. He said it was a consideration with poor men who talked of migrating West that here shellfish and eels were abundant and easily obtained. Spoke of the large tract of wood running down the centre of the Cape from Sandwich, three miles wide and thirty long, and he declared repeatedly, since I looked surprised, that there was more wood in Barnstable County than in Ohio *County*. His father-in-law owned $75,000 worth thereabouts. Wood was worth six dollars per cord.

June 17. This morning had for breakfast fresh eels from Herring River, caught in an eel-pot baited with horseshoe clams [*sic*] cut up.

Crossed Herring River, and went down to the shore

tary heath am at once exhilarated. This is a common experience in my travelling. I plod along, thinking what a miserable world this is and what miserable fellows we that inhabit it, wondering what it is tempts men to live in it; but anon I leave the towns behind and am lost in some boundless heath, and life becomes gradually more tolerable, if not even glorious.

After passing the centre of Harwich, with its seminary, I struck north to the ponds between Harwich and Brewster. Saw some white pond-lilies open that had been dropped by the roadside. Disturbed a very large water snake sunning on the bank of a pond-hole.

At what is called on the map Hinckley's Pond, in Harwich, met with the first cranberry-patch. A man told me there were twelve acres here in all, in one body, owned by Albert Clark of Boston, and by others, and this was the largest patch on that part the Cape. They formed a handsome, perfectly level bed, a field, a redeemed meadow, adjoining the pond, the plants in perfectly straight rows eighteen inches apart, in coarse white sand which had been carted in. What with the runners and the moss, etc., between, they made a uniform green bed, very striking and handsome. Baker had complained that the cranberry vines were seriously injured by worms, would be, perhaps, destroyed. He and some others had turned theirs into English grass. They also are apt to become too thick and cease to bear well. They then sell them to others to set out for $5.00 a square rod, as another informed me by the pond. This was a large and interesting pond.

A little further, I came to Long Pond, and passed be-

and walked a mile or more eastward along the beach. This beach seems to be laid down too long on the map. The sea never runs very much here, since this shore is protected from the swell by Monomoy. The Harbor (?) of West Harwich is merely some wharves protected by a shoal offshore. Passed a place where they had been taking bluefish with a seine and, as usual, had left their backbones on the beach. There was a scup also, a good fish. A fish hawk (?) or eagle sailed low directly over my head as I sat on the bank. The bank is quite low there. I could see Monomoy, very low and indistinct, stretching much further south than I expected. The wooded portions of this, and perhaps of Nauset Beach further north, looked like islets on the water. You could not distinguish much without a glass, but the lighthouse and fishermen's houses at the south end loomed very large to the naked eye.

I soon turned inland through the woods and struck north to the centre of Harwich. At a retired house where I inquired the road to Brewster, a woman told me that if I wanted to go to Brewster I had come a good deal out of my way, and yet she did not know where I had come from, and I was certainly taking the right course to keep in the way. But they presume that a traveller inquiring the way wishes to be anywhere but where he is. They take me for a roadster, and do not know where *my* way is. They take it for granted that my way is a direct one from village to village.

I go along the settled road, where the houses are interspersed with woods, in an unaccountably desponding mood, but when I come out upon a bare and soli-

tween it and Bangs Pond by a low beach, and took my lunch on a pine hill with a flat summit, on the Brewster side of Long Pond, near the house of one Cohoon. This is a noble lake some two miles long, as a man there told me (the Historical Collections say the chain of ponds is three and two thirds miles long), with high, steep, sliding sand-banks, more or less wooded, and is the source of Herring River, which empties into the sound on the south. Connected with Bangs and Hinckley's Ponds. This high hill with a flat summit, on which was an open pitch pine wood, very suitable for picnics, appeared to be the best point to view it from. You could see at least three ponds at once. Situated about halfway between the two seas, on the shore of this noble lake, it appeared to be the best place for an *inland* hotel on the Cape. What was that slender, succulent, somewhat samphire-like plant in the sand-bank by this pond? After bathing, I abandoned the road and struck across the country northeast by chart and compass, for Orleans, passing between this and another large pond called Sheep Pond, on the north, the country being at first woody, then open.

After passing Sheep Pond I knocked at a house near the road from Brewster to Chatham to inquire the way to Orleans. This house was about a quarter of a mile from the road, in the fields, and the usual Sabbath-like serenity reigned around it. There was no beaten path through the grass to the front door, so I approached the back side. As I stood at the door while the woman was getting me a glass of water, I was struck by the peculiar neatness of the yellow painted floor, so clean, perhaps, because the husband was gone to sea with his dirty boots. I inquired the way of another woman who lived on the road near by, who was just setting her dinner-table when I thought it must be mid-afternoon. She directed me by a road or cart-path through the woods that ran due southeast, but I knew better than to follow this long. Concluded she meant the south part of Orleans, and so I struck off northeast by fainter cart-paths through the woods. I kept on through uninterrupted wood by various paths somewhat east of north for about an hour, avoiding those that ran southeast, because I knew by the map that there were large ponds east of me which I must go round on the north. At length, seeing no end to the woods, laying down my pack, I climbed an oak and looked off; but the woods bounded the horizon as far as I could see on every side, and eastward it was several miles, for on that side I observed a great depression where a large pond lay concealed in the forest. All the life I could see was a red-tailed or hen hawk circling not far above my head. This gave me a new idea of the extent of Cape Cod woodland. After a while, travelling by compass alone, without path, I fell into a more beaten path than I had left, and came very unexpectedly upon a house on the shore of the pond, in the midst of the woods, in the most secluded place imaginable. There was a small orchard even. It was mid-afternoon, and, to judge from appearances and from the sounds, you would have supposed that only the hens and chickens were at home; but after my first knock I heard a slight stir within, and though all was

still immediately, they being afraid, I knew better than [to] give it up, but knocked all round the house at five doors in succession, there being two to a stoop, and by the time I got round to the first again there was a woman with a child in her arms there ready to answer my questions.

I found that I had not come out of my way.

Of the woods of the Cape which I walked through in Yarmouth, Dennis, Harwich, and Brewster, it is to be said that they are dry pine and oak woods, extensive but quite low, commonly, with an abundance of bear-berry and checkerberry in the more open parts, the latter forming an almost uninterrupted bed for great distances.

I soon came out on the open hills in the northeast part of Brewster, from which I overlooked the Bay, some two miles distant. This was a grand place to walk. There were two or three more of those peculiar ponds with high, shiny sand-banks, by which you detected them before you saw the water, as if freshly scooped out of the high plains or a table-land. The banks were like those of the sea on the Back Side, though on a smaller scale, and they had clear sandy shores. One pond would often be separated from another by low curving beaches or necks of land. The features of the surrounding landscape simple and obvious. The sod, so short and barren, affords the best ground for walking. Brewster is much more hilly than Eastham. The latter is, indeed, quite flat. In short, Brewster, with its noble ponds, its bare hills, gray with poverty-grass and lichens, and its secluded cottages, is a

very interesting town to an inlander. Saw a woman mending a fence nearly a mile from a house, using an axe.

Barber appears to be mistaken about seeing both seas from the county road in this town, — to have misunderstood the Massachusetts Historical Collections. I passed over some hills there where pine seed had recently been planted with a hoe only, about four feet apart. At first I thought the turtles had been laying their eggs there, but I observed them in straight lines and detected some little pines an inch high just up. Some of the Cape roads are repaired with the coarsest bushes and roots, with such earth as adheres to them.

Jeremiah's Gutter is what is called Boat Meadow River on the map. I saw the town bounds there. There, too, was somebody's Folly, who dug a canal, which the sand filled up again. About a mile north of this, I left the road and struck across west of the road to near the Eastham Meeting-house, crossing a part of that "beach" where once wheat grew, and by Great Pond, where a canal has been talked of. Passed some large tupelo trees. The greater part of Eastham an open plain, and also the southwest part of Wellfleet. Put up at the Traveller's Home (Cobb's), so called, at the Camp Ground, just within the woods.

Cobb says he has known formerly one man in Eastham export twelve hundred bushels of grain from his own farm. Twenty of corn to an acre is an average crop in a fair year in his neighborhood, which is better soil than usual. Thought likely there was not more raised in the town now than used. Cobb thought the

Nauset lights not of much use, because so often you could not see them, and if you could they would not prevent your coming ashore. Sailors preferred to depend on the "blue pigeon" (lead). He said that the inhabitants lived on the West or Bay Side, though no more fertile or fishy, because their harbors were there. On the Back Side they could not get off to fish more than once a fortnight, but on the West almost every day. He thought the Cape wasting on both sides there. That the Truro Insurance Company had a hard time to meet their payments. They import cedar posts from Maine, which, with rails, make a fence costing about seventy-five cents a rod, but they are not so durable as formerly, being made of younger trees.

According to Pratt's History, first camp-meeting in 1828.

June 18. Thursday. From Traveller's Home to Small's in Truro.

A mizzling and rainy day with thick driving fog; a drizzling rain, or "drisk," as one called it. I struck across into the stage-road, a quarter of a mile east, and followed that a mile or more into an extensive bare plain tract called Silver Springs, in the southwest part of Wellfleet, — according to Pratt, one third of Wellfleet was covered mostly with pines in 1844, — then turned off northeast through the bushes, to the Back Side, three quarters of a mile distant. The desert was about one hundred and fifteen rods wide on the bank where I struck it. You might safely say it was from thirty to one hundred rods or more in width. But the bank was apparently not so high as in Truro. This was on that long Table-Land in Wellfleet. Where the bank was covered with coarse pebbles, however high, I judged that it could not have been formed by the wind, but rather the small sand-hills on the west edge of the desert were formed of its finer particles and remains, leaving the coarser parts here. However, I afterwards saw where, in the hollows more or less deep, the sand blown up from the beach had covered the dark stratum of the original surface ten feet deep with *fine sand*, which was now densely covered with bushes.

As I walked on the top of the bank for a mile or two before I came to a hollow by which to descend, though it rained but little, the strong wind there drove that and the mist against my unprotected legs so as to wet me through and plaster over the legs of my pants with sand. The wind was southeasterly.

I observed, in a few stiller places behind a bar, a yellowish scum on the water close to the shore, which I suspect was the pollen of the pine, lately in full bloom, which had been wafted on to the ocean. Small thought at first that I referred to a scum like that which collects on salt-vats.

Stopped to dry me about 11 A. M. at a house near John Newcomb's, who they told me died last winter, ninety-five years old (or would have been now had he lived?). I had shortly before picked up a Mother-Carey's-chicken, which was just washed up dead on the beach. This I carried tied to the tip of my umbrella, dangling outside. When the inhabitants saw me come up from the beach this stormy day, with this emblem

dangling from my umbrella, and saw me set it up in a corner carefully to be out of the way of cats, they may have taken me for a crazy man. It is remarkable how wet the grass will be there in a misty day alone; more so than after a rain with us.

The Mother-Carey's-chicken was apparently about thirteen inches in alar extent, black-brown, with seven primaries, the second a little longer than the third; rump and vent white, making a sort of ring of white, breast ashy-brown, legs black with yellowish webs, bill black with a protuberance above.

I think there were more boat-houses in the hollows along the Back Side than when I first walked there. These are the simplest and cheapest little low, narrow, and long sheds, just enough to cover a boat, within the line of the bank at some hollow. But in my three walks there I never chanced to see a man about one of them, or any boating there.

Soon after leaving Newcomb's Hollow, I passed a hulk of a vessel about a hundred feet long, which the sea had cast up in the sand. She lay at high-water mark high up the beach, the ribs at her bows rising higher than my head above the sand; then for sixty or seventy feet there was *nothing* to be seen of her, and at last only the outline of her stern ribs projecting slightly above the sand for a short distance. Small suggested that this might be the hulk of the Franklin, lost there seven or eight years ago. They sometimes buy and break them up and carry them piecemeal up the bank, all which is a great job; or they burn them down to the sand and get out the iron alone. It was

an impressive sight to see, lying thus insignificant, the hulk of a large (? I walked five rods beside it) vessel which had been lost for years, now cast up and half buried in the sand, like a piece of driftwood. Apparently no longer regarded. It looked very small and insignificant under that impending bank.

In Newcomb's Hollow I had already entered a Humane house. A sign over the door said "For Cases of Distress only," and directed where the key of the life-boat was to be obtained. Mine was a case of distress. Within was a simple apartment containing the boat, a bench, a fireplace and chimney, an india-rubber bucket, a few armfuls of wood, a keg of rags, a tin case with matches and two candles and a candlestick over the fireplace, etc. Also an extract from the laws of the State to protect the property of the Humane Society. I did not look closely for oil or food. I actually sought the Humane house for shelter. It was with peculiar reflections that I contemplated these two candles and those matches prepared to keep the spark of life in some suffering fellow-creature. This was before I went to the house by Newcomb's.

The waves ran pretty well on account of the easterly wind. I observed how merely undulatory was the motion of the waves. A floating chip or the like on the back of the largest wave often was not advanced in the least toward the shore, however great the undulation.

I noticed dor-bugs washed up many miles south of the Highland Light.

I think it was north of Newcomb's Hollow that I

passed a perpendicular promontory of clay in the bank, which was conspicuous a good way through the fog.

Reached the Highland Light about 2 P. M. The *Smilacina racemosa* was *just* out of bloom on the bank. They call it the "wood lily" there. Uncle Sam called it "snake-corn," and said it looked like corn when it first came up.

Small says that the lighthouse was built about sixty years ago. He knows by his own age. A new lighthouse was built some twenty-five years ago. They are now building another still on the same spot.

He once drove some cattle up the beach on the Back Side from Newcomb's Hollow to Pamet River Hollow, — a singular road by which to drive cows, yet well fenced! They were rather wild and gave him some trouble by trying to get up the bank at first, though in vain. He could easily head them off when they turned. And also they wanted to drink the salt water. They did not mind the waves, and if the sea had been the other side, where they had belonged and wanted to go, would have taken to it.

The sea was not frozen there exactly as I had inferred from the papers last winter. Small never knew it to be frozen smooth there so as to bear, but there was last winter a mere brash of pieces several inches thick reaching out half a mile or more, but you cannot go out on it. It is worth the while to see the ice piled up on the shore.

Small says that the Truro fishermen who were lost in the great shipwreck were on the Nantucket Shoals. Four or five vessels were lost with all aboard. They

Shrub Oak Leaves

Highland Light, Cape Cod

may have been endeavoring to reach Provincetown Harbor. He spoke of one of his neighbors who was drowned in Truro, and very soon after his bones were found picked clean by the beach-fleas. Thinks you could get off in a boat from the Back Side one day out of three at *the right tide*. He thinks that what we thought a shark may have been a big bass, since one was taken just alive soon after in that cove.

A youngish man came into Small's with a thick outside coat, when a girl asked where he got that coat. He answered that it was taken off a man that came ashore dead, and he had worn it a year or more. The girls or young ladies expressed surprise that he should be willing to wear [it] and said, "You'd not dare to go to sea with that coat on." But he answered that he might just as well embark in that coat as any other.

They brought me an *Attacus Cecropia* which a boy had found in a swamp near by on the 17th. Its body was large like the one I have preserved, while the two I found to have come out in my chamber meanwhile, and to have laid their eggs, had comparatively small bodies.

One said there was a little bit of a rill of fresh water near Small's, though it could not be called a brook.

June 19. *Friday.* Fog still, but I walked about a mile north onward on the beach.

The sea was still running considerably. It is surprising how rapidly the water soaks into the sand, and is even dried up between each undulation. The sand has many holes in it, about an eighth of an inch over, which

seem to have been made by the beach-flea. These have a firm and as if artificial rim or curb, and it is remarkable that the waves flow two or three feet over them with force without obliterating them. They help soak up the water. As I walked along close to the edge of the water, the sea oscillating like a pendulum before me and each billow flowing with a flat white foaming edge and a rounded outline up the sand, it reminded me of the white toes of blue-stockinged feet thrust forward from under the garments in an endless dance. It was a contra-dance to the shore. Some waves would flow unexpectedly high and fill my shoes with water before I was aware of it. It is very exciting for a while to walk where half the floor before you is thus incessantly fluctuating.

There is frequently, if not for the most part, a bar just off the shore on which the waves first break and spend more or less of their violence, and I saw that the way to land in a boat at such a time would be to row along outside this bar and its breakers, till you came to an opening in it, then enter and row up or down within the bar to a comparatively safe place to land.

I turned up the first hollow. A piping plover peeped around me there, and feigned lameness, — though I at first thought that she was dusting herself on the sand, — to attract me away from her nest evidently.

Returned inland. The poverty-grass was fully out, in bright-yellow mounds or hillocks, more like painted clods than flowers, or, on the bare sandy hills and plains of the Cape, they looked like tufts of yellow

Vol. IX

lichens on a roof. They indicate such soil as the cladonia lichen with us. If the soil were better they would not be found there. These hillocks are about as big as a large ant-hill — some have spread to eight or ten feet in diameter, but are flat and broken more or less — and commonly dead in the middle or perhaps one side, but I saw many perfect dense hemispheres of yellow flowers. As the sand gathers around them, they rise above it, and they seemed to bloom and flourish better when thus nearly buried in sand. A hemisphere eighteen inches in diameter would rest flat on the surface for six inches in width on the outside and be rather loosely rooted in the middle, for you could easily lift it all up. The *Hudsonia ericoides* was the most common, and the *tomentosa* appeared to be less in hillocks, *i. e.* more broken and dead. The poverty-grass emits a common sweetish scent as you walk over the fields. It blossoms on the edges first. You meet with it in Plymouth as you approach the peculiar soil of the Cape.

June 20. *Saturday.* Fog still.

A man working on the lighthouse, who lives at the Pond Village, says that he raised potatoes and pumpkins there where a vessel once anchored. That was when they let the salt water into the pond. Says the flags there now are barrel flags; that the chair flag is smaller, partly three-sided, and has no bur; perhaps now all gone. Speaking of the effect of oil on the water, this man said that a boat's crew came ashore safely from their vessel on the Bay Side of Truro some time

ago in a storm, when the wind blowed square on to the land, only by heaving over oil. The spectators did not think they would reach the shore without being upset. When I expressed some doubt of the efficacy of this, he observed in the presence of Small and others, "We always take a bottle of oil when looking for sea clams, and, pouring out a few drops, can look down six or seven feet."

We dined on halibut caught on the ledges some three miles off the Back Side.

There was a carpenter who worked on the lighthouse boarding at Small's, who had lived sixteen years on the extremity of Cape Ann. When I asked him about Salvages, he said it was a large bare rock, perhaps fifty yards long and a dozen feet high, about two miles from the shore at Sandy Bay, outside Avery's Rock. That he and all the inhabitants of the Cape always called it "Selvaygias." Did not know but it had something to do with salvage for wrecks. This man, who is familiar with the shore of New England north of Cape Cod, thought that there was no beach equal to this for grandeur. He thought August the most foggy month.

Small thought that the shore at the mouth of Pamet River about held its own.

I saw an extract in a Cape (*Yarmouth Register*) paper from a promised History of the Cape by Dr. Dix, an Englishman, who was owing Small for board, etc. (page 136 of it). There was also advertised "The Annals of Barnstable County and its several Towns," etc., by Frederick Freeman, to be in two volumes, 8vo, $4.00. This will probably be out first.

A child asked concerning a bobolink, "What makes he sing so sweet, Mother? Do he eat flowers?"

Talked with an old lady who thought that the beach plums were better than cherries.

Visited the telegraph station, tended by one Hall, just north of the light. He has a small volume called the "Boston Harbor Signal Book," containing the names of some three thousand vessels, their owners, etc., and a code of signals. There were also the private signals of more than a hundred merchants on a large sheet on the wall. There was also a large volume called "The Universal Code of Signals," Marryat (Richardson, London), 1854, containing the names of some twenty thousand vessels of all nations, but chiefly English, and an extensive system of signalling, by which he could [carry on] a long conversation with a vessel on almost any subject. He said that he could make out the name seven miles off and the signal sometimes twenty miles.[1] Thought there would be a fog as long as the wind was southwest. "How is it in Boston?" I asked. "I will ask," said he. *Tick tick tick* — "Wind northeast and cloudy." (Here it was southwest and thick fog.) He thought that there [were] more vessels to be seen passing this point than any other in the United States. One day when telegraphing the passing vessels he put in "a fox passing," for there was one running between the station and the edge of the bank. I observed the name of the brig Leader displayed on

[1] The man at Hull July 24, 1851, said they could tell the kind of vessel thirty miles off, the number at masthead ten or twelve miles, name on hull six or seven miles

Vol. IX

a flag for me. The report was, "Brig Leader in." It *may* be a month before the vessel reaches Boston.

The operator said that last winter the wind between his station and the bank blew him three rods through the air, and he was considerably hurt when he fell. A boy was blown head over heels. The fences were blown up, post and rail. There was no wind just this side the edge of the bank, but if you lay down there and extended your hand over the edge of the bank it would be blown suddenly upward, or if you cast off a large piece of wood it would be blown up thirty or forty feet high. Both boys and men often amuse themselves by running and trying to jump off the bank with their jackets spread, and being blown back. (Small confirmed this.) Hall said that he could not possibly jump off. *Sometimes* and in *some* places, pebbles as big as chestnuts are blown far over the bank.

Hall said that he saw very large flocks of geese; had counted as many as six hundred go by at once, reaching three miles; and sometimes alight on the water.

Talked with Uncle Sam, who was picking gooseberries on the bank, — for the sun shone a short time. He showed me some fossil shells imbedded in stone which he had picked up on the *high* bank, just south of the light, and laid on his pile of driftwood. He wanted to know something about them. Said that a lecturer down at Pamet River had said, as he was told, that the Norwegians who formerly came to this country cemented them together. He had come down to watch a piece of driftwood, perhaps a stump, which had been

lodged on a bar for a day or two. He was trying to make out what it was. There is something picked up on the shore of the Cape and advertised in every paper.

This was the third foggy day. It cleared up the next day noon, but the night after and the next day was foggy again. It is a serious objection to visiting or living on the Cape that you lose so many days by fog. Small said that a week of fog at this season would be nothing remarkable. You can see that the fog is local and of no great thickness. From time to time the sun almost or quite shines, and you can see half a mile, or to Provincetown even, and then, against all your rules, it thickens up again. An inlander would think [it] was going to clear up twenty times when it may last a week. Small said that they were very common with southerly winds, being blown up from Nantucket Shoals; that they were good for almost everything but corn, yet there was probably less rain there at this season than on the mainland. I have now visited the Cape four times in as many different years, once in October, twice in June, and once in July, having spent in all about one month there, and about one third the days were foggy, with or without rain. According to Alden (in Massachusetts Historical Collections, vol. v, First Series, page 57), Nantucket was discovered by a famous old Indian giant named Maushop, who waded the sea to it, and there filling his pipe with "poke," his smoke made fog. Whence that island is so much in the fog, and the aborigines on the opposite portion of the Cape, seeing a fog over the water at a distance, would say,

"There comes old Maushop's smoke." The Gloucester carpenter thought August the worst month for fog on the coast.

The fog lasted this time, with the exception of one afternoon and one or two slight breakings away, five days, or from Thursday morning till I reached Minot's Ledge, Monday noon. How much longer it continued on the Cape I do not know. The Cape people with whom I talked very generally denied that it [was] a phenomenon in any degree peculiar to the Cape. They said that it was just such weather at Boston. Indeed, some denied that it was fog at all. They said with some asperity that it was rain. Yet more rain would have fallen in a smart shower in the country in twenty minutes than in these five days on the Cape. When I got home I found that there had been an abundance [of] cloudy weather and rain within a week, but not one foggy day in Concord.

Small thought that Lieutenant Davis might have misunderstood him. He meant to say that the offshore current (three miles off) set down the Cape, and wrecks in it went down the coast, the inshore one sets up.

I noticed several lengths of fence hereabouts made chiefly of oars, very long ones.

A Cape Cod house is low, unpainted, shingled on the sides. They have many windows, even under the roofs to light the closets there, and as the chambers can only be lighted at one end, there are commonly two windows there. Once I saw a triangular blind under the peak, though there was no window beneath it. The windows commonly afford a view of the bay or ocean, though the house may be sheltered by some hill, or they are very snugly placed in a hollow, apparently as secluded as among the New Hampshire hills.

June 21. Sunday. About noon it cleared up, and after dinner I set out for Provincetown, straight across the country to the Bay where the new road strikes it, directly through the pine plantation about one mile from the lighthouse. The pines have apparently not done so well here as in some other places on the Cape. I observed a tuft of crow-berry, together with poverty-grass, about one mile west of the light. This part of Truro affords singularly interesting and cheering walks for me, with regular hollows or dimples shutting out the sea as completely as if in the midst of the continent, though when you stand on the plain you commonly see the sails of vessels standing up or down the coast on each side of you, though you may not see the water. At first you may take them for the roofs of barns or houses. It is plain for miles without a tree, where the new telegraph-wires are a godsend to the birds, affording them something to perch upon. That solitude was sweet to me as a flower. I sat down on the boundless level and enjoyed the solitude, drank it in, the medicine for which I had pined, worth more than the bear-berry so common on the Cape. As I was approaching the Bay through a sandy hollow a mile east of High Head, I found two or three arrow-points and a rude axe or hammer, a flattish stone from the beach with a deep groove chipped around it.

The beach on the Bay Side was completely strewn

with seaweed (the grassy kind), which does not grow on the Atlantic side, as if the Bay were a meadow compared with the Atlantic. The beach was harder than the Back Side, the hardest part being on the weed at high-water line. The skulls and backbones of black-fish, their vertebræ and spinal processes, and disk-shaped bones, five inches in diameter, from the spine were strewn all along. These looked like rough crack-ers.[1]

Also the ribs of whale (probably humpbacked), — they get humpback and finback and right whales, I heard, — six feet long, lay under the bank, hardly to be distinguished from their gray rails. Some of those whale ribs, ten inches wide, were from time to time set up in the sand, like mile stones (or bones); they seemed to answer that purpose along the new road. They had taken a whale in Provincetown Harbor on the previous 17th, and stripped off the blubber at one of the wharves. I saw many dogfish whose livers had been extracted.

At East Harbor River, as I sat on the Truro end of the bridge, I saw a great flock of mackerel gulls, one hundred at least, on a sandy point, whitening the

[1] The old traveller Lawson, in his account of the fishes of Carolina, says of the "Bottle-Nose," referring apparently to this fish, though this is the popular name for a different species in England, that "They are never seen to swim leisurely, as sometimes all other fish do, but are continually running after their prey in great shoals, like wild horses, leaping now and then above the water."

If those disk-shaped bones with nothing but muscle between them were really inserted between the vertebræ as it appeared, they must make the spine very flexible as well as wonderfully elastic and strong.

Vol. IX

shore there like so many white stones on the shore and in the water, uttering all together their vibrating shrill note. They had black heads, light bluish-slate wings, and light rump and tail and beneath. From time to time all or most would rise and circle about with a clamor, then settle again on the same spot close together.

Soon after crossing the bridge, I turned off and ascended Mt. Ararat. It exhibited a remarkable landscape: on the one side the desert, of smooth and spotless palest fawn-colored sand, slightly undulating, and beyond, the Atlantic; on the other, the west, side, a few valleys and hills, *densely* clothed with a short, almost moss-like (to look down at) growth of huckleberry, blueberry, bear-berry, josh-pear (which is so abundant in Provincetown), bayberry, rose, checkerberry, and other bushes, and beyond, the Bay. All these bushes formed an even and dense covering to the sand-hills, much as bear-berry alone might. It was a very strange scenery. You would think you might be in Labrador, or some other place you have imagined. The shrubbery at the very summit was swarming with mosquitoes, which troubled me when I sat down, but they did not rise above the level of the bushes.

At the Pilgrim House, though it was not crowded, they put me into a small attic chamber which had two double beds in it, and only one window, high in a corner, twenty and a half inches by twenty-five and a half, in the alcove when it was swung open, and it required a chair to look out conveniently. Fortunately it was not

a cold night and the window could be kept open, though at the risk of being visited by the cats, which appear to swarm on the roofs of Provincetown like the mosquitoes on the summits of its hills. I have spent four memorable nights there in as many different years, and have added considerable thereby to my knowledge of the natural history of the cat and the bedbug. Sleep was out of the question. A night in one of the attics of Provincetown! to say nothing of what is to be learned in entomology. It would be worth the while to send a professor there, one who was also skilled in entomology. Such is your *Pilgerruhe* or Pilgrims'-Rest. Every now and then one of these animals on its travels leaped from a neighboring roof on to mine, with such a noise as if a six-pounder had fallen within two feet of my head, — the discharge of a catapult, — a twelve-pounder discharged by a catapult, — and then followed such a scrambling as banished sleep for a long season, while I watched lest they came in at the open window. A kind of foretaste, methought, of the infernal regions. I did n't wonder they gave quit-claim deeds of their land here. My experience is that you fare best at private houses. The barroom may be defined a place to spit.

> "Soon as the evening shades prevail,
> The *cats take* up the wondrous tale."

At still midnight, when, half awake, half asleep, you seem to be weltering in your own blood on a battle-field, you hear the stealthy tread of padded feet belonging to some animal of the cat tribe, perambulating the roof within a few inches of your head.

I had already this evening called on Mr. Atwood, the Representative of the town and one of the commissioners appointed by the legislature to superintend the experiments in the artificial breeding of fishes. He said that he knew (I think) eighty-two kinds of fishes there.

When Mr. Pool, the Doorkeeper of the House of Representatives, — if that is his name and title, — who makes out a list of the Representatives and their professions, asked him his business, he answered, "Fisherman." At which Pool was disturbed and said that no representative had ever called himself a fisherman before. It would not do to print it so. And so Atwood is put down as "Master Mariner"!! So much for American democracy. I reminded him that Fisherman had been a title of honor with a large party ever since the Christian Era at least. When next we have occasion to speak of the apostles I suppose we should call them "Master Mariners"!

Atwood said that his brother here took the bone shark recently which I read was thirty feet long. Fog again at night.

June 22. Monday. Took the steamer Acorn [?] about 9 A. M. for Boston, in the fog. The captain said that the mate to the whale taken on the 17th had been about the steamer all night. It was a thick fog with some rain, and we saw no land nor a single sail, till near Minot's Ledge. The boat stopped and whistled once or twice. The monotony was only relieved by the numerous petrels, those black sea-swallows, incessantly

found the first still in the chamber. This, too, she says, went right to laying eggs. I am not sure whether this, too, came from the other cocoon. Neither was quite so large as the one I had. The second had broken off the better part of its wings. Their bodies were quite small, perhaps because they were empty of eggs. I let them go. The eggs are large, pretty close together, glued to the wood or paper.

June 23. Skinner, the harness-maker, tells me that he found a black duck's nest Sunday before the last, *i. e.* the 14th, with perhaps a dozen eggs in it, a mere hollow on the top of a tussock, four or five feet within a clump of bushes forming an islet (in the spring) in Hubbard's great meadow. He scared up the duck when within a few feet. Pratt says he knows of a black walnut at Hunt's on Ponkawtasset.

P. M. — Looked for the black duck's nest, but could find no trace of it. Probably the duck led her young to the river as soon as hatched. What with gunners, dogs, pickerel, bullfrogs, hawks, etc., it is a wonder if any of them escape.

Small rudbeckia, *i. e. hirta*, at Hubbard's Bath.

June 24. Wednesday. P. M. — To Farmer's Owl-Nest Swamp.

Melvin thinks there cannot be many black ducks' nests in the town, else his dog would find them, for he will follow their trail as well as another bird's, or a fox. The dog once caught five black ducks here but partly grown. Farmer was hoeing corn with his Irishmen.

skimming over the undulating [surface], a few inches above and parallel with it, and occasionally picking some food from it. Now they dashed past our stern and now across our bows, as if we were stationary, though going at the rate of a dozen knots an hour. It is remarkable what great solitudes there may be on this bay, notwithstanding all its commerce, and going from Boston to Provincetown you might be wrecked in clear weather, without being seen by any passing vessel. Once, when the fog lifted a little and the boat was stopped, and the engine whistled, I thought that I saw an open sea without an object for three or four miles at least. We held on, and it suddenly thickened up again, and yet in three minutes, notwithstanding the fog, we saw the light-boat right ahead. This shows how deceptive and dangerous fogs are. I should have said we might have run half an hour without danger of striking any object.

The greatest depth in the Bay between Long Point, Provincetown, and Manomet, Plymouth, according to Coast Survey charts, is about twenty-five fathoms.

Get home at 5 P. M.[1]

It seems that Sophia found an *Attacus Cecropia* out in my chamber last Monday, or the 15th. It soon went to laying eggs on the window-sill, sash, books, etc., of which *vide* a specimen. Though the window was open (blinds closed), it did not escape. Another was seen at the window outside the house on the south side (mother's chamber) on the 21st, which S. took in, supposing it the first which had got out, but she

[1] *Vide* July 7th.

The crows had got much of it, and when he came to a vacant hill he took a few beans from his pocket — for each hoer had a pocketful — and dropped them there, so making his rows complete. Melvin was there with his dog, which had just caught a woodchuck. M. said that he once saw a fox jump over a wall with something in his mouth, and, going up, the fox dropped a woodchuck and a mouse, which he had caught and was carrying home to his young. He had eaten the head of the woodchuck. When M. looked there the next morning they were gone.

Went to Farmer's Swamp to look for the screech owl's[1] nest Farmer had found. You go about forty-five rods on the first path to the left in the woods and then turn to the left a few rods. I found the nest at last near the top of a middling-sized white pine, about thirty feet from the ground. As I stood by the tree, the old bird dashed by within a couple of rods, uttering a peculiar mewing sound, which she kept up amid the bushes, a blackbird in close pursuit of her. I found the nest empty, on one side of the main stem but close to it, resting on some limbs. It was made of twigs rather less than an eighth of an inch thick and was almost flat above, only an inch lower in the middle than at the edge, about sixteen inches in diameter and six or eight inches thick, with the twigs in the midst, and beneath was mixed sphagnum and sedge from the swamp beneath, and the lining or flooring was coarse strips of grape-vine bark; the whole pretty firmly matted together.

[1] [The situation of the nest and Thoreau's description of the notes indicate a long-eared owl rather than a screech owl.]

How common and important a material is grape-vine bark for birds' nests! Nature wastes nothing. There were white droppings of the young on the nest and one large pellet of fur and small bones two and a half inches long. In the meanwhile, the old bird was uttering that hoarse worried note from time to time, somewhat like a partridge's, flying past from side to side and alighting amid the trees or bushes. When I had descended, I detected one young one two thirds grown perched on a branch of the next tree, about fifteen feet from the ground, which was all the while staring at me with its great yellow eyes. It was gray with gray horns and a dark beak. As I walked past near it, it turned its head steadily, always facing me, without moving its body, till it looked directly the opposite way over its back, but never offered to fly. Just then I thought surely that I heard a puppy faintly barking at me four or five rods distant amid the bushes, having tracked me into the swamp, — *what what, what what what.* It was exactly such a noise as the barking of a very small dog or perhaps a fox. But it was the old owl, for I presently saw her making it. She repeated [*sic*] perched quite near. She was generally reddish-brown or partridge-colored, the breast mottled with dark brown and fawn-color in downward strings [*sic*], and had plain fawn-colored thighs.

Found there the *Calla palustris*, out of bloom, and the naumbergia, now in prime, which was hardly begun on the 9th at Bateman Pond Swamp. This was about four or five rods southerly of the owl tree. The large hastate tear-thumb is very common there; and

what is that large, coarse, flag-like sedge, with two ridges to its blade? Just out of bloom. In dense fields in water, like the flag.

I think that this is a cold swamp, *i. e.* it is springy and shady, and the water feels more than usually cold to my feet.

Returning, heard a fine, clear note from a bird on a white birch near me, — *whit whit, whit whit, whit whit,* (very fast) *ter phe phe phe,* — sounding perfectly novel. Looking round, I saw it was the huckleberry-bird, for it was near and plain to be seen.

Looked over Farmer's eggs and list of names. He has several which I have not. Is not his "chicklisee," after all, the Maryland yellow-throat? The eggs were numbered with a pen, — 1, 2, 3, etc., — and corresponding numbers written against the names on the cover of the pasteboard box in which were the eggs. Among the rest I read, "*Fire never redder.*" That must be the tanager. He laughed and said that this was the way he came to call it by that name: Many years ago, one election-day, when he and other boys, or young men, were out gunning to see how many birds they could kill, Jonathan Hildreth, who lived near by, saw one of these birds on the top of a tree before him in the woods, but he did not see a deep ditch that crossed his course between him and it. As he raised his gun, he exclaimed, " Fire never redder!" and, taking a step or two forward, with his eye fixed on the bird, fell headlong into the ditch, and so the name became a byword among his fellows.

Vol. IX

June 25. Most of the mountain-ash trees on the street are the European, as Prichard's, Whiting's, etc. The American ones (*Pyrus Aucuparia* is the European) in Cheney's (from Winchendon) row have only opened within a day or two; that American one in Mrs. Hoar's yard, apparently a week. The fruit of the European one is as large as small peas already.

P. M. — To Gowing's Swamp. White pine effete. *Gaylussacia dumosa* apparently in a day or two.[1]

June 26. Friday. Stand over a bream's nest close to the shore at Hubbard's rear wood. At length she ventures back into it, after many approaches. The apparent young bream, hardly half an inch long, are hovering over it all the while in a little school, never offering to swim away from over that yellow spot; such is their instinct. The old one at length returns and takes up her watch beneath, but I notice no recognition of each other.[2]

The largest tupelo I remember in Concord is on the northerly edge of Staples's clearing. See a pack of partridges as big as robins at least. I must be near bobolinks' nests many times these days, — in E. Hosmer's meadow by the garlic and here in Charles Hubbard's, — but the birds are so overanxious, though you may be pretty far off, and so shy about visiting their nests while you are there, that you watch them in vain. The female flies close past and perches near you on a rock or stump and chirps *whit tit, whit tit, whit it tit tit te* incessantly.

[1] Not quite in prime July 2d.
[2] Some nests are high and dry July 5th.

Some of the *Salix Torreyana* by railroad is cordate and some not. The sterile one there is not, nor those near it.

June 27. P. M. — Up Assabet.
See apparently a young bobolink fluttering over the meadow. The garlic not even yet quite.

In the Wheeler meadow, the bushy one southwest of Egg Rock, the coarse sedge[1] — I think the same with that in the Great Meadows — evidently grows in patches with a rounded outline; *i. e.,* its edge is a succession of blunt, rounded capes, with a very distinct outline amid the other kinds of grass and weeds.

I cannot find one of the three bits of white cotton string which I tied to willows in that neighborhood in the spring, and I have no doubt that the birds, perhaps crow blackbirds, have got every one for their nests. I must drive down a stake for a mark next time.

June 28. Geum Virginianum some time, apparently, past its prime by red cohosh. It was not nearly out June 7th; say, then, the 18th.

I hear on all hands these days, from the elms and other trees, the twittering peep of young gold robins, which have recently left their nests, and apparently indicate their locality to their parents by thus incessantly peeping all day long.

Observed to-night a yellow wasps' (?) nest, made of the same kind of paper with the hornets', in horizontal strips, some brownish, some white. It was broad

[1] Wool-grass.

cone-shape, some two inches in its smallest diameter, with a hole at the apex beneath about one half inch [in] diameter, and was suspended to the sheathing overhead within the recess at Mrs. Brown's front door. She was afraid of the wasps, and so I brushed it off for her. It was apparently the same kind of nest that I observed first a few days since, of the same size, under the peak of our roof, just over my chamber windows. (The last is now five inches in diameter, July 7th.) It contained only one comb about one and one eighth inches in diameter suspended from above, and this was surrounded by about two thin coverings of paper an eighth of an inch or more apart. The wasps looked at first like bees, with yellow rings on the abdomen. The cells contain what look and move like white grubs.

(July 7th, watching the nest over my window, I see that the wasps are longer than honey-bees and have a white place between the abdomen and breast. There are commonly three or four visible at once about the nest, and they are continually bringing down new layers of paper from the top about a sixth of an inch distant from the last, building downward on all sides at once evenly and beginning, or starting, a new one before they have finished the first.[1] They have turned the entrance a little outward; i. e., have built the successive layers a little over its inner side, i. e. that toward the house, so that it partly faces outward. They are continually arriving and departing, and one or two commonly are at work at once on the edge of the

[1] July 14, these new layers are coming down like new leaves, investing it.

Vol. IX

new curtain or layer. What becomes of the first layers surrounding the comb within? Do they steadily cut them away and use them on the outside, and build new and larger combs beneath? Some that come forth appear to have something white like the paper in their mouths, at any rate.)

There is one in Mr. Smith's bank, one side open and flat against the ground. One of his men thinks they will not sting him if he holds his breath.

June 29. A. M. — Up Assabet with Blake.

Allium Canadense in house and probably in field.[1] The river is now whitened with the down of the black willow, and I am surprised to see a minute plant abundantly springing from its midst and greening it, — where it has collected in denser beds against some obstacle as a branch on the surface, — like grass growing in cotton in a tumbler.[2]

P. M. — Walk to Lee's Cliff.

Small rough sunflower, the common, at Bittern Cliff. Where I took shelter under the rock at Lee's Cliff, a phœbe has built her nest, and it now has five eggs in it, nearly fresh.

June 30. A. M. — To Ball's Hill.

Yesterday afternoon it was remarkably cool, with

[1] Possibly earlier in field, for I find it all withered there July 7th, though none visibly out before, — as if frost-bitten even.

[2] It is the young willow. *Vide* July 9th. On July 7th I see scarcely any left on the water. June 26, 1860.

wind, it being *easterly*, and I anticipated a sea-turn. There was a little, a blue mistiness, ere long. The coolness continues, and this morning the sky is full of clouds, but they look to me like dog-day clouds and not rain-threatening. It does not rain.

XII

JULY, 1857

(ÆT. 39–40)

July 2. P. M. — To Gowing's Swamp.

Flannery says that there was a frost this morning in Moore's Swamp on the Bedford road, where he has potatoes. He observed something white on the potatoes about 3.30 A. M. and, stooping, breathed on and melted it. Minott says he has known a frost every month in the year, but at this season it would be a *black* frost, which bites harder than a white one.

The *Gaylussacia dumosa* var. *hirtella*, not yet quite in prime. This is commonly an inconspicuous bush, eight to twelve inches high, half prostrate over the sphagnum in which it grows, together with the andromedas, European cranberry, etc., etc., but sometimes twenty inches high quite on the edge of the swamp. It has a very large and peculiar bell-shaped flower, with prominent *ribs* and a rosaceous tinge, and is not to be mistaken for the edible huckleberry or blueberry blossom. The flower deserves a more particular description than Gray gives it. But Bigelow says well of its corolla that it is "remarkable for its distinct, five angled form." Its segments are a little recurved. The calyx-segments are acute and pink at last; the racemes, elongated, about one inch long, one-sided; the corolla, narrowed at the mouth, but very wide above; the calyx, with its segments, pedicels, and the whole raceme (and indeed the leaves somewhat), glandular-hairy.

Calla palustris (with its convolute point like the cultivated) at the south end of Gowing's Swamp. Having found this in one place, I now find it in another. Many an object is not seen, though it falls within the range of our visual ray, because it does not come within the range of our intellectual ray, i. e., we are not looking for it. So, in the largest sense, we find only the world we look for.

I hear many Maryland yellow-throats about the edge of this swamp, and even [?] near their nests. Indeed, I find one or two old ones *suspended much like a red-wing's* amid the water andromeda. They are quite small and of such material as *this* bird chooses.

I see amid the *Andromeda Polifolia* pure bright crimson leaves, and, looking closely, find that in many instances one branch, affected by a kind of disease, bears very handsome light-crimson leaves, two or three times as wide as usual, of the usual white color beneath, which contrast strangely with the slender green and glaucous ones on the contiguous branches. The water andromeda has similar crimson leaves, only proportionally larger and coarser, showing the dots. These are very common. Those of the *Polifolia* far more delicate.

Pogonia ophioglossoides apparently in a day or two.

July 3. Minott says that old Joe Merriam used to tell of his shooting black ducks in the Dam meadows

---

and what luck he had. One day he had shot a couple of ducks and was bringing them home by the legs, when he came to a ditch. As he had his gun in the other hand, and the ditch was wide, he thought he would toss the ducks over before he jumped, but they had no sooner struck the ground than they picked themselves up and flew away, which discouraged him with respect to duck-shooting.

M. says that my pool in Gowing's Swamp used to be called Duck Pond, though he does not know of ducks settling there. Perhaps they did anciently. He once fell into a deep hole when going after blueberries in the town (?) swamp beyond his own meadow. He stepped on to some "water-brush" (probably water andromeda), and suddenly sank very deep, spraining his hand, which he put out to save himself. He once killed a black duck in Beck Stow's Swamp, but could not get it on account of the water. Somebody else got a boat and got it. Thus the ducks and geese will frequent a swamp where there is considerable water, in the spring.

Minott was sitting in his shed as usual, while his handsome pullets were perched on the wood within two feet of him, the rain having driven them to this shelter.

There always were poor and rich as now, — in that first year when our ancestors lived on pumpkins and raccoons, as now when flour is imported from the West.

July 4. P. M. — Up Assabet with Brown and Rogers. Saw many pickerel near the boat. At length, near

---

the upper Assabet bath place, I observed, "Stop! Was that a big pickerel we just passed?" for it was so large I could hardly believe my eyes and thought it must have been a stake. We dropped back and found it to be a pickerel, which apparently would weigh four pounds, and it appeared slightly wounded about the head. We struck him three times with a paddle, and once he nearly jumped into the boat, but at last we could not find him. It seemed out of proportion to the small stream. We ought to have used a pointed or hooked stick to secure him; might have hooked him under the gills. I have heard of small fishes being caught in a slip-noose of grass. Close by I detected in the weeds the back of a large mud turtle exposed and, after ascertaining which end was his tail, — for he lay perfectly still, — I took him into the boat. His back was singularly gibbous or bulged up, he having been evidently wounded once. His approach and aspect drove my companions to the end of the boat.

To-day is warm again, but for nearly a week many people have sat by a fire.

July 5. A. M. — To Lee's Cliff by boat.

Potentilla arguta abundantly out. Partridges big as quails. At Clamshell I found three arrowheads and a small Indian chisel for my guests. Rogers determined the rate of the boat's progress by observing by his second-hand how long the boat was going its length past a pad, calling the boat's length so much.

For some days I have seen great numbers of blackish spiny caterpillars stripping the black willows, some

---

full-grown on June 30th and some now not more than three quarters of an inch long. When looking at a blackbird's nest I pricked my hand smartly on them several times; in fact the nest was pretty well protected by this *chevaux-de-frise*. Are they the caterpillars of the *Vanessa Antiopa?*[1]

That new ravine at Clamshell is so enlarged that bank swallows already use its sides, and I feel some young there. After leaving my companions at the Lee Bridge road, I pushed up Well Meadow Brook a few rods, through the weeds. I saw by the commotion that great numbers of fishes fled before me and concealed themselves amid the weeds or in the mud. The mud was all stirred up by them. Some ran partly ashore. Higher up, when I had left the boat and walked up the brook on the quaking shore, I found a bay and pool connected with the brook all alive with them, and observed two or three caught partly high and dry by their heedless haste, in a shallow and very weedy place. These were young pickerel two or three inches long. I suspect that all, or the greater part, were pickerel, and that they commonly breed in such still weedy basins in deep muddy meadows.

Comara palustris apparently in prime.

A phœbe's nest with four eggs half hatched, at stone bridge.

There has been, amid the chips where a wood-pile stood, in our yard, a bumblebee's nest for ten days or more. Near it there was what I should have called a mouse's nest of withered grass, but this was mainly

[1] Yes; according to Harris's description, they are.

of different material and *perhaps* was made by the bee. It was a little heap two inches high, six long, and four wide, made of old withered grass and *small bits* of rags, brown paper, cotton-wool, strings, lint, and whole feathers, with a small half-closed hole at one end, at which the [bee] buzzed and showed himself if you touched the nest. I saw the cat putting out her paw there and starting back, and to-day I find the remains, apparently, of the bee dead at the entrance. On opening, I find nothing in the nest.

There came out this morning, apparently from one of those hard *stem-wound* cocoons on a black birch in my window, a moth whose wings are spread four and a quarter inches, and it is about an inch and three quarters long. It is black, wings and body, with two short, broad feathery antennæ. The wings all have a clay-colored border behind, with a distinct black waving line down the middle of it, and, about midway the wings, a less distinct clay-colored line. Near the point of each forward wing, a round black spot or eye, with a bluish crescent within its forward edge, and beyond this spot, a purple tinge with a short whitish waving line continued through it from the crescent. The rear wings have a row of oblong roundish black spots along the clay-colored border, within the black line. There is a very faint light line on the fore wings on each side of the head. Beneath, on wings and body, dark purplish brown takes the place of the black above. It is rather handsomer and higher-colored beneath than above. There is a very small light or clay-colored triangular spot near the middle of wing beneath; also a

row of brown spots on a white band along each side of the body. This is evidently the male *Attacus Promethea*. The rich purplish brown beneath — a sort of chocolate purple — makes the figure of a smaller moth of different form.

The cocoon, about an inch long, is surrounded by the now pale withered leaf of the birch, which is wrapped almost quite around it and extends beneath, and it is very hard and firm, the light silk being wound thickly about the petiole, and also, afterward, the twig itself for half an inch or more both above and beneath the petiole. Sometimes there is no real petiole for a core, but the silky sheath can be slid up and down the twig.

July 6. Rubus triflorus well ripe. The beach plums have everywhere the crescent-shaped mark made by the curculio, — the few that remain on.

July 7. Some of the inhabitants of the Cape think that the Cape is theirs and all occupied by them, but in my eyes it is no more theirs than it is the blackbirds', and in visiting the Cape there is hardly more need of my regarding or going through the villages than of going through the blackbirds' nests. I am inclined to leave them both on one side, or perchance I just glance into them to see how they are built and what they contain. I know that they have *spoken for* the whole Cape, and lines are drawn on their maps accordingly, but I know that these are imaginary, having perambulated many such, and they would have to get me or one of

my craft to find them for them. For the most part, indeed with very trifling exceptions, there were no human beings there, only a few imaginary lines on a map.

July 8. P. M. — To Laurel Glen.

A chewink's nest with four young just hatched, at the bottom of the pyrola hollow and grove, where it is so dry, about seven feet southwest of a white pine.

Counted the rings of a white pine stump, sawed off last winter at Laurel Glen. It was three and a half feet [in] diameter and has one hundred and twenty-six rings. *Chimaphila umbellata*, apparently a day or two. I find the *Pyrola secunda* only on the point of expanding. Hear apparently redstarts there, — so they must have nests near, — also pine warblers and *till tilts*.

Later. — To Gowing's Swamp.

The *Gaylussacia dumosa* is now in prime at least. The drosera, round and spatulate leafed, is very abundant and handsome on the sphagnum in the open spaces, amid the *Andromeda calyculata* and *Polifolia*. Find a *Pogonia ophioglossoides* with a third leaf and second flower an inch above the first flower.

Edith Emerson shows me *Oldenlandia purpurea* var. *longifolia*, which she saw very abundantly in bloom on the Blue Hills (Bigelow's locality) on the 29th of June. Says she has seen the pine-sap this year in Concord.

July 9. Could see no yellow wasps about the nest over my window at 6 A. M., but did just before 6.30.[1] I hear of still a second nest at Mrs. Brown's and one at Julius Smith's.

Another *Attacus Promethea*, a male from the same young black birch, was out and on the window this morning. *Q. v.* I dipped the *body* into alcohol before it had fairly spread its wings, but so discolored it, *i. e.* the white line with dots on the side of the abdomen.

I see that the seeds of the *Salix nigra* gathered on the catkins on the 7th, or two days since, put in tumblers of water in my window, have already germinated! and show those two little roundish green leaves.

P. M. — Up Assabet with Sophia.

There is now but little black willow down left on the trees. They will be handsomest somewhat later than this, when there is no down on them, and the new growth has more invested the stems. I think I see how this tree is propagated by its seeds. Its countless minute brown seeds, just perceptible to the naked eye in the midst of their cotton, are wafted with the cotton to the water, — most abundantly about a fortnight ago, — and there they drift and form a thick white scum together with other matter, especially against some alder or other fallen or drooping shrub where there is less current than usual. There, within two or three days, a great many germinate and show their two little roundish leaves, more or less tingeing with green the surface of the scum, — somewhat like grass

[1] *Vide* 10th.

seed in a tumbler of cotton. Many of these are drifted in amid the button-bushes, willows, and other shrubs, and the sedge, along the riverside, and the water falling just at this time, when they have put forth little fibres, they are deposited on the mud just left bare in the shade, and thus probably a great many of them have a chance to become perfect plants. But if they do not drift into sufficiently shallow water and are not left on the mud just at the right time, probably they perish. The mud in many such places is now green with them, though perhaps the seed has often *blown directly through the air* to such places.

I am surprised to see dense groves of young maples an inch or more high from seed of this year. They have sprung in pure sand, where the seed has been drifted and moisture enough supplied at the water's edge. The seed (now effete) commonly lies on the surface, having sent down its rootlet into the sand.

I see no flowers on the bass trees by this river this year, nor at Conantum.

Am surprised to find how much carburetted hydrogen gas there is in the beds of sawdust by the side of this stream, as at the "Narrows." If I thrust in my paddle and give it a twist, great bubbles two inches or more in diameter rush up with great force and sound, lifting the water an inch or two, as if it were violently boiling, and filling the air with that strong gunpowder scent. The bubbles, being lighter than atmospheric air, burst at once, and give me [no] opportunity to see myself in them, as those which the boat makes in sluggish water.

July 10. Put some more black willow seed in a tumbler of water at 9.30 A. M.

P. M. — To Pratt's and Peter's.

One flower on the *Solanum nigrum* at Pratt's, which he says opened the 7th. He found, about a week ago, the *Botrychium Virginianum* in bloom, about the bass in Fever-bush Swamp.[1] I see some lupine still in bloom, though many pods have been ripe some time.

The tephrosia, which grows by Peter's road in the woods, is a very striking and interesting, if I may not say beautiful, flower, especially when, as here, it is seen in a cool and shady place, its clear rose purple contrasting very agreeably with yellowish white, rising from amidst a bed of finely pinnate leaves. Bigelow calls the flowers " very beautiful."

At evening I watch to see when my yellow wasps cease working. For some time before sunset there are but few seen going and coming, but for some time after, or as long as I could easily see them ten feet off, I saw one go forth or return from time to time.

July 11. P. M. — To Corner Spring and Cliffs.

Haying is fairly begun, and for some days I have heard the sound of the mowing-machine, and now the lark must look out for the mowers. The flowering fern, which is so much larger in the copses, though much is brown and effete, is still perhaps in prime. *Vaccinium Pennsylvanicum* ripe. Their dark blue with a bloom is a color that surprises me. The cymbidium is really a splendid flower, with its spike two or three inches long,

[1] *Done* on the 13th.

of commonly three or five large, irregular, concave, star-shaped purple flowers, amid the cool green meadow-grass. It has an agreeable fragrance withal. I see more berries than usual of the *Rubus triflorus* in the open meadow near the southeast corner of the Hubbard meadow blueberry swamp. Call it, perhaps, Cymbidium Meadow. They are dark shining red and, when ripe, of a very agreeable flavor and somewhat of the raspberry's *spirit*. Petty morel not yet, by the bars this side Corner Spring; nor is the helianthus there budded yet. *Apocynum cannabinum*, with its *small white* flowers and *narrow* sepals half as long as whole corolla, apparently two or three days. The trumpet-weed is already as high as my head, with a rich glaucous bloom on its stem. Indeed, looking off into the vales from Fair Haven Hill, where a thin blue haze now rests almost universally, I see that the earth itself is invested with a glaucous bloom at this season like some fruits and rapidly growing stems.

Thermometer at 93° + this afternoon.

Am surprised to find the water of Corner Spring spoiled for the present, however much I clear it out, by the numbers of dead and dying frogs in it (*Rana palustris*). There is a mortality among [them] which has made them hop to this spring to die.

There is an abundance of corydalis on the top of the Cliffs, but most of it is generally out of bloom, *i. e.* excepting a twig or two, and it is partly withered, not so fresh as that in our garden; but some in the shade is quite green and fresh and abundantly blooming still.

July 12. P. M. — To *Equisetum hyemale*.

Those little minnows, a third or half inch long or more, which I catch when bathing, hovering over open sandy spaces, as here at Clamshell, appear to be little shiners. When left dry on my hand, they can toss themselves three or four inches with a spring of their tails, and so often get into the water again. Small as they are, it is rather difficult to catch them, they dodge your hands so fast.

I drink at every cooler spring in my walk these afternoons and love to eye the bottom there, with its pebbly caddis-cases, or its white worms, or perchance a luxurious frog cooling himself next my nose. Sometimes the farmer, foreseeing haying, has been prudent enough to sink a tub in one, which secures a clear deep space. It would be worth the while, methinks, to make a map of the town with all the good springs on it, indicating whether they were cool, perennial, copious, pleasantly located, etc. The farmer is wont to celebrate the virtues of some one on his own farm above all others. Some cool rills in the meadows should be remembered also, for some such in deep, cold, grassy meadows are as cold as springs. I have sometimes drank warm or foul water, not knowing such cold streams were at hand. By many a spring I know where to look for the dipper or glass which some mower has left. When a spring has been allowed to fill up, to be muddied by cattle, or, being exposed to the sun by cutting down the trees and bushes, to dry up, it affects me sadly, like an institution going to decay. Sometimes I see, on one side the tub, — the tub overhung with various wild plants and flowers, its edge almost completely concealed even from the searching eye, — the white sand freshly cast up where the spring is bubbling in. Often I sit patiently by the spring I have cleaned out and deepened with my hands, and see the foul water rapidly dissipated like a curling vapor and giving place to the cool and clear. Sometimes I can look a yard or more into a crevice under a rock, toward the sources of a spring in a hillside, and see it come cool and copious with incessant murmuring down to the light. There are few more refreshing sights in hot weather.

I find many strawberries deep in the grass of the meadow near this Hosmer Spring; then proceed on my way with reddened and fragrant fingers, till it gets washed off at new springs. It is always pleasant to go over the bare brow of Lupine Hill and see the river and meadows thence. It is exceedingly sultry this afternoon, and few men are abroad. The cows stand up to their bellies in the river, lashing their sides with their tails from time to time.

A strong and wholesome fragrance now from the vegetation as I go by overgrown paths through the swamp west of Nut Meadow. *Equisetum hyemale* has been out a good while; is mostly effete, but some open yet. Some have several flower-spikes on the sides near the top, but most one at top, of the last year's plant. This year's shoots a foot high, more or less. All the *Pyrola secunda* I can find is out of bloom. The *Chimaphila umbellata* flower-*buds* make a very pretty umbel, of half a dozen small purple balls surmounted by

a green calyx. They contrast prettily with the glossy green leaves.

A song sparrow's nest in a small clump of alder, two feet from ground! Three or four eggs.

I hear the occasional *link* note from the earliest bobolinks of the season, — a day or two.

July 13. Very hot weather.
P. M. — To Rattlesnake Fern Swamp.

I hear before I start the distant mutterings of thunder in the northwest, though I see no cloud. The haymakers are busy raking their hay, to be ready for a shower. They would rather have their grass wet a little than not have the rain. I keep on, regardless of the prospect. See the indigo-bird still, chirping anxiously on the bushes in that sprout-land beyond the red huckleberry. *Vaccinium Pennsylvanicum* berries pretty thick there, and one lass is picking them with a dipper tied to her girdle. The first thought is, What a good school this lass goes to! Rattlesnake fern just done.

I make haste home, expecting a thunder-shower, which we need, but it goes by. The grass by the roadside is burnt yellow and is quite dusty. This, with the sultry air, the parched fields, and the languid inhabitants, marks the season. Already the elms with denser foliage begin to hang dark against the glaucous mist.

The price of friendship is the total surrender of yourself; no lesser kindness, no ordinary attentions and offerings will buy it. There is forever that purchase to be made with that wealth which you possess, yet only once in a long while are you *advertised* of such a

commodity. I sometimes awake in the night and think of friendship and its possibilities, a new life and revelation to me, which perhaps I had not experienced for many months. Such transient thoughts have been my nearest approach to realization of it, thoughts which I know of no one to communicate to. I suddenly erect myself in my thoughts, or find myself erected, infinite degrees above the possibility of ordinary endeavors, and see for what grand stakes the game of life may be played. Men, with their indiscriminate attentions and ceremonious good-will, offer you trivial baits, which do not tempt; they are not serious enough either for success or failure. I wake up in the night to these higher levels of life, as to a day that begins to dawn, as if my intervening life had been a long night. I catch an echo of the great strain of Friendship played somewhere, and feel compensated for months and years of commonplace. I rise into a diviner atmosphere, in which simply to exist and breathe is a triumph, and my thoughts inevitably tend toward the grand and infinite, as aeronauts report that there is ever an upper current hereabouts which sets toward the ocean. If they rise high enough they go out to sea, and behold the vessels seemingly in mid-air like themselves. It is as if I were serenaded, and the highest and truest compliments were paid me. The universe gives me three cheers.

Friendship is the fruit which the year should bear; it lends its fragrance to the flowers, and it is in vain if we get only a large crop of apples without it. This experience makes us unavailable for the ordinary cour-

tesy and intercourse of men. We can only recognize them when they rise to that level and realize our dream.

July 14. P. M. — Up Assabet with Loomis and Wilde.

Set fire to the carburetted hydrogen from the sawdust shoal with matches, and heard it flash. It must be an interesting sight by night.

July 15. Tephrosia is generally considerably past its prime. *Vaccinium vacillans* berries. Scare up a snipe (?) by riverside, which goes off with a dry *crack*, and afterward two woodcocks in the shady alder marsh at Well Meadow, which go off with a whistling flight. *Rhus glabra* under Cliffs, not yet.

When I entered the woods there, I was at once pursued by a swarm of those wood flies which gyrate around your head and strike your hat like rain-drops. As usual, they kept up with me as I walked, and gyrated about me still, as if I were stationary, advancing at the same time and receiving reinforcements from time to time. Though I switched them smartly for half a mile with some indigo-weed, they did not mind it in the least, nor a better switch of *Salix tristis;* but though I knocked down many of them, they soon picked themselves up and came on again. They had a large black spot on their wings and some yellowish rings about their abdomens. They keep up a smart buzzing all the while. When I descended into the swamp at Well Meadow, they deserted me, but soon pursued me again when I came out. Apparently the same swarm followed me quite through the wood (with this exception), or for two miles, and they did not leave me till I had got some twenty rods from the woods toward Hayden's. They did not once sting, though they endeavored sometimes to alight on my face. What they got by their perseverance I do not know, — unless it were a switching.

July 16. Thursday. P. M. — To Hemlocks.
Geum album, apparently well out.

As I walked through the pasture side of the hill, saw a mouse or two glance before me in faint galleries in the grass. They are seldom seen, for these small deer, like the larger, disappear suddenly, as if they had exploded before your eyes.

Lechea thymifolia of Gray is the large-podded one according to plate in his "Genera." G., in same, shows five petals to *Portulaca* and says. it "has from early times been naturalized around gardens almost everywhere . . . is said to be truly wild in Arkansas and Texas."

I hear of the first early blueberries brought to market. What a variety of rich blues their berries present, *i. e.* the earliest kind! Some are quite black and without bloom. What innocent flavors!

July 17. P. M. — To Lee's Cliff.
The young leaves of the slippery elm are a yellowish green and large, and the branches recurved or drooping. *Hypericum corymbosum.* Am caught in the rain and take shelter under the thick white pine

by Lee's Cliff. I see thereunder an abundance of chimaphila in bloom. It is a beautiful flower, with its naked umbel of crystalline purplish-white flowers, their disks at an angle with the horizon. On its lower side a ring of purple (or crimson) scales at the base of its concave petals, around the large, green, sticky ovary.

The *Sagina procumbens* continues to flower sparingly. It agrees with Gray's plate.

I found yesterday, at and above the Hemlocks on the Assabet, the dicksonia, apparently in prime; *Aspidium Noveboracense; Aspidium marginale*, apparently in prime; *Osmunda Claytoniana* and *cinnamomea*, done.

I find to-day, at Bittern Cliff and at Lee's, *Asplenium ebeneum* (the larger), apparently nearly in prime, and *A. Trichomanes*, apparently just begun. This very commonly occurs in tufts at the base of the last, like radical leaves to it. At Lee's Cliff, *Polypodium vulgare*, not yet brown fruit. *Aspidium Noveboracense* at Corner Spring, not yet brown; also *Aspidium Filixfœmina* (?), with lunar-shaped fruit, not yet brown; also apparently a chaffy-stemmed dicksonia, densely brown-fruited; also an almost thrice pinnate fern with a very chaffy stipe, in prime, already yellowish above, somewhat *A. cristatum*-like, some of the dots confluent.

Ampelopsis out of bloom at Lee's. *Aralia racemosa*, not in bloom, at Corner Spring.

July 18. Minott says that old Sam Nutting used to pinch off the first leaves of his melon vines as soon as

they had three or four leaves, because they only attracted the bugs, and he was quite successful.

George Bradford says he finds in Salem striped maple and *Sambucus pubens*. He (and Tuckerman?) found the *Utricularia resupinata* once in Plymouth, and it seems to correspond with mine at Well Meadow.

July 19. Smooth sumach out since the 16th.

July 20. To BOSTON ON WAY TO MAINE WOODS.
At Natural History Library. Holbrook makes the *Emys terrapin* to be found from Rhode Island to Florida and South America. "The only Emys common to North and South America." So did not know it was found at New Bedford. Was not my Freetown turtle (*vide* April 13th) Holbrook's *Kinosternon Pennsylvanicum?* In his plate the edges of the scales are of more *waving* lines than those of the *Sternothœrus;* it has more brown or reddish yellow both above and below; its tail appears more sharply horny. There is no yellow line on its neck. The sternum is considerably larger (in proportion to carapax) as well as broader behind, and the plates connecting it with the upper shell are much wider. In the generic account the difference from the *Sternothœrus* is that the jaws are hooked (I see no difference in the plates) and the "sternum subdivided into three sections, anterior and posterior movable; " and the "supplemental plates very large." Under this species he says the shell is "ecarinate;" "vertebral plates depressed, sub-imbricate." "Length of shell, $3\frac{1}{2}$ inches; breadth of shell, 2 inches 10 lines;

elevation, $1\frac{3}{4}$ inches; length of sternum, 3 inches 2 lines." "The living animal has a slight odour of musk that is not disagreeable." Found in Atlantic States from Florida to latitude 41°. Thinks Hitchcock mistook it for *Sternothœrus* in his Geology. Found in the West, and Say says, high up the Missouri.

According to De Kay, it is found sparingly in the southern counties of New York, and he says, "It has a strong musky smell." Of the *Sternothœrus* he says, "There appear to be two varieties, of which one is smooth on the shell, while the other is sub-carinate." Length of shell of *Sternothœrus*, $2\frac{5}{10}$ inches; height, $1\frac{2}{10}$; of *Kinosternon*, 4 and $1\frac{8}{10}$. (*Vide* April 13th.)

De Kay does not describe the *Cistuda Blandingii* as found in New York.

5 P. M. — Take cars for Portland. Very hot and dusty; as much need of a veil in the cars to exclude cinders as in the woods to keep off mosquitoes. Riding in the cars this weather like sitting in the flue of a chimney.

Take steamer at Portland. Delayed by fog in night off coast of Maine.[1]

July 21. Tuesday. 1 P. M. At Bangor. — Thatcher's moose-horns hanging in his barn spread two feet eight inches. There is one more prong on one side than the other. This is small.

[1] [The account of this journey appears in *The Maine Woods* under the title of "The Allegash and East Branch." In the following pages only those passages of the Journal which were not reproduced in that account are included.]

July 22. Wednesday. I am struck by the appearance of large canoe birch trees, even about houses, as an ornamental tree, and they are very enlivening, their trunks white as if whitewashed, though they rarely escape being barked and so disfigured more or less by mischievous fingers. Their white boles are in keeping with the fresh, cool air.

At a mile and a half north of Bangor, passed the spot, at Treat's Falls, where the first settler and fur-trader, one Treat, lived. . . .

We wanted to get one [1] who was temperate and reliable, an older man than we had before, well skilled in Indian lore. I was warned not to employ an Indian on account of their obstinacy and the difficulty of understanding one another, and on account of their dirty habits in cooking, etc., but it was partly the Indian, such as he was, that I had come to see. The difficulty is to find one who will not get drunk and detain you wherever liquor is to be had. Some young white men of Oldtown named Pond were named as the very ones for us. But I was bent on having an Indian at any rate.

While we were talking with Polis, a young, very dark-complexioned Indian, named something like Nicholai Orson, came up, and Polis said, "He go with you." We found that the latter wanted to go very much, said he knew the country and all about it. But I said, "We don't know you." He was too dark-colored, as if with African blood, — P. said they did not mix with them, — and too young for me. While I was

[1] [An Indian guide.]

talking with him, Thatcher [1] took Polis aside and inquired the other's character, when P. frankly told him that he would n't do for us at all, that he was a very good fellow except that he would get drunk whenever he had a chance. . . . T. said he would get away from Nicholai with as few words as possible. So T. saying to N. that if we wanted him we would call again in a couple of hours, we departed.[2] . . .

A *light* india-rubber coat is useful, but you cannot work in it in warm weather, for your underclothes will be just as wet with perspiration as if dipped in water before you know it, and, beside, I wore off the rubber against the cross-bars behind my back. You could not wear india-rubber pants in addition unless you sat perfectly still in cool weather.

The only india-rubber bags we could find in Bangor were no better than a canvas bag, the rubber rapidly cracking and peeling off, letting in water and dirtying the contents. They would have been an imposition if the seller had not admitted that they would not hold water, and asserted that he could not make one that would. Doubted; far better ones could be home-made of good india-rubber cloth.

Called on a Mr. Coe, part proprietor (?) of the Chamberlain Farm, so called, on Chamberlain Lake (spoke of it as "our farm"), who gave us some advice as to our outfit. Said he should like to have the making up of our packs, thinking we should take too

[1] [Mr. Thatcher of Bangor was Thoreau's companion on his Chesuncook excursion in 1853.]
[2] [Joe Polis was the Indian finally engaged for the expedition.]

Vol. IX

many things. Told of one who, having to *walk* a few days through the woods, began by loading himself with some fifteen pounds of shot. The rule is to carry as little as possible. Advised us to go on foot, carry but few supplies, and replenish at the different camps we might find. He hastily scribbled this memorandum for us: —

"Axe
Canoe
Blankets
Fry-pan
Teakettle
Dippers
Tea
Salt
Hard-bread and pork
Pepper
Matches
Ammunition and lines and hooks
Camphor "

July 23. Thursday. Some fifteen caribou were taken by one (?) man about Moosehead last winter. . . .

[Mr. Leonard, of Bangor, a sportsman,] said that the horns of a moose would spread four feet, sometimes six; would weigh thirty or forty pounds (the hide, fifty); squirrels and mice ate the horns when shed. (They told me that the horns were not grown at this season.) . . . [Leonard told] also of some panthers which appeared near a house in Foxcroft. . . .

I observed from the stage many of the *Fringilla hyemalis* flitting along the fences, even at this season, whence I conclude that they must breed here. Also,

between Monson and the lake, the now very handsome panicles of the red elder-berry, so much earlier than the black, the most showy objects by the roadside. In one place the tree-cranberry in a yard, already *reddening*, though nowhere else after was it nearly so early. . . .

There were two public houses near together,[1] and they wanted to detain us at the first, even took off some of our baggage in spite of us; but, on our protesting, shouted, "Let them go! let them go!" as if it was any of their business. Whereupon we, thanking them for the privilege, rode on, leaving P. behind, who, I knew, would follow his canoe. Here we found a spacious house, quite empty, close to the lake, with an attentive landlord, which was what we wanted. A bright wood fire soon burned in the ample barroom, very comfortable in that fresh and cool atmosphere, and we congratulated ourselves on having escaped the crowd at the other house.

Fogg, the landlord, said that there was scarcely any hemlock about the lake. Here was an Indian who came to talk with Polis, who made canoes, had made those two for Leonard. . . . He said that he used the red cedar of uplands (*i. e.* arbor-vitæ?) for ribs, etc.

July 24. Friday. As we paddled along, we saw many peetweets, also the common iris or blue flag, along the rocky shore, and here and afterwards great fields of epilobium or fire-weed, a mass of color. . . .

P. said that *Bematinichtik* meant high land generally and no particular height. . . .

[1] [At Moosehead Lake.]

Near this island, or rather some miles southwest of it, on the mainland, where we stopped to stretch our legs and look at the vegetation, I measured a canoe birch, five and a half feet in circumference at two and a half from the ground. . . .

I was disappointed to find my clothes under my india-rubber coat as completely wetted by perspiration as they could have been by rain, and that this would always be the consequence of *working* in such a garment, at least in warm weather. . . .

We looked down on the unpretending buildings and grounds of the Kineo House, as on a little flat map, oblong-square, at our feet. . . .

It [1] suggested to me how unexplored still are the realms of nature, that what we know and have seen is always an insignificant portion. We may any day take a walk as strange as Dante's imaginary one to L' Inferno or Paradiso.

July 25. Saturday. Very early this morning we heard the note of the wood thrush, on awaking, though this was a poor singer. I was glad to find that this prince of singers was so common in the wilderness. . . .

The shores of this lake are rocky, rarely sandy, and we saw no good places for moose to come out on, *i. e.* no meadows. What P. called Caucomgomoc Mountain, with a double top, was seen north over the lake in mid-forenoon. Approaching the shore, we scared up some young dippers with the old bird. Like the

[1] [Phosphorescent wood. See *Maine Woods*, pp. 198–201; Riv. 245–248.]

shecorways, they ran over the water very fast. Landing on the east side, four or five miles north of Kineo, I noticed roses (*R. nitida*) in bloom, and, as usual, an abundance of rue (*Thalictrum Cornuti*) along the shore. The wood there was arbor-vitæ, spruce, fir, white pine, etc. The ground and rotting trunks, as usual, covered with mosses, some strange kinds, — various wild feather and leaf-like mosses, of rank growth, that were new or rare to me, — and an abundance of *Clintonia borealis*. . . .

The Indian started off first with the canoe and was soon out of sight, going much faster than an ordinary walk. We could see him a mile or more ahead, when his canoe against the sky on the height of land between Moosehead and the Penobscot was all that was to be seen about him. . . .

Here, among others, were the *Aster Radula*, just in bloom; large-flowered bellwort (*Uvularia grandiflora*), in fruit. The great purple orchis (*Platanthera fimbriata*), very splendid and perfect ones close to the rails. I was surprised to see it in bloom so late. *Vaccinium Canadense; Dalibarda repens*, still in bloom; *Pyrola secunda*, out of bloom; *Oxalis Acetosella*, still occasionally in flower; Labrador tea (*Ledum latifolium*), out of bloom; *Kalmia glauca*, etc., etc., close to the track.

A cousin of mine and his son met with a large male moose on this carry two years ago, standing within a few rods of them, and at first mistook him for an ox. They both fired at him, but to no purpose.

As we were returning over the track where I had passed but a few moments before, we started a par-

Vol. IX

tridge with her young partly from beneath the wooden rails. While the young hastened away, she sat within seven feet of us and plumed herself, perfectly fearless, without making a noise or ruffling her feathers as they do in our neighborhood, and I thought it would be a good opportunity to observe whether she flew as quietly as other birds when not alarmed. We observed her till we were tired, and when we compelled her to get out of our way, though she took to wing as easily as if we had not been there and went only two or three rods, into a tree, she flew with a considerable *whir*, as if this were unavoidable in a rapid motion of the wings. . . .

Here was a canoe on the stocks, in an earlier stage of its manufacture than I had seen before, and I noticed it particularly. The St. Francis Indian was paring down the long cedar strips, or lining, with his crooked knife.

As near as I could *see*, and *understand* him and Polis, they first lay the bark flat on the ground, outside up, and two of the top rails, the inside and thickest ones, already connected with cross-bars, upon it, in order to get the form; and, with logs and rocks to keep the bark in place, they bend up the birch, cutting down slits in the edges from within three feet of the ends and perpendicularly on all sides about the rails, making a square corner at the ground; and a row of stakes three feet high is then driven into the ground all around, to hold the bark up in its place. They next lift the frame, *i. e.* two rails connected by cross-bars, to the proper height, and sew the bark strongly to the rails with spruce roots every six inches, the thread passing

around the rail and also *through* the ends of the cross-bars, and sew on strips of bark to protect the sides in the middle. The canoe is as yet carried out square down at the ends (not), and is perfectly flat on the bottom. (This canoe had advanced thus far.)

Then, as near as I could learn, they shape the ends (?), put in all the lining of long thin strips, so shaped and shaved as just to fit, and fill up the bark, pressing it out and shaping the canoe. Then they put in the ribs and put on the outer or thinnest rail over the edge of the bark. . . .

Our path up the bank here led by a large dead white pine, in whose trunk near the ground were great square-cornered holes made by the woodpeckers, probably the red-headed. They were seven or eight inches long by four wide and reached to the heart of the tree through an inch or more of sound wood, and looked like great mortise-holes whose corners had been somewhat worn and rounded by a loose tenon. The tree for some distance was quite honeycombed by them. It suggested woodpeckers on a larger scale than ours, as were the trees and the forest.[1] . . .

Returning, we found the tree cranberry in one place still in bloom. The stream here ran very swiftly and was hard to paddle against.

July 26. Sunday. I distinguished more plainly than formerly the very sharp and regular dark tops of the fir trees, shaped like the points of bodkins. These give a

[1] [The holes were doubtless the work of the pileated woodpecker.]

peculiarly dark and sombre look to the forest. The spruce-top has a more ragged outline. . . .

Here were many raspberries on the site of an old logging-camp, but not yet ripe. . . .

In the meanwhile I observed the plants on the shore: white and black spruce, *Hypericum ellipticum*, *Smilax herbacea*, sium, and a strange-looking polygonum. . . .

As we sat on the bank, two canoes, containing men, women, and children, probably from Chesuncook, returned down the stream. We supposed that they had been a-berrying this Sunday morning. . . .

The canoe implies a long antiquity in which its manufacture has been gradually perfected. It will ere long, perhaps, be ranked among the lost arts. . . .

July 27. Monday. There were some yellow lilies (*Nuphar*), *Scutellaria galericulata*, clematis (abundant), sweet-gale, "great smilacina" (did I mean *S. racemosa?*), and beaked hazel, the only hazel I saw in Maine.

July 28. Tuesday. As I remember, Hodge mistakes when he says[1] that "it is erroneously represented on the charts, for it extends in a north-northeasterly, south-southwesterly direction about twelve miles." He appears to be thinking of the easterly part. On the north side there is quite a clearing, and we had been advised to ascend the bare hill there for the sake of the prospect. . . .

Great trunks of trees stood dead and bare far out in the lake, making the impression of ruined piers of

[1] [Of Chamberlain Lake.]

Vol. IX

probe employed in a new direction, and a wise man will attend to each one's report.

July 30. Thursday. I saw thus early the slate-colored snowbird (*Fringilla hyemalis*) here. As I walked along the ridge of the island, through the woods, I heard the rush and clatter of a great many ducks which I had alarmed from the concealed northern shore beneath me. . . .

I heard here, at the foot of the lake, the cawing of a crow, which sounded so strangely that I suspected it might be an uncommon species. . . .

To a philosopher there is in a sense no great and no small, and I do not often submit to the criticism which objects to comparing so-called great things with small. It is often a question which is most dignified by the comparison, and, beside, it is pleasant to be reminded that ancient worthies who dealt with affairs of state recognized small and familiar objects known to ourselves. We are surprised at the permanence of the relation. Loudon in his "Arboretum," vol. iv, page 2038, says, "Dionysius the geographer compares the form of the Morea in the Levant, the ancient Peloponnesus, to the leaf of this tree [the Oriental plane]; and Pliny makes the same remark in allusion to its numerous bays. To illustrate this comparison, Martyn, in his Virgil (vol. ii, page 149), gives a figure of the plane tree leaf, and a map of the Morea," both which Loudon copies.[1]

Loudon says ("Arboretum," vol. iv, page 2323,

[1] [See *Excursions*, p. 280; Riv. 343.]

a city that had been, while behind, the timber lay criss-a-cross for half a dozen rods or more over the water. . . .

We were glad to find on this carry some raspberries, and a few of the *Vaccinium Canadense* berries, which had begun to be ripe here.

July 29. Wednesday. I noticed there[1] *Aralia racemosa*, and *Aster macrophyllus in bloom*, with bluish rays and quite fragrant (!), like some medicinal herb, so that I doubted at first if it were that. . . .

I found on the edge of this clearing the *Cirsium muticum*, or swamp thistle, abundantly in bloom. I think we scared up a black partridge just beyond. . . .

I am interested in an indistinct prospect, a distant view, a mere suggestion often, revealing an almost wholly new world to me. I rejoice to get, and am apt to present, a new view. But I find it impossible to present my view to most people. In effect, it would seem that they do not wish to take a new view in any case. Heat lightning flashes, which reveal a distant horizon to our twilight eyes. But my fellows simply assert that it is not broad day, which everybody knows, and fail to perceive the phenomenon at all. I am willing to pass for a fool in my often desperate, perhaps foolish, efforts to persuade them to lift the veil from off the possible and future, which they hold down with both their hands, before their eyes. The most valuable communication or news consists of hints and suggestions. When a truth comes to be known and accepted, it begins to be bad taste to repeat it. Every individual constitution is a

[1] [Telos Lake.]

apparently using the authority of Michaux, whom see in my books) of the hemlock that "in Nova Scotia, New Brunswick, the district of Maine, the state of Vermont, and the upper parts of New Hampshire, it forms three quarters of the evergreen woods, of which the remainder consists of the black spruce." (!) Speaks of its being "constantly found at the foot of the hills."

The events attending the fall of Dr. Johnson's celebrated willow at Lichfield, — a *Salix Russelliana* twenty-one feet in circumference at six feet from the ground, — which was blown down in 1829, were characteristic of the Briton, whose whole island, indeed, is a museum. While the neighbors were lamenting the fate of the tree, a coachmaker remembered that he had used some of the twigs for pea-sticks the year before and made haste to see if any of these chanced to be alive. Finding that one had taken root, it was forthwith transplanted to the site of the old tree, "a band of music," says Loudon, "and a number of persons attending its removal, and a dinner being given afterwards by Mr. Holmes [the coachmaker][1] to his friends, and the admirers of Johnson."

July 31. Friday. This morning heard from the camp the red-eye, robin (P. said it was a sign of rain), tweezer-bird, *i. e.* parti-colored warbler, chickadee, wood thrush, and soon after starting heard or saw a blue jay. . . .

I saw here my sweet-scented *Aster macrophyllus* (?) just out, also, near end of carry in rocky woods, a new

[1] [Thoreau's brackets.]

plant, the halenia or spurred gentian, which I observed afterward on the carries all the way down to near the mouth of the East Branch, eight inches to two feet high.

I also saw here, or soon after, the red cohosh berries, ripe, (for the first time in my life); spikenard, etc. The commonest aster of the woods was *A. acuminatus*, not long out, and the commonest solidago on the East Branch, *Solidago squarrosa*. . . .

P. said that his mother was a Province woman and as white as anybody, but his father a pure-blooded Indian. I saw no trace of white blood in his face, and others, who knew him well and also his father, were confident that his mother was an Indian and suggested that she was of the Quoddy tribe (belonged to New Brunswick), who are often quite light-colored. . . .

I got there[1] one (apparently) *Lilium superbum* flower, with strongly revolute sepals and perfectly smooth leaves beneath, otherwise not large nor peculiar. On this East Branch we saw many of the *small* purple fringed orchis (*Platanthera psycodes*), but no *large* ones (*P. fimbriata*), which alone were noticed on the West Branch and Umbazookskus. Also saw often the *Lysimachia ciliata*, and once white cohosh berries, and at one place methinks the *Vaccinium Pennsylvanicum* (?) with the other. . . .

On a small bare sand or gravel bar,[2] I observed that same *Prunus* which grows on the rocks at Bellows

[1] [Where he gathered lily roots, on the East Branch, below Bowlin Stream. See *Maine Woods*, p. 309; Riv. 384.]
[2] [On the East Branch.]

XIII

AUGUST, 1857

(ÆT. 40)

Aug. 1. I saw at the end of this carry[1] small *Apocynum cannabinum* on the rocks, also more of the spurred gentian. . . .

Here were many Canada blueberries and, on the rocks, a new *Allium* or garlic, with purple flowers, and the *Lobelia Kalmii*, both on bare rocks just below the falls. On the main land were Norway pines and a sandy soil, and *Bæomyces roseus* and *Desmodium Canadense*, — a new soil for this river.[2]

Aug. 2. Sunday. At a small river coming in from the south a few miles below Nicketow, the Penobscot is crooked and the place is called *Payt-gum-kiss*, or Petticoat, according to P.

Aug. 3. Monday. This was the midst of the raspberry season. We found them abundant on every carry on the East Branch and below, and children were carrying them from all sides into Bangor. I observed that they were the prominent dish on the tables, once a low scarlet mountain, garnishing the head of the table in a dish two feet across. Earlier the strawberries are

[1] [That mentioned on p. 314 of *Maine Woods* (Riv. 390).]
[2] [See *Maine Woods*, p. 315; Riv. 392.]

Falls, whose leaf might at first sight be mistaken for that of a willow. It is evidently the *Prunus depressa* (sand cherry) of Pursh, and distinct, as a variety at least, from the common allied one (*P. pumila* of Pursh), which is not *depressed* even when it grows, as it often does abundantly, in river meadows (*e. g.* Edmund Hosmer's on Assabet). The leaf of the former is more lanceolate-spatulate, and I have never seen it in Concord, though the *P. pumila* is very common here. Gray describes but one kind.

Jackson, being some miles below this, in the East Branch, the 6th of October, twenty years ago, says, "There are several small gravelly islands covered with a profusion of deep purple beach plums, but since they had been frozen they were found to be tasteless and insipid." We did not see any of these.

Vol. IX

equally abundant, and we even found a few still deep in the grass. Neither of these abound about Boston, and we saw that they were due to the peculiar air of this higher latitude. Though for six weeks before leaving home we had been scarcely able to lie under more than a single sheet, we experienced no hot weather in Maine. The air was uniformly fresh and bracing like that of a mountain to us, and, though the inhabitants like to make it out that it is as warm there as in Massachusetts, we were not to be cheated. It is so much the more desirable at this season to breathe the raspberry air of Maine.

P. wanted to sell us his canoe. Said it would last seven or eight years, or, with care, perhaps ten.

It was P. who commonly reminded us that it was dinner-time on this excursion, sometimes by turning the prow to the shore. He once made an indirect but lengthy apology, by saying that we might think it strange, but one who worked hard all day was very particular to have his dinner in good season.

Aug. 4. Tuesday. A. M. — Rode to Pushaw Lake with Thatcher and Hoar.

Duck-meat, apparently a new kind, there. T. thinks there's little if any red cedar about Bangor.

Aug. 5. Wednesday. To my surprise found on the dinner-table at Thatcher's the *Vaccinium Oxycoccus*. T. did not know it was anything unusual, but bought it at such a rate per bushel of Mr. Such-a-one, who brought it to market. They call it the "bog cranberry." I did not perceive that it differed from the common, unless that it was rather more skinny.

T. has four rude pictures which belonged to Reuben Brown, on which is printed, "*A. Doolittle sculpt,*" and these titles: —

"Plate I. The Battle of Lexington April 19, 1775."

"Plate II. A View of the Town of Concord."

"Plate III. The Engagement at the North Bridge in Concord."

"Plate IV. A View of the South Part of Lexington."

Plate II is like that at Mr. Brooks's. In Plate III (you look westward) what appears to be the old Buttrick house has the upper story projecting over the lower. The French (Hoar's) house appears on the left. Another house is seen on the right of Buttrick's (?), perhaps Jarvis's. There is a wall on the south or town side of the road, where the British stood, and a large upright tree on the south side there, at the Bridge.

P. M. — Rode to Old Fort Hill at the bend of the Penobscot some three miles above Bangor, to look for the site of the Indian town, — perhaps the ancient Negas?[1] Found several arrowheads and two little dark and crumbling fragments of Indian earthenware, like black earth.

Aug. 6. Thursday. A. M. — To the high hill and ponds in Bucksport, some ten or more miles out.

A withdrawn, wooded, and somewhat mountainous country. There was a little trout-pond just over the highest hill, very muddy, surrounded by a broad belt

[1] Willis puts it on the Kenduskeag.

Vol. IX

of yellow lily pads. Over this we pushed with great difficulty on a rickety raft of small logs, using poles thirty feet long, which stuck in the mud. The pond was about twenty-five feet deep in the middle, and our poles would stick up there and hold the raft. There was no apparent inlet, but a small outlet. The water was not clear nor particularly cold, and you would have said it was the very place for pouts, yet T. said that the only fish there caught were brook trout, at any time of day. You fish with a line only, sinking twenty feet from the raft. The water was full of insects, which looked very much like the little brown chips or bits of wood which make coarse sawdust, with legs, running over the submerged part of the raft, etc. I suppose this pond owed its trout to its elevation and being fed by springs. It seems they do not require swift or clear water, sandy bottom, etc. Are caught like pouts without any art. We had many bites and caught one.

Aug. 7. Friday. P. M. — Take cars for Portland, and at evening the boat for Boston. A great deal of cat-tail flag by railroad between Penobscot and Kennebec. Fine large ponds about Belgrade.

END OF VOLUME IX

The Journal of Henry D. Thoreau

VOLUME X

(August, 1857 — June, 1858)

In the Easterbrooks Country

CONTENTS

Vol. X

Vol. X

AUGUST, 1857 (ÆT. 40)

Aug. 8. Saturday. Get home at 8.30 A. M.

I find that B. M. Watson sent me from Plymouth, July 20th, six glow-worms, of which two remain, the rest having escaped. He says they were found by his family on the evenings of the 18th and 19th of July. "They are very scarce, these being the only ones we have found as yet. They were mostly found on the way from the barn to James's cottage, under the wild cherry trees on the right hand, in the grass where it was very dry, and at considerable distance from each other. We have had no rain for a month."

Examining them by night, they are about three quarters of an inch long as they crawl. Looking down on *one*, it shows two bright dots near together on the head, and, along the body, nine transverse lines of light, succeeded by two more bright dots at the other extremity, wider apart than the first. There is also a bright dot on each side opposite the transverse lines. It is a greenish light, growing more green as the worm

is brought into more light. A slumbering, glowing, *inward* light, as if shining for itself inward as much as outward. The other worm, which was at first curled up still and emitted a duller light, was one and one twentieth inches in length and also showed two dots of light only on the forward segment. When stretched out, as you look down on them, they have a square-edged look, like a row of buns joined together. Such is the ocular illusion. But whether stretched out or curled up, they look like some kind of rare and precious gem, so regularly marked, far more beautiful than a uniform mass of light would be.

Examining by day, I found the smallest to be seven eighths to one inch long, and the body about one sixth of an inch wide and from one thirteenth to one twelfth of an inch deep, convex above, pointed at head, broader at tail; head about one twentieth of an inch wide. Yet these worms were more nearly linear, or of a uniform breadth (being perhaps broadest at forward extremity), than the *Lampyre* represented in my French book, which is much the broadest behind and has also two rows of dots down the back. They have six light-brown legs within a quarter of an inch of the forward extremity. The worm is composed of twelve segments or overlapping scales, like the abdominal plates of a snake, and has a slight elastic projection (?) beneath at tail. It has also six short antennæ-like projections from the head, the two outer on each side the longest, the two inner very short. The general color above was a pale brownish yellow or buff; the head small and dark-brown; the antennæ chestnut and white; white or

whitish on sides and beneath. You could see a faint dorsal line. They were so transparent that you could see the internal motions when looking down on them.

I kept them in a sod, supplying a fresh one each day. They were invariably found underneath it by day, next the floor, still and curled up in a ring, with the head within or covered by the tail. Were apt to be restless on being exposed to the light. One that got away in the yard was found again ten feet off and down cellar.

What kind are these?

In the account of the Glow-worm in Rees's Cyclopædia it is said, "The head is small, flat, hard, and black, and sharp towards the mouth; it has short antennæ, and six moderately long legs; the body is flat and is composed of twelve rings, whereas the body of the male consists only of five; it is of a dusky color, with a streak of white down the back."

Knapp, in "Journal of a Naturalist," speaks of "the luminous caudal spot" of the *Lampyris noctiluca*.[1]

Speaking with Dr. Reynolds about the phosphorescence which I saw in Maine, etc., etc., he said that he had seen the will-o'-the-wisp, a small blue flame, like burning alcohol, a few inches in diameter, over a bog, which moved when the bog was shaken.

Aug. 9. Sunday. I see the blackbirds flying in flocks (which did not when I went away July 20th) and hear the shrilling of my alder locust.

[1] *Vide* Sept. 16th for an account of another kind. *Vide* Jan. 15, 1858.

Aug. 10. Monday. P. M. — In Clintonia Swamp I see a remarkable yellow fungus about the base of some grass growing in a tuft. It is a jelly, shaped like a bodkin or a pumpkin's stigma, two inches long, investing the base of the grass blades, a quarter to a half inch thick, tapering to the grass each way and covered with a sort of moist meal. It was strong-scented and disagreeable.

Cat-tail commonly grows in the hollows and boggy places where peat has been dug.

How meanly and miserably we live for the most part! We escape fate continually by the skin of our teeth, as the saying is. We are practically desperate. But as every man, in respect to material wealth, aims to become independent or wealthy, so, in respect to our spirits and imagination, we should have some spare capital and superfluous vigor, have some margin and leeway in which to move. What kind of gift is life unless we have spirits to enjoy it and taste its true flavor? if, in respect to spirits, we are to be forever cramped and in debt? In our ordinary estate we have not, so to speak, quite enough air to breathe, and this poverty qualifies our piety; but we should have more than enough and breathe it carelessly. Poverty is the rule. We should first of all be full of vigor like a strong horse, and beside have the free and adventurous spirit of his driver; *i. e.*, we should have such a reserve of elasticity and strength that we may at any time be able to put ourselves at the top of our speed and go beyond our ordinary limits, just as the invalid hires a horse. Have the gods sent us into this world, — to this *muster,*

Vol. X

— to do chores, hold horses, and the like, and not given us any spending money?

The poor and sick man keeps a horse, often a hostler; but the well man is a horse to himself, is horsed on himself; he feels his own oats. Look at the other's shanks. How spindling! like the timber of his gig! First a sound and healthy life, and then spirits to live it with.

I hear the neighbors complain sometimes about the peddlers selling their help *false* jewelry, as if they themselves wore *true* jewelry; but if their help pay as much for it as they did for theirs, then it is just as *true* jewelry as theirs, just as becoming to them and no more; for unfortunately it is the cost of the article and not the merits of the wearer that is considered. The money is just as well spent, and perhaps better earned. I don't care how much false jewelry the peddlers sell, nor how many of the eggs which you steal are rotten. What, pray, is *true* jewelry? The hardened tear of a diseased clam, murdered in its old age. Is that fair play? If not, it is no jewel. The mistress wears this in her ear, while her help has one made of paste which you cannot tell from it. False jewelry! Do you know of any shop where *true* jewelry can be bought? I always look askance at a jeweller and wonder what *church* he can belong to.

I heard some ladies the other day laughing about some one of their *help* who had *helped* herself to a real hoop from off a hogshead for her gown. I laughed too, but which party do you think I laughed at? Is n't hogshead as good a word as crinoline?

Aug. 11. Tuesday. Red cohosh berries well ripe in front of Hunt's, perhaps a week or more, — a round, conical spike, two and a half inches long by one and three quarters, of about thirty cherry-red berries. The berries oblong, seven sixteenths of an inch by six sixteenths, with a seam on one side, on slender pedicels about five eighths of an inch long.

Aug. 13. J. Farmer saw some days ago a black-headed gull, between a kingfisher and common gull in size, sailing lightly on Bateman's Pond. It was very white beneath and bluish-white above. *Corallorhiza multiflora* and *Desmodium rotundifolium,* how long?

Aug. 15. Lycopodium lucidulum, how long?

Aug. 16. Myriophyllum ambiguum, apparently var. *limosum,* except that it is not nearly linear-leafed but pectinate, well out how long?

Aug. 20. Thursday. P. M. — To Hubbard's Close.

The hillside at Clintonia Swamp is in some parts quite shingled with the rattlesnake-plantain (*Goodyera pubescens*) leaves overlapping one another. The flower is now apparently in its prime. As I stand there, I hear a peculiar sound which I mistake for a woodpecker's tapping, but I soon see a cuckoo hopping near suspiciously or inquisitively, at length within twelve feet, from time to time uttering a hard, dry note, very much like a woodpecker tapping a dead dry tree rapidly,

its *full* clear white throat and breast toward me, and slowly lifting its tail from time to time. Though somewhat allied to that throttled note it makes by night, it was quite different from that.

I go along by the hillside footpath in the woods about Hubbard's Close. The *Goodyera repens* grows behind the spring where I used to sit, amid the dead pine leaves. Its leaves partly concealed in the grass. It is just done commonly.

Helianthus, *strumosus*-like, at the south end of Stow's *cold* pool; how long?

Aug. 22. Saturday. Channing has brought me from Plymouth and Watson *Drosera filiformis,* just out of bloom, from Great South Pond, *Solidago tenuifolia* in bloom, *Sabbatia chloroides,* and *Coreopsis rosea.*

Edward Hoar shows me *Lobelia Kalmii,* which he gathered in flower in Hopkinton about the 18th of July. (I found the same on the East Branch and the Penobscot); staphylea (in fruit) from Northampton, plucked within a week or so (Bigelow says it grows in Weston); also the leaves of a tree growing in Windsor, Vt., which they call the pepperidge, quite unlike our tupelo. Is it not the *Celtis crassifolia?* He says he found the *Uvularia perfoliata* on the Stow road, he thinks within Concord bounds.

Aug. 23. P. M. — To Conantum.
Hear the mole cricket nowadays. Collinsonia (very little left) not out.

Aug. 24. A. M. — Ride to Austin Bacon's, Natick.

On the left hand, just this side the centre of Wayland, I measure the largest, or northernmost, of two large elms standing in front of an old house. At four feet from the ground, where, looking from *one* side, is the smallest place between the ground and the branches, it is seventeen feet in circumference, but there is a bulge on the north side for five feet upward. At five feet it divides to two branches, and each of these soon divides again.

A. Bacon showed me a drawing apparatus which he said he invented, very simple and convenient, also microscopes and many glasses for them which he made. Showed me an exotic called "cypress," which he said had spread from the cemetery over the neighboring fields. Did not know what it was. Is it not *Euphorbia Cyparissias?* and does it not grow by the north roadside east of Jarvis's?[1]

I measured a scarlet oak northeast of his house, on land of the heirs of John Bacon, which at seven feet from the ground, or the smallest place below the branches, was ten feet eight inches in circumference, at one foot from ground sixteen and one fourth feet in circumference. It branched at twelve feet into three. Its trunk tapered or lessened very gradually and regularly from the ground to the smallest place, after the true Eddystone Lighthouse fashion. It has a large and handsome top, rather high than spreading (spreads about three and a half rods), but the branches often

[1] Also at J. Moore's front yard.

dead at the ends. This has grown considerably since Emerson measured; *vide* his account. Bacon says that E. pronounced it the largest oak in the State.

Showed us an elm on the north side of the same field, some ten feet in circumference, which he said was as large in 1714, his grandmother having remembered it nearly so long. There was a dead *Rhus radicans* on it two inches in diameter.

In the meadow south of this field, we looked for the *Drosera filiformis*, which formerly grew there, but could not find it. Got a specimen of very red clover, said to be from the field of Waterloo, in front of the house near the schoolhouse on the hill. Returned eastward over a bare hill with some walnuts on it, formerly called Pine Hill, from whence a very good view of the new town of Natick. On the northeast base of this hill Bacon pointed out to me what he called Indian corn-hills, in heavy, moist pasture ground where had been a pine wood. The hillocks were in irregular rows four feet apart which ran along the side of the hill, and were much larger than you would expect after this lapse of time. I was confident that if Indian, they could not be very old, perhaps not more than a century or so, for such could never have been made with the ancient Indian hoes, — clamshells, stones, or the like, — but with the aid of plows and white men's hoes. Also pointed out to me what he thought the home site of an Indian squaw marked by a buckthorn bush by the wall.

These hillocks were like tussocks with lichens thick on them, and B. thought that the rows were not running as a white man['s] with furrow.

Vol. X

We crossed the road which runs east and west, and, in the low ground on the south side, saw a white oak and a red maple, each forty or fifty feet high, which had fairly grown together for three or more feet upward from the ground. Also, near by, a large white ash which though healthy bore a mark or scar where a branch had been broken off and stripped down the trunk. B. said that one of his ancestors, perhaps his grandfather, before the Revolution, went to climb this tree, and reached up and took hold of this branch, which he stripped down, and this was the scar!

Under the dead bark of this tree saw several large crickets of a rare kind. They had a peculiar naked and tender look, with *branched* legs and a rounded incurved front.

Red cohosh grows along a wall in low ground close by. We ascended a ridge hill northeast of this, or east by south of Bacon's house, on the north end of which Squaw Poquet, as well as her father, who was a powwow, before her, lived. Bacon thought that powwows commonly withdrew at last to the northeast side of a hill and lived alone. We saw the remains of apple trees in the woods, which she had planted. B. thought apple trees did not now grow so large in New England as formerly, that they only grew to be one foot in diameter and then began to decay, whereas they formerly grew to be two or three and even sometimes four feet in diameter.

The *Corallorhiza multiflora* was common in these woods, and out.

The *Galium circæzans* leaves taste very much like

licorice and, according to B., produce a great flow of water, also make you perspire and are good for a cold.

We came down northward to the Boston and Worcester turnpike, by the side of which the *Malaxis liliifolia* grows, though we did not find it.

We waded into Coos Swamp on the south side the turnpike to find the ledum, but did not succeed. B. is sure it grows there. This is a large swamp with a small pond, or pond-hole, in the midst and the usual variety of shrubs. I noticed small spruces, high blueberry, the water andromeda, rhodora, *Vaccinium dumosum* (hairy) ripe, *Kalmia glauca, Decodon verticillatus*, etc. B. says that the arbor-vitæ grows indigenously in pretty large patches in Needham; that Cochituate Pond is only between three and four miles long, or five including the meadows that are flowed, yet it has been called even ten miles long.

B. gave me a stone with very pretty black markings like jungermannias, from a blasting on the aqueduct in Natick. Some refer it to electricity.

According to Guyot at the Montreal meeting the other day, Mt. Washington is 6285 feet above high-water mark at Portland.

Aug. 25. Tuesday. P. M. — To Hill and meadow.
Plucked a *Lilium Canadense* at three-ribbed goldenrod wall, six and eight twelfths feet high, with a pyramid of seed-vessels fourteen inches long by nine wide, the first an irregular or *diagonal* whorl of six, surmounted by a whorl of three. The upper two whorls of leaves are diagonal or *scattered*. It agrees with Gray's *L. Can-*

adense except in size, also with G.'s *superbum* except that the leaves of my specimen are rough on the edges and veins beneath (but I have not the flowers!). Bigelow says that the leaves of the *L. superbum* are twice as long as the internodes. These are only *as* long. This, as well as most that I saw on the Penobscot, is probably only a variety of the *L. Canadense*.

Aug. 26. Wednesday. P. M. — Up Assabet with Bradford and Hoar.

B. tells me he found the *Malaxis liliifolia* on Kineo. Saw there a tame gull as large as a hen, brown dove-color. A lumberer called some timber "frowy." B. has found *Cassia Chamæcrista* by the side of the back road between Lincoln and Waltham, about two miles this side of Waltham.

Aug. 27. Thursday. P. M. — To Conantum, high-blackberrying.

Detected a, to me, *new* kind of high blackberry on the edge of the cliff beyond Conant's wall on Lee's ground, — a long-peduncled (or pedicelled), *leafy-racemed* (somewhat panicled), *erect* blackberry. It has the aspect of *R. Canadensis* become erect, three or four feet high. The racemes (or panicles?) leafy, with simple ovate and broad-lanceolate leaves; *loose, few flowered* (ten or twelve); peduncles (or pedicels) *one to two or more inches long*, often branched, with *bracts midway*, in fruit, at least, drooping. Perhaps the terminal flowers open first. Stem angular and furrowed much like that of *R. villosus*, leaf-stalks more prickly; leaves broader,

thinner, and less pointed, smooth above; beneath, as well as young branches, much smoother than *R. villosus;* lower leaves ternate and, if I remember, sometimes quinate. Berries of good size, globular, of very few, large grains, very glossy, of a lively flavor, when young of a peculiar light pink; sepals less recurved when ripe than those of *villosus*. It is apparently Bigelow's *R. frondosus* made a variety by Gray; *but see flowers.*

Aug. 28. Polygonum Pennsylvanicum by bank, how long?

R. W. E. says that he saw *Asclepias tuberosa* abundant and in bloom on Naushon last week; also a sassafras stump three feet across. The deer escape by running to the mainland, and in winter cross on the ice. The last winter they lost about one hundred and fifty sheep, whose remains have never been found. Perhaps they were carried off on the ice by the sea. Looking through a glass, E. saw vessels sailing near Martha's Vineyard with full sails, yet the water about them appeared perfectly smooth, and reflected the vessels. They thought this reflection a mirage, *i. e.* from a haze.

As we were riding by Deacon Farrar's lately, E. Hoar told me in answer to my questions, that both the young Mr. Farrars, who had now come to man's estate, were excellent young men, — their father, an old man of about seventy, once cut and corded seven cords of wood in one day, and still cut a double swath at haying time, and was a man of great probity, — and to show the unusual purity of one of them, at least, he said that, his

brother Frisbie, who had formerly lived there, inquiring what had become of a certain hired man whom he used to know, young Mr. Farrar told him that he was gone, "that the truth was he one day let drop a prophane word, and after that he thought that he could not have him about, and so he got rid of him." It was as if he had dropped some filthy thing on the premises, an intolerable nuisance, only to be abated by removing the source of it. I should like to hear as good news of the New England farmers generally. It to some extent accounts for the vigor of the father and the successful farming of the sons.

I read the other day in the *Tribune* that a man apparently about seventy, and smart at that, went to the police in New York and asked for a lodging, having been left by the cars or steamboat when on his way to Connecticut. When they asked his age, native place, etc., he said his name was McDonald; he was born in Scotland in 1745, came to Plymouth, Mass., in 1760, was in some battles in the Revolution, in which he lost an eye; had a son eighty-odd years old, etc.; but, seeing a reporter taking notes, he was silent. Since then I heard that an old man named McDonald, one hundred and twelve years old, had the day before passed through Concord and was walking to Lexington, and I said at once he must be a humbug. When I went to the post-office to-night (August 28), G. Brooks asked me if I saw him and said that he heard that he told a correct story, except he said that he remembered Braddock's defeat! He had noticed that Dr. Heywood's old house, the tavern, was gone since he was here in the Revolution.

Just then Davis, the postmaster, asked us to look at a letter he had received. It was from a Dr. Curtis of Newton asking if this McDonald belonged about Concord as he said, and saying that his story appeared to be a correct one. Davis had never heard of him, and, as we presumed him to be a humbug, we advised Davis to write accordingly. But I afterward remembered reading nearly a year ago of a man of this name and age in St. Louis, who said he had married a wife in Concord before the Revolution, and then began to think that his story might be all true. So it seems that a veteran of a hundred and twelve, after an absence of eighty-seven years, may come back to the town where he married his wife in order to hunt up his relatives, and not only have no success, but be pronounced a humbug!![1]

Aug. 29. Saturday. P. M. — To Owl-Nest Swamp with C.

Gerardia tenuifolia, a new plant to Concord, apparently in prime, at entrance to Owl-Nest Path and generally in that neighborhood. Also on Conantum height above orchard, two or three days later. This species grows on dry ground, or higher than the *purpurea*, and is more delicate. Got some ferns in the swamp and a small utricularia not in bloom, apparently different from that of Pleasant Meadow (*vide*

[1] [These last two paragraphs appear in the manuscript journal under date of July 28, having been written at the time when he was writing up his recent Maine excursion. The date in the second paragraph indicates this as their proper place.]

August 18). The proserpinaca leaves are very interesting in the water, so finely cut. *Polygonum arifolium* in bloom how long?

We waded amid the proserpinaca south of the wall and stood on a small bed of sphagnum, three or four feet in diameter, which rose above the surface. Some kind of water rat had its nest or retreat in this wet sphagnum, and being disturbed, swam off to the shore from under us. He was perhaps half as large again as a mole, or nearly, and somewhat grayish. The large and broad-leafed sium which grows [here] is, judging from its seed, the same with the common. I find the calla going to seed, but still the seed is green. That large, coarse, flag-like reed is apparently *Carex comosa;* now gone to seed, though only one is found with seed still on it, under water.

The Indian Rock, further west, is upright, or overhanging two feet, and a dozen feet high. Against this the Indians camped. It has many very large specimens of the *Umbilicaria Dillenii,* some six or eight inches in diameter, dripping with moisture to-day, like leather aprons hanging to the side of the rock, olive-green (this moist day), curled under on the edges and showing the upper side; but when dry they curl upward and show the crocky under sides. Near by, north, is a rocky ridge, on the east slope of which the *Corallorhiza multiflora* is very abundant. Call that Corallorhiza Rocks.

Aug. 30. Sunday. P. M. — To Conantum.

Small botrychium, not long. The flower of *Cicuta maculata* smells like the leaves of the golden senecio.

mon there, wholly immersed and without floating leaves, which rises erect from the sandy bottom in curving rows four or five feet long. On digging I find it to rise from a subterranean shoot which is larger than any part above ground. It may be one I have, whose floating leaves the high water has destroyed or prevented. The leaves of it have small bits of that fresh-water sponge, so strong-scented, on them.

Collinsonia has been out apparently three or four days. *Polygonum tenue* at Bittern Cliff, how long?

Aug. 31. Monday. P. M. — To Flint's Pond.

An abundance of fine high blackberries behind Britton's old camp on the Lincoln road, now in their prime there, which have been overlooked. Is it not our richest fruit?

Our first muskmelon to-day.

Lycopodium complanatum out, how long? I have seen for several days amphicarpæa with perfectly white flowers, in dense clusters.

At Flint's Pond I waded along the edge eight or ten rods to the wharf rock, carrying my shoes and stockings. Was surprised to see on the bottom and washing up on to the shore many little farinaceous roots or tubers like very small potatoes, in strings. I saw these at every step for more than a dozen rods and thought they must have been washed up from deeper waters. Examining very closely, I traced one long string through the sandy soil to the root of a ground-nut which grew on the edge of the bank, and afterwards saw many more, whose tuberous roots lying in the sand were washed bare, the pond being unusually high. I could have gathered quarts of them. I picked up one string floating loose, about eighteen inches long, with as usual a little greenness and vitality at one end, which had thirteen nuts on it about the size of a walnut or smaller. I never saw so many ground-nuts before, and this made on me the impression of an unusual fertility.

Bathing there, I see a small potamogeton, very com-

II

SEPTEMBER, 1857

(ÆT. 40)

Sept. 1. Tuesday. P. M. — To Fair Haven Pond by boat.

Landing at Bittern Cliff, I see that fine purple grass; how long? At Baker's shore, I at length distinguished fairly the *Sagittaria simplex,* which I have known so long, the small one with simple leaves. But this year there are very few of them, being nearly drowned out by the high water.

On the west side of Fair Haven Pond, an abundance of the *Utricularia purpurea* and of the whorled, etc., whose finely dissected leaves are a rich sight in the water. Again I observe that the heart-leaf, as it decays, preserves fresh and green for some time within, or in its centre, a finely dissected green leaf, suggesting that it has passed through this stage in its development. Immersed leaves often present this form, but [it] seems that even emersed ones remember it. High blackberries are still in their prime on Lee's Cliff, but huckleberries soft and wormy, many of them.

I have finally settled for myself the question of the two varieties of *Polygonum amphibium.* I think there are not even two varieties. As formerly, I observe again to-day a *Polygonum amphibium* extending from the shore six feet into the water. In the water, of course, the stem is prostrate, rank, and has something serpent-like in its aspect. From the shore end rise erect flowering branches whose leaves are more or less roughish and prickly on the midrib beneath. On the water end the leaves are long-petioled, *heart-shaped*, and perfectly smooth. *Vide* a specimen pressed. I have seen this same plant growing erect in the *driest* soil, by the roadside, and it ranges from this quite into the water.

Sept. 2. Wednesday. P. M. — To Yellow Birches.
Measured the thorn at Yellow Birch Swamp. At one foot from ground it is a foot and ten inches in circumference. The first branch is at two feet seven inches. The tree spreads about eighteen feet. The height is about seventeen feet.

A yellow birch some rods north was, at three feet from ground, four feet plus in circumference. A second, northeast of it, was, at four feet, five feet five inches in circumference. It branched at eight feet, the branches extending north two and a third rods, but south only one and a half. Was some fifty or sixty feet high. The third, or largest, yellow birch, at the cellar, was, at three feet from the ground on the inside or at the ground on the outside, just below the branches, ten feet nine inches in circumference. It divides to three branches at ground on the upper side, and these almost immediately to three more, so low and horizontal that you can easily step into it. It extends two rods east and one west, the ends of the branches coming down to height of head all round, nearly. It is about

two thirds as high as wide, or thirty-three feet high. Looking from the west, of an irregular diamond shape resting on the ground. The roots inclose some cellar stones. All these birches were measured at the smallest place between the ground and branches. Large yellow birches branch low and form a dense broom-like head of many long tapering branches.

In the botrychium swamp, where the fever-bush is the prevailing underwood, I see a *Rhus radicans* running up a buttonwood which is some forty feet high. It first makes a complete circle about it horizontally at the ground, then goes winding up it in a serpentine manner on the southwest (?) side, thirty feet at least, or as far as I could see, beginning to put out a few twigs at seven or eight feet. It is a vine one and a half and two inches wide, somewhat flattened, clinging close and flat to the tree by innumerable brown fibres which invest itself and adhere to the bark on each side in a thick web. You can hardly tell if it is alive or dead with[out] looking upward. Remembering that it was poisonous to some to handle, it had altogether a venomous look. It made me think of a venomous beast of prey which had sprung upon the tree and had it in its clutches, as the glutton is said to cling to the deer while it sucks its blood. It had fastened on it, as a leopard or panther on a deer and there was no escape. It was not married to the buttonwood, as the vine to the poplar. I saw a still larger one the other day in Natick on an elm.

Some bass trees blossomed sparingly after all, for I see some fruit.

Sept. 3. P. M. — Rode to Prospect Hill, Waltham.
The *Polygonum Pennsylvanicum* there. One *Chimaphila maculata* on the hill. Tufts of *Woodsia Ilvensis*. *Hedyotis longifolia* still flowering commonly, near the top, in a *thin* wood. *Gerardia tenuifolia* by the road in Lincoln, and a slate-colored snowbird back.

Sept. 4. P. M. — To Bateman's Pond.
Rudbeckia laciniata (?) by Dodge's Brook, north of the road; how long? *Cornus sericea* berries begin to ripen. The leaves of the *light-colored* spruce in the spruce swamp are erect like the white!

Penetrating through the thicket of that swamp, I see a great many very straight and slender upright shoots, the slenderest and tallest that I ever saw. They are the *Prinos lævigatus*. I cut one and brought it home in a ring around my neck, — it was flexible enough for that, — and found it to be seven and a half feet long and quite straight, eleven fortieths of an inch in diameter at the ground and three fortieths [in] diameter at the other end, only the last foot or so of this year's growth. It had a light-grayish bark, rough-dotted. Generally they were five or six feet high and not bigger than a pipe-stem anywhere. This comes of its growing in dense dark swamps, where it makes a good part of the underwood.

At the cleft rock by the hill just west of this swamp, — call it Cornel Rock, — I found apparently *Aspidium cristatum* (?), *q. v.* That is an interesting spot. There is the handsomest and most perfect *Cornus circinata* there that I know, now apparently its fruit

in prime, hardly light-blue but delicate bluish-white. It is the richest-looking of the cornels, with its large round leaf and showy cymes; a slender bush seven or eight feet high. There is quite a collection of rare plants there, — petty morel, *Thalictrum dioicum*, witch-hazel, etc., *Rhus radicans*, maple-leaved viburnum, polypody, *Polygonum dumetorum*, anychia. There was a strawberry vine falling over the perpendicular face of the rock, — or more than perpendicular, — which hung down dangling in the air five feet, not yet reaching the bottom, with leaves at intervals of fifteen inches. Various rocks scattered about in these woods rising just to the surface with smooth rounded surfaces, showing a fine stratification *on its edges*.

The sides of Cornus florida Ravine at Bateman's Pond are a good place for ferns. There is a *Woodsia Ilvensis*, a new one to Concord. Petty morel in the ravine, and large cardinal-flowers.

I see prenanthes radical leaf turned pale-yellow. Arum berries ripe.

Already, long before sunset, I feel the dew falling in that cold calla swamp.

Sept. 5. Saturday. I now see those brown shaving-like stipules [1] of the white pine leaves, which are falling, *i. e.* the stipules, and caught in cobwebs.
River falls suddenly, having been *high* all summer.

Sept. 6. Sunday. P. M. — To Assabet, west bank.
Turned off south at Derby's Bridge and walked
_____
[1] ? Sheaths.

through a long field, half meadow, half upland. Soapwort gentian, out not long, and dwarf cornel again. There is a handsome crescent-shaped meadow on this side, opposite Harrington's. A good-sized black oak in the pasture by the road half-way between the schoolhouse and Brown's. Walked under Brown's hemlocks by the railroad. How commonly hemlocks grow on the north slope of a hill near its base, with only bare reddened ground beneath! This bareness probably is not due to any peculiar quality in the hemlocks, for I observe that it is the same under pitch and white pines when equally thick. I suspect that it is owing more to the shade than to the fallen leaves. I see one of those peculiarly green locusts with long and slender legs on a grass stem, which are often concealed by their color. What green, herbaceous, graminivorous ideas he must have! I wish that my thoughts were as *seasonable* as his! Some haws *begin* to be ripe.

We go along under the hill and woods north of railroad, west of Lord's land, about to the west of the swamp and to the Indian ditch. I see in the swamp black chokeberries twelve feet high at least and in fruit.

C. says that they use high blueberry wood for tholepins on the Plymouth ponds.

I observe to-day, away at the south end of our dry garden, a moist and handsome *Rana halecina*. It is the only frog that I ever see in such localities. He is quite a traveller. A very cool day.

Sept. 7. Monday. P. M. — To Dodge Brook Wood.

It occurred to me some weeks ago that the river-banks

were not *quite* perfect. It is too late then, when the mikania is in bloom, because the pads are so much eaten then. Our first slight frost in some places this morning. Northwest wind to-day and cool weather; such weather as we have not had for a long time, a new experience, which arouses a corresponding breeze in us. *Rhus venenata* berries are whitening. Its leaves appear very fresh, of a rich, dark, damp green, and very little eaten by insects.

Go round by the north side of Farmer's (?) Wood, turn southeast into the shut-in field, and thence to Spencer Brook, a place for hawks. *Bidens chrysanthemoides* there; how long? There are three or four larch trees near the east edge of the meadows here. One measures two feet and seven inches in circumference at six feet from ground; begins to branch there, but is dead up to ten feet from ground, where its diameter is apparently about twelve feet; and from this it tapers regularly to the top, which is about forty-five feet from the ground, forming a regular, sharp pyramid, yet quite airy and thin, so that you could see a hawk through it pretty well. These are young and healthy trees.

Measured that large tupelo behind Merriam's, which now is covered with green fruit, and its leaves begin to redden. It is about thirty feet high, with a round head and equally broad near the ground. At one foot from the ground, it is four and a third feet in circumference; at seven feet, three and a third in circumference. The principal [branches] diverge at about fifteen or sixteen feet from the ground and tend upward; the lower

Vol. X

ones are small and partly dead. The lowest, at about thirteen or fourteen feet from the ground, are three or four inches in diameter, and first grow out horizontally about six feet, then, making an abrupt angle, straggle downward nearly to the ground, fifteen feet from the tree. This leaves the tree remarkably open in the middle.

Returning to my boat, at the white maple, I see a small round flock of birds, perhaps blackbirds, dart through the air, as thick as a charge of shot, — now comparatively thin, with regular intervals of sky between them, like the holes in the strainer of a watering-pot, now dense and dark, as if closing up their ranks when they roll over one another and stoop downward.

Sept. 9. Wednesday. P. M. — To the Hill for white pine cones.

Very few trees have any. I can only manage small ones, fifteen or twenty feet high, climbing till I can reach the dangling green pickle-like fruit in my right hand, while I hold to the main stem with my left. The cones are now all flowing with pitch, and my hands are soon so covered with it that I cannot easily cast down the cones where I would, they stick to my hands so. I cannot touch the basket, but carry it on my arm; nor can I pick up my coat, which I have taken off, unless with my teeth, or else I kick it up and catch it on my arm. Thus I go from tree to tree, from time to time rubbing my hands in brooks and mud-holes, in the hope of finding something that will remove pitch

like grease, but in vain. It is the stickiest work I ever did. I do not see how the squirrels that gnaw them off and then open them scale by scale keep their paws and whiskers clean. They must know of, or possess, some remedy for pitch that we know nothing of. How fast I could collect cones, if I could only contract with a family of squirrels to cut them off for me! Some are already brown and dry and partly open, but these commonly have hollow seeds and are worm-eaten. The cones collected in my chamber have a strong spirituous scent, almost rummy, or like a molasses hogshead, agreeable to some. They are far more effectually protected than the chestnut by its bur.

Going into the low sprout-land north of the Sam Wheeler orchard, where is a potato-field in new ground, I see the effects of the frost of the last two or three nights. The ferns and tall erechthites showing its pappus are drooping and blackened or imbrowned on all sides, also *Eupatorium pubescens*, tender young *Rhus glabra*, etc., and the air is full of the rank, sour smell of freshly withering vegetation. It is a great change produced in one frosty night. What a sudden period put to the reign of summer!

On my way home, caught one of those little red-bellied snakes in the road, where it was rather sluggish, as usual. Saw another in the road a week or two ago. The whole length was eight inches; tail alone, one and four fifths. The plates about one hundred and nineteen; scales forty and upward. It was a dark ash-color above, with darker longitudinal lines, light brick-red beneath. There were three triangular buff spots just behind the head, one above and one each side. It is apparently *Coluber amœnus*, and perhaps this is the same with Storer's *occipito-maculatus.*

C. brings me a small *red* hypopytis. It has a faint sweet, earthy, perhaps checkerberry, scent, like that sweet mildewy fragrance of the earth in spring.

Aunts have just had their house shingled, and amid the rubbish I see sheets of the paper birch bark, which have lain on the roof so long. The common use of this formerly shows that it must have been abundant here.

Sept. 10. Thursday. P. M. — To Cardinal Ditch and Peter's.

Cardinal-flower, nearly done. Beach plum, almost ripe. Squash vines on the Great Fields, *generally* killed and blackened by frost (though not so much in our garden), revealing the yellow fruit, perhaps prematurely. Standing by Peter's well, the white maples by the bank of the river a mile off now give a rosaceous tinge to the edge of the meadow. I see lambkill ready to bloom a second time. Saw it out on the 20th ; how long ?

Sept. 11. Friday. Up railroad and to Clamshell.

Solidago puberula apparently in prime, with the *S. stricta*, near gerardia oaks. Red choke-berry ripe; how long ? On the east edge of Dennis Swamp, where I saw the strange warbler once.

To my surprise I find, by the black oaks at the sand-hole east of Clamshell, the *Solidago rigida*, apparently

in prime or a little past. The heads and rays were so large I thought at first it must be a hieracium. The rays are from ten to fourteen, and three to three and a half fortieths of an inch wide. The middle leaves are *clasping* by a heart-shaped base. The heads are seven fortieths of an inch wide and seventeen fortieths long, in recurved panicles, — these. Eaton says truly, "Scales of the calyx round-obtuse, nerved, membranous at the edges."

My old *S. stricta* (early form) must be *S. arguta* var. *juncea.* It is now done.

Sept. 12. Saturday. P. M. — To Owl Swamp (Farmer's).

In an open part of the swamp, started a very large wood frog, which gave one leap and squatted still. I put down my finger, and, though it shrank a little at first, it permitted me to stroke it as long as I pleased. Having passed, it occurred to me to return and cultivate its acquaintance. To my surprise, it allowed me to slide my hand under it and lift it up, while it squatted cold and moist on the middle of my palm, panting naturally. I brought it close to my eye and examined it. It was very beautiful seen thus nearly, not the dull dead-leaf color which I had imagined, but its back was like burnished bronze armor defined by a varied line on each side, where, as it seemed, the plates of armor united. It had four or five dusky bars which matched exactly when the legs were folded, showing that the painter applied his brush to the animal when in that position, and reddish-orange soles to its delicate feet.

There was a conspicuous dark-brown patch along the side of the head, whose upper edge passed directly through the eye horizontally, just above its centre, so that the pupil and all below were dark and the upper portion of the iris golden. I have since taken up another in the same way.[1]

Round-leaved cornel berries nearly all fallen.

Crossing east through the spruce swamp, I think that I saw a female redstart.

What is that running herbaceous vine which forms a dense green mat a rod across at the bottom of the swamp northwest of Corallorhiza Rock ?[2] It is of the same form, stem and leaves, with the more brown hairy and woolly linnæa. It also grows in the swamp by the beech trees in Lincoln.

Sept. 13. Sunday. Nabalus Fraseri, top of Cliffs, — a new plant, — yet in *prime* and not long out. The nabalus family generally, apparently now in prime.

Sept. 16. A. M. — To Great Yellow Birch, with the Watsons.

Solidago latifolia in prime at Botrychium Swamp. Barberries very handsome now. See boys gathering them in good season. Some fever-bush berries already ripe. Watson has brought me apparently *Artemisia vulgaris*, growing naturally close to Austin's house in Lincoln ; hardly in bloom.

Walked through that beautiful soft white pine grove

[1] Indeed they can generally be treated so. Some are reddish, as burnished copper.   [2] It is chrysosplenium.

on the west of the road in John Flint's pasture. These trees are large, but there is ample space between them, so that the ground is left grassy. Great pines two or more feet in diameter branch sometimes within two feet of the ground on each side, sending out large horizontal branches on which you can sit. Like great harps on which the wind makes music. There is no finer tree. The different stages of its soft glaucous foliage completely concealing the trunk and branches are separated by dark horizontal lines of shadow, the flakes of pine foliage, like a pile of light fleeces.

I see green and closed cones beneath, which the squirrels have thrown down. On the trees many are already open. Say within a week have begun. In one small wood, all the white pine cones are on the ground, generally unopened, evidently freshly thrown down by the squirrels, and then the greater part have already been stripped. They begin at the base of the cone, as with the pitch pine. It is evident that they have just been very busy throwing down the white pine cones in all woods. Perhaps they have stored up the seeds separately. This they can do before chestnut burs open.

Watson gave me three glow-worms which he found by the roadside in Lincoln last night. They exhibit a greenish light, only under the caudal extremity, and intermittingly, or at will. As often as I touch one in a dark morning, it stretches and shows its light for a moment, only under the last segment. An average one is five eighths of an inch long, exclusive of the head, when still ; four fifths of an inch, or more, with the head, when moving ; one fourth of an inch wide, broadest forward; and from one tenth to one eighth inch deep, nearly (at middle). They have six brown legs within about one fourth of an inch of the forward extremity. This worm is apparently composed of twelve scale-like segments, including the narrow terminal one or tail, and not including the head, which at will is drawn under the foremost scale or segment like a turtle's. (I do not remember if the other species concealed its head thus, completely.) Looking down on it, I do not see *distinctly* more than two antennæ, one on each side, whitish at base, dark-brown at tip, and apparently about the same length with the longest of the other species. The general color above is black, or say a very dark brown or blackish; the head the same. On each side two *faint* rows of light-colored dots. The first segment is *broadly* conical, and much the largest; the others very narrow in proportion to their breadth transversely, and successively narrower, slightly recurved at tip and bristle-pointed and also curved upward at the thin outer edge, while the rounded dorsal ridge is slightly elevated above this. Beneath, dirty white with two rows of black spots on each side.

They always get under the sod by day and bury themselves. They are not often much curled up, never in a ring, nor nearly so much as the other kind. They are much more restless when disturbed, both by day and night, than the others. They are a much coarser insect than the other and approach more nearly to the form of a sow-bug. I kept them more than a week.

Vide back, August 8th.

were round still and preserved the same relation to the wind and other elements that they held twenty years ago. I suggested that they were birds of the season.

Coming home through the street in a thunder-shower at ten o'clock this night, it was exceedingly dark. I met two persons within a mile, and they were obliged to call out from a rod distant lest we should run against each other. When the lightning lit up the street, almost as plain as day, I saw that it was the same *green* light that the glow-worm emits. Has the moisture something to do with it in both cases?

Sept. 19. *Saturday.* Still somewhat rainy, — since last evening.

Solidago arguta variety done, say a week or more.

Sept. 20. *Sunday.* Another mizzling day.

P. M. — To beach plums behind A. Clarke's.

We walked in some trodden path on account of the wet grass and leaves, but the fine grass overhanging paths, weighed down with dewy rain, wet our feet nevertheless. We cannot afford to omit seeing the beaded grass and wetting our feet. This is our first fall rain, and makes a dividing line between the summer and fall. Yet there has been no drought the past summer. Vegetation is unusually fresh. Methinks the grass in some shorn meadows is even greener than in the spring. You are soon wet through by the underwood if you enter the woods, — ferns, aralia, huckleberries, etc. Went through the lower side of the wood west of Peter's.

Sept. 17. *Thursday.* I go to Fair Haven Hill, looking at the varieties of nabalus, which have a singular prominence now in all woods and roadsides. The lower leaves are very much eaten by insects. How perfectly each plant has its turn! — as if the seasons revolved for it alone. Two months ago it would have taken a sharp eye to have detected this plant. One of those great puffballs, three inches in diameter, ripe.

Sept. 18. *Friday.* P. M. — Round Walden with C. We find the water cold for bathing. Coming out on to the Lincoln road at Bartlett's path, we found an abundance of haws by the roadside, just fit to eat, quite an agreeable subacid fruit. We were glad to see anything that could be eaten so abundant. They must be a supply depended on by some creatures. These bushes bear a profusion of fruit, rather crimson than scarlet when ripe.

I hear that "Uncle Ned" of the Island told of walking along the shore of a pond where the "shells" of the mosquitoes were washed up in winrows.

As I was going through the Cut, on my way, I saw what I thought a rare high-colored flower in the sun on the sandy bank. It was a *Trifolium arvense* whose narrow leaves were turned a bright crimson, enhanced by the sun shining through it and lighting it up. Going along the low path under Bartlett's Cliff, the *Aster lævis* flowers, when seen toward the sun, are very handsome, having a purple or lilac tint.

We started a pack of grouse, which went off with a whir like cannon-balls. C. said he did not see but they

Vol. X

The *early* decaying and variegated spotted leaves of the *Aralia nudicaulis*, which spread out flat and of uniform height some eighteen (?) inches above the forest floor, are very noticeable and interesting in our woods in early autumn, now and for some time. For more than a month it has been changing. The outlines of trees are more conspicuous and interesting such a day as this, being seen distinctly against the near misty background, — distinct and dark.

The branches of the alternate cornel are spreading and flat, somewhat cyme-like, as its fruit. Beach plums are now perfectly ripe and unexpectedly good, as good as an average cultivated plum. I get a handful, dark-purple with a bloom, as big as a good-sized grape and but little more oblong, about three quarters of an inch broad and a very little longer. I got a handkerchief full of elder-berries, though I am rather late about it, for the birds appear to have greatly thinned the cymes.

A great many small red maples in Beck Stow's Swamp are turned quite crimson, when all the trees around are still perfectly green. It looks like a gala day there.

A pitch pine and birch wood is rapidly springing up between the Beck Stow Wood and the soft white pine grove. It is now just high and thick enough to be noticed as a young wood-lot, if not mowed down.[1]

Sept. 21. *Monday.* P. M. — To Corallorhiza Rock and Tobacco-pipe Wood, northeast of Spruce Swamp.

Peaches are now in their prime. Came through that

[1] Cut down in '59.

thick white pine wood on the east of the spruce swamp.

This is a very dense white pine grove, consisting of tall and slender trees which have been thinned, yet they are on an average only from three to six feet asunder. Perhaps half have been cut. It is a characteristic white pine grove, and I have seen many such. The trees are some ten inches in diameter, larger or smaller, and about fifty feet high. They are bare for thirty-five or forty feet up, — which is equal to at least twenty-five years of their growth, or with only a few dead twigs high up. Their green crowded tops are mere oval spear-heads in shape and almost in proportionate size, four to eight feet wide, — not enough, you would think, to keep the tree alive, still less to draw it upward. In a dark day the wood is not only thick but dark with the boles of the trees. Under this dense shade, the red-carpeted ground is almost bare of vegetation and is dark at noon. There grow *Goodyera pubescens* and *repens, Corallorhiza multiflora* (going to seed), white cohosh *berries, Pyrola secunda,* and, on the low west side and also the east side, an abundance of tobacco-pipe, which has begun to turn black at the tip of the petals and leaves.

The *Solidago cœsia* is very common and fresh in copses, perhaps the prevailing solidago now in woods. *Rudbeckia laciniata* done, probably some time. The warmth of the sun is just beginning to be appreciated again on the advent of cooler days.

Measured the large white willow north the road near Hildreth's. At a foot and a half from the ground

it is fourteen feet in circumference; at five feet, the smallest place, it is twelve feet in circumference. It was once still larger, for it has lost large branches.[1]

Sept. 23. Wednesday. P. M. — To chestnut oaks.

Varieties of nabalus grow along the Walden road in the woods; also, still more abundant, by the Flint's Pond road in the woods. I observe in these places only the *N. alba* and *Fraseri;* but these are not well distinguished; they seem to be often alike in the color of the pappus. Some are very tall and slender, and the largest I saw was an *N. Fraseri!* One *N. alba* had a panicle three feet long!

The Ripley beeches have been cut. I can't find them. There is one large one, apparently on Baker's land, about two feet in diameter near the ground, but fruit hollow. I see yellow pine-sap, in the woods just east of where the beeches used to stand, just done, but the red variety is very common and quite fresh generally there.[2]

Sept. 24. Thursday. A. M. — Up the *Assabet.*

The river is considerably raised and also muddied by the recent rains.

I saw a red squirrel run along the bank under the hemlocks with a nut in its mouth. He stopped near the foot of a hemlock, and, hastily pawing a hole with his fore feet, dropped the nut, covered it up, and retreated part way up the trunk of the tree, all in a few moments. I approached the shore to examine the

[1] Cut down in '59.   [2] Oct. 14, 1858.

Vol. X

deposit, and he, descending betrayed no little anxiety for his treasure and made two or three motions to recover the nut before he retreated. Digging there, I found two pignuts joined together, with their green shells on, buried about an inch and a half in the soil, under the red hemlock leaves.[1] This, then, is the way forests are planted. This nut must have been brought twenty rods at least and was buried at just the right depth. If the squirrel is killed, or neglects its deposit, a hickory springs up.[2]

P. M. — I walked to that very dense and handsome white pine grove east of Beck Stow's Swamp. It is about fifteen rods square, the trees large, ten to twenty inches in diameter. It is separated by a wall from another pine wood with a few oaks in it on the southeast, and about thirty rods north and west are other pine and oak woods. Standing on the edge of the wood and looking through it, — for it is quite level and free from underwood, *mostly* bare, red-carpeted ground, — you would have said that there was not a hardwood tree in it, young or old, though I afterward found on one edge a middling-sized sassafras, a birch, a small tupelo, and two little scarlet oaks, but, what was more interesting, I found, on looking closely over its floor, that, alternating with thin ferns and small blueberry bushes, there was, as often as every five feet, a little oak, three to twelve inches high, and in one place I found a green acorn dropped by the base of a tree. I

[1] *Vide* Patent Office Reports, 1856, p. 59.
[2] These nuts were there Oct. 8th. Gone Nov. 21st.

was surprised, I confess, to find my own theory so perfectly proved. These oaks, apparently, find such a locality unfavorable to their growth as long as the pines stand. I saw that some had been browsed by the cows which resort to the wood for shade. As an evidence that hardwood trees would not flourish under those circumstances, I found a red maple twenty-five feet high recently prostrated, as if by the wind, but still covered with green leaves, the only maple in the wood, and also two birches decaying in the same position.[1] The ground was completely strewn with white pine cones, apparently thrown down by the squirrels, still generally green and closed, but many stripped of scales, about the base of almost every pine, sometimes all of them. Now and for a week a good time to collect them. You can hardly enter such a wood but you will hear a red squirrel chiding you from his concealment in some pine-top. It is the sound most native to the locality.

Minott tells of their finding near a bushel of chestnuts in a rock, when blasting for the mill brook, at that ditch near Flint's Pond. He said it was a gray squirrel's depot.

I find the *Lycopodium dendroideum,* not quite out, just northwest of this pine grove, in the grass. It is not the variety *obscurum,* which grows at Trillium Wood, is more upright-branched and branches round.

Sept. 25. Friday. P. M. — To tupelo on Daniel B. Clark's land.

[1] [*Excursions,* pp. 190–192; Riv. 233–236.]

Stopping in my boat under the Hemlocks, I hear singular bird-like chirruping from two red squirrels. One sits high on a hemlock bough with a nut in its paws. A squirrel seems always to have a nut at hand ready to twirl in its paws. Suddenly he dodges behind the trunk of the tree, and I hear some birds in the maples across the river utter a peculiar note of alarm of the same character with the hen's (I think they were robins), and see them seeking a covert. Looking round, I see a marsh hawk beating the bushes on that side.

You notice now the dark-blue dome of the soapwort gentian in cool and shady places under the bank.

Pushing by Carter's pasture, I see, deep under water covered by the rise of the river, the cooper's poles a-soak, held down by planks and stones.

Fasten to the white maple and go inland. Wherever you may land, it would be strange if there were not some alder clump at hand to hide your oars in till your return.

The red maple has fairly begun to blush in some places by the river. I see one, by the canal behind Barrett's mill, all aglow against the sun. These first trees that change are most interesting, since they are seen against others still freshly green, — such brilliant red on green. I go half a mile out of my way to examine such a red banner. A single tree becomes the crowning beauty of some meadowy vale and attracts the attention of the traveller from afar. At the eleventh hour of the year, some tree which has stood mute and inglorious in some distant vale thus proclaims its character as effectually as [if] it stood by the highway-side,

and it leads our thoughts away from the dusty road into those brave solitudes which it inhabits. The whole tree, thus ripening in advance of its fellows, attains a singular preëminence. I am thrilled at the sight of it, bearing aloft its scarlet standard for its regiment of green-clad foresters around. The forest is the more spirited.[1]

I remember that brakes had begun to decay as much as six weeks ago. Dogwood (*Rhus venenata*) is yet but pale-scarlet or yellowish. The *R. glabra* is more generally turned.

Stopped at Barrett's mill. He had a buttonwood log to saw. In an old grist-mill the festoons of cobwebs revealed by the white dust on them are an ornament. Looking over the shoulder of the miller, I drew his attention to a mouse running up a brace. "Oh, yes," said he, "we have plenty of them. Many are brought to the mill in barrels of corn, and when the barrel is placed on the platform of the hopper they scamper away."

As I came round the island, I took notice of that little ash tree on the opposite shore. It has been cut or broken off about two feet from the ground, and seven small branches have shot up from its circumference, all together forming a perfectly regular oval head about twenty-five feet high and very beautiful. With what harmony they work and carry out the idea of the tree, one twig not straying farther on this side than its fellow on that! That the tree thus has its idea to be lived up to, and, as it were, fills an invisible mould in the

[1] [*Excursions*, pp. 260, 261; Riv. 318–320.]

Vol. X

air, is the more evident, because if you should cut away one or all but one, the remaining branch or branches would still in time form a head in the main similar to this.

Brought home my first boat-load of wood.

Sept. 26. Saturday. A. M. — Apparently *Hypericum prolificum* in Monroe's garden, still out.

The season is waning. A wasp just looked in upon me. A very warm day for the season.

P. M. — Up river to Clamshell.

These are warm, serene, bright autumn afternoons. I see far off the various-colored gowns of cranberry-pickers against the green of the meadow. The river stands a little way over the grass again, and the summer is over. The pickerel-weed is brown, and I see musquash-houses. *Solidago rigida*, just done, within a rod southwest of the oak. I see a large black cricket on the river, a rod from shore, and a fish is leaping at it. As long as the fish leaps, it is motionless as if dead; but as soon as it feels my paddle under it, it is lively enough. I sit on Clamshell bank and look over the meadows. Hundreds of crickets have fallen into a sandy gully and now are incessantly striving to creep or leap up again over the sliding sand. This their business this September afternoon. I watch a marsh hawk circling low along the edge of the meadow, looking for a frog, and now at last it alights to rest on a tussock.

Coming home, the sun is intolerably warm on my left cheek. I perceive it is because the heat of the re-

flected sun, which is as bright as the real one, is added to that of the real one, for when I cover the reflection with my hand the heat is less intense.

That cricket seemed to know that if he lay quietly *spread out* on the surface, either the fishes would not suspect him to be an insect, or if they tried to swallow him would not be able to.

What blundering fellows these crickets are, both large and small! They were not only tumbling into the river all along shore, but into this sandy gully, to escape from which is a Sisyphus labor. I have not sat there many minutes watching two foraging crickets which have decided to climb up two tall and slender weeds almost bare of branches, as a man shins up a liberty-pole sometimes, when I find that one has climbed to the summit of my knee. They are incessantly running about on the sunny bank. Their still larger cousins, the mole crickets, are creaking loudly and incessantly all along the shore. Others have eaten themselves cavernous apartments, sitting-room and pantry at once, in windfall apples.

Speaking to Rice of that cricket's escape, he said that a snake [*sic*] in like manner would puff itself up when a snake was about to swallow him, making right up to him. He once, with several others, saw a small striped snake swim across a piece of water about half a rod wide to a half-grown bullfrog which sat on the opposite shore, and attempt to seize him, but he found that he had caught a Tartar, for the bullfrog, seeing him coming, was not afraid of him, but at once seized his head in his mouth and closed his jaws upon it, and he thus held the snake a considerable while before the latter was able by struggling to get away.

When that cricket felt my oar, he leaped without the least hesitation or perhaps consideration, trusting to fall in a pleasanter place. He was evidently trusting to drift against some weed which would afford him a *point d'appui.*

Sept. 27. I am surprised to find that, yesterday having been a sudden very warm day, the peaches have mellowed suddenly and wilted, and I find many more fallen than even after previous rains. Better if ripened more gradually.

How out of all proportion to the *value* of an idea, when you come to one, — in Hindoo literature, for instance, — is the historical fact about it, — the when, where, etc., it was actually expressed, and what precisely it might signify to a sect of worshippers! Anything that is called history of India — or of the world — is impertinent beside any real poetry or inspired thought which is dateless.

P. M. — To Lee's Cliff by land.

Small red maples in low ground have fairly begun to burn for a week. It varies from scarlet to crimson. It looks like training-day in the meadows and swamps. They have run up their colors. A small red maple has grown, perchance, far away on some moist hillside, a mile from any road, unobserved. It has faithfully discharged the duties of a maple there, all winter and summer, neglected none of its economies, added

to its stature in the virtue which belongs to a maple, by a steady growth all summer, and is nearer heaven than in the spring, never having gone gadding abroad; and now, in this month of September, when men are turned travellers, hastening to the seaside, or the mountains, or the lakes, — in this month of travelling, — this modest maple, having ripened its seeds, still without budging an inch, travels on its reputation, runs up its scarlet flag on that hillside, to show that it has finished its summer work before all other trees, and withdraws from the contest. Thus that modest worth which no scrutiny could have detected when it was most industrious, is, by the very tint of its maturity, by its very blushes, revealed at last to the most careless and distant observer. It rejoices in its existence; its reflections are unalloyed. It is the day of thanksgiving with it. At last, its labors for the year being consummated and every leaf ripened to its full, it flashes out conspicuous to the eye of the most casual observer, with all the virtue and beauty of a maple, — *Acer rubrum.* In its hue is no regret nor pining. Its leaves have been asking their parent from time to time in a whisper, "When shall we redden?" It has faithfully husbanded its sap, and builded without babbling nearer and nearer to heaven. Long since it committed its seeds to the winds and has the satisfaction of knowing perhaps that a thousand little well-behaved and promising maples of its stock are already established in business somewhere. It deserves well of Mapledom. It has afforded a shelter to the wandering bird.[1] Its

[1] [*Excursions*, pp. 260 261; Riv. 319, 320.]

autumnal tint shows how it has spent its summer; it is the hue of its virtue.

These burning bushes stand thus along the edge of the meadows, and I distinguish them afar upon all the hillsides, here and there.[1] Her *virtues* are as scarlet.[2]

The large common ferns (either cinnamon or interrupted) are yellowish, and also many as rich a deep brown now as ever. White birches have fairly begun to yellow, and blackberry vines here and there in sunny places look like a streak of blood on the grass. Bass, too, fairly begun to yellow. *Solidago nemoralis* nearly done. I sit on the hillside at Miles Swamp. A woodbine investing the leading stem of an elm in the swamp quite to its top is seen as an erect slender red column through the thin and yellowing foliage of the elm, — a very pretty effect. I see some small woodbine leaves in the shade of a delicate cherry-color, bordering on pink.

As I sit there I see the shadow of a hawk flying above and behind me. I think I see more hawks nowadays. Perhaps it is both because the young are grown and their food, the small birds, are flying in flocks and are abundant. I need only sit still a few minutes on any spot which overlooks the river meadows, before I see some black circling mote beating along, circling along the meadow's edge, now lost for a moment as it turns edgewise in a peculiar light, now reappearing further or nearer.

[1] [*Excursions*, p. 259; Riv. 317.]
[2] [*Excursions*, p. 261; Riv. 320.]

Witch-hazel two thirds yellowed.

Huckleberries are still abundant and quite plump on Conantum, though they have a somewhat dried taste.

It is most natural, *i. e.* most in accordance with the natural phenomena, to suppose that North America was discovered from the northern part of the Eastern Continent, for a study of the range of plants, birds, and quadrupeds points to a connection on that side. Many birds are common to the northern parts of both continents. Even the passenger pigeon has flown across there. And some European plants have been detected on the extreme northeastern coast and islands, which do not extend inland. Men in their migrations obey in the main the same law.

Sept. 28. I planted six seeds sent from the Patent Office and labelled, I think, "*Poitrine jaune grosse*" (large yellow pumpkin (or squash?)). Two came up, and one bore a squash which weighs the other bore four,

and one bore a squash which weighs			$123\frac{1}{2}$ lbs.
the other bore four,	1	weighing	$72\frac{3}{4}$
	2d	"	54
	3d	"	$37\frac{3}{4}$
	4th	"	$21\frac{3}{4}$
			$309\frac{3}{4}$

Who would have believed that there was 310 pounds of *poitrine jaune grosse* in that corner of our garden? Yet that little seed found it. Other seeds would find something else every year for successive ages, until the crop more than filled our whole garden; which suggests that the various fruits are the product of the same elements differently combined, and those elements are in continual revolution around the globe. This *poitrine* found here the air of France, and measurably its soil too.[1]

Looking down from Nawshawtuct this afternoon, the white maples on the Assabet and below have a singular light glaucous look, almost hoary, as if curled and showing the under sides of the leaves, and they contrast with the fresh green pines and hemlocks. The swamp white oaks present some of the same crisped whitish appearance.

I see that E. Wood has sent a couple of Irishmen, with axe and bush-whack, to cut off the natural hedges of sumach, Roxbury waxwork, grapes, etc., which have sprung up by the walls on this hill farm, in order that his cows may get a little more green. And they have cut down two or three of the very rare celtis trees, not found anywhere else in town. The Lord deliver us from these vandalic proprietors! The botanist and lover of nature has, perchance, discovered some rare tree which has sprung up by a farmer's wall-side to adorn and bless it, sole representative of its kind in these parts. Strangers send for a seed or a sprig from a distance, but, walking there again, he finds that the farmer has sent a raw Irishman, a hireling just arrived on these shores, who was never there before, — and, we trust, will never be let loose there again, — who knows not whether he is hacking at the upas tree or the Tree of Knowledge, with axe and stub-scythe to exterminate it, and he will know it no

[1] [*Excursions*, p. 203; Riv. 249.]

that they do not regard him. It has got to be so cool, then, that tender chickens seek a shelter at night; but I saw the hens at Clark's (the R. Brown house) were still going to roost in the apple trees. M. asks the peddlers if they've got anything that'll cure the rheumatism, and often buys a wash of them.

I was telling him how some crows two or three weeks ago came flying with a scolding caw toward me as I stood on "Cornel Rock," and alighted within fifty feet on a dead tree above my head, unusually bold. Then away go all but one, perchance, to a tall pine in the swamp, twenty rods off; anon he follows. Again they go quite out of sight amid the tree-tops, leaving one behind. This one, at last, quite at his leisure, flaps away cawing, knowing well where to find his mates, though you might think he must winter alone.

Minott said that as he was going over to Lincoln one day thirty or forty years ago, taking his way through Ebby Hubbard's woods, he heard a great flock of crows cawing over his head, and one alighted just within gunshot. He raised his little gun marked London, which he knew would fetch down anything that was within gunshot, and down came the crow; but he was not killed, only so filled with shot that he could not fly. As he was going by John Wyman's at the pond, with the live crow in his hand, Wyman asked him what he was going to do with that crow, to which he answered, "Nothing in particular," — he happened to alight within gunshot, and so he shot him. Wyman said that he'd like to have him. "What do you want to do with him?" asked M. "If you'll give

more forever. What is trespassing? This Hessian, the day after he was landed, was whirled twenty miles into the interior to do this deed of vandalism on our favorite hedge. I would as soon admit a living mud turtle into my herbarium. If some are prosecuted for abusing children, others deserve to be prosecuted for maltreating the face of nature committed to their care.

Had one of those sudden cool gusts, which filled the air with dust from the road, shook the houses, and caused the elms to labor and drop many leaves, early in afternoon. No such gust since spring.

Sept. 29. All sorts of men come to Cattle-Show. I see one with a blue hat.

I hear that some have gathered fringed gentian. Pines have begun to be parti-colored with yellow leaves.

Sept. 30. Ground white with frost this morning.
P. M. — To Walden.
Young oaks generally reddening, etc., etc. *Rhus Toxicodendron* turned yellow and red, handsomely dotted with brown.

At Wheeler's Wood by railroad, heard a cat owl hooting at 3.30 P. M., which was repeatedly answered by another some forty rods off.

Talked with Minott, who was sitting, as usual, in his wood-shed. His hen and chickens, finding it cold these nights on the trees behind the house, had begun last night to roost in the shed, and one by one walked or hopped up a ladder within a foot of his shoulder to the loft above. He sits there so much like a fixture

Vol. X

him to me, I'll tell you," said the other. To which Minott said, "You may have him and welcome." Wyman then proceeded to inform him that the crows had eaten a great space in Josh Jones the blacksmith's corn-field, which Minott had passed just below the almshouse, and that Jones had told him that if he could kill a crow in his corn-field he would give him half a bushel of rye. He could guess what he wanted the crow for. So Wyman took the crow and the next time he went into town he tossed him over the wall into the corn-field and then shot him, and, carrying the dead crow to Jones, he got his half-bushel of rye.

[Here, and at several following points, matter relative to the recent Maine excursion is omitted as having been already used in "The Maine Woods."]

The mist and mizzling rain there[1] was like the sparkling dust of amethysts.

The Watsons tell me that Uncle Ned uses the expression "a glade" for the sheen of the moon on the water, which is, I see, according to Bailey, being from κλάδος, a branch. Helps thinks "a glade" such a path through a forest as an army would cut with a sword. . . .

What poor crack-brains we are! easily upset and unable to take care of ourselves! If there were a precipice at our doors, some would be found jumping off to-day for fear that, if they survived, they might jump off to-morrow. . . .

Consider what actual phenomena await us. To say nothing of life, which may be rare and difficult to detect, and death, which is startling enough, we cannot begin

[1] [At Mt. Kineo, Moosehead Lake.]

to conceive of anything so surprising and thrilling but that something more surprising may be actually presented to us.[1] . . .

According to the Upanishads, "As water, when rained down on elevated ground, runs scattered off in the valleys, so ever runs after difference a person who beholds attributes different (from the soul)."

"As pure water, which is thrown down on pure ground, remains alike, so also, O Gautama, is the soul of the thinker who knows."

Minott says he is seventy-five years old.

Minott said he had seen a couple of pigeons go over at last, as he sat in his shed. At first he thought they were doves, but he soon saw that they were pigeons, they flew so straight and fast.

He says that that tall clock which still ticks in the corner belonged to old John Beatton, who died before he was born; thought it was two hundred years old!! Some of the rest of the furniture came from the same source. His gun marked London was one that Beatton sent to England for, for a young man that lived with him. I read on John Beatton's tombstone near the powder-house that he died in 1776, aged seventy-four.

[1] [Apropos of the phosphorescent wood of *Maine Woods*, pp. 198–201 (Riv. 245–248).]

III

OCTOBER, 1857

(ÆT. 40)

Oct. 1. P. M. — To second stone bridge and down Assabet home.

The ash trees are a dull red, and some quite mulberry-color. Methinks it has to do with the smart frost of yesterday morning; *i. e.*, that after the maples have fairly begun, the *young* red oaks, ash trees, etc., begin with the first smart frost. The pines now half turned yellow, the needles of this year are so much the greener by contrast. The arbor-vitæ changes with them so completely that it looks as if the lower parts were dead. All very much exposed button-bushes are brown and sere; so their yellowish season does not amount to much away from the river.[1] . . .

It seemed to me that it was no compliment to their god to suppose that he would not let them go to Ktaadn without so much ado.[2] They'd better have put their shoulders to the wheel and stumped it along at a good round pace. . . .

I boiled some rice at the carry, for our dinner, in cooking which I consider myself adept, having had a good deal of experience in it. P. said that he sometimes used it, but boiled it till it all fell apart, and,

[1] *Vide* [4] pages forward [Oct. 4].
[2] [See *Maine Woods*, pp. 214, 215; Riv. 265.]

---

finding this mess unexpectedly soft though quickly prepared, he asked if it had not been cooked before.

Washing the dishes, especially the greasy ones, is the most irksome duty of the camp, and it reminded me of that sacred band in Fourier's scheme, who took upon themselves the most disagreeable services. The consequence is that they do not often get washed.

Oct. 2. P. M. — To Hubbard's Close and Swamp. *Veronica scutellaria* still. Sitting on a rock east of Trillium Woods, I perceive that, generally speaking, it is only the edge or *pediment* of the woods that shows the bright autumnal tints yet (while the superstructure is green), the birches, very young oaks and hickories, huckleberry bushes, blackberries, etc., etc., that stand around the edges, though here and there some taller maple flames upward amid the masses of green, or some other riper and mellower tree.

The chief incidents in Minott's life must be more distinct and interesting to him now than immediately after they occurred, for he has recalled and related them so often that they are stereotyped in his mind. Never having travelled far from his hillside, he does not suspect himself, but tells his stories with fidelity and gusto to the minutest details, — as much as Herodotus his histories.

The leaves of some trees merely wither, turn brown, and drop off at this season, without any conspicuous flush of beauty, while others now first attain to the climax of their beauty.

There is a more or less general reddening of the leaves

---

at this season, down to the cinquefoil and mouse-ear, sorrel and strawberry under our feet. White oaks are still quite green, with a few distinct *red* leaves intermixed. A great many red maples are merely yellow; more, scarlet, in some cases deepening to crimson.

Looking at the pines of Trillium Woods, I see that the pitch pines have generally a rounded head, composed of countless distinct small rounded masses of foliage, the tops of their plumes, while the white pines are more smooth, or only flaky.

Since the cooler weather many crickets are seen clustered on warm banks and by sunny wall-sides. It is evident from their droppings that the woodchucks (?)[1] eat many of them these evenings.

I go through Stow's Wood and up Laurel Glen eastward. The chickadees of late have winter ways, flocking after you.

This changing of the leaves — their brighter tints — must have to do with cold, for it begins in the low meadows and in frosty hollows in the woods. There is where you must look as yet for the bright tints. I see the sprouts at the base of an old red oak for four or five feet upward, investing its trunk, all clear bright red, while all above is green. The shrub oak leaves around are more yellow or scarlet than the red. At the bottom of this hollow, the young walnut leaves have just been killed by the frosts while still green, and generally the hazel leaves also, but not the oaks, cherries, etc., etc. Many little maples in those coldest places have already dropped all their leaves. Gener-

[1] Skunks?

ally in low ground many maple and birch and locust leaves have fallen. Grape leaves were killed and crisped by the last frost.

The fringed gentian at Hubbard's Close has been out some time, and most of it already withered.

In the clintonia swamp I see where some animal has been getting the seeds of the skunk-cabbage out of their pericarp. You may take a dry walk there for a quarter of a mile along the base of the hill through this open swamp, where there is no underwood, all the way in a field of cinnamon fern four or five feet high and level, brushing against its light fronds, which offer now no serious obstacle. They are now generally imbrowned or crisp. In the more open swamp beyond, these ferns, recently killed by the frost and exposed to the sun, fill the air with a very strong sour scent, as if your nose [were] over a hogshead of vinegar. When I strip off a handful of the frond I find it is the cinnamon fern. I perceive it afterward in different parts of the town.

The erechthites down (fire-weed) is conspicuous in sprout-lands of late, since its leaves were killed.

Oct. 3. The *Rhus radicans* also turns yellow and red or scarlet, like the *Toxicodendron.* Asters, and still more goldenrods, look quite rare now. See a cowbird alone.

Getting over the wall near Sam Barrett's the other day, I had gone a few rods in the road when I met Prescott Barrett, who observed, "Well, you take a walk round the square sometimes." So little does he

know of my habits. I go across lots over his grounds every three or four weeks, but I do not know that I ever walked round the square in my life.

How much more agreeable to sit in the midst of old furniture like Minott's clock and secretary and looking-glass, which have come down from other generations, than in [*sic*] that which was just brought from the cabinet-maker's and smells of varnish, like a coffin! To sit under the face of an old clock that has been ticking one hundred and fifty years, — there is something mortal, not to say immortal, about it! A clock that began to tick when Massachusetts was a province. Meanwhile John Beatton's heavy tombstone is cracked quite across and widely opened.[1]

Oct. 4. A. M. — By boat to Conantum.

River fallen again. Barberrying and graping. Many of the grapes shrivelled and killed by frost now, and the leaves mostly fallen. The yellow leaves of the white willow thickly strew the bottom of my boat. Willows, elms, etc., shed their oldest leaves first, even like pines.[2] The recent and green ones are seen mottling a yellowish ground, especially in the willow; and, in the case of the willow, at least, these green ones wither and fall for the most part without turning yellow at all.

The button-bushes are generally greenish-yellow now; only the highest and most exposed points brown and crisp in some places. The black willow, rising above them, is crisped yellowish-brown, so that the

[1] It has fallen also and has been set up.
[2] [Altered in pencil so as to read, " These willows shed," etc.]

Vol. X

general aspect of the river's brim now is a modest or sober ripe yellowish-brown, — generally no bright colors. When I scare up a bittern from amid the weeds, I say it is the color of that bird's breast, — or body generally, for the darker part of its wings correspond to the sere pickerel-weed. Now that the pontederia is brown, the humble, weedy *green* of the shore is *burweed*, polygonum, wool-grass, and, in some places, rushes. Such is the river's border ordinarily, — either these weeds mingled with the sere and dark-brown pontederia or a convex raised rim of button-bushes, two to four feet high by a rod wide, through [which] the black willows rise one to a dozen feet higher. Here and there, to be sure, are the purple-leaved *Cornus sericea,* yellowish sweet-gale, reddish rose bushes, etc., etc.

Alders are still a fresh green. The grape leaves are generally crisp and curled, having a very light-colored appearance, but where it is protected by other foliage it is still a dense canopy of greenish-yellow shields.

From the midst of these yellowing button-bushes, etc., I hear from time to time a half-warbled strain from some young sparrow who thinks it is spring.

Scared up from the low shore at the bend, on the south side, opposite Clamshell, a flock of seventy-five or one hundred of what appeared solitary tattlers (??), that went off with a *rippling* note, wheeled, and alighted there again.[1]

Now again, when other trees prove so fickle, the steadfast evergreenness of the pines is appreciated.

[1] Henry Haynes next year thought they might be " Black-backs."

Bright-tinted flaming scarlet or yellow maples amid pines show various segments of bright cones embosomed in green.

At Potter's Swamp, where they are all maples, it adds to the beauty of the maple swamp at this season that it is not seen as a simple mass of color, but, different trees being of different tints, — green, yellow, scarlet, crimson, and different shades of each, — the outline of each tree is distinct to where one laps on to another. Yet a painter would hardly venture to make them thus distinct a quarter of a mile off.[1]

Hear a catbird and chewink, both faint.

Fever-bush has begun to yellow. *Some* nightshade leaves are a very dark purple.

See a grackle on the shore, so near I see the light mark about the eye.

While I lived in the woods I did various jobs about the town, — some fence-building, painting, gardening, carpentering, etc., etc. One day a man came from the east edge of the town and said that he wanted to get me to brick up a fireplace, etc., etc., for him. I told him that I was not a mason, but he knew that I had built my own house entirely and would not take no for an answer. So I went.

It was three miles off, and I walked back and forth each day, arriving early and working as late as if I were living there. The man was gone away most of the time, but had left some sand dug up in his cow-yard for me to make mortar with. I bricked up a fireplace, papered a chamber, but my principal work was whitewashing

[1] [*Excursions,* p. 262; Riv. 321.]

ceilings. Some were so dirty that many coats would not conceal the dirt. In the kitchen I finally resorted to yellow-wash to cover the dirt. I took my meals there, sitting down with my employer (when he got home) and his hired men. I remember the awful condition of the sink, at which I washed one day, and when I came to look at what was called the towel I passed it by and wiped my hands on the air, and thereafter I resorted to the pump. I worked there hard three days, charging only a dollar a day.

About the same time I also contracted to build a wood-shed of no mean size, for, I think, exactly six dollars, and cleared about half of it by a close calculation and swift working. The tenant wanted me to throw in a gutter and latch, but I carried off the board that was left and gave him no latch but a button. It stands yet, — behind the Kettle house. I broke up Johnny Kettle's old "trow," in which he kneaded his bread, for material. Going home with what nails were left in a flower [sic] bucket on my arm, in a rain, I was about getting into a hay-rigging, when my umbrella frightened the horse, and he kicked at me over the fills, smashed the bucket on my arm, and stretched me on my back; but while I lay on my back, his leg being caught over the shaft, I got up, to see him sprawling on the other side. This accident, the sudden bending of my body backwards, sprained my stomach so that I did not get quite strong there for several years, but had to give up some fence-building and other work which I had undertaken from time to time.

Vol. X

I go north by Jarvis's lane from the old pump-maker's house. There is not that profusion and consequent confusion of events which belongs to a summer's walk. There are few flowers, birds, insects, or fruits now, and hence what does occur affects us as more simple and significant. The cawing of a crow, the scream of a jay. The latter seems to scream more fitly and with more freedom now that some fallen maple leaves have made way for his voice. The jay's voice resounds through the vacancies occasioned by fallen maple leaves.

The mulberry [1] was perhaps the first tree that was conspicuously turned after the maples. Many maples are still quite green; so that their gala-day will be prolonged. I see some hickories now a crisped mass of imbrowned yellow, green in the recesses, sere brown on the prominences, though the eye does not commonly thus discriminate. The smooth sumach is very important for its mass of clear red or crimson. Some of it is now a very dark crimson.

In the old Carlisle road I see a great many pitch pine twigs or plumes, cast down, evidently, by squirrels, — but for what?

Many are now gathering barberries.

Am surprised to see a large sassafras tree, with its rounded umbrella-like top, without limbs beneath, on the west edge of the Yellow Birch Swamp, or east of Boulder Field. It is some sixteen inches in diameter. There are seven or eight within two rods. Leaves curled, but not changed. See a red squirrel cast down a chest-

[1] Or ash??

I built the common slat fence for $1.50 per rod, or worked for $1.00 per day. I built six fences.

Minott and Rice are apt to tell me the same story many times over. Minott told me the other day again of his peach tree. John Richardson was going by with a basket full of peach-stones. "What are you going to do with them?" asked M. He said he was going to plant. "Well, give me two or three of them, and I'll try too." So he raised one fine tree, which bore first-rate rare-ripes as big as an apple, but after bearing once or twice something got into it and the tree died. They're short-lived things.

Oct. 5.[1] P. M. — To Yellow Birch Swamp.

I go by the river and Hunt's Bridge. A warm and bright October afternoon. One man is making a gutter, to be prepared for rains, in his piece recently laid down in Merrick's pasture, where the grass is just springing up. I see many haws still green and hard, though their leaves are mostly fallen. Do they ever turn red and edible? Their leaves are a very dull reddish cast. The surface of the river sparkles in this air here and there. I see in most orchards the apples in heaps under the trees, and ladders slanted against their twiggy masses. The earth shines now as much as, or more than, ever in spring, especially the bare and somewhat faded fields, pastures, stubble, etc. The light is reflected as from a ripe surface, no longer absorbed to secure maturity.

[1] Begins now ten days of perfect Indian summer without rain; and the eleventh and twelfth days equally warm, though rainy.

nut bur. The pigeon woodpecker utters his whimsical *ah-week ah-week*, etc., as in spring. The yellow birch is somewhat yellowed. See a cherry-bird. Many robins feeding on poke berries on Eb Hubbard's hill. There is a great abundance of poke there. That lowest down the hill, killed by frost, drooping and withered, no longer purple-stemmed, but faded; higher up it is still purple.

I hear the alarum of a small red squirrel. I see him running by fits and starts along a chestnut bough toward me. His head looks disproportionately large for his body, like a bulldog's, perhaps because he has his chaps full of nuts. He chirrups and vibrates his tail, holds himself in, and scratches along a foot as if it were a mile. He finds noise and activity for both of us. It is evident that all this ado does not proceed from fear. There is at the bottom, no doubt, an excess of inquisitiveness and caution, but the greater part is make-believe and a love of the marvellous. He can hardly keep it up till I am gone, however, but takes out his nut and tastes it in the midst of his agitation. "*See there, see there,*" says he, "who's that? O dear, what shall I do?" and makes believe run off, but doesn't get along an inch, — lets it all pass off by flashes through his tail, while he clings to the bark as if he were holding in a race-horse. He gets down the trunk at last on to a projecting knot, head downward, within a rod of you, and chirrups and chatters louder than ever. Tries to work himself into a fright. The hind part of his body is urging the forward part along, snapping the tail over it like a whip-lash, but the fore part, for the most part, clings fast to the bark with desperate energy. *Squirr,* "to throw with a jerk," seems to have quite as much to do with the name as the Greek *skia oura,* shadow and tail.

The lower limbs of trees often incline downwards as if from sympathy with the roots; the upper tend upwards with the *leading* stem.

I found on the 4th, at Conantum, a half-bushel of barberries on one clump about four feet in diameter at base, falling over in wreaths on every side. I filled my basket, standing behind it without being seen by other pickers only a dozen rods off. Some great clumps on Melvin's preserve, no doubt, have many more on them.

I hear nowadays again the small woodpecker's sharp, shrill note from high on the trees. . . .

It is evident that some phenomena which belong only to spring and autumn here, lasted through the summer in that latitude, as the peeping of hylodes and blossoming of some flowers that long since withered here were there still freshly in bloom, in that fresher and cooler atmosphere, — the calla for instance. To say nothing of the myrtle-bird and *F. hyemalis* which breed there, but only transiently visit us in spring and fall. Just as a river which here freezes only a certain distance from the shore, follow it further north, is found to be completely bridged over. The toads, too, as I have said, rang at this season. What is summer where Indian corn will not ripen?

Oct. 6. P. M. — To Saw Mill Brook *via* Hubbard's Close.

A beautiful bright afternoon, still warmer than yesterday. I carry my coat on my arm. This weather makes the locust to be heard, — many of them. I go along the hill from the old burying-ground and descend at Minott's. Everything — all fruits and leaves, the reddish-silvery feathery grass in clumps,[1] even the surfaces of stone and stubble — are all ripe in this air. Yes, the hue of maturity has come even to that fine silver-topped feathery grass, two or three feet high, in clumps on dry places. I am riper for thought, too.

Of trees which are numerous here and form considerable masses or groups, those now sufficiently changed in their color to attract the eye generally are red maple (in prime), — *N. B.,* the *white maples* began in water long ago, but are rare, — white birch (perhaps in prime), *young* oaks in sprout-lands, etc. (especially young scarlet oaks), white ash, white pines (when near), elms, buttonwoods, and perhaps walnuts. Some others are equally changed, but so rare or distant from the village as to make less impression on me.

The shrubs now generally conspicuous from some distance, from their changed color and mass, are huckleberries and blueberries (high and low), smooth sumach and *Rhus venenata,* woodbine, button-bush, and grape perhaps.

I observe too that the ferns of a rich brown (being sere), about swamps, etc., are an important feature. A broad belt of rich brown (and crisp) ferns stands about many a bright maple swamp.

Some maples are in form and *color* like hickories,

¹ *Andropogon scoparius.*

tall and irregular. It, indeed, admits of singular variety in form and color. I see one now shaped like a hickory which is a very rich yellow with a tinge of brown, which, when I turn my head slightly, concealing the trunk, looks like a mass of yellow cloud, wreath upon wreath, drifting through the air, stratified by the wind.[1]

The trumpet-weeds are perfectly killed sere brown along the fences.

Think what a change, unperceived by many, has within a month come over the landscape! Then the general, the universal, hue was green. Now see those brilliant scarlet and glowing yellow trees in the lowlands a mile off! I see them, too, here and there on the sides of hills, standing out distinct, mere bright [an indecipherable word] and squads perchance, often in long broken lines, and so apparently elevated by their distinct color that they seem arranged like the remnants of a morning mist just retreating in a broken line along the hillsides. Or see that crowd in the swamp half a mile through, all vying with one another, a blaze of glory. See those crimson patches far away on the hillsides, like dense flocks of crimson sheep, where the huckleberry reminds of recent excursions. See those patches of rich brown in the low grounds, where the ferns stand shrivelled. See the greenish-yellow phalanxes of birches, and the crisped yellowish elm-tops here and there. We are not prepared to believe that the earth is now so parti-colored, and would present to a bird's eye such distinct masses of bright color. A great painter is at work. The very pumpkins yellow-

¹ [*Excursions,* p. 262; Riv. 321.]

ing in the fields become a feature in the landscape, and thus they have shone, maybe, for a thousand years here.

I have just read Ruskin's "Modern Painters." I am disappointed in not finding it a more out-of-door book, for I have heard that such was its character, but its title might have warned me. He does not describe Nature as Nature, but as Turner painted her, and though the work betrays that he has given a close attention to Nature, it appears to have been with an artist's and critic's design. How much is written about Nature as somebody has portrayed her, how little about Nature as she is, and chiefly concerns us, *i. e.* how much prose, how little poetry!

Going through Ebby Hubbard's woods, I see thousands of white pine cones on the ground, fresh light brown, which lately opened and shed their seeds and lie curled up on the ground. The seeds are rather pleasant or nutritious tasting, taken in quantity, like beechnuts, methinks. I see a great quantity of hypopitys, now all sere, along the path in the woods beyond. Call it Pine-Sap Path. It seems to have been a favorable season for it. It was evidently withered earlier than the tobacco-pipe, which is still *pretty* white!

Going through the Ministerial sprout-lands, I see the *young* oaks generally turning scarlet, and chestnuts, too, the young and also the old.

The lower chestnut leaves are among the most interesting now when closely inspected, varying from green to yellow, very finely and richly peppered with brown and green spots, at length turning brown with a tinge of crimson; but they, like others, must be seen on the twig, for they fade immediately, or in one night, if plucked. These brilliant leaves are as tender and inclined to wilt and fade as flowers, indeed are more transitory.

The amelanchier is yellowing and reddening a little, and also falling. I see *Lobelia inflata* leaves in the shade, a peculiar hoary white.

I see one or two chestnut burs open on the trees. The squirrels, red and gray, are on all sides throwing them down. You cannot stand long in the woods without hearing one fall.

As I came up the Turnpike, I smelt that strong-scented — like carrion, etc. — obscene fungus at the mossy bank, and I saw a dozen of those large flat oval black bugs with light-colored shoulder-pieces, such as, methinks, I see on carrion, feeding on its remnants. . . .

The frontier houses [1] preserve many of the features of the logging-camp. . . .

Looking up Trout Stream, it seemed as wild a place for a man to live as we had seen. What a difference between a residence there and within five minutes' walk of the depot! What different men the two lives must turn out!

Oct. 7. P. M. — To Cliffs and Walden.

Little chincapin oaks are partly turned, dull scarlet or yellow as it may happen, nearly in prime, not fallen. Some of their leaves (as well as of the white oak) are gnawed into lace regularly about the edges. Horn-

[1] [In Maine.]

Vol. X

beam generally green still, but becoming yellowish-brown and falling. Black alder still green. Elder is greenish-yellow. I see *some* panicled andromeda dark-red or crimson. Swamp-pink a *dark* reddish purple where exposed. Beach plum begins to turn a clear pale yellow in dry places. Sage willow is fairly yellowing and some even falling.

Crossing Depot Brook, I see many yellow butterflies fluttering about the *Aster puniceus*, still abundantly in bloom there.

I go across Bartonia Meadow direct to Bear Garden Hill-side. Approaching the sand-slide, I see, some fifty rods off, looking toward the sun, the top of the maple swamp just appearing over the sheeny russet edge of the hill, — a strip, apparently twenty rods long and ten feet deep, of the most intensely brilliant scarlet, orange, and yellow, equal to any flowers or fruits or any tints ever painted. As I advance, lowering the edge of the hill, which makes the firm foreground or lower frame to the picture, the depth of this brilliant grove revealed steadily increases, suggesting that the whole of the concealed valley is filled with such color.[1] As usual, there is one tree-top of an especially brilliant scarlet, with which the others contrast.

One wonders that the tithing-men and fathers of the town are not out to see what the trees mean by their high colors and exuberance of spirits, fearing that some mischief is brewing. I do not see what the Puritans did at that season when the maples blazed out in scarlet. They certainly could not have worshipped

[1] [*Excursions*, p. 262; Riv. 321, 322.]

in groves then. Perhaps that is what they built meeting-houses and surrounded them with horse-sheds for.[1]

No wonder we must have our annual cattle-show and fall training and perhaps Cornwallis, our September courts, etc. Nature holds her annual fair and gala-days in October in every hollow and on every hill-side.

Look into that hollow all aglow, where the trees are clothed in their vestures of most dazzling tints. Does it not suggest a thousand gypsies beneath, rows of booths, and that man's spirits should rise as high, that the routine of his life should be interrupted by an analogous festivity and rejoicing? [2]

It is the reign of crickets now. You see them gliding busily about over all sunny surfaces. They sometimes get into my shoes; but oftener I have to empty out the seeds of various shrubs and weeds which I have been compelled to transport.

Looking toward the sun from Lupine Bank, I see bloody patches of blackberry vines amid the fine hoary and sheeny grass of the pasture. Since the frosts such pastures are already a hoary russet.

Some shrub oaks are yellow, others reddish.

When I turn round half-way up Fair Haven Hill, by the orchard wall, and look northwest, I am surprised for the thousandth time at the beauty of the landscape, and I sit down to behold it at my leisure. I think that Concord affords no better view. It is always incred-

[1] [*Excursions*, pp. 262, 263; Riv. 322.]
[2] [*Excursions*, p. 275; Riv. 337, 338.]

ibly fair, but ordinarily we are mere objects in it, and not witnesses of it. I see, through the bright October air, a valley extending southwest and northeast and some two miles across, — so far I can see distinctly, — with a broad, yellow meadow tinged with brown at the bottom, and a blue river winding slowly through it northward, with a regular edging of low bushes on the brink, of the same color with the meadow. Skirting the meadow are straggling lines, and occasionally large masses a quarter of a mile wide, of brilliant scarlet and yellow and crimson trees, backed by and mingled with green forests and green and hoary russet fields and hills; and on the hills around shoot up a million scarlet and orange and yellow and crimson fires amid the green; and here and there amid the trees, often beneath the largest and most graceful of those which have brown-yellow dome-like tops, are bright white or gray houses; and beyond stretches a forest, wreath upon wreath, and between each two wreaths I know lies a similar vale; and far beyond all, on the verge of the horizon, are half a dozen dark-blue mountain-summits. Large birds of a brilliant blue and white plumage are darting and screaming amid the glowing foliage a quarter of a mile below, while smaller blue birds warble faintly but sweetly around me.[1]

Such is the dwelling-place of man; but go to a caucus in the village to-night or to a church to-morrow, and see if there is anything said to suggest that the inhabitants of those houses know what kind of world they live in. But hark! I hear the tolling of a distant

[1] The autumnal tints were more generally diffused there Oct. 10th.

funeral bell, and they are conveying a corpse to the churchyard from one of the houses that I see, and its serious sound is more in harmony with this scenery than any ordinary bustle could be. It suggests that a man must die to his present life before he can appreciate his opportunities and the beauty of the abode that is appointed him.

I do not know how to entertain one who can't take long walks. The first thing that suggests itself is to get a horse to draw them, and that brings us at once into contact with stablers and dirty harness, and I do not get over my ride for a long time. I give up my forenoon to them and get along pretty well, the very elasticity of the air and promise of the day abetting me, but they are as heavy as dumplings by mid-afternoon. If they can't walk, why won't they take an honest nap and let me go in the afternoon? But, come two o'clock, they alarm me by an evident disposition to sit. In the midst of the most glorious Indian-summer afternoon, there they sit, breaking your chairs and wearing out the house, with their backs to the light, taking no note of the lapse of time.

As I sat on the high bank at the east end of Walden this afternoon, at five o'clock, I saw, by a peculiar intention or dividing of the eye, a very striking subaqueous rainbow-like phenomenon. A passer-by might, perhaps would, have noticed that the bright-tinted shrubs about the high shore on the sunny side were reflected from the water; but, unless on the alert for such effects, he would have failed to perceive the full beauty of the phenomenon. Unless you look for re-

flections, you commonly will not find them. Those brilliant shrubs, which were from three to a dozen feet in height, were all reflected, dimly so far as the details of leaves, etc., were concerned, but brightly as to color, and, of course, in the order in which they stood, — scarlet, yellow, green, etc.; but, there being a slight ripple on the surface, these reflections were not true to their height though true to their breadth, but were extended downward with mathematical perpendicularity, three or four times too far, forming sharp pyramids of the several colors, gradually reduced to mere dusky points. The effect of this prolongation of the reflection was a very pleasing softening and blending of the colors, especially when a small bush of one bright tint stood directly before another of a contrary and equally bright tint. It was just as if you were to brush firmly aside with your hand or a brush a fresh line of paint of various colors, or so many lumps of friable colored powders. There was, accordingly, a sort of belt, as wide as the whole height of the hill, extending downward along the whole north or sunny side of the pond, composed of exceedingly short and narrow inverted pyramids of the most brilliant colors intermixed. I have seen, indeed, similar inverted pyramids in the old drawings of tattooing about the waists of the aborigines of this country. Walden, too, like an Indian maiden, wears this broad rainbow-like belt of brilliant-colored points or cones round her waist in October. The color seems to be reflected and re-reflected from ripple to ripple, losing brightness each time by the softest possible gradation, and tapering toward the

beholder, since he occupies a mere point of view. This is one of the prettiest effects of the autumnal change.

The harvest of leaves is at hand in some valleys, and generally the young deciduous trees on hillsides have the brilliant tint of ripe fruits. Already many windfalls strew the ground under the maples and elms, etc. I see one or two maple shrubs quite bare, while many large maples are still quite green.

In that rainbow belt we have color, which is commonly so rare and precious and confined to precious stones, in the utmost profusion. The ripples convey the reflection toward us, till all the color is winnowed out and spilled between them and only the dusky points reach near to this side where we stand. It is as if a broad belt (or waist-cloth) of sharp and narrow inverted cones or pyramids of bright colors, softly blended like fairy worsted work, their bases rising to a line mathematically level about the waist of the pond. That fall river Indian, like the Almouchicois generally, wore a belt of hollow tubes.

It was strange that only the funeral bell was in harmony with that scene, while other sounds were too frivolous and trivial, as if only through the gate of death would man come to appreciate his opportunities and the beauty of the world he has abused. In proportion as death is more earnest than life, it is better than life.

The sun set just before I reached the railroad causeway on my return, but then there was not a cloud to be seen in the horizon. Coming through the Irish [*sic*]

field, the mountains were purple, much redder than a grape. . . .

That simple and mild nasal chant [1] affected me like the dawn of civilization to the wilderness. I thought of "Lo, the poor Indian! whose untutored mind," etc. There is always a slight haze or mist on the brow of the Indian. The white man's brow is clear and distinct. It is eleven o'clock in the forenoon with him. It is four o'clock in the morning with the Indian.

Oct. 8. **P. M. — Up Assabet.**

Hemlock leaves are copiously falling. They cover the hillside like some wild grain. The changing red maples along the river are past their prime now, earlier than generally elsewhere. They are much faded, and many leaves are floating on the water. Those white maples that were so early to change in the water have more than half lost their leaves.

Walking through the Lee farm swamp, a dozen or more rods from the river, I found a large box trap closed. I opened it and found in it the remains of a gray rabbit, — skin, bones, and mould, — closely fitting the right-angled corner of one side. It was wholly inoffensive, as so much vegetable mould, and must have been dead some years. None of the furniture of the trap remained, but the box itself, with a lid which just moved on two rusty nails; the stick which held the bait, the string, etc., etc., were all gone. The box had the appearance of having been floated off in an upright position by a freshet. It had been a rabbit's

[1] [See *Maine Woods*, pp. 197, 198; Riv. 244.]

living tomb. He had gradually starved to death in it. What a tragedy to have occurred within a box in one of our quiet swamps! The trapper lost his box, the rabbit its life. The box had not been gnawed. After days and nights of moaning and struggle, heard for a few rods through the swamp, increasing weakness and emaciation and delirium, the rabbit breathes its last. They tell you of opening the tomb and finding by the contortions of the body that it was buried alive. This was such a case. Let the trapping boy dream of the dead rabbit in its ark, as it sailed, like a small meeting-house with its rude spire, slowly, with a grand and solemn motion, far amid the alders.

Four dark-colored ducks (white beneath), *maybe* summer, or teal (??), with a loud *creaking* note of alarm, flew away from near the shore and followed the bend of the river upward.

I see and hear white-throated sparrows on the swamp white oaks by the river's edge, uttering a faint sharp *cheep*.

The chipmunk,[1] the wall-going squirrel, that will cross a broad pasture on the wall, now this side, now that, now on top, and lives under it, — as if it were a track laid for him expressly.

Oct. 9. P. M. — To Dugan Desert and Ministerial Swamp.

The elms are now at the height of their change. As I look down our street, which is lined with them, now clothed in their very rich brownish-yellow dress, they

[1] An allied one is called the wall-mouse in the West.

Vol. X

about as birches; many ash trees are a mere finely divided dull-reddish color; swamp white oaks are green, yellow, and brown, much less ripe than elms, not much yellowed yet.

Under the pines by the Clamshell, that fine purple grass is now withered and faded to a very light brown which reflects the autumnal light. Patches of rabbit's clover amid the blackberry vines are now quite hoary if not silvery. I thought it a mass of *Aster Tradescanti* at first, but they are not so common. Many plants, like them, remind you by their color of the frosts.

Sprout-lands, with their oaks, chestnuts, etc., etc., are now at their height of color.

From Lupine Hill, not only the maples, etc., have acquired brighter tints at this season, but the pines, by contrast, appear to have acquired a new and more liquid green, and to some extent this is true, — where their old leaves have chiefly fallen, which is not yet generally the case, however.

I see now that, near the river and low on the meadows, the maple stands with paled fires, burned out, thin-leaved, a salmon or faint cherry tint, ready to surrender to the first smart frost.

It has come to this, — that the lover of art is one, and the lover of nature another, though true art is but the expression of our love of nature. It is monstrous when one cares but little about trees but much about Corinthian columns, and yet this is exceedingly common.

Scarlet oaks have fairly begun to blaze, — especially their lower limbs, — in low places which have

remind me of yellowing sheaves of grain, as if the harvest had come to the village itself, and we might expect to find some maturity and *flavor* in the thoughts of the villagers at last. Under those light-rustling yellow piles, just ready to fall on the heads of the walker, how can any crudity or greenness of thought or act prevail? The street is a great harvest-home. It would be worth the while to set out these trees, if only for their autumnal value. Think of these great yellow canopies or parasols held over our heads and houses by the mile together, making the village all one and compact, an *ulmarium*. And then how gently and unobserved they drop their burdens and let in the sun when it is wanted, their leaves not heard when they fall on our roofs and in our streets.

I see the traveller driving into the village under its canopy of elm-tops, with his crop, as into a great granary or barn-yard. I am tempted to go thither as to a husking of thoughts, now dry and ripe and ready to be separated from their integuments, but I foresee that it will be chiefly husks and little thought, blasted pig-corn, fit only for cob-meal.[1] Is there, then, indeed, no thought under this ample husk of conversation and manners? There is the sermon husk, the lecture husk, and the book husk, and are they all only good to make mats of and tread under foot?

Looking from railroad bridge, birches are perhaps at the height of their change now; hickories are about the color of elms or a little browner; balm-of-Gileads,

[1] [*Excursions*, pp. 263, 264; Riv. 322-324.]

most felt the frost. Hazels at their height, varying from green through dull crimson to dull scarlet.

Going along the mill road, the common shrub oaks make a dull-red or salmon impression in the mass at a little distance, from which brighter scarlet oaks stand out.

On F. Wheeler's clearing, over the swamp, many shrub oak leaves fallen, laying bare the acorns, which are browned. Many leaves already thickly strew the dry, sandy ground.

In the swamp, some twenty-foot maples are already bare, and some white pines are as yellow as birches. The spruces appear unchanged, even close at hand, though many leaves have fallen and are falling. The *Viburnum nudum* in the swamp is a clear handsome crimson. The young cherry yellow, with a faint cherry tinge. The mulberry is browned and falling, though it is but slightly tinged with yellow.

I see an Irishman digging mud at Harrington's mud-hole. He digs it out rapidly, — a hole four feet wide by eight long, — leaving a water-tight partition, eighteen or twenty inches wide, on two sides next the water. At three feet it is clear white sand, whiter than common sand-hills. Why? Why is there no stain of vegetation in it? It requires some skill to save much of the partition at last. This man first pares off the top nearly to the level of the water, then, standing on it, digs it away as the water rushes in, — though it fills it before he has got a foot, — and he thus saves about half its depth. No doubt his work is the more amusing for requiring this exercise of thought.

Saw a jay stealing corn from a stack in a field.

Oct. 10. P. M. — To Walden over Fair Haven Hill.

Some *Prinos verticillatus* yellowing and browning at once, and in low ground just falling and leaving the bright berries bare.

From the upper side of Wheeler's clearing on Fair Haven Hill, I see five smokes, now at 3.30 P. M., — one toward Lexington, one over Bedford, one over Billerica, one, very copious, as much further north, and one over Carlisle. These are all dark, seen against the sky and from the sun, and, except the first, apparently beyond the respective towns. Going over to the southwest side of the hill, I see one large widespread smoke toward Wachusett and rising against it, apparently beyond the height of land between the Concord and Nashua, and another much nearer, toward Stow. These two are light, or smoke-colored, because seen more toward the sun, perhaps; or is it solely because seen against the mountain and woods? There is another, the eighth, a little south of west, nearly under the sun, but this, being very distant and seen against the sky, is dusky. I could not see south and southwest.

I think that these smokes are the most distant sign of the presence of man on the globe that I detect with my unarmed eye, — of man's cohabitancy. I see the evidence that so many farmers with their hired men and boys are at work in their clearings from five to fifteen miles off. I see this smoky telegraph for hours marking the locality and occupation of some farmer and suggesting peaceful rural enterprises and improvements which I may yet see described in the agricul-

tural reports, though I may never have seen, and perhaps never shall see, that farm or farmer. Considering the slight evidence I have of their existence, they are as far away as if in another quarter of the globe. Sometimes the smoke is seen beyond a distant range of hills, spreading along, low and bluish, seen against a more distant hill or mountain; at others it is a column faintly and dimly seen against the horizon, but more distinctly revealed by a dusky but cloud-like expansion above. It may be a dusky almost level bar, slanting upward a little, like a narrow banner. The smokes from a dozen clearings far and wide, from a portion of the earth thirty miles or more in diameter, reveal the employment of many husbandmen at this season. Thus I see the woods burned up from year to year. The telltale smokes reveal it. The smokes will become rarer and thinner year by year, till I shall detect only a mere feathery film and there is no more brush to be burned.

Generally speaking, the autumnal tints affect the color of the landscape for only two or three miles, but I distinguish maples by their color half a mile north of Brooks Clark's, or some three miles distant, from this hill, — one further east very bright. Also I see them in the northeast, or on or near, apparently, a road between Bedford and Billerica, at least four or five miles distant!! This is the furthest I can see them.

Descend from Fair Haven Hill through Stow's sprout-land to railroad. See chincapin oaks in frosty places sere brown and ready to fall, while in others

they are still green, in woods. They turn of various colors, some quite handsome clear scarlet or red. Many young white oaks in similar frosty places are all withered and shrivelled. I see in the woods some *Smilacina racemosa* leaves, — which are usually a uniform pale-brown, — very wildly and remarkably marked, — *weirdly.* They are pale-brown, almost white, and somewhat curled, varied with rectilinear broad black (brown, seen close to) marks along the veins, say one inch, more or less, long by one tenth inch wide, with square corners. (Suppose you were to have a neckerchief after this pattern!) The whole plant gracefully bent almost horizontally with the weight of its dense raceme of bright cherry-red berries at the end.

Generally speaking, chestnuts, hickories, aspens, and some other trees attain a fair clear yellow only in small specimens in the woods or sprout-lands, or in their lower leaves.

You see now in sprout-lands young scarlet oaks of every degree of brightness from green to dark scarlet. It is a beautifully formed leaf, with its broad, free, open sinuses, — worthy to be copied in sculpture. A very agreeable form, a bold, deep scallop, as if the material were cheap. Like tracery. The color is more mingled with light than in the less deeply scalloped oak leaves. It is a less simple form. Though the connected outline is a broad oval, it is much improved by deep bays of light, as a simple oval pond would be improved by four or five broad, rounded promontories extending far into it on different sides, while the watery

bays, instead of being rounded at bottom, extended far inland in sharp friths. The leaf suggests a lavish expense in the creation of those deep scallops, as if so much material had been cut out and thrown away.[1]

This is the end of the sixth day of glorious weather, which I am tempted to call the finest in the year, so bright and serene the air and such a sheen from the earth, so brilliant the foliage, so pleasantly warm (except, perhaps, this day, which is cooler), too warm for a thick coat, — yet not sultry nor oppressive, — so ripe the season and our thoughts. Certainly these are the most brilliant days in the year, ushered in, perhaps, by a frosty morning, as this. As a dewy morning in the summer compared with a parched and sultry, languid one, so a frosty morning at this season compared with a merely dry or foggy one. These days you may say the year is ripened like a fruit by frost, and puts on brilliant tints of maturity but not yet of decay. It is not sere and withered as in November. See the heaps of apples in the fields and at the cider-mill, of pumpkins in the fields, and the stacks of corn-stalks and the standing corn. Such is the season. The morning frosts have left a silvery hue on the fine pasture grasses. They have faded to a kindred color.

Oct. 11. *Sunday.* P. M. — Up Assabet.

River lower than before since winter at least; very low. Another frost last night, although with fog, and this afternoon the maple and other leaves strew the water, and it is almost a leaf harvest. I see some fine clear

[1] [*Excursions*, pp. 279, 280; Riv. 342, 343.]

yellows from the *Rhus Toxicodendron* on the bank by the hemlocks and beyond. The osmunda ferns are generally withered and brown except where very much protected from frost. The *O. regalis* is the least generally withered of them. The onoclea is much later and still generally green along the bank, or faded white here and there.

Looking at the reflection of the bank by the Hemlocks, the reflected sun dazzles me, and I approach nearer to the bank in order to shut it out (of course it disappears sooner in the reflection than the substance, because every head is raised above the level of the water), and I see in the reflection the fine, slender grasses on the sharp or well-defined edge of the bank all glowing with silvery light, a singularly silvery light to be seen in the water [?], and whose substance I cannot see to advantage with my head thus high, since the sun is in the way.

This is the seventh day of glorious weather. Perhaps these might be called Harvest Days. Within the week most of the apples have been gathered; potatoes are being dug; corn is still left in the fields, though the stalks are being carried in. Others are ditching and getting out mud and cutting up bushes along fences, — what is called "brushing up," — burning brush, etc.

These are cricket days.

The river is so low that I run against several rocks, which I must have floated over three or four days ago, and I see many snags and water-logged trunks on the bottom or partly exposed, which were then invisible.

Vol. X

Oct. 12. P. M. — To Annursnack.

The eighth fine day, warmer than the last two. I find one or two house-leek blossoms even yet fresh, and all the rest crisp. The fringed gentian by the brook opposite is in its prime, and also along the north edge of the Painted-Cup Meadows. The stems of the blue vervain, whose flowers and leaves are withered and brown, are nearly as handsome and clear a purple as those of the poke have been, from top to bottom.

Looking from the Hill. The autumnal tints generally are much duller now than three or four days ago, or before the last two frosts. I am not sure but the yellow now prevails over the red in the landscape, and even over the green. The general color of the landscape from this hill is now russet, *i. e.* red, yellow, etc., mingled. The maple fires are generally about burnt out. Yet I can see very plainly the colors of the sproutland, chiefly oak, on Fair Haven Hill, about four miles distant, and also yellows on Mt. Misery, five miles off, also on Pine Hill, and even on Mt. Tabor, indistinctly. Eastward, I distinguish red or yellow in the woods as far as the horizon, and it is most distant on that side, — six miles, at least.

The huckleberries on Nagog Hill are *very* red. The smaller and tenderer weeds were in their prime, methinks, some weeks ago. They have felt the frosts earlier than the maples and other trees, and are now withered generally.

I see a very distant mountain house in a direction a little to the west of Carlisle, and two elms in the horizon on the right of it. Measuring carefully on the map

It is remarkable how many trees — maple and swamp white [oak], etc. — which stand on the bank of the river, being undermined by the water or broken off by the ice or other cause, fall into the stream and finally sink to the bottom and are half buried there for many years. A great deal of wood, especially of the kinds named, is thus lost. They last longer there probably than in *favorable* localities out of water. I see still the timber foundation of an old dam just above Spencer Brook, extending across the river on the bottom, though there has been nothing above water within my recollection. The large black oaks in front of Prescott Barrett's are one by one falling into the river, and there are none to succeed them. They were probably left to skirt the stream when the other wood was cut, and now, when they are undermined, there are none behind to supply their places.

Mr. Conant of Acton tells me that there was a gristmill built over the river there by Sam Barrett's grandfather, and that he remembers going to it when he was fourteen. He went in at the Lee house and crossed the river by a bridge at the mill. He says that it is as much as sixty years since the mill was standing. Minott thinks it is not quite so long since. He remembers the bridge there, not a town one, nor strong enough for a horse and cart. Thinks the mill was discontinued because Dr. Lee complained of its flowing his woodland. They used to stop with their carts this side and carry their bags back and forth over the bridge on their shoulders. Used a small and poor road across to Lee's farm.

of the county, I think it must be the Baptist Church in North Tewksbury, within a small fraction of fourteen miles from me. I think that this is the greatest distance at which I have seen an elm without a glass. There is another elm in the horizon nearly north, but not so far. It looks very much larger than it is. Perhaps it looms a little. The elm, I think, can be distinguished further than any other tree, and, however faintly seen in the distant horizon, its little dark dome, which the thickness of my nail will conceal, just rising above the line of the horizon, apparently not so big as a prominence on an orange, it suggests ever the same quiet rural and domestic life passing beneath it. It is the vignette to an unseen idyllic poem. Though that little prominence appears so dark there, I know that it is now a rich brownish-yellow canopy of rustling leaves, whose harvest-time is already come, sending down its showers from time to time. Homestead telegraphs to homestead through these distant elms seen from the hilltops. I fancy I hear the house-dog's bark and lowing of the cows asking admittance to their yard beneath it. The tea-table is spread; the master and mistress and the hired men now have just sat down in their shirt-sleeves. Some are so lifted up in the horizon that they seem like portions of the earth detached and floating off by themselves into space. Their dark masses against the sky can be seen as far, at least, as a white spire, though it may be taller. Some of these trees, seen through a glass, are not so large. . . .

This was what those scamps did in California. The trees were so grand and venerable that they could not afford to let them grow a hair's breadth bigger, or live a moment longer to reproach themselves. They were so big that they resolved they should never be bigger. They were so venerable that they cut them right down. It was not for the sake of the wood; it was only because they were very grand and venerable.

Oct. 13. P. M. — To Poplar Hill.

Maple fires are burnt out generally, and they have fairly begun to fall and look smoky in the swamps. When my eyes were resting on those smoke-like bare trees, it did not at first occur to me why the landscape was not as brilliant as a few days ago. The outside trees in the swamps lose their leaves first.

The brilliancy of young oaks, especially scarlet oaks, in sprout-lands is dulled. These red maples and young scarlet oaks, etc., have been the most conspicuous and important colors, or patches of color, in the landscape. Those *most* brilliant days, then, so far as the autumnal tints are concerned, are over; *i. e.*, when we may be surprised at any turn by the sight of some incredibly bright and dazzling tree or grove of trees.

I noticed the first *large* white oaks wholly changed to a salmon-color, but not brilliant like those sprout-land fires. Are very large oaks never brilliant in their tints?[1]

The hickories on Poplar Hill have not lost any of their brilliancy, generally speaking. Some are quite green even. I look down into a mocker-nut, whose recesses and greater part are pure yellow, and from

[1] Yes.

this you pass through a ruddy orange in the more exposed leaves to a rich crispy brown in the leaves of the extreme twigs about the clusters of round green nuts.

The red of oaks, etc., is far more general now than three or four days ago, but it is also much duller, so that some maples that were a bright scarlet can now hardly be distinguished by their color from oaks, which have just turned red.

The Great Fields from this hill are pale-brown, often hoary — there is not yellow enough for russet — pastures, with very large red or purple patches of blackberry vines. You can only appreciate the effect of these by a strong and peculiar intention of the eye. We ordinarily do not see what is before us, but what our prejudices presume to be there.

The pitch and white pines on the north of Sleepy Hollow, *i. e.* north side the hill, are at the height of their change and are falling. Maybe they are later than on the south side of hills. They are at the height of their change, generally, though many needles fallen, carpeting the ground. Pinweeds are brown; how long? Some of the large ash trees, both *a* black and white, are quite bare of leaves already. With the red maples, then. Looking from this hill, green begins to look as rare and interesting as any color, — you may say begins to be a color by itself, — and I distinguish green streaks and patches of grass on most hillsides.

See a pretty large flock of tree sparrows, very lively and tame, drifting along and pursuing each other along a bushy fence and ditch like driving snow. Two

Vol. X

pursuing each other would curve upward like a breaker in the air and drop into the hedge again.

Some white willows are very fresh and green yet. This has been the ninth of those wonderful days, and one of the warmest. I am obliged to sit with my window wide open all the evening as well as all day. It is the earlier Indian summer.

Our cherry trees have now turned to mostly a red-orange color.

Oct. 14. P. M. — To White Pond.

Another, the tenth of these memorable days. We have had some fog the last two or three nights, and this forenoon it was slow to disperse, dog-day-like, but this afternoon it is warmer even than yesterday. I should like it better if it were not so warm. I am glad to reach the shade of Hubbard's Grove; the coolness is refreshing. It is indeed a golden autumn. These ten days are enough to make the reputation of any climate. A tradition of these days might be handed down to posterity. They deserve a notice in history, in the history of Concord. All kinds of crudities have a chance to get ripe this year. Was there ever such an autumn? And yet there was never such a panic and hard times in the commercial world. The merchants and banks are suspending and failing all the country over, but not the sand-banks, solid and warm, and streaked with bloody blackberry vines. You may run upon them as much as you please,[1] — even as the

[1] You cannot break them. If you should slump, 't is to a finer sand.

crickets do, and find their account in it. They are the stockholders in these banks, and I hear them creaking their content. You may see them on change any warmer hour. In these banks, too, and such as these, are my funds deposited, a fund of health and enjoyment. Their (the crickets) prosperity and happiness and, I trust, mine do not depend on whether the New York banks suspend or no. We do not rely on such slender security as the thin paper of the Suffolk Bank. To put your trust in such a bank is to be swallowed up and undergo suffocation. Invest, I say, in these country banks. Let your capital be simplicity and contentment. Withered goldenrod (*Solidago nemoralis*) is no failure, like a broken bank, and yet in its most golden season nobody counterfeits it. Nature needs no counterfeit-detector. I have no compassion for, nor sympathy with, this miserable state of things. Banks built of granite, after some Grecian or Roman style, with their porticoes and their safes of iron, are not so permanent, and cannot give me so good security for capital invested in them, as the heads of withered hardhack in the meadow. I do not suspect the solvency of these. I know who is their president and cashier.

I take all these walks to every point of the compass, and it is always harvest-time with me. I am always gathering my crop from these woods and fields and waters, and no man is in my way or interferes with me. My crop is not their crop. To-day I see them gathering in their beans and corn, and they are a spectacle to me, but are soon out of my sight. I am not gathering beans and corn. Do they think there are no fruits but such as these? I am a reaper; I am not a gleaner. I go reaping, cutting as broad a swath as I can, and bundling and stacking up and carrying it off from field to field, and no man knows nor cares. My crop is not sorghum nor Davis seedlings. There are other crops than these, whose seed is not distributed by the Patent Office. I go abroad over the land each day to get the best I can find, and that is never carted off even to the last day of November, and I do not go as a gleaner.

The farmer has always come to the field after some material thing; that is not what a philosopher goes there for.

I see, in Hubbard's Grove, a large black birch at the very height of its change. Its leaves a clear, rich yellow; many strew the ground. Near by is a tupelo which is all a distinct yellow with a little green. Within a couple of rods a single hyla peeps interruptedly, bird-like.

Large oaks appear to be now generally turned or turning. The white, most conspicuous in sunny places, say a reddish salmon; began to change at lower limbs. Black oaks a brownish yellow. These large trees are not brilliant.

On the causeway I pass by maples here and there which are bare and smoke-like, having lost their brilliant clothing; but there it lies, nearly as bright as ever, on one side on the ground, making nearly as regular a figure as lately on the tree. I should rather say that I first observed the trees thus flat on the ground like a permanent colored and substantial shadow, and they

alone suggested to look for the trees that had borne them. They preserve these bright colors on the ground but a short time, a day or so, especially if it rains.[1]

I see a large flock of grackles, probably young birds, quite near me on William Wheeler's apple trees, pruning themselves and trying to sing. They *never* succeed; make a sort of musical spluttering. Most, I think, have brownish heads and necks, and some purple reflections from their black bodies.

There is a very little gossamer, mostly blowing off in large loops from the south side the bridge, the loose end having caught. I also see it here and there stretched across lanes from side to side, as high as my face.

Sat in the old pasture beyond the Corner Spring Woods to look at that pine wood now at the height of its change, pitch and white. Their change produces a very singular and pleasing effect. They are regularly parti-colored. The last year's leaves, about a foot beneath the extremities of the twigs on all sides, now changed and ready to fall, have their period of brightness as well as broader leaves. They are a clear yellow, contrasting with the fresh and liquid green of the terminal plumes, or this year's leaves. These two quite distinct colors are thus regularly and equally distributed over the whole tree. You have the warmth of the yellow and the coolness of the green. So it should be with our own maturity, not yellow to the very extremity of our shoots, but youthful and untried green ever putting forth afresh at the extremities, foretelling a maturity as yet unknown. The ripe leaves fall to the ground

[1] [*Excursions*, p. 265; Riv. 325.]

and become nutriment for the green ones, which still aspire to heaven. In the fall of the leaf, there is no fruit, there is no true maturity, neither in our science and wisdom.

Some aspens are a very fair yellow now, and trembling as in summer. I think it is they I see a mile off on Bear Garden Hill, amid the oaks and pines.

There is a very thick haze this afternoon and almost a furnace-like heat. I cannot see far toward the sun through it.

Approaching White Pond by the path, I see on its perfectly smooth surface what I at first mistake for a large raft of dead and black logs and limbs, but it soon elevates itself in the form of a large flock of black ducks, which go off with a loud quacking.

This, as other ponds now, when it is still, has a fine sparkle from skaters on it. I go along near the shore in the woods to the hill recently cleared on the east side. The clethra as an under-bush has an exceedingly pale yellow leaf. The nemopanthes on the hillside is like the amelanchier, yellowish with considerable ruddiness; the total effect is russet.

Looking now toward the north side of the pond, I perceive that the reflection of the hillside seen from an opposite hill is not so broad as the hillside itself appears, owing to the different angle at which it is seen. The reflection exhibits such an aspect of the hill, *apparently*, as you would get if your eye were placed at that part of the surface of the pond where the reflection seems to be. In this instance, too, then, Nature avoids repeating herself. Not even reflections in still water are like

their substances as seen by us. This, too, accounts for my seeing portions of the sky through the trees in reflections often when none appear in the substance. Is the reflection of a hillside, however, such an aspect of it as can be obtained by the eye directed to the hill itself from any single point of view? It plainly is not such a view as the eye would get looking upward from the immediate base of the hill or water's edge, for there the first rank of bushes on the lower part of the hill would conceal the upper. The reflection of the top appears to be such a view of it as I should get with my eye at the water's edge above the edge of the reflection; but would the lower part of the hill also appear from this point as it does in the reflection? Should I see as much of the under sides of the leaves there? If not, then the reflection is never a true copy or repetition of its substance, but a new composition, and this may be the source of its novelty and attractiveness, and of this nature, too, may be the charm of an echo. I doubt if you can ever get Nature to repeat herself exactly.

The occasional dimples on this pure sheeny surface in which the sky is reflected make you suspect as soon some mote fallen from the sky as risen from beneath, to disturb it.

Next to the scarlet, methinks the white shrub oaks make, or have made, the most brilliant show at a distance on hillsides. The latter is not very bright, unless seen between you and the sun, but there its abundant inward color is apparent.

At the head of the path by the pond, I saw a red squirrel, only a rod off in a white pine, eating a toadstool. It was a slightly convex white disk, (then) two inches in diameter. I saw where he had bitten off its white stump within a few feet of the base of the tree. I should not have called it an edible one; but he knows. He held it vertically with a paw on each side and what had been the lower side toward him, and was nibbling off the inside edge very fast, turning it round from time to time and letting some fragments drop, pausing to look at me. As a boy might nibble a biscuit. Are nuts scarce? I think it was not the edible one; was too big.

Veronica serpyllifolia in bloom.

Oct. 15. Rain at last, and end of the remarkable days. The springs and rivers have been very low. Millers have not water enough to grind their grists.

There has been a great fall of leaves in the night on account of this moist and rainy weather; but hardly yet that touch that brings down the rock maple. The streets are thickly strewn with elm and buttonwood and other leaves, *feuille-morte* color. Some elms and butternuts are quite bare. Yet the sugar maples in our streets are now in their prime and show unexpectedly bright and delicate tints, while some white maples by the river are nearly bare. I see, too, that all locusts did not become crisp and fall before this without acquiring a bright color. In the churchyard they are unwithered, just turning a pale yellow. How many plants are either yellow or scarlet! Not only maples, but rose bushes, hazel bushes, etc., etc. Rue is a conspicuous pale yellow for a weed.[1]

---

[1] *Vide* 20th, 1858.

I saw the other day a cricket standing on his head in a chocolate-colored (inside) fungus, only his tail-yards visible. He had sunk a well an inch deep, and was even then sinking it, perpendicularly, unconscious of what was going on above.

The ten days — at least — before this were plainly Indian summer. They were remarkably pleasant and warm. The latter half I sat and slept with an open window, though the first part of the time I had a little fire in the morning. These succeeded to days when you had worn thick clothing and sat by fires for some time.

Our staghorn sumach has just become a very rich scarlet. So, apparently, has the large one at Mrs. Simmonds's. They are later than the others; a yellower scarlet, almost orange.

It is another example of the oddity of the Orientals that yellow "is in the east a regal color, more especially so in China, where it is exclusively royal." (Field on Colors, 139.) Further west it was purple, regal and imperial.

The river lower this morning than before this year. Concord Bank has suspended.

Oct. 16. *Friday.* P. M. — Up Assabet.
It clears up *entirely* by noon, having been cloudy in the forenoon, and is as warm as before now. I stop a while at Cheney's shore to hear an incessant musical twittering from a large flock of young goldfinches which have dull-yellow and drab and black plumage, on maples, etc., while the leaves are falling. Young birds can hardly restrain themselves, and if they did not leave us, might

perchance burst forth into song in the *later* Indian-summer days.

I see dwarf cornel leaves on the hemlock bank, some green, some bright crimson. The onoclea has faded whiter still. Hemlock leaves are falling now faster than ever, and the trees are more parti-colored. The falling leaves look pale-yellow on the trees, but become reddish on the ground. The large poplar (*P. grandidentata*) is now at the height of its change, — clear yellow, but many leaves have fallen. The ostrya still holds its leaves. It is about the color of the elm at its height. I see red oaks now turned various colors, — red-brown or yellow-brown or scarlet-brown, — not commonly bright. The swamp white are greener yet.

Melvin is fishing for pickerel. Thinks this the best day for fishing we have had this long time; just wind enough. Says there are some summer ducks up the stream, the same I saw here the other day. Thinks they are here after acorns. He once caught seven summer ducks by baiting his steel traps with acorns under water. They dove for them, and he caught them by the neck. He saw yesterday a green chestnut bur on the Great Meadows (now bare), fifty rods from the Holt. Could not tell how it came there.

Am surprised to find an abundance of witch-hazel, now at the height of its change, where S. Wheeler cut off, at the bend of the Assabet. The tallest bushes are bare, though in bloom, but the lowest are full of leaves, many of them green, but chiefly clear and handsome yellow of various shades, from a pale lemon in the shade or within the bush to a darker and warmer yellow with-

out. Some are even a hue of crimson; some green, with bright yellow along the veins. This reminds me that, generally, plants exposed turn early, or not at all, while the same species in the shade of the woods at a much later date assume very pure and delicate tints, as more withdrawn from the light.

You notice now many faded, almost white dicksonia ferns, and some brakes about as white.

A great part of the pine-needles have just fallen. See the carpet of pale-brown needles under this pine. How light it lies up on the grass, and that great rock, and the wall, resting thick on its top and its shelves, and on the bushes and underwood, hanging lightly! They are not yet flat and reddish, but a more delicate pale brown, and lie up light as joggle-sticks just dropped. The ground is nearly concealed by them. How beautifully they die, making cheerfully their annual contribution to the soil! They fall to rise again; as if they knew that it was not one annual deposit alone that made this rich mould in which pine trees grow. They live in the soil whose fertility and bulk they increase, and in the forests that spring from it.

The leaves that were floating before the rain have now sunk to the bottom, being wetted above as well as below.

I see a delicate pale brown-bronze wood frog. I think I can always take them up in my hand. They, too, vary in color, like the leaves of many species of plants at present, having now more yellow, now more red; and perhaps for the same reason.

I saw some blackbirds, apparently grackles, singing,

after their fashion, on a tree by the river. Most had those grayish-brown heads and necks; some, at least, much ferruginous or reddish brown reflected. They were pruning themselves and splitting their throats in vain, trying to sing as the other day. All the melody flew off in splinters.[1] Also a robin sings once or twice, just as in spring!

I think that the principal stages in the autumnal changes of trees are these, thus far, as I remember, this year: —

First, there were in September the few prematurely blushing white maples, or blazing red ones in water, that reminded us of October. Next, the red maple swamps blazed out in all their glory, attracting the eyes of all travellers and contrasting with other trees. And hard upon these came the ash trees and yellowing birches, and walnuts, and elms, and the sprout-land oaks, the last streaking the hillsides far off, often occupying more commanding positions than the maples. All these add their fires to those of the maples. But even yet the summer is unconquered. Now the red maple fires are gone out (very few exceptions), and the brightness of those accompanying fires is dulled, their leaves falling; but a general, though duller, fire, yellowish or red, growing more reddish, has seized the masses of the forest, and betrays the paucity of the evergreens, but mingled with it are the delicate tints of aspens, etc., and, beneath, of protected underwoods whose exposed specimens gave us such promise.

What is acorn-color! Is it not as good as chestnut?[2]

[1] [Channing, p. 105.]   [2] [Channing, p. 106.]

Vol. X

Oct. 17. Saturday. Very high wind in the night, shaking the house. I feel it taking hold under the eaves, which project at the end of the house, each time with a jerk. Some rain also, and these two bring down the leaves. A great many more ash trees, elms, etc., are bare now.

What a new beauty the blue of the river acquires, seen at a distance in the midst of the various-tinted woods, great masses of red and yellow, etc.! It appears as color, which ordinarily it does not, — elysian.

The trainers are out with their band of music, and I find my account in it, though I have not subscribed for it. I am walking with a hill between me and the soldiers. I think, perhaps, it will be worth the while to keep within hearing of these strains this afternoon. Yet I hesitate. I am wont to find music unprofitable; it is a luxury. It is surprising, however, that so few habitually intoxicate themselves with music, so many with alcohol. I think, perchance, I may risk it, it will whet my senses so; it will reveal a glory where none was seen before. It is remarkable that men too must dress in bright colors and march to music once in the year. Nature, too, assumes her bright hues now, and think you a subtile music may not be heard amid the hills? No doubt these strains do sometimes suggest to Abner, walking behind in his red-streaked pants, an ideal which he had lost sight of, or never perceived. It is remarkable that our institutions can stand before music, it is so revolutionary.

P. M. — To Clintonia Swamp.

Glossy-brown white oak acorns strew the ground thickly, many of them sprouted. How soon they have sprouted! I find some quite edible, but they too, like

wild apples, require an outdoor appetite. I do not admit their palatableness when I try them in the house. Is not the outdoor appetite the one to be prayed for?

The cinnamon ferns surrounding the swamp have just lost their leafets, except the terminal ones. They have acquired their November aspect, and the wool now adheres to my clothes as I go through them. The protected ones are not yet bare. The dicksonia ferns are killed sere and brown where exposed, but in woods are still pretty green even, only some faded white. They grow in patches.

The swamp floor is covered with red maple leaves, many yellow with bright-scarlet spots or streaks. Small brooks are almost concealed by them. The *Lycopodium lucidulum* looks suddenly greener amid the withered leaves.[1]

It is cooler to-day, and a fire is necessary, which I have not had for about a week. The mountains are more distinct in the horizon, and as I come home the sunset sky is white and cold; recently it was a warm orange (?) tint.

Oct. 18. P. M. — To Conantum.

Clear and pleasant afternoon, but cooler than before. At the brook beyond Hubbard's Grove, I stand to watch the water-bugs (*Gyrinus*). The shallow water appears now more than usually clear there, as the weather is cooler, and the shadows of these bugs on the bottom, half a dozen times as big as themselves, are very distinct and interesting, with a narrow and well-defined

[1] [*Excursions*, p. 266; Riv. 326.]

halo about them. But why are they composed, as it were, of two circles run together, the foremost largest? Is it owing to the manner in which the light falls on their backs, in two spots? You think that the insect must be amused with this pretty shadow. I also see plainly the shadows of ripples they make, which are scarcely perceptible on the surface.

Many alders and birches just bare.

I should say that the autumnal change and brightness of foliage began fairly with the red maples (not to speak of a very few premature trees in water) September 25th, and ends this year, say generally October 22d, or maybe two or three days earlier. The fall of the leaf, in like way, began fairly with the fall of the red maple leaves, October 13th, and ended at least as early as when the pitch pines had *generally* fallen, November 5th (the larches are about a week later). The red maples are now fairly bare, though you may occasionally see one full of leaves.

So gradually the leaves fall, after all, — though individuals will be completely stripped in one short windy rain-storm, — that you scarcely miss them out of the landscape; but the earth grows more bare, and the fields more hoary, and the heavy shadows that began in June take their departure, November being at hand.

I go along the sunny west side of the Holden wood. Snakes lie out now on sunny banks, amid the dry leaves, now as in spring. They are chiefly striped ones. They crawl off a little into the bushes, and rest there half-concealed till I am gone.

The bass and the black ash are completely bare;

how long? Red cedar is fallen and falling. Looking across to the sprout-land beneath the Cliffs, I see that the pale brown of withered oak leaves begins to be conspicuous, amid the red, in sprout-lands.

In Lee's Wood, white pine leaves are now fairly fallen (not pitch pine yet), — a pleasant, soft, but slippery carpet to walk on. They sometimes spread leafy twigs on floors. Would not these be better? Where the pines stand far apart on grassy pasture hillsides, these tawny patches under each tree contrast singularly with the green around. I see them under one such tree completely and evenly covering and concealing the grass, and more than an inch deep, as they lie lightly. These leaves, like other, broader ones, pass through various hues (or shades) from green to brown, — first yellow, giving the tree that parti-colored look, then pale brown when they fall, then reddish brown after lying on the ground, and then darker and darker brown when decaying.

I see many robins on barberry bushes, probably after berries. The red oaks I see to-day are full of leaves, — a brownish yellow (with more or less green, but no red or scarlet). I find an abundance of those small, densely clustered grapes, — not the smallest quite, — still quite fresh and full on green stems, and leaves crisp but not all fallen; so much later than other grapes, which were further advanced October 4th when it was too late to get many. These are not yet ripe and may fairly be called frost grapes. Half-way up Blackberry Steep, above the rock. The huckleberries on Conantum appear to have been softened and spoilt by

the recent rain, for they are quite thick still on many bushes. Their leaves have fallen. So many leaves have now fallen in the woods that a squirrel cannot run after a nut without being heard.

As I was returning over Hubbard's stump fence pasture, I heard some of the common black field crickets [1] (three quarters of an inch long), two or three rods before me, make, as I thought, a peculiar shrilling, like a clear and sharp twittering of birds, [so that I looked up for some time to see a flock of small birds going over, but they did not arrive. These fellows were, one or two, at the mouth of their burrows, and as I stood over one I saw how he produced the sound, by very slightly lifting his wing-cases (if that is the name of them), and shuffling them (transversely of course) over each other about an eighth of an inch, perhaps three or four times, and then stopping. Thus they stand at the mouths of their burrows, in the warm pastures, near the close of the year, shuffling their wing-cases over each other (the males only), and produce this sharp but pleasant creaking sound, — helping to fetch the year about. Thus the sounds of human industry and activity — the roar of cannon, blasting of rocks, whistling of locomotives, rattling of carts, tinkering of artisans, and voices of men — may sound to some distant ear like an earth-song and the creaking of crickets. The crickets keep about the mouths of their burrows as if apprehending cold.

The fringed gentian closes every night and opens every morning in my pitcher.

[1] *Acheta abbreviata.*

Vol. X

Oct. 19. Mr. Sanborn tells me that he looked off from Wachusett last night, and that he saw the shadow of the mountain gradually extend itself eastward not only over the earth but finally *on to the sky* in the horizon. Thought it extended as much as two diameters of the moon on to the sky, in a small cone. This was like the spectre of the Brocken.

Harris says the crickets produce their shrilling by shuffling their wing-covers together *lengthwise*. I should have said it was sidewise, or transversely to the insect's length, as I looked down on it. You may see these crickets now everywhere in the ruts, as in the cross-road from the Turnpike to the Great Road, creeping along, or oftenest three or four together, absorbed in feeding on, *i. e.* sucking the juices of, a crushed companion. There are two broad ruts made by ox-carts loaded with muck, and a cricket has been crushed or wounded every four or five feet in each. It is one long slaughter-house. But as often as a cart goes by, the survivors each time return quickly to their seemingly luscious feast. At least two kinds there.

Oct. 20. P. M. — To the Easterbrooks Country.

I go along the riverside and by Dakin the pump-maker's. There is a very strong northwest wind, Novemberish and cool, raising waves on the river and admonishing to prepare for winter.

I see two *Chenopodium album* with stems as bright purple and fair as the poke has been, and the calyx-lobes enveloping the seeds the same color.

Apples are gathered; only the ladders here and there, left leaning against the trees.

I had gone but little way on the old Carlisle road when I saw Brooks Clark, who is now about eighty and bent like a bow, hastening along the road, barefooted, as usual, with an axe in his hand; was in haste perhaps on account of the cold wind on his bare feet. It is he who took the *Centinel* so long. When he got up to me, I saw that besides the axe in one hand, he had his shoes in the other, filled with knurly apples and a dead robin. He stopped and talked with me a few moments; said that we had had a noble autumn and might now expect some cold weather. I asked if he had found the robin dead. No, he said, he found it with its wing broken and killed it. He also added that he had found some apples in the woods, and as he hadn't anything to carry them in, he put 'em in his shoes. They were queer-looking trays to carry fruit in. How many he got in along toward the toes, I don't know. I noticed, too, that his pockets were stuffed with them. His old tattered frock coat was hanging in strips about the skirts, as were his pantaloons about his naked feet. He appeared to have been out on a scout this gusty afternoon, to see what he could find, as the youngest boy might. It pleased me to see this cheery old man, with such a feeble hold on life, bent almost double, thus enjoying the evening of his days. Far be it from me to call it avarice or penury, this childlike delight in finding something in the woods or fields and carrying it home in the October evening, as a trophy to be added to his winter's store. Oh, no;

he was happy to be Nature's pensioner still, and bird-like to pick up his living. Better his robin than your turkey, his shoes full of apples than your barrels full; they will be sweeter and suggest a better tale. He can afford to tell how he got them, and we to listen. There is an old wife, too, at home, to share them and hear how they were obtained. Like an old squirrel shuffling to his hole with a nut. Far less pleasing to me the loaded wain, more suggestive of avarice and of spiritual penury.

This old man's cheeriness was worth a thousand of the church's sacraments and *memento mori*'s. It was better than a prayerful mood. It proves to me old age as tolerable, as happy, as infancy. I was glad of an occasion to suspect that this afternoon he had not been at "work" but living somewhat after my own fashion (though he did not explain the axe), — had been out to see what nature had for him, and now was hastening home to a burrow he knew, where he could warm his old feet. If he had been a young man, he would probably have thrown away his apples and put on his shoes when he saw me coming, for shame. But old age is manlier; it has learned to live, makes fewer apologies, like infancy. This seems a very manly man. I have known him within a few years building stone wall by himself, barefooted. I keep along the old Carlisle road. The leaves having mostly fallen, the country now seems deserted, and you feel further from home and more lonely. I see where squirrels, apparently, have gnawed the apples left in the road. The barberry bushes are now alive with, I should say, thousands

of robins feeding on them. They must make a principal part of their food now. I see the yellowish election-cake fungi. Those large chocolate-colored ones have been burst some days (at least).

Warren Brown, who owns the Easterbrooks place, the west side the road, is picking barberries. Allows that the soil thereabouts is excellent for fruit, but it is so rocky that he has not patience to plow it. That is the reason this tract is not cultivated. The yellow birches are generally bare. The sassafras in Sted Buttrick's pasture near to E. Hubbard's Wood, nearly so; leaves all withered. Much or most of the fever-bush still green, though somewhat wrinkled.[1]

There was Melvin, too, a-barberrying and nutting. He had got two baskets, one in each hand, and his game-bag, which hung from his neck, all full of nuts and barberries, and his mouth full of tobacco. Trust him to find where the nuts and berries grow. He is hunting all the year and he marks the bushes and the trees which are fullest, and when the time comes, for once leaves his gun, though not his dog, at home, and takes his baskets to the spot. It is pleasanter to me to meet him with his gun or with his baskets than to meet some portly caterer for a family, basket on arm, at the stalls of Quincy Market. Better Melvin's pignuts than the others' shagbarks. It is to be observed that the best things are generally most abused, and so are not so much enjoyed as the worst. Shagbarks are eaten by epicures with diseased appetites; pignuts by the country boys who gather them. So

[1] Fever-bush in '61, Oct. 9th, at height of change!!

fagots and rubbish yield more comfort than sound wood.

Melvin says he has caught partridges in his hands. If there's only one hole, knows they've not gone out. Sometimes shoots them through the snow.

What a wild and rich domain that Easterbrooks Country! Not a cultivated, hardly a cultivatable field in it, and yet it delights all natural persons, and feeds more still. Such great rocky and moist tracts, which daunt the farmer, are reckoned as unimproved land, and therefore worth but little; but think of the miles of huckleberries, and of barberries, and of wild apples, so fair, both in flower and fruit, resorted to by men and beasts; Clark, Brown, Melvin, and the robins, these, at least, were attracted thither this afternoon. There are barberry bushes or clumps there, behind which I could actually pick two bushels of berries without being seen by you on the other side. And they are not a quarter picked at last, by all creatures together. I walk for two or three miles, and still the clumps of barberries, great sheaves with their wreaths of scarlet fruit, show themselves before me and on every side, seeming to issue from between the pines or other trees, as if it were they that were promenading there, not I.

That very dense and handsome maple and pine grove opposite the pond-hole on this old Carlisle road is Ebby Hubbard's.[1] Melvin says there are those alive who remember mowing there. Hubbard loves to come with his axe in the fall or winter and trim up his woods.

[1] Sted Buttrick's, according to Melvin.

Melvin tells me that Skinner says he thinks he heard a wildcat scream in E. Hubbard's Wood, by the Close. It is worth the while to have a Skinner in the town; else we should not know that we had wildcats. They had better look out, or he will skin them, for that seems to have been the trade of his ancestors. How long Nature has manœuvred to bring our Skinner within ear-shot of that wildcat's scream! Saved Ebby's wood to be the scene of it! Ebby, the *wood-saver*.

Melvin says that Sted sold the principal log of one of those pasture oaks to Garty for ten dollars and got several cords besides. What a mean bribe to take the life of so noble a tree!

Wesson is so gouty that he rarely comes out-of-doors, and is a spectacle in the street; but he loves to tell his old stories still! How, when he was stealing along to get a shot at his ducks, and was just upon them, a red squirrel sounded the alarm, *chickaree chickaree chickaree*, and off they went; but he turned his gun upon the squirrel to avenge himself.

It would seem as if men generally could better appreciate honesty of the John Beatton stamp, which gives you your due to a mill, than the generosity which habitually throws in the half-cent.

Oct. 21. First ice that I've seen or heard of, a tenth of an inch thick in yard, and the ground is slightly frozen.

I see many myrtle-birds now about the house this forenoon, on the advent of cooler weather. They keep flying up against the house and the window and fluttering there, as if they would come in, or alight on the wood-pile or pump. They would commonly be mistaken for sparrows, but show more white when they fly, beside the yellow on the rump and sides of breast seen near to and two white bars on the wings. Chubby birds.

P. M. — Up Assabet.

Cool and windy. Those who have put it off thus long make haste now to collect what apples were left out and dig their potatoes before the ground shall freeze hard. Now again, as in the spring, we begin to look for sheltered and sunny places where we may sit.

I see, hanging over an alder bough above the hemlocks, five inches above the water, a great eel, over two feet long and two inches wide or thick horizontally (more vertically) in the forward part of its body. It must weigh two and a half pounds; the biggest I ever saw. What a repulsive and gluttonous-looking creature, with its vomer made to plow the mud and wallow in filth, and its slimy skin (I had forgotten it was scaly, it is so fine). It was somewhat bloated, perhaps, and its skin distended, but at any rate it had got its skin full. It is more repulsive to me than a snake, and I think must be less edible. Its dead-white eye-spots — for the eyes were closed flat on its black and shiny vomer — and the fringed gelatinous kind of alga or what-not that covered like a lichen the parts submerged made it yet more repulsive.

I cannot go by a large dead swamp white oak log this cool evening, but with no little exertion get it aboard, and some blackened swamp white oak stumps, whose

earthy parts are all gone. I see a robin eating prinos berries. Is not the robin the principal berry-eating bird nowadays? There must be more about the barberry bushes in Melvin's Preserve than anywhere.

As I am paddling home swiftly before the northwest wind, absorbed in my wooding, I see, this cool and grayish evening, that peculiar yellow light in the east, from the sun a little before its setting. It has just come out beneath a great cold slate-colored cloud that occupies most of the western sky, as smaller ones the eastern, and now its rays, slanting over the hill in whose shadow I float, fall on the eastern trees and hills with a thin yellow light like a clear yellow wine, but somehow it reminds me that now the hearth-side is getting to be a more comfortable place than out-of-doors. Before I get home the sun has set and a cold white light in the west succeeded.

I saw wood tortoises coupled, up the Assabet, the back of the upper above water. It held the lower with its claws about the head, and they were not to be parted.

It is pitiful to see a man of sixty, a philosopher, perchance, inquiring for a bearing apple orchard for sale. If he must have one, why did he not set it out when he was thirty? How mean and lazy, to be plucking the fruit of another man's labor. The old man I saw yesterday lives on peaches and milk in their season, but then he planted them.

Is not the poet bound to write his own biography? Is there any other work for him but a good journal? We do not wish to know how his imaginary hero, but how he, the actual hero, lived from day to day.

Vol. X

That big swamp white oak limb or tree which I found prostrate in the swamp was longer than my boat and tipped it well. One whole side, the upper, was covered with green hypnum, and the other was partly white with fungi. That green coat adhered when I split it. Immortal wood! that had begun to live again. Others burn unfortunate trees that lose their lives prematurely. These old stumps stand like anchorites and yogees, putting off their earthy garments, more and more sublimed from year to year, ready to be translated, and then they are ripe for my fire. I administer the last sacrament and purification. I find old pitch pine sticks which have lain in the mud at the bottom of the river, nobody knows how long, and weigh them up, — almost as heavy as lead, — float them home, saw and split them. Their pitch, still fat and yellow, has saved them for me, and they burn like candles at last. I become a connoisseur in wood at last, take only the best.

Oct. 22. 6 A. M. — To Hill.

Ground pretty white with frost. The stiffened and frosted weeds and grass have an aggrieved look. The lately free-flowing blades of grass look now like mourning tresses sculptured stiffly in marble; they lie stiff and dishevelled. A very narrow strip of ice has formed along the riverside, in which I see a pad or two, wearing the same aggrieved look, like the face of the child that cried for spilt milk, its summer irrevocably gone. Going through the stiff meadow-grass, I collect the particles of white frost on the top of my shoes. Under

the ash trees their peculiar club-shaped leaf-stems thickly strew the ground. The bright tints of autumn are now fairly and generally over. Perhaps the brightest *trees* I see this moment are some aspens. Large oaks are already generally brown. Reddish brown is the prevailing color of deciduous woods. The swamp white oaks are greener than the rest yet. The black willows along the river are about as bare as in November. The button-bushes are completely bare, letting in more light to the water, and these days I see on their stems the ribbed reflections of the waves I have made. Blackbirds go over, chattering, and a small hawk — pigeon or sparrow — glides along and alights on an elm.

P. M. — To and round Flint's Pond.

Crossing my old bean-field, I see the blue pond between the green white pines in the field and am reminded that we are almost reduced to the russet (*i. e.* pale-brown grass tinged with red blackberry vines) of such fields as this, the blue of water, the green of pines, and the dull reddish brown of oak leaves. The sight of the blue water between the now perfectly green white pines, seen over the light-brown pasture, is peculiarly Novemberish, though it may be like this in early spring.

As I go through the woods now, so many oak and other leaves have fallen the rustling noise somewhat disturbs my musing. However, Nature in this may have intended some kindness to the ducks, which are now loitering hereabouts on their migration southward, mostly young and inexperienced birds, for, as they are feeding [in] Goose Pond, for instance, the rustling of the leaves betrays the approach of the sportsman and his dog, or other foe; so perhaps the leaves on the ground protect them more than when on the trees.

There is scarcely a square rod of sand exposed, in this neighborhood, but you may find on it the stone arrowheads of an extinct race. Far back as that time seems when men went armed with bows and pointed stones here, yet so numerous are the signs of it. The finer particles of sand are blown away and the arrow-point remains. The race is as clean gone — from here — as this sand is clean swept by the wind. Such are our antiquities. These were our predecessors. Why, then, make so great ado about the Roman and the Greek, and neglect the Indian? We [need] not wander off with boys in our imaginations to Juan Fernandez, to wonder at footprints in the sand there. Here is a print still more significant at our doors, the print of a race

 that has preceded us, and this the little symbol that Nature has transmitted to us. Yes, *this* arrow-headed character is probably more ancient than any other, and to my mind it has not been deciphered. Men should not go to New Zealand to write or think of Greece and Rome, nor more to New England. New earths, new themes expect us. Celebrate not the Garden of Eden, but your own.

I see what I call a hermit thrush on the bushes by

Vol. X

the shore of Flint's Pond; pretty tame. It has an olive-brown back, with a more ferruginous tail, which [is] very narrowly tipped with whitish; an apparently cream-colored throat; and dusky cream-color beneath. The breast is richly spotted with black. The legs are flesh-colored and transparent; the bill black. Yet Wilson says the legs are dusky. Can it be the *Turdus olivaceus* of Giraud?

Chestnut trees are almost bare. Now is just the time for chestnuts. The white oak generally withers earlier than other large oaks. On the north side of the chestnut oak hill, in the woods, I see a scarlet oak and even a white one, still almost entirely green! The chestnut oak there is also generally green still, some leaves turned yellow-brown and withering so.

Look from the high hill, just before sundown, over the pond. The mountains are a mere cold slate-color. But what a perfect crescent of mountains we have in our northwest horizon! Do we ever give thanks for it? Even as pines and larches and hemlocks grow in communities in the wilderness, so, it seems, do mountains love society and form a community in the horizon. Though there may be two or more ranges, one behind the other, and ten or twelve miles between them, yet if the farthest are the highest, they are all seen as one group at this distance. I look up northwest toward my mountains, as a farmer to his hill lot or rocky pasture from his door. I drive no cattle to Ipswich hills. I own no pasture for them there. My eyes it is alone that wander to those blue pastures, which no drought affects. They are my flocks and herds. See how they

look. They are shaped like tents, inclining to sharp peaks. What is it lifts them upward so? Why not rest level along the horizon? They seem not perfect, they seem not satisfied, until their central parts have curved upward to a sharp summit. They are a succession of pickets with scallops between. That side my pasture is well fenced. This being their upper side, I fancy they must have a corresponding under side and roots also. Might they not be dug up like a turnip? Perhaps they spring from seeds which some wind sowed. Can't the Patent Office import some of the seed of Himmaleh with its next rutabagas? Spore of mountains has fallen there; it came from the gills of an agaric. Ah, I am content to dwell there and see the sun go down behind my mountain fence.

It is just about nine miles, as I walk, from here around Flint's Pond.

The hickory leaves, now after they have fallen, are often if not oftenest a dark rich yellow, very conspicuous upon the brown leaves of the forest floor, seeming to have more life in them than those leaves which are brown. I saw some hickory sprouts above the perfoliate bellwort near the pond, with very large leaves. One of five leafets had the terminal one fourteen inches long by ten and three quarters wide, and the general leaf-stalk was ten and a half inches long.

The leaf-stalk commonly adheres to the leaf when fallen, but in the case of the ash, hickory, and probably other compound leaves, it separates from them and by its singular form puzzles the uninitiated.

What a perfect chest the chestnut is packed in! I

now hold a green bur in my hand which, round, must have been two and a quarter inches in diameter, from which three plump nuts have been extracted. It has a straight, stout stem three sixteenths of an inch in diameter, set on strongly and abruptly. It has gaped in four segments or quarters, revealing the thickness of its walls, from five eighths to three quarters of an inch. With such wonderful care Nature has secluded and defended these nuts, as if they were her most precious fruits, while diamonds are left to take care of themselves. First it bristles all over with sharp green prickles, some nearly half an inch long, like a hedgehog rolled into a ball; these rest on a thick, stiff, bark-like rind, one sixteenth to one eighth of an inch thick, which, again, is most daintily lined with a kind of silvery fur or velvet plush one sixteenth of an inch thick, even rising in a ridge between the nuts, like the lining of a casket in which the most precious commodities are kept. I see the brown-spotted white cavities where the bases of the nuts have rested and sucked up nourishment from the stem. The little stars on the top of the nuts are but shorter and feebler spines which mingle with the rest. They stand up close together, three or more, erecting their tiny weapons, as an infant in the brawny arms of its nurse might put out its own tiny hands, to fend off the aggressor. There is no waste room. The chest is packed quite full; half-developed nuts are the waste paper used in the packing, to fill the vacancies. At last Frost comes to unlock this chest; it alone holds the true key. Its lids straightway gape open, and the October air rushes in, dries the ripe nuts, and then with a ruder gust shakes them all out in a rattling shower down upon the withered leaves.

Such is the cradle, thus daintily lined, in which they have been rocked in their infancy. With what steadiness the nuts must be held within these stout arms, — there can be no motion on their base, — and yet how tenderly, by a firm hold that relaxes only as they grow, the walls that confine them, superfluously strong as they seem, expanding as they grow!

The chestnut, with its tough shell, looks as if it were able to protect itself, but see how tenderly it has been reared in its cradle before its green and tender skin hardened into a shell. The October air comes in, as I have said, and the light too, and proceed to paint the nuts that clear, handsome reddish (?) brown which we call chestnut. Nowadays the brush that paints chestnuts is very active. It is entering into every open bur over the stretching forests' tops for hundreds of miles, without horse or ladder, and putting on rapid coats of this wholesome color. Otherwise the boys would not think they had got perfect nuts. And that this may be further protected, perchance, both within the bur and afterward, the nuts themselves are partly covered toward the top, where they are first exposed, with that same soft velvety down. And then Nature drops it on the rustling leaves, a *done* nut, prepared to begin a chestnut's course again. Within itself, again, each individual nut is lined with a reddish velvet, as if to preserve the seed from jar and injury in falling and, perchance, from sudden damp and cold, and, within that, a thin white skin enwraps the germ. Thus it is lining

within lining and unwearied care, — not to count closely, six coverings at least before you reach the contents!

But it is a barbarous way to jar the tree, and I trust I do repent of it. Gently shake it only, or let the wind shake it for you. You are gratified to find a nut that has in it no bitterness, altogether palatable.

Oct. 23. P. M. — Up Assabet.

The ferns which I can see on the bank, apparently all evergreens, are polypody at rock, marginal shield fern, terminal shield fern, and (I think it is) *Aspidium spinulosum*, which I had not identified. Apparently *Aspidium cristatum* elsewhere.[1]

I can find no bright leaves now in the woods. Witch-hazel, etc., are withered, turned brown, or yet green. See by the droppings in the woods where small migrating birds have roosted.

I see a squirrel's nest in a white pine, recently made, on the hillside near the witch-hazels.

The high bank-side is mostly covered with fallen leaves of pines and hemlocks, etc. The above-named evergreen ferns are so much the more conspicuous on that pale-brown ground. They stand out all at once and are seen to be evergreen; their character appears. The fallen pine-needles, as well as other leaves, now actually paint the surface of the earth brown in the woods, covering the green and other colors, and the few evergreen plants on the forest floor stand out distinct and have a rare preëminence.

Sal Cummings, a thorough countrywoman, conversant

[1] *Vide* pp. [134] and [149].

with nuts and berries, calls the soapwort gentian "blue vengeance," mistaking the word. A masculine wild-eyed woman of the fields. Somebody has her daguerreotype. When Mr. —— was to lecture on Kansas, she was sure "she wa'n't going to hear him. None of her folks had ever had any."

Oct. 24. P. M. — To Smith's chestnut grove.

Rain last night, raising the springs a little. To-day and yesterday still, gray days, but not cold. The sugar maple leaves are now falling fast.

I get a couple of quarts of chestnuts by patiently brushing the thick beds of leaves aside with my hand in successive concentric circles till I reach the trunk; more than half under one tree. I believe I get more by resolving, where they are reasonably thick, to pick all under one tree first. Begin at the tree and brush the leaves with your right hand in toward the stump, while your left holds the basket, and so go round and round it in concentric circles, each time laying bare about two feet in width, till you get as far as the boughs extend. You may presume that you have got about all then. It is best to reduce it to a system. Of course you will shake the tree first, if there are any on it. The nuts lie commonly two or three together, as they fell.

I find on a chestnut tree, while shaking it, fifteen or twenty feet high, on the bark of the trunk, a singular green kind of slug nearly half an inch long, of this form, and about three sixteenths high from the paper up, narrower on back, as appears in sketch; a brown mark across middle of

back and near tail as drawn (only full). It can elongate itself and also run out its head a little from beneath this soft kind of shell. Beneath, quite flat and fleshy-ribbed. Climbs up glass slowly but easily. Reminds me of a green beechnut, but flat-backed. Would hardly suspect it to have life at first sight. Sticks very firmly to the bark or glass; hard to be pushed aside.

I find one of those small, hard, dark-brown millipede worms partly crawled into a hole in a chestnut.

I read of an apple tree in this neighborhood that had blossomed again about a week ago.

I find my account in this long-continued monotonous labor of picking chestnuts all the afternoon, brushing the leaves aside without looking up, absorbed in that, and forgetting better things awhile. My eye is educated to discover anything on the ground, as chestnuts, etc. It is probably wholesomer to look at the ground much than at the heavens. As I go stooping and brushing the leaves aside by the hour, I am not thinking of chestnuts merely, but I find myself humming a thought of more significance. This occupation affords a certain broad pause and opportunity to start again afterward, — turn over a new leaf.

I hear the dull thump of heavy stones against the trees from far through the rustling wood, where boys are ranging for nuts.

Oct. 25. Rain in night.
P. M. — By boat to Battle-Ground.
A rainy day and easterly wind, — an easterly storm.

I see flying very high over the meadow, from the east, eleven large birds, leisurely circling a little by the way, surveying the bare meadow. I think they must be fish hawks.

I am amused to see that Varro tells us that the Latin *e* represents the vowel sound in the bleat of a sheep (*Bee*). If he had said in any word pronounced by the Romans we should be not the wiser, but we do not doubt that sheep bleat to-day as they did then.

The fresh clamshells opened by the musquash begin to be conspicuous.

Oct. 26. Hard rain in the night and almost steady rain through the day, the second day. Wind still easterly or northeasterly.

P. M. — Round by Puffer's *via* Clamshell.

A driving east or northeast storm. I can see through the drisk only a mile. The river is getting partly over the meadows at last, and my spirits rise with it. Methinks this rise of the waters must affect every thought and deed in the town. It qualifies my sentence and life. I trust there will appear in this Journal some flow, some gradual filling of the springs and raising of the streams, that the accumulating grists may be ground. A storm is a new, and in some respects more active, life in nature. Larger migrating birds make their appearance. They, at least, sympathize with the movements of the watery element and the winds. I see two great fish hawks (*possibly* blue herons) slowly beating northeast against the storm, by what a curious tie circling ever near each other and in the same direction,

as if you might expect to find the very motes in the air to be paired; two long undulating wings conveying a feathered body through the misty atmosphere, and this inseparably associated with another planet of the same species. I can just glimpse their undulating lines. Damon and Pythias they must be. The waves beneath, which are of kindred form, are still more social, multitudinous, ἀνήριθμον. Where is my mate, beating against the storm with me? They fly according to the valley of the river, northeast or southwest.

I start up snipes also at Clamshell Meadow. This weather sets the migratory birds in motion and also makes them bolder.

These regular phenomena of the seasons get at last to be — they were *at first*, of course — simply and plainly phenomena or phases of my life. The seasons and all their changes are in me. I see not a dead eel or floating snake, or a gull, but it rounds my life and is like a line or accent in its poem. Almost I believe the Concord would not rise and overflow its banks again, were I not here. After a while I learn what my moods and seasons are. I would have nothing subtracted. I can imagine nothing added. My moods are thus periodical, not two days in my year alike. The perfect correspondence of Nature to man, so that he is at home in her!

Going along the road toward the bæomyces, I see, as I think, a space a yard or two square where the bank has been [burnt] over by accident, by some traveller or sportsman. Even as I stand within four or five feet I take it to be so. It was the fallen leaves of the

Salix tristis, thickly covering the ground, so black, with an ashy reflection, that they look exactly like cinders of leaves. And the small twigs were also blackened and inconspicuous; I could hardly detect them. Just the right mingling of black and ash-color. It was a wet day, which made them look blacker. Mere evergreen mossy banks, as that by this road in the woods, now more attract us when greenness is so rare.

At the hewing-place on the flat above, many sparrows are flitting past amid the birches and sallows. They are chiefly *Fringilla hyemalis*. How often they may be [seen] thus flitting along in a straggling manner from bush to bush, so that the hedgerow will be all alive with them, each uttering a faint *chip* from time to time, as if to keep together, bewildering you so that you know not if the greater part are gone by or still to come. One rests but a moment on the tree before you and is gone again. You wonder if they know whither they are bound, and how their leader is appointed.

The pitch pine leaves not yet quite fallen. Yellowish leaves still adhere to the very tops of the birches.

Those sparrows, too, are thoughts I have. They come and go; they flit by quickly on their migrations, uttering only a faint *chip*, I know not whither or why exactly. One will not rest upon its twig for me to scrutinize it. The whole copse will be alive with my rambling thoughts, bewildering me by their very multitude, but they will be all gone directly without leaving me a feather. My loftiest thought is somewhat like an eagle that suddenly comes into the field of view, sug-

gesting great things and thrilling the beholder, as if it were bound hitherward with a message for me; but it comes no nearer, but circles and soars away, growing dimmer, disappointing me, till it is lost behind a cliff or a cloud.

Spring is brown; summer, green; autumn, yellow; winter, white; November, gray.

Oct. 27. P. M. — Up river.

The third day of steady rain; wind northeast. The river has now risen so far over the meadows that I can *just* cross Hubbard's Great Meadow in my boat.

Stedman Buttrick tells me that a great many ducks and large yellow-legs have been killed within a day or two. It is rather late for ducks generally. He says that the spruce swamp beyond Farmer's is called Fox Castle Swamp and has been a great place for foxes. Some days ago he was passing under a black oak on his land, when he saw the *dust* of acorn shells (or cups?) falling about him. Looking up, he saw as many as twenty (!) striped squirrels busily running out to ends of the twigs, biting off the nuts, running back and taking off the shells (cups?) and stowing the nuts away in their cheeks.

I go up the river as far as Hubbard's Second Grove, in order to share the general commotion and excitement of the elements, — wind and waves and rain. A half-dozen boats at the landing were full, and the waves beating over them. It was hard work getting at and hauling up and emptying mine. It was a rod and a half from the water's edge. Now look out for your rails and other fencing-stuff and loose lumber, lest it be floated off. I sailed swiftly, standing up and tipping my boat to make a keel of its side, though at first it was hard to keep off a lee shore. I looked for cranberries drifted up on the lee side of the meadows, but saw few. It was exciting to feel myself tossed by the dark waves and hear them surge about me. The reign of water now begins, and how it gambols and revels! Waves are its leaves, foam its blossoms. How they run and leap in great droves, deriving new excitement from each other! Schools of porpoises and blackfish are only more animated waves and have acquired the gait and game of the sea itself. The high wind and the dashing waves are very inspiriting. The clumps of that "west of rock" willow and a *discolor* are still thinly leaved, with peculiar silvery-yellow leaves in this light. The rising water is now rolling and washing up the river wreck of sparganium, etc., etc. Wool-grass tops appear thickly above the flood.

When I turn about, it requires all my strength and skill to push the boat back again. I must keep it pointed directly in the teeth of the wind. If it turns a little, the wind gets the advantage of me and I lose ground. The wind being against the stream makes it rise the faster, and also prevents the driftwood from coming down. How many a meadow my boat's bottom has rubbed over! I might perhaps consult with it respecting cranberry vines, cut-grass, pitcher-plant, etc., etc. I hear that Sammy Hoar saw geese go over to-day.

The fall (strictly speaking) is approaching an end in this probably annual northeast storm. Thus the

summer winds up its accounts. The Indians, it is said, did not look for winter till the springs were full. Long-continued rain and wind come to settle the accounts of the year, filling the springs for winter. The ducks and other fowl, reminded of the lateness thus, go by. The few remaining leaves come fluttering down. The snow-flea (as to-day) is washed out of the bark of meadow trees and covers the surface of the flood. The winter's wood is bargained for and being hauled. This storm reminds men to put things on a winter footing. There is not much more for the farmer to do in the fields.

The real facts of a poet's life would be of more value to us than any work of his art. I mean that the very scheme and form of his poetry (so called) is adopted at a sacrifice of vital truth and poetry. Shakespeare has left us his fancies and imaginings, but the truth of his life, with its becoming circumstances, we know nothing about. The writer is reported, the liver not at all. Shakespeare's house! how hollow it is! No man can conceive of Shakespeare in that house. But we want the basis of fact, of an actual life, to complete our Shakespeare, as much as a statue wants its pedestal. A poet's life with this broad actual basis would be as superior to Shakespeare's as a lichen, with its base or thallus, is superior in the order of being to a fungus.

The Littleton Giant brought us a load of coal within the week. He appears deformed and weakly, though naturally well formed. He does not nearly stand up straight. His knees knock together; they touch when

Vol. X

he is standing most upright, and so reduce his height at least three inches. He is also very round-shouldered and stooping, probably from the habit of crouching to conceal his height. He wears a low hat for the same purpose. The tallest man looks like a boy beside him. He has a seat to his wagon made on purpose for him. He habitually stops before all doors. You wonder what his horses think of him, — that a strange horse is not afraid of him. His voice is deep and full, but mild, for he is quite modest and retiring, — really a worthy man, 't is said. Pity he could n't have been undertaken by a committee in season and put through, like the boy Safford, been well developed bodily and also mentally, taught to hold up his head and not mind people's eyes or remarks. It is remarkable that the giants have never correspondingly great hearts.

Oct. 28. P. M. — To Conantum.

To-day it does not rain, but is cloudy all the day. Large oak leaves have been falling for a week at least, but the oaks are not yet reduced to their winter state. On the causeway I see fox-colored sparrows flitting along in the willows and alders, uttering a faint *cheep*, and tree sparrows with them. On a black willow, a single grackle with *the bright iris*. (I doubt if some of the brown-headed blackbirds I have seen within three weeks *were* grackles.)

As I sat at the wall-corner, high on Conantum, the sky generally covered with continuous cheerless-looking slate-colored clouds, except in the west, I saw, through the hollows of the clouds, here and there the

blue appearing. All at once a low-slanted glade of sunlight from one of heaven's west windows behind me fell on the bare gray maples, lighting them up with an incredibly intense and pure white light; then, going out there, it lit up some white birch stems south of the pond, then the gray rocks and the pale reddish young oaks of the lower cliffs, and then the very pale brown meadow-grass, and at last the brilliant white breasts of two ducks, tossing on the agitated surface far off on the pond, which I had not detected before. It was but a transient ray, and there was no sunshine afterward, but the intensity of the light was surprising and impressive, like a halo, a glory in which only the just deserved to live.

It was as if the air, purified by the long storm, reflected these few rays from side to side with a complete illumination, like a perfectly polished mirror, while the effect was greatly enhanced by the contrast with the dull dark clouds and sombre earth. As if Nature did not dare at once to let in the full blaze of the sun to this combustible atmosphere. It was a serene, elysian light, in which the deeds I have dreamed of but not realized might have been performed. At the eleventh hour, late in the year, we have visions of the life we might have lived. No perfectly fair weather ever offered such an arena for noble acts. It was such a light as we behold but dwell not in! In each case, every recess was filled and lit up with this pure white light. The maples were Potter's, far down stream, but I dreamed I walked like a liberated spirit in their maze. The withered meadow-grass was as soft and glorious as paradise. And then it was remarkable that the light-giver should have revealed to me, for all life, the heaving white breasts of those two ducks within this glade of light. It was extinguished and relit as it travelled.

Tell me precisely the value and significance of these transient gleams which come sometimes at the end of the day, before the close of the storm, final dispersion of the clouds, too late to be of any service to the works of man for the day, and notwithstanding the whole night after may be overcast! Is not this a language to be heard and understood? There is, in the brown and gray earth and rocks, and the withered leaves and bare twigs at this season, a purity more correspondent to the light itself than summer offers.

These two ducks, as near as I could see with my glass, were all dark above, back and wings, but had bright white breasts and necks. They were swimming and tacking about in the midst of the pond, with their heads half the time plunged beneath the surface. Were they grebes? or young sheldrakes? Even at this distance they warily withdraw still further off till I am gone.

Both aspleniums and the small botrychium are still fresh, as if they were evergreen. The latter sheds pollen. The former are most fresh under the shelter of rocks.

I look up and see a male marsh hawk with his clean-cut wings, that has just skimmed past above my head, — not at all disturbed, only tilting his body a little, now twenty rods off, with demi-semi-quaver of his wings. He is a very neat flyer. Again, I hear the scream

Vol. X

of a hen-hawk, soaring and circling onward. I do not often see the marsh hawk thus. What a regular figure this fellow makes on high, with his broad tail and broad wings! Does he perceive me, that he rises higher and circles to one side? He goes round now one full circle without a flap, tilting his wing a little; then flaps three or four times and rises higher. Now he comes on like a billow, screaming. Steady as a planet in its orbit, with his head bent down, but on second thought that small sprout-land seems worthy of a longer scrutiny, and he gives one circle backward over it. His scream is somewhat like the whinnering of a horse, if it is not rather a *split squeal*. It is a hoarse, tremulous breathing forth of his winged energy. But why is it so regularly repeated at that height? Is it to scare his prey, that he may see by its motion where it is, or to inform its mate or companion of its whereabouts? Now he crosses the at present broad river steadily, deserving to have one or two rabbits at least to swing about him. What majesty there is in this small bird's flight! The hawks are large-souled.

Those late grapes on Blackberry Steep are now as ripe as ever they will be. They are sweet and shrivelled but on the whole poor. They ripen there the latter part of October.

The white pine needles on the ground are already turned considerably redder. The pitch pines, which are yellower than the white when they fall, are three quarters fallen. I see some which look exactly like bamboo, very prettily barred with brown every tenth of an inch or so.

Going up the cliffy hillside, just north of the witch-hazel, I see a vigorous young apple tree, which, planted by birds or cows, has shot up amid the rocks and woods, and has much fruit on it and more beneath it, uninjured by the frosts, now when all other fruits are gathered. It is of a rank, wild growth, with many green leaves on it still, and makes an impression, at least, of thorniness. The fruit is hard and green, but looks like palatable winter fruit; some dangling on the twigs, but more half buried in the wet leaves, or rolled far down the hill amid the rocks. The owner, Lee, knows nothing of it. There is no hand to pluck its fruit; it is only gnawed by squirrels, I perceive. It has done double duty, — not only borne this crop, but each twig has grown a foot into the air. And this is such a fruit! Bigger than *many* berries, and carried home will be sound and palatable, perchance, next spring. Who knows but this chance wild fruit may be equal to those kinds which the Romans and the English have so prized, — may yet become the favorite of the nations? When I go by this shrub, thus late and hardy, and its dangling fruit strikes me, I respect the tree and am grateful for Nature's bounty.

Even the sourest and crabbedest apple, growing in the most unfavorable position, suggests such thoughts as these, it [is] so noble a fruit. Planted by a bird on a wild and rocky hillside, it bears a fruit, perchance, which foreign potentates shall hear of and send for, though the virtues of the owner of the soil may never be heard of beyond the limits of his village. It may be the choicest fruit of its kind. Every wild apple

shrub excites our expectation thus. It is a prince in disguise, perhaps.[1]

There is, apparently, limestone just above this apple tree.

I see pignuts which squirrels have industriously gnawed, the thick rind closely adhering, so that at last they are left brown and very rough; but in no case is the shell cut quite through, for, as I find, they contain no meat, but, under a shell of double thickness, a mere dry brown skin, and it seems the squirrels knew this!

Is that small fern (still partly green) *Aspidium cristatum*, at Lee's Cliff, northwest of the witch-hazel?

Suppose I see a single green apple, brought to perfection on some thorny shrub, far in a wild pasture where no cow has plucked it. It is an agreeable surprise. What chemistry has been at work there? It affects me somewhat like a work of art. I see some shrubs which cattle have browsed for twenty years, keeping them down and compelling them to spread, until at last they are so broad they become their own fence and some interior shoot darts upward and bears its fruit! What a lesson to man! So are human beings, referred to the highest standard, the celestial fruit which they suggest and aspire to bear, browsed on by fate, and only the most persistent and strongest genius prevails, defends itself, sends a tender scion upward at last, and drops its perfect fruit on the ungrateful earth; and that fruit, though somewhat smaller, perchance, is

[1] [*Excursions*, pp. 299–301, 307; Riv. 368, 369, 376, 377.]

essentially the same in flavor and quality as if it had grown in a garden. That fruit seems all the sweeter and more palatable even for the very difficulties it has contended with.

Here, on this rugged and woody hillside, has grown an apple tree, not planted by man, no relic of a former orchard, but a natural growth like the pines and oaks. Most fruits we prize and use depend entirely on our care. Corn and grain, potatoes, peaches (*here*), and melons, etc., depend altogether on our planting, but the apple emulates man's independence and enterprise. Like him to some extent, it has migrated to this new world and is ever here and there making its way amid the aboriginal trees. It accompanies man like the ox and dog and horse, which also sometimes run wild and maintain themselves.

Spite of wandering kine and other adverse circumstance, that scorned shrub, valued only by small birds as a covert, a shelter from hawks, has its blossom week, and in course its harvest, sincere, though small.[1]

> 'T was thirty years ago,
> In a rocky pasture field
> Sprang an infant apple grove
> Unplanted and concealed.
> I sing the wild apple, theme enough for me.
> I love the racy fruit and I reverence the tree.

In that small family there was one that loved the sun, which sent its root down deep and took fast hold on life, while the others went to sleep.

[1] [*Excursions*, pp. 300, 305–307; Riv. 369, 374–377.]

> In two years' time 't had thus
> Reached the level of the rocks,
> Admired the stretching world,
> Nor feared the wandering flocks.
> But at this tender age
> Its sufferings began:
> There came a browsing ox
> And cut it down a span.
> Its heart did bleed all day,
> And when the birds were hushed, —

Oct. 29. P. M. — Down river in boat.

Though it did not rain yesterday, as I remember, it was overcast all day, — did n't clear up, — and this forenoon it has rained again. The sun only comes out once or twice for a moment this afternoon.[1] Accordingly, this being the seventh day of cloud and the fourth of rain (skipping yesterday), the river is very high for the season and all over the meadow in front of the house, and still rising. Many are out (as yesterday) shooting musquash.

I see evidently what Storer calls the little brown snake (*Coluber ordinatus*), driven out of the grass of the meadow by the flood. Its head is raised to the surface for air, and it appears sluggish and enfeebled by the water. Putting out my paddle, it immediately coils about it and is raised into the boat. It has a distinct pale-pink abdomen, slightly bluish forward. Above it is pale-brown, with a still lighter brown stripe running down the middle of the back, on each side of

[1] This is the fall storm.

Vol. X

which is a line of dark-brown spots about an eighth of an inch apart, as the two lines are also an eighth of an inch apart. This snake is about one foot long. I hold it in my hand, and it is quite inoffensive.

The sun comes out once or twice, the water is smooth, and the cocks crow as in spring. As I am picking cranberries below Flint's Bridge, they being drifted against the shore together with much loose meadow wreck, I notice many crickets wrecked with them and half drowned, as well as snails' shells. Spiders, however, are in their element.

A flock of about eighty crows flies ramblingly over toward the sowing, cawing and loitering and making a great ado, apparently about nothing. I meet Goodwin and afterward Melvin. They are musquash-shooting. The latter has killed nineteen to-day downstream, thirty-one yesterday up the Assabet. He has also a coot, which he calls a little black dipper! It has some clear white under its tail. Is this, then, the name of that dipper? and are the young dippers of Moosehead different?[1] The latter were in flocks and had some white in front, I have said. Melvin asked if I had seen "Pink-eye," meaning Goodwin.

There is a large square-sided black rock, say five or six feet high, eight long, and five wide, on Mrs. Ripley's shore, wedged close between two small elms, and your first thought on seeing it is that it has according to some law occupied that space between the trees, not reflecting that it is more ancient than the trees by a geological period, and that the latter have but re-

[1] *Vide* Nov. 27, 1857.

cently sprung up under its protection. I thought the rock had been accurately fitted into that space.

There are some things of which I cannot at once tell whether I have dreamed them or they are real; as if they were just, perchance, establishing, or else losing, a real basis in my world. This is especially the case in the early morning hours, when there is a gradual transition from dreams to waking thoughts, from illusions to actualities, as from darkness, or perchance moon and star light, to sunlight. Dreams are real, as is the light of the stars and moon, and theirs is said to be a *dreamy* light. Such early morning thoughts as I speak of occupy a debatable ground between dreams and waking thoughts. They are a sort of permanent dream in my mind. At least, until we have for some time changed our position from prostrate to erect, and commenced or faced some of the duties of the day, we cannot tell what we have dreamed from what we have actually experienced.

This morning, for instance, for the twentieth time at least, I thought of that mountain in the easterly part of our town (where no high hill actually is) which once or twice I had ascended, and often allowed my thoughts alone to climb. I now contemplate it in my mind as a familiar thought which I have surely had for many years from time to time, but whether anything could have reminded me of it in the middle of yesterday, whether I ever before remembered it in broad daylight, I doubt. I can now eke out the vision I had of it this morning with my old and yesterday forgotten dreams.

My way up used to lie through a dark and unfrequented wood at its base, — I cannot now tell exactly, it was so long ago, under what circumstances I first ascended, only that I shuddered as I went along (I have an indistinct remembrance of having been out overnight alone), — and then I steadily ascended along a rocky ridge half clad with stinted trees, where wild beasts haunted, till I lost myself quite in the upper air and clouds, seeming to pass an imaginary line which separates a hill, mere earth heaped up, from a mountain, into a superterranean grandeur and sublimity. What distinguishes that summit above the earthy line, is that it is unhandselled, awful, grand. It can never become familiar; you are lost the moment you set foot there. You know no path, but wander, thrilled, over the bare and pathless rock, as if it were solidified air and cloud. That rocky, misty summit, secreted in the clouds, was far more thrillingly awful and sublime than the crater of a volcano spouting fire.

This is a business we can partly understand. The perfect mountain height is already thoroughly purified. It is as if you trod with awe the face of a god turned up, unwittingly but helplessly, yielding to the laws of gravity. And are there not such mountains, east or west, from which you may look down on Concord in your thought, and on all the world? In dreams I am shown this height from time to time, and I seem to have asked my fellow once to climb there with me, and yet I am constrained to believe that I never actually ascended it. It chances, now I think of it,[1] that

[1] Now *first think of it*, at this stage of my description, which makes

Vol. X

it rises in my mind where lies the Burying-Hill. You might go through its gate to enter that dark wood,[1] but that hill and its graves are so concealed and obliterated by the awful mountain that I never thought of them as underlying it. Might not the graveyards of the just always be hills, ways by which we ascend and overlook the plain?

But my old way down was different, and, indeed, this was another way up, though I never so ascended. I came out, as I descended, breathing the thicker air. I came out the belt of wood into a familiar pasture, and along down by a wall. Often, as I go along the low side of this pasture, I let my thoughts ascend toward the mount, gradually entering the stinted wood (Nature subdued) and the thinner air, and drape themselves with mists. There are ever two ways up: one is through the dark wood, the other through the sunny pasture. That is, I reach and discover the mountain only through the dark wood, but I see to my surprise, when I look off between the mists from its summit, how it is ever adjacent to my native fields, nay, imminent over them, and accessible through a sunny pasture. Why is it that in the lives of men we hear more of the dark wood than of the sunny pasture?

A hard-featured god reposing, whose breath hangs about his forehead.

it the more singularly symbolical. The interlineations on the last page were made before this. [The interlineations referred to comprise the words "only that I shuddered . . . overnight alone" in the last paragraph.]

[1] Perchance that was the grave.

Though the pleasure of ascending the mountain is largely mixed with awe, my thoughts are purified and sublimed by it, as if I had been translated.

I see that men may be well-mannered or conventionally polite toward men, but skeptical toward God.

Forever in my dream and in my morning thought,
    Eastward a mount ascends;
But when in the sunbeam its hard outline is sought,
    It all dissolves and ends.
The woods that way are gates; the pastures too slope
        up
    To an unearthly ground;
But when I ask my mates to take the staff and cup,
    It can no more be found.
Perhaps I have no shoes fit for the lofty soil
    Where my thoughts graze,
No properly spun clues, nor well-strained mid-day oil,
    Or must I mend my ways?
It is a promised land which I have not yet earned.
    I have not made beginning
With consecrated hand, nor have I ever learned
    To lay the underpinning.
The mountain sinks by day, as do my lofty thoughts,
    Because I'm not high-minded.
If I could think alway above these hills and warts,
    I should see it, though blinded.
It is a spiral path within the pilgrim's soul
    Leads to this mountain's brow;
Commencing at his hearth he climbs up to this goal
    He knows not when nor how.

We see mankind generally either (from ignorance or avarice) toiling too hard and becoming mere machines in order to acquire wealth, or perhaps inheriting it or getting it by other accident, having recourse, for relaxation after excessive toil or as a mere relief to their idle ennui, to artificial amusements, rarely elevating and often debasing. I think that men generally are mistaken with regard to amusements. Every one who deserves to be regarded as higher than the brute may be supposed to have an earnest purpose, to accomplish which is the object of his existence, and this is at once his work and his supremest pleasure; and for diversion and relaxation, for suggestion and education and strength, there is offered the never-failing amusement of getting a living, — never-failing, I mean, when temperately indulged in. I know of no such amusement, — so wholesome and in every sense profitable, — for instance, as to spend an hour or two in a day picking some berries or other fruits which will be food for the winter, or collecting driftwood from the river for fuel, or cultivating the few beans or potatoes which I want. Theatres and operas, which intoxicate for a season, are as nothing compared to these pursuits. And so it is with all the true arts of life. Farming and building and manufacturing and sailing are the greatest and wholesomest amusements that were ever invented (for God invented them), and I suppose that the farmers and mechanics know it, only I think they indulge to excess generally, and so what was meant for a joy becomes the sweat of the brow. Gambling, horse-racing, loafing, and rowdyism generally, after all tempt but few. The mass are tempted by those other amusements, of farming, etc. It is a great amusement, and more profitable than I could have invented, to go and spend an afternoon hour picking cranberries. By these various pursuits your experience becomes singularly complete and rounded. The novelty and significance of such pursuits are remarkable. Such is the path by which we climb to the heights of our being; and compare the poetry which such simple pursuits have inspired with the unreadable volumes which have been written about art.

Who is the most profitable companion? He who has been picking cranberries and chopping wood, or he who has been attending the opera all his days? I find when I have been building a fence or surveying a farm, or even collecting simples, that these were the true paths to perception and enjoyment. My being seems to have put forth new roots and to be more strongly planted. This is the true way to crack the nut of happiness. If, as a poet or naturalist, you wish to explore a given neighborhood, go and live in it, *i. e.* get your living in it. Fish in its streams, hunt in its forests, gather fuel from its water, its woods, cultivate the ground, and pluck the wild fruits, etc., etc. This will be the surest and speediest way to those perceptions you covet. No amusement has worn better than farming. It tempts men just as strongly to-day as in the day of Cincinnatus. Healthily and properly pursued, it is not a whit more grave than huckleberrying, and if it takes any airs on itself as superior there's something wrong about it.

I have aspired to practice in succession all the honest arts of life, that I may gather all their fruits. But then, if you are intemperate, if you toil to raise an unnecessary amount of corn, even the large crop of wheat becomes as a small crop of chaff.

If our living were once honestly got, then it would be time to invent other amusements.

After reading Ruskin on the love of Nature, I think, "Drink deep, or taste not the Pierian spring." He there, to my surprise, expresses the common infidelity of his age and race. He has not implicitly surrendered himself to her. And what does he substitute for that Nature? I do not know, unless it be the Church of England. Questioning whether that relation to Nature was of so much value, after all! It is sour grapes! He does not speak to the condition of foxes that have more spring in their legs. The love of Nature and fullest perception of the revelation which she is to man is not compatible with the belief in the peculiar revelation of the Bible which Ruskin entertains.

Oct. 30. Another, the eighth, day of cloudy weather, though no rain to-day.

P. M. — Near the island, in my boat, I scare up a bittern (*Ardea minor*), and afterward half a dozen ducks, probably summer ducks. Saw a large flock of blackbirds yesterday.

There's a very large and complete circle round the moon this evening, which part way round is a faint rainbow. It is a clear circular space, sharply and mathematically cut out of a thin mackerel sky. You

see no mist within it, large as it is, nor even a star.

I find thousands of ants now apparently gone into winter quarters in my stumps, large black ones, red in the middle, partly dormant even this warm weather, yet with white grubs or young. Some are winged. . . .

The clintonia was perfectly at home there.[1] Its leaves were just as handsomely formed and green and disposed commonly in triangles about its stem, and its berries were just as blue and glossy as if they grew by some botanist's favorite walk in Concord. . . .

Oct. 31. Cloudy still and, in the afternoon, rain, the ninth day. The sugar maple and elm leaves are fallen, but I still see many large oaks, especially scarlet ones, which have lost very few leaves. Some scarlet oaks are pretty bright yet. The white birches, too, still retain many yellow leaves at their very tops, having a lively flame-like look when seen against the woods. River probably at its height, higher than before since spring.

I see some of those great chocolate-colored fungi already emptied. They burst open and expand into a saucer, and the dust blows out, leaving a distinct spongy bottom or base, often more than an inch thick. Like sponge to the eye, but how unlike it in its repugnance to water! Many small grubs, covered and disguised with the dust, are feeding on these fungi. What primitive and simple bread or manna these are!

Out of a natural curiosity, the growth of the woods,

[1] [In the Maine woods.]

we walked into the dark and musty log house there,[1] trampling down the rank herd's-grass three feet high which grew close up to the door, and the hunter followed us as if to see us put the house on as he had done. He behaved as if he were the latest comer, and was so absorbed in us that he did not appear to own the newly baked loaf of bread in a blackened Yankee baker on the counter by his side, and I thought at first it had lain over from another season.

In the Lee farm swamp, by the old Sam Barrett mill site, I see two kinds of ferns still green and much in fruit, apparently the *Aspidium spinulosum* (?) and *cristatum* (?).[2] They are also common in other swamps now. They are quite fresh in those cold and wet places and almost flattened down now. The atmosphere of the house is less congenial to them. In the summer you might not have noticed them. Now they are conspicuous amid the withered leaves. You are inclined to approach and raise each frond in succession, moist, trembling, fragile greenness. They linger thus in all moist clammy swamps under the bare maples and grape-vines and witch-hazels, and about each trickling spring which is half choked with fallen leaves. What means this persistent vitality, invulnerable to frost and wet? Why were these spared when the brakes and osmundas were stricken down? They stay as if to keep up the spirits of the cold-blooded frogs which have not yet gone into the mud; that the summer may die with decent and graceful moderation,

[1] [At Telos Lake. See *Maine Woods*, pp. 268, 269; Riv. 333, 334.]
[2] *Vide* page [117].

gradually. Is not the water of the spring improved by their presence? They fall back and droop here and there, like the plumes of departing summer, — of the departing year. Even in them I feel an argument for immortality. Death is so far from being universal. The same destroyer does not destroy all. How valuable they are (with the lycopodiums) for cheerfulness. Greenness at the end of the year, after the fall of the leaf, as in a hale old age. To my eyes they are tall and noble as palm groves, and always some forest nobleness seems to have its haunt under their umbrage. Each such green tuft of ferns is a grove where some nobility dwells and walks. All that was immortal in the swamp's herbage seems here crowded into smaller compass, — the concentrated greenness of the swamp. How dear they must be to the chickadee and the rabbit! The cool, slowly retreating rear-guard of the swamp army. What virtue is theirs that enables them to resist the frost?

If you are afflicted with melancholy at this season, go to the swamp and see the brave spears of skunk-cabbage buds already advanced toward a new year. Their gravestones are not bespoken yet. Who shall be sexton to them? Is it the winter of their discontent? Do they seem to have lain down to die, despairing of skunk-cabbagedom? "Up and at 'em," "Give it to 'em," "Excelsior," "Put it through," — these are their mottoes. Mortal human creatures must take a little respite in this fall of the year; their spirits do flag a little. There is a little questioning of destiny, and thinking to go like cowards to where the "weary shall

Vol. X

be at rest." But not so with the skunk-cabbage. Its withered leaves fall and are transfixed by a rising bud. Winter and death are ignored; the circle of life is complete. Are these false prophets? Is it a lie or a vain boast underneath the skunk-cabbage bud, pushing it upward and lifting the dead leaves with it? They rest with spears advanced; they rest to shoot!

I say it is good for me to be here, slumping in the mud, a trap covered with withered leaves. See those green cabbage buds lifting the dry leaves in that watery and muddy place. There is no can't nor cant to them. They see over the brow of winter's hill. They see another summer ahead.

IV

NOVEMBER, 1857

(ÆT. 40)

Nov. 1. P. M. — To Fair Haven Pond over Cliffs. Another cloudy afternoon after a clear morning.

When I enter the woods I notice the drier crispier rustle of withered leaves on the oak trees, — a sharper susurrus.

Going over the high field west of the cut, my foot strikes a rattle-pod in the stubble, and it is betrayed. From that faint sound I knew it must be there, and went back and found it. I could have told it as well in the dark. How often I have found pennyroyal by the fragrance it emitted when bruised by my feet!

The lowest and most succulent oak sprouts *in exposed places* are red or green longest. Large trees quite protected from sun and wind will be greener still. The larches are at the height of their change.

I see much witch-hazel in the swamp by the south end of the Abiel Wheeler grape meadow. Some of it is quite fresh and bright. Its bark is alternate white and smooth reddish-brown, the small twigs looking as if gossamer had lodged on and draped them. What a lively spray it has, both in form and color! Truly it looks as if it would make divining-rods, — as if its twigs knew where the true gold was and could point to it. The gold is in their late blossoms. Let them

alone and they never point down to earth. They impart to the whole hillside a speckled, parti-colored look.

I see the common prinos berries partly eaten about the hole of a mouse under a stump.

As I return by the Well Meadow Field and then Wheeler's large wood, the sun shines from over Fair Haven Hill into the wood, and I see that the sun, when low, will shine into a thick wood, which you had supposed always dark, as much as twenty rods, lighting it all up, making the gray, lichen-clad stems of the trees all warm and bright with light, and a distinct black shadow behind each. As if every grove, however dense, had its turn.

A higher truth, though only dimly hinted at, thrills us more than a lower expressed.

Jersey tea has perhaps the most green leaves of any shrub at present.

Nov. 2. P. M. — To Bateman's Pond.

Row up Assabet as far as the Pokelogan, thence on foot. It is very pleasant and cheerful nowadays, when the brown and withered leaves strew the ground and almost every plant is fallen or withered, to come upon a patch of polypody on some rocky hillside in the woods, — as in abundance on hillside between Calla Swamp and Bateman's Pond, and still more same hillside east of the callas, — where, in the midst of the dry and rustling leaves, defying frost, it stands so freshly green and full of life. The mere greenness, which was not remarkable in the summer, is positively interesting now. My thoughts are with the polypody a long time after my body has passed. The brakes, the sarsaparilla, the osmundas, the Solomon's-seals, the lady's-slippers have long since withered and fallen. The huckleberries and blueberries, too, have lost their leaves. The forest floor is covered with a thick coat of moist brown leaves. But what is that perennial and springlike verdure that clothes the rocks, of small green plumes pointing various ways? It is the cheerful community of the polypody. It survives at least as the type of vegetation, to remind us of the spring which shall not fail. These are the green pastures where I browse now. Why is not this form copied by our sculptors instead of the foreign acanthus leaves and bays? The sight of this unwithering green leaf excites me like red at some seasons. Are not the wood frogs the philosophers who walk (?) in these groves?[1] Methinks I imbibe a cool, composed, frog-like philosophy when I behold them. I don't care for acanthus leaves; they are far-fetched. I do love this form, however, and would like to see it painted or sculptured, whether on your marble or my butter. How fit for a tuft about the base of a column!

I come to a black snake in the wood-path, with its crushed head resting on a stone and its uninjured body trailing thence. How often I see where thus some heel has bruised the serpent's head! I think it an unnatural antipathy.

Crossed over that high, flat-backed rocky hill, where the rocks, as usual thereabouts, stand on their edges, and the grain, though usually running northeasterly

[1] [Channing, p. 103.]

and southwesterly, — by compass east-northeast, west-southwest, — is frequently kinked up in a curious manner, reminding me of a curly head. Call the hill Curly-pate.

Bateman's Pond is agitated by the strong wind, — a slate-colored surface under the cloudy sky. I find some good blue pearmains under their tree in a swamp, amid the huckleberry bushes, etc., all fallen. They lie with a rich bloom on them still, though half of them are gnawed by squirrels or rabbits; low in the sedge, with decayed leaves adhering to them.

How contagious are boys' games! A short time ago they were spinning tops, as I saw and heard, all the country over. Now every boy has a stick curved at the end, a *hawkie* (?), in his hand, whether in yards or in distant lanes I meet them.

The evergreen ferns and lycopodiums now have their day; now is the *flower* of their age, and their greenness is appreciated. They are much the clearest and most liquid green in the woods, more yellow and brown specked in the open places.

The form of the polypody is *strangely* interesting; it is even outlandish. Some forms, though common in our midst, are thus perennially foreign as the growths of other latitudes; there being a greater interval between us and their kind than usual. We all feel the ferns to be further from us, essentially and sympathetically, than the phænogamous plants, the roses and weeds, for instance. It needs no geology nor botany to assure us of that. We feel it, and told *them* of it first. The bare outline of the polypody thrills me strangely. It

is a strange type which I cannot read. It only piques me. Simple as it is, it is as strange as an Oriental character. It is quite independent of my race, and of the Indian, and all mankind. It is a fabulous, mythological form, such as prevailed when the earth and air and water were inhabited by those extinct fossil creatures that we find. It is contemporary with them, and affects as the sight of them.

As I stood on Curly-pate, the air had become gradually thick with mist in the southwest. The sky was overcast, and a cool, strong wind blew from the same quarter, and in the mist I perceived the strong scent of smoke from some burning. Standing on one of those curly-headed rocks, whose strata are vertical, gives me a sense of elevation like a mountain-top. In fact, they are on the axis of elevation.

There are no fresh — or blue — fringed gentians by the swamp-side by Bateman's now.

Wild apples have lost some of their brilliancy now and are chiefly fallen.

Returning, I see the red oak on R. W. E.'s shore reflected in the bright sky water. In the reflection the tree is black against the clear whitish sky, though as I see it against the opposite woods it is a warm greenish yellow. But the river sees it against the bright sky, and hence the reflection is like ink. The water tells me how it looks to it seen from below. I think that most men, as farmers, hunters, fishers, etc., walk along a river's bank, or paddle along its stream, without seeing the reflections. Their minds are not abstracted from the surface, from surfaces generally. It is only

a reflecting mind that sees reflections. I am aware often that I have been occupied with shallow and commonplace thoughts, looking for something superficial, when I did not see the most glorious reflections, though exactly in the line of my vision. If the fisherman was looking at the reflection, he would not know when he had a nibble! I know from my own experience that he may cast his line right over the most elysian landscape and sky, and not *catch* the slightest notion of them. You must be in an abstract mood to see reflections however distinct. I was even startled by the sight of that reflected red oak as if it were a black water-spirit. When we are enough abstracted, the opaque earth itself reflects images to us; *i. e.*, we are imaginative, see visions, etc. Such a reflection, this inky, leafy tree, against the white sky, can only be seen at this season.

The water is falling fast, and I push *direct* over the meadow this evening, probably for the last time this fall, scraping the cranberry vines and hummocks from time to time with my flat-bottomed boat.

Nov. 3. P. M. — To the Easterbrooks moraine *via* Ponkawtasset-top.

Islands, pale-brown grassy isles, are appearing again in the meadow as the water goes down. From this hilltop, looking down-stream over the Great Meadows away from the sun, the water is rather dark, it being windy, but about the shores of the grassy isles is a lighter-colored smooth space.

Pitch pine needles are almost all fallen.

There is a wild pear tree on the east side of Ponkaw-tasset, which I find to be four and a half feet in circumference at four feet from the ground.

Looking westward now, at 4 P. M., I see against the sunlight, where the twigs of a maple and black birch intermingle, a little gossamer or fine cobwebs, but much more the twigs, especially of the birch, waving slightly, reflect the light like cobwebs. It is a phenomenon peculiar to this season, when the twigs are bare and the air is clear. I cannot easily tell what is cobweb and what twig, but the latter often curve upward more than the other.

I see on many rocks, etc., the seeds of the barberry, which have been voided by birds, — robins, no doubt, chiefly. How many they must thus scatter over the fields, spreading the barberry far and wide! That has been their business for a month.

Follow up the Boulder Field northward, and it terminates in that moraine. As I return down the Boulder Field, I see the now winter-colored — i. e. reddish (of oak leaves) — horizon of hills, with its few white houses, four or five miles distant southward, between two of the boulders, which are a dozen rods from me, a dozen feet high, and nearly as much apart, — as a landscape between the frame of a picture. But what a picture-frame! These two great slumbering masses of rock, reposing like a pair of mastodons on the surface of the pasture, completely shutting out a mile of the horizon on each side, while between their adjacent sides, which are nearly perpendicular, I see to the now purified, dry, reddish, leafy horizon, with a faint tinge of

blue from the distance. To see a remote landscape between two near rocks! I want no other gilding to my picture-frame. There they lie, as perchance they tumbled and split from off an iceberg. What better frame could you have? The globe itself, here named pasture, for ground and foreground, two great boulders for the sides of the frame, and the sky itself for the top! And for artists and subject, God and Nature! Such pictures cost nothing but eyes, and it will not bankrupt one to own them. They were not stolen by any conqueror as spoils of war, and none can doubt but they are really the works of an old master. What more, pray, will you see between any two slips of gilded wood in that pasture you call Europe and browse in sometimes? It is singular that several of those rocks should be thus split into twins. Even very low ones, just appearing above the surface, are divided and parallel, having a path between them.

It would be something to own that pasture with the great rocks in it! And yet I suppose they are considered an incumbrance only by the owner.

I came along the path that comes out just this side the lime-kiln.

Coming by Ebby Hubbard's thick maple and pine wood, I see the rays of the sun, now not much above the horizon, penetrating quite through it to my side in very narrow and slender glades of light, peculiarly bright. It seems, then, that no wood is so dense but that the rays of the setting sun may penetrate twenty rods into it. The other day (November 1st), I stood on the sunny side of such a wood at the same season,

or a little earlier. Then I saw the lit sides of the tree stems all aglow with their lichens, and observed their black shadows behind. Now I see chiefly the dark stems massed together, and it is the warm sunlight that is reduced to a pencil of light; i. e., then light was the rule and shadow the exception, now shadow the rule and light the exception.

I notice some old cow-droppings in a pasture, which are decidedly pink. Even these trivial objects awaken agreeable associations in my mind, connected not only with my own actual rambles but with what I have read of the prairies and pampas and Eastern land of grass, the great pastures of the world.

Nov. 4. P. M. — To Pine Hill *via* Spanish Brook.

I leave the railroad at Walden Crossing and follow the path to Spanish Brook. How swift Nature is to repair the damage that man does! When he has cut down a tree and left only a white-topped and bleeding stump, she comes at once to the rescue with her chemistry, and covers it decently with a fresh coat of gray, and in course of time she adds a thick coat of green cup and bright cockscomb lichens, and it becomes an object of new interest to the lover of nature! Suppose it were always to remain a raw stump instead! It becomes a shell on which this humble vegetation spreads and displays itself, and we forget the death of the larger in the life of the less.

I see in the path some rank thimble-berry shoots covered with that peculiar hoary bloom very thickly. It is only rubbed off in a few places down to the purple

skin, by some passing hunter perchance. It is a very singular and delicate outer coat, surely, for a plant to wear. I find that I can write my name in it with a pointed stick very distinctly, each stroke, however fine, going down to the purple. It is a new kind of enamelled card. What is this bloom, and what purpose does it serve? Is there anything analogous in animated nature? It is the *coup de grace*, the last touch and perfection of any work, a thin elysian veil cast over it, through which it may be viewed. It is breathed on by the artist, and thereafter his work is not to be touched without injury. It is the evidence of a ripe and completed work, on which the unexhausted artist has breathed out of his superfluous genius, and his work looks through it as a veil. If it is a poem, it must be invested with a similar bloom by the imagination of the reader. It is the subsidence of superfluous ripeness. Like a fruit preserved in its own sugar. It is the handle by which the imagination grasps it.

I frequently see a spreading pitch pine on whose lower and horizontal limbs the falling needles have lodged, forming thick and unsightly masses, where anon the snow will collect and make a close canopy. The evergreens, with their leaves, are, of course, more likely to catch this litter than the deciduous trees, and the pines especially, because their lower branches are oftener horizontal and flat, beside being unyielding to the wind. Robins build there.

I notice the new and as yet unswollen scales of willow catkins or buds (the first [?] by the pond) quite yellow in the sun, but nearer I find that half are turned black.

Nature's Decoration of an Old Pine Stump

Curly-pate Hill, above Bateman's Pond

The evergreen ferns and lycopodiums, etc., on the forest floor, though partly fallen, represent the evergreen trees among humbler plants.

I climb Pine Hill just as the sun is setting, this cool evening. Sitting with my back to a thick oak sprout whose leaves still glow with life, Walden lies an oblong square endwise to, beneath me. Its surface is slightly rippled, and dusky prolonged reflections of trees extend wholly across its length, or half a mile, — I sit high. The sun is once or twice its diameter above the horizon, and the mountains north of it stand out grand and distinct, a decided purple. But when I look critically, I distinguish a whitish mist — such is the color of the denser air — about their lower parts, while their tops are dark-blue. (So the mountains too have a bloom on them; and is not the bloom on fruits equivalent to that blue veil of air which distance gives to many objects?) I see one glistening reflection on the dusky and leafy northwestern earth, seven or eight miles off, betraying a window there, though no house can be seen. It twinkles incessantly, as from a waving surface. This, probably, is the undulation of the air. Now that the sun is actually setting, the mountains are dark-blue from top to bottom. As usual, a small cloud attends the sun to the portals of the day and reflects this brightness to us, now that he is gone. But those grand and glorious mountains, how impossible to remember daily that they are there, and to live accordingly! They are meant to be a perpetual reminder to us, pointing out the way.

him to follow; it was safe enough. Minott followed half a dozen rods and then decided that he would n't risk it and went back; he 'd go ten miles round sooner than cross. "But," said Minott, "the fellow kept on and I 'll be hanged if he did n't get safe across."

The pitch pines generally have lost their leaves now, and the larches are fast falling. The elms have been bare some time.

Sometimes I would rather get a transient glimpse or side view of a thing than stand fronting to it, — as those polypodies. The object I caught a glimpse of as I went by haunts my thoughts a long time, is infinitely suggestive, and I do not care to front it and scrutinize it, for I know that the thing that really concerns me is not there, but in my relation to that. That is a mere reflecting surface. It is not the polypody in my pitcher or herbarium, or which I may possibly persuade to grow on a bank in my yard, or which is described in botanies, that interests me, but the one that I pass by in my walks a little distance off, when in the right mood. Its influence is sporadic, wafted through the air to me. Do you imagine its fruit to stick to the back of the leaf all winter? At this season polypody is in the air.[1] It is worth the while to walk in swamps now, to bathe your eyes with greenness. The terminal shield fern is the handsomest and glossiest green.

Start up a snipe feeding in a wet part of the Dam Meadows.

I think that the man of science makes this mistake, and the mass of mankind along with him: that you

[1] [Channing, p. 103.]

Nov. 5. P. M. — To the Dam Meadows.

But little corn is left in the field now, and that looks rather black. There is an abundance of cat-tail in the Dam Meadows.

Returning, talked with Minott. He told me how he and Harry Hooper used to go to Howard's meadow (Heywood's, by the railroad) when it was flowed and kill fishes through the ice. They would cut a long stick and go carefully over the ice when it was only a couple of inches thick, and when they saw a fish, strike the ice smartly, cracking it in all directions, right over him, and when he turned his belly, being stunned, would cut him out quickly before he came to. These were little fishes which he called "prods." He did n't know much more about them. They were somewhat like a small pout, but had different heads. They got so many once that he told Harry to cut a stick and string them and they 'd give them to Zilpha as they went by. He has caught pickerel in the brook there which weighed two or three pounds.

He went to Bateman's Pond once in the winter to catch minnows with a net through the ice, but did n't get any. He went — rode — with Oliver Williams first into Acton and then round to this pond on this errand.

Minott was rather timid. One day early in the winter he had been over to Fair Haven Hill after a fox with John Wyman, but they did n't get him. The pond was frozen about two inches thick, but you could easily see the water through the ice, and when they came back, Wyman said he was going straight across because it was nearer, but Minott objected. But Wyman told

should coolly give your chief attention to the phenomenon which excites you as something independent on you, and not as it is related to you. The important fact is its effect on me. He thinks that I have no business to see anything else but just what he defines the rainbow to be, but I care not whether my vision of truth is a waking thought or dream remembered, whether it is seen in the light or in the dark. It is the subject of the vision, the truth alone, that concerns me. The philosopher for whom rainbows, etc., can be explained away never saw them. With regard to such objects, I find that it is not they themselves (with which the men of science deal) that concern me; the point of interest is somewhere *between* me and them (*i. e.* the objects). . . .

And where does your Eastern stuff go to?[1] Whose houses does it build? It has built Bangor, and what is the precise value of Bangor, omitting the lumber on its wharves? Western stuff is good enough for me. I think that this craving a better material than we deserve, and wasting what we get, is the secret of bankruptcy. And what is it, after all, but lumber? I do not wish to see any more poor men in rich houses. I would rather see one rich man in a poor house. No more cripples on stilts. . . .

For a man to pride himself on this kind of wealth, as if it enriched him, is as ridiculous as if one struggling in the ocean with a bag of gold on his back should gasp out, "I am worth a hundred thousand dollars!"

[1] [Refers, of course, to the lumbering operations of the Maine woods.]

I see his ineffectual struggles just as plainly, and what it is that sinks him.

Nov. 6. Very warm but rather cloudy weather, after rain in the night. Wind southwest. Thermometer on north of the house 70° at 12 M. Indian summer. The cocks crow in the soft air. They are very sensitive to atmospheric changes.

P. M. — To Curly-pate *via* old Carlisle road.

Stedman Buttrick tells me that Dr. Ripley used to have his pork packed with the best pieces at the top of the barrel, and when some parishioner wondered at it, that he should thus eat these first, he answered that when packed thus the topmost were the best all the way through.

He said that his grandfather lived in the Jarvis house, and that the other old house whose upper story projected over the lower like the Hunt house, and which I saw in the picture of Concord Fight, stood close to his own house, and he pulled it down when he was sixteen.

I passed through that chestnut wood in the hollow southeast of Curly-pate. Turning over the wet chestnut leaves in the hollows, looking for nuts, I found a red-backed salamander, between three and four inches long, bluish-gray beneath (*Salamandra erythronota*). It jerked itself about in a lively manner, trying to hide itself under the leaves, and would quickly slip out of my fingers. Its motions appeared to partake of those of a snake and a frog, — between a squirm and a hop. It was not particularly swift, yet, from the character

Vol. X

all open. This road was the new one; the bridle-road the old one.

Minott is a very pleasing figure in nature. He improves every scenery, — he and his comrades, Harry Hooper, John Wyman, Oliver Williams, etc. If he gets into a pondhole he disturbs it no more than a water-spirit for me.

Nov. 7. You will sometimes see a sudden wave flow along a puny ditch of a brook, inundating all its shores, when a musquash is making his escape beneath. He soon plunges into some hole in the bank under water, and all is still again.

P. M. — To Bateman's Pond with R. W. E.

Stedman Buttrick, speaking of R. W. E.'s cow that was killed by lightning and not found for some days, said that they heard a "bellering" of the cows some days before they found her, and they found the ground much trampled about the dead cow; that that was the way with cows in such cases; if such an accident happened to one of their number, they would have spells of gathering around her and "bellering."

Minott adorns whatever part of nature he touches; whichever way he walks he transfigures the earth for me. If a common man speaks of Walden Pond to me, I see only a shallow, dull-colored body of water without reflections or peculiar color, but if Minott speaks of it, I see the green water and reflected hills at once, for he *has been* there. I hear the rustle of the leaves from woods which he goes through.

This has been another Indian-summer day. Thermometer 58° at noon.

of the motion and its glossiness, it was *glancing.* A dozen rods further I turned [up] another, very similar but without a red back, but rather slightly clay-colored. I did not observe any transverse bands; else it might be the *S. fasciata.*

When I came out on to the old Carlisle road in the dusk on my return, I saw Brooks Clark coming homeward, with his axe in his hand and both hands behind his back, being bent almost double. He said he was over eighty. Some years ago he bought some land up that way, and, the birches having sprung up there, he called it his birch pasture. There was enough birch wood there to carry him through the winter, and he was now cutting it. He remembered when they began to burn lime there, and bought the right to get out stone of Easterbrooks more than sixty years ago. It was Peter Barrett that began it. The lime sold for $5.00 a cask (larger casks than now). But the stone was difficult to get out. He remembers seeing the mowers at work in the meadow where Stedman Buttrick's handsome pine and maple wood is, seventy years ago, and where there was a large old chestnut by the roadside there, which being cut, two sprouts came up which have become the largest chestnut trees by the wall now. As for the yellow birch cellar-hole, Ephraim Brown told him that old Henry Flint (an ancestor of Clark's wife) dug it, and erected the frame of a house there, but never finished it, selling out, going to live by the river. It was never finished. Clark's father told him that he remembered when there were no fences between his house and Lawrence's; it was

Nov. 8. A warm, cloudy, rain-threatening morning.

About 10 A. M. a long flock of geese are going over from northeast to southwest, or parallel with the general direction of the coast and great mountain-ranges. The sonorous, quavering sounds of the geese are the voice of this cloudy air, — a sound that comes from directly between us and the sky, an aerial sound, and yet so distinct, heavy, and sonorous, a clanking chain drawn through the heavy air. I saw through my window some children looking up and pointing their tiny bows into the heavens, and I knew at once that the geese were in the air. It is always an exciting event. The children, instinctively aware of its importance, rushed into the house to tell their parents. These travellers are revealed to you by the upward-turned gaze of men. And though these undulating lines are melting into the southwestern sky, the sound comes clear and distinct to you as the clank of a chain in a neighboring stithy. So they migrate, not flitting from hedge to hedge, but from latitude to latitude, from State to State, steering boldly out into the ocean of the air. It is remarkable how these large objects, so plain when your vision is rightly directed, may be lost in the sky if you look away for a moment, — as hard to hit as a star with a telescope.

It is a sort of encouraging or soothing sound to assuage their painful fears when they go over a town, as a man moans to deaden a physical pain. The direction of their flight each spring and autumn reminds us inlanders how the coast trends. In the afternoon I met Flood, who had just endeavored to draw my attention to a flock of geese in the mizzling air, but encountering me he lost sight of them, while I, at length, looking that way, discerned them, though he could not. This was the third flock to-day. Now if ever, then, we may expect a change in the weather.

P. M. — To the swamp in front of the C. Miles house.

The great white pines on the hill south of it were cut, apparently last winter. I count on two stumps about one hundred and twenty-five rings, and the sap averages in each case about three inches thick.

In a thick white pine wood, as in that swamp at the east end, where the ground is level, the ground now (and for some time) is completely covered with a carpet of pale-brown leaves, completely concealing the green mosses and even some lycopodiums. The effect is exactly as [if] a uniform pale-brown matting had been spread over the green and russet floor. It is even soothing to walk over this soft and springy bed. How silently and unobserved by most do these changes take place! This additional warm matting is tucked about their roots to defend them from the frost. It is interesting to see the green of mosses peeping out here and there. You hear only the soft crisped sound of sinking needles under your feet.

I find in the swamp there by the larches the *Kalmia glauca*, good specimens.

I have no doubt that a good farmer, who, of course, loves his work, takes exactly the same kind of pleasure in draining a swamp, seeing the water flow out in his newly cut ditch, that a child does in its mud dikes and water-wheels. Both alike love to play with the natural forces.

There is quite a ravine by which the water of this swamp flows out eastward, and at the bottom of it many prinos berries are conspicuous, now apparently in their prime. These are appointed to be an ornament of this bare season between leaves and snow. The swamp-pink's large yellowish buds, too, are conspicuous now. I see also the swamp pyrus buds, expanded sometimes into small leaves. This, then, is a regular phenomenon. It is the only shrub or tree that I know which so decidedly springs again in the fall, in the Indian summer. It might be called the Indian-summer shrub. The clethra buds, too, are decidedly expanded there, showing leafets, but very small. Some of the new pyrus leaves are nearly full-grown. Would not this be a pretty device on some hale and cheery old man's shield, — the swamp pyrus unfolding its leaves again in the fall? Every plant enjoys some preëminence, and this is its. The most forward to respond to the warmer season. How much spring there is in it! Its sap is most easily liquefied. It takes the least sun and mildness to thaw it and develop it. It makes this annual sacrifice of its very first leaves to its love for the sun. While all other shrubs are reserved, this is open and confiding. I see it not without emotion. I too have my spring thoughts even in November. This I see in pleasant October and November days, when rills and birds begin to tinkle in winter fashion through the more open aisles of the swamps.

I do not know exactly what that sweet word is which the chickadee says when it hops near to me now in those ravines.

The chickadee
Hops near to me.

When the air is thick and the sky overcast, we need not walk so far. We give our attention to nearer objects, being less distracted from them. I take occasion to explore some near wood which my walks commonly overshoot.

What a difference it makes between two ravines in other respects exactly similar that in the one there is a stream which drains it, while the other is dry!

I see nowadays in various places the scattered feathers of robins, etc., where some hawk or beast of prey has torn them to pieces.

I step over the slip-noose snares which some woodling has just set. How long since men set snares for partridges and rabbits?

Ah, my friends, I know you better than you think, and love you better, too. The day after never, we will have an explanation.

Nov. 9. Surveying for Stedman Buttrick and Mr. Gordon.

Jacob Farmer says that he remembers well a particular bound (which is the subject of dispute between the above two men) from this circumstance: He, a boy, was sent, as the representative of his mother, to witness the placing of the bounds to her lot, and he remembers that, when they had fixed the stake and stones, old Mr. Nathan Barrett asked him if he had a knife about him, upon which he pulled out his knife and gave it to him. Mr. Barrett cut a birch switch and

trimmed it in the presence of young Farmer, and then called out, "Boy, here's your knife;" but as the boy saw that he was going to strike him when he reached his hand for the knife, he dodged into a bush which alone received the blow. And Mr. Barrett said that if it had not been for that, he would have got a blow which would have made him remember that bound as long as he lived, and explained to him that that was his design in striking him. He had before told his mother that since she could not go to the woods to see what bounds were set to her lot, she had better send Jacob as a representative of the family. This made Farmer the important witness in this case. He first, some years ago, saw Buttrick trimming up the trees, and told him he was on Gordon's land and pointed out this as the bound between them.

One of the company to-day told of George Melvin once directing Jonas Melvin, for a joke, to go to the widow Hildreth's lot (along which we were measuring) and gather the chestnuts. They were probably both working there. He accordingly took the oxen and cart and some ladders and another hired man, and they worked all day and got half a bushel.

Mr. Farmer tells me that one Sunday he went to his barn, having nothing to do, and thought he would watch the swallows, republican swallows. The old bird was feeding her young, and he sat within fifteen feet, overlooking them. There were five young, and he was curious to know how each received its share; and as often as the bird came with a fly, the one at the door (or opening) took it, and then they all hitched round one notch, so that a new one was presented at the door, who received the next fly; and this was the invariable order, the same one never receiving two flies in succession. At last the old bird brought a very small fly, and the young one that swallowed it did not desert his ground but waited to receive the next, but when the bird came with another, of the usual size, she commenced a loud and long scolding at the little one, till it resigned its place, and the next in succession received the fly.

Bigelow, the tavern-keeper, once, wrote C., put up this advertisement in the streets of Concord, "All those who are in favor of the universal salvation of mankind, are requested to meet at the school-house (?) next Saturday evening (?), to choose officers."

Very warm to-day; rainy in forenoon.

Nov. 11. Clear and fine Indian-summer day.

P. M. — To Lincoln limestone with E. Hoar.

Hoar showed me last evening the large fossil tooth of a shark, such as figured in Hitchcock, which he bought at Gay Head the other day. He also bought one or more other species.

I heard, day before yesterday, much firing of guns in the chestnut woods by Curly-pate Hill, probably at gray squirrels. George Buttrick says it is late for them; were thickest in chestnut time.

That cellar-hole off northwest of Brooks Clark's is where Boaz Brown used to live, and the andromeda swamp behind is "Boaz's (pronounced Boze's) meadow," says Jacob Farmer, who has seen corn growing in the

Vol. X

meadow. The Lincoln limestone dips east by north, strikes north by west; the hornblende slate (?) on Bare Hill, northeast and northwest.

Nov. 13. Some rain in the night.

I see, on a white oak on Egg Rock, where the squirrels have lately made a nest for the winter of the dry oak leaves, probably using those on the tree before they fell. Now that the top of the oak is bare, this is a dark round mass against the sky, as big as a peck measure, very conspicuous. There are considerable many still hanging on the lower parts. I suspect it is a gray squirrel's nest.

I observed on the 7th, between the site of Paul Adams's and Bateman's Pond, in quite open land, some very prominent Indian corn-hills. I should say that they were higher above the intermediate surface than when they were first made. It was a pasture, and they were thickly covered with grass and lichens. Perhaps the grass had grown better on the hillocks, and so they had grown while the intermediate spaces had been more trodden by the cows. These very regular round grassy hillocks, extending in straight rows over the swells and valleys, had a singular effect, like the burial-ground of some creatures.

I find that I can see the sun set from almost any hill in Concord, and some within the confines of the neighboring towns, and though this takes place at just about 5 P. M., when the cows come in, get to the post-office by the time the mail is distributed. See the sun rise or set if possible each day. Let that be your pill. How

speedily the night comes on now! There is some duskiness in the afternoon light before you are aware of it, the cows have gathered about the bars, waiting to be let out, and, in twenty minutes, candles gleam from distant windows, and the walk for this day is ended. It remains only to get home again. Who is weary? Why do we cease work and go to bed? Who taught men thus to spend their nights and days? Yet I must confess that I am surprised when I find that particular wise and independent persons conform so far as regularly to go to bed and get up about the same time with their neighbors.

My assistants and company in surveying on the 9th were, Gordon and Buttrick, the principals in the dispute; Jacob Farmer, the principal witness; George Buttrick, son of Stedman; and French, son-in-law of Gordon. I had the most to do with Gordon, who came after me. He was quite eloquent at our house on the subject of two neighbors disputing at his time of life about a "pelfry" sum or a few rods of land; seemed really to have a very good heart; thought that the main thing in this life was to keep up friendly relations; and as he rode along, would quote Scripture in a low tone, and put his whole soul into some half-whispered expression which I could not hear, but nevertheless nodded assent to. He thought it was too bad that he should have spent his seventy-third birthday settling that dispute in the woods. Apparently did not know it till afterwards.

Buttrick is a rather large man, in more senses than one. His portly body as he stood over the bound was

the mark at which I sighted through the woods, rather too wide a one for accuracy. He did not cease to regret for a day or two that I should have had no dinner, but Gordon detained me. Buttrick said that he had a piece of meat cooked and expected me at his house. Thought it too bad in Gordon to make a man go without his dinner, etc. He offered me a glass of gin, or wine, as I chose. Lamented the cutting down of apple orchards and scarcity of cider-mills. Told of an orchard in the town of Russell, on the side of a hill, where the apples rolled down and lay four feet deep (?) against a wall on the lower side, and this the owner cut down.

Farmer, half a dozen years since, saw Buttrick trimming up the trees there and observed [to] him, "You are on Mr. Gordon's land." This was the beginning of the trouble. Buttrick adhered to the bounds which Abel Brooks, who sold to him, had pointed out. Farmer was sure of the bounds between them, because when Jacob Brown's Bateman wood-lot was divided between Mrs. Farmer (his mother) and her sister, the mother of Mrs. Gordon, he had witnessed the setting of the bounds as the representative of his mother, and came near being whipped at this one.

Nov. 14. P. M. — Ride to limestone quarries on old Carlisle road with E. Hoar.

This morning it was considerably colder than for a long time, and by noon very much colder than heretofore, with a pretty strong northerly wind. The principal flight of geese was November 8th, so that the bulk of them preceded this cold turn five days. You need greatcoat and buffalo and gloves now, if you ride. I find my hands stiffened and involuntarily finding their way to my pockets. No wonder that the weather is a standing subject of conversation, since we are so sensitive. If we had not gone through several winters, we might well be alarmed at the approach of cold weather. With this keener blast from the north, my hands suddenly fail to fulfill their office, as it were begin to die. We must put on armor against the new foe. I am almost world-ridden suddenly. I can hardly tie and untie my shoe-strings. What a story to tell an inhabitant of the tropics, — perchance that you went to walk, after many months of warmth, when suddenly the air became so cold and hostile to your nature, that it benumbed you so that you lost the use of some of your limbs, could not untie your shoe-strings or un-button your clothes! This cold weather makes us step more briskly.[1]

I hear that the Indians say we are to have a hard win-ter, because of the abundance of acorns, also because of the unusual thickening of corn-husks in the summer!

The stone at those quarries strikes northeasterly and southwesterly, or apparently with the rocks of Curly-pate, a third of a mile off. The strata appear to be nearly vertical. In the most southwesterly quarry, I noticed in the side of an upright sliver of rock, where the limestone had formerly been blasted off, the bot-tom of the nearly perpendicular hole which had been drilled for that purpose, two or three inches deep and about two and a half feet from the ground. In this

[1] *Vide* forward.

I found two fresh chestnuts, a dozen or more amphi-carpæa seeds, as many apparently either prinos (?) or rose (?) seeds (single seeds and fresh), and several fresh barberry seeds mixed with a little earth and rub-bish. What placed them there? Squirrel, mouse, jay, or crow? At first I thought that a quadruped could hardly have reached this hole, but probably it could easily, and it was a very cunning place for such a deposit.[1] I brought them all home in order to ascertain what the seeds were and how they came there. Examining the chestnuts carefully in the even-ing and wondering if so small a bird as a chickadee could transport one, I observed near the larger end of one some very fine scratches, which it seemed to me might have been made by the teeth of a very small animal when carrying it, but certainly not by the bill of a bird, since they had pricked sharply into the shell, rucking it up one way. I then looked to see where the teeth of the other jaw had scratched it, but could discover no marks and was therefore still somewhat in doubt. Coming up-stairs an hour afterward, I ex-amined those scratches with a microscope, and saw plainly that they had been made by some fine and sharp cutting instrument like a fine chisel, a little con-cave, and had plowed under the surface of the shell a little, toward the big end of the nut, raising it up; and, looking farther, I now discovered, on the larger end of the nut, at least two corresponding marks made by the lower incisors, plowing toward the first and about a quarter of an inch distant. These were a little

[1] *Vide* Nov. 19th.

Vol. X

less obvious to the unarmed eye, but no less plain through the glass. I now had no doubt that they were made by the incisors of a mouse, and, comparing them with the incisors of a deer mouse (*Mus leucopus*) whose skull I have, I found that one or two of the marks were just the width of its two incisors combined (a twentieth of an inch), and the others, though finer, might have been made by them. On one side, at least, it had taken fresh hold once or twice. I have but little doubt that these seeds were placed there by a *Mus leucopus*, our most common wood mouse. The other nut, which had no marks on it, I suppose was carried by the star end, which was gone from both. There was no chest-nut tree within twenty rods. These seeds thus placed in this recess will account for chestnut trees, barberry bushes, etc., etc., growing in chinks and clefts where we do not see how the seeds could have fallen. There was earth enough even in this little hole to keep some very small plant alive.

I hear that Gardiner Heywood caught a trout in Wal-den Pond the other day and that it weighed five pounds.[1]

It seems that the Abel Davis who caught the pickerel in Temple Brook, which would make such a meal for his "Lavinia" and himself, was addicted to talking to himself, thinking aloud. He was once talked of for captain of the company, and about that time, they say, was overheard saying to himself, "Captain Abel Davis! What a fine-looking man!"

[1] And a little over. Speared it about a week ago, and saw another not quite so large. Henry and John Bigelow put a couple into the pond some ten years ago. Were these the ones?

Can those straight ridges running north by west and south by east over the most level part of Curly-pate have anything to do with diluvial furrows?

Returning along the edge of Calla Swamp, under the fern-clad hill, I feel the crunching sound [*sic*] of frost-crystals in the heaving mud under my feet, and see and feel the sphagnum already stiffened into a crust, and what probably in the forenoon was water trickling from a fern-clad rock is now half a dozen icicles, six or eight inches long. Such is the first freez-ing day. Such phenomena are first observed under the north side of a hill in a cold swamp like this. Such are the first advances of winter. Ice-crystals shoot in the mud, the sphagnum becomes a stiffened mass, and dropping water in these cold places, a rigid icicle.

E. Hoar tells me that his partner, having a new adobe house, or perhaps roof to it, built in Santa Bar-bara, on the California coast, corrected the bad level-ling of his carpenters by taking such a position as to make the ridge-pole coincide with the horizon line where the Pacific appeared to meet the sky.

The thermometer is 27° at 6 P. M. The mud in the street is stiffened under my feet this evening.

Where there is a wall near a pitch pine wood, I see the scales of the cones which the squirrels have carried to the wall and stripped, strewn all along the wall on the ground.

Nov. 15. The obvious falling of leaves (*i. e.*, not to include the fall of the pitch pines and larches and the complete fall of the birches, white willows, etc.) ended about the first of November. A very few bright-colored leaves on small shrubs, such as oak sprouts, black cherry, blueberry, etc., have lingered up to this time in favorable places. By the first of November, or at most a few days later, the trees generally wear, in the main, their winter aspect, their leaves gradually falling until spring.

P. M. — To Holden Swamp and C. Miles Swamp.

Where the earth has been freshly exposed and so lies light, it is now heaved up and white with asbestos-like crystals two or three inches long, which sink and are crunched by my feet. Cold pools in shady woods and under the north sides of walls are now skimmed over. Ice a quarter of an inch thick. I see its large flaky crystals like low undulations, a mosaic of slightly concave, perhaps triangular pieces. The paths whose surface was frozen each night are now thawing and wet.

The water of the brook beyond Hubbard's Grove, where it spreads out a little, though not frozen, is clear, cold, and deserted of life. There are no water-bugs nor skaters on it. Rennie, in "Library of Entertaining Knowledge," says they are seen all winter on some pools in England, i. e. the *Gyrinus natator*. I see no ants on the great ant-hills, and methinks I have not for three weeks at least. There is but little insect-life abroad now. You wonder what nourishment the cattle can extract from the withered and bleached grass. This cold blast has swept the water-bugs from the pools. My walk is the more lonely when I perceive that there are no ants now upon their hillocks in field or wood. These are deserted mounds. They have

Vol. X

commenced their winter's sleep. I break my way into the midst of Holden Swamp to get a specimen of *Kalmia glauca* leaf. The surface is composed of great porous tussocks, or hummocks, of sphagnum, fifteen or twenty inches high or more, about the stems of blueberry bushes, choke-berry, water andromeda, swamp-pink, spruce, etc., etc., in which my feet sink five or six inches, and my shoes are filled with the rubbish. The water is frozen solid in the leaves of the pitcher-plants. This is the thickest ice I've seen. This water was most exposed in the cool swamp. I part the scraggy bushes with my hands and press my way through them. I come out covered with the fragments of lichens and rotten twigs and sphagnum.

Going by my owl-nest oak, I saw that it had broken off at the hole and the top fallen, but, seeing in the cavity some leaves, I climbed up to see what kind of nest it was and what traces of the owls were left. Having shinned up with some difficulty to the top of this great stump some fifteen or eighteen feet high, I took out the leaves slowly, watching to see what spoils had been left with them. Some were pretty green, and all had evidently been placed there this fall. When I had taken all out with my left hand, holding on to the top of the stump with my right, I looked round into the cleft, and there I saw, sitting nearly erect at the bottom in one corner, a little *Mus leucopus*, panting with fear and with its large black eyes upon me. I held my face thus within seven or eight inches of it as long as I cared to hold on there, and it showed no sign of retreating. When I put in my hand, it merely withdrew

downward into a snug little nest of hypnum and apparently the dirty-white wool-like pappus of some plant as big as a batting-ball. Wishing to see its tail, I stirred it up again, when it suddenly rushed up the side of the cleft, out over my shoulder and right arm, and leaped off, falling down through a thin hemlock spray some fifteen or eighteen feet to the ground, on the hillside, where I lost sight of it, but heard it strike. It will thus make its nest at least sixteen feet up a tree, improving some cleft or hollow, or probably bird's nest, for this purpose. These nests, *I suppose*, are made when the trees are losing their leaves, as those of the squirrels are.

At C. Miles Swamp, I see that the larches have finished falling since the 8th (say the 12th?). Find plenty of *Andromeda Polifolia* there, where you can walk dry-shod in the spruce wood, together with *Kalmia glauca*. The former is linear, about twice as long and two thirds as broad as the latter, alternate mucronate, round-stemmed. The *Kalmia glauca* has fewer leaves now, opposite, glossy above; a very sharp two-edged twig, the edges springing from the base of the leaves and decussating like them, so that when the twig is held up to the light it appears alternately thicker and thinner. This plant is commonly seen now with only a few narrow and erect young leaves in a tuft near the end of the twigs, but in many cases older, broader, and nearly horizontal ones, half a dozen of them along the last four or five inches of the twig. The andromeda is most white beneath; the other is more greenish.

The white willows, which retain many of their leaves even yet, are of a peculiar buff (?) or fawn (?) color.

Raspberry shoots, too, have their bloom like the thimble-berry, but they are not so rank nor smooth.

Of the evergreen trees described by Loudon, methinks these it would be worth the while to have on one's premises: —

Pinus sylvestris, Scotch pine or fir; the most valuable pine of Europe. Looks like our pitch pine.

Pinus Pinaster, which is planted on the sands in France.

Abies excelsa, the lofty or Norway spruce fir.

Perhaps *Picea pectinata*, the comb-like-leaved silver fir.

The Scotch larch, which is not indigenous in Britain, but on the mountains of the middle of Europe. I have,

Of western American trees: —

The *Pinus Lambertiana*, the gigantic or Lambert's pine, Columbia River, one hundred and fifty to two hundred feet high, twenty to near sixty in circumference, allied closely to *P. Strobus*.

Abies Douglassii, northwestern America, one hundred to one hundred and eighty feet high.

Picea grandis, great silver fir, northern California, one hundred and seventy to two hundred feet high.

Nov. 17. Rain last night.

Nov. 18. P. M. — To Dam Meadows.

Going along the Bedford road at Moore's Swamp, I hear the dry rustling of seedy rattlesnake grass in the wind, a November sound, within a rod of me.

The sunlight is a peculiarly thin and clear yellow, falling on the pale-brown bleaching herbage of the fields at this season. There is no redness in it. This is November sunlight. Much cold, slate-colored cloud, bare twigs seen gleaming toward the light like gossamer, pure green of pines whose old leaves have fallen, reddish or yellowish brown oak leaves rustling on the hillsides, very pale brown, bleaching, almost hoary fine grass or hay in the fields, akin to the frost which has killed it, and flakes of clear yellow sunlight falling on it here and there, — such is November.

The fine grass killed by the frost, withered and bleached till it is almost silvery, has clothed the fields for a long time.

Now, as in the spring, we rejoice in sheltered and sunny places. Some corn is left out still even.

What a mockery to turn cattle out into such pastures! Yet I see more in the fields now than earlier.

I hear a low concert from the edge of Gowing's Swamp, amid the maples, etc., — suppressed warblings from many flitting birds. With my glass I see only tree sparrows, and suppose it is they.

What I noticed for the thousandth time on the 15th was the waved surface of thin dark ice just frozen, as if it were a surface composed of large, perhaps triangular pieces raised at the edges; *i. e.*, the filling up between the original shooting of the crystals — the midribs of the icy leaves — is on a lower plane.

Flannery is the hardest-working man I know. Before sunrise and long after sunset he is taxing his unweariable muscles. The result is a singular cheerfulness. He is always in good spirits. He often overflows with his joy when you perceive no occasion for it. If only the gate sticks, some of it bubbles up and overflows in his passing comment on that accident. How much mere industry proves! There is a sparkle often in his passing remark, and his voice is really like that of a bird.

Crows will often come flying much out of their way to caw at me.

In one light, these are old and worn-out fields that I ramble over, and men have gone to law about them long before I was born, but I trust that I ramble over them in a new fashion and redeem them.

I noticed on the 15th that that peculiar moraine or horseback just this side of J. P. Brown's extends southerly of Nut Meadow Brook in the woods, maybe a third or a half a mile long in all.

The rocks laid bare here and there by ditching in the Dam Meadows are very white, having no lichens on them.

The musquash should appear in the coat of arms of some of the States, it is so common. I do not go by any permanent pool but, sooner or later, I hear its plunge there. Hardly a bit of board floats in any ditch or pond-hole but this creature has left its traces on it.

How singularly rivers in their sources overlap each other! There is the meadow behind Brooks Clark's and at the head of which Sted Buttrick's handsome

maple lot stands, on the old Carlisle road. The stream which drains this empties into the Assabet at Dove Rock. A short distance west of this meadow, but a good deal more elevated, is Boaz's meadow, whose water finds its way, naturally or artificially, northeastward around the other, crossing the road just this side the lime-kiln, and empties into the Saw Mill Brook and so into the main river.

There are many ways of feeling one's pulse. In a healthy state the constant experience is a pleasurable sensation or sentiment. For instance, in such a state I find myself in perfect connection with nature, and the perception, or remembrance even, of any natural phenomena is attended with a gentle pleasurable excitement. Prevailing sights and sounds make the impression of beauty and music on me. But in sickness all is deranged. I had yesterday a kink in my back and a general cold, and as usual it amounted to a cessation of life. I lost for the time my *rapport* or relation to nature. Sympathy with nature is an evidence of perfect health. You cannot perceive beauty but with a serene mind. The cheaper your amusements, the safer and saner. They who think much of theatres, operas, and the like, are beside themselves. Each man's necessary path, though as obscure and apparently uneventful as that of a beetle in the grass, is the way to the deepest joys he is susceptible of; though he converses only with moles and fungi and disgraces his relatives, it is no matter if he knows what is steel to his flint.

Many a man who should rather describe his dinner imposes on us with a history of the Grand Khan.

Nov. 19. P. M. — To Cliffs.

In Stow's sprout-land west of railroad cut, I see where a mouse which has a hole under a stump has eaten out clean the insides of the little *Prinos verticillatus* berries. These may be the doubtful seeds of the 14th. What pretty fruit for the mice, these bright prinos berries! They run up the twigs in the night and gather this shining fruit, take out the small seeds, and eat their kernels at the entrance to their burrows. The ground is strewn with them there.

Turning up a stone on Fair Haven Hill, I find many small dead crickets about the edges, which have endeavored to get under it and apparently have been killed by the frost; quite under it and alive, two or three small purplish-brown caterpillars; and many little ants, quite active, with their white grubs, in spacious galleries, somewhat semicylindrical, whose top often was the bottom of the stone. You would think they had been made by a worm.

Going along close under the Cliffs, I see a dozen or more low blackberry vines dangling down a perpendicular rock at least eight feet high, and blown back and forth, with leaves every six inches, and one or two have reached the ground and taken firm root there. There are also many of the common cinquefoil with its leaves five inches asunder, dangling down five or six feet over the same rock. I see many acorn and other nut shells which in past years have been tucked into clefts in the rocks.

Nov. 20. High wind in the night, shaking the house, apparently from the northwest.

About 9.30 A. M., though there is very little cloud, I see a few flakes of snow, two or three only, like flocks of gossamer, straggling in a slanting direction to the ground, unnoticed by most, in a rather raw air. At ten there is a little more. The children in the next yard have seen it and are excited. They are searching to see if any rests on the ground.

In books, that which is most generally interesting is what comes home to the most cherished private experience of the greatest number. It is not the book of him who has travelled the farthest over the surface of the globe, but of him who has lived the deepest and been the most at home. If an equal emotion is excited by a familiar homely phenomenon as by the Pyramids, there is no advantage in seeing the Pyramids. It is on the whole better, as it is simpler, to use the common language. We require that the reporter be very permanently planted before the facts which he observes, not a mere passer-by; hence the facts cannot be too homely. A man is worth most to himself and to others, whether as an observer, or poet, or neighbor, or friend, where he is most himself, most contented and at home. There his life is the most intense and he loses the fewest moments. Familiar and surrounding objects are the best symbols and illustrations of his life. If a man who has had deep experiences should endeavor to describe them in a book of travels, it would be to use the language of a wandering tribe instead of a universal language. The poet has made the best roots in his native soil of any man, and is the hardest to transplant. The man

who is often thinking that it is better to be somewhere else than where he is excommunicates himself. If a man is rich and strong anywhere, it must be on his native soil. Here I have been these forty years learning the language of these fields that I may the better express myself. If I should travel to the prairies, I should much less understand them, and my past life would serve me but ill to describe them. Many a weed here stands for more of life to me than the big trees of California would if I should go there. We only need travel enough to give our intellects an airing. In spite of Malthus and the rest, there will be plenty of room in this world, if every man will mind his own business. I have not heard of any planet running against another yet.

P. M. — To Ministerial Swamp.

Some bank swallows' nests are exposed by the caving of the bank at Clamshell. The very smallest hole is about two and a half inches wide horizontally, by barely one high. All are much wider than high (vertically). One nest, with an egg in it still, is completely exposed. The cavity at the end is shaped like a thick hoe-cake or lens, about six inches wide and two plus thick, vertically. The nest is a regular but shallow one made simply of stubble, about five inches in diameter, and three quarters of an inch deep.

I see many pollywogs in cold pools now.

I enter the Ministerial Swamp at the road below Tarbell's. The water andromeda leaves are brown now, except where protected by trees. In some places

where many of the bright-crimson shoots of high blueberry are seen together, they have a very pretty effect, a crimson vigor to stand above the snow. Where the larches stand thick with their dark boles and stems, the ground is thickly strewn with their fine and peculiarly dark brown leaves, chaff-like, i. e. darker than those of other *pines*, perhaps like black walnut or cherry shavings. As where other evergreens stand thick, little or nothing grows beneath. I see where squirrels (apparently) have eaten and stripped the spruce cones. I distinguished where the earth was cast out in cutting ditches through this swamp long ago, and this earth is covered and concealed with a thick growth of cup and cockscomb lichens. In this light-lying earth, in one place, I see where some creature some time ago has pawed out much comb of some kind of bee (probably for the honey?), making a hole as big as my head, and this torn comb lies about.

Returning through Harrington's land, I see, methinks, two gentlemen plowing a field, as if to try an agricultural experiment, — for, it being cold and windy, both plowman and driver have their coats on, — but when I get closer, I hear the driver speak in a peculiarly sharp and petulant manner to the plowman as they are turning the land furrow, and I know at once that they belong to those two races which are so slow to amalgamate. Thus my little idyl is disturbed.

I see a partridge on the ground under a white oak by Tarbell's black birches, looking just like a snag.

This is the second time I have seen them in such a place. Are they not after acorns?

In the large Tommy Wheeler field, *Ranunculus bulbosus* in full bloom!

I hear again the soft rippling of the Assabet under those black birches, which Tappan once remarked on. It is not so steep a fall as to be hoarse.

The hardy tree sparrow has taken the place of the chipping and song sparrow, so much like the former that most do not know it is another. His faint lisping chip will keep our spirits up till another spring.

I observed this afternoon how some bullocks had a little sportiveness forced upon them. They were running down a steep declivity to water, when, feeling themselves unusually impelled by gravity downward, they took the hint even as boys do, flourished round gratuitously, tossing their hind quarters into the air and shaking their heads at each other, but what increases the ludicrousness of it to me is the fact that such capers are never accompanied by a smile. Who does not believe that their step is less elastic, their movement more awkward, for their long domesticity?

Nov. 21.[1] P. M. — Up Assabet.

Paddling along, a little above the Hemlocks, I hear, I think, a boy whistling upon the bank above me, but immediately perceive that it is the whistle of the locomotive a mile off in that direction. I perceived that it was distant, and therefore the locomotive, the moment that the key was changed from a very high

[1] Dates between Nov. 17th and 21st doubtful, a day or two.

to a low one. Was it because distant sounds are commonly on a low key?

Just above the grape-hung birches, my attention was drawn to a singular-looking dry leaf or parcel of leaves on the shore about a rod off. Then I thought it might be the dry and yellowed skeleton of a bird with all its ribs; then the shell of a turtle, or possibly some large dry oak leaves peculiarly curved and cut; and then, all at once, I saw that it was a woodcock, perfectly still, with its head drawn in, standing on its great pink feet. I had, apparently, noticed only the yellowish-brown portions of the plumage, referring the dark-brown to the shore behind it. May it not be that the yellowish-brown markings of the bird correspond somewhat to its skeleton? At any rate with my eye steadily on it from a point within a rod, I did not for a considerable time suspect it to be a living creature. Examining the shore after it had flown with a whistling flight, I saw that there was a clear space of mud between the water and the edge of ice-crystals about two inches wide, melted so far by the lapse of the water, and all along the edge of the ice, for a rod or two at least, there was a hole where it had thrust its bill down, probing, every half-inch, frequently closer. Some animal life must be collected at that depth just in that narrow space, savory morsels for this bird.

I was paddling along slowly, on the lookout for what was to be seen, when my attention was caught by a strange-looking leaf or bunch of leaves on the shore, close to the water's edge, a rod distant. I thought to

myself, I may as well investigate that, and so pushed slowly toward it, my eyes resting on it all the while. It then looked like a small shipwrecked hulk and, strange to say, like the bare skeleton of a fowl that has been picked and turned yellowish, resting on its breast-bone, the color of a withered black or red oak leaf. Again I thought it must be such a leaf or cluster of leaves peculiarly curved and cut or torn on the upper edges.

The chubby bird dashed away zigzag, carrying its long tongue-case carefully before it, over the witch-hazel bushes. This is its walk, — the portion of the shore, the narrow strip, still kept open and unfrozen between the water's edge and the ice. The sportsman might discover its neighborhood by these probings.

Nov. 23. Monday. P. M. — To Gowing's Swamp.
Garfield, who was working in what was Moore's Swamp, tells me that he sometimes digs up frogs in the winter, when ditching in springy places, one at a time. He is very much troubled by the short-tailed meadow mouse in that meadow. They live under the stumps, and gnaw his potatoes in the fall. He thought that his little dog, a terrier, had killed a bushel of them the past year.

At the back of Gowing's hillside, just west of his swamp, in the midst of shrub oaks and other dry upland trees, the ground slopes regularly on all sides to a deep round hollow, perhaps fifteen feet lower than the lowest side and thirty feet in diameter at the bot-

tom. The bottom is rather wet and covered with sphagnum, and many stiff and dead-looking button-bushes stand in it, while all around a dense high hedge of high blueberry curves over it. So sudden a change there will be in the vegetation with a change of soil. Many such a dimple with its peculiar vegetations have I seen in a dry wood-lot. The *Vaccinium corymbosum* and panicled andromeda in a dense hedge, in a circular or oval or other curved form, surrounding and slanting over it so as almost to conceal it; and in the same manner the blueberry, etc., will grow around and overhang the largest ponds.

Walked through Gowing's Swamp from west to east. You may say it is divided into three parts, — first, the thin woody; second, the coarse bushy or gray; and third, the fine bushy or brown.

First: The trees are larch, white birch, red maple, spruce, white pine, etc.

Second: The coarse bushy part, or blueberry thicket, consists of high blueberry, panicled andromeda, *Amelanchier Canadensis* var. *oblongifolia*, swamp-pink, choke-berry, *Viburnum nudum*, rhodora, (and probably prinos, holly, etc., etc., not distinguishable easily now), but chiefly the first two. Much of the blueberry being dead gives it a very gray as well as scraggy aspect. It is a very bad thicket to break through, yet there are commonly thinner places, or often opens, by which you may wind your way about the denser clumps. Small specimens of the trees are mingled with these and also some water andromeda and lambkill.

Third: There are the smooth brown and wetter spaces where the water andromeda chiefly prevails, together with purplish lambkill about the sides of them, and hairy huckleberry; but in the midst and wettest part the narrow revolute and glaucous (beneath) leaves of the *Andromeda Polifolia* and *Kalmia glauca* are seen, and in the sphagnum the *Vaccinium Oxycoccus*. In one of the latter portions occurs that open pool.

Sphagnum is found everywhere in the swamp.

First, there is the dark wooded part; second, the scraggy gray blueberry thicket; third, the rich brown water andromeda spaces.

The high blueberry delights singularly in these localities. You distinguish it by its gray spreading mass; its light-gray bark, rather roughened; its thickish shoots, often crimson; and its plump, roundish red buds. Think of its wreaths and canopies of cool blue fruit in August, thick as the stars in the Milky Way! The panicled andromeda is upright, light-gray, with a rather smoother bark, more slender twigs, and small, sharp red buds lying close to the twig. The blueberry is particularly hard to break through, it is so spreading and scraggy, but a hare can double swiftly enough beneath it. The ground of sphagnum is now thickly strewn with the leaves of these shrubs.

The water andromeda makes a still more uniformly dense thicket, which must be nearly impervious to some animals; but as man lifts his head high above it, [he] finds but little difficulty in making his way through it, though it sometimes comes up to his middle, and if his eye scans its surface it makes an impression of smoothness and denseness, — its rich brown, wholesome surface, even as grass or moss.

Ascending the high land on the south, I looked down over the large open space with its *navel* pool in the centre. This green stagnant pool, rayed with the tracks or trails of musquash and making but a feeble watery impression, reminded me of portions of the map of the moon.

This swamp appears not to have had any natural outlet, though an artificial one has been dug. The same is perhaps the case with the C. Miles Swamp. And is it so with Beck Stow's? These three are the only places where I have found the *Andromeda Polifolia.* The *Kalmia glauca* in Gowing's, C. Miles's, and Holden's swamps. The latter has no outlet of any kind.

I am interested in those plants, like panicled andromeda, shrub oak, etc., for which no use that I know has been discovered. The panicled andromeda, instead of the date tree, might be my coat-of-arms.

Fresh slender shoots of the *Viburnum nudum* make very good withes, I find.

Austin Bacon told me that the worst swamp he ever found was not in Vermont or up country where he had surveyed, but in Newton (?), where he surveyed for a road once. The water was about two feet deep, and you jumped from tussock to tussock; these generally tipped over with you into the water.

Vol. X

etc., with a few small birches, maples, pines, etc. As I remember, it lies *somewhat* thus: —

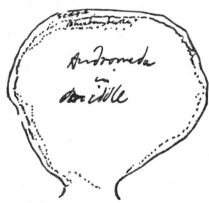

The southerly continuation of this and the other two ponds are much more wet, — have open water and less andromeda, much more sedge in proportion. Why does the sedge grow thus around the andromeda in a regular ring next the hill? I think it is because it is more wet there. It would be open water there all the way round if it were not for the sedge, but I could walk through the andromeda if I could get to it. Why should it be more wet there? I do not know, unless the springs are at the base of the hills. The sedge can evidently bear more water than the andromeda, and the andromeda than the blueberry bushes, etc. Perhaps the sedge prepares the ground for the andromeda sometimes, furnishing a base and support for it. I see the latter, as it were, making its way out thinly into the

There is a strong and warm southwest wind, which brings the frost out of the ground, — more than I thought was in it, — making the surface wet.

Walking along the top of Gowing's hill wood-lot, I see from time to time large ant-hills amid the young oaks. Often their tops have been disturbed and flattened, by some creature apparently. Some may be deserted. The sedge-grass has sprung up long and thick about the sides of these mounds, though there may be none amid the oaks around. The working of the ants keeps clear a little space amid the bushes.

In the evening heavy rain and some thunder and lightning, and rain in the night.

Nov. 24. P. M. — To Andromeda Ponds.

Cold Thanksgiving weather again, the pools freezing. The first or northernmost Andromeda Pond, considering the main portion north of the isthmus, is surrounded, except at the isthmus, by dry hills, twenty-five to forty [feet] high perhaps, covered with young oaks. Its interior, or far the greater part of the whole, is filled with a uniformly dense and level bed of brown andromeda, in which I detect nothing else from the hills except some white cotton-grass waving over it. Between the andromeda and the hills, there is a border, from one to two rods wide, of coarse and now yellowish sedge all the way round, except, of course, at the isthmus, and part of the way, just within the edge of the andromeda, mixed with it, a second inner border of gray bushes, chiefly, I suppose, blueberry,

sedge here and there. Perhaps the sedge once covered the whole or greater part. The sphagnum, *apparently*, having some slight solid core to grow around, like an andromeda or blueberry stem, builds itself up a foot or more and may make a soil for noble plants thus.

On the dry hillside next the water, there is another belt, *i. e.* of lambkill, pretty dense, running apparently quite round the pond a rod or more in width. Probably it occurs very far off, or high, thinly, but here it is a thick growth and has relation to the swamp.

According to this, then, you have clear open water, but shallow; then, in course of time, a shallow lake with much sedge standing in it; then, after a while, a dense andromeda bed with blueberry bushes and perhaps a wet border of sedge (as here at present); and finally, a maple swamp.

Spruce and larch appear to flourish very well at the same time with the andromeda.

Looking toward the sun, the andromeda in front of me is a very warm red brown and on either side of me, a pale silvery brown; looking from the sun, a uniform pale brown.

Perhaps the *Andromeda Polifolia* and *Kalmia glauca* prefer stagnant water.

These andromeda swamps charmed me more than twenty years ago, — I knew not why, — and I called them "a moccasin-print."

The *Fringilla hyemalis* appear to be flitting about in a more lively manner on account of the cold. They go off with a twitter from the low weeds and bushes. Nowadays birds are so rare I am wont to mistake them at first for a leaf or mote [?] blown off from the trees or bushes.

Some poets have said that writing poetry was for youths only, but not so. In that fervid and excitable season we only get the impulse which is to carry us onward in our future career. Ideals are then exhibited to us distinctly which all our lives after we may aim at but not attain. The mere vision is little compared with the steady corresponding endeavor thitherward. It would be vain for us to be looking ever into promised lands toward which in the meanwhile we were not steadily and earnestly travelling, whether the way led over a mountain-top or through a dusky valley. In youth, when we are most elastic and there is a spring to us, we merely receive an impulse in the proper direction. To suppose that this is equivalent to having travelled the road, or obeyed the impulse faithfully throughout a lifetime, is absurd. We are shown fair scenes in order that we may be tempted to inhabit them, and not simply tell what we have seen.

Nov. 25. P. M. — To Hubbard's Close and thence through woods to Goose Pond and Pine Hill.

A clear, cold, windy afternoon. The cat crackles with electricity when you stroke her, and the fur rises up to your touch.

This is November of the hardest kind, — bare frozen ground covered with pale-brown or straw-colored herbage, a strong, cold, cutting northwest wind which makes me seek to cover my ears, a perfectly clear and cloudless sky. The cattle in the fields have a cold,

shrunken, shaggy look, their hair standing out every way, as if with electricity, like the cat's. Ditches and pools are fast skimming over, and a few slate-colored snowbirds, with thick, shuffling twitter, and fine-chipping tree sparrows flit from bush to bush in the otherwise deserted pastures. This month taxes a walker's resources more than any. For my part, I should sooner think of going into quarters in November than in the winter. If you do feel any fire at this season out of doors, you may depend upon it, it is your own. It is but a short time, these afternoons, before the night cometh, in which no man can walk. If you delay to start till three o'clock, there will be hardly time left for a long and rich adventure, — to get fairly out of town. November Eat-heart, — is that the name of it?[1] Not only the fingers cease to do their office, but there is often a benumbing of the faculties generally. You can hardly screw up your courage to take a walk when all is thus tightly locked or frozen up and so little is to be seen in field or wood. I am inclined to take to the swamps or woods as the warmest place, and the former are still the openest. Nature has herself become like the few fruits which she still affords, a very thick-shelled nut with a shrunken meat within. If I find anything to excite or warm my thoughts abroad, it is an agreeable disappointment, for I am obliged to go abroad willfully and against my inclinations at first. The prospect looks so barren, so many springs are frozen up, not a flower perchance and but few birds left, not a companion abroad in all these fields for me, I am slow to go forth. I seem to antici-

[1] [Channing, p. 107.]

pate a fruitless walk. I think to myself hesitatingly, Shall I go there, or there, or there? and cannot make up my mind to any route, all seem so unpromising, mere surface walking and fronting the cold wind, so that I have to force myself to it often and at random. But then I am often unexpectedly compensated, and the thinnest yellow light of November is more warming and exhilarating than any wine they tell of; and then the mite which November contributes becomes equal in value to the bounty of July. I may meet with something which interests me, and immediately it is as warm as in July, as if it were the south instead of the northwest wind that blowed.

I do not know if I am singular when I say that I believe there is no man with whom I can associate who will not, comparatively speaking, spoil my afternoon. That society or encounter may at last yield a fruit which I am not aware of, but I cannot help suspecting that I should have spent those hours more profitably alone.

Pools under the north sides of hills are frozen pretty thick. That cold one of Stow's is nearly an inch and a half thick. It is already dusty, though the ice is but a day or two old. That of Jarvis's, opposite Breed's, is also skimmed over thinly, but Goose Pond very little way as yet. The main crystals of this new ice remind me where massed together sometimes of spiny cactus leaves. Meeting each other, they inclose figures of a more or less triangular form rather than squarish. Sometimes many are closely parallel, half an inch apart, and in favorable lights you see a resemblance to large feathers. Sometimes those large spiny crystals ray

from a centre, star-like, somewhat like the folds of a garment taken up by a point. The plaited ice. Also you may say the waved ice, — still speaking of the first thin ice of the season.

I notice a thimble-berry vine forming an arch four feet high, which has firmly rooted itself at the small end.

The roar of the wind in the trees over my head sounds as cold as the wind feels.

I come to what seems an old ditch a dozen feet long, in Hubbard's Close. It is skinned over, but I see where a spring wells up from its bottom under the ice. When I come to it, small *black-looking* fishes (?), four or five inches long, apparently trout, dart about it with incredible velocity, trying to escape or to bury themselves in the mud. It is some time before all have succeeded in burying themselves to their minds, but when I shake the bog they start again.

Ascending the hill on the east of the Close, I find, in the pine wood on its top, some fragments of a frozen white fungus or toadstool, which apparently a squirrel has eaten, for he has also dropped some at the base of a pine. These look almost exactly like asbestos, so white and stringy to the eye.

Methinks there has been more pine-sap than usual the past summer. I never saw a quarter part so much. It stands there withered in dense brown masses, six or eight inches high, partly covered with dead leaves. The tobacco-pipes are a darker brown.

You see here and there, under pitch pines, bits of gray bark which have fallen, reminding you very strongly of the scaly armor, perhaps, of fossil fishes or other creatures. I see, under a large white pine, three quarts at least of scales in a heap, where a squirrel has sat on the instep of the tree and stripped the cones. Further in Ebby Hubbard's wood, I see a great two-storied mass of black spunk which has fallen.

I shiver about awhile on Pine Hill, waiting for the sun to set. Methinks the air is dusky soon after four these days. The landscape looks darker than at any season, — like arctic scenery. There is the sun a quarter of an hour high, shining on it through a perfectly clear sky, but to my eye it is singularly dark or dusky. And now the sun has disappeared, there is hardly less light for half a minute. I should not know when it was down, but by looking for [it] as I stand at this height.

Returning, I see a fox run across the road in the twilight from Potter's into Richardson's woods. He is on a canter, but I see the whitish tip of his tail. I feel a certain respect for him, because, though so large, he still maintains himself free and wild in our midst, and is so original so far as any resemblance to our race is concerned. Perhaps I like him better than his tame cousin the dog for it.

It is surprising how much, from the habit of regarding writing as an accomplishment, is wasted on form. A very little information or wit is mixed up with a great deal of conventionalism in the style of expressing it, as with a sort of preponderating paste or vehicle. Some life is not simply expressed, but a long-winded speech is made, with an occasional attempt to put a little life into it.

Vol. X

Nov. 26.[1] Speaking of those long, dry, barren hollows in the Richardson wood-lot with Ebby Hubbard, he says that the reason why no trees have sprung up in them is because the trees were very old when they were cut, and no sprouts came up from the stumps. Otherwise the lowest ground is the best-timbered. I have referred it to frost.

Rice tells me he remembers that Nathan Barrett's father used to stutter. He went round collecting the direct taxes soon after the Revolution, — on carriages, watches, dogs, etc., etc. It was perhaps a dollar on a dog. Coming to Captain Bent's, who kept tavern in Sudbury where Israel Rice lives, he collected his tax and then said, "I want you to may-ma-ma-ma-make me a ha-ha-ha-ha-ha — to make me a ha-ha-ha — a *whole* mug o' flip."

Got my boat up this afternoon. (It is Thanksgiving Day.) One end had frozen in. I see that already some eager urchins have been able to try their skates on a short and narrow strip of ice by the riverside there.

Minott's is a small, square, one-storied and unpainted house, with a hipped roof and at least one dormer-window, a third the way up the south side of a long hill which is some fifty feet high and extends east and west. A traveller of taste may go straight through the village without being detained a moment by any dwelling, either the form or surroundings being objectionable, but very few go by this house without being agreeably impressed, and many are therefore led to inquire

[1] [The manuscript journal volume which begins here has "The Open Winter" on its first fly-leaf.]

who lives in it. Not that its form is so incomparable, nor even its weather-stained color, but chiefly, I think, because of its snug and picturesque position on the hillside, fairly lodged there, where all children like to be, and its perfect harmony with its surroundings and position. For if, preserving this form and color, it should be transplanted to the meadow below, nobody would notice it more than a schoolhouse which was lately of the same form. It is there because somebody was independent or bold enough to carry out the happy thought of placing it high on the hillside. It is the locality, not the architecture, that takes us captive. There is exactly such a site, only of course less room on either side, between this house and the next westward, but few if any, even of the admiring travellers, have thought of this as a house-lot, or would be bold enough to place a cottage there.

Without side fences or gravelled walks or flower-plats, that simple sloping bank before it is pleasanter than any front yard, though many a visitor — and many times the master — has slipped and fallen on the steep path. From its position and exposure, it has shelter and warmth and dryness and prospect. He overlooks the road, the meadow and brook, and houses beyond, to the distant woods. The spring comes earlier to that dooryard than any, and summer lingers longest there.

Nov. 27. Mr. Wesson says that he has seen a striped squirrel eating a white-bellied mouse on a wall — had evidently caught [it]; also that the little dipper is not

a coot, — but he appears not to know a coot, and did not recognize the lobed feet when I drew them. Says the little dipper has a bill like a hen, and will not dive at the flash so as to escape, as he has proved.[1] Says that a loon can run but little way and very awkwardly, falling on its belly, and cannot rise from the ground. Makes a great noise running on the water before it rises.

Standing before Stacy's large glass windows this morning, I saw that they were gloriously ground by the frost. I never saw such beautiful feather and fir-like frosting. His windows are filled with fancy articles and toys for Christmas and New-Year's presents, but this delicate and graceful outside frosting surpassed them all infinitely. I saw countless feathers with very distinct midribs and fine pinnæ. The half of a trunk seemed to rise in each case up along the sash, and these feathers branched off from it all the way, sometimes nearly horizontally. Other crystals looked like pine plumes the size of life. If glass could be ground to look like this, how glorious it would be!

You can tell which shopman has the hottest fire within by the frost being melted off. I was never so struck by the gracefulness of the curves in vegetation, and wonder that Ruskin does not refer to frostwork.

P. M. — Rode to the kiln and quarry by William Farrar's, Carlisle, and to gorge behind Melvin's.

The direction of the strata at this quarry is like that of Curly-pate and the Easterbrooks quarries, east-

[1] *Vide* Dec. 26, 1857.

northeast by west-southwest, though the latter are very nearly two miles southeast.

Was struck by the appearance of a small hickory near the wall, in the rocky ravine just above the trough. Its trunk was covered with loose scales unlike the hickories near it and as much as the shagbark; but probably it is a shaggy or scaly-barked variety of *Carya glabra*. It may be well to observe it next fall. The husk is not thick, like that of the shagbark, but quite thin, and splits into four only part way down. The shell is not white nor sharply four-angled like the other, but it is rather like a pignut.

The stratification trends there as at Curly-pate, or perhaps more north and south.

That trough placed on the side of the rocky valley to catch the trickling spring for the sake of the cattle, with a long slab cover to the trough that leads to it to fend off the feet of cattle that come to drink, is an agreeable object and in keeping with the circumstances, amid the hickories and perhaps ash trees. It reminds me of life sometimes in the pasture, — that other creatures than myself quench their thirst at this hillside.

I think that Ruskin is wrong about reflections in his "Elements of Drawing," page 181. He says the reflection is merely the substance "reversed" or "topsy-turvy," and adds, "Whatever you can see from the place in which you stand, of the solid objects so reversed under the water, you will see in the reflection, always in the true perspective of the solid objects so reversed."

Nov. 28. P. M. — Around Ebby Hubbard's wood-lot.

On the hillside above his swamp, near the Ministerial land, I found myself walking in one of those shelf-like hillside paths made by Indians, hunters, cows, or what-not, and it was beset with fresh snares for partridges, this wise:  Upright twigs are stuck in the ground across the path, a foot or more in height and just close enough together to turn a partridge aside, leaving a space about four inches wide in the middle, and some twigs are stretched across above to prevent the birds hopping over. Then a sapling about an inch in diameter or less is bent over, and the end caught under one of the twigs which has a notch or projection on one side, and a free-running noose, attached to the sapling, hangs in the opening and is kept spread by being hung on some very slight nicks in the two twigs. This seems to suppose the bird to be going one way only, but perhaps if it cannot escape one way it will turn and try to go back, and so spring the trap.

I saw one that was sprung with nothing in it, another whose slip-noose was blown or fallen one side, and another with a partridge still warm in it. It was a male bird hanging dead by the neck, just touching its toes to the ground. It had a collar or ruff about its neck, of large and conspicuous black feathers with a green reflection. This black is peculiar to the male, the female's being brown. Its feet, now clinched in its agony,

Vol. X

were the strangest-looking pale blue, with a fine fringe, of scales or the like, on each side of each toe. The small black feathers were centred with gray spots. The scapulars were darker brown, dashed with large clear pale-brown spots; the breast-feathers light with light-brown marks. The tail-feathers had each a broad black bar, except the middle one, which was more mixed or grayish there. The bands of the females are said to be more brown, as is their collar. There were a few droppings of the bird close by the snare in two instances. Were they dropped after it was caught? Or did they determine the locality of the snare?

These birds appear to run most along the sides of wooded banks around swamps. At least these paths and snares occur there oftenest. I often scare them up from amid or near hemlocks in the woods.

The general color of the bird is that of the ground and dry leaves on it at present. The bird hanging in the snare was very inconspicuous. I had gone close by it once without noticing it. Its wings are short and stout and look as if they were a little worn by striking the ground or bushes, or perhaps in drumming. I observed a bare bright-red or scarlet spot over each eye.

Spoke to Skinner about that wildcat which he says he heard a month ago in Ebby Hubbard's woods. He was going down to Walden in the evening, to see if geese had not settled in it (with a companion), when they heard this sound, which his companion at first thought made by a coon, but S. said no, it was a wildcat. He says he has heard them often in the Adiron-

dack region, where he has purchased furs. He told him he would hear it again soon, and he did. Somewhat like the domestic cat, a low sort of growling and then a sudden quick-repeated caterwaul, or *yow yow yow*, or *yang yang yang*. He says they utter this from time to time when on the track of some prey.

Nov. 29. Sophia called on old lady Hayden yesterday, and she told her of somebody's twin infants of whom one died for want of air. The father, therefore, was advised to take the survivor with him each morning to the barn, and hold it up to the muzzle of each of the cattle in succession as they got up, that it might catch their first morning breath, and then lay it on the hay while he foddered them. He did so, and there never was a healthier child than this, three months afterward.

P. M. — To Assabet Bath and down bank.

This and yesterday remarkably warm days. In John Hosmer's low birch sprout-land, a few rods beyond Tortoise Hollow, or Valley, I find, on raking aside the withered leaves on the ground, one of those fuzzy caterpillars, black at each end and rust-colored in middle, curled up in a ring, — the same kind that I find on the ice and snow, frozen, in winter. I think that the river *might* rise so high as to wash this out of the withered grass and leaves here. Soon after I find another in a catbird's nest, nearly three feet from the ground, in a thorn, together [with] half a nestful of freshly nibbled acorn shells and a few hazelnut shells, the work, probably, of a mouse or a squirrel; but this caterpillar was dead and apparently partly eaten. So I am still inclined to think that most of them are washed out of the meadows by the freshets. Several times before I have seen nests half filled with nutshells, and as the *Mus leucopus* adds to and after occupies old nests, am inclined to think that he does it. It may be a convenient deposit for him (or for a striped squirrel??), or else he likes it for concealment and protection against hawks, — in the midst of a thorn bush, before the leaves fall. I do not know, however, that the mouse has this habit of perching while it nibbles, as the squirrel has.

Again I am struck by the singularly wholesome colors of the withered oak leaves, especially the shrub oak, so thick and firm and unworn, without speck or fret, clear reddish-brown (sometimes paler or yellowish brown), its whitish under sides contrasting with it in a very cheerful manner. So strong and cheerful, as if it rejoiced at the advent of winter, and exclaimed, "Winter, come on!" It exhibits the fashionable colors of the winter on the two sides of its leaves. It sets the fashions, colors good for bare ground or for snow, grateful to the eyes of rabbits and partridges. This is the extent of its gaudiness, red brown and misty white, and yet it is gay. The colors of the brightest flowers are not more agreeable to my eye. Then there is the now rich, dark brown of the black oak's large and somewhat curled leaf on sprouts, with its lighter, almost yellowish, brown under side. Then the salmonish hue of white oak leaves, with the under sides less distinctly lighter. Many, however, have quite faded already.

was said, had also got a letter from his son Silas in Framingham, to whom he had written, which confirmed the report. As Wild went down-town, he met Meeks the carpenter and inquired in a significant way if he got anything new. Meeks simply answered, "Well, David Loring won't eat another Thanksgiving dinner." A child at school wrote to her parents at Northboro, telling the news. Mrs. Loring's sister lives there, and it chances that her husband committed suicide. They were, therefore, slow to communicate the news to her, but at length could not contain themselves longer and told it. The sister was terribly affected; wrote to her son (L.'s nephew) in Worcester, who immediately took the cars and went to Framingham and when he arrived there met his uncle just putting his family into the cars. He shook his hand very heartily indeed, looking, however, hard at his throat, but said not a word about his errand. Already doubts had arisen, people were careful how they spoke of it, the expressmen were mum, Adams and Wetherbee never said Loring. The Framingham expressman used the same room with Adams in Boston. A. simply asked, "Any news from Framingham this morning? Seen Loring lately?" and learned that all was well.

Nov. 30. A still, warm, cloudy, rain-threatening day.
Surveying the J. Richardson lot.
The air is full of geese. I saw five flocks within an hour, about 10 A. M., containing from thirty to fifty each, and afterward two more flocks, making in all

Going through a partly frozen meadow near the meadow [*sic*], scraping through the sweet-gale, I am pleasantly scented with its odoriferous fruit.

A week or so ago, as I learn, Miss Emeline Barnett told a little boy who boards with her, and who was playing with an open knife in his hand, that he must be careful not to fall down and cut himself with it, for once Mr. David Loring, when he was a little boy, fell down with a knife in his hand and cut his throat badly. It was soon reported, among the children at least, that little David Loring, the grandson of the former, had fallen down with a knife in his hand as he was going to school, and nearly cut his throat; next, that Mr. David Loring the grandfather (who lives in Framingham) had committed suicide, had cut his throat, was not dead, indeed, but was not expected to live; and in this form the story spread like wildfire over the town and county. Nobody expressed surprise. His oldest acquaintances and best friends, his legal adviser, all said, "Well, I can believe it." He was known by many to have been speculating in Western lands, which, owing to the hard times, was a failure, and he was depressed in consequence. Sally Cummings helped spread the news. Said there was no doubt of it, but there was Fay's wife (L.'s daughter) knew nothing of it yet, they were as merry as crickets over there. Others stated that Wetherbee, the expressman, had been over to Northboro, and learned that Mr. Loring had taken poison in Northboro. Mr. Rhodes was stated to have received a letter from Mr. Robbins of Framingham giving all the particulars. Mr. Wild, it

from two hundred and fifty to three hundred at least, all flying southwest over Goose and Walden Ponds. The former was apparently well named Goose Pond. You first hear a faint honking from one or two in the northeast and think there are but few wandering there, but, looking up, see forty or fifty coming on in a more or less broken harrow, wedging their way southwest. I suspect they honk more, at any rate they are more broken and alarmed, when passing over a village, and are seen falling into their ranks again, assuming the perfect harrow form. Hearing only one or two honking, even for the seventh time, you think there are but few till you see them. According to my calculation a thousand or fifteen hundred may have gone over Concord to-day. When they fly low and near, they look very black against the sky.[1]

Northwest of Little Goose Pond, on the edge of Mrs. Bigelow's wood-lot, are several hornbeams (*Carpinus*). Looking into a cleft in one of them about three feet from the ground, which I thought might be the scar of a blazing, I found some broken kernels of corn, probably placed there by a crow or jay. This was about half a mile from a corn-field.

[1] I hear that one was killed by Lee in the Corner about this time.

DECEMBER, 1857

(ÆT. 40)

Dec. 1. P. M. — Walking in Ebby Hubbard's woods, I hear a red squirrel barking at me amid the pine and oak tops, and now I see him coursing from tree to tree. How securely he travels there, fifty feet from the ground, leaping from the slender, bending twig of one tree across an interval of three or four feet and catching at the nearest twig of the next, which so bends under him that it is at first hard to get up it. His travelling a succession of leaps in the air at that height without wings! And yet he gets along about as rapidly as on the ground.

I hear the faintest possible quivet from a nuthatch, quite near me on a pine. I thus always begin to hear this bird on the approach of winter,[1] as if it did not breed here, but wintered here.

I hear of two more flocks of geese going over to-day.

Dec. 2. Measuring Little Goose Pond, I observed two painted tortoises moving about under the thin transparent ice. When I broke it with my fist over each in succession, it was stunned by the blow. I put them back through the hole; else they might have frozen outside. There was a brown leech spread broad

[1] Hear it all the fall (and occasionally through the summer of '59).

and flat and roundish on the sternum of one, nearly an inch and a half across, apparently going to winter with it.

Where are the respectabilities of sixty years ago, the village aristocracy, the Duncan Ingrahams who lived in the high house? An Englishman lived in the Vose house. How poor and short-lived a distinction to strive after!

I find that, according to the deed of Duncan Ingraham to John Richardson in 1797, my old bean-field on Walden Pond then belonged to George Minott. (Minott thinks he bought it of an Allen.) This was Deacon George Minott, who lived in the house next below the East Quarter schoolhouse, and was a brother of my grandfather-in-law. He was directly descended from Thomas Minott, who, according to Shattuck, was secretary of the Abbot of Walden (!) in Essex and whose son George was born at Saffron Walden (!) and afterwards was one of the early settlers of Dorchester.

Roads were once described as leading to a meetinghouse, but not so often nowadays.

Dec. 3. *Thursday.* Surveying the Richardson lot, which bounds on Walden Pond, I turned up a rock near the pond to make a bound with, and found under it, attached to it, a collection of black ants (say a quarter of an inch long) an inch in diameter, collected around one monster black ant as big as four or five at least, and a small parcel of yellowish eggs (?). The large ant had no wings and was probably their queen. The ants were quite lively, though but little way under the

edge of the rock. The eggs (?) adhered to the rock when turned up.

Dec. 4. Surveying the Richardson Fair Haven lot. Rufus Morse, who comes to find his bounds on R., accounts for his deed being tattered by saying that some tame flying squirrels got loose and into a chest where he kept his papers and nibbled them, though the lid was not raised enough to get in a cent! They are so flat. I survey to a white oak called in '91 "a small white oak."

Dec. 5. At noon a few flakes fall.

Dec. 6. *Sunday.* Flannery tells me he is cutting in Holbrook's Swamp, in the Great Meadows, a lonely place. He sees a fox repeatedly there, and also a white weasel, — once with a mouse in its mouth, in the swamp.

Dec. 7. Running the long northwest side of Richardson's Fair Haven lot.

It is a fair, sunny, and warm day in the woods for the season. We eat our dinners on the middle of the line, amid the young oaks in a sheltered and very unfrequented place. I cut some leafy shrub oaks and cast them down for a dry and springy seat. As I sit there amid the sweet-fern, talking with my man Briney, I observe that the recent shoots of the sweet-fern — which, like many larger bushes and trees, have a few leaves in a tuft still at their extremities — toward the sun are densely covered with a bright, warm, silvery down,

which looks like frost, so thick and white. Looking the other way, I see none of it, but the bare reddish twigs. Even this is a cheering and compensating discovery in my otherwise barren work. I get thus a few positive values, answering to the bread and cheese which make my dinner. I owe thus to my weeks at surveying a few such slight but positive discoveries.

Briney, who has been in this country but few years, says he has lost three children here. His eldest boy fell on the deck in rough weather and struck his knee on the anchor-chain, and though he did not mind it then, his whole body ran out of the wound within two or three months.

I would rather sit at this table with the sweet-fern twigs between me and the sun than at the king's.

Dec. 8. Staples says he came to Concord some twenty-four years ago a poor boy with a dollar and three cents in his pocket, and he spent the three cents for drink at Bigelow's tavern, and now he's worth "twenty hundred dollars clear." He remembers many who inherited wealth whom he can buy out to-day. I told him that he had done better than I in a pecuniary respect, for I had only earned my living. "Well," said he, "that's all I've done, and I don't know as I've got much better clothes than you." I was particularly poorly clad then, in the woods; my hat, pants, boots, rubbers, and gloves would not have brought fourpence, and I told the Irishman that it wasn't everybody could afford to have a fringe round his legs, as I had, my corduroys not preserving a selvage.

Staples said there was one thing he liked. "What is that?" "An honest man." If he lent a man money, and when it became due he came and asked for more time because he could not pay, he excused him, but if, after it had become due, he went to the man, and he then made the same excuse, he lost all confidence in him.

Dec. 13. P. M. — To Goose Pond.

This and the like ponds are just covered with virgin ice just thick enough to bear, though it cracks about the edges on the sunny sides. You may call it virgin ice as long as it is transparent. I see the water-target leaves frozen in under the ice in Little Goose Pond. I see those same two tortoises (of Dec. 2d), moving about in the same place under the ice, which I cannot crack with my feet. The Emerson children see six under the ice of Goose Pond to-day. Apparently many winter in the mud of these ponds and pond-holes.

In sickness and barrenness it is encouraging to believe that our life is dammed and is coming to a head, so that there seems to be no loss, for what is lost in time is gained in power. All at once, unaccountably, as we are walking in the woods or sitting in our chamber, after a worthless fortnight, we cease to feel mean and barren.

I go this afternoon thinking I may find the stakes set for auction lots on the Ministerial Lot in December, '51. I find one white birch standing and two fallen. The latter were faced at one end, for the numbers, and at the other *rotten* and broken off as short, appar-

ently, as if sawed, because the bark so tears. At first I did not know but they had been moved, but thinking that if they had fallen where they stood I should find some hole or looseness in the ground at the rotten end, I felt for it and in each case found it; in one, also, the rotten point of the stake. Thus in six years two out of three stout (two-and-a-half-inch) birch stakes were flat. The hickory stake I set on R. W. E.'s town line in March, '50, was flat this last summer, or seven years, but a white [*sic*] stake set in '49–'50 on Moore and Hosmer's lot was standing aslant this month. A surveyor should know what stakes last longest.

I hear a characteristic anecdote respecting Mrs. Hoar, from good authority. Her son Edward, who takes his father's place and attends to the same duties, asked his mother the other night, when about retiring, "Shall I put the cat down cellar?" "No," said she, "you may put her outdoors." The next night he asked, "Shall I put the cat outdoors?" "No," answered she, "you may put her down cellar." The third night he asked, "Shall I put the cat down cellar or outdoors?" "Well," said his mother, "you may open the cellar door and then open the front door, and let her go just which way she pleases." Edward suggested that it was a cold night for the cat to be outdoors, but his mother said, "Who knows but she has a little kitten somewhere to look after?" Mrs. H. is a peculiar woman, who has her own opinion and way, a strong-willed, managing woman.

Dec. 15. Within a day or two, I saw another partridge in the snare of November 28th, frozen stiff.

To-day I see that some creature has torn and disembowelled it, removing it half a rod, leaving the head in snare, which has lifted it three or four feet in the air on account of its lightness. This last bird was either a female or young male, its ruff and bar on tail being rather dark-brown than black.

Dec. 16. Begins to snow about 8 A. M., and in fifteen minutes the ground is white, but it soon stops. Plowed grounds show white first.

Dec. 20. A. M. — To Easterbrooks Country with Ricketson.

A hen-hawk circling over that wild region. See its red tail.

The cellar stairs at the old Hunt house are made of square oak timbers; also the stairs to the chamber of the back part of apparently square maple (?) timber, much worn. The generous cellar stairs!

Dec. 21. Walking over the Andromeda Ponds between Walden and Fair Haven, which have only frozen just enough to bear me, I see in springy parts, where the ice is thin, good-sized pollywogs wiggling away, scared by the sound of my steps and cracking of the ice. They appear to keep in motion in such muddy pond-holes, where a spring wells up from the bottom till midwinter, if not all winter.

Dec. 25. Surveying for heirs of J. Richardson, G. Heywood and A. Brooks accompanying.

Skate on Goose Pond. Heywood says that some who have gone into Ebby Hubbard's barn to find him have seen the rats run over his shoulders, they are so familiar with him. This because I stopped to speak with Hubbard in his barn about bounds. I find the true line between Richardson and Mrs. Bigelow, which Captain Hubbard overlooked in 1840, and yet I find it by his own plan of 1827. Bigelow had set a split stone far into Richardson. After making the proper allowance for variation since 1827, I set my stake exactly on an old spotted line, which was overlooked in 1840 and is probably as old as the survey of '27, or thirty years. It is on good-sized white pines, and is quite distinct now, though not blazed into the wood at first. It would not be detected unless you were looking for it.

Dec. 26. Snows all day, — first snow of any consequence, three or four inches in all.

Humphrey Buttrick tells me that he has shot little dippers. He also saw the bird which Melvin shot last summer (a coot), but he never saw one of them before. The little dipper must, therefore, be different from a coot. Is it not a grebe?

Dec. 27. Sunday. A clear, pleasant day.

P. M. — To Goose Pond.

Tree sparrows about the weeds in the yard. A snowball on every pine plume, for there has been no wind to shake it down. The pitch pines look like trees heavily laden with snow oranges. The snowballs on their plumes are like a white fruit. When I thought-

lessly strike at a limb with my hatchet, in my surveying, down comes a sudden shower of snow, whitening
my coat and getting into my neck. You must be careful how you approach and jar the trees thus supporting a light snow.

Partridges dash away through the pines, jarring
down the snow.

Mice have been abroad in the night. We are almost
ready to believe that they have been shut up in the
earth all the rest of the year because we have not seen
their tracks. I see where, by the shore of Goose Pond,
one has pushed up just far enough to open a window
through the snow three quarters of an inch across,
but has not been forth. Elsewhere, when on the pond,
I see in several places where one has made
a circuit out on to the pond a rod or more,
returning to the shore again. Such a track
may, by what we call accident, be preserved
for a geological period, or be obliterated by
the melting of the snow.

Goose Pond is not thickly frozen yet. Near the north
shore it cracks under the snow as I walk, and in many
places water has oozed out and spread over the ice,
mixing with the snow and making dark places. Walden
is almost entirely skimmed over. It will probably be
completely frozen over to-night.[1]

I frequently hear a dog bark at some distance in
the night, which, strange as it may seem, reminds me
of the cooing or *crowing* of a ring dove which I heard
every night a year ago at Perth Amboy. It was sure

[1] Yes.

to coo on the slightest noise in the house; as good as
a watch-dog. The crowing of cocks, too, reminds me
of it, and, now I think of it, it was precisely the intona-
tion and accent of the cat owl's *hoo' hoo-hoo-oo*, dwelling in each case sonorously on the last syllable. They
get the pitch and break ground with the first note, and
then prolong and swell it in the last. The commonest
and cheapest sounds, as the barking of a dog, produce
the same effect on fresh and healthy ears that the rarest
music does. It depends on your appetite for sound. Just
as a crust is sweeter to a healthy appetite than confectionery to a pampered or diseased one. It is better that these
cheap sounds be music to us than that we have the rarest
ears for music in any other sense. I have lain awake
at night many a time to think of the barking of a dog
which I had heard long before, bathing my being again
in those waves of sound, as a frequenter of the opera
might lie awake remembering the music he had heard.

As my mother made my pockets once of Father's
old fire-bags, with the date of the formation of the Fire
Society on them, — 1794, — though they made but
rotten pockets, — so we put our meaning into those
old mythologies. I am sure that the Greeks were commonly innocent of any such *double-entendre* as we attribute to them.

One while we do not wonder that so many commit
suicide, life is so barren and worthless; we only live
on by an effort of the will. Suddenly our condition is
ameliorated, and even the barking of a dog is a pleasure to us. So closely is our happiness bound up with
our physical condition, and one reacts on the other.

Vol. X

Do not despair of life. You have no doubt force
enough to overcome your obstacles. Think of the fox
prowling through wood and field in a winter night
for something to satisfy his hunger. Notwithstanding
cold and the hounds and traps, his race survives. I
do not believe any of them ever committed suicide. I
saw this afternoon where probably a fox had rolled
some small carcass in the snow.

I cut a blueberry bush this afternoon, a venerable-
looking one bending over Goose Pond, with a gray,
flat, scaly bark, the bark split into long, narrow, closely
adhering scales, the inner bark dull-reddish. At several feet from the ground it was one and five sixteenths
inches in diameter, and I counted about twenty-nine
indistinct rings. It seems a very close-grained wood.
It appears, then, that some of those old gray blueberry
bushes which overhang the pond-holes have attained
half the age of man.

I am disappointed by most essays and lectures. I
find that I had expected the authors would have some
life, some very private experience, to report, which
would make it comparatively unimportant in what
style they expressed themselves, but commonly they
have only a talent to exhibit. The new magazine which
all have been expecting may contain only another love
story as naturally told as the last, perchance, but without the slightest novelty in it. It may be a mere vehicle
for Yankee phrases.

What interesting contrasts our climate affords! In
July you rush panting into [a] pond, to cool yourself
in the tepid water, when the stones on the bank are

so heated that you cannot hold one tightly in your hand,
and horses are melting on the road. Now you walk
on the same pond frozen, amid the snow, with numbed
fingers and feet, and see the water-target bleached and
stiff in the ice.

Dec. 31. P. M. — Surveying Goose Pond.

After some rain yesterday and in the night, there
was a little more snow, and the ground is still covered.
I am surprised to find Walden still closed since Sunday night, notwithstanding the warm weather since it
skimmed over, and that Goose Pond bears, though
covered with slosh; but ice under water is slow to thaw.
It does not break up so soon as you would expect.
Walking over it, I thought that I saw an old glove on
the ice or slosh, but, approaching, found it to be a bullfrog, flat on its belly with its legs stretched out. Touching it, I found it to be alive, though it could only partially open its eyes, and it hung motionless and flimsy
like a rag in my hands. It was evidently nearly chilled
to death and could not jump, though there was then no
freezing. I looked round a good while and finally
found a hole to put it into, squeezing it through. Perhaps in such a warm rain the surface water becomes
warmer than at the bottom, and so tempts the frogs
up on to the ice through a hole. This one was wholly
unscathed by any animal, but would surely have frozen
stiff in the night.

It is remarkable that in ordinary winter weather you
will commonly find some of these small holes called air
or breathing holes, in most ponds. But of whatever

service they may be to the inhabitants of the water, they are not commonly formed by any undulation or upwelling from below, but as far as I have observed, by surface water flowing in through a crevice and wearing away the ice.

Warm as it is, underneath all this slosh the ice seems as solid as ever.

Under and attached to one of the lowermost branches of a white pine sapling in my old potato-field, I see a large hornet's nest, *close to the ground.*

I have been surveying most of the time for a month past and have associated with various characters: —

First there was Staples, quick, clear, downright, and on the whole a good fellow, especially good to treat with rougher and slower men than himself, always meaning well.

An Irishman, rather slow and dull but well-meaning.

A rustic innkeeper, evidently rather close-fisted.

George Heywood, a quiet, efficient man, very gentlemanly and agreeable to deal with; no pretense nor bluster, but simple, direct, and even sweet.

—— ——, a crooked stick, not readily apprehending your drift, referring to old deeds or places which he can't find, thinking he is entitled to many more acres than belong to him, but never leaving his work or his cattle to attend to you. To be found commonly in his barn, if you come upon him suddenly before he can hide. Has some complaint or injury which deforms him somewhat, — has crooked his body, so that when you meet him in the street he looks as if he was going across the road.

ferred to being left. He said he did n't want to make bounds, and asked me if I should have set it there, to which I answered, "Yes, of course," that was what I had been doing all my life, making bounds, or rather finding them, remaking what had been unmade, where they were away. He listened to me as if I were an oracle. He did not in the least understand my instrument, or "spy-glass," as he called it, but had full faith that it knew the way straight through the thickest wood to missing bounds. He was so deaf I had to shout to him, and there were two more in his house deafer than he, — and I think only one other. The passers-by commonly hear them talking to one another within. I could never communicate with him when setting a stake or carrying the chain but by signs, and must first get his attention to the signs. This I accomplished, when he had hold of the chain, by giving it several smart jerks. When he paid me at his house, I observed that all his money was in silver. He said he told H—— that we had been cutting off some of his land, and H—— said, "Is that right?" H—— has a good deal of large old wood which he will not cut. —— says that he goes into it with his axe, and striking on an old tree says, "That's sound," and so lets it stand, though when cut it turns out to be false-hearted.

—— says that Rice worked two days on only two sides of his lot, but that he told him he would not charge him but two dollars if it took him a week. I found and used one of Rice's poles, left on the ground all planed for the purpose, for he worked not without tools.

Another Irishman, one of the worst of his race, full of blarney, one of the would-be gentlemen, who, when treated according to his deserts, having complained unreasonably of my price, apologizes by saying that he meant nothing. "What's the use of having a tongue in your head if you don't use it?"

A common specimen of the Yankee, who commonly answers me with "exactly" or "just so."

—— ——, who was so afraid he should lose some land belonging to him that, though he had employed Rice to survey his small wood-lot of three acres, within a year, he working two or three days at it and setting at least fifty stakes about it, having also two plans of it, yet, seeing that I had by chance set a stake a foot or two one side of his line, thought there was some mistake and would have me measure his lot anew. It was but little labor, the lines were so open, — for a path was actually worn round the whole lot. He appears to go round it every day or two. When I wanted a straight pole, he was very scrupulous not to cut it from his neighbor's side of the line. He did not seem able to understand a plan or deed, and had sold some of his land because he did not know that he had a good title to it. Everything I told him about his deed and plan seemed to surprise him infinitely and make him laugh with excess of interest. When I pointed out anything in the plan, he did not look at it, only at my finger and at me, and took my word for it. I told him that I wondered his last surveyor had not set a stake and stone in one place, according to his plan and deed, a perfectly plain case, the stump of the pitch pine re-

VI

JANUARY, 1858

(ÆT. 40)

Jan. 1. There are many words which are genuine and indigenous and have their root in our natures, not made by scholars, and as well understood by the illiterate as others. There are also a great many words which are spurious and artificial, and can only be used in a bad sense, since the thing they signify is not fair and substantial, — such as the *church,* the *judiciary,* to *impeach,* etc., etc. They who use them do not stand on solid ground. It is in vain to try to preserve them by attaching other words to them as the *true* church, etc. It is like towing a sinking ship with a canoe.

I have lately been surveying the Walden woods so extensively and minutely that I now see it mapped in my mind's eye — as, indeed, on paper — as so many men's wood-lots, and am aware when I walk there that I am at a given moment passing from such a one's wood-lot to such another's. I fear this particular dry knowledge may affect my imagination and fancy, that it will not be easy to see so much wildness and native vigor there as formerly. No thicket will seem so unexplored now that I know that a stake and stones may be found in it. In these respects those Maine woods differed essentially from ours. There you are never

reminded that the wilderness which you are threading is, after all, some villager's familiar wood-lot from which his ancestors have sledded their fuel for generations, or some widow's thirds, minutely described in some old deed, which is recorded, of which the owner has got a plan, too, and old bound marks may be found every forty rods if you will search.[1] What a history this Concord wilderness which I affect so much may have had! How many old deeds describe it, — some particular wild spot, — how it passed from Cole to Robinson, and Robinson to Jones, and Jones finally to Smith, in course of years! Some have cut it over three times during their lives, and some burned it and sowed it with rye, and built walls and made a pasture of it, perchance. All have renewed the bounds and reblazed the trees many times. Here you are not reminded of these things. 'T is true the map informs you that you stand on land granted by the State to such an academy, or on Bingham's Purchase, but these names do not impose on you, for you see nothing to remind you of the academy or of Bingham.[2]

Jan. 3. Sunday. I see a flock of *F. hyemalis* this afternoon, the weather is hitherto so warm.

About, in his lively "Greece and the Greeks," says, "These are the most exquisite delights to be found in Greece, next to, or perhaps before, the pleasure of admiring the masterpieces of art, — a little cool water under a genial sun." I have no doubt that this is true.

[1] [*Maine Woods*, p. 168; Riv. 206, 207.]
[2] [*Maine Woods*, pp. 168, 169; Riv. 207.]

Why, then, travel so far when the same pleasures may be found near home?

The slosh on Walden had so much water in it that it has now frozen perfectly smooth and looks like a semitransparent marble. Being, however, opaque, it reminds one the more of some vast hall or corridor's floor, yet probably not a human foot has trodden it yet. Only the track-repairers and stokers have cast stones and billets of wood on to it to prove it.

Going to the Andromeda Ponds, I was greeted by the warm brown-red glow of the *Andromeda calyculata* toward the sun. I see where I have been through, the more reddish under sides apparently being turned up. It is long since a human friend has met me with such a glow.

Jan. 4. P. M. — The weather still remarkably warm; the ice too soft for skating. I go through by the Andromeda Ponds and down river from Fair Haven. I am encouraged by the sight of men fishing in Fair Haven Pond, for it reminds me that they have animal spirits for such adventures. I am glad to be reminded that any go a-fishing. When I get down near to Cardinal Shore, the sun near setting, its light is wonderfully reflected from a narrow edging of yellowish stubble at the edge of the meadow ice and foot of the hill, an edging only two or three feet wide, and the stubble but a few inches high. (I am looking east.) It is remarkable because the ice is but a dull lead-color (it is so soft and sodden), reflecting no light, and the hill beyond is a dark russet, here and there patched with snow,

Vol. X

but this narrow intermediate line of stubble is all aglow. I get its true color and brightness best when I do not look directly at it, but a little above it toward the hill, seeing it with the lower part of my eye more truly and abstractly. It is as if all the rays slid over the ice and lodged against and were reflected by the stubble. It is surprising how much sunny light a little straw that survives the winter will reflect.

The channel of the river is open part of the way. The *Cornus sericea* and some quite young willow shoots are the red-barked twigs so conspicuous now along the riversides.

That bright and warm reflection of sunlight from the insignificant edging of stubble was remarkable. I was coming down-stream over the meadows, on the ice, within four or five rods of the eastern shore. The sun on my left was about a quarter of an hour above the horizon. The ice was soft and sodden, of a dull lead-color, quite dark and reflecting no light as I looked eastward, but my eyes caught by accident a singular sunny brightness reflected from the narrow border of stubble only three or four inches high (and as many feet wide perhaps) which rose along the edge of the ice at the foot of the hill. It was not a mere brightening of the bleached stubble, but the warm and yellow light of the sun, which, it appeared, it was peculiarly fitted to reflect. It was that amber light from the west which we sometimes witness after a storm, concentrated on this stubble, for the hill beyond was merely a dark russet spotted with snow. All the yellow rays seemed to be reflected by this insignificant stubble

alone, and when I looked more generally a little above it, seeing it with the under part of my eye, it appeared yet more truly and more bright; the reflected light made its due impression on my eye, separated from the proper color of the stubble, and it glowed almost like a low, steady, and serene fire. It was precisely as if the sunlight had mechanically slid over the ice, and lodged against the stubble. It will be enough to say of something warmly and sunnily bright that it glowed like lit stubble. It was remarkable that, looking eastward, this was the only evidence of the light in the west.

Here and there in the meadow, etc., near springy places, you see where the thinner ice has been pushed up tentwise ( ) and cracked, either for want of room, two fields crowding together, or expanding with heat from below.

Jan. 5. P. M. — I see one of those fuzzy winter caterpillars, black at the two ends and brown-red in middle, crawling on a rock by the Hunt's Bridge causeway.

Mr. Hosmer is loading hay in his barn. It is meadow-hay, and I am interested in it chiefly as a botanist. If meadow-hay is of less worth in the market, it is more interesting to the poet. In this there is a large proportion of *Osmunda regalis*. But I fear that in the long run it is not so interesting to the cattle to contemplate and chew this as English hay and clover. How completely a load of hay in the winter revives the memory of past summers! Summer in us is only a little dried like it. The rowen in Hosmer's barn has a finer and greener look than the first crop. And so the ferns in coal remind us of summer still longer past.

Jan. 6. The first snow-storm of much importance. By noon it *may be* six inches deep.

P. M. — Up railroad to North River.

The main stream, barely skimmed over with snow, which has sunk the thin ice and is saturated with water, is of a dull-brown color between the white fields.

I detect a very tall and slender tupelo by its thorny-looking twigs. It is close by a white oak, at the yellow gerardia up railroad. It is nearly fifty feet high and only one foot through at the ground. I derive a certain excitement, not to be refused, even from going through Dennis's Swamp on the opposite side of the railroad, where the poison-dogwood abounds. This simple-stemmed bush is very full of fruit, hanging in loose, dry, pale-green drooping panicles. Some of them are a foot long. It impresses me as the most fruitful shrub thereabouts. I cannot refrain from plucking it and bringing home some pretty sprigs. Other fruits there are there which belong to the hard season, the enduring paniced andromeda and a few partly decayed prinos berries. I walk amid the bare midribs of cinnamon ferns, with at most a terminal leafet, and here and there I see a little dark water at the bottom of a dimple in the snow, over which the snow has not yet been able to prevail.

I was feeling very cheap, nevertheless, reduced to

make the most of dry dogwood berries. Very little evidence of God or man did I see just then, and life not as rich and inviting an enterprise as it should be, when my attention was caught by a snowflake on my coat-sleeve. It was one of those perfect, crystalline, star-shaped ones, six-rayed, like a flat wheel with six spokes, only the spokes were perfect little pine trees in shape, arranged around a central spangle. This little object, which, with many of its fellows, rested unmelting on my coat, so perfect and beautiful, reminded me that Nature had not lost her pristine vigor yet, and why should man lose heart? Sometimes the pines were worn and had lost their branches, and again it appeared as if several stars had impinged on one another at various angles, making a somewhat spherical mass. These little wheels came down like the wrecks of chariots from a battle waged in the sky. There were mingled with these starry flakes small downy pellets also. This was at mid-afternoon, and it has not quite ceased snowing yet (at 10 P. M.). We are rained and snowed on with gems. I confess that I was a little encouraged, for I was beginning to believe that Nature was poor and mean, and I was now convinced that she turned off as good work as ever. What a world we live in! Where are the jewellers' shops? There is nothing handsomer than a snowflake and a dewdrop. I may say that the maker of the world exhausts his skill with each snowflake and dewdrop that he sends down. We think that the one mechanically coheres and that the other simply flows together and falls, but in truth they are the product of *enthu-*

siasm, the children of an ecstasy, finished with the artist's utmost skill.[1]

The North River is not frozen over. I see tree sparrows twittering and moving with a low creeping and jerking motion amid the chenopodium in a field, upon the snow, so chubby or puffed out on account of the cold that at first I took them for the arctic birds, but soon I see their bright-chestnut crowns and clear white bars; as the poet says, " a thousand feeding like one," [2] — though there are not more than a dozen here.

Jan. 7. The storm is over, and it is one of those beautiful winter mornings when a vapor is seen hanging in the air between the village and the woods. Though the snow is only some six inches deep, the yards appear full of those beautiful crystals (star or wheel shaped flakes), lying light, as a measure is full of grain.

9 A. M. — To Hill.

It snowed so late last night, and so much has fallen from the trees, that I notice only one squirrel, and a fox, and perhaps partridge track, into which the snow has blown. The fox has been beating the bush along walls and fences. The surface of the snow in the woods is thickly marked by the snow which has fallen from the trees on to it. The mice have not been forth since the snow, or perhaps in some places where they have, their tracks are obliterated.

By 10.30 A. M. it begins to blow hard, the snow comes down from the trees in fine showers, finer far than ever

[1] [Channing, pp. 72, 73.]
[2] ["There are forty feeding like one." — WORDSWORTH.]

falls direct from the sky, completely obscuring the view through the aisles of the wood, and in open fields it is rapidly drifting. It is too light to make good sleighing.

By 10 o'clock I notice a very long level stratum of cloud not very high in the southeastern sky, — all the rest being clear, — which I suspect to be the vapor from the sea. This lasts for several hours.

These are true mornings of creation, original and poetic days, not mere repetitions of the past. There is no lingering of yesterday's fogs, only such a mist as might have adorned the first morning.

P. M. — I see some tree sparrows feeding on the fine grass seed above the snow, near the road on the hillside below the Dutch house. They are flitting along one at a time, their feet commonly sunk in the snow, uttering occasionally a low sweet warble and seemingly as happy there, and with this wintry prospect before them for the night and several months to come, as any man by his fireside. One occasionally hops or flies toward another, and the latter suddenly jerks away from him. They are reaching or hopping up to the fine grass, or oftener picking the seeds from the snow. At length the whole ten have collected within a space a dozen feet square, but soon after, being alarmed, they utter a different and less musical chirp and flit away into an apple tree.

Jan. 8. P. M. — To that small meadow just above the Boaz Brown meadow.

Going through the swamp, the snow balled so as to raise me three inches higher than usual.

Jan. 9. Snows again.

P. M. — To Deep Cut.

The wind is southwest, and the snow is very moist, with large flakes. Looking toward Trillium Wood, the nearer flakes appear to move quite swiftly, often making the impression of a continuous white line. They are also seen to move directly and nearly horizontally, but the more distant flakes appear to loiter in the air, as if uncertain how they will approach the earth, or even to cross the course of the former, and are always seen as simple and distinct flakes. I think that this difference is simply owing to the fact that the former pass quickly over the field of view, while the latter are much longer in it.

This moist snow has affected the yellow sulphur parmelias and others. They have all got a green hue, and the fruit of the smallest lichen looks fresh and fair. And the wet willow bark is a brighter yellow.

Some chickadees come flitting close to me, and one utters its spring note, *phe-be*, for which I feel under obligations to him.

Jan. 10. Sunday. P. M. — To Goose Pond across Walden.

The north side of Walden is a warm walk in sunny weather. If you are sick and despairing, go forth in winter and see the red alder catkins dangling at the extremities of the twigs, all in the wintry air, like long,

hard mulberries, promising a new spring and the fulfillment of all our hopes. We prize any tenderness, any softening, in the winter, — catkins, birds' nests, insect life, etc., etc. The most I get, perchance, is the sight of a mulberry-like red catkin which I know has a dormant life in it, seemingly greater than my own.

Jan. 11. Monday. Rain, rain — washes off almost every vestige of snow.

Jan. 13. Wednesday. Go to Lynn to lecture, *via* Cambridge.

4.30 P. M. — At Jonathan Buffum's, Lynn. Lecture in John B. Alley's parlor. Mr. J. Buffum describes to me ancient wolf-traps, made probably by the early settlers in Lynn, perhaps after an Indian model; one some two miles from the shore near Saugus, another more northerly; holes say seven feet deep, about as long, and some three feet wide, stoned up very smoothly, and perhaps converging a little, so that the wolf could not get out. Tradition says that a wolf and a squaw were one morning found in the same hole, staring at each other.

Jan. 14. Mr. Buffum says that in 1817 or 1819 he saw the sea-serpent at Swampscott, and so did several hundred others. He was to be seen off and on for some time. There were many people on the beach the first time, in carriages partly in the water, and the serpent came so near that they, thinking that he might come ashore, involuntarily turned their horses to the shore

Vol. X

as with a general consent, and this movement caused him to shear off also. The road from Boston was lined with people directly, coming to see the monster. Prince came with his spy-glass, saw, and printed his account of him. Buffum says he has seen him twenty times, once alone, from the rocks at Little Nahant, when he passed along close to the shore just beneath the surface, and within fifty or sixty feet of him, so that he could have touched him with a very long pole, if he had dared to. Buffum is about sixty, and it should be said, as affecting the value of his evidence, that he is a firm believer in Spiritualism.

This forenoon I rode to Nahant with Mr. Buffum. All the country bare. A fine warm day; neither snow nor ice, unless you search narrowly for them. On the way we pass Mr. Alonzo Lewis's cottage. On the top of each of his stone posts is fastened a very perfectly egg-shaped pebble of sienite from Kettle Cove, fifteen to eighteen inches long and of proportionate diameter. I never saw any of that size so perfect. There are some fifteen of them about his house, and on one flatter, circular one he has made a dial, by which I learned the hour (9.30 A. M.). Says he was surveying once at Kettle Cove, where they form a beach a third of a mile long and two to ten feet deep, and he brought home as many as his horse could draw. His house is clapboarded with hemlock bark; now some twenty years old. He says that he built it himself.

Called at the shop where lately Samuel Jillson, now of Feltonville, set up birds, — for he is a taxidermist and very skillful; kills his own birds and with blow-

guns, which he makes and sells, some seven feet long, of glass, using a clay ball. Is said to be a dead shot at six rods!

Warm and fall-like as it is, saw many snow buntings at the entrance to the beach. Saw many black ducks (so Lewis said; may they not have been velvet ducks, *i. e.* coot?) on the sea. Heard of a flock of geese (!) (may they not have been brant, or some other species?), etc.; ice [?] divers. On the south side of Little Nahant a large mass of *fine* pudding-stone. Nahant is said to have been well-wooded, and furnished timber for the wharves of Boston, *i. e.* to build them. Now a few willows and balm-of-Gileads are the only trees, if you except two or three small cedars. They say others will not grow on account of wind. The rocks are porphyry, with dykes of dark greenstone in it, and, at the extremity of Nahant, argillaceous slate, very distinctly stratified, with fossil corallines in *it* (?), looking like shells. Egg Rock, it seems, has a fertile garden on the top.

P. M. — Rode with J. Buffum, Parker Pillsbury, and Mr. Mudge, a lawyer and geologist of Lynn, into the northwest part of Lynn, to the Danvers line. After a mile or two, we passed beyond the line of the porphyry into the sienite. The sienite is more rounded. Saw some furrows in sienite. On a ledge of sienite in the woods, the rocky woods near Danvers line, saw many boulders of sienite, part of the same flock of which Ship Rock (so called) in Danvers is one. One fifteen feet long, ten wide, and five or six deep rested on four somewhat rounded (at least water-worn) stones, eighteen inches in diameter or more, so that you could crawl under it, on the top of a cliff, and projected about eight feet over it, — just as it was dropped by an iceberg. A fine broad-backed ledge of sienite just beyond, north or northwest, from which we saw Wachusett, Watatic, Monadnock, and the Peterboro Hills.

Also saw where one Boyse (if that is the spelling), a miller in old times, got out millstones in a primitive way, so said an old man who was chopping there. He pried or cracked off a piece of the crust of the ledge, lying horizontal, some sixteen or eighteen inches thick, then made a fire on it about its edges, and, pouring on water, cracked or softened it, so that he could break off the edges and make it round with his sledge. Then he picked a hole through the middle and hammered it as smooth as he could, and it was done. But this old man said that he had heard old folks say that the stones were so rough in old times that they made a noise like thunder as they revolved, and much grit was mixed with the meal.

Returning down a gully, I thought I would look for a new plant and found at once what I suppose to be *Genista tinctoria*, dyers'-green-weed, — the stem is quite green, with a few pods and leaves left. It is said to have become naturalized on the hills of Essex County. Close by was a mass of sienite some seven or eight feet high, with a cedar some two inches thick springing from a mere crack in its top.

Visited Jordan's or the Lynn Quarry (of sienite) on our return, more southerly. The stone cracks very squarely and into very large masses. In one place was

a dyke of dark greenstone, of which, joined to the sienite, I brought off two specimens, *q. v.* The more yellowish and rotten surface stone, lying above the hard and grayer, is called the sap by the quarrymen.

From these rocks and wooded hills three or four miles inland in the northwest edge of Lynn, we had an extensive view of the ocean from Cape Ann to Scituate, and realized how the aborigines, when hunting, berrying, might perchance have looked out thus on the early navigators sailing along the coast, — thousands of them, — when they little suspected it, — how patent to the inhabitants their visit must have been. A vessel could hardly have passed within half a dozen miles of the shore, even, — at one place only, in pleasant weather, — without being seen by hundreds of savages.

Mudge gave me Saugus jasper, graywacke, amygdaloid (greenstone with nodules of feldspar), asbestos, hornstone (?); Buffum some porphyry, epidote, argillaceous slate from end of Nahant.

Mr. Buffum tells me that they never eat the sea-clams without first taking out "the worm," as it is called, about as large as the small end of a pipe-stem. He supposes it is the penis.

Jan. 15. At Natural History Rooms, Boston.

Looked at the little grebe. Its feet are not webbed with lobes on the side like the coot, and it is quite white beneath. Saw the good-sized duck — velvet duck, with white spot on wing — which is commonly called "coot" on salt water. They have a living young bald eagle in the cellar. Talked with Dr. Kneeland. They

have a golden eagle from Lexington, which K. obtained two or three years since, the first Dr. Cabot has heard of in Massachusetts. Speaking to him of my night-warbler, he asked if it uttered such a note, making the note of the myrtle-bird, *ah, te-te-te te-te-te te-te-te*, exactly, and said that that was the note of the white-throated sparrow, which he heard at Lake Superior, at night as well as by day.[1] *Vide* his report, July 15, 1857.

Same afternoon, saw Dr. Durkee in Howard Street. He has not seen the common glow-worm, and called his a variety of *Lampyris noctiluca*. Showed to Agassiz, Gould, and Jackson, and it was new to them. They thought it a variety of the above. His were luminous throughout, mine only in part of each segment.

Saw some beautiful painted leaves in a shop window, — maple and oak.

Jan. 17. *Sunday.* P. M. — To Conantum.

The common birch fungus, which is horizontal and turned downward, splits the bark as it pushes out very simply, thus:[2] I see a large downy owl's feather adhering to a sweet-fern twig, looking like the down of a plant blowing in the wind. This is near where I have found them before, on Conantum, above first Cliff. They would be very ornamental to a bonnet, so soft and fine with their reflections that the eye hardly rests on the down.

[1] [Concerning Thoreau's confusion as to the authorship of this song of the white-throated sparrow, see *Journal*, vol. v, p. 119.]
[2] *Vide* 26th.

Jan. 18. At the Dugan Desert, I notice, under the overhanging or nearly horizontal small white oaks and shrub oaks about the edge, singular little hollows in the sand, evidently made by drops of rain or melting snow falling from the same part of the twig, a foot or two, on the same spot a long time. They are very numerous under every such low horizontal bough, on an average about three quarters of an inch apart or more. They are a third of an inch wide and a quarter to even three quarters of an inch deep; made some days ago evidently.

The *F. hyemalis* about. I hear that the Emerson children found ladies'-delights out yesterday.

Jan. 19. *F. hyemalis.*

Jan. 23. *Saturday.* The wonderfully mild and pleasant weather continues. The ground has been bare since the 11th. This morning was colder than before. I have not been able to walk up the North Branch this winter, nor along the channel of the South Branch at any time.

P. M. — To Saw Mill Brook.

A fine afternoon. There has been but little use for gloves this winter, though I have been surveying a great deal for three months. The sun, and cockcrowing, bare ground, etc., etc., remind me of March.

Standing on the bridge over the Mill Brook on the Turnpike, there being but little ice on the south side, I see several small water-bugs (*Gyrinus*) swimming about, as in the spring.

I see the terminal shield fern very fresh, as an evergreen, at Saw Mill Brook, and (I think it is) the marginal fern and *Lycopodium lucidulum.*

I go up the brook, walking on it most of the way, surprised to find that it will bear me. How it falls from rock to rock, as down a flight of stairs, all through that rocky wood, from the swamp which is its source to the Everett farm! The bays or more stagnant parts are thickest frozen, the channel oftenest open, and here and there the water has overflowed the ice and covered it with a thickening mass of glistening spiculæ. The white markings on the under side are very rich and varied, — the currency of the brook, the impression of its fleeting bubbles even. It comes out of a meadow of about an acre.

I go near enough to Flint's Pond, about 4 P. M., to hear it thundering. In summer I should not have suspected its presence an eighth of a mile off through the woods, but in such a winter day as this it speaks and betrays itself.

Returning through Britton's field, I notice the stumps of chestnuts cut a dozen years ago. This tree grows rapidly, and one layer seems not to adhere very firmly to another. I can easily count the concentric circles of growth on these old stumps as I stand over them, for they are worn into conspicuous furrows along the lines of the pores of the wood. One or more rings often gape an eighth of an inch or more, at about their twenty-fourth or twenty-fifth year, when the growth, in three or four cases that I examined, was most rapid.

Looking toward the woods in the horizon, it is seen to be very hazy.

At Ditch Pond I hear what I suppose to be a fox barking, an exceedingly husky, hoarse, and ragged note, prolonged perhaps by the echo, like a feeble puppy, or even a child endeavoring to scream, but choked with fear, yet it is on a high key. It sounds so through the wood, while I am in the hollow, that I cannot tell from which side it comes. I hear it bark forty or fifty times at least. It is a peculiar sound, quite unlike any other woodland sound that I know.

Walden, I think, begins to crack and boom first on the south side, which is first in the shade, for I hear it cracking there, though it is still in the sun around me. It is not so sonorous and like the dumping of frogs as I have heard it, but more like the cracking of crockery. It suggests the very brittlest material, as if the globe you stood on were a hollow sphere of glass and might fall to pieces on the slightest touch. Most shivering, splintery, screeching cracks these are, as if the ice were no thicker than a tumbler, though it is probably nine or ten inches. Methinks my weight sinks it and helps to crack sometimes.

Who can doubt that men are by a certain fate what they are, contending with unseen and unimagined difficulties, or encouraged and aided by equally mysterious auspicious circumstances? Who can doubt this essential and innate difference between man and man, when he considers a whole race, like the Indian, inevitably and resignedly passing away in spite of our efforts to Christianize and educate them? Indi-

viduals accept their fate and live according to it, as the Indian does. Everybody notices that the Indian retains his habits wonderfully, — is still the same man that the discoverers found. The fact is, the history of the white man is a history of improvement, that of the red man a history of fixed habits of stagnation.

To insure health, a man's relation to Nature must come very near to a personal one; he must be conscious of a friendliness in her; when human friends fail or die, she must stand in the gap to him. I cannot conceive of any life which deserves the name, unless there is a certain tender relation to Nature. This it is which makes winter warm, and supplies society in the desert and wilderness. Unless Nature sympathizes with and speaks to us, as it were, the most fertile and blooming regions are barren and dreary.

Mrs. William Monroe told Sophia last evening that she remembered her (Sophia's) grandfather very well, that he was taller than Father, and used to ride out to their house — she was a Stone and lived where she and her husband did afterward, now Darius Merriam's — when they made cheeses, to drink the whey, being in consumption. She said that she remembered Grandmother too, Jennie Burns, how she came to the schoolroom (in Middle Street (?), Boston) once, leading her little daughter Elizabeth, the latter so small that she could not tell her name distinctly, but spoke thick and lispingly, — " Elizabeth Orrock Thoreau." [1]

The dog is to the fox as the white man to the red. The former has attained to more clearness in his bark;

[1] *Vide* Feb. 7th.

it is more ringing and musical, more developed; he explodes the vowels of his alphabet better; and beside he has made his place so good in the world that he can run without skulking in the open field. What a smothered, ragged, feeble, and unmusical sound is the bark of the fox! It seems as if he scarcely dared raise his voice lest it should catch the ear of his tame cousin and inveterate foe.

I observe that the ice of Walden is heaved up more than a foot over that bar between the pond and Cyrus Hubbard's basin. The gravelly bank or bar itself is also heaved up considerably where exposed. So that I am inclined to think that such a tilting is simply the result of a thawing beneath and not merely of a crowding or pressure on the two sides.

I do not see that I can live tolerably without affection for Nature. If I feel no softening toward the rocks, what do they signify?

I do not think much of that chemistry that can extract corn and potatoes out of a barren [soil], but rather of that chemistry that can extract thoughts and sentiments out of the life of a man on any soil. It is in vain to write on the seasons unless you have the seasons in you.

Jan. 24. Sunday. P. M. — Nut Meadow Brook.

The river is broadly open, as usual this winter. You can hardly say that we have had any sleighing at all this winter, though five or six inches of snow lay on the ground five days after January 6th. But I do not quite like this warm weather and bare ground at this season. What is a winter without snow and ice in this latitude? The bare earth is unsightly. This winter is but unburied summer.

At that gully or ravine in the Clamshell bank, methinks the sides fall away faster in the winter; and such a winter as this, when the ground is bare, [faster] than ever. The subsoil and sand keeps freezing and thawing, and so bursts off, and the larger stones roll down on each side and are collected in a row at the bottom, so that there will be a sort of wall there of stones as big as a hen's egg propped up and finally covered with sand.

The inside of the swallow-holes there appears quite firm yet and regular, with marks where it was pecked or scratched by the bird, and the top is mottled or blotched, almost as if made firm in spots by the saliva of the bird. There is a low oven-like expansion at the end, and a good deal of stubble for the nest. I find in one an empty black cherry stone and the remains of a cricket or two. Probably a mouse left them there.

I see two of those black and red-brown fuzzy caterpillars in a mullein leaf on this bare edge-hill, which could not have blown from any tree, I think. They apparently take refuge in such places. One on the railroad causeway where it is high, in the open meadow.

I see a couple of broken small turtle eggs here which have been trodden out of the banks by cows going to drink in the river.

At Hosmer's tub spring a small frog is active!

At Nut Meadow Brook the small-sized water-bugs are as abundant and active as in summer. I see forty

Vol. X

or fifty circling together in the smooth and sunny bays all along the brook. This is something new to me. What must they think of this winter? It is like a child waked up and set to playing at midnight. Methinks they are more ready to dive to the bottom when disturbed than usual. At night, of course, they dive to the bottom and bury themselves, and if in the morning they perceive no curtain of ice drawn over their sky, and the pleasant weather continues, they gladly rise again and resume their gyrations in some sunny bay amid the alders and the stubble. I think that I never noticed them more numerous, but the fact is I never looked for them so particularly. But I fear for their nervous systems, lest this be too much activity, too much excitement. The sun falling thus warmly for so long on the open surface of the brook tempts them upward gradually, till there is a little group gyrating there as in summer. What a funny way they have of going to bed! They do not take a light and retire up-stairs; they go below. Suddenly it is heels up and heads down, and they go down to their muddy bed and let the unresting stream flow over them in their dreams. They go to bed in another element. What a deep slumber must be theirs, and what dreams, down in the mud there! So the insect life is not withdrawn far off, but a warm sun would soon entice it forth. Sometimes they seem to have a little difficulty in making the plunge. Maybe they are too dry to slip under. I saw one floating on its back, and it struggled a little while before it righted itself. Suppose you were to plot the course of one for a day; what kind of a figure would it

make? Probably this feat too will one day be performed by science, that maid of all work. I see one chasing a mote, and the wave the creature makes always causes the mote to float away from it. I would like to know what it is they communicate to one another, they who appear to value each other's society so much. How many water-bugs make a quorum? How many hundreds does their Fourier think it takes to make a complete bug? Where did they get their backs polished so? They will have occasion to remember this year, that winter when we were waked out of our annual sleep! What is their precise hour for retiring?

I see stretching from side to side of this smooth brook, where it is three or four feet wide, apparently an invisible waving line like a cobweb, against which the water is heaped up a very little. This line is constantly swayed to and fro, as by the current or wind bellying forward here and there. I try repeatedly to catch and break it with my hand and let the water run free, but still, to my surprise, I clutch nothing but fluid, and the imaginary line keeps its place. Is it the fluctuating edge of a lighter, perhaps more oily, fluid, overflowing a heavier? I see several such lines. It is somewhat like the slightest conceivable smooth fall over a dam. I must ask the water-bug that glides across it.

Ah, if I had no more sins to answer for than a water-bug! They are only the small water-bugs that I see. They are earlier in the spring and apparently hardier.

I walked about the long pond-hole beyond the wooded moraine. There are prinos bushes with much moss on them, such as grows on the button-bush around.

There is considerable rattlesnake grass there, which, with its drooping end above the ice, reminds me of wild rice meadows.

On every old oak stump the ends of the pores are the prominent part, while only the scale-like silver ray is left between their circles.

The sprouts of the canoe birch are not reddish like the white, but a yellowish brown. The small white begin to cast off their red cuticle the third or fourth year and reveal a whitish one.

The poison sumach, with its recurved panicles of pale-greenish fruit massed together in profusion at the base of last year's stout blunt twigs, is very interesting and handsome. It is one of the chief ornaments of the swamps, dry and durable, befitting the season, and always attracts me. It might be the symbol of a vigorous swamp. The wood is very brittle to split down in the forks, and, just broken, has a strong, somewhat liquorice-like scent. I do not know that any bird eats them.

I see a few fishes dart in the brooks.

Between winter and summer there is, to my mind, an immeasurable interval. As, when I pry into the old bank swallows' holes to-day, — see the marks of their bills and even whole eggs left at the bottom, — it affects me as the phenomena of a former geological period. Yet perchance the very swallow which laid those eggs will revisit this hole next spring. The upper side of his gallery is a low arch, quite firm and durable. Like the water-bugs the dormant buds and catkins which overhang the brook *might* be waked up in midwinter, but these bugs are much the most susceptible to the genial influences.

In fact, there was a succession of these invisible cables or booms stretched across the stream, though it ran quite swiftly.

I noticed at Walden yesterday that, when the ice cracked, one part was frequently left an eighth of an inch, perhaps, higher than another, and afterward frozen to it in this position. You could both see and with your feet feel the inequality.

Jan. 25. Monday. A warm, moist day. Thermometer at 6.30 P. M. at 49°.

What a rich book might be made about buds, including, perhaps, sprouts! — the impregnable, vivacious willow catkins, but half asleep under the armor of their black scales, sleeping along the twigs; the birch and oak sprouts, and the rank and lusty dogwood sprouts; the round red buds of the blueberries; the small pointed red buds, close to the twig, of the panicled andromeda; the large yellowish buds of the swamp-pink, etc. How healthy and vivacious must he be who would treat of these things!

You must love the crust of the earth on which you dwell more than the sweet crust of any bread or cake. You must be able to extract nutriment out of a sand-heap. You must have so good an appetite as this, else you will live in vain.

The creditor is servant to his debtor, especially if he is about paying his due. I am amused to see what airs men take upon themselves when they have money

to pay me. No matter how long they have deferred it, they imagine that they are my benefactors or patrons, and send me word graciously that *if I will come to their houses* they will pay me, when it is their business to come to me.

Jan. 26. A warm rain from time to time.

P. M. — To Clintonia Swamp down the brook.

When it rains it is like an April shower. The brook is quite open, and there is no snow on the banks or fields. From time to time I see a trout glance, and sometimes, in an adjoining ditch, quite a school of other fishes, but I see no tortoises. In a ditch I see very light-colored and pretty large lizards moving about, and I suspect I may even have heard a frog drop into the water once or twice. I like to sit still under my umbrella and meditate in the woods in this warm rain.

On the side-hill at the swamp, I see how the common horizontal birch fungus is formed. I see them in all stages and of all sizes on a dead *Betula alba*, both on the upper and under sides, but always facing the ground. At first you perceive the bark merely raised into a nub and perhaps begun to split, and, removing a piece of the bark, you [find] a fibrous whitish germ like a mildew in the bark, as it were of a fungus beneath, in the bark and decayed wood. Next you will see the fungus pushed out like a hernia, about the size as well as form of a pea. At first it is of a nearly uniform convex and homogeneous surface, above and below, but very soon, or while yet no larger than a pea,

Vol. X

it begins to show a little horizontal flat disk, always on the under side, which you would not suspect without examining it, and the upper surface already begins to be water. So it goes on, pushing out through the bark further and further, spreading and flatting out more and more, till it has attained its growth, with a more or less elongated neck to its peninsula. The fungus as it grows fills the rent in the bark very closely, and the edges of the bark are recurved, lip-like. They commonly break off at the junction of the true bark with the wood, bringing away some of the woody fibre. Apparently the spongy decayed bark and wood is their soil.

This is a lichen day. The white lichens, partly encircling aspens and maples, look as if a painter had touched their trunks with his brush as he passed.

The yellow birch tree is peculiarly interesting. It might be described as a tree whose trunk or bole was covered with golden and silver shavings glued all over it and dangling in curls. The edges of the curls, like a line of breakers, form commonly diagonal lines up and down the tree, corresponding to the twist of the nerve or grain.

Nature loves gradation. Trees do not spring abruptly from the earth. Mosses creep up over the insteps of the trees and endeavor to reclaim them. Hence the propriety of lacing over the instep.

Is not the moccasin a more picturesque and fitter sort of shoe than ours in which to move amid the herbage?

How protean is life! One may eat and drink and

sleep and digest, and do the ordinary duties of a man, and have no excuse for sending for a doctor, and yet he may have reason to doubt if he is as truly alive or his life is as valuable and divine as that of an oyster. He may be the very best citizen in the town, and yet it shall occur to him to prick himself with a pin to see if he is alive. It is wonderful how quiet, harmless, and ineffective a living creature may be. No more energy may it have than a fungus that lifts the bark of a decaying tree. I raised last summer a squash which weighed 123½ pounds. If it had fallen on me it would have made as deep and lasting an impression as most men do. I would just as lief know what it thinks about God as what most men think, or are said to think. In such a squash you have already got the bulk of a man. My man, perchance, when I have put such a question to him, opes his eyes for a moment, essays in vain to think, like a rusty firelock out of order, then calls for a plate of that same squash to eat and goes to sleep, as it is called, — and that is no great distance to go, surely.

Melvin would have sworn he heard a bluebird the other day if it had n't been January. Some say that this particularly warm weather within a few days is the January thaw, but there is nothing to thaw. The sand-banks in the Deep Cut are as dry as in summer.

Some men have a peculiar taste for bad words, mouthing and licking them into lumpish shapes like the bear her cubs, — words like "tribal" and "ornamentation," which drag a dead tail after them. They will pick you out of a thousand the still-born words, the falsettos, the wing-clipped and lame words, as if only the false notes caught their ears. They cry encore to all the discords.

The cocks crow in the yard, and the hens cackle and scratch, all this winter. Eggs must be plenty.

Jan. 27. Wednesday. P. M. — To Hill and beyond.

It is so mild and moist as I saunter along by the wall east of the Hill that I remember, or anticipate, one of those warm rain-storms in the spring, when the earth is just laid bare, the wind is south, and the cladonia lichens are swollen and lusty with moisture, your foot sinking into them and pressing the water out as from a sponge, and the sandy places also are drinking it in. You wander indefinitely in a beaded coat, wet to the skin of your legs, sit on moss-clad rocks and stumps, and hear the lisping of migrating sparrows flitting amid the shrub oaks, sit long at a time, still, and have your thoughts. A rain which is as serene as fair weather, suggesting fairer weather than was ever seen. You could hug the clods that defile you. You feel the fertilizing influence of the rain in your mind. The part of you that is wettest is fullest of life, like the lichens. You discover evidences of immortality not known to divines. You cease to die. You detect some buds and sprouts of life. Every step in the old rye-field is on virgin soil.

And then the rain comes thicker and faster than before, thawing the remaining frost in the ground, detaining the migrating bird; and you turn your back to it, full of serene, contented thought, soothed by the steady dropping on the withered leaves, more at home

for being abroad, more comfortable for being wet, sinking at each step deep into the thawing earth, gladly breaking through the gray rotting ice. The dullest sounds seem sweetly modulated by the air. You leave your tracks in fields of spring rye, scaring the fox-colored sparrows along the wood-sides. You cannot go home yet; you stay and sit in the rain. You glide along the distant wood-side, full of joy and expectation, seeing nothing but beauty, hearing nothing but music, as free as the fox-colored sparrow, seeing far ahead, a courageous knight [?], a great philosopher, not indebted to any academy or college for this expansion, but chiefly to the April rain, which descendeth on all alike; not encouraged by men in your walks, not by the divines nor the professors, and to the lawgiver an outlaw; not encouraged (even) when you are reminded of the government at Washington.

Time never passes so quickly and unaccountably as when I am engaged in composition, *i. e.* in writing down my thoughts. Clocks seem to have been put forward.

The ground being bare this winter, I attend less to buds and twigs. Snow covering the ground secures our attention to twigs, etc., which rise above it.

I notice a pretty large rock on the Lee farm, near the site of the old mill over the Assabet, which is quite white and bare, with the roots of a maple, cut down a few years ago, spreading over it, and a thin dark-green crust or mould, a mere patch of soil as big as a dollar, in one or two places on it. It is evident that that rock was covered as much as three inches deep with soil

Vol. X

a few years since, for the old roots are two inches thick, and that it has been burnt and washed off since, leaving the surface bare and white. There are a few lichens started at one end.

As I came home day before yesterday, over the railroad causeway, at sunset, the sky was overcast, but beneath the edge of the cloud, far in the west, was a narrow stripe of clear amber sky coextensive with the horizon, which reached no higher than the top of Wachusett. I wished to know how far off the cloud was by comparing it with the mountain. It had somewhat the appearance of resting on the mountain, concealing a part of its summit. I did not suppose it did, because the clouds over my head were too high for that, but when I turned my head I saw the whole outline of the mountain distinctly. I could not tell how far the edge of the cloud was beyond it, but I think it likely that that amber light came to me through a low narrow skylight, the upper sash of whose frame was forty miles distant. The amount of it is that I saw a cloud more distant than the mountain.

Steadily the eternal rain falls, — drip, drip, drip, — the mist drives and clears your sight, the wind blows and warms you, sitting on that sandy upland by the edge of the wood that April day.

Jan. 28. Minott has a sharp ear for the note of any migrating bird. Though confined to his dooryard by the rheumatism, he commonly hears them sooner than the widest rambler. Maybe he listens all day for them, or they come and sing over his house, — report

themselves to him and receive their season ticket. He is never at fault. If he says he heard such a bird, though sitting by his chimney-side, you may depend on it. He can swear through glass. He has not spoiled his ears by attending lectures and caucuses, etc. The other day the rumor went that a flock of geese had been seen flying north over Concord, midwinter as it was, by the almanac. I traced it to Minott, and yet I was compelled to doubt. I had it directly that he had heard them within a week. I saw him, — I made haste to him. His reputation was at stake. He said that he stood in his shed, — it was one of the late warm, muggy, April-like mornings, — when he heard one short but distinct *honk* of a goose. He went into the house, he took his cane, he exerted himself, or that sound imparted strength to him. Lame as he was, he went up on to the hill, — he had not done it for a year, — that he might hear all around. He saw nothing, but he heard the note again. It came from over the brook. It was a wild goose, he was sure of it. And hence the rumor spread and grew. He thought that the back of the winter was broken, — if it had any this year, — but he feared such a winter would kill him too.

I was silent; I reflected; I drew into my mind all its members, like the tortoise; I abandoned myself to unseen guides. Suddenly the truth flashed on me, and I remembered that within a week I had heard of a box at the tavern, which had come by railroad express, containing three wild geese and directed to his neighbor over the brook. The April-like morning had excited one so that he honked; and Minott's reputation acquired new lustre.

He has a propensity to tell stories which you have no ears to hear, which you cut short and return unfinished upon him.

I notice much cotton-like down attached to the long curled-up seed-vessels of the *Epilobium angustifolium*, such as I think I have seen used in some birds' nests.

It has been spitting a little snow to-day, and we were uncertain whether it would increase or turn to rain. Coming through the village at 11 P. M., the sky is completely overcast, and the (perhaps thin) clouds are very distinctly pink or reddish, somewhat as if reflecting a distant fire, but this phenomenon is universal all round and overhead. I suspect there is a red aurora borealis behind.

Jan. 29. P. M. — To Great Meadows at Copan.

It is considerably colder. I go through the northerly part of Beck Stow's, north of the new road. For a great distance it is an exceedingly dense thicket of blueberry bushes, and the shortest way is to bend down bushes eight feet high and tread on them. The small red and yellow buds, the maze of gray twigs, the green and red sphagnum, the conspicuous yellowish buds of the swamp-pink with the diverging valves of its seed-vessels, the dried choke-berries still common, these and the like are the attractions.

The cranberry rising red above the ice is seen to be allied to the water andromeda, but is yet redder.

In the ditches on Holbrook's meadow near Copan,

I see a *Rana palustris* swimming, and much conferva greening all the water. Even this green is exhilarating, like a spring in winter. I am affected by the sight even of a mass of conferva in a ditch. I find some radical potamogeton leaves six inches long under water, which look as if growing.

Found some splendid fungi on old aspens used for a fence; quite firm; reddish-white above and bright-vermilion beneath, or perhaps more scarlet, reflecting various shades as it is turned. It is remarkable that the upper side of this fungus, which must, as here, commonly be low on decaying wood, so that we look down on it, is not bright-colored nor handsome, and it was only when I had broken it off and turned it over that I was surprised by its brilliant color. This intense vermilion (?) face, which would be known to every boy in the town if it were turned upward, faces the earth and is discovered only by the curious naturalist. Its ear is turned down, listening to the honest praises of the earth. It is like a light-red velvet or damask. These silent and motionless fungi, with their ears turned ever downward toward the earth, revealing their bright colors perchance only to the prying naturalist who turns them upward, remind me of the "Hear-all" of the story.

Jan. 30. P. M. — To Gowing's Swamp.

I thought it would be a good time to rake in the mud of that central pool, and see what animal or vegetable life might be there, now that it is frozen. I supposed

Vol. X

that tortoises and frogs might be buried in the mud. The pool, where there is nothing but water and sphagnum to be seen and where you cannot go in the summer, is about two rods long and one and a half wide, with that large-seeded sedge in a border a rod wide about it. Only a third of this (on one side) appears as water now, the rest a level bed of green sphagnum frozen with the water, though rising three or four inches above the general level here and there. I cut a hole through the ice, about three inches thick, in what alone appeared to be water, and, after raking out some sphagnum, found that I could not fairly reach the mud and tortoises, — if there are any there, — though my rake was five feet and nine inches long; but with the sphagnum I raked up several kinds of bugs, or insects. I then cut a hole through the frozen sphagnum nearer the middle of the pool, though I supposed it would be a mere mass of sphagnum with comparatively little water, and more mud nearer the surface. To my surprise, I found clear water under this crust of sphagnum to about five feet in depth, but still I could not reach the mud with my rake through the more decayed sphagnum beneath.

I returned to the thicket and cut a maple about eighteen feet long. This dropped down five or six feet, and then, with a very slight pressure, I put it down the whole length. I then went to the thicket again, searched a long while for a suitable pole, and at last cut another maple thirty feet long and between four and five inches thick at the butt, sharpened and trimmed and carried it on my shoulder to the spot, and, rough

as it was, it went down with very little pressure as much as twenty feet, and with a little more pressure *twenty-six feet and one inch;* and there I left it, for I had measured it first. If the top had not been so small that it bent in my hands, I could probably have forced it much further. I suspect that the depth of mud and water under where I walk in summer on the water andromeda, *Andromeda Polifolia, Kalmia glauca,* sphagnum, etc., is about the same. The whole swamp would flow off down an inclined plane. Of course there is room enough for frogs and turtles, safe from frost.

I noticed that the sap flowed very freely from one of the maples which I cut.

In the meanwhile the hole which I had first cut had skimmed over. I stooped to look at the ice-crystals. The thin skimming, which did not yet cover the whole surface, was minutely marked with feathers, as in the frost on windows in the morning. The crystallization was, as usual, in deep furrows, some a third of an inch wide and finely grained or channelled longitudinally. These commonly intersected each other so as to form triangles of various sizes, and it was remarkable that there was an elevated space between the sides of the triangles, which in some cases was not yet frozen, while you could see and feel the furrow where the crystals had shot on each side much lower. The water crystallizes in certain planes only.

It seems, then, that sphagnum will grow on the surface of water five feet deep! [1]

[1] *Vide* [pp. 271, 272].

What means the maple sap flowing in pleasant days in midwinter, when you must wait so late in the spring for it, in warmer weather? It is a very encouraging sign of life now.

Jan. 31. I notice in one place that the last six or more inches of the smooth sumach's lusty twigs are dead and withered, not having been sufficiently matured, notwithstanding the favorable autumn. This is attaining one's growth through difficulties.

Saw one faint tinge of red on red ice pond-hole, six inches over.

VII

FEBRUARY, 1858

(ÆT. 40)

Feb. 1. Measured Gowing's Swamp two and a half rods northeast of the middle of the hole, *i. e.* in the andromeda and sphagnum near its edge, where I stand in the summer; also five rods northeast of the middle of the open hole, or in the midst of the andromeda. In both these places the pole went hard at first, but broke through a crust of roots and sphagnum at about three feet beneath the surface, and I then easily pushed the pole down just twenty feet. This being a small pole, I could not push it any further holding it by the small end; it bent then. With a longer and stiffer pole I could probably have fathomed thirty feet. It seems, then, that there is, over this andromeda swamp, a crust about three feet thick, of sphagnum, andromeda (*calyculata* and *Polifolia*), and *Kalmia glauca*, etc., beneath which there is almost clear water, and, under that, an exceedingly thin mud. There can be no soil above that mud, and yet there were three or four larch trees three feet high or more between these holes, or over exactly the same water, and there were small spruces near by. For aught that appears, the swamp is as deep under the andromeda as in the middle. The two andromedas and the *Kalmia glauca* may be more

truly said to grow in water than in soil there. When the surface of a swamp shakes for a rod around you, you may conclude that it is a network of roots two or three feet thick resting on water or a very thin mud. The surface of that swamp, composed in great part of sphagnum, is really floating. It evidently begins with sphagnum, which floats on the surface of clear water, and, accumulating, at length affords a basis for that large-seeded sedge (?), andromedas, etc. The filling up of a swamp, then, in this case at least, is not the result of a deposition of vegetable matter washed into it, settling to the bottom and leaving the surface clear, so filling it up from the bottom to the top; but the vegetation first extends itself over it as a film, which gradually thickens till it supports shrubs and completely conceals the water, and the under part of this crust drops to the bottom, so that it is filled up first at the top and the bottom, and the middle part is the last to be reclaimed from the water.

Perhaps this swamp is in the process of becoming peat. This swamp has been partially drained by a ditch.

I fathomed also two rods within the edge of the blueberry bushes, in the path, but I could not force a pole down more than eight feet five inches; so it is much more solid there, and the blueberry bushes require a firmer soil than the water andromeda.

This is a regular *quag,* or shaking surface, and in this way, evidently, floating islands are formed. I am not sure but that meadow, with all its bushes in it, would float a man-of-war.

Feb. 2. Still rains, after a rainy night with a little snow, forming slosh. As I return from the post-office, I hear the hoarse, robin-like chirp of a song sparrow on Cheney's ground, and see him perched on the topmost twig of a heap of brush, looking forlorn and drabbled and solitary in the rain.

Feb. 3. P. M. — To Conantum.

I notice that the corner posts of the old Conantum house, which is now being pulled down, were all set butt up, and are considerably larger at that end.

I do not see this year, and I do not know that I ever have seen, any unseasonable swelling of the buds of *indigenous* plants in mild winters. I think that herbaceous plants show less greenness than usual this winter, having been more exposed for want of a snowy covering.

Feb. 4. P. M. — To C. Miles Swamp.

Discover the *Ledum latifolium,* quite abundant over a space about six rods in diameter just east of the small pond-hole, growing with the *Andromeda calyculata,* [A.] *Polifolia, Kalmia glauca,* etc. The *A. Polifolia* is very abundant about the pond-hole, some of it very narrow-leaved and dark, even black, above, as if burnt.

The ledum bears a *general* resemblance to the water andromeda, with its dark reddish-purplish, or rather mulberry, leaves, reflexed; but nearer it is distinguished by its coarseness, the perfect tent form of its upper leaves, and the *large, conspicuous* terminal *roundish* (strictly oval) red buds, nearly as big as the swamp-pink's, but rounded. The woolly stem for a couple of inches beneath the bud is frequently bare and conspicuously club-shaped. The rust on the under sides of the leaves seems of a lighter color than that of Maine. The seed-vessels (which open at the base first) still hold on. This plant might easily be confounded with the water andromeda by a careless observer. When I showed it to a teamster, he was sure that he had seen it often in the woods, but the sight of the woolly under side staggered him.

There are many small spruce thereabouts, with small twigs and leaves, an abnormal growth, reminding one of strange species of evergreen from California, China, etc. I brought some home and had a cup of tea made, which, in spite of a slight piny or turpentine flavor, I thought unexpectedly good.

An abundance of nesæa on the east edge of the pond-hole (call it Ledum Pond-hole); and is that a lysimachia mingled with it? [1]

The ledum does not grow amid the maples, — nor, indeed, does the *A. Polifolia, Kalmia glauca,* nor *even* the water andromeda abundantly. It bears no more shade than that of the spruce trees, which do not prevail over the above-named shrubbery. As usual with the finding of new plants, I had a presentiment that I should find the ledum in Concord. It is a remarkable fact that, in the case of the most interesting plants which I have discovered in this vicinity, I have anticipated finding them perhaps a year before the discovery.

[1] Elodea.

Feb. 5. P. M. — To Boaz's Meadow.

There is a plenty of that handsome-seeded grass which I think Tarbell called goose grass [1] in the meadow south of the roadway, at Boaz's Meadow, also in the meadows far north in the woods, and some .in Minot Pratt's meadow.

Feb. 7. Aunt Louisa has talked with Mrs. Monroe, and I can correct or add to my account of January 23d. She says that she was only three or four years old, and that she went to school, with Aunt Elizabeth and one other child, to a woman named Turner, somewhere in Boston, who kept a spinning-wheel a-going while she taught these three little children. She remembers that one sat on a lignum-vitæ mortar turned bottom up, another on a box, and the third on a stool; and then repeated the account of Jennie Burns bringing her little daughter to the school, as before.

I observed yesterday in that oak stump on the ditch-bank by Trillium Wood (which I counted the rings of once) that between the twentieth and twenty-seventh rings there was only about three sevenths of an inch, though before and after this it grew very fast and seven spaces would make nearly two inches. The tree was growing lustily till twenty years old, and then for seven years it grew only one fourth or one fifth part as fast as before and after. I am curious to know what happened to it.

P. M. — To Cliffs through Wheeler's pasture on the hill.

[1] Probably glyceria.

This new pasture, with gray stumps standing thickly in the now sere sward, reminds me of a graveyard. And on these monuments you can read each tree's name, when it was born (if you know when it died), how it throve, and how long it lived, whether it was cut down in full vigor or after the infirmities of age had attacked it.

I am surprised to find the epigæa on this hill, at the northwest corner of C. Hubbard's (?) lot, *i. e.* the large wood. It extends a rod or so and is probably earlier there than where I have found it before. Some of the buds show a very little color. The leaves have lately been much eaten, I suspect by partridges. Little mounds or tufts of yellowish or golden moss in the young woods look like sunlight on the ground.

If possible, come upon the top of a hill unexpectedly, perhaps through woods, and then see off from it to the distant earth which lies behind a bluer veil, before you can see directly down it, *i. e.* bringing its own near top against the distant landscape.

In the Fair Haven orchard I see the small botrychium still fresh, but quite dark reddish. The bark of the *Populus grandidentata* there is a green clay-color.

Feb. 8. P. M. — To Walden and Goose Pond.

The ground is so completely bare this winter, and therefore the leaves in the woods so dry, that on the 5th there was a fire in the woods by Walden (Wheeler's), and two or three acres were burned over, set probably by the engine. Such a burning as commonly occurs in the spring.

The ice which J. Brown is now getting for his ice-house from S. Barrett's is from eight to nine plus inches thick, but I am surprised to find that Walden ice is only six inches thick, or even a little less, and it has not been thicker. You can almost drive an axe through it at one blow. In many places about the shore it is open a dozen feet wide, as when it begins to break up in the spring.

I observe, as usual, the shore heaved up near where my house was. It is evidently the result of its thawing. It is lifted up with an abrupt, nearly perpendicular edge nearly a foot high (but looks as if it had been crowded up by the ice), while the part under water probably has not been frozen, or has not been thawed. But in the water close to the shore I observe singular dimples in the sand, sometimes perfectly circular tunnels, etc., as if a stone had been turned round and round and then lifted out. Perhaps this ridge thus lifted up remains somewhat loose through the summer, not falling entirely back, and the next winter, therefore, freezes yet deeper and is heaved up yet higher, and so gains a little from year to year. Thus a pond may create a barrier for itself along an adjacent meadow. When it thus lifts up the shore, it lifts the trees with it, and they are upset.

At Little Goose Pond, where I am surprised to find the ice no thicker than at Walden, I raked in the middle and brought up the branches of white pines two inches thick, but perfectly sound, four rods or more from the shore. The wood has been cut about seventeen years on one side, and at least twelve or fourteen on the other, and the present growth is oak. These were the tops of pines that formerly fell into the pond. They would long since [have] decayed on land.

I walked about Goose Pond, looking for the large blueberry bushes. I see many which have thirty rings of annual growth. These grow quite on the edge, where they have escaped being cut with the wood, and have all the appearance of age, gray and covered with lichens, commonly crooked, zigzag, and intertwisted with their neighbors, — so that when you have cut one off it is hard to extract it, — and bending over nearly to the ice, with lusty young shoots running up straight by their sides. I cut one, which measured eight and a half inches in circumference at the butt, and I counted pretty accurately forty-two rings. From another I cut a straight and sound club, four feet long and six and a half inches in circumference at the small end. It is a heavy and close-grained wood.

This is the largest of the *Vaccinieæ* which grows here, or is described in Gray's Botany. Some may have borne fruit before I was born, or forty and odd years ago. Older than my cultivated fruit trees. Nobody could tell me what kind of wood it was. The biggest panicled andromeda that I saw thereabouts was only a little more than an inch in diameter and apparently not half as old. It has a much more yellow wood, with a twist to its grain.

Mrs. Monroe says that her mother respected my grandfather very much, because he was a religious man. She remembers his calling one day and inquiring where blue vervain grew, which he wanted, to make a

syrup for his cough, and she, a girl, happening to know, ran and gathered some.

Feb. 9. A. M. — To old Hunt house with Thatcher. The stairs of the old back part are white pine or spruce, each the half of a square log; those of the cellar in front, oak, of the same form. There is no ridge-pole whatever, — not even a board, — but a steep roof; and some of the rafters are oak saplings, hewn and showing a good deal of bark, and scarcely three inches diameter at the small end; yet they have sufficed.

Saw at Simon Brown's a sketch, apparently made with a pen, on which was written, "Concord Jail, near Boston America," and on a fresher piece of paper on which the above was pasted, was written, "The jail in which General Sir Arch[ld] Campbell & —— Wilson were confined when taken off Boston in America by a French Privateer." A letter on the back side, from Mr. Lewis of Framingham to Mr. Brown, stated that he, Lewis, had received the sketch from the grandson of Wilson, who drew it.

You are supposed to be in the jail-yard, or close to it westward, and see the old jail, gambrel-roofed, the old Hurd house (partly) west of the graveyard, the graveyard, and Dr. Hurd house, and, over the last and to the north of it, a wooded hill, apparently Windmill Hill, and just north of the Hurd house, beyond it, apparently the court-house and schoolhouse, each with belfries, and the road to the Battle-Ground, and a distant farmhouse on a hill, French's or Buttrick's, perhaps.

Vol. X

Begins to snow at noon, and about one inch falls, whitening the ground.

Feb. 10. Grows cold toward night, and windy.

Feb. 11. At 3 P. M. it is 11° and windy.

I think it is the coldest day of this winter. The river channel is now suddenly and generally frozen over for the first time.

P. M. — To Hill.

The water in the pitcher-plant leaves is frozen, but I see none burst. They are very tightly filled and smooth, apparently stretched.

The leaves of the round-leaved pyrola, so exposed this winter, look not only dark but as if frozen. I am not sure that they are stiffened however.[1] I see that the hemlock leaves also have this frozen or frozen-thawed, cadaverous look, dark and slightly imbrowned, especially the most exposed twigs, while some sheltered ones are still a bright green. The same is the case even with the white pines and, as far as I observe, other evergreens. There is a change in their leaves with cold weather, corresponding to the reddening and darkening of checkerberry and pyrola leaves. They change, though they do not fall, and are to some extent affected, even as those trees which, like the oaks, retain a part of their leaves during the winter in a withered state; i. e., they have begun to wither or be killed. I have often before noticed that the pines, when cold weather came, were of a darker and duller green, somewhat

[1] I think not.

like a frozen apple. In the hemlock, at least, there is a positive tendency to redness. The evergreens, then, though they do not fall the first year, lose their original summer greenness; they are changed and partially killed by the cold, like pyrola and checkerberry and lambkill, and even, in a degree, like oak leaves. Perhaps the pitch pine is the least affected.

Cut a club of celtis wood. It is hard but, I think, brittle.

The celastrus (waxwork) is a soft, spongy, and flexible wood, though of very slow growth. You can easily sink your knife into it. I count twenty-five rings in the heart-wood of one which is not quite an inch in diameter. In the sap there is no evidence of rings at all.

Feb. 12. Colder than yesterday morning; perhaps the coldest of the winter.

P. M. — To Ledum Pond.

Those small holes in the ground, — musquash, mice, etc., — thickly beset with crystals of frost, remind me of the invisible vapor issuing thence which may be called Earth's breath, though you might think it were the breath of a mouse. In cold weather you see not only men's beards and the hair about the muzzles of oxen whitened with their frozen breath, but countless holes in the banks, which are the nostrils of the earth, white with the frozen earth's breath.

About the ledum pond-hole there is an abundance of that abnormal growth of the spruce. Instead of a regular, free, and open growth, you have a multitude of slender branches crowded together, putting out from the summit or side of the stem and shooting up nearly perpendicularly, with dense, fine, wiry branchlets and fine needles, which have an impoverished look, altogether forming a broom-like mass, very much like a heath.

There is, apparently, more of the *Andromeda Polifolia* in that swamp than anywhere else in Concord.

Feb. 13. Last night said to have been a little colder than the night before, and the coldest hitherto.

P. M. — Ride to Cafferty's Swamp.

The greatest breadth of the swamp appears to be northeasterly from Adams's.

There is much panicled andromeda in it, some twelve feet high, and, as I count, seventeen years old, with yellowish wood. I saw three tupelos in the swamp, each about one foot in diameter and all within two rods. In those parts of the swamp where the bushes were not so high but that I could look over them, I observed that the swamp was variously shaded, or painted even, like a rug, with the sober colors running gradually into each other, by the colored recent shoots of various shrubs which grow densely, as the red blueberry, and the yellowish-brown panicled andromeda, and the dark-brown or blackish *Prinos verticillatus*, and the choke-berry, etc. Standing on a level with those shrubs, you could see that these colors were only a foot or so deep, according to the length of the shoots. So, too, oftener would the forests appear if we oftener stood above them.

How often vegetation is either yellow or red! as the

buds of the swamp-pink, the leaves of the pitcher-plant, etc., etc., and to-day I notice yellow-green recent shoots of high blueberry.

Observed a coarse, dense-headed grass in the meadow at Stow's old swamp lot.

What did the birds do for horsehair here formerly?

Feb. 14. About one inch of snow falls.

Feb. 15. To Cambridge and Boston.

Saw, at a menagerie, a Canada lynx, said to have been taken at the White Mountains. It looked much like a monstrous gray cat standing on stilts, with its tail cut down to five inches, a tuft of hair on each ear and a ruff under the throat.

Feb. 18. I find Walden ice to be nine and a half plus inches thick, having gained three and a half inches since the 8th.

The *Rubus hispidus* (*sempervirens* of Bigelow) is truly evergreen. There has been so little snow this winter that I have noticed it the more, — red, glossy, and, as it were, plaited.

I see the ice, three inches thick, heaved up tentwise eighteen inches or more in height, near the shore, yet where the water is too deep for the bottom to have been heaved, as if some steam had heaved it.

At Brister's further spring, the water which trickles off in various directions between and around little mounds of green grass half frozen, when it reaches the more mossy ground runs often between two per-

Vol. X

pendicular walls of ice, as at the bottom of a cañon, the top of these perfectly square-edged banks being covered with the moss that originally covered the ground (otherwise undisturbed) and extending several feet on each side at the same level. These icy cliffs are of a loose crystalline composition, with many parallel horizontal seams, as if built up. I suppose that the water flows just under the moss, and, freezing, heaves it one stage; then the next night, perchance, new water, flowing underneath, heaves the whole another stage; and so on, steadily lifting it up.

Far from here, I see the surface of weeds and mud lifted up in like manner where there is no cañon or rill, but a puddle.

George Minott tells me that he, when young, used often to go to a store by the side of where Bigelow's tavern was and kept by Ephraim Jones, — the Goodnow store. That was probably the one kept by my old trader. Told me how Casey, who was a slave to a man — Whitney — who lived where Hawthorne owns, — the same house, — before the Revolution, ran off one Sunday, was pursued by the neighbors, and hid himself in the river up to his neck till nightfall, just across the Great Meadows. He ran through Gowing's Swamp and came back that night to a Mrs. Cogswell, who lived where Charles Davis does, and got something to eat; then cleared far away, enlisted, and was freed as a soldier after the war. Whitney's boy threw snowballs at him the day before, and finally C., who was chopping in the yard, threw his axe at him, and W. said he was an ugly nigger and he must put him in

jail. He may have been twenty years old when stolen from Africa; left a wife and one child there. Used to say that he went home to Africa in the night and came back again in the morning; *i. e.*, he dreamed of home. Lived to be old. Called Thanksgiving "Tom Kiver."

Feb. 19. Coldest morning this winter by our thermometer, — 3° at 7.30.

The traveller is defended and calloused. He deals with surfaces, has a greatcoat on. But he who stays at home and writes about homely things gives us naked and tender thoughts and sentiments.

Feb. 20. Snows all day. The most wintry day of the winter; yet not more than three inches on a level is fallen.

We hear the names of the worthies of Concord, — Squire Cuming and the rest, — but the poor slave Casey seems to have lived a more adventurous life than any of them. Squire Cuming probably never had to run for his life on the plains of Concord.

Feb. 24. I see, at Minot Pratt's, rhodora in bloom in a pitcher with water andromeda.

Went through that long swamp northeast of Boaz's Meadow. Interesting and peculiar are the clumps, or masses, of panicled andromeda, with light-brown stems, topped uniformly with very distinct yellow-brown recent shoots, ten or twelve inches long, with minute red buds sleeping close along them. This uniformity in such masses gives a pleasing tinge to the swamp's surface. Wholesome colors, which wear well. I see quite a number of emperor moth cocoons attached to this shrub, some hung round with a loose mass of leaves as big as my two fists. What art in the red-eye to make these two adjacent maple twigs serve for the rim of its pensile basket, inweaving them! Surely it finds a place for itself in nature between the two twigs of a maple.

On the side of the meadow moraine just north of the boulder field, I see barberry bushes three inches in diameter and ten feet high. What a surprising color this wood has! It splits and splinters very much when I bend it. I cut a cane and, shaving off the outer bark, it is of imperial yellow, as if painted, fit for a Chinese mandarin.

Feb. 25. Ice at Walden eleven inches thick and very soggy, sinking to a level with the water, though there is but a trifling quantity of snow on it. Does it not commonly begin to be soggy even thus early, and thick, sinking deeper? I hear of sudden openings in ponds — as at Cochituate — this year.

Feb. 27. A. M. — To Hill.

The hedges on the Hill are all cut off. The journals think they cannot say too much on improvements in husbandry. It is a safe theme, like piety. But for me, as for one of these farms brushed up, — a model farm, — I had as lief see a patent churn and a man turning it. It is simply a place where somebody is making money.[1]

¹ [*Maine Woods*, p. 171 ; Riv. 210.]

Vol. X

I see a snow bunting, though it is pleasant and warm.

Feb. 28. P. M. — To White Pond.

I see twenty-four cones brought together under one pitch pine in a field, evidently gnawed off by a squirrel, but not opened. Rice says he saw a whistler (?) duck to-day.

VIII

MARCH, 1858

(ÆT. 40)

March 1. The divergent open capsules (?) of the rhodora, yellowish-brown, are quite interesting when the sun falls on them. We have just had a winter with absolutely no sleighing, which I do not find that any one distinctly remembers the like of. It may have been as warm before, but with more snow. It was wonderfully warm and pleasant up to the 10th of February, and since then the greatest degree of cold I have heard of was − 4°. The ground has been partially covered or whitened only since the 20th. It has been an excellent winter for walking in the swamps, or walking anywhere, and for lumbering operations in Maine, there being not too much snow, and yet the swamps, etc., frozen there.

March 2. Snowed last night and this morning, about seven inches deep, much more than during the winter, the first truly wintry-looking day so far as snow is concerned; but the snow is quite soft or damp, lodging in perpendicular walls on the limbs, white on black. But it is as yet neither wheeling nor sleighing, the ground being muddy.

I remember to have seen these wood-lots being cut this winter: a little on the southwest edge of R. W. E.'s

Pinnacle; Stow's, up to east end of cold pool; northwest corner of Gowing's, next Great Fields and Moore; an acre or more of the southwest part of the Dennis swamp by railroad; Cyrus Hosmer's, southwest of Desert; and west of Marlborough road; except north part of last.

I walk through the Colburn farm pine woods by railroad and thence to rear of John Hosmer's. See a large flock of snow buntings, the white birds of the winter, rejoicing in the snow. I stand near a flock in an open field. They are trotting about briskly over the snow amid the weeds, — apparently pigweed and Roman wormwood, — as it were to keep their toes warm, hopping up to the weeds. Then they restlessly take to wing again, and as they wheel about one, it is a very rich sight to see them dressed in black and white uniforms, alternate black and white, very distinct and regular. Perhaps no colors would be more effective above the snow, black tips (considerably more) to wings, then clear white between this and the back, which is black or very dark again. One wonders if they are aware what a pleasing uniform appearance they make when they show their backs thus. They alight again equally near. Their track is much like a small crow's track, showing a long heel and furrowing the snow between with their toes.

The last new journal thinks that it is very liberal, nay, bold, but it dares not publish a child's thought on important subjects, such as life and death and good books. It requires the sanction of the divines just as surely as the tamest journal does. If it had been published at the time of the famous dispute between Christ and the doctors, it would have published only the opinions of the doctors and suppressed Christ's. There is no need of a law to check the license of the press. It is law enough, and more than enough, to itself. Virtually, the community have come together and agreed what things shall be uttered, have agreed on a platform and to excommunicate him who departs from it, and not one in a thousand dares utter anything else. There are plenty of journals brave enough to say what they think about the government, this being a free one; but I know of none, widely circulated or well conducted, that dares say what it thinks about the Sunday or the Bible. They have been bribed to keep dark. They are in the service of hypocrisy.

March 4. Thermometer 14° this morning, and this makes decent sleighing of the otherwise soft snow.

Father Rasle's dictionary of the Abenaki language amounts to a very concentrated and trustworthy natural history of that people, though it was not completed. What they have a word for, they have a thing for. A traveller may tell us that he *thinks* they used a pavement, or built their cabins in a certain form, or soaked their seed corn in water, or had no beard, etc., etc.; but when one gives us the word for these things, the question is settled, — that is a clincher. Let us know what words they had and how they used them, and we can infer almost all the rest. The lexicographer not only *says* that a certain people have or do a certain thing, but, being evidently a disinterested party, it

may be allowed that he brings sufficient evidence to prove it. He does not so much assert as exhibit. He has no transient or private purpose to serve.

The snow *balls* particularly when, as now, colder weather comes after a damp snow has fallen on muddy ground, and it is soft beneath while just freezing above.

I grow so fast and am so weighed down and hindered, that I have to stop continually and look for a rock where I may kick off these newly acquired heels and soles.

March 5. Went to hear a Chippeway Indian, a Doctor Mung-somebody, — assisted by a Penobscot, who said nothing. He made the audience laugh unintentionally by putting an *m* after the word *too*, which he brought in continually and unnecessarily, and almost after this word alone, emphasizing and prolonging that sound, as, "They carried them home toom-ah," as if it were a necessity for bringing in so much of the Indian language for a relief to his organs or a compensation for "twisting his jaws about," as he said, in his attempt to speak English. So Polis and the Penobscots continually put the *um* or *em* to our words, — as *paddlum*, *littlum*, etc. There was so much of unsubdued Indian accent resounding through his speech, so much of the "bow-arrow tang!" I have no doubt it was a great relief to him and seemed the word best pronounced.[1]

He thought his ancestors came from Asia, and was sure that Behring's Strait was no obstacle, since Indians of his tribe cross Lakes Huron and Superior in

[1] [*Maine Woods*, p. 187; Riv. 230, 231.]

Vol. X

birch-bark canoes. Thought Indians might be Jews, because of a similarity of customs. When a party of his warriors wish to tell an advanced party concealed in a dangerous position to retreat, they shoot an arrow close past them; if to stay, they shoot an arrow over their heads; and exactly this, he declared, the Jews did. I inferred from his statement that the totem (a deer in his case) takes the place of the surname with us, for he said that his children would have the same totem. He did not use this word. Said they had a secret fraternity like the Masonic, by which they knew and befriended members anywhere.

Had some ornaments of snake-skins, four or five inches broad, with a bead edging, — broad belts, — worn diagonally across the breast or for a garter, or for a very large and broad string handle to a bag, passing round the neck. Also an otter-skin pouch. The head left on was evidently very convenient as well as important, to hold it when caught under the belt. It was thus very quickly returned to its place. Had head, feet, and all. Had on an eagle-feather cap, *i. e.* a band with long black eagles' feathers standing from it. This not worn every day. A buffalo-skin blanket, worked with porcupine quills.

Showed the cradle. The mother cuts a notch in the lower end for each day that passes and one at the top for each moon. If it falls into the water it floats on this. Said the first poetry made at Plymouth was suggested by the sight of this cradle swinging from a tree, *viz.* "Rock-a-by, baby," etc.

Exhibited very handsome birch-bark trays, orna-

mented with moose-hair inworked in the false bottom and side, representing strawberries, etc., very well. Only the white hair was not dyed. These were made without communication with the whites.

They place the feet of the child in the cradle straight, or as they would have them. Indians step with the feet straight, but whites, who toe out, seem to have no use for any toes but the great one in walking. Indian women are brought up to toe in. It is improper for them to toe out. Shot small arrows through a blow-gun very straight at an apple a rod off, lodging them all in it. The gun was of elder with the pith out, about six feet long; the arrows, quite slender, of hard wood, with a large and dense cylindrical mass of thistle-down at what is commonly the feathered end.

The Penobscot, who chanced to be Joe Polis's brother, told me that the *shecorway* of the Maine lakes was the sheldrake, and that when they call out the moose at night they imitate the voice of the cow moose. That of the bull is very different.

The former carried the cradle low down on his back with a strap round his head, and showed how the mother had both hands free and could chop wood, etc., with her infant on her back. The same blanket covered both if necessary, and the child was prevented from being smothered by the bow over its face holding up the blanket. He regretted that their marriage customs were not so good as ours, that they did not choose for themselves but their parents for them.

We read the English poets; we study botany and zoölogy and geology, lean and dry as they are; and it is rare that we get a new suggestion. It is ebb-tide with the scientific reports, Professor —— in the chair. We would fain know something more about these animals and stones and trees around us. We are ready to skin the animals alive to come at them. Our scientific names convey a very partial information only; they suggest certain thoughts only. It does not occur to me that there are other names for most of these objects, given by a people who stood between me and them, who had better senses than our race. How little I know of that *arbor-vitæ* when I have learned only what science can tell me! It is but a word. It is not a *tree* of *life*. But there are twenty words for the tree and its different parts which the Indian gave, which are not in our botanies, which imply a more practical and vital science. He used it every day. He was well acquainted with its wood, and its bark, and its leaves. No science does more than arrange what knowledge we have of any class of objects. But, generally speaking, how much more conversant was the Indian with any wild animal or plant than we are, and in his language is implied all that intimacy, as much as ours is expressed in our language. How many words in his language about a moose, or birch bark, and the like! The Indian stood nearer to wild nature than we. The wildest and noblest quadrupeds, even the largest fresh-water fishes, some of the wildest and noblest birds and the fairest flowers have actually receded as *we* advanced, and we have but the most distant knowledge of them. A rumor has come down to us that the skin of a lion was seen and his roar heard

Vol. X

here by an early settler. But there was a race here that slept on his skin. It was a new light when my guide gave me Indian names for things for which I had only scientific ones before. In proportion as I understood the language, I saw them from a new point of view.

A dictionary of the Indian language reveals another and wholly new life to us. Look at the word "canoe," and see what a story it tells of outdoor life, with the names of all its parts and modes of using it, as our words describing the different parts and seats of a coach, — with the difference in practical knowledge between him who rides and him who walks; or at the word "wigwam," and see how close it brings you to the ground; or "Indian corn," and see which race was most familiar with it. It reveals to me a life within a life, or rather a life without a life, as it were threading the woods between our towns still, and yet we can never tread in its trail. The Indian's earthly life was as far off from us as heaven is.

I saw yesterday a musquash sitting on thin ice on the Assabet, by a hole which it had kept open, gnawing a white root. Now and then it would dive and bring up more. I waited for it to dive again, that I might run nearer to it meanwhile, but it sat ten minutes all wet in the freezing wind while my feet and ears grew numb, so tough it is; but at last I got quite near. When I frightened it, it dove with a sudden slap of its tail. I feel pretty sure that this is an involuntary movement, the tail by the sudden turn of the body being brought down on the water or ice like a whip-lash.

March 6. P. M. — Up river on ice to Fair Haven Pond.

The river is frozen more solidly than during the past winter, and for the first time for a year I could cross it in most places. I did not once cross it the past winter, though by choosing a safe place I might have done so, without doubt, once or twice. But I have had no river walks before.

I see the first hen-hawk, or hawk of any kind, methinks, since the beginning of winter. Its scream, even, is inspiring as the voice of a spring bird.

That light spongy bark about the base of the nesæa appears to be good tinder. I have only to touch one end to a coal, and it all burns up slowly, without blazing, in whatever position held, and even after being dipped in water.

March 7. Walking by the river this afternoon, it being half open and the waves running pretty high, — the black waves, yellowish where they break over ice, — I inhale a fresh, meadowy, spring odor from them which is a little exciting. It is like the fragrance of tea to an old tea-drinker.

March 8. Went to a concert of instrumental music this evening. The imitations of the horn and the echo by the violoncello were very good, but the sounds of the clarinet were the most liquid and melodious. It is a powerful instrument and filled the hall, realizing my idea of the shepherd's pipe. It was a conduit of gurgling melody, but it apparently required a great

effort of the lungs. Its sounds entered every cranny of the hall and filled it to repletion with sweet liquid melody. There was no squeaking, no jarring string, no fuzzy breathing, no rattling stops; but pure melody, flowing in its own invisible and impalpable channels.

March 9. About three inches more of snow fell last night, which, added to about five of the old, makes eight, or more than before since last spring. Pretty good sleighing.

The State commonly grants a tract of forest to make an academy out of,[1] for such is the material of which our institutions are made, though only the crudest part of it is used, but the groves of the academy are straightway cut down, and that institution is built of its lumber, its coarsest and least valuable part. Down go the groves of the academy and up goes its frame, — on some bare common far away. And as for the public domains, if anybody neglected his civil duties during the last war, he is privileged to cut and slash there, — he is let loose against one hundred and sixty acres of well-behaved trees, as if the liberty he had defended was derived from *liber, bark,* and meant the liberty to bark the trees.

March 14. P. M. — I see a *Fringilla hyemalis,* the first bird, perchance, — unless one hawk, — which is an evidence of spring, though they lingered with us the past unusual winter, at least till the 19th of January. They are now getting back earlier than our per-

[1] [*Maine Woods,* p. 252; Riv. 312.]

manent summer residents. It flits past with a rattling or grating chip, showing its two white tail-feathers.

The sleighing which began the 4th of March is now done, the only sleighing since the winter of '56–7.

I hear that many cherry-birds have been seen. I think I have seen many more tracks of skunks within two or three weeks than all the winter before; as if they were partially dormant here in the winter, and came out very early, i. e., perhaps some of them are more or less dormant.

March 16. P. M. — To Conantum.

A thick mist, spiriting away the snow. Very bad walking. This fog is one of the first decidedly spring signs; also the withered grass bedewed by it and wetting my feet. A still, foggy, and rather warm day. I heard this morning, also, quite a steady warbling from tree sparrows on the dripping bushes, and that peculiar drawling note of a hen, who has this peevish way of expressing her content at the sight of bare ground and mild weather. The crowing of cocks and the cawing of crows tell the same story. The ice is soggy and dangerous to be walked on.

How conversant the Indian who lived out of doors, who lay on the ground, must have been with mouse-ear leaves, pine-needles, mosses, and lichens, which form the crust of the earth. No doubt he had names accordingly for many things for which we have no popular names.

I walk in muddy fields, hearing the tinkling of new-born rills. Where the melted snow has made a swift rill in the rut of a cart-path, flowing over an icy bottom

and between icy banks, I see, just below a little fall of one inch, a circular mass of foam or white bubbles nearly two inches in diameter, slowly revolving but never moving off. The swift stream at the fall appears to strike one side, as it might the side of a water-wheel, and so cause it to revolve, but in the angle between this and the fall, and half an inch distant, is another circle of bubbles, individually larger and more evanescent, only half an inch in diameter, revolving very rapidly in the opposite direction. The laws, perchance, by which the world was made, and according to which the systems revolve, are seen in full operation in a rill of melted snow.

March 17. Hear the first bluebird.
P. M. — To the Hill.

A remarkably warm and pleasant day with a south or southwest wind, but still very bad walking, the frost coming out and the snow that was left going off. The air is full of bluebirds. I hear them far and near on all sides of the hill, warbling in the tree-tops, though I do not distinctly see them.

I stand by the wall at the east base of the hill, looking over the alder meadow, lately cut off. I am peculiarly attracted by its red-brown maze, seen in this bright sun and mild southwest wind. It has expression in it as a familiar freckled face. Methinks it is about waking up, though it still slumbers. See the still, smooth pools of water in its midst, almost free from ice. I seem to hear the sound of the water soaking into it, — as it were its voice.

We must not expect it to blow warm long at a time. Even to-day, methinks, there are cool veins in the air, as if some puffs came over snow and ice and others not, like the meat which consisted alternately of a streak of fat and a streak of lean.

I sit on the bank at the Hemlocks and watch the great white cakes of ice going swiftly by. Now one strikes a rock and swings round in an eddy. They bear on them the wrecks and refuse of the shore where they were formed. Even the shade is agreeable to-day. You hear the buzzing of a fly from time to time, and see the black speck zigzag by.

Ah! there is the note of the first flicker, a prolonged, monotonous *wick-wick-wick-wick-wick-wick*, etc., or, if you please, *quick-quick*, heard far over and through the dry leaves. But how that single sound peoples and enriches all the woods and fields! They are no longer the same woods and fields that they were. This note really *quickens* what was dead. It seems to put a life into withered grass and leaves and bare twigs, and henceforth the days shall not be as they have been. It is as when a family, your neighbors, return to an empty house after a long absence, and you hear the cheerful hum of voices and the laughter of children, and see the smoke from the kitchen fire. The doors are thrown open, and children go screaming through the hall. So the flicker dashes through the aisles of the grove, throws up a window here and cackles out it, and then there, airing the house. It makes its voice ring up-stairs and down-stairs, and so, as it were, fits it for its habitation and ours, and takes possession.

It is as good as a housewarming to all nature. Now I hear and see him louder and nearer on the top of the long-armed white oak, sitting very upright, as is their wont, as it were calling for some of his kind that may also have arrived.

As usual, I have seen for some weeks on the ice these peculiar (perla?) insects with long wings and two tails.

The withered vegetation, seed-vessels of all kinds, etc., are peculiarly handsome now, having been remarkably well preserved the past winter on account of the absence of snow.

How indulgent is Nature, to give to a few common plants, like checkerberry, this aromatic flavor to relieve the general insipidity! Perhaps I am most sensible of the presence of these plants when the ground is first drying at this season and they come fairly out. Also mouse-ear and pyrola.

Sitting under the handsome scarlet oak beyond the hill, I hear a faint note far in the wood which reminds me of the robin. Again I hear it; it is he, — an occasional peep. These notes of the earliest birds seem to invite forth vegetation. No doubt the plants concealed in the earth hear them and rejoice. They wait for this assurance.

Now I hear, when passing the south side of the hill, or first when threading the maple swamp far west of it, the *tchuck tchuck* of a blackbird, and after, a distinct *conqueree*. So it is a red-wing?

Thus these four species of birds have all come in one day, no doubt to almost all parts of the town.

March 18. 7 A. M. — By river.

Almost every bush has its song sparrow this morning, and their tinkling strains are heard on all sides. You see them just hopping under the bush or into some other covert, as you go by, turning with a jerk this way and that, or they flit away just above the ground, which they resemble. It is the prettiest strain I have heard yet. Melvin is already out in his boat for all day, with his white hound in the prow, bound up the river for musquash, etc., but the river is hardly high enough to drive them out.

P. M. — To Fair Haven Hill *via* Hubbard's Bath.

How much more habitable a few birds make the fields! At the end of winter, when the fields are bare and there is nothing to relieve the monotony of the withered vegetation, our life seems reduced to its lowest terms. But let a bluebird come and warble over them, and what a change! The note of the first bluebird in the air answers to the purling rill of melted snow beneath. It is eminently soft and soothing, and, as surely as the thermometer, indicates a higher temperature. It is the accent of the south wind, its vernacular. It is modulated by the south wind. The song sparrow is more sprightly, mingling its notes with the rustling of the brash along the watersides, but it is at the same time more *terrene* than the bluebird. The first woodpecker comes screaming into the empty house and throws open doors and windows wide, calling out each of them to let the neighbors know of its return. But heard further off it is very suggestive of ineffable

associations which cannot be distinctly recalled, — of long-drawn summer hours, — and thus it, also, has the effect of music. I was not aware that the capacity to hear the woodpecker had slumbered within me so long. When the blackbird gets to a *conqueree* he seems to be dreaming of the sprays that are to be and on which he is to perch. The robin does not come singing, but utters a somewhat anxious or inquisitive peep at first. The song sparrow is immediately most at home of any that I have named. I see this afternoon as many as a dozen bluebirds on the warm side of a wood.

At Hubbard's shore, where a strong but warm westerly wind is blowing, the shore is lined for half a rod in width with pulverized ice, or "brash," driven against it.

At Potter's sand-hill (Bear Garden), I see, on the southeast side of the blue-curls, very distinct and regular arcs of circles (about a third of a circle), scored deep in the sand by the tops of these weeds, which have been blown about by the wind, and these marks show very surely and plainly how the wind has been blowing and with what force and flawiness.

The rather warm but strong wind now roars in the wood — as in the maple swamp — with a novel sound. I doubt if the same is ever heard in the winter. It apparently comes at this season, not only to dry the earth but to wake up the trees, as it were, as one would awake a sleeping man with a smart shake. Perchance they need to be thus wrung and twisted, and their sap flows the sooner for it.

Perfectly dry sand even is something attractive now,

and I am tempted to tread on and to touch it, as a curiosity. Skunks' tracks are everywhere now, on the sand, and the little snow that is left.

The river is still closed with ice at Cardinal Shore, so Melvin must have stopped here at least; but there is a crescent of "brash" there, which the waves blown up-stream have made, half a dozen rods wide. It is even blown a rod on to the solid ice. The noise made by this brash undulating and grating upon itself, at a little distance, is very much like the rustling of a winrow of leaves disturbed by the winds. A little farther off it is not to be distinguished from the roar of the wind in the woods.

Each new year is a surprise to us. We find that we had virtually forgotten the note of each bird, and when we hear it again it is remembered like a dream, reminding us of a previous state of existence. How happens it that the associations it awakens are always pleasing, never saddening; reminiscences of our sanest hours? The voice of nature is always encouraging.

The blackbird — probably grackle this time — wings his way direct above the swamp northward, with a regular *tchuck*, carrier haste, calling the summer months along, like a hen her chickens.

When I get two thirds up the hill, I look round and am for the hundredth time surprised by the landscape of the river valley and the horizon with its distant blue scalloped rim. It is a spring landscape, and as impossible a fortnight ago as the song of birds. It is a deeper and warmer blue than in winter, methinks. The snow is off the mountains, which seem even to

have come again like the birds. The undulating river is a bright-blue channel between sharp-edged shores of ice retained by the willows. The wind blows strong but warm from west by north, so that I have to hold my paper tight when I write this, making the copses creak and roar; but the sharp tinkle of a song sparrow is heard through it all. But ah! the needles of the pine, how they shine, as I look down over the Holden wood and westward! Every third tree is lit with the most subdued but clear ethereal light, as if it were the most delicate frostwork in a winter morning, reflecting no heat, but only light. And as they rock and wave in the strong wind, even a mile off, the light courses up and down there as over a field of grain; *i. e.*, they are alternately light and dark, like looms above the forest, when the shuttle is thrown between the light woof and the dark web, weaving a light article, — spring goods for Nature to wear. At sight of this my spirit is like a lit tree. It runs or flashes over their parallel boughs as when you play with the teeth of a comb. The pine-tops wave like squirrels' tails flashing in the air. Not only osiers but pine-needles, methinks, shine in the spring, and arrowheads and railroad rails, etc., etc. Anacreon noticed the same. Is it not the higher sun, and cleansed air, and greater animation of nature? There is a warmer red to the leaves of the shrub oak, and to the tail of the hawk circling over them.

I sit on the Cliff, and look toward Sudbury. I see its meeting-houses and its common, and its fields lie but little beyond my ordinary walk, but I never played on its common nor read the epitaphs in its graveyard, and many strangers to me dwell there. How distant in all important senses may be the town which yet is within sight! We see beyond our ordinary walks and thoughts. With a glass I might perchance read the time on its clock. How circumscribed are our walks, after all! With the utmost industry we cannot expect to know well an area more than six miles square, and yet we pretend to be travellers, to be acquainted with Siberia and Africa!

Going by the epigæa on Fair Haven Hill, I thought I would follow down the shallow gully through the woods from it, that I might find more or something else. There was an abundance of checkerberry, as if it were a peculiar locality for shrubby evergreens. At first the checkerberry was green, but low down the hill it suddenly became dark-red, like a different plant, as if it had been more subject to frost there, it being more frosty lower down. Where it was most turned, that part of the leaf which was protected by another overlapping it was still pure bright-green, making a pretty contrast when you lifted it. Eight or ten rods off I noticed an evergreen shrub with the aspect or habit of growth of the juniper, but, as it was in the woods, I already suspected it to be what it proved, the American yew, already strongly budded to bloom. This is a capital discovery. I have thus found the ledum and the taxus this winter and a new locality of the epigæa.

March 19. P. M. — To Hill and Grackle Swamp.
Another pleasant and warm day. Painted my boat

this afternoon. These spring impressions (as of the apparent waking up of the meadow described day before yesterday) are not repeated the same year, at least not with the same force, for the next day the same phenomenon does not surprise us. Our appetite has lost its edge. The other day the face of the meadow wore a peculiar appearance, as if it were beginning to wake up under the influence of the southwest wind and the warm sun, but it cannot again this year present precisely that appearance to me. I have taken a step forward to a new position and must see something else. You perceive, and are affected by, changes too subtle to be described.

I see little swarms of those fine fuzzy gnats in the air. I am behind the Hemlocks. It is their wings which are most conspicuous, when they are in the sun. Their bodies are comparatively small and black, and they have two mourning plumes in their fronts. Are not these the winter gnat? They keep up a circulation in the air like water-bugs on the water. They people a portion of the otherwise vacant air, being apparently fond of the sunshine, in which they are most conspicuous. Sometimes a globular swarm two feet or more in diameter, suggesting how genial and habitable the air is become.

I hear turkeys gobble. This too, I suppose, is a spring sound. I hear a steady sigh of the wind, rising and swelling into a roar, in the pines, which seems to tell of a long, warm rain to come.

I see a white pine which has borne fruit in its ninth year. The cones, four in number, which are seven

Vol. X

eighths of an inch long, have stems about two and a half inches long! — not yet curving down; so the stem probably does not grow any more.

Met Channing and walked on with him to what we will call Grackle Swamp, admiring the mosses; those bright-yellow hypnums (?), like sunlight on decaying logs, and jungermannia, like sea-mosses ready spread.

Hear the phebe note of a chickadee. In the swamp, see grackles, four or five, with the light ring about eye, — their bead eyes. They utter only those ineffectual *split* notes, no *conqueree*.

Might I not call that Hemlock Brook? and the source of it *Horse-skull* Meadow?

Hear the pleasant *chill-lill* of the *F. hyemalis*, the first time have heard this note. This, too, suggests pleasant associations.

By the river, see distinctly red-wings and hear their *conqueree*. They are not associated with grackles. They are an age before their cousins, have attained to clearness and liquidity. They are officers, epauletted; the others are rank and file. I distinguish one even by its flight, hovering slowly from tree-top to tree-top, as if ready to utter its liquid notes. Their whistle is very clear and sharp, while the grackle's is ragged and split.

It is a fine evening, as I stand on the bridge. The waters are quite smooth; very little ice to be seen. The red-wing and song sparrow are singing, and a flock of tree sparrows is pleasantly warbling. A new era has come. The red-wing's *gurgle-ee* is heard when smooth waters begin; they come together. One or two boys

are out trying their skiffs, even like the fuzzy gnats in the sun, and as often as one turns his boat round on the smooth surface, the setting sun is reflected from its side.

I feel reproach when I have spoken with levity, when I have made a jest, of my own existence. The makers have thus secured seriousness and respect for their work in our very organization. The most serious events have their ludicrous aspect, such as death; but we cannot excuse ourselves when we have taken this view of them only. It is pardonable when we spurn the proprieties, even the sanctities, making them stepping-stones to something higher.

March 20. A. M. — By river.
The tree sparrow is perhaps the sweetest and most melodious warbler at present and for some days. It is peculiar, too, for singing in concert along the hedge-rows, much like a canary, especially in the mornings. Very clear, sweet, melodious notes, between a twitter and a warble, of which it is hard to catch the strain, for you commonly hear many at once. The note of the *F. hyemalis*, or *chill-lill*, is a jingle, with also a shorter and drier *crackling* or shuffling chip as it flits by. I hear now, at 7 A. M., from the hill across the water, probably the note of a woodpecker, I know not what species; not that very early *gnah gnah*, which I have not heard this year. Now first I hear a very short robin's song.

P. M. — To Clematis Brook *via* Lee's with C.

We cross the Depot Field, which is fast becoming dry and hard. At Hubbard's wall, how handsome the willow catkins! Those wonderfully bright silvery buttons, so regularly disposed in oval schools in the air, or, if you please, along the seams which their twigs make, in all degrees of forwardness, from the faintest, tiniest speck of silver, just peeping from beneath the black scales, to lusty pussies which have thrown off their scaly coats and show some redness at base on a close inspection. These fixed swarms of arctic buds spot the air very prettily along the hedges. They remind me somewhat by their brilliancy of the snow-flecks which are so bright by contrast at this season when the sun is high. Is not this, perhaps, the earliest, most obvious, awakening of vegetable life?[1]

Farmer told me this morning that he found a bay-wing's egg yesterday, dropped in a footpath! I have not seen that bird yet.

In low grounds we feel from time to time the icy crust in the soil sink beneath us, but it is so dry that we need no rubbers now. A small ant fallen on water and swimming. A small brown grasshopper jumps into a brook at our approach and, drifting down, clings to a stubble. I see another just like it two hours later. We look into that pool on the south side of Hubbard's Grove, and admire the green weeds, water purslane (?), at the bottom. There is, slowly moving along in it near the bottom, one of those bashaws with two tails, — in this case *red* tails, — something devil's-needle-like.

[1] They are grayish and not nearly so silvery a week or ten days later, when more expanded, showing the dark scales.

Vol. X

The whole pool is full of a small gyrating insect. I took up from a weed within it, by a chance sweep of my hand, a minute bivalve clam-like shell hardly one twentieth of an inch long. Yet this dries up in summer. The other pool near by, within the woods, is still covered with black soggy ice.

The herbaceous plants have evidently suffered far more than usual the past wonderfully mild and snowless winter. Not only is there less green in the fields, but even less at the bottoms of the pools and ditches.

The foul flanks of the cattle remind me how early it is still in the spring.

On that same tree by Conant's orchard, I see a flock of cherry-birds with that alert, chieftain-like look, and hear their *seringo* note, as if made by their swift flight through the air. They have been seen a week or two.

Fair Haven is still closed. Near the open water where the river is eating up into it, the ice is very *black*, even *sooty*, here and there, from this point of view. You would not believe that mere water-logged ice could be so black. You cannot now get on to it, but you see the holes which pickerel-fishers cut in it a month ago.

We go looking in vain for ducks, — a semiriparial walk. From time to time we are deceived a moment by a shining cake of ice on its edge at a distance.

We go along behind Lee's, looking out over the Sudbury meadows. I see a distant roof at Round Hill. It is pleasant when we see thus only the roof of a house at a distance, a mere gray scale, diamond-shape, against the side of a hill, while all the lower part is lost in shade. It is more interesting than a full view.

The river but yesterday was a bright-blue artery between straight edgings of ice held by the bushes, but beyond, on each side, was a clear canal. To-day most of this ice is drifted down the stream or blown across it, so that often the straight edge is presented to the opposite meadow and is at first sight unaccountable.

The wind shifts to east or southeast, but still its rawness is agreeable. As C. says of the water insects, we too come out of our shells in the spring. Yes, we take off our greatcoats.

I had noticed from the Cliff by Lee's road an elevated sandy point above Pole Brook which I said must be Indian ground, and, walking there, I found a piece of a soapstone pot.

In the sluiceway of Pole Brook, by the road just beyond, I found another kind of Indian pot. It was an eel-pot (?) or creel, a wattled basket or wickerwork, made of willow osiers with the bark on, very artfully. It was about four feet long and shaped thus:

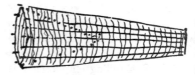 Moore says that he used to find them in the brooks when he was trout-fishing, stopping them up so closely with sticks and stones on the sides that not a trout could pass, and he would cut them from end to end with his knife. About a dozen (or more) willow sticks, as big [as] one's finger or larger, being set small end down in a circle, in a thin round board which made the bottom, and then smaller osiers interwoven at right angles with them, close and firm. Another funnel-shaped basket was

secured within this, extending about half-way down it, as represented by the dotted lines, with an opening hardly two inches wide at the bottom, where only a dozen sharped sticks approached each other. There was a square door in the board bottom, by which the fishes could be taken out. This was set in that sluiceway, with the mouth or broad end down-stream, all sunk beneath the surface, the fishes being now evidently running up the brooks from the river and ponds, the ice being mostly gone out of the meadows and brooks. We raised this and found eight or ten small pickerel in it, the biggest a foot long, and one good-sized perch. It was pleasant to find that any were practicing such cunning art in the outskirts.[1] I am not sure whether this invention is Indian or derived from our own ancestors. "Creel" appears to be an old English word. But I have no doubt that the Indians used something very like this. How much more we might have learned of the aborigines if they had not been so reserved! Suppose they had generally become the laboring class among the whites, that my father had been a farmer and had an Indian for his hired man, how many aboriginal ways we children should have learned from them! It was very pleasant to meet with this kind of textile or basket in our walk, to know that some had leisure for other things than farming and town meeting, and that they felt the spring influence in their way. That man was not fitting for the State prison when he was weaving that creel. He was meditating a small poem

[1] Minott has known them to be set for musquash, and sometimes the musquash gnaw out, if not drowned.

Willow Catkins

A Turtle Dove's Nest

in his way. It was equal to a successful stanza whose subject was spring.

The fishes are going up the brooks as they open. They are dispersing themselves through the fields and woods, imparting new life into them. They are taking their places under the shelving banks and in the dark swamps. The water running down meets the fishes running up. They hear the latest news. Spring-aroused fishes are running up our veins too. Little fishes are seeking the sources of the brooks, seeking to disseminate their principles. Talk about a revival of religion! and business men's prayer-meetings! with which all the country goes mad now! What if it were as true and wholesome a *revival* as the little fishes feel which come out of the sluggish waters and run up the brooks toward their sources? All Nature *revives* at this season. With her it is really a *new life*, but with these churchgoers it is only a revival of religion or hypocrisy. They go downstream to still muddier waters. It cheers me more to behold the swarms of gnats which have revived in the spring sun. The fish lurks by the mouth of its native brook, watching its opportunity to dart up the stream by the cakes of ice.

Do the fishes stay to hold prayer-meetings in Fair Haven Bay, while some monstrous pike gulps them down? Or is it not rather each one privately, or with its kindred spirits, as soon as possible stemming the current of its native brook, making its way to more ethereal waters, burnishing his scaly armor by his speed, ofttimes running into osier creels and finding its salvation there even, as in the discharge of its duty?

No wonder we feel the spring influences. There is a motion in the very ground under our feet. Each rill is peopled with new life rushing up it.

If a man do not revive with nature in the spring, how shall he revive when a white-collared priest prays for him?

Small water-bugs in Clematis Brook.

We had turned in at the old Minott house. We kept on by Heron Pool and through the pitch pine wood behind Baker's, down the path to Spanish Brook, and came out on to the railroad at Walden. Channing thought it was a suitably long stretch to wind up with, like one of our old Nashoba walks, so long drawn and taxing our legs so, in which it seemed that the nearer you got to home the farther you had to go.

That is a very handsome descent by the path to Spanish Brook, seeing the path below, between the trunks of the trees. How important the hemlock amid the pines, for its darker and wilder green!

We, too, are out, obeying the same law with all nature. Not less important are the observers of the birds than the birds themselves.[1]

At last I see a small, straight flock of ducks going northeast in the distance.

In order that a house and grounds may be picturesque and interesting in the highest degree, they must suggest the idea of necessity, proving the devotion of the builder, not of luxury. We need to see the honest and naked life here and there protruding. What is a fort without any foe before it, that is not now sus-

[1] [Channing, p. 94.]

Vol. X

taining and never has sustained a siege? The gentleman whose purse is always full, who can meet all demands, though he employs the most famous artists, can never make a very interesting seat. He does not carve from near enough to the bone. No man is rich enough to keep a poet in his pay.

March 21. Warm rain, April-like, the first of the season, holding up from time to time, though always completely overcast.

P. M. — To Ministerial Swamp *via* Little River.

Standing by the mud-hole in the swamp, I hear the pleasant phebe note of the chickadee. It is, methinks, the most of a wilderness note of any yet. It is peculiarly interesting that this, which is one of our winter birds also, should have a note with which to welcome the spring.

Standing by that pool, it is pleasant to see the dimples made on its smooth surface by the big drops, after the rain has held up a quarter of an hour.

The skunk-cabbage at Clamshell is well out, shedding pollen. It is evident that the date of its flowering is very fluctuating, according to the condition in which the winter leaves the crust of the meadow.

This first spring rain is very agreeable. I love to hear the pattering of the drops on my umbrella, and I love also the wet scent of the umbrella. It helps take the remaining frost out and settles the ways, but there is yet frost and ice in meadows and swamps.

March 22. P. M. — Launch my boat and row downstream.

There is a strong and cool northwest wind. Leaving our boat just below N. Barrett's, we walk down the shore. We see many gulls on the very opposite side of the meadow, near the woods. They look bright-white, like snow on the dark-blue water. It is surprising how far they can be seen, how much light they reflect, and how conspicuous they are. Being strung along one every rod, they made me think of a fleet in line of battle. We go along to the pitch pine hill off Abner Buttrick's, and, finding a sheltered and sunny place, we watch the ducks from it with our glass. There are not only gulls, but about forty black ducks and as many sheldrakes and, I think, two wood ducks. The gulls appear considerably the largest and make the most show, they are so uniformly light-colored. At a distance, as I have said, they look like snowy masses, and even nearer they have a lumpish look, like a mass of cotton, the head being light as well as the breast. They are seen sailing about in the shallow water, or standing motionless on a clod that just rises above the surface, in which position they have a particularly clumsy look; or one or two may be seen slowly wheeling about above the rest. From time to time the whole flock of gulls suddenly rises and begins circling about, and at last they settle down in some new place and order. With these were at first associated about forty black ducks, pretty close together, sometimes apparently in close single lines, some looking lumpish like decoys of wood, others standing on the bottom and reminding me of penguins. They were constantly diving with great energy, making the water fly apparently two feet upward in a thick shower. Then away they all go, circling about for ten minutes at least before they can decide where to alight.

The black heads and white breasts, which may be golden-eyes, for they are evidently paired, male and female, for the most part,[1] — and yet I thought that I saw the red bill of the sheldrake, — these are most incessantly and skillfully plunging and from time to time apparently pursuing each other. They are much more active, whether diving or swimming about, than you expect ducks to be. Now, perchance, they are seen changing their ground, swimming off, perhaps, two by two, in pairs, very steadily and swiftly, without diving. I see two of these very far off on a bright-blue bay where the waves are running high. They are two intensely white specks, which yet you might mistake for the foaming crest of waves. Now one disappears, but soon is seen again, and then its companion is lost in like manner, having dived.

I see those peculiar spring (?) clouds, scattered cumuli with dark level bases. No doubt the season is to be detected by the aspect of the clouds no less than by that of the earth.

March 23. Surveying Mr. Gordon's farm.

See something stirring amid the dead leaves in the water at the bottom of a ditch, in two or three places, and presently see the back of a yellow-spotted turtle. Afterward a large flock of fox-colored sparrows flits by along an alder-row, uttering a faint chip like that of the tree sparrow.

[1] They are sheldrakes.

Vol. X

above, rusty-brown behind, and darker, ash or slate, with purplish-brown reflections, forward; legs, black; and bill, blue-black. Common to the Old and New Worlds.

March 25. P. M. — To bank of Great Meadows by Peter's.

Cold northwest wind as yesterday and day before. Large skaters (*Hydrometra*) on a ditch.

Going across A. Clark's field behind Garfield's, I see many fox-colored sparrows flitting past in a straggling manner into the birch and pitch pine woods on the left, and hear a sweet warble there from time to time. They are busily scratching like hens amid the dry leaves of that wood (not swampy), from time to time the rearmost moving forward, one or two at a time, while a few are perched here and there on the lower branches of a birch or other tree; and I hear a very clear and sweet whistling strain, commonly half-finished, from one every two or three minutes. It is too irregular to be readily caught, but methinks begins like *ar tche tche tchear, te tche tchear,* etc., etc., but is more clear than these words would indicate. The whole flock is moving along pretty steadily.

There are so many sportsmen out that the ducks have no rest on the Great Meadows, which are not half covered with water. They sit uneasy on the water, looking about, without feeding, and I see one man endeavor to approach a flock crouchingly through the meadow for half a mile, with india-rubber boots on, where the water is often a foot deep. This has been

March 24. P. M. — To Fair Haven Pond, east side.

The pond not yet open. A cold north-by-west wind, which must have come over much snow and ice. The chip of the ground-bird[1] resembles that of a robin, *i. e.*, its expression is the same, only fainter, and reminds me that the robin's peep, which sounds like a note of distress, is also a *chip*, or call-note to its kind.

Returning about 5 P. M. across the Depot Field, I scare up from the ground a flock of about twenty birds, which fly low, making a short circuit to another part of the field. At first they remind me of bay-wings, except that they are in a flock, show no white in tail, are, I see, a little larger, and utter a faint *sveet sveet* merely, a sort of sibilant *chip*. Starting them again, I see that they have black tails, very conspicuous when they pass near. They fly in a flock somewhat like snow buntings, occasionally one surging upward a few feet in pursuit of another, and they alight about where they first were. It [is] almost impossible to discover them on the ground, they squat so flat and so much resemble it, running amid the stubble. But at length I stand within two rods of one and get a good view of its markings with my glass. They are the *Alauda alpestris,* or shore lark,[2] quite a sizable and handsome bird; delicate pale-lemon-yellow line above the [eye], with a dark line through the eye; the yellow again on the sides of the neck and on the throat, with a black crescent below the throat; with a buff-ash breast and reddish-brown tinges; beneath, white;

[1] That is, song sparrow.
[2] Did I not see them on Nantucket?

going on, on these meadows, ever since the town was settled, and will go on as long as ducks settle here.

You might frequently say of a poet away from home that he was as mute as a bird of passage, uttering a mere *chip* from time to time, but follow him to his true habitat, and you shall not know him, he will sing so melodiously.

March 27. P. M. — Sail to Bittern Cliff.

Scare up a flock of sheldrakes just off Fair Haven Hill, the conspicuous white ducks, sailing straight hither and thither. At first they fly low up the stream, but, having risen, come back half-way to us, then wheel and go up-stream. Soon after we scare up a flock of black ducks. We land and steal over the hill through the woods, expecting to find them under Lee's Cliff, as indeed we do, having crawled over the hill through the woods on our stomachs; and there we watched various water-fowl for an hour. There are a dozen sheldrakes (or goosanders) and among them four or five females. They are now pairing. I should say one or two pairs are made. At first we see only a male and female quite on the alert, some way out on the pond, tacking back and forth and looking every way. They keep close together, headed one way, and when one turns the other also turns quickly. The male appears to take the lead. Soon the rest appear, sailing out from the shore into sight. We hear a squeaking note, as if made by a pump, and presently see four or five great herring gulls wheeling about. Sometimes they make a sound like the scream of a hen-hawk.

They are shaped somewhat like a very thick white rolling-pin, sharpened at both ends. At length they alight near the ducks.

The sheldrakes at length acquire confidence, come close inshore and go to preening themselves, or it may be they are troubled with lice. They are all busy about it at once, continually thrusting their bills into their backs, still sailing slowly along back and forth offshore. Sometimes they are in two or three straight lines. Now they will all seem to be crossing the pond, but presently you see that they have tacked and are all heading this way again. Among them, or near by, I at length detect three or four whistlers, by their wanting the red bill, being considerably smaller and less white, having a white spot on the head, a black back, and altogether less white, and also keeping more or less apart and not diving when the rest do. Now one half the sheldrakes sail off southward and suddenly go to diving as with one consent. Seven or eight or the whole of the party will be under water and lost at once. In the meanwhile, coming up, they chase one another, scooting over the surface and making the water fly, sometimes three or four making a rush toward one.

At length I detect two little dippers, as I have called them, though I am not sure that I have ever seen the male before. They are male and female close together, the common size of what I have called the little dipper.[1] They are incessantly diving close to the button-bushes.

[1] Rice says that the little dipper has a hen bill and is not lobe-footed. He and his brother Israel also speak of another water-fowl of the river with a hen bill and some bluish feathers on the wings.

The female is apparently uniformly black, or rather dark brown, but the male has a conspicuous crest, with, apparently, white on the hindhead, a white breast, and white line on the lower side of the neck; i. e., the head and breast are black and white conspicuously. Can this be the *Fuligula albeola*, and have I commonly seen only the female? Or is it a grebe?

Fair Haven Pond four fifths clear. C. saw a phœbe, i. e. pewee, the 25th.

The sheldrake has a peculiar long clipper look, often moving rapidly straight forward over the water. It sinks to very various depths in the water sometimes, as when apparently alarmed, showing only its head and neck and the upper part of its back, and at others, when at ease, floating buoyantly on the surface, as if it had taken in more air, showing all its white breast and the white along its sides. Sometimes it lifts itself up on the surface and flaps its wings, revealing its whole rosaceous breast and its lower parts, and looking in form like a penguin. When I first saw them fly up-stream I suspected that they had gone to Fair Haven Pond and would alight under the lee of the Cliff. So, creeping slowly down through the woods four or five rods, I was enabled to get a fair sight of them, and finally we sat exposed on the rocks within twenty-five rods. They appear not to observe a person so high above them.

It was a pretty sight to see a pair of them tacking about, always within a foot or two of each other and heading the same way, now on this short tack, now on that, the male taking the lead, sinking deep and

looking every way. When the whole twelve had come together they would soon break up again, and were continually changing their ground, though not diving, now sailing slowly this way a dozen rods, and now that, and now coming in near the shore. Then they would all go to preening themselves, thrusting their bills into their backs and keeping up such a brisk motion that you could not get a fair sight of one's head. From time to time you heard a slight titter, not of alarm, but perhaps a breeding-note, for they were evidently selecting their mates. I saw one scratch its ear or head with its foot. Then it was surprising to see how, briskly sailing off one side, they went to diving, as if they had suddenly come across a school of minnows. A whole company would disappear at once, never rising high as before. Now for nearly a minute there is not a feather to be seen, and the next minute you see a party of half a dozen there, chasing one another and making the water fly far and wide.

When returning, we saw, near the outlet of the pond, seven or eight sheldrakes standing still in a line on the edge of the ice, and others swimming close by. They evidently love to stand on the ice for a change.

I saw on the 22d a sucker which apparently had been dead a week or two at least. Therefore they must begin to die late in the winter.

March 28. P. M. — To Cliffs.

After a cloudy morning, a warm and pleasant afternoon. I hear that a few geese were seen this morning.

Israel Rice says that he heard two brown thrashers sing this morning! Is sure because he has kept the bird in a cage. I can't believe it.

I go down the railroad, turning off in the cut. I notice the hazel stigmas in the warm hollow on the right there, just beginning to peep forth. This is an unobserved but very pretty and interesting evidence of the progress of the season. I should not have noticed it if I had not carefully examined the fertile buds. It is like a crimson star first dimly detected in the twilight. The warmth of the day, in this sunny hollow above the withered sedge, has caused the stigmas to show their lips through their scaly shield. They do not project more than the thirtieth of an inch, some not the sixtieth. The staminate catkins are also considerably loosened. Just as the turtles put forth their heads, so these put forth their stigmas in the spring. How many accurate thermometers there are on every hill and in every valley! Measure the length of the hazel stigmas, and you can tell how much warmth there has been this spring. How fitly and exactly any season of the year may be described by indicating the condition of some flower!

I go by the springs toward the epigæa. It is a fine warm day with a slight haziness. It is pleasant to sit outdoors now, and, it being Sunday, neighbors walk about or stand talking in the sun, looking at and scratching the dry earth, which they are glad to see and smell again. In the sunny epigæa wood I start up two *Vanessa Antiopa*, which flutter about over the dry leaves before, and are evidently attracted toward me, settling at last within a few feet. The same warm and placid day calls out men and butterflies.

It is surprising that men can be divided into those who lead an indoor and those who lead an outdoor life, as if birds and quadrupeds were to be divided into those that lived a within nest or burrow life and [those] that lived without their nests and holes chiefly. How many of our troubles are house-bred! He lives an outdoor life; *i. e.*, he is not squatted behind the shield of a door, he does not keep himself *tubbed*. It is such a questionable phrase as an "honest man," or the "naked eye," as if the eye which is not covered with a spyglass should properly be called naked.

From Wheeler's plowed field on the top of Fair Haven Hill, I look toward Fair Haven Pond, now quite smooth. There is not a duck nor a gull to be seen on it. I can hardly believe that it was so alive with them yesterday. Apparently they improve this warm and pleasant day, with little or no wind, to continue their journey northward. The strong and cold northwest wind of about a week past has probably detained them. Knowing that the meadows and ponds were swarming with ducks yesterday, you go forth this particularly pleasant and still day to see them at your leisure, but find that they are all gone. No doubt there are some left, and many more will soon come with the April rains. It is a wild life that is associated with stormy and blustering weather. When the invalid comes forth on his cane, and misses improve the pleasant air to look for signs of vegetation, that wild life has withdrawn itself.

But when one kind of life goes, another comes. This

Vol. X

plowed land on the top of the hill — and all other fields as far as I observe — is covered with cobwebs, which every few inches are stretched from root to root or clod to clod, gleaming and waving in the sun, the light flashing along them as they wave in the wind. How much insect life and activity connected with this peculiar state of the atmosphere these imply! Yet I do not notice a spider. Small cottony films are continually settling down or blown along through the air.[1] Does not this gossamer answer to that of the fall? They must have sprung to with one consent last night or this morning and bent new cables to the clods and stubble all over this part of the world.

The little fuzzy gnats, too, are in swarms in the air, peopling that uncrowded space. They are not confined by any fence. Already the distant forest is streaked with lines of thicker and whiter haze over the successive valleys.

Walden is open. When? On the 20th it was pretty solid. C. sees a very little ice in it to-day, but probably it gets entirely free to-night. Fair Haven Pond is open.[2]

Sitting on the top of the Cliffs, I look through my glass at the smooth river and see the long forked ripple made by a musquash swimming along over the meadow. While I sit on these warm rocks, turning my glass toward the moun-

[1] A gossamer day. I see them also for a week after.
[2] This and Flint's and Walden all open together this year, the latter was so thinly frozen! (For C. says Flint's and Walden were each a third open on the 25th.)

tains, I can see the sun reflected from the rocks on Monadnock, and I know that it would be pleasant to be there too to-day as well as here. I see, too, warm and cosy seats on the rocks, where the flies are buzzing, and probably some walker is enjoying the prospect.

From this hilltop I overlook, again bare of snow, putting on a warm, hazy spring face, this seemingly concave circle of earth, in the midst of which I was born and dwell, which in the northwest and southeast has a more distant blue rim to it, as it were of more costly manufacture. On ascending the hill next his home, every man finds that he dwells in a shallow concavity whose sheltering walls are the convex surface of the earth, beyond which he cannot see. I see those familiar features, that large type, with which all my life is associated, unchanged.

Cleaning out the spring on the west side of Fair Haven Hill, I find a small frog, apparently a bullfrog, just come forth, which must have wintered in the mud there. There is very little mud, however, and the rill never runs more than four or five rods before it is soaked up, and the whole spring often dries up in the summer. It seems, then, that two or three frogs, the sole inhabitants of so small a spring, will bury themselves at its head. A few frogs will be buried at the puniest spring-head.

Coming home, I hear the croaking frogs in the pool on the south side of Hubbard's Grove. It is sufficiently warm for them at last.

Near the sand path above Potter's mud-hole I find what I should call twenty and more mud turtles'

eggs close together, which appear to have been dug from a hole close by last year. They are all broken or cracked and more or less indented and depressed, and they look remarkably like my pigeon's egg fungi, a dirty white covered thickly with a pure white roughness, which through a glass is seen to be oftenest in the form of minute but regular rosettes of a very pure white substance. If these are turtles' eggs, — and there is no stem mark of a fungus, — it is remarkable that they should thus come to resemble so closely another natural product, the fungus.

The first lark of the 23d sailed through the meadow with that peculiar prolonged chipping or twittering sound, perhaps sharp clucking.

March 29. Monday. Hear a phœbe early in the morning over the street. Considerable frost this morning, and some ice formed on the river. The white maple stamens are very apparent now on one tree, though they do not project beyond the buds.

P. M. — To Ball's Hill.

Nearly as warm and pleasant as yesterday.

I see what I suppose is the female rusty grackle; black body with green reflections and purplish-brown head and neck, but I notice no light iris. By a pool southeast of Nathan Barrett's, see five or six painted turtles in the sun, — probably some were out yesterday, — and afterward, along a ditch just east of the pine hill near the river, a great many more, as many as twenty within a rod. I must have disturbed this afternoon one hundred at least. They have crawled out on to the grass on the sunny side of the ditches where there is a sheltering bank. I notice the scales of one all turning up on the edges. It is evident that great numbers lie buried in the mud of such ditches and mud-holes in the winter, for they have not yet been crawling over the meadows. Some have very broad yellow lines on the back; others are almost uniformly dark above. They hurry and tumble into the water at your approach, but several soon rise to the surface and just put their heads out to reconnoitre. Each trifling weed or clod is a serious impediment in their path, catching their flippers and causing them to tumble back. They never lightly skip over it. But then they have patience and perseverance, and plenty of time. The narrow edges of the ditches are almost paved in some places with their black and muddy backs. They seem to come out into the sun about the time the phœbe is heard over the water.

At the first pool I also scared up a snipe. It rises with a single *cra-a-ck* and goes off with its zigzag flight, with its bill presented to the earth, ready to charge bayonets against the inhabitants of the mud.

As I sit two thirds the way up the sunny side of the pine hill, looking over the meadows, which are now almost completely bare, the crows, by their swift flight and scolding, reveal to me some large bird of prey hovering over the river. I perceive by its markings and size that it cannot be a hen-hawk, and now it settles on the topmost branch of a white maple, bending it down. Its great armed and feathered legs dangle helplessly in the air for a moment, as if feeling for the

perch, while its body is tipping this way and that. It sits there facing me some forty or fifty rods off, pluming itself but keeping a good lookout. At this distance and in this light, it appears to have a rusty-brown head and breast and is white beneath, with rusty leg-feathers and a tail black beneath. When it flies again it is principally black varied with white, regular light spots on its tail and wings beneath, but chiefly a conspicuous white space on the forward part of the back; also some of the upper side of the tail or tail-coverts is white. It has broad, ragged, buzzard-like wings, and from the white of its back, as well as the shape and shortness of its wings and its not having a gull-like body, I think it must be an eagle. It lets itself down with its legs somewhat helplessly dangling, as if feeling for something on the bare meadow, and then gradually flies away, soaring and circling higher and higher until lost in the downy clouds. This lofty soaring is at least a grand recreation, as if it were nourishing sublime ideas. I should like to know why it soars higher and higher so, whether its thoughts are really turned to earth, for it seems to be more nobly as well as highly employed than the laborers ditching in the meadow beneath or any others of my fellow-townsmen.

Hearing a quivering note of alarm from some bird, I look up and see a male hen-harrier, the neatly built hawk, sweeping over the hill.

While I was looking at the eagle (?), I saw, on the hillside far across the meadow by Holbrook's clearing, what I at first took for a red flag or handkerchief

Vol. X

carried along on a pole, just above the woods. It was a fire in the woods, and I saw the top of the flashing flames above the tree-tops. The woods are in a state of tinder, and the smoker and sportsman and the burner must be careful now.

I do not see a duck on the Great Meadows to-day, as I did not up-stream yesterday. It is remarkable how suddenly and completely those that were here two days ago have left us. It is true the water has gone down still more on the meadows. I infer that waterfowl travel in pleasant weather.

With many men their fine manners are a lie all over, a skim-coat or finish of falsehood. They are not brave enough to do without this sort of armor, which they wear night and day.

The trees in swamps are streaming with gossamer at least thirty feet up, and probably were yesterday.

I see at Gourgas's hedge many tree sparrows and fox-colored sparrows. The latter are singing very loud and sweetly. Somewhat like *ar, tea, — twe'-twe, twe'-twe,* or *ar te, ter twe'-twe, twe'-twe,* variously. They are quite tame.

March 30. P. M. — To my boat at Cardinal Shore and thence to Lee's Cliff.

Another fine afternoon, warmer than before, I think.

I walk in the fields now without slumping in the thawing ground, or there are but few soft places, and the distant sand-banks look dry and warm. The frogs are now heard leaping into the ditches on your approach,

and their dimple is seen. I find a smallish bullfrog [1] under my boat.

Approaching carefully the little pool south of Hubbard's Grove, I see the dimples where the croakers which were on the surface have dived, and I see two or three still spread out on the surface, in the sun. They are very wary, and instantly dive to the bottom on your approach and bury themselves in the weeds or mud. The water is quite smooth, and it is very warm here, just under the edge of the wood, but I do not hear any croaking. Later, in a pool behind Lee's Cliff, I hear them, — the waking up of the leafy pools. The last was a pool amid the blueberry and huckleberry and a few little pines. I do not remember that I ever hear this frog in the river or ponds. They seem to be an early frog, peculiar to pools and small ponds in the woods and fields.

I notice, scampering over this water, two or three brown spiders, middling-sized. They appear to be the ones which have spun this gossamer.

There is at the bottom of this pool much of the ludwigia, that evergreen weed seen in winter at the bottom of pools and ditches. Methinks those peculiar bulbs, some of which I see near it, are of this plant.

Landing at Bittern Cliff, I went round through the woods to get sight of ducks on the pond. Creeping down through the woods, I reached the rocks, and saw fifteen or twenty sheldrakes scattered about. The full-plumaged males, conspicuously black and white and often swimming in pairs, appeared to be the most wary,

[1] [Queried in pencil.]

keeping furthest out. Others, with much less white and duller black, were very busily fishing just north the inlet of the pond, where there is about three feet of water, and others still playing and preening themselves. These ducks, whose tame representatives are so sluggish and deliberate in their motions, were full of activity. A party of these ducks fishing and playing is a very lively scene. On one side, for instance, you will see a party of eight or ten busily diving and most of the time under water, not rising high when they come up, and soon plunging again. The whole surface will be in commotion there, though no ducks may be seen. I saw one come up with a large fish, whereupon all the rest, as they successively came to the surface, gave chase to it, while it held its prey over the water in its bill, and they pursued with a great rush and clatter a dozen or more rods over the surface, making a great furrow in the water, but, there being some trees in the way, I could not see the issue. I saw seven or eight all dive together as with one consent, remaining under half a minute or more. On another side you see a party which seem to be playing and pluming themselves. They will run and dive and come up and dive again every three or four feet, occasionally one pursuing another; will flutter in the water, making it fly, or erect themselves at full length on the surface like a penguin, and flap their wings. This party make an incessant noise. Again you will see some steadily tacking this way or that in the middle of the pond, and often they rest there asleep with their heads in their backs. They readily cross the pond, swimming from this side to that.

chink is filled. While the waves toss this bright day, the ducks, asleep, are drifting before it across the ponds. Every now and then one or two lift their heads and look about, as if they watched by turns. I see also two ducks, perhaps a little larger than these, I am pretty sure without red bills and therefore not sheldrakes (and they are not nearly as white as sheldrakes ordinarily), with more elevated heads and gibbous (?) bills. The heads, bills, and upper parts of neck, black;[1] breast, white or whitish; but back sober-colored. Can they be brant or mallards? The leaves are now so dry and loose that it is almost impossible to approach the shore of the pond without being heard by the ducks.

I am not sure but I heard a pine warbler day before yesterday, and from what a boy asks me about a yellow bird which he saw there I think it likely. Just after sundown I see a large flock of geese in a perfect harrow cleaving their way toward the northeast, with Napoleonic tactics splitting the forces of winter.

C. says he saw a great many wood turtles on the bank of the Assabet to-day. The painted and wood turtles have seemed to be out in surprising abundance at an unusually early date this year, but I think I can account for it. The river is remarkably low, almost at summer level. I am not sure that I remember it so low at this season. Now, probably, these tortoises would always lie out in the sun at this season, if there were any bank at hand to lie on. Ordinarily at this season, the meadows being flooded, together with the pools and ditches in which the painted turtles lie, there

[1] Were they geese?

While I am watching the ducks, a mosquito is endeavoring to sting me.

At dusk I hear two flocks of geese go over.

March 31. P. M. — To Flint's Pond.

A fresh south or southeast wind.

The most forward willow catkins are not so silvery now, more grayish, being much enlarged and the down less compact, revealing the dark scales.

Flint's, Fair Haven, and Walden Ponds broke up just about the same time, or March 28th, this year. This is very unusual. It is because on account of the mildness of the winter Walden did not become so cold as the others, or freeze so thick, and there was proportionally less thawing to be done in it.

They are burning brush nowadays. You see a great slanting column of dun smoke on the northeast of the town, which turns out to be much farther off than you suppose. It is Sam Pierce burning brush. Thus we are advertised of some man's occupation in a neighboring town. As I walk I smell the smoke of burnings, though I see none.

In the wood-paths now I see many small red butterflies, I am not sure of what species, not seeing them still. The earliest butterflies seem to be born of the dry leaves on the forest floor.

I see about a dozen black ducks on Flint's Pond, asleep with their heads in their backs and drifting across the pond before the wind. I suspect that they are nocturnal in their habits and therefore require much rest by day. So do the seasons revolve and every

is no bank exposed near their winter quarters for them to come out on, and I first noticed them under water on the meadow. But this year it is but a step for them to the sunny bank, and the shores of the Assabet and of ditches are lined with them.

C. heard hylas to-day.

IX

APRIL, 1858

(ÆT. 40)

April 1. White-bellied swallows.

P. M. — Paddle up Assabet.

The river is at summer level; has not been up this spring, and has fallen to this. The lowermost willow at my boat is bare. The white maples are abundantly out to-day. Probably the very first bloomed on the 29th. We hold the boat beneath one, surprised to hear the resounding hum of honey-bees, which are busy about them. It reminds me of the bass and its bees. The trees are conspicuous with dense clusters of light-colored stamens. The alders above the Hemlocks do not yet shed pollen. What I called yellow wasps, which built over my window last year, have come, and are about the old nest; numbers have settled on it.[1]

I observed night before last, as often before, when geese were passing over in the twilight quite near, though the whole heavens were still light and I knew which way to look by the honking, I could not distinguish them. It takes but a little obscurity to hide a bird in the air. How difficult, even in broadest daylight, to discover again a hawk at a distance in the sky when you have once turned your eyes away!

Pleasant it is to see again the red bark of the *Cornus*

[1] Were they not the common kind looking at it?

sericea shining in the warm sun at the hill swamp, above the spring. Walking through the maple [*sic*] there, I see a squirrel's nest twenty-three or twenty-four feet high in a large maple, and, climbing to it, — for it was so peculiar, having a basketwork of twigs about it, that I did not know but it was a hawk's nest, — I found that it was a very perfect (probably) red squirrel's nest, made entirely of the now very dark or blackish green moss such as grows on the button-bush and on the swampy ground, — a dense mass of it about one foot through, matted together, — with an inobvious hole on the east side and a tuft of loose moss blowing up above it, which seemed to answer for a door or porch covering. The cavity within was quite small, but very snug and warm, where one or two squirrels might lie warmly in the severest storm, the dense moss walls being about three inches thick or more. But what was most peculiar was that this nest, though placed over the centre of the tree, where it divided into four or five branches, was regularly and elaborately hedged about and supported by a basketwork of strong twigs stretched across from bough to bough, which twigs I perceived had been gnawed green from the maple itself, the stub ends remaining visible all around.

Near by I saw another much smaller and less perfect nest of the same kind, which had fallen to the ground. This had been made in a birch, and the birch twigs had been gnawed off, but in this case I noticed a little fine broken grass within it, mixed with the moss.

I notice large water-bugs.

It is remarkable that the river seems rarely to rise

or fall gradually, but rather by fits and starts, and hence the water-lines, as indicated now by the sawdust, are very distinct parallel lines four or five or more inches apart. It is true the wind has something to do with it, and might waft to a certain place much more dust than was left on another where the water stood much longer at the same level. Surely the saw-miller's is a trade which cannot be carried on in secret. Not only this sawdust betrays him, but at night, especially, when the water is high, I hear the tearing sound of his saw a mile or more off, borne down the stream.

I see six *Sternothærus odoratus* in the river thus early. Two are fairly out sunning. One has crawled up a willow. It is evident, then, that they may be earlier in other places or towns than I had supposed, where they are not concealed by such freshets as we have. I took up and smelt of five of these, and they emitted none of their peculiar scent! It would seem, then, that this may be connected with their breeding, or at least with their period of greatest activity. They are quite sluggish now.

At Hemlock Brook, a dozen or more rods from the river, I see on the wet mud a little snapping turtle evidently hatched last year. It does not open its eyes nor mouth while I hold it. Its eyes appear as if sealed up by its long sleep. In our ability to contend with the elements what feeble infants we are to this one. Talk of great heads, look at this one! Talk of Hercules' feats in the cradle, what sort of cradle and nursing has this infant had? It totters forth confident and victorious when it can hardly carry its shield. It looked

so much like the mud or a wet muddy leaf, it was a wonder I saw it.

I start, under the hemlocks there, a butterfly (call it the tawny-orange single-white-spotted) about the size of *Vanessa Antiopa*, tawny-orange, with black spots or eyes, and pale-brown about them, a white spot near the corner of each front wing, a dark line near the edge behind, a small sharp projecting angle to the hind wings, a green-yellow back to body.[1]

See wood turtles coupled on their edges at the bottom, where the stream has turned them up.

Far up in still shallows, disturb pickerel and perch, etc. They apparently touch the muddy bottom as they dart out, muddying the water here and there.

A *Rana halecina* on the bank.

When I started to walk that suddenly pleasant afternoon, the 28th of March, I crossed the path of the two brothers R., who were walking direct to the depot as if they had special business there that Sunday, the queer short-legged dog running ahead. I talked with them an hour there in the hope that the one who is not a stranger to me would let something escape from his wise head. But he was very moderate; all I got out of him to be remembered was that in some town up-country where he lived when young, they called the woodchuck "squash-belly," — with reference to his form I suggested, but so far he had not advanced. This he communicated very seriously, as an important piece of information with which he labored. The other told me

[1] [*Vanessa j-album*, to judge by the date and the general description.]

how to raise a dog's dander, — any the gentlest dog's, — by looking sternly in his face and making a peculiar sound with your mouth. I then broke short the conference, continued my walk, while these gentlemen wheeled directly about and walked straight back again.

It is evident that the date of the first general revival of the turtles, excepting such as are generally seen in ditches, i. e. the yellow-spotted, depends on the state of the river, whether it is high or low in the spring.

April 2. P. M. — To yew and R. W. E.'s Cliff.

At Hubbard's Grove I see a woodchuck. He waddles to his hole and then puts out his gray nose within thirty feet to reconnoitre. It is too windy, and the surface of the croaker pool is too much ruffled, for any of the croakers to be lying out, but I notice a large mass of their spawn there well advanced. At the first little sluiceway just beyond, I catch a large *Rana halecina*, which puffs itself up considerably, as if it might be full of spawn. I must look there for its spawn. It is rather sluggish; cannot jump much yet. It allows me to stroke it and at length take it up in my hand, squatting still in it.

Who would believe that out of these dry and withered banks will come violets, lupines, etc., in profusion? At the spring on the west side of Fair Haven Hill, I startle a striped snake. It is a large one with a white stripe down the dorsal ridge between two broad black ones, and on each side the last a buff one, and then blotchy brown sides, darker toward tail; beneath,

greenish-yellow. This snake generally has a pinkish cast. There is another, evidently the same species but not half so large, with its neck lying affectionately across the first, — I may have separated them by my approach, — which, seen by itself, you might have thought a distinct species. The dorsal line in this one is bright-yellow, though not so bright as the lateral ones, and the yellow about the head; also the black is more glossy, and this snake has no pink cast. No doubt on almost every such warm bank now you will find a snake lying out. The first notice I had of them was a slight rustling in the leaves, as if made by a squirrel, though I did not see them for five minutes after. The biggest at length dropped straight down into a hole, within a foot of where he lay. They allowed me to lift their heads with a stick four or five inches without stirring, nor did they mind the flies that alighted on them, looking steadily at me without the slightest motion of head, body, or eyes, as if they were of marble; and as you looked hard at them, you continually forgot that they were real and not imaginary.

The hazel has just begun to shed pollen here, perhaps yesterday in some other places. This loosening and elongating of its catkins is a sufficiently pleasing sight, in dry and warm hollows on the hillsides. It is an unexpected evidence of life in so dry a shrub.

On the side of Fair Haven Hill I go looking for bay-wings, turning my glass to each sparrow on a rock or tree. At last I see one, which flies right up straight from a rock eighty [or] one hundred feet and warbles a peculiar long and pleasant strain, after the manner

of the skylark, methinks, and close by I see another, apparently a bay-wing, though I do not see its white in tail, and it utters while sitting the same subdued, rather peculiar strain.

See how those black ducks, swimming in pairs far off on the river, are disturbed by our appearance, swimming away in alarm, and now, when we advance again, they rise and fly up-stream and about, uttering regularly a *crack cr-r-rack* of alarm, even for five or ten minutes, as they circle about, long after we have lost sight of them. Now we hear it on this side, now on that.

The yew shows its bundles of anthers plainly, as if it might open in four or five days.

Just as I get home, I think I see crow blackbirds about a willow by the river.[1]

It is not important that the poet should say some particular thing, but should speak in harmony with nature. The tone and pitch of his voice is the main thing.

It appears to me that the wisest philosophers that I know are as foolish as Sancho Panza dreaming of his Island. Considering the ends they propose and the obstructions in their path, they are even. One philosopher is feeble enough alone, but observe how each multiplies his difficulties, — by how many unnecessary links he allies himself to the existing state of things. He girds himself for his enterprise with fasting and prayer, and then, instead of pressing forward like a light-armed soldier, with the fewest possible hindrances,

[1] Yes.

he at once hooks himself on to some immovable institution, as a family, the very rottenest of them all, and begins to sing and scratch gravel *towards* his objects. Why, it is as much as the strongest man can do decently to bury his friends and relations without making a new world of it. But if the philosopher is as foolish as Sancho Panza, he is also as wise, and nothing so truly makes a thing so or so as thinking it so.

Approaching the side of a wood on which were some pines, this afternoon, I heard the note of the pine warbler, calling the pines to life, though I did not see it. It has probably been here as long as I said before. Returning, I saw a sparrow-like bird flit by in an orchard, and, turning my glass upon it, was surprised by its burning yellow. This higher color in birds surprises us like an increase of warmth in the day.

April 3. Going down-town this morning, I am surprised by the rich strain of the purple finch from the elms. Three or four have arrived and lodged against the elms of our street, which runs east and west across their course, and they are now mingling their loud and rich strains with that of the tree sparrows, robins, bluebirds, etc. The hearing of this note implies some improvement in the acoustics of the air. It reminds me of that genial state of the air when the elms are in bloom. They sit still over the street and make a business of warbling. They advertise me surely of some additional warmth and serenity. How their note rings over the roofs of the village! You wonder that even the sleepers are not awakened by it to inquire who is there, and yet probably not another than myself in all the town observes their coming, and not half a dozen ever distinguished them in their lives. And yet the very mob of the town know the hard names of Germanians or Swiss families which once sang here or elsewhere.

About 9 A. M., C. and I paddle down the river. It is a remarkably warm and pleasant day. The shore is alive with tree sparrows sweetly warbling, also blackbirds, etc. The crow blackbirds which I saw last night are hoarsely clucking from time to time. Approaching the island, we hear the air full of the hum of bees, which at first we refer to the near trees. It comes from the white maples across the North Branch, fifteen rods off. We hear it from time to time, as we paddle along all day, down to the Bedford line. There is no pause to the hum of the bees all this warm day. It is a very simple but pleasing and soothing sound, this susurrus, thus early in the spring.

When off the mouth of the Mill Brook, we hear the stertorous *tut tut tut* of frogs from the meadow, with an occasional faint bullfrog-like *er er er* intermingled. I land there to reconnoitre. The river is remarkably low, quite down to summer level, and there is but very little water anywhere on the meadows. I see some shallow lagoons (west of the brook), whence the sound comes. There, too, are countless painted turtles out, around on the banks and hummocks left by the ice. Their black and muddy backs shine afar in the sun, and though now fifteen to twenty rods off, I see through my glass that they are already alarmed, have their necks stretched out and are beginning to slip into the

water, where many heads are seen. Resolved to identify this frog, one or two of whose heads I could already see above the surface with my glass, I picked my way to the nearest pool. Close where I landed, an *R. halecina* lay out on some sedge. In went all the turtles immediately, and soon after the frogs sank to the bottom, and their note was heard only from more distant pools. I stood perfectly still, and ere long they began to reappear one by one, and spread themselves out on the surface. They were the *R. halecina*. I could see very plainly the two very prominent yellow lines along the sides of the head and the large dark ocellated marks, even under water, on the thighs, etc. Gradually they begin to recover their voices, but it is hard to say at first which one of the dozen within twenty feet is speaking. They begin to swim and hop along the surface toward each other. Their note is a hard dry *tut tut tut tut*, not at all ringing like the toad's, and produced with very little *swelling* or motion of the throat, but as much trembling of the whole body; and from time to time one makes that faint somewhat bullfrog-like *er er er*. Both these sounds, then, are made by one frog, and what I have formerly thought an early bullfrog note was this. This, I think, is the first frog sound I have heard from the river meadows or anywhere, except the croaking leaf-pool frogs and the hylodes. They are evidently breeding now like toads, and probably are about the water as exclusively as the toads will soon be.

This sound we continue to hear all day long, especially from the broad meadows in Bedford. Close at hand a single one does not sound loud, yet it is

Vol. X

surprising how far a hundred or thousand croaking (?) at once can be heard. It comes borne on the breeze from north over the Bedford meadows a quarter of a mile off, filling the air. It is like the rattling of a wagon along some highway, or more like a distant train on a railroad, or else of many rills emptying in, or more yet like the sound of a factory, and it comes with an echo which makes it seem yet more distant and universal. At this distance it is a soft and almost purring sound, yet with the above-named bullfrog-like variation in it. Sometimes the meadow will be almost still; then they will begin in earnest, and plainly excite one another into a general snoring or eructation over a quarter of a mile of meadow. It is unusually early to hear them so numerously, and by day, but the water, being so very low and shallow on the meadows, is unusually warm this pleasant day. This might be called the Day of the Snoring Frogs, or the Awakening of the Meadows. Probably the frost is out of the meadows very early this year. It is a remarkable spring for reptile life. It remains now to detect the note of the *palustris*, wood frog, and *fontinalis*. I am not sure but I heard one kind of bullfrog's note along the river once or twice. I saw several middle-sized frogs with green noses and dark bodies, small, bullfrog-like (??), sitting along the shore.

At what perhaps is called the Holt just below N. Barrett's, many grackles and red-wings together flit along the willows by our side, or a little ahead, keeping up a great chattering, while countless painted turtles are as steadily rustling and dropping into the water from the willows, etc., just ahead.

We land at Ball's Hill and eat our dinners. It is so warm we would fain bathe. We seek some shade and cannot easily find it. You wonder that all birds and insects are not out at once in such a heat. We find it delicious to take off our shoes and stockings and wade far through the shallows on the meadow to the Bedford shore, to let our legs drink air.

How pretty the white fibrous roots of the eriocaulon, floating in tufts on the meadow, like beaded chains!

In the hazy atmosphere yesterday we could hardly see Garfield's old unpainted farmhouse. It was only betrayed by its elms. This would be the right color for painters to imitate. When the sun went into a cloud we detected the outlines of the windows only.

When returning, we discovered, on the south side of the river, just at the old crossing-place from the Great Meadows, north of the ludwigia pool, a curious kind of spawn. It was white, each ovum about as big as a robin-shot or larger, with mostly a very minute white core, no black core, and these were agglutinated together in the form of zigzag hollow cylinders, two or three inches in diameter and one or two feet long, looking like a lady's ruff or other muslin work, on the bottom or on roots and twigs of willow and button-bush, where the water was two or three feet deep. The greater part lay on the bottom, looking like a film, these cylinders being somewhat coiled about there. When you took it up, the two sides fell together, and it was flat in your hand like the leg of a stocking. In one place there were a dozen very large red-bellied and brown-backed leeches in it, evidently battening on it. This must be frog or fish spawn. If frog-spawn, I think it must be that of the *Rana halecina*,[1] the only ones fairly awake along the river; but how are leeches propagated? There was a great abundance of it, many bushels, for at least a dozen rods along the shore, and it must afford food to many creatures. The consistency of a jelly we eat. We saw one perch there. Some on the ruts was quite up to the surface, but most lower. When you had taken up a handful and broken it, on dropping it into the water it recovered its form for the most part. I noticed that the fine willow root-fibres and weeds, potamogeton, etc., there were thickly covered with a whitish film or fuzz, an eighth to a quarter of an inch deep, or long, apparently connected with this spawn, which made them look like plants covered with frost in a winter morning, though it was a duller white; but out of water you did not perceive anything. Probably this was the milt.

When I have been out thus the whole day and spend the whole afternoon returning, it seems to me pitiful and ineffectual to be out as usual only in the afternoon, — as if you had come late to a feast, after your betters had done. The afternoon seems coarse and reversed, or at best a long twilight, after the fresh and bright forenoon.

The gregariousness of men is their most contemptible and discouraging aspect. See how they follow each other like sheep, not knowing why. Day & Martin's

[1] No. *Vide* April 5th. Is it not fish-spawn?

Vol. X

blacking was preferred by the last generation, and also is by this. They have not so good a reason for preferring this or that religion as in this case even. Apparently in ancient times several parties were nearly equally matched. They appointed a committee and made a compromise, agreeing to vote or believe so and so, and they still helplessly abide by that. Men are the inveterate foes of all improvement. Generally speaking, they think more of their hen-houses than of any desirable heaven. If you aspire to anything better than politics, expect no coöperation from men. They will not further anything good. You must prevail of your own force, as a plant springs and grows by its own vitality.

Hear the *Rana halecina* in the evening also, from my window.

April 4. P. M. — Go to the cold pond-hole south of J. P. Brown's, to hear the croaking frogs. They are in full blast on the southwest side, where there have been some birches, etc., cut the past winter, and there is much brush fallen in the water, whose shelter they evidently like, and there they have dropped their spawn on the twigs. I stand for nearly an hour within ten feet on the bank overlooking them. You see them lying spread out, or swimming toward one another, sometimes getting on to the brush above the water, or hopping on to the shore a few feet. I see one or two pairs coupled, now sinking, now rising to the surface. The upper one, a male, quite dark brown and considerably smaller than the female, which is reddish —

such part of her as I can see — and has quite distinct dark bars on its posterior extremities, while I cannot discern any on the male. But the greatest commotion comes from a mass of them, five or six inches in diameter, where there are at least a dozen or fifteen clinging to one another and making a queer croaking. From time to time a newcomer adds himself to the mass, turning them over and over.[1] The water is all alive with them for a couple of rods, and from time to time they croak much more generally than at others, evidently exciting one another to it, as do the *R. halecina*. Before I caught any of them I was only struck with the fact that the males were much smaller and very much darker, though I could see only one female partially. At length, when all the rest had been scared to the bottom by nearer approach, I got near to the struggling mass. They were continually dropping off from it, and when at length I reached out to seize it, there were left but two. Lifting the female, the male still clung to her with his arms about her body, and I caught them both, and they were perfectly passive while I carried them off in my hand. To my surprise the female was the ordinary light-reddish-brown *wood frog* (*R. sylvatica*), with legs distinctly barred with dark, while the male, whose note alone I have heard, methinks, was not only much smaller, but of a totally different color, a dark brown above with dark-slate-colored sides, and the yet darker bars on its posterior extremities and the dark line from its snout only to be

[1] It was an incessantly struggling mass. You could have *taken up* a *dozen* or fifteen in your two hands.

distinguished [on] a close inspection. Throat and beneath, a cream white, like but clearer than the female. In color, a small bullfrog [1] which I had caught, and any other frog that I know, was more like the female than these males were. I have caught the female in previous years, as last spring in New Bedford, but could find no description of him and suspected it to be an undescribed frog. It seems they were all (of this mass) about one female, and I saw only one other in the pool, but apparently only one had possession of her. There was a good deal of spawn firmly attached to the brush close to the surface, and, as usual, in some lights you could not see the jelly, only the core. I brought these frogs home and put them in a pan of water.[2]

Sophia has brought home the early large-catkinned willow, well out; probably some yesterday at least.

April 5. What I call the young bullfrog, about two and a half inches long, — though it has no yellow on throat. It has a bright-golden ring outside of the iris as far as I can see round it. Is this the case with the bullfrog? May it not be a young *Rana fontinalis?* No yellow to throat. I found it on the shore of the Clamshell Hill ditch. Can jump much better than the others, and easily gets out of the deep pan.[3]

Those to whom I showed the two *R. sylvatica* could not believe that they were one species, but this morn-

[1] Probably *R. fontinalis*.   [2] *Vide* below.
[3] *Vide* three pages forward. *Vide* also June 8, 1858. Probably a *Rana fontinalis*.

ing, on taking them out of the water to examine minutely, they changed so rapidly, chameleon-like, that I could only describe their first appearance from memory. The male grew a lighter brown and the female darker, till in ten minutes there was but a slight shade of difference, and their whole aspect, but especially that of the male, *seemed* altered also, so that it was not easy to distinguish them. Yet they would readily be recognized for rather dark-colored wood frogs, the posterior extremities of both having distinct dark bars. The female was two and one tenth inches long, the male one and four fifths inches long. The female was (apparently involuntarily) dropping a little spawn in the pan this morning, and the black core was as big as the head of a pin when it issued from the body. The only difference in color that I now noticed, except that the male was a shade the darkest (both a pale brown), was that there was a very distinct dark mark on the front side at the base of the anterior extremities of the female, while there was but the slightest trace of it in the male. Also the female was more green on the flanks and abdomen; also she had some dusky spots beneath. What is described as a yellow line along the lower edge of the dark one through the eyes, *i. e.* along the upper jaw, and which I observed to be such last spring, was in both these at all times a broad silvery or bright cream-colored line. Putting them into the water, after an hour they again acquired distinct colors, but not quite so distinct at first. It is singular that at the breeding-season, at least, though both are immersed in water, they are of a totally different color, —

the male **a** very dark brown for a frog, darker than the ordinary color of any Massachusetts frog, without distinct bars to his posterior extremities or a distinct dark line along the snout, while the female is a light reddish brown or lively dead-leaf color, — and that, taken out of water, they rapidly approximate each other till there is only a shade of difference if any. At their breeding-season, then, the colors of the male are not livelier, as in the case of birds, but darker and more sombre.

Considering how few of these or of the *R. halecina* you meet with in the summer, it is surprising how many are now collected in the pools and meadows. The woods resound with the one, and the meadows day and night with the other, so that it amounts to a general awakening of the pools and meadows.

I hear this morning the seringo sparrow.

In the proceedings of the Natural History Society for December, 1856, there were presented by Dr. H. R. Storer, "a globular concretion of grass said to have been formed by the action of waves upon the seashore." Were not these some obtained by the Hoars or Emersons from Flint's Pond?

P. M. — I go to the meadow at the mouth of the Mill Brook to find the spawn of the *R. halecina*. They are croaking and coupling there by thousands, as before, though there is a raw east wind to-day. I see them coupled merely, in a few instances, but no such balls or masses of them about one female as in the case of the *R. sylvatica,* though this may occur. You can easily

get close to them and catch them by wading. The first lagoon within the meadow was not a foot deep anywhere, and I found the spawn where it was about eight inches deep, with a grassy and mossy bottom. It was principally in two collections, which were near together and each about a yard in diameter. The separate masses of this were from two to six, or commonly three or four, inches in diameter, and generally looked quite black and dense or fine-egged in the water. But it really on a closer inspection presented quite an interesting variety of appearances. The black core is about the size of a pin-head, and one half of it is white. It commonly lies with the black side up, and when you look directly down on it, has a rich, very dark blue-purple appearance. When with the white or wrong side up, it looks like a mass of small silvery points or bubbles, and you do not notice the jelly. But it lies also at all intermediate angles, and so presents a variety of appearances. It is attached pretty firmly to the grass and rises just to the surface. There are very fine froth-like bubbles more or less mingled with it. I am not sure that I can distinguish it from that of the *R. sylvatica*.

I caught several of the first. The dark blotches on the back were generally more or less roundish with a crenate edge. There were distinct, raised, light bronze-colored ridges from the snout along the side-head and body, which were conspicuous at a distance. They were, all that I caught, distinctly *yellow*-white beneath, and some had green buttocks.[1] And now, standing over them, I saw that there were considerable *lateral*

[1] Were they not males?

bubbles formed when they croaked, *i. e.*, the throat was puffed out *on each side* quite far behind the snout. The tympanum was very convex and prominent.

At evening I find that the male *R. sylvatica* couples with or fastens himself to the back of the young bull-frog (?), or whatever it is,[1] and the latter meanwhile *croaks*, in short croaks four or five times repeated, much like the *R. sylvatica*, methinks.

I hear the hylodes peeping now at evening, being at home, though I have not chanced to hear any during the day. They prefer the evening.

April 6. A moist, foggy, and very slightly drizzly morning. It has been pretty foggy for several mornings. This makes the banks look suddenly greener, apparently making the green blades more prominent and more vividly green than before, prevailing over the withered ones.

P. M. — Ride to Lee's Cliff and to Second Division Brook.

It begins to grow cold about noon, after a week or more of generally warm and pleasant weather. They with whom I talk do not remember when the river was so low at this season. The top of the bathing-rock, above the island in the Main Branch, was more than a foot out of water on the 3d, and the river has been falling since. On examining the buds of the elm at Helianthus Bank, I find it is not the slippery elm, and therefore I know but one.

At Lee's Cliff I find no saxifrage in bloom above

[1] *R. fontinalis.*

the rock, on account of the ground having been so exposed the past exceedingly mild winter, and no *Ranunculus fascicularis* anywhere there, but on a few small warm shelves under the rocks the saxifrage makes already a pretty white edging along the edge of the grass sod [?] on the rocks; has got up three or four inches, and may have been out four or five days. I also notice one columbine, which may bloom in a week if it is pleasant weather.

The *Ulmus Americana* is apparently just out here, or possibly yesterday. The *U. fulva* not yet, of course. The large rusty blossom-buds of the last have been extensively eaten and mutilated, probably by birds, leaving on the branches which I examine mostly mere shells.

I see, in [one] or two places in low ground, elder started half an inch, before any other shrub or tree. The *Turritis stricta* is four to six inches high. No mouse-ear there yet.

I hear hylas in full blast 2.30 P. M.

It is remarkable how much herbaceous and shrubby plants, some which are decidedly evergreen, have suffered the past very mild but open winter on account of the ground being bare. Accordingly the saxifrage and crow-foot are so backward, notwithstanding the warmth of the last ten days. Perhaps they want more moisture, too. The asplenium ferns of both species are very generally perfectly withered and shrivelled, and in exposed places on hills the checkerberry has not proved an evergreen, but is completely withered and a dead-leaf color. I do not remember when it has suffered so much.

Such plants require to be covered with snow to protect them.

At Second Division, the *Caltha palustris*, half a dozen well out. The earliest may have been a day or two.

The frost is but just coming out in cold wood-paths on the north sides of hills, which makes it very muddy, there only.

Returned by the Dugan Desert and stopped at the mill there to get the aspen flowers. The very earliest aspens, such as grow in warm exposures on the south sides of hills or woods, have begun to be effete. Others are not yet out.

Talked a moment with two little Irish (?) boys, eight or ten years old, that were playing in the brook by the mill. Saw one catch a minnow. I asked him if he used a hook. He said no, it was a "dully-chunk," or some such word. "*Dully* what?" [I] asked. "Yes, *dully*," said he, and he would not venture to repeat the whole word again. It was a small horsehair slip-noose at the end of a willow stick four feet long. The horsehair was twisted two or three together. He passed this over the fish slowly and then jerked him out, the noose slipping and holding him. It seems they are sometimes made with wire to catch trout. I asked him to let me see the fish he had caught. It was a little pickerel five inches long, and appeared to me strange, being *transversely* barred, and reminded me of the Wrentham pond pickerel; but I could not remember surely whether this was the rule or the exception; but when I got home I found that this was the

one which Storer does not name nor describe, but only had heard of. Is it not the brook pickerel? Asking what other fish he had caught, he said a pike. "That," said I, "is a large pickerel." He said it had "a long, long neb like a duck's bill."

It rapidly grows cold and blustering.

April 7. A cold and gusty, blustering day. We put on greatcoats again.

P. M. — Down the Great Meadows.

The river is low, even for summer. The ground about the outmost willow at my boat's place is high and dry. I cross the meadows and step across the Mill Brook near Mrs. Ripley's. You hear no stertorous sounds of the *Rana halecina* this cold and blustering day, unless a few when you go close to their breeding-places and listen attentively. Scarcely one has his head out of water, though I see many at the bottom. I wear india-rubber boots and wade through the shallow water where they were found. In a shallow sheet of water on the meadow, with a grassy bottom, the spawn will commonly all be collected in one or two parcels in the deepest part, if it is generally less than eight or ten inches deep, to be prepared for a further fall. You will also find a little here and there in weedy ditches in the meadow. One of the first-named parcels will consist of even a hundred separate deposits about three or four inches in diameter crowded together. The frogs are most numerous to-day about and beneath the spawn. Each little mass of ova is pretty firmly attached to the stubble, — not accidentally,

but designedly and effectually, — and when you pull it off, leaves some of the jelly adhering to the stubble. If the mass is large it will run out of your hand this side or that, like a liquid, or as if it had life, — like "sun-squall." It is not injured by any ordinary agitation of the water, but the mass adheres well together. It bears being carried any distance in a pail. When dropped into the water again, it falls wrong side up, showing the white sides of the cores or yolks (?). On the Great Meadows, I stand close by two coupled. The male is very much the smallest, an inch, *at least*, the shortest, and much brighter-colored. The line, or "halo" (?), or margin about its blotches is a distinct yellow or greenish yellow. The female has a distended paunch full of spawn.

Snipes rise two or three times as I go over the meadow.

The remarkable spawn of the 3d, just below the Holt (?), does not show its cylindrical form so well as before; appears to have been broken up considerably, perhaps by creatures feeding on it.

I see the remains of a duck which has died on this meadow, and the southeast edge of the meadow is strewn with the feathers of the water-fowl that plumed themselves here before the water went down. There is no water anywhere on these meadows now — except the one or two permanent pools — which I cannot walk through in my boots.

Where they have been digging mud the past winter in Beck Stow's Swamp, I perceive that the crust, for one foot deep at least, consists chiefly, or perhaps half of it, — the rest mainly sphagnum, — of the dead and fallen stems of water andromeda which have accumulated in course of time.

I brought home the above two kinds of spawn in a pail. Putting some of the *Rana halecina* spawn in a tumbler of water, I cannot see the gelatinous part, but only the dark or white cores, which are kept asunder by it at regular intervals.

The other (probably fish) spawn is seen to be arranged in perfect hexagons; *i. e.*, the ova so impinge on each other; but where there is a vent or free side, it is a regular arc of a circle. Is not this the form that spheres pressing on each other equally on all sides assume? I see the embryo, already fish-like (?), curved round the yolk, with a microscope.[1]

April 8. Surveying Kettell farm.

Could I have heard *Fringilla socialis* along the street this morning?[2] Or may it have been the *hyemalis?*

Polly Houghton comes along and says, half believing it, of my compass, "This is what regulates the moon and stars."

April 9. April rain at last, but not much; clears up at night.

At 4.30 P. M. to Well Meadow Field.

[1] The greater part of the fish-spawn, being left out in a firkin, was apparently killed by the cold, the water freezing half an inch thick April 7th.
[2] Possibly, for I hear it the 14th, and perhaps the 12th. *Vide* 12th.

The yew looks as if it would bloom in a day or two, and the staminate *Salix humilis* in the path in three or four days.[1] Possibly it is already out elsewhere, if, perchance, that was not it just beginning on the 6th on the Marlborough road. The pistillate appear more forward. It must follow pretty close to the earliest willows.

I hear the booming of snipe this evening, and Sophia says she heard them on the 6th. The meadows having been bare so long, they may have begun yet earlier. Persons walking up or down our village street in still evenings at this season hear this singular *winnowing* sound in the sky over the meadows and know not what it is. This "booming" of the snipe is our regular village serenade. I heard it this evening for the first time, as I sat in the house, through the window. Yet common and annual and remarkable as it is, not one in a hundred of the villagers hears it, and hardly so many know what it is. Yet the majority know of the Germanians who have only been here once. Mr. Hoar was almost the only inhabitant of this street whom I had heard speak of this note, which he used annually to hear and listen for in his sundown or evening walks.

R. Rice tells me that he has seen the pickerel-spawn hung about in strings on the brush, especially where a tree had fallen in. He thinks it was the pickerel's because he has seen them about at the time. This seems to correspond with mine of April 3d, though he did [not] recognize the peculiar form of it.

I doubt if men do ever simply and naturally glorify

[1] *Vide* 13th.

God in the ordinary sense, but it is remarkable how sincerely in all ages they glorify nature. The praising of Aurora, for instance, under some form in all ages is obedience to as irresistible an instinct as that which impels the frogs to peep.

April 11. P. M. — To Lee's Cliff.

The black spheres (rather dark brown) in the *Rana sylvatica* spawn by Hubbard's Grove have now opened and flatted out into a rude broad pollywog form. (This was an early specimen.)

Yesterday saw moles working in a meadow, throwing up heaps.

I notice at the Conantum house, of which only the chimney and frame now stand, a triangular mass of rubbish, more than half a bushel, resting on the great mantel-tree against an angle in the chimney. It being mixed with clay, I at first thought it a mass of clay and straw mortar, to fill up with, but, looking further, I found it composed of corn-cobs, etc., and the excrement probably of rats,   of this form and size, and of pure clay,   looking like the cells of an insect. Either   the wharf rat or this country rat. They had anciently chosen this warm place for their nest and carried a great store of eatables thither, and the clay of the chimney, washing down, had incrusted the whole mass over. So this was an old rats' nest as well as human nest, and so it is with every old house. The rats' nest may have been a hundred and fifty years old. Wherever you see an old house, there look for an old rats' nest. In hard times they had, ap-

parently, been compelled to eat the clay, or it may be that they love it. It is a wonder they had not set the house on fire with their nest. Conant says this house was built by Rufus Hosmer's great-grandfather.

Slippery elm. Crowfoot (*Ranunculus fascicularis*) at Lee's *since* the 6th, apparently a day or two before this. Mouse-ear, not yet. What that large frog, bullfrog-like but with brown spots on a dirty-white throat, in a pool on Conantum? See thimble-berry and rose bush leafing under the rocks.

April 12. A. M. — Surveying part of William P. Brown's wood-lot in Acton, west of factory.

Hear the huckleberry-bird and, I think, the *Fringilla socialis.*[1] The handsomest pails at the factory are of oak, white and some "gray" (perhaps scarlet), but these are chiefly for stables. The woods are all alive with pine warblers now. Their note is the music to which I survey. Now the early willows are in their prime, methinks. At angle H of the lot, on a hillside, I find the mayflower, but not in bloom. It appears to be common thereabouts.

Returning on the railroad, the noon train down passed us opposite the old maid Hosmer's house. In the woods just this side, we came upon a partridge standing on the track, between the rails over which the cars had just passed. She had evidently been run down, but, though a few small feathers were scattered along for a dozen rods beyond her, and she looked a little ruffled, she was apparently more disturbed in mind than body.

[1] Probably, for I hear it the 14th.

I took her up and carried her one side to a safer place. At first she made no resistance, but at length fluttered out of my hands and ran two or three feet. I had to take her up again and carry and drive her further off, and left her standing with head erect as at first, as if beside herself. She was not lame, and I suspect no wing was broken. I did not suspect that this swift wild bird was ever run down by the cars. We have an account in the newspapers of every cow and calf that is run over, but not of the various wild creatures who meet with that accident. It may be many generations before the partridges learn to give the cars a sufficiently wide berth.

April 13. Began to rain last evening, and still rains.

The tree sparrows sing sweetly, canary-like, still. Hear the first toad in the rather cool rain, 10 A. M.

See through the dark rain the first flash of lightning, in the west horizon, doubting if it was not a flash of my eye at first, but after a very long interval I hear the low rumbling of the first thunder, and now the summer is baptized and inaugurated in due form. Is not the first lightning the forerunner or warranty of summer heat? The air now contains such an amount of heat that it emits a flash.

Speaking to J. B. Moore about the partridges being run down, he says that he was told by Lexington people some years ago that they found a duck lying dead under the spire of their old meeting-house (since burned) which stood on the Battle-Ground. The weathercock — and it was a cock in this case — was

considerably bent, and the inference was that the duck had flown against it in the night.

P. M. — To the yew.

Shepherd's-purse already going to seed; in bloom there some time. Also chickweed; how long? I had thought these would be later, on account of the ground having been so bare, and indeed they did suffer much, but early warm weather forwarded them. That unquestionable staminate *Salix humilis* beyond yew will not be out for three or four days. Its old leaves on the ground are turned cinder-color, as are those under larger and doubtful forms. Epigæa abundantly out, *maybe* four or five days. It was apparently in its winter state March 28th.

April 14. Rains still, with one or two flashes of lightning, but soon over.

The yew plucked yesterday blossoms in house to-day.

P. M. — Up Assabet.

The river is a little higher on account of rain. I see much sweet flag six or eight inches long, floating, it having been cut up apparently by musquash. (The 17th I see much of the sparganium cut up close to the bottom along a musquash-path at the bottom of a meadow where there was one foot of water.)

My *Rana halecina* spawn in tumbler is now flatted out and begins to betray the pollywog form. I had already noticed a little motion in it from time to time, but nothing like the incessant activity of the embryo fishes.

I find no suckers'[1] nests yet. There has been no rise of the river of any consequence.

At Ed. Hoar's in the evening. I look at one of his slides through a microscope, at the infusorial skeletons of the navicula and dumb-bell infusoria, etc., etc. With his microscope I see the heart beating in the embryo fish and the circulations distinctly along the body.

April 15. P. M. — To sedge-path *Salix humilis.*

I see many planting now.

See a pair of woodpeckers on a rail and on the ground a-courting. One keeps hopping near the other, and the latter hops away a few feet, and so they accompany one another a long distance, uttering sometimes a faint or short *a-week.*

I go to find hylodes spawn. I hear some now peeping at mid-afternoon in Potter's meadow, just north of his swamp. It is hard to tell how far off they are. At a distance they often appear to be nearer than they are; when I get nearer I think them further off than they are; and not till I get their parallax with my eyes by going to one side do I discover their locality. From time to time one utters that peculiar quavering sound, I suspect of alarm, like that which a hen makes when she sees a hawk. They peep but thinly at this hour of a bright day. Wading about in the meadow there, barelegged, I find the water from time to time, though no deeper than before, exceedingly cold,

[1] [A pencilled interrogation-point in parentheses here.]

evidently because there is ice in the meadow there still.

Having stood quite still on the edge of the ditch close to the north edge of the maple swamp some time, and heard a slight rustling near me from time to time, I looked round and saw a mink under the bushes within a few feet. It was pure reddish-brown above, with a blackish and somewhat bushy tail, a blunt nose, and somewhat innocent-looking head. It crept along toward me and around me, *within two feet*, in a semicircle, snuffing the air, and pausing to look at me several times. Part of its course when nearest me was in the water of the ditch. It then crawled slowly away, and I saw by the ripple where it had taken to the ditch again. Perhaps it was after a frog, like myself. It may have been attracted by the peeping. But how much blacker was the creature I saw April 28th, 1857! A very different color, though the tail the same form.

The naturalist accomplishes a great deal by patience, more perhaps than by activity. He must take his position, and then wait and watch. It is equally true of quadrupeds and reptiles. Sit still in the midst of their haunts.

Saw flitting silently through the wood, near the yew, two or three thrushes, much like, at least, the *Turdus Wilsonii;* a light ring about eyes, and whitish side of throat (?); rather fox-colored or cinnamon tail, with ashy reflections from edges of primaries; flesh-colored legs. Did not see the breast. Could it have been what I have called *T. solitarius?* Soon after *methought* I heard one faint wood thrush note (??).[1]

[1] *Vide* 21st.

Catch a peeper at Hayden's Pool. I suspect it may have been a female, for, though I kept it a day at home, it did not peep. It was a pale fawn-color out of water, nine tenths of an inch long, marked with dusky like this, though not so distinctly. It could easily climb up the side of a tumbler, and jumped eighteen inches at once.

Equisetum arvense out by railroad, and probably I saw it out on the 12th, near the factory.

April 16. My fish ova in a tumbler has [sic] gradually expanded till it is some three sixteenths of an inch in diameter, and for more than a week the embryos have been conspicuously active, hardly still enough to be observed with a microscope. Their tails, eyes, pectoral fins, etc., were early developed and conspicuous. They keep up a regular jerking motion as they lie curved in the egg, and so develop themselves. This morning I set them in the sun, and, looking again soon after, found that they were suddenly hatched, and more than half of them were free of the egg. They were nearly a quarter of an inch long, or longer than the diameter of a perfect egg. The substance of the egg-shell seemed to have expanded and softened, and the embryo by its incessant quirking elongated it so that it was able to extend itself at full length. It then almost incessantly kept up a vibratory motion of its tail and its pectoral fins, and every few moments it bunted against the side of the egg, wearing it away and extending it, till it broke through. Sometimes it got its head

out first and then struggled many minutes before it escaped completely. It was a pretty sight to see them all rising immediately to the surface by means of the tail and pectoral fins, the first vibrating from one twentieth to one thirtieth of an inch, at an angle of about forty-five degrees, and then, ceasing their motions, they steadily settled down again. Think of the myriads of these minnows set free of a warm morning, and rising and falling in this wise in their native element!! (Some are still in the egg on the 18th.)

The incessant activity of these minnows, and apparent vigor, are surprising. Already they dart swiftly an inch one side like little pickerel, tender as they are, carrying the yolk with them, which gradually diminishes, as I notice, in a day or two after. They have no snouts yet, or only blunt and rounded ones. I have not detected any general resting even at night, though they often rest on the bottom day or night. They are remarkably aroused when placed in the morning sun. This sets them all in motion. Looking at them through a jar between you and the sun, a hundred at once, they reflect the colors of the rainbow, — some purple, others violet, green, etc., etc. It is a wonder how they survive the accidents of their condition. By what instinct do they keep together in a school?

I think that the spawn could not have been laid long when I found it April 3d, it was so perfect and the embryo so slightly, if at all, developed. That was a sudden very warm day. In that case, they may be hatched in a fortnight. That appeared to have been a general breeding-place for this species of fish. I

Vol. X

looked a good while on the 14th, but could find none near home.

My hylodes in the tumbler will always hop to the side toward the window as fast as I turn it.

We may think these days of the myriads of fishes just hatched which come rising to the surface. The water swarms with them as with the mosquito.

P. M. — To Conantum.

The *Rana sylvatica* spawn at Hubbard's Grove begins to kick free. This is early. I put some in a bottle, which being shaken in my walk, I find the embryos all separated from the ova when I get home. These are now regular little pollywogs and wiggle about in a lively manner when the water is shaken. They are chiefly tail and head. They look like the samara of the ash, and in both cases this winged or feather-like tail it is that transports them. I can already see their little feet or fins.

The bodkin-like bulb, considerably grown, in my tumbler and elsewhere, is probably the water-purslane. I see it floating free and sending out many rootlets, on pools and ditches. In this way it spreads itself.

The earliest red maple I can see in this walk is well out, on the Hubbard Bridge causeway. Probably some was yesterday.

I sat a long time by the little pool behind Lee's, to see the hylodes. Not one was heard there; only the skater insects were slightly rippling the surface, pursuing one another and breeding amid the grass. The bottom is covered with pretty proserpinaca. At length

I see one hylodes with heels up, burying itself at the bottom. How wary they are! After nearly half an hour I see one sitting out on a blade of the floating purple grass, but down he goes again. They see or hear you three or four rods off. They are more active toward night.

April 17. P. M. — *Via* Assabet to Coral Rock.

See several kingfishers. Red-wings still in flocks, and crow blackbirds feeding amid leaves by Assabetside, half a dozen together. The female flowers of the alder are now very pretty when seen against the sun, bright-crimson. I take up a wood turtle on the shore, whose sternum is covered with small ants. The sedge is shooting up in the meadows, erect, rigid, and sharp, a glaucous green unlike that of the grass on banks. The linnæa-like plant turns out to be golden saxifrage. Its leaf is the same form, but smooth and not shrubby.

The *Rana halecina* spawn in tumbler begins to struggle free of the ova, but it is not so much developed as the *R. sylvatica*. Some of the first may be a little more forward in the meadows. I see some to-day, probably this kind, flatted out, though I do not see the frog. It made the same sound, however. The *R. sylvatica* is probably generally the earliest.

April 18. P. M. — To Hubbard's Grove.

A dandelion open; will shed pollen to-morrow.

The *Rana sylvatica* tadpoles have mostly wiggled away from the ova. Put some *R. halecina* spawn which has flatted out in a ditch on Hubbard's land. I saw in those ditches many small pickerel, landlocked, which appeared to be transversely barred! They bury themselves in the mud at my approach.

Examined the pools and ditches in that neighborhood, *i. e.* of Skull-Cap Ditch, for frogs. All that I saw distinctly, except two *R. fontinalis*, were what I have considered young bullfrogs, middling-sized frogs with a greenish-brown back and a throat commonly white or whitish. I saw in a deep and cold pool some spawn placed just like that of the *R. sylvatica* and the *R. halecina*, — it was in the open field, — and the only frog I could distinguish near it was a middling-sized one, or larger, with a yellow throat, not distinctly green, but brown or greenish-brown above, but green along each upper jaw. A small portion of bright-golden ring about the eye was to be seen in front.

In the spring near by, I see two unquestionable *R. fontinalis*, one much the largest and with brighter mottlings, probably on account of the season. The upper and forward part of their bodies distinct green, but their throats, white or whitish, not yellow. There were also two small and dark-colored frogs, yet with a little green tinge about the snouts, in the same spring.

I suspect that all these frogs may be the *R. fontinalis*, and none of them bullfrogs. Certainly those two unquestionable *R. fontinalis* had no yellow to throats, and probably they vary very much in the greenness of the back. Those two were not so much barred on the legs as mottled, and in one the mottlings had quite bright halos. They had the yellow segment in front part of eye, as also had the two smallest. Have the bullfrogs this? I doubt if I have seen a bullfrog yet.

I should say, with regard to that spawn, that I heard in the neighboring pool the stertorous *tut tut tut* like the *R. halecina*, and also one dump sound.

Frogs are strange creatures. One would describe them as peculiarly wary and timid, another as equally bold and imperturbable. All that is required in studying them is patience. You will sometimes walk a long way along a ditch and hear twenty or more leap in one after another before you, and see where they rippled the water, without getting sight of one of them. Sometimes, as this afternoon the two *R. fontinalis*, when you approach a pool or spring a frog hops in and buries itself at the bottom. You sit down on the brink and wait patiently for his reappearance. After a quarter of an hour or more he is sure to rise to the surface and put out his nose quietly without making a ripple, eying you steadily. At length he becomes as curious about you as you can be about him. He suddenly hops straight toward [you], pausing within a foot, and takes a near and leisurely view of you. Perchance you may now scratch its nose with your finger and examine it to your heart's content, for it is become as imperturbable as it was shy before. You conquer them by superior patience and immovableness; not by quickness, but by slowness; not by heat, but by coldness. You see only a pair of heels disappearing in the weedy bottom, and, saving a few insects, the pool becomes as smooth as a mirror and apparently as uninhabited. At length, after half an hour, you detect a frog's snout and a pair of eyes above the green slime, turned toward you, — etc.

It is evident that the frog spawn is not accidentally

placed, simply adhering to the stubble that may be nearest, but the frog chooses a convenient place to deposit it; for in the above-named pool there was no stout stubble rising above the surface except at one side, and there the spawn was placed.

It is remarkable how much the musquash cuts up the weeds at the bottom of pools and ditches, — burreed, sweet flags, pontederia, yellow lily, fine, grass-like rushes, and now you see it floating on the surface, sometimes apparently where it has merely burrowed along the bottom.

I see where a ditch was cut a few years ago in a winding course, and now a young hedge of alders is springing up from the bottom on one side, winding with the ditch. The seed has evidently been caught in it, as in a trap.

April 19. Spend the day hunting for my boat, which was stolen. As I go up the riverside, I see a male marsh hawk hunting. He skims along exactly over the edge of the water, on the meadowy side, not more than three or four feet from the ground and winding with the shore, looking for frogs, for in such a tortuous line do the frogs sit. They probably know about what time to expect his visits, being regularly decimated. Particular hawks farm particular meadows. It must be easy for him to get a breakfast. Far as I can see with a glass, he is still tilting this way and that over the water-line.

At Fair Haven Pond I see, half a mile off, eight large water-fowl, which I thought at first were large ducks, though their necks appeared long. Studying them

patiently with a glass, I found that they had gray backs, black heads and necks with perhaps green reflections, white breasts, dark tips to tails, and a white spot about eyes on each side of bill. At first the whole bird had looked much darker, like black ducks. I did not know but they might be brant or some very large ducks, but at length inclined to the opinion that they were geese. At 5.30, being on the Common, I saw a small flock of geese going over northeast. Being reminded of the birds of the morning and their number, I looked again and found that there were eight of them, and probably they were the same I had seen.

Viola ovata on bank above Lee's Cliff. Edith Emerson found them there yesterday; also columbines and the early potentilla April 13th!!!

I hear the pine warbler there, and also what I thought a variation of its note, quite different, yet I thought not unfamiliar to me. Afterwards, along the wall under the Middle Conantum Cliff, I saw many goldfinches, male and female, the males singing in a very sprightly and varied manner, sitting still on bare trees. Also uttered their watery twitter and their peculiar mewing. In the meanwhile I heard a faint thrasher's note, as if faintly but perfectly imitated by some bird twenty or thirty rods off. This surprised me very much. It was equally rich and varied, and yet I did not believe it to be a thrasher. Determined to find out the singer, I sat still with my glass in hand, and at length detected the singer, a goldfinch sitting within gunshot all the while. This was the most varied and sprightly performer of any bird I have heard this year, and it is strange that I never heard the strain before. It may be this note which is taken for the thrasher's before the latter comes.

P. M. — Down river.

I find that my *Rana halecina* spawn in the house is considerably further advanced than that left in the meadows. The latter is not only deeper beneath the surface now, on account of the rain, but has gathered dirt from the water, so that the jelly itself is now plainly seen; and some of it has been killed, probably by frost, being exposed at the surface. I hear the same *tut tut tut*, probably of the *halecina*, still there, though not so generally as before.

See two or three yellow lilies nearly open, showing most of their yellow, beneath the water; say in two or three days.

Rice tells me of winging a sheldrake once just below Fair Haven Pond, and pursuing it in a boat as it swam down the stream, till it went ashore at Hubbard's Wood and crawled into a woodchuck's hole about a rod from the water on a wooded bank. He could see its tail and pulled it out. He tells of seeing cartloads of lamprey eels in the spawning season clinging to the stones at a dam in Saco, and that if you spat on a stone and cast it into the swift water above them they would directly let go and wiggle down the stream and you could hear their tails snap like whips on the surface, as if the spittle was poison to them; but if you did not spit on the stone, they would not let go. He thinks that a flock of geese will sometimes stop for a wounded one to get well.

Hear of bluets found on Saturday, the 17th; how long?

Hear a toad ring at 9 P. M. Perhaps I first hear them at night, though cooler, because it is still. R. W. E. saw an anemone on the 18th.

April 20. P. M. — Rain-storm begins, with hail.

April 21. George Melvin says that Joshua Haynes once saw a perch depositing her spawn and the male following behind and devouring it! (?) Garlick in his book on pisciculture says that the perch spawn in May. Melvin says that those short-nosed brook pickerel are caught in the river also, but rarely weigh more than two pounds.

The puddles have dried off along the road and left thick deposits or water-lines of the dark-purple anthers of the elm, coloring the ground like sawdust. You could collect great quantities of them.

The arbor-vitæ is apparently effete already. Ed. Hoar says he heard a wood thrush the 18th.

P. M. — To Easterbrooks's and Bateman's Pond.

The benzoin yesterday and possibly the 19th, so much being killed. It might otherwise have been earlier yet. *Populus grandidentata* some days at least. The *Cornus florida* flower-buds are killed.

The rocks on the east side of Bateman's Pond are a very good place for ferns. I see some very large leather-apron umbilicaria there. They are flaccid and unrolled now, showing most of the olivaceous-fuscous upper side. This side feels cold and damp, while the other,

the black, is dry and warm, notwithstanding the warm air. This side, evidently, is not expanded by moisture. It is a little exciting even to meet with a rock covered with these *livid* (?) green aprons, betraying so much life. Some of them are three quarters of a foot in diameter. What a growth for a bare rock!

April 22. Hear martins about a box.

P. M. — To Hubbard's Great Meadow.

The spawn of April 18th is gone! It was fresh there and apparently some creature has eaten it. I see spawn (*R. halecina*-like) in the large pool southeast of this and catch one apparently common-sized (!) *R. halecina* near it. The general aspect dark-brown, with bronze-colored stripes along sides of back one tenth of an inch wide; spots, roundish with a dull-green halo; a roundish spot on each orbit; no bright spots. I catch apparently another in the Great Meadow, and I think some *R. halecina* are still spawning, for I see some fresh spawn there.

Andromeda, apparently a day or two, — at least at edge of Island Wood, which I have not seen.

I walk along several brooks and ditches, and see a great many yellow-spotted turtles; several couples copulating. The uppermost invariably has a depressed sternum while the other's is full. The *Emys picta* are evidently breeding also. See two apparently coupled on the shore. You see both kinds now in little brooks not more than a foot wide, slowly and awkwardly moving about one another. They can hardly make their way against the swift stream. I see one *E. picta* hold-

ing on to a weed with one of its fore feet. Meanwhile a yellow-spotted turtle shoots swiftly down the stream, carried along by the current, and is soon out of sight. The *E. picta* are also quite common in the shallows on the river meadows. I see many masses of empty or half-empty *R. halecina* spawn.

April 23. I receive to-day *Sanguinaria Canadensis* from Brattleboro, well in bloom, — how long? — in a large box full of mayflowers.

The toads ring now by day, but not very loud nor generally.

I see the large head apparently of a bullfrog, by the riverside. Many middle-sized frogs, apparently bullfrogs, green above and more or less dark-spotted, with either yellow or white throats, sitting along the water's edge now.

Catch two *Rana palustris* coupled.[1] They jump together into the river. The male is two and a quarter inches long. This I find to be about an average-sized one of four or five that I distinguish. Above, pale-brown or fawn-brown (another, which I think is a male from the size and the equally bright yellow of the abdomen and inside of limbs, is *dusky*-brown, and next day both the males are of this color; so you must notice the change of color of frogs), with two rows of very oblong, two or three or more times as long as broad, squarish-ended dark-brown spots with a light-brown edge, the rear ones becoming smaller and roundish; also a similar row along each side, and, beneath it, a

[1] *Vide* May 1st and 2d.

row of smaller roundish spots; as Storer says, a large roundish spot on the upper and inner side of each orbit and one on the top of the head before it; the throat and forward part of the belly, cream-colored; abdomen and inside of the limbs bright ochreous-yellow, part of which is seen in looking at the back of the frog. Tympanum slightly convex in middle. The female is about an eighth of an inch longer (another one is three quarters of an inch longer), beside being now fuller (probably of spawn). The pale brown, or fawn-brown, is more brassy or bronze-like and does not become darker next day. She has no very oblong squarish spots on back, but smaller and roundish ones and many fine dusky spots interspersed; is thickly dark-spotted on sides. Throat and belly, white or pale cream-color; sides of abdomen only and inside of limbs, much paler yellow than the male; has no dark spots on orbits or on head in front (another specimen has).

Saw a *Viola blanda* in a girl's hand.

April 24. A cold northwest wind. I go at 8 A. M. to catch frogs to compare with the *R. palustris* and bullfrog which I have, but I find it too cold for them. Though I walk more than a mile along the river, I do not get sight of one, and only of one or two turtles. Neither do I find any more frogs (though many *Emys picta*) at 4 P. M., it being still cold. Yet the frogs were quite numerous yesterday. This shows how sensitive they are to changes of temperature. Hardly one puts its head out of the water, if ever he creeps out the grassy

or muddy bottom this cold day. That proserpinaca deserves to be named after the frog, — *ranunculus*, or what-not, — it is so common and pretty at the bottom [of] the shallow grassy pools where I go looking for spawn. It is remarkable that I see many *E. picta* dead along the shore, dead within a few weeks apparently, also a sternothærus. One of the last, alive, emitted no odor to-day.

I find washed up by the riverside part of a pale-greenish egg-shell bigger than a hen's egg, which was probably the egg of a duck laid on the meadow last year or lately.

There is an abundance of the *R. halecina* spawn near the elm at the hill shore north of Dodd's. It is now semiopaque, greenish, and flatted down and run together, mostly hatched; and a good deal has been killed, apparently by the cold. The water thereabouts is swarming with the young pollywogs for a rod about, but where have all the frogs hidden themselves?

E. Hoar saw the myrtle-bird to-day.

The pollywogs must be a long time growing, for I see those of last year not more than two inches long, also some much larger.

The hatched frog-spawn is quite soft and apparently dissolving at last in the water. Yet possibly that mass of jelly once brought me on a stake was this jelly consolidated.

I find that my fish ova were not all killed some weeks ago in the firkin, as I supposed, for many that were accidentally left in it have hatched, and they bore the cold of last night better than those hatched earlier

and kept in the larger vessel (tub), which froze but thinly, while the firkin froze a quarter of an inch thick last night.

April 25. P. M. — To Assabet.

Approaching the Island, I hear the *phe phe, phe phe, phe phe, phe phe, phe*, the sharp whistling note, of a fish hawk, and, looking round, see him just afterward launching away from one of the swamp white oaks southwest of the Island. There is about half a second between each note, and he utters them either while perched or while flying. He shows a great proportion of wing and some white on back. The wings are much curved. He sails along some eighty feet above the water's edge, looking for fish, and alights again quite near. I see him an hour afterward about the same spot.

See a barn swallow. Also see one myrtle-bird, and Goodwin says he heard a stake-driver several days ago.

April 26. A little snow in the night, which is seen against the fences this morning. See a chewink (male) in the Kettell place woods.

April 27. It has been so cold since the 23d that I have not been able to catch a single frog, have hardly seen where one jumped, as I walked through the meadows looking for them, though in some warmer places I heard a low stertorous *R. halecina*-like note from a few. The tortoises are stirring much more. Frogs appear to love warm and moist weather, rainy or

cloudy. They will sit thickly along the shore, apparently small bullfrogs, etc., *R. palustris*.

My young fishes had the pectoral fins and tail very early developing, but not yet can I detect any other fins with my glass. They had mouths, which I saw them open as soon as hatched, and more and more a perch-like head. I think that with Hoar's microscope I detected two dorsal fins such as the perch have. When I put them suddenly in the sun they sink and rest on the bottom a moment.

In the French work for schools of Edwards and Comte, it is said that the perch spawns not till the age of three years, and in the spring. " The ova are joined together by some glutinous matter in long strings (*cordons*) intertwined with the reeds." (Page 36.)

I noticed yesterday that again the newly laid spawn at the cold pool on Hubbard's land was all gone, and that in the larger pool south of it was much diminished. What creature devours it?

Snows hard in afternoon and evening. Quite wintry. About an inch on ground the next morning.

April 28. Blustering northwest wind and wintry aspect.

A. M. — Down river to look at willows.

The common *S. cordata* apparently not yet within two days at least. This salix is not *always* conspicuously double-scaled, nor is the scale carried up on the catkin. It is not always even on that of the *S. Torreyana.*

I see the fish hawk again [two or three indecipherable words] Island. As it flies low, directly over my head,

I see that its body is white beneath, and the white on the forward side of the wings beneath, if extended across the breast, would form a regular crescent. Its wings do not form a regular curve in front, but an abrupt angle. They are loose and broad at tips. This bird goes fishing slowly down one side of the river and up again on the other, forty to sixty feet high, continually poising itself almost or quite stationary, with its head to the northwest wind and looking down, flapping its wings enough to keep its place, sometimes stationary for about a minute. It is not shy. This boisterous weather is the time to see it.

I see the myrtle-bird in the same sunny place, south of the Island woods, as formerly. Thus are the earliest seen each spring in some warm and calm place by the waterside, when it is cool and blustering elsewhere. The barn swallows and a martin are already skimming low over that small area of smooth water within a few feet of me, never leaving that spot, and I do not observe them thus playing elsewhere. Incessantly stooping back and forth there.

P. M. — To Ledum Swamp.

At Clamshell Ditch, one *Equisetum sylvaticum* will apparently open to-morrow. Strawberries are abundantly out there; how long?

Some Salix tristis, bank near bæomyces. Did I not put it too early in last year's list of willows? Probably earlier elsewhere?

It is much warmer, and now for the first time since April 23d I find frogs out. (Perhaps I could have found some yesterday.)

I noticed one of the large scroll ferns, with its rusty wool, up eight inches on the 28th. See a white-throated sparrow by Cheney's wall, the stout, chubby bird.

After sundown. By riverside. — The frogs and toads are now fairly awake. Both are most musical now at evening. I hear now on various sides, along the river and its meadows, that low, stertorous sound, — *like* that of the *Rana halecina*, — which I have heard occasionally for a few days. (I also hear it in Stow's field by railroad, with toads' ringing.) It is exceedingly like the note of the *R. halecina*, yet I fancy it is somewhat more softly purring, with frequently a low quivering, chuckling, or inquisitive croak, which last takes the place of the bullfrog-like *er er er* of the *halecina*. This is the only difference between it and the *halecina* that I am sure of. The short quivering croak reminds me of the alarm (?) note of the hylodes. I suspect it is the *R. palustris*, now breeding.[1] I hear no snipe.

Frogs, etc., are perfect thermometers. Some that I had in a firkin were chilled to stiffness, while their fellows buried themselves again in the mud of the meadows; *i. e.*, in a cold night at this season they are stiffened in a tub of water, the small *R. palustris*, not being able to bury themselves in mud. They appear to lose their limbs or portions of them, which slough off in consequence.

[1] *Vide* May 1st.

The snow was generally gone about 10 A. M., except in circular patches in the shadow of the still leafless trees.

April 29. Storrow Higginson plucked the uva-ursi fully out the 25th; perhaps two or three days, for it was nearly out, he says, the 18th!!! By his account it was on Pine Hill.

I heard yesterday at Ledum Swamp the lively, sweet, yet somewhat whimsical note of the ruby-crowned wren, and had sight of him a moment. Did I not hear it there the 10th?

Noticed a man killing, on the sidewalk by Minott's, a little brown snake with blackish marks along each side of back and a pink belly. Was it not the *Coluber amœnus*?

April 30. P. M. — I carry the rest of my little fishes, fifteen or twenty, to the cold pool in Hubbard's ground. They are about a quarter-inch long still, and have scarcely increased in length.

I learn that one farmer, seeing me standing a long time still in the midst of a pool (I was watching for hylodes), said that it was his father, who had been drinking some of Pat Haggerty's rum, and had lost his way home. So, setting out to lead him home, he discovered that it was I.

I find a *Fringilla melodia* nest with five eggs. Part, at least, must have been laid before the snow of the 27th, but it is perfectly sheltered under the shelving turf and grass on the brink of a ditch. The snow would not even have touched the bird sitting on them.

Vol. X

X

MAY, 1858

(ÆT. 40)

May 1. A warm and pleasant day, reminding me of the 3d of April when the *R. halecina* waked up so suddenly and generally, and now, as then, apparently a new, allied frog is almost equally wide awake, — the one of last evening (and before).

When I am behind Cheney's this warm and still afternoon, I hear a voice calling to oxen three quarters of a mile distant, and I know it to be Elijah Wood's. It is wonderful how far the *individual* proclaims himself. Out of the thousand millions of human beings on this globe, I know that this sound was made by the lungs and larynx and lips of E. Wood, am as sure of it as if he nudged me with his elbow and shouted in my ear. He can impress himself on the very atmosphere, then, can launch himself a mile on the wind, through trees and rustling sedge and over rippling water, associating with a myriad sounds, and yet arrive distinct at my ear; and yet this creature that is felt so far, that was so noticeable, lives but a short time, quietly dies and makes no more noise that I know of. I can tell him, too, with my eyes by the very gait and motion of him half a mile distant. Far more wonderful his purely spiritual influence, — that after the lapse of thousands of years you may still detect the individual in the turn of a sentence or the tone of a thought!! E. Wood has a peculiar way of modulating the air, imparts to it peculiar vibrations, which several times when standing near him I have noticed, and now a vibration, spreading far and wide over the fields and up and down the river, reaches me and maybe hundreds of others, which we all know to have been produced by Mr. Wood's pipes. However, E. Wood is not a match for a little peeping hylodes in this respect, and there is no peculiar divinity in this.

The inhabitants of the river are peculiarly wide awake this warm day, — fishes, frogs, and toads, from time to time, — and quite often I hear a tremendous rush of a pickerel after his prey. They are peculiarly active, maybe after the *Rana palustris*, now breeding. It is a perfect frog and toad day. I hear the stertorous notes of last evening from all sides of the river at intervals, but most from the grassiest and warmest or most sheltered and sunniest shores. I get sight of ten or twelve *Rana palustris* and catch three of them. One apparent male utters one fine, sharp squeak when caught. Also see by the shore one apparent young bullfrog (?), with bright or vivid light green just along its jaws, a dark line between this and jaws, and a white throat; head, brown above. This is the case with one I have in the firkin, which I think was at first a dull green. These are the only kinds I find sitting along the river. The *Rana palustris* is the prevailing one, and I suppose it makes the *halecina*-like sound described last night.[1] They will be silent for a long time. You

[1] It does. *Vide* May 2d.

Vol. X

ear as the rippling breeze or the circulations of the air itself, for when it dies away on one side it swells again on another, and if it should suddenly cease all men would exclaim at the pause, though they might not have noticed the sound itself.

It occurs to me that that early purple grass on pools corresponds to the color of leaves acquired after the frosts in the fall, as if the cold had, after all, more to do with it than is supposed. As the tops of the *Juncus filiformis* are red, and the first *Lysimachia quadrifolia* red-brown.

As I sit above the Island, waiting for the *Rana palustris* to croak, I see many minnows from three quarters to two inches long, but mostly about one inch. They have that distinct black line along each side from eye to tail on a somewhat transparent brownish body, dace-like, and a very sharply forked tail. When were they hatched? Certainly two or three months ago, at least; perhaps last year. Is it not the brook minnow?

I also hear the myrtle-birds on the Island woods. Their common note is somewhat like the *chill-lill* or jingle of the *F. hyemalis*. Ephemeræ quite common over the water.

Suddenly a large hawk sailed over from the Assabet, which at first I took for a hen-harrier, it was so neat a bird and apparently not very large. It was a fish hawk, with a very conspicuous white crown or head and a uniform brown above elsewhere; beneath white, breast and belly. Probably it was the male, which is the smaller and whiter beneath. A wedge-shaped tail.

will see perhaps one or two snouts and eyes above the surface, then at last may hear a coarsely purring croak, often rapid and as if it began with a *p*, at a distance sounding softer and like *tut tut, tut tut, tut*, lasting a second or two; and then, perchance, others far and near will be excited to utter similar sounds, and all the shore seems alive with them. However, I do not as yet succeed to see one make this sound. Then there may be another pause of fifteen or thirty minutes.

The *Rana palustris* leaves a peculiar strong scent on the hand, which reminds me of days when I went a-fishing for pickerel and used a frog's leg for bait. When I try to think what it smells like, I am inclined to say that it might be the bark of some plant. It is disagreeable. Some are in the water, others on the shore.

I do not see a single *R. halecina*. What has become of the thousands with which the meadows swarmed a month ago? They have given place to the *R. palustris*. Only their spawn, mostly hatched and dissolving, remains, and I expect to detect the spawn of the *palustris* soon.

I find many apparent young bullfrogs in the shaded pools on the Island Neck.[1] There is one good-sized bullfrog among them.[2]

The toads are so numerous, some sitting on all sides, that their ring is a continuous sound throughout the day and night, if it is warm enough, as it now is, except perhaps in the morning. It is as uninterrupted to the

[1] Probably *R. fontinalis*.
[2] This probably the first bullfrog of the season.

He alighted on a dead elm limb on Prichard's ground, and at this distance, with my glass, I could see some dark of head above the white of throat or breast. He was incessantly looking about as if on his guard. After fifteen minutes came a crow from the Assabet and alighted cawing, about twenty rods from him, and ten minutes later another. How alert they are to detect these great birds of prey! They do not thus pursue ordinary hawks, and their attendance alone might suggest to unskillful observers the presence of a fish hawk or eagle. Some crows up the Assabet evidently knew that he was sitting on that elm far away. He sailed low almost directly over my boat, fishing. His wings had not obviously that angular form which I thought those of another had the other day.

The old *Salix sericea* is now all alive with the hum of honey-bees. This would show that it is in bloom. I see and hear one humblebee among them, inaugurating summer with his deep bass. May it be such a summer to me as it suggests. It sounds a little like mockery, however, to cheat me again with the promise of such tropical opportunities. I have learned to suspect him, as I do all fortune-tellers. But no sound so brings round the summer again. It is like the drum of May training. This reminds me that men and boys and the most enlightened communities still love to march after the beating of a drum, as do the most aboriginal of savages.

Two sternothæruses which I catch emit no scent yet. Hear a thrasher.

Hear that a shad-bush is out at Lee's Cliff.

May 2. Sit without fire to-day and yesterday.

I compare the three *Rana palustris* caught yesterday with the male and female of April 23d. The males agree very well. What I have regarded as the groundwork varies from pale brown to dusky brown, even in the same specimen at different times. The present female is larger than that of April 23d, more than half an inch longer than her male, and she has the round dark spots on the orbits and one in front on head and also oblong-square spots on back. She is also dusky-brown like male. None of all have any green. I at last hear the note, for two are coupled in a firkin in my chamber, under my face. It is made by the male alone, and is, as I supposed, the sound of April 30th and May 1st, — the *tut tut tut*, more or less rapidly repeated, and a frequent querulous or inquisitive *cr-r-rack*, half a second long. It makes these sounds only when I excite it by putting others of its kind near it. Its pouches are distended laterally, apparently beneath and behind the eye, and not very conspicuous. Close by, it sounds like a dry belching sound, the bursting of little bubbles more or less rapidly, and the querulous note may be the same very rapidly repeated.

I doubt if I have heard any sound from a bullfrog in river yet.

P. M. — Down river.

The *Salix Babylonica* (fertile) behind Dodd's is more forward than the *alba* by my boat. Put it just before it. See stake-driver. At mouth of the Mill Brook, I hear, I should say, the true *R. halecina* croak, *i. e.* with the faint bullfrog-like *er-er-er* intermixed. Are they

still breeding? Peetweet on a rock. See and hear the red-wings in flocks yet, making a great noise.

If I were to be a frog hawk for a month I should soon know some things about the frogs. How patiently they skim the meadows, occasionally alighting, and fluttering as if it were difficult ever to stand still on the ground. I have seen more of them than usual since I too have been looking for frogs. Hear a tree-toad.

May 3. P. M. — Ride to Flint's Pond to look for *Uvularia perfoliata. Salix purpurea* in Monroe's garden effete. Apparently blooms with our early willows; say 10th of April?

At Hosmer's medicinal (?) spring, Everett's farm, *Ranunculus repens*, abundantly out, apparently several days.

Hear of a peach out in Lincoln.

Probably I heard the black and white creeper April 25th. I hear it and see it well to-day.

Comptonia well out, how long? *Viola cucullata,* how long? Hear of robins' nests with four eggs. See no signs of the *Uvularia perfoliata* yet; apparently will not bloom within ten days.

E. Hoar brings me a twig of a willow plucked in Newton, which was killed some weeks ago, when it had just begun to bloom. The catkins look peculiarly woolly, and the scales peculiarly rounded or blunt. Is it the *eriocephala*? Our earliest gooseberry not yet, perhaps because there will be but few blossoms on it this year. Partridges have been heard drumming.

In the woods near the *Uvularia perfoliata*, see and hear a new bird to me. At first it was silent, and I took

it for the common pewee, but, bringing my glass to bear on it, found it to be pure white throat and beneath, yellow on sides of body or wings, greenish-yellow back and shoulders, a white or whitish ring about eyes, and a light mark along side of head, two white bars on wings, apparently black bill and dark or perhaps slate-colored (?) wings and above tail. It surprised me by singing in a novel and powerful and rich strain. Yet it may be the white-eyed vireo (which I do not know), if it comes so early.[1] Nuttall says it comes to Cambridge about the middle of April.

May 4. The *Salix pedicellaris* by railroad, apparently not for two or three days. The Missouri currant, probably to-day.

P. M. — By boat to Holden Swamp.

To go among the willows now and hear the bees hum is equal to going some hundreds of miles southward toward summer.

I see along the sides of the river, *i. e.*, where the bottom is permanently covered, what I have heretofore called the oat spawn, attached to old pontederia stems, etc.,[2] now some foot or eighteen inches under the surface. It is not black and white, like that of the *Rana halecina, sylvatica,* and *palustris,* which I cannot distinguish from one another, but a pale brown or fawn-color. Some is pretty fresh or recently laid, others already flatted out. Hence, from comparison with my earlier *sylvatica* and *halecina* spawn, I judge that it may have been laid ten days.[3]

[1] *Vide* the 9th.   [2] *Vide* the 8th.
[3] Is it not that of the *R. fontinalis*? *Vide* June 8th.

Vol. X

At Clamshell Shore, I see a clam lying up with open valves.

Salix pedicellaris at Holden's Swamp, staminate, out apparently two days.

It is still warmer than May 1st, yet I hear the stertorous *tut tut tut* of hardly so many frogs (*R. palustris* chiefly, I suppose) as then. As with the *halecina,* it is the first sudden heats that excite them most, methinks.

I find hopping in the meadow a *Rana halecina,* much brighter than any I have seen this year. There is not only a vivid green halo about each spot, but the back is vivid light-green between the spots. I think this was not the case with any of the hundreds I saw a month ago!! Why?? The brassy lines along the sides of the back are narrower (only about one sixteenth of an inch) and more prominent than the more fawn-colored lines of the *R. palustris.* In this one, which I carry home and compare with the *palustris,* there is a large spot on each orbit, but none on the top of the head in front. It is all white beneath, except a tinge of greenish yellow on the abdomen.

Witherell speaks of the *R. palustris* as the yellow-legged frog, very properly. See several bullfrogs along the river, but silent.

I go into Holden Swamp to hear warblers. See a little blue butterfly (or moth) — saw one yesterday — fluttering about over the dry brown leaves in a warm place by the swamp-side, making a pleasant contrast. From time to time have seen the large *Vanessa Antiopa* resting on the black willows, like a leaf still adhering.

As I sit there by the swamp-side this warm summery afternoon, I hear the crows cawing hoarsely, and from time to time see one flying toward the top of a tall white pine. At length I distinguish a hen-hawk perched on the top. The crow repeatedly stoops toward him, now from this side, now from that, passing near his head each time, but he pays not the least attention to it.

I hear the *weese wese wese* of the creeper continually from the swamp. It is the prevailing note there. And methought I heard a redstart's note (?), but oftener than the last I heard the tweezer note, or *screeper* note, of the parti-colored warbler, bluish above, yellow or orange throat and breast, white vent, and white on wings, neck *above* yellowish, going restlessly over the trees — maples, etc. — by the swamp, in creeper fashion, and as you may hear at the same time the true creeper's note without seeing it, you might think it uttered the creeper's note also.

The red-wings, though here and there in flocks, are apparently beginning to build. I judge by their shyness and alarm in the bushes along the river and their richer, solitary warbling.

Coming back, I talk with Witherell at William Wheeler's landing. He comes pushing Wheeler's square-ended boat down-stream with a fish-spear. Says he caught a snapping turtle in the river May 1st. He sits on the side of my boat by the shore a little while, talking with me. There is a hole in the knee of his pants as big as your hand, and he keeps passing his hand

over this slowly, to hide his bare skin, which is sunburnt and the color of his face, though the latter is reddened by rum, of which his breath smells. But how intimate he is with mud and its inhabitants. He says he caught a large pickerel the other night with spawn in it yet; that Henry Bigelow put many little trout into that round pond (Green Pond he calls it) on the Marlborough road, which Elbridge Haynes caught a few years after, weighing two or three pounds apiece. A man told him that he saw a trout weighing about a pound and a half darting at a pickerel, and every time he darted he took a bit off a fin, and at last the man walked in and caught the pickerel, and it weighed five pounds. This was in Spectacle Pond in Littleton. A fisherman told him once that the common eel "gendered" into the river clam, and the young fed on the clam till they were big enough to get other food, and hence you found so many dead clams in the river. I asked him if he knew what fish made the stone-heaps in the river. He said the lamprey eel. He saw one making one last spring about this time, as he was going across the fields by the river near Tarbell's to get seed corn. It was a single lamprey piling up the stones. He used to see thousands of them where he lived a boy, where the lead pipe factory was.

Agassiz says in his Introduction (page 175), "I have known it [the *Chelonura serpentina*] snapping in the same fierce manner [which somebody else had described at a later period when it was very young] as it does when full grown, at a time it was still a pale almost colorless embryo, wrapped up in its fœtal

envelopes, with a yolk larger than itself hanging from its sternum, three months before hatching."

May 5. The two *Rana palustris* which I caught May 1st have been coupled ever since in a firkin in my chamber. They were not coupled when I caught them. Last night I heard them hopping about, for the first time, as if trying to get out. Perhaps the female was trying to find a good place to deposit her spawn. As soon as I get up I find that she has dropped her spawn, a globular mass, wrong or white side up, about two inches in diameter, which still adheres to her posterior, and the male still lies on her back. A few moments later they are separate. The female moves about restlessly from time to time, the spawn still attached, but soon it is detached from her posterior, still adhering to her right leg, as if merely sticking to it. In the course of the forenoon it becomes quite detached. At night they are coupled again. The spawn was not dropped at 10 P. M. the evening before, but apparently in the night. The female now looked long and lank. This is the first spawn I have known to be dropped by the *R. palustris*. I should not know it by its appearance from that of the *sylvatica* and *halecina*. The only frogs hereabouts whose spawn I do not know are the bullfrogs, *R. fontinalis*, and hylodes. The first have not begun to trump, and I conclude are not yet breeding; the last, I think, must be nearly done breeding, and probably do not put their spawn in the river proper; possibly, therefore, the oat spawn of yesterday may be that of the *R. fontinalis*.[1]

[1] *Vide* June 8th.

Saw and heard the small pewee yesterday. The aspen leaves at Island to-day appear as big as a ninepence suddenly.

May 6. I heard from time to time a new note from my *Rana palustris* in the firkin in my chamber. It was that strong vibratory purr or *prr-r-r-a-a-a*, as if it began with a *p*, lasting two or three seconds and sometimes longer. In the firkin near my bed, it sounded just like a vibrating sliver which struck hard and rapidly against the rail [it] belonged to, — *dry*, like a fine and steady watchman's rattle sounding but [a] little while. I recognized it as a sound I hear along the riverside. It was like the *tut tut tut* more sharply and very rapidly or closely sounded perchance; perhaps even like the tapping of a woodpecker. Yes, quite like it thus close by.

This morning that spawn laid night before last has expanded to three and a half inches in diameter.

P. M. — To Trillium Wood.

It is a muggy and louring afternoon, and I go looking for toad spawn and for frogs. In all cases in which I have noticed frogs coupled this year, — the *sylvatica, halecina,* and *palustris,* — the female has been considerably the largest. The most common frog that I get sight of along the brooks and ditches this afternoon, and indeed for some weeks in similar localities and even in some parts of the river shore, is what I have called the young *R. pipiens,* with commonly a dull-green head and sides of head, sometimes bright green, and back dusky-spotted. Can this be the bullfrog? Is it not the *fontinalis* with less bright green and a white throat? Sometimes it is yellow-throated. I saw lately in the river a full-grown bullfrog, with, *I think*, a white throat.

I see a *Rana sylvatica* by a ditch in Stow's meadow, fifteen rods from the (Trillium) Wood. The *Salix rostrata* staminate flowers are of very peculiar yellow, — a bright, what you might call *yellow* yellow.

A boy brings me to-day an *Attacus Cecropia* moth which has come out of a cocoon in his trunk. It is, I think, the male, a dark brown above, and considerably larger than mine. It must be about seven inches in alar extent.

Minott remembers the *Rana palustris*, or yellow-legged one, as "the one that stinks so," as if that scent were peculiar to it. I suppose it is. He says that the white-legged one (the *halecina*) was preferred for invalids, *i. e.* their legs, as being sweeter. He says that there used to be a great many more bullfrogs than there are now, and what has got them he does not know.

About 9 P. M. I went to the edge of the river to hear the frogs. It was a warm and moist, rather foggy evening, and the air full of the ring of the toad, the peep of the hylodes, and the low *growling* croak or stertoration of the *Rana palustris*. Just there, however, I did not hear much of the toad, but rather from the road, but I heard the steady peeping of innumerable hylodes for a background to the *palustris* snoring, further over the meadow. There was a universal snoring of the *R. palustris* all up and down the river on each side, the very sounds that mine made in my

chamber last night, and probably it began in earnest last evening on the river. It is a hard, dry, unmusical, *fine* watchman's-rattle-like stertoration, swelling to a speedy conclusion, lasting say some four or five seconds usually. The rhythm of it is like that of the toads' ring, but not the sound. This is considerably like that of the tree-toad, when you think of it critically, after all, but is not so musical or sonorous as that even. There is an occasional more articulate, querulous, or rather quivering, alarm note such as I have described (May 2d). Each shore of the river now for its whole length is all alive with this stertorous purring. It is such a sound as I make in my throat when I imitate the growling of wild animals. I have heard a little of it at intervals for a week, in the warmest days, but now at night it [is] universal all along the river. If the note of the *R. halecina*, April 3d, was the first awakening of the river meadows, this is the second, — considering the hylodes and toads less (?) peculiarly of the river meadows. Yet how few distinguished this sound at all, and I know not one who can tell what frog makes it, though it is almost as universal as the breeze itself. The sounds of those three reptiles now fill the air, especially at night. The toads are most regardless of the light, and regard less a cold day than the *R. palustris* does. In the mornings now, I hear no *R. palustris* and no hylodes, but a few toads still, but now, at night, all ring together, the toads ringing through the day, the hylodes beginning in earnest toward night and the *palustris* at evening. I think that the different epochs in the revolution of the seasons

may perhaps be best marked by the notes of reptiles. They express, as it were, the very feelings of the earth or nature. They are perfect thermometers, hygrometers, and barometers.

One of our cherries opens.

I heard a myrtle-bird's[1] *tull-lull* yesterday, and that somebody else heard it four or five days ago.

Many are catching pouts this louring afternoon, in the little meadow by Walden.

The thinker, he who is serene and self-possessed, is the brave, not the desperate soldier. He who can deal with his thoughts as a material, building them into poems in which future generations will delight, he is the man of the greatest and rarest vigor, not sturdy diggers and lusty polygamists. He is the man of energy, in whom subtle and poetic thoughts are bred. Common men can enjoy partially; they can go a-fishing rainy days; they can *read* poems perchance, but they have not the vigor to beget poems. They can enjoy feebly, but they cannot create. Men talk of freedom! How many are free to think? free from fear, from perturbation, from prejudice? Nine hundred and ninety-nine in a thousand are perfect slaves. How many can exercise the highest human faculties? He is the man truly — courageous, wise, ingenious — who can use his thoughts and ecstasies as the material of fair and durable creations. One man shall derive from the fisherman's story more than the fisher has got who tells it. The mass of men do not know how to cultivate the fields they traverse. The mass glean only a scanty pittance

[1] White-throat sparrow.

where the thinker reaps an abundant harvest. What is all your building, if you do not build with thoughts? No exercise implies more real manhood and vigor than joining thought to thought. How few men can tell what they have thought! I hardly know half a dozen who are not too lazy for this. They cannot get over some difficulty, and therefore they are on the long way round. You conquer fate by thought. If you think the fatal thought of men and institutions, you need never pull the trigger. The consequences of thinking inevitably follow. There is no more Herculean task than to think a thought about this life and then get it expressed.

Horticulturalists think that they make flower-gardens, though in their thoughts they are barren and flowerless, but to the poet the earth is a flower-garden wherever he goes, or thinks. Most men can keep a horse or keep up a certain fashionable style of living, but few indeed can keep up great expectations. They justly think very meanly of themselves.

May 7. Plant melons. Hear young bluebirds in the box. Did I not see a bank swallow fly by?

Cousin Charles says that he drove Grandmother over to Weston the 2d of May; on the 3d it snowed and he rode about there in a sleigh; on the 4th and the 5th, when he returned in a chaise to Concord, it was considered dangerous on account of the drifts.

P. M. — To Assabet by Tarbell's.

I see the second amelanchier well out by railroad. How long elsewhere? The wild gooseberry here and there along the edge of river in front of Tarbell's, like our second one, apparently as early as in garden, and will open in a few days.

I see a wood tortoise by the river there, half covered with the old withered leaves. Taking it up, I find that it must have lain perfectly still there for some weeks, for though the grass is all green about it, when I take it up, it leaves just such a bare cavity, in which are seen the compressed white roots of the grass only, as when you take up a stone. This shows how sluggish these creatures are. It is quite lively when I touch it, but I see that it has some time lost the end of its tail, and possibly it has been sick. Yet there was another crawling about within four or five feet. It seems, then, that it will lie just like a stone for weeks immovable in the grass. It lets the season slide. The male yellow-spotted and also wood turtle have very distinctly depressed sternums, but not so the male *Emys picta* that I have noticed. The earliest apple trees begin to leave and to show green veils against the ground and the sky. See already a considerable patch of *Viola pedata* on the dry, bushy bank northeast of Tarbell's.

May 8. P. M. — To stone-heaps.

Mr. Wright of the factory village, with whom I talked yesterday, an old fisherman, remembers the lamprey eels well, which he used to see in the Assabet there, but thinks that there have been none in the river for a dozen years and that the stone-heaps are not made by them. I saw one apparently just formed yesterday. Could find none April 15th. This after-

Vol. X

noon I overhaul two new ones in the river opposite Prescott Barrett's, and get up more than a peck of stones. The nests are quite large and very high, rising to within a foot of the surface where the water is some three feet deep. I cannot detect any ova or young fishes or eels in the heap, but a great many insects, pashas with two tails, and, I think, some little leeches only. The larger stones are a little larger than a hen's egg, but the greater part of the heap is merely a coarse gravel.

I see a great deal of the oat spawn, generally just flatted out, in that long pokelogan by the Assabet Bath-Place. It is over the coarse, weedy (pontederia and yellow lily stubble), and not the grassy bottom, commonly where there is more or less water all summer.

The herb-of-St.-Barbara. Broke off a twig of Prichard's Canada plum in the evening, from which I judge that it may have opened to-day.

May 9. P. M. — To Holden and to Ledum Swamp.

See two *Rana halecina.* They have the green halo, but are plain brown between the spots on the back and not vivid light-green like the one of May 4th.

See in *Ludwigia palustris* ditch on Hubbard's land evidently toad-spawn already hatched, or flatted out. I distinguish the long strings, now straighter than usual and floating thin on the surface. It is less obvious than frog-spawn, and might easily be overlooked on a slimy surface. I can distinguish the little pollywog while yet in the ova by their being quite small and

very black. This makes the fifth kind of frog or toad spawn that I have detected this year.

See, in the Holden Swamp wood, the bird of May 3d. It has sly and inquisitive ways, holding down its head and looking at me at some distance off. It has a distinct white line along the bill and about the eyes, and no yellow there, as is said of the white-eyed vireo, and I am now inclined to think it the *solitary vireo* (?), whose song is not described, and which is considered rare. I should say it had a blue-slate head, and, I note, a distinct yellowish *vent*, which none of the vireos are allowed to have!! The sides of the body are distinctly yellow, but there is none at all on the throat or breast.

Vaccinium Pennsylvanicum, — how long? — by owl-nest tree. The parti-colored warbler is very common and musical there, — my tweezer-bird, — making the *screep screep screep* note. It is an almost incessant singer and a very handsomely marked bird. It frequents the spruce trees, at regular intervals pausing as it flits, hops, and creeps about from limb to limb or up the main stem, and holding up its head, utters its humble notes, like *ah twze twze twze,* or *ah twze twze twze twze.*

I notice very large clams, apparently the *Unio complanatus* (*vide* two specimens in drawer), or common, in West Meadow Brook near the road, one more than four and a half inches long. I have before seen them very large in brooks.

A dandelion perfectly gone to seed, a complete globe, a system in itself.

My *Rana palustris* spawn, laid in house May 5th, in the sun this afternoon swells and rises to the surface in the jar, so that the uppermost ova project slightly above it.

May 10. A rather warm and pleasant day. Going down-town in the morning, I hear the warbling vireo, golden robin, catbird, and summer yellowbird. For some days the *Salix alba* have shown their yellow wreaths here and there, suggesting the coming of the yellowbird, and now they are alive with them.

About 8.30 A. M., I go down the river to Ball's Hill.

As I paddle along, hear the Maryland yellow-throat, the bobolink, the oven-bird, and the yellow-throated vireo.

That early glaucous, sharp-pointed, erect sedge, grass-like, by the riverside is now apparently in prime. Is it the *Carex aquatilis?*

I hear in several places the low dumping notes of awakened bullfrogs, what I call their *pebbly* notes, as if they were cracking pebbles in their mouths; not the plump *dont dont* or *ker dont,* but *kerdle dont dont.* As if they sat round mumbling pebbles. At length, near Ball's Hill, I hear the first regular bullfrog's trump. Some fainter ones far off are very like the looing [*sic*] of cows. This sound, heard low and far off over meadows when the warmer hours have come, grandly inaugurates the summer. I perspire with rowing in my thick coat and wish I had worn a thin one. This trumpeter, marching or leaping in the van of advancing summer, whom I now hear coming on over the green meadows, seems to say, "*Take off your coat, take off your coat, take off your coat!*" He says, "Here comes a gale that I can breathe. This is something like; this is what I call summer." I see three or four of them sitting silent in one warm meadow bay. Evidently their breeding-season now begins. But they are soon silent as yet, and it is only an occasional and transient trump that you hear. That season which is bounded on the north, on the spring side at least, by the trump of the bullfrog. This note is like the first colored petals within the calyx of a flower. It conducts us toward the germ of the flower summer. He knows no winter. I hear in his tone the rumors of summer heats. By this note he reassures the season. Not till the air is of that quality that it can support this sound does he emit it. It requires a certain sonorousness. The van is led by the croaking wood frog and the little peeping hylodes, and at last comes this pursy trumpeter, the air growing more and more genial, and even sultry, as well as sonorous. As soon as Nature is ready for him to play his part, she awakens him with a warmer, perchance a sultry, breath and excites him to sound his trombone. It reminds me at once of tepid waters and of bathing. His trump is to the ear what the yellow lily or spatter-dock is to the eye. He swears by the powers of mud. It is enough for the day to have heard only the first half-trump of an early awakened one from far in some warm meadow bay. It is a certain revelation and anticipation of the livelong summer to come. It gives leave to the corn to grow and to the heavens to thunder and lighten. It gives leave

to the invalid to take the air. Our climate is now as tropical as any. It says, Put out your fires and sit in the fire which the sun has kindled.

I hear from some far meadow bay, across the Great Meadows, the half-sounded trump of a bullfrog this warm morning. It is like the tap of a drum when human legions are mustering. It reminds me that summer is now in earnest mustering her forces, and that ere long I shall see their waving plumes and glancing armor and hear the full bands and steady tread. The bullfrog is earth's trumpeter, at the head of the terrene band. He replies to the sky with answering thunder. I see still five or six ducks, which I scare from the Great Meadows. Some may be going to breed here.

How much expression there is in the *Viola pedata!* I do not know on the whole but it is the handsomest of them all, it is so large and grows in such large masses. Yet I have thought there was a certain shallowness in its expression. Yet it spreads so perfectly open with its face turned upward that you get its whole expression.

P. M. — To Walden.

R. W. E. is sure that he heard a cuckoo to-day. A hair-bird's nest in his yard with one egg.

The northern wild red cherry by Everett's, apparently to-morrow. Hear in various woods the yorrick note of the veery. So the bird seen long since probably was not the veery. A boy found yesterday one or two of the fringed polygala out.

It is remarkable how many new birds have come all at once to-day. The hollow-sounding note of the

oven-bird is heard from the depth of the wood. The warbling vireo cheers the elms with a strain for which they must have pined. The trees, in respect to these new arrivers, have been so many empty music-halls. The oriole is seen darting like a bright flash with clear whistle from one tree-top to another over the street. The very catbird's mew in the copse harmonizes with the bare twigs, as it were shaming them into life and verdure, and soon he mounts upon a tree and is a new creature. Toward night [the] wood thrush ennobles the wood and the world with his strain.

May 11. P. M. — Wishing to get one of the little brook (?) pickerel, of Hubbard's ditches, in the arethusa meadow, I took a line in my pocket, and, baiting with a worm and cutting a pole there, I caught two directly. The biggest was nine inches long and thickly barred transversely with broken dark greenish-brown lines, alternating with golden ones. The back was the dark greenish brown with a pale-brown dorsal line. Both have the vertical dark or black line beneath the eyes and appearing, with the pupil and a mark above, to pass through it. Noticed the same in the *reticulatus* the other day. The head, *i. e.* to the rear of the gills, just one fourth the whole length. From the front of the eye to the end of the lower jaw about one ninth the whole length. In the largest specimen the lower jaw projects one eleventh of an inch beyond the upper. I put the small one, six or seven inches long, in spirits. Opening the larger, I found that it was a female, and that the ova were few and small as yet!!

I also found that apparently its last food was another pickerel two thirds as big as itself, the tail end not yet digested. So it appears that you may dig a ditch in the river meadow, for the sake of peat, and though it have no other connection with brook or river except that it is occasionally overflowed, though only twenty or thirty feet long by three or four wide and one to three deep, you may have pickerel in it nine inches long, at least, and these live in part by devouring one another. Surely it cannot be many pickerel that the bigger ones find to devour there. You might think they would have more sympathy with their fellow-prisoners. This ditch, or these ditches — for I caught one in two ditches — have not been overflowed or connected with the brook or river since the spring of '57, I think, — certainly not any of them since last fall. Yet you may find a few sizable pickerel in such narrow quarters. I have seen them several together in much smaller and shallower ditches there, and they will bury themselves in the mud at your approach. Yet, opening one, you may perchance discover that he has just swallowed his sole surviving companion! You can easily distinguish the transverse bars a rod off, when the fish is in the water. Melvin says they get to weigh about two pounds.[1]

May 12. Chimney swallows.

P. M. — Up Assabet.

On the 8th I noticed a little pickerel recently dead in the river with a slit in its upper lip three quarters of an inch long, apparently where a hook had pulled

[1] It appears to be the *Esox fasciatus. Vide* May 27.

out. There was a white fuzzy swelling at the end of the snout accordingly, and this apparently had killed it.

It rained last night, and now I see the elm seed or samaræ generally fallen or falling. It not only strews the street but the surface of the river, floating off in green patches to plant other shores. The rain evidently hastened its fall. This must be the earliest of trees and shrubs to go to seed or drop its seed. The white maple keys have not fallen. The elm seed floats off down the stream and over the meadows, and thus these trees are found bordering on the stream. By the way, I notice that birches near meadows, where there is an exceedingly gentle inclination, grow in more or less parallel lines a foot or two apart, parallel with the shore, apparently the seed having been dropped there either by a freshet or else lodged in the parallel waving hollows of the snow.

It clears off in the forenoon and promises to be warm in the afternoon, though it at last becomes cool. I see now, as I go forth on the river, the first summer shower coming up in the northwest, a dark and well-defined cloud with rain falling sheaf-like from it, but fortunately moving off northeast along the horizon, or down the river. The peculiarity seems to be that the sky is not generally overcast, but elsewhere, south and northeast, is a fair-weather sky with only innocent cumuli, etc., in it. The thunder-cloud is like the ovary of a perfect flower. Other showers are merely staminiferous or barren. There are twenty barren to one fertile. It is not commonly till thus late in the season that the fertile are seen. In the thunder-cloud, so

Vol. X

distinct and condensed, there is a positive energy, and I notice the first as the bursting of the pollen-cells in the flower of the sky.

Waded through the west-of-rock, or Wheeler, meadow,[1] but I find no frog-spawn there!! I do not even notice tadpoles. Beside that those places are now half full of grass, some pools where was spawn are about dried up (!), as that in Stow's land by railroad. Where are the tadpoles? There is much less water there than a month ago. Where, then, do the *Rana palustris* lay their spawn? I think in the river, because it is there I hear them, but I cannot see any. Perhaps they choose pretty deep water, now it is so warm. Now and for a week I have noticed a few pads with wrinkled edges blown up by the wind. Already the coarse grass along the meadow shore, or where it is wettest, is a luxuriant green, answering in its deep, dark color to the thunder-cloud, — both summer phenomena, — as if it too had some lightning in its bosom.

Some early brakes at the Island woods are a foot high and already spread three or four inches. The *Polygonatum pubescens* is strongly budded. The *Salix lucida* above Assabet Spring will not open for several days. The early form of the cinquefoil is now apparently in prime and very pretty, spotting the banks with its clear bright yellow.

See apparently young toad tadpoles now, — judging from their blackness, — now quite free from the eggs or spawn. If I remember rightly, the toad is colored

[1] And the next day over the large meadow south.

and spotted more like a frog at this season when it is found in the water.

Observed an *Emys insculpta*, as often before, with the rear edge on one side of its shell broken off for a couple of inches, as if nibbled by some animal. Do not foxes or musquash do this? In this case the under jaw was quite nervy.

Found a large water adder by the edge of Farmer's large mud-hole, which abounds with tadpoles and frogs, on which probably it was feeding. It was sunning on the bank and would face me and dart its head toward me when I tried to drive it from the water. It is barred above, but indistinctly when out of water, so that it then appears almost uniformly dark-brown, but in the water broad reddish-brown bars are seen, very distinctly alternating with very dark brown ones. The head was very flat and suddenly broader than the neck behind. Beneath it was whitish and reddish flesh-color. It was about two inches in diameter at the thickest part. They are the biggest and most formidable-looking snakes that we have. The inside of its mouth and throat was pink. It was awful to see it wind along the bottom of the ditch at last, raising wreaths of mud, amid the tadpoles, to which it must be a very sea-serpent. I afterward saw another running under Sam Barrett's grist-mill the same afternoon. He said that he saw a water snake, which he distinguished from a black snake, in an apple tree near by, last year, with a young robin in its mouth, having taken it from the nest. There was a cleft or fork in the tree which enabled it to ascend.

Find the *Viola Muhlenbergii* abundantly out (how long?), in the meadow southwest of Farmer's Spring.

The cinnamon and interrupted ferns are both about two feet high in some places. The first is more uniformly woolly down the stem, the other, though very woolly at top, being partly bare on the stem. The wool of the last is coarser.

George, the carpenter, says that he used to see a great many stone-heaps in the Saco in Bartlett, near the White Mountains, like those in the Assabet, and that there were no lampreys there and they called them "snake-heaps."

Saw some unusually broad chestnut planks, just sawed, at the mill. Barrett said that they came from Lincoln; whereupon I said that I guessed I knew where they came from, judging by their size alone, and it turned out that I was right. I had often gathered the nuts of those very trees and had observed within a year that they were cut down. So it appears that we have come to this, that if I see any peculiarly large chestnuts at the sawmill, I can guess where they came from, even know them in the log. These planks were quite shaky, and the heart had fallen out of one. Barrett said that it was apt to be the case with large chestnut. They use this wood for coffins, instead of black walnut.

May 13. P. M. — To Island.

Uvularia sessilifolia is well out in Island woods, opposite Bath Rock; how long?

The early willows now show great green wands a foot or two long, consisting of curled worm-like catkins three inches long, now in their prime. They present conspicuous masses of green now before the leaves are noticeable, like the fruit of the elm at present. Some have begun to show their down. So this is apparently the next tree (or shrub?) after the elm to shed its seeds.

I wade through the great Lee farm meadow. Many *Emys picta* which I see have perfectly fresh and clear black scales now. I can even see the outlines of the bony plates beneath impressed in the scales. These turtles abound now in the shallow pools in the meadows with grassy or weedy bottoms. I notice on one, part of whose rear marginal plate is broken, two small claw-like horny appendages on the skin, just over the tail.

Viola lanceolata, how long?

As I sat in my boat near the Bath Rock at Island, I saw a red squirrel steal slyly up a red maple, as if he were in search of a bird's nest (though it is early for most), and I thought I would see what he was at. He crept far out on the slender branches and, reaching out his neck, nibbled off the fruit-stems, sometimes bending them within reach with his paw; and then, squatting on the twig, he voraciously devoured the half-grown keys, using his paws to direct them to his mouth, as a nut. Bunch after bunch he plucked and ate, letting many fall, and he made an abundant if not sumptuous feast, the whole tree hanging red with fruit around him. It seemed like a fairy fruit as I sat looking toward the sun and saw the red keys made all glowing and transparent by the sun between me and the body of the squirrel. It was certainly a cheering sight, a cunning red squirrel perched on a slender

twig between you and the sun, feasting on the handsome red maple keys. He nibbled voraciously, as if they were a sweet and luscious fruit to him. What an abundance and variety of food is now ready for him! At length, when the wind suddenly began to blow hard and shake the twig on which he sat, he quickly ran down a dozen feet.

The large globular masses of oat spawn, often on the very top of the old pontederia stems and also on the shooting *Equisetum limosum*, of the same color with the weeds and bottom, look like a seedy fruit which is divested of its rind.

May 14. 5.30 A. M. — Up railroad.

Hear and see the red-eye on an oak. The tail is slightly forked and apparently three quarters of an inch beyond wings; all whitish beneath. Hear and see a redstart. Methinks I did also on the 10th? The rhythm a little way off is *ah, tche tche tche'-ar.*

10 A. M. — To Hill.

A kingbird. Saw a young robin dead. Saw the *Viola palmata*, early form, yesterday; how long? Look at White Avens Shore. See what I call vernal grass in bloom in many places.

The *Salix sericea*, large and small, and the *petiolaris* or loose-catkinned (so far as I know their staminate flowers) are now out of bloom. The *rostrata* not quite done. Some of its catkins now three and a half inches long. The *alba* not quite done. *S. pedicellaris* by railroad about done, and the *Torreyana* done.

Vol. X

Picked up, floating, an *Emys picta*, hatched last year. It is an inch and one twentieth long in the upper shell and agrees with Agassiz's description at that age. Agassiz says he could never obtain a specimen of the *insculpta* only one year old, it is so rarely met with, and young *Emydidæ* are so aquatic. I have seen them frequently.

To-day, for the first time, it appears to me summer-like and a new season. There is a tender green on the meadows and just leafing trees. The blossoms of the cherry, peach, pear, etc., are conspicuous, and the air is suddenly full of fragrance. Houses are seen to stand amid blossoming fruit trees, and the air about them is full of fragrance and the music of birds.

As I go down the railroad at evening, I hear the incessant evening song of the bay-wing from far over the fields. It suggests pleasant associations. Are they not heard chiefly at this season?

The fruit of the early aspen is almost as large — its catkins — as those of the early willow. It will soon be ripe. The very common puffed-up yellow ovaries make quite a show, like some normal fruit; even quite pretty.

I discovered this morning that a large rock three feet in diameter was partially hollow, and broke into it at length with a stone in order to reach some large black crystals which I could partly see. I found that it had been the retreat of a squirrel, and it had left many nuts there. It had entered a small hole bristling with crystals, and there found a chamber or grotto a foot long at least, surrounded on all sides by crystals.

They thus explore and carry their nuts into every crevice, even in the rocks.

Celandine by cemetery. One tells me he saw to-day the arum flower.[1]

May 15. 7.30 A. M. — Ride to the Shawsheen in the northeast of Bedford. Meadow saxifrage well out, many of them, at the tan-yard meadow. The *Equisetum limosum* will apparently (?) open there in two or three days. *Thalictrum dioicum* abundant, apparently in prime; how long? It is a very interesting, graceful, and delicate plant, especially the sterile, with its pretty, commonly purple, petal-like sepals, and its conspicuous long yellow anthers in little bare clusters (?), trembling over the meadow. Yet a frail and rather inobvious plant. It grows on moist, commonly rocky slopes next to meadows at the base of hills, or by rocks in rather swampy woods. The meadows are now full of sedges in bloom, which shed clouds of pollen and cover my shoes with it. The cassia has not come up yet. High blueberries well out.

Hear the evergreen-forest note. Also, in rather low ground in Bedford, a note much like the summer yellowbird's, or between that and the redstart, and see the bird quite near, but hopping quite low on the bushes. It looked like the yellowbird with a bluish-ash top of head. What was it?[2]

The shad-bush in bloom is now conspicuous, its white flags on all sides. Is it not the most massy and

---

[1] I find it *well out* the 16th. See diœcious specimens.
[2] Probably parti-colored warbler. *Vide* [p. 423].

conspicuous of any wild plant now in bloom? I see where the farmer mending his fence has just cut one to make part of the fence, and it is stretched out horizontally, a mass of white bloom.

Measured two apple trees by the road from the middle of Bedford and Fitch's mill. One, which divided at the ground, was thirteen and a half feet in circumference there, around the double trunk; but another, in a field on the opposite side of the road, was the most remarkable tree for size. This tree was exceedingly low for the size of its trunk, and the top rather small. At three feet from the ground it measured ten and a quarter feet in circumference, and immediately above this sent off a branch as big as a large apple tree. It was hollow, and on one side part of the trunk had fallen out. These trees mark the residence of an old settler evidently.

May 16. A. M. — Up Assabet.

Aralia nudicaulis at Island. The leaf-stalks are often eaten off, probably by some quadruped. The flower-buds of the *Cornus florida* are five eighths of an inch in diameter. The *Salix lucida* will hardly bloom within two days. The *S. Torreyana* catkins are so reddish that at a little distance it looks somewhat like the common black cherry now leafing.

A hummingbird yesterday came into the next house and was caught. Flew about our parlor to-day and tasted Sophia's flowers. In some lights you saw none of the colors of its throat. In others, in the shade the throat was a clear bright scarlet, but in the sun it glowed

with splendid metallic, *fiery* reflections about the neck and throat. It uttered from time to time, as it flew, a faint squeaking chirp or chirrup. The hum sounded more hollow when it approached a flower. Its wings fanned the air so forcibly that you felt the cool wind they raised a foot off, and nearer it was very remarkable. Does not this very motion of the wings keep a bird cool in hot weather?

The only indigenous willow I noticed yesterday on the Shawsheen — a mile below Fitch's mill — was the small *sericea*, such as by Assabet white maple. What was that loud but distant note of a bird, apparently in the low land, somewhat like the guinea-hen note, also reminding me a little of the plover about Truro light, but apparently a hawk? Got quite a view down the valley of the Shawsheen below the junction of Vine Brook, northeast, from a hill in the extreme northeast of Bedford.

P. M. — To Uvularia perfoliata at Flint's Pond.

See again the warbler of yesterday. All bright yellow beneath and apparently bluish-slate above, but I do not see it well. Its note, with little variation, is like *twit twit, twit twit, twitter twitter twe.* It must be the parti-colored warbler.[1]

Sat down in the sun in the path through Wright's wood-lot above Goose Pond, but soon, hearing a slight rustling, I looked round and saw a very large black snake about five feet long on the dry leaves, about a rod off. When I moved, it vibrated its tail very rapidly

[1] [Probably the Nashville warbler.]

and smartly, which made quite a loud rustling or rattling sound, reminding me of the rattlesnake, as if many snakes obeyed the same instinct as the rattlesnake when they vibrate their tails. Once I thought I heard a low hiss. It was on the edge of a young wood of oaks and a few white pines from ten to eighteen feet high, the oaks as yet bare of leaves. As I moved toward the snake, I thought it would take refuge in some hole, but it appeared that it was out on a scout and did not know of any place of refuge near. Suddenly, as it moved along, it erected itself half its length, and when I thought it was preparing to strike at me, to my surprise it glided up a slender oak sapling about an inch in diameter at the ground and ten feet high. It ascended this easily and quickly, at first, I think, slanting its body over the lowest twig of the next tree. There were seven little branches for nine feet, averaging about the size of a pipe-stem. It moved up in a somewhat zigzag manner, availing itself of the branches, yet also in part spirally about the main stem. It finds a rest (or hold if necessary) for its neck or forward part of its body, moving crosswise the small twigs, then draws up the rest of its body. From the top of this little oak it passed into the top of a white pine of the same height an inch and a half in diameter at the ground and two feet off; from this into another oak, fifteen feet high and three feet from the pine; from this to another oak, three feet from the last and about the same height; from this to a large oak about four feet off and three or four inches in diameter, in which it was about fourteen feet from the ground; thence through two more oaks, a little lower, at

intervals of four feet, and so into a white pine; and at last into a smaller white pine and thence to the ground. The distance in a straight line from where it left the ground to where it descended was about twenty-five feet, and the greatest height it reached, about fourteen feet. It moved quite deliberately for the most part, choosing its course from tree to tree with great skill, and resting from time to time while it watched me, only my approach compelling it to move again. It surprised me very much to see it cross from tree to tree exactly like a squirrel, where there appeared little or no support for such a body. It would glide down the proper twig, its body resting at intervals of a foot or two, on the smaller side twigs, perchance, and then would easily cross an interval of two feet, sometimes in an ascending, sometimes a descending, direction. If the latter, its weight at last bent the first twig down nearer to the opposite one. It would extend its neck very much, as I could see by the increased width of the scales exposed, till its neck rested across the opposite twig, hold on all the while tightly to some part of the last twig by the very tip of its tail, which was curled round it just like a monkey's. I have hardly seen a squirrel *rest* on such slight twigs as it would rest on in mid-air, only two or three not bigger than a pipe-stem, while its body stretched *clear* a foot at least between two trees. It was not at all like creeping over a coarse basketwork, but suggested long practice and skill, like the rope-dancer's. There were no limbs for it to use comparable for size with its own body, and you hardly noticed the few slight twigs it rested on, as it glided through the air. When its neck rested on the opposite twig, it was, as it were, glued to it. It helped itself over or up them as surely as if it grasped with a hand. There were, no doubt, rigid kinks in its body when they were needed for support. It is a sort of endless hook, and, by its ability to bend its body in every direction, it finds some support on every side. Perhaps the edges of its scales give it a hold also. It is evident that it can take the young birds out of a sapling of any height, and no twigs are so small and pliant as to prevent it. Pendulous sprays would be the most difficult for it, where the twigs are more nearly parallel with the main one, as well as nearly vertical, but even then it might hold on by its tail while its head hung below. I have no doubt that this snake could have reached many of the oriole-nests which I have seen. I noticed that in its anger its rigid neck was very much flattened or compressed vertically. At length it coiled itself upon itself as if to strike, and, I presenting a stick, it struck it smartly and then darted away, running swiftly down the hill toward the pond.

Yellow butterflies. Nabalus leaves are already up and coming up in the wood-paths. Also the radical leaves of one variety of *Solidago arguta*, and apparently of *S. altissima*, are conspicuously up.

A golden-crowned thrush hops quite near. It is quite small, about the size of the creeper, with the upper part of its breast thickly and distinctly pencilled with black, a tawny head; and utters now only a sharp cluck for a *chip*. See and hear a redstart, the rhythm of whose strain is *tse'-tse, tse'-tse, tse'*, emphasizing the last syllable of all and not ending with the common *tsear*. Hear the night-warbler.

The *Uvularia perfoliata*, which did not show itself at all on the 3d, is now conspicuous, and one is open but will not shed pollen before to-morrow. It has shot up about ten inches in one case and bloomed within thirteen days!!

Ranunculus repens at Brister's Spring; how long? Was that *R. repens* at the Everett Spring on the 3d?[1] The whip-poor-will heard.

E. Hoar detected the other day two ovaries under one scale of a *Salix rostrata*, and, under another, a stamen and another stamen converted into an ovary.

May 17. Louring and more or less rainy.
P. M. — To Ledum Swamp.

Near Bæomyces Bank, I see the *Salix humilis* showing its down or cotton, and also the *S. tristis*.[2] Probably the last is wholly out of bloom some time. These, then, have ripe seed before the white maple.

It rains gently from time to time as I walk, but I see a farmer with his boys, John Hosmer, still working in the rain, bent on finishing his planting. He is slowly getting a soaking, quietly dropping manure in the furrows. This rain is good for thought. It is especially agreeable to me as I enter the wood and hear the soothing dripping on the leaves. It domiciliates me in nature. The woods are the more like a house for the rain; the few slight noises sound more hollow in them; the birds hop nearer; the very trees seem still and pensive. The clouds are but

[1] Yes.
[2] As I see the last still in bloom on the 20th on a north side-hill, *perhaps* this was a very small *humilis?*

Vol. X

a higher roof. The clouds and rain confine me to near objects, the surface of the earth and the trees. On the first holdings up in the intervals of the rain, the chewink is heard again, and the huckleberry-bird, and the evergreen-forest note, etc. I am coming in sight of the Charles Miles house. What a pleasant sandy road, soaking up the rain, that from the woods to the Miles house! The house becomes a controlling feature in the landscape when there is but one or two in sight.

The red maple tops ten days ago looked like red paint scaling off, when seen against houses. Now they have acquired a browner red. The *Populus grandidentata* now shows large, silvery, downy, but still folded, leafets.

You are more than paid for a wet coat and feet, not only by the exhilaration that the fertile moist air imparts, but by the increased fragrance and more gem-like character of expanding buds and leafets in the rain. All vegetation is now fuller of life and expression, somewhat like lichens in wet weather, and the grass. Buds are set in syrup or amber.

Measured the large apple tree in front of the Charles Miles house. It is nine feet and ten inches in circumference at two and a half feet from the ground, the smallest place below the branches, which are now four, — once five, one being cut, — starting at about five feet from the ground, and each as big as a good-sized modern tree. The top is large. The trunk looks healthy and is scarcely larger at the ground than where measured. It is large for an oak, a sturdy-looking tree, reminding one of the portly bodies of some of our grandfathers. It is not grafted. Once stood by the fence.

While I was measuring the tree, Puffer came along, and I had a long talk with him, standing under the tree in the cool sprinkling rain till we shivered. He said that he had seen pout-spawn attached to the under side of the white lily pads!! He thought he knew it from having seen it in their bodies. He thought that the pickerel-spawn was dropped in deep water and was devoured by pouts and eels. Wondered where eels bred, and how, for he never detected any spawn in them. Had been told (like Witherell) that they gendered into, *i. e.* copulated with, the clam. Told of a winter some fifteen years ago when there was a freshet in February, and the snapping turtles thought it was spring and came up with it on to the meadows; but it froze, and the ice settled on them and killed them when the water went down, and — they were found dead in great numbers in the spring, — one that must have weighed one hundred pounds. Had seen pickerel that had been frozen four or five hours brought to life in water. Said that the black snake laid eight or ten eggs in a field. Once killed a very large water adder, and counted over sixty little snakes in it an inch or two long, and that was not all. Once he was going along, saw a water adder and heard a low sound which it made with its mouth, and he saw as many as twenty-five little snakes run into its mouth. Says the foxes eat the *Emys picta*, which I believe he called grass turtles. He had seen where they had opened them. But they could not get at the box turtle. Found some young stake-drivers as he was mowing.

When the hummingbird flew about the room yesterday, his body and tail hung in a singular manner between the wings, swinging back and forth with a sort of oscillating motion, not hanging directly down, but yet pulsating or teetering up and down.

I see a chewink flit low across the road with its peculiar flirting, undulating motion.

I thought yesterday that the view of the mountains from the bare hill on the Lincoln side of Flint's Pond was very grand. Surely they do not look so grand anywhere within twenty miles of them. And I reflected what kind of life it must be that is lived always in sight of them. I looked round at some windows in the middle of Lincoln and considered that such was the privilege of the inhabitants of these chambers; but their blinds were closed, and I have but little doubt that they are *blind* to the beauty and sublimity of this prospect. I doubt if in the landscape there can be anything finer than a distant mountain-range. They are a constant elevating influence.

Ranunculus acris, apparently in a day or two. Rhodora at Clamshell well out.

Just after hearing my night-warbler I see two birds on a tree. The one which I examined — as well as I could without a glass — had a white throat with a white spot on his wings, was dark above and moved from time to time like a creeper, and it was about the creeper's size.[1] The other bird, which I did not examine particularly, was a little larger and more tawny.[2]

It is remarkable how little way most men get in their

[1] The plate of *Sylvia Canadensis* in New York Reports has since reminded me of this.
[2] Perhaps golden-crowned thrush.

account of the mysteries of nature. Puffer, after describing the habits of a snake or turtle, — some peculiarity which struck him in its behavior, — would say with a remarkable air as if he were communicating or suggesting something, possibly explaining something, "Now I take it *that* is Nature; Nature did that."

May 18. Set an arbor-vitæ hedge fifteen inches east of our line; about twenty inches high.

May 19. A. M. — Surveying (by the eye) for Warner the meadow surveyed for John Hosmer in June, '56.

The black currant near southwest corner of his Saw Mill field (*Ribes floridum*) perfectly out; how long?

P. M. — To Everett Spring.

There appears to be quite a variety in the colors of the *Viola cucullata*. Some dark-blue, if not lilac (?), some with a very dark blue centre and whitish circumference, others dark-blue within and dark without, others all very pale blue. *Stellaria borealis* well out, apparently several days. What I called the *Ranunculus bulbosus* there May 3d proves to be the *R. repens*. It would appear then to be the earliest ranunculus. It is a dense bed of yellow now. I am struck by the light spot in the sinuses of the leaves. The *Equisetum sylvaticum* there is now of a reddish cast.

R. W. E. says that Pratt found yesterday out the trientalis, *Trillium cernuum*, and *Smilacina bifolia*.

Four rods plus south of the cross-fence over Everett's hill, on the west slope, I find the *Ranunculus aborti-*

vus, two plants open only; but will not shed pollen till to-morrow. A rod or two further the *Equisetum hyemale*, apparently a little past bloom, or effete, all the heads open.

Looking with my glass into the Gourgas pond-hole, I see three or four buck-bean blossoms. Two birds about the size and of the appearance of a pigeon or turtle dove start up with a loud alarm note from the shallow muddy flat there, — with a harsh shrill cry, *phil phil phil* or the like. At first I could not guess what they were, but since concluded that they were the larger yellow-legs. Could this bird have made the sound heard on the 15th? There remained feeding on the mud along the water's edge two peetweet-like birds, but apparently larger and less teetering. I thought they were *T. solitarius*.

Heard the night-warbler *begin* his strain just like an oven-bird! I have noticed that when it drops down into the woods it darts suddenly *one side* to a perch when low.

May 20. P. M. — Up Assabet.

A cloudy afternoon, with a cool east wind, producing a mist. Hundreds of swallows are now skimming close over the river, at its broadest part, where it is shallow and runs the swiftest, just below the Island, for a distance of twenty rods. There are bank, barn, cliff, and chimney swallows, all mingled together and continually scaling back and forth, — a very lively sight. They keep descending or stooping to within a few inches of the water on a curving wing,

without quite touching it, and I suppose are attracted by some small insects which hover close over it. They also stoop low about me as I stand on the flat island there, but I do not perceive the insects. They rarely rise more than five feet above the surface, and a general twittering adds to the impression of sociability. The principal note is the low grating sound of the bank swallow, and I hear the *vit vit* of the barn swallow. The cliff swallow, then, is here. Are the insects in any measure confined to that part of the river? Or are they congregated for the sake of society? I have also in other years noticed them over another swift place, at Hubbard's Bath, and also, when they first come, in smaller numbers, over the still and smooth water under the lee of the Island wood. They are thick as the gnats which perhaps they catch. Swallows are more confident and fly nearer to man than most birds. It may be because they are more protected by the sentiment and superstitions of men.

The season is more backward on account of the cloudy and rainy weather of the last four or five days and some preceding. The *Polygonatum pubescens*, not quite. The red oak is not out.

Hear a quail whistle.

I notice that the sugar maple opposite Barrett's does not bloom this year, nor does the canoe birch by the Hemlocks bear sterile catkins. Perhaps they more or less respect the alternate years.

3.30 P. M. — To Brister's Hill.

Going along the deep valley in the woods, just before entering the part called Laurel Glen, I heard a noise, and saw a fox running off along the shrubby side-hill. It looked like a rather small dirty-brown fox, and very clumsy, running much like a wood-chuck. It had a dirty or dark brown tail, with very little white to the tip. A few steps further I came upon the remains of a woodchuck, yet warm, which it had been eating. Head, legs, and tail, all remained, united by the skin, but the bowels and a good part of the flesh were eaten. This was evidently a young fox, say three quarters grown, or perhaps less, and appeared as full as a tick. There was a fox-hole within three rods, with a very large sand-heap, several cartloads, before it, much trodden. Hearing a bird of which I was in search, I turned to examine it, when I heard a bark behind me, and, looking round, saw an old fox on the brow of the hill on the west side of the valley, amid the bushes, about ten rods off, looking down at me. At first it was a short, puppy-like bark, but afterward it began to bark on a higher key and more prolonged, very unlike a dog, a very ragged half-screaming *bur-ar-r-r*. I proceeded along the valley half a dozen rods after a little delay (the fox being gone), and then looked round to see if it returned to the woodchuck. I then saw a full-grown fox, perhaps the same as the last, cross the valley through the thin low wood fifteen or twenty rods behind me, but from east to west, pausing and looking at me anxiously from time to time. It was rather light tawny (not fox-colored) with dusky-brown bars, and looked very large, wolf-like. The full-grown fox stood much higher on its legs and was longer, but

the body was apparently not much heavier than that of the young. Going a little further, I came to another hole, and ten feet off was a space of a dozen square feet amid some little oaks, worn quite bare and smooth, apparently by the playing of the foxes, and the ground close around a large stump about a rod from the hole was worn bare and hard, and all the bark and much of the rotten wood was pawed or gnawed off lately. They had pawed a deep channel about one and in between the roots, perhaps for insects. There lay the remains of another woodchuck, now dry, the head, skin, and legs being left, and also part of the skin of a third, and the bones of another animal, and some partridge feathers. The old foxes had kept their larder well supplied. Within a rod was another hole, apparently a back door, having no heap of sand, and five or six rods off another in the side of the hill with a small sand-heap, and, as far down the valley, another with a large sand-heap and a back door with none. There was a well-beaten path from the one on the side-hill five or six rods long to one in the valley, and there was much blackish dung about the holes and stump and the path. By the hole furthest down the valley was another stump, which had been gnawed (?) very much and trampled and pawed about like the other. I suppose the young foxes play there. There were half a dozen holes or more, and what with the skulls and feathers and skin and bones about, I was reminded of Golgotha. These holes were some of them very large and conspicuous, a foot wide vertically, by eight or ten inches, going into the side-hill with a curving stoop,

and there was commonly a very large heap of sand before them, trodden smooth. It was a sprout-land valley, cut off but a year or two since.

As I stood by the last hole, I heard the old fox bark, and saw her (?) near the brow of the hill on the north-west, amid the bushes, restless and anxious, overlook-ing me a dozen or fourteen rods off. I was, on doubt, by the hole in which the young were. She uttered at very short intervals a prolonged, shrill, screeching kind of bark, beginning lower and rising to a very high key, lasting two seconds; a very broken and ragged sound, more like the scream of a large and angry bird than the bark of a dog, trilled like a piece of vibrating metal at the end. It moved restlessly back and forth, or approached nearer, and stood or sat on its haunches like a dog with its tail laid out in a curve on one side, and when it barked it laid its ears flat back and stretched its nose forward. Sometimes it uttered a short, puppy-like, snappish bark. It was not fox-colored now, but a very light tawny or wolf-color, dark-brown or dusky beneath in a broad line from its throat; its legs the same, with a broad dusky perpendicular band on its haunches and similar ones on its tail, and a small whitish spot on each side of its mouth. There it sat like a chief-tain on his hills, looking, methought, as big as a prairie wolf, and shaggy like it, anxious and even fierce, as I peered through my glass. I noticed, when it with-drew, — I too withdrawing in the opposite direction, — that as it had descended the hill a little way and wanted to go off over the pinnacle without my seeing which way it went, it ran one side about ten feet, till it was behind

a small white pine, then turned at a right angle and ascended the hill directly, with the pine between us. The sight of it suggested that two or three might at-tack a man. The note was a shrill, vibrating scream or cry; could easily be heard a quarter of a mile. How many woodchucks, rabbits, partridges, etc., etc., they must kill, and yet how few of them are seen! A very wolfish color. It must have been a large fox, and, if it is true that the old are white on the sides of the face, an old one. They evidently used more than a half dozen holes within fifteen rods. I withdrew the sooner for fear by his barking he would be betrayed to some dog or gunner.

It was a very wild sight to see the wolf-like parent circling about me in the thin wood, from time to time pausing to look and bark at me. This appears to be nearest to the cross fox of Audubon, and is considered a variety of the red by him and most others, not white beneath as the red fox of Harlan. Emmons says of the red fox, "In the spring the color appears to fade," and that some are "pale yellow," but does not de-scribe minutely. This was probably a female, for Bell says of the English fox that the female "loses all her timidity and shyness when suckling her young;" also that they are a year and a half in attaining their full size.[1]

Hear the pe-pe. See tanagers, male and female, in

[1] I find afterward three or four more fox-holes near by, and see where they have sat on a large upturned stump, which had heaved up earth with it. Many large pieces of woodchuck's skin about these holes. They leave the head and feet. A scent of carrion about the holes.

the top of a pine, one red, other yellow, from below. We have got to these high colors among birds.

Saw in the street a young cat owl, one of two which Skinner killed in Walden Woods yesterday. It was almost ready to fly, at least two and a half feet in alar extent; tawny with many black bars, and darker on wings. Holmes, in Patent Office Report, says they "pair early in February." So I visited the nest. It was in a large white pine close on the north side of the path, some ten rods west of the old Stratton cellar in the woods. This is the largest pine thereabouts, and the nest is some thirty-five feet high on two limbs close to the main stem, and, according to Skinner, was not much more than a foot across, made of small sticks, nearly flat, "without fine stuff!" There were but two young. This is a path which somebody travels every half-day, at least, and only a stone's throw from the great road. There were many white droppings about and large rejected pellets containing the vertebræ and hair of a skunk. As I stood there, I heard the crows making a great noise some thirty or forty rods off, and immediately suspected that they were pestering one of the old owls, which Skinner had not seen. It proved so, for, as I approached, the owl sailed away from amidst a white pine top, with the crows in full pursuit, and he looked very large, stately, and heavy, like a seventy-four among schooners. I soon knew by the loud cawing of the crows that he had alighted again some forty rods off, and there again I found him perched high on a white pine, the large tawny fellow with black dashes and large erect horns. Away he goes again, and the crows after him.

Vol. X

May 21. P. M. — To Boulder Field.

Horse-chestnut in bloom. *Actæa spicata* var. *rubra* will bloom, apparently, in four or five days. It is now fifteen inches high. Lilac in bloom. Pratt shows me what I take to be *Genista tinctoria* (not budded) from the Boulder Field. It has leafed; when? Also a ranunculus from his land, — which has been out how long? — which is very near to *R. repens*, but has small flowers, petals less than the calyx, and leaves, methinks, more divided, but I did not see it open. It may be a variety of *repens*.[1]

His daughter has found in bloom: huckleberry on the 19th; *Viola pubescens*, 16th; *Geranium maculatum*, 18th. I notice that the old indigo-bird path behind Pratt's is for some distance distinctly defined by young birches, three or four feet high, which are now clothed with tender leaves before the young oaks, etc., on each side. They are especially thick in the ruts, while there are but few here and there in the sprout-land generally. I suspect that the seed was blown and lodged there in the winter.

E. Hoar saw *Silene Pennsylvanica* out in Lincoln to-day, in a warm cleft of a rock; also *Cerasus pumila* between here and Newton.

May 22. Saturday. Ed. Emerson brings me the egg of a hawk, dirty bluish-white,[2] just found, with three other eggs not much developed, in a nest on the ground. Probably a hen-harrier's.

[1] When I look May 29th, the flower open is of usual size and true *R. repens*.   [2] *Vide* May 30th.

P. M. — By cars to Worcester, on way to New York.

We have had much rainy weather for about a week, and it has just cleared up. I notice, as I glide along, that the sun coming out shines brightly on smooth waters, ponds, and flooded meadows raised by the rain, and is reflected from the new lily pads, which most now first generally notice, spread out on the surface, the foul weather having prevented our observing their growth. Something like this annually occurs. After this May storm the sun bursts forth and is reflected brightly in some placid hour from the new leaves of the lily spread out on the surface in the ponds and pools raised [by] the rain, and we seem to have taken a long stride into summer. So was it also in a former geological age, when water and water-plants prevailed and before man was here to behold them. The sun was then reflected from the lily pad after the May storm as brightly as now.

May 23. In Worcester.

5 A. M. — Walk with Blake, Brown, and Rogers to Quinsigamond Pond, carrying our breakfast. Paddled up the pond northerly three quarters of a mile from the bridge, and lunched in Shrewsbury on the east side. See some quite fresh frog-spawn of the dark kind, like the *Rana palustris*, for instance. Cross and ascend Wigwam Hill. Krigia and comandra out there. Brown thrasher's nest on ground, under a small tree, with four eggs.

Found in the water, eight or ten inches deep, just behind the Lake House, a nasturtium not quite open, which I think must be a variety of the horse-radish (*N. Armoracia*). Yet *such* a variety is not described by

Gray, for the immersed stem leaves were all narrowly dissected and pinnate (*vide* pressed specimen), and I saw similar ones in the streets in Worcester in dry ground. The lowest portion — for I had not the root — had the true horse-radish taste. It seemed to be the result of its growing at some time in water. Has the *N. lacustre* the common horse-radish taste?

A little south of the Boston and Worcester turnpike, and six rods from the west side of the pond, I saw a chestnut about eighteen inches in diameter which was struck by lightning in the night some ten days ago. There was left standing only a splinter of the stump, some seven feet high, with the main limbs fallen upon and around it. The bark and thin slivers or strips of the wood had been cast to a dozen rods around in all directions, the ground being strewn with them, and some rested on the top of an adjacent wood[-pile]. Also one or two large limbs were thrown to a distance. But what was most remarkable and peculiar, there was a trench somewhat more than two rods long, five feet wide at top, and more than two feet deep, leading perfectly straight from the foot of the tree toward the pond, large old roots being burst through, in the gravelly soil, and masses of the earth cast a rod each way, yet most of the dirt formed a bank to the trench. It would have taken an Irishman at least three hours to have dug this. Then, after an interval of three or four rods, where the ground was a little higher, the trench reappeared at the water's edge, though quite short there, exactly in the line of the first ditch continued, and there some two cartloads of gravelly soil were thrown out, and the water stood in it.

I counted in all nine places within eight or ten rods along the water's edge, or six or eight rods from the tree, where it had made a short furrow in the ground; and in some cases there were slight furrows here and there between these and the tree, as if the lightning had diverged in rays from the base of the tree, perhaps (?) at first along the roots to the pond. Did it pass *through* the ground when it did not break the surface? The bark was not so much stripped off as I have seen, but the wood was finely splintered.

May 24. Monday. To New York by railroad.

All through Connecticut and New York the white involucres of the cornel (*C. florida*), recently expanded, some of them reddish or rosaceous, are now conspicuous. It is not quite expanded in Concord. It is the most showy indigenous tree now open. (One plant at Staten Island on the 25th had but just begun to *flower, i. e.* the true flowers to open.) After entering the State of New York I observed, now fully in bloom, what I call the *Viburnum prunifolium*, looking very like our *V. Lentago* in flower at a little distance. It is thorny, as they told me at Staten Island, and the same I dealt with at Perth Amboy, and is insufficiently described. It grows on higher and drier ground than our *V. nudum*, but its fruit, which is called "nanny berries," resembles that rather than the *V. Lentago*. It shows now rich, dense, rounded masses of white flowers; i. e., the surface of the bushes makes the impression of regular curves or convex masses of bloom, bearing a large proportion to the green leaves. The pink azalea, too, not yet out at home, is

generally out, with the cornel. (I see it also next day at Staten Island.)

I saw a musquash swimming across a pool, I think after entering upon Manhattan Island!

In the evening, looked at the aquarium at Barnum's. The glass boxes with nothing but water (labelled fresh or salt) and pebbles seemed sufficiently interesting. There were breams only two inches long, probably hatched only last year. The sea-anemones were new and interesting to me. The ferns, etc., under glass a fine parlor ornament.

May 25. Visited the Egyptian Museum.
The chariot wheel might have been picked out of a ditch in Carlisle, and the infant's shoe have been found with it.

P. M. — To Staten Island.
See an abundance of *Ranunculus abortivus* in the wood-path behind Mr. E.'s house, going to seed and in bloom. The branches are fine and spreading, about eight or ten inches high. (*Vide* pressed plants.) Also some *R. recurvatus;* and, well out, what appears to be *Thaspium trifoliatum* (?) in flower, in path to house. (*Vide* pressed.) Potatoes just hoed; ours not fairly up.

May 26. 3 P. M. — Return to Boston.

May 27. At Boston, Cambridge, and Concord.
De Kay describes the *Esox fasciatus*, which is apparently mine of May 11th. As I count, the rays are the same in number, *viz.* "P. 13, V. 9, D. 14, A. 13, C. 20."

He says it is from six to eight inches long and abundant in New York; among other things is distinguished by "a muddy tinge of the roundish pectoral, abdominal, and ventral fins; and by a broad concave or lunated tail." I do not observe the peculiarity in the tail in mine, now it is in spirits.

Ed. Emerson shows me an egg of a bittern (*Ardea minor*) from a nest in the midst of the Great Meadows, which four boys found, scaring up the bird, last Monday, the 24th. It was about a foot wide on the top of a tussock, where the water around was about one foot deep. I will measure the egg.[1] They were a little developed. Also an egg of a turtle dove, one of two in a nest in a pitch pine, about six feet from the ground, in Sleepy Hollow Cemetery, by the side of a frequented walk, on a fork on a nearly horizontal limb. The egg is milk-white, elliptical, one and three sixteenths inches long by seven eighths wide.

May 28. I get the nest of the turtle dove above named, it being deserted and no egg left. It appears to have been built on the foundation of an old robin's nest and consists of a loose wisp of straw and pinweed, the seedy ends projecting, ten inches long, laid across the mud foundation of the robin's nest, with a very slight depression. Very loose and coarse material is artificially disposed, without any lining or architecture. It was close to a frequented path of the cemetery and within reach of the hand.

[1] It is clay-colored, one and seven eighths inches long by one and nine sixteenths, about the same size at each end.

Hear the wood pewee.
P. M. — By boat to Great Meadows to look for the bittern's nest.

The *Cornus florida* involucres are partly expanded, but not yet very showy. *Salix nigra* apparently one day in one place. The *Salix pedicellaris*, which abounds in the Great Meadows, is a peculiar and rather interesting willow, some fifteen inches high and scarcely rising above the grass even now. With its expanded reddish ovaries, it looks like the choke-berry in bud at a little distance. The *Ranunculus Purshii* is now abundant and conspicuous in river.

I see common in these meadows what appears to be that coarse grass growing in circles, light or yellowish green, with dense wool-grass-like heads and almost black involucres, just begun to bloom. Is it the *Scirpus sylvaticus* var. *atrovirens?* (*Vide* pressed.) As I look far over the meadow, which is very wet, — often a foot of water amid the grass, — I see this yellowish green interspersed with irregular dark-green patches where it is wettest, just like the shadow of a cloud, — and mistook it for that at first. *That* was a dark-green and fine kind of sedge. These various shades of grass remind me of June, now close at hand. From time to time I hear the sound of the bittern, concealed in the grass, indefinitely far or near, and can only guess at the direction, not the distance. I fail to find the nest.

I come, in the midst of the meadow, on two of the *Emys meleagris*, much larger than I have found before. Perhaps they are male and female, the one's sternum being decidedly depressed an eighth of an inch, the other's not at all. They are just out of the water, partly concealed by some withered grass, and hiss loudly and run out their long necks very far and struggle a good deal when caught. They continue to scratch my hand in their efforts to escape as I carry them, more than other turtles do. The dorsal shield of each is just seven inches long; the sternum of what appears to be the female is about an eighth inch shorter, of the male near a quarter of an inch longer, yet in both the projection of the sternum is chiefly forward. Breadth of shell in the male four and seven eighths, of female four and a half, in middle, but the female widens a little behind. Height of each about two and three quarters inches. The smoothish dark-brown shells, high, regularly rounded, are very thickly but not conspicuously spotted (unless in water) with small oval or elongated yellow spots, as many as fifty or sixty to a scale, and more or less raying from the origin of the scale, becoming larger and horn-colored on the marginal scales especially of *one*. The thickly and evenly distributed yellow marks of the head and neck correspond to those of the shell pretty well. They are high-backed turtles. The sternum is horn-color, with a large dark or blackish spot occupying a third or more of the rear outer angle of each scale. The throat is clear light-yellow and much and frequently exposed. Tail, tapering and sharp. The claws are quite sharp and perfect. One closes its forward valve to within an eighth of an inch, but the posterior not so much, and evidently they are not inclined to shut up close, if indeed they can at this season, or at all. The sternum

Vol. X

of the male, notwithstanding the depression, curves upward at each extremity much more than the female's. They run out their heads remarkably far and have quite a harmless and helpless expression, yet, from the visible length of neck, the more snake-like. About the size of the wood tortoise. Very regularly and smoothly rounded shells. Voided many fragments of common snail-shells and some insect exuviæ.

Hear for a long time, as I sit under a willow, a summer yellowbird sing, without knowing what it is. It is a rich and varied singer with but few notes to remind me of its common one, continually hopping about.

See already one or two (?) white maple keys on the water. Saw the mouse-ear going to seed in Worcester the 23d. The red actæa is fully expanded and probably has been open two or three days, but there will be no pollen till to-morrow. What kind of cherry tree is that, now rather past prime, wild-red-cherry-like, if not it, between the actæa and river near wall? Some ten inches in diameter. Hear the night[hawk?] and see a bat to-night. The earliest cinnamon fern, apparently not long.

E. Hoar finds the *Eriophorum vaginatum* at Ledum Swamp, with lead-colored scales; how long?

May 29. P. M. — To Bateman's Pond *via* Pratt's.
Buttonwood, one tree, not for two or three days. *Rubus triflorus*, well out, at Calla Swamp, how long? Calla apparently in two or three, or three or four days, the very earliest. *Arethusa bulbosa*, well out. *Cornus*

Canadensis blooms apparently with *C. florida;* not quite yet. I mistook dense groves of little barberries in the droppings of cows in the Boulder Field for apple trees at first. So the cows eat barberries, and help disperse or disseminate them exactly as they do the apple! That helps account for the spread of the barberry, then. See the genista, winter-killed at top, some seven or eight rods north of the southernmost large boulder in the Boulder Field. Cannot find any large corydalis plants where it has been very plenty. A few of the *Cornus florida* buds by the pond have escaped after all.

Farmer describes an animal which he saw lately near Bateman's Pond, which he thought would weigh fifty or sixty pounds, color of a she fox at this season, low but very long, and ran somewhat like a woodchuck. I think it must have been an otter, though they are described as dark glossy-brown.

May 30. Hear of lady's-slipper seen the 23d; how long? I saw the *Nuphar advena* above water and yellow in Shrewsbury the 23d.
P. M. — To hen-harrier's nest and to Ledum Swamp.
Edward Emerson shows me the nest which he and another discovered. It is in the midst of the low wood, sometimes inundated, just southwest of Hubbard's Bath, the island of wood in the meadow. The hawk rises when we approach and circles about over the wood, uttering a note singularly like the common one of the flicker. The nest is in a more bushy or open place in this low wood, and consists of a large mass of

sedge and stubble with a very few small twigs, as it were accidentally intermingled. It is about twenty inches in diameter and remarkably flat, the slight depression in the middle not exceeding three quarters of an inch. The whole opening amid the low bushes is not more than two feet in diameter. The thickness of it raises the surface about four inches above the ground. The inner and upper part is uniformly rather fine and pale-brown sedge. There are two dirty, or rather dirtied, white eggs left (of four that were), one of them one and seven tenths inches long, and not "spherical," as Brewer says, but broad in proportion to length.[1]

Ledum, one flower out, but perhaps if Pratt had not plucked some last Sunday it might have bloomed here yesterday? It is decidedly leafing also. *Andromeda Polifolia* by the ditch well out, how long? I perceive the turpentine scent of the ledum in the air as I walk through it.

As I stand by the riverside some time after sundown, I see a light white mist rising here and there in wisps from the meadow, far and near, — less visible within a foot of me, — to the height of three or four or ten feet. It does not rise generally and evenly from every part of the meadow, but, as yet, over certain spots only, where there is some warm breath of the meadow turned into cloud.

May 31. A. M. — To Island.

[1] Another is one and seven eighths inches long by one and a half inches. *Vide* the last (which was addled).

Choke-cherry, a day or two. *Cornus florida*, not yet for two or three days. I saw some in Connecticut with involucres much more rosaceous than ours. A yellowbird's nest of that grayish milkweed fibre, one egg, in alder by wall west of Indian burying(?)-ground.

P. M. — To Laurel Glen.

I see, running along on the flat side of a railroad rail on the causeway, a wild mouse with an exceedingly long tail. Perhaps it would be called the long-tailed meadow mouse. It has no white, only the feet are light flesh-color; but it is uniformly brown as far as I can see, — for it rests a long time on the rail within a rod, — but when I look at it from behind in the sun it is a very tawny almost golden brown, quite handsome. It finally runs, with a slight hop, — the tarsus of the hind legs being very long while the fore legs are short and its head accordingly low, — down the bank to the meadow.

I saw on the 29th *white Viola pedata*, and to-day a white *V. cucullata*.

There were severe frosts on the nights of the 28th and 29th, and now I see the hickories turned quite black, and in low ground the white oak shoots, though they do not show black in drying. Also many ferns are withered and black and some *Prinos lævigatus* tips, etc.

I find a chewink's nest with four eggs (fresh) on the side-hill at Jarvis's wood-lot, twenty feet below woodchuck's hole at canoe birch. The nest is first of withered leaves, then stubble, thickly lined with withered grass

XI

JUNE, 1858

(ÆT. 40)

June 2. 8.30 A. M. — Start for Monadnock.

Between Shirley Village and Lunenburg, I notice, in a meadow on the right hand, close to the railroad, the *Kalmia glauca* in bloom, as we are whirled past. The conductor says that he has it growing in his garden. Blake joins me at Fitchburg. Between Fitchburg and Troy saw an abundance of wild red cherry, now apparently in prime, in full bloom, especially in burnt lands and on hillsides, a small but cheerful lively white bloom.

Arrived at Troy Station at 11.5 and shouldered our knapsacks, steering northeast to the mountain, some four miles off, — its top. It is a pleasant hilly road, leading past a few farmhouses, where you already begin to snuff the mountain, or at least up-country, air. By the roadside I plucked, now apparently in prime, the *Ribes Cynosbati*, rather downy leaved, and, near by, the same with smooth berries. I noticed, too, the *Salix lucida*, by the roadside there on high land; the *S. rostrata*, etc., were common.

Almost without interruption we had the mountain in sight before us, — its sublime gray mass — that antique, brownish-gray, Ararat color. Probably these crests of the earth are for the most part of one color in all lands,

and partly sheltered by dead leaves, shoved [?] up a huckleberry bush.

There was a slight sea-turn, the wind coming cool and easterly this morning, which at first I mistook for the newly leafing deciduous trees investing the evergreens, which is a kind of sea-turn in harmony with the other. I remember that the stage-drivers riding back and forth daily from Concord to Boston and becoming weather-wise perforce, often meeting the sea-breeze on its way into the country, were wont to show their weather wisdom by telling anxious travellers that it was nothing but a sea-turn.

At 5 P. M., go to see a gray squirrel's nest in the oak at the Island point. It is about fifteen feet from the ground, — the entrance, — where a limb has been broken off, and the tree is hollow above and below. One young one darted past downward under my face, with the speed of a bird. There is much short brown dung about, and a smell of urine, and the twigs around have been gnawed.

Does not the voice of the toad along the river sound differently now from what it did a month ago? I think it is much less sonorous and ringing, a more croaking and inquisitive or *qui vive* sound. Is it not less prolonged also?

that gray color of antiquity, which nature loves; color of unpainted wood, weather-stain, time-stain; not glaring nor gaudy; the color of all roofs, the color of things that endure, and the color that wears well; color of Egyptian ruins, of mummies and all antiquity; baked in the sun, done brown. Methought I saw the same color with which Ararat and Caucasus and all earth's brows are stained, which was mixed in antiquity and receives a new coat every century; not scarlet, like the crest of the bragging cock, but that hard, enduring gray; a terrene sky-color; solidified air with a tinge of earth.[1]

The red elder was in full bloom by the road, apparently in prime.

We left the road at a schoolhouse, and, crossing a meadow, began to ascend gently through very rocky pastures. Previously an old man, a mile back, who lived on a hilltop on the road, pointed out the upper corner of his pasture as a short way up. Said he had not been up for seven years and, looking at our packs, asked, "Are you going to carry them up?" "Well," said he, with a tone half of pity and half regret, adding, "I shall never go up again."

Here, at the base, by the course of a rocky rill, where we paused in the shade, in moist ground, I saw the *Tiarella cordifolia*, abundant and apparently in prime, with its white spike sometimes a foot and more high; also the leaves of the *Geranium Robertianum*, emitting their peculiar scent, with the radical reddish tinge, not yet budded. The cress in the water there was quite

[1] Best view of mountain about two and a half miles this side of summit.

agreeable to our taste, and methinks would be good to eat fresh with bread.

The neighboring hills began to sink, and entering the wood we soon passed Fassett's shanty, — he so busily at work inside that he did not see us, — and we took our dinner by the rocky brook-side in the woods just above. A dozen people passed us early in the afternoon, while we sat there, men and women on their way down from the summit, this suddenly very pleasant day after a louring one having attracted them. We met a man (apparently an Indian or Canadian half-breed) and a boy, with guns, who had been up after pigeons but only killed five crows.

Thereabouts first I noticed the *Ribes prostratum*, abundantly in bloom, apparently in prime, with its pretty erect racemes of small flowers, sometimes purplish with large leaves. There, too, the *Trillium erythrocarpum*, now in prime, was conspicuous, — three white lanceolate waved-edged petals with a purple base. This the handsomest flower of the mountain, coextensive with the wooded sides. Also the *Viburnum lantanoides*, apparently in prime, with its large and showy white outer florets, reminding me by its marginal flowering of the tree-cranberry, coextensive with last; and *Uvularia grandiflora*, not long begun to bloom. Red elder-berry not open, apparently, there; and *Amelanchier Canadensis* var. *Botryapium* not long in bloom.

Having risen above the dwarfish woods (in which mountain-ash was very common), which reached higher up along this ravine than elsewhere, and nearly all the visitors having descended, we proceeded to find a place

Vol. X

for and to prepare our camp at mid-afternoon. We wished it to be near water, out of the way of the wind, which was northwest, and of the path, and also near to spruce trees for a bed. (There is a good place if you would be near the top within a stone's throw of the summit, on the north side, under some spruce trees.) We chose a sunken yard in a rocky plateau on the southeast side of the mountain, perhaps half a mile from the summit, by the path, a rod and a half wide by many more in length, with a mossy and bushy floor about five or six feet beneath the general level, where a dozen black spruce trees grew, though the surrounding rock was generally bare. There was a pretty good spring within a dozen rods, and the western wall shelved over a foot or two. We slanted two scraggy spruce trees, long since bleached, from the western wall, and, cutting many spruce boughs with our knives, made a thick bed and walls on the two sides to keep out the wind. Then, putting several poles transversely across our two rafters, we covered [them] with a thick roof of spruce twigs, like shingles. The spruce, though harsh for a bed, was close at hand, we cutting away one tree to make room. We crawled under the low eaves of this roof, about eighteen inches high, and our extremities projected about a foot.

Having left our packs here and made all ready for the night, we went up to the summit to see the sun set. Our path lay through a couple of small swamps and then up the rocks. Some forty or fifty rods below the very apex southeast, or quite on the top of the mountain, I saw a little bird flit out from beneath a rock close by the path on the left of it, where there were only very few scattered

dwarf black spruce about, and, looking, I found a nest with three eggs. It was the *Fringilla hyemalis*, which soon disappeared around a projecting rock. It was near by a conspicuous spruce, six or eight feet high, on the west edge of a sort of hollow, where a vista opened south over the precipice, and the path ascended at once more steeply. The nest was sunk in the ground by the side of a tuft of grass, and was pretty deep, made of much fine dry grass or sedge (?) and lined with a little of a delicate bluish hair-like fibre (?) (*q. v.*) two or three inches long. The eggs were three, of a regular oval form, faint bluish-white, sprinkled with fine pale-brown dots, in two of the three condensed into a ring about the larger end. They had apparently just begun to develop. The nest and tuft were covered by a projecting rock. Brewer says that only one nest is known to naturalists.[1] We saw many of these birds flitting about the summit, perched on the rocks and the dwarf spruce, and disappearing behind the rocks. It is the prevailing bird now up there, *i. e.* on the summit. They are commonly said to go to the fur countries to breed, though Wilson says that some breed in the Alleghanies. The New York Reports make them breed on the mountains of Oswego County and the Catskills.[2] This was a quite interesting discovery. They probably are never seen in the surrounding low grounds at this season. The ancestors of this bird had evidently perceived on their flight northward that here was a small piece of arctic region, containing all the conditions they

[1] [Dr. T. M. Brewer, in his "Synopsis of the Birds of North America," appended to his edition of Wilson's *American Ornithology*.]
[2] Prevail in Nova Scotia according to Bryant and Cabot.

require, — coolness and suitable food, etc., etc., — and so for how long have builded here. For ages they have made their home here with the *Arenaria Grœnlandica* and *Potentilla tridentata*. They discerned arctic isles sprinkled in our southern sky. I did not see any of them below the rocky and generally bare portion of the mountain. It finds here the same conditions as in the north of Maine and in the fur countries, — Labrador mosses, etc. Now that the season is advanced, migrating birds have gone to the extreme north or gone to the mountain-tops. By its color it harmonized with the gray and brownish-gray rocks. We felt that we were so much nearer to perennial spring and winter.

I observed rabbit's dung commonly, quite to the top and all over the rocky portion, and where they had browsed the bushes. For the last fifteen or twenty rods the ground between the rocks is pretty thickly clothed or carpeted with mountain cranberry and *Potentilla tridentata*, only the former as yet slightly budded, but much lower than this the mountain cranberry is not common. The former grows also in mere seams on the nearly upright sides of rocks, and occasionally I found some of last year's cranberries on the latter, which were an agreeable acid. These were the prevailing plants of a high order on the very summit. There was also on the same ground considerable fine grass,[1] and radical leaves of a sericocarpus-like aster (?),[2] — I saw some withered heads, — springing up commonly, and a little (hardly yet conspicuously budded except in the warmest places)

[1] Was it not *Juncus trifidus*?
[2] Was it not the *Solidago thyrsoidea* of Aug., 1860?

Arenaria Grœnlandica in dense tufts, succulent. There were a few very dwarfish black spruce there, and a very little dry moss, and, on the rocks, many of that small leather-colored lichen, and *Umbilicaria pustulata*, and the two common (?) kinds of cladonia, white and green, between them.[1]

Scarcely, if at all, lower than the above-named plants, grew the *Vaccinium Pennsylvanicum*, also *Pyrus arbutifolia*, very minute and but just budded, and minute mountain-ashes, a few inches high only. From these one may judge what plants, among others, grow far north.

We heard the hylodes peeping from a rain-water pool a little below the summit toward night.

As it was quite hazy, we could not see the shadow of the mountain well, and so returned just before the sun set to our camp. We lost the path coming down, for nothing is easier than to lose your way here, where so little trail is left upon the rocks, and the different rocks and ravines are so much alike. Perhaps no other equal area is so bewildering in this respect as a rocky mountain-summit, though it has so conspicuous a central point.

Notwithstanding the newspaper and egg-shell left by visitors, these parts of nature are still peculiarly un-handselled and untracked. The natural terraces of rock are the steps of this temple, and it is the same whether it rises above the desert or a New England village. Even the inscribed rocks are as solemn as most ancient gravestones, and nature reclaims them with bog and lichens. They reminded me of the grave and pass of Ben Waddi (?). These sculptors seemed to me to court such

[1] *Vide* specimens of Aug., 1860.

alliance with the grave as they who put their names over tombstones along the highway. One, who was probably a blacksmith, had sculptured the emblems of his craft, an anvil and hammer, beneath his name. Apparently a part of the regular outfit of mountain-climbers is a hammer and cold-chisel, and perhaps they allow themselves a supply of garlic also. Certainly you could not hire a stone-cutter to do so much engraving for less than several thousand dollars. But no Old Mortality will ever be caught renewing these epitaphs. It reminds what kinds of steeps do climb the false pretenders to fame, whose chief exploit is the carriage of the tools with which to inscribe their names. For speaking epitaphs they are, and the mere name is a sufficient revelation of the character. They are all of one trade, — stone-cutters, defacers of mountain-tops. " Charles & Lizzie ! " Charles carried the sledge-hammer, and Lizzie the cold-chisel. Some have carried up a paint-pot, and painted their names on the rocks.

We returned to our camp and got our tea in our sunken yard. While one went for water to the spring, the other kindled a fire. The whole rocky part of the mountain, except the extreme summit, is strewn with the relics of spruce trees, a dozen or fifteen feet long, and long since dead and bleached, so that there is plenty of dry fuel at hand. We sat out on the brink of the rocky plateau near our camp, taking our tea in the twilight, and found it quite dry and warm there, though you would not have thought of sitting out at evening in the surrounding valleys. It was evidently warmer and drier there than below. I have often perceived the warm air

high on the sides of hills late into the night, while the valleys were filled with a cold damp night air, as with water, and here the air was warmer and drier the greater part of the night. We perceived no dew there this or the next night. This was our parlor and supper-room; in another direction was our wash-room. The chewink sang before night, and this, as I have before observed, is a very common bird on mountain-tops. It seems to love a cool atmosphere, and sometimes lingers quite late with us. And the wood thrush, indefinitely far or near, a little more distant and unseen, as great poets are. Early in the evening the nighthawks were heard to spark and boom over these bare gray rocks, and such was our serenade at first as we lay on our spruce bed. We were left alone with the nighthawks. These withdrawn bare rocks must be a very suitable place for them to lay their eggs, and their dry and unmusical, yet supramundane and spirit-like, voices and sounds gave fit expression to this rocky mountain solitude. It struck the very key-note of the stern, gray, barren solitude. It was a thrumming of the mountain's rocky chords; strains from the music of Chaos, such as were heard when the earth was rent and these rocks heaved up. Thus they went sparking and booming, while we were courting the first access of sleep, and I could imagine their dainty limping flight, circling over the kindred rock, with a spot of white quartz in their wings. No sound could be more in harmony with that scenery. Though common below, it seemed peculiarly proper here. But ere long the nighthawks were stilled, and we heard only the sound of our companion's breathing

or of a bug in our spruce roof. I thought I heard once faintly the barking of a dog far down under the mountain, and my companion thought he heard a bullfrog.

A little after 1 A. M., I woke and found that the moon had risen, and heard some little bird near by sing a short strain of welcome to it, somewhat song-sparrow-like. But every sound is a little strange there, as if you were in Labrador. Before dawn the nighthawks commenced their sounds again, and these sounds were as good as a clock to us, telling how the night got on.

June 3. At length, by 3 o'clock, the signs of dawn appear, and soon we hear the robin and the *Fringilla hyemalis*, — its prolonged jingle, — sitting on the top of a spruce, the chewink, and the wood thrush. Whether you have slept soundly or not, it is not easy to lie abed under these circumstances, and we rose at 3.30, in order to see the sun rise from the top and get our breakfast there. Concealing our blankets under a shelving rock near the camp, we set out.

It was still hazy, and we did not see the shadow of the mountain until it was comparatively short. We did not get the most distant views, as of the Green and White Mountains, while we were there. We carried up fuel for the last quarter of a mile. A *Fringilla hyemalis* seemed to be attracted by the smoke of our fire, and flew quite near to us. They are the prevailing bird of the summit, and perhaps are baited by the crumbs left by visitors. It was flitting about there, and it would sit and sing, on the *top* of a dwarf spruce, the strain I have often heard. I saw just beneath the summit, and commencing some fifteen or twenty rods from it, dwarfish *Rhodora Cana-densis*, not yet anywhere quite out, much later than in the valley, very common; lambkill; and checkerberry; and, in slightly boggy places, quite dwarfish specimens of *Eriophorum vaginatum*, quite common in similar localities all over the rocky part, six inches high or more. A little water andromeda with it, scarcely out, and Labrador tea, scarcely suggesting flowers. (This I observed only in two or three places on the northerly side.) A viburnum (probably *nudum* or a form of it) was quite common, just begun to leaf, and with nemopanthes, showing its *transparent* leafets not yet expanded, a little behind the other, was quite sizable, especially the latter. These two, with the spruce, the largest shrubs at this height. In the little thickets made by these bushes, grew the two-leaved Solomon's-seal, not nearly out, and *Clintonia borealis*, not budded, though out in the valley. Within the folded leaves of the last, was considerable water, as within the leaves of the seaside goldenrod on the sands of the Cape. *Cornus Canadensis*, *along* the base of the rocks, not out. Diervilla. And, on the moist ground or in the small bogs, *Lycopodium annotinum*, resembling at first sight the *L. lucidulum*, but running, was very common in boggy places, sometimes forming quite conspicuous green patches.

The above plants of the mountain-top, except perhaps the mountain cranberry, extended downward over the whole top or rocky part of the mountain and were there mingled with a little *Polypodium vulgare;* a peculiar *Amelanchier Canadensis*, apparently variety *oligocarpa*, just begun to bloom, with few flowers, short

Vol. X

roundish petals, and *finely* serrate leaves; red cherry, not out; *Populus tremuliformis*, not common and quite small; small willows, apparently *discolor*, etc., also *rostrata*, and maybe *humilis;* canoe birch and yellow birch, for the most part scrubby, largest in swampy places; meadow-sweet; *Lycopodium clavatum; Amelanchier Canadensis* var. *oblongifolia*, not quite out, a little of it; and also a little very dwarfish hemlock and white pine (two or three feet high); a *little* mayflower and *Chiogenes hispidula.*

We concluded to explore the whole rocky part of the mountain in this wise, to saunter slowly about it, about the height and distance from the summit of our camp, or say half a mile, more or less, first going north from the summit and returning by the western semicircle, and then exploring the east side, completing the circle, and return over the summit at night.

To sum up, these were the *Plants of the Summit, i. e.* within a dozen rods of it: *Potentilla tridentata* (and lower); *Vaccinium Vitis-Idæa;* fine grass;[1] sericocarpus-like radical leaves;[2] *Arenaria Grœnlandica;* dwarf black spruce; a little dry moss; the two kinds of cladonia, white and green, and the small leather-colored lichen of rocks,[3] mingled with the larger *Umbilicaria pustulata.* All these but the *V. Vitis-Idæa* generally dispersed over the rocky part.[4]

[1] Was it not *Juncus trifidus* of August, 1860?
[2] Was it not *Solidago thyrsoidea* of August, 1860?
[3] *U. erosa* (?) or *hyperborea* (?). *Vide* Sept. 21, 1858, and a specimen from Lafayette. *Vide* specimen of August, 1860.
[4] The *Vaccinium Vitis-Idæa* also in patches lower down. *Vide* August, 1860.

Within fifteen or twenty rods of it, or scarcely, if at all, lower than the last: Vaccinium Pennsylvanicum *and perhaps the variety* angustifolium *(?);* Pyrus arbutifolia; *mountain-ash. Generally distributed.*

Commencing fifteen or twenty rods below it: Rhodora; lambkill; checkerberry; *Eriophorum vaginatum;* water andromeda; Labrador tea; *Viburnum (nudum?);* nemopanthes; two-leaved Solomon's-seal; clintonia; *Cornus Canadensis; Lycopodium annotinum;* diervilla.

Generally lower than the above, on the rest of the bare rocky part, with all of the above: *Ribes prostratum; Polypodium vulgaris; Amelanchier Canadensis* var. *oligocarpa* (?); red cherry; *Populus tremuliformis; Salix* apparently *discolor*, perhaps also *humilis*, certainly *rostrata;* meadow-sweet; canoe birch; yellow birch; *Lycopodium clavatum; Amelanchier oblongifolia;* a little red elder; hemlock; white pine; mayflower; chiogenes.[1]

Did not examine particularly the larger growth of the swamps, but think it was chiefly spruce, white and yellow birch, mountain-ash, etc.

The *Vaccinium Pennsylvanicum* and the *Abies nigra* are among the most prevailing conspicuous plants.

We first descended somewhat toward the north this forenoon, then turned west over a ridge by which some ascend from the north. There are several large ponds not far from the mountain on the north, and I thought there was less forest to be seen on this side than on the south. We crossed one or two now dry watercourses, where, however, judging from the collections of rubbish

[1] Saw the raspberry in '52 and '60.

or drift, much water must have flown at some other season.

Jackson in his map in the Report on the Geology of Massachusetts calls this mountain "mica slate and porphyritic granite," and [says] that the rocks on the summit are "a hard variety of gneiss filled with small crystals of garnets."

We observed that the rocks were remarkably smoothed, almost polished and rounded, and also scratched. The scratches run from about north-northwest to south-southeast. The sides of the rocks often straight, upright walls, several rods long from north to south and five to ten feet high, with a very smooth, rounded edge. There were many of these long, straight, rounded walls of rock, especially on the northwest and west. Some smaller or lower ones were so rounded and smooth as to resemble at a little distance long-fallen trunks of trees. The rocks were, indeed, singularly worn on a great scale. Often a vertical cross-section would show some such profile as this:

as if they had been grooved with a tool of a corresponding edge. There were occasionally conspicuous masses and also veins of white quartz, and very common were bright-purple or wine-colored garnets imbedded in the rock, looking like berries in a pudding. In many parts, as on the southeast plateau especially, the rocks were regularly stratified, and split into regular horizontal slabs about a foot in thickness, projecting one beyond another like steps.

The little bogs or mosses, sometimes only a rod in diameter, are a singular feature. Ordinarily the cladonia and other lichens are crackling under your feet, when suddenly you step into a miniature bog filling the space between two rocks and you are at a loss to tell where the moisture comes from. The amount of it seems to be that some spongy moss is enabled to grow there and retain some of the clouds which rest on it. Moisture and aridity are singularly near neighbors to each other up there. The surface is made up of masses of rock more or less smoothed and rounded, or else jagged, and the little soil between is a coarse, gravelly kind, the ruins of the rocks and the decayed vegetation that has grown there. You step unexpectedly from Arabia Petræa, where the dry lichens crackle under your feet, into a miniature bog, say Dismal Swamp, where you suddenly sink a foot in wet moss, and the next step carries you into Arabia Petræa again. In more extensive swamps I slumped through moss to water sometimes, though the bottom was of rock, while a fire would rapidly spread in the arid lichens around. Perhaps the mosses grow in the wettest season chiefly, and so are enabled to retain some moisture through the driest. Plants of the bogs and of the rocks grow close to each other. You are surprised to see a great many plants of bogs growing close to the most barren and driest spots, where only cladonias cover the rocks. Often your first notice of a bog in the midst of the arid waste, where the lichens crackle under your feet, is your slumping a foot into wet moss. Methinks there cannot be so much evaporation going on up there, — witness the water in the clintonia leaves, as in the solidago by the sandy seashore, — and this (which is owing to the coolness),

rather than the prevalence of mist, may account for the presence of this moisture forming bogs.

In a shallow rain-water pool, or rock cistern, about three rods long by one or one and a half wide, several hundred feet below the summit, on the west side, but still on the bare rocky top and on the steepest side of the summit, I saw toad-spawn (black with white bellies), also some very large spawn new to me. There were four or five masses of it, each three or four inches in diameter and of a peculiar light misty bluish white as it lay in the water near the surface, attached to some weed or stick, as usual. Each mass consisted of but few large ova, more than a quarter of an inch in diameter, in which were pale-brown tadpoles flattened out. The outside of the mass when taken up was found to consist of large spherical or rounded gelatinous projections three quarters of an inch wide, and blue in the light and air, while the ova within were greenish. This rain-water pool was generally less than a foot deep, with scarcely a weed in it, but considerable mud concealing its rocky bottom. The spawn was unusually clean and clear. I suspect it to be that of bullfrogs,[1] though not a frog was to be seen; they were probably lurking beneath the rocks in the water at that hour. This pool was bounded on one or two sides by those rounded walls of rock five or six feet high. My companion had said that he heard a bullfrog the evening before. Is it likely that these toads and frogs ever hopped up there? The hylodes peeped regularly toward night each day in a similar pool much nearer the summit. Agassiz might say that

[1] Probably *Rana fontinalis. Vide* August, 1860.

Vol. X

they originated on the top. Perhaps they fell from the clouds in the form of spawn or tadpoles or young frogs. I think it more likely that they fell down than that they hopped up. Yet how can they escape the frosts of winter? The mud is hardly deep enough to protect them.

Having reached the neighborhood of our camp again and explored the wooded portion lower down along the path up the mountain, we set out northeast along the east side of the mountain. The southeast part of the mountain-top is an extended broad rocky *almost* plateau, consisting of large flat rocks with small bogs and rain-water pools and easy ascents to different levels. The black spruce tree which is scattered here and there over it, the prevailing tree or shrub of the mountain-top, evidently has many difficulties to contend with. It is generally of a yellowish green, its foliage. The most exposed trees are very stout and spreading close to the rock, often much wider close to the rock than they are high, and these lower, almost their only, limbs completely filling and covering openings between the rocks. I saw one which grew out of a narrow crack in the rock, which was three feet high, five inches in diameter at the ground, and six feet wide on the rock. It was shaped like a bodkin, — the main stem. The spruce commonly grows in clefts of the rocks; has many large limbs, and longer than the tree is high, perhaps, spreading close and flat over the rock in every direction, sometimes eight or ten within a foot of the rock; then, higher up the stem, or midway for three or six feet, though perfectly perpendicular, is quite bare on the north side and commonly smooth, showing no trace of a limb, no stubs, but the

limbs at this height all ray out southward, and the top is crowned with a tuft of tender twigs. This proves the violence of the storms which they have to contend with. Its branches love to run along flat on the rocks, filling the openings between the rocks. It forms dense coverts and forms, apparently, for the rabbits, etc. A single spruce tree of this habit would sometimes make a pretty good shelter, while the rocks on each side were your walls.

As I walked over this plateau, I first observed, looking toward the summit, that the steep angular projections of the summit and elsewhere and the brows of the rocks were the parts chiefly covered with dark-brown lichens, — umbilicaria, etc., — as if they were to grow on the ridge and slopes of a man's nose only. It was the 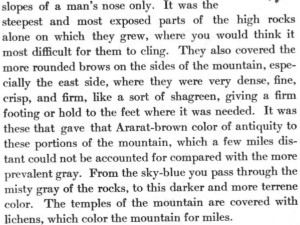 steepest and most exposed parts of the high rocks alone on which they grew, where you would think it most difficult for them to cling. They also covered the more rounded brows on the sides of the mountain, especially the east side, where they were very dense, fine, crisp, and firm, like a sort of shagreen, giving a firm footing or hold to the feet where it was needed. It was these that gave that Ararat-brown color of antiquity to these portions of the mountain, which a few miles distant could not be accounted for compared with the more prevalent gray. From the sky-blue you pass through the misty gray of the rocks, to this darker and more terrene color. The temples of the mountain are covered with lichens, which color the mountain for miles.

The west side descends steeply from the summit, but there is a broad almost plateau on the southeast and east, not much beneath the summit, with a precipitous termination on the east, and the rounded brows of the last are covered with the above-named lichens. A spur of moderate length runs off northerly; another, but lower, southwesterly; another, much longer, a little higher than the last, southerly; and one longer and higher than these, one or two miles long, northeasterly. As you creep down over those eastern brows to look off the precipice, these rough and rigid lichens, forming a rigid crust, as it were baked, done brown, in the sun of centuries, afford a desirable hand and foot hold.

They seemed to me wild robins that placed their nests in the spruce up there. I noticed one nest. William Emerson, senior, says they do not breed on Staten Island. They do breed at least at Hudson's Bay. They are certainly a hardy bird, and are at home on this cool mountain-top.

We boiled some rice for our dinner, close by the edge of a rain-water pool and bog, on the plateau southeast from the summit. Though there was so little vegetation, our fire spread rapidly through the dry cladonia lichens on the rocks, and, the wind being pretty high, threatened to give us trouble, but we put it out with a spruce bough dipped in the pool.[1] I thought that if it had spread further, it must soon have come to a bog. Though you could hardly tell what was moist and what dry till the fire came to it. Nothing could be drier than the cladonia, which was often adjacent to a mass of moss saturated with moisture.

[1] And wet the ground with it. You cook beside such a moss for the sake of water.

Vol. X

These rain-water pools or cisterns are a remarkable feature. There is a scarcity of bubbling springs, but this water was commonly cool enough in that atmosphere and warm as the day was. I do not know why they were not warmer, for they were shallow and the nights were not cold. Can there be some concealed snow or ice about? Hardly. They are quite shallow, but sometimes four or five rods over and with considerable mud at the bottom at first, decayed lichens, and disintegrated rock. Apparently these were the origin of the bogs, *Eriophorum vaginatum*, moss, and a few other boggy plants springing up in them and gradually filling them; yet, though sometimes filled with sedge (?) or fine grass, and generally the dwarfish *Eriophorum vaginatum* in the moss, they were singularly barren, and, unless they were fairly converted into swamps, contained very little variety. You never have to go far to find water of some kind. On the top, perhaps, of a square half-acre of almost bare rock, as in what we called our wash-room by our camp, you find a disintegrated bog, wet moss alternating with dry cladonia (sign and emblem of dryness in our neighborhood), and water stands in little holes, or if you look under the edges of a boulder there, you find standing water, yet cool to drink.

After dinner we kept on northeast over a high ridge east of the summit, whence was a good view of that part of Dublin and Jaffrey immediately under the mountain. There is a fine, large lake extending north and south, apparently in Dublin, which it would be worth the while to sail on. When on the summit of this, I heard the ring of toads from a rain-pool a little lower

and northeasterly. It carried me back nearly a month into spring (though they are still ringing and copulating in Concord), it sounded so springlike in that clear, fresh air. Descending to that pool we found toads copulating at the bottom of the water.

In one or two places on this side of the mountain, which, as I have said, terminated in an abrupt precipice, I saw bogs or meadows four or six rods wide or more, but with only grass and moss and eriophorum, without bushes, in them, close to the edge of the mountain or precipice, where, if you stood between the meadow and the summit, looking east, there would appear to be a notch in the rim of the cup or saucer on the east and the meadow ready to spill over and run down the mountain

on that side; but when you stood on this notched edge, the descent was seen to be much less precipitous than you had expected. Such spongy mountain bogs, however, are evidently the sources of rivers. Lakes of the clouds when they are clear water. Between this and the northeast spur or ridge was the largest swamp or bog that I saw, consisting, perhaps, of between one and two acres, as I remember. It was a grassy and mossy bog without large bushes, in which you sank a foot, with a great many fallen trees in it, showing their bleached

upper side here and there but almost completely buried in the moss. This must once have been a dense swamp, full of pretty large trees. The trees buried in the moss were much larger than any now standing at this height. The outlet of this, if it had any, must have been northwesterly. This was a wild place enough.

Having ascended the highest part of the northeastern ridge north of this bog, we returned to the summit, first to the ridge of the plateau, and west on it to the summit, crossing a ravine between. I noticed, in many places upon the mountain, sandy or gravelly spaces from a few feet to a rod in diameter, where the thin sward and loam appeared to have been recently removed or swept away. I was inclined to call them scars, and thought of very violent winds and tempests of rain as the cause, perhaps, but do not know how to account for them.

We had thus made a pretty complete survey of the top of the mountain. It is a very unique walk, and would be almost equally interesting to take though it were not elevated above the surrounding valleys. It often reminded me of my walks on the beach, and suggested how much both depend for their sublimity on solitude and dreariness. In both cases we feel the presence of some vast, titanic power. The rocks and valleys and bogs and rain-pools of the mountain are so wild and unfamiliar still that you do not recognize the one you left fifteen minutes before. This rocky region, forming what you may call the top of the mountain, must be more than two miles long by one wide in the middle, and you would need to ramble about it many times before it would begin to be familiar. There may be twenty little swamps so much alike in the main that [you] would not know whether you had seen a particular one before, and the rocks are trackless and do not present the same point. So that it has the effect of the most intricate labyrinth and artificially extended walk.

This mountain is said in the Gazetteer to extend northeast [and] southwest five miles, by three wide, and the streams on the east to empty into the Contoocook and Merrimack, on the west into the Ashuelot and Connecticut; is 3718 feet high; and, judging from its account, the top was wooded fifty years ago.

We proceeded to get our tea on the summit, in the very place where I had made my bed for a night some fifteen years before. There were a great many insects of various kinds on the topmost rocks at this hour, and among them I noticed a yellow butterfly and several large brownish ones fluttering over the apex.

It was interesting to watch from that height the shadows of fair-weather clouds passing over the landscape. You could hardly distinguish them from forests. It reminded me of the similar shadows seen on the sea from the high bank of Cape Cod beach. There the perfect equality of the sea atoned for the comparatively slight elevation of the bank. We do not commonly realize how constant and amusing a phenomenon this is in a summer day to one standing on a sufficiently elevated point. In the valley or on the plain you do not commonly notice the shadow of a cloud unless you are in it, but on a mountain-top, or on a lower elevation in a plain country or by the seaside, the shadows of clouds flitting over the landscape are a never-failing source of

amusement. It is commonly easy to refer a shadow to its cloud, since in one direction its form is preserved with sufficient accuracy. Yet I was surprised to observe that a long, straggling downy cumulus extending north and south a few miles east of us, when the sun was perhaps an hour high, cast its shadow along the base of the Peterboro Hills, and did not fall on the other side, as I should have expected. It proved the clouds not so high as I supposed. It suggested how with tolerable accuracy you might easily calculate the height of a cloud with a quadrant and a good map of the country; e. g., observe at what distance the shadow of a cloud directly overhead strikes the earth, and then take the altitude of the sun, and you may presume that you have the base and two angles of a right-angled triangle, from which the rest may be calculated; or you may allow for the angle of elevation of the mountain as seen from the place where the shadow falls. Also you might determine the breadth of a cloud by observing the breadth of the shadow at a given distance, etc., etc. Many such calculations would be easy in such a locality. It was pleasant enough to see one man's farm in the shadow of a cloud, — which perhaps he thought covered all the Northern States, — while his neighbor's farm was in sunshine. It was still too hazy to allow of our seeing the shadow of the mountain, so we descended a little before the sun set, but already the hylodes had been peeping for some time.

Again the wood thrush, chewink, etc., sang at eve. I had also heard the song sparrow.

As the sky was more cloudy this evening, we looked out a shelving rock near our camp, where we might take

shelter from the rain in the night if necessary, i. e., if our roof did not prove tight enough. There were plenty of clefts and small caverns where you might be warm and dry. The mosquitoes troubled us a little this night.

Lying up there at this season, when the nighthawk is most musical, reminded me of what I had noticed before, that this bird is crepuscular in its habits. It was heard by night only up to nine or ten o'clock and again just before dawn, and marked those periods or seasons like a clock. Its note very conveniently indicated the time of night. It was sufficient to hear the nighthawk booming when you awoke to know how the night got on, though you had no other evidence of the hour. I did not hear the sound of any beast. There are no longer any wolves to howl or panthers to scream. One man told me that many foxes took refuge from dogs and sportsmen on this mountain.

The plants of cold northern bogs grow on this mountain-top, and even they have a boreal habit here, more dwarfish than such of them as grow in our swamps. The more memorable and peculiar plants of the mountain-top were the mountain cranberry and the *Potentilla tridentata*, the *dwarfish* spruce, *Arenaria Grœnlandica* (not now conspicuous). The *Ribes prostratum*, or fetid currant, was very abundant from quite near the summit to near the base, and its currant-acid fragrance was quite agreeable to me, partly, perhaps, from its relation to the currant of the gardens. You also notice many small weed-like mountain-ashes, six or eight inches high, which, on trying to pull up, you find to be very firmly rooted, having an old and large root out of proportion to

their top. I might also name in this connection not only the blueberry but the very common but dwarfish *Eriophorum vaginatum* and the *Lycopodium annotinum*, also the amelanchier, variety *oligocarpa*. I was not prepared to find vegetation so much later there than below or with us, since I once found blueberries ripe on Wachusett unexpectedly early. However, it was a pleasing lateness, and gives one a chance to review some of his lessons in natural history. On the rocky part, the only plants, as I noticed, which were or had been in bloom were the salix, now generally done; *Ribes prostratum*, in prime; *Eriophorum vaginatum ; Vaccinium Pennsylvanicum*, just begun; *Amelanchier oligocarpa*, little, not long; water andromeda, ditto, ditto; and *probably* (?) the populus, birches (?), mayflower, and spruce.

June 4. Friday. At 6 A. M. we began to descend. Near the upper edge of the wood, I heard, as I had done in ascending, a very peculiar lively and interesting strain from some bird, which note was new to me. At the same time I caught sight of a bird with a very conspicuous deep-orange throat and otherwise dark, with some streaks along the head. This may have been the Blackburnian warbler, if it was not too large for that, and may have been the singer. We descended or continued along the base of the mountain southward, taking the road to the State Line Station and Winchendon, through the west part of Rindge.

It is remarkable how, as you are leaving a mountain and looking back at it from time to time, it gradually gathers up its slopes and spurs to itself into a regular whole, and makes a new and total impression. The lofty beaked promontory which, when you were on the summit, appeared so far off and almost equal to it, seen now against the latter, scarcely deepens the tinge of bluish, misty gray on its side. The mountain has several spurs or ridges, bare and rocky, running from it, with a considerable depression between the central peak and them; *i. e.*, they attain their greatest height half a mile or more from the central apex. There is such a spur, for instance, running off southward about a mile. When we looked back from four or five miles distant on the south, this, which had appeared like an independent summit, was almost totally lost to our view against the general misty gray of the side of the principal summit. We should not have suspected its existence if we had not just come from it, and though the mountain ranges northeasterly and southwesterly, or not far from north and south, and is much the longest in that direction, it now presented a pretty regular pyramidal outline· with a broad base, as if it were broadest east and west. That is, when you are on the mountain, the different peaks and ridges appear more independent; indeed, there is a bewildering variety of ridge and valley and peak, but when you have withdrawn a few miles, you are surprised at the more or less pyramidal outline of the mountain and that the lower spurs and peaks are all subordinated to the central and principal one. The summit appears to rise and the surrounding peaks to subside, though some new prominences appear. Even at this short distance the mountain has lost most of its rough and jagged

outline, considerable ravines are smoothed over, and large boulders which you must go a long way round make no impression on the eye, being swallowed up in the air.

We had at first thought of returning to the railroad at Fitzwilliam, passing over Gap Mountain, which is in Troy and Fitzwilliam quite near Monadnock, but concluded to go to Winchendon, passing through the western part of Rindge to the State Line Station, the latter part of the road being roundabout. We crossed the line between Jaffrey and Rindge three or four miles from the mountain. Got a very good view of the mountain from a high hill over which the road ran in the western part of Rindge.

But the most interesting part of this walk was the three miles along the railroad between State Line and Winchendon Station. It was the best timbered region we saw, though its trees are rapidly falling. The railroad runs very straight for long distances here through a primitive forest. To my surprise I heard the *tea-lea* of the myrtle-bird [1] here, as in Maine, and suppose that it breeds in this primitive wood. There was no house near the railroad but at one point, and then a quarter of a mile off. The red elder was in full bloom and filled the air with its fragrance. I saw some of the handsomest white pines here that I ever saw, — even in Maine, — close by the railroad. One by which I stood was at least three and a half feet in diameter at two feet from the ground, and, like several others about it, rose perfectly straight without any kind of limb to the height of sixty feet at least. What struck

[1] White-throat, probably.

me most in these trees, as I was passing by, was not merely their great size, for they appeared less than they were, but their perfect perpendicularity, roundness, and apparent smoothness, tapering very little, like artificial columns of a new style. Their trunks were so very round that for that reason they appeared smoother than they were, marked with interrupted bands of light-colored lichens. Their regular beauty made such an impression that I was forced to turn aside and contemplate them. They were so round and perpendicular that my eyes slid off, and they made such an impression of finish and even polish as if they had had an enamelled surface. Indeed they were less rough than I might have expected. Beneath them grew the *Trillium pictum* and clintonia, both in bloom.

For last expedition to Monadnock, *vide* September, 1852.

I find the *Cornus florida* out in my pitcher when I get home June 4th, though it was not out on Island May 31st, and it is well out on Island when I look June 6th. I will say, therefore, that it opened June 3d.

June 5. A. M. — Surveying a blueberry and maple swamp belonging to Thomas Brooks in the northeast part of Lincoln, burned over in fall of '57. The fire spread across a ditch about four feet wide, catching the dry grass. The maples are killed part way or entirely round, near the ground, as you find on cutting the bark, being most protected on the inside of a clump toward each other, but less and less as you try higher up. Yet, generally, they have leaved out. Will they,

when thus girdled, live more than one year? The effect on the alders has been that the bark for a foot or two next the ground is now in loose curls turned back or outward, showing the yellowish wood and yellowish inner side of the bark, evidently owing to the drying and contracting of the outside. The principal loss appears to have been of blueberries. Brooks *says* he has got twenty-five (??) bushels there in a year.

P. M. — Surveying, for Warner, wood bought of John Brown near Concord line.

I now see a painted turtle in a rut, crossing a sandy road. They are now laying, then. When they get into a rut they find it rather difficult to get out, and, hearing a wagon coming, they draw in their heads, lie still, and are crushed.

Clasping hound's-tongue in garden.

Can our second gooseberry in garden be the *R. rotundifolium?*

June 6. P. M. — *Cornus florida* at Island well out, say the 3d. I hear of linnæa out in a pitcher and probably (?) in woods.

Go to Painted-Cup Meadow *via* Assabet Bath.

See three or four *Emys insculpta* about, making their holes in the gravelly bank south of Assabet Bath, and a few holes which must have been made a day or two, probably by the same. Golden senecio is not uncommon now. Am surprised to find that the buckbean flowers are withered, being killed by the recent frosts. Yellow Bethlehem-star.

Edith Emerson has found, in the field (Merriam's) just south of the Beck Stow pine grove, *Lepidium campestre*, which may have been out ten days.

June 7. P. M. — To Walden.

Warm weather has suddenly come, beginning yesterday. To-day it is yet warmer, 87° at 3 P. M., compelling me to put on a thin coat, and I see that a new season has arrived. June shadows are moving over waving grass-fields, the crickets chirp uninterruptedly, and I perceive the agreeable acid scent of high blueberry bushes in bloom. The trees having leaved out, you notice their rounded tops, suggesting shade. The nighthawk sparks and booms over arid hillsides and sprout-lands.

It is evidence enough against crows and hawks and owls, proving their propensity to rob birds' nests of eggs and young, that smaller birds pursue them so often. You do not need the testimony of so many farmers' boys when you can see and hear the small birds daily crying "Thief and murder" after these spoilers. What does it signify, the kingbird, blackbird, swallow, etc., etc., pursuing a crow? They say plainly enough, "I know you of old, you villain; you want to devour my eggs or young. I have often caught you at it, and I'll publish you now." And probably the crow pursuing the fish hawk and eagle proves that the latter sometimes devour their young.

The *Salix tristis* is now generally going or gone to seed. *Oxalis violacea* in garden.

I see toads copulating and toad-spawn freshly laid

in the Wyman meadow at Walden. *Utricularia vulgaris* out there. The water colored or dusted with the pollen of the pitch pine.

As I was wading in this Wyman meadow, looking for bullfrog-spawn, I saw a hole at the bottom, where it was six or eight inches deep, by the side of a mass of mud and weeds which rose just to the surface three or four feet from the shore. It was about five inches in diameter, with some sand at the mouth, just like a musquash's hole. As I stood there within two feet, a pout put her head out, as if to see who was there, and directly came forth and disappeared under the target-weed; but as I stood perfectly still, waiting for the water which I had disturbed to settle about the hole, she circled round and round several times between me and the hole, cautiously, stealthily approaching the entrance but as often withdrawing, and at last mustered courage to enter it. I then noticed another similar hole in the same mass, two or three feet from this. I thrust my arm into the first, running it in and downward about fifteen inches. It was a little more than a foot long and enlarged somewhat at the end, the bottom, also, being about a foot beneath the surface, — for it slanted downward, — but I felt nothing within; I only felt a pretty regular and rounded apartment with firm walls of weedy or fibrous mud. I then thrust my arm into the other hole, which was longer and deeper, but at first discovered nothing; but, trying again, I found that I had not reached the end, for it turned a little and descended more than I supposed. Here I felt a similar apartment or enlarge-

Vol. X

ment, some six inches in diameter horizontally but not quite so high nor nearly so wide at its throat. Here, to my surprise, I felt something soft, like a gelatinous mass of spawn, but, feeling a little further, felt the horns of a pout. I deliberately took hold of her by the head and lifted her out of the hole and the water, having run my arm in two thirds its length. She offered not the slightest resistance from first to last, even when I held her out of water before my face, and only darted away suddenly when I dropped her in the water. The entrance to her apartment was so narrow that she could hardly have escaped if I had tried to prevent her. Putting in my arm again, I felt, under where she had been, a flattish mass of ova, several inches in diameter, resting on the mud, and took out some. Feeling again in the first hole, I found as much more there. Though I had been stepping round and over the second nest for several minutes, I had not scared the pout. The ova of the first nest already contained white wiggling young. I saw no motion in the others. The ova in each case were dull-yellowish and the size of small buckshot. These nests did not communicate with each other and had no other outlet.

Pouts, then, make their nests in shallow mud-holes or bays, in masses of weedy mud, or probably in the muddy bank; and the old pout hovers over the spawn or keeps guard at the entrance. Where do the Walden pouts breed when they have not access to this meadow? The first pout, whose eggs were most developed, was the largest and had some slight wounds on the back. The

other may have been the male in the act of fertilizing the ova.[1]

I sit in my boat in the twilight by the edge of the river. Toads are now in full blast along the river. Some sit quite out at the edge of the pads, and hold up their heads so high when they ring, and make such a large bubble, that they look as if they would tumble over backward. Bullfrogs now are in full blast. I do not hear other frogs; their notes are probably drowned. I perceive that this generally is the rhythm of the bullfrog: *er | er-r | er-r-r |* (growing fuller and fuller and more tremendous) and then doubling, *er, er | er, err | er, er, er | er, er, er |* and finally *er, er, er, er | er, er, er, er.* Or I might write it *oorar | oorar | oorar | oorar-hah | oorar-hah hah | oorar hah hah hah.* Some of these great males are yellow or quite yellowish over the whole back. Are not the females oftenest white-throated? What lungs, what health, what terrenity (if not serenity) it suggests! At length I hear the faint stertoration of a *Rana palustris* (if not *halecina*). Seeing a large head, with its prominent eyes, projecting above the middle of the river, I found it was a bullfrog coming across. It swam under water a rod or two, and then came up to see where it was, or its way. It is thus they cross when sounds or sights attract them to more desirable shores. Probably they prefer the night for such excursions, for fear of large pickerel, etc. I thought its throat was not yellow nor baggy. Was it not the female attracted by the note of the male?

Fireflies pretty numerous over the river, though we

[1] The ova in jar had mostly turned quite white and dead on the 8th; perhaps could not bear the light.

have had no thunder-showers of late. Mosquitoes quite troublesome here.

The ledum is a very good plant to bloom in a pitcher, lasting a week or more.

June 8. P. M. — To marsh hawk's nest near Hubbard's Bath.

I see many breams' nests made, and in one or two in which I look, I find, on taking out the stones and the gravel, the small yellowish ova about one twentieth of an inch in diameter. This is not, at least ordinarily, visible now as you look down on the nest, but, on taking up portions of the bottom of the concave nest, you find it scattered (not crowded) over the sand, stones, clamshells, weeds, etc., which form the bottom of the nest. It studs the little gray and brown stones, rather scatteredly, like some kind of gem adhering pretty firmly, and the bream is steadily poised over her treasures. You see the bream poised over her large concave nest in the sand, and, taking up a part of the bottom, as some brown stone, you find it studded with the small gem-like ova, loosely dispersed. Apparently it has not been laid long.

The *Salix nigra* is still in bloom. I see red-wing blackbirds hatched. In several places I see where dead suckers have been at last partly devoured by some animal, and their great bladders are seen floating off.

Thomas Bell, in his "British Reptiles," says of "the *Terrapene Europæa*, the common lacustrine tortoise of the Continent," "As they live principally upon small fish, the air-bags of which they reject, it is said that the people are wont to judge of the quantity of tortoises to

be found in a lake or pond, by the number of air-bags which are seen swimming on the surface of the water."

The marsh hawk's eggs are not yet hatched. She rises when I get within a rod and utters that peculiar cackling or scolding note, much like, but distinct from, that of the pigeon woodpecker. She keeps circling over the nest and repeatedly stoops within a rod of my head in an angry manner. She is not so large as a hen-hawk, and is much more slender. She will come sailing swiftly and low over the tops of the trees and bushes, etc., and then stoop as near to my head as she dares, in order to scare me away. The primaries, of which I count but five, are very long and loose, or distant, like fingers with which she takes hold of the air, and form a very distinct part of the wing, making an angle with the rest. Yet they are not broad and give to the wing a long and slender appearance. The legs are stretched straight back under the tail. I see nothing of the male, nor did I before. A red-wing and a kingbird are soon in pursuit of the hawk, which proves, I think, that she meddles with their nests or themselves. She circles over me, scolding, as far as the edge of the wood, or fifteen rods.

The early potentilla is now in some places erect. The sidesaddle-flower is out, — how long? — and the sweet flag, how long?

I see quite common, on the surface in deep water wherever there are weeds, *misty white strings* of spawn, reminding one of toad-spawn without the ova, only whiter, or more opaque. But these strings turn on themselves, forming small masses four to eight inches long, attached to the weeds, — *Ranunculus Purshii*, potamo-

geton, etc., etc. These strings are full of minute ova, like seeds, pale-brown, oval or elliptical, about one fiftieth of an inch long.

I perceive distinctly to-day that there is no articular line along the sides of the back of the bullfrog, but that there is one along the back of that bullfrog-like, smaller, widely dispersed and early frog so common about fountains, brooks, ditches, and the river, of which I probably have one small one bottled and have heard the croak (*vide* April 5th, 1858). That pale-brown or oat spawn must belong, then, I think, to the *Rana fontinalis*.

A kingbird's nest with three eggs, lined with some hair, in a fork — or against upright part — of a willow, just above near stone bridge. Is that small spiked rush from a few inches to a foot or more in height *Eleocharis palustris?* or *tenuis?* In early aster meadow and elsewhere common, along meadow-paths. Whiteweed is getting to be common.

June 9. P. M. — To Beck Stow's.

High blackberry, not long. I notice by the roadside at Moore's Swamp the very common *Juncus effusus*, not quite out, one to two and a half feet high. See a yellow spotted turtle digging her hole at 5 P. M., in a pasture near Beck Stow's, some dozen rods off. It is made under one side like the *picta's*.

Potamogetons begin to prevail in the river and to catch my oar. The river is weedy. White maple keys are abundantly floating.

June 10. Smilacina racemosa well out, how long?

Sophia has received the whorled arethusa from Northampton to-day.

P. M. — To Assabet Bath and return by stone bridge.

A Maryland yellow-throat's nest near apple tree by the low path beyond the pear tree. Saw a bird flit away low and stealthily through the birches, and [it] was soon invisible. Did not discover the nest till after a long search. Perfectly concealed under the loose withered grass at the base of a clump of birches, with no apparent entrance. The usual small deep nest (but not raised up) of dry leaves, fine grass stubble, and lined with a little hair. Four eggs, white, with brown spots, chiefly at larger end, and some small black specks or scratches. The bird flits out very low and swiftly and does not show herself, so that it is hard to find the nest or to identify the bird.

See a painted turtle digging her nest in the road at 5.45 P. M.

At the west bank, by the bathing-place, I see that several turtles' holes have already been opened and the eggs destroyed by the skunk or other animal. Some of them — I judge by the size of the egg — are *Emys insculpta's* eggs. (I saw several of them digging here on the 6th.) Among the shells at one hole I find one minute egg left unbroken. It is not only very small, but broad in proportion to length. *Vide* collection. One *E. insculpta* is digging there about 7 P. M. Another great place for the last-named turtle to lay her eggs is that rye-field of Abel Hosmer's just north of the stone bridge, and also the neighboring pitch pine wood. I saw them here on the 6th, and also I do this afternoon, in various parts of the field and in the rye, and two or three crawling up the very steep sand-bank there, some eighteen feet high, steeper than sand will lie, — for this keeps caving. They must often roll to the bottom again. Apparently the *E. insculpta* are in the very midst of their laying now. As we entered the north end of this rye-field, I saw what I took to be a hawk fly up from the south end, though it may have been a crow. It was soon pursued by small birds. When I got there I found an *E. insculpta* on its back with its head and feet drawn in and motionless, and what looked like the track of a crow on the sand. Undoubtedly the bird which I saw had been pecking at it, and perhaps they get many of the eggs.[1]

Common blue flag, how long?

June 11. P. M. — To Assabet Bath.

The fertile *Salix alba* is conspicuous now at a distance, in fruit, being yellowish and drooping. Hear the parti-colored warbler. Examine the stone-heaps. One is now a foot above water and quite sharp. They contain, apparently freshly piled up, from a wheelbarrow to a cartload of stones; but I can find no ova in them. I see a musquash dive head foremost (as he is swimming) in the usual way, being scared by me, but without making any noise.

Saw a painted turtle on the gravelly bank just south of the bath-place, west side, and suspected that she had just laid (it was mid-afternoon). So, examining the ground, I found the surface covered with loose lichens,

[1] *Vide* June 11th, 1860.

etc., about one foot behind her, and digging, found five eggs just laid one and a half or two inches deep, under one side. It is remarkable how firmly they are packed in the soil, rather hard to extract, though but just buried. I notice that turtles which have just commenced digging will void considerable water when you take them up. This they appear to have carried up to wet the ground with.

Saw half a dozen *Emys insculpta* preparing to dig now at mid-afternoon, and one or two had begun at the most gravelly spot there; but they would not proceed while I watched, though I waited nearly half an hour, but either rested perfectly still with heads drawn partly in, or, when a little further off, stood warily looking about with their necks stretched out, turning their dark and anxious-looking heads about. It seems a very earnest and pressing business they are upon. They have but a short season to do it in, and they run many risks.

Having succeeded in finding the *E. picta's* eggs, I thought I would look for the *E. insculpta's* at Abel Hosmer's rye-field. So, looking carefully to see where the ground had been recently disturbed, I dug with my hand and could directly feel the passage to the eggs, and so discovered two or three nests with their large and long eggs, — five eggs in one of them. It seems, then, that if you look carefully soon after the eggs are laid in such a place, you can find the nests, though rain or even a dewy night might conceal the spot. I saw half a dozen *E. insculpta* digging at mid-afternoon.

Near a wall thereabouts, saw a little woodchuck,

Vol. X

about a third grown, resting still on the grass within a rod of me, as gray as the oldest are, but it soon ran into the wall.

Edward Hoar has seen the triosteum out, and *Euphorbia Cyparissias* (how long?), and a *Raphanus Raphanistrum*, the last at Waltham; also *Eriophorum polystachyon*.

June 12. Rains all day. Much water falls.

June 13. Louring all day.
P. M. — To Ledum Swamp.
Lambkill, maybe one day. Strawberries. In the great apple tree front of the Miles house I hear young pigeon woodpeckers.

The ledum is apparently past prime. The *Kalmia glauca* and the *Andromeda Polifolia* are done, the kalmia just done. The ledum has grown three or four inches (as well as the andromeda). It has a rather agreeable fragrance, between turpentine and strawberries. It is rather strong and penetrating, and sometimes reminds me of the peculiar scent of a bee. The young leaves, bruised and touched to the nose, even make it smart. It is the young and expanding ledum leaves which are so fragrant. There is a yellow fungus common on its leaves, and a black one on the andromeda. The *Vaccinium Oxycoccus* grows here and is abundantly out; some days certainly. I hear and see the parti-colored warbler, blue yellow-backed, here on the spruce trees. It probably breeds here. Also, within three feet of the edge of the pond-hole, where

I can hardly stand in india-rubber shoes without the water flowing over them, a large ant-hill swarming with ants, — though not on the surface because of the mizzling rain. One of the prevailing front-rank plants here, standing in the sphagnum and water, is the elodea.

I see a song sparrow's nest here in a little spruce just by the mouth of the ditch. It rests on the thick branches fifteen inches from the ground, firmly made of coarse sedge without, lined with finer, and then a little hair, small within, — a very thick, firm, and portable nest, an inverted cone; — four eggs. They build them in a peculiar manner in these sphagnous swamps, elevated apparently on account of water and of different materials. Some of the eggs have quite a blue ground.

Go to Conantum end. The *Rubus frondosus* will not bloom apparently for a day or two, though the *villosus* is apparently in prime there. I hear the peculiar notes of young bluebirds that have flown. *Arenaria lateriflora*, how long?

The *Scheuchzeria palustris*, now in flower and going to seed, grows at Ledum Pool, as at Gowing's Swamp. See now in meadows, for the most part going to seed, *Carex scoparia*, with its string of oval beads; and *C. lupulina*,[1] with its inflated perigynia; also what I take to be *C. stipata*, with a dense, coarse, somewhat sharp triangular mass of spikelets; also *C. stellulata*, with a string of little star-like burs. The delicate, pendulous, slender-peduncled *C. debilis*.

Catbirds hatched.

[1] [Two interrogation-points in pencil here.]

June 14. Miss Pratt brings me the fertile barberry from northeast the great yellow birch. The staminate is apparently effete. Young partridges, when?

P. M. — To Gowing's Swamp.

I notice interrupted ferns, which were killed, fruit and all, by the frosts of the 28th and 29th of May, now coming up afresh from the root. The barren fronds seem to have stood it better.

See in a meadow a song sparrow's nest with three eggs, and another egg just buried level with the bottom of the nest. Probably it is one of a previous laying, which the bird considered addled. I find it to be not at all developed, nor yet spoiled.

Common garden columbine, broad and purple, by roadside, fifty rods below James Wright's.

The river is raised surprisingly by the rain of the 12th. The Mill Brook has been over the Turnpike.

June 15. Rains steadily again, and we have had no clear weather since the 11th. The river is remarkably high, far higher than before, this year, and is rising. I can paddle into and all about the willowy meadow southwest of Island. I had, indeed, anticipated this on account of the remarkable lowness of the river in the spring.

That coarse grass in the Island meadow which grows in full circles, as on the Great Meadows, is wool-grass, though but little blooms. Some is now fairly in bloom and it has the dark bracts of what I observed on the Great Meadows. The peculiarly circular form of the patches, sometimes their projecting edges being the

arcs of circles, is very obvious now that the lower and different grass around is under water. Many plants have a similar habit of growth. The *Osmunda regalis*, growing in very handsome hollow circles, or sometimes only crescents or arcs of circles, is now generally a peculiarly tender green, — its delicate fronds, — but some has begun to go to seed and look brown. Hollow circles, one or two feet to a rod in diameter. These two are more obvious when, as now, all the rest of the meadow is covered with water. That large grass, five feet high, of the river brink is now just begun. Can it be blue-joint, or *Calamagrostis Canadensis?*[1]

June 16. P. M. — To Staples's Meadow Wood.

It is pleasant to paddle over the meadows now, at this time of flood, and look down on the various meadow plants, for you can see more distinctly quite to the bottom than ever. A few sedges are very common and prominent, one, the tallest and earliest, now gone and going to seed, which I do not make out, also the *Carex scoparia* and the *C. stellulata*. How will the water affect these plants, standing thus long over them? The head of every sedge that now rises above the surface is swarming with insects which have taken refuge from the flood on it, — beetles, grasshoppers, spiders, caterpillars, etc. How many must have been destroyed! No doubt thousands of birds' nests have been destroyed by the flood, — blackbirds', bobolinks', song sparrows', etc. I see a robin's nest high above the water with the young just dead and the old bird in the water,

[1] Probably phalaris.

apparently killed by the abundance of rain, and afterward I see a fresh song sparrow's nest which has been flooded and destroyed. Two sternothærus which I smell of have no scent to-day.

Looking into Hubbard's Pool, I at length see one of the minims which I put into it. I brought the last here April 30th. It is now a little perch about an inch and a quarter long; it was then about a quarter of an inch long. I can now see the transverse bars a rod off. It is swimming actively round and round the pool, but avoids the quite shallow water of the edges, so it does not get landlocked or lost in the weedy overflowed edges. I put twenty or thirty into this pool in all. They grow very fast, then, at last.

Carrion-flower, how long? Not long. How agreeable and wholesome the fragrance of the low blackberry blossom, reminding me of all the rosaceous fruit-bearing plants, so near and dear to our humanity! It is one of the most deliciously fragrant flowers, reminding of wholesome fruits.

I see a yellow-spotted turtle digging its hole at mid-afternoon, but, like the last of this species I saw, it changed its place after I saw it, and I did not get an egg; it is so wary. Some turtles must lay in pretty low fields, or else make a much longer excursion than I think they do, the water in which they dwell is so far from high land.

Among the geraniums which now spot the wood or sprout-land paths, I see some with very broad, short, rounded petals, making a smaller but full round flower.

The *Salix nigra* appears to be quite done.

Edward Emerson, Edward Bartlett, and Storrow Higginson come to ask me the names of some eggs to-night. They have the egg of the warbling vireo,[1] — much like the pepe's, but smaller. They tell of a hen-hawk's nest seen the 6th, with two eggs. They have also, undoubtedly, the egg of the purple finch, seen first two or three weeks ago, and they bring me two nests and one egg. Both these nests were in small fir trees, one by the Lee house (that was), Joe Barrett's, and the other in the New Burying-Ground. The last appeared to have been spoiled by the rain and was against the main stem and contained four fresh eggs, they say, the 14th; the other had five eggs two days earlier; both near the top. The egg is a little more than three quarters of an inch long by nearly five eighths at the bigger end, and so of another from the other nest, rather more slender, — a tapering pale bluish-green egg, with blackish-brown and also dull slate-colored spots and streaks about the larger end and a few very fine spots on the other parts. The Lee nest is somewhat like a hair-bird's, though larger. They are both about four inches wide, outside to outside, and two and a half high, two and a quarter to two and a half [in] diameter within, and one and a quarter to one and a half deep. The Lee house one (which had the egg in it) is composed externally of many small weed stems — apparently lepidium, lechea — and root-fibres, and the inner part is very thick and substantial, of root-fibres and bark-shreds and a little

[1] Or is it not yellow-throated vireo's? *Vide* nest. From a maple near Hemlocks, Assabet.

cow's hair, lined with much horsehair. The other is a little less substantial, externally of pinweed and apparently hypericum stems and root-fibres and within of root-fibres lined with much fine and soft bark-shreds.

Edward Bartlett brings me a crow's nest, one of several which he found in maple trees, twenty or thirty feet from ground, in a swamp near Copan, and in this he found an addled egg. The mass of twigs which was its foundation were too loose and bulky to be brought away, — half a wheelbarrow-load, at least, chiefly maple, eighteen inches long and a quarter of an inch wide. The rest or inner portion of the nest, which part is ten or twelve inches in diameter, about two inches thick, and slightly concave, is composed almost wholly of coarse strips of grape-vine bark, with some finer, apparently maple, bark-shreds and some hair and hog's bristles, perhaps of carrion carried to its young heretofore; and the under part is loosely earthy to some extent.

June 17. P. M. — To hawk's nest.

One egg is hatched since the 8th, and the young bird, all down, with a tinge of fawn or cinnamon, lies motionless on its breast with its head down and is already about four inches long! An hour or two after, I see the old hawk pursue a stake-driver which was flying over this spot, darting down at him and driving him off.

The stake-driver comes beating along, like a long, ungainly craft, or a revenue cutter, looking into the harbors, and if it finds a fisherman there, standing out again.

See a painted turtle digging at mid-afternoon. I have only to look at dry fields or banks near water to find the turtles laying there afternoons.

June 18. How dogs will resort to carrion, a dead cow or horse, half buried, no matter how stale, — the best-bred and petted village dogs, and there gorge themselves with the most disgusting offal by the hour, as if it were a season of famine! Surely they are foul creatures that we make cossets of.

P. M. — To Walden to see a bird's nest, a red-eye's, in a small white pine; nest not so high as my head; still laying. A boy climbs to the cat owl's nest and casts down what is left of it, — a few short sticks and some earthy almost turfy foundation, as if it were the accumulation of years. Beside much black and white skunk-hair, there are many fishes' scales (!) intimately mixed with its substance, and some skunk's bones.

E. Bartlett has found three bobolinks' nests. One or more of them he thinks has been covered by the recent flood. A little boy brings me an egg of Wilson's thrush, which he found in a nest in a low bush about a foot from the ground.

Coming across the level pasture west of E. Hubbard's swamp, toward Emerson's, I find a young *Emys insculpta*, apparently going to lay, though she had not dug a hole. It was four and a quarter inches long by three and a half wide, and altogether the handsomest turtle of this species, if not of any, that I have ever seen. It was quite fresh and perfect, without wound or imperfection; its claws quite sharp and slender, and the

Vol. X

annual striæ so distinct on all the scales above and below that I could count them with ease. It was nine years old, though it would be like an infant among turtles, the successive striæ being perfectly parallel at equal distances apart. The sternum, with a large black spot on the rear angle of each scale and elsewhere a rich brown color, even reminded me of the turtle-shell of commerce. While its upper shell was of a uniform wholesome brown, very prettily marked indeed, not only by the outlines of the scales, but more distinctly by the lines of prominences raying out from the starting-point of each scale, perfectly preserved in each year's growth, a most elaborate coat of mail, worthy the lifelong labor of some reptilian Vulcan. This must have been a belle among the *E. insculpta*. Nevertheless I did discover that all the claws but one of one hind foot were gone! Had not a bird pecked them off? So liable are they to injury in their long lives. Then they are so well-behaved; can be taken up and brought home in your pocket, and make no unseemly efforts to escape. The upper shell was remarkably spreading and curving upward on the rear edges.

June 19. *Saturday.* I do not hear the night-warbler so often as a few weeks ago. Birds generally do not sing so tumultuously.

Storrow Higginson and other boys have found this forenoon at Flint's Pond one or more veery-nests on the ground. Also showed me one of five eggs, far advanced, they found there in a nest some fourteen feet high in a slender maple sapling, placed between many

upright shoots, many dry leaves outside. It is a slender clear-blue egg, more slender and pointed at the small end than the robin's, and he says the bird was thrush-like with a pencilled breast. It is probably the wood thrush.[1] He saw one or two other similar nests, he thought, not yet completed. Also showed me an egg, which answers to the description of the tanager's. Two fresh eggs in small white oak sapling, some fourteen feet from ground.[2] They saw a tanager near.[3]

P. M. — To Bateman's Pond.

The swamp-pink, apparently not long, and the maple-leaved viburnum, a little longer, but quite early. Some of the calla is going to seed.

See an oven-bird's nest with two eggs and one young one just hatched. The bird flits out low, and is, I think, the same kind that I saw flit along the ground and trail her wings to lead me off day before yesterday.

June 20. P. M. — By boat to Holden Swamp.

I heard that snapping sound against a pad on the surface, and at the same time saw a pad knocked up several inches, and a ripple in the water there as when a pickerel darts away. I should say without doubt some fish had darted there against the pad, perhaps at an insect on the under side.

Got the marsh hawk's egg, which was addled. I

[1] Saw it the 23d, and it is apparently this bird. It is some ten rods south along path beyond the clearing, opposite a stone turned over. *Vide* 23d. *Vide* July 31st.

[2] Similarly placed to the hermit (?) thrush's of three pages forward.

[3] I have one egg. *Vide* 23d.

noticed on the 17th that the hawk (my marsh hawk) was off her nest and soaring above the wood late in the afternoon, as I was returning.

I notice that when turtles are floating dead their necks and legs are stretched out. I have seen them this year of every kind but the *meleagris* and cistudo, including a snapping turtle with shell some nine inches long, floating or lying dead. What kills them?

I wade about Holden Swamp, looking for birds' nests. The spruce there are too thin-foliaged for nests, though I hear a pepe expressing anxiety, and also song sparrows. See the redstart and hear many; also *hear* the blue yellow-backs.

Walking in the white pine wood there, I find that my shoes and, indeed, my hat are covered with the greenish-yellow pollen of the white pines, which is now being shed abundantly and covers like a fine meal all the plants and shrubs of the forest floor. I never noticed it in such abundance before. My shoes are green-yellow, or yellow-green, even the next day with it.

Dangle-berry well out, how long? *Potentilla Norvegica*, how long? What is that sedge with a long *beak*, some time out of bloom, now two feet high, common just north of new stone bridge? *Vide* pressed one.

I see that the French have a convenient word, *aunaie*, also spelt *aulnaie* and *aulnage*, etc., signifying a grove of alders. It reminds me of their other convenient word used by Rasle, *cabanage*.

June 21. *Vide* at Cambridge, apparently in prime, *Silene inflata;* also, in a rich grass-field on Sacramento

Street, what may be *Turritis glabra* (?), also in prime, the last three or four feet high. Both pressed.

Talked with Mr. Bryant at the Natural History Rooms. He agrees with Kneeland in thinking that what I call the myrtle-bird's is the white-throat sparrow's note. Bryant killed one Down East in summer of '56. He has lived the last fifteen years at Cohasset, and also knows the birds of Cambridge, but talks of several birds as rare which are common in Concord, such as the stake-driver, marsh hawk (have neither of their eggs in the collection), Savannah sparrow, the *passerina* much rarer, and I think purple finch, etc. Never heard the *tea-lee* note of myrtle-bird (?) in this State. Their large hawk is the red-shouldered, not hen-hawk. He thinks that the sheldrake of the Maine lakes is the *merganser*, the *serrator* belonging rather to the seacoast. Of the two little dippers or grebes, he thought the white-breasted one would be the commonest, which has also a slender bill, while the other has a brownish breast and a much thicker bill.

The egg of the *Turdus solitarius* in the collection is longer, but marked very much like the tanager's, only paler-brown. They have also the egg of the *T. brunneus*, the other hermit thrush, not common here.

June 22. Edward Bartlett found what he calls two bobolinks' nests some weeks ago, with each six eggs. I have one of the nests. There is but little of it, composed simply of some flexible grass without and finer within, kept in form by the thick tussock or tuft of meadow-grass at the bottom and in the midst of which it is placed.

He shows me, also, one of three eggs found the 20th in Gourgas's wood-lot, within a rod of the roadside, in a small slender oak (eighteen feet high), about fourteen feet from the ground, about fifteen rods north of Britton's corner, in a grove, where two or three small branches left the main stem; eggs somewhat advanced. Says the bird was a thrush of some kind. The egg is one inch by five eighths, rather slender, faint-blue, and quite generally spotted with distinct rather reddish brown, inclining to small streaky blotches, though especially at the larger end; not *pale*-brown like that described [on the preceding] page. Can it be the *Turdus solitarius?* [1]

Mowing the June grass about our house a few days ago, I disturbed several toads squatted deep in the rankest grass near the house, and wounded one or two with the scythe. They appear to love such cool and shady retreats by day, hopping out at night and in the rain.

I see in the river a little pickerel, not quite two inches long, which must have been hatched this year, and probably as early as the perch, since they have more to grow.

I notice, after tipping the water out of my boat under the willows, much evidently pine pollen adhering to the inside of the boat along the water-line. Did it fall into it during my excursion to Holden's Swamp the 20th, or has it floated through the air thus far? [2]

[1] I have the egg. *Vide* Dec. 7th, 1858. *Vide* my note to Wilson's hermit thrush.
[2] *Vide* June 21st, 1860.

About the grassy island in front of the Rock, grows abundantly, apparently the *Carex crinita*, with about four long pendulous fertile spikes and one barren, two and a half feet high and long since done. I think that I first noticed willow down floating on the river about the 16th.

Observe a painted turtle laying or digging at 5 P. M. She has not excavated any hole, but has already watered the ground, and, as usual when I take her up under these circumstances, passes more water.

June 23. P. M. — With some boys to Flint's Pond, to see the nests mentioned on last [two pages]. The hermit (?) thrush's nest referred to on last page is a rather shallow nest of loose construction, though sufficiently thick-bottomed, about five inches in diameter and hardly one deep within, externally of rather coarse and loosely arranged stubble, chiefly everlasting stems with the flowers yet emitting some fragrance, some whorled loosestrife with the seed-vessels, etc., etc.; within, finer grass and pine-needles. Yet the grass is as often bent angularly as curved regularly to form the nest.

The tanager's nest of the 19th is four and a half to five inches wide and an inch or more deep, considerably open to look through; the outside, of many very slender twigs, apparently of hemlock, some umbelled pyrola with seed-vessels, everlasting, etc.; within, quite round and regular, of very slender or fine stems, apparently pinweed or the like, and pine-needles; hardly any grass stubble about it. The egg is a regular oval nine tenths of an inch long by twenty-seven fortieths, pale-blue, sprinkled with purplish-brown spots, thickest on the larger end. To-day there are three rather fresh eggs in this nest. Neither going nor returning do we see anything of the tanager, and conclude it to be deserted, but perhaps she stays away from it long.

That rather low wood along the path which runs parallel with the shore of Flint's Pond, behind the rock, is evidently a favorite place for veery-nests. I have seen three there. One lately emptied I got to-day, amid the dry leaves by some withered ferns. It is composed externally of a mass of much withered oak leaves, thick and pretty well stuck together, plastered or stuck down over the rim, is five to six inches in diameter and four high, two and a half wide within, and very deep, more than two inches. Next to the leaves come bark-shreds, apparently maple bark, and the lining is of a little fine grass, pine-needles, apparently a little hypnum root-fibre. A very deep well-shaped and rounded cavity. Saw another with two eggs in it, one a much lighter blue than the other. This was by the path leading toward the rock, amid some sprouts at the base of a sapling oak, elevated about six inches above the general level (the veery's). It was a deep, firm nest three quarters of an inch thick, outwardly oak and chestnut leaves, then rather coarse bark-shreds, maple or oak, lined with the same and a few dark root-fibres.

What that empty nest partly of mud, with conspicuous saliva, on a middle-sized maple, against main stem, near wood thrush's?

In the case of the hermit (?) thrush, wood thrush, and tanager's, each about fourteen feet high in slender saplings, you had to climb an adjacent tree in order to reach them.

A male redstart seen, and often heard. What a little fellow!

Lysimachia quadrifolia, how long? and veiny-leaved hawkweed, how long? Get an egg out of a deserted bank swallow's nest, in a bank only about four feet high dug in the spring for a bank wall near Everett's. The nest is flattish and lined abundantly with the small, somewhat downy, naturally curved feathers of poultry. Egg pure white, long, oval, twenty-seven fortieths by eighteen fortieths of an inch.

Take two eggs out of the oviduct of an *E. insculpta*, just run over in the road.

They have lately cooked a snapping turtle at Mrs. Wetherbee's, eggs and all, and she thinks there were just forty-two of them!

June 24. Very hot weather.
Aralia hispida at Cliffs. Epilobium, how long?
Storrow Higginson gives me a bobolink's egg. It is a regular oval, seven eighths by five eighths inch. It is a dark cream-color with pretty large spots of brown, sometimes blackish, chiefly at the large end, and very faint, more internal pale-purplish spots equally dispersed.

June 25. P. M. — To Conantum.
Hotter than yesterday and, like it, muggy or close.

Vol. X

So hazy can see no mountains. In many spots in the road and by edge of rye-fields the reflected heat is almost suffocating. 93° at 1 P. M.

At my perch pool I hear the pebbly sound of frogs, and some, perhaps below the middle size, hop in before I see them. I suspect that this sound is not made by the bullfrog, but by the *fontinalis* or *palustris*.

In the meadow or partly included in the west end of Hubbard's Grove, a smooth, rather flaccid rush with roundish spikes, say twenty inches high, apparently fresh, somewhat *flava*-like.

Sitting on the Conantum house sill (still left), I see two and perhaps three young striped squirrels, two-thirds grown, within fifteen or twenty feet, one or more on the wall and another on the ground. Their tails are rather imperfect, as their bodies. They are running about, yet rather feebly, nibbling the grass, etc., or sitting upright, looking very cunning. The broad white line above and below the eye make it look very long as well as large, and the black and white stripes on its sides, curved as it sits, are very conspicuous and pretty. Who striped the squirrel's side? Several times I saw two approach each other and playfully and, as it were, affectionately put their paws and noses to each other's faces. Yet this was done very deliberately and affectionately. There was no rudeness nor excessive activity in their sport. At length the old one appears, larger and much more bluish, and shy, and, with a sharp cluck or chip, calls the others gradually to her and draws them off along the wall, they from time to time frisking ahead of her, then she ahead of

them. The hawks must get many of these inexperienced creatures.

The *Rubus frondosus* is hardly past prime, while the *villosus* is almost wholly done here. Just south the wall at Bittern Cliff, the *Panicum latifolium*, hardly yet, with some leaves almost an inch and a half wide.

We bathe at Bittern Cliff. The water is exceedingly warm near the surface, but refreshingly cold four or five feet beneath. There must be twenty degrees difference at least.[1] The ground under the white pines is now strewn with the effete flowers, like an excrement.[2] I notice an apparent female bullfrog, with a lustrous greenish (not yellow) throat.

June 27. Sunday. P. M. — Up Assabet.
Land at old mill-site and walk through the Lee Woods looking for birds' nests. See an *Attacus luna* in the shady path, smaller than I have seen before. At first it appears unable or unwilling to fly, but at length it flutters along and upward two or three rods into an oak tree, and there hangs inconspicuous amid the leaves.

Find two wood pewees' nests, made like the one I have. One on a dead horizontal limb of a small oak, fourteen feet from ground, just on a horizontal fork and looking as old as the limb, color of the branch, three eggs far advanced. The other, with two eggs, was in a similar position exactly over a fork, but on a living branch of a slender white oak, eighteen feet

[1] [Queried in the margin.]
[2] Also July 4th, 1860, turned reddish, as the pitch pine earlier.

from ground; lichens without, then pine-needles, lined with usnea, willow down. Both nests three to five feet from main stem.

June 28. P. M. — To broom.

The erect potentilla is a distinct variety, with differently formed leaves as well as different time of flowering, and not the same plant at a different season. Have I treated it as such?

The *Genista tinctoria* has been open apparently a week. It has a pretty and lively effect, reminding me for some reason of the poverty-grass. Mountain laurel on east side of the rocky Boulder Field wood is apparently in prime.

I see in many places little barberry bushes just come up densely in the cow-dung, like young apple trees, the berries having been eaten by the cows. Here they find manure and an open space for the first year at least, when they are not choked by grass or weeds. In this way, evidently, many of these clumps of barberries are commenced.

I notice that the ostrya, when growing in woods, has a remarkable spread for the size of its trunk, more than any tree, methinks.

Cymbidium, how long? *Epilobium coloratum*, how long? We find in the Botrychium Swamp fine wiry asparagus plants, six inches high, with the seeds at bottom, apparently planted by birds, but no plants two years old. There are fertile bayberry bushes fifteen rods east of yellow birch and six south of apple tree.

Vol. X

June 29. P. M. — To Walden.

Bathing in the cove by railroad. When I hold my head near the surface and look down, in two or three feet of water, the bottom appears concave, just as the sky does. How interesting the water-target's slender gelatinous stem and leaves, reminding me of the plants in aquaria!

END OF VOLUME X

The Journal of Henry D. Thoreau

VOLUME XI

(July, 1858 — February, 1859)

October Reflections

CONTENTS

Vol. XI

vi   CONTENTS

CONTENTS   vii

Vol. XI

THE JOURNAL OF
HENRY DAVID THOREAU

VOLUME XI

I

JULY, 1858 (ÆT. 40–41)

July 2. A. M. — Start for White Mountains in a private carriage with Edward Hoar.

Notice in a shallow pool on a rock on a hilltop, in road in North Chelmsford, a rather peculiar-looking *Alisma Plantago*, with long reddish petioles, just budded.

Spent the noon close by the old Dunstable graveyard, by a small stream north of it. Red lilies were abundantly in bloom in the burying-ground and by the river. Mr. Weld's monument is a large, thick, naturally flat rock, lying flat over the grave. Noticed the monument of Josiah Willard, Esq., "Captain of Fort Dummer." Died 1750, aged 58.

Walked to and along the river and bathed in it. There were harebells, well out, and much *Apocynum cannabinum*, well out, apparently like ours, prevailing along the steep sandy and stony shore. A marked peculiarity in this species is that the upper branches rise above the flowers. Also get the *A. androsæmifolium*, quite downy beneath. The *Smilacina stellata* going to seed, quite common in the copse on top of the bank.

What a relief and expansion of my thoughts when I come out from that inland position by the graveyard to this broad river's shore! This vista was incredible there. Suddenly I see a broad reach of blue beneath, with its curves and headlands, liberating me from the more terrene earth. What a difference it makes whether I spend my four hours' nooning between the hills by yonder roadside, or on the brink of this fair river, within a quarter of a mile of that! Here the earth is fluid to my thought, the sky is reflected from beneath, and around yonder cape is the highway to other continents. This current allies me to all the world. Be careful to sit in an elevating and inspiring place. There my thoughts were confined and trivial, and I hid myself from the gaze of travellers. Here they are expanded and elevated, and I am charmed by the beautiful river-reach. It is equal to a different season and country and creates a different mood. As you travel northward from Concord, probably the reaches of the Merrimack River, looking up or down them from the bank, will be the first inspiring sight. There is something in the scenery of a broad river equivalent to culture and civilization. Its channel conducts our thoughts as well as bodies to classic and famous ports, and allies us to all that is fair and great. I like to remember that at the end of half a day's walk I can stand on the bank of the Merrimack. It is just wide enough to interrupt the land and lead my eye and thoughts down its channel to the sea. A river is superior to a lake in its liberating influence. It has motion and indefinite length. A river touching the back of a town is like a wing, it may be unused as yet, but

ready to waft it over the world. With its rapid current it is a slightly fluttering wing. River towns are winged towns.

I returned through the grass up the winding channel of our little brook to the camp again. Along the brook, in the rank grass and weeds, grew abundantly a slender umbelliferous plant mostly just out of bloom, one and a half to four feet high. Either *Thaspium aureum* or *Cryptotænia Canadensis* (Sison).[1] Saw also the scouring-rush, apparently just beginning to bloom!

In the southern part of Merrimack, passed a singular "Horseshoe Pond" between the road and the river on the interval. Belknap says in his History, speaking of the changes in river-courses, "In some places these ancient channels are converted into ponds, which, from their curved form, are called horseshoe ponds."

Put up at tavern in Merrimack, some miles after passing over a pretty high, flat-topped hill in road, whence we saw the mountains (with a steep descent to the interval on right).

7 P. M. — I walked by a path through the wood northeast to the Merrimack, crossing two branches of Babboosuck Brook, on which were handsome rocky falls in the woods.

The wood thrush sings almost wherever I go, eternally reconsecrating the world, morning and evening, for us. And again it seems habitable and more than habitable to us.[2]

[1] *Vide* June 3d, 1852, and May 11th, 1859.
[2] *Vide* next page.

July 3. Continued along in a slight rain through Bedford, crossing to Manchester, and driving by a brook in Hookset just above Pinnacle. Then through Allenstown and Pembroke, with its long street, to Loudon, leaving Concord on the left. Along the sandy roadside in a pitch pine wood in Loudon, much apparent *Calystegia spithamœa* in bloom, but I think with reddish flowers. Probably same with my New Bedford plant.

July 4. *Sunday*. A. M. — Clears up after a rainy night. Get our breakfast apparently in the northern part of Loudon, where we find, in a beech and maple wood, *Panax quinquefolium*, apparently not quite out, *Osmorrhiza brevistylis* (or hairy uraspermum), gone to seed, which Bigelow refers to woods on Concord Turnpike, *i. e.* hairy sweet cicely. Also ternate polypody (?). Saw a chestnut tree in Loudon.

Leaving Loudon Ridge on the right we continued on by the Hollow Road — a long way through the forest without houses — through a part of Canterbury into Gilmanton Factory village. I see the *Ribes prostratum*, or fetid currant, by roadside, already red, as also the red elder-berries, ripe or red.[1] Strawberries were abundant by the roadside and in the grass on hillsides everywhere, with the seeds conspicuous, sunk in pits on the surface. (*Vide* a leaf of same kind pressed.)

The Merrimack at Merrimack, where I walked, — half a mile or more below my last camp on it in '39, — had gone down two or three feet within a few days, and the muddy and slimy shore was covered with the tracks

[1] This only in the northern part of New Hampshire.

of many small animals, apparently three-toed sandpipers, minks, turtles, squirrels, perhaps mice, and some much larger quadrupeds. The *Solidago lanceolata*, not out, was common along the shore. Wool-grass without black sheaths, and a very slender variety with it; also *Carex crinita*.

We continue along through Gilmanton to Meredith Bridge, passing the Suncook Mountain on our right, a long, barren rocky range overlooking Lake Winnepiseogee. Turn down a lane five or six miles beyond the bridge and spend the midday near a bay of the lake. *Polygonum cilinode*, apparently not long. I hear song sparrows there among the rocks, with a totally new strain, ending *whit whit, whit whit, whit whit whit*. They had also the common strain. We had begun to see from Gilmanton, from high hills in the road, the sharp rocky peak of Chocorua in the north, to the right of the lower Red Hill. It was of a pale-buff color, with apparently the Sandwich Mountains west of it and Ossipee Mountain on the right. The goldfinch was more common than at home, and the fragrant fern was perceived oftener. The evergreen-forest note frequently heard.

It is far more independent to travel on foot. You have to sacrifice so much to the horse. You cannot choose the most agreeable places in which to spend the noon, commanding the finest views, because commonly there is no water there, or you cannot get there with your horse. New Hampshire being a more hilly and newer State than Massachusetts, it is very difficult to find a suitable place to camp near the road, affording water, a good prospect, and retirement. We several

times rode on as much as ten miles with a tired horse, looking in vain for such a spot, and then almost invariably camped in some low, unpleasant spot. There are very few, scarcely any, lanes, or even paths and bars along the road. Having got beyond the range of the chestnut, the few bars that might be taken down are long and heavy planks or slabs, intended to confine sheep, and there is no passable road behind. And beside, when you have chosen a place one must stay behind to watch your effects, while the other looks about. I frequently envied the independence of the walker, who can spend the midday hours and take his lunch in the most agreeable spot on his route. The only alternative is to spend your noon at some trivial inn, pestered by flies and tavern loungers.

Camped within a mile south of Senter Harbor, in a birch wood on the right near the lake. Heard in the night a loon, screech owl, and cuckoo, and our horse, tied to a slender birch close by, restlessly pawing the ground all night and whinnering to us whenever we showed ourselves, asking for something more than meat to fill his belly with.

July 5. *Monday*. Continue on through Senter Harbor and ascend Red Hill in Moultonboro. On this ascent I notice the *Erigeron annuus*, which we have not, methinks, *i. e. purple* fleabane (for it is commonly purplish), hairy with thin leaves and broader than the *strigosus*. Notice the *Comandra umbellata*, with leaves in three very regular spiral lines. Dr. Jackson says that Red Hill is so called from the uva-ursi on it turning red in

the fall. On the top we boil a dipper of tea for our dinner and spend some hours, having carried up water the last half-mile.

Enjoyed the famous view of Winnepiseogee and its islands southeasterly and Squam Lake on the west, but I was as much attracted at this hour by the wild mountain view on the northward. Chocorua and the Sandwich Mountains a dozen miles off seemed the boundary of cultivation on that side, as indeed they are. They are, as it were, the impassable southern barrier of the mountain region, themselves lofty and bare, and filling the whole northerly horizon, with the broad vale or valley of Sandwich between you and them; and over their ridges, in one or two places, you detected a narrow, blue edging or a peak of the loftier White Mountains proper (or so called). Ossipee Mountain is on the east, near by; Chocorua (which the inhabitants pronounce She-corway or Corway), in some respects the wildest and most imposing of all the White Mountain peaks, north of northeast, bare rocks, slightly flesh-colored; some large mountains, perhaps the Franconia, far northwesterly; Ragged (??) Mountain, south of west; Kearsarge, southwest; Monadnock (?), dim and distant blue, and some other mountains as distant, more easterly; Suncook Mountain, south-southeast, and, beyond the lake, south of southeast, Copple-Crown Mountain (?). When I looked at the near Ossipee Mountain (and some others), I saw first smooth pastures around the base or extending part way up, then the light green of deciduous trees (probably oak, birch, maple, etc.), looking dense and shrubby, and above all the rest, looking like permanent shadows, dark saddles of spruce or fir or both on the summits. Jackson says larch, spruce, and birch reach to the summit of Ossipee Mountain. The landscape is spotted, like a leopard-skin, with large squarish patches of light-green and darker forests and blue lakes, etc., etc.

On the top I found *Potentilla tridentata*, out a good while, choke-berry, red lily, dwarfish red oaks, *Carex Novæ-Angliæ* (?), and a carex *scoparia*-like. Apparently the common *Vaccinium Pennsylvanicum*, and just below, in the shrubbery, the *Vaccinium Canadense* was the prevailing one. Just below top, a clematis, and, as you descended, the red oak, growing larger, canoe birch, some small white birch, red maple, rock maple, *Populus tremuliformis*,[1] diervilla (very common), etc., etc.[2]

Heard the chewink on the summit, and saw an ant-hill there, within six rods of apex, about seven by six feet in diameter and sixteen inches high, with grass growing on all sides of it. This reminded me of the great ant-hills I saw on Chesterfield Mountain, opposite Brattleboro.

Descended, and rode along the west and northwest side of Ossipee Mountain. Sandwich, in a large level space surrounded by mountains, lay on our left. Here first, in Moultonboro, I heard the *tea-lee* of the white-throated sparrow. We were all the afternoon riding along under Ossipee Mountain, which would not be left

[1] The common species afterward on sides and about the mountains.
[2] Diervilla and checkerberry common after on mountainsides.

behind, unexpectedly large still, louring over your path. Crossed Bearcamp River, a shallow but unexpectedly sluggish stream, which empties into Ossipee Lake. Have new and memorable views of Chocorua, as we get round it eastward. Stop at Tamworth village for the night.

We are now near the edge of a wild and unsettlable mountain region, lying northwest, apparently including parts of Albany and Waterville. The landlord said that bears were plenty in it; that there was a little interval on Swift River that might be occupied, and that was all. Norcross gets his lumber in that region, on Mad and Swift Rivers, as I understood; and on Swift River, as near as I could learn, was the only road leading into it.

July 6. Tuesday. 5.35 A. M. — Keep on through North Tamworth, and breakfast by shore of one of the Ossipee Lakes. Chocorua north-northwest. Hear and see loons and see a peetweet's egg washed up. A shallow-shored pond, too shallow for fishing, with a few breams seen near shore; some pontederia and target-weed in it.

Travelling thus toward the White Mountains, the mountains fairly begin with Red Hill and Ossipee Mountain, but the White Mountain scenery proper on the high hillside road in Madison before entering Conway, where you see Chocorua on the left, Mote Mountain ahead, Doublehead, and some of the White Mountains proper beyond, *i. e.* a sharp peak.

We fished in vain in a small clear pond by the roadside in Madison.

Vol. XI

Chocorua is as interesting a peak as any to remember. You may be jogging along steadily for a day before you get round it and leave it behind, first seeing it on the north, then northwest, then west, and at last southwesterly, ever stern, rugged and inaccessible, and omnipresent. It was seen from Gilmanton to Conway, and from Moultonboro was the ruling feature.

The scenery in Conway and onward to North Conway is surprisingly grand. You are steadily advancing into an amphitheatre of mountains. I do not know exactly how long we had seen one of the highest peaks before us in the extreme northwest, with snow on its side just below the summit, but a little beyond Conway a boy called it Mt. Washington. I think it was visible just before entering Conway village. If Mt. Washington, the snow must have been in Tuckerman's Ravine, which, methinks, is rather too low. Perhaps it was that we afterward saw on Mt. Adams. There was the regular dark pyramid of Kearsarge at first in front, then, as you proceed to North Conway, on our right, with its deserted hotel on the summit, and Mote Mountain accompanies you on the left, and high, bare rocky precipices at last on the same side. The road, which is for the most part level, winds along the Saco through groves of maples, etc., on the level intervals, with so little of rugged New Hampshire under your feet, often soft and sandy road. The scenery is remarkable for this contrast of level interval with soft and shady groves, with mountain grandeur and ruggedness. Often from the midst of level maple groves, which remind you only of classic lowlands, you look out through a vista to the most

rugged scenery of New England. It is quite unlike New Hampshire generally, quite unexpected by me, and suggests a superior culture. We at length crossed the Saco from the left to the right side of the valley, going over or through three channels. After leaving North Conway, the higher White Mountains were less seen, if at all. They had not appeared in pinnacles, as sometimes described, but broad and massive. Only one of the higher peaks or summits (called by the boy Mt. Washington) was conspicuous. The snow near the top was conspicuous here thirty miles off. The summit appeared dark, the rocks just beneath pale-brown (forenoon) (not flesh-colored like Chocorua), and below, green, wooded.

The road to-day from Tamworth almost to the base of Mt. Washington was better on the whole, less hilly, than through Gilmanton to Tamworth; *i. e.*, the hills were not so long and tedious.

At Bartlett Corner we turned up the Ellis River and took our nooning on the bank of the river, by the bridge just this side of Jackson Centre, in a rock maple grove. Saw snow on Mt. Carter (?) from this road. There are but few *narrow* intervals on this road, — two or three only after passing Jackson, — and each is improved by a settler. We see the handsome *Malva sylvestris*, an introduced flower, by roadside, apparently in prime, and also in Conway, and hear the night-warbler all along thus far.

Saw the bones of a bear at Wentworth's house, and camped, rather late, on right-hand side of road just beyond, or a little more than four miles from Jackson.

The wood was canoe birch and some yellow (see little of the small white birch as far as to the neighborhood of the mountains), rock maple, spruce, fir, *Populus tremuliformis*, and one *grandidentata*, etc. In this deep vale between the mountains, the sun set very early to us, but we saw it on the mountains long after. Heard at evening the wood thrush, veery, white-throated sparrow, etc., and I found a fresh nest in a fir, made of hemlock twigs, etc., when I was getting twigs for a bed. The mosquitoes troubled us in the evening and just before dawn, but not seriously in the middle of the night. This, I find, is the way with them generally.

Wentworth said he was much troubled by the bears. They killed his sheep and calves and destroyed his corn when in the milk, close by his house. He has trapped and killed many of them and brought home and reared the young. When we looked up in the night we saw that the stars were bright as in winter, owing to the clear cold air.

July 7. Wednesday. Having engaged the services of Wentworth to carry up some of our baggage and to keep our camp, we rode onward to the Glen House, eight miles further, sending back our horse and wagon to his house. This road passes through what is called the Pinkham Notch, in Pinkham's Grant, the land, a large tract, having been given away to Pinkham for making the road a good while since. Wentworth has lived here thirty years and is a native. Have occasional views of Mt. Washington or a spur of it, etc.

Get by roadside, in bloom some time, *Geum macrophyllum;* also, in a damp place, *Platanthera dilatata,* a narrow white spike. Turned off a little to the right to see Glen Ellis Falls.

Began the ascent by the mountain road at 11.30 A. M.

For about the first three quarters of a mile of steady (winding) ascent the wood was spruce, yellow birch (some, generally the largest, with a very rough, coarse, scaly bark, but other trees equally large had a beautifully smooth bark, and Wentworth called these "silver birch;" it appeared not to depend on age merely), hemlock, beech, canoe birch (according to Willey, "most abundant in the districts formerly burnt"), rock maple, fir, mountain maple (called by Wentworth bastard maple), northern wild cherry, striped maple, etc. At about a mile and three quarters spruce prevails, and rock maple, beech, and hemlock, etc., disappear. At three miles, or near the limit of trees, fir (increasing) and spruce chiefly prevail. And near by was the foot of the ledge and limit of trees, only their dead trunks standing, probably fir and spruce, about the shanty where we spent the night with the colliers.

I went on nearly a mile and a half further, and found many new alpine plants and returned to this shanty. A merry collier and his assistant, who had been making coal for the summit and were preparing to leave the next morning, made us welcome to this shanty and entertained us with their talk. We here boiled some of our beef-tongues, a very strong wind pouring in gusts down the funnel and scattering the fire about through the cracked stove. This man, named Page, had im-

ported goats on to the mountain, and milked them to supply us with milk for our coffee. The road here ran north and south to get round the ledge. The wind, blowing down the funnel, set fire to a pile of dirty bed-quilts when I was out, and came near burning up the building. There were many barrels of spoiled beef in the cellar, and he said that a person coming down the mountain some time ago looked into the cellar and saw five wildcats (*loups-cerviers*) there. Page had heard two fighting like cats near by a few nights before. The wind blowed very strong and in gusts this night, but he said it was nothing to what it was sometimes, when the building rocked four inches.

July 8. Though a fair day, the sun did not rise clear. I started before my companions, wishing to secure a clear view from the summit, while they accompanied the collier and his assistant, who were conducting up to the summit for the first time his goats. He led the old one, and the rest followed.

I noticed these plants this morning and the night before at and above the limit of trees: *Oxalis Acetosella,* abundant and in bloom near the shanty and further down the mountain, all over the woods; *Cornus Canadensis,* also abundantly in bloom about the shanty and far above and below it. At shanty, or limit of trees. began to find *Alsine Grœnlandica* abundant and in prime, the first mountain flower.[1] Noticed one returning, in carriage-road more than half-way down the mountain. It extended to within a mile of summit

[1] Durand in Kane puts it at 73° + in Greenland.

along path,[1] and grew about our camp at Hermit Lake. The second mountain plant I noticed was the ledum,[2] growing in dense continuous patches or fields, filling broad spaces between the rocks, but dwarfish compared with ours in Concord. It was still in bloom. It *prevailed* about two miles below the summit. At the same elevation I noticed the *Vaccinium uliginosum,* a prevailing plant from the ledge to perhaps one mile or more below summit, almost entirely out of bloom, a procumbent bilberry, growing well, not dwarfish, with peculiar glaucous roundish-obovate leaves.[3] About the same time and locality, *Salix Uva-ursi,* the prevailing willow of the alpine region, completely out of bloom and going or gone to seed, a flat, trailing, glossy-leaved willow with the habit of the bearberry, spreading in a close mat over the rocks or rocky surface. I saw one spreading flat for three or four feet over a rock in the ravine (as low as I saw it).[4] *Diapensia Lapponica* (*Menziesia cœrulea*),[5] beginning about same time, or just over the ledge, reached yet higher, or to within last mile. Quite out of bloom; only one flower seen. It grows in close, *firm*, and dense rounded tufts, just like a moss but harder, between the rocks, the flowers con-

[1] Aye, to summit.
[2] Loudon makes three (!) species, and says bees are very fond of the flower.
[3] According to Durand at 78° N. in Smith's Sound.
[4] Durand in Kane places this at 65° N. in Greenland, but Kane (vol. i, p. 462) says that Morton and Hans saw it along the shore of Kennedy Channel, the furthest coast reached, and that with the southern Esquimaux it is reputed to cure scurvy.
[5] According to Durand, at 73° in Greenland.

siderably elevated above its surface. *Empetrum nigrum*, growing somewhat like *Corema*, with berries green and some turning black.[1] Mountain cranberry was abundant and in bloom, a very pretty flower, with, say, the *Vaccinium uliginosum* and to within last mile. Gold-thread in bloom, was abundant to within last mile. As high as the above, on this side or that extended dwarf shrubby canoe birches and almost impassable thickets of dwarf fir and spruce. The latter when dead exhibited the appearance of deer's horns, their hard, gnarled, slow-grown branches being twisted in every direction. Their roots were singularly knotted and swollen from time to time, from the size of the finger into oval masses like a ship's block, or a rabbit made of a handkerchief. *Epigæa*.[2] At this height, too, was a *Lycopodium annotinum*, a variety; and, probably, there, too, *L. Selago*, as at edge of ravine;[3] sedges, sorrel, moss, and lichens. Was surprised not to notice the *Potentilla tridentata* in bloom till quite high, though common on low mountains southward.[4] Here it was above the trailing spruce, answering to top of Monadnock, and with it came more sedge, *i. e.* a more grassy surface without many larger plants. (George Bradford says he has found this potentilla on Cape Ann, at Eastern Point, east side Gloucester Harbor.[5]) About a mile below top, *Geum radiatum* var. *Peckii* in prime, and

[1] According to Durand, as far as Disco Island, 70° N.; "the ordinary food of deer and rabbits."
[2] And after pretty high on Lafayette.
[3] Both, according to Durand, at 64° N. in Greenland.
[4] According to Durand at 79° N.
[5] And Russell says in the college yard at Amherst.

a little *Silene acaulis* (moss campion), still in bloom, a pretty little purplish flower growing like a moss in dense, hard tufts.[1]

The rocks of the alpine portion are of about uniform size, not large nor precipitous. Generally there is nothing to prevent ascending in any direction, and there is no climbing necessary on the summit. For the last mile the rocks are generally smaller and more bare and the ascent easier, and there are some rather large level grassy spaces. The rocks are not large and flat enough to hold water, as on Monadnock. I saw but little water on this summit, though in many places, commonly in small holes on the grassy flats, and I think the rocky portion under your feet is less interesting than at Monadnock. I sweated in a thick coat as I ascended. About half a mile below top I noticed dew on the mossy, tufted surface, with mountain cranberry in the sedge.

On the very summit I noticed moss, sedge (the kind I have tied together),[2] forming what is now to be called the Great Pasture there, they say; a little alsine and diapensia; a bright-green crustaceous lichen;[3] and that small dark-brown umbilicaria-like one (of Monadnock), of which I have a specimen. The rocks, being small and not precipitous, have no such lichen-clad angles as at Monadnock, yet the general aspect of the rocks about you is dark-brown. All over the summit there is

[1] Durand says at 73° + in Greenland.
[2] *Carex rigida*, with a black spike.
[3] Is this *Lecida geographica*? Oakes (in "Scenery," etc.) speaks of the geographic lichen as found on the summit; *viz.* "the yellow of the beautiful geographic lichen."

Vol. XI

a great deal of that sedge grass, especially southeast and east amid the smallish rocks. There was a solidago (or aster) quite near summit (not out), perhaps *S. Virgaurea*.

The only bird I had seen on the way up, above the limit of trees, was the *Fringilla hyemalis*. Willey says the swallow flies over the summit and that a bear has been seen there.

I got up about half an hour before my party and enjoyed a good view, though it was hazy, but by the time the rest arrived a cloud invested us all, a cool driving mist, which wet you considerably, as you squatted behind a rock. As I looked downward over the rock surface, I saw tinges of blue sky and a light as of breaking away close to the rocky edge of the mountain far below me instead of above, showing that there was the edge of the cloud. It was surprising to look down thus under the cloud at an angle of thirty or forty degrees for the only evidences of a clear sky and breaking away. There was a ring of light encircling the summit, thus close to the rocks under the thick cloud, and the evidences of a blue sky in that direction were just as strong as ordinarily when you look upward.

On our way up we had seen all the time, before us on the right, a large patch of snow on the southeast side of Mt. Adams, the first large summit north of Washington. I observed that the enduring snow-drifts were such as had lodged under the southeast cliffs, having been blown over the summit by the northwest wind. They lie up under such cliffs and at the head of the ravines on the southeast slopes.

A Mr. White, an artist taking views from the summit, had just returned from the Gulf of Mexico with the pretty purple-flowered *Phyllodoce taxifolia* and *Cassiope hypnoides*.

The landlords of the Tiptop and Summit Houses, Spaulding and Hall, assured me that my (Willey's) map was wrong, both in the names and height of Adams and Jefferson, — that the order should be reversed, Adams being the sharp peak, the second large one north of Washington, — but Boardman's map also calls this Jefferson.

About 8.15 A.M., being still in a dense fog, we started direct for Tuckerman's Ravine, I having taken the bearing of it before the fog, but Spaulding also went some ten rods with us and pointed toward the head of the ravine, which was about S. 15° W. Hoar tried to hire Page to go with us, carrying part of our baggage, — as he had already brought it up from the shanty, — and he professed to be acquainted with the mountain; but his brother, who lived at the summit, warned him not to go, lest he should not be able to find his way back again, and he declined. The landlords were rather anxious about us. I looked at my compass every four or five rods and then walked toward some rock in our course, but frequently after taking three or four steps, though the fog was no more dense, I would lose the rock I steered for. The fog was very bewildering. You would think that the rock you steered for was some large boulder twenty rods off, or perchance it looked like the brow of a distant spur, but a dozen steps would take you to it, and it would suddenly have sunk into the ground. I discovered this illusion. I said to my companions, "You see that boulder of a peculiar form, slanting over another. Well, that is in our course. How large do you think it is, and how far?" To my surprise, one answered three rods, but the other said nine. I guessed four, and we all thought it about eight feet high. We could not see beyond it, and it looked like the highest part of a ridge before us. At the end of twenty-one paces or three and a half rods, I stepped upon it, — less than two feet high, — and I could not have distinguished it from the hundred similar ones around it, if I had not kept my eye on it all the while.

It is unwise for one to ramble over these mountains at any time, unless he is prepared to move with as much certainty as if he were solving a geometrical problem. A cloud may at any moment settle around him, and unless he has a compass and knows which way to go, he will be lost at once. One lost on the summit of these mountains should remember that if he will travel due east or west eight or nine miles, or commonly much less, he will strike a public road. Or whatever direction he might take, the average distance would not be more than eight miles and the extreme distance twenty. Follow some water-course running easterly or westerly. If the weather were severe on the summit, so as to prevent searching for the summit houses or the path, I should at once take a westward course from the southern part of the range or an eastward one from the northern part. To travel there with security, a person must know his bearings at every step, be it fair weather or foul. An ordinary rock in a fog, being in the apparent horizon.

Vol. XI

is exaggerated to, perhaps, at least ten times its size and distance. You will think you have gone further than you have to get to it.

Descending straight by compass through the cloud, toward the head of Tuckerman's Ravine, we found it an easy descent over, for the most part, bare rocks, not very large, with at length moist springy places, green with sedge, etc., between little sloping shelves of green meadow, where the hellebore grew, within half a mile of top, and the *Oldenlandia cœrulea* was abundantly out (!) and very large and fresh, surpassing ours in the spring. And here, I think, *Juncus trifidus* (?),[1] and *Lycopodium Selago*, and *Lonicera cœrulea*, or mountain fly-honeysuckle, in bloom, only two specimens; it is found in the western part of Massachusetts.[2] Saw a few little ferns of a narrow triangular form, somewhat like the *Woodsia Ilvensis*, but less hairy and taller; small clintonias in bloom, and *Viola palustris*, in prime, from three quarters of a mile below summit down to snow; and a fine juncus or scirpus, *cœspitosus*-like, i. e. a single-headed or spiked rush; and trientalis, still in bloom, rather depauperate; and, I think, a few small narrow-leaved blueberry bushes; at least one minute mountain-ash. Also the *Geum radiatum* var. *Peckii* was conspicuous in prime hence down to the snow in the ravine. These chiefly in those peculiar moist and mossy sloping shelves on the mountain-side, on way to the ravine, or within a mile of the summit.

[1] Yes.
[2] Oakes makes the plain above the ravine twelve hundred feet or more below summit.

Some twenty or thirty rods above the edge of the ravine, where it was more level and wet and grassy under low cliffs, grew the *Phyllodoce taxifolia*, not in tufts, under the jutting rocks and in moss, somewhat past prime.[1] The *Uvularia grandiflora* apparently in prime, and, part way down into ravine, *Loiseleuria (Azalea) procumbens*, on rocks, still in bloom,[2] and *Cassiope hypnoides*, about done. These four on a moist southeast slope. Also *Rubus triflorus*, reaching to camp, in prime.

Just on the edge of the ravine I began to see the *Heracleum lanatum* in prime, and the common archangelica, not out; and as I descended into the ravine on the steep side moist with melted snows, *Veronica alpina*, apparently in prime, and *Nabalus Boottii* (?) budded, down to snow, and *Epilobium alpinum* in prime, and *Platanthera dilatata* in prime, and the common rue and the first *Castilleja septentrionalis* (*Bartsia pallida*), apparently not long, which was more common about our camp. I recollect seeing all the last eight (except the rue and veronica and nabalus, which I do not remember) about our camp and yet more flourishing there and *Solidago Virgaurea* var. *alpina*, not quite out, edge of ravine. Should have included *Arnica mollis* among those on side of ravine reaching to camp, and, according to Hoar, raspberry and linnæa.

We crossed a narrow portion of the snow, but found it unexpectedly hard and dangerous to traverse. I tore up my nails in my efforts to save myself from sliding

[1] According to Durand, at Disco, 70° N.
[2] According to Durand, at 69° in Greenland.

down its steep surface. The snow-field now formed an irregular crescent on the steep slope at the head of the ravine, some sixty rods wide horizontally, or from north to south, and twenty-five rods wide from upper to lower side. It may have been half a dozen feet thick  in some places, but it diminished sensibly in the rain while we were there. Is said to be all gone commonly by end of August. The surface was hard, difficult to work your heels into, and a perfectly regular steep slope, steeper than an ordinary roof from top to bottom. A considerable stream, a source of the Saco, was flowing out from beneath it, where it had worn a low arch a rod or more wide. Here were the phenomena of winter and earliest spring, contrasted with summer. On the edge of and beneath the overarching snow, many plants were just pushing up as in our spring. The great plaited elliptical buds of the hellebore had just pushed up there, even under the edge of the snow, and also bluets. Also, close to edge of snow, the bare upright twigs of a willow, with small silvery buds not yet expanded, of a satiny lustre, one to two feet high (apparently *Salix repens*),[1] but not, as I noticed, procumbent, while a rod off on each side, where it had been melted some time, it was going to seed and fully leaved out. The surface of the snow was dirty, being covered with cinder-like rubbish of vegetation, which had blown on to it. Yet from the camp it looked quite white and pure. For thirty or forty rods, at least,

[1] Also apparently *S. phylicifolia*. *Vide* Sept. 21.

down the stream, you could see the point where the snow had recently melted. It was a dirty-brown flattened stubble, not yet at all greened, covered with a blackish slimy dirt, the dust of the snow-crust. Looking closely, I saw that it was composed in great part of the stems and flowers apparently of last year's goldenrods (if not asters), — perhaps large *thyrsoidea*, for they grew there on the slides, — now quite flattened, with other plants. A pretty large dense-catkined willow grew in the upper part of the ravine, *q. v.* Also, near edge of snow, vanilla grass, a vaccinium,[1] budded, with broad obovate leaves (*q. v.*), *Spiræa salicifolia* (and *on slides*), and nabalus (*Boottii ?*) leaves.

From the edge of the ravine, I should have said that, having reached the lower edge of the cloud, we came into the sun again, much to our satisfaction, and discerned a little lake called Hermit Lake, about a mile off, at the bottom of the ravine, just within the limit of the trees. For this we steered, in order to camp by it for the sake of the protection of the wood. But following down the edge of the stream, the source of Ellis River, which was quite a brook within a stone's throw of its head, we soon found it very bad walking in the scrubby fir and spruce, and therefore, when we had gone about two thirds the way to the lake, decided to camp in the midst of the dwarf firs, clearing away a space with our hatchets.

[1] This is apparently *V. cæspitosum*, for the anthers are two-awned, though I count but ten stamens in the flower I open, and I did not notice that the plant was tufted. Apparently the same, with thinner leaves, by Peabody River at base, but noticed no flowers there. Yet Gray refers it only to the alpine region!

Having cleared a space with some difficulty where the trees were seven or eight feet high, Wentworth kindled a fire on the lee side, without — against my advice — removing the moss, which was especially dry on the rocks and directly ignited and set fire to the fir leaves, spreading off with great violence and crackling over the mountain, and making us jump for our baggage; but fortunately it did not burn a foot toward us, for we could not have run in that thicket. It spread particularly fast in the procumbent creeping spruce, scarcely a foot deep, and made a few acres of deer's horns, thus leaving our mark on the mountainside. We thought at first it would run for miles, and W. said that it would do no harm, the more there was burned the better; but such was the direction of the wind that it soon reached the brow of a ridge east of us and then burned very slowly down its east side. Yet Willey says (page 23), speaking of the dead trees or "buck's horns," "Fire could not have caused the death of these trees; for fire will not spread here, in consequence of the humidity of the whole region at this elevation;" and he attributes their death to the cold of 1816. Yet it did spread above the limit of trees in the ravine.

Finally we kept on, leaving the fire raging, down to the first little lake, walking in the stream, jumping from rock to rock with it. It may have fallen a thousand feet within a mile below the snow, and we camped on a slight rising ground between that first little lake and the stream, in a dense fir and spruce wood thirty feet high, though it was but the limit of trees there. On our way we found the *Arnica mollis* (recently begun to bloom),

a very fragrant yellow-rayed flower, by the side of the brook (also half-way up the ravine). The *Alnus viridis* was a prevailing shrub all along this stream, seven or eight feet high near our camp near the snow. It was dwarfish and still in flower, but in fruit only below; had a glossy, roundish, wrinkled, green, sticky leaf. Also a little *Ranunculus abortivus* by the brook, in bloom.

Close by our camp, the *Heracleum lanatum*, or cow-parsnip, masterwort, grew quite rankly, its great leaves eighteen inches wide and umbels eight or nine inches wide; the petioles had inflated sheaths. I afterward saw it, I think in Campton, as much as seven feet high. It was quite common and conspicuous in the neighborhood of the mountains, especially in Franconia Notch. Our camp was opposite a great slide on the south, apparently a quarter of a mile wide, with the stream between us and it, and I resolved if a great storm should occur that we would flee to higher ground northeast. The little pond by our side was perfectly clear and cool, without weeds, and the meadow by it was dry enough to sit down in. When I looked up casually toward the crescent of snow I would mistake it for the sky, a white glowing sky or cloud, it was so high, while the dark earth on [the] mountainside above it passed for a dark cloud.

In the course of the afternoon we heard, as we thought, a faint shout, and it occurred to me that Blake, for whom I had left a note at the Glen House, might possibly be looking for me; but soon Wentworth decided that it must be a bear, for they make a noise like a woman in distress. He has caught many of them.

Nevertheless, we shouted in return and waved a light coat on the meadow. After an hour or two had elapsed, we heard the voice again, nearer, and saw two men, and I went up the stream to meet Blake and Brown, wet, ragged, and bloody with black flies. I had told Blake to look out for a smoke and a white tent, and we had made a smoke sure enough. They were on the edge of the ravine when they shouted and heard us answer, or about a mile distant, — heard over all the roar of the stream!! You could hear one shout from Hermit Lake to the top of the ravine above snow, back and forth, which I should think was a mile. They also saw our coat waved and ourselves. We slept five in the tent that night, and it rained, putting out the fire we had set. It was quite warm at night in our tent.

The wood thrush, which Wentworth called the nightingale, sang at evening and in the morning, and the same bird which I heard on Monadnock, I think, and then thought might be the Blackburnian warbler; also the veery.[1]

July 9. Friday. Walked to the Hermit Lake, some forty rods northeast. *Listera cordata* abundant and in prime in the woods, with a little *Platanthera obtusata*, also apparently in prime. (The last also as far up as the head of the ravine sparingly.) This was a cold, clear lake with scarcely a plant in it, of perhaps half an acre, and from a low ridge east of it was a fine view up the ravine. Hoar tried in vain for trout here. The *Vaccinium Canadense* was the prevailing one here and by our

[1] *Vide* Apr. 15th, 1859, about going up a mountain.

camp. Heard a bullfrog in the lake, and afterward saw a large toad part way up the ravine. Our camp was about on the limit of trees here, and may have been from twenty-five hundred to three thousand feet below the summit.

I was here surprised to discover, looking down through the fir-tops, a large, bright, downy fair-weather cloud covering the lower world far beneath us, and there it was the greater part of the time we were there, like a lake, while the snow and alpine summit were to be seen above us on the other side, at about the same angle. The pure white crescent of snow was our sky, and the dark mountainside above, our permanent cloud.

We had the *Fringilla hyemalis* with its usual note about our camp, and Wentworth said it was common and bred about his house. I afterward saw it in the valleys about the mountains. I had seen the white-throated sparrow near his house. This also, he said, commonly bred there, on the ground.

The wood we were in was fir and spruce. Along the brook grew the *Alnus viridis*, *Salix Torreyana* (?), canoe birch, red cherry, mountain-ash, etc., and prominent among lesser plants, *Heracleum lanatum*, *Castilleja septentrionalis*, the swamp gooseberry in flower and in green fruit, and a sort of *Ribes floridum* without resinous-dotted leaves! The *Hedyotis cœrulea* was surprisingly large and fresh, in bloom, looking as much whiter than usual as late snows do. I thought they must be a variety. And on a sand-bar by the brook, *Oxyria digyna*, the very pretty mountain sorrel, apparently in

prime.[1] Apparently *Viola blanda*, as well as wool-grass, in the meadow, and apparently *Aster prenanthes* and *Juncus filiformis*; also rhodora, fetid currant, amelanchier (variety *oligocarpa*), trientalis, mountain maple, tree-cranberry with green fruit, *Aster acuminatus*, and *Aralia nudicaulis* a salix *humilis*-like, and *Polystichum aculeatum* (? ?), and *Lycopodium annotinum* (variety).

I ascended the stream in the afternoon and got out of the ravine at its head, after dining on chiogenes tea, which plant I could gather without moving from my log seat. We liked it so well that Blake gathered a parcel to carry home. In most places it was scarcely practicable to get out of the ravine on either side on account of precipices. I judged it to be one thousand or fifteen hundred feet deep, but with care you could ascend by some slides. I found that we might have camped in the scrub firs above the edge of the ravine, though it would have been cold and windy and comparatively unpleasant there, for we should have been most of the time in a cloud.

The dense patches of dwarf fir and spruce scarcely rose above the rocks which they concealed, and you would often think the trees not more than a foot or two deep, — as, indeed, they might not be generally, — but, searching within, you would find hollow places six or eight feet deep between the rocks, where they filled up all level, and by clearing a space here with your hatchet you could find a shelter for your tent, and also fuel, and water was close by above the head of the ravine. Nevertheless, at a glance, looking over, or even walking

[1] Seen in Kane's expedition by Hans, etc., at the furthest north point, or 80° +.

over, this dense shrubbery, you would have thought it nowhere more than a foot or two deep, and the trees at most only an inch or two in diameter; but by searching you would find deep hollow places in it, as I have said, where the firs were from six to ten inches in diameter. The strong wind and the snow are said to flatten these trees down thus. Such a shrubbery would begin with a thin and shallow but dense edge of spruce, not more than a foot thick, like moss upon a rock, on which you could walk, but in many places in the middle of it, though its surface was of a uniform slope, it would be found to be six or eight feet deep. So that these very thickets of which the traveller complains afford at the same time an indispensable shelter. I noticed that this shrubbery just above the ravine, as well as in it, was principally fir, while the yet more dwarfish and prostrate portion on the edge was spruce.

Returning, I sprained my ankle in jumping down the brook, so that I could not sleep that night, nor walk the next day.[1] We had commonly clouds above and below us, though it was clear where we were. These clouds commonly reached about down to the edge of the ravine.

The black flies, which pestered us till into evening, were of various sizes, the largest more than an eighth of an inch long. There were scarcely any mosquitoes here, it was so cool.

[1] [He had found the *Arnica mollis* the day before (*see ante*, pp. 24 and 27), not at the time of spraining his foot, as Emerson has it in his Biographical Sketch. Channing's account of the incident (p. 44) is correct.]

A small owl came in the evening and sat within twelve feet of us, turning its head this way and that and peering at us inquisitively. It was apparently a screech owl.[1]

July 10. *Saturday.* Wentworth says he once collected one hundred pounds of spruce gum and sold it at Biddeford for forty cents per pound. Says there are "sable lines" about here. They trap them, but rarely see them. His neighbor, who lives on the hill behind where we camped on the 6th, has four hours more sun than he. He can, accordingly, make hay better, but W. beats him in corn. The days are about forty minutes longer on top of Mt. Washington than at seashore, according to guide-book. The sun set to us here at least an hour earlier than usual.

This ravine at the bottom of which we were, looking westward up it, had a rim somewhat like that of the crater of a volcano. The head of it bore from camp about N. 65° W., looking nearer than it was; the highest rock, with the outline of a face on it on the south rim, S. 32° W.; a very steep cliff on the opposite side, N. 20° W.; and over the last we judged was the summit of Mt. Washington. As I understood Wentworth, this was in Pingree's Grant; the Glen House in Pinkham's Grant. To-day and yesterday clouds were continually drifting over the summit, commonly extending about down to the edge of the ravine. When we looked up that way, the black patch made by our fire looked like a shadow on the mountainside.

[1] Or *Acadica* ? ? Saw-whet?

When I tasted the water under the snow arch the day before, I was disappointed at its warmth, though it was in fact melted snow; but half a mile lower it tasted colder. Probably, the ice being cooled by the neighborhood of the snow, it seemed thus warmer by contrast.

The only animals we saw about our camp were a few red squirrels. W. said there were striped ones about the mountains. The *Fringilla hyemalis* was most common in the upper part of the ravine, and I saw a large bird of prey, perhaps an eagle, sailing over the head of the ravine. The wood thrush and veery sang regularly, especially morning and evening. But, above all, the peculiar and memorable songster was that Monadnock-like one, keeping up an exceedingly brisk and lively strain. It was remarkable for its incessant twittering flow. Yet we never got sight of the bird, at least while singing, so that I could not identify it, and my lameness prevented my pursuing it. I heard it afterward, even in the Franconia Notch. It was surprising for its steady and uninterrupted flow, for when one stopped, another appeared to take up the strain. It reminded me of a fine corkscrew stream issuing with incessant lisping tinkle from a cork, flowing rapidly, and I said that he had pulled out the spile and left it running.[1] That was the rhythm, but with a sharper tinkle of course. It had no more variety than that, but it was more remarkable for its continuance and monotonousness than any bird's note I ever heard. It evidently belongs only to cool mountainsides, high up amid the fir and spruce. I saw once flitting through the fir-tops restlessly a small white

[1] [He seems to be describing the song of the winter wren.]

and dark bird, sylvia-like, which may have been it. Sometimes they appeared to be attracted by our smoke. The note was so incessant that at length you only noticed when it ceased.

The black flies were of various sizes here, much larger than I noticed in Maine. They compelled me most of the time to sit in the smoke, which I preferred to wearing a veil. They lie along your forehead in a line, where your hat touches it, or behind your ears, or about your throat (if not protected by a beard), or into the rims of the eyes, or between the knuckles, and there suck till they are crushed. But fortunately they do not last far into the evening, and a wind or a fog disperses them. I did not mind them much, but I noticed that men working on the highway made a fire to keep them off. I find many of them accidentally pressed in my botany and plant book. A botanist's books, if he has ever visited the primitive northern woods, will be pretty sure to contain these specimens of the black fly. Anything but mosquitoes by night. Plenty of fly-blowing flies, but I saw no ants in the dead wood; some spiders.

In the afternoon, Hoar, Blake, and Brown ascended the slide on the south to the highest rock. They were more than an hour getting up, but we heard them shout distinctly from the top. Hoar found near the edge of the ravine there, between the snow there and edge, *Rhododendron Lapponicum*, some time out of bloom,[1] growing in the midst of empetrum and moss; *Arctostaphylos alpina*, going to seed; *Polygonum viviparum*, in prime;[2]

[1] According to Durand, at 68° in Greenland.
[2] According to Durand, at all Kane's stations.

Vol. XI

and *Salix herbacea*,[1] a pretty, trailing, roundish-leaved willow, going to seed, but apparently not so early as the *S. Uva-ursi*.

July 11. Sunday. Mizzling weather. Were visited by three men from Glen House, who thought it was well named " *Tucker's* Ravine," because it tuckered a man out to get to it!

It rained hard all Sunday night, wetting us but little, however. One of the slender spruce trees by our camp, which we cut down, though it looked young and thrifty, being twenty-eight feet high and only six and a half inches in diameter, had about eighty rings, and the firs were at least as old.

Wentworth said that he had five hundred acres, and would sell the whole with buildings for $2000. He knew a dead log on the fire to be spruce, and not fir, because the stubs of the lower part slanted downward, and also by its "straight rift." He called a rotten cane "dozy." After some observation I concluded that it was true that the *base* of the lower limbs of the spruce slanted downward more generally than those of the fir.

July 12. Monday. It having cleared up, we shouldered our packs and commenced our descent, by a path about two and a half or three miles to carriage-road, not descending a great deal.

The prevailing under-plants at first, as we descended, were *Oxalis Acetosella* (abundantly in bloom), *Cornus Canadensis, Clintonia borealis*, chiogenes, *Vaccinium*

[1] According to Durand, at 73° in Greenland.

Canadense, gold-thread, *Listera cordata, Smilacina bifolia. Solidago thyrsoidea*, large and prevalent, on more open and grassy parts, from top of ravine to base of mountain, where it was in prime, three feet high and spikes eighteen inches long. Trees, at first, fir and spruce; then canoe birches[1] increased, and after two miles yellow birch began. Half-way down the mountain, on the road, saw a whiteweed and one *Alsine Grœnlandica*. It [is] surprising how much of that white froth, the nidus of an insect, there was on the grass and weeds on and about the mountains. They were white with it. *Carex trisperma* (?), three-quarters down. Hear the oven-bird near base. Dined by Peabody River, three quarters of a mile south of Glen House. Found *Lonicera ciliata* in fruit there[2] and saw a little white pine, and *Alnus incana* was common, and that large, fragrant *Aster macrophyllus* (?) was budded.

I had noticed that the trees at the ravine camp — fir and spruce — did not stand firmly. Two or three of us could have pulled over one thirty feet high and six or seven inches thick. They were easily rocked, lifting the horizontal roots each time, which reminded me of what is said about the Indians sometimes bending over a young tree, burying a chief under its roots, and letting it spring back for his monument and protection. W. said they had found the fir the best material for bridge planking in his town, outlasting other woods!

In the afternoon we rode along, three of us, northward

[1] Oakes says the white birch (here, meaning the canoe) come in after a burning.
[2] Found in Essex woods.

and northwestward on our way round the mountains, going through Gorham. We camped about a mile and a half west of Gorham, by the roadside, on the bank of Moose River.

July 13. Tuesday. This morning it rained, keeping us in camp till near noon, for we did not wish to lose the view of the mountains as we rode along.

We dined at Wood's tavern in Randolph, just over Randolph Hill, and here had a pretty good view of Madison and Jefferson, which rose from just south the stream there, but a cloud rested on the summits most of the time.

As we rode along in the afternoon, I noticed that when finally it began to rain hard, the clouds settling down, we had our first distinct view of the mountain outline for a short time.

Wood said they had no spruce but white spruce there, though I called it black, and that they had no white pine nor oak.

It rained steadily and soakingly the rest of the afternoon, as we kept on through Randolph and Kilkenny and Jefferson Hill, so that we had no clear view of the mountains.

We put up at a store just opposite the town hall on Jefferson Hill. It here cleared up at sunset, after two days' rain, and we had a fine view of the mountains, repaying us for our journey and wetting, Mt. Washington being some thirteen miles distant southeasterly. Southwestward we looked down over a very extensive, uninterrupted, and level-looking forest, which our host said

was very valuable on account of its white pine, their most valuable land, indeed. Over this the fog clouds were rolling beneath us, and a splendid but cloudy sunset was preparing for us in the west. By going still higher up the hill, in the wet grass north of the town house, we could see the whole White Mountain range from Madison to Lafayette.

The alpine, or rocky, portion of Mt. Washington and its neighbors was a dark chocolate-brown, the extreme summits being dark topped or edged, — almost invariably this dark saddle on the top, — and, as the sun got lower, a very distinct brilliant and beautiful green, as of a thick mantle, was reflected from the vegetation in the ravines, as from the fold of a mantle, and on the lower parts of the mountains. They were chiefly Washington and the high northern peaks that we attended to. The waifs of fog-like cloud skirting the sides of Cherry Mountain and Mt. Deception in the south had the appearance of rocks, and gave to the mountainsides a precipitous look. I saw a bright streak looking like snow, a narrow bright ribbon where the source of the Ammonoosuc, swollen by the rain, leaped down the side of Mt. Washington from the Lake of the Clouds. The shadows on Lafayette betrayed ridges running toward us. That brilliant green on the northern mountains was reflected but a moment or two, for the atmosphere at once became too misty. It several times disappeared and was then brought out again with wonderful brilliancy, as it were an invisible writing, or a fluid which required to be held to the sun to be brought out.

After the sun set to us, the bare summits were of a

delicate rosaceous color, passing through violet into the deep dark-blue or purple of the night which already invested their lower parts, for this night-shadow was wonderfully blue, reminding me of the blue shadows on snow. There was an afterglow in which these tints and variations were repeated. It was the grandest mountain view I ever got. In the meanwhile, white clouds were gathering again about the summits, first about the highest, appearing to form there, but sometimes to send off an emissary to initiate a cloud upon a neighboring peak. You could tell little about the comparative distance of a cloud and a peak till you saw that the former actually impinged on the latter. First Washington, then Adams, then Jefferson put on their caps, and you saw the latter, as it were, send off one small nucleus to gather round the head of Madison.

This was the best point from which to observe these effects that we *saw* in our journey, but it appeared to me that from a hill a few miles further westward, perhaps in Whitefield, the view might be even finer. I made the accompanying two sketches of the mountain outline here, as far south only as what the landlord called Mt. Pleasant, the route from the Notch house being visible no further.

View of White Mountains *proper* from town house and store in Jefferson. Other mountains and Franconia Mountains further to the right. N. B. — Oakes puts Jefferson next to Washington, but makes it lower than the third.

This was said to be a fine farming town. I heard the ring of toads and saw a remarkable abundance of butter-

cup (the tall) yellowing the fields in this town and the next, somewhat springlike.

July 14. Wednesday. This forenoon we rode on through Whitefield to Bethlehem, clouds for the most part concealing the higher mountains. Found the *Geum strictum* in bloom in Whitefield; also common flax by a house. Got another fine view of the mountains — the higher ones much more distant than before — from a hill just south of the public house in Bethlehem, but might have got a better view from a higher hill a little more east, which one said was the highest land between the Green and the White Mountains, of course on that line. Saw the Stratford Peaks, thirty or forty miles north, and many mountains east of them. Climbed the long hill from Franconia to the Notch, passed the Profile House, and camped half a mile up the side of Lafayette.

Loudon says of the *Vaccinium uliginosum* that it is "taller than the common bilberry," *i. e. Vaccinium Myrtillus*, and is "a shrub about 2 ft. high; a native of Sweden, Germany, Siberia, Switzerland, Savoy, Scotland, and the north of England; as well as in the more northern parts of America, and on its west coast; and on the island of Sitcha, and in the north of Asia, in marshy mountain heaths and alpine bogs." High on the mountains in Scotland. "It is said to cover extensive tracts of land on the west coast of Greenland, along with *Andromeda tetragona*. . . . The berries are agreeable, but inferior in flavor to those of *V. Myrtillus*: eaten in large quantities, they occasion giddiness, and a slight headache." Called "the bog Whortleberry, or great Bilberry."

Vaccinium angustifolium Ait. "Berries large, and known by the name of bluets. . . . A shrub, nearly 2 ft. high; a native of Canada, about Hudson's Bay and Labrador; and of the high alpine woods of the Rocky Mountains, from the Atlantic to the Pacific. . . . The fruit is large, globose, blackish purple," highly esteemed.

Vaccinium Vitis-Idæa. "The berries of this plant form an important article of commerce in the seaports bordering the Gulf of Bothnia, whence they are sent to the south of Europe along with cranberries." "Mount Ida Whortleberry, or Cowberry."

Vaccinium Oxycoccus. Bankers in Russia whiten silver money by boiling it in their juice. "In Russia, and in some parts of Sweden, the long filiform shoots of the oxycoccus are collected in spring, after most of the leaves have dropped off, and are dried, and twisted into ropes, which are used to tie on the thatch of houses, and even for harnessing horses."

Cassiope hypnoides "A native of Lapland, Denmark, and Siberia, on the mountains, where it covers whole tracts of land; and on the northwest coast of North America."

Phyllodoce taxifolia. "A native of Europe, North America, and Asia. In Europe: in Scotland on dry heathy moors, rare;" etc., etc. Cultivated in British gardens.

Arctostaphylos Uva-Ursi. "In Sweden, Russia, and America, they [the berries] form a principal part of the food of bears."

Arctostaphylos alpina. "Native of Denmark, Switzerland, Dauphiné, Savoy, Siberia, etc." Berries scarcely

edible. According to Linnæus very common about the White Sea.

(Pursh says of the *Chiogenes hispidulum* that it is growing always amidst sphagnum.)

Rhododendron Lapponicum. "A native of the arctic regions of Europe, Asia, and North America, where it forms a procumbent shrub, flowering in July."

Salix Urva-ursi Pursh. "A native of Labrador." His (Loudon's) leaves are blunt-obovate!

S. herbacea L. "A native of Britain on the Welsh and Highland Mountains." "In the *Companion to the Botanical Magazine*, it is stated that S. herbacea exceeds in the elevation of its habitat every other shrub in Britain." "S. herbacea is the least of British willows, and according to Sir J. E. Smith, the least of all shrubs. Dr. Clarke, in his Scandinavia, calls it a perfect tree in miniature; so small that it may be taken up, and root, trunk, and branches, spread out in a small pocket-book." But it has a considerable prostrate stem and root. Leaves used for tanning in Iceland.

S. repens (of Linnæus) has in plate pointed (!) lanceolate leaves, which Loudon says are from one quarter to three quarters of an inch long, while the plant rises "only a finger's length"! Can it be mine?

Loiseleuria procumbens. "Plentiful on the tops of mountains in Scotland."

Alnus viridis D. C. Belongs to the continent of Europe.

Empetrum nigrum. The north of Europe and of Asia, abundant in Scotland. "The Scotch Highlanders and Russian peasants eat the berries." One of the

Vol. XI

plants that would prevail in England with ling, etc., if let alone, or ground not cultivated.

Willey says of Jackson, "The great number of sheep scattered upon the mountains make it the principal place of resort for what bears and wolves are yet left among these hills." Wentworth said that he had trapped and killed a number of them. They killed many of his sheep and calves, and destroyed much of his corn when in the milk, close to his house. A sheep could run faster than a bear, but was not so long-winded, especially going up a mountainside. The bear, when pursued, would take directly to some distant and impenetrable thicket, as these dark fir thickets on the mountainside. He once found some young bears on a nest made of small dry sticks collected under a ledge, and raising them five or six inches from the ground. He carried home the young and reared them. The voice of a bear was like that of a woman in distress. It was in Gilead, the first town (in Maine) northeast from Jackson, that Bean killed his bear, thrusting his arm down her throat.

July 15. *Thursday.* Continued the ascent of Lafayette, also called the Great Haystack. It is perhaps three and a half miles from the road to the top by path along winding ridge.

At about a mile and a half up by path, the spruce began to be small. Saw there a silent bird, dark slate and blackish above, especially head, with a white line over the brows, then dark slate next beneath, white

throat and reddish belly, black bill. A little like a nuthatch. Also saw an *F. hyemalis* on top of a dead tree. The wood was about all spruce here, twenty feet high, together with *Vaccinium Canadense*, lambkill in bloom, mountain-ash, *Viburnum nudum*, rhodora, *Amelanchier oligocarpa*, nemopanthes. As I looked down into some very broad and deep ravines from this point, their sides appeared to be covered chiefly with spruce, with a few bodkin points of fir here and there (had seen two days before some very handsome firs on low ground which were actually concave on sides of cone), while the narrow bottom or middle of the ravine, as far up and down as trees reached, where, of course, there was most water, was almost exclusively hardwood, apparently birch chiefly.

As we proceeded, the number of firs began to increase, and the spruce to diminish, till, at about two miles perhaps, the wood was almost pure fir about fourteen feet high; but this suddenly ceased at about half a mile further and gave place to a very dwarfish fir, and to spruce again, the latter of a very dwarfish, procumbent form, dense and flat, one to two feet high, which crept yet higher up the mountain than the fir, — over the rocks beyond the edge of the fir, — and with this spruce was mixed *Empetrum nigrum*, dense and matted on the rocks, partly dead, with berries already blackening, also *Vaccinium uliginosum*. Though the edges all around and the greater part of such a thicket high up the otherwise bare rocks might be spruce, yet the deeper hollows between the rocks, in the midst, would invariably be filled with fir, rising only to the same level, but much larger round. These firs especially made the stag-horns when dead.

The spruce was mostly procumbent at that height, but the fir upright, though flat-topped. In short, spruce gave place to fir from a mile and a half to a mile below the top, — so you may say firs were the highest trees, — and then succeeded to it in a very dwarfish and procumbent form yet higher up.

At about one mile or three quarters below the summit, just above the limit of trees, we came to a little pond, maybe of a quarter of an acre (with a yet smaller one near by), the source of one head of the Pemigewasset, in which grew a great many yellow lilies (*Nuphar advena*) and I think a potamogeton. In the flat, dryish bog by its shore, I noticed the *Empetrum nigrum* (1), ledum (2), *Vaccinium Oxycoccus*, *Smilacina trifolia*, *Kalmia glauca* (3) (in bloom still), *Andromeda calyculata* (4) (and I think *Polifolia ? ?*), *Eriophorum vaginatum*, *Vaccinium uliginosum* (5), *Juncus filiformis*, four kinds of sedge (*e. g. Carex pauciflora?*), *C. irrigua* with dangling spikes, and a *C. lupulina*-like, and the *Scirpus cæspitosus* (?) of Mt. Washington, brown lichens (*q. v.*), and cladonias, all low and in a moss-like bed in the moss of the bog; also rhodora of good size. 1, 2, 3, 4, and 5 were quite dwarfish. The outlet of the pond was considerable, but soon lost beneath the rocks. A willow, *rostrata*-like but not downy, grew there. In the dwarf

fir thickets above and below this pond, I saw the most beautiful linnæas that I ever saw. They grew quite densely, full of rose-purple flowers, — deeper reddish-purple than ours, which are pale, — perhaps nodding over the brink of a spring, altogether the fairest mountain flowers I saw, lining the side of the narrow horse-track through the fir scrub. As you walk, you overlook the top of this thicket on each side. There also grew near that pond red cherry, *Aster prenanthes* (??) and common rue.

We saw a line of fog over the Connecticut Valley. Found near summit apparently the *Vaccinium angustifolium* of Aitman (variety of *Vaccinium Pennsylvanicum*, Gray), bluets, and a broad-leaved vaccinium lower down (*q. v.*). Just below top, reclined on a dense bed of *Salix Uva-ursi*, five feet in diameter by four or five inches deep, a good spot to sit on, mixed with a rush, amid rocks. This willow was generally showing its down.

We had fine weather on this mountain, and from the summit a good view of Mt. Washington and the rest, though it was a little hazy in the horizon. It was a wild mountain and forest scene from south-southeast round easterwardly to north-northeast. On the northwest the country was half cleared, as from Monadnock, — the leopard-spotted land. I saw, about west-northwest, a large *Green* Mountain, perhaps Mansfield Mountain, though the compass was affected here.

The *Carex scirpoidea* (?) grew at top, and it was surprising how many large bees, wasps, butterflies, and other insects were hovering and fluttering about the very

apex, though not particularly below. What attracts them to such a locality [1]

Heard one white-throated sparrow above the trees, and also saw a little bird by the pond. Think I heard a song sparrow about latter place. Saw a toad near limit of trees, and many pollywogs in the pond above trees.

Boiled tea for our dinner by the little pond, the head of the Pemigewasset. Saw tracks in the muddy bog by the pond-side, shaped somewhat like a small human foot *sometimes*, perhaps made by a bear.

We made our fire on the moss and lichens, by a rock, amid the shallow fir and spruce, burning the dead fir twigs, or "deer's-horns." I cut off a flourishing fir three feet high and not flattened at top yet. This was one and a quarter inches in diameter and had thirty-four rings. One, also flourishing, fifteen inches high, had twelve rings at ground. One, a dead one, was twenty-nine inches in circumference, and at four feet from ground branched horizontally as much as five feet each way, making a flat top, curving upward again into stag-horns, with branches very large and stout at base, thus:

Another fir, close by and dead, was thirty inches in circumference at ground and only half an inch in diameter at four and a half feet. Another fir, three feet high, fresh and vigorous, without a flat

---

[1] In an account of C. Piazzi Smyth's scientific mission under the English Government to the Peak of Teneriffe, in 1856, it is said,

top as yet, had its woody part an inch and an eighth thick (or diameter) at base (the bark being one eighth inch thick) and sixty-one rings. There was no sign of decay, though it was, as usual, mossy, or covered with lichens.

I cut off at ground one of the little procumbent spruce trees, which spread much like a juniper, but not curving upward. This rose about nine inches above the ground, but I could not count the rings, they were so fine. (*Vide* piece.) The smallest diameter of the *wood* is forty-one eightieths of an inch. The number of rings, as near as I can count with a microscope, taking much pains, is about seventy, and on one side these are included within a radius of nine fortieths of an inch, of which a little more than half is heart-wood, or each layer on this side is less than one three-hundredth of an inch thick. The bark was three fortieths of an inch thick. It was quite round and easy to cut, it was so fresh.

If the fir thirty inches in circumference grew no faster than that an inch and an eighth in diameter, then it was about five hundred and forty-nine years old. If as fast as the *little* spruce, it would be nearly fourteen hundred years old.

When half-way down the mountain, amid the spruce,

"In the hollow of this crater [the topmost] 12,200 feet above the sea level, though at a lesser altitude they had left all signs of animal life, they found a population of bees, flies, spiders, as well as swallows and linnets — the birds and insects flying about in numbers."

And of a lower altitude, speaking of the flowers, it is said that during the early summer "the townspeople [of Orotava] find it worth their while to pack their hives of bees on mules and bring them to these upper regions to gather honey from the myriads of mountain flowers."

we saw two pine grosbeaks, male and female, close by the path, and looked for a nest, but in vain. They were remarkably tame, and the male a brilliant red orange, — neck, head, breast beneath, and rump, — blackish wings and tail, with two white bars on wings. (Female, yellowish.) The male flew nearer inquisitively, uttering a low twitter, and perched fearlessly within four feet of us, eying us and pluming himself and plucking and eating the leaves of the *Amelanchier oligocarpa* on which he sat, for several minutes. The female, meanwhile, was a rod off. They were evidently breeding there. Yet neither Wilson nor Nuttall speak of their breeding in the United States.

At the base of the mountain, over the road, heard (and saw), at the same place where I heard him the evening before, a splendid rose-breasted grosbeak singing. I had before mistaken him at first for a tanager, then for a red-eye, but was not satisfied; but now, with my glass, I distinguished him sitting quite still, high above the road at the entrance of the mountain-path in the deep woods, and singing steadily for twenty minutes. It was remarkable for sitting so still and where yesterday. It was much richer and sweeter and, I think, more powerful than the note of the tanager or red-eye. It had not the hoarseness of the tanager, and more sweetness and fullness than the red-eye. Wilson does not give their breeding-place. Nuttall quotes Pennant as saying that some breed in New York but most further north. They, too, appear to breed about the White Mountains.

Heard the evergreen-forest note on the sides of the

mountains often. Heard no robins in the White Mountains.

Rode on and stopped at Morrison's (once Tilton's) Inn in West Thornton. *Heracleum lanatum* in Notch and near, very large, some seven feet high. Observed, as we rode south through Lincoln, that the face of cliffs on the hills and mountains east of the river, and even the stems of the spruce, reflected a pink light at sunset.

July 16. Friday. Continue on through Thornton and Campton. The butternut is first noticed in these towns, a common tree. *Urtica Canadensis* in Campton.

About the mountains were wilder and rarer birds, more or less arctic, like the vegetation. I did not even *hear* the robin on them, and when I had left them a few miles behind, it was a great change and surprise to hear the lark, the wood pewee, the robin, and the bobolink (for the last had not done singing). On the mountains, especially at Tuckerman's Ravine, the notes even of familiar birds sounded strange to me. I hardly knew the wood thrush and veery and oven-bird at first. They sing differently there.[1] In two instances, — going down the Mt. Jefferson road and along the road in the Franconia Notch, — I started an *F. hyemalis* within two feet, close to the roadside, but looked in vain for a nest. They alight and sit thus close. I doubt if the chipping sparrow is found about the mountains.

We were not troubled at all by black flies after leaving the Franconia Notch. It is apparently only in primitive

[1] [His wood thrush and veery were probably the olive-backed thrush and the Bicknell thrush.]

Vol. XI

woods that they work. We had grand views of the Franconia Mountains from Campton, and were surprised by the regular pyramidal form of most of the peaks, including Lafayette, which we had ascended. I think that there must be some ocular illusion about this, for no such regularity was observable in ascending Lafayette. I remember that when I got more than half a mile down it I met two men walking up, and perspiring very much, one of whom asked me if a cliff within a stone's throw before them was the summit. Indeed the summit of a mountain, though it may appear thus regular at a distance, is not, after all, the easiest thing to find, even in clear weather. The surface was so irregular that you would have thought you saw the summit a dozen times before you did, and in one sense the nearer you got to it, the further off it was. I told the man it was seven or eight times as far as that. I suspect that such are the laws of light that our eye, as it were, leaps from one prominence to another, connecting them by a straight line when at a distance and making one side balance the other. So that when the summit viewed is fifty or a hundred miles distant, there is but very general and very little truth in the impression of its outline conveyed to the mind. Seen from Campton and lower, the Franconia Mountains show three or four sharp and regular blue pyramids, reminding you of pictures of the Pyramids of Egypt, though when near you suspected no such resemblance. You know from having climbed them, most of the time out of sight of the summit, that they must be at least of a scalloped outline, and it is hardly to be supposed that a nearer or more distant prominence

always is seen at a distance filling up the irregularities. It would seem as if by some law of light and vision the eye inclined to connect the base and apex of a peak in the horizon by a straight line. Twenty-five miles off, in this case, you might think that the summit was a smooth inclined plane, though you can reach it only over a succession of promontories and shelves.

Cannon Mountain on the west side of the Franconia Notch (on whose side is the profile) is the most singularly lumpish mass of any mountain I ever saw, especially so high. It looks like a behemoth or a load of hay, and suggests no such pyramid as I have described. So my theory does not quite hold together, and I would say that the eye needs only a hint of the general form and completes the outline from the slightest suggestion. The huge lumpish mass and curving outline of Cannon Mountain is yet more remarkable than the pyramidal summits of the others. It would be less remarkable in a mere hill, but it is, in fact, an elevated and bald rocky mountain.

My last view of these Franconia Mountains was from a hill in the road just this side of Plymouth village. Campton apparently affords the best views of them, and some artists board there.

Gathered the *Carex straminea* (?), some three feet high, *scoparia*-like, in Bridgewater. Nooned on west bank of the Pemigewasset, half a mile above the New Hampton covered bridge. Saw first pitch pines in New Hampton. Saw chestnuts first and frequently in Franklin and Boscawen, or about 43½° N., or half a degree higher than Emerson put it. It was quite common in

Hollis. Of oaks, I saw and heard only of the red in the north of New Hampshire. The witch-hazel was very abundant and large in the north part of New Hampshire and about the mountains.

Lodged at tavern in Franklin, west side of river.

July 17. Saturday. Passed by Webster's place, three miles this side of the village. Some half-dozen houses there; no store nor public buildings. A very quiet place. Road lined with elms and maples. Railroad between house and barn. The farm apparently a level and rather sandy interval, nothing particularly attractive about it. A plain public graveyard within its limits. Saw the grave of Ebenezer Webster, Esq., who died 1806, aged sixty-seven, and of Abigail, his wife, who died 1816, aged seventy-six, probably Webster's father and mother; also of other Websters, and Haddocks. Now belongs to one Fay [?] of Boston. W. was born two or more miles northwest, but house now gone.

Spent the noon on the bank of the Contoocook in the northwest corner of Concord, there a stagnant river owing to dams. Began to find raspberries ripe. Saw much elecampane by roadsides near farmhouses, all the way through New Hampshire.

Reached Weare and put up at a quiet and agreeable house, without any sign or barroom. Many Friends in this town. Know Pillsbury and Rogers here. The former lived in Henniker, next town.

July 18. Sunday. Keep on through New Boston, the east side of Mount Vernon, Amherst to Hollis, and noon

Vol. XI

by a mill-pond in the woods, on Pennichook Brook, in Hollis, or three miles north of village. At evening go on to Pepperell. A marked difference when we enter Massachusetts, in roads, farms, houses, trees, fences, etc., — a great improvement, showing an older-settled country. In New Hampshire there is a greater want of shade trees, but long bleak or sunny roads from which there is no escape. What barbarians we are! The convenience of the traveller is very little consulted. He merely has the privilege of crossing somebody's farm by a particular narrow and maybe unpleasant path. The individual retains all other rights, — as to trees and fruit, and wash of the road, etc. On the other hand, these should belong to mankind inalienably. The road should be of ample width and adorned with trees expressly for the use of the traveller. There should be broad recesses in it, especially at springs and watering-places, where he can turn out and rest, or camp if he will. I feel commonly as if I were condemned to drive through somebody's cow-yard or huckleberry pasture by a narrow lane, and if I make a fire by the roadside to boil my hasty pudding, the farmer comes running over to see if I am not burning up his stuff. You are barked along through the country, from door to door.

July 19. Get home at noon.

For such an excursion as the above, carry and wear: —

Three strong check shirts.
Two pairs socks.
Neck ribbon and handkerchief.
Three pocket-handkerchiefs.

One thick waistcoat.
One thin (or half-thick) coat.
One thick coat (for mountain).
A large, broad india-rubber knapsack, with a *broad* flap.
A flannel shirt.
India-rubber coat.
Three bosoms (to go and come in).
A napkin.
Pins, needles, thread.
A blanket.
A cap to lie in at night.
Tent (or a large simple piece of india-rubber cloth for the mountain tops?).
Veil and *gloves* (or enough millinet to cover all at night).
Map and compass.
Plant book and paper.
Paper and stamps.
Botany, spy-glass, microscope.
Tape, insect-boxes.
Jack-knife and clasp-knife.
Fish-line and hooks.
Matches.
Soap and dish-cloths.
Waste-paper and twine.
Iron spoon.
Pint dipper with a pail-handle added (not to put out the fire), and perhaps a bag to carry water in.
Frying-pan, only if you ride.
Hatchet (sharp), if you ride, and perhaps in any case on mountain, with a sheath to it.
Hard-bread (sweet crackers good); a moist, sweet plum cake very good and lasting; pork, corned beef or tongue, sugar, tea or coffee, and a little salt.

As I remember, those dwarf firs on the mountains grew up straight three or four feet without diminishing much if any, and then sent forth every way very stout

branches, like bulls' horns or shorter, horizontally four or five feet each way. They were stout because they grew so slowly. Apparently they were kept flat-topped by the snow and wind. But when the surrounding trees rose above them, they, being sheltered a little, apparently sent up shoots from the horizontal limbs, which also were again more or less bent, and this added to the horn-like appearance.

We might easily have built us a shed of spruce bark at the foot of Tuckerman's Ravine. I thought that I might in a few moments strip off the bark of a spruce a little bigger than myself and seven feet long, letting it curve as it naturally would, then crawl into it and be protected against any rain. Wentworth said that he had sometimes stripped off birch bark two feet wide, and put his head through a slit in the middle, letting the ends fall down before and behind, as he walked.

The slides in Tuckerman's Ravine appeared to be a series of deep gullies side by side, where sometimes it appeared as if a very large rock had slid down without turning over, plowing this deep furrow all the way, only a few rods wide. Some of the slides were streams of rocks, a rod or more in diameter each. In some cases which I noticed, the ravine-side had evidently been undermined by water on the lower side.

It is surprising how much more bewildering is a mountain-top than a level area of the same extent. Its ridges and shelves and ravines add greatly to its apparent extent and diversity. You may be separated from your party by only stepping a rod or two out of the path. We turned off three or four rods to the pond on our way up Lafayette, knowing that Hoar was behind, but so we lost him for three quarters of an hour and did not see him again till we reached the summit. One walking a few rods more to the right or left is not seen over the ridge of the summit, and, other things being equal, this is truer the nearer you are to the apex.

If you take one side of a rock, and your companion another, it is enough to separate you sometimes for the rest of the ascent.

On these mountain-summits, or near them, you find small and almost uninhabited ponds, apparently without fish, sources of rivers, still and cold, strange as condensed clouds, weird-like, — of which nevertheless you make tea! — surrounded by dryish bogs, in which, perchance, you may detect traces of the bear or *loup-cervier.*

We got the best views of the mountains from Conway, Jefferson, Bethlehem, and Campton. Conway combines the Italian (?) level and softness with Alpine peaks around. Jefferson offers the completest view of the range a dozen or more miles distant; the place from which to behold the manifold varying lights of departing day on the summits. Bethlehem also afforded a complete but generally more distant view of the range, and, with respect to the highest summits, more diagonal. Campton afforded a fine distant view of the pyramidal Franconia Mountains with the lumpish Profile Mountain. The last view, with its smaller intervals and partial view of the great range far in the north, was somewhat like the view from Conway.

Belknap in his "History of New Hampshire," third

volume, page 33, says: "On some mountains we find a shrubbery of hemlock [?][1] and spruce, whose branches are knit together so as to be impenetrable. The snow lodges on their tops, and a cavity is formed underneath. These are called by the Indians, Hakmantaks."

Willey quotes some one[2] as saying of the White Mountains, "Above this hedge of dwarf trees, which is about 4000 feet above the level of the sea, the scattered fir and spruce bushes, shrinking from the cold mountain wind, and clinging to the ground in sheltered hollows by the sides of the rocks, with a few similar bushes of white and yellow [?][3] birch, reach almost a thousand feet high."

Willey says that "the tops of the mountains are covered with snow from the last of October to the end of May;" that the alpine flowers spring up under the shelter of high rocks. Probably, then, they are most abundant on the southeast sides?

To sum up (omitting sedges, etc.), plants prevailed thus on Mt. Washington:—

1st. *For three quarters of a mile:* Black (?) spruce, yellow birch, hemlock, beech, canoe birch, rock maple, fir, mountain maple, red cherry, striped maple, etc.

2d. *At one and three quarters miles:* Spruce prevails, with fir, canoe and yellow birch. Rock maple, beech, and hemlock disappear. (On Lafayette, lambkill, *Viburnum nudum,* nemopanthes, mountain-ash.) Hardwoods in bottom of ravines, above and below.

[1] [The query is Thoreau's.]
[2] This is Oakes in his "Scenery," etc.
[3] [The query is Thoreau's.]

Vol. XI

3d. *At three miles, or limit of trees* (colliers' shanty and Ravine Camp): Fir prevails, with *some spruce* and canoe birch; mountain-ash, *Alnus viridis* (in moist ravines), red cherry, mountain maple, *Salix (humilis-*like and *Torreyana-*like, etc.), *Vaccinium Canadense, Ribes lacustre, prostratum,* and *floridum* (?), rhodora, *Amelanchier oligocarpa,* tree-cranberry, chiogenes, *Cornus Canadensis, Oxalis Acetosella,* clintonia, gold-thread, *Listera cordata, Smilacina bifolia, Solidago thyrsoidea, Ranunculus abortivus, Platanthera obtusata* and *dilatata, Oxyria digyna, Viola blanda, Aster prenanthes* (?), *A. acuminatus, Aralia nudicaulis, Polystichum aculeatum* (?), wool-grass, etc.

4th. *Limit of trees to within one mile of top,* or as far as dwarf firs: Dwarf fir, spruce, and some canoe birch, *Vaccinium uliginosum* and *Vitis-Idæa, Salix Uva-ursi,* ledum, *Empetrum nigrum, Oxalis Acetosella, Linnæa borealis, Cornus Canadensis, Alsine Grœnlandica, Diapensia Lapponica,* gold-thread, epigæa, sorrel, *Geum radiatum* var. *Peckii, Solidago Virgaurea* var. *alpina, S. thyrsoidea* (not so high as last), hellebore, oldenlandia, clintonia, *Viola palustris,* trientalis, a little *Vaccinium angustifolium* (?), ditto of *Vaccinium cœspitosum,*[1] *Phyllodoce taxifolia, Uvularia grandiflora, Loiseleuria procumbens, Cassiope hypnoides, Rubus triflorus, Heracleum lanatum,* archangelica, *Rhododendron Lapponicum, Arctostaphylos alpina, Salix herbacea, Polygonum viviparum, Veronica alpina, Nabalus Boottii, Epilobium alpinum, Platanthera dilatata,* common rue, *Castilleja septentrionalis, Arnica mollis, Spiræa salicifolia,*

[1] *Vide* June 14, 1859.

Salix repens,[1] *Solidago thyrsoidea,* raspberry (Hoar), *Lycopodium annotinum* and *Selago,* small fern, grass, sedges, moss and lichens.[2] (On Lafayette, *Vaccinium Oxycoccus, Smilacina trifolia, Kalmia glauca, Andromeda calyculata,* red cherry, yellow (water) lily, *Eriophorum vaginatum.*)

5th. *Within one mile of top: Potentilla tridentata,* a very little fir, spruce, and canoe birch, one mountain-ash, *Alsine Grœnlandica,* diapensia, *Vaccinium Vitis-Idæa,* gold-thread, *Lycopodium annotinum* and *Selago,* sorrel, *Silene acaulis, Solidago Virgaurea* var. *alpina,* helebore, oldenlandia, *Lonicera cœrulea,* clintonia, *Viola palustris,* trientalis, *Vaccinium angustifolium* (?), a little fern, *Geum radiatum* var. *Peckii,* sedges, rush, moss, and lichens, and probably more of the last list.

6th. *At apex:* Sedge, moss, and lichens, and a little alsine, diapensia, *Solidago Virgaurea* var. *alpina* (?), etc.

The 2d may be called the Spruce Zone; 3d, the Fir Zone; 4th, the Shrub, or Berry, Zone; 5th, the Cinquefoil, or Sedge, Zone; 6th, the Lichen, or Cloud, Zone.

Durand in Kane (page 444, 2d vol.) thinks that plants suffer more in alpine regions than in the polar zone. Among authorities on northern plants, names E. Meyer's "Plantæ Labradoricæ" (1830) and Giesecke's list of Greenland plants in Brewster's Edinburgh Encyclopedia (1832).

It is remarkable that what you may call trees on the White Mountains, *i. e.* the forests, cease abruptly with

[1] And apparently *S. phylicifolia* (?). *Vide* Sept. 21.
[2] *Vide* Sept. 21.

those about a dozen feet high, and then succeeds a distinct kind of growth, quite dwarfish and flattened and confined almost entirely to fir and spruce, as if it marked the limit of *almost* perpetual snow, as if it indicated a zone where the trees were peculiarly oppressed by the snow, cold, wind, etc. The transition from these flattened firs and spruces to shrubless rock is not nearly so abrupt as from upright or slender trees to these dwarfed thickets.

July 21. Wednesday. CONCORD. P. M. — To Walden, with E. Bartlett and E. Emerson.

The former wished to show me what he thought an owl's nest he had found. Near it, in Abel Brooks's wood-lot, heard a note and saw a small hawk fly over. It was the nest of this bird. Saw several of the young flitting about and occasionally an old bird. The nest was in a middling-sized white pine, some twenty feet from the ground, resting on two limbs close to the main stem, on the south side of it. It was quite solid, composed entirely of twigs about as big round as a pipe-stem and less; was some fifteen inches in diameter and one inch deep, or nearly flat, and perhaps five inches thick. It was very much dirtied on the sides by the droppings of the young. As we were standing about the tree, we heard again the note of a young one approaching. We dropped upon the ground, and it alighted on the edge of the nest; another alighted near by, and a third a little further off. The young were apparently as big as the old, but still lingered about the nest and returned to it. I could hear them coming some distance off. Their note was a kind

Vol. XI

the *F. fuscus*, and had not the white bars on tail of the *F. Pennsylvanicus.* It also had the fine sharp shin.[1]

But what then is my hawk killed by Farrar, with so stout a leg? Had that any white bars on tail?[2]

July 22. The nest of the marsh hawk is empty. It has probably flown. C. and I took refuge from a shower under our boat at Clamshell; staid an hour at least. A thunderbolt fell close by. A mole ran under the boat. The wind canted round as usual (is not this owing to the circular manner of storms?) more easterly, and compelled us to turn the boat over. Left a little too soon, but enjoyed a splendid rainbow for half an hour.

July 23. Neottia gracilis, how long?

July 26. Button-bush in prime. Edward Bartlett shows me a nest in the Agricultural ground which had four eggs, yet pretty fresh, but the bird has now deserted it. (*Vide* one.) It is like Farmer's seringo. It is a broad egg, white with large reddish and purplish brown spots chiefly about large end. The nest is small and deep and low in the grass of this pasture. (*Vide* nest out of order.) Could not see the bird; only saw bay-wings and huckle-berry-birds. I suspect it may be the *Fringilla passerina?* He says the bird had a clear yellowish-white breast!

July 28. P. M. — To Conantum.

From wall corner saw a pinkish patch on side-hill west

[1] *Vide* Aug. 29th.
[2] *Vide* Aug. 29th.

of peeping squeal, which you might at first suspect to be made by a jay; not very loud, but as if to attract the old and reveal their whereabouts. The note of the old bird, which occasionally dashed past, was somewhat like that of the marsh hawk or pigeon woodpecker, a cackling or clattering sound, chiding us. The old bird was anxious about her inexperienced young, and was trying to get them off. At length she dashed close past us, and appeared to fairly strike one of the young, knocking him off his perch, and he soon followed her off. I saw the remains of several birds lying about in that neighborhood, and saw and heard again the young and old thereabouts for several days thereafter. A young man killed one of the young hawks, and I saw it. It was the *Falco fuscus,* the American brown or slate-colored hawk. Its length was thirteen inches; alar extent, twenty-three. The tail reached two or more inches beyond the closed wings. Nuttall says the upper parts are "a deep slate-color" (these were very dark brown); also that the nest is yet unknown. But Wilson describes his *F. velox* (which is the same as Nuttall's *F. fuscus*) as "whole upper parts very dark brown," but legs, greenish-yellow (these were yellow). The toes had the peculiar pendulous lobes which W. refers to. As I saw it in the woods, I was struck by its dark color above, its tawny throat and breast, brown-spotted, its clean, slender, long yellow legs, feathered but little below the knee, its white vent, its wings distinctly and rather finely dark-barred beneath, short, black, much curved bill, and slender black sharp claws. Its tail with a dark bar near edge beneath. In hand I found it had the white spots on scapulars of

of Baker Farm, which turned out to be epilobium, a rod across. Through the glass it was as fine as a moss, but with the naked eye it might have been mistaken for a dead pine bough. This pink flower was distinguished perhaps three quarters of a mile.[1]

Heard a kingfisher, which had been hovering over the river, plunge forty rods off.

The under sides of maples are very bright and conspicuous nowadays as you walk, also of the curled [?] panicled andromeda leaves. Some grape leaves, also, are blown up.

July 29. P. M. — To Pine Hill, looking for the *Vaccinium Pennsylvanicum* berries. I find plenty of bushes, but these bear very sparingly. They appear to bear but one or two years before they are overgrown. Also they probably love a cool atmosphere, for they bear annually on mountains, as Monadnock. Where the woods have been cut a year or two they have put forth fresh shoots of a livelier green. The *V. vacillans* berries are in dense clusters, raceme-like, as huckleberries are not.

I see nowadays young martins perched on the dead tops of high trees; also young swallows on the telegraph-wire.

In the Chinese novel "Ju-Kiao-Li, or The Two Fair Cousins," I find in a motto to a chapter (quoted): "He who aims at success should be continually on his guard against a thousand accidents. How many preparations are necessary before the sour plum begins to sweeten! . . . But if supreme happiness was to be attained in

[1] *Vide* Aug. 21.

the space of an hour, of what use would be in life the noblest sentiments?" (Page 227.) Also these verses on page 230: —

"Nourished by the study of ten thousand different works,
The pen in hand, one is equal to the gods.
Let not humility take its rank amongst virtues:
Genius never yields the palm that belongs to it."

Again, page 22, vol. ii: —

"If the spring did not announce its reign by the return of the leaves,
The moss, with its greenish tints, would find favor in men's eyes."

July 31. P. M. — To Flint's Pond.

I see much eriocaulon floating, with its mass of white roots uppermost, near the shore in Goose Pond. I suspect it may have been loosened up by the musquash, which either feeds on it, or merely makes its way through its dense mats. I also see small fishes, apparently shiners, four or five inches long, in this pond. Yet I have seen this almost all dried up.

I have smelled fungi in the thick woods for a week, though they are not very common. I see tobacco-pipes now in the path. You are liable to be overtaken by a thunder-shower these afternoons. The anychia already shows green seed-vessels on its lower branches. Petty morel has begun to bloom in shady swamps, how long?

Got the wood thrush's nest of June 19th (now empty). It was placed between many small upright shoots, against the main stem of the slender maple, and measures four and a half to five inches in diameter from out-

side to outside of the rim, and one and three quarters deep within. It is quite firm (except the external leaves falling off), the rim about three quarters of an inch thick, and it is composed externally of leaves, apparently chiefly chestnut, very much decayed, beneath which, in the place of the grass and stubble of which most nests are composed, are apparently the midribs of the same leaves, whose whole pulp, etc., is gone, arranged as compactly and densely (in a curving manner) as grass or stubble could be, upon a core, not of mud, but a pale-brown composition quite firm and smooth (within), looking like inside of a cocoanut-shell, and apparently composed of decayed leaf pulp (?), which the bird has perhaps mixed and cemented with its saliva. This is about a quarter of an inch thick and about as regular as a half of a cocoanut-shell. Within this, the lower part is lined with considerable rather coarse black root-fibre and a very little fine stubble. From some particles of fine white sand, etc., on the pale-brown composition of the nest, I thought it was obtained from the pond shore. This composition, viewed through a microscope, has almost a cellular structure.

II

AUGUST, 1858

(ÆT. 41)

Aug. 1. P. M. — Up Assabet.

The radical or immersed leaves of the pontederia are linear and grass-like, and I see that I have mistaken them for vallisneria just springing from the bottom. The leaves of new plants are just reaching and leaving the surface now, like spoons on the end of long handles.

Edward Bartlett and another brought me a green bittern, this year's bird, apparently full grown but not full plumaged, which they caught near the pool on A. Heywood's land behind Sleepy Hollow. They caught it in the woods on the hillside. It had not yet acquired the long feathers of the neck. The neck was bent back on itself an inch or more, — that part being bare of feathers and covered by the long feathers from above, — so that it did not appear very long until stretched out. This doubling was the usual condition and not apparent, but could be felt by the hand. So the green bitterns are leaving the nest now.

Aug. 2. P. M. — Up Assabet.

Landed at the Bath-Place and walked the length of Shad-bush Meadow. I noticed meandering down that meadow, which is now quite dry, a very broad and distinct musquash-trail, where they went and came con-

tinually when it was wet or under water in the winter or spring. These trails are often nine or ten inches wide and half a dozen deep, passing under a root and the lowest overhanging shrubs, where they glided along on their bellies underneath everything. I traced one such trail forty rods, till it ended in a large cabin three feet high, with blueberry bushes springing still from the top; and other similar trails led off from it on opposite sides. Near the cabin they had burrowed or worn them out nine or ten inches deep, as if this now deserted castle had been a place of great resort. Their skins used to be worth fifty cents apiece.

I see there what I take to be a marsh hawk of this year, hunting by itself. It has not learned to be very shy yet, so that we repeatedly get near it. What a rich brown bird! almost, methinks, with purple reflections.

What I have called the *Panicum latifolium* has now its broad leaves, striped with red, abundant under Turtle Bank, above Bath-Place.

Aug. 3. Savory-leaved aster.

Aug. 5. *Thursday.* 9.30 A. M. — Up river to Pantry Brook.

It clears up this morning after several cool, cloudy, and rainy dog-days. The wind is westerly and will probably blow us part way back. The river is unusually full for the season, and now quite smooth. The pontederia is apparently in its prime; the button-bush perhaps a little past, the upper halves of its balls in the sun looking brown generally. The late rose is still conspicuous, in clumps advanced into the meadow here and there. See the mikania only in one or two places beginning. The white lilies are less abundant than usual, methinks, perhaps on account of the high water. The water milkweed flower is an interesting red, here and there, like roses along the shore. The gratiola begins to yellow the shore in some places, and I notice the unobtrusive red of dense fields of stachys on the flat shores. The sium has begun to lift its umbels of white flowers above most other plants. The purple utricularia tinges the pools in many places, the most common of all its tribe.

The best show of lilies is on the west side of the bay, in Cyrus Hosmer's meadow, above the willow-row. Many of them are not open at 10 o'clock A. M. I noticed one with the sepals perfectly spread flat on the water, but the petals still held together in a sharp cone, being held by the concave, slightly hooked points. Touching this with an oar, it opens quickly with a spring. The same with many others, whose sepals were less spread. Under the influence of the light and warmth, the petals elevate or expand themselves in the middle, becoming more and more convex, till at last, being released at their overlapping points, they spring open and quickly spread themselves equally, revealing their yellow stamens. How satisfactory is the fragrance of this flower! It is the emblem of purity. It reminds me of a young country maiden. It is just so simple and unproved. Wholesome as the odor of the cow. It is not a highly refined odor, but merely a fresh youthful morning sweetness. It is merely the unalloyed sweetness of the earth and the water; a fair opportunity and field for

life; like its petals, uncolored by any experience; a simple maiden on her way to school, her face surrounded by a white ruff. But how quickly it becomes the prey of insects!

As we paddle slowly along the edge of the pads, we can see the weeds and the bottom distinctly in the sun, in this still August air, even five or six feet deep, — the countless utricularias, potamogetons, etc., etc., and hornwort standing erect with its reddish stems. Countless schools of little minnows of various species, chubby little breams not an inch long, and lighter-colored banded minnows are steadily passing, partly concealed by the pads, and ever and anon we see the dimple where some larger pickerel has darted away, for they lie just on the outer edge of the pads.

The foliage is apparently now in the height of its beauty, this wet year, now dense enough to hide the trunks and stems. The black willows are perhaps in their best condition, — airy, rounded masses of light green rising one above another, with a few slender black stems, like umbrella handles, seen here and there in their midst, low spreading cumuli of slender falcate leaves, buttressed by smaller sallows, button-bushes, cornels, and pontederias, — like long green clouds or wreaths of vapor resting on the riverside. They scarcely leave the impression of leaves, but rather of a low, swelling, rounded bank, even as the heaviest particles of alluvium are deposited nearest the channel. It is a peculiarity of this, which I think is our most interesting willow, that you rarely see the trunk and yet the foliage is never dense. They generally line one side of the river

Vol. XI

only, and that is the meadow, a concave, passive, female side.[1] They resound still with the sprightly twitter of the kingbird, that aerial and spirited bird hovering over them, swallow-like, which loves best, methinks, to fly where the sky is reflected beneath him. Also now from time to time you hear the chattering of young blackbirds or the *link* of bobolinks there, or see the great bittern flap slowly away. The kingbird, by his activity and lively note and his white breast, keeps the air sweet. He sits now on a dead willow twig, akin to the flecks of mackerel sky, or its reflection in the water, or the white clamshell, wrong side out, opened by a musquash, or the fine particles of white quartz that may be found in the muddy river's sand. He is here to give a voice to all these. The willow's dead twig is aerial perch enough for him. Even the swallows deign to perch on it. These willows appear to grow best on elevated sand-bars or deep sandy banks, which the stream has brought down, leaving a little meadow behind them, at some bend, often mixed with sawdust from a mill. They root themselves firmly here, and spread entirely over the sand.

The rose, which grows along with the willows and button-bushes, has a late and rare look now.

From off Rainbow Rush Shore I pluck a lily more than five inches in diameter. Its sepals and petals are long and slender or narrow (others are often short, broad, and rounded); the thin white edges of the four sepals are, as usual, or often, tinged with red. There are some twenty-five petals in about four rows. Four alternate ones of the outmost row have a reddish or

[1] *Vide* Aug. 7th and 15th.

rosaceous line along the middle between the sepals, and both the sepals and the outmost row of petals have seven or eight parallel darkish lines from base to tip. As you look down on the lily, it is a pure white star centred with yellow, — with its short central anthers orange-yellow.

The *Scirpus lacustris* and rainbow rush are still in bloom and going to seed. The first is the tule of California.

Landed at Fair Haven Pond to smell the *Aster macrophyllus*. It has a slight fragrance, somewhat like that of the Maine and northern New Hampshire one. Why has it no more in this latitude? When I first plucked it on Webster Stream I did not know but it was some fragrant garden herb. Here I can detect some faint relationship only by perseveringly smelling it.

The purple utricularia is *the* flower of the river to-day, apparently in its prime. It is very abundant, far more than any other utricularia, especially from Fair Haven Pond upward. That peculiar little bay in the pads, just below the inlet of the river, I will call Purple Utricularia Bay, from its prevalence there. I count a dozen within a square foot, one or two inches above the water, and they tinge the pads with purple for more than a dozen rods. I can distinguish their color thus far. The buds are the darkest or deepest purple. Methinks it is more abundant than usual this year.

I notice a commotion in the pads there, as of a musquash making its way along, close beneath the surface, and at its usual rate, when suddenly a snapping turtle puts its snout out, only up to the eyes. It

Water-lily

Cobwebs in Barrett's Mill

looks exactly like a sharp stake with two small knots on it, thus: _ .⌃• - - _

While passing there, I heard what I should call my night-warbler's note, and, looking up, saw the bird dropping to a bush on the hillside. Looking through the glass, I saw that it was the Maryland yellow-throat!! and it afterward flew to the button-bushes in the meadow.

I notice no polygonum out, or a little of the front-rank only. Some of the polygonums not only have leaves like a willow, especially like the *S. lucida*, but I see that their submerged leaves turn, or give place, to fibrous pink roots which might be mistaken for those of the willow.

Lily Bay is on the left, just above the narrow place in the river, which is just above Bound Rock. There are but few lilies this year, however; but if you wish to see how many there are, you must be on the side toward the sun.

Just opposite this bay, I heard a peculiar note which I thought at first might be that of a kingbird, but soon saw for the first time a wren within two or three rods perched on the tall sedge or the wool-grass and making it, — probably the short-billed marsh wren. It was peculiarly brisk and rasping, not at all musical, the rhythm something like *shar te dittle ittle ittle ittle ittle*, but the last part was drier or less liquid than this implies. It was a small bird, quite dark above and apparently plain ashy-white beneath, and held its head up when it sang, and also commonly its tail. It dropped into the deep sedge on our approach, but did not go off, as we saw by the motion of the grass; then reappeared and uttered its brisk notes quite near us, and, flying off, was lost in the sedge again.

We ate our dinner on the hill by Rice's. This forenoon there were no hayers in the meadow, but before we returned we saw many at work, for they had already cut some grass next to the upland, on the drier sides of the meadow, and we noticed where they had stuck up green bushes near the riverside to mow to.

While bathing at Rice's landing, I noticed under my arm, amid the potamogeton, a little pickerel between two and a half and three inches long, with a little silvery minnow about one inch long in his mouth. He held it by the tail, as it was jerking to and fro, and was slowly taking it in by jerks. I watched to see if he turned it, but to my surprise he at length swallowed it tail foremost, the minnow struggling to the last and going alive into his maw. Perhaps the pickerel learn by experience to turn them head downward. Thus early do these minnows fall on fate, and the pickerel too fulfill his destiny.

Several times on our return we scared up apparently two summer ducks, probably of this year, from the side of the river, first, in each case, seeing them swimming about in the pads; also, once, a great bittern, — I suspect also a this year's bird, for they are probably weaned at the same time with the green one.

Though the river was high, we pushed through many beds of potamogeton, long leafy masses, slanting downward and waving steadily in the stream, ten feet or more in length by a foot wide. In some places it looked as if the new sparganium would fairly choke up the stream.

Huckleberries are not quite yet in their prime.

Vol. XI

Aug. 6. P. M. — Walk to Boulder Field.

The broom is quite out of bloom; probably a week or ten days. It is almost ripe, indeed. I should like to see how rapidly it spreads. The dense roundish masses, side by side, are three or four feet over and fifteen inches high. They have grown from near the ground this year. The whole clump is now about eighteen feet from north to south by twelve wide. Within a foot or two of its edge, I detect many slender little plants springing up in the grass, only three inches high, but, on digging, am surprised to find that they are two years old. They have large roots, running down straight as well as branching, much stouter than the part above ground. Thus it appears to spread slowly by the seed falling from its edge, for I detected no runners. It is associated there with indigo, which is still abundantly in bloom.

I then looked for the little groves of barberries which some two months ago I saw in the cow-dung thereabouts, but to my surprise I found some only in one spot after a long search. They appear to have generally died, perhaps dried up. These few were some two inches high; the roots yet longer, having penetrated to the soil beneath. Thus, no doubt, some of those barberry clumps are formed; but I noticed many more small barberry plants standing single, most commonly protected by a rock.

Cut a couple of those low scrub apple bushes, and found that those a foot high and as wide as high, being clipped by the cows, as a hedge with shears, were about twelve years old, but quite sound and thrifty.[1]

---

[1] [*Excursions*, pp. 304, 305; Riv. 374.]

If our sluggish river, choked with potamogeton, might seem to have the slow-flying bittern for its peculiar genius, it has also the sprightly and aerial kingbird to twitter over and lift our thoughts to clouds as white as its own breast.

Emerson is gone to the Adirondack country with a hunting party. Eddy says he has carried a double-barrelled gun, one side for shot, the other for ball, for Lowell killed a bear there last year. But the story on the Mill-Dam is that he has taken a gun which throws shot from one end and ball from the other!

I think that I speak impartially when I say that I have never met with a stream so suitable for boating and botanizing as the Concord, and fortunately nobody knows it. I know of reaches which a single country-seat would spoil beyond remedy, but there has not been any important change here since I can remember. The willows slumber along its shore, piled in light but low masses, even like the cumuli clouds above. We pass haymakers in every meadow, who may think that we are idlers. But Nature takes care that every nook and crevice is explored by some one. While they look after the open meadows, we farm the tract between the river's brinks and behold the shores from that side. We, too, are harvesting an annual crop with our eyes, and think you Nature is not glad to display her beauty to us?

Early in the day we see the dewdrops thickly sprinkled over the broad leaves of the potamogeton. These cover the stream so densely in some places that a web-footed bird can almost walk across on them.

Nowadays we hear the *squealing* notes of young

hawks. The kingfisher is seen hovering steadily over one spot, or hurrying away with a small fish in his mouth, sounding his alarum nevertheless. The note of the wood pewee is now more prominent, while birds generally are silent.

This is pure summer; no signs of fall in this, though I have seen some maples, as above the Assabet Spring, already prematurely reddening, owing to the water, and for some time the *Cornus sericea* has looked brownish-red.

Every board and chip cast into the river is soon occupied by one or more turtles of various sizes. The sternothærus oftenest climbs up the black willows, even three or more feet.

I hear of pickers ordered out of the huckleberry-fields, and I see stakes set up with written notices forbidding any to pick there. Some let their fields, or allow so much for the picking. *Sic transit gloria ruris.* We are not grateful enough that we have lived part of our lives before these evil days came. What becomes of the true value of country life? What if you must go to market for it? Shall things come to such a pass that the butcher commonly brings round huckleberries in his cart? It is as if the hangman were to perform the marriage ceremony, or were to preside at the communion table. Such is the inevitable tendency of *our* civilization, — to reduce huckleberries to a level with beef-steak. The butcher's item on the door is now "calf's head and huckleberries." I suspect that the inhabitants of England and of the Continent of Europe have thus lost their natural rights with the increase of population and of

Vol. XI

monopolies. The wild fruits of the earth disappear before civilization, or are only to be found in large markets. The whole country becomes, as it were, a town or beaten common, and the fruits left are a few hips and haws.

Aug. 7. Saturday. P. M. — Up Assabet.

The most luxuriant groves of black willow, *as I recall them,* are on the inside curves, or on sandy capes between the river and a bay, or sandy banks parallel with the firmer shore, *e. g.* between Lee's and Fair Haven on north side, point of Fair Haven Island, opposite Clamshell and above, *just below stone bridge,* Lee Meadow or opposite house, below Nathan Barrett's at Bay, sandy bank below Dove Rock. They also grow on both sides sometimes, where the river runs straight through stagnant meadows or swamps, — *e. g.* above Hollowell Bridge, — or on one side, though straight, along the edge of a swamp, — as above Assabet Spring, — but rarely ever against a firm bank or hillside, the positive male shore, *e. g.* east shore of Fair Haven Pond, east side above railroad bridge, etc.[1] Measured the two largest of three below Dove Rock. The southernmost is three feet nine inches in circumference at ground, and it branches there. The westernmost is four feet two inches in circumference at ground and three feet two inches at three feet above ground. Or the largest is one foot and four inches in diameter at ground. They all branch at the ground, dividing within four or five feet into three or four main stems. The three here have the effect of

[1] *Vide* Aug. 15.

one tree, seen from the water, and are twenty-five feet high or more, and, all together, broader than high. They are none of them upright, but in this case, close under a higher wood of maples and swamp white oak, slant over the stream, and, taken separately or viewed from the land side, are very imperfect trees. If you stand at their base and look upward or outward, you see a great proportion of naked trunk but thinly invested with foliage even at the summit, and they are among the most unsightly trees. The lower branches slant downward from the main divisions so as commonly to rest on the water. But seen from the water side no tree of its height, methinks, so completely conceals its trunk. They meet with many hard rubs from the ice and from driftwood in freshets in the course of their lives, and whole trees are bent aside or half broken off by these causes, but they soon conceal their injuries.

The *Sternothærus odoratus* knows them well, for it climbs highest up their stems, three or four feet or more nowadays, sometimes seven or eight along the slanting branches, and is frequently caught and hung by the neck in its forks. They do not so much jump as tumble off when disturbed by a passer. The small black mud tortoise, with its muddy shell, eyes you motionless from its resting-place in a fork of the black willow. They will climb four feet up a stem not more than two inches in diameter, and yet undo all their work in an instant by tumbling off when your boat goes by. The trunk is covered with coarse, long, and thick upraised scales. It is this turtle's castle and path to heaven. He is on the upward road along the stem of the willow, and by its

dark stem it is partially concealed. Yes, the musquash and the mud tortoise and the bittern know it well.

But not these sights alone are now seen on our river, but the sprightly kingbird glances and twitters above the glossy leaves of the swamp white oak. Perchance this tree, with its leaves glossy above and whitish beneath, best expresses the life of the kingbird and is its own tree.

How long will it be after we have passed before the mud tortoise has climbed to its perch again?

The author of the Chinese novel "Ju-Kiao-Li," some eight hundred years ago, appears to have appreciated the beauty of willows. Pe, his principal character, moved out of the city late in life, to a stream bordered with willows, about twenty miles distant, in order to spend the rest of his days drinking wine and writing verses there. He describes the eyebrow of his heroine as like a willow leaf floating on the surface of the water.

In the upper part of J. Farmer's lane I find huckleberries which are distinctly pear-shaped, all of them. These and also other roundish ones near by, and apparently huckleberries generally, are dotted or apparently dusted over with a yellow dust or meal, which looks as if it could be rubbed off. Through a glass it looks like a resin which has exuded, and on the small green fruit is of a bright orange or lemon-color, like small specks of yellow lichens. It is apparently the same as that on the leaves.

Monarda fistula is now apparently in prime, four and more, eight or ten rods behind red oak on Emerson's Assabet field.

Aug. 8. P. M. — To Ledum Swamp.

I see at Clamshell Hill a yellow-browed sparrow sitting quite near on a haycock, pluming itself. Observe it a long time in all positions with my glass, within two rods. It is probably a this year's bird. I think it must be the *Fringilla passerina*, for its breast and beneath is the clear pale ochreous white which Wilson speaks of, and its wing-shoulder is distinctly yellow when not concealed in the feathers of the side. Its legs and bill, except the upper side of the upper mandible, are quite a reddish flesh-color. The yellow on its temple is quite bright, and the pale-brownish cheeks. The crown is blackish with a distinct white line along the midst. I see what I call chestnut with the black and whitish on the back and wings. It stands very upright, so that I can see all beneath. It utters no note, *i. e.* song, only a faint, short, somewhat cricket-like or *trilled* chip.

I see that handsome fine purple grass now, on Hosmer's hillside, above where he has mowed; not yet in perfection.

You see now in the meadows where the mower's scythe has cut in two the great oval and already black fruit of the skunk-cabbage, rough as a nutmeg-grater, exposing its numerous nuts. I had quite forgotten the promise of this earliest spring flower, which, deep in the grass which has sprung up around it, its own leaves for the most part decayed, unremembered by us, has been steadily maturing its fruit. How far we have wandered, in our thoughts at least, since we heard the bee humming in its spathe! I can hardly recall or believe now that for every such black and rather unsightly (?) capsule there

was a pretty freckled horn which attracted our attention in the spring. However, most of them lie so low that they escape or are not touched by the scythe.[1]

Saw yesterday a this year's (?) marsh hawk, female, flying low across the road near Hildreth's. I took it to be a young bird, it came so near and looked so fresh. It is a fine rich-brown, full-breasted bird, with a long tail. Some hens in the grass beneath were greatly alarmed and began to run and fly with a cackling to the shelter of a corn-field. They which did not see the hawk and were the last to stir expressed the most alarm. Meanwhile, the hawk sails low and steadily over the field away, not thinking of disturbing them.

I find at Ledum Swamp, near the pool, the white fringed orchis, quite abundant but past prime, only a few, yet quite fresh. It seems to belong to this sphagnous swamp and is some fifteen to twenty inches high, quite conspicuous, its white spike, amid the prevailing green. The leaves are narrow, half folded, and almost insignificant. It loves, then, these cold bogs.

The rusty wool-grass is in bloom there with very short wool. Is it ever long? The *Gaylussacia dumosa* var. *hirtella* is the prevailing low shrub, perhaps. I see one ripe berry. This is the only inedible species of *Vaccinieæ* that I know in this town.

The peculiar plants of this swamp are, then, as I re-

[1] My friends can rarely guess what fruit it is, but think of pineapples and the like. After lying in the house a week, and being wilted and softened, on breaking it open it has an agreeable sweetish scent, perchance like a banana, and suggests that it may be edible. But a long while after slightly tasting it, it bites my palate.

Vol. XI

member, these nine: spruce, *Andromeda Polifolia, Kalmia glauca, Ledum latifolium, Gaylussacia dumosa* var. *hirtella, Vaccinium Oxycoccus, Platanthera blephariglottis, Scheuchzeria palustris, Eriophorum vaginatum.*[1]

I see there, especially near the pool, tall and slender huckleberry bushes of a peculiar kind. Some are seven feet high. They are, for the most part, three or four feet high, very slender and drooping, bent like grass to one side. The berries are round and glossy-black, with resinous dots, as usual, and in flattish-topped racemes, sometimes ten or twelve in a raceme, but generally more scattered. Call it, perhaps, the tall swamp huckleberry.

The nesæa is fairly begun.

Looking north from Hubbard's Bridge about 4 P. M., the wind being southeasterly, I am struck by the varied lights of the river. The wind, which is a considerable breeze, strikes the water by a very irregular serrated edge about mid-channel, and then abruptly leaves it on a distinct and regular meandering line, about eight feet from the outer edge of the pads on the west side. The rippled portion of the river is blue, the rest smooth, silvery. Thus to my eye the river is divided into five portions, — first the weedy and padded borders, then a smooth, silvery stripe, eight or ten feet wide, and next the blue rippled portion, succeeded by the broader silver, and the pads of the eastern side. How many aspects the river wears, depending on the height of the water, the season of the year and state of vegetation, the wind, the position of the sun and condition of the heavens, etc., etc.! Apparently such is the angle at which the

[1] *Woodsia Virginica. Vide* Sept. 6th.

wind strikes the river from over the bushes that it falls about mid-channel, and then it is either obliged to leave

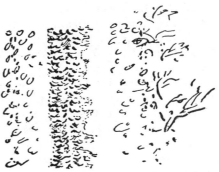

it at a nearly similar angle on account of the opposite shore and bushes, or, perchance, the smoothing influence of the pads is felt to some distance beyond their edges. The line which separates the smooth from the rippled portion is as distinct and continuous as that which marks the edge of the pads. I think that there is more oily matter floating on the stiller sides of the river, and this too may have something to do with the above phenomenon. Then there is the watered appearance of the surface in a shower.

Aug. 9. Edward Bartlett shows me this morning a nest which he found yesterday. It is saddled on the lowest horizontal branch of an apple tree in Abel Heywood's orchard, against a small twig, and answers to Nuttall's description of the goldfinch's nest, which it probably is. The eggs were five, pure white or with a faint bluish-green tinge, just begun to be developed. I did not see the bird.[1]

It is but little you learn of a bird in this irregular way, — having its nest and eggs shown you. How much more suggestive the sight of the goldfinch going off on a jaunt over the hills, twittering to its plainer consort by its side!

It is surprising to what extent the world is ruled by cliques. They who constitute, or at least lead, New England or New York society, in the eyes of the world, are but a clique, a few "men of the age" and of the town, who work best in the harness provided for them. The institutions of almost all kinds are thus of a sectarian or party character. Newspapers, magazines, colleges, and all forms of government and religion express the superficial activity of a few, the mass either conforming or not attending. The newspapers have just got over that eating-fullness or dropsy which takes place with the annual commencements and addresses before the Philomathean or Alpha Beta Gamma societies. Neither they who make these addresses nor they who attend to them are representative of the latest age. The boys think that these annual recurrences are part and parcel of the annual revolution of the system. There are also regattas and fireworks and "surprise parties" and horse-shows. So that I am glad when I see or hear of a man anywhere who does not know of these things nor recognizes these particular fuglers. I was pleased to hear the other day that there were two men in Tamworth, N. H., who had been fishing for trout there ever since May; but it was a

[1] *Vide* next page but one.

Vol. XI

scrap, not omitting what they did at New Rochelle and Evansville. And all the speeches are reported, and some think of collecting them into a volume ! ! !

You say that you have travelled far and wide. How many men have you seen that did not belong to any sect, or party, or clique? Did you go further than letters of introduction would avail?

The goldfinch nest of this forenoon is saddled on a horizontal twig of an apple, some seven feet from ground and one third of an inch in diameter, supported on one side by a yet smaller branch, also slightly attached to another small branch. It measures three and one half inches from outside to outside, one and three quarters inside, two and one half from top to bottom, or to a little below the twig, and one and one half inside. It is a very compact, thick, and warmly lined nest, slightly incurving on the edge within. It is composed of fine shreds of bark — grape-vine and other — and one piece of twine, with, more externally, an abundance of pale-brown slender catkins of oak (?) or hickory (?), mixed with effete apple blossoms and their peduncles, showing little apples, and the petioles of apple leaves, sometimes with half-decayed leaves of this year attached, last year's heads of lespedeza, and some other heads of weeds, with a little grass stem or weed stem, all more or less disguised by a web of white spider or caterpillar silk, spread over the outside. It is thickly and very warmly lined with (apparently) short thistle-down, mixed with which you see some grape-vine bark, and the rim is composed of the same shreds of bark, catkins, and some fine fibrous stems, and two or three hairs (of

serious drawback to be told that they sent their fish to Boston and so catered for the few. The editors of newspapers, the popular clergy, politicians and orators of the day and office-holders, though they may be thought to be of very different politics and religion, are essentially one and homogeneous, inasmuch as they are only the various ingredients of the froth which ever floats on the surface of society.

I see a pout this afternoon in the Assabet, lying on the bottom near the shore, evidently diseased. He permits the boat [to] come within two feet of him. Nearly half the head, from the snout backward diagonally, is covered with an inky-black kind of leprosy, like a crustaceous lichen. The long feeler on that side appears to be wasting, and there stands up straight in it, about an inch high, a little black tree-like thorn or feeler, branched at top. It moves with difficulty.

Edith Emerson gives me an *Asclepias tuberosa* from Naushon, which she thinks is now in its prime there.

It is surprising what a tissue of trifles and crudities make the daily news. For one event of interest there are nine hundred and ninety-nine insignificant, but about the same stress is laid on the last as on the first. The newspapers have just told me that the transatlantic telegraph-cable is laid. That is important, but they instantly proceed to inform me how the news was received in every larger town in the United States, — how many guns they fired, or how high they jumped, — in New York, and Milwaukee, and Sheboygan; and the boys and girls, old and young, at the corners of the streets are reading it all with glistening eyes, down to the very last

horse) mixed with wool (?); for only the hollow is lined with the looser or less tenacious thistle-down. This nest shows a good deal of art.

The mind tastes but few flavors in the course of a year. We are visited by but few thoughts which are worth entertaining, and we chew the cud of these unceasingly. What ruminant spirits we are! I remember well the flavor of that rusk which I bought in New York two or three months ago and ate in the cars for my supper. A fellow-passenger, too, pretended to praise it, and yet, O man of little faith! he took a regular supper at Springfield. They cannot make such in Boston. The mere fragrance, rumor, and reminiscence of life is all that we get, for the most part. If I am visited by a thought, I chew that cud each successive morning, as long as there is any flavor in it. Until my keepers shake down some fresh fodder. Our genius is like a brush which only once in many months is freshly dipped into the paint-pot. It becomes so dry that though we apply it incessantly, it fails to tinge our earth and sky. Applied to the same spot incessantly, it at length imparts no color to it.

Aug. 10. P. M. — To yew, etc.

It is cloudy and misty dog-day weather, with a good deal of wind, and thickening to occasional rain this afternoon. This rustling wind is agreeable, reminding me, by its unusual sound, of other and ruder seasons. The most of a storm you can get now is rather exhilarating. The grass and bushes are quite wet, and the pickers are driven from the berry-field. The rabbit's-foot clover is very wet to walk through, holding so much water. The fine grass falls over from each side into the middle of the woodland paths and wets me through knee-high.

I see many tobacco-pipes, now perhaps in their prime, if not a little late, and hear of pine-sap. The Indian-pipe, though coming with the fungi and suggesting, no doubt, a close relation to them, — a sort of connecting link between flowers and fungi, — is a very interesting flower, and will bear a close inspection when fresh. The whole plant has a sweetish, earthy odor, though Gray says it is inodorous. I see them now on the leafy floor of this oak wood, in families of twelve to thirty sisters of various heights, — from two to eight inches, — as close together as they can stand, the youngest standing close up to the others, all with faces yet modestly turned downwards under their long hoods. Here is a family of about twenty-five within a diameter of little more than two inches, lifting the dry leaves for half their height in a cylinder about them. They generally appear bursting up through the dry leaves, which, elevated around, may serve to prop them. Springing up in the shade with so little color, they look the more fragile and delicate. They have very delicate pinkish half-naked stems with a few semitransparent crystalline-white scales for leaves, and from the sinuses at the base of the petals without (when their heads are drooping) more or less dark purple is reflected, like the purple of the arteries seen on a nude body. They appear not to flower only when upright. Gray says they are upright in fruit. They soon become black-specked, even before flowering.

Am surprised to find the yew with ripe fruit (how

long?), — though there is a little still small and green, — where I had not detected fertile flowers. It fruits very sparingly, the berries growing singly here and there, on last year's wood, and hence four to six inches below the extremities of the upturned twigs. It is the most surprising berry that we have: first, since it is borne by an evergreen, hemlock-like bush with which we do not associate a soft and bright-colored berry, and hence its deep scarlet contrasts the more strangely with the pure, dark evergreen needles; and secondly, because of its form, so like art, and which could be easily imitated in wax, a very thick scarlet cup or mortar with a dark-purple (?) bead set at the bottom. My neighbors are not prepared to believe that such a berry grows in Concord.

I notice several of the hylodes hopping through the woods like wood frogs, far from water, this mizzling [day]. They are probably common in the woods, but not noticed, on account of their size, or not distinguished from the wood frog. I also saw a young wood frog, with the dark line through the eye, no bigger than the others. One hylodes which I bring home has a perfect cross on its back, — except one arm of it.

The wood thrush's was a peculiarly woodland nest, made solely of such materials as that unfrequented grove afforded, the refuse of the wood or shore of the pond. There was no horsehair, no twine nor paper nor other relics of art in it.

Aug. 11. P. M. — To Beck Stow's.

I see of late a good many young sparrows (and old) of

Vol. XI

different species flitting about. That blackberry-field of Gowing's in the Great Fields, this side of his swamp, is a famous place for them. I see a dozen or more, old and young, perched on the wall. As I walk along, they fly up from the grass and alight on the wall, where they sit on the alert with outstretched necks. Nearest and unalarmed sit the huckleberry-birds; next, quite on the alert, the bay-wings, with which and further off the yellow-browed sparrows, of whom one at least has a clear yellowish breast; add to which that I heard thereabouts the seringo note. If made by this particular bird, I should infer it was *Fringilla passerina*. I still hear there at intervals the bay-wing, huckleberry-bird, and seringo.

Now is our rainy season. It has rained half the days for ten days past. Instead of dog-day clouds and mists, we have a rainy season. You must walk armed with an umbrella. It is wettest in the woods, where the air has had no chance to dry the bushes at all.

The *Myriophyllum ambiguum*, apparently variety *natans*, is now apparently in its prime. Some buds have gone to seed; others are not yet open. It is floating all over the surface of the pool, by the road, at the swamp, — long utricularia-like masses without the bladders. The emersed part, of linear or pectinate leaves, rises only about half an inch; the rest, eighteen inches more or less in length, consists of an abundance of capillary pinnate leaves, covered with slime or conferva (?) as a web. Evidently the same plant, next the shore and creeping over the mud, only two or three inches long, is without the capillary leaves, having roots instead, and appar-

ently is the variety *limosum* (?), I suspect erroneously so called.

Heard a fine, sprightly, richly warbled strain from a bird perched on the top of a bean-pole. It was at the same time novel yet familiar to me. I soon recognized it for the strain of the purple finch, which I have not heard lately. But though it appeared as large, it seemed a different-colored bird. With my glass, four rods off, I saw it to be a goldfinch. It kept repeating this warble of the purple finch for several minutes. A very surprising note to be heard now, when birds generally are so silent. Have not heard the purple finch of late. I conclude that the goldfinch is a very fine and powerful singer, and the most successful and remarkable mocking-bird that we have. In the spring I heard it imitate the thrasher exactly, before that bird had arrived, and now it imitates the purple finch as perfectly, after the latter bird has ceased to sing! It is a surprising vocalist. It did not cease singing till I disturbed it by my nearer approach, and then it went off with its usual *mew*, succeeded by its watery twitter in its *ricochet* flight. Have they not been more common all summer than formerly?

I go along plum path behind Adolphus Clark's. This is a peculiar locality for plants. The *Desmodium Canadense* is now apparently in its prime there and very common, with its rather rich spikes of purple flowers, — the most (?) conspicuous of the desmodiums. It might be called Desmodium Path. Also the small rough sunflower (now abundant) and the common apocynum (also in bloom as well as going and gone to seed) are very common. I smell the fragrant everlasting concealed in the higher grass and weeds there, some distance off. It reminds me of the lateness of the season. Saw the elodea (not long) and a dangle-berry ripe (not long) at Beck Stow's.

See a small variety of helianthus growing with the *divaricatus*, on the north side of Peter's path, two rods east of bars southeast of his house. It is an imperfect flower, but apparently answers best to the *H. trachelii-folius*. There is evidently a great variety in respect to form, petiole, venation, roughness, thickness, and color of the leaves of helianthuses.

Saw yesterday the *Utricularia vulgaris*, apparently in its prime, yellowing those little pools in Lincoln at the town bound by Walden. Their stems and leaves seem to half fill them. Some pools, like that at bath-place by pond in R. W. E.'s wood, will have for all vegetation only the floating immersed stems and leaves, light-brown, of this plant, without a flower, perhaps on account of shade.

The great bullfrogs, of various colors from dark brown to greenish yellow, lie out on the surface of these slimy pools or in the shallow water by the shore, motionless and philosophic. Toss a chip to one, and he will instantly leap and seize and drop it as quick. Motionless and indifferent as they appear, they are ready to leap upon their prey at any instant.

Aug. 12. When I came down-stairs this morning, it raining hard and steadily, I found an Irishman sitting with his coat on his arm in the kitchen, waiting to see me. He wanted to inquire what I thought the weather

would be to-day! I sometimes ask my aunt, and she consults the almanac. So we shirk the responsibility.

P. M. — To the Miles blueberry swamp and White Pond.

It clears up before noon and is now very warm and clear. When I look at the sparrows on the fences, yellow-browed and bay-wings, they all have their bills open and are panting with heat. Apparently the end of the very wet weather we have had about a fortnight.

At Clamshell I see more of, I think, the same clear-breasted, yellow-browed sparrows which I saw there the other day and thought the *Fringilla passerina*, and now I hear, from some thereabouts, the seringo note.

As I stand on the bank there, I find suddenly that I hear, low and steady, under all other sounds, the creak of the mole cricket by the riverside. It has a peculiarly late sound, suggestive of the progress of the year. It is the voice which comes up steadily at this season from that narrow sandy strip between the meadow and the water's edge. You might think it issued from that small frog, the only living thing you see, which sits so motionless on the sand. But the singer is wholly out of sight in his gallery under the surface. *Creak creak, creak creak, creak creak, creak creak.* It is a sound associated with the declining year and recalls the moods of that season. It is so unobtrusive yet universal a sound, so underlying the other sounds which fill the air, — the song of birds, rustling of leaves, dry hopping sound of grasshoppers, etc., — that now, in my chamber, I can hardly be sure whether I hear it still, or remember it, it so rings in my ears.

It is surprising how young birds, especially sparrows of all kinds, abound now, and bobolinks and wood pewees and kingbirds. All weeds and fences and bare trees are alive with them. The sparrows and bobolinks are seen surging over or falling behind the weeds and fences, even as grasshoppers now skip from the grass and leaves in your path.

That very handsome high-colored fine purple grass grows particularly on dry and rather unproductive soil just above the edge of the meadows, on the base of the hills, where the hayer does not deign to swing his scythe. He carefully gets the meadow-hay and the richer grass that borders it, but leaves this fine purple mist for the walker's harvest. Higher up the hill, perchance, grow blackberries and johnswort and neglected and withered and wiry June-grass. Twenty or thirty rods off it appears as a high-colored purple border above the meadow, like a berry's stain laid on close and thick, but if you pluck one plant you will be surprised to find how thin it is and how little color it has. What puny causes combine to produce such decided effects! There is ripeness in its color as in the poke stem. It grows in waste places, perhaps on the edge of blackberry-fields, a thin, fine, spreading grass, left by the mower. It oftenest grows in scattered rounded tufts a foot in diameter, especially on gentle slopes.[1]

I see a hen-harrier (female) pursued by a red-wing, etc., circling low and far off over the meadow. She is a peculiar and distinct reddish brown on the body beneath.

[1] [*Excursions*, pp. 252, 253; Riv. 309, 310.]

All farmers are complaining of the catching weather. I see some of their hay, which is spread, afloat in the meadow.

This year the fields have not yet worn a parched and withered look.

I perceive that some high blueberries have a peculiar and decided bitter taste, which makes them almost inedible. Some of the blueberries growing sparingly on recent sprouts are very large. I eat the blueberry, but I am also interested in the rich-looking glossy black choke-berries which nobody eats, but which bend down the bushes on every side, — sweetish berries with a dry, and so choking, taste. Some of the bushes are more than a dozen feet high.

The note of the wood pewee is a prominent and common one now. You see old and young together.

As I sit on the high bank overlooking White Pond, I am surprised at the number of birds about me, — wood pewees, singing so sweetly on a pine; chickadees, uttering their *phebe* notes, apparently with their young too; the pine warbler, singing; robins, restless and peeping; and a Maryland yellow-throat, hopping within a bush closely. Some boys bathing shake the whole pond. I see the undulations a third across it though they are out of sight, and, if it were smooth, might perhaps see them quite across.

Hear what I have called the alder locust (?) as I return over the causeway, and probably before this.

It is pleasant enough, for a change, to walk in the woods without a path in a wet and mizzling afternoon, as we did the 10th, winding amid the wet bushes, which wet our legs through, and seeing ever and anon a wood frog skip over the dead and wet leaves, and the various-colored fungi, — rejoicing in fungi. (I saw some large ones, green, that afternoon.) We are glad to come to more open spaces where we can walk dry on a carpet of pine leaves.

Saw a *Viola pedata* blooming again.

Aug. 13. This month thus far has been quite rainy. It has rained more or less at least half the days. You have had to consider each afternoon whether you must not take an umbrella. It has about half the time either been dogdayish or mizzling or decided rain. It would rain five minutes and be fair the next five, and so on, alternately, a whole afternoon. The farmers have not been able to get much of their hay. On the whole it has been rather cool. It has been still decidedly summer, with some reminiscences of autumn. The last week has been the heart of the huckleberry season.

P. M. — Up Assabet.

The dullish-blue or lead-colored *Viburnum dentatum* berries are now seen, not long, overhanging the side of the river, amid cornels and willows and button-bushes. They make a dull impression, yet held close in some lights they are glossy. The umbelled fruits — viburnums and cornels, aralias, etc. — have begun.

As I am paddling up the north side above the Hemlocks, I am attracted by the singular shadows of the white lily pads on the rich-brown muddy bottom. It is remarkable how light tends to prevail over shadow there. It steals in under the densest curtain of pads

and illustrates the bottom. The shadows of these pads, seen (now at 3 P. M.) a little one side, where the water is eighteen inches or two feet deep, are rarely orbicular or entire-edged or resembling the leaf, but are more or less perfect rosettes, generally of an oval form, with five to fifteen or more regularly rounded petals, open half-way to the centre: You cannot commonly refer the shadow to its substance but by touching the leaf with your paddle. Light knows a thousand tricks by which it prevails. Light is the rule, shadow the exception. The leaf fails to cast a shadow equal in area to itself. While it is a regular and almost solid disk, the shadow is a rosette or palmate, as if the sun, in its haste [to] illustrate every nook, shone round the shortest corner. Often if you connect the extremities of the petals, you have the general outline and size of the leaf, and the shadow is less than the substance by the amount of the openings. These petals seem to depend for their existence on the somewhat scalloped, waved, or undulating edge of the pad, and the manner in which the light is reflected from it. Generally the two sharp angles of the pad are almost entirely eroded in the shadow. The shadows, too, have a slight halo about them. Such endless and varied play of light and shadow is on the river bottom! It is protean and somewhat weird even. The shadow of the leaf might be mistaken for that of the flower. The sun playing with a lily leaf draws the outline of a lily on the bottom with its shadow.

The broad-leaved helianthus on bank opposite Assa-

bet Spring is not nearly out, though the *H. divaricatus* was abundantly out on the 11th.

I landed to get the wood pewee nest in the Lee Wood. Perhaps those woods might be called Mantatukwet's, for he says he lived at the foot of Nawshawtuct about fifty years before 1684.[1]

Hypopytis abundantly out (how long?), apparently a good while, in that long wood-path on the left side, under the oak wood, before you begin to rise, going from the river end. Very little indeed is yet erect, and that which is not is apparently as forward as the rest. Not generally quite so high as the *Monotropa uniflora* which grows with it. I see still in their midst the dry upright brown spikes of last year's seed-vessels. The chimaphila is more of an umbel: Where that dense young birch grove, four to eight feet high, was burned over in the spring, — I am pretty sure it was early in May, — I see now a yet more dense green crop of *Solidago altissima*, three or four feet high and budded to bloom. Where did all the seed come from? I think the burning was too late for any seed to have blown on since. Did it, then, lie in the ground so low as to escape the fire? The seed may have come from plants which grow in the old path along the fence on the west side. It is a singular fact, at any rate, that a dense grove of young white birches, covering half a dozen acres, may be burned over in May, so as to kill nearly all, and now, amid the dead brown trees, you see [a] dense green crop of *Solidago*

[1] Call it Woodis Park.

altissima covering the ground like grass, four feet high. Nature practices a rotation of crops, and always has some seed ready in the ground.

Young white maples below Dove Rock are an inch and a half high, and red maples elsewhere about one inch high.

I come to get the now empty nests of the wood pewees found June 27th. In each case, on approaching the spot, I hear the sweet note of a pewee lingering about, and this alone would have guided me within four or five rods. I do not know why they should linger near the empty nest, but perhaps they have built again near there or intend to use the same nest again (?). Their full strain is *pe-ah-ee'* (perhaps repeated), rising on the last syllable and emphasizing that, then *pe'-ee*, emphasizing the first and falling on the last, all very sweet and rather plaintive, suggesting innocence and confidence in you. In this case the bird uttered only its last strain, regularly at intervals.

These two pewee nests are remarkably alike in their position and composition and form, though half a mile apart. They are both placed on a horizontal branch of a young oak (one about fourteen, the other about eighteen, feet from ground) and three to five feet from main trunk, in a young oak wood. Both rest directly on a horizontal fork, and such is their form and composition that they have almost precisely the same color and aspect from below and from above.

The first is on a dead limb, very much exposed, is three inches in diameter outside to outside, and two inches in diameter within, the rim being about a quarter

Vol. XI

of an inch thick, and it is now one inch deep within. Its framework is white pine needles, especially in the rim, and a very little fine grass stem, covered on the rim and all without closely with small bits of lichen (cetraria?), slate-colored without and blackish beneath, and some brown caterpillar (?) or cocoon (?) silk with small seed-vessels in it. They are both now thin and partially open at the bottom, so that I am not sure they contain all the original lining. This one has no distinct lining, unless it is a very little green usnea amid the loose pine-needles. The lichens of the nest would readily be confounded with the lichens of the limb. Looking down on it, it is a remarkably round and neat nest.

The second nest is rather more shallow now and half an inch wider without, is lined with much more usnea (the willow down which I saw in it June 27 is gone; perhaps they cast it out in warm weather!), and shows a little of some slender brown catkin (oak?) beneath, without.

These nests remind me of what I suppose to be the yellow-throat vireo's and hummingbird's. The lining of a nest is not in good condition — perhaps is partly gone — when the birds have done with it.

The remarkable difference between the two branches of our river, kept up down to the very junction, indicates a different geological region for their channels.

Aug. 14. P. M. — To the one-arched bridge. Hardhacks are probably a little past prime.

Stopped by the culvert opposite the centaurea, to look at the sagittaria leaves. Perhaps this plant is in its

Vol. XI

prime (?). Its leaves vary remarkably in form. I see, in a thick patch six or eight feet in diameter, leaves nearly a foot long of this form: and others, this form: as long or longer, of with all the various intermediate ones, perhaps, around the edge of the patch, not distinguished at first, but mistaken for grass.

Suggesting to C. an Indian name for one of our localities, he thought it had too many syllables for a place so near the middle of the town, — as if the more distant and less frequented place might have a longer name, less understood and less alive in its syllables.

The Canada thistle down is now begun to fly, and I see the goldfinch upon it. *Carduelis.* Often when I watch one go off, he flies at first one way, rising and falling, as if skimming close over unseen billows, but directly makes a great circuit as if he had changed his mind, and disappears in the opposite direction, or is seen to be joined there by his mate.

We walked a little way down the bank this side the Assabet bridge. The broad-leaved panic grass, with its hairy sheaths or collars, attracts the eye now there by its perfectly fresh broad leaf. We see from time to time many bubbles rising from the sandy bottom, where it is two or more feet deep, which I suspect to come from clams there letting off air. I think I see the clams, and it is often noticed there.

I see a pickerel nearly a foot long in the deep pool under the wooden bridge this side the stone one, where it has been landlocked how long?

There is brought me this afternoon *Thalictrum Cornuti*, of which the club-shaped filaments (and sepals?) and seed-vessels are a bright purple and quite showy.

To speak from recollection, the birds which I *have chanced to hear* of late are (running over the whole list): —

The squealing notes of young hawks.
Occasionally a red-wing's *tchuck*.
The *link* of bobolinks.
The *chickadee* and *phebe* note of the chickadees, five or six together occasionally.
The *fine* note of the cherry-bird, pretty often.
The twitter of the kingbird, pretty often.
The wood pewee, with its young, peculiarly common and prominent.
Only the *peep* of the robin.
The pine warbler, occasionally.
The bay-wing, pretty often.
The seringo, pretty often.
The song sparrow, often.
The field sparrow, often.
The goldfinch, a prevailing note, with variations into a fine song.
The ground-robin, *once* of late.
The flicker's cackle, *once* of late.
The nighthawk, as usual.

I have not been out early nor late, nor attended particularly to the birds. The more characteristic notes would appear to be the wood pewee's and the goldfinch's, with the squeal of young hawks. These might be called the pewee-days.[1]

[1] *Vide* [p. 107].

Aug. 15. P. M. — Down river to Abner Buttrick's.

Rain in the night and dog-day weather again, after two clear days. I do not like the name "dog-days." Can we not have a new name for this season? It is the season of mould and mildew, and foggy, muggy, often rainy weather.

The front-rank polygonum is apparently in prime, or perhaps not quite.[1] Wild oats, apparently in prime. This is quite interesting and handsome, so tall and loose. The lower, spreading and loosely drooping, dangling or blown one side like a flag, staminate branches of its ample panicle are of a lively yellowish green, contrasting with the very distant upright pistillate branches, suggesting a spear with a small flag at the base of its head. It is our wild grain, unharvested.

The black willows are already being imbrowned. It must be the effect of the water, for we have had no drought.

The smaller white maples are very generally turned a dull red, and their long row, seen against the fresh green of Ball's Hill, is very surprising. The leaves evidently come to maturity or die sooner in water and wet weather. They are redder now than in autumn, and set off the landscape wonderfully. The Great Meadows are not a quarter shorn yet. The swamp white oaks, ash trees, etc., which stand along the shore have horizontal lines and furrows at different heights on their trunks, where the ice of past winters has rubbed against them.

Might not the potamogeton be called *waving weed?*

[1] *Vide* 19th.

I notice the black willows from my boat's place to Abner Buttrick's, to see where they grow, distinguishing ten places. In seven instances they are on the concave or female side distinctly. Then there is one clump just below mouth of Mill Brook on male side, one tree at Simmonds's boat-house, male side, and one by oak on Heywood Shore. The principal are on the sand-bars or points formed along the concave side. Almost the only exceptions to their growing on the concave side exclusively are a few mouths of brooks and edges of swamps, where, apparently, there is an eddy or slow current. Similar was my observation on the Assabet as far up as Woodis Park. The localities I noticed to-day were: mouth of Mill Brook (and up it); sand-bar along shore just below, opposite; opposite Simmonds's boat-house; one at boat-house; Hornbeam Cape; Flint's meadow, along opposite boys' bath-place; one by oak below bath-place on south side; at meadow fence, south side; point of the diving ash; south side opposite bath-place by wall. Up Assabet the places were (the 13th): south side above Rock; Willow Swamp; Willow Bay (below Dove Rock); Willow Island; swift place, south side; mouth of Spencer Brook.

Wars are not yet over. I hear one in the outskirts learning to drum every night; and think you there will be no field for him? He relies on his instincts. He is instinctively meeting a demand.

Aug. 16. Hear it raining again early when I awake, as it did yesterday, still and steady, as if the season were troubled with a diabetes.

I hear these birds on my way thither, between two and three o'clock: goldfinches twitter over; the song sparrow sings several times; hear a low warble from bluebirds, with apparently their young, the *link* of many bobolinks (and see large flocks on the fences and weeds; they are largish-looking birds with yellow throats); a large flock of red-wings goes *tchucking* over; a lark twitters; crows caw; a robin peeps; kingbirds twitter, as ever.

At sunset I hear a low short warble from a golden robin, and the notes of the wood pewee.

In my boating of late I have several times scared up a couple of summer ducks of this year, bred in our meadows. They allowed me to come quite near, and helped to people the river. I have not seen them for some days. Would you know the end of our intercourse? Goodwin shot them, and Mrs. ——, who never sailed on the river, ate them. Of course, she knows not what she did. What if I should eat her canary? Thus we share each other's sins as well as burdens. The lady who watches admiringly the matador shares his deed. They belonged to me, as much as to any one, when they were alive, but it was considered of more importance that Mrs. —— should taste the flavor of them dead than that I should enjoy the beauty of them alive.

A three-ribbed goldenrod on railroad causeway, two to three feet high, abundantly out before *Solidago nemoralis*.

I notice that when a frog, a *Rana halecina*, jumps, it drops water at the same instant, as a turtle often when touched as she is preparing to lay. I see many frogs

jump from the side of the railroad causeway toward the ditch at its base, and each drops some water. They apparently have this supply of water with them in warm and dry weather, at least when they leave the water, and, returning to it, leave it behind as of no further use.

Thalictrum Cornuti is now generally done.

The hardhack commonly grows in low meadow-pastures which are uneven with grassy clods or hummocks, such as the almshouse pasture by Cardinal Ditch.

I am surprised to find that where of late years there have been so many cardinal-flowers, there are now very few. So much does a plant fluctuate from season to season. Here I found nearly white ones once. Channing tells me that he saw a white bobolink in a large flock of them to-day. Almost all flowers and animals may be found white. As in a large number of cardinal-flowers you may find a white one, so in a large flock of bobolinks, also, it seems, you may find a white one.

Talked with Minott, who sits in his wood-shed, having, as I notice, several seats there for visitors, — one a block on the sawhorse, another a patchwork mat on a wheelbarrow, etc., etc. His half-grown chickens, which roost overhead, perch on his shoulder or knee. According to him, the Holt is at the "diving ash," where is some of the deepest water in the river. He tells me some of his hunting stories again. He always lays a good deal of stress on the kind of gun he used, as if he had bought a new one every year, when probably he never had more than two or three in his life. In this case it was a "half-stocked" one, a little "cocking-piece," and whenever he finished his game he used the word

"gavel," I think in this way, "gave him gavel," *i. e.* made him bite the dust, or settled him. Speaking of foxes, he said: "As soon as the nights get to be cool, if you step outdoors at nine or ten o'clock when all is still, you'll hear them bark out on the flat behind the houses, half a mile off, or sometimes *whistle* through their noses. I can tell 'em. I know what that means. I know all about that. They are out after something to eat, I suppose." He used to love to hear the goldfinches sing on the hemp which grew near his gate.

At sunset paddled to Hill.

Goodwin has come again to fish, with three poles, hoping to catch some more of those large eels.

A blue heron, with its great undulating wings, prominent cutwater, and leisurely flight, goes over southwest, cutting off the bend of the river west of our house. Goodwin says he saw one two or three days ago, and also that he saw some black ducks. A muskrat is swimming up the stream, betrayed by two long diverging ripples, or ripple-lines, two or three rods long each, and inclosing about seventy-five degrees, methinks. The rat generally dives just before reaching the shore and is not seen again, probably entering some burrow in the bank.

Am surprised to see that the snapping turtle which I found floating dead June 16th, and placed to rot in the cleft of a rock, has been all cleaned, so that there is no smell of carrion. The scales have nearly all fallen off, and the sternum fallen apart, and the bony frame of the back is loose and dropping to pieces, as if it were many years old. It is a wonderful piece of dovetailing, the ends of the ribs (which are narrow and rib-like) set into sockets in the middle of the marginal bones, whose joints are in each case *between* the ribs. There are many large fish-bones within the shell. Was it killed by the fish it swallowed? The bones not being dispersed, I suppose it was cleaned by insects.

Aug. 17. Still hear the chip-bird early in the morning, though not so generally as earlier in the season.

Minott has only lately been reading Shattuck's "History of Concord," and he says that his account is not right by a jugful, that he does not come within half a mile of the truth, not as he has heard tell.

Some days ago I saw a kingbird twice stoop to the water from an overhanging oak and pick an insect from the surface.

C. saw pigeons to-day.

P. M. — To Annursnack *via* swimming-ford.

The river is twelve to eighteen inches deeper there than usual at this season. Even the slough this side is two feet deep.

There has been so much rain of late that there is no curling or drying of the leaves and grass this year. The foliage is a pure fresh green. The aftermath on early-mown fields is a very beautiful green.

Being overtaken by a shower, we took refuge in the basement of Sam Barrett's sawmill, where we spent an hour, and at length came home with a rainbow over-arching the road before us.

The dog-days, the foggy and mouldy days, are not over yet. The clouds are like a mildew which over-

Vol. XI

spreads the sky. It is sticky weather, and the air is filled with the scent of decaying fungi.

Aug. 18. P. M. — To Fair Haven Hill.

Miss Caroline Pratt saw the white bobolink yesterday where Channing saw it the day before, in the midst of a large flock.[1] I go by the place this afternoon and see very large flocks of them, certainly several hundreds in all, and one has a little white on his back, but I do not see *the* white one. Almost every bush along this brook is now alive with these birds. You wonder where they were all hatched, for you may have failed to find a single nest. I know eight or ten active boys who have been searching for these nests the past season quite busily, and they have found but two at most. Surely but a small fraction of these birds will ever return from the South. Have they so many foes there? Hawks must fare well at present. They go off in a straggling flock, and it is a long time before the last loiterer has left the bushes near you.

I also see large flocks of blackbirds, blackish birds with chattering notes. It is a fine sight when you can look down on them just as they are settling on the ground with outspread wings, — a hovering flock.

Having left my note-book at home, I strip off a piece of birch bark for paper. It begins at once to curl up, yellow side out, but I hold that side to the sun, and as soon as it is dry it gives me no more trouble.

[1] I hear also of a swallow (probably barn swallow), perfectly white, killed by John Flint's son this year and set up by some one in the North Quarter.

I sit under the oaks at the east end of Hubbard's Grove, and hear two wood pewees singing close by. They are perched on dead oak twigs four or five rods apart, and their notes are so exactly alike that at first I thought there was but one. One appeared to answer the other, and sometimes they both sung together, — even as if the old were teaching her young. It was not the usual spring note of this bird, but a simple, clear *pe-e-eet*, rising steadily with one impulse to the end.[1] They were undistinguishable in tone and rhythm, though one which I thought might be the young was feebler. In the meanwhile, as it was perched on the twig, it was incessantly turning its head about, looking for insects, and suddenly would dart aside or downward a rod or two, and I could hear its bill snap as it caught one. Then it returned to the same or another perch.

Heard a nuthatch.[2]

Last evening one of our neighbors, who has just completed a costly house and front yard, the most showy in the village, illuminated in honor of the Atlantic telegraph. I read in great letters before the house the sentence "Glory to God in the highest." But it seemed to me that that was not a sentiment to be illuminated, but to keep dark about. A simple and genuine sentiment of reverence would not emblazon these words as on a signboard in the streets. They were exploding countless crackers beneath it, and gay company, passing in and out, made it a kind of housewarming. I felt a kind of shame for [it], and was inclined to pass quickly by,

[1] Not heard for a long time, Oct. 15, 1859.
[2] And a week later. Not heard since spring.

the ideas of indecent exposure and cant being suggested. What is religion? That which is never spoken.

Aug. 19. P. M. — Sail to Baker Farm shore.

It is cool with a considerable northwesterly wind, so that we can sail to Fair Haven. The dog-day weather is suddenly gone and here is a cool, clear, and elastic air. You may say it is the first day of autumn. You notice the louder and clearer ring of crickets, and the large, handsome red spikes of the *Polygonum amphibium* are now generally conspicuous along the shore. The *P. hydropiperoides* fairly begins to show. The front-rank polygonum is now in prime.

We scare up a stake-driver several times. The blue heron has within a week reappeared in our meadows, and the stake-driver begins to be seen oftener, and as early as the 5th I noticed young summer ducks about; the same of hawks, owls, etc. This occurs as soon as the young birds can take care of themselves, and some appear to be very early on the return southward, with the very earliest prospect of fall. Such birds are not only more abundant but, methinks, more at leisure now, having reared their family, and perhaps they are less shy. Yes, bitterns are more frequently seen now to lift themselves from amid the pontederia or flags, and take their sluggish flight to a new resting-place, — bitterns which either have got through the labors of breeding or are now first able to shift for themselves. And likewise blue herons, which have bred or been bred not far from us (plainly), are now at leisure, or are impelled to revisit our slow stream. I have not seen the last since spring.

When I see the first heron, like a dusky blue wave undulating over our meadows again, I think, since I saw them going northward the other day, how many of these forms have been added to the landscape, complete from bill to toe, while, perhaps, I have idled! I see two herons. A small bird is pursuing the heron as it does a hawk. Perhaps it is a blackbird and the herons gobble up their young!

I see thistle-down, grayish-white, floating low quite across Fair Haven Pond. There is wont to be just water [sic] enough above the surface to drive it along. The heads of the wool-grass are now brown and, in many meadows, lodged. The button-bush is about done. Can hardly see a blossom. The mikania not yet quite in prime. Pontederia has already begun to wane; i. e., the fields of them are not so dense, many seed-vessels having turned down; and some leaves are already withered and black, but the remaining spikes are as fair as ever. It chances that I see no yellow lilies. They must be scarce now. The water is high for the season. Water cool to bathe.

We have our first green corn to-day, but it is late. The saw-grass (*Paspalum ?*) of mown fields, not long.

I noticed the localities of black willows as far up as the mouth of the river in Fair Haven Pond, but not so carefully as elsewhere, and from the last observations I infer that the willow grows especially and almost exclusively in places where the drift is most likely to lodge, as on capes and points and concave sides of the river, though I noticed a few exceptions to my rule.

It is so cool, some apprehend a frost to-night.

Aug. 20. Edward Hoar has found in his garden two or three specimens of what appears to be the *Veronica Buxbaumii*, which blossomed at least a month ago. Yet I should say the pods were turgid, and, though obcordate enough, I do not know in what sense they are "obcordate-triangular." He found a *Viburnum dentatum* with leaves somewhat narrower than common and wedge-shaped at base. He has also the *Rudbeckia speciosa*, cultivated in a Concord garden.

Flannery tells me that at about four o'clock this morning he saw white frost on the grass in the low ground near Holbrook's meadow. Up early enough to see a frost in August!

P. M. — To Poplar Hill and the Great Fields.

It is still cool weather with a northwest wind. This weather is a preface to autumn. There is more shadow in the landscape than a week ago, methinks, and the creak of the cricket sounds cool and steady.

The grass and foliage and landscape generally are of a more thought-inspiring color, suggest what some perchance would call a pleasing melancholy. In some meadows, as I look southwesterly, the aftermath looks a bright yellowish-green in patches. Both willows and poplars have leaves of a light color, at least beneath, contrasting with most other trees.

Generally there has been no drought this year. Nothing in the landscape suggests it. Yet no doubt these leaves are, compared with themselves six or eight weeks ago, as usual, "horny and dry," as one remarks by my side.

You see them digging potatoes, with cart and barrels,

Vol. XI

in the fields on all hands, before they are fairly ripe, for fear of rot or a fall in the price, and I see the empty barrels coming back from market already.

Polygonum dumetorum, how long?

Aug. 21. P. M. — A-berrying to Conantum.

I notice hardhacks clothing their stems now with their erected leaves, showing the whitish under sides. A pleasing evidence of the advancing season.

How yellow that kind of hedgehog (?) sedge,[1] in the toad pool by Cyrus Hubbard's corner.

I still see the patch of epilobium on Bee Tree Hill as plainly as ever, though only the pink seed-vessels and stems are left.

Aug. 22. P. M. — I have spliced my old sail to a new one, and now go out to try it in a sail to Baker Farm. It is a "square sail," some five feet by six. I like it much. It pulls like an ox, and makes me think there's more wind abroad than there is. The yard goes about with a pleasant force, almost enough, I would fain imagine, to knock me overboard. How sturdily it pulls, shooting us along, catching more wind than I knew to be wandering in this river valley! It suggests a new power in the sail, like a Grecian god. I can even worship it, after a heathen fashion. And then, how it becomes my boat and the river, — a simple homely square sail, all for use not show, so low and broad! *Ajacean.* The boat is like a plow drawn by a winged bull. If I had had this a dozen years ago, my voyages would have been performed more

[1] *Cyperus phymatodes.*

quickly and easily. But then probably I should have lived less in them. I land on a remote shore at an unexpectedly early hour, and have time for a long walk there. Before, my sail was so small that I was wont to raise the mast with the sail on it ready set, but now I have had to rig some tackling with which to haul up the sail.

As for the beauty of the river's brim: now that the mikania begins to prevail the button-bush has done, the pontederia is waning, and the willows are already somewhat crisped and imbrowned (though the last may be none the worse for it); lilies, too, are as good as gone. So perhaps I should say that the brim of the river was in its prime about the 1st of August this year, when the pontederia and button-bush and white lilies were in their glory. The cyperus (*phymatodes*, etc.) now yellows edges of pools and half-bare low grounds.

See one or two blue herons every day now, driving them far up or down the river before me. I see a mass of bur-reed, etc., which the wind and waves are sweeping down-stream. The higher water and wind thus clear the river for us.

At Baker Farm a large bird rose up near us, which at first I took for a hen-hawk, but it appeared larger. It screamed the same, and finally soared higher and higher till it was almost lost amid the clouds, or could scarcely be distinguished except when it was seen against some white and glowing cumulus. I think it was at least half a mile high, or three quarters, and yet I distinctly heard it scream up there each time it came round, and with my glass saw its head steadily bent toward the ground, looking for its prey. Its head, seen in a proper light, was distinctly whitish, and I suspect it may have been a white-headed eagle. It did not once flap its wings up there, as it circled and sailed, though I watched it for nearly a mile. How fit that these soaring birds should be haughty and fierce, not like doves to our race!

Aug. 23. Cooler than ever. Some must have fires, and I close my window.

P. M. — Britton's camp *via* Hubbard's Close.

The rhexia in the field west of Clintonia Swamp makes a great show now, though a little past prime. I go through the swamp, wading through the luxuriant cinnamon fern, which has complete possession of the swamp floor. Its great fronds, curving this way and that, remind me [of] a tropical vegetation. They are as high as my head and about a foot wide; may stand higher than my head without being stretched out. They grow in tufts of a dozen, so close that their fronds interlace and form one green waving mass. There in the swamp cellar under the maples. A forest of maples rises from a forest of ferns. My clothes are covered with the pale-brown wool which I have rubbed off their stems.[1]

See an abundance of pine-sap on the right of Pine-sap Path. It is almost all erect, some eight to nine inches high, and all effete there. Some stems are reddish. It lifts the leaves with it like the Indian-pipe, but is not so delicate as that. The Indian-pipe is still pushing up.

Everywhere in woods and swamps I am already reminded of the fall. I see the spotted sarsaparilla leaves

[1] *Vide* Sept. 24, 1859.

Vol. XI

the purpose, which he says received much commendation, — all parties thought it a very pretty piece. Think of Emerson shooting a peetweet (with shot) for Agassiz, and cracking an ale-bottle (after emptying it) with his rifle at six rods! They cut several pounds of lead out of the tree. It is just what Mike Saunders, the merchant's clerk, did when he was there.

The writer needs the suggestion and correction that a correspondent or companion is. I sometimes remember something which I have told another as worth telling to myself, *i. e.* writing in my Journal.

Channing, thinking of walks and life in the country, says, "You don't want to discover anything new, but to discover something old," *i. e.* be reminded that such things still are.

Aug. 24. Edward Hoar brings *Cassia Chamæcrista* from Greenport, L. I., which must have been out a good while.

P. M. — Sail to Ball's (?) Hill.

It is a strong but fitful northwest wind, stronger than before. Under my new sail, the boat dashes off like a horse with the bits in his teeth. Coming into the main stream below the island, a sudden flaw strikes me, and in my efforts to keep the channel I run one side under, and so am compelled to beach my boat there and bail it.

They are haying still in the Great Meadows; indeed, not half the grass is cut, I think.

I am flattered because my stub sail frightens a haymakers' horse tied under a maple while his masters are loading. His nostrils dilate; he snorts and tries to break

and brakes, and, in swamps, the withering and blackened skunk-cabbage and hellebore, and, by the river, the already blackening pontederias and pipes. There is no plateau on which Nature rests at midsummer, but she instantly commences the descent to winter.

I see a golden-crowned thrush, but it is silent except a chip; sitting low on a twig near the main stem of a tree, in these deep woods.

High blackberries now in their prime, their great racemes of shining black fruit, mixed with red and green, bent over amid the sweet-fern and sumach on sunny hillsides, or growing more rankly with larger fruit by rich roadsides and in lower ground.

The *chewink* note of a chewink (not common), also a cuckoo's note.

Smooth sumach berries all turned crimson. This fruit is now erect spear-heads, rising from the ample dark-green, unspotted leaves, pointing in various directions. I see dense patches of the pearly everlasting, maintaining their ground in the midst of dense green sweet-fern, a striking contrast of snow-white and green. *Viburnum nudum* berries, apparently but a day or two. *Epilobium angustifolium* is abundantly shedding its downy seed, — wands of white and pink.

Emerson says that he and Agassiz and Company broke some dozens of ale-bottles, one after another, with their bullets, in the Adirondack country, using them for marks! It sounds rather Cockneyish. He says that he shot a peetweet for Agassiz, and this, I think he said, was the first game he ever bagged. He carried a double-barrelled gun, — rifle and shotgun, — which he bought for

loose. He eyes with terror this white wind steed. No wonder he is alarmed at my introducing such a competitor into the river meadows. Yet, large as my sail is, it being low I can scud down for miles through the very meadows in which dozens of haymakers are at work, and they may not detect me.

The zizania is the greater part out of bloom; *i. e.*, the yellowish-anthered (?) stamens are gone; the wind has blown them away. The *Bidens Beckii* has only begun a few days, it being rather high water. No hibiscus yet.

The white maples in a winding row along the river and the meadow's edge are rounded hoary-white masses, as if they showed only the under sides of their leaves. Those which have been changed by water are less bright than a week ago. They now from this point (Abner Buttrick's shore) are a pale lake, mingling very agreeably with the taller hoary-white ones. This little color in the hoary meadow edging is very exhilarating to behold and the most memorable phenomenon of the day. It is as when quarters of peach of this color are boiled with white apple-quarters. Is this anything like *murrey* color? In some other lights it is more red or scarlet.

Climbing the hill at the bend, I find *Gerardia Pedicularia*, apparently several days, or how long?

Looking up and down the river this sunny, breezy afternoon, I distinguish men busily haying in gangs of four or five, revealed by their white shirts, some two miles below, toward Carlisle Bridge, and others still further up the stream. They are up to their shoulders in the grassy sea, almost lost in it. I can just discern a few white specks in the shiny grass, where the most distant are at work. What an adventure, to get the hay from year to year from these miles on miles of river meadow! You see some carrying out the hay on poles, where it is too soft for cattle, and loaded carts are leaving the meadows for distant barns in the various towns that border on them.

I look down a straight reach of water to the hill by Carlisle Bridge, — and this I can do at any season, — the longest reach we have. It is worth the while to come here for this prospect, — to see a part of earth so far away over the water that it appears islanded between two skies. If that place is real, then the places of my imagination are real.

Desmodium Marylandicum apparently in prime along this Ball's (?) Hill low shore, and apparently another kind, *Dillenii* (??) or *rigidum* (??), the same. These and lespedezas now abound in dry places. Carrion-flower fruit is blue; how long? Squirrels have eaten hazelnuts and pitch pine cones for some days.

Now and of late we remember hazel bushes, — we become aware of such a fruit-bearing bush. They have their turn, and every clump and hedge seems composed of them. The burs begin to look red on their edges.

I notice, in the river, opposite the end of the meadow-path, great masses of ranunculus stems, etc., two or three feet through by a rod or more long, which look as if they had been washed or rolled aside by the wind and waves, amid the potamogeton.

I have just read of a woodchuck that came to a boat on Long Island Sound to be taken in!

Pipes (*Equisetum limosum*) are brown and half-with-

ered along the river, where they have been injured by water.

Aug. 25. It has been cool and especially windy from the northwest since the 19th, inclusive, but is stiller now.

The note of a warbling vireo sounds very rare.

P. M. — To Lupine Hill and beyond.

I see a mouse on the dry hillside this side of Clamshell. It is evidently the short-tailed meadow mouse, or *Arvicola hirsuta*. Generally above, it is very dark brown, almost blackish, being browner forward. It is also dark beneath. Tail but little more than one inch long. Its legs must be very short, for I can hardly glimpse them. Its nose is not sharp. It endeavors to escape down the hill to the meadow, and at first glides along in a sort of path (?), methinks. It glides close to the ground under the stubble and tries to conceal itself.

I gather from Nut Meadow Brook, not far below the road, a potamogeton (perhaps *P. Claytoni* (*heterophyllus* of Gray), which Russell said was the one by road at Jenny Dugan's). It is still out. Has handsome broad, grassy immersed leaves and somewhat elliptic floating ones.

I distinguish these plants this afternoon: *Cyperus filiculmis* (*Mariscoides*, or tuberous cyperus of Bigelow) in arid, sandy pastures, with globular green heads and slender, commonly slanting culms, five to twelve inches long. It is perhaps getting stale. The prevalent grass in John Hosmer's meadow I take to be cut-grass? [1] Long since done, and the leaves now commonly purplish, re-

[1] No.

flecting that color in the sun from a distance. The *Paspalum setaceum* (*ciliatifolium*), my saw-grass, which I have seen for some time, commonly cut off by the mowers, apparently in prime or past. *Eragrostis capillaris* [1] (*Poa hirsuta*), hair spear-grass, perhaps not quite so bright as heretofore. Money-Diggers' Hollow has the most of it. Say a week in prime. *Fimbrystilis capillaris* (*Scirpus capillaris*), that little scirpus turning yellowish in sandy soil, as our garden and Lupine Hill sand. Some time in prime. *Cyperus strigosus* under Clamshell Hill, that yellowish fuzzy-headed plant, five to twelve inches high, now apparently in prime. Also in Mrs. Hoar's garden. Also *Cyperus phymatodes*, very much like last, in Mrs. Hoar's garden, which has little tubers at a distance from the base; apparently in prime. *Cyperus dentatus* (?), with flat spikelets, under Solidago rigida Bank, apparently in prime; also [at] Pout's Nest, with round fascicles of leaves amid spikes. *Juncus scirpoides* [2] (?) (*polycephalus*, many-headed of Bigelow), at Alder Ditch and in Great Meadows, etc., perhaps some time. *Andropogon furcatus*, forked beard grass, Solidago rigida Bank, a slender grass three to seven feet high on dry soil, apparently in prime with digitate purple spikes, all over hillside behind Cæsar's. *Setaria glauca*, glaucous panic grass, bottle grass, sometimes called fox-tail, tawny yellow, going to seed, Mrs. Hoar's garden. *Setaria viridis*, green bottle grass, in garden, some going to seed, but later than the last. These two I have called millet grass. *Aristida*

[1] [*Capillaris* is crossed out in pencil and *pectinacea* substituted.]

[2] Is it not *paradoxus*? *Vide* Aug. 30.

dichotoma,[1] poverty grass, slender, curving, purplish, in tufts on sterile soil, looking white fuzzy as it goes to seed; apparently in prime.

Aug. 26. P. M. — To Great Meadows.

The *Solidago arguta* is apparently in its prime. Hips of moss rose not long scarlet. The *Juncus effusus*, a long [time] withered (the upper part). The liatris is about (or nearly) in prime. *Aster lævis*, how long?

Two interesting tall purplish grasses appear to be the prevailing ones now in dry and sterile neglected fields and hillsides, — *Andropogon furcatus*, forked beard grass, and apparently *Andropogon scoparius*,[2] purple wood grass, though the last appears to have three awns like an *Aristida*. The first is a very tall and slender-culmed grass, with four or five purple finger-like spikes, raying upward from the top. It is very abundant on the hillside behind Peter's. The other is also quite slender, two to three or four feet high, growing in tufts and somewhat curving, also commonly purple and with pretty purple stigmas like the last, and it has purple anthers.[3] When out of bloom, its appressed spikes are recurving and have a whitish hairy or fuzzy look.

These are the prevailing conspicuous flowers where I walk this afternoon in dry ground. I have sympathy with them because they are despised by the farmer and

[1] *Andropogon scoparius*, purple wood grass?

[2] Put with this *Andropogon*, i. e. *Sorghum, nutans. Vide* Sept. 6th.

[3] Broom grass, perhaps.

occupy sterile and neglected soil. They also by their rich purple reflections or tinges seem to express the ripeness of the year. It is high-colored like ripe grapes, and expresses a maturity which the spring did not suggest. Only the August sun could have thus burnished these culms and leaves. The farmer has long since done his upland haying, and he will not deign to bring his scythe to where these slender wild grasses have at length flowered thinly. You often see the bare sand between them. I walk encouraged between the tufts of purple wood grass, over the sandy fields by the shrub oaks, glad to recognize these simple contemporaries. These two are almost the first grasses that I have learned to distinguish. I did not know by how many friends I was surrounded. The purple of their culms excites me like that of the pokeweed stems.

Think what refuge there is for me before August is over, from college commencements and society that isolates me! I can skulk amid the tufts of purple wood grass on the borders of the Great Fields! Wherever I walk this afternoon the purple-fingered grass stands like a guide-board and points my thoughts to more poetic paths than they have lately travelled.

A man shall, perchance, rush by and trample down plants as high as his head, and cannot be said to know that they exist, though he may have cut and cured many tons of them for his cattle. Yet, perchance, if he ever favorably attend to them, he may be overcome by their beauty.

Each humblest plant, or weed, as we call it, stands there to express some thought or mood of ours, and yet

how long it stands in vain! I have walked these Great Fields so many Augusts and never yet distinctly recognized these purple companions that I have there. I have brushed against them and trampled them down, forsooth, and now at last they have, as it were, risen up and blessed me. Beauty and true wealth are always thus cheap and despised. Heaven, or paradise, might be defined as the place which men avoid. Who can doubt that these grasses which the farmer says are of no account to him find some compensation in my appreciation of them? I may say that I never saw them before, or can only recall a dim vision of them, and now wherever I go I hardly see anything else. It is the reign and presidency only of the andropogons.[1]

I walk down the Great Meadows on the upland side. They are still mowing, but have not got more than half, and probably will not get nearly all. I see where the tufts of *Arum peltandrum* have been cut off by the mower, and the leaves are all gone, but the still green fruit, which had curved downward close to the ground on every side amid the stubble, was too low for his scythe, and so escaped. Thus this plant is perpetuated in such localities, though it may be cut before the seed is mature.

The wool-grass, black-bracted, of these meadows long since went out of bloom, and is now not merely withered at top but wasted half away, and is quite gray, while that which I examine in another meadow, green-bracted, has but recently ceased to bloom. Looking from this side, the meadow appears to be filled almost exclusively with wool-grass, yet very little has any culm or has blossomed

[1] [*Excursions*, pp. 255-257; Riv. 313-316.]

this year. I notice, however, one tract, in the midst of the rest, an oblong square with perfectly straight sides, reaching from the upland toward the river, where it has quite generally blossomed and the culms still stand as high as my head. This, plainly, is because the land of a particular proprietor has been subjected to a peculiar treatment.

Minott tells me that once, one very dry summer, when but part of these meadows had been cut, Moore and Hosmer got the owners to agree to have them burnt over, in the expectation that it would improve the quality of the grass, and they made quite an affair of it, — had a chowder, cooked by Moore's boys, etc.; but the consequence was that this wool-grass came in next year more than ever.

Some come a good way for their meadow-grass, even from Lincoln. George Baker has some in this meadow and some in the Sudbury meadows. But Minott says they want to get rid of their river meadow now, since they can get more and very much better grass off their redeemed swamps, or meadows of their own making, near home. Hardhack, meadow-sweet, alders, maples, etc., etc., appear to be creeping into the meadow. M. says they used to mow clean up to the ditch by the hard land. He remembers how he used to suffer from the heat, working out in the sun on these broad meadows, and when they took their luncheon, how glad he was to lie along close to the water, on the wet ground under the white maples by the riverside. And then one would swim a horse over at the Holt,[1] go up to Jack Buttrick's

[1] Goodwin puts the "Holt" lower down, where I did.

(now Abner's), where there was a well of cool water, and get one or two great jugs full, with which he recrossed on the horse. He tells of one fellow who trod water across there with a jug in each hand!

He has seen young woodcocks in the nest there, *i. e.* on the ground where he had mowed, the middle of August; and used to see the summer ducks perched on the maples, on some large limb close up to the main stem, since they cannot cling to a small twig.

Aug. 27. P. M. — To Walden.

Dog-day weather again to-day, of which we had had none since the 18th, — *i. e.* clouds without rain. Wild carrot on railroad, apparently in prime. *Hieracium Canadense*, apparently in prime, and perhaps *H. scabrum*. *Lactuca*, apparently much past prime, or nearly done. The *Nabalus albus* has been out some ten days, but *N. Fraseri* at Walden road will not open, apparently, for some days yet.

I see round-leaved cornel fruit on Heywood Peak, now half China-blue and half white, each berry. *Rhus Toxicodendron* there is half of it turned scarlet and yellow, as if we had had a severe drought, when it has been remarkably wet. It seems, then, that in such situations some plants will always assume this prematurely withered autumnal aspect. *Orchis lacera*, probably done some time. Robins fly in flocks.

Apparently *Juncus tenuis*, some time out of bloom, by depot wood-piles, *i. e.* between south wood-shed and good apple tree; some fifteen inches high. More at my boat's shore.

Aug. 28. Soaking rain last night, straight down. When the wind stirs after the rain, leaves that were prematurely ripe or withered begin to strew the ground on the leeward side. Especially the scarlet leaves of the cultivated cherry are seen to have fallen. Their change, then, is not owing to drought, but commonly a portion of them ripens thus early, reminding us of October and November. When, as I go to the post-office this morning, I see these bright leaves strewing the moist ground on one side of the tree and blown several rods from it into a neighboring yard, I am reminded that I have crossed the summit ridge of the year and have begun to descend the other slope. The prospect is now toward winter. These are among the first-fruits of the leafy harvest.

The sharp whistling note of a downy woodpecker, which sounds rare; perhaps not heard since spring.

Aug. 29. I hear this morning one *eat it potter* from a golden robin. They are now rarely seen.

The ghost-horse (*Spectrum*) is seen nowadays, — several of them. All these high colors in the stems and leaves and other portions of plants answer to some maturity in us. I presume if I am the wiser for having lived this season through, such plants will emblazon the truth of my experience over the face of nature, and I shall be aware of a beauty and sweetness there.

Has not the mind, too, its harvest? Do not some scarlet leaves of thought come scatteringly down, though it may be prematurely, some which, perchance, the summer's drought has ripened, and the rain loosened? Are there

no purple reflections from the culms of thought in my mind?

I remember when boiled green corn was sold piping hot on a muster-field in this town, and my father says that he remembers when it used to be carried about the streets of Boston in large baskets on the bare heads of negro women, and gentlemen would stop, buy an ear, and eat it in the street.

Ah! what a voice was that hawk's or eagle's of the 22d! Think of hearing, as you walk the earth, as usual in leaden shoes, a fine, shrill scream from time to time, which you would vainly endeavor to refer to its true source if you had not watched the bird in its upward flight. It comes from yonder black spot on the bosom of a cloud. I should not have suspected that sound to have issued from the bosom of a cloud if I had not seen the bird. What motive can an eagle have for screaming among the clouds, unobserved by terrestrial creatures? We walk invested by sound, — the cricket in the grass and the eagle in the clouds. And so it circled over, and I strained my eyes to follow it, though my ears heard it without effort.

Almost the very sands confess the ripening influence of the August sun, and, methinks, with the slender grasses waving over them, reflect a purple tinge. The empurpled sands. Such is the consequence of all this sunshine absorbed into the pores of plants and of the earth. All sap or blood is wine-colored. The very bare sands, methinks, yield a purple reflection. At last we have not only the purple sea, but the purple land.[1]

[1] [*Excursions*, pp. 257, 258; Riv. 316.]

Vol. XI

P. M. — To J. Farmer's *via* Assabet.

As, standing up in my boat, I am watching some minnows at the Prichard bend steadily stemming the current in the sunny water between the waving potamogeton, right under my face, I see a musquash gliding along above the sand directly beneath them, a perfect denizen of the water as much as they. This rat was a pale brown, as light as pale-brown paper or perfectly withered white oak leaves. Its coat is never of this color out of water, and I suppose it was because it was completely coated with air. This makes it less visible on a sandy bottom.

Is not that *Eleocharis tenuis*, long since out of bloom, growing in the water along the Merrick shore, near the oak; round culms, fifteen inches to two feet high? A spiked rush, without a leaf, and round. I can hardly find a head left on it. Yet Flint says this blooms in August! It grows in dense fields like pipes. Did I find it before this year?

The mikania is apparently in prime or a little past. Perhaps the front-rank polygonum is in prime now, for there is apparently more than before.

I look along Mantatuket Field hedge to see if there are hazelnuts there, but am surprised to find that thereabouts the bushes have been completely stripped by squirrels already and the rich brown burs are strewn on the ground beneath. What a fine brown these dried burs have already acquired, — not chestnut nor hazel! I fear it is already too late for me, though I find some yet quite green in another place. They must have been very busy collecting these nuts and husking them for a

fortnight past, climbing to the extremities of the slender twigs. Who witnesses the gathering of the hazelnuts, the hazel harvest? Yet what a busy and important season to the striped squirrel! Now, if ever, he needs to get up a bee. Every nut that I could find left in that field was a poor one. By more frequented paths the squirrels have not worked yet. Take warning from the squirrel, which is already laying up his winter store.

I see some *Cornus sericea* berries turning. The Assabet helianthus (apparently variety of *decapetalus*), well out some days at least. Are not the petals peculiarly reflexed? Small botrychium in the bobolink meadow, not yet. *Gentiana Andrewsii*, one not quite shedding pollen.

Before bathing at the Pokelogan, I see and hear a school of large suckers, which have come into this narrow bay and are swiftly dashing about and rising to the surface, with a bubbling sound, as if to snatch something from the surface. They agitate the whole bay. They [are] great ruddy-looking fellows, limber with life. How intelligent of all watery knowledge! They seem to measure the length, breadth, and depth of that cove — which perhaps they never entered before — with every wave of their fins. They feel it all at once. With what superfluous vigor they seem to move about restlessly in their element! Lift them but six inches, and they would quirk their tails in vain. They are poor, soft fish, however, large as they are, and taste when cooked at present much like boiled brown paper.

The wild *Monarda fistulosa* is apparently nearly done. *Cicuta maculata*, apparently generally done.

J. Farmer shot a sharp-shinned hawk this morning,

which was endeavoring to catch one of his chickens. I bring it home and find that it measures seventeen inches in length and thirty in alar extent, and the tail extends four inches beyond the closed wings. It has a very large head, and the wing is six and a half inches wide at the secondaries. It is dark-brown above, skirted with ferruginous; scapulars, with white spots; legs, bright-yellow; iris, yellow. Has those peculiar pendulous lobes to the feet, which Farmer thinks are to enable it to hold a small bone of its prey between the nail and the lobe, as it feeds, while perching. The breast and belly feathers are shafted with dark-brown pointed spots. Vent white. There are three obvious slate-colored bars to tail, alternating with the black.[1]

F. says that he has seen the nest of a smaller hawk, the pigeon hawk, heretofore, on an oak (in Owl-Nest Swamp), made of sticks, some fifteen feet from ground. R. Rice says that he has found the nest of the pigeon hawk hereabouts.

We go to see a bittern nest by Spencer Brook. F. says they call the cardinal-flower "slink-weed," and say that the eating it will cause cows to miscarry. He calls the *Viburnum nudum* "withe-wood," and makes a withe by treading on one end and twisting by the other till he cracks it and makes it flexible so that it will bend without breaking. The bittern's nest was close to the edge of the brook, eighteen inches above the water, and was made of the withered sedge that had grown close by (*i. e.* wool-grass, etc.) and what I have called [two] pages back *Eleocharis tenuis*. It was quite a deep nest, like

[1] I have the wing, legs, and tail of this specimen. *Vide* next page.

and as big as a hen's nest, deep in the grass. He or his son saw the young about it a month ago.

He hears — heard a week ago — the sound of a bird flying over, like *cra-a-ack*, *cr-r-r-a-k*, only in the night, and thinks it may be a blue heron.[1]

We saw where many cranberries had been frost-bitten, F. thinks the night of the 23d. They are much injured. *Spiranthes cernua*, how long? Near the bittern-nest, grows what F. calls blue-joint grass; out of bloom.

Returning, rather late afternoon, we saw some forty martins sitting in a row and twittering on the ridge of his *old* house, apparently preparing to migrate. He had never seen it before. Soon they all took to flight and filled the air in the neighborhood.

The sharp-shinned hawk of to-day is much larger than that of July 21st, though the colors, etc., etc., appear to be essentially the same. Yet its leg is not so stout as that which Farrar[2] gave me, but is at least half an inch longer.[3] The toes, especially, are longer and more slender, but I am not sure whether Farrar's hawk has those pendulous lobes, the foot is so dry, nor if it had sharp-edged shin, it being eaten away by worms. The inner vanes of the primaries of Farrar's bird are brighter white with much narrower bars of blackish. The longest primary of Farrar's bird is about ten inches; that of to-day, about eight inches. I find the outside tail-feathers of to-day's bird much harder to pull than the inside ones![4]

[1] *Vide* three pages forward.
[2] *Vide* Oct. 11, 1856.
[3] Which makes me think Farrar's another species. He said it had not a white rump.
[4] *Vide* July 21st. *Vide* May 17, 1860.

Our black willow is of so peculiar and light a green, so ethereal, that, as I look back forty rods at those by the Heron Rock, their outlines are seen with perfect distinctness against the darker green of maples, etc., three or four rods behind them, as if they were a green cloud or smoke blown by. They are seen as distinctly against these other trees as they would be against the sky.

Rice tells me a queer story. Some twenty-five years ago he and his brother William took a journey in their wagon into the northwest part of Maine, carrying their guns and fishing-tackle with them. At Fryeburg they visited the scene of Lovewell's Fight, and, seeing some trout in the stream there, they tried to dig some fishworms for bait, but they could not find any. So they asked a boy where they got fishworms, but he did not know what they meant. "Long, slender worms, angleworms," said they; but he only answered that he had seen worms in their manure-heap (which were grubs). On inquiring further, they found that the inhabitants had never seen nor heard of angleworms, and one old settler, who had come from Massachusetts and had lived there thirty years, declared that there was no such worm in that neighborhood.

Mr. Farmer gave me a turtle-shaped bug found by Melvin on a board by the river, some time ago.

I hear A—— W—— complained of for overworking his cattle and hired men, but there is this to be said in his favor, that he does not spare himself. They say that he made his horse "Tom" draw twenty-nine hundred of hay to Boston the other day, — or night, — but then he

put his shoulder to the wheel at every hill. I hear that since then the horse has died, but W—— is alive and working.

How hard one must work in order to acquire his language, — words by which to express himself! I have known a particular rush, for instance, for at least twenty years, but have ever been prevented from describing some [of] its peculiarities, because I did not know its name nor any one in the neighborhood who could tell me it. With the knowledge of the name comes a distincter recognition and knowledge of the thing. That shore is now more describable, and poetic even. My knowledge was cramped and confined before, and grew rusty because not used, — for it could not be used. My knowledge now becomes communicable and grows by communication. I can now learn what others know about the same thing.

Aug. 30. P. M. — To bayonet rush by river.

Find at Dodd's shore: *Eleocharis obtusa*, some time out of bloom (fresh still at Pratt's Pool); also *Juncus acuminatus* (?), just done (also apparently *later* and yet in bloom at Pout's Nest); also what I called *Juncus scirpoides*, but which appears to be *Juncus paradoxus*, with seeds tailed at both ends, (it is fresher than what I have seen before, and smaller), not done. Some of it with few flowers! A terete leaf rises above the flower. It looks like a small bayonet rush.

The *Juncus militaris* has been long out of bloom. The leaf is three feet long; the whole plant, four or five.

It grows on edge of Grindstone Meadow and above. It would look more like a bayonet if the leaf were shorter than the flowering stem, which last is the bayonet part. This is my rainbow rush.

All over Ammannia Shore and on bare spots in meadows generally, *Fimbristylis autumnalis*, apparently in prime; minute, two to five inches high, with aspect of *F. capillaris*.

As I am now returning over Lily Bay, I hear behind me a singular loud stertorous sound which I thought might have been made by a cow out of order, twice sounded. Looking round, I saw a blue heron flying low, about forty rods distant, and have no doubt the sound was made by him. Probably this is the sound which Farmer hears.[1]

Aug. 31. P. M. — To Flint's Pond.

A hot afternoon. We have had but few warmer. I hear and see but few bobolinks or blackbirds for several days past. The former, at least, must be withdrawing. I have not heard a seringo of late, but I see to-day one golden robin. The birches have lately lost a great many of their lower leaves, which now cover and yellow the ground. Also some chestnut leaves have fallen. Many brakes in the woods are perfectly withered.

At the Pout's Nest, Walden, I find the *Scirpus debilis*, apparently in prime, generally aslant; also the *Cyperus dentatus*, with some spikes changed into leafy tufts; also here less advanced what I have called *Juncus acuminatus*.

[1] *Vide* three pages back.

Ludwigia alternifolia still. Sericocarpus about done.

High blackberries are abundant in Britton's field. At a little distance you would not suspect that there were any, — even vines, — for the racemes are bent down out of sight, amid the dense sweet-ferns and sumachs, etc. The berries still not more than half black or ripe, keeping fresh in the shade. Those in the sun are a little wilted and insipid.

The smooth sumach's lower leaves are bright-scarlet on dry hills. *Lobelia Dortmanna* is not quite done. Some ground-nuts are washed out.

The Flint's Pond rush appears to be *Cladium mariscoides*, twig rush, or, in Bigelow, water bog rush, a good while out of bloom; style three-cleft. It is about three feet high. This, with *Eleocharis palustris*, which is nearest the shore, forms the dense rushy border of the pond. It extends along the whole of this end, at least about four rods wide, and almost every one of the now dry and brown flower-heads has a cobweb on it. I perceive that the slender semicircular branchlets so fit to the grooved or flattened culm as still, when pressed against it, to make it cylindrical! — very neatly.

The monotropa is still pushing up. Red choke-berry, apparently not long.

At Goose Pond I scare up a small green bittern. It plods along low, a few feet over the surface, with limping flight, and alights on a slender water-killed stump, and voids its excrement just as it starts again, as if to lighten itself.

Edward Bartlett brings me a nest found three feet from the ground in an arbor-vitæ, in the New Burying-

Vol. XI

Ground,[1] with one long-since addled egg in it. It is a very thick, substantial nest, five or six inches in diameter and rather deep; outwardly of much coarse stubble with its fine root-fibres attached, loose and dropping off, around a thin casing of withered leaves; then finer stubble within, and a lining of fine grass stems and horsehair. The nest is most like that found on Cardinal Shore with an addled pale-bluish egg, which I thought a wood thrush's at first, except that that has no casing of leaves. It is somewhat like a very large purple finch's nest, or perchance some red-wing's with *a hair lining*. The egg is three quarters of an inch long, rather broad at one end (or for length), greenish-white with brown dashes or spots, becoming a large conspicuous purple-brown blotch at the large end; almost exactly like — but a little greener (or bluer) and a little smaller — the egg found on the ground in R. W. E.'s garden. Do the nest and egg belong together?. Was not the egg dropped by a bird of passage in another's nest? Can it be an indigo-bird's nest? I take it to be too large.

[1] *Vide* the nest.

III

SEPTEMBER, 1858

(ÆT. 41)

Sept. 1. P. M. — To Botrychium Swamp.

Aster miser not long, but the leaves turned red. At the pool by the oaks behind Pratt's, I see the *Myriophyllum ambiguum* still, and going to seed, greening the surface of the water. The *Leersia oryzoides*, false rice, or rice cut-grass, is abundant and in prime on the shore there. Also find it on the shore of Merrick's pasture. It has very rough sheaths. Am surprised to see frog(?)-spawn *just laid*, neither in spherical masses nor in a string, but flatted out thin *on the surface*, some eight or nine inches wide, — a small black spawn, white one side, as usual. I saw one or two *F.* [*sic*] *fontinalis* on the shore. Was it toad-spawn?

Ranunculus repens in bloom — as if begun again? — at the violet wood-sorrel spring. *Chelone glabra* well out, how long? In the same meadow, *Aster longifolius* well out, not long. That meadow is white with the *Eriophorum polystachyon*, apparently var. *angustifolium* (?). *Vide* it pressed. On dry land, common, but apparently getting stale, *Panicum clandestinum*. Dangle-berries now ready for picking. At Botrychium Swamp, *Nabalus altissimus*. Of twenty plants (all in shade) only one out, apparently two or three days. Elsewhere, in open land, *N. Fraseri*, apparently several days, say five; but not a very rough one. *Ledum Telephium*, how long? In the evening, by the roadside, near R. W. E.'s gate, find a glow-worm of the common kind. Of two men, Dr. Bartlett and Charles Bowen, neither had ever seen it!

Sept. 2. Up Assabet.

The common light-sheathed *Scirpus Eriophorum* still. At the Pokelogan, apparently *Cinna arundinacea* (?) in prime (one stamen); also *Elymus Virginicus* (?). Lyme grass or wild rye, apparently lately done. That rich, close, erect-panicled grass of the meadows, apparently for a month in bloom, seems to be *Glyceria obtusa*. Very common in the meadow west of Brooks Clark's.

Sept. 3. P. M. — Up Assabet a-hazelnutting.

I see a small striped snake, some fifteen or eighteen inches long, swallowing a toad, all but the head and one fore leg taken in. It is a singular sight, that of the little head of the snake directly above the great, solemn, granitic head of the toad, whose eyes are open, though I have reason to think that he is not alive, for when I return some hours after I find that the snake has disgorged the toad and departed. The toad had been swallowed with the hind legs stretched out and close together, and its body is compressed and elongated to twice its length, while the head, which had not been taken in, is of the original size and full of blood. The toad is quite dead, apparently killed by being so far crushed; and its eyes are still open. The body of the snake was enlarged regularly from near the middle to its jaws. It appeared to have given up this attempt at the

eleventh hour. Probably the toad is very much more elongated when perfectly swallowed by a small snake. It would seem, then, that snakes undertake to swallow toads which are too big for them.

I see where the bank by the Pokelogan is whitewashed, *i. e.* the grass, for a yard or two square, by the thin droppings of some bird which has roosted on a dead limb above. It was probably a blue heron, for I find some slate-blue feathers dropped, apparently curving breast-feathers, broadly shafted with white.

I hear a faint warble from time to time from some young or old birds, from my window these days. Is it the purple finch again, — young birds practicing?[1]

Zizania still.

The hazelnut bushes up this way are chiefly confined to the drier river-bank. At least they do not extend into the lower, somewhat meadowy land further inland. They appear to be mostly stripped. The most I get are left hanging over the water at the swimming-ford.

How important the hazelnut to the ground squirrel! They grow along the walls where the squirrels have their homes. They are the oaks that grow before their doors. They have not far to go to their harvesting. These bushes are generally stripped, but isolated ones in the middle of fields, away from the squirrel-walks, are still full of burs. The wall is highway and rampart to these little beasts. They are almost inaccessible in their holes beneath it, and on either side of it spring up, also defended by the wall, the hazel bushes on whose fruit the squirrels in a great measure depend. Notwithstanding

[1] *Vide* Sept. 6th.

the abundance of hazelnuts here, very little account is made of them, and I think it is because pains is not taken to collect them before the squirrels have done so. Many of the burs are perfectly green yet, though others are brightly red-edged. The squirrel lives in a hazel grove. There is not a hazel bush but some squirrel has his eye on its fruit, and he will be pretty sure to anticipate you. As we say, "The tools to those who can use them," so we may say, "The nuts to those who can get them."

That floating grass by the riverside whose lower leaves, so flat and linear, float on the surface of the water, though they are not now, at least, lake-colored, is apparently the *Glyceria fluitans*, floating fescue grass, still blooming and for a good while. I got it yesterday at Merrick's shore.

At the sand-bar by the swimming-ford, I collect two small juncuses, not knowing but I have pressed them before. One appears to be *Juncus scirpoides* (?), small as it is; the other, *Juncus articulatus* (??).

At Prichard's shore I see where they have plowed up and cast into the river a pile of elm roots, which interfered with their laying down the adjacent field. One which I picked up I at first thought was a small lead pipe, partly coiled up and muddy in the water, it being apparently of uniform size. It was just nineteen feet and eight inches long; the biggest end was twenty-one fortieths of an inch in diameter, and the smallest nineteen fortieths. This difference was scarcely obvious to the eye. No doubt it might have been taken up very much longer. It looked as if, when green and flexible, it might answer

the purpose of a rope, — of a cable, for instance, when you wish to anchor in deep water. The wood is very porous.

The narrow brown sheaths from the base of white pine leaves now strew the ground and are washed up on the edge of puddles after the rain.

Sept. 4. Much rain, with thunder and lightning.

Our large-fruited sparganium is evidently *S. ramosum*, still a little, at least, in flower.

My large grass of the riverside with a narrow or spike-like appressed panicle, long since out, at the end of a long bare culm, leafy below, is apparently *Phalaris arundinacea*.

Piper grass is apparently *Triticum repens;* now done.

What I called *Panicum capillare* (after Hoar, without examining) is *P. sanguinale*, crab grass, finger grass, or purple panic grass. *Panicum capillare* (very different and like *Eragrostis capillaris*, the fine purple grass) is now in prime in garden.

Sept. 5. P. M. — To Walden.

Prinos verticillatus berries reddening.

I hear two or more wood pewees this afternoon, but had not before for a fortnight or more. The *pewee days* are over for some time.

Went down to the pond-hole behind where I used to live. It is quite full of water. The middle or greater part is densely covered with target leaves, crowding one another and curling up on their edges. Then there is a space or canal of clear water, five to twenty feet wide, quite around them, and the shore is thickly covered with rattlesnake grass, now ripe.

I find many high blueberries, quite fresh, overhanging the south shore of Walden.

I find, all about Walden, close to the edge on the steep bank, and at Brister's Spring, a fine grass now generally past prime, *Agrostis perennans*,[1] thin grass, or hair grass, on moist ground or near water. The branches of the panicle are but slightly purplish.

Sept. 6. 6 A. M. — To Merrick's shore.

Hear a warbling vireo, sounding very rare and rather imperfect. I think this is what I have mistaken for the young purple finch note.

Also hear apparently a yellow-throated vireo.

That fine spreading-panicled dark-purple grass, now rising all along the river near the waterside, is *Panicum agrostoides;* in prime. That finer and narrower-panicled, now out of bloom, is red-top, or else white bent; with the former.

River risen still higher, and weeds covered.

P. M. — To Ledum Swamp.

Going over Clamshell Plain, I see a very large flock of a hundred or more cowbirds about some cows. They whirl away on some alarm and alight on a neighboring rail fence, close together on the rails, one above another. Then away they whirl and settle on a white oak top near me. Half of them are evidently quite young birds, hav-

[1] *Vide* Sept. 7.

ing glossy black breasts with a drab line down middle. The heads of all are light-colored, perhaps a slaty drab, and some apparently wholly of this color.

On the hillside above Clamshell Ditch, grows that handsome grass of Sept. 1st (*vide* September 4th), evidently *Sorghum nutans* (*Andropogon* of Bigelow), chestnut beard grass, Indian grass, wood grass. It is much larger than what I saw before; is still abundantly in flower; four and a half feet high; leaves, perhaps arundinaceous, eighteen inches long; panicle, nine inches long. It is a very handsome, wild-looking grass, well enough called Indian grass, and I should have named it with the other andropogons, August 26th. With its narrow one-sided panicle of bright purple and yellow (I include the yellow anthers) often waving [?], raised high above the leaves, it looks like a narrow banner. It is of more vivid colors than its congeners, and might well have caught an Indian's eye. These bright banners are now advanced on the distant hillsides, not in large armies, but scattered troops or single file, like the red men themselves. They stand thus fair and bright in our midst, as it were representative of the race which they are named after, but for the most part unobserved. It stands like an Indian chief taking a last look at his beloved hunting-grounds. The expression of this grass haunted me for a week after I first passed and noticed it, like the glance of an eye.[1]

Aster patens past prime at Money-Diggers' Hill. *Polygonum tenue*, how long? *Solidago nemoralis* is apparently in prime on Lupine Hill; some of it past. It

[1] [*Excursions*, p. 258; Riv. 316.]

is swarming with butterflies, — yellow, small red, and large, — fluttering over it. At Ledum Pool edge, I find the *Woodwardia Virginica* fern, its fruit mostly turned deep reddish-brown. It appears to grow only close to the pool, part of the fruit forming two lines parallel with the midrib. A third part of the nesæa there is turned scarlet. *Kalmia glauca* is again in bloom. The hairy huckleberries are rather scarce and soft. They are insipid and leave a hairy skin in the mouth.

That swamp is a singularly wild place, without any natural outlet. I hear of a marsh hawk's nest there this summer. I see great spiders there of an uncommon kind, whose webs — the main supporting line — stretch six feet in the clear from spruce to spruce, as high as my head, with a dense web of the usual form some fifteen inches in diameter beneath.

Stopped and talked with W—— W—— and ate a watermelon with him on the grass. Once his senseless democracy appeared. He spoke with an ignorant pride of Buchanan's telegraphic message, of which most of us were ashamed; said he supposed he had more learning than Victoria! But the less said about them the better. Seeing a stake-driver flying up the river, he observed that when you saw that bird flying about it was a never-failing sign of a storm approaching. How many of these sayings like this arise not from a close and frequent observation of the phenomena of nature, but from a distant and casual one!

I find very common in prime by roadsides, in dry ground, etc., *Vilfa vaginæflora*, rush grass, hidden-flowered vilfa; also by Corner roadside, beyond brooks,

Panicum filiforme with and like *P. sanguinale*, apparently in prime, and with last fills the old mullein-field in front of Bear Garden Hill.

Is that narrowly-linear-leaved potamogeton, all immersed and now forming dense beds in the Assabet, a distinct species, or only the immersed leaves of one? *Vide* pressed.

A year ago last spring I gave to Edith Emerson and to Sophia some clasping hound's-tongue seeds, it being very rare hereabouts, wishing to spread it. Now and for a long time it has been a pest in the garden (it does not bloom till the second year), by its seeds clinging to our clothes. Mrs. E. has carried it to Boston thus, and I have spent twenty minutes at once in clearing myself of it. So it is in a fair way to be dispersed.

Sept. 7. P. M. — To Assabet Bath.

I turn Anthony's corner. It is an early September afternoon, melting warm and sunny; the thousands of grasshoppers leaping before you reflect gleams of light; a little distance off the field is yellowed with a Xerxean army of *Solidago nemoralis* between me and the sun; the earth-song of the cricket comes up through all; and ever and anon the hot z-ing of the locust is heard. (Poultry is now fattening on grasshoppers.) The dry deserted fields are one mass of yellow, like a color shoved to one side on Nature's palette. You literally wade in yellow flowers knee-deep, and now the moist banks and low hollows are beginning to be abundantly sugared with *Aster Tradescanti*.[1]

[1] [Channing, pp. 104, 105.]

J. Farmer calls those *Rubus sempervirens* berries, now abundant, "snake blackberries."

Looking for my Maryland yellow-throat's nest, I find that apparently a snake has made it the portico to his dwelling, there being a hole descending into the earth through it!

In Shad-bush Meadow the prevailing grasses (not sedges) now are the slender *Panicum clandestinum*, whose seeds are generally dropped now, *Panicum virgatum*, in large tufts, and blue-joint, the last, of course, long since done. These are all the grasses that I notice there.

What a contrast to sink your head so as to cover your ears with water, and hear only the confused noise of the rushing river, and then to raise your ears above water and hear the steady creaking of crickets in the aerial universe!

While dressing, I see two small hawks, probably partridge hawks, soaring and circling about one hundred feet above the river. Suddenly one drops down from that height almost perfectly perpendicularly after some prey, till it is lost behind the bushes.

Near the little bridge at the foot of Turtle Bank, *Eragrostis capillaris* in small but dense patches, apparently in prime (the *Poa capillaris* of Bigelow). What I have thus called in press is *E. pectinacea* (*P. hirsuta* of Bigelow). On the flat hill south of Abel Hosmer, *Agrostis scabra*, hair grass, flyaway grass, tickle grass, out of bloom; branches purplish. That of September 5th was the *A. perennans*, in lower ground.

On the railroad between tracks above Red House,

Aristida dichotoma, half a dozen inches high, hardly yet out; forked aristida, or poverty grass.

Storrow Higginson brings from Deerfield this evening some eggs to show me, — among others apparently that of the Virginian rail. It agrees in color, size, etc., according to Wilson, and is like (except, *perhaps*, in form) to one which E. Bartlett brought me a week or ten days ago, which dropped from a load of hay carried to Stow's barn! So perhaps it breeds here.[1] Also a smaller egg of same form, but dull white with very pale dusky spots, which may be that of the Carolina rail. He had also what I think the egg of the *Falco fuscatus*, it agreeing with MacGillivray's sparrow hawk's egg.

Sept. 8. 6 A. M. — On river.

It flows with a full tide. When it is thus deep its current is swift, and then its surface (commonly smooth and dark) is freckled with ripples, or rather I should say that swifter currents are here and there bursting up from below and spreading out on every side, as if the river were breaking over a thousand concealed rocks. The surface is broken and dimpled with upswelling currents.

Red oak acorns, yet green, are abundantly cut off by the squirrels.

The yellow-legs is nodding its head along the edge of the meadow. I hear also its creaking *te te te*.[2]

[1] Yes. *Vide* Sept. 9th. *Vide* Sept. 21st and Dec. 7th, and June 1st, 1859.

[2] *Vide* 18th.

Gather half my grapes, which for some time have perfumed the house.

P. M. — To Owl Swamp.

I perceive the dark-crimson leaves, quite crisp, of the white maple on the meadows, recently fallen. This is their first fall, *i. e.* of those leaves which changed long ago. They fall, then, with birches and chestnuts, etc. (lower leaves), before red maples generally begin to turn.

It is good policy to be stirring about your affairs, for the reward of activity and energy is that if you do not accomplish the object you had professed to yourself, you do accomplish something else. So, in my botanizing or natural history walks, it commonly turns out that, going for one thing, I get another thing. "Though man proposeth, God disposeth all."

Sept. 9. P. M. — To Waban Cliff.

A very hot day, — 90°, as I hear. Yesterday was hot, too. Now it is about time to gather elder-berries. Many *Viola cucullata* have opened again.

What is that short squeaking note heard from time to time from amid the weeds on the west side the river at Hubbard's Bath? There are broad patches, sometimes of several acres, on the edge of the meadow, where it is wettest and weediest, which the farmers do not mow. There especially stands the brown-headed wool-grass. There are small tracts still, as it were, in their primitive condition, — wild tracts where the bittern rises and where, no doubt, the meadow-hen lurks. (Was it the note of the last I heard?)

Heard a short plover-like note from a bird flying high across the river.

Watched a little dipper[1] some ten rods off with my glass, but I could see no white on the breast. It was all black and brownish, and head not enlarged. Who knows how many little dippers are sailing and sedulously diving now along the edge of the pickerel-weed and the button-bushes on our river, unsuspected by most? This hot September afternoon all may be quiet amid the weeds, but the dipper, and the bittern, and the yellow-legs, and the blue heron, and the rail are silently feeding there. At length the walker who sits meditating on a distant bank sees the little dipper sail out from amid the weeds and busily dive for its food along their edge. Yet ordinary eyes might range up and down the river all day and never detect its small black head above the water.

It requires a different intention of the eye in the same locality to see different plants, as, for example, *Juncaceæ* and *Gramineæ* even; *i. e.*, I find that when I am looking for the former, I do not see the latter in their midst. How much more, then, it requires different intentions of the eye and of the mind to attend to different departments of knowledge! How differently the poet and the naturalist look at objects! A man sees only what concerns him. A botanist absorbed in the pursuit of grasses does not distinguish the grandest pasture oaks. He as it were tramples down oaks unwittingly in his walk.

Bidens cernua, how long?

[1] ?? *Vide* 30th.

The river is about at its height to-day or yesterday. Much bur-reed and heart-leaf is floating and washed up, apparently the first important contribution to the river wrack.

The sportsman will paddle a boat now five or six miles, and wade in water up to his knees, being out all day without his dinner, and think himself amply compensated if he bags two or three yellow-legs. The most persistent and sacrificing endeavors are necessary to success in any direction.

Woodbine scarlet, like a brilliant scarf on high, wrapped around the stem of a green tree. By a blush betrays where it hangs upon an elm.

I find an abundance of beaked hazelnuts at Blackberry Steep, one to three burs together, but, gathering them, I get my fingers full of fine shining bristles, while the common hazel burs are either smooth or covered with a softer glandular down; i. e., its horns are *brazen-tipped*.

Under the rocks near the slippery elm, the *Gymnostichum Hystrix*, bottle-brush grass, hedgehog grass, long done.

Rice says he saw two meadow-hens when getting his hay in Sudbury some two months ago, and that they breed there. They kept up a peculiar note. My egg (named Sept. 7th) was undoubtedly a meadow-hen's *Rallus Virginiana*. R. says that he has caught pigeons which had ripe grapes in their crops long before any were ripe here, and that they came from the southwest.

We live in the same world with the Orientals, far off

as they may seem. Nature is the same here to a chemist's tests. The weeping willow (*Salix Babylonica*) will grow here. The peach, too, has been transplanted, and is agreeable to our palates. So are their poetry and philosophy near and agreeable to us.

Sept. 10. Tower-mustard in bloom again. A musquash-house begun.

Sept. 12. *Sunday.* P. M. — To Cliffs.
The handsome crimson-tipped hazelnut burs now and for some time have reminded us that it was time to gather these nuts. They are worth gathering, if only to see the rich color of the fruit brought together in a quantity.

Lycopodium complanatum, how long? Have seen the pigeon's-egg fungus in pastures some time. Yew berries still hold on. The cinnamon fern has begun to yellow and wither. How rich in its decay! *Sic transit gloria mundi!* Die like the leaves, which are most beautiful in their decay. Thus gradually and successively each plant lends its richest color to the general effect, and in the fittest place, and passes away. Amid the October woods we hear no funereal bell, but the scream of the jay. Coming to some shady meadow's edge, you find that the cinnamon fern has suddenly turned this rich yellow. Thus each plant surely acts its part, and lends its effect to the general impression. See petty morel berries ripe.

Woodsia Ilvensis under the cave at Cliffs in fruit.
Very heavy rain all yesterday afternoon, and to-day it is somewhat cooler and clearer and the wind more

northwesterly, and I see the unusual sight of ripples or waves curving up-stream off Cardinal Shore, so that the river might seem to be flowing that way. The mountains are of a darker blue.

The spring on the west side of Fair Haven Hill is nearly dry; there is no stream flowing from it. What a disappointment to a herd of cows to find their accustomed spring dry! Even in that little hollow on the hillside, commonly moistened by the spring, grow the soft rush, rhyncospora, etc. What an effect a little moisture on a hillside produces, though only a rod square! The *Juncaceæ* and *Cyperaceæ* soon find it out and establish themselves there.

The *Panicum filiforme* is very abundant in that old mullein-field of Potter's, by the Corner road. Its slender culms are purple, and, seen in the right light, where they stand thick, they give a purple gleam to the field. More purple far than the *P. sanguinale*. Some small red maples by water begun to redden.

In Hubbard's ditched meadow, this side his grove, I see a great many large spider's webs stretched across the ditches, about two feet from bank to bank, though the thick woven part is ten or twelve inches. They are parallel, a few inches or a foot or more apart, and more or less vertical, and attached to a main cable stretched from bank to bank. They are the yellow-backed spider, commonly large and stout but of various sizes. I count sixty-four such webs there, and in each case the spider occupies the centre, head downward. This is enough,

methinks, to establish the rule. They are not afraid of turning their brains then. Many insects must be winging their way over this small river. It reminds me of the Indians catching ducks at Green Bay with nets in old times.

Sept. 13. P. M. — To Annursnack.
Solidago puberula, apparently in prime and handsome, roadside, Colburn's Hill.
I noticed the black willows quite imbrowned on the 10th, and the button-bushes beginning to look yellowish.

A. Hosmer is pleased because from the cupola of his new barn he can see a new round-topped mountain in the northwest. Is curious to know what one it is. Says that if he lived as near Annursnack as Heywood does, he should go up it once a week, but he supposes that Heywood does not go up it more than once a year. What is that grass still in bloom a foot or more in height in Heywood's potato-field, some fifty rods west of house-leek? It is somewhat like what I have wrongly called *Danthonia spicata*, but with a longer and a round spike, etc., etc. *Vide* press. There is a man there mowing the *Panicum Crus-galli*, which is exceedingly rank and dense, completely concealing the potatoes, which have never been hoed, it was so wet. He saves this grass and says the cattle like it well.

I notice that the large ant-hills, though they prevent bushes and ferns from growing where they are built, keeping open a space four to seven feet wide in their midst, do not keep out grass, but they are commonly little grassy mounds with bare tops.

Looking from the top of Annursnack, the aspect of the earth generally is still a fresh green, especially the woods, but many dry fields, where apparently the June-grass has withered uncut, are a very pale tawny or lighter still. It is fit that some animals should be nearly of this color. The cougar would hardly be observed stealing across these plains. In one place I still detect the ruddiness of sorrel.

Euphorbia hypericifolia still, and gone to seed, on the top of Annursnack.

From many a barn these days I hear the sound of the flail. For how many generations this sound will continue to be heard here! At least until they discover a new way of separating the chaff from the wheat.

Saw *one* raking cranberries on the 10th; rather early.

A small dense flock of wild pigeons dashes by over the side of the hill, from west to east, — perhaps from Wetherbee's to Brooks's, for I see the latter's pigeon-place. They make a dark slate-gray impression.

Fringed gentian out well, on easternmost edge of the Painted-Cup Meadows, by wall.[1]

Saw a striped snake run into the wall, and just before it disappeared heard a loud sound like a hiss! I think it could hardly have been made by its tail among leaves.

The squirrels know better than to open unsound hazelnuts. At most they only peep into them. I see some on the walls with a little hole gnawed in them, enough to show that they are empty.

Muskmelons and squashes are turning yellow in the

[1] Caroline Pratt tells me the 20th that her father found it out full a fortnight before that date!

gardens, and ferns in the swamps. Hear many warbling vireos these mornings. Many yellow butterflies in road and fields all the country over.

Sept. 14. Half a dozen *Bidens chrysanthemoides* in river, not long. Picked eleven of those great potato-worms, caterpillars of the sphinx moth, off our privet. The *Glyceria obtusa*, about eighteen inches high, quite common, in the meadow west of Brooks Clark's, has turned a dull purple, probably on account of frosts.

Sept. 15. I have not seen nor heard a bobolink for some days at least, numerous as they were three weeks ago, and even fifteen days. They depart early. I hear a nuthatch occasionally, but it reminds me of winter.

P. M. — To Walden.

I paddle about the pond, for a rarity. The eriocaulon, still in bloom there, standing thinly about the edge, where it is stillest and shallowest, in the color of its stem and radical leaves is quite in harmony with the glaucous water. Its radical leaves and fine root-fibres form a peculiar loose but thick and continuous carpet or rug on the sandy bottom, which you can lift up in great flakes, exposing the fine white beaded root-fibres. This evidently affords retreats for the fishes, musquash, etc., etc., and you can see where it has been lifted up into galleries by them. I see one or two pickerel poised over it. They, too, are singularly greenish and transparent, so as not to be easily detected, only a little more yellowish than the water and the eriocaulon; ethereal fishes, not far from

the general color of heart-leaf and target-weed, unlike the same fish out of water.

I notice, as I push round the pond close to the shore, with a stick, that the weeds are eriocaulon, two or three kinds of potamogeton, — one with a leaf an inch or two long, one with a very small, floating leaf, a third all immersed, four or five inches high and yellowish-green (this (*vide* press) is apparently an immersed form of *P. hybridus*), — target-weed, heart-leaf, and a little callitriche. There is but little of any of them, however, in the pond itself. It is truly an ascetic pond, and lives very sparingly on vegetables at any rate.

I gather quite a lot of perfectly fresh high blueberries overhanging the south side, and there are many green ones among them still. They are all shrivelled now in swamps commonly.

The target-weed still blooms a little in the Pout's Nest, though half the leaves have turned a reddish orange, are sadly eaten, and have lost nearly all their gelatinous coating. But perfect fresh green leaves have expanded and are still expanding in their midst. The whole pool is covered, as it were, with one vast shield of reddish and green scales. As these leaves change and decay, the firmer parts along the veins retain their life and color longest, as with the heart-leaf. The leaves are eaten in winding lines about a tenth of an inch wide, scoring them all over in a curious manner, and also in spots. These look dark or black because they rest on the dark water.

Looking closely, I am surprised to find how many frogs, mostly small, are resting amid these target leaves,

with their green noses out. Their backs and noses are exactly the color of this weed. They retreat, when disturbed, under this close shield. It is a frog's paradise.

I see, in the paths, pitch pine twigs gnawed off, where no cones are left on the ground. Are they gnawed off in order to come at the cones better?

I find, just rising above the target-weed at Pout's Nest, *Scirpus subterminalis*, apparently recently out of bloom. The culms two to three feet along, *appearing* to rise half an inch above the spikes. The long, linear immersed leaves coming off and left below.

At entrance of the path (on Brister's Path) near Staples and Jarvis bound, apparently the true *Danthonia spicata*, still green. It is generally long out of bloom and turned straw-color. I will call the other (which I had so named), of Hosmer's meadow, *for the present*, meadow oat grass, as, indeed, I did at first.

A hummingbird in the garden.

There is a southeast wind, with clouds, and I suspect a storm brewing. It is very rare that the wind blows from this quarter.

Sept. 16. When I awake I hear the sound of steady heavy rain. A southeast storm. Our peach tree limbs are broken off by it. It lasts all day, rains a great deal, and scatters many elm boughs and leaves over the street. This wind does damage out of proportion to its strength. The fact is, the trees are unprepared to resist a wind from this quarter and, being loaded with foliage and fruit, suffer so much the more. There will be many windfalls, and fruit [will] be cheap for awhile.

It rained as hard as I remember to have seen it for about five minutes at six o'clock P. M., when I was out, and then suddenly, as it were in an instant, the wind whirled round to the westward, and clear sky appeared there and the storm ended, — which had lasted all day and part of the previous night. All this occurred while I was coming from the post-office. The street is strewn with a great many perfectly green leaves, especially of elms, and branches, large and small, also for the most part quite sound. It is remarkable that these tough and slender limbs can be thus twisted off.

Sept. 17. P. M. — Ride to Beaver Pond and beyond.

I see several apple trees that were blown down yesterday and some pretty large elm limbs. The orchards are strewn with windfalls, mostly quite green.

Paddle round Beaver Pond in a boat, which I calked with newspaper. It has a very boggy and generally inaccessible shore, now more inaccessible than usual on account of the rain and high water. A singularly muddy hole.

See elecampane, quite out of bloom. Also the *Solidago odora*, which I see has just done.

River rising fast, from yesterday's rain. Cooler weather now for two or three days, so that I am glad to sit in the sun on the east side of the house mornings. Methinks, too, that there are more sparrows in flocks now about in garden, etc.

Sept. 18. P. M. — Sail to Fair Haven Pond.

It is a fine September day. The river is still rising on

account of the rain of the 16th and is getting pretty well over the meadows. As we paddle westward, toward College Meadow, I perceive that a new season has come. The air is incredibly clear. The surface of both land and water is bright, as if washed by the recent rain and then seen through a much finer, clearer, and cooler air. The surface of the river sparkles. I am struck by the soft yellow-brown or brown-yellow of the black willows, stretching in cloud-shaped wreaths far away along the edges of the stream, of a so much mellower and maturer tint than the elms and oaks and most other trees seen above and beyond them. It is remarkable that the button-bushes beneath and mingling with them are of exactly the same tint and in perfect harmony with them. They are like two interrupted long brown-yellow masses of verdure resting on the water, a peculiarly soft and warm yellow. This is, perhaps, the most interesting autumnal tint as yet.

Above the railroad bridge, with our sail set, wind north-northwest, we see two small ducks, dusky, — perhaps dippers,[1] or summer ducks, — and sail within four rods before they fly. They are so tame that for a while we take them for tame ducks.

The pads are drowned by the flood, but I see one pontederia spike rising blue above the surface. Elsewhere the dark withered pontederia leaves show themselves, and at a distance look like ducks, and so help conceal them. For the ducks are now back again in numbers, since the storm and freshet.

We can just go over the ammannia meadow.

[1] Too large. *Vide* 30th.

It is a wonderful day. As I look westward, this fine air — "gassy," C. calls it — brings out the grain of the hills. I look into the distant sod. This air and sun, too, bring out all the yellow that is in the herbage. The very grass or sedge of the meadow is the same soft yellow with the willows, and the button-bush harmonizes with them. It is as if the earth were one ripe fruit, like a muskmelon yellowed in the September sun; *i. e.*, the sedges, being brought between me and the sun, are seen to be ripe like the cucumbers and muskmelons in the garden. The earth is yellowing in the September sun. It occurs to me to put my knee on it, press it gently, and hear if it does not crack within as if ripe. Has it not, too, a musty fragrance, as a melon?

At Clamshell we take the wind again, and away we glide. I notice, along the edge of the eastern meadow wood, some very light-colored and crisped-looking leaves, apparently on small maples, or else swamp white oaks, as if some vine ran over the trees, for the leaves are of a different color from the rest. This must be the effect of frost, I think.

The sedge and wool-grass all slant strongly southward or up the stream now, which makes a strange impression on the sailor, but of late the wind has been north and stronger than the sluggish current of the river.

The small white pines on the side of Fair Haven Hill now look remarkably green, by contrast with the surrounding shrubbery, which is recently imbrowned. You are struck by their distinct liquid green, as if they had but just sprung up there. All bright colors seem brighter now for the same reason, *i. e.* from contrast with the

duller browns and russets. The very cows on the hillside are a brighter red amid the pines and the brown hazels. The perfectly fresh spike of the *Polygonum amphibium* attracts every eye now. It is not past its prime. C. thinks it is exactly the color of some candy. Also the *Polygala sanguinea* on the bank looks redder than usual.

Many red maples are now partly turned dark crimson along the meadow-edge.

Near the pond we scare up twenty or thirty ducks, and at the pond three blue herons. They are of a hoary blue. One flies afar and alights on a limb of a large white pine near Well Meadow Head, bending it down. I see him standing there with outstretched neck.

Finding grapes, we proceeded to pluck them, tempted more by their fragrance and color than their flavor, though some were very palatable. We gathered many without getting out of the boat, as we paddled back, and more on shore close to the water's edge, piling them up in the prow of the boat till they reached to the top of the boat, — a long sloping heap of them and very handsome to behold, being of various colors and sizes, for we even added green ones for variety. Some, however, were mainly green when ripe. You cannot touch some vines without bringing down more single grapes in a shower around you than you pluck in bunches, and such as strike the water are lost, for they do not float. But it is a pity to break the handsome clusters.

Thus laden, the evening air wafting the fragrance of the cargo back to us, we paddled homeward. The cooler air is so clear that we see Venus plainly some time before sundown. The wind had all gone down, and the water was perfectly smooth. The sunset was uncommonly fair. Some long amber clouds in the horizon, all on fire with gold, were more glittering than any jewelry. An Orient city to adorn the plates of an annual could not be contrived or imagined more gorgeous. And when you looked with head inverted the effect was increased tenfold, till it seemed a world of enchantment. We only regretted that it had not a due moral effect on us scapegraces.

Nevertheless, when, turning my head, I looked at the willowy edge of Cyanean Meadow and onward to the sober-colored but fine-grained Clamshell Hills, about which there was no glitter, I was inclined to think that the truest beauty was that which surrounded us but which we failed to discern, that the forms and colors which adorn our daily life, not seen afar in the horizon, are our fairest jewelry. The beauty of Clamshell Hill, near at hand, with its sandy ravines, in which the cricket chirps. This is an Occidental city, not less glorious than that we dream of in the sunset sky.

It chanced that all the front-rank polygonum, with its rosaceous spikes, was drowned by the flood, but now, the sun having for some time set, with our backs to the west we saw the light reflected from the slender clear white spikes of the *P. hydropiperoides* (now in its prime), which in large patches or masses rise about a foot above the surface of the water and the other polygonum. Under these circumstances this polygonum was very pretty and interesting, only its more presentable part rising above the water.

Mr. Warren brings to me three kinds of birds which he has shot on the Great Meadows this afternoon, *viz.*

two *Totanus flavipes*, such as I saw the 8th (there were eight in the flock, and he shot seven), one *Rallus Carolinus*, and one peetweet. I doubt if I have seen any but the *T. flavipes* here, since I have measured this.[1] Wilson says that this does not penetrate far inland, though he sees them near Philadelphia after a northeast storm.

The above rail corresponds to the land rail or corncrake of Europe in form and habits. In Virginia is called the sora; in South Carolina, the coot. It is the game rail of the South, and the only species of the genus *Crex* in America. Note *kuk kuk kuk*. Go to Hudson's Bay and thereabouts to breed. This was a male, having a black throat and black about base of bill. Peabody says that they are seen here only in the autumn on their return from the north, though Brewer thinks their nest may be found here. In the genus *Crex*, the bill is stout and shorter than the head. In *Rallus* (as in *R. Virginianus*), it is longer than the head and slender. In the latter, too, the crown and whole upper parts are black, streaked with brown; the throat, breast, and belly, orange-brown; sides and vent, black tipped with white; legs and feet, dark red-brown; none of which is true of the *R. Carolinus*.

I notice that the wing of the peetweet, which is about two inches wide, has a conspicuous and straight-edged white bar along its middle on the under side for half its length. It is seven eighths of an inch wide and, being quite parallel with the darker parts of the wing, it produces that singular effect in its flying which I have noticed. This line, by the way, is not mentioned by Wil-

[1] Or very likely I have. *Vide* 25th.

son, yet it is, perhaps, the most noticeable mark of the bird when flying! The under side of the wings is commonly slighted in the description, though it is at least as often seen by us as the upper. Wilson says that "the whole lower parts are beautifully marked with roundish spots of black, . . . but the young are pure white below." May I not have made the young the *T. solitarius?* But the young are white-spotted on wings.

I think that I see a white-throated sparrow this afternoon.

Sept. 19. Sunday. P. M. — To Cassandra Ponds.

We go through Sedge Hollow. See a small hole, perhaps a skunk's, in that hollow, and, about the mouth, fragments of a hornets' or wasps' nest. I knew that foxes were said to tear in pieces these nests for the sake of the grubs or old hornets left in them. Perhaps the skunk does.

These dry, sedgy hollows are peculiar and interesting to me. The fine, thick sedge makes a soft bed to recline on, and is recurved and lodging like a curly head. These dry hollows, side by side with the deeper and wet ones, are surrounded by hazel bushes and panicled andromeda instead of alders and willows. There is this sort of analogy to the wet ones, or ponds. In the lowest part, even here, I perceive that a different and coarser kind of sedge grows. Along the middle and bottom of the hollows is the indistinct trail of wild animals — foxes, etc. — and sportsmen. C. thinks this might be called Fox Path.

As I stand on the shore of the most westerly Cassandra Pond but one, I see in the air between me and the sun

those interesting swarms of minute light-colored gnats,[1] looking like motes in the sun. These may be allied to the winter gnat of Kirby and Spence. Do they not first appear with cooler and frosty weather, when we have had a slight foretaste of winter? Then in the clear, cool air they are seen to dance. These are about an eighth of an inch long, with a greenish body and two light-colored plumes in front; the wings not so long as the body. So I think they are different from those over the river in the spring. I see a dozen of these choirs within two or three rods, their centres about six feet above the surface of the water andromeda. These separate communities are narrow horizontally and long vertically, about eighteen inches wide and densest in the middle, regularly thinning to nothing at the edges. These individuals are constantly gyrating up and down, cutting figures of 8 like the water-bug, but keeping nearly about the same place.

It is to me a very agreeable reminder of cooler weather.

Hear a chewink's *chewink*. But how ineffectual is the note of a bird now! We hear it as if we heard it not, and forget it immediately. In spring it makes its due impression, and for a long time will not have done echoing, as it were, through our minds. It is even as if the atmosphere were in an unfavorable condition for this kind of music. Every musician knows how much depends on this. Going through low woods I see a white, dusty or mealy-looking mildew on the leaves, — oaks, etc., — the effects of the dog-days or mould season.

[1] Apparently male *Tipulidæ* or crane-flies. *Vide Library of Entertaining Knowledge*, "Insect Transformations," p. 363.

Sept. 20. The river probably reaches its highest since June to-day. The Maryland yellow-throat is here. Hear warbling vireos still, in the elms.

Miss Pratt shows me a small luminous bug found on the earth floor of their shed (I think a month ago). Had two bright points in its tail, as bright or brighter than the glow-worm. *Vide* it in paper. It is now dried, three eighths of an inch long by somewhat more than one eighth wide, ovate-oblong with a broad and blunt head, dull straw-color, clear rose-red on the sides, composed of many segments, which give it a dentate appearance on the edges. A broad flattish kind of shield in front, also red and straw-color.

Sept. 21. Go to Cape Ann.

A very warm day.

A. M. — Go with Russell to the rooms of the Essex Institute, — if that is the name. See some Indian pottery from the Cayuga Reservation, fragments, very pale brick-color three eighths of an inch thick, with a rude ornament (apparently made with the end of a stick) of this form and size: the lines representing slight hollows in a row around it. Saw a stone, apparently slate, shaped like small "sinkers," but six inches by three and a half with a small handle, found near here. Was it a sinker or pestle?

(On the 24th, at the East India Marine Hall, saw a circular stone mortar about six inches in diameter, and a stone exactly like the above in it, described as pestle and mortar found in making Salem Turnpike. Were they

together? Also, at the last place, what was called the blade of an Indian knife found on Governor Endicott's farm, broken, three or four inches long, of a light-colored kind of slate, quite thin, with a back. It might have been for skinning.)

At the Essex Institute (?), — if that's the name, — the eggs of the *Rallus Virginianus*, labelled by Brewer, but much smaller than those I have seen, and nearly white, with dull-brown spots! Can mine be the egg of the *R. crepitans*, though larger than mine? Their eggs of the *Sterna hirundo* look like mine which I have so called; also do those of the black-headed gull, which I do not perceive in Peabody. Looked over the asters, goldenrods, and willows in their herbarium, collected and named by Oakes, Lapham, Russell, and *Cassi* — something. Oakes's *Salix sericea*, also Marshall's, and what O. calls *grisea* of Willdenow, is the same I so call, by the white maple at Assabet. What O. calls *S. phyllicifolia* from White Mountains, having only sterile catkins, — his specimen, — is apparently the one I have from there together with the *repens*.

P. M. — Walked with Russell to Marblehead above railroad.

Saw, in Salem, *Solidago Canadensis*, considerably past prime; our three-ribbed one done; *Spartina cynosuroides;* (was that the *S. juncea*, seven feet high, with a broad leaf, which I mistook for the above? Very common on edge of marshes); apparently *Scirpus pungens*, two to four feet high; *Polygonum aviculare*, appar-

Vol. XI

ently peculiar; swamp thistle, still abundant; *Trifolium procumbens*, still abundant; *Aster Novæ-Angliæ*, dark-violet or lilac-purple, in prime or a little past, three quarters of a mile down railroad; also by shore in Manchester, the 22d; *Ruppia maritima*, in a ditch. In Marblehead, *Aster cordifolius*, abundant, railroad; *Woodsia Ilvensis*. R. pointed out *Juncus bufonius* (??) (but did not know it); it was *tenuis*-like and probably that. *Juncus Greenii* (?) (*tenuis*-like), dense-flowered, on high sea-bank, sea side of Marblehead. Herb-robert, near shore, done. *Datura Stramonium* var. *Tatula*, done there, but out at Rockport; got seeds. Also various lichens. Got *Parmelia parietina*, *elegans*, and *rubina* on the rocks. Saw, but did not get, *P. murorum*. *Cetraria Islandica*. R. said that that I saw at the White Mountains was bitter. *Endocarpon miniatum* (which we have) on rocks. *Peltigera polydactyla*. *Umbilicaria Muhlenbergii*, rocks by sea. That common crustaceous lichen on rocks, — black fruit prettily scattered on a white ground, — which reminds me of maps, is *Lecidea atroalba*. R. thought that my small umbilicaria on Monadnock and Lafayette was *U. erosa* or *hyperborea*.

He knew a *Carex lupulina* because the beaks were recurved.

Called Marblehead coast greenstone generally with dykes in sienite.

Saw artichokes out in several places, at some time. Have a sort of Spouting Horn by shore. Returned by some very deep hollows in Salem (like the Truro ones) called the Dungeons ! ! as our Dunge Hole.

R. gave me from his garden corns of the true [?]

squirrel-corn corydalis, which I plant, and what Tracy gave him for *Utricularia intermedia* from ——, not in flower, though he says that T. has examined the flowers. It looks like mine. What I have called the clustered blackberry he has raised from the seed he got here, and this second year (or third) it has run as long as the common, but, perhaps because in rich soil and the shade, no flowers or fruit.

Saw no *Aster Tradescanti* in this walk, but an abundance of *A. multiflorus* in its prime, in Salem and Marblehead.

Sept. 22. A clear cold day, wind northwest. Leave Salem for the Cape on foot.

Near Beverly Bridge, crossed over that low and flat part of Salem where the first settlement was made and Arabella Stewart [*sic*] [1] is supposed to have been buried.

Soon struck off to the shore in Beverly. See the *discolor* thistle on a sandy beach, and *Phaseolus diversifolius* (three-lobed bean vine), with pretty terete long pods, some ripe, but a few flowers still. *Aster linifolius*, perhaps still in prime, — though it has a flexuous stem, — in a marsh, and lyme-grass, apparently like ours, along edge of marsh. Dined on the edge of a high rocky cliff, quite perpendicular, on the west side of entrance of Manchester Harbor.

One mile southeast of the village of Manchester, struck the beach of "musical sand," just this side of a large, high, rocky point called Eagle Head. This is a curving sandy beach, maybe a third of a mile long by

[1] [The Lady Arbella Johnson?]

some twelve rods wide. (We also found it on a similar but shorter beach on the east side of Eagle Head.) We first perceived the sound when we scratched with our umbrella or finger swiftly and forcibly through the sand; also still louder when we struck forcibly with our heels "scuffing" along. The wet or damp sand yielded no peculiar sound, nor did that which lay loose and deep next the bank, but only the more compact and dry. The sound was not at all musical, nor was it loud. Fishermen might walk over it all their lives, as indeed they have done, without noticing it. R., *who had not heard it*, was about right when he said it was like that made by rubbing on wet glass with your fingers. I thought it as much like the sound made in waxing a table as anything. It was a squeaking sound, as of one particle rubbing on another. I should say it was merely the result of the friction of peculiarly formed and constituted particles. The surf was high and made a great noise, yet I could hear the sound made by my companion's heels two or three rods distant, and if it had been still, probably could have heard it five or six rods.

We kept thence along the rocky shore to Kettle Cove, where, however, I did not find any rocks like Lewis's.

Somewhere thereabouts *Scirpus maritimus*, with its great spikes now withered. In the marsh at Kettle Cove, *Gerardia maritima*, apparently in prime, four or five inches high; *Euphorbia polygonifolia*, six inches in diameter. *Spartina glabra* in the salt water of the cove.

The shore, thus far, from Beverly Bridge had been a succession of bold rocky points half a mile apart, with sometimes curving sandy beaches between, or else rocks.

We now kept the road to Gloucester, leaving the shore a mile or more to the right, wishing to see the magnolia swamp. This was perhaps about a mile and a half beyond Kettle Cove. After passing over a sort of height of land in the woods, we took a path to the left, which within a few rods became a corduroy road in the swamp. Within three or four rods on the west side of this, and perhaps ten or fifteen from the highroad, was the magnolia. It was two to seven or eight feet high, but distinguished by its large and still fresh green leaves, which had not begun to fall. I saw last year's shoots which had died down several feet, and probably this will be the fate of most which has grown this year. The swamp was an ordinary one, not so wet but we got about very well. The bushes of this swamp were not generally more than six feet high. There was another locality the other side of the road.

Cooked our supper in a salt marsh some two miles this side of Gloucester, in view of the town. We had cooked our tea for dinner with dead bayberry bushes; now we used the chips and bark which the tide had deposited in little parcels on the marsh, having carried water in our dippers from a brook, a quarter of a mile. There was a large patch of samphire turned a bright crimson, very conspicuous, near by on the flat marsh, the more conspicuous because large and in the midst of the liquid green of the marsh. We sat on some stones which we obtained flat in the marsh till starlight.

I had seen in this day's walk an abundance of *Aster cordifolius* (but no *A. undulatus*); also saw *A. corymbosus*, which is a handsome white wood aster; and, very

common, what I called *A. longifolius*, with shorter thick, clasping leaves and growing in drier ground than ours, methinks; also, all along the road, the up-country hard, small, mulberry-shaped high blackberry, and many still holding on. This may be due to the cool air of the Cape. They were quite sweet and good. *Vide* a specimen. The foliage had but just fairly begun to change.

Put up in Gloucester.

Sept. 23. Another fair day and wind northwest, but rather warmer. We kept along the road to Rockport, some two miles or more, to a "thundering big ledge" by the road, as a man called it; then turned off toward the south shore, at a house with two very large and old pear trees before it. Part of the house was built by a Witham, one of the first settlers, and the place or neighborhood used to be called "the Farms." Saw the *F. hyemalis* flitting along the walls, and it was cool enough for them on this cape. In a marsh by the shore, where was a very broad curving sandy beach, the shore of a cove, found the *Ranunculus Cymbalaria*, still in bloom, but mostly in fruit. *Glaux maritima* (?), nearly prostrate, with oblong leaves. *Triglochin palustris* in fruit.

An eleocharis, apparently marine, with lenticular fruit and a wrinkled mitre-shaped beak. *Spergularia rubra*, etc., samphire, etc.

The narrow road — where we followed it — wound about big boulders, past small, often *bevel*-roofed cottages where sometimes was a small flag flying for a vane. The number and variety of bevelled roofs on the

Cape is surprising. Some are so nearly flat that they reminded me of the low brows of monkeys.

We had already seen a sort of bare rocky ridge, a bare boulder-covered back of the Cape, running northeasterly from Gloucester toward Rockport and for some three miles quite bare, the eastern extremity of the Cape being wooded. That would be a good place to walk.

In this marsh, saw what I thought the solitary tattler, quite tame.

Having reached the shore, we sat under the lee of the rocks on the beach, opposite Salt Island. A man was carting seaweed along the shore between us and the water, the leather-apron kind, which trailed from his cart like the tails of oxen, and, when it came between us and the sun, was of a warm purple-brown glow. Half a mile further, beyond a rocky head, we came to another curving sandy beach, with a marsh between it and the Cape on the north. Saw there, in the soft sand, with beach-grass, apparently *Juncus Balticus* (?), very like but not so stout (!) as *Juncus effusus*.

Met a gunner from Lynn on the beach, who had several pigeons which he had killed in the woods by the shore. Said that they had been blown off the mainland. Second, also a kingfisher. Third, what he called the "ox-eye," about size of peetweet but with a short bill and a blackish-brown crescent on breast, and wing above like peetweet's, but no broad white mark below. Could it be *Charadrius semipalmatus*? Fourth, what he called a sandpiper, very white with a long bill. Was this *Tringa arenaria*? Fifth, what I took to be a solitary tattler, but possibly it was the pectoral sandpiper, which I have seen since.

On the edge of the beach you see small dunes, with white or fawn-colored sandy sides, crowned with now yellowish smilax and with bayberry bushes. Just before reaching Loblolly Cove, near Thacher's Island, sat on a beach composed entirely of small paving-stones lying very loose and deep.

We boiled our tea for dinner on the mainland opposite Straitsmouth Island, just this side the middle of Rockport, under the lee of a boulder, using, as usual, dead bayberry bushes for fuel. This was, indeed, all we could get. They make a very quick fire, and I noticed that their smoke covered our dippers with a kind of japan which did not crock or come off nearly so much as ordinary soot.

We could see the Salvages very plainly, apparently extending north and south, the Main Rock some fifteen or twenty rods long and east-northeast of Straitsmouth Island, apparently one and a half or two miles distant, with half-sunken ledges north and south of it, over which the sea was breaking in white foam. The ledges all together half a mile long. We could see from our dining-place Agamenticus, some forty miles distant in the north. Its two sides loomed thus: so that about a third of the whole was lifted up, while a small elevation close to it on the east, which afterward was seen to be a part of it, was wholly lifted up.

Rockport well deserves its name, — several little rocky harbors protected by a breakwater, the houses at Rockport Village backing directly on the beach. At Folly Cove, a wild rocky point running north, covered with

beach-grass. See now a mountain on the east of Agamenticus. Isles of Shoals too low to be seen. Probably land at Boar's Head, seen on the west of Agamenticus, and then the coast all the way from New Hampshire to Cape Ann plainly, Newburyport included and Plum Island. Hog Island looks like a high hill on the mainland.

It is evident that a discoverer, having got as far west as Agamenticus, off the coast of Maine, would in clear weather discern the coast trending southerly beyond him as far round as Cape Ann, and if he did not wish to be embayed would stand across to Cape Ann, where the Salvages would be the outmost point.

At Annisquam we found ourselves in the midst of boulders scattered over bare hills and fields, such as we had seen on the ridge northerly in the morning, i. e., they abound chiefly in the central and northwesterly part of the Cape. This was the most peculiar scenery of the Cape. We struck inland southerly, just before sundown, and boiled our tea with bayberry bushes by a swamp on the hills, in the midst of these great boulders, about halfway to Gloucester, having carried our water a quarter of a mile, from a swamp, spilling a part in threading swamps and getting over rough places. Two oxen feeding in the swamp came up to reconnoitre our fire. We could see no house, but hills strewn with boulders, as if they had rained down, on every side, we sitting under a shelving one. When the moon rose, what had appeared like immense boulders half a mile off in the horizon now looked by contrast no larger than nutshells or buri-nut against the moon's disk, and she was the biggest boulder of all. When we had put out our bayberry fire, we heard

Vol. XI

a squawk, and, looking up, saw five geese fly low in the twilight over our heads. We then set out to find our way to Gloucester over the hills, and saw the comet very bright in the northwest. After going astray a little in the moonlight, we fell into a road which at length conducted us to the town.

As we bought our lodging and breakfast, a pound of good ship-bread, which cost seven cents, and six herring, which cost three cents, with sugar and tea, supplied us amply the rest of the two days. The selection of suitable spots to get our dinner or supper led us into interesting scenery, and it was amusing to watch the boiling of our water for tea. There is a scarcity of fresh water on the Cape, so that you must carry your water a good way in a dipper.

Sept. 24. What that singular spiny plant, otherwise like chenopodium, which I found on a wharf in Salem?

Saw at the East India Marine Hall a bay lynx killed in Danvers July 21st (I think in 1827); another killed in Lynnfield in March, 1832. These skins were, now at any rate, quite light dirty-whitish or white wolfish color, with small pale-brown spots. The animals much larger than I expected. Saw a large fossil turtle, some twenty inches in diameter, with the plates distinct, in a slate-colored stone from western New York; also a sword in its scabbard, found in the road near Concord April 19, 1775, and supposed to have belonged to a British officer.

Cape Ann, from Beverly round to Squam, is bristling with little capes, projecting from the main one and similar to it.

Sept. 25. A smart white frost last night, which has killed the sweet potato vines and melons.

P. M. — Go a-graping up Assabet with some young ladies.

The zizania fruit is green yet, but mostly dropped or plucked. Does it fall, or do birds pluck it? The *Gentiana Andrewsii* are now in prime at Gentian Shore. Some are turned dark or reddish-purple with age. There is a very red osier-like cornel on the shore by the stone-heaps.

Edward Hoar says he found last year *Datura Stramonium* in their garden. Add it, then, to our plants.

In the evening Mr. Warren brings me a snipe and a pectoral sandpiper. This last, which is a little less than the snipe but with a longer wing, must be much like *T. solitarius*, and I may have confounded them. The shaft of the first primary is conspicuously white above. The catbird still mews occasionally, and the chewink is heard faintly.

Melvin says he has found the pigeon hawk's nest here (distinct from partridge hawk's); also that he sometimes sees the larger yellow-legs here. Goodwin also says the last.

Sept. 26. Another smart frost, making dry walking amid the stiffened grass in the morning. The purple grass (*Eragrostis pectinacea*) done. Perhaps the first smart frost finished its purple.

I observe that the seeds of the *Panicum sanguinale* and *filiforme* are perhaps half fallen, evidently affected by the late frosts, as chestnuts, etc., will be by later ones;

and now is the time, too, when flocks of sparrows begin to scour over the weedy fields, especially in the morning. Methinks they are attracted to some extent by this their harvest of panic seed. The spikes of *P. Crus-galli* also are partially bare. Evidently the small granivorous birds abound more after these seeds are ripe. The seeds of pigweed are yet apparently quite green. Maybe they are somewhat peculiar for hanging on all winter.

Sept. 27. P. M. — By boat to Fair Haven Pond.

Wind northeast. Sail most of the way. The river has gone down from its height on the 20th, and is now some eighteen inches lower, or within its banks. The front-rank polygonum is uncovered and in bloom still, but its leaves generally turned a dull red. The *P. hydropiperoides* is apparently past prime. The *P. amphibium* spikes still in prime.[1]

When close to the bushes you do not notice any mark of the recent high water, but at a little distance you see a perfectly level line on the button-bushes and willows, about eighteen inches above the present surface, it being all dark below and warm sunny yellow above. The leaves that have been immersed are generally fallen or withered. Though the bushes may be loose and open, this water-line is so perfectly level that it appears continuous.

The farmers digging potatoes on shore pause a moment to watch my sail and bending mast. It is pleasant to see your mast bend in these safe waters. It is rare that the wind is so northeast that I can sail well from the railroad bridge to Clamshell Hill, as to-day.

[1] [Two interrogation-points in pencil here.]

Vol. XI

Acalypha is killed by frost, and rhexia.

Liatris done, apparently some time. When Gosnold and Pring and Champlain coasted along our shores, even then the small shrub oak grew on the mainland, with its pretty acorns striped dark and light alternately.[1]

Sept. 29. Fine weather.

P. M. — To White Pond.

One or two myrtle-birds in their fall dress, with brown head and shoulders, two whitish bars on wings, and bright-yellow rump. Sit on Clamshell, looking up the smooth stream. Two blue herons, or "herns," as Goodwin calls them, fly sluggishly up the stream. Interesting even is a stake, with its reflection, left standing in the still river by some fisherman.

Again we have smooth waters, yellow foliage, and faint warbling birds, etc., as in spring. The year thus repeats itself. Catch some of those little fuzzy gnats dancing in the air there over the shelly bank, and these are black, with black plumes, unlike those last seen over the Cassandra Pond.

Brushed a spectrum, ghost-horse, off my face in a birch wood, by the J. P. Brown cold Heart-Leaf Pond. Head somewhat like a striped snake.

That pond is drier than I ever saw it, *perhaps,*[2] — all but a couple of square rods in the middle, — and now covered with cyperus, etc. The mud is cracked into large polygonal figures of four to six sides and six to twelve inches across, with cracks a half to three quarters of an inch wide.

[1] The black oak acorns also slightly marked thus.
[2] No, have seen it so before.

Red maples now fairly glow along the shore. They vary from yellow to a peculiar crimson which is more red than common crimson.[1] But these particular trees soon fade. It is the first blush which is the purest. See men raking cranberries now, or far away squatting in the meadows, where they are picking them. Grapes have begun to shrivel on their stems. They drop off on the slightest touch, and if they fall into the water are lost, going to the bottom. You see the grape leaves touched with frost curled up and looking crisp on their edges.

The fisherman Haynes thinks that the large flock of peetweet-like birds which I saw on the meadow one fall were what he calls "black-backs."

What are those little birds in flocks in the garden and on the peach trees these mornings, about size of chip-birds, without distinct chestnut crowns?[2]

Sept. 28. *Tuesday.* P. M. — To Great Fields *via* Gentian Lane.

The gentian (*Andrewsii*), now generally in prime, loves moist, shady banks, and its transcendent blue shows best in the shade and suggests coolness; contrasts there with the fresh green; — a splendid blue, light in the shade, turning to purple with age. They are particularly abundant under the north side of the willow-row in Merrick's pasture. I count fifteen in a single cluster there, and afterward twenty at Gentian Lane near Flint's Bridge, and there were other clusters below. Bluer than the bluest sky, they lurk in the moist and shady recesses of the banks.

[1] [*Excursions,* p. 261; Riv. 320.]
[2] Probably are chip-birds. *Vide* Oct. 5.

See what must be a solitary tattler feeding by the water's edge, and it has tracked the mud all about. It cannot be the *Tringa pectoralis,* for it has no conspicuous white chin, nor black dashes on the throat, nor brown on the back and wings, and I think I see the round white spots on its wings. It has not the white on wing of the peetweet, yet utters the *peetweet* note! — *short* and *faint,* not protracted, and not the "sharp whistle" that Wilson speaks of.

The lespedeza leaves are all withered and ready to fall in the frosty hollows near Nut Meadow, and [in] the swamps the ground is already strewn with the first maple leaves, concealing the springiness of the soil, and many plants are prostrate there, November-like. High up in Nut Meadow, the very brook — push aside the half-withered grass which (the farmer disdaining to cut it) conceals it — is as cool as a spring, being near its sources.

Take perhaps our last bath in White Pond for the year. Half a dozen *F. hyemalis* about. Looking toward the sun, some fields reflect a light sheen from low webs of gossamer which thickly cover the stubble and grass.

On our way, near the Hosmer moraine, let off some pasture thistle-down. One steadily rose from my hand, freighted with its seed, till it was several hundred feet high, and then passed out of sight eastward. Its down was particularly spreading or open. Is not here a hint to balloonists? Astronomers can calculate the orbit of that thistle-down called the comet, now in the northwest sky, conveying its nucleus, which may not be so solid as a thistle's seed, somewhither, but what astronomer can calculate the orbit of my thistle-down and tell where it will deposit its precious freight at last? It may still be travelling when I am sleeping.

Some *Lobelia inflata* leaves peculiar hoary-white.

Sept. 30. A large flock of grackles amid the willows by the riverside, or chiefly concealed low in the button-bushes beneath them, though quite near me. There they keep up their spluttering notes, though somewhat less loud, methinks, than in spring. These are the first I have seen, and now for some time, I think, the red-wings have been gone. These are the first arrivers from the north where they breed.

I observe the peculiar steel-bluish purple of the night-shade, *i. e.* the tips of the twigs, while all beneath is green, dotted with bright berries, over the water. Perhaps this is the most singular color of any autumnal tint. It is almost black in some lights, distinctly steel-blue in the shade and contrasting with the green beneath, but, seen against the sun, it is a rich purple, its veins full of fire. The form of the leaf, too, is peculiar.

The pearly everlasting is an interesting white at present. Though the stem and leaves are still green, it is dry and unwithering like an artificial flower. Its white flexuous

stem and branches, too, like wire wound with cotton. Its amaranthine quality is instead of high color. Neither is there any scent to betray it. Its very brown centre now affects us as a fresh and original color. It monopolizes a small circle, in the midst of sweet-fern perchance, on a dry hillside.

I see undoubtedly the little dipper by the edge of the pads this afternoon, and I think I have not seen it before this season. It is much smaller than I have seen this season, and is hard to detect even within four or five rods. It warily dives and comes up a rod or two further off amid the pads, scarcely disturbing the surface.

The wind is northerly these afternoons, blowing pretty strong early in the afternoon, so that I can sail up the stream; but later it goes down, leaving the river glassy smooth, and only a leaping fish or an insect dimples it or makes a sparkle on it.

Some young black cherry leaves are completely changed some time to their deep cherry-red. Also they are rather dull, but beneath quite lively, like the juice of a freshly crushed cherry.

In our late walk on the Cape, we entered Gloucester each time in the dark at mid-evening, travelling partly across lots till we fell into a road, and as we were simply seeking a bed, inquiring the way of villagers whom we could not see, the town seemed far more homelike to us than when we made our way out of it in the morning. It was comparatively still, and the inhabitants were sensibly or poetically employed, too, and then we went straight to our chamber and saw the moonlight reflected

Vol. XI

from the smooth harbor and lighting up the fishing vessels, as if it had been the harbor of Venice. By day we went remarking on the peculiar angles of the bevelled roofs, of which there is a remarkable variety there. There are also many large, square, three-story houses with short windows in the upper story, as if the third story were as good as a gig for respectability. When entering the town in the moonlight we could not always tell whether the road skirted the back yards or the front yards of the houses, and the houses did not so impertinently stare after the traveller and watch his coming as by day.

Walking early in the day and approaching the rocky shore from the north, the shadows of the cliffs were very distinct and grateful and our spirits were buoyant. Though we walked all day, it seemed the days were not long enough to get tired in. Some villages we went through or by without communicating with any inhabitant, but saw them as quietly and distantly as in a picture.

IV

OCTOBER, 1858

(ÆT. 41)

Oct. 1. P. M. — To Hubbard's Close. Clintonia Maple Swamp is very fair now, especially a quarter of a mile off, where you get the effect of the light colors without detecting the imperfections of the leaves. Look now at such a swamp, of maples mixed with the evergreen pines, at the base of a pine-clad hill, and see their yellow and scarlet and crimson fires of all tints, mingled and contrasted with the green. Some maples are yet green, only yellow-tipped on the edges of their flakes, as the edges of a hazelnut bur. Some are wholly brilliant scarlet, raying out regularly and finely every way. Others, of more regular form, seem to rest heavily, flake on flake, like yellow or scarlet snow-drifts.[1]

The cinnamon ferns are crisp and sour [?] in open grounds.

The fringed gentians are now in prime. These are closed in the afternoon,[2] but I saw them open at 12 M. a day or two ago, and they were exceedingly beautiful, especially when there was a single one on a stem. They who see them closed, or in the afternoon only, do not suspect their beauty.

Viola lanceolata again.

[1] [*Excursions*, pp. 261, 262; Riv. 320, 321.]
[2] No. *Vide* forward.

See larks in small flocks.

Was overtaken by a sudden gust and rain from the west. It broke off some limbs and brought down many leaves. Took refuge in Minott's house at last. He told me his last duck-shooting exploit for the fifth or sixth time. Says that Jake Potter, who died over eighty some dozen years since, told him that when he was a boy and used to drive his father Ephraim's cows to pasture in the meadows near Fair Haven, after they were mown in the fall, returning with them at evening, he used to hear the wildcats yell in the Fair Haven woods.

Minott tells of a great rise of the river once in August, when a great many "marsh-birds," as peeps, killdees, yellow-legs, etc., came inland, and he saw a flock of them reaching from Flint's Bridge a mile down-stream over the meadows, and making a great noise. Says the "killdees" used to be common here, and the yellow-legs, called "humilities," used commonly to breed here on the tussocks in the meadows. He has often found their nests.

Let a full-grown but young cock stand near you. How full of life he is, from the tip of his bill through his trembling wattles and comb and his bright eye to the extremity of his clean toes! How alert and restless, listening to every sound and watching every motion! How various his notes, from the finest and shrillest alarum as a hawk sails over, surpassing the most accomplished violinist on the short strings, to a hoarse and terrene voice or cluck! He has a word for every occasion; for the dog that rushes past, and partlet cackling in the barn. And then how, elevating himself and flapping his wings, he gathers

impetus and air and launches forth that world-renowned ear-piercing strain! not a vulgar note of defiance, but the mere effervescence of life, like the bursting of a bubble in a wine-cup. Is any gem so bright as his eye?

The elms are now great brownish-yellow masses hanging over the street. Their leaves are perfectly ripe. I wonder if there is any answering ripeness in the lives of those who live beneath them.[1] The harvest of elm leaves is come, or at hand.

The cat sleeps on her head! What does this portend? It is more alarming than a dozen comets. How long prejudice survives! The big-bodied fisherman asks me doubtingly about the comet seen these nights in the northwest, — if there is any danger to be apprehended from that side! I would fain suggest that only he is dangerous to himself.

Oct. 2. A dark and windy night the last. It is a new value when darkness amounts to something positive. Each morning now, after rain and wind, is fresher and cooler, and leaves still green reflect a brighter sheen.

Minott told me yesterday that he had never seen the seashore but once, and that was Noddle's Island in the War of 1812.

The garden is alive with migrating sparrows these mornings. The cat comes in from an early walk amid the weeds. She is full of sparrows and wants no more breakfast this morning, unless it be a saucer of milk, the dear creature. I saw her studying ornithology between the corn-rows.[2]

[1] [*Excursions,* p. 263; Riv. 322.]   [2] [Channing, p. 298.]

As I approached Perch Pool the other day, half a dozen frogs leaped into it and buried themselves in the mass of callitriche at the bottom. I stood looking for perch a minute or two, when one after another up came the frogs from out the callitriche, just as a piece of cork would rise by mere buoyancy to the surface; and then, by a distinct effort, they let go all, drop anchor, elevate or let float up their heels, and lie spread out on the surface. They were probably *Rana fontinalis.*

Sailed to Baker Farm with a strong northwest wind. Got a peck of the small long-bunched grapes now turned purple under Lee's Cliff. One or two vines bear very plentifully. The bunches are about six inches long by one and a half, and quite dense and cylindrical commonly. They are now apparently just in their prime, to judge from color. Considerably later than the *Vitis Labrusca,* but are not good.[1] A large chocolate-colored puffball "smokes."

Oct. 3. One brings me this morning a Carolina rail alive, this year's bird evidently from its marks. He saved it from a cat in the road near the Battle-Ground. On being taken up, it pecked a little at first, but was soon quiet. It staggers about as if weak on my window-sill and pecks at the glass, or stands with its eyes shut, half asleep, and its back feathers hunched up. Possibly it is wounded. I suspect it may have been hatched here. Its feet are large and spreading, qualifying it to run on mud or pads. Its crown is black, but chin white, and its back feathers are distinctly edged with white in streaks.

[1] Mother [made] a nice jelly of them afterward.

I compare my hazelnuts gathered some time ago. The beaked are pointed nuts, while the common are blunt; and the former are a much paler brown, also have a yellower and much sweeter meat.

A fringed gentian, plucked day before yesterday, at length, this forenoon, untwists and turns its petals partially, in my chamber.

Have noticed a very brilliant scarlet blackberry patch within a week.

The red maples which changed first, along the river, are now faded and partly fallen. They look more pink. But others are lit, and so there is more color than before. Some particular maple among a hundred will be of a peculiarly bright and pure scarlet, and, by its difference of tint and intenser color, attract our eyes even at a distance in the midst of the crowd.[1] Looking all around Fair Haven Pond yesterday, where the maples were glowing amid the evergreens, my eyes invariably rested on a particular small maple of the purest and intensest scarlet.

P. M. — Paddle about Walden.

As I go through the Cut, I discover a new locality for the crotalaria, being attracted by the pretty blue-black pods, now ripe and dangling in profusion from these low plants, on the bare sandy and gravelly slope of the Cut. The vines or plants are but half a dozen times longer (or higher) than the pods. It was the contrast of these black pods with the yellowish sand which betrayed them.

[1] [*Excursions,* p. 261; Riv. 320.]

How many men have a fatal excess of manner! There was one came to our house the other evening, and behaved very simply and well till the moment he was passing out the door. He then suddenly put on the airs of a well-bred man, and consciously described some arc of beauty or other with his head or hand. It was but a slight flourish, but it has put me on the alert.

It is interesting to consider how that crotalaria spreads itself, sure to find out the suitable soil. One year I find it on the Great Fields and think it rare; the next I find it in a new and unexpected place. It flits about like a flock of sparrows, from field to field.

The maples about Walden are quite handsome now. Standing on the railroad, I look across the pond to Pine Hill, where the outside trees and the shrubs scattered generally through the wood glow through the green, yellow, and scarlet, like fires just kindled at the base of the trees, — a general conflagration just fairly under way, soon to envelop every tree. The hillside forest is all aglow along its edge and in all its cracks and fissures, and soon the flames will leap upward to the tops of the tallest trees. About the pond I see maples of all their tints, and black birches (on the southwest side) clear pale yellow; and on the peak young chestnut clumps and walnuts are considerably yellowed.

I hear, out toward the middle, or a dozen rods from me, the plashing made apparently by the shiners, — for they look and shine like them, — leaping in schools on the surface. Many lift themselves quite out for a foot or two, but most rise only part way out, — twenty black points at once. There are several schools indulging in

this sport from time to time as they swim slowly along. This I ascertain by paddling out to them. Perhaps they leap and dance in the water just as gnats dance in the air at present. I have seen it before in the fall. Is it peculiar to this season?

Hear a hylodes peeping on shore.

A general reddening now of young and scrub oaks. Some chinquapin bright-red. White pines fairly begin to change. The large leaves of some black oak sprouts are dark-purple, almost blackish, above, but greenish beneath. See locust leaves all crisped by frost in Laurel Glen Hollow, but only part way up the bank, as on the shore of a lake.

Oct. 4. Going by Dr. Barrett's, just at the edge of evening, I saw on the sidewalk something bright like fire, as if molten lead were scattered along, and then I wondered if a drunkard's spittle were luminous, and proceeded to poke it on to a leaf with a stick. It was rotten wood. I found that it came from the bottom of some old fence-posts which had just been dug up near by and there glowed for a foot or two, being quite rotten and soft, and it suggested that a lamp-post might be more luminous at bottom than at top. I cut out a handful and carried it about. It was quite soft and spongy and a very pale brown — some almost white — in the light, quite soft and flaky; and as I withdrew it gradually from the light, it began to glow with a distinctly blue fire in its recesses, becoming more universal and whiter as the darkness increased. Carried toward a candle, it is quite a blue light. One man whom I met in the street was able

Vol. XI

to tell the time by his watch, holding it over what was in my hand. The posts were oak, probably white. Mr. Melvin, the mason, told me that he heard his dog barking the other night, and, going out, found that it was at the bottom of an old post he had dug up during the day, which was all aglow.

P. M. (before the above). — Paddled up the Assabet. Strong north wind, bringing down leaves.

Many white and red maple, bass, elm, and black willow leaves are strewn over the surface of the water, light, crisp colored skiffs. The bass is in the prime of its change, a mass of yellow.

See B—— a-fishing notwithstanding the wind. A man runs down, fails, loses self-respect, and goes a-fishing, though he were never seen on the river before. Yet methinks his "misfortune" is good for him, and he is the more mellow and humane. Perhaps he begins to perceive more clearly that the object of life is something else than acquiring property, and he really stands in a truer relation to his fellow-men than when he commanded a false respect of them. There he stands at length, perchance better employed than ever, holding communion with nature and himself and coming to understand his real position and relation to men in this world. It is better than a poor debtors' prison, better than most successful money-getting.

I see some rich-weed in the shade of the Hemlocks, for some time a clear, almost ivory, white, and the boehmeria is also whitish. *Rhus Toxicodendron* in the shade is a pure yellow; in the sun, more scarlet or reddish.

Grape leaves apparently as yellow as ever. Witch-hazel apparently at height of change, yellow below, green above, the yellow leaves by their color concealing the flowers. The flowers, too, are apparently in prime. The leaves are often richly spotted reddish and greenish brown. The white maples that changed first are about bare. The brownish-yellow clethra leaves thickly paint the bank. *Salix lucida* leaves are one third clear yellow. The *Osmunda regalis* is yellowed and partly crisp and withered, but a little later than the cinnamon, etc.

Scare up two ducks, which go off with a sharp creaking *ar-r-week, ar-r-week, ar-r-week.* Is not this the note of the wood duck?

Hornets are still at work in their nests.

Ascend the hill. The cranberry meadows are a dull red. See crickets eating the election-cake toadstools. The Great Meadows, where not mown, have long been brown with wool-grass.

The hickories on the northwest side of this hill are in the prime of their color, of a rich orange; some intimately mixed with green, handsomer than those that are wholly changed. The outmost parts and edges of the foliage are orange, the recesses green, as if the outmost parts, being turned toward the sunny fire, were first baked by it.

Oct. 5. I still see large flocks, apparently of chipbirds, on the weeds and ground in the yard; without very distinct chestnut crowns, and they are divided by a light line. They are eating seeds of the *Amaranthus hybridus*, etc.

8 A. M. — I go to Hubbard's Close to see when the

fringed gentians open. They begin to open *in the sun* about 8.30 A. M., or say 9.

Chewink note still. Grackles in flocks. *Phebe* note of chickadee often these days.

Much green is indispensable for maples, hickories, birches, etc., to contrast with, as of pines, oaks, alders, etc. The former are fairest when seen against these. The maples, being in their prime, say yesterday, before the pines, are conspicuously parti-colored.

P. M. — To Easterbrooks Country.

White pines in low ground and swamps are the first to change. Some of these have lost many needles. Some on dry ground have so far changed as to be quite handsome, but most only so far as to make the misty glaucous (green) leaves more soft and indefinite. The fever-bush is in the height of its change and is a showy clear lemon-yellow, contrasting with its scarlet berries. The yellow birch is apparently at the height of its change, clear yellow like the black. I think I saw a white ash which was all turned clear yellowish, and no mulberry, in the Botrychium Swamp.

Looking on the Great Meadows from beyond Nathan Barrett's, the wool-grass, where uncut, is very rich brown, contrasting with the clear green of the portions which are mown; all rectangular.

The staghorn sumach apparently in the prime [1] of its change.

In the evening I am glad to find that my phosphorescent wood of last night still glows somewhat, but I im-

[1] [Queried in pencil.]

prove it much by putting it in water. The little chips which remain in the water or sink to the bottom are like so many stars in the sky.

The comet makes a great show these nights. Its tail is at least as long as the whole of the Great Dipper, to whose handle, till within a night or two, it reached, in a great curve, and we plainly see stars through it. [1]

Huckleberry bushes generally red, but dull Indian-red, not scarlet.

The red maples are generally past their prime (of color). They are duller or faded. Their first fires, like those of genius, are brightest. In some places on the edges of swamps many of their tops are bare and smoky. The dicksonia fern is for the most part quite crisp and brown along the walls.

Oct. 6. P. M. — To Saw Mill Brook and Flint's Pond.

Now, methinks, the autumnal tints are brightest in our streets and in the woods generally. In the streets, the *young* sugar maples make the most show. The street is never more splendid. As I look up the street from the Mill-Dam, they look like painted screens standing before the houses to celebrate a gala-day. [2] One half of each tree glows with a delicate scarlet. But only one of the large maples on the Common is yet on fire. The butternuts on the street are with, or a little later than, the walnuts. The three-thorned acacias have turned (one half) a pe-

[1] It finally reaches between one fourth and one third from the horizon to the zenith.

[2] [*Excursions*, p. 271; Riv. 332.]

culiarly clear bright and delicate yellow, peculiar also for the smallness of the leaf. Asparagus-beds are a soft mass of yellow and green. Buttonwoods have no bright colors, but are a brownish and yellowish green, somewhat curled and crisp and looking the worse for the wear. Stand where half a dozen large elms droop over a house. It is as if you stood within a ripe pumpkin rind, and you feel as mellow as if you were the pulp. [1]

In Saw Mill Brook Path, and in most wood-paths, the *Aster undulatus* is now very fair and interesting. Generally a tall and slender plant with a very long panicle of middle-sized lilac or paler purple flowers, bent over to one side the path. The *Rhus Toxicodendron* leaves are completely changed and of very various colors, pale yellow to deep scarlet and delicate. The leaf-stalks are commonly drooping, being bent short downward near the base in a peculiar manner. Several species of ferns are faded quite white in the swamp, — dicksonia and another, and some brakes, — for in moist woods and swamps they are preserved longer than in dry places. *Solidago latifolia* in bloom still, but always sparingly. Cinnamon ferns are generally crisped, but in the swamp I saw some handsomely spotted green and yellowish, and one clump, the handsomest I ever saw, perfect in outline, falling over each way from the centre, of a very neat drab color, quaker-like, fit to adorn an Oriental drawing-room. The evergreens seem positively greener, owing to the browning of other leaves. I should not suspect that the white birches had changed so much and

[1] [*Excursions*, pp. 263; Riv. 323.]

lost so many leaves, if I did not see them against the unchanged pitch pines on the hillside. I notice *Hieracium paniculatum* and *scabrum* in dark, low wood-paths, turned a hoary white. The medeola leaves are a pale straw-color with a crimson centre; perhaps getting stale now. The tupelo at Wharf Rock is completely scarlet, with blue berries amid its leaves.

Leaves now have fairly begun to rustle under foot in wood-paths, especially in chestnut woods, scaring the ducks as you approach the ponds. And what is that common scent there so much like fragrant everlasting?

The smooth sumachs, which are in their prime, or perhaps a little past, are, methinks, the most uniform and intense scarlet of any shrub or tree. They stand perfectly distinct amid the pines, with slender spreading arms, their leafets drooping and somewhat curled though fresh. Yet, high-colored as they are, from their attitude and drooping, like scarfs, on rather bare and dark stems, they have a funereal effect, as if you were walking in the cemetery of a people who mourned in scarlet.

Most *S. nemoralis*, and most other goldenrods, now look hoary, killed by frost.

The corn stands bleached and faded — quite white in the twilight — in the fields. No greenness there has the frost and sun left. Seen against the dark earth.

My phosphorescent wood still glows a little, though it has lain on my stove all day, and, being wet, it is much improved still.

Oct. 8. Fine pasture grass, seen in the sun, begins to look faded and bleached like the corn.

Strong northwest wind. The button-bushes and black willows are rapidly losing leaves, and the shore begins to look Novemberish.

Mulberry leaves of ash are apparently dulled.

Oct. 9. Cold and northwest wind still. The maple swamps begin to look smoky, they are already so bare. Their fires, so faded, are pale-scarlet or pinkish. Some *Cornus sericea* looks quite greenish yet. Huckleberry leaves falling fast.

I go to the Cliffs. The air is clear, with a cold northwest wind, and the trees beginning to be bare. The mountains are darker and distincter, and Walden, seen from this hill, darker blue. It is quite Novemberish. People are making haste to gather the remaining apples this cool evening.[1] Bay-wings flit along road.

Crows fly over and caw at you now.

Methinks hawks are more commonly seen now, — the slender marsh hawk for one. I see four or five in different places. I watch two marsh hawks which rise from the woods before me as I sit on the Cliff, at first plunging at each other, gradually lifting themselves as they come round in their gyrations, higher and higher, and floating toward the southeast. Slender dark motes they are at last, almost lost to sight, but every time they come round eastward I see the light of the westering sun reflected from the under sides of their wings.

Those little bits of phosphorescent wood which I picked up on the 4th have glowed each evening since, but required wetting to get the most light out of them.

[1] And for some time after.

This evening only one, about two inches long, shows any light. This was wet last evening, but is now apparently quite dry. If I should wet it again, it would, no doubt, glow again considerably.

Oct. 10. *Sunday.* P. M. — To Annursnack.

November has already come to the river with the fall of the black willow and the button-bush, and the fall and blackening of the pontederia. The leaves of the two former are the greater part fallen, letting in the autumn light to the water, and the ducks have less shelter and concealment.

As I go along the Groton road, I see afar, in the middle of E. Wood's field, what looks like a stone jug or post, but my glass reveals it a woodchuck, a great, plump gray fellow, and when I am nearly half a mile off, I can still see him nibbling the grass there, and from time to time, when he hears, perchance, a wagon on the road, sitting erect and looking warily around for approaching foes. I am glad to see the woodchuck so fat in the orchard. It proves that is the same nature that was of yore.

The autumnal brightness of the foliage generally is less, or faded, since the fading of the maples and hickories, which began about the 5th.[1] Oak leaves generally (perhaps except scarlet?) begin to wither soon after they begin to turn, and large trees (except the scarlet) do not generally attain to brilliancy.[2]

Apparently *Fringilla pusilla* yet.

[1] But the oaks became brighter. *Vide* 15th.
[2] [Queried in pencil.]

Vol. XI

The *Salix humilis* leaves are falling fast in Wood Turtle Path (A. Hosmer's), a dry wood-path, looking curled and slaty-colored about the half-bare stems. Thus each humble shrub is contributing its mite to the fertility of the globe. I find the under sides of the election-cake fungi there covered with pink-colored fleas, apparently poduras, skipping about when it is turned up to the light.

The simplest and most lumpish fungus has a peculiar interest to us, compared with a mere mass of earth, because it is so obviously organic and related to ourselves, however mute. It is the expression of an idea; growth according to a law; matter not dormant, not raw, but inspired, appropriated by spirit. If I take up a handful of earth, however separately interesting the particles may be, their relation to one another appears to be that of mere juxtaposition generally. I might have thrown them together thus. But the humblest fungus betrays a life akin to my own. It is a successful poem in its kind. There is suggested something superior to any particle of matter, in the idea or mind which uses and arranges the particles.

Genius is inspired by its own works; it is hermaphroditic.

I find the fringed gentian abundantly open at 3 and at 4 P. M., — in fact, it must be all the afternoon, — open to catch the cool October sun and air in its low position. Such a dark blue! surpassing that of the male bluebird's back, who must be encouraged by its presence.[1]

[1] Inclosing it in a mass of the sphagnum near or in which it often grows, I carry it home, and it opens for several days in succession.

The indigo-weed, now partly turned black and broken off, blows about the pastures like the flyaway grass.

I find some of those little rooty tubers (?), now woody, in the turtle field of A. Hosmer's by Eddy Bridge.

Pulling up some *Diplopappus linariifolius*, now done, I find many *bright-purple* shoots, a half to three quarters of an inch long, freshly put forth underground and ready to turn upward and form new plants in the spring.

Oct. 11. P. M. — To Conantum.

The autumnal tints have not been so bright as usual this year,[1] but why it is hard to say. The summer has been peculiarly cool, as well as wet, and it may be that the leaves have been the more inclined to decay before coming to maturity. Also, apparently, many leaves are killed by the mere frosts before ripening, the locust for instance, — and the frost came early this year, — just as melons and squashes before they have turned yellow; *i. e.*, the leaves fall while they are still green.

I observe the small cornel or bunch-berry conspicuously green now, like wintergreen and evergreen in the woods, amid the changed or withered foliage of the forest floor. Yet I have seen it purple (?) in the winter, methinks.

See a small flock of cowbirds (?), with at any rate conspicuously *drab* head and shoulders, — the rest black. What were those slender sparrow-like birds which went off singly from the sides of Conantum hills, with a sharp *chit chit*, a peculiar note, flying *somewhat* like a goldfinch but not quite so ricochet? They are quite shy.

[1] ?? Perhaps they were later (?).

Witch-hazel, grape, smooth sumach, and common hazel are partly fallen, — some of the first-named wholly, — yet full of bloom. It is a cool seat under the witch-hazel in full bloom, which has lost its leaves! The leaves are greenish and brownish yellow. White pines are apparently ready to fall. Some are much paler brown than others. The small botrychium has shed pollen apparently within ten days. The *Viburnum Lentago* is generally a dull red on a green ground, but its leaves are yet quite fresh.

See a white-throat sparrow ?[1]

Oct. 12. P. M. — Up Assabet.

Most exposed button-bushes and black willows are two thirds bare, and the leaves which remain on the former are for the most part brown and shrivelled. The balls stand out bare, ruddy or brown. The coarse grass of the riverside (*Phalaris ?*) is bleached as white as corn. The *Cornus sericea* begins to fall, though some of it is green; and the *C. florida* at Island shows some scarlet tints, but it is not much exposed. I believe that this was quite showy at Perth Amboy.

There are many maple, birch, etc., leaves on the Assabet, in stiller places along the shore, but not yet a leaf harvest. Many swamp white oaks look crisp and brown.

I land at Pinxter Swamp. The leaves of the azaleas are falling, mostly fallen, and revealing the large blossom-buds, so prepared are they for another year. With man all is uncertainty. He does not confidently look forward to another spring. But examine the root of the

[1] Yes.

savory-leaved aster, and you will find the new shoots, fair purple shoots, which are to curve upward and bear the next year's flowers, already grown half an inch or more in earth. Nature is confident.

The river is lower than before this year, or at least since spring, yet not remarkably low, and meadows and pools generally are drier.

The oak leaves generally are duller than usual this year.[1] I think it must be that they are killed by frost before they are ripe. Some small sugar maples are still as fair as ever. You will often see one, large or small, a brilliant and almost uniform scarlet, while another close to it will be perfectly green.

The *Osmunda regalis* and some of the small or middle-sized ferns, not evergreens, in and about the swamps, are generally brown and withered, though with green ones intermixed. They are still, however, interesting, with their pale brown or cinnamon-color and decaying scent. Hickories are for the most part being rapidly browned and crisp. Of the oaks, the white is apparently the most generally red at present. I see a scarlet oak still quite green.

Brakes are fallen in the pastures. They lie flat, still attached to the ground by their stems, and in sandy places they blow about these and describe distinct and perfect circles there. The now fallen dark-brown brake lies on or across the old brake, which fell last year and is quite gray but remarkably conspicuous still. They have fallen in their ranks, as they stood, and lie as it were with a winding-sheet about them.

[1] *Vide* 15th.

Young sweet-fern, where it had been burned in the spring, is quite green. Exposed clethra is crisp and brown. Some bass trees are quite bare, others but partly. The hop hornbeam is in color and falling like the elm. Acorns, red and white (especially the first), appear to be fallen or falling. They are so fair and plump and glossy that I love to handle them, and am loath to throw away what I have in my hand.

I see a squirrel-nest of leaves, made now before the leaves are fallen.

I have heard of judges, accidentally met at an evening party, discussing the efficacy of the laws and courts, and deciding that, with the aid of the jury system, "substantial justice was done." But taking those cases in which honest men refrain from going to law, together with those in which men, honest and dishonest, do go to law, I think that the law is really a "humbug," and a benefit principally to the lawyers. This town has made a law recently against cattle going at large, and assigned a penalty of five dollars. I am troubled by an Irish neighbor's cow and horse, and have threatened to have them put in the pound. But a lawyer tells me that these town laws are hard to put through, there are so many quibbles. He never knew the complainant to get his case if the defendant were a-mind to contend. However, the cattle were kept out several days, till a Sunday came, and then they were all in my grounds again, as I heard, but all my neighbors tell me that I cannot have them impounded on that day. Indeed, I observe that very many of my neighbors do *for this reason* regularly turn their cattle loose on Sundays. The judges may discuss the question

of the courts and law over their nuts and raisins, and mumble forth the decision that "substantial justice is done," but I must believe they mean that they do really get paid a "substantial" salary.

Oct. 13. Rain, all day, more or less, which the cloudy and rather still yesterday threatened. Elm leaves thickly strew the street now and rattle underfoot, — the dark-brown pavement. The elms are at least half bare.

Oct. 14. P. M. — Sail to Ball's Hill.

The white maples are now apparently in their autumnal dress. The leaves are much curled and of a pale hoary or silvery yellow, with often a rosaceous cheek, though not so high-colored as two months ago. They are beginning to lose their leaves. Though they still hold on, they have lost much of their vitality.

On the top of Ball's Hill, nearly half-way its length, the red pine-sap, quite fresh, apparently not long in bloom, the flower recurved. As last year, I suspect that this variety is later than the yellowish one, of which I have seen none for a long time. The last, in E. Hubbard's wood, is all brown and withered. This is a clear and distinct deep-red from the ground upward, all but the edges and tips of the petals, and is very handsome amid the withered lower leaves, as it were the latest flower of the year. The roots have not only a sweet earthy, but decidedly checkerberry, scent. At length this fungus-like plant bursts red-ripe, stem and all, from the ground. Its deep redness reminds me of the deeper colors of the western sky after the sun has set, — a sort of afterglow in the flowery year. I suspect that it is eminently an autumnal flower.

The tufts of *Andropogon scoparius*, which is common on the sandy shore under Ball's Hill and yet more on the hill just behind Reuben Brown's place, are now in their autumnal state,—recurved [?] culms adorned with white fuzzy spikes. The culms still are of a dull-red color, quite agreeable in the sun.

Paddling slowly back, we enjoy at length very perfect reflections in the still water. The blue of the sky, and indeed all tints, are deepened in the reflection.

Oct. 15. The balm-of-Gileads are half bare. I see a few red maples still bright, but they are commonly yellow ones.[1] White pines are in the midst of their fall. The Lombardy poplars are still quite green and cool. Large rock maples are now perhaps in their prime,—later than I supposed,—though some small ones have begun to fall. Some that were green a week ago are now changed. The large white oak by path north of Sleepy Hollow is now all red and at height. Perhaps half the white ash trees are yellow, and if the mulberry ones were dulled (?) a week ago, the yellow ones, methinks, are fresher or brighter than ever, but fast falling. White birches, though they have lost many leaves, are still, perhaps, as soft a yellow as ever, a fine yellow imbrication seen against the greener forest. They change gradually and last long.

P. M. — To Walden.

White oaks are rapidly withering,—the outer leaves.

[1] No.   [2] Rather the 18th, *q. v.*

tinged under sides of the outmost leaves, blown up by the wind and perhaps partly crisped.[1]

I notice thorn bushes in sprout-lands quite bare. The lower leaves of huckleberry bushes and young wild black cherries fall first, but for the most part the upper leaves of apple trees. The high blueberries are still a bright or red scarlet. Goldenrods now pretty generally show their dirty-white pappus together with the still yellow scales, the last preserving some semblance of the flowers. Small hickories are the clearest and most delicate yellow in the shade of the woods. Cinnamon ferns in Clintonia Swamp are fast losing their leafets. Some large dicksonias on the moist hillside there are quite green yet, though nearly prostrate in a large close patch slanting down the hill, and with some faded nearly white.

The yellow lily in the brook by the Turnpike is still expanding fresh leaves with wrinkled edges, as in the spring.

The *Salix humilis* falls, exposing its great cones like a fruit.

On the sandy slope of the cut, close by the pond, I notice the chips which some Indian fletcher has made. Yet our poets and philosophers regret that we have no antiquities in America, no ruins to remind us of the past. Hardly can the wind blow away the surface anywhere, exposing the spotless sand, even though the thickest woods have recently stood there, but these little stone chips made by some aboriginal fletcher are revealed. With them, too, this time, as often, I find the white man's arm, a conical bullet, still marked by the groove

[1] For shrub oak color *vide* Oct. 2d, 1857.

The small black oaks, too, are beginning to wither and turn brown. *Small* red oaks, at least, and small scarlet ones, are apparently in their prime in sprout-lands and young woods. The large leaves of the red oaks are still fresh, of mingled reddish or scarlet, yellow, and green, striking for the size of the leaf, but not so uniformly dark and brilliant as the scarlet. The black oak is yellowish, a half-decayed or brownish yellow, and already becoming brown and crisp, though not so much so as the white. The scarlet is the most brilliant of the oaks, finely fingered, especially noticeable in sprout-lands and young woods. The larger ones are still altogether green, or show a deep cool green in their recesses.

If you stand fronting a hillside covered with a variety of young oaks, the brightest scarlet ones, uniformly deep, dark scarlet, will be the scarlet oaks; the next most uniformly reddish, a peculiar dull crimson (or salmon?) red, are the white oaks; then the large-leaved and variously tinted red oaks, scarlet, yellow, and green; and finally the yellowish and half-decayed brown leaves of the black oak.

The colors of the oaks are far more distinct now than they were before. See that white and that black oak, side by side, young trees, the first that peculiar dull crimson (or salmon) red, with crisped edges, the second a brownish and greenish yellow, much sun still in its leaves. Looking at a young white oak, you see two distinct colors, the brighter or glossier red of the upper surfaces of the inner leaves, as yet not much affected by frost and wind, contrasting with the paler but still crimson-

Vol. XI

of the rifle, which has been roughened or rucked up like a thimble on the side by which it struck the sand. As if, by some [un]explained sympathy and attraction, the Indian's and the white man's arrowheads sought the same grave at last.

Oct. 16. P. M. — Sail up river.

There is less wind these days than a week or fortnight ago; calmer and more Indian-summer-like days. I now fairly begin to see the brown balls of the button-bush (which is about bare) reflected in smooth water, looking black against the sky, also the now withered straw-colored coarse grass (*Phalaris*); and the musquash-houses rapidly rising of late are revealed by the fall of the button-bush, willows, pontederia, etc.

In the reflection the button-bushes and their balls appear against the sky, though the substance is seen against the meadow or distant woods and hills; *i. e.*, they appear in the reflection as they would if viewed from that point on the surface from which they are reflected to my eye, so that it is as if I had another eye placed there to see for me. Hence, too, we are struck by the prevalence of sky or light in the reflection, and at twilight dream that the light has gone down into the bosom of the waters; for in the reflection the sky comes up to the very shore or edge and appears to extend under it, while, the substance being seen from a more elevated point, the actual horizon is perhaps many miles distant over the fields and hills. In the reflection you have an infinite number of eyes to see for you and report the aspect of things each from its point of view. The statue in the meadow which actually is seen obscurely against the meadow, in the reflection appears dark and distinct against the sky.

The mikania, goldenrods, and *Andropogon scoparius* have now their November aspect, the former showing their dirty-white pappus, the last its white plumose hairs. The year is thus acquiring a grizzly look before the snows of winter. I see some *Polygonum amphibium*, front-rank, and *hydropiperoides* still.

At Clamshell the large black oaks are brownish and greenish yellow; the swamp white, at a distance, a yellowish green; though many of the last (which are small) are already withered pale-brown with light under sides.

Willows generally turn yellow, even to the little sage willow, the smallest of all our species, but a foot or two high, though the *Salix alba* hardly attains to more than a sheeny polish.[1] But one willow, at least, the *S. cordata*, varies from yellow to a light scarlet in wet places, which would be deeper yet were it not for its lighter under sides. This is seen afar in considerable low patches in the meadow. It is remarkable among our willows for turning scarlet, and I can distinguish this species now by this, *i. e.* part of it, in perhaps the wettest places; the rest is yellow. It is as distinctly scarlet as the gooseberry, though it may be lighter.

[1] *Vide* 18th.

Vol. XI

ceal the river, unless in some quiet coves, yet they remind me of ditches in swamps, whose surfaces are often quite concealed by leaves now. The waves made by my boat cause them to rustle, and both by sounds and sights I am reminded that I am in the very midst of the fall.

Methinks the reflections are never purer and more distinct than now at the season of the fall of the leaf, just before the cool twilight has come, when the air has a finer grain. Just as our mental reflections are more distinct at this season of the year, when the evenings grow cool and lengthen and our winter evenings with their brighter fires may be said to begin. And painted ducks, too, often come and sail or float amid the painted leaves.

Cattle are seen these days turned into the river meadows and straying far and wide. They have at length reached those "pastures new" they dreamed of.

I see one or two large white maples quite bare. Some late red maples are unexpectedly as fair and bright as ever, both scarlet and yellow, and still distance all competitors. There is no brighter and purer scarlet (often running into crimson) and no softer and clearer yellow than theirs now, though the greater part have quite lost their leaves. The fires I thought dulled, if not put out, a week ago seem to have burst forth again. This accounts for those red maples which were seen to be green while all around them were scarlet. They but bided their time. They were not so easily affected.

I distinguish one large red oak — the most advanced one — from black ones, by its *red* brown, though some

[1] [*Excursions*, p. 268; Riv. 328.]

The oak sprout-land on the hillside north of Puffer's is now quite brilliant red. There is a pretty dense row of white birches along the base of the hill near the meadow, and their light-yellow spires are seen against the red and set it off remarkably, the red being also seen a little below them, between their bare stems. The green white pines seen here and there amid the red are equally important.

The tupelo by Staples's meadow is completely bare. Some high blueberry is a deep dark crimson. In sprout-lands you see great mellow yellowish leaves of aspen sprouts here and there.

See a large flock of grackles steering for a bare elm-top near the meadows. As they fly athwart my view, they appear successively rising half a foot or a foot above one another, though the flock is moving straight forward. I have not seen red-wings [for] a long while, but these birds, which went so much further north to breed, are still arriving from those distant regions, fetching the year about.

Oct. 17. P. M. — Up Assabet.

There are many crisped but colored leaves resting on the smooth surface of the Assabet, which for the most part is not stirred by a breath; but in some places, where the middle is rippled by a slight breeze, no leaves are seen, while the broad and perfectly smooth portions next the shore will be covered with them, as if by a current they were prevented from falling on the other parts. These leaves are chiefly of the red maple, with some white maple, etc. To be sure, they hardly begin to con-

others are yellow-brown and greenish. The *large* red oaks are about in their prime. Some are a handsome light scarlet, with yellow and green.[1]

The *Cornus sericea* is a very dark crimson, though it has lost some leaves. The *Salix lucida* lower leaves are all fallen (the rest are yellow). So, too, it is the lower leaves of the willows generally which have fallen first.

Saw a small hawk come flying over the Assabet, which at first I mistook for a dove, though it was smaller. It was blunt or round-shouldered like a dove. It alighted on a small elm and did not mind a wagon passing near by. Seen through my glass twenty rods off, it had a very distinct black head, with apparently a yellowish-brown breast and beneath and a brown back, — both, however, quite light, — and a yellowish tail with a distinct broad black band at the tip. This I saw when, in pruning itself, it was tilted or flirted up. Could it have been a sparrow hawk?

One reason why I associate perfect reflections from still water with this and a later season may be that now, by the fall of the leaves, so much more light is let in to the water. The river reflects more light, therefore, in this twilight of the year, as it were an afterglow.

Oct. 18. P. M. — To Smith's chestnut grove and Saw Mill Brook.

The large sugar maples on the Common are now at the height of their beauty. One, the earliest to change, is partly bare. This turned so early and so deep a scarlet that some thought that it was surely going to die.

[1] *Vide* 28th.

Also that one at the head of the Turnpike reveals its character now as far as you can see it. Yet about ten days ago all but one of these was quite green, and I thought they would not acquire any bright tints. A delicate but warmer than golden yellow is the prevailing color, with scarlet cheeks.[1] They are great regular oval masses of yellow and scarlet. All the sunny warmth of the season seems to be absorbed in their leaves. There is an auction on the Common, but its red flag is hard to be discerned amid this blaze of color. The lowest and inmost leaves next the bole are of the most delicate yellow and green, as usual, like the complexion of young men brought up in the house.

Little did the fathers of the town anticipate this brilliant success when they caused to be imported from further in the country some straight poles with the tops cut off, which they called sugar maple trees, — and a neighboring merchant's clerk, as I remember, by way of jest planted beans about them. Yet these which were then jestingly called bean-poles are these days far the most beautiful objects noticeable in our streets. They are worth all and more than they have cost, — though one of the selectmen did take the cold which occasioned his death in setting them out, — if only because they have filled the open eyes of children with their rich color so unstintedly so many autumns. We will not ask them to yield us sugar in the spring, while they yield us so fair a prospect in the autumn. Wealth may be the inheritance of few in the houses, but it is equally distributed on the Common. All children alike can

[1] Vide [pp. 226, 227].

revel in this golden harvest. These trees, throughout the street, are at least equal to an annual festival and holiday, or a week of such, — not requiring any special police to keep the peace, — and poor indeed must be that New England village's October which has not the maple in its streets. This October festival costs no powder nor ringing of bells, but every tree is a liberty-pole on which a thousand bright flags are run up. Hundreds of children's eyes are steadily drinking in this color, and by these teachers even the truants are caught and educated the moment they step abroad. It is as if some cheap and innocent gala-day were celebrated in our town every autumn, — a week or two of such days.

What meant the fathers by establishing this *living* institution before the church, — this institution which needs no repairing nor repainting, which is continually "enlarged and repaired" by its growth? Surely trees should be set in our streets with a view to their October splendor. Do you not think it will make some odds to these children that they were brought up under the maples? Indeed, neither the truant nor the studious are at present taught colors in the schools. These are instead of the bright colors in apothecary shops and city windows. It is a pity we have not more red maples and some hickories in the streets as well. Our paint-box is very imperfectly filled. Instead of, or besides, supplying paint-boxes, I would supply these natural colors to the young.[1]

I know of one man at least, called an excellent and peculiarly successful farmer, who has thoroughly re-

[1] [Excursions, pp. 271–274, 277; Riv. 333–337, 340.]

Vol. XI

paired his house and built a new barn with a barn cellar, such as every farmer seems fated to have, who has not a single tree or shrub of any kind about his house or within a considerable distance of it.

No annual training or muster of soldiery, no celebration with its scarfs and banners, could import into the town a hundredth part of the annual splendor of our October. We have only to set the trees, or let them stand, and Nature will find the colored drapery, — flags of all her nations, some of whose private signals hardly the botanist can read. Let us have a good many maples and hickories and scarlet oaks, then, I say. Blaze away! Shall that dirty roll of bunting in the gunhouse be all the colors a village can display? A village is not complete unless it has these trees to mark the season in it. They are as important as a town clock. Such a village will not be found to work well. It has a screw loose; an essential part is wanting. Let us have willows for spring, elms for summer, maples and walnuts and tupelos for autumn, evergreens for winter, and oaks for all seasons. What is a gallery in a house to a gallery in the streets! I think that there is not a picture-gallery in the country which would be worth so much to us as is the western view under the elms of our main street. They are the frame to a picture, and we are not in the dilemma of the Irishman who, having bought a costly gilt picture-frame at an auction, found himself obliged to buy a picture at private sale to put into it, for our picture is already painted with each sunset behind it. An avenue of elms as large as our largest, and three miles long, would seem to lead to some admirable place,

though only Concord were at the end of it. Such a street as I have described would be to the traveller, especially in October, an ever-changing panorama.

A village needs these innocent stimulants of bright and cheery prospects to keep off melancholy and superstition. Show me two villages, one embowered in trees and blazing with all the glories of October, the other a merely trivial and treeless waste, and I shall be sure that in the latter will be found the most desperate and hardest drinkers. What if we were to take half as much pains in protecting them as we do in setting them out, — not stupidly tie our horses to our dahlia stems? They are cheap preachers, permanently settled, which preach their half-century, and century, aye, and century and a half sermons, with continually increasing influence and unction, ministering to many generations of men, and the least we can do is to supply them with suitable colleagues as they grow infirm.[1]

Children are now everywhere playing with the brown and withered leaves of elms and buttonwoods, which strew the streets and are collected into heaps in the sluiceways. In the woods even the little pea-vine turns a delicate yellow and is more conspicuous than ever, and in the now neglected gardens the asparagus-beds, greenish without, glow yellow within, as if a fire were bursting out there.

As I go down the Turnpike past Clintonia Swamp, I am struck by the magical change which has taken place in the red maple swamps, which just a fortnight ago were splendid masses of scarlet and yellow and crimson,

[1] [Excursions, pp. 275–278; Riv. 338–341.]

rising amid the yet green trees, — pines and oaks, etc., — like immense flower-beds on one side of the town, visible for miles, attracting the eyes of all travellers; now, — though a few late ones are bright as ever in some places, — all their splendor gone, wafted away, as it were, by a puff of wind, and they are the mere ghosts of trees, unnoticed by any, or, if noticed at all, like the smoke that is seen where a blaze is extinguished, or as the red clouds at evening change suddenly to gray and black, — so suddenly their glory departs, — desolate gray twigs.

The *Salix alba* is a light and silvery green. Since the red maples generally fell, the chestnuts have been yellowing, and the oaks reddening and yellowing. The chestnuts are now in their prime, though many leaves are fallen. The forest, which showed but little ripeness ten days ago, except about its edges and here and there as you looked down on it from a height, is now seen to be generally of a mellow brownish yellow, like perfectly ripe fruit, which we know to be more perfectly ripe for being a little specked. By the brook, witch-hazel, as an underwood, is in the height of its change, but elsewhere exposed large bushes are bare. *Rhus Toxicodendron* is fallen. The hornbeam is a greenish yellow, or yellow as it were dusted with green. The maple-leaved viburnum, now at its height, varies, with more or less of shade, from dark crimson through a delicate pale crimson to whitish. The sage willow, a light yellow, in prime, though hardly noticed amid the more conspicuous oaks. Larches have begun to change in water.

As I come through Hubbard's Woods I see the winter-

green, conspicuous now above the freshly fallen white pine needles. Their shining green is suddenly revealed above the pale-brown ground. I hail its cool unwithering green, one of the humbler allies by whose aid we are to face the winter.

Saw, October 14th, a snake at Ball's Hill, like a striped snake, but apparently yellow-spotted above and with a flatter head? Noticed a little snake, eight or nine inches long, in the rut in the road in the Lincoln woods. It was brown above with a paler-brown dorsal stripe, which was bounded on each side by a row of dark-brown or blackish dots one eighth inch apart, the opposite rows alternating thus: beneath, light cream-color or yellowish white. Evidently Storer's *Coluber ordinatus*. It ran along in the deep sandy rut and would probably be run over there.

See larks, with their white tail-feathers, fluttering low over the meadows these days.

Minott was sitting outside, as usual, and inquired if I saw any game in my walks these days; since, now that he cannot go abroad himself, he likes to hear from the woods. He tried to detain me to listen to some of his hunting-stories, especially about a slut that belonged to a neighbor by the name of Billings, which was excellent for squirrels, rabbits, and partridges, and would always follow him when he went out, though Billings was "plaguy mad about it;" however, he had only to go by Billings's to have the dog accompany him. B. afterward carried her up country and gave her away, the news of which almost broke Minott's heart. He said he

could have cried when he heard of it, for he had dreamed of her several nights. She was a plaguy good dog for squirrels, etc., but her pups were none of them equal to herself. It was not time for squirrels now, because the leaves were not off enough. He used sometimes to take his old king's-arm on these excursions. It was heavy, but it was sure. His present gun has a flint lock and has often been repaired, and he said he didn't suppose it would fetch more than a dollar if put up at auction now. But he wouldn't take twenty dollars for it. He didn't want to part with it. He liked to look at it.

As leaves fall along the river and in the woods, the squirrels and musquash make haste to shelter and conceal themselves by constructing nests and cabins.

Oct. 19. A remarkably warm day. I have not been more troubled by the heat this year, being a *little* more thickly clad than in summer. I walk in the middle of the street for air. The thermometer says 74° at 1 P. M. This must be Indian summer.

P. M. — Ride to Sam Barrett's mill.

Am pleased again to see the cobweb drapery of the mill. Each fine line hanging in festoons from the timbers overhead and on the sides, and on the discarded machinery lying about, is covered and greatly enlarged by a coating of meal, by which its curve is revealed, like the twigs under their ridges of snow in winter. It is like the tassels and tapestry of counterpane and dimity in a lady's bedchamber, and I pray that the cobwebs may not have been brushed away from the mills which I visit. It is as if I were aboard a man-of-war, and this

were the fine "rigging" of the mill, the sails being taken in. All things in the mill wear the same livery or drapery, down to the miller's hat and coat. I knew Barrett forty rods off in the cranberry meadow by the meal on his hat.

Barrett's apprentice, it seems, makes trays of black birch and of red maple, in a dark room under the mill. I was pleased to see this work done here, a wooden tray is so handsome. You could count the circles of growth on the end of the tray, and the dark heart of the tree was seen at each end above, producing a semicircular ornament. It was a satisfaction to be reminded that we may so easily make our own trenchers as well as fill them. To see the tree reappear on the table, instead of going to the fire or some equally coarse use, is some compensation for having it cut down. The wooden tray is still in demand to chop meat in, at least. If taken from the bench to the kitchen, they are pretty sure to crack, being made green. They should be placed to season for three months on the beams in a barn, said the miller.

Hosmer says that the rill between him and Simon Brown generally runs all night and in the fore part of the day, but then dries up, or stops, and runs again at night, or it will run all day in cloudy weather. This is perhaps because there is less evaporation then. It would be interesting to study the phenomena of this rill, so slight that it does not commonly run all day at this season, nor quite run across the road. In the scale of rivers it is at the opposite extreme to the Mississippi, which overflows so widely and makes "crevasses," and yet it interests out of proportion to its size, and I have no doubt that I might learn some of the laws of the Mississippi more easily by attending to it.

Standing on Hunt's Bridge at 5 o'clock, the sun just ready to set, I notice that its light on my note-book is quite rosy or purple, though the sun itself and its halo are merely yellow, and there is no purple in the western sky. Perhaps I might have detected a purple tinge already in the eastern sky, had I looked, and I was exactly at that distance this side the sunset where the foremost of the rosy waves of light roll in the wake of the sun, and the white page was the most suitable surface to reflect it.[1]

The lit river, purling and eddying onward, was spotted with recently fallen leaves, some of which were being carried round by eddies. Leaves are now falling all the country over: some in the swamps, concealing the water; some in woods and on hillsides, where perhaps Vulcan may find them in the spring; some by the wayside, gathered into heaps, where children are playing with them; and some are being conveyed silently seaward on rivers; concealing the water in swamps, where at length they flat out and sink to the bottom, and we never hear of them again, unless we shall see their impressions on the coal of a future geological period. Some add them to their manure-heaps; others consume them with fire. The trees repay the earth with interest for what they have taken from it. The trees are discounting.[2]

Standing on the east of the maples on the Common

[1] *Vide* Sept. 24, 1851.
[2] [*Excursions*, pp. 268, 269; Riv. 329.]

I see that their yellow, compared with the pale lemon-yellow of the elms close by, amounts to a scarlet, without noticing the bright-scarlet cheeks.[1]

Some *Chenopodium album* are purple-stemmed now, like poke long ago; some handsomely striped, purple and green.

There is no handsomer shingling and paint than the woodbine at present, covering a whole side of some houses, *viz.* the house near the almshouse and the brick house.[2]

I was the more pleased with the sight of the trays because the tools used were so simple, and they were made by hand, not by machinery. They may make equally good pails, and cheaper as well as faster, at the pail-factory with the home-made ones, but that interests me less, because the man is turned partly into a machine there himself. In this case, the workman's relation to his work is more poetic, he also shows more dexterity and is more of a man. You come away from the great factory saddened, as if the chief end of man were to make pails; but, in the case of the countryman who makes a few by hand, rainy days, the relative importance of human life and of pails is preserved, and you come away thinking of the simple and helpful life of the man, — you do not turn pale at the thought, — and would fain go to making pails yourself. We admire more the man who can use an axe or adze skillfully than him who can merely tend a machine. When labor is reduced to turning a crank it is no longer amusing nor truly profit-

[1] [*Excursions*, p. 271; Riv. 333.]
[2] [*Excursions*, p. 276; Riv. 338.]

able; but let this business become very profitable in a pecuniary sense, and so be "driven," as the phrase is, and carried on on a large scale, and the man is sunk in it, while only the pail or tray floats; we are interested in it only in the same way as the proprietor or company is.

Walked along the dam and the broad bank of the canal with Hosmer. He thought this bank proved that there were strong men here a hundred years ago or more, and that probably they used wooden shovels edged with iron, and perchance home-made, to make that bank with, for he remembered and had used them. Thus rapidly we skip back to the implements of the savage. Some call them "shod shovels."

Oct. 20. Indian summer this and the 19th. I hear of apple trees in bloom again in Waltham or Cambridge.

P. M. — To White Pond.

Another remarkably warm and pleasant day, if not too hot for walking; 74° at 2 P. M. Thought I would like to see the glassy gleaming surface of White Pond. I think that this is the acme of the fall generally,[1] — not quite of sugar maples perhaps, — and it is this remarkable heat which this time, more than anything, methinks, has caused the leaves to fall.[2] It has suddenly perfectly ripened and wilted them, and now, with a puff of wind, they come showering down on land and water, making a sound like rain. They are thickly strewn under their respective trees in the Corner road, and wagons roll over

[1] Or say the 21st.
[2] There has been no frost for some days.

them as a shadow. Rain and frost and unusual heat, succeeded by wind, all have to do with the fall of the leaf. No doubt the leaves suddenly ripen to their fall in intense heat, such as this, just as peaches, etc., over softened and ripened, fall.[1] As I go through Hubbard's fields, I see that the cows have got into the shade of trees as in July. The black birch in this grove is in the midst of its fall, perfectly yellow.[2] But these delicately tinted leaves will wilt and fade even in your hat on your way home. Their colors are very fugacious. They must be seen on the tree or under it. You cannot easily carry this splendor home.

The tupelos appear to fall early. I have not seen one with leaves since the 16th.

It is so warm that even the tipulidæ appear to prefer the shade. There they continue their dance, balancing to partners, as it seems, and by a fine hum remind me of summer still, when now the air generally is rather empty of insect sounds. Also I see yellow butterflies chasing one another, taking no thought for the morrow, but confiding in the sunny day as if it were to be perpetual. There is a haze between me and the nearest woods, as thick as the thickest in summer. My black clothes are white with the gossamer they have caught in coming through the fields, for it streams from every stubble, though it is not remarkably abundant. Flocks of this gossamer, like tangled skeins, float gently through

[1] [*Excursions*, pp. 265, 266; Riv. 325, 326.]
[2] 22d, 1855. As I pass this grove, I see the open ground strewn and colored with the yellow leaves which have been wafted from a large black birch.

the quiet air as high as my head, like white parachutes to unseen balloons.

From the higher ground west of the stump-fence field. The stagnant river gleams like liquid gossamer in the sun, and I can hardly distinguish the sparkle occasioned by an insect from the white breast of a duck. Methinks the jay, panting with heat, is silenced for a time.

Green leaves are doubtless handsome in their season, but now that we behold these ripe ones, we are inclined to think that the former are handsome somewhat as green fruits are, as green apples and melons. It would give our eyes the dysentery to look only on green leaves always. At this season each leaf becomes a laboratory in which the fairest and brightest colors are compounded.

There is one advantage in walking eastward these afternoons, at least, that in returning you may have the western sky before you.

Hickories, and some oaks even, are now overdone. They remind me of a loaf of brown bread perfectly baked in the oven, in whose cracks I see the yellowish inside contrasting with the brown crust. Some small red maples still stand yellow within the woods.

As I look over the smooth gleaming surface of White Pond, I am attracted by the sun-sparkles on it, as if fiery serpents were crossing to and fro. Yet if you were there you would find only insignificant insects.

As I come up from the pond, I am grateful for the fresh easterly breeze at last thickening the haze on that side and driving it in on us, for Nature must preserve her equilibrium. However, it is not much cooler.

As I approached the pond, I saw a hind in a potato-

field (digging potatoes), who stood stock-still for ten minutes to gaze at me in mute astonishment, till I had sunk into the woods amid the hills about the pond, and when I emerged again, there he was, motionless still, on the same spot, with his eye on me, resting on his idle hoe, as one might watch at the mouth of a fox's hole to see him come out. Perchance he may have thought *nihil humanum*, etc., or else he was transfixed with thought, — which is worth a bushel or two of potatoes, whatever his employer may say, — contrasting his condition with my own, and though he stood so still, civilization made some progress. But I must hasten away or he'll lose his day. I was as indifferent to his eyeshot as a tree walking, for I am used to such things. Perchance he will relate his adventure when he gets home at night, and what he has seen, though he did not have to light a candle this time. I am in a fair way to become a valuable citizen to him, as he is to me. He raises potatoes in the field for me; I raise curiosity in him. He stirs the earth; I stir him. What a power am I! I cause the potatoes to rot in the ground. I affect distant markets surely. But he shall not spoil my day; I will get in my harvest nevertheless. This will be nuts to him when the winter evenings come; he will tell his dream then. Talk of reaping-machines! I did not go into that field at all. I did not meddle with the potatoes. He was the only crop I gathered at a glance. Perchance he thought, "I harvest potatoes; he harvests me!"

W. W. introduced me to his brother in the road. The latter was not only a better-dressed but a higher-cultured man than the other, yet looking remarkably like him, —

his brother! In all cases we esteem rather the suggested ideal than the actual man, and it is remarkable that so many men have an actual brother, an improved edition of themselves, to whom we are introduced at last. Is he his brother, or his other self? I expect to be introduced to the ideal Mr. W. one of these days and then cut the acquaintance of the actual one.

It is remarkable that yellow and bright scarlet in the autumnal tints are generally interchangeable. I see it now even in the case of the scarlet oak, for here is a yellow one. Shade turns scarlet to yellow. So you would say that scarlet was intense yellow, more cooked, nearer the sun, like Mars. Red maple is either scarlet or yellow,[1] *Rhus Toxicodendron*, etc., etc. So with black scrub oaks, etc., etc.[2] Many plants which in the summer show a few red or scarlet leaves at length are all yellow only, as horehound now.[3] Others begin with yellow and end with a brilliant scarlet.[4]

The large crickets now swarm in dry paths, each at the mouth of its burrow, as I notice when crossing to Martial Miles's.

The broad hairy leaves or blades of the *Panicum clandestinum* are turned to a very dark purple in cultivated potato-fields.

A white-throated sparrow.

[1] *Vide* 15th, 1857.
[2] As meadow-sweet, tupelo even, high blueberry in shade, the 31st, red oak; and the russet leaves, as barberry, apple, etc.
[3] *Diplopappus linariifolius* in shade yellow, in sun purple, last of October.
[4] *Vide* 24th. Some blue-stemmed goldenrod yellow, some purple, Nov. 10th.

On Money-Diggers' Hill-side, the *Andropogon scoparius* now stands in tufts two feet high by one wide, with little whitish plumes along the upper half of its reddish fawn-colored (?) culms. Now in low grounds the different species of bidens or beggar's-ticks adhere to your clothes. These bidents, tridents, quadridents are shot into you by myriads of unnoticed foes.

Oct. 21. Cooler to-day, yet pleasant.

6 A. M. — Up Assabet.

Most leaves now on the water. They fell yesterday, — white and red maple, swamp white oak, white birch, black and red oak, hemlock (which has begun to fall), hop-hornbeam, etc., etc. They cover the water thickly, concealing all along the south side for half a rod to a rod in width, and at the rocks, where they are met and stopped by the easterly breeze, form a broad and dense crescent quite across the river.

On the hilltop, the sun having just risen, I see on my note-book that same rosy or purple light, when contrasted with the shade of another leaf, which I saw on the evening of the 19th, though perhaps I can detect a *little* purple in the eastern horizon.

The *Populus grandidentata* is quite yellow and leafy yet,[1] — the most showy tree thereabouts.

P. M. — Up Assabet, for a new mast, the old being broken in passing under a bridge.

Talked with the lame Haynes, the fisherman. He feels sure that they were not "suckers" which I saw rise to

[1] *Vide* 16th, 1857.

the shad-flies, but chivin, and that suckers do not rise to a fly nor leap out. He has seen a great many little lamprey eels come down the rivers, about as long as his finger, attached to shad. But never knew the old to come down. Thinks they die attached to roots. Has seen them half dead thus. Says the spawn is quite at the bottom of the heap. Like Witherell, he wonders how the eels increase, since he could never find any spawn in them.

The large sugar maples on the Common are in the midst of their fall to-day.

Oct. 22. P. M. — To Cliffs and Walden.

A thickly overcast yet thick and hazy day.

I see a Lombardy poplar or two yellowing at last; many leaves clear and handsome yellow. They thus, like the balm-of-Gilead and aspens, show their relation to the willows. Horse-chestnuts are yellow and apparently in prime. I see locusts are generally yellow but thinly leaved, and those at extremities.

Going by Farrar's field bought of John Reynolds, I examined those singular barren spots produced by putting on too much meadow mud of a certain quality. In some places the sod was entirely gone; there was no grass and only a small sandy desert with the yellowish *Fimbristylis capillaris* and sorrel on it. In most places this sand was quite thickly covered with sarothra, now withered and making a dark show at a distance, and sorrel, which had not risen from the surface. These are both sour-juiced plants. It was surprising how completely the grass had been killed.

I see the small narrow leaves of the *Aster dumosus* and also the yet finer ones of the *Diplopappus linariifolius* in wood-paths, turned a clear light-yellow. The sagittate leaves of the *Viola ovata*, too, now flat in the path, and the prettily divided leaves or fingers of the *V. pedata*, with purple petioles (also fallen flatter than usual ?), are both turned a clear handsome light-yellow. Also the *V. cucullata* is turned yellow. These are far more conspicuous now than ever before, contrasted with the green grass; so that you do not recognize them at first on account of their very conspicuousness or brightness of color.

Many other small plants have changed now, whose color we do not notice in the midst of the general changing. Even the *Lycopodium complanatum* (evergreen) is turned a light yellow (a part of it) in its season, like the pines (or evergreen trees).

I go up the hill from the spring. Oaks (except the scarlet), especially the small oaks, are generally withered or withering, yet most would not suspect it at a little distance, they have so much color yet. Yet, this year at least, they must have been withered more by heat than frost, for we have had very hot weather and little if any frost since the oaks generally changed. Many of the small scarlet ones are withered too, but the larger scarlet appear to be in their prime now. Some large white, black, and red are still pretty fresh.

It is very agreeable to observe now from an eminence the different tints of red and brown in an oak sprout-land or young woodland, the brownish predominating. The chocolate is one. Some will tell you that they prefer these more sober colors which the landscape wears

Vol. XI

at present to the bright ones it exhibited a few days ago, as some prefer the sweet brown crust to the yellow inside. It is interesting to observe how gradually but steadily the woods advance through deeper and deeper shades of brown to their fall. You can tell the young white oak in the midst of the sprout-land by its light-brown color, almost like that of the russet fields seen beyond, also the scarlet by its brighter red,[1] but the pines are now the brightest of them all.

Apple orchards throughout the village, or on lower and rich ground, are quite green, but on this drier Fair Haven Hill all the apple trees are yellow, with a sprinkling of green and occasionally a tinge of scarlet, *i. e.* are russet.

I can see the red of young oaks as far as the horizon on some sides.

I think that the yellows, as birches, etc., are the most distinct this very thick and cloudy day in which there is no sun, but when the sun shines the reds are lit up more and glow.

The oaks stand browned and crisped (amid the pines), their bright colors for the most part burnt out, like a loaf that is baked, and suggest an equal wholesomeness. The whole tree is now not only ripe but, as it were, a fruit perfectly cooked by the sun. That same sun which called forth its leaves in the spring has now, aided by the frost, sealed up their fountains for the year and withered them. The order has gone forth for them to rest. As each tree casts its leaves it stands careless and free, like a horse freed from his harness, or like one who

[1] *Vide* 25th.

has done his year's work and now stands unnoticed, but with concentrated strength and contentment, ready to brave the blasts of winter without a murmur.

You get very near wood ducks with a boat nowadays.

I see, from the Cliffs, that color has run through the shrub oak plain like a fire or a wave, not omitting a single tree, though I had not expected it, — large oaks do not turn so completely, — and now is for the most part burnt out for want of fuel, *i. e.* excepting the scarlet ones. The brown and chocolate colors prevail there. That birch swamp under the Cliff is very interesting. The birches are now but thinly clad and that at top, its flame-shaped top more like flames than ever now. At this distance their bare slender stems are very distinct, dense, and parallel, apparently on a somewhat smoky ground (caused by the bare twigs), and this pretty thicket of dense parallel stems is crowned or surmounted by little cones or crescents of golden spangles.

Hear a cuckoo and grackles.

The birches have been steadily changing and falling for a long, long time. The lowermost leaves turn golden and fall first; so their autumn change is like a fire which has steadily burned up higher and higher, consuming the fuel below, till now it has nearly reached their tops. These are quite distinct from the reddish misty maze below, if they are young trees (*vide* sketch), or the fine and close parallel white stems if they are larger. Nevertheless the topmost leaves at the extremities of the leaves [*sic*] are still *green*.[1]

[1] *Vide* Nov. 3d.

I am surprised to find on the top of the Cliff, near the dead white pine, some small staghorn sumachs. (Mother says she found them on the hill behind Charles Davis's!) These are now at the height of their change,[1] as is ours in the yard, turned an *orange* scarlet, not so dark as the smooth, which is now apparently fallen.[2] But ours, being in a shady and cool place, is probably later than the average, for I see that one at Flood's cottage has fallen. I *guess* that they may have been at height generally some ten days ago.

Near by, the *Aralia hispida*, turned a very clear dark red.

I see Heavy Haynes fishing in his old gray boat, sinking the stern deep. It is remarkable that, of the four fishermen who most frequent this river, — Melvin, Goodwin, and the two Hayneses, — the last three have all been fishermen of the sea, have visited the Grand Banks, and are well acquainted with Cape Cod. These fishermen who sit thus alone from morning till night must be greater philosophers than the shoemakers.

You can still pluck a variegated and handsome nose-gay on the top of the Cliff. I see a mullein freshly out, very handsome *Aster undulatus*, and an abundance of the little blue snapdragon, and some *Polygonum Persicaria*, etc., etc.

The black shrub oak on the hillside below the bear-berry fast falling and some quite bare. Some chinquapin there not fallen. Notice a chestnut quite bare. The leaves of the hickory are a very rich yellow, though they

[1] *Vide* the 5th, and the 15th, 1857.
[2] It is generally, but I see some (one or two) the 24th.

Vol. XI

These bright leaves are not the exception but the rule, for I believe that *all* leaves, even grasses, etc., etc., — *Panicum clandestinum*, — and mosses, as sphagnum, under favorable circumstances acquire brighter colors just before their fall. When you come to observe faithfully the changes of each humblest plant, you find, it may be unexpectedly, that each has sooner or later its peculiar autumnal tint or tints, though it may be rare and unobserved, as many a plant is at all seasons. And if you undertake to make a complete list of the bright tints, your list will be as long as a catalogue of the plants in your vicinity.[1]

Think how much the eyes of painters, both artisans and artists, and of the manufacturers of cloth and paper, and the paper-stainers, etc., are to be educated by these autumnal colors. The stationer's envelopes may be of very various tints, yet not so various as those of the leaves of a single tree sometimes. If you want a different shade or tint of a particular color, you have only to look further within or without the tree, or the wood.[2] The eye might thus be taught to distinguish color and appreciate a difference of tint or shade.

Oct. 23. P. M. — To Ledum Swamp.

One tells me that he saw geese go over Wayland the 17th.

Large wild cherries are half fallen or more, the few remaining leaves yellowish. Choke-cherries are bare; how long? Amelanchier bare. *Viburnum nudum* half

[1] [*Excursions*, pp. 288, 289; Riv. 354, 355.]
[2] [*Excursions*, p. 273; Riv. 335.]

may be quite withered and fallen, but they become brown. Looking to Conantum, the huckleberries are apparently fallen.

The fields are now perhaps truly and most generally russet, especially where the blackberry and other small reddish plants are seen through the fine bleached grass and stubble, — like a golden russet apple. This occurs to me, going along the side of the Well Meadow Field.

Apparently the scarlet oak, large and small (not shrubby), is in prime now, after other oaks are generally withered or withering. The clumps of *Salix tristis*, half yellow, spotted with dark-brown or blackish and half withered and turned dark ash-colored, are rather interesting. The *S. humilis* has similar dark spots.

Hornets' nests are now being exposed, deserted by the hornets; and little wasp (?) nests, one and a half inches wide, on huckleberry (?) and sweet-fern (?). White pines have for the most part fallen. All the underwood is hung with their brown fallen needles, giving to the woods an untidy appearance.

C. tells of hearing after dark the other night frequent raucous notes which were new to him, on the ammannia meadow, in the grass. Were they not meadow-hens? Rice says he saw one within a week. Have they not lingered to feed in our meadows the late warm and pleasant nights?

The haze is still very thick, though it is comparatively cool weather, and if there were no moon to-night, I think it would be very dark. Do not the darkest nights occur about this time, when there is a haze produced by the Indian-summer days, succeeded by a moonless night?

fallen or more; when wet and in shade, a light crimson. Hardhack, in low ground, where it has not withered too soon, inclines to a very light scarlet. Sweet-gale is not fallen, but a *very dull* yellowish and scarlet. You see in woods many black (?) oak sprouts, forming low bushes or clumps of green and dark crimson. (C. says they are handsome, like a mahonia.) The meadow-sweet is yellowish and yellow-scarlet. In Ledum Swamp the white azalea is a *dirty brown scarlet*, half fallen, or more. Panicled andromeda reddish-brown and half fallen. Some young high blueberry, or sprouts, never are a deeper or brighter crimson-scarlet than now. Wild holly fallen. Even the sphagnum has turned brownish-red on the exposed surfaces, in the swamp, looking like the at length blushing pellicle of the ripe globe there. The ledum is in (the midst of?) its change, rather conspicuous, yellow and light-scarlet and falling. I detect but few *Andromeda Polifolia* and *Kalmia glauca* leaves turned a light red or scarlet. The spruce is changed and falling, but is brown and inconspicuous.

A man at work on the Ledum Pool, draining it, says that, when they had ditched about six feet deep, or to the bottom, near the edge of this swamp, they came to old flags, and he thought that the whole swamp was once a pond and the flags grew by the edge of it. Thought the mud was twenty feet deep near the pool, and that he had found three growths of spruce, one above another, there. He had dug up a hard-pan with iron in it (as he thought) under a part of this swamp, and in what he cast out sorrel came up and grew, very rankly indeed.

I notice some late rue turned a very clear light yellow. I see some rose leaves (the early smooth) turned a handsome clear yellow, — and some (the *R. Carolina*) equally clear and handsome scarlet or dark red. This is the rule with it. Elder is a dirty greenish yellow and apparently mostly fallen. Beach plum is still green with some dull-red leaves, but apparently hardly any fallen. Butternuts are bare. Mountain-ash of both kinds either withered or bare.

Oct. 24. A northeast storm, though not much rain falls to-day, but a fine driving mizzle or "drisk." This, as usual, brings the geese, and at 2.30 P. M. I see two flocks go over. I hear that some were seen two or three weeks ago (??), faintly honking. A great many must go over to-day and also alight in this neighborhood. This weather warns them of the approach of winter, and this wind speeds them on their way. Surely, then, while geese fly overhead we can live here as contentedly as they do at York Factory on Hudson's Bay. We shall perchance be as well provisioned and have as good society as they. Let us be of good cheer, then, and expect the annual vessel which brings the spring to us without fail.[1]

P. M. — To Woodis Park over Hill.

The celtis has just fallen. Its leaves were apparently a yellow green. The sassafras trees are bare, — how long? — and the white ash apparently just bared. The locusts are bare except the tops, and in this respect those on the hills, at least, are as peculiar as birches. Some trees

[1] [Channing, p. 106.]

lose their lower leaves first, as birches and locusts; some the upper, as apples (though a few green leaves may remain on the very tips of the twigs) and generally maples, though the last fall fast. Hickories are two thirds fallen, at least.[1]

This rain and wind too bring down the leaves very fast. The yard is strewn with the yellow leaves of the peach and the orange and scarlet ones of the cherry. You could not spread a cloth but it would soon be strewn with them.

Thorns and balm-of-Gilead and red mulberries bare.

The brilliant autumnal colors are red and yellow and the various tints, hues, and shades of these. Blue is reserved to be the color of the sky, but yellow and red are the colors of the earth flower. Every fruit, on ripening, and just before its fall, acquires a bright tint. So do the leaves; so the sky before the end of the day, and the year near its setting. October is the red sunset sky, November the later twilight. Color stands for all ripeness and success. We have dreamed that the hero should carry his color aloft, as a symbol of the ripeness of his virtue. The noblest feature, the eye, is the fairest-colored, the jewel of the body. The warrior's flag is the flower which precedes his fruit. He unfurls his flag to the breeze with such confidence and brag as the flower its petals. Now we shall see what kind of fruit will succeed.

The very forest and herbage, the pellicle of the earth as it were, must acquire a bright color, an evidence of

[1] Apparently mocker-nut later.

its ripeness, as if the globe itself were a fruit on its stem, with ever one cheek toward the sun.

Our appetites have commonly confined our views of ripeness and its phenomena — color and mellowness and perfectness — to the fruits which we eat, and we are wont to forget that an immense harvest which we do not eat, hardly use at all, is annually ripened by nature. At our annual cattle-shows and horticultural exhibitions we make, as we think, a great show of fair fruits, destined, however, to a rather ignoble fate, fruits not worshipped for this chiefly; but round about and within our towns there is annually another show of fruits, on an infinitely grander scale, fruits which address our taste for beauty alone.

The scarlet oak, which was quite green the 12th, is now completely scarlet and apparently has been so a few days. This alone of our indigenous deciduous trees (the pitch pine is with it) is now in its glory. (I have not seen the beech, but suppose it past.[1] The *Populus grandidentata* [2] and sugar maple come nearest to it, but they have lost the greater part of their leaves.) Look at one, completely changed from green to bright dark-scarlet, every leaf, as if it had been dipped into a scarlet dye, between you and the sun. Was not this worth waiting for? Little did you think ten days ago that that cold green tree could assume such color as this. Its leaves still firmly attached while those of other trees are falling around it. I am the last to blush, but I blush deeper than any of ye. I bring up the rear in my red coat. The

[1] It is. *Vide* 25th.
[2] *Vide* 16th, 1857. And *P. tremuloides* (*vide* Nov. 2d).

scarlet oaks, alone of oaks, have not given up the fight. Perchance their leaves, so finely cut, are longer preserved partly because they present less surface to the elements, and for a long time, if I remember rightly, some scarlet oak leaves will "hold out to burn."

Now in huckleberry pastures you see only here and there a few bright scarlet or crimson (for they vary) leaves amid or above the bare reddish stems, burning as if with condensed brightness, — as if the few that remained burned with the condensed brightness of all that have fallen. In sheltered woods you [see] some dicksonia still straw-color or pale-yellow. Some thoroughwort the same color. In the shade generally you find paler and more delicate tints, fading to straw-color and white. The deep reds and scarlets and purples show exposure to the sun. I see an intensely scarlet high blueberry — but where one leaf has overlapped another it is yellow — with a regular outline.

That large hornets' nest which I saw on the 4th is now deserted, and I bring it home. But in the evening, warmed by my fire, two or three come forth and crawl over it, and I make haste to throw it out the window.

Oct. 25. P. M. — To the Beeches.

I look at the willows by the causeway, east side, as I go, — *Salix discolor, Torreyana, rostrata,* and *lucida* are all almost quite bare, and the remaining leaves are yellow or yellowish. Those of the last the clearest and most conspicuous yellow. *S. pedicellaris* is merely yellowish, being rather green and not fallen. The *S. alba* at a distance looks very silvery in the light.

Now that the leaves are fallen (for a few days), the long yellow buds (often red-pointed) which sleep along the twigs of the *S. discolor* are very conspicuous and quite interesting, already even carrying our thoughts forward to spring. I noticed them first on the 22d. They may be put with the azalea buds already noticed. Even bleak and barren November wears these *gems*[1] on her breast in sign of the coming year. How many thoughts lie undeveloped, and as it were dormant, like these buds, in the minds of men!

This is the coolest day thus far, reminding me that I have only a half-thick coat on. The easterly wind comes cold into my ear, as yet unused to it. Yet this first decided coolness — not to say wintriness — is not only bracing but exhilarating and concentrating [to] our forces. So much the more I have a hearth and heart *within* me. We step more briskly, and brace ourselves against the winter.

I see some alders about bare. Aspens (*tremuliformis*) generally bare.

Near the end of the causeway, milkweed is copiously discounting. This is much fairer than the thistle-down. It apparently bursts its pods after rain especially (as yesterday's), opening on the under side, away from succeeding rains. Half a dozen seeds or more, attached by the tips of their silks to the core of the pod, will be blown about there a long time before a strong puff launches

[1] [Thoreau underscored this word doubtless to emphasize its etymology, — from the Latin *gemma*, a bud.]

them away, and in the meanwhile they are expanding and drying their silk.

In the cut the *F. hyemalis*, which has been here for a month, flits away with its sharp twitter amid the falling leaves. This is a fall sound.

At the pond the black birches are bare; how long?

Now, as you walk in woods, the leaves rustle under your feet as much as ever. In some places you walk pushing a mass before you. In others they half cover pools that are three rods long. They make it slippery climbing hills.

Now, too, for the different shades of brown, especially in sprout-lands. I see [three] kinds of oaks now, — the whitish brown of the white oak, the yellowish brown of the black oak, and the red or purplish brown [of the scarlet oak][1] (if it can be called brown at all, for it is not faded to brown yet and looks full of life though really withered (*i. e.* the shrubs) for the most part, excepting here and there leading shoots or spring twigs, which glow as bright a scarlet as ever). There is no red here, but perhaps that may be called a lighter, yellowish brown,[2] and so distinguished from the black in color. It has more life in it now than the white and black, not withered so much. These browns are very pure and wholesome colors, far from spot and decay, and their rustling leaves call the roll for a winter campaign. How different now the rustling of these sere leaves from the soft, fluttering murmur of the same when alive! This

[1] [A loose sheet of Thoreau's manuscript, apparently of one of his lectures, in reproducing this passage supplies these missing words.]
[2] *Vide* Oct. 31st.

sharp rustle warns all to go home now who are not prepared for a winter campaign.[1]

The scarlet oak shrubs are as distinct amid the other species as before they had withered, and it is remarkable how evenly they are distributed over the hills, by some law not quite understood. Nature ever plots against Baker and Stow, Moore and Hosmer.

The black scrub oak, seen side by side with the *white*, is yet lighter than that.

How should we do without this variety of oak leaves, — the forms and colors? On many sides, the eye requires such variety (seemingly infinite) to rest on.

Chestnut trees are generally bare, showing only a thin crescent of burs, for they are very small this year. I climb one on Pine Hill, looking over Flint's Pond, which, indeed, I see from the ground. These young chestnuts growing in clumps from a stump are hard to climb, having few limbs below, far apart, and they dead and rotten.

The brightest tint of the black oaks that I remember was some yellow gleams from half green and brownish leaves; *i. e.*, the tops of the large trees have this yellowish and green look. It is a mellow yellow enough, without any red. The brightest of the red oaks were a pretty delicate scarlet, inclining to a brownish yellow, the effect enhanced by the great size of the leaf.

When, on the 22d, I was looking from the Cliffs on

[1] The fields are russet now when the oaks are brown, especially where the red blackberry vine tinges [?], and continue so to be for a week or two, as Nov. 3d.

the shrub oak plain, etc., calling some of the brightest tints flame-like, I saw the flames of a burning — for we see their smokes of late — two or three miles distant in Lincoln rise above the red shrubbery, and saw how in intensity and brilliancy the real flame distanced all colors, even by day.

Now, especially, we notice not only the silvery leaves of the *Salix alba* but the silvery sheen of pine-needles; *i. e.*, when its old leaves have fallen and trees generally are mostly bare, in the cool Novemberish air and light we observe and enjoy the trembling shimmer and gleam of the pine-needles. I do not know why we perceive this more at this season, unless because the air is so clear and all surfaces reflect more light; and, besides, all the needles now left are fresh ones, or the growth of this year. Also I notice, when the sun is low, the light reflected from the parallel twigs of birches recently bare, etc., like the gleam from gossamer lines. This is another Novemberish phenomenon. Call these November Lights. Hers is a cool, silvery light.

In November consider the sharp, dry rustle of withered leaves; the cool, silvery, and shimmering gleams of light, as above; the fresh bright buds formed and exposed along the twigs; walnuts.

The leaves of the *Populus grandidentata*, though half fallen and turned a pure and handsome yellow, are still wagging as fast as ever. These do not lose their color and wither on the tree like oaks and beeches and some of their allies, and hickories, too, and buttonwood, neither do maples, nor birches quite, nor willows (except the *Salix tristis* and perhaps some of the next allied);[1] — but they are fresh and unwilted, full of sap and fair as ever when they are first strewn on the ground. I do not think of any tree whose leaves are so fresh and fair when they fall.

The beech has just fairly turned brown of different shades, but not yet crisped or quite withered. Only the young in the shade of the woods are yet green and yellow. Half the leaves of the last are a light yellow with a green midrib, and are quite light and bright seen through the woods. The lower parts, too, of the large tree are yellow yet. I should put this tree, then, either with the main body of the oaks or between them and the scarlet oak. I have not seen enough to judge of their beauty.

Returning in an old wood-path from top of Pine Hill to Goose Pond, I see many goldenrods turned purple — all the leaves. Some of them are *Solidago cæsia* and some (I think) *S. puberula*. Many goldenrods, as *S. odorata*, turn yellow or paler. The *Aster undulatus* is now a dark purple (its leaves), with brighter purple or crimson under sides. The *Viburnum dentatum* leaves, which are rather thin now, are drooping like the *Cornus sericea* (although fresh), and are mixed purplish and light green.

Oct. 26. The sugar maples are about bare, except a few small ones.

Minott remembers how he used to chop beech wood. He says that when frozen it is hard and brittle just like glass, and you must look out for the chips, for, if they strike you in the face, they will cut like a knife.

[1] *Vide* 27th *inst.*

He says that some call the stake-driver "belcher-squelcher," and some, "wollerkertoot." I used to call them "pump-er-gor'." Some say "slug-toot."

The largest scarlet oak that I remember hereabouts stands by the penthorum pool in the Sleepy Hollow cemetery, and is now in its prime. I found the sap was flowing fast in it.[1] White birches, elms, chestnuts, *Salix alba* (small willows), and white maple are a long time falling. The scarlet oak generally is not in prime till now, or even later.

I wear a thicker coat, my single thick fall coat, at last, and begin to feel my fingers cool early and late.

One shopkeeper has hung out woollen gloves and even thick buckskin mittens by his door, foreseeing what his customers will want as soon as it is finger-cold, and determined to get the start of his fellows.

Oct. 27. P. M. — Sail to Fair Haven Pond.

A moderate northerly wind and pleasant, clear day. There is a slight rustle from the withered pontederia. The *Scirpus lacustris*, which was all conspicuously green on the 16th, has changed to a dull or brownish yellow. The bayonet rush also has partly changed, and now, the river being perhaps lower than before this season, shows its rainbow colors, though dull. It depends, then, on the river being low at an earlier period, say a month ago at least, when this juncus is in its full vigor, — though then, of course, you would not get the yellow! — that the colors may be bright. I distinguish four colors now, perfectly horizontal and parallel bars, as it were, six or

[1] Also in another Nov. 2d. It had a pleasant acorn-like taste.

eight inches wide as you look at the side of a dense patch along the shallow shore. The lowest is a dull red, the next clear green, then dull yellowish, and then dark brown. These colors, though never brilliant, are yet noticeable, and, when you look at a long and dense patch, have a rainbow-like effect. The red (or pinkish) is that part which has been recently submerged; the green, that which has not withered; the yellowish, what has changed; and the brown, the withered extremity, since it dies downward gradually from the tip to the bottom. The amount of it is that it decays gradually, beginning at the top, and throughout a large patch one keeps pace with another, and different parts of the plant being in different stages or states at the same time and, moreover, the whole being of a uniform height, a particular color in one plant corresponds exactly to the same in another, and so, though a single stalk would not attract attention, when seen in the mass they have this singular effect. I call it, therefore, the rainbow rush. When, moreover, you see it reflected in the water, the effect is very much increased.

The leaves of the *Salix cordata* are now generally withered and many more fallen. They are light-brown, and many remain on the twigs, so many that this willow and the *tristis* I think must be peculiar in this respect [1] as well as its [*sic*] turning scarlet. Some others, as the *sericea*, are still yellow and greenish and have not been touched by frost. They must be tougher.

At the east shore of Fair Haven Pond I see that clams have been moving close to the water's edge. They have

[1] Yes.

just moved a few feet toward the deeper water, but they came round a little, like a single wheel on its edge.

Alders are fallen without any noticeable change of color. The leaves of young oaks are now generally withered, but many leaves of large oaks are greenish or alive yet. Many of them fall before withering. I see some now three quarters bare, with many living leaves left. Is it not because on larger trees they are raised above the effect of frost?

We have a cool, white sunset, Novemberish, and no redness to warm our thoughts.

Not only the leaves of trees and shrubs and flowers have been changing and withering, but almost countless sedges and grasses. They become pale-brown and bleached after the frost has killed them, and give that peculiar light, almost silvery, sheen to the fields in November. The colors of the fields make haste to harmonize with the snowy mantle which is soon to invest them and with the cool, white twilights of that season which is itself the twilight of the year. They become more and more the color of the frost which rests on them. Think of the interminable forest of grasses which dies down to the ground every autumn! What a more than Xerxean army of wool-grasses and sedges without fame lie down to an ignominious death, as the mowers esteem it, in our river meadows each year, and become "old fog" to trouble the mowers, lodging as they fall, that might have been the straw beds of horses and cattle, tucked under them every night!

The fine-culmed purple grass, which lately we admired so much, is now bleached as light as any of them.

Culms and leaves robbed of their color and withered by cold. This is what makes November — and the light reflected from the bleached culms of grasses and the bare twigs of trees! When many hard frosts have formed and melted on the fields and stiffened grass, they leave them almost as silvery as themselves. There is hardly a surface to absorb the light.

It is remarkable that the autumnal change of our woods has left no deeper impression on our literature yet.[1] There is no record of it in English poetry, apparently because, according to all accounts, the trees acquire but few bright colors there. Neither do I know any adequate notice of it in our own youthful literature, nor in the traditions of the Indians. One would say it was the very phenomenon to have caught a savage eye, so devoted to bright colors. In our poetry and science there are many references to this phenomenon, but it has received no such particular attention as it deserves. High-colored as are most political speeches, I do not detect any reflection, even, from the autumnal tints in them. They are as colorless and lifeless as the herbage in November.

The year, with these dazzling colors on its margin, lies spread open like an illustrated volume. The preacher does not utter the essence of its teaching.

A great many, indeed, have never seen this, the flower, or rather ripe fruit, of the year, — many who have spent their lives in towns and never chanced to come into the country at this season. I remember riding with one such citizen, who, though a fortnight too late for the most

[1] [Excursions, p. 249; Riv. 305.]

Vol. XI

merely indicate faintly our good intentions, giving them in our despair a terminal twist toward our mark, — such as reddish, yellowish, purplish, etc. We cannot make a hue of words, for they are not to be compounded like colors, and hence we are obliged to use such ineffectual expressions as reddish brown, etc. They need to be ground together.

Oct. 28. Cattle coming down from up country.

P. M. — Up Assabet to Cedar Swamp.

Here is an Indian-summer day. Not so warm, indeed, as the 19th and 20th, but warm enough for pleasure.

The majority of the white maples are bare, but others are still thickly leaved, the leaves being a greenish yellow. It appears, then, that they hold their leaves longer than our other maples, or most trees. The majority of them do not acquire a bright tint at all, and, though interesting for their early summer blush, their autumnal colors are not remarkable.

The dogwood on the island is perhaps in its prime,[1] — a distinct scarlet, with half of the leaves green in this case. Apparently none have fallen. I see yet also some *Cornus sericea* bushes with leaves turned a clear dark but dull red, rather handsome. Some large red oaks are still as bright as ever, and that is here a brownish yellow, with leaves partly withered; and some are already quite bare.[2] Swamp white oak withers apparently with the white. Some of both are still partly greenish, while others of both are bare.

[1] *Vide* Nov. 5th.   [2] *Vide* 31st.

brilliant tints, was taken by surprise, and would not believe that the tints had been any brighter. He had never heard of this phenomenon before.

October has not *colored* our poetry yet.

Not only many have never witnessed this phenomenon, but it is scarcely remembered by the majority from year to year.[1]

It is impossible to describe the infinite variety of hues, tints, and shades, for the language affords no names for them, and we must apply the same term monotonously to twenty different things. If I could exhibit so many different trees, or only leaves, the effect would be different. When the tints are the same they differ so much in purity and delicacy that language, to describe them truly, would have not only to be greatly enriched, but as it were dyed to the same colors herself, and speak to the eye as well as to the ear. And it is these subtle differences which especially attract and charm our eyes. Where else will you study color under such advantages? What other school of design can vie with this?[2] To describe these colored leaves you must use colored words. How tame and ineffectual must be the words with which we attempt to describe that subtle difference of tint which so charms the eye? Who will undertake to describe in words the difference in tint between two neighboring leaves on the same tree? or of two thousand? — for by so many the eye is addressed in a glance. In describing the richly spotted leaves, for instance, how often we find ourselves using ineffectually words which

[1] [Excursions, p. 249; Riv. 305, 306.]
[2] [Excursions, p. 273; Riv. 335.]

How handsome the great red oak acorns now! I stand under the tree on Emerson's lot. They are still falling. I heard one fall into the water as I approached, and thought that a musquash had plunged. They strew the ground and the bottom of the river thickly, and while I stand here I hear one strike the boughs with force as it comes down, and drop into the water. The part that was covered by the cup is whitish-woolly. How munificent is Nature to create this profusion of wild fruit, as it were merely to gratify our eyes! Though inedible they are more wholesome to my immortal part, and stand by me longer, than the fruits which I eat. If they had been plums or chestnuts I should have eaten them on the spot and probably forgotten them. They would have afforded only a momentary gratification, but being acorns, I remember, and as it were *feed* on, them still. They are untasted fruits forever in store for me. I know not of their flavor as yet. That is postponed to some still unimagined winter evening. These which we admire but do not eat are nuts of the gods. When time is no more we shall crack them. I cannot help liking them better than horse-chestnuts, which are of a similar color, not only because they are of a much handsomer form, but because they are indigenous. What hale plump fellows they are! They can afford not to be useful to me, nor to know me or be known by me. They go their way, I go mine, and it turns out that sometimes I go *after* them.

The hemlock is in the midst of its fall, and the leaves strew the ground like grain. They are inconspicuous on the tree.

The *Populus grandidentata* leaves are not all fallen yet. This, then, is late to lose its leaves, later, rather, than the sugar maple. Its leaves are large and conspicuous on the ground, and from their freshness make a great show there. It is later to fall than the *tremuliformis*,[1] as it was later to bloom.

I now begin to notice the evergreen ferns, when the others are all withered or fallen. The black willows have been bare some time. Panicled andromeda and winterberry are about bare. Pitch pines are falling; and white cedars are apparently in the midst of their fall, turning a pale brown and strewing the ground.

There are now but few bright leaves to be seen,[2] *viz.*: —

3. Pitch pine (though most is faded on the trees).
2. Larch.
1. Scarlet oak.
4. *Populus grandidentata*[3] (thin-leaved).[4]
6. A few yellow leaves on young willows, coniferous ones and *S. sericea* especially, still holding on to the extremity of the twigs.
8. Some crimson *Viburnum nudum* (thin-leaved).
9. Meadow-sweet.
10. Some *Viburnum dentatum*, greenish purple (thin-leaved, not conspicuous).
5. Some small white birch tops.
5. High blueberry (more common than last).

[1] No. *Vide* [p. 261].
[2] *Vide* the 9th and onward.
[3] Some on the 5th.
[4] (4) *P. tremuloides*, thicker-leaved, but rather duller than last.

7. Some silky cornel.
14. Flowering dogwood.[1]
11. Gooseberry.
12. Common wild rose, yellow inclining to scarlet.
12. *Rosa Carolina* (clear dark red) and sweet-briar.
13. Staghorn sumach, in cool places and shaded.

Numbered in the order of their importance, most being either very thin-leaved now, or rare.

Oct. 29. 6.30 A. M. — Very hard frost these mornings; the grasses, to their finest branches, clothed with it.

The cat comes stealthily creeping towards some prey amid the withered flowers in the garden, which being disturbed by my approach, she runs low toward it with an unusual glare or superficial light in her eye, ignoring her oldest acquaintance, as wild as her remotest ancestor; and presently I see the first tree sparrow hopping there. I hear them also amid the alders by the river, singing sweetly, — but a few notes.

Notwithstanding the few handsome scarlet oaks that may yet be found, and the larches and pitch pines and the few thin-leaved *Populus grandidentata*, the brightness of the foliage, generally speaking, is past.

P. M. — To Baker Farm, on foot.

The *Salix Torreyana* on the right has but few leaves near the extremities (like the *S. sericea* of the river), and is later to fall than the *S. rostrata* near by. Its leaves turn merely a brownish yellow, and not scarlet like the *cordata*, so that it is not allied to that in this respect.

[1] Not yet at height. *Vide* Nov. 5.

Vol. XI

(In *S. tristis* path about Well Meadow Field the *S. tristis* is mostly fallen or withered on the twigs, and the curled leaves lie thickly like ashes about the bases of the shrubs.)

Notice the fuzzy black and reddish caterpillars on ground.

I look north from the causeway at Heywood's meadow. How rich some scarlet oaks imbosomed in pines, their branches (still bright) intimately intermingled with the pine! They have their full effect there. The pine boughs are the green calyx to its [*sic*] petals. Without these pines for contrast the autumnal tints would lose a considerable part of their effect.

The white birches being now generally bare, they stand along the east side of Heywood's meadow slender, parallel white stems, revealed in a pretty reddish maze produced by their fine branches. It is a lesser and denser smoke (?) than the maple one. The branches must be thick, like those of maples and birches, to give the effect of smoke, and most trees have fewer and coarser branches, or do not grow in such dense masses.

Nature now, like an athlete, begins to strip herself in earnest for her contest with her great antagonist Winter. In the bare trees and twigs what a display of muscle!

Looking toward Spanish Brook, I see the white pines, a clear green, rising amid and above the pitch pines, which are parti-colored, glowing internally with the warm yellow of the old leaves. Of our Concord evergreens, only the white and pitch pines are interesting in their change, for only their leaves are bright and conspicuous enough.

I notice a barberry bush in the woods[1] still thickly clothed, but merely yellowish-green, not showy. Is not this commonly the case with the introduced European plants? Have they not European habits? And are they not also late to fall, killed before they are ripe? — *e. g.* the quince, apple, pear(?), barberry, silvery abele, privet, plum(?), white willow, weeping willow, lilac, hawthorn (the horse-chestnut and European mountain-ash are distincter yellow, and the Scotch larch is at least as bright as ours at same time; the Lombardy poplar is a handsome yellow (some branches early), and the cultivated cherry is quite handsome orange, often yellowish), which, with exceptions in parenthesis, are inglorious in their decay.

As the perfect winged and usually bright-colored insect is but short-lived, so the leaves ripen but to fall.

I go along the wooded hillside southwest of Spanish Brook. With the fall of the white pine, etc., the *Pyrola umbellata* and the lycopodiums, and even evergreen ferns, suddenly emerge as from obscurity. If these plants are to be evergreen, how much they require this brown and withered carpet to be spread under them for effect. Now, too, the light is let in to show them. Cold(?)-blooded wood frogs hop[2] about amid the cool ferns and lycopodiums.

Am surprised to see, by the path to Baker Farm, a very tall and slender large *Populus tremuliformis* still thickly clothed with leaves which are merely yellowish-green, later than any *P. grandidentata* I know. It must

[1] And elsewhere the same.
[2] Or earlier?

be owing to its height above frosts, for the leaves of sprouts are fallen and withered some time, and of young trees commonly. Afterwards, when on the Cliff, I perceive that, birches being bare (or as good as bare), one or two poplars — I am not sure which species — take [1] their places on the Shrub Oak Plain, and are brighter than they were, for they hold out to burn longer than the birch. The birch has now generally dropped its golden spangles, and those oak sprout-lands where they glowed are now an almost uniform brown red. Or, strictly speaking, they are pale-brown, mottled with dull red where the small scarlet oak stands.[2]

I find the white pine cones, which have long since opened, hard to come off.

The thickly fallen leaves make it slippery in the woods, especially climbing hills, as the Cliffs. The late wood tortoise and squirrel betrayed.

Apple trees, though many are thick-leaved, are in the midst of their fall. Our English cherry has fallen. The silvery abele is still densely leaved, and green, or at most a yellowish green. The lilac still thickly leaved; a yellowish green or greenish yellow as the case may be. Privet thickly leaved, yellowish-green.

If these plants acquire brighter tints in Europe, then one would say that they did not fully ripen their leaves here before they were killed. The orchard trees are not for beauty, but use. English plants have English habits here: they are not yet acclimated; they are early or late as if ours were an English spring or autumn; and no

[1] *Tremuloides*, bright at distance. *Vide* Nov. 2d.
[2] Shrub oaks withered. *Vide* Nov. 2d.

doubt in course of time a change will be produced in their constitutions similar to that which is observed in the English man here.

Oct. 30. Rain and wind, bringing down the leaves and destroying the little remaining brilliancy. The buttonwoods are in the midst of their fall. Some are bare. They are late among the trees of the street.

I see that Prichard's mountain-ash (European) has lately put forth new leaves when all the old have fallen, and they are four or five inches long! But the American has not started. It knows better.

Beware how you meddle with a buttonwood stump. I remember when one undertook to dig a large one up that he might set a front-yard post on the spot, but I forget how much it cost, or how many weeks one man was about it before it was all cut up and removed. It would have been better to set the post *in* it. One man who has just cut down a buttonwood had it disposed of, all but eight feet of the butt, when a neighbor offered him five cents for it, and though it contained a cord of wood, he, as he says, "took him up mighty quick," for if a man's time were of value he could not afford to be splitting it.

In Rees's Cyclopædia, under the head of the Fall of the Leaf, mention is made of the leaves at this season "changing their healthy green color to more or less of a yellow, sometimes a reddish hue." And after speaking of the remarkable brilliancy of the American forests, he says that some European plants allied to the brilliant American ones assume bright hues in the fall.

What is commonly described as the autumnal tints of the oaks generally, is for the most part those tints or hues which they have when partially withered, corresponding to those which those of more truly deciduous trees have when freshly fallen, and not merely the tints of their maturity, as in the maple, etc. It may account for this to say that the scarlet oak especially withers very slowly and gradually, and retains some brightness to the middle of November, and large red and black and swamp white oaks, especially the two last (or excepting some of the first), are not commonly so interesting in the maturity of their leaves as before or after.

Oct. 31. P. M. — To Conantum.

Our currants bare; how long?

The Italian poplars are now a dull greenish yellow, not nearly so fair as the few leaves that had turned some time ago. Some silvery abeles are the same color.[1] I go over the Hubbard Bridge causeway. The young *Salix alba* osiers are just bare, or nearly so, and the yellow twigs accordingly begin to show.

It is a fine day, Indian-summer-like, and there is considerable gossamer on the causeway and blowing from all trees. That warm weather of the 19th and 20th was, methinks, the same sort of weather with the most pleasant in November (which last alone some allow to be Indian summer), only more to be expected.

I see many red oaks, thickly leaved, fresh and at the height of their tint. These are pretty clear yellow. It is much clearer yellow than any black oak, but some others

[1] But both turn more yellow.

are about bare. These and scarlet oaks, which are yet more numerous, are the only oaks not withered that I notice to-day, except one middle-sized white oak probably protected from frost under Lee's Cliff.

Between the absolutely deciduous plants and the evergreens are all degrees, not only those which retain their withered leaves all winter, but those, commonly called evergreen, which, though slow to change, yet acquire at last a ruddy color while they keep their leaves, as the lambkill and water andromeda (?).

Get a good sight on Conantum of a sparrow (such as I have seen in flocks some time), which utters a sharp *te-te-te* quickly repeated as it flies, sitting on a wall three or four rods off. I see that it is rather long and slender, is perhaps dusky-ash above with some black backward; has a pretty long black bill, a white ring about eye, white chin and line under cheek, a black (or dark) spotted breast and dirty cream-color beneath; legs long and slender and perhaps reddish-brown, two faint light bars on wings; but, what distinguishes it more, it keeps gently jerking or tossing its tail as it sits, and when a flock flies over you see the tails distinctly black beneath. Though I detected no yellow, yet I think from the note that it must be the shore lark (such as I saw March 24th) in their fall plumage. They are a common bird at this season, I think.[1]

I see a middle-sized red oak side by side with a black one under Lee's Cliff. The first is still pretty fresh, the latter completely withered. The withered leaves of the first are flat, apparently thin, and a yellowish brown;

[1] [Titlarks?]

those of the black are much curled and a very different and dark brown, and look thicker.

Barberry generally is thickly leaved and only somewhat yellowish or scarlet, say russet.

I tasted some of the very small grapes on Blackberry Steep, such as I had a jelly made of. Though shrivelled, and therefore ripe, they are very acid and inedible.

The slippery elm has a few scattered leaves on it, while the common close by is bare. So I think the former is later to fall. You may well call it bare.

The cedar at Lee's Cliff has apparently just fallen, — almost.

As I sit on the Cliff there, the sun is now getting low, and the woods in Lincoln south and east of me are lit up by its more level rays, and there is brought out a more brilliant redness in the scarlet oaks, scattered so equally over the forest, than you would have believed was in them. Every tree of this species which is visible in these directions, even to the horizon, now stands out distinctly red. Some great ones lift their red backs high above the woods near the Codman place, like huge roses with a myriad fine petals, and some more slender ones, in a small grove of white pines on Pine Hill in the east, in the very horizon, alternating with the pines on the edge of the grove and shouldering them with their red coats, — an intense, burning red which would lose some of its strength, methinks, with every step you might take toward them, — look like soldiers in red amid hunters in green. This time it is *Lincoln* green, too. Until the sun thus lit them up you would not have believed that there were so many redcoats in the forest army. Looking

westward, their colors are lost in a blaze of light, but in other directions the whole forest is a flower-garden, in which these late roses burn, alternating with green, while the so-called "gardeners," working here and there, perchance, beneath, with spade and water-pot, see only a few little asters amid withered leaves, for the shade that lurks amid their foliage does not report itself at this distance. They are unanimously red. The focus of their reflected [color] is in the atmosphere far on this side. Every such tree, especially in the horizon, becomes a nucleus of red, as it were, where, with the declining sun, the redness grows and glows like a cloud. It only has some comparatively dull-red leaves for a nucleus and to start it, and it becomes an intense scarlet or red mist, or fire which finds fuel for itself in the very atmosphere. I have no doubt that you would be disappointed in the brilliancy of those trees if you were to walk to them. You see a redder tree than exists. It is a strong red, which gathers strength from the air on its way to your eye. It is partly borrowed fire, borrowed of the sun. The scarlet oak asks the clear sky and the brightness of the Indian summer. These bring out its color. If the sun goes into a cloud they become indistinct.

These are my China asters, my late garden flowers. It costs me nothing for a gardener. The falling leaves, all over the forest, are protecting the roots of my plants. Only look at what is to be seen, and you will have garden enough, without deepening the soil of your yard. We have only to elevate our view a little to see the whole forest as a garden.[1]

[1] [*Excursions*, pp. 282–284; Riv. 346–349.]

To my surprise, the only yellow that I see amid the universal red and green and chocolate is one large tree-top in the forest, a mile off in the east, across the pond, which by its form and color I know to be my late acquaintance the tall aspen (*tremuliformis*) of the 29th. It, too, is far more yellow at this distance than it was close at hand, and so are the Lombardy poplars in our streets. The *Salix alba*, too, looks yellower at a distance now. Their dull-brown and green colors do not report themselves so far, while the yellow *crescit eundo*, and we see the sun reflected in it. After walking for a couple of hours the other day through the woods, I came to the base of a tall aspen, which I do not remember to have seen before, standing in the midst of the woods in the next town, still thickly leaved and turned to greenish yellow. It is perhaps the largest of its species that I know. It was by merest accident that I stumbled on it, and if I had been sent to find it, I should have thought it to be, as we say, like looking for a needle in a haymow. All summer, and it chances for so many years, it has been concealed to me; but now, walking in a different direction, to the same hilltop from which I saw the scarlet oaks, and looking off just before sunset, when all other trees visible for miles around are reddish or green, I distinguish my new acquaintance by its yellow color. Such is its fame, at last, and reward for living in that solitude and obscurity. It is the most distinct tree in all the landscape, and would be the cynosure of all eyes here. Thus it plays its part in the choir. I made a minute of its locality, glad to know where so large an aspen grew. Then it seemed peculiar in its solitude and

obscurity. It seemed the obscurest of trees. Now it was seen to be equally peculiar for its distinctness and prominence. Each tree (in October) runs up its flag and we know [what] colors it sails under. The sailor sails, and the soldier marches, under a color which will report his virtue farthest, and the ship's "private signals" must be such as can be distinguished at the greatest distance. The eye, which distinguishes and appreciates color, is itself the seat of color in the human body.

It is as if it recognized me too, and gladly, coming half-way to meet me, and now the acquaintance thus propitiously formed will, I trust, be permanent.

Of the three (?) mocker-nuts on Conantum top only the southernmost is bare, the rest are thickly leaved yet. The *Viburnum Lentago* is about bare.

That hour-glass apple shrub near the old Conantum house is full of small yellow fruit. Thus it is with them. By the end of some October, when their leaves have fallen, you see them glowing with an abundance of wild fruit, which the cows cannot get at over the bushy and thorny hedge which surrounds them.[1] Such is their pursuit of knowledge through difficulties.[2] Though they may have taken the hour-glass form, think not that their sands are run out. So is it with the rude, neglected genius from amid the country hills; he suffers many a check at first, browsed on by fate, springing in but a rocky pasture, the nursery of other creatures there, and he grows broad and strong, and scraggy and thorny, hopelessly stunted, you would say, and not like a sleek orchard tree

[1] [*Excursions*, p. 306; Riv. 376.]
[2] [*Excursions*, p. 307; Riv. 377.]

all whose forces are husbanded and the precious early years not lost, and when at first, within this rind and hedge, the man shoots up, you see the thorny scrub of his youth about him, and he walks like an hour-glass, aspiring above, it is true, but held down and impeded by the rubbish of old difficulties overcome, and you seem to see his sands running out. But at length, thanks to his rude culture, he attains to his full stature, and every vestige of the thorny hedge which clung to his youth disappears, and he bears golden crops of Porters or Baldwins, whose fame will spread through all orchards for generations to come, while that thrifty orchard tree which was his competitor will, perchance, have long since ceased to bear its engrafted fruit and decayed.[1]

The beach plum is withering green, say with the apple trees, which are half of them bare. Larches fairly begun to fall; so they are at height.

[1] [See *Excursions*, p. 307; Riv. 377.]

V

NOVEMBER, 1858

(ÆT. 41)

Nov. 1. P. M. — To Poplar Hill.

Many black oaks are bare in Sleepy Hollow. Now you easily detect where larches grow, *viz.* in the swamp north of Sleepy Hollow. They are far more distinct than at any other season. They are very regular soft yellow pyramids, as I see them from the Poplar Hill. Unlike the pines there is no greenness left to alternate with their yellow, but they are a uniform yellow, and they differ from other yellow trees in the generally regular pyramidal outline, *i. e.* these middling-sized trees. These trees now cannot easily be mistaken for any other, because they are the only conspicuously yellow trees now left in the woods, except a very few aspens of both kinds, not one in a square mile, and these are of a very different hue as well as form, the birches, etc., having fallen. The larch, apparently, will soon be the only yellow tree left in the woods. It is almost quite alone now. But in the summer it is not easy to distinguish them either by their color or form at a distance.

If you wish to count the scarlet oaks, do it now. Stand on a hilltop in the woods, when the sun is an hour high and the sky is clear, and every one within range of your vision will be revealed. You might live

to the age of Methusaleh and never find a tithe of them otherwise.[1]

We are not wont to see our dooryard as a part of the earth's surface. The gardener does not perceive that some ridge or mound in his garden or lawn is related to yonder hill or the still more distant mountain in the horizon, is, perchance, a humble spur of the last. We are wont to look on the earth still as a sort of chaos, formless and lumpish. I notice from this height that the curving moraine forming the west side of Sleepy Hollow is one of several arms or fingers which stretch away from the hill range that runs down the north side of the Boston road, turning northward at the Court-House; that this finger-like moraine is continued northward by itself almost to the river, and points plainly enough to Ponkawtasset Hill on the other side, even if the Poplar Hill range itself did not indicate this connection; and so the sloping cemetery lots on the west of Sleepy Hollow are related to the distant Ponkawtasset. The smooth-shaven knoll in the lawn, on which the children swing, is, perchance, only a spur of some mountains of the moon, which no traveller has reached, heaved up by the same impulse.

The hawthorn is but three-quarters fallen and is a greenish yellow or yellowish green.

I hear in the fields just before sundown a shriller chirping of a few crickets, reminding me that their song is getting thin and will soon be quenched.

As I stood on the south bank of the river a hundred rods southwest of John Flint's, the sun being just about to enter a long and broad dark-blue or slate-colored

[1] [*Excursions*, p. 283; Riv. 348.]

cloud in the horizon, a cold, dark bank, I saw that the reflection of Flint's white house in the river, prolonged by a slight ripple so as to reach the reflected cloud, was a very distinct and luminous light blue.

As the afternoons grow shorter, and the early evening drives us home to complete our chores, we are reminded of the shortness of life, and become more pensive, at least in this twilight of the year. We are prompted to make haste and finish our work before the night comes. I leaned over a rail in the twilight on the Walden road, waiting for the evening mail to be distributed, when such thoughts visited me. I seemed to recognize the November evening as a familiar thing come round again, and yet I could hardly tell whether I had ever known it or only divined it. The November twilights just begun! It appeared like a part of a panorama at which I sat spectator, a part with which I was perfectly familiar just coming into view, and I foresaw how it would look and roll along, and prepared to be pleased. Just such a piece of art merely, though infinitely sweet and grand, did it appear to me, and just as little were any active duties required of me. We are independent on all that we see. The hangman whom I have *seen* cannot hang me. The earth which I have *seen* cannot bury me. Such doubleness and distance does sight prove. Only the rich and such as are troubled with ennui are implicated in the maze of phenomena. You cannot see anything until you are clear of it. The long railroad causeway through the meadows west of me, the still twilight in which hardly a cricket was heard,[1] the dark bank of

[1] Probably too cool for any these evenings; only in the afternoon.

clouds in the horizon long after sunset, the villagers crowding to the post-office, and the hastening home to supper by candle-light, had I not seen all this before! What new sweet was I to extract from it? Truly they mean that we shall learn our lesson well. Nature gets thumbed like an old spelling-book. The almshouse and Frederick were still as last November. I was no nearer, methinks, nor further off from my friends. Yet I sat the bench with perfect contentment, unwilling to exchange the familiar vision that was to be unrolled for any treasure or heaven that could be imagined. Sure to keep just so far apart in our orbits still, in obedience to the laws of attraction and repulsion, affording each other only steady but indispensable starlight. It was as if I was promised the greatest novelty the world has ever seen or shall see, though the utmost possible novelty would be the difference between me and myself a year ago. This alone encouraged me, and was my fuel for the approaching winter. That we may behold the panorama with this slight improvement or change, this is what we sustain life for with so much effort from year to year.

And yet there is no more tempting novelty than this new November. No going to Europe or another world is to be named with it. Give me the old familiar walk, post-office and all, with this ever new self, with this infinite expectation and faith, which does not know when it is beaten. We'll go nutting once more. We'll pluck the nut of the world, and crack it in the winter evenings. Theatres and all other sightseeing are puppet-shows in comparison. I will take another walk to the Cliff, an-

other row on the river, another skate on the meadow, be out in the first snow, and associate with the winter birds. Here I am at home. In the bare and bleached crust of the earth I recognize my friend.

One actual Frederick that you know is worth a million only read of. Pray, am I altogether a bachelor, or am I a widower, that I should go away and leave my bride? This Morrow that is ever knocking with irresistible force at our door, there is no such guest as that. I will stay at home and receive company.

I want nothing new, if I can have but a tithe of the old secured to me. I will spurn all wealth beside. Think of the consummate folly of attempting to go away from *here!* When the constant endeavor should be to get nearer and nearer *here.* Here are all the friends I ever had or shall have, and as friendly as ever. Why, I never had any quarrel with a friend but it was just as sweet as unanimity could be. I do not think we budge an inch forward or backward in relation to our friends. How many things can you go away from? They see the comet from the northwest coast just as plainly as we do, and the same stars through its tail. Take the shortest way round and stay at home. A man dwells in his native valley like a corolla in its calyx, like an acorn in its cup. *Here,* of course, is all that you love, all that you expect, all that you are. Here is your bride elect, as close to you as she can be got. Here is all the best and all the worst you can imagine. What more do you want? Bear here-away then! Foolish people imagine that what they imagine is somewhere else. That stuff is not made in any factory but their own.

Nov. 2. P. M. — To Cliff.

A cool gray November afternoon; sky overcast.

Looking back from the causeway, the large willow by Mrs. Bigelow's and a silvery abele are the only leafy trees to be seen in and over the village, the first a yellowish mass, also some Lombardy poplars on the outskirts. It is remarkable that these (and the weeping willow, *yet green*) and a few of our *Populus tremuloides* (lately the *grandidentata* also[1]), all closely allied, are the only trees now (except the larch and perhaps a very few small white birches) which are conspicuously yellow, almost the only deciduous ones whose leaves are not withered, *i. e.* except scarlet oaks, red oaks, and some of the others, etc.

I see here and there yet some middle-sized coniferous willows, between *humilis* and *discolor,* whose upper leaves, left on, are quite bright lemon-yellow in dry places. These single leaves brighter than their predecessors which have fallen. The pitch pine is apparently a little past the midst of its fall. In sprout-lands some young birches are still rather leafy and bright-colored. Going over the newly cleared pasture on the northeast of Fair Haven Hill, I see that the scarlet oaks are more generally bright than on the 22d *ult.* Even the little sprouts in the russet pasture and the high tree-tops in the yew wood burn now, when the middle-sized bushes in the sprout-lands have mostly gone out. The large scarlet oak trees and tree-tops in woods, perhaps especially on hills, apparently are late because raised above the influence of the early frosts. Methinks they are as bright, even this dark day, as I ever saw them. The blossoming of the

[1] Still one.

scarlet oak! the forest-flower, surpassing all in splendor (at least since the maple)! I do not know but they interest me more than the maples, they are so widely and equally dispersed throughout the forest; they are so hardy, a nobler tree on the whole, lasting into November; our chief November flower, abiding the approach of winter with us, imparting warmth to November prospects. It is remarkable that the latest bright color that is general should be this deep, dark scarlet and red, the intensest of colors, the ripest fruit of the year, like the cheek of a glossy red ripe apple from the cold Isle of Orleans, which will not be mellow for eating till next spring! When I rise to a hilltop, a thousand of these great oak roses, distributed on every side as far as the horizon! This my unfailing prospect for a fortnight past as surely as I rose to a hilltop! This late forest-flower surpasses all that spring or summer could do. Their colors were but rare and dainty specks, which made no impression on a distant eye. Now it is an extended forest or a mountain-side that bursts into bloom, through or along which we may journey from day to day. I admire these roses three or four miles off in the horizon. Comparatively, our gardening is on a petty scale, the gardener still nursing a few asters amid dead weeds, ignorant of the gigantic asters and roses which, as it were, overshadow him and ask for none of his care. Comparatively, it is like a little red paint ground on a teacup and held up against the sunset sky. Why not take more elevated and broader views, walk in the greater garden, not skulk in a little "debauched" nook of it? Consider the beauty of the earth, and not merely of a few impounded herbs? However, you will not see these splendors, whether you stand on the hilltop or in the hollow, unless you are prepared to see them. The gardener can see only the gardener's garden, wherever he goes. The beauty of the earth answers exactly to your demand and appreciation.[1]

Apples in the village and lower ground are now generally killed brown and crisp, without having turned yellow, especially the upper parts, while those on hills and [in] warm places turned yellowish or russet, and so ripened to their fall. Of quince bushes the same, only they are a little later and are greener yet.

The sap is now frequently flowing fast in the scarlet oaks (as I have not observed it in the others), and has a pleasant acorn-like taste. Their bright tints, now that most other oaks are withered, are connected with this phenomenon. They are full of sap and life. They flow like a sugar maple in the spring. It has a pleasantly astringent taste, this strong oak wine.[2]

That small poplar seen from Cliffs on the 29th is a *P. tremuloides*. It makes the impression of a bright and clear yellow at a distance, though it is rather dingy and spotted.

It is later, then (this and the Baker Farm one), than any *P. grandidentata* that I know.

Looking down on the oak wood southeast of Yew Wood, I see some large black oak tops a brown yellow still; so generally it shows life a little longer than the white and swamp white apparently. One just beyond the smallpox burying-ground is generally greenish in-

[1] [*Excursions*, pp. 284–286; Riv. 349–351.]
[2] [*Excursions*, pp. 281, 282; Riv. 346.]

clining to scarlet, looking very much like a scarlet oak not yet completely changed, for the leaf would not be distinguished. However, the nuts, with yellow meat, and the strong bitter yellow bark betrayed it. Yet it did not amount to scarlet.

I see a few shrub oak leaves still fresh where sheltered. The little chinquapin has fallen.

I go past the Well Meadow Field. There is a sympathy between this cold, gray, overcast November afternoon and the grayish-brown oak leaves and russet fields.

The Scotch larch is changed at least as bright as ours.

Nov. 3. Colder weather, true November weather comes again to-night, and I must rekindle my fire which I had done without of late. I must walk briskly in order to keep warm in my thin coat.

P. M. — To Annursnack.

I am inclined to think that pignuts fall earlier than mocker-nuts, *i. e.* the leaves, and that the first are now about fallen (?). Those on Nawshawtuct are bare, but I see a great many hickories of some kind not nearly bare.

Monroe's arbor-vitæ hedge has fallen. Put it with the white pine. The jay is the bird of October. I have seen it repeatedly flitting amid the bright leaves, of a different color from them all and equally bright, and taking its flight from grove to grove. It, too, with its bright color, stands for some ripeness in the bird harvest. And its scream! it is as if it blowed on the edge of an October leaf. It is never more in its element and at home than when flitting amid these brilliant colors. No doubt it delights in bright color, and so has begged for itself a bril-

liant coat. It is not gathering seeds from the sod, too busy to look around, while fleeing the country. It is wide awake to what is going on, on the *qui vive*. It flies to some bright tree and bruits its splendors abroad.

By fall I mean literally the falling of the leaves, though some mean by it the changing or the acquisition of a brighter color. This I call the autumnal tint, the ripening to the fall.

The only white birch leaves now seen are those lingering green terminal leaves of the 23d, now at last turned yellow,[1] for they are now burnt upward to the last spark and glimmering. Methinks the birch ripens its leaves very perfectly though gradually.

I should say that that tree which ripened its leaves well, like this, was better suited to the climate than one like the locust and most apples, — which was mostly killed by frost first annually. Perhaps this tells at last on the constitution of the tree, and that variety would be safest to cultivate which matured its leaves best.

The pitch pine fallen and falling leaves now and for some time have not been bright or yellow, but brown.

At base of Annursnack I find one or two fringed gentians yet open, but even the stems are generally killed. I notice that the cows lately admitted to the meadows and orchards have browsed the grass, etc., closely, on that strip between the dry hillside and the wet meadow, where it is undoubtedly sweetest and freshest yet, and where it chances that this late flower the gentian grows. There, too, grows the herbage which is now the most grateful to the cattle. Also *Aster undulatus* is still

[1] And at least seven days later.

freshly in bloom; yarrow, etc., etc. Much *Lycopodium complanatum* not open yet.

Returning, I see at the very northwest end of the White Cedar Swamp a little elder, still quite leafy and green, near the path on the edge of the swamp. Its leaflets are commonly nine, and the lower two or more are commonly divided. This seemed peculiarly downy beneath, even "sub-pubescent," as Bigelow describes the *Sambucus pubens* to be. Compare it with the common.[1] Also by it is *Viburnum nudum*, still quite fresh and green, the slender shoots from starting plants very erect and straight.

The lower leaves of the water andromeda are now red,[2] and the lambkill leaves are drooping (is it more than before?) and purplish from the effect of frost in low swamps like this.

Though I listen for them, I do not hear a cricket this afternoon. I think that I heard a few in the afternoon of November 1st. They then sounded peculiarly distinct, being but few here and there on a dry and warm hill, bird-like. Yet these seemed to be singing a little louder and in a little loftier strain, now that the chirp of the cricket generally was quenched.

How long we will follow an illusion! On meeting that one whom I call my friend, I find that I had imagined something that was not there. I am sure to depart sadder than I came. Nothing makes me so dejected as to

[1] It is apparently only a more downy common one, and this may have preserved it from frost.
[2] So at Potter's Swamp, — pretty commonly a dark scarlet, — Nov. 5, 1855.

have met my friends, for they make me doubt if it is possible to have any friends. I feel what a fool I am. I cannot conceive of persons more strange to me than they actually are; not thinking, not believing, not doing as I do; interrupted by me. My only distinction must be that I am the greatest bore they ever had. Not in a single thought agreed; regularly balking one another. But when I get far away, my thoughts return to them. That is the way I *can* visit them. Perhaps it is unaccountable to me why I care for them. Thus I am taught that my friend is not an actual person. When I have withdrawn and am alone, I forget the actual person and remember only my ideal. Then I have a friend again. I am not so ready to perceive the illusion that is in Nature. I certainly come nearer, to say the least, to an actual and joyful intercourse with her. Every day I have more or less communion with her, *as I think.* At least, I do not feel as if I must withdraw out of nature. I feel like a welcome guest. Yet, strictly speaking, the same must be true of nature and of man; our ideal is the only real. It is not the finite and temporal that satisfies or concerns us in either case.

I associate the idea of friendship, methinks, with the person the most foreign to me. This illusion is perpetuated, like superstition in a country long after civilization has been attained to. We are attracted toward a particular person, but no one has discovered the laws of this attraction. When I come nearest to that other *actually*, I am wont to be surprised at my selection. It may be enough that we have met *some time*, and now can never forget it. Some time or other we paid each other

this wonderful compliment, looked largely, humanly, divinely on one another, and now are fated to be acquaintances forever. In the case of nature I am not so conscious of this unsatisfied yearning.

Some oak woods begin to look bare, and even smoky, after their fashion.

Nov. 4. A rainy day.

Called to C. from the outside of his house the other afternoon in the rain. At length he put his head out the attic window, and I inquired if he didn't want to take a walk, but he excused himself, saying that he had a cold. "But," added he, "you can take so much the longer walk. Double it."

On the 1st, when I stood on Poplar Hill, I saw a man, far off by the edge of the river, splitting billets off a stump. Suspecting who it was, I took out my glass, and beheld Goodwin, the one-eyed Ajax, in his short blue frock, short and square-bodied, as broad as for his height he can afford to be, getting his winter's wood; for this is one of the phenomena of the season. As surely as the ants which he disturbs go into winter quarters in the stump when the weather becomes cool, so does G. revisit the stumpy shores with his axe. As usual, his powder-flask peeped out from a pocket on his breast, his gun was slanted over a stump near by, and his boat lay a little further along. He had been at work laying wall still further off, and now, near the end of the day, betook himself to those pursuits which he loved better still. It would be no amusement to me to see a gentleman buy his winter wood. It is to see G. get his. I

helped him tip over a stump or two. He said that the owner of the land had given him leave to get them out, but it seemed to me a condescension for him to ask any man's leave to grub up these stumps. The stumps to those who can use them, I say, — to those who will split them. He might as well ask leave of the farmer to shoot the musquash and the meadow-hen, or I might as well ask leave to look at the landscape. Near by were large hollows in the ground, now grassed over, where he had got out white oak stumps in previous years. But, strange to say, the town does not like to have him get his fuel in this way. They would rather the stumps would rot in the ground, or be floated down-stream to the sea. They have almost without dissent agreed on a different mode of living, with their division of labor. They would have him stick to laying wall, and buy corded wood for his fuel, as they do. He has drawn up an old bridge sleeper and cut his name in it for security, and now he gets into his boat and pushes off in the twilight, saying he will go and see what Mr. Musquash is about.

When the Haverhill fishermen told me that they could distinguish the Concord River stuff (*i. e.* driftwood) I see they were right, for much of it is chestnut rails, and of these they have but few, and those in the southern part of New Hampshire.

If, about the last of October, you ascend any hill in the outskirts of the town and look over the forest, you will see, amid the brown of other oaks, which are now withered, and the green of the pines, the bright-red tops or crescents of the scarlet oaks, very equally and thickly distributed on all sides, even to the horizon. Complete

trees standing exposed on the edges of the forest, where you have never suspected them, or their tops only in the recesses of the forest surface, or perhaps towering above the surrounding trees, or reflecting a warm rose red from the very edge of the horizon in favorable lights. All this you will see, and much more, if you are prepared to see it, — if you *look* for it. Otherwise, regular and universal as this phenomenon is, you will think for threescore years and ten that all the wood is at this season sere and brown. Objects are concealed from our view not so much because they are out of the course of our visual ray (continued) as because there is no intention of the mind and eye toward them. We do not realize how far and widely, or how near and narrowly, we are to look. The greater part of the phenomena of nature are for this reason concealed to us all our lives. Here, too, as in political economy, the supply answers to the demand. Nature does not cast pearls before swine. There is just as much beauty visible to us in the landscape as we are prepared to appreciate, — not a grain more. The actual objects which one person will see from a particular hilltop are just as different from those which another will see as the persons are different. The scarlet oak must, in a sense, be in your eye when you go forth. We cannot see anything until we are possessed with the idea of it, and then we can hardly see anything else. In my botanical rambles I find that first the idea, or image, of a plant occupies my thoughts, though it may at first seem very foreign to this locality, and for some weeks or months I go thinking of it and expecting it unconsciously, and at length I surely see it, and it is henceforth an actual neighbor of mine. This is the history of my finding a score or more of rare plants which I could name.

Take one of our selectmen and put him on the highest hill in the township, and tell him to look! What, probably, would he see? What would he *select* to look at? Sharpening his sight to the utmost, and putting on the glasses that suited him best, aye, using a spy-glass if he liked, straining his optic nerve to its utmost, and making a full report. Of course, he would see a Brocken spectre of himself. Now take Julius Cæsar, or Emanuel Swedenborg, or a Fiji-Islander, and set him up there! Let them compare notes afterward. Would it appear that they had enjoyed the same prospect? For aught we know, as strange a man as any of these is always at our elbows. It does not appear that anybody saw Shakespeare when he was about in England looking off, but only some of his raiment.

Why, it takes a sharpshooter to bring down even such trivial game as snipes and woodcocks; he must take very particular aim, and know what he is aiming at. He would stand a very small chance if he fired at random into the sky, being told that snipes were flying there. And so it is with him that shoots at beauty. Not till the sky falls will he catch larks, unless he is a trained sportsman. He will not bag any if he does not already know its seasons and haunts and the color of its wing, — if he has not dreamed of it, so that he can *anticipate* it; then, indeed, he flushes it at every step, shoots double and on the wing, with both barrels, even in corn-fields. The sportsman trains himself, dresses, and watches unweariedly, and loads and primes for his particular game.

He prays for it, and so he gets it. After due and long preparation, schooling his eye and hand, dreaming awake and asleep, with gun and paddle and boat, he goes out after meadow-hens, — which most of his townsmen never saw nor dreamed of, — paddles for miles against a head wind, and therefore he gets them. He had them half-way into his bag when he started, and has only to shove them down. The fisherman, too, dreams of fish, till he can almost catch them in his sink-spout. The hen scratches, and finds her food right under where she stands; but such is not the way with the hawk.

The true sportsman can shoot you almost any of his game from his windows. It comes and perches at last on the barrel of his gun; but the rest of the world never see it, with the feathers on. He will keep himself supplied by firing up his chimney. The geese fly exactly under his zenith, and honk when they get there. Twenty musquash have the refusal of each one of his traps before it is empty.[1]

Nov. 5. Humphrey Buttrick says that he finds old and young of both kinds of small rails, and that they breed here, though he never saw their nests.

P. M. — Up Assabet.

The river has risen somewhat, on account of rain yesterday and the 30th. So it was lowest the 30th.

That great fleet of leaves of the 21st October is now sunk to the bottom, near the shore, and are [*sic*] flatted out there, paving it thickly, and but few recently fallen are to be seen on the water; and in the woods the leaves do not lie up so crisp since the rain.

[1] [*Excursions*, pp. 285–288; Riv. 350–354.]

Vol. XI

Saw Stewart shoot a Carolina rail, which was standing on the side of a musquash-cabin off Prichard's, within two rods of him. This has no black throat and is probably the female.

The large shallow cups of the red oak acorns look like some buttons I have seen which had lost their core.

The *Cornus florida* on the Island is still full-leafed, and is now completely scarlet, though it was partly green on the 28th. It is apparently in the height of its color there now, or, if more exposed, perhaps it would have been on the 1st of November. This makes it the latest tree to change. The leaves are drooping, like the *C. sericea*, while those of some sprouts at its base are horizontal. Some incline to crimson.

A few white maples are not yet bare, but thinly clothed with dull-yellow leaves which still have life in them. Judging from the two aspens, this tree, and the willows, one would say that the earliest trees to leaf were, perhaps, the last to lose their leaves.

Little dippers were seen yesterday.

The few remaining topmost leaves of the *Salix sericea*, which were the last to change, are now yellow like those of the birch.

Water milkweed has been discounting some days, with its small upright pods.

I hear one cricket this louring day. Since but one is heard, it is the more distinct and therefore seems louder and more musical. It is a clearer note, less creaking than before.

A few *Populus grandidentata* leaves are still left on. The common smooth rose leaves are pretty conspicu-

ously yellow yet along the river, and some dull-reddish high blackberry is seen by the roads. Also meadow-sweet is observed yet with the rose. It is quite still; no wind, no insect hum, and no note of birds, but one hairy woodpecker. That lake grass, *Glyceria fluitans*, is, methinks, more noticeable now than in summer on the surface of the fuller stream, green and purple. Meadow-sweet is a prominent yellow yet.

Nov. 6. Yesterday was a still and cloudy day. This is another rainy day. On the whole, we have had a good deal of fair weather the last three months. Mr. Buttrick, the marketman, says he has been to Boston twenty-seven times since the first of August, and has not got wet till to-day, though he rides in an open wagon.

I guessed at Goodwin's age on the 1st. He is hale and stout and looks younger than he is, and I took care to set him high enough. I guessed he was fifty-five, and he said that if he lived two or three months longer he would be fifty-six. He then guessed at my age, thought I was forty. He thought that Emerson was a very young-looking man for his age, "But," said he, "he has not been out o' nights as much as you have."

Some horse-chestnuts are still thickly leaved and yellow, not withered.

Nov. 7. P. M. — To Bateman's Pond.

It cleared up this forenoon. I leave my boat opposite the Hemlocks. I see the cold sunlight from some glade between the clouds falling on distant oak woods, now nearly bare, and as I glance up the hill between them, seeing the bare but bright hillside beyond, I think, Now we are left to the hemlocks and pines with their silvery light, to the bare trees and withered grass. The very rocks and stones in the rocky roads (that beyond Farmer's) look white in the clear November light, especially after the rain. We are left to the chickadee's familiar notes, and the jay for trumpeter. What struck me was a certain emptiness beyond, between the hemlocks and the hill, in the cool, washed air, as if I appreciated even here the absence of insects from it. It suggested agreeably to me a mere space in which to walk briskly. The fields are bleak, and they are, as it were, vacated. The very earth is like a house shut up for the winter, and I go knocking about it in vain. But just then I heard a chickadee on a hemlock, and was inexpressibly cheered to find that an old acquaintance was yet stirring about the premises, and was, I was assured, to be there all winter. All that is evergreen in me revived at once.

The very moss, the little pine-tree moss, in Hosmer's meadow is revealed by its greenness amid the withered grass and stubble.

Hard frosts have turned the cranberry vines to a dark purple.

I hear one faint cricket's chirp this afternoon.

Going up the lane beyond Farmer's, I was surprised to see fly up from the white, stony road, two snow buntings, which alighted again close by, one on a large rock, the other on the stony ground. They had pale-brown or tawny touches on the white breast, on each side of the head, and on the top of the head, in the last place with some darker color. Had light-yellowish bills. They sat

quite motionless within two rods, and allowed me to approach within a rod, as if conscious that the white rocks, etc., concealed them. It seemed as if they were attracted to surfaces of the same color with themselves, — white and black (or quite dark) and tawny. One squatted *flat*, if not both. Their soft rippling notes as they went off reminded me [of] the northeast snow-storms to which ere long they are to be an accompaniment.

I find in a swamp witch-hazel buds still opening, for here they are sheltered, but I can find no fringed gentian, blue, near Bateman's Pond. But *Aster undulatus* and several golden rods, at least, may be found yet. I see *Lycopodium dendroideum*[1] which has not yet shed pollen. In and about Fox Castle Swamp, lambkill is reddened about as much as ever. Round-leaved cornel is bare.

The nuthatch is another bird of the fall which I hear these days and for a long time, — apparently ever since the young birds grew up.

The *Cornus florida* by the pond is quite bare; how long? (That at Island still thickly leaved.) So that I can only say that the sheltered *C. florida* change much later than the scarlet oak *generally*, and perhaps the former is to be considered later on the whole.

Methinks those scarlet oaks, those burning bushes, begin to be rare in the landscape. They are about Bateman's Pond, at any rate.

My apple harvest! It is to glean after the husbandman and the cows, or to gather the crop of those wild trees far away on the edges of swamps which have escaped their notice. Now, when it is generally all fallen,

[1] Var. *obscurum.*

if indeed any is left, though you would not suppose there were any on the first survey, nevertheless with experienced eyes I explore amid the clumps of alder (now bare) and in the crevices of the rocks full of leaves, and prying under the fallen and decaying ferns which, with apple and alder leaves, thickly strew the ground. From amid the leaves anywhere within the circumference of the tree, I draw forth the fruit, all wet and glossy, nibbled by rabbits and hollowed out by crickets, but still with the bloom on it and at least as ripe and well kept, if not better than those in barrels, while those which lay exposed are quite brown and rotten. Showing only a blooming cheek here and there between the wet leaves, or fallen into hollows long since and covered up with the leaves of the tree, — a proper kind of packing. I fill my pockets on each side, and as I retrace my steps, I eat one first from this side, and then from that, in order to preserve my balance. And here and there is one lodged as it fell between the bases of the suckers which spring thickly from a horizontal limb. In the midst of an alder clump, covered by leaves, there it lies, safe from cows which might smell it out and unobserved by the husbandman; reserved for me.[1]

It is too late, generally, to look for the handsome ones now. The exposed are decayed or decaying.

Looking southwest toward the pond just before sunset, I saw against the light what I took to be a shad-bush in full bloom, but without a leafet. I was prepared for this sight after this very warm autumn, because this tree frequently puts forth new leaves in October. Or it

[1] [*Excursions*, pp. 317, 318; Riv. 390, 391.]

might be a young wild apple. Hastening to it, I found it was only the feathery seeds of the virgin's-bower, whose vine, so close to the branches, was not noticeable. They looked just like dense umbels of white flowers, and in this light, three or four rods off, were fully as white as white apple blossoms. It is singular how one thing thus puts on the semblance of another. I thought at first I had made a discovery more interesting than the blossoming of apple trees in the fall. This, I thought, which I never saw nor heard of before, must be the result of that wonderfully warm weather about the 19th and 20th of October. It carried me round to spring again, when the shad-bush, almost leafless, is seen waving its white blossoms amid the yet bare trees. The feathery masses at intervals along the twigs, just like umbels of apple bloom, so caught and reflected the western light.

The *small* beeches are still covered with withered leaves, but the larger are three-quarters bare.

The *Diplopappus linariifolius*, which was yellow in the shade, in open and sunny places is purple.

I see the small botrychium leaf in Hosmer's meadow still firm, but a reddish brown or leather-color.

Rounding the Island just after sunset, I see not only the houses nearest the river but our own reflected in the river by the Island. From what various points of view and in what unsuspected lights and relations we sooner or later see the most familiar objects! I see houses reflected in the river which stand a mile from it, and whose inhabitants do not consider themselves near the shore.

I pass a musquash-house, apparently begun last night. The first mouthfuls of weeds were placed between some small button-bush stems which stood amid the pads and pontederia, for a support and to prevent their being washed away. Opposite, I see some half concealed amid the bleached phalaris grass (a tall coarse grass), or, in some places, the blue-joint.

Nov. 8. P. M. — To Boulder Field.

Goodwin, laying wall at Miss Ripley's, observed to me going by, "Well, it seems that —— thought that he had lived long enough." He committed suicide within a week, at his sister's house in Sudbury. A boy slept in the chamber with him, and, hearing a noise, got [up] and found —— on the floor with both his jugular veins cut, but his windpipe whole. He said to the boy, "Take the razor and cut deeper," but the boy ran, and —— died, and Garfield said it was about time, for ——, in revenge for being sent to the house of correction, had set fire to a pile of wood of his, that long pile by the roadside beyond William Wheeler's, that I stood under in a rain once. —— probably burned Witherell's house too, and perhaps Boynton's stable.

The red osier at Mrs. Simmons's is quite bare; how long? Her hawthorn is still quite leafy and pretty, yellow-brown, dotted. A thorn at Hall's fence is dark scarlet and pretty. There are many leaves on the buckthorn still.

Common thorn bushes, long since bare, when many grow together in clumps, make another such a smoke, though smaller, as the maples, — the same color. I can often distinguish the bush by this. Alders are a very dark gray, sort of iron gray, and, if near enough, you see

Vol. XI

dark lines (the stems) and specks (the fruit) like cinders, like a very dense, dark, and unconsumed uliginous smoke, in which many cinders rise.

Those trees and bushes which grow in dense masses and have many fine twigs, being bare, make an agreeable misty impression where there are a myriad retreating points to receive the eye, not a hard, abrupt wall; just as, in the sky, the visual ray is cushioned on clouds, unless it is launched into the illimitable ether. The eye is less worn and wearied, not to say wounded, by looking at these mazes where the seer is not often conscious of seeing anything. It is well that the eye is so rarely caught and detained by any object in one whole hemisphere of its range, *i. e.* the sky. It enjoys everlasting holiday on this side. Only the formless clouds and the objectless ether are presented to it. For they are nervous who see many faces in the clouds. Corresponding to the clouds in the sky are those mazes now on the earth. Nature disposes of her naked stems so softly as not to put our eyes out. She makes them a smoke, or stationary cloud, on this side or that, of whose objective existence we rarely take cognizance. She does not expect us to notice them. She calls our attention to the maple swamp more especially in October.

There is also the coarse maze produced by an oak wood (when nearly all the leaves are fallen), in which, however, the large boughs reflecting the light have considerable distinctness, and that of the forest in general. I thought, from a small specimen, that the brushy yellow birch tops were of the same hue with the alders.[1]

[1] *Vide* Nov. 11th.

Nature has many scenes to exhibit, and constantly draws a curtain over this part or that. She is constantly repainting the landscape and all surfaces, dressing up some scene for our entertainment. Lately we had a leafy wilderness, now bare twigs begin to prevail, and soon she will surprise us with a mantle of snow.[1] Some green she thinks so good for our eyes, like blue, that she never banishes it entirely, but has created evergreens.

It is remarkable how little any but a lichenist will observe on the bark of trees. The mass of men have but the vaguest and most indefinite notion of mosses, as a sort of shreds and fringes, and the world in which the lichenist dwells is much further from theirs than one side of this earth from the other. They see bark as if they saw it not. These objects which, though constantly visible, are rarely looked at are a sort of eye-brush.

Each phase of nature, while not invisible, is yet not too distinct and obtrusive. It is there to be found when we look for it, but not demanding our attention. It is like a silent but sympathizing companion in whose company we retain most of the advantages of solitude, with whom we can walk and talk, or be silent, naturally, without the necessity of talking in a strain foreign to the place.

I know of but one or two persons with whom I can afford to walk. With most the walk degenerates into a mere vigorous use of your legs, ludicrously purposeless, while you are discussing some mighty argument, each one having his say, spoiling each other's day, worrying one another with conversation, hustling one another

[1] I read that snow fell two or three inches deep in Bangor yesterday morning.

with our conversation. I know of no use in the walking part in this case, except that we may seem to be getting on together toward some goal; but of course we keep our original distance all the way. Jumping every wall and ditch with vigor in the vain hope of shaking your companion off. Trying to kill two birds with one stone, though they sit at opposite points of [the] compass, to see nature and do the honors to one who does not.

Animals generally see things in the vacant way I have described. They rarely see anything but their food, or some real or imaginary foe. I never saw but one cow looking into the sky.

Lichens as they affect the scenery, as picturesque objects described by Gilpin or others, are one thing; as they concern the lichenist, quite another.

These are the various grays and browns which give November its character. There are also some red mazes, like the twigs of the white maple and our *Cornus sericea*, etc. (the red osier, too, further north), and some distinct yellow ones, as willow twigs, which are most interesting in spring. The silvery abeles are steadily falling nowadays. The chalky white under side of these leaves is remarkable. None of our leaves is so white.

I think I admire again about this time the still bright-red or crimson fruit of the sumach, now when not only its own but most other leaves have fallen and there are few bright tints, it is now so distinct on its twigs. Your attention is not distracted by its brilliant leaves now.

I go across N. Barrett's land and over the road beyond his house. The aspect of the Great Meadows is now nearly uniform, the new and exposed grass being nearly as brown and sere as that which was not cut. Thus Nature has been blending and harmonizing the colors here where man had interfered.

I wandered over bare fields where the cattle, lately turned out, roamed restless and unsatisfied with the feed; I dived into a rustling young oak wood where not a green leaf was to be seen; I climbed to the geological axis of elevation and clambered over curly-pated rocks whose strata are on their edges, amid the rising woods; and again I thought, They are all gone surely, and left me alone. Not even a man Friday remains. What nutriment can I extract from these bare twigs? Starvation stares me in the face. "*Nay, nay!*" said a nuthatch, making its way, head downward, about a bare hickory close by. "The nearer the bone the sweeter the meat. Only the superfluous has been swept away. Now we behold the naked truth. If at any time the weather is too bleak and cold for you, keep the sunny side of the trunk, for there is a wholesome and inspiring warmth such as the summer never afforded. There are the winter mornings, with the sun on the oak wood tops. While buds sleep, thoughts wake." ("Hear! hear!" screamed the jay from a neighboring copse, where I had heard a tittering for some time.) "Winter has a concentrated and nutty kernel if you know where to look for it." And then the speaker shifted to another tree, further off, and reiterated his assertions, and his mate at a distance confirmed them; and I heard a suppressed chuckle from a red squirrel that heard the last remark, but had kept silent and invisible all the while. Is that you? "Yes-sir-ee," said he. Then, running down a slanting

bough, he called out rather impudently, "Look here! just get a snug-fitting fur coat and a pair of fur gloves like mine, and you may laugh at a northeast storm," and then he wound up with a slang phrase, in his own lingo, accompanied by a flourish of his tail, just as a newsboy twirls his fingers with his thumb on his nose and inquires, "Does your mother know you are out?"

The wild pear tree on Ponkawtasset has some yellow leaves still. The now more noticeable green radical leaves of the buttercup in the russet pastures remind me of the early spring to come, of which they will offer the first evidence. Now, too, I can *see* (for the same reason) where grows our only patch of broom, a quarter of a mile off, it [is] such a distinct, somewhat yellowish, green. Already the creeping juniper is a ripe glaucous green, with a distinct ruddy tinge to the upper surface, — the whole bush a ripe tint like a fruit.

I stand in Ebby Hubbard's yellow birch swamp, admiring some gnarled and shaggy picturesque old birches there, which send out large knee-like limbs near the ground, while the brook, raised by the late rain, winds fuller than usual through the rocky swamp. I thought with regret how soon these trees, like the black birches that grew on the hill near by, would be all cut off, and there would be almost nothing of the old Concord left, and we should be reduced to read old deeds in order to be reminded of such things, — deeds, at least, in which some old and revered bound trees are mentioned. These will be the only proof at last that they ever existed. Pray, farmers, keep some old woods to match the old deeds. Keep them for history's sake, as specimens of

Vol. XI

what the township was. Let us not be reduced to a mere paper evidence, to deeds kept in a chest or secretary, when not so much as the bark of the paper birch will be left for evidence, about its decayed stump.

The sides of the old Carlisle road where it is low and moist are (and have for a long time been), for many rods together and a rod in width, brown or cinnamon-colored with the withered dicksonia fern, not like the brown of trees (their withered leaves), but a peculiar cinnamon-brown. The bare huckleberry bushes and the sweet-ferns are draped with them as a kind of mourning.

Solidago puberula still out, for you see a few bright-yellow solidago flowers long after they are generally turned to a dirty-white fuzzy top. Pratt says he saw a few florets on a *Polygala sanguinea* within a week. He shows me samphire, plucked three weeks ago in Brighton, when it was a very brilliant crimson still.

Looking from Pratt's window at sunset, I saw that purple or rosy light reflected from some old chestnut rails on the hilltop before his house. Methinks it is pinkish, even like the old cow-droppings in the pastures. So universally does Nature blush at last. The very herbage which has gone through the stomachs and intestines of the cow acquires at last a faint pinkish tinge.

The button-bush balls are now blackish (really dark-brown) and withered, looking much blacker against the light than a month ago.

Nov. 9. It is remarkable that the only deciduous *trees* in the town which now make any show with their living leaves are: (1) scarlet oaks, perhaps only

one (2) *Populus tremuliformis*, one (3) dogwood, (the *small* white birch (*i. e.* young trees) spangles hardly deserved to be named), weeping willows, *Salix alba*, silvery abele, poplars (Italian), some apples, some horse-chestnuts, rarely wild pear trees, some English cherries (orange or yellow), — the first three alone being indigenous, to eight foreign.

And of shrubs, there are Jersey tea, gooseberry, two kinds of rose, *perhaps* sweet-fern, meadow-sweet, and high blackberry; also the lilac, quince, buckthorn, broom, privet, hawthorn, and barberry, well leaved. The very few leaves on sallows, *Viburnum nudum*, high blueberry, and perhaps *Cornus sericea*, do not deserve to be named, and hardly the five [*sic*] above. I have not seen the bayberry or beach plums. And add, *perhaps*, a few other shrubs. Sweet-briar pretty (?) well leaved. (Is it foreign?) Or of shrubs, seven foreign to about six native, and the last much the least noticeable and much the thinnest-leaved.

There are a very few living yellow leaves on young wild cherries yet, but these are not nearly so much to be named as the birch spangles.[1]

The newspaper tells me that Uncannunuc was white with snow for a short time on the morning of the 7th. Thus steadily but unobserved the winter steals down from the north, till from our highest hills we can discern its vanguard. Next week, perchance, our own hills will be white. Little did we think how near the winter was. It is as if a scout had brought in word that an enemy were approaching in force only a day's march

[1] Also leaves on green-briar, according to Nov. 11, 1855.

distant. Manchester was the spy this time, which has a camp at the base of that hill. We had not thought seriously of winter; we dwelt in fancied security yet.

P. M. — To Great Fields and Walden.

The scarlet oak by Agricultural Ground (and no doubt generally) is falling fast, and has been for some days, and they have now generally grown dull — before the leaves have lost their color. Other oaks may be said [to] have assumed their true November aspect; i. e., the larger ones are about bare. Only the latest black oaks are leafy, and they just withered. The trees on the hill just north of Alcott's land, which I saw yesterday so distinctly from Ponkawtasset, and thought were either larches or aspens, prove to be larches. On a hill like this it seems they are later to change and brighter now than those in the Abel Heywood swamp, which are brownish-yellow. The first-named larches were quite as distinct amid the pines seen a mile off as near at hand.

Oak sprouts — white and black, at least — are a deeper and darker red than the trees. Here is a white oak sprout, for example, far brighter red than any tree of the kind I ever saw. I do not find that black oaks get to be quite scarlet or red at all, yet the very young and sprouts often are, and are hard to distinguish from the scarlet oak.

Garfield shot a hen-hawk just as I came up on the hillside in front of his house. He has killed three within two years about his house, and they have killed two hens for him. They will fly off with a hen. In this case the hen was merely knocked over. I was surprised to find that this bird had not a red tail, and guessed it must be

like in the river? In this respect, also, Walden is a small ocean.

We had a true November sunset after a dark, cloudy afternoon. The sun reached a clear stratum just before setting, beneath the dark cloud, though ready to enter another on the horizon's edge, and a cold, yellow sunlight suddenly illumined the withered grass of the fields around, near and far, eastward. Such a phenomenon as, when it occurs later, I call the afterglow of the year.

It is of no use to plow deeper than the soil is, unless you mean to follow up that mode of cultivation persistently, manuring highly and carting on muck at each plowing, — making a soil, in short. Yet many a man likes to tackle mighty themes, like immortality, but in his discourse he turns up nothing but yellow sand, under which what little fertile and available surface soil he may have is quite buried and lost. He should teach frugality rather, — how to postpone the fatal hour, — should plant a crop of beans. He might have raised enough of these to make a deacon of him, though never a preacher. Many a man runs his plow so deep in heavy or stony soil that it sticks fast in the furrow. It is a great art in the writer to improve from day to day just that soil and fertility which he has, to harvest that crop which his life yields, whatever it may be, not be straining as if to reach apples or oranges when he yields only ground-nuts. He should be digging, not soaring. Just as earnest as your life is, so deep is your soil. If strong and deep, you will sow wheat and raise bread of life in it.

Now the young hen-hawks, full-grown but inexperi-

a young one. I brought it home and found that it was so, the same which Wilson called "Falco leverianus American Buzzard or White-breasted Hawk," it differed so much from the old. There [was] little if any rufous brown about this bird. It had a white breast and prettily barred (with blackish or dark-brown) white tail-coverts;[1] was generally dark-brown with white spots above. He says that he killed the others also at this season, and that they were marked like this. They were all young birds, then, and hence so bold or inexperienced, perhaps. They take his hens from between the house and the barn. When the hawk comes, all the hens and roosters run for the barn.

I see catnep turned at top to a crimson purple.

As I stood upon Heywood's Peak, I observed in the very middle of the pond, which was smooth and reflected the sky there, what at first I took to be a sheet of very thin, dark ice two yards wide drifting there, the first ice of the season, which had formed by the shore in the morning, but immediately I considered that it was too early and warm for that. Then I wondered for a moment what dark film could be floating out there on the pure and unruffled lake. To be sure, it was not a very conspicuous object, and most would not have noticed it! But, suspecting what it was, I looked through my glass and could plainly see the dimples made by a school of little fishes continually coming to the surface there together. It was exactly analogous to the dark rippled patches on the sea made by the menhaden as seen from Cape Cod. Why have I never observed the

[1] Vide the 11th.

enced, still white-breasted and brown (not red)-tailed, swoop down after the farmer's hens, between the barn and the house, often carrying one off in their clutches, and all the rest of the pack half fly, half run, to the barn. Unwarrantably bold, one ventures to stoop before the farmer's eyes. He clutches in haste his trusty gun, which hangs, ready loaded, on its pegs; he pursues warily to where the marauder sits teetering on a lofty pine, and when he is sailing scornfully away he meets his fate and comes fluttering head forward to earth. The exulting farmer hastes to secure his trophy. He treats the proud bird's body with indignity. He carries it home to show to his wife and children, for the hens were his wife's special care. He thinks it one of his best shots, full thirteen rods. This gun is "an all-fired good piece" — nothing but robin-shot. The body of the victim is delivered up to the children and the dog and, like the body of Hector, is dragged so many times round Troy.

But alas for the youthful hawk, the proud bird of prey, the tenant of the skies! We shall no more see his wave-like outline against a cloud, nor hear his scream from behind one. He saw but a pheasant in the field, the food which nature has provided for him, and stooped to seize it. This was his offense. He, the native of these skies, must make way for those bog-trotters from another land, which never soar. The eye that was conversant with sublimity, that looked down on earth from under its sharp projecting brow, is closed; the head that was never made dizzy by any height is brought low; the feet that were not made to walk on earth now lie useless along it. With those trailing claws for grapnels it dragged the lower sky. Those wings which swept the sky must now dust the chimney-corner, perchance. So weaponed, with strong beak and talons, and wings, like a war-steamer, to carry them about. In vain were the brown-spotted eggs laid, in vain were ye cradled in the loftiest pine of the swamp. Where are your father and mother? Will they hear of your early death? before ye had acquired your full plumage, they who nursed and defended ye so faithfully?

Nov. 10. A pleasant day, especially the forenoon. Thermometer 46° at noon. Some would call it Indian summer, but it does not deserve to be called summer; grows cool in afternoon when I go —

To Baker Farm aspen *via* Cliffs.

Some very handsome *Solidago nemoralis* in bloom on Fair Haven Hill. (Look for these late flowers — November flowers — on hills, above frost.)

I think I may say that about the 5th the white, swamp white, and black, and perhaps red, oaks (the last *may* be later) were in their November condition, *i. e.* for the most part fallen. The few *large* black oak tops, still covered with leaves above the forest (*i. e.* just withered), are brownish-yellow.

The brilliancy of the scarlet oak being generally dulled, the season of brilliant leaves may be considered over, — say about the 10th; and now a new season begins, the pure November season of the russet earth and withered leaf and bare twigs and hoary withered goldenrods, etc.

From Fair Haven Hill, using my glass, I think that I

can see some of the snow of the 7th still left on the brow of Uncannunuc. It is a light line, lying close along under the edge of a wood which covers the summit, which has protected it. I can understand how much nearer they must feel to winter who live in plain sight of that than we do. I think that I could not have detected the edge of the forest if it had not been for the snow.

In the path below the Cliff, I see some blue-stemmed goldenrod turned yellow as well as purple. The Jersey tea is fallen, all but the terminal leaves. These, however, are the greenest and apparently least changed of any indigenous plant, unless it be the sweet-fern. Withered leaves generally, though they remain on the trees, are drooping. As I go through the hazel bushes toward the sun, I notice the silvery light reflected from the fine down on their tender twigs, this year's growth. This apparently protects them against the winter. The very armor that Nature puts on reminds you of the foe she would resist. This a November phenomenon, — the silvery light reflected from a myriad of downy surfaces.

A true November seat is amid the pretty white-plumed *Andropogon scoparius*, the withered culms of the purple wood grass which covers so many dry knolls. There is a large patch at the entrance to Pleasant Meadow. It springs from pink-brown clumps of radical leaves, which make good seats. Looking toward the sun, as I sit in the midst of it rising as high as my head, its countless silvery plumes are a very cheerful sight. At a distance they look like frost on the plant.

I look out westward across Fair Haven Pond. The warmer colors are now rare. A cool and silvery light is

the prevailing one; dark-blue or slate-colored clouds in the west, and the sun going down in them. All the light of November may be called an afterglow.

Hornbeam bare; how long? Perhaps with the ostrya and just after elms? There are still a few leaves on the large *Populus tremuliformis*, but they will be all gone in a day or two. They have turned quite yellow.

Hearing in the oak and near by a sound as if some one had broken a twig, I looked up and saw a jay pecking at an acorn. There were several jays busily gathering acorns on a scarlet oak. I could hear them break them off. They then flew to a suitable limb and, placing the acorn under one foot, hammered away at it busily, looking round from time to time to see if any foe was approaching, and soon reached the meat and nibbled at it, holding up their heads to swallow, while they held it very firmly with their claws. (Their hammering made a sound like the woodpecker's.) Nevertheless it sometimes dropped to the ground before they had done with it.

Aphides on alder.

Sap still flows in scarlet oak.

Returned by Spanish Brook Path. Notice the glaucous white bloom on the thimble-berry of late, as there are fewer things to notice. So many objects are white or light, preparing us for winter.

By the 10th of November we conclude with the scarlet oak dulled (and the colors of October generally faded), with a few golden spangles on the white birches and on a lingering *Populus tremuliformis* and a few sallows, a few green leaves on the Jersey tea, and a few

lingering scarlet or yellow or crimson ones on the flowering dogwood in a sheltered place, the gooseberry, the high blueberry, *Cornus sericea*, the late rose and the common smooth one, and the sweet-briar,[1] meadow-sweet, sweet-fern, and *Viburnum nudum*.[2] But they are very rare or uninteresting. To these may be added the introduced plants of November 9th, which are more leafy. Of them the silvery abele, English cherry, and broom have been of the most interesting colors.

Nov. 11. Goodwin brings me this forenoon a this year's loon, which he just killed on the river, — great northern diver, but a smaller specimen than Wilson describes and somewhat differently marked. It is twenty-seven inches long to end of feet by forty-four, and bill three and three-quarters to angle of mouth; above blackish-gray with small white spots (two at end of each feather).[3] Beneath, pure white, throat and all, except a dusky bar across the vent. Bill chiefly pale-bluish and dusky. You are struck by its broad, flat, sharp-edged legs, made to cut through the water rather than to walk with, set far back and naturally stretched out backward, its long and powerful bill, conspicuous white throat and breast. Dislodged by winter in the north, it is slowly travelling toward a warmer clime, diving in the cool river this morning, which is now full of light, the trees and bushes on the brink having long

[1] English?

[2] And green-briar, according to Nov. 7th and 11th, 1855; and perhaps a *few* other shrubs.

[3] [It must have been a red-throated loon.]

since lost their leaves, and the neighboring fields are white with frost. Yet this hardy bird is comfortable and contented there if the sportsman would let it alone.

P. M. — To Island and J. P. Brown's cold pond.

A cold day. Now seek sunny and sheltered places as in early spring, the south side the island, for example. Certain localities are thus distinguished. And they retain this peculiarity permanently, unless it depends on a wood which may be cut. Thousands of years hence this may still be the warmest and sunniest spot in the spring and fall.

I hear here a faint creaking of two or three crickets or locustæ, but it is a steady sound, — not the common cricket's, — long-continued, and when one pauses, generally another continues the strain, so that it seems absolutely continuous. They are either in the grass or on the bushes by the edge of the water, under this sunny wood-side. I afterward hear a few of the common cricket on the side of Clamshell. Thus they are confined now to the sun on the south sides of hills and woods. They are quite silent long before sunset.

Snow-fleas are skipping on the surface of the water at the edge, and spiders running about. These become prominent now.

The waters look cold and empty of fish and most other inhabitants now. Here, in the sun in the shelter of the wood, the smooth shallow water, with the stubble standing in it, is waiting for ice. Indeed, ice that formed last night must have recently melted in it. The sight of such water now reminds me of ice as much as of

water. No doubt many fishes have gone into winter quarters.[1]

The flowering dogwood, though still leafy, is uninteresting and partly withered.

Gossamer reflecting the light is another November phenomenon (as well as October). I see here, looking toward the sun, a very distinct silvery sheen from the cranberry vines, as from a thousand other November surfaces, though, looking down on them, they are dark purple.

Speaking of twiggy mazes, the very stubble and fine pasture grasses unshorn are others reflecting the light too, like twigs; but these are of a peculiar bleached brownish color, a principal ingredient in the russet of the earth's surface.[2]

Going by the willow-row above railroad, scare up small duck, — perhaps teal, — and, in the withered grass at Nut Meadow Brook, two black ducks, which rise black between me and the sun, but, when they have circled round to the east, show some silvery sheen on the under side of their wings. Am surprised to see a little ice in this brook in the shade, as I push far up it through a dense field of withered blue-joint, — a spot white with frost, a few inches over. Saw a small pool in the woods also skimmed over, and many ice-crystals heaved up in low ground. Scare up a bird which at first ran in the grass, then flew, — a snipe. See only a very few small water-bugs in the brook, but no large ones nor skaters.

[1] *Vide* account of eels in *Tribune* for Nov. 9th.
[2] *Vide* Nov. 8th.

As a general rule, the leaves hold on longest on our indigenous trees and shrubs which were the first to leaf out, *e. g.* aspen, white birch, meadow-sweet, gooseberry, roses, sallows.

In the shade of the wood, on the hillside just west of the cold pond, am surprised to see the frost about the cistus not in the least melted. This, at least, is an evidence that cold weather is come. Looking closely at it, it reminds me by its form and position of the decodon bark half cracked open. It consists of four or five thin curled shavings of frost, so to speak horizontally

  grained, placed vertically and based on the stem, one within another, and curling toward the same side, forming a sort of fool's cap of different

thicknesses, or cockles, or sugar-plums. It seems it is so cool that the frost about the cistus does not melt all day, in the shade. Coming home I have cold fingers, and must row to get warm.

In the meadows the pitcher-plants are bright-red.

This is the month of nuts and nutty thoughts, — that November whose name sounds so bleak and cheerless. Perhaps its harvest of thought is worth more than all the other crops of the year. Men are more serious now.

I find, in the wood-path this side that pond, thirteen kernels of corn close together, and five of them have the germ uncovered, the thin husk that was over them torn off. This might have been done accidentally by the

squirrel (?) in separating it from the ear or in transporting it. And this may be the origin of some account of their eating out the germ to prevent its sprouting. If they do eat it, perhaps it is because it is the softest (as it is) and perhaps the most savory part. These were at least a third of a mile from a corn-field.[1]

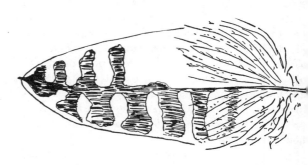

The tail-coverts of the young hen-hawk, *i. e.* this year's bird, at present are white, very handsomely barred or watered with dark brown in an irregular manner somewhat as above, the bars on opposite sides of the midrib alternating in an agreeable manner. Such natural objects have suggested the "watered" figures or colors in the arts. Few mortals ever look down on the tail-coverts of a young hen-hawk, yet these are not only beautiful, but of a peculiar beauty, being differently marked and colored (to judge from Wilson's account of the old) from those of the old bird. Thus she finishes her works above men's sight.

[1] *Vide* fall of '59.

The scarlet oak leaf! What a graceful and pleasing outline! a combination of graceful curves and angles.

These deep bays in the leaf are agreeable to us as the thought of deep and smooth and secure havens to the mariner. But both your love of repose and your spirit of adventure are addressed, for both bays and headlands are represented, — sharp-pointed rocky capes and rounded bays with smooth strands. To the sailor's eye is a much indented shore, and in his casual glance he thinks that if he doubles its sharp capes he will find a haven in its deep rounded bays. If I were a drawing-master, I would set my pupils to copying these leaves, that they might learn to draw firmly and gracefully. It is a shore to the aerial ocean, on which the windy surf beats. How different from the white oak leaf with its rounded headlands, on which no lighthouse need be placed![1]

[1] [Excursions, p. 280; Riv. 344.]

Some white oak leaves retain a smothered inward crimson fire long after they have fallen very pure and complete, more interesting to me than their fresher glow, because more indestructible, — an evening glow.

Nov. 12. I hear from Ricketson to-day that on the 10th the following trees, *which I had not seen lately,* were leafy and, as I infer, more or less unwithered. His words are, "Horse-chestnut quite full of yellow and green foliage. English walnut ditto.[1] Beech, linden (1), hawthorn (nearly perfect in green foliage, only a little decayed at the top, but in a sheltered place), silver linden, copper beech (2), elm (3), weeping ash,[2] *Euonymus Europæus* (4)."[3] Also "the guelder-rose"[4] and "*Bignonia radicans*[5] and *acuminata*" and "numerous shrubs in full leaf." Of those not European, "Osage orange (*Maclura*), *Cornus florida* (handsome), tulip, three-thorned acacia,[6] Mexican cypress."

He sent me specimens of those numbered above which were fresh, especially the fourth, and the third next, the second least so; but then what he sends for the American linden is greener than the European!! I find that E. Hoar observed the English elms with leaves or leafy still November 2d, near Salisbury.

It is much the coldest day yet, and the ground is a little frozen and resounds under my tread. All people move the brisker for the cold, yet are braced and a little

[1] Persian, according to Loudon.
[2] Variety of English *Fraxinus excelsior,* according to L.
[3] English, according to L.   [4] English.
[5] American.   [6] American.

Vol. XI

elated by it. They love to say, "Cold day, sir." Though the days are shorter, you get more work out of a hired man than before, for he must work to keep warm.

P. M. — To Hill.

The riverside is skimmed over and presents a wintry aspect, — those great plaits, or folds, as it were, where the crystals have shot, wool-grass frozen in, and the thin white ice where the water has gone down.

Now for a brisk and energetic walk, with a will and a purpose. Have done with sauntering, in the idle sense. You must rush to the assault of winter. Make haste into the outskirts, climb the ramparts of the town, be on the alert and let nothing escape your observation. The army is all van.

The cold alone has brought down a good part of the remaining leaves of abeles and white willows. I see the handsome leaves of the last thickly strewn over the ice and reminding of grain even, half upside down. Pitch pine leaves are about all fallen.

The very common redness of the recent shoots, as white maples, huckleberries, etc., now that the twigs are bare, and on many sides masses of them are run together in a maze, adds to the general russet of nature. The black willow shoots are a very pale brownish yellow.

We are now reduced to browsing on buds and twigs, and methinks, with this diet and this cold, we shall look to the stall-fed thinkers like those unkempt cattle in meadows now, grazing the withered grass.

Examining closely the base of some frost-weed, I find in each case a little frost firmly attached to the naked woody stem just under the bark, having burst the last

for about an inch along the stem and elevated it. Perhaps this weed dies down slowly, since it blossoms a second time, and there is more sap now in the stem near its base than usual, which escapes in a vapor from the stem, and, being frozen, forms this kind of icicle.

I think that the change to some higher color in a leaf is an evidence that it has arrived at a late and more perfect and final maturity, answering to the maturity of fruits, and not to that of green leaves, etc., etc., which merely serve a purpose.[1] The word "ripe" is thought by some to be derived from the verb "to reap," according to which that is ripe which is ready to be reaped. The fall of the leaf is preceded by a ripe old age.

Nov. 13. 8.30 A. M. — To Hill.

I notice of late the darker green (livid?) of the arbor-vitæ and other evergreens, the effect of cold. So they are never so purely bright a green as immediately after their fall. They are not perfectly *ever*-green.

I hear go over, not far from the house, goldfinches, as I think, — their mewing note and ricochet flight, — I think not redpolls, for I hear no rattling notes. Also hear a robin's note.

Last night was quite cold, and the ground is white with frost. Thus gradually, but steadily, winter approaches. First there is the bleached grass, then the frost, then snow, the fields growing more and more hoary. There is frost not only on all the withered grass and stubble, but it is particularly thick and white and handsome around the throat of every hole and chink in

[1] [Excursions, p. 250; Riv. 306.]

the earth's surface, the congealed breath of the earth as it were, so that you would think at first it was the entry to some woodchuck's, or squirrel's, or mouse's, retreat. But it is the great dormant earth gone into winter quarters here, the earth letting off steam after the summer's work is over.

As I stand on the hill at 9 A. M., it looks like snow; the sky is overcast; smokes go up thickly from the village, answering to the frost in the chinks; and there is a remarkable stillness, as if it were earlier, the effect of the colder weather merely, as it were stiffening things. Leaves, twigs, birds (except the chickadee, and its feeble note seems to enhance the stillness), and insects are hushed. The few tinkling sounds — the chopping, or the like — are heard far and distinctly. It is like the calm before a hurricane or an earthquake, this stillness which precedes the winter's setting in.

Larches now look dark or brownish yellow.

Now, on the advent of much colder weather, the last *Populus tremuliformis* has lost its leaves, the sheltered dogwood is withered, and even the scarlet oak may be considered as extinguished, and the larch looks brown and nearly bare, and the few leaves left here and there on the indigenous shrubs named on the 9th are being rapidly killed by the same cause, and are falling.

Now for twinkling light reflected from unseen windows in the horizon in the early twilight.

One hickory at least (on the hill) has not lost its leaves yet, *i. e.*, has a good many left. So they are a month falling.

I see some feathers of a blue jay scattered along a

wood-path, and at length come to the body of the bird. What a neat and delicately ornamented creature, finer than any work of art in a lady's boudoir, with its soft light purplish-blue crest and its dark-blue or purplish secondaries (the narrow half) finely barred with dusky. It is the more glorious to live in Concord because the jay is so splendidly painted.[1]

A large flock of geese go over just before night.

After expecting snow all day, — though we did not know but it would prove rain, — we looked out the window at 9 P. M. and saw the ground for the most part white with the first sugaring, which at first we could hardly tell from a mild moonlight, — only there was no moon. Thus it comes stealthily in the night and changes the whole aspect of the earth.

Of course frozen ground, ice, and snow have now banished the few remaining skaters (if there were any?), crickets, and water-bugs.

It is wonderful what gradation and harmony there is in nature. The light reflected from bare twigs at this season — *i. e.*, since they began to be bare, in the latter part of October — is not only like that from gossamer, but like that which will ere long be reflected from the ice that will incrust them. So the bleached herbage of the fields is like frost, and frost like snow, and one prepares for the other.

Nov. 14. It is very cold and windy; thermometer 26. I walk to Walden and Andromeda Ponds. It is all at once perfect winter. I walk on frozen ground two-

[1] [Channing, p. 300.]

thirds covered with a sugaring of dry snow, and this strong and cutting northwest wind makes the oak leaves rustle dryly enough to set your heart on edge. A great many have fallen, even since the snow last evening. Take a citizen out into an oak sprout-land when there is a sugaring of dry snow and a cold, cutting northwest wind rustles the leaves. A sympathetic shiver will seize him. He will know of no fire to warm his wits by. He has no pleasing pursuit to follow through these difficulties, no traps to inspect, no chopping to do. Every resounding step on the frozen earth is a vain knocking at the door of what was lately genial Nature, his bountiful mother, now turned a stepmother. He is left outside to starve. The rustling leaves sound like the fierce breathing of wolves, — an endless pack, half famished, from the north, impelled by hunger to seize him. Of birds only the chickadees seem really at home. Where they are is a hearth and a bright fire constantly burning. The tree sparrows must be very lively to keep warm. The rest keep close to-day.

You will see where a mouse (or mole?) has run under the thinnest snow, like this. Such humble paths they prefer, perhaps to escape nocturnal foes.

Now I begin to notice the silver downy twigs of the sweet-fern in the sun (lately bare), the red or crimson twigs and buds of the high blueberry. The different colors of the water andromeda in different lights.

If he looks into the water, he gets no comfort there, for that is cold and empty, expecting ice.

Now, while the frosty air begins to nip your fingers and your nose, the frozen ground rapidly wears away

the soles of your shoes, as sandpaper might; the old she wolf is nibbling at your very extremities. The frozen ground eating away the soles of your shoes is only typical of the vulture that gnaws your heart this month.

Now all that moves migrates, or has migrated. Ducks are gone by. The citizen has sought the town. Probably the witch-hazel and many other flowers lingered till the 11th, when it was colder. The last leaves and flowers (?) may be said to fall about the middle of November.

Snow and cold drive the doves to your door, and so your thoughts make new alliances.

Nov. 15. P. M. — To Grackle Swamp.

A very fine snow falling, just enough to whiten the bare spots a little. I go to look for evergreen ferns before they are covered up.[1] The end of last month and the first part of this is the time. I do not know that I find more than one kind now in that swamp, and of that the fertile fronds are mostly decayed. All lie flat, ready to be buried in snow.

Slight as the snow is, you are now reminded occasionally in your walks that you have contemporaries, and perchance predecessors. I see the track of a fox which was returning from his visit to a farmyard last night, and, in the wood-path, of a man and a dog. The dog must have been a large one. I see their shadows before me. In another place, where the snow is so slight and lifted up on the withered grass that no track is left, I see by the cakes or balls of snow that have dropped from

[1] For ferns *vide* 17th.

his shoes that a man has passed. This would be known for a man and a dog's track in any part of the world. Five toes in a bundle, somewhat diamond-shape, forming a sort of rosette, are the print of the dog, whether on the sands of Africa or the snow of New England. The track of his master is somewhat more variable, yet reducible within certain limits.

The *Lycopodium dendroideum* var. *obscurum* appears to be just in bloom in the swamp about the Hemlocks (the regular one (not variety) is apparently earlier), — later than the *Lycopodium complanatum*, which is done there.

Gossamer, methinks, belongs to the latter part of October and first part of November; also the frost-weed and evergreen ferns. Buds and twigs (like gossamer), and the mazes made by twigs, and the silvery light on this down, and the silver-haired andropogon grass to the first half of November.

The water andromeda leaves have fallen, and the persistent turned that red brown; how long?

Nov. 16. P. M. — To Hubbard's Close.

A cold and blustering afternoon; sky for the most part overcast.

The *Cornus Canadensis* is called by Loudon "a deciduous herbaceous plant," the pyrolas "ever-green herbaceous plants." The bunchberry leaves are now little if any withered,[1] but generally drooping, the four hanging together as is the habit of the *sericea* and *florida*, the lambkill, etc. The plant dies down to its perennial

[1] I see, next day, that in exposed places they are.

root each year, and a fresh one shoots up in the spring. You can see its pink bud already strongly formed. But this year's plant is very slow to die, and I suspect many of the leaves remain green all winter under the snow. They are now generally purplish-tinged. Let me observe in what respect the pyrolas are more evergreen. The new bud is formed between the present two leaves, the old leaves, lower on the stem or vine, being mostly decayed.

There are many large limbs strewn about the woods, which were broken off by that strong southeast wind in peach time. These are now thickly leaved, the dead wood not being able to cast off the withered leaves; but the leaves having died thus prematurely are of a different color from that their companions changed to, — a peculiar yellow-brown (*i. e.* chestnuts and oaks) with more or less green in it.

I see a gray squirrel, eight or ten rods off in Hubbard's large wood, scamper over the leaves and run up an oak. From the oak it crosses ascending into a tall white pine top, and there lies concealed, and I can see no more of him.

The earth half covered with this slight snow, merely grayed with [it], is the more like the bare gray limbs of oak woods now, and such woods and the earth make the more uniform impression.

Methinks the wintergreen, pipsissewa, is our handsomest evergreen, so liquid glossy green and dispersed almost all over the woods. The mountain laurel, the *Lycopodium dendroideum, complanatum,* and *lucidulum,* and the terminal shield fern are also very interesting.

Preaching? Lecturing? Who are ye that ask for these things? What do ye want to hear, ye puling infants? A trumpet-sound that would train you up to mankind, or a nurse's lullaby? The preachers and lecturers deal with men of straw, as they are men of straw themselves. Why, a free-spoken man, of sound lungs, cannot draw a long breath without causing your rotten institutions to come toppling down by the vacuum he makes. Your church is a baby-house made of blocks, and so of the state. It would be a relief to breathe one's self occasionally among men. If there were any magnanimity in us, any grandeur of soul, anything but sects and parties undertaking to patronize God and keep the mind within bounds, how often we might encourage and provoke one another by a free expression! I will not consent to walk with my mouth muzzled, not till I am rabid, until there is danger that I shall bite the unoffending and that my bite will produce hydrophobia.

Freedom of speech! It hath not entered into your hearts to conceive what those words mean. It is not leave given me by your sect to say this or that; it is when leave is given to your sect to withdraw. The church, the state, the school, the magazine, think they are liberal and free! It is the freedom of a prison-yard. I ask only that one fourth part of my honest thoughts be spoken aloud. What is it you tolerate, you church to-day? Not truth, but a lifelong hypocrisy. Let us have institutions framed not out of our rottenness, but out of our soundness. This factitious piety is like stale gingerbread. I would like to suggest what a pack of fools and cowards we mankind are. They want me to agree not to breathe

too hard in the neighborhood of their paper castles. If I should draw a long breath in the neighborhood of these institutions, their weak and flabby sides would fall out, for my own inspiration would exhaust the air about them. The church! it is eminently the timid institution, and the heads and pillars of it are constitutionally and by principle the greatest cowards in the community. The voice that goes up from the monthly concerts is not so brave and so cheering as that which rises from the frog-ponds of the land. The best "preachers," so called, are an effeminate class; their bravest thoughts wear petticoats. If they have any manhood they are sure to forsake the ministry, though they were to turn their attention to baseball. Look at your editors of popular magazines. I have dealt with two or three the most liberal of them. They are afraid to print a whole sentence, a *round* sentence, a free-spoken sentence. They want to get thirty thousand subscribers, and they will do anything to get them. They consult the D.D.'s and all the letters of the alphabet before printing a sentence.[1] I have been into many of these cowardly New England towns where they *profess* Christianity, — invited to speak, perchance, — where they were trembling in their shoes at the thought of the things you might say, as if they knew their weak side, — that they were weak on all sides. The devil they have covenanted with is a timid devil. If they would let their sores alone they might heal, and they could to the wars again like men; but instead of that they get together in meeting-house cellars, rip off the bandages and poultice them with sermons.

[1] [See *Cape Cod, and Miscellanies,* p. 469 ; *Misc.,* Riv. 271.]

One of our New England towns is sealed up hermetically like a molasses-hogshead, — such is its sweet Christianity, — only a little of the sweet trickling out at the cracks enough to daub you. The few more liberal-minded or indifferent inhabitants are the flies that buzz about it. It is Christianity bunged up. I see awful eyes looking out through a bull's-eye at the bung-hole. It is doubtful if they can fellowship with me.

The further you go up country, I think the worse it is, the more benighted they are. On the one side you will find a barroom which holds the " Scoffers," so called, on the other a vestry where is a monthly concert of prayer. There is just as little to cheer you in one of these companies as the other. It may be often the truth and righteousness of the barroom that saves the town. There is nothing to redeem the bigotry and moral cowardice of New-Englanders in my eyes. You may find a cape which runs six miles into the sea that has not a man of moral courage upon it. What is called faith is an immense prejudice. Like the Hindoos and Russians [?] and Sandwich-Islanders (that were), they are the creatures of an institution. They do not think; they adhere like oysters to what their fathers and grandfathers adhered to. How often is it that the shoemaker, by thinking over his last, can think as valuable a thought as he makes a valuable shoe?

I have been into the town, being invited to speak to the inhabitants, not valuing, not having read even, the Assembly's Catechism, and I try to stimulate them by reporting the best of my experience. I see the craven priest looking round for a hole to escape at, alarmed

because it was he that invited me thither, and an awful silence pervades the audience. They think they will never get me there again. But the seed has not all fallen in stony and shallow ground.

The following are our shrubby evergreen plants (not including *Coniferæ*) : [1] —

> *Mitchella repens*
> Linnæa
> *Andromeda Polifolia*
> *Cassandra calyculata*
> Mayflower
> Checkerberry
> Mountain laurel
> Lambkill
> *Kalmia glauca*
> Labrador tea
> Common cranberry
> European cranberry

To which I will add the herbaceous : —

> *Chimaphila umbellata*
>   *maculata*

N. B. — *Rubus hispidus* leaves last through the winter, turning reddish.[2]

It is no compliment to be invited to lecture before the rich Institutes and Lyceums. The settled lecturers are as tame as the settled ministers. The audiences do not want to hear any prophets; they do not wish to be stimulated and instructed, but entertained. They, their wives and daughters, go to the Lyceum to suck a sugar-plum. The little of medicine they get is disguised with

[1] Genista is *not* evergreen. *Vide Mar.* 6, 1859.
[2] Gold-thread. *Vide* 25th.

sugar. It is never the reformer they hear there, but a faint and timid echo of him only. They seek a passtime merely. Their greatest guns and sons of thunder are only wooden guns and great-grandsons of thunder, who give them smooth words well pronounced from manuscripts well punctuated, — they who have stolen the little fire they have from prophets whom the audience would quake to hear. They ask for orators that will entertain them and leave them where they found them. The most successful lecturing on Washington, or what-not, is an awful scratching of backs to the tune, it may be, of fifty thousand dollars. Sluggards that want to have a lullaby sung to them! Such manikins as I have described are they, alas, who have made the greatest stir (and what a shallow stir) in the church and Lyceum, and in Congress. They want a medicine that will not interfere with their daily meals.

There is the Lowell Institute with its restrictions, requiring a certain faith in the lecturers. How can any freethinking man accept its terms? It is as if you were to resolve that you would not eat oysters that were not of a particular faith, — that, for instance, did not believe the Thirty-Nine Articles, — for the faith that is in an oyster is just as valuable as the faith referred to in Mr. Lowell's will. These popular lecturers, our preachers, and magazines are for women and children *in the bad sense.*

The curators have on their lists the names of the men who came before the Philomathean Institute in the next large town and did no harm; left things *in statu quo,* so that all slept the better for it; only confirmed the audience in their previous badness; spoke a good word for

God; gave the clergy, that heavy set, a lift; told the youngsters to be good boys. A man may have a good deal to say who has not any desk to thump on, who does not thunder in bad air.

They want all of a man but his truth and independence and manhood.

One who spoke to their condition would of course make them wince, and they would retaliate, *i. e.* kick him out, or stop their ears.

The cold weather which began on the 12th, with the snow of the 13th and since, suddenly killed the few remaining living leaves, without any exceptions to speak of. Most foreign plants at once dropped their leaves, though pretty thick before, but there are many still on the privet. The sweet-fern in some places has still many green, more than any indigenous shrub or tree, though far the greater part of them (the sweet-ferns) are bare or withered. Probably the larch about fallen.

Nov. 17. The ground has remained frozen since the morning of the 12th.

P. M. — Up Assabet.

The polypody on the rock is much shrivelled by the late cold. The edges are curled up, and it is not nearly so fair as it was ten days ago. I see a small botrychium in the swampy wood west of river, opposite Emerson's field, quite fresh, not at all injured.

The musquash are more active since the cold weather. I see more of them about the river now, swimming back and forth across the river, and diving in the middle, where I lose them. They dive off the round-backed, black mossy stones, which, when small and slightly exposed, look much like themselves. In swimming show commonly three parts with water between. One sitting in the sun, as if for warmth, on the opposite shore to me looks quite reddish brown. They avail themselves of the edge of the ice now found along the sides of the river to feed on.

Much *Lycopodium complanatum* did not shed pollen on the 3d, and the *Lycopodium dendroideum* var. *obscurum* sheds it only within a very few days [1] (was apparently in its prime yesterday). So it would seem that *these* lycopodiums, at least, which have their habitat on the forest floor and but lately attracted my attention there (since the withered leaves fell around them and revealed them by the contrast of their color and they emerged from obscurity), — it would seem that they at the same time attained to their prime, their flowering season. It was coincident with this prominence.[2]

Leaving my boat, I walk through the low wood west of Dove Rock, toward the scarlet oak. The very sunlight on the pale-brown bleached fields is an interesting object these cold days. I naturally look toward [it] as to a wood-fire. Not only different objects are presented to our attention at different seasons of the year, but we are in a frame of body and of mind to appreciate different objects at different seasons. I see one thing when it is cold and another when it is warm.

Looking toward the sun now when an hour high, there being many small alders and birches between me and it for half a dozen rods, the light reflected from their

[1] Nov. 2, 1853.   [2] *Vide* 30th.

twigs has the appearance of an immense cobweb with closely concentric lines, of which I see about one fourth, on account of the upward curve of the twigs on each side, and the light not being reflected to me at all from one side of the trees directly in front of me. The light is thus very pleasantly diffused.

We are interested at this season by the manifold ways in which the light is reflected to us. Ascending a little knoll covered with sweet-fern, shortly after, the sun appearing but a point above the sweet-fern, its light was reflected from a dense mass of the bare downy twigs of this plant in a surprising manner which would not be believed if described. It was quite like the sunlight reflected from grass and weeds covered with hoar frost. Yet in an ordinary light these are but dark or dusky looking twigs with scarcely a noticeable downiness. Yet as I saw it, there was a perfect halo of light resting on the knoll as I moved to right or left. A myriad of surfaces are now prepared to reflect the light. This is one of the hundred silvery lights of November. The setting sun, too, is reflected from windows more brightly than at any other season. "November Lights" would be a theme for me.

I am surprised to see a stake-driver fly up from the weeds within a stone's throw of my boat's place. It drops its excrement from thirty feet in the air, and this falling, one part being heavier than another, takes the form of a snake, and suggests that this may be the origin of some of the stories of this bird swallowing a snake or eel which passed through it.

Nature is moderate and loves degrees. Winter is not all

Vol. XI

white and sere. Some trees are evergreen to cheer us, and on the forest floor our eyes do not fall on sere brown leaves alone, but some evergreen shrubs are placed there to relieve the eye. Mountain laurel, lambkill, checkerberry, wintergreen, etc., etc., etc., and a few evergreen ferns scattered about keep up the semblance of summer still.

As for the evergreen ferns, I see now —

> Common polypody (though shrivelled by cold where exposed).
> *Asplenium trichomanes.*
> *A. ebeneum.*
> *Aspidium spinulosum* (?), large frond, small-fruited, in swamp southeast Brister's Spring, on 16th.
> *A. cristatum* (?), Grackle Swamp on the 15th, with oftener what I take to be the narrower and more open sterile frond.
> *A. marginale* (common).
> *A. achrostichoides* (terminal shield).

The first one and the last two are particularly handsome, the last especially, it has so thick a frond.

Nov. 18. P. M. — To Conantum.

Notice the short bright-yellow willow twigs on Hubbard's Causeway. They are prominent now, first, because they are bare; second, because high-colored always and [because of] this rarity of bright colors at present; third, because of the clear air and November light. For the same reason I notice nowadays the red twigs of the silky cornel by the river. The black willow twigs are tawny in the mass, almost cinnamon.

The fruitless enterprise of some persons who rush helter-skelter, carrying out their crazy scheme, — merely "putting it through," as they phrase it, — reminds me

of those thistle-downs which, not being detained nor steadied by any seed at the base, are blown away at the first impulse and go rolling over all obstacles. They may indeed go fastest and farthest, but where they rest at last not even a thistle springs. I meet these useless barren thistle-downs driving over the fields. They remind me of busy merchants and brokers on 'change doing business on credit, gambling with fancy stocks, that have failed over and over again, assisted to get a-going again to no purpose, — a great ado about nothing, — all in my eye, — with nothing to deposit, not of the slightest use to the great thistle tribe, not even tempting a jackass. When you right or extricate one of these fellows and set him before the wind again, it is worth the while to look and see if he has any seed of success under him. Such a one you may know afar — he floats more slowly and steadily — and of his enterprise expect results.

Am surprised to see Fair Haven Pond completely frozen over during the last four days. It will probably open again. Thus, while all the channel elsewhere is open and a mere edging of ice amid the weeds is seen, this great expansion is completely bridged over, thus early.

Some mocker-nuts, and I think some hickories, on Conantum are not yet bare. Their withered leaves hold on almost like the oaks. Now is the time to gather the mocker-nuts.

I go along under the east side of Lee's Cliff, looking at the evergreen ferns. The marginal fern is the commonest. How pretty the smallest asplenium sometimes, in a recess under a shelving rock, as it were pinned on rosettewise, as if it were the head of a breastpin.

I look south from the Cliff. The westering sun just out of sight behind the hill. Its rays from those bare twigs across the pond are bread and cheese to me. So many oak leaves have fallen that the white birch stems are more distinct amid the young oaks; I see to the bone. See those brave birches prepared to stand the winter through on the hillsides. They never sing, "What's this dull town to me?" The maples skirting the meadows (in dense phalanxes) look like light infantry advanced for a swamp fight. Ah, dear *November*, ye must be sacred to the *Nine* surely.[1]

The early willow catkins already peep out a quarter of an inch. Early crowfoot is reddened at Lee's.

Nov. 19. P. M. — Mocker-nutting, to Conantum.

The lambkill and water andromeda are turned quite dark red where much exposed; in shelter are green yet.

Those long mocker-nuts appear not to have got well ripe this year. They do not shed their husks, and the meat is mostly skinny and soft and flabby. Perhaps the season has been too cold. I shook the trees. It is just the time to get them. How hard they rattle down, like stones! There is a harmony between this stony fruit and these hard, tough limbs which bear it. I was surprised to see how much the hickory-tops had been bent and split, apparently by ice, tough as they are. They seem to have suffered more than evergreens do. The husks of one tree scarcely gaped open at all, and could

[1] [Channing, p. 107.]

Vol. XI

not be removed. I did not think at first why these nuts had not been gathered, but I suspect it may be because Puffer, who probably used to get them, has committed suicide.

Nov. 20. P. M. — To Ministerial Swamp.

I have seen more gray squirrels of late (as well as musquash); I think not merely because the trees are bare but because they are stirring about more, — nutting, etc.

Martial Miles tells me of a snapping turtle caught in the river at Waltham, about October 1st, he thinks, which weighed fifty-five pounds (?). He saw it. There were two fighting.

He says that a marsh hawk had his nest in his meadow several years, and though he shot the female three times, the male with but little delay returned with a new mate. He often watched these birds, and saw that the female could tell when the male was coming a long way off. He thought that he fed her and the young all together (?). She would utter a scream when she perceived him, and, rising into the air (before or after the scream?), she turned over with her talons uppermost, while he passed some three rods above, and caught without fail the prey which he let drop, and then carried it to her young. He had seen her do this many times, and always without failing.

The common milkweed (*Asclepias Cornuti*) and some thistles still discounting.

I go across the great Tony Wheeler pasture. It is a cool but pleasant November afternoon. The glory of

November is in its silvery, sparkling lights. I think it is peculiar among the months for the amount [of] sparkling white light reflected from a myriad of surfaces. The air is so clear, and there are so many bare, polished, bleached or hoary surfaces to reflect the light. Few things are more exhilarating, if it is only moderately cold, than to walk over bare pastures and see the abundant sheeny light like a universal halo, reflected from the russet and bleached earth. The earth shines perhaps more than in spring, for the reflecting surfaces are less dimmed now. It is not a red but a white light. In the woods and about swamps, as Ministerial, also, there are several kinds of twigs, this year's shoots of shrubs, which have a slight down or hairiness, hardly perceptible in ordinary lights though held in the hand, but which, seen toward the sun, reflect a cheering silvery light. Such are not only the sweet-fern, but the hazel in a less degree, alder twigs, and even the short huckleberry twigs, also lespedeza stems. It is as if they were covered with a myriad fine spiculæ which reflect a dazzling white light, exceedingly warming to the spirits and imagination. This gives a character of snug warmth and cheerfulness to the swamp, as if it were a place where the sun consorted with rabbits and partridges. Each individual hair on every such shoot above the swamp is bathed in glowing sunlight and is directly conversant with the day god.

The cinnamon-brown of withered pinweeds (how long?) colors whole fields. It may be put with the now paler brown of hardhack heads and the now darker brown of the dicksonia fern by walls.

I notice this afternoon that the pasture white oaks have commonly a few leaves left on the lower limbs and also next the trunk.

Winter-rye is another conspicuous green amid the withered grass fields.

The rubuses are particularly hardy to retain their leaves. Not only low blackberry and high blackberry leaves linger still fresh, but the *Rubus hispidus* leaves last all winter like an evergreen. The great round-leaved pyrola, dwarf cornel, checkerberry, and lambkill have a lake or purplish tinge on the under side at present, and these last two are red or purplish above. It is singular that a blush should suffuse the under side of the thick-leaved pyrola while it is still quite green above.

When walnut husks have fairly opened, showing the white shells within, — the trees being either quite bare or with a few withered leaves at present, — a slight jar with the foot on the limbs causes them to rattle down in a perfect shower, and on bare, grass-grown pasture ground it is very easy picking them up.

As I returned over Conantum summit yesterday, just before sunset, and was admiring the various rich browns of the shrub oak plain across the river, which seemed to me more wholesome and remarkable, as more permanent, than their late brilliant colors, I was surprised to see a broad halo travelling with me and always opposite the sun to me, at least a quarter of a mile off and some three rods wide, on the shrub oaks.

The rare wholesome and permanent beauty of withered oak leaves of various hues of brown mottling a hillside, especially seen when the sun is low, — Quaker colors, sober ornaments, beauty that quite satisfies the eye. The richness and variety are the same as before, the colors different, more incorruptible and lasting.[1]

Sprague of Cohasset states to the Natural History Society, September 1st, '58, that the light under the tail of the common glow-worm "remained for 15 minutes after death."

Who are bad neighbors? They who suffer their neighbors' cattle to go at large because they don't want their ill will,— are afraid to anger them. They are abettors of the ill-doers.

Who are the religious? They who do not differ much from mankind generally, except that they are more conservative and timid and useless, but who in their conversation and correspondence talk about kindness of Heavenly Father. Instead of going bravely about their business, trusting God ever, they do like him who says "Good sir" to the one he fears, or whistles to the dog that is rushing at him.[2] And because they take His name in vain so often they presume that they are better than you. Oh, their religion is a rotten squash.

Nov. 21. P. M. — To Hubbard's place.

See small water-bugs in Nut Meadow Brook in one place. Probably they were not to be found in the late cold weather, 12th, 13th, etc.

See from Clamshell apparently two little dippers, one up-stream, the other down, swimming and diving in the perfectly smooth river this still, overcast day.

Probably the bulk of the scarlet oak leaves are fallen.

[1] *Vide* four pages forward.   [2] [Channing, p. 89.]

I find very handsome ones strewn over the floor of Potter's maple swamp. They are brown above, but still purple beneath. These are so deeply cut and the middle and lobes of the leaf so narrow that they look like the remnant of leafy stuff out of which leaves have been cut, or like scrap-tin. The lobes are remarkably sharp-pointed and armed with long bristles. Yes, they lie one above another like masses of scrap-tin.[1]

Nov. 22. In surveying Mr. Bigelow's wood-lot today I found at the northeasterly angle what in the deed from the Thayers in '38 was called "an old stump by the wall." It is still quite plain and may last twenty years longer. It is oak.

This is quite a pleasant day, but hardly amounting to Indian summer. I see swarms of large mosquito-like insects dancing in the garden. They may be a large kind of *Tipulidæ.* Had slender ringed abdomens and no plumes. The river is quite low, — about as low as it has been, for it has not been very low.

About the first of November a wild pig from the West, said to weigh three hundred pounds, jumped out of a car at the depot and made for the woods. The owner had to give up the chase at once, not to lose his passage, while some railroad employees pursued the pig even into the woods a mile and a half off, but there the pig turned and pursued them so resolutely that they ran for their lives and one climbed a tree. The next day being Sunday, they turned out in force with a gun and a large mastiff, but still the pig had the best of it, — fairly

[1] [*Excursions*, p. 279; Riv. 342.]

frightened the men by his fierce charges, — and the dog was so wearied and injured by the pig that the men were obliged to carry him in their arms. The pig stood it better than the dog. Ran between the gun man's legs, threw him over, and hurt his shoulder, though pierced in many places by a pitchfork. At the last accounts, he had been driven or baited into a barn in Lincoln, but no one durst enter, and they were preparing to shoot him. Such pork might be called venison.[1]

Nov. 23. A northeasterly storm, with occasional sugarings of snow.

Nov. 24. P. M. — To Cliffs and Walden.

There is a slight sugaring of snow on the ground. On grass ground there is much the less, and that is barely perceptible, while plowed ground is quite white, and I can thus distinguish such fields even to the horizon. It is dark, drizzling still from time to time, sprinkling or snowing a little. I see more snow in the north and northwest horizon. I can not only distinguish plowed fields — regular white squares in the midst of russet — but even cart-paths, and foot or cow paths a quarter of a mile long, as I look across to Conantum. It is pleasant to see thus revealed as a feature, even in the distant landscape, a cow-path leading from far inland down to the river.

The young oaks on the plain under the Cliffs are of a more uniform color than a fortnight ago, — a reddish brown.

Fair Haven Pond is closed still.

[1] Caught him at last in a snare, and so conveyed him to Brighton.

It is a lichen day, with a little moist snow falling. The great green lungwort lichen shows now on the oaks, — strange that there should be none on the pines close by, — and the fresh bright chestnut fruit of other kinds, glistening with moisture, brings life and immortality to light.[1] That side of the trunk on which the lichens are thickest is the side on which the snow lodges in long ridges.

When I looked out this morning, the landscape presented a very pretty wintry sight, little snow as there was. Being very moist, it had lodged on every twig, and every one had its counterpart in a light downy white one, twice or thrice its own depth, resting on it.

I hear a screech owl in Wheeler's wood by the railroad, and I heard one a few evenings ago at home.

Saw a scarlet oak some sixteen inches in diameter at three feet from ground blown down evidently in that southeast wind some months ago. It stood on the southerly edge of Wheeler's wood, and had fallen north-north-west, breaking off a white oak nine inches in diameter and a small white pine in its fall. It was a perfectly sound oak. I was surprised to see how little root it had. Very few roots reached deeper than two feet, — the thickness of the crust of earth turned up by its fall, — and those that did were not bigger than one's finger; and there was not a root bigger than your finger at four feet from the centre on any side of the more than semi-circle exposed. No wonder it was uprooted!

Here is an author who contrasts love for "the beauties of the person" with that for "excellences of the mind,"

[1] [Channing, pp. 111, 112.]

as if these were the alternatives. I must say that it is for neither of these that I should feel the strongest affection. I love that one with whom I sympathize, be she "beautiful" or otherwise, of excellent mind or not.

Nov. 25. P. M. — To Ministerial Swamp.

I go through the Dennis Swamp by railroad. See a few high blueberry buds which have fairly started, expanded into small red leaves, apparently within a few weeks.[1]

The *Rubus hispidus* is now very common and conspicuous amid the withered grass and leaves of the swamp, with its green or reddened leaves; also the gold-thread. The prinos berries on their light-brown twigs are quite abundant and handsome.

While most keep close to their parlor fires this cold and blustering Thanksgiving afternoon, and think with compassion of those who are abroad, I find the sunny south side of this swamp as warm as their parlors, and warmer to my spirit. Aye, there is a serenity and warmth here which the parlor does not suggest, enhanced by the sound of the wind roaring on the northwest side of the swamp a dozen or so rods off. What a wholesome and inspiring warmth is this! I see aspen (*tremuliformis*) leaves, which have long since fallen, turned black, which also shows the relation of this tree to the willow, many species of which also turn black.

Pass Tarbell's behind. The farmer, now on the

[1] *Vide* Oct. 13, 1859.

Vol. XI

round northeast I am greatly surprised by the very brilliant sunlight of which I speak, surpassing the glare of any noontide, it seems to me.

Nov. 26. The various evergreens, large and small, may be said generally to turn green or to have turned reddish about the middle of November. Got in boat on account of Reynolds's new fence going up (earlier than usual). A good many leaves of the sweet-fern, though withered now, still hold on; so that this shrub may be put with the oaks in this respect. So far as I remember, it is peculiar among shrubs in this.

Walden is very low, compared with itself for some years. The bar between pond and Hubbard's pond-hole is four feet wide, but the main bar is not *bare*. There is a shore at least six feet wide inside the alders at my old shore, and what is remarkable, I find that not only Goose Pond also has fallen correspondingly within a month, but even the smaller pond-holes only four or five rods over, such as Little Goose Pond, shallow as they are. I begin to suspect, therefore, that this rise and fall extending through a long series of years is not peculiar to the Walden system of ponds, but is true of ponds generally, and perhaps of rivers, though in their case it may be more difficult to detect. Even around Little Goose Pond the shore is laid bare for a space even wider than at Walden, it being less abrupt. The Pout's Nest, also, has lost ten feet on all sides.

Those pouts' nests which I discovered in the spring are high and dry six feet from the water. I overhauled one, ripping up the frozen roof with my hands. The

down-hill of life, at length gets his new barn and barn-cellar built, far away in some unfrequented vale. This for twoscore years he has struggled for. This is his poem done at last, — to get the means to dig that cavity and rear those timbers aloft. How many millions have done just like him! — or failed to do it! There is so little originality, and just so little, and just as much, fate, so to call it, in literature. With steady struggle, with alternate failure and success, he at length gets a barn-cellar completed, and then a tomb. You would say that there was a tariff on thinking and originality.

I pass through the Ministerial Swamp and ascend the steep hill on the south cut off last winter. In the barren poplar hollow just north of the old mountain cranberry is another, the largest, patch of it (*i. e.* bear-berry) that I remember in Concord. How often I see these aspens standing dead in barren, perhaps frosty, valleys in the woods!

Most shrub oaks there have lost their leaves (*Quercus ilicifolia*), which, very fair and perfect, cover the ground.

You are surprised, late these afternoons, a half an hour perhaps before sunset, after walking in the shade or on looking round from a height, to see the singularly bright yellow light of the sun reflected from pines, especially pitch pines, or the withered oak leaves, through the clear, cold air, the wind, it may be, blowing strong from the northwest. Sunlight in summer falling on green woods is not, methinks, such a noticeable phenomenon. I stand on that high hill south of the swamp cut off by C. (?) Wheeler last winter, and when I look

roof was only three inches thick, then a cavity and a bottom of wet mud. In this mud I found two small frogs, one apparently a *Rana palustris* less than an inch long, the other apparently a young *R. pipiens* an inch and a half long. They were quite sluggish and had evidently gone into winter quarters there, but probably some mink would have got them.

The Pout's Nest was frozen just enough to bear, with two or three breathing-places left. The principal of these was a narrow opening about a rod long by eighteen inches wide within six feet of the southwest side of the pond-hole, and the immediately adjacent ice was darker and thinner than the rest, having formed quite recently. I observed that the water at this breathing-chink was all alive with pollywogs, mostly of large size, though some were small, which apparently had collected there chiefly, as the water-surface was steadily contracted, for the sake of the air (?). There [were] more than a hundred of them there, or ten or a dozen in a square foot, and many more under the ice. I saw one firmly frozen in and dead. One had legs, and his tail was half eaten off by some creature, yet he was alive. There were also one or two frogs stirring among them. Here was evidently warmer water, probably a spring, and they had crowded to it. Looking more attentively, I detected also a great many minnows about one inch long either floating dead there or frozen into the ice, — at least fifty of them. They were shaped like bream, but had the transverse bars of perch. There were more pollywogs in other parts of the pond-hole, and at the north end I saw two perch about seven inches long, dead, close to the shore, and turned a *bright green*,— which are commonly yellow, — as if poisoned by the water or something they had eaten. Perhaps the fishes had suffered by the falling of this pond-hole and consequent isolation from the main pond, which has left this part still more shallow and stagnant than before. It is full of the target-weed. If the pond continues to fall, undoubtedly all the fishes thus landlocked will die. I noticed at the above-named chink tracks which looked like those of an otter, where some animal had entered and come out of the water, leaving weeds and fragments of ice at the edge of the hole. No doubt several creatures, like otter and mink and foxes, know where to resort for their food at this season. This is now a perfect otter's or mink's preserve. Perhaps such a mass of decaying weeds is fatal to the fishes here.

It is evident that those frogs would have been frozen stiff the first colder night in such a shallow retreat. It is very likely that that hole (*i. e.* pout's hole) was under water when they took refuge there, and, the water going down, they were chilled. In such cases, then, pollywogs and fishes, and even frogs, resort to the last part to freeze, the warmest water, where it is open longest.

Examining those minnows by day, I find that they are one and one sixth inches long by two fifths of an inch wide (this my largest); in form like a bream; of a very pale golden like a perch, or more bluish. Have but one dorsal fin and, as near as I can count, rays, dorsal 19 (first, 9 stouter and stiff and more distinctly pointed, then 10 longer and flexible, whole fin about three times as long as average height), caudal 17 [?], anal 13 or 14, ventral 6, pectoral 10 (?). They have about seven trans-

verse dusky bars like a perch (!). Yet, from their form and single dorsal fin, I think they are breams. Are they not a new species? Have young breams transverse bars? A little narrower than this.[1]

Nov. 27. Those barren hollows and plains in the neighborhood of Walden are singular places.

I see many which were heavily wooded fifteen or thirty years ago now covered only with fine sedge, sweet-fern, or a few birches, willows, poplars, small wild cherries, panicled cornels, etc. They need not amount to hollows at all: many of them are glades merely, and all that region is elevated, but the surrounding higher ground, though it may be only five or ten feet higher, will be covered with a good growth. One should think twice before he cut off such places. Perhaps they had better never be laid bare, but merely thinned out. We do not begin to understand the treatment of woodland yet. On such spots you will see various young trees — and some of them which I have named — dead as if a fire had run through them, killed apparently by frost.

I find scarlet oak acorns like this; in form not essentially different from those of the black oak, except that the scales of the black stand out more loose and bristling about the fruit. So all scarlet oak acorns do not regularly taper to a point from a broad base, and

Scarlet Oak

[1] *Vide* [next page].

Emerson represents but one form of the fruit.[1] The leaf of this was not very deeply cut, was broad for its length.

I got seventeen more of those little bream of yesterday. As I now count, the dorsal fin-rays are 9–10 (Girard says 9–11), caudal 17 (with apparently 4 short on each side), anal 3–11, pectoral 11, ventral 1–5.[2] They have about seven transverse dark bars, a vertical dark mark under eye, and a dark spot on edge of operculum. They appear to be the young of the *Pomotis obesus*, described by Charles Girard to the Natural History Society in April, '54, obtained by Baird in fresh water about Hingham and [in] Charles River in Holliston.[3] I got more perfect specimens than the bream drawn above. They are exceedingly pretty seen floating dead on their sides in a bowl of water, with all their fins spread out. From their size and form and position they cannot fail to remind you of coins in the basin. The conspicuous transverse bars distinguish them at once. This is the form of the dorsal fin, which consists of two parts, the foremost of shorter stiff, spiny rays, the

[1] *Vide* Jan. 19th, 1859.

[2] *Vide* Dec. 3d. *Vide* also Mar. 26.

[3] [A newspaper clipping pasted into the Journal contains the following extract from a report of the proceedings of the Boston Society of Natural History: —

"Specimens of *Pomotis* and *Esox*, and of amphibians, were presented by Mr. H. D. Thoreau, from Concord, Mass. Mr. Putnam was of opinion that one of the *Pomotis* would prove a new species. There are with us two varieties of pickerel commonly known as the long or shovel-nosed, and the short or trout-nosed; these specimens were of the latter. Mr. Putnam was inclined to think these were distinct species, unless the differences should prove to be sexual. Drs. D. H. and

other eleven at least half as long again and quite flexible and waving, falling together like a wet rag *out of water*. So, with the anal fin, the three foremost rays are short and spiny, as I see, and one of each of the ventral (according to Girard, and to me). These foremost rays in each case look like slender raking masts, and their points project beyond the thin web of the fin, whose edge looks like the ropes which stretch from masthead to masthead, loopwise. The stiff and spiny foremost part of the fins evidently serves for a cut-water which bears the brunt of any concussion and perhaps may serve for weapons of offense, while the more ample and gently waving flexible after part more especially guides the motions of the fish. The transverse bars are continued across these parts of the dorsal and anal fins, as the markings of a turtle across its feet or flippers; methinks the fins of the minnows are peculiarly beautiful.

How much more remote the newly discovered species seems to dwell than the old and familiar ones, though

H. R. Storer considered them varieties of the same species; Messrs. Baird and Girard think them (*Esox reticulatus* and *E. ornatus*) distinct."

Another clipping says: —

"Mr. F. W. Putnam at a previous meeting stated that possibly the young *Pomotis* presented by Mr. Thoreau were the *P. obesus* of Girard. He had since then examined Girard's original specimens, and he finds that they are the same. The *P. guttatus* recently described in the Proceedings of the Academy of Natural Sciences at Philadelphia is identical with *P. obesus*. Having teeth on the palatines, and consequently belonging to the genus *Bryttus*, the proper name for the species is *B. obesus* (Putnam). He had also satisfied himself that the *Esox ornatus* of Girard is the same as the *E. fasciatus* of De Kay."]

both inhabit the same pond! Where the *Pomotis obesus* swims must be a new country, unexplored by science. The seashore may be settled, but aborigines dwell unseen only thus far inland. This country is so new that species of fishes and birds and quadrupeds inhabit it which science has not yet detected. The water which such a fish swims in must still have a primitive forest decaying in it.

Nov. 28. A gray, overcast, still day, and more small birds — tree sparrows and chickadees — than usual about the house. There have been a very few fine snowflakes falling for many hours, and now, by 2 P. M., a regular snow-storm has commenced, fine flakes falling steadily, and rapidly whitening all the landscape. In half an hour the russet earth is painted white even to the horizon. Do we know of any other so silent and sudden a change?

I cannot now walk without leaving a track behind me; that is one peculiarity of winter walking. Anybody may follow my trail. I have walked, perhaps, a particular wild path along some swamp-side all summer, and thought to myself, I am the only villager that ever comes here. But I go out shortly after the first snow has fallen, and lo, here is the track of a sportsman and his dog in my secluded path, and probably he preceded me in the summer as well. Yet my hour is not his, and I may never meet him!

I asked Coombs the other night if he had been a-hunting lately. He said he had not been out but once this fall. He went out the other day with a companion, and

they came near getting a fox. They broke his leg. He has evidently been looking forward to some such success all summer. Having done thus much, he can afford to sit awhile by the stove at the post-office. He is plotting now how to break his head.

Goodwin cannot be a very bad man, he is so cheery.

And all the years that I have known Walden these striped breams have skulked in it without my knowledge! How many new thoughts, then, may I have?

Nov. 29. P. M. — To Hill.

About three inches of snow fell last evening, and a few cows on the hillside have wandered about in vain to come at the grass. They have at length found that place high on the south side where the snow is thinnest.

How bright and light the day now! Methinks it is as good as half an hour added to the day. White houses no longer stand out and stare in the landscape. The pine woods snowed up look more like the bare oak woods with their gray boughs. The river meadows show now far off a dull straw-color or pale brown amid the general white, where the coarse sedge rises above the snow; and distant oak woods are now more distinctly reddish. It is a clear and pleasant winter day. The snow has taken all the November out of the sky. Now blue shadows, green rivers, — both which I see, — and still winter life.

I see partridge and mice tracks and fox tracks, and crows sit silent on a bare oak-top. I see a living shrike caught to-day in the barn of the Middlesex House.

Nov. 30. The shrike was very violent for a long time, beating itself against the bars of its cage at Stacy's. To-day it is quiet and has eaten raw meat. Its plain dark ash-colored crown and back are separated by a very distinct line from the black wings. It has a powerful hawk-like beak, but slender legs and claws. Close to, it looks more like a muscicapa than anything.

P. M. — To Walden with Channing, and Fair Haven Hill.

It is a pleasant day and the snow melting considerably. We stand on the Pout's Nest, now frozen, with snow ice added to the old, so that it will bear, — a coarse frozen white batter, — and the hills around are covered with snow, though Walden is open. It is a perfect winter scene. This withdrawn but ample recess in the woods, with all that is necessary for a human residence, yet never referred to by the London *Times* and *Galignani's Messenger*, as some of those arctic bays are. Some are hastening to Europe and some to the West Indies, but here is a bay never steered for. These nameless bays where the *Times* and *Tribune* have no correspondent are the true bays of All Saints for me. Green pines on this side, brown oaks on that, the blue sky overhead, and this white counterpane all around. It is an insignificant fraction of the globe which England and Russia and the filibusters have overrun. The open pond close by, though considerably rippled to-day, affects me as a peculiarly mild and genial object by contrast with this frozen pool and the snow-covered shore, and I sit down on the shore in the sun, on the bare rocks. There seems to be a milder air above it, as the water within it is milder.

Going westward through Wheeler's Owl Wood toward Weird Dell, Well Meadow Field, I beheld a peculiar winter scene, seen many times before but forgotten. The sun, rather low, is seen through the wood with a cold, dazzling white lustre, like that of burnished tin reflected from the silvery needles of the pines. No powerful light streams through, but you stand in the quiet and somewhat sombre aisles of a forest cathedral, where cold green masses alternate with pale-brown but warm leather-colored ones, almost ruddy (you are inclined to call them red).[1] These are the internal decorations, while dark trunks, streaked with snow, rise on all sides, and a pure white floor stretches around, and perhaps a single patch of yellow sunlight is seen on the white shaded floor.

The short afternoons are come. Yonder dusky cloud-mass in the northwest will not be wafted across the sky before yonder sun that lurks so low will be set. We see purple clouds in the east horizon.

But did ever clouds flit and change, form and dissolve, so fast as in this clear, cold air? For it is rapidly growing colder, and at such a time, with a clear air and wind and shifting clouds, I never fail to see mother-o'-pearl tints abundant in the sky.

We see the tracks of a hunter and his hounds who have gone along the path from the Dell to the Cliffs. The dog makes a genuine track with his five toes, an honest dog's track, and if his master went barefoot we should count five toe-prints in his track too, and they would be seen to resemble each other remotely; but now we see only

[1] Reddish-tawny (?).

Walden in Early Winter

Alder Catkins in Winter

the track of a boot, and I thought the dog must be disgusted to tread in it. Walking thus where a man and two dogs had recently passed along, making a trail only a few inches wide, treading in one another's tracks alternately, the impression was that they had constantly crowded on one another, though in fact the dogs may have been a quarter of a mile ahead [of] or behind their master. The dog rosette identical [with that] which is spotted all over Greece. They go making these perfect imperfect [*sic*] impressions faster than a Hoe's cylinder power-press.

Coming over the side of Fair Haven Hill at sunset, we saw a large, long, dusky cloud in the northwest horizon, apparently just this side of Wachusett, or at least twenty miles off, which was snowing, when all the rest was clear sky. It was a complete snow-cloud. It looked like rain falling at an equal distance, except that the snow fell less directly and the upper outline of a part of the cloud [was] more like that of a dusky mist. It was [not] much of a snow-storm, just enough to partially obscure the sight of the mountains about which it was falling, while the cloud was apparently high above them, or it may have been a little this side. The cloud was of a dun color, and at its south end, near where the sun was just about to set, it was all aglow on its under side with a salmon fulgor, making it look warmer than a furnace at the same time that it was snowing. In short, I saw a cloud, quite local in the heavens, whose south end rested over the portals of the day, twenty and odd miles off, and was lit by the splendor of the departing sun, and from this lit cloud snow was falling. It was merely

an extensive flurry, though it may have lasted twenty minutes.

I have seen a dark cloud as wide as the sky rolling up from the northwest and blasting all my hopes, at sight of which I have dismissed the sun for three weeks and resigned myself to my fate. But when, after being absorbed in other meditations, I have looked round for that cloud half an hour after, I have distinguished only an indistinct white film far in the southeast which only added to the glory of the day by reflecting its light.

The river may be said to have frozen generally last night.

That was a remarkable prospect from the side of Fair Haven Hill just before the sun set, a strong cold northwest wind blowing, and as good a winter prospect as the arctic regions present, — the brilliant Blessed Isles already gathered about the portals of the day, and mother-o'-pearl clouds forming and dissolving in the crisped air between the zenith and the west horizon, while at least twenty miles off (at first thirty) in the northwest a vast dark dun-colored cloud whose southern end overlapped the setting sun, a glowing canopy, was snowing on the mountains seen dimly beneath it. It was a rare and strange sight, that of a snow-storm twenty miles off on the verge of a perfectly clear sky. Thus local is all storm, surrounded by serenity and beauty. The terrestrial mountains were made ridiculous beneath that stupendous range. I said to my companion, "There comes a storm which will cover the earth four feet deep. Make haste and do your necessary work before the night comes." But before we had got home I saw it in the

east still further off, — not having seen it pass us, — a pale ethereal film, almost dissolved in the sky, as indistinct as a fabulous island. In these clear, cold days fear no cloud. They vanish and dissolve before the cloud-consuming air. This air snaps them up like a dog his meat.

Bare hickories now seen over the shining surface of the snow suggest a cold equal to that of the Cold Friday. As I go up the hill eastward while the sun is setting, I see a tinge of green reflected from its surface under my face, and the scattered clouds in the east are greener yet.

C. thought that if he lived in Weird Dell — which I talked of buying — he should come and sit on the northwest side every night and see the shadows steal gradually across it.

Just before the sun disappeared we saw, just in the edge of the horizon westward from Acton, maybe eight miles off, a very brilliant fire or light, just like a star of the first magnitude or a house burning without smoke, and this, though so far and so brilliant, was undoubtedly only the sun reflected from some gilt weathercock there. So incredibly brilliant are all surfaces now. It was pure flame, larger than a house, precisely as if the planet Venus rested in the horizon's edge. Possibly the weathercock was nearer, but we both concluded that it was not.

The sun seen setting through the snow-carpeted woods, with shimmering pine-needles or dark-green masses and warm brown oak leaves for screens. With the advent of snow and ice, so much cold white, the

browns are warmer to the eye. All the red that is in oak leaves and huckleberry twigs comes out.

A cloud, then, which glows high above the portals of the day seven or eight minutes before the sun disappears, may be some twenty miles off only.

Neither England nor America have [*sic*] any right to laugh at that sentence in the rare book called "The Blazon of Gentry," written by a zealous student of heraldry, which says after due investigation that "Christ was a gentleman, as to the flesh, by the part of his mother, . . . and might have borne coat-armor. The apostles also were gentlemen of blood, and many of them descended from that worthy conqueror Judas Machabeus; but, through the tract of time, and persecution of wars, poverty oppressed the kindred and they were constrayned to servile workes." Whatever texts we may quote or commentaries we may write, when we consider the laws and customs of these two countries we cannot fail to perceive that the above sentence is perfectly of a piece with our practical commentary on the New Testament. The above is really a pertinent reason offered why Christianity should be embraced in England and America. Indeed, it is, accordingly, only what may be called "respectable Christianity" that is at all generally embraced in the two countries.

I read that a woman picked a pint of ripe red raspberries at Bunker Hill Cliff, where they get the Quincy granite, October 1st, this year.[1]

There is a late greenness accompanied by a few yellow flowers, a November greenness, methinks, corre-

[1] Was it not Nov. 1st?

sponding to the early greenness of the spring and its blossoms. Early in November (and late in October) lycopodiums and evergreen ferns (the small botrychium sheds pollen then, as well as several lycopodiums) have their day, under the yellow flowers of the witch-hazel and amid a few lingering goldenrods, as in spring green radical leaves are associated with alder and willow blossoms. The cold greens have their day so late in the fall. I do not speak so much of a lingering verdure, but of one which then is most flourishing and, you may say, greenest before the lichen days have come.

I cannot but see still in my mind's eye those little striped breams poised in Walden's glaucous water. They balance all the rest of the world in my estimation at present, for this is the bream that I have just found, and for the time I neglect all its brethren and am ready to kill the fatted calf on its account. For more than two centuries have men fished here and have not distinguished this permanent settler of the township. It is not like a new bird, a transient visitor that may not be seen again for years, but there it dwells and has dwelt permanently, who can tell how long? When my eyes first rested on Walden the striped bream was poised in it, though I did not see it, and when Tahatawan paddled his canoe there. How wild it makes the pond and the township to find a new fish in it! America renews her youth here. But in my account of this bream I cannot go a hair's breadth beyond the mere statement that it exists, — the miracle of its existence, my contemporary and neighbor, yet so different from me! I can only poise my thought there by its side and try to think

Vol. XI

dering along the shore of the ocean of truth, with their backs to that ocean, ready to seize on the shells which are cast up. You would say that the scientific bodies were terribly put to it for objects and subjects. A dead specimen of an animal, if it is only well preserved in alcohol, is just as good for science as a living one preserved in its native element.

What is the amount of my discovery to me? It is not that I have got one in a bottle, that it has got a name in a book, but that I have a little fishy friend in the pond. How was it when the youth first discovered fishes? Was it the number of their fin-rays or their arrangement, or the place of the fish in some system that made the boy dream of them? Is it these things that interest mankind in the fish, the inhabitant of the water? No, but a faint recognition of a living contemporary, a provoking mystery.[1] One boy thinks of fishes and goes a-fishing from the same motive that his brother searches the poets for rare lines. It is the poetry of fishes which is their chief use; their flesh is their lowest use. The beauty of the fish, that is what it is best worth the while to measure. Its place in our systems is of comparatively little importance. Generally the boy loses some of his perception and his interest in the fish; he degenerates into a fisherman or an ichthyologist.[2]

[1] [Channing, p. 300.]
[2] *Vide* [pp. 363, 364].

like a bream for a moment. I can only think of precious jewels, of music, poetry, beauty, and the mystery of life. I only see the bream in its orbit, as I see a star, but I care not to measure its distance or weight. The bream, appreciated, floats in the pond as the centre of the system, another image of God. Its life no man can explain more than he can his own. I want you to perceive the mystery of the bream. I have a contemporary in Walden.[1] It has fins where I have legs and arms. I have a friend among the fishes, at least a new acquaintance. Its character will interest me, I trust, not its clothes and anatomy. I do not want it to eat. Acquaintance with it is to make my life more rich and eventful. It is as if a poet or an anchorite had moved into the town, whom I can see from time to time and think of yet oftener. Perhaps there are a thousand of these striped bream which no one had thought of in that pond, — not their mere impressions in stone, but in the full tide of the bream life.

Though science may sometimes compare herself to a child picking up pebbles on the seashore, that is a rare mood with her; ordinarily her practical belief is that it is only a few pebbles which are *not* known, weighed and measured. A new species of fish signifies hardly more than a new name. See what is contributed in the scientific reports. One counts the fin-rays, another measures the intestines, a third daguerreotypes a scale, etc., etc.; otherwise there's nothing to be said. As if all but this were done, and these were very rich and generous contributions to science. Her votaries may be seen wan-

[1] [Channing, pp. 299, 300.]

VI

DECEMBER, 1858

(ÆT. 41)

Dec. 2. When I first saw that snow-cloud **it** stretched low along the northwest horizon, perhaps one quarter round and half a dozen times as high as the mountains, and was remarkably horizontal on its upper edge, but that edge was obviously for a part of the way very thin, composed of a dusky mist which first suggested snow. When, soon after, it had risen and advanced and was plainly snowing, it was as if some great dark machine was sifting the snow upon the mountains. There was at the same time the most brilliant of sunsets, the clearest and crispiest of winter skies. We have had every day since similar slight flurries of snow, we being in their midst.

Dec. 3. P. M. — To Walden.
A deliciously mild afternoon, though the ground **is** covered with snow. The cocks crowed this morning **as** of yore.

I carry hatchet and rake in order to explore the Pout's Nest for frogs and fish, — the pond not being frozen. A small part of that chink of the 26th is not yet frozen, and is crowded with pollywogs, mostly of large size, and very many have legs more or less developed. With my small iron rake, about a foot long by four inches wide, I jerk on to the ice at one jerk forty-five pollywogs, and more than as many more fall into the water. Many of the smallest pollywogs have bright copper-red bellies, prettily spotted, while the large are commonly pale-yellow, either clear or spotted. Many are dying. They have crowded so thickly along the open chink three or four inches wide by the side of a boat in the ice that, when I accidentally rock it, about a hundred are washed out on to the ice. One salamander among them, and four of the new breams, much larger, darker, and richer-colored than any I had found. I have often seen pollywogs in small numbers in the winter, in spring-holes, etc., but never such crowding to air-holes in the ice. All that is peculiar in this case is that this small pond has recently been cut off from the main pond by the falling of the water and that it is crowded with vegetable matter, chiefly target-weed, so that apparently the stagnant water has not only killed the breams and perch (of which last I find three dead) but many pollywogs, and compels others to seek the surface.

As I return home by the Shanty Field and the railroad, I cannot help contrasting this evening with the 30th (on Fair Haven Hill-side). Now there is a genial, soft air, and in the west many clouds of purplish dove-color. I walk with unbuttoned coat, taking in the influences of the hour. Coming through the pitch pines east of the Shanty Field, I see the sun through the pines very yellow and warm-looking, and every twig of the pines and every weed is lit with yellow light (not silvery). The other night the few cloudy islets about [the] setting sun (where it had set) were glitter-

ingly bright afar through the cold air. Now (when I get to the causeway) all the west is suffused with an extremely rich, warm purple or rose-color, while the edges of what were dove-colored clouds have a warm saffron glow, finally deepening to rose or damask when the sun has set. The other night there was no reddening of the clouds after sunset, no afterglow, but the glittering clouds were almost immediately snapped up in the crisped air.

I improve every opportunity to go into a grist-mill, any excuse to see its cobweb-tapestry. I put questions to the miller as an excuse for staying, while my eye rests delighted on the cobwebs above his head and perchance on his hat.

The salamander above named, found in the water of the Pout's Nest, is the *Salamandra symmetrica*.[1] It is some three inches long, brown (not dark-brown) above and yellow with small dark spots beneath, and the same spots on the sides of the tail; a row of very minute vermilion spots, not detected but on a close examination, on each side of the back; the tail is waved on the edge (upper edge, at least); has a pretty, bright eye. Its tail, though narrower, reminds me of the pollywog. Why should not it lose its tail as well as that?[2]

The largest of the four breams (*vide* November 26th) two and nine twentieths inches long, by one inch broad and nine twentieths thick. The back, sides forward, tail, and anal fin black or blackish or very dark; the trans-

---

[1] Probably *dorsalis*. *Vide* Apr. 18, 1859.
[2] See one with much larger vermilion spots, Apr. 18, 1859. Are they not larger in the spring?

verse dark bars few and indistinct except in middle of fish; sides toward tail yellowish-olive. Rear of abdomen has violet reflections (and about base of anal fin). Operculums tinged, streaked, and spotted with golden, coppery, greenish, and violet reflections. A vertical dark mark or line, corresponding to the stripes, through the eye. Iris copper-color or darker. The others, about two inches long, are differently colored, not so dark, more olive, and distinctly barred. The smallest are the lightest-colored, but the larger on the whole richer, as well as darker. The fins, especially the dorsal, caudal, and anal, are remarkably pretty, in color a fine network of light and dark. The lower jaw extends about three fortieths of an inch beyond the upper. The rich dark, almost black, back, with dark-barred sides alternating with yellowish olive, and the fine violet-purple reflections from the sides of the abdomen, like the nacre of a shell, as coin-like they lie flat in a basin, — such jewels they swam between the stems (clothed in transparent jelly) of the target-weed.

R. W. E. saw quite a flock of ducks in the pond (Walden) this afternoon.

Dec. 5. Some sugar maples, both large and small, have still, like the larger oaks, a few leaves about the larger limbs near the trunk.

P. M. — To Walden.

Snowed yesterday afternoon, and now it is three or four inches deep and a fine mizzle falling and freezing to the twigs and stubble, so that there is quite a glaze. The stiffened ice-coated weeds and grasses on

the causeway recall past winters. These humble withered plants, which have not of late attracted your attention, now arrest it by their very stiffness and exaggerated size. Some grass culms eighteen inches or two feet high, which nobody noticed, are an inexhaustible supply of slender ice-wands set in the snow. The grasses and weeds bent to the crusty surface form arches of various forms. It is surprising how the slenderest grasses can support such a weight, but the culm is buttressed by another icy culm or column, and the load gradually taken on. In the woods the drooping pines compel you to stoop. In all directions they are bowed down, hanging their heads. The large yellowish leaves of the black oak (young trees) are peculiarly conspicuous, rich and warm, in the midst of this ice and snow, and on the causeway the yellowish bark of the willows gleams warmly through the ice. The birches are still upright, and their numerous parallel white ice-rods remind me of the recent gossamer-like gleams which they reflected.

How singularly ornamented is that salamander! Its brightest side, its yellow belly, sprinkled with fine dark spots, is turned downward. Its back is indeed ornamented with two rows of bright vermilion spots, but these can only be detected on the very closest inspection, and poor eyes fail to discover them even then, as I have found.

Dec. 6. Go out at 9 A. M. to see the glaze. It is already half fallen, melting off. The dripping trees and wet falling ice will wet you through like rain in the woods. It is a lively sound, a busy tinkling, the incessant brattling and from time to time rushing, crashing sound of this falling ice, and trees suddenly erecting themselves when relieved of their loads. It is now perfect only on the north sides of woods which the sun has not touched or affected. Looking at a dripping tree between you and the sun, you may see here or there one or another rainbow color, a small brilliant point of light. Yesterday it froze as it fell on my umbrella, converting the cotton cloth into a thick stiff glazed sort of oilcloth, so that it was impossible to shut it.

Dec. 7. To Boston.
At Natural History Rooms.

The egg of *Turdus solitarius* is light-bluish with pale-brown spots. This is apparently mine which I call hermit thrush, though mine is [sic] redder and distincter brown spots.

The egg of *Turdus brunneus* (called hermit thrush) is a clear blue.

The rail's egg (of Concord, which I have seen) is not the Virginia rail's, which is smaller and nearly pure white, nor the clapper rail's, which is larger. Is it the sora rail's (of which there is no egg in this collection)?

My egg found in R. W. E.'s garden is not the white-throated sparrow's egg.

Dr. Bryant calls my seringo (*i. e.* the faint-noted bird) Savannah sparrow. He says Cooper's hawk is just like the sharp-shinned, only a little larger commonly. He could not tell them apart. Neither he nor Brewer can

identify eggs always. Could match some gulls' eggs out of another basket full of a different species as well as out of the same basket.

Dec. 9. At New Bedford.

See a song sparrow and a pigeon woodpecker. Dr. Bryant tells of the latter picking holes in blinds, and also in his barn roof and sides in order to get into it; holes in the window sashes or casings as if a nail had been driven into them.

Asked a sailor at the wharf how he distinguished a whaler. He said by the "davits," large upright timbers with sheaves curving over the sides, thus: to hold up the boats (a merchantman has only a few and small at the stern); also by the place for the man to stand at masthead (crosstrees, I should say they were) and look out for whales, which you do not see on a merchant-ship; *i. e.*, the crosstrees of the latter are very slight, of the whaler somewhat like this:

Dec. 11. P. M. — To Walden.

An overcast afternoon and rather warm. The snow on the ground in pastures brings out the warm red in leafy oak woodlands by contrast. These are what Thomson calls "the tawny copse." So that they suggest both shelter and warmth. All browns, indeed, are warmer now than a week ago. These oak woodlands half a mile off, commonly with pines intermingled, look like warm coverts for birds and other wild animals. How much warmer our woodlands look and *are* for

these withered leaves that still hang on! Without them the woods would be dreary, bleak, and wintry indeed. Here is a manifest provision for the necessities of man and the brutes. These leaves remain to keep us warm, and to keep the earth warm about their roots. While the oak leaves look redder and warmer, the pines look much darker since the snow has fallen (the hemlocks darker still). A mile or two distant they are dark-brown, or almost black, as, still further, is all woodland, and in the most distant horizon have a blue tinge like mountains, from the atmosphere. The boughs of old and bare oak woods are gray and in harmony with the white ground, looking as if snowed on.

Already, in hollows in the woods and on the sheltered sides of hills, the fallen leaves are collected in small heaps on the snow-crust, simulating bare ground and helping to conceal the rabbit and partridge, etc. They are not equally diffused, but collected together here and there as if for the sake of society.

I find at the Pout's Nest, now quite frozen over, air-holes and all, twenty-two pollywogs frozen in and dead within a space of two and a half feet square, also a minnow — apparently a young shiner, but it has a dark longitudinal line along side (about an inch and a half long) — with the bream.[1]

The terminal shoots of the small scarlet oaks are still distinctly red, though withered.

A "swirl," applied to leaves suddenly caught up by a sort of whirlwind, is a good word enough, methinks.

Walden is about one-third skimmed over. It is frozen

[1] *Vide* 25th.

nearly half the way out from the northerly shore, excepting a very broad open space on the northwest shore and a considerable space at the pines at the northeast end; but the ice, thin as it is, extends quite across from the northwest side to the southwest cape (west side of the railroad bay) by an isthmus only two or three rods wide in its narrowest part. It is evident that whether a pond shall freeze this side or that first depends much on the wind. If it is small and lies like Walden between hills, I should expect that in perfectly calm weather it would freeze soonest along the south shore, but in this case there was probably wind from the north or northwest, and the more sheltered and smooth north side froze first. The warmth reflected from the pines at the northeast corner may account for the open water there, but I cannot account for the open space of the northwest end.[1] It is remarkable that the south edge of the ice projects southward in a cape corresponding to the deep triangular bay in the south side, though it is in the middle of the pond, and there is even a rude correspondence elsewhere along the edge of the ice to the opposite shore. This might seem to indicate that the ice to some extent formed first over deepest water.

When the ice was melting and the trees dripping, on the morning of the 6th, I noticed that the snow was discolored, — stained yellow by this drip, — as if the trees were urinating.

[1] It must be because it is there open to the rake of the north wind, the shore being flat and gently sloping backward a long way, while the protection of Heywood's Peak may account for the ice-isthmus being met by the break-wind of the west railroad cape.

The large scarlet oak in the cemetery has leaves on the lower limbs near the trunk just like the large white oaks now. So has the largest black oak which I see. Others of both, and all, kinds are bare.

Some, being offended, think sharp and satirical things, which yet they are not prepared consciously to utter. But in some unguarded moment these things escape from them, when they are as it were unconscious. They betray their thoughts, as it were by talking in their sleep, for the truth will out, under whatever veil of civility.

Dec. 12. P. M. — Up river on ice to Fair Haven Hill.

Crossing the fields west of our Texas house, I see an immense flock of snow buntings, I think the largest that I ever saw. There must be a thousand or two at least. There is but three inches, at most, of crusted and dry frozen snow, and they are running amid the weeds which rise above it. The weeds are chiefly *Juncus tenuis* (?), but its seeds are apparently gone. I find, however, the glumes of the piper grass scattered about where they have been. The flock is at first about equally divided into two parts about twenty rods apart, but birds are incessantly flitting across the interval to join the pioneer flock, until all are united. They are very restless, running amid the weeds and continually changing their ground. They will suddenly rise again a few seconds after they have alighted, as if alarmed, but after a short wheel settle close by. Flying from you, in some positions, you see only or chiefly the black part of their bodies, and then, as they wheel, the white comes into

view, contrasted prettily with the former, and in all together at the same time. Seen flying higher against a cloudy sky they look like large snowflakes. When they rise all together their note is like the rattling of nuts in a bag, as if a whole binful were rolled from side to side. They also utter from time to time — *i. e.*, individuals do — a clear rippling note, perhaps of alarm, or a call. It is remarkable that their notes above described should resemble the lesser **redpolls'**! Away goes this great wheeling, rambling flock, rolling through the air, and you cannot easily tell where they will settle. Suddenly the pioneers (or a part not foremost) will change their course when in full career, and when at length they know it, the rushing flock on the other side will be fetched about as it were with an undulating jerk, as in the boys' game of snap-the-whip, and those that occupy the place of the snapper are gradually off after their leaders on the new tack. As far as I observe, they confine themselves to upland, not alighting in the meadows. Like a snow-storm they come rushing down from the north. The extremities of the wings are black, while the parts next their bodies are black [*sic*]. They are unusually abundant now.

See a shrike on a dead pine at the Cliffs.

The pitch pines have not done falling, considerable having fallen on the snow.

The river meadows, where they were not cut, are conspicuous brown-straw-colored now,— in the sun almost a true straw-color. November lingers still there.

I should like to know where all those snowbirds will

Vol. XI

roost to-night, for they will probably roost together. And what havoc an owl might make among them![1]

Dec. 13. P. M. — To Walden.

There is a fine mizzling rain, which rests in small drops on your coat, but on most surfaces is turning to a glaze. Yet it is not cold enough for gloves even, and I think that the freezing may be owing to the fineness of the rain, and that, if it should rain much harder, even though it were colder, it would not freeze to what it fell on. It freezes on the railroad rails when it does not on the wooden sleepers. Already I begin to see, on the storm side of every twig and culm, a white glaze (reflecting the snow or sky), rhyming with the vegetable core. And on those fine grass heads which are bent over in the path the fine dew-like drops are frozen separately like a string of beads, being not yet run together. There is little if any wind, and the fine rain is visible only against a dark ground.

There is not so much ice in Walden as on the 11th.

A damp day brings out the color of oak leaves, somewhat as of lichens. They are of a brighter and deeper leather-color, richer and more wholesome, hanging more straightly down than ever. They look peculiarly clean and wholesome, their tints brought out and their lobes more flattened out, and they show to great advantage, these trees hanging still with leather-colored leaves in this mizzling rain, seen against the misty sky.

[1] Melvin tells me that he saw a thousand feeding a long time in the Great Meadows, — he thinks on the seeds of the wool-grass (!!), — about same time.

They are again as it were full-veined with some kind of brown sap.

Dec. 14. I see at Derby's shop a barred owl (*Strix nebulosa*), taken in the woods west of the factory on the 11th, found (with its wing broke [*sic*]) by a woodchopper. It measures about three and a half feet in alar extent by eighteen to twenty inches long, or *nearly* the same as the cat owl, but is small and without horns. It is very mild and quiet, bears handling perfectly well, and only snaps its bill with a loud sound at the sight of a cat or dog. It is apparently a female, since it is large and has white spots on the wings. The claws are quite dark rather than dark horn-color. It hopped into the basin of the scales, and I was surprised to find that it weighed only one pound and one ounce. It may be thin-fleshed on account of its broken wing, but how light-bodied these fliers are! It has no yellow iris like the cat owl, and has the bristles about its yellow bill which the other has not. It has a very smooth and handsome round head, a brownish gray. Solemnity is what they express, — fit representatives of the night.

Dec. 18. P. M. — To Walden.

The pond is merely frozen a little about the edges. I see various little fishes lurking under this thin, transparent ice, close up to the edge or shore, especially where the shore is flat and water shoal. They are little shiners[1] with the dark longitudinal stripe, about an inch and a half long, perch, and one pickerel about a foot long. They are all a peculiar rich-brown color seen thus

[1] ? ? *Vide* 25th.

through the ice. They love to get up as close to the shore as possible, and when you walk along you scare them out. I cast a stone on the ice over a perch six inches long, thinking only to stun it, but killed it so. The ice is about one inch thick. I notice that it is firmly frozen to the shore, so that there is no rise and fall as when it was water, or at least nothing equal to that, but the ice has been cracked with a great many parallel cracks six inches to a foot from the shore. Yet apparently no water has oozed out there.

Minott tells how he used to love to walk through swamps where great white pines grew and hear the wind sough in their tops. He recalls this now as he crouches over his stove, but he adds that it was dangerous, for even a small dead limb broken off by the wind and falling from such a height would kill a man at once.

Dec. 20. Walden is frozen over, except two small spots, less than half an acre in all, in middle.

Dec. 22. P. M. — To Walden.

I see in the cut near the shanty-site quite a flock of *F. hyemalis* and goldfinches together, on the snow and weeds and ground. Hear the well-known mew and watery twitter of the last and the drier *chill chill* of the former. These burning yellow birds with a little black and white on their coat-flaps look warm above the snow. There may be thirty goldfinches, very brisk and pretty tame. They hang head downwards on the weeds. I hear of their coming to pick sunflower seeds in Melvin's garden these days.

Vol. XI

The pond is no more frozen than on the 20th. I see where a rabbit has hopped across it in the slosh last night, making a track larger than a man's ordinarily is.

Dec. 23. P. M. — To Eddy Bridge.
Colder last night. Walden undoubtedly frozen at last, — what was left to freeze.[1]

See a shrike on the top of an oak. It sits still, pluming itself. At first, when it was flying, I thought it a hairy woodpecker.

How perfectly at home the musquash is on our river. And then there is an abundance of clams, a wholesome diet for him, to be had for the diving for them. I do not know that he has any competition in this chase, unless it is an occasional otter. The clams are a sizable fish and in time of scarcity would not be contemptible food for man.

Dec. 24. Those two places in middle of Walden not frozen over yet, though it was quite cold last night!

See another shrike this afternoon, — the fourth this winter! It looks much smaller than a jay.

Dec. 25. P. M. — Up river on ice to Fair Haven Pond and across to Walden.

The ground is still for the most part bare. Such a December is at least as hard a month to get through as November. You come near eating your heart now.

There is a good deal of brown or straw-color in the landscape now, especially in the meadows, where the

[1] No.

ranker grasses, many of them uncut, still stand. They are bleached a shade or two lighter. Looking from the sun, there is a good deal of warm sunlight in them. I see where one farmer has been getting this withered sedge on the ice within a day or two for litter, in a meadow which had not been cut. Of course he could not cut very close.

The ice on the river is about half covered with light snow, it being drifted thus, as usual, by the wind. (On Walden, however, which is more sheltered, the ice is uniformly covered and white.) I go running and sliding from one such snow-patch to another. It is easiest walking on the snow, which gives a hold to my feet, but I walk feebly on the ice. It is so rough that it is but poor sliding withal.

I see, in the thin snow along by the button-bushes and willows just this side of the Hubbard bridge, a new track to me, looking even somewhat as if made by a row of large rain-drops, but it is the track of some small animal. The separate tracks are at most five eighths of an inch in diameter, nearly round, and one and three quarters to two inches apart, varying perhaps half an inch from a straight line, thus: • - - - • - - - • - - - • . Sometimes they are three or four inches apart. The size is but little larger than that of a mouse, but it is never ⟨ ⟨ thus, or like a mouse. Goodwin, to whom I described it, did not know what it could be.

The sun getting low now, say at 3.30, I see the ice green, southeast.

Goodwin says that he once had a partridge strike a

twig or limb in the woods as she flew, so that she fell and he secured her.

Going across to Walden, I see that the fuzzy purple wool-grass is now bleached to a dark straw-color without any purple.

I notice that a fox has taken pretty much my own course along the Andromeda Ponds. The sedge which grows in tufts eighteen or twenty inches high there is generally recurving, thus: —

I see that the shiners which Goodwin is using for bait to-day have no longitudinal dark bar or line on their sides, such as those minnows of the 11th and 18th had. Yet I thought that by the position of their fins, etc., the latter could not be the banded minnow.

Walden at length skimmed over last night, *i. e.* the two holes that remained open. One was very near the middle and deepest part, the other between that and the railroad.

Now that the sun is setting, all its light seems to glance over the snow-clad pond and strike the rocky shore under the pitch pines at the northeast end. Though the bare rocky shore there is only a foot or a foot and a half high as I look, it reflects so much light that the rocks are singularly distinct, as if the pond showed its teeth.

I stayed later to hear the pond crack, but it did not much. How full of soft, pure light the western sky now, after sunset! I love to see the outlines of the pines against it. Unless you watch it, you do not know when the sun goes down. It is like a candle extinguished without smoke. A moment ago you saw that glittering orb amid the dry oak leaves in the horizon, and now you can detect no trace of it. In a pensive mood I enjoy the complexion of the winter sky at this hour.

Those small sphagnous mountains in the Andromeda Ponds are grotesque things. Being frozen, they bear me up like moss-clad rocks and make it easy getting through the water-brush.

But for all voice in that serene hour I hear an owl hoot. How glad I am to hear him rather than the most eloquent man of the age!

I saw a few days ago the ground under a swamp white oak in the river meadow quite strewn with brown dry galls about as big as a pea and quite round, like a small fruit which had fallen from it.

Dec. 26. P. M. — To Jenny Dugan's.

I walk over the meadow above railroad bridge, where the withered grass rises above the ice, the river being low. I notice that water has oozed out over the edge of this ice or next the meadow's edge on the west, not having come from the river but evidently from springs in the bank. This thin water is turned to a slush of crystals as thick as mortar nearly, and will soon be solid ice.

Call at a farmer's this Sunday afternoon, where I surprise the well-to-do masters of the house lounging in very ragged clothes (for which they think it necessary to apologize), and one of them is busy laying the supper-table (at which he invites me to sit down at last), bringing up cold meat from the cellar and a lump of butter

on the end of his knife, and making the tea by the time his mother gets home from church. Thus sincere and homely, as I am glad to know, is the actual life of these New England men, wearing rags indoors there which would disgrace a beggar (and are not beggars and paupers they who *could be* disgraced so?) and doing the indispensable work, however humble. How much better and more humane it was than if they had imported and set up among their Penates a headless torso from the ruins of Ireland! I am glad to find that our New England life has a genuine humane core to it; that inside, after all, there is so little pretense and brag. Better than that, methinks, is the hard drinking and quarrelling which we must allow is not uncommon there. The middle-aged son sits there in the old unpainted house in a ragged coat, and helps his old mother about her work when the field does not demand him.

Dec. 27. Talk of fate! How little one can know what is fated to another! — what he can do and what he can not do! I doubt whether one can give or receive any very pertinent advice. In all important crises one can only consult his genius. Though he were the most shiftless and craziest of mortals, if he still recognizes that he has any genius to consult, none may presume to go between him and her [*sic*]. They, methinks, are poor stuff and creatures of a miserable fate who can be advised and persuaded in very important steps. Show me a man who consults his genius, and you have shown me a man who cannot be advised. You may know what a thing costs or is worth to you; you can

never know what it costs or is worth to me. All the community may scream because one man is born who will not do as it does, who will not conform because conformity to him is death, — he is so constituted. They know nothing about his case; they are fools when they presume to advise him. The man of genius knows what he is aiming at; nobody else knows. And he alone knows when something comes between him and his object. In the course of generations, however, men will excuse you for not doing as they do, if you will bring enough to pass in your own way.

Dec. 28. P. M. — To Walden.

The earth is bare. I walk about the pond looking at the shores, since I have not paddled about it much of late years. What a grand place for a promenade! Methinks it has not been so low for ten years, and many alders, etc., are left dead on its brink. The high blueberry appears to bear this position, alternate wet and dry, as well as any shrub or tree. I see winterberries still abundant in one place.

That rocky shore under the pitch pines which so reflects the light, is only three feet wide by one foot high; yet there even to-day the ice is melted close to the edge, and just off this shore the pickerel are most abundant. This is the warm and sunny side to which any one — man, bird, or quadruped — would soonest resort in cool weather. I notice a few chickadees there in the edge of the pines, in the sun, lisping and twittering cheerfully to one another, with a reference to me, I think, — the cunning and innocent little birds. One a

little further off utters the phœbe note. There is a foot more or less of clear open water at the edge here, and, seeing this, one of these birds hops down as if glad to find any open water at this season, and, after drinking, it stands in the water on a stone up to its belly and dips its head and flirts the water about vigorously, giving itself a good washing. I had not suspected this at this season. No fear that it will catch cold.

The ice cracks suddenly with a shivering jar like crockery or the brittlest material, such as it is. And I notice, as I sit here at this open edge, that each time the ice cracks, though it may be a good distance off toward the middle, the water here is very much agitated. The ice is about six inches thick.

Aunt Jane says that she was born on Christmas Day, and they called her a Christmas gift, and she remembers hearing that her Aunt Hannah Orrock was so disconcerted by the event that she threw all the spoons outdoors, when she had washed them, or with the dish-water.

Father says that he and his sisters (except Elizabeth) were born in Richmond Street, Boston, between Salem and Hanover Streets, on the spot where a bethel now stands, on the left hand going from Hanover Street. They had milk of a neighbor, who used to drive his cows to and from the Common every day.

Dec. 29. P. M. — Skate to Israel Rice's.

I think more of skates than of the horse or locomotive as annihilators of distance, for while I am getting along with the speed of the horse, I have at the same time the satisfaction of the horse and his rider, and far more adventure and variety than if I were riding. We never cease to be surprised when we observe how swiftly the skater glides along. Just compare him with one walking or running. The walker is but a snail in comparison, and the runner gives up the contest after a few rods. The skater can afford to follow all the windings of a stream, and yet soon leaves far behind and out of sight the walker who cuts across. Distance is hardly an obstacle to him. I observe that my ordinary track is like this:

the strokes being seven to ten feet long. The new stroke is eighteen or twenty inches one side of the old. The briskest walkers appear to be stationary to the skater. The skater has wings, *talaria*, to his feet. Moreover, you have such perfect control of your feet that you can take advantage of the narrowest and most winding and sloping bridge of ice in order to pass between the button-bushes and the open stream or under a bridge on a narrow shelf, where the walker cannot go at all. You can glide securely within an inch of destruction on this the most slippery of surfaces, more securely than you could walk there, perhaps, on any other material. You can pursue swiftly the most intricate and winding path, even leaping obstacles which suddenly present themselves.

I saw, on the ice off Pole Brook, a small caterpillar curled up as usual (over the middle of the river) but wholly a light yellow-brown. Just above south entrance

to Farrar Cut, a large hornets' nest thirty feet high on a maple over the river.

Heavy Haynes was fishing a quarter of a mile this side of Hubbard's Bridge. He had caught a pickerel, which the man who weighed it told me (he was apparently a brother of William Wheeler's, and I saw the fish at the house where it was) weighed four pounds and three ounces. It was twenty-six inches long. It was a very handsome fish, — dark-brown above, yellow and brown on the sides, becoming at length almost a clear golden yellow low down, with a white abdomen and reddish fins. They are handsome fellows, both the pikes in the water and tigers in the jungle. The shiner and the red-finned minnow (a dace) are the favorite bait for them.

What tragedies are enacted under this dumb icy platform in the fields! What an anxious and adventurous life the small fishes must live, liable at any moment to be swallowed by the larger. No fish of moderate size can go sculling along safely in any part of the stream, but suddenly there may come rushing out this jungle or that some greedy monster and gulp it down. Parent fishes, if they care for their offspring, how can they trust them abroad out of their sight? It takes so many young fishes a week to fill the maw of this large one. And the large ones! Heavy Haynes and Company are lying in wait for them.

VII

JANUARY, 1859

(ÆT. 41)

Jan. 2. P. M. — To Cliffs and Walden.

Going up the hill through Stow's young oak woodland, I listen to the sharp, dry rustle of the withered oak leaves. This is the voice of the wood now. It would be comparatively still and more dreary here in other respects, if it were not for these leaves that hold on. It sounds like the roar of the sea, and is enlivening and inspiriting like that, suggesting how all the land is seacoast to the aerial ocean. It is the sound of the surf, the rut of an unseen ocean, billows of air breaking on the forest like water on itself or on sand and rocks. It rises and falls, wells and dies away, with agreeable alternation as the sea surf does. Perhaps the landsman can foretell a storm by it. It is remarkable how universal these grand murmurs are, these backgrounds of sound, — the surf, the wind in the forest, waterfalls, etc., — which yet to the ear and in their origin are essentially one voice, the earth-voice, the breathing or snoring of the creature. The earth is our ship, and this is the sound of the wind in her rigging as we sail. Just as the inhabitant of Cape Cod hears the surf ever breaking on its shores, so we country-men hear this kindred surf on the leaves of the forest. Regarded as a voice, — though it is not articulate, —

as our articulate sounds are divided into vowels (but this is nearer a consonant sound), labials, dentals, palatals, sibilants, mutes, aspirate, etc., so this may be called *folial* or *frondal*, produced by air driven against the leaves, and comes nearest to our sibilants or aspirate.

The color of young oaks of different species is still distinct, but more faded and blended, becoming a more uniform brown. Michaux said that white oaks would be distinguished by their retaining their leaves in the winter, but as far as my observation goes they cannot be so distinguished. All our large oaks may retain a few leaves at the base of the lower limbs and about the trunks, though only a few, and the white oak scarcely more than the others, while the same trees when young are all alike thickly clothed in the winter, but the leaves of the white oaks are the most withered and shrivelled of them all.

Why do young oaks retain their leaves while old ones shed them? Why do they die on the stem, having some life at the base in the one case, while they wither through at the base in the other case? Is it because in the former case they have more sap and vigor?

There being some snow on the ground, I can easily distinguish the forest on the mountains (the Peterboro Hills, etc.) and tell which are forested, those parts and those mountains being dark like a shadow. I cannot distinguish the forest thus far in the summer.

The white pines, etc., as I look down on them from this hill, are now darker, as becomes the sterner season, like a frost-bitten apple, — a sombre green.

When I hear the hypercritical quarrelling about grammar and style, the position of the particles, etc., etc., stretching or contracting every speaker to certain rules of theirs, — Mr. Webster, perhaps, not having spoken according to Mr. Kirkham's rule, — I see that they forget that the first requisite and rule is that expression shall be vital and natural, as much as the voice of a brute or an interjection: first of all, mother tongue; and last of all, artificial or father tongue. Essentially your truest poetic sentence is as free and lawless as a lamb's bleat. The grammarian is often one who can neither cry nor laugh, yet thinks that he can express human emotions. So the posture-masters tell you how you shall walk, — turning your toes out, perhaps, excessively, — but so the beautiful walkers are not made.

Mediæval, or law, Latin seems to have invented the word "forest," not being satisfied with *silva*, *nemus*, etc. Webster makes it from the same root with "L. *foris*, Fr. *hors*, and the Saxon *faran*, to go, to depart." The allied words "all express distance from cities and civilization, and are from roots expressing departure or wandering," — as if this newer term were needed to describe those strange, wild woods furthest from the centres of civilization.

The earth, where quite bare, is now, and for five or six weeks, russet without any lively red, — not golden-russet.

I notice on the top of the Cliffs that the extremities of the smooth sumach are generally dead and withered, while those of the staghorn, which are so downy, are

alive. Is this a prevailing difference? Which extends furthest north?

The outside bark-scales of some large pitch pines in the midst of the woods having dropped off gives a peculiar flatness to the ridges, as if it had been shaved or scraped.

Minott says that a fox will lead a dog on to thin ice in order that he may get in. Tells of Jake Lakin losing a hound so, which went under the ice and was drowned below the Holt; was found afterward by Sted. Buttrick, his collar taken off and given to Lakin. They used to cross the river there on the ice, going to market, formerly.

Looking from the southwest side of Walden toward Heywood's Peak before sunset, the brown light on the oak leaves is almost dazzling.

Jan. 3. Having had rain within a few days on the four or five inches of snow there was, making slosh of it without melting the hard frozen ground, the slosh and surface water have now frozen, making it pretty good skating in the roads generally. I walked to Acton, but might have skated well half or two thirds the way.

Many of the clusters of the smooth sumach are now a very dark crimson.

Jan. 4. A northeast snow-storm, or rather a north snow-storm, very hard to face. P. M. to Walden in it. It snows very hard, driving along almost horizontally, falling but a foot or two in a rod. Nobody is in the

Vol. XI

street, or thinks of going out far except on important business. Most roads are trackless. The snow may be now fifteen to eighteen inches deep. As I go along the causeway, I find it is one thing to go south, or from the wind, another to face it. I can see through the storm a house or large tree only a quarter of a mile; beyond all is white falling snow. Woods and single trees seen through this air are all dark or black. The surface of the snow is in great waves whose ridges run from east to west, about a rod apart, or generally less, — say ten feet, — low and gentle swells. The small white pines stand thus, the lower branches loaded and bent down the ground, while the upper are commonly free and erect: —

But the pitch pines near Thrush Alley are the most interesting objects, for they hold much more snow. The snow lodges on their plumes, and, bending them down, it accumulates more and more on the angle generally at the base of the several plumes, in little conical heaps shaped somewhat like this: —

or

differing according to the number and position of the plumes. They look as if a child had stuck up its elbow under a white sheet. Some small ones stand stiffly up-right like a soldier's plume. Several trees will be so fallen together and inter-mingled that you do not see them dis-tinctly. At the same time the lowermost small black and dead horizontal limbs near the ground, where there is least wind and jar, — these almost exclusively, — say for six or eight feet up, are covered with upright walls of snow five or six times their own height and zigzagging with them like the Wall of China; or like great white caterpillars they lie along them, these snowy sloths; or rather it is a labyrinth, a sort of cobweb, of broad white belts in the air. Only a dim twilight struggles through to this lower region, and the sight of these snowy walls or labyrinths suggests a rare stillness, freedom from wind and jar. If you try to stoop and wind your way there, you get your neck and ears full of snow.

I can't draw it. That is, for each dead pine branch you have a thin flat branch of snow resting on it, an exaggeration of the former. It is a still white labyrinth of snowy purity, and you can look far into its recesses under the green and snowy canopy, — a labyrinth of which, perchance, a rabbit may have the clue. I noticed one pitch pine about three feet high so snowed up, and its branches all drooping, it looked like a draped statue or a white-ant hill.

In the woods the snow is often two feet deep, and you must walk at a very deliberate pace if you would keep it up. Still the withered hoary goldenrods (chiefly *S. nemoralis*) and asters (perhaps oftenest *A. dumosus*) rise above the snow here and there, — gray weeds, sufficiently dry and everlasting. The oak leaves, especially the black oak leaves, are very agreeable and wholesome colors. The deeper the snow, the more universal the whiteness, the more agreeable is this color.

Your breath causes the snow to turn to ice in your beard; a shaggy mass of icicles it becomes, which makes you look like a man from the extreme north.

When it grew late, the air being thick and unelastic in this storm, I mistook the distant sound of the locomotive whistle for the hoot of an owl. It was quite like it. I see, nevertheless, a few tree sparrows about, looking chubbier than ever, their feathers being puffed up, and flitting and twittering merrily along the fence.

Turning north, the large rather moist flakes actually put out your eyes, and you must manage to look through the merest crack. Even in the midst of the storm I see where great clouds of fine snow roll down the wood-side,

the wind shaking the snow from the trees. It looks like the vapor from the locomotive.

Jan. 5. As I go over the causeway, near the railroad bridge, I hear a fine busy twitter, and, looking up, see a nuthatch hopping along and about a swamp white oak branch, inspecting every side of it, as readily hanging head-downwards as standing upright, and then it utters a distinct *gnah*, as if to attract a companion. Indeed, that other, finer twitter seemed designed to keep some companion in tow, or else it was like a very busy man talking to himself. The companion was a single chickadee, which lisped six or eight feet off. There were, perhaps, no other birds than these two within a quarter of a mile. And when the nuthatch flitted to another tree two rods off, the chickadee unfailingly followed.

Jan. 6. P. M. — To M. Miles's.
Near Nut Meadow Brook, on the Jimmy Miles road, I see a flock of snow buntings. They are feeding exclusively on that ragged weed which I take to be Roman wormwood.[1] Their tracks where they sink in the snow are very long, *i. e.*, have a very long heel, thus:

or sometimes almost in a single straight line. They made notes when they went, — sharp, rippling, like a vibrating spring. They had run about to every such such [*sic*], leaving distinct tracks raying from and to them, while the snow immediately about the weed was

[1] ["Which I take to be" is crossed out in pencil.]

so tracked and pecked where the seeds fell that no track was distinct.

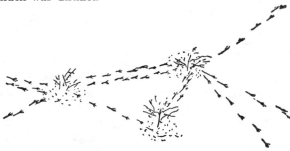

And much more tracked up

Miles had hanging in his barn a little owl (*Strix Acadica*) which he caught alive with his hands about a week ago. He had forced it to eat, but it died. It was a funny little brown bird, spotted with white, seven and a half inches long to the end of the tail, or eight to the end of the claws, by nineteen in alar extent, — not so long by considerable as a robin, though much stouter. This one had three (not two)[1] *white* bars on its tail, but no noticeable white at the tip. Its cunning feet were feathered quite to the extremity of the toes, looking like whitish (or tawny-white) mice, or as when one pulls stockings over his boots. As usual, the white spots on the upper sides of the wings are smaller and a more distinct white, while those beneath are much larger, but a subdued, satiny white. Even a bird's wing has an upper and under side, and the last admits only of more subdued and tender colors.

[1] Nuttall says three.

Jan. 9. At sundown to Walden.
Standing on the middle of Walden I see with perfect distinctness the form and outlines of the low hills which surround it, though they are wooded, because they are quite white, being covered with snow, while the woods are for the most part bare or very thin-leaved. I see thus the outline of the hills eight or ten rods back through the trees. This I can never do in the summer,

when the leaves are thick and the ground is nearly the same color with them. These white hills are now seen as through a veil of stems. Immediately after the wood was cut off, this outline, of course, was visible at all seasons, but the wood, springing up again, concealed it, and now the snow has come to reveal the lost outline.

The sun has been set some minutes, and as I stand on the pond looking westward toward the twilight sky, a soft, satiny light is reflected from the ice in flakes here and there, like the light from the under side of a bird's wing. It is worth the while to stand here at this hour and look into the soft western sky, over the pines whose outlines are so rich and distinct against the clear sky. I am inclined to measure the angle at which [a] pine bough meets the stem. That soft, still, cream-colored sky seems the scene, the stage or field, for some rare drama to be acted on.

C. says the winter is the sabbath of the year. The perfect winter days are cold, but clear and bright.

Jan. 10. P. M. — Up Assabet to Sam Barrett's Pond.

Cold weather at last; — 8° this forenoon. This is much the coldest afternoon to bear as yet, but, cold as it is, — four or five below at 3 P. M., — I see, as I go round the Island, much vapor blowing from a bare space in the river just below, twenty rods off. I see, in the Island wood, where squirrels have dug up acorns in the snow, and frequently where they have eaten them on the trees and dropped the shells about on the snow.

Hemlock is still falling on the snow, like the pitch pine. The swamp white oaks apparently have fewer leaves — are less likely to have any leaves, even the small ones — than any oaks except the chinquapin, methinks. Here is a whole wood of them above Pinxter Swamp, which you may call bare.

Even the tawny (?) recent shoots of the black willow, when seen thickly and in the sun along the river, are a warm and interesting sight. These gleaming birch and alder and other twigs are a phenomenon still perfect, — that gossamer or cobweb-like reflection.

The middle of the river where narrow, as south side Willow Island, is lifted up into a ridge considerably higher than on the sides and cracked broadly.

The alder is one of the prettiest of trees and shrubs in the winter, it is evidently so full of life, with its conspicuous pretty red catkins dangling from it on all sides. It seems to dread the winter less than other plants. It has a certain heyday and cheery look, and less stiff than most, with more of the flexible grace of summer. With those dangling clusters of red catkins which it switches in

the face of winter, it brags for all vegetation. It is not daunted by the cold, but hangs gracefully still over the frozen stream.

At Sam Barrett's Pond, where Joe Brown is now getting his ice, I think I see about ten different freezings in ice some fifteen or more inches thick. Perhaps the successive cold nights might be discovered recorded in each cake of ice.

See, returning, amid the Roman wormwood in front of the Monroe place by the river, half a dozen goldfinches feeding just like the sparrows. How warm their yellow breasts look! They utter the goldfinches' watery twitter still.

I come across to the road south of the hill to see the pink on the snow-clad hill at sunset.

About half an hour before sunset this intensely clear cold evening (thermometer at five — 6°), I observe all the sheets of ice (and they abound everywhere now in the fields), when I look from one side about at right angles with the sun's rays, reflect a green light. This is the case even when they are in the shade. I walk back and forth in the road waiting to see the pink. The windows on the skirts of the village reflect the setting sun with intense brilliancy, a dazzling glitter, it is so cold. Standing thus on one side of the hill, I begin to see a pink light reflected from the snow there about fifteen minutes before the sun sets. This gradually deepens to purple and violet in some places, and the pink is very distinct, especially when, after looking at the simply white snow on other sides, you turn your eyes to the hill. Even after all direct sunlight is withdrawn from the hill-

top, as well as from the valley in which you stand, you see, if you are prepared to discern it, a faint and delicate tinge of purple or violet there. This was in a very clear and cold evening when the thermometer was — 6°. This is one of the phenomena of the winter sunset, this distinct pink light reflected from the brows of snow-clad hills on one side of you as you are facing the sun.

The cold rapidly increases; it is — 14° in the evening.

I hear the ground crack with a very loud sound and a great jar in the evening and in the course of the night several times. It is once as loud and heavy as the explosion of the Acton powder-mills. This cracking is heard all over New England, at least, this night.

Jan. 11. At 6 A. M. — 22° and how much more I know not, ours having gone into the bulb; but that is said to be the lowest.

Going to Boston to-day, I find that the cracking of the ground last night is the subject of conversation in the cars, and that it was quite general. I see many cracks in Cambridge and Concord. It would appear then that the ground cracks on the advent of very severe cold weather. I had not heard it before, this winter. It was so when I went to Amherst a winter or two ago.

Jan. 12. Mr. Farmer brings me a hawk which he thinks has caught thirty or forty of his chickens since summer, for he has lost so many, and he has seen a hawk *like* this catch some of them. Thinks he has seen this same one sitting a long time upright on a tree, high

or low, about his premises, and when at length a hen or this year's chicken had strayed far from the rest, it skimmed along and picked her up without pausing, and bore her off, the chicken not having seen him approaching. He found this, caught by one leg and frozen to death, in a trap which he had set for mink by a spring and baited with fish.

This measures nineteen by forty-two inches and is, according to Wilson and Nuttall, a young *Falco lineatus*, or red-shouldered hawk. It might as well be called red or rusty breasted hawk.[1] Nuttall says it lives on frogs, crayfish, etc., and does not go far north, — not even to Massachusetts, he thought. Its note, *kee-oo*. He never saw one soar, at least in winter. According to all accounts Wilson's *Falco hyemalis* is the old of this bird, for there is a remarkable difference between old and young.

Mine agrees with Wilson's *F. lineatus*, or the young, except that the greater wing-coverts and secondaries are hardly what I should call "pale olive brown thickly spotted," etc., but rather dusky-brown, somewhat indistinctly barred with whitish (which is pure white on each edge of the feathers) and edged with rusty; that the shafts of the breast-feathers are only dark-brown; that the tail is not quite black, but very dark brown, and is not "broadly tipped" with white, but only with a quarter of an inch of it; vent not "pale ochre," but white; legs and feet hardly fine yellow, but dull greenish-yellow; femorals as bright rusty as the breast. It differs from Wilson's winter falcon, which is considered by Audubon and Brewer the same as the *lineatus*,

[1] According to *Birds of Long Island*, mine is the old bird (??).

in not having what I should call a "tooth in the upper mandible;" head, sides of neck, etc., hardly "streaked with white;" above, all primaries and exterior tail-feathers not "brownish orange," and tail not "barred alternately with dark and pale brown," its inner veins and coverts not "white;" and what is very important, the breast and beneath is not "white."

Since Nuttall makes it a southern bird, and it is not likely to come north in the winter, it would seem that it breeds here.

Farmer says that he saw what he calls the common hen-hawk, one soaring high with apparently a chicken in its claws, while a young hawk circled beneath, when former suddenly let drop the chicken, but the young failing to catch, he shot down like lightning and caught and bore off the falling chicken before it reached the earth.

Jan. 13. The cold spell is over, and here this morning is a fog or mist; the wind, if there is any, I think, northerly; and there is built out horizontally on the north side of every twig and other surface a very remarkable sort of hoar frost, the crystallized fog, which is still increasing. Mr. Edwin Morton was telling me night before last of a similar phenomenon witnessed in central New York, the fog of highlands or mountains crystallizing in this way and forming a white fringe or frost on the trees even to an inch and a half. This is already full an inch deep on many trees, and gets to be much more, perhaps an inch and a half even, on some in the course of the day. It is quite rare here, at least on

this scale. The mist lasts all this day, though it is **far** from warm (+ 11° at 8 A. M.), and till noon of the 14th, when it becomes rain, and all this time there is exceedingly little if any wind.

I go to the river this morning and walk up it to see the trees and bushes along it. As the frostwork (which is not thin and transparent like ice, but white and snow-like, or between the distinctly leaf with veins and a mere aggregation of snow, though you easily distinguish the distinct leaves) is built out northward from each surface, spreading at an angle of about forty-five degrees, *i. e.* some twenty-odd each side of the north, you must stand on the north side and look south at the trees, etc., when they appear, except the large limbs and trunk, wholly of snow or frostwork, mere ghosts of trees, seen softly against the mist for a background. It is mist on mist. The outline and character of each tree is more distinctly exhibited, being exaggerated, and you notice any peculiarity in the disposition of the twigs. Some elm twigs, thus enlarged into snowy fingers, are strikingly regular and handsome, thus:

In the case of most evergreens, it amounts to a very rich sugaring, being so firmly attached. The weeping willow seems to weep with more remarkable and regular curve than ever, and stands still and white with thickened twigs, as if carved in white marble or alabaster. Those trees, like alders, which have not

grown much the past year — which have short and angular twigs — are the richest in effect. The end of each alder twig is recurved where the drooping catkin is concealed. On one side you see the dark-brown fruit, but on the north that too is concealed.

I can see about a quarter of a mile through the mist, and when, later, it is somewhat thinner, the woods, the pine woods, at a distance are a dark-blue color.

Jan. 14. The fog-frosts and the fog continue, though considerable of the frostwork has fallen.

This forenoon I walk up the Assabet to see it. The hemlocks are perhaps a richer sight than any tree, — such Christmas trees, thus sugared, as were never seen. On [*sic*] side you see more or less greenness, but when you stand due north they are unexpectedly white and rich, so beautifully still, and when you look under them you see some great rock, or rocks, all hoary with the same, and a finer frost on the very fine dead hemlock twigs there and on hanging roots and twigs, quite like the cobwebs in a grist-mill covered with meal, — and it implies a stillness like that; or it is like the lightest down glued on. The birch, from its outline and its numerous twigs, is also one of the prettiest trees in this dress.

The fog turns to a fine rain at noon, and in the evening and night it produces a glaze, which this morning, —

Jan. 15, — is quite handsome. Instead of that soft, white, faery-like mantle of down with which the trees

were thickly powdered, they are now cased in a coat of mail, of icy mail, built out in many cases about as far from the twig with icy prominences. Birches, tree-tops, and especially slender-twigged willows or osiers are bent over by it, as they were not by the snow-white and light frost of yesterday and the day before, so that the character or expression of many trees and shrubs is wholly altered. I might not guess what the pollard willow row at Merrick's shore, with twigs one or two years old, was, — instead of

The fog still continues through, and succeeding to, the rain. The third day of fog. The thermometer at 7.30 or 8 A. M. is at 33°.

Jan. 16. P. M. — To Walden and thence *via* Cassandra Ponds to Fair Haven and down river.

There is still a good deal of ice on the north sides of woods and in and about the sheltered swamps. As we go southwestward through the cassandra hollows toward the declining sun,[1] they look successively, both by their form and color, like burnished silvery shields in the midst of which we walked, looking toward the sun. The whole surface of the snow the country over, and of the ice, as yesterday, is rough, as if composed of hailstones half melted together. This being the case, I noticed yesterday, when walking on the river, that where there was little or no snow and this rough sur-

[1] [Channing, p. 111.]

face was accordingly dark, you might have thought that the ice was covered with cinders, from the innumerable black points reflecting the dark water. My companion thought that cinders had fallen on that part of the ice.

The snow which three-quarters conceals the cassandra in these ponds, and every twig and trunk and blade of withered sedge, is thus covered or cased with ice, and accordingly, as I have said, when you go facing the sun, the hollows look like a glittering shield set round with brilliants.[1] That bent sedge in the midst of the shield, each particular blade of it being married to an icy wire twenty times its size at least, shines like polished silver rings or semicircles. It must have been far more splendid here yesterday, before any of the ice fell off. No wonder my English companion[2] says that our scenery is more spirited than that of England. The snow-crust is rough with the wreck of brilliants under the trees, — an inch or two thick with them under many trees, where they last several days.

When, this evening, I took a split hickory stick which was very slightly charred or scorched, but quite hot, out of my stove, I perceived a strong scent precisely like that of a burnt or roasted walnut, — as was natural enough.

Jan. 18. That wonderful frostwork of the 13th and 14th was too rare to be neglected, — succeeded as it

[1] [Channing, p. 111.]
[2] [Thomas Cholmondeley. In his letter of Jan. 19, 1859, to Mr. Blake, Thoreau says "Cholmondeley has been here again," etc. (*Familiar Letters*, p. 349; Riv. 406).]

was, also, by two days of glaze, — but, having company, I lost half the advantage of it. It was remarkable to have a fog for four days in midwinter without wind. We had just had sudden severe cold weather, and I suspect that the fog was occasioned by a warmer air, probably from the sea, coming into contact with our cold ice-and-snow-clad earth. The hoar frost formed of the fog was such a one as I do not remember on such a scale. Apparently as the fog was coarser and far more abundant, it was whiter, less delicate to examine, and of far greater depth than a frostwork formed of dew. We did not have an opportunity to see how it would look in the sun, but seen against the mist or fog it was too fair to be remembered. The trees were the ghosts of trees appearing in their winding-sheets, an intenser white against the comparatively dusky ground of the fog. I rode to Acton in the afternoon of the 13th, and I remember the wonderful avenue of these faery trees which everywhere over-arched my road. The elms, from their form and size, were particularly beautiful. As far as I observed, the frostwork was deepest in the low grounds, especially on the *Salix alba* there. I learn from the papers that this phenomenon prevailed all over this part of the country and attracted the admiration of all. The trees on Boston Common were clad in the same snow-white livery with our Musketaquid trees.

Perhaps the most unusual thing about this phenomenon was its duration. The air seemed almost perfectly still the first day, and I did not perceive that the frosting lost anything; nay, it evidently grew during the first

half of the day at least, for it was cold at the same time that it was foggy.

Every one, no doubt, has looked with delight, holding his face low, at that beautiful frostwork which so frequently in winter mornings is seen bristling about the throat of every breathing-hole in the earth's surface. In this case the fog, the earth's breath made visible, was in such abundance that it invested all our vales and hills, and the frostwork, accordingly, instead of being confined to the chinks and crannies of the earth, covered the mightiest trees, so that we, walking beneath them, had the same wonderful prospect and environment that an insect would have in the former case. We, going along our roads, had such a prospect as an insect would have making its way through a chink in the earth which was bristling with hoar frost.

That glaze! I know what it was by my own experience; it was the frozen breath of the earth upon its beard.

But to remember still that frostwork, I do not know why it should build out northward alone, while the

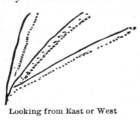

Looking from East or West

Cross-Section of a Twig

twig is perfectly bare on the south side. Is not the phenomenon electrical? You might have guided yourself night or day by observing on which side the twigs it was. Closely examined, it is a coarse aggregation of thin flakes or leafets.

Standing a little east or west of an evergreen, you saw considerable of its greenness, especially the second day, when much had fallen; but in each case successively you were agreeably disappointed when you arrived exactly north of the tree and saw it to best advantage.

Take the most rigid tree, the whole effect is peculiarly soft and spirit-like, for there is no marked edge or outline. How could you draw the outline of these snowy fingers seen against the fog, without exaggeration? There is no more a boundary-line or circumference that can be drawn, than a diameter. Hardly could the New England farmer drive to market under these trees without feeling that his sense of beauty was addressed. He would be aware that the phenomenon called beauty was become visible, if one were at leisure or had had the right culture to appreciate it. A miller with whom I rode actually remarked on the beauty of the trees; and a farmer told me in all sincerity that, having occasion to go into Walden Woods in his sleigh, he thought he never saw anything so beautiful in all his life, and if there had been men there who knew how to write about it, it would have been a great occasion for them.

Many times I thought that if the particular tree, commonly an elm, under which I was walking or riding were the only one like it in the country, it would [be] worth a journey across the continent to see it. Indeed, I have no doubt that such journeys would be undertaken on hearing a true account of it. But, instead of being confined to a single tree, this wonder was as cheap and common as the air itself. Every man's wood-lot was a miracle and surprise to him, and for those who could not go so far there were the trees in the street and the weeds in the yard. It was much like (in effect) that snow that lodges on the fine dead twigs on the lower part of a pine wood, resting there in the twilight commonly only till it has done snowing and the wind arises. But in this case it did not rest *on* the twig, but grew out from it horizontally, and it was not confined to the lowest twigs, but covered the whole forest and every surface.

Looking down the street, you might say that the scene differed from the ordinary one as frosted cake differs from plain bread. In some moods you might suspect that it was the work of enchantment. Some magician had put your village into a crucible and it had crystallized thus. The weeping willow, with its thickened twigs, seemed more precise and regularly curved than ever, and as still as if it were carved of alabaster. The maples, with their few long shoots, were rather set and still. It was remarkable that when the fog was a little thinner, so that you could see the pine woods a mile or more off, they were a distinct dark blue. If any tree is set and stiff, it was now more stiff, if airy and graceful, it was now more graceful. The birches especially were a great ornament. As usual in the winter, where a rock rises above the ice it was a mere hillock covered with a white counterpane, and often where one end, perhaps the higher, of the rock was bare on one side it looked like a seal or walrus slowly lifting itself above the surface, or resting there. One

Vol. XI

suggested a bonfire under the elms in the street at night.

P. M. — Up Assabet to bridge.

Two or more inches of snow fell last night. In the expanse this side Mantatuket Rock I see the tracks of a crow or crows in and about the button-bushes and willows. They have trampled and pecked much in some spots under the button-bushes where these seeds are still left and dibbled into the snow by them. It would seem, then, that they eat them. The only other seeds there can be there are those of the mikania, for I look for them. You will see a crow's track beginning in the middle of the river, where one alighted. I notice such a track as this, where one alighted, and apparently struck its spread tail into the snow at the same time with its feet. I see afterward where a wing's quills have marked the snow much like a partridge's. The snow is very light, so that the tracks are rarely distinct, and as they often advance by hops some might mistake it for a squirrel's or mink's track. I suspect that they came here yesterday after minnows when the fishermen were gone, and that has brought them here to-day in spite of the snow. They evidently look out sharp for a morsel of fish. I see where, by the red maple above Pinxter Swamp, they have picked over the fine dark-greenish moss from button-bush, and the leaves which had formed a squirrel's nest, knocking it down on to the river and there

treading about and pecking a small piece, apparently for some worms or insects that were in it, as if they were hard pushed.

I am pretty sure to find tracks under the last-named bank, in the edge of the low swamp white oak wood, either of rabbits or mice, crows or fox. The two former generally keep close under the bank, as the safest beat for them, but sometimes I see where they hopped across the river several times last night, and I can imagine how shyly they looked back from the opposite side. The mice occasionally hop out a rod and back, making a semicircle; more rarely quite across.

In my walk of the 16th, I noticed that almost all the way after leaving the railroad till I reached the highway near Hubbard's Bridge I was on the track of a fox. My beat was nearly identical with its (or there may have been several), — lengthwise through the Cassandra Ponds and Hollows by the lowest and most open path, along the narrow grown-up hillside path to Pleasant Meadow, and just along the edge of the button-bushes, visiting every musquash-house, and crossing the river from time to time.

I notice in midstream, opposite the cooper's shore, where an opening has been made for ice, some eighteen feet square, and has not frozen over again, but the water is seen passing with a swift current and disappearing quickly under the thin edge of the newly formed ice. I notice one of those fine unaccountable cobweb-like lines, nearly straight though undulating, stretched from side to side of this opening, about eight inches from the edge of the ice on the lower side. It looked

at first as if the water, compared with the ice, was higher, in fact heaped up at that point on account of the obstruction which the lower side offered, and that it then suddenly descended and passed under the thin edge of the newly formed ice! The ridge of the watery dam was a narrow light line, and there were on the upper side, parallel with it, eight or ten other light lines or ripples alternating with dark within the breadth of three or four inches, growing less and less distinct; and on the lower side there was a sudden slope (apparently to the level of the water below) about one inch wide. It was remarkable that the current and all that it carried with it passed incessantly through and over these lines without in the least disturbing them, or rather breaking them, only producing that slight undulation. I describe it as it appears.

Of the large black oaks on the north bank near Prescott Barrett's, some are quite bare, others have about as many leaves on their lower parts as a white oak. The swamp white oaks opposite are all bare. I notice in two places where a musquash has been out on the snow-covered ice, and has travelled about a rod or less, leaving the sharp mark of its tail.

To-day, an average winter day, I notice no vapor over the open part of the river below the Island, as I did the very cold afternoon of the 10th. The air and water are probably now too nearly of the same temperature. That, then, in the winter, is a phenomenon of very cold weather.

Jan. 19. Wednesday. P. M. — To Great Meadows *via* Sleepy Hollow.

It is a remarkably warm, still, and pleasant afternoon for winter, and the wind, as I discover by my hand-kerchief, southwesterly. I noticed last night, just after sunset, a sheet of mackerel sky far in the west horizon, very finely imbricated and reflecting a coppery glow, and again I saw still more of it in the east this morning at sunrise, and now, at 3.30 P. M., looking up, I perceive that almost the entire heavens are covered with a very beautiful mackerel sky. This indicates a peculiar state of the atmosphere. The sky is most wonderfully and beautifully mottled with evenly distributed cloudlets, of indescribable variety yet regularity in their form, suggesting fishes' scales, with perhaps small fish-bones thrown in here and there. It is white in the midst, or most prominent part, of the scales, passing into blue in the crannies. Something like this blue and white mottling, methinks, is seen on a mackerel, and has suggested the name.[1] Is not the peculiar propriety of this term lost sight of by the meteorologists? It is a luxury for the eye to rest on it. What curtains, what tapestry to our halls! Directly overhead, of course, the scales or cloudlets appear large and coarse, while far on one side toward the horizon they appear very fine. It is as if we were marching to battle with a shield, a testudo, over our heads. I thus see a *flock* of small clouds, like sheep, some twenty miles in diameter, distributed with wonderful regularity. But they are being steadily driven to

[1] *Vide* Feb. 28, 1859.

some new pasture, for when I look up an hour afterward not one is to be seen and [the] sky is beautifully clear. The form of these cloudlets is, by the way, like or akin to that of waves, of ripple-marks on sand, of small drifts, wave-like, on the surface of snow, and to the first small openings in the ice of the midstream.

I look at a few scarlet and black oaks this afternoon. Our largest scarlet oak (by the Hollow), some three feet [in] diameter at three feet from ground, has more leaves than the large white oak close by (which has more than white oaks generally). As far as I observe to-day, the scarlet oak has more leaves now than the black oak. Gathered a scarlet oak acorn of this form, and with distinct fine dark stripes or rays, such as a *Quercus ilicifolia* has.

By the swamp between the Hollow and Peter's I see the tracks of a crow or crows, chiefly in the snow, two or more inches deep, on a broad frozen ditch where mud has been taken out. The perpendicular sides of the ditch expose a foot or two of dark, sooty mud which had attracted the crows, and I see where they have walked along beneath it and pecked it. Even here also they have alighted on any bare spot where a foot of stubble was visible, or even a rock. Where one walked yesterday, I see, notwithstanding the effect of the sun on it, not only the foot-tracks, but the distinct impression of its tail where it alighted, counting distinctly eleven (of probably twelve) feathers, — about four inches of each, — the whole mark being some ten inches wide and six deep, or more like a semicircle than that of yester-

day. The same crow, or one of the same, has come again to-day, and, the snow being sticky this warm weather, has left a very distinct track. The width of the whole track is about two and three quarters inches, length of pace about seven inches, length of true track some two inches (not including the nails), but the mark made in setting down the foot and withdrawing it is in each case some fifteen or eighteen inches long, for its hind toe makes a sharp scratch four or five inches long before it settles, and when it lifts its foot again, it makes two other fine scratches with its middle and outer toe on each side, the first some nine inches long, the second six. The inner toe is commonly close to the middle one. It makes a peculiar curving track (or succession of curves), stepping round the planted foot each time with a sweep, thus: —

You would say that it toed in decidedly and walked feebly. It must be that they require but little and glean that very assiduously.

The sweet-fern retains its serrate terminal leaves.

Walking along the river eastward, I notice that the twigs of the black willow, many of which were broken off by the late glaze, only break at base, and only an inch higher up bend without breaking.

I look down the whole length of the meadows to Ball's Hill, etc. In a still, warm winter day like this, what warmth in the withered oak leaves, thus far away, mingled with pines! They are the redder for the warmth and the sun. At this season we do not want any more color.

A mile off I see the pickerel-fisher returning from the Holt, taking his way across the frozen meadows before sunset toward his hut on the distant bank. I know him (looking with my glass) by the axe over his shoulder, with his basket of fish and fish-lines hung on it, and the tin pail of minnows in his hand. The pail shines brightly more than a mile off, reflecting the setting sun. He starts early, knowing how quickly the sun goes down.

To-night I notice, this warm evening, that there is most green in the ice when I go directly from the sun. There is also considerable when I go directly toward it, but more than that a little one side; but when I look at right angles with the sun, I see none at all. The water (where open) is also green. I see a rosy tinge like dust on the snow when I look directly toward the setting sun, but very little on the hills. Methinks this pink on snow (as well as blue shadows) requires a clear, cold evening. At least such were the two evenings on which I saw it this winter.

Coming up the street in the twilight, it occurs to me that I know of no more agreeable object to bound our view, looking outward through the vista of our elm-lined streets, than the pyramidal tops of a white pine forest in the horizon. Let them stand so near at least.

Jan. 20. A second remarkably pleasant day like the last.

P. M. — Up river.

I see a large white oak perfectly bare.

Among four or five pickerel in a "well" on the river,

I see one with distinct transverse bars as I look down on its back, — not quite across the back, but plain as they spring from the side of the back, — while all the others are uniformly dark above. Is not the former *Esox fasciatus*? There is no marked difference when I look at them on their sides.

I see in various places on the ice and snow, this very warm and pleasant afternoon, a kind of mosquito perhaps, a feeble flyer, commonly resting on the ice.

The green of the ice and water begins to be visible about half an hour before sunset. Is it produced by the reflected blue of the sky mingling with the yellow or pink of the setting sun?

What a singular element is this water! I go shaking the river from side to side at each step, as I see by its motion at the few holes.

I learn from J. Farmer that he saw to-day in his wood-lot, on removing the bark of a dead white pine, an immense quantity of mosquitoes, moving but little, in a cavity between the bark and the wood made probably by some other insect. These were probably like mine. There were also wasps and what he calls lightning-bugs there.

Jan. 21. A January thaw, with some fog, occasioned as yet wholly by warm weather, without rain; high wind in the night; wind still south. The last two days have been remarkably pleasant and warm, with a southerly wind, and last night was apparently warmer yet (I think it was 46° this morning); and this morning I am surprised to see much bare ground and ice where

Vol. XI

was snow last evening, and though last evening it was good sleighing and the street was not wet at all, — though the snow was moist, — now it is almost entirely bare ice except for the water. The sluices are more than full, rushing like mill-streams on each side the way and often stretching in broad lakes across the street. It is the worst or wettest of walking, requiring india-rubber boots. Great channels, eight inches deep and a foot or more wide, are worn in the ice across the street, revealing a pure, clear ice on the sides, contrasting with the dirty surface. I do not remember so sudden a change, the effect of warmth without rain. Yesterday afternoon it was safe sledding wood along the riverside on the ice, — Hubbard was doing so, — and I saw at the bridges that the river was some eight inches lower than it had been when it froze, the ice adhering to the piers, and all held up there so much higher than the surrounding surface; and now it is rapidly rising, and the river is forbidden ground.

It is surprising how suddenly the slumbering snow has been melted, and with what a rush it now seeks the lowest ground on all sides. Yesterday, in the streets and fields, it was all snow and ice and rest; now it is chiefly water and motion. Yesterday afternoon I walked in the merely moist snow-track of sleds and sleighs, while all the sides of the road and the ditches rested under a white mantle of snow. This morning I go picking my way in rubbers through broad puddles on a slippery icy bottom, stepping over small torrents which have worn channels six or eight inches deep, and on each side rushes past with a loud murmur a stream large enough

to turn a mill, occasionally spreading out into a sizable mill-pond.

It begins to rain by afternoon, and rains more or less during the night. Before night I heard of the river being over the road in one place, though it was rather low before. Saw Melvin buying an extra quantity of shot in anticipation of the freshet and musquash-shooting to-morrow.

Jan. 22. Apparently the wind south two or three days or thermometer so long above 40° will make a freshet, if there is snow enough on the ground.

8.30 A. M. — Go to the riverside.

It is over the meadows. Hear Melvin's gun. The thick white ice is seen lifted up and resting over the channel several rods from the present shore on the high bank side.

As I stand there looking out to that white ice, about four rods distant (at my boat's place), I notice countless narrow light lines, a third of an inch wide, in or on the very thin, dark, half-cemented ice (hardly so thick as pasteboard) which has formed since midnight on the surface of the risen water between the old ice and the shore. At first I thought that these light lines were cracks in that thin ice or crystallization (it is now 34°), occasioned, perhaps, by the mere rising of the water. But observing that some of them were peculiarly meandering, returning on themselves loopwise, I looked at them more attentively, and at length I detected at the inner end of one such line a small black speck about a rod from me. Suspecting this to be a caterpillar, I took steps to ascer-

tain if it were, at any rate, a living creature, by discovering if it were in motion. It appeared to me to move, but it was so slowly that I could not be certain until I set up a stick on the shore or referred it to a fixed point on the ice, when I was convinced that it was a caterpillar slowly crawling toward the shore, or rather to the willows. Following its trail back with my eye, I found that it came pretty directly from the edge of the old or thick white ice (*i. e.* from where the surface of the flood touched its sloping surface) toward the willows, from northeast to southwest, and had come about three rods. Looking more sharply still, I detected seven or eight such caterpillars within a couple of square rods on this crystallization, each at the end of its trail and headed toward the willows in exactly the same direction. And there were the distinct trails of a great many more which had reached the willows or disappeared elsewhere. These trails were particularly distinct when I squatted low and looked over the ice, reflecting more light then. They were generally pretty direct toward the shore, or toward any clump of willows if within four or five rods. I saw one which led to the willows from the old ice some six rods off. Slowly as they crawled, this journey must have been made within a few hours, for undoubtedly this ice was formed since midnight. Many of the lines were very meandering, like this: —

and apparently began and ended within the thin ice. There was not enough ice to support even a caterpillar within three or four feet of the shore, for the water was still rapidly rising and not now freezing, and I noticed no caterpillars on the ice within several feet, but with a long stick I obtained quite a number. Among them were three kinds. Probably the commonest were, first, a small flat (beneath) black one with a dark shell head and body consisting of numerous rings, like dark velvet, four or five eighths of an inch long;[1] second, a black caterpillar about same length, covered with hairy points or tufts, (remind me somewhat of that kind I see on the black willows, which is larger and partly yellow); thirdly, one all brown fuzzy and six or seven eighths of an inch long. The last lay at the bottom, but was alive. All curled up when I rescued them.

There were also many small brown grasshoppers (not to mention spiders of various sizes and snow-fleas) on the ice, but none of these left any perceptible track.

These tracks, thus distinct, were quite innumerable, — there was certainly one for each foot of shore, — many thousands (?) within half a dozen rods, — leading commonly from the channel ice to or toward the shore or a tree, but sometimes wandering parallel to the shore. Yet comparatively few of the caterpillars were now to be seen. You would hardly believe that there had been caterpillars enough there to leave all these trails within so short a time.

It may be a question how did they come on the channel ice. I answer that they were evidently drowned out of the meadow-grass by the rise of the water, i. e., if

[1] Vide [p. 442].

there is sufficient thaw to lay the ground bare (as the musquash are, which I now hear one shooting from a boat), and that they either swam or were washed on to that channel ice by the rising water (while probably others were washed yet higher up the bank or meadow and were not obliged to make this journey?), and so, as soon as the water froze hard enough to bear, they commenced their slow journey toward the shore, or any other dark terrestrial-looking object, like a tree, within half a dozen rods. At first I thought they left a trail because the ice was so very thin and watery, but perhaps the very slight snow that whitened the ground a little had melted on it. Possibly some were washed from adjacent fields and meadows into the river, for there has been a great wash, a torrent of water has rushed downward over these fields to the river. There was, perhaps, a current setting from the shore toward the middle, which floated them out. How is it when a river is rising?

At any rate, within twenty-four hours this freshet has invaded the Broadways or lower streets of the caterpillar towns, and, within some six hours probably, these innumerable journeys have been performed by wrecked caterpillars over a newly formed ice-bridge, — more such adventurers in our town alone than there are human beings in the United States, — and their trails are there to be seen, every one of them. Undespairing caterpillars, determined to reach the shore. What risks they run who go to sleep for the winter in our river meadows!

Perhaps the insects come up from their winter re-

treats in the roots of the grass in such warm and sunny days as we have had, and so are the more washed away, and also become food for crows, which, as I noticed, explore the smallest bare tufts in the fields.

I notice where a musquash has lately swam under this thin ice, breaking it here and there, and his course for many rods is betrayed by a continuous row of numerous white bubbles as big as a ninepence under the ice. J. Farmer tells me that he once saw a musquash rest three or four minutes under the ice with his nose against the ice in a bubble of air about an inch in diameter, and he thinks that they can draw air through the ice, and that one could swim across Nagog Pond under the ice.

I think that the greater part of the caterpillars reaching the few feet of open water next the shore must sink to the bottom, and perhaps they survive in the grass there. A few may crawl up the trees. One which I took off the bottom was alive.

A freshet, then, even in midwinter, is a most momentous event to the insect world.

Perhaps the caterpillars, being in the water, are not frozen in, but crawl out on the ice and steer for the land from wherever they may be. Apparently those which started from the edge of the channel ice must have been drifted there either by the current or wind, because they could not have risen directly up to it from the bottom, since it slopes toward the shore for a rod under water. It is remarkable that the caterpillars know enough to steer for the shore, though four or five rods off.

I notice that, the river thus breaking up in this freshet, this body of ice over the channel cracks on each side near the line of the willows, a little outside of them, two great rents showing the edge and thickness of the ice, making many a jounce or thankee-marm for the skater when all is frozen again, while between them the ice of the channel is lifted up level, while outside these rents the ice slopes downward for a rod, the shore edge still fastened to the bottom; i. e., the fuller tide, rushing downward, lifts up the main body of the ice, cracking it on each side of the channel, the outside strips remaining attached to the bottom by their shore edges and sloping upward to the rents, so that the freshet runs through, and nearly overflows these two strips, creeping far up the bank or over the meadows on each side.

P. M. — I see many caterpillars on the ice still, and those glow-worm-like ones. I see several of the black fuzzy (with distinct tufts) caterpillars described above, on the open water next the shore, but none of them is moving; also, in the water, common small black crickets (one alive) and other bugs (commonly alive), which have been washed out of their winter quarters. And in the fields generally, exposed on bare, hard ice, the snow being gone and more than half the earth bare, are a great many caterpillars (still two other kinds than yet described), many naked and fishworm-color, four to six inches long, and those glow-worm-like ones (some more brown). They have evidently been washed out of their retreats in the grass by the great flow of water, and left on the ice. They must afford abundant food [for] birds.

Crows which fared hard ten days ago must fare sump-tuously now. This will account for their tracks which I saw the other day leading to every little bare strip [?] or exposed tuft of grass, — those warm days. Perhaps the caterpillars, etc., crawl forth in sunny and warm days in midwinter when the earth is bare, and so supply the birds, and are ready to be washed away by a flow of water! I find thus a great variety of living insects now washed out. Four kinds of caterpillars, and also the glow-worm-like creature so common, grasshoppers, crickets, and many bugs, not to mention the mosquito-like insects which the warm weather has called forth (flying feebly just over the ice and snow a foot or two), spiders, and snow-fleas. A sudden thaw is, then, a great relief to crows and other birds that may have been put to it for food. Their larders are now overstocked.

Can that glow-worm-like creature, so common on the ice by the riverside and in the fields now, be the female of the lightning-bug? It is about half an inch long by one eleventh of an inch wide, dusky reddish-brown above, lighter beneath, with a small black flat-tish head and about four short antennæ, six legs under the forward part of the body, which last consists of twelve ring-like segments. There is one row of mi-nute light-colored dots down the middle of the back, and perhaps (?) others, fainter, on the side.

Many are out in boats, steering outside the ice of the river over the newly flooded meadows, shooting mus-quash. Cocks crow as in spring.

The energy and excitement of the musquash-hunter even, not despairing of life, but keeping the same rank

and savage hold on it that his predecessors have for so many generations, while so many are sick and despair-ing, even this is inspiriting to me. Even these deeds of death are interesting as evidences of life, for life will still prevail in spite of all accidents. I have a certain faith that even musquash are immortal and not born to be killed by Melvin's double-B (?) shot.

Methinks the breadth of waves, whether in water or snow or sand or vapor (in the mackerel sky), is deter-mined generally by the force of the wind or other current striking the water, etc. It depends on how much water, etc., the wind has power to displace.

The musquash-hunter (last night), with his increased supply of powder and shot and boat turned up some-where on the bank, now that the river is rapidly rising, dreaming of his exploits to-day in shooting musquash, of the great pile of dead rats that will weigh down his boat before night, when he will return wet and weary and weather-beaten to his hut with an appetite for his supper and for much sluggish (punky) social inter-course with his fellows, — even he, dark, dull, and bat-tered flint as he is, is an inspired man to his extent now, perhaps the most inspired by this freshet of any, and the Musketaquid Meadows cannot spare him. There are poets of all kinds and degrees, little known to each other. The Lake School is not the only or the principal one. They love various things. Some love beauty, and some love rum. Some go to Rome, and some go a-fishing, and are sent to the house of correc-tion once a month. They keep up their fires by means unknown to me. I know not their comings and goings.

How can I tell what violets they watch for? I know them wild and ready to risk all when their muse invites. The most sluggish will be up early enough then, and face any amount of wet and cold. I meet these gods of the river and woods with sparkling faces (like Apollo's) late from the house of correction, it may be carrying whatever mystic and forbidden bottles or other vessels concealed, while the dull regular priests are steering their parish rafts in a prose mood. What care I to see galleries full of representatives of heathen gods, when I can see natural living ones by an infinitely superior artist, without perspective tube? If you read the Rig Veda, oldest of books, as it were, describing a very primitive people and condition of things, you hear in their prayers of a still older, more primitive and abo-riginal race in their midst and round about, warring on them and seizing their flocks and herds, infesting their pastures. Thus is it in another sense in all communities, and hence the prisons and police.

I hear these guns going to-day, and I must confess they are to me a springlike and exhilarating sound, like the cock-crowing, though each one may report the death of a musquash. This, methinks, or the like of this, with whatever mixture of dross, is the real morning or evening hymn that goes up from these vales to-day, and which the stars echo. This is the best sort of glori-fying of God and enjoying him that at all prevails here to-day, without any clarified butter or sacred ladles.

As a mother loves to see her child imbibe nourish-ment and expand, so God loves to see his children thrive on the nutriment he has furnished them. In the

musquash-hunters I see the Almouchicois still pushing swiftly over the dark stream in their canoes. These aboriginal men cannot be repressed, but under some guise or other they survive and reappear continually. Just as simply as the crow picks up the worms which all over the fields have been washed out by the thaw, these men pick up the musquash that have been washed out the banks. And to serve such ends men plow and sail, and powder and shot are made, and the grocer exists to retail them, though he may think himself much more the deacon of some church.

From year to year the snow has its regular retreat and lurking-places when a thaw comes (laying bare the earth), under the southeastward banks. I see it now resting there in broad white lines and deep drifts (from my window), as I have seen it for many years, — as it lay when the Indian was the only man here to see it.

Jan. 23. The freshet is now frozen over, but not thick enough to bear without cracking, and that pecul-iar whitish ice like bread or mortar that has run over is seen four to six feet in width all along the shore and about trees, posts, rocks, etc. It is produced by the water, probably, still rising after the freezing in the night and flowing back over the ice in a semiliquid state, or like soft solder, — a rough or wrinkled or rippled dirty-white surface, often stained with the bank, yellowish or brown.

There is a cold northwest wind, and I notice that the snow-fleas which were so abundant on this water yesterday have hopped to some lee, *i. e.*, are collected like powder under the southeast side of posts or trees or sticks or ridges in the ice. You are surprised to see that they manage to get out of the wind. On the southeast side of every such barrier along the shore there is a dark line or heap of them. I see one of those glow-worm-like creatures frozen in, sticking up perpendicular, half above the ice.

Going over the Hosmer pasture this side Clamshell southwestward, I thought I saw much gossamer on the grass, but was surprised to find that it was the light reflected from the withered grass stems which had been bent or broken by the snow (now melted). It looked just like gossamer even within ten [?] feet, — most would have taken it for that, — also these fine gleaming lines (like those of the alders and birch twigs, etc.) were very distinctly parts of an arc of a large circle, — the lower side of it, — as you looked toward the sun, the light being necessarily so reflected. This is a remarkable instance of the November, or rather winter, light reflected from twigs and stubble. The grass stood thus: —

It was just like an abundant gossamer.

The earth being generally bare, I notice on the ice where it slopes up eastward a little, a distinct rosy light (or pink) reflected from it generally, half an hour before sunset. This is a colder evening than of late, and there is so much the more of it.

Jan. 24. An abundance of excellent skating, the freshet that covered the meadows being frozen. Many boys and girls are skating on Mantatuket Meadow and on Merrick's. Looking from this shore, they appear decidedly elevated, — not by their skates merely. What is the cause? Do we take the ice to be air?

I see an abundance of caterpillars of various kinds on the ice of the meadows, many of those large, dark, hairy, with longitudinal light stripes, somewhat like the common apple one. Many of them are frozen in yet, some for two thirds their length, yet all are alive. Yet it has been so cold since the rise that you can now cross the channel almost anywhere. I also see a great many of those little brown grasshoppers and one perfectly green one, some of them frozen in, but generally on the surface, showing no signs of life; yet when I brought them home to experiment on, I found them all alive and kicking in my pocket. There were also a small kind of reddish wasp, quite lively, on the ice, and other insects; those naked, or smooth, worms or caterpillars. This shows what insects have their winter quarters in the meadow-grass. This ice is a good field for an entomologist.

I experimented on the large bubbles under the ice. Some, the oldest and nearest the surface, were white; others, the newest and against the present under surface, were of a bluish or slate color, more transparent. I found that the whiteness of the first was owing to the great quantity of little bubbles above and below the great one produced by the heat of this "burning-glass," while those of recent formation have not had time to

accomplish this. When I cut through with my knife an inch or two to one of the latter kind, making a very slight opening, the confined air, pressed by the water, burst up with a considerable hissing sound, sometimes spurting a little water with it, and thus the bubble was contracted, almost annihilated; but frequently, when I cut into one of the old or white ones, there was no sound, the air did not rush out because there was no pressure, there being ice below as well as above it; but when I also pierced the lower ice it did rush out with a sound like the others.

My object at first was to ascertain if both kinds of bubbles contained air. But that was plain enough, for when the water rushed in the bluish, or new, ones wholly beneath the ice wholly or nearly disappeared, while the white ones, giving place to water, were no longer white. It would seem, then, that a considerable pressure, such as the water exerts on an air-bubble under the ice, does not force it through the ice, certainly not for a considerable time. How, then, can the musquash draw air through the ice as is asserted? He might, however, come to breathe in such a bubble as this already existing.

The larger spiders generally rest on the ice with all their legs spread, but on being touched they gather them up.

Jan. 25. The river has gone down about eight inches, and the ice still adhering to the shore all about the meadows slants downward for some four or five feet till it meets the water, and it is there cracked, often

letting the water up to overflow it, so that it is hard to get off and on in some places.

That channel ice of the 22d (*q. v.*), lifted up, looks thin, thus: —

The edges of the outside portions are more lifted up now, apparently by the weight of the water on them.

Jan. 26. P. M. — Over Cyanean Meadow on ice. These are remarkably warm and pleasant days. The water is going down, and the ice is rotting. I see some insects — those glow-worm-like ones — sunk half an inch or more into the ice by absorbed heat and yet quite alive in these little holes, in which they alternately freeze and thaw. At Willow Bay I see for many rods black soil a quarter of an inch deep, covering and concealing the ice (for several rods). This, I find, was blown some time ago from a plowed field twenty or more rods distant. This shows how much the sediment of the river may be increased by dust blown into it from the neighboring fields. Any ice begins immediately after it is formed to look dusty in the sun anywhere. This black soil is rapidly sinking to the bottom through the ice, by absorbing heat, and, water overflowing and freezing, it is left deep within thick ice. Or else, lying in wavelets on the ice, the surface becomes at last full of dark-bottomed holes alternating with clear ice.

The ice, having fairly begun to decompose, is very

handsomely marked, more or less internally as it appears, with a sort of graphic character, or bird-tracks, very agreeable and varied. It appears to be the skeleton of the ice revealed, the original crystals (such as we see shoot on very thin ice just beginning) revealed by the rotting. Thus the peculiar knotty grain or knurliness of the ice is shown, — white marks on dark. These white waving lines within it look sometimes just like some white, shaggy wolf-skin.

The meadow which makes up between Hubbard's mainland and his swamp wood is very handsomely marked, or marbled, with alternate white and dark ice. The upper surface appears to be of one color and consistency, like a hard enamel, but very interesting white figures are seen through it.

What various kinds of ice there are! This which lately formed so suddenly on the flooded meadows, from beneath which the water has in a great measure run out, letting it down, while a warm sun has shone on it, is perhaps the most interesting of any. It might be called graphic ice.

It is a very pleasant and warm day, and when I came down to the river and looked off to Merrick's pasture, the osiers there shone as brightly as in spring, showing that their brightness depends on the sun and air rather than the season.

Jan. 27. I see some of those little cells, perhaps, of a wasp or bee, made of clay or clayey mud. It suggests that these insects were the first potters. They look somewhat like small stone jugs.

Vol. XI

less varied than the other, but still is very peculiar and interesting. You notice the polished surface much more, as if it were the marble floor of some stupendous hall. Yet such is its composition it is not quite so hard and metallic, I think. The skater probably makes more of a scratch. The other was hard and crystalline.

As I look south just before sunset, over this fresh and shining ice, I notice that its surface is divided, as it were, into a great many contiguous tables in different planes, somewhat like so many different facets of a polyhedron as large as the earth itself. These tables or planes are bounded by cracks, though without any appreciable opening, and the different levels are betrayed by the reflections of the light or sky being interrupted at the cracks. The ice formed last night is a day old, and these cracks, as I find, run generally from northeast to southwest across the entire meadow, some twenty-five or thirty rods, nearly at right angles with the river, and are from five to fifteen feet apart, while there are comparatively few cracks crossing them in the other direction. You notice this phenomenon looking over the ice some rods before you; otherwise might not observe the cracks when upon them. It is as if the very globe itself were a crystal with a certain number of facets.

When I look westward now to the flat snow-crusted shore, it reflects a strong violet color. Also the pink light reflected from the low, flat snowy surfaces amid the ice on the meadows, just before sunset, is a constant phenomenon these clear winter days. Whole fields and sides of hills are often the same, but it is more distinct on

Jan. 28. Melvin tells me that one with whom he deals below says that the best musquash skins come from Concord River, and it is because our musquash are so fat. M. says that they eat apples, and he has seen where they have eaten acorns, and Isaiah Green told him and convinced him that they ate his seed-corn in the hill. He weighed a very large one the other day, and it weighed five pounds. Thinks they would not commonly weigh more than three.

When you have been deprived of your usual quantity of sleep for several nights, you sleep much more soundly for it, and wake up suddenly like a bullet that strikes a wall.

Jan. 30. How peculiar the hooting of an owl! It is not shrill and sharp like the scream of a hawk, but full, round, and sonorous, waking the echoes of the wood.

The surface of the snow, especially on hillsides, has a peculiarly combed or worn appearance where water has run in a thaw; *i. e.*, the whole surface shows regular furrows at a distance, as if it had been scraped with an immense comb.

Jan. 31. P. M. — Up river across Cyanean Meadow.

Now we have quite another kind of ice. It has rained hard, converting into a very thin liquid the snow which had fallen on the old ice, and this, having frozen, has made a perfectly smooth but white snow ice. It is white like polished marble (I call it marble ice), and the trees and hill are reflected in it, as not in the other. It is far

these flat islands of snow scattered here and there over the meadow ice. I also see this pink in the dust made by the skaters. Perhaps the green seen at the same time in ice and water is produced by the general yellow or amber light of this hour, mingled with the blue of the reflected sky? ?

Surely the ice is a great and absorbing phenomenon. Consider how much of the surface of the town it occupies, how much attention it monopolizes! We do not commonly distinguish more than one kind of water in the river, but what various kinds of ice there are!

Young Heywood told me that the trout which he caught in Walden was twenty-seven inches long and weighed five pounds, but was thin, not in good condition. (He saw another.) It was in the little cove between the deep one and the railroad.

FEBRUARY, 1859

(ÆT. 41)

Feb. 1. P. M. — Up Assabet.

The river having suddenly gone down since the freshet, I see cakes of ice eight or ten feet across left two feet high or more above the banks, frozen to four or five maples or oaks. Indeed, each shore is lined with them, where wooded, a continuous row attached to alders, maples, swamp white oaks, etc., which grow through them or against their edges. They are somewhat like tables of a picnic party or a muster-field dinner. Rustic tables and seats. Sometimes a little inclined, having settled on one side. Also an ice-belt adheres to the steep shores, and the rain and melted snow, running down, has drifted over the edge of it, forming abundant and pretty icicles, and you see where this hard and thick ice has bent under its own weight.

As for large oak leaves now, I think there is not much difference between the white and scarlet oaks; then come black, red, and swamp white, but the last one has scarcely any.

Feb. 2. I see Peter Hutchinson cutting down a large red oak on A. Heywood's hillside, west of the former's house. He points out to me what he calls the "gray oak" there, with "a thicker bark" than the red. It is the scarlet oak.

Feb. 3. Five minutes before 3 P. M., Father died.[1]

After a sickness of some two years, going down-town in pleasant weather, doing a little business from time to time, hoeing a little in the garden, etc., Father took to his chamber January 13th, and did not come down again. Most of the time previously he had coughed and expectorated a great deal. Latterly he did not cough, but continued to raise. He continued to sit up in his chamber till within a week before he died. He sat up for a little while on the Sunday four days before he died. Generally he was very silent for many months. He was quite conscious to the last, and his death was so easy that we should not have been aware that he was dying, though we were sitting around his bed, if we had not watched very closely.[2]

I have touched a body which was flexible and warm, yet tenantless, — warmed by what fire? When the spirit that animated some matter has left it, who else, what else, can animate it?

How enduring are our bodies, after all! The forms of our brothers and sisters, our parents and children and wives, lie still in the hills and fields round about us, not to mention those of our remoter ancestors, and the matter which composed the body of our first human father still exists under another name.

When in sickness the body is emaciated, and the ex-

[1] [This sentence (with the date) has a full page to itself in the original Journal.]

[2] [See *Familiar Letters*, pp. 350, 351; Riv. 407, 408.]

pression of the face in various ways is changed, you perceive unexpected resemblances to other members of the same family; as if within the same family there was a greater general similarity in the framework of the face than in its filling up and clothing.

Father first came to this town to live with his father about the end of the last century, when he was about twelve years old. (His father died in 1801.) Afterward he went to the Lexington Academy (Parker's?) a short time, perhaps a year, then into Deacon White's store as clerk; then learned the dry-goods business in a store in Salem. (Aunt J. shows me a letter from him directly after his going there, dated 1807.) Was with a Hathaway. When about twenty-one, opened a store for himself on the corner where the town house stands of late years, a yellow building, now moved and altered into John Keyes's house. He did so well there that Isaac Hurd went into partnership with him, to his injury. They soon dissolved, but could not settle without going to law, when my father gained the case, bringing his books into court. Then, I think, he went to Bangor and set up with Billings, selling to Indians (among others); married; lived in Boston; writes thence to aunts at Bangor in 1815 with John on his knee; moved to Concord (*where I was born*), then to Chelmsford, to Boston, to Concord again, and here remained. Mother first came to Concord about the same age that father did, but a little before him.

As far as I know, Father, when he died, was not only one of the oldest men in the middle of Concord, but the

one perhaps best acquainted with the inhabitants, and the local, social, and street history of the middle of the town, for the last fifty years. He belonged in a peculiar sense to the village street; loved to sit in the shops or at the post-office and read the daily papers. I think that he remembered more about the worthies (and unworthies) of Concord village forty years ago, both from dealing as a trader and from familiar intercourse with them, than any one else. Our other neighbors, now living or very recently dead, have either come to the town more recently than he, or have lived more aloof from the mass of the inhabitants.

Some have spoken slightingly of the Indians, as a race possessing so little skill and wit, so low in the scale of humanity, and so brutish that they hardly deserved to be remembered, — using only the terms "miserable," "wretched," "pitiful," and the like. In writing their histories of this country they have so hastily disposed of this refuse of humanity (as they might have called it) which littered and defiled the shore and the interior. But even the indigenous animals are inexhaustibly interesting to us. How much more, then, the indigenous man of America! If wild men, so much more like ourselves than they are unlike, have inhabited these shores before us, we wish to know particularly what manner of men they were, how they lived here, their relation to nature, their arts and their customs, their fancies and superstitions. They paddled over these waters, they wandered in these woods, and they had their fancies and beliefs connected with the sea and the forest, which concern us quite as much as the fables of Oriental nations do. It frequently happens that the historian, though he professes more humanity than the trapper, mountain man, or gold-digger, who shoots one as a wild beast, really exhibits and practices a similar inhumanity to him, wielding a pen instead of a rifle.

One tells you with more contempt than pity that the Indian had no religion, holding up both hands, and this to all the shallow-brained and bigoted seems to mean something important, but it is commonly a distinction without a difference. Pray, how much more religion has the historian? If Henry Ward Beecher knows so much more about God than another, if he has made some discovery of truth in this direction, I would thank him to publish it in *Silliman's Journal*, with as few flourishes as possible.

It is the spirit of humanity, that which animates both so-called savages and civilized nations, working through a man, and not the man expressing himself, that interests us most. The thought of a so-called savage tribe is generally far more just than that of a single civilized man.

I perceive that we partially die ourselves through sympathy at the death of each of our friends or near relatives. Each such experience is an assault on our vital force. It becomes a source of wonder that they who have lost many friends still live. After long watching around the sick-bed of a friend, we, too, partially give up the ghost with him, and are the less to be identified with this state of things.

The writer must to some extent inspire himself. Most

of his sentences may at first lie dead in his essay, but when all are arranged, some life and color will be reflected on them from the mature and successful lines; they will appear to pulsate with fresh life, and he will be enabled to eke out their slumbering sense, and make them worthy of their neighborhood. In his first essay on a given theme, he produces scarcely more than a frame and groundwork for his sentiment and poetry. Each clear thought that he attains to draws in its train many divided thoughts or perceptions. The writer has much to do even to create a theme for himself. Most that is first written on any subject is a mere groping after it, mere rubble-stone and foundation. It is only when many observations of different periods have been brought together that he begins to grasp his subject and can make one pertinent and just observation.

Feb. 5. When we have experienced many disappointments, such as the loss of friends, the notes of birds cease to affect us as they did.

I see another butcher-bird on the top of a young tree by the pond.

Feb. 7. Evidently the distant woods are more blue in a warm and moist or misty day in winter, and is not this connected with the blue in snow in similar days?

Going along the Nut Meadow or Jimmy Miles road, when I see the sulphur lichens on the rails brightening with the moisture I feel like studying them again as a relisher or tonic, to make life go down and digest well, as we use pepper and vinegar and salads. They are a

Vol. XI

sort of winter greens which we gather and assimilate with our eyes.[1] That's the true use of the study of lichens. I expect that the lichenist will have the keenest relish for Nature in her every-day mood and dress. He will have the appetite of the worm that never dies, of the grub. To study lichens is to get a taste of earth and health, to go gnawing the rails and rocks. This product of the bark is the essence of all times. The lichenist extracts nutriment from the very crust of the earth. A taste for this study is an evidence of titanic health, a sane earthiness. It makes not so much blood as soil of life. It fits a man to deal with the barrenest and rockiest experience. A little moisture, a fog, or rain, or melted snow makes his wilderness to blossom like the rose. As some strong animal appetites, not satisfied with starch and muscle and fat, are fain to eat that which eats and digests, — the contents of the crop and the stomach and entrails themselves, — so the lichenist loves the tripe of the rock, — that which eats and digests the rocks. He eats the eater. "Eat-all" may be his name. A lichenist fats where others starve. His provender never fails. What is the barrenest waste to him, the barest rocks? A rail is the sleekest and fattest of coursers for him.[2] He picks anew the bones which have been picked a generation since, for when their marrow is gone they are clothed with new flesh for him. What diet drink can be compared with a tea or soup made of the very crust of the earth? There is no such collyrium or salve for sore eyes as these brightening lichens in a moist day. Go and

[1] [Channing, p. 112.]
[2] [Channing, p. 73.]

bathe and screen your eyes with them in the softened light of the woods.

Feb. 11. P. M. — To Ball's Hill over ice.

Among the common phenomena of the ice are those triangular points of thick ice heaved up a couple of feet where the ice has recently settled about a rock. The rock looks somewhat like a dark fruit within a gaping shell or bur. Also, now, as often after a freshet in cold weather, the ice which had formed around and frozen to the trees and bushes along the shore, settling, draws them down to the ground or water, often breaking them extensively. It reminds you of an alligator or other evil genius of the river pulling the trees and bushes which had come to drink into the water. If a maple or alder is unfortunate enough to dip its lower limbs into the freshet, dallying with it, their fate is sealed, for the water, freezing that night, takes fast hold on them like a vise, and when the water runs out from beneath, an irresistible weight brings them down to the ground and holds them there. Only the spring sun will soften the heart of this relentless monster, when, commonly, it is too late. How the ice far in the meadows, thus settling, spreads the clumps of willows, etc., on every side!

Nature works by contraries. That which in summer was most fluid and unresting is now most solid and motionless. If in the summer you cast a twig into the stream it instantly moved along with the current, and nothing remained as it was. Now I see yonder a long row of black twigs standing erect in mid-channel where two months ago a fisherman set them and fastened his lines to them. They stand there motionless as guide-posts while snow and ice are piled up about them.

Such is the cold skill of the artist. He carves a statue out of a material which is fluid as water to the ordinary workman. His sentiments are a quarry which he works.[1]

I see only the chain of sunken boats passing round a tree above the ice.

The south side of Ball's Hill, which is warm and half bare, is tracked up with partridges, and I start several there. So is it next Sunday with the Hill shore, east of Fair Haven Pond. These birds are sure to be found now on such slopes, where only the ground and dry leaves are exposed.

The water lately went down, and the ice settled on the meadows, and now rain has come, and cold again, and this surface is alternate ice and snow. Looking from this hill toward the sun, they are seen to be handsomely watered all over with alternate waves of shining ice and white snow-crust, literally "watered" on the grandest scale, — this palace floor.

Feb. 12. Saturday. You may account for that ash by the Rock having such a balanced and regular outline by the fact that in an open place their branches are equally drawn toward the light on all sides, and not because of a mutual understanding through the trunk.

[1] [Channing, p. 301.]

For there is Cheney's abele, which stands just south of a large elm. It grows wholly southward, and in form is just half a tree. So with the tupelos under the Hill shore, east of Fair Haven Pond. They terminate abruptly like a bull's horn, having no upward leading shoot, and bend off over the water, — are singularly one-sided. In short, trees appear to grow regularly because the sky and diffusion of light are commonly regular.

There is a peculiarly drooping elm at George Prescott's great gate just north of his house, very different from the common or upright stiff-branched ones near by it.

Feb. 13. P. M. — On ice to Fair Haven Pond.

Yesterday there was no skating, unless you swept the snow from the ice; but to-day, though there has been no rain nor thaw, there is pretty good skating. Yesterday the water which had flowed, and was flowing, back over the ice on each side of the river and the meadows, a rod or two in width, was merely skimmed over, but last night it froze so that there is good skating there. Also the wind will generally lay bare some portion of the ice, unless the snow is very deep.

This yellowish ice which froze yesterday and last night is thickly and evenly strewn with fibrous frost-crystals very much like bits of asbestos, an inch or more long, sometimes arranged like a star or rosette, one for every inch or two; but where I broke in yesterday, and

Vol. XI

apparently wherever the water overflowed the thin ice late in the day, there are none. I think that this is the vapor from the water which found its way up through the ice and froze in the night. It is sprinkled like some kind of grain, and is in certain places much more thickly strewn, as where a little snow shows itself above the ice.

The old ice is covered with a dry, powdery snow about one inch deep, from which, as I walk toward the sun, this perfectly clear, bright afternoon, at 3.30 o'clock, the colors of the rainbow are reflected from a myriad fine facets. It is as if the dust of diamonds and other precious stones were spread all around. The blue and red predominate. Though I distinguish these colors everywhere toward the sun, they are so much more abundantly reflected to me from two particular directions that I see two distant rays, or arms, so to call them, of this rainbow-like dust, one on each side of the sun, stretching away from me and about half a dozen feet wide, the two arms including an angle of about sixty degrees. When I look from the sun, I see merely dazzling white points. I can easily see some of these dazzling grains fifteen or twenty rods distant on any side, though the facet which reflects this light cannot be more than a tenth or twelfth of an inch at most. Yet I might easily, and commonly do, overlook all this.

Winter comes to make walking possible where there was no walking in summer. Not till winter do we take possession of the whole of our territory. I have three great highways raying out from one centre, which is near my door. I may walk down the main river or up either of its two branches. Could any avenues be con-

trived more convenient? With this river I am not compelled to walk in the tracks of horses.

Never is there so much light in the air as in one of these bright winter afternoons, when all the earth is covered with new-fallen snow and there is not a cloud in the sky. The sky is much the darkest side, like the bluish lining of an egg-shell. There seems nothing left to make night out of. With this white earth beneath and that spot[less] skimmed-milk sky above him, man is but a black speck inclosed in a white egg-shell.

Sometimes in our prosaic moods, life appears to us but a certain number more of days like those which we have lived, to be cheered not by more friends and friendship but probably fewer and less. As, perchance, we anticipate the end of this day before it is done, close the shutters, and with a cheerless resignation commence the barren evening whose fruitless end we clearly see, we despondingly think that all of life that is left is only this experience repeated a certain number of times. And so it would be, if it were not for the faculty of imagination.

I see, under this ice an inch thick, a large bubble with three cracks across it, yet they are so fine — though quite distinct — that they let no air up, and I release it with my knife. An air-bubble very soon makes the ice look whitish above it. It is whitest of all when it is fairly inclosed, with ice beneath it. When, by treading above it, I dislodge a bubble under this ice which formed only last night, I see that it leaves the outline of its form behind, the ice being a little thinner above it.

Here is the track of one who walked here yesterday. The age of the track is betrayed by a certain smoothness or shininess produced by the sun shining on the raw and disturbed edges and melting them. The fresh track is evidently made in a dry, powdery substance; that of yesterday, as if it were made in a slightly glutinous matter, or which possessed considerable tenacity.

Then there is the wonderful stillness of a winter day. The sources of sound, as of water, are frozen up; scarcely a tinkling rill of it is to be heard. When we listen, we hear only that sound of the surf of our internal sea, rising and swelling in our ears as in two seashells. It is the sabbath of the year, stillness audible, or at most we hear the ice belching and crackling as if struggling for utterance.

A transient acquaintance with any phenomenon is not sufficient to make it completely the subject of your muse. You must be so conversant with it as to *remember* it and be reminded of it long afterward, while it lies remotely fair and elysian in the horizon, approachable only by the imagination.

Feb. 14. P. M. — On ice up Assabet to railroad.

The ice-belt which I still see along the steep bank of the Assabet is now some three weeks old, and though it was then six or eight inches thick, it is now only two or three, or much less, in many places nearly wasted away, and those once horizontal tables are often fallen aslant, like shields pierced with many holes. That belt, at first

consisting of more or less blunt triangles projecting four or five feet from the bank, was at first, of course,

perfectly horizontal and level (I see where dogs and foxes have run along on it for half a mile together), but now, such is the flexibility of the ice, it is bent downward by its own weight, thus: or if you stand in front of it, it is a waving or undulating line instead of a

level one, *i. e.* on its edge. I see one table, where the ice is a little more than one inch thick, which is curved downward on the sides eighteen inches within a horizontal distance of two and a half feet, thus: There is nothing like a crack at this bend. Some of the belt itself, where three inches thick, has bent downward eighteen inches at four or five feet from the bank. I also see on Sunset Interval a large cake a rod square and a foot thick with more than a foot of soil attached beneath, which, by its own weight resting high and dry there, has bent very considerably. In one great cake there just like this, I see a fence-post with three holes in it standing upright, and perhaps the whole of it has been brought away in the soil beneath. It does not appear where it came from. Looking at the edge of one of these cakes, I notice some bubbles, seen edgewise, in the form of some buttons or of an inverted Moorish dome. These are they which when you look down on them appear thus:

As I walk over thin ice, settling it down, I see great bubbles under, three or four feet wide, go waddling or wobbling away like a scared lady impeded

---

by her train.[1] I have but little doubt that the musquash gets air from these bubbles, which are probably very conspicuous under the ice. They are its reservoirs.

Feb. 15. P. M. — Up river to Fair Haven Pond.

I thought, by the peculiar moaning sound of the wind about the dining-room at noon, that we should have a rain-storm. I heard only one blast through some crack, but no doubt that betrayed a *pluvious* breath.

I am surprised to find how much it has thawed in the street, though there has been no rain, only a south wind. There is already water standing over an icy foundation, and the dirt of the street is more obvious, the snow having partly melted away from it. We walk through almost invisible puddles on the river and meadows, in which we see the trees, etc., reflected.

I see some remarkable overflowed ice. Here is one shield of an oval form, some twenty feet long, very regularly and interestingly mottled with yellowish or deadleaf color, the stain of the mead, which by some law has been regularly distributed through the white, yet so delicately shaded off that it almost makes you dizzy to look at it. It reminds me of the beginning of a higher organization, or bony structure in a molluscous fish. The overflow must have been from the centre, where it burst up and flowed each way. In the proper light I am surprised to detect very fine and perfectly regular curving rays within the ice, just like the veins of some

[1] [Channing, p. 301.]

leaves, only finer and more regular, bilateral, perhaps a trace of the water as it flowed, — say like the lines of a cowry shell. It is but imperfectly suggested in the drawing.

Against the thickening air, trees are more and more distinct. The apple trees, so moist, are blacker than ever. A distant white birch, erect on a hill against the white, misty sky, looks, with its fine twigs, so distinct and black, like a millipede crawling up to heaven. The white oak leaves against the darker green of pines, now moist, are far more reddish.

Against Bittern Cliff I feel the first drop strike the right slope of my nose and run down the ravine there. Such is the origin of rivers.[1] Not till half a mile further my doubting companion feels another on his nose also, and I get one [in] my eye, and soon after I see the countless dimples in the puddles on the ice. So measured and deliberate is Nature always. Then the gentle, spring-like rain begins, and we turn about.

The sound of it pattering on the dry oak leaves, where young oaks thickly cover a hillside, is just like that of wind stirring them, when first heard, but is steady and monotonous and so betrayed. We rejoice to be wetted, and the very smell of wet woollen clothes exhilarates us.

I forgot to say (the 14th) that there are two of those ice-belts, a narrower and thinner one about twenty inches below the first, often connected with it by icicles at the edge. Thus each rise was recorded.

[1] [Channing, p. 118.]

Feb. 16. P. M. — From the entrance of the Mill road I look back through the sun, this soft afternoon, to some white pine tops near Jenny Dugan's. Their flattish boughs rest stratum above stratum like a cloud, a green mackerel sky, hardly reminding me of the concealed earth so far beneath. They are like a flaky crust of the earth,[1] a more ethereal, terebinthine, evergreen earth. It occurs to me that my eyes rest on them with the same pleasure as do those of the hen-hawk which has been nestled in them.

My eyes nibble the piny sierra which makes the horizon's edge, as a hungry man nibbles a cracker.

The hen-hawk and the pine are friends. The same thing which keeps the hen-hawk in the woods, away from the cities, keeps me here. That bird settles with confidence on a white pine top and not upon your weathercock. That bird will not be poultry of yours, lays no eggs for you, forever hides its nest. Though willed, or *wild*, it is not willful in its wildness. The unsympathizing man regards the wildness of some animals, their strangeness to him, as a sin; as if all their virtue consisted in their tamableness. He has always a charge in his gun ready for their extermination. What we call wildness is a civilization other than our own. The hen-hawk shuns the farmer, but it seeks the friendly shelter and support of the pine. It will not consent to walk in the barn-yard, but it loves to soar above the clouds. It has its own way and is beautiful, when we would fain subject it to our will. So any surpassing work of art is strange and wild to the mass of men, as is genius itself.

¹ [Channing, p. 114.]

No hawk that soars and steals our poultry is wilder than genius, and none is more persecuted or above persecution. It can never be poet laureate, to say "Pretty Poll" and "Polly want a cracker."[1]

Feb. 20. Have just read "Counterparts, or The Cross of Love," by the author of "Charles Auchester." It is very interesting — its illustration of Love and Friendship — as showing how much we can know of each other through sympathy merely, without any of the ordinary information. You know about a person who deeply interests you more than you can be told. A look, a gesture, an act, which to everybody else is insignificant tells you more about that one than words can. (How language is always found to serve best the highest moods, and expression of the highest truths!) If he wished to conceal something from you it would be apparent. It is as if a bird told you. Something of moment occurs. Your friend designs that it shall be a secret to you. Vain wish! You will know it, and his design. He says consciously nothing about it, yet as he is necessarily affected by it, its effect is visible to you. From this effect you infer the cause. Have you not already anticipated a thousand possible accidents? Can you be surprised? You unconsciously through sympathy make the right supposition. No other will account for precisely this behavior. You are disingenuous, and yet your knowledge exceeds the woodcraft of the cunningest hunter. It is as if you had a sort of trap, knowing the haunts of your game, what lures attract it

¹ [Channing, p. 114.]

Vol. XI

---

and its track, etc. You have foreseen how it will behave when it is caught, and now you only behold what you anticipated.

Sometimes from the altered manner of our friend, which no cloak can possibly conceal, we know that something has happened, and what it was, all the essential particulars, though it would be a long story to tell, — though it may involve the agency of four or five persons who never breathed it to you. Yet you are sure, as if you had detected all their tracks in the wood. You are the more sure because, in the case of love, effects follow their causes more inevitably than usual, this being a controlling power. Why, a friend tells all with a look, a tone, a gesture, a presence, a friendliness. He is present when absent.

In the composition it is the greatest art to find out as quickly as possible which are the best passages you have written, and tear the rest away to come at them. Even the poorest parts will be most effective when they serve these, as pediments to the column.

How much the writer lives and endures in coming before the public so often! A few years or books are with him equal to a long life of experience, suffering, etc. It is well if he does not become hardened. He learns how to bear contempt and to despise himself. He makes, as it were, *post-mortem* examinations of himself before he is dead. Such is art.

P. M. — The rain ceases, and it clears up at 5 P. M. It is a warm west wind and a remarkably soft sky, like plush; perhaps a lingering moisture there. What a reve[la]tion the blue and the bright tints in the west

---

again, after the storm and darkness! It is the opening of the windows of heaven after the flood!

Feb. 22. Go to Worcester to lecture in a parlor.

Feb. 23. P. M. — Walk to Quinsigamond Pond, where was good skating yesterday, but this very pleasant and warm day it is suddenly quite too soft. I was just saying to Blake that I should look for hard ice in the shade, or [on the] north side, of some wooded hill close to the shore, though skating was out of the question elsewhere, when, looking up, I saw a gentleman and lady very gracefully gyrating and, as it were, courtesying to each other in a small bay under such a hill on the opposite shore of the pond. Intervening bushes and shore concealed the ice, so that their swift and graceful motions, their bodies inclined at various angles as they gyrated forward and backward about a small space, looking as if they would hit each other, reminded me of the circling of two winged insects in the air, or hawks receding and approaching.

I first hear and then see eight or ten bluebirds going over. Perhaps they have not reached Concord yet. One boy tells me that he saw a bluebird in Concord on Sunday, the 20th.[1]

I see, just caught in the pond, a brook pickerel which, though it has no transverse bars, but a much finer and slighter reticulation than the common, is very distinct from it in the length and form of the snout. This is

¹ *Vide* March 9th. According to newspaper, they were seen 23d February also in Connecticut, and March 3d in West Roxbury.

much shorter and broader as you look down on it, thus:

In Bell Pond (once Bladder Pond) on the same road, near to Worcester, they were catching little shiners, only, at most, two inches long, for perch bait. (The perch and pickerel they commonly catch at Quinsigamond are small.) They cut a round hole about three feet in diameter and let down a simple net of this form, with only a stone to sink it in the bottom, then cast Indian meal or bits of cracker into the water, and the minnows swim forward after the bait, and the fisherman, without seeing them, pulls up the net at a venture.

Feb. 25. Heard Staples, Tuttle, E. Wood, N. Barrett, and others this morning at the post-office talking about the profit of milk-farming. The general conclusion seemed to be that it was less profitable than it was three years ago. Yet Staples thought he could name half a dozen who had done well. He named one. He thought he could name eight or ten who had paid off the mortgages on their farms by this means within a few years. Tuttle said he would give him a good supper if he would name three. Staples named only the one referred to above, David Buttrick, but he added, looking at Tuttle, "There is yourself. You know you came to town with nothing in your pocket but an old razor, a few pennies, and a damned dull jack-knife, and

now you are richer than David Buttrick." "Well," answered Tuttle, "I shouldn't have been, if I hadn't used the razor so much."

When it snowed yesterday very large flakes, an inch in diameter, Aunt said, "They are picking geese." This, it seems, is an old saying.

Measure your health by your sympathy with morning and spring. If there is no response in you to the awakening of nature, — if the prospect of an early morning walk does not banish sleep, if the warble of the first bluebird does not thrill you, — know that the morning and spring of your life are past. Thus may you feel your pulse.

I heard this morning a nuthatch on the elms in the street. I think that they are heard oftener and again [*sic*] at the approach of spring, just as the *phœbe* note of the chickadee is; and so their *gnah gnah* is a herald of the spring.

Joe Smith says that he saw blackbirds this morning. I hear that robins were seen a week or more ago. So the birds are quite early this year.

P. M. — Up river on ice.

I see a handful of the scarlet *Rosa Carolina* hips in the crotch of a willow on some mud, a foot or more above the ice. They are partly eaten, and I think were placed there by a musquash. The rose bush, with a few hips on it, still stands in the ice within a few feet. Goodwin says he has seen their tracks eight or ten rods long to an apple tree near the water, where they have been for apples.

Along edge of Staples's meadow sprout-land, the young maples, some three years old, are stripped down,

i. e. the lower branches for a foot or two, by the ice falling. This barks and wounds the young trees severely.

The ice over the middle of the river is now alternately dark and whitish. I see the river beginning to show dark through the thinnest parts, in broad crescents convex up-stream, single or connected.

A good book is not made in the cheap and offhand manner of many of our scientific Reports, ushered in by the message of the President communicating it to Congress, and the order of Congress that so many thousand copies be printed, with the letters of instruction for the Secretary of the Interior (or rather exterior); the bulk of the book being a journal of a picnic or sporting expedition by a brevet Lieutenant-Colonel, illustrated by photographs of the traveller's footsteps across the plains and an admirable engraving of his native village as it appeared on leaving it, and followed by an appendix on the palæontology of the route by a distinguished savant who was not there, the last illustrated by very finely executed engravings of some old broken shells picked up on the road.

There are several men of whose comings and goings the town knows little. I mean the trappers. They may be seen coming from the woods and river, perhaps with nothing in their hands, and you do not suspect what they have been about. They go about their business in a stealthy manner for fear that any shall see

where they set their traps, — for the fur trade still flourishes here. Every year they visit the out-of-the-way swamps and meadows and brooks to set or examine their traps for musquash or mink, and the owners of the land commonly know nothing of it. But, few as the trappers are here, it seems by Goodwin's accounts that they steal one another's traps.

All the criticism which I got on my lecture on Autumnal Tints at Worcester on the 22d was that I assumed that my audience had not seen so much of them as they had. But after reading it I am more than ever convinced that they have not seen much of them, — that there are very few persons who do see much of nature.

Feb. 27. P. M. — To Cliffs.

Though it was a dry, powdery snow-storm yesterday, the sun is now so high that the snow is soft and sticky this afternoon. The sky, too, is soft to look at, and the air to feel on my cheek.

Health makes the poet, or sympathy with nature, a good appetite for his food, which is constantly renewing him, whetting his senses. Pay for your victuals, then, with poetry; give back life for life.

Feb. 28. To Cambridge and Boston.

Saw a mackerel in the market. The upper half of its sides is mottled blue and white like the mackerel sky, as stated January 19th, 1858.

END OF VOLUME XI

The Journal of Henry D. Thoreau

VOLUME XII

(March, 1859 — November, 1859)

View from Pine Hill over Walden Pond, toward Mt. Wachusett

CONTENTS

vi   CONTENTS

CONTENTS   vii

Vol. XII

THE JOURNAL OF
HENRY DAVID THOREAU

VOLUME XII

I

MARCH, 1859 (ÆT. 41)

March 2. Wednesday. P. M. — To Cassandra Ponds and down river.

It is a remarkably cold day for March, and the river, etc., are frozen as solidly as in the winter and there is no water to be seen upon the ice, as usually in a winter day, apparently because it has chiefly run out from beneath on the meadows and left the ice, for often, as you walk over the meadows, it sounds hollow under your tread.

I see in the Deep Cut, on the left-hand, or east, side, just beyond the clay, a ravine lately begun, in a slightly different manner from the Clamshell one. The water running down the steep sand-bank (which is some thirty or thirty-five feet high), it being collected from the field above, had worn a channel from four to six inches wide, gradually, through the frozen crust of the sand, which was one to two feet thick, and, reaching the loose unfrozen sand beneath, had washed it downward, and out through the narrow channel lower

down, until quite a cavern was formed, whose bottom was eight or ten feet below the surface, while it was five or six feet wide. But within a few days the crust, thawing, had fallen in, and so the cavern, with its narrow "crack," or skylight, was turned into an open ravine, and there is no telling where the mischief will end.

The willow catkins by the railroad where you first come in sight of the [*sic*] have now all (on one or two bushes) crept out about an eighth of an inch, giving to the bushes already a very pretty appearance when you stand on the sunny side, the silvery-white specks contrasting with the black scales. Seen along the twigs, they are somewhat like small pearl buttons on a waistcoat. Go and measure to what length the silvery willow catkins have crept out beyond their scales, if you would know what time o' the year it is by Nature's clock.

As I go through the Cassandra Ponds, I look round on the young oak woods still clad with rustling leaves as in winter, with a feeling as if it were their last rustle before the spring, but then I reflect how far away still is the time when the new buds swelling will cause these leaves to fall. We thus commonly antedate the spring more than any other season, for we look forward to it with more longing. We talk about spring as at hand before the end of February, and yet it will be two good months, one sixth part of the whole year, before we can go a-maying. There may be a whole month of solid and uninterrupted winter yet, plenty of ice and good sleighing. We may not even see the bare ground, and hardly the water, and yet we sit down and warm our spirits an-

nually with this distant prospect of spring. As if a man were to warm his hands by stretching them toward the rising sun and rubbing them. We listen to the February cock-crowing and turkey-gobbling as to a first course, or prelude.

The bluebird which some woodchopper or inspired walker is said to have seen in that sunny interval between the snow-storms is like a speck of clear blue sky seen near the end of a storm, reminding us of an ethereal region and a heaven which we had forgotten. Princes and magistrates are often styled serene, but what is their turbid serenity to that ethereal serenity which the bluebird embodies? His Most Serene Birdship! His soft warble melts in the ear, as the snow is melting in the valleys around. The bluebird comes and with his warble drills the ice and sets free the rivers and ponds and frozen ground. As the sand flows down the slopes a little way, assuming the forms of foliage where the frost comes out of the ground, so this little rill of melody flows a short way down the concave of the sky. The sharp whistle of the blackbird, too, is heard like single sparks or a shower of them shot up from the swamps and seen against the dark winter in the rear.[1]

Under the alders at Well Meadow I see a few skunk-cabbage spathes fairly open on the side, and these may bloom after a day or two of pleasant weather. But for the most part, here and generally elsewhere, the spathes are quite small, slender, and closed as yet, or frost-bitten. The caltha leaves have grown decidedly. They

[1] [Channing, pp. 286, 287.]

make nearly a handful in one place, above the surface of the springy water, the leaves not yet quite flatted out, but curled up into a narrow ellipse. They barely peep above the water. Also what I take to be a kind of cress is quite fresh-looking, as if it had grown a little there. The chrysosplenium may have looked as it does, even under the snow, or all winter (?). It already, at any rate, makes pretty (dirty) green beds, about level with the surface of the water. These plants (*i. e.* first ones) are earlier than any pads, for the brooks, and ditches even, are generally frozen over still, firmly.

March 3. Going to Acton this morning, I saw some sparrows on the wall, which I think must have been the *F. hyemalis* (?).

P. M. — Up river to Nut Meadow Brook.

It is nearly as cold as yesterday. The piers of the bridge by the railroad bridge are adorned with very handsome salver or waiter shaped ice three or four feet in diameter (bottom upward), the crenate edges all around being adorned with bell-shaped pendants (produced by the melting (?) or perchance the water dashed against them).

Going by the solidago oak at Clamshell Hill bank, I heard a faint rippling note and, looking up, saw about fifteen snow buntings sitting in the top of the oak, all with their breasts toward me, — sitting so still and quite white, seen against the white cloudy sky, they did not look like birds but the ghosts of birds, and their

boldness, allowing me to come quite near, enhanced this impression. These were almost as white as snowballs, and from time [to time] I heard a low, soft rippling note from them. I could see no features, but only the general outline of plump birds in white. It was a very spectral sight, and after I had watched them for several minutes, I can hardly say that I was prepared to see them fly away like ordinary buntings when I advanced further. At first they were almost concealed by being almost the same color with the cloudy sky.

I see in that ditch (call it Grassy Ditch) near John Hosmer's second spring south of Nut Meadow Brook much grass which has lately grown an inch or more and lies flat on the water. Is it the *Glyceria fluitans*? It is somewhat frost-bitten too. It fills the ditch like moss, as seen at a little distance. It must be a very springy ditch to be thus open entirely. Also, pretty near the spring, I see a tuft of carex (?) whose stiff glaucous points have risen several inches above the surface.

See two small water-bugs at the spring; none elsewhere.

I see apparently some callitriche, fresh, in the spring. We recross the river at Grindstone Meadow, but probably cannot to-morrow or next day there. The ice is spotted with dark crescents, — we tread on the white parts, — and it is puffed up along the middle, being at least six inches high in the middle where we cross.

All the lower part of steep southern slopes of hills is now commonly bare, — though the snow may be pretty deep on the brow, — especially the springy bases where the skunk-cabbage, etc., grow.

How imperceptibly the first springing takes place! In some still, muddy springs whose temperature is more equable than that of the brooks, while brooks and ditches are generally thickly frozen and concealed and the earth is covered with snow, and it is even cold, hard, and nipping winter weather, some fine grass which fills the water like a moss begins to lift its tiny spears or blades above the surface, which directly fall flat for half an inch or an inch along the surface, and on these (though many are frost-bitten) you may measure the length to which the spring has advanced, — has *sprung*. Very few indeed, even of botanists, are aware of this growth. Some of it appears to go on even under ice and snow, or, in such a place as I have described, if it is also sheltered by alders, or the like, you may see (as March 2d) a little green crescent of caltha leaves, raised an inch or so above the water, with leaves but partially unrolled and looking as if it would withdraw beneath the surface again at night. This, I think, must be the most conspicuous and forward greenness of the spring. The small reddish radical leaves of the dock, too, are observed flat on the moist ground as soon as the snow has melted there, as if they had grown beneath it.

The mossy bank along the south side of Hosmer's second spring ditch is very interesting. There are many coarse, hair-like masses of that green and brown moss on its edge, hanging over the ditch, alternating with withered-looking cream-colored sphagnum tinged with rose-color, in protuberances, or mammæ, a foot across on the perpendicular side of the ditch. Cast water

on their cheeks, and they become much more reddish, yet hardly so interesting. This is while the top of the bank and all the hillside above is covered deep with snow. The pretty fingers of the *Lycopodium clavatum*, peeping out here and there amid the snow and hanging down the ditch-side, contrasting with the snow, are very interesting.

Channing tells me he has met with a sassafras tree in New Bedford woods, which, according to a string which he put round it, is eleven and three quarters feet in circumference at about three feet from the ground. They consider them very good for rails there, they are so light and durable.

Talk about reading! — a good reader! It depends on how he is heard. There may be elocution and pronunciation (recitation, say) to satiety, but there can be no good reading unless there is good hearing also. It takes two at least for this game, as for love, and they must coöperate. The lecturer will read best those parts of his lecture which are best heard. Sometimes, it is true, the faith and spirits of the reader may run a little ahead and draw after the good hearing, and at other times the good hearing runs ahead and draws on the good reading. The reader and the hearer are a team not to be harnessed tandem, the poor wheel horse supporting the burden of the shafts, while the leader runs pretty much at will, while the lecture lies passive in the painted curricle behind. I saw some men unloading molasses-hogsheads from a truck at a depot the other day, rolling them up an inclined plane. The truckman stood behind and shoved, after putting a couple of ropes one round each end of the hogshead, while two men standing in the depot steadily pulled at the ropes. The first man was the lecturer, the last was the audience. It is the duty of the lecturer to team his hogshead of sweets to the depot, or Lyceum, place the horse, arrange the ropes, and shove; and it is the duty of the audience to take hold of the ropes and pull with all their might. The lecturer who tries to read his essay without being abetted by a good hearing is in the predicament of a teamster who is engaged in the Sisyphean labor of rolling a molasses-hogshead up an inclined plane alone, while the freight-master and his men stand indifferent with their hands in their pockets. I have seen many such a hogshead which had rolled off the horse and gone to smash, with all its sweets wasted on the ground between the truckman and the freight-house, — and the freight-masters thought that the loss was not theirs.

Read well! Did you ever know a full well that did not yield of its refreshing waters to those who put their hands to the windlass or the well-sweep? Did you ever suck cider through a straw? Did you ever know the cider to push out of the straw when you were not sucking, — unless it chanced to be in a complete ferment? An audience will draw out of a lecture, or enable a lecturer to read, only such parts of his lecture as they like. A lecture is like a barrel half full of some palatable liquor. You may tap it at various levels, — in the sweet liquor or in the froth or in fixed air above. If it is pronounced good, it is partly to the credit of the hearers; if bad, it is partly their fault. Some,

times a lazy audience refuses to coöperate and pull on the ropes with a will, simply because the hogshead is full and therefore heavy, when if it were empty, or had only a little sugar adhering to it, they would whisk it up the slope in a jiffy. The lecturer, therefore, desires of his audience a long pull, a strong pull, and all pull together. I have seen a sturdy truckman, or lecturer, who had nearly broken his back with shoving his lecture up such an inclined plane while the audience were laughing at him, at length, as with a last effort, set it a-rolling in amid the audience and upon their toes, scattering them like sheep and making them cry out with pain, while he drove proudly away. Rarely it is a very heavy freight of such hogsheads stored in a vessel's hold that is to be lifted out and deposited on the public wharf, and this is accomplished only after many a hearty pull all together and a good deal of heave-yo-ing.

March 4. Began to snow last evening, and it is now (early in the morning) about a foot deep, and raining.

P. M. — To E. Hosmer Spring. Down Turnpike and back by E. Hubbard's Close.

We stood still a few moments on the Turnpike below Wright's (the Turnpike, which had no wheel-track beyond Tuttle's and no track at all beyond Wright's), and listened to hear a spring bird. We heard only the jay screaming in the distance and the cawing of a crow. What a perfectly New England sound is this voice of the crow! If you stand perfectly still anywhere in the outskirts of the town and listen, stilling the almost

Vol. XII

incessant hum of your own personal factory, this is perhaps the sound which you will be most sure to hear rising above all sounds of human industry and leading your thoughts to some far bay in the woods where the crow is venting his disgust. This bird sees the white man come and the Indian withdraw, but it withdraws not. Its untamed voice is still heard above the tinking of the forge. It sees a race pass away, but it passes not away. It remains to remind us of aboriginal nature.

I find near Hosmer Spring in the wettest ground, which has melted the snow as it fell, little flat beds of light-green moss, soft as velvet, which have recently pushed up, and lie just above the surface of the water. They are scattered about in the old decayed trough. And there are still more and larger at Brister's Spring.) They are like little rugs or mats and are very obviously of fresh growth, such a green as has not been dulled by winter, a very fresh and living, perhaps slightly glaucous, green. The myosotis and bitter cress are hardly clean and fresh enough for a new growth.[1] The radical leaves of the *Ranunculus repens* are conspicuous, but the worse for the wear; but the golden saxifrage has in one or two places decidedly and conspicuously grown, like the cowslip at Well Meadow and still more, rising in dense beds a half to three quarters of an inch above the water, the leaves, like those of the cowslip, only partly concealed and flatted out. This distinguishes the fresh-springing leaves of these two. Probably there is more of the chrysosplenium thus ad-

[1] But the last *is*, at Well Meadow. *Vide* [Mar. 5].

vanced in Concord than of the caltha.[1] I see none of the last here.

The surface of the snow thus rapidly melting and sinking (there are commonly some inches of water under it, the rain having soaked through), though still very fresh and pure white, is all cracked, as it were, like that of some old toadstools. It has sunk so much that every inequality in the surface of the ground beneath is more distinctly shown than when bare. The ruts of old wood-paths are represented in the surface a foot above, and the track of the man and of the dog that ran by the side of the team (in the old snow), — the *thread*, in short, of every valley. The surface of the snow, though so recent, is therefore, on account of the rain, very diversified. On steep slopes it is regularly furrowed, apparently by water that has flowed down it.

In the brook in Hubbard's Close I see the grass pushing up from the bottom four or five inches long and waving in the current, which has not yet reached the surface.

C. thinks this is called a *sap* snow, because it comes after the sap begins to flow.

The story goes that at the Social Club the other night Cyrus Stow, hearing that the lecture before the Lyceum by Alger was to be on "The Sophistry of Ennui" and not knowing what that was, asked in good faith if it went by wind or water.

March 5. Going down-town this forenoon, I heard a white-bellied nuthatch on an elm within twenty feet,

[1] There is also at Well Meadow on the 5th.

uttering peculiar notes and more like a song than I remember to have heard from it.[1] There was a chickadee close by, to which it may have been addressed. It was something like *to-what what what what what*, rapidly repeated, and not the usual *gnah gnah;* and this instant it occurs to me that this may be that earliest spring note which I hear, and have referred to a woodpecker! (This is before *I* have chanced to see a bluebird, blackbird, or robin in Concord this year.) It is the spring note of the nuthatch. It paused in its progress about the trunk or branch and uttered this lively but peculiarly inarticulate song, an awkward attempt to warble almost in the face of the chickadee, as if it were one of its kind. It was thus giving vent to the spring within it. If I am not mistaken, it is what I have heard in former springs or winters long ago, fabulously early in the season, when we men had but just begun to anticipate the spring, — for it would seem that we, in our anticipations and sympathies, include in succession the moods and expressions of all creatures. When only the snow had begun to melt and no rill of song had broken loose, a note so dry and fettered still, so inarticulate and half thawed out, that you might (and would commonly) mistake for the tapping of a woodpecker. As if the young nuthatch in its hole had listened only to the tapping of woodpeckers and learned that music, and now, when it would sing and give vent to its spring ecstasy, it can modulate only some notes like that. That is its theme still. That is its ruling idea of song and music, — only a little clangor and liquidity added

[1] Also the 21st March.

Vol. XII

minutes after, two more, and so many more at intervals of a few minutes. This is apparently their spring movement. Turkeys gobble in some distant farmyard at the same time. At length the sun is seen to have come out and to be shining on the oak leaves on the south side of Bear Garden Hill, and its light appears to be exactly limited to them.

I saw on the ice, quite alive, some of those black water-beetles, which apparently had been left above by a rise of the river. Were they a *Gyrinus?* [1]

When I was last at Well Meadow, I saw where apparently a dozen hounds had all crossed the brook at exactly one point, leaving a great trail in the slosh above the ice, though there was but one track of a man. It reminded me of a buffalo-trail. Every half-mile, as you go up the river, you come to the tracks of one or two dogs which have recently crossed it without any man.

Those skunk-cabbage buds which are most advanced have cast off their outmost and often frost-bitten sheaths, and the spathe is broader and slightly opened (some three quarters of an inch or more already) and has acquired brighter and more variegated colors. The outside of the spathe shows some ripeness in its colors and markings, like a melon-rind, before the spadix begins to bloom. I find that many of the most forward spathes, etc., have been destroyed since I was here three days ago. Some animal has nibbled away a part of the spathes (or sometimes only a hole in it) — and

[1] No.

to the tapping of the woodpecker. It was the handle by which my thoughts took firmly hold on spring.

This herald of spring is commonly unseen, it sits so close to the bark.

P. M. — Up river to Well Meadow.

The snow melts and sinks very rapidly. This spring snow is peculiarly white and blinding. The inequalities of the surface are peculiar and interesting when it has sunk thus rapidly. I see crows walking about on the ice half covered with snow in the middle of the meadows, where there is no grass, apparently to pick up the worms and other insects left there since the midwinter freshet. We see one or two little gnats or mosquitoes in the air.

See a large light-colored hawk circling a long time over Fair Haven Hill, and another, probably its mate, starts away from Holden Wood and circles toward it. The last being nearest, I distinguished that its wings were black tipped. (I have no glass.) What can they be? I think that I have seen the same in previous springs. They are too light-colored for hen-hawks, and for a *pair* of marsh hawks, — being apparently alike. Then the fish hawk is said by the books not to get here nearly so early, and, beside, they would not circle about *so much* over the hill. The goshawk, which I next think of, has no black tip to wings that I can learn. May it not be the winter hawk of Wilson? for he says its primaries are black at the tips, and that [it] is lighter than the red-shouldered, of same species.

At the same time I see a crow going north or northeast, high over Fair Haven Hill, and, two or three

I see the fragments scattered about — and then eaten out the whole of the spadix. Indeed, but few forward ones are left. Is this a mouse or musquash? or a bird? The spadix is evidently a favorite titbit to some creature.

That more entire-leaved plant amid the early skunk-cabbage which I called a cress on the 3d has the bitter taste of cress. The common cress has in one place grown considerably, and is fresh and clean and very good to eat. I wonder that I do not see where some creatures have eaten it.

The sweet-gale brush seen in a mass at a little distance is considerably darker than the alders above it. This will do for the sweet-gale maze in November.

The cowslip there is very prominently flower-budded, lifting its yellow flower-buds above water in one place. The leaves are quite inconspicuous when they first come up, being rolled up tightly.

March 6. Sunday. P. M. — To Yellow Birch Swamp.

We go through the swamp near Bee-Tree, or Oak, Ridge, listening for blackbirds or robins and, in the old orchards, for bluebirds. Found between two of the little birches in the path (where they grow densely), in Indigo-bird Sprout-land, a small nest suspended between one and two feet above the ground, between two of the little birches. This is where I have seen the indigo-bird in summer, and the nest apparently answers to Wilson's account of that bird's, being fastened with saliva to the birch on each side. Wilson says it is "built in a low bush . . . suspended between two twigs, one passing up each side." This is about the diameter of a hair-bird's nest within, composed chiefly of fine bark-shreds looking like grass and one or two strips of grape-vine bark, and very securely fastened to the birch on each side by a whitish silk or cobweb and saliva. It is thin, the lining being probably gone.

There is a very picturesque large black oak on the Bee-Tree Ridge, of this form:—

The genista is not evergreen, having turned brown, though it is still quite leafy. I could not find a single green shoot. It is correctly represented in Loudon's "Arboretum," in '44, as "a deciduous under-shrub." Yet in his "Encyclopædia," in '55, it is represented as "an evergreen shrub."

Measured a thorn which, at six inches from the ground, or the smallest place below the branches, — for it branches soon, — was two feet three inches in circumference. Cut off a barberry on which I counted some twenty-six rings, the broadest diameter being about three and a half inches. Both these were on the west side the Yellow Birch Swamp.

The slender black birches, with their catkined twigs gracefully drooping on all sides, are very pretty. Like the alders, with their reddish catkins, they express more life than most trees. Most trees look completely at rest, if not dead, now, but these look as if

the sap must be already flowing in them, — and in winter as well.

In woodland roads you see where the trees which were bent down by ice, and obstructed the way, were cut off the past winter; their tops lie on one side.

March 7. 6.30 A. M. — To Hill.

I come out to hear a spring bird, the ground generally covered with snow yet and the channel of the river only partly open. On the Hill I hear first the tapping of a small woodpecker. I then see a bird alight on the dead top of the highest white oak on the hilltop, on the topmost point. It is a shrike. While I am watching him eight or ten rods off, I hear robins down below, west of the hill. Then, to my surprise, the shrike begins to sing. It is at first a wholly ineffectual and inarticulate sound without any solid tone to it, a mere hoarse breathing, as if he were clearing his throat, unlike any bird that I know, — a shrill hissing. Then he uttered a kind of mew, a very decided mewing, clear and wiry, between that of a catbird and the note of the nuthatch, as if to lure a nuthatch within his reach; then rose into the sharpest, shrillest vibratory or tremulous whistling or chirruping on the very highest key. This high gurgling jingle was like some of the notes of a robin singing in summer. But they were very short spurts in all these directions, though there was all this variety. Unless you saw the shrike it would be hard to tell what bird it was. This variety of notes covered considerable time, but were sparingly uttered with intervals. It was a decided chinking sound — the

Vol. XII

clearest strain — suggesting much ice in the stream. I heard this bird sing once before, but that was also in early spring, or about this time. It is said that they imitate the notes of the birds in order to attract them within their reach. Why, then, have I never heard them sing in the winter? (I have seen seven or eight of them the past winter quite near.) The birds which it imitated — if it imitated any this morning — were the catbird and the robin, neither of which probably would it catch, — and the first is not here to be caught. Hearing a peep, I looked up and saw three or four birds passing rather [*sic*], which suddenly descended and settled on this oak-top. They were robins, but the shrike instantly hid himself behind a bough and in half a minute flew off to a walnut and alighted, as usual, on its very topmost twig, apparently afraid of its visitors. The robins kept their ground, one alighting on the very point which the shrike vacated. Is not this, then, probably the spring note or pairing note or notes of the shrike?

The first note which I heard from the robins, far under the hill, was *sveet sveet*, suggesting a certain haste and alarm, and then a rich, hollow, somewhat plaintive *peep* or *peep-eep-cep*, as when in distress with young just flown. When you first see them alighted, they have a haggard, an anxious and hurried, look.

I hear several jays this morning.

I think that many of the nuts which we find in the crevices of bark, firmly wedged in, may have been placed there by jays, chickadees, etc., to be held fast while they crack them with their bills.

A lady tells me that she saw, last Cattle-Show Day, —— —— putting up a specimen of hairwork in a frame (by his niece) in the exhibition hall. I think it represented flowers, and underneath was written "this Hare was taken from 8 different heads." She made some sort of exclamation, betraying that there was some mistake in the writing, whereupon —— —— took it down and carried it off, but soon came back with a new description or label, "this hare was taken from 8 different heads," and thus it stood through the exhibition.

P. M. — To Ministerial Swamp.

I hear of two who saw bluebirds this morning, and one says he saw one yesterday.[1] This seems to have been the day of their general arrival here, but I have not seen one in Concord yet.

It is a good plan to go to some old orchard on the south side of a hill, sit down, and listen, especially in the morning when all is still. You can thus often hear the distant warble of some bluebird lately arrived, which, if you had been walking, would not have been audible to you. As I walk, these first mild spring days, with my coat thrown open, stepping over tinkling rills of melting snow, excited by the sight of the bare ground, especially the reddish subsoil, where it is exposed by a cutting, and by the few green radical leaves, I stand still, shut my eyes, and listen from time to time, in order to hear the note of some bird of passage just arrived.

There are few, if any, so coarse and insensible that

[1] *Vide* 9th.

they are not interested to hear that the bluebird has
come. The Irish laborer has learned to distinguish
him and report his arrival. It is a part of the news of
the season to the lawyer in his office and the mechanic
in his shop, as well as to the farmer. One will remember, perchance, to tell you that he saw one a week ago
in the next town or county. Citizens just come into
the country to live put up a bluebird box, and record
in some kind of journal the date of the first arrival
observed, — though it may be rather a late one. The
farmer can tell you when he saw the first one, if you
ask him within a week.

I see a great many of those glow-worm-like caterpillars observed in the freshet in midwinter, on the
snowy ice in the meadows and fields now; also small
beetles of various kinds, and other caterpillars. I think
this unusual number is owing to that freshet, which
washed them out of their winter quarters so long ago,
and they have never got back to them. I also see —
but their appearance is a regular early spring, or late
winter, phenomenon — a great many of those slender
black-bodied insects from one quarter to (with the
feelers) one inch long, with six legs and long gray wings,
two feelers before, and two forks or tails like feelers

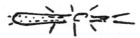

behind. The last are sometimes concealed by the wings.
This is what I have called
for convenience *Perla*. They are crawling slowly
about over the snow. I have no doubt that crows
eat some of the above-named caterpillars, but do other
birds?

whilst that of the other side remains turgid with fluid;
the stem makes a bend, therefore, until its growing
point becomes opposite to the light, and then increases
in that direction." (C.'s "Vegetable Physiology," page
174.)

There is no ripeness which is not, so to speak, something ultimate in itself, and not merely a perfected
means to a higher end. In order to be ripe it must serve
a transcendent use. The ripeness of a leaf, being perfected, leaves the tree at that point and never returns
to it. It has nothing to do with any other fruit which
the tree may bear, and only the genius of the poet can
pluck it.

The fruit of a tree is neither in the seed nor the timber, — the full-grown tree, — but it is simply the highest
use to which it can be put.

March 8. A rainy day.
P. M. — To Hill in rain.

To us snow and cold seem a mere delaying of the
spring. How far we are from understanding the value
of these things in the economy of Nature!

The earth is still mostly covered with ice and snow.
As usual, I notice large pools of greenish water in the
fields, on an icy bottom, which cannot owe their greenness
to the reflected blue mingled with the yellowish light
at sundown, as I supposed in the case of the green ice
and water in clear winter days, for I see the former
now at midday and in a rain-storm, when no sky is
visible. I think that these green pools over an icy bottom must be produced by the yellow or common earth-

The mystery of the life of plants is kindred with
that of our own lives, and the physiologist must not
presume to explain their growth according to mechanical laws, or as he might explain some machinery of
his own making. We must not expect to probe with
our fingers the sanctuary of any life, whether animal
or vegetable. If we do, we shall discover nothing but
surface still. The ultimate expression or fruit of any
created thing is a fine effluence which only the most
ingenuous worshipper perceives at a reverent distance
from its surface even. The cause and the effect are
equally evanescent and intangible, and the former
must be investigated in the same spirit and with the
same reverence with which the latter is perceived.
Science is often like the grub which, though it may
have nestled in the germ of a fruit, has merely blighted
or consumed it and never truly tasted it. Only that
intellect makes any progress toward conceiving of the
essence which at the same time perceives the effluence.
The rude and ignorant finger is probing in the rind
still, for in this case, too, the angles of incidence and
excidence [*sic*] are equal, and the essence is as far on
the other side of the surface, or matter, as reverence
detains the worshipper on this, and only reverence can
find out this angle instinctively. Shall we presume to
alter the angle at which God chooses to be worshipped?

Accordingly, I reject Carpenter's explanation of the
fact that a potato vine in a cellar grows toward the light,
when he says, "The reason obviously is, that, in consequence of the loss of fluid from the tissue of the stem,
on the side on which the light falls, it is contracted,

stain in the water mingling with the blue which is reflected from the ice. Many pools have so large a proportion of this yellow tinge as not to look green but yellow.
The stain, the tea, of withered vegetation — grass and
leaves — and of the soil supplies the yellow tint.

But perhaps those patches of emerald sky, sky just
tinged with green, which we sometimes see, far in the
horizon or near it, are produced in the same way as I
thought the green ice was, — some yellow glow reflected
from a cloud mingled with the blue of the atmosphere.

One might say that the yellow of the earth mingled
with the blue of the sky to make the green of vegetation.

I see, under the pitch pines on the southwest slope
of the hill, the reddish bud-scales scattered on the snow
which fell on the 4th, and also settled an inch into it,
and, examining, I find that in a great many cases the
buds have been eaten by some creature and the scales
scattered about, or, being opened, have closed over
a cavity. Many scales rest amid the needles. There
is no track on the snow, which is soft, but the scales
must have been dropped within a day or two. I see
near one pine, however, the fresh track of a partridge
and where one has squatted all night. Tracks might
possibly have been obliterated by the rapid melting
of the snow the last day or two. Yet I am inclined to
think that these were eaten by the red squirrel; or was
it the crossbill? for this is said to visit us in the winter.
Have I ever seen a squirrel eat the pine buds? [1]

There is a fine freezing rain with strong wind from
the north; so I keep along under shelter of hills and

[1] Farmer does not know of squirrels eating pine buds.

woods, along their south sides, in my india-rubber coat and boots. Under the south edge of Woodis Park, in the low ground, I see many radical leaves of the *So-lidago altissima* and another — I am pretty sure it is the *S. stricta* — and occasionally also of the *Aster undulatus*, and all are more or less lake beneath. The first, at least, have when bruised a strong scent. Some of them have recently grown decidedly. So at least several kinds of goldenrods and asters have radical leaves lake-colored at this season. The common straw-berry leaves, too, are quite fresh and a handsome lake-color beneath in many cases. There are also many little rosettes of the radical leaves of the *Epilobium coloratum*, half brown and withered, with bright-green centres, at least. And even the under side of some mul-lein leaves is lake or crimson also.

There is but a narrow strip of bare ground reach-ing a few rods into the wood along the south edge, but the less ground there is bare, the more we make of it. Such a day as this, I resort where the partridges, etc., do — to the bare ground and the sheltered sides of woods and hills — and there explore the moist ground for the radical leaves of plants, while the storm blows overhead, and I forget how the time is passing. If the weather is thick and stormy enough, if there is a good chance to be cold and wet and uncomfortable, in other words to feel weather-beaten, you may consume the afternoon to advantage thus browsing along the edge of some near wood which would scarcely detain you at all in fair weather, and you will [be] as far away there as at the end of your longest fair-weather walk, and

come home as if from an adventure. There is no better fence to put between you and the village than a storm into which the villagers do not venture out.

I go looking for green radical leaves. What a dim and shadowy existence have now to our memories the fair flowers whose localities they mark! How hard to find any trace of the stem now, after it has been flattened under the snows of the winter! I go feeling with wet and freezing fingers amid the withered grass and the snow for these prostrate stems, that I may reconstruct the plant. But greenness so absorbs our attention that sometimes I do not see the former rising from the midst of those radical leaves when it almost puts my eyes out. The shepherd's-purse radical leaves are particu-larly bright.

I see there a dead white pine, some twenty-five feet high, which has been almost entirely stripped of its bark by the woodpeckers. Where any bark is left, the space between it and the wood is commonly closely packed with the gnawings of worms, which appear to have consumed the inner bark. But where the bark is gone, the wood also is eaten to some depth, and there are numerous holes penetrating deep into the wood. Over all this portion, which is almost all the tree, the wood-peckers have knocked off the bark and enlarged the holes in pursuit of the worms.

The fine rain with a strong north wind is now form-ing a glaze on my coat. When I get home the ther-mometer is at 29°. So a glaze seems to be formed when a fine rain is falling with the thermometer very little below the freezing-point.

Men of science, when they pause to contemplate "the power, wisdom, and goodness" of God, or, as they sometimes call him, "the Almighty Designer," speak of him as a total stranger whom it is necessary to treat with the highest consideration. They seem suddenly to have lost their wits.

March 9. P. M. — To Lee's Cliff with C.

C. says that he heard and saw a bluebird on the 7th, and R. W. E. the same. This was the day on which they were generally observed. I am doubtful about one having been seen on the 20th of February by a boy, as stated February 23d. C. also saw a skater-insect on the 7th, and a single blackbird flying over Cassandra Ponds, which he thought a grackle.

A true spring day, not a cloud in the sky. The earth shines, its icy armor reflecting the sun, and the rills of melting snow in the ruts shine, too, and water, where exposed in the right light on the river, is a remarkably living blue, just as the osiers appear brighter. Yet it is cool and raw and very windy. The ice over the chan-nel of the river, when not quite melted, is now gener-ally mackerelled (the water representing the blue por-

tions) with parallel openings, riddling it or leaving a sort of network of ice over it, answering to the ridges of the waves. You can best observe them from bridges. In some cases the snow upon the ice, having lain in

successive drifts, might also assist or modify this phe-nomenon.

The rain of yesterday has been filling the meadows again, flowing up under the dry ice of the winter freshet, which for the most part rested on the ground, and so this rise is at first the less observed until it shows itself beyond the edge of the ice.

At Corner Spring Brook the water reaches up to the crossing and stands over the ice there, the brook being open and some space on each side of it. When I look, from forty or fifty rods off, at the yellowish water covering the ice about a foot here, it is decidedly purple (though, when close by and looking down on it, it is yellowish merely), while the water of the brook-channel and a rod on each side of it, where there is no ice beneath, is a beautiful very dark blue. These colors are very distinct, the line of separation being the edge of the ice on the bottom, and this apparent juxtaposi-tion of different kinds of water is a very singular and pleasing sight. You see a light-purple flood, about the color of a red grape, and a broad channel of dark-pur-ple water, as dark as a common blue-purple grape, sharply distinct across its middle.

I see at Lee's the long, narrow radical leaves of the *Turritis stricta* just beginning to push their shoots, — the most forward-looking plant there.

We cross Fair Haven Pond on the ice, though it is difficult getting on and off, it being melted about the edges, as well as overflowed there.

It is worth while to hear the wind roar in the woods to-day. It sounds further off than it is.

Came across a stout and handsome woodchopper with a full dark or black beard, but that on his upper lip was a distinct sandy color. It was a very pleasing contrast, suggesting a sympathy with the centre of light and intelligence nearer to which it grew.

March 10. 6 A. M. — To Hill.

I see at near [*sic*] the stone bridge where the strong northwest wind of last night broke the thin ice just formed, and set the irregular triangular pieces on their edges quite perpendicular and directed northwest and southeast and pretty close together, about nine inches high, for half a dozen rods, like a dense fleet of schooners with their mainsails set.

And already, when near the road, I hear the warble of my first *Concord* bluebird, borne to me from the hill through the still morning air, and, looking up, I see him plainly, though so far away, a dark speck in the top of a walnut.

When I reach the Assabet above the Hemlocks, I hear a loud crashing or brattling sound, and, looking through the trees, see that it is the thin ice of the night, half an hour after sunrise, now swiftly borne down the stream in large fleets and going to wreck against the thick old ice on each side. This evidently is a phenomenon of the morning. The river, too, has just waked up, and, no doubt, a river in midsummer as well as in winter recognizes the advent of the morning as much as a man or an animal does. They retire at night and awake in the morning.

Looking northeast over Hosmer's meadow, I see

still the rosy light reflected from the low snow-spits, alternating with green ice there. Apparently because the angles of incidence and excidence are equal, therefore we see the green in ice at sundown when we look aslant over the ice, our visual ray making such an angle with it as the yellow light from the western horizon does in coming to it.

P. M. — To Witherell Vale.

There are some who never do nor say anything, whose life merely excites expectation. Their excellence reaches no further than a gesture or mode of carrying themselves. They are a sash dangling from the waist, or a sculptured war-club over the shoulder. They are like fine-edged tools gradually becoming rusty in a shop-window. I like as well, if not better, to see a piece of iron or steel, out of which many such tools will be made, or the bush-whack in a man's hand.[1]

When I meet gentlemen and ladies, I am reminded of the extent of the inhabitable and uninhabitable globe; I exclaim to myself, Surfaces! surfaces! If the outside of a man is so variegated and extensive, what must the inside be? You are high up the Platte River, traversing deserts, plains covered with soda, with no deeper hollow than a prairie-dog hole tenanted also by owls and venomous snakes.

As I look toward the woods (from Wood's Bridge), I perceive the spring in the softened air.[2] This is to me the most interesting and affecting phenomenon of the season as yet. Apparently in consequence of the very

[1] [Channing, p. 330.]   [2] *Vide* April 15.

warm sun, this still and clear day, falling on the earth four fifths covered with snow and ice, there is an almost invisible vapor held in suspension, which is like a thin coat or enamel applied to every object, and especially it gives to the woods, of pine and oak intermingled, a softened and more living appearance. They evidently stand in a more genial atmosphere than before. Looking more low, I see that shimmering in the air over the earth which betrays the evaporation going on. Looking through this transparent vapor, all surfaces, not osiers and open waters alone, look more vivid. The hardness of winter is relaxed.

There is a fine effluence surrounding the wood, as if the sap had begun to stir and you could detect it a mile off. Such is the difference between an object seen through a warm, moist, and soft air and a cold, dry, hard one. Such is the genialness of nature that the trees appear to have put out feelers by which our senses apprehend them more tenderly. I do not know that the woods are ever more beautiful, or affect me more.

I feel it to be a greater success as a lecturer to affect uncultivated natures than to affect the most refined, for all cultivation is necessarily superficial, and its roots may not even be *directed toward* the centre of the being.

Rivers, too, like the walker, unbutton their icy coats, and we see the dark bosoms of their channels in the midst of the ice. Again, in pools of melted snow, or where the river has risen, I look into clear, placid water, and see the russet grassy bottom in the sun.

Look up or down the open channel now, so smooth, like a hibernating animal that has ventured to come out to the mouth of its burrow. One way, perhaps, it is like melted silver alloyed with copper. It goes nibbling off the edge of the thick ice on each side. Here and there I see a musquash sitting in the sun on the edge of the ice, eating a clam, and the clamshells it has left are strewn along the edge. Ever and anon he drops into the liquid mirror, and soon reappears with another clam. This clear, placid, silvery water is evidently a phenomenon of spring. Winter could not show us this.

A broad channel of water separates the dry land from the ice, and the musquash-hunter finds it hard to reach the game he has shot on the ice.

Fine red-stemmed mosses have begun to push and bud on Clamshell bank, growing in the Indian ashes where surface taken off. Carpenter says, "The first green crust upon the cinders with which the surface of Ascension Island was covered, consisted of minute mosses."

We sit in the sun on the side of Money-Diggers' Hill, amid the crimson low blueberry shoots and the withered *Andropogon scoparius* and the still erect *Solidago arguta* (var. the common) and the tall stubble thickly hung with fresh gleaming cobwebs. There are some grayish moths out, etc. ; some gnats.

I see the bridge far away over the ice resting on its black piers above the ice which is lifted around it. It is short-legged now. This level or horizontal line resting on perpendicular black ones is always an interesting sight to me.

As we sit in this wonderful air, many sounds — that of woodchopping, for one — come to our ears agreeably blunted or muffled, even like the drumming of a partridge, not sharp and rending as in winter and recently. If a partridge should drum in winter, probably it would not reverberate so softly through the wood and sound indefinitely far. Our voices, even, sound differently and betray the spring. We speak as in a house, in a warm apartment still, with relaxed muscles and softened voices. The voice, like a woodchuck in his burrow, is met and lapped in and encouraged by all genial and sunny influences. There may be heard now, perhaps, under south hillsides and the south sides of houses, a slight murmur of conversation, as of insects, out of doors.

These earliest spring days are peculiarly pleasant. We shall have no more of them for a year. I am apt to forget that we may have raw and blustering days a month hence. The combination of this delicious air, which you do not want to be warmer or softer, with the presence of ice and snow, you sitting on the bare russet portions, the south hillsides, of the earth, this is the charm of these days. It is the summer beginning to show itself like an old friend in the midst of winter. You ramble from one drier russet patch to another. These are your stages. You have the air and sun of summer, over snow and ice, and in some places even the rustling of dry leaves under your feet, as in Indian-summer days.

The bluebird on the apple tree, warbling so innocently to inquire if any of its mates are within call, —

the angel of the spring! Fair and innocent, yet the offspring of the earth. The color of the sky above and of the subsoil beneath. Suggesting what sweet and innocent melody (terrestrial melody) may have its birthplace between the sky and the ground.

Two frogs (may have been *Rana fontinalis;* did not see them) jumped into Hosmer's grassy ditch.

See in one place a small swarm of insects flying or gyrating, dancing like large tipulidæ. The dance within the compass of a foot always above a piece of snow of the same size in the midst of bare ground.

The most ornamental tree I have seen this spring was the willow full of catkins now showing most of their down, in front of Puffer's house.

March 11. 6 A. M. — By riverside I hear the song of many song sparrows, the most of a song of any yet. And on the swamp white oak top by the stone bridge, I see and hear a red-wing. It sings almost steadily on its perch there, sitting all alone, as if to attract companions (and I see two more, also solitary, on different tree-tops within a quarter of a mile), calling the river to life and tempting ice to melt and trickle like its own sprayey notes. Another flies over on high, with a *tchuck* and at length a clear whistle. The birds anticipate the spring; they come to melt the ice with their songs.

But methinks the sound of the woodpecker tapping is as much a spring note as any these mornings; it echoes peculiarly in the air of a spring morning.

Vol. XII

P. M. — To Hunt house.

I go to get one more sight of the old house which Hosmer is pulling down, but I am too late to see much of it. The chimney is gone and little more than the oblong square frame stands. E. Hosmer and Nathan Hosmer are employed taking it down. The latter draws all the nails, however crooked, and puts them in his pockets, for, being wrought ones, he says it is worth the while.

It appears plainly, now that the frame is laid bare,

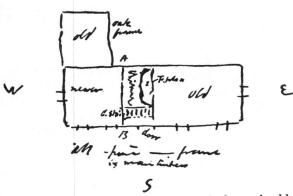

that the eastern two-thirds of the main house is older than the western third, for you can see where the west part has been added on, at the line A B. All the joists in the old part are hewn; in the newer, sawn. But very extensive repairs had been made in the old part, probably at the same time with the addition. Also the back part had been added on to the new part, merely

butted on at one side without tenant or mortise. The peculiar cedar laths were confined to the old part. The whole has oak sills and pine timbers. The two Hosmers were confident that the chimney was built at the same time with the new part, because, though there were flues in it from the new part, there was no break in the courses of brick about them. On the chimney was the date 1703 (?), — I think that was it, — and if this was the date of the chimney, it would appear that the old part belonged to the Winthrops, and it may go back to near the settlement of the town. The laths long and slender of white cedar split. In the old part the ends of the timbers were not merely mortised into the posts, but rested on a shoulder thus: twelve by four mantellong and inches The fireplace measures feet wide by three deep and a half high. The tree is log, fourteen feet some fifteen to sixteen square at the ends, but one half cut away diagonally between the ends, and now charred. It would take three men to handle it easily. The timbers of the old part had been cased and the joists plastered over at some time, and, now that they were uncovered, you saw many old memorandums and scores in chalk on them, as " May ye 4th," " Ephraim Brown," " 0—3s—4d," " oxen ╫╫╫," — so they kept their score or tally, — such as the butcher and baker sometimes make. Perhaps the occupant had let his neighbor have the use of his oxen so many days. I asked if they had found any old coins. N. Hosmer answered, Yes, he had, and showed it me, — took it out of his pocket. It was about as big as a quarter of a dollar, with "Britain," etc., legible, "Geo II," and date "1742," but it was of lead. But there was no manuscript, — not a copy of verses, only these chalk records of butter and cheese, oxen and bacon, and a counterfeit coin, out of the smoky recesses. Very much such relics as you find in the old rats' nests in which these houses abound.[1]

My mother says that she has been to the charitable society there. One old jester of the town used to call it "the *chattable* society."

Mrs. A. takes on dolefully on account of the solitude in which she lives, but she gets little consolation. Mrs. B. says she envies her that retirement. Mrs. A. is aware that she does, and says it is as if a thirsty man should envy another the river in which he is drowning. So goes the world. It is either this extreme or that. Of solitude one gets too much and another not enough.

E. Hosmer says that a man told him that he had seen my uncle Charles take a twelve-foot ladder, set it up straight, and then run up and down the other side, kicking it from behind him as he went down. E. H. told of seeing him often at the tavern toss his hat to the ceiling, twirling it over, and catch it on his head every time.

Large flocks of blackbirds to-day in the elm-tops and other trees. These are the first conspicuous large

[1] *Vide* [pp. 46–48]. [See *Excursions*, p. 201; Riv. 247.]

flocks of birds. J. Farmer says he saw ducks this morning and has seen larks some days. Channing saw geese to-day.

Find out as soon as possible what are the best things in your composition, and then shape the rest to fit them. The former will be the midrib and veins of the leaf.

There is always some accident in the best things, whether thoughts or expressions or deeds. The memorable thought, the happy expression, the admirable deed are only partly ours. The thought came to us because we were in a fit mood; also we were unconscious and did not know that we had said or done a good thing. We must walk consciously only part way toward our goal, and then leap in the dark to our success. What we do best or most perfectly is what we have most thoroughly learned by the longest practice, and at length it falls from us without our notice, as a leaf from a tree. It is the *last* time we shall do it, — our unconscious leavings.

March 12. Saturday. P. M. — Walk in rain to Ministerial Swamp.

Going up the railroad in this rain, with a south wind, I see a pretty thick low fog extending across the railroad only against Dennis's Swamp. There being much more ice and snow within the swamp, the vapor is condensed and is blown northward over the railroad. I see these local fogs with always the same origin, *i. e.*, large masses of snow or ice, in swamps or woods, perhaps the north sides of hills, in several places after-

ward. The air is warm. As often as we came to a particularly icy or snowy place, as Harrington's road in woods, we found ourselves in a fog.

It is a regular spring rain, such as I remember walking in, — windy but warm. It alternately rains hard and then holds up a little. A similar alternation we see in the waves of water and all undulating surfaces, — in snow and sand and the clouds (the mackerel sky). Now you walk in a comparative lull, anticipating fair weather, with but a slight drizzling, and anon the wind blows and the rain drives down harder than ever. In one of these lulls, as I passed the Joe Hosmer (rough-cast) house, I thought I never saw any bank so handsome as the russet hillside behind it. It is a very barren, exhausted soil, where the cladonia lichens abound, and the lower side is a flowing sand, but this russet grass with its weeds, being saturated with moisture, was in this light the richest brown, methought, that I ever saw. There was the pale brown of the grass, red browns of some weeds (sarothra and pinweed probably), dark browns of huckleberry and sweet-fern stems, and the very visible green of the cladonias thirty rods off, and the rich brown fringes where the broken sod hung over the edge of the sand-bank. I did not see the browns of withered vegetation so rich last fall, and methinks these terrestrial lichens were never more fair and prominent. On some knolls these vivid and rampant lichens as it were dwarf the oaks. A peculiar and unaccountable light seemed to fall on that bank or hillside, though it was thick storm all around. A sort of Newfoundland sun seemed to be shining on

it. It was such a light that you looked around for the sun that might be shining on it. Both the common largest and the very smallest hypericums (*Sarothra*) and the pinweeds were very rich browns at a little distance, coloring whole fields, and also withered and fallen ferns, reeking wet. It was a prospect to excite a reindeer. These tints of brown were as softly and richly fair and sufficing as the most brilliant autumnal tints.[1] In fair and dry weather these spots may be commonplace, but now they are worthy to tempt the painter's brush. The picture should be the side of a barren lichen-clad hill with a flowing sand-bank beneath, a few blackish huckleberry bushes here and there, and bright white patches of snow here and there in the ravines, the hill running east and west and seen through the storm from a point twenty or thirty rods south. This kind of light, the air being full of rain and all vegetation dripping with it, brings out the browns wonderfully.[2]

I notice now particularly the sallows by the railroad, full of dark cones, as a fruit. The broad radical leaves of (apparently) water dock are very fresh and conspicuous.

See two ducks flying over Ministerial Swamp.

In one place in the meadow southeast of Tarbell's, I find on the ice, about a couple of holes an inch across where a little stubble shows itself, a great many small ants dead, — say a thousand. They are strewn about the holes for six or eight inches, and are collected in a dense heap about the base of the stubble. I take up

[1] [Channing, p. 294.]   [2] *Vide* [p. 45].

a mass of them on my knife, each one entire, but now, of course, all wet and adhering together. It looks as if they had been tempted out by the warmth of the sun and had been frozen or drowned; or is it possible that they were killed by the frost last fall and now washed up through the ice? I think, from their position around the base of the stubble in that little hole in the ice, that they came out of the earth and clustered there since the ice melted to that extent. There are many other insects and worms and caterpillars (and especially spiders, dead) on the ice, there as well as elsewhere.

I perceive that a freshet which washes the earth bare in the winter and causes a great flow of water over it in that state — when it is not soaked up — must destroy a great many insects and worms. I find a great many that appear to have been drowned rather than frozen. May not this have tempted the bluebirds on early this year?

March 13. 7 A. M. — *F. hyemalis* in yard.

Going down railroad, listening *intentionally*, I hear, far through the notes of song sparrows (which are very numerous), the song of one or two larks. Also hearing a coarse *chuck*, I look up and see four blackbirds, whose size and long tails betray them crow blackbirds.[1] Also I hear, I am pretty sure, the cackle of a pigeon woodpecker.

The bright catkins of the willow are the springing most generally observed.

¹ [Two interrogation-points in pencil here.]

P. M. — To Great Fields.

Water rising still. Winter-freshet ice on meadows still more lifted up and partly broken in some places. The broad light artery of the river (and some meadows, too) very fair in the distance from Peter's.

Talking with Garfield to-day about his trapping, he said that mink brought three dollars and a quarter, a remarkably high price, and asked if I had seen any. I said that I commonly saw two or three in a year. He said that he had not seen one alive for eight or ten years. "But you trap them?" "O yes," he said. "I catch thirty or forty dollars' worth every winter." This suggests how little a trapper may see of his game. Garfield caught a skunk lately.

In some meadows I see a great many dead spiders on the ice, where apparently it has been overflowed — or rather it was the heavy rain, methinks — when they had no retreat.

Hear a ground squirrel's sharp chirrup, which makes you start, it is so sudden; but he is probably earthed again, for I do not see him.

On the northeast part of the Great Fields, I find the broken shell of a *Cistuda Blandingii*, on very dry soil. This is the fifth, then, I have seen in the town. All the rest were three in the Great Meadows (one of them in a ditch) and one within a rod or two of Beck Stow's Swamp.

It is remarkable that the spots where I find most arrowheads, etc., being light, dry soil, — as the Great Fields, Clamshell Hill, etc., — are among the first to be bare of snow, and the frost gets out there first. It

Vol. XII

is very curiously and particularly true, for the only parts of the northeast section of the Great Fields which are so dry that I do not slump there are those small in area, where perfectly bare patches of sand occur, and there, singularly enough, the arrowheads are particularly common. Indeed, in some cases I find them only on such bare spots a rod or two in extent where a single wigwam might have stood, and not half a dozen rods off in any direction. Yet the difference of level may not be more than a foot, — if there is any. It is as if the Indians had selected precisely the driest spots on the whole plain, with a view to their advantage at this season. If you were going to pitch a tent to-night on the Great Fields, you would inevitably pitch on one of these spots, or else lie down in water or mud or on ice. It is as if they had chosen the site of their wigwams at this very season of the year.

I see a small flock of blackbirds flying over, some rising, others falling, yet all advancing together, one flock but many birds, some silent, others tchucking, — incessant alternation. This harmonious movement as in a dance, this agreeing to differ, makes the charm of the spectacle to me. One bird looks fractional, naked, like a single thread or ravelling from the web to which it belongs. Alternation! Alternation! Heaven and hell! Here again in the flight of a bird, its ricochet motion, is that undulation observed in so many materials, as in the mackerel sky.

If men were to be destroyed and the books they have written [were to] be transmitted to a new race of creatures, in a new world, what kind of record would be

found in them of so remarkable a phenomenon as the rainbow?

I cannot easily forget the beauty of those terrestrial browns in the rain yesterday. The withered grass was not of that very pale hoary brown that it is to-day, now that it is dry and lifeless, but, being perfectly saturated and dripping with the rain, the whole hillside seemed to reflect a certain yellowish light, so that you looked around for the sun in the midst of the storm. All the yellow and red and leather-color in the fawn-colored weeds was more intense than at any other season. The withered ferns which fell last fall — pinweeds, sarothra, etc. — were actually a *glowing* brown for the same reason, being all dripping wet. The cladonias crowning the knolls had visibly expanded and erected themselves, though seen twenty rods off, and the knolls appeared swelling and bursting as with yeast. All these hues of brown were most beautifully blended, so that the earth appeared covered with the softest and most harmoniously spotted and tinted tawny fur coat of any animal. The very bare sand slopes, with only here and there a thin crusting of mosses, was [*sic*] a richer color than ever it is.

In short, in these early spring rains, the withered herbage, thus saturated, and reflecting its brightest withered tint, seems in a certain degree to have revived, and sympathizes with the fresh greenish or yellowish or brownish lichens in its midst, which also seem to have withered. It seemed to me — and I think it may be the truth — that the abundant moisture, bringing out the highest color in the brown surface of the earth, generated a certain degree of light, which, when the rain held up a little, reminded you of the sun shining through a thick mist.

Oak leaves which have sunk deep into the ice now are seen to be handsomely spotted with black (of fungi or lichens?), which spots are rarely perceived in dry weather.

All that vegetable life which loves a superfluity of moisture is now rampant, cold though it is, compared with summer. Radical leaves are as bright as ever they are.

The barrenest surfaces, perhaps, are the most interesting in such weather as yesterday, when the most terrene colors are seen. The wet earth and sand, and especially subsoil, are very invigorating sights.

The Hunt house, to draw from memory, — though I have given its measures within two years in my Journal, — looked like this: —

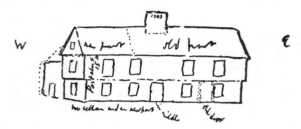

This is only generally correct, without a scale.

Probably grackles have been seen some days. I think I saw them on the 11th? Garfield says he saw black ducks yesterday.

Vol. XII

March 14. P. M. — To Hunt house.

I thought from the above drawing that the original door must have been in the middle of the old part and not at one end, and that I should detect it in the manner in which the studs were set in. I really did so and found some other traces of the old door (where I have dotted it) when I got there. Some of the chalk-marks which have been preserved under the casing of the timbers so long have been completely washed off in yesterday's rain, as the frame stood bare. Also read in chalk on a chamber floor joist (which had been plastered over beneath) "enfine Brown," so many s. and d., and what most read for "Feb 1666," but, being written over a rough knot, it is doubtful. "Hides 3."

Saw E. Hosmer take up the cellar stairs. They are of white oak, in form like one half of a squared white oak log sawed diagonally. These lie flat on their broadest sides on the slanting earth, resting near each end on a horse, which is a white oak stick with the bark on, hewed on the upper side and sunk in the earth, and they are fastened to this by two pins of wood placed as I have indicated.

I judge by my eye that the house is fifteen feet high to the eaves. The posts are remarkably sawn and hewn away on account of the projection of the upper story, so that they are more than twice as large above

as below, thus: the corner posts being cut on two sides or more than half away (six inches off them) below the sec-ond story. The chimney was laid in clay. "T. B." were perhaps the initials of Thomas Brown; also "I. [?] H. D."

The cowslip in pitcher has fairly blossomed to-day.

I see a large flock of grackles searching for food along the water's edge, just below Dr. Bartlett's. Some wade in the water. They are within a dozen rods of me and the road. It must be something just washed up that they are searching for, for the water has just risen and is still rising fast. Is it not insects and worms washed out of the grass? and perhaps the snails? When a grackle sings, it is as if his mouth were full of cotton, which he was trying to spit out.

The river is still rising. It is open [?] and generally over the meadows. The meadow ice is rapidly breaking up. Great cakes half a dozen rods long are drifted down against the bridges. There is a strong current on the meadow, not only north along the causeway, but south along the north end of the causeway, the water thus rushing both ways toward the only outlet at the bridge. This is proved by great cakes of ice floating swiftly along parallel with the causeway, but in opposite directions, to meet at the bridge. They are there soon broken up by the current after they strike the abutments. I see a large cake eight feet wide and ten inches thick, just broken off, carried under the bridge in a vertical position and wholly under water, such is the pressure there. This shows to what an extent the causeways and bridges act as dams to the flood.

March 15. Rainy day and southerly wind.

I come home in the evening through a very heavy rain after two brilliant rainbows at sunset, the first of the year.

March 16. 6 A. M. — The water is just over the slanting iron truss, four feet from its east end, and still rising.

P. M. — Launch my boat and sail to Ball's Hill.

It is fine clear weather and a strong northwest wind. What a change since yesterday! Last night I came home through as incessant heavy rain as I have been out in for many years, through the muddiest and wettest of streets, still partly covered with ice, and the rain-water stood over shoes in many places on the sidewalks. I heard of several who went astray in this water and had adventures in the dark. You require india-rubber boots then. But to-day I see the children playing at hop-scotch on those very sidewalks, with a bed marked in the dry sand. So rapid are the changes of weather with us, and so porous our soil.

With a strong wind we sail over the Red Bridge road. The water is falling over the lower side of the road as over a dam. For the road really operates as a dam, the water being much lower on the east side.

A new phase of the spring is presented; a new season has come. By the soaking rain and the wind of yesterday especially, the remaining snow and ice has been almost entirely swept away, and the ice has been broken, floated off, and melted, and much frost taken out of the ground; and now, as we glide over the Great

Meadows before this strong wind, we no longer see dripping, saturated russet and brown banks through rain, hearing at intervals the alarm notes of the early robins, — banks which reflect a yellowish light, — but we see the bare and now pale-brown and dry russet hills. The earth has cast off her white coat and come forth in her clean-washed sober russet early spring dress. As we look over the lively, tossing blue waves for a mile or more eastward and northward, our eyes fall on these shining russet hills, and Ball's Hill appears in this strong light at the verge of this undulating blue plain, like some glorious newly created island of the spring, just sprung up from the bottom in the midst of the blue waters. The fawn-colored oak leaves, with a few pines intermixed, thickly covering the hill, look not like a withered vegetation, but an ethereal kind, just expanded and peculiarly adapted to the season and the sky.

Look toward the sun, the water is yellow, as water in which the earth has just washed itself clean of its winter impurities; look from the sun and it is a beautiful dark blue; but in each direction the crests of the waves are white, and you cannot sail or row over this watery wilderness without sharing the excitement of this element. Our sail draws so strongly that we cut through the great waves without feeling them. And all around, half a mile or a mile distant, looking over this blue foreground, I see the bare and peculiarly neat, clean-washed, and bright russet hills reflecting the bright light (after the storm of yesterday) from an infinite number of dry blades of withered grass. The russet

surfaces have now, as it were, a combed look, — combed by the rain. And the leather-color of withered oak leaves covering Ball's Hill, seen a mile or two off in the strong light, with a few pines intermixed, as if it were an island rising out of this blue sea in the horizon. This sight affects me as if it were visible at this season only. What with the clear air and the blue water and the sight of the pure dry withered leaves, that distant hill affects me as something altogether ethereal.

After a day of soaking rain, concluded with a double rainbow the evening before, — not to mention the rain of the evening, — go out into the sparkling spring air, embark on the flood of melted snow and of rain gathered from all hillsides, with a northwest wind in which you often find it hard to stand up straight, and toss upon a sea of which one half is liquid clay, the other liquid indigo, and look round on an earth dressed in a home-spun of pale sheeny brown and leather-color. Such are the blessed and fairy isles we sail to!

We meet one great gull beating up the course of the river against the wind, at Flint's Bridge. (One says they were seen about a week ago, but there was very little water then.) Its is a very leisurely sort of limping flight, tacking its way along like a sailing vessel, yet the slow security with which it advances suggests a leisurely contemplativeness in the bird, as if it were working out some problem quite at its leisure. As often as its very narrow, long, and curved wings are lifted up against the light, I see a very narrow distinct light edging to the wing where it is thin. Its black-tipped wings. Afterwards, from Ball's Hill, looking

Vol. XII

north, I see two more circling about looking for food over the ice and water.

There is an unexpected quantity of ice in that direction, not on the channel, but the meadows east of it, all the way from Ball's Hill to Carlisle Bridge, — large masses, which have drifted from the channel and from above, for there the wind has blown more directly across the river. These great masses have been driven and wedged one against another, and ground up on the edges. This first sight of the bare tawny and russet earth, seen afar, perhaps, over the meadow flood in the spring, affects me as the first glimpse of land, his native land, does the voyager who has not seen it a long time. But in a week or two we get used to it.

I look down over Tarbell's Bay, just north of Ball's Hill. Not only meadows but potato and rye fields are buried deep, and you see there, sheltered by the hills on the northwest, a placid blue bay having the russet hills for shores. This kind of bay, or lake, made by the freshet — these deep and narrow " fiords " — can only be seen along such a stream as this, liable to an annual freshet. The water rests as gently as a dewdrop on a leaf, laving its tender temporary shores. It has no strand, leaves no permanent water-mark, but though you look at it a quarter of a mile off, you know that the rising flood is gently overflowing a myriad withered green blades there in succession. There is the magic of lakes that come and go. The lake or bay is not an institution, but a phenomenon. You plainly see that it is so much water poured into the hollows of the earth

March 17. 6.30 A. M. — River risen still higher. It is seven and a half inches below the highest part of the truss and about fifteen and a half inches below the middle of the lower stone step of the railroad. It is not quite over Wood's road.

I hear a robin fairly singing.

A great many musquash have been killed within a week. One says a cartload have been killed in Assabet. Perhaps a dozen gunners have been out in this town every day. They get a shilling apiece for their skins. One man getting musquash and one mink earned five or six dollars the other day. I hear their guns early and late long before sunrise and after sunset, for those are the best times.

P. M. — To Flint's Bridge by water.

The water is very high, and smooth as ever it is. It is very warm. I wear but one coat on the water. The town and the land it is built on seem to rise but little above the flood. This bright smooth and level surface seems here the prevailing element, as if the distant town were an island. I realize how water predominates on the surface of the globe. I am surprised to see new and unexpected water-lines, drawn by the level edge of the flood about knolls in the meadows and in the woods, — waving lines, rarely if ever recognized or thought of by the walker or any, which mark the boundary of a possible or probable freshet any spring.[1] Even if the highest water-mark were indicated at one point, the surveyor could not, with any labor short of infinite, draw these lines for us which

[1] [Channing, pp. 294, 295.]

wind about every elevation of earth or rock. Yet, though this slight difference of level which the water so simply and effectually points out, is so unobservable by us ordinarily, no doubt Nature never forgets it for a moment, but plants grow and insects, etc., breed in conformity to it. Many a kingdom of nature has its boundaries parallel with ·this waving line. By these freshets, the relation of some field, usually far from the stream, to future or past deluge is suggested. I am surprised and amused, at least, to walk in such a field and observe the nice distinctions which the great water-level makes there. So plants and animals and thoughts have their commonly unseen shores, and many portions of the earth are, with reference to them, islands or peninsulas or capes, shores or mountains.

We are stiff and set in our geography because the level of water is comparatively, or within short periods, unchangeable. We look only in the sea for islands and continents and their varieties. But there are more subtle and invisible and fluctuating floods which island this or that part of the earth whose geography has never been mapped. For instance, here is Mantatuket Rock, commonly a rocky peninsula with a low or swampy neck and all covered with wood. It is now a small rocky island, and not only the swampy neck but a considerable portion of the upland is blotted out by the flood, covered and concealed under water; and what surprises me is that the water should so instantly know and select its own shore on the upland, though I could not have told with my eye whether it

would be thirty feet this way or as many that. A distinction is made for me by the water in this case which I had never thought of, revealing the relation of this surface to the flood ordinarily far from it, and which I now begin to perceive that every tree and shrub and herbaceous plant growing there knew, if I did not.

How different to-day from yesterday! Yesterday was a cool, bright day, the earth just washed bare by the rain, and a strong northwest wind raised respectable billows on our vernal seas and imparted remarkable life and spirit to the scene. To-day it is perfectly still and warm. Not a ripple disturbs the surface of these lakes, but every insect, every small black beetle struggling on it, is betrayed; but, seen through this air, though many might not notice the difference, the russet surface of the earth does not shine, is not bright. I see no *shining* russet islands with dry but flushing oak leaves. The air is comparatively dead when I attend to it, and it is as if there were the veil of a fine mist over all objects, dulling their edges. Yet this would be called a clear day. These aerial differences in the days are not commonly appreciated, though they affect our spirits.

When I am opposite the end of the willow-row, seeing the osiers of perhaps two years old all in a mass, they are seen to be very distinctly yellowish beneath and scarlet above. They are fifty rods off. Here is the same chemistry that colors the leaf or fruit, coloring the bark. It is generally, probably always, the upper part of the twig, the more recent growth, that is the

higher-colored and more flower or fruit like. So leaves are more ethereal the higher up and further from the root. In the bark of the twigs, indeed, is the more permanent flower or fruit. The flower falls in spring or summer, the fruit and leaves fall or wither in autumn, but the blushing twigs retain their color throughout the winter and appear more brilliant than ever the succeeding spring. They are winter fruit. It adds greatly to the pleasure of late November, of winter, or of early spring walks to look into these mazes of twigs of different colors.

As I float by the Rock, I hear rustling amid the oak leaves above that new water-line, and, there being no wind, I know it to be a striped squirrel, and soon see its long-unseen striped sides flirting about the instep of an oak. Its lateral stripes, alternate black and yellowish, are a type which I have not seen for a long time, or rather a punctuation-mark, the character to indicate where a new paragraph commences in the revolution of the seasons. Double lines.

I find by measurement that there is from two to three inches fall in the middle between the piers of Flint's Bridge, on the two sides of the bridge, supposing the planking to be level; but there is much more close to the abutments, for the water is very conspicuously heaped up in the middle in each case, or between each two piers, thus: —

If you look from above, it is somewhat thus: —
If I land now on any knoll which is left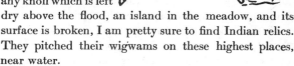
dry above the flood, an island in the meadow, and its surface is broken, I am pretty sure to find Indian relics. They pitched their wigwams on these highest places, near water.

I was speaking yesterday of the peculiarity of our meadow-bays in time of flood, — a shore where there are no shore-marks; for in time trees, rocks, etc., arrange themselves parallel with the water's edge, and the water by its washing makes for itself a strand, washing out the soil from the bank and leaving the sand and stones, and paths of animals and men conform to the permanent shore, but in this case all is abrupt and surprising. Rocky islands covered with green lichens and with polypody half submerged rise directly from the water, and trees stand up to their middles in it. Any eye would perceive that a rock covered with green lichens quite down to the water's edge was something unusual.

March 18. 8 A. M. — To stone bridge.
The water has fallen three or four inches. It was at its height last night, and was then about five inches below the highest part of the truss. This is quite high water. But it has now begun to rain, and the river will probably rise again.

Along the shores you see now much coarse wrack

of green and black pontederia stems which have been torn up by the ice. The ice and the wrack are also dotted with cranberries here and there.

What a variety of weather! What a difference in the days! Three days ago, the 15th, we had steady rain with a southerly wind, with a clear interval and a brilliant double rainbow at sunset, — a day when all the russet banks were dripping, saturated with wet, and the peep of the robin was heard through the drizzle and the rain. In the evening it rained again much harder than before. The next day it was clear and cool, with a strong northwest wind, and the flood still higher on the meadows; the dry russet earth and leather-colored oak reflected a flashing light from far; the tossing blue waves with white crests excited the beholder and the sailer. In short, the tables were completely turned; snow and ice were for the most part washed and blown away from both land and water. Yesterday it was very warm, without perceptible wind, with a comparatively lifeless [air], yet such as invalids like, with no flashing surfaces, but, as it were, an invisible mist sobering down every surface; and the water, still higher than before, was perfectly smooth all day. This was a weather-breeder. To-day comes a still, steady rain again, with warm weather and a southerly wind, which threatens to raise the river still higher, though it had begun to fall.[1]

One would say that frost in the ground, though it may be melted for several inches (as now), bred rain, if, indeed, its evaporations do not create it. Expect

[1] *Vide* [p. 65].

rain after rain till the frost is completely out. The melted frost, rising in the form of vapor, returns, perhaps, in rain to liberate its kind still imprisoned in the earth.

Consider how I discovered where the Winthrop family in this town placed their front door some two hundred years ago, without any verbal or written or ocular evidence. I first suspected [?] and then verified it. I, with others, saw by the frame of the old Hunt house that an addition had been made to its west end in 1703. This brought the front door, which was in the middle of the present, near one end of the original or Winthrop house. I, sitting at home, said to myself, having an occult sympathy with the Winthrops of that date, "The front door must originally have been in the middle of the old house, for symmetry and convenience required it, and if it was, I shall find traces of it; I shall find there where studs have been set into the frame in a different manner from the rest." I went to the house and looked where the door should have been, and I found precisely the evidence I sought, and, beside, where the timber above had been cut out just the width of the door. Indeed, if I had found no traces of the old door, I should have known that the present door was placed where it is after the house was built, for at this corner of the house the end of the sill chanced to be nearly round, the stick tapering, and the post was fitted upon [it] in a remarkable manner, thus: Oak wood had been thus laboriously fitted to it, but within three feet of the corner this sill had been wholly cut away under the

door to make room for it, for they certainly had not put in a piece of sill only three feet long and *of that form* there originally.

Flood, who is saving rails, etc., at the stone bridge, remarks that old settlers say this stream is highest the third day after a rain. But of course this depends on the amount of the rain, the direction and force of the wind, etc., etc. A southwest wind will take the water out sooner, and any strong wind will evaporate it fast.

Rice thinks that he has seen two gulls on the Sudbury meadows, — the white and the gray gulls. He has often seen a man shoot the large gull from Cambridge bridge by heading him off, for the gull flies slowly. He would first run this way, and when the gull turned aside, run that, till the gull passed right over his head, when he shot him. Rice saw Fair Haven Pond still covered with ice, though open along the shore, yesterday. I frequently see the gulls flying up the course of the stream, or of the river valley, at least. R. thinks that the ducks will be seen more numerous, gathering on our waters, just before a storm, like yesterday's.

March 19. 7 A. M. — Fair weather and a very strong southwest wind, the water not quite so high as day before yesterday, — just about as high as yesterday morning, — notwithstanding yesterday's rain, which was pretty copious.

P. M. — To Tarbell's *via* J. P. Brown's.

The wind blows very strongly from the southwest, and, the course of the river being northeast, it must help the water to run off very much. If it blew with

equal violence from the north, the river would probably have risen on account of yesterday's rain. On the northeast sides of the broadest expanses the waves run very high, quite sea-like, and their tumult is exciting both [to] see and [to] hear. All sorts of lumber is afloat. Rails, planks, and timber, etc., which the unthrifty neglected to secure now change hands. Much railroad lumber is floated off. While one end rests on the land, it is the railroad's, but as soon as it is afloat it is made the property of him who saves it. I see some poor neighbors as earnest as the railroad employees are negligent, to secure it. It blows so hard that you walk aslant against the wind. Your very beard, if you wear a full one, is a serious cause of detention. Or if you are fortunate enough to go before the wind, your carriage can hardly be said to be natural to you.

A new ravine has begun at Clamshell this spring. That other, which began with a crack in the frozen ground, I stood at the head of and looked down and out through the other day. It not only was itself a new feature in the landscape, but it gave to the landscape seen through [it] a new and remarkable character, as does the Deep Cut on the railroad. It faces the water, and you look down on the shore and the flooded meadows between its two sloping sides as between the frame of a picture. It affected me like the descriptions or representations of much more stupendous scenery, and to my eyes the dimensions of this ravine were quite indefinite, and in that mood I could not have guessed if it were twenty or fifty feet wide. The landscape has a strange and picturesque appearance seen through it, and it is itself no mean feature in it. But a short time ago I detected here a crack in the frozen ground. Now I look with delight as it were at a new landscape through a broad gap in the hill.

Walking afterward on the side of the hill behind Abel Hosmer's, overlooking the russet interval, the ground being bare where corn was cultivated last year, I see that the sandy soil has been washed far down the hill for its whole length by the recent rains combined with the melting snow, and it forms on the nearly level ground at the base very distinct flat yellow sands, with a convex edge, contrasting with the darker soil there.

Such slopes must lose a great deal of this soil in a single spring, and I should think that was a sound reason in many cases for leaving them woodland and never exposing and breaking the surface. This, plainly, is one reason why the brows of such hills are commonly so barren. They lose much more than they gain annually. It is a question whether the farmer will not lose more by the wash in such cases than he will gain by manuring.

The meadows are all in commotion. The ducks are now concealed by the waves, if there are any floating there. While the sun is behind a cloud, the surface of

the flood is almost uniformly yellowish or blue, but when the sun comes out from behind the cloud, a myriad dazzling white crests to the waves are seen. The wind makes such a din about your ears that conversation is difficult; your words are blown away and do not strike the ear they were aimed at. If you walk by the water, the tumult of the waves confuses you. If you go by a tree or enter the woods, the din is yet greater. Nevertheless this universal commotion is very interesting and exciting. The white pines in the horizon, either single trees or whole woods, a mile off in the southwest or west, are particularly interesting. You not only see the regular bilateral form of the tree, all the branches distinct like the frond of a fern or a feather (for the pine, even at this distance, has not merely beauty of outline and color, — it is not merely an amorphous and homogeneous or continuous mass of green, — but shows a regular succession of flattish leafy boughs or stages, in flakes one above another, like the veins of a leaf or the leafets of a frond; it is this richness and symmetry of detail which, more than its outline, charms us), but that fine silvery light reflected from its needles (perhaps their under sides) incessantly in motion. As a tree bends and waves like a feather in the gale, I see it alternately dark and light, as the sides of the needles, which reflect the cool sheen, are alternately withdrawn from and restored to the proper angle,[1] and the light appears to flash upward from the base of the tree incessantly. In the intervals of the flash it is often as if the tree were withdrawn

[1] [Channing, p. 296.]

altogether from sight. I see one large pine wood over whose whole top these cold electric flashes are incessantly passing off harmlessly into the air above. I thought at first of some fine spray dashed upward, but it is rather like broad flashes of pale, cold light. Surely you can never see a pine wood so expressive, so speaking. This reflection of light from the waving crests of the earth is like the play and flashing of electricity. No deciduous tree exhibits these fine effects of light. Literally incessant sheets, not of heat- but cold-lightning, you would say were flashing there. Seeing some just over the roof of a house which was far on this side, I thought at first that it was something like smoke even — though a rare kind of smoke — that went up from the house. In short, you see a play of light over the whole pine, similar in its cause, but far grander in its effects, than that seen in a waving field of grain. Is not this wind an awaking to life and light [of] the pines after their winter slumber? The wind is making passes over them, magnetizing and electrifying them. Seen at midday, even, it is still the light of dewy morning alone that is reflected from the needles of the pine. This is the brightening and awakening of the pines, a phenomenon perchance connected with the flow of sap in them. I feel somewhat like the young Astyanax at sight of his father's flashing crest.[1] As if in this wind-storm of March a certain electricity was passing from heaven to earth through the pines and calling them to life.

That first general exposure of the russet earth, March

[1] [Channing, p. 296.]

16th, after the soaking rain of the day before, which washed off most of the snow and ice, is a remarkable era in an ordinary spring. The earth casting off her white mantle and appearing in her homely russet garb. This russet — including the leather-color of oak leaves — is peculiar and not like the russet of the fall and winter, for it reflects the spring light or sun, as if there were a sort of sap in it. When the strong northwest winds first blow, drying up the superabundant moisture, the withered grass and leaves do not present a merely weather-beaten appearance, but a washed and combed springlike face. The knolls forming islands in our meadowy flood are never more interesting than then. This is when the earth is, as it were, re-created, raised up to the sun, which was buried under snow and ice.

To continue the account of the weather [seven] pages back: To-day it has cleared off to a very strong southwest wind, which began last evening, after the rain, — strong as ever blows all day, stronger than the northwest wind of the 16th and hardly so warm, with flitting wind-clouds only. It differs from the 16th in being yet drier and barer, — the earth, — scarcely any snow or ice to be found, and, such being the direction of the wind, you can hardly find a place in the afternoon which is both sunny and sheltered from the wind, and there is a yet greater commotion in the water.

We are interested in the phenomena of Nature mainly as children are, or as we are in games of chance. They are more or less exciting. Our appetite for novelty is insatiable. We do not attend to ordinary things, though they are most important, but to extraordinary ones.

While it is only moderately hot or cold, or wet or dry, nobody attends to it, but when Nature goes to an extreme in any of these directions we are all on the alert with excitement. Not that we care about the philosophy or the effects of this phenomenon. *E. g.*, when I went to Boston in the early train the coldest morning of last winter, two topics mainly occupied the attention of the passengers, Morphy's chess victories and Nature's victorious cold that morning. The inhabitants of various towns were comparing notes, and that one whose door opened upon a greater degree of cold than any of his neighbors' doors chuckled not a little. Almost every one I met asked me almost before our salutations were over "how the glass stood" at my house or in my town, — the librarian of the college, the registrar of deeds at Cambridgeport, — a total stranger to me, whose form of inquiry made me think of another sort of glass, — and each rubbed his hands with pretended horror but real delight if I named a higher figure than he had yet heard. It was plain that one object which the cold was given us for was our amusement, a passing excitement. It would be perfectly consistent and American to bet on the coldness of our respective towns, of [*sic*] the morning that is to come. Thus a greater degree of cold may be said to warm us more than a less one. We hear with ill-concealed disgust the figures reported from some localities, where they never enjoy the luxury of severe cold. This is a perfectly legitimate amusement, only we should know that each day is peculiar and has its kindred excitements.

In those wet days like the 12th and the 15th when the browns culminated, the sun being concealed, I was drawn toward and worshipped the brownish light in the sod, — the withered grass, etc., on barren hills. I felt as if I could eat the very crust of the earth; I never felt so terrene, never sympathized so with the surface of the earth. From whatever source the light and heat come, thither we look with love.

The newspapers state that a man in Connecticut lately shot ninety-three musquash in one day.

Melvin says that in skinning a mink you must cut round the parts containing the musk, else the operation will be an offensive one; that Wetherbee has already baited some pigeons (he hears); that he last year found a hen-hawk's egg in March and thinks that woodcocks are now laying.

March 20. 7 a. m. — River no higher than three days ago, notwithstanding the rain of two days ago, the wind being southwest and very strong.

P. M. — I see under the east side of the house, amid the evergreens, where they were sheltered from the cold northwest wind, quite a parcel of sparrows, chiefly *F. hyemalis*, two or three tree sparrows, and one song sparrow, quietly feeding together. I watch them through a window within six or eight feet. They evidently love to be sheltered from the wind, and at least are not averse to each other's society. The tree sparrows *sing* a little. One perches on a bush to sing, while others are feeding on the ground, but he is very restless on his perch, hopping about and stooping as if dodging

Vol. XII

those that fly over. He must perch on some bit of stubble or twig to sing. They are evidently picking up the seeds of weeds which lie on the surface of the ground invisible to our eyes. They suffer their wings to hang rather loose. The *F. hyemalis* is the largest of the three. They have remarkably distinct light-colored bills, and when they stretch, show very distinct clear-white lateral tail-feathers. This stretching seems to be contagious among them, like yawning with us. They have considerable brown on the quill-feathers. The tree sparrows are much brighter brown and white than the song sparrow. The latter alone scratches once or twice, and is more inclined to hop or creep close to the ground, under the fallen weeds. Perhaps it deserves most to be called the *ground*-bird.

P. M. — Up Assabet. Very strong northwest wind.

When I get opposite the end of the willow-row, the sun comes out and they are very handsome, like a rosette, pale-tawny or fawn-colored at base and a rich yellow or orange yellow in the upper three or four feet. This is, methinks, the brightest object in the landscape these days. Nothing so betrays the spring sun. I am aware that the sun has come out of a cloud first by seeing it lighting up the osiers. Such a willow-row, cut off within a year or two, might be called a heliometer, or measure of the sun's brightness.

The last year's shoots of many trees—as maples, both white and red—retain a permanent bright color, red or scarlet, all winter and spring, till new ones

grow. The top of the forest is thus very agreeably tinged.

The river is so high that I leave it at Pinxter Swamp, and come into it again only at the swift narrow place above, near the road.

March 21. 6 a. m. — The water has fairly begun to fall. It was at its height the 17th; fell a little — two or three inches — the morning of the 18th. On the 18th it rained very considerably all day, which would ordinarily have raised the river a foot, or perhaps two, but, the wind being very strong from the southwest, it only prevented its falling any more until this morning. It did not probably raise it more than two inches. Of course, there could not have been much melted snow and ice to be added to the last rain about the sources of the river, since they are considerably further south, where the ground must have been much more bare than here.

A crow blackbird.

P. M. — Sail to Fair Haven Pond.

A strong northwest wind. Draw my boat over the road on a roller. Raising a stone for ballast from the south side of the railroad causeway, where it is quite sunny and warm, I find the under sides very densely covered with little ants, all stirring and evidently ready to come out, if some have not already. They feel the heat through the stone on the ground. It blowed very smartly in gusts, and my boat scud along this way and that, not minding its helm much, as if it were lifted partly out of water. I went from point to point as quickly as you could say "here" and "there."

I see a female marsh hawk sailing and hunting over
Potter's Swamp. I not only see
the white rump but the very peculiar crescent-shaped curve of
its wings.

Fair Haven Pond is only two thirds open. The east
end is frozen still, and the body of the ice has drifted
in to shore a rod or two, before the northwest wind,
and its edge crumbled against the trees.

I see, on a yellow lily root washed up, leaf-buds grown
five or six inches, or even seven or eight, with the stems.

Everywhere for several days the alder catkins have
dangled long and loose, the most alive apparently of
any tree. They seem to welcome the water which half
covers them. The willow catkins are also very conspicuous, in silvery masses rising above the flood.

I see several white pine cones in the path by Wheildon's which appear to have fallen in the late strong
winds, but perhaps the ice in the winter took them off.
Others still hold on.

From the evening of March 18th to this, the evening of the 21st, we have had uninterrupted strong
wind, — till the evening of the 19th very strong southwest wind, then and since northwest, — three days
of strong wind.

March 22. P. M. — The wind changes to easterly
and is more raw, *i. e.* cool and moist, and the air thickens as if it would rain.

Returning from Poplar Hill through the west end
of Sleepy Hollow, it is very still, the air thick, just ready

to rain, and I hear there, on the apple trees and small
oaks, the tree sparrows and hyemalis singing very
pleasantly. I hear the lively jingle of the hyemalis and
the sweet notes of the tree sparrow, canary-like, —
svar svar, svit vit vit vit vit, the last part with increasing rapidity. Both species in considerable numbers,
singing together as they flit along, make a very lively
concert. They sing as loud and full as ever now. There
has been no sweeter warble than this of the tree sparrow as yet.

It is a peculiarly still hour now, when the first drops
of rain begin to be heard on the dry leaves around me,
and, looking up, I see very high in the air two large
birds, which, at that height, with their narrow wings,
flying southeast, looked, *i. e.* were shaped, like nighthawks. I think they were gulls.

The great scarlet oak has now lost almost every leaf,
while the white oak near it still retains them.

C. says he saw fox-colored sparrows this afternoon.

March 23. P. M. — Walk to Cardinal Shore and
sail to Well Meadow and Lee's Cliff.

It clears up at 2 P. M.

The *Lycoperdon stellatum* are numerous and blossomed out widely in Potter's Path by Bare Hill, after
the rain of the night.

As we sail upward toward the pond, we scare up
two or three golden-eyes, or whistlers, showing their
large black heads and black backs, and afterward I
watch one swimming not far before us and see the white
spot, amid the black, on the side of his head. I have

now no doubt that I saw some on the 21st flying here,
and it is very likely that Rice saw them here on the
17th, as he says.

The pond may be said to be open to-day. There is,
however, quite a large mass of ice, which has drifted,
since the east wind arose yesterday noon, from the
east side over to the north of the Island. This ice, of
which there may be eight or ten acres, is so very dark,
almost black, that it is hard to discern till you are just
upon it, though some little pieces which we broke off
and left on its edge were very visible for half a mile.
When at the edge of this field of ice, it was a very dark
gray in color, had none of the usual whiteness of ice.
It was about six inches thick, but was most completely
honeycombed. The upper surface was not only thus
dark, dusky, or blackish, but full of little hollows three
to six inches across, and the whole mass undulated
with the waves very much, irregular cracks alternately
opening and closing in it, yet it was well knitted together. With my paddle I could depress it six inches
on the edge, and cause it to undulate like a blanket
for a rod or more, and yet it bore us securely when we
stepped out upon it, and it was by no means easy to
break off or detach a piece a foot wide. In short, it was
thoroughly honeycombed and, as it were, saturated
with water. The masses broken off reminded me of
some very decayed and worm-eaten interiors of trees.
Yet the small cakes into which it visibly cracked
when you bent it and made it undulate were knitted
together or dovetailed somewhat like the plates of a
tortoise-shell, and immediately returned to their places.

Though it would bear you, the creaking of one such
part on another was a quite general and considerable
noise, and one detached mass, rubbed in your hand
upon the edge of the field, yielded a singular metallic
or ringing sound, evidently owing to its hollowness or
innumerable perforations. It had a metallic ring. The
moment you raised a mass from the water, it was very
distinctly white and brilliant, the water running out
from it. This was the relic of that great mass which
I saw on the 21st on the east side.

There was a great quantity of bayonet rush, also,
drifted over here and strewn along the shore. This
and the pontederia are the coarsest of the wrack. Now
is the time, then, that it is added to the wrack, probably being ripped up by the ice. It reminds you of the
collections of seaweed after a storm, — this river-weed
after the spring freshets have melted and dispersed the
ice. The ice thus helps essentially to clear the shore.

I am surprised to see one of those sluggish ghost-
horses alive on the ice. It was probably drifted from
the shore by the flood and here lodged.

That dark, uneven ice has a peculiarly coarse-grained
appearance, it is so much decomposed. The pieces
are interlocked by the irregularities of the perpendicular combing. The under side presents the most continuous surface, and it is held together chiefly on that
side. One piece rings when struck on another, like a
trowel on a brick, and as we rested against the edge
of this ice, we heard a singular wheezing and grating
sound, which was the creaking of the ice, which was
undulating under the waves and wind.

As we entered Well Meadow, we saw a hen-hawk perch on the topmost plume of one of the tall pines at the head of the meadow. Soon another appeared, probably its mate, but we looked in vain for a nest there. It was a fine sight, their soaring above our heads, presenting a perfect outline  and, as they came round, showing their rust-colored tails with a whitish rump, or, as they sailed away from us, that slight teetering or quivering motion of their dark-tipped wings seen edgewise, now on this side, now that, by which they balanced and directed themselves. These are the most eagle-like of our common hawks. They very commonly perch upon the very topmost plume of a pine, and, if motionless, are rather hard to distinguish there.

The cowslip and most of the skunk-cabbage there have been and are still drowned by flood; else we should find more in bloom. As it is, I see the skunk-cabbage in bloom, but generally the growth of both has been completely checked by the water.

While reconnoitring there, we hear the peep of one hylodes somewhere in this sheltered recess in the woods. And afterward, on the Lee side, I hear a single croak from a wood frog.

We cross to Lee's shore and sit upon the bare rocky ridge overlooking the flood southwest and northeast. It is quite sunny and sufficiently warm. I see one or two of the small fuzzy gnats in the air. The prospect thence is a fine one, especially at this season, when the water

is high. The landscape is very agreeably diversified with hill and vale and meadow and cliff. As we look southwest, how attractive the shores of russet capes and peninsulas laved by the flood! Indeed, that large tract east of the bridge is now an island. How fair that low, undulating russet land! At this season and under these circumstances, the sun just come out and the flood high around it, russet, so reflecting the light of the sun, appears to me the most agreeable of colors, and I begin to dream of a russet fairyland and elysium. How dark and terrene must be green! but this smooth russet surface reflects almost all the light. That broad and low but firm island, with but few trees to conceal the contour of the ground and its outline, with its fine russet sward, firm and soft as velvet, reflecting so much light, — all the undulations of the earth, its nerves and muscles, revealed by the light and shade, and even the sharper ridgy edge of steep banks where the plow has heaped up the earth from year to year, — this is a sort of fairyland and elysium to my eye. The tawny couchant island! Dry land for the Indian's wigwam in the spring, and still strewn with his arrow-points. The sight of such land reminds me of the pleasant spring days in which I have walked over such tracts, looking for these relics. How well, too, this smooth, firm, light-reflecting, tawny earth contrasts with the darker water which surrounds it, — or perchance lighter sometimes! At this season, when the russet colors prevail, the contrast of water and land is more agreeable to behold. What an inexpressibly soft curving line is the shore! Or if the water is perfectly smooth and

yet rising, you seem to see it raised an eighth of an inch with swelling lip above the immediate shore it kisses, as in a cup or the of [sic] a saucer. Indian isles and promontories. Thus we sit on that rock, hear the first wood frog's croak, and dream of a russet elysium. Enough for the season is the beauty thereof. Spring has a beauty of its own which we would not exchange for that of summer, and at this moment, if I imagine the fairest earth I can, it is still russet, such is the color of its blessed isles, and they are surrounded with the phenomena of spring.

The qualities of the land that are most attractive to our eyes now are dryness and firmness. It is not the rich black soil, but warm and sandy hills and plains which tempt our steps. We love to sit on and walk over sandy tracts in the spring like cicindelas. These tongues of russet land tapering and sloping into the flood do almost speak to one. They are alternately in sun and shade. When the cloud is passed, and they reflect their pale-brown light to me, I am tempted to go to them.

I think I have already noticed within a week how very agreeably and strongly the green of small pines contrasts with the russet of a hillside pasture now. Perhaps there is no color with which green contrasts more strongly.

I see the shadow of a cloud — and it chances to be a hollow ring with sunlight in its midst — passing over the hilly sprout-land toward the Baker house, a sprout-land of oaks and birches; and, owing to the color of the birch twigs, perhaps, this shadow turns all from

russet to a decided dark-purplish color as it moves along. And then, as I look further along eastward in the horizon, I am surprised to see strong purple and violet tinges in the sun, from a hillside a mile off densely covered with full-grown birches. It is the steep old corn-field hillside of Jacob Baker's. I would not have believed that under the spring sun so many colors were brought out. It is not the willows only that shine, but, under favorable circumstances, many other twigs, even a mile or two off. The dense birches, so far that their white stems are not distinct, reflect deep, strong purple and violet colors from the distant hillsides opposite to the sun. Can this have to do with the sap flowing in them?

As we sit there, we see coming, swift and straight, northeast along the river valley, not seeing us and therefore not changing his course, a male goosander, so near that the green reflections of his head and neck are plainly visible. He looks like a paddle-wheel steamer, so oddly painted up, black and white and green, and moves along swift and straight like one. Ere long the same returns with his mate, the red-throated, the male taking the lead.

The loud *peop* (?) of a pigeon woodpecker is heard in our sea [?], and anon the prolonged loud and shrill *cackle*, calling the thin-wooded hillsides and pastures to life. It is like the note of an alarm-clock set last fall so as to wake Nature up at exactly this date. *Up up up up up up up up!* What a rustling it seems to make among the dry leaves!

You can now sit on sunny sheltered sprout-land

hillsides and enjoy the sight and sound of rustling dry leaves.

Then I see come slowly flying from the southwest  a great gull, of voracious form, which at length by a sudden and steep descent alights in Fair Haven Pond, scaring up a crow which was seeking its food on the edge of the ice. This shows that the crows get along the meadow's edge also what has washed up.

It is suggested that the blue is darkest when reflected from the most agitated water, because of the shadow (occasioned by the inequalities) mingled with it.

Some Indians of the north have but one word for blue and black, and blue is with us considered the darkest color, though it is the color of the sky or air. Light, I should say, was white; the absence of it, black. Hold up to the light a perfectly opaque body and you get black, but hold up to it the least opaque body, such as air, and you get blue. Hence you may say that blue is light seen through a veil.

March 24. P. M. — Down railroad.

Southeast wind. Begins to sprinkle while I am sitting in Laurel Glen, listening to hear the earliest wood frogs croaking. I think they get under weigh a little earlier, *i. e.*, you will hear many of them sooner than you will hear many hylodes. Now, when the leaves get to be dry and rustle under your feet, dried by the March winds, the peculiar dry note, *wurrk wurrk wur-r-r-k wurk* of the wood frog is heard faintly by ears on the

alert, borne up from some unseen pool in a woodland hollow which is open to the influences of the sun. It is a singular sound for awakening Nature to make, associated with the first warmer days, when you sit in some sheltered place in the woods amid the dried leaves. How moderate on her first awakening, how little demonstrative! You may sit half an hour before you will hear another. You doubt if the season will be long enough for such Oriental and luxurious slowness. But they get on, nevertheless, and by to-morrow, or in a day or two, they croak louder and more frequently. Can you ever be sure that you have heard the very first wood frog in the township croak? Ah! how weather-wise must he be! There is no guessing at the weather with him. He makes the weather in his degree; he encourages it to be mild. The weather, what is it but the temperament of the earth? and he is wholly of the earth, sensitive as its skin in which he lives and of which he is a part. His life relaxes with the thawing ground. He pitches and tunes his voice to chord with the rustling leaves which the March wind has dried. Long before the frost is quite out, he feels the influence of the spring rains and the warmer days. His is the very voice of the weather. He rises and falls like quicksilver in the thermometer. You do not perceive the spring so surely in the actions of men, their lives are so artificial. They may make more fire or less in their parlors, and their feelings accordingly are not good thermometers. The frog far away in the wood, that burns no coal nor wood, perceives more surely the general and universal changes.

Vol. XII

In the ditch under the west edge of Trillium Wood I see six yellow-spot turtles. They surely have not crawled from far. Do they go into the mud in this ditch? A part of the otherwise perfectly sound and fresh-looking scales of one has been apparently eaten away, as if by a worm.

There sits also on the bank of the ditch a *Rana fontinalis*, and it is altogether likely they were this species that leaped into a ditch on the 10th. This one is mainly a bronze brown, with a very dark greenish snout, etc., with the raised line down the side of the back. This, methinks, is about the only frog which the marsh hawk could have found hitherto.

Returning, above the railroad causeway, I see a flock of goldfinches, first of *spring*, flitting along the causeway-bank. They have not yet the bright plumage they will have, but in some lights might be mistaken for sparrows. There is considerable difference in color between one and another, but the flaps of their coats are black, and their heads and shoulders more or less yellow. They are eating the seeds of the mullein and the large primrose, clinging to the plants sidewise in various positions and pecking at the seed-vessels. Wilson says, "In the month of April they begin to change their winter dress, and, before the middle of May, appear in brilliant yellow."

C. sees geese go over again this afternoon. How commonly they are seen in still rainy weather like this! He says that when they had got far off they looked like a black ribbon almost perpendicular waving in the air.

March 25. A rainy day.

P. M. — To Clamshell.

I heard the *what what what what* of the nuthatch this forenoon. Do I ever hear it in the afternoon? It is much like the cackle of the pigeon woodpecker and suggests a relation to that bird.

Again I walk in the rain and see the rich yellowish browns of the moist banks. These Clamshell hills and neighboring promontories, though it is a dark and rainy day, reflect a certain yellowish light from the wet withered grass which is very grateful to my eyes, as also the darker more reddish browns, as the radical leaves of the *Andropogon scoparius* in low tufts here and there. (Its culms, where they stand, are quite light yellow.) Surely russet is not the name which describes the fields and hillsides now, whether wet or dry. There is not red enough in it. I do not know a better name for this (when wet) yellowish brown than "tawny." On the south side of these warm hills, it may perhaps be called one of the fawn-colors, *i. e.* brown inclining to green. Much of this peculiar yellowish color on the surface of the Clamshell plain is due to a little curled sedge or grass growing at short intervals, loosely covering the ground (with green mosses intermixed) in little tufts like curled hair.

I saw yesterday, in Laurel Glen, where the early sedge had been grazed very close to the ground, and the same, perhaps digested, fine as green-paint dust, lay around. Was it the work of a mouse?

Day before yesterday, in clear, dry weather, we had

pale-brown or fawn-colored earth, *i. e.*, a dry, withered grass blade [color]; to-day, a more yellow brown or tawny, the same being wet. The wet brings out an agreeable yellow light, as if the sun were shining through a mist on it. The earth is more truly russet in November, when there is more redness left in the withered and withering vegetation. Such is the change in the color of the bare portions of the earth (*i. e.* bare of trees and bushes) produced by rain. Also the oak leaves are much redder. In fair weather the light color of these objects was simply a light reflected from them, originating in the sun and sky; now it is a more proper and inward light, which attracts and confines our attention to moist sward itself.

A snipe flies away from the moist Clamshell shore, uttering its *cr-a-ack c-r-r-rack.*

I thought the other day, How we enjoy a warm and pleasant day at this season! We dance like gnats in the sun.

A score of my townsmen have been shooting and trapping musquash and mink of late. Some have got nothing else to do. If they should strike for higher wages now, instead of going to the clam-banks, as the Lynn shoemakers propose, they would go to shooting musquash. They are gone all day; early and late they scan the rising tide; stealthily they set their traps in remote swamps, avoiding one another. Am not I a trapper too, early and late scanning the rising flood, ranging by distant wood-sides, setting my traps in solitude, and baiting them as well as I know how, that I may catch life and light, that my intellectual part

may taste some venison and be invigorated, that my nakedness may be clad in some wild, furry warmth?

The color of spring hitherto, — I should say that in dry weather it was fawn-colored, in wet more yellowish or tawny. When wet, the green of the fawn is supplied by the lichens and the mosses.

March 26. P. M. — To Conantum *via* Cardinal Shore and boat.

The river has gone down considerably, but the rain of yesterday and to-day has checked its fall somewhat.

Much earth has been washed away from the roots of grasses and weeds along the banks of the river, and many of those pretty little bodkin bulbs are exposed and so transported to new localities. This seems to be the way in which they are spread.

I see many smallish ants on the red carcass of a musquash just skinned and lying on the bank, cold and wet as the weather is. They love this animal food. On the top of the hill at Lee's Cliff much wintergreen has been eaten; at least a great many leaves are lying loose, strewn about.

I find washed up on the (Cardinal) shore a little bream about an inch and an eighth long, very much like those found at Walden last fall. It has about seven transverse bars, a similar dorsal fin, a reddish-copper iris, with the black vertical dash through the eye. I think it must be one of the common breams of the river, — though I see only the black spot on the operculum and not any red one, — and apparently all the young are thus striped (?).

Vol. XII

What was that large rather grayish duck on Fair Haven Pond this afternoon? It was far off. Was it a last year's male sheldrake, or a female, or another?

March 27. 7 A. M. — Was that the *Alauda*, shore lark (?), which flew up from the corn-field beyond Texas house, and dashed off so swiftly with a peculiar note, — a small flock of them?

P. M. — Sail from Cardinal Shore up Otter Bay, close to Deacon Farrar's.

I see a gull flying over Fair Haven Pond which appears to have a much duskier body beneath than the common near by, though about the same size. Can it be another species?

The wind is so nearly west to-day that we sail up from Cardinal Shore to the pond, and from the road up what I will call Otter Bay, behind Farrar's, and, returning, sail from the road at Creel (or Pole) Brook to Pond Island and from Hallowell willows to railroad. The water is quite high still, and we sail up Otter Bay, I think, more than half a mile, to within a very short distance of Farrar's. This is an interesting and wild place.

There is an abundance of low willows whose catkins are now conspicuous, rising four to six or seven feet above the water, thickly placed on long wand-like osiers. They look, when you look from the sun, like dead gray twigs or branches (whose wood is exposed) of bushes in the light, but, nearer, are recognized for the pretty bright buttons of the willow. We sail by masses of these silvery buttons two or three rods long,

rising above the water. By their color they have relation to the white clouds and the sky and to the snow and ice still lingering in a few localities. In order to see these silvery buttons in the greatest profusion, you must sail amid them on some flooded meadow or swamp like this. Our whole course, as we wind about in this bay, is lined also with the alder, whose pretty tassels, now many of them in full bloom, are hanging straight down, suggesting in a peculiar manner the influence of gravity, or are regularly blown one side.

It is remarkable how modest and unobtrusive these early flowers are. The musquash and duck hunter or the farmer might and do commonly pass by them with[out] perceiving them. They steal into the air and light of spring without being noticed for the most part. The sportsman seems to see a mass of weather-stained dead twigs showing their wood and partly covered with gray lichens and moss, and the flowers of the alder, now partly in bloom, maybe half, make the impression at a little distance of a collection of the brown twigs of winter — also are of the same color with many withered leaves.

Twenty rods off, masses of alder in bloom look like masses of bare brown twigs, last year's twigs, and would be taken for such.

Of our seven indigenous flowers which begin to bloom in March, four, *i. e.* the two alders, the aspen, and the hazel, are not generally noticed so early, if at all, and most do not observe the flower of a fifth, the white maple. The first four are yellowish or reddish brown at a little distance, like the banks and sward moistened by the spring rain. The browns are the prevailing shades as yet, as in the withered grass and sedge and the surface of the earth, the withered leaves, and these brown flowers.

I see from a hilltop a few very bright green spots a rod in diameter in the upper part of Farrar's meadow, which the water has left within a day or two. Going there, I find that a very powerful spring is welling up there, which, with water warm from the bowels of the earth, has caused the grass and several weeds, as *Cardamine rhomboidea*, etc., to grow thus early and luxuriantly, and perhaps it has been helped by the flood standing over it for some days. These are bright liquid green in the midst of brown and withered grass and leaves. Such are the spots where the grass is greenest now.

C. says that he saw a turtle dove on the 25th.

It is remarkable how long many things may be preserved by excluding the air and light and dust, moisture, etc. Those chalk-marks on the chamber-floor joists and timbers of the Hunt house, one of which was read by many "Feb. 1666," and all of which were in an ancient style of writing and expression, — "ye" for " the," etc., "enfine Brown," — were as fresh when exposed (having been plastered and cased over) as if made the day before. Yet a single day's rain completely obliterated some of them. Cousin Charles says that, on the timbers of a very old house recently taken down in Haverhill, the chalk-marks made by

the framers, numbering the sticks, [were] as fresh as if just made.

I saw a large timber over the middle of the best room of the Hunt house which had been cased, according to all accounts, at least a hundred years ago, the casing having just been taken off. I saw that the timber appeared to have been freshly hewn on the under side, and I asked the carpenter who was taking down the house what he had been hewing that timber for, — for it had evidently been done since it was put up and in a very inconvenient position, and I had no doubt that he had just done it, for the surface was as fresh and distinct from the other parts as a fresh whittling, — but he answered to my surprise that he had not touched it, it was so when he took the casing off. When the casing was put on, it had been roughly hewn by one standing beneath it, in order to reduce its thickness or perhaps to make it more level than it was. So distinct and peculiar is the weather-stain, and so indefinitely it may be kept off if you do not allow this painter to come [?] to your wood.

Cousin Charles says that he took out of the old Haverhill house a very broad panel from over the fireplace, which had a picture of Haverhill at some old period on it. The panel had been there perfectly sheltered in an inhabited house for more than a hundred years. It was placed in his shop and no moisture allowed to come near it, and yet it shrunk a quarter of an inch in width when the air came to both sides of it.

He says that his men, who were digging a cellar last week on a southwest slope, found fifty-one snakes

of various kinds and sizes — green, black, brown, etc. —about a foot underground, within two feet square (or cube?). The frost was out just there, but not in many parts of the cellar. They could not run, they were so stiff, but they ran their tongues out. They did [not] take notice of any hole or cavity.

March 28. P. M. — Paddle to the Bedford line.

It is now high time to look for arrowheads, etc. I spend many hours every spring gathering the crop which the melting snow and rain have washed bare. When, at length, some island in the meadow or some sandy field elsewhere has been plowed, perhaps for rye, in the fall, I take note of it, and do not fail to repair thither as soon as the earth begins to be dry in the spring. If the spot chances never to have been cultivated before, I am the first to gather a crop from it. The farmer little thinks that another reaps a harvest which is the fruit of his toil. As much ground is turned up in a day by the plow as Indian implements could not have turned over in a month, and my eyes rest on the evidences of an aboriginal life which passed here a thousand years ago perchance. Especially if the knolls in the meadows are washed by a freshet where they have been plowed the previous fall, the soil will be taken away lower down and the stones left, — the arrowheads, etc., and soapstone pottery amid them, — somewhat as gold is washed in a dish or tom. I landed on two spots this afternoon and picked up a dozen arrowheads. It is one of the regular pursuits of the spring. As much as sportsmen go in pursuit of ducks, and

gunners of musquash, and scholars of rare books, and travellers of adventures, and poets of ideas, and all men of money, I go in search of arrowheads when the proper season comes round again. So I help myself to live worthily, and loving my life as I should. It is a good collyrium to look on the bare earth, — to pore over it so much, getting strength to all your senses, like Antæus. If I did not find arrowheads, I might, perchance, begin to pick up crockery and fragments of pipes, — the relics of a more recent man. Indeed, you can hardly name a more innocent or wholesome entertainment. As I am thus engaged, I hear the rumble of the bowling-alley's thunder, which has begun again in the village. It comes before the earliest natural thunder. But what its lightning is, and what atmospheres it purifies, I do not know. Or I might collect the various bones which I come across. They would make a museum that would delight some Owen at last, and what a text they might furnish me for a course of lectures on human life or the like! I might spend my days collecting the fragments of pipes until I found enough, after all my search, to compose one perfect pipe when laid together.

I have not decided whether I had better publish my experience in searching for arrowheads in three volumes, with plates and an index, or try to compress it into one. These durable implements seem to have been suggested to the Indian mechanic with a view to my entertainment in a succeeding period. After all the labor expended on it, the bolt may have been shot but once perchance, and the shaft which was devoted to it decayed, and there lay the arrowhead, sinking into the ground, awaiting me. They lie all over the hills with like expectation, and in due time the husbandman is sent, and, tempted by the promise of corn or rye, he plows the land and turns them up to my view. Many as I have found, methinks the last one gives me about the same delight that the first did. Some time or other, you would say, it had rained arrowheads, for they lie all over the surface of America. You may have your peculiar tastes. Certain localities in your town may seem from association unattractive and uninhabitable to you. You may wonder that the land bears any money value there, and pity some poor fellow who is said to survive in that neighborhood. But plow up a new field there, and you will find the omnipresent arrow-points strewn over it, and it will appear that the red man, with other tastes and associations, lived there too. No matter how far from the modern road or meeting-house, no matter how near. They lie in the meeting-house cellar, and they lie in the distant cow-pasture. And some collections which were made a century ago by the curious like myself have been dispersed again, and they are still as good as new. You cannot tell the third-hand ones (for they are all second-hand) from the others, such is their persistent out-of-door durability; for they were chiefly made to be lost. They are sown, like a grain that is slow to germinate, broadcast over the earth. Like the dragon's teeth which bore a crop of soldiers, these bear crops of philosophers and poets, and the same seed is just as good to plant again. It is a stone fruit. Each one yields me a thought. I come nearer to the maker

of it than if I found his bones. His bones would not prove any wit that wielded them, such as this work of his bones does. It is humanity inscribed on the face of the earth, patent to my eyes as soon as the snow goes off, not hidden away in some crypt or grave or under a pyramid. No disgusting mummy, but a clean stone, the best symbol or letter that could have been transmitted to me.

The Red Man, his mark ⟶

At every step I see it, and I can easily supply the "Tahatawan" or "Mantatuket" that might have been written if he had had a clerk. It is no single inscription on a particular rock, but a footprint — rather a mind-print — left everywhere, and altogether illegible. No vandals, however vandalic in their disposition, can be so industrious as to destroy them.

Time will soon destroy the works of famous painters and sculptors, but the Indian arrowhead will balk his efforts and Eternity will have to come to his aid. They are not fossil bones, but, as it were, fossil thoughts, forever reminding me of the mind that shaped them. I would fain know that I am treading in the tracks of human game, — that I am on the trail of mind, — and these little reminders never fail to set me right. When I see these signs I know that the subtle spirits that made them are not far off, into whatever form transmuted. What if you do plow and hoe amid them, and swear that not one stone shall be left upon another? They are only the less like to break in that case. When

you turn up one layer you bury another so much the more securely. They are at peace with rust. This arrow-headed character promises to outlast all others. The larger pestles and axes may, perchance, grow scarce and be broken, but the arrowhead shall, perhaps, never cease to wing its way through the ages to eternity. It was originally winged for but a short flight, but it still, to my mind's eye, wings its way through the ages, bearing a message from the hand that shot it. Myriads of arrow-points lie sleeping in the skin of the revolving earth, while meteors revolve in space. The footprint, the mind-print of the oldest men. When some Vandal chieftain has razed to the earth the British Museum, and, perchance, the winged bulls from Nineveh shall have lost most if not all of their features, the arrowheads which the museum contains will, perhaps, find themselves at home again in familiar dust, and resume their shining in new springs upon the bared surface of the earth then, to be picked up for the thousandth time by the shepherd or savage that may be wandering there, and once more suggest their story to him. Indifferent they to British Museums, and, no doubt, Nineveh bulls are old acquaintances of theirs, for they have camped on the plains of Mesopotamia, too,[1] and were buried *with* the winged bulls.

They cannot be said to be lost nor found. Surely their use was not so much to bear its fate to some bird or quadruped, or man, as it was to lie here near the surface of the earth for a perpetual reminder to the generations that come after. As for museums. I think

[1] [Channing, p. 295.]

it is better to let Nature take care of our antiquities. These are our antiquities, and they are cleaner to think of than the rubbish of the Tower of London, and they are a more ancient armor than is there. It is a recommendation that they are so inobvious, — that they occur only to the eye and thought that chances to be directed toward them. When you pick up an arrowhead and put it in your pocket, it may say: "Eh, you think you have got me, do you? But I shall wear a hole in your pocket at last, or if you put me in your cabinet, your heir or great-grandson will forget me or throw me out the window directly, or when the house falls I shall drop into the cellar, and there I shall lie quite at home again. Ready to be *found* again, eh? Perhaps some new red man that is to come will fit me to a shaft and make me do his bidding for a bow-shot. What reck I?"

As we were paddling over the Great Meadows, I saw at a distance, high in the air above the middle of the meadow, a very compact flock of blackbirds advancing against the sun. Though there were more than a hundred, they did not appear to occupy more than six feet in breadth, but the whole flock was dashing first to the right and then to the left. When advancing straight toward me and the sun, they made but little impression on the eye, — so many fine dark points merely, seen against the sky, — but as often as they wheeled to the right or left, displaying their wings flatwise and the whole length of their bodies, they were a very conspicuous black mass. This fluctuation in the amount of dark surface was a very pleasing phenomenon. It reminded me [of] those blinds whose sashes [sic] are made to move all together by a stick, now admitting nearly all the light and now entirely excluding it; so the flock of blackbirds opened and shut. But at length they suddenly spread out and dispersed, some flying off this way, and others that, as, when a wave strikes against a cliff, it is dashed upward and lost in fine spray. So they lost their compactness and impetus and broke up suddenly in mid-air.

We see eight geese floating afar in the middle of the meadow, at least half a mile off, plainly (with glass) much larger than the ducks in their neighborhood and the white on their heads very distinct. When at length they arise and fly off northward, their peculiar *heavy* undulating wings, blue-heron-like and unlike any duck, are very noticeable. The black, sheldrake, etc., move their wings rapidly, and remind you of paddle-wheel steamers. Methinks the wings of the black duck appear to be set very far back when it is flying. The meadows, which are still covered far and wide, are quite alive with black ducks.

When walking about on the low east shore at the Bedford bound, I heard a faint honk, and looked around over the water with my glass, thinking it came from that side or perhaps from a farmyard in that direction. I soon heard it again, and at last we detected a great flock passing over, quite on the other side of us and pretty high up. From time to time one of the company uttered a short note, that peculiarly metallic, clangorous sound. These were in a single undulating line, and, as usual, one or two were from time to time crowded out of the line, apparently by the

crowding of those in the rear, and were flying on one side and trying to recover their places, but at last a second short line was formed, meeting the long one at the usual angle and making a figure somewhat like a hay-hook. I suspect it will be found that there is really some advantage in large birds of passage flying in the wedge form and cleaving their way through the air, — that they really do overcome its resistance best in this way, — and perchance the direction and strength of the wind determine the comparative length of the two sides.

The great gulls fly generally up or down the river valley, cutting off the bends of the river, and so do these geese. These fly sympathizing with the river, — a stream in the air, soon lost in the distant sky.

We see these geese swimming and flying at midday and when it is perfectly fair.

If you scan the horizon at this season of the year you are very likely to detect a small flock of dark ducks moving with rapid wing athwart the sky, or see the undulating line of migrating geese against the sky.

Perhaps it is this easterly wind which brings geese, as it did on the 24th.

Ball's Hill, with its withered oak leaves and its pines, looks very fair to-day, a mile and a half off across the water, through a very thin varnish or haze. It reminds me of the isle which was called up from the bottom of the sea, which was given to Apollo.

How charming the contrast of land and water, espe-

cially a temporary island in the flood, with its new and tender shores of waving outline, so withdrawn yet habitable, above all if it rises into a hill high above the water and contrasting with it the more, and if that hill is wooded, suggesting wildness! Our vernal lakes have a beauty to my mind which they would not possess if they were more permanent. Everything is in rapid flux here, suggesting that Nature is alive to her extremities and superficies. To-day we sail swiftly on dark rolling waves or paddle over a sea as smooth as a mirror, unable to touch the bottom, where mowers work and hide their jugs in August; coasting the edge of maple swamps, where alder tassels and white maple flowers are kissing the tide that has risen to meet them. But this particular phase of beauty is fleeting. Nature has so many shows for us she cannot afford to give much time to this. In a few days, perchance, these lakes will have all run away to the sea. Such are the pictures which she paints. When we look at our masterpieces we see only dead paint and its vehicle, which suggests no liquid life rapidly flowing off from beneath. In the former case — in Nature — it is constant surprise and novelty. In many arrangements there is a wearisome monotony. We know too well what [we] shall have for our Saturday's dinner, but each day's feast in Nature's year is a surprise to us and adapted to our appetite and spirits. She has arranged such an order of feasts as never tires. Her motive is not economy but satisfaction.

As we sweep past the north end of Poplar Hill, with a sand-hole in it, its now dryish, pale-brown mottled

sward clothing its rounded slope, which was lately saturated with moisture, presents very agreeable hues. In this light, in fair weather, the patches of now dull-greenish mosses contrast just regularly enough with the pale-brown grass. It is like some rich but modest-colored Kidderminster carpet, or rather the skin of a monster python tacked to the hillside and stuffed with earth. These earth colors, methinks, are never so fair as in the spring. Now the green mosses and lichens contrast with the brown grass, but ere long the surface will be uniformly green. I suspect that we are more amused by the effects of color in the skin of the earth now than in summer. Like the skin of a python, greenish and brown, a fit coat for it to creep over the earth and be concealed in. Or like the skin of a pard, the great leopard mother that Nature is, where she lies at length, exposing her flanks to the sun. I feel as if I could land to stroke and kiss the very sward, it is so fair. It is homely and domestic to my eyes like the rug that lies before my hearth-side.[1] Such ottomans and divans are spread for us to recline on. Nor are these colors mere thin superficial figures, vehicles for paint, but wonderful living growths, — these lichens, to the study of which learned men have devoted their lives, — and libraries have been written about them. The earth lies out now like a leopard, drying her lichen and moss spotted skin in the sun, her sleek and variegated hide. I know that the few raw spots will heal over. Brown is the color for me, the color of our coats and our daily lives, the color of the poor man's loaf.

[1] [Channing, p. 95.]

Ripples on Goose Pond

Ball's Hill and River Flood from Ponkawtasset Hill

The bright tints are pies and cakes, good only for October feasts, which would make us sick if eaten every day.

One side of each wave and ripple is dark and the other light blue, reflecting the sky, — as I look down on them from my boat, — and these colors (?) combined produce a *dark* blue at a distance. These blue spaces ever remind me of the blue in the iridescence produced by oily matter on the surface, for you are slow to regard it as a reflection of the sky. The rippling undulating surface over which you glide is like a changeable blue silk garment.

Here, where in August the bittern booms in the grass, and mowers march *en échelon* and whet their scythes and crunch / / / / / the ripe wool-grass, raised now a few feet, you scud before the wind in your tight bark and listen to the surge (or sough?) of the great waves sporting around you, while you hold the steering-oar and your mast bends to the gale and you stow all your ballast to windward. The crisped sound of surging waves that rock you, that ceaseless roll and gambol, and ever and anon break into your boat.

Deep lie the seeds of the rhexia now, absorbing wet from the flood, but in a few months this mile-wide lake will have gone to the other side of the globe; and the tender rhexia will lift its head on the drifted hummocks in dense patches, bright and scarlet as a flame, — such succession have we here, — where the wild goose and countless wild ducks have floated and dived above them. So Nature condenses her matter. She

is a thousand thick. So many crops the same surface bears.

Undoubtedly the geese fly more numerously over rivers which, like ours, flow northeasterly, — are more at home with the water under them. Each flock runs the gantlet of a thousand gunners, and when you see them steer off from you and your boat you may remember how great their experience in such matters may be, how many such boats and gunners they have seen and avoided between here and Mexico, and even now, perchance (though you, low plodding, little dream it), they see one or two more lying in wait ahead. They have an experienced ranger of the air for their guide. The echo of one gun hardly dies away before they see another pointed at them. How many bullets or smaller shot have sped in vain toward their ranks! Ducks fly more irregularly and shorter distances at a time. The geese rest in fair weather by day only in the midst of our broadest meadow or pond. So they go, anxious and earnest to hide their nests under the pole.

The gulls seem used to boats and sails and will often fly quite near without manifesting alarm.

March 29. Driving rain and southeast wind, etc. Walden is first clear after to-day.

Garfield says he saw a woodcock about a fortnight ago. Minott thinks the middle of March is as early as they come and that they do not then begin to lay.

March 30. 6 A. M. — To Hill (across water).
Hear a red squirrel chirrup at me by the hemlocks

Vol. XII

(running up a hemlock), all for my benefit; not that he is excited by fear, I think, but so full is he of animal spirits that he makes a great ado about the least event. At first he scratches on the bark very rapidly with his hind feet without moving the fore feet. He makes so many queer sounds, and so different from one another, that you would think they came from half a dozen creatures. I hear now two sounds from him of a very distinct character, — a low or base inward, worming, screwing, or brewing, kind of sound (very like that, by the way, which an anxious partridge mother makes) and at the same time a very sharp and shrill bark, and clear, on a very high key, totally distinct from the last, — while his tail is flashing incessantly. You might say that he successfully accomplished the difficult feat of singing and whistling at the same time.

P. M. — To Walden *via* Hubbard's Close.

The green-bodied flies out on sheds, and probably nearly as long as the other; the same size as the house-fly.

I see numerous large skaters on a ditch. This may be the *Gerris lacustris*, but its belly is not white, only whitish in certain lights. It has six legs, two feelers (the two foremost legs being directed forward), a stoutish body, and brown above. The belly looks whitish when you look at it edgewise, but turned quite over (on its back), it is brown.

A very small brown grasshopper hops into the water.

I notice again (in the spring-holes in Hubbard's Close) that water purslane, being covered with water, is an evergreen, — though it is reddish.

Little pollywogs two inches long are lively there.

See on Walden two sheldrakes, male and female, as is common. So they have for some time paired. They are a hundred rods off. The male the larger, with his black head and white breast, the female with a red head. With my glass I see the long red bills of both. They swim at first one way near together, then tack and swim the other, looking around incessantly, never quite at their ease, wary and watchful for foes. A man cannot walk down to the shore or stand out on a hill overlooking the pond without disturbing them. They will have an eye upon him. The locomotive-whistle makes every wild duck start that is floating within the limits of the town. I see that these ducks are not here for protection alone, for at last they both dive, and remain beneath about forty pulse-beats, — and again, and again. I think they are looking for fishes. Perhaps, therefore, these divers are more likely to alight in Walden than the black ducks are.

Hear the hovering note of a snipe.

March 31. The frost is out of our garden, and I see one or two plowing early land. You walk dry now over this sandy land where the frost is melted, even after heavy rain, and there is no slumping in it, for there is no hard-pan and ice to hold the water and make a batter of the surface soil. This is a new condition of things when the surface of the earth generally begins to be dry. But there is still much frost in cold ground, and I often feel the crust which was heaved by it sink under me, and for some time have noticed the chinks where the frozen ground has gaped and erected itself from and over stones and sleepers.

P. M. — To Holbrook's improvements.

Many painted turtles out along a ditch in Moore's Swamp. These the first I have seen, the water is so high in the meadows. One drops into the water from some dead brush which lies in it, and leaves on the brush two of its scales. Perhaps the sun causes the loosened scales to curl up, and so helps the turtle to get rid of them.

Humphrey Buttrick says that he has shot two kinds of little dippers, — the one black, the other with some white.

I see, on a large ant-hill, largish ants at work, front half reddish, back half black, but on another, very large ant-hill near by (a rod to left of Holbrook's road, perhaps fifty rods this side of his clearing on the north side), five feet through, there [are] none out.

It will show how our prejudices interfere with our perception of color, to state that yesterday morning, after making a fire in the kitchen cooking-stove, as I sat over it I thought I saw a little bit of red or scarlet flannel on a chink near a bolt-head on the stove, and I tried to pick it out, — while I was a little surprised that I did not smell it burning. It was merely the reflection of the flame of the fire through a chink, on the dark stove. This showed me what the true color of the flame was, but when I knew what this was, it was not very easy to perceive it again. It appeared now more yellowish. I think that my senses made the truest report the first time.

Vol. XII

II

APRIL, 1859

(ÆT. 41)

April 1. Some have planted peas and lettuce.

Melvin, the sexton, says that when Loring's Pond was drained once — perhaps the dam broke — he saw there about all the birds he has seen on a salt marsh. Also that he once shot a mackerel gull in Concord, — I think he said it was in May; that he sees the two kinds of yellow-legs here; that he has shot at least two kinds of large gray ducks, as big (one, at least) as black ducks.

He says that one winter (it may have been the last) there were caught by him and others at one place in the river below Ball's Hill, in sight of Carlisle Bridge, about two hundred pounds of pickerel within a week, — something quite unprecedented, at least of late years. This was about the last of February or first of March. No males were caught! and he thinks that they had collected there in order to spawn. Perhaps perch and pickerel collect in large numbers for this purpose.

P. M. — To Assabet over meadows in boat; a very strong and a cold northwest wind.

I land again at the (now island) rock, on Simon Brown's land, and look for arrowheads, and picked [*sic*] up two pieces of soapstone pottery. One was probably part of the same which C. found with me there

The wood frogs lie spread out on the surface of the sheltered pools in the woods, cool and windy as it is, dimpling the water by their motions, and as you approach you hear their lively *wurk wurrk wur-r-k*, but, seeing you, they suddenly hist and perhaps dive to the bottom.

It is a very windy afternoon, wind northwest, and at length a dark cloud rises on that side, evidently of a windy structure, a dusky mass with lighter intervals, like a parcel of brushes lying side by side, — a parcel of "mare's-tails" perhaps. It winds up with a flurry of rain.

the other day. C.'s piece was one side of a shallow dish, say an inch and a half deep, four eighths to six eighths of an inch thick, with a sort of ear for handle on one side, — almost a leg. His piece, like mine, looks as if it had been scratched all over on the outside by a nail,  and it is evident that this is the way it was fashioned. It was scratched with some hard, sharp-pointed stone and so crumbled and worn away.

This little knoll was half plowed (through its summit) last fall in order to be cultivated this spring, and the high water standing over all but the apex has for a fortnight been faithfully washing away the soil and leaving the stones — Indian relics and others — exposed. The very roots of the grass, yellowish-brown fibres, are thus washed clean and exposed in considerable quantity there. You could hardly have contrived a better way to separate the arrowheads that lay buried in that sod between the rocks from the sod and soil.

At the Pokelogan up the Assabet, I see my first phœbe, the mild bird. It flirts its tail and sings *pre vit, pre vit, pre vit, pre vit* incessantly, as it sits over the water, and then at last, rising on the last syllable, says *pre-*VEE, as if insisting on that with peculiar emphasis.

The villagers remark how dark and angry the water looks to-day. I think it is because it is a clear and very windy day and the high waves cast much shadow.

Crow blackbirds common.

April 2. P. M. — To Lee's Cliff (walking).

Alders generally appear to be past prime.[1] I see a little snow ice in one place to-day. It is still windy and cool, but not so much so as yesterday. I can always sail either up or down the river with the rudest craft, for the wind always blows more or less with the river valley. But where a blunt wooded cape or hill projects nearly in the direction to which the wind is blowing, I find that it blows in opposite directions off that shore, while there may be quite a lull off the centre. This makes a baffling reach. Generally a high wood close upon the west side of our river, the prevailing winds being northwest, makes such a reach.

There are many fuzzy gnats now in the air, windy as it is. Especially I see them under the lee of the middle Conantum cliff, in dense swarms, all headed one way, but rising and falling suddenly all together as if tossed by the wind. They appear to love best a position just below the edge of the cliff, and to rise constantly high enough to feel the wind from over the edge, and then sink suddenly down again. They are not, perhaps, so thick as they will be, but they are suddenly much thicker than they were, and perhaps their presence affects the arrival of the phœbe, which, I suspect, feeds on them.

From near this cliff, I watch a male sheldrake in the river with my glass. It is very busily pluming itself while it sails about, and from time to time it raises itself upright almost entirely out of water, showing

[1] *Incana* on causeways, *i. e.* the earliest ones. See some same [?] species not open, the 10th.

its rosaceous breast. It is some sixty rods off, yet I can see the red bill distinctly when it is turned against its white body. Soon after I see two more, and one, which I think is not a female, is more gray and far less distinctly black and white than the other. I think it is a young male and that it might be called by some a gray duck. However, if you show yourself within sixty rods, they will fly or swim off, so shy are they. Yet in the fall I sometimes get close upon a young bird, which dashes swiftly across or along the river and dives.

In the wood on top of Lee's Cliff, where the other day I noticed that the chimaphila leaves had been extensively eaten and nibbled off and left on the ground, I find under one small pitch pine tree a heap of the cones which have been stripped of their scales, evidently by the red squirrels, the last winter and fall, they having sat upon some dead limbs above. They were all stripped regularly from the base upward, excepting the five to seven uppermost and barren scales, making a pretty figure like this:—

I counted two hundred and thirty-nine cones under this tree alone, and most of them lay within two feet square upon a mass of the scales one to two inches deep and three or four feet in diameter. There were also many cones under the surrounding pines. Those I counted

Vol. XII

would have made some three quarts or more. These had all been cut off by the squirrels and conveyed to this tree and there stripped and eaten. They appeared to have devoured all the fruit of that pitch pine grove, and probably it was they that nibbled the wintergreen. No fruit grows in vain. The red squirrel harvests the fruit of the pitch pine. His body is about the color of the cone. I should like to get his recipe for taking out pitch, for he must often get his chaps defiled, methinks. These were all fresh cones, the fruit of last year, perhaps. There was a hole in the ground where they lodged by that tree.

I see fly across the pond a rather large hawk, and when at length it turns up am surprised to see a large blackish spot on the under side of each wing, reminding me of the nighthawk. Its wings appeared long and narrow, but it did not show the upper or under side till far off, — sailing [?] so level. What was it?

The bass recently cut down at Miles Swamp, which averages nearly two and a half feet in diameter at the ground, has forty-seven rings, and has therefore grown fast. The black ash is about eighteen inches in diameter and has forty-eight rings. The white ash is about fifteen inches in diameter and has seventy-eight rings.

I see the small botrychium still quite fresh in the open pasture, only a reddish or leathery brown, — some, too, yellow. It is therefore quite evergreen and more than the spleenworts.

As I go down the street just after sunset, I hear many snipe to-night. This sound is annually heard by the

villagers, but always at this hour, *i. e.* in the twilight, — a hovering sound high in the air, — and they do not know what to refer it to. It is very easily imitated by the breath. A sort of shuddering with the breath. It reminds me of calmer nights. Hardly one in a hundred hears it, and perhaps not nearly so many know what creature makes it. Perhaps no one dreamed of snipe an hour ago, but the air seemed empty of such as they; but as soon as the dusk begins, so that a bird's flight is concealed, you hear this peculiar spirit-suggesting sound, now far, now near, heard through and above the evening din of the village. I did not hear one when I returned up the street half an hour later.

April 3. An easterly wind and rain.

P. M. — To White Pond.

C. says he saw a striped snake on the 30th. We go by Clamshell. The water on the meadows is now visibly lowered considerably, and the tops of bushes begin to appear. The high water has stood over and washed down the base of that avalanche of sand from my new ravine, leaving an upright edge a foot high, and as it subsided gradually, it has left various parallel shore-lines, with stones arranged more or less in rows along them, thus forming a regular beach of four or five rods' length.

The bæomyces is in its perfection this rainy day. I have for some weeks been insisting on the beauty and richness of the moist and saturated crust of the earth. It has seemed to me more attractive and living than ever, — a very sensitive cuticle, teeming with life, especially in the rainy days. I have looked on it as the skin of a pard. And on a more close examination I am borne out by discovering, in this now so bright bæomyces and in other earthy lichens and in cladonias, and also in the very interesting and pretty red and yellow stemmed mosses, a manifest sympathy with, and an expression of, the general life of the crust. This early and hardy cryptogamous vegetation is, as it were, a flowering of the crust of the earth. Lichens and these mosses, which depend on moisture, are now most rampant. If you examine it, this brown earth-crust is not dead. We need a popular name for the bæomyces. C. suggests " pink mould." Perhaps " pink shot " or " eggs " would do.

A great many oak leaves have been blown off in the late windy weather. When I disturb a leaf in the woods I find it quite dry within this rainy day. I saw the other day a long winrow of oak leaves, a foot high, washed up on the meadow-edge a quarter of a mile off, opposite Ball's Hill, whence they partly came.

It does not rain hard to-day, but mizzles, with considerable wind, and your clothes are finely bedewed with it even under an umbrella. The rain-drops hanging regularly under each twig of the birches, so full of light, are a very pretty sight as you look forth through the mizzle from under your umbrella. In a hard rain they do not lodge and collect thus.

I hear that Peter Hutchinson hooked a monstrous pickerel at the Holt last winter. It was so large that he could not get his head through the hole, and so they cut another hole close by, and then a narrow channel

from that to the first to pass the line through, but then, when they came to pull on the line, the pickerel gave a violent jerk and escaped. Peter thinks that he must have weighed ten pounds.

Men's minds run so much on work and money that the mass instantly associate all literary labor with a pecuniary reward. They are mainly curious to know how much money the lecturer or author gets for his work. They think that the naturalist takes so much pains to collect plants or animals because he is paid for it. An Irishman who saw me in the fields making a minute in my note-book took it for granted that I was casting up my wages and actually inquired what they came to, as if he had never dreamed of any other use for writing. I might have quoted to him that the wages of sin is death, as the most pertinent answer. "What do you get for lecturing now?" I am occasionally asked. It is the more amusing since I only lecture about once a year out of my native town, often not at all; so that I might as well, if my objects were merely pecuniary, give up the business. Once, when I was walking on Staten Island, looking about me as usual, a man who saw me would not believe me when I told him that I was indeed from New England but was not looking at that region with a pecuniary view, — a view to speculation; and he offered me a handsome bonus if I would sell his farm for him.

I see by the White Pond path many fox-colored sparrows apparently lurking close under the lee side of a wall out of the way of the storm. Their tails near the base are the brightest things of that color — a rich

Vol. XII

cinnamon-brown — that I know. Their note to-day is the *chip* much like a tree sparrow's. We get quite near them.

Near to the pond I see a small hawk, larger than a pigeon hawk, fly past, — a deep brown with a light spot on the side. I think it probable it was a sharp-shinned hawk.

The pond is quite high (like Walden, which, as I noticed the 30th *ult.*, had risen about two feet since January, and perhaps within a shorter period), and the white sand beach is covered. The water being quite shallow on it, it is very handsomely and freshly ripple-marked for a rod or more in width, the ripples only two or three inches apart and very regular and parallel, but occasionally there is a sort of cell a foot long (a split closed at each end) in one. In some parts, indeed, it reminded me of a cellular tissue, but the last foot next the shore had no ripple-marks; apparently they were constantly levelled there. These were most conspicuous where a dark sediment, the dead wood or crumbled leaves, perchance, from the forest, lay in the furrows and contrasted with the white sand. The

cells were much more numerous and smaller in proportion than I represent them.

I find in drawing these ripple-marks that I have drawn precisely such lines as are used to represent a shore on maps, and perchance the sight of these parallel ripple-marks may have suggested that method of drawing a shore-line. I do not believe it, but if we were

to draw such a lake-shore accurately it would be very similar.

April 4. Clear, cold, and very windy; wind northwest.

For a fortnight past, or since the frost began to come out, I have noticed the funnel-shaped holes of the skunk in a great many places and their little mincing tracks in the sand. Many a grub and beetle meets its fate in their stomachs.

Methinks the peculiar and interesting *Brown Season* of the spring lasts from the time the snow generally begins to go off — as this year the fore part of March — till the frost is generally (or entirely?) out. Perhaps it will be through the first week of April this year. Ordinary years it must be somewhat later. The surface of the earth is never so completely saturated with wet as during this period, for the frost a few inches beneath holds all the ice and snow that are melted and the rain, and an unusual amount of rain falls. All plants, therefore, that love moisture and coolness, like mosses and lichens, are in their glory, but also [?] I think that the very withered grass and weeds, being wet, are *blooming* at this season. The conspicuous reddish brown of the fallen brakes is very rich, contrasting with the paler brown of oak leaves.

Such an appetite have we for new life that we begin by nibbling the very crust of the earth. We betray our vegetable and animal nature and sympathies by our delight in water. We rejoice in the full rills, the melting snow, the copious spring rains and the freshets, as if we were frozen earth to be thawed, or lichens and mosses, expanding and reviving under this influence.

The osier bark now, as usual, looks very yellow when wet, and the wild poplar very green.

P. M. — To Cliffs.

Those striped snakes of the 30th were found (several in all) on west side the railroad causeway, on the sand, which is very warm. It would seem, then, that they come out in such places soon after the frost is out. The railroad men who were cutting willows there to set on the sides of the Deep Cut, to prevent the gullying there, came across them.

The epigæa looks as if it would open in two or three days at least,[1] — showing much color and this form: The flower-buds are protected by the withered leaves, oak leaves, which partly cover them, so that you must look pretty sharp to detect the first flower. These plants blossom by main strength, as it were, or the virtue that is in them, — not growing by water, as most early flowers, — in dry copses.

I see several earthworms to-day under the shoe of the pump, on the platform. They may have come up through the cracks from the well where the warm air has kept them stirring.

On the barren railroad causeway, of pure sand, grow chiefly sallows, a few poplars, and sweet-fern and blackberry vines.

When I look with my glass, I see the cold and sheeny snow still glazing the mountains. This it is which makes

[1] *Vide* 12th.

the wind so piercing cold. There are dark and windy clouds on that side, of that peculiar brushy or wispy character — or rather like sheafs — which denotes wind. They only spit a little snow at last, thin and scarcely perceived, like falling gossamer.

April 5. In running a line through a wood-lot in the southwest part of Lincoln to-day, I started from an old pine stump, now mostly crumbled away, though a part of the wood was still hard above ground, which was described in his [*sic*] deed of 1813 (forty-six years ago) as a pine stump. It was on the side of a hill above Deacon Farrar's meadow.

As I stood on a hill just cut off, I saw, half a dozen rods below, the bright-yellow catkins of a tall willow just opened on the edge of the swamp, against the dark-brown twigs and the withered leaves. This early blossom looks bright and rare amid the withered leaves and the generally brown and dry surface, like the early butterflies. This is the most conspicuous of the March flowers (*i. e.* if it chances to be so early as March). It suggests unthought-of warmth and sunniness. It takes but little color and tender growth to make miles of dry brown woodland and swamp look habitable and home-like, as if a man could dwell there.

Mr. Haines, who travelled over the lots with us this very cold and blustering day, was over eighty.

"What raw, blustering weather!" said I to my employer to-day. "Yes," answered he. "Did you see those two sun-dogs on Saturday?" They are a pretty sure sign of cold and windy weather.

Vol. XII

April 6. Another remarkably windy day; cold northwest wind and a little snow spitting from time to time, yet so little that even the traveller might not perceive it.

For nineteen days, from the 19th of March to the 6th of April, both inclusive, we have had remarkably windy weather. For ten days of the nineteen the wind has been remarkably strong and violent, so that each of those days the wind was the subject of general remark. The first one of these ten days was the warmest, the wind being southwest, but the others, especially of late, were very cold, the wind being northwest, and for the most part icy cold. There have also been five days that would be called windy and only four which were moderate. The last seven, including to-day, have all been windy, five of them remarkably so; wind from northwest.[1]

The sparrows love to flit along any thick hedge, like that of Mrs. Gourgas's. Tree sparrows, *F. hyemalis*, and fox-colored sparrows in company.

A fish hawk sails down the river, from time to time almost stationary one hundred feet above the water, notwithstanding the very strong wind.

I see where moles have rooted in a meadow and cast up those little piles of the black earth.

April 7. The Cheney elm looks as if it would shed pollen to-morrow,[2] and the *Salix purpurea* will perhaps within a week.[3]

P. M. — Up Assabet with Pratt.

[1] *Vide* 10th, forward.   [2] No.   [3] *Vide* 13th.

Standing under the north side of the hill, I hear the rather innocent *phe phe, phe phe, phe phe, phe'* of a fish hawk (for it is not a scream, but a rather soft and innocent note), and, looking up, see one come sailing from over the hill. The body looks quite short in proportion to the spread of the wings, which are quite dark or blackish above. He evidently has something in his talons. We soon after disturb him again, and, at length, after circling around over the hill and adjacent fields, he alights in plain sight on one of the half-dead white oaks on the top of the hill, where probably he sat before. As I look through my glass, he is perched on a large dead limb and is evidently standing on a fish (I had noticed something in his talons as he flew), for he stands high and uneasily, finding it hard to keep his balance in the wind. He is disturbed by our neighborhood and does not proceed at once to eat his meal. I see the tail of the fish hanging over the end of the limb. Now and then he pecks at it. I see the white on the crown of the hawk. It is a very large black bird as seen against the sky. Soon he sails away again, carrying his fish, as before, horizontally beneath his body, and he circles about over the adjacent pasture like a hawk hunting, though he can only be looking for a suitable place to eat his fish or waiting for us to be gone.

Looking under the limb on which he was perched, we find a piece of the skin of a sucker (?) or some other scaly fish which a hawk had dropped there long since.

No doubt many a fish hawk has taken his meal on that sightly perch.

It seems, then, that the fish hawk which you see soaring and sailing so leisurely about over the land — for this one soared quite high into the sky at one time — may have a fish in his talons all the while and only be waiting till you are gone for an opportunity to eat it on his accustomed perch.

I told Pratt my theory of the formation of a swamp on a hillside, but he thought that the growth of the alders, etc., there would not make the ground any more moist there, but less so, and stated that the soil (as he had noticed) was drier under rank grass in a mowing-field than at the same depth under a surface of bare and hot sand, because the grass took up the moisture from the soil.

I saw a hole (probably of a woodchuck) partly dug on the east side of the hill, and three or four large stones lay on the fresh sand-heap thrown out, which the woodchuck had pushed up from below. One was about six inches long by four or more wide and might weigh four pounds, and, looking into the hole, whose bottom I could not see, I saw another nearly as large about three feet down, on its way up. I have seen their holes dug in much worse places than this. This hole sloped downward at a considerable angle, so that the stones had to be pushed up a steep slope.

A small hawk flies swiftly past on the side of the hill, swift and low, apparently the same as that of April 3d, a deep rusty brown.

The woodchuck probably digs in a stony place that he may be the more secure.

Vol. XII

I hear there the hovering note of a snipe at 4.30 P. M., — unusually early in the day.[1]

Find a *Sternothærus odoratus* so far from water on Simon Brown's knoll, where water has not been since about March 20th, that I think he was then washed and left there and has since lain in the ground. There are two or three small leeches on him, which may have adhered to him all winter. The white man's relics in the fields are like the Indian's, — pipes, pottery, and (instead of arrowheads) bullets.

April 8. *Friday.* I believe that I rarely hear the nuthatch's note from the elms toward evening, for when I heard it yesterday evening I was surprised.

P. M. — To epigæa and Well Meadow.

I see on the west side of the railroad causeway a peculiar early willow, now just beginning to bloom with the common *Salix discolor* there, perhaps (as I remember) some thirty rods beyond the wall, against A. Wheeler's land. The catkins (sterile) are peculiarly long and tapering, and grayish or mouse-color, beginning to open low on one side, while the points have comparatively little down on  them. I find no description of it. Perhaps rather more than one inch long. The most decidedly opening first on one side near the base of any. Call it the gray bodkin-pointed.

As I stood by the foot of a middling-sized white pine

[1] Also the next day at 9 A. M. as much as ever, through the wind !

the other day, on Fair Haven Hill, one of the very windy days, I felt the ground rise and fall under my feet, being lifted by the roots of the pine, which was waving in the wind; so loosely are they planted.

We have had two more windy days, this and yesterday, though less so than the previous ones. We have had, most of the time, during this windy weather for a month past, when the wind was northwest, those peculiar brushy clouds which look as if a little snow or rain was falling in the northwest, but they prove to be wind chiefly. It has not rained, I think, with the wind in that quarter.

These windy days the sparrows resort to the pines and peach trees on the east side of our house for shelter, and there they sing all together, — tree sparrows, fox-colored sparrows, and song sparrows. The *F. hyemalis* with them do not sing so much of late. The first two are most commonly heard together, the fine canary-like twitter of the tree sparrow appearing to ripen or swell from time to time into the clear, rich whistle of the fox-colored sparrow, so that most refer both notes to one bird.

What a pitiful business is the fur trade, which has been pursued now for so many ages, for so many years by famous companies which enjoy a profitable monopoly and control a large portion of the earth's surface, unweariedly pursuing and ferreting out small animals by the aid of all the loafing class tempted by rum and money, that you may rob some little fellow-creature of its coat to adorn or thicken your own, that you may get a fashionable covering in which to hide your head,

or a suitable robe in which to dispense justice to your fellow-men ! Regarded from the philosopher's point of view, it is precisely on a level with rag and bone picking in the streets of the cities. The Indian led a more respectable life before he was tempted to debase himself so much by the white man. Think how many musquash and weasel skins the Hudson's Bay Company pile up annually in their warehouses, leaving the bare red carcasses on the banks of the streams throughout all British America, — and this it is, chiefly, which makes it *British* America. It is the place where Great Britain goes a-mousing. We have heard much of the wonderful intelligence of the beaver, but that regard for the beaver is all a pretense, and we would give more for a beaver hat than to preserve the intelligence of the whole race of beavers.

When we see men and boys spend their time shooting and trapping musquash and mink, we cannot but have a poorer opinion of them, unless we thought meanly of them before. Yet the world is imposed on by the fame of the Hudson's Bay and Northwest Fur Companies, who are only so many partners more or less in the same sort of business, with thousands of just such loafing men and boys in their service to abet them. On the one side is the Hudson's Bay Company, on the other the company of scavengers who clear the sewers of Paris of their vermin. There is a good excuse for smoking out or poisoning rats which infest the house, but when they are as far off as Hudson's Bay, I think that we had better let them alone. To such an extent do time and distance, and our imaginations, consecrate at last not only the most ordinary, but even vilest pursuits. The efforts of legislation from time to time to stem the torrent are significant as showing that there is some sense and conscience left, but they are insignificant in their effects. We will fine Abner if he shoots a singing bird, but encourage the army of Abners that compose the Hudson's Bay Company.

One of the most remarkable sources of profit opened to the Yankee within a year is the traffic in skunk-skins. I learn from the newspapers — as from other sources (*vide* Journal of Commerce in *Tribune* for April 5, 1859) — that "the traffic in skunk-skins has suddenly become a most important branch of the fur trade, and the skins of an animal which three years ago were deemed of no value whatever, are now in the greatest demand." "The principal markets are Russia and Turkey, though some are sent to Germany, where they are sold at a large profit." Furs to Russia! "The black skins are valued the most, and during the past winter the market price has been as high as one dollar per skin, while mottled skins brought only seventy cents." "Upward of 50,000 of these skins have been shipped from this city [New York] alone within the past two months." Many of them "are designed for the Leipsic sales, Leipsic being next to Novgorod, in Russia, the most important fur *entrepôt* in Europe. The first intimation received in this market of the value of this new description of fur came from the Hudson's Bay Company, which, having shipped a few to London at a venture, found the returns so profitable that

they immediately prosecuted the business on an extensive scale." "The heaviest collections are made in the Middle and Eastern States, in some parts of which the mania for capturing these animals seems to have equalled the Western Pike's Peak gold excitement, men, women, and children turning out *en masse* for that purpose." And beside, " our fur dealers also receive a considerable sum for the *fat* of these animals!!"

Almost all smile, or otherwise express their contempt, when they hear of this or the rat-catching of Paris, but what is the difference between catching and skinning the skunk and the mink? It is only in the name. When you pass the palace of one of the managers of the Hudson's Bay Company, you are reminded that so much he got for his rat-skins. In such a snarl and contamination do we live that it is almost impossible to keep one's skirts clean. Our sugar and cotton are stolen from the slave, and if we jump out of the fire, it is wont to be into the frying-pan at least. It will not do to be thoughtless with regard to any of our valuables or property. When you get to Europe you will meet the most tender-hearted and delicately bred lady, perhaps the President of the Antislavery Society, or of that for the encouragement of humanity to animals, marching or presiding with the scales from a tortoise's back — obtained by laying live coals on it to make them curl up — stuck in her hair, rat-skin fitting as close to her fingers as erst to the rat, and, for her cloak, trimmings perchance adorned with the spoils of a hundred skunks, — rendered inodorous, we trust. Poor mis-

guided woman! Could she not wear other armor in the war of humanity?

When a new country like North America is discovered, a few feeble efforts are made to Christianize the natives before they are all exterminated, but they are not found to pay, in any sense. But the energetic traders of the discovering country organize themselves, or rather inevitably crystallize, into a vast rat-catching society, tempt the natives to become mere vermin-hunters and rum-drinkers, reserving half a continent for the field of their labors. Savage meets savage, and the white man's only distinction is that he is the chief.

She says to the turtle basking on the shore of a distant isle, " I want your scales to adorn my head" (though fire be used to raise them); she whispers to the rats in the wall, " I want your skins to cover my delicate fingers; " and, meeting an army of a hundred skunks in her morning walk, she says, " worthless vermin, strip off your cloaks this instant, and let me have them to adorn my robe with; " and she comes home with her hands muffled in the pelt of a gray wolf that ventured abroad to find food for its young that day.

When the question of the protection of birds comes up, the legislatures regard only a low use and never a high use; the best-disposed legislators employ one, perchance, only to examine their crops and see how many grubs or cherries they contain, and never to study their dispositions, or the beauty of their plumage, or listen and report on the sweetness of their song. The legislature will preserve a bird professedly not because it is a beautiful creature, but because it is a good sca-

venger or the like. This, at least, is the defense set up. It is as if the question were whether some celebrated singer of the human race — some Jenny Lind or another — did more harm or good, should be destroyed, or not, and therefore a committee should be appointed, not to listen to her singing at all, but to examine the contents of her stomach and see if she devoured anything which was injurious to the farmers and gardeners, or which they cannot spare.[1]

Cold as it is, and has been for several weeks, in all exposed places, I find it unexpectedly warm in perfectly sheltered places where the sun shines. And so it always is in April. The cold wind from the northwest seems distinct and separable from the air here warmed by the sun, and when I sit in some warm and sheltered hollow in the woods, I feel the cold currents drop into it from time to time, just as they are seen to ripple a small lake in such a situation from time to time.

The epigæa is not quite out. The earliest peculiarly woodland herbaceous flowers are epigæa, anemone, thalictrum, and — by the first of May — *Viola pedata*. These grow quite in the woods amid dry leaves, nor do they depend so much on water as the very earliest flowers. I am, perhaps, more surprised by the growth of the *Viola pedata* leaves, by the side of paths amid the shrub oaks and half covered with oak leaves, than by any other growth, the situation is so dry and the surrounding bushes so apparently lifeless.

I noticed the other day a leaf on a young oak very

[1] *Vide* April 21st.

rapidly revolving like a windmill, in the wind, not around its midrib for an axis, but about its broken stem, and I saw that this was the way those curiously broken and twisted and splintered petioles were made. It went round so fast as almost to appear like a circular figure.

I find that the cress (*Cardamine hirsuta*) which was so forward at Well Meadow a fortnight ago has been almost entirely browsed off by some creature, so that, if I had not detected it, I might have been surprised that it made no more show. The skunk-cabbage leaf-buds, which have just begun to unroll, also have been extensively eaten off as they were yet rolled up like cigars. These early greens of the swamp are thus kept down. Is it by the rabbit? I could see the tracks of some animal, apparently as large, very indistinct in the mud and water. Also an early kind of sedge there was cropped. The only animals at all likely to have done this are rabbits, musquash, woodchuck (though I doubt if the last has been about here long enough), and geese. Of these, I think it most likely to have been the first, and probably it was the same that gnawed the spathes and ate up the spadix of the cabbage some weeks ago. Woodchucks might nibble some plants now in warmer and drier places. These earliest greens must be very acceptable to these animals. Do partridges ever eat these things?

The *Alnus serrulata* is evidently in its prime considerably later than the *incana*, for those of the former which I notice to-day have scarcely begun, while the latter chance to be done. The fertile flowers are an interesting bright crimson in the sun.

C. says that he found a musquash's skull (which he showed me) at the fox-burrow in Laurel Glen, from which it would appear that they kill the musquash.

See the first bay-wing hopping and flitting along the railroad bank, but hear no note as yet.

I saw Heavy Haynes fishing for trout down the Mill Brook this morning, cold and blustering as it was. He caught two. He is splitting pine-knots at the almshouse door for spearing. Has already been spearing in Walden, and got some pickerel, all in the two little meadows there, and saw some pouts and perch. So the pickerel have come into those meadows, probably since January, for the bars were dry before. Perhaps they lie in shallow water, not for warmth, — for it is coldest there by night now, — but for food, the early insects and frogs which may soonest be found there!

April 9. P. M. — To Goose Pond.

The wind is as strong, and yet colder, being more from the north, than before. Through, I think, all this windy weather, or at least for about three weeks, the wind has regularly gone down with the sun, strong as it has been each day.

As we go up the hill in the woods east of Hubbard's Close, I hear a singular sound through the roaring of the wind amid the trees, which I think at first some creature forty rods off, but it proves to be the creaking of one bough on another. When I knew what it was I was surprised to find it so near, even within a rod. It was occasioned by two little dead limbs, an inch or less in diameter, on two different white pines

which stood four or five feet apart, — such limbs as are seen on every white pine below the living ones, some twelve feet from the ground. These with every motion of the trees in the wind were grating back and forth on each other, and had worn into one another, and this produced, not a mere coarse, grating sound, but a perfect viol sound, such as I never heard from trees before, — a jarring or vibratory creak, as if the bow leaped on the strings, for one limb was bow and the other string. It was on one key or note when the trees approached, and quite another and very fine and sharp when they receded. I raised one limb with a pole, and the music ceased. This was as musical as a viol, a forest viol, which might have suggested that instrument to some Orpheus wandering in the wood. He would only have to place a box of resonant wood beneath to complete a simple viol. We heard several others afterward which made a coarse, squeaking noise like a bird, but this would have suggested music to any one. It was mythologic, and an Indian might have referred it to a departed spirit. The fiddles made by the trees whose limbs cross one another, — played on by the wind! When we listened, in the wood, we heard all kinds of creaking and groaning sounds from the laboring trees.

We go seeking the south sides of hills and woods, or deep hollows, to walk in this cold and blustering day. We sit by the side of Little Goose Pond, which C. calls Ripple Lake or Pool, to watch the ripples on it. Now it is nearly smooth, and then there drops down on to it, deep as it lies amid the hills, a sharp and nar-

row blast of the icy north wind careering above, striking it, perhaps, by a point or an edge, and swiftly spreading along it, making a dark-blue ripple. Now four or five windy bolts, sharp or blunt, strike it at once and spread different ways. The boisterous but playful north wind evidently stoops from a considerable height to dally with this fair pool which it discerns beneath. You could sit there and watch these blue shadows playing over the surface like the light and shade on changeable silk, for hours. It reminds me, too, of the swift Camilla on a field [of] grain. The wind often touches the water only by the finest points or edges. It is thus when you look in some measure from the sun, but if you move round so as to come more opposite to him, then all these dark-blue ripples are all sparkles too bright to look at, for you now see the sides of the wavelets which reflect the sun to you.

A large fox-hole in Britton's hollow, lately dug; an ox-cartload of sand, or more, thrown up on the hillside.

Watching the ripples fall and dash across the surface of low-lying and small woodland lakes is one of the amusements of these windy March and April days. It is only on small lakes deep sunk in hollows in the woods that you can see or study them these days, for the winds sweep over the whole breadth of larger lakes incessantly, but they only touch these sheltered lakelets by fine points and edges from time to time.

And then there is such a fiddling in the woods, such a viol-creaking of bough on bough, that you would think music was being born again, as in the days of

Orpheus. Orpheus and Apollo are certainly there taking lessons; aye, and the jay and the blackbird, too, learn now where they stole their "thunder." They are perforce silent, meditating new strains.

When the playful breeze drops on the pool, it springs to right and left, quick as a kitten playing with dead leaves, clapping her paw on them. Sometimes it merely raises a single wave at one point, as if a fish darted near the surface. While to you looking down from a hillside partly from the sun, these points and dashes look thus dark-blue, almost black, they are seen by another, standing low and more opposite to the sun, as the most brilliant sheeny and sparkling surface, too bright to look at. Thus water agitated by the wind is both far brighter and far darker than smooth water, seen from this side or that, — that is, as you look at the inclined surface of the wave which reflects the sun, or at the shaded side. For three weeks past, when I have looked northward toward the flooded meadows they have looked dark-blue or blackish, in proportion as the day was clear and the wind high from the northwest, making high waves and much shadow.

We can sit in the deep hollows in the woods, like Frosty Hollow near Ripple Lake, for example, and find it quite still and warm in the sun, as if a different atmosphere lurked there; but from time to time a cold puff from the rude Boreas careering overhead drops on us, and reminds us of the general character of the day. While we lie at length on the dry sedge, nourishing spring thoughts, looking for insects, and counting the rings on old stumps.

These old gray or whitish stumps, with their porous structure where the ducts are seen, are very much like bones, — the bones of trees. I break a little cube out of this old oak stump, which was sawed off some thirty years ago, and which has about one hundred rings, — a piece sharply square-cornered and exactly the form of a square bunch of matches; and, the sawed end being regularly channelled by time in the direction of the ducts and of the silver grain, it looks precisely like the loose ends, or dipped end of the bunch, and would be mistaken for such on any shelf.

Those ripple lakes lie now in the midst of mostly bare brown or tawny dry woodlands, themselves the most living objects. They may say to the first woodland flowers, We played with the north winds here before ye were born.[1]

April 10. A calm day at last, the water almost smooth and now so low that I cannot cross the meadows. So ends the spring freshet (apparently), which began (not to include the winter one) March 8th and was at its height the 17th and 18th. It has lasted a month, and to-day, too, ends the windy spell. Since the 6th (*q. v.*) there have been two days, the 7th and 8th, of strong northwest wind, and one, the 9th, of very strong and yet colder and more northerly wind than before. This makes twenty-two days of windy weather in all, reckoning only from the last still days (the 17th and 18th of March) and not including to-day. Of these, eleven days have been of very strong and cold northwest wind,

[1] [Channing, p. 95.]

Vol. XII

the last, or yesterday, more northerly, — except the first, when the wind was southwest, — seven of strong wind and generally northwest, and four only of moderate wind. We had rain on the 18th, 22d, 24th, 25th, 29th of March, and 3d of April, and always with an easterly or southerly wind; or as often as the wind came from the east or south it brought rain, with generally considerable wind driving it, and it invariably cleared off cold with a wind from the northwest. The wind has regularly gone down with the sun, and risen again with it. It has been so strong as to interfere with all outdoor occupations. Yet I have not observed a single tree which was blown down by it.

P. M. — Paddle to Well Meadow.

I see some remarkable examples of meadow-crust floated off on the A. Wheeler meadow and above, densely covered with button-bushes and willows, etc. One sunk in five feet of water on a sandy shore, which I must examine again.

I hear of a cinquefoil found in bloom on the 8th. It was in this sprout-land, where it was protected. This, with bluets, mouse-ear, and *Viola ovata* (of the herbaceous plants), I should call pasture flowers (among those of March and April).

I might class the twenty-two herbaceous flowers which I have known to be open before the first of May thus: —

Garden flowers	Chickweed and shepherd's-purse.
Meadow flowers	Skunk-cabbage, caltha, chrysosplenium, dandelion, strawberry, *Viola cucullata*, *Ranunculus repens* (?).
Rock flowers	Saxifrage, crowfoot, columbine, and tower-mustard.

Woodland flowers	Epigæa, anemone, and thalictrum.
Pasture flowers	Cinquefoil, bluets, mouse-ear, and *Viola sagittata*.
Water flowers	*Callitriche verna* and nuphar.

The woody plants — trees and shrubs — might be arranged under three heads, *viz.* : —

Wet Land		*Dry Land*	*Intermediate*
Alders, both (?)		Aspens	Elms
White maple		Hazels	Red maple
Most willows		Arbutus	Peach
Sweet-gale	(?)	Arbor-vitæ	Abele
Benzoin		Red cedar	Cultivated cherry
Cassandra		Fir-balsam	
White alder [?]		(?) Sweet-fern	
Larch		Shad-bush	
		Salix humilis	
		S. tristis	
		S. rostrata	
		Yew	

The hellebore buds [?] are quite conspicuous and interesting to-day, but not at all unrolled, though six or eight inches high.

The *Alnus serrulata* appears to grow on drier land than the other sometimes.

See a kingfisher flying very low, in the ricochet manner, across the water. Sheldrakes and gulls and black ducks still.

Hear the first stuttering frog croak — probably *halecina* — in the last Cassandra Pond.

April 11. Rain all day.

April 12. Clears up in afternoon.
P. M. — Paddle to Cliffs.
I saw a minnow on the 10th which looked like a

young brook minnow, not one inch long. When was it spawned?

The small alder (*A. serrulata*) is sometimes yellow-flowered, sometimes reddish-flowered. It grows with the *incana* at Cardinal Shore.

I see where the musquash has eaten the white base of the pontederia leaves. I first perceived the pickerel dart on the 10th, the river having gone down so much that you could not cross the meadows, and that being the first really warm and pleasant day since March 17th.

Saw a duck, apparently a sheldrake, at the northeast end of Cyanean Meadow. It disappeared at last by diving, and I could not find it. But I saw what looked like a ripple made by the wind, which moved slowly down the river at least forty rods toward the shore and there disappeared. Though I saw no bird there, I suspect that the ripple was made by it. Two sheldrakes flew away from this one when first observed. Why did this remain? Was it wounded? Or can those which dart so swiftly across the river and dive be another species and not the young of the season or females of the common one? Is it not, after all, the red-breasted merganser, and did I not see them in Maine?

I see half a dozen sheldrakes very busily fishing around the base of Lupine Hill or Promontory. There are two full-plumaged males and the rest females, or perhaps some of them young males. They are coasting along swiftly with their bodies sunk low and their heads half under, looking for their prey, one behind another, frequently turning and passing over the same ground

again. Their crests are very conspicuous, thus: When one sees a fish he at first swims rapidly after it, and then, if necessary, flies close over the water after it, and this excites all the rest to follow, swimming or flying, and if one seizes the fish, which I suspect is commonly a pickerel, they all pursue the lucky fisher, and he makes the water fly far in his efforts to get away and gulp down his fish. I can see the fish in his bill all the while, and he must swallow it very skillfully and quickly, if at all. I was first attracted to them by seeing these great birds rushing, shooting, thus swiftly through the air and water and throwing the water high about them. Sometimes they dive and swim quietly beneath, looking for their game. At length they spy me or my boat, and [I] hear a faint quack indicative of alarm, and suddenly all arise and go off. In the meanwhile I see two black ducks sailing with them along the shore. These look considerably smaller, and of course carry their heads more erect. They have a raw, gosling look beside the others, and I see their light bills against their dusky necks and heads. At length, when I get near them, I hear their peculiar quack also, and off they go. The sheldrakes appear to be a much more lively bird than the black duck. How different from the waddling domestic duck! The former are all alive, eagerly fishing, quick as thought, as they need to be to catch a pickerel.

I look again at the meadow-crust carried off by the ice. There is one by the railroad bridge, say three rods by one, covered with button-bushes and willows. Another, some five rods by three, at the south end of

Vol. XII

Potter Swamp Meadow, also covered densely with button-bushes, etc. It is far from the river, by the edge of the wood. Another, and the most interesting one, lies up high some thirty rods north of this near the wood-side and fifteen rods from the river. I measure it with a tape. It is rudely triangular and about four rods on a side, though the sides are longer on the convex line. As well as the other, it is from one to three feet thick and very densely covered with button-bushes, with a few black and other willows and late roses from four to seven feet high. As dense and impassable as any kind of thicket that we have, and there are, besides, countless great yellow and white lily and pontederia roots in it. It is a large and densely bushy island in the meadow. It would surprise any one to behold it. Suppose that you were to find in the morning such a slice of the earth's crust with its vegetation dropped in your front yard, if it could contain it. I think we should not soon hear the last of it. It is an island such as might almost satisfy Sancho Panza's desires. It is a forest, in short, and not a very small one either. It is Birnam wood come to Dunsinane. It contained at least eight square rods.

There was another piece covered in like manner, some five rods long and three wide, sunk off Cardinal Shore on a hard sandy bottom, and so deep that its whole size did not appear above water. I could not touch the bottom with my oars on the outside. This no one would have detected for an immigrant or new-come land unless very familiar with the shore, for if the raw edge is concealed it looks exactly as if it grew

there like the others near by. There was a strip without anything but grass on it, some five rods long by twenty feet wide, and two pieces making as much more in length end to end with it on the [*sic*]. In all there must have been from a third to half an acre on this single meadow, which came from far up-stream, I could not tell from where. I saw more up the stream, and they were all dropped nearly in a line on the east side for half a mile or more.

Such revolutions can take place and none but the proprietor of the meadow notice it, for the traveller passing within sight does not begin to suspect that the bushy island which he sees in the meadow has floated from elsewhere, or if he saw it when on its voyage, he would not know it for a voyager. In one year all the raw edge is concealed, and the vegetation thus transplanted does not appear to find it out. These must have been carried off about the 16th of March or when the river broke up, perhaps in that strong southwest wind of the 19th. The ice, being eighteen or twenty inches thick and having ten thousand strong handles to take hold by, aided too often by the lightness of the frozen meadow, can easily lift these masses, and if there were rocks imbedded in them, would move them also. For the cake of ice may be a dozen rods or more in breadth. These have generally grounded high on the meadows, where the lilies, etc., will all die. Indeed, most of them have already been killed by frost, and probably the button[-bush] will much of it die too. Also that which has sunk in deep water will die. I saw one piece a rod wide nearly in the middle of the river, and detected it only by the top [of] a few twigs seen above the surface. The willows or osiers will do well, and the roses, wherever they may lodge on the banks or in the meadow, but the button-bush must stand immediately on the edge of the river or other water, and there they are most likely to be placed.

The present islands, bushy or wooded, in the meadow have no doubt commonly had this origin. The soil is there doubled, and so elevated, and the plants set out at the same time. The surface being at once elevated one to three feet for four rods or more, though the button-bush dies, willows will live and maples and alders, etc., spring up there. When the flood comes with icy hands you have got a mighty lifter at work. Black willows ten feet high and these four or five rods of button-bushes are all taken up together with their soil and carried upright and without jarring to a new locality half a mile or more distant.

I observe that different meadows are at different levels above the river. The great Sudbury meadows are low. Cyanean Meadow is generally higher than the ammannia meadow. I can cross the last still, but not the first. The surface has been much taken off the last by the ice, and perhaps more has lodged on the other. Mantatuket Meadow appears to be about the height of Cyanean Meadow generally, or hardly so low. The Potter Swamp Meadow is lower than any that I have named in Concord. Perhaps those valleys parallel with the river are where the water has swept off the meadow-crust the most, and not old channels? It is evident that this transportation of the meadow

surface affects the relative height of the meadows very much.

Some meadows are now saved by the causeways and bridges and willow-rows. Though there were a hundred pieces in Potter Swamp Meadow, there were none in the meadow this side the causeway. Probably more meadow, etc., was transported two hundred years ago than to-day there, when the river, at high water especially, was less obstructed. This is the origin of almost all inequalities of surface in the meadows, and it is impossible to say how many of the clumps of bushes you see there have been thus transplanted.

As for that mass which sunk in deep water off Cardinal Shore, the cake of ice which transported it may have struck the shore many rods from its burden and melted in that position.

Consider what a new arrangement of the clumps in the mead is thus made every year. The revolution from each source is now confined to the space between two causeways and bridges, or two willow-rows, while formerly it was only confined by the form or dimensions of the meadow.

I find, on that most interesting mass of meadow and button-bushes, or the top of a sort of musquash-mound, a very peculiar stercus, precisely like a human one in size and form and color externally, so that I took it for such. But it was nearly inodorous and contained some fish-scales, and it was about the color of fireproof-brick dust within. I think it was that of an otter, quite fresh.

I hear that the epigæa is no more forward than on the 8th.

Vol. XII

Pine warblers heard in the woods by C. to-day. This, except the pigeon woodpecker and pigeon and hawks, as far as they are migratory, is the first that I should call woodland (or dry woodland) birds that arrives. The red-wings generally sit on the black willows and the swamp white oaks and maples by the water, and sing *o-gurgle-ee* this evening, as if glad to see the river's brink appearing again and smooth waters also. The grackles are feeding on the meadow-edge.

April 13. A little snow fell on the 11th with the rain, and on some very warm banks, the south sides of houses and hills, the grass looked quite green by contrast in spots.

The streets are strewn with the bud-scales of the elm, which they, opening, have lost off, and their tops present a rich brown already. I hear a purple finch on one, and did I not hear a martin's[1] rich warble also? The birds are not so early now as I should have expected. Were they not deterred from coming north by the very strong and cold northwest wind, notwithstanding that the ground has been bare so long? The *Salix purpurea* will hardly open for five days yet.[2]

P. M. — Paddle to Ball's Hill and sail back.

I see the small botrychium fresh and yellow still, so it is as much an evergreen as any fern.

It is pleasant and pretty warm. To-day is the awakening of the meadows now partly bare. I hear the stuttering note of probably the *Rana halecina* (see one by shore) come up from all the Great Meadow,

[1] Probably a white-bellied swallow.   [2] *Vide* 22d.

especially the sedgy parts, or where the grass was not cut last year and now just peeps above the surface. There is something soothing and suggestive of halcyon days in this low but universal breeding-note of the frog. Methinks it is a more unmistakable evidence of warmer weather — of the warmest we have at this date — than almost anything else. The hylodes and wood frogs are other degrees on the thermometer of the season, indicating that the weather has attained a higher temperature than before and winter fairly ended, but *this* note marks what you may call April heat (or spring heat).

I see no ducks on the meadows to-day, perhaps because there is so much less water and it is so fair.

Saw a great bird flying rather low and circling more or less over the Great Meadows, which I at first thought was a fish hawk, having a fair sight of it from Ball's Hill, but with my glass I saw that it was a gull, but, I should say, wholly slate-color and dark at that, — though there may have been small spots which made no impression of another color. It was at least as large, maybe larger than the herring gull. Was it the saddle-back gull?

Is that a potamogeton, or a pontederia, or a sium, coming up so thickly now on the bottom of the river near the shore, especially on a grassy bottom, with two little roundish leafets becoming spatulate, and a seed triangular and pointed with one side more flat than the others?

April 14. Wind was easterly yesterday; hence snow

and rain to-day. I think that this is the seventh rain-storm (as I reckon), beginning with the 18th of March, which resulted from the wind becoming easterly on the previous day, after having been in each instance but one northwest the day before, and that once the previous day was quite calm.

There are many worm holes or piles in the door-yard this forenoon. How long?

Transplanting currant bushes to-day, I find that, though the leaf-buds have not begun to open, white shoots have shot up from the bottom of the stocks two to four inches, far below the surface as yet, and I think that they have felt the influence of the season, not merely through the thawed ground, but through that portion of the plant above ground. There is this growth at the root in early spring, preceding any visible growth above ground.

April 15. Ground white with snow this morning, but it melts in a few hours, and, the sun coming out, I observe, after it is gone, much bluish vapor curling up from plowed ground, looking like a smoke there, but not from ground not recently plowed or from grass ground. Is it that the plowed ground is warmer, or merely that it has absorbed more moisture? Perhaps the sun penetrates it and so warms it more, since it lies up lighter. It is a very noticeable phenomenon, at any rate, that only the ground just plowed thus smokes.

P. M. — To Cliffs and Well Meadow.

There is quite a shimmer in the air, the day being

pretty warm, but methinks it is a little greater over plowed ground than over sod, but I see it in woods as high as the tree-tops. M. [?] Pratt refers it chiefly to heat, as about a stove, and thinks I should [see] the most over the driest sand, and it occurs to me that if it is chiefly owing to evaporation I ought to see considerable over water, but I believe that I do not. Carpenter refers it (in part, at least) to the exhalation of plants, but they are not now exhaling, — not leafed or leafing as yet. I am uncertain, therefore, whether to regard [*sic*] the earliest shimmer in the spring, on pleasant days, to heated air in motion or to vapor raised by heat into the air. (*Vide* back to April 10th.)

I see and hear white-bellied swallows as they are zigzagging through the air with their loud and lively notes. I am pretty sure it was these and not the martin I heard on the 13th.

The bay-wing now sings — the first I have been able to hear — both about the Texas house and the fields this side of Hayden's, both of them similar dry and open pastures. I heard it just before noon, when the sun began to come out, and at 3 P. M., singing loud and clear and incessantly. It sings with a pleasing deliberation, contrasting with the spring vivacity of the song sparrow, whose song many would confound it with. It comes to revive with its song the dry uplands and pastures and grass-fields about the skirts of villages. Only think how finely our life is furnished in all its details, — sweet wild birds provided to fill its interstices with song! It is provided that while we are employed in our corporeal, or intellectual, or other,

Vol. XII

exercises we shall be lulled and amused or cheered by the singing of birds. When the laborer rests on his spade to-day, the sun having just come out, he is not left wholly to the mercy of his thoughts, nature is not a mere void to him, but he can hardly fail to hear the pleasing and encouraging notes of some newly arrived bird. The strain of the grass finch is very likely to fall on his ear and convince him, whether he is conscious of it or not, that the world is beautiful and life a fair enterprise to engage in. It will make him calm and contented. If you yield for a moment to the impressions of sense, you hear some bird giving expression to its happiness in a pleasant strain. We are provided with singing birds and with ears to hear them. What an institution that! Nor are we obliged to catch and cage them, nor to be bird-fanciers in the common sense. Whether a man's work be hard or easy, whether he be happy or unhappy, a bird is appointed to sing to a man while he is at his work.

Consider how much is annually spent on the farmer's life: the beauty of his abode, which has inspired poets since the world was made; the hundreds of delicate and beautiful flowers scattered profusely under his feet and all around him, as he walks or drives his team afield, — he cannot put his spade into uncultivated, nor into much cultivated, ground without disturbing some of them; a hundred or two of equally beautiful birds to sing to him morning and evening, and some at noonday, a good part of the year; a perfect sky arched over him, a perfect carpet spread under him, etc., etc.! And can the farmer speak or think carelessly

of these gifts? Will he find it in his heart to curse the flowers and shoot the birds?

Hear a goldfinch, after a loud mewing on an apple tree, sing in a rich and varied way, as if imitating some other bird.

Observe in the small shallow rills in the sandy road beyond the Smallpox Burying-Ground, made by the snow of the morning, now melted, very interesting ripples over a pebbly or uneven bottom on this side or that. The beauty of these little ripples was occasioned by their shadows amid the bright water. They were so arranged with remarkable order as to resemble the bright scales of a portion of a snake's skin, thus: with geometrical regularity, seven or eight parallel rows in a triangular form, successively diminishing in size. The ripple is occasioned merely by the impetuosity of the water meeting some slight obstacle. Thus you see in the very ripples on a rill a close resemblance in arrangement to the bright scales of a fish, and it [would] greatly help to conceal a fish if it could lie under them. The water was generally less than an inch deep on a sandy bottom.

The warm pine woods are all alive this afternoon with the jingle of the pine warbler, the for the most part invisible minstrel. That wood, for example, at the Punk Oak, where we sit to hear it. It is surprising how quickly the earth, which was covered half an inch deep this morning, and since so wet, has become comparatively dry, so that we sit on the ground or on the dry leaves in woods at 3 P. M. and smell the pines and see and hear the flies, etc., buzz about, though the sun did not come out till 12 m. This morning, the aspect of winter; at mid-forenoon, the ground reeking with moisture; at 3 p. m., sit on dry leaves and hear the flies buzz and smell the pines! That wood is now very handsome seen from the westerly side, the sun falling far through it, though some trunks are wholly in shade. This warbler impresses me as if it were calling the trees to life. I think of springing twigs. Its jingle rings through the wood at short intervals, as if, like an electric shock, it imparted a fresh spring life to them.[1] You hear the same bird, now here now there, as it incessantly flits about, commonly invisible and uttering its simple jingle on very different keys, and from time to time a companion is heard farther or nearer. This is a peculiarly summer-like sound. Go to a warm pine wood-side on a pleasant day at this season after storm, and hear it ring with the jingle of the pine warbler.

As I sit on the stump of a large white pine which was sawed off, listening to these warblers, in a warm sun, I see a fair-weather cloud going over rather low, and hear the flies buzz about me, and it reminds me of those long-drawn summer days when you lie out-of-doors and are more related to the clouds travelling over. The summer clouds, the thunder-cloud especially, are nearer to us than the clouds of winter.

When we go huckleberrying, the clouds are our fellow-travellers, to greet or avoid. I might say the clouds have come. I perceive that I am in the same apartment with them.

[1] [Channing, p. 95.]

Going up a mountain is like travelling half a day through a tan-yard, till you get into a fog, and then, when the fog blows away, you discover yourself and a buzzing fly on the sunny mountain-top.

The wood thrush! At Well Meadow Head. Not being prepared to hear it, I thought it a boy whistling at first. Also a catbird mews?[1]

The epigæa opened, apparently, the 13th.

April 16. Sheldrakes yet on Walden, but I have not identified a whistler for several weeks, — three or more.

April 17. *Sunday.* P. M. — Up Assabet.

The river, which had got down on the 10th so that I could not cross the meadows, is up again on account of snow and rain, so that I push with difficulty straight to Mantatuket's Rock, but, I believe, is already falling. Many grackles and robins are feeding on those strips of meadow just laid bare. It is still rather cold and windy, and I listen for new birds under the lee of the Rock woods in vain; but I hear the hum of bees on a willow there, and this fine susurrus makes the weather seem warmer than it is. At the same time I hear the low stuttering of the *Rana halecina* from the Hunt meadow (call it the Winthrop meadow).

How pleasing and soothing are some of the first and least audible sounds of awakened nature in the spring, as this first humming of bees, etc., and the stuttering of frogs! They cannot be called musical, — are no

[1] Could this have been a goldfinch? (Not seen.)

Vol. XII

more even than a noise, so slight that we can endure it. But it is in part an expression of happiness, an ode that is sung and whose burden fills the air. It reminds me of the increased genialness of nature. The air which was so lately void and silent begins to resound as it were with the breathing of a myriad fellow-creatures, and even the unhappy man, on the principle that misery loves company, is soothed by this infinite din of neighbors. I have listened for the notes of various birds, and now, in this faint hum of bees, I hear as it were the first twittering of the bird Summer. Go ten feet that way, to where the northwest wind comes round the hill, and you hear only the dead mechanical sound of the blast and your thoughts recur to winter, but stand as much this way in the sun and in the lee of this bush, and your charmed ears may hear this faint susurrus weaving the web of summer. The notes of birds are interrupted, but the hum of insects is incessant. I suppose that the motion of the wings of the small tipulidæ which have swarmed for some weeks produced a humming appreciated by some ears. Perhaps the phœbe heard and was charmed by it. Thus gradually the spaces of the air are filled. Nature has taken equal care to cushion our ears on this finest sound and to inspire us with the strains of the wood thrush and poet. We may say that each gnat is made to vibrate its wings for man's fruition. In short, we hear but little music in the world which charms us more than this sound produced by the vibration of an insect's wing and in some still and sunny nook in spring.

A wood tortoise on bank; first seen, water so high.

I heard lately the voice of a hound hunting by itself. What an awful sound to the denizens of the wood! That relentless, voracious, demonic cry, like the voice of a fiend! At hearing of which, the fox, hare, marmot, etc., tremble for their young and themselves, imagining the worst. This, however, is the sound which the lords of creation love to accompany and follow, with their bugles and "mellow horns" conveying a similar dread to the hearers instead of whispering peace to the hare's palpitating breast.

A partridge drums.

April 18. 8 a. m. — To the south part of Acton, surveying, with Stedman Buttrick.

When B. came to see me the other evening, and stood before the door in the dark, my mother asked, "Who is it?" to which he replied, quite seriously, "Left-tenant [*sic*] Stedman Buttrick."

B. says that he shot some crossbills which were opening pine cones in the neighborhood of the Easterbrook place some years ago, that he saw two *dildees* [*sic*] here as much as a month ago at least, and that they used to breed on that island east of his house, — I think he called it Burr's Island. He sees the two kinds of telltale here. Once shot an eider duck here. Has often shot the pintail (he calls it spindle-tail) duck here. Thinks he has killed four (?!) kinds of teal here. Once shot a sheldrake which had a good-sized sucker in its throat, the tail sticking out its bill, so that, as he thought, it could not have flown away with it. It was a full-plumaged male. Once, in the fall, shot a mackerel gull on what I call Dove Rock. Once shot a *whole flock* of little ducks not more than two thirds the size of a pigeon, yet full-grown, near the junction of the two rivers. Also got two ducks, the female *all* white and the male with a long and conspicuous bottle-green crest above the white. Looked through Audubon, but could find no account of them. Sees two kinds of gray ducks, one larger than a black duck. Has seen the summer duck here carrying its young to the water in her bill, as much as thirty rods. Says that teal have bred here.

His boy found, one February, as much as a peck of chestnuts in different parcels within a short distance of one another, just under the leaves in Hildreth's chestnut wood, placed there, as he says, by the chip-squirrel, which they saw eating them. He has seen the cross fox here.

I am looking for acorns these days, to sow on the Walden lot, but can find very few sound ones. Those which the squirrels have not got are mostly worm-eaten and quite pulverized or decayed. A few which are cracked at the small [end], having started last fall, have yet life in them, perhaps enough to plant. Even these look rather discolored when you cut them open, but Buttrick says they will do for pigeon-bait. So each man looks at things from his own point of view. I found by trial that the last or apparently sound acorns would always sink in water, while the rotten ones would float, and I have accordingly offered five cents a quart for such as will sink. You can thus separate the good from the bad in a moment. I am not sure,

however, but the germs of many of the latter [1] have been injured by the frost.

Hear a field sparrow.

Ed. Emerson shows me his aquarium. He has two minnows from the brook, which I think must be the banded minnow; a little more than an inch long with very conspicuous broad black transverse bars. Some *Rana sylvatica* spawn just begun to flat out. Also several kinds of larvæ in the water, — one very like a dragon-fly, with three large feather-like appendages to the tail, small gyrinus, which he says nibbled off the legs of the skater (?), etc., etc., but no dragon-fly grubs. Two salamanders, one from Ripple Lake and the other from the pool behind my house that was. One some four inches long, with a carinated and waved (crenated) edged tail as well as light-vermilion spots on the back, evidently the *Salamandra dorsalis*. (This I suspect is what I called *S. symmetrica* last fall.) (This is pale-brown above.) The other two thirds as large, a very handsome bright orange salmon, also with vermilion spots, which must be the true *S. symmetrica*. Both thickly sprinkled with black dots. The latter's tail comparatively thick and straight-edged.

Haynes (Heavy) says that trout spawn twice in a year, — once in October and again in the spring.

[1] [That is, such as will sink. The sentence "You . . . moment" was written afterward and inserted over a caret.]

Vol. XII

Saw snow ice a yard across to-day under the north side of a wood.

April 19. Was it a vireo I heard this forenoon on the elms?

Channing sees the same small flock of sheldrakes, three birds, in Walden still. They have been there a week or two, but I cannot see them the 22d.

P. M. — Began to set white pines in R. W. E.'s Wyman lot.

April 20. Hear and see my ruby-crowned or crested wren singing at 6 A. M. on Wheildon's pines.

Setting pines all day.

April 21. Setting pines all day. This makes two and a half days, with two men and a horse and cart to help me. We have set some four hundred trees at fifteen feet apart diamondwise, covering some two acres. I set every one with my own hand, while another digs the holes where I indicate, and occasionally helps the other dig up the trees. We prefer bushy pines only one foot high which grow in open or pasture land, yellow-looking trees which are used to the sun, instead of the spindling dark-green ones from the shade of the woods. Our trees will not average much more than two feet in height, and we take a thick sod with them fifteen to eighteen inches in diameter. There are a great many more of these plants to be had along the edges and in the midst of any white pine wood than one would suppose. One man charged us five or six cents for them

about a mile and a half distant! Got about one hundred and twenty from George Heywood's land and the rest from the Brister lot and this Wyman lot itself.

R. W. E. has bought a quarter of a pound of white pine seed at $4.00 per pound.

We could not dig up pines on the north side of the wood on the Brister lot to-day on account of frost! Though we had quite forgotten it, and put the winter so far behind us.

See the *Vanessa Antiopa*. C. has seen it a week or so. C. sees a cicindela to-day. I hear of a robin's nest begun, and that geese go over to-day.

Put out a fire in the woods, the Brister lot. Quite a warm day.

Storer's account of the salamanders concludes with these words, " All the salamanders here described, feed upon insects, which they devour in very large numbers, and hence their utility cannot be questioned." The same might be said in behalf of the creatures that devour the salamanders.

In those little Ripple Lakes in the cool hollows in the woods, there you find these active bright-spotted salamanders, — *S. dorsalis*, the brown (olive-brown or palish-brown), with carinated and wave-crenate thin tail, and the *S. symmetrica*, the bright orange salmon, with a thick, straight-edged tail, — both with vermilion spots on back and countless fine black dots above and beneath. The first-named is quite voracious, catching many of the larvæ in the aquarium, in fact depopulating it. He gulps them down very deliberately after catching them. What pretty things go to make up the sum of life in any valley! This Ripple Lake with the wind playing over it, the bright spotted butterflies that flutter from time to time over the dry leaves, and the minnows and salamanders that dart in the water itself. Beneath this play of ripples which reflect the sky, — a darker blue than the real, — the vermilion-spotted salamanders are darting at the various grotesque-formed larvæ of the lake.

April 22. The *Salix purpurea* in prime, out probably three or four days; say 19th. Arbor-vitæ, how long?
P. M. — In a fine rain, around Walden.

I go by a *Populus grandidentata* on the eastern sand slope of the Deep Cut just after entering, whose aments (which apparently here began to shed pollen yesterday) in scattered clusters at the ends of the bare twigs, but just begun to shed their pollen, not hanging loose and straight yet, but curved, are a very rich crimson, like some ripe fruit, as mulberries, seen against the sand. I cannot represent the number in a single cluster, but they are much the handsomest now before the crimson anthers have burst, and are all the more remarkable for the very open and bare habit of the tree.

When setting the pines at Walden the last three days, I was sung to by the field sparrow. For music I heard their jingle from time to time. That the music the pines were set to, and I have no doubt they will build many a nest under their shelter. It would seem as if such a field as this — a dry open or half-open pasture in the woods, with small pines scattered in it — was well-nigh, if not quite, abandoned to this one alone

among the sparrows. The surface of the earth is portioned out among them. By a beautiful law of distribution, one creature does not too much interfere with another. I do not hear the song sparrow here. As the pines gradually increase, and a wood-lot is formed, these birds will withdraw to new pastures, and the thrushes, etc., will take their place. Yes, as the walls of cities are fabled to have been built by music, so my pines were established by the song of the field sparrow. They commonly place their nests here under the shelter of a little pine in the field.

As I planted there, wandering thoughts visited me, which I have now forgotten. My senses were busily suggesting them, though I was unconscious of their origin. *E. g.*, I first *consciously* found myself entertaining the thought of a carriage on the road, and directly after I was aware that I heard it. No doubt I had heard it before, or rather my ears had, but I was quite unconscious of it, — it was not a fact of my then state of existence; yet such was the force of habit, it affected my thoughts nevertheless, so double, if not treble, even, are we. Sometimes the senses bring us information quicker than we can receive it. Perhaps these thoughts which run in ruts by themselves while we are engaged in some routine may be called automatic. I distinctly entertained the idea of a carriage, without the slightest suspicion how it had originated or been suggested to my mind. I have no doubt at all that my ears had heard it, but my mind, just then preoccupied, had refused to attend to it. This suggests that most, if not all, indeed, of our ideas may be due

Vol. XII

to some sort of sensuous impression of which we may or may not be conscious.

This afternoon there is an east wind, and a rain-storm accordingly beginning, the eighth of the kind with this wind.

I still see a large flock of grackles.

Within a few days I pricked my fingers smartly against the sharp, stiff points of some sedge coming up. At Heywood's meadow, by the railroad, this sedge, rising green and dense with yellow tips above the withered clumps, is very striking, suggesting heat, even a blaze, there.

Scare up partridges feeding about the green springy places under the edge of hills. See them skim or scale away for forty rods along and upward to the woods, into which they swiftly scale, dodging to right and left and avoiding the twigs, yet without once flapping the wings after having launched themselves.

April 23. Rain, rain.

Hear seringo, by chance the first, and while it rains. The tree sparrows abundant and singing in the yard, but I have not noticed a *hyemalis* of late. The field sparrow sings in our yard in the rain.

The sidewalk is all strewn with fishworms this forenoon, up and down the street, and many will evidently die in the cold rain. Apparently the rain tempted them to remain on the surface, and then the cold and wet benumbs and drowns them. Some of them are slowly crawling across the paths. What an abundant supply of food for the birds lately arrived! From Gil-

bert White, and the notes by others to his last edition, I should infer that these were worms which, having been tempted out in unusual numbers by the rain, lost their way back to their holes. They say that they never take their tails out of their holes.

In about five quarts of scarlet oak acorns gathered the other day there [were] only some three gills that had life in them, or say one in seven. I do not know how many the squirrels had got, but as it was quite near a house, a tree by itself, I think not a great many. The rest were apparently destroyed by worms; so that I should say the worms destroyed before spring three fourths of them. As the grub is already in the acorn, it may be just as well (except for the squirrels) to sow them now as in the fall, whatever you can get.

Clears up at 3 P. M., and a very strong south wind blows.

I go on the water. I frequently observe that the waves do not always run high in proportion to the strength of the wind. The wind seems sometimes to flat them down, perhaps when it blows very hard in gusts, which interrupt a long roll.

What is that small willow on the north side of S. Brown's stump, which apparently began to open two days ago?

A large hickory by the wall on the north side (or northeast side) of the hill apparently just blown down, the one I saw the screech owl go into two or three years ago. I think it may have fallen in this very high wind which arose within an hour; at any rate it has fallen since the grass began to spring, for the owl-hole contains a squirrel's nest made of half-green grass somewhat withered, which could only have been found quite recently, and also the limbs have been driven so deep into the ground that I cannot pull them out, which shows that the ground was thawed when it fell; also the squirrel's nest, which is perfectly sheltered, now the tree is fallen, was quite wet through with rain, that of the morning, as I think. This nest, which I suppose was that of a red squirrel, was at the bottom of a large hole some eighteen inches deep and twenty-five feet from the ground, where a large limb had been broken off formerly. An opening on the side had been stopped with twigs as big as a pipe-stem and larger, some of them the hickory twigs quite green and freshly gnawed off with their buds, forming a rude basketwork which kept up and in the grass and rotten wood, four or five handfuls of which, mixed with the rotten wood of the inside, composed the nest. This was the half old and withered and half green grass gathered a few days since about the base of the tree.

April 24. Sunday. P. M. — To Pine Hill and Heywood's meadow.

The weather is windy still and cool. I see for several days past tipulidæ of larger size dancing like the small.

A great many oak leaves have their petioles broken off half an inch or more from the base, so that the leaves fall before they are regularly cast off by the tree. I see many young oaks — a scarlet one this afternoon — the half of whose petioles have been thus broken

mechanically by the force of the wind on the blade of the leaf in the winter. These stub ends will, [of] course, be cast soon, like the entire leaves. Thus you may have small trees entirely divested of their leaves excepting a fragment of the petioles by merely mechanical means or violence, long before they have all fallen regularly. They are whirled about by the wind till they break off, and these broken and stringy petioles give to the tree a ragged appearance.

I notice that the white pine cones in Wheildon's grove have now almost entirely fallen.

There is a season for everything, and we do not notice a given phenomenon except at that season, if, indeed, it can be called the same phenomenon at any other season. There is a time to watch the ripples on Ripple Lake, to look for arrowheads, to study the rocks and lichens, a time to walk on sandy deserts; and the observer of nature must improve these seasons as much as the farmer his. So boys fly kites and play ball or hawkie at particular times all over the State. A wise man will know what game to play to-day, and play it. We must not be governed by rigid rules, as by the almanac, but let the season rule us. The moods and thoughts of man are revolving just as steadily and incessantly as nature's. Nothing must be postponed. Take time by the forelock. Now or never! You must live in the present, launch yourself on every wave, find your eternity in each moment. Fools stand on their island opportunities and look toward another land. There is no other land; there is no other life but this, or the like of this. Where the good husbandman is,

there is the good soil. Take any other course, and life will be a succession of regrets.[1] Let us see vessels sailing prosperously before the wind, and not simply stranded barks. There is no world for the penitent and regretful.

On the Mill-Dam a man is unmanned. I love best to meet them in the outskirts. They remind me of wharf rats in the other place. Let me see man a-farming, a-hunting, a-fishing, a-walking, — anything but a-shopping. Farmers' coats are ugly in the shops and on the Mill-Dam, but become them in the fields.

Dr. B. asked me what I found that was new these days, if I was still looking after the beautiful. I told [him] yes, and that I wished to hire two or three good observers.

With what energy Nature carries out her plans! I see white birches six or eight feet high growing in the seams of rocks three or four feet from the ground, in the midst of a sprout-land. If men will not let them grow on the surface of the earth, Nature can still maintain the species by dropping seeds into the seams of the rocks. By their growth, probably, they help to split the rocks. How often seeds appear to catch and take root in what we should have deemed the most unfavorable place! Deep in the seam of a rock the seed is out of the way of birds and squirrels.

For several weeks past I have noticed stumps which had had their bark stripped off, I think by skunks on their nightly rounds.

Sitting on Lightning Hillside and looking over Hey-

[1] [Channing, p. 85.]

wood's meadow, I am struck by the vivid greenness of the tips of the sedge just pushing up out of its dry tussocks in the water. I observed it here on the 22d. It is some six inches high or more.[1] All the lower, or the greater, part of the tussock is  brown and sere and prostrate withered blades of last year, while from the top spring up ranks of green life like a fire, from amid the withered blades. This new grass is green beneath, but yellow-tipped, perhaps on account of the recent snow or higher water. It is the renewal of life. The contrast of life with death, spring with winter, is nowhere more striking. Such is the regularity [of] the growth and of the fallen grass that it affects you like a geometrical figure. The fallen dead and decaying last year's grass is dead past all resurrection, perfectly brown and lifeless, while this vivid green that has shot up from its midst close upon the heels of winter, even through snow, is like the first phalanx of Spring's forces.

The green has the regularity of a parapet or rampart to a fortress. It winds along the irregular lines of tussocks like the Wall of China over hill and dale.[2]

April 25. P. M. — To Kalmia Swamp.
First notice martins.

Carex stricta. Vide June 19th.   [2] [Channing, p. 104.]

I got to-day and yesterday the first decided impression of greenness beginning to prevail, summer-like. It struck me as I was going past some opening and by chance looked up some valley or glade, — greenness just beginning to prevail over the brown or tawny. It is a sudden impression of greater genialness in the air, when this greenness first makes an impression on you at some turn, from blades of grass decidedly green, though thin, in the sun and the still, warm air, on some warm orchard-slope perhaps. It reminds you of the time, not far off, when you will see the dark shadows of the trees there and buttercups spotting the grass. Even the grass begins to wave, in the 19th-of-April fashion.[1] When the wind is still cool elsewhere, I glance up some warm southern slope, sunny and still, where the thinly scattered blades of green grass, lately sprung, already perchance begin to wave, and I am suddenly advertised that a new season has arrived. This is the beginning of that season which, methinks, culminates with the buttercup and wild pink and *Viola pedata.* It begins when the first toad is heard.

Methinks I hear through the wind to-day — and it was the same yesterday — a very faint, low ringing of toads, as if distant and just begun. It is an indistinct undertone, and I am far from sure that I hear anything. It may be all imagination.

I see the meadow-sweet, thimble-berry (even in a swamp), high blackberry, and (on a dry rock in the woods in a sunny place) some *Vaccinium Pennsylvanicum* leafing (even the last) apparently two or three

[1] [See *Journal*, vol. xiii, p. 303.]

days. Fern scrolls are eight inches high, — beyond Hubbard Bridge on the north bank of road.

A mosquito endeavors to sting me.

Ranunculus repens at Corner Spring apparently yesterday; five of them out now. Thus early now because exposed to light. The *Viola blanda* are numerously open there, say two days at least. Also bluets and potentilla are first noticed by me, and *V. sagittata.* The more yellowish red maples of this afternoon are one, barked, northeast corner Hubbard's Dracæna Grove, the easternmost tree of the row south of Hubbard's Grove, the larger about ten rods this side Hubbard Bridge, south side. The two at this end of bridge are quite red.

I hear still the *what what what* of a nuthatch, and, directly after, its ordinary winter note of *gnah gnah,* quite distinct. I think the former is its spring note or breeding-note.

E. Bartlett has found a crow's nest with four eggs a little developed in a tall white pine in the grove east of Beck Stow's.

The snipe have hovered commonly this spring an hour or two before sunset and also in the morning. I can see them flying very high over the Mill-Dam, and they appear to make that sound when descending, — one quite by himself.

Toads have been observed or disturbed in gardens for a week. One saw a striped snake the 3d of April on a warm railroad sand-bank, — a similar place to the others I heard of.

Young Stewart tells me that he saw last year a pout's

nest at Walden in the pond-hole by the big pond. The spawn lay on the mud quite open and uncovered, and the old fish was tending it. A few days after, he saw that it was hatched and little pouts were swimming about.

April 26. Start for Lynn.

Rice says that he saw a large mud turtle in the river about three weeks ago, and has seen two or three more since. Thinks they come out about the first of April. He saw a woodchuck the 17th; says he heard a toad on the 23d.

P. M. — Walked with C. M. Tracy in the rain[1] in the western part of Lynn, near Dungeon Rock. Crossed a stream of stones ten or more rods wide, reaching from top of Pine Hill to Salem. Saw many *discolor*-like willows on hills (rocky hills), but apparently passing into *S. humilis;* yet no *eriocephala,* or distinct form from *discolor.* Also one *S. rostrata.* Tracy thought his neighborhood's a depauperated flora, being on the porphyry. Is a marked difference between the vegetation of the porphyry and the sienite.

Got the *Cerastium arvense* from T.'s garden; said to be abundant on Nahant and to have flowers big as a five-cent-piece; very like a dianthus, — the leaf. Also got the *Nasturtium officinale,* or common brook cress, from Lynn, and set it in Depot Field Brook. Neither of these in bloom. His variety *Virginica* of *Cardamine* grows on dry ground.

[1] This is the last of the rains (spring rains!) which invariably followed an east wind. *Vide* back.

April 27. Walk along Swampscott Beach from Red Rock northeast. The beach is strewn with beautifully colored purple and whitish algæ just left by the tide. Hear and see the seringo in fields next the shore. No noticeable yellow shoulder, pure whitish beneath, dashed throat and a dark-brown line of dashes along the sides of the body.[1]

Struck inland and passed over the west end of High Rock, through the cemetery, and over Pine Hill, where I heard a strange warbler, methought, a dark-colored, perhaps reddish-headed bird. Thence through East Saugus and Saugus to Cliftondale, I think in the southern part of Saugus.

The little brown snake with the light line along the back just killed in the road.

Saw at the Aquarium in Bromfield Street apparently brook minnows with the longitudinal dark lines bordered with light. A little pout incessantly nibbles at the dorsal fin of the common perch, also at apparently the mucus on its back. See the sea-raven.

Toads ring and, no doubt, in Concord also.

April 28. 8.30 A. M. — Row to Carlisle Bridge with Blake and Brown.

See black ducks and sheldrakes still. The first myrtle-bird that I have noticed. A small hawk, perhaps

[1] Ours examined the 30th is apparently or perhaps a little smaller and less distinctly whitish beneath and with a less distinct dark line on the sides, but breast equally dashed with brown. Did not see the yellow shoulder, and the head was a little less yellow. Also note of ours apparently more feeble, first part like a watch-spring, last more ringing and clear in both birds.

pigeon hawk. A gull. Sit on Ball's Hill. The water partly over the Great Meadows. The wind is northeast, and at the western base of the hill we are quite sheltered; yet the waves run quite high there and still further up the river, — waves raised by the wind beyond the hill, — while there are very slight waves or ripples over the meadow south of the hill, which is much more exposed, evidently because the water is shallow there and large waves are not so easily formed on account of friction.

S. Higginson brought me the arbutus in bloom on the 26th, one twig only out.

See a shad-fly, one only, on water.

A little snake, size of little brown snake, on pine hill, but uniformly grayish above as far as I could see. E. Emerson's *Salamandra dorsalis* has just lost its skin.

April 29. 7 A. M. — To Walden, and set one hundred larch trees from England, all two years from seed, about nine inches high, just begun to leaf.

See and hear a black and white creeper.

First observe the dandelion well out in R. W. E.'s yard; also anemone at Sassafras Shore. Interrupted fern scrolls there, four to five inches high.

Those red maples are reddest in which the fertile flowers prevail.

Haynes was fishing for pickerel with a pole yesterday, and said that he caught several the day before, *i. e.* 27th.

April 30. P. M. — Sail to Holden Swamp.

The warmest afternoon yet. Sat in sun without fire this forenoon.

The wind has at length been easterly without rain following. Fishes, especially pickerel, lie up in greater numbers, though Haynes thinks the water is still too cold for them. See a bream. A small willow some ten rods north of stone bridge, east side, bloomed yesterday. *Salix alba* leafing, or stipules a quarter of an inch wide; probably began a day or two [ago]. *Luzula campestris* is almost out at Clamshell. Its now low purplish and silky-haired leaves are the blooming of moist ground and early meadow-edges. See two or three strawberry flowers at Clamshell.

The 27th and to-day are weather for a half-thick single coat. This old name is still useful. There is scarcely a puff of wind till I get to Clamshell; then it rises and comes from the northwest instead of northeast and blows quite hard and fresher. See a stake-driver.

Land at Holden Wood. That interesting small blue butterfly (size of small red) is apparently just out, fluttering over the warm dry oak leaves within the wood in the sun. Channing also first sees them to-day. The moment it rests and closes its wings, it looks merely whitish-slate, and you think at first that the deeper blue was produced by the motion of its wings, but the fact is you now see only their under sides which thus [*sic*] whitish spotted with black, with a dark waved line next the edge. This first *off-coat* warmth just preceding the advent of the swamp warblers (parti-colored, redstart, etc.) brings them out. I come here to listen for

warblers, but hear or see only the black and white creeper and the chickadee.

Did I not hear a tree sparrow this forenoon?

The *Viburnum nudum* around the edge of the swamp, on the northern edge of the warm bays in sunny and sheltered places, has just expanded, say two days, the two diverging leafets being an inch long nearly, — pretty yellowish-brown leafets in the sun, the most noticeable leafiness here now, just spotting and enlivening the dead, dark, bare twigs, under the red blossoms of the maples.

It is a day for many small fuzzy gnats and other small insects. Insects swarm about the expanding buds.

The viburnum buds are so large and long, like a spear-head, that they are conspicuous the moment their two leafets diverge and they are lit up by the sun. They unfold their wings like insects and arriving warblers. These, too, mark the season well. You see them a few rods off in the sun, through the stems of the alders and maples.

That small curled grass in tufts in dry pastures and hills, spoken of about a month ago, is not early sedge.

I notice under the southern edge of the Holden Wood, on the Arrowhead Field, a great many little birches in the grass, apparently seedlings of last year, and I take up a hundred and ten from three to six or seven inches high. They are already leafed, the little rugose leafets more than half an inch wide, or larger than any wild shrubs or trees, while the larger white

birches have not started. I could take up a thousand in two or three hours. I set ten in our yard.

Channing saw ducks — he thinks female sheldrakes! — in Walden to-day.

Julius Smith says he saw a little hawk kill a robin yesterday.

III

MAY, 1859

(ÆT. 41)

May 1. Hear the ruby-crowned wren.

We accuse savages of worshipping only the bad spirit, or devil, though they may distinguish both a good and a bad; but they regard only that one which they fear and worship the devil only. We too are savages in this, doing precisely the same thing. This occurred to me yesterday as I sat in the woods admiring the beauty of the blue butterfly. We are not chiefly interested in birds and insects, for example, as they are ornamental to the earth and cheering to man, but we spare the lives of the former only on condition that they eat more grubs than they do cherries, and the only account of the insects which the State encourages is of the "Insects *Injurious* to Vegetation." We too admit both a good and a bad spirit, but we worship chiefly the bad spirit, whom we fear. We do not think first of the good but of the harm things will do us.

The catechism says that the chief end of man is to glorify God and enjoy him forever, which of course is applicable mainly to God as seen in his works. Yet the only account of its beautiful insects — butterflies, etc. — which God has made and set before us which the State ever thinks of spending any money on is the account of those which are injurious to vegetation!

This is the way we glorify God and enjoy him forever. Come out here and behold a thousand painted butterflies and other beautiful insects which people the air, then go to the libraries and see what kind of prayer and glorification of God is there recorded. Massachusetts has published her report on "Insects Injurious to Vegetation," and our neighbor the "Noxious Insects of New York." We have attended to the evil and said nothing about the good. This is looking a gift horse in the mouth with a vengeance. Children are attracted by the beauty of butterflies, but their parents and legislators deem it an idle pursuit. The parents remind me of the devil, but the children of God. Though God may have pronounced his work good, we ask, "Is it not poisonous?"

Science is inhuman. Things seen with a microscope begin to be insignificant. So described, they are as monstrous as if they should be magnified a thousand diameters. Suppose I should see and describe men and houses and trees and birds as if they were a thousand times larger than they are! With our prying instruments we disturb the balance and harmony of nature.

P. M. — To Second Division.

Very warm. Looking from Clamshell over Hosmer's meadow, about half covered with water, see hundreds of turtles, chiefly *picta*, now first lying out in numbers on the brown pieces of meadow which rise above the water. You see their black backs shine on these hummocks left by the ice, fifty to eighty rods off. They would rapidly tumble off if you went much nearer.

Vol. XII

This heat and stillness draws them up. It is remarkable how surely they are advertised of the first warm and still days, and in an hour or two are sure to spread themselves over the hummocks. There is to-day a general resurrection of them, and there they bask in the sun. It is their sabbath. At this distance, if you are on the lookout, especially with a glass, you can discover what numbers of them there are, but they are shy and will drop into the water on a near approach. All up and down our river meadows their backs are shining in the sun to-day. It is a turtle day.

As we sat on the steep hillside south of Nut Meadow Brook Crossing, we noticed a remarkable whirlwind on a small scale, which carried up the oak leaves from that Island copse in the meadow. The oak leaves now hang thinly and are very dry and light, and these small whirlwinds, which seem to be occasioned by the sudden hot and calm weather (like whirlpools or dimples in a smooth stream), wrench them off, and up they go, somewhat spirally, in countless flocks like birds, with a rustling sound; and higher and higher into the clear blue deeps they rise above our heads, till they are fairly lost to sight, looking, when last seen, mere light specks against the blue, like stars by day, in fact. I could distinguish some, I have no doubt, five or six hundred feet high at least, but if I looked aside a moment they were lost. The largest oak leaves looked not bigger than a five-cent-piece. These were drifting eastward, — to descend where? Methought that, instead of decaying on the earth or being consumed by fire, these were being translated and would soon be taken in at

the windows of heaven. I had never observed this phenomenon so remarkable. The flight of the leaves. This was quite local, and it was comparatively still where we sat a few rods on one side. Thousands went up together in a rustling flock.

Many of the last oak leaves hang thus ready to go up. I noticed two or more similar whirlwinds in the woods elsewhere this afternoon. One took up small twigs and clusters of leaves from the ground, matted together. I could easily see where it ran along with its nose (or point of its tunnel) close to the ground, stirring up the leaves as it travelled, like the snout of some hunting or rooting animal.

See and hear chewink.

See a little snake on the dry twigs and chips in the sun, near the arbutus, uniformly brown (or reddish-brown) above except a yellowish ring on the occiput, the head also lighter than the body; beneath vermilion, with apparently a row of light dots along each side. It is apparently *Coluber amœnus* (?), except that it has the yellowish ring.

Luzula campestris. Also the *Oryzopsis Canadensis* by the Major Heywood path-side, say a day, or April 30th, six inches high or more, with fine bristle-like leaves. See a thrasher.

What is that rush at Second Division? It now forms a dense and very conspicuous mass some four rods long and one foot high. The top for three inches is red, and the impression at a little distance is like that made by sorrel. Certainly no plant of this character exhibits such a growth now, *i. e.* in the mass. It surprises you to see it, carries your thoughts on to June.

The climbing fern is persistent, *i. e.* retains its greenness still, though now partly brown and withered.

May 2. Small pewee and young lackey caterpillars.

I see on the *Salix rostrata* by railroad many honey-bees laden with large and peculiarly orange-colored pellets of its pollen.

P. M. — Up Assabet.

Those swarms of small miller-like insects which fly low over the surface of the river, sometimes constantly falling to and touching the surface and then rising again. When at rest they are seen to be blackish-winged, but flying they look light-colored. They flutter low and continuously over the same place. Theirs is a sort of dance.

A peetweet and its mate at Mantatuket Rock. The river seems really inhabited when the peetweet is back and those little light-winged millers (?). This bird does not return to our stream until the weather is decidedly pleasant and warm. He is perched on the accustomed rock. Its note peoples the river, like the prattle of children once more in the yard of a house that has stood empty.

I am surprised by the tender yellowish green of the aspen leaf just expanded suddenly, even like a fire, seen in the sun, against the dark-brown twigs of the wood, though these leafets are yet but thinly dispersed. It is very enlivening.

I heard yesterday, and perhaps for several days, the

soft purring sound of what I take to be the *Rana palustris*, breeding, though I did not this time see the frog.

I feel no desire to go to California or Pike's Peak, but I often think at night with inexpressible satisfaction and yearning of the *arrowheadiferous* sands of Concord. I have often spent whole afternoons, especially in the spring, pacing back and forth over a sandy field, looking for these relics of a race. This is the gold which our sands yield. The soil of that rocky spot on Simon Brown's land is quite ash-colored — now that the sod is turned up — by Indian fires, with numerous pieces of coal in it. There is a great deal of this ash-colored soil in the country. We do literally plow up the hearths of a people and plant in their ashes. The ashes of their fires color much of our soil.

May 3. Surveying the Bedford road.

Hear the *te-e-e* of a white-throat sparrow.

I hear of phœbes', robins', and bluebirds' nests and eggs. I have not heard any snipes boom for about a week, nor seen a tree sparrow *certainly* since April 30 (??), nor *F. hyemalis* for several days.

May 4. *Wednesday.* P. M. — To Lee's Cliff on foot.

This the fourth warm day.

The cassandra (in full bloom) swarms with little bees, and amid them is one bumblebee which they appear to molest from time to time, and afterward I see one flying high overhead at Holden Swamp.

Notice the white willows on Hubbard's Bridge cause-

way, — quite a mass of green when seen aslant from this side, and have been two or three days, but as yet no bloom there nor hum of bees. Also their freshest osiers are very bright, yet I think most of it is due to the height at which the sun runs. They are priests of the sun, report his brightness, — heliometers. We do not realize how much more light there is in the day than in winter. If the ground should be covered with snow, the reflection would dazzle us and blister our faces. This willow begins to be green before the aspens, — say five or six days ago.

It is now quite dry, especially the leaves in the woods, and this is the time for fires in the woods. I have seen the smoke of several within a week or ten days.

A small willow inside wall just beyond Conant's bars has begun to leaf two or three days. It is either *discolor* or *humilis*, having large and old fertile catkins.

Crossing that first Conantum field, I perceive a peculiar fragrance in the air (not *the* meadow fragrance), like that of vernal flowers or of expanding buds. The ground is covered with the mouse-ear in full bloom, and it may be that in part. It is a temperate southwest breeze, and this is a scent as of willows (flowers and leafets), bluets, violets, shad-bush, mouse-ear, etc., combined; or perhaps the last chiefly; at any rate it is very perceptible. The air is more genial, laden with the fragrance of spring flowers. I, sailing in the spring ocean, getting in from my winter voyage, begin to smell the land. Such a scent perceived by a mariner would be very exciting. I not only smell the land breeze, but I

perceive in it the fragrance of spring flowers. I draw near to the land; I begin to lie down and stretch myself on it. After my winter voyage I begin to smell the land.

I came out expecting to see the redstart or the parti-colored warbler, and as soon as I get within a dozen rods of the Holden wood I hear the screeper note of the tweezer-bird, *i. e.* parti-colored warbler, which also I see, but not distinctly. Two or three are flitting from tree-top to tree-top about the swamp there, and you have only to sit still on one side and wait for them to come round. The water has what you may call a summer ripple and sparkle on it; *i. e.*, the ripple does not suggest coldness in the breeze that raises it. It is a hazy day; the air is hazed, you might fancy, with a myriad expanding buds.

After crossing the Arrowhead Fields, we see a woodchuck run along and climb to the top of a wall and sit erect there, — our first. It is almost exactly the color of the ground and the wall and the bare brown twigs, all together. And when in the Miles Swamp Field we see two, one chasing the other, coming very fast down the lilac field hill straight toward [us], while we squat still in the middle of the field. The foremost is a small gray or slaty-colored one, the other two or three times as heavy and a warm tawny, decidedly yellowish in the sun, a very large and fat one, pursuing the first. I think this must be the male in pursuit of the female. Suddenly the foremost, when thirty or forty rods off, perceives us, and tries as it were to sink into the earth, and finally gets behind a low tuft of grass and peeps out. Also the other (which at first appears to fondle the earth, inclining his cheek to it and dragging his body a little along it) tries to hide himself, and at length gets behind an apple tree and peeps out on one side in an amusing manner. This makes three that we see. They are clumsy runners, with their short legs and heavy bodies, — run with an undulating or wobbling motion, jerking up the hind quarters. Their tails were dark-tipped. They can run pretty fast, however. Their tails are low when running.

Looking up through this soft and warm southwest wind, I notice the conspicuous shadow of Middle Conantum Cliff, now at 3 P. M., and elsewhere the shade of a few apple trees, — their trunks and boughs. Through this warm and hazy air the sheeny surface of the hill, now considerably greened, looks soft as velvet, and June is suggested to my mind. It is remarkable that shadow should only be noticed now when decidedly warm weather comes, though before the leaves have expanded, i. e., when it begins to be grateful to our senses. The shadow of the Cliff is like a dark pupil on the side of the hill. This first shadow is as noticeable and memorable as a flower. I observe annually the first shadow of this cliff. When we begin to pass from sunshine into shade for our refreshment; when we look on shade with yearning as on a friend. That cliff and its shade suggests dark eyes and eyelashes and overhanging brows. Few things are more suggestive of heat than this first shade, though now we see only the tracery of tree-boughs on the greening grass and the sandy street. This I notice at the same time with the first

bumblebee, when the *Rana palustris* purrs in the meadow generally, the white willow and aspen display their tender green full of yellow light, the particolored warbler is first heard over the swamp, the woodchuck, who loves warmth, is out on the hillsides in numbers, the jingle of the chip-bird is incessantly heard, the thrasher sings incessantly, the first cricket is heard in a warm rocky place, and that scent of vernal flowers is in the air. This is an intenser expression of that same influence or aspect of nature which I began to perceive ten days ago (*vide* 25th), — the same *lieferung.*

These days we begin to think in earnest of bathing in the river, and to sit at an open window. Life out of doors begins.

It would require a good deal of time and patience to study the habits of woodchucks, they are so shy and watchful. They hear the least sound of a footstep on the ground, and are quick to see also. One should go clad in a suit somewhat like their own, the warp of tawny and the woof of green, and then, with a painted or well-tanned face, he might lie out on a sunny bank till they appeared.

We hear a thrasher sing for half an hour steadily, — a very rich singer and heard a quarter of a mile off very distinctly. This is first heard commonly at planting-time. He sings as if conscious of his power.

See little apple trees just springing up in cow-dung. Under Lee's Cliff, a phœbe's nest and one egg, with apparently a cowbird's egg, — which is here, then, — but unusually long with a very broad ring of chestnut-

Vol. XII

brown about the larger end, contrasting with the smaller flesh-colored egg of the phœbe.

The grass of the river meadows shooting up is now a glaucous green, while that of the uplands is dark-green. The former, or sedge, is [a] very erect and stiff spear, while the latter is an inclined and flexible blade.

Hear the exact note of the pe-pe once, but at the same time with the thrasher at Bittern Cliff. Could it have been the last??

A carex at Lee's, say May 1st, at least, with broadish flaccid glaucous leaves. Call it *C. laxiflora*-like. I can find but one tuft that has not been nibbled off by rabbits or woodchucks, so fond are they of this early grass. Two grasses are almost in flower there.[1] Gather an apparent *Viola cucullata* (*vide* press), but close under the rocks. Can it be a distinct variety?

May 5. Thursday. P. M. — To Melvin's Preserve.

Red-wings fly in flocks yet. Near the oak beyond Jarvis land, a yellow butterfly, — how hot! this meteor dancing through the air. Also see a *scalloped*-edge dark-colored butterfly resting on the trunk of a tree, where, both by its form and color, its wings being closed, it resembles a bit of bark, or rather a lichen. Evidently their forms and colors, especially of the under sides of their wings, are designed to conceal them when at rest with their wings closed.

Am surprised to find the *Viola Muhlenbergii* quite abundant beyond the bayberry and near the wall. According to my observation this year, it now stands thus

[1] Is one the sweet-scented vernal?

with the violets: the *V. ovata* is the commonest, but not abundant in one spot; the *V. Muhlenbergii* is most abundant in particular spots, coloring the hummocks with its small pale flowers; the *V. blanda* and *cucullata* are, equally, less abundant than the former, or rather rare; *V. pedata* and *lanceolata* rarer yet, or not seen.

I noticed lately where middle-sized ants, half black and half sorrel, had completely removed the pine-needles from the crown of their large hills, leaving them bare like a mountain-top.

Am struck by the beauty of the yellow birches, now fairly begun to be in bloom, at Yellow Birch, or Botrychium, Swamp. It is perhaps the handsomest tree or shrub yet in bloom (apparently opened yesterday), of similar character to the alders and poplars, but larger and of higher color. You see a great tree all hung with long yellow or golden tassels at the end of its slender, drooping spray, in clusters at intervals of a few inches or a foot. These are all dangling and incessantly waving in the wind, — a great display of lively blossoms (lively both by their color and motion) without a particle of leaf. Yet they are dense enough to reveal the outline of the tree, seen against the bare twigs of itself and other trees. The tassels of this one in bloom are elongated to two or three times the length of those of another not in bloom by its side. These dancing tassels have the effect of the leaves of the tremble. Those not quite open have a rich, dark, speckled or braided look, almost equally handsome. Golden tassels all trembling in the gentlest breeze, the only signs of life on the trees. A careless observer might not notice them at all. The reawakened springy life of the swamp, the product of its golden veins. These graceful pendants, not in too heavy or dense masses, but thinly dispersed with a noble moderation. Great vegetable chandeliers they stand in the swamps. The unopened catkins, some more golden, others brown or coppery, are like living worms ready to assume a winged life. These trees, which cannot stir their stumps, thus annually assume this lively color and motion.

I see and am bitten by little black flies, — I should say the same with those of Maine, — here on the Melvin Preserve. One eighth of an inch long.

Brakes are five inches high. *Poa annua* (small and flat spreading in Pratt's garden), say a week.

The sun sets red (first time), followed by a very hot and hazy day.

The wilderness, in the eyes of our forefathers, was a vast and howling place or *space*, where a man might roam naked of house and most other defense, exposed to wild beasts and wilder men. They who went to war with the Indians and French were said to have been "out," and the wounded and missing who at length returned after a fight were said to have "got in," to Berwick or Saco, as the case might be.

Veronica peregrina, Pratt's garden.

May 6. Surveying for Willis & Damon at the factory. Hear the *tea-lee* of the white-throat sparrow. It is suddenly very warm and oppressive, especially in the woods with thick clothing. *Viola pedata* begins to be common about white pine woods there.

While surveying this forenoon behind Willis's house on the shore of the mill-pond, I saw remarkable swarms of that little fuzzy gnat (*Tipulidæ*). Hot as it was, — oppressively so, — they were collected in the hollows in the meadow, apparently to be out of the way of the little breeze that there was, and in many such places in the meadow, within a rod of the water, the ground was perfectly concealed by them. Nay, much more than that. I saw one shallow hollow some three feet across which was completely filled with them, all in motion but resting one upon another, to the depth, as I found by measurement with a stick, of more than an inch, — a living mass of insect life. There were a hundred of these basins full of them, and I then discovered that what I had mistaken for some black dye on the wet shore was the bodies of those that were drowned and washed up, blackening the shore in patches for many feet together like so much mud. We were also troubled by getting them into our mouths and throats and eyes. This insect resembles the plate of the *Chironomus plumosus* ("Library of Entertaining Knowledge, Insect Transformations," page 305), also the *Corethra plumicornis* (page 287), both of which live at first in the water, like the mosquito.

Young red maples suddenly bursting into leaf are very conspicuous now in the woods, among the most prominent of all shrubs or trees. The sprouts are reddish.

Hear yellow-throat vireo, and probably some new warblers. See the strong-scented wood ants in a stump.

Black suckers, so called, are being speared at the factory bridge.

This is about the last of the very dry leaves in the woods, for soon the ground will be shaded by expanded green leaves. It is quite hazy, if not smoky, and I smell smoke in the air, this hot day. My assistants, being accustomed to work indoors in the factory, are quite overcome by this sudden heat. The old leaves and earth are driest now, just before the new leaves expand and when the heat is greatest. I see the black traces of many a recent fire in the woods, especially in young woods.

At evening I hear the first sultry buzz of a fly in my chamber, telling of sultry nights to come.

May 7. Saturday. Surveying Damon's Acton lot.

It is hotter still, — 88° or more, as I hear in the afternoon. I frequently see pigeons dashing about in small flocks, or three or four at a time, over the woods here. Theirs is a peculiarly swift, dashing flight. The mayflower is still sparingly in bloom on what I will call Mayflower Path in this lot. It is almost the prevailing undershrub here. I think I hear the redstart.

To-day and yesterday the sunlight is peculiarly yellow, on account of the smoky haze. I notice its peculiar yellowness, almost orange, even when, coming through a knot-hole in a dark room, it falls on the opposite wall. Such is the first hot weather.

May 8. Sunday. Hotter still than the last two days, — 90° and more. Summer yellowbird. C. sees a chimney swallow. Indeed, several new birds have come, and many new insects, with the expanding leafets. Catbird. The swollen leaf-buds of the white pine — and

yet more the pitch pine — look whitish, and show life in the tree.

Go on the river.

The sweet flags, both pads, and equisetum and pontederia are suddenly becoming conspicuous, also the *Arum peltandrum*. Grackles here yet. Tree-toad is heard. Apple trees begin to make a show with their green. See two great devil's-needles go by coupled, the foremost blue, the second brown.

Hear a dor-bug in the house at evening.

May 9. Surveying for Stow near Flint's Pond.

Hear the warbling vireo and oven-bird; yellow-throat vireo (?). One helping me says he scared up a whip-poor-will from the ground.

See black birch bloom fallen effete.

The first thunder this afternoon.

May 11. Wednesday. Golden robin yesterday. Fir-balsam well out in the rain; so say 9th.

P. M. — To Flint's Pond.

Arum triphyllum out. Almost every one has a little fly or two concealed within. One of the handsomest-formed plants when in flower. Sorrel out in rain, apparently a day or two, — say 9th. A blue heron flies away from the shore of the pond.

Scirpus planifolius in bloom on Smith's wooded hill, side of Saw Mill Brook.

A partridge-nest, with eleven fresh eggs, at foot of a chestnut, one upon another. It is quite a deep cavity amid the leaves, with some feathers of the bird in it.

Young, or fresh-expanding, oak leaves are very hand-some now, showing their colors. It is a leafy mist throughout the forest.

Uvularia perfoliata out in rain; say, then, the 9th. Just after plucking it I perceived what I call the *meadow* fragrance, though in the woods; but I afterward found that this flower was peculiarly fragrant, and its fra-grance like that, so it was probably this which I had perceived. S. was reminded of the lily-of-the-valley by it.

The witch-hazel has one of the broadest leaves now.

In the path in Stow's wood-lot, I find apparently *Thaspium aureum* (*Zizia aurea*), which will open the first fair day.[1] Shows quite yellow now.

Found in the path in the woods by the Mill Brook ditch, Flint's Pond, dead, the *Coluber punctatus*, 13¼ inches long, but no row of spots in middle of abdomen. The head above blackish with a blackish ring behind the yellow. Tail 3 inches long; breadth of body $\frac{5}{16}$; plates 162; scales 55. Above, uniform glossy slate-color, with a yellowish-white band across the occiput; the head above blackish, and a blackish band close behind the yellowish one. Beneath, yellow or buff (whitish under head), with a row of small slanting black spots, one on each side of each abdominal plate except the first ¾ inch behind the head. In the midst of the path in the woods. I admired the iridescence from its glossy belly. It differs from Storer's *C. punctatus*, for it is not brown above, nor "reddish yellow" beneath, and has no row of spots in middle of the abdomen.

In that first thunder-shower, the evening of the 9th,

[1] 13th in house and probably abroad.

Sarsaparilla flower. *Salix discolor* seed, or down, begins to blow.

A woodcock starts up with whistling sound.

I have been struck of late with the prominence of the *Viburnum nudum* leaf in the swamps, reddish-brown and one inch over, a peculiarly large and mature-looking, firm-looking leaf.

Swamp white oak leafed several days, but generally appears as in winter at a little distance. *Salix lucida* well out, how long? Nemopanthes flower, apparently a day or two.

Now, when the warblers begin to come in numbers with the leafing of the trees, the woods are so open that you can easily see them. They are scarce and silent in a cool and windy day, or found only in sheltered places.

I see an oak shoot (or sprout) already grown ten inches, when the buds of oaks and of most trees are but just burst generally. You are surprised to see such a sudden and rapid development when you had but just begun to think of renewed life, not yet of growth. Very properly these are called shoots. This plant has, per-haps, in four or five days accomplished one fourth part [of] its whole summer's growth. (So on the 4th of June I notice the shoots of the white pine, five to nine inches long, arranged raywise about the terminal one and the end of their branches, having in about a fortnight ac-complished one quarter to one third their whole sum-mer growth. Thus they may be properly said to *shoot* when their season comes, and then stand to harden and mature before the winter.)

the grass evidently erected itself and grew darker, as it were instantaneously. Was it the effect of electricity in the air? It looked very differently from what it had ten minutes before.

May 12. Dug up to-day the red-brown dor-bugs. My red oak acorns have sent down long radicles under-ground. A parti-colored warbler hangs dead downward like a goldfinch on our gooseberries, within a few feet of me, apparently about the blossoms.

May 13. *Friday.* Surveying Damon's Acton lot. Hear the pe-pe and evergreen-forest note, also night-warbler (the last perhaps the 11th). Apple in bloom.

May 14. *Saturday.* Surveying for Damon. Rhodora out, says C. Yorrick heard the 12th. Did I hear a bobolink this morning? C. says he heard a yellow-legs yesterday.

Bought a black sucker (?), just speared at the factory dam, fifteen inches long, blacker than I am used to, I think; at any rate a very good fish to eat, as I proved, while the other common sucker there is said not to be. This had very conspicuous corrugations on the lips. I suspect that their other one is the horned chub. They have speared the former a long time there, and it is getting late for them.

Vernal grass quite common at Willis Spring now.

May 15. *Sunday.* Observe *Cornus florida* involucres.

Vol. XII

May 16. *Monday.* Surveying Damon's farm and factory lot.

Our corydalis was out the 13th. Hear a tanager to-day, and one was seen yesterday. Sand cherry out. *Ranunculus abortivus* well out (when?), southwest angle of Damon's farm. Hear a bobolink and kingbird, and find sparrows' nests on the ground.

At eve the first *spark* of a nighthawk.

May 18. Surveying for Stow in Lincoln. Two-leaved Solomon's-seal. I hear of young song sparrows and young robins since the 16th. That hand-some spawn of Ed. Emerson's aquarium — minute transparent ova in a double row on the glass or the stones — turns out to be snail-spawn, it having just hatched, and there was no salamander-spawn, as I thought on the 18th of April. Not *Paludina decisa*, but the smaller and simpler one.

May 19. Our *Azalea nudiflora* flowers. It is a warm, muggy, rainy evening, when the night-hawks commonly *spark* and the whip-poor-will is heard.

May 22. *Sunday.* A warm, drizzling day, the tender yellow leafets now generally conspicuous, and contrast-ing with the almost black evergreens which they have begun to invest. The foliage is never more conspicuously a tender yellow than now. This lasts a week from this date, and then begins to be confounded with the older green. We have had rain for three or four days, and hence the tender foliage is the more yellow.

Swallows fly low. The *Ranunculus bulbosus* is abundant.

I see that by the very severe frost of about the 15th, or full of the moon, a great many leaves were killed, as young oaks, cultivated grapes,[1] butternuts, ferns, etc., etc., which now show brown or blackish.[2]

May 24. What that brilliant warbler on the young trees on the side of the Deep Cut? Orange throat and beneath, with distinct black stripes on breast (*i. e.* on each side?), and, I think, some light color on crown. Was [it] Blackburnian? or *maculosa??*[3]

Hear the wood pewee.

Sand cherry flower is apparently at its height. I see (the 9th of June) that its fruit is an abortive puff, like that of some plums.

May 25. Dragon-flies have begun to come out of their larva state in numbers, leaving the cases on the weeds, etc. See one tender and just out this forenoon.

Meadow fox-tail grass abundantly out (how long?), front of E. Hosmer's by bars and in E. Hubbard's meadow, front of meeting-house.

The *Salix petiolaris* is either entire or serrate, and generally, I should now say, was becoming serrate, the later leaves, *e. g.* that one, a fertile one, nearly opposite the Shattuck oak. The river is quite high for the season, on account of the late rains. Hear within a day or two

[1] And some native.
[2] White ash; ferns generally; apparently *Polygala verticillata*, for it is not leafed again the 24th.
[3] Probably first.

Vol. XII

Now first I notice a linty dust on the surface of the dark river at the Hemlocks, evidently from the new and downy leaves. These expressions of the face of Nature are as constant and sure to recur as those of the eyes of maidens, from year to year, — sure to be repeated as long as time lasts. It is a new and peculiar season when this phenomenon is observed. Rivers flow already bearing the dust of summer on their bosoms. The dark river, now that shades are increased, is like the dark eye of a maiden.

Azalea nudiflora blooms generally.

Hear a black and white creeper sing, *ah vee vee, vee vee, vitchet vitchet vitchet vitchet.*

A peculiarity of these days is the first hearing of the crickets' creak, suggesting philosophy and thought. No greater event transpires now. It is the most interesting piece of news to be communicated, yet it is not in any newspaper.[1]

Melvin and Skinner tell me of three wild geese, to their surprise seen within a week down the river, — a gander and two geese, — which must be breeding here. Melvin got near them a fortnight ago. They are too much disturbed to rear a brood, I think.

Melvin tells of seeing once in June dead shad-flies washed up on the North Branch in windrows, along the shore.

Golden senecio, at least to-morrow.

Went by Temple's. For rural interest, give me the houses of the poor, with simply a cool spring, a good deal of weather-stained wood, and a natural door-stone;

[1] [Channing, p. 296.]

what I call the *sprayey* note of the toad, different and later than its early *ring.*

May 26. Thursday. P. M. — To Ledum Swamp and Lee's Cliff.

Eleocharis tenuis in bloom, apparently the earliest eleocharis. The rhodora at Ledum Swamp is now in its perfection, brilliant islands of color. *Eriophorum vaginatum*, how long? Ledum out apparently two or three days. *Andromeda Polifolia* out, how long? Tall swamp huckleberry just budded to bloom. Do I not hear the nuthatch note in the swamp? Do not detect the scheuchzeria there yet.[1]

The air is full of terebinthine odors to-day, — the scent of the sweet-fern, etc. The reddish leaves (and calyx) of the *Vaccinium vacillans*, just leafed, are interesting and peculiar now, perhaps more or less crimson. See a flock of cowbirds, the first I have seen. Cows in water, so warm has it got to be. Geranium (how long?), behind Bittern Cliff, and wild pink. Pitch pine pollen at Lee's. Cherry-birds. Ascendant potentilla abundant, how long? *Juniperus repens* pollen, how long? Interrupted fern pollen [*sic*]. The dicksonia fern is one foot high, but not fairly unfolded. The tender white-downy stems of the meadow saxifrage, seen toward the westering sun, are very conspicuous and thick in the meadows now.

A purple finch's nest in one of our firs.

May 27. Friday. P. M. — Up Assabet.

[1] *Vide* 30th.

a house standing somewhere in nature, and not merely in an atmosphere of art, on a measured lot; on a hillside, perchance, obviously not made by any gardener, amid rocks not placed there by a landscape gardener for effect; with nothing "pretty" about it, but life reduced to its lowest terms and yet found to be beautiful. This is a good foundation or board to spring from. All that the natives erect themselves above that will be a genuine growth.

Blue-eyed grass out.

May 28. Saturday. P. M. — To Cliffs.

Some *Salix rostrata* seed begins to fly. Low blackberry in bloom on railroad bank. Also *S. Torreyana* seed, just begun to fly. *S. pedicellaris* long out of bloom there.

At the extreme east side of Trillium Wood, come upon a black snake, which at first keeps still prudently, thinking I may not see him, — in the grass in open land, — then glides to the edge of the wood and darts swiftly up into the top of some slender shrubs there — *Viburnum dentatum* and alder — and lies stretched out, eying me, in horizontal loops eight feet high. The biggest shrub was not over one inch thick at the ground. At first I thought its neck was its chief member, — as if it drew itself up by it, — but again I thought that it rather (when I watched it ascending) extended its neck and a great part of its body upward, while the lower extremity was more or less coiled and rigid on the twigs from a *point d'appui.* Thus it lifted itself quickly to higher forks. When it moved along more horizontally, it extended its neck far, and placed it successively between the slender forks. This snake, some four feet long, rested there at length twelve feet high, on twigs, not one so big as a pipe-stem, in the top of a shad-bush; yet this one's tail was broken off where a third of an inch thick, and it could not cling with that. It was quick as thought in its motions there, and perfectly at home in the trees, so far was it from making the impression of a snake in an awkward position.

Cinnamon fern pollen [*sic*]. Lady's-slipper pollen. These grow under pines even in swamps, as at Ledum Swamp.

The lint from leaves sticks to your clothes now. Hear a rose-breasted grosbeak.

Methinks every tree and shrub is started, or more, now, but the *Vaccinium dumosum*, which has not burst.

May 29. Sunday. Thorn bushes and the *Ranunculus bulbosus* are apparently in prime.

Coming out of Sleepy Hollow Cemetery to-day, where I had just been to deposit the corpse of a man, I picked up an oak three inches high with the acorn attached. They are just springing up now on all sides.

The republican swallow at Hosmer's barn just begun to lay.

May 30. P. M. — To Gowing's Swamp.

Sorrel begins to redden fields. The peculiarly tender foliage (yellowish) which began to invest the dark evergreens on the 22d lasts a week or more, growing darker. No American mountain-ash out.

When I entered the interior meadow of Gowing's Swamp I heard a slight snort, and found that I had suddenly come upon a woodchuck amid the sphagnum, lambkill, *Kalmia glauca*, andromeda, cranberry, etc., there. It was only seven feet off, and, being surprised, would not run. It would only stand erect from time to time, — perfectly erect with its blackish paws held like hands near together in front, — just so as to bring its head, or eyes, above the level of the lambkill, kalmia, etc., and look round, turning now this ear toward me, then that; and every now and then it would make a short rush at me, half a foot or so, with a snort, and then draw back, and also grit its teeth — which it showed — very audibly, with a rattling sound, evidently to intimidate me. I could not drive it, but it would steadily face me and rush toward me thus. Also it made a short motion occasionally as if to bury itself by burrowing there. It impressed me as a singularly wild and grizzly [*sic*] native, survivor of the red man. He may have thought that no one but he came to Gowing's Swamp these afternoons.

Its colors were gray, reddish brown, and blackish, the gray-tipped wind hairs giving it a grizzly look above, and when it stood up its distinct rust-color beneath was seen, while the top of its head was dark-brown, becoming black at snout, as also its paws and its little rounded ears. Its head from snout to ears, when it stood up erect, made a nearly horizontal line. It did much looking round. When thus erect, its expression and posture were very bear-like, with the clumsiness of the bear. Though I drew off three or four rods, it

would not retreat into the thicket (which was only a rod off) while I was there so near.

The scheuchzeria is at height or past. E. Emerson's *Calla palustris* out the 27th. *Eleocharis palustris*, R. W. E.'s meadow, not long. Hear of linnæa out, the 28th.

May 31. Tuesday. Small black flies or millers over river, with long feelers, flying low in swarms now.

IV

JUNE, 1859

(ÆT. 41)

June 1. Wednesday. Some boys found yesterday, in tussock of sedge amid some flags in a wet place in Cyrus Hosmer's meadow, west of the willow-row, six inches above the water, the nest evidently of a rail, with seven eggs. I got one to-day. It is cream-colored, sprinkled with reddish-brown spots and more internal purplish ones, on most eggs (not on mine) chiefly about the larger end. *Vide* September 7th and 9th and 21st and December 7th, '58, and June 13th, '59. The nest (which I have) is made of old sedge, five or six inches [in] diameter and one or two deep.

There has been an abundance of meadow sedges (*carices*) flowering and fruiting in May, but from the end of May to the middle of June is apparently the best time to study them.

Eleocharis palustris not quite open yesterday in river.[1]

June 2. I hear that Farmer shot on the 28th *ult.* two marsh hawks, male and female, and got their four eggs, in which the young were moving.

P. M. — To Flint's Pond.

Red maple seed is partly blown off. Some of it is conspicuously whitish or light-colored on the trees.

[1] Open on the 3d.

Examine a small striped snake, some sixteen inches long. Dark-brown above, with a grayish dorsal line and squarish black spots in the brown; then lighter-brown or dead-leaf color on the sides, chocolate-brown still lower, and light or pale-cream brown beneath. A dark-brown spot on each side of each abdominal plate. The sides yellowish forward. This is apparently a striped snake, but not yellow-striped as described.

Strawberries reddening on some hills.

Found within three rods of Flint's Pond a rose-breasted grosbeak's nest.[1] It was in a thicket where there was much cat-briar, in a high blueberry bush, some five feet from the ground, in the forks of the bush, and of very loose construction, being made of the dead gray extremities of the cat-briar, with its tendrils (and some of this had dropped on the ground beneath), and this was lined merely with fine brown stems of weeds like pinweeds, without any leaves or anything else, — a slight nest on the whole. Saw the birds. The male uttered a very peculiar sharp clicking or squeaking note of alarm while I was near the nest. The egg is thickly spotted with reddish brown on a pale-blue ground (not white ground as Buonaparte and the New York ornithologist say), like a hermit thrush's, but rounder; very delicate.

June 3. Friday. P. M. — Up Assabet.
A large yellow butterfly (somewhat Harris *Papilio Asterias* like but not *black*-winged) three and a half to four inches in expanse. Pale-yellow, the front wings

[1] And one fresh egg (three on the 4th).

crossed by three or four black bars; rear, or outer edge, of all wings widely bordered with black, and some yellow behind it; a short black tail to each hind one, with two blue spots in front of two red-brown ones on the tail.[1]

Arenaria laterifiora well out, how long? Common rum cherry out yesterday, how long? *Carex crinita* out a good while. *Carex lanuginosa*, Smith's shore, green fruit. *Carex pallescens*, Smith's shore (higher up bank), green fruit.

Nighthawk, two eggs, fresh. Quail heard.

June 4. P. M. — To Flint's Pond.
Cornus alternifolia well out, apparently three or four days. Yellow-eyed grass, how long? *Poa compressa* not quite out.

June 5. Sunday. P. M. — To Ball's Hill.
Cat-briar in flower, how long? Allium not out.
See several ducks, I think both summer and black.
A yellowbird's nest; four eggs, developed. Pigeon woodpecker's nest in a hollow black willow over river; six eggs, almost hatched.
The new white maple leaves look reddish, and at a distance brown, as if they had not put out yet.

June 6. P. M. — To Well Meadow.
Yellow wood-sorrel out. Umbelled thesium, how long? Red avens, how long? *Stellaria longifolia*, at Well Meadow Head, how long? *Cardamine rhomboidea* has green seed.

[1] *P. Turnus?*

Hear of a kingfisher's nest, just found in a sand-bank behind Abner Buttrick's, with six fresh eggs, of which I have one. The boy said it was six or seven feet deep in the bank.

June 8. Wednesday. Notice that one of these little silvery scales on a stone is now empty of eggs; how long? See a painted turtle beginning to lay. She has merely scratched the ground a little, and moistened it very much. This must be to make it adherent. It is at the same time beginning to rain. See lightning-bugs to-night.

Noticed yesterday, dancing before our chamber windows, swarms of little plumed gnats with white wings and a reddish body forward. One on my book at night incessantly leaps backward. It seems to be a kind of *Chironomus.*

June 9. Thursday. A boy shows me one of three (apparent) hen-hawk's eggs, fresh, obtained on the 6th from a pine near Breed's house site.

June 10. Friday. Surveying for D. B. Clark on "College Road," so called in Peter Temple's deed in 1811, Clark thought from a house so called once standing on it. Cut a line, and after measured it, in a thick wood, which passed within two feet of a blue jay's nest which was about four feet up a birch, beneath the leafy branches and quite exposed. The bird sat perfectly still with its head up and bill open upon its pretty large young, not moving in the least, while we drove a stake

close by, within three feet, and cut and measured, being about there twenty minutes at least.

June 11. P. M. — To Owl Swamp.
Lambkill flower. Carrion-flower up a day or two. *Panicum latifolium* (not out) grows by riverside at Dakin's Brook. Ferns generally were killed by the frost of last month, *e. g.* brakes, cinnamon fern, flowering and sensitive ferns, and no doubt others. I smell the strong sour scent of their decaying. *Galium triflorum,* how long?

In one grove pitch pine shoots are from seven to nine tenths as long as last year's growth.

When I return, about 5 P. M., the shad-flies swarm over the river in considerable numbers, but there are very few at sundown. Hemlocks are about at height of their beauty, with their fresh growth.

June 12. Sunday. P. M. — To Gowing's Swamp.
I am struck with the beauty of the sorrel now, *e. g. Lepidium campestre* field. What a wholesome red! It is densest in parallel lines according to the plowing or cultivation. There is hardly a more agreeable sight at this season.

Maryland yellow-throat four eggs, fresh, in sphagnum in the interior *omphalos.*

June 13. To Boston.
My rail's egg of June 1st looks like that of the Virginia rail in the Boston collection. A boy brought me a remarkably large cuckoo's egg on the 11th. Was it not

that of the yellow-billed? The one in the collection looks like it. This one at B. is not only larger but lighter-colored.

In the plates of Hooker's "Flora Boreali-Americana," the leaves of *Vaccinium cæspitosum* are not so wide as the fruit; yet mine of Tuckerman's Ravine may be it.

June 14. P. M. — To Flint's Pond.
Early strawberries begin to be common. The lower leaves of the plant are red, concealing the fruit. Violets, especially of dry land, are scarce now.

Eleocharis palustris abundant in Stow's meadow, by railroad. See a rose-bug.

A pout's nest (at Pout's Nest) with a straight en-

trance some twenty inches long and a simple round nest at end. The young just hatched, all head, light-colored, under a mass of weedy hummock which is all under water.

The common utricularia out. Hear the *phebe* note of a chickadee. Cow-wheat, how long? A rose-breasted grosbeak betrays itself by that peculiar squeak, on the Britton path. It is evident that many breed in the low woods by Flint's Pond. Catbird's nest with four eggs in a swamp-pink, three and a half feet up.

The rose-breasted grosbeak is common now in the Flint's Pond woods. It is not at all shy, and our richest

singer, perhaps, after the wood thrush. The rhythm is very like that of the tanager, but the strain is perfectly clear and sweet. One sits on the bare dead twig of a chestnut, high over the road, at Gourgas Wood, and over my head, and sings clear and loud at regular intervals, — the strain about ten or fifteen seconds long, rising and swelling to the end, with various modulations. Another, singing in emulation, regularly answers it, alternating with it, from a distance, at least a quarter of a mile off. It sings thus long at a time, and I leave it singing there, regardless of me.

June 15. A. M. — To lead-mill, Acton.
Suddenly hot weather, — 90° — after very cool days. Yarrow out, how long? Blue flag abundant. Blue-eyed grass at height.

Saw near mill, on the wooded hillside, a regular old-fashioned country house, long and low, one story unpainted, with a broad green field, half orchard, for all yard between it and the road, — a part of the hillside, — and much June-grass before it. This is where the men who save the country are born and bred. Here is the pure fountain of human life.

Walked over a rocky hill there in the midst of the heat. How interesting a thin patch of strawberry vines now on a rocky hillside, though the fruit is quite scarce! Good for suggestion and intention, at least.

Herd's-grass spikes just appear; not in bloom. (My notes on this hitherto not to be trusted.)

Sitting by Hubbard Bath [?] swamp wood and looking

north, at 3 P. M., I notice the now peculiar glaucous color of the very water, as well as the meadow-grass (*i. e.* sedge), at a dozen or twenty rods' distance, seen through the slight haze which accompanies this first June heat. A sort of leaden color, as if the fumes of lead floated over it.

Young crow blackbirds which have left the nest, with great heads and bills, the top of the head covered with a conspicuous raised light-colored down.

A fly (good-sized) with a large black patch on the wing and a reddish head alights on my hand. (A day or two after, one with a greenish head.)

Birds *shoot* like twigs. The young are as big as the old when they leave the nest; have only got to harden and mature.

June 16. P. M. — Paddle to Great Meadows.
Small snapdragon, how long?
Examined a kingfisher's nest, — though there is a *slight* doubt if I found the spot. It was formed singularly like that of the bank swallow, *i. e.* flat-elliptical, thus: ⬭ some eight inches, as I remember, in the largest diameter, and located just like a swallow's, in a sand-bank, some twenty inches below the surface. Could feel nothing in it, but it may have been removed. Have an egg from this.

Walked into the Great Meadows from the angle on the west side of the Holt, in order to see what were the prevailing sedges, etc.

On the dry and hard bank by the river, grows June-grass, etc., *Carex scoparia, stellulata, stricta,* and *Bux-*

baumii; in the wet parts, pipes two and a half feet high, *C. lanuginosa, C. bullata* (?), [*C.*] *monile, Eleocharis palustris, Panicum virgatum* [1] (a little just begins to show itself), and *Glyceria fluitans* here and there and out. There was a noble sea of pipes, — you may say pipes exclusively, — a rich dark green, quite distinct from the rest of the meadow and visible afar, a broad stream of this valuable grass growing densely, two and a half feet high in water. Next to this, south, where it was quite as wet, or wetter, grew the tall and slender *C. lanuginosa,* the prevailing sedge in the wetter parts where I walked. This was a sheeny glaucous green, bounding the pipes on each side, of a dry look. Next in abundance in the wet parts were the inflated sedges above named.[2] Those pipes, in such a mass, are, methinks, the richest mass of uniform dark liquid green now to be seen on the surface of the town [?]. You might call this meadow the "Green Sea."

Phalaris Americana, Canary grass, just out. The island by Hunt's Bridge is densely covered with it.

Saw, in the midst of the Great Meadows, the trails or canals of the musquash running an indefinite distance, now open canals full of water, in which ever minnows dart constantly, deep under the grass; and here and there you come to the stool of a musquash, where it has flatted down the tufts of sedge and perhaps gnawed them off.

June 17. Rain, especially heavy rain, raising the river in the night of the 17th.

[1] Blue-joint.   [2] *Vide* July 7th, '59, also June 22d, '60.

June 18. P. M. — Sail up river.

Rain again, and we take shelter under a bridge, and again under our boat, and again under a pine tree. It is worth the while to sit or lie through a shower thus under a bridge or under a boat on the bank, because the rain is a much more interesting and remarkable phenomenon under these circumstances. The surface of the stream betrays every drop from the first to the last, and all the variations of the storm, so much more expressive is the water than the comparatively brutish face of earth. We no doubt often walk between drops of rain falling thinly, without knowing it, though if on the water we should have been advertised of it. At last the whole surface is nicked with the rebounding drops as if the surface rose in little cones to accompany or meet the drops, till it looks like the back of some spiny fruit or animal, and yet the different-colored currents, light and dark, are seen through it all; and then, when it clears up, how gradually the surface of the water becomes more placid and bright, the dimples growing fewer and finer till the prolonged reflections of trees are seen in it, and the water is lit up with a joy which is in sympathy with our own, while the earth is comparatively dead. I saw swarms of little gnats, light-winged, dancing over the water in the midst of the rain, though you would say any drop would end one's days.

The swamp white oaks and red maples and willows, etc., now first begin to show a slight silveriness on the under edges of their flakes, where the under sides of the new leaves are shown.

Vol. XII

hatched, yet they fly. The old one in the woods near makes a chuckling sound just like a red squirrel's bark, also mewing.

Flies rain about my head.

Notice green berries, — blueberries and huckleberries.

Is that red-top, nearly out on railroad bank? *Eriophorum polystachyon* of Torrey, Bigelow, and Gray, the apparently broadish-leaved, but Gray makes the wool too long. In Pleasant and Well Meadow; at height.

Carex polytrichoides in fruit and a little in flower, Heywood Meadow in woods and Spanish Meadow Swamp. *Trisetum palustre* (?), Well Meadow Head, in wet; apparently at height.

June 20. River, on account of rain, some two feet above summer level.

Great purple fringed orchis.

What that colored-flowered locust in Deacon Farrar's yard and house this side Lincoln?

June 21. *Tuesday.* P. M. — To Derby's pasture behind and beyond schoolhouse.

Meadow-sweet. Hedge-hyssop out. In that little pool near the Assabet, above our bath-place there, *Glyceria pallida* well out in water and *Carex lagopodioides* just beginning. That grass covering dry and dryish fields and hills, with curled or convolute radical leaves, is apparently *Festuca ovina*, and not *Danthonia* as I thought it. It is now generally conspicuous. Are any of our simpler forms the *F. tenella*? [1]

¹ *Vide* July 2d, 1860.

June 19. *Sunday.* P. M. — To Heywood Meadow and Well Meadow.

In Stow's meadow by railroad, *Scirpus Eriophorum*, with blackish bracts, not long out.

A flying squirrel's nest and young on Emerson's hatchet path, south of Walden, on hilltop, in a covered hollow in a small old stump at base of a young oak, covered with fallen leaves and a portion of the stump; nest apparently of dry grass. Saw three young run out after the mother and up a slender oak. The young half-grown, very tender-looking and weak-tailed, yet one climbed quite to the top of an oak twenty-five feet high, though feebly. Claws must be very sharp and early developed. The mother rested quite near, on a small projecting stub big as a pipe-stem, curled crosswise on it. Have a more rounded head and snout than our other squirrels. The young in danger of being picked off by hawks.

Find by Baker Rock the (apparently) *Carex Muhlenbergii* gone to seed, dark-green, as Torrey says. Resembles the *stipata*.

Blackbirds nest in the small pond there, and generally in similar weedy and bushy pond-holes in woods.

The prevailing sedge of Heywood Meadow by Bartlett Hill-side, that which showed yellow tops in the spring, is the *Carex stricta*. On this the musquash there commonly makes its stools. A tall slender sedge with conspicuous brown staminate spikes. Also some *C. lanuginosa* with it. *C. canescens*, too, grows there, less conspicuous, like the others gone to seed.

Scare up young partridges; size of chickens just

You see now the *Eupatoreum purpureum* pushing up in rank masses in the low grounds, and the lower part of the uppermost leaves, forming a sort of cup, is conspicuously purplish.

June 22. Paddle up the river to Lee's, measuring the bridges.

The sun coming out at intervals to-day, after a long rainy and cloudy spell in which the weeds have grown much, I observe that the rough goldenrods and one other, which have grown one to two feet high, have many of them in various parts of the town immediately drooped their tops, hanging down five or six inches. This weed appears to be particularly tender in this respect, having probably grown very rapidly in the rain.

Comara palustris, how long? *Scirpus lacustris* is freshly out.

I notice a black willow top a foot above water, a dozen rods from shore, near the outlet of Fair Haven Pond, or just off the point of the Island, where the water is ten feet deep by my measure, and it is alive and green. Yet one who was not almost daily on the river would not perceive this revolution constantly going on. Only in very few cases [1] can I discover where the surface has been taken up, since the water stands over and conceals the scar till it is healed, and for similar reasons it is hard to tell what is a fresh deposit and what an old growth. I should say that the largest masses, or islands, of button-bushes standing in the

¹ And at lowest water a month later.

meadows had drifted there. Even the owner of the meadow and the haymakers may not always detect what was imported thus the previous spring, these transplanted plants look so at home there. So the revolution is almost an imperceptible one. Many seeing the green willow-tops rising above the surface in deep water think that there is a rock there on which they grow. There is a very large mass of bushes thus moved on the right shore, some way above Sherman's Bridge, and a large mass above Heard's Bridge some distance, on the east side (having drifted across).

I hear now that snapping sound under the pads, or probably as soon as the pads are thickly spread over the surface. Also I hear it made by a fish darting to the surface in midstream where are no weeds, — a dry, snapping sound.

June 23. Ride to Wayland, surveying the bridges. Veiny-leaved hawkweed freshly out.

At Heard's Bridge the white maple is the prevailing one, and I do not notice a red one there nor at Bridle Point Bridge. I think I saw the white as far down as the Sudbury causeway.[1]

A foggy, Cape-Cod day, with an easterly wind.

June 24. To Billerica dam, surveying the bridges. Another foggy [sic], amounting from time to time to a fine rain, and more, even to a shower, though the grass was thickly covered with cobwebs in the morning. Yet

[1] The next day saw the white maple and hibiscus in Billerica on the river, — the maple at least as far down as the falls.

it was a condensed fog, I should say. Its value appeared to be as a veil to protect the tender vegetation after the long rainy and cloudy weather.

The 22d, 23d, and 24th, I have been surveying the bridges and river from Heard's Bridge to the Billerica dam. I hear of two places in Wayland where there was formerly what was called a hay bridge, but no causeway, at some narrow and shallow place, a hundred years ago or more. Have looked after all the swift and the shallow places also.

The testimony of the farmers, etc., is that the river thirty to fifty years ago was much lower in the summer than now. Deacon Richard Heard spoke of playing when a boy on the river side of the bushes where the pads are, and of wading with great ease at Heard's Bridge, and I hear that one Rice (of Wayland or Sudbury), an old man, remembers galloping his horse through the meadows to the edge of the river. The meadow just above the causeway on the Wayland side was spoken of as particularly valuable. Colonel David Heard, who accompanied me and is best acquainted of any with the details of the controversy, — has worked at clearing out the river (I think about 1820), — said that he did not know of a rock in the river from the falls near the Framingham line to perhaps the rear of Hubbard's in Concord.

The grass not having been cut last year, the ice in the spring broke off great quantities of pipes, etc., immense masses of them, which were floated and drifted down against the causeways and bridges; and there they lie still, almost concealing any green grass,

Vol. XII

like a raft on the meadows, along the south side the causeways. The inhabitants of Wayland used a good deal for mulching trees. One told me that at Sherman's Bridge they stretched quite across the river above the bridge, so that a man "could walk across on them," — perhaps "did walk across on them," — but on inquiring of one who lived by the bridge I learned that "a dog could not have walked across on them."

Daniel Garfield, whom I met fishing on the river, and who has worked on Nine-Acre Corner and Lee's Bridges for fifty years or more, could remember one year when Captain Wheeler dug much mud from the river, when the water was so low that he could throw out pickerel on each side outside the bushes (where the pads now are). Says that his old master with whom he lived in Lincoln when he was young told him that he wheeled the first barrow-load at the building of Lee's Bridge and road, and that if he were alive now he would be a good deal over a hundred years old. Yet Shattuck says that bridge was a new bridge in 1660.

Ebenezer Conant remembers when the Canal dam was built, and that before that it used to be dry at midsummer outside the bushes on each side.

Lee says that about 1819 the bridge near him was rebuilt and the mud-sills taken up. These are said to remain sound an indefinite while. When they put in a new pile (Buttrick the carpenter tells me) they find the mortise in the mud-sill and place it in that. Deacon Farrar says that he can remember Lee's Bridge seventy-five years ago, and that it was not a new bridge then. That it is sometimes obstructed by hay in the spring.

That he has seen a chip go faster up-stream there than ever down. His son said this was the case considerably further up in the meadows toward Rice's, and he thought it the effect of Stow River backing up.

Deacon Farrar thought the hay bridge called Farrar's Bridge was for foot-passengers only.

I found the water in Fair Haven Pond on the 22d twelve to thirteen feet deep in what I thought the channel, but in Purple Utricularia Bay, half a dozen rods from the steep hill, twenty-two and a half feet was the most I found.

John Hosmer tells me that he remembers Major Hosmer's testifying that the South Bridge was carried up-stream, before the court, at the beginning of the controversy.

Simonds of Bedford, who is measuring the rapidity of the current at Carlisle Bridge, says that a board with a string attached ran off there one hundred yards in fifteen minutes at the height of water (in May, and pretty high), when the Commissioners were here. That he has found it to be swiftest just after the water has begun to fall.

The character of the river valley changes about at Hill's Bridge. The meadows are quite narrow and of a different character, — higher and firmer, — a long hill bounds the meadow, and almost the river, on the west for a good way, and high land on the east, and the bottom is harder and said to be often rocky (?).

The water was about four and a half feet deep — sounded with a paddle and guessed at — at the Fordway, and at that stage so swift and strong that you could not row a boat against it in the swiftest part of the falls.[1]

June 26. Sunday. P. M. — Up Assabet.

The black willow down is now quite conspicuous on the trees, giving them a parti-colored or spotted white and green look, quite interesting, like a fruit. It also rests on the water by the sides of the stream, where caught by alders, etc., in narrow crescents ten and five feet long, at right angles with the bank, so thick and white as to remind me of a dense mass of hoar-frost crystals.

June 27. I find that the tops of my stakes in Moore's Swamp are nearly two feet lower than a fortnight ago, or when Garfield began to fill it.

P. M. — To Walden.

At the further Brister's Spring, under the pine, I find an *Attacus luna*, half hidden under a skunk-cabbage leaf, with its back to the ground and motionless, on the edge of the swamp. The under side is a particularly pale hoary green. It is somewhat greener above with a slightly purplish brown border on the front edge of its front wings, and a brown, yellow, and whitish eye-spot in the middle of each wing. It is very sluggish and allows me to turn it over and cover it up with another leaf, — sleeping till the night come. It has more rela-

[1] July 22d, the average depth of water at the Fordway was two feet, it having fallen in Concord two feet nine and three fourths inches since June 23d; so that the water fell possibly as much in this month at the Fordway as at Concord, — I think surely within half a foot as much.

Vol. XII

tion to the moon by its pale hoary-green color and its sluggishness by day than by the form of its tail. A frail creature, rarely met with, though not uncommon.

June 29. P. M. — To Walden.

Very hot. The piper grass bloom in prime. Examined the flying squirrel's nest at the base of a small white [oak] or two (sprouts), four inches through, in a small old white oak stump, half open above, just below the level of the ground, composed of quite a mass of old withered oak leaves and a few fresh green ones, and the inside wholly of fine, dry sedge and sedge-like bark-fibres. The upper side of the nest was half visible from above. It was eight or nine inches across. In it I found the wing of an *Attacus luna*, — and July 1st another wing near Second Division, which makes three between June 27th and July 1st.

At the railroad spring in Howard's meadow, I see two chestnut-sided warblers hopping and chipping as if they had a nest, within six feet of me, a long time. No doubt they are breeding near. Yellow crown with a fine dark longitudinal line, reddish-chestnut sides, black triangle on side of head, white beneath.

River falls several inches.

June 30. Cooler, with a northerly wind. The pads blown up by it already show crimson, it is so strong, but this not a fall phenomenon yet.

V

JULY, 1859

(ÆT. 41–42)

July 1. P. M. — To Second Division Brook.

Have heard the peculiar peep of young tailless golden robins for a day or more.

White water ranunculus in full bloom at least a week, in Second Division Brook, near the dam, in the shade of the bank, a clear day. Its leaves and stems waving in the brook are interesting, — much cut and green.

The *Holcus lanatus*, past prime, near J. P. Brown's little meadow beyond end of his moraine; also grows near southwest end of Hubbard's Grove. *Agrostis*, either *vulgaris* or *alba* (or both), now generally coming into bloom in fields both moist and dry, but I should say with considerable ligules and rather roughish sheaths.

July 2. P. M. — To Stow's chestnut and *Thaspium aureum*.

Vetch, morning-glory, *Andromeda ligustrina*, how long?

Waded out thirteen rods from rock in Flint's Pond, and was only up to my middle.

Mitchella repens is abundantly out. *Pyrola elliptica* out. Cladium not quite.

July 3. P. M. — To Hubbard's Grove.

You see in rich moist mowing the yet slender, recurving unexpanded panicles or heads of the red-top (?), mixed with the upright, rigid herd's-grass. Much of it is out in dry places. *Glyceria fluitans* is very abundant in Depot Field Brook. *Hypericum ellipticum* out.

I noticed the other day, I think the 30th, a large patch of *Agrostis scabra* in E. Hosmer's meadow, — the firmer ridges, — a very interesting purple with its fine waving top, mixed with blue-eyed grass.

The *Mitchella repens*, so abundant now in the northwest part of Hubbard's Grove, emits a strong astringent cherry-like scent as I walk over it, now that it is so abundantly in bloom, which is agreeable to me, — spotting the ground with its downy-looking white flowers.

Eleocharis obtusa and *acicularis* are now apparently in prime at water's edge by Hubbard's Grove bridge path. Also *Juncus bufonius* is very abundant in path there, fresh quite, though some shows seed. *Juncus tenuis*, though quite fresh, is also as much gone to seed.

July 4. June 28th, I observed up the Assabet some exceedingly handsome amelanchier leaves, bright-crimson, regularly striped with green on the veins and with scattered yellow spots. The shrub probably dying. *Vide* some in press.

P. M. — To Fair Haven Pond, measuring depth of river.

As you walk beside a ditch or brook, you see the frogs which you alarm launching themselves from a considerable distance into the brook. They spring considerably upward, so as to clear all intervening obstacles, and seem to know pretty well where the brook is. Yet no doubt they often strike, to their chagrin and perhaps sorrow, on a pebbly shore or rock. Their noses must be peculiarly organized to resist accidents of this kind, and allow them to cast themselves thus heedlessly into the air, trusting to fall into the water, for they come down nose foremost. A frog reckons that he knows where the brook is. I shudder for them when I see their soft, unshielded proboscis falling thus heedlessly on whatever may be beneath.

I observe at Well Meadow Head that the fall has already come conspicuously to the hellebore, and they are mostly turned yellow, while their large green seed-vessels are ripening; but the skunk-cabbage is still green.

The front-rank polygonum, having been submerged by the unusually high water of the last fortnight, is a conspicuous red or purple color; and this is evidently the effect of the water alone, as, I think, it is the water which turns the early maples.[1] All the river's edge is now tinged with this purplish streak, yet they are healthy-looking leaves.

Johnswort is just fairly begun. *Hypericum ellipticum* and Jersey tea first observed.

The deepest place I find in the river to-day is off Bittern Cliff, answering to the bold shore. There is an uninterrupted deep and wide reach of the river from Fair Haven Pond to Nut Meadow Brook.

July 5. P. M. — To Ball's Hill, sounding river.

[1] Both white and red, when the leaves are not half developed, long ago.

Having sounded the river yesterday and to-day from entrance to Fair Haven Pond to oak at Ball's Hill, the water being to-day three inches lower than yesterday, — or now a foot and a quarter above what I call summer level, — I make these observations: [1] —

Calling any place above Ball's Hill where the water is eleven feet deep or more at summer level a deep hole, I find six such deep holes within the above limits, *viz.*: 1st, under the steep hill at southwest part of Fair Haven Pond; 2d, at Bittern Cliff; 3d, four rods below French's Rock, or opposite mouth of Mill Brook; 4th, deep hole at ash; 5th, deep hole at sharp bend; 6th, deep hole at northeast angle of the Holt. In the order of depth they stand thus: —

1. Purple Utricularia Bay	19¼ feet
2. Sharp bend by Holt	17
3. Northeast angle of Holt	16¼
4. French's Rock	12¼
5. Bittern Cliff	11
6. Deep hole by ash	11

These "holes" appear to be of two kinds. In two, if not three, of the above instances they appear to be a trace of the original formation of the river valley, and to be independent of the river and not necessarily at an

[1] [From now till the middle of August Thoreau devoted much of his time to a study of the physiography of Concord River, and the Journal contains many tables of statistics concerning its depth, its rise and fall, its meanders, the rapidity of its current, and the like. Such details could be of no interest to the general reader, and the editors are assured on expert authority that they are now without scientific value. Most of them are therefore omitted, enough being retained to show something of the method of the work and the painstaking spirit in which it was carried on.]

Vol. XII

angle. No. 1 is evidently traceable to a very steep and high hill half a dozen rods off, and No. 5 to a small rocky cliff some three rods off. There is a part of the bare, precipitous cliff under water at lowest level. No. 4 appears to be of a similar character with the last.

The others (or 2, 3, and 6) are of a different character, — where there is meadow on each side and they are not betrayed by any elevation of the shore. In each case they are close to the positive side at an angle in the river. The deepest (and also the deepest of any in the river proper), which will serve for a sample, is at the sharpest bend in the river in Concord, and, I think, at the narrowest part of the river in the town. The stream, not deep and rather more than ordinarily swift above, here strikes square (or worse [?]) against the easterly bank (which is only some three feet above summer level), and has eaten out a channel to that depth, so near the bank (some twelve feet) that you could jump from the bank into the deepest place in the river proper in the town. Thence it shoals regularly to the opposite shore. The bottom exactly in the deepest holes of this last description is not muddy but sandy. In each of these three instances there is a muddy, stagnant expansion on the opposite side just below (or else about opposite), betraying a reaction to this force. There is also a low meadow or point on the opposite side where the river has flowed at a comparatively recent period. The river is not particularly swift at these places.

Calling all places which are four or less feet deep at summer level shallows, there are at least seven such between Fair Haven Pond and Ball's Hill.

Potamogetons begin to prevail below four and a half [feet] (five and a half in sluggish water), and reach quite across the river at three feet. They invariably occupy these shoals, except the one below ash tree with a bottom of shifting sand, though they are densest on broad sand-bars occupying the midstream, on which there is one to two and a half or three feet [of] water and a clearer channel on one or both sides or in the middle.

With one exception (*i. e.* Barrett's Bar) these shoals are just below (?) considerable bends. Also the river is generally narrower than the average at the shoals.

The river (in Concord) is much more variable in depth below the junction of the two rivers than above it.

The great bends in Concord above Ball's Hill are about nine. The only remarkable, or Great, Bend in Concord is the Holt, where a new channel might be cut, saving nearly two thirds the distance.

All these bends in C. (except perhaps the Holt in part (?)) are occasioned by the river striking firmer land or a hill or cliff and being turned by it. It is like the wriggling of a snake controlled between two fences. It is not so with the Sudbury Meadow bends.

From a rude estimate I should say about one mile, or say one eighth (?) part the river in Concord, is weedy.

There is a peculiarly long, sluggish, wide, deep, and lake-like reach, muddy in the broadest parts (for Concord), from Fair Haven Pond to Nut Meadow Brook. Though in meadows, it is pretty straight. Not enough current to make a meander.

Many a farmer living near the river will tell you of some deep hole which he thinks the deepest in all the river, and which he says has never been sounded (which may have been true, and hence its reputation), where he has chanced to fish, or possibly bathed, or somebody has been drowned. It only need to be considerably over his head to acquire this reputation. If you tell him you have sounded it, and it was not very deep, he will think that you did not find the right spot.

The deep places in the river are not so obvious as the shallow ones and can only be found by carefully probing it. So perhaps it is with human nature.

Fair Haven Pond, though not very deep generally, is a kind of deep hole, to be referred to Fair Haven and Lee's Cliff, etc.

The deepest part of the river is generally rather toward one side, especially where the stream is energetic. On a curve it is generally deepest on the inside bank, and the bank most upright.

Those deep holes in the Great Meadows are somewhat like trout-holes under the bank in Second Division Brook.

The principal weedy place for length (in Concord) is from boat's place to oak; for density, shallowness, and length, all together, is Barrett's Bar.

The swifter places *that I remember*, between Fair Haven Pond and Ball's Hill, *leaving out bridges*,[1] are: —

> Clamshell
> Hubbard's Bath
> Merrick's
> Island shoal, etc.

[1] Aug. 4th. I do not remember any of consequence above except amid weeds at Rice's Bend.

> French Rock, etc., the shoal below
> Rocks below Old North Bridge
> Barrett's Bar
> Sharp Bend Reach
> Holt's Ford

That is, generally the shoal and weedy places, but also where the obstruction is a sharp bend or rocks.

July 6. My English cress (*Nasturtium officinale*) at Depot Field Brook is in bloom, and has already begun to go to seed, turning purplish, as it withers (from white).

P. M. — To Lee's Cliff.

The fields are now purplish with the anthers of the herd's-grass, which is apparently at its height.

Grass now for a week or more has been seriously in the way of the walker, but already I take advantage of the few fields that are mowed. It requires skillful tacking, a good deal of observation, and experience to get across the country now.

At Lee's Cliff, pellitory apparently not long, yet I see small green fruit. The gymnostichum grass just begun.

The heart-leaf flower is now very conspicuous and pretty (3 P. M.) in that pool westerly of the old Conantum house. Its little white five-petalled flower, about the size of a five-cent-piece, looks like a little white lily. Its perfectly heart-shaped floating leaf, an inch or more long, is the smallest kind of pad. There is a single pad to each slender stem (which is from one to several feet long in proportion to the depth of the water), and these padlets cover sometimes, like an imbrication, the whole

surface of a pool. Close under each leaf or pad is concealed an umbel of ten to fifteen flower-buds of various ages, and of these one at a time (and sometimes more) curls upward between the lobes of the base, and expands its corolla to the light and air about half an inch above the water, and so on successively till all have flowered. Over the whole surface of the shallow pool you see thus each little pad with its pretty lily between its lobes, turned toward the sun. It is simply leaf and flower.

Galium pilosum, how long?

July 7. P. M. — To Great Meadows.

P. Hutchinson says he once found a wood duck's nest in a hollow maple by Heywood's meadow (now by railroad), and tried to get the young as soon as hatched, but they were gone too soon for him.

On the first, or westerly, part of the Great Meadows, *i. e.* the firmer parts and the bank, I find, mixed with sedges of different kinds, much red-top (coloring the surface extensively), fowl-meadow (just begun to bloom and of a purplish lead-color, taller than the red-top), the slender purple-spiked panic, *Agrostis* (*perennans?* or *scabra??*). In the wet, or main, part, beside various other sedges, — as [*Carex*] *stellulata, lanuginosa, stricta*, etc., etc., — wool-grass, now in flower, a sedge (apparently *C. ampullacea* var. *utriculata* toward Holbrook's) thicker-culmed than wool-grass, but softer and not round, with fertile spikes often three inches long, and slender. A great part of the meadow is covered with, I think, either this or wood grass (not in flower). I am not

certain which prevails, but I think wool-grass, which does not flower. Also, mixed with these and lower, dulichium, *Eleocharis palustris*, etc., etc.[1]

First notice pontederia out; also tephrosia, how long?

The note of the bobolink has begun to sound rare?

Do not young nighthawks run pretty soon after being hatched? I hear of their being gone very soon.

Bathing at Barrett's Bay, I find it to be composed in good part of sawdust, mixed with sand. There is a narrow channel on each side, deepest on the south. The potamogeton is eight feet long there in eighteen inches of water.

I learn from measuring on Baldwin's second map that the river (*i. e.* speaking of that part below Framingham) is much the straightest in the lower part of its course, or from Ball's Hill to the Dam.

It winds most in the broad meadows. The greatest meander is in the Sudbury meadows.

From upper end of Sudbury Canal to Sherman's Bridge direct is 558 rods (1 mile 238 rods); by thread of river, 1000 rods (3 miles 40 rods), or nearly twice as far.

But, though meandering, it is straighter in its general course than would be believed. These nearly twenty-three miles in length (or 16 + direct) are contained within a breadth of two miles twenty-six rods; *i. e.*, so much it takes to meander in. It can be plotted by the scale of one thousand feet to an inch on a sheet of paper seven feet one and one quarter inches long by eleven inches wide.

[1] *Vide* back, June 16th.

The deep and lake-like are the straightest reaches. The straightest reach within these limits above Ball's Hill is from Fair Haven Pond to Clamshell Hill.

I observed in Maine that the dam at the outlet of Chesuncook Lake, some twenty miles off, had raised the water so as to kill the larches on the Umbazookskus extensively. They were at least four or five miles up the Umbazookskus.

July 8. Friday. I see an emperor moth (*Attacus Cecropia*), which came out the 6th.

P. M. — To Clamshell by river.

The *Carex Muhlenbergii* is common on Clamshell slope, just beyond the ravine.

Thimble-berries have begun.

The islands of the river, below the Assabet especially, — as Hosmer's, and the one just below French's Rock, — are now covered with canary grass, which has almost entirely done and closed up; fowl-meadow (*Poa serotina*), now fairly begun to bloom (first noticed the middle of June its slender green panicles shaped like a green red-top); *Glyceria fluitans*, going out of bloom; also the sensitive fern (the "hand leaf" of haymakers); pipes; (and sedges, which might be named as soon as any, as the *crinita* which overhangs the water).

I judge that in a freshet the water rises higher as you go down the river, both from the height to which it rose last March, as shown me at several bridges, and from the height of the bridges themselves, which the builders have been gradually compelled to raise, for the most part just above high-water mark.

July 9. Paddle up river and sound a little above Fair Haven Pond.

See young kingbirds which have lately flown perched in a family on the willows, — the airy bird, lively, twittering.

The water having gone down, I notice a broad red base to the bayonet rush, apparently the effect of the water, even as the maples (of both kinds) and the polygonums are reddened. The bayonet rush is not quite out.

I see, at length, where the floated meadow (on Hubbard's meadow) came from last spring, — from opposite Bittern Cliff, and some below. There is a pond created in the meadow there, some five rods by four and three to three and a half feet deep, water being eleven and a half inches above summer level, — a regular oval pond, where nothing rises above water, but I see pontederia grass-like leafets springing up all over the bottom. The piece taken out here probably contained no button-bushes. So much of the meadow which has been moved [?] is thus converted into a pool. Close by, south, are still larger scars, where masses of button-bush thicket have been ripped up. No doubt some of those on Hubbard's meadow came from here. The water where they stood is about the same depth as in the other place. I see a piece of floated button-bush on the south side of Fair Haven Pond, west of the old boat place of Baker Shore, which is twelve rods long by one rod wide, and, in two or three pieces [*sic*] where it is several thicknesses, it is full three feet thick of solid earth. The whole is set in a straight line separating the meadow in the rear

Vol. XII

from the pond, forming, in fact, just such a brink there as exists in perfection on the west side of the pond. This might be called brink-bush, or drift-bush, river-fence. It is the floating fencing-stuff of the river. Possibly that (in the spring) island south of the mouth of Well Meadow Brook, and even the large island in the pond, had its beginning thus, not only willows but maples and alders having at length sprung up on it and built it up.

The next day (10th) I see, just above Sherman's Bridge, on the east side, a piece, some eight rods long by one rod wide, arranged as a brink separating a meadow from the river in the same manner, and, a quarter of a mile higher up on the same side, a more or less broken piece which I estimated by my eye to be five rods by twelve, the largest mass or collection of the kind moved together that I ever saw. I have seen six pieces moved last March, or spring, which contained all together more than half an acre. There was more than a quarter of an acre in the last piece alone.

The button-bush and black willow generally grow together, especially on the brink of the stagnant parts of the river. (Very little comparatively in the great Sudbury meadow and in our Great Meadows.) Perhaps they are there carried off by the ice. They stand generally in line (sometimes half a dozen rods wide) on the brink of the river, separating it from some (commonly narrow) meadow behind, and at high water are a distinct line of separation, rising above the surface and indicating the summer boundary. The best example is at Fair Haven Pond, west side. It is often pretty deep water quite up to the bushes, or there are pads, etc., out-

side them. There they stand in massive and regular straight or curving lines, and you suppose that they have stood there for ages. But I have seen twelve rods together (*i. e.* in one piece) of such fence, the whole width of it transplanted half a mile to some shore where there was none, and forming a fence to the pond or river there. We are accustomed to refer changes in the shore and the channel to the very gradual influence of the current washing away and depositing matter which was held in suspension, but certainly in many parts of our river the ice which moves these masses of bushes and meadow is a much more important agent. It will alter the map of the river in one year. The whole shore for forty rods on the east side below Bittern Cliff was stripped of its button-bushes and willows, etc., etc., last spring, and as I floated over the river there to-day, I could not at first account for the remarkable breadth of the river there, like a bay. I got a very novel impression of the size of the river, though it is now low water. In fact the width of the river has been increased fully three or four rods for more than forty rods in length, and is three to four feet deep on that side now. You cannot tell, of any clump or row of button-bushes, whether it grew up where it stands or was thus set out there. I have seen these masses, sunk in midstream, produce a small weedy spot the same year, and possibly a large mass might thus form an extensive shallow and weedy place or island.

Potamogetons begin to prevail at five and a half feet in sluggish water (at summer level), though they will still be visible when the water rises higher, rising with it. They appear at four and a half, if more rapid, and are densest at three feet, if the stream is not exceedingly rapid.

The kalmiana lily grows to seven and a half feet (summer level) where it is sluggish (and is still atop when it is a foot or two deeper), and you see this, the heart-leaf, utricularia, and potamogeton, all together, in five feet [of] water (also in same place when a foot or two higher). The front-rank polygonum grows outside the pontederia, next to the potamogeton, and, near the causeway bridge, in Wayland, reaches (except four or five feet) quite across the river (three feet [of] water).

We have not only the Assabet uniting with the main stream about in the middle of the township, but three highways thus raying out in different directions, — as great an amount of river within these limits as could well be. Neither stream runs direct through the town. The main stream runs first northerly or northwesterly and then northeasterly, and perhaps this is as convenient for sailing in flat-bottomed boats as any arrangement could be, the prevailing winds being northwest and southwest, but sailing is much affected by hills, woods, etc.

To-day, July 9th, water is eleven and a half inches above summer level.

July 10. Water ten and a half inches above summer level.

8 A. M. — Take boat at Fair Haven Pond and paddle up to Sudbury Causeway, sounding the river.

To-day, like yesterday, is very hot, with a blue haze concealing the mountains and hills, looking like hot dust in the air.

Hearing a noise, I look up and see a pigeon woodpecker pursued by a kingbird, and the former utters loud shrieks with fear.

Paddling through the wild Sudbury meadows, I am struck with the regularity with which the phalanxes of bulrushes (*Scirpus lacustris*) occur. They do not grow in a continuous line, like pipes or pontederia, but in small isolated patches. At each bend, though it does not appear on Baldwin's map, there is a bay-like expansion of the river, now half emerged, thus: —

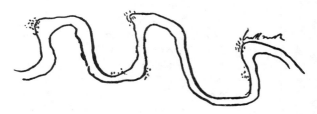

where the more stagnant water has deposited mud, and in each such place, with remarkable regularity, a phalanx of bulrushes presents itself as you ascend. It occasionally occupies a corresponding place as you descend, and also intermediate shores of a similar character. Yet it so constantly occurs in just this position as to be remarkable. It is not very common along our river, being mainly confined to the larger and wilder meadows, — at any rate to the expansions, be they larger or smaller. These phalanxes are from one to three or more rods wide, and the rush is of a glaucous green, very interesting with its shafts slanting different ways. At one bend,

especially, grows — and I have not noticed it elsewhere except in this meadow — the great *Scirpus fluviatilis* (how long out?). Yet the leaves are not so roughish nor so long as described.

The *Arundo Phragmites* is not nearly out, though quite tall. *Spartina cynosuroides* well out. The green pipes border the stream for long distances.

The high water of the last month has left a whitish scum on the grass.

We scare up eight or a dozen wood ducks, already about grown. The meadow is quite alive with them.

What was that peculiar loud note from some invisible water-fowl near the Concord line? Any kind of plover? or clapper rail?

H. Buttrick says he has shot a meadow-hen much larger than the small one here. I hear in the ridge the peculiar notes of, I think, the meadow-hen, — same *e. g.* [*sic*] where I got an egg and nest. The young are probably running there. Often hear it in the great Sudbury meadow.

See many young birds now, — blackbirds, swallows, kingbirds, etc., in the air. Even hear one *link* from a bobolink.

I notice at Bittern Cliff that the sparganium floats upstream, probably because the wind has blown thus.

The bottom of Fair Haven Pond is very muddy. I can generally thrust a pole down three feet into it, and it may be very much deeper.

Young pouts are an inch long, and in some ditches left high and dry and dead with the old.

July 11. Another hot day with blue haze, and the sun sets red, threatening still hotter weather, and the very moon looks through a somewhat reddish air at first.

The position of the button-bushes determines the width of the river, no less than the width or depth of the water determines the position of the button-bushes. We call that all river between the button-bushes, though sometimes they may have landed or sprung up in a regular brink fashion three or four rods further from, or nearer to, the channel.

That mass (described on the 9th, seen the 10th) in the Wayland meadows above Sherman's Bridge was, I think, the largest mass drifted or growing at all on that great meadow. So this transplantation is not on an insignificant scale when compared with [the] whole body that grows by our river. The largest single mass on the Wayland meadows, considering both length and breadth, was the recently drifted one. To-day the farmer owns a meadow slightly inclined toward the river and generally (*i. e.* taking the year together) more or less inundated on that side. To-morrow it is a meadow quite cut off from the river by a fence of button-bush and black willow, a rod or more in width and four to seven or eight feet high, set along the inundated side and concealing the river from sight.

I hear that Mr. and Mrs. Such-a-one are "going to the beach" for six weeks. What a failure and defeat this suggests their lives to be! Here they live, perchance, the rest of the year, trying to do as they would be done by and to exercise charity of all kinds, and now at last, the parents not having realized their aspirations in the married state, and the misses now begun to be old maids without having found any match at all, succumb and slope to the beach for six weeks. Yet, so far from being felt to be a proof of failure in the lives of these Christians, it is thought to be the culminating-point of their activity. At length their season of activity is arrived, and they go to the beach, they energetically keep cool. They bathe daily and are blown on by the sea-breeze. This keeps their courage up for the labors of the year. This recess which the Sabbath-school teachers take! What if they were to abide, instead, with the caravan of sweltering pilgrims making their way over this Sahara to their Mecca?

We hear at length that Miss Such-a-one, now well advanced in years, has at length shut up house and gone to the beach. Man servant and maid servant went long ago to prepare the way for her, — to get the bottles of all kinds ready. She has fought the good fight here until at length no shield nor pretense will serve, and now she has gone to the beach, and have not her principles gone with her? She has flitted to Swallow Cave, where, perchance, no duties lurk.

Ah, shall we not go to the beach after another fashion some of us one day? Think of the numbers who are imbeached by this time! How they flutter like devil's-needles and butterflies commingled along our pontederia'd shores!

They have gone and left an empty house. The silver is cached, as prairie travellers leave behind provisions which they expect to return to. But the rent of the last house goes on nevertheless, and is to be added to the

board at the great watering-place. So is it with every domicil we rent; the rent never ceases, but enlarges from year to year. They have gone to the beach to get a few pebbles, which help digestion for the rest of the year.

July 12. Another hot day. 96° at mid-afternoon.
P. M. — To Assabet Bath.

The elm avenue above the Wheeler farm is one of the hottest places in the town; the heat is reflected from the dusty road. The grass by the roadside begins to have a dry, hot, dusty look. The melted ice is running almost in a stream from the countryman's covered wagon, containing butter, which is to be conveyed hard to Boston market. He stands on the wheel to relieve his horses at each shelf in the ascent of Colburn Hill.

I think I have distinguished our eriophorums now. There is the *E. vaginatum*, the earliest, out long ago; the *E. polystachyon*, well out June 19th; and to-day I see the *E. gracile*, which apparently has not been out quite so long as the last. Its leaves are channelled triangular. Saw yesterday the *E. Virginicum*, apparently in bloom, though very little woolly or reddish as yet, — a dense head.

The taller dark rhynchospora is well out.

In the evening, the moon being about full, I paddle up the river to see the moonlight and hear the bullfrogs. The toads and the pebbly *dont dont* are most common. There are fireworks in the village, — rockets, blue lights, etc. I am so far off that I do not hear the rush of the

Vol. XII

rocket till it has reached its highest point, so that it seems to be produced there. So the villagers entertain themselves this warm evening. Such are the[ir] aspirations.

I see at 9.30 P. M. a little brood of four or five barn swallows, which have quite recently left the nest, perched close together for the night on a dead willow twig in the shade of the tree, about four feet above the water. Their tails not yet much grown. When I passed up, the old bird twittered about them in alarm. I now float within four feet, and they do not move or give sign of awaking. I could take them all off with my hand. They have been hatched in the nearest barn or elsewhere, and have been led at once to roost here, for coolness and security. There is no cooler nor safer place for them. I observe that they take their broods to the telegraph-wire for an aerial perch, where they teach them to fly. They have gone to their beach.

July 14. P. M. — Sounded river from Ball's Hill (*i. e.* off Squaw [?] Harbor) to Atkins's boat-house corner.

The river, in all the above distance, nowhere washes the base of an isolated (*i. e.* to except long, lowish hill-banks like Clamshell, etc.) steep hill, without a greater depth off it.

The average depth between Sudbury Causeway and Atkins's boat-house bend at wall, or for fifteen miles two hundred and eighty-two rods, is eight and one eighth feet.

There extends from Tarbell Hill to Skelton Bend what I will call the Straight Reach, a mile and a third

long and quite straight. This is the finest *water* view, making the greatest impression of size, of any that I know on the river. It is very broad, deep, and clear of weeds. Average depth 11+ feet (and at highest water some 19 feet). The bottom is almost everywhere muddy. No weeds in the middle. Measuring on the plan by Baldwin, it is three to four hundred feet wide. The depth is also very uniform, varying but little (in the thread) from the average 11+ (except a deep hole and channel at the commencement off Tarbell Hill).

Yesterday (the 13th) Frank Adams brought me a bird's nest and egg from an apple tree near the road by Addison Fay's house. He says it was about twelve feet high in the tree, and it appears to have been in a fork. The nest is most like a kingbird's, or a stout, thick cherry-bird's, or even a very thick tanager's, or a purple finch's half as large again as usual. The egg is the size and form of the phœbe's, but blue-white. The nest is three inches high and five inches wide outside, two inches deep and two and a half wide inside; composed of coarse stubble, strings, coarse root-fibre, etc., externally, and neatly lined with fine withered grass. The egg is pale blue-white, four tenths of an inch long by three tenths wide at the larger end, being broad at one end like a phœbe's. Can it be a cherry-bird's without spots and of the form described by Wilson?

He also has a very large cuckoo's egg, which again makes me suspect that we have the yellow-billed cuckoo.

July 15. P. M. — To Ledum Swamp.

First notice Canada thistle, *Aralia hispida*, *Stachys aspera*, and *Asclepias pulchra*. The *Eriophorum vaginatum* done. The white orchis not yet, apparently, for a week or more. Hairy huckleberry still in bloom, but chiefly done.

Gather a few *Vaccinium Pennsylvanicum*. Raspberries, in one swamp, are quite abundant and apparently at their height.

July 16 and 18. Afternoons, I sounded the Assabet as far up as the stone bridge.

This bridge, as I see by the town records, was talked about (*i. e.* the building) in 1807, and was probably built that year or the next (though E. Wood says that the Turnpike Company, who then proposed to build it, did not fulfill their contract). Shattuck's date, 1802, is wrong. Accordingly, by building this narrow bridge here, twenty-five feet in width, or contracting the stream to about one fourth its average width, the current has been so increased as to wash away about a quarter of an acre of land which rises a dozen or fourteen feet above water (or at least an acre four feet in depth) and dig a hole six times the average depth of the stream, twenty-two and a half feet deep, or considerable, *i. e.* three feet, deeper than any place in the main stream from Sudbury Causeway to Atkins's boat-house bend, and all this in fifty years.[1] Yet the depth under the bridge is only two and a half feet plus. It falls in four rods from two and a half to twenty-two and a half.

A considerable island has been formed there, at least

[1] *Vide* July 20th.

Vol. XII

black willow loves to grow. I know of no such banks on the main stream.

Again there are comparatively few of the large floating potamogetons here. (I do not remember any of the very largest species.) The weeds are chiefly bur-reeds and a slenderer potamogeton and an immersed species (I speak of weeds in the middle). You wonder what makes the difference between this stream and the other. It seems impossible that it should be a geological difference in the beds of the streams so near together. Is it not owing simply to the greater swiftness of this stream? Does not this produce a sandy and gravelly and stony bottom, and so invite a different fauna and flora? I suspect that a fall of two or three inches more in a mile will produce a different fauna and flora to some extent, — the fresh-water sponge, the wood tortoise, the sucker, the kingfisher, the stone-heaps.

It is remarkable how the stones are separated from the sand at the Eddy Bridge and deposited in a bar or islands by themselves a few rods lower down. The sand-bar there, partly under water, looks exactly like a snow-drift. It is a narrow, sharp ridge, extending southwest from the island, with deep water on each side. The sand carried round by the eddy falls there where the ice is observed to loiter most. The large stones are perhaps swept away by a stronger current beneath.

The bars and banks of this stream are peculiar, *i. e.* of fine sand without mud. This indicates a fall and swifter water, and consequently it is on such a stream the mills are built and sawdust and shavings are mixed with such sand to form the bank. One such bank at the

three feet and a half above low water, composed of sand, and, two or three rods lower, are deposited the stones, generally larger than a hen's egg, without sand, forming bars and islands quite distinct from the former. This is much the swiftest place on the stream thus far and deeper than any for twenty-five miles of [the] other stream, and consequently there is a great eddy, where I see cakes of ice go round and round in the spring, and, as usual, the shoal water and islands formed by the ruins of the bank and of the bottom are close by. As usual, the shoal water is produced by the rapidity of the current close by.

The sand and gravel are deposited chiefly in the immediate neighborhood of the swiftest water, the swift water producing an eddy. Hence, apparently, the sandy islands at the junction of the rivers, the sand-bar at the swift place on the Assabet, etc. Contract the stream and make it swift, and you will wear a deep hole and make sand-bars and islands below.

The stream is remarkably different from the other. It is not half so deep. It is considerably more rapid. The bottom is not muddy but sandy and occasionally stony. Though far shallower, it is less weedy than the other. In the above distance weeds do not anywhere grow quite across it. A shallowness of two and a half feet does not necessarily bring in weeds, and for long distances three feet is clear of weeds. This is owing, perhaps, not only to the greater swiftness of the current, but to the want of mud under the sand. The banks and bars are peculiar. They are commonly composed of a fine sand mixed with sawdust, shavings, etc., in which the

swift place has been recently raised four or five feet above the present level by freshets. It is apparently advancing down-stream.

What is deposited by the eddy occasioned by the narrows is building it up, and so the stream is being narrowed further down. Eddies are the great builders of sand-bars and islands and banks. Any agent that stops the progress of the water downward builds up the bottom in some place.

At the bottom of the deep hole at Eddy Bridge, I felt several water-logged trunks of trees and saw some, which probably were carried round and round by the eddy until they became water-logged and sank.

July 18. One tells me that he stopped at Stedman Buttrick's on the 10th, and found him sitting under a cherry tree ringing a bell, in order to keep the birds off!

If you get on to a rock in the river, *rock* the boat, while you keep steadily pushing, and thus there will be moments when the boat does not rest on the rock at all, and you will rapidly get it off. The river is getting low, so that the entrances to musquash-holes in the bank are revealed and often laid bare, with fresh green rushes or flags, etc., in them.

Nathan Hosmer remembers that when the two new

stone piers at Hunt's Bridge were built, about 1820, one Nutting went under water to place the stones, and he was surprised to see how long he would remain under about this business. Nothing has got built without labor. Past generations have spent their blood and strength for us. They have cleared the land, built roads, etc., for us. In all fields men have laid down their lives for us. Men are industrious as ants.

I find myself very heavy-headed these days. It occurs to me that probably in different states of what we call health, even in morbid states, we are peculiarly fitted for certain investigations, — we are the better able to deal with certain phenomena.

N. Barrett says that he has formerly cut six cocks of hay on his bar.

July 19. P. M. — Up Assabet.

The architect of the river builds with sand chiefly, not with mud. Mud is deposited very slowly, only in the stagnant places, but sand is the ordinary building-material.

It is remarkable how the river, while it may be encroaching on the bank on one side, preserves its ordinary breadth by filling up the other side. Generally speaking, up and down this and the other stream, where there is a swift place and the bank worn away on one side, — which, other things being equal, would leave the river wider there, — a bank or island or bar is being built up on the other, since the eddy where, on one side, sand, etc., are deposited is produced by the rapidity of the current, thus: —

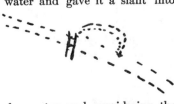

e. g. north side of Egg Rock, at Hemlocks, at Pigeon Rock Bend, at Swift Place Bank, etc., and on main stream at Ash Tree Bend. The eddy occasioned by the swiftness deposits sand, etc., close by on one side and a little offshore, leaving finally a low meadow outside where was once the bed of the river. There are countless places where the one shore is thus advancing and, as it were, dragging the other after it.

I dug into that sand-bank, once sand-bar, at the narrow and swift place off Hildreth's, five and a half feet deep, this afternoon. It is more than a rod wide and covered with willows and alders, etc. It is built up four or five feet above the summer level. It is uniformly fine sand, more or less darkened with decayed vegetation, probably much of it sawdust, and it has been deposited this depth here by the eddy at high water within a very recent period. The same agent is in a great many places steadily advancing such a bar or bank down the stream a rod or more from the old shore. The more recent and lower extremity of this bank or bar is composed of sawdust and shavings, almost entirely so to a depth of two feet. Before it reaches the surface, pads spring up in it; when [it] begins to appear, pontederia shows itself, and bulrushes, and next black willows, button-bushes, etc. The finest black willows on the river grow on these sand-banks. They are also much resorted to by the turtles for laying their eggs. I dug up

Vol. XII

three or four nests of the *Emys insculpta* and *Sternothærus odoratus* while examining the contents of the bank this afternoon. This great pile of dry sand in which the turtles now lay was recently fine particles swept down the swollen river.

Indeed, I think that the river once ran from opposite Merriam's to Pinxter Swamp and thence along Hosmer's hard land toward the bridge, and all the firm land north of Pinxter Swamp is such a sand-bank which the river has built (leaving its old bed a low meadow behind) while following its encroaching northeast side. That extensive hard land which the river annually rises over, and which supports a good growth of maples and swamp white oaks, will probably be found to be all alluvial and free from stones.

The land thus made is only of a certain height, say four to six feet above summer level, or oftener four or five feet. At highest water I can still cut off this bend by paddling through the woods in the old bed of the river. Islands are formed which are shaped like the curving ridge of a snow-drift.

Stagnant rivers are deep and muddy; swift ones shallow and sandy.

Scirpus subterminalis, river off Hoar's and Cheney's, not long.

July 20. The little Holbrook boy showed me an egg which I unhesitatingly pronounced a peetweet's, given him by Joe Smith. The latter, to my surprise, declares it a meadow-hen's; saw the bird and young, and says the latter were quite black and had hen bills. Can it be so?

Humphrey Buttrick says he finds snipes' nests in our meadows oftener than woodcocks'.

P. M. — To Eddy Bridge.

Abel Hosmer says that the Turnpike Company did not fulfill their engagement to build a new bridge over the Assabet in 1807; that the present stone bridge was not built till about the time the Orthodox meeting-house was built. (That was in 1826.) Benjamin says it was built soon after the meeting-house, or perhaps 1827, and was placed some fifty feet higher up-stream than the old wooden one.

Hosmer says that the eddy and wearing away of the bank has been occasioned wholly by the bridge; that there was only the regular bend there before. He had thought that it was in consequence of the bridge being set askew or diagonally with the stream, so that the abutments turned the water and gave it a slant into the banks, thus: I think that this did not create, only increased, the evil. The bank which it has worn away rises some sixteen feet above low water, and, considering the depth of the water, you may say that it has removed the sand to a depth of twenty-five feet over an area of a quarter of an acre, or say to the depth of three feet or a yard over two acres, or 9680 cubic yards or cartloads, which, at twenty-five cents per load, it would have cost $2420 to move in the ordinary manner, or enough to fill the present river for a quarter of a mile, calling it six rods wide and twelve feet deep. Beside creating some small islands and bars close by, this sand and gravel has, of course, been distributed along in the river and on the adjacent meadows below. Hosmer complains that his interval has accordingly been very much injured by the sand washed on to it below, — "hundreds of dollars" damage done to him. All this within some thirty-five[1] years.

It may well be asked what has become of all this sand? Of course it has contributed to form sand-bars below, possibly a great way below.

Jacob Farmer tells me that he remembers that when about twenty-one years old he and Hildreth were bathing in the Assabet at the mouth of the brook above Winn's, and Hildreth swam or waded across to a sandbar (now the island there), but the water was so deep on that bar that he became frightened, and would have been drowned if he had not been dragged out and resuscitated by others. This was directly over where that island is now, and was then only a bar beginning under water. That island, as he said, had been formed within thirty-five years,[2] or since the Eddy Bridge was built; and I suggest that it may have been built mainly of the ruins of that bank. It is the only island in the Assabet for two and a half miles.

There is a perfect standstill in the eddy at Eddy Bridge now, and there is a large raft of grass, weeds, and lumber perfectly at rest there, against Hosmer's bank. The coarser materials — stones as big as a hen's egg —

[1] Or thirty-two?
[2] Farrar (blacksmith) does not remember such a change.

are dropped close by, but the sand must have been carried far down-stream.

Hosmer says that when he digs down in his millet-field, twenty rods or more from the river, in his interval, at three or four feet depth he comes to coarse stones which look like an old bed of the river. I see them at each of the small wooden bridges, and very likely they underlie the whole of that interval, covered with sand. Such is the character of a river-bottom, — the stones from a hen's egg to the size of your head dropped down to one level, the sand being washed away, and now found in one stratum.

So completely emasculated and demoralized is our river that it is even made to observe the Christian Sabbath, and Hosmer tells me that at this season on a Sunday morning[1] (for then the river runs lowest, owing to the factory and mill gates being shut above) little gravelly islands begin to peep out in the channel below. Not only the operatives make the Sunday a day of rest, but the river too, to some extent, so that the very fishes feel the influence (or want of *influence*) of man's religion. The very rivers run with fuller streams on Monday morning. All nature begins to work with new impetuosity on Monday.

I see where turtles' eggs are still being dug up!

July 21. P. M. — To Assabet, above factory.

For about one third the way from the factory dam to the powder-mills the river is broad and deep, in short a mill-pond.

[1] He should rather say Monday morning.

Harrington has what he calls his Elm Hole, where he thinks he finds the old bed of the river some ten rods from the present. The river in many places evidently once washed the base of hills, from which it is now separated by fifty rods of meadow.

The pontederia on the Assabet is a very fresh and clear blue to-day, and in its early prime, — very handsome to see. The nesæa grows commonly along the river near the powder-mills, one very dense bed of it at the mouth of the powder-mill canal.

The canal is still cluttered with the wreck of the mills that have been blown up in times past, — timber, boards, etc., etc., — and the steep hill is bestrewn with the fragments of the mills, which fell on it more than half a dozen years ago (many of them), visible half a mile off. As you draw near the powder-mills, you see the hill behind bestrewn with the fragments of mills which have been blown up in past years, — the fragments of the millers having been removed, — and the canal is cluttered with the larger ruins. The very river makes greater haste past the dry-house, as it were for fear of accidents.

July 22. Start just before 8 A.M. and sail to the Falls of Concord River.

Water $2\frac{1}{4}$+ inches above summer level. A southwest wind rises and blows us rapidly along.

We are early enough to see the light reflected from the sides of the gyrating water-bugs. Heard from a bittern above the factory yesterday, too large for the small one and too small, perhaps, for the large one, a peculiar hoarse, grating note, lazily uttered, — a bit-

tern's croak, — at 1 P. M., as it flew over the meadows, — a sound perfectly becoming the bird, far as possible from music.

Some have just begun to get the hay on our Great Meadows.

The peetweet, our only beach-bird, teeters along the shore, reminding me that this is an arm of the ocean stream.

At Hill's Bridge we begin to find ourselves shut in by hills, and the character of the shores is fairly changed. There is very little meadow along the stream henceforward, but commonly a firm bank and pastures and cultivated fields — corn and potatoes — down to the shore, for it is commonly a firm shore, though it may be subject to inundation. The shores are still uninhabited, — the road being remote, — especially on the west side, and in the neighborhood of Middle Bridge we find ourselves off the middle of Billerica, the quiet town, and see its rural spire rising above the trees. Many handsome elm-tops and groves of elms are visible in Billerica. There is a fine grove of elms about the first house of the Atkins boat-house. Jug Island is a peculiar one, the only one of the kind that I know in the river, — except the small one at Falls, — firm and rocky, not made by the river, with deep water about it, especially on the east side, always separated from the shore, rising to a considerable height above the surface, — a part of the adjacent rocky range cut off by the river. The interval becomes more and more narrow and sandy or firm below this island and range of hills, and you see red-top and corn on it and woods.

For the last mile above the Falls the river becomes rocky, the rocks gradually increasing in number, until at the Falls its bed is crowded with them. Some of the rocks are curiously water-worn. They are, as usual in our black river, almost as black as ink, — the parts much submerged, — and I notice that bricks and white crockery on the bottom acquire the same color from the water, as if painted black. The water of this river is a black paint-brush which coats all things with fast colors. Rocks half a dozen feet in diameter which were originally of the usual lumpish form

are worn thus ⌢ by the friction of the pebbles, etc., washed ⌣ against them by the stream at high water. Several of them have this peculiar sheaf-like form; and black as ink. But, though evidently worn into this form by the rush of water, they are by no means worn smooth, but are as rough as a grater, such being their composition. These are just above the Fordway. There are two pleasant old houses near the Fordway on the east side.

I was surprised to see on the upright sides of these rocks, one or two feet above the present water, very distinct white spots, looking like white paint across the river. Examining, I found them to be three fourths to one inch in diameter of an oval or circular form; the white coating spreading

on to the rock in an irregular fringe like the feet of an insect, increasing their resemblance to a bug, and they were raised one eighth or one tenth of an inch and finely dotted with the contained ova, reminding me of coins, — shaped like bugs or coins, — and I at first bent to read the inscriptions as if they were a work of art. They were full of ova with much water in them or other liquid.[1]

Subtracting two and a quarter inches, I find the water at the Fordway, west side, two and one fourth feet deep, but generally not quite two feet.

Apparently the stream has been cleared of rocks and deepened on the westerly side at the Falls. At the narrowest place, where there is a willow in the middle, there is a clear channel on the west about thirty-five feet wide and four and a quarter feet deep (at deepest), or to the willow thirty-eight and a quarter feet, to opposite shore fifty-four feet more, and about two feet deep at deepest, with many rocks; in all say ninety-two feet.

We lunched about 12 o'clock (having got to the Falls about eleven), sitting on the largest rocky islet there, which, as I remember, may have been four to six rods long, but though it was not six feet above the water, if so much, there was no trace of the water ever having washed over it. Indeed, I *think* it does not rise more than five feet there ever, to judge from appearances. The obvious water-marks were about four feet above the present water. On this rock were dense trees and bushes, grass and soil, etc., etc., only five feet above the

[1] *Vide* Aug. 8th.

Vol. XII

present surface and evidently not disturbed by water or ice.

In the very midst of the Falls, on the rocky ridge where is some earth, only a foot or two above the water, grows the nesæa, as also abundantly on the sides. The hibiscus is very common along the neighboring shores.

When I was here a month ago, the water being high, the current was very strong here, so that I could not paddle, perhaps could not have rowed a boat against it at the narrowest place; but now I can paddle against it there, and easily push about anywhere. When the water is high, then, it is strong and hard to resist at all falls and rapids. Now there is not so much of a rush as at the bridge near the powder-mills.

The shores at the Falls are firm and rocky, though for the most part covered densely with bushes, — maples, alders, grape-vines, cat-briars, etc. There is no space for the river to expand in, and it is withal very much contracted in capacity by the rocks in it. Its bed is more or less strewn with rocks for some sixty rods, the largest forming rocky isles with soil and bushes and trees on them, though only some five or maybe six (?) feet high. There is water six and a half feet deep between the Fordway and the narrowest place below.

I was surprised to see on the rocks, densely covering them, though only in the midst of the fall, where was the swiftest water, a regular seaweed, growing just like rockweed and of the same olive-green color, — "*Podostemon Ceratophyllum*, River-weed," — still in bloom, though chiefly gone to seed. Gray says it is "attached to loose stones," and Torrey says it "adheres to pebbles," but

here it covered the rocks under water in the swiftest place only, and was partly uncovered by the fall of the water. I found, in what I gathered, a little pout which had taken refuge in it. Though the botanist, in obedience to his rules, puts it among phænogamous plants, I should not hesitate to associate it with the rockweed. It is the rockweed of our river. I have never seen it elsewhere in the river, though possibly it grows at the factory or other swift places. It seemed as if our river had there for a moment anticipated the sea, suffered a sea-change, mimicked the great ocean stream. I did not see it a few rods above or below, where the water is more sluggish. So far as I know, then, it grows only in the swiftest water, and there is only one place, and that the Falls, in Concord River where it can grow. Gray only speaks of it as growing at "the bottom of shallow streams," Torrey says "at the bottom of shallow pebbly streams," and Bigelow only says it is attached to stones at the bottom. Yet apparently our sluggish river is only a stream, and sufficiently like ordinary rippling streams to admit of its growth at this one spot. A careless observer might confound it with the rockweed of the sea. It covers the rocks in exactly the same manner, and when I tore it off, it brought more or less of the thin, scaly surface of the rocks with it. It is a foretaste of the sea. It is very interesting and remarkable that at this one point we have in our river a plant which so perfectly represents the rockweed of the seashore. This is from four to eight or nine inches long. It has the peculiar strong fresh-water scent.

The west end of Hill's Bridge is (upper side of planking) eight feet eleven inches above summer level, under side of string-piece seven feet eight inches. I cannot hear that it ever rises on to this bridge, but there is a good deal of fresh drift stuff on the top of the abutment under the string-piece at seven feet eight inches above summer level, apparently washed on in the spring. The upper side of planking at east end is about nine feet eight inches above summer level.

At Turnpike Bridge the water has apparently washed away a part of the abutment some seven and a half feet above summer level.

At Middle Bridge, judging from water-marks on the piers, I should think the water might have risen there seven feet seven inches (more or less) above summer level, i. e. up to the timber which rests crosswise on the piers, twenty-two inches below top of planks.

A carpenter who lives (?) at Billerica Corner says the water stood all around the nearest inhabited two-story house to the bridge last spring, so that you could go round it in a boat. (It is the opposite side the road to the river.) I think that this proves a rise here of at least seven feet above summer level and perhaps more.

Therefore, as far as my observation goes, the rise of the river last spring from Sherman's Bridge to Billerica Corner Bridge was very uniform and to about the same height above summer level, but it must fall off rapidly two or three feet or more at the Falls.

I see neither of the small islands which are on Baldwin's map below the Atkins house.

It is a question if the river has as much created the shoal places as found them.

The shallowest place in all the river above described — also from Pelham Pond — is at the Fordway above the Falls, where it is not two and a half [feet] at deepest to-day, and generally only two feet, with a hard bottom and numerous rocks in its bed. It is quite fordable in a carriage.

The weediest place is at the Sudbury causeway. The most of a sand-bar *visibly* formed or forming is Barrett's Bar. If a large piece of meadow should lodge on this, it would help make an island of it rapidly.

The deepest and broadest place is in Fair Haven Pond. I think that the river proper is nowhere so wide as in some parts between Squaw [?] Harbor and Skelton Bend.

The presence or absence of weeds at a given shallowness is a good gauge of the rapidity of the current. At the Fordway they do not grow where it is only two feet on an average, owing to the swiftness of the current (as well as stoniness), and in the very swiftest and narrowest part of the Falls occurs one species, the podostemon, which I have not found in any other part of the river.

The muddiest are the most stagnant parts. The hibiscus and white maple do not occur on the main stream for a long distance above the mouth of the Assabet, maybe ten miles.

It is remarkable how the river, even from its very source to its mouth, runs with great bends or zigzags regularly recurring and including many smaller ones, first northerly, then northeasterly, growing more and more simple and direct as it descends, like a tree; as

if a mighty current had once filled the valley of the river, and meandered in it according to the same law that this small stream does in its own meadows.

A river of this character can hardly be said to fall at all: it rather runs over the extremity of its trough, being filled to overflowing. Its only fall at present (above *the* Falls and this side Framingham) is like the fall produced by a dam, the dam being in this case the bottom in a shallow. If, after flowing twenty miles, all the water has got to rise as high as it was when it started, or rather if it has got to pass over a bottom which is as high as that was where it started, it cannot be said to have gained anything or have fallen at all. It has not got down to a lower level. You do not produce a fall in the channel or bottom of a trough by cutting a notch in its edge. The bottom may lose as much as the surface gains.

Rocks which are covered by freshets a week or more will have lichens on them, as that on my old plan just below the Hemlocks.

If our river had been dry a thousand years, it would be difficult to *guess* even where its channel had been without a spirit level. I should expect to find water-worn stones and a few muddy pools and small swamps.

July 23. P. M. — To Walden.

Going through Thrush Alley and beyond, I am pestered by flies about my head, — *not till now* (though I may have said so before). They are perfect imps, for they gain nothing for their pains and only pester me. They do not for the most part attempt to settle on me,

never sting me. Yet they seriously interfere with walking in the wood. Though I may keep a leafy twig constantly revolving about my head, they too constantly revolve, nevertheless, and appear to avoid it successfully. They leave you only when you have got fairly out of the wood. They seem to do it for deviltry and sport.

The second and fourth, or lake-like, reaches of the river are those in which there is the least fall, if indeed there can be said to be any much of the year. A slight northerly wind, or a shower at the lower end, will make it easier to row up stream than down.

Low blackberries have begun.

I notice the scarlet leaves of the sand cherry, which grows in dry places, and skunk-cabbage leaves have now begun to decay, turning black, and the angelica fall has commenced along the brooks.

Rhexia in bloom, how long? What I call *Juncus scirpoides* is common at Hubbard's Close, and also what I call *Juncus marginatus* (somewhat like the luzula). *Prenanthes alba*, how long? See an early kind of wool-grass, done, of various sizes, and another with larger reflexed sheaths, not begun *Aster Radula*, how long?

July 24. P. M. — To Ledum Swamp.

The hairy huckleberry still lingers in bloom, — a few of them. The white orchis will hardly open for a week. Mulgedium, how long?

Near the ditch beyond Dennis's Lupine Hill, a vaccinium near to *Pennsylvanicum*, perhaps a variety of it, with ripe fruit, little or no bloom, broader-leaved than that, and not shining beneath but somewhat glaucous.

July 25. The Rice boy brings me what he thought a snipe's egg, recently taken from a nest in the Sudbury meadows. It is of the form of a rail's egg, but is not whitish like mine, but olive-colored with dark-brown spots. Is it the sora rail? He has also a little egg, as he says taken out of a thrasher's nest, apparently one third grown.

Flagg says that the chimney swallow is sometimes abroad "the greater part of the night;" is informed by Fowler that the rose-breasted grosbeak often sings in the light of the moon.

P. M. — Water three and a half inches above summer level. I measure the rapidity of the river's current. At my boat's place behind Channing's, a bottle sunk low in the water floats one hundred feet in five minutes; one hundred feet higher up, in four and a half minutes. (I think the last the most correct.) It came out a rod and a half ahead of two chips.

July 26. P. M. — To Great Meadows.

I see in Clark's (?) land, behind Garfield's, a thick growth of white birches, apparently three years old, blown from the wood on the west and southwest.

Looking from Peter's, the meadows are somewhat glaucous, with a reddish border, or bank, by the river, where the red-top and *Agrostis scabra* grow, and a greener stream where the pipes are, in the lowest part, by the

Holt, and in some places yellowish-green ferns and now brown-topped wool-grass.

There is much of what I call *Juncus scirpoides* now in its prime in the wetter parts, as also the *Eleocharis palustris*, long done, and *Rhyncospora alba* lately begun. Also buck-bean by itself in very wet places which have lost their crust.

Elodea, how long?

Now observe the darker shades, and especially the apple trees, square and round, in the northwest landscape. Dogdayish.

Methinks the hardhack leaves always stand up, for now they do, and have as soon as they blossomed at least.

July 28. P. M. — Up Assabet.

I see what I take to be young purple finches eating mountain-ash berries (ours). The kingbirds eat currants.

I notice that the common greenish rock lichen (*Parmelia*) grows on the rocks of the Assabet down to within two feet of summer level; *i. e.*, it is submerged perhaps one fourth part of the year.

The black willows are the children of the river. They do not grow far from the water, not on the steep banks which the river is wearing into, not on the unconverted shore, but on the bars and banks which the river has made. A bank may soon get to be too high for it. It grows and thrives on the river-made shores and banks, and is a servant which the river uses to build up and defend its banks and isles. It is married to the river.

Vol. XII

Where an eddy is depositing a sand-bar, anon to be elevated into an island or bank, there especially the black willow flourishes. There are certain trees and other plants, as this, the white maple, mikania, etc., which do not grow away from the riverside. The river has not simply to [*sic*] their base, but they accompany *it*, wherever it goes.

The season has now arrived when I begin to see further into the water, — see the bottom, the weeds, and fishes more than before. I can see the bottom when it is five and a half feet deep even, see the fishes, especially the perch, scuttling in and out amid the weeds. Has this clarity anything to do with the greater sluggishness of the water when low? Perhaps you can see furthest into the most sluggish water.

If a tree is undermined and swept down-stream, it lodges in some shallow place, with its branches downstream, and its butt on the surface, pointing up.

The sweet and plaintive note of the pewee (wood pewee) is now prominent, since most other birds are more hushed. I hear probably young families of them answering each other from a considerable distance, especially about the river. Hear also part of the song of what sounds and looks like a rose-breasted grosbeak. Saw young martins being fed on a bridge-rail yesterday.

July 29. P. M. — To Fair Haven Hill shore.

Ranunculus Flammula var. *reptans* out, also impatiens, noli-me-tangere. The *Cyperus dentatus* in bloom on hard sandy parts of meadows now is very interesting and handsome on being inspected now, with its

bright chestnut purple *sided* flat spikelets, — a plant and color looking toward autumn. Very neat and handsome on a close inspection. *Vide* about Hubbard's brook pickerel ditches. Also in dry sandy soil the little tufts of *Fimbristylis capillaris* in bloom are quite brown and withered-looking now, — another yet more autumnal-suggesting sight. In dry pastures see also the round green heads of the *Cyperus filiculmis*.

The river is very nearly down to summer level now, and I notice there, among other phenomena of low water by the river, the great yellow lily pads flat on bare mud, the *Ranunculus Flammula* (just begun), a close but thin green matting now bare for five or six feet in width, bream nests bare and dried up, or else bare stones and sand for six or eight feet. The white lilies are generally lifted an inch or two above water by their stems; also the *Utricularia vulgaris* and *purpurea* are raised higher above the surface than usual. Rails are lodged amid the potamogetons in midstream and have not moved for ten days. Dog-days and fogs. Rocks unsuspected peep out and are become visible. The water milfoil (the *ambiguum* var. *natans*), otherwise not seen, shows itself. This is observed only at lowest water.

I examined some of these bream nests left dry at Cardinal Shore. These were a foot or two wide and excavated five inches deep (as I measured) in hard sand. The fishes must have worked hard to make these holes. Sometimes they are amid or in pebbles, where it is harder yet. There are now left at their bottoms, high and dry, a great many snails (*Paludina decisa*, also ⟲), young and old, some very minute. They either wash into them or take refuge there as the water goes down. I suspect they die there. The fishes really work hard at making their nests — these, the stone-heaps, etc. — when we consider what feeble means they possess.

Vaccinium vacillans begin to be pretty thick and some huckleberries. See large flocks of red-wings now, the young grown. *Bartonia tenella*, how long?

July 30. A. M. — On river to ascertain the rate of the current.

This dog-day weather I can see the bottom where five and a half feet deep. At five feet it is strewn clear across with sium, heart-leaf, *Ranunculus Purshii*, etc. It is quite green and verdurous, especially with the first. I see the fishes moving leisurely about amid the weeds, their affairs revealed, especially perch, — some large ones prowling there; and pickerel, large and small, lie imperturbable.

I see more moss(?)-covered rocks on the bottom and some rising quite near the surface, — three or four between my boat's place and thirty rods above, — and a good many three feet over on the bottom, revealed in the sunny water, and little suspected before. Indeed, the bottom may be considered rocky from above Dodd's to my boat's place, though you would suspect it only when looking through this clear water. They are so completely covered with moss-like weeds or tresses that you do not see them, — like the heads of mermaids. A rock there is a nucleus or hard core to a waving mass of weeds, and you must probe it hard with a paddle to detect the hard core. No doubt many a

reach is thus rock-strewn which is supposed to have an uninterruptedly muddy bottom. They sleep there concealed under these long tresses on the bottom, suggesting a new kind of antiquity. There is nothing to wear on and polish them there. They do not bear the paint rubbed off from any boat. Though unsuspected by the oldest fisher, they have eyed Concord for centuries through their watery veil without ever parting their tresses to look at her.

Perchance the increased stagnancy of the river at this season makes the water more transparent, it being easier to look into stagnant water than when the particles are in rapid motion.

The outside heart-leaves above Dodd's grow in six feet of water, and also the kalmiana lily. Trying the current there, there being a very faint, chiefly side, wind, commonly not enough to be felt on the cheek or to ripple the water, — what would be called by most a calm, — my bottle floats about seventy-five feet in forty minutes, and then, a very faint breeze beginning to drive it back, I cannot wait to see when it will go a hundred. It is, in short, an exceedingly feeble current, almost a complete standstill. My boat is altogether blown up-stream, even by this imperceptible breath. Indeed, you can in such a case feel the pulse of our river only in the shallowest places, where it preserves some slight passage between the weeds. It faints and gives up the ghost in deeper places on the least adverse wind, and you would presume it dead a thousand times, if you did not apply the nicest tests, such as a feather to the nostrils of a drowned man. It is a mere

string of lakes which have not made up their minds to be rivers. As near as possible to a standstill.

Yet by sinking a strawberry box beneath the surface I found that there was a slight positive current there, that when a chip went pretty fast up-stream in this air, the same with the box sunk one foot and tied to it went slowly down, at three feet deep or more went faster than when the box was sunk only one foot. The water flowed faster down at three feet depth than at one, there where it was about seven feet deep, and though the surface for several inches deep may be flowing up in the wind, the weeds at bottom will all be slanted down. Indeed, I suspect that at four or five feet depth the weeds will be slanted downward in the strongest wind that blows up, in that the current is *always* creeping along downward underneath. After my first experiments I was surprised to find that the weeds at bottom slanted down-stream.

I have also been surprised to find that in the clear channel between the potamogetons, though it looked almost stagnant, it was hard to swim against it; as at Rice's Bend.

See many cowbirds about cows.

P. M. — Left boat at Rice's Bend. I spoke to him of the clapper rail. He remembered that his father once killed a bird, a sort of mud-hen, which they called the tinker, since he made [a] noise just like a tinker on brass, and they used to set it agoing in the meadows by striking two coppers together. His father stuffed it and did not know what it was. It had a long body.

Yet the river in the middle of Concord is swifter than

above or below, and if Concord people are slow in consequence of their river's influence, the people of Sudbury and Carlisle should be slower still.

July 31. 7.30 A. M. — Up river.

C. and I, having left our boat at Rice's Bend last night, walk to it this forenoon on our way to Saxonville.

Water three quarters of an inch above summer level.

It is emphatically one of the dog-days. A dense fog, not clearing off till we are far on our way, and the clouds (which did not let in any sun all day) were the dog-day fog and mist, which threatened no rain. A muggy but comfortable day.

As we go along the Corner road, the dense fog for a background relieves pleasantly the outlines of every tree, though only twenty rods off, so that each is seen as a new object, especially that great oak scrag behind Hubbard's, once bent into a fence, now like a double-headed eagle, dark on the white ground. We go in the road to Rice's on account of the heavy dew, yet the fine tops of red-top, drooping with dew over the path, with a bluish hue from the dew, — blue with dew, — wet our shoes through. The roads are strewn with meadow-hay, which the farmers teamed home last evening (Saturday).

The grass is thickly strewn with white cobwebs, tents of the night, which promise a fair day. I notice that they are thickest under the apple trees. Within the woods the mist or dew on them is so very fine that they look smoke-like and dry, yet even there, if you put your finger under them and touch them, you take off the dew and they become invisible. They are revealed by the dew, and perchance it is the dew and fog which they reveal which are the sign of fair weather. It is pleasant to walk thus early in the Sunday morning, while the dewy napkins of the cobwebs are visible on the grass, before the dew evaporates and they are concealed.

Returning home last evening, I heard that exceedingly fine z-ing or creaking of crickets (?), low in the grass in the meadows. You might think it was a confused ringing in your head, it is so fine. Heard it again toward evening. Autumnalish.

On the 26th I saw quails which had been picking dung in a cart-path. Probably their broods are grown.

The goldfinch's note, the cool watery twitter, is more prominent now.

We had left our paddles, sail, etc., under one of Rice's buildings, on some old wagon-bodies. Rice, who called the big bittern "cow-poke, baked-plum-pudding."

It is worth the while to get at least a dozen miles on your journey before the dew is off. Stopped at Weir Hill Bend to cut a pole to sound with, and there came two real country boys to fish. One little fellow of seven or eight who talked like a man of eighty, — an old head, who had been, probably, brought up with old people. He was not willing to take up with my companion's jesting advice to bait the fish by casting in some of his worms, because, he said, "It is too hard work to get them where we live."

Begin to hear the sharp, brisk *dittle-ittle-ittle* of the wren amid the grass and reeds, generally invisible.

I only hear it between Concord line and Framingham line.

What a variety of weeds by the riverside now, in the water of the stagnant portions! Not only lilies of three kinds, but heart-leaf, *Utricularia vulgaris* and *purpurea*, all (at least except two yellow lilies) in prime. Sium in bloom, too, and *Bidens Beckii* just begun, and *Ranunculus Purshii* still.

The more peculiar features of Concord River are seen in these stagnant, lake-like reaches, where the pads and heart-leaf, pickerel-weed, button-bush, utricularias, black willows, etc., abound.

Above the Sudbury causeway, I notice again that remarkable large and tall typha, apparently *T. latifolia* (yet there is at least more than an inch interval between the two kinds of flowers, judging from the stump of the sterile bud left on).[1] It is seven or eight feet high (its leaves), with leaves flat on one side (only concave at base, the sheathing part) and regularly convex on the other. They are so much taller than any I see elsewhere as to appear a peculiar species. Long out of bloom. They are what you may call the tallest reed of the meadows, unless you rank the arundo with them, but these are hardly so tall.

The button-bush, which is, perhaps, at the height of its bloom, resounds with bees, etc., perhaps as much as the bass has. It is remarkable that it is these late flowers about which we hear this susurrus. You notice it with your back to them seven or eight rods off.

See a blue heron several times to-day and yesterday.

[1] *Vide* [p. 273].

Vol. XII

They must therefore breed not far off. We also scare up many times green bitterns, perhaps young, which utter their peculiar note in the Beaver Hole Meadows and this side.

For refreshment on these voyages, [we] are compelled to drink the warm and muddy-tasted river water out of a clamshell which we keep, — so that it reminds you of a clam soup, — taking many a sup, or else leaning over the side of the boat while the other leans the other way to keep your balance, and often plunging your whole face in at that, when the boat dips or the waves run.

At about one mile below Saxonville the river winds from amid high hills and commences a great bend called the Ox-Bow. Across the neck of this bend, as I paced, it is scarcely twenty rods, while it must be (as I judged by looking, and was told) a mile or more round. Fishermen and others are accustomed to drag their boats overland here, it being all hard land on this neck. A man by the bridge below had warned us of this cut-off, which he said would save us an hour!

A man fishing at the Ox-Bow said without hesitation that the stone-heaps were made by the sucker, at any rate that he had seen them made by the sucker in Charles River, — the large black sucker (not the horned one). Another said that the water rose five feet above its present level at the bridge on the edge of Framingham, and showed me about the height on the stone. It is an arched stone bridge, built some two years ago.

About the Sudbury line the river becomes much narrower and generally deeper, as it enters the first large

meadows, the Sudbury meadows, and is very winding, — as indeed the Ox-Bow was. It is only some thirty or forty feet wide, yet with firm upright banks a foot or two high, — canal-like. This canal-like reach is the transition from the Assabet to the lake-like or Musketaquid portion. At length, off Pelham Pond, it is almost lost in the weeds of the reedy meadow, being still more narrowed and very weedy, with grassy and muddy banks. This meadow, which it enters about the Sudbury line, is a very wild and almost impenetrable one, it is so wet and muddy. It is called the Beaver-Hole Meadows and is a quite peculiar meadow, the chief growth being, not the common sedges, but great bur-reed, five or six feet high and all over it, mixed with flags, *Scirpus fluviatilis*, and wool-grass, and rank canary grass. Very little of this meadow can be worth cutting, even if the water be low enough. This great sparganium was now in fruit (and a very little in flower). I was surprised by the sight of the great bur-like fruit, an inch to an inch and a half in diameter, the fruit-stems much branched and three or four feet high. It is a bur of sharp-pointed cones; stigmas linear. I can hardly believe that this is the same species that grows in C. It is apparently much earlier than ours. Yet ours may be a feeble growth from its very seeds floated down.

Can it be that in this wild and muddy meadow the same plant grows so rankly as to look like a new species? It is decidedly earlier as well as larger than any I find in C. It does not grow in water of the river, but densely, like flags, in the meadow far and wide, five or six feet high, and this, with the *Scirpus fluviatilis*, etc., makes a very novel sight. Where there are rare, wild, rank plants, there too some wild bird will be found. The marsh wrens and the small green bitterns are especially numerous there. Doubtless many rails here. They lurk amid these reeds. Behind the reeds on the east side, opposite the pond, was a great breadth of pontederia. Zizania there just begun.

This wren (excepting, perhaps, the red-wing black-bird) is the prevailing bird of the Sudbury meadows, yet I do not remember to have heard it in Concord. I get a nest,[1] suspended in a patch of bulrush (*Scirpus lacustris*) by the river's edge, just below the Sudbury causeway, in the afternoon. It is a large nest (for the bird), six inches high, with the entrance on one side, made of coarse material, apparently withered bulrush and perhaps pipes and sedge, and no particular lining; well woven and not very thick; some two and a half or three feet above water. The bird is shy and lurks amid the reeds.

We could not now detect any passage into Pelham Pond, which at the nearest, near the head of this reach, came within thirty rods of the river.

Do not the lake-like reaches incline to run more north and south?

The potamogetons do not abound anywhere but in shallows, hence in the swifter places. The lake-like reaches are too deep for them.

[1] Rice saw one in his meadow (at the Dam Meadows) in Concord half a dozen years ago. I hear of another in Nine-Acre Corner this year.

Vol. XII

VI

AUGUST, 1859

(ÆT. 42)

Aug. 1. 6 A. M. — River is at summer level.

This being Monday morning, the river is probably lower than at any other time in the week.

Am surprised to see in water opposite between Monroe's and Dodd's the *Myriophyllum ambiguum* var. *natans*, amid the *Bidens Beckii*. It must have been out (under water) a fortnight. A pretty sprig of pectinate leafets above the capillary-leafed and slimy mass. The *B. Beckii* (just beginning to bloom) just shows a few green leafets above its dark and muddy masses, now that the river is low. Evidently the above two and lilies, cardinal-flowers, etc., depend on the state of the river in June. After a very wet June I think there is less bloom on them. Some years the first two are not noticed at all.

We have now got down to the water milfoil and the *B. Beckii*. These might be called *low-water plants*.[1]

The bottom is occasionally — though quite rarely in Concord — of soft shifting sand, ripple-marked, in which the paddle sinks, under four or five feet of water (as below the ash tree hole), and few weeds grow on such a shallow.

Evidently the hill at Hemlocks would be a flowing sand-hill, if it were not held together by the hemlocks.

[1] *Vide* Aug. 4th.

Cardinal-flower. Have seen it formerly much earlier. Perhaps the high water in June kept it back.

This sixteen miles up, added to eleven down, makes about twenty-seven that I have boated on this river, to which may be added five or six miles of the Assabet.

The common cat-tail (about five feet high by railroad, beyond the South Bridge) has no interval between the two kinds of flowers, but mine of yesterday (*vide* [six] pages back) has, and yet it is much larger than the common. Can it, then, be the *Typha angustifolia*, which is described as smaller and rare?

I see a kingbird hovering within six inches above the potamogetons, front of Cheney's, and repeatedly snapping up some insects, perhaps a devil's-needle.[1]

The west edge of the Rock above Island is eleven and a half inches above summer level.

Now, at 5 P. M., the river has risen an inch and a half since 6 A. M., though we have not had a drop of rain for three days, and then but a few drops, and it fell three quarters of an inch between yesterday (Sunday) morning and this morning. Is this rise owing to the water let on from various mill-ponds this Monday morning?

Aug. 2. I try the current above Dodd's.

There is a southwest breeze. A loose board moves faster than one with a sunk box, but soon drifts diagonally across and lodges at fifty feet.

The box, sunk fourteen inches below the board, floats one hundred feet in nine minutes; sunk two and a half feet, in nine and a quarter minutes; sunk five and a half feet, it is not half-way in thirteen minutes, or, allowing for its starting this time a little out of the wind and current, say it is twenty minutes in going a hundred feet.

I should infer from this that the swiftest and most un-

[1] Often afterward for weeks; stoops from the willows.

nterrupted current under all conditions was neither at he surface nor the bottom, but nearer the surface than he bottom. If the wind is down-stream, it is at the surace; if up-stream, it is beneath it, and at a depth proortionate to the strength of the wind. I think that there never ceases to be a downward current.

Rudely calculating the capacity of the river here and omparing it with my boat's place, I find it about as wo to one, and such is the slowness of the current, viz. nine minutes to four and a half to a hundred feet. If ou are boating far it is extremely important to know he direction of the wind. If it blows strong up-stream, here will be a surface current flowing upward, another beneath flowing downward, and a very feeble one (in he lake-like parts) creeping downward next the bottom. A wind in which it is not worth the while to raise a sail vill often blow your sailless boat up-stream.

The sluggishness of the current, I should say, must e at different places as the areas of cross-sections at hose places.

That fine z-ing of locusts in the grass which I have heard for three or four days is, methinks, an August sound and is very inspiriting. It is a certain maturity n the year which it suggests. My thoughts are the less rude for it. There is a certain moral and physical slugishness and standstill at midsummer.

I think that clams are chiefly found at shallow and lightly muddy places where there is a gradually shelving shore. Are not found on a very hard bottom, nor n deep mud.

All of the river from the southwest of Wayland to off

the Height of Hill [sic] below Hill's Bridge is meadowy. This is the true Musketaquid.

The buttonwood bark strews the streets, — curled pieces. Is it not the effect of dry weather and heat? As birds shed their feathers, or moult, and beasts their hair. Neat rolls of bark (like cinnamon, but larger), light and dark brown.

Aug. 3. 6 A. M. — River fallen one inch since 2.30 P. M. yesterday; i.e., it is now a quarter of an inch above summer level. Juncus Greenei grows in river meadow opposite Dodd's; long done.

I saw (the 31st ult.) that the river was narrowed to a third its width by a large mass of button-bushes sunk in the middle of it above the Sudbury causeway. The low water reveals a mass of meadow sunk under the railroad bridge. Both this and Lee's Bridge are thus obstructed this year.

I should say the origin of these holes was that the river, being shallow and therefore crowded, runs swiftly and digs into the bank and so makes a deep hole and a bend. The three large lakes may perhaps be considered as three deep holes made by a larger river or ocean current in former ages.

The almost constant occurrence of a bay, or stagnant expansion, on the convex side at the bends is remarkable. It seems to be a place where the river has formerly flowed, but which, by wearing into the opposite bank, it has left.

There are about twenty-one weedy places (i. e., where the weeds extend quite across), all together about two

Vol. XII

miles in length. These weedy places, you may say (notwithstanding the frequent winding of the river), generally occur at bends (the Island shoal, perhaps, and Barrett's Bar, and above Middlesex Turnpike Bridge re exceptions).

The most remarkable bend between Framingham and he Dam is the Ox-Bow in Framingham.

Since our river is so easily affected by wind, the fact hat its general course is northeast and that the prevailing winds in summer are southwest is very favorable to ts rapid drainage at that season.

If by fall you mean a swifter place occasioned by the ottom below for a considerable distance being lower han the bottom above for a considerable distance, I do not know of any such between Pelham Pond and the Falls. These swifter places are produced by a contraction of the stream, — chiefly by the elevation of the ottom at that point, — also by the narrowing of the tream.

The depths are very slight compared with the lengths. The average depth of this twenty-five miles is about one seventeen thousandth the length; so that if this portion of the river were laid down on a map four feet long the depth would be about equal to the thickness of ordinary letter paper, of which it takes three hundred and fifty o an inch. Double the thickness of the letter paper, and it will contain the deep holes which are so unfathomed and mysterious, not to say bottomless, to the wimmers and fishermen.

Methinks the button-bushes about Fair Haven indiate a muddy but not deep pond.

The deepest reach of this twenty-five miles is from E. Davis Hill to Skelton Bend.

Methinks I saw some of the fresh-water sponge in the river in Framingham.

Undoubtedly, in the most stagnant parts of the river, when the wind blows hard up-stream, a chip will be drifted faster up-stream than ever it floats downward there in a calm.

P. M. — I see two or three birds which I take to be rose-breasted grosbeaks of this year. They are speckled brown and white (with considerable white) birds, and no rose on breast that I see. I hear them singing a little in a grosbeak-like strain, but a more partial warble. Heard one July 28th on an oak high up Assabet, and to-day on an apple tree near Brister's.

Warren Miles tells me that in mowing lately he cut in two a checkered "adder," — by his account it was the chicken snake, — and there was in its stomach a green snake, dead and partly digested, and he was surprised to find that they ate them.

Water-bugs are collected in dense swarms about my boat, at its stagnant harbor. They gyrate in a very leisurely manner under my face, occasionally touching one another by their edges a moment. When I move or disturb the water, they at once begin to gyrate rapidly. After the evening has set in, I perceive that these water-bugs, which all day were collected in dense swarms in the stagnant water amid the weeds at the sides, are dispersed over the river (quite across it here) and gyrating rapidly in the twilight.

The haymakers are quite busy on the Great Meadows, it being drier than usual. It being remote from public view, some of them work in their shirts or half naked.

As I wade through the middle of the meadows in sedge up to my middle and look afar over the waving and rustling bent tops of the sedge (all are bent northeast by the southwest wind) toward the distant mainland, I feel a little as if caught by a rising tide on flats far from the shore. I am, as it were, cast away in the midst of the sea. It is a level sea of waving and rustling sedge about me. The grassy sea. You feel somewhat as you would if you were standing in water at an equal distance from the shore. To-day I can walk dry over the greater part of the meadows, but not over the lower parts, where pipes, etc., grow; yet many think it has not been so dry for ten years! Goodwin is there after snipes. I scare up one in the wettest part.

High blackberries begin to be ripe.

A novel phenomenon of dry weather and a low stage of water is the sight of dense green beds of *Eleocharis acicularis*, still in bloom, which grows at the bottom of muddy pools, but now, they being dry, looks like a dense fine bed of green moss, denser than grass. I recline on such a bed, perfectly dry and clean, amid the flags and pontederia, where lately was water and mud. It covers the mud with a short dense green mat of culms fine as a hair, quite agreeable to rest on and a rather novel sight.

Aug. 5. See many yellowed peach leaves and butter-nut leaves, which have fallen in the wind yesterday and the rain to-day.

Vol. XII

The lowest dark-colored rocks near the water at the stone bridge (*i. e.* part of the bridge) are prettily marked with (apparently) mosses, which have adhered to them at higher water and [are] now withered and bleached on, — in fact are transferred, — and by their whitish color are seen very distinctly on the dark stone and have a very pretty effect. They are quite like sea-mosses in their delicacy, though not equally fine with many. These are very permanently and closely fastened to the rock. This is a phenomenon of low water. Also see them transferred to wood, as pieces of bridges.

Aug. 8. P. M. — Up Assabet.

I perceive that rocks on the bottom stretch across from Mantatuket Point to the Island, and probably make the ancient core of the shoals and islands, and the river has cut through above and between them and made them islands, just as it at high water cuts off and makes an island of Mantatuket Rock itself; *i. e.*, the shallows below the junction are to be considered as the point of the hill, at least the rocky portion of them.

I find the same curious eggs (which I saw at the Fordway on the 22d) on the rocks and trees on the Assabet, always on the upright, or steep, sides of rocks in the water or on bare-barked (or perhaps denuded of bark) trees on the edge of the river and overhanging

it. Are they to be found up the main stream? They are not yet hatched.[1]

Peetweets take their flight over the water, several together, apparently the old with their young now grown, the former (?) uttering a peculiarly soft rippling call. That is, it is not now a sharp, ringing note.

The river, now that it is so clear and sunny, is better than any aquarium. Standing up and pushing gently up the stream, or floating yet more quietly down it, I can, in some places, see the secrets of half the river and its inhabitants, — the common and familiar bream with the dusty light reflected from its fins, the vigorous-looking perch, tiger-like among fishes (I notice that many of the perch are poised head downward, peeping under the rocks), the motionless pickerel with reticulated back and sides, as it were the seed-vessel of a water-plant, eyes set far back. It is an enchanter's wand ready to surprise you with life.

The weeds are as indispensable to the fishes as woods and shrubbery to us. I saw a perch conceal himself from my sight under a tuft of weeds at the bottom not much wider than its own length. That potamogeton (is it *P. Robbinsii?*) growing in dense beds under water, all immersed in shallow places, like a bed of brown and muddy ostrich-feathers, alternating with darker beds of *Bidens Beckii*, which show but a particle of green above the surface (I think of the latter in the South Branch), — what concealment these afford to turtles, frogs, fishes, etc.! The potamogetons are so thick in some places in the main stream that a frog might hop

[1] *Vide* Aug. 11th.

quite across the river on them without getting in over his head.

Rice has had a little experience once in pushing a canal-boat up Concord River. Says this was the way they used to get the boat off a rock when by chance it had got on to one. If it had run quite on, so that the rock was partly under the main bottom of the boat, they let the boat swing round to one side and placed a stout stake underneath, a little aslant, with one end on the bottom of the river and the other ready to catch the bows of the boat, and while one held it, perhaps, the other pushed the boat round again with all his force, and so drove it on to the stake and lifted it up above the rock, and so it floated off.

Aug. 9. I see under the railroad bridge a mass of meadow which lodged there last spring, not revealed till this low water, and this is now dense with a thrifty growth of bulrushes.

Minott says that some used to wonder much at the windings of the Mill Brook and could not succeed in accounting for them, but his Uncle Ben Prescott settled the difficulty by saying that a great eel came out of Flint's Pond and rooted its way through to the river and so made the channel of the Mill Brook.

Minott says that he can remember when (it may be forty or fifty years ago) the Great Meadows were so dry one year that, they having got off all the grass and cut it quite smoothly, they talked seriously of having a regimental muster there. He assured me it would have been a good place, for the grass was cut smooth, and the earth was baked so hard that you could ride in a carriage right through the middle from the west end clear to Neck. Cannon could have been dragged about there perfectly well. I was thinking it would be rather *tussocky* ground for soldiers to wheel and manœuvre on, and rather damp to camp on, but he declared not. This appeared to be good evidence for the river meadow proprietors. But when I asked him if he thought the meadows were more wet now than fifty years ago, he answered that he did "not think they were," nor the grass any poorer. As he remembered, in one of those years, not far from the dry one referred to, there came a rain in August, when the meadows were partly cut, which raised the water so that it floated off what was left cut and went over the tops of the standing grass, and you could have gone all over the meadows in a boat, and he saw there on the meadows such an immense swarm of sea-birds of various kinds — peeps, plover, yellow-legs, etc. — as he never saw before nor since. He thinks he saw so many in one flock as could not have been packed into his kitchen. He had never seen anything at all like it but once since, and that was the day after he had been to a muster with his company at Waltham — when he was a young man — and had saved the greater part of his allowance of powder on the field. The next day, after getting home, the yellow-legs were so thick on the Mill Brook meadows that he killed a bushel of them.

I saw the tortoises shedding their scales a week ago. Many of the scales two-thirds off, turned up all around.

Aug. 11. A. M. — Up Assabet to stone bridge.

This river is so shallow that you can easily push up it with a paddle, but the other is commonly too deep for this.

As I paddle up this stream this forenoon, the river gently rising as usual in the forenoon (in consequence of raising the gates of the various mill-ponds on and near to it, which had been shut in the night), I meet with many a clam which comes floating down in midstream, nicely poised on the water with its pearly concave side uppermost. These have been opened and left by the musquash during the night on the shore, or often on rocks in the stream, and now the water rising gently sets them afloat, as with care you can float an iron pot. But soon a stronger wind or eddy will cause the water to break over them and they will at once sink to the bottom. Last night it lay half buried in mud and sand at the bottom. The musquash has devoured its tenant, and now it floats seaward, a pearly skiff set afloat by the industrious millers. I met with as many as a dozen of them coming down the stream this forenoon, ∨ the valves at an angle of 45° [*sic*], sometimes a single valve, but the least touch of my oars would sink them.

The musquash are eating clams quite fast there. Those lately opened are generally quite small. Is it because of the season or the stream? When I raked the river the other day, all the clams I caught had closed their shells on the teeth of the rake which entered them, just as they catch sea clams with a pointed stick.

Vol. XII

Those singular eggs which I saw at the Falls of Concord River in July (*vide* August 8) are far more numerous at the Assabet stone bridge, and many are hatched. They are sprinkled all over the stones of the arch just within it on the sides, and overhead, but extending only [a] few feet under the bridge on either side.

Aug. 14. P. M. — To Barrett's Bar.

The zizania now makes quite a show along the river, overtopping the withered heads of the early canary grass.

When I reached the upper end of this weedy bar, at about 3 P. M., this warm day, I noticed some light-colored object in mid-river, near the other end of the bar. At first I thought of some large stake or board standing amid the weeds there, then of a fisherman in a brown holland sack, referring him to the shore beyond. Supposing it the last, I floated nearer and nearer till I saw plainly enough the motions of the person, whoever it was, and that it was no stake. Looking through my glass thirty or forty rods off, I thought certainly that I saw C., who had just bathed, making signals to me with his towel, for I referred the object to the shore twenty rods further. I saw his motions as he wiped himself, — the movements of his elbows and his towel. Then I saw that the person was nearer and therefore smaller, that it stood on the sand-bar in midstream in shallow water and must be some maiden [in] a bathing-dress, — for it was the color of brown holland web, — and a very peculiar kind of dress it seemed. But about this time I discovered with my naked eye that it

was a blue heron standing in very shallow water amid the weeds of the bar and pluming itself. I had not noticed its legs at all, and its head, neck, and wings, being constantly moving, I had mistaken for arms, elbows, and towel of a bather, and when it stood stiller its shapely body looked like a peculiar bathing-dress. I floated to within twenty-five rods and watched it at my leisure. Standing on the shallowest part of the bar at that end, it was busily dressing its feathers, passing its bill like a comb down its feathers from base to tip. From its form and color, as well as size, it was singularly distinct. Its great spear-shaped head and bill was very conspicuous, though least so when turned toward me (whom it was eying from time to time). It coils its neck away upon its back or breast as a sailor might a rope, but occasionally stretches itself to its full height, as tall as a man, and looks around and at me. Growing shy, it begins to wade off, until its body is partly immersed amid the weeds, — potamogetons, — and then it looks more like a goose. The neck is continually varying in length, as it is doubled up or stretched out, and the legs also, as it wades in deeper or shallower water.

Suddenly comes a second, flying low, and alights on the bar yet nearer to me, almost high and dry. Then I hear a note from them, perhaps of warning, — a short, coarse, frog-like purring or eructating sound. You might easily mistake it for a frog. I heard it half a dozen times. It was not very loud. Anything but musical. The last proceeds to plume himself, looking warily at me from time to time, while the other continues to edge off through the weeds. Now and then the latter holds its neck as if it were ready to strike its prey, — 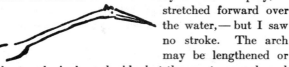 stretched forward over the water, — but I saw no stroke. The arch may be lengthened or shortened, single or double, but the great spear-shaped bill and head are ever the same. A great hammer or pick, prepared to transfix fish, frog, or bird. At last, the water becoming too deep for wading, this one takes easily to wing — though up to his body in water — and flies a few  rods to the shore. It rather flies, then, than swims. It was evidently scared. These were probably birds of this season. I saw some distinct ferruginous on the angle of the wing. There they stood in the midst of the open river, on this shallow and weedy bar in the sun, the leisurely sentries, lazily pluming themselves, as if the day were too long for them. They gave a new character to the stream. Adjutant they were to my idea of the river, these two winged men.

You have not seen our weedy river, you do not know the significance of its weedy bars, until you have seen the blue heron wading and pluming itself on it. I see that it was made for these shallows, and they for it. Now the heron is gone from the weedy shoal, the scene appears incomplete. Of course, the heron has sounded the depth of the water on every bar of the river that is fordable to it. The water there is not so many feet deep,

but so many heron's tibiæ. Instead of a foot rule you should use a heron's leg for a measure. If you would know the depth of the water on these few shoalest places of Musketaquid, ask the blue heron that wades and fishes there. In some places a heron can wade across.

How long we may have gazed on a particular scenery and think that we have seen and known it, when, at length, some bird or quadruped comes and takes possession of it before our eyes, and imparts to it a wholly new character. The heron uses these shallows as I cannot. I give them up to him.

By a gauge set in the river I can tell about what time the millers on the stream and its tributaries go to work in the morning and leave off at night, and also can distinguish the Sundays, since it is the day on which the river does not rise, but falls. If I had lost the day of the week, I could recover it by a careful examination of the river. It lies by in the various mill-ponds on Sunday and keeps the Sabbath. What its *persuasion* is, is another question.

In 1677 the town's "brandmarke" as fixed by the State was ⌇⌇⌇ .

David Heard says that the cattle liked the pipes so well that they distinguished their rustle from that of other grass as he was bringing them to them, and were eager to get them. The cattle distinguished the peculiar rustle of the pipes in the meadow-hay which was being brought to them, and were eager to get them.

Aug. 17. *Wednesday.* Frost in low ground this morning.

That was purple grass which I saw to-day. I see also the saw-grass in the shorn fields.

Aug. 18. *Thursday.* Half the leaves of some cherries in dry places are quite orange now and ready to fall.

Aug. 21. *Sunday.* P. M. — Walk over the Great Meadows and observe how dry they are. There is quite a drought, and I can walk almost anywhere over these meadows without wetting my feet. It is much drier than it was three weeks ago there. It is like the summer of '54. Almost all the grass has been cut and carried off. It is quite dry crossing the neck of the Holt. In many holes in the meadow, made by the ice, the water having dried up, I see many small fishes — pouts and pickerel and bream — left dead and dying. In one place there were fifty or one hundred pouts from four to five inches long with a few breams, all dead and dry. It is remarkable that these fishes have not all been devoured by birds or quadrupeds. The blue herons must find it easy to get their living now. Are they not more common on our river such years as this?

In holes where the water has just evaporated, leaving the mud moist, I see a hundred little holes near together, with occasionally an indistinct track of a bird between. Measuring these holes, I find them to be some two inches deep, or about the length of a snipe's bill, and doubtless they were made by them. I start one snipe.

People now (at this low stage of water) dig mud for

their compost-heaps, deepen wells, build bank walls, perchance, along the river, and in some places make bathing-places by raking away the weeds. Many are ditching.

Aug. 22. *Monday.* The circles of the blue vervain flowers, now risen near to the top, show how far advanced the season is.

The savory-leaved aster (*Diplopappus linariifolius*) out; how long? Saw the *Aster corymbosus* on the 19th.

Have seen where squirrels have eaten, *i. e.* stripped, many white pine cones, for a week past, though quite green.

That young pitch pine whose buds the crossbills (?) plucked has put out shoots close by them, but they are rather feeble and late.

Riding to the factory, I see the leaves of corn, planted thick for fodder, so rolled by the drought that I mistook one row in grass for some kind of rush or else reed, small and terete.

At the factory, where they were at work on the dam, they showed large and peculiar insects which they were digging up amid the gravel and water of the dam, nearly two inches long and half an inch wide, with six legs, two large shield-like plates on the forward part of the body, — under which they apparently worked their way through wet sand, — and two large claws, somewhat lobster-like, forward. The abdomen long, of many rings, and fringed with a kind of bristles on each side.

The other day, as I was going by Messer's, I was

struck with the pure whiteness of a tall and slender buttonwood before his house. The southwest side of it for some fifty or more feet upward, as far as the outer bark had recently scaled off, was as white, as distinct and bright a white, as if it had been painted, and when I put my finger on it, a white matter, like paint not quite dry, came off copiously, so that I even suspected it was paint. When I scaled off a piece of bark, the freshly exposed surface was brown. This white matter had a strong fungus-like scent, and this color is apparently acquired after a little exposure to the air. Nearly half the tree was thus uninterruptedly white as if it had been rounded and planed and then painted. No birch presents so uniformly white a surface.

It is very dry now, but I perceive that the great star-shaped leaves of the castor bean plants in Mr. Rice's garden at twilight are quite cold to the touch, and quite shining and wet with moisture wherever I touch them. Many leaves of other plants, as cucumbers, feel quite dry.

Aug. 23. P. M. — To Laurel Glen to see the effect of the frost of the 17th (and perhaps 18th).

As for autumnal tints, the *Smilacina racemosa* is yellowed, spotted brown in streaks, and half withered; also two-leaved Solomon's-seal is partly yellowed and withered. Birches have been much yellowed for some time; also young wild cherry and hazel, and some horse-chestnuts and larches on the street. The scarlet lower leaves of the choke-berry and some brakes are the handsomest autumnal tints which I see to-day.

At Laurel Glen, these plants were touched by frost, in the lowest places, *viz.,* the very small white oaks and hickories; dogsbane very generally; ferns generally, — especially *Aspidium Thelypteris* (?), the revolute one at bottom of hollow, — including some brakes; some little chinquapin oaks and chestnuts; some small thorns and blueberry (*Vaccinium vacillans* shoots); aspen, large and tender leaves and shoots; even red maple; many hazel shoots; geraniums; indigo-weed; lespedeza (the many-headed) and desmodium (one of the erect ones); a very little of the lowest locust leaves. These were very small plants and low, and commonly the most recent and tender growth. The bitten part, often the whole, was dry and shrivelled brown or darker. In the river meadows the blue-eyed grass was very generally cut off and is now conspicuously black, — I find but one in bloom, — also small flowering ferns. The cranberries (not vines) are extensively frost-bitten and spoiled.

In Moore's Swamp the potatoes were extensively killed, the greenest or tenderest vines. One says that the driest part suffered the most. They had not nearly got ripe. One man had his squash vines killed.[1]

Aug. 24. P. M. — To Conantum.
The small sempervirens blackberry in prime in one

[1] At frosty hollows by Ripple Lake on the 28th, see the effects of the same frost of 17th, — little chinquapin oaklets and the tenderest shoots of *Cornus alba,* the gray dead twigs of the cornel of past years, all their tops; and these two are almost the only shrubs at the bottom. The older cornel leaves have been turned to dark purple, plainly by the frost. Erechthites not touched even Aug. 30th (*vide* Sept. 2d).

Vol. XII

place. *Aster puniceus* and *Diplopappus umbellatus,* how long? *Calamagrostis coarctata* not quite, end of Hubbard's meadow wood-path. *Panicum virgatum,* say two or three weeks. Leersia, or cut-grass, some time, roadside, Corner road, by brook.

Aug. 25. Copious rain at last, in the night and during the day.
A. M. — Mountain-ash berries partly turned. Again see, I think, purple finch eating them.

I see, after the rain, when the leaves are rustling and glistening in the cooler breeze and clear air, quite a flock of (apparently) *Fringilla socialis* in the garden.

Aug. 26. The dust is laid, the streets washed, the leaves — the first ripe crop — fallen, owing to yesterday's copious rain. It is clearer weather, and the creak of the crickets is more distinct, just as the air is clearer.

The trees look greener and fresher, not only because their leaves are washed and erected, but because they have for the most part shed their yellow and sere leaves.

The front-rank polygonum is now perhaps in its prime. Where it forms an island in the river it is surmounted in the middle or highest part by the *P. hydropiperoides.*
P. M. — To Fair Haven Hill.
Elder-berries have fairly begun to be ripe, as also the *Cornus sericea* berries, and the dull-reddish leaves of the last begin to be conspicuous.

The creak of the mole cricket has a very *afternoon* sound.

Potato vines are generally browning and rank. Roman wormwood prevails over them; also erechthites, in new and boggy ground, and butterweed. These lusty natives prevail in spite of the weeding hoe, and take possession of the field at last. Potato vines have taken a veil of wormwood. The barn-yard grass and various *panics* (*sanguinale, capillare,* and bottle-grass) now come forward with a rush and take possession of the cultivated fields, partly abandoned for the present by the farmer and gardener.

How singular that the *Polygonum aviculare* should grow so commonly and densely about back doors where the earth is trodden, bordering on paths! Hence properly called door-grass. I am not aware that it prevails in any other places.

The pontederia leaves are already slightly imbrowned, though the flowers are still abundant.

The river is a little cooled by yesterday's rain, and considerable heart-leaf (the leaves mainly) is washed up.

I begin to think of a thicker coat and appreciate the warmth of the sun. I see sun-sparkles on the river, such as I have not seen for a long time. At any rate, they surprise me. There may be cool veins in the air now, any day.

Now for dangle-berries. Also *Viburnum nudum* fruit has begun.

I saw a cherry-bird peck from the middle of its upright (vertical) web on a bush one of those large

(I think yellow-marked) spiders within a rod of me. It dropped to the ground, and then the bird picked it up. It left a hole or rent in the middle of the web. The spider cunningly spreads his net for feebler insects, and then takes up his post in the centre, but perchance a passing bird picks him from his conspicuous station.

I perceived for the first time, this afternoon, in one place, a slight mouldy scent. There are very few fungi in a dry summer like this.

The *Uvularia sessilifolia* is for the most part turned yellow, with large green fruit, or even withered and brown. Some medeola is quite withered. Perhaps they are somewhat frost-bitten.

I see a goldfinch eating the seeds of the coarse barn-yard grass, perched on it. It then goes off with a cool twitter.

Notice arrowhead leaves very curiously eaten by some insect. They are dotted all over in lines with small roundish white scales, — which your nail will remove, and then a scar is seen beneath, — as if some juice had exuded from each puncture and then hardened.

The first fall rain is a memorable occasion, when the river is raised and cooled, and the first crop of sere and yellow leaves falls. The air is cleared; the dog-days are over; sun-sparkles are seen on water; crickets sound more distinct; saw-grass reveals its spikes in the shorn fields; sparrows and bobolinks fly in flocks more and more. Farmers feel encouraged about their late potatoes and corn. Mill-wheels that have rested for want of water begin to revolve again. Meadow-haying is over.

Vol. XII

The first significant event (for a long time) was the frost of the 17th. That was the beginning of winter, the first summons to summer. Some of her forces succumbed to it. The second event was the rain of yesterday.

My neighbor told me yesterday that about four inches of rain had fallen, for he sent his man for a pail that was left in the garden during the rain, and there was about four inches depth of water in it. I inquired if the pail had upright sides. "No," he said, "it was flaring !!" However, according to another, there was full four inches in a tub.

Leersia or cut-grass in prime at Potter's holes.

That first frost on the 17th was the first stroke of winter aiming at the scalp of summer. Like a stealthy and insidious aboriginal enemy, it made its assault just before daylight in some deep and far-away hollow and then silently withdrew. Few have seen the drooping plants, but the news of this stroke circulates rapidly through the village. Men communicate it with a tone of warning. The foe is gone by sunrise, but some fearful neighbors who have visited their potato and cranberry patches report this stroke. The implacable and irresistible foe to all this tender greenness is not far off, nor can we be sure, any month in the year, that some scout from his low camp may not strike down the tenderest of the children of summer. The earliest and latest frosts are not distinguishable. This foe will go on steadily increasing in strength and boldness, till his white camps will be pitched over all the fields, and we shall be compelled to take refuge in our strongholds,

with some of summer's withered spoils stored up in barns, maintaining ourselves and our herds on the seeds and roots and withered grass which we have *em-barned*. Men in anticipation of this time have been busily collecting and curing the green blades all the country over, while they have still some nutriment in them. Cattle and horses have been dragging homeward their winter's food.

A *new plant*, apparently *Lycopodium inundatum*, Hubbard's meadow-side, Drosera Flat, not out.

Aug. 27. A little more rain last night.

What were those insects, some winged, with short backs and say half an inch long, others wingless and shorter, like little coils of brass wire (so marked), in dense droves together on trees and fences, — apparently harmless, — especially a week or ten days ago?

I was telling Jonas Potter of my lameness yesterday, whereat he says that he "broke" both his feet when he was young, — I imagined how they looked through his wrinkled cowhides, — and he did not get over it for four years, nay, even now he sometimes felt pains in them before a storm.

All our life, *i. e.* the living part of it, is a persistent dreaming awake. The boy does not camp in his father's yard. That would not be adventurous enough, there are too many sights and sounds to disturb the illusion; so he marches off twenty or thirty miles and there pitches his tent, where stranger inhabitants are tamely sleeping in their beds just like his father at home, and camps in *their* yard, perchance. But then he

dreams uninterruptedly that he is anywhere but where he is.

I often see yarrow with a delicate pink tint, very distinct from the common pure-white ones.

What is often called poverty, but which is a simpler and truer relation to nature, gives a peculiar relish to life, just as to be kept short gives us an appetite for food.

Vilfa vaginæflora (?) well out.

The first notice I have that grapes are ripening is by the rich scent at evening from my own native vine against the house, when I go to the pump, though I thought there were none on it.

The children have done bringing huckleberries to sell for nearly a week. They are suspected to have berries [*sic*] in them.

On the 23d I gathered perfectly fresh and large low blackberries, peculiarly sweet and soft, in the shade of the pines at Thrush Alley, long after they are done in open fields. They seem like a different variety from the common, they are so much sweeter, tenderer, and larger. They do not grow densely but sparingly, now resting on the ground in the shade of their leaves, perfectly ripe. These that have ripened slowly and perfectly in the shade are the sweetest and tenderest, have the least of the *bramble* berry about them.

Elder-berry clusters swell and become heavy and therefore droop, bending the bushes down, just in proportion as they ripen. Hence you see the green cymes perfectly erect, the half-ripe drooping, and the perfectly ripe hanging straight down on the same bush.

I think that some summer squashes had turned yellow in our yard a fortnight or more ago.

There are various ways in which you can tell if a watermelon is ripe. If you have had your eye on the patch much from the first, and so know which formed first, you may presume that these will ripen soonest; or else you may incline to those which lie nearest the centre of the hill or root, as the oldest. Next the dull dead color and want of bloom are as good signs as any. Some look green and livid and have a very fog or mildew of bloom on them, like a fungus. These are as green as a leek through and through, and you'll find yourself in a pickle if you open one. Others have a dead dark greenness, the circulations being less rapid in their cuticles and their blooming period passed, and these you may safely bet on. If the vine is quite green and lively, the death of the quirl at the root of the stem is almost a sure sign. For fear we should not discover it before, this is placed for a sign that there is redness and ripeness (if not mealiness) within. Of two otherwise similar, take that which yields the lowest tone when struck with your knuckles, i. e., which is hollowest. The old or ripe ones sing base; the young, tenor or falsetto. Some use the violent method of pressing to hear if they crack within, but this is not to be allowed. Above all no tapping on the vine is to be tolerated, suggestive of a greediness which defeats its own purpose. It is very childish. One man told me that he could n't raise melons because his children would cut them all up. I thought that he convicted himself out of his own mouth, and was not fit to be the ruler of a country according to Confucius'

standard, that at any rate he could not raise children in the way they should go. I once saw one of his boys astride of my earliest watermelon, which grew near a broken paling, and brandishing a case-knife over it, but I instantly blowed him off with my voice from a neighboring window before serious damage was done, and made such an ado about [it] as convinced him that he was not in his father's dominions, at any rate. This melon, though it lost some of its bloom then, grew to be a remarkably large and sweet one, though it bore to the last a triangular scar of the tap which the thief had designed on it.

I served my apprenticeship and have since done considerable journey-work in the huckleberry-field, though I never paid for my schooling and clothing in that way. It was itself some of the best schooling I got, and paid for itself. Occasionally in still summer forenoons, when perhaps a mantua-maker was to be dined, and a huckleberry pudding had been decided on, I, a lad of ten, was dispatched to the huckleberry hills, all alone. My scholastic education could be thus far tampered with and an excuse might be found. No matter how few and scarce the berries on the near hills, the exact number necessary for a huckleberry pudding could surely be collected by 11 o'clock. My rule in such cases was never to eat one till my dish was full. At other times when I had companions, some used to bring such curiously shaped dishes that I was often curious to see how the berries disposed of themselves in them. Some brought a coffee-pot to the huckleberry-field, and such a vessel possessed this advantage at least,

that if a greedy boy had skimmed off a handful or two on his way home, he had only to close the lid and give his vessel a shake to have it full again. This was done all round when we got as far homeward as the Dutch house. This can probably be done with any vessel that has much side to it.

I once met with a whole family — father and mother and children — ravaging a huckleberry-field in this wise: they cut up the bushes, and, as they went, beat them over the edge of a bushel basket, till they had it full of berries, ripe and green, leaves, sticks, etc., and so they passed along out of my sight like wild men.

See *Veratrum viride* completely withered and brown from top to bottom, probably as early as skunk-cabbage.

Aug. 28. P. M. — To Walden.

A cool day; wind northwest. Need a half-thick coat. Thus gradually we withdraw into winter quarters. It is a clear, flashing air, and the shorn fields now look bright and yellowish and cool, tinkled and twittered over by bobolinks, goldfinches, sparrows, etc. You feel the less inclined to bathing this weather, and bathe from principle, when boys, who bathe for fun, omit it.

Thick fogs these mornings. We have had little or no dog-days this year, it has been so dry.

Pumpkins begin to be yellow. White cornel berries mostly fallen.

The arrowhead is still a common flower and an important one. I see some very handsome ones in Cardinal Ditch, whose corollas are an inch and a half in diameter. The greater part, however, have gone to

seed. The flowers I see at present are autumn flowers, such as have risen above the stubble in shorn fields since it was cut, whose tops have commonly been clipped by the scythe or the cow; or the late flowers, as asters and goldenrods, which grow in neglected fields and along ditches and hedgerows.

The rhexia in Ebby Hubbard's field is considerably past prime, and it is its reddish chalices which show most at a distance now. I should have looked ten days ago. Still it is handsome with its large yellow anthers against clear purple petals. It grows there in large patches with hardhack.

I hear that some of the villagers were aroused from their sleep before light by the groans or bellowings of a bullock which an unskillful butcher was slaughtering at the slaughter-house. What morning or Memnonian music was that to ring through the quiet village? What did that clarion sing of? What a comment on our village life! Song of the dying bullock! But no doubt those who heard it inquired, as usual, of the butcher the next day, "What have you got to-day?" "Sirloin, good beefsteak, rattleran," etc.

I saw a month or more ago where pine-needles which had fallen (old ones) stood erect on low leaves of the forest floor, having stuck in, or passed through, them. They stuck up as a fork which falls from the table. Yet you would not think that they fell with sufficient force.

The fruit of the sweet-gale is yellowing.

Aug. 29. I hear in the street this morning a goldfinch sing part of a sweet strain.

It is so cool a morning that for the first time I move into the entry to sit in the sun. But in this cooler weather I feel as if the fruit of my summer were hardening and maturing a little, acquiring color and flavor like the corn and other fruits in the field. When the very earliest ripe grapes begin to be scented in the cool nights, then, too, the first cooler airs of autumn begin to waft my sweetness on the desert airs of summer. Now, too, poets nib their pens afresh. I scent their first-fruits in the cool evening air of the year. By the coolness the experience of the summer is condensed and matured, whether our fruits be pumpkins or grapes. Man, too, ripens with the grapes and apples.

I find that the water-bugs (*Gyrinus*) keep amid the pads in open spaces along the sides of the river all day, and, at dark only, spread thence all over the river and gyrate rapidly. For food I see them eating or sucking at the wings and bodies of dead devil's-needles which fall on the water, making them too gyrate in a singular manner. If one gets any such food, the others pursue him for it.

There was a remarkable red aurora all over the sky last night.

P. M. — To Easterbrooks Country.

The vernonia is one of the most conspicuous flowers now where it grows, — a very rich color. It is somewhat past its prime; perhaps about with the red eupatorium. *Botrychium lunarioides* now shows its fertile frond above the shorn stubble in low grounds, but not shedding pollen. See the two-leaved Solomon's-seal berries, many of them ripe; also some ripe mitchella

berries, contrasting with their very fresh green leaves. White cohush berries, apparently in prime, and the arum fruit. The now drier and browner (purplish-brown) looking rabbit's clover, whose heads collected would make a soft bed, is an important feature in the landscape; pussies some call them; more puffed up than before. The thorn bushes are most sere and yellowish-brown bushes now.

I see more snakes of late, methinks, both striped and the small green.

The slate-colored spots or eyes — fungi — on several kinds of goldenrods are common now. The knife-shaped fruit of the ash has strewn the paths of late.

Aug. 30. P. M. — Up Assabet.

The river began to fall perhaps yesterday, after rising perhaps fourteen or fifteen inches. It is now about one foot higher than before the rain of the 25th. A rise of one foot only from low water gives an appearance of fullness to the stream, and though the meadows were dry before, it would now be difficult to work on them. The potamogetons, etc., are drowned, and you see a full rippling tide where was a sluggish and weedy stream but four or five days ago. Now, perhaps, will be the end of quite a number of plants which culminate in dry weather when the river is low, as some potamogetons, limnanthemum (in the river), etc. Sparganium and heart-leaf are washed up, and the first driftwood comes down; especially portions of bridges that have been repaired take their way slowly to the sea, if they are not saved by some thrifty boatman. The river is fuller,

with more current; a cooler wind blows; the reddish *Panicum agrostoides* stands cool along the banks; the great yellow flowers of the *Bidens chrysanthemoides* are drowned, and now I do not see to the bottom as I paddle along.

The pasture thistle, though past its prime, is quite common, and almost every flower (*i. e.* thistle), wherever you meet with it, has one or more bumblebees on it, clambering over its mass of florets. One such bee which I disturb has much ado before he can rise from the grass and get under weigh, as if he were too heavily laden, and at last he flies but low. Now that flowers are rarer, almost every one of whatever species has bees or butterflies upon it.

Now is the season of rank weeds, as *Polygonum Careyi*, tall rough goldenrod, *Ambrosia elatior*, primrose, erechthites (some of this seven feet high), *Bidens frondosa* (also five feet high). The erechthites down has begun to fly.

We start when we think we are handling a worm, and open our hands quickly, and this I think is designed rather for the protection of the worm than of ourselves.

Acorns are not fallen yet. Some haws are ripe.

The plants now decayed and decaying and withering are those early ones which grow in wet or shady places, as hellebore, skunk-cabbage, the two (and perhaps three) smilacinas, uvularias, polygonatum, medeola, *Senecio aureus* (except radical leaves), and many brakes and sarsaparillas, and how is it with trilliums [1] and arums? [2]

[1] Many fallen, Aug. 19, 1852.
[2] Trientalis and arums are decayed and decaying.

The prevailing flowers, considering both conspicuousness and numbers, at present time, as I think now: [1]

Solidagos, especially large three-ribbed, *nemoralis*, tall rough, etc.
Asters, especially *Tradescanti, puniceus, corymbosus, dumosus, Diplopappus umbellatus*
Tansy
Helianthuses, as *Helianthus decapetalus, divaricatus, annuus*, etc.
Eupatoriums, as *perfoliatum, purpureum*
Mikania
Polygonums, as *P. Careyi, dumetorum*, front-rank, *Persicaria, sagittatum*, etc.
Gnaphalium, as *polycephalum* and pearly
Bidens, as *frondosa* and *chrysanthemoides*
Gerardias, as *purpurea* and *pediculata*
Hieraciums, as *Canadense, scabra*, and *paniculatum*
Vernonia
Polygala sanguinea, etc.
Liatris
Nabalus albus
Mints, as lycopuses, white mint, pycnanthemums
Hypericums, the small ones of all kinds
Leontodon autumnalis (prevailing, open in forenoon)
Pontederia
Sagittaria variabilis
Desmodiums
Spiranthes cernua
Lespedeza violacea
Cuscuta
Rhexia
Lobelia cardinalis
Cirsium pumilum
Chenopodiums
Scutellaria lateriflora
Impatiens
Apios
Linaria vulgaris
Gratiola aurea

[1] Imperfect list.

Aug. 31. P. M. — To Fair Haven Hill.

Was caught in five successive showers, and took refuge in Hayden's barn, under the cliffs, and under a tree. A thunder-cloud, seen from a hilltop, as it is advancing rapidly across the sky on one side, whose rear at least will soon strike us. The dark-blue mass (seen edgewise) with its lighter upper surface and its copious curving rain beneath and behind, like an immense steamer holding its steady way to its port, with tremendous mutterings from time to time, a rush of cooler air, and hurried flight of birds.

These later weeds, — chenopodiums, Roman wormwood, amaranth, etc., — now so rank and prevalent in the cultivated fields which were long since deserted by the hoers, now that the potatoes are for the most part ripened, are preparing a crop for the small birds of the fall and winter, those pensioners on civilization. These weeds require cultivated ground, and Nature perseveres each year till she succeeds in producing a bountiful harvest by their seeds, in spite of our early assiduity. Now that the potatoes are cared for, Nature is preparing a crop of chenopodium and Roman wormwood for the birds.

Now especially the crickets are seen and heard on dry and sandy banks and fields, near their burrows, and some hanging, back down, to the stems of grass, feeding. I entered a dry grassy hollow where the cricket alone seemed to reign, — open like a bowl to the sky.

While I stand under a pine for shelter during the rain, on Fair Haven Hill-side, I see many sarsaparilla plants fallen and withering green, *i. e.* before changing. It is

as if they had a weak hold on the earth, on the subterranean stocks.

The nightshade berries are handsome, not only for their clear red, but the beautifully regular form of their drooping clusters, suggesting a hexagonal arrangement for economy of room.

There was another shower in the night (at 9 P. M.), making the sixth after 1.30 P. M. It was evidently one cloud thus broken into six parts, with some broad intervals of clear sky and fair weather. It would have been convenient for us, if it had been printed on the first cloud, "Five more to come!" Such a shower has a history which has never been written. One would like to know how and where the cloud first gathered, what lands and water it passed over and watered, and where and when it ceased to rain and was finally dissipated.

VII

SEPTEMBER, 1859

(ÆT. 42)

Sept. 1. P. M. — To Saw Mill Brook and Flint's Pond.

That reach in the road this side Britton's Camp might be called Nabalus Road, they are so abundant there. Some of them are fully six feet high, — a singularly tall and slender plant.

See, I think, my first tobacco-pipe this afternoon, now that they are about done, and have seen no pinesap this year, abundant as both the above were last year. Like fungi, these plants are apparently scarce in a dry year, so that you might at first think them rare plants. This is a phenomenon of drought.

I see in different places small grubs splitting leaves now, and so marking them curiously with light brown or whitish on the green. Here are two at work in a *Rhus Toxicodendron* leaf. They appear to have been hatched within the leaf at the apex, and each has eaten upward on its own side of the midrib and equally fast, making a light-colored figure shaped like a column of smoke in the midst of the green. They perfectly split the leaf, making no visible puncture in it, even at the ribs or veins. Some creatures are so minute that they find food enough for them between the two sides of a thin leaf, without injuring the cuticle. The ox requires

the meadows to be shorn for him, and cronches both blade and stalk, even of the coarsest grass, as corn; but these grubs do their browsing in narrower pastures, pastures not so wide as their own jaws, between fences (inviolable to them) of their own establishing, or along narrow lanes. There, secure from birds, they mine, and no harm can they do now that the green leaf has so commonly done its office.

If you would study the birds now, go where their food is, *i. e.* the berries, especially to the wild black cherries, elder-berries, poke berries, mountain-ash berries, and ere long the barberries, and for pigeons the acorns. In the sprout-land behind Britton's Camp, I came to a small black cherry full of fruit, and then, for the first time for a long while, I see and hear cherry-birds — their shrill and fine seringo — and the note of robins, which of late are scarce. We sit near the tree and listen to the now unusual sounds of these birds, and from time to time one or two come dashing from out the sky toward this tree, till, seeing us, they whirl, disappointed, and perhaps alight on some neighboring twigs and wait till we are gone. The cherry-birds and robins seem to know the locality of every wild cherry in the town. You are as sure to find them on them now, as bees and butterflies on the thistles. If we stay long, they go off with a fling, to some other cherry tree, which they know of but we do not. The neighborhood of a wild cherry full of fruit is now, for the notes of birds, a little spring come back again, and when, a mile or two from this, I was plucking a basketful of elder-berries (for which it was rather early yet), there too, to my surprise,

I came on a flock of golden robins and of bluebirds, apparently feeding on them. Excepting the vacciniums, now past prime and drying up, the cherries and elder-berries are the two prevailing fruits now. We had remarked on the general scarcity and silence of the birds, but when we came to the localities of these fruits, there again we found the berry-eating birds assembled, — young (?) orioles and bluebirds at the elder-berries.

Green white pine cones are thrown down. An unusual quantity of these have been stripped for some time past, and I see the ground about the bases of the trees strewn with them.

The spikenard berries in the shade at Saw Mill have but just begun to turn. The *Polygonatum biflorum* with its row of bluish-green berries (the blue a bloom), pendulous from the axils of the recurved stem, apparently now in its prime. Red choke-berry ripe. Smooth sumach probably hardly ripe yet generally.

The fruit of the arum is the most remarkable that I see this afternoon, such its brilliancy, color, and form; perhaps in prime now. It is among the most easily detected now on the floor of the swamp, its bright-scarlet cone above the fallen and withered leaves and amid its own brown or whitish and withering leaves. Its own leaves and stem perhaps soft and decaying, while it is perfectly fresh and dazzling. It has the brightest gloss of any fruit I remember, and this makes the green ones about as remarkable as the scarlet. With, perchance, a part of the withered spathe still investing and veiling it. The scarlet fruit of the arum spots the swamp floor.

Vol. XII

and burnished copper from another. Yet there was nothing in its form to recommend this bug.

You must be careful not to eat too many nuts. I one winter met a young man whose face was broken out into large pimples and sores, and when I inquired what was the matter, he answered that he and his wife were fond of shagbarks, and therefore he had bought a bushel of them, and they spent their winter evenings eating them, and this was the consequence.

Sept. 2. P. M. — To Ledum Swamp.

The pontederia leaves are now decidedly brown or brownish, and this may be the effect of frost, since we have had some considerable in low places. Perhaps they occupy particularly cold places.

The farmer is obliged to hide his melon-patch in the midst of his corn or potatoes, far away. I sometimes stumble on it as I am going across lots. I see one to-day where the watermelons are intermixed with carrots in a carrot-bed, and so concealed by the general resemblance of leaf, etc., at a little distance.

Going along Clamshell Hill, I look over the meadows. Now, after the first rain raising the river, the first assault on the summer's sluggishness, the air is of late cooler and clearer, autumnal, and the meadows and low grounds, which, of course, have been shorn, acquire a fresh yellowish green as in the spring. This is another phase of the second spring, of which the peeping of hylas by and by is another.[1]

[1] One reason for this in some even dry fields is owing to the cyperuses — which are yellow and low and late — being revealed by cutting the grass and still growing.

Now, also, bright-colored fungi of various colors on the swamp floor begin to compete with these fruits. I see a green one.

The elder-berry cyme, held erect, is of very regular form, four principal divisions drooping toward each quarter around an upright central one. Are said to make a good dye. They fill your basket quickly, the cymes are so large and lie up so light.

The autumnal dandelion is a prevailing flower now, but since it shuts up in the afternoon it might not be known as common unless you were out in the morning or in a dark afternoon. Now, at 11 A. M., it makes quite a show, yet at 2 P. M. I do not notice it.

Bought a pair of shoes the other day, and, observing that as usual they were only wooden-pegged at the toes, I required the seller to put in an extra row of iron pegs there while I waited for them. So he called to his boy to bring those zinc pegs, but I insisted on iron pegs and no zinc ones. He gave me considerable advice on the subject of shoes, but I suggested that even the wearer of shoes, of whom I was one, had an opportunity to learn some of their qualities. I have learned to respect my own opinion in this matter. As I do not use blacking and the seller often throws in a box of blacking when I buy a pair of shoes, they accumulate on my hands.

Saw this afternoon, on a leaf in the Saw Mill wood-path, a very brilliant beetle a quarter or a third of an inch in length with brilliant green and copper reflections.[1] The same surface, or any part of the upper surface, of the bug was green from one point of view

[1] *Vide* June 28th, 1860.

I once did some surveying for a man who remarked, *but not till the job was done*, that he did not know when he should pay me. I did not pay much heed to this, though it was unusual, supposing that he meant to pay me some time or other. But after a while he sent to me a quart of red huckleberries, and this I thought was ominous and he distinguished me altogether too much by this gift, since I was not his particular friend. I saw it was the first installment, which would go a great way toward being the last. In course of years he paid a part of the debt in money, and that is the last I have heard of it.

The sarothra grows thickly, and is now abundantly in bloom, on denuded places, *i. e.*, where the sod and more or less soil has been removed, by sandy roadsides.

At Ledum Swamp the frosts have now touched the *Polygonum Careyi* pretty extensively, the leaves and stem, leaving the red spikes; also some erechthites and poke and the tenderest high blueberry shoots, their tips (from where the bushes were cut down). But the *Woodwardia Virginica* is not touched. (*Vide* back, August 23d.)

Poke berries begin at Corner Spring.

Sept. 3. A strong wind, which blows down much fruit. R. W. E. sits surrounded by choice windfall pears.

Sept. 4. P. M. — To Well Meadow and Walden.

The purple culms and spikes of the crab-grass or finger-grass, spreading and often almost prostrate

under our feet in sandy paths and causeways, are where the purple cuticle of the earth again shows itself, and we seem to be treading in our vintage whether we will or not. Earth has donned the purple. When, walking over some dry field (some time since), I looked down and saw the yellowish tuft of the *Fimbristylis capillaris*, with its spreading inverted cone of capillary culms, like the upper half of an hour-glass, but still more, when, pacing over the sandy railroad causeway, I look down and find myself treading on the purple culms of the crab-grass, I am reminded of the maturity of the year. We have now experienced the full effects of heat such as we have in this latitude. The earth itself appears to me as a ripe purple fruit, — though somewhat dusty here, — and I may have rubbed the bloom off with my feet. But if Bacchus can ever stand our climate, this must be his season.

Topping the corn, which has been going on some days, now reveals the yellow and yellowing pumpkins. This is a genuine New England scene. The earth blazes not only with sun-flowers but with sun-fruits.

The four-leaved loosestrife, which is pretty generally withering and withered, seems to have dried up, — to suffer peculiarly from the annual drought, — perhaps both on account of its tenuity and the sandiness or dryness of its locality.

The *Lycopodium complanatum* sheds pollen [*sic*].

Where are the robins and red-wing blackbirds of late? I see no flocks of them; not *one* of the latter, and only a few solitary robins about wild cherry trees, etc.

A few yew berries, but they appear (?) to be drying

up. The most wax-like and artificial and surprising of our wild berries, — as surprising as to find currants on hemlocks.

In the Well Meadow Swamp, many apparent *Aster miser*, yet never inclining to red there (in the leaf) and sometimes with larger flowers (five eighths of an inch [in] diameter) and slenderer cauline leaves than common, out apparently almost as long as *miser* elsewhere.

The swamp thistle (*Cirsium muticum*) is apparently in its prime. One or two on each has faded, but many more are to come. Some are six feet high and have radical leaves nearly two feet long. Even these in the shade have humblebees on them.

You see small flocks of ducks, probably wood ducks, in the smaller woodland ponds now and for a week, as I at Andromeda Ponds, and can get nearer to them than in the spring.

The *Cornus sericea* and *C. paniculata* are rather peculiar for turning to a dull purple on the advent of cooler weather and frosts, in the latter part of August and first part of September. The latter, which grows at the bottom of our frostiest hollows, turns a particularly clear dark purple, an effect plainly attributable to frost. I see it this afternoon in the dry, deep hollow just west of the middle Andromeda Pond.

I think I see two kinds of three-ribbed goldenrod (beside *Canadensis*), both being commonly smooth-stemmed below and downy above, but one has very fine or small rays as compared with the other. They appear to be both equally common now. The fine-rayed at Sedge Path.

Vol. XII

 See a very large mass of spikenard berries fairly ripening, eighteen inches long.

Three kinds of thistles are commonly out now, — the pasture, lanceolate, and swamp, — and on them all you are pretty sure to see one or two humblebees. They become more prominent and interesting in the scarcity of purple flowers. (On many you see also the splendid goldfinch, yellow and black (?) like the humblebee.) The thistles beloved of humblebees and goldfinches.

Three or four plants are peculiar now for bearing plentifully their fruit in drooping cymes, *viz.* the elderberry and the silky cornel and the *Viburnum Lentago* and *Solanum Dulcamara*. The other cornels do not generally come to droop before they lose their fruit. Nor do the viburnums droop much. The fruit of the *Cornus sericea* is particularly interesting to me, and not too profuse, — small cymes of various tints half concealed amid the leaves.

Sept. 5. Spent a part of the forenoon in the woods in the northwest part of Acton, searching for a stone suitable for a millstone for my lead-mill.

Sept. 6. Hear the sounds nowadays — the lowing, tramp, and calls of the drivers — of cows coming down from up-country.

Staghorn sumach berries probably some time, but ours are injured by worms. The fever-bush leaves

are remarkably round and entire yet, as if by their odor defended from insects.[1]

The feverwort berries are apparently nearly in their prime, of a clear "corn yellow" and as large as a small cranberry, in whorls at the axils of the leaves of the half-prostrate plants.

I hear occasionally a half-warbled strain from a warbling vireo in the elm-tops, as I go down the street nowadays. There is about as much life in their notes now as in the enfeebled and yellowing elm tree leaves at present.

The liatris is, perhaps, a little past prime. It is a very rich purple in favorable lights and makes a great show where it grows. Any one to whom it is new will be surprised to learn that it is a wild plant. For prevalence and effect it may be put with the vernonia, and it has a general resemblance to thistles and knapweed, but is a handsomer plant than any of them.

Sept. 8. The 7th, 8th, and 9th, the State muster is held here. The only observation I have to make is that [Concord] is fuller of dust and more uninhabitable than I ever knew it to be before. Not only the walls, fences, and houses are thickly covered with dust, but the fields and meadows and bushes; and the pads in the river for half a mile from the village are white with it. From a mile or two distant you see a cloud of dust over the town and extending thence to the muster-field. I went to the store the other day to buy a bolt for our front door, for, as I told the storekeeper, the Governor

[1] It is eaten or cut by them. *Vide* Sept. 4th, 1856.

was coming here. "Aye," said he, "and the Legislature too." "Then I will take two bolts," said I. He said that there had been a steady demand for bolts and locks of late, for our protectors were coming. The surface of the roads for three to six inches in depth is a light and dry powder like ashes.

P. M. — To Fair Haven Pond.

Grapes are turning purple, but are not ripe.

I see the black head and neck of a little dipper in midstream, a few rods before my boat. It disappears, and though I search carefully, I cannot detect it again. It is undoubtedly hidden mid the weeds — pads, flags, and pontederia, etc. — along the shore. Ducks more common.

Sept. 9. I start many pigeons now in a sprout-land.

I have noticed for a week or more some swarms of light-colored and very small fuzzy gnats in the air, yet not in such concentrated swarms as I shall see by and by.

Now for hazelnuts, — where the squirrels have not got them.

Within a week I think I have heard screech owls at evening from over the river once or twice.

Sept. 10. See wasps, collected in the sun on a wall, at 9 A. M.

Sept. 11. P. M. — To Conantum-end.

The prinos berries are now seen, red (or scarlet), clustered along the stems, amid the as yet green leaves. A cool red.

Vol. XII

By the pool in Hubbard's Grove, I see tall tupelos, all dotted with the now ripe (apparently in prime) small oval purple berries, two or three together on the end of slender peduncles, amid the reddening leaves. This fruit is very acid and has a large stone, but I see several robins on the trees, which appear to have been attracted by it. Neither tree nor fruit is generally known, and many liken the former when small to a pear. The trees are quite full of fruit.

The wax-like fruit of *Cornus paniculata* still holds on abundantly.

This being a cloudy and somewhat rainy day, the autumnal dandelion is open in the afternoon.

The *Rhus Toxicodendron* berries are now ripe and greenish-yellow, and some already shrivelled, over bare rocks.

September is the month when various small, and commonly inedible, berries in cymes and clusters hang over the roadsides and along the walls and fences, or spot the forest floor. The clusters of the *Viburnum Lentago* berries, now in their prime, are exceedingly and peculiarly handsome, and edible withal. These are drooping, like the *Cornus sericea* cymes. Each berry in the cyme is now a fine, clear red on the exposed side and a distinct and clear green on the opposite side. Many are already purple, and they turn in your hat, but they are handsomest when thus red and green.

The large clusters of the *Smilacina racemosa* berries, four or five inches long, of whitish berries a little smaller than a pea, finely marked and dotted with vermilion

or bright red, are very conspicuous. I do not chance to see any ripe.

No fruit is handsomer than the acorn. I see but few fallen yet, and they are all wormy. Very pretty, especially, are the white oak acorns, three raying from one centre.

I see dill and saffron still, commonly out at R. W. E.'s.

Sept. 12. P. M. — To Moore's Swamp and Great Fields.

Elder-berries are apparently in prime, generally black, though many have been plucked by birds.

The four kinds of bidens (*frondosa, connata, cernua,* and *chrysanthemoides*) abound now, but much of the *Beckii* was drowned by the rise of the river. Omitting this, the first two are inconspicuous flowers, cheap and ineffectual, commonly without petals, like the erechthites, but the third and fourth are conspicuous and interesting, expressing by their brilliant yellow the ripeness of the low grounds.

Most of the late flowers are already associated in my mind with cooler and clearer, flashing weather, as the witch-hazel, the gentians, the *Bidens cernua, Spiranthes cernua, Polygonum amphibium* and *hydropiperoides* in its prime, and the *Polygala sanguinea,* still prevalent.

I stand in Moore's Swamp and look at Garfield's dry bank, now before the woods generally are changed at all. How ruddy ripe that dry hillside by the swamp, covered with goldenrods and clumps of hazel bushes here and there, now more or less scarlet. The golden-

rods on the top and the slope of the hill are the *Solidago nemoralis,* at the base the taller *S. altissima.* The whole hillside is perfectly dry and ripe.

Many a dry field now, like that of Sted Buttrick's on the Great Fields, is one dense mass of the bright-golden recurved wands of the *Solidago nemoralis* (a little past prime), waving in the wind and turning upward to the light hundreds, if not a thousand, flowerets each. It is the greatest mass of conspicuous flowers in the year, and uniformly from one to two feet high, just rising above the withered grass all over the largest fields, now when pumpkins and other yellow fruits begin to gleam, now before the woods are noticeably changed. Some field where the grass was too thin and wiry to pay for cutting, with great purplish tufts of *Andropogon furcatus,* going to seed, interspersed. Such a mass of yellow for this field's last crop! Who that had botanized here in the previous month could have foretold this more profuse and teeming crop? All ringing, as do the low grounds, with the shrilling of crickets and locusts and frequented by honey-bees (*i. e.* the goldenrod *nemoralis*). The whole field turns to yellow, as the cuticle of a ripe fruit. This is the season when the prevalence of the goldenrods gives such a ripe and teeming look to the dry fields and to the swamps. They are now (the *arguta* being about done) the *nemoralis* and *altissima,* both a little past prime. The *S. nemoralis* spreads its legions over the dry plains now, as soldiers muster in the fall. It is a muster of all its forces, which I review, eclipsing all other similar shows of the year. Fruit of August and September, sprung from the sun-dust. The fields and hills appear in their yellow uniform. There are certain fields so full of them that they might give their name to the town or region, as one place in England is called Saffron Walden. Perhaps the general prevalence of yellow is greater now when many individual plants are past prime.

I notice in Moore's Swamp that though the potato vines were killed long since, few if any weeds are. They survive to perpetuate their race, until severer frosts come.

The beach plums are about ripe; the black cherries nearly gone.

I start a flock of five turtle doves from the dry Great Fields, near buckwheat. They go off with a whistling note.

A profusion of wild fruits, agreeable to the eye if not palate, is seen along some walls and hedges now. Take this dry wall-side by Sted Buttrick's field now, though probably not remarkably rich. Here I find elder-berries, panicled cornel, acorns of various kinds, black cherry (nearly gone), green-briar berries, grapes, hazelnuts (the pale-brown nuts now peeping between the husks), alternate cornel (which is about done), sumach, chokeberry, and haws; and earlier there were shad-berries, thimble-berries, and various kinds of huckle- and blackberries, etc. Some shrub oak acorn cups are empty, but they have not many fallen. Large yellowish caterpillars, heaped on the leaves, have so stripped some shrub oaks as to expose and reveal the acorns.

The other day a tender-hearted man came to the depot and informed Neighbor Wild that there was a

Maltese cat caught in a steel trap near the depot, which perhaps was his. Wild thought it must be his or " Min Thoreau." She had tried to jump over a fence with the trap on her leg, but had lodged one side while the trap hung the other. The man could not stand to open the trap, the cat scratched so, but at length he threw the trap over, and so the cat went home, dragging it to Wild's (for it was his cat), and the man advised him to keep the trap to pay the one who set it for his inhumanity. I suspect, however, that the cat had wandered off to Swamp Bridge Brook and there trod in a trap set for mink or the like. It is a wonder it does not happen oftener.

I saw a star-nosed mole dead in the path on Conantum yesterday, with no obvious wound.

Sept. 13. P. M. — Up Assabet.

The *Bidens chrysanthemoides,* now apparently in its prime by the river, now almost dazzles you with its great sunny disk. I feast my eyes on it annually. It grows but sparingly near the village, but those few never fail to make their appearance at last. The yellow lily's is a cool yellow in comparison, but in this is seen the concentrated heat of autumn.

Now, while other fruits are ripe or ripening, I see the great peduncle of the peltandra, eighteen or twenty-four inches long, curving downward, with its globular mass of green fruit, often two inches in diameter, at the end, looking like slung shot. This mass of viscid seeds or nuts must be the food of many creatures. Also the pontederia spike is now generally turned downward

Vol. XII

beneath the water and increased in size, though some have flowers still at their tips. So, too, probably (for I do not see them) the yellow and white lilies are ripening their seeds in the water and mud beneath the surface.[1]

The bloom and freshness of the river was gone as soon as the pickerel-weed began to be imbrowned, in the latter part of August. It is fall and harvest there now.

I remember my earliest going a-graping. (It was a wonder that we ever hit upon the ripe season.) There was more fun in finding and eying the big purple clusters high on the trees and climbing to them than in eating them. We used to take care not to chew the skins long lest they should make our mouths sore.

Some haws of the scarlet thorn are really a splendid fruit to look at now and far from inedible. They are not only large, but their beauty is enhanced by the persistent calyx relieving the clear scarlet of the fruit.

There are various degrees of living out-of-doors. You must be outdoors long, early and late, and travel far and earnestly, in order to perceive the phenomena of the day. Even then much will escape you. Few live so far outdoors as to hear the first geese go over.

I see some shrub oak acorns turned dark on the bushes and showing their meridian lines, but generally acorns of all kinds are green yet. The great red oak acorns have not fallen. It is a wonder how pigeons can swallow acorns whole, but they do.

Many hemlock leaves which had prematurely ripened and withered in the dry weather have fallen in

[1] Yes, I see them, — the former urn-shaped. *Vide* 14th.

the late winds and washed up along the side of the river, — already red there.

Sept. 14. High, gusty winds, with dust and a little rain (more or less for two or three days).

These powerful gusts fill all the air with dust, concealing the earth and sky.

P. M. — To Cliffs *via* Hubbard's Bath.

The *Spiranthes cernua* has a sweet scent like the clethra's.

The mountain sumach appears to bear quite sparingly. Its berries are a hoary crimson and not bright like those of the smooth. Also they are in looser masses. They are, *perhaps,* a little later, but I think ripe now.

I see in the swamp under the Cliffs the dark, decaying leaves of the skunk-cabbage, four or five spreading every way and so flat and decayed as to look like a fungus or mildew, making it doubtful at first what plant it is; but there is the sharp green bud already revealed in the centre between the leaf-stalks, ready to expand in the spring.

This wind has strewn the Fair Haven Hill-side with apples. I think that fully three quarters of all are on the ground. Many trees are almost entirely stripped, the whole crop lying in a circular form beneath, yet hard and green. Others on the hillside have rolled far down. The farmers will be busy for some time gathering these windfalls. The winds have come to shake the apple trees prematurely, making fruit (for pies) cheap, I trust, against Thanksgiving or Cattle-Show.[1] Not

[1] [*Excursions,* p. 296; Riv. 364.]

only apples and other fruit, but a great many green as well as withered leaves, strew the ground under almost all kinds of trees.

I notice of late the green or ripe pods of the *Orchidaceæ*, — some for a long time, — including gymnodenia, lady's-slipper, etc.; pods full of a fine, dust-like seed. The dusty-seeded *Orchidaceæ*.

The yellow lily (*Nuphar advena*) fruit, now green and purplish, is ripening under water, of this form and size: full of yellow seeds: The white lily, when stripped of the blackened and decaying petals, etc., is of this form:

Even the tough-twigged mocker-nut, yet green, is blown off in some places. I bring home a twig with three of its great nuts together, as big as small apples, and children follow and eye them, not knowing what kind of fruit it is.

Like the fruits, when cooler weather and frosts arrive, we too are braced and ripened. When we shift from the shady to the sunny side of the house, and sit there in an extra coat for warmth, our green and leafy and pulpy thoughts acquire color and flavor, and perchance a sweet nuttiness at last, worth your cracking. Now all things suggest fruit and the harvest, and flowers look *late*, and for some time the sound of the flail has been heard in the barns.

They are catching pigeons nowadays. Coombs has a stand west of Nut Meadow, and he says that he has

just shot fourteen hawks there, which were after the pigeons. I have one which he has shot within a day or two and calls a pigeon hawk. It is about twenty inches in alar extent. Above dark-slate or brownish with the edges, *i. e.* tips, of the feathers (especially of wing-coverts) rufous. The primaries and secondaries dark or blackish brown, barred with black, and only a [*sic*] some white concealed on the inner vanes near the base. Wings beneath white or whitish, thickly barred with dark. Scapulars with white spots. Head much mutilated, but no "black spots" visible, but apparently the dark brown mixed or edged with rufous. Cere, etc., said to have been green. Beneath brownish-white, centred with brown, with a darker line through that. Femorals still more rustyish brown, with central dashes. Legs yellowish. Tail slate, with four black bars half an inch or more wide; the edge slate, with a very narrow edging of white; beneath the slate is almost white.

What kind of hawk is this? I can learn nothing from Wilson and Nuttall. The latter thinks that neither the pigeon nor sparrow hawk is found here!!![1]

Sept. 15. Yesterday was very cold, with northwest wind, and this morning the first frost in the garden, killing some of our vines.

W. Ricketson says that, when looking for insects this morning under the loose bark of an apple tree on Nawshawtuct, he found a bat hanging there which measured eleven feet [*sic*], alar extent.

[1] Dr. Kneeland, to whom I showed the tail and wings, thought it a pigeon hawk.

P. M. — To Annursnack.

Dense flocks of pigeons hurry-skurry over the hill. Pass near Brooks's pigeon-stands. There was a flock perched on his poles, and they sat so still and in such regular order there, being also the color of the wood, that I thought they were wooden figures at first. They were perched not only in horizontal straight lines one above the other, which the cross-bars required, but at equal distances apart on these perches, which must be their own habit; and it struck me that they made just such a figure seen against the sky as pigeonholes cut in a doves' house do, *i. e.* a more or less triangular figure, thus: and possibly the seeing them thus perched might have originally suggested this arrangement of the holes.

Pigeons dart by on every side, — a dry slate color, like weather-stained wood (the weather-stained birds), fit color for this aerial traveller, a more subdued and earthy blue than the sky, as its field (or path) is between the sky and the earth, — not black or brown, as is the earth, but a terrene or slaty blue, suggesting their aerial resorts and habits.

The Emersons tell me that their Irishman, James, held his thumb for the calf to suck, after dipping it in a pitcher of milk, but, the milk not coming fast enough, [the calf] butted (or bunted) the pitcher to make the milk come down, and broke it.

The grain of the wild rice is all green yet.

I find that Temple raises his own tobacco. The great leaves were spread over the bottom and sides of a hay-

rigging in his barn, by the open door, to dry. He smokes them. He says that the season is rather short for it here, but I saw some still growing and in bloom abundantly. What kind is it? "Cuby, they call it." He smokes it and thinks it better than any he can buy.

Sept. 16. Another and severer frost, which cut off all our vines, etc., lespedeza, corn, etc.

P. M. — By the roadside, forty or fifty rods east of the South Acton station, I find the *Aster Novæ-Angliæ*, apparently past prime. I must call it a plant of this vicinity, then. I thought it "in prime or a little past" at Salem, September 21, 1858. I will venture to put it with the *A. puniceus*.

Young Nealy says that there are blue-winged teal about now. Others are out after ducks. Nealy says he shot the first golden plover he has seen, this morning.[1]

How unpromising are promising men! Hardly any disgust me so much. I have no faith in them. They make gratuitous promises, and they break them gratuitously.

When an Irishwoman tells me that she wouldn't tell a lie for her life (because I appear to doubt her), it seems to me that she has already told a lie. She holds herself and the truth very cheap to say that so easily.

What troubles men lay up for want of a little energy and precision! A man who steps quickly to his mark leaves a great deal of filth behind. There's many a well-meaning fellow who thinks he has a hard time of it who will not put his shoulder to the wheel, being spell-

[1] Does he know it??

bound, — who sits about, as if he were hatching his good intentions, and every now and then his friends get up a subscription for him, and he is cursed with the praise of being "a clever fellow." It would really be worth his while to go straight to his master the devil, if he would only shake him up when he got there. Men who have not learned the value of time, or of anything else; for whom an infant school and a birchen rod is still and forever necessary. A man who is not prompt affects me as a creature covered with slime, crawling through mud and lying dormant a great part of the year. Think of the numbers — men and women — who want and *will* have and *do* have (how do they get it?!) what they will not earn! The non-producers. How many of these bloodsuckers there are fastened to every helpful man or woman in this world! They constitute this world. It is a world full of snivelling prayers, — whose very religion is a prayer! As if beggars were admirable, were respectable, to anybody!

Again and again I am surprised to observe what an interval there is, in what is called civilized life, between the shell and the inhabitant of the shell, — what a disproportion there is between the life of man and his conveniences and luxuries. The house is neatly painted, has many apartments. You are shown into the sitting-room, where is a carpet and couch and mirror and splendidly bound Bible, daguerreotypes, ambrotypes, photographs of the whole family even, on the mantelpiece. One could live here more deliciously and improve his divine gifts better than in a cave surely. In the bright and costly saloon man will not be starv-

ing or freezing or contending with vermin surely, but he will be meditating a divine song or a heroic deed, or perfuming the atmosphere by the very breath of his natural and healthy existence. As the parlor is preferable to the cave, so will the life of its occupant be more godlike than that of the dweller in the cave. I called at such a house this afternoon, the house of one who in Europe would be called an operative. The woman was not in the third heavens, but in the third kitchen, as near the wood-shed or to outdoors and to the cave as she could instinctively get, for there she belonged, — a coarse scullion or wench, not one whit superior, but in fact inferior, to the squaw in a wigwam, — and the master of the house, where was he? He was drunk somewhere, on some mow or behind some stack, and I could not see him. He had been having a spree. If he had been as sober as he may be to-morrow, it would have been essentially the same; for refinement is not in him, it is only in his house, — in the appliances which he did not invent. So is it in the Fifth Avenue and all over the civilized world. There is nothing but confusion in our New England life. The hogs are in the parlor. This man and his wife — and how many like them! — should have sucked their claws in some hole in a rock, or lurked like gypsies in the outbuildings of some diviner race. They've got into the wrong boxes; they rained down into these houses by mistake, as it is said to rain toads sometimes. They wear these advantages helter-skelter and without appreciating them, or to satisfy a vulgar taste, just as savages wear the dress of civilized men, just as that Indian chief

Vol. XII

walked the streets of New Orleans clad in nothing but a gaudy military coat which his Great Father had given him. Some philanthropists trust that the houses will civilize the inhabitants at last. The mass of men, just like savages, strive always after the outside, the clothes and finery of civilized life, the blue beads and tinsel and centre-tables. It is a wonder that any load ever gets moved, men are so prone to put the cart before the horse.

We do everything according to the fashion, just as the Flatheads flatten the heads of their children. We conform ourselves in a myriad ways and with infinite pains to the fashions of our time. We mourn for our lost relatives according to fashion, and as some nations hire professed mourners to howl, so we hire stone-masons to hammer and blast by the month and so express our grief. Or if a public character dies, we get up a regular wake with eating and drinking till midnight.

Grasshoppers have been very abundant in dry fields for two or three weeks. Sophia walked through the Depot Field a fortnight ago, and when she got home picked fifty or sixty from her skirts, — for she wore hoops and crinoline. Would not this be a good way to clear a field of them, — to send a bevy of fashionably dressed ladies across a field and leave them to clean their skirts when they get home? It would supplant anything at the patent office, and the motive power is cheap.

I am invited to take some party of ladies or gentlemen on an excursion, — to walk or sail, or the like, — but by all kinds of evasions I omit it, and am thought to

be rude and unaccommodating therefore. They do not consider that the wood-path and the boat are my studio, where I maintain a sacred solitude and cannot admit promiscuous company. I will see them occasionally in an evening or at the table, however. They do not think of taking a child away from its school to go a-huckleberrying with them. Why should not I, then, have my school and school hours to be respected? Ask me for a certain number of dollars if you will, but do not ask me for my afternoons.

Sept. 18. Considerable rain yesterday, raising the streams at last somewhat.

The frost of the 16th was very severe for the season, killing all our vines, and to-day I see the corn, much of which was not yet topped, all withered and white, and the lespedeza withered in the paths, etc., etc., grape-vines very generally, and the ground-nut.

P. M. — To Grape Cliff.

There is an abundant crop of cones on the white pines this year,[1] and they are now for the most part brown and open. They make a great show even sixty rods off. The tops of the high trees for six or ten feet downward are quite browned with them, hanging straight downward. It is worth the while to observe this evidence of fertility, even in the white pine, which commonly we do not regard as a fruit-bearing tree. It is worth a long walk to look from some favorable point over a pine forest whose tops are thus covered with the brown cones just opened, — from which the

[1] Not only here, but as far off as Worcester, I observe.

winged seeds have fallen or are ready to fall. It is really a rich and interesting sight. How little observed are the fruits which we do not use! How few attend to the ripening and dispersion of the pine seed!

From the observation of this year I should say that the fringed gentian opened before the witch-hazel, for though I know many more localities of the last than the first, I do not find the last out till to-day, and it cannot have been out but a day or two.

Grape-vines are cut off, *i. e.* the leaves, before they have generally turned, this year.

The witch-hazel fruit appears to be now opening. The double-fruited stone splits and reveals the two shining black oblong seeds. It has a peculiarly formed nut, in pretty clusters, clothed, as it were, in close-fitting buckskin, amid the now yellowing leaves.

I hear the *chewink* note now more than a month ago, and it sounds cool and solitary.

Rice, who walks with me, thinks that that fine early sedge grass would be a capital thing to stuff cushions and beds with, it is so tough. (In hollows in woods.)

See checkerberries not yet fully grown nor ripe, somewhat pear-shaped, and whitish at the blossom end. A bear-berry ripe.

One might at first expect that the earth would bear its best men within the tropics, where vegetation is most luxuriant and there is the most heat. But the temperate zone is found to be most favorable to the growth and ripening of men. This fruit attains to the finest flavor there. So, methinks, it is neither the stem nor blossom end of a fruit that is sweetest and maturest, but its

blossom cheek or temperate zone, the portion that lies under its temperate zone. I suspect that the south pole is the stem end of the globe and that Europe and America are on its rosy cheek, and fortunate are we who live in America, where the bloom is not yet rubbed off.

I have seen no *Viburnum nudum* berries for some time. They are considerably earlier than the *V. Lentago.*

Dr. Bartlett handed me a paper to-day, desiring me to subscribe for a statue to Horace Mann. I declined, and said that I thought a man ought not any more to take up room in the world after he was dead. We shall lose one advantage of a man's dying if we are to have a statue of him forthwith. This is probably meant to be an opposition statue to that of Webster. At this rate they will crowd the streets with them. A man will have to add a clause to his will, "No statue to be made of me." It is very offensive to my imagination to see the dying stiffen into statues at this rate. We should wait till their bones begin to crumble — and then avoid too near a likeness to the living.

See large flocks, apparently of chip-birds,[1] rise from the weeds in the garden, now after it clears up. Has the storm driven them from the north? Robins are eating the mountain-ash berries very fast. The robins are more seen than a fortnight ago.

Cistus, some gone to seed and open several days.

Sept. 19. A. M. — To Stow.

Hear the note of the goldfinch on all sides this fine day after the storm. Butternuts have been falling for two

[1] And Sept. 26th.

or three weeks, — now mostly fallen, — but must dry and lose their outer shells before cracking them.

They say that kittens' tails are brittle, and perhaps the tip of that one's was *broken* off.

The young gentleman who travels abroad learns to *pronounce,* and makes acquaintance with foreign lords and ladies, — among the rest perchance with Lord Ward, the inventor and probably consumer of the celebrated Worcestershire Sauce.

See many yellow butterflies in the road this very pleasant day after the rain of yesterday. One flutters across between the horse and the wagon safely enough, though it looks as if it would be run down.

Sept. 20. P. M. — To White Pond.

The button-bushes by the river are generally overrun with the mikania. This is married to the button-bush as much as the vine to the elm, and more. I suspect that the button-bushes and black willows have been as ripe as ever they get to be.

I get quite near to a blackbird on an apple tree, singing with the grackle note very earnestly and not minding me. He is all alone. Has a (rustyish) brown head and shoulders and the rest black. I think it is a grackle. Where are the red-wings now? I have not seen nor heard one for a long time. Is this a grackle come from its northern breeding-place?

Sept. 21. Heard in the night a snapping sound and the fall of some small body on the floor from time to time. In the morning I found that it was produced by

the witch-hazel nuts on my desk springing open and casting their seeds quite across the chamber, hard and stony as these nuts are.[1]

It is overcast, like yesterday, and yet more rain-promising.[2]

Methinks the 19th was such a day (the second after rain) as the 18th in '58, — a peculiarly fine September day, looking toward the fall, warm and bright, with yellow butterflies in the washed road, and early-changed maples and shrubs adorning the low grounds. The red nesæa blazing along the Assabet above the powder-mills. The apple crop, red and yellow, more conspicuous than ever amid the washed leaves.

The farmers on all sides are digging their potatoes, so prone to their work that they do not see me going across lots.

I sat near Coombs's pigeon-place by White Pond. The pigeons sat motionless on his bare perches, from time to time dropping down into the bed and uttering a *quivet* or two. Some stood on the perch; others squatted flat. I could see their dove-colored breasts. Then all at once, being alarmed, would take flight, but ere long return in straggling parties. He tells me that he has fifteen dozen baited, but does not intend to catch any more at present, or for two or three weeks, hoping to attract others. Rice says that white oak acorns pounded up, shells and all, make the best bait for them.

I see now in the wood-paths where small birds and

[1] For several days they are shooting their shining black seeds about my chamber. *Vide* [next page].
[2] Rains in afternoon and night.

partridges, etc., have been destroyed, — only their feathers left, — probably by hawks. Do they not take their prey often to a smooth path in the woods?

White Pond is being dimpled here and there all over, perhaps by fishes; and so is the river. It is an overcast day. Has that anything to do with it? I see some of the rainbow girdle reflected around its edge. Looking with the proper intention of the eye, I see it is ribbed with the dark prolonged reflections of the pines almost across. But why are they bent one side? Is it the effect of the wind?

We are having our dog-days now and of late, methinks, having had none to speak of in August; and now at last I see a few toadstools, — the election-cake (the yellowish, glazed over) and the taller, brighter-yellow above. Those shell-less slugs which eat apples eat these also.

Jays are more frequently heard of late, maybe because other birds are more silent.

Considerable many acorns are fallen (black oak chiefly) in the path under the south edge of Conant's Wood, this side of White Pond. Acorns have been falling very sparingly ever since September 1, but are mostly wormy. They are as interesting now on the shrub oak (green) as ever.

I suspect that it is not when the witch-hazel nut first gapes open that the seeds fly out, for I see many (if not most of them) open first with the seeds in them; but when I release a seed (it being still held by its base), it flies as I have said. I think that its slippery base is compressed by the unyielding shell, which at length expels

it, just as I can make one fly by pressing it and letting it slip from between my thumb and finger. It appears to fit close to the shell at its base, even after the shell gapes.

The ex-plenipotentiary refers in after[-dinner] speeches with complacency to the time he spent abroad and the various lords and distinguished men he met, as to a *deed done* and an ever-memorable occasion! Of what account are titles and offices and opportunities, if you do no memorable deed?

I perceive that a spike of arum berries which I gathered quite green September 1 is now turned completely scarlet, and though it has lain on my desk in a dry and warm chamber all the while, the berries are still perfectly plump and fresh (as well as glossy) to look at, — as much so as any.

The greater part [of], almost all, the mikania was killed by the frost of the 15th and 16th. Only that little which was protected by its position escaped and is still in bloom. And the button-bush too is generally browned above by the same cause. This has given a considerably brown look to the side of the river.

Saw bæomyces (lately opened, probably with the rain of the 17th) by roadside.

Yesterday was a still, overcast, rain-promising day, and I saw this morning (perhaps it was yesterday) the ground about the back door all marked with worm-piles. Had they not come out for water after the dry weather?

See a St. Domingo cuckoo (black-billed) still.

Sept. 22. A mizzling day, with less rain than yesterday, filling the streams.

Vol. XII

As I went past the Hunt cellar, where Hosmer pulled down the old house in the spring, I thought I would see if any new or rare plants had sprung up in that place which had so long been covered from the light. I was surprised to find there *Urtica urens* (?), very fresh and in bloom, one to three feet high, with ovate deeply cut leaves, which I never saw before; also *Nicotiana*, probably *Tabacum* (not the wild one), in flower, and *Anethum graveolens* (?), or dill, also in flower. I had not seen either of the last two growing spontaneously in Concord before. It is remarkable that tobacco should have sprung up there. Could the seed have been preserved from a time when it was cultivated there?[1] Also the *Solanum nigrum*, which is rare in Concord, with many flowers and green fruit. The prevailing plants in and about this cellar were mallows, *Urtica urens*, rich-weed (very rank), catnep, *Chenopodium Botrys*, *Solanum nigrum*, chickweed, *Bidens frondosa*, etc.[2]

It is remarkable what a curse seems to attach to any place which has long been inhabited by man. Vermin of various kinds abide with him. It is said that the site of Babylon is a desert where the lion and the jackal prowl. If, as here, an ancient cellar is uncovered, there springs up at once a crop of rank and noxious weeds, evidence of a certain unwholesome fertility, — by which perchance the earth relieves herself of the poisonous qualities which have been imparted to her.

[1] I learn that it was formerly cultivated in Concord, but Temple, who has raised a little for two years past a mile and a quarter west of this, thinks he is the only one who has cultivated any in C. of late years.

[2] [See *Excursions*, p. 201; Riv. 247.]

As if what was foul, baleful, grovelling, or obscene in the inhabitants had sunk into the earth and infected it. Certain qualities are there in excess in the soil, and the proper equilibrium will not be attained until after the sun and air have purified the spot. The very shade breeds saltpetre. Yet men value this kind of earth highly and will pay a price for it, as if it were as good a soil for virtue as for vice.

In other places you find henbane and the Jamestown-weed and the like, in cellars, — such herbs as the witches are said to put into their caldron.

It would be fit that the tobacco plant should spring up on the house-site, aye on the grave, of almost every householder of Concord. These vile weeds are sown by vile men. When the house is gone they spring up in the corners of cellars where the cider-casks stood always on tap, for murder and all kindred vices will out. And that rank crowd which lines the gutter, where the wash of the dinner dishes flows, are but more distant parasites of the host. What obscene and poisonous weeds, think you, will mark the site of a Slave State? — what kind of Jamestown-weed?

There are mallows for food, — for cheeses, at least; rich-weed for high living; the nettle for domestic felicity, — a happy disposition; black nightshade, tobacco, henbane, and Jamestown-weed as symbols of the moral atmosphere and influences of that house, the idiocy and insanity of it; dill and Jerusalem-oak and catnep for senility grasping at a straw; and beggar-ticks for poverty.[1]

[1] *Vide* next page.

I see the fall dandelions all closed in the rain this afternoon. Do they, then, open only in fair or cloudy forenoons and cloudy afternoons?

There is mallow with its pretty little button-shaped fruit, which children eat and call cheeses, — eaten green. There are several such fruits discoverable and edible by children.

The mountain-ash trees are alive with robins and cherry-birds nowadays, stripping them of their fruit (in drooping clusters). It is exceedingly bitter and *austere* to my taste. Such a tree fills the air with the watch-spring-like note of the cherry-birds coming and going.

Sept. 23. Pretty copious rain in the night.

11 A. M. — River risen about fourteen inches above lowest this year (or thirteen and three quarters above my mark by boat).

What an army of non-producers society *produces*, — ladies generally (old and young) and gentlemen *of leisure*, so called! Many think themselves well employed as charitable dispensers of wealth which somebody else earned, and these who produce nothing, being of the most luxurious habits, are precisely they who want the most, and complain loudest when they do not get what they want. They who are literally paupers maintained at the public expense are the most importunate and insatiable beggars. They cling like the glutton to a living man and suck his vitals up. To every locomotive man there are three or four deadheads clinging to him, as if they conferred a great favor on society by living

upon it. Meanwhile they fill the churches, and die and revive from time to time. They have nothing to do but sin, and repent of their sins. How can you expect such bloodsuckers to be happy?[1]

Not only foul and poisonous weeds grow in our tracks, but our vileness and luxuriance make simple and wholesome plants rank and weed-like. All that I ever got a premium for was a monstrous squash, so coarse that nobody could eat it. Some of these bad qualities will be found to lurk in the pears that are invented in and about the purlieus of great towns. "The evil that men do lives after them." The corn and potatoes produced by excessive manuring may be said to have, not only a coarse, but a poisonous, quality. They are made food [for] hogs and oxen too. What creatures is the grain raised on the corn-fields of Waterloo food for, unless it be for such as prey upon men? Who cuts the grass in the graveyard? I can detect the site of the shanties that have stood all along the railroads by the ranker vegetation. I do not go there for delicate wild-flowers.

It is important, then, that we should air our lives from time to time by removals, and excursions into the fields and woods, — starve our vices. Do not sit so long over any cellar-hole as to tempt your neighbor to bid for the privilege of digging saltpetre there.

So live that only the most beautiful wild-flowers will spring up where you have dwelt, — harebells, violets, and blue-eyed grass.[2]

[1] *Vide* back, Sept. 16th.
[2] *Vide* Oct. 13th.

Sept. 24. P. M. — To Melvin's Preserve.

Was that a flock of grackles on the meadow? I have not seen half a dozen blackbirds, methinks, for a month.

I have many affairs to attend to, and feel hurried these days. Great works of art have endless leisure for a background, as the universe has space. Time stands still while they are created. The artist cannot be in [a] hurry. The earth moves round the sun with inconceivable rapidity, and yet the surface of the lake is not ruffled by it. It is not by a compromise, it is not by a timid and feeble repentance, that a man will save his soul and *live*, at last. He has got to *conquer* a clear field, letting Repentance & Co. go. That's a well-meaning but weak firm that has assumed the debts of an old and worthless one. You are to fight in a field where no allowances will be made, no courteous bowing to one-handed knights. You are expected to do your duty, not in spite of every thing but *one*, but in spite of *everything*.

See a green snake.

Stedman Buttrick's handsome maple and pine swamp is full of cinnamon ferns. I stand on the elevated road, looking down into it. The trees are very tall and slender, without branches for a long distance. All the ground, which is perfectly level, is covered and concealed, as are the bases of the trees, with the tufts of cinnamon fern, now a pale brown. It is a very pretty sight, these northern trees springing out of a groundwork of ferns. It is like pictures of the tropics, except that here the palms are the undergrowth. You could not have arranged a nosegay more tastefully. It is a rich

groundwork, out of which the maples and pines spring.[1] But outside the wood and by the roadside, where they are exposed, these ferns are withered, shrivelled, and brown, for they are tenderer than the dicksonia. The fern, especially if large, is so foreign and tropical that these remind me of artificial groundworks set in sand, to set off other plants. These ferns (like brakes) begin to decay, *i. e.* to turn yellow or brown and ripen, as here, before they are necessarily frost-bitten. Theirs is another change and decay, like that of the brake and sarsaparilla in the woods and swamps, only later, while the exposed ones are killed before they have passed through all their changes. The exposed ones attained to a brighter yellow early and were then killed; the shaded ones pass through various stages of rich, commonly pale brown, as here, and last much longer. The brown ones are the most interesting.

Going along this old Carlisle road, — road for walkers, for berry-pickers, and no more worldly travellers; road for Melvin and Clark, not for the sheriff nor butcher nor the baker's jingling cart; road where all wild things and fruits abound, where there are countless rocks to jar those who venture there in wagons; which no jockey, no wheelwright in his right mind, drives over, no little spidery gigs and Flying Childers; road which leads to and through a great but not famous garden, zoölogical and botanical garden, at whose *gate* you never arrive,[2] — as I was going along there, I perceived the grateful scent of the dicksonia fern, now

[1] *Vide* Aug. 23d, 1858.
[2] *Vide* forward.

partly decayed, and it reminds me of all up-country with its springy mountainsides and unexhausted vigor. Is there any essence of dicksonia fern, I wonder? Surely that giant who, my neighbor expects, is to bound up the Alleghanies will have his handkerchief scented with that. In the lowest part of the road the dicksonia by the wall-sides is more than half frost-bitten and withered, — a sober Quaker-color, brown crape! — though not so tender or early [?] as the cinnamon fern; but soon I rise to where they are more yellow and green, and so my route is varied. On the higher places there are very handsome tufts of it, all yellowish outside and green within. The sweet fragrance of decay! When I wade through by narrow cow-paths, it is as if I had strayed into an ancient and decayed herb-garden. Proper for old ladies to scent their handkerchiefs with. Nature perfumes her garments with this essence now especially. She gives it to those who go a-barberrying and on dank autumnal walks. The essence of this as well as of new-mown hay, surely! The very scent of it, if you have a decayed frond in your chamber, will take you far up country in a twinkling. You would think you had gone after the cows there, or were lost on the mountains. It will make you as cool and well as a frog, — a wood frog, *Rana sylvatica*. It is the scent the earth yielded in the saurian period, before man was created and fell, before milk and water were invented, and the mints. Far wilder than they. *Rana sylvatica* passed judgment on it, or rather that peculiar-scented *Rana palustris*. It was in his reign it was introduced. That is the scent of the Silurian Period precisely,

and a modern beau may scent his handkerchief with it. Before man had come and the plants that chiefly serve him. There were no *Rosaceæ* nor mints then. So the earth smelled in the Silurian (?) Period, before man was created and any soil had been debauched with manure. The saurians had their handkerchiefs scented with it. For all the ages are represented still and you can smell them out.

A man must attend to Nature closely for many years to know when, as well as where, to look for his objects, since he must always anticipate her a little. Young men have not learned the phases of Nature; they do not know what constitutes a year, or that one year is like another. I would know when in the year to expect certain thoughts and moods, as the sportsman knows when to look for plover.

Though you may have sauntered near to heaven's gate, when at length you return toward the village you give up the enterprise a little, and you begin to fall into the old ruts of thought, like a regular roadster. Your thoughts very properly fail to report themselves to headquarters. Your thoughts turn toward night and the evening mail and become begrimed with dust, as if you were just going to put up at (with?) the tavern, or even come to make an exchange with a brother clergyman here on the morrow.

Some eyes cannot see, even through a spy-glass. I showed my spy-glass to a man whom I met this afternoon, who said that he wanted to see if he could look through it. I tried it carefully on him, but he failed. He said that he tried a lot lately on the muster-field

but he never could see through them, somehow or other everything was all a blur. I asked him if he considered his eyes good. He answered that they were good to see far. They looked like two old-fashioned china saucers. He kept steadily chewing his quid all the while he talked and looked. This is the case with a great many, I suspect. Everything is in a blur to them. He enjoys the distinction of being the only man in the town who raises his own tobacco. Seeing is not in them. No focus will suit them. You wonder how the world looks to them, — if those are *eyes* which they have got, or bits of old china, familiar with soap-suds.

As I stood looking over a wall this afternoon at some splendid red sumach bushes, now in their prime, I saw Melvin the other side of the wall and hailed him. "What are *you* after there?" asked he. "After the same thing that you are, perhaps," answered I. But I mistook, this time, for he said that he was looking amid the huckleberry bushes for some spectacles which a woman lost there in the summer. It was his mother, no doubt.

Road — that old Carlisle one — that leaves towns behind; where you put off worldly thoughts; where you do not carry a watch, nor remember the proprietor; where the proprietor is the only trespasser, — looking after *his* apples! — the only one who mistakes his calling there, whose title is not good; where fifty may be a-barberrying and you do not see one. It is an endless succession of glades where the barberries grow thickest, successive yards amid the barberry bushes where you

do not see out. There I see Melvin and the robins, and many a nut-brown maid *sashé*-ing [sic] to the barberry bushes in hoops and crinoline, and none of them see me. The world-surrounding hoop! faery rings! Oh, the jolly cooper's trade it is the best of any! Carried to the furthest isles where civilized man penetrates. This the girdle they've put round the world! Saturn or Satan set the example. Large and small hogsheads, barrels, kegs, worn by the misses that go to that lone schoolhouse in the Pinkham notch. The lonely horse in its pasture is glad to see company, comes forward to be noticed and takes an apple from your hand. Others are called *great* roads, but this is greater than they all. The road is only laid out, offered to walkers, not *accepted* by the town and the travelling world. To be represented by a dotted line on charts, or drawn in lime-juice, undiscoverable to the uninitiated, to be held to a warm imagination. No guide-boards indicate it. No odometer would indicate the miles a wagon had run there. Rocks which the druids *might* have raised — if they could. There I go searching for malic acid of the right quality, with my tests. The process is simple. Place the fruit between your jaws and then endeavor to make your teeth meet. The very earth contains it. The Easterbrooks Country contains malic acid.

To my senses the dicksonia fern has the most wild and primitive fragrance, quite unalloyed and untamable, such as no human institutions give out, — the early morning fragrance of the world, antediluvian, strength and hope imparting. They who scent it can never faint. It is ever a new and untried field where it grows, and only when we think original thoughts can we perceive it. If we keep that on [*sic*] our boudoir we shall be healthy and evergreen as hemlocks. Older than, but related to, strawberries. Before strawberries were, it was, and it will outlast them. Good for the trilobite and saurian in us; death to dandies. It yields its scent most morning and evening. Growing without manure; older than man; refreshing him; preserving his original strength and innocence. When the New Hampshire farmer, far from travelled roads, has cleared a space for his mountain home and conducted the springs of the mountain to his yard, already it grows about the sources of that spring, before any mint is planted in his garden. There his sheep and oxen and he too scent it, and he realizes that the world is new to him. There the pastures are rich, the cattle do not die of disease, and the men are strong and free. The wild original of strawberries and the rest.

Nature, the earth herself, is the only panacea. They bury poisoned sheep up to the necks in earth to take the poison out of them.

After four days cloud and rain we have fair weather. A great many have improved this first fair day to come a-barberrying to the Easterbrooks fields. These bushy fields are all alive with them, though I scarcely see one. I meet Melvin loaded down with barberries, in bags and baskets, so that he has to travel by stages and is glad to stop and talk with me. It is better to take thus what Nature offers, in her season, than to buy an extra dinner at Parker's.

The sumach berries are probably past their beauty. Fever-bush berries are scarlet now, and also green.

They have a more spicy taste than any of our berries, carrying us in thought to the spice islands. Taste like lemon-peel. The panicled andromeda berries (?) begin to brown. The bayberry berries are apparently ripe, though not so gray as they will be, — more lead-colored. They bear sparingly here. Leaves not fallen nor changed, and I the more easily find the bushes amid the changed huckleberries, brakes, etc., by their greenness.

The poke on Eb. Hubbard's hillside has been considerably frost-bitten before the berries are one-third ripe. It is in flower still. Great drooping cylindrical racemes of blackish-purple berries, six inches or more in length, tapering a little toward the end; great flat blackish and ripe berries at base, with green ones and flowers at the other end; all on brilliant purple or crimson-purple peduncle and pedicels.[1]

Those thorns by Shattuck's barn, now nearly leafless, have hard green fruit as usual.

The shrub oak is apparently the most fertile of our oaks. I count two hundred and sixty-six acorns on a branch just two feet long. Many of the cups are freshly empty now, showing a pretty circular pink scar at the bottom, where the acorn adhered. They are of various forms and sizes on different shrubs; are now turning dark-brown and showing their converging meridional light-brown lines. Never fear for striped squirrels in our shrub oak land.

Am surprised to find, by Botrychium Swamp, a *Rhus*

[1] [The word "poke" appears here, drawn across the page in large characters now (1906) of a dirty light-brown color. The stain is doubtless what remains of the poke berry's purple juice.]

radicans which is quite a tree by itself. It is about nine feet high by nine in width, growing in the midst of a clump of barberry bushes, which it overhangs. It is now at the height of its change, very handsome, scarlet and yellow, and I did not at first know what it was. I found it to consist of three or four branches, each nearly two inches thick and covered with those shaggy fibres, and these are twined round some long-since rotted barberry stems, and around one another, and now make a sizable-looking trunk, which rises to the height of four feet before it branches, and then spreads widely every way like an oak. It was, no doubt, indebted to the barberry for support at first, but now its very branches are much larger than that, and it far overtops and overspreads all the barberry stems.

Sept. 25. P. M. — To Emerson's Cliff.

Holding a white pine needle in my hand, and turning it in a favorable light, as I sit upon this cliff, I perceive that each of its three edges is notched or serrated with minute forward-pointing bristles. So much does Nature avoid an unbroken line that even this slender leaf is serrated; though, to my surprise, neither Gray nor Bigelow mention it. Loudon, however, says, "Scabrous and inconspicuously serrated on the margin; spreading in summer, but in winter contracted, and lying close to the branches." Fine and smooth as it looks, it is serrated after all. This is its concealed wildness, by which it connects itself with the wilder oaks.

Prinos berries are fairly ripe for a few days. Moles work in meadows.

I see at Brister Spring Swamp the (apparently) *Aspidium Noveboracense*, more than half of it turned white. Also some dicksonia is about equally white. These especially are the white ones. There is another, largish, and more generally decayed than either of these, with large serrated segments, rather far apart, — perhaps the *Asplenium Filix-fœmina* (?). The first may be called now the white fern, — with rather small entirish and flat segments close together. In shade is the laboratory of white. Color is produced in the sun. The cinnamon ferns are all a decaying brown there. The sober brown colors of those ferns are in harmony with the twilight of the swamp. The terminal shield fern and the *Aspidium spinulosum* (?) are still fresh and green, the first as much so as the polypody.

At 2 P. M. the river is sixteen and three quarters inches above my hub[?] by boat.

Nabalus albus still common, though much past prime. Though concealed amid trees, I find three humble-bees on one.

As when Antæus touched the earth, so when the mountaineer scents the fern, he bounds up like a chamois, or mountain goat, with renewed strength. There is no French perfumery about it. It has not been tampered with by any perfumer to their majesties. It is the fragrance of those plants whose impressions we see on our coal. Beware of the cultivation that eradicates it.

The very crab-grass in our garden is for the most part a light straw-color and withered, probably by the frosts of the

15th and 16th, looking almost as white as the corn; and hundreds of sparrows (chip-birds?) find their food amid it. The same frosts that kill and whiten the corn whiten many grasses thus.

Sept. 26. P. M. — To Clamshell by boat.

The *Solanum dulcamara* berries are another kind which grows in drooping clusters. I do not know any clusters more graceful and beautiful than these drooping cymes of scarlet or translucent cherry-colored elliptical berries with steel-blue (or lead?) purple pedicels (not peduncles) like those leaves on the tips of the branches. These in the water at the bend of the river are peculiarly handsome, they are so long an oval or ellipse. No berries, methinks, are so well spaced and agreeably arranged in their drooping cymes, — somewhat hexagonally like a honeycomb. Then what a variety of color! The peduncle and its branches are green, the pedicels and sepals only that rare steel-blue purple, and the berries a clear translucent cherry red. They hang more gracefully over the river's brim than any pendants in a lady's ear. The cymes are of irregular yet regular form, not too crowded, elegantly spaced. Yet they are considered poisonous! Not to look at, surely. Is it not a reproach that so much that is beautiful is poisonous to us? Not in a stiff, flat cyme, but in different stages above and around, finding ample room in space. But why should they not be poisonous? Would it not be in bad taste to eat these berries which are ready to feed another sense? A drooping berry should always be of an oval or pear shape. Nature not

only produces good wares, but puts them up handsomely. Witness these pretty-colored and variously shaped skins in which her harvests, the seeds of her various plants, are now being packed away. I know in what bags she puts her nightshade seeds, her cranberries, viburnums, cornels, by their form and color, often by their fragrance; and thus a legion of consumers find them.

The celtis berries are still green. The pontederia is fast shedding its seeds of late. I saw a parcel suddenly rise to the surface of their own accord, leaving the axis nearly bare. Many are long since bare. They float, at present, but probably sink at last. There are a great many floating amid the pads and in the wreck washed up, of these singular green spidery(?)-looking seeds. Probably they are the food of returning water-fowl. They are ripe, like the seeds of different lilies, at the time the fowl return from the north.

I hear a frog or two, either *palustris* or *halecina*, croak and *work* faintly, as in spring, along the side of the river. So it is with flowers, birds, and frogs a renewal of spring.

Hearing a sharp *phe-phe* and again *phe-phe-phe*, I look round and see two (probably larger) yellow-legs, like pigeons, standing in the water by the bare, flat ammannia shore, their whole forms reflected in the water. They allow me to paddle past them, though on the alert.

Heavy Haynes says he has seen one or two fish hawks within a day or two. Also that a boy caught a very large snapping turtle on the meadow a day or two

ago. He once dug one up two or three feet deep in the meadow in winter when digging mud. He was rather dormant. Says he remembers a fish-house that stood by the river at Clamshell.

Observed the spiders at work at the head of Willow Bay. Their fine lines are extended from one flag or bur-reed to another, even six or eight feet, perfectly parallel with the surface of the water and only a few inches above it. I see some,—though it requires a very favorable light to detect them, they are so fine, — blowing off perfectly straight horizontally over the water, only half a dozen inches above it, as much as seven feet, one end fastened to a reed, the other free. They look as stiff as spears, yet the free end waves back and forth horizontally in the air several feet. They work thus in calm and fine weather when the water is smooth. Yet they can run over the surface of the water readily.

The savage in man is never quite eradicated. I have just read of a family in Vermont who, several of its members having died of consumption, just *burned* the lungs, heart, and liver of the last deceased, in order to prevent any more from having it.

How feeble women, or rather ladies, are! They cannot bear to be shined on, but generally carry a parasol to *keep off* the sun.

Sept. 28. At Cattle-Show to-day I noticed that the ladies' apple (small, one side green, the other red, glossy) and maiden's-blush (good size, yellowish-white with a pink blush) were among the handsomest. The pumpkin-sweet one of the largest exhibited. The ram's-

horn was a handsome uniformly very dark purple or crimson.

The white pine seed is very abundant this year, and this must attract more pigeons. Coombs tells me that he finds the seed in their crops. Also that he found within a day or two a full-formed egg with shell in one.

In proportion as a man has a poor ear for music, or loses his ear for it, he is obliged to go far for it or fetch it from far, and pay a great price for such as he *can* hear. Operas, ballet-singers, and the like only affect him. It is like the difference between a young and healthy appetite and the appetite of an epicure, between a sweet crust and a mock-turtle soup.

As the lion is said to lie in a thicket or in tall reeds and grass by day, slumbering, and sallies at night, just so with the cat. She will ensconce herself for the day in the grass or weeds in some out-of-the-way nook near the house, and arouse herself toward night.

Sept. 29. Down railroad and to Fair Haven Hill.

In Potter's maple swamp I see the (apparently) *Aspidium Thelypteris* (revolute segments) about half decaying or whitish, but later than the flowering fern and the osmunda, which are almost entirely withered and brown there.

Dogwood (poison) berries are ripe, and leaves begun to fall.

Juniperus repens berries are quite green yet. I see some of last year's *dark*-purple ones at the base of the branchlets. There is a very large specimen on the side of Fair Haven Hill, above Cardinal Shore. This is very handsome this bright afternoon, especially if you stand on the lower and sunny side, on account of the various ways in which its surging flakes and leafets, green or silvery, reflect the light. It is as if we were giants, and looked down on an evergreen forest from whose flaky surface the light is variously reflected. Though so low, it is so dense and rigid that neither men nor cows think of wading through it. We get a bird's-eye view of this evergreen forest, as a hawk sailing over, looking into its unapproachable clefts and recesses, reflecting a green or else a cheerful silvery light.

Horse-chestnuts strew the roadside, very handsome-colored but simply formed nuts, looking like mahogany knobs, with the waved and curled grain of knots.

Having just dug my potatoes in the garden, — which did not turn out very well, — I took a basket and trowel and went forth to dig my wild potatoes, or ground-nuts, by the railroad fence. I dug up the tubers of some half a dozen plants and found an unexpected yield. One string weighed a little more than three quarters of a pound. There were thirteen which I should have put with the large potatoes (this year) if they had been the common kind. The biggest was two and three quarters inches long and seven inches in circumference the smallest way. Five would have been called good-sized potatoes. It is but a slender vine now, killed by frost, and not promising such a yield, but deep in the soil (or sand), five or six inches or sometimes a foot, you come to the string of brown and commonly *knubby* nuts. The cuticle of the tuber is more or less cracked longitudinally, forming meridional furrows, and the roots (?), or shoots,

bear a large proportion to the tuber. In case of a famine I should soon resort to these roots. If they increased in size, on being cultivated, as much as the common potato has, they would become monstrous.[1]

Saw a warbler in Potter's Swamp, light-slate head and above and no bars on wings; yellow all beneath, except throat, which was lighter ash, and perhaps upper part of breast; a distinct light ring about eye, iris-like; light bill, and apparently flesh-color legs, etc. Very inquisitive, hopping within ten feet, with a *chip*. It is somewhat like the Nashville warbler.[2]

Sept. 30. P. M. — Up Assabet.

Ever since the unusually early and severe frost of the 16th, the evergreen ferns have been growing more and more distinct amid the fading and decaying and withering ones, and the sight of those suggests a cooler season. They are greener than ever, by contrast. The terminal shield fern is one of the handsomest. The most decidedly evergreen are the last, polypody, *Aspidium marginale*, and *Aspidium spinulosum* of Woodis Swamp and Brister's. *Asplenium Filix-fœmina* (?) is decaying, maybe a little later than the dicksonia, — the largish fern with long, narrow pinnules deeply cut and toothed, and reniform fruit-dots.

Of the twenty-three ferns which I seem to know here, seven may be called evergreens. As far as I know, the earliest to wither and fall are the brake (mostly fallen),

[1] *Vide* Oct. 15th.
[2] Was it a yellow-rump warbler? [A surprising question. The bird may have been a Connecticut warbler.]

the *Osmunda cinnamomea* (begun to be stripped of leaves), *O. Claytoniana*, and *O. regalis* (the above four generally a long time withered, or say since the 20th); also (5th), as soon, the exposed onoclea; then (6th) the dicksonia, (7th) *Aspidium Noveboracense*, (8th) *Thelypteris*, (9th) *Filix-fœmina* (the last four now fully half faded or decayed or withered). Those not seen are *Adiantum pedatum, Woodwardia Virginica, Asplenium thelypteroides, Woodsia Ilvensis, Aspidium cristatum, Lygodium palmatum, Botrychium Virginicum.*

Some acorns (swamp white oak) are browned on the trees, and some bass berries. Most shrub oak acorns browned.

The wild rice is almost entirely fallen or eaten, apparently by some insect, but I see some green and also black grains left.[1]

[1] For more of September, *vide* [p. 362].

VIII

OCTOBER, 1859

(ÆT. 42)

Oct. 1. P. M. — To the beeches.

Looking down from Pine Hill, I see a fish hawk over Walden.

The shrub oaks on this hill are now at their height, both with respect to their tints and their fruit. The plateaus and little hollows are crowded with them three to five feet high, the pretty fruit, varying in size, pointedness, and downiness, being now generally turned brown, with light, converging meridional lines. Many leading shoots are perfectly bare of leaves, the effect of the frost, and on some bushes half the cups are empty, but these cups generally bear the marks of squirrels' teeth, and probably but few acorns have fallen of themselves yet. However, they are just ready to fall, and if you bend back the peduncles on these bare and frost-touched shoots, you find them just ready to come off, separating at the base of the peduncle, and the peduncle remaining attached to the fruit. The squirrels, probably striped, must be very busy here nowadays. Though many twigs are bare, these clusters of brown fruit in their grayish-brown cups are unnoticed and almost invisible, unless you are looking for them, above the ground, which is strewn with their similarly colored leaves; *i. e.*, this leaf-strewn earth has the same general gray and brown color with the twigs and fruit, and you may

Tufts of Andropogon lighted by the Sun

Large Juniper on Fair Haven Hill

brush against great wreaths of fruit without noticing them. You press through dense groves full of this interesting fruit, each seeming prettier than the last. Now is the time for shrub oak acorns, then, if not for others. I see where the squirrels have left the shells on rocks and stumps. They take the acorn out of its cup on the bush, leaving the cup there with a piece bit out of its edge.

The little beechnut burs are mostly empty, and the ground is strewn with the nuts mostly empty and abortive. Yet I pluck some apparently full grown with meat. This fruit is apparently now at its height.

Oct. 2. Rain in the night and cloudy this forenoon.

We had all our dog-days in September this year. It was too dry before, even for fungi. Only the last three weeks have we had any fungi to speak of. Nowadays I see most of the election-cake fungi, with crickets and slugs eating them. I see a cricket feeding on an apple, into which he has eaten so deep that only his posteriors project, but he does not desist a moment though I shake the apple and finally drop it on the ground.

P. M. — To lygodium.

One of the large black birches on Tarbell's land is turned completely brownish-yellow and has lost half its leaves; the other is green still.

I see in the corn-field above this birch, collected about the trunk of an oak, on the ground, fifty to a hundred ears of corn which have been stripped to the cob, evidently by the squirrels. Apparently a great

part of the kernels remain on the ground, but in every case the germ has been eaten out. It is apparent that the squirrel prefers this part, for he has not carried off the rest.

I perceive in various places, in low ground, this afternoon, the sour scent of cinnamon ferns decaying. It is an agreeable phenomenon, reminding me of the season and of past years.

So many maple and pine and other leaves have now fallen that in the woods, at least, you walk over a carpet of fallen leaves.

As I sat on an old pigeon-stand, not used this year, on the hill south of the swamp, at the foot of a tree, set up with perches nailed on it, a pigeon hawk, as I take it, came and perched on the tree. As if it had been wont to catch pigeons at such places.

That large lechea, now so freshly green and sometimes scarlet, looks as if it would make a pretty edging like box, as has been suggested. The *Aster undulatus* and *Solidago cæsia* and often *puberula* are particularly prominent now, looking late and bright, attracting bees, etc. I see the *S. cæsia* so covered with the little fuzzy gnats as to be whitened by them. How bright the *S. puberula* in sprout-lands, — its yellow wand,[1] — perhaps in the midst of a clump of little scarlet or dark-purple black oaks! The *A. undulatus* looks fairer than ever, now that flowers are more scarce.

The climbing fern is perfectly fresh, — and apparently therefore an evergreen, — the more easily found amid the withered cinnamon and flowering ferns.

[1] Quite generally withered and fuzzy Oct. 14th, 1861.

Vol. XII

Acorns generally, as I notice, — swamp white, shrub, black, and white, — are turned brown; but few are still green. Yet few, except of shrub oaks, have fallen. I hear them fall, however, as I stand under the trees. This would be the time to notice them.

How much pleasanter to go along the edge of the woods, through the field in the rear of the farmhouse, whence you see only its gray roof and its haystacks, than to keep the road by its door! This we think as we return behind Martial Miles's. I observed that many pignuts had fallen yesterday, though quite green.

Some of the *Umbelliferæ*, now gone to seed, are very pretty to examine. The *Cicuta maculata*, for instance, the concave umbel is so well spaced, the different umbellets (?) like so many constellations or separate systems in the firmament.

Hear a hylodes in the swamp.

Oct. 3. P. M. — To Bateman's Pond; back by hog-pasture and old Carlisle road.

Some faces that I see are so gross that they affect me like a part of the person improperly exposed, and it occurs to me that they might be covered, and, if necessary, some other, and perhaps better-looking, part of the person be exposed.

It is somewhat cooler and more autumnal. A great many leaves have fallen and the trees begin to look thin. You incline to sit in a sunny and sheltered place. This season, the fall, which we have now entered on, commenced, I may say, as long ago as when the first frost was seen and felt in low ground in August. From that

time, even, the year has been gradually winding up its accounts. Cold, methinks, has been the great agent which has checked the growth of plants, condensed their energies, and caused their fruits to ripen, in September especially. Perchance man never ripens within the tropics.[1]

I see on a wall a myrtle-bird in its October dress, looking very much like a small sparrow. Also everywhere about the edge of the woods this afternoon, sylvias rather large and of a greenish yellow above and beneath, perhaps white vent, and much dark brown above, getting their food on the white birches. The same in very distant places. Perhaps it is the birch louse they eat. What bird is this?[2] It is quite unlike the sparrow-like myrtle-bird above described, unless some of them are of this color now.

The *Woodsia Ilvensis* is partly withering or withered on the rocks, but not so much as the dicksonia. Yet it is evidently not evergreen.

I see the ground strewn with *Populus grandidentata* leaves in one place on the old Carlisle road, where one third are fallen. These yellow leaves are all thickly brown-spotted and are very handsome, somewhat leopard-like. It would seem that they begin to decay in spots at intervals all over the leaf, producing a very pretty effect. Think of the myriad variously tinted and spotted and worm-eaten leaves which now combine to produce the general impression of autumn! The ground is here strewn with thousands, any one of which,

[1] *Vide* [pp. 368, 369, 373, and 375].
[2] [Probably the black-poll warbler.]

if you carry it home, it will refresh and delight you to behold. If we have not the leopard and jaguar and tiger in our woods, we have all their spots and rosettes and stripes in our autumn-tinted leaves.

The ash trees are at their height now, if not earlier. Many of their leaves have fallen.

The dicksonia ferns by the old Carlisle road-side are now almost all withered to dark cinnamon, and the large cinnamon ferns in Buttrick's wood are no longer noticed.

Looking from the hog-pasture over the valley of Spencer Brook westward, we see the smoke rising from a huge chimney above a gray roof amid the woods, at a distance, where some family is preparing its evening meal. There are few more agreeable sights than this to the pedestrian traveller. No cloud is fairer to him than that little bluish one which issues from the chimney. It suggests all of domestic felicity beneath. There beneath, we suppose, that life is lived of which we have only dreamed. In our minds we clothe each unseen inhabitant with all the success, with all the serenity, which we can conceive of. If old, we imagine him serene; if young, hopeful. Nothing can exceed the perfect peace which reigns there. We have only to see a gray roof with its plume of smoke curling up amid the trees to have this faith. There we suspect no coarse haste or bustle, but serene labors which proceed at the same pace with the declining day. *There* is no hireling in the barn nor in the kitchen. Why does any distant prospect ever charm us? Because we instantly and inevitably imagine a life to be lived there such as is not lived else-

where, or where we **are**. We presume that success **is** the rule. We forever **carry a** perfect sampler in our minds. Why are distant valleys, why lakes, why mountains in the horizon, ever fair to us? Because we realize for a moment that they may be the home of man, and that man's life may be in harmony with them. Shall I say that we thus forever delude ourselves? We do not suspect that *that* farmer goes to the depot with his milk. *There* the milk is not watered. We are constrained to imagine a life in harmony with the scenery and the hour. The sky and clouds, and the earth itself, with their beauty forever preach to us, saying, Such an abode we offer you, to such and such a life we encourage you. *There* is not haggard poverty and harassing debt. There is not intemperance, moroseness, meanness, or vulgarity. Men go about sketching, painting landscapes, or writing verses which celebrate man's opportunities. To go into an actual farmer's family at evening, see the tired laborers come in from their day's work thinking of their wages, the sluttish help in the kitchen and sink-room, the indifferent stolidity and patient misery which only the spirits of the youngest children rise above, — that suggests one train of thoughts. To look down on that roof from a distance in an October evening, when its smoke is ascending peacefully to join the kindred clouds above, — that suggests a different train of thoughts. We think that we see these fair abodes and are elated beyond all speech, when we see only our own roofs, perchance. We are ever busy hiring house and lands and peopling them in our imaginations. There is no beauty in the sky, but in the eye that sees

it. Health, high spirits, serenity, these are the great landscape-painters. Turners, Claudes, Rembrandts are nothing to them. We never see any beauty but as the garment of some virtue. Men love to walk in those picture-galleries still, because they have not quite forgotten their early dreams. When I see only the roof of a house above the woods and do not know whose it is, I presume that one of the worthies of the world dwells beneath it, and for a season I am exhilarated at the thought. I would fain sketch it that others may share my pleasure. But commonly, if I see or know the occupant, I am affected as by the sight of the almshouse or hospital.

Wild apples are perhaps at their height, or perhaps only the earlier ones.

Those *P. grandidentata* leaves are wildly rich. So handsomely formed and floridly scalloped, to begin with, — a fine chrome yellow now richly spotted with dark brown like a leopard's skin, — they cover the still green sward by the roadside and the gray road thick as a pavement, each one worthy to be admired as a gem or work of Oriental art.

Among sound leaves I think of the fever-bush, *Rhus radicans*, beech, and shrub oak.

It was mainly the frost of September 15 and 16 that put an end to the summer, that put the finishing stroke to the already withering grass, and left it to bleach in the fields, turning russet with blackberry vines intermixed, earlier than usual. The same frost suddenly cut off the mikania and browned the button-bushes, causing the upper leaves at length to fall. It must be the frost that

ripens nuts, — acorns, for example, — browning them. Frost and cold paint the acorn and the chestnut.

The hickory has spots with a central ring, evidently produced by an insect.

Consider the infinite promise of a man, so that the sight of his roof at a distance suggests an idyll or pastoral, or of his grave an Elegy in a Country Churchyard. How all poets have idealized the farmer's life! What graceful figures and unworldly characters they have assigned to them! Serene as the sky, emulating nature with their calm and peaceful lives. As I come by a farmer's to-day, the house of one who died some two years ago, I see the decrepit form of one whom he had engaged to "carry through," taking his property at a venture, feebly tying up a bundle of fagots with his knee on it, though time is fast loosening the bundle that he is. When I look down on that roof I am not reminded of the mortgage which the village bank has on that property, — that that family long since sold itself to the devil and wrote the deed with their blood. I am not reminded that the old man I see in the yard is one who has lived beyond his calculated time, whom the young one is merely "carrying through" in fulfillment of his contract; that the man at the pump is watering the milk. I am not reminded of the idiot that sits by the kitchen fire.

Oct. **4.** When I have made a visit where my expectations are not met, I feel as if I owed my hosts an apology for troubling them so. If I am disappointed, I find that I have no right to visit them.

I have always found that what are called the best of manners are the worst, for they are simply the shell without the meat. They cover no life at all. *They* are the universal slaveholders, who treat men as things. Nobody holds you more cheap than the man of manners. They are marks by the help of which the wearers ignore you and remain concealed themselves. Are they such great characters that they feel obliged to make the journey of life incognito? Sailors swear; gentlemen make their manners to you.

All men sympathize by their lower natures; the few, only, by their higher. The appetites of the mistress are commonly the same as those of her servant, but her society is commonly more select. The help may have some of the tenderloin, but she must eat it in the kitchen.

P. M. — To Conantum.

How interesting now, by wall-sides and on open springy hillsides, the large, straggling tufts of the dicksonia fern above the leaf-strewn greensward, the cold fall-green sward! They are unusually preserved about the Corner Spring, considering the earliness of this year. Long, handsome lanceolate green fronds, pointing in every direction, recurved and full of fruit, intermixed with yellowish and sere brown and shrivelled ones. The whole clump, perchance, strewn with fallen and withered maple leaves and overtopped by now withered and unnoticed osmundas. Their lingering greenness so much the more noticeable now that the leaves (generally) have changed. They affect us as if they were evergreen, such persistent life and greenness in the midst of their own decay. I do not notice them

so much in summer. No matter how much withered they are, with withered leaves that have fallen on them, moist and green they spire above them, not fearing the frosts, fragile as they are. Their greenness so much the more interesting because so many have already fallen and we know that the first severer frost will cut off them too. In the summer greenness is cheap; now it is something comparatively rare and is the emblem of life to us.

It is only when we forget all our learning that we begin to know. I do not get nearer by a hair's breadth to any natural object so long as I presume that I have an introduction to it from some learned man. To conceive of it with a total apprehension I must for the thousandth time approach it as something totally strange. If you would make acquaintance with the ferns you must forget your botany. You must get rid of what is commonly called *knowledge* of them. Not a single scientific term or distinction is the least to the purpose, for you would fain perceive something, and you must approach the object totally unprejudiced You must be aware that *no thing* is what you have taken it to be. In what book is this world and its beauty described? Who has plotted the steps toward the discovery of beauty? You have got to be in a different state from common. Your greatest success will be simply to perceive that such things are, and you will have no communication to make to the Royal Society. If it were required to know the position of the fruit-dots or the character of the indusium, nothing could be easier than to ascertain it; but if it is required that

you be affected by ferns, that they amount to anything, signify anything, to you, that they be another sacred scripture and revelation to you, helping to redeem your life, this end is not so surely accomplished. In the one case, you take a sentence and analyze it, you decide if it is printed in large [*sic*] primer or small pica; if it is long or short, simple or compound, and how many clauses it is composed of; if the i's are all dotted, or some for variety without dots; what the color and composition of the ink and the paper; and it is considered a fair or mediocre sentence accordingly, and you assign its place among the sentences you have seen and kept specimens of. But as for the meaning of the sentence, that is as completely overlooked as if it had none. This is the Chinese, the Aristotelean, method. But if you should ever perceive the meaning you would disregard all the rest. So far science goes, and it punctually leaves off there, — tells you finally where it is to be found and its synonyms, and rests from its labors.

This is a fine and warm afternoon, Indian-summer-like, but we have not had cold enough before it.

Birds are now seen more numerously than before, as if called out by the fine weather, probably many migrating birds from the north. I see and hear probably flocks of grackles with their split and shuffling note, but no red-wings for a long time; chip-birds (but without chestnut crowns; is that the case with the young?), bay-wings on the walls and fences, and the yellow-browed sparrows. Hear the pine warblers in the pines, about the needles, and see them on the ground and on rocks, with a yellow ring round the eye (!), reddish legs,

slight whitish bar on wings. Going over the large hillside stubble-field west of Holden Wood, I start up a large flock of shore larks; hear their *sveet sveet* and *sveet sveet sveet*, and see their tails dark beneath. They are very wary, and run in the stubble for the most part invisible, while one or two appear to act the sentinel on rock, peeping out behind it perhaps, and give their note of alarm, when away goes the whole flock. Such a flock circled back and forth several times over my head, just like ducks reconnoitring before they alight. If you look with a glass you are surprised to see how alert these spies are. When they alight in some stubbly hollow they set a watch or two on the rocks to look out for foes. They have dusky bills and legs.

The birds seem to delight in these first fine days of the fall, in the warm, hazy light, — robins, bluebirds (in families on the almost bare elms), phœbes, and probably purple finches. I hear half-strains from many of them, as the song sparrow, bluebird, etc., and the sweet *phe-be* of the chickadee.

Now the year itself begins to be ripe, ripened by the frost, like a persimmon.[1]

The maidenhair fern at Conantum is apparently unhurt by frost as yet.

Oct. 6. A. M. — To Boston.

Examine the pigeon and sparrow hawks in the Natural History collection. My wings and tail are apparently the pigeon hawk's. The sparrow hawks are decidedly red-brown with bluish heads and blue or

[1] *Vide* bottom of 11th.

slate sides; also are much more thickly barred with dark on wing-coverts, back, and tail than the pigeon hawk.

Oct. 7. The pontederia seeds which I dropped into a pitcher of water have now mostly sunk. As the outside decays they become heavier than water.

Oct. 9. P. M. — Boston.

Read a lecture to Theodore Parker's society.

Aster cordifolius abundant and commonly in bloom in Roxbury. See the privet everywhere with dense pyramidal clusters of berries. *Salsola kali* common in bloom, with pretty crimson flowers. *Chenopodium maritimum* perhaps in bloom. *Senecio vulgaris* still in bloom.

Oct. 10. White-throated sparrows in yard and close up to house, together with myrtle-birds (which fly up against side of house and alight on window-sills) and, I think, tree sparrows?

Colder weather, and the cat's fur grows.

Oct. 11. P. M. — To Cliffs.

Looking under large oaks, black and white, the acorns appear to have fallen or been gathered by squirrels, etc. I see in many *distant* places stout twigs (black or scarlet oak) three or four inches long which have been gnawed off by the squirrels, with four to seven acorns on each, and left on the ground. These twigs have been gnawed off on each side of the nuts in

order to make them more portable, I suppose. The nuts all abstracted and sides of the cups broken to get them out.

The note of the chickadee, heard now in cooler weather and above many fallen leaves, has a new significance.

There was a very severe frost this morning (ground stiffened), probably a chestnut-opening frost, a season-ripener, opener of the burs that inclose the Indian summer. Such is the cold of early or middle October. The leaves and weeds had that stiff, hoary appearance.

Oct. 12. P. M. — To Hubbard's Close.

The common goldenrods on railroad causeway have begun to look hoary or gray, the down showing itself, — that November feature.

I see scattered flocks of bay-wings amid the weeds and on the fences.

There are now apparently very few ferns left (except the evergreen ones), and those are in sheltered places. This morning's frost will nearly finish them. Now for lycopodiums (the *dendroideum* not yet apparently in bloom), the *dendroideum* and *lucidulum*, etc., — how vivid a green! — lifting their heads above the moist fallen leaves.

We have now fairly begun to be surrounded with the brown of withered foliage, since the young white oaks have withered. This phenomenon begins with the very earliest frost (as this year August 17th), which kills some ferns and other most sensitive plants; and so gradually the plants, or their leaves, are killed and withered that we

scarcely notice it till we are surrounded with the scenery of November.[1]

I see quinces commonly left out yet, though apples are gathered. Probably their downy coats defend them.

Going through Clintonia Swamp, I see many of those buff-brown puffballs one to two inches [in] diameter on the ground, partly open and with water in them and partly entire as yet, with a cracked surface.

The willows on the Turnpike resound with the hum of bees, almost as in spring! I see apparently yellow wasps, hornets, and small bees attracted by something on their twigs.

Oct. 13. P. M. — Up Assabet.

Many of the small hypericums, *mutilum* and *Canadense*, have survived the frosts as yet, after all. The hemlock seed is now in the midst of its fall, some of it, with the leaves, floating on the river. The cones, being thus expanded, are more conspicuous on the trees. Many feverwort berries are fresh yet, though the leaves are quite withered. They are remarkable for their peculiar color. The thorn fruit on the hill is considerably past prime, though abundant and reddening the bushes still. The common alder up the Assabet is nerved like the hornbeam. I see no acorns on the trees. They appear to have all fallen before this.

The swamp amelanchier is leafing again, as usual. What a pleasing phenomenon, perhaps an Indian-summer growth, an anticipation of the spring, like the notes of birds and frogs, etc., an evidence of warmth and

[1] Yet these same plants will wither and fall without frost.

genialness. Its buds are annually awakened by the October sun as if it were spring. The shad-bush is leafing again by the sunny swamp-side. It is like a youthful or poetic thought in old age. Several times I have been cheered by this sight when surveying in former years. The chickadee seems to lisp a sweeter note at the sight of it. *I* would not fear the winter more than the shad-bush which puts forth fresh and tender leaves on its approach. In the fall I will take this for my coat-of-arms. It seems to detain the sun that expands it. These twigs are so full of life that they can hardly contain themselves. They ignore winter. They anticipate spring. What faith! Away in some warm and sheltered recess in the swamp you find where these leaves have expanded. It is a foretaste of spring. In my latter years, let me have some *shad-bush* thoughts.[1]

I perceive the peculiar scent of the witch-hazel in bloom for several rods around, which at first I refer to the decaying leaves. I see where dodder was killed, with the button-bush, perhaps a week.

British naturalists very generally apologize to the reader for having devoted their attention to natural history to the neglect of some important duty.

Among plants which spring in cellars (*vide* September 22d) might be mentioned funguses. I remember seeing in an old work a plate of a fungus which grew in a wine-cellar and got its name from that circumstance. It is related in *Chambers's Journal* that Sir Joseph Banks, having caused a cask of wine to be placed in a cellar in order to improve it, " at the end of three years

[1] *Vide* Nov. 25th, 1858. *Vide* mountain-ash, Oct. 30th, 1858.

he directed his butler to ascertain the state of the wine, when, on attempting to open the cellar door, he could not affect it, in consequence of some powerful obstacle; the door was consequently cut down, when the cellar was found to be completely filled with a fungous production, so firm that it was necessary to use an axe for its removal. This appeared to have grown from, or to have been nourished by, the decomposing particles of the wine, the cask being empty, and carried up to the ceiling, where it was supported by the fungus." Perhaps it was well that the fungus instead of Sir Joseph Banks drank up the wine. The life of a wine-bibber is like that of a fungus.

Oct. 14. 9 A. M. — To and around Flint's Pond with Blake.

A fine Indian-summer day. The 6th and 10th were quite cool, and any particularly warm days since may be called Indian summer (?), I think.

We sit on the rock on Pine Hill overlooking Walden. There is a thick haze almost entirely concealing the mountains.

There is wind enough to raise waves on the pond and make it bluer. What strikes me in the scenery here now is the contrast of the unusually blue water with the brilliant-tinted woods around it. The tints generally may be about at their height. The earth appears like a great inverted shield painted yellow and red, or with imbricated scales of that color, and a blue navel in the middle where the pond lies, and a distant circumference of whitish haze. The nearer woods, where chestnuts

grow, are a mass of warm, glowing [yellow] (though the larger chestnuts have lost the greater part of their leaves and generally you wade through rustling chestnut leaves in the woods), but on other sides the red and yellow are intermixed. The red, probably of scarlet oaks on the south of Fair Haven Hill, is very fair.

The beech tree at Baker's fence is past prime and many leaves fallen.

The shrub oak acorns are now all fallen, — only one or two left on, — and their cups, which are still left on, are apparently somewhat incurved at the edge as they have dried, so that probably they would not hold the acorn now. The ground is strewn also with red oak acorns now, and, as far as I can discover, acorns of all kinds have fallen.

At Baker's wall two of the walnut trees are bare but full of green nuts (in their green cases), which make a very pretty sight as they wave in the wind. So distinct you could count every one against the sky, for there is not a leaf on these trees, but other walnuts near by are yet full of leaves. You have the green nut contrasted with the clean gray trunks and limbs. These are pig-nut-shaped.

The chestnuts generally have not yet fallen, though many have. I find under one tree a great many burs, apparently not cast down by squirrels — for I see no marks of their teeth — and not yet so opened that any of the nuts fall out. They do not all wait till frosts open the burs before they fall, then.

I see a black snake, and also a striped snake, out this warm day.

Vol. XII

I see and hear many hawks for some weeks past. On the 11th I saw one as small as I ever saw, — I thought not larger than a kingbird, — as I stood on the Cliffs, hovering over the wood about on a level with me. It sailed directly only a rod or two, then flapped its wings fast and sailed on a rod or two further. Was it not a sparrow hawk? Dr. Kneeland says he sees it hereabouts and distinguishes it partly by its smaller size.

See great numbers of crickets in the cross-road from Tuttle's to Alcott's.

Populus grandidentata up Assabet yellow, but not quite at height.

Of my list of fruits for '54, all those named before August 15th were done this year by August 1st at least, except that the sumach berries still hold on, and bunch-berries undoubtedly, where they grow, also Jersey tea fruit, waxwork, privet common in gardens. Possibly some poke berries, still green, may turn, though the vines [*sic*] are killed. The birds may not have gathered quite all the mountain-ash (ours was stripped in about one day by them a week or two ago), and uva-ursi, of course, holds on. Perhaps trientalis fruit holds on. I have not noticed *Aralia nudicaulis* berries for some weeks, nor high blackberries for two or three weeks. Wild apples are perhaps now at height. Cat-tail ripe before July 31st. Alternate cornel fell long ago. Elder-berries are gone, how long? Muskmelons and watermelons with the early frosts of September 16th this year, except those up to this time in cellar. *Viburnum dentatum* probably done before October 1st.

Those on that list after October 15th (inclusive) stand thus: —

Barberries are gathered.

Thorn-apples much past prime, but many bushes still red with them.

Prinos berries fair as ever.

Red choke-berries done (though they may dry on).

Spikenard (not seen).

Fever-bush (not seen).[1]

Arum probably done (?).[2]

Vaccinium Oxycoccus (not seen).

Grapes all fallen, probably a week or more; generally before October.

Acorns of all kinds fallen (been falling for three or four weeks); can find none on the trees.[3]

Rose hips (not noticed).[4]

Viburnum Lentago probably done several weeks.

Poison-dogwood all ripe some time.

Cornus sericea generally fallen by September 30th; all probably by the 12th.

Waxwork (not seen).

Woodbine (not seen).

Fever-wort many still fresh, their peculiar corn-yellow, along the withering stems, October 13th; all leaves withered.

Zizania, some black left (and green) September 30th.

Checkerberries; see none yet full grown and colored, but there are very few this year.

Shrub oak acorns all fallen (can find but one or two left).[5]

The smilacina berries of both kinds more or less shrivelled for some weeks.

Yew probably done some time.

Maple viburnum (not seen), probably done several weeks.

[1] Oct. 14th, can't find any.
[2] Oct. 14th, see none.
[3] Yes; black oak and a great many shrub oak.
[4] Some sweet-briar hips frost-bitten before complete change.
[5] ! Hardly half fallen in another place.

Mitchella ripe a good while.
Medeola probably fallen several weeks.
Common cranberry (not seen).
Pontederia seeds are still falling, a few.
Asclepias Cornuti apparently not yet generally discounts.[1]
Pignuts generally still green on trees.
Wild pears (not seen).
Button-bush balls (now too brown for beauty).
Green-briar (condition not noticed).
Sweet-briar (some hips apparently frost-bitten!).
Bass berries mostly dry and brown September 30th.
Tupelo (not seen of late).
Bayberries (picked by birds?).

Of the above-named list, etc., those still persistent and interesting, then, are: —

     * Sumach berries of different kinds.
       Bunchberries where found.
       Privet berries   "   "
     * Waxwork (?).
       Possibly a little poke (?).
       Mountain-ash (??).
     * Amphicarpæa, some time.
     * Uva-ursi.
     * Wild apples.
     * Barberries left.
     * Some thorn-apples.
     * Celtis, how long?
     * Prinos.
       Is there any spikenard?
       "   "   "   fever-bush?[2]
       "   "   "   arum?[3]
     * Cranberries, two kinds.[4]

[1] See one.
[2] Can see none the 15th.
[3] Can see none the 15th.
[4] The *Vaccinium Oxycoccus* mostly quite ripened by frost the 17th.

Vol. XII

I hear a man laughed at because he went to Europe twice in search of an imaginary wife who, he thought, was there, though he had never seen nor heard of her. But the majority have gone further while they stayed in America, have actually allied themselves to one whom they thought their wife and found out their mistake too late to mend it. It would be cruel to laugh at these.

Wise, the balloonist, says that he lost a balloon "in a *juniper bog* in the State of Maine," which he mistook for a "prairie." Does he mean a larch swamp?[1] Balloonists speak of hearing dogs bark at night and wagons rumbling over bridges.

Arbor-vitæ falling (seeds), how long?

Oct. 15. P. M. — To Botrychium Swamp.
A cold northwest wind.

I see some black oak acorns on the trees still and in some places at least half the shrub oak acorns. The last are handsomer now that they have turned so much darker.

I go along the east edge of Poplar Hill. This very cold and windy day, now that so many leaves have fallen, I begin to notice the silveriness of willows blown up in the wind, — a November sight.

The hickories at Poplar Hill (and elsewhere, as far as I perceive) are all past prime now and most half-withered or bare, very different from last year. In warmer autumns, if I remember rightly, they last several weeks later than this in some localities, one succeeding another with its splendid glow, an evidence of the genial-

[1] [Larch swamps are called "juniper bogs" in some parts of Maine.]

     * Rose hips, all kinds.
     * Poison-dogwood.
     * *R. Toxicodendron.*
     * Some fever-wort.
     * Checkerberries, hardly ripe.
     * Ground-nut.
       Smilacina (two kinds, at least), shrivelled.
     * Mitchella, fair.
     * Mallows.
       Asclepiases.
     * Hickory-nuts.
     * Green-briar (?).
     * Bayberries.

Of which those starred are the only noticeable ones, and only the following probably are in their mellow prime now: —

     Uva-ursi.
     Wild apples.
     Prinos.
     Cranberries.
     Rose hips.
     Mitchella.
     Hickory-nuts (*hardly yet*).
     Bayberries.
     Mallows.

Some *Rhus radicans* was leafless on the 13th, and some tupelos bare maybe a week or more, and button-bushes nearly bare.

My little white pines by Walden are now conspicuous in their rows, the grass, etc., having withered to tawny and the blackberry turned to scarlet. They have been almost inobvious through the summer. The dark evergreen leaves of the checkerberry also attract us now amid the shrub oaks, as on the southwest of Pine Hill.

ness of the season. In cool and moist places, in a genial year, some are preserved green after others have changed, and by their later change and glow they prolong the season of autumnal tints very agreeably.

This is a cold fall.

The larches in A. Heywood's swamp, though a yellower green than the white pines, are not yet sharply distinguished from them by their form, as they will be.

The oaks generally are very fair now at a distance. Standing on this hilltop this cold and blustering day, when dark and slate-colored clouds are flitting over the sky, the beauty of the scenery is enhanced by the contrast in the short intervals of sunshine. The whole surface of the country, both young woodlands and full-grown forests, whether they clothe sides of hills or their lit tops are seen over a ridge, — the birch phalanxes and huckleberry flocks [?], etc., — even to the horizon, is like a rug of many brilliant colors, with the towns in the more open and tawny spaces. The beauty or effect of the scene is enhanced, if, standing here, you see far in the horizon the red regiments of oaks alternately lit up by the sun and dimmed by the passing shadow of a cloud. As the shadows of these cold clouds flit across the landscape, the red banners of distant forests are lit up or disappear like the colors of a thousand regiments.

Pratt says that he planted a ground-nut in his garden in good soil, but they grew no bigger than a bean. He did not know but it would take more than one year, even if he planted the tuber.

The yellow birches are generally bare. *Juniperus repens* leaves have fallen, perhaps with red cedar.

The ash trees I see to-day are quite bare, apparently several or some days.

The little leaves of the mitchella, with a whitish midrib and veins, lying generally flat on the mossy ground, perhaps about the base of a tree, with their bright-scarlet twin berries sprinkled over them, may properly be said to *checker* the ground. Now, particularly, they are noticed amid the fallen leaves.

The bayberry leaves have fallen, and all the berries are gone. I suppose the birds have eaten them. Mountain laurel leaves are fallen. The yellow birches are bare, revealing the fruit (the short, thick brown catkins) now ripe and ready to scale off. How full the trees are! About as thick as the leaves were. The fever-bush is for the most part bare, and I see no berries. *Rhus radicans* too is bare. The maidenhair is for the most part withered. It is not evergreen, then. The mountain sumach which I see is bare, and some smooth ditto.

That appears to be *Aspidium cristatum* which I find evergreen in swamps, but no fertile fronds now. It is broader and denser than the plate of the English one. It cannot be a described variety of *spinulosum*, for it is only once pinnate.

I think I see myrtle-birds on white birches, and that they are the birds I saw on them a week or two ago, — apparently, or probably, after the birch lice. See a *Fringilla hyemalis*. The chickadees sing as if at home. They are not travelling singers hired by any Barnum. Theirs is an honest, homely, heartfelt melody. Shall not the voice of man express as much content as the note of a bird?

Botrychium Lunaria has shed pollen, how long? The little larches in midst of Gowing's Swamp already changed, before others elsewhere.

Each town should have a park, or rather a primitive forest, of five hundred or a thousand acres, where a stick should never be cut for fuel, a common possession forever, for instruction and recreation. We hear of cow-commons and ministerial lots, but we want *men*-commons and lay lots, inalienable forever. Let us keep the New World *new*, preserve all the advantages of living in the country. There is meadow and pasture and wood-lot for the town's poor. Why not a forest and huckleberry-field for the town's rich? All Walden Wood might have been preserved for our park forever, with Walden in its midst, and the Easterbrooks Country, an unoccupied area of some four square miles, might have been our huckleberry-field. If any owners of these tracts are about to leave the world without natural heirs who need or deserve to be specially remembered, they will do wisely to abandon their possession to all, and not will them to some individual who perhaps has enough already. As some give to Harvard College or another institution, why might not another give a forest or huckleberry-field to Concord? A town is an institution which deserves to be remembered. We boast of our system of education, but why stop at schoolmasters and schoolhouses? We are all schoolmasters, and our schoolhouse is the universe. To attend chiefly to the desk or schoolhouse while we neglect the scenery in which it is placed is absurd. If we do not look out we shall find our fine schoolhouse standing in a cow-yard at last.

The *Kalmia glauca*, now falling, is quite a brilliant scarlet. In this case you have the fresh liquid-green leaves of this year above the brilliant scarlet ones of last year. Most other evergreens exhibit only a contrast of green with yellow or yellowish.

The balm-of-Gileads by Mrs. Ripley's bare. Those beyond Barrett's Bridge green and full of leaves. The spruce leaves have fallen, — how long? — and its seeds are falling. Larch seeds falling. Celtis berries ripe, how long? *Solanum Dulcamara* berries linger over water but mostly are shrivelled. Canoe birch is now at least half fallen or more, apparently with the small white; looks in color like an aspen.

Oct. 16. Sunday. P. M. — Paddle to Puffer's and thence walk to Ledum Swamp and Conant's Wood.

A cold, clear, Novemberish day. The wind goes down and we do not sail. The button-bushes are just bare, and the black willows partly so, and the mikania all fairly gray now. I see the button-bush balls reflected on each side, and each wool-grass head and recurved withered sedge or rush is also doubled by the reflection. The *Scirpus lacustris* is generally brown, the *Juncus militaris* greener. It is rather too cool to sit still in the boat unless in a sunny and sheltered place. I have not been on the river for some time, and it is the more novel to me this cool day.

When I get to Willow Bay I see the new musquash-houses erected, conspicuous on the now nearly leafless shores. To me this is an important and suggestive sight, as, perchance, in some countries new haystacks

in the yards; as to the Esquimaux the erection of winter houses. I remember this phenomenon annually for thirty years. A more constant phenomenon here than the new haystacks in the yard, for they were erected here probably before man dwelt here and may still be erected here when man has departed. For thirty years I have annually observed, about this time or earlier, the freshly erected winter lodges of the musquash along the riverside, reminding us that, if we have no gypsies, we have a more indigenous race of furry, quadrupedal men maintaining their ground in our midst still. This may not be an annual phenomenon to you. It may not be in the Greenwich almanac or ephemeris, but it has an important place in my Kalendar. So surely as the sun appears to be in Libra or Scorpio, I see the conical winter lodges of the musquash rising above the withered pontederia and flags. There will be some reference to it, by way of parable or otherwise, in *my* New Testament. Surely, it is a defect in our Bible that it is not truly ours, but a Hebrew Bible. The most pertinent illustrations for us are to be drawn, not from Egypt or Babylonia, but from New England.

Talk about learning our *letters* and being *literate!* Why, the roots of *letters* are *things*. Natural objects and phenomena are the original symbols or types which express our thoughts and feelings, and yet American scholars, having little or no root in the soil, commonly strive with all their might to confine themselves to the imported symbols alone. All the true growth and experience, the living speech, they would fain reject as

"Americanisms." It is the old error, which the church, the state, the school ever commit, choosing darkness rather than light, holding fast to the old and to tradition. A more intimate knowledge, a deeper experience, will surely originate a word. When I really know that our river pursues a serpentine course to the Merrimack, shall I continue to describe it by referring to some other river no older than itself which is like it, and call it a *meander?* It is no more *meandering* than the Meander is *musketaquidding.* As well sing of the nightingale here as the Meander. What if there were a tariff on words, on language, for the encouragement of home manufactures? Have we not the genius to coin our own? Let the schoolmaster distinguish the true from the counterfeit.

They go on publishing the "chronological cycles" and "movable festivals of the Church" and the like from mere habit, but how insignificant are these compared with the annual phenomena of your life, which fall within your experience! The signs of the zodiac are not nearly of that significance to me that the sight of a dead sucker in the spring is. That is the occasion for an *im*movable festival in my church. Another kind of Lent then begins in my thoughts than you wot of. I am satisfied then to live on fish alone for a season.

Men attach a false importance to celestial phenomena as compared with terrestrial, as if it were more respectable and elevating to watch your neighbors than to mind your own affairs. The nodes of the stars are not the knots we have to untie. The phenomena of our year are one thing, those of the almanac another.

Vol. XII

the westering sun, the glittering white tufts of the *Andropogon scoparius*, lit up by the sun, were affectingly fair and cheering to behold. It was already a cheerful Novemberish scene. A narrow glade stretching east and west between a dense birch wood, now half bare, and a ruddy oak wood on the upper side, a ground covered with tawny stubble and fine withered grass and cistuses. Looking westward along it, your eye fell on these lit tufts of andropogon,[1] their glowing half raised a foot or more above the ground, a lighter and more brilliant whiteness than the downiest cloud presents (though seen on one side they are grayish).[2] Even the lespedezas stand like frost-covered wands, and now hoary goldenrods and some bright-red blackberry vines amid the tawny grass are in harmony with the rest; and if you sharpen and rightly intend your eye you see the gleaming lines of gossamer (stretching from stubble to stubble over the whole surface) which you are breaking. How cheerful these cold but bright white waving tufts! They reflect all the sun's light without a particle of his heat, or yellow rays. A thousand such tufts now catch up the sun and send to us its light but not heat. His heat is being steadily withdrawn from us. Light without heat is getting to be the prevailing phenomenon of the day now. We economize all the warmth we get now.

The frost of the 11th, which stiffened the ground, made new havoc with vegetation, as I perceive. Many

[1] *Vide* Nov. 8th.
[2] *Vide* (by chance) same date, or Oct. 16th, 1858.

For October, for instance, instead of making the sun enter the sign of the scorpion, I would much sooner make him enter a musquash-house. Astronomy is a fashionable study, patronized by princes, but not fungi. "Royal Astronomer." The snapping turtle, too, must find a place among the constellations, though it may have to supplant some doubtful characters already there. If there is no place for him overhead, he can serve us bravely underneath, supporting the earth.

This clear, cold, Novemberish light is inspiriting. Some twigs which are bare and weeds begin to glitter with hoary light. The very edge or outline of a tawny or russet hill has this hoary light on it. Your thoughts sparkle like the water surface and the downy twigs. From the shore you look back at the silver-plated river.

Every rain exposes new arrowheads. We stop at Clamshell and dabble for a moment in the relics of a departed race.

Where we landed in front of Puffer's, found a jug which the haymakers had left in the bushes. Hid our boat there in a clump of willows, and though the ends stuck out, being a pale green and whitish, they were not visible or distinguishable at a little distance.

Passed through the sandy potato-field at Witherell's cellar-hole. Potatoes not dug; looking late and neglected now; the very vines almost vanished on some sandier hills.

When we emerged from the pleasant footpath through the birches into Witherell Glade, looking along it toward

plants have ceased to bloom, no doubt. Many *Diplopappus linariifolius* are gone to seed, and yellowish globes. Such are the stages in the year's decline. The flowers are at the mercy of the frosts. Places where erechthites grows, more or less bare, in sproutlands, look quite black and white (black withered leaves and white down) and wintry.

At Ledum Swamp, feeling to find the *Vaccinium Oxycoccus* berries, I am struck with the coldness of the wet sphagnum, as if I put my hands into a moss in Labrador, — a sort of winter lingering the summer through there. To my surprise, now at 3.30 P. M., some of the sphagnum in the shade is still stiff with frost, and when I break it I see the glistening spiculæ. This is the most startling evidence of winter as yet. For only on the morning of the 11th was there any stiffening of the ground elsewhere. Also in the high sedgy sprout-land south of this swamp, I see hoary or frost-like patches of sedge amid the rest, where all is dry; as if in such places (the lowest) the frost had completely bleached the grass so that it now looks like frost. I think that that is the case.

It is remarkable how, when a wood has been cut (perhaps where the soil was light) and frosts for a long while prevent a new wood from springing up there, that fine sedge (*Carex Pennsylvanica?*) will densely cover the ground amid the stumps and dead sprouts. It is the most hardy and native of grasses there. This is *the* grass of the sprout-lands and woods. It wants only the sun and a reasonably dry soil. Then there are the grasses and sedges of the meadows, but the cultivated fields and the pastures are commonly clothed with introduced grasses.

The nesæa is all withered, also the woodwardia. The ledum and *Andromeda Polifolia* leaves have fallen. The *Kalmia glauca* is still falling. The spruce, also, has fallen.

The ledum smells like a bee, — that peculiar scent they have. C., too, perceives it.

See a hairy woodpecker on a burnt pitch pine. He distinctly rests on his tail constantly. With what vigor he taps and bores the bark, making it fly far and wide, and then darts off with a sharp whistle!

I remark how still it is to-day, really Sabbath-like. This day, at least, we do not hear the rattle of cars nor the whistle. I cannot realize that the country was often as still as this twenty years ago.

Returning, the river is perfectly still and smooth. The broad, shallow water on each side, bathing the withered grass, looks as if it were ready to put on its veil of ice at any moment. It seems positively to invite the access of frost. I seem to hear already the creaking, shivering sound of ice there, broken by the undulations my boat makes. So near are we to winter. Then, nearer home, I hear two or three song sparrows on the button-bushes sing as in spring, — that memorable tinkle, — as if it would be last as it was first.

The few blackish leaves of pontederia rising above the water now resemble ducks at a distance, and so help to conceal them now that they are returning.

The weeds are dressed in their frost jackets, naked down to their close-fitting downy or flannel shirts. Like

athletes they challenge the winter, these bare twigs. This cold refines and condenses us. Our spirits are strong, like that pint of cider in the middle of a frozen barrel.

The cool, placid, silver-plated waters at even coolly await the frost. The musquash is steadily adding to his winter lodge. There is no need of supposing a peculiar instinct telling him how high to build his cabin. He has had a longer experience in this river-valley than we. Evergreens, I should say, fall early, both the coniferous and the broad-leaved.

That election-cake fungus which is still growing (as for some months) appears to be a *Boletus*.

I love to get out of cultivated fields where I walk on an imported sod, on English grass, and walk in the fine sedge of woodland hollows, on an American sward. In the former case my thoughts are heavy and lumpish, as if I fed on turnips. In the other I nibble ground-nuts.

Your hands begin to be cool, rowing, now. At many a place in sprout-lands, where the sedge is peculiarly flat and white or hoary, I put down my hand to feel if there is frost on it. It must be the *trace* of frost. Since the frost of the 11th, the grass and stubble has received another coat of tawny.

That andropogon bright feathery top may be put with the clematis seed and tail. Only this cold, clear sky can light them up thus.

The farmer begins to calculate how much longer he can safely leave his potatoes out.

Each ball of the button-bush reflected in the silvery

water by the riverside appears to me as distinct and important as a star in the heavens viewed through " optic glass." This, too, deserves its Kepler and Galileo.

As nature generally, on the advent of frost, puts on a russet and tawny dress, so is not man clad more in harmony with nature in the fall in a tawny suit or the different hues of Vermont gray? I would fain see him glitter like a sweet-fern twig between me and the sun.

A few green yellow lily pads lie on the surface waiting to be frozen in. All the *Lycopodium complanatum* I see to-day has shed its pollen.

Oct. 17. A smart frost this morning. Ground stiffened. Hear of ice in a tub.

P. M. — To Gowing's Swamp.

The water standing over the road at Moore's Swamp, I see the sand spotted black with many thousands of little snails with a shell, and two feelers out, slowly dragging themselves over the bottom. They reminded me by their color, number, and form of the young tadpoles.

I look for *Vaccinium Oxycoccus* in the swamp. The uneven surface of the sphagnum in which the slender vine grows comes up to my idea of a mountainous country better than many actual mountains that I have seen. Labrador mountains these are at least. The higher patches of sphagnum are changed to a dark purple, which shows a crude green where you crack it by your weight. The lower parts are yet yellowish-green merely. These interesting little cranberries are quite scarce, the vine bearing (this year, at least) only amid the higher

and drier sphagnous mountains amid the lowest bushes about the edge of the open swamp. There the dark-red berries (quite ripe) now rest, on the shelves and in the recesses of the red sphagnum. There is only enough of these berries for sauce to a botanist's Thanksgiving dinner.

What I put into my pocket, whether berry or apple, generally has to keep company with an arrowhead or two. I hear the latter chinking against a key as I walk. These are the perennial crop of Concord fields. If they were sure it would pay, we should see farmers raking the fields for them.

The rain drives me from my berrying and we take shelter under a tree. It is worth the while to sit under the lee of an apple tree trunk in the rain, if only to study the bark and its inhabitants. I do not disturb the father-long-legs which to avoid the storm has merely got round to the lee side, or under the shelter of an excrescence. Thus easily insects find their roof ready for them. Man's very size compels him to build a house. Caves and recesses big enough are too rare.

Why should we not stay at home? This is the land and we are the inhabitants so many travellers come to see. Why should we suffer ourselves to drift outside and lose all our advantages? They were bold navigators once who merely sighted these shores. We were born and bred further in the land than Captain John Smith got.

I hear that ten geese went over New Bedford some days ago.

When La Mountain and Haddock dropped down in

the Canada wilderness the other day, they came near starving, or dying of cold and wet and fatigue, not knowing where to look for food nor how to shelter themselves. Thus far we have wandered from a simple and independent life. I think that a wise and independent, self-reliant man will have a complete list of the edibles to be found in a primitive country or wilderness, a bill of fare, in his waistcoat pocket at least, to say nothing of matches and warm clothing, so that he can commence a systematic search for them without loss of time. They might have had several frogs apiece if they had known how to find them. Talk about tariffs and protection of home industry, so as to be prepared for wars and hard times!! Here we are, deriving our breadstuffs from the West, our butter stuffs from Vermont, and our tea and coffee and sugar stuffs, and much more with which we stuff ourselves, from the other side of the globe. Why, a truly prudent man will carry such a list as the above, in his mind at least, even though he walk through Broadway or Quincy Market. He will know what are the permanent resources of the land and be prepared for the hardest of times. He will go behind cities and their police; he will see through them. Is not the wilderness of mould and dry-rot forever invading and threatening them? They are but a camp abundantly supplied to-day, but gnawing their old shoes to-morrow.[1]

    [1] Why, a philosopher who soars higher than usual in his thoughts from time to time drops down into what is just such a wilderness to him as that was to La Mountain and Haddock, where he finds hardly one little frog gone into winter quarters to sustain him and runs screaming toward the climes of the sun.

Vol. XII

pity, nor sympathy, in the common sense, but that he should emit and communicate to me his essential fragrance, that he should not be forever repenting and going to church (when not otherwise sinning), but, as it were, going a-huckleberrying in the fields of thought, and enrich all the world with his visions and his joys.

Why do you flee so soon, sir, to the theatres, lecture-rooms, and museums of the city? If you will stay here awhile I will promise you strange sights. You shall walk on water; all these brooks and rivers and ponds shall be your highway. You shall see the whole earth covered a foot or more deep with purest white crystals, in which you slump or over which you glide, and all the trees and stubble glittering in icy armor.

Oct. 19.[1] When a government puts forth its strength on the side of injustice, as ours (especially to-day) to maintain slavery and kill the liberators of the slave, what a merely brute, or worse than brute, force it is seen to be! A demoniacal force! It is more manifest than ever that tyranny rules. I see this government to be effectually allied with France and Austria in oppressing mankind.

One comment I heard of by the postmaster of this village on the news of Brown's death:[2] "He died as the

    [1] [Here begin Thoreau's notes for his first address on John Brown, delivered in Concord, Oct. 30 of this year (*Cape Cod, and Miscellanies*, pp. 409–440; *Misc.*, Riv. 197–236).]
    [2] [It had been reported that Brown was killed at the time of his capture. (See *Cape Cod, and Miscellanies*, p. 417; *Misc.*, Riv. 207.) For matter in relation to Thoreau's John Brown speeches see *Familiar Letters*, pp. 358–360; Riv. 413–415.]

I see all the farmers' old coats spread over the few squashes and pumpkins still left out in a pile. The arbor-vitæ sheds seeds; how long?

Oct. 18. Rains till 3 P. M., but is warmer.
P. M. — To Assabet, front of Tarbell's.
Going by Dennis Swamp on railroad, the sour scent of decaying ferns is now very strong there. *Rhus venenata* is bare, and maples and some other shrubs, and more are very thin-leaved, as alder and birches, so that the swamp, with so many fallen leaves and migrating sparrows, etc., flitting through it, has a very late look.

For falling, put the canoe birch with the small white. The beach plum is almost quite bare. The leaves of a chinquapin oak have not fallen. The long, curved, yellowish buds of the *Salix discolor* begin to show, the leaves falling; even the down has peeped out from under some.

In the ditch along the west side of Dennis Swamp I see half a dozen yellow-spot turtles moving about. Probably they are preparing to go into winter quarters.

I see one of the smaller thrushes to-day.

Saw a tree-toad on the ground in a sandy wood-path. It did not offer to hop away, may have been chilled by the rain (?). It is marked on the back with black, somewhat in the form of the hylodes.

Why can we not oftener refresh one another with original thoughts? If the fragrance of the dicksonia fern is so grateful and suggestive to us, how much more refreshing and encouraging — re-creating — would be fresh and fragrant thoughts communicated to us fresh from a man's experience and life! I want none of his

fool dieth." I should have answered this man, "He did not live as the fool liveth, and he died as he lived."

Treason! where does treason take its rise? I cannot help thinking of you as you deserve, ye governments. Can you dry up the fountains of thought? High treason which is resistance to *tyranny* here below has its origin in, and is first committed by, the power that makes and forever re-creates man. When you have caught and hung all of these human rebels, you have accomplished nothing but your own guilt, for you have not struck at the fountainhead. You presume to contend with a foe against whom West Point cadets and rifled cannon *point* not. Can all the arts of the cannon-founder tempt matter to turn against its Maker? Is the form in which he casts it more essential than the constitution of it and of himself?

I see that the same journal that contains this pregnant news from Harper's Ferry is chiefly filled, in parallel columns, with the reports of the political conventions that are now being held. But the descent is too steep to them; they should have been spared this contrast. To turn from the voices and deeds of earnest men to the cackling of political conventions! Office-seekers and speechmakers, who do not so much as lay an egg, but wear their breasts bare upon an egg of chalk. Their great game is the game of straws, or rather that universal and aboriginal game of the platter, at which the Indians cried, *Hub-bub*. Some of them generals forsooth!

It galls me to listen to the remarks of craven-hearted neighbors who speak disparagingly of Brown because he resorted to violence, resisted the government, threw his life away! — what way have they thrown their lives, pray? — neighbors who would praise a man for attacking singly an ordinary band of thieves or murderers. Such minds are not equal to the occasion. They preserve the so-called peace of their community by deeds of petty violence every day. Look at the policeman's billy and handcuffs! Look at the jail! Look at the gallows! Look at the chaplain of the regiment! We are hoping only to live safely on the outskirts of *this* provisional army. So they defend themselves and our hen-roosts, and maintain slavery.

There sits a tyrant holding fettered four millions of slaves. Here comes their heroic liberator; if he falls, will he not still live?

C. says that he saw a loon at Walden the 15th.

P. M. — To Lee's Cliff.

The tupelo berries have all fallen; how long? Alternate cornel about bare. Hardhack half bare. Many witch-hazel nuts are not yet open. The bushes just bare. The slippery elm is nearly bare, like the common near it. Cedar berries, how long? 14th at least; probably by the time they lost their leaves. There is one sizable tree west by north of Lee's Cliff, near the wall. *Lycopodium dendroideum* (not variety) is just shedding pollen near this cedar. I see asparagus in the woods there near the cedar, four or five feet high!

Find the seedling archangelica grown about two feet high and still quite green and growing, though the full-grown plants are long since dead, root and stalk. This suggests that no doubt much of the radical spring green-

ness is of this character, — seedlings of biennials, and perhaps more of them a persistent or late growth from a perennial root, as crowfoot, whiteweed, five-finger, etc. The scent of the archangelica root is not agreeable to me. The scent of my fingers after having handled it reminds me strongly of the musquash and woodchuck, though the root itself does not; so its odor must be allied to theirs.

I find at Lee's Cliff, on the shelves and sides of the rocks, a new fern, apparently *Cystopteris fragilis*, more than half decayed or withered, though some fresher and shorter fronds at the base of the others are still quite green. It curls up so in my hat that I have difficulty in examining it. It is abundant thereabouts.

Paddling up the river the other day, those (probably canoe) birches on Mt. Misery on the edge of the hill a mile in front looked like little dark clouds, for [I] could not distinguish their white trunks against the sky.

Though the dark-blue, or ripe, creeping juniper berries are chiefly on the lower part of the branches, I see fresh green ones on old wood as big as a pipe-stem and often directly opposite to purple ones (!). They are strangely mixed up. I am not sure but some of this year's berries are already ripe. See a black and rusty hedgehog (?) caterpillar in the path.

The remarks of my neighbors upon Brown's death and supposed fate, with very few exceptions, are, "He is undoubtedly insane," "Died as the fool dieth," "Served him right;" and so they proceed to live their sane, and wise, and altogether admirable lives, reading their Plutarch a little, but chiefly pausing at that feat

Vol. XII

of Putnam, who was let down into a wolf's den (that is quite the strongest pap that Young America is fed on); and so they nourish themselves for brave and patriotic deeds.

What is the character of that calm which follows when the law and the slaveholder prevail?

A government that pretends to be Christian and crucifies a million Christs every day!

Our foes are in our midst and all about us. Hardly a house but is divided against itself. For our foe is the all but universal woodenness (both of head and heart), the want of vitality, of man, — the effect of vice, — whence are begotten fear and superstition and bigotry and persecution and slavery of all kinds. Mere figure-heads upon a hulk, with livers in the place of hearts. A church that can never have done with excommunicating Christ while it exists. Our plains were overrun the other day with a flock of adjutant-generals, as if a brood of cockerels had been let loose there, waiting to use their spurs in what sort of glorious cause, I ask. What more probable in the future, what more certain heretofore, than in grinding in the dust four hundred thousands of feeble and timid men, women, and children? The United States exclaims: "Here are four millions of human creatures which we have stolen. We have abolished among them the relations of father, mother, children, wife, and we mean to keep them in this condition. Will you, O Massachusetts, help us to do so?" And Massachusetts promptly answers, "Aye!"

The cause is the worship of idols, which at length changes the worshiper into a stone image himself.

Every man worships his ideal of power and goodness, or God, and the New-Englander is just as much an idolater as the Hindoo.

The momentary charge at Balaclava, in obedience to a blundering command, — proving what a perfect machine the soldier is — has been celebrated by a poet laureate; but the steady and for the most part successful charge against the legions of Slavery kept up for some years in Kansas by John Brown in obedience to an infinitely higher command is unsung, — as much more memorable than that as an intelligent and conscientious man is superior to a machine.

The brutish, thick-skinned herd, who do not know a *man* by sympathy, make haste home from their ballot-boxes and churches to their Castles of Indolence, perchance to cherish their valor there with some nursery talk of knights and dragons. A whole nation will for ages cling to the memory of its Arthur, or other imaginary hero, who perhaps never assailed its peculiar institution or sin, and, being imaginary, never failed, when they are themselves the very freebooters and craven knights whom he routed, while they forget their real heroes.

The publishers and the various boards of wooden-heads can afford to reprint that story of Putnam's. You might open the district schools with the reading of it, because there is nothing about slavery or the church in it; unless it occurs to the reader that the *pastors* are *wolves* in sheep's clothing.

I have seen no hearty approbation for this man in any Abolition journal; as if it were not consistent with their policy to express it, or maybe they did not feel it. And as for the herd of newspapers, I do not chance to know one in the country that will deliberately print anything that will ultimately and permanently reduce the number of its subscribers. They do not believe it would be *expedient*. If we do not say pleasant things, they argue, nobody will attend to us. And so they are like some auctioneers, who sing an obscene song in order to draw a crowd around them.

Another neighbor asks, Yankee-like, "What will *he* gain by it?" as if he expected to fill his pockets by this enterprise. They have no idea of gain but in this worldly sense. If it does not lead to a surprise party, if he does not get a new pair of boots and a vote of thanks, it must be a failure. Such do not know that like the seed is the fruit, and that, in the moral world, when good seed is planted, good fruit is inevitable and does not depend on our watering and cultivating; that when you plant, or bury, a hero in this field, a crop of heroes is sure to spring up. This is a seed of such force and vitality that it does not ask our leave to germinate.

Some eighteen hundred years ago Christ was crucified; this morning, perhaps, John Brown was hung. These are the two ends of a chain which I rejoice to know is not without its links.

The Republican editors, obliged to get their sentences ready for the morning edition, — and their dinner ready before afternoon, — speak of these men, not in a tone of admiration for their disinterestedness and heroism, not of sorrow even for their fate, but calling

them "deluded fanatics," "mistaken men," "insane," or "crazed." Did it ever occur to you what a *sane* set of editors we are blessed with? — not "mistaken men;" who know very well on which side their bread is buttered!

The *noble* Republican Party is in haste to exculpate itself from all sympathy with these "misguided men." Even the very men who would rejoice if he had succeeded, though in spite of all odds, are estranged from and deny him because he failed. A "dangerous man"! All the worthies and martyrs were such dangerous men. We wish that these editors and ministers were a little more *dangerous*.

It is mentioned against him and as an evidence of his insanity, "a conscientious man, very modest in his demeanor, that he was apparently inoffensive, until the subject of slavery was introduced, when he would exhibit a feeling of indignation unparalleled." (*Boston Journal*, October 21, 1859.)

If Christ should appear on earth he would on all hands be denounced as a mistaken, misguided man, insane and crazed.

The Liberator calls it "a misguided, wild, and apparently insane . . . effort."

"The American Board of Commissioners for Foreign Missions," which have just met in Philadelphia, did not dare as a body to protest even against the foreign slave-trade, which even many domestic slave-traders are ready to do. And I hear of Northern men, women, and children by families buying a life-membership in this society. A life-membership in the grave! You can get buried cheaper than that.

He was a superior man. He did not value his bodily life in comparison with ideal things; he did not recognize unjust human laws, but resisted them, as he was bid; and now he is called insane by all who cannot appreciate such magnanimity. He needed no babbling lawyer, making false issues, to defend him. He was more than a match for all judges that American voters, or office-holders of whatever grade, can create. He could not have been tried by a jury of his peers, because his peers did not exist.

When a man stands up serenely against the condemnation and vengeance of mankind, rising above them literally by a whole body, — though he were a slave, though he were a freeman, though he were of late the vilest murderer, who has settled that matter with himself, — the spectacle is a sublime one! — didn't ye know it, ye Garrisons, ye Buchanans, ye politicians, attorney-generals? — and we become criminal in comparison. Do yourselves the honor to recognize him. *He* needs none of your respect. What though he did not belong to your clique!

I do not believe in erecting statues to those who still live in our minds and hearts, whose bones have not yet crumbled in the earth around us, but I would rather see the statue of John Brown in the Massachusetts State-House yard than that of any other man whom I know.

What a contrast, when we turn to that political party which is so anxiously shaking its skirts clean of him and his friends and looking round for some available slaveholder to be its candidate!

The evil is not merely a stagnation of blood, but a

stagnation of spirit. Of course, the mass of men, even the well-disposed but sluggish souls who are ready to abet when their conscience or sympathies are reached, cannot conceive of a man who is actuated by higher motives than they are. Accordingly they pronounce him insane, for they know that they would never act as he does as long as they are themselves.

This most hypocritical and diabolical government looks up from its seat upon four millions of gasping slaves and inquires with an assumption of innocence, "What do you assault me for? Am I not an honest man?" "Ah, sir, but your seat — your footstool — my father and mother — get off! — get off!" But there sits the incubus with all his weight, and stretching ever more and more, and for all reply answers, "Why won't you cease agitation upon this subject?"

The only government that I recognize is that power that establishes justice in the land, never that which establishes injustice. Suppose that there is a private company in Massachusetts that out of its own purse and magnanimity saves all the fugitive slaves that run to us, and protects our colored fellow-citizens, and leaves the other work to the government, so called. Is not that government fast losing its occupation and becoming contemptible to mankind? If private men are obliged to perform the offices of government, to protect the weak and dispense justice, then the government becomes only a hired man, or clerk, to perform menial or indifferent services. Of course, that is but the shadow of a government, whose existence necessitates a Vigilance Committee. But such is the character of our Northern

States generally; each has its Vigilance Committee. And, to a certain extent, these crazy governments recognize and accept this relation. They say, virtually, "We'll be glad to work for you on these terms, only don't make a noise about it." Such a government is losing its power and respectability as surely as water runs out of a leaky vessel and is held by one that can contain it.

Oct. 20. P. M. — To Ripple Lake.

Dug some artichokes behind Alcott's, the largest about one inch in diameter. Now apparently is the time to begin to dig them, the plant being considerably frost-bitten. Tried two or three roots. The main root ran down straight about six inches and then terminated abruptly, thus: They have quite a nutty taste eaten raw.

What is that flat, spreading festuca-like grass, just killed, behind A.'s house?

As I go to Clintonia Swamp along the old cross-road, I see a large and very straggling flock of crows fly[ing] southwest from over the hill behind Bull's and contending with the strong and cold northwest wind. This is the annual phenomenon. They are on their migrations.

The beach plum is nearly bare, and so is the woodbine on the brick house. The wild red cherry by A. Brooks's Hollow is completely fallen; how long? The sand cherry in my field path is almost entirely bare. Some chinquapin is half fallen.

Scare up a yellow-legs, apparently the larger, on the

shore of Walden. It goes off with a sharp *phe phe, phe phe.*

This is the coldest day as yet; wind from the northwest. It is finger-cold as I come home, and my hands find their way to my pocket. I learn the next day that snow fell to-day in northern New York and New Hampshire, and that accounts for it. We feel the cold of it here as soon as the telegraph can inform us. La Mountain's adventure has taught us how swiftly the wind may travel to us from that quarter.

Oct. 21. P. M. — To Mason's pasture.

The brook between John Flint's house and the river is half frozen over.

The clump of mountain laurel in Mason's pasture is of a triangular form, about six rods long by a base of two and a third rods, — or seven or eight square rods, — beside some separate clumps.

It is very cold and blustering to-day. It is the breath of winter, which is encamped not far off to the north.

A great many shrub oak acorns hold on, and are a darker brown than ever.

Insane! A father and seven sons, and several more men besides, — as many, at least, as twelve disciples, — all struck with insanity at once; while the sane tyrant holds with a firmer gripe than ever his four millions of slaves, and a thousand sane editors, his abettors, are saving their country and their bacon! Just as insane as were their efforts in Kansas. Ask the tyrant who is his most dangerous foe, the sane man or the insane.

If some Captain Ingraham threatens to fire into an

Vol. XII

Austrian vessel, we clap our hands all along the shore. It won't hit us; it won't disturb our tyranny. But let a far braver than he attack the Austria within us, we turn, we actually *fire* those same guns upon him, and cry, "Insane."

The government, its salary being insured, withdraws into the back shop, taking the Constitution with it, as farmers in the winter contrive to turn a penny by following the coopering business. When the reporter to the *Herald* (!) reports the conversation "*verbatim*," he does not know of what undying words he is made the vehicle.

Read his admirable answers to Mason and others. How they are dwarfed and defeated by the contrast! On the one side half-brutish, half-timid questioning; on the other, truth, clear as lightning, crashing into their obscene temples. They are made to stand with Pilate, and Gessler, and the Inquisition. How ineffectual their speech and action! and what a void their silence!

I speak to the stupid and timid chattels of the north, pretending to read history and their Bibles, desecrating every house and every day they breathe in! True, like the clods of the valley, they are incapable of perceiving the light, but I would fain arouse them by any stimulus to an intelligent life.

Throughout the land they, not of equal magnanimity, talk of vengeance and insanity.

Away with your broad and flat churches, and your narrow and tall churches! Take a step forward and invent a new style of outhouses. Invent a salt that will save you and defend our nostrils.

The slave-ship is on her way, crowded with its dying hundreds; a small crew of slaveholders is smothering four millions under the hatches; and yet the politician asserts that the only proper way by which deliverance is to be obtained is by "the quiet diffusion of sentiments of humanity," without any "outbreak"! And in the same breath they tell us that all is *quiet* now at Harper's Ferry. What is that that I hear cast overboard? The bodies of the dead, who have found deliverance. That is the way we are diffusing humanity, and all its sentiments with it.

Prominent and influential editors, accustomed to deal with politicians, men of an infinitely lower grade, say, in their ignorance, that he acted "on the principle of revenge." They do not know the man. They must enlarge themselves to conceive of him. I have no doubt that, if that is of any importance, the time will come when they will begin to see him as he was. They have got to conceive of a man of *ideas* and of *principle*, hard as it may be for them, and not a politician or an Indian; of a man who did not wait till he was personally interfered with or thwarted in some harmless business before he gave his life to the cause of the oppressed.

I know that there have been a few heroes in the land, but no man has ever stood up in America for the dignity of human nature so devotedly, persistently, and so effectively as this man. Ye need not trouble yourselves, Republican or any other party, to wash your skirts of him. No intelligent person will ever be convinced that he was any creature of yours. He went and came, as he informs us, "under the auspices of John Brown, and nobody else."

Ethan Allen and Stark, though worthy soldiers in their day, were rangers in a far lower field and in a less important cause.

Insane! Do the thousands who knew him best, who have rejoiced at his deeds in Kansas and have afforded him material aid, think him insane?

It costs us nothing to be just. It enriches us infinitely to recognize greater qualities than we possess in another. We can at least express our sympathy with, and admiration for, John Brown and his companions, and this is what I now propose to do.

What has Massachusetts and the North sent a few *sane* senators to Congress for of late years? — to declare with effect what kind of sentiments? All their speeches put together and boiled down — and probably they themselves will allow it — do not match for simple and manly directness, force, and effectiveness the few casual remarks of *insane* John Brown on the floor of the Harper's Ferry engine-house. To be sure, he was not our representative. He is too fair a specimen of a man to represent the like of us. In his case there is no idle eloquence, no *made* speech. Truth is his inspirer, and earnestness his critic and polisher of his sentences. He could afford to lose his Sharp's rifles, while he retained his faculty of speech, — a Sharp's rifle of infinitely surer and longer range.

"But he won't gain anything." Well, no! I don't suppose he could get four-and-sixpence a day for being hung, take the year round. But then he stands a chance

to save a considerable part of his soul, — and such a soul! — when you do not. No doubt you can get more in your market for a quart of milk than for a quart of blood, but that is not the market that heroes carry their blood to.

So ye write in your easy-chairs, and thus he, wounded, responds from the floor of the Harper's Ferry engine-house: "No man sent me here; it was my own prompting and that of my Maker. I acknowledge no master in human form."

And in what a sweet, kindly strain he proceeds, addressing those who held him prisoner: "I think, my friends, you are guilty of a great wrong against God and humanity, and it would be perfectly right for any one to interfere with you so far as to free those you willfully and wickedly hold in bondage."

And, referring to his movement: "It is, in my opinion, the greatest service a man can render to God!"

"I pity the poor in bondage that have none to help them; that is why I am here; not to gratify any personal animosity, revenge, or vindictive spirit. It is my sympathy with the oppressed and the wronged, that are as good as you, and as precious in the sight of God."

"I want you to understand that I respect the rights of the poorest and weakest of colored people, oppressed by the slave system, just as much as I do those of the most wealthy and powerful."

Thus the *insane* man preaches, while the representatives of so-called Christians (I refer to the Board of Commissioners for Foreign Missions), who pretend to

be interested in the heathen, dare not so much as protest against the foreign slave-trade!

"I wish to say, furthermore, that you had better, all you people at the South, prepare yourselves for a settlement of that question, that must come up for settlement sooner than you are prepared for it. The sooner you are prepared the better. You may dispose of me very easily. I am nearly disposed of now; but this question is still to be settled, — this negro question, I mean; the end of that is not yet."

You will perceive that not a single forcible or noticeable word is uttered by his questioners; they stand there the helpless tools in this great work. It was no human power that gathered them about this preacher.

What should we think of the Oriental Cadi behind whom worked in secret a Vigilance Committee? What shall we think of a government to which all the truly brave and just men in the land are enemies, standing between it and those whom it oppresses? Do not we Protestants know the likeness of Luther, Fox, Bunyan, when we see it? Shall we still be put to bed with our story-books, not knowing day from night?

We talk about a *representative* government, but what a monster of a government is that where the noblest faculties of the mind and the *whole* heart are not represented. A semihuman tiger or ox stalking over the earth, with its heart taken out and the top of its brain shot away.

In California and Oregon, if not nearer home, it is common to treat men exactly like deer which are hunted, and I read from time to time in Christian newspapers

how many "bucks," that is, Indian men, their sportsmen have killed.

Who is here so base, that would be a bondman? Who is here so vile, that will not love his country? If any, speak; for him have I offended. I pause for a reply.

We dream of foreign countries, of other times and races of men, placing them at a distance in history or in space; but let some significant event like the present occur in our midst, and we discover, often, this distance and this strangeness between us and our nearest neighbors. *They* are our Austrias, and Chinas, and South Sea Islands. Our crowded society becomes well spaced all at once, clean and handsome to the eye, — a city of magnificent distances. We discover why it was that we never got beyond compliments and surfaces with them before; we become aware of as many versts between us and them as there are between a wandering Tartar or Pawnee and a Chinese or American town. The thoughtful man becomes a hermit in the thoroughfares of the market-place. Impassable seas suddenly find their level between us, or dumb steppes stretch themselves out there.

I do not complain of any tactics that are effective of good, whether one wields the quill or the sword, but I shall not think him mistaken who quickest succeeds to liberate the slave. I will judge of the tactics by the fruits.

It is the difference of constitution, of intelligence, and faith, and not streams and mountains, that makes the true and impassable boundaries between individuals and states. None but the like-minded can come plenipotentiary to our court.

They who are continually shocked by slavery have some right to be shocked by the violent death of the slaveholder, but no others. Such will be more shocked by his life than by his death.

Oct. 22. P. M. — To Cliffs and Fair Haven.

I am surprised to find in the field behind the top of the Cliffs a little vetch still perfectly fresh and *blooming*, where Wheeler had grain a year or two since, with numerous little plump pods four or five eighths of an inch long and commonly four roundish seeds to each. It must be, I think, Gray's *Vicia tetrasperma*, though he makes that have white flowers (apparently same as Bigelow's *V. pusilla*, also made to have white flowers, but Dewey calls them "bluish white"), while these are purple. Otherwise it corresponds.

A marsh hawk sails over Fair Haven Hill. In the wood-path below the Cliffs I see perfectly fresh and fair *Viola pedata* flowers, as in the spring, though but few together. No flower by its second blooming more perfectly brings back the spring to us.

In my blustering walk over the Mason and Hunt pastures yesterday, I saw much of the withered indigo-weed which was broken off and blowing about, and the seeds in its numerous black pods rattling like the rattlepod though not nearly so loud.

The very surface of the earth itself has been rapidly imbrowned of late, like the acorns in their cups, in consequence of cold and frost; and the evergreens and few

deciduous plants which are slow to wither, like Jersey tea, are more and more distinct.

F. hyemalis quite common for a week past.

One would say that the modern Christian was a man who had consented to say all the prayers in their liturgy, provided you would let him go straight to bed and sleep quietly afterward. All his prayers begin with "Now I lay me down to sleep." He has consented to perform certain old-established charities, too, after a fashion, but he does n't wish to hear of any new-fangled ones; he does n't want to have any codicils added to the contract, to fit it to the present time, — unexpected demands made on him, after he has said his prayers. He shows the whites of his eyes on the Sabbath and the blacks all the rest of the week.

It was evidently far from being a wild and desperate and insane attempt. It was a well-matured plan.

The very fact that he had no rabble or troop of hirelings about him would alone distinguish him from ordinary heroes. His company was small indeed, because few could be found worthy to pass muster. He would have no rowdy or swaggerer, no profane swearer, for, as he said, he always found these men to fail at last. He would have only men of principle, and they are few. When it was observed that if he had had a chaplain his would have been a perfect Cromwellian company, he said that he would have had a chaplain if he could [have] found one who could perform that service suitably.

Each one who there laid down his life for the poor and oppressed was thus a picked man, culled out of many

Vol. XII

thousands, if not millions; a man of principle, of rare courage, and of devoted humanity; ready to lay down their lives any moment for the weak and enslaved. It may be doubted if there were any more their equals in all the land, for their leader scoured the land far and wide, seeking to swell his troop. These alone stood forward, prepared to step between the oppressor and the oppressed. Surely they were the very best men you could select to be hung. That was the greatest compliment this country could pay them. They were ripe for the gallows.

I regard this event as a touchstone designed to bring out with glaring distinctness the character of this government.

A man of Spartan habits, who at sixty has scruples about his diet at your table, must eat sparingly and fare hard, as becomes a soldier, he says, and one who is ever fitting himself for difficult enterprises.

A man of rare common sense and directness of speech, as of action; a Transcendentalist above all, a man of ideals and principles, — that was what distinguished him. Of unwavering purposes, not to be dissuaded but by an experience and wisdom greater than his own. Not yielding to a whim or transient impulse, but carrying out the purpose of a life.

He did not go to the college called Harvard; he was not fed on the pap that is there furnished. As he phrased it, "I know no more of grammar than one of your calves." But he went to the great university of the West, where he sedulously pursued the study of Liberty, for which he had early betrayed a fondness,

and, having taken many degrees, he finally commenced the practice of Humanity, as you all know.

I see now that it was necessary that the bravest and humanest man in all the country should be hung. Perhaps he saw it himself. If any leniency were shown him, any compromise made with him, any treating with him at all, by the government, he might be suspected.

We needed to be thus assisted to see our government by the light of history. It needed to see itself.

Compare the platform of any or all of the political parties, which deem themselves sane, with the platform on which he lay and uttered these things!!

I foresee the time when the painter will paint that scene, the poet will sing it, the historian record it, and, with the Landing of the Pilgrims and the Declaration of Independence, it will be the ornament of some future national gallery, when the present form of slavery shall be no more. We shall then be at liberty to weep for John Brown. Then and not till then we will take our revenge.

I rejoice that I live in this age, that I was his contemporary.

When I consider the spectacle of himself, and his six sons, and his son-in-law, enlisted for this fight, proceeding coolly, reverently, humanely to work, while almost all America stood ranked on the other side, I say again that it affects me as a sublime spectacle. For months if not years, sleeping and waking upon it, summering and wintering the thought, without expecting any reward but a good conscience and the gratitude of those made free.

If he had had any journal advocating "his cause," it would have been fatal to his efficiency, — any "organ," as the phrase is, monotonously and wearisomely playing that same old tune, and then passing round the hat. If he had acted in any way so as to gain the respect or toleration of the government, he might have been suspected. It was the fact that the tyrant must give place to him, or he to the tyrant, that distinguished him from all other reformers that I know.

For once the Sharp's rifle and the revolver were employed in a righteous cause. The tools were in the hands of one who could use them. I know that the mass of my neighbors think that the only righteous use that can be made of them is to fight duels with them when we are insulted by other nations, or hunt Indians, or shoot fugitive slaves with them.

Talk of political parties and their platforms! he could not have any platform but that of the Harper's Ferry engine-house.

I am aware that I anticipate a little, — that he was still, at the last accounts, alive in the hands of his foes; but that being the case, I find myself most naturally thinking and speaking of him as physically dead.

The same indignation that cleared the temple once will clear it again. The question is not about the weapon, but the spirit in which you use it. No man has appeared in America as yet who loved his fellow-man so well and treated him so tenderly. He lived for him; he took up his life and he laid it down for him.

Though you may not approve of his methods or his

principles, cease to call names, to cry mad dog. The method is nothing; the spirit is all in all. It is the deed, the devotion, the soul of the man. For you this is at present a question of magnanimity. If the schoolboy, forgetting himself, rushed to the rescue of his drowning playmate, what though he knock down somebody on his way, what though he does not go to the same church with you, or his father belong to the same political party! Would you not like to claim kindred with him in this, though in no other thing he is like, or likely, to you?

Heroes have fought well on their stumps when their legs were shot off, but I never heard of any good done by a government that had no heart, or at least had not brains of a high order.

This is not the time to hear what Tom, Dick, or Harry is doing, or in such a case would have done. We shall have time enough to find that out in, if we do not know it already. We ask you to the extent of your ability to appreciate *this man* and *his deed*, in spite of the difference between you and him. Who cares whether he belonged to your clique, or party, or sect, or not?

A man does a brave and humane deed, and at once, on all sides, we hear people and parties declaring: "I did n't do it, nor countenance *him* to do it, in any conceivable way. It can't fairly be inferred from my past career." Now, I am not interested to hear you define your position. I don't know that I ever was, or ever shall be. I am not now, at any rate. I think [it] is mere egotism, and impertinent.

On the whole my respect for my fellow-men, except

as one may outweigh a million, is not being increased these days. I have noticed the cold-blooded way in which newspaper-writers and men generally speak of this event, as if an ordinary malefactor, though one of unusual pluck, — as the Governor of Virginia says, using the language of the cockpit, "the *gamest* man he ever saw," — had been caught and were about to be hung. He was not dreaming of his foes when the Governor thought he looked so brave.

Think of him, — of his rare qualities! — such a man as it takes ages to make, and ages to understand; no mock hero, not the representative of any party. A man such as the sun may never rise upon again in this benighted land, to whose making went the costliest material, the finest adamant, the purest gold; sent to be the redeemer of those in captivity; — and the only use to which you can put him, after mature deliberation, is to hang him at the end of a rope. I need not describe him. He has stood where I now stand; you have all seen him. You who pretend to care for Christ crucified, consider what you are about to do to him who offered himself to be the savior of four millions of men!

I wish to correct the tone and some of the statements of the newspapers respecting the life and character and last action of John Brown. The newspapers seem to ignore, or perhaps they are really ignorant of, the fact that there are at least as many as one or two individuals to a town throughout the North who think much as I do about him and his enterprise. I do not hesitate to assert that they are an important and growing party.

I speak for the slave when I say that I prefer the philanthropy of John Brown to that philanthropy which neither shoots me nor liberates me.

Talk of failure and throwing his life away! he is not dead yet in any sense, and if he were dead he would still live. Were the battles of Black Jack and Ossawatomie and many encounters of less note useless and a failure? I think that it was he more than any other who made Kansas as free as she is, who taught the slaveholder that it was not safe for him to carry his slaves thither. None of the political parties have ever accomplished anything of the sort. It was he who taught Missouri that it was not profitable to hold slaves in that neighborhood. Was it a failure to deliver from bondage thirteen human beings and walk off with them by broad daylight, for weeks if not months, at a leisurely pace, through one State after another, for half the length of the North, conspicuous to all parties, with a price set upon his head, going into a court-room on his way and telling what he had done? To face singly in his work of righteousness the whole power of this unrighteous government, and successfully too! Who has gained the most ground within five years, — Brown or the Slave Power?

And this, not because the government was lenient, but because none of its menials dared to touch him. They counted the cost and concluded that a thousand dollars was not enough.

There are a few — there are more than you suppose — who cannot help thinking of that man now in the clutches of the enraged slaveholder.

He is one of that class of whom we hear a great deal, but, for the most part, see nothing at all, — the Puritans. It is in vain to kill him. He died lately in the time of Cromwell, but he reappeared here. Why should he not ? Some of the Puritan stock are said to have come over and settled in New England. They were a class that did something else than celebrate their forefathers' day and eat parched corn in remembrance of their ancestors. They were neither Democrats nor Republicans. They were men of simple habits, straightforward, prayerful; not thinking much of rulers who did not fear God, not making many compromises, or seeking after available candidates.

He is of the same age with the century. He is what is called a thin and wiry-looking man, being composed of nerves instead of flesh, some five feet nine or ten inches high, with a sharp eye, and the last time he was hereabouts wore a long white beard; with a very soldierlike bearing.

I understand his grandfather was an officer in the Revolution; that he himself was born in Connecticut, but early went to Ohio with his father. His father was a contractor who furnished beef to the army there in the last war, and young Brown, accompanying his father to the camp and assisting him in his employment, saw considerable of military life, — more perhaps than he would if he had been a soldier, for he was sometimes present at the councils of the officers. He saw enough, at any rate, to disgust him with war and excite in him a great abhorrence of it; so much so that, though he was offered some petty office in the army, he not

only refused it, but also refused to train when he was warned, and was fined for it. He was then about eighteen. He said that few persons had any conception of the cost, even the pecuniary cost, of firing a single bullet in war. Above all, he learned by experience how armies were collected, supplied, and maintained in the field for a length of time, — a work which required at least as much experience and skill as to lead them in battle. And he then resolved that he would never have anything to do with war, unless it were a war for liberty. I should say that he was an old-fashioned man in his respect for the Constitution and the Declaration of Independence, and his faith in the permanence of this Union. Slavery he saw to be wholly opposed to all of these, and he was its determined foe.

When the troubles first broke out in Kansas, he sent several of his sons thither to strengthen the party of the Free State men, fitting them out with such weapons as he had, telling them if the troubles should increase, and there should be need of him, he should follow, to assist them with his hand and counsel. It was not long before he felt it to be his duty to give the Free State men of Kansas, who had no leader of experience, the benefit of what experience he had had.

At a time when scarcely a man from the Free States was able to reach Kansas by any direct route, at least without having his arms taken from him, he, carrying what imperfect firelocks and other weapons he could collect, openly drove an ox-cart through Missouri, with his surveyor's compass exposed in it, and, passing for a simple surveyor, who by his very profession must

Vol. XII

be neutral, he met with no resistance and in the course of his leisurely journey became thoroughly acquainted with the plans of the Border Ruffians. For some time after his arrival he pursued, before he was known, similar tactics. When, for instance, he saw a knot of the Ruffians on the prairie, discussing, of course, the single topic that then occupied their minds, he would take his compass and one of his sons, and perhaps proceed to run an imaginary line which passed through the very spot on which that conclave had assembled, and then of course he would have some talk with them, learn their news and their plans, and when he had heard all they had to impart, he would resume his surveying, and run on his line till he was out of sight. This is enough to show that his plans were not crazily laid.

For a good part of his life he was a surveyor, part of the time, I think, in Illinois. At one time he was engaged in wool-growing, and went to Europe once as the agent of some wool-growers; and there too he carried his common sense with him. I have been told, for instance, that he made such a remark as this, — that he saw why the soil of England was so rich and that of Germany (or a part of it at least) so exhausted, and he thought of writing to some of the crowned heads about it. It was because in England the peasantry lived on the soil which they cultivated, while in Germany they were gathered into villages at night. It would be worth the while to have collected all the remarks of such a traveller.

Of course, he is not so foolish as to ask or expect

any favors from the government, nor probably will his friends for him.

No wonder it struck the politicians and preachers generally very forcibly that either he was insane or they, and they, being the painters, or judges, this time, decided, naturally enough, that it must be he. Such, however, as far as I learn, has not been nor is likely to be the decision of those who have recently stood face to face to him and who are now about to hang him. They have not condescended to such insult. The slaveholders and the slaves who have really dealt with him are not likely sincerely to question his sanity, but rather political or religious parties, who stand further off from a living man.

I almost fear to hear of his deliverance, doubting if a prolonged life, if any life, can do as much good as his death.

No doubt many of you have seen the little manuscript book which he carried about him, during the Kansas troubles, — his "orderly book," as I think he called it, — containing the names of his small company, a score at most, and half of them his own family, and the rules which bound them together, — a contract which many of them have sealed with their blood. There was one rule, as I remember, which prohibited prophane swearing in his camp.

I believe that he never was able to find more than a score or so of recruits whom he would accept, and only ten or a dozen in whom he had perfect faith.

Perhaps anxious politicians may prove that only seventeen white men and five negroes were concerned in this enterprise, but the anxiety to prove this might suggest to themselves that all is not told. Why do they still dodge the truth? Do they not realize why they are so anxious? It is because of a dim consciousness of the fact, which they do not distinctly face, that at least five millions of the inhabitants of the United States who were not pining to attempt, would have rejoiced if it had succeeded. They at most only criticise the tactics.

He said that if any man offered himself to be a soldier under him who was forward to tell what he could or would do if he could only get sight of the enemy, he had but little confidence in him.

One writer says, I know not with what motive, that it is a fact "illustrative of Brown's insanity, that he has charts of nearly all the great battle-fields of Europe." I fear that his collection is not to be compared for completeness with that which this government possesses, however his sanity may be compared with its, though it did not make them itself, but there are two or three fields in Kansas of which he did not need to make any chart.

At any rate, I do not think it is sane to spend one's whole life talking or writing about this matter, and I have not done so. A man may have other affairs to attend to.

The murderer always knows that he is justly punished; but when a government takes the life of a man without the consent of his conscience, it is an audacious government, and is taking a step toward its own dissolution. Is it not possible that an individual may be right and a government wrong? Are laws to be enforced

simply because they were made, and declared by any number of men to be good, when they are *not* good? Is there any necessity for a man's being a tool to perform a deed of which he disapproves? Is it the intention of lawmakers that good men shall be hung ever? Are judges to interpret the law according to the letter, and not the spirit? Who is it whose safety requires that Captain Brown be hung? Is it indispensable to any Northern man? If you do not wish it, say so distinctly. What right have you to enter into a compact with yourself (even) that you *will* do thus or so, against your better nature? Is it for *you* to *make up* your mind, — to *form* any resolution whatever, — and not accept the convictions that are forced upon you, and which even pass your *understanding?*

Any man knows when he is justified, and not all the wits in the world can enlighten him on that point.

I do not believe in lawyers, — in that mode of defending or attacking a man,— because you descend to meet the judge on his own ground, and, in cases of the highest importance, it is of no consequence whether a man breaks a human law or not. Let lawyers decide trivial cases. If they were interpreters of the everlasting laws which rightfully bind man, that would be another thing.

Just as we are doing away with duelling or fighting one another with pistols, I think that we may in course of time do away with fighting one another with lawyers. Such improvements are not altogether unheard of. A counterfeiting law-factory, standing half in a slave land and half in a free! What kind of laws for freemen can

Vol. XII

you expect from that? Substantial justice!! There's nothing substantial about it, but the Judge's salary and the lawyer's fee.

The thought of that man's position and probable fate is spoiling many a man's day here at the North for other thinking. We do not think of buying any crape this time.

It seems that one of his abettors had lived there for years, and Brown took all his measures deliberately. The country was mountainous, and it was given out that they were concerned in mining operations, and to play this part required very little invention on his part, such had been his previous pursuits and habits. Having been a surveyor, he would not make a strange figure in the fields and woods; this, too, would account [for] quantities of spades and pickaxes, and strangers from time to time visiting and conferring with him in a somewhat mysterious manner.

I have no respect for the judgment of any man who can read the report of that conversation and still call the principal *insane*. It has the ring of a saner sanity than an ordinary discipline and habits of life, than an ordinary organization, secures. Take any sentence of it, — "Any questions that I can honorably answer, I will; not otherwise. So far as I am myself concerned, I have told everything truthfully. I value my word, sir."

He never overstated anything, but spoke within bounds. I remember particularly how, in his speech here, he referred to what his family had suffered in Kansas, never giving the least vent to his pent-up fire. It was a volcano with an ordinary chimney-flue. Also,

referring to the deeds of certain Border Ruffians, he said, rapidly paring away his speech, like an experienced soldier keeping a reserve of force and meaning, "They had a perfect right to be hung."

I would fain do my best to correct, etc., little as I know of him.

But I believe, without having any outward evidence, that many have already silently retracted their words.

They (Allen and Stark) may have possessed some of his love of liberty, indignation, and courage to face their country's foes, but they had not the rare qualities — the peculiar courage and self-reliance — which could enable them to face their country itself, and all mankind, in behalf of the oppressed.

He could give you information on various subjects, for he had travelled widely and observed closely. He said that the Indians with whom he dealt in Kansas were perhaps the richest people in a pecuniary sense on the earth. The money that this government annually paid them gave so much to each member of the community. They were, moreover, more intelligent than the mass of the Border Ruffians, or that class of the inhabitants of Missouri.

Much of the time of late years he has had to skulk in the swamps of Kansas with a price set upon his head, suffering from sickness and poverty and exposure, befriended only by Indians and [a] few white men. When surprise was expressed that he was not taken, he accounted for it by saying that it was perfectly well understood that he would not be taken alive. He would even show himself openly in towns which were half composed of Border Ruffians, and transact some business, without delaying long, and yet nobody attempted to arrest [him], because, as he said, a small party did not like to undertake it, and a large one could not be got together in season.

I thought the same of his speech which I heard some years ago, — that he was not in the least a rhetorician, was not talking to Buncombe or his constituents anywhere, who had no need to invent anything, but to tell the simple truth and communicate his resolution. Therefore he appeared incomparably strong, and eloquence in Congress or elsewhere was at a discount. It was like the speeches of Cromwell compared with those of an ordinary king.

They have tried a long time; they have hung a good many, but never found the right one before.

Dispersing the sentiments of humanity! As if they were ever found unaccompanied by its deeds! as if you could disperse them as easily as water with a watering-pot and they were good only to lay the dust with!

A few ministers are doing their duty in New York. This use of the word "insane" has got to be a mere trope.

Newspaper-editors talk as if it were impossible that a man could be "divinely appointed" in these days to do any work whatever, as if vows and religion were out of date as connected with any man's daily work, and as if a man's death were a failure and his continued life, be it of whatever character, were a success. They argue that it is a proof of his *insanity* that he thought he was appointed to do this work which he did, — that he did not suspect himself for a moment!

If they do not mean this, then they do not speak the truth and say what they mean. They are simply at their old tricks still.

He said truly that the reason why such greatly superior numbers quailed before him with a handful of men only was, as some of his prisoners stated, that the former *lacked a cause*, — a kind of armor which he and his party never lacked. He said that when the time arrived, few men were found willing to lay down their lives in defense of what they knew to be wrong. They did not like that this should be their last act in this world.

As if the agent to abolish slavery could only be somebody "appointed" by the President or some political party.

All this — his insanity (monomania, says one), etc. — made him to be "dreaded by the Missourians as a supernatural being." Sure enough, a hero in the midst of us cowards is always so dreaded. He is just that thing. He shows himself superior to nature. He has a spark of divinity in him.

> "Unless above himself he can
> Erect himself, how poor a thing is man!"

I have read all the newspapers I could get within a week, and I do not remember in them a single expression of sympathy for these men.

Most of them decided not to print the full report of Brown's words in the armory "to the exclusion of other matter." Why, they have *mattered*, and there is no safety for them but in excluding the dead part and

Vol. XII

giving place to the living and healthy. But I object not so much to what they have not done as to what they have done.

He was by descent and birth a New England farmer, a man of great common sense, deliberate and practical as that class, and tenfold more so. He was like the best of those who stood at our bridge once, on Lexington Common, and on Bunker Hill, only he was firmer and higher-principled than any that I chance to have heard of as there. It was no Abolition lecturer that converted him.

A Western paper says, to account for his escape from so many perils, that he was concealed under a "rural exterior," as if in that prairie land a hero should by good rights wear a citizen's dress only. It would appear from published letters that the women of the land are where the men should be. What sort of violence is that which is encouraged not by soldiers but by citizens, not so much by laymen as by ministers of the Gospel, not so much by the fighting sects as by Quakers, and not so much by Quaker men as Quaker women? The enemy may well "quake" at the thought of it. Is not that a righteous war where the best are thus opposed to the worst?

Governor Wise speaks far more justly and admiringly of him than any Northern editor that I have heard of. "They are themselves mistaken who take him to be a madman. . . . He is cool, collected, and indomitable, and it is but just to him to say that he was humane to his prisoners. . . . And he inspired me with great trust in his integrity as a man of truth. He is a

fanatic, vain and garrulous (!!), but firm, truthful, and intelligent. His men, too, who survive, are like him. . . . Colonel Washington says that he was the coolest and firmest man he ever saw in defying danger and death. With one son dead by his side, and another shot through, he felt the pulse of his dying son with one hand, and held his rifle with the other, and commanded his men with the utmost composure, encouraging them to be firm, and to sell their lives as dear as they could. Of the three white prisoners, Brown, Stevens, and Coppoc, it was hard to say which was the most firm." There is another man with whom the South and a good part of the North heartily sympathize. His name is Walker.

I subscribed a trifle when he was here three years ago, I had so much confidence in the man, — that he would do right, — but it would seem that he had not confidence enough in me, nor in anybody else that I know, to communicate his plans to us.

I do not wish to kill or to be killed, but I can foresee circumstances in which both of these things would be by me unavoidable. In extremities I could even be killed.

This event advertises me that there is such a fact as death, — the possibility of a man's dying. It seems as if no man had ever died in America; for in order to die you must first have lived. I don't believe in the hearses and palls and funerals that they have had. There was no death in the case, because there had been no life; they merely rotted or sloughed off, pretty much as they had rotted or sloughed along. No temple's veil was rent, only a hole dug somewhere. The best of them fairly ran down like a clock. I hear a good many pretend that they are going to die; or that they have died, for aught I know. Nonsense! I'll defy them to do it. They have n't got life enough in them. They 'll deliquesce like fungi, and keep a hundred eulogists mopping the spot where they left off. Only half a dozen or so have died since the world began. *Memento mori!* they don't understand that sublime sentence which some worthy got sculptured on his gravestone once. They 've understood it in a grovelling and snivelling sense. They 've wholly forgotten how to die. Be sure you die. Finish your work. Know when to leave off. Men make a needless ado about taking lives, — capital punishment. Where is there any life to take? You don't know what it means to let the dead bury the dead.

Beauty stands veiled the while, and music is a screeching lie.

These men, in teaching us how to die, have at the same time taught us how to live. If this man's acts and words do not create a revival, it will be the severest possible satire on the acts and words of those who are said to have effected such things.

Do you ever think you have died, or are going to die, sir? No! there is no hope of you, sir. You have n't got your lesson yet. You 've got to stay after school.

It is the best news that America has ever heard.

Franklin, — Washington, — they were let off without dying; these were merely missing one day.

It has already quickened the public pulse of the North; it has infused more, and more generous, blood

into her veins and heart than any number of years of what is called commercial and political prosperity could. How many a man who was lately contemplating suicide has now something to live for!

Mr. Giddings says of them that "their sad fate will occupy a brief page in the history of our nation." Does he think that the history of the Republican Party — hitherto, for it may be re-created by his death — will be in the proportion of a sentence to that page?

When I reflect to what a cause this man devoted himself, and how religiously, and then reflect to what cause his judges and all who condemn him so angrily and fluently devote themselves, I see that they are as far apart as the heavens and earth are asunder. The amount of it is our "leading men" are a harmless kind of folk, and they know well enough that *they* were not divinely appointed, but elected by the votes of their party.

The most sensible of the apparently editorial articles on this event that I have met with is in the *Wheeling Intelligence. Vide* Supplement to Journal, October 29th.[1]

Swamp-pink and waxwork were bare October 23d; how long?

Oct. 28. Goldenrods and asters have been altogether *lingering* some days. Walnuts commonly fall, and the black walnuts at Smith's are at least half fallen.

[1] [This "supplement" does not appear among the manuscript volumes of the journal.]

Vol. XII

They are of the form and size of a small lemon and — what is singular — have a rich nutmeg fragrance. They are now turning dark-brown. Gray says it is rare in the Eastern but very common in the Western States. Is it indigenous in Massachusetts?[1] If so, it is much the most remarkable nut that we have.

[1] Emerson says it is, but rare.

IX

NOVEMBER, 1859

(ÆT. 42)

Nov. 5. In Boston. — The first Indian-summer day, after an unusually cold October. Sat at the end of Long Wharf for coolness, but it was very warm, with scarcely a breath of wind, and so thick a haze that I could see but little way down the harbor.

Nov. 6. The river is quite low, about four inches lower than the hub [?] I used in the summer, or lower than before, this year. Yet there is more water in the mill-streams; the mill-wheels are supplied now which were stationary in the summer.

C. thinks that he saw bats last evening.

Nov. 8. A pleasant day.

P. M. — To Nut Meadow and Fair Haven Hill.

I hear a small z-ing cricket.

Coombs says that quite a little flock of pigeons bred here last summer. He found one nest in a small white pine near his pigeon-stand (where he baited them in the summer), so low he could put his hand in it (!?). I saw, while talking with him, a trout playing about in the open roadside watering-place, on the Jimmy Miles road (*i. e.* in Nut Meadow Brook), which was apparently fifteen inches long; not lurking under the bank **but** openly swimming up and down in midstream.

How richly and exuberantly downy are many golden-rod and aster heads now, their seed just on the point of falling or being blown away, before they are in the least weather-beaten! They are now puffed up to their utmost, clean and light.[1]

The tufts of purplish withered andropogon in With-erell Glade are still as fair as ever, soft and trembling and bending from the wind; of a very light mouse-color seen from the side of the sun, and as delicate as the most fragile ornaments of a lady's bonnet; but looking toward the sun they are a brilliant white, each polished hair (of the pappus?) reflecting the November sun without its heats, not in the least yellowish or brown like the goldenrods and asters.

Nov. 9. A fine Indian-summer day. Have had pleasant weather about a week.[2]

Nov. 10. Rain; warm.

Nov. 11. Windy and cooler.

I observed, October 23d, wood turtles copulating in the Assabet, and a flock of goldfinches on the top of a hemlock, — as if after its seeds?

Also, October 24th, riding home from Acton, I saw the withered leaves blown from an oak by the roadside dashing off, gyrating, and surging upward into the air, so exactly like a flock of birds sporting with one another that, for a minute at least, I could not be sure they were

[1] *Vide* back, Oct. 16th.
[2] *Vide* Nov. 1st.

not birds; and it suggested how far the motions of birds, like those of these leaves, might be determined by currents of air, *i. e.*, how far the bird learns to conform to such currents.

The flat variety of *Lycopodium dendroideum* shed pollen on the 25th of October. That's a lycopodium path on north side of Colburn Hill.

Nov. 12. The first sprinkling of snow, which for a short time whitens the ground in spots.

I do not know how to distinguish between our waking life and a dream. Are we not always living the life that we imagine we are? Fear creates danger, and courage dispels it.

There was a remarkable sunset, I think the 25th of October. The sunset sky reached quite from west to east, and it was the most varied in its forms and colors of any that I remember to have seen. At one time the clouds were most softly and delicately rippled, like the ripple-marks on sand. But it was hard for me to see its beauty then, when my mind was filled with Captain Brown. So great a wrong as his fate implied overshadowed all beauty in the world.

Nov. 15. A very pleasant Indian-summer day.
P. M. — To Ledum Swamp.

I look up the river from the railroad bridge. It is perfectly smooth between the uniformly tawny meadows, and I see several musquash-cabins off Hubbard Shore distinctly outlined as usual in the November light.

Vol. XII

I hear in several places a faint cricket note, either a fine z-ing or a distincter creak, also see and hear a grasshopper's crackling flight.

The clouds were never more fairly reflected in the water than now, as I look up the Cyanean Reach from Clamshell.

A fine gossamer is streaming from every fence and tree and stubble, though a careless observer would not notice it. As I look along over the grass toward the sun at Hosmer's field, beyond Lupine Hill, I notice the shimmering effect of the gossamer, — which seems to cover it almost like a web, — occasioned by its motion, though the air is so still. This is noticed at least forty rods off.

I turn down Witherell Glade, only that I may bring its tufts of andropogon between me and the sun for a moment. They are pretty as ever.[1]

In the midst of Ledum Swamp I came upon a white cat under the spruces and the water brush, which evidently had not seen me till I was within ten feet. There she stood, quite still, as if hoping to be concealed, only turning her head slowly away from and toward me, looking at me thus two or three times with an extremely worried expression in her eyes, but not moving any other part of her body. It occurred to me from her peculiar anxious expression and this motion, as if spellbound, that perhaps she was deaf; but when I moved toward her she found the use of her limbs and dashed off, bounding over the andromeda by successive leaps like a rabbit, no longer making her way through or beneath it.

[1] *Vide* Oct. 16th and Nov. 8th.

I noticed on the 3d, in Worcester,[1] that the white pines had been as full of seed there as here this year. Also gathered half a pocketful of shagbarks, of which many still hung on the trees though most had fallen.

All through the excitement occasioned by Brown's remarkable attempt and subsequent behavior, the Massachusetts Legislature, not taking any steps for the defense of her citizens who are likely to be carried to Virginia as witnesses and exposed to the violence of a slaveholding mob, is absorbed in a liquor-agency question. That has, in fact, been the all-absorbing question with it!! I am sure that no person up to the occasion, or who perceived the significance of the former event, could at present attend to this question at all. As for the Legislature, bad spirits occupied their thoughts.[2]

If any person, in a lecture or a conversation, should now cite any ancient example of heroism, such as Cato, or Tell, or Winkelried, passing over the recent deeds and words of John Brown, I am sure that it would be felt by any intelligent audience of Northern men to be tame and inexcusably far-fetched. I do not know of *such* words, uttered under such circumstances, in Roman, or English, or any, history.[3]

It is a fact proving how universal and widely related any transcendent greatness is, like the apex of a

[1] [He had been to Worcester to read his address on John Brown there. See *Familiar Letters*, pp. 358, 359; Riv. 413, 414.]
[2] [*Cape Cod, and Miscellanies*, p. 446; *Misc.*, Riv. 243.]
[3] [*Cape Cod, and Miscellanies*, p. 441; *Misc.*, Riv. 237.]

pyramid to all beneath it, that when I now look over my extracts of the noblest poetry the best is oftenest applicable in part or wholly to this man's position. Almost any noble verse may be read either as his elegy or eulogy or be made the text of an oration on him. Indeed, such are now first discerned to be the parts of a divinely established liturgy, applicable to those rare cases for which the ritual of no church has provided, — the case of heroes, martyrs, and saints. This is the formula established on high, their burial service, to which every great genius has contributed its line or syllable. Of course the ritual of no church which is wedded to the state can contain a service applicable to the case of a state criminal unjustly condemned, — a martyr.

The sense of grand poetry read by the light of this event is brought out distinctly like an invisible writing held to the fire.[1]

About the 23d of October I saw a large flock of goldfinches[2] (judging from their motions and notes) on the tops of the hemlocks up the Assabet, apparently feeding on their seeds, then falling. They were collected in great numbers on the very tops of these trees and flitting from one to another. Rice has since described to me the same phenomenon as observed by him there since (says he saw the birds picking out the seeds), though he did not know what birds they were. William Rice says that these birds get so much of the lettuce seed that you can hardly save any. They get sunflower seeds also. Are called "lettuce-birds" in the books.

[1] [Cape Cod, and Miscellanies, pp. 451, 452; Misc., Riv. 249, 250.]
[2] Vide Nov. 11th.

A lady who was suitably indignant at the outrage on Senator Sumner, lamenting to me to-day the very common insensibility to such things, said that one woman to whom she described the deed and on whom she thought that she had made some impression, lately inquired of her with feeble curiosity: "How is that young man who had his head hurt? I have n't heard anything about him for a good while."

As I returned over the Corner Bridge I saw cows in the sun half-way down Fair Haven Hill next the Cliff, half a mile off, the declining sun so warmly reflected from their red coats that I could not for some time tell if they were not some still bright-red shrub oaks, — for they had no more form at that distance.

Nov. 17. Another Indian-summer day, as fair as any we 've had. I go down the railroad to Andromeda Ponds this afternoon.

Captain Hubbard is having his large wood — oak and white pine, on the west of the railroad this side the pond — cut. I see one white oak felled with one hundred and fifteen rings to it; another, a red, oak has about the same number. Thus disappear the haunts of the owls. The time may come when their aboriginal *hoo-hoo-hoo* will not be heard hereabouts.

I have been so absorbed of late in Captain Brown's fate as to be surprised whenever I detected the old routine running still, — met persons going about their affairs indifferent. It appeared strange to me that the little dipper should be still diving in the river as of yore; and this suggested that this grebe might be diving here

when Concord shall be no more. Any affecting human event may blind our eyes to natural objects.[1]

At the pond-side I see titmice alighting on the now hoary gray goldenrod and hanging back downward from it, as if eating its seeds; or could they have been looking for insects? There were three or four about it.

I sit in the sun on the northeast side of the first Andromeda Pond, looking over it toward the sun. How fair and memorable this prospect when you stand opposite to the sun, these November afternoons, and look over the red andromeda swamp! — a glowing, warm brown red in the Indian-summer sun, like a bed of moss in a hollow in the woods, with gray high blueberry and straw-colored grasses interspersed. And when, going round it, you look over it in the opposite direction, it presents a gray aspect.

The musquash are active, swimming about in the further pond to-day, — this Indian-summer day. Channing also sees them thus stirring in the river this afternoon.

Nov. 18. A fog this morning and yesterday morning, lasting till about 10 A. M.

I looked into the Church of England liturgy, printed near the beginning of the last century, to find a service applicable to the case of Captain Brown. The only martyr recognized and provided for by it was King Charles the First!! Of all the inhabitants of England and of the world, he was the only one whom that church made a martyr and saint of!! And now for more than

[1] [Cape Cod, and Miscellanies, p. 441; Misc., Riv. 237.]

half a century it had celebrated his martyrdom by an annual service! What a satire on the church is that!![1]

An apothecary in New Bedford told R.[2] the other day that a man (a Mr. Leonard) of Springfield told him that he once attended a meeting in Springfield where a woman was exhibited as in a mesmeric state, insensible to pain, — a large and fleshy woman, — and the spectators were invited to test her condition with pins or otherwise. After some had tried, one among them came forward with a vial of cowage, and, after stating to the company that it would produce intolerable irritation in the skin, he proceeded to rub a little on the woman's bare arm and on her neck. She immediately winced under it, whereupon he took out another vial containing sweet oil, and, applying a little of that, relieved her. He then stated that any one present might apply to his skin as much as he pleased. Some came forward and he laid bare his breast and when they applied it sparingly and hesitatingly, he said, "Rub away, gentlemen, — as much as you like," and he betrayed no sign of irritation. That man was John Brown.

Nov. 22. Ground white with snow a few hours. C. says that he saw to-day a procession of minnows (one to two inches long) some three or four feet wide, about forty abreast, passing slowly along northerly, close to the shore, at Wharf Rock, Flint's Pond. They were fifteen minutes passing!

[1] [Cape Cod, and Miscellanies, p. 446; Misc., Riv. 243, 244.]
[2] [Mr. Ricketson was in Concord from Nov. 19th to 24th, 1859. He walked and supped with Thoreau on the 20th and went to visit him the next day. See *Daniel Ricketson and his Friends*, pp. 312–314.]

Nov. 24. The river has risen considerably, at last, owing to the rain of the 22d. Had been very low before.

See, on the railroad-slope by the pond, and also some days ago, a flock of goldfinches eating the seed of the Roman wormwood. At Spanish Brook Path, the witch-hazel (one flower) lingers.

I observe that ferns grow especially where there is an abrupt or broken bank, as where, in the woods, sand has been anciently dug out of a hillside to make a dam with and the semicircular scar has been covered with a sod and shrubs again. The shelter and steepness are favorable when there is shade and moisture.

How pretty amid the downy and cottony fruits of November the heads of the white anemone, raised a couple of feet from the ground on slender stalks, two or three together, — small heads of yellowish-white down, compact and regular as a thimble beneath, but, at this time, diffusive and bursting forth above, somewhat like a little torch with its flame, — a very neat object!

Nov. 25. P. M. — Paddle to Baker Farm.

The weeds of water-plants have decayed and fallen long since, and left the water along the sides of the river comparatively clear. In this clear, cold water I see no fishes now, and it is as empty as the air. But for some days, at least, or since colder weather, I have noticed the snow-fleas skipping on the surface next the shore. These are rather a cool-weather phenomenon. I see them to-day skipping by thousands in the wet clamshells left by the muskrats.[1]

    [1] Probably washed out by rise of river.

Landing at the ash tree above the railroad, I thought I heard the peculiar note of grackles toward the willow-row across the field, and made a memorandum of it, never doubting; but soon after I saw some farmers at work there, and found that it was the squeaking of the wheel that rolled before their plow. It perfectly resembled the grackle's note, and I never should have suspected it if I had not seen the plowers. It is fit that the creaking of the farmer's plow who is working by the riverside should resemble the note of the blackbirds which frequent those fields.

There is a thin ice for half a rod in width along the shore, which shivers and breaks in the undulations of my boat. Those bayonet rushes still standing are much curved.

See but few ducks, — two of them, — and generally few in the fall compared with the spring.

A large whitish-breasted bird is perched on an oak under Lee's Cliff, for half an hour at least. I think it must be a fish hawk (?).

We hear the clattering sound of two ducks — which rise and fly low at first — before we can see them though quite far off by the side of the pond. Our hands and feet are quite cold, and the water freezes on the paddles, but about sundown it grows sensibly warmer and a little misty. Is not this common at this season?

Nov. 26. P. M. — Walk over the Colburn Farm wood-lot south [of] the road.

I find, sometimes, after I have been lotting off a large wood-lot for auction, that I have been cutting new paths to walk in. I cut lines an inch [*sic*] or two long in arbitrary directions, in and around some dense wood-lot which perhaps is not crossed once a month by any mortal, nor has been for thirty or fifty years, and thus I open to myself new works [*sic*], — enough in a lot of forty acres to occupy me for an afternoon. A forty-acre wood-lot which otherwise would not detain a walker more than half an hour, being thus opened and carved out, will entertain him for half a day.

In this case there was a cultivated field here some thirty years ago, but, the wood being suffered to spring up, from being open and revealed this part of the earth became a covert and concealed place. Excepting an occasional hunter who crossed it maybe once in several months, nobody has walked there, nobody has penetrated its recesses. The walker habitually goes round it, or follows the single cart-path that winds through it. Woods, both the primitive and those which are suffered to spring up in cultivated fields, thus preserve the mystery of nature. How private and sacred a place a grove thus becomes! — merely because its denseness excludes man. It is worth the while to have these thickets on various sides of the town, where the rabbit lurks and the jay builds its nest.

When I ran out the boundary lines of this lot, I could commonly distinguish the line, not merely by the different growth of wood, but often by a kind of ditch which I think may have been produced by the plow, which heaped up the soil along the side of the field when it was

cultivated. I could also detect trees variously bent and twisted, which probably had made part of a hedge fence when young, and others which were scarred by the fencing-stuff that had been fastened to them.

The chickadee is the bird of the wood the most unfailing. When, in a windy, or in any, day, you have penetrated some thick wood like this, you are pretty sure to hear its cheery note therein. At this season it is almost their sole inhabitant.

I see here to-day one brown creeper busily inspecting the pitch pines. It begins at the base, and creeps rapidly upward by starts, adhering close to the bark and shifting a little from side to side often till near the top, then suddenly darts off downward to the base of another tree, where it repeats the same course. This has no black cockade, like the nuthatch.

In the midst of this wood there occur less valuable patches, of an eighth of an acre or more, where there is much grass, and cladonia, shrub oaks, and lichen-covered birches, and a few pitch pines only, — places of a comparatively sterile character, as if the soil had been run out. The birches will have much of the birch fungus on them, and their fallen dead tops strew the ground.

Nov. 27. P. M. — To Colburn Farm wood-lot north of C. Hill.

I traverse this wood-lot back and forth by the lines cut by those who have lotted it off. Thus I scare up the partridges in it. A dozen long lines four rods apart are cut through it. Walking through these, I am pretty sure to scare up what partridges there are in it, and there are few wood-lots of this size which have not some in them at present.

Come upon a large ant-hill in the midst of the wood, but no ants on it. It has made an open and bare spot in the woods, ten or twelve feet in diameter. Its mound is partly grassed over, as usual, and trees have been prevented from springing up by the labors of the ants beneath. As this wood is about thirty years old, it may prove that the ant-hill is of the same age!

On the 22d the ground was white with snow for a few hours only. Yet, though you saw no more of it generally the latter part of that day, I still see some of it in cold, wet, shaded places, as amid andromeda and cranberry vines.

This wood-lot, especially at the northwest base of the hill, is extensively carpeted with the *Lycopodium complanatum* and also much *dendroideum* and *Chimaphila umbellata*. The former, methinks, abounds especially in shady and rather moist, and I think old, or rather diseased, and *cold* (?), woods. It covers the earth densely, even under the thickest white pine groves, and equally grows under birches. It surprises you as if the trees stood in green grass where you commonly see only withered leaves.

The Greeks and Romans made much of honey because they had no sugar; olive oil also was very important. Our poets (?) still sing of honey, though we have sugar, and oil, though we do not produce and scarcely use it.

The principal flight of geese is said to have been a few days before the 24th. I have seen none.

taking a walk for exercise as some are. It is one thing to *own* a wood-lot as he does who perambulates its bounds almost daily, so as to have worn a path about it, and another to own one as many another does who hardly knows where it is. Evidently the quantity of chips in his basket is not essential; it is the chippy idea which he pursues. It is to him an unaccountably pleasing occupation. And no doubt he loves to see his pile grow at home.

Think how variously men spend the same hour in the same village! The lawyer sits talking with his client in the twilight; the trader is weighing sugar and salt; while Abel Brooks is hastening home from the woods with his basket half full of chips. I think I should prefer to be with Brooks. He was literally as smiling as a basket of chips. A basket of chips, therefore, must have been regarded as a singularly pleasing (if not pleased) object.

We make a good deal of the early twilights of these November days, they make so large a part of the afternoon.

Nov. 29. P. M. — To Copan.

There is a white birch on Copan which has many of the common birch fungus of a very peculiar and remarkable form, not flat thus: but shaped like a bell or short horn, thus: 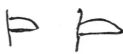 as if composed of a more flowing material which had settled downward like a drop. As C. said, they were shaped like icicles, especially those short and spreading ones about bridges.

Nov. 28. P. M. — To E. Hubbard's Wood.

Goodwin tells me that Therien, who lives in a shanty of his own building and alone in Lincoln, uses for a drink only checkerberry-tea. (G. also called it "ivory-leaf.") Is it not singular that probably only one *tea*-drinker in this neighborhood should use for his beverage a plant which grows here? Therien, really drinking his checkerberry-tea from motives of simplicity or economy and saying nothing about it, deserves well of his country. As he does now, we may all do at last.

There is scarcely a wood of sufficient size and density left now for an owl to haunt in, and if I hear one hoot I may be sure where he is.

Goodwin is cutting out a few cords of dead wood in the midst of E. Hubbard's old lot. This has been Hubbard's practice for thirty years or more, and so, it would seem, they are all dead before he gets to them.

Saw Abel Brooks there with a half-bushel basket on his arm. He was picking up chips on his and neighboring lots; had got about two quarts of old and blackened pine chips, and with these was returning home at dusk more than a mile. Such a petty quantity as you would hardly have gone to the end of your yard for, and yet he said that he had got more than two cords of them at home, which he had collected thus and sometimes with a wheelbarrow. He had thus spent an hour or two and walked two or three miles in a cool November evening to pick up two quarts of pine chips scattered through the woods. He evidently takes real satisfaction in collecting his fuel, perhaps gets more heat of all kinds out of it than any man in town. He is not reduced to

Saw quite a flock of snow buntings not yet very white. They rose from the midst of a stubble-field unexpectedly. The moment they settled after wheeling around, they were perfectly concealed, though quite near, and I could only hear their rippling note from the earth from time to time.

Nov. 30. I am one of a committee of four, *viz.* Simon Brown (Ex-Lieutenant-Governor), R. W. Emerson, myself, and John Keyes (late High Sheriff), instructed by a meeting of citizens to ask liberty of the selectmen to have the bell of the first parish tolled at the time Captain Brown is being hung, and while we shall be assembled in the town house to express our sympathy with him. I applied to the selectmen yesterday. Their names are George M. Brooks, Barzillai Hudson, and Julius Smith. After various delays they at length answer me to-night that they "are uncertain whether they have any control over the bell, but that, *in any case*, they will not give their consent to have the bell tolled." Beside their private objections, they are influenced by the remarks of a few individuals. Dr. Bartlett tells me that Rockwood Hoar said he "hoped no such foolish thing would be done," and he also named Stedman Buttrick, John Moore, Cheney (and others added Nathan Brooks, senior, and Francis Wheeler) as strongly opposed to it; said that he had heard "five hundred" (!) damn me for it, and that he had no doubt that if it were done some counter-demonstration would be made, such as firing minute-guns. The doctor himself is more excited than anybody, for he has the minister under his wing. Indeed, a considerable part of Concord are in the condition of Virginia to-day, — afraid of their own shadows.

I see in E. Hubbard's gray oak wood, four rods from the old wall line and two or three rods over the brow of the hill, an apparent downy woodpecker's nest in a dead white oak stub some six feet high. It is made as far as I can see, like that which I have, but looks quite fresh, and I see, by the very numerous fresh white chips of dead wood scattered *over* the recently fallen leaves beneath, that it must have been made since the leaves fell. Could it be a nuthatch or chickadee's work? [1]

This has been a very pleasant month, with quite a number of Indian-summer days, — a pleasanter month than October was. It is quite warm to-day, and as I go home at dusk on the railroad causeway, I hear a hylodes peeping.

[1] [Probably a downy woodpecker's winter quarters.]

END OF VOLUME XII

Vol. XII

The Journal of Henry D. Thoreau

VOLUME XIII

(December, 1859 — July, 1860)

Houstonia

CONTENTS

Vol. XIII

Vol. XIII

THE JOURNAL OF
HENRY DAVID THOREAU

VOLUME XIII

I

DECEMBER, 1859 (ÆT. 42)

Nov. 30, *Dec.* 1 *and* 2 were remarkably warm and springlike days, — a moist warmth. The crowing of cocks and other sounds remind you of spring, such is the state of the air. I wear only one coat.

Dec. 3. Suddenly quite cold, and freezes in the house.

Rode with a man this forenoon who said that if he did not clean his teeth when he got up, it made him sick all the rest of the day, but he had found by late experience that when he had not cleaned his teeth for several days they cleaned themselves. I assured him that such was the general rule, — that when from any cause we were prevented from doing what we had commonly thought indispensable for us to do, things *cleaned* or took care of themselves.

X [1] was betrayed by his eyes, which had a glaring

[1] [X, whom Thoreau drove this morning to Acton, was literally an unknown quantity to him at the time. He did not learn till afterward

---

film over them and no serene depth into which you could look. Inquired particularly the way to Emerson's and the distance, and when I told him, said he knew it as well as if he saw it. Wished to turn and proceed to his house. Told me one or two things which he asked me not to tell S. [1] Said, "I know I am insane," — and I knew it too. Also called it "nervous excitement." At length, when I made a certain remark, he said, "I don't know but *you* are Emerson; are you? You look somewhat like him." He said as much two or three times, and added once, "But then Emerson would n't lie." Finally put his questions to me, of Fate, etc., etc., as if I *were* Emerson. Getting to the woods, I remarked upon them, and he mentioned my name, but never to the end suspected who his companion was. Then "proceeded to business," — "since the time was short," — and put to me the questions he was going to put to Emerson. His insanity exhibited itself chiefly by his incessant excited talk, scarcely allowing me to interrupt him, but once or twice apologizing for his behavior. What he said was for the most part connected and sensible enough.

When I hear of John Brown and his wife weeping at length, it is as if the rocks sweated.

Dec. 4. Awake to winter, and snow two or three inches deep, the first of any consequence.

that it was Francis Jackson Merriam, one of John Brown's men, on his way to Canada. See the account in *Familiar Letters*, pp. 365–367; Riv. 422–425.]

[1] [Mr. F. B. Sanborn.]

Dec. 5. P. M. — Down Turnpike to Smith's Hill.

Rather hard walking in the snow. There is a slight mist in the air and accordingly some glaze on the twigs and leaves, and thus suddenly we have passed from Indian summer to winter. The perfect silence, as if the whispering and creaking earth were muffled (her axle), and the stillness (motionlessness) of the twigs and of the very weeds and withered grasses, as if they were sculptured out of marble, are striking. It is as if you had stepped from a withered garden into the yard of a sculptor or worker in marble, crowded with delicate works, rich and rare. I remark, half a mile off, a tall and slender pitch pine against the dull-gray mist, peculiarly monumental. I noticed also several small white oak trees full of leaves by the roadside, strangely interesting and beautiful. Their stiffened leaves were very long and deeply cut, and the lighter and glazed under sides being almost uniformly turned vertically toward the northwest, as a traveller turns his back to the storm, though enough of the redder and warmer sides were seen to contrast with them, it looked like an artificial tree hung with many-fingered gauntlets. Such was the disposition of the leaves, often nearly in the same plane, that it looked like a brown arbor-vitæ.

See four quails running across the Turnpike. How they must be affected by this change from warm weather and bare ground to cold and universal snow!

Returning from the post-office at early candle-light, I noticed for the first time this season the peculiar effect of lights in offices and shops seen over the snowy streets, suggesting how withdrawn and inward the life in the former, how exposed and outward in the latter.

His late career — these six weeks, I mean — has been meteor-like, flashing through the darkness in which we live. I know of nothing more miraculous in all history.[1]

Nothing could his enemies do but it redounded to his infinite advantage, the advantage of his cause. They did not hang him at once; they reserved him to preach to them. And here is another great blunder: they have not hung his four followers with him; that scene is still to come, and so his victory is prolonged.

No theatrical manager could have arranged things so wisely to give effect to his behavior and words. And who, think you, *was* the Manager? Who placed the slave-woman and her child between his prison and the gallows?[2]

The preachers, the Bible men, they who talk about principle and doing to others as you would that they should do unto you, —how could they fail to recognize him, by far the greatest preacher of them all, with the Bible on his lips, and in his acts, the embodiment of principle, who actually carried out the golden rule? All whose moral sense is aroused, who have a calling from on high to preach, have sided with him. It may prove the occasion, if it has not proved it already, of a new sect of *Brownites* being formed in our midst.[3]

I see now, as he saw, that he was not to be pardoned or rescued by men. That would have been to disarm

[1] [*Cape Cod, and Miscellanies*, p. 441; *Misc.*, Riv. 237.]
[2] [*Cape Cod, and Miscellanies*, p. 448; *Misc.*, Riv. 246.]
[3] [*Cape Cod, and Miscellanies*, pp. 442, 443; *Misc.*, Riv., 239.]

Vol. XIII

him, to restore to him a material weapon, a Sharp's rifle, when he had taken up the sword of the spirit, — the sword with which he has really won his greatest and most memorable victories. Now he has not laid aside the sword of the spirit. He is pure spirit himself, and his sword is pure spirit also.

On the day of his translation, I heard, to be sure, that he was hung, but I did not know what that meant, —and I felt no sorrow on his account; but not for a day or two did I even *hear* that he was dead, and not after any number of days shall I believe it. Of all the men who are said to be my contemporaries, it seems to me that John Brown is the only one who *has not* died. I meet him at every turn. He is more alive than ever he was. He is not confined to North Elba nor to Kansas. He is no longer working in secret only. John Brown has earned immortality.[1]

Men have been hung in the South before for attempting to rescue slaves, and the North was not much stirred by it. Whence, then, this wonderful difference? We were not so sure of their devotion to principle. We have made a subtle distinction, have forgotten human laws, and do homage to an idea. The North is suddenly all Transcendental. It goes behind the human law, it goes behind the apparent failure, and recognizes eternal justice and glory.

It is more generous than the spirit which actuated our forefathers, for it is a revolution in behalf of another, and an oppressed, people.[2]

[1] [*Cape Cod, and Miscellanies*, pp. 448–450; *Misc.*, Riv. 246–248.]
[2] [*Cape Cod, and Miscellanies*, p. 443; *Misc.*, Riv. 239, 240.]

Dec. 6. P. M. — To Walden and Baker Bridge, in the shallow snow and mizzling rain.

It is somewhat of a lichen day. The bright-yellow sulphur lichens on the walls of the Walden road look novel, as if I had not seen them for a long time. Do they not require cold as much as moisture to enliven them? What surprising forms and colors! Designed on every natural surface of rock or tree. Even stones of smaller size which make the walls are so finished, and piled up for what use? How naturally they adorn our works of art! See where the farmer has set up his post-and-rail fences along the road. The sulphur lichen has, as it were, at once leaped to occupy the northern side of each post, as in towns handbills are pasted on all bare surfaces, and the rails are more or less gilded with them as if it had rained gilt. The handbill which nature affixes to the north side of posts and trees and other surfaces. And there are the various shades of green and gray beside.

Though it is melting, there is more ice left on the twigs in the woods than I had supposed.

The mist is so thick that we cannot quite see the length of Walden as we descend to its eastern shore. The reflections of the hillsides are so much the more unsubstantial, for we see even the reflected mist veiling them. You see, beneath these whitened wooded hills and shore sloping to it, the dark, half mist-veiled water. For two rods in width next the shore, where the water is shallowest and the sand bare, you see a strip of light greenish two or three rods in width, and then dark brown (with a few green streaks only) where

the dark sediment of ages has accumulated. And, looking down the pond, you see on each side successive wooded promontories — with their dim reflections — growing dimmer and dimmer till they are lost in the mist. The more distant shores are a mere dusky line or film, a sort of concentration of the mistiness.

In the pure greenish stripe next the shore I saw some dark-brown objects above the sand, which looked very much like sea turtles in various attitudes. One appeared holding its great head up toward the surface. They were very weird-like and of indefinite size. I supposed that they were stumps or logs on the bottom, but was surprised to find that they were a thin and *flat* collection of sediment on the sandy bottom, like that which covered the bottom generally further out.

When the breeze rippled the surface some distance out, it looked like a wave coming in, but it never got in to the shore.

No sooner has the snow fallen than, in the woods, it is seen to be dotted almost everywhere with the fine seeds and scales of birches and alders, — no doubt an ever-accessible food to numerous birds and perhaps mice. Thus it is alternate snow and seeds.

Returning up the railroad, I see the great tufts of sedge in Heywood's meadow curving over like locks of the meadow's hair, above the snow.  These browned the meadow considerably. Then came a black maze, of alders moistened by the rain, which made a broad black belt between the former brown and the red-brown oaks higher up the hillside.

The white pines now, seen through the mist, the ends of their boughs drooping a little with the weight of the glaze, resemble very much hemlocks, for the extremities of their limbs always droop thus, while pines are commonly stiffly erect or ascendant.

Came upon a round bed of tansy, half a dozen feet in diameter, which was withered quite black, as seen above the snow, — blacker than any plant I remember. This reminded me that its name was by some thought to be from ἀθανασία, or immortality, from its not withering early, but in this case it suggested its funereal reputation.

What a transit that of his horizontal body alone, but just cut down from the gallows-tree! We read that at such a time it passed through Philadelphia, and by Saturday night had reached New York. Thus like a meteor it passed through the Union from the Southern regions toward the North. No such freight have the cars borne since they carried him southward alive.[1]

What avail all your scholarly accomplishments and learning, compared with wisdom and manhood? To omit his other behavior, see what a work this comparatively unread and unlettered man has written within six weeks! Where is our professor of belles-lettres, or of logic and rhetoric, who can write so well? He has written in prison, not a History of the World like Raleigh, for his time was short, but an American book which shall live longer than that.

[1] [Cape Cod, and Miscellanies, p. 449; Misc., Riv. 247.]

The death of Irving, which at any other time would have attracted universal attention, having occurred while these things were transpiring, goes almost unobserved. Literary gentlemen, editors, and critics think that they know how to write because they have studied grammar and rhetoric; but the art of composition is as simple as the discharge of a bullet from a rifle, and its masterpieces imply an infinitely greater force behind it. This unlettered man's speaking and writing is standard English. Some words and phrases deemed vulgarisms and Americanisms before, he has made standard American. "It will pay." It suggests that the one great rule of composition — and if I were a professor of rhetoric I should insist on this — is to speak the truth. This first, this second, this third. This demands earnestness and manhood chiefly.[1]

I felt that he, a prisoner in the midst of his enemies and under sentence of death, if consulted as to his next step, could answer more wisely than all his countrymen beside. He best understood his position; he contemplated it most calmly. All other men, North and South, were beside themselves. Our thoughts could not revert to any greater or wiser or better men with whom to compare him, for he was above them all. The man this country was about to hang was the greatest and best in it.[2]

Commonly men live according to a formula, and are satisfied if the order of law is observed, but in this instance they returned to original perceptions and there was a revival of old religion; and they saw that what

[1] [Cape Cod, and Miscellanies, pp. 446–448; Misc., Riv. 244, 245.]
[2] [Cape Cod, and Miscellanies, pp. 441, 442; Misc., Riv. 237, 238.]

Vol. XIII

was called order was confusion, what was called justice, injustice, that the best was deemed the worst.

Most Northern men, and not a few Southern ones, have been wonderfully stirred by Brown's behavior and words. They have seen or felt that they were great, heroic, noble, and that there has been nothing quite equal to them in this country, if in the recent history of the world. But the minority have been unmoved by them. They have only been surprised and provoked by the attitude of their neighbors. They have seen that Brown was brave and believed that he had done right, but they have not detected any further peculiarity in him. Not being accustomed to make fine distinctions or to appreciate noble sentiments, they have read his speeches and letters as if they read them not, — they have not known when they burned. They have not felt that he spoke with authority, and hence they have only remembered that the law must be executed. They remember the old formula; they do not hear the new revelation. The man who does not recognize in Brown's words a wisdom and nobleness, and therefore an authority, superior to our laws, is a modern Democrat. This is the test by which to try him. He is not willfully but constitutionally blind, and he is consistent with himself. Such has been his past life. In like manner he has read history and his Bible, and he accepts, or seems to accept, the last only as an established formula, and not because he has been convicted by it. You will not find kindred sentiments in his commonplace-book.[1]

[1] [Cape Cod, and Miscellanies, pp. 443, 444; Misc., Riv. 240, 241.]

And in these six weeks what a variety of themes he has touched on! There are words in that letter to his wife, respecting the education of his daughters, which deserve to be framed and hung over every mantelpiece in the land. Compare their earnest wisdom with that of Poor Richard![1]

"He nothing common did or mean
Upon that memorable scene,
.   .   .   .
Nor called the gods with vulgar spite,
To vindicate his helpless right;
But bowed his comely head
Down, as upon a bed."[2]

Years are no longer required for a revolution of public opinion; days, nay hours, produce marked changes. Fifty who were ready to say, on going into some meeting in honor of him, that he ought to be hung, will not say it when they come out. They hear his words read, every one of which "conveys the perfect charm;" they see the earnest faces of the congregation; and perhaps they join in singing the hymn in his praise.

What confessions it has extorted from the cold and conservative! Witness the Newton letter.

The order of instruction has been reversed. I hear that the preacher says that his act was a failure, while to some extent he eulogizes the man. The class-teacher, after the services, tells his grown-up pupils that at first he thought as the preacher does now, but now he thinks that John Brown was right. But it is under-

[1] [Cape Cod, and Miscellanies, p. 447; Misc., Riv. 244, 245.]
[2] [Cape Cod, and Miscellanies, p. 449; Misc., Riv. 247.]

stood that the pupils are as much ahead of the teacher as he is ahead of the priest; and the very little boys at home ask their parents why God did not save him.

They, whether in the church or out of it, who adhere to the spirit and abandon the letter, and who are accordingly called infidel, have been foremost in this movement.[1]

I took out my boots, which I have not worn since last spring, with the mud and dust of spring still on them, and went forth in the snow. That is an era, when, in the beginning of the winter, you change from the shoes of summer to the boots of winter.

Dec. 8. Here is a better *glaze* than we have yet had, for it snowed and rained in the night.

I go to Pleasant Meadow, — or rather toward the sun, for the glaze shows best so. The wind has risen and the trees are stiffly waving with a brattling sound. The birches, seen half a mile off toward the sun, are the purest dazzling white of any tree, probably because their stems are not seen at all. It is only those seen at a particular angle between us and the sun that appear thus.

Day before yesterday the ice which had fallen from the twigs covered the snow beneath in oblong pieces one or two inches long, which C. well called lemon-drops.

When a noble deed is done, who is likely to appreciate it? They who are noble themselves. I am not surprised that certain of my neighbors speak of John Brown as an ordinary felon. Who are they? They

[1] [*Cape Cod, and Miscellanies*, pp. 442, 443; *Misc.*, Riv. 238, 239.]

Vol. XIII

have much flesh, or at least much coarseness of some kind. They are not ethereal natures, or the dark qualities predominate in them, or they have much office. Several of them are decidedly pachydermatous. How can a man behold the light who has no answering inward light? They are true to their *sight*, but when they look this way they *see* nothing, they are blind. For the children of the light to contend with them is as if there should be a contest between eagles and owls. Show me a man who feels bitterly toward John Brown, and then let me hear what noble verse he can repeat.[1]

Certain persons disgraced themselves by hanging Brown in effigy in this town on the 2d. I was glad to know that the only four whose names I heard mentioned in connection with it had not been long resident here, and had done nothing to secure the respect of the town.

It is not every man who can be a Christian, whatever education you give him. It is a matter of constitution and temperament. I have known many a man who pretended to be a Christian, in whom it was ridiculous, for he had no genius for it.[2]

The expression "a *liberal* education" originally meant one worthy of freemen. Such is education simply in a true and broad sense. But education ordinarily so called — the learning of trades and professions which is designed to enable men to earn their living, or to fit them for a particular station in life — is *servile*.[3]

[1] [*Cape Cod, and Miscellanies*, pp. 444, 445; *Misc.*, Riv. 241, 242.]
[2] [*Cape Cod, and Miscellanies*, p. 445; *Misc.*, Riv. 242.]
[3] [*Cape Cod, and Miscellanies*, p. 448; *Misc.*, Riv. 245.]

Two hundred years ago is about as great an antiquity as we can comprehend or often have to deal with. It is nearly as good as two thousand to our imaginations. It carries us back to the days of aborigines and the Pilgrims; beyond the limits of oral testimony, to history which begins already to be enamelled with a gloss of fable, and we do not quite believe what we read; to a strange style of writing and spelling and of expression; to those ancestors whose names we do not know, and to whom we are related only as we are to the race generally. It is the age of our very oldest houses and cultivated trees. Nor is New England very peculiar in this. In England also, a house two hundred years old, especially if it be a wooden one, is pointed out as an interesting relic of the past.

When we read the history of the world, centuries look cheap to us and we find that we had doubted if the hundred years preceding the life of Herodotus seemed as great an antiquity to him as a hundred years does to us. We are inclined to think of all Romans who lived within five hundred years B. C. as *contemporaries* to each other. Yet Time moved at the same deliberate pace then as now. Pliny the Elder, who died in the 79th year of the Christian era, speaking of the paper made of papyrus which was then used, — how carefully it was made, — says, *just as we might say*, as if it were something remarkable: "There are, thus, ancient memorials in the handwriting of Caius and Tiberius Gracchus, almost two hundred years old, which I have seen in the possession of Pomponius Secundus the poet, a very illustrious citizen. As for

the handwriting of Cicero, Augustus, and Virgil, we very often meet with it still." This too, according to Pliny, was the age of the oldest wines. "In one year the quality of all kinds of wine was peculiarly good. In the consulship of Lucius Opimius, when Caius Gracchus, disturbing the people with seditions, was killed, there was that bright and serene weather (*ea caeli temperies fulsit*) which they call a *cooking* (of the grape) by the heat of the sun. This was in the year of the city 634. And some of those wines have lasted to this day, almost two hundred years, now reduced to the appearance of candied honey (*in speciem redacta mellis asperi*)." [1]

How is it that what is actually present and transpiring is commonly perceived by the common sense and understanding only, is bare and bald, without halo or the blue enamel of intervening air? But let it be past or to come, and it is at once idealized. As the man dead is spiritualized, so the fact remembered is idealized. It is a deed ripe and with the bloom on it. It is not simply the understanding now, but the imagination, that takes cognizance of it. The imagination requires a long range. It is the faculty of the poet to see present things as if, in this sense, also past and future, as if distant or universally significant. We do not know poets, heroes, and saints for our contemporaries, but we locate them in some far-off vale, and, the greater and better, the further off we [are] accustomed to consider them. We believe in spirits, we believe in beauty,

[1] Bohn's translation says, "have assumed the consistency of honey with a rough taste !!"

but not now and here. They have their abode in the remote past or in the future.

Dec. 9. Suddenly cold last night. The river and Fair Haven Pond froze over *generally* (I see no opening as I walk) last night, though they were only frozen along the edges yesterday. This is unusually sudden.

How prominent the late or fall flowers are, now withered above the snow, — the goldenrods and asters, Roman wormwood, etc., etc.! These late ones have a sort of life extended into winter, hung with icy jewelry.

I observe at mid-afternoon, the air being very quiet and serene, that peculiarly softened western sky, which perhaps is seen commonly after the first snow has covered the earth. There are many whitish filmy clouds a third of the way to the zenith, generally long and narrow, parallel with the horizon, with indistinct edges, alternating with the blue. And there is just enough *invisible* vapor, perhaps from the snow, to soften the blue, giving it a slight greenish tinge. Thus, methinks, it often happens that as the weather is harder the sky seems softer. It is not a cold, hard, glittering sky, but a warm, soft, filmy one.

The prosaic man sees things baldly, or with the bodily sense; but the poet sees them clad in beauty, with the spiritual sense.

Editors are still pretty generally saying that Brown's was a "crazy scheme," and their one only evidence and proof of it is that it cost him his life. I have no doubt that, if he had gone with five thousand men, liberated a thousand slaves, killed a hundred or two

slaveholders, and had as many more killed on his own side, but not lost his own life, such would have been prepared to call it by another name. Yet he has been far more successful than that. They seem to know nothing about living or dying for a principle.[1]

Abel Brooks told me this anecdote on the 28th *ult.:* —

"I don't know as you remember Langley Brown. Dr. Ripley asked him to bring him a load of the best oak wood he could get. So Langley he picked out a first-rate load of white oak, and teamed it to his door. But when the doctor saw it he said at once that it would n't do, he did n't want any such stuff as that. Langley next picked out a load of yellow oak and carried that to the doctor; but the latter answered, as quickly as before, that that was not what he wanted at all. Then Langley selected a load of red oak, very straight and smooth, and carted that to the doctor's, and the moment he saw it he exclaimed, 'Ah, that 's what I want, Mr. Brown!'"

Dec. 10. Get in my boat, in the snow. The bottom is coated with a glaze.

Dec. 11. At 2 P. M. begins to snow, and snows till night. Still, normal storm, large flakes, warm enough, lodging.

See one sheldrake in Walden. As I stand on the railroad at Walden, at R. W. E.'s crossing, the sound of the snowflakes falling on the dry oak leaves (which

[1] [*Cape Cod, and Miscellanies*, pp. 445, 446; *Misc.*, Riv. 242, 243.]

Vol. XIII

hold on) is exactly like a rustling produced by a steady but slight breeze. But there is no wind. It is a gentle and uninterrupted susurrus.

This light snow, which has been falling for an hour, resting on the horizontal spray of the hemlocks, produces the effect of so many crosses, or checker or lattice work.

Dec. 12. P. M. — To Pine Hill and round Walden.

Seeing a little hole in the side of a dead white birch, about six feet from the ground, I broke it off and found it to be made where a rotten limb had broken off. The hole was about an inch over and was of quite irregular and probably natural outline, and, within, the rotten wood had been removed to the depth of two or three inches, and on one side of this cavity, under the hole, was quite a pile of bird-droppings. The diameter of the birch was little more than two inches, — if at all. Probably it was the roosting-place of a chickadee. The bottom was an irregular surface of the rotten wood, and there was nothing like a nest.

There is a certain Irish woodchopper who, when I come across him at his work in the woods in the winter, never fails to ask me what time it is, as if he were in haste to take his dinner-pail and go home. This is not as it should be. Every man, and the woodchopper among the rest, should love his work as much as the poet does his. All good political arrangements proceed on this supposition. If labor mainly, or to any considerable degree, serves the purpose of a police, to

keep men out of mischief, it indicates a rottenness at the foundation of our community.

The night comes on early these days, and I soon see the pine tree tops distinctly outlined against the dun (or amber) but cold western sky.

The snow having come, we see where is the path of the partridge, — his comings and goings from copse to copse, — and now first, as it were, we have the fox for our nightly neighbor, and countless tiny deer mice. So, perchance, if a still finer substance should fall from heaven (iodine?), something delicate enough to receive the trace of their footsteps, we should see where unsuspected spirits and faery visitors had hourly crossed our steps, had held conventions and transacted their affairs in our midst. No doubt such subtle spirits transact their affairs in our midst, and we may perhaps invent some sufficiently delicate surface to catch the impression of them.

If in the winter there are fewer men in the fields and woods, — as in the *country* generally, — you see the tracks of those who had preceded you, and so are more reminded of them than in summer.

As I talked with the woodchopper who had just cleared the top of Emerson's I got a new view of the mountains over his pile of wood in the foreground. They were very grand in their snowy mantle, which had a slight tinge of purple. But when afterward I looked at them from a higher hill, where there was no wood-pile in the foreground, they affected me less. It is now that these mountains, in color as well as form, most resemble the clouds.

I am inclined to think of late that as much depends on the state of the bowels as of the stars. As are your bowels, so are the stars.

Dec. 13. P. M. — On river to Fair Haven Pond.

My first true winter walk is perhaps that which I take on the river, or where I cannot go in the summer. It is the walk peculiar to winter, and now first I take it. I see that the fox too has already taken the same walk before me, just along the edge of the button-bushes, where not even he can go in the summer. We both turn our steps hither at the same time.

There is now, at 2.30 P. M., the melon-rind arrangement of the clouds. Really parallel columns of fine mackerel sky, reaching quite across the heavens from west to east, with clear intervals of blue sky, and a fine-grained vapor like spun glass extending in the same direction beneath the former. In half an hour all this mackerel sky is gone.

What an ever-changing scene is the sky with its drifting cirrhus and stratus! The spectators are not requested to take a recess of fifteen minutes while the scene changes, but, walking commonly with our faces to the earth, our thoughts revert to other objects, and as often as we look up the scene has changed. Now, I see, it is a column of white vapor reaching quite across the sky, from west to east, with locks of fine hair, or tow that is carded, combed out on each side, — surprising touches here and there, which show a peculiar state of the atmosphere. No doubt the best weather-signs are in these forms which the vapor takes. When

I next look up, the locks of hair are perfect fir trees with their recurved branches. (These trees extend at right angles from the side of the main column.) This appearance is changed all over the sky in one minute. Again it is pieces of asbestos, or the vapor takes the curved form of the surf or breakers, and again of flames.

But how long can a man be in a mood to watch the heavens? That melon-rind arrangement, so very common, is perhaps a confirmation of Wise the balloonist's statement that at a certain height there is a current of air moving from west to east. Hence we so commonly see the clouds arranged in parallel columns in that direction.

What a spectacle the subtle vapors that have their habitation in the sky present these winter days! You have not only ever-varying forms of a given type of cloud, but various types at different heights or hours. It is a scene, for variety, for beauty and grandeur, out of all proportion to the attention it gets. Who watched the forms of the clouds over this part of the earth a thousand years ago? Who watches them to-day?

Now that the river is frozen we have a sky under our feet also. Going over black ice three or four inches thick, only reassured by seeing the thickness at the cracks, I see it richly marked internally with large whitish figures suggesting rosettes of ostrich-feathers or coral. These at first appear to be a dust on the surface, but, looking closely, are found to be at various angles with it internally, in the grain. The work of crystallization. Often you see as it were a sheaf of feathered arrows

five or six feet long, very delicate but perfectly straight, their planes making a very slight angle with the surface of the ice, and yet no seam is to be detected. The black floor is by these divided into polygonal segments, for the most part geometrically straight-sided. Their position merely suggests a cleavage which has no existence. Perhaps it is the angle of excidence answering to the angle of incidence at which the sun's light and heat strikes the ice at different hours!!

I walk thus along the riverside, perhaps between the button-bushes and the meadow, where the bleached and withered grass — the *Panicum virgatum* and blue-joint and wool-grass — rustle amid the osiers which have saved them from the scythe.

When the snow is only thus deep, the yellowish straw-color of the sedge in the meadows rising above the snow is now first appreciated, seen between the ice and the snow-clad land.

Near the mouth of Well Meadow Brook, I see a musquash under the black ice of the pond. It is ten or twelve rods from a cabin, which must be the nearest open place, and it moves off slowly, pushing against the ice with its feet, toward the middle of the pond, and as I follow, it at length sinks to the bottom and is lost. Did it go down for concealment or for air? Here was a musquash at least a dozen rods from any hole, and it did not swim toward its cabin.

I see, in the Pleasant Meadow field near the pond, some little masses of snow, such as I noticed yesterday in the open land by the railroad causeway at the Cut. I could not account for them then, for I did not

go to them, but thought they might be the remainders of drifts which had been blown away, leaving little perpendicular masses six inches or a foot higher than the surrounding snow in the midst of the fields. Now I detect the cause. These (which I see to-day) are the remains of snowballs which the wind of yesterday rolled up in the moist snow. The morning was mild, and the snow accordingly soft and moist yet light, but in the middle of the day a strong northwest wind arose, and before night it became quite hard to bear.

These masses which I examined in the Pleasant Meadow field were generally six or eight inches high — though they must have wasted and settled considerably — and a little longer than high, presenting a more or less fluted appearance externally. They were hollow cylinders about two inches in diameter within, like muffs. Here were a dozen within two rods square, and I saw them in three or four localities miles apart, in almost any place exposed to the sweep of the northwest wind. There was plainly to be seen the furrow in the snow produced when they were rolled up, in the form of a very narrow pyramid, commencing perhaps two inches wide, and in the course of ten feet (sometimes of four or five only) becoming six or eight inches wide, when the mass was too heavy to be moved further. The snow had been thus rolled up even, like a carpet. This occurred on perfectly level ground and also where the ground rose gently to the southeast. The ground was not laid bare. That wind must have rolled up masses thus till they were a foot in diameter. It is certain, then, that a sudden strong wind when the snow

is moist but light (it had fallen the afternoon previous) will catch and roll it up as a boy rolls up his ball. These white balls are seen far off over the fields.

When I reach the causeway at the Cut, returning, the sun has just set, — a perfect winter sunset, so fair and pure, with its golden and purple isles. I think the summer rarely equals it. There are real damask-colored isles or continents north of the sun's place, and further off northeast they pass into bluish purple. Hayden's house, over which I see them, seems the abode of the blessed. The east horizon also is purple. But that part of the parallel cloud-columns overhead is now invisible. At length the purple travels westward, as the sun sinks lower below the horizon, the clouds overhead are brought out, and so the purple glow glides down the western sky.

Virgil's account of winter occupations in the First Georgic, line 291, applies well enough to New England: —

"Some keep at work by the late light of the winter
  Fire, and point torches with a sharp iron.
In the meanwhile the wife, relieving her long labor with her

Singing, thickens the webs with the shrill slay;
Or boils down the liquor of sweet must with fire,
And skims off the foam of the boiling kettle with leaves.
  . . . .
   . . Winter is an idle time to the husbandman.
In cold weather they commonly enjoy what they have laid up,
And jovial they give themselves up to mutual feasting:
Genial winter invites this and relaxes their cares;
As when now the laden keel has touched its port,
And the joyful sailors have placed a crown on the stern.
However, now is the time to gather acorns,
And laurel berries, and the olive, and bloody (colored) myrtle berries;
Now to set snares for cranes,[1] and deer,
And chase the long-eared hares;
  . . . .
When the snow lies deep, and the rivers are full of drifting ice."

I saw yesterday where fox-hunters with a sleigh and hounds had improved the first shallow snow to track their game. They thread the woods by old and grown-up and forgotten paths, where no others would think to drive.

Dec. 14. At 2 P. M. begins to snow again. I walk to Walden.

Snow-storms might be classified. This is a fine, dry snow, drifting nearly horizontally from the north, so that it is quite blinding to face, almost as much so as sand. It is cold also. It is drifting but not accumulating fast. I can see the woods about a quarter of a mile distant through it. That of the 11th was a still storm, of large flakes falling gently in the quiet air, like so many white feathers descending in different directions when seen against a wood-side, — the regular snow-storm such as is painted. A myriad falling flakes weaving a coarse

[1] Say partridges.

garment by which the eye is amused. The snow was a little moist and the weather rather mild. Also I remember the perfectly crystalline or *star* snows, when each flake is a perfect six(?)-rayed wheel. This must be the *chef-d'œuvre* of the Genius of the storm. Also there is the pellet or shot snow, which consists of little dry spherical pellets the size of robin-shot. This, I think, belongs to cold weather. Probably never have much of it. Also there is sleet, which is half snow, half rain.

The *Juncus tenuis*, with its conspicuous acheniums, is very noticeable now, rising above the snow in the wood-paths, commonly aslant.

Dec. 15. The first kind of snow-storm, or that of yesterday, which ceased in the night after some three inches had fallen, was that kind that makes handsome drifts behind the walls. There are no drifts equal to these behind loosely built stone walls, the wind passing between the stones. Slight as this snow was, these drifts now extend back four or five feet and as high as the wall, on the north side of the Corner Bridge road. The snow is scooped out in the form of easy-chairs, or of shells or *plinths*, if that is the name for them.

The backs of the chairs often inclining to fall off.

A man killed a wild goose a day or two since in Spencer Brook, near Legross's.

I hear from J. [?] Moore that one man in Bedford has got eighteen minks the last fall.[1]

Philosophy is a Greek word by good rights, and it stands almost for a Greek thing. Yet some rumor of it has reached the commonest mind. M. Miles, who came to collect his wood bill to-day, said, when I objected to the small size of his wood, that it was necessary to split wood fine in order to cure it well, that he had found that wood that was more than four inches in diameter would not dry, and moreover a good deal depended on the manner in which it was corded up in the woods. He piled his high and tightly. If this were not well done the stakes would spread and the wood lie loosely, and so the rain and snow find their way into it. And he added, "I have handled a good deal of wood, and I think that I understand the *philosophy* of it."

Dec. 16. A. M. — To Cambridge, where I read in Gerard's Herbal.[2] His admirable though quaint descriptions are, to my mind, greatly superior to the modern more scientific ones. He describes not according to rule but to his natural delight in the plants. He brings them vividly before you, as one who has seen and delighted in them. It is almost as good as to see the plants themselves. It suggests that we cannot too often get rid of the barren assumption that is

[1] Farmer says he probably bought most of them.
[2] *Vide* extracts from preface made in October, 1859.

in our science. His leaves are leaves; his flowers, flowers; his fruit, fruit. They are green and colored and fragrant. It is a man's knowledge added to a child's delight. Modern botanical descriptions approach ever nearer to the dryness of an algebraic formula, as if $x + y$ were $=$ to a love-letter. It is the keen joy and discrimination of the child who has just seen a flower for the first time and comes running in with it to its friends. How much better to describe your object in fresh English words rather than in these conventional Latinisms! He has really seen, and smelt, and tasted, and reports his sensations.

Bought a book at Little & Brown's, paying a ninepence more on a volume than it was offered me for elsewhere. The customer thus pays for the more elegant style of the store.

Dec. 17. P. M. — To Walden.

The snow being some three or four inches deep, I see rising above it, *generally*, at my old bean-field, only my little white pines set last spring in the midst of an immense field of *Solidago nemoralis*, with a little sweet-fern (*i. e.* a large patch of it on the north side). What a change there will be in a few years, this little forest of goldenrod giving place to a forest of pines!

By the side of the Pout's Nest, I see on the pure white snow what looks like dust for half a dozen inches under a twig. Looking closely, I find that the twig is hardhack and the dust its slender, light-brown, chaffy-

Vol. XIII

I observe, then, eaten by birds to-day, the seed of hardhack and meadow-sweet, sumach, and probably lespedeza, and even seed-box.

Under the hill, on the southeast side of R. W. E.'s lot, where the hemlock stands, I see many tracks of squirrels. The dark, thick green of the hemlock (amid the pines) seems to attract them as a covert. The snow under the hemlock is strewn with the scales of its cones, which they (and *perhaps* birds?) have stripped off, and some of its little winged seeds. It is pleasant to see the tracks of these squirrels (I am not sure whether they are red or gray or both, for I see none) leading straight from the base of one tree to that of another, thus leaving untrodden triangles, squares, and polygons of every form, bounded by much trodden highways. One, two, three, and the track is lost on the upright bole of a pine, — as if they had played at base-running from goal to goal, while pine cones were thrown at them on the way. The tracks of two or three suggest a multitude. You come thus on the tracks of these frisky and volatile (semivolitant) creatures in the midst of perfect stillness and solitude, as you might stand in a hall half an hour after the dancers had departed.

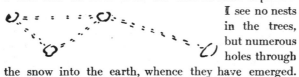

I see no nests in the trees, but numerous holes through the snow into the earth, whence they have emerged. They have loitered but little on the snow, spending their time chiefly on the trees, their castles, when abroad. The snow is strewn not only with hemlock

looking seed, which falls still in copious showers, dusting the snow, when I jar it; and here are the tracks of a sparrow which has jarred the twig and picked the minute seeds a long time, making quite a hole in the snow. The seeds are so fine that it must have got more snow than seed at each peck. But they probably look large to its microscopic eyes. I see, when I jar it, that a meadow-sweet close by has quite similar, but larger, seeds. This the reason, then, that these plants rise so high above the snow and retain their seed, dispersing it on the least jar over each successive layer of snow beneath them; or it is carried to a distance by the wind. What abundance and what variety in the diet of these small granivorous birds, while I find only a few nuts still! These stiff weeds which no snow can break down hold their provender. What the cereals are to men, these are to the sparrows. The only threshing they require is that the birds fly against their spikes or stalks. A little further I see the seed-box (?) (*Ludwigia*) full of still smaller yellowish seeds. And on the ridge north is the track of a partridge amid the shrubs. It has hopped up to the low clusters of smooth sumach berries, sprinkled the snow with them, and eaten all but a few. Also, here only, or where it has evidently jarred them down — whether intentionally or not, I am not sure — are the large oval seeds of the stiff-stalked lespedeza, which suspect it ate, with the sumach berries. There is much solid food in them. When the snow is deep the birds could easily pick the latter out of the heads as they stand on the snow.

scales, but, under other trees, with the large white pine scales for rods together where there is no track the wind having scattered them as they fell, and also the shells of hickory-nuts. It reminds me of the platform before a grocery where nuts are sold. You see many places where they have probed the snow for these white pine cones, evidently those which they cut off green and which accordingly have not opened so as to drop the seeds. This was perhaps the design in cutting them off so early, — thus to preserve them under the snow (not dispersed). Do they find them by the scent? At any rate they will dig down through the snow and come right upon a pine cone or a hickory-nut or an acorn, which you and I cannot do.

Two or three acres of Walden, off the bar, not yet frozen. Saw in [it] a good-sized black duck, which did not dive while I looked. I suspect it must have been a *Fuligula*, though I saw no white.

Dec. 18. Rains.

P. M. — To Assabet opposite Tarbell's, *via* Abel Hosmer's.

It rains but little this afternoon, though there is no sign of fair weather. Only the mist appears thinner here and there from time to time. It is a lichen day. The pitch pines on the south of the road at the Colburn farm are very inspiriting to behold. Their green is as much enlivened and freshened as that of the lichens. It suggests a sort of sunlight on them, though not even a patch of clear sky is seen to-day. As dry and olive or slate-colored lichens are of a fresh and living green so the already green pine-needles have acquired a far livelier tint, as if they enjoyed this moisture as much as the lichens do. They seem to be lit up more than when the sun falls on them. Their trunks, and those of trees generally, being wet, are very black, and the bright lichens on them are so much the more remarkable.

I see three shrikes in different places to-day, — two on the top of apple trees, sitting still in the storm, on the lookout. They fly low to another tree when disturbed, much like a bluebird, and jerk their tails once or twice when they alight.

Apples are thawed now and are very good. Their juice is the best kind of bottled cider that I know. They are all good in this state, and your jaws are the cider-press.[1]

The thick, low cloud or mist makes novel prospects for us. In the southwest horizon I see a darker mass of it stretched along, seen against itself. The oak woods a quarter of a mile off appear more uniformly red than ever. They are not only redder for being wet, but, through the obscurity of the mist, one leaf runs into another and the whole mass makes one impression. The withered oak leaves, being thoroughly saturated with moisture, are of a livelier color. Also some of the most withered white oak leaves with roundish black spots like small lichens are quite interesting now.

Dec. 19. Yarrow [2] too is full of seed now, and the common johnswort has some seed in it still.

¹ [*Excursions*, pp. 319, 320; Riv. 393.]   ² Tansy?

Farmer has lately been riding about in the neighboring towns west and northwest, as far as Townsend, buying up their furs, — mink, musquash, and fox. Says that Stow is as good a town for mink as any, but none of them have more musquash than Concord. He, however, saw but one mink-track in all his rides, and thinks that they are scarce this year.

When a man is young and his constitution and body have not acquired firmness, *i. e.*, before he has arrived at middle age, he is not an assured inhabitant of the earth, and his compensation is that he is not quite earthy, there is something peculiarly tender and divine about him. His sentiments and his weakness, nay, his very sickness and the greater uncertainty of his fate, seem to ally him to a noble race of beings, to whom he in part belongs, or with whom he is in communication. The young man is a demigod; the grown man, alas! is commonly a mere mortal. He is but half here, he knows not the men of this world, the powers that be. They know him not. Prompted by the reminiscence of that other sphere from which he so lately arrived, his actions are unintelligible to his seniors. He bathes in light. He is interesting as a stranger from another sphere. He really thinks and talks about a larger sphere of existence than this world. It takes him forty years to accommodate himself to the carapax of this world. This is the age of poetry. Afterward he may be the president of a bank, and go the way of all flesh. But a man of settled views, whose thoughts are few and hardened like his bones, is truly mortal, and his only resource is to say his prayers.

Vol. XIII

Dec. 20. A. M. — To T. Wheeler wood-lot.

Snows very fast, large flakes, a very lodging snow, quite moist; turns to rain in afternoon. If we leave the sleigh for a moment, it whitens the seat, which must be turned over. We are soon thickly covered, and it lodges on the twigs of the trees and bushes, — there being but little wind, — giving them a very white and soft, spiritual look. Gives them a still, soft, and light look. When the flakes fall thus large and fast and are so moist and melting, we think it will not last long, and this turned to rain in a few hours, after three or four inches had fallen.

To omit the first mere whitening, —

There was the snow of the 4th December.

11th was a lodging snow, it being mild and still, like to-day (only it was not so moist). Was succeeded next day noon by a strong and cold northwest wind.

14th, a fine, dry, cold, driving and drifting storm.

20th (to-day's), a very lodging, moist, and large-flaked snow, turning to rain. To be classed with the 11th in the main. This wets the woodchopper about as much as rain.

Dec. 21. A. M. — A fine winter day and rather mild. Ride to T. Wheeler's lot. See a red squirrel out in two places. Do they not come out chiefly in the forenoon? Also a large flock of snow buntings, fair and pleasant as it is. Their whiteness, like the snow, is their most remarkable peculiarity.

The snow of yesterday having turned to rain in the afternoon, the snow is no longer (now that it is frozen)

---

a uniformly level white, as when it had just fallen, but on all declivities you see it, even from a great distance, strongly marked with countless furrows or channels. These are about three inches deep, more or less parallel where the rain ran down. On hillsides these reach from top to bottom and give them a peculiar combed appearance. Hillsides around a hollow are thus very regularly marked by lines converging toward the centre at the bottom. In level fields the snow is not thus furrowed, but dimpled with a myriad little hollows where the water settled, and perhaps answering slightly to the inequalities of the ground. In level woods I do not see this regular dimpling — the rain being probably conducted down the trunks — nor the furrows on hillsides; the rain has been differently distributed by the trees.[1]

This makes a different impression from the fresh and uniformly level white surface of recently fallen snow. It is now, as it were, wrinkled with age. The incipient slosh of yesterday is now frozen, and makes good sleighing and a foundation for more.

Dec. 22. Another fine winter day.
P. M. — To Flint's Pond.

C. is inclined to walk in the road, it being better walking there, and says: "You don't wish to see anything but the sky to-day and breathe this air. You could walk in the city to-day, just as well as in the country. You only wish to be out." This was because I inclined to walk in the woods or by the river.

¹ *Vide* plate [*sic*] [three] pages forward.

As we passed under the elm beyond George Heywood's, I looked up and saw a fiery hangbird's nest dangling over the road. What a reminiscence of summer, a fiery hangbird's nest dangling from an elm over the road when perhaps the thermometer is down to −20 (?), and the traveller goes beating his arms beneath it! It is hard to recall the strain of that bird then.

We pause and gaze into the Mill Brook on the Turnpike bridge. C. says that in Persia they call the ripple-marks on sandy bottoms "chains" or "chain-work." I see a good deal of cress there, on the bottom, for a rod or two, the only green thing to be seen. No more slimy than it usually is beneath the water in summer. Is not this the plant which most, or most conspicuously, preserves its greenness in the winter? Is it not now most completely in its summer state of any plant? So far as the water and the mud and the cress go, it is a summer scene. It is green as ever, and waving in the stream as in summer.

How nicely is Nature adjusted! The least disturbance of her equilibrium is betrayed and corrects itself. As I looked down on the surface of the brook, I was surprised to see a leaf floating, as I thought, up the stream, but I was mistaken. The motion of a particle of dust on the surface of any brook far inland shows which way the earth declines toward the sea, which way lies the constantly descending route, and the only one.

I see in the chestnut woods near Flint's Pond where squirrels have collected the small chestnut burs left on the trees and opened them, generally at the base of

the trunks on the snow. These are, I think, all small and imperfect burs, which do not so much as open in the fall and are rejected then, but, hanging on the tree, they have this use at least, as the squirrels' winter food.

Three men are fishing on Flint's Pond, where the ice is seven or eight inches thick. I look back to the wharf rock shore and see that rush (cladium I have called it), the warmest object in the landscape, — a narrow line of warm yellow rushes — for they reflect the western light, — along the edge of the somewhat snowy pond and next the snow-clad and wooded shore. This rush, which is comparatively inconspicuous in the summer, becomes thus in the winter afternoons a conspicuous and interesting object, lit up by the westering sun.

The fisherman stands erect and still on the ice, awaiting our approach, as usual forward to say that he has had no luck. He has been here since early morning, and for some reason or other the fishes won't bite. You won't catch him here again in a hurry. They all tell the same story. The amount of it is he has had "fisherman's luck," and if you walk that way you may find him at his old post to-morrow. It is hard, to be sure, — four little fishes to be divided between three men, and two and a half miles to walk; and you have only got a more ravenous appetite for the supper which you have not earned. However, the pond floor is not a bad place to spend a winter day.

On what I will call Sassafras Island, in this pond, I notice the largest and handsomest high blueberry bush that I ever saw, about ten feet high. It divides

at the ground into four stems, all very large and the largest three inches in diameter (one way) at three feet high, and at the ground, where they *seem* to form one trunk (at least *grown* together), nine inches in diameter. These stems rise upward, spreading a little in their usual somewhat zigzag manner, and are very handsomely clothed with large gray and yellow lichens with intervals of the (*smoothish?* and) finely divided bark. The bark is quite reddish near the ground. The top, which is spreading and somewhat flattish or corymbose, consists of a great many fine twigs, which give it a thick and dark appearance against the sky compared with the more open portion beneath. It was perfectly sound and vigorous.

In a (apparently kingbird's?) nest on this island I saw three cherry-stones, as if it had carried home this fruit to its young. It was, outside, of gnaphalium and saddled on a low limb. Could it have been a cherry-bird?

The cladium (?) retains its seeds over the ice, little conical, sharp-pointed, flat-based, dark-brown, shining seeds. I notice some seeds left on a large dock, but see none of parsnips or other umbelliferous plants.

The furrows in the snow on the hillsides look somewhat like this: —

Dec. 23. The third fine, clear, bright, and rather mild winter day.

P. M. — To Ball's Hill across meadow.

The gardener at Sleepy Hollow says that they caught many small pouts and some pickerel that weighed half a pound (!) in the little pond lately dug there.[1] I think this pond, say a third of an acre, was commenced about three years ago and completed last summer. It has no inlet and a very slight outlet, a shallow ditch that previously existed in the meadow, but in digging they have laid open two or three very deep spring-holes, and the pickerel were found in them. These fishes, no doubt, came up the shallow ditch. This proves that if you dig a pond in a meadow and connect it by the smallest rill or ditch with other water in which fishes live, however far off, the pond will be at once stocked with fishes. They are always ready to extend their territory.

The Great Meadows are more than half covered with ice, and now I see that there was a very slight fall of snow last night. It is only betrayed here, having covered the ice about an eighth of an inch thick, except where there are cracks running quite across the meadow, where the water has oozed a foot or two each way and dissolved the snow, making conspicuous dark lines.

In this slight snow I am surprised to see countless tracks of small birds, which have run over it in every direction from one end to the other of this great meadow since morning. By the length of the hind toe I know them to be snow buntings. Indeed, soon after I see them running still on one side of the meadow.

[1] *Vide* Oct. 10, 1860.

I was puzzled to tell what they got by running there. Yet I [saw them] stopping repeatedly and picking up something. Of course I thought of those caterpillars which are washed out by a rain and freshet at this season, but I could not find one of them. It rained on the 18th and again the 20th, and over a good part of the meadow the top of the stubble left by the scythe rises a little above the ice, *i. e.* an inch or two, not enough to disturb a skater. The birds have run here chiefly, visiting each little collection or tuft of stubble, and found their food chiefly in and about this thin stubble. I examined such places a long time and very carefully, but I could not find there the seed of any plant whatever. It was merely the stubble of sedge, with never any head left, and a few cranberry leaves projecting. All that I could find was pretty often (in some places very often) a little black, or else a brown, spider (sometimes quite a large one) motionless on the snow or ice; and therefore I am constrained to think that they eat them, for I saw them running and picking in exactly such places a little way from me, and here were their tracks all around. Yet they are called graminivorous [*sic*]. Wilson says that he has seen them feeding on the seeds of aquatic plants on the Seneca River, clinging to their heads. I think he means wool-grass. Yet its seeds are too minute and involved in the wool. Though there was wool-grass hereabouts, the birds did not go near it. To be sure, it has but little seed now. If they are so common at the extreme north, where there is so little vegetation but perhaps a great many spiders, is it not likely that they feed on these insects?

It is interesting to see how busy this flock is, exploring this great meadow to-day. If it were not for this slight snow, revealing their tracks but hardly at all concealing the stubble, I should not suspect it, though I might see them at their work. Now I see them running briskly over the ice, most commonly near the shore, where there is most stubble (though very little); and they explore the ground so fast that they are continually changing their ground, and if I do not keep my eye on them I lose the direction. Then here they come, with a stiff *rip* of their wings as they suddenly wheel, and those peculiar rippling notes, flying low quite across the meadow, half a mile even, to explore the other side, though that too is already tracked by them. Not the fisher nor skater range the meadow a thousandth part so much in a week as these birds in a day. They hardly notice me as they come on. Indeed, the flock, flying about as high as my head, divides, and half passes on each side of me. Thus they sport over these broad meadows of ice this pleasant winter day. The spiders lie torpid and plain to see on the snow, and if it is they that they are after they never know what kills them.

I have loitered so long on the meadow that before I get to Ball's Hill those patches of bare ice (where water has oozed out and frozen) already reflect a green light which advertises me of the lateness of the hour. You may walk eastward in the winter afternoon till the ice begins to look green, half to three quarters of an hour before sunset, the sun having sunk behind you to the proper angle. Then it is time to turn your steps home-

Vol. XIII

ward. Soon after,[1] too, the ice began to boom, or fire its evening gun, another warning that the end of the day was at hand, and a little after the snow reflected a distinct rosy light, the sun having reached the grosser atmosphere of the earth. These signs successively prompt us once more to retrace our steps. Even the fisherman, who perhaps has not observed any sign but that the sun is ready to sink beneath the horizon, is winding up his lines and starting for home; or perhaps he leaves them to freeze in.

In a clear but pleasant winter day, I walk away till the ice begins to look green and I hear it boom, or perhaps till the snow reflects a rosy light.

I ascended Ball's Hill to see the sun set. How red its light at this hour! I covered its orb with my hand, and let its rays light up the fine woollen fibres of my glove. They were a dazzling rose-color. It takes the gross atmosphere of earth to make this redness.

You notice the long and slender light-brown or grayish downy racemes of the clethra seeds about the edges of ponds and pond-holes. The pods contain many very minute chaffy-looking seeds.

You find in the cluster of the sweet-fern fruit now one or two rather large flattish conical hard-shelled seeds with a small meat.

The pinweed — the larger (say *thymifolia*) — pods open, showing their three pretty leather-brown inner divisions open like a little calyx, a third or half containing still the little hemispherical or else triangular reddish-brown seeds. They are hard and abundant. That

[1] About same time, as noticed two or three days.

large juncus (*paradoxus*-like?) of the river meadows — long white-tailed seed — just rising above the ice is full of seed now, glossy, pale-brown, white-tailed, chaffy to look at. The wool-grass wool is at least half gone, and its minute almost white [?] seed or achenium in it; but a *little* is left, not more than the thirtieth of an inch long. It looks too minute and involved in the wool for a snow bunting to eat. The above plants are all now more or less recurved, bent by the cold and the blasts of autumn.

The now bare or empty heads of the liatris look somewhat like dusky daisies surmounted by a little button instead of a disk. The last, a stiff, round, parchment-like skin, the base on which its flowerets stood, is pierced by many little round holes just like the end of a thimble, where the cavities are worn through, and it is convex like that. It readily scales off and you can look through it.

I noticed on the 18th that the plumes of the pine which had been covered with snow and glaze and were *then* thawed and wet with the mist and rain were very much contracted or narrowed, —

not   — and this gave a peculiar and more
               open character to the tree.

Dec. 24. P. M. — To Flint's Pond.

A strong and very cold northwest wind. I think that

the cold winds are oftenest not northwest, but northwest by west. There is, in all, an acre or two in Walden not yet frozen, though half of it has been frozen more than a week.

I measure the blueberry bush on Flint's Pond Island. The five stems are united at the ground, so as to make one round and solid trunk thirty-one inches in circumference, but probably they have grown together there, for they become separate at about six inches above. They may have sprung from different seeds of one berry. At three feet from the ground they measure eleven inches, eleven, eleven and a half, eight, and six and a half, or, on an average, nine and a half. I climbed up and found a comfortable seat with my feet four feet above the ground, and there was room for three or four more there, but unfortunately this was not the season for berries.

There were several other clumps of large ones there. One clump close by the former contained twenty-three stems within a diameter of three feet, and their average diameter at three feet from the ground was about two inches. These had not been cut, because they stood on this small island which has little wood beside, and therefore had grown the larger. The two prevailing lichens on them were *Parmelia caperata* and *saxatilis*, extending quite around their trunks; also a little of a parmelia more glaucous than the last one, and a little green usnea and a little ramalina.[1]

This island appears to be a mere stony ridge three or four feet high, with a very low wet shore on each side,

[1] *Vide* specimens in drawer.

even as if the water and ice had shoved it up, as at the other end of the pond.

I saw the tracks of a partridge more than half an inch deep in the ice, extending from this island to the shore, she having walked there in the slosh. They were quite perfect and reminded me of bird-tracks in stone. She may have gone there to bud on these blueberry trees. I saw where she spent the night at the bottom of that largest clump, in the snow.

This blueberry grove must be well known to the partridges; no doubt they distinguish their tops from afar.

Perhaps yet larger ones were seen here before we came to cut off the trees. Judging from those whose rings I have counted, the largest of those stems must be about sixty years old. The stems rise up in a winding and zigzag manner, one sometimes resting in the forks of its neighbor. There were many more clumps of large ones there.

Dec. 25. The last our coldest night, as yet. No doubt Walden froze over last night entirely.

P. M. — To Carlisle Bridge on river and meadow.

I now notice a great many flat, annular, glow-worm-like worms frozen in the ice of the Great Meadow, which were evidently washed out of the meadow-grass lately; but they are almost all within the ice, inaccessible to birds; are only in certain parts of the meadow, especially about that island in it, where it is shallow. It is as if they were created only to be frozen, for this must be their annual fate. I see one which seems to

be a true glow-worm.[1] The transparent ice is specked black with them, as if they were cranberry leaves in it. You can hardly get one out now without breaking it, they are so brittle. The snow buntings are about, as usual, but I do not think that they were after *these* insects the other day.

Standing by the side of the river at Eleazer Davis's Hill, — prepared to pace across it, — I hear a sharp fine *screep* from some bird, which at length I detect amid the button-bushes and willows. The *screep* was a note of recognition meant for me. I saw that it was a novel bird to me. Watching it a long time, with my glass and without it, I at length made out these marks: It was slate-colored above and dirty-white beneath, with a broad and very conspicuous bright-orange crown, which in some lights was *red*-orange, along the middle of the head; this was bounded on each side by a black segment, beneath which was a yellow or whitish line. There was also some yellow and a black spot on the middle of the closed wings, and yellow within the tail-feathers. The ends of the wings and the tail above were dusky, and the tail forked.

It was so very active that I could not get a steady view of it. It kept drifting about behind the stems of the button-bushes, etc., half the time on the ice, and again on the lower twigs, busily looking for its prey, turning its body this way and that with great restlessness, appearing to hide from me behind the stems of the button-bush and the withered coarse grass. When I

[1] No. I compare it with description Sept. 16, 1857, and find it is not the glow-worm, though somewhat like it.

came nearest it would utter its peculiar *screep*, or *screep screep*, or even *screep screep screep*. Yet it was unwilling to leave the spot, and when I cornered it, it hopped back within ten feet of me. However, I could see its brilliant crown, even between the twigs of the button-bush and through the withered grass, when I could detect no other part.

It was evidently the golden-crested wren, which I have not made out before. This little creature was contentedly seeking its food here alone this cold winter day on the shore of our frozen river. If it does not visit us often it is strange that it should choose such a season.

I see that the strong wind of yesterday has blown off quite a number of white pine cones, which lie on the ice opposite E. Davis's Hill.

As I crossed Flint's about 4 P. M. yesterday on my way home, when it was bitter cold, the ice cracked with an exceedingly brittle shiver, as if all the pond's crockery had gone to smash, suggesting a high degree of tension, even of dryness, — such as you hear only in very cold weather, — right under my feet, as if I had helped to crack it. It is the report of the artillery which the frost foe has discharged at me. As you are swiftly pacing homeward, taking your way across the pond, with your mittened hands in your pocket and your cap drawn down over your ears, the pond loves to give a rousing crack right under your feet, and you hear the whole pond titter at your surprise. It is bracing its nerves against the unheard-of cold that is at hand, and it snaps some of them. You hear this best where there is considerable depth and breadth of water, — on ponds rather than on the river and meadow. The cold strains it up so tight that some of the strings snap. On hearing that sound you redouble your haste toward home, where vestal virgins keep alive a little fire still. In the same manner the very surface of the earth cracks in frosty weather.

To-night, when I get just below Davis's Hill the ice displays its green flag and fires its evening gun as a warning to all walkers to return home.

Consider how the pickerel-fisher lives. G., whom I saw at Flint's Pond on the 22d, had been there all day, eaten all the dinner he had brought, and caught only four little fish, hardly enough for his supper, if he should cook them. His companion swore that he would not go a-fishing again for ten years. But G. said nothing of that sort. The next day I found him five miles from here on the other side of the town, with his lines set in the bay of the river off Ball's Hill. There, too, he had been tramping about from hole to hole, — this time alone, — and he had done a trifle better than the day before, for he had caught three little fish and one great one. But instead of giving up here, he concluded to leave his lines in overnight, — since his bait would die if he took them off, — and return the next morning. The next was a bitter cold day, but I hear that Goodwin had some fish to dispose of. Probably not more than a dollar's worth, however.

You may think that you need take no care to preserve your woodland, but every tree comes either from the stump of another tree or from a seed. With the present management, will there always be a fresh stump,

or a nut in the soil, think you? Will not the nobler kinds of trees, which bear comparatively few seeds, grow more and more scarce? What is become of our chestnut wood? There are but few stumps for sprouts to spring from, and, as for the chestnuts, there are not enough for the squirrels, and nobody is planting them.

The sweet-gale rises above the ice of the meadow on each side of the river, with its brown clusters of little aments (some of its seeds begun to fall) amid its very dark colored twigs. There is an abundance of bright-yellow resin between its seeds, and the aments, being crushed between the fingers, yield an odoriferous, perhaps terebinthine (piney) fragrance and stain the fingers yellow. It is worth the while, at this season especially, when most plants are inexpressive, to meet with one so pronounced.

I see the now withered spikes of the chelone here and there, in which (when diseased?) a few of its flat winged seeds are still found.

How different are men and women, e. g. in respect to the adornment of their heads! Do you ever see an old or jammed bonnet on the head of a woman at a public meeting? But look at any assembly of men with their hats on; how large a proportion of the hats will be old, weather-beaten, and indented, but I think so much the more picturesque and interesting! One farmer rides by my door in a hat which it does me good to see, there is so much character in it, — so much independence to begin with, and then affection for his old friends, etc., etc. I should not wonder if there were lichens on it. Think of painting a hero in a bran-new

hat! The chief recommendation of the Kossuth hat is that it looks old to start with, and almost as good as new to end with. Indeed, it is generally conceded that a man does not look the worse for a somewhat dilapidated hat. But go to a lyceum and look at the bonnets and various other headgear of the women and girls, — who, by the way, keep their hats on, it being too dangerous and expensive to take them off!! Why, every one looks as fragile as a butterfly's wings, having just come out of a bandbox, — as it will go into a bandbox again when the lyceum is over. Men wear their hats for use; women theirs for ornament. I have seen the greatest philosopher in the town with what the traders would call "a shocking bad hat" on, but the woman whose bonnet does not come up to the mark is at best a "bluestocking." The man is not particularly proud of his beaver and musquash, but the woman flaunts her ostrich and sable in your face.

Ladies are in haste to dress *as if* it were cold or *as if* it were warm, — though it may not yet be so, — merely to display a new dress.

Again, what an ado women make about trifles! Here is one tells me that she cannot possibly wear india-rubber boots in sloshy weather, because they have heels. Men have been wearing boots with heels from time immemorial; little boys soon learn the art, and are eager to try the experiment. The woodchoppers and teamsters, and the merchants and lawyers, go and come quietly the livelong day, and though they may meet with many accidents, I do not remember any that originated in the heels of their boots. But not so

with women; they bolt at once, recklessly as runaway horses, the moment they get the boots on, before they have learned the wonderful art of wearing them. My informant tells me of a friend who has got a white swelling from coming down-stairs imprudently in boots, and of another seriously injured on the meeting-house steps, — for when you deal with steps, then comes the rub, — and of a third who involuntarily dashed down the front stairs, knocked a hat-tree through the side-lights, and broke I do not know how many ribs. Indeed, that quarter-inch obstruction about the heels seems to be an insuperable one to the women.

Dec. 26. P. M. — Skate to Lee's Bridge and there measure back, by pacing, the breadth of the river. After being uniformly overcast all the forenoon, still and moderate weather, it begins to snow very gradually, at first imperceptibly, this afternoon, — at first I thought I imagined it, — and at length begins to snow in earnest about 6 p. m., but lasts only a few minutes.

I see a brute with a gun in his hand, standing motionless over a musquash-house which he has destroyed. I find that he has visited every one in the neighborhood of Fair Haven Pond, above and below, and broken them all down, laying open the interior to the water, and then stood watchful, close by, for the poor creature to show its head there for a breath of air. There lies the red carcass of one whose pelt he has taken on the spot, flat on the bloody ice. And for his afternoon's cruelty that fellow will be rewarded with a ninepence, perchance. When I consider what are the opportunities of the civilized man for getting ninepences and getting light, this seems to me more savage than savages are. Depend on it that whoever thus treats the musquash's house, his refuge when the water is frozen thick, he and his family will not come to a good end. So many of these houses being broken open, — twenty or thirty I see, — I look into the open hole, and find in it, in almost every instance, many pieces of the white root with the little leaf-bud curled up which I take to be the yellow lily root, — the leaf-bud unrolled has the same scent with the yellow lily. There will be half a dozen of these pointed buds, more or less green, coming to  a point at the end of the root : Also I see a little coarser, what I take to be green leaf-stalk of the pontederia, for I see a little of the stipule sheathing the stalk from within it? The first unrolls to something like:[1]

In one hole there was a large quantity of this root, and these buds attached or bitten off, the root generally five or six eighths inch in diameter and one to four inches long. I think, therefore, that this root must be their principal food at this time. If you open twenty cabins you will find it in at least three quarters of them, and nothing else, unless a very little pontederia leaf-stem. I see no fresh clamshells in them, and scarcely any on the ice anywhere on the edge of open

[1] Of course it is yellow lily.

places, nor are they probably deposited in a heap under the ice. It may be, however, that the shells are opened in this hole and then dropped in the water near by!! By eating or killing at least so many lily buds they must thin out that plant considerably.

Twice this winter I have noticed a musquash floating in a placid open place in the river when it was frozen for a mile each side, looking at first like a bit of stump or frozen meadow, but showing its whole upper outline from nose to end of tail; perfectly still till he observed me, then suddenly diving and steering under the ice toward some cabin's entrance or other retreat half a dozen or more rods off.

As some of the tales of our childhood, the invention of some Mother Goose, will haunt us when we are grown up, so the race itself still believes in some of the fables with which its infancy was amused and imposed on, e. g. the fable of the cranes and pygmies, which learned men endeavored to believe or explain in the last century.

Aristotle, being almost if not quite the first to write systematically on animals, gives them, of course, only popular names, such as the hunters, fowlers, fishers, and farmers of his day used. He used no scientific terms. But he, having the priority and having, as it were, created science and given it its laws, those popular Greek names, even when the animal to which they were applied cannot be identified, have been in great part preserved and make those learned far-fetched and commonly unintelligible names of genera to-day, e. g. Ὁλοθούριον, etc., etc. His History of Animals has thus become a very storehouse of scientific nomenclature.

Vol. XIII

Dec. 27. Grows cold in the evening, so that our breaths condense and freeze on the windows and in the morning, —

Dec. 28, — they are like ground glass (covered with frost), and we cannot see out. Sleds creak or squeak along the dry and hard snow-path. Crows come near the houses. These are among the signs of cold weather.

The open places in the river yesterday between Lee's Bridge and Carlisle Bridge were: 1st, below Nut Meadow Brook, a rather shoal place; 2d, at Clamshell Bend, longer; 3d, at Hubbard's Bath Bend; (3½, was there not a little open at ash tree?[1]); 4th, I think there was a short opening at Lee's Bend;[2] 5th, from Monroe's to Merrick's pasture; 6th, below junction to bridge; 7th, below French's Rock; 8th, Barrett's Bar. *N. B.* — Did not observe or examine between this and the shoal below the Holt.[3] It was no doubt open at the last place and perhaps more. There was no opening between the Holt shoal and Carlisle Bridge, for there was none on the 25th.

The most solidly frozen portions are the broad and straight reaches. All broad bays are frozen hard. When you come to where the river is winding, there is shallower and swifter water — and open places as yet.

[1] Yes.

[2] Or, rather, I think it was thinly frozen?

[3] Perhaps ice between 8th and ash opening; 9th, west side Holt Bend; 10th, north side ditto; 11th, east side ditto; 12th, Holt Ford *was* open almost round the Holt. *N. B.* — But slight intervals between the last four.

It is remarkable that the river should so suddenly contract at Pelham Pond. It begins to be Musketaquid there.

The places where the river was *certainly* (i. e. except 4th) open yesterday were all only five feet or less in depth, according to my map, and all except 8th at bends or else below the mouth of a brook. And all places not more than five and a quarter feet deep were open (I am doubtful only about behind Rhodes) except above Holt Bend and *perhaps* Pad Island, or possibly none need be excepted.

Hence, I should say, if you wish to ascertain where the river is five feet, or less than five feet, deep in Concord, wait till it is open for not more than half a dozen rods below Nut Meadow (it was probably some twenty the 27th), and then all open places will be five or less than five feet deep.

Dec. 29. A very cold morning, — about − 15° at 8 A. M. at our door.

I went to the river immediately after sunrise. I could [see] a little greenness in the ice, and also a little rose-color from the snow, but far less than before the sun set. Do both these phenomena require a gross atmosphere? Apparently the ice is greenest when the sun is twenty or thirty minutes above the horizon.

From the smooth open place behind Cheney's a great deal of vapor was rising to the height of a dozen feet or more, as from a boiling kettle. This, then, is a phenomenon of quite cold weather. I did not notice it yesterday afternoon. These open places are a sort of breathing-holes of the river. When I look toward the sun, now that they are smooth, they are hardly to be distinguished from the ice. Just as cold weather reveals the breath of a man, still greater cold reveals the breath of, *i. e.* warm, moist air over, the river.

I collect this morning the little shining black seeds of the amaranth, raised above the snow in its solid or dense spike.

P. M. — To Ball's Hill, skating.

Walked back, measuring the river and ice by pacing.[1]

The first open place in the main stream in Concord, or no doubt this side Carlisle Bridge, coming up-stream, were [*sic*] : —

1st, Holt Ford, 10 rods by 1 (extreme width).

2d, east side Holt Bend, near last, 8 by 1½.

3d, west side Holt Bend (midway), 3 by ½.

(On the 28th it must have been open nearly all round to Holt Bend.)

4th, Barrett's Bar, 42 rods by 6 at west end, where it reaches 12 rods above ford; extends down the north side *very narrow* to the rock and only little way down the south side; can walk in middle half-way.

5th, a bar above Monument, 10 by 3.

6th, from Hunt's Bridge to Island, or say 54 rods by 4.

7th, from 8 below willow-row to 5 below boat's place, or 80+ rods by 3.

This as far as I looked to-day, but no doubt[2] the next was : —

8th, just above ash tree, probably three or four rods long.

[1] Feb. 15, 1860, when the river was much more open than Dec. 29, 1859, it was scarcely open at the narrowest place above Bound Rock, only puffed up in the channel, and the first decided opening was at Rice's Bend; all below Bound Rock to Fair Haven Pond, etc., was quite solid. Hence the statements below are true.

[2] Proved by looking the 30th.

9th, at Hubbard's Bath Bend.

10th, Clamshell Bend.

11th, below Nut Meadow, probably two or three rods long.

This is the last in Concord. (I do not include the small openings which are to be found now at bridges.) The longest opening is that below my boat's place; next, at junction next Barrett's Bar; next, either Clamshell or Hubbard's Bath. But for area of water that below the junction is considerably the largest of all.[1]

When I went to walk it was about 10° above zero, and when I returned, 1°. I did not notice any vapor rising from the open places, as I did in the morning, when it was − 16° and also − 6°. Therefore the cold must be between + 1° and − 6° in order that vapor may rise from these places. It takes a greater degree of cold to show the breath of the river than that of man. Apparently, the river is not enough warmer than the air to permit of its rising into it, *i. e.*, evaporating, unless the air is of a very low temperature. When the air is say four or five degrees below, the water being + 32°, then there is a visible evaporation. Is there the same difference, or some 40°, between the heat of the human breath and that air in which the moisture in the breath becomes visible in vapor? This has to do with the dew-point. Next, what makes the water of those open places thus warm? and is it any warmer than elsewhere? There is considerable heat reflected from a sandy bottom where the water is shallow, and at these places it is always sandy and shallow, but I doubt if this actually makes the water warmer, though it may

[1] *Vide* Jan. 22.

Vol. XIII

melt the more opaque ice which absorbs it. The fact that Holt Bend, which is deep, is late to freeze, being narrow, seems to prove it to be the swiftness of the water and not reflected heat that prevents freezing. The water is apparently kept warm under the ice and down next to the unfrozen earth, and by a myriad springs from within the bowels of the earth.

I notice that, on the thin black ice lately formed on these open places, the breath of the water has made its way up through and is frozen into a myriad of little rosettes, which nearly cover its surface and make it white as with snow. You see the same on pretty thick ice. This occurs whenever the weather is coldest in the night or very early in the morning. Also, where these open places have lately closed, the ice for long distances over the thread of the river will often be heaved up

roofwise a foot high and a rod wide, apparently pushed up by the heat of this breath beneath.

As I come home, I observe much thin ice, just formed as it grows colder, drifting in gauze-like masses down these open places, just as I used to see it coming down the open river when it began to freeze. In this case it is not ice which formed last night, but which is even now forming.

The musquash make a good deal of use of these open spaces. I have seen one four times in three several places this winter, or within three weeks. They improve all the open water they can get. They occasionally leave their clamshells upon the edges of them

now. This is all the water to reflect the sky now, whether amber or purple. I sometimes see the musquash dive in the midst of such a placid purple lake.

Where the channel is broad the water is more sluggish and the ice accordingly thick, or it will answer just as well if the channel is deep, *i. e.*, if its capacity is the same, though it be very narrow. The ice will be firm there too, *e. g.* at Ash Tree Rock (though it was lately open off the willows eight or ten rods above, being less deep and narrower); and even at the deeper hole next below the opening is not where it is deep, though very narrow, but half a dozen rods below, where it is much wider.

To-night I notice the rose-color in the snow and the green in the ice *at the same time*, having been looking out for them.

The clouds were very remarkable this cold afternoon, about twenty minutes before sunset, consisting of very long and narrow white clouds converging in the horizon (melon-rind-wise) both in the west and east. They looked like the skeletons and backbones of celestial sloths, being pointed at each end, or even like porcupine quills or ivory darts sharp at each end. So long and slender, but pronounced, with a manifest backbone and marrow. It looked as if invisible giants were darting them from all parts of the sky at the setting sun. These were long darts indeed. Well underneath was an almost invisible rippled vapor whose grain was exactly at right angles with the former, all over the sky, yet it was so delicate that it did not prevent your seeing the former at all. Its filmy arrows all pointed athwart the others. I know that in fact those slender white cloud sloths were nearly parallel across the sky, but how much handsomer are the clouds because the sky is made to appear concave to us! How much more beautiful an arrangement of the clouds than parallel lines ! At length those white arrows and bows, slender and sharp as they were, gathering toward a point in the west horizon, looked like flames even, forked and darting flames of ivory-white, and low in the west there was a piece of rainbow but little longer than it was broad.

Taking the river in Concord in its present condition, it is, with one exception, only the shallowest places that are open. Suppose there were a dozen places open a few days ago, if it has grown much colder since, the deepest of them will be frozen over ; and the shallowest place in all in Concord is the latest of all to freeze, e. g. at the junction. So, if you get into the river at this season, it is most likely to be at the shallowest places, they being either open or most thinly frozen over. That is one consolation for you.

The exception is on the west side of the Holt (and the depth is *one side* from the opening), but that is on account of the narrowness of the river there. Indeed, the whole of Holt Bend is slow to freeze over, on account of the great narrowness and consequent swiftness of the stream there; but the two narrowest points of it are among the first to freeze over, because they are much the deepest, the rush of waters being either below or above them, where it is much shallower, though broader.

Vol. XIII

To be safe a river should be straight and deep, or of nearly uniform depth.

I do not remember any particular swiftness in the current above the railroad ash tree, where there is still an opening (seen December 30th), and it may be owing to the very copious springs in the high bank for twenty rods. There is not elsewhere so long a high and springy bank bounding immediately on the river in the town. To be sure, it is not deep.

Dec. 30. I awake to find it snowing fast, but it slackens in a few hours. Perhaps seven or eight inches have fallen, — the deepest snow yet, and almost quite level. At first the flakes (this forenoon) were of middling size. At noon, when it was leaving off, they were of a different character. I observed them on my sleeve, — little slender spiculæ about one tenth of an inch long, little dry splinters, sometimes two forking, united at one end, or two or three lying across one another, quite dry and fine; and so it concluded.

P. M. — Going by Dodd's, I see a shrike perched on the tip-top of the topmost upright twig of an English cherry tree before his house, standing square on the topmost bud, balancing himself by a slight motion of his tail from time to time. I have noticed this habit of the bird before. You would suppose it inconvenient for so large a bird to maintain its footing there. Scared by my passing [?] in the road, it flew off, and I thought I would see if it alighted on a similar place. It flew toward a young elm, whose higher twigs were much more slender, though not quite so upright as

those of the cherry, and I thought he might be excused if he alighted on the side of one; but no, to my surprise, he alighted without any trouble upon the very top of one of the highest of all, and looked around as before.

I spoke to the barber to-day about that whirl of hair on the occiput of most (if not all) men's heads. He said it was called the crown, and was of a spiral form, a beginning spiral, when cut short; that some had two, one on the right, the other on the left, close together. I said that they were in a sense double-headed. He said that it was an old saying that such were bred under two crowns.

I noticed the other day that even the golden-crested wren was one of the winter birds which have a black head, — in this case divided by yellow.

Those who depend on skylights found theirs but a dim, religious light this forenoon and hitherto, owing to the thickness of snow resting on them. Also cellar windows are covered, and cellars are accordingly darkened.

What a different phenomenon a musquash now from what it is in summer! Now if one floats, or swims, its whole back out, or crawls out upon the ice at one of those narrow oval water spaces in the river, some twenty rods long (in calm weather, smooth mirrors), in a broad frame of white ice or yet whiter snow, it is seen at once, as conspicuous (or more so) as a fly on a window-pane or a mirror. But in summer, how many hundreds crawl along the weedy shore or plunge in the long river unsuspected by the boatman! Even if the musquash is not there I often see the open clam-

shell on the edge of the ice, perfectly distinct a long way off, and he is betrayed. However, the edges of these silver lakes, — winter lakes, late freezers, swift-waters, musquash mirrors, breathing-holes, — to-day, after the morning's snow, are, by the water flowing back over the thin edges and staining the snow, a distinct yellow (brown-yellow) tinge for a rod or two on every side. This shows what and how much coloring matter there is in the river water. I doubt if it would be so at Walden. No doubt, however, we here get the impurer parts of the river, the scum as it were, repeatedly washed over at these places.

Dec. 31. Thermometer at 7.45 A. M., — 1°, yet even more vapor is rising from the open water below my boat's place than on the 29th, when it was − 15°. The wind is southwesterly, *i. e.* considerably south of west. This shows that fog over the water is a phenomenon of the morning chiefly, as well in winter as in summer. You will see a fog over the water in a winter morning, though the temperature may be considerably higher than at midday when no fog is seen.

There has evidently been a slight fog generally in the night, and the trees are white with it. The crystals are directed southwesterly, or toward the wind. I think that these crystals are particularly large and numerous, and the trees (willows) particularly white, next to the open water spaces, where the vapor even now is abundantly rising. Is this fog in the night occasioned by the cold earth condensing the moisture which a warmer wind has brought to us?

At 10 A. M., thermometer 18°. I see no vapor from the water.

Crows yesterday flitted silently, if not ominously, over the street, just after the snow had fallen, as if men, being further within, were just as far off as usual. This is a phenomenon of both cold weather and snowy. You hear nothing; you merely see these black apparitions, though they come near enough to look down your chimney and scent the boiling pot, and pass between the house and barn.

Just saw moved a white oak, Leighton's, some five inches in diameter, with a frozen mass of earth some five or five and a half feet in diameter and two plus thick. It was dug round before the frost, — a trench about a foot wide and filled with stalks, etc., — and now pried up with levers till on a level with the ground, then dragged off. It would not have cost half so much if a sloping path had been dug to it on one side so that the drag could have been placed under it in the hole and another dug at the hole it was removed to, — unless the last were planked over and it was dragged on to it.

They were teaming ice before sunrise (from Sam Barrett's Pond) on the morning of the 29th, when the thermometer was 16 or 20 degrees below. Cold work, you would say. Yet some say it is colder in thawing weather, if you have to *touch* the ice.

P. M. — To the sweet-gale meadow or swamp up Assabet.

I notice that one or more of the terminal leafets remain on the branches of the flowering fern commonly.

See where probably a shrike (do I ever see a small

hawk in winter?) has torn a small bird in pieces and its slate-colored down and its feathers have been blown far and wide over the snow.

There is a great deal of hemlock scales scattered over the recent snow (at the Hemlocks), evidently by birds on the trees, and the wind has blown them southeast, — scales, seeds, and cones, — and I see the tracks of small birds that have apparently picked the seeds from the snow also. It may have been done by goldfinches. I see a tree sparrow hopping close by, and perhaps they eat them on the snow. Some of the seeds have blown at least fifteen rods southeast. So the hemlock seed is important to some birds in the winter.

All the sound witch-hazel nuts that I examine are empty.

How vain to try to teach youth, or anybody, truths! They can only learn them after their own fashion, and when they get ready. I do not mean by this to condemn our system of education, but to show what it amounts to. A hundred boys at college are drilled in physics and metaphysics, languages, etc. There *may* be one or two in each hundred, prematurely old perchance, who approaches the subject from a similar point of view to his teachers, but as for the rest, and the most promising, it is like agricultural chemistry to so many Indians. They get a valuable drilling, it *may* be, but they do not learn what you profess to teach. They at most only learn where the arsenal is, in case they should ever want to use any of its weapons. The young men, being young, necessarily listen to the lecturer in history, just as they do to the singing of a bird.

Vol. XIII

They expect to be affected by something he may say. It is a kind of poetic pabulum and imagery that they get. Nothing comes quite amiss to their mill.

I think it will be found that he who speaks with most authority on a given subject is not ignorant of what has been said by his predecessors. He will take his place in a regular order, and substantially add his own knowledge to the knowledge of previous generations.

The oblong-conical sterile flower-buds or catkins of the sweet-gale, half a dozen at the end of each black twig, dark-red, oblong-conical, spotted with black, and about half an inch long, are among the most interesting buds of the winter. The leaf-buds are comparatively minute. The white edges of their scales and their regular red and black colors make the imbrication of the bud very distinct. The sterile and fertile flowers are not only on distinct plants, but they commonly grow in distinct patches. Sometimes I detect the one only for a quarter of a mile, and then the other begins to prevail, or both may be found together. It grows along the wet edge of banks and the river and in open swamps.

The mulleins are full of minute brown seeds, which a jar sprinkles over the snow, and [they] look black there; also the primrose, of larger brown seeds, which rattle out in the same manner.

One of the two large docks, perhaps *obtusifolius*, commonly holds its seeds now, but they are very ready to fall. (Mainly one-seeded; *vide* three-ribbed goldenrod meadow.)

There appears to be not much (compared with the fall) seed left on the common or gray goldenrod, its down being mostly gone, and the seed is attached to that.

Potentilla Norvegica appears to have some sound seed in its closed heads.

The very gray flattish heads of the calamint are quite full of minute dark-brown seed.

The conical heads of the cone-flower also are full of long blackish seeds. Both the last drop their seeds on being inverted and shaken.

I see also the yellow lily (*L. Canadense*) pods with its three now gray divisions spreading open like the petals of a flower, and more than half the great red flattish triangularish or semicircularish seeds gone. The pod boys throw with a humming sound.

Even the sidesaddle-flower, where it shows its head above the snow, now gray and leathery, dry, is covered beneath its cap with pretty large close-set light-brown seeds.

I see one or more sedges with seeds yet, one apparently the *Carex debilis*, if it is not *flava*?

A man may be old and infirm. What, then, are the thoughts he thinks? what the life he lives? They and it are, like himself, infirm. But a man may be young, athletic, active, beautiful. Then, too, his thoughts will be like his person. They will wander in a living and beautiful world. If you are well, then how brave you are! How you hope! You are conversant with joy! A man thinks as well through his legs and arms as his brain. We exaggerate the importance and exclusiveness of the headquarters. Do you suppose they were a race of consumptives and dyspeptics who invented Grecian mythology and poetry? The poet's words are, "You would almost say the body thought!" I quite say it. I trust we have a good body then.

II

JANUARY, 1860

(ÆT. 42)

Jan. 2. 8 A. M. — 15° below.

Take the whole day, this is probably the coldest thus far.

The past December has been remarkable for steady cold, or coldness, and sleighing.

Jan. 3. P. M. — To Baker's Bridge *via* Walden.

As we passed the almshouse brook this pleasant winter afternoon, at 2.30 P. M. (perhaps 20°, for it was 10° when I got home at 4.45), I saw vapor curling along over the open part by the roadside.

The most we saw, on the pond and after, was a peculiar track amid the men and dog tracks, which we took to be a fox-track, for he trailed his feet, leaving a mark, in a peculiar manner, and showed his wildness by his turning off the road.

Saw four snow buntings by the railroad causeway, just this side the cut, quite tame. They arose and alighted on the rail fence as we went by. Very stout for their length. Look very pretty when they fly and reveal the clear white space on their wings next the body, — white between the blacks. They were busily eating the seed of the piper grass on the embankment there, and it was strewn over the snow by them like

oats in a stable. Melvin speaks of seeing flocks of them on the river meadows in the fall, when they are of a different color.

Melvin thinks that the musquash eat more clams now than ever, and that they leave the shells in heaps under the ice. As the river falls it leaves them space enough under the ice along the meadow's edge and bushes. I think he is right. He speaks of the mark of the tail, which is dragged behind them, in the snow, — as if made by a case-knife.

He does not remember that he ever sees the small hawk, *i. e.* pigeon hawk, here in winter. He shot a large hawk the other day, when after quails. Had just shot a quail, when he heard another utter a peculiar note which indicated that it was pursued, and saw it dodge into a wall, when the hawk alighted on an apple tree. Quails are very rare here, but where they are is found the hunter of them, whether he be man or hawk.

When a locomotive came in, just before the sun set, I saw a small cloud blown away from it which was a very rare but distinct violet purple.

I hear that one clearing out a well lately, perhaps in Connecticut, found one hundred and seventy and odd frogs and some snakes in it.

Jan. 4. P. M. — To second stone bridge and down river.

It is frozen directly under the stone bridge, but a few feet below the bridge it is open for four rods, and over that exceedingly deep hole, and again at that very swift and shallow narrow place some dozen rods lower.

These are the only places open between this bridge and the mouth of the Assabet, except here and there a crack or space a foot wide at the springy bank just below the Pokelogan.

It is remarkable that the deepest place in either of the rivers that I have sounded should be open, simply on account of the great agitation of the water there. This proves that it is the swiftness and not warmth that makes the shallow places to be open longest.

In Hosmer's pitch pine wood just north of the bridge, I find myself on the track of a fox — as I take it — that has run about a great deal. Next I come to the tracks of rabbits, see where they have travelled back and forth, making a well-trodden path in the snow; and soon after I see where one has been killed and apparently devoured. There are to be seen only the tracks of what I take to be the fox. The snow is much trampled, or rather flattened by the body of the rabbit. It is somewhat bloody and is covered with flocks of slate-colored and brown fur, but only the rabbit's tail, a little ball of fur, an inch and a half long and about as wide, white beneath, and the contents of its paunch or of its entrails are left, — nothing more. Half a dozen rods further, I see where the rabbit has been dropped on the snow again, and some fur is left, and there are the tracks of the fox to the spot and about it. There, or within a rod or two, I notice a considerable furrow in the snow, three or four inches wide and some two rods long, as if one had drawn a stick along, but there is no other mark or track whatever; so I conclude that a partridge, perhaps scared by the fox, had dashed swiftly along so low as to plow the snow. But two or three rods further on one side I see more sign, and lo! there is the remainder of the rabbit, — the whole, indeed, but the tail and the inward or soft parts, — all frozen stiff; but here there is no distinct track of any creature, only a few scratches and marks where some great bird of prey — a hawk or owl — has struck the snow with its primaries on each side, and one or two holes where it has stood. Now I understand how that long furrow was made, the bird with the rabbit in its talons flying low there, and now I remember that at the first bloody spot I saw some of these quill-marks; and therefore it is certain that the bird had it there, and probably he killed it, and he, perhaps disturbed by the fox, carried it to the second place, and it is certain that he (probably disturbed by the fox again) carried it to the last place, making a furrow on the way.

If it had not been for the snow on the ground I probably should not have noticed any signs that a rabbit had been killed. Or, if I had chanced to see the scattered fur, I should not have known what creature did it, or how recently. But now it is partly certain, partly probable, — or, supposing that the bird could not have taken it from the fox, it is almost all certain, — that an owl or hawk killed a rabbit here last night (the fox-tracks are so fresh), and, when eating it on the snow, was disturbed by a fox, and so flew off with it half a dozen rods, but, being disturbed again by the fox, it flew with it again about as much further, trailing it in the snow for a couple of rods as it flew, and there

it finished its meal without being approached. A fox would probably have torn and eaten some of the skin.

When I turned off from the road my expectation was to see some tracks of wild animals in the snow, and, before going a dozen rods, I crossed the track of what I had no doubt was a fox, made apparently the last night, — which had travelled extensively in this pitch pine wood, searching for game. Then I came to rabbit-tracks, and saw where they had travelled back and forth in the snow in the woods, making a perfectly trodden path, and within a rod of that was a hollow in the snow a foot and a half across, where a rabbit had been killed. There were many tracks of the fox about that place, and I had no doubt then that he had killed that rabbit, and I supposed that some scratches which I saw might have been made by his frisking some part of the rabbit back and forth, shaking it in his mouth. I thought, Perhaps he has carried off to his young, or buried, the rest. But as it turned out, though the circumstantial evidence against the fox was very strong, I was mistaken. I had made him kill the rabbit, and shake and tear the carcass, and eat it all up but the tail (almost); but it seems that he did n't do it at [all], and apparently never got a mouthful of the rabbit. Something, surely, must have disturbed the bird, else why did it twice fly along with the heavy carcass?

The tracks of the bird at the last place were two little round holes side by side, the dry snow having fallen in and concealed the track of its feet.

It was most likely an owl, because it was most likely that the fox would be abroad by night.

Vol. XIII

The sweet-gale has a few leaves on it yet in some places, partly concealing the pretty catkins.

Again see what the snow reveals. Opposite Dodge's Brook I see on the snow and ice some fragments of frozen-thawed apples under an oak. How came they there? There are apple trees thirty rods off by the road. On the snow under the oak I see two or three tracks of a crow, and the droppings of several that were perched on the tree, and here and there is a perfectly round hole in the snow under the tree. I put down my hand and draw up an apple [out] of each, from beneath the snow. (There are no tracks of squirrels about the oak.) Crows carried these frozen-thawed apples from the apple trees to the oak, and there ate them, — what they did not let fall into the snow or on to the ice.

See that long meandering track where a deer mouse hopped over the soft snow last night, scarcely making any impression. What if you could witness with owls' eyes the revelry of the wood mice some night, frisking about the wood like so many little kangaroos? Here is a palpable evidence that the woods are nightly thronged with little creatures which most have never seen, — such populousness as commonly only the imagination dreams of.

The circumstantial evidence against that fox was very strong, for the deed was done since the snow fell and I saw no other tracks but his at the first places. Any jury would have convicted him, and he would have been hung, if he could have been caught.

Jan. 5. P. M. — *Via* Turnpike to Smith's and back by Great Road.

How much the snow reveals! I see where the downy woodpecker has worked lately by the chips of bark and rotten wood scattered over the snow, though I rarely see him in the winter. Once to-day, however, I hear his sharp voice, even like a woodchuck's. Also I have occasionally seen where (probably) a flock of goldfinches in the morning had settled on a hemlock's top, by the snow strewn with scales, literally blackened or darkened with them for a rod. And now, about the hill in front of Smith's, I see where the quails have run along the roadside, and can count the number of the bevy better than if I saw them. Are they not peculiar in this, as compared with partridges, — that they run in company, while at this season I see but [one] or two partridges together?

A man receives only what he is ready to receive, whether physically or intellectually or morally, as animals conceive at certain seasons their kind only. We hear and apprehend only what we already half know. If there is something which does not concern me, which is out of my line, which by experience or by genius my attention is not drawn to, however novel and remarkable it may be, if it is spoken, we hear it not, if it is written, we read it not, or if we read it, it does not detain us. Every man thus *tracks himself* through life, in all his hearing and reading and observation and travelling. His observations make a chain. The phenomenon or fact that cannot in any wise be linked with the rest which he has observed, he does not observe. By and by we may be ready to receive what we cannot receive now. I find, for example, in Aristotle something about the spawning, etc., of the pout and perch, because I know something about it already and have my attention aroused; but I do not discover till very late that he has made other equally important observations on the spawning of other fishes, because I am not interested in those fishes.

I see the dead stems of the water horehound just rising above the snow and curving outward over the bank of the Assabet, near the stone-heaps, with its brown clusters of dry seeds, etc., every inch or two. These, stripped off or rubbed between the fingers, look somewhat like ground coffee and are agreeably aromatic. They have the fragrance of lemon-peel.

Jan. 7. A thaw begins, with a southerly wind. From having been about 20° at midday, it is now (the thermometer) some 35° quite early, and at 2 p. m. 45°. At once the snow, which was dry and crumbling, is softened all over the country, not only in the streets, but in the remotest and slightest sled-track, where the farmer is hauling his wood; not only in yards, but in every woodland hollow and on every hill. There is a softening in the air and a softening underfoot. The softness of the air is something tangible, almost gross. Some are making haste to get their wood home before the snow goes, sledding, *i. e.* sliding, it home rapidly. Now if you take up a handful, it holds together and is readily fashioned and compressed into a ball, so that an endless supply of one kind of missiles is at hand.

I find myself drawn toward this softened snow, even that which is stained with dung in the road, as

to a friend. I see where some crow has pecked at the now thawing dung here. How provident is Nature, who permits a few kernels of grain to pass undigested through the entrails of the ox, for the food of the crow and dove, etc.!

As soon as I reach the neighborhood of the woods I begin to see the snow-fleas, more than a dozen rods from woods, amid a little goldenrod, etc., where, methinks, they must have come up through the snow. Last night there was not one to be seen. The frozen apples are thawed again.

You hear (in the house) the unusual sound of the eaves running.

Saw a large flock of goldfinches [1] running and feeding amid the weeds in a pasture, just like tree sparrows. Then flitted to birch trees, whose seeds probably they eat. [2] Heard their twitter and mew.

Nature so fills the soil with seeds that I notice, where travellers have turned off the road and made a new track for several rods, the intermediate narrow space is soon clothed with a little grove which just fills it.

See, at White Pond, where squirrels have been feeding on the fruit of a pignut hickory, which was quite full of nuts and still has many on it. The snow for a great space is covered with the outer shells, etc.; and, especially, close to the base of this and the neighboring trees of other species, where there is a little bare ground, there is a very large collection of the shells, most of which have been gnawed quite in two.

[1] These *were* goldfinches [see p. 82].
[2] So it is possible that they *also* eat hemlock seed.

Vol. XIII

The white pine cones show still as much as ever, hanging sickle-wise about the tops of the trees.

I saw yesterday the track of a fox, and in the course of it a place where he had apparently pawed to the ground, eight or ten inches, and on the just visible ground lay frozen a stale-looking mouse, probably rejected by him. A little further was a similar hole with some fur in it. Did he smell the dead or living mouse beneath and paw to it, or rather, catching it on the surface, make that hollow in his efforts to eat it? It would be remarkable if a fox could smell and catch a mouse passing under the snow beneath him! You would say that he need not make such a hole in order to eat the mouse.

Jan. 8. Began to rain last evening, and rained some in the night. To-day it is very warm and pleasant.

2 p. m. — Walk to Walden.

Thermometer 48 at 2 p. m. We are suddenly surrounded by a warm air from some other part of the globe. What a change! Yesterday morning we walked on dry and squeaking snow, but before night, without any rain, merely by the influence of that warm air which had migrated to us, softening and melting the snow, we began to slump in it. Now, since the rain of last night, the softest portions of the snow are dissolved in the street, revealing and leaving the filth which has accumulated there upon the firmer foundation, and we walk with open coats, charmed with the trickling of ephemeral rills.

After December all weather that is not wintry is

springlike. How changed are our feelings and thoughts by this more genial sky!

When I get to the railroad I listen from time to time to hear some sound out of the distance which will express this mood of Nature. The cock and the hen, that pheasant which we have domesticated, are perhaps the most sensitive to atmospheric changes of any domestic animals. You cannot listen a moment such a day as this but you will hear, from far or near, the clarion of the cock celebrating this new season, yielding to the influence of the south wind, or the drawling note of the hen dreaming of eggs that are to be. These are the sounds that fill the air, and no hum of insects. They are affected like voyagers on approaching the land. We discover a new world every time that we see the earth again after it has been covered for a season with snow.

I see the jay and hear his scream oftener for the thaw.

Walden, which was covered with snow, is now covered with shallow puddles and slosh of a pale glaucous slate-color. The sloshy edges of the puddles are the frames of so many wave-shaped mirrors in which the leather-colored oak leaves, and the dark-green pines and their stems, on the hillside, are reflected.

We see no fresh tracks. The old tracks of the rabbit, now after the thaw, are shaped exactly like a horseshoe, an unbroken curve. Those of the fox which has run along the side of the pond are now so many white snowballs, raised as much above the level of the water-darkened snow as at first they sank beneath it. The snow, having been compressed by their weight, resists the melting longer. Indeed, I see far across the pond, half a mile distant, what looks like a perfectly straight row of white stones, — some fence or other work of art, — stretching twenty rods along the bare shore. There are a man's tracks, perhaps my own, along the pond-side there, looking not only larger than reality, but more elevated owing to the looming, and are referred to the dark background against which they are seen. When I know that they are on the ice, they look like white stepping-stones.

I hear the goldfinch notes (they *may* be linarias), and see a few on the top of a small black birch by the pond-shore, of course eating the seed. Thus they distinguish its fruit from afar. When I heard their note, I looked to find them on a birch, and lo, it was a black birch![1]

We have a fine moonlight evening after, and as by day I have noticed that the sunlight reflected from this moist snow had more glitter and dazzle to it than when the snow was dry, so now I am struck by the brighter sheen from the snow in the moonlight. All the impurities in the road are lost sight of, and the melting snow shines like frostwork.

When returning from Walden at sunset, the only cloud we saw was a small purplish one, exactly conforming to the outline of Wachusett, — which it concealed, — as if on that mountain only the universal moisture was at that moment condensed.

The commonest difference between a public speaker who has not enjoyed the advantage of the highest

[1] Were they not linarias? *Vide* Jan. 24, 27, 29.

education in the popular sense, at school and college, and one who has, is that the former will pronounce a few words, and use a few more, in a manner in which the scholars have agreed not to, and the latter will occasionally quote a few Latin and even Greek words with more confidence, and, if the subject is the derivation of words, will maintain a wise silence.

Jan. 9. Another fine warm day, — 48° at 2 P. M.
P. M. — To Walden.

I call that ice marbled when shallow puddles of melted snow and rain, with perhaps some slosh in them, resting on old ice, are frozen, showing a slightly internal marbling, or alternation of light and dark spots or streaks.

I see, on a slender oak (not white oak) overhanging the pond, two knots which, though near, I at first mistook for vireo nests. One was in a fork, too, and both were just the right size and color, if not form. Thus, too, the nests may be concealed to some eyes.

I am interested by a clump of young canoe birches on the hillside shore of the pond. There is an interesting variety in the colors of their bark, passing from bronze at the earth, through ruddy and copper colors to white higher up, with shreds of different color from that beneath peeling off. Going close to them, I find that at first, or till ten feet high, they are a dark bronze brown, a wholly different-looking shrub from what they afterward become, with some ruddy tinges, and, of course, regular white specks; but when they get to be about two inches in diameter, the outmost

Vol. XIII

cuticle bursts up and down the tree on the south side, and peels off each way, under the influence, probably, of the sun and rain and wind, and perhaps aided sometimes by birds. It is as if the tree unbuttoned a thin waistcoat and suffered it to blow aside, revealing its bosom or inner garment, which is a more ruddy brown, or sometimes greenish or coppery; and thus one cuticle peels off after another till it is a ruddy white, as if you saw to a red ground through a white wash; and at length it is snow-white, about five or six feet from the ground, for it is first white there, while the top, where it is smaller and younger, is still dark-brown. It may be, then, half a dozen years old before it assumes the white toga which is its distinctive dress.

After the January thaw our thoughts cease to refer to autumn and we look forward to spring.

I hear that R. M——, a rich old farmer who lives in a large house, with a male housekeeper and no other family, gets up at three or four o'clock these winter mornings and milks seventeen cows regularly. When asked why he works so hard he answers that the poor are obliged to work hard. Only think, what a creature of fate he is, this old Jotun, milking his seventeen cows though the thermometer goes down to − 25°, and not knowing why he does it, — draining sixty-eight cows' teats in the dark of the coldest morning! Think how helpless a rich man who can only do as he has done, and as his neighbors do, one or all of them! What an account he will have to give of himself! He spent some time in a world, alternately cold and warm, and every winter morning, with lantern in hand, when the frost

goblins were playing their tricks, he resolutely accomplished his task and milked his seventeen cows, while the man housekeeper prepared his breakfast! If this were original with him, he would be a hero to be celebrated in history. Think how tenaciously every man does his deed, of some kind or other, though it be idleness! He is rich, dependent on nobody, and nobody is dependent on him; has as good health as the average, at least, can do as he pleases, as we say. Yet he gravely rises every morning by candle-light, dons his cowhide boots and his frock, takes his lantern and wends to the barn and milks his seventeen cows, milking with one hand while he warms the other against the cow or his person. This is but the beginning of his day, and his Augean stable work. So serious is the life he lives.

Jan. 12. The very slight rain of yesterday afternoon turned to snow in the night, and this morning considerable has fallen and is still falling. At noon it clears up. About eight inches deep.

I go forth to walk on the Hill at 3 P. M. Thermometer about 30°.

It is a very beautiful and spotless snow now, it having just ceased falling. You are struck by its peculiar tracklessness, as if it were a thick white blanket just spread. As it were, each snowflake lies as it first fell, or there is a regular gradation from the denser bottom up to the surface, which is perfectly light, and as it were fringed with the last flakes that fell. This was a star snow, dry, but the stars of considerable size. It lies up light as down. When I look closely it seems to be chiefly composed of crystals in which the six rays or leafets are more or less perfect, with a cottony powder intermixed. It is not yet in the least melted by the sun. The sun is out very bright and pretty warm, and, going from the sun, I see a myriad sparkling points scattered over its surface, — little mirror-like facets, which on examination I find to be one of those star wheels (more or less entire) from an eighth to a third of an inch in diameter, which has fallen in the proper position, reflecting an intensely bright little sun, as if it were a thin and uninterrupted scale of mica. Such is the glitter or sparkle on the surface of such a snow freshly fallen when the sun comes out and you walk from it, the points of light constantly changing. I suspect that these are good evidence of the freshness of the snow. The sun and wind have not yet destroyed these delicate reflectors.

The aspect of the pines now, with their plumes and boughs bent under their burden of snow, is what I call *glyphic*, like lumpish forms of sculpture, — a certain dumb sculpture.

There is a wonderful stillness in the air, so that you hear the least fall of snow from a bough near you, suggesting that perhaps it was of late equally still in what you called the snow-*storm*, except for the motion of the falling flakes and their rustling on the dry leaves, etc.

Looking from the hilltop, the pine woods half a mile or a mile distant north and northwest, their sides and brows especially, snowed up like the fronts of houses, look like great gray or grayish-white lichens, cetrarias maybe, attached to the sides of the hills. Those oak

Vol. XIII

woods whose leaves have fallen have caught the snow chiefly on their lower and more horizontal branches, and these look somewhat like ramalina lichens.

As I stand by the hemlocks, I am greeted by the lively and unusually prolonged *tche de de de de de* of a little flock of chickadees. The snow has ceased falling, the sun comes out, and it is warm and still, and this flock of chickadees, little birds that perchance were born in their midst, feeling the influences of this genial season, have begun to flit amid the snow-covered fans of the hemlocks, jarring down the snow, — for there are hardly bare twigs enough for them to rest on, — or they plume themselves in some snug recess on the sunny side of the tree, only pausing to utter their *tche de de de*.

The locust pods, which were abundant, are still, part of them, unopened on the trees.

I notice, as I am returning half an hour before sunset, the thermometer about 24°, much vapor rising from the thin ice which has formed over the snow and water to-day by the riverside. Here, then, I actually see the vapor rising *through* the ice.

Jan. 13. Tuttle was saying to-day that he did remember a certain man's living with him once, from something that occurred. It was this: The man was about starting for Boston market for Tuttle, and Mrs. Tuttle had been telling him what to get for her. The man inquired if that was all, and Mrs. Tuttle said no, she wanted some nutmegs. "How many," he asked. Tuttle, coming along just then, said, "Get a bushel."

When the man came home he said that he had had a good deal of trouble about the nutmegs. He could not find so many as were wanted, and, besides, they told him that they did not sell them by the bushel. But he said that he would take a bushel by the weight. Finally he made out to get a peck of them, which he brought home. It chanced that nutmegs were very high just then, so Tuttle, after selecting a few for his own use, brought the remainder up to town and succeeded in disposing of them at the stores for just what he gave for them.

One man at the post-office said that a crow would drive a fox. He had seen three crows pursue a fox that was crossing the Great Meadows, and he fairly ran from [them] and took refuge in the woods.

Farmer says that he remembers his father's saying that as he stood in a field once, he saw a hawk soaring above and eying something on the ground. Looking round, he saw a weasel there eying the hawk. Just then the hawk stooped, and the weasel at the same instant sprang upon him, and up went the hawk with the weasel; but by and by the hawk began to come down as fast as he went up, rolling over and over, till he struck the ground. His father, going up, raised him up, when out hopped the weasel from under his wing and ran off none the worse for his fall.

The surface of the snow, now that the sun has shone on it so long, is not so light and downy, almost impalpable, as it was yesterday, but is somewhat flattened down and looks even as if [it] had had a skim-coat of some whitewash. I can see sparkles on it, but they are finer than at first and therefore less dazzling.

The thin ice of the Mill Brook sides at the Turnpike bridge is sprinkled over with large crystals which look like asbestos or a coarse grain. This is no doubt the vapor of last evening crystallized. I see vapor rising from and curling along the open brook and also rising from the end of a plank in the sun, which is wet with melted snow, though the thermometer was 16° only when I left the house.

I see in low grounds numerous heads of bidens, with their seeds still.

I see under some sizable white pines in E. Hubbard's wood, where red squirrels have run about much since this snow. They have run chiefly, perhaps, under the surface of the snow, so that it is very much undermined by their paths under these trees, and every now and then they have come to the surface, or the surface has fallen into their gallery. They seem to burrow under the snow about as readily as a meadow mouse. There are also paths raying out on every side from the base of the trees. And you see many holes through the snow into the ground where they now are, and other holes where they have probed for cones and nuts. The scales of the white pine cones are scattered about here and there. They seek a dry place to open them, — a fallen limb that rises above the snow, or often a lower dead stub projecting from the trunk of the tree.

Jan. 14. About an inch more snow fell this morning. An average snow-storm is from six to eight inches deep on a level.

The snow having ceased falling this forenoon, I go

to Holden Wood, Conantum, to look for tracks. It is too soon. I see none at all but those of a hound, and also where a partridge waded through the light snow, apparently while it was falling, making a deep gutter.

Yesterday there was a broad field of bare ice on each side of the river, *i. e.* on the meadows, and now, though it is covered with snow an inch deep, as I stand on the river or even on Fair Haven Hill a quarter to half a mile off, I can see where the ice is through the snow, *plainly*, trace its whole outline, it being quite dark compared with where the snow has fallen on snow. In this case a mantle of light snow even an inch thick is not sufficient to conceal the darkness of the ice beneath it, where it is contrasted with snow on snow.

Those little groves of sweet-fern still thickly leaved, whose tops now rise above the snow, are an interesting warm brown-red now, like the reddest oak leaves. Even this is an agreeable sight to the walker over snowy fields and hillsides. It has a wild and jagged leaf, alternately serrated. A warm reddish color revealed by the snow.

It is a mild day, and I notice, what I have not observed for some time, that blueness of the air only to be perceived in a mild day. I see it between me and woods half a mile distant. The softening of the air amounts to this. The mountains are quite invisible. You come forth to see this great blue presence lurking about the woods and the horizon.

Jan. 16. P. M. — Down Boston road around Quail Hill.

Very warm, — 45° at 2 p. m.

There is a tender crust on the snow, and the sun is brightly reflected from it. Looking toward Billerica from the cross-road near White's, the young oaks on the top of a hill in the horizon are very red, perhaps seven or eight miles off and directly opposite to the sun, far more red, no doubt, than they would appear near at hand, really bright red; but nowhere else that I perceive. It is an aerial effect, depending on their distance and elevation and being opposite to the sun, and also contrasted with the snowy ground.

Looking from Smith's Hill on the Turnpike, the hills eight or ten miles west are white, but the mountains thirty miles off are blue, though both may be equally white at the same distance.

I see a flock of tree sparrows busily picking something from the surface of the snow amid some bushes. I watch one attentively, and find that it is feeding on the very fine brown chaffy-looking seed of the panicled andromeda. It understands how to get its dinner, to make the plant *give down*, perfectly. It flies up and alights on one of the dense brown panicles of the hard berries, and gives it a vigorous shaking and beating with its claws and bill, sending down a shower of the fine chaffy-looking seed on to the snow beneath. It lies very distinct, though fine almost as dust, on the spotless snow. It then hops down and briskly picks up from the snow what it wants. How very clean and agreeable to the imagination, and withal abundant, is this kind of food! How delicately they fare! These dry persistent seed-vessels hold their crusts of bread

Vol. XIII

until shaken. The snow is the white table-cloth on which they fall. No anchorite with his water and his crust fares more simply. It shakes down a hundred times as much as it wants at each shrub, and shakes the same or another cluster after each successive snow. How bountifully Nature feeds them! No wonder they come to spend the winter with us, and are at ease with regard to their food. These shrubs ripen an abundant crop of seeds to supply the wants of these immigrants from the far north which annually come to spend the winter with us. How neatly and simply it feeds!

This shrub grows unobserved by most, only known to botanists, and at length matures its hard, dry seed-vessels, which, if noticed, are hardly supposed to contain seed. But there is no shrub nor weed which is not known to some bird. Though you may have never noticed it, the tree sparrow comes from the north in the winter straight to this shrub, and confidently shakes its panicle, and then feasts on the fine shower of seeds that falls from it.

Jan. 17. Another mild day.
P. M. — To Goose Pond and Walden.
Sky overcast, but a crescent of clearer in the northwest. I see on the snow in Hubbard's Close one of those rather large flattish black bugs some five eighths of an inch long, with feelers and a sort of shield at the forward part with an orange mark on each side of it. In the spring-hole ditches of the Close I see many little water-bugs (*Gyrinus*) gyrating, and some under

water. It must be a common phenomenon there in mild weather in the winter.

I look again at that place of squirrels (of the 13th). As I approach, I have a glimpse of one or two red squirrels gliding off silently along the branches of the pines, etc. They are gone so quickly and noiselessly, perhaps keeping the trunk of the tree between you and them, that [you] would not commonly suspect their presence if you were not looking for them. But one that was on the snow ascended a pine and sat on a bough with its back to the trunk as if there was nothing to pay. Yet when I moved again he scud up the tree, and glided across on some very slender twigs into a neighboring tree, and so I lost him. Here is, apparently, a settlement of these red squirrels. There are many holes through the snow into the ground, and many more where they have probed and dug up a white pine cone, now pretty black and, for aught I can see, with abortive or empty seeds; yet they patiently strip them on the spot, or at the base of the trees, or at the entrance of their holes, and evidently find some good seed. The snow, however, is strewn with the empty and rejected seeds. They seem to select for their own abode a hillside where there are half a dozen rather large and thick white pines near enough together for their aerial travelling, and then they burrow numerous holes and depend on finding (apparently) the pine cones which they cast down in the summer, before they have opened. In the fall they construct a nest of grass and bark-fibres, moss, etc., in one of the trees for winter use, and so apparently have two resources.

I walk about Ripple Lake and Goose Pond. I see the old tracks of some foxes and rabbits about the edge of these ponds (over the ice) within a few feet of the shore. I think that I have noticed that animals thus commonly go round by the shore of a pond, whether for fear of the ice, or for the shelter of the shore, *i. e.* not to be seen, or because their food and game is found there. But a dog will oftener bolt straight across.

When I reached the open railroad causeway returning, there was a splendid sunset. The northwest sky at first was what you may call a lattice sky, the fair weather establishing itself first on that side in the form of a long and narrow crescent, in which the clouds, which were uninterrupted overhead, were broken into long bars parallel to the horizon, thus: —

Alcott said well the other day that this was his definition of heaven, "A place where you can have a little conversation."

Jan. 18. 2 P. M. — To Fair Haven Pond, on river. Thermometer 46; sky mostly overcast.

The temperature of the air and the clearness or serenity of the sky are indispensable to a knowledge of a day, so entirely do we sympathize with the moods of nature. It is important to know of a day that is past whether it was warm or cold, clear or cloudy, calm or windy, etc.

Vol. XIII

winter began. It is the swifter though *deeper*, but not *deep*, channels on each side that remain open.

When I reached the lowest part of the Great Meadows, the neck of the Holt, I saw that the ice, thickly covered with snow, before me was of two shades, white and darker, as far as I could see in parallel sections. This was owing to fine snow blown low over the first — hence white — portion. I noticed it when I was returning toward the sun. This snow looks just like vapor curling along over the surface, — long waving lines producing the effect of a watered surface, very interesting to look at, when you face the sun, waving or curving about swellings in the ice like the grain of wood, the whole surface in motion, like a low, thin, but infinitely broad stream made up of a myriad meandering rills of vapor flowing over the surface. It *seemed* to rise a foot or two, yet when I laid my finger on the snow I did not perceive that any of the drifting snow rose above it or passed over it; it rather turned and went round it. It was the snow, probably the last light snow of the morning (when half an inch fell), blown by the strong northwest wind just risen, and apparently blown only where the surface beneath was smooth enough to let it slide. On such a surface it would evidently be blown a mile very quickly. Here the distance over which it was moving may have been half a mile. As you look down on it around you, you only see it moving straight forward in a thin sheet; but when you look at it several rods off in the sun, it has that waving or devious motion like vapor and flames, very agreeable and surprising.

They are very different seasons in the winter when the ice of the river and meadows and ponds is bare, — blue or green, a vast glittering crystal, — and when it is all covered with snow or slosh; and our moods correspond. The former may be called a crystalline winter.

Standing under Lee's Cliff, several chickadees, uttering their faint notes, come flitting near to me as usual. They are busily prying under the bark of the pitch pines, occasionally knocking off a piece, while they cling with their claws on any side of the limb Of course they are in search of animal food, but I see one suddenly dart down to a seedless pine seed wing on the snow, and then up again. C. says that he saw them busy about these wings on the snow the other [day], so I have no doubt that they eat this seed.

There is a springy place in the meadow near the Conantum elm.

The sky in the reflection at the open reach at Hubbard's Bath is more green than in reality, and also darker-blue, and the clouds are blacker and the purple more distinct.

Jan. 19. P. M. — Down river.
2 P. M. — Thermometer 38. Somewhat cloudy at first.

The open water at Barrett's Bar is very small compared with that at Hubbard's Bath yesterday, and I think it could not have frozen much last night.

It is evident mere shallowness is not enough to prevent freezing, for that shallowest space of all, in middle of river at Barrett's Bar, has been frozen ever since the

Jan. 20. 2 P. M. — 39°. Up Assabet.

The snow and ice under the hemlocks is strewn with cones and seeds and tracked with birds and squirrels. What a bountiful supply of winter food is here provided for them! No sooner has fresh snow fallen and covered up the old crop than down comes a new supply all the more distinct on the spotless snow. Here comes a little flock of chickadees, attracted by me as usual, and perching close by boldly; then, descending to the snow and ice, I see them pick up the hemlock seed which lies all around them. Occasionally they take one to a twig and hammer at it there under their claws, perhaps to separate it from the wing, or even the shell. The snowy ice and the snow on shore have been blackened with these fallen cones several times over this winter. The snow along the sides of the river is also all dusted over with birch and alder seed, and I see where little birds have picked up the alder seed.

At R. W. E.'s red oak I see a gray squirrel, which has been looking after acorns there, run across the river. The half-inch snow of yesterday morning shows its tracks plainly. They are much larger and more like a rabbit's than I expected.

The squirrel runs in an undulating manner, though it is a succession of low leaps of from two and a half to three feet. Each four tracks occupy a space some six

A Concert of Blackbirds

Sedges by the River

or seven inches long. Each foot-track is very distinct, showing the toes and protuberances of the foot, and is from an inch and a half to an inch and three quarters long. The clear interval between the hind and fore feet is four to five inches. The fore feet are from one and a half to three inches apart in the clear; the hind, one to two inches apart. I see that what is probably the track of the same squirrel near by is sometimes in the horseshoe form, i. e., when its feet are all brought close together: the open side still forward. I must have often mistaken this for a rabbit. But is not the bottom of the rabbit's foot so hairy that I should never see these distinct marks or protuberances?

This squirrel ran up a maple till he got to where the stem was but little bigger than his body, and then, getting behind the gray-barked stem, which was almost exactly the color of its body, it clasped it with its fore feet and there hung motionless with the end of its tail blowing in the wind. As I moved, it steadily edged round so as to keep the maples always between me and it, and I only saw its tail, the sides of its body projecting, and its little paws clasping the tree. It remained otherwise perfectly still as long as I was thereabouts, or five or ten minutes. There was a leafy nest in the tree.

Jan. 22. P. M. — Up river to Fair Haven Pond; return *via* Andromeda Ponds and railroad.

Overcast, but some clear sky in southwest horizon; mild weather still.

Where the sedge grows rankly and is uncut, as along the edge of the river and meadows, what fine coverts

are made for mice, etc., at this season! It is arched over, and the snow rests chiefly on its ends, while the middle part is elevated from six inches to a foot and forms a thick thatch, as it were, even when all is covered with snow, under which the mice and so forth can run freely, out of the way of the wind and of foxes. After a pretty deep snow has just partially melted, you are surprised to find, as you walk through such a meadow, how high and lightly the sedge lies up, as if there had been no pressure upon it. It grows, perhaps, in dense tufts or tussocks, and when it falls over, it forms a thickly thatched roof.

Nature provides shelter for her creatures in various ways. If the musquash, etc., has no longer extensive fields of weed and grass to crawl in, what an extensive range it has under the ice of the meadows and riversides! for, the water settling directly after freezing, an icy roof of indefinite extent is thus provided for it, and it passes almost its whole winter under shelter, out of the wind and invisible to men.

The ice is so much rotted that I observe in many places those lunar-shaped holes, and dark places in the ice, convex up-stream, sometimes double-lunar.

I perceive that the open places in the river do not preserve the same relative importance that they had December 29th. Then the largest four or five stood in this order: (1) below boat's place, (2) below junction, (3) Barrett's Bar, (4) Clamshell or else Hubbard's Bath. Now it is (1) below junction, (2) Hubbard's Bath or else Clamshell. I do not know but Clamshell is as

Vol. XIII

large as Hubbard's Bath. Which of the others is largest I am not quite sure. In other words, below junction and Hubbard's Bath (if not also Clamshell, not seen) retain about their former size, while below boat's place and Barrett's Bar have been diminished, especially below boat's place.

Birds are commonly very rare in the winter. They are much more common at some times than at others. I see more tree sparrows in the beginning of the winter (especially when snow is falling) than in the course of it. I think that by observation I could tell in what kind of weather afterward these were most to be seen. Crows come about houses and streets in very cold weather and deep snows, and they are heard cawing in pleasant, thawing winter weather, and their note is then a pulse by which you feel the quality of the air, i. e., when cocks crow. For the most part, lesser redpolls and pine grosbeaks do not appear at all. Snow buntings are very wandering. They were quite numerous a month ago, and now seem to have quit the town. They seem to ramble about the country at will.

C. says that he followed the track of a fox all yesterday afternoon, though with some difficulty, and then lost it at twilight. I suggested that he should begin next day where he had left off, and that following it up thus for many days he might catch him at last. "By the way," I asked, "did you go the same way the fox did, or did you take the back track?" "Oh," said he, "I took the back track. It would be of no use to go the other way, you know."

Minott says that a hound which pursues a fox by

scent cannot tell which way he is going; that the fox is very cunning and will often return on its track over which the dog had already run. It will ascend a high rock and then leap off very far to one side; so throw the dogs off the scent for a while and gain a breathing-spell.

I see, in one of those pieces of drifted meadow (of last spring) in A. Wheeler's cranberry meadow, a black willow thus transplanted more than ten feet high and five inches in diameter. It is quite alive.

The snow-fleas are thickest along the edge of the wood here, but I find that they extend quite across the river, though there are comparatively few over the middle. There are generally fewer and fewer the further you are from the shore. Nay, I find that they extend quite across Fair Haven Pond. There are two or three inches of snow on the ice, and thus they are revealed. There are a dozen or twenty to a square rod on the very middle of the pond. When I approach one, it commonly hops away, and if it gets a good spring it hops a foot or more, so that it is at first lost to me. Though they are scarcely the twentieth of an inch long they make these surprising bounds, or else conceal themselves by entering the snow. We have now had many days of this thawing weather, and I believe that these fleas have been gradually hopping further and further out from the shore. To-day, perchance, it is water, a day or two later ice, and no fleas are seen on it. Then snow comes and covers the ice, and if there is no thaw for a month, you see no fleas for so long. But, at least soon after a thaw, they are to be seen on the centre of ponds at least half a mile across. Though this is my opinion, it is by no means certain that they come here thus, for I am prepared to believe that the water in the middle may have had as many floating on it, and that these were afterward on the surface of the ice, though unseen, and hence under the snow when it fell, and ready to come up through it when the thaw came. But what do they find to eat in apparently pure snow so far from any land? Has their food come down from the sky with the snow? They must themselves be food for many creatures. This must be as peculiarly a winter animal as any. It may truly be said to live in snow.

I see some insects of about this form on the snow: ————————

I scare a partridge that was eating the buds and ends of twigs of the *Vaccinium vacillans* on a hillside.

At the west or nesæa end of the largest Andromeda Pond, I see that there has been much red ice, more than I ever saw, but now spoiled by the thaw and snow.

The leaves of the water andromeda are evidently more appressed to the twigs, and showing the gray under sides, than in summer.

Jan. 23. 8 A. M. — On river.

Walking on the ice by the side of the river this very pleasant morning, I see many minnows (may be dace) from one and a half to four inches long which have come out, through holes or cracks a foot wide more or less, where the current has worn through and shows

the dark stream, and the water has flown over the adjacent ice, sinking it down so as to form a shallow water four or five feet wide or more, and often several rods long, and four or five inches deep on the side next the crack, or deepest side. This water has a yellowish color, and a fish or anything else in it is at once seen. I think that they come out into this thin water overlying the ice for the sake of the sun's warmth. Much heat must be reflected from the icy bottom this sunny morning, — a sort of anticipation of spring to them. This shallow surface water is also thinly frozen over, and I can sometimes put my hand close over the minnow. When alarmed they make haste back to the dark water of the crack, and seek the depths again.

Each pleasant morning like this all creatures recommence life with new resolutions, — even these minnows, methinks.

That snow which in the afternoons these days is thawing and dead — in which you slump — is now hard and crisp, supporting your weight, and has a myriad brilliant sparkles in the sunlight.

When a thaw comes, old cracks are enlarged in every direction, so that an ordinary man's track will look like the track of a snow-shoe, and a hound's track will sometimes have spread to a foot in diameter (when there is a thin snow on ice), with all the toes distinct, looking like the track of a behemoth or megalonyx.

Minott says that pigeons alight in great flocks on the tops of hemlocks in March, and he thinks they eat the seed. (But he also thought for the same reason

that they ate the white pine seed at the same season, when it is not there! They might find a little of the last adhering to the pitch.)

Says he used to shoot the gray squirrel thus: he put his hat or coat upon a stick while the squirrel hung behind an upright limb, then, going round to the side, he shot him, for the squirrel avoided exposing himself to the coat as much as to the man.

He has stood on the steep hill southwest side of Moore's Swamp and seen two foxes chase a white rabbit all about it. The rabbit would dodge them in the thicket, and now and then utter a loud cry of distress. The foxes would burst out on the meadow and then dash into the thicket again. This was when the wood had been cut and he could see plainly. He says that the white rabbit loves to sit concealed under the overarching cinnamon ferns (which he calls "buck-horns") on the sunny side of a swamp, or under a tuft of brakes which are partly fallen over. That a hound in its headlong course will frequently run over the fox, which quickly turns and gets off three or four rods before the former can stop himself.

For Spring and Blossoming *vide* Pliny, vol. ii, page 163.

Jan. 24. 2 P. M. — To Tarbell, river, *via* railroad.

Thermometer 46. Sky thinly overcast, growing thicker at last as if it would rain. Wind northwest.

See a large flock of lesser redpolls, eating the seeds of the birch (and perhaps alder [1]) in Dennis Swamp

[1] *Vide* the 29th.

by railroad. They are distinct enough from the goldfinch, their note more shelly and general as they fly, and they are whiter, without the black wings, beside that some have the crimson head or head and breast. They alight on the birches, then swarm on the snow beneath, busily picking up the seed in the copse.

The Assabet is open above Derby's Bridge as far as I go or see, probably to the factory, and I know not how far below Derby's. It opens up here sooner than below the Assabet Bath to its mouth.

The blue vervain stands stiffly and abundant in one place, with much rather large brown seed in it. It is in good condition.

Scare a shrike from an apple tree. He flies low over the meadow, somewhat like a woodpecker, and alights near the top twig of another apple tree. See a hawk sail over meadow and woods; not a hen-hawk; possibly a marsh hawk. A grasshopper on the snow. The droppings of a skunk left on a rock, perhaps at the beginning of winter, were full of grasshoppers' legs.

As I stand at the south end of J. P. B.'s moraine, I watch six tree sparrows, which come from the wood and alight and feed on the ground, which is there bare. They are only two or three rods from me, and are incessantly picking and eating an abundance of the fine grass (short-cropped pasture grass) on that knoll, as a hen or goose does. I see the stubble an inch or two long in their bills, and how they stuff it down. Perhaps they select chiefly the green parts. So they vary their fare and there is no danger of their starving. These six hopped round for five minutes over a space a rod square before I put them to flight, and then I noticed, in a space only some four feet square in that rod, at least eighteen droppings (white at one end, the rest more slate-colored). So wonderfully active are they in their movements, both external and internal. They do not suffer for want of a good digestion, surely. No doubt they eat some earth or gravel too. So do partridges eat a great deal. These birds, though they have bright brown and buff backs, hop about amid the little inequalities of the pasture almost unnoticed, such is their color and so humble are they.

Solomon thus describes the return of Spring (Song of Solomon, ii, 10–12): —

"Rise up, my love, my fair one, and come away.

"For, lo, the winter is past, the rain is over and gone;

"The flowers appear on the earth; the time of the singing of birds is come, and the voice of the turtle is heard in our land."

Jan. 25. In keeping a journal of one's walks and thoughts it seems to be worth the while to record those phenomena which are most interesting to us at the time. Such is the weather. It makes a material difference whether it is foul or fair, affecting surely our mood and thoughts. Then there are various degrees and kinds of foulness and fairness. It may be cloudless, or there may be sailing clouds which threaten no storm, or it may be partially overcast. On the other hand it may rain, or snow, or hail, with various degrees of intensity. It may be a transient thunder-storm, or a shower, or a flurry of snow, or it may be a prolonged

storm of rain or snow. Or the sky may be overcast or rain-threatening. So with regard to temperature. It may be warm or cold. Above 40° is warm for winter. One day, at 38 even, I walk dry and it is good sleighing; the next day it may have risen to 48, and the snow is rapidly changed to slosh. It may be calm or windy. The finest winter day is a cold but clear and glittering one. There is a remarkable life in the air then, and birds and other creatures appear to feel it, to be excited and invigorated by it. Also warm and melting days in winter are inspiring, though less characteristic.

I will call the weather fair, if it does not threaten rain or snow or hail; foul, if it rains or snows or hails, or is so overcast that we expect one or the other from hour to hour. To-day it is fair, though the sky is slightly overcast, but there are *sailing* clouds in the southwest.

The river is considerably broken up by the recent thaw and rain, but the Assabet much the most, probably because it is swifter and, owing to mills, more fluctuating.

When the river begins to break up, it becomes clouded like a mackerel sky, but in this case the blue portions are where the current, clearing away the ice beneath, begins to show dark. The current of the water, striking the ice, breaks it up at last into portions of the same form with those which the wind gives to vapor. First, all those open places which I measured lately much enlarge themselves each way.

Saw A. Hosmer approaching in his pung. He cal-

Vol. XIII

culated so that we should meet just when he reached the bare planking of the causeway bridge, so that his horse might as it were stop of his own accord and no other excuse would be needed for a talk. He says that he has seen that little bird (evidently the shrike) with mice in its claws. Wonders what has got all the rabbits this winter. Last winter there were hundreds near his house; this winter he sees none.

Jan. 26. Fair, but overcast. Thermometer about 32°. Pretty good skating on the Great Meadows, slightly raised and smoothed by the thaw and also the rain of (I think) the 23d–24th.

Great revolutions of this sort take place before you are aware of it. Though you walk every day, you do not foresee the kind of walking you will have the next day. Skating, crusted snow, slosh, etc., are wont to take you by surprise.

P. M. — To Eleazer Davis's Hill, and made a fire on the ice, merely to see the flame and smell the smoke. We soon had a slender flame flashing upward some four feet, — so many parallel undulating tongues. The air above and about it was all in commotion, being heated so that we could not see the landscape distinctly or steadily through it. If only to see the *pearl* ashes and hear the brands sigh.

Jan. 27. 2 P. M. — Up river to Fair Haven Pond, and return by Walden.

Half a dozen redpolls busily picking the seeds out of the larch cones behind Monroe's. They are pretty

tame, and I stand near. They perch on the slender twigs which are beaded with cones, and swing and teeter there while they perseveringly peck at them, trying now this one, now that, and sometimes appearing to pick out and swallow them quite fast. I notice no redness or carmine at first, but when the top of one's head comes between me and the sun it unexpectedly glows.

Fair and hardly a cloud to be seen. Thermometer 28. (But it is overcast from the northwest before sunset.)

After the January thaw we have more or less of crusted snow, i. e. more consolidated and crispy. When the thermometer is not above 32 this snow for the most part bears, — if not too deep.

Now I see, as I am on the ice by Hubbard's meadow, some wisps of vapor in the west and southwest advancing. They are of a fine, white, thready grain, curved

like skates at the end. Have we not more finely divided clouds in winter than in summer? flame-shaped, asbestos-like? I doubt if the clouds show as fine a grain in warm weather. They are wrung dry now. They are not expanded but contracted, like spiculæ. What hieroglyphics in the winter sky!

Those wisps in the west advanced and increased like white flames with curving tongues, — like an aurora by day. Now I see a few hard and distinct ripple-marks at right angles with them, or parallel with the horizon, the

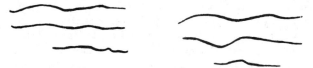

lines indicating the ridges of the ripple-marks. These are like the abdominal plates of a snake. This occupies only a very small space in the sky. Looking right up overhead, I see some gauzy cloud-stuff there, so thin as to be grayish, — brain-like, finely reticulated; so thin yet so firmly drawn, membranous. These, methinks, are always seen overhead only. Now, underneath the flamy asbestos part, I detect an almost imperceptible rippling in a thin lower vapor, — an incipient mackerel-ling (in *form*). Now, nearly to the zenith, I see, not a mackerel sky, but blue and thin, blue-white, finely mixed, like fleece finely picked and even strewn over a blue ground. The white is in small roundish flocks. In a mackerel sky there is a parallelism of oblongish scales. This is so remote as to appear stationary, while a lower vapor is rapidly moving eastward.

Such clouds as the above are the very thin advance-guard of the cloud behind. It soon comes on more densely from the northwest, and darkens all.

No bright sunset to-night.

What fine and pure reds we see in the sunset sky! Yet earth is not ransacked for dye-stuffs. It is all accomplished by the sunlight on vapor at the right angle, and the sunset sky is constant if you are at the

right angle. The sunset sky is sometimes more northerly, sometimes more southerly. I saw one the other day occupying only the south horizon, but very fine, and reaching more than half-way to the zenith from west to east. This may either be for want of clouds or from excess of them on certain sides.

As I go along the edge of Hubbard's Wood, on the ice, it is very warm in the sun — and calm there. There are certain spots I could name, by hill and wood sides, which are always thus sunny and warm in fair weather, and have been, for aught I know, since the world was made. What a distinction they enjoy!

How many memorable localities in a river walk! Here is the warm wood-side; next, the good fishing bay; and next, where the old settler was drowned when crossing on the ice a hundred years ago. It is all storied.

I occasionally hear a musquash plunge under the ice next the shore.

These winter days I occasionally hear the note of a goldfinch, or maybe a redpoll, unseen, passing high overhead.

When you think that your walk is profitless and a failure, and you can hardly persuade yourself not to return, it is on the point of being a success, for then you are in that subdued and knocking mood to which Nature never fails to open.

Jan. 29. Colder than before, and not a cloud in the sky to-day.

P. M. — To Fair Haven Pond and return *via* Andromeda Ponds and railroad.

Half an inch or more of snow fell last night, the ground being half bare before. It was a snow of small flakes not star-shaped.

As usual, I now see, walking on the river and river-meadow ice, thus thinly covered with the fresh snow, that conical rainbow, or parabola of rainbow-colored reflections, from the myriad reflecting crystals of the snow, *i. e.*, as I walk toward the sun, —

always a little in advance of me, of course, angle of reflection being equal to that of incidence.

To-day I see quite a flock of the lesser redpolls eating the seeds of the alder, picking them out of the cones just as they do the larch, often head downward; and I see, under the alders, where they have run and picked up the fallen seeds, making chain-like tracks, two parallel lines.

Not only the Indian, but many wild birds and quadrupeds and insects, welcomed the apple tree to these shores. As it grew apace, the bluebird, robin, cherry-bird, kingbird, and many more came with a rush and built their nests in it, and so became orchard-birds.

The woodpecker found such a savory morsel under its bark that he perforated it in a ring quite round the tree, a thing he had never done before. It did not take the partridge long to find out how sweet its buds were, and every winter day she flew and still flies from the wood to pluck them, much to the farmer's sorrow. The rabbit too was not slow to learn the taste of its twigs and bark. The owl crept into the first one that became hollow, and fairly hooted with delight, finding it just the place for him. He settled down into it, and has remained there ever since. The lackey caterpillar saddled her eggs on the very first twig that was formed, and it has since divided her affections with the wild cherry; and the canker-worm also in a measure abandoned the elm to feed on it. And when the fruit was ripe, the squirrel half carried, half rolled, it to his hole, and even the musquash crept up the bank and greedily devoured it; and when it was frozen and thawed, the crow and jay did not disdain to peck it.[1] And the beautiful wood duck, having made up her mind to stay a while longer with us, has concluded that there is no better place for her too.

Jan. 30. 2 P. M. — To Nut Meadow and White Pond road.

Thermometer 45°. Fair with a few cumuli of indefinite outline in the north and south, and dusky under sides. A gentle west wind and a blue haze. Thaws.

The river has opened to an unusual extent, owing to the very long warm spell, — almost all this month.

[1] [*Excursions*, pp. 293, 294; Riv. 360, 361.]

Even from Hubbard's Bridge up and down it is breaking up, is all mackerelled, with lunar-shaped openings and some like a thick bow. They [are] from one to twelve feet long.

Yesterday's slight snow is all gone, leaving the ice, old snow, and bare ground; and as I walk up the riverside, there is a brilliant sheen from the wet ice toward the sun, instead of the crystalline rainbow of yesterday. Think of *that* (of yesterday), — to have constantly before you, receding as fast as you advance, a bow formed of a myriad crystalline mirrors on the surface of the snow!! What miracles, what beauty surrounds us! Then, another day, to do all your walking kneedeep in perfect six-rayed crystals of surpassing beauty but of ephemeral duration, which have fallen from the sky.

The ice has so melted on the meadows that I see where the musquash has left his clamshells in a heap near the riverside, where there was a hollow in the bank.

The small water-bugs are gyrating abundantly in Nut Meadow Brook. It is pleasant also to see the very distinct ripple-marks in the sand at its bottom, of late so rare a sight.

I go through the piny field northwest of M. Miles's. There are no more beautiful natural parks than these pastures in which the white pines have sprung up spontaneously, standing at handsome intervals, where the wind chanced to let the seed lie at last, and the grass and blackberry vines have not yet been killed by them.

There are certain sounds invariably heard in warm

and thawing days in winter, such as the crowing of cocks, the cawing of crows, and sometimes the gobbling of turkeys. The crow, flying high, touches the tympanum of the sky for us, and reveals the tone of it. What does it avail to look at a thermometer or barometer compared with listening to his note? He informs me that Nature is in the tenderest mood possible, and I hear the very flutterings of her heart.

Crows have singular wild and suspicious ways. You will [see] a couple flying high, as if about their business, but lo, they turn and circle and caw over your head again and again for a mile; and this is their business, — as if a mile and an afternoon were nothing for them to throw away. This even in winter, when they have no nests to be anxious about. But it is affecting to hear them cawing about their ancient seat (as at F. Wheeler's wood) which the choppers are laying low.

I saw the other day (apparently) mouse(?)-tracks which had been made in slosh on the Andromeda Ponds and then frozen, — little gutters about two inches wide and nearly one deep, looking very artificial with the nicks on the sides.

I sit on the high hilltop south of Nut Meadow, near the pond. This hazy day even Nobscot is so blue that it looks like a mighty mountain. See how man has cleared commonly the most level ground, and left the woods to grow on the more uneven and rocky, or in the swamps. I see, when I look over our landscape from any eminence as far as the horizon, certain rounded hills, amid the plains and ridges and cliffs, which have

Vol. XIII

a marked family likeness, like eggs that belong to one nest though scattered. They suggest a relation geologically. Such are, for instance, Nashoba, Annursnack, Nawshawtuct, and Ponkawtasset, all which have Indian names, as if the Indian, too, had regarded them as peculiarly distinct. There is also Round Hill in Sudbury, and perhaps a hill in Acton. Perhaps one in Chelmsford. They are not apparently rocky.

The snow-flea seems to be a creature whose summer and prime of life is a thaw in the winter. It seems not merely to enjoy this interval like other animals, but then chiefly to exist. It is the creature of the thaw. Moist snow is its element. That thaw which merely excites the cock to sound his clarion as it were calls to life the snow-flea.

Jan. 31. 2 P. M. — To Bedford Level.

Thermometer 45. Fair but all overcast. Sun's place quite visible. Wind southwest.

Went to what we called Two-Boulder Hill, behind the house where I was born. There the wind suddenly changed round 90° to northwest, and it became quite cold (had fallen to 24° or 24° [*sic*] at 5.30). Called a field on the east slope Crockery Field, there were so many bits in it. Saw a pitch pine on a rock about four feet high, but two limbs flat on the ground. This spread much and had more than a hundred cones of different ages on it. Such are always the most fertile.

Can look a great way northeast along the Bedford Swamp. Saw a large hawk, probably hen-hawk.

The ice that has been rotting and thawing from time

to time on the meadows — the water run out from below — has many curious marks on it. There are many ingrained waving lines more or less parallel. Often they make circular figures, or oval, and are concentric, as if they marked the edge of a great bubble or the like.

I notice the ice on a ditched brook so far worn by the current as to be mackerelled in color, white and dark, all along the middle, making a figure two or three rods long which reminds me forcibly of the flat skin of a boa-constrictor, — marked just like it.

III

FEBRUARY, 1860

(ÆT. 42)

Feb. 1. 2 P. M. — 5°. A cold day.

Two or three inches of dry snow last night.

Grows colder apace toward night. Frost forms on windows.

Feb. 2. 6° below at about 8 A. M.

Clock has stopped. Teams squeak.

2 P. M. — To Fair Haven Pond.

The river, which was breaking up, is frozen over again. The new ice over the channel is of a yellow tinge, and is covered with handsome rosettes two or three inches in diameter where the vapor which rose through froze and crystallized. This new ice for forty rods together is thickly covered with these rosettes, often as thick as snow, an inch deep, and sometimes in ridges like frozen froth three inches high. Sometimes they are

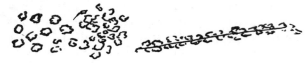

in a straight line along a crack. The frozen breath of the river at a myriad breathing-holes.

Vol. XIII

The many distinct firm ridges on a slope of the drift — as if the edges of so many distinct layers cropped out — form undulating parallel lines of great interest. Sometimes yet smaller hollows or cradles, not reaching to the ice and at right angles with the low ridges of the drift, remind you of panelling. Again these oval hollows produce a regular reticulation.

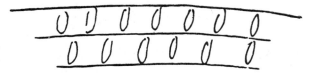

One hour you have bare ice; the next, a level counterpane of snow; and the next, the wind has tossed and sculptured it into these endless and varied forms. It is such a scene as Boothia Felix may present, — if that is any wilder than Concord. I go sliding over the few bare spots, getting a foothold for my run on the very thin sloping and ridged snow. The snow is not thus drifted in fields and meadows generally, but chiefly where there was an icy foundation on which it slid readily. The whole of the snow has evidently shifted, perhaps several times, and you cannot tell whether some slight ridges an inch high are the foundation of a drift just laid or the relics of one removed. Behind

A thaw began the 7th of January, and it was mild and thawing most of the time for the rest of that month; but with February we have genuine winter again. Almost all the openings in the river are closed again, and the new ice is covered with rosettes.

It blowed considerably yesterday, though it is very still to-day, and the light, dry snow, especially on the meadow ice and the river, was remarkably plowed and drifted by it, and now presents a very wild and arctic scene. Indeed, no part of our scenery is ever more arctic than the river and its meadows now, though the snow was only some three inches deep on a level. It is cold and perfectly still, and you walk over a level snowy tract. It is a sea of white waves of nearly uniform shape and size. Each drift is a low, sharp promontory directed toward the northwest, and showing which way the wind blowed with occasional small patches of bare ice amid them. It is exactly as if you walked over a solid sea where the waves rose about two feet high. These promontories have a general resemblance to one another. Many of them are perfect tongues of snow more or less curving and sharp.

Commonly the wind has made a little hollow in the snow directly behind this tongue, it may be to the ice, spoon-shaped or like a tray, — if small, a cradle in the snow. Again it is a complete canoe, the tongue being its bows.

a tuft of bushes it is collected deep, thus:

I forgot to say that all the ice between the rosettes was thinly sprinkled with very slender grain-like spiculæ, sometimes two together.

The sky was all overcast, but the sun's place quite distinct.

The cloud about the sun had a cold, dry, windy look, as if the cloud, elsewhere homogeneous cold slaty, were there electrified and arranged like iron-filings about the sun, its fibres, so to speak, more or less raying from the sun as a centre.

About 3 P. M. I noticed a distinct fragment of rainbow, about as long as wide, on each side of the sun, one north and the [other] south and at the same height above the horizon with the sun, all in a line parallel with the horizon; and, as I thought, there was a slight appearance of a bow.

The sun-dogs, if that is their name, were not so distinctly bright as an ordinary rainbow, but were plainly orange-yellow and a peculiar light violet-blue, the last color looking like a hole in the cloud, or a thinness through which you saw the sky. This lasted perhaps half an hour, and then a bow about the sun became quite distinct, but only those parts where the sun-dogs were were distinctly rainbow-tinted, the rest being merely reddish-brown and the clouds within finely raying from the sun more or less. But higher up, so that its centre would have been in the zenith

or apparently about in the zenith, was an arc of a distinct rainbow. A rainbow right overhead. Is this what is called a parhelion?

It is remarkable that the straw-colored sedge of the meadows, which in the fall is one of the least noticeable colors, should, now that the landscape is mostly covered with snow, be perhaps the most noticeable of all objects in it for its color, and an agreeable contrast to the snow.

I frequently see where oak leaves, absorbing the heat of the sun, have sunk into the ice an inch in depth and afterward been blown out, leaving a perfect type of the leaf with its petiole and lobes sharply cut, with perfectly

upright sides, so that I can easily tell the species of oak that made it. Sometimes these moulds have been evenly filled with snow while the ice is dark, and you have the figure of the leaf in white.

I see where some meadow mouse — if not mole — just came to the surface of the snow enough to break it with his back for three or four inches, then put his head out and at once withdrew it.

We walked, as usual, on the fresh track of a fox, peculiarly pointed, and sometimes the mark of two toe-nails in front separate from the track of the foot in very thin snow. And as we were kindling a fire on the pond by the side of the island, we saw the fox himself at the inlet of the river. He was busily examining along the sides of the pond by the button-bushes and willows, smelling in the snow. Not appearing to regard us much, he slowly explored along the shore of the pond thus, half-way round it; at Pleasant Meadow, evidently looking for mice (or moles?) in the grass of the bank, smelling in the shallow snow there amid the stubble, often retracing his steps and pausing at particular spots. He was eagerly searching for food, intent on finding some mouse to help fill his empty stomach. He had a blackish tail and blackish feet. Looked lean and stood high. The tail peculiarly large for any creature to carry round. He stepped daintily about, softly, and is more to the manor born than a dog. It was a very arctic scene this cold day, and I suppose he would hardly have ventured out in a warm one.

Vol. XIII

The fox seems to get his living by industry and perseverance. He runs smelling for miles along the most favorable routes, especially the edge of rivers and ponds, until he smells the track of a mouse beneath the snow or the fresh track of a partridge, and then follows it till he comes upon his game. After exploring thus a great many quarters, after hours of fruitless search, he succeeds. There may be a dozen partridges resting in the snow within a square mile, and his work is simply to find them with the aid of his nose. Compared with the dog, he affects me as high-bred, unmixed. There is nothing of the mongrel in him. He belongs to a noble family which has seen its best days, — a younger son. Now and then he starts, and turns and doubles on his track, as if he heard or scented danger. (I watch him through my glass.) He does not mind us at the distance of only sixty rods. I have myself seen one place where a mouse came to the surface to-day in the snow. Probably he has smelt out many such galleries. Perhaps he seizes them *through* the snow.

I had a transient vision of one mouse this winter, and that the first for a number of years.

I have seen a good many of those snails left on the ice during the late thaw, as the caterpillars, etc., were.

Feb. 3. 3 P. M. — To Gowing's Swamp.

I accurately pace the swamp in two directions and find it to be shaped thus: —

Gowing's Swamp. (Scale of forty paces to an inch)

When I read some of the rules for speaking and writing the English language correctly, — as that a sentence must never end with a particle, — and perceive how implicitly even the learned obey it, I think —

> Any fool can make a rule
> And every fool will mind it.

Feb. 5. P. M. — Up Assabet.

2 P. M., 40°.

I see where crows have pecked the tufts of cladonia lichens which peep out of the snow, pulling them to pieces, no doubt looking for worms. Also have eaten the frozen-thawed apples under the trees, tracking all the ground over there.

February 1st, though so cold and the snow so dry, as it blowed pretty hard, was a day of drift behind northerly walls, and when those shell-like drifts were formed, as well as the wild drifts of Hubbard's meadow described on the 3d.

I see at the Assabet stone bridge where, apparently, one or two otters travelled about on the ice last night in the thin snow. The river is open eight or ten rods there, and I noticed their tracks all about the river and close to the edge of the ice, thin as it was, for a dozen rods above and below the bridge. At first, being at a distance, I thought them dog-tracks, but I might have known that no dogs would ever have run about so there, on that thin ice and so near the edge of it. They were generally like this, each four being from fifteen to twenty-four inches apart. Occasionally the track was somewhat like a rabbit's. I saw where one had apparently dragged himself along the ice. They had entered the water in many places, also travelled along under the slanting ice next the bank long distances. They were evidently attracted by that open water. There was no distinct sliding place.

Coming home last night in the twilight, I recognized a neighbor a dozen rods off by his walk or carriage, though it was so dark that I could not see a single feature of his person. Indeed, his person was all covered up excepting his face and hands, and I could not possibly have distinguished these at this distance from another man's. Nor was it owing to any peculiarity in his dress, for I should have known him though he had had on a perfectly new suit. It was because the man within the clothes moved them in a peculiar manner that I knew him thus at once at a distance and in the twilight. He made a certain figure in any clothes he might wear, and moved in it in a peculiar manner. Indeed, we have a very intimate knowledge of one another; we see through thick and thin; spirit meets spirit. A man hangs out innumerable signs by which we may know him. So, last summer, I knew another neighbor half a mile off up the river, though I did not see him, by the manner in which the breath from his lungs and mouth, *i. e.* his voice, made the air strike my ear. In that manner he communicated himself to all his acquaintance within a diameter of one mile (if it were all up and down the river). So I remember to have been sure once in a very dark night who was preceding me on the sidewalk, — though I could not see him, — by the sound of his tread. I was surprised to find that I knew it.

And to-day, seeing a peculiar very long track of a man in the snow, who has been along up the river this morning, I guessed that it was George Melvin, because it was accompanied by a hound's track. There was a

thin snow on the ice, and I observed that he not only furrowed the snow for a foot before he completed his step, but that the (toe) of his track was always indefinite, as if his boot had been worn out and prolonged at the toe. I noticed that I and my companion made a clear and distinct track at the toe, but when I experimented, and tried to make a track like this by not lifting my feet but gliding and partly scuffing along, I found myself walking just like Melvin, and that perfectly convinced me that it was he.[1]

We have no occasion to wonder at the instinct of a dog. In these last two instances I surpassed the instinct of the dog.

It may always be a question how much or how little of a man goes to any particular act. It is not merely by taking time and by a conscious effort that he betrays himself. A man is revealed, and a man is concealed, in a myriad unexpected ways; *e. g.*, I can hardly think of a more effectual way of disguising neighbors to one another than by stripping them naked.

Feb. 6. To Cambridge.
A rainy day.

Feb. 7. 2 P. M. — To Walden and Flint's.
Thermometer 43°. Fair, with many clouds, mostly obscuring the sun. Wind northwest, growing cooler.

The sand has begun to flow on the west side of the cut, the east being bare. Nature has some bowels at last.

[1] I told him of it afterward, and he gave a corresponding account of himself.

I notice over the ditch near the Turnpike bridge, where water stands an inch or two deep over the ice, that the dust which had blown on to the ice from the road is now very regularly and handsomely distributed over the ice by the water, *i. e.*, is broken into prettily shaped small black figures equally distant from one another, — so that what was a deformity is now a beauty. Some kinds of worms or caterpillars have apparently crawled over it and left their trails on it, white or clear trails.

Feb. 8. 2 P. M. — Up river to Fair Haven Hill.
Thermometer 43. 40° and upward may be called a *warm* day in the winter.

We have had much of this weather for a month past, reminding us of spring. February may be called *earine* (springlike). There is a peculiarity in the air when the temperature is thus high and the weather fair, at this season, which makes sounds more clear and pervading, as if they trusted themselves abroad further in this genial state of the air. A different sound comes to my ear now from iron rails which are struck, as from the cawing crows, etc. Sound is not abrupt, piercing, or rending, but softly sweet and musical. It will take a yet more genial and milder air before the bluebird's warble can be heard.

Walking over Hubbard's broad meadow on the softened ice, I admire the markings in it. The more interesting and prevailing ones now appearing ingrained and giving it a more or less marbled look, — one, what you may call *checkered* marbling (?), consisting of small polygonal figures three quarters  [of an inch in] diameter, bounded by whitish lines more or less curved within the ice, and apparently covered with an entire thin surface ice, and so on for rods (these when five or six inches wide make a mackerel-sky ice); the other apparently passing from this into a sort of fibrous structure of waving lines, hair-like or rather flame-like, — call it *phlogistic*: — only

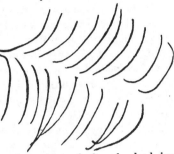

far more regular and beautiful than I can draw. Sometimes like perhaps a cassowary's feathers, the branches being very long and fine. This fibrous or phlogistic structure is evidently connected with the flow of the surface water, for I see some old holes, now smoothly frozen over, where these rays have flowed from all sides into the hole in the midst of the checked ice,

making a circular figure which reminded me of a jellyfish: only far more beautiful than this. The whitish lines which bound these figures and form the parallel fibres are apparently lines of fine bubbles more dense than elsewhere.  I am not sure that these markings always imply a double or triple ice, *i. e.* a thinner surface ice, which contains them.

The ice is thus marked under my feet somewhat as the heavens overhead; there is both the mackerel sky and the fibrous flame or asbestos-like form in both. The mackerel spotted or marked ice is very common, and also reminds me of the reticulations of the pickerel.

I see some quite thin ice which had formed on puddles on the ice, now soaked through, and in these are very interesting figures bounded by straight and crinkled 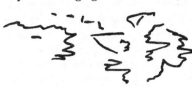 particularly white lines. I find, on turning the ice over, that these lines correspond to the raised edges of and between bubbles which have occupied a place in the ice, *i. e.* upward [?] in it.

Then there is occasionally, where puddles on the ice have frozen, that triangular rib-work of crystals, — a beautiful casting in alto[*sic*]-relievo of low crystal prisms with one edge up, — so meeting and cross-

Vol. XIII

ing as to form triangular and other figures. Shining splinters in the sun. Giving a rough hold to the feet.

One would think that the forms of ice-crystals must include all others.

I see hundreds of oak leaves which have sunk deep into the ice. Here is a scarlet oak leaf which has sunk one inch into the ice, and the leaf still rests at the bottom of this mould. Its stem and lobes and all their bristly points are just as sharply cut there as is the leaf itself, fitting the mould closely and tightly, and, there being a small hole or two in the leaf, the ice stands up through them half an inch high, like so many sharp tacks. Indeed, the leaf is sculptured thus in bas-relief [*sic*], as it were, as sharply and exactly as it could be done by the most perfect tools in any material. But as time has elapsed since it first began to sink into the ice, the upper part of this mould is enlarged by melting more or less, and often shows the outline of the leaf exaggerated and less sharp and perfect. You see these leaves at various depths in the ice, — many quite concealed by new ice formed over them, for water flows into the mould and thus a cast of it is made in ice. So fragments of rushes and sedge and cranberry leaves have on all sides sunk into the ice in like manner. The smallest and lightest-colored object that falls on the ice begins thus at once to sink through it, the sun as it were driving it; and a great many, no doubt, go quite through.

This is especially common after a long warm spell like this. I see, even, that those colored ridges of froth which have bounded the water that overflowed the ice, since they contain most of the impurities or coloring matter, sink into the ice accordingly, making rough furrows an inch or more deep often.

The proper color of water is perhaps best seen when it overflows white ice.

Pliny could express a natural wonder.

About an old boat frozen in, I see a great many little gyrinus-shaped bugs swimming about in the water above the ice.

Feb. 9. A hoar frost on the ground this morning — for the open fields are mostly bare — was quite a novel sight. I had noticed some vapor in the air late last evening.

Feb. 10. A very strong and a cold northwest wind to-day, shaking the house, — thermometer at 11 A. M., 14°, — consumes wood and yet we are cold, and drives the smoke down the chimney.

I see that Wheildon's pines are rocking and showing their silvery under sides as last spring, — their first awakening, as it were.

P. M. — The river, where open, is very black, as usual when the waves run high, for each wave casts a shadow.[1] Theophrastus notices that the roughened water is black, and says that it is because fewer rays fall on it and the light is dissipated.

It is a day for those rake and horn icicles; the water,

[1] Call it Black Water.

dashing against the southeast shores where they chance to be open, *i. e.* free of ice, and blown a rod inland, freezes to the bushes, forming rakes and oftener horns. If twigs project above the ice-belt thus: the water freezes over them thus: —

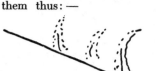

The very grass stubble is completely encased for a rod in width along the shore, and the trunks of trees for two or three feet up.

Any sprig lying on the edge of the ice is completely crusted. Sometimes the low button-bush twigs with their few remaining small dark balls, and also the drooping corymbs of the late rose hips, are completely encased in an icicle, and you see their bright scarlet reflected through the ice in an exaggerated manner. If a hair is held up above the ice where this spray is blowing, it is sufficient to start a thick icicle rake or horn, for the ice forming around it becomes at once its own support, and gets to be two or three inches thick. Where the open water comes within half a dozen feet of the shore, the spray has blown over the intervening ice and covered the grass and stubble, looking like a glaze, — countless loby fingers and horns over some fine stubble core, — and when the grass or stem is horizontal you

have a rake. Just as those great organ-pipe icicles

Vol. XIII

that drip from rocks have an annular structure growing downward, so these on the horizontal stubble and weeds, when directed to the point toward which the wind was blowing; *i. e.*, they grow thus southeast.

Then there is the thickened edge of the ice, like a cliff, on the southeast sides of openings against which the wind has dashed the waves, especially on the southeast side of broad meadows.

No finer walking in any respect than on our broad meadow highway in the winter, when covered with bare ice. If the ice is wet, you slip in rubbers; but when it is dry and cold, rubbers give you a firm hold, and you walk with a firm and elastic step. I do not know of any more exhilarating walking than up or down a broad field of smooth ice like this in a cold, glittering winter day when your rubbers give you a firm hold on the ice.

I see that the open places froze last night only on the windward side, where they were less agitated, the waves not yet running so high there.

A little snow, however, even the mere shavings or dust of ice made by skaters, hinders walking in rubbers very much, for though the rubber may give a good hold on clear ice, when you step on a little of the ice dust or snow you slide on that.

Those little gyrinus-shaped bugs of the 8th, that had come out through a crevice in the ice about a boat frozen in, and were swimming about in the shallow

water above the ice, I see are all gone now that that water is frozen, — have not been frozen in; so they must have returned back under the ice when it became cold, and this shows that they were not forced up accidentally in the first place, but attracted by the light and warmth, probably as those minnows were some time ago. That is, in a thaw in the winter some water-insects — beetles, etc. — will come up through holes in the ice and swim about in the sun.

Feb. 11. Saturday. 2 P. M., 20°.

Feb. 12. Sunday. 2 P. M., 22°.
Walk up river to Fair Haven Pond. Clear and windy, — northwest.

About a quarter of an inch of snow fell last evening. This scarcely colors that part of the ground that was bare, and on all icy surfaces which are exposed to the sweep of the wind it is already distributed very regularly in thin drifts. It lies on the ice in waving lines or in lunar or semicircular, often spread-eagle, patches with very regular intervals, quite like the openings lately seen in the river when breaking up. The whole surface of the icy field is thus watered. That is, it is not collected in one place more than another, but very evenly distributed in these patches over the whole surface. I speak of what lies on the open ice. It comes flowing like a vapor from the northwest, low over the ice and much faster than a man walks, and a part is ever catching and lodging here and there and building a low drift, the northwest side of which will be abrupt

with a sharp, beetling edge an inch or a half-inch high. No doubt these drifts are constantly changing their ground or rolling over. I see now that this vapor-like snow-dust is really sometimes blown up six or eight feet into the air, though for the most part it merely slides low over the ice.

The greater part of this snow is lodged a foot deep amid the button-bushes, and there it continues to accumulate as long as the wind blows strong.

In this cold, clear, rough air from the northwest we walk amid what simple surroundings! Surrounded by our thoughts or imaginary objects, living in our *ideas*, not one in a million ever sees the objects which are actually around him.

Above me is a cloudless blue sky; beneath, the sky-blue, *i. e.* sky-reflecting, ice with patches of snow scattered over it like mackerel clouds. At a distance in several directions I see the tawny earth streaked or spotted with white where the bank or hills and fields appear, or else the green-black evergreen forests, or the brown, or russet, or tawny deciduous woods, and here and there, where the agitated surface of the river is exposed, the blue-black water. That dark-eyed water, especially when I see it at right angles with the direction of the sun, is it not the first sign of spring? How its darkness contrasts with the general lightness of the winter! It has more life in it than any part of the earth's surface. It is where one of the arteries of the earth is palpable, visible.

Those are peculiar portions of the river which have thus always opened first, — been open latest and longest. In winter not only some creatures, but the very earth is partially dormant; vegetation ceases, and rivers, to some extent, cease to flow. Therefore, when I see the water exposed in midwinter, it is as if I saw a skunk or even a striped squirrel out. It is as if the woodchuck unrolled himself and snuffed the air to see if it were warm enough to be trusted.

It excites me to see early in the spring that black artery leaping once more through the snow-clad town. All is tumult and life there, not to mention the rails and cranberries that are drifting in it. Where this artery is shallowest, i. e., comes nearest to the surface and runs swiftest, there it shows itself soonest and you may see its pulse beat. These are the wrists, temples, of the earth, where I feel its pulse with my eye. The living waters, not the dead earth. It is as if the dormant earth opened its dark and liquid eye upon us.

But to return to my walk. I proceed over the sky-blue ice, winding amid the flat drifts as if amid the clouds, now and then treading on that thin white ice (much marked) of absorbed puddles (of the surface), which crackles somewhat like dry hard biscuit. Call it biscuit ice. Some of it is full of internal eyes like bird's-eye maple, little bubbles that *were* open above, and

elsewhere I tread on ice in which are traced all kinds of characters, Coptic and Syriac, etc. How curious those crinkled lines in ice that has been partly rotted, reaching down half an inch perpendicularly, or else at an angle with the surface, and with a channel that may be felt above!

There are places (a few), like that at Hubbard's Grove, commonly thin or open, leading to the shore, with the ice puffed up, *as if* kept open by a musquash, where apparently a spring comes in. Only betrayed by its being slow to freeze, or by the rottenness of the ice there. This is the least observed of all tributaries, the first evidence of a tributary.

On the east side of the pond, under the steep bank, I see a single lesser redpoll picking the seeds out of the alder catkins, and uttering a faint mewing note from time to time on account of me, only ten feet off. It has a crimson or purple front and breast.

How unexpected is one season by another! Off Pleasant Meadow I walk amid the tops of bayonet rushes frozen in, as if the summer had been overtaken by the winter.

Returning just before sunset, I see the ice beginning to be green, and a rose-color to be reflected from the

Vol. XIII

low snow-patches. I see the color from the snow first where there is some shade, as where the shadow of a maple falls afar over the ice and snow. From this is reflected a purple tinge when I see none elsewhere. Some shadow or twilight, then, is necessary, umbra mixed with the reflected sun. Off Holden Wood, where the low rays fall on the river from between the fringe of the wood, the snow-patches are not rose-color, but a very dark purple like a grape, and thus there are all degrees from pure white to black. When crossing Hubbard's broad meadow, the snow-patches are a most beautiful crystalline purple, like the petals of some flowers, or as if tinged with cranberry juice. It is quite a faery scene, surprising and wonderful, as if you walked amid those rosy and purple clouds that you see float in the evening sky. What need to visit the crimson cliffs of Beverly?

I thus find myself returning over a green sea, winding amid purple islets, and the low sedge of the meadow on one side is really a burning yellow.

The hunter may be said to invent his game, as Neptune did the horse, and Ceres corn.

It is twenty above at 5.30, when I get home.

I walk over a smooth green sea, or *aequor*, the sun just disappearing in the cloudless horizon, amid thousands of these flat isles as purple as the petals of a flower. It would not be more enchanting to walk amid the purple clouds of the sunset sky. And, by the way, this is but a sunset sky under our feet, produced by the same law, the same slanting rays and twilight. Here the clouds are these patches of snow or frozen

vapor, and the ice is the greenish sky between them. Thus all of heaven is realized on earth. You have seen those purple fortunate isles in the sunset heavens, and that green and amber sky between them. Would you believe that you could ever walk amid those isles? You can on many a winter evening. I have done so a hundred times. The ice is a solid crystalline sky under our feet.

Whatever aid is to be derived from the use of a scientific term, we can never begin to see anything as it is so long as we remember the scientific term which always our ignorance has imposed on it. Natural objects and phenomena are in this sense forever wild and unnamed by us.

Thus the sky and the earth sympathize, and are subject to the same laws, and in the horizon they, as it were, meet and are seen to be one.

I have walked in such a place and found it hard as marble.

Not only the earth but the heavens are made our footstool. That is what the phenomenon of ice means. The earth is annually inverted and we walk upon the sky. The ice reflects the blue of the sky. The waters become solid and make a sky below. The clouds grow heavy and fall to earth, and we walk on them. We live and walk on solidified fluids.

We have such a habit of looking away that we see not what is around us. How few are aware that in winter, when the earth is covered with snow and ice, the phenomenon of the sunset sky is double! The one is on the earth around us, the other in the horizon. These snow-clad hills answer to the rosy isles in the west. The winter is coming when I shall walk the sky. The ice is a solid sky on which we walk. It is the inverted year. There is an annual light in the darkness of the winter night. The shadows are blue, as the sky is forever blue. In winter we are purified and translated. The earth does not absorb our thoughts. It becomes a Valhalla.

Next above Good Fishing Bay and where the man was drowned, I pass Black Rock Shore, and over the Deep Causeway I come to Drifted Meadow.

North of the Warm Woodside (returning) is Bulrush Lagoon, — off Grindstone Meadow, — a good place for lilies; then Nut Meadow Mouth; Clamshell Bend, or Indian Bend; Sunset Reach, where the river flows nearly from west to east and is a fine sparkling scene from the hills eastward at sunset; then Hubbard's Bathing-Place, and the swift place, and Lily Bay, or Willow Bay.

Feb. 13. 2 P. M. — Down river.

Thermometer 38°. Warm; a cloud just appearing in the west.

That hard meadow just below the boys' bathing-place below the North Bridge is another elfin burial-ground. It would be a bad place to walk in a dark night. The mounds are often in ridges, even as if turned up by the plow.

Water overflowing the ice at an opening in the river, and mixing with thin snow, saturating it, seen now on one side at right angles with the sun's direction, is as

Vol. XIII

black as black cloth. It is surprising what a variety of distinct colors the winter can show us, using but few pigments, so to call them. The principal charm of a winter walk over ice is perhaps the peculiar and pure colors exhibited.

There is the *red* of the sunset sky, and of the snow at evening, and in rainbow flocks during the day, and in sun-dogs.

The *blue* of the sky, and of the ice and water reflected, and of shadows on snow.

The *yellow* of the sun and the morning and evening sky, and of the sedge (or straw-color, bright when lit on edge of ice at evening), and *all three* in hoar frost crystals.

Then, for the secondary, there is the *purple* of the snow in drifts or on hills, of the mountains, and clouds at evening.

The *green* of evergreen woods, of the sky, and of the ice and water toward evening.

The *orange* of the sky at evening.

The *white* of snow and clouds, and the *black* of clouds, of water agitated, and water saturating thin snow on ice.

The *russet* and *brown* and *gray*, etc., of deciduous woods.

The *tawny* of the bare earth.

I suspect that the green and rose (or purple) are not noticed on ice and snow unless it is pretty cold, and perhaps there is less greenness of the ice now than in December, when the days were shorter. The ice may now be too old and white.

Those horn, knob, and rake icicles on the southeast

sides of all open places — or that were open on the 10th near enough to the bushes — are suddenly softening and turning white on one side to-day, so that they remind me of the alabaster (?) or plaster images on an Italian's board. All along the ice belt or shelf — for the river has fallen more than a foot — countless white figures stand crowded, their minute cores of sedge or twigs being concealed. Some are like beaks of birds, — cranes or herons. Having seen this phenomenon in one place, I know with certainty in just how many places and where, throughout the town, — four or five, — I shall find these icicles, on the southeast sides of the larger open places which approached near enough to a bushy or reedy shore.

The grass comes very nearly being completely encrusted in some places, but commonly rounded knobs stand up.

The ground being bare, I pick up two or three arrow-heads in Tarbell's field near Ball's Hill.

There is nothing more affecting and beautiful to man, a child of the earth, than the sight of the naked soil in the spring. I feel a kindredship with it.

The sun being in a cloud, partly obscured, I see a very dark purple tinge on the flat drifts on the ice earlier than usual, and when afterward the sun comes out below the cloud, I see no purple nor rose. Hence it seems that the twilight has as much or more to do with this phenomenon, supposing the sun to be low, than the slight angle of its rays with the horizon.

Always you have to contend with the stupidity of men. It is like a stiff soil, a hard-pan. If you go deeper than usual, you are sure to meet with a pan made harder even by the superficial cultivation. The stupid you have always with you. Men are more obedient at first to words than ideas. They mind names more than things. Read to them a lecture on "Education," naming that subject, and they will think that they have heard something important, but call it "Transcendentalism," and they will think it moonshine. Or halve your lecture, and put a psalm at the beginning and a prayer at the end of it and read it from a pulpit, and they will pronounce it good without thinking.

The Scripture rule, "Unto him that hath shall be given," is true of composition. The more you have thought and written on a given theme, the more you can still write. Thought breeds thought. It grows under your hands.

Feb. 15.[1] As in the expression of moral truths we admire any closeness to the physical fact which in all language is the symbol of the spiritual, so, finally, when natural objects are described, it is an advantage if words derived originally from nature, it is true, but which have been turned (*tropes*) from their primary signification to a moral sense, are used, *i. e.*, if the object is personified. The one who loves and understands a thing the best will incline to use the personal pronouns in speaking of it. To him there is no *neuter*

[1] [The manuscript journal volume that begins with this date bears the legend "The early spring" at the beginning.]

gender. Many of the words of the old naturalists were in this sense doubly tropes.

P. M. — About 30° at 2 P. M. Skated to Bound Rock.

Frequently, the same night that it first freezes, or perhaps in the morning, the ice over the thread of the river will be puffed up for many rods a foot or more, evidently by expanding vapors beneath, and also over the channel of some warm spring emptying in. Also at Walden where it is very shallow or the ice rests on a bar between the pond and a bay.

When lately the open parts of the river froze more or less in the night after that windy day, they froze by  stages, as it were, many feet wide, and the water dashed and froze against the edge of each successive strip of ice, leaving so many parallel ridges.

The river is rapidly falling, is more than a foot lower than it was a few days ago, so that there is an ice-belt left where the bank is steep, and on this I skate in many places; in others the ice slants from the shore for a rod or two to the water; and on the meadows for the most part there is no water under the ice, and it accordingly rumbles loudly as I go over it, and I rise and fall as I pass over hillocks or hollows.

From the pond to Lee's Bridge I skated so swiftly before the wind, that I thought it was calm, for I kept pace with it, but when I turned about I found that quite a gale was blowing.

Occasionally one of those puffs (making a pent-roof

of ice) runs at right angles across the river where there is no spring or stream emptying in. A crack may have started it.

Feb. 16. 2 P. M. — To Walden.

A snow-storm, which began in the night, — and is now three or four inches deep. The ground, which was more than half bare before, is thus suddenly concealed, and the snow lodges on the trees and fences and sides of houses, and we have a perfect wintry scene again. We hear that it stormed at Philadelphia yesterday morning.

As I [look] toward the woods beyond the poorhouse, I see how the trees, especially apple trees, are suddenly brought out relieved against the snow, black on white, every twig as distinct as if it were a pen-and-ink drawing the size of nature. The snow being spread for a background, while the storm still raging confines your view to near objects, each apple tree is distinctly outlined against it.

Suddenly, too, where of late all was tawny-brown in pastures I see a soft snowy field with the pale-brown lecheas just peeping out of it.

It is a moist and starry snow, lodging on trees, — leaf, bough, and trunk. The pines are well laden with it. How handsome, though wintry, the side of a high pine wood, well grayed with the snow that has lodged on it, and the smaller pitch pines converted into marble or alabaster with their lowered plumes like rams' heads!

The character of the wood-paths is wholly changed

Vol. XIII

by the new-fallen snow. Not only all tracks are concealed, but, the pines drooping over it and half concealing or filling it, it is merely a long chink or winding open space between the trees.

This snow, as I have often noticed before, is composed of stars and other crystals with a very fine cotton intermixed. It lodges and rests softly on the horizontal limbs of oaks and pines. On the fruit and dry leafets (?) of the alders that slant over the pond it is in the form of little cones two inches high, making them snowball plants. So many little crystalline wheels packed in cotton.

When we descend on to Goose Pond we find that the snow rests more thickly on the numerous zigzag and horizontal branches of the high blueberries that bend over it than on any deciduous shrub or tree, producing a very handsome snowy maze, and can thus distinguish this shrub, by the manner in which the snow lies on it, quite across the pond. It is remarkable also how very distinct and *white* every plane surface, as the rocks which lie here and there amid the blueberries or higher on the bank, — a place where no twig or weed rises to interrupt the pure white impression. In fact, this crystalline snow lies up so light and downy that it evidently admits more light than usual, and the surface is more white and glowing for it. It is semitransparent. This is especially the case with the snow lying upon rocks or musquash-houses, which is elevated and brought between you and the light. It is partially transparent, like alabaster. Also all the birds' nests in the blueberry bushes are revealed, by the great snow-balls they hold.

Feb. 17. P. M. — Cold and northwest wind, drifting the snow. 3 P. M., thermometer 14°.

A perfectly clear sky except one or two little cloud-flecks in the southwest, which, when I look again after walking forty rods, have entirely dissolved. When the sun is setting the light reflected from the snow-covered roofs is quite a clear pink, and even from white board fences.

Grows colder yet at evening, and frost forms on the windows.

I hear that some say they saw a bluebird and heard it sing last week ! ! It was probably a shrike.

Minott says that he hears that Heard's testimony in regard to Concord River in the meadow case was that "it is dammed at both ends and cursed in the middle," *i. e.* on account of the damage to the grass there.

We cannot spare the very lively and lifelike descriptions of some of the old naturalists. They sympathize with the creatures which they describe. Edward Topsell in his translation of Conrad Gesner, in 1607, called "The History of Four-footed Beasts," says of the antelopes that "they are bred in India and Syria, near the river Euphrates," and then — which enables you to realize the living creature and its habitat — he adds, "and delight much to drink of the cold water thereof." The beasts which most modern naturalists describe do not *delight* in anything, and their water is neither hot nor cold. Reading the above makes you want to go and drink of the Euphrates yourself, if it is warm weather. I do not know how much of his spirit he owes to Gesner, but he proceeds in his translation to say that "they have horns growing forth of the crown of their head, which are very long and sharp; so that Alexander affirmed they pierced through the shields of his soldiers, and fought with them very irefully: at which time his company slew as he travelled to India, eight thousand five hundred and fifty, which great slaughter may be the occasion why they are so rare and seldom seen to this day."

Now here *something* is described at any rate; it is a real account, whether of a real animal or not. You can plainly see the horns which "grew forth" from their crowns, and how well that word "irefully" describes a beast's fighting! And then for the number which Alexander's men slew "as he travelled to India," — and what a travelling was that, my hearers! — eight thousand five hundred and fifty, just the number you would have guessed after the thousands were given, and [an] easy one to remember too. He goes on to say that "their horns are great and made like a saw, and they with them can cut asunder the branches of osier or small trees, whereby it cometh to pass that many times their necks are taken in the twists of the falling boughs, whereat the beast with repining cry, bewrayeth himself to the hunters, and so is taken." The artist too has done his part equally well, for you are presented with a drawing of the beast with serrated horns, the tail of a lion, a cheek tooth (canine?) as big as a boar's, a stout front, and an exceedingly "ireful" look, as if he were facing all Alexander's army.

Though some beasts are described in this book which have no existence as I can learn but in the imagination

of the writers, they really have an existence there, which is saying not a little, for most of our modern authors have not imagined the actual beasts which they presume to describe. The very frontispiece is a figure of "the gorgon," which looks sufficiently like a hungry beast covered with scales, which you may have dreamed of, apparently just fallen on the track of you, the reader, and snuffing the odor with greediness.

These men had an adequate idea of a beast, or what a beast should be, a very *bellua* (the translator makes the word *bestia* to be "*a vastando*"); and they will describe and will draw you a cat with four strokes, more beastly or beast-like to look at than Mr. Ruskin's favorite artist draws a tiger. They had an adequate idea of the wildness of beasts and of men, and in their descriptions and drawings they did not always fail when they *surpassed* nature.

Gesner says of apes that "they are held for a subtil, ironical, ridiculous and unprofitable beast, whose flesh is not good for meat as a sheep, neither his back for burthen as an asses, nor yet commodious to keep a house like a dog, but of the Grecians termed gelotopoios, made for laughter." As an evidence of an ape's want of "discretion," he says: "A certain ape after a shipwreck, swimming to land, was seen by a countryman, who thinking him to be a man in the water gave him his hand to save him, yet in the mean time asked him what countryman he was, to which he answered that he was an Athenian: Well, said the man, dost thou know Piræus (a port in Athens)? Very well, said the ape, and his wife, friends and children. Whereat the

Vol. XIII

man being moved, did what he could to drown him." "They are best contented to sit aloft although tied with chains. . . . They bring forth young ones for the most part by twins, whereof they love the one and hate the other; that which they love they bear on their arms, the other hangeth at the dam's back, and for the most part she killeth that which she loveth, by pressing it too hard: afterward, she setteth her whole delight upon the other."

Feb. 18. A snow-storm, falling all day; wind northeast.

The snow is fine and drives low; is composed of granulated masses one sixteenth to one twentieth of an inch in diameter. Not in flakes at all. I think it is not those large-flaked snow-storms that are the worst for the traveller, or the deepest.

It would seem as if the more odd and whimsical the conceit, the more credible to the mass. They require a surprising truth, though they may well be surprised at any truth. For example, Gesner says of the beaver: "The biting of this beast is very deep, being able to crash asunder the hardest bones, and commonly he never loseth his hold until he feeleth his teeth gnash one against another. Pliny and Solinus affirm, that the person so bitten cannot be cured, except he hear the crashing of the teeth, which I take to be an opinion without truth."

Gesner (unless we owe it to the translator) has a livelier conception of an animal which has no existence, or of an action which was never performed, than most naturalists have of what passes before their eyes. The

ability to report a thing *as if* [*it*] *had occurred*, whether it did or not, is surely important to a describer. They do not half tell a thing because you might expect them to but half believe it. I feel, of course, very ignorant in a museum. I know nothing about the things which they have there, — no more than I should know my friends in the tomb. I walk amid those jars of bloated creatures which they label frogs, a total stranger, without the least froggy thought being suggested. Not one of them can croak. They leave behind all life they that enter there, both frogs and men. For example, Gesner says again, "The tree being down and prepared, they take one of the oldest of their company, whose teeth could not be used for the cutting, (or, as others say, they constrain some strange beaver whom they meet withal, to fall flat on his back), . . . and upon his belly lade they all their timber, which they so ingeniously work and fasten into the compass of his legs that it may not fall, and so the residue by the tail draw him to the water side, where those buildings are to be framed, and this the rather seemeth to be true, because there have been some such taken that had no hair on their backs, but were pilled, which being espied by the hunters, in pity of their slavery or bondage, they have let them go away free." Gives Albertus and Olaus Magnus as authorities for this.

Melvin tells me that he went a day or two ago to where G. M. Barrett had placed a dead cow of his, and that he found the snow thickly tracked by foxes to within five feet around the carcass, and they appeared to have sat down there, but so suspicious of some trick were they that they had not touched it.

Sometimes, when I go forth at 2 P. M., there is scarcely a cloud in the sky, but soon one will appear in the west and steadily advance and expand itself, and so change the whole character of the afternoon and of my thoughts. The history of the sky for that afternoon will be but the development of that cloud.

I think that the most important requisite in describing an animal, is to be sure and give its character and spirit, for in that you have, without error, the sum and effect of all its parts, known and unknown. You must tell what it is to man. Surely the most important part of an animal is its *anima*, its vital spirit, on which is based its character and all the peculiarities by which it most concerns us. Yet most scientific books which treat of animals leave this out altogether, and what they describe are as it were phenomena of dead matter. What is most interesting in a dog, for example, is his attachment to his master, his intelligence, courage, and the like, and not his anatomical structure or even many habits which affect us less.

If you have undertaken to write the biography of an animal, you will have to present to us the living creature, *i. e.*, a result which no man can understand, but only in his degree report the impression made on him.

Science in many departments of natural history does not pretend to go beyond the shell; *i. e.*, it does not get to animated nature at all. A history of animated nature must itself be animated.

The ancients, one would say, with their gorgons,

sphinxes, satyrs, mantichora, etc., could imagine more than existed, while the moderns cannot imagine so much as exists.

In describing brutes, as in describing men, we shall naturally dwell most on those particulars in which they are most like ourselves, — in which we have most sympathy with them.

We are as often injured as benefited by our systems, for, to speak the truth, no human system is a true one, and a name is at most a mere convenience and carries no information with it. As soon as I begin to be aware of the life of any creature, I at once forget its name. To know the names of creatures is only a convenience to us at first, but so soon as we have learned to distinguish them, the sooner we forget their names the better, so far as any true appreciation of them is concerned. I think, therefore, that the best and most harmless names are those which are an imitation of the voice or note of an animal, or the most poetic ones. But the name adheres only to the accepted and conventional bird or quadruped, never an instant to the real one. There is always something ridiculous in the name of a great man, — as if he were named John Smith. The name is convenient in communicating with others, but it is not to be remembered when I communicate with myself.

If you look over a list of medicinal recipes in vogue in the last century, how foolish and useless they are seen to be! And yet we use equally absurd ones with faith to-day.

When the ancients had not found an animal wild and

strange enough to suit them, they created one by the mingled [traits] of the most savage already known, — as hyenas, lionesses, pards, panthers, etc., etc., — one with another. Their beasts were thus of wildness and savageness all compact, and more *ferine* and *terrible* than any of an unmixed breed could be. They allowed nature great license in these directions. The most strange and fearful beasts were by them supposed to be the offspring of two different savage kinds. So fertile were their imaginations, and such fertility did they assign to nature. In the modern account the fabulous part will be omitted, it is true, but the portrait of the real and living creature also.

The old writers have left a more lively and lifelike account of the gorgon than modern writers give us of real animals.

Feb. 19. Snow maybe near a foot deep, and now drifting.

· *Feb.* 20. P. M. — I see directly in front [of] the Depot Lee [?] house, on the only piece of bare ground I see hereabouts, a large flock of lesser redpolls feeding. They must be picking up earth, sand, or the withered grass. They are so intent on it that they allow me to come quite near. This, then, is one use for the drifting of snow which lays bare some spots, however deep it may be elsewhere, — so that the birds, etc., can come at the earth. I never thought of this use before. First the snow fell deep and level on the 18th, then, the 19th, came high wind and plowed it out here and there to

the ground; and so it will always be in some places, however deep it may have been.

J. Farmer tells me that his grandfather once, when moving some rocks in the winter, found a striped squirrel frozen stiff. He put him in his pocket, and when he got home laid him on the hearth, and after a while he was surprised to see him running about the room as lively as ever he was.

I notice a very pale pink reflection from snowy roofs and sides of white houses at sunrise. So both the pink and the green are phenomena of the morning, but in a much less degree, which shows that they depend more on the twilight and the grossness of the atmosphere than on the angle at which the sunlight falls.

Feb. 21. 2 P. M. — Thermometer forty-six and snow rapidly melting. It melts first and fastest where the snow is so thin that it feels the heat reflected from the ground beneath.

I see now, in the ruts in sand on hills in the road, those interesting ripples which I only notice to advantage in very shallow running water, a phenomenon almost, as it were, confined to melted snow running in ruts in the road in a thaw, especially in the spring. It is a spring phenomenon. The water, meeting with some slight obstacle, ever and anon appears to shoot across diagonally to the opposite side, while ripples from

the opposite side intersect the former, producing countless regular and sparkling diamond-shaped ripples.

If you hold your head low and look along up such a stream in a right light, it is seen to have a regularly braided surface, tress-like, preserving its figures as if it were solid, though the stream is seen pulsing high through the middle ripples in the thread of the stream. The ripples are as rectilinear as ice-crystals. When you see the sparkling stream from melting snow in the ruts, know that then is to be seen this braid of the spring.

It was their very admiration of nature that made the ancients attribute those magnanimous qualities which are rarely to be found in man to the lion as her master-piece, and it is only by a readiness, or rather prepared-ness, to see more than appears in a creature that one can appreciate what is manifest.

It is remarkable how many berries are the food of birds, mice, etc. Perhaps I may say that all are, how-ever hard or bitter. This I am inclined to say, judging of what I do not know from what I do. For example, mountain-ash, prinos, skunk-cabbage, sumach, choke-cherry, cornels probably, elder-berry, viburnums, rose hips, arum, poke, thorn, barberry, grapes, tupelo, am-phicarpæa, thistle-down, bayberry (?), *Cornus florida*, checkerberry, hemlock, larch, pines, etc., birch, alder, juniper. The berries and seeds of wild plants generally, however little it is suspected by us, are the food of birds, squirrels, or mice.

Feb. 23. 2 P. M. — Thermometer 56°. Wind south. 3 P. M. — Thermometer 58° and snow almost gone. River rising. We have not had such a warm day since the beginning of December (which was remarkably warm).

Vol. XIII

Would it not apply to the crows searching for their food in our meadows, along the water's edge, a little later?

A fact stated barely is dry. It must be the vehicle of some humanity in order to interest us. It is like giving a man a stone when he asks you for bread. Ultimately the moral is all in all, and we do not mind it if inferior truth is sacrificed to superior, as when the moralist fables and makes animals speak and act like men. It must be warm, moist, incarnated, — have been breathed on at least. A man has not seen a thing who has not felt it.

Feb. 24. 2 P. M. — Thermometer 42. A very spring-like day, so much sparkling light in the air.

The clouds reflecting a dazzling brightness from their edges, and though it is rather warm (the wind raw) there are many, finely divided, in a stream southwest to northeast all the afternoon, and some most brilliant mother-o'-pearl. I never saw the green in it more dis-tinct. This on the thin white edges of clouds as if it were a small piece of a rainbow. Some of the finest imaginable rippling, and some fine strings of clouds, narrow ant-eater skeletons, stretching from southwest to northeast, with the wind, looking like a little cotton

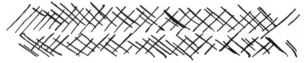

caught on a crooked telegraph-wire, the spine is so distinct.

A great part of the very finely divided cloud, one stratum above another, had the appearance of a woven

I walk over the moist Nawshawtuct hillside and see the green radical leaves of the buttercup, shepherd's-purse (circular), sorrel, chickweed, cerastium, etc., re-vealed.

About 4 P. M. a smart shower, ushered in by thunder and succeeded by a brilliant rainbow and yellow light from under the dark cloud in the west. Thus the first remarkable heat brings a thunder-shower.

The words "pardall" and "libbard," applied by Ges-ner to the same animal, express as much of the wild beast as any.

I read in Brand's "Popular Antiquities" that "Bishop Stillingfleet observes, that among the Saxons of the northern nations, the Feast of the New Year was observed with more than ordinary jollity: thence, as Olaus Wormius and Scheffer observe, they reckoned their age by so many Iolas." (*Iola*, to make merry. — Gothic.) So may we measure our lives by our joys. We have lived, not in proportion to the number of years that we have spent on the earth, but in proportion as we have enjoyed.

February is pronounced the coldest month in the year. In B.'s "Popular Antiquities" is quoted this from the Harleian Manuscripts: —

> "Février de tous les mois,
> Le plus court et moins courtois."

In the same work it is said that this saying is still current in the north of England: —

> "On the first of March,
> The crows begin to search."

web, the fibres crossing each other in a remarkable man-ner right overhead.

The river risen and quite over the meadows yesterday and to-day, and musquash begun to be killed.

Feb. 25. P. M. — Round *via* Clamshell to Hubbard's Bridge.

Colder, and frozen ground; strong wind, northwest.

I noticed yesterday in the street some dryness of stones at crossings and in the road and sidewalk here and there, and even two or three boys beginning to play at marbles, so ready are they to get at the earth.

The fields of open water amid the thin ice of the meadows are the spectacle to-day. They are especially dark blue when I look southwest. Has it anything to do with the direction of the wind? It is pleasant to see high dark-blue waves half a mile off running inces-santly along the edge of white ice. There the motion of the blue liquid is the most distinct. As the waves

rise and fall they seem to run swiftly along the edge of the ice.

The white pine cones have been blowing off more

or less in every high wind ever since the winter began, and yet perhaps they have not more than half fallen yet.

For a day or two past I have seen in various places the small tracks apparently of skunks. They appear to come out commonly in the warmer weather in the latter part of February.

I noticed yesterday the first conspicuous silvery sheen from the needles of the white pine waving in the wind. A small one was conspicuous by the side of the road more than a quarter of a mile ahead. I suspect that those plumes which have been appressed or contracted by snow and ice are not only dried but opened and spread by the wind.

Those peculiar tracks which I saw some time ago, and still see, made in slosh and since frozen at the Andromeda Ponds, I think must be mole-tracks, and those "nicks" on the sides are where they shoved back the snow with their vertical flippers. This is a very peculiar track, a broad channel in slosh, and at length in ice.

Feb. 26. Sunday. 2 P. M. — Thermometer 30; cold northwest wind.

The water is about six inches above Hoar's steps. That well covers the meadows generally. Cold and strong northwest wind this and yesterday.

Feb. 27. 2 P. M. — Thermometer 50.
To Abner Buttrick's Hill.
The river has been breaking up for several days,

and I now see great cakes lodged against each of the bridges, especially at Hunt's and the North Bridge, where the river flows with the wind. For a week or more you could not go to Ball's Hill by the south side of the river. The channel is now open, at least from our neighborhood all the way to Ball's Hill,[1] except the masses of ice moving in it; but the ice generally rests on the bottom of the meadows, — such as was there before the water rose, — and the freshet is for the most part covered with a thin ice except where the wind has broke[n] it up. The high wind for several days has prevented this water from freezing hard.

There are many cranberries washed far on to a large cake of ice which stretches across the river at Hunt's Bridge. The wind subsiding leaves them conspicuous on the middle of the cake.

I noticed yesterday that the skunk-cabbage had not started yet at Well Meadow, and had been considerably frost-bitten.

Heywood says that when the ground is regularly descending from the north to the railroad, a low fence a quarter of a mile off has been found to answer perfectly; if it slopes upward, it must be very near the road.

I walk down the river below Flint's on the north side. The sudden apparition of this dark-blue water on the surface of the earth is exciting. I must now walk where I can see the most water, as to the most living part of nature. This is the blood of the earth, and we see its blue arteries pulsing with new life now. I see, from

[1] Yes, and upward as far as Cardinal Shore, the reach above Hubbard's Bridge being open; thence it is mackerelled up to the pond.

Vol. XIII

far over the meadows, white cakes of ice gliding swiftly down the stream, — a novel sight. They are whiter than ever in this spring sun.

The abundance of light, as reflected from clouds and the snow, etc., etc., is more springlike than anything of late.

For several days the earth generally has been bare. I see the tawny and brown earth, the fescue- and lichen-clad hills behind Dakin's and A. Buttrick's.

Among the radical leaves most common, and therefore early-noticed, are the veronica and the thistle, — green in the midst of brown and decayed; and at the bottom of little hollows in pastures, now perhaps nearly covered with ice and water, you see some greener leafets of clover.

I find myself cut off by that arm of our meadow sea which makes up toward A. Buttrick's. The walker now by the river valley is often compelled to go far round by the water, driven far toward the farmers' door-yards.

I had noticed for some time, far in the middle of the Great Meadows, something dazzlingly white, which I took, of course, to be a small cake of ice on its end, but now that I have climbed the pitch pine hill and can overlook the whole meadow, I see it to be the white breast of a male sheldrake accompanied perhaps by his mate (a darker one). They have settled warily in the very midst of the meadow, where the wind has blown a space of clear water for an acre or two. The aspect of the meadow is sky-blue and dark-blue, the former a thin ice, the latter the spaces of open water which the

wind has made, but it is chiefly ice still. Thus, as soon as the river breaks up or begins to break up fairly, and the strong wind widening the cracks makes at length open spaces in the ice of the meadow, this hardy bird appears, and is seen sailing in the first widened crack in the ice, where it can come at the water. Instead of a piece of ice I find it to be the breast of the sheldrake, which so reflects the light as to look larger than it is, steadily sailing this way and that with its companion, who is diving from time to time. They have chosen the opening farthest removed from all shores. As I look I see the ice drifting in upon them and contracting their water, till finally they have but a few square rods left, while there are forty or fifty acres near by. This is the first bird of the spring that I have seen or heard of.

C. saw a skater-insect on E. Hubbard's Close brook in woods to-day.

Feb. 28. 2 P. M. — Thermometer 52; wind easterly. To Conantum.

I am surprised to see how my English brook cress has expanded or extended since I saw it last fall to a bed four feet in diameter, as if it had grown in the water, though it is quite dirty or muddied with sediment. Many of the sprigs turn upwards and just rest on the water at their ends, as if they might be growing. It has also been eaten considerably by some inhabitant of the water. I am inclined to think it must grow in the winter.

What is that bluish bulb now apparently beginning to shoot in the water there, floating loose (not the water-purslane)?

I suppose they are linarias which I still see flying about.

Passed a very little boy in the street to-day, who had on a home-made cap of a woodchuck-skin, which his father or elder brother had killed and cured, and his mother or elder sister had fashioned into a nice warm cap. I was interested by the sight of it, it suggested so much of family history, adventure with the chuck, story told about [it], not without exaggeration, the human parents' care of their young these hard times. Johnny was promised many times, and now the work has been completed, — a perfect little idyl, as they say. The cap was large and round, big enough, you would say, for the boy's father, and had some kind of cloth visor stitched to it. The top of the cap was evidently the back of the woodchuck, as it were expanded in breadth, contracted in length, and it was as fresh and handsome as if the woodchuck wore it himself. The great gray-tipped wind hairs were all preserved, and stood out above the brown only a little more loosely than in life. As if he put his head into the belly of a woodchuck, having cut off his tail and legs and substituted a visor for the head. The little fellow wore it innocently enough, not knowing what he had on, forsooth, going about his small business pit-a-pat; and his black eyes sparkled beneath it when I remarked on its warmth, even as the woodchuck's might have done. Such should be the history of every piece of clothing that we wear.

As I stood by Eagle Field wall, I heard a fine rattling sound, produced by the wind on some dry weeds at my

elbow. It was occasioned by the wind rattling the fine seeds in those pods of the indigo-weed which were still closed, — a distinct rattling din which drew my attention to it, — like a small Indian's calabash. Not a mere rustling of dry weeds, but the shaking of a rattle, or a hundred rattles, beside.

Looking from Hubbard's Bridge, I see a great water-bug even on the river, so forward is the season.

I take up a handsomely spread (or blossomed) pitch pine cone, but I find that a squirrel has begun to strip it first, having gnawed off a few of the scales at the base. The squirrel always begins to gnaw a cone thus at the base, as if it were a stringent law among the squirrel people, — as if the old squirrels taught the young ones a few simple rules like this.

C. saw a dozen robins to-day on the ground on Ebby Hubbard's hill by the Yellow Birch Swamp.

One tells me that George Hubbard told him he saw blackbirds go over this forenoon.

One of the Corner Wheelers feels sure that he saw a bluebird on the 24th, and says he saw a sheldrake in the river at the factory "a month ago." I should say that the sheldrake was our hardiest duck.

It suggests from what point of view Gesner (or his translator) describes an animal, — how far he takes into account man's relation to it, — that he commonly gives the "epithets" which have been applied to it. He deals in description, and epithets are a short description. And the translator says to the reader, "All these rows and ranks of living four-footed beasts are as letters and midwives to save the reverence which is

Vol. XIII

due to the Highest (that made them) from perishing within you."

I hear this account of Austin: —

An acquaintance who had bought him a place in Lincoln took him out one day to see it, and Austin was so smitten with the quiet and retirement and other rural charms that he at once sold his house in Concord, bought a small piece of rocky pasture in an out-of-the-way part of this out-of-the-way town, and with the funds raised by the sale of his old house built him a costly stone house upon it. Now he finds that this retirement (or country life) is the very thing which he does not want, but, his property being chiefly invested in the house, he is caught in a trap, as it were, for he cannot sell it, though he advertises it every year. As for society, he has none; his neighbors are few and far between, and he never visits them nor they him. They can do without him, being old settlers, *adscripti glebae*. He found one man in the next town who got his living by sporting and fishing, and he has built him a little hut and got him to live on his place for society and helpfulness. He cannot get help either for the outdoor or indoor work. There are none thereabouts who work by the day or job, and servant-girls decline to come so far into the country. Surrounded by grain-fields, he sends to Cambridge for his oats, and, as for milk, he can scarcely get any at all, for the farmers all send it to Boston, but he has persuaded one to leave some for him at the depot half a mile off.

As it is important to consider Nature from the point of view of science, remembering the nomenclature and

system of men, and so, if possible, go a step further in that direction, so it is equally important often to ignore or forget all that men presume that they know, and take an original and unprejudiced view of Nature, letting her make what impression she will on you, as the first men, and all children and natural men still do. For our science, so called, is always more barren and mixed up with error than our sympathies are.

As I go down the Boston road, I see an Irishman wheeling home from far a large damp and rotten pine log for fuel. He evidently sweats at it, and pauses to rest many times. He found, perhaps, that his wood-pile was gone before the winter was, and he trusts thus to contend with the remaining cold. I see him unload it in his yard before me and then rest himself. The piles of solid oak wood which I see in other yards do not interest me at all, but this looked like *fuel*. It warmed me to think of it. He will now proceed to split it finely, and then I fear it [will] require almost as much heat to dry it, as it will give out at last. How rarely we are encouraged by the sight of simple actions in the street! We deal with banks and other institutions, where the life and humanity are concealed, — what there is. I like at least to see the great beams half exposed in the ceiling or the corner.

IV

MARCH, 1860

(ÆT. 42)

March 1. Rain all day. This will apparently take the frost out very much and still further settle the ways. It was already yesterday pretty good bare-ground walking on the north side the street. Yesterday was a dark, louring, moist day and still. The afternoon before, the wind was east, and I think that a storm (snow or rain) always succeeds. To-day is a still, dripping *spring* rain, but more fell in the night. It makes the walking worse for the time, but if it does not freeze again, will greatly help to settle the ways.

I have thoughts, as I walk, on some subject that is running in my head, but all their pertinence seems gone before I can get home to set them down. The most valuable thoughts which I entertain are anything but what *I* thought. Nature abhors a vacuum, and if I can only walk with sufficient carelessness I am sure to be filled.

March 2. Notice the brightness of a row of osiers this morning. This phenomenon, whether referable to a change in the condition of the twig or to the spring air and light, or even to our imaginations, is not the less a real phenomenon, affecting us annually at this

season. This is one compensation for having them lopped so often along the causeways, that it is only these new and vigorous growths which shine thus.

Frequently within ten days it has been uncomfortable walking in a greatcoat.

2 P. M. — Thermometer 50°. To Witherell Glade *via* Clamshell; thence to Hubbard's Close.

Thinking to look at the cabbage as I pass under Clamshell, I find it very inconspicuous. Most would have said that there was none there. The few tallest and slenderest but tender ones were frost-bitten and far from blooming, but I found three or four more, broad and stout, — a hardy mahogany-colored one, but very low, half covered with the withered sedge, which it lifted up with it, and not apparently open. Putting my finger into one, the broadest and lowest, which opened about half an inch and stood with its back to the west (while they are all sheltered by the hill on the north), I was surprised when I drew it forth to see it covered with pollen. It was fairly in bloom, and probably yesterday too. Evidently some buds are further advanced than others even when the winter comes, and then these are further expanded and matured in advance of the others in the very warm days in the winter. No doubt it may have bloomed in some places in this neighborhood in the last day or two of February this year. Unusually warm weather in February, with bare ground where they grow, may cause them to bloom before February is over. Most would not have detected any change in it since the fall.

Vol. XIII

The grass has evidently sprung and grown a little, a very little, of late, say the very last of February, in warm wet places at the south base of hills, like this. It has a healthy but dark-green look. The (apparently) *Epilobium coloratum* has conspicuous green radical leaves there.

I see several minute glaucous sort of grasshoppers skipping over the grass and water. Men shooting musquash these days.

All the grass-stubble in fields not mown is conspicuous pointed eastward, and reflects the light from a thousand parallel lances.

Probably blown thus by the prevailing winds through the winter. Now and for some days look for arrowheads where it is not too soft.

There is a strong westerly wind to-day, though warm, and we sit under Dennis's Lupine Promontory, to observe the water. The great phenomenon these days is the sparkling blue water, — a richer blue than the sky ever is. The flooded meadows are ripple lakes on a large scale. The landscape, though no growth is visible in it, is bright and springlike.

There is the tawny earth (almost completely bare) of different shades, lighter or darker, the light very light in this air, more so than the surface of the earth ever is (*i. e.* without snow), bleached as it were; and, in the hollows of it, set round by the tawny hills and banks, is this copious living and sparkling blue water of various shades. It is more dashing, rippling, sparkling, living, this windy but clear day; never smooth, but ever varying in its degree of motion and depth of blue as the wind is

more or less strong, rising and falling. All along the shore next us is a strip a few feet wide of very light and smooth sky-blue, for so much is sheltered even by the lowest shore, but the rest is all more or less agitated and dark-blue. In it are, floating or stationary, here and there, cakes of white ice, the least looking like ducks, and large patches of water have a dirty-white or even tawny look, where the ice still lies on the bottom of the meadow. Thus even the meadow flood is *parded*, and of various patches of color. Ever and anon the wind seems to drop down from over the hill in strong puffs, and then spread and diffuse itself in dark fan-shaped figures over the surface of the water. It is glorious to see how it sports on the watery surface. You see a hundred such nimble-footed puffs drop and spread on all sides at once, and dash off, sweeping the surface of the water for forty rods in [a] few seconds, as if so many invisible spirits were playing tag there. It even suggests some fine dust swept along just above the surface, and reminds me of snow blowing over ice and vapor curling along a roof, — meandering like that, often. Like hair, like the crown of the head, curling various ways. The before dark blue is now diversified with much darker or blackish patches with a suggestion of red, — purplish even.

Then the wind blows with stronger gust down the Nut Meadow valley on our right, and I am surprised to see that the billows which it makes are concentric curves apparently reaching round from shore to shore of this broad bay, forty rods wide or more: —

This is conspicuously the form of them. For which two things may account, — the greater force of the wind in the middle and the friction of the shores. And when it blows hardest, each successive billow (four or five feet apart or more) is crowned with yellowish or dirty-white foam. The wind blows around each side of the hill, the opposite currents meeting perchance, or it falls over the hill. So you have a field of ever-varying color, — dark blue, blackish, yellowish, light blue, and smooth sky-blue, and purplish, and yellowish foam, all at once. Sometimes the wind visibly catches up the surface and blows it along and about in spray four or five feet high. Now and then, when the gust increases, there comes a top of fly-away grass from over the hill, goes dancing over the waves, and soon is lost. The requisites are high water mostly clear of ice, ground bare and sufficiently dry, weather warm enough, and wind strong and gusty; then you may sit or stand on a hill and watch this play of the wind with the water. I know of no checker-board more interesting to watch. The wind, the gusts, comb the hair of the water-

nymphs. You never tire of seeing it drop, spread, and sweep over the yielding and sensitive surface. The water is so full of life, now rising into higher billows which would make your mast crack if you had any, now subsiding into lesser, dashing against and wearing away the still anchored ice, setting many small cakes adrift. How they entertain us with ever-changing scenes, in the sky above or on the earth below! If the plowman lean on his plow-handle and look up or down, there is danger that he will forget his labor on that day.

These are ripple days begun, — not yet in woodland pools, where is ice yet.

I see a row of white pines, too, waving and reflecting their silvery light. The red maple sap flows freely, and probably has for several days. I begin to notice the reddish stems of moss on low ground, not bright yet.

C. has seen good bæomyces (?) lately. There is none however at Bæomyces Bank. In Hosmer's ditches in the moraine meadow, the grass just peeps above the surface, apparently begun to grow a little.

I see on [sic] a small round last year's turtle with a yellowish spot on each scale and a yellow-pink breast centred with black. Also see a yellow-spot turtle there.

Some of those tufts of andropogon radical leaves make excellent seats now when the earth is moist.

We see one or two gnats in the air.

See thirty or more crows come flying in the usual irregular zigzag manner in the strong wind, from over M. Miles's, going northeast, — the first migration of them, — without cawing.

Vol. XIII

See a little conferva in ditches.

Looking up a narrow ditch in a meadow, I see a modest brown bird flit along it furtively, — the first song sparrow, — and then alight far off on a rock. Ed. Hoar says he heard one February 27th.

Hayden thinks he has seen bluebirds for a *fortnight !!* Say that he has possibly for a week (?), and that will agree with Wheeler. Ed. Hoar says he heard one February 27th.[1]

At Brister Spring, and especially below, at the cowslip, the dense bedded green moss is very fresh and handsome, and the cowslip leaves, though unfolded, rise to the surface.

See a little frog in one of the spring-holes.

See a hen-hawk.

Two or three tufts of carex have shot up in Hosmer's cold spring ditch and been frost-bitten.

Ed. Hoar says he heard a phœbe February 27th.

March 3. 2 P. M. — 50°; overcast and somewhat rain-threatening; wind southwest.

To Abner Buttrick and Tarbell Hills.

See a flock of large ducks in a line, — maybe black? — over Great Meadows; also a few sheldrakes.

It was pleasant to hear the tinkling of very coarse brash — broken honeycombed dark ice — rattling one piece against another along the northeast shores, to which it has drifted.

Scarcely any ice now about river except what rests on the bottom of the meadows, dirty with sediment.

[1] I first hear one March 3d.

The first song sparrows are very inconspicuous and shy on the brown earth. You hear some weeds rustle, or think you see a mouse run amid the stubble, and then the sparrow flits low away.

When I read Topsell's account of the ichneumon eating his way out of the crocodile, I think that, though it be not true in fact, it is very true in fancy, and it is no small gift to be able to give it so good a setting-forth. What a pity that our modern naturalists cannot tell their truths with half this zest and spirit!

Nowadays we have rain, and then high wind directly after it.

C. says that Walden began to be hard to get on to the first of March.

I saw this afternoon a meadow below Flint's willow-row still frozen over (at 3 P. M.), — frozen last night, — and the frozen part corresponded generally to the anchor ice on the bottom, while there was an open canal all around and beyond the edge of the anchor ice; but when I returned two hours later, the wind had broken up and dissipated every vestige of this surface ice; *i. e.*, it was an ice formed last night which it took the whole day with a strong wind to break up in this rather sheltered place.

Our muddiest and wettest walking thus far was the last week of February. I should have launched my boat ere this if it had been ready. The last skating was on Walden the 26th February. The next day it was soft. Sleighing ended February 22d, and there had not been much a long time before.

I see one of those gray-winged (long and slender) perla-like insects by the waterside this afternoon.

March 4. Sunday. 2 P. M. — To Conantum *via* Clamshell.

Thermometer 44; very strong and gusty northwest wind, with electric-looking wind-clouds. One spits a little rain, but mostly clear.

The frost is all out of the upper part of the garden.

These wind-clouds come up and disappear fast, and have a more or less perpendicular fibre.

Sit under Lupine Promontory again, to see the ripples. The wind is too strong, the waves run too high and incessantly, to allow the distinct puffs or gusts that drop from over the hill to be seen distinctly enough on tumultuous surface. Yet it is interesting. It spreads and runs as a bird spreads its tail suddenly, or it is as if a gust fell on a head of dark hair and made dimples or "crowns" in it, or it is as when dust before a brisk sweeper curls along over a floor.

There is much less of that yellowish anchor ice than on the 2d. Cakes of it successively rise, being separated by warmth from the bottom, and are driven off to the leeward shore. In some places that shore is lined with such cakes now, which have risen and been blown clear across the meadow and river, — large masses. Some portions of them are singularly saturated, of a yellowish or clay-color, and an uneven upper surface, with a finely divided perpendicular grain, looking (in form) just like some kinds of fungi (that commonly yellowish kind). There the smaller

pieces, of irregular form, strike against one another and make a pleasant musical, or tinkling, sound. Some of the ice will occasionally be lifted up on its edge two feet high and very conspicuous afar.

That reddish-purple tinge in the meadow ripples appears to be owing to a reflection in some cases from the somewhat russet bottom.

I see some curled dock, just started.

The earth is never lighter-colored than now, — the hillsides reflecting the sun when first dried after the winter, — especially, methinks, where the sheep's fescue grows (?). It contrasts finely with the rich blue of the water.

I saw half a dozen crows on a cake of ice in the middle of the Great Meadows yesterday, evidently looking for some favorite food which is washed on to it, — snails, or cranberries perhaps.

I see a bush of the early willow — by wall far in front of the C. Miles house — whose catkins are conspicuous thirty rods off, very decidedly green, three eighths of an inch by measure. The bush at this distance had quite a silvery look, and the catkins show some redness within. Many of the scales as usual had fallen.

A hen-hawk rises and sails away over the Holden Wood as in summer. Saw and heard one scream the 2d.

I notice, where (ice or) snow has recently melted, a very thin dirty-white web like a dense cobweb, left flat on the grass, such as I saw some years ago.

There is a broad and very black space extending through Fair Haven Pond over the channel, visible

Vol. XIII

half a mile off, where the ice is thinnest and saturated with water. The channel is already open a little way at the upper end of the pond. This pond at its outlet contracts gradually into the river, so that you could hardly tell where the pond left off and the river began. I see that the ice at present extends that way only so far as I last year assumed that the pond did. In this sense the river hence to the Hubbard Bridge is pond-like compared with the portion below.

See two apparently sternothærus eggs dropped in a slight hollow in the grass, evidently imperfectly planted by the turtle; still whole.

The last three have been true March days for wind.

The handsome and neat brown (pale-brown yet distinct on the lighter withered sod) of the lechea is now conspicuous as a shading in the drying fields.

See no ducks to-day, though much water. Nights too cold?

Aspen down a quarter of an inch out.

March 5. The meadows skim over at night.

White pine cones half fallen.

The old naturalists were so sensitive and sympathetic to nature that they could be surprised by the ordinary events of life. It was an incessant miracle to them, and therefore gorgons and flying dragons were not incredible to them. The greatest and saddest defect is not credulity, but our habitual forgetfulness that our science is ignorance.

Chickweed and shepherd's-purse in bloom in C.'s garden, and probably all winter, or *each month*.

The song sparrows begin to sing hereabouts.

I see some tame ducks in the river, six of them. It is amusing to see how exactly perpendicular they will stand, with their heads on the bottom and their tails up, plucking some food there, three or four at once. Perhaps the grass, etc., is a little further advanced there for them.

George Buttrick thinks that forty musquash have been killed this spring between Hunt's and Flint's Bridge. The best time to hunt them is early morning and evening. His father goes out at daybreak, and can kill more in one hour after that than from that time to near sunset. He says that *he* has found eleven young in one musquash, and that Joel Barrett observed that one pair near his house bred five times in one year. Thought it would hardly pay to shoot them for their fur alone, but would if you owned river-meadow banks, they undermine them so.

So far as the natural history is concerned, you often have your choice between uninteresting truth and interesting falsehood.

As the ancients talked about "hot and cold, moist and dry," so the moderns talk about "electric" qualities.

As we sat under Lupine Promontory the other day, watching the ripples that swept over the flooded meadow and thinking what an eligible site that would be for a cottage, C. declared that we did not live in the country as long as we lived on that village street and only took walks into the fields, any more than if we lived in Boston or New York. We enjoyed none of the immortal quiet of the country as we might here, for instance, but perchance the first sound that we hear in the morning, instead of the tinkling of a bird, is your neighbor hawking and spitting.

Our spiræas have been considerably unfolded for several days.

Ways fairly settled generally.

March 6. 3 P. M. 44°. Fair and springlike, *i. e.* rather still for March, with some raw wind. Pleasant in sun.

Going by Messer's, I hear the well-known note and see a flock of *F. hyemalis* flitting in a lively manner about trees, weeds, walls, and ground, by the roadside, showing their two white tail-feathers. They are more fearless than the song sparrow. These attract notice by their numbers and incessant twittering in a social manner.

The linarias have been the most numerous birds the past winter.

Mr. Stacy tells me that the flies buzzed about him as he was splitting wood in his yard to-day.

I can scarcely see a heel of a snow-drift from my window.

Jonas Melvin says he saw hundreds of "speckled" turtles out on the banks to-day in a voyage to Billerica for musquash. Also saw gulls. Sheldrakes and black ducks are the only ones he has seen this year. They are fishing on Flint's Pond to-day, but find it hard to get on and off.

C. hears the nuthatch.

Jonas Melvin says that he shot a sheldrake in the river late last December.

A still and mild moonlight night and people walking about the streets.

March 7. Frost this morning, though completely overcast.

3 P. M. — 34°.

A little sleety snow falling all day, which does not quite cover the ground, — a sugaring. Song sparrow heard through it; not bluebird.

White maple buds partly opened, so as to admit light to the stamens, some of them, yesterday at least.

C. says that he saw a swarm of very small gnats in the air yesterday.

March 8. 2.30 P. M. — 50°. To Cliffs and Walden.

See a small flock of grackles on the willow-row above railroad bridge. How they sit and make a business of chattering! for it cannot be called singing, and no improvement from age to age perhaps. Yet, as *nature* is a *becoming*, their notes may become melodious at last. At length, on my very near approach, they flit suspiciously away, uttering a few subdued notes as they hurry off.

This is the first *flock* of blackbirds I have chanced to see, though Channing saw one the 6th. I suspect that I have seen only grackles as yet.

I saw, in Monroe's well by the edge of the river, the other day, a dozen frogs, chiefly shad frogs, which had been dead a good while. It may be that they get into that sort of spring-hole in the fall to hibernate, but for some reason die; or perhaps they are always

jumping into it in the summer, but at that season are devoured by some animal before they infest the water.

Now and for some days I see farmers walking about their fields, knocking to pieces and distributing the cow-dung left there in the fall, that so, with the aid of the spring rains, they fertilize a larger surface and more equally.

To say nothing of fungi, lichens, mosses, and other cryptogamous plants, you cannot say that vegetation absolutely ceases at any season in this latitude; for there is grass in some warm exposures and in springy places, always growing more or less, and willow catkins expanding and peeping out a little further every warm day from the very beginning of winter, and the skunk-cabbage buds being developed and actually flowering sometimes in the winter, and the sap flowing [in] the maples in midwinter in some days, perhaps some cress growing a little (?), certainly some pads, and various naturalized garden weeds steadily growing if not blooming, and apple buds sometimes expanding. Thus much of vegetable life or motion or growth is to be detected every winter. There is something of spring in all seasons. There is a large class which is evergreen in its radical leaves, which make such a show as soon as the snow goes off that many take them to be new growth of the spring.

At the pool on the south side of Hubbard's Grove, I notice that the crowfoot, *i. e.* buttercup, leaves which are at the bottom of the water stand up and are much more advanced than those two feet off in the air, for

there they receive warmth from the sun, while they are sheltered from cold winds.

Nowadays we separate the warmth of the sun from the cold of the wind and observe that the cold does not pervade all places, but being due to strong northwest winds, if we get into some sunny and sheltered nook where they do not penetrate, we quite forget how cold it is elsewhere.

In some respects our spring, in its beginning, fluctuates a whole month, so far as it respects ice and snow, walking, sleighing, etc., etc.; for some years winter may be said to end about the first of March, and other years it may extend into April.

That willow-clump by railroad at Walden looks really silvery.

I see there that moles have worked for several days. There are several piles on the grass, some quite fresh and some made before the last rain. One is as wide as a bushel-basket and six inches high; contains a peck at least. When I carefully remove this dirt, I cannot see, and can scarcely detect by feeling, any looseness in the sod beneath where the mole came to the surface and discharged all this dirt. I do feel it, to be sure, but it is scarcely perceptible to my fingers. The mole must have filled up this doorway very densely with earth, perhaps for its protection.

Those small green balls in the Pout's-Nest — and in the river, etc. — are evidently the buds by which the *Utricularia vulgaris* are propagated. I find them attached to the root as well as adrift.

I noticed a very curious phenomenon in this pond.

It is melted for two or three rods around the open side, and in many places partly filled with a very slender thread-like spike-rush (apparently *Eleocharis tenuis?*) which is matted more or less horizontally and floating, and is much bleached, being killed. In this fine matting I noticed perfectly straight or even cuts a rod or more in length, just as if one had severed this mass of fine rush as it lay [?] with some exceeding sharp instrument. However, you could not do it with a scythe, though you might with scissors, if it were ruled. It is as if you were to cover a floor with very fine flaccid grass and tread it to one inch in thickness, and then cut this web straight across. The fact is, this floating matting (it also rests partly on soft mud) was not cut at all, but pulled apart on a straight line, producing the exact appearance of a cut, as if you were to pull a piece of felt apart by a force on each side and yet leave the edge as straight as if it had been cut. It had been frozen in, and when the ice cracked it was in an instant thus pulled apart, without further disturbing the relative position of the fibres. I first conjectured this, and then saw the evidence of it, for, glancing my eye along such a cut, which ran at right angles with the shore, I saw that it exactly corresponded at its termination to an old crack in the ice which was still unmelted and which continued its course exactly. This in the ice had been filled and cemented so as to look like a white seam. Would this account for such a crack being continued into the meadow itself, as I have noticed?

I meet some Indians just camped on Brister's Hill. As usual, they are chiefly concerned to find where black

ash grows, for their baskets. This is what they set about to ascertain as soon as they arrive in any strange neighborhood.

March 9. Snows this forenoon, whitening the ground again.

2 and 3 P. M. — Thermometer 41°.

I have seen three or four pieces of coral in the fields of Concord, and Mr. Pratt has found three or four on his farm. How shall they be accounted for? Who brought them here? and when?

These barns shelter more beasts than oxen and horses. If you stand awhile in one of them now, especially where grain is piled, you will hear ever and anon a rustling in it made by the mice, which take the barn to be their home, as much as the house is yours.

As I recall it, February began cold, with some dry and fine driving snow, making those shell-shaped drifts behind walls, and some days after were some wild but low drifts on the meadow ice. I walked admiring the winter sky and clouds.

After the first week, methinks, it was much milder, and I noticed that some sounds, like the tinkling of railroad rails, etc., were springlike. Indeed, the rest of the month was *earine*, river breaking up a part and closing again, and but little snow.

About 8th and 12th, the beauty of the ice on the meadows, partly or slightly rotted, was noticeable, with the curious figures in it, and, in the coolest evenings, the green ice and rosy isles of flat drifts.

About the 9th, noticed the very black water of some open reaches, in a high wind and cold.

About the middle of the month was a moist, lodging snow, and the 18th a fine granular one, making about a foot, — the last. Then sudden warm weather and rain come and dissolve it all at once, and the ruts, flowing with melted snow, shone in the sun, and the little sleighing was all gone. And from the 25th to 27th the river *generally* broke up.

March began warm, and I admired the ripples made by the gusts on the dark-blue meadow flood, and the light-tawny color of the earth, and was on the alert for several days to hear the first birds. For a few days past it has been generally colder and rawer, and the ground has been whitened with snow two or three times, but it has all been windy.

You incline to walk now along the south side of hills which will shelter you from the blustering northwest and north winds. The sidewalks are wet in the morning from the frost coming out.

March 10. 2 P. M. — About 30°.

March 11. Sunday. 2 P. M. — About 40°.

It is cold and blustering walking in the wind, though the thermometer is at 40; *i. e.*, though the temperature is thus high, the strong and blustering northwest winds of March make this notorious March weather, which is worse to bear than severe cold without wind.

The farmers say that there is nothing equal to the March winds for drying wood. It will dry more this month than it has in all the winter before.

I see a woodchuck out on the calm side of Lee's Hill (Nawshawtuct). He has pushed away the withered leaves which filled his hole and come forth, and left his tracks in those slight patches of the recent snow which are left about his hole.

I was amused with the behavior of two red squirrels as I approached the hemlocks. They were as gray as red, and white beneath. I at first heard a faint, sharp chirp, like a bird, within the hemlock, on my account, and then one rushed forward on a descending limb toward me, barking or chirruping at me after his fashion, within a rod. They seemed to vie with one another who should be most bold. For four or five minutes at least, they kept up an incessant chirruping or squeaking bark, vibrating their tails and their whole bodies and frequently changing their position or point of view, making a show of rushing forward, or perhaps darting off a few feet like lightning and barking still more loudly, *i. e.* with a yet sharper exclamation, as if frightened by their own motions; their whole bodies quivering, their heads and great eyes on the *qui vive.* You are uncertain whether it is not half in sport after all.

March 12. Sleet, turning soon to considerable rain, — a rainy day. Thermometer about 40, yet it seems a warm rain to walk in, it being still, while yesterday, of the same temperature, with that raw northwest wind, was cold and blustering. It is the wind of March that makes it unpleasant often, and to seem much colder than it is.

March 13. Quite overcast all day. Thermometer 36.

March 14. 2 P. M. — Thermometer 39. Overcast, with a flurry of snow and a little rain, till 4.30 P. M. To Walden and Cliffs.

I am surprised to find Walden almost entirely open. There is only about an acre of ice at the southeast end, north of the Lincoln bound, drifted there, and a little old and firm and snowy in the bottom of the deep south bay. I may say it opens to-morrow.[1] I have not observed it to open before before the 23d of March.[2] But Fair Haven Pond has not yet a channel through it, nor half through, though it is wholly clear, on an average, two or three days before Walden. However, it is clear enough why Walden has broken up thus early this year. It does not ordinarily freeze till near the end of December (average of twelve observations, December 25th[3]), while Fair Haven Pond freezes about December 2d. But this past winter our cold weather was mostly confined to December, which was remarkable for its uniform cold, while January and February were very open and pleasant. So that Fair Haven Pond, having more than three weeks the start, and that being almost all the cold weather that we had, froze much the thickest. Walden did not freeze so thick as usual. If we have an average winter up to January, but a particularly warm one afterward, Walden will break up early, not having had any chance to freeze thick.

You must look sharp to see if the pond is wholly clear of ice. Standing on the northerly shore, I did not

---

[1] *Vide* 17th.
[2] March 19, 1856, it was twenty-six inches thick!!
[3] Also it froze over the 25th in '59.

for budding. One eye will mark how much the twigs grew last year, another the lichens on the trunk.

Standing on the Cliffs, I see that the young oaks on the plain beneath now look thin-leaved, showing the upright gray stems. The steady March winds have blown off so many leaves.

The Peterboro Hills are covered with snow, though this neighborhood is bare. We thus see winter retiring for some time after she [*sic*] has left us, commonly.

I see that the Indians have got their black ash and made a basket or two, the large kind, — one a bushel-basket, the rim of white oak, — and they have hung them on the trees, as if to exhibit their wares. May not that size and style of basket be an Indian invention?

March 15. I hear that there was about one acre of ice only at the southwest corner (by the road) of Flint's Pond on the 13th. It will probably, then, open entirely to-day, with Walden.

Though it is pretty dry and settled travelling on open roads, it is very muddy still in some roads through woods, as the Marlborough road or Second Division road.

2 P. M. — To Lee's Cliff.

Thermometer 50°. On the whole the finest day yet (the thermometer was equally high the 3d),[1] considering the condition of the earth as well as the temperature of the air. Yet I think I feel the heat as much if not more than I did on the 23d of February, when the

---

[1] 2d and 8th. *Vide* next page.

detect any, but, having ascended the peak, I saw a field of an acre which had drifted to the southeast corner beside some in the deep south bay.

As I stand there, I see some dark ripples already drop and sweep over the surface of the pond, as they will ere long over Ripple Lake and other pools in the wood. No sooner has the ice of Walden melted than the wind begins to play in dark ripples over the surface of the virgin water. It is affecting to see Nature so tender, however old, and wearing none of the wrinkles of age. Ice dissolved is the next moment as perfect water as if it had been melted a million years. To see that which was lately so hard and immovable now so soft and impressible! What if our moods could dissolve thus completely? It is like a flush of life in a cheek that was dead. It seems as if it must rejoice in its own newly acquired fluidity, as it affects the beholder with joy. Often the March winds have no chance to ripple its face at all.

I see on the peak several young English cherry trees six or eight feet high, evidently planted by birds and growing well. I have seen a pretty large one formerly on Fair Haven Hill. If the stone falls in a sprout-land like this they may attain to be sizable trees. These grew nearly a foot last year and look quite healthy. The bird must have brought the stone far to this locality.

Every craftsman looks at his own objects with peculiar eyes. I thought of this on seeing these young cherry trees and remembering how I used to distinguish the erect and lusty shoots when I cultivated a small nursery,

thermometer rose to 58°. Is it because there was more snow lying about then? The comparative stillness, as well as the absence of snow, has an effect on our imaginations, I have no doubt. Our cold and blustering days this month, thus far, have averaged about 40°. Here is the first fair, and at the same time calm and warm, day.

Looking over my Journal, I find that the —

		1st of March was rainy.
2	at 2 P. M.	56°
3		50
4		44
5	(probably as low)	
6	at 3 P. M.	44
7	" " " "	34
8	2 P. M.	50
9	" " "	41
10		30
11		40
12		40
13		36
14		39
15		50

The temperature has been as high on three days this month, and on the 3d [*sic*] considerably higher, and yet this has seemed the warmest and most summer-like, evidently owing to the calmness and greater absence of snow. How admirable in our memory lies a calm warm day amid a series of cold and blustering ones! The 11th was cold and blustering at 40; to-day delightfully warm and pleasant (being calm) at 50°.

I see those devil's-needle-like larvæ in the warm pool south of Hubbard's Grove (with two tails) swimming about and rising to the top.

What a difference it makes whether a pool lies open to the sun or is within a wood, — affecting its breaking-up. This pool has been open at least a week, while that three or four rods from it in the woods is still completely closed and dead.

It is very warm under the south edge of the wood there, and the ground, as for some time, — since snow went off, — is seen all strewn with the great white pine cones which have been blown off during the winter, — part of the great crop of last fall, — of which apparently as many, at least, still remain on the trees.

A hen-hawk sails away from the wood southward. I get a very fair sight of it sailing overhead. What a perfectly regular and neat outline it presents! an easily recognized figure anywhere. Yet I never see it represented in any books. The exact correspondence of the marks on one side to those on the other, as the black or dark tip of one wing to the other, and the dark line midway the wing. I have no idea that one can get as correct an idea of the form and color of the under sides of a hen-hawk's wings by spreading those of a dead specimen in his study as by looking up at a free and living hawk soaring above him in the fields. The penalty for obtaining a petty knowledge thus dishonestly is that it is less interesting to men generally, as it is less significant. Some, seeing and admiring the neat figure of the hawk sailing two or three hundred feet above their heads, wish to get nearer and hold it in their hands, perchance, not

realizing that they can see it best at this distance, better now, perhaps, than ever they will again. What is an eagle in captivity! — screaming in a courtyard! I am not the wiser respecting eagles for having seen one there. I do not wish to know the length of its entrails.

How neat and all compact this hawk! Its wings and body are all one piece, the wings apparently the greater part, while its body is a mere fullness or protuberance between its wings, an inconspicuous pouch hung there. It suggests no insatiable maw, no corpulence, but looks like a larger moth, with little body in proportion to its wings, its body naturally more etherealized as it soars higher.

These hawks, as usual, began to be common about the first of March, showing that they were returning from their winter quarters.

I see a little ice still under water on the bottom of the meadows by the Hubbard's Bridge causeway.

The frost is by no means out in grass upland.

I see to-day in two places, in mud and in snow, what I have no doubt is the track of the woodchuck that has lately been out, with peculiarly spread toes like a little hand.

Am surprised to hear, from the pool behind Lee's Cliff, the croaking of the wood frog. It is all alive with them, and I see them spread out on the surface. Their note is somewhat in harmony with the rustling of the now drier leaves. It is more like the note of the classical frog, as described by Aristophanes, etc. How suddenly they awake! yesterday, as it were, asleep and dormant, to-day as lively as ever they are. The awakening of the

leafy woodland pools. They must awake in good condition. As Walden opens eight days earlier than I have known it, so this frog croaks about as much earlier.

Many large fuzzy gnats and other insects in air.

It is remarkable how little certain knowledge even old and weather-wise men have of the comparative earliness of the year. They will speak of the passing spring as earlier or later than they ever knew, when perchance the third spring before it was equally early or late, as I have known.

March 16. 2 P. M. — Thermometer 55; wind slight, west by south. To Abner Buttrick's Hill.

The buttercup radical leaves are many of them now a healthy dark green, as if they had acquired new life. I notice that such are particularly downy, and probably that enables them to endure the cold so well, like mulleins. Those and thistles and shepherd's-purse, etc., have the form of rosettes on the brown ground.

Here is a flock of red-wings. I heard one yesterday, and I see *a female* among these. These are easily distinguished from grackles by the richness and clarity of their notes, as if they were a more developed bird. How handsome as they go by in a checker, each with a bright-scarlet shoulder! They are not so very shy, but mute when we come near. I think here are four or five grackles with them, which remain when the rest fly. They cover the apple trees like a black fruit. The air is full of song sparrows and bluebirds to-day.

The minister asked me yesterday: "What birds are

they that make these little tinkling sounds? I have n't seen one." Song sparrows.

C. saw a green fly yesterday.

Saw a flock of sheldrakes a hundred rods off, on the Great Meadows, mostly males with a few females, all intent on fishing. They were coasting along a spit of bare ground that showed itself in the middle of the meadow, sometimes the whole twelve apparently in a straight line at nearly equal distances apart, with each its head under water, rapidly coasting along back and forth, and ever and anon one, having caught something, would be pursued by the others. It is remarkable that they find their finny prey on the middle of the meadow now, and even on the very inmost side, as I afterward saw, though the water is quite low. Of course, as soon as they are seen on the meadows there are fishes there to be caught. I never see them fish thus in the channel. Perhaps the fishes lie up there for warmth already.

I also see two gulls nearly a mile off. One stands still and erect for three quarters of an hour, or till disturbed, on a little bit of floated meadow-crust which rises above the water, — just room for it to stand on, — with its great white breast toward the wind. Then another comes flying past it, and alights on a similar perch, but which does not rise quite to the surface, so that it stands in the water. Thus they will stand for an hour, at least. They are not of handsome form, but look like great wooden images of birds, bluish-slate and white. But when they fly they are quite another creature.

The grass is covered with gossamer to-day, though I notice no floating flocks. This, then, is a phenomenon of the first warm and calm day after the ground is bare.

See larks about, though I have heard of them in the winter.

March 17. P. M. — To Walden and Goose Pond.

Thermometer 56; wind south, gentle; somewhat overcast.

There is still perhaps a half-acre of ice at the bottom of the deep south bay of Walden. Also a little at the southeast end of Goose Pond. Ripple Lake is mostly covered yet.

I see a large flock of sheldrakes, which have probably risen from the pond, go over my head in the woods. A dozen large and compact birds flying with great force and rapidity, spying out the land, eyeing every traveller, fast and far they "steam it" on clipping wings, over field and forest, meadow and flood; now here, and you hear the whistling of their wings, and in a moment they are lost in the horizon. Like swift propellers of the air. Whichever way they are headed, that way their wings propel them. What health and vigor they suggest! The life of man seems slow and puny in comparison, — reptilian.

The cowslip leaves are now expanded.

The rabbit and partridge can eat wood; therefore they abound and can stay here all the year.

The leaves on the woodland floor are already getting to be dry.

How handsome a flock of red-wings, ever changing its oval form as it advances, by the rear birds passing the others!

Vol. XIII

Was not that a marsh hawk, a slate-colored one which I saw flying over Walden Wood with long, slender, *curving* wings, with a diving, zigzag flight ? [1]

March 18. Sunday. Quite a fog, — after three warm days, — lasting till 8 A. M.

2 P. M. — Thermometer 56. Wind south, but soon changes to southeast, making the air fresh and hazy and rippling the before smooth water. The water is low on the meadows. The Mantatuket Meadow nearly half bare.

Go [to] Cold Pool (J. P. B.'s).

When we start it is stiller, *i. e.* calmer, than the last two days, and therefore seems warmer. Let there be a strong northwest wind with the thermometer at 40 at this season, and we shall call it cold and blustering; but let the thermometer rise only ten degrees, or to 50, and, if it is quite fair and calm, we shall call it a summer day. The thermometer does not give account of the wind, but our moods are very obedient to it.

I examine the skunk-cabbage, now generally and abundantly in bloom all along under Clamshell. It is a flower, as it were, without a leaf. All that you see is a stout beaked hood just rising above the dead brown grass in the springy ground now, where it has felt the heat, under some south bank. The single enveloping leaf, or "spathe," is all the flower that you see commonly, and those are as variously colored as tulips and of similar color, — from a very dark almost black mahogany to a light yellow streaked or freckled

[1] No doubt it was, for I see another, a brown one, the 19th.

with mahogany. It is a leaf simply folded around the flower, with its top like a bird's beak bent over it for its further protection, evidently to keep off wind and frost, with a sharp angle down its back. These various colors are seen close together, and their beaks are bent in various directions.

All along under that bank I heard the hum of honey-bees in the air, attracted by this flower. Especially the hum of one within a spathe sounds deep and loud. They circle about the bud at first hesitatingly, then alight and enter at the open door and crawl over the spadix, and reappear laden with the yellow pollen. What a remarkable instinct it is that leads them to this flower! This bee is said to have been introduced by the white man, but how much it has learned! This is the only indigenous flower in bloom in this town at present,[1] and probably I and my companion are the only men who have detected it this year; yet this foreign fly has left its home, probably a mile off, and winged its way to this warm bank to the only indigenous flower that has been in flower for a fortnight past. (Probably the chickweed and shepherd's-purse are of no use to it.)

There is but one indigenous flower in bloom in the town, and has been but one for sixteen days past, and probably this is the only one which the honey-bee can use, and this has only been detected hitherto by the botanist; yet this imported insect knows where to find it, and is sure to be heard near it. Six weeks hence children will set forth a-maying and have indifferent luck; but

[1] Possibly the very first alder and white maple open to-day. *Vide* 19th and 20th.

the first sunny and warmer day in March the honey-[bee] comes forth, stretches its wings, and goes forth in search of the earliest flower.

The curled dock has grown the most of any plant I have noticed yet. It had begun the 2d.

Turning over a log, I see a fishworm out, and plenty of sow-bugs running about, and ant-like creatures, also a wireworm. Black spiders are more numerous than before, and it must be they that have shot these webs of late on all the stubble and bushes.

You see a fly come forth from its hibernaculum in your yard, stretch its wings in the sun, and set forth on its flowery journey. You little think that it knows the locality of early flowers better than you. You have not dreamed of them yet. It knows a spot a mile off under a warm bank-side where the skunk-cabbage is in bloom. No doubt this flower, too, has learned to expect its winged visitor knocking at its door in the spring. The bee sees their low roofs in the brown and springy ground.

It is very warm on the sandy slopes of Clamshell now. The buzzing fly describes an unseen arc in that calm air, reminding us of far-off sultry heats to come. A brown cicindela (green beneath) runs on the sand. I see a brown grasshopper, also a green one, each about three quarters of an inch long, *hop* at a ditch.

C. picks up at Clamshell a very thin piece of pottery about one eighth of an inch thick, which appears to contain much pounded shell.

See middling-sized frogs at Hosmer's early ditch, brown above, whitish beneath. Are they not *Rana fontinalis?* — though neither green nor yellow. Also a great many similar-colored small ones, which may be male sylvaticas.

Callitriche has decidedly started.

I see that simplest form shell snail of the water copulating.

We sit on the withered sedge, on a warm and sheltered hillside, in the sprout-land toward J. P. B.'s Cold Pool, and observe the hazel catkins around us already very much loosened and elongated. No doubt, this being the fourth of these warm days, they began to be so on the 15th. As I sit there, I notice on a bush four feet off, between me and the sun, the little fiery-crimson stars where the stigmas have just begun to peep (one thirtieth of an inch), minute points of crimson not half so big as the head of a pin, yet making a large impression, they so fill your imagination.

Pratt says that his bees come out in a pleasant day at any time in the winter; that of late they have come out and eased themselves, the ground being covered around the hives with their yellow droppings. Were not these the little yellow pellets I saw in a skunk-cabbage flower some years ago?[1] He says they come home now all yellow. I tell him it is skunk-cabbage pollen. I think there would be no surer way to tell when this flower had bloomed than to keep bees and watch when they first returned laden with pollen. Let them search for you, — a swarm of bees. Probably with a microscope you could tell exactly when each of the bee-frequented flowers began to bloom throughout the year.

[1] No, for Farmer says the former are liquid.

The elm buds are expanded, partly opened.

The first day in March when, the ground being bare, the temperature rises to 58° and the weather is clear and calm is a memorable one. Is it not commonly a bluebird day?

On the 16th, going behind Flint's, the water on the meadow quite low, I observed that portions were *clear* water, — it being calm, — while in other parts the stubble of the sedge rose just above the surface, and this sedge was seen thus to grow in rounded patches with a regular curved edge. The water being just at this height, you could easily see the boundary of a particular kind of sedge. I think that many kinds of sedge spread in this manner.

The sweet-fern grows in large, dense, more or less rounded or oval patches in dry land. You will see three or four such patches in a single old field. It is now quite perfect in my old bean-field.

March 19. Early willows in their silvery state.

2 P. M. — Thermometer 51; wind easterly, blowing slightly. To Everett's Spring.

Going along the Turnpike, I look over to the pitch pines on Moore's hillside, — ground bare as it has been since February 23, except a slight whitening or two, — and it strikes me that this pine, take the year round, is the most cheerful tree and most living to look at and have about your house, it is so sunny and full of light, in harmony with the yellow sand there and the spring sun. The deciduous trees are apparently dead, and the white pine is much darker, but the pitch pine has an ingrained

sunniness and is especially valuable for imparting warmth to the landscape at this season. Yet men will take pains to cut down these trees and set imported larches in their places! The pitch pine shines in the spring somewhat as the osiers do.

I see in the ditch by the Turnpike bridge a painted tortoise, and, I think, a small shiner or two, also several suckers which swiftly dart out of sight, rippling the water. We rejoice to see the waters inhabited again, for a fish has become almost incredible.

Myriads of water-bugs of various sizes are now gyrating, and they reflect the sun like silver. Why do they cast a *double* orbicular shadow on the bottom?

I see some monstrous yellow lily roots in the ditch there just beyond the bridge on the right hand, — great branching roots, three or four of them from one base, two feet long (or more) and as big as my arm, all covered with muddy sediment. I know of no herbaceous plant which suggests so much vigor. They taper at the extremity, down (or up) to the green leaf-bud, and, regularly marked as they are with the bases of the leaf-stalks, they look like pineapples there.

Holding by an alder, I get my hand covered with those whitish lice, which I suppose will cover themselves with down.

The *Rana halecina* sits on the bank there.

The *Alnus incana* is out,[1] near Everett's Spring, but

[1] Probably yesterday in some places.

not the *Alnus serrulata*, i. e. the smaller one, which grows south of scouring-rush.

The plants which have grown the most there — and they are very conspicuous now — are the forget-me-not, the *Ranunculus repens* (much more than any *bulbosus*), and a common sedge which already begins to yellow the top of some tussocks.[1]

The lower part of the hill at Minott's is decidedly green now.

The road and paths are perfectly dry and settled in the village, except a very little frost still coming out on the south side the street.

March 20. Worm-piles in dooryard this morning.

A foggy morning; turns to some April-like rain, after east wind of yesterday.

A. Buttrick says he saw and heard woodcocks the 5th of March this year, or much earlier than ever before. Thinks they are now laying. His dog put them up at the brushy point below Flint's, — one pair there. Is another pair at Hunt's Pond, another at Eleazer Davis's Hill. He says that he caught three skunks and a crow last week in his traps baited with muskrat for mink. Says a fox will kill a skunk and eat him greedily before he smells, but nothing will eat a mink.

2 P. M. — Thermometer about 49.

This is a slight, dripping, truly April-like rain. You hardly know whether to open your umbrella or not. More mist than rain; no wind, and the water perfectly

[1] Just fairly begun at Heywood meadow the 25th.

smooth and dark, but ever and anon the cloud or mist thickens and darkens on one side, and there is a sudden rush of warm rain, which will start the grass. I stand on Hunt's Bridge and, looking up-stream, see now first, in this April rain, the water being only rippled by the current, those alternate dark and light patches on the surface, all alike dimpled with the falling drops. (The ground now soaks up the rain as it falls, the frost being pretty commonly out.) It reminds me of the season when you sit under a bridge and watch the dimples made by the rain.

I see where some one has lately killed a striped snake.

The white maple by the bridge is abundantly out, and of course did not open this rainy day. Yesterday, at least, it began.

I observed on the 18th a swarm of those larger tipulidæ, or fuzzy gnats, dancing in a warm sprout-land, about three feet above a very large white pine stump which had been sawed off quite smoothly and was conspicuous. They kept up their dance directly over this, only swaying to and fro slightly, but always recovering their position over it. This afternoon, in the sprinkling rain, I see a very small swarm of the same kind dancing in like manner in a garden, only a foot above the ground but directly over a bright tin dish, — apparently a mustard-box, — and I suspect that they select some such conspicuous fixed point on the ground over which to hover and by which to keep their place, finding it for their convenience to keep the same place. These gyrate in the air as water-bugs on the water.[1]

[1] For same, *vide* March 10, 1859.

Fair Haven Pond was seen entirely open the 20th. (I saw it the 15th, and thought it would open in four or five days; the channel was not then open.) Say, then, 20th. Channel open, say 17th.

The phenomena of an average March are increasing warmth, melting the snow and ice and, gradually, the frost in the ground; cold and blustering weather, with high, commonly northwest winds for many days together; misty and other rains taking out frost, and whitenings of snow, and winter often back again, both its cold and snow; bare ground and open waters, and more or less of a freshet; some calm and pleasant days reminding us of summer, with a blue haze or a thicker mist wreathing the woods at last, in which, perchance, we take off our coats awhile and sit without a fire a day; ways getting settled, and some greenness appearing on south bank; April-like rains, after the frost is chiefly out; plowing and planting of peas, etc., just beginning, and the old leaves getting dry in the woods.

Vegetation fairly begins, — conferva and mosses, grass and carex, etc., — and gradually many early herbaceous plants start, and noticed radical leaves; *Stellaria media* and shepherd's-purse bloom; maple and buttonwood sap (6th) flow; spiræas start, cladonias flush, and bæomyces handsome; willow catkins become silvery, aspens downy; osiers, etc., look bright, white maple and elm buds expand and open, oak woods thin-leaved; alder and hazel catkins become relaxed and elongated. First perceptible greenness on south banks, 22d. The skunk-cabbage begins to bloom (23d); plant peas, etc., 26th; spring rye, wheat, lettuce; maple

Methinks this gentle rainy day reminds me more of summer than the warmest fair day would.

A. Buttrick said to-day that the black ducks come when the grass begins to grow in the meadows, *i. e.* in the water.

Perhaps calm weather and thermometer at about 50, the frost being commonly out and ground bare, may be called an April-like rain.

The 15th, 16th, 17th, 18th, and 19th were very pleasant and warm days, the thermometer standing at 50°, 55°, 56°, 56°, and 51° (average 53½°), — quite a spell of warm weather (succeeding to cold and blustering), in which the alders and white maples, as well as many more skunk-cabbages, bloomed, and the hazel catkins became relaxed and elongated.

A. Buttrick says he has seen ground squirrels some time. I hear that the first alewives have been caught in the Acushnet River.

Our own mistakes often reveal to us the true colors of objects better than a conscious discrimination. Coming up the street the other afternoon, I thought at first that I saw a smoke in Mr. Cheney's garden. It was his white tool-house.

March 21. Colder and overcast. Did not look at thermometer; probably not far from 40°.

March 22. Colder yet, and a whitening of snow, some of it in the form of pellets, — like my pellet frost! — but melts about as fast as it falls. At 4 P. M., 28; probably about 30 at 2 P. M.

swamps red-tinged (?) 28th, and lake grass; and perchance the gooseberry and lilac begin to show a little green. That is, *one indigenous native flower* blooms. (*Vide* if the early sedge does.)

About twenty-nine migratory birds arrive (including hawks and crows), and two or three more utter their spring notes and sounds, as nuthatch and chickadee, turkeys, and woodpecker tapping, while apparently the snow bunting, lesser redpoll, shrike, and doubtless several more — as owls, crossbills (?) — leave us, and woodcocks and hawks begin to lay.

Many insects and worms come forth and are active, — and the perla insects still about ice and water, — as tipula, grubs, and fuzzy caterpillars, minute hoppers on grass at springs; gnats, large and small, dance in air; the common and the green fly buzz outdoors; the gyrinus, large and small, on brooks, etc., and skaters; spiders shoot their webs, and at last gossamer floats; the honey-bee visits the skunk-cabbage; fishworms come up, sow-bugs, wireworms, etc.; various larvæ are seen in pools; small green and also brown grasshoppers begin to hop, small ants to stir (25th); *Vanessa Antiopa* out 29th; cicindelas run on sand; and small reddish butterflies are seen in wood-paths, etc., etc., etc.

Skunks are active and frolic; woodchucks and ground squirrels come forth; moles root; musquash are commonly drowned out and shot, and sometimes erect a new house, and at length are smelled; and foxes have young (?).

As for fishes, etc., trout glance in the brooks, brook minnows are seen; see furrows on sandy bottoms, and small shell snails copulate; dead suckers, etc., are seen floating on meadows; pickerel and perch are running up brooks, and suckers (24th) and pickerel begin to dart in shallows.

And for reptiles, not only salamanders and polly-wogs are more commonly seen, and also those little frogs (*sylvatica* males?) at spring-holes and ditches, the yellow-spot turtle and wood turtle, *Rana fontinalis*, and painted tortoise come forth, and the *Rana sylvatica* croaks.

Our river opened in 1851, much before February 25; 1852, March 14 at least; 1853, say March 8 at least; 1854, say March 9; average March 5. Hudson River opened, according to Patent Office Reports, 1854, page 435: 1851, February 25; 1852, March 28; 1853, March 23; 1854, March 17; average March 16. According to which our river opens some eleven days the soonest. Perhaps this is owing partly to the fact that our river is nearer the ocean and that it rises southward instead of northward.

March 23. 2 P. M. — 40°; rather windy. Small dark-based cumuli spring clouds, mostly in rows parallel with the horizon.

I see one field which was plowed before the 18th and spring rye sowed. The earlier the better, they say. Some fields might have been plowed earlier, but the ground was too wet. Farmer says that some fifty years ago he plowed and sowed wheat in January, and never had so good a crop.

I hear that Coombs has killed half a dozen ducks,

one of them a large gray duck in Goose Pond. He tells me it weighed five and a half pounds, — while his black ducks weigh only three and a half, — and was larger than a sheldrake and very good to eat. Simply gray, and was alone, and had a broad flat bill. Was it the gadwall? or a kind of goose?

It will be seen by the annexed scrap[1] that March is the fourth coldest month, or about midway between December and November. The same appears from the fifteen years' observation at Mendon. ("American Almanac," page 86.) The descent to extreme cold occupies seven months and is therefore more gradual (though a part of it is more rapid) than the ascent to extreme heat, which takes only five months. The mean average temperature of the coldest month (February) being 23.25, and of the warmest (July) being 72.35, the whole ascent from extreme cold to extreme heat is 49.10°, and in March (32.73) we have accomplished 8.48°, or a little less than one sixth the ascent. (According to the Mendon fifteen years' average the whole ascent is 47.5, and in March we have advanced 9.2, a little more than one fifth.) It appears (from the scrap) that December, January, and February, the three winter months, differ very little in temperature, and the three summer months and September are next most alike, though they differ considerably more. (Same from Mendon tables.) The greatest or abruptest change is from November to December (in Mendon tables from September to October), the next most abrupt from

[1] [Tables from the Patent Office Reports, 1853, p. 332 ; 1854, p. 427; 1855, p. 375.]

Vol. XIII

April to May (in Mendon tables from March to April). The least change (according to the above tables) is from December to January. (According to Mendon tables, the same from December to January as from January to February.) The three spring months, and also October and November, are transition months, in which the temperature rapidly changes.

March 24. Cold and rather blustering again, with flurries of snow.

The boatman, when the chain of his boat has been broken with a stone by some scamp, and he cannot easily transport his boat to the blacksmith's to have it mended, gets the latter to bend him a very stout iron wire in the form of an S, then, hooking this to the two broken ends and setting it upright on a rock, he hammers it down till it rests on itself in the form of an 8, which is very difficult to pry open.

2 P. M. — About 39. To Copan.

I see a male frog hawk beating a hedge, scarcely rising more than two feet from the ground for half a mile, quite below the level of the wall within it. How unlike the hen-hawk in this!

They are real wind-clouds this afternoon; have an *electric*, fibry [*sic*] look. Sometimes it is a flurry of snow falling, no doubt. Peculiar cold and windy cumuli are mixed with them, not black like a thunder-cloud, but cold dark slate with very bright white crowns and prominences.

I find on Indian ground, as to-day on the Great Fields, very regular oval stones like large pebbles,

sometimes five or six inches long, water-worn, of course, and brought hither by the Indians. They commonly show marks of having been used as hammers. Often in fields where there is not a stone of that kind in place for a mile or more.

From Holbrook's clearing I see five large dark-colored ducks, probably black ducks, far away on the meadow, with heads erect, necks stretched, on the alert, only one in water. Indeed, there is very little water on the meadows. For length of neck those most wary look much like geese. They appear quite large and heavy. They probably find some sweet grass, etc., where the water has just receded.

There are half a dozen gulls on the water near. They are the large *white* birds of the meadow, the whitest we have. As they so commonly stand above water on a piece of meadow, they are so much the more conspicuous. They are *very* conspicuous to my naked eye a mile off, or as soon as I come in sight of the meadow, but I do not detect the sheldrakes around them till I use my glass, for the latter are not only less conspicuously white, but, as they are fishing, sink very low in the water. Three of the gulls stand together on a piece of meadow, and two or three more are standing solitary half immersed, and now and then one or two circle slowly about their companions.

The sheldrakes appear to be the most native to the river, briskly moving along up and down the side of the stream or the meadow, three-fourths immersed and with heads under water, like cutters collecting the revenue of the river bays, or like pirate crafts peculiar to the stream. They come the earliest and seem to be most at home.

The water is so low that all these birds are collected near the Holt. The inhabitants of the village, poultry-fanciers, perchance, though they be, [know not] these active and vigorous wild fowl (the sheldrakes) pursuing their finny prey ceaselessly within a mile of them, in March and April. Probably from the hen-yard fence with a good glass you can see them at it. They are as much at home on the water as the pickerel is within it. Their serrated bill reminds me of a pickerel's snout. You see a long row of these schooners, black above with a white stripe beneath, rapidly gliding along, and occasionally one rises erect on the surface and flaps its wings, showing its white lower parts. They are the duck most common and most identified with the stream at this season. They appear to get their food wholly within the water. Less like our domestic ducks.

I saw two red squirrels in an apple tree, which were rather small, had simply the tops of their backs red and the sides and beneath gray!

Fox-colored sparrows go flitting past with a faint, sharp chip, amid some oaks.

According to a table in the "American Almanac" for '49, page 84, made at Cambridge, from May, '47, to May, '48, the monthly mean force of the wind for the twelve months (I putting January, February, March, and April, '48, before May, etc., of '47), numbering them 1, 2, 3, etc., from the highest force downward, was —

Vol. XIII

1848				1847							
Jan.	Feb.	Mar.	Apr.	May	June	July	Aug.	Sept.	Oct.	Nov.	Dec.
6	5	3	3	3	2	1	4	4	6	5	4

For quantity of clouds, they stood —

4	9	7	10	7	5	8	6	3	11	2	1

For depth of rain in inches, —

7	6	9	12	10	2	8	3	1	11	4	5

That is, for force of wind, March, April, and May were equal, and were inferior to July and June; for quantity of clouds March and May were equal, and were preceded by December, November, September, January, June, and August. For depth of rain, September stood first, and March ninth, succeeded only by May, October, and April. The wind's force was observed at sunrise, 9 A. M., 3 P. M., and 9 P. M., and in March the greatest force was at 3 P. M., the least at 9 P. M. So, for the whole year the greatest force was at 3 P. M., but the least at sunrise and 9 P. M. both alike. The clouds were observed at the same time, and in March there was the greatest quantity at 9 P. M. and the least at sunrise, but for the year the greatest quantity at 3 P. M. and the least at sunrise and 9 A. M. alike.

At Mendon, Mass., for the whole year 1847 alone (i. e. a different January, February, March, and April from the last) it stood, for force of wind, —

Jan.	Feb.	Mar.	Apr.	May	June	July	Aug.	Sept.	Oct.	Nov.	Dec.
3	5	3	1	4	1	3	2	3	2	3	3

For clouds

5	1	6	8	7	9	11	8	3	10	4	2

According to which, for force of wind, March, July, September, November, and December were equal, and

were inferior to April, June, August, and October; and for clouds March was sixth. The wind's force for March was greatest at 9 A.M. and 3 P. M., which were equal; but for the year greatest at 9 A. M. and least at sunrise. For March there was the greatest quantity of clouds at 9 A. M., but for the year at both sunrise and 9 A. M.

In the last table eight points of the wind were noticed, viz. northwest, north, northeast, east, southeast, south, southwest, west. During the year the wind was southwest 130 days, northwest 87, northeast 59, south 33, west 29, east 14, southeast 10, north 3 days. In March it was northwest 9 days, southwest 8, northeast 5, south 4, west 3, north 2.

March 25. Cold and blustering.

2 P. M. — 35°. To Well Meadow and Walden.

See first cloud of dust in street.

One early willow on railroad, near cowcatcher, just sheds pollen from one anther, but probably might find another more forward.

I notice on hillside in Stow's wood-lot on the west of the Cut what looks like a rope or hollow semicylinder of sawdust around a large white pine stump, just over its instep. There are two or three mouse-holes between the prongs, and the mice have evidently had a gallery through this duct. Much of it is very coarse and fibry [*sic*],—fibres of wood an inch or more long mixed with finer. This is probably the work of the mice in the winter on the roots below, making rooms for themselves. Some of the fine dust is formed into a pellet a quarter of an inch wide and

flat, of a regular form, half as thick as wide. If not so large they had passed through the creature. you might think

The ring of this dust or chewings is not more than two inches wide, and yet it is a hollow semicylinder, more or less regular. I think that I can explain it thus: The mice — of course deer mice — had a gallery in the snow around the stump, from hole to hole. When they began to gnaw away the stump underground they brought up their gnawings, and, of course, had no place to cast them but in the gallery through which they ran. Can it be that they eat any of this wood? The gnawings and dust were abundant and fresh, while that made by worms under the bark was old and dirty and could not have been washed into this position, though some of it might have been made by worms beneath the ground.

At Well Meadow I notice, as usual, that the common cress has been eaten down close, and the uncertain coarse sedge there, etc. The skunk-cabbage leaf-buds have just begun to appear, but not yet any hellebore. The senecio is considerably grown, and I see many little purplish rosettes of *Viola pedata* leaves in sandy paths well grown. One *Caltha palustris* flower, just on the surface of the water, is perfectly out.[1]

See no ducks on Fair Haven Pond, but, sailing over it and at length hovering very long in one place with head stretched downward, a fish hawk.

It is hard descending steep north hillsides as yet, because the ground is yet frozen there and you cannot get a hold by sinking your heels into it.

[1] None out at Second Division Brook the next day, or 26th.

The grass is dense and green as ever, and the caltha blooms in sheltered springy places, being protected from frosts in the night, probably, by a vapor arising from the warm water.

Though the meadow flood is low, methinks they [the meadows] must be covered with a sweet grass which has lately grown under water (parts of them at least), so much the more accessible to such ducks as feed on shore. Probably many ducks as well as geese do feed on shore in the night.

Windy as it is, you get along comfortably enough in the woods, and see the chill-lills and cinnamon sparrows flitting along from bush to bush. Methought on the 18th, a warm day, that the chill-lills and tree sparrows haunted rather the shaded and yet snowy hollows in the woods. The deep [sic] some thirty rods behind where I used to live is mostly covered with ice yet, but no doubt such are generally open now, -- Ripple Lake, for example.

To speak of the general phenomena of March: When March arrives, a tolerably calm, clear, sunny, spring-like day, the snow is so far gone that sleighing ends and our compassion is excited by the sight of horses laboriously dragging wheeled vehicles through mud and water and slosh. We shall no longer hear the jingling of sleigh-bells. The sleigh is housed, or, perchance, converted into a wheeled vehicle by the travelling peddler caught far from home. The wood-sled is perhaps abandoned by the roadside, where the snow ended, with two sticks put under its runners, — there to rest, it may be, while

the grass springs up green around it, till another winter comes round. It may be near where the wagon of the careless farmer was left last December on account of the drifted snow. As March approaches, at least, peddlers will do well to travel with wheels slung under their sleighs, ready to convert their sleighs into wheeled vehicles at an hour's warning. Even the boy's sled gets put away by degrees, or when it is found to be in the way, and his thoughts are directed gradually to more earthy games. There are now water privileges for him by every roadside.

The prudent farmer has teamed home, or to market, his last load of wood from the lot, nor left that which was corded a year ago to be consumed by the worms and the weather. He will not have to sell next winter oak wood rotted an inch deep all round, at a reduction in the price if he deals with knowing customers. He has hauled his last logs to mill. No more shall we see the sled-track shine or hear the sled squeak along it.

The boy's sled gets put away in the barn or shed or garret, and there lies dormant all summer, like a wood-chuck in the winter. It goes into its burrow just before woodchucks come out, so that you may say a woodchuck never sees a sled, nor a sled a woodchuck, — unless it were a prematurely risen woodchuck or a belated and unseasonable sled. Before the woodchuck comes out the sled goes in. They dwell at the antipodes of each other. Before sleds rise woodchucks have set. The ground squirrel too shares the privileges and misfortunes of the woodchuck. The sun now passes from the constellation of the sled into that of the woodchuck.

Vol. XIII

The snow-plow, too, has now nothing more to do but to dry-rot against another winter, like a thing whose use is forgotten, incredible to the beholder, its vocation gone.

I often meet with the wood-sled by the path, carefully set up on two sticks and with a chip under the cop to prevent its getting set, as if the woodman had waited only for another snow-storm to start it again, little thinking that he had had his allowance for the year. And there it rests, like many a human enterprise postponed, sunk further than he thought into the earth after all, its runners, by which it was to slide along so glibly, rotting and its ironwork rusting. You question if it will ever start again.

If we must stop, says the schemer, leave the enterprise so that we can start again under the best possible circumstances. But a scheme at rest begins at once to rust and rot, though there may be two sticks under the runner and a chip under the cop. The ineradicable [?] grass will bury it, and when you hitch your forces to it a year hence it is a chance if it has not lost its cohesion. Examine such a scheme, and see if it rests on two sticks and can be started again. Examine also its joints, and see if it will cohere when it is started.

You can easily find sticks and chips, but who shall find snow to put under it? There it slumbers, sinking into the ground, willingly returning to the earth from which it came. Mortises and tenons and pins avail not to withhold it.

All things decay,
And so must our sleigh.

The sleighing, the sledding, or sliding, is gone. We now begin to wheel or roll ourselves and commodities along, which requires more tractile power. The ponderous cart and the spruce buggy appear from out their *latebrœ* like the dusty flies that have wintered in a crevice, and we hear the buzzing of their wheels. The high-set chaise, the lumbering coach like wasps and gnats and bees come humming forth.

The runners have cut through to the earth; they go in search of the snow into the very gutters, or invade the territory of the foot-passenger. The traveller, when he returns the hired horse to his stable, concludes at last that it is worse sleighing than wheeling. To be sure, there was one reach where he slid along pretty well under the north side of a wood, but for the most part he cut through, as when the cook cuts edgings of dough for her pies, and the grating on the gravel set his teeth on edge.

You see where the teamster threw off two thirds his load by the roadside, and wonder when he will come back for it.

Last summer I walked behind a team which was ascending the Colburn Hill, which was all dripping with melting ice, used to cool the butter which it held. In January, perchance I walk up the same hill behind a sled-load of frozen deer between snow-drifts six feet high.

To proceed with March: Frost comes out of warm sand-banks exposed to the sun, and the sand flows down in the form of foliage. But I see still adhering to the bridges the great chandelier icicles formed in yesterday's cold and windy weather.

By the 2d, ice suddenly softens and skating ends. This warmer and springlike day, the inexperienced eagerly revisit the pond where yesterday they found hard and glassy ice, and are surprised and disappointed to find it soft and rotten. Their aching legs are soon satisfied with such sport. Yet I have in such a case found a strip of good skating still under the north side of a hill or wood. I was the more pleased because I had foreseen it.[1] Skates, then, have become useless tools and follow sleds to their winter quarters. They are ungratefully parted with, not like old friends surely. They and the thoughts of them are shuffled out of the way, and you will probably have to hunt long before you find them next December.

It is too late to get ice for ice-houses, and now, if I am not mistaken, you cease *to notice* the green ice at sunset and the rosy snow, the air being warmer and softer. Yet the marks and creases and shadings and bubbles, etc., in the rotting ice are still very interesting.

If you walk under cliffs you see where the melted snow which trickled down and dripped from their perpendicular walls has frozen into huge organ-pipe icicles.

The water going down, you notice, perchance, where the meadow-crust has been raised and floated off by the superincumbent ice, *i. e.*, if the water has been high in the winter, — often successive layers of ice and meadow-crust several feet in thickness. The most

[1] *Vide* skating at Quinsigamond, Feb., 1859.

Now you admire the various brown colors of the parded earth, the plump cladonias, etc., etc. Perchance you notice the bæomyces in fruit and the great chocolate-colored puffball still losing its dust, and, on bare sandy places, the *Lycoperdon stellatum*, and then your thoughts are directed to arrowheads and you gather the first Indian relics for the season. The open spaces in the river are now long reaches, and the ice between is mackerelled, and you no longer think of crossing it except at the broadest bay. It is, perhaps, lifted up by the melted snow and the rain.

The 8th, it is clear again, but a very cold and blustering day, yet the wind is worse than the cold. You calculate your walk beforehand so as to take advantage of the shelter of hills and woods; a very slight elevation is often a perfect fence. If you must go forth facing the wind, bending to the blast, and sometimes scarcely making any progress, you study how you may return with it on your back. Perchance it is suddenly cold, water frozen in your chamber, and plants even in the house; the strong draft consumes your fuel rapidly, though you have but little left. You have had no colder walk in the winter. So rapidly is the earth dried that this day or the next perhaps you see a cloud of dust blown over the fields in a sudden gust.

The 9th, it is quite warm, with a southwest wind. The first lightning is seen in the horizon by one who is out in the evening. It is a dark night.

The 10th, you first notice frost on the tawny grass. The river-channel is open, and you see great white cakes going down the stream between the still icy

sudden and greatest revolution in the condition of the earth's surface, perhaps, that ever takes place in this town.

The air is springlike. The milkman closes his ice-house doors against the milder air.

By the 3d, the snow-banks are softened through to earth. Perchance the frost is out beneath in some places, and so it melts from below upward and you hear it sink as it melts around you as you walk over it. It is soft, saturated with water, and glowing white.

The 4th is very wet and dirty walking; melted snow fills the gutters, and as you ascend the hills, you see bright braided streams of it rippling down in the ruts. It glances and shines like burnished silver. If you walk to sandy cliffs you see where new ravines have formed and are forming. An east wind to-day, and maybe brings rain on —

The 5th, a cold mizzling rain, and, the temperature falling below zero [*sic*], it forms a thin glaze on your coat, the last glaze of the year.

The 6th, it clears off cold and windy. The snow is chiefly gone; the brown season begins. The tawny frozen earth looks drier than it is. The thin herd's- or piper-grass that was not cut last summer is seen all slanting southeast, as the prevailing wind bent it before the snow came, and now it has partly sprung up again. The bleached grass white.

The 7th is a day of misty rain and mistling, and of moist brown earth into which you slump as far as it is thawed at every step. Every now and then the mist thickens and the rain drives in upon you from one side.

meadows, and the wind blows strong from the northwest, as usual. The earth begins to look drier and is whiter or paler-brown than ever, dried by the wind. The very russet oak leaves mixed with pines on distant hills look drier too.

The 11th is a warmer day and fair, with the first considerable bluish haze in the air. It reminds you of the azure of the bluebird, which you hear, which perhaps you had only *heard of* before.

The morning of the 12th begins with a snow-storm, snowing as seriously and hard as if it were going to last a week and be as memorable as the Great Snow of 1760, and you forget the haze of yesterday and the bluebird. It tries hard but only succeeds to whiten the ground, and when I go forth at 2 P. M. the earth is bare again. It is much cooler and more windy than yesterday, but springlike and full of life. It is, however, warm in the sun, and the leaves already dry enough to sit on. Walden is melted on the edge on the northerly side. As I walk I am excited by the living dark-blue color of the open river and the meadow flood (?) seen at a distance over the fields, contrasting with the tawny earth and the patches of snow. In the high winds in February, at open reaches in the river it was positively angry and black; now it is a cold, dark blue, like an artery. The storm is not yet over. The night sets in dark and rainy, — the first considerable rain, taking out the frost. I am pleased to hear the sound of it against the windows, for that copious rain which made the winter of the Greeks and Romans is the herald of summer to us.

The 13th, the ways are getting settled in our sandy village. The river is rising fast. I sit under some sheltering promontory and watch the gusts ripple the meadow flood.

14th. This morning it snows again, and this time it succeeds better, is a real snow-storm, — by 2 o'clock, three or four inches deep, — and winter is fairly back again. The early birds are driven back or many of them killed. The river flood is at its height, looking dark amid the snow.

15th. The ice is all out of the river proper and the meadow, except ground ice or such as lies still at the bottom of the meadow, under water.

16th. The ice of the night fills the river in the morning, and I hear it go grating downward at sunrise. As soon as I can get it painted and dried, I launch my boat and make my first voyage for the year up or down the stream, on that element from which I have been debarred for three months and a half. I taste a spring cranberry, save a floating rail, feel the element fluctuate beneath me, and am tossed bodily as I am in thought and sentiment. Than longen folk to gon on *voyages.* The water freezes on the oars. I wish to hear my mast crack and see my rapt [?] boat run on her side, so low her deck drinks water and her keel plows air. My only competitors or fellow-voyagers are the musquash-hunters. To see a dead sucker washing on the meadows! The ice has broken up and navigation commenced. We may set sail for foreign parts or expect the first arrival any day. To see the phenomena of the water and see the earth from the *water side,* to stand outside of it on

another element, and so get a pry on it in thought at least, that is no small advantage. I make more boisterous and stormy voyages now than at any season. Every musquash-shooter has got his boat out ere this. Some improvident fellows have left them out, or let them freeze in, and now find them in a leaking condition. But the solid ice of Fair Haven as yet bars all progress in that direction. I vastly increase my sphere and experience by a boat.

17th. The last night, perhaps, we experience the first wind of the spring that shakes the house. Some who sleep in attics expect no less than that the roof will be taken off. They calculate what chance there is for the wind to take hold of the overlapping roof or eaves. You hear that your neighbor's chimney is blown down. The street is strewn with rotten limbs, and you notice here and there a prostrate pine on the hills. The frozen sidewalks melt each morning. When you go to walk in the afternoon, though the wind is gone down very much, you watch from some hilltop the light flashing across some waving white pines. The whole forest is waving like a feather in the wind. Though the snow is gone again here, the mountains are seen to be still covered, and have been ever since the winter. With a spy-glass I can look into such a winter there as it seems to me I have only read of. No wonder the northwest wind is so cold that blows from them to us.

18th. A warm day. I perceive, on some warm wooded hillsides half open to the sun, the dry scent of the withered leaves, gathered in piles here and there by the wind. They make dry beds to recline on, and

Vol. XIII

remind me of fires in the woods that may be expected ere long.

The 19th, say 56 or 60 and *calm,* is yet warmer, a really warm day. Perhaps I wear but one coat in my walk, or sweat in two. The genial warmth is the universal topic. Gnats hum; the early birds warble. Especially the calmness of the day is admirable. The wind is taking a short respite, locked up in its cave somewhere. We admire the smoothness of the water, the shimmering over the land. All vegetation feels the influence of the season. Many first go forth to walk and sit outdoors awhile. The river falling, I notice the coarse wrack left along the shore, dotted with the scarlet spring cranberries. Before night a sudden shower, and some hear thunder, a single low rumble.

The 21st is warm too by the thermometer, but more windy.

The 23d, a channel is worn through Fair Haven Pond.

24th. The winds are let out of their cave, and have fairly resumed their sway again, with occasional flurries of snow which scarcely reach the earth. Gusty electric clouds appear here and there in the sky, like charges of cavalry on a field of battle. It is icy cold, too, and you need all your winter coats at least. The fresh spray, dashed against the alders and willows, makes rake and horn icicles along the causeways.

25th. Colder yet. Considerable ice forms. The river skims over along the side. The river is down again, lower than any time this month.

26th. Warm again. The frost is at length quite out

of early gardens. A few begin to plow, and plant peas and rye, etc. In the afternoon a thick haze conceals the mountains and wreathes the woods, the wind going east.

27th. Steady, pattering, April-like rain, dimpling the water, foretold by the thick haze of yesterday, and soaked up by the ground for the most part, the frost being so much out.

28th. Some sit without a fire in afternoon, it is so warm. I study the honeycombed black ice of Fair Haven Pond.

29th. See a pellet frost in the morning, — or snow. Fair Haven Pond is open.

30th. You see smokes rising above the woods in the horizon this dry day, and know not if it be burning brush or an accidental fire.

31st. The highways begin to be dusty, and even our minds; some of the dusty routine of summer even begins to invade them. A few heels of snow may yet be discovered, or even seen from the window.

March 26. A pleasant day.

I think I heard the last lesser redpolls near the beginning of this month; say about 7th.

The top of a white maple swamp had a reddish tinge at a distance day before yesterday. Was it owing to any expansion of the buds?

2 P. M. — Thermometer 4 [*sic*]. To Second Division Brook.

Though there is very considerable greenness on the warmest southerly banks, there is no change perceptible in the aspect of the earth's surface generally, or at a little distance. It is as bare and dead a brown as ever. When the sun comes out of a cold slate-colored cloud, these windy days, the bleached and withered pastures reflect its light so brightly that they are almost white. They are a pale tawny, or say fawn-color, without any redness. The brown season extends from about the 6th of March ordinarily into April. The first part of it, when the frost is rapidly coming out and transient snows are melting, the surface of the earth is saturated with moisture. The latter part is dry, the whitish-tawny pastures being parded with brown and green mosses (that commonest one) and pale-brown lecheas, which mottle it very pleasingly. This dry whitish-tawny or drab color of the fields — withered grass lit by the sun — is the color of a teamster's coat. It is one of the most interesting effects of light now, when the sun, coming out of clouds, shines brightly on it. It is the *fore*-glow of the year. There is certainly a singular propriety in that color for the coat of a farmer or teamster or shepherd or hunter, who is required to be much abroad in our landscape at this season. It is in harmony with nature, and you are less conspicuous in the fields and can get nearer to wild animals for it. For this reason I am the better satisfied with the color of my hat, a drab, than with that of my companion, which is black, though his coat is of the exact tint and better than mine; but again my dusty boots harmonize better with the landscape than his black and glossy india-rubbers.

I had a suit once in which, methinks, I could glide across the fields unperceived half a mile in front of a farmer's windows. It was such a skillful mixture of

browns, dark and light properly proportioned, with even some threads of green in it by chance. It was of loose texture and about the color of a pasture with patches of withered sweet-fern and lechea. I trusted a good deal to my invisibility in it when going across lots, and many a time I was aware that to it I owed the near approach of wild animals.

No doubt my dusty and tawny cowhides surprise the street walkers who wear patent-leather or Congress shoes, but they do not consider how absurd such shoes would be in my vocation, to thread the woods and swamps in. Why should I wear *Congress* who walk alone, and not where there is any congress of my kind?

C. was saying, properly enough, the other day, as we were making our way through a dense patch of shrub oak: "I suppose that those villagers think that we wear these old and worn hats with holes all along the corners for oddity, but Coombs, the musquash hunter and partridge and rabbit snarer, knows better. He understands us. He knows that a new and square-cornered hat would be spoiled in one excursion through the shrub oaks."

The walker and naturalist does not wear a hat, or a shoe, or a coat, to be looked at, but for other uses. When a citizen comes to take a walk with me I commonly find that he is lame, — disabled by his shoeing. He is sure to wet his feet, tear his coat, and jam his hat, and the superior qualities of my boots, coat, and hat appear. I once went into the woods with a party for a fortnight. I wore my old and common clothes, which were of Vermont gray. They wore, no doubt, the best they had for such an occasion, — of a fashionable color and qual-

ity. I thought that they were a little ashamed of me while we were in the towns. They all tore their clothes badly but myself, and I, who, it chanced, was the only one provided with needles and thread, enabled them to mend them. When we came out of the woods I was the best dressed of any of them.

One of the most interesting sights this afternoon is the color of the yellow sand in the sun at the bottom of Nut Meadow and Second Division Brooks. The yellow sands of a lonely brook seen through the rippling water, with the shadows of the ripples like films passing over it.

By degrees you pass from heaven to earth up the trunk of the white pine. See the flash of its boughs reflecting the sun, each light or sunny above and shaded beneath, even like the clouds with their dark bases, a sort of mackerel sky of pine boughs.

The woodchoppers are still in the woods in some places, splitting and piling at least.

I hear that mayflowers brought from Fitchburg last Thursday (22d) have blossomed *here*. They are evidently much earlier than any of ours. Ours at Second Division (first lot) are under the icy snow.

The rare juncus there is five and six inches high and red (from the cold?) on the bare meadow, — much the most growth of anything of the kind hereabouts. Very little water; only at the cowslip. The equisetum has risen above water at first Nut Meadow crossing. The earliest willows are now in the gray, too advanced to be silvery, — mouse or maltese-cat color.

The Second Division Spring is all covered with a brown floating gelatinous substance of the consistency

of frog-spawn, but with nothing like spawn visible in it. It is of irregular longish, or rather ropy, form, and is of the consistency of frog-spawn without the ova. I think it must be done with. It quite covers the surface.

I also find near by a green zigzag, wormy, spawn-like substance in strings under the water, in which I feel a sort of granule, spawn-like. Can this be the excrement of any creature? Can it turn and swell to that brown and floating jelly? Are these the productions of lizards or the *Rana fontinalis*?

Tried by various tests, this season fluctuates more or less. For example, we may have absolutely no sleighing during the year. There was none in the winter months of '58 (only from March 4 to 14). '52–'53 was an open winter. Or it may continue uninterrupted from the beginning of winter to the 3d of April, as in '56, and the dependent phenomena be equally late. The river may be either only transiently closed, as in '52–'53 and '57–'58, or it may not be open entirely (up *to* pond) till April 4th.

As for cold, some years we may have as cold days in March as in any winter month. March 4, 1858, it was −14, and on the 29th, 1854, the pump froze so as to require thawing.

The river may be quite high in March or at summer level.

Fair Haven Pond may be open by the 20th of March, as this year, or not till April 13 as in '56, or twenty-three days later.

Tried by the skunk-cabbage, this may flower March 2 ('60) or April 6 or 8 (as in '55 and '54), or some five weeks later, — say thirty-six days.

The bluebird may be seen February 24, as in '50, '57, and '60, or not till March 24, as in '56, — say twenty-eight days.

The yellow-spotted tortoise may be seen February 23, as in '57, or not till March 28, as in '55, — thirty-three days.

The wood frog may be heard March 15, as this year, or not till April 13, as in '56, — twenty-nine days.

That is, tried by the last four phenomena, there may be about a month's fluctuation, so that March may be said to have receded half-way into February or advanced half-way into April, i. e., it borrows half of February or half of April.

March 27 and 28. Surveying Ed. Hoar's farm in Lincoln.

Fair, but windy and rather cool.

Louis Minor tells me he saw some geese about the 23d.

March 29. Calm, warmer, and pleasant at once.

March 30. A very warm and pleasant day (at 2 P. M., 63° and rising).

More worm-piles in yard (not seen since morning of 20th, on account of cold, etc.). You will see these earlier on warm banks, as at Clamshell, earlier than in our yard. Do not woodcock, etc., feed on them at night? They come out just before the toads which feed on them. These little piles on the bare earth, like dimples on water, remind you of April.

The afternoon so warm — wind southwest — you take off coat. The streets are quite dusty for the first time.

The earth is more dry and genial, and you seem to be crossing the threshold between winter and summer. At eve I go listening for snipe, but hear none. The inhabitants come forth from their burrows such an afternoon as this, as the woodchuck and ground squirrels have, as the toads do.

I hear of the first fire in the woods this afternoon.[1]

As I walk the street I realize that a new season has arrived. It is time to begin to leave your greatcoat at home, to put on shoes instead of boots and feel light-footed.

March 31. Surveying again for Ed. Hoar the woodland adjoining his farm.

A yet warmer day. A very thick haze, concealing mountains and all distant objects like a smoke, with a strong but warm southwest wind. Your outside coat is soon left on the ground in the woods, where it first becomes quite intolerable. The small red butterfly in the wood-paths and sprout-lands, and I hear at mid-afternoon a very faint but positive ringing sound rising above the susurrus of the pines, — of the breeze, — which I think is the note of a distant and perhaps solitary toad; not loud and ringing, as it will be. Toward night I hear it more distinctly, and am more confident about it. I hear this faint first reptilian sound added to the sound of the winds thus each year a little in advance of the unquestionable note of the toad. Of constant sounds in the warmer parts of warm days there now begins to be added to the rustling or crashing, waterfall-like

[1] Was a small one the 28th.

sound of the wind this faintest imaginable prelude of the toad. I often draw my companion's attention to it, and he fails to hear it at all, it is so slight a departure from the previous monotony of March. This morning you walked in the warm sprout-land, the strong but warm southwest wind blowing, and you heard no sound but the dry and mechanical susurrus of the wood; now there is mingled with or added to it, to be detected only by the sharpest ears, this first and faintest imaginable voice. I heard this under Mt. Misery. Probably they come forth earlier under the warm slopes of that hill.

The pewee sings in earnest, the first I have heard; and at even I hear the first real robin's song.

I hear that there has been a great fire in the woods this afternoon near the factory. Some say a thousand acres have been burned over. This is the dangerous time, — between the drying of the earth, or say when dust begins to fly, and the general leafing of the trees, when it is shaded again. These fires are a perfectly regular phenomenon of this season. Many refer to them this thick haze, but, though in the evening I smell the smoke (no doubt) of the Concord fire, I think that the haze generally is owing to the warm southwest wind having its vapor condensed by our cooler air. An engine sent from town and a crowd of boys; and I hear that one man had to swim across a pond to escape being burnt.

One tells me he found the saxifrage out at Lee's Cliff this afternoon, and another, Ellen Emerson, saw a yellow or little brown snake, evidently either the *Coluber ordinatus* or else *amœnus*, probably the first.

Sit without fire.

V

APRIL, 1860

(ÆT. 42)

April 1. Sunday. Warm, with the thick haze still concealing the sun.

Worm-piles abundant this morning.

Our gooseberry begins to show a little green, but not our currant.

3 P. M. — Up Assabet in boat.

There is another fire in the woods this afternoon. It is yet more hazy than before, — about as thick as a fog, and apparently clouds behind it. Still warmer than yesterday, — 71 at 3 P. M.

The river was lowest for March yesterday, *viz.* just three feet below Hoar's wall. It is so low that the mouths of the musquash-burrows in the banks are exposed with the piles of shells before them.

Willows about the stump on S. Brown's land are very well out. Are they *discolor?* The red maple buds are considerably expanded, and no doubt make a greater impression of redness.

A kingfisher seen and heard.

As we paddle up the Assabet we hear the wood turtles — the first I have noticed — and painted turtles rustling down the bank into the water, and see where they have travelled over the sand and the mud. This and the previous two days have brought them out in numbers. Also see the sternothærus on the bottom.

The river being so low, we see lines of sawdust perfectly level and parallel to one another on the side of the steep dark bank at the Hemlocks, for thirty rods or more visible at once, reminding you of a coarse chalk-line made by snapping a string, not more than half an inch wide much of it, but more true than that would be. The sawdust adheres to the perfectly upright bank and probably marks the standstill or highest water for the time. This level line drawn by Nature is agreeable to behold.

The large *Rana fontinalis* sits enjoying the warmth on the muddy shore. I hear the first hylodes by chance, but no doubt they have been heard some time. Hear the hum of bees on the maples. Rye-fields look green. Pickerel dart, and probably have some time. The sweet-gale is almost in bloom; say next pleasant day.[1]

The fruit a thinker bears is *sentences*, — statements or opinions. He seeks to affirm something as true. I am surprised that my affirmations or utterances come to me ready-made, — not fore-thought, — so that I occasionally awake in the night simply to let fall ripe a statement which I had never consciously considered before, and as surprising and novel and agreeable to me as anything can be. As if we only thought by sympathy with the universal mind, which thought while we were asleep. There is such a necessity [to] make a definite statement that our minds at length do it without our consciousness, just as we carry our food to our mouths. This occurred to me last night, but I was so surprised

[1] It sheds its pollen the same night in my chamber, — from the old mill-site, north side.

Vol. XIII

creatures live and run under the leaves in the woods, out of the way of cold and of hawks. The fire has burned off the top and half-way down their galleries. Every now and then we saw an oblong square mark of pale-brown or fawn-colored ashes amid the black cinders, where corded wood had been burned.

In one place, though at the north edge of a wood, I saw white birch and amelanchier buds (the base of whose stems had been burned or scorched) just bursting into leaf, — evidently the effect of the fire, for none of their kind is so forward elsewhere.

This fire ran before the wind, which was southwest, and, as nearly as I remember, the fires generally at this season begin on that side, and you need to be well protected there by a plowing or raking away the leaves. Also the men should run ahead of the fire before the wind, most of them, and stop it at some cross-road, by raking away the leaves and setting back fires.

Look out for your wood-lots between the time when the dust first begins to blow in the streets and the leaves are partly grown.

The earliest willows are apparently in prime.[1]

I find that the signs of the weather in Theophrastus are repeated by many more recent writers without being referred to him or through him; *e. g.*, by an authority quoted by Brand in his "Popular Antiquities," who evidently does not know that they are in Theophrastus.

Talking with a farmer who was milking sixteen cows in a row the other evening, an ox near which we stood,

[1] *Vide* forward.

by the fact which I have just endeavored to report that I have entirely forgotten what the particular observation was.

April 2. Cold and windy.

2 P. M. — Thermometer 31°, or fallen 40° since yesterday, and the ground slightly whitened by a flurry of snow. I had expected rain to succeed the thick haze. It was cloudy behind the haze and rained a little about 9 P. M., but, the wind having gone northwest (from southwest), it turned to snow.

The shrubs whose buds had begun to unfold yesterday are the spiræa, gooseberry, lilac, and Missouri currant, — the first much the most forward and green, the rest in the order named.

Walked to the Mayflower Path and to see the great burning of the 31st.

I smelled the burnt ground a quarter of a mile off. It was a very severe burn, the ground as black as a chimney-back. The fire is said to have begun by an Irishman burning brush near Wild's house in the south part of Acton, and ran north and northeast some two miles before the southwest wind, crossing Fort Pond Brook. I walked more than a mile along it and could not see to either end, and crossed it in two places. A thousand acres must have been burned. The leaves being thus cleanly burned, you see amid their cinders countless mouse-galleries, where they have run all over the wood, especially in shrub oak land, these lines crossing each other every foot and at every angle. You are surprised to see by these traces how many of these

at the end of the row, suddenly half lay, half fell, down on the hard and filthy floor, extending its legs helplessly to one side in a mechanical manner while its head was uncomfortably held between the stanchions as in a pillory. Thus man's fellow-laborer the ox, tired with his day's work, is compelled to take his rest, like the most wretched slave or culprit. It was evidently a difficult experiment each time to lie down at all without dislocating his neck, and his neighbors had not room to try the same at the same time.

April 4. Wednesday morning. Lodged at Sanborn's last night after his *rescue*, he being away.

It is warmer, an April-like morning after two colder and windy days, threatening a moist or more or less showery day, which followed.

The birds sing quite numerously at sunrise about the villages, — robins, *tree sparrows*, and methinks I heard the purple finch. The birds are eager to sing, as the flowers to bloom, after raw weather has held them in check.

April 5. P. M. — Row to Clamshell and walk beyond.

Fair but windy and cool.

When I stand more out of the wind, under the shelter of the hill beyond Clamshell, where there is not wind enough to make a noise on my person, I hear, or think that I hear, a very faint distant ring of toads, which, though I walk and walk all the afternoon, I never come nearer to. It is hard to tell if it is not a ringing in my ears; yet I think it is a solitary and distant toad called to life by some warm and sheltered pool or hill, its note having, as it were, a chemical affinity with the air of the spring. It merely gives a slightly more ringing or sonorous sound to the general rustling of inanimate nature. A sound more ringing and articulate my ear detects, under and below the noise of the rippling wind. Thus gradually and moderately the year begins. It creeps into the ears so gradually that most do not observe it, and so our ears are gradually accustomed to the sound, and perchance we do not perceive it when at length it has become very much louder and more general.

It is to be observed that we heard of fires in the woods in various towns, and more or less distant, on the same days that they occurred here, — the last of March and first of April. The newspapers reported many. The same cause everywhere produced the same effect.

April 6. Rainy, more or less, — April weather.

I am struck by the fact that at this season all vegetable growth is confined to the warm days; during the cold ones it is stationary, or even killed. Vegetation thus comes forward rather by fits and starts than by a steady progress. Some flowers would blossom to-morrow if it were as warm as to-day, but cold weather intervening may detain them a week or more. The spring thus advances and recedes repeatedly, — its pendulum oscillates, — while it 'is carried steadily forward. Animal life is to its extent subject to a similar

law. It is in warm and calm days that most birds arrive and reptiles and insects and men come forth.

A toad has been seen dead on the sidewalk, flattened.

April 7. The purple finch, — if not before.

P. M. — To Annursnack.

This is the *Rana halecina* day, — awakening of the meadows, — though not very warm. The thermometer in Boston to-day is said to be 49. Probably, then, when it is about 50 at this season, the river being low, they are to be heard in calm places.

Fishes now lie up abundantly in shallow water in the sun, — pickerel, and I see several bream. What was lately motionless and lifeless ice is a transparent liquid in which the stately pickerel moves along. A novel sight is that of the first bream that has come forth from I know not what hibernaculum, moving gently over the still brown river-bottom, where scarcely a weed has started. Water is as yet only melted ice, or like that of November, which is ready to become ice.

As we were ascending the hill in the road beyond College Meadow, we saw the dust, etc., in the middle of the road at the top of the hill taken up by a small whirlwind. Pretty soon it began to move northeasterly through the balm-of-Gilead grove, taking up a large body of withered leaves beneath it, which were whirled about with a great rustling and carried forward with it into the meadow, frightening some hens there. And so they went on, gradually, or rather one after another, settling to the ground, and looking at last almost exactly like a flock of small birds dashing about in sport, till

Vol. XIII

they were out of sight forty or fifty rods off. These leaves were chiefly only a rod above the ground (I noticed some taken up last spring very high into the air), and the diameter of the whirl may have been a rod, more or less.

Early potentilla out, — how long? — on side of Annursnack.

April 8 *and* 9. More or less rainy.

April 10. Cheney elm, many anthers shed pollen, probably 7th. Some are killed. *Salix purpurea* apparently will not open for four or five days.

2 P. M. — 44° and east wind (followed by some rain still the next day, as usual).

April 11. P. M. — To Cliffs.

The hills are now decidedly greened as seen a mile off, and the road or street sides pretty brightly so. I have not seen any lingering heel of a snow-bank since April came in.

Acer rubrum west side Deep Cut, some well out, some killed by frost; probably a day or two at least. Hazels there are all done; were in their prime, methinks, a week ago at least. The early willow still in prime. *Salix humilis* abundantly out, how long?

Epigæa abundantly out (probably 7th at least).

Stow's cold pool three quarters full of ice.

My early sedge, which has been out at Cliffs apparently a few days (not yet quite generally), the highest only two inches, is probably *Carex umbellata.*

April 12. White-bellied swallows. Elm bud-scales have begun to strew the ground, and the trees look richly in flower. 60 at 2 P. M.

Hear a pigeon woodpecker's prolonged cackle.

April 13. P. M. — I go up the Assabet to look at the sweet-gale, which is apparently [?] out at Merrick's shore. It is abundantly out at Pinxter Swamp, and has been some time; so I think I may say that the very first opened April 1st (*q. v.*). This may be not only because the season was early and warm, but because the water was so low, — or would that be favorable?

At first I had felt disinclined to make this excursion up the Assabet, but it distinctly occurred to me that, perhaps, if I came against my will, as it were, to look at the sweet-gale as a matter [of] business, I might discover something else interesting, as when I discovered the sheldrake. As I was paddling past the uppermost hemlocks I saw two peculiar and plump birds near me on the bank there which reminded me of the cow blackbird and of the oriole at first. I saw at once that they were new to me, and guessed that they were crossbills, which was the case, — male and female. The former was dusky-greenish (through a glass), orange, and red, the orange, etc., on head, breast, and rump, the vent white; dark, large bill; the female more of a dusky slate-color, and yellow instead of orange and red. They were very busily eating the seeds of the hemlock, whose cones were strewn on the ground, and they were very fearless, allowing me to approach quite near.

When I returned this way I looked for them again, and at the larger hemlocks heard a peculiar note, *cheep, cheep, cheep, cheep,* in the rhythm of a fish hawk but faster and rather loud, and looking up saw them fly to the north side and alight on the top of a swamp white oak, while I sat in my boat close under the south bank. But immediately they recrossed and went to feeding on the bank within a rod of me. They were very parrot-like both in color (especially the male, greenish and orange, etc.) and in their manner of feeding, — holding the hemlock cones in one claw and rapidly extracting the seeds with their bills, thus trying one cone after another very fast. But they kept their bills a-going [so] that, near as they were, I did not distinguish the cross. I should have looked at them in profile. At last the two hopped within six feet of me, and one within four feet, and they were coming still nearer, as if partly from curiosity, though nibbling the cones all the while, when my chain fell down and rattled loudly, — for the wind shook the boat, — and they flew off a rod. In Bechstein I read that "it frequents fir and pine woods, but only when there are abundance of the cones." It may be that the abundance of white pine cones last fall had to do with their coming here. The hemlock cones were very abundant too, methinks.

April 14. A strong westerly wind in forenoon, shaking the house.

2 p. m. — 44°. To Easterbrooks's.

Benzoin not for two or three days at least. Goldfinches the 11th and in winter.

Vol. XIII

is, connected by crosspieces and lying on the cellar-bottom against one side, the whole length, with concavities cut in them to receive the barrels and prevent their rolling. There were places for eight barrels. It

suggests how much more preparation was made in those days for the storing of liquors. We have at most one keg in our cellar for which such a horse would be a convenient place; yet in this now remote and uncovered cellar-hole lies a horse with places for eight barrels of liquor. It would make a toper's mouth water to behold it. You wonder how they got apples and cider-mills a-going so early, say a hundred and fifty years ago. No doubt they worked hard and sweated a good deal, and perhaps they required, or could bear, more strong drink than the present generation. This horse is a fixture, framed with the house, or rather with the cellar; a first thought it must have been, perchance made by a separate contract, since it comes below the sills. The barrels and their contents, and they who emptied them, and the house above, are all gone, and still the scalloped logs remain now in broad daylight to testify to the exact number of barrels of liquor which the former occupant expected to, and probably did, lay in. His gravestone somewhere tells one sober story no doubt, and this his barrel-horse tells another, — and the only one that I hear. For twenty and odd years only the woodchucks and wild mice to my knowledge have occupied this cellar. Such is the lowest stick of timber in an old New England man's house. He dug a hole

April 15. Strong northwest wind and cold. Thin ice this forenoon along meadow-side, and lasts all day.

2 p. m. — Thermometer 37. To Conantum.

At Conantum pitch pines hear the first pine warbler. Have not heard snipe yet. Is it because the meadows, having been bare, have not been thawed?

See ripples spread fan-like over Fair Haven Pond, from Lee's Cliff, as over Ripple Lake.

Crowfoot abundant; say in prime. A cedar under the Cliff abundantly out; how long? Some still not out. Say 13th. Mouse-ear. Turritis about out; say 16th.

Some little ferns already fairly unfolded, four or five inches long, there close under the base of the rocks, apparently *Woodsia Ilvensis?*

See and hear the seringo, — rather time [*sic*] compared with song sparrow. Probably see bay-wing (surely the 16th) about walls.

The arbor-vitæ *appears* to be much of it effete.

At this season of the year, we are continually expecting warmer weather than we have.

April 16. Rather warm.

In afternoon a true April rain, dripping and soaking into the earth and heard on the roof, which continuing, in the night it is very dark. This is owing to both the absence of the moon and the presence of the clouds.

I observed yesterday, in the cellar of the old Conantum house, a regular frame or "horse" to rest barrels (of cider, vinegar, etc.) on. It was probably made before the house was built, being exactly the length of the cellar, — two pieces of timber framed together, that

six feet into the earth and laid down a timber to hold his cider-barrel. Then he proceeded to build a house over it, with kitchen and sitting and sleeping rooms. It reminds me of travellers' stories of the London docks, of rows of hogsheads, of bonded liquors. Every New England cellar was once something like it. It is a relic of old England with her ale. The first settlers made preparations to drink a good deal, and they did not disappoint themselves.

April 17. I hear this forenoon the soothing and simple, though monotonous, notes of the chip-bird, telling us better than our thermometers what degree of summer warmth is reached; adds its humble but very pleasant contribution to the steadily increasing quire of the spring. It perches on a cherry tree, perchance, near the house, and unseen, by its steady *che-che-che-che-che-che,* affecting us often without our distinctly hearing it, it blends all the other and previous sounds of the season together. It invites us to walk in the yard and inspect the springing plants.

The evenings are very considerably shortened. We begin to be more out of doors, the less housed, think less, stir about more, are fuller of affairs and chores, come in chiefly to eat and to sleep. The amelanchier flower-buds are conspicuously swollen. Willows (*Salix alba*) probably (*did not* four or five days ago).

P. M. — Sail to Ball's Hill.

It is quite warm — 67 at 2 p. m. — and hazy, though rather strong and gusty northwest wind.

We land at the Holt and walk a little inland. It is

unexpectedly very warm on lee side of hilltop just laid bare and covered with dry leaves and twigs. See my first *Vanessa Antiopa*.

Looking off on to the river meadow, I noticed, as I thought, a stout stake aslant in the meadow, three or more rods off, sharp at the top and rather light-colored on one side, as is often the case; yet, at the same time, it occurred to me that a stake-driver often resembled a stake very much, but I thought, nevertheless, that there was no doubt about this being a stake. I took out my glass to look for ducks, and my companion, seeing what I had, and asking if it was not a stake-driver, I suffered my glass at last to rest on it, and I was much surprised to find that it was a stake-driver after all. The bird stood in shallow water near a tussock, perfectly still, with its long bill pointed upwards in the same direction with its body and neck, so as perfectly to resemble a stake aslant. If the bill had made an angle with the neck it would have been betrayed at once. Its resource evidently was to rely on its form and color and immobility solely for its concealment. This was its instinct, whether it implies any conscious artifice or not. I watched it for fifteen minutes, and at length it relaxed its muscles and changed its attitude, and I observed a slight motion; and soon after, when I moved toward it, it flew. It resembled more a piece of a rail than anything else, — more than anything that would have been seen here before the white man came. It is a question whether the bird consciously coöperates in each instance with its Maker, who contrived this concealment. I can never believe that this resemblance

is a mere coincidence, not designed to answer this very end — which it does answer so perfectly and usefully.

The meadows are alive with purring frogs.

J. Brown says that he saw martins on his box on the 13th and 14th, and that his son saw one the 8th (?).

I notice now and of late holes recently dug, — woodchuck? or fox?

Lake grass was very long — a foot or two — and handsome, the 15th.

Heard a pigeon woodpecker on the 16th.

April 18. Cold, and still a strong wind. 46 at 2 P. M.

The *Salix discolor* peels well; also the aspen (early) has begun to peel.

Melvin says he has heard snipe some days, but thinks them scarce.

As I go by the site of Staples's new barn on the Kettle place, I see that they have just dug a well on the hillside and are bricking it up. They have dug twenty-four feet through sand (no stones of any size or consequence in it; I see none at all in what was thrown out; should say it was pure sand), and have some four feet of water in the well. This is probably as low as water in the meadow in front. It is just as far to water as in Messer's well east of it, and about as high up the hill. The whole range appears to be strictly a sandhill. Humphrey Buttrick, the sportsman, was at the bottom, bricking up the well; a Clark who had been mining lately in California, and who had dug the well, was passing down brick and mortar to him; and Melvin, with a bundle of apple scions in his hand, was sitting

Vol. XIII

close by and looking over into the well from time to time.

Melvin said he feared that, the water being so low, the snipes would be overtaken by it and their nests broken up when it rose; that Josh Haynes told him that he found a woodcock's nest, and afterward he sailed over the nest in a boat, and yet, when the water went down, the bird went on and hatched the eggs.

Melvin has seen a dandelion in bloom.

Clark has heard a partridge drum.

I find that the side-hill just below the Dutch house is more loose and sandy than half a dozen years ago, and I attribute it to the hens wallowing in the earth and dusting themselves, and also pecking the grass and preventing its growing.

April 19. Surveying J. B. Moore's farm.

Hear the field sparrow sing on his dry upland, it being a warm day, and see the small blue butterfly hovering over the dry leaves.

Toward night, hear a partridge drum. You will hear at first a single beat or two far apart and have time to say, " There is a partridge," so distinct and deliberate is it often, before it becomes a rapid roll.

Part of the Bedford road in Moore's Swamp had settled a few days ago so much more that the water was six inches deep over it, when they proceeded to cart on more sand; and about the 17th, when they had carted on considerable, half a dozen rods in length suddenly sank before their eyes, and only water and sand was seen where the road had been. One said that the water

was six feet deep over the road. It certainly was four or five. The road was laid out fifty feet wide, and without this, one ach side, a broad ditch had been dug, thus: —

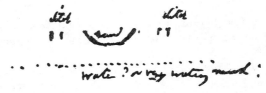

As I calculate, at least ten feet in thickness of sand have been placed on this swamp, and the firm mud could not have been less than a dozen more. The weight of the sand has now at last pressed down the mud and broken through it, causing the sides to turn up suddenly, *i. e.*, a thickness of six feet or more to turn, indeed, completely over and bottom side up on to the middle of the road a part of the way. The weight of sand suddenly jerked this tremendous weight of mud right back on to the road, bottom up.

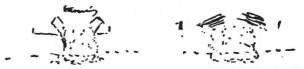

The evening of the 21st a few rods more, with the culvert, went down, so that it was full four feet under water, making some seven or eight rods in all.

Up to about the 17th it had settled gradually, but then it sank *instantly* some five feet. This shows that the weight of sand had burst through the mud, and that therefore it must have been comparatively liquid beneath. Perhaps it was water. In the deepest part of many a seemingly firm swamp which is cultivated, there is an exceedingly thin and liquid mud, or perhaps water. Here was probably once a pond, which has filled up and grown over, but still a relic of it survives deep under the mud in the deepest part.

There are thus the relics of ponds concealed deep under the surface, where they are little suspected, perchance, as under cleared and cultivated swamps or under roads and culverts. The two walls of the culvert must have been ten or twelve feet high, of heavy rocks, and yet they had not broken through in all this time till now!

April 20. The *Salix purpurea* in prime; began, say, 18th.

A warm day. Now begin to sit without fires more commonly, and to wear but one coat commonly.

Moore tells me that last fall his men, digging sand in that hollow just up the hill, dug up a parcel of snakes half torpid. They were both striped and black together, in a place somewhat porous, he thought where a horse had been buried once. The men killed them, and laid them all in a line on the ground, and they measured several hundred feet. This seems to be the common practice when such collections are found; they are at once killed and stretched out in a line, and the sum of their lengths measured and related.

It is a warm evening, and I hear toads ring distinctly for the first time.

C. sees bluets and some kind of thrush to-day, size of wood thrush, — *he* thought probably hermit thrush.

April 22. Row to Fair Haven.
Thermometer 56° or 54°.

See shad-flies. Scare up woodcock on the shore by my boat's place, — the first I had seen. It was feeding within a couple of rods, but I had not seen or thought of it. When I made a loud and sharp sound driving in my rowlocks, it suddenly flew up. It is evident that we very often come quite near woodcocks and snipe thus concealed on the ground, without starting them and so without suspecting that they are near. These marsh-birds, like the bittern, have this habit of keeping still and trusting to their resemblance to the ground.

See now hen-hawks, a pair, soaring high as for pleasure, circling ever further and further away, as if it were midsummer. The peculiar flight of a hawk thus fetches the year about. I do not see it soar in this serene and leisurely manner very early in the season, methinks.

The early luzula is almost in bloom; makes a show, with its budded head and its purplish and downy, silky leaves, on the warm margin of Clamshell Bank. Two or three dandelions in bloom spot the ground there.

Land at Lee's Cliff. The cassandra (water-brush) is well out, — how long?[1] — and in one place we dis-

[1] One found it the 20th.

turb great clouds of the little fuzzy gnats that were resting on the bushes, as we push up the shallow ditch there. The *Ranunculus fascicularis* is now in prime, rather than before. The columbine is hardly yet out.

I hear that the *Viola ovata* was found the 17th and the 20th, and the bloodroot in E. Emerson's garden the 20th.

J. B. Moore gave me some mineral which he found being thrown out of [a] drain that was dug between Knight's factory and his house. It appears to me to be red lead and quartz, and the lead is quite pure and marks very well, or freely, but is pretty dark.

April 24. The river is only half an inch above summer level. The meadow-sweet and hardhack have begun to leaf.

April 25. A cold day, so that the people you meet remark upon it, yet the thermometer is 47 at 2 P. M. We should not have remarked upon it in March. It is cold for April, being windy withal.

I fix a stake on the west side the willows at my boat's place, the top of which is at summer level and is about ten and a half inches below the stone wharf there. The river is one and one fourth inches above summer level to-day. That rock northwest of the boat's place is about fifteen inches (the top of it) below summer level. Heron Rock top (just above the junction of the rivers) is thirteen inches above summer level. I judge by my eye that the rock on the north side,

where the first bridge crossed the river, is about four inches lower than the last.

Mr. Stewart tells me that he has found a gray squirrel's nest up the Assabet, in a maple tree. I resolve that I too will find it. I do not know within less than a quarter of a mile where to look, nor whether it is in a hollow tree, or in a nest of leaves. I examine the shore first and find where he landed. I then examine the maples in that neighborhood to see what one has been climbed. I soon find one the bark of which has been lately rubbed by the boots of a climber, and, looking up, see a nest. It was a large nest made of maple twigs, with a centre of leaves, lined with finer, about twenty feet from the ground, against the leading stem of a large red maple. I noticed no particular entrance. When I put in my hand from above and felt the young, they uttered a dull croak-like squeak, and one clung fast to my hand when I took it out through the leaves and twigs with which it was covered. It was yet blind, and could not have been many days old, yet it instinctively clung to my hand with its little claws, as if it knew that there was danger of its falling from a height to the ground which it never saw. The idea of clinging was strongly planted in it. There was quite a depth of loose sticks, maple twigs, piled on the top of the nest. No wonder that they become skillful climbers who are born high above the ground and begin their lives in a tree, having first of all to descend to reach the earth. They are cradled in a tree-top, in but a loose basket, in helpless infancy, and there slumber when their mother is away. No wonder that they are never made dizzy by high climbing, that were born in the top of a tree, and learn to cling fast to the tree before their eyes are open.

On my way to the Great Meadows I see boys a-fishing, with perch and bream on their string, apparently having good luck, the river is so low.

The river appears the lower, because now, before the weeds and grass have grown, we can see by the bare shore of mud or sand and the rocks how low it is. At midsummer we might imagine water at the base of the grass where there was none.

I hear the greatest concerts of blackbirds — red-wings and crow blackbirds — nowadays, especially of the former (also the 22d and 29th). The maples and willows along the river, and the button-bushes, are all alive with them. They look like a black fruit on the trees, distributed over the top at pretty equal distances. It is worth while to see how slyly they hide at the base of the thick and shaggy button-bushes at this stage of the water. They will suddenly cease their strains and flit away and secrete themselves low amid these bushes till you are past; or you scare up an unexpectedly large flock from such a place, where you had seen none.

I pass a large quire in full blast on the oaks, etc., on the island in the meadow northwest of Peter's. Suddenly they are hushed, and I hear the loud rippling rush made by their wings as they dash away, and, looking up, I see what I take to be a sharp-shinned hawk just alighting on the trees where they were, having failed to catch one. They retreat some forty rods off, to another tree, and renew their concert there. The hawk plumes him-

self, and then flies off, rising gradually and beginning to circle, and soon it joins its mate, and soars with it high in the sky and out of sight, as if the thought of so terrestrial a thing as a blackbird had never entered its head. It appeared to have a plain reddish-fawn breast. The size more than anything made me think it a sharp-shin.

When looking into holes in trees to find the squirrel's nest, I found a pout partly dried, with its tail gone, in one maple, about a foot above the ground. This was probably left there by a mink. Minott says that, being at work in his garden once, he saw a mink coming up from the brook with a pout in her mouth, half-way across his land. The mink, observing him, dropped her pout and stretched up her head, looking warily around, then, taking up the pout again, went onward and went under a rock in the wall by the roadside. He looked there and found the young in their nest, — so young that they were all "red" yet.

April 26. Hear the ruby-crowned wren in the morning, near George Heywood's.

We have had no snow for a long long while, and have about forgotten it. Dr. Bartlett, therefore, surprises us by telling us that a man came from Lincoln after him last night on the wheels of whose carriage was an inch of snow, for it snowed there a little, but not here. This is connected with the cold weather of yesterday; the chilling wind came from a snow-clad country. As the saying is, the cold was in the air and had got to come down.

To-day it is 53° at 2 P. M., yet cold, such a difference is there in our feelings. What we should have called a

Vol. XIII

warm day in March is a cold one at this date in April. It is the northwest wind makes it cold.

Out of the wind it is warm. It is not, methinks, the same air at rest in one place and in motion in another, but the cold that is brought by the wind seems not to affect sheltered and sunny nooks.

P. M. — To Cliffs and Well Meadow.

Comptonia. There are now very few leaves indeed left on the young oaks below the Cliffs. Sweet-briar, thimble-berry, and blackberry on warm rocks leaf early.

Red maples are past prime. I have noticed their handsome crescents over distant swamps commonly for some ten days. At height, then, say the 21st. They are especially handsome when seen between you and the sunlit trees.

The *Amelanchier Botryapium* is leafing; will apparently bloom to-morrow or next day. Sweet-fern (that does not flower) leafing.

The forward-rank sedge of Well Meadow which is so generally eaten (by rabbits, or possibly woodchucks), cropped close, is allied to that at Lee's Cliff, which is also extensively browsed now. I have found it difficult to get whole specimens. Certain tender early greens are thus extensively browsed now, in warm swamp-edges and under cliffs, — the bitter cress, the *Carex varia* (?) at Lee's, even skunk-cabbage.

The hellebore now makes a great garden of green under the alders and maples there, five or six rods long and a foot or more high. It grows thus before these trees have begun to leaf, while their numerous stems serve only to break the wind but not to keep out the sun. It is the

greatest growth, the most massive, of any plant's; now ahead of the cabbage. Before the earliest tree has begun to leaf it makes conspicuous green patches a foot high.

The river is exactly at summer level.

April 27. River five eighths of an inch below summer level.

P. M. — Row to Conantum.

At the stone bridge the lower side outer end of the stone is about a quarter of an inch above summer level.

I saw yesterday, and see to-day, a small hawk which I take to be a pigeon hawk. This one skims low along over Grindstone Meadow, close to the edge of the water, and I see the blackbirds rise hurriedly from the button-bushes and willows before him. I am decided by his size (as well as color) and his low, level skimming.[1]

The river meadows are now so dry that E. Wood is burning the Mantatuket one. Fishes are rising to the shad-flies, probably because the river is so low.

Luzula a day or two at Clamshell. Strawberry well out; how long? *Viola ovata* common. One dandelion white, as if going to seed! *Thalictrum anemonoides* are abundant, maybe two or three days, at Blackberry Steep.

I see where a robin has been destroyed, probably by a hawk. I think that I see these traces chiefly in the spring and fall. Why so? Columbine, but perhaps earlier, for I hear that it has been plucked here.

[1] Methinks I saw a yet smaller hawk, perhaps sparrow hawk, fly or skim over the village about the 12th.

I see, close under the rocks at Lee's, some *new* poly-pody flatted out.

I stand under Lee's Cliff. There is a certain summeriness in the air now, especially under a warm cliff like this, where you smell the very dry leaves, and hear the pine warbler and the hum of a few insects, — small gnats, etc., — and see considerable growth and greenness. Though it is still windy, there is, nevertheless, a certain serenity and long-lifeness in the air, as if it were a habitable place and not merely to be hurried through. The noon of the year is approaching. Nature seems meditating a siesta. The hurry of the duck migration is, methinks, over. But the woods generally, and at a distance, show no growth yet.

There is a large fire in the woods northwest of Concord, just before night. A column of smoke is blown away from it far southeast, and as the twilight approaches, it becomes more and more dun. At first some doubted if it was this side the North River or not, but I saw that Annursnack was this side of it, but I expected our bells would ring presently. One who had just come down in the cars thought it must be in Groton, for he had left a fire there. And the passengers in the evening train from Boston said that they began to see the smoke of it as soon as they left the city! So hard is it to tell how far off a great fire is.[1]

April 28. P. M. — To Ed. Hoar's, Lincoln. Warm. 65°.

[1] I learn afterward that it was just this side of Groton Junction in Groton. Some seven hundred acres burned. *Vide* Apr. 30th.

The common *Salix rostrata* on east side railroad, yesterday at least. *S. Torreyana* a day or two longer. These willows are full of bees and resound with their hum. I see honey-bees laden with large pellets of the peculiar yellow pollen of the *S. rostrata*. Methinks I could tell when that was in bloom by catching the bees on their return to the hive. Here are also much smaller bees and flies, etc., etc., all attracted by these flowers. As you stand by such a willow in bloom and resounding with the hum of bees in a warm afternoon like this, you seem nearer to summer than elsewhere.

Again I am advertised of the approach of a new season, as yesterday. The air is not only warmer and stiller, but has more of meaning or smothered voice to it, now that the hum of insects begins to be heard. You seem to have a great companion with you, are reassured by the scarcely audible hum, as if it were the noise of your own thinking. It is a voiceful and significant stillness, such as precedes a thunder-storm or a hurricane. The boisterous spring winds cease to blow, the waves to dash, the migrating ducks to vex the air so much. You are sensible of a certain repose in nature.

Sitting on Mt. Misery, I see a very large bird of the hawk family, blackish with a partly white head but no white tail, — probably a fish hawk; sailed quite near, looking very large.

Large ants at work; how long?

April 29. River two and seven eighths inches below summer level at 6 A. M. Three plus inches below at night.

Peetweet. I see this above Dodd's, and in the afternoon another up Assabet. As if they had come together from the south, — those bound to this river valley, — for they are not a numerous bird. I have in other instances noticed that birds which are not seen flying in flocks will yet arrive in a town generally, in all parts of it, the same day.

We have had but little fire for two or three weeks past. A few bits of old board, which make a quick blaze, suffice to take off the chill of your chamber in the morning. You now look on heaps of fuel with indifference. One old plank, well husbanded, is sufficient shield against all the cold that is to come.

The frost melting at 6 A. M. wets my feet. It is almost a dew then.

The only change in the distant forest is the red crescents to the red maples of late.

 I see the downy tall anemone heads yet, and, in some cases, the cotton which remains is entirely free of seed, and is very prettily recurved, in the form of a fool's-cap or short cone. You could not do it with your fingers.

P. M. — Up Assabet.

The earliest aspen is just bursting into bloom, but none is quite flatted out.

I listen to a concert of red-wings, — their rich sprayey notes, amid which a few more liquid and deep in a lower tone or undertone, as if it bubbled up from the very water beneath the button-bushes; as if those singers sat lower. Some old and skillful performer

touches these deep and liquid notes, and the rest seem to get up a concert just to encourage him. Yet it is ever a prelude or essay with him, as are all good things, and the melody he is capable of and which we did not hear this time is what we remember. The future will draw him out. The different individuals sit singing and pluming themselves and not appearing to have any conversation with one another. They are only tuning all at once; they never seriously perform; the hour has not arrived. Then all go off with a hurried and perhaps alarmed *tchuck tchuck*.

A clam lies up.

I stepped ashore behind Prichard's to examine a dead mud turtle, and when I had done, and turned round toward my boat again, behold, it was half-way across the river, blown by the southwest wind! The wind had risen after I landed, and perhaps I had given it a slight impulse with my foot when I landed. It lodged against a clump of willows on the other side, and I was compelled to return up-stream to borrow another boat to get it with. When I had borrowed a boat, I came near making the mistake of simply crossing the stream at once and running down the opposite shore; as if I could release my own boat and return on the same side to the borrowed one, return that, and so have got over my difficulties. I had to pause a moment and cipher it out in my mind.

It was remarkable how rapidly this large snapping turtle, which was killed last fall, had decayed. There [was] very little indeed of offensive odor about it. The shell contained only skin and bones now, and the prevailing odor was a peculiarly salt one, like strong dry salt fish. But a small dead dog of apparently the same age near by was much more offensive.

I have noticed before that turtles and snakes are decomposed rapidly. Perhaps it is so with all reptiles.

It was remarkable what a bar the river had become to me, being between me and my boat, — how comparatively helpless I was. I have rarely looked at it in that light. There was no way but to row quite down to my boat, bring it over to this side, row back with the borrowed boat, and return on the bank to my own. It reminded me of the man crossing the bridge with a fox, a goose, and a peck of corn. By the time I got under weigh again the afternoon was too far spent for a long excursion.

The turtle's scales were more than half of them off, and its long framework loosened, and the very bones of its head seemed somewhat decayed.

The river being very low, I notice, up the Assabet, where the muddy shore has been probed either by a peetweet (do they feed thus?) or a woodcock or snipe, — I am inclined to think the peetweet, for I see them along the river just arrived. According to this, this bird is so confined in its range that perhaps I could tell if it had come by finding its track on the mud or sand.

When I examine a flat sandy shore on which the ripples now break, I find the tracks of many little animals that have lately passed along it close to the water's edge. Some, indeed, have come out of the water and gone into it again. Minks, squirrels, and birds; they it is that walk these inland strands. The moist sand and mud which

the water has but just ceased to dash over retains the most delicate impressions. It is the same with all our rivers. I have noticed it on the sandy shore of the broad Merrimack. Many little inhabitants of the wood and of the water have walked there, though probably you will not see one. They make tracks for the geologists. I now actually see one small-looking rusty or brown black mink scramble along the muddy shore and enter a hole in the bank.

I see swarms of water-bugs at rest in still bays under the willows and button-bushes, but when I approach near they begin to gyrate rapidly, and this evidently is their resource to avoid capture.

On the west side, just at the bend of the river by Dove Rock, where the ripples have caused the sandy strand to cave and made a perpendicular cliff an inch high, I notice, rising above the sand and waving in the water, what look at first like stubble of rye or pipes. With my finger I dig some up, two or three inches long and half in the sand. They look even like earthworms coated with sand, are hollow cylinders of sand, and have a certain toughness, breaking when drawn apart just as if there was a skin to them. They are both simple, more or less upright, flexible and waving, and also are branched sometimes. I bring some home, which, dried and half flattened, look just like dead fishworms that have fallen in the sand. When I place a piece in the palm of my hand and rub it with my finger, it is reduced at once to pure sand and there is no vestige of a skin. The man of the Aquarium tells me, after this, that he finds

exactly similar things by the salt water, with worms in them.

I detect a new water-plant which I must have often seen before and confounded with the ranunculuses, utricularias, and potomogetons. It *appears* to be the *Naias flexilis*, said to bloom in July and August. Much of it is covered with a whitish mealy-looking substance. It forms dense beds on the bottom in muddy places, *e. g.* west side just above sawed maple. I see its buds plainly now.

April 30. Cattle begin to go up-country, and every week day, especially Mondays, to this time [*sic*] May 7th,[1] at least, the greatest droves to-day. Methinks they will find slender picking up there for a while. Now many a farmer's boy makes his first journey, and sees something to tell of, — makes acquaintance with those hills which are mere blue warts in his horizon, finds them solid and *terra firma*, after all, and inhabited by herdsmen, partially befenced and measurable by the acre, with cool springs where you may quench your thirst after a dusty day's walk.

Surveying Emerson's wood-lot to see how much was burned near the end of March, I find that what I anticipated is exactly true, — that the fire did not burn hard on the northern slopes, there being then frost in the ground, and where the bank was very steep, say at angle of forty-five degrees, which was the case with more than a quarter of an acre, it did not run down at all, though no man hindered it.

[1] And 14th; thereafter few.

That fire in the woods in Groton on the 27th, which was seen so far, so very dun and extensive the smoke, so that you looked to see the flames too, proves what slight burnings it is, comparatively, that we commonly see making these cloud-like or bluish smokes in the horizon, and also how very far off they may often be. Those whitish columns of smoke which we see from the hills, and count so many of at once, are probably often fifty or sixty miles off or more. I can now believe what I have read of a traveller making such a signal on the slope of the Rocky Mountains a hundred miles off, to save coming back to his party. Yet, strange to say, I did not see the smoke of the still larger fire between Concord and Acton in March at all, I being in Lincoln and outdoors all the time. This Groton fire did not seem much further off than a fire in Walden Woods, and, as I believe and hear, in each town the inhabitants supposed it to be in the outskirts of their own township.

VI

MAY, 1860

(ÆT. 42)

May 1. Plant potatoes; the very *midst* of early potato planting.

I now, as usual, turn up numerous yellow dor-bugs, which are as yet a very pale yellow, not having been exposed to the light. Also those great white potato-worms.

The sugar maple keys (or buds?) hang down one inch, quite.

Ed. Emerson's snails (the simplest kind) spawned March 28. I see young now as big as the head of a pin. The stones in his aquarium are covered with very minute green polypuses, some of them budded. The incipient ones are like a fine forest. You can only see them against a strong light.

May 2. River three and five sixteenths below summer level.

I observed on the 29th that the clams had not only been moving much, furrowing the sandy bottom near the shore, but generally, or almost invariably, had moved toward the middle of the river. Perhaps it had something to do with the low stage of the water. I saw one making his way — or perhaps it had rested since

low. (But since — May 8th — I notice them, and perhaps I overlooked them before.)

I notice on the east bank by the stone-heaps, amid the bushes, what I supposed to be two woodchucks' holes, with a well-worn path from one to the other, and the young trees close about them, aspen and black cherry, had been gnawed for a foot or more upward for a year or two. There were some fresh wounds, and also old and extensive scars of last year partially healed.

The naked viburnum is leafing. The sedge apparently *Carex Pennsylvanica* has now been out on low ground a day or two.

A crowd of men seem to generate vermin even of the human kind. In great towns there is degradation undreamed of elsewhere, — gamblers, dog-killers, rag-pickers. Some live by robbery or by luck. There was the Concord muster (of last September). I see still a well-dressed man carefully and methodically searching for money on the muster-fields, far off across the river. I turn my glass upon him and notice how he proceeds. (I saw them searching there in the fall till the snow came.) He walks regularly and slowly back and forth over the ground where the soldiers had their tents, — still marked by the straw, — with his head prone, and poking in the straw with a stick, now and then turning back or aside to examine something more closely. He is dressed, methinks, better than an average man whom you meet in the streets. How can he pay for his board thus? He dreams of finding a few coppers, or perchance a half-dime, which have fallen from the soldiers' pockets, and no doubt he *will* find something

morning — over that sawdust bar just below Turtle Bar, toward the river, the surface of the bar being an inch or two higher than the water. Probably the water, falling, left it thus on dry (moist) land.

I notice this forenoon (11.30 A. M.) remarkably round-topped white clouds just like round-topped hills,

on all sides of the sky, often a range of such, such

as I do not remember to have seen before. There was considerable wind on the surface, from the north-east, and the above clouds were moving west and southwest, — a generally distributed cumulus. What added to the remarkableness of the sight was a very fine, fleecy cirrhus, like smoke, narrow but of indefinite length, driving swiftly eastward beneath the former, proving that there were three currents of air, one above the other. (The same form of cloud prevailed to some extent the next day.)

Salix alba apparently yesterday.

The early potentillas are now quite abundant.

P. M. — To stone-heaps and stone bridge.

Since (perhaps) the middle of April we have had much easterly (northeast chiefly) wind, and yet no rain, though this wind rarely fails to bring rain in March. (The same is true till 9th of May at least; *i. e.*, in spite of east winds there is no rain.)

I find no stone-heaps made yet, the water being very

of the kind, having dreamed of it, — having knocked, this door will be opened to him.

Walking over the russet interval, I see the first red-winged grasshoppers. They rise from the still brown sod before me, and I see the redness of their wings as they fly. They are quite shy and hardly let me come within ten feet before they rise again, — often before I have seen them fairly on the ground.

It was 63° at 2 P. M., and yet a good deal of coolness in the wind, so that I can scarcely find a comfortable seat. (Yet a week later, with thermometer at 60 and but little wind, it seems much warmer.)

We have had cool nights of late.

May 3. To Cambridge and Boston.

I see at the Aquarium many of my little striped or barred breams, now labelled *Bryttus obesus*. Compared with the common, they have rounded tails, larger dorsal and anal fins, and are fuller or heavier forward. I observe that they incline to stand on their heads more.

The proprietor said that some little fishes one and a half to two inches long, with a very distinct black line along the sides, which I should have called brook minnows, Agassiz was confident were young suckers, but Mr. Putnam thought that they were the *Leuciscus atronarus*, *i. e.* my brook minnow. I observe that a leuciscus (probably *pulchellus*, if not *argenteus*), five inches long, also has a broad line along the side, but not nearly so dark. He shows me the eudora (water-plant), which he has not seen east of the Connecticut.

Young Shoots on Pitch Pine

The Great Meadows in Spring

May 4. River three and one fourth inches below summer level. Scales of turtles are coming off (painted turtle). Quite a warm day, — 70 at 6 P. M. Currant out a day or two at least, and our first gooseberry a day later.

P. M. — To Great Meadows by boat.

I see Haynes with a large string of pickerel, and he says that he caught a larger yesterday. There were none of the brook pickerel in this string. He goes every day, and has good luck. It must be because the river is so low. Fishing, then, has fairly commenced. It is never any better pickerel-fishing than now. He has caught three good-sized trout in the river within a day or [two]; one would weigh a pound and a half. One above the railroad bridge, and one off Abner Buttrick's, Saw Mill Brook. He has caught them in the river before, but very rarely. He caught these as he was fishing for pickerel. This, too, may be because the river is low and it is early in the season. He says that he uses the *Rana halecina* for bait; that a pickerel will spit out the yellow-legged one.

Walking over the river meadows to examine the pools and see how much dried up they are, I notice, as usual, the track of the musquash, some five inches wide always, always exactly in the lowest part of the muddy hollows connecting one pool with another, winding as they wind, as if loath to raise itself above the lowest mud. At first he swam there, and now, as the water goes down, he follows it steadily, and at length travels on the bare mud, but as low and close to the water as he can get. Thus he first traces the channel of the future brook and river, and deepens it by dragging his belly along it.

He lays out and engineers its road. As our roads are said to follow the trail of the cow, so rivers in another period follow the trail of the musquash.

They are perfect rats to look at, and swim fast against the stream. When I am talking on a high bank I often see one swimming along within half a dozen rods and land openly, as if regardless of us. Probably, being under water at first, he did not hear us.

When the locomotive was first introduced into Concord, the cows and horses ran in terror to [the] other sides of their pastures as it passed along, and I suppose that the fishes in the river manifested equal alarm at first; but I notice (to-day, the 11th of May) that a pickerel by Derby's Bridge, poised in a smooth bay, did not stir perceptibly when the train passed over the neighboring bridge and the locomotive screamed remarkably loud. The fishes have, no doubt, got used to the sound.

I see a bullfrog under water.

Land at the first angle of the Holt. Looking across the Peninsula toward Ball's Hill, I am struck by the bright blue of the river (a deeper blue than the sky), contrasting with the fresh yellow green of the meadow (*i. e.* of coarse sedges just starting), and, between them, a darker or greener green next the edge of the river, especially where that small sand-bar island is, — the green of that early rank river-grass. This is the first painting or coloring in the meadows. These several colors are, as it were, daubed on, as on chinaware, or as distinct and simple as a child's painted [*sic*]. I am struck by the amount and variety of color after so much brown.

Vol. XIII

As I stood there I heard a thumping sound, which I referred to Peter's, three quarters of a mile off over the meadow. But it was a pigeon woodpecker excavating its nest within a maple within a rod of me. Though I had just landed and made a noise with my boat, he was too busy to hear me, but now he hears my tread, and I see him put out his head and then withdraw it warily and keep still, while I stay there.

Pipes (*Equisetum limosum*) are now generally three to seven inches high, but so brown as yet that I mistook them at a little distance for a dead brown stubble amid the green of springing sedge, and not a fresh growth at all. They are at last a very dark green still, if I remember.

The river is very low, but I find that the meadows, though bare, are not very dry, except for the season, and I am pretty sure that within two or three years, and at this season, I have seen the pools on the meadows drier when there was more water in the river.

The Great Meadows are wet to walk over, after all, and the great pools on them are rather unapproachable, even in india-rubber boots. Apparently it is impossible for the meadows to be so dry at this season, however low the river may be, as they may be at midsummer and later. Their own springs are fuller now.

A *Nuphar advena* in one of these pools what you may call out, for it is rather stale, though no pollen is shed.

What little water there is amid the pipes and sedge is filled and swarming with apparently the larva of some insect, perhaps ephemeræ. They keep up an undulating motion, and have many feathery fringes on the sides.

I observe fishes close inshore, active and rippling the water when not scared, as if breeding; often their back fins out.

The sun sets red, shorn of its beams.

Those little silvery beetles in Ed. Emerson's aquarium that dash about are evidently the *Notonecta*, or water-boatmen. I believe there is a larger and somewhat similar beetle, which does not swim on its back, called *Dytiscus*.

Missouri currant out; how long?

May 5. Cobwebs on the grass, — half green, half brown, — this morning; certainly not long, perhaps this the first time; and dews.

2 P. M. — 76°. Warm and hazy (and yesterday warm also); my single thick coat too much. Wind southeast. A fresher and cooler breeze is agreeable now. The wind becomes a breeze at this season.

The yellowish (or common) winged grasshoppers are quite common now, hopping and flying before me. *Viola blanda*, how long?

Clams lie up abundantly.

Bluets have spotted the fields for two or three days mingled with the reddish luzula, as in Conant's field north of Holden Wood toward the brook. They fill the air with a sweet and innocent fragrance at a few rods' distance.

I have not worn my outside coat since the 19th of April and now it is the 13th of May; nor, I think, had any fire in my chamber. Latterly have sat with the window open, even at evening.

Anemone and *Thalictrum anemonoides* are apparently in prime about the 10th of May. The former abounds in the thin young wood behind Lee's Cliff. Tent caterpillar nest an inch and a half over. Dicksonia fern up six inches in a warm place. Yellow butter-flies. *Veronica serpyllifolia*, say yesterday.

There are some dense beds of houstonia in the yard of the old Conantum house. Some parts of them show of a distinctly bluer shade two rods off. They are most interesting now, before many other flowers are out, the grass high, and they have lost their freshness I sit down by one dense bed of them to examine it. It is about three feet long and two or more wide. The flowers not only crowd one another, but are in several tiers, one above another, and completely hide the ground, — a mass of white. Counting those in a small place, I find that there are about three thousand flowers in a square foot. They are all turned a little toward the sun, and emit a refreshing odor. Here is a lumbering humblebee, probing these tiny flowers. It is a rather ludicrous sight. Of course they will not support him, except a little where they are densest; so he bends them down rapidly (hauling them in with his arms, as it were), one after another, thrusting his beak into the tube of each. It takes him but a moment to dispatch one. It is a singular sight, a humblebee clambering over a bed of these delicate flowers. There are various other bees about them.

See at Lee's a pewee (phœbe) building. She has just woven in, or laid on the edge, a fresh sprig of saxifrage in flower. I notice that phœbes will build in the same

The dog's-tooth violet was sent from Cambridge in flower, May 1st.

2 P. M. — To Second Division.

74°; wind southeast; and hazy.

A goldfinch apparently not quite in summer dress; with a dark-brown, not black, front.

See a song sparrow's nest with four eggs in the side of a bank, or rather ditch. I commonly find the earliest ones in such sheltered and concealed places. What did they do before the white man came here with his ditches and stone walls? (Methinks by the 13th I hear the bay-wing sing the oftenest.)

As I go down the warm sandy path in the gully behind J. P. Brown's, I see quite a number of *Viola pedata*, indigo-weed shoots six inches high, a prenanthes leaf eight inches high, and two-leaved Solomon's-seal pushing up, — all signs of warm weather. As the leaves are putting forth on the trees, so now a great many herbaceous plants are springing up in the woods and fields.

There is a peculiar stillness associated with the warmth, which the cackling of a hen only serves to deepen, increasing the Sabbath feeling.

In the Major Heywood path see many rather small (or middle-sized) blackish butterflies. The *Luzula campestris* is apparently in prime.

Oryzopsis grass well out, how long?

Now at last we seek the shade these days, as the most grateful. Sit under the pines near the stone guide-post on the Marlborough road. The note of the pine warbler, which sounded so warm in March, sounds equally cool now.

recess in a cliff year after year. It is a constant thing here, though they are often disturbed. Think how many pewees must have built under the eaves of this cliff since pewees were created and this cliff itself built!! You can possibly find the crumbling relics of how many, if you should look carefully enough! It takes us many years to find out that Nature repeats herself annually. But how perfectly regular and calculable all her phenomena must appear to a mind that has observed her for a thousand years!

Vernal grass at this cliff (common at Damon's Spring the 12th). The marginal shield fern is one foot high here. *Amelanchier Botryapium* flower in prime.

Have seen no ducks for a week or more.

Knawel some time. *Vaccinium Pennsylvanicum* flowers against rocks, not long.

Sun goes down red. Hear of bear-berry well out the 29th of April at Cliffs, and there probably some days.

The peepers and toads are in full blast at night.

May 6. River three and one fourth inches below summer level. Why is it only three eighteenths of an inch lower than last Sunday (April 29)? For we are in the midst of a remarkable drought, and I think that if there had been any rain within a week near the sources of the river I should have heard of it. Is it that these innumerable sources of the river which the springs in the meadows are, are able to keep up the supply? The river had been falling steadily a good while before. Why, then, has it not fallen more the past week?

The Second Division rush is not yet out. It is the greatest growth of what you may call the grass kind as yet, the reddish tops, say sixteen inches high (above the now green), trembling in the wind very agreeably. The dark beds of the white ranunculus in the Second Division Brook are very interesting, the whitish stems seen amid and behind the dark-brown old leaves.

The white-throated sparrow, and probably the 28th of April. The large osmunda ferns, say one foot high, some of them; also a little brake one foot high. Hear probably a yellow-throated vireo in the woods. A creeper (black and white) yesterday.

Sit on the steep north bank of White Pond. The *Amelanchier Botryapium* in flower now spots the brown sprout-land hillside on the southeast side, across the pond, very interestingly. Though it makes but a faint impression of color, I see its pink distinctly a quarter of a mile off. It is seen now in sprout-lands half a dozen years old, where the oak leaves have just about all fallen except a few white oaks. (It is in prime about the 8th.) Others are seen directly under the bank on which we sit, on this side, very white against the blue water.

Many at this distance would not notice those shad-bush flowers on the hillside, or [would] mistake them for whitish rocks. They are the more interesting for coming thus between the fall of the oak leaves and the expanding of other shrubs and trees. Some of the larger, near at hand, are very light and elegant masses of white bloom. The white-fingered flower of the sprout-lands. In sprout-lands, having probably the start or preëminence over the other sprouts, from not being commonly, or [at] all, cut down with the other trees and shrubs, they are as high or higher than any of them for five or six years, and they are so early that they feel almost the full influence of the sun, even amid full-grown deciduous trees which have not leafed, while they are considerably sheltered from the wind by them.

There is so fine a ripple on White Pond that it amounts to a mere imbrication, very regular.

The song of the robin heard at 4.30 P. M., this still and hazy day, sounds already vespertinal. Maple keys an inch and a half long.

Mists these mornings.

Our second shad-bush out, how long? It is generally just beginning in the woods.

My chamber is oppressively warm in the evening.

May 7. River one eighth of an inch lower than yesterday.

Chimney swallow. Catbird sings. Hear the white-throat sparrow's *peabody* note in gardens.

Canada plum in full bloom, or say in prime. Also common plum in full bloom?

It is very hazy, as yesterday, and I smell smoke.

P. M. — To Assabet stone bridge.

Find in the road beyond the Wheeler cottages a little round, evidently last year's, painted turtle. Has no yellow spots, but already little red spots on the edges of the sides. The sternum a sort of orange or pinkish-red.

This warm weather, I see many new beetles and other

insects. *Ribes florida* by bridge (flower). Cultivated cherry flowered yesterday at least, not yet ours.

Myrtle-bird.

Met old Mr. Conant with his eye and half the side of his face black and blue, looking very badly. He said he had been jerked down on to the barn-floor by a calf some three weeks old which he was trying to lead. The strength of calves is remarkable. I saw one who had some difficulty in pulling along a calf not a week old. With their four feet they have a good hold on the earth. The last one was sucking a cow that had sore teats, and every time it bunted, the cow kicked energetically, raking the calf's head and legs, but he stood close against the cow's belly and never budged in spite of all her kicks, though a man would have jumped out of the way. Who taught the calf to bunt?

I saw bluets whitening the fields yesterday a quarter of a mile off. They are to the sere brown grass what the shad-bush is now to the brown and bare sprout-lands or young woods.

When planting potatoes the other day, I found small ones that had been left in the ground, perfectly sound!

May 8. A cloudy day.

The small pewee, how long. The night-warbler's note. River four and seven eighths inches below summer level. Stone-heaps, how long?

I see a woodchuck in the middle of the field at Assabet Bath. He is a [an indecipherable word] heavy fellow with a black tip to his tail, poking about almost

Vol. XIII

on his belly, — where there is but little greenness yet, — with a great heavy head. He is very wary, every minute pausing and raising his head, and sometimes sitting erect and looking around. He is evidently nibbling some green thing, maybe clover. He runs at last, with an undulating motion, jerking his lumbering body along, and then stops when near a hole. But on the whole he runs and stops and looks round very much like a cat in the fields.

The cinquefoil is closed in a cloudy day, and when the sun shines it is turned toward it.

The simple *peep peep* of the peetweet, as it flies away from the shore before me, sounds hollow and rather mournful, reminding me of the seashore and its wrecks, and when I smell the fresh odor of our marshes the resemblance is increased.

How the marsh hawk circles or skims low, round and round over a particular place in a meadow, where, perhaps, it has seen a frog, screaming once or twice, and then alights on a fence-post! How it crosses the causeway between the willows, at a gap in them with which it is familiar, as a hen knows a hole in a fence! I lately saw one flying over the road near our house.

I see a gray squirrel ascend the dead aspen at the rock, and enter a hole some eighteen feet up it. Just below this, a crack is stuffed with leaves which project. Probably it has a nest within and has filled up this crack.

Now that the river is so low, the bared bank, often within the button-bushes, is seen to be covered with that fine, short, always green *Eleocharis acicularis* (?).

C. has seen a brown thrasher and a republican swallow to-day.

May 9. River five and three fourths inches below summer level.

I think I heard a bobolink this forenoon.

A boy brought me what I take to be a very red *Rana sylvatica*, caught on the leaves the 6th.

Have had no fire for more than a fortnight, and no greatcoat since April 19th.

Fir balsam bloom. Sugar maple blossoms are now a tender yellow; in prime, say 11th. Thousands of dandelions along the meadow by the Mill Brook, behind R. W. E.'s, in prime, say 10th.[1]

P. M. — To Flint's Pond.

It is a still, cloudy, thoughtful day.

Oven-bird, how long? In Ebby Hubbard's wood, I climb to a hole in a dead white pine, a dozen feet up, and see by the gray fur about the edge of the hole that it probably has been used by the gray squirrel. Maryland yellow-throat.

We sit by the shore of Goose Pond. The tapping of a woodpecker sounds distinct and hollow this still cloudy day, as not before for a long time, and so do the notes of birds, as if heard against a background for a relief, *e. g.* the cackle of the pigeon woodpecker, the note of the jay, the scratching in the dry leaves of three or four chewinks near us (for they are not shy), about the pond, under the blueberry bushes. The water is smooth. After sitting there a little while, I count the

[1] By the 18th are much concealed by grass.

noses of twenty frogs within a couple of rods, which have ventured to come to the surface again, — so quietly that I did not see one come up. At the fox-hole by Britton's Hollow there are some three cart-buck-loads of sand cast out.

That large pine-tree moss that makes beds on the ground, now fruiting, when I brush my hand over its fruit is surprisingly stiff and elastic like wires.

Yellow lily pads begun to spread out on some pools, but hardly yet on the river; say 10th on river.

Golden robin.

The wall by the road at the bars north of Cyrus Smith's chestnut grove is very firmly bound together by the *Rhus Toxicodendron* which has overrun it, for twenty feet in length. Would it not be worth the while to encourage its growth for this purpose, if you are not afraid of being poisoned? It runs up by small root-like stems, which cling close and flat to the wall, and which intertwine and seem to take a new start from the top of the wall (as from the ground), where the stems are generally larger than below, so that it is in fact a row of this rhus growing on the top of the wall to some three or four feet above it, and by its rooty stems binding the stones very firmly together. How much better this than sods on a wall!

Of that *early* sedge in Everett's meadow,[1] the topmost spikes are already effete; say a week, then. I see a second amelanchier with a distinct pink or rosaceous tinge like an apple blossom. Elm seed has begun to fall.

[1] *Carex stricta.*

Vol. XIII

quantity at once — attracted my attention and I found they were the work of bees. The bees were hovering low over the surface, and were continually entering and issuing from the holes. They were about the size of a honey-bee, black bodied, with, I thought, yellow thighs, — if it was not pollen. Many of the holes appeared to have been freshly stopped up with granules of moist sand. These holes were made close together in the dry and sandy soil there, with very little grass on it, sloping toward the west, between the roads, and covered a triangular space some seven rods by three. I counted twenty-four in a square foot. There must have been some twenty-five thousand of these nests in all. The surface was yellowed with them. Evidently a kind of mining bee.

I see in roadside hard sward, by the brook beyond, a sedge darker than the *stricta* and not in tufts, quite short. Is it the *C. vulgaris?* Its leading spikes are effete.

Evergreen-forest note.

Some very young oaks — white oak, etc. — in woods begin to leaf.

Hear the first cricket.

The red maples, fruiting now, are in the brick-red state.

I heard yesterday one or two warblers. One's note was, in rhythm, like a very feeble field sparrow. Was it the redstart? Probably one or two strange warblers now. Was it not the parti-colored warbler, — with bluish head and yellow beneath, but not the screeper note, but note ending with a jingle slightly like the field sparrow?

Meadow fox-tail grass out several days.

Cattle going up country for ten days past.[1] You must keep your gate shut.

May 10. River six and one eighth inches below summer level.

Thermometer at 2 P. M., 71. The winds died away with April.

In the midst of a remarkable drought. Hear of great fires in the woods up country the past week, it is so dry. Some farmers plowed around their houses to save them.

P. M. — To Bateman's Pond.

Salix alba flower in prime and resounding with the hum of bees on it. The sweet fragrance fills the air for a long distance. How much the planting of this willow adds to the greenness and cheerfulness of our landscape at this season!

As I stand on Hunt's Bridge, I notice the now comparatively dark green of the canary grass (*Phalaris*), the coarse grass vigorously spring[ing] up on the muddy islands and edges, the glaucous green of *Carex stricta* tufts, and the light yellowish green of the very coarse sedges of the meadow.

Going over the hill behind S. Brown's, when we crossed the triangular space between the roads beyond the pump-maker's, I saw countless little heaps of sand like the small ant-hills, but, looking more closely, the size of the holes (a little less than a quarter of an inch) and the comparative irregularity of the heaps — as if the sand had been brought forth and dropped in greater

[1] Yes, and the 14th.

May 11. The river no lower than yesterday.

Warbling vireo.

2 P. M. — 77°. Very warm. To factory village.

Redstart. Red-wings do not fly in flocks for ten days past, I think.

I see at Damon's Spring some dandelion seeds all blown away, and other perfectly ripe spheres (much more at Clamshell the 13th). It is ripe, then, several days, or say just before elm seed, but the mouse-ear not on the 13th anywhere.

The senecio shows its yellow.

The warmth makes us notice the shade of houses and trees (even before the last have leafed) falling on the greened banks, as Harrington's elm and house. June-like.

See some large black birch stumps all covered with pink scum from the sap.

The *Ranunculus abortivus* well out; say five days? Red cherry in bloom, how long? Yellow violet, almost; say to-morrow.

William Brown's nursery is now white (fine white) with the shepherd's-purse, some twelve to eighteen inches high, covering it under his small trees, like buckwheat, though not nearly so white as that. I never saw so much. It also has green pods. Say it is in prime.

E. Hosmer, as a proof that the river has been lower than now, says that his father, who was born about the middle of the last century, used to tell of a time, when he was a boy, when the river just below Derby's Bridge did not run, and he could cross it dry-shod on the rocks, the water standing in pools when Conant's mill (where the factory now is) was not running. I noticed the place to-day, and, low as the river is for the season, it must be at least a foot and a half deep there.

May 12. Celandine. Very hot.

2.30 P. M. — 81°.

We seek the shade to sit in for a day or two. The neck-cloth and single coat is too thick; wear a half-thick coat at last [?].

The sugar maple blossoms on the Common resound with bees.

Ostrya flower commonly out on Island, how long? Maybe a day or two.

First bathe in the river. Quite warm enough.

River five and one half plus inches below summer level.

Very heavy dew and mist this morning; plowed ground black and moist with it. The earth is so dry it drinks like a sponge.

May 13. I observe this morning the dew on the grass in our yard, — literally sparkling drops, which thickly stud it. Each dewdrop is a beautiful crystalline sphere just below (within an eighth of an inch more or less) the tip of the blade. Sometimes there are two or three, one beneath the other, the lowest the largest. Each dewdrop takes the form of the planet itself.

What an advance is this from the sere, withered, and flattened grass, at most whitened with frost, which we have lately known, to this delicate crystalline drop trembling at the tip of a fresh green grass-blade. The surface of the globe is thus tremblingly alive.

A great many apple trees out, and probably some for two days.

2 P. M. — 82°; warmest day yet.

This and the last two days remarkably warm. Need a half-thick coat; sit and sleep with open window, the 13th.

Row to Bittern Cliff.

The celtis is not yet in bloom.

The river is now six and fifteen sixteenths inches below summer level.

At Clamshell, one cerastium flower quite done and dry. *Ranunculus bulbosus* abundant, spotting the bank; maybe a week. Tall buttercup. Horsemint seen springing up for a week, and refreshing scent.

Hear several bobolinks distinctly to-day.

Hear the *pebbly* notes of the frog.

See the coarse green rank canary grass, springing up amid the bare brown button-bushes and willows. Redwings are evidently busy building their nests. They are sly and anxious, the females, about the button-bushes.

See two crows pursuing and diving at a hen-hawk very high in the air over the river. He is steadily circling and rising. While they, getting above, dive down toward him, passing within a foot or two, making a feint, he merely winks, as it were, bends or jerks his wings slightly as if a little startled, but never ceases soaring, nor once turns to pursue or shake them off. It seemed as if he was getting uncomfortably high for them.

At Holden Swamp, hear plenty of parti-colored warblers (tweezer-birds) and redstarts. *Uvularia sessilifolia* abundant, how long? The swamp is so dry that

Vol. XIII

I walk about it in my shoes, and the *Kalmia glauca* is apparently quite backward accordingly, — can scarcely detect any buds of it, — while the rhodora on shore will apparently bloom to-morrow. Hear the *yorrick.*

The intermediate ferns and cinnamon, a foot and a half high, have just *leafeted* out. The sensitive fern is only six inches high, — apparently the latest of all. Sorrel.

It is a remarkable day for this season. You have the heat of summer before the leaves have expanded. The sky is full of glowing summer cumuli. There is no haze; the mountains are seen with perfect distinctness. It is so warm that you can lie on the still brownish grass in a thin coat, and will seek the shade for this purpose.

What is that fern so common at Lee's Cliff, now sprung up a foot high with a very chaffy stem? Marginal shield? Is that *Polypodium Dryopteris* in the bank behind the slippery elm? Now six or seven inches high. There is no mouse-ear down even there. Those heads which have looked most expanded and downy are invariably cut off by some creature (probably insect) and withered. The crickets creak steadily among the rocks. The *Carex varia* (?) at Lee's all gone to seed. Barberry in bloom. *Myosotis stricta. Arum triphyllum,* how long? *Cardamine rhomboidea,* apparently to-morrow, just above Bittern Cliff.

It is so warm that I hear the peculiar *sprayey* note of the toad generally at night. The third sultry evening in my chamber. A faint lightning is seen in the north horizon.

The tender yellow green of birches is now the most

noticeable of any foliages in our landscape, as looking across the pond from Lee's Cliff. The poplars are not common enough. The white birches are now distinguished simply by being clothed with a tender and yellow green, while the trees generally are bare and brown, — upright columns of green dashing the brown hillsides.

May 14. The heat continues.

It is remarkably hazy; wind still northeast. You can hardly see the horizon at all a mile off. The mornings for some time past have been misty rather than foggy, and now it lasts through the day and becomes a haze. The sunlight is yellow through it.

In the afternoon it is cooler, much cooler at about 60, and windier.

Some *Salix discolor* down shows itself before mouse-ear. The order is, then, dandelion, elm seed, willow, and next, probably, mouse-ear down, *i. e.* of the more noticeable seeds.

At Stow's meadow by railroad I see *Carex stipata,* maybe five days out. *C. vulgaris,* five to eight inches high and done [1] (the short scattered dark-scaled one). At Smith's shore the *C. Buxbaumii* is nearly done. Put, then, in the order (the meadow carices observed) till I know better: *C. vulgaris,* May 1st; *C. stricta,* May 3d; [2] *Buxbaumii,* May 6th; *C. stipata,* say 9th; or perhaps the first two together. Flowering fern is a foot high.

---

[1] Still out near English cress, May 16th.
[2] Still out near English cress, May 16th.

C. sees the chestnut-sided warbler and the tanager to-day, and heard a whip-poor-will last night.

The early sedges, even in the meadows, have blossomed before you are aware of it, while their tufts and bases are still mainly brown.

May 15. P. M. — To sedge path and Cliffs.

Yesterday afternoon and to-day the east wind has been quite cool, if not cold, but the haze thicker than ever. Too cool, evidently, and windy for warblers, except in sheltered places; too cool in tops of high exposed trees.

The *Carex stricta* and *C. vulgaris* both are common just beyond the English brook cress, and many of both are still in bloom.

I noticed on the 13th my middle-sized orange butterfly with blackish spots.

Noticed on the 6th the largest shrub oak that I know in the road by White Pond, just before getting to the lane.

The *Salix humilis* is going to seed as early as the *discolor*, for aught I see; now downy.

Oaks are just coming into the gray.

Deciduous woods now swarm with migrating warblers, especially about swamps.

Did I not hear part of a grosbeak's strain?

Lousewort flower some time, and frost-bitten.

Under the Cliffs, edge of Gerardia quercifolia Path, the *C. varia*, gone to seed (*vide* press), and, on top of Cliffs near staghorn sumach, *C. Pennsylvanica*, gone to seed and ten or more inches high, also still apparently in bloom (*vide* press).

Looking from the Cliffs through the haze, the deciduous trees are a mist of leafets, against which the pines are already darkened. At this season there is thus a mist in the air and a mist on the earth.

Rye is a foot or more high, and some [?] two feet, — the early. The springing sorrel, the expanding leafets, the already waving rye tell of June.

Sun goes down red, and did last night. A hot day does not succeed, but the very dry weather continues. It is shorn of its beams in the mist-like haze.

Ranunculus bulbosus begins in churchyard to-day.

May 16. P. M. — To Copan and Beck Stow's.

2 P. M. — 56°, with a cold east wind. Many people have fires again.

Near Peter's I see a small creeper hopping along the branches of the oaks and pines, ever turning this way and that as it hops, making various angles with the bough; then flies across to another bough, or to the base of another tree, and traces that up, zigzag and prying into the crevices. Think how thoroughly the trees are thus explored by various birds. You can hardly sit near one for five minutes now, but either a woodpecker or creeper comes and examines its bark rapidly, or a warbler — a summer yellowbird, for example — makes a pretty thorough exploration about all its expanding leafets, even to the topmost twig. The whole North American forest is being thus explored for insect food now by several hundred (?) species of birds. Each is visited by many

kinds, and thus the equilibrium of the insect and vegetable kingdom is preserved. Perhaps I may say that each opening bud is thus visited before it has fully expanded.

The golden robin utters from time to time a hoarse or grating *cr-r-ack*. The creepers are very common now.

Now that the warblers are here in such numbers is the very time on another account to study them, for the leaf-buds are generally but just expanding, and if you look toward the light you can see every bird that flits through a small grove, but a few weeks hence the leaves will conceal them.

The deciduous trees are just beginning to invest the evergreens, and this, methinks, is the very midst of the leafing season, when the oaks are getting into the gray.

A lupine will open to-day. One wild pink out. Red cherry apparently in prime.

A golden-crowned thrush keeps the trunks of the young trees between me and it as it hops away.

Are those poplars the *tremuliformis* which look so dead south of Holbrook's land, not having leafed out?

Menyanthes, apparently a day or two. *Andromeda Polifolia*, how long? *Andromeda calyculata* much past prime.

Nemopanthes, maybe a day or two out.

The swamps are exceedingly dry. On the 13th I walked wherever I wanted to in thin shoes in Kalmia Swamp, and to-day I walk through the middle of Beck Stow's. The river meadows are more wet, comparatively.

I pass a young red maple whose keys hang down three inches or more and appear to be nearly ripe.

This, being in a favorable light (on one side from the sun) and being of a high color, — a pink scarlet, — is a very beautiful object, more so than when in flower. Masses of double samaræ unequally disposed along the branches, trembling in the wind. Like the flower of the shad-bush, so this handsome fruit is seen for the most part now against bare twigs, it is so much in advance of its own and of other leaves. The peduncles gracefully rise a little before they curve downward. They are only a little darker shade than the samaræ. There are sometimes three samaræ together. Sun goes down red.

May 17. Quite a fog till 8 A. M., and plowed ground blackened with the moisture absorbed.

J. Farmer sends me to-day what is plainly Cooper's hawk. It is from eighteen to nineteen inches long, and from flexure of wing eleven inches (alar extent thirty-four). The tail extends four or five inches beyond the wings. Tarsus about three inches long and with feet yellow. The bird above is nearly a uniform dark brown, or dark chocolate-brown, with bluish reflections; head darker. Tail with four blackish bands, and narrowly tipped with whitish. Cere greenish. Breast transversely barred with pale rusty, centred longitudinally with darker-brown lines. Under wing-coverts like breast, without the transverse bars. Vent white. Wings beneath (secondaries and primaries) thickly barred with blackish brown and light, — white. Iris yellow. There is attached to the breast fragments of a bluish-white egg. No ruff about eye as in the harrier. (*Vide* the large

Falco fuscus of August 29, 1858.) It was shot on its nest (a female, then) in a white pine north of Ponkawtasset, on the 16th, and had four eggs which may have been sat on one week.[1]

It agrees very well with Nuttall's account (*q. v.* in my scrap in Giraud), except that the second primary is not equal to the sixth and the tail is *full* nine inches long; also sufficiently with Giraud's account, except that the tarsus is about three inches long. It is a large bird, but rather slender, with a very long tail. This makes the tenth species of the hawk kind that I have seen in Concord. The egg which Farmer saved is one and ten twelfths inches by one and five and a half twelfths, of a regular oval form, bluish-white with a few large, rough dirty spots.

P. M. — To J. Farmer's.

Is not that little fern which I have seen unrolling four or five days, scattered along the low meadow-edge next the river, the *Aspidium Thelypteris?* Now five or six inches high.

A nighthawk with its distinct white spots.

Early aspen down has just begun (before mouse-ear).

Carex crinita just out, or say a day, on the grassy island. The *C. stricta* is common yet there, and interesting, in large thick tufts with its brown spikes. That island is thickly covered with white violets. Common cress out, how long? Many flowers fallen, showing minute pods.

The river is seven and one eighth inches below summer level.

[1] *Vide* May 29th.

See the sium pushing up near the waterside. It smells, when broken off, like a parsnip.

Standing in the meadow near the early aspen at the island, I hear the first fluttering of leaves, — a peculiar sound, at first unaccountable to me. The breeze causes the now fully expanded aspen leaves there to rustle with a pattering sound, striking on one another. It is much like a gentle surge breaking on a shore, or the rippling of waves. This is the first softer music which the wind draws from the forest, the woods generally being comparatively bare and just bursting into leaf. It was delicious to behold that dark mass and hear that soft rippling sound.

Tupelo buds just expanding, but inconspicuous as yet. Round-leafed cornel leafets, one inch wide. *Salix sericea*, half an inch wide. Lambkill leaf, a day or two. Sarsaparilla flower, apparently yesterday. *Polygala paucifolia* common, how long? Rhodora generally out. *Eleocharis tenuis*, probably two or three days (some of it) in river meadows, as near mouth of Dakin's Brook. May be earlier in midst of Hubbard's Close.

By Sam Barrett's meadow-side I see a female Maryland yellow-throat busily seeking its food amid the dangling fruit of the early aspen, in the top of the tree. Also a chestnut-sided warbler, — the handsome bird, — with a bright-yellow crown and yellow and black striped back and bright-chestnut sides, not shy, busily picking about the expanding leaves of a white birch. I find some minute black flies on them.

Rye two and a half to three feet high. It is so dry that much of the sidesaddle leaf has no water in it.

Vol. XIII

Old brown rocks in the river and mill-ponds show by their water-lines how high the water has formerly stood.

Hear of a hummingbird on the 12th.

Willow (*alba*) catkins are in the midst of their fall.

Hear the first bullfrog's *trump*.

May 18. P. M. — To Walden.

The creak of the cricket has been common on all warm, dry hills, banks, etc., for a week, — inaugurating the summer.

Gold-thread out, — how long? — by Trillium Woodside. Trientalis.

The green of the birches is fast losing its prominence amid the thickening cloud of reddish-brown and yellowish oak leafets. The last and others [?] are now like a mist enveloping the dark pines. Apple trees, now, for two or three days, generally bursting into bloom (not in full bloom), look like whitish rocks on the hillsides, — somewhat even as the shad-bush did.

The sand cherry flower is about in prime. It grows on all sides of short stems, which are either upright or spreading, forming often regular solid cylinders twelve to eighteen inches long and only one and a half inches in diameter, the flowers facing out every way, of uniform diameter, determined by the length of the peduncles. Pretty wands of white flowers, with leafets intermingled.

The remarkably dry weather has been both very favorable and agreeable weather to walkers. We have had almost constant east winds, yet generally accompanied with warmth, — none of the rawness of the

east wind commonly. We have, as it were, the bracing air of the seashore with the warmth and dryness of June in the country.

The night-warbler is a powerful singer for so small a bird. It launches into the air above the forest, or over some hollow or open space in the woods, and challenges the attention of the woods by its rapid and impetuous warble, and then drops down swiftly into the tree-tops like a performer withdrawing behind the scenes, and he is very lucky who detects where it alights.

That large fern (is it *Aspidium spinulosum?*) of Brister Spring Swamp is a foot or more high. It is partly evergreen.

A hairy woodpecker betrays its hole in an apple tree by its anxiety. The ground is strewn with the chips it has made, over a large space. The hole, so far as I can see, is exactly like that of the downy woodpecker, — the entrance (though not so round) and the conical form within above, — only larger.

The bird scolds at me from a dozen rods off.

Now for very young and tender oak leaves and their colors.

May 19. A. M. — River seven inches below summer level.

Wind south, and a gentle intermittent warm rain at last begins. This has been the longest drought that I remember. The last rain was April 16th, except that some detected a few drops falling on the 9th; was literally the last drop we had. If this had occurred a month later, after the crops were fairly growing, it would have been a great calamity. As it is, there has been very little growth. My potatoes, planted May 1st, are but just beginning to peep here and there. My corn, planted the 2d, has not a quarter part showed itself, and grass seed sown ten days ago has not germinated. But weeds have not grown as much as usual. It must have been a severe trial for young fruit and other trees. Plowing and planting have been uncommonly dirty work, it has been so dusty.

2 p. m. — To Second Division. Thermometer 72°.

It cleared up at noon, to our disappointment, and very little rain had fallen.

There is a strong southwest wind after the rain, rather novel and agreeable, blowing off some apple blossoms. The grass, especially the meadow-grasses, are seen to wave distinctly, and the shadows of the bright fair-weather cumuli are sweeping over them like the shades of a watered or changeable stuff, — June-like. The grass and the tender leaves, refreshed and expanded by the rain, are peculiarly bright and yellowish-green when seen in a favorable light.

This occurrence of pretty strong southwest winds near the end of May, three weeks after the colder and stronger winds of March and April have died away, after the first heats and perhaps warm rain, when the apple trees and upland buttercups are in bloom, is an annual phenomenon. Not being too cold, they are an agreeable novelty and excitement now, and give life to the landscape.

Sorrel just begins to redden some fields.

I have seen for a week a smaller and redder butterfly

than the early red or reddish one. Its hind wings are chiefly dark or blackish. It is quite small. The forward wings, a pretty bright scarlet red with black spots.

See a green snake, a very vivid yellow green, of the same color with the tender foliage at present, and as if his colors had been heightened by the rain.

White thorn in bloom at Tarbell's Spring, considerable of it; possibly a little yesterday.

What they say of the 19th of April, '75, — that "the apple trees were in bloom and grass was waving in the fields," — could only have been said within a week past this early year. This is the season when the meadow-grass is seen waving in the wind at the same time that the shadows of clouds are passing over it.

At the Ministerial Swamp I see a *white* lady's-slipper almost out, fully grown, with red ones.

By the path-side near there, what I should call a veery's nest with four light-blue eggs, but I have not heard the veery note this year, only the *yorrick*. It is under the projecting edge or bank of the path, — a large mass of fine grass-stubble, pine-needles, etc., but not leaves, and lined with pine-needles.

In Second Division Meadow, *Eriophorum polystachyon*, apparently two or three days, though only six or eight inches high at most. The Second Division rush is not quite in bloom yet. The panicle is quite fresh, one eighth to one quarter inch long, but the sepals are not green but light-brown. Is it a new species?

Going along the Second Division road, this side the brooks, where the woods have been extensively cut off, I smell now, the sun having come out after the rain of

the morning, the scent of the withered pine boughs which cover and redden the ground. They part with their tea now.

You see now, on all sides, the gray-brown, lumbering woodchucks running to their subterranean homes. They are but poor runners, and depend on their watchfulness and not being caught far from their burrows.

The reddish-brown loosestrife is seen springing up in dry woods, six or eight inches high.

Now, sitting on the bank at White Pond, I do not see a single shad-bush in bloom across the pond, where they had just fairly begun on the 6th. The small *Populus grandidentata*, with their silvery leafets not yet generally flattened out, represent it there now, — are the most like it. I see some tall shad-bush without the reddish leaves — what I think I have thought a variety of the *Botryapium* — still well in bloom apparently with the *oblongifolium*. Is it the last?

The largest shrub oak that I have noticed grows by the north side of the White Pond road, not far from the end of the lane. It measures sixteen inches in circumference at two feet from the ground, and looks like a Cape Cod red oak in size and form, — a scraggly small tree (*maybe* a dozen feet high).

Pyrus arbutifolia out. Beach plum by Hubbard's wall, perhaps a day. Lilac, the 17th. The fresh shoots of the white pine are now perpendicular whitish marks about two inches long, about six inches apart on a glaucous-green ground.

I measure a bear's foot which F. Monroe brought

from Vermont, where it was killed in a trap within a few years. It was formed very much like a boy's foot, with its five toes, and the solid part measured seven and one half inches in length by three and three quarters. The claws extended one inch further, and *with the fur* (not allowing anything for shrinkage all this while) it must have made a track nine by four and a half inches at least. The fur came down thick all around to the ground. There was a seam or joint across the middle of the sole.

River raised one and a half inches at night by rain of forenoon, — *i. e.* five and a half inches below summer level.

May 20. A strong, cold west wind. 60° at 2 p. m. To Walden.

The *Carex vulgaris* is more glaucous than the *stricta*. Mouse-ear down at last.

Scirpus planifolius — how long? — apparently in prime in woods about the bottom of the long south bay of Walden, say two rods southwest.

Judging from Hind's Report of his survey of the region between the Assiniboine and Saskatchewan Rivers, the prevailing trees — and they are small — are aspens and willows, which, if let alone, *i. e.*, if the prairies were not burned by the Indians, might at last make a soil for nobler forests. No wonder that these small trees are so widely dispersed; their abundant fine and light seed, being buoyed up and wafted far through the atmosphere, speedily clothe the burnt tracts of British America. Heavy-seeded trees are slow to spread themselves, but both air and water combine to transport the seeds of these trees.

May 21. Cold, — at 11 A. M. 50°; and sit by a fire. At 12 it begins to rain.

P. M. — To Cambridge.

All vegetation is refreshed by the rain. The grass appears to stand perfectly erect and on tiptoe, several inches higher, all [at] once in every field, the fresh green prevailing over the brown ground in every field. The color of the new leaves is surprising. The birches by the railroad, as I am whirled by them in the cars, flash upon me yellow as gamboge, their leaves more like flowers than foliage.

Wintergreen had started the 18th at least. Noticed the shadows of apple trees yesterday.

May 22. Another cold and wet day, requiring fire. Ceases to rain at midday, but continues foul. The principal rain was during last night, and was quite considerable.

C. hears a cuckoo, and appears, by his account, to have seen the *Sylvia maculosa*.

I see the effects of frost (probably the morning of the 21st) on squashes that sowed themselves.

May 23. 6 A. M. — To Junction.

River four and one sixth inches below summer level, having risen about three inches since the morning of the 19th.

See hopping along the limbs of a black willow and inspecting its leafets for insects, in all positions, often

head downward, the *Sylvia striata*, black-poll warbler. Black crown or all top of head; a broad white space along side-head and reaching less distinctly over the neck, in a ring; beneath this, from base of mandibles, a streak of black, becoming a stream or streams of black spots along the sides; beneath white; legs yellow; back above slaty-brown, streaked with black; primaries yellowish-dusky, with two white bars or marks; inner tail-feathers more or less white; tail forked; bill black. Not particularly lively. The female is said to be considerably different. This at first glance was a chickadee-like bird. It was rather tame.

I distinguish well the red-eye and the yellow-throat vireo at the Island. It would not be easy to distinguish them always by the note, and I may have been mistaken sometimes, and before this year, in speaking of the yellow-throat vireo. The red-eye sings as slightly and feebly here now as the other. You can see these here to advantage now on the sunny side of the woods, the sun just bursting forth in the morning after the rain, for they [are] busily preening themselves, and, though incessantly moving their heads and bodies, remain in the same spot.

Myrtle-bird here still.

Notice the first lint from new leafets, evidently washed off by the rain, and covering the water like dust.

P. M. — 69. By boat to Ball's Hill.

Say the sweet-scented vernal grass is in its prime. Interrupted fern fruit probably a day or two, and cinnamon, say the same or just after.

I see on the white maples, and afterward running along the shore close to the water, at different times, three or four water-thrushes (water wagtails, *Turdus Noveboracensis*). By its lurking along the waterside it might be mistaken by some at first for the song sparrow. It is considerably like the golden-crowned thrush, but it has a distinct buffish-white line over the eye and the breast and sides distinctly striped with dark. All above uniform olive-brown. It may be distinguished at a distance from a sparrow by its wagging motion, teetering on its perch. It persistently runs along the shore, peetweet- and song-sparrow-like, running like a rail around the tussocks and other obstacles and appearing again at the water's edge. It was not very shy. We very easily kept along two rods off it, while it was amid the button-bushes.

Started up two (probably) *Totanus solitarius* (?), (possibly small yellow-legs ? ? ?). They utter a faint yellow-leg note, rather than peetweet note, *viz. phe, phe, pheet pheet pheet*. Are not shy; stand still [on] or beside a tussock to be looked at. Have peculiarly long, slender, curving wings. Fly like a peetweet, but are considerably larger and apparently uniformly dark-brown above. The belly and vent very bright white; breast (upper part) grayish-brown. When they flew from me saw considerable white, apparently on tail-coverts or sides of tail. Watched one still within three rods, with glass. There was a little speckling of whitish perhaps amid the brown above. I think they were too small for the lesser yellow-legs.

Eleocharis palustris, say three or four days.

Critchicrotches some two or three days; now tender to eat.

How agreeable and surprising the peculiar fragrance of the sweet flag when bruised! That this plant alone should have extracted this odor surely for so many ages each summer from the moist earth!

The pipes in the Great Meadows now show a darker green amid the yellowish of the sedges, like the shadow of a passing cloud. From a hilltop half a mile off you can easily distinguish the limits of the pipes by their dark green. They do not terminate abruptly, but are gradually lost in the sedge.

There is very little white maple seed this year, so that I cannot say surely how far advanced it is. What I notice appears to be fully grown, but is on the trees yet, always surprisingly large, like the wings of some lusty moth. Possibly it ripens with mouse-ear.

I get sight for a moment of a large warbler on a young oak, — only the under side, which is a clear bright lemon-yellow, *all* beneath, with a sort of crescent of black spots on the breast. Is it not the *Sylvia pardalina*? Methinks it was a rather dark brown above.[1]

The quarter-grown red oak leaves between you and the sun, how yellow-green!

Now, if you look over our Great Meadow from Ball's Hill, in a warm, fair day like this, you will receive the same impression as from the English grass fields in the middle of June, the sedges are so much more dense and forward. I mark the large white maples, now conspicuous and pretty densely leaved,

[1] *Vide* 28th.

stand up over the green sea on this edge of the river, so still, with each a speck of shade at its base, as in the noon of a summer day, and a dark *line* merely of shadow runs along at the base of the hill on the south of the meadow, — the June shadows beginning here. A green canopy held still above the already waving grass. It reminds you of warm, still noons, high grass, and the whetting of the scythe.

Most of the corn is planted.

Distinguish plainly a swamp sparrow (two to-day) by the riverside, a peculiarly glossy deep-chestnut crown, ash side-head and throat, and a dark or black line through the eye.

I find, in skunk hedge below Flint's, *Carex rosea*, not long, say three or four days. I should have thought it *C. stellulata*, but it is plainly staminate above, fertile below.[1] Also *C. gracillima*, same place, apparently four or five days.

River at 6 P. M. about one and two thirds inches below summer level; risen some two and a half inches since 6 A. M.

Notice the flags eaten off, probably by musquash.

May 24. 6 A. M. — Water fallen about one inch. P. M. — To Cliffs.

I see in a ditch a painted turtle nibbling the edge of a frost-bitten yellow lily pad (in the water), which has turned white. Other pads have evidently been nibbled by him, having many scallops or notches in their edges, just the form of his jaws.

[1] Also seen at calamint wall, Annursnack, June 10th.

That earliest little slender-leaved panic grass will bloom, say in a day (if not now).

About a rod from the west spring on Fair Haven Hill, by the wall, stands an English cherry tree three feet high. I think that this was planted there by a bird which came to the spring for water after feeding on cherries in the town (?), for I frequently find the stones dropped in the springs.

Those red cedars now ten feet high or more on Fair Haven Hill have all the regular form of the leaf, except a small bunch or two in their midst, yet I remember that when four or five feet high they had only the acetate [*sic;* = acicular?] form. It seems, then, that you will see small trees which have only leaves of the acetate [*sic*] form, but when they get larger they have leaves of the usual form.

Looking into the northwest horizon, I see that Wachusett is partially concealed by a haze. It is suddenly quite a cool southeast wind. (When I started, at two, it was also southeast, and thermometer 69.) This is one of the values of mountains in the horizon, that they indicate the state of the atmosphere. I should not have noticed this haze if I had not looked toward the mountains.

How perfectly new and fresh the world is seen to be, when we behold a myriad sparkles of brilliant white sunlight on a rippled stream! So remote from dust and decay, more bright than the flash of an eye.

I noticed the first shadows of hickories, — not dense and dark shade, but open-latticed, a network of sun and shadow. Just begun to describe their semicircles on the north sides of the trees. The first demonstrations that

it will shade the ground, unobserved as yet by the cows in the pasture.

I saw yesterday a herd of cows standing in the water of the river, though it was rather cold water. They begin their bathing about the same time that we do. They splash about till they get into a convenient place, about up to their bellies, and chew the cud there.

As I sit just above the northwest end of the Cliff, I see a tanager perched on one of the topmost twigs of a hickory, holding by the tender leafets, now five inches long, and evidently come to spy after me, peeping behind a leafet. He is between me and the sun, and his plumage is incredibly brilliant, all aglow. It is our highest-colored bird, — a deep scarlet (with a yellower reflection when the sun strikes him), in the midst of which his pure-black wings look high-colored also. You can hardly believe that a living creature can wear such colors. A hickory, too, is the fittest perch for him.

Hear a wood pewee.

A pincushion gall on a black shrub oak (not yet crimson-spotted). Yesterday saw oak-apples (now yellow) on a black shrub oak, two-thirds grown.

May 25. Frost last night in low ground.

The yards are now full of little spires of June-grass, with a brownish tinge but not quite in flower, trembling in the breeze. You see a myriad of fine parallel perpendicular stems about a foot high against the lighter green ground. It has shot up erect suddenly, and gives a new aspect to our yards. The earth wears a new and greener vest.

The trees I notice which look late now are not only locusts and Holbrook Hollow aspens but tupelos, white ash, swamp white oaks, buttonwoods, and some elms, and even some red maples.

P. M. — To Gowing's Swamp and Copan.

Quite warm, and I see in the east the first summer shower cloud, a distinct cloud above, and all beneath to the horizon the general slate-color of falling rain, though distant, deepest in the middle.

The scheuchzeria out some days apparently, but only in the open pool in the midst of the swamp.

I see half a dozen heads of tortoises above the sphagnum there in the pool, and they have vermilion spots on the neck or hindhead, — a sort of orange vermilion. Are they the yellow-spot or wood tortoise?

The European cranberry budded to bloom and grown one inch. Comandra out, not long. Red and white oak leafets handsome now.

Pe-pe heard, and probably considerably earlier.

It is remarkable that the aspen on Holbrook's road, though in most places it is the earliest indigenous tree to leaf, is the very latest, and the buds are hardly yet swollen at all. Can it be a distinct variety?

See the effect of frost on the sweet-fern either this morning or the 21st.

It evidently rains around us, and a little falls here, and the air is accordingly cooled by it, and at 5 P. M. the toads ring loud and numerously, as if invigorated by this little moisture and coolness.

Euphorbia cyparissias. Cherry-birds.

7 P. M. — River one inch below summer level.

May 26. Overcast, rain-threatening; wind northeast and cool.

9 A. M. — To Easterbrooks Country.

Carex lanuginosa, Smith's shore, say three or four days. *C. pallescens* (?), long-stalked, staminate, Channing's shore, high. *C. pallescens* var. *undulata*, rather spreading, common, as in Clark's field from opposite my old house. *C. polytrichoides* well out, say a few days, Botrychium Swamp. Melons have peeped out two or three days. Our pink azalea.

5 P. M. — River five eighths of an inch below summer level.

May 27. Fire in house again.

The *Sylvia striata* are the commonest bird in the street, as I go to the post-office, for several days past. I see six (four males, two females) on one of our little fir trees; are apparently as many more on another close by. The white bars on the wings of both sexes are almost horizontal. I see them thus early and late on the trees about our houses and other houses the 27th and 28th and 29th also, — peach trees, etc., but especially on the firs. They are quite tame. I stand within seven or eight feet while they are busily pecking at the freshly bursting or extending glaucous fir twigs, deliberately examining them on all sides, and from time to time one utters a very fine and sharp, but faint *tse tse*, *tse tse*, *tse tse*, with more or less of these notes. I hear the same in the woods. Examining the freshly starting fir twigs, I find that there are a great many lice or aphides amid the still appressed leafets or leaves of the buds, and

no doubt they are after these. Occasionally a summer yellowbird is in company with them, about the same business. They, the black-polls, are very numerous all over the town this spring. The female has not a black, but rather, methinks, a slate-colored crown, and is a very different bird, — more of a yellowish brown.

Eleocharis acicularis, not long, on the low exposed bank of the river; if [?] it is that that greens the very low muddy banks.

J. Farmer found a marsh hawk's nest on the 16th, — near the Cooper's hawk nest, — with three fresh eggs.

May 28. P. M. — To Deep Cut.

Carex debilis, not long.

Along the edge of Warren's wood east of the Cut, see not only the chestnut-sided warbler but the splendid *Sylvia pardalina*. It is a bright yellow beneath, with a broad black stripe along each side of the throat, becoming longish black marks crescentwise on the fore part of the breast, leaving a distinct clear bright-yellow throat, and all the rest beneath bright-yellow; a distinct bright-yellow ring around eye; a dark bluish brown apparently all above; yellowish legs. Not shy; on the birches. Probably saw it the 23d.

I see apparently a vireo, much like the red-eye (no yellow throat), with the white or whitish line above eye but a head differently formed, *i. e.*, a crest erectile at will and always prominent.

Solid white fog over meadow in evening.

I notice to-night that the potamogetons have just reached the surface of the river and begun to spread

Vol. XIII

out there. The surface of the water in shallow places begins to be interrupted or dimpled with small brown leaves. First, from the 9th to 13th the first pads began [to] spread, and the pontederia, etc., showed themselves. Now the appearance of the potamogetons marks a new era in the vegetation of the river, the commencement of its summer stage. Its spring ends now; its time of freshet (generally) is over.

The river is now some three inches below summer level.

May 29. P. M. — After hawks with Farmer to Easterbrooks Country.

He tells me of a sterile bayberry bush between his house and Abel Davis, opposite a ledge in the road, say half a dozen rods off in the field, on the left, by a brook.

Hearing a warbling vireo, he asked me what it was, and said that a man who lived with him thought it said, "Now I have caught it, O how it is sweet!" I am sure only of the last words, or perhaps, "Quick as I catch him I eat him. O it is very sweet."

Saw male and female wood tortoise in a meadow in front of his house, — only a little brook anywhere near. They are the most of a land turtle except the box turtle.

We proceeded [to] the Cooper's hawk nest[1] in an oak and pine wood (Clark's) north of Ponkawtasset. I found a fragment [of] one of the eggs which he had thrown out. Farmer's egg, by the way, was a dull or dirty white, *i. e.* a rough white with large dirty spots, perhaps in the grain, but not surely, of a regular oval

[1] *Vide* 17th.

form and a little larger than his marsh hawk's egg. I climbed to the nest, some thirty to thirty-five feet high in a white pine, against the main stem. It was a mass of bark-fibre and sticks about two and a half feet long by eighteen inches wide and sixteen high. The lower and main portion was a solid mass of fine bark-fibre such as a red squirrel uses. This was surrounded and surmounted by a quantity of dead twigs of pine and oak, etc., generally the size of a pipe-stem or less. The concavity was very slight, not more than an inch and a half, and there was nothing soft for a lining, the bark-fibres being several inches beneath the twigs, but the bottom was floored for a diameter of six inches or more with flakes of white oak and pitch pine bark one to two inches long each, a good handful of them, and on this the eggs had lain. We saw nothing of the hawk. This was a dozen rods south of the oak meadow wall.

Saw, in a shaded swamp beyond, the *Stellaria borealis*, still out, — large, broadish leaves.

Some eighteen feet high in a white pine in a swamp in the oak meadow lot, I climbed to a red squirrel's nest. The young were two-thirds grown, yet feeble and not so red as they will be. One ran out and along a limb, and finally made off into another tree. This was a mass of rubbish covered with sticks, such as I commonly see (against the main stem), but not so large as a gray squirrel's.

We next proceeded to the marsh hawk's nest from which the eggs were taken a fortnight ago and the female shot.[1] It was in a long and narrow cassandra

[1] *Vide* June 4th.

swamp northwest of the lime-kiln and some thirty rods from the road, on the side of a small and more open area some two rods across, where were few if any bushes and more [?] sedge with the cassandra. The nest was on a low tussock, and about eighteen inches across, made of dead birch twigs around and a pitch pine plume or two, and sedge grass at bottom, with a small cavity in the middle.

The female was shot and eggs taken on the 16th; yet here was the male, hovering anxiously over the spot and neighborhood and scolding at us. Betraying himself from time to time by that peculiar *clacking* note reminding you of a pigeon woodpecker. We thought it likely that he had already got another mate and a new nest near by. He would not quite withdraw though fired at, but still would return and circle near us. They are said to find a new mate very soon.

In a tall pine wood on a hill, say southwest of this, or northwest of Boaz's Lower Meadow, I climbed to a nest high in a white pine, apparently a crow's just completed, as it were on a squirrel's nest for a foundation, but finished above in a deep concave form, of twigs which had been gnawed off by the squirrel.

In another white pine near by, some thirty feet up it, I found a gray squirrel's nest, with young about as big as the red squirrels were, but yet blind. This was a large mass of twigs, leaves, bark-fibre, etc., with a mass of loose twigs on the top of it, which was conical. Perhaps the twigs are piled on the warmer part of the nest to prevent a hawk from pulling it to pieces.

I have thus found three squirrels' nests this year, two

gray and one red, in these masses of twigs and leaves and bark exposed in the tree-tops and not in a hollow tree, and methinks this is the rule and not the exception.

Farmer says that he finds the nests or holes or forms of the gray rabbit in holes about a foot or a foot and a half deep, made sideways into or under a tussock, especially amid the sweet-fern, in rather low but rather open ground. Has found seven young in one. Has found twenty-four eggs in a quail's nest.

In many places in the woods where we walk to-day we notice the now tender branches of the brakes eaten off, almost in every case, though they may be eighteen or more inches from the ground. This was evidently done by a rabbit or a woodchuck.

The wild asparagus beyond Hunt's Bridge will apparently open in two days.[1]

C. has seen to-day an orange-breasted bird which may be the female (?) Blackburnian warbler.

The leaves now conceal the warblers, etc., considerably. You can see them best in white oaks, etc., not maples and birches.

I hear that there was some frost last night on Hildreth's plain; not here.

On the 28th, the *latest* trees and shrubs start thus in order of leafing:[2] —

---

[1] Front of Whiting's shop, the 30th.

[2] June 3d. The deciduous trees which look late are, *in order of lateness*, bayberry latest, button-bush, poison-dogwood, black ash, buttonwood (mountain rhus, *Vaccinium dumosum*, and Holbrook aspen not being seen). The locust is pretty green. The first three look dead at a little distance, but the bayberry showed growth (including flower-buds) before button-bush. *Vide* June 4th.

Vol. XIII

1.	Locust	
2.	Dangle-berry	21st
3.	Mountain rhus	22d
4.	Poison-dogwood	23d
5.	Black spruce	23d
6.	Black ash	24th
7.	Button-bush	26th
8.	Hemlock	27th
9.	Bayberry	28th
10.	*Vaccinium dumosum*[1]	
11.	Holbrook aspens	

I hear from vireos (probably red-eyes) in woods a fine harsh note, perhaps when angry with each other.

May 30. P. M. — To Second Division.

A washing southwest wind. George Melvin said yesterday that he was still grafting, and that there had been a great blow on the apple trees this year, and that the blossoms had held on unusually long. I suggested that it might be because we had not had so much wind as usual.

On the wall, at the brook behind Cyrus Hosmer's barn, I start a nighthawk within a rod or two. It alights again on his barn-yard board fence, sitting diagonally. I see the white spot on the edge of its wings as it sits. It flies thence and alights on the ground in his corn-field, sitting flat, but there was no nest under it. This was unusual. Had it not a nest near by?

I observed that some of the June-grass was white and withered, being eaten off by a worm several days ago, or considerably before it blossoms. June-grass fills the field south of Ed. Hosmer's ledge by the road, and gives

---

[1] June 13th, grown half an inch to an inch.

it now a very conspicuous and agreeable brown or ruddy(?)-brown color, about as ruddy as chocolate, perhaps. This decided color stretching afar with a slightly undulating surface, like a mantle, is a very agreeable phenomenon of the season. The brown panicles of the June-grass now paint some fields with the color of early summer.

Front-yard grass is mowed by some. The stems of meadow saxifrage are white now. The *Salix tristis* generally shows its down now along dry wood-paths.

The *Juncus filiformis* not out yet, though some panicles are grown nearly half an inch. Much of it seems to be merely chaffy or effete, but much also plumper, with green sepals and minute stamens to be detected within. It arises, as described, from matted running rootstocks. Perhaps will bloom in a week.

A succession of moderate thunder and lightning storms from the west, two or three, an hour apart.

Saw some devil's-needles (the first) about the 25th.

I took refuge from the thunder-shower this afternoon by running for a high pile of wood near Second Division, and while it was raining, I stuck three stout cat-sticks into the pile, higher than my head, each a little lower than the other, and piled large flattish wood on them and tossed on dead pine-tops, making a little shed, under which I stood dry.

May 31. Rained hard during the night. At 6 P. M. the river has risen to half an inch below summer level, having been three to four inches below summer level yesterday morning. I hear the sprayey note of toads now more than ever, after the rain.

VII

JUNE, 1860

(ÆT. 42)

June 1. 2 P. M. — River $1\frac{3}{8}$ *above* summer level.
6 P. M. $1\frac{6}{8}$ "   "   "

Farmer has heard the quail a fortnight. Channing yesterday. The barberry flower is now in prime, and it is very handsome with its wreaths of flowers. Many low blackberry flowers at Lee's Cliff. June-grass there well out. Krigia, how long?

Breams' nests begun at Hubbard's Grove shore. They have carefully cleaned the bottom, removing the conferva, small weeds, etc., leaving the naked stems of some coarse ones, as the bayonet rush, bare and red.

Young Stewart tells me that when he visited again that gray squirrel's nest which I described about one month ago up the Assabet, the squirrels were gone, and he thought that the old ones had moved them, for he saw the old about another nest. He found another, similar nest with three dead blind gray squirrels in it, the old one probably having been killed. This makes three gray squirrels' nests that I have seen and heard of (*seen* two of them) this year, made thus of leaves and sticks open in the trees, and I hear of some more similar ones found in former years, so that I think this mode of nesting their young may be the rule with them

Vol. XIII

here. Add to this one red squirrel's nest of the same kind.

June 2. *Saturday.* The past has been Anniversary Week in Boston, and there have been several rainy or cloudy days, as the 30th, afternoon and especially night, and 31st, and night of June 1st. Cleared up at noon to-day. This Anniversary Week is said to be commonly rainy.

P. M. — To river behind Hubbard's Grove.

Red clover first seen. A boy brought me yesterday a nest with two Maryland yellow-throats' eggs and two cowbirds' eggs in it, and said that they were all found together. Saw a pigeon yesterday; a turtle dove to-day.

You see now, in suitable shallow and warm places where there is a sandy bottom, the nests of the bream begun, — circular hollows recently excavated, weeds, confervæ, and other rubbish neatly removed, and many whitish root-fibres of weeds left bare and exposed.

There is a lively and washing northwest wind after the rain, it having cleared up at noon. The waves are breaking on this shore with such a swash that sometimes I cannot distinguish the bream poised over her nest within ten feet of me. The air is cleansed and clear, and therefore the waves, as I look toward the sun, sparkle with so bright and white a light, — so peculiarly fresh and bright. The impurities have all come down out of the air.

The yellow Bethlehem-star is pretty common now. The poison-dogwood is so late, and has such a proportion of thick gray stems, that at a little distance

they look like dead trees amid the green birches and alders.

8 P. M. — Up Assabet.

The river is four inches above summer level.

A cool evening. A cold, white twilight sky after the air has been cleared by rain, and now the trees are seen very distinctly against it, — not yet heavy masses of verdure, but a light openwork, the leaves being few and small yet, as regularly open as a sieve.

Cool as it is, the air is full of the ringing of toads, peeping of hylodes, and purring of (probably) *Rana palustris.* The last is especially like the snoring of the river. In the morning, when the light is similar, you will not hear a peeper, I think, and scarcely a toad. Bats go over, and a kingbird, very late. Mosquitoes are pretty common. Ever and anon we hear the stake-driver from a distance. There is more distinct sound from animals than by day, and an occasional bullfrog's trump is heard. Turning the island, I hear a very faint and slight screwing or working sound once, and suspect a screech owl, which I after see on an oak. I soon hear its mournful scream, probably to its mate, not loud now, but, though within twenty or thirty rods, sounding a mile off. I hear it louder from my bed in the night.

Water-bugs dimple the surface now quite across the river, in the moonlight, for it is a full moon. The evergreens are very dark and heavy.

Hear the sound of Barrett's sawmill, at first like a drum, then like a train of cars. The water has been raised a little by the rain after the long drought, and so he [is] obliged to saw by night, in order to finish his jobs before the sun steals it from him again.

June 3. 6 A. M. — River three and three sixteenth inches above summer level; *i. e.*, the river has begun to fall within twenty-four hours and less after the rain ceased.

2 P. M. — To bayberry.

These are the clear breezy days of early June, when the leaves are young and few and the sorrel not yet in its prime. Perceive the meadow fragrance.

Am surprised to [see] some twenty or more crows in a flock still, cawing about us.

The roads now strewn with red maple seed. The pines' shoots have grown generally from three to six inches, and begin to make a distinct impression, even at some distance, of white and brown above their dark green. The foliage of deciduous trees is still rather yellow-green than green.

There are in the Boulder Field several of the creeping juniper which grow quite flat on the ground, somewhat like the empetrum, most elevated in the middle.

Not only brakes, many of them tall, and branching two feet at least from the ground, have their branches nibbled off, but the carrion-flower has very commonly lost its leaves, either by rabbits or woodchucks.

Tree-toads heard. See a common toad three quarters of an inch long.

There are various sweet scents in the air now. Especially, as I go along an arbor-vitæ hedge, I perceive a very distinct fragrance like strawberries from it.

Vol. XIII

June 4. Leave off flannel. Yesterday and to-day uncomfortably warm when walking.

The foliage of the elms over the street impresses me as dense and heavy already, — comparatively.

The black-poll warblers (*Sylvia striata*) appear to have left, and some other warblers, if not generally, with this first clear and bright and warm, peculiarly June weather, immediately after the May rain. About a month ago, after the strong and cold winds of March and April and the (in common years) rain and high water, the ducks, etc., left us for the north. Now there is a similar departure of the warblers, on the expansion of the leaves and advent of yet warmer weather. Their season with us, *i. e.* those that go further, is when the buds are bursting, till the leaves are about expanded; and probably they follow these phenomena northward till they get to their breeding-places, flying from tree to tree, *i. e.* to the next tree which contains their insect prey.

2 P. M. — To Fair Haven Hill.

They began to carry round ice about the 1st.

What I called *Carex conoidea* in '59, was seen June 2d this year in fruit, and may have flowered with *C. pallescens*. C. Hubbard's first meadow, south side of Swamp Brook willows. *Glyceria fluitans*, say two or three days, Depot Brook.

I see the great blue devil's-needles coasting along the river now, and coupled.

Carex retrorsa (much of it going to seed), Hubbard's Bath shore, say ten days. Has the general aspect of *pallescens*.

At Staples Meadow I observe that a great deal of the pitcher-plant is quite dry, dead, and slate-colored, with some green flower-buds pushing up, perhaps. I think it was thus half killed by the drought of April and May.

The clear brightness of June was well represented yesterday by the buttercups (*Ranunculus bulbosus*) along the roadside. Their yellow so glossy and varnished within; but not without. Surely there is no reason why the new butter should not be yellow now.

The time has come now when the laborers, having washed and put on their best suits, walk into the fields on the Sabbath, and lie on the ground at rest.

Aphides on alders, which dirty your clothes with their wool as you walk.

A catbird has her nest in our grove. We cast out strips of white cotton cloth, all of which she picked up and used. I saw a bird flying across the street with so long a strip of cloth, or the like, the other day, and so slowly, that at first I thought it was a little boy's kite with a long tail. The catbird sings less now, while its mate is sitting, or maybe taking care of her young, and probably this is the case with robins and birds generally.

At the west spring of Fair Haven Hill I cast a bit of wood against a pitch pine in bloom (perhaps not yet in prime generally), and I see the yellow pollen-dust blown away from it in a faint cloud, distinctly for three rods at least, and gradually rising all the while (rising five or six feet perhaps).

I hear that the nest of that marsh hawk which we saw on the 29th (*q. v.*) has since been found with five

eggs in it. So that bird (male), whose mate was killed on the 16th of May, has since got a new mate and five eggs laid.

One asks me to-day when it is that the leaves are fully expanded, so that the trees and woods look dark and heavy with leaves. I answered that there were leaves on many if not on most trees already fully expanded, but that there were not many on a tree, the shoots having grown only some three inches, but by and by they will have grown a foot or two and there will be ten times as many leaves. Each tree (or most trees) now holds out many little twigs, some three inches long, with two or three fully expanded leaves on it, between us and the sun, making already a grateful but thin shade, like a coarse sieve, so open that we see the fluttering of each leaf in its shadow; but in a week or more the twigs will have so extended themselves, and the number of fully expanded leaves be so increased, that the trees will look heavy and dark with foliage and the shadow be dark and opaque, — a gelid shade.

Hazy, and mountains concealed.

I notice to-day, for example, that most maple, birch, willow, alder, and elm leaves are fully expanded, but most oaks and hickories, ash trees, etc., are not quite.

You may say that now, when most trees have fully expanded leaves and the black ash fairly shows green, the leafy season has fairly commenced. (I see that I so called it May 31 and 27, 1853.)

June 5. A. M. — Northeast wind and rain, steady rain.

Hemlock bead-work handsome, but hardly yet large ones.

When I open my window at night I hear the peeping of hylodes distinctly through the rather cool rain (as also some the next morning), but not of toads; more hylodes than in the late very warm evenings when the toads were heard most numerously. The hylodes evidently love the cooler nights of spring; the toads, the warm days and nights of May. Now it requires a cool (and better if wet) night, which will silence the toads, to make the hylodes distinct.

June 6. Rain still (the second day), — clears up before night, — and so cool that many have fires.

The grass began to look fairly green or summer-like generally about the 1st.

6.30 P. M. — On river, up Assabet, after the rain.

The water has risen to eight and three quarters inches above summer level, and is rising fast. But little rain has fallen this afternoon.

The hemlocks generally have not grown quite enough to be handsomest, but the younger and lower growths are seen now in the dark and cavernous recesses, very fair with so many bright eyes on their green.

Saw those swarms of black moths fluttering low over the water on the 2d and to-night.

The *Salix nigra* is now getting stale. It is a very densely flowered willow, perhaps the most so of any. The sterile ones seen afar (even by moonlight on the 2d) are dense masses of yellow (now more pale) against the

green of trees in the rear. They have but little leafiness themselves as yet.

Not only the foliage begins to look dark and dense, but many ferns are fully grown, as the cinnamon and interrupted, perfectly recurved over the bank and shore, adding to the leafy impression of the season. The *Osmunda regalis* looks later and more tender, reddish-brown still. It preserves its habit of growing in circles, though it may be on a steep bank and one half the circle in the water.

The new leaves are now very fair, pure, unspotted green, commonly more or less yellowish. The swamp white oak leaf looks particularly tender and delicate. The red maple is much harder and more matured. Yet the trees commonly are not so densely leaved but that I can see through them; *e. g.*, I see through the red oak and the bass (below Dove Rock), looking toward the sky. They are a mere network of light and shade after all. The oak may be a little the thickest. The white ash is considerably thinner than either.

The grass and foliage are particularly fresh and green after the two days of rain, and we mark how the darkening elms stand along the highways. Like wands or wreaths seen against the horizon, they streak the sky with green.

How full the air of sound at sunset and just after, especially at the end of a rain-storm! Every bird seems to be singing in the wood across the stream, and there are the hylodes and the sounds of the village. Beside, sounds are more distinctly heard.

Ever and anon we hear a few *sucks* or strokes from

the bittern, the stake-driver, wherever we lie to, as if he had taken the job of extending all the fences into the river to keep cows from straying round. We hear but three or four toads in all, to-night, but as many hylodes as ever. It is too cool, both water and air (especially the first), after the rain, for the toads. At 9 A. M. it is 58. This temperature now, after a rain-storm has cooled the water, will silence the toads generally but make the hylodes more musical than ever.

As the light is obscured after sunset, the birds rapidly cease their songs, and the swallows cease to flit over the river. And soon the bats are seen taking the places of the swallows and flying back and forth like them, and commonly a late kingbird will be heard twittering still in the air. After the bats, or half an hour after sunset, the water-bugs begin to spread themselves over the stream, though fifteen minutes earlier not one was seen without the pads, — now, when it is difficult to see them or the dimples they make, except you look toward the reflected western sky. It is evident that they dare not come out thus by day for fear of fishes, and probably the nocturnal or vespertinal fishes, as eels and pouts, do not touch them. I think I see them all over Walden by day, and, if so, it may be because there is not much danger from fishes in that very deep water. I wonder if they spread thus over the whole breadth of Flint's Pond. It would be a measure of the size of a lake to know that it was so large that these insects did not cross it.

See to-night three dead (fresh) suckers on the Assabet. What has killed them?

June 7. 6 A. M. — River nine and fifteen sixteenths above summer level; has risen one and three sixteenths inches since last evening at 6.30. Thus, it having rained two days most of the time, though not much the last afternoon, the river had risen some six inches at the end of the last afternoon, by the time it cleared up, and only some one and a quarter inches in the next twelve hours of night.

P. M. — To Gowing's Swamp and Copan.

Red maple seed is still in the midst of its fall; is blown far from the trees.

This is a southwest-breezy day, after the rain of the last two days. There is on the whole a fresh and breezy coolness in June thus far, perhaps owing to the rains and the expanded foliage.

White clover already whitens some fields and resounds with bees.

Am surprised to find that in that frosty Holbrook Road Hollow (call it Frosty Poplar Hollow) none of the poplars (*P. tremuliformis*) less than ten feet high (or parts of others less than ten feet above the ground) in the bottom of the hollow have burst their buds yet, making this which in some localities is perhaps the earliest conspicuous tree, in others the latest to leaf. Also the shrub oaks are but just begun to leaf here, and many maples and white birches have but lately leafed, having yet very small and tender leaves. These poplars, and I think the oaks (for I detect no dead and withered leafets on them), etc., have here acquired a new habit, and are retarded in their development, just as if they grew in a colder latitude, like the plants by the snow in Tuckerman's Ravine. They have not put forth and then been frost-bitten, as in most hollows, but the spring has come later to them. The poplars generally look quite dead still amid the verdure that surrounds the hollow; only those that rise about ten feet are unfolded at the top. The amount of development is a matter of elevation here. Generally speaking, all poplar buds above a certain level have burst, and all below are inert. The line of separation is very distinct now, because the tops of the tallest are already leafed out and are green. This level line extends to the hillsides all around, and above it all trees are leafed out. This is true of the shrub oaks also, except that a great many of them which stand much higher have already leafed and been frost-bitten, which makes them look about as late as those which apparently have not leafed. This hollow seems to be peculiar, — a dry depression between Beck Stow's and the Great Meadows, — to be steadily cold and late, and not warm by day so that the buds burst and are then killed by frost, as usual. Perhaps it is not so much a frosty hollow as a cold one. It is most open north and south.

Standing at Holbrook's barrel spring, a female chestnut-sided warbler hops within four feet of me, inquisitively holding its head down one side to me and peeping at me.

Seeing house-leek on several rocks in the fields and by roadside in the neighborhood of Brooks Clark's, Farmer told me that it was the work of Joe Dudley, a simple fellow who lives at one of the Clarks; that, though half-witted, he knew more medicinal plants

Vol. XIII

than almost anybody in the neighborhood. Is it necessary that the simpler should be a simpleton?

I noticed rye (winter rye) just fairly begun to bloom, May 29th.

A painted turtle beginning her hole for eggs at 4 p. m.

Yellow bugs have come by thousands this clear and rather warm day after the rain; also squash-bugs have come. When, in a warm day after rain, the plants are tender and succulent, this is the time they work most.

River at 6 p. m., twelve and five eighths inches above summer level.

To-night the toads ring loudly and generally, as do hylodes also, the thermometer being at 62 at 9 p. m. Four degrees more of warmth, the earth being drier and the water warmer, makes this difference. It appears, then, that the evening just after a rain-storm (as the last), thermometer 58, the toads will be nearly silent, but the hylodes wide awake; but the next evening, with thermometer at 62, both will be wide awake.

Dor-bugs come humming by my head to-night.

The peculiarities of the new leaves, or young ones, are to be observed. *As I now remember*, there is the whitish shoot of the white pine; the reddish brown of the pitch pine, giving a new tinge to its tops; the bead-work of the hemlock; the now just conspicuous bursting lighter glaucous-green buds of the black spruce in cold swamps; the frizzly-looking glaucous-green shoots and leafets of the fir (and fragrant now or soon); the thin and delicate foliage of the larch; the inconspicuous and fragrant arbor-vitæ; the bead-work of the *Juniperus repens* (red cedar inconspicuous); probably the bead-

work of the yew;[1] the tented leaves of the white oak; the crimson black and white oaks and black shrub lately, and now, in hollows, the downy grayish (at first) of black and white, etc.; the now tender, delicate green of swamp white and chincapin; the large and yellowish, rapidly expanding (at first), of the nut trees; the gamboge-yellow of the birches (now as dark as most, for leaves are acquiring one shade at present); the thick darker green of alders; the downyish of buttonwood *still small;* the soon developed and darkened and fluttering early aspens and Gileads; the still silvery *Populus grandidentata ;* the small-leafeted and yellowish locust; the early yellow of *Salix alba ;* the fine-leaved *S. nigra ;* the wreath-and-column-leaved elm; the suddenly expanding but few-leaved ash trees, showing much stalk, or stem, and branch; the button-bush, with shoots before leaves; the reddish-leafed young checkerberry; the suddenly developed and conspicuous viburnums (sweet and naked); the unequal-leafing panicled andromeda; the purplish-brown stipules of the *Amelanchier Botryapium ;* the downy stipules of the *A. oblongifolia.* The red maples now become darker and firm, or hard. The large-leafed sumachs.

June 8. River at 6 a. m. twelve and seven eighths inches above summer level.

2 p. m. — To Well Meadow *via* Walden.

Within a day or two has begun that season of summer when you see afternoon showers, maybe with thunder, or the threat of them, dark in the horizon, and are

[1] June 8th, grown one inch or more, but not very distinct in color.

uncertain whether to venture far away or without an umbrella. I noticed the very first such cloud on the 25th of May, — the dark iris of June. When you go forth to walk at 2 p. m. you see perhaps, in the southwest or west or maybe east horizon, a dark and threatening mass of cloud showing itself just over the woods, its base horizontal and dark, with lighter edges where it is rolled up to the light, while all beneath is the kind of dark slate of falling rain. These are summer showers, come with the heats of summer.

June-grass just begun to bloom in the village.

A great yellow and dark butterfly (C. saw something like it a week ago).[1]

What delicate fans are the great red oak leaves now just developed, so thin and of so tender a green! They hang loosely, flaccidly, down at the mercy of the wind, like a new-born butterfly or dragon-fly. A strong and cold wind would blacken and tear them now. They remind me of the frailest stuffs hung around a dry-goods shop. They have not been hardened by exposure yet, these raw and tender lungs of the tree. The white oak leaves are especially downy, and lint your clothes.

This is truly June when you begin to see brakes (dark green) fully expanded in the wood-paths.

That sedge which grows in the Fox Path Hollow (by the Andromeda Ponds), the coarser one, rather around the sides or slopes than at the very bottom, is a slender *Carex siccata*, almost all out of bloom, — all except that which is at the bottom of the hollow. For I see here

[1] *Papilio Turnus.*

on a smaller scale the same phenomena as at Holbrook Poplar Hollow (*vide* yesterday). The panicled cornel looks generally dead, just beginning to leaf; young white and black oaks are in the red; and the second amelanchier is in the flower still here. Indeed, shrub oaks, and young oaks generally and conspicuously, are quite late — just in the red — now in hollows and other cold parts of the woods; and *generally* these shrubs, including hazel even, have not been frost-bitten, but have not put forth till now.

Carex bromoides may have been out a fortnight at Well Meadow; and *C. scabrata*, say ten days. *C. tenella* (near the earliest cowslip) all in seed and much seed fallen and no sterile flower; say three weeks. *C. intumescens*, say five or six days (*e. g.*, just south of earliest cowslip).

Hoed potatoes first time two or three days ago; my corn to-day.

All stagnant water is covered with the lint from the new leaves, — harmless to drink, — especially after rain. If you [take] a scarlet oak leaf and rub the under side on your coat-sleeve, it will not whiten it, but a white oak leaf will color it as with meal.

Carex polytrichoides grows at Well Meadow.

I see a small mist of cobweb, globular, on a dead twig eight inches above the ground in the wood-path. It is from an inch and a half to two inches in diameter, and when I disturb it I see it swarming with a mass of a thousand minute spiders. A spider-nest lately hatched.

In early June, methinks, as now, we have clearer days, less haze, more or less breeze, — especially after rain, —

and more sparkling water than before. (I look from Fair Haven Hill.) As there is more shade in the woods, so there is more shade in the sky, *i. e.* dark or heavy clouds contrasted with the bright sky, — not the gray clouds of spring.

The leaves generally are almost fully expanded, *i. e.* some of each tree.

You seek the early strawberries in any the most favorable exposure, — on the sides [of] little knolls or swells, or in the little sandy hollows where cows have pawed, settling the question of superiority and which shall lead the herd, when first turned out to pasture.

As I look at the mountains in the horizon, I am struck by the fact that they are all pyramidal — pyramids, more or less low — and have a peak. Why have the mountains usually a peak? This is not the common form of hills. They do not so impress us at least.

River at 7 P. M. fourteen and a half above summer level.

June 9. 7 A. M. — River fourteen and one eighth above summer level only, though after considerable rain in the night.

We have had half a dozen showers to-day, distinct summer showers from black clouds suddenly wafted up from the west and northeast; also some thunder and hail, — large white stones.

Standing on the Mill-Dam this afternoon, after one of these showers, I noticed the air full of some kind of

Vol. XIII

down, which at first I mistook for feathers or lint from some chamber, then for light-winged insects, for it rose and fell just like the flights of may-flies. At length I traced it to the white willow behind the blacksmith's shop, which apparently the rain has released. The wind was driving it up between and over the buildings, and it was flying all along the Mill-Dam in a stream, filling the air like a flight of bright-colored gauze-winged insects, as high as the roofs. It was the willow down with a minute blackish seed in the midst or beneath. In the moist air, seen against the still dark clouds, like large white dancing motes, from time to time falling to earth. The rain had apparently loosened them, and the slight breeze succeeding set them a-going.

As I stood talking with one on the sidewalk, I saw two yellow dor-bugs fall successively to the earth from the elm above. They were sluggish, as usual by day, and appeared to have just lost their hold, perhaps on account of the rain or the slight wind arising. I also see them floating in the river, into which they have fallen, or perhaps they have been carried off by its rising. They might be called blunderers.

6 P. M. — Paddle to Flint's hedge.

River fourteen and three quarters above summer level.

Viburnum Lentago nearly in prime.

An abundance of *Carex scoparia* now conspicuously browns the shores, especially below Flint's willows. The *C. lagopodioides* is apparently in prime (out say one week or less) at Flint's hedge. That is apparently the *C. rosea* there under the hickory; observed the 23d of

May. The *C. monile* is now quite conspicuous along the river, as well as the *C. bullata*.

A kingbird's nest and one egg.

C. says that a fox stood near, watching him, in Britton's Hollow to-day. No doubt she had young.

The water-bugs begin to venture out on to the stream from the shadow of a dark wood, as at the Island. So soon as the dusk begins to settle on the river, they begin to steal out, or to extend their circling from amid the bushes and weeds over the channel of the river. They do not simply then, if ever, venture forth, but then invariably, and at once, the whole length of the stream, they one and all sally out and begin to dimple its broad surface, as if it were a necessity so to do.

June 10. Another showery day, or rather shower-threatening.

2 P. M. — To Annursnack.

A very strong northwest wind, and cold. At 6 P. M. it was 58°. This, with wind, makes a very cold day at this season. Yet I do not need fire in the house.

This violent and cool wind must seriously injure the just developed tender leaves. I never observed so much harm of this kind done. Leaves of all kinds are blown off and torn by it, as oak, maple, birch, etc. As I sit under a white oak, I see the fragments torn off — a quarter or half the leaf — filling the air and showering down at each ruder blast, and the ground is spotted green with them. There are not many whole leaves of the white oak blown off, but these torn fragments rather. At the Assabet stone bridge, the water along the shore is lined with a broad green mass of them, which have been blown into it, three or four feet wide, washed against the shore. Such a wind makes tearing work with them, now that they are so tender.

There is much handsome interrupted fern in the Painted-Cup Meadow, and near the top of one of the clumps we noticed something like a large cocoon, the color of the rusty cinnamon fern wool. It was a red bat, the New York bat, so called. It hung suspended, head directly downward, with its little sharp claws or hooks caught through one of the divisions at the base of one of the pinnæ, above the fructification. It was a delicate rusty brown in color, very like the wool of the cinnamon fern, with the whiter bare spaces seen through it early in the season. I thought at first glance it was a broad brown cocoon, then that it was the plump body of a monstrous emperor moth. It was rusty or reddish brown, white or hoary within or beneath the tips, with a white apparently triangular spot beneath, about the insertion of the wings. Its wings were very compactly folded up, the principal bones (darker-reddish) lying flat along the under side of its body, and a hook on each meeting its opposite under the chin of the creature. It did not look like fur, but more like the plush of the ripe cat-tail head, though more loose, — all trembling in the wind and with the pulsations of the animal. I broke off the top of the fern and let the bat lie on its back in my hand. I held it and turned it about for ten or fifteen minutes, but it did not awake. Once or twice it opened its eyes a little, and even it raised its head, opened its mouth, but soon drowsily dropped its head and fell

Vol. XIII

asleep again. Its ears were rounded and nearly bare. It was more attentive to sounds than to motions. Finally, by shaking it, and especially by hissing or whistling, I thoroughly awakened it, and it fluttered off twenty or thirty rods to the woods. I cannot but think that its instinct taught it to cling to the interrupted fern, since it might readily be mistaken for a mass of its fruit. Raised its old-haggish head. Unless it showed its head wide awake, it looked like a tender infant.

June 11. 6 A. M. — River twelve inches above summer level at 10.30 A. M. Sail to Tall's Island.

Wind northwest, pretty strong, and not a warm day.

I notice the patches of bulrushes (*Scirpus lacustris*) now generally eighteen inches high and very dark green, but recently showing themselves.

The evergreens are now completely invested by the deciduous trees, and you get the full effect of their dark green contrasting with the yellowish green of the deciduous trees.

The wind does not blow through our river-valley just as the vanes indicate at home, but conformably to the form of the valley somewhat. It depends on whether you have a high and hilly shore to guide it, or a flat one which it may blow across. With a northwest wind, it is difficult to sail from the willow-row to Hubbard's Bath, yet I can sail more westerly from the island point in Fair Haven Bay to the bath-place above; and though I could not do the first to-day, I did sail all the way from Rice's Bar to half a mile above Sherman's Bridge by all the windings of the river.

If the bend is due east and the wind northwest I can sail round it. Again, as I was approaching Bittern Cliff, I had but little wind, but I said to myself, As soon as I reach the cliff I shall find myself in a current of wind blowing into the opening of the pond valley; and I did. Indeed, the wind flows through that part of the river-valley above the water-line somewhat as the water does below it.

I see from time to time a fish, scared by our sail, leap four to six feet through the air above the waves. See many small blue devil's-needles to-day, but no mates with them, and is it not they that the kingbird stoops to snap up, striking the water each time?

I find the Sudbury meadows unexpectedly wet. There is at least one foot of water on the meadows generally. I cut off the principal bends, pushing amid the thin sedge and pipes, and land on Tall's Island. I had carried india-rubber boots to look for wrens' nests, but the water was very much too deep, and I could not have used them except on the very edge in some places. Yet the river in Concord this morning was but just one foot above summer level and about eighteen inches above where it was just before the middle of May, when everybody remarked on its extreme lowness, and Ebby Conant observed to me, "It is lower than ever it was known to be, is n't it?" I told him that I had seen it as low, *in the summer*, about every other year. If you should lower it eighteen inches now here, there would still be much water on the Sudbury meadows. The amount of it is, the Sudbury meadows are so low, referred to the river, that when the river is nineteen and

one eighth inches above extreme low water (the lowest we have had this year) you can push over the greater part of the Sudbury meadows in a boat. Accordingly, on far the greater part of these meadows there is now very little grass, *i. e.* sedge, but thin pipes and sedge, — the *Carex stricta* and *monile* commonly (too wet for *scoparia* and *stellulata*). I do not see the great *Scirpus fluviatilis* there yet. The greater part of the meadows are evidently too wet for the *C. stricta* (occasionally some large tussocks surrounded by water) and *monile* even, and the pipes are but thin. There are many large spaces of pads, — two at Tall's Island, — showing that they are wet all summer. The sedges, even, are thick and rank only on the more elevated and drier edges of the meadow. This is more like a lagoon than a meadow, in fact. It is too wet even for sedges to flourish, for they are not dense, as on other meadows, except on the higher parts near the hills or shores. *C. stricta* grows thinly (with thin pipes) or occasionally in large tufts. On dry parts only, the *C. monile*, etc., etc.

Landing on Tall's Island, I perceive a sour scent from the wilted leaves and scraps of leaves which were blown off yesterday and strew the ground in all woods.

Just within the edge of the wood there, I see a small painted turtle on its back, with its head stretched out as if to turn over. Surprised by the sight, I stooped to investigate the cause. It drew in its head at once, but I noticed that its shell was partially empty. I could see through it from side to side as it lay, its entrails having been extracted through large openings just before the hind legs. The dead leaves were flattened for a foot over, where it had been operated on, and were a little bloody. Its paunch lay on the leaves, and contained much vegetable matter, — old cranberry leaves, etc. Judging by the striæ, it was not more than five or six years old, — or four or five. Its fore parts were quite alive, its hind legs apparently dead, its inwards gone; apparently its spine perfect. The flies had entered it in numbers. What creature could have done this which it would be difficult for a man to do? I thought of a skunk, weazel, mink, but I do not believe that they could have got their snouts into so small a space as that in front of the hind legs between the shells. The hind legs themselves had not been injured nor the shell scratched. I thought it most likely that it was done by some bird of the heron kind which has a long and powerful bill. And probably this accounts for the many dead turtles which I have found and thought died from disease. Such is Nature, who gave one creature a taste or yearning for another's entrails as its favorite tidbit!! I thought the more of a bird, for, just as we were shoving away from this isle, I heard a sound just like a small dog barking hoarsely, and, looking up, saw it was made by a bittern (*Ardea minor*), a pair of which were flapping over the meadows and probably had a nest in some tussock thereabouts. No wonder the turtle is wary, for, notwithstanding its horny shell, when it comes forth to lay its eggs it runs the risk of having its entrails plucked out. That is the reason that the box turtle, which lives on the land, is made to shut itself up entirely within the shell, and I suspect that the

mud tortoise only comes forth by night. What need the turtle has of some horny shield over those tender parts and avenues to its entrails! I saw several of these painted turtles dead on the bottom.[1]

Already I see those handsome fungi spots on the red maple leaves, yellow within, with a green centre, then the light-red ring deepening to crimson. The largest a quarter of an inch in diameter.

Heard many redstarts on the Island. Saw creepers and one wood pewee nest on a swamp white oak, not quite done.

On our way up, we ate our dinner at Rice's shore, and looked over the meadows, covered there with waving sedge, light-glaucous as it is bent by the wind, reflecting a grayish or light-glaucous light from its under side. That meadow opposite Rice's Bath is comparatively well covered with sedge, as the *great* Sudbury meadow is not.

I now first begin to notice the silvery under sides of the red maple and swamp white oak leaves, turned up by the wind. Looking at a hillside of young trees, what various shades of green! The oaks generally are a light and tender and yellowish green; the white birches, dark green now; the maples, dark and silvery.

Notice pads and pontederias are now pretty thick. The white lily pads reddish, and showing their crimson under sides from time to time when the wind blows hardest.

The potamogeton (the large common one) is remark-

[1] *Vide* June 10, 1858.

Vol. XIII

able as a *brown* leaf, — fit color for the brown water on which it floats, — but the potamogetons are few and scarcely obvious yet on the river.

A painted turtle laying, at 5 P. M.

Saw a sphinx moth night before last.

The *Carex tentaculata* at Clamshell in prime, say one week. It abounds at Forget-me-not Shore, — dense-flowered, spreading spikes.

At 9 P. M., 54°, and no toads nor peepers heard.

Some fields began to be white with whiteweed on the 9th.

June 12. P. M. Up Assabet.

I find several *Emys insculpta* nests and eggs, and see two painted turtles going inland to lay at 3 P. M. At this moment these turtles are on their way inland to lay their eggs all over the State, warily drawing in their heads and waiting when you come by. Here is a painted turtle just a rod inland, its back all covered with the fragments of green leaves blown off and washed up yesterday, which now line the shore. It has come out through this wrack. As the river has gone down, these green leaves mark the bank in lines just like sawdust.

I see a young yellow-spot turtle in the Assabet, still quite broad and roundish though I count about seven striæ. It is very handsome.

At 7.30 P. M. I hear many toads, it being a warm night, but scarcely any hylodes.[1]

River ten and one third above summer level.

[1] 17th, have heard no more hylodes

June 13. 2 P. M. To M. Miles's *via* Clamshell.

Hear of a snapping turtle which had begun to lay her eggs last night in Cyrus Hosmer's corn-field, this side of Clamshell. He found it by its scaring his horse as he was plowing between his corn. The horse started and stopped at it. I saw its track. I see how I can find them. Select a cultivated field, especially a sandy one near the river or a brook, and walk along its edge, parallel with the stream, at this season, and you will see by the track if a turtle has recently been out that way, — can follow it and find the eggs.

I first heard that *tchuck* sound — as of a fish striking a pad — on the 2d of June, when there were very few weeds in the river, and have since heard it repeatedly.

I noticed as I sat in my boat by the riverside last evening, half an hour after sunset, a very low and local, yet dense, fog close to the shore, under the edge of the sedge on one side, a foot high by three or four wide for several rods. It occupied such a space as a shadow does under a hedge. It occurred to me that perhaps the water was cooler there than elsewhere.

I find, on the face of Clamshell Hill, *Carex Muhlenbergii* about ripe, the perigynia nerved distinctly on both sides. I think that this is the same with that of May 26 and June 10, etc., — all that I may have thought *cephalophora* this year, — though I did not find them distinctly nerved on both sides. They were younger. The achenium of this is orbicular. It grows, then, here and probably at Lee's south slope, Annursnack Hill (very common), and is generally long done.

I see, at Martial Miles's, two young woodchucks,

taken sixteen days ago, when they were perhaps a fortnight old. There were four in all, and they were dug out by the aid of a dog. The mother successively *pushed out* her little ones to the dog to save herself, and one was at once killed by the dog. These two are now nearly one-third grown. They have found a hole within the house, into which they run, and whither they have carried shavings, etc., and made a nest. Thence they run outdoors, and feed close along about the house, lurking behind barrels, etc. They eat yarrow, clove[r], catnep, etc., and are fed with milk and bread. They do not drink the milk like a dog or like a cat, but simply suck it, taking the sharp edge of the shallow tin dish in their mouths. They are said to spit like a cat. They eat bread sitting upright on their haunches and holding it in their fore paws, just like a squirrel. That is their common and natural mode of eating. They are as gray — or grayer (or hoary) — as the old. Mrs. Miles says they sleep on their heads, *i. e.*, curling their heads right under them; also that they can back as straight into their hole as if they went head foremost. I saw a full-grown one this afternoon which stood so erect and still, its paws hanging down and inobvious as its ears, that it might be mistaken for a short and very stout stake.

At Ledum Swamp the woodwardia is recent; generally not yet expanded; one of the latest ferns. The *Eriophorum vaginatum* is generally gone to seed. The *Carex canescens* (the glaucous *scoparia*-like) is the prevailing *Carex* there, hanging over the ditches and the pool.

I find in J. Hosmer's spring a seedling skunk-cabbage

Vol. XIII

with the nut attached. It had fallen into the spring, perhaps, from a mouse's store, and a single green leaf two or three inches long had grown from it while a root had penetrated the mud. The strawberry about Hosmer's tub spring has its seeds in pits and is therefore *Fragaria Virginiana*.

The *Eriophorum polystachyon* is well cottoned out.

Now perceive the smell of red clover blossoms.

This afternoon the streets are strewn with the leaves of the buttonwood, which are still falling. Looking up, I see many more hanging wilted or withered, — half-formed leaves. I think that the leaves of these trees were especially injured by the cold wind of the 10th, as the other trees, and are just now falling in consequence. I can tell when I am under a buttonwood by the number of leaves on the ground. With the other trees it was mainly a mechanical injury, done rather by the wind than the cold, but the tender shoots of this tree were killed.

Yesterday I could still see through the bass and the red oak up the Assabet, and the last was a little the densest.

On the 11th I saw, swimming near me on the Sudbury meadows, apparently the *Bryttus obesus*, judging from its stripes and form. It was quite tame and apparently rather sluggish.

June 14. I see near at hand two of those large yellow (and black) butterflies which I have probably seen nearly a month. They rest on the mud near a brook. Two and three quarters to three inches in alar

extent; yellow with a broad black border, outside of which a row of small yellow spots; three or four black marks transversely to the fore wings, and two fine lines parallel with the body on the hinder (?) wings; a small and slender swallow tail with reddish brown and blue at the tail; body black above and yellow along the sides.[1]

P. M. — To Second Division.

At Dugan Desert many fresh turtle-tracks. They generally steer for some more elevated and perhaps bushy place. The tail makes a serpentine track, the tracks of the flippers and claws quite distinct, and you see where the turtle rested on its shell, flatting the sand, from time to time. You can easily trace one to where the sand has been disturbed, and dig up its eggs, as I did, — six eggs, about two and a half to three inches deep. *Emys insculpta.*

The juncus of Second Division is just beginning[2] at the west or northwesterly edge, next the higher ground. It may be that most of it does not bloom. The stigmas are prominent [on] a few plants, the anthers scarcely perceptible yet. The sepals are rather a green [?] purple, with a green centre, than green.

The slender grass mixed with the above, apparently *Trisetum palustre*, is now very commonly in bloom, apparently several days; also the smaller (fifteen-inch) festuca two or three days, in dry ground.

The white water ranunculus is abundant in the brook; out say a week, and well open in the sunshine. It is [a]

[1] C. says it is the *Papilio Turnus* of Say.
[2] Say, rather, in a day or two.

pretty white flower (with yellow centre) seen above the dark brown-green leaves in the rapid water, its peduncle recurved so as to present the flower erect half an inch to an inch above the surface, while the buds are submerged.

See a pigeon. A brood of little partridges in the wood-paths. The old bird utters a loud wiry, mewing sound of alarm, the young a very fine sharp sound like cherry-birds. For a week at least have seen cowbirds about cows.

The common cress gone to seed; only a little lingers.

I felt that the season of storms, *i. e.* of two days' rain, was past about June 1st.

Saw a rainbow in afternoon of 7th.

June 15. 2 P. M. — River four and one half above summer level.

For some time I have not heard toads by day,[1] and not for a long time in numbers; yet they still ring at night. Perhaps it is entirely a matter of temperature, — that in June and maybe the latter half of May (?) they require the coolness of the evening to arouse them. The hylodes appear to have done.

I paddle to Clamshell.

Notice the down of the white willow near the bridge, twenty rods off, whitening Sassafras Shore for two or three rods like a dense white foam. It is all full of little seeds not sprouted, is as dense as fur, and has first blown fifteen rods overland. This is a late willow to ripen, but the black willow shows no down yet, *as I notice.* It is very conspicuously white along the shore,

[1] But rarely.

a foot or two wide, — a dense downy coat or fleece on the water. Has blown northeast.

See froth about the base of some grass in a meadow. The large early wool-grass of the meadows will shed pollen in a day or two — can *see* stamens — on Hosmer's Flat shore. This it is grows in circles.

As I stood there I heard that peculiar hawk-like (for rhythm) but more resonant or clanging kind of scream which I may have heard before this year, plover-like, indefinitely far, — over the Clamshell plain. After proceeding half a dozen rods toward the hill, I heard the familiar willet note of the upland plover and, looking up, saw one standing erect — like a large telltale, or chicken with its head stretched up — on the rail fence. After a while it flew off southwest and low, then wheeled and went a little higher down the river. Of pigeon size, but quick quivering wings. Finally rose higher and flew more or less zigzag, as if uncertain where it would alight, and at last, when almost out of sight, it pitched down into a field near Cyrus Hubbard's. It was the same note I heard so well on Cape Cod in July, '55, and probably the same I heard in the Shawsheen valley, May 15, 1858. I suspect, then, that it breeds here.

The button-bush is now fairly green.

The *Carex stricta* tufts are now as large as ever, and, the culms falling over, they are like great long-haired

heads, now drooping around the great tussocks. I know of no other sedge that make so massive and conspicuous a tussock, yet with a slender leaf. This the one that reflects the peculiar glaucous sheen from its bent surfaces.

The turtles are apparently now in the midst of their laying. I go looking for them, to see where they have left the water for this purpose. See a snapping turtle whose shell is about ten inches long making her hole on the top of the sand-bank at the steam-mill site, within four rods of the road. She pauses warily at sound of my boat, but I should have mistaken her for a dark stone if she had [not] lifted her snout above her shell. I went to her as she lay and hissed by the hole at 4 P. M. It was about three and a half inches across, and not perpendicular but chiefly on one side; say five inches deep (as yet), and four plus inches wide beneath, but only about one inch of the bottom exposed when you looked straight down, — in short, like the common *Emys picta's* hole. She had copiously wet the ground before or while digging, as the *picta* does. Saw two or three similar holes made by her afterward. There was her broad track (some ten inches wide) up the sandy or gravelly bank, and I saw where she had before dug, or begun to dig, within a rod of this, but had retreated to the river. I withdrew to the bridge to observe her (not having touched her), but she took the occasion to hasten to the river.

A thunder-shower in the north goes down the Merrimack.

We have had warmer weather for several days, say

Vol. XIII

since 12th. A new season begun, — daily baths, thin coat, etc.[1]

The bullfrogs now *commonly* trump at night, and the mosquitoes are now really troublesome.

June 16. I notice this forenoon, about my melons, an excrement five to six eighths of an inch long, narrowed and with a sort of stem at one end, full of wing-cases of beetles, etc., and black, looking at first like the cocoon of some insect, but moist and fresh. Also saw four or five on the sidewalk as I went to the post-office (after a warm night). It is probably the excrement of the toad, of which I have seen no account.

I saw great puffs on the andromeda the 14th.

At 2 P. M. 85°, and about same for several days past. I have heard no hylodes since the 12th, and no purring frogs (*Rana palustris*). Think they ceased about the same time, or with the 85° heat, *i. e.* with ribbon for neck and thinnest sack.

Thunder-showers show themselves about 2 P. M. in the west, but split at sight of Concord and go east on each side, we getting only a slight shower.

At evening paddle to Clamshell.

The meadows full of lightning-bugs to-night; first seen the 14th. (There had then been a thunder-shower *in the north*.)

Rose-bugs two or three days at least.

It appears to me that these phenomena occur simultaneously, say June 12th, *viz. :* —

[1] Heat probably about 85° at 2 P. M. *Vide* [below].

Heat about 85° at 2 P. M. True summer.
Hylodes cease to peep.
Purring frogs (*Rana palustris*) cease.
Lightning-bugs first seen.
Bullfrogs trump *generally*.
Mosquitoes begin to be really troublesome.
Afternoon thunder-showers almost regular.[1]
Sleep with open window (10th), and wear thin coat and ribbon on neck.
Turtles fairly and generally begun to lay.

As I stand at Clamshell, it occurs to me that I never see the stinkpot laying its eggs on land by day; that therefore it must lay its eggs by night.[2] Where, then, shall I look for them now by night with a lantern? Why not here as well as anywhere? And I turn my eyes in the twilight to the shore there, when I see a turtle just entering the water. Running to it with haste, I see it (after it has entered the river) to be a stinkpot, which probably was frightened by us. Had come forth to lay, or, possibly, was returning. I think I never see the *picta* and *insculpta* and yellow-spot ashore by night.

The pickerel-weed appears to have suddenly shot up to about its final height, but it is mainly owing to the river having rapidly fallen a foot within a few days. So far as the height of this plant is concerned, the river now reaches its summer régime. Not yet the potamogetons.

Channing found a marsh hawk's nest on the Great Meadows this afternoon, with three eggs considerably developed. This is the third I have heard of this year.[3]

[1] 15th, 16th, 17th.
[2] No. *Vide* back in Journal to when Ricketson here once.
[3] *Vide* July 3d.

June 17. Quite a fog this morning.

About 1 P. M., notice thunder-clouds in west and hear the muttering. As yesterday, it splits at sight of Concord and goes south and north. Nevertheless about 3 P. M. begins a steady gentle rain here for several hours, and in the night again, the thunder, as yesterday, mostly forerunning or superficial to the shower.

This the third day of thunder-showers in afternoon, though the 14th it did not rain here.

Carex flava out, possibly a week.

June 18. The tumultuous singing of birds, a burst of melody, wakes me up (the window being open) these mornings at dawn. What a *matinade* to have poured into your slumber!

2 P. M. — To Walden and Cliffs.

Rabbit clover is now two or three inches high.

I see in the southerly bays of Walden the pine pollen now washed up thickly; only at the bottom of the bays, especially the deep long bay, where it is a couple of rods long by six to twenty-four inches wide and one inch deep; pure sulphur-yellow, and now has no smell. It has come quite across the pond from where the pines stand, full half a mile, probably washed across most of the way.

I have scarcely seen a warbler for a fortnight, or since the leaves have been developed, though I hear plenty of them in the tree-tops.

Standing on Emerson's Cliff, I see very distinctly the redness of a luxuriant field of clover on the top of Fair Haven Hill, some two thirds of a mile off, the day being

cloudy and misty, the sun just ready to break out. You might have mistaken the redness for that of withered pine boughs where wood was cut last winter.

On this Emerson hill I notice, among other growths after the cutting two years ago, — the huckleberry and blueberry, — that the sedge *P. Pennsylvanica* has shot up into large and luxuriant and densely set tufts, giving to the spaces between the little oak sprouts and clumps quite a grassy appearance.

Notice those remarkable galls on a shrub oak, two or three together, or hardly so broad as this, each with a grub in it.

June 19. Dewy clouds in the air to-day and yesterday, yet not threatening rain; somewhat dog-day-like.

Let an oak be hewed and put into the frame of a house, where it is sheltered, and it will last several centuries. Even as a sill it may last one hundred and fifty years. But simply cut it down and let it lie, though in an open pasture, and it will probably be thoroughly rotten in twenty-five years. There is the oak cut down at Clamshell some twenty years ago, the butt left on the ground. It has about two-thirds wasted away, and is hardly fit for fuel.

The leading shoot of one of my young white pines (not the rankest, but easily reached) has grown sixteen and a quarter inches. Let me measure it again in a few days.[1]

[1] *Vide* 27th and July 4th.

Vol. XIII

2 P. M. — To Flint's Pond.

Going through the cold hollows at Ripple Lake, where the wood was cut some twenty-two years ago, I observe that they are still almost entirely sedge, — bare grassy hollows, — while at a certain height all around the wood rises abruptly and densely to the height of fifteen or twenty feet. These portions are kept bare and are likely to be an indefinite time longer. The sedge of these hollows is the *Pennsylvanica*, slender *siccata*, and some *vestita*, as well as grass. There are numberless chocolate-colored and other devil's-needles coursing up and down these hollows now.

Observe a nest crowded full with four young brown thrashers half fledged. You would think they would die of heat, so densely packed and overflowing. Three head one way, and the other lies across. How quickly a fox would gobble them up!

Ripple Lake northeast shore is lined with a pale-yellowish pine pollen, though there are no pines within a dozen rods, and those (white pines) on the east. Half of the pool is gray with the dust, as with meal. Is not this paler yellow that of the white pine? So of Goose Pond. Thus these ponds and pools in the woods catch the pine pollen that may be floating in the atmosphere, and it is washed up to one side (the northeast side). At Flint's also. They are *pollen-ometers*. I see at Flint's a great many winged insects collected on it.

The devil's-needles now abound in wood-paths and about the Ripple Lakes. Even if your eyes were shut you would know they were there, hearing the rustling

of their wings as they flit by or wheel in pursuit of one another. Very various colors and sizes.

I observe that the water-bugs confine themselves to the shore, even of Ripple Lake, now by *day*, though I doubt if there are fishes that would disturb them in the middle here.

The eriocaulon shows white heads two to five inches high.

I follow a distinct fox-path amid the grass and bushes for some forty rods beyond Britton's Hollow, leading from the great fox-hole. It branches on reaching the peach-orchard. No doubt by these routes they oftenest go and return to their hole. As broad as a cart-wheel, and at last best seen when you do not look too hard for it.

Some tall rough goldenrod is three feet high, and generally in rich ground it is two or more. Also some fragrant goldenrod is two feet high. The *Carex tentaculata* is peculiar whitish-spiked. The clethra has a peculiarly fresh, shining leaf. The red oak leaf has a hard gloss to it.

Some large round oak-apples on small trees or bushes are interesting and handsome even as a fruit, — a lemon or orange. Here are some five inches in circumference, glossy-green on one side (pale on the other) with whitish prominences.

Those two pointed ones of yesterday are a pale dull green, with similar whitish points.

Pads already eaten for some time, in straight lines as if racked by shot; and I see that they are thus eaten from the upper side, for here is one place begun but not eaten through.

Is not that the *Glyceria pallida* now out a day or two in the small fen just south of Lincoln bound on the Turnpike? *Eriophorum gracile* (the triangular-leafed) well out, same place with the last, probably some days. Redstarts are common here now. Sugar maple keys are falling on the Common. The green sarsaparilla berries make quite a show as you catch sight of them half concealed by their leaves.

June 20. No dew this *morning*, but early in the forenoon.

Heavy rain (with holdings up) all day and part of the following night. Very little wind, and that northeast. (This the result of the two days of dewy clouds, dogdayish.) It comes down perpendicularly. Nearly an inch and a quarter falls into a large tin pail with upright sides (which I had placed in the garden for the purpose) between 8 A. M. and 12, and by the next morning there is two and one eighth inches, — which is the whole of it. More rain falls to-day than any day since March, if not this year. It is a warm rain, and I sit all the day and evening with my window open. It beats down the potatoes, grass, etc., and so weighs down the luxuriant shoots of the currant that they either break off or require to be broken off at a great sacrifice of growth, — eighteen to twenty-four inches long.

June 21. 6 A. M. — The river has risen to seven and a half inches above summer level (probably from

about two or three above in the morning of yesterday). At 7 P. M. it is eleven and a half inches above summer level.

The wind is still northeast, and the air is now so cold (cooled by the rain) that most have fires, and it is uncomfortably cool out of the sun, which does not shine much this forenoon.

Phalaris Americana (some probably two or three days). It is the rankest and for its size most conspicuous common grass. You see great dark-green islets of it by the side of, or even in, the river, where it is muddy, with the large whitish panicles (?) lifted above the broad rank leaves. These are four or five feet high, very luxuriant.

I first noticed elms full of *dark* shade at a distance some three or four days ago. As soon as they are well leafed it is seen how gracefully they droop.

At 12 M. it is only 59° above zero, and I am surprised to hear some toads ring, which I have not heard lately by day; as if this degree of coolness even (at midday) was agreeable to them, corresponding to 62 or more at evening.

At noon the sun comes fairly out and the wind rises. June has been quite a breezy month thus far. I have waited in vain for perfectly smooth water in which to watch the bream poised over her nest. There has been almost a steady breeze or breeziness with the waving of new-leafed boughs.

2 P. M. — To Little Truro.

Carex flava grows up the railroad, about as far as the spring on the north side. I see, on the railroad track,

Vol. XIII

young partridges about as big as my fist, while the old bird in grass does not see me at first. The young now make a sound not so fine, more like some of the notes of little chickens. The old bird steps about alarmed with swollen throat, or neck-feathers puffed up.

Crossing William Brown's dry field in front of the schoolhouse, I see a young thrasher which has just left the nest, and the old bird about it. I oftenest find them in half-open dry fields where there are scattered birches, pines, and shrub oaks.

The earliest cinquefoil grows abundantly in Brown's dry pastures, but I scarcely see one in bloom now. The silvery cinquefoil is abundant.

Having noticed the pine pollen washed up on the shore of three or four ponds in the woods lately and at Ripple Lake, a dozen rods from the nearest pine, also having seen the pollen carried off visibly half a dozen rods from a pitch pine which I had jarred, and rising all the while when there was very little wind, it suggested to me that the air must be full of this fine dust at this season, that it must be carried to great distances, when dry, and falling at night perhaps, or with a change in the atmosphere, its presence might be detected remote from pines by examining the edges of pretty large bodies of water, where it would be collected to one side by the wind and waves from a large area.

So I thought over all the small ponds in the township in order to select one or more most remote from the woods or pines, whose shores I might examine and so test my theory. I could think of none more favorable

than this little pond only four rods in diameter, a watering-place in John Brown's pasture, which has but few pads in it. It is a small round pond at the bottom of a hollow in the midst of a perfectly bare, dry pasture. The nearest wood of any kind is just thirty-nine rods distant northward, and across a road from the edge of the pond. Any other wood in other directions is five or six times as far. I knew it was a bad time to try my experiment, — just after such heavy rains and when the pines are effete, — a little too late. The wind was now blowing quite strong from the northeast, whereas all the pollen that I had seen hitherto had been collected on the northeast sides of ponds by a southwest wind. I approached the pond from the northeast and, looking over it and carefully along the shore there, could detect no pollen. I then proceeded to walk round it, but still could detect none. I then said to myself, If there was any here before the rain and northeast wind, it must have been on the northeast side and then have been washed over and now up high quite at or on the shore. I looked there carefully, stooping down, and was gratified to find, after all, a distinct yellow line of pollen dust about half an inch in width — or washing off to two or three times that width — quite on the edge, and some dead twigs which I took up from the wet shore were completely coated with it, as with sulphur. This yellow line reached half a rod along the southwest side, and I then detected a little of the dust slightly graying the surface for two or three feet out there. (Many little snow(?)-fleas on it.)

When I thought I had failed, I was much pleased to detect, after all, this distinct yellow line, revealing unmistakably the presence of pines in the neighborhood and thus confirming my theory. As chemists detect the presence of ozone in the atmosphere by exposing to it a delicately prepared paper, so the lakes detect for us thus the presence of the pine pollen in the atmosphere. They are our *pollinometers*. How much of this invisible dust must be floating in the atmosphere, and be inhaled and drunk by us at this season!! Who knows but the pollen of some plants may be unwholesome to inhale, and produce the diseases of the season?[1]

Of course a large pond will collect the most, and you will find most at the bottom of long deep bays into which the wind blows.

I do not believe that there is any part of this town on which the pollen of the pine may not fall. The time to examine the ponds this year was, I should say, from the 15th to the 20th of this month. Looking at the trees to-day, I find that the pines are now effete, especially the pitch pine, the sterile flowers now turned reddish. The white pine is lighter-colored, and all but a very little indeed is effete. In the white pine it is a dense cluster of twenty or thirty little flowers about the base of this year's shoot.

I did not expect to find any pollen, the pond was so small and distant from any wood, but I thought that I would examine. Who knows but the pollen of various kinds floating through the air at this season may be the

[1] *Vide* June 20 and 22, 1858.

source of some of the peculiar perfumes which are not traceable to their sources?

Noticed a dead *Emys picta* on its back, — dead a month or two. The head was gone, and of course all the insides, and there was a hole in front of its hind legs on each side; the legs left. Was not this killed just as the one at Tall's Island?

That meadow-grass which emits the peculiar glaucous sheen from its bent and waving surface is the *Carex stricta*, either in tufts or growing thinly. (*Vide* 15th.) *Carex lupulina*, say four or five days, or maybe a week, at Little Truro Pond-hole. This in plenty just at the Hill Landing old bridge site.

Saw the pigeon-egg puffball formed on the 19th.

Started up a nighthawk in the dry field near the pond-hole. Probably they affect these dry and gravelly fields, as at Truro, where the small fescue grass grows and some tufts of *Carex scoparia* (?).

Tall fescue grass.

Eleocharis, the two small still in bloom, especially the smallest.

June 22. River at 6 A. M. eleven and fifteen sixteenths inches above summer level, having risen only seven sixteenths in the night. At 7 P. M. it is fifteen and one eighth above summer level.

I see minnows by the shore half an inch long.

Rice tells me that he saw in a mud-hole near the river in Sudbury, about a fortnight ago, a pout protecting her ova, which were in a ball about as big as an apple, all exposed, not at all hatched (I think he said on a stick),

under which she swam. There were also pouts of various sizes about there, some only two inches long (!), says his son William.

Hear the peculiar peep of young golden robins on the elms this morning.

What is that great toothless, thin-shelled green clam which Rice brought from the same mud-hole mentioned above, — just six inches long, three inches high, and two and three quarters broad? Very green, with rays. A handsome shell.[1]

There is a strong northeast wind this afternoon, the thermometer 60° only at 12.30 P. M. and 65 at 5 P. M. But it is remarkably cold in the wind, and you require a thick coat. 65° now, with wind, is uncomfortably cold. I hear that it has killed some birds. Martins, etc., found dead in neighbors' yards.

The heavy rain of the 20th with the cold of the 21st has killed some birds. A martin and another bird were found dead in Wheildon's garden.

The leaves are now rapidly becoming hard and glazed, acquiring firmness as well as a darker color.

2 P. M. — To Great Meadows.

At Moore's Swamp the *Carex comosa* (?).

A painted turtle digging to lay in wood-path at 3.30 P. M. The throat of the hole in this hard ground is only seven eighths of an inch to an inch wide, and the hole is now about two inches deep and about the same in width beneath, expanding in all directions beneath, but chiefly toward the head of the turtle.

On the northeast side of the Great Fields there are

[1] *Anodon fluviatilis.*

two or three little patches of sand one to two rods across with a few slivers of arrowhead stone sprinkled over them. It is easy to find an arrowhead if it is exposed. These spots are plowed only by the wind and rain, and yet I rarely cross them but I find a new arrowhead exposed.

The latest aspens at Holbrook's Hollow probably did not leaf till about a week ago, or the middle of June. I saw them on the 7th as well as to-day. They have now grown an inch.

Observe the tops of the flowering fern killed by frost along the south edge of the Great Meadows last night. These ferns are very tender and betray it.

I walk straight across the meadow from west of Holbrook's to the river, and the prevailing grasses were *Scirpus Eriophorum* (out several days), *Carex stellulata*, *C. bullata*, with oftenest two *fertile* spikes, methinks; this the order of their prevalence.[1] *Alopecurus geniculatus* in the Great Meadow path quite fresh, say several (three or four) days.

The pretty new moon in the west is quite red this evening.

June 23. River at 7 A. M. fifteen inches above summer level, having fallen.

A sparrow's nest with three fresh eggs in a hollow of a willow, two and a half feet from ground, at my boat's place. The bird has the usual marks, except perhaps the spot on the breast is more obvious, and the lines over the eyes more white and distinct. The eggs have a

[1] *Vide* June 16, 1859.

much *bluer*-white ground than those I have, and beside are but slightly spotted with brown except toward the larger end. The chip of the bird is metallic, not the hoarse chip of the spring song sparrow. *Vide* eggs in collection.[1]

2 P. M. — To Bare Hill road.

This is a decidedly dogdayish day,[2] foretold by the red moon of last evening. The sunlight, even this forenoon, was peculiarly yellow, passing through misty clouds, and this afternoon the atmosphere is decidedly blue. I see it in the street within thirty rods, and perceive a distinct musty odor.

First *bluish, musty* dog-day, and sultry. Thermometer at two only 85°, however, and wind comes easterly soon and rather cool.[3]

The foliage is now thick and for the most part dark, and this kind of weather is probably the result of this amount of shadow; but it grows cooler with easterly wind before night.

I suspect that it may be true, as said, that the first half of June is cooler than the last half of May, on this account.

Smilacina racemosa, how long? *Agrostis scabra*,[4] pond path at east end of Walden. *Poa compressa* may fairly begin on the railroad at Walden; also piper grass just begun.

I see a young *Rana sylvatica* in the woods, only

---

[1] *Vide* June 25, 1856.
[2] And the 24th also.
[3] As it does the 24th.
[4] Probably *vulgaris*.

five eighths of an inch long. Or is it a hylodes? — for I see a faint cross-like mark on the back and yet the black dash on the sides of the face.

At 7 P. M. the river is fifteen and three fourths inches above summer level.[1]

It rained hard on the 20th and part of the following night, — two and one eighth inches of rain in all, there being no drought, — raising the river from some two or three inches above summer level to seven and a half inches above summer level at 7 A. M. of the 21st.

At 7 P. M. of the 21st, 11½ inches above summer level.

6 A. M.	22d,	11⅝
7 P. M.	22d,	15⅛
7 A. M.	23d,	15
7 P. M.	23d,	15¾

Thus two and one eighth inches of rain at this season, falling in one day, with little or no wind, raises the river while it is falling some four inches; on the next day it rises four more; the next night it rises seven sixteenths inch more; the next day (second after the rain) it rises three and three sixteenths inches; the next night it falls one eighth of an inch; it rises again three fourths of an inch, or five eighths absolutely; *i. e.*, it rises still the third day after the rain. That is, after a remarkably heavy rain of one day it does not rise as much in a night as it ordinarily falls in a day at this season.

June 24. 2 P. M. — To Clamshell.
The dogdayish weather continues.

---

[1] At height for this rise.

Vol. XIII

The leaves generally are eaten when young and tender, as the leaves of melons (squashes) as soon as they expand a little. When they become more hard and glazed they are less edible. Hence this and earlier is the season for galls of various kinds. The pads are already extensively eaten. I do not know what eats those shot-like lines, but I see the pads, especially of the yellow lilies, with many little black or dark-brown grubs on them (no doubt hatched on them), annular, and yellow beneath, and now eating them but not eating through, making crinkled lines all over them.

Notice no young breams in the nests yet.[1]

That hilly road through Baker's land to Bare Hill is a true up-country road with the scent of ferns along it. There are birches, etc., enough in the road for bean-poles and to stick your peas with, and the man who has just built him a true country-house there is now indulging himself with pea-brush probably for the first time. The brush five times as high as his peas, which are now in bloom.

Have seen the flowering fern ripe for some days.

Saw young bluebirds fully grown yesterday, but with a feeble note and dull colors.

Start a woodcock from amid ferns.

Common curled dock, some time. Notice the red cups of the tops of trumpet-weed a foot [or] two high.

All plants leafed, say the middle of June, and summer commenced. River begins then to wear its summer aspect.

---

[1] *Perhaps* I do July 2d.

I perceive the rank, dog-like scent of meadow-rue. See white lily buds.

June 25. 2 P. M. — To Dugan Desert.

I see a female marsh hawk, beating along a wall, suddenly give chase to a small bird, dashing to right and left twenty feet high about a pine.

There are no turtle-tracks now on the desert, but I see many crow-tracks there, and where they have pecked or scratched in the sand in many places, possibly smelling the eggs!? Also the track of a fox over the sand, and find his excrement *buried* in the sand, and the crows have dabbled in the sand over it. It is full of fur as usual. What an unfailing supply of small game it secures that its excrement should be so generally of fur!

As near as I can make out with my glass, I see and hear the parti-colored warbler[1] at Ledum Swamp on the larches and pines. A bluish back, yellow breast with a reddish crescent above, and white belly, and a continuous *screeping* note to the end.

At evening up the Assabet.

7 P. M., river twelve and a half inches above summer level.

The water of the Assabet is now generally whitened with the down of the black willow floating on it, yet it is not yet collected in very dense masses, not quite in the prime of its fall. The coarsest kind of lint that falls on the stream. The phalaris grass, now maybe in its prime, is, with its great white spike lifted over [?] its rank

---

[1] Yes.

blades, eighteen inches above, perhaps the most conspicuous grass we have in Concord (or hereabouts, except the phragmites). Will soon close up into a narrow spike.

Scirpus lacustris, some days.

Hear four or five screech owls on different sides of the river, uttering those peculiar low screwing or working, ventriloquial sounds. Probably young birds, some of them, lately taken flight.

Farmers are just beginning their June-grass haying.

The *Glyceria pallida* (?)[1] grows in that ditch at the little brook on the Corner road, close to the road on the south side in A. Wheeler's (?) land.

June 26. Still hazy and dogdayish.

Go to the menagerie in the afternoon.

At 5 p. m., — river ten and a half inches above summer level, — cross the meadow to the Hemlocks.

The blue-eyed grass, now in its prime, occupies the drier and harder parts of the meadow, where I can walk dry-shod, but where the coarser sedge grows and it is lower and wetter there is none of it. I keep dry by following this blue guide, and the grass is not very high about it. You cross the meadows dry-shod by following the winding lead of the blue-eyed grass, which grows only on the firmer, more elevated, and drier parts.

The hemlocks are too much grown now and are too dark a green to show the handsomest bead-work by contrast.

Under the Hemlocks, on the bare bank, apparently the *Aira flexuosa*, not long.

[1] No. Torrey's *Poa dentata*.

Young black willows have sprouted and put forth their two minute round leafets where the cottony seeds have lodged in a scum against the alders, etc. Leafets from one fortieth to one twenty-fifth of an inch in diameter. When separated from the continuous film of down they have a tendency to sink.

The Canada naiad (?), which I gathered yesterday, had perhaps bloomed. Thought I detected with my glass something like stamens about the little balls.

June 27. — 2 p. m. — Up Assabet to Farmer's.

See on the open grassy bank and shore, just this side the Hemlocks, a partridge with her little brood. Being in my boat, I went within three rods, and they were hardly scared at all. The young were but little bigger than chickens four or five days old, yet could fly two or three rods. The partridge now takes out her brood to feed, all the country over; and what an extensive range they have! — not confined to a barn-yard.

To-day it is cool and clear and quite windy, and the black willow down is now washed up and collected against the alders and weeds; the river mostly swept of its dust and looking more sparkling.

Farmer says that he found on the 24th a black snake laying her eggs on the side of the hill between his peach-orchard and the ledge in the woods. He showed me the place to-day. The hole was about three inches long by one wide and four or five inches deep, in a slanting direction. ━━━━ ◠ He found the snake lying with her head and tail both

at once in the hole, occupied with laying; and she had then layed twelve eggs. He pressed out two more, — fourteen in all. They were not connected together, and were twice as large as the sternothærus' egg; soft-shelled. He left them on the ground, but when he went there this morning he saw some crows devour them before his eyes. This hole was not in sand, but in rather lean pasture sod, and hard, freshly made. It bore a general resemblance to a turtle's hole. Was close by where his uncle (?) tried to dig through to the other side of the world. Dug more or less for three years. Used to dig nights, as long as one candle lasted. Left a stone just between him and the other side, not to be removed till he was ready to marry Washington's sister. The foxes now occupy his hole.

Holcus lanatus, a week or ten days, Hosmer's field on Assabet, north of Poke-logan. *Juncus tenuis*, three or four days.

Farmer calls the flowering fern "staghorn;" says it is the common name with farmers.

His bees are swarming, all collected over the outside of the hive.

River at 6 p. m. seven and five eighths inches above summer level.

The pine shoot which on the 19th had grown sixteen and a quarter inches is now twenty and three quarters long, or has grown four and a half inches in eight days, a little more than half an inch a day. It had evidently grown much faster before.[1]

[1] *Vide* July 4th.

Get from Farmer specimens of barley and wheat, and, in the former, apparently *Bromus secalinus*[1] (?); none of them yet out.

June 28. — Assabet Bath and Sunset Interval.

On the 25th I first noticed that the black willows — the sterile ones, not whitened with down — were just begun to be handsome, with their light ethereal green against other trees. They are now getting to be sufficiently thick.

This month, it must be 85° at 2 p. m. and *still* to make hot weather. 80° with wind is quite comfortable.

June-grass is now generally browned atop, its spikes being out of bloom and old. Herd's-grass out, two or three days.

I now see and hear many young birds about; young barn swallows on telegraph-wire, etc.

Farmer said yesterday that he thought foxes did not live so much in the depth of the woods as on open hill-sides, where they lay out and overlooked the operations of men, — studied their ways, — which made them so cunning.

The 21st I began to notice the *Festuca ovina* in dry pastures, prevailing and so marking a season. Fowl-meadow grass, though not quite in bloom, has now begun to make an impression on the inlands and in the meadows, with its dense-growing recurved or drooping green tops. *Panicum latifolium*, how long?

I see no tortoises laying nowadays, but I meet to-day with a wood tortoise which is eating the leaves of the

[1] *Vide* 30th.

early potentilla, and, soon after, another in Hosmer's sandy bank field north of Assabet Bridge, deliberately eating *sorrel*. It was evidently quite an old one, its back being worn quite smooth, and its motions peculiarly sluggish. It continued to eat when I was within a few feet, holding its head high and biting down at it, each time bringing away a piece of a leaf. It made you think of an old and sick tortoise eating some salutary herb to cure itself with, and reminded me of the stories of the ancients, who, I think, made the tortoises thus cure themselves with dittany or origanum when bitten by a venomous snake. That is, it impressed me as if it must know the virtues of herbs well and could select the one best suited [to] its condition of body. When I came nearer, it at once drew in its head. Its back was smooth and yellowish, — a venerable tortoise. When I moved off, it at once withdrew into the woods.

See two of those remarkably brilliant beetles near the caving edge here, with copper and green reflections (head green), and blue ones. They are sluggish and can be transported on a leaf.

On the alder leaves by the riverside in Sunset Interval, I see countless small black miller-like insects three eighths of an inch and of this form: but all of them had not feelers.

I think they were the same that hover in a swarm over the water at evening.

June 29. Dogdayish and showery, with thunder.

At 6 P. M. 91°, the hottest yet, though a thunder-

shower has passed northeast and grazed us, and, in consequence, at 6.30 or 7, another thunder-shower comes up from the southwest and there is a sudden burst from it with a remarkably strong, gusty wind, and the rain for fifteen minutes falls in a blinding deluge. I think I never saw it rain so hard. The roof of the depot shed is taken off, many trees torn to pieces, the garden flooded at once, corn and potatoes, etc., beaten flat.[1] You could not see distinctly many rods through the rain. It was the very strong gusts added to the weight of the rain that did the mischief. There was little or no wind before the shower; it belonged wholly to it. Thus our most violent thunder-shower followed the hottest hour of the month.

June 30. Try the temperature of the springs and pond. At 2.15 P. M. the atmosphere north of house is 83° above zero, and the same afternoon, the water of the Boiling Spring, 45°; our well after pumping, 49°; Brister's Spring, 49°; Walden Pond (at bottom, in four feet water), 71°; river at one rod from shore, 77°.[2] I see that the temperature of the Boiling Spring on the 6th of March, 1846, was also 45°, and I suspect it varies very little throughout the year.

If you paw into sand, both by day and night, you find the heat to be permanently greatest some three inches (to-day) below the surface, and this is about [the] depth at which the tortoises place their eggs. Where the tem-

[1] There was the same sudden and remarkably violent storm about two hours earlier all up and down the Hudson, and it struck the Great Eastern at her moorings in New York and caused some damage.

[2] 2 P. M., the 1st of July, the air is 77° and the river 75°

perature is highest permanently and changes least between night and day.

At 2 P. M. the river is six inches above summer level.

Generally speaking, the fields are not imbrowned yet, but the freshness of the year is preserved. Standing on the side of Fair Haven Hill the verdure generally appears at its height, the air clear, and the water sparkling (after the rain of yesterday), and it is a world of glossy leaves and grassy fields and meads.

The foliage of deciduous trees is now so nearly as dark as evergreens that I am not struck by the contrast.

I think that the shadows under the edge of woods are less noticed now because the woods themselves are darker. So, too, with the darkness and shadows of elms.

Seen through this clear, sparkling, breezy air, the fields, woods, and meadows are very brilliant and fair. The leaves are now hard and glossy (the oldest), yet still comparatively fresh, and I do not see a single acre of grass that has been cut yet. The river meadows on each side the stream, looking toward the light, have an elysian beauty. A light-yellow plush or velvet, as if some gamboge had been rubbed into them. They are by far the most bright and sunny-looking spots, such is the color of the sedges which grow there, while the pastures and hillsides are dark-green and the grain-fields glaucous-green. It is remarkable that the meadows, which are the lowest part, should have this lightest, sunniest, yellowest look.

Now that season begins when you see the river to be so regularly divided longitudinally into pads, smooth water, and sparkling ripples between, in a clear day.

The older white oak leaves have now a blue or dark-purplish bloom on their cheeks or prominences, which you can rub off, leaving them green.

The grasses of Sedge Path are the early sedge (which is much of it turned by a smut), *Festuca ovina*, and the *Carex siccata*. *Bromus secalinus* by Walden, say yesterday. This and that in Farmer's barley the same, though some is downy and some smooth, and it does not open much in bloom because the glume does not reach beyond middle of second flower.

I hear no toads to speak of, of late, except a few at evening.

See in the garden the hole in which a toad sits by day. It is a round hole about the width of his body across, and extending under one side about the length of my little finger; in the main, indeed, shaped like a turtle's nest, but not so broad beneath and not quite so deep. There sits the toad, in the shade, and concealed completely under the ground, with its head toward the entrance, waiting for evening. This was on the side of a corn-hill.

They are now cutting clover. *Scirpus subterminalis* is apparently just beginning at the Pout's Nest, the water being very low.

There is a turnip-like weed now in flower and going to [seed], a pest in grain-fields; same as I noticed formerly in Stow's field; say six weeks. Is it *Brassica campestris*?[1]

[1] *Vide* Aug. 19th.

JULY, 1860

(ÆT. 42–43)

July 1. 2 P. M. — To Well Meadow.

River three and seven eighths above summer level.

Rattlesnake grass is just beginning. The slender and leafy panic of the meadows (tall for size), say a week. Saw a large black and blue (edged) butterfly yesterday. Fowl-meadow grass.

Notice those slate-colored spots on a rough goldenrod leaf, answering to the crimson on red maples, surrounded by a light ring and centred with greenish.

The hellebore fall is now conspicuous and fairly under weigh. The cabbage but just begun to fall. I see one leaf of the last fully eighteen inches by thirteen.

Brachyelytrum grass, apparently just begun, or a day.

While reclining on the sedge at end of town-bound path, by the *scoparia*, I see a warbler deliberately investigating the smooth sumachs and their old berry-bunches, in various positions. It is a slaty blue above, with a bright-yellow front-head and much yellow on the wings (at angle, etc.), a very distinct black throat, triangularwise, with a broad black line through the eyes or side-head, a forked tail which is dark beneath; belly and vent white or whitish. It is undoubtedly the *Sylvia chrysoptera*, or golden-winged warbler, which I think must be breeding here.

I see young partridges not bigger than robins fly three or four rods, not squatting fast, now.

Returning over the causeway, the light of the sun was reflected from the awns of a grain-field (probably wheat) [1] by Abiel Wheeler's house so brightly and in such a solid mass as to far surpass in amount of light the densest whiteweed thereabouts, and at first impress you as if it were whiter than whiteweed, but in fact it was *not* white, but a very bright sunny gleam from the waving phalanx of awns, more calculated to reflect the light than any object in the landscape.

July 2. A. M. — To lilies above Nut Meadow.

The phalaris heads are now closed up, and it looks like another kind of grass, — those heads which stood so whitish some eighteen inches above their broad green leaves. The bayonet rush is not quite out.

The lilies are not yet in prime. A large one measures six and a half inches over by two and a half high.

Nowadays hear from my window the constant tittering of young golden robins, and by the river fields the alarm note of the peetweets, concerned about their young.

Does not the summer régime of the river begin say about July 1st, when the black willow is handsome and the beds of front-rank polygonum are formed above water?

Yesterday I detected the smallest grass that I know, apparently *Festuca tenella* (?), apparently out of bloom, in the dry path southwest of the yew, — only two to four inches high, like a moss.

[1] Yes.

July 3. 2 P. M. — To Holbrook's meadow and Turnpike to try springs.

Looked for the marsh hawk's nest (of June 16th, *q. v.*) in the Great Meadows. It was in the very midst of the sweet-gale (which is three feet high), occupying an opening only a foot or two across. We had much difficulty in finding it again, but at last nearly stumbled on to a young hawk. There was one as big as my fist, resting on the bare, flat nest in the sun, with a great head, staring eyes, and open gaping or panting mouth, yet mere down, grayish-white down, as yet; but I detected another which had crawled a foot one side amid the bushes for shade or safety, more than half as large again, with small feathers and a yet more angry, hawk-like look. How naturally anger sits on the young hawk's head! It was 3.30 P. M., and the old birds were gone and saw us not. Meanwhile their callow young lie panting under the sweet-gale and rose bushes in the swamp, waiting for their parents to fetch them food.

June is an up-country month, when our air and landscape is most like that of a more mountainous region, full of freshness, with the scent of ferns by the wayside.

The scheuchzeria is full of green fruit fully grown at Gowing's. It forms the upright grass-like plant next the more open pool, rising amid the floating sphagnum, with the spatulate sundew interspersed with it, and a very little of the leaden-sheathed eriophorum and a sprig or two of cassandra. The *Glyceria aquatica* has been out some time and is now apparently done at

Holbrook's meadow. The *Agrostis scabra*, the fine, long, slender branched fly-away grass, almost out, in what was Moore's Swamp by Bedford road. Also, in the ditch on the south side the road there, partly procumbent at base, a rather delicate and pale rough-flowered grass with (in this case) the paleæ so projecting at tip as to give it a dentate appearance. I called it last year the *Poa dentata* of Torrey. Now in its prime here, and larger specimens in the ditch by the Corner road, south side, southwest of stump fence, say ten days. The paleæ have a white or scarious tip and just below it a dark transverse line.

July 4. Gentle rain in the night (last).

The white pine shoot which on the 19th of June had grown sixteen and a quarter inches and on the 27th twenty and three quarters is now twenty-three and an eighth inches long.

2 P. M. — Look at springs toward Dugan's and White Pond.

Standing on J. P. Brown's land, south side, I observed his rich and luxuriant uncut grass-lands northward, now waving under the easterly wind. It is a beautiful Camilla, sweeping like waves of light and shade over the whole breadth of his land, like a low steam curling over it, imparting wonderful life to the landscape, like the light and shade of a changeable garment, waves of light and shade pursuing each other over the whole breadth of the landscape like waves hastening to break on a shore. It is an interesting feature, very easily overlooked, and suggests that we are wading and navigating at present in a sort of sea of grass, which yields and undulates under the wind like water; and so, perchance, the forest is seen to do from a favorable position.

None of his fields is cut yet.

Early, there was that flashing light of waving pine in the horizon; now, the Camilla on grass and grain.

Juncus bufonius, probably several days in some places.

The sedgy hollows, table-lands, and frosty places in the woods now most beautiful, the sedge most fresh and yellowish-green, a soft, dry bed to recline on. For example, that place south of Ledum Swamp, the sedge, especially in the old path, falling every way like cowlicks on an unkempt head. When we enter it from the west, with the sun shining between thundery clouds, it is all lit with a blaze of yellow light, like a pasture on Mt. Washington, nearer the sun than usual.

How beautiful the dark-green oak leaves now! How dark the chincapin oak leaves! Now the pines are almost indistinguishable by color amid the deciduous trees.

The large johnswort now begins to be noticed generally, — a July yellow.

Scared up a young bobolink, which flies a couple of rods only.

A few toads still ring at evening, and I still notice, on the rocks at White Pond, the pine pollen yellowing them, though it fell some time ago.

7 P. M., river is one and three eighths above summer level.

July 5. Rain last night and all to-day.

I notice of late the *Osmunda regalis* fully grown, fresh and handsome.

July 6. Rained last night, as well as all yesterday and some of the night before. Three quarters of an inch has fallen.

6 A. M., river two and seven sixteenths above summer level. 7 P. M., three and five eighths above summer level. Thus three quarters of an inch has raised it only two and a quarter inches.

July 7. 7 A. M. River two and a half above summer level.

East wind and hazy.

I see a flock of some twenty-five crows. Probably the young are just grown.

Agrostis scabra. Cyperus filiculmis, a day. *Rhyncospora fusca*, apparently beginning (see stigmas). *Glyceria elongata* at little snapping turtle or Hemlock ditch, apparently done, say ten days; panicle not narrow now, more than *G. fluitans*.

Have begun to gather currants three or four days. Notice few ripe blueberries.

June 30th, July 3d, 4th, 6th, and 7th, I carried round a thermometer in the afternoon and ascertained the temperature of the springs, brooks, etc.

The springs, in the order of coldness, stand thus: —

1	Boiling Spring	45°	June 30
2	Dennis's railroad	46½°	July 7
3 & 4	Henry Shattuck's two	48°	July 6

5	Violet Sorrel (N. Barrett's)	48°	July 6
6	E. Hosmer's dam	48°	July 3
7	J. Farmer's	48°	July 6
8	Beyond Peter's	48° to 49°	July 3
9	Brister's	49°	June 30
10	Corner Spring (W. Wheeler's)	49°	July 4
11	Minot Pratt's	49°	July 6
12	Dugan's	50°	July 4
13	Cheney's	50°	July 3, 6 P. M., (air 72°) (July 4, 2 P. M., air 83 and spring 50 + still)
14	Garfield's (Moore's Swamp)	52°	July 3
15	John Hosmer's	54°	July 4
16	Assabet	54°	July 7
17	Oak Meadow	54°	July 6
18	Wheeler's	56° +	July 7

Omitting the last, as too much enlarged artificially and so warmed, the average temperature of seventeen is 49½°. Omitting also the 1st, 2d, 14th, 15th, 16th, and 17th, *i. e.* the extremes, the average of the remaining eleven is 48.7°, and they do not differ more than 2° from one another. On the whole, then, where I had expected to find great diversity I find remarkable uniformity. The temperature of good or cool springs in this town at this season varies very little indeed from 49°, and I should be surprised to meet with one considered cold which varied more than 3° from this.

The temperature of our well was 49°, June 30th; E. Hosmer's northernmost 49°, July 6; southernmost 49½°, July 6. 49° would seem to be the temperature at present very generally of water at a certain depth in the ground. This is very near the mean annual temperature of the air here.

The temperature of the air in the meanwhile was as follows, on the north side of our house: —

June 30	July 3	July 4	July 6	July 7
2.15 P. M., 83°	2 P. M., 82°	2 P. M., 83°	6 A. M., 57° to 60°	7 A. M., 56°
	6 P. M., 72°		2 P. M., 75°	2.30 P. M., 76°
			7 P. M., 75°	

The average temperature of the air at 2 P. M. for the five days of my observations was 80°, and the greatest variation during the observations was some 10° in the course of the afternoon. But I presume that this made no odds with the temperature of the springs, for Cheney's Spring stood 50° + both at 6 P. M., the 3d, when the thermometer was at 72°, and at 2 P. M., the 4th, when it had risen 11° higher. I should say, then, that a spring colder than 48° was remarkably cold; 48° to 50°, inclusive, quite cold, a very good cold spring; above 50° and not above 54°, cold; above that and not above 58°, *tolerable* merely. Or, I should rather say that only 50° and below was *cold* for a *spring;* say below 48°, remarkably cold; between that and 50°, inclusive, cold; 50° to 54°, inclusive, *pretty* cold; thence to 58°, inclusive, merely tolerable to drink.

Of the above springs, all but Nos. 1, 4, 7, 11 (?), and 17 are distinctly just at the base of a hill or bank and on the edge of a meadow or river. Apparently the water which percolates through the hill or upland, having reached a stratum saturated with water and impervious to it, bursts out in a spring. No. 1 (the coldest) only bursts out higher up a hillside, and 4, 7, and 17, a little *within* meadows. No. 11 should perhaps be included among the mass.

Of course an indefinite number of such springs may be found and cleared out along the bases of the hills, as wells dug anywhere are pretty sure to come to water of a similar character. The above are such as have been discovered and used, — been kept open, — or which have kept themselves clear. Frequently, in ditching his meadow, the farmer strikes on a powerful spring, and if it is cold enough and convenient to his house or work, he stones it up or sinks a tub or barrel there.

Of the above, Nos. 3, 6, 8, 13, 15 are, or have been, barrelled or tubbed; Nos. 5 and 13 stoned about (the last with steps down to it); Nos. 1 and 18 much deepened and enlarged and more or less covered. The remaining ten are in a natural state, only kept open more or less by use. 8, 9, and 14 have, or have had, a box for minnows in or near them. Perhaps the most natural well of them all is No. 11, Minot Pratt's, filling an oblong angular cavity between upright rocks.

Where the bottom is gravelly, and they are made deep by being barrelled or stoned up, they are a peculiarly clear and crystalline-looking water, Walden-Pond-like, quite unlike the river and brooks, — a peculiar clearness with whitish sands at the bottom, — perhaps because too cold for vegetation to defile them.

Each farmer values his spring and takes pride in it. He is inclined to think it the coldest in the neighborhood.

Each one is the source of a streamlet which finds its

way into the river, though possibly one or two of them may dry up some seasons. Only one to my knowledge visibly bubbles up, — or did before interfered with, — *viz.* the Boiling Spring, which is the coldest. This would indicate that its reservoir is still higher considerably and deep within the hill. You commonly see the water coming in more or less copiously through the gravel on the upper side, sometimes from under a rock in a considerable stream and with a tinkling sound.

The coldest, as I notice, have the clearest and most crystalline or Walden-Pond-like look.

Henry Shattuck's two were of the same temperature, though one was in the open meadow at the head of a ditch, and the other in the bank and covered or boxed over. This shows that they come at once from a considerable depth in the earth and have no time to be warmed before they flow off. A rail standing on its end in one of his ditches was almost concealed, so deep is the mud in his meadow. He pointed out two or three in his ditches "as big as your body" and of unknown depth.

No. 1 is at the head of them all, and no doubt was used by the Indians. It is used by the Fitchburg Railroad for their locomotives. No. 2 was made in cutting for the railroad, and is used by the track-repairers. Some are far away and only used by hunters and walkers and berry-pickers. Some are used in haying-time only. Some are so cold and clear, and so near withal, as to be used daily by some family, who "turn up their noses" at the well. Others, as Dugan's, is instead of the well. One, as Wheeler's, has had five

---

hundred dollars expended on it. No. 6 was found by Hosmer when he built his dam, and he imagines that it has medicinal properties, and used accordingly to come to drink at it often, though half a mile from his house. Some will have a broken tumbler hid in the grass near, or a rusty dipper hung on a twig near by. Others, again, drink through some hollow weed's stem. None are too cold for the *Rana fontinalis*, which will hardly make room for your face when you stoop to drink. Some are only known to myself and friends, and I clear them out annually.

I suspect that most of them never freeze entirely over.

The brooks stood thus, the temperature of the [atmosphere] at 2 p. m. being (as before) about 80°: —

July 7	Hemlock Brook (Grackle Swamp), where I saw the little snapping turtle	61	1
3	Saw Mill Brook, at Turnpike	62	2
4	Nut Meadow, at Brown s fence	64	3
4	" " (road by Dugan's)	65	4
3	Brook between Emerson and Connor	65	5
9	Swamp Bridge (back road) (air 80½ at 2 p. m.)	70	6
9	Miles Swamp Brook (Conantum)	70½	7
6	Dakin's, in road beyond Winn's	73	8
6	Below Francis Jarvis's, in road	74	9
3	Mill Brook (Turnpike Bridge)	75	10
3	Mill Brook (East Quarter schoolhouse)	78	11

$$11\overline{)757\tfrac{1}{2}}$$
$$68\tfrac{9}{11}$$
say 69

The first five may be considered cold brooks. The 1st, 2d, and 5th come directly out of cold, peaty, or else

---

shady, swamps. This suggests that the soil of such swamps, though cleared and cultivated, must be many degrees cooler than that of dry, open uplands, and demand different crops and treatment.

The river stood thus at my boat's place: —

June 30, 2 p. m., air 83°, one rod from shore, 77°
July 1, 2 p. m., air 77°, " " " " 75°
July 3, 2 p. m., air 82°,
        6 p. m., air 72°, " " " " 75°
July 4, 2 p. m., air 83°, " " " " 78° (at Clamshell)
                    in middle,   76° ("   "   )
                    four feet from shore, 79° ("   "   )
July 6,[1] 6 a. m., air 57° to 60°, one rod from shore, 67°
                    in middle,   69°
        2 p. m., air 75°, one rod from shore, 76°
        7 p. m., air 75°, one rod off, 73°
July 7, 7 a. m., air 56°, one rod off, 69°
                    in middle,   70½°
        2.30 p. m., air 76°, in middle, 75°
                    one rod off,   74° to 75°

Average temperature of river at one rod from shore at 2 p. m., 76°, or 7° more than that of the brooks tried. As the brooks are larger they approach nearer to the river in temperature.

It will be seen by the observations of the 4th, 6th, and 7th that there is from one and a half to two degrees difference between the temperature of the river at one rod from shore and in the middle, and that in the morning the middle is the warmest, at 2 p. m. the coldest. If the weather is colder than usual, the difference between the side and middle is less. Hence,

[1] After ¾ inch rain on the 5th.

evidently, fishes will change their ground every day and night, as they prefer warmer or cooler water.[1]

The temperature of the Assabet at the stone-heaps, in the middle (both at top and bottom, it being only some three feet deep), on the 7th of July, at 4.30 P. M., was 75°, or the same as the main stream at 2.30 P. M.

The following water also was tested : [2] —

June 30,	Walden Pond, at bottom in four feet water,	71°
July 4,	White Pond, top, five feet from shore,	76°
July 3,	Gowing's Swamp (edge of middle pool),	78°
" "	in the sphagnum generally,	77°
July 3,	Merriam's cow-watering place, beyond Gowing's Swamp,	83°
July 3,	Spring in Holbrook's ditch,	58°

Places where cows drink were apparently at this date from 75° up to 83°.

In the afternoon of July 3d, when the air at our house at 2 o'clock was 82°, a breezy afternoon, [on] the little arrowhead desert on Sted Buttrick's land on the Great Fields, the thermometer, being buried an inch and three quarters deep, rose to 90°; at three inches deep, to 86°; lying flat on the surface, back up, to 86°; held in air above to 84°. That is, at this time of day, say mid-afternoon, it is warmer at two to three inches beneath the surface in such sand (where turtles bury their eggs) than in the air above. Indeed, I should think that in the hottest weather the eggs would be half cooked here.

At two to three inches deep in a half-deserted large

[1] *Vide* June 22d and 30th, 1855; also July 2d and 3d, 1855.

[2] *Vide* Aug. 23d and 24th and Aug. 10th; and Aug. 22d for Bittern Cliff.

ant-hill on Holbrook's path, it rose to 102°, — this was loose and gravelly, — or some 18° higher than in the air. This shows how much heat a sandy and porous soil may detain.

N. B. — My experiments were vitiated by my having to cover the thermometer with the sand which was taken up both from the surface and from below, and not waiting for the whole to acquire the same temperature with the surrounding soil of the same depth.

It appears that in a cold day at present the water of the river at 6 A. M. will be ten to fourteen degrees warmer than the air, and accordingly feels warm to the touch. In the translation into English of Cranz's "Greenland" from High Dutch (1767) I find "an elve or mountain spring," and again "Salmon elves, or the little streams from the hills."

July 8. Yesterday was quite hazy, with an east wind. This morning there is a cold mist, which soon becomes rain, — at 2.30 P. M. The thermometer is at 66°, and some sit by fires.

July 9. Clears up at noon.

See two handsome rose-breasted grosbeaks on the Corner causeway. One utters a peculiar squeaking or snapping note, and, both by form of bill and this note, and color, reminds me of some of those foreign birds with great bills in cages.

There is a smart shower at 5 P. M., and in the midst of it a hummingbird is busy about the flowers in the garden, unmindful of it, though you would think that

Vol. XIII

each big drop that struck him would be a serious accident.

July 10. 2 P. M. — To Pleasant Meadow *via* Lincoln Bridge.

The *Festuca ovina* is a peculiar light-colored, whitish grass, as contrasted with the denser dark-green sod of pastures; as on the swells by the tin-hole near Brister's.

Entering J. Baker's great mud-hole, this cloudy, cool afternoon, I was exhilarated by the mass of cheerful bright-yellowish light reflected from the sedge (*Carex Pennsylvanica*) growing densely on the hillsides laid bare within a year or two there. It is of a distinct cheerful yellow color even this overcast day, even as if they were reflecting a bright sunlight, though no sun is visible. It is surprising how much this will light up a hillside or upland hollow or plateau, and when, in a clear day, you look toward the sun over it late in the afternoon, the scene is incredibly bright and elysian. These various lights and shadows of the grass make the charm of a walk at present.

I find in this mud-hole a new grass, *Eatonia Pennsylvanica*, two and a half feet high.

Juncus, apparently *marginatus*, say ten days.

July 11. Heavy rain in the night [of the] 10th–11th. An unusual quantity of rain within a week past; too much now for our garden. The lower leaves of vines yellowed.

To-day and yesterday are cool and comfortable days, with a breeze. Thermometer at 2 P. M., 70 to 77.

2 P. M. — To Pine Hill.

Herd's-grass and red-top in prime. I often notice them growing in parallel rows of reddish and green, the seed apparently having fallen so.

Haying is now generally under way.

As I go along the railroad causeways, I am interested now, and of late, by those patches a rod or two over — amid the red-top, herd's-grass, etc., of A. Wheeler's meadow — of *Agrostis scabra*, that exceedingly fine slender-branched grass drooping and waving in the wind. It gives a pale pinkish(?)-purple sheen to those parts, completely monopolizing (apparently) the ground there. It makes the most purple impression of any grass. Call it early purple grass, as compared with the *Eragrostis pectinacea*. Probably it is not quite in prime. It is the most finely branched and slender-culmed for its size, and near at hand the most invisible of any grass at present, and less noticeable close at hand than in a favorable light at a distance. You will see, thus, scattered over a meadow, little flecks and patches of it, almost like a flat purplish cobweb of the morning, and it seems to recline on the other grasses. It is the finest hair that waves in the fields now; Proserpine's hair.

Find a yellow butterfly about dead, probably in consequence of the heavy rain of last night.

In the pool in Laurel Glen, *Glyceria acutiflora* almost.[1]

I look at a young fox at Derby's. You would say from his step and motions that his legs were as elastic

[1] Out long since and now going to seed generally and very abundant, in wettest part of Great Meadows, about Holt.

as india-rubber, — all springs, ready at any instant to bound high into the air. Gravity seems not enough to keep him in contact with the earth. There seems to be a peculiar principle of resiliency constantly operating in him.

River at 7 P. M. eight and a half inches above summer level.

July 12. Hear a nuthatch in the street. So they breed here.

The best way to drink, especially at a shallow spring, or one so sunken below the surface as to be difficult to reach, is through a tube. You can commonly find growing near a spring a hollow reed or weed of some kind suitable for this purpose, such as rue or touch-me-not or water saxifrage, or you can carry one in your pocket.

Juncus militaris.

The river at 8 P. M. is eight and three quarters inches above summer level.

Just after the sun is set I observe the dewdrops on the pontederia leaves. (Do not know how early they begin to form.) Even when the leaf stands perpendicular, the drop is collected at the uppermost point, and then, on a slight jar or agitation of the water, runs down the leaf. This is the only broad and thick leaf that rises above the water, and therefore it appears to be the only one that collects the dew thus early.

A Mr. Bradshaw, taxidermist, carpenter, etc., etc., of Wayland, tells me that he finds the long-eared owl there in summer, and has set it up.

Vol. XIII

willows over the river, and for some days have seen them on the telegraph-wires.

Observed a huckleberry bush springing from the top of a large and high white pine stump that had been sawed off. It stood in the chink between the bark and the wood, and had evidently come from a seed dropped by a bird, which had blown into this crack.

A heavy shower (with thunder) just before noon this morning, and more in the west of us in the afternoon.

July 14. 2 P. M. — To Botrychium Swamp.

Botrychium Virginianum apparently in prime. *Alopecurus aristulatus* past prime. Pratt's Pond side. Perceive now the light-colored tops of chestnuts in bloom, and, when I come near them, an offensive, sickening odor, somewhat like that of the barberry blossoms, but worse.

Returning, I notice on a large pool of water in A. Heywood's cow-yard a thick greenish-yellow scum mantling it, an exceedingly rich and remarkable color, as if it were covered with a coating of sulphur. This sort of scum seems to be peculiar to cow-yards, and contrasts with that red one by the Moore's Swamp road last summer. Out of foulness Nature thus extracts beauty. These phenomena are observed only in summer or warm weather, methinks.

7 P. M. — On river.

Water ten and five eighths above summer level; probably about done rising.

The spartina grass.

July 13. 2 P. M. — To Little Truro.

You now especially notice some very red fields where the red-top grass grows luxuriantly and is now in full bloom, — a red purple, passing into brown, looking at a distance like a red-sandstone soil. The different cultivated fields are thus like so many different-colored checkers on a checker-board. First we had the June-grass reddish-brown, and the sorrel red, of June; now the red-top red of July. For a week — and if you look very closely, for a fortnight or more — past, the season has had a more advanced look, from the reddening, imbrowning, or yellowing, and ripening of many grasses, as the sweet-scented vernal (for some time generally withered) and the June-grass, and some grain, — rye, wheat, etc., — so that the fields and hillsides present a less liquid green than they did. The vernal freshness of June is passed. Our mowing-fields new laid down with herds'-grass, red-top, and clover — *i. e.* the second year — are red or reddish squares divided regularly with greener herd's-top [*sic*] in parallel lines, probably the seed, of different weight, having fallen thus, the red spaces often eight or ten feet wide. The various colors or tints of grasses, in some large pasture for instance, especially in cloudy weather, supply the place of light and shade. The pasture is distinctly parded with them half a mile off, — the very light, whitish *Festuca ovina*, the dark-green *Poa compressa*, and rounded yellow patches of sedge (*Carex scoparia*, etc.).

Observed last night young swallows roosting on the

I look for dewdrops on the pontederia, but see none at first; but finally, looking in a still and shady place behind some willows, I see many drops fully formed sparkling in the light, at just eight minutes after seven by my watch (the sun sets at thirty-five minutes after seven; say, then, half an hour before sunset). But, it being windy, I did not notice any *generally*, even long after sunset.

Also looked to see if the lilies withdraw under water at night, as stated in Mrs. Lincoln's Botany. The buds which opened and closed to-day, and other buds, now rest half an inch or more deep in the water, which they would naturally do by their form and weight. When they open in the morning they will probably rest more buoyantly on the surface, but I have never discovered that they withdrew under water.

The fowl-meadow grass is now in prime and covering the islands very densely. It has a purplish tinge and a very green culm contrasting with its panicle.

The surface of the earth in summer is painted of various shades of green in mowing and pasture and meadow and some waste land by the grasses. The *Agrostis vulgaris* of pastures and hilltops is a dark green, the *Festuca ovina* a very light (even whitish) green. How rich some fields of red-top at present! Perfect squares, it may be, like rich carpets spread out, and contrasting with very different tints of green next to them.

The true grasses (excepting the grains) which thus at a distance paint the landscape *generally* at this season or earlier are (1) herd's-grass, (2) red-top, (3) *Agrostis scabra*, (4) blue-joint (?), (5) June-grass, (6) *Poa com-*

pressa, (7) fowl-meadow, (8) sheep's fescue, (9) piper grass (?), (10) vernal grass, (11) canary grass, especially Nos. 5, 2, 8, 6, 1; but of these only one (8), probably, is indigenous, and Nos. 5, 6, 10, 11 are now generally done.

The *Cyperaceæ* which now or earlier color the landscape generally by their mass are (1) *Carex Pennsylvanica*, (2) *C. scoparia*, (3) *monile*, (4) *stellulata*, (5) *lanuginosa*, (6) *bullata*, (7) *siccata*, (8) *crinita*, (9) *lupulina*, (10) *Scirpus eriophorum*, (11) *Eleocharis acicularis*, (12) *Scirpus lacustris*, (13) eriophorums, etc. Nos. 1 and 7 give a yellow hue to upland open wilds or woodlands and dry hollows, where the forest has recently stood, — *not pastured*. 3, 4, 5, 6, 9, 10 make the mass of the sedge on the river meadows, of a general yellow hue; 2 and 8 flourish more about their edges; 11 greens the muddy banks at low water; and 12 stands in dark-green patches here and there along the muddy shores of the river.

July 15. It seemed to me yesterday that the foliage had attained its maximum of darkness, and as I ascended the hill at eve the hickories looked even autumnal. Especially I was struck by the dark but still perfect green leaf of the swamp white oak.

I hear this forenoon the *link link* of the first bobolink going over our garden, — though I hear several full strains of bobolinks to-day, as in May, carrying me back to Apple Sunday, but they have been rare a long time. Now as it were the very cope of the dark-glazed heavens yields a slightly metallic sound when struck.

I hear on all sides these days the loud tinkling rattle of the mowing-machine, but, alas, the mower goes to the blacksmith's to whet his scythe only every second or third day!

P. M. — To Hill and Assabet Bath.

On Hill. — No crops clothe the earth with richer hues and make a greater impression of luxuriousness than the cultivated grasses. Field after field, densely packed like the squares of a checker-board, all through and about the villages, paint the earth with various shades of green and other colors. There is the rich glaucous green of young grain now, of various shades, depending on its age and kind; the flashing blades of corn which does not yet hide the bare ground; the yellowing tops of ripening grain; the dense uniform red of red-top, the most striking and high-colored of all (that is, cultivated); the very similar purple of the fowl-meadow (the most deep-piled and cumulous-looking, like down) along the low river-banks; the very dark and dusky, as it were shadowy, green of herd's-grass at a distance, as if clouds were always passing over it, — close at hand it is of a dark purplish or slaty purple, from the color of its anthers; the fresh light green where June-grass has been cut, and the fresh dark green where clover has been cut; and the hard, dark green of pastures (red-top) generally, — not to speak of the very light-colored wiry fescue there.

The solid square fields of red-top look singularly like bare ground at a distance, but when you know it to be red-top you see it to be too high-colored for that. Yet it thus suggests a harmony between itself and the

Vol. XIII

ground. Look down on a field of red-top now in full bloom, a quarter of a mile west of this hill, — a very dense and red field, — at 2.30 P. M. of this very warm and slightly hazy but not dogdayish day, in a blazing sun. I am surprised to see a very distinct white vapor, like a low cloud in a mountainous country, or a smoke, drifting along close over the red-top. Is it not owing to the contrast between this hot noontide air and the moist coolness of that dense grass-field?

Then there is the cheerful yellowish green of the meadows, where the sedges prevail, *i. e.* yellowest where wettest, with darker patches and veins of grass, etc., in the higher and drier parts. I can just distinguish with my naked eye — knowing where to look — the darker green of pipes on the peat meadows two miles from the hill.

The potato-fields are a very dark green.

July 16. 2 P. M. — To Great Meadows by boat.

You notice now along the river, on the muddy shores, the dry (and closed) whitish heads of the canary grass, standing high above its yet fresh green leaves. It forms only narrow, dense patches a few rods in length. The banks of the Great Meadows are red-top, and (is it not?) *Agrostis scabra* (the fine long-branched, yet branching again often below the middle) and fowl-meadow on the lower parts of the bank commonly. The *Glyceria acutiflora* is abundant and now going to seed in the wettest part of the Holt portion of the meadow. That which I have called the *Poa dentata* of Torrey is a very common grass in ditches and other wet places, especially

with the last-named at the Holt, and is now mostly done. I should think it might be an undescribed species of *Glyceria*.

Setaria viridis, Channing's garden, probably two or three days.

I notice the fruit of the bur-reed (opposite Prichard Shore), now large, pickle-green, and about as big as that of the upper Sudbury meadows; so I think it is the same, though not so rank.

In the bays by the riverside where the pads have been least eaten, I see at least three times as many of the three kinds mixed as can lie on that surface, one overlapping and crowding another and the more exposed curled up on their edges; but they are so much riddled already and eaten by insects that this abundant supply is needed. It is an abundant vegetable food apparently for many kinds. I see a large tuft of pontederia whose leaves have been slit longitudinally into a dozen parallel slits, — not always clear out, — and so they hang in ribbons; and there is a downy feather of a bird attached to one. Could it have been done by some water-fowl?

Pipes have been out of bloom apparently a long time.

Standing amid the pipes of the Great Meadow, I hear a very sharp creaking *peep*, no doubt from a rail quite near me, calling to or directing her young, who are meanwhile uttering a very faint, somewhat similar peep, which you would not hear if not very much inclined to hear it, in the grass close around me. Sometimes the old bird utters two short, sharp creaks. I look sharp, but can see nothing of them. She sounds now here, now there, within two or three rods of me, incessantly running in the grass. I had already heard, more distant, a more prolonged note from some water-fowl, perhaps a plover, if not possibly a male rail, here-abouts.

The *Ailantus glandulosus* (Warren's yard), in its height probably on Saturday, 14th, filled the streets with a disagreeable sickish odor much like that of the chestnut. I should put this, the chestnut, and the barberry together.

July 17. 2 P. M. — To Walden.

The soft sand on the bottom of Walden, as deep as I can wade, feels very warm to my feet, while the water feels cold. This may be partly a mere sensation, but I suspect that the sand is really much warmer than the water and that some creatures take refuge in it accordingly, that much heat passes through the water and is absorbed in the sand. Yet when I let a thermometer lie on the bottom and draw it up quickly I detect no difference between the temperature of the bottom and of the water at the surface. Probably it would have been different if the thermometer had been buried in the sand.

The air at 2 P. M. was 77; Walden near the shore is 76, in the middle, 74°; and when I let down a thermometer some sixty feet and draw it up quickly, I get no lower than 74°, but it may have risen as it came up.

The nighthawk's ripping sound, heard overhead these days, reminds us that the sky is, as it were, a roof, and that our world is limited on that side, it being reflected as from a roof back to earth. It does not suggest an

Vol. XIII

grayish light beneath it, — which so darkened the streets and houses that seamstresses complained that they could not see to thread a needle, and for a few minutes rain fell in a deluge, the gutters ran full, and there was a whirlpool at every grating. This month has been remarkably wet, and the haymakers are having very catching weather.

2 P. M. — Up river in boat.

The pontederia is now generally conspicuous and handsome, — a very fresh blue, — with no stale flowers.

You now see great beds of polygonums above the surface getting ready to bloom, and the dulichium stands thick in shallow water, while in the cultivated ground the pigweed, butterweed, and Roman wormwood, and amaranth are now rank and conspicuous weeds. One troublesome rank weed in the garden now is the *Panicum Crus-galli*, — its great rather flat spreading branches. I see one just out.

I hear now that very fine pittering sound of a locust or cricket in the grass.

The *Juncus militaris* is commonly, but freshly, out.

We come to a standstill and study the pads in the J. Hosmer bulrush bog. There are on the pads, eating them, not only many black slugs or grubs, but a great many small dark-brown beetles, a quarter of an inch long, with a pale-brown edge, copulating; also other beetles, skaters, and flies (small brownish, large-winged flies in numbers together), and a variety of eggs are fastened to the pads, many in little round pinkish patches. I see one purplish patch exactly in the form of the point of a leaf, with a midrib, veins, and a bristle-

infinite depth in the sky, but a nearness to the earth, as of a low roof echoing back its sounds.

Eleocharis acicularis still blooms.

The sternothærus in Walden has a smooth, clean shell, rather prettily marked, it is so clean, and would by many be taken for a different species from that of the river, which is commonly colored with mud and moss. I take two into the boat, and they think it enough when they have merely hidden their *heads* in a corner.

Also the great bullfrogs which sit out on the stones every two or three rods all around the pond are singularly clean and handsome bullfrogs, with fine yellow throats sharply separated from their pickle-green heads by their firmly shut mouths, and with beautiful eyes. They sit thus imperturbable, often under a pile of brush, at nearly regular intervals. An English taxidermist of Wayland (a cockney) told me the other day that he would have set up a bullfrog, it has so beautiful a "hie," but he could not buy a bullfrog's "hie" in the market.

July 18. 2 P. M. — To Second Division.

The *Asclepias Cornuti* is abundantly visited nowadays by a large orange-brown butterfly with dark spots and with silver spots beneath. Wherever the asclepias grows you see them.

The Second Division juncus is already withering and is considerably browned, so early is it. It appears not to ripen any seed.

July 19. A very dark cloud came up from the west this forenoon, — a dark curtain rolled up, with a

like point, calculated to deceive; this lying on the pad. Some small *erect* pontederia leaves are white with eggs on the under side as if painted.

There are small open spaces amid the pads, — little deeps bottomed and surrounded with brown and ruddy hornwort like coral, — whose every recess is revealed in the sunlight. Here hundreds of minnows of various sizes and species are poised, comparatively safe from their foes, and commonly a red spider is seen making its way from side to side of the deep.

The rich crimson under sides (with their regularly branching veins) of some white lily pads surpasses the color of most flowers. No wonder the spiders are red that swim beneath; and think of the fishes that swim beneath this crimson canopy, — beneath a crimson sky. I can frequently trace the passage of a boat, a pickerel-fisher, perhaps, by the crimson under sides of the pads upturned.

The pads crowd and overlap each other in most amicable fashion. Sometimes one lobe of a yellow lily pad is above its neighbor, while the other is beneath, and frequently I see where a little heart-leaf (now showing its green spidery rays) has emerged by the stem, in the sinus of a great nuphar leaf, and is outspread in the very midst of it. The pads are rapidly consumed, but fresh ones are all the while pushing up and unrolling. They push up and spread out in the least crevice that offers.

Upland haying is past prime, and they are working into the low ground. None mowing on the Great Meadows yet.

I noticed on the 16th that the darkness of the pipes was not obvious, the sedge is now comparatively so dark.

Minott, who sits alone confined to his room with dropsy, observed the other day that it was a cold summer. He knew it was cold; the whip-poor-will told him so. It sung once and then stopped.

July 20. 2 P. M. — To Walden.

Warm weather, — 86 at 2 P. M. (not so warm for a good while).

Emerson's lot that was burnt, between the railroad and the pond, has been cut off within the last three months, and I notice that the oak sprouts have commonly met with a check after growing one or two feet, and small reddish leafets have again put forth at the extremity within a week or so, as in the spring. Some of the oak sprouts are five to six feet high already.

On his hill near by, where the wood was cut about two years ago, this second growth of the oaks, especially white oaks, is much more obvious, and commenced longer ago. The shoots of this year are generally about two feet long, but the first foot consists of large dark-green leaves which expanded early, before the shoot met with a check. This is surmounted by another foot of smaller yellowish-green leaves. This is very generally the case, and produces a marked contrast. Dark-green bushes surmounted by a light or yellowish-green growth.

Sometimes, in the first-mentioned sprout-land, you see where the first shoot withered, as if frost-bitten at

the end, and often only some large buds have formed there as yet. Many of these sprouts, the rankest of them, are fated to fall, being but slightly joined to the stump, riddled by ants there; and others are already prostrated.

Bathing on the side of the deep cove, I noticed just below the high-water line (of rubbish) quite a number of little pines which have just sprung up amid the stones and sand and wreck, some with the seed atop. This, then, is the state of their coming up naturally. They have evidently been either washed up, or have blown across the ice or snow to this shore. If pitch pine, they were probably blown across the pond, for I have often seen them on their way across.

Both *Scirpus subterminalis* and *debilis* are now in bloom at the Pout's Nest, the former the longest time, the water being very low and separated from the pond. The former out for some time, the latter not long.

Great numbers of pollywogs have apparently just changed into frogs. At the pondlet on Hubbard's land, now separated from the main pond by a stony bar, hundreds of small frogs are out on the shore, enjoying their new state of existence, masses of them, which, with constant plashing, go hopping into the water a rod or more before me, where they are very swift to conceal themselves in the mud at the bottom. Their bodies may be one and a half inches long or more. I have rarely seen so many frogs together. Yet I hardly see one pollywog left in this pool.

Yet at the shore against Pout's Nest I see many pollywogs, and some, with hind legs well grown beside

their tails, lie up close to the shore on the sand with their heads out like frogs, apparently already breathing air before losing their tails. They squat and cower there as I come by, just like frogs.

July 21. A rainy day; half an inch of rain falls, spoiling much hay. This is so wet a season that the grass is still growing fast and most things are very fresh.

The leaves generally do not get to be perfect till the middle of July, when they are of a dark, hard, glossy green, *e. g.* the swamp white oak.

6 P. M. — Up Assabet.

Now, after the rain, the sun coming forth brightly, the swallows in numbers are skimming low over the river just below the junction.

Considerable bur-reed, vallisneria, and heart-leaf has been washed up against the weeds and pads along the sides of the river of late.

The canary grass standing so high and densely, with its now very light-brown closed heads, looks more like grain at a distance than any of our wild grasses, as you look down the river from the junction.

July 22. 2 P. M. — 70°, and, with a breeze, cool. To Annursnack.

See in the ditch by the roadside on Colburn Hill a box turtle which was crushed some time ago, and there is the mark of the wheel that passed over him. It is remarkable that, though I have seen but four or five of these turtles in this town, two at least of them had been crushed by a wheel, — that, few as they are, they

should have got in the way of a wheel. I found another on the railroad once, southeast of this, on a part of the same dry region, and one on the dry plain under Fair Haven Hill.

In the path through Hosmer's pines beyond the Assabet, see a wood turtle — whose shell has apparently had one or two mouthfuls taken out of it on the sides — eating in a leisurely manner a common pink-topped toadstool some two inches in diameter, which it had knocked down and half consumed. Its jaws were covered with it.

The butterflies at present are chiefly on the Canada thistle and the mayweed. I see on the last, in the road beyond Colburn Hill, a surprising number of the small reddish (small copper) butterflies, for a dozen rods.

The leek will apparently bloom very soon. I see the stigmas, I think. What a surprising and stately plant! Its great flower-stem stands now a little aslant, some fifteen or eighteen inches high, regular[ly] beset with its great thick leaves, gradually lessening upward to its massy head. It has a peculiarly columnar appearance, like the Leaning Tower of Pisa.

Yesterday having been a rainy day, the air is now remarkably clear and cool and you rarely see the horizon so distinct. The surface of the earth, especially looking westward, — grass grounds, pastures, and meadows, — is remarkably beautiful. I stand in Heywood's pasture west of the leek and, leaning over the wall, look westward. All things — grass, etc. — are peculiarly fresh this season on account of the copious rains.

The next field on the west slopes gently from both east and west to a meadow in the middle. So, as I look over the wall, it is first dark-green, where white clover has been cut (still showing a myriad low white heads which resound with the hum of bees); next, along the edge of the bottom or meadow, is a strip or belt three or four rods wide of red-top, uncut, perfectly distinct; then the cheerful bright-yellow sedge of the meadow, yellow almost as gamboge; then a corresponding belt of red-top on its upper edge, quite straight and rectilinear like the first; then a glaucous-green field of grain still quite low; and, in the further corner of the field, a much darker square of green than any yet, all brilliant in this wonderful light. You thus have **a sort of terrestrial rainbow, thus:** —

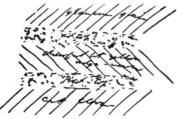

The farmer accustomed to look at his crops from a mercenary point of view is not aware how beautiful they are. This prospect was really exciting, even as a rainbow is. Then the next pasture on the northwest, where it sloped toward me gently, a smooth velvet or impalpable green slope, with here and there the lightest cobwebby touch of lighter green like a dew on it, where a little fescue grass still made an impression in spite of

the cows. These soft, indefinite lighter touches on the dark-green enamelled slope! It was like a delicately watered surface, and here and there stood on it a few young hickories, their stems and their umbrage both as black as a coal; and further, just this side the wall over which the clear light came, some low bushes, probably sumach, reflected a hoary, silvery light. You can tell the crops afar off by their color. The next, more springy pasture on the north was all lit up with yellow ferns.

Smooth sumach apparently in prime, and handsome as a spiræa. The flies that rain about your head in woods, how long? Hills (not so far off as to be blue) are now a yellowish brown from the withered heads of grass. Pastures generally a brownish tinge. First locust heard.

July 23. The button-bush is but just fairly beginning here and there.

Still more rain this forenoon, but chiefly clouds. We have had several thunder-showers this month in the forenoon, it clearing off bright by the afternoon.

I saw the other day where the lightning on the 12th or 13th had struck the telegraph-posts at Walden Pond. It had shattered five posts in succession, they being a dozen rods apart, spoiling them entirely; though all of them *stood* but one, yet they were a mere wrack of splinters through which you could look. It had omitted a great many more posts and struck half a dozen more at a great distance from these on each side. The furthest I noticed was near by the second mile-post, the nearest midway the causeway. And at the same time

there was a smart shock, an explosion, at the operating office at the depot, two miles off from the furthest point. I should think, speaking from memory, that the posts struck were the oldest and dampest, or most rotten. At one or two posts it had plainly entered the ground and plowed toward the railroad-track, slightly injuring it. It struck a pitch pine standing within four or five feet of the wire, leaving a white seam down one side of it, also two large oaks a little further off. This was where the telegraph ran parallel to, and a few feet only from, a wood. It also struck a small oak on the opposite side of the track. The lightning struck for two miles (!!) at least.

2 P. M. — By boat to Conantum.

It has cleared up fairly.

The late rose is now in prime along the river, a pale rose-color but very delicate, keeping up the memory of roses. Also the *Lilium Canadense* is apparently in prime and very abundant in College Meadow.

So far as leaves are concerned, one of the most noticeable phenomena of this green-leaf season is the conspicuous reflection of light in clear breezy days from the silvery under sides of some.

All trees and shrubs which have light-colored or silvery under sides to their leaves, but especially the swamp white oak and the red maple, are now very bright and conspicuous in the strong wind after the rain of the morning. Indeed, now that the leaves are so numerous they are more noticeable than ever, but you must be on the windward side. Some, as the *Salix alba*, are thus silvered only at the top and extremities, the

younger leaves alone being sufficiently appressed to show their under sides. But the two kinds first mentioned are the most generally conspicuous, and these forming commonly the front rank, — especially at the base of hills, — behind which grow other oaks, and birches, pines, etc., you see the whole outline of these trees, waving and rustling in the breeze against that darker green, suggesting frostwork, or as if etched in silver on a green ground. To be sure, most, if not all leaves, not to mention grasses, are a paler green beneath, and hence the oaks and other trees behind show various shades of green, which would be more observed if it were not for these stronger contrasts. Though the wind may not be very strong nor incessant, you appear to see *only* the under sides of those first named, and they make a uniform impression, as if their leaves, having been turned up, were permanently held so. Before the wind arose, the wooded shore and hillsides were an almost uniform green, but now the whole outline of the swamp white oaks and maples is revealed by the wind — a sort of magic, a "presto change" — distinctly against trees whose leaves are nearly of the same color with the upper sides of these.

Some of the swamp white oaks, whose leaves are but slightly turned up, look as if crisped by frost. The grape leaf also, where it occurs, is sufficiently conspicuous. Thus the leaves take an airing. It is like etching on silverware. If you look sharply, you perceive also the paler under sides of the oaks and birches in the background contrasting with the darker upper sides of their lower leaves. In a maple swamp every maple-top stands now distinguished thus from the birches in their midst. Before they were confounded, but a wind comes and lifts their leaves, showing their lighter under sides, and suddenly, as by magic, the maple stands out from the birch. There is a great deal of life in this landscape. What an airing the leaves get! Perchance it is necessary that their under sides be thus exposed to the light and air in order that they may be hardened and darkened by it.

At the same time with this, and indeed for about a week, I have seen some maples of both kinds just beginning to show a ruddy tinge, and I think that this is really for the most part an evidence of feebleness, for I see that one or two white maples standing in wet places, which have been thus premature, have finally died.

I see a snake crossing the river at Hubbard's Bridge as swiftly as a muskrat could, which, indeed, I at first took it for, — faster than a muskrat would.

I find the ripest blueberries (*Vaccinium vacillans*) not on the very top nor on the lower slope, but on the brow, or what is called the "pitch," of the hill (Conantum) toward the light. The ripest are of course the largest, and this year very large and hard and bead-like.

Slender early spiranthes noticed.

I read of the Amazon that its current, indeed, is strong, but the wind always blows up the stream. This sounds too good to be true.

July 24. The carpenter working for Edward Hoar in Lincoln caught, two or three days ago, an exhausted or half-famished golden-winged warbler alive in their

yard. It was within half a mile that I saw one a few weeks ago. It is a sufficiently well-marked bird, by the large yellow spot on the wing (the greater coverts), yellow front and crown, and the very distinct black throat and, I should say, upper breast, above which white divided by a broad black line through the eye. Above blue-gray, with much yellowish-green dusting or reflection, *i. e.* edging, to the feathers.

Many a field where the grass has been cut shows now a fresh and very lit-up light green as you look toward the sun. This is a remarkably cool day. Thermometer 72° at 2 P. M.

The song of the field sparrow sounds more prominent of late, and quite rich and varied, and methinks I begin to hear the warbling vireo more?

July 25. P. M. — To Mr. Bradshaw's, Wayland, with Ed. Hoar.

I was surprised to see among the birds which Bradshaw has obtained the little auk of Nuttall (*Mergulus alle*, or common sea-dove), which he says that he shot in the fall on the pond of the Assabet at Knight's factory. There were two, and the other was killed with a paddle. It is said in Wilson, though apparently not *by* him, that "with us it is a very rare bird, and when seen it is generally in the vicinity of the sea." One was sent to him from Great Egg Harbor in December, 1811, as a great curiosity, and this is the one described. Rarely visits Great Britain; is found as far north as Spitzbergen at least. "The Greenlanders call it the Ice-bird from the circumstance of its being the harbinger of ice." "It

grows fat in the stormy season, from the waves bringing plenty of crabs and small fish within its reach." Nuttall says its appearance here is always solitary; driven here by stress of weather; that it has been seen in Fresh Pond, and Audubon found a few breeding in Labrador. Giraud says, "In the United States it is rare." "I am informed [it] [1] is occasionally seen by the fishermen of Egg Harbor." Is that on Long Island? [2] Says one was killed at "Raynor South," and it is said to breed on the arctic coast. Ross's party fed on them on the west coast of Greenland. Peabody says: "In hardiness and power of enduring cold, no bird exceeds them. . . . In Newfoundland they are called the Ice-bird, from the presumption that, unless extreme cold were approaching, they would not come so far from home. Those that are found in this state are generally exhausted by their long flight; some have quietly submitted to be taken by the hand. They are not regular visitants, but occasional solitary wanderers."

Was also surprised to see the fork-tailed stormy petrel (*Thalassidroma Leachii*) in his collection, which he caught exhausted near his house, and I think that he said his boy found another dead. Brewer says, "Habitat from Massachusetts to Newfoundland." Wilson says that one of the other species (*T. Wilsonii*) was shot on the Schuylkill near Philadelphia, and that they are sometimes found in the interior of Great Britain. Giraud says that the former, like the last, "is of rare

[1] [The brackets are Thoreau's.]
[2] [Great Egg Harbor and Little Egg Harbor are on the New Jersey coast.]

occurrence on the shores of Long Island," and, under the *T. Wilsonii*, that "the Petrel is never seen inland except when driven in, as it occasionally happens, by severe storms." Baird wrote to him shortly after the gale in August, 1842. "You have probably seen an account in the papers of the Petrels which had been driven inland by the storm of August. They were nearly all the Fork-tailed Petrel, Thalassidroma Leachii. I saw about half a dozen specimens killed near Washington. They were killed in Petersburgh and Bewfort, Va., and many other places." According to Peabody, Audubon makes the fork-tailed to be much more abundant on the coast of Massachusetts than the *T. Wilsonii*, and about vessels to be the most suspicious of the three. P. says, "I have had one brought to me which was taken near Chicopee River in Springfield, 70 miles from the shore."

He had also the *Ardea exilis*, or least bittern, which he obtained on his river meadow. He sees it there occasionally and has set it up before, though it is not so common as the *viridis*. He sees it stand on the pads. It is considerably less than the *viridis* and more tawny or tawny-brown. Wilson says it "is the smallest known species of the whole tribe," and that, like the *viridis*, they skulk by day and feed by night. Peabody says, "They are seldom seen, as they rise only in sudden alarm."

He also has the long-eared owl (*Strix otus*), which he killed in the woods behind his house. Wilson says, "Except in size, this species has more resemblance to the Great Horned Owl than any other of its tribe." Probably the same with the European. Peabody says it "is never common" in Massachusetts. Giraud has seen it in his neighborhood only in the winter.

He has the *Rallus Carolinianus*, and says that he sees another kind as common as this on the river meadows there, — a true rail, but with a much longer bill. He is very confident about it and has killed and set them up. It is undoubtedly the *R. Virginianus*, or lesser clapper rail, which, as he had already said, corresponded to an English rail which he knew. So we have this in Concord, no doubt.

He has the *Sylvia maculosa*, shot near his house. Bluish-ash above, I believe, head or crown the same, yellow throat and beneath, with many blackish spots and marks [?] on sides and breast, and white spots on inner vanes of tail-feathers, the tail being blackish.

Has two specimens of what he called the crow black-bird, shot by his house in the spring. They appeared to me surprisingly large, and he had furnished them with yellow irides, which he says are like the original ones. Nuttall says that the *Quiscalus major* has a yellow iris, the other a silvery iris. Brewer says that the former resembles the latter "to a great degree, differing from it principally in size and in its concave tail." This of Bradshaw's measured about fourteen inches long. He says these two were larger than others with them. The vertical depth of bill at base was that assigned to the *Q. versicolor* by Nuttall. As set up, I think that the tail was not convex.

Passed a field in Wayland occupied by so worthless a crop to *the farmer* as to attract attention, — a very undulating gravelly and stony field filled with johns-

wort (in its prime), sorrel (still red-seeded), and mulleins, between which, however, you saw the gravel, — yet very pleasant to the naturalist.

July 26. 2 P. M. — To Walden.

Rhyncospora alba, perhaps as long as *fusca*, toward east part of Hubbard's Close, *i. e.* arethusa part. Rusty cotton-grass abundant, but also going and gone to seed, say a fortnight, in same place. Common cranberry still lingers in bloom there, though berries are half grown.

Methinks the leaves begin to rustle generally, *i. e.* with a harder rustle, about June 11th, when they begin to show light under sides in the breeze.

I saw a bream swimming about in that smaller pool by Walden in Hubbard's Wood, though entirely cut off from the pond now. So they may be well off in the Wyman meadow or Pout's Nest.

July 27. A. M. — Pretty heavy rain last night.

The day after a heavy rain, I can detect all the poor or sappy shingles on my neighbor's low roof which I overlook, for they, absorbing much water and not drying for a long time, are so many black squares spotting the gray roof.

2 P. M. — Sail and paddle down river.

The water has begun to be clear and sunny, revealing the fishes and countless minnows of all sizes and colors, this year's brood.

I see healthy blossoms of the front-rank polygonum just fairly begun.

Vol. XIII

I see running on the muddy shore under the pontederia a large flat and thin-edged brown bug (with six legs), some seven eighths of an 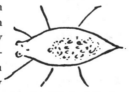 inch long, pointed behind; with apparently its eggs, fifty or sixty in number, large and dark-colored, standing side by side on their ends and forming a very conspicuous patch which covers about a third of its flat upper surface. I remove one with my knife, and it appears to stand in a thick glutinous matter. It runs through the water and mud, and falls upon its back a foot or more from my hand without dislodging them.

See, twenty rods or more down-stream, four or five young ducks, which appear already to be disturbed by my boat. So, leaving that to attract their attention, I make my way alongshore in the high grass and behind the trees till I am opposite to them. At a distance they appear simply black and white, as they swim deep, — black backs and white throats. Now I find that they have retreated a little into the pontederia, and are very busily diving, or dipping, not immersing their whole bodies, but their heads and shoulders while their bodies are perfectly perpendicular, just like tame ducks. All of them close together will be in this attitude at the same moment. I now see that the throat, and probably upper part, at least, of breast, is clear-white, and there is a clear line of white above eye and on neck within a line of black; and as they stand on their heads, the tips apparently of their tails (possibly wings??) are conspicuously white or whitish; the upper part, also, is

seen to be brownish rather than black. I presume these to be young summer ducks, though so dark; say two thirds grown.

How easy for the young ducks to hide amid the pickerel-weed along our river, while a boat goes by! and this plant attains its height when these water-fowl are of a size to need its shelter. Thousands of them might be concealed by it along our river, not to speak of the luxuriant sedge and grass of the meadows, much of it so wet as to be inaccessible. These ducks are diving scarcely two feet within the edge of the pickerel-weed, yet one who had not first seen them exposed from a distance would never suspect their neighborhood.

See very great flocks of young red-wing blackbirds.

July 28. 2 P. M. — Up Assabet to Annursnack.

Dulichium spathaceum apparently some days. *Holcus lanatus* long done; very abundant on the west and northwest side of Painted-Cup Meadow.

A man shows me in the street a single bunch of potato-balls (*i. e.* on one stem) twenty in number, several of them quite an inch in diameter and the whole cluster nearly five inches in diameter as it hangs, to some extent emulating a cluster of grapes. The very sight of them supplies my constitution with all needed potash.

Scirpus subterminalis in the Assabet at island above Dove Rock, how long?

July 29. Rain, more or less, by day, and more in the night.

2 p. m. — To Lincoln Bridge by railroad.

Cyperus filiculmis, how long? Some time.

July 30. 2 p. m. — To Martial Miles's Swamp.

Fimbristylis capillaris, probably several days in some places. See very pretty pink yarrow, roadside opposite Whiting's orchard.

See hen-hawks perched. Are they not more at liberty now, their young being better able to shift for themselves, some of them?

Am glad to press my way through Miles's Swamp. Thickets of choke-berry bushes higher than my head, with many of their lower leaves already red, alternating with young birches and raspberry, high blueberry andromeda (high and low), and great dense flat beds of *Rubus sempervirens*. Amid these, perhaps in cool openings, stands an island or two of great dark-green high blueberry bushes, with big cool blueberries, though bearing but sparingly this year.

In a frosty hollow in the woods west of this and of the blackberry field, find a patch of amelanchier, probably *oblongifolia* (??), full of fruit now in its prime. Comparing it with the *Botryapium* of the Cliffs, it appears to be the oblong, being much more obtuse and very little serrate, and not heart-shaped like the *Botryapium*. It is an open sedge hollow surrounded by woods, with some shrubs in it rising above the sedge which have been killed by frost formerly. Here grows a pretty thick patch of the shad-bush, about a rod and a half long, the bushes about three feet high, and quite interesting now, in fruit. Firm dark-green leaves with short, broad,

irregular racemes (cluster-like) of red and dark dull-purplish berries intermixed, making considerable variety in the color, — of peculiar color among our small fruits. The ripest and largest dark-purple berries are just half an inch in diameter. You are surprised and delighted to see this handsome profusion in hollows so dry and usually so barren and bushes commonly so fruitless. These berries are peculiar in that the red are nearly as pleasant-tasted as the more fully ripe dark-purple ones. I think this crop is due to the wetness and coolness of the summer.

Though an agreeable berry, they are hardly so grateful to my palate as huckleberries and blueberries. These conspicuous red — for most are red — [berries] on rather high and thin-leaved bushes, growing open and airy, remind you a little of the wild holly, the berry so contrasts with the dark leaf.

Returning, we come through the midst of the nearly quite dry J. P. B.'s Cold Pool. Excepting a little pool in the middle, this is now one great dense bed of *Cyperus diandrus*, well out, and *Juncus Conradi*, as I call it, now in prime (together with *Juncus acuminatus*). The lower and internal part of this bed is yellow, bright-yellow like sedge, *i. e.* the cyperus stems and leaves, while the spikes of this and the rest form a soft reddish-brown crust, as it were, over all. Mixed with these over the whole area is literally a myriad of gratiola (say in its prime); a most remarkable sight, — countless yellow dots, and occasionally you see a perfectly white one among them.

Quite a sultry day, and smells mustyish, as if dog-days

were beginning. Is it not the height of summer when the locust is heard?

Hear the sound of the first flail, — some farmer, perchance, wishing to make room in his barn, or else wanting the grain. Is it wheat or rye? It may be either.

As I come through Hosmer's potato-field, I see the great clusters of potato-balls on the sandy ground, bespattered with sand, on each side. Methinks they are unusually abundant this year. Somebody has hung up one great cluster at the post-office. Is it owing to the wet and coolness?

July 31. Foggy morning.

M. Pratt sends me *Trifolium agrarium* (a long time out) from a ditch-side on his land, — yellow hop clover. This specimen is two feet high or long. He had not seen it there for some years.

Mr. Bradford finds and brings to me what I judge from a plate in Loudon to be *Potentilla recta* of southern Europe; a long time out. *Vide* press. I find the base of the plant by the east wall, in the road, about six rods south of John Flint's house.

I copy this account of *P. recta* from Persoon: " Fol. septenatis quinatisque, foliol. lanceolatis grosse dentatis, petalis obcordatis cal. majoribus, caule erecto. . . . Ad muros et ad agrorum margines. Pet. magna pallida, calyce submajora." This is under his division with digitate leaves and a naked *receptacle* (?), if this is his word.[1]

But in this the outside of the calyx or receptacle is

[1] It is.

shortly pubescent, and the petals are much longer than the calyx. *Vide* Persoon's other division.[1]

P. M. — Up Assabet.

Decidedly dog-days, and a strong musty scent, not to be wondered at after the copious rains and the heat of yesterday.

At mid-afternoon I am caught in another deluging rain[2] as I stand under a maple by the shore. Looking on a water surface, you can see as well as hear when it rains very hard. At first we had a considerable shower which but slightly dimpled the water, and I saw the differently shaded or lit currents of the river through it all; but anon it began to rain very hard, and there were a myriad white globules dancing or rebounding an inch or two from the surface, where the big drops fell, and I heard a sound as if it rained pebbles or shot. At this season the sound of a gentler rain than this, *i. e.* the sound of the dripping rain on the leaves, which are now dark and *hard*, yields a dry sound as if the drops struck on paper, but six weeks ago, when the leaves were so yellowish and tender, methinks it was a softer sound, as was the rustling.

Now, in the still moonlight, the dark foliage stands almost stiff and dark against the sky.

At 5 p. m. the river is nine and seven eighths inches above summer level.

We may expect to see any common small-seeded European plant springing up by our roadsides in course of time.

[1] Do not find another so much like it.
[2] A great deal fell.

Before it rained hardest I could see in the midst of the dark and smoother water a lighter-colored and rougher surface, generally in oblong patches, which moved steadily down the stream, and this, I think, was the new water from above welling up and making its way downward amid the old. The water or currents of a river are thus not homogeneous, but the surface is seen to be of two shades, the smoother and darker water which already fills its bed [?] and the fresh influx of lighter-colored and rougher, probably more rapid, currents which spot it here and there; *i. e.,* some water seems to occupy it as a lake to some extent, other is passing through it as a stream, — the lacustrine and the fluviatile water. These lighter reaches without reflections (?) are, as it were, water wrong side up. But do I ever see these except when it rains? And are they not the rainwater which has not yet mingled with the water of the river?

END OF VOLUME XIII

Vol. XIII

The Journal of Henry D. Thoreau

VOLUME XIV

(August, 1860 — 1861)

Along the Old Marlborough Road in November

Mt. Monadnock from the Troy Road

CONTENTS

Vol. XIV

Aug. 1. P. M. — To Cliffs.

The earliest corn has shed its pollen, say a week or ten days. Rye, wheat, and oats and barley have bloomed, say a month.

I stand at the wall-end on the Cliffs and look over the Miles meadow on Conantum. It is an unusually clear day after yesterday's rain.

How much of beauty — of color, as well as form — on which our eyes daily rest goes unperceived by us! No one but a botanist is likely to distinguish nicely the different shades of green with which the open surface of the earth is clothed, — not even a landscape-painter if he does not know the species of sedges and grasses which paint it. With respect to the color of grass, most of those even who attend peculiarly to the aspects of Nature only observe that it is more or less dark or light, green or brown, or velvety, fresh or parched, etc. But if you are studying grasses you look for another and different beauty, and you find it, in the wonderful variety of color, etc., presented by the various species.

Take the bare, unwooded earth now, and consider the beautiful variety of shades (or tints?) of green that clothe it under a bright sun. The pastured hills of Conantum, now just imbrowned (probably by the few now stale flowering tops of the red-top which the cows have avoided as too wiry), present a hard and solid green or greenish brown, just touched here and there delicately with light patches of sheep's fescue (though it may be only its radical leaves left), as if a dew lay on it there, — and this has some of the effect of a watered surface, — and the whole is dotted with a thousand little shades of projecting rocks and shrubs. Then, looking lower at the meadow in Miles's field, that is seen as a bright-yellow and sunny stream (yet with a slight tinge of glaucous) between the dark-green potato-fields, flowing onward with windings and expansions, and, as it were, with rips and waterfalls, to the river meadows.

Again, I sit on the brow of the orchard, and look northwest down the river valley (at mid-afternoon). There flows, or rests, the calm blue winding river, lake-like, with its smooth silver-plated sides, and wherever weeds extend across it, there too the silver plate bridges it, like a spirit's bridge across the Styx; but the rippled portions are blue as the sky. This river reposes in the midst of a broad brilliant yellow valley amid green fields and hills and woods, as if, like the Nanking or Yang-ho (or what-not), it flowed through an Oriental Chinese meadow where yellow is the imperial color. The immediate and raised edge of the river, with its willows and button-bushes and polygonums, is a light

green, but the immediately adjacent low meadows, where the sedge prevails, is a brilliant and cheerful yellow, intensely, incredibly bright, such color as you never see in pictures; yellow of various tints, in the lowest and sedgiest parts deepening to so much color as if gamboge had been rubbed into the meadow there; the most cheering color in all the landscape; shaded with little darker isles of green in the midst of this yellow sea of sedge. Yet it is the bright and cheerful yellow, as of spring, and with nothing in the least autumnal in it. How this contrasts with the adjacent fields of red-top, now fast falling before the scythe!

When your attention has been drawn to them, nothing is more charming than the common colors of the earth's surface. See yonder flashing field of corn through the *shimmering* air. (This was said day before yesterday.)

The deciduous woods generally have now and for a long time been nearly as dark as the pines, though, unlike the pines, they show a general silveriness.

For some days have seen stigmas of what I have called *Cyperus dentatus*, but it is evidently later than the *diandrus.*

See a berry (not ripe) of the two-leaved Solomon's-seal dropped at the mouth of a mouse or squirrel's hole, and observe that many are gone from these plants, as if plucked by mice.

The sphagnum shows little black-balled drumsticks now. The nuthatch is active now. Meadow-haying commenced. *Cinna arundinacea* (?) almost.

Looked in two red maple swamps to find the young plants. If you look carefully through a dense red maple swamp now, you find many little maples a couple of inches high which have sprung up chiefly on certain spots alone, especially where the seed has fallen on little beds of sphagnum, which apparently have concealed the seed at the same time that they supplied the necessary moisture. There you find the little tree already deeply rooted, while the now useless winged seed lies empty near by, with its fragile wing half wasted away, as if wholly unrelated to that plant, — not visibly attached, but lying empty on one side. But so far as I look, I see only one maple to a seed, but, indeed, I see only a single seed at a time. You do not find dense groves of them generally, as you might expect from the abundance of seed that falls.

Nevertheless, you will be surprised, on looking through a large maple swamp which two months ago was red with maple seed falling in showers around, at the very small number of maple seeds to be found there, and probably every one of these will be empty. The little maples appear oftenest to have sprung from such as fell into crevices in the moss or leaves and so escaped. Indeed, almost every seed that falls to the earth is picked up by some animal or other whose favorite and perhaps peculiar food it is. They are daily busy about it in the season, and the few seeds which escape are exceptions. There is at least a squirrel or mouse to a tree. If you postpone your search but for a short time, you find yourself only gleaning after them. You may find several of their holes under every tree, if not within it. They ransack the woods. Though the seed may be almost microscopic, it is nuts to them; and this apparently is

one of the principal ends which these seeds were intended to serve.

Look under a nut tree a month after the nuts have fallen, and see what proportion of sound nuts to the abortive ones and shells you will find ordinarily. They have been dispersed, and many effectually planted, far and wide by animals. You have come, you would say, after the feast was over, and are presented with shells only. It looks like a platform before a grocery. These little creatures must live, and, pray, what are they to eat if not the fruits of the earth? — i. e. the graminivorous [sic] ones.[1]

Aug. 2. The wing of the sugar maples is dry and ripe to look at, but the seed end and seed are quite green. I find, as Michaux did, one seed always abortive.

P. M. — Up Assabet.

The young red maples have sprung up chiefly on the sandy and muddy shores, especially where there is a bay or eddy.

At 2 P. M. the river is twelve and seven eighths above summer level, higher than for a long time, on account of the rain of the 31st. Seed of hop-hornbeam not ripe. The button-bush is about in prime, and white lilies considerably past prime. Mikania begun, and now, perhaps, the river's brink is at its height. The black willow down is even yet still seen here and there on the water.

The river, being raised three or four inches, looks quite full, and the bur-reed, etc., is floating off in con-

[1] *Vide* below.

siderable masses. See those round white patches of eggs on the upright sides of dark rocks.

There is now and of late a very thin, in some lights purplish, scum on the water, outside of coarser drift that has lodged, — a brown scum, somewhat gossamer-like as it lies, and browner still on your finger when you take it up. What is it? The pollen of some plant?

As we rest in our boat under a tree, we hear from time to time the loud snap of a wood pewee's bill overhead, which is incessantly diving to this side and that after an insect and returning to its perch on a dead twig. We hear the sound of its bill when it catches one.

In huckle-berry fields I see the seeds of berries recently left on the rocks where birds have perched. How many of these small fruits they may thus disseminate!

Aug. 3. The knotty-rooted cyperus out some days at least.

Aug. 4. 8.30 A. M. — Start for Monadnock.[1]

Begins to rain at 9 A. M., and rains from time to time thereafter all day, the mountain-top being constantly enveloped in clouds.

Notice in Troy much of the *cyperinus* variety of wool-grass, now done, of various heights. Also, by roadside, the *Ribes Cynosbati,* with its prickly berries now partly reddened but hardly ripe. Am exhilarated by the peculiar raspberry scent by the roadside this wet day — and of the dicksonia fern. Raspberries still quite common,

[1] [See account of the Monadnock excursion in *Familiar Letters,* pp. 368–372; Riv. 428–433.]

though late. The high blackberries, the mulberry kind, all still green and red; and also on the 9th, except one berry on a rock.

There was a little sunshine on our way to the mountain, but the cloud extended far down its sides all day, so that one while we mistook Gap Monadnock for the true mountain, which was more to the north.

According to the guide-board it is two and one fourth miles from Troy to the first fork in the road near the little pond and schoolhouse, and I should say it was near two miles from there to the summit, — all the way up-hill from the meadow.

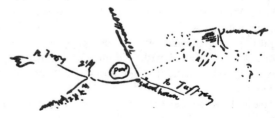

We crossed the immense rocky and springy pastures, containing at first raspberries, but much more hard-hack in flower, reddening them afar, where cattle and horses collected about us, sometimes came running to us, as we thought for society, but probably not. I told Bent of it, — how they gathered about us, they were so glad to see a human being, — but he said I might put it in my book so, it would do no harm, but then the fact was they came about me for salt. "Well," said I, "it was probably because I had so much salt in my constitution." Said he, "If you had had a little salt with you [you]

could hardly have got away from them." "Well," said I, "[I] had some salt in my pocket." "That's what they smelt," said he. Cattle, young and old, with horns in all stages of growth, — young heifers with budding horns, —and horses with a weak [?] Sleepy-David look, though sleek and handsome. They gathered around us while we took shelter under a black spruce from the rain.

We were wet up to our knees before reaching the woods or steep ascent where we entered the cloud. It was quite dark and wet in the woods, from which we emerged into the lighter cloud about 3 P. M., and proceeded to construct our camp, in the cloud occasionally amounting to rain, where I camped some two years ago.

Choosing a place where the spruce was thick in this sunken rock yard, I cut out with a little hatchet a space for a camp in their midst, leaving two stout ones six feet apart to rest my ridge-pole on, and such limbs of these as would best form the gable ends. I then cut four spruces as rafters for the gable ends, leaving the stub ends of the branches to rest the cross-beams or girders on, of which there were two or three to each slope; and I made the roof very steep. Then cut an abundance of large flat spruce limbs, four or five feet long, and laid them on, shingle-fashion, beginning at the ground and covering the stub ends. This made a foundation for two or three similar layers of smaller twigs. Then made a bed of the same, closed up the ends somewhat, and all was done. All these twigs and boughs, of course, were dripping wet, and we were wet through up to our middles. But we made a good fire at the door, and in an hour or two were completely dried.

The most thickly leaved and flattest limbs of the spruce are such as spread flat over the rocks far and wide (while the upper ones were more bushy and less flat); not the very lowest, which were often partly under the surface and but meagrely leafed, but those close above them.

Standing and sitting before the fire which we kindled under a shelving rock, we could dry us much quicker than at any fireside below, for, what with stoves and reduced fireplaces, they could not have furnished such blaze or heat in any inn's [?] kitchen or parlor. This fire was exactly on the site of my old camp, and we burned a hole deep into the withered remains of its roof and bed.

It began to clear up and a star appeared at 8 P. M. Lightning was seen far in the south. Cloud, drifting cloud, alternated with moonlight all the rest of the night. At 11.30 P. M. I heard a nighthawk. Maybe it hunted then because prevented by the cloud at evening.

I heard from time to time through the night a distant sound like thunder or a falling of a pile of lumber, and I suspect that this may have been the booming of nighthawks at a distance.

Aug. 5. The wind changed to northerly toward morning, falling down from over the summit and sweeping through our camp, open on that side, and we found it rather cold!

About an hour before sunrise we heard again the nighthawk; also the robin, chewink, song sparrow,

Fringilla hyemalis; and the wood thrush from the woods below.

Had a grand view of the summit on the north now, it being clear. I set my watch each morning by sunrise, and this morning the lichens on the rocks of the southernmost summit (south of us), just lit by the rising sun, presented a peculiar yellowish or reddish brown light (being wet) which they did not any morning afterward. The rocks of the main summit were olive-brown, and C. called it the Mount of Olives.

I had gone out before sunrise to gather blueberries, — fresh, dewy (because wet with yesterday's rain), almost crispy blueberries, just in prime, much cooler and more grateful at this hour, — and was surprised to hear the voice of people rushing up the mountain for berries in the wet, even at this hour. These alternated with bright light-scarlet bunchberries not quite in prime.

The sides and angles of the cliffs, and their rounded brows (but especially their southeast angles, for I saw very little afterward on the north side; indeed, the cliffs or precipices are not on that side), were clothed with these now lively olive-brown lichens (umbilicaria), alike in sun and shade, becoming afterward and generally dark olive-brown when dry. *Vide* my specimens. Many of the names inscribed on the summit were produced by merely rubbing off the lichens, and they are thus distinct for years.

At 7.30 A. M. for the most part in cloud here, but the country below in sunshine. We soon after set out to walk to the lower southern spur of the mountain. It is chiefly a bare gray and extremely diversified rocky sur-

face, with here and there a spruce or other small tree or bush, or patches of them, or a little shallow marsh on the rock; and the whole mountain-top for two miles was covered, on countless little shelves and in hollows between the rocks, with low blueberries of two or more species or varieties, just in their prime. They are said to be later here than below. Beside the kinds (black and blue *Pennsylvanicum*) common with us, there was the downy *Vaccinium Canadense* and a form or forms intermediate between this and the former, *i. e.* of like form but less hairy. The *Vaccinium Canadense* has a larger leaf and more recurved and undulating on its surface, and generally a lighter green than the common. There were the blue with a copious bloom, others simply black (not shiny, as ours commonly) and on largish bushes, and others of a peculiar blue, as if with a skim-coat of blue, hard and thin, as if glazed, such as we also have. The black are scarce as with us.

These blueberries grew and bore abundantly almost wherever anything else grew on the rocky part of the mountain, — except perhaps the very wettest of the little swamps and the thickest of the little thickets, — quite up to the summit, and at least thirty or forty people came up from the surrounding country this Sunday to gather them. When we behold this summit at this season of the year, far away and blue in the horizon, we may think of the blueberries as blending their color with the general blueness of the mountain. They grow alike in the midst of the cladonia lichens and of the lambkill and moss of the little swamps. No shelf amid the piled rocks is too high or dry for them, for everywhere they enjoy the cool and moist air of the mountain. They are evidently a little later than in Concord, — say a week or ten days later. Blueberries of every degree of blueness and of bloom. There seemed to be fewer of them on the more abrupt and cold westerly and northwesterly sides of the summit, and most in the hollows and shelves of the plateau just southeast of the summit.

Perhaps the prettiest berry, certainly the most novel and interesting to me, was the mountain cranberry, now grown but yet hard and with only its upper cheek red. They are quite local, even on the mountain. The vine is most common close to the summit, but we saw very little fruit there; but some twenty rods north of the brow of this low southern spur we found a pretty little dense patch of them between the rocks, where we gathered a pint in order to make a sauce of them. They here formed a dense low flat bed, covering the rocks for a rod or two, some lichens, green mosses, and the mountain potentilla mingled with them; and they rose scarcely more than one inch above the ground. These vines were only an inch and a half long, clothed with small, thick, glossy leaves, with two or three berries together, about as big as huckleberries, on the recurved end, with a red cheek uppermost and the other light-colored. It was thus a dense, firm sward [?] of glossy little leaves dotted with bright-red berries. They were very easy to collect, for you only made incessant dabs at them with all your fingers together and the twigs and leaves were so rigid that you brought away only berries and no leaves.

Vol. XIV

P. M. — Walked to the wild swamp at the northeast spur. That part is perhaps the most interesting for the wild confusion of its variously formed rocks, and is the least, if at all, frequented. We found the skull and jaws of a large rodent, probably a hedgehog, — larger than a woodchuck's, — a considerable quantity of dry and hard dark-brown droppings, of an elliptical form, like very large rat-droppings, somewhat of a similar character but darker than the rabbit's, and I suspect that these were the porcupine's.

Returned over the top at 5 p. m., after the visitors, men and women, had descended, and so to camp.

Aug. 6. The last was a clear, cool night. At 4 a. m. see local lake-like fogs in some valleys below, but there is none here.

This forenoon, after a breakfast on cranberries, leaving, as usual, our luggage concealed under a large rock, with other rocks placed over the hole, we moved about a quarter of a mile along the edge of the plateau eastward and built a new camp there. It was [a] place which I had noticed the day before, where, sheltered by a perpendicular ledge some seven feet high and close to the brow of the mountain, grew five spruce trees. Two of these stood four feet from the rock and six or more apart; so, clearing away the superfluous branches, I rested stout rafters from the rock-edge to limbs of the two spruces and placed a plate beam across, and, with two or three cross-beams or girders, soon had a roof which I could climb and shingle. After filling the inequalities with rocks and rubbish, I soon had a sloping floor on

I noticed two other patches where the berries were thick, *viz.* one a few rods north of the little rain-water lake of the rocks, at the first, or small, meadow (source of Contoocook) at northeast end of the mountain, and another not more than fifty rods northwest of the summit, where the vines were much ranker and the berries larger. Here the plants were four or five inches high, and there were three or four berries of pretty large huckleberry size at the end of each, and they branched like little bushes. In each case they occupied almost exclusively a little sloping shelf between the rocks, and the vines and berries were especially large and thick where they lay up against the sloping sunny side of the rock.

We stewed these berries for our breakfast the next morning, and thought them the best berry on the mountain, though, not being quite ripe, the berry was a little bitterish — but not the juice of it. It is such an acid as the camper-out craves. They are, then, somewhat earlier than the common cranberry. I do not know that they are ever gathered hereabouts. At present they are very firm berries, of a deep, dark, glossy red. Doubtless there are many more such patches on the mountain.[1]

We heard the voices of many berry-pickers and visitors to the summit, but neither this nor the camp we built afterward was seen by any one.

[1] Brought some home, and stewed them the 12th, and all thought them quite like, and as good as, the common cranberry. Yet George Emerson speaks of it as "austere" and inferior to the common cranberry.

which to make our bed. Lying there on that shelf just on the edge of the steep declivity of the mountain, we could look all over the south and southeast world without raising our heads. The rock running east and west was our shelter on the north.

Our huts, being built of spruce entirely, were not noticeable two or three rods off, for we did [not] cut the spruce amid which they were built more than necessary, bending aside their boughs in order to enter. My companion, returning from a short walk, was lost when within two or three rods, the different rocks and clumps of spruce looked so much alike, and in the moonlight we were liable to mistake some dark recess between two neighboring spruce ten feet off for the entrance to our house. We heard this afternoon the tread of a blueberry-picker on the rocks two or three rods north of us, and saw another as near, south, and, stealing out, we came round from another side and had some conversation with them, — two men and a boy, — but they never discovered our house nor suspected it. The surface is so uneven that ten steps will often suffice to conceal the ground you lately stood on, and yet the different shelves and hollows are so much alike that you cannot tell if one is new or not. It is somewhat like travelling over a huge fan. When in a valley the nearest ridge conceals all the others and you cannot tell one from another.

This afternoon, again walked to the larger northeast swamp, going directly, *i. e.* east of the promontories or part way down the slopes. Bathed in the small rocky basin above the smaller meadow. These two swamps are about the wildest part of the mountain and most interesting to me. The smaller occurs on the north-east side of the main mountain, *i. e.* at the northeast end of the plateau. It is a little roundish meadow a few rods over, with cotton-grass in it, the shallow bottom of a basin of rock, and out the east side there trickles a very slight stream, just moistening the rock at present and collecting enough in one cavity to afford you a drink. This is evidently a source of the Contoocook, the one I noticed two years ago as such.

The larger swamp is considerably lower and more northerly, separating the northeast spur from the main mountain, probably not far from the line of Dublin. It extends northwest and southeast some thirty or forty rods, and probably leaked out now under the rocks at the northwest end, — though I found water only half a dozen rods below, — and so was a source probably of the Ashuelot. The prevailing grass or sedge in it, growing in tufts in the green moss and sphagnum between the fallen dead spruce timber, was the *Eriophorum vaginatum* (long done) and the *E. gracile*. Also the *Epilobium palustre*, apparently in prime in it, and common wool-grass (*Scirpus Eriophorum*). Around its edge grew the *Chelone glabra* (not yet out), meadow-sweet in bloom, black choke-berry just ripening, red elder (its fruit in prime), mountain-ash, *Carex trisperma* and *Deweyana* (small and slender), and the fetid currant in fruit (in a torrent of rocks at the east end), etc., etc.

I noticed a third, yet smaller, quite small, swamp, yet more southerly, on the edge of the plateau, evidently another source of a river, where the snows melt.

At 5 P. M. we went to our first camp for our remain-

ing baggage. From this point at this hour the rocks of the precipitous summit (under whose south side that camp is placed), lit by the declining sun, were a very light gray, with reddish-tawny touches from the now drying *Aira flexuosa* on the inaccessible shelves and along the seams. Returned to enjoy the evening at the second camp.

Evening and morning were the most interesting seasons, especially the evening. Each day, about an hour before sunset, I got sight, as it were accidentally, of an elysium beneath me. The smoky haze of the day, suggesting a furnace-like heat, a trivial dustiness, gave place to a clear transparent enamel, through which houses, woods, farms, and lakes were seen as in [a] picture indescribably fair and expressly made to be looked at. At any hour of the day, to be sure, the surrounding country looks flatter than it is. Even the great steep, furrowed, and rocky pastures, red with hardhack and raspberries, which creep so high up the mountain amid the woods, in which you think already that you are half-way up, perchance, seen from the top or brow of the mountain are not for a long time distinguished for elevation above the surrounding country, but they look smooth and tolerably level, and the cattle in them are not noticed or distinguished from rocks unless you search very particularly. At length you notice how the houses and barns keep a respectful, and at first unaccountable, distance from these near pastures and woods, though they *are* seemingly flat, that there is a broad neutral ground between the roads and the mountain; and yet when the truth flashes upon you, you have to imagine the long, ascending path through them.

To speak of the landscape generally, the open or cleared land looks like a thousand little swells or tops of low rounded hills, — tent-like or like a low hay-cap spread, — tawny or green amid the woods. As you look down on this landscape you little think of the hills where the traveller walks his horse. The woods have not this swelling look. The most common color of open land (from apex at 5 P. M.) is tawny brown, the woods dark green. At midday the darker green of evergreens amid the hardwoods is quite discernible half a dozen miles off. But, as the most interesting view is at sunset, so it is the part of [the] landscape nearest to you and most immediately beneath the mountain, where, as usual, there is that invisible gelid haze to glass it.

The nearest house to the mountain which we saw from our camp — one on the Jaffrey road — was in the shadow even of the low southern spur of the mountain which we called the Old South, just an hour before the sun set, while a neighbor on a hill within a quarter of a mile eastward enjoyed the sunlight at least half an hour longer. So much shorter are their days, and so much more artificial light and heat must they obtain, at the former house. It would be a serious loss, methinks, one hour of sunlight every day. *We* saw the sun so much longer. Of course the labors of the day were brought to an end, the sheep began to bleat, the doors were closed, the lamps were lit, and preparations for the night were made there, so much the earlier.

The landscape is shown to be not flat, but hilly, when the sun is half an hour high, by the shadows of the hills.

But, above all, from half an hour to two hours before sunset many western mountain-ranges are revealed, as the sun declines, one behind another, by their dark outlines and the intervening haze; *i. e.*, the ridges are dark lines, while the intervening valleys are a cloud-like haze. It was so, at least, from 6 to 6.30 P. M. on the 6th; and, at 5 P. M. on the 8th, it being very hazy still, I could count in the direction of Saddleback Mountain eight distinct ranges, revealed by the darker lines of the ridges rising above this cloud-like haze. And I might have added the ridge of Monadnock itself within a quarter of a mile of me.

Of course, the last half of these mountain-ridges appeared successively higher and seemed higher, all of them (*i. e.* the last half), than the mountain we were on, as if you had climbed to the heights of the sky by a succession of stupendous terraces reaching as far as you could see from north to south. The Connecticut Valley was one broad gulf of haze which you were soon over. They were the Green Mountains that we saw, but there was no greenness, only a bluish mistiness, in what we saw; and all of Vermont that lay between us and their summit was but a succession of parallel ranges of mountains. Of course, almost all that we mean commercially and agriculturally by Vermont was concealed in those long and narrow haze-filled valleys. I never saw a mountain that looked so high and so melted away at last cloud-like into the sky, as Saddleback this eve, when your eye had clomb to it by these eight successive terraces. You had to begin at this end and ascend step by step to recognize it for a mountain at all. If you had first rested your eye on *it*, you would have seen it for a cloud, it was so incredibly high in the sky.

After sunset the ponds are white and distinct.[1] Earlier we could distinguish the reflections of the woods perfectly in ponds three miles off.

I heard a cock crow very shrilly and distinctly early in the evening of the 8th. This was the most distinct sound from the lower world that I heard up there at any time, not excepting even the railroad whistle, which was louder. It reached my ear perfectly, to each note and curl, — from some submontane cock. We also heard at this hour an occasional bleat from a sheep in some mountain pasture, and a lowing of a cow. And at last we saw a light here and there in a farmhouse window. We heard no sound of man except the railroad whistle and, on Sunday, a church-bell. Heard no dog that I remember. Therefore I should say that, of all the sounds of the farmhouse, the crowing of the cock could be heard furthest or most distinctly under these circumstances. It seemed to wind its way through the layers of air as a sharp gimlet through soft wood, and reached our ears with amusing distinctness.

Aug. 7. Morning — dawn and sunrise — was another interesting season. I rose always by four or half past four to observe the signs of it and to correct my watch. From our first camp I could not see the sun rise, but only when its first light (yellowish or, rather, pink-

 [1] At 5 P. M. the 5th, being on the apex, the small pond by the schoolhouse is mostly smooth plated, with a darker rippled portion in the middle.

Vol. XIV

ish) was reflected from the lichen-clad rocks of the southern spur. But here, by going eastward some forty rods, I could see the sun rise, though there was invariably a low stratum or bar of cloud in the horizon. The sun rose about five. The tawny or yellowish pastures about the mountain (below the woods; what was the grass?) reflected the auroral light at 4.20 A. M. remarkably, and they were at least as distinct as at any hour.

There was every morning more or less solid white fog to be seen on the earth, though none on the mountain. I was struck by the localness of these fogs. For five mornings they occupied the same place and were about the same in extent. It was obvious that certain portions of New Hampshire and Massachusetts were at this season commonly invested with fog in the morning, while others, or the larger part, were free from it. The fog lay on the lower parts only. From our point of view the largest lake of fog lay in Rindge and southward; and southeast of Fitzwilliam, *i. e.* about Winchendon, very large there. In short, the fog lay in great spidery lakes and streams answering to the lakes, streams, and meadows beneath, especially over the sources of Miller's River and the region of primitive wood thereabouts; but it did [not] rest on lakes always, *i. e.*, where they were elevated, as now some in Jaffrey were quite clear. It suggested that there was an important difference, so far as the health and spirits of the inhabitants were concerned, between the town where there was this regular morning fog and that where there was none. I shall always remember the inhabitants of State Line as dwellers in the fog. The geography and statistics of fog have

not been ascertained. If we awake into a fog, it does not occur to us that the inhabitants of a neighboring town which lies higher may have none, neither do they, being ignorant of this happiness, inform us of it. Yet, when you come to look down thus on the country every morning, you see that here this thick white veil of fog is spread and not there. It was often several hundred feet thick, soon rising, breaking up, and drifting off, or rather seeming to drift away, as it evaporated. There was commonly such a risen fog drifting through the interval between this mountain and Gap Monadnock.

One morning I noticed clouds as high as the Peterboro Hills, — a lifted fog, — ever drifting easterly but making no progress, being dissipated. Also long rolls and ant-eaters of cloud, at last reduced by the sun to mere vertebræ. That morning (the 8th) the great and general cloud and apparently fog combined over the lowest land running southwest from Rindge was apparently five hundred or more feet deep, but our mountain was above all.

This forenoon I cut and measured a spruce on the north side the mountain, and afterward visited the summit, where one of the coast surveyors had been signalling, as I was told, to a mountain in Laconia, some fifty-five miles off, with a glass reflector.

After dinner, descended into the gulf and swamp beneath our camp. At noon every roof in the southern country sloping toward the north was distinctly revealed, — a lit gray.

In the afternoon, walked to the Great Gulf and

meadow, in the midst of the plateau just east of and under the summit.

Aug. 8. *Wednesday.* 8.30 A. M. Walk round the west side of the summit. Bathe in the rocky pool there, collect mountain cranberries on the northwest side, return over the summit, and take the bearings of the different spurs, etc. Return to camp at noon.

Toward night, walk to east edge of the plateau.

Aug. 9. At 6 A. M., leave camp for Troy, where we arrive, after long pauses, by 9 A. M., and take the cars at 10.5.

I observed these plants on the rocky summit of the mountain, above the forest: —

Raspberry, not common.
Low blueberries of two or three varieties.[1]
Bunchberry.
Solidago thyrsoidea.
Fetid currant, common; leaves beginning to be scarlet; grows amid loose fallen rocks.
Red cherry, some ripe, and handsome.
Black choke-berry.
Potentilla tridentata, still lingering in bloom.
Aralia hispida, still lingering in bloom.
Cow-wheat, common, still in bloom.
Mountain cranberry, not generally abundant; full grown earlier than lowland ditto.[2]
Black spruce.
Lambkill, lingering in flower in cool and moist places.
Aster acuminatus, abundant; not generally open, but fairly begun to bloom.

[1] *Vide* p. [11].   [2] *Vide* p. [12].

Red elder, ripe, apparently in prime, not uncommon.
Arenaria Grœnlandica, still pretty common in flower.
Solidago lanceolata, not uncommon; just fairly begun.
Epilobium angustifolium, in bloom; not common, however.
Epilobium palustre, some time, common in mosses, small and slender.
Wild holly, common; berries not quite ripe.
Viburnum nudum, common; berries green.
White pine; saw three or four only, mostly very small.
Mountain-ash, abundant; berries not ripe; generally very small, largest in swamps.
Diervilla, not uncommon, still.
Rhodora, abundant; low, *i. e.* short.
Meadow-sweet, abundant, apparently in prime.
Hemlocks; two little ones with rounded tops.
Chelone glabra, not yet; at northeast swamp-side.
Yarrow.
Canoe birch, very small.
Clintonia borealis, with fruit.
Checkerberry.
Gold-thread.
One three-ribbed goldenrod, northwest side (not *Canadense*).
Tall rough goldenrod, not yet; not uncommon.
Populus tremuliformis, not very common.
Polygonum cilinode, in bloom.
Yellow birch, small.
Fir, a little; four or five trees noticed.
Willows, not uncommon, four or five feet high.
Red maple, a very little, small.
Water andromeda, common about the bogs.
Trientalis.
Pearly everlasting, out.
Diplopappus umbellatus, in bloom, not common (?); northeast swamp-side, also northwest side of mountain.
Juncus trifidus.
Some *Juncus paradoxus?* } about edge of marshes.
Some *Juncus acuminatus?* }

CYPERACEÆ

Eriophorum gracile, abundant, whitening the little swamps.
Eriophorum vaginatum, abundant, little swamps, long done, (this the coarse grass in tufts, in marshes).
Wool-grass, not uncommon, (common kind).
Carex trisperma (?) or *Deweyana*, with large seeds, slender and drooping, by side of northeast swamp. *Vide* press.
Carex scoparia? or *straminea?* a little.
C. debilis.
Carex, small, rather close-spiked, *C. canescens*-like (?), common.
A fine grass-like plant very common, perhaps *Eleocharis tenuis;* now without heads, but marks of them.

GRASSES

Aira flexuosa.
Glyceria elongata, with appressed branches (some purplish), in swamp.
Blue-joint, apparently in prime, one place.
Festuca ovina, one place.
Cinna arundinacea, one place.
Agrostis scabra (?), at our spring, *q. v.*

FERNS AND LICHENS, ETC.

A large greenish lichen flat on rocks, of a peculiarly concentric growth, *q. v.*
Some common sulphur lichen.
The very bright handsome crustaceous yellow lichen, as on White Mts., *q. v.*
Two or three umbilicaria lichens, *q. v.*, giving the dark brown to the rocks.
A little, in one place, of the old hat umbilicaria, as at Flint's Pond Rock.
Green moss and sphagnum in the marshes.
Two common cladonias, white and greenish.
Stereocaulon.
Lycopodium complanatum, one place.
Lycopodium annotinum, not very common.
Common polypody.

Vol. XIV

Dicksonia fern, *q. v.*
Sensitive fern, and various other common ones.

I see that in my last visit, in June, '58, I also saw here Labrador tea (on the north side), two-leaved Solomon's-seal, *Amelanchier Canadensis* var. *oligocarpa* and var. *oblongifolia*, one or two or three kinds of willows, a little mayflower, and chiogenes, and *Lycopodium clavatum*.

The prevailing trees and shrubs of the mountain-top are, in order of commonness, etc., low blueberry, black spruce, lambkill, black choke-berry, wild holly, *Viburnum nudum*, mountain-ash, meadow-sweet, rhodora, red cherry, canoe birch, water andromeda, fetid currant.

The prevailing and characteristic smaller plants, excepting grasses, cryptogamic, etc.: *Potentilla tridentata*, *Solidago thyrsoidea*, bunchberry, cow-wheat, *Aster acuminatus*, *Arenaria Grœnlandica*, mountain cranberry, *Juncus trifidus*, *Clintonia borealis*, *Epilobium palustre*, *Aralia hispida*.

Of *Cyperaceæ* the most common and noticeable now were *Eriophorum gracile* and *vaginatum*, a few sedges, and perhaps the grass-like *Eleocharis tenuis*.

The grass of the mountain now was the *Aira flexuosa*, large and abundant, now somewhat dry and withered, on all shelves and along the seams, quite to the top; a pinkish tawny now. Most would not have noticed or detected any other. The other kinds named were not common. You would say it was a true mountain grass. The only grass that a careless observer would notice. There was nothing like a sod on the mountain-top. The tufts of *J. trifidus*, perhaps, came the nearest to it.

The black spruce is the prevailing tree, commonly six or eight feet high; but very few, and those only in the most sheltered places, as hollows and swamps, are of regular outline, on account of the strong and cold winds with which they have to contend. Fifteen feet high would be unusually large. They cannot grow here without some kind of lee to start with. They commonly consist of numerous flat branches close above one another for the first foot or two, spreading close over the surface and filling and concealing the hollows between the rocks; but exactly at a level with the top of the rock which shelters them they cease to have any limbs on the north side, but all their limbs now are included within a quadrant between southeast and southwest, while the stem, which is always perfectly perpendicular, is bare and smooth on the north side; yet it is led onward at the top by a tuft of tender branches a foot in length and spreading every way as usual, but the northern part of these successively die and disappear. They thus remind you often of masts of vessels with sails set on one side, and sometimes one of these almost bare masts is seen to have been broken short off at ten feet from the ground, such is the violence of the wind there. I saw a spruce, healthy and straight, full sixteen feet without a limb or the trace of a limb on the north side. When building my camp, in order to get rafters six feet long and an inch and a half in diameter at the small end, I was obliged to cut down spruce at least five inches in diameter at one foot from the ground. So stout and tapering do they grow. They spread so close to the rocks that the lower branches are often half worn away for a foot in length by their rubbing on the rocks in the wind, and I sometimes mistook the creaking of such a limb for the note of a bird, for it is just such a note as you would expect to hear there. The two spruce which formed the sides of my second camp had their lower branches behind the rock so thick and close, and, on the outsides of the quadrant, so directly above one another perpendicularly, that they made two upright side walls, as it were, very convenient to interlace and make weather-tight.

I selected a spruce growing on the highest part of the plateau east of the summit, on its north slope, about as high as any tree of its size, to cut and count its rings. It was five feet five inches high. As usual, all its limbs except some of the leading twigs extended toward the south. One of the lowermost limbs, so close to the ground that I thought its green extremity was a distinct tree, was ten feet long. There were ten similar limbs (though not so long) almost directly above one another, within two feet of the ground, the largest two inches thick at the butt. I cut off this tree at one foot from the ground. It was there five inches in diameter and had forty-four rings, but four inches of its growth was on the south side the centre and only one inch on the north side. I cut it off again nineteen inches higher and there there were thirty-five rings.

Our fuel was the dead spruce — apparently that which escaped the fire some forty years ago!! — which lies spread over the rocks in considerable quantity still, especially at the northeast spur. It makes very good dry fuel, and some of it is quite fat and sound. The

spruce twigs were our bed. I observed that, being laid bottom upward in a hot sun, as at the foot of our bed, the leaves turned pale-brown, as if boiled, and fell off very soon.

The black spruce is certainly a very wild tree, and loves a primitive soil just made out of disintegrated granite.

After the low blueberry I should say that the lamb-kill was the commonest shrub. The black choke-berry also was very common, but this and the rhodora were both dwarfish. Though the meadow-sweet was very common, I did not notice any hardhack; yet it was exceedingly prevalent in the pastures below.

The *Solidago thyrsoidea* was the goldenrod of the mountain-top, from the woods quite to the summit. Any other goldenrod was comparatively scarce. It was from two inches to two feet high. It grew both in small swamps and in the seams of the rocks everywhere, and was now in its prime.

The bunchberry strikes one from these parts as much as any, — about a dozen berries in a dense cluster, a lively scarlet on a green ground.

Spruce was the prevailing tree; blueberry, the berry; *S. thyrsoidea*, the goldenrod; *A. acuminatus*, the aster (the only one I saw, and very common); *Juncus tri-fidus*, the juncus; and *Aira flexuosa*, the grass, of the mountain-top.

The two cotton-grasses named were very common and conspicuous in and about the little meadows.

The *Juncus trifidus* was the common grass (or grass-

like plant) of the very highest part of the mountain, — the peak and for thirty rods downward, — growing on the shelves and especially on the edges of the *scars* rankly, and on this part of the mountain almost alone had it fruited, — for I think that I saw it occasionally lower and elsewhere on the rocky portion without fruit.

The apparently common green and white cladonias, together with yet whiter stereocaulon, grew all over the flat rocks in profusion, and the apparently common greenish rock lichen (*q. v.* in box) grew concentricwise in large circles on the slopes of rocks also, not to mention the common small umbilicaria (*q. v.*) of one or two kinds which covered the brows and angles of the rocks.

The berries now ripe were: blueberries, bunchberries, fetid currant, red cherry, black choke-berry (some of them), mountain cranberry (red-cheeked and good cooked), red elder (quite showy), *Clintonia borealis*, raspberry (not common). And berries yet green were: *Aralia hispida* (ripe in Concord, *much* of it), wild holly (turning), *Viburnum nudum* (green), mountain-ash.

The birds which I noticed were: robins, chewinks, *F. hyemalis*, song sparrow, nighthawk, swallow (a few, probably barn swallow, one flying over the extreme summit), crows (sometimes flew over, though mostly heard in the woods below), wood thrush (heard from woods below); and saw a warbler with a dark-marked breast and yellowish angle to wing and white throat,

and heard a note once like a very large and powerful nuthatch. Some small hawks.

The bird peculiar to the mountain was the *F. hyemalis*, and perhaps the most common, flitting over the rocks, unless the robin and chewink were as common. These, with the song sparrow and wood thrush, were heard regularly each morning. I saw a robin's nest in one of the little swamps. The wood thrush was regularly heard late in the afternoon, its strain coming up from the woods below as the shadows were lengthening.

But, above all, this was an excellent place to observe the habits of the nighthawks. They were heard and seen regularly at sunset, — one night it was at 7.10, or exactly at sunset, — coming upward from the lower and more shaded portion of the rocky surface below our camp, with their *spark spark*, soon answered by a companion, for they seemed always to hunt in pairs, — yet both would dive and boom and, according to Wilson, only the male utters this sound. They pursued their game thus a short distance apart and some sixty or one hundred feet above the gray rocky surface, in the twilight, and the constant *spark spark* seemed to be a sort of call-note to advertise each other of their neighborhood. Suddenly one would hover and flutter more stationarily for a moment, somewhat like a kingfisher, and then dive almost perpendicularly downward with a rush, for fifty feet, frequently within three or four rods of us, and the loud booming sound or rip was made just at the curve, as it ceased to fall, but whether voluntarily or involuntarily I know not. They appeared to be diving for their insect prey. What eyes they must have to be able to discern it *beneath* them against the rocks in the twilight! As I was walking about the camp, one flew low, within two feet of the surface, about me, and lit on the rock within three rods of me, and uttered a harsh note like *c-o-w, c-o-w,* — hard and gritty and allied to their common notes, — which I thought expressive of anxiety, or to alarm me, or for its mate.

I suspect that their booming on a distant part of the mountain was the sound which I heard the first night which was like very distant thunder, or the fall of a pile of lumber.

They did not fly or boom when there was a cloud or fog, and ceased pretty early in the night. They came up from the same quarter — the shaded rocks below — each night, two of them, and left off booming about 8 o'clock. Whether they then ceased hunting or withdrew to another part of the mountain, I know not. Yet I heard one the first night at 11.30 P. M., but, as it had been a rainy day and did not clear up here till some time late in the night, it may have been compelled to do its hunting then. They began to boom again at 4 A. M. (other birds about 4.30) and ceased about 4.20. By their color they are related to the gray rocks over which they flit and circle.

As for quadrupeds, we saw none on the summit and only one small gray rabbit at the base of the mountain, but we saw the droppings of rabbits all over the mountain, and they must be the prevailing large animal, and we heard the motions probably of a mouse about our camp at night. We also found the skull of a rodent

larger than a woodchuck or gray rabbit, and the tail-bones (maybe of the same) some half-dozen inches long, and saw a large quantity of dark-brown oval droppings (*q. v.*, preserved). I think that this was a porcupine, and I hear that they are found on the mountain. Mr. Wild saw one recently dead near the spring some sixteen years ago. I saw the ordure of some large quadruped, probably this, on the rocks in the pastures beneath the wood, composed chiefly of raspberry seeds.

As for insects: There were countless ants, large and middle-sized, which ran over our bed and inside our clothes. They swarmed all over the mountain. Had young in the dead spruce which we burned. Saw but half a dozen mosquitoes. Saw two or three common yellow butterflies and some larger red-brown ones, and moths. There were great flies, as big as horse-flies, with shining black abdomens and buff-colored bases to their wings. Disturbed a swarm of bees in a dead spruce on the ground, but they disappeared before I ascertained what kind they were. On the summit one noon, *i. e.* on the very apex, I was pestered by great swarms of small black wasps or winged ants about a quarter of an inch long, which fluttered about and settled on my head and face. Heard a *fine* (in the sod) cricket, a dog-day locust once or twice, and a *creaking* grasshopper.

Saw two or three frogs, — one large *Rana fontinalis* in that rocky pool on the southwest side, where I saw the large spawn which I supposed to be bullfrog spawn two years ago, but now think must have been *R. fontinalis*

Vol. XIV

spawn; and there was a dark pollywog one inch long. This frog had a raised line on each side of back and was as large as a common bullfrog. I also heard the note once of some familiar large frog. The one or two smaller frogs which I saw elsewhere were perhaps the same.

There were a great many visitors to the summit, both by the south and north, *i. e.* the Jaffrey and Dublin paths, but they did not turn off from the beaten track. One noon, when I was on the top, I counted forty men, women, and children around me, and more were constantly arriving while others were going. Certainly more than one hundred ascended in a day. When you got within thirty rods you saw them seated in a row along the gray parapets, like the inhabitants of a castle on a gala-day; and when you behold Monadnock's blue summit fifty miles off in the horizon, you may imagine it covered with men, women, and children in dresses of all colors, like an observatory on a muster-field. They appeared to be chiefly mechanics and farmers' boys and girls from the neighboring towns. The young men sat in rows with their legs dangling over the precipice, squinting through spy-glasses and shouting and hallooing to each new party that issued from the woods below. Some were playing cards; others were trying to see their house or their neighbor's. Children were running about and playing as usual. Indeed, this peak in pleasant weather is the most trivial place in New England. There are probably more arrivals daily than at any of the White Mountain houses. Several were busily engraving their names on the rocks with cold-chisels, whose inces-

sant clink you heard, and they had but little leisure to look off. The mountain was not free of them from sunrise to sunset, though most of them left about 5 P. M. At almost any hour of the day they were seen wending their way single file in various garb up or down the shelving rocks of the peak. These figures on the summit, seen in relief against the sky (from our camp), looked taller than life. I saw some that camped there, by moonlight, one night. On Sunday, twenty or thirty, at least, in addition to the visitors to the peak, came up to pick blueberries, and we heard on all sides the rattling of dishes and their frequent calls to each other.

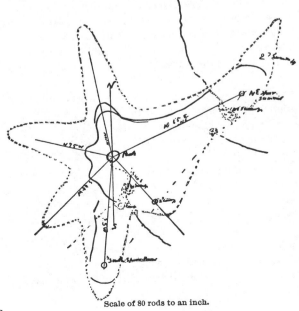

Scale of 80 rods to an inch.

The rocky area — or summit of the mountain above the forest — which I am describing is of an irregular form from a mile and a half to two miles long, north and south, by three quarters to a mile wide at the widest part, in proportion as you descend lower on the rocks.

There are three main spurs, *viz.* the northeast, or chief, one, toward Monadnock Pond and the village of Dublin; the southerly, to Swan's [?]; and the northerly, over which the Dublin path runs. These afford the three longest walks. The first is the longest, wildest, and least-frequented, and rises to the greatest height at a distance from the central peak. The second affords the broadest and smoothest walk. The third is the highest of all at first, but falls off directly. There are also two lesser and lower spurs, on the westerly side, — one quite short, toward Troy, by which you might come up from that side, the other yet lower, but longer, from north 75° west. But above all, for walking, there is an elevated rocky plateau, so to call it, extending to half a mile east of the summit, or about a hundred rods east of the ravine. This slopes gently toward the south and east by successive terraces of rock, and affords the most amusing walking of any part of the mountain.

The most interesting precipices are on the south side of the peak. The greatest abruptness of descent (from top to bottom) is on the west side between the two lesser ravines.

The northeast spur (of two principal summits beyond the swamp) has the most dead spruce on it.

The handsome ponds near the mountain are a long pond chiefly in Jaffrey, close under the mountain on the

east, with a greatly swelling knoll extending into it on the east side; Monadnock Pond in Dublin, said to be very deep, about north-northeast (between the northeast spur and Dublin village); a large pond with a very white beach much further off in Nelson, about north (one called it Breed's?); Stone Pond, northwesterly, about as near as Monadnock Pond. Also large ponds in Jaffrey, Rindge, Troy; and many more further off.

The basis of my map was the distance from the summit to the second camp, measured very rudely by casting a stone before. Pacing the distance of an easy cast, I found it about ten rods, and thirteen such stone's throws, or one hundred and thirty rods, carried me to the camp. As I had the course, from the summit and from the camp, of the principal points, I could tell the rest nearly enough. It was about fifty rods from the summit to the ravine and eighty more to the camp.

It was undoubtedly Saddleback Mountain which I saw about S. 85° W. What was that elevated part of the Green Mountains about N. 50° W., which one called falsely Camel's Hump? — the next elevated summit north of Saddleback.

It would evidently be a noble walk from Watatic to Goffstown perchance, over the Peterboro mountains, along the very backbone of this part of New Hampshire, — the most novel and interesting walk that I can think of in these parts.

They who simply climb to the peak of Monadnock have seen but little of the mountain. I came not to look *off from* it, but to look *at* it. The view of the pinnacle itself from the plateau below surpasses any view which

you get from the summit. It is indispensable to see the top itself and the sierra of its outline from one side. The great charm is not to look off from a height but to walk over this novel and wonderful rocky surface. Moreover, if you would enjoy the prospect, it is, methinks, most interesting when you look from the edge of the plateau immediately down into the valleys, or where the edge of the lichen-clad rocks, only two or three rods from you, is seen as the lower frame of a picture of green fields, lakes, and woods, suggesting a more stupendous precipice than exists. There are much more surprising effects of this nature along the edge of the plateau than on the summit. It is remarkable what haste the visitors make to get to the top of the mountain and then look away from it.

Northward you see Ascutney and Kearsarge Mountains, and faintly the White Mountains, and others more northeast; but above all, toward night, the Green Mountains.

But what a study for rocks does this mountain-top afford! The rocks of the pinnacle have many regular nearly right-angled slants to the southeast, covered with the dark-brown (or olivaceous) umbilicaria. The rocks which you walk over are often not only worn smooth and slippery, but grooved out, as if with some huge rounded tool, or they are much oftener convex:
You see huge buttresses or walls put up by Titans, with true joints, only recently loosened by an earthquake as if ready to

topple down. Some of the lichen-clad rocks are of a rude brick-loaf form or small cottage form:
You see large boulders, left just on the edge of the steep descent of the plateau, commonly resting on a few small stones, as if the Titans were in the very act of transporting them when they were interrupted; some left standing on their ends, and almost the only convenient rocks in whose shade you can sit sometimes. Often you come to a long, thin rock, two or three rods long, which has the appearance of having just been split into underpinning-stone, — perfectly straight-edged and parallel pieces, and lying as it fell, ready for use, just as the mason leaves it. Post-stones, door-stones, etc. There were evidences of recent motion as well as ancient.

I saw on the flat sloping surface of rock a fresher white space exactly the size and form of a rock which was lying by it and which had lately covered it. What had upset it? There were many of these whitish marks where the dead spruce had lain but was now decayed or gone.

The rocks were not only coarsely grooved but finely scratched from northwest to southeast, commonly about S. 10° E. (but between 5° and 20° east, or, by the true meridian, more yet).[1] I could have steered myself in a fog by them.

Piles of stones left as they were split ready for the

[1] Hitchcock, p. 387, calls the rock of Monadnock granite, and says the scratches are north and south, nearly, and very striking. *Vide* three pages forward.

builder. I saw one perfect triangular hog-trough — except that it wanted one end — and which would have been quite portable and convenient in a farmer's yard. The core, four or five feet long, lay one side.

The rocks are very commonly in terraces with a smooth rounded edge to each. The most remarkable of these terraces that I noticed was between the second camp and the summit, say some forty rods from the camp. These terraces were some six rods long and six to ten feet wide, but the top slanting considerably back into the mountain, and they were about four or five feet high each. There were four such in succession here, running S. 30° E. The edges of these terraces, here and commonly, were rounded and grooved like the rocks at a waterfall, as if water and gravel had long washed over them.

Some rocks were shaped like huge doughnuts: The edges of cliffs were frequently lumpishly rounded, covered with lichens, so that you could not stand near the edge. The extreme east and northeast parts of the plateau, especially near the little meadow, are the most interesting for the forms of rocks. Sometimes you see where a huge oblong square stone has been taken out from the edge of a terrace, leaving a space which looks like a giant's grave unoccupied.

On the west side the summit the strata ran north and

south and dipped to east about 60° with the horizon. There were broad veins of white quartz (sometimes one foot wide) running directly many rods.

Near the camp there was a succession of great rocks, their corners rounded semi-circularly and grooved at the same time like the capital of a column reversed. The most rugged walking is on the steep westerly slope.

We had a grand view, especially after sunset, as it grew dark, of the *sierra* of the summit's outline west of us, — the teeth of the sierra often turned back toward the summit, — when the rocks were uniformly black in the shade and seen against the twilight.

In Morse's Gazetteer (1797) it is said, "Its base is five miles in diameter north to south, and three from east to west. . . . Its summit is a bald rock." By the summit he meant the very topmost part, which, it seems, was always a "bald rock."

There were all over the rocky summit peculiar yellowish gravelly spots which I called scars, commonly of an oval form, not in low but elevated places, and looking as if a little mound had been cut off there. The edges of these, on the very pinnacle of the mountain, were formed of the *Juncus trifidus*, now gone to seed. If they had been in hollows, you would have said that they were the bottom of little pools, now dried up, where the gravel and stones had been washed bare. I am not certain about their origin. They suggested some force which had suddenly cut

off and washed or blown away the surface there, like a thunder-spout [*sic*], or lightning, or a hurricane. Such spots were very numerous, and had the appearance of a fresh scar.

Much, if not most, of the rock appears to be what Hitchcock describes and represents as graphic granite (*vide* his book, page 681).

Hitchcock says (page 389) that he learns from his assistant, Abraham Jenkins, Jr., that "on the sides of and around this mountain [Monadnock][1] diluvial grooves and scratches are common; having a direction about N. 10° W. and S. 10° E. The summit of the mountain, which rises in an insulated manner to the height of 3250 feet, is a naked rock of gneiss of several acres in extent, and this is thoroughly grooved and scored. One groove measured fourteen feet in width, and two feet deep; and others are scarcely of less size. Their direction at the summit, by a mean of nearly thirty measurements with a compass, is nearly north and south."

According to Heywood's Gazetteer, the mountain is "talc, mica, slate, distinctly stratified," and is 3718 feet high.

Though there is little or no soil upon the rocks, owing apparently to the coolness, if not moisture, you have rather the vegetation of a swamp than that of sterile rocky ground below. For example, of the six prevailing trees and shrubs — low blueberry, black spruce, lamb-kill, black choke-berry, wild holly, and *Viburnum nudum* — all but the first are characteristic of swampy and low

[1] [The brackets are Thoreau's.]

ground, to say nothing of the commonness of wet mosses, the two species of cotton-grass, and some other plants of the swamp and meadow. Little meadows and swamps are scattered all over the mountain upon and amid the rocks. You are continually struck with the proximity of gray and lichen-clad rock and mossy bog. You tread alternately on wet moss, into which you sink, and dry, lichen-covered rocks. You will be surprised to see the vegetation of a swamp on a little shelf only a foot or two over, — a bog a foot wide with cotton-grass waving over it in the midst of cladonia lichens so dry as to burn like tinder. The edges of the little swamps — if not their middle — are commonly white with cotton-grass. The *Arenaria Grœnlandica* often belies its name here, growing in wet places as often as in dry ones, together with eriophorum.

One of the grandest views of the summit is from the east side of the central meadow of the plateau, which I called the Gulf, just beneath the pinnacle on the east, with the meadow in the foreground.

Water stands in shallow pools on almost every rocky shelf. The largest pool of open water which I found was on the southwest side of the summit, and was four rods long by fifteen to twenty feet in width and a foot deep. Wool- and cotton-grass grew around it, and there was a dark green moss and some mud at the bottom. There was a smoother similar pool on the next shelf above it. These were about the same size in June and in August, and apparently never dry up. There was also the one in which I bathed, near the northeast little meadow. I had a delicious bath there, though the water was warm, but there was a pleasant strong and drying wind blowing over the ridge, and when I had bathed, the rock felt like plush to my feet.

The cladonia lichens were so dry at midday, even the day after rain, that they served as tinder to kindle our fire, — indeed, we were somewhat troubled to prevent the fire from spreading amid them, — yet at night, even before sundown, and morning, when we got our supper and breakfast, they would not burn thus, having absorbed moisture. They had then a cool and slightly damp feeling.

Every evening, excepting, perhaps, the Sunday evening after the rain of the day before, we saw not long after sundown a slight scud or mist begin to strike the summit above us, though it was perfectly fair weather generally and there were no clouds over the lower country.

First, perhaps, looking up, we would see a small scud not more than a rod in diameter drifting just over the apex of the mountain. In a few minutes more a somewhat larger one would suddenly make its appearance, and perhaps strike the topmost rocks and invest them for a moment, but as rapidly drift off northeast and disappear. Looking into the southwest sky, which was clear, we would see all at once a small cloud or scud a rod in diameter beginning to form half a mile from the summit, and as it came on it rapidly grew in a mysterious manner, till it was fifty rods or more in diameter, and draped and concealed for a few moments all the summit above us, and then passed off and disappeared northeastward just as it had come on. So that it ap-

Vol. XIV

peared as if the clouds had been attracted by the summit. They also seemed to rise a little as they approached it, and endeavor to go over without striking. I gave this account of it to myself. They were not attracted to the summit, but simply generated there and not elsewhere. There would be a warm southwest wind blowing which was full of moisture, alike over the mountain and all the rest of the country. The summit of the mountain being cool, this warm air began to feel its influence at half a mile distance, and its moisture was rapidly condensed into a small cloud, which expanded as it advanced, and evaporated again as it left the summit. This would go on, apparently, as the coolness of the mountain increased, and generally the cloud or mist reached down as low as our camp from time to time, in the night.

One evening, as I was watching these small clouds forming and dissolving about the summit of our mountain, the sun having just set, I cast my eyes toward the dim bluish outline of the Green Mountains in the clear red evening sky, and, to my delight, I detected exactly over the summit of Saddleback Mountain, some sixty miles distant, its own little cloud, shaped like a parasol and answering to that which capped our mountain, though in this case it did not rest on the mountain, but was considerably above it, and all the rest of the west horizon for forty miles was cloudless.
I was convinced that it was the local cloud of that mountain because it was directly over the summit, was of small size and of umbrella form answering to the summit, and there was no other cloud to be seen in that horizon. It was a beautiful and serene

object, a sort of fortunate isle, — like any other cloud in the sunset sky.

That the summit of this mountain is cool appears from the fact that the days which we spent there were remarkably warm ones in the country below, and were the common subject of conversation when we came down, yet we had known nothing about it, and went warmly clad with comfort all the while, as we had not done immediately before and did not after we descended. We immediately perceived the difference as we descended. It was warm enough for us on the summit, and often, in the sheltered southeast hollows, too warm, as we happened to be clad, but on the summits and ridges it chanced that there was always wind, and in this wind it was commonly cooler than we liked. Also our water, which was evidently rain-water caught in the rocks and retained by the moss, was cool enough if it were only in a little crevice under the shelter of a rock, *i. e.* out of the sun.

Yet, though it was thus cool, and there was this scud or mist on the top more or less every night, there was, as we should say, no dew on the summit any morning. The lichens, blueberry bushes, etc., did not feel wet, nor did they wet you in the least, however early you walked in them. I rose [?] to observe the sunrise and picked blueberries every morning before sunrise, and saw no dew, only once some minute dewdrops on some low grass-tips, and that was amid the wet moss of a little bog, but the lambkill and blueberry bushes above it were not wet. Yet the Thursday when we left, we found that though there was no dew on the summit there

was a very heavy dew in the pastures below, and our feet and clothes were completely wet with it, as much as if we had stood in water.

I should say that there were no true springs (?) on the summit, but simply rain-water caught in the hollows of the rocks or retained by the moss. I observed that the well which we made for washing — by digging up the moss with our hands — half dried up in the sun by day, but filled up again at night.

The principal stream on the summit, — if not the only one, — in the rocky portion described, was on the southeast side, between our two camps, though it did not distinctly show itself at present except a little below our elevation. For the most part you could only see that water had flowed there between and under the rocks.

I fancied once or twice that it was warmer at 10 P. M. than it was immediately after sunset.

The voices of those climbing the summit were heard remarkably far. We heard much of the ordinary conversation of those climbing the peak above us a hundred rods off, and we could hear those on the summit, or a hundred and thirty rods off, when they shouted. I heard a party of ladies and gentlemen laughing and talking there in the night (they were camping there), though I did not hear what they said. We heard, or imagined that we heard, from time to time, as we lay in our camp by day, an occasional chinking or clinking sound as if made by one stone on another.

In clear weather, in going from one part of the summit to another it would be most convenient to steer by distant objects, as towns or mountains or lakes, rather than by features of the summit itself, since the former are most easily recognized and almost always in sight.

I saw what I took to be a thistle-down going low over the summit, and might have caught it, though I saw no thistle on the mountain-top nor any other plant from which this could have come. (I have no doubt it was a thistle by its appearance and its season.) It had evidently come up from the country below. This shows that it may carry its seeds to higher regions than it inhabits, and it suggests how the seeds of some mountain plants, as the *Solidago thyrsoidea*, may be conveyed from mountain to mountain, also other solidagos, asters, epilobiums, willows, etc.

The descent through the woods from our first camp to the site of the shanty is from a third to half a mile. You then come to the raspberry and fern scented region. There were some raspberries still left, but they were fast dropping off.

There was a good view of the mountain from just above the pond, some two miles from Troy. The varying outline of a mountain is due to the crest of different spurs, as seen from different sides. Even a small spur, if you are near, may conceal a much larger one and give its own outline to the mountain, and at the same time one which extends directly toward you is not noticed at all, however important, though, as you travel round the mountain, this may gradually come into view and finally its crest may be one half or more of the outline presented. It may partly account for the peaked or pyramidal form of mountains that one crest may be

seen through the gaps of another and so fill up the line.

Think I saw leersia or cut-grass in bloom in Troy.

I carried on this excursion the following articles (beside what I wore), *viz. :* —

> One shirt.
> One pair socks.
> Two pocket-handkerchiefs.
> One *thick* waistcoat.
> One flannel shirt (had no occasion to use it).
> India-rubber coat.
> Three bosoms.
> Towel and soap.
> Pins, needles, thread.
> A blanket (would have been more convenient if stitched up in the form of a bag).
> Cap for the night.
> Map and compass.
> Spy-glass and microscope and tape.
> Saw and hatchet.
> Plant-book and blotting-paper.
> Paper and stamps.
> Botany.
> Insect and lichen boxes.
> Jack-knife.
> Matches.
> Waste paper and twine.
> Iron spoon and pint dipper with handle.
> > All in a knapsack.
> Umbrella.

N. B. — Add to the above next time a small bag, which may be stuffed with moss or the like for a pillow.

For provision for one, six days, carried : —

2½ lbs. of salt beef and tongue.	Take only salt beef next time, 2 to 3 lbs.

Vol. XIV

18 hard-boiled eggs.	Omit eggs.
2½ lbs. sugar and a little salt.	2 lbs. of sugar would have done.
About ¼ lb. of tea.	⅔ as much would have done.
2 lbs. hard-bread.	The right amount of bread, but might have taken more home-made and more *solid* sweet cake.
½ loaf home-made bread and a piece of cake.	

N. B. — Carry salt (or some of it) in a wafer-box. Also some sugar in a small box.

N. B. — Observe next time: the source of the stream which crosses the path; what species of swallow flies over mountain; what the grass which gives the pastures a yellowish color seen from the summit.

The morning would probably never be ushered in there by the chipping of the chip-bird, but that of the *F. hyemalis* instead, — a dry, hard occasional chirp, more in harmony with the rocks. There you do not hear the *link* of the bobolink, the chatter of red-wings and crow blackbirds, the wood pewee, the twitter of the kingbird, the half [*sic*] strains of the vireo, the passing goldfinch, or the occasional plaintive note of the bluebird, all which are now commonly heard in the lowlands.

That area is literally a chaos, an example of what the earth was before it was finished.[1]

Do I not hear the mole cricket at night?

Aug. 10. 2 P. M. — Air, 84°; Boiling Spring this afternoon., 46°; Brister's, 49°; or where there is little or no

[1] *Vide* Aug. 26 and 28, and Sept. 1.

surface water the same as in spring. Walden is at surface 80° (air over it 76).

Aster dumosus and pennyroyal out; how long? Sand cherry is well ripe — some of it — and tolerable, better than the red cherry or choke-cherry. *Juncus paradoxus*, that large and late juncus (tailed), as in Hubbard's Close and on island above monument and in Great Meadows, say ten days.

Saw yesterday in Fitzwilliam from the railroad a pond covered with white lilies uniformly about half the size of ours!

Saw this evening, behind a picture in R. W. E.'s dining-room, the hoary bat. First heard it fluttering at dusk, it having hung there all day. Its rear parts covered with a fine hoary down.

Aug. 11. Panicum capillare; how long? *Cyperus strigosus;* how long?

Aug. 12. The river-bank is past height. The buttonbush is not common now, though the clethra is in prime. The black willow hardly ceases to shed its down when it looks yellowish. *Setaria glauca*, some days. *Elymus Virginicus*, some days. *Andropogon furcatus* (in meadow); how long? Probably before *scoparius*. Zizania several days.

River at 5 P. M. three and three quarters inches below summer level.

Panicum glabrum (not *sanguinale?* — our common); how long? The upper glume equals the flower, yet it has many spikes.

Aug. 13. P. M. — To Great Meadows and Gowing's Swamp.

Purple grass (*Eragrostis pectinacea*), two or three days. *E. capillaris*, say as much. *Andropogon scoparius*, a day or two. *Calamagrostis coarctata*, not quite. *Glyceria obtusa*, well out; say several days.

Some of the little cranberries at Gowing's Swamp appear to have been frost-bitten. Also the blue-eyed grass, which is now black-topped.

Hear the steady shrill of the alder locust.

Rain this forenoon; windy in afternoon.

Aug. 14. Heavy rain.

Aug. 15. Fair weather.
See a blue heron.

Aug. 16. 2 P. M. — River about ten and a half inches above summer level.

Apparently the Canada plum began to be ripe about the 10th.

Aug. 17. We have cooler nights of late.

See at Pout's Nest two solitary tattlers, as I have seen them about the muddy shore of Gourgas Pond-hole and in the Great Meadow pools. They seem to like a muddier shore than the peetweet.

Hear a whip-poor-will sing to-night.

Aug. 18. The note of the wood pewee sounds prominent of late.

Aug. 19. Examine now more at length that smooth, turnip-scented brassica which is a pest in some grain-fields. Formerly in Stow's land; this year in Warren's, on the Walden road. To-day I see it in Minot Pratt's, with the wild radish, which is a paler yellow and a rougher plant. I thought it before the *B. campestris*, but Persoon puts that under brassicas with *siliquis tetraedris*, which this is not, but, for aught that appears, it agrees with his *B. Napus*, closely allied, *i. e.* wild rape. Elliot speaks of this as introduced here. *Vide* Patent Office Report for 1853 and "Vegetable Kingdom," page 179. The *B. campestris* also is called rape.[1]

Leersia (cut-grass) abundantly out, apparently several days.

Aug. 21. Soaking rains, and in the night.
A few fireflies still at night.

Aug. 22. P. M. — Row to Bittern Cliff.

Now, when the mikania is conspicuous, the bank is past prime,[2] for lilies are far gone, the pontederia is past prime, willows and button-bushes begin to look the worse for the wear thus early, — the lower or older leaves of the willows are turned yellow and decaying, — and many of the meadows are shorn. Yet now is the time for the cardinal-flower. The already, *methinks*, yellowing willows and button-bushes, the half-shorn meadows, the higher water on their edges, with wool-grass standing over it, with the notes of flitting bobolinks and red-wings of *this year*, in rustling flocks, all tell of the fall.

[1] *Vide* Sept. 8.   [2] *Vide* Sept. 5.

I hear two or three times behind me the loud *creaking* note of a wood duck which I have scared up, which goes to settle in a new place.

Some deciduous trees are now at least as dark as evergreens, the alders are darker than white pines, and as dark as pitch, as I now see them.

I try the temperature of the river at Bittern Cliff, the deep place. The air over river at 4.30 is 81°; the water at the top, 78°; poured from a bottle (into a dipper) which I let lie on the bottom half an hour, 73°, — or 5° difference. When I merely sunk the thermometer and pulled it up rapidly it stood 73½, though not in exactly the same place, — say two rods off.

When I used to pick the berries for dinner on the East Quarter hills I did not eat one till I had done, for going a-berrying implies more things than eating the berries. They at home got only the pudding: I got the forenoon out of doors, and the appetite for the pudding.

It is true, as is said, that we have as good a right to make berries private property as to make grass and trees such; but what I chiefly regret is the, in effect, dog-in-the-manger result, for at the same time that we exclude mankind from gathering berries in our field, we exclude them from gathering health and happiness and inspiration and a hundred other far finer and nobler fruits than berries, which yet we shall not gather ourselves there, nor even carry to market. We strike only one more blow at a simple and wholesome relation to nature. As long as the berries are free to all comers they are beautiful, though they may be few and small, but tell me that is a blueberry swamp which somebody has

hired, and I shall not want even to look at it. In laying claim for the first time to the spontaneous fruit of our pastures we are, accordingly, aware of a little meanness inevitably, and the gay berry party whom we turn away naturally look down on and despise us. If it were left to the berries to say who should have them, is it not likely that they would prefer to be gathered by the party of children in the hay-rigging, who have come to have a good time merely?

I do not see clearly that these successive losses are ever quite made up to us. This is one of the taxes which we pay for having a railroad. Almost all our improvements, so called, tend to convert the country into the town.

This suggests what origin and foundation many of our laws and institutions have, and I do not say this by way of complaining of this particular custom. Not that I love Cæsar less, but Rome more.

Yes, and a potato-field is a rich sight to me, even when the vines are half decayed and blackened and their decaying scent fills the air, though unsightly to many; for it speaks then more loudly and distinctly of potatoes than ever. I see their weather-beaten brows peeping out of the hills here and there, for the earth cannot contain them, when the creak of the cricket and the shrilling of the locust prevail more and more, in the sunny end of summer. There the confident husbandman lets them lie for the present, even as if he knew not of them, or as if that property were insured, so carelessly rich he is. He relaxes now his labors somewhat, seeing to their successful end, and takes long mornings, perchance, stretched in the shade of his ancestral elms.

Returning down the river, when I get to Clamshell I see great flocks of the young red-wings and some crow blackbirds on the trees and the ground. They are not very shy, but only timid, as inexperienced birds are. I do not know what they find to eat on this half bare, half grassy bank, but there they hop about by hundreds, while as many more are perched on the neighboring trees; and from time to time they all rise from the earth and wheel and withdraw to the trees, but soon return to the ground again. The red-wings are almost reddish about the throat. The crow blackbirds have some notes now just like the first croaks of the wood frog in the spring.

Sorghum nutans well out (behind the birch); how long? Paspalum ditto.

The recent heavy rains have washed away the bank here considerably, and it looks and smells more mouldy with human relics than ever. I therefore find myself inevitably exploring it. On the edge of the ravine whose beginning I witnessed, one foot beneath the surface and just over a layer some three inches thick of pure shells and ashes, — a gray-white line on the face of the cliff. — I find several pieces of Indian pottery with a rude ornament on it, not much more red than the earth itself. Looking farther, I find more fragments, which have been washed down the sandy slope in a stream, as far as ten feet. I find in all thirty-one pieces, averaging an inch in diameter and about a third of an inch thick. Several of them made part of the upper edge of the vessel, and have a rude ornament encircling them in three rows, as if pricked with a stick in the soft clay, and also an-

other line on the narrow edge itself. At first I thought to match the pieces again, like a geographical puzzle, but I did not find that any I [got] belonged together. The vessel must have been quite large, and I have not got nearly all of it. It appears to have been an impure clay with much sand and gravel in it, and I think a little pounded shell. It is [of] very unequal thickness, some of the unadorned pieces (probably the bottom) being half an inch thick, while near the edge it is not more than a quarter of an inch thick. There was under this spot and under the layer of shells a manifest hollowness in the ground, not yet filled up. I find many small pieces of bone in the soil of this bank, probably of animals the Indians ate.

In another part of the bank, in the midst of a much larger heap of shells which has been exposed, I found a delicate stone tool of this form and size: of a soft slate-stone. It is very thin and sharp on each side edge, and in the middle is not more than an eighth of an inch thick. I suspect that this was used to open clams with.

It is curious that I had expected to find as much as this, and in this very spot too, before I reached it (I mean the pot). Indeed, I never find a remark-

able Indian relic — and I find a good many — but I have first divined its existence, and planned the discovery of it. Frequently I have told myself distinctly what it was to be before I found it.

The river is fifteen and three quarters inches above summer level.[1]

Aug. 24. This and yesterday very foggy, dogdayish days. Yesterday the fog lasted till nine or ten, and to-day, in the afternoon, it amounts to a considerable drizzling rain.

P. M. — To Walden to get its temperature. The air is only 66 (in the mizzling rain the 23d it was 78); the water at top, 75° (the 23d also 75). What I had sunk to the bottom in the middle, where a hundred feet deep by my line, left there half an hour, then pulled up and poured into a quart dipper, stood at 53°.[2] I tried the same experiment yesterday, but then in my haste was uncertain whether it was not 51°; certain that a little later it was 54°. So 53° it must be for the present. I may have been two or more minutes pulling up the line so as to prevent its snarling. Therefore I think the water must have acquired a temperature two or three degrees higher than it had at the bottom by the time I tried it. So it appears that the bottom of Walden has, in fact, the temperature of a genuine and cold spring, or probably is of the same temperature with the average mean temperature of the earth, and, I *suspect*, the same all the year. This shows that springs need not come from a very great depth in order to be cold. What various tem-

[1] And about the same the 25th. [2] *Vide* 28th.

peratures, then, the fishes of this pond can enjoy! They require no other refrigerator than their deeps afford. They can in a few moments sink to winter or rise to summer. Walden, then, must be included among the springs, but it is one which has no outlet, — is a well rather. It reaches down to where the temperature of the earth is unchanging. It is not a superficial pond, — not in the mere skin of the earth. It goes deeper. How much this varied temperature must have to do with the distribution of the fishes in it! The few trout must oftenest go down below in summer.

At the bottom of the deep cove I see much black birch and red maple just sprung up, and their seeds have evidently been drifted to this shore. The little birches are already fragrant.

Aug. 25. 2 P. M. — To Clamshell.

See a large hen-hawk sailing over Hubbard's meadow and Clamshell, soaring at last very high and toward the north. At last it returns southward, at that height impelling itself steadily and swiftly forward with its wings set in this wise: *i. e.* more curved, or, as it were, trailing behind, without apparent motion. It thus moves half a mile directly.

The front-rank polygonum is apparently in prime; low, solid, of a pinkish rose-color. Notice the small botrychium's leaf.

As I row by, see a green bittern near by standing erect on Monroe's boat. Finding that it is observed, it draws in its head and stoops to conceal itself. When it flies it seems to have no tail. It allowed me to approach so near, apparently being deceived by some tame ducks there.

Aug. 26. 2 p. m. — To White Pond.

The leersia or cut-grass in the old pad ditch by path beyond Hubbard's Grove.

As I cross the upland sprout-land south of Ledum Swamp, I see that the fine sedge there is half withered and brown, and it is too late for that cheerful yellow gleam.

Thread my way through the blueberry swamp in front of Martial Miles's. The high blueberries far above your head in the shade of the swamp retain their freshness and coolness a long time. Little blue sacks full of swampy nectar and ambrosia commingled, like schnapps or what-not, that you break with your teeth. Is not this the origin of the German name as given by Gerard? But there is far the greatest show of choke-berries there, rich to see. I wade and press my way through endless thickets of these untasted berries, their lower leaves now fast reddening. Yet they have an agreeable juice, — though the pulp may be rejected, — and perhaps they might be made into wine.

The shrilling of the alder locust is the solder that welds these autumn days together. All bushes (*arbusta*) resound with their song, and you wade up to your ears in it. Methinks the burden of their song is the countless harvests of the year, — berries, grain, and other fruits.

I am interested by the little ridge or cliff of foam which the breeze has raised along the White Pond shore, the westerly breeze causing the wavelets to lapse on the

shore and mix the water with the air gradually. Though this is named *White* Pond from the whiteness of its sandy shore, the line of foam is infinitely whiter, far whiter than any sand. This reminds me how far a white pond-shore, *i. e.* the sand, may be seen. I saw from Monadnock the north shore of a large pond in Nelson which was some eight miles north by the map, very distinct to every one who looked that way. Perhaps in such cases a stronger light is reflected from the water on to the shore. The highest ridge of foam is where it is held or retained and so built up gradually behind some brush or log on the shore, by additions below, into a little cliff, like a sponge. In other places it is rolled like a muff. It is all light and trembling in the air.

Thus we are amused with foam, a hybrid between two elements. A breeze comes and gradually mingles some of the water with the air. It is, as it were, the aspiration of the pond to soar into the air. The debatable ground between two oceans, the earth, or shore, being only the point of resistance, where they are held to mingle.

See nowadays the pretty little Castile-soap galls on the shrub oaks. Their figure is like the Indian girdle of triangular points. Also other galls, yellowish and red on different sides.

The pussy clover heads were most interesting, large, and puffy, say ten days ago.

I notice milkweed in a hollow in the field by the cove at White Pond, as if the seed had settled there, owing to the lull of the wind.

It is remarkable how commonly you see the thistle-down sailing just over water (as I do after this — the 2d

of September — at Walden). I see there, *i. e.* at Walden, at 5 p. m., September 2d, many seedless thistle-downs sailing about a foot above the water, and some in it, as if there was a current just above the surface which prevented their falling or rising. They are probably wafted to the water because there is more air over water.

Aug. 27. P. M. — To Ministerial Swamp.

Clear weather within a day or two after the thick dog-days. The nights have been cooler of late, but the heat of the sun by day has been more local and palpable, as it were. It is as if the sun touched your shoulder with a hot hand while there are cool veins in the air. That is, I am from time to time surprised and oppressed by a melting heat on my back in the sun, though I am sure of a greater general coolness. The heat is less like that of an apartment equably warmed, and more like that [of] a red-hot iron carried about and which you occasionally come near.

See one of the shrilling green alder locusts on the under side of a grape leaf. Its body is about three quarters of an inch or less in length; antennæ and all, two inches. Its wings are at first perpendicular above its shoulders, it apparently having just ceased shrilling. Transparent, with lines crossing them.

Notice now that sour-tasting white (creamy, for consistence) incrustation between and on the berries of the smooth sumach, like frostwork. Is it not an exudation? or produced by the bite of an insect?

Calamagrostis coarctata grass by Harrington's Pool, Ministerial Swamp, say one week (not in prime).

Muhlenbergia glomerata, same place, say ten days, or past prime.

Gather some of those large and late low blackberries (as at Thrush Alley) which run over the thin herbage, green moss, etc., in open pitch pine woods.

Aug. 28. About 6.20 p. m. paddled on Walden. Near the shore I see at least one little skater to a foot, further off one to a yard, and in middle not more than one to a rod; but I see no gyrinus at all here to-night.

At first the sky was completely overcast, but, just before setting, the sun came out into a clear space in the horizon and fell on the east end of the pond and the hillside, and this sudden blaze of light on the still very fresh green leaves was a wonderful contrast with the previous and still surrounding darkness. Indeed, the bright sunlight was at this angle reflected from the water at the east end — while I in the middle was in the shade of the east woods — up under the verdure of the bushes and trees on the shore and on Pine Hill, especially to the tender under sides and to the lower leaves not often lit up. Thus a double amount of light fell on them, and the most vivid and varied shades of green were revealed. I never saw such a green *glow* before. The outline of each shrub and tree was a more or less distinct downy or silvery crescent, where the light was reflected from the under side of the most downy, or newest, leaves, — as I should not have seen it at midday, — either because the light fell more on the under sides of the leaves, being so horizontal and also reflected upward, or because the leaves stood more erect at this hour and after a cloudy day, or for both reasons. The lit water at the east end was invisible to me, or no more than a line, but the shore itself was a very distinct whitish line. When the sun fell lower, and the sunlight no longer fell on the pond, the green blaze of the hillside was at once very much diminished, because the light was no longer reflected upward to it.

At sunset the air over the pond is 62 + ; the water at the top, 74°; poured from a stoppled bottle which lay at the bottom where one hundred feet deep, twenty or thirty minutes, 55° (and the same when drawn up in an open bottle which lay five minutes at the bottom); in an open bottle drawn up from about fifty feet depth (*there*) or more, after staying there five minutes, 63°. This about half the whole difference between the top and bottom, so that the temperature seems to fall regularly as you descend, at the rate of about one degree to five feet. When I let the stoppled bottle down *quickly*, the cork was forced out before it got to the bottom, when [?] the water drawn up stood at 66°. Hence it seemed to be owing to the rising of the warmer water and air in the bottle. Five minutes with the open bottle at the bottom was as good as twenty with it stoppled.

I found it 2° warmer than the 24th, though the air was then 4° warmer than now. Possibly, comparing one day with the next, it is warmer at the bottom in a cold day and colder in a warm day, because when the surface is cooled it mixes more with the bottom, while the average temperature is very slightly changed.

The *Lycopodium inundatum* common by Harrington's mud-hole, Ministerial Swamp.

Hear the night-warbler and whip-poor-will.

There was no prolonged melody of birds on the summit of Monadnock. They for the most part emitted sounds there more in harmony with the silent rocks, — a faint chipping or *chink*ing, often somewhat as of two stones struck together.

Aug. 30. Surveying Minott's land.

Am surprised to find on his hard land, where he once raised potatoes, the hairy huckleberry, which before I had seen in swamps only. Here, too, they are more edible, not so insipid, yet not quite edible generally. They are improved, you would say, by the firmer ground. The berries are in longer racemes or clusters than any of our huckleberries. They are the prevailing berry all over this field. They are oblong and black, and the thick, shaggy-feeling coats left in the mouth are far from agreeable to the palate. Are now in prime.

Also find, in one of his ditches where peat was dug (or mud), the *Lemna polyrhiza;* not found in Concord before, and said not to blossom in this country. I found it at Pushaw. Also the *Muhlenbergia glomerata* near the lemna, or southeast of it.

The hairy huckleberry and muhlenbergia, I think, grow here still because Minott is an old-fashioned man and has not scrubbed up and improved his land as many, or most, have. It is in a wilder and more primitive condition. The very huckleberries are shaggy there. There was only one straight side to his land, and that I cut through a dense swamp. The fences are all meandering, just as they were at least in 1746, when it was described.

Vol. XIV

The lemna reminds me strongly of that greenish or yellowish scum which I see mantling some barn-yard pools. It makes the same impression on the eye at a little distance. You would say it was the next higher stage of vegetation. The smallest of *pads*, one sixth of an inch in diameter and, like the white lily pad, crimson beneath. It completely covers two or three ditches under the edge of the wood there, except where a frog has jumped in and revealed the dark water, — and maybe there rests, his green snout concealed amid it; but it soon closes over him again when he has dived. These minute green scales completely cover some ditches, except where a careless frog has leapt in or swam across, and rent the veil.

There is also, floating in little masses, a small ranunculus-like plant, flattish-stemmed with small forks, some of it made into minute caddis-cases. Perhaps it was cut up by some creature at the bottom. *Vide* press.

II

SEPTEMBER, 1860

(ÆT. 43)

Sept. 1. P. M. — To Walden.

Saw a fish hawk yesterday up the Assabet. In one position it flew just like a swallow; of the same form as it flew.

We could not judge correctly of distances on the mountain, but greatly exaggerated them. That surface was so novel, — suggested so many thoughts, — and also so uneven, a few steps sufficing to conceal the least ground, as if it were half a mile away, that we would have an impression as if we had travelled a mile when we had come only forty rods. We no longer thought and reasoned as in the plain.

Now see many birds about E. Hubbard's elder hedge, — bobolinks, kingbirds, pigeon woodpeckers, — and not elsewhere.

Many pine stipules fallen yesterday. Also see them on Walden to-day.

Hear that F. Hayden saw and heard geese a fortnight ago!

I see within an oak stump on the shore of Walden tomato plants six or eight inches high, as I found them formerly about this pond in a different place. Since they do not bear fruit the seed must be annually brought here by birds, yet I do not see them pecking the tomatoes in our gardens, and this is a mile and a half from the village and half a mile from the nearest house in Lincoln.

River about eight inches above summer level yesterday.

We are so accustomed to see another forest spring up immediately as a matter of course, whether from the stump or from the seed, when a forest is cut down, never troubling about the succession, that we hardly associate the seed with the tree, and do not anticipate the time when this regular succession will cease and we shall be obliged to plant, as they do in all old countries. The planters of Europe must have a very different, a much correcter, notion of the value of the seed of forest trees than we. To speak generally, they know that the forest trees spring from seeds, as we do of apples and pears, but we know only that they come out of the earth.

See how artfully the seed of a cherry is placed in order that a bird may be compelled to transport it. It is placed in the very midst of a tempting pericarp, so that the creature that would devour a cherry must take a stone into its mouth. The bird is bribed with the pericarp to take the stone with it and do this little service for Nature. Cherries are especially birds' food, and many kinds are called birds' cherry, and unless we plant the seeds occasionally, I shall think the birds have the best right to them. Thus a bird's wing is added to the cherry-stone which was wingless, and it does not wait for winds to transport it. If you ever ate a cherry, and did not make two bites of it, you must have perceived it. There it is, right in the midst of the luscious morsel,

an earthy residuum left on the tongue. And some wild men and children instinctively swallow it, like the birds, as the shortest way to get rid of it. And the consequence is that cherries not only grow here but there, and I know of some handsome young English cherries growing naturally in our woods, which I think of transplanting back again to my garden. If the seed had been placed in a leaf, or at the root, it would not have got transported thus. Consider how many seeds of plants we take into our mouths. Even stones as big as peas, a dozen at once.

The treatment of forests is a very different question to us and to the English. There is a great difference between replanting the cleared land from the superabundance of seed which is produced in the forest around it, which will soon be done by nature alone if we do not interfere, and the planting of land the greater part of which has been cleared for more than a thousand years.

Sept. 2. P. M. — To Annursnack.
Solidago nemoralis apparently in prime, and *S. stricta.* The former covers A. Hosmer's secluded turtle field near the bridge, together with johnswort, now merely lingering.

Sept. 3. P. M. — To Bateman's Pond.
2 P. M. — River six and seven eighths above [summer level].
Here is a beautiful, and perhaps *first* decidedly autumnal, day, — a cloudless sky, a clear air, with,

[1] [*Excursions*, p. 188; Riv. 230, 231.]

maybe, veins of coolness. As you look toward the sun, the [*sic*] shines more than in the spring. The dense fresh green grass which has sprung up since it was mowed, on most ground, reflects a blaze of light, as if it were morning all the day. The meads and slopes are enamelled with it, for there has been no drought nor withering. We see the smokes of burnings on various sides. The farmers are thus clearing up their pastures, — some, it may be, in preparation for plowing. Though it is warm enough, I notice again the swarms of fuzzy gnats dancing in the cooler air, which also is decidedly autumnal.

See on the two pear trees by the Boze cellar ripe pears, some ripe several days. Most are bitter, others mealy, but one was quite sweet and good, of middling size, and prettier than most cultivated ones. It had a few faint streaks of red and was exceeding wax-like.

Sept. 4. P. M. — To Conantum.
At my Swamp Brook crossing at Willow Bay, I see where a great many little red maples have sprung up in a potato-field, apparently since the last plowing or cultivating this year. They extend more or less thickly as much as eleven rods in a northwest direction from a small tree, the only red maple in that neighborhood. And it is evidently owing to the land having been cultivated this year that the seed vegetated there; otherwise there would now be no evidence that any such seeds had fallen here. Last year and for many years it has been a pasture. It is evident that land may be kept as a pasture and covered with grass any number of years, and though there are maples adjacent to it, none of the

seed will catch in it; but at last it is plowed, and this year the seed which falls on it germinates, and if it chances not to be plowed again, and cattle are kept out, you soon have a maple wood there. So of other light-seeded trees.

It is cooler these days and nights, and I move into an eastern chamber in the morning, that I may sit in the sun. The water, too, is cooler when I bathe in it, and I am reminded that this recreation has its period. I feel like a melon or other fruit laid in the sun to ripen. I grow, not gray, but yellow.

Saw flocks of pigeons the 2d and 3d. I see and hear on Conantum an upland plover. The goldfinch is very busy pulling the thistle to pieces.

What I have called *Muhlenbergia sobolifera* is in prime (say a week); the *M. Mexicana* not quite (say in two or three days).

Sept. 5. P. M. — To Ball's Hill.
The brink of the river [1] is still quite interesting in some respects, and to some eyes more interesting than ever. Though the willows and button-bushes have already assumed an autumnal hue, and the pontederia is extensively crisped and blackened, the dense masses of mikania, now, it may be, paler than before, are perhaps more remarkable than ever. I see some masses of it, overhanging the deep water and completely concealing the bush that supports them, which are as rich a sight as any flower we have, — little terraces of contiguous corymbs, like mignonette (?). Also the dodder is

[1] *Vide* Aug. 22d.

more revealed, also draping the brink over the water. The mikania is sometimes looped seven or eight feet high to a tree above the bushes, — a manifest vine, with its light-colored corymbs at intervals.

See the little dippers back. Did I not see a marsh hawk in imperfect plumage? Quite brown, with some white midway the wings, and tips of wings black?

What further adds to the beauty of the bank is the hibiscus, in prime, and the great bidens.

Having walked through a quantity of desmodium under Ball's Hill, by the shore there (*Marilandicum* or *rigidum*), we found our pants covered with its seeds to a remarkable and amusing degree. These green scales closely covering and greening my legs reminded me of the lemna on a ditch. It amounted to a kind of coat of mail. It was the event of our walk, and we were proud to wear this badge, as if he were the most distinguished who had the most on his clothes. My companion expressed a certain superstitious feeling about it, for he said he thought it would not be right to walk intentionally amid the desmodium so as to get more of the ticks on us, nor yet to pick them off, but they must be carried about till they are rubbed off accidentally. I saw that Nature's design was furthered even by his superstition.

Sept. 6. The willows and button-bushes have very rapidly yellowed since I noticed them August 22d. I think it was the 25th of August that I found the lower or older leaves of the willow twigs decidedly and rapidly yellowing and decaying on a near inspection. Now the change is conspicuous at a distance.

Sept. 7. P. M. — To Cardinal Shore.

I see many seedling shrub oaks springing up in Potter's field by the swamp-side, some (of last year) in the open pasture, but many more in the birch wood half a dozen rods west from the shrub oaks by the path. The former were dropped by the way. They plant in birch woods as in pines. This small birch wood has been a retreat for squirrels and birds. When I examine the little oaks in the *open* land there is always an effete acorn with them.

Common rose hips as handsome as ever.

Sept. 8. To Lowell *via* Boston.

Rainy day.

Pursh's [*sic*] [1] *Brassica Napus* is "radice caulescente fusiformi, fol. laevibus, superioribus cordato-lanceolatis amplexicaulibus, inferioribus lyratis dentatis." Frequently found wild. The lower leaves of mine are considerably bristly. Sowerby's Botany at Cambridge says of *B. campestris*, "Pods upright, cylindrical, or very obscurely quadrangular, veiny, the seeds slightly projecting, the beak awl-shaped, striated, square at its base." *B. Napus*, — "Pod on a slender stalk, spreading, round, beaded, with an angular point." Mine is apparently *B. Napus*, judging from pods, for the lower leaves are all eaten. *Vide* young plants in spring.[2]

Sept. 9. In Lowell. — My host says that the thermometer was at 80° yesterday morning, and this morning is at 52°. Sudden coolness.

[1] [The quotation is from Persoon's *Synopsis Plantarum*.]
[2] *Vide* back, Aug. 19th.

Vol. XIV

Clears up in afternoon, and I walk down the Merrimack on the north bank. I see very large plants of the lanceolate thistle, four feet high and very branching. Also *Aster cordata* with the *corymbosus*.

Concord River has a high and hard bank at its mouth, maybe thirty feet high on the east side; and my host thinks it was originally about as high on the west side, where now it is much lower and flat, having been dug down. There is a small isle in the middle of the mouth. There are rips in the Merrimack just below the mouth of the Concord. There is a fall and dam in the Concord at what was Hurd's factory, — the principal fall on the Concord, in Lowell, — one at a bleachery above, and at Whipple's, — three in all below Billerica dam.

Sept. 10. Lowell to Boston and Concord.

There was a frost this morning, as my host, who keeps a market, informed me.

Leaving Lowell at 7 A. M. in the cars, I observed and admired the dew on a fine grass in the meadows, which was almost as white and silvery as frost when the rays of the newly risen sun fell on it. Some of it *was* probably the frost of the morning melted. I saw that this phenomenon was confined to one species of grass, which grew in narrow curving lines and small patches along the edges of the meadows or lowest ground, — a grass with very fine stems and branches, which held the dew; in short, that it was what I had falsely called *Eragrostis capillaris*, but which is probably the *Sporobolus serotinus*, almost the only, if not the only, grass there in its prime. And thus this plant has its day. Owing to the number of its

very fine branches, now in their prime, it holds the dew like a cobweb, — a clear drop at the end and lesser drops or beads all along the fine branches and stems. It grows on the higher parts of the meadows, where other herbage is thin, and is the less apt to be cut; and, seen toward the sun not long after sunrise, it is very conspicuous and bright a quarter of a mile off, like frostwork. Call it dew-grass. I find its *hyaline* seed.[1]

Almost every plant, however humble, has thus its day, and sooner or later becomes the characteristic feature of some part of the landscape or other.

Almost all other grasses are now either cut or withering, and are, beside, so coarse comparatively that they can never present this phenomenon. It is only a grass that is in its full vigor, as well as fine-branched (capillary), that can thus attract and uphold the dew. This is noticed about the time the first frosts come.

If you sit at an open attic window almost anywhere, about the 20th of September, you will see many a milkweed down go sailing by on a level with you, — though commonly it has lost its freight, — notwithstanding that you may not know of any of these plants growing in your neighborhood.

My host, yesterday, told me that he was accustomed once to chase a *black* fox [2] from Lowell over this way and lost him at Chelmsford. Had heard of him within about six years. A Carlisle man also tells me since that this fox used to turn off and run northwest from Chelmsford, but that he would soon after return.

[1] Also saw it the 16th.
[2] Like the silver, made a variety of the red by Baird.

Sept. 11. George Melvin came to tell me this forenoon that a strange animal was killed on Sunday, the 9th, near the north line of the town, and it was not known certainly what it was. From his description I judged it to be a Canada lynx. In the afternoon I went to see it. It was killed on Sunday morning by John Quincy Adams, who lives in Carlisle about half a mile (or less) from the Concord line, on the Carlisle road.

Some weeks ago a little girl named Buttrick, who was huckleberrying near where the lynx was killed, was frightened by a wild animal leaping out of the bushes near her — *over* her, as she said — and bounding off. But no one then regarded her story. Also a Mr. Grimes, who lives in Concord just on the line, tells me that some month ago he heard from his house the loud cry of an animal in the woods northward, and told his wife that if he were in Canada he should say it was a bob-tailed cat. He had lived seven years in Canada and seen a number of this kind of animal. Also a neighbor of his, riding home in the night, had heard a similar cry. Jacob Farmer saw a strange animal at Bateman's Pond a year ago, which he thinks was this.

Adams had lost some of his hens, and had referred it to a fox or the like. He being out, his son told me that on Sunday he went out with his gun to look after the depredator, and some forty or fifty rods from his house northwesterly [1] (on Dr. Jones's lot, which I surveyed) in the woods, this animal suddenly dropped within two feet of him, so near that he could not fire. He had heard a loud hiss, but did not mind it. He accordingly struck

[1] *Vide* forward.

Vol. XIV

hair. A principal claw was ¾ inch long measured directly, but it was very curving.

For color: It was, above, brownish-gray, with a dark-brown or black line down the middle of the back. Sides gray, with small dark-brown spots, more or less within the hair. Beneath, lighter, *hoary*, and long-haired. Legs gray, like the sides, but more reddish-brown behind, especially the hind legs, and these, like the belly and sides, were indistinctly spotted with dark brown, having the effect more of a dark-brown tinge at a little distance than of spots. General aspect brownish-hoary. Tail, above, more reddish than rest of back, much, and conspicuously black at end. Did not notice any white at tip. Throat pretty white. Ears, without, broadly edged with black half an inch or more wide, the rest being a triangular white. There

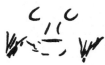

was but a small muffler, chiefly a triangular whitish and blackish tuft on the sides of the face or neck, not noticeably under the chin.

It weighed, by their account, nineteen pounds. This was a female, and Farmer judged from his examination of the mammæ — two or more of them being enlarged, and the hair worn off around them — that it had suckled young this year. The fur was good for nothing now.

I cannot doubt that this is a Canada lynx; yet I am somewhat puzzled by the descriptions of the two lynxes. Emmons says of the Canada lynx that it has "no naked

it with the butt of his gun, and it then bounded off fifteen feet [1] or more, turned about, and faced him, whereupon he fired directly into its eyes, putting them out. His gun was loaded with small shot, No. 9. The creature then bounded out of sight, and he had a chance to reload, by which time it appeared again, crawling toward him on its belly, fiercely seeking him. He fired again, and, it still facing him, he fired a third time also, and finally finished it with the butt of his gun.

It was now skinned and the skin stuffed with hay, and the skull had been boiled, in order to be put into the head.

I measured the stuffed skin carefully. From the forehead (the nose pointing down) to end of tail, 3 feet 4½ [inches]. Tail stout and black at the abrupt end, 5 inches. Extreme length from fore paws to hind paws, 4 feet 8 inches, when stretched out, the skin being *stiff*. (They said it measured 5 feet before it was skinned, which is quite likely.) Forehead to extremity of hind feet, 50½ inches. It stood, as nearly as I could measure, holding it up, 19 to 20 inches high from ground to shoulder. From midway between the legs beneath, the hind legs measured 19 inches, within; the fore legs, 16 inches, within. From skull to end of tuft on ear, 4½ inches; tuft on ear (black and thin), 1½ inches. The width of fore paw gently pressed was 3½ inches; would have made a track perhaps four inches wide in snow. There was a small *bare* brown tubercle of flesh to each toe, and also a larger one for the sole, amid the grayish-white

[1] Another says he told him thirty feet and that they went and measured it. *Vide* forward.

spots or tubercles [on the soles of its feet] like the other species of the feline race;" and Audubon says, "Soles, hairy;" but of the *Lynx rufus*, "Soles . . . naked." It is Audubon's *L. rufus* in the naked soles, also in "ears, outer surface, a triangular spot of dull white, . . . bordered with brownish-black," not described in his *Canadensis*. It is his *L. Canadensis* in size, in color generally, in length of ear-tuft (his *L. rufus* tufts being only half an inch), in "upper surface of the tail, to within an inch of the tip, and exterior portion of the thighs, rufous," in tail being stout, not "slender" like *rufus*. Audubon says that the *L. rufus* is easily distinguished from small specimens of the female *L. Canadensis* by "the larger feet and more tufted ears of the latter, . . . as well as its grayer color." This is four inches longer than his smaller Canada lynx and exactly as long as his larger one, — both his being males. Emmons's one is also just 37 inches, or the same length. Emmons's largest *L. rufus* is, thus measured, only 29 inches long and Audubon's "fine specimen" only 30 inches.

Grimes, who had lived seven years in Canada, called this a "bob-tailed cat," and said that the Canada lynx was as dark as his dog, which would be called a black dog, though somewhat brownish.

They told me there that a boy had seen another, supposed to be its mate,[1] this morning, and that they were going out to hunt it toward night.[2]

The water is cold to-day, and bathing begins to be questionable.

[1] Only a stone.   [2] *Vide* next page.

The turtles, painted and sternothærus, are certainly less timid than in the spring. I see a row of half a dozen or more painted turtles on a slanting black willow, so close together that two or three of them actually have their fore feet on the shells of their predecessors, somewhat like a row of bricks that is falling. The scales of some are curled up and just falling.

Sept. 12. Very heavy rain to-day (equinoctial), raising the river suddenly. I have said, within a week, that the river would rise this fall because it did not at all in the spring, and now it rises. A very dark and stormy night (after it); shops but half open. Where the fence is not painted white I can see nothing, and go whistling for fear I run against some one, though there is little danger that any one will be out. I come against a stone post and bruise my knees; then stumble over a bridge, — being in the gutter. You walk with your hands out to feel the fences and trees. There is no vehicle in the street to-night.

The thermometer at 4 P. M. was 54°.

There was pretty high wind in the night.

Sept. 13. I go early to pick up my windfalls. Some of them are half buried in the soil, the rain having spattered the dirt over them.

The river this morning, about 7 A. M., is already twenty-eight and a half inches above summer level, and more than twenty inches of this is owing to the rain of yesterday and last night!! By 1.30 P. M., when it has risen two or three inches more, I can just cross the

meadow in a straight line to the Rock. I see a snake swimming on the middle of the tide, far from shore, washed out of the meadow, and myriads of grasshoppers and beetles, etc., are wrecked or clinging to the weeds and stubble that rises above the flood. At evening the river is five inches higher than in the morning.

There is very little current at my boat's place this evening, yet a chip floats down (and next morning, the 14th, I see that a large limb has been carried up-stream during the night, from where it lay at evening, some twenty rods above the junction, to a place thirty rods above the junction). Yet, when I try the current (in the evening of the 13th) with a chip, it goes down at Heron Rock, but the limb was large and irregular, and sank very deep in the water; so I think that the Assabet water was running up beneath while the Musketaquid flowed down over it slowly.

A Carlisle man tells me of a coon he killed in Carlisle which weighed twenty-three and a half pounds and dressed fourteen pounds. He frequently sees and hears them at present.

On the 13th I go to J. Q. Adams's again to see the lynx. Farmer said that if the skin was tainted the hair would come off.

The tail is black at extremity for one inch, and no white at tip; the rest of it above is rust-color (beneath it is white), with the slightest possible suggestion of white rings, *i. e.* a few white hairs noticed. When stretched or spread the fore foot measured just 5 inches in width, the hind foot scarcely less than 6 inches. The

black border on the ear was broadest on the inner (*i. e.* toward the other ear) and forward side, — ½ inch and more. The tufts on the ears only about ⅛+ inch wide.

Adams went to show me the carcass. It was quite sweet still (13th, in afternoon), only a little fly-blown. No quadruped or bird had touched it. Remarkably long and slender, made for jumping. The muscles of the thigh were proportionately very large. I thought the thigh would measure *now* 9 inches in circumference. I had heard that there was nothing in its stomach, but he opened the paunch and found it full of rabbits' fur. I cut off a fore leg.

He said that he had lost two or three hens only, and apparently did not think much of that. The first he knew the animal was within three feet of him, so that he could hardly turn his gun to strike him. He did not know where he came from, — whether from over the wall, to which he was near, or from a chestnut, for he was in the midst of the woods of Jones's lot, *not cut.* He felt somewhat frightened. Struck him with the butt of his gun, but did not hurt him much, he was so quick. He jumped at once *thirty feet*, turned round, and faced him. He then fired, about thirty feet, at his eyes, and destroyed one, — perhaps put out the other, too. He then bounded out of sight. When he had loaded he found him crawling toward him on his belly as if to spring upon him; fired again, and thinks he mortally wounded him then. After loading, approached, and the lynx faced him, all alive. He then fired, and the lynx leapt up fifteen feet, fell, and died. Either at the second or last shot

leapt within ten feet of him. He was much impressed by his eyes and the ruff standing out on the sides of his neck.

This was about one hundred and thirty rods easterly from his house.

The skinned tail measured 5 inches. I boiled the leg on the 14th (five days after it was killed) for the bone. It smelled and looked like very good meat, like mutton.

Vide Salem lynxes, September 23d, 1858.[1]

It is remarkable how slow people are to believe that there are any wild animals in their neighborhood. They who have seen this generally suppose that it got out of a menagerie; others that it strayed down from far north. At most they call it *Canada* lynx. In Willey's White Mountain book the same animal is spoken of as a terror to the hunter and called the "Siberian Lynx." What they call it I know not.

I do not think it necessary even to suppose it a straggler, but only very rare hereabouts. I have seen two lynxes that were killed between here and Salem since '27. Have heard of another killed in or near Andover. There may have been many more killed as near within thirty years and I not have heard of it, for they who kill one commonly do not know what it is. They are nocturnal in their habits, and therefore are the more rarely seen, yet a strange animal is seen in this town by somebody about every year, or its track. I have heard of two or three such within a year, and of half a dozen within fifteen years. Such an animal might range fifteen to twenty miles back and forth from Acton to Tewksbury

[1] *Vide* extract from Richardson, Nov. 10, 1860.

and find more woodland than in the southern part of New Hampshire generally.

Farmer says that a farmer in Tewksbury told him two or three years ago that he had seen deer lately on the pine plain thereabouts.

Adams got a neighbor to help him skin the lynx, a middle-aged man; but he was "so nervous" and unwilling to touch even the dead beast, when he came to see it, that he gave him but little assistance.

Dr. Reynolds tells me of a lynx killed in Andover, in a swamp near Haggerty's Pond, one winter when he kept school in Tewksbury, about 1820. At first it was seen crossing the Merrimack into Tewksbury, and there was accordingly a story of an animal about that was ten feet long. They turned out, all the hunters of the neighborhood, and tracked it in the snow, across Tewksbury to the swamp in Andover and back again to Tewksbury. One old hunter bet something that they could not show him a track which he did not know, but when they showed him this he gave up. Finally they tracked it to the Andover swamp, and a boy shot it on a tree, though it leapt and fell within a few feet of him when shot.

Rice tells of a common wildcat killed in Sudbury some forty years ago, resting on some ice as it was crossing the Sudbury meadows amid ice and water.

Mr. Boutwell of Groton tells me that a lynx was killed in Dunstable within two or three years. Thinks it is in the State Museum.[1]

This makes five that I have heard of (and seen three)

[1] *Vide* "New England's Prospect" near beginning of Indian Book No. 9.

Vol. XIV

linen bag, said to have been brought from England. They were oval stones or pebbles from the shore, — or *might* have been picked up at Walden. There was a pound, a half-pound, a quarter, a two-ounce, and several one-ounce weights, now all rather dark and ancient to look at, like the bag. This was to me the most interesting relic in his collection. I love to see anything that implies a simpler mode of life and greater nearness to the earth.

Sept. 16. 7 A. M. — River fallen one and a half inches. Is three feet and seven eighths of an inch above summer level, *i. e.* at notch on tree. I mark a willow eight feet above summer level.

See no zizania seed ripe, or black, yet, but almost all is fallen.

Sept. 17. 6.30 A. M. — River thirty-four and an eighth above summer level, or fallen about four inches since evening of 15th. It flows now (a sunk bottle) one hundred feet in two minutes at boat's place, there being no wind.

P. M. — Up river.

Pontederia seeds falling.

See a flock of eight or ten wood ducks on the Grindstone Meadow, with glass, some twenty-five rods off, — several drakes very handsome. They utter a creaking scream as they sail there, — being alarmed, — from time to time, shrill and loud, very unlike the black duck. At last one sails off, calling the others by a short creaking note.

killed within some fifteen or eighteen miles of Concord within thirty years past, and no doubt there have been three times as many of them killed here.[1]

Sept. 14. A. M. — River still rising; at 4 P. M. one and an eighth inches higher than in morning.

Sept. 15. In morning river is three feet two and a half plus inches above summer level. 6 P. M., river is slightly higher than in morning, or at height. Thus it reached its height the third day after the rain; had risen on the morning of the third day about thirty inches on account of the rain of one day (the 12th).

Joe Smith's man brings me this forenoon a fish hawk which was shot on George Brooks's pigeon-stand last evening. It is evidently a female of this year, full grown. Length 23 inches; alar extent 5 feet 6½ inches. It probably lit there merely for a perch.

Looked at Mr. Davis's museum. Miss Lydia Hosmer (the surviving maiden lady) has given him some relics which belonged to her (the Hosmer) family. A small lead or pewter sun-dial, which she told him was brought over by her ancestors and which has the date 1620 scratched on it. Also some *stone* weights in an ancient

[1] *Vide* Sept. 29, 1856. Walcott [?] saw a lynx of some kind which was killed in (his father's?) barn in Bolton [?] some twenty-five years ago; not so big as mine. Bradford says the Essex Institute have another killed in that neighborhood more recently.

Oct. 15. — Channing reads in papers that within a few days a wild cat was killed in Northampton weighing twenty-two pounds and another in Tyringham, Berkshire County, of thirty-six pounds (of course *L. Canadensis* both).

Sept. 18. According to all accounts, very little corn is fit to grind before October 1st (though I have one kind ripe and fit to grind September 1st). It becomes hard and dry enough in the husk in the field by that time, much of it. But long before this, or say by the 1st of September, it begins to glaze (or harden on the surface), when it begins to be too hard to boil.

P. M. — To beeches.

This is a beautiful day, warm but not too warm, a harvest day (I am going down the railroad causeway), the first unquestionable and conspicuous autumnal day, when the willows and button-bushes are a yellowed bower in parallel lines along the swollen and shining stream. The first autumnal tints (of red maples) are now generally noticed. The shrilling of the alder locust fills the air. A brightness as of spring is reflected from the green shorn fields. Both sky and earth are bright. The first clear blue and shining white (of clouds). Cornstalk-tops are stacked about the fields; potatoes are being dug; smokes are seen in the horizon. It is the season of agricultural fairs. If you are not happy to-day you will hardly be so to-morrow.

Leaving Lowell on the morning of the 10th, after the rain of the day before, I passed some heaps of brush in an opening in the woods, — a pasture surrounded by woods, — to which the owner was just setting fire, wet as they were, it being the safest time to burn them. Hence they make so much smoke sometimes. Some farmer, perhaps, wishes to plow this fall there, and sow rye perchance, or merely to keep his pasture clear. Hence the smokes in the horizon at this season. The rattle-pod (in Deep Cut) has begun to turn black and rattle for three or four days.

Notice some green pods of lady's-slipper still, full of chaffy seed.

The beechnut burs are browned but not falling. They open directly in my chamber. The nuts are all empty.

White pine cones (a small crop), and all open that I see.[1]

The toadstools in wood-paths are perforated (almost like pepper-boxes) by flattish slippery insects, bronze and black, which are beneath and within it. Or you see their heads projecting and the dust (or exuviæ) they make like a curb about the holes.

Smooth sumach berries are about past their beauty and the white creamy incrustation mostly dried up.

I see in the Walden road two dead shrews and some fox-dung by them. They look as if bitten and flatted by the fox. Were they not dropped there by him? Perhaps they will not eat one.[2]

Sept. 19. 4 P. M. — River fallen about one foot.

Sept. 20. Cattle-Show.
Rainy in forenoon.

Sept. 21. Hard rain last night. About one and seven eighths inches fallen since yesterday morning, and river rising again.

See, at Reynolds's, Hungarian millet raised by

[1] Are they not last year's?
[2] *Vide* 24th.

Everett. It is smaller and more purple than what is commonly raised here.

P. M. — To Easterbrooks Country.

The fever-bush berries have begun some time, — say one week; are not yet in prime. Taste almost exactly like lemon-peel. But few bushes bear any.

The bayberries are perhaps ripe, but not so light a gray and so rough, or wrinkled, as they will be.

The pods of the broom are nearly half of them open. I perceive that one, just ready to open, opens with a slight spring on being touched, and the pods at once twist and curl a little. I suspect that such seeds as these, which the winds do not transport, will turn out to be more sought after by birds, etc., and so transported by them than those lighter ones which are furnished with a pappus and are accordingly transported by the wind; *i. e.*, that those which the wind takes are less generally the food of birds and quadrupeds than the heavier and wingless seeds.

Muhlenbergia Mexicana by wall between E. Hosmer and Simon Brown, some time. Some large thorn bushes quite bare.

Sept. 22. P. M. — To Clamshell by boat.
Find more pieces of that Indian pot. Have now thirty-eight in all.

Evidently the recent rise of the river has caused the lower leaves of the button-bush to fall. A perfectly level line on these bushes marks the height to which the water rose, many or most of the leaves so high having fallen.

The clematis yesterday was but just beginning to be feathered, but its feathers make no show. Feathers out next day in house.

See a large flock of crows.

The sweet-gale fruit is yet quite green, but perhaps it is ripe. The button-bush balls are hardly reddened.

Moreover the beach plum appears to prefer a sandy place, however far inland, and one of our patches grows on the only desert which we have.

Some of the early botanists, like Gerard, were prompted and compelled to *describe* their plants, but most nowadays only measure them, as it were. The former is affected by what he sees and so inspired to portray it; the latter merely fills out a schedule prepared for him, — makes a description *pour servir*. I am constantly assisted by the books in identifying a particular plant and learning some of its humbler uses, but I rarely read a sentence in a botany which reminds me of flowers or living plants. Very few indeed write as if they had seen the thing which they pretend to describe.

Sept. 23. P. M. — To Cliffs.
Some small botrychium ripe.

I see on the top of the Cliffs to-day the dung of a fox, consisting of fur, with part of the jaw and one of the long rodent teeth of a woodchuck in it, and the rest of it huckleberry seeds with some whole berries. I saw exactly the same beyond Goose Pond a few days ago, on a rock, — except that the tooth (a curved rodent) was much smaller, probably of a mouse. It is evident,

then, that the fox eats huckleberries and so contributes very much to the dispersion of this shrub, for there were a number of entire berries in its dung, — in both the last two I chanced to notice. To spread these seeds, Nature employs not only a great many birds but this restless ranger the fox. Like ourselves, he likes two courses, rabbit and huckleberries.

I see everywhere in the shady yew wood those pretty round-eyed fungus-spots on the upper leaves of the blue-stemmed goldenrod (*vide* press), contrasting with the few bright-yellow flowers above them, — yellowish-white rings (with a slate-colored centre), surrounded by green and then dark.

Red pine-sap by north side of Yew Path some ten rods east of yew, not long done. The root of the freshest has a decided checkerberry scent, and for a long time — a week after — in my chamber, the bruised plant has a very pleasant earthy sweetness.

I hear that a large owl, probably a cat owl, killed and carried off a full-grown turkey in Carlisle a few days ago.

Sept. 24. P. M. — To Flint's Pond *via* Smith's chestnut grove.

See a dead shrew in road on Turnpike Hill. (Had hard rain the night of the 20th.) *Vide* back, 18th.

It is remarkable how persistently Nature endeavors to keep the earth clothed with wood of some kind, — how much vitality there is in the stumps and roots of some trees, though small and young. For example, examined the little hickories on the bare slope of Smith's

Hill. I have observed them endeavoring to cover that slope for a dozen years past, and have wondered how the seed came there, planted on a bare pasture hillside, but I now see that the nuts were probably planted just before the pine wood (the stumps of which remain) was cut down, and, having sprung up about that time, have since been repeatedly cut down to keep the pasture clear, till now they are quite feeble or dying, though many are six feet high. When a part of the hill has been plowed and cultivated I examine the roots which have been turned out, and find that they are two inches thick at the ground though only one to three feet high above. I *judge* that it is fifteen years since the pine wood was cut, and if the hickories had not been cut down and cattle been kept out, there would have been a dense hickory wood there now fifteen to twenty feet high at least. You see on an otherwise perfectly bare hillside or pasture where pines were cut, say fifteen years before, remote from any hickories, countless little hickories a foot high or little more springing up every few feet, and you wonder how they came there, but the fact that they preserve their vitality, though cut down so often and so long, accounts for them.

This shows how heedlessly wood-lots are managed at present, and suggests that when one is cut (if not before) a provident husbandman will carefully examine the ground and ascertain what kind of wood is about to take the place of the old and how abundantly, in order that he may act understandingly and determine if it is best to clear the land or not. I have seen many a field perfectly barren for fifteen or twenty years, which, if

properly managed, or only let alone, would naturally have yielded a crop of birch trees within that time.

In Wood Thrush Path at Flint's Pond, a great many of the geiropodium fungus now shed their dust. When closed it is [a] roundish or conical orange-colored fungus three quarters of an inch in diameter, covered with a mucilaginous matter. The thick outer skin of many (it is pink-red inside) had already curled back (it splits into segments and curls parallel to the axis of the plant) and revealed the pinkish fawn-colored puffball capped with a red dimple or crown. This is a hollow bag, which, when you touch it, spurts forth a yellowish-white powder three or four inches through its orifice.

See two very handsome butterflies on the Flint's Pond road in the woods at Gourgas lot, which C. had not seen before. I find that they are quite like the *Vanessa Atalanta*, or red admiral, of England.

2 P. M. — The river risen about thirty-three inches above summer level.

Sept. 25. Hard, gusty rain (with thunder and lightning) in afternoon. About seven eighths of an inch falls.

Sept. 26. P. M. — Round Walden and Pleasant Meadow.

Small oaks in hollows (as under Emerson Cliff) have fairly begun to change.

The taller grass and sedge is now generally withered and brown, and reveals the little pines in it.

Vol. XIV

I see that acorns — white oak, etc. — have fallen after the rain and wind, just as leaves and fruit have.

I see, just up, the large light-orange toadstools with white spots, — at first: then:

Sept. 27. A. M. — Sawing up my raft by river.

River about thirty-five inches above summer level, and goes no higher this time.

Monroe's tame ducks sail along and feed close to me as I am working there. Looking up, I see a little dipper, about one half their size, in the middle of the river, evidently attracted by these tame ducks, as to a place of security. I sit down and watch it. The tame ducks have paddled four or five rods down-stream along the shore. They soon detect the dipper three or four rods off, and betray alarm by a tittering note, especially when it dives, as it does continually. At last, when it is two or three rods off and approaching them by diving, they all rush to the shore and come out on it in their fear, but the dipper shows itself close to the shore, and when they enter the water again joins them within two feet, still diving from time to time and threatening to come up in their midst. They return up-stream, more or less alarmed, and pursued in this wise by the dipper, who does not know what to make of their fears, and soon the dipper is thus tolled along to within twenty feet of where I sit, and I can watch it at my leisure. It has a dark bill and considerable white on the sides of the head or neck, with black between it, no tufts, and no observable white on back or tail. When at last disturbed by me, it suddenly sinks low (all its body) in the water without diving.

Thus it can float at various heights. (So on the 30th I saw one suddenly dash along the surface from the meadow ten rods before me to the middle of the river, and then dive, and though I watched fifteen minutes and examined the tufts of grass, I could see no more of it).

Sept. 28. Butternuts still on tree and falling, as all September.

This morning we had a very severe frost, the first to kill our vines, etc., in garden; what you may call a black frost, — making things look black. Also ice under pump.

Sept. 29. Another hard frost and a very cold day.

Sept. 30. Frost and ice.

III

OCTOBER, 1860

(ÆT. 43)

Oct. 1. Remarkable frost and ice this morning; quite a wintry prospect. The leaves of trees stiff and white at 7 A. M. I hear it was 21° this morning early. I do not remember such cold at this season. This is about the full of the moon (it fulled at 9 P. M. the 29th) in clear, bright moonlight nights. We have fine and bright but cold days after it. One man tells me that he regretted that he had not taken his mittens with him when he went to his morning's work, — mowing in a meadow, — and when he went to a spring at 11 A. M., found the dipper with two inches of ice in it frozen solid.

P. M. — Rain again.

Button-bush balls were fairly reddened yesterday, and the *Andropogon scoparius* looked silvery in sun. Gossamer was pretty thick on the meadows, and noticed the round green leafy buds of the utricularia in the clear, cold, smooth water. Water was prepared for ice, and C. saw the first *Vanessa Antiopa* since spring.

Oct. 3. See *Vanessa Antiopa*.

The hard frost of September 28th, 29th, and 30th, and especially of October 1st, has suddenly killed, crisped, and caused to fall a great many leaves of ash, hickory, etc., etc. These (and the locusts, *generally*) look shriv-

elled and hoary, and of course they will not ripen or be bright. They are killed and withered green, — all the more tender leaves. Has killed all the burdock flowers and no doubt many others.

Sam Barrett says that last May he waded across the Assabet River on the old dam in front of his house without going over his india-rubber boots, which are sixteen and a half inches high. I do not believe you could have done better than this a hundred years ago, or before the canal dam was built.

Bay-wings about.

I have seen and heard sparrows in *flocks*, more as if flitting by, within a week, or since the frosts began.

Gathered to-day my apples at the Texas house. I set out the trees, fourteen of them fourteen years ago and five of them several years later, and I now get between ten and eleven barrels of apples from them.

Oct. 5. Rain, more or less, yesterday afternoon and this forenoon.

P. M. — To Walden.

The frosts have this year killed all of Stow's artichokes before one of them had blossomed, but those in Alcott's garden had bloomed probably a fortnight ago. This suggests that this plant could not have grown much further north than this. I see a great many young hickories fifteen feet high killed, turned brown, almost black, and withering in the woods, as I do not remember to have seen them before. Indeed, the woods have a strong decaying scent in consequence. Also much indigo-weed is killed and turned black and broken off, as well as

ferns generally. The butternut is also killed, turned dark-brown, and the leaves mostly fallen, — not turning yellow at all. The maples generally are what Gerard would have called an "over-worn" scarlet color.

About 4 P. M. it is fast clearing up, the clouds withdrawing, with a little dusky scud beyond their western edges against the blue. We came out on the east shore of Walden. The water is tolerably smooth. The smooth parts are dark and dimpled by many rising fishes. Where it is rippled it is light-colored, and the surface thus presents three or four alternate light and dark bars. I see a fish hawk, skimming low over it, suddenly dive or stoop for one of those little fishes that rise to the surface so abundantly at this season. He then sits on a bare limb over the water, ready to swoop down again on his finny prey, presenting, as he sits erect, a long white breast and belly and a white head. No doubt he well knows the habits of these little fishes which dimple the surface of Walden at this season, and I doubt if there is any better fishing-ground for him to resort to. He can easily find a perch overlooking the lake and discern his prey in the clear water.

The sporobolus grass in the meadows is now full of rain (as erst of dew) and would wet you through if you walked there.

Apparently all the celtis and horse-chestnut leaves are killed, turned dark-brown and withering, before changing or ripening, so severe has been the frost, and, looking from hills over huckleberry-fields, the sweet-fern patches are turned a dark brown, almost black (mulberry black) amid the crimson blueberry and

huckleberry, so that the surface is parded black and scarlet from the same cause.

Oct. 6. P. M. — Over hill to Woodis Park.

I see not one hemlock cone of this year at the Hemlocks, but very many of last year holding on. Apparently they bore so abundantly last year that they do not bear at all this year.

I hear that the late cold of September 29 and 30 and October 1 froze all Bull's grapes (papers say some fifty bushels), the thermometer going down to 20°.

As I go over the hill, I see a large flock of crows on the dead white oak and on the ground under the living one. I find the ground strewn with white oak acorns, and many of these have just been broken in two, and their broken shells are strewn about, so that I suppose the crows have been eating them. Some are merely scratched, as if they had been pecked at without being pierced; also there are two of the large swamp white oak acorn-cups joined together dropped under this oak, perhaps by a crow, maybe a quarter of a mile from its tree, and that probably across the river. Probably a crow had transported one or more swamp white oak acorns this distance. They must have been too heavy for a jay.

The crow, methinks, is our only large bird that hovers and circles about in flocks in an irregular and straggling manner, filling the air over your head and sporting in it as if at home here. They often burst up above the woods where they were perching, like the black fragments of a powder-mill just exploded.

One crow lingers on a limb of the dead oak till I am

within a dozen rods. There is strong and blustering northwest wind, and when it launches off to follow its comrades it is blown up and backward still nearer to me, and it is obliged to tack four or five times just like a vessel, a dozen rods or more each way, very deliberately, first to the right, then to the left, before it can get off; for as often as it tries to fly directly forward against the wind, it is blown upward and backward within gunshot, and it only advances directly forward at last by stooping very low within a few feet of the ground where the trees keep off the wind. Yet the wind is not remarkably strong.

Horace Mann tells me that he saw a painted turtle in this town eating a unio, in our river, in the shell, it evidently having just caught and opened it. He has been collecting shells in Ohio recently, and was obliged to wade at least knee-deep into the streams for mussels, the hogs, which run at large there, having got them all in the shallower water.

Oct. 7. P. M. — To Hubbard's Bath and Grove.

Now and for a week the chip-birds in flocks; the withered grass and weeds, etc., alive with them.

Rice says that when a boy, playing with darts with his brother Israel, one of them sent up his dart when a flock of crows was going over. One of the crows followed it down to the earth, picked it up, and flew off with it a quarter of a mile before it dropped it. He has observed that young wood ducks swim faster than the old, which is a fortunate provision, for they can thus retreat and hide in the weeds while their parents fly off. He says

Vol. XIV

thousand in this field, — and he shows some one the ear in his granary. Also his rye in barrels and his seed-corn tucked into the mow as he was husking, — the larger and fuller ears picked out, with the husk on. But all this corn will be given to his pigs and other stock. Three great hogs weighing twelve hundredweight lie asleep under his barn already sold. Hears of one man who sold his fat hog for $75.00. He has two high and very spreading apple trees, looking like one, they are so close together, from which he gathered one year twenty-one barrels of sound Hubbardston's nonesuch and five barrels of windfalls, grafted on to it within a few years.

If we have not attended to the subject, we may think that the activity of the animals is not enough to account for the annual planting of such extensive tracts; just as we wonder where all the flies and other insects come from in the spring, because we have not followed them into their winter quarters and counted them there. Yet nature does preserve and multiply the race of flies while we are inattentive and sleeping.

Many people have a foolish way of talking about small things, and apologize for themselves or another having attended to a small thing, having neglected their ordinary business and amused or instructed themselves by attending to a small thing; when, if the truth were known, their ordinary business was the small thing, and almost their whole lives were misspent, but they were such fools as not to know it.

Oct. 8. P. M. — To Damon's wood-lot, part of the burnt district of the spring.

that you must shoot the little dipper as soon as it comes up, — before the water is fairly off its eyes, — else it will dive at the flash.

I see one small but spreading white oak full of acorns just falling and ready to fall. When I strike a limb, great numbers fall to the ground. They are a very dark hazel, looking black amid the still green leaves, — a singular contrast. Some that have fallen have already split and sprouted, an eighth of an inch. This when, on *some* trees, far the greater part have not yet fallen.

Probably the blueberry and huckleberry, amelanchier, and other bushes which spring up immediately when the woods are cut have been already planted and started annually, as the little oaks have. Nature thus keeps a supply of these plants in her nursery (*i. e.* under the larger wood), always ready for casualties, as fires, windfalls, and clearings by man. Birds and foxes, etc., are annually conveying the seed into the woods.

Rice reminds me that when the maples in a blueberry swamp have got up high, the blueberries die, and you have at length a maple wood clear of underwood.

Remarking to old Mr. B—— the other day on the abundance of the apples, "Yes," says he, "and fair as dollars too." That's the kind of beauty they see in apples.

Looked over Hayden's farm and granary. He now takes pleasure in his field of corn just ready for harvesting, — the rather small ears fully filled out and rounded at the end, setting low and many on one stalk. He loves to estimate the number of bushels he will have; has already calculated the number of hills, — some forty

Am surprised to see how green the forest floor and the sprout-land north of Damon's lot are already again, though it was a very severe burn. In the wood-lot the trees are *apparently* killed for twenty feet up, especially the smaller, then six or ten feet of green top, while very vigorous sprouts have shot up from the base below the influence of the fire. This shows that they will die, I think. The top has merely lived for the season while the growth has been in their sprouts around the base. This is the case with oaks, maples, cherry, etc. Also the blueberry (*Vaccinium vacillans*) has sent up very abundant and vigorous shoots all over the wood from the now more open and cleaned ground. These are evidently from stocks which were comparatively puny before. The adjacent oak sprout-land has already sprung up so high that it makes on me about the same impression that it did before, though it [was] from six to ten feet high and was generally killed to the ground. The fresh shoots from the roots are very abundant and three to five feet high, or half as high as before. So vivacious are the roots and so rapidly does Nature recover herself. You see myriads of little shrub oaks and others in the woods which look as if they had just sprung from the seed, but on pulling one up you find it to spring from a long horizontal root which has survived perhaps several burnings or cuttings. Thus the stumps and roots of young oak, chestnut, hickory, maple, and many other trees retain their vitality a very long time and after many accidents, and produce thrifty trees at last.

In the midst of the wood, I noticed in some places, where the brush had been more completely burned and the ground laid bare, some fire-weed (*Senecio*), golden-rods, and ferns.

Standing by a pigeon-place on the north edge [of] Damon's lot, I saw on the dead top of a white pine four or five rods off — which had been stripped for fifteen feet downward that it might die and afford with its branches a perch for the pigeons about the place, like the more artificial ones that were set up — two woodpeckers that were new to me. They uttered a peculiar sharp *kek kek* on alighting (not so sharp as that of the hairy or downy woodpecker) and appeared to be about the size of the hairy woodpecker, or between that and the golden-winged. I had a good view of them with my glass as long as I desired. With the back to me, they were clear black all above, as well as their feet and bills, and each had a yellow or orange (or possibly orange-scarlet?) front (the anterior part of the head at the base of the upper mandible). A long white line along the side of the head to the neck, with a black one below it. The breast, as near as I could see, was gray specked with white, and the under side of the wing expanded was also gray, with small white spots. The throat white and vent also white or whitish. Is this the arctic three-toed? [1] Probably many trees dying on this large burnt tract will attract many woodpeckers to it.

I find a great many white oak acorns already sprouted, although they are but half fallen, and can easily believe that they sometimes sprout before they fall. It is a good year for them. It is remarkable how soon and unac-

---

[1] *Not* of Nuttall. [The birds must have been arctic three-toed woodpeckers, though Thoreau misplaces the yellow crown-patch.]

countably they decay. Many which I cut open, though they look sound without, are discolored and decaying on one side or throughout within, though there is no worm in them. Perhaps they are very sensitive to moisture. Those which I see to-day are merely hazel and not nearly so black as what I saw yesterday. Trees that stand by themselves without the wood bear the most.

The sugar maple seeds are now browned — the seed end as well as wing — and are ripe. The severe frosts about the first of the month ripened them.

Oct. 9. P. M. — Up Assabet.

See one crow chasing two marsh hawks over E. Hosmer's meadow. Occasionally a hawk dives at the crow, but the crow perseveres in pestering them. Can it *now* have anything to do with the hawk's habit of catching young birds? In like manner smaller birds pursue crows. The crow is at length joined by another.

See several squirrels' nests of leaves formed in the maples lately.

Though the red maples have not their common brilliancy on account of the very severe frost about the end of September, some are very interesting. You cannot judge a tree by seeing it from one side only. As you go round or away from it, it may overcome you with its mass of glowing scarlet or yellow light. You need to stand where the greatest number of leaves will transmit or reflect to you most favorably. The tree which looked comparatively lifeless, cold, and merely parti-colored, seen in a more favorable light as you are floating away

Vol. XIV

from it, may affect you wonderfully as a warm, glowing drapery. I now see one small red maple which is all a pure yellow within and a bright red scarlet on its outer surface and prominences. It is a remarkably distinct painting of scarlet on a yellow ground. It is an indescribably beautiful contrast of scarlet and yellow. Another is yellow and green where this was scarlet and yellow, and in this case the bright and liquid green, now getting to be rare, is by contrast as charming a color as the scarlet.

I met in the street afterward a young lady who rowed up the river after me, and I could tell exactly where she plucked the maple twig which she held in her hand. It was the one so conspicuous for a quarter of a mile in one reach of the river.

I wonder that the very cows and the dogs in the street do not manifest a recognition of the bright tints about and above them. I saw a terrier dog glance up and down the painted street before he turned in at his master's gate, and I wondered what he thought of those lit trees, — if they did not touch his philosophy or spirits, — but I fear he had only his common doggish thoughts after all. He trotted down the yard as if it were a matter of course after all, or else as if he deserved it all.

Wood ducks are about now, amid the painted leaves.

For two or more nights past we have had remarkable glittering golden sunsets as I came home from the post-office, it being cold and cloudy just above the horizon. There was the most intensely bright golden light in the west end of the street, extending under the elms, and the very dust a quarter of a mile off was like gold-dust. I

wondered how a child could stand quietly in that light, as if it had been a furnace.

This haste to kill a bird or quadruped and make a skeleton of it, which many young men and some old ones exhibit, reminds me of the fable of the man who killed the hen that laid golden eggs, and so got no more gold. It is a perfectly parallel case. Such is the knowledge which you may get from the anatomy as compared with the knowledge you get from the living creature. Every fowl lays golden eggs for him who can find them, or can detect alloy and base metal.

Oct. 10. In August, '55, I levelled for the artificial pond at Sleepy Hollow. They dug gradually for three or four years and completed the pond last year, '59. It is now about a dozen rods long by five or six wide and two or three deep, and is supplied by copious springs in the meadow. There is a long ditch leading into it, in which no water now flows, nor has since winter at least, and a short ditch leading out of it into the brook. It is about sixty rods from the very source of the brook. Well, in this pond thus dug in the midst of a meadow a year or two ago and supplied by springs in the meadow, I find to-day several small patches of the large yellow and the kalmiana lily already established. Thus in the midst of death we are in life. The water is otherwise apparently clear of weeds. The river, where these abound, is about half a mile distant down the little brook near which this pond lies, though there *may* be a few pads in the ditched part of it at half that distance. How, then, did the seed get here? I learned last winter (*vide* December 23, 1859) that many small pouts and some sizable pickerel had been caught here, though the connection with the brook is a very slight and shallow ditch. I think, therefore, that the lily seeds have been conveyed into this pond from the river immediately, or perchance from the meadow between, either by fishes, reptiles, or birds which fed on them, and that the seeds were not lying dormant in the mud. You have only to dig a pond anywhere in the fields hereabouts, and you will soon have not only water-fowl, reptiles, and fishes in it, but also the usual water-plants, as lilies, etc. You will no sooner have got your pond dug than nature will begin to stock it. I suspect that turtles eat these seeds, for I often see them eating the decayed lily leaves. If there is any water communication, perhaps fishes arrive first, and then the water-plants for their food and shelter.

Horace Mann shows me the skeleton of a blue heron. The neck is remarkably strong, and the bill. The latter is 5 + inches long to the feathers above and $6\frac{1}{2}$ to the gape. A stake-driver which he has, freshly killed, has a bill 3 inches long above and $4\frac{1}{8}$ to the gape and between $\frac{5}{8}$ and $\frac{6}{8}$ deep vertically at the base. This bird weighs a little over two pounds, being quite large and fat. Its nails are longer and less curved than those of the heron. The sharp bill of the heron, like a stout pick, wielded by that long and stout neck, would be a very dangerous weapon to encounter. He has made a skeleton of the fish hawk which was brought to me within a month. I remark the great eye-sockets, and the claws, and perhaps the deep, sharp breast-bone. Including its strong hooked bill it is clawed at both ends, harpy-like.

Vol. XIV

There is a remarkably abundant crop of white oak acorns this fall, also a fair crop of red oak acorns; but not of scarlet and black, very few of them. Which is as well for the squirrel. The acorns are now in the very midst of their fall. The white oak acorn is about the prettiest of ours. They are a glossy hazel (while the red and black are more or less downy at first) and of various forms, — some nearly spherical but commonly oblong and pointed, some more *slender* oval or elliptical; and of various shades of brown, — some almost black, but generally a wholesome hazel. Those which have fallen longest, and been exposed to the severe frosts on the ground, are partly bleached there. The white oak acorns are found chiefly on trees growing in the open or on the edge of the wood, and on the most exposed side of these trees. They grow either singly or in twos and threes.

This afternoon (11th) the strong wind which arose at noon has strewn the ground with them. I could gather many bushels in a short time. This year is as good for white oak acorns as for apples and pears. What pleasant picking on the firm, green pasture sod which is browned with this glossy fruit! The worms are already at work in them, — sometimes three or four in one, — and some are already decayed and decaying on the tree without a worm. The fibery [*sic*] inner bark of the nut appears to retain moisture and hasten rot, especially when the fruit has once been swollen by the wet. The best time to gather these nuts is now, when a strong wind has arisen suddenly in the day, before the squirrels have preceded you; and so of chestnuts.

Of red oak acorns, some are short and broad, others

P. M. — Went to a fire — or smoke — at Mrs. Hoar's. There is a slight blaze and more smoke. Two or three hundred men rush to the house, cut large holes in the roof, throw many hogsheads of water into it, — when a few pails full well directed would suffice, — and then they run off again, leaving your attic three inches deep with water, which is rapidly descending through the ceiling to the basement and spoiling all that can be spoiled, while a torrent is running down the stairways. They were very forward to put out the [fire], but they take no pains to put out the water, which does far more damage. The first was amusement; the last would be mere work and utility. Why is there not a little machine invented to throw the water out of a house?

They are hopelessly cockneys everywhere who learn to swim with a machine. They take neither disease nor health, nay, nor life itself, the natural way. I see dumbbells in the minister's study, and some of their dumbness gets into his sermons. Some travellers carry them round the world in their carpetbags. Can he be said to travel who requires still this exercise? A party of school-children had a picnic at the Easterbrooks Country the other [day], and they carried bags of beans from their gymnasium to exercise with there. I cannot be interested in these extremely artificial amusements. The traveller is no longer a wayfarer, with his staff and pack and dusty coat. He is not a pilgrim, but he travels in a saloon, and carries dumb-bells to exercise with in the intervals of his journey.

Oct. (10 *and*) 11. P. M. — To Sleepy Hollow and north of M. Pratt's.

longer. I see some pretty shrub oak acorns longitudinally striped. Chestnuts also are frequently striped, but before they have been exposed to the light, and are completely ripe.

The season is as favorable for pears as for apples. R. W. E.'s garden is strewn with them. They are not so handsome as apples, — are of more earthy and homely colors, — yet they are of a wholesome color enough. Many, inclining to a rough russet or even ferruginous, both to touch (rusty) and eye, look as if they were proof against frost. After all, the few varieties of wild pears here have more color and are handsomer than the many celebrated varieties that are cultivated. The cultivated are commonly of so dull a color that it is hard to distinguish them from the leaves, and if there are but two or three left you do not see them revealing themselves distinctly at a distance amid the leaves, as apples do, but I see that the gatherer has overlooked half a dozen large ones on this small tree, which were concealed by their perfect resemblance to the leaves, — a yellowish green, spotted with darker-green rust or fungi (?). Yet some have a fair cheek, and, generally, in their form they are true pendants, as if shaped expressly to hang from the trees.

They are a more aristocratic fruit. How much more attention they get from the proprietor! The hired man gathers the apples and barrels them. The proprietor plucks the pears at odd hours for a pastime, and his daughter wraps them each in its paper. They are, perchance, put up in the midst of a barrel of Baldwins as if something more precious than these. They are spread on the floor of the best room. They are a gift to the most distinguished guest. Judges and ex-judges and honorables are connoisseurs of pears, and discourse of them at length between sessions. I hold in my hand a Bonne Louise which is covered with minute brown specks or dots one twelfth to one sixteenth [of an inch] apart, largest and most developed on the sunny side, quite regular and handsome, as if they were the termination or operculum of pores which had burst in the very thin pellicle of the fruit, producing a slight roughness to the touch. Each of these little ruptures, so to call them, is in form a perfect star with five rays; so that, if the apple is higher-colored, reflecting the sun, on the duller surface of this pear the whole firmament with its stars shines forth. They whisper of the happy stars under whose influence they have grown and matured. It is not the case with all of them, but only the more perfect specimens.

Pears, it is truly said, are less poetic than apples. They have neither the beauty nor the fragrance of apples, but their excellence is in their flavor, which speaks to a grosser sense. They are *glouts-morceaux*. Hence, while children dream of apples, ex-judges realize pears. They are named after emperors and kings and queens and dukes and duchesses. I fear I shall have to wait till we get to pears with American names, which a republican can swallow.

Looking through a more powerful glass, those little brown dots are stars with from four to six rays, — commonly five, — where a little wart-like prominence (perhaps the end of a pore or a thread) appears to have

burst through the very thin pellicle and burst it into so many rays.

Oct. 13. P. M. — Up river.

I find no new cones on Monroe's larch by the river, but many old ones (the same was the case with the hemlocks on Assabet), unless those imperfect ones with a twig growing from their extremity were this year's, — but I think they were last year's. Last year both white pine, hemlock, and larches bore abundantly and there were very few white oak acorns. This year, so far as I observe, there are scarcely any white pine cones (were there any?) or hemlock or larch, and a great abundance of white oak acorns in all parts of the town. So far as I have observed, if pines or oaks bear abundantly one year they bear little or nothing the next year. This is a white oak year, not a pine year. It is also an apple and a potato year. I should think that there might be a bushel or two of acorns on and under some single trees. There are but few in the woods. Those spreading trees that stand in open pastures fully exposed to the light and air are the most fertile ones. I rejoice when the white oaks bear an abundant crop. I speak of it to many whom I meet, but I find few to sympathize with me. They seem to care much more for potatoes. The Indians say that many acorns are a sign of a cold winter. It is a cold fall at any rate.

The shore at Clamshell is greened with pontederia seed which has floated up and been left there, with some button-bush seed and some of those slender bulbs of the lysimachia and those round green leaf-buds of the

Utricularia vulgaris. Thus, probably, are all these dispersed. I also see large masses of the last-named weed lodged against the bridges, etc., with the conspicuous greener leaf-buds attached. I find no yellow lily seeds, only a few white lily seed-pods. These are full of seeds the color of apple seeds and but a quarter as big. They sink in water as soon as the slimy matter which invests them is washed off. I see a white lily stem coiled up with many whorls like a wire spring. They are almost only white lily pads that are left now.

There is some of the fresh-water sponge in this the main stream too.

The *F. hyemalis* back, and I think I see and hear the shore larks.

The shrub oaks on J. Hosmer's hillside this side of Hollowell place have already passed the height of their beauty. Is it not early on account of frost?

At Holden Swamp. — Now, as soon as the frost strips the maples, and their leaves strew the swamp floor and conceal the pools, the note of the chickadee sounds cheerfully wintryish.

I see many pine and oak tree tops in the woods that were blown off last spring. They lie many rods from their trunks, so that I have to look a little while to tell where they came from. Moreover, the butt of the piece over which I stand looks so large compared with the broken shaft up there so high that I at first feel sure it did not come from there, — which [?] it did, — and so am puzzled to locate it.

The lentago fruit is quite sweet and reminds me of

dates in their somewhat mealy pulp. It has large flat black seeds, somewhat like watermelon seeds, but not so long.

The scientific differs from the poetic or lively description somewhat as the photographs, which we so weary of viewing, from paintings and sketches, though this comparison is too favorable to science. All science is only a makeshift, a means to an end which is never attained. After all, the truest description, and that by which another living man can most readily recognize a flower, is the unmeasured and eloquent one which the sight of it inspires. No scientific description will supply the want of this, though you should count and measure and analyze every atom that seems to compose it.

Surely poetry and eloquence are a more universal language than that Latin which is confessedly dead. In science, I should say, all description is postponed till we know the whole, but then science itself will be cast aside. But unconsidered expressions of our delight which any natural object draws from us are something complete and final in themselves, since all nature is to be regarded as it concerns man; and who knows how near to absolute truth such unconscious affirmations may come? Which are the truest, the sublime conceptions of Hebrew poets and *seers*, or the guarded statements of modern geologists, which we must modify or unlearn so fast?

As they who were present early at the discovery of gold in California, and observed the sudden fall in its value, have most truly described that state of things, so it is commonly the old naturalists who first received American plants that describe them best. A scientific description is such as you would get if you should send out the scholars of the polytechnic school with all sorts of metres made and patented to take the measures for you of any natural object. In a sense you have got nothing new thus, for every object that we see mechanically is mechanically daguerreotyped on our eyes, but a true description growing out [of] the perception and appreciation of it is itself a new fact, never to be daguerreotyped, indicating the highest quality of the plant, — its relation to man, — of far more importance than any merely medicinal quality that it may possess, or be thought to-day to possess. There is a certainty and permanence about this kind of observation, too, that does not belong to the other, for every flower and weed has its day in the medical pharmacopœia, but the beauty of flowers is perennial in the taste of men.

Truly this is a world of vain delights. We think that men have a substratum of common sense but sometimes are peculiarly frivolous. But consider what a value is seriously and permanently attached to gold and so-called precious stones almost universally. Day and night, summer and winter, sick or well, in war and in peace, men speak of and believe in gold as a great treasure. By a thousand comparisons they prove their devotion to it. If wise men or true philosophers bore any considerable proportion to the whole number of men, gold would be treated with no such distinction. Men seriously and, if possible, religiously believe in and worship gold. They hope to earn golden opinions, to celebrate their golden wedding. They dream of the golden

age. Now it is not its intrinsic beauty or value, but it? rarity and arbitrarily attached value, that distinguishe? gold. You would think it was the reign of shams.

The one description interests those chiefly who hav? not seen the thing; the other chiefly interests those wh? have seen it and are most familiar with it, and bring? it home to the reader. We like to read a good descrip tion of no thing so well as of that which we already kno? the best, as our friend, or ourselves even. In proportio? as we get and are near to our object, we do without th? measured or scientific account, which is like the measur? they take, or the description they write, of a man whe? he leaves his country, and insert in his passport for th? use of the detective police of other countries. The me? of science merely look at the object with sinister eye, t? see if [it] corresponds with the passport, and merel? visé or make some trifling additional mark on its pass port and let it go; but the real acquaintances and friend? which it may have in foreign parts do not ask to see n? think of its passport.

Gerard has not only heard of and seen and raised ? plant, but felt and smelled and tasted it, applying all hi? senses to it. You are not distracted from the thing to th? system or arrangement. In the true natural order th? order or system is not insisted on. Each is first, an? each last. That which presents itself to us this momen? occupies the whole of the present and rests on the ver? topmost point of the sphere, under the zenith. Th? species and individuals of all the natural kingdoms as? our attention and admiration in a round robin. W? make straight lines, putting a captain at their head and ?

Vol. XIV

lieutenant at their tails, with sergeants and corporals all along the line and a flourish of trumpets near the beginning, insisting on a particular uniformity where Nature has made curves to which belongs their own sphere-music. It is indispensable for us to square her circles, and we offer our rewards to him who will do it.

Who [sic] describes the most familiar object with a zest and vividness of imagery as if he saw it for the first time, the novelty consisting not in the strangeness of the object, but in the new and clearer perception of it.

Oct. 14. This year, on account of the very severe frosts, the trees change and fall early, or fall before fairly changing. The willows have the bleached look of November. Consider how many leaves there are to fall each year and how much they must add to the soil. Coultas (in " What may be Learned from a Tree ") finds that a single beech twig twenty-seven inches and three lines long and six years old was " the leaf-labor of one hundred and fifty-five leaves," and quotes from Asa Gray's " First Lessons in Botany " that " the Washington Elm at Cambridge — a tree of no extraordinary size — was some years ago estimated to produce a crop of seven millions of leaves, exposing a surface of 200,000 square feet, or about five acres, of foliage." Supposing this to be true, and that the horizontal spread of this (like other the largest elms) is one hundred feet, then, if all its leaves should be spread evenly on the ground directly under it, there would be about twenty-five thicknesses. An ordinary forest would probably cover the ground as thickly as this tree would. Supposing a

leaf to be of the same thickness with an ordinary shee? of letter-paper, and that the mass is compressed as muc? as paper packed in a ream, the twenty-five would b? about one sixteenth of an inch thick. This is a rud? calculation.

We have had a remarkably fertile year. Let us se? now if we have a cold winter after it.

P. M. — Up Groton Turnpike.

If you examine a wood-lot after numerous fires an? cuttings, you will be surprised to find how extreme? vivacious are the roots of oaks, chestnuts, hickories? birches, cherries, etc. The little trees which look lik? seedlings of the year will be found commonly to sprin? from an older root or horizontal shoot or a stump. Thos? layers which you may have selected to transplant wil? be found to have too much of old stump and root under ground to be removed. They have commonly met wit? accidents and seen a good deal of the world already? They have learned to endure and bide their time. Whe? you see an oak fully grown and of fair proportions, yo? little suspect what difficulties it may have encountered i? its early youth, what sores it has overgrown, how fo? years it was a feeble layer lurking under the leaves an? scarcely daring to show its head above them, burnt an? cut, and browsed by rabbits. Driven back to earth agai? twenty times, — as often as it aspires to the heavens? The soil of the forest is crowded with a mass of thes? old and tough fibres, annually sending up their shoot? here and there. The underground part survives an? holds its own, though the top meets with countless acci? dents; so that, although seeds were not to be supplie?

or many years, there would still spring up shoots enough to stock it. So with the old and feeble huckleberry roots. Nay, even the sedge (*Carex Pennsylvanica*) is already rooted in most woods, and at once begins to spread and prevail when the wood is cut, especially if a frost or fire keeps down the new wood.

I examine the John Hosmer wood-lot (sprout-land) cut off last winter on the north side at Colburn Hill. Next to the conspicuous sprouts from the large stumps (of which the white birch have here grown the most, — commonly four or five feet) you notice an increased growth of weeds, as goldenrods (especially *S. puberula*), the two fire-weeds, asters, everlasting (fragrant), hawk-weeds, yarrow, low blackberry, cinquefoil, etc. All of these, I believe, except the erechthites, are perennials, and those which blossomed this year (with this exception) must have sprung up before the wood was cut. The others were probably planted last fall or in the winter, unless their seed endures in the soil. I see, for example, what I consider seedling goldenrods, everlasting, and yarrow, *i. e.* mere radical leaves without any stem, which will bloom next year. The seedling trees of this year, of course, will be scarcely noticed among the sprouts and weeds. I chance to see none. I see, however, many young black cherry trees, three to six inches high, which are just three years old, with roots partly coiled up (as if they had met with difficulties in their upward growth) and much larger than their stems. These, then, were planted in the midst of this pine and oak and birch wood at least two years before it was cut, though the tree they came from is so far off that I know

not where it is, and they have not effectually risen above the surface till this year. If you look through a sprout-land you will find no tree, not strictly speaking a forest tree, and which at the same time did not attain to its growth there before, so common as these little black cherries, the birds having conveyed the stones into the midst of the woods and dropped them there; *i. e.* they are planted chiefly before the wood is cut. *These* cherry trees are, however, short-lived. They live a few years and bear large and pleasant-tasted fruit, but when the forest trees have grown up around them they die.

I see that a great part of the club-moss (*Lycopodium complanatum*) which was so abundant in the lower part of this wood has already been killed, and is completely withered and bleached white, probably by the cold last winter, if not also by exposure to the light and heat of the summer.

This lot is thickly covered with the rubbish or tops. I suspect that it is, on the whole, better to leave this than to clear the ground, — that when it is not too thick (as masses of pine-tops) it is an important protection to the seedling trees (gardeners find that seedling pines require shade in their nurseries), and of course the soil is enriched by its decay.

Under one white oak where, on the 8th, the ground was strewn with acorns, I find but a single sound one left to-day, and under another, though many acorns are left, all of them are decayed, so rapidly are they gathered by the squirrels. I take them from the tree already decayed without a worm in them. Far the greater part that you find destroyed (this does not include those

eaten by animals) have thus decayed, and I think that the cause was the severe frost of about October 1st, which especially injured those on the ground. It is surprising that any escape the winter. I am not sure that white oak acorns do (as I am that many scarlet and red oak, etc., do). These are not protected by any downiness, and their shoots and leaves I know are the most tender in the spring. Probably almost all the white oak acorns would be destroyed by frost if left on the surface in pastures, and so it may be that more escape because the squirrels carry them off and bury them, or leave them under the shelter of the woods and leaves, though they consume so many, than would if they were not disturbed. Also I find many full-grown worms in them, and the acorn all powder, on the tree.

Do I not see yellow-crowned warblers? Much yellow on shoulders or sides, and white in wings when they fly.[1]

Acorns that fall in open pastures decay so fast that you might wonder how any survived the winter, but the fact is that they are not suffered to lie long, but are picked up and carried off by animals, and either deposited in holes or buried under the leaves in the forest, or consumed; and so, probably, more of these survive than would if they were not carried off.

Oct. 16. P. M. — To White Pond and neighborhood.

As a consequence of the different manner in which trees which have winged seeds and those which have not are planted, — the [former] being blown together in one direction by the wind, the latter being dispersed ir-

[1] Yes. They fly up against the windows the next day.

regularly by animals, — I observe that the former, as pines (which (the white) are said in the primitive wood to grow in communities), white birches, red maples, alders, etc., often grow in more or less regular rounded or oval or conical patches, as the seeds fell, while oaks, chestnuts, hickories, etc., simply form woods of greater or less extent whether by themselves or mixed; *i. e.*, they do not naturally spring up in an oval form (or elliptical) unless they derive it from the pines under which they were planted.

For example, take this young white pine wood half a dozen years old, which has sprung up in a pasture adjacent to a wood of oaks and pines mixed. It has the form of a broad crescent, or half-moon, with its diameter resting on the old wood near where a large white pine stood. It is true most such groves are early squared by our plows and fences, for we square these circles every day in our rude practice. And in the same manner often they fall in a sprout-land amid oaks, and I, looking from a hilltop, can distinguish in distant old woods still, of pine and oak mixed, these more exclusive and regular communities of pine, a dozen or more rods wide, while it is the oak commonly that fills up the irregular crevices, beside occupying extensive spaces itself. So it happens that, as the pines themselves and their fruit have a more regularly conical outline than deciduous trees, the groves they form also have.

Our wood-lots, of course, have a history, and we may often recover it for a hundred years back, though we *do* not. A small pine lot may be a side of such an oval, or a half, or a square in the inside with all the curving sides cut off by fences. Yet if we attended more to the history of our lots we should manage them more wisely.

Looking round, I observe at a distance an oak wood-lot some twenty years old, with a dense narrow edging of pitch pines about a rod and a half wide and twenty-five or thirty years old along its whole southern side, which is straight and thirty or forty rods long, and, next to it, an open field or pasture. It presents a very singular appearance, because the oak wood is broad and has no pines within it, while the narrow edging is perfectly straight and dense, and pure pine. It is the more remarkable at this season because the oak is all red and yellow and the pine all green. I understand it and read its history easily before I get to it. I find, as I expected, a fence separating the pines from the oaks, or that they belong to different owners. I also find, as I expected, that eighteen or twenty years ago a pitch pine wood had stood where the oaks are, and was then cut down, for there are their old stumps. But before they were cut, their seeds were blown into the neighbor's field, and the little pines came up all along its edge, and they grew so thickly and so fast that that neighbor refrained at last from plowing them up or cutting them off, for just this rod and a half in width, where they were thickest, and moreover, though there are no sizable oaks mixed with these pines, the whole surface even of this narrow strip is as usual completely stocked with little seedling oaks less than a foot high. But I ask, if the neighbor so often lets this narrow edging grow up, why not often, by the same rule, let them spread over the whole of his field? When at length he sees how they have grown, does he not often

regret that he did not do so? Or why be dependent even to this extent, on these windfalls from our neighbors' trees, or an accident? Why not control our own woods and destiny more? (This was north from the lane beyond Conant's handsome wood.) There are many such problems in forest geometry to be solved.

Again, I read still further back a more varied story. Take the line between Rice and Conant (?) or Garfield (?). Here is a green strip of dense pitch and white pine some thirty or forty rods long by four wide and thirty years old. On the east side is a large red and yellow [sic] oak wood-lot, the nearest part of it some dozen or more years old, and on the west a strip three rods wide of little white and pitch pines four to ten feet high that have sprung up in the open land, and next to these is an open field occasionally cultivated. Given these facts, to find the wall. If you think a moment you will know without my telling you that it is between the pine wood and the oak. Some dozen or more years ago there was a large pine wood extending up to the wall on the west, and then an open field belonging to another man. But, as before, the pine seed had blown over the wall and taken so well that for four rods in width it was suffered to grow, or rather may be said to have defended itself and crowded the farmer back (no thanks to him). But when, some fifteen years ago, the old pine wood was cut by its owner, the other

was not ready to cut his younger one. This is now about thirty years old and for many years it has been endeavoring to spread into the open land by its side, as its parents did, but for a long time the proprietor, not taking the hint, blind to his own interests, plowed quite up to the edge of the wood, as I noticed, — and got a few beans for his pains. But the pines (which he did not plant) grew while he slept, and at length, one spring, he gave up the contest and concluded at last to plow only within three rods of the wood, the little pines were so thick and promising. He concluded not to cut his own fingers any more, i. e. not further than up to the last joint, and hence this second row of little pines. They would have covered the half or perhaps the whole of his barren field before this if he had let them.

I examined these pine lots. The strip of little pines contained also a little white birch, much sweet-fern, and thin open sod, but scarcely one oak, and that very small. The strip of large pines contained countless oaks of various kinds, — white, red, black, and shrub oak, — which had come from the young oak lot, many little pines of both kinds, and *little* wild cherry, — white [sic], — and some hazel and high blueberry. (It was rather elevated as well as dry soil.)

I dug up some of the little oaks to see how old they were and how they had fared. The largest in the lot were about one foot high. First, a red or scarlet oak, apparently four years old. The acorn was about one inch below the surface of the pine leaves. It rose five inches above the leaves, and the root extended about one foot below the surface. It had died down once.

The second was a black oak which rose six inches above the leaves (or eight, measured along the stem). It was apparently four years old. It was much branched and its tops had been cut off by rabbits last year. The root ran straight down about one inch, then nearly horizontally five or six inches, and when I pulled it up it broke off where less than one eighth inch thick, at sixteen inches below the surface. This tree was one fourth of an inch in diameter at the surface and nearly three fourths of an inch in diameter at five inches below (along the root). At the same height above the surface it was hardly one fifth of an inch in diameter.

The third was a white oak ten inches high, apparently seven years old. It also had been browsed by a rabbit and put out a new shoot accordingly. Two years' growth was buried in the leaves. The root was very similar, both in direction and form, to the last, only not quite so thick.

Fourth, a shrub oak also quite similar, though less thick still and with two or more shoots from one stock.

In all these cases, or especially the first three [?], there was one main and an unexpectedly great, fusiform root, altogether out of proportion to the top, you would say tapering both ways, but of course largest and sharpest downward, with many fine stringy fibres extending on every side from it perhaps a foot. Just as a biennial plant devotes its energies the first year to producing a stock on which it can feed the next, so these little oaks in their earliest years are forming great fusiform vigorous roots on which they can draw when they are suddenly left to seek their fortunes in a sprout-land.

Thus this double forest was advancing to conquer new (or old) land, sending forward their children on the wings of the wind, while already the oak seedlings from the oak wood behind had established themselves beneath the old pines ready to supplant them. The pines were the vanguard. They stood up to fire with their children before them, while the little oaks kneeled behind and between them. The pine is the pioneer, the oak the more permanent settler who lays out his improvements. Pines are by some considered lower in the scale of trees — in the order of development — than oaks.

While the pines were blowing into the pasture from this narrow edging, the animals were planting the acorns under the pines. Even the small pine woods are thus perfectly equipped.

There was even under these dark, dense pines, thirty years old, a pretty thick bed of blueberry and huckleberry bushes next the wall, ten feet wide, the relics of a still denser and higher one that grew there when it was an open field. The former had thus been driven back three times, first by the blueberry hedge, then by the pines of thirty years ago, and lastly by the young pines that sprang from them. Thus a wood-lot had been forced upon him, and yet perhaps he will talk of it as a creation of his own.

I have come up here this afternoon to see ——'s dense white pine lot beyond the pond, that was cut off last winter, to know how the little oaks look in it. To my surprise and chagrin, I find that the fellow who calls himself its owner has burned it all over and sowed winter-rye here. He, no doubt, means to let it grow up

again in a year or two, but he thought it would be clear gain if he could extract a little rye from it in the meanwhile. What a fool! Here nature had got everything ready for this emergency, and kept them ready for many years, — oaks half a dozen years old or more, with fusiform roots full charged and tops already pointing skyward, only waiting to be touched off by the sun, — and he thought he knew better, and would get a little rye out of it first, which he could feel at once between his fingers, and so he burned it, and dragged his harrow over it. As if oaks would bide *his* time or come at his bidding. Or as if he preferred to have a pine or a birch wood here possibly half a century hence — for the land is "pine sick" — rather than an oak wood at once. So he trifles with nature. I am chagrined for him. That he should call himself an agriculturalist! He needs to have a guardian placed over him. A forest-warden should be appointed by the town. Overseers of poor husbandmen.

He has got his dollars for the pine timber, and now he wishes to get his bushels of grain and finger the dollars that they will bring; and then, Nature, you may have your way again. Let us purchase a mass for his soul. A greediness that defeats its own ends.

I examined a little lot of his about a dozen rods square just this side, cut off last winter, apparently two thirds white pine and one third white oak. Last year the white pine seed was very abundant, but there was little or no white oak seed. Accordingly I noticed twenty or more seedling white pines of this year on the barest spots, but not a single seedling oak. This suggests how much the

species of the succeeding forest may depend on whether the trees were fertile the year before they were cut, or not.

I see a very large white oak acorn which has a double meat with a skin between. There is a very young grub in it.

They appear to be last year's hemlock and larch cones that still hold on in great numbers!

As time elapses, and the resources from which our forests have been supplied fail, we shall of necessity be more and more convinced of the significance of the seed.

I see in a thick pitch pine wood half a dozen stout pine twigs five eighths of an inch thick that have been gnawed off with their plumes. Why?

Hear the alder locust still. Robins apparently more numerous than a month ago. See grackles in cornfields in two places to-day.

It chanced that here were two proprietors within half a mile who had done exactly the same, i. e., accepted part of a wood-lot that was forced on them, and I have no doubt that there are several more exactly similar cases within that half-mile diameter.

The history of a wood-lot is often, if not commonly, *here*, a history of cross-purposes, — of steady and consistent endeavor on the part of Nature, of interference and blundering with a glimmering of intelligence at the eleventh hour on the part of the proprietor. The proprietor of wood-lots commonly treats Nature as an Irishman drives a horse, — by standing before him and beating him in the face all the way across a field.

If I find any starved pasture in the midst of our woods, — and I remember many such, and they are

the least valuable tracts we have, — I know that it has commonly had such a history as this wood-lot (above). It was burned over when cut, and perhaps cultivated a year or two, often because the owner thought it was what the soil needed in order that it might produce trees. In some cases there may be sense in such a course if he can afford to wait a century instead of a third of that time for a crop. It depends on what the trees are, the locality, etc. But commonly the owner who adopts this course makes a move in the dark and in ninety-nine cases in a hundred [an indecipherable word] his own fingers.

The time will soon come, if it has not already, when we shall have to take special pains to secure and encourage the growth of white oaks, as we already must that of chestnuts for the most part. These oaks will become so scattered that there will be not seed enough to seed the ground rapidly and completely.

Horace Mann tells me that he found in the crop or inside of the stake-driver killed the other day one grasshopper, several thousand-legs one to one and a half inches long, and not much else.

It commonly happens in settled countries like this that the new community of pines, sprung from seeds blown off from an older one, is very youthful compared with the trees it sprang from because many successive crops of trees or seeds have been plowed up or cut before the owner allowed Nature to take her course. Naturally the pines spread more steadily and with no such abrupt descents. In the wildwood at least there are commonly only fires and insects or blight, and not the axe and plow and the cattle, to interrupt the regular progress of things.

Oct. 17. P. M. — To Walden Woods.

The trees which *with us* grow in masses, *i. e.* not merely scattering, are: —

       1, 2. White and pitch pine
         3. Oaks
         4. White birch
         5. Red maple
         6. Chestnut
         7. Hickory
           Alder
           Hemlock, spruce, and larch
           Cedar (white and red)
           Willow
           Locust
           Apple
           Red cherry (in neighboring towns) W. [*sic*]
           Sugar maple (rare)

Of these only white and pitch pine, oaks, white birch, and red maple are *now* both important and abundant. (Chestnut and hickory have become rare.)

It is an interesting inquiry what determines which species of these shall grow on a given tract. It is evident that the soil determines this to some extent, as of the oaks only the swamp white stands in our meadows, and, so far as these seven trees are concerned, swamps will be composed only of red maples, swamp white oaks, white birch, and white pine. By removing to upland we get rid of the swamp white oak and red maples in *masses*, and are reduced to white and pitch pine, oaks, and white birch only, *i. e.* of those that are abundant and important.

Secondly, ownership, and a corresponding difference

Vol. XIV

of treatment of the land as to time of cutting, etc. decides the species.

Third, age, as, if the trees are one hundred years old they may be chestnut, but if sprout-land are less likely to be; etc., etc., etc.

The noblest trees and those which it took the longest to produce, and which are the longest-lived, as chestnuts, hickories (?), oaks, are the first to become extinct under our present system and the hardest to reproduce, and their place is taken by pines and birches, of feebler growth than the primitive pines and birches, for want of a change of soil.

There is many a tract now bearing a poor and decaying crop of birches, or perhaps of oaks, dying when a quarter grown and covered with fungi and excrescences where two hundred years ago grew oaks or chestnuts of the largest size.

I look through a lot of young oaks twenty or twenty-five years old (Warren's, east of the Deep Cut, exclusively oak, the eastern part). There are plenty of little oaks from a few inches to a foot in height, but on examination I find fewer seedlings in proportion to the whole (*i. e.* manifestly seedlings) and they have much older and larger and poorer or more decayed roots than the oaks in dense pine woods. Oftenest they are shoots from the end of a horizontal twig running several feet under the leaves and leading to an old stump [?] under the surface. But I must examine again and further.

Looking through this wood and seeking very carefully for oak seedlings and anything else of the kind, I am surprised to see where the wood was chiefly oak a

cluster of little chestnuts six inches high and close together. Working my hand underneath, I easily lift them up with all their roots, — four little chestnuts two years old, which partially died down the first year, — and to my surprise I find still attached four great chestnuts from which they sprang and four acorns which have also sent up puny little trees beneath the chestnuts. These eight nuts all lay within a diameter of two inches about an inch and a half beneath the present leafy surface, in a very loose soil of but [?] half decayed leaves in the midst of this young oak wood. If I had not been looking for something of the kind, I should never have seen either the oaks or the chestnuts. Such is the difference between looking for a thing and waiting for it to attract your attention. In the last case you will probably never see it [at] all. They were evidently planted there two or three years ago by a squirrel or mouse. I was surprised at the sight of these chestnuts, for there are not *to my knowledge* any chestnut trees — none, at least, nearly large enough to bear nuts — within about half a mile of that spot, and I should about as soon have expected to find chestnuts in the artificial pine grove in my yard. The chestnut trees old enough to bear fruit are near the Lincoln line about half a mile east of this through the woods and over hill and dale. No one acquainted with these woods — not the proprietor — would have believed that a chestnut lay under the leaves in that wood or within a quarter of a mile of it, and yet from what I saw then and afterward I have no doubt that there were hundreds, which were placed there by quadrupeds and birds. This wood lies on the south of

the village, separated from it by a mile of open fields and meadows. It is the northern part of an extensive pine and oak forest which half a mile eastward, near the Lincoln line, begins to contain a few chestnuts. These little chestnuts were growing well, but the oaks appeared to be dead and dying.[1]

It is well known that the chestnut timber of this vicinity has rapidly disappeared within fifteen years, having been used for railroad sleepers, for rails, and for planks, so that there is danger that this part of our forest will become extinct.

The last chestnut tracts of any size were on the side of Lincoln. As I advanced further through the wood toward Lincoln, I was surprised to see how many little chestnuts there were, mostly two or three years old and some even ten feet high, scattered through them and also under the dense pines, as oaks are. I should say there was one every half-dozen rods, made more distinct by their yellow leaves on the brown ground, which surprised me because I had not attended to the spread of the chestnut, and it is certain that every one of these came from a chestnut placed there by a quadruped or bird which had brought it from further east, where alone it grew.

You would say that the squirrels, etc., went further for chestnuts than for acorns in proportion as they were a greater rarity. I suspect that a squirrel may convey them sometimes a quarter or a half a mile even, and no doubt as soon as a young chestnut fifteen or twenty feet

[1] I dug up three or four more a few days after, and found that they had not the very large roots that young oaks have.

high, far advanced beyond the chestnut woods, bears a single bur, which no man discovers, a squirrel or bird is almost sure to gather it and plant it in that neighborhood or still further forward. A squirrel goes a-chestnutting perhaps as far as the boys do, and when he gets there he does not have to shake or club the tree or wait for frost to open the burs; he walks [?] up to the bur and cuts it off, and strews the ground with them before they have opened. And the fewer they are in the wood the more certain it is that he will appropriate every one, for it is no transient afternoon's picnic with him, but the pursuit of his life, a harvest that he gets as surely as the farmer his corn.

Now it is important that the owners of these wood-lots should know what is going on here and treat them and the squirrels accordingly. They little dream of what the squirrels are about; know only that they get their seed-corn in the adjacent fields, and encourage their boys to shoot them every day, supplying them with powder and shot for this purpose. In newer parts of the country they have squirrel-hunts on a large scale and kill many thousands in a few hours, and all the neighborhood rejoices.

Thus it appears that by a judicious letting Nature alone merely we might recover our chestnut wood in the course of a century.

This also suggests that you cannot raise one kind of wood alone in a country unless you are willing to plant it yourself. If no oaks grow within miles of your pines, the ground under the pines will not be filled with little oaks, and you will have to plant them. Better have

your wood of different kinds in narrow lots of fifty acres, and not one kind covering a township.

I took up a red oak seedling of this year five inches high. In this case the top is larger, putting length and breadth together, than the root, and the great acorn is still perfectly sound, lying on its side, and the plant this first year evidently derives a great part of its nourishment from it. The root is abruptly curved back under the acorn, and I find that seedling or young oaks generally have roots which slant off more or less horizontally from where the acorn lay two to five or six inches, and then, having acquired their greatest thickness, descend straight downward. To this irregularity is sometimes added a half-turn or spiral in the upper part of the root: or, looking down on it: The acorn is still so sound that I think it must continue to furnish nourishment to the plant a part of next year.

Apparently the pine woods are a natural nursery of oaks, from whence we might easily transplant them to our grounds, and thus save some of those which annually decay, while we let the pines stand. Experience has proved, at any rate, that these oaks will bear exposure to the light. It is remarkable that for the most part there are no seedling oaks in the open grassy fields and pastures. The acorns are little likely to succeed if dropped there. Those springing up in such places appear to have been dropped or buried by animals when on their way with them to another covert.

Vol. XIV

I examine under the pitch pines by Thrush Alley to see how long the oaks live under dense pines. The oldest oaks there are about eight or ten years old. I see none older under these and other dense pines, even when the pines are thirty or more years old, though I have no doubt that oaks began to grow there more than twenty years ago. Hence they must have died, and I suppose I could find their great roots in the soil if I should dig for them. I should say that they survived under a very dense pine wood only from six to ten years. This corresponds exactly with the experience of the English planters, who begin to shred the branches of the nursing pines when the oaks are six or seven years old and to remove the pines altogether when the oaks are eight to ten years old.

But in openings amid the pines, though only a rod in diameter, or where the pines are thin, and also on their edges, the oaks shoot up higher and become trees, and this shows how mixed woods of pine and oak are produced. If the pines are quite small or grow but thinly, fewer acorns will be planted amid them, it is true, but more will come to trees, and so you have a mixed wood. Or when you thin out a pine wood, the oaks spring up here and there; or when you thin an oak wood, the pines plant themselves and grow up in like manner.

It is surprising how many accidents these seedling oaks will survive. We have seen [?] that they commonly survive six to ten years under the thickest pines and acquire stout and succulent roots. Not only they bear the sudden exposure to the light when the pines are cut,

but, in case of a more natural succession, when a fire runs over the lot and kills pines and birches and maples, and oaks twenty feet high, these little oaks are scarcely injured at all, and they will still be just as high the next year, if not in the fall of the same year if the fire happens early in the spring. Or if in the natural course of events a fire does not occur nor a hurricane, the soil may at last be exhausted for pines, but there are always the oaks ready to take advantage of the least feebleness and yielding of the pines.

Hereabouts a pine wood, or even a birch wood, is no sooner established than the squirrels and birds begin to plant acorns in it. First the pines, then the oaks; and coniferous trees, geologists tell us, are older, as they are lower in the order of development, — were created before oaks.

I observe to-day a great many pitch pine plumes cut off by squirrels and strewn under the trees, as I did yesterday.[1]

I count the rings of a great white pine sawed off in Laurel Glen a few years ago, —about one hundred and thirty. This, probably, was really of the second growth, at least, but probably now even the second growth is all gone in this town. We may presume that any forest tree here a hundred and thirty years old belongs to the second growth, at least. We may say that all pines and oaks of this age or *growth* are now extinct in this town,

[1] The next day (18th) I see twenty pine twigs, some three-plumed, at Beck Stow's, recently gnawed off and lying under one tree. This is to be seen now on all sides of the town. Why so? Saw the same last fall and before.

and the present generation are not acquainted with large trees of these species.

A month ago I saw the smoke of many burnings in the horizon (even now see one occasionally), and now in my walks I occasionally come to a field of winter-rye already greening the ground in the woods where such a fire was then kindled.

If any one presumes that, after all, there cannot be so many nuts planted as we see oaks spring up at once when the pines are cut, he must consider that *according to the above calculation* (two pages back) there are some ten years for the animals to plant the oak wood in; so that, if the tract is ten rods square or contains one hundred square rods, it would only be necessary that they should plant ten acorns in a year which should not be disturbed, in order that there might be one oak to every square rod at the end of ten years.[1] This, or anything like this, does not imply any very great activity among the squirrels. A striped squirrel could carry enough in his cheeks at one trip.

While the man that killed my lynx (and many others) thinks it came out of a menagerie, and the naturalists call it the Canada lynx, and at the White Mountains they call it the Siberian lynx,—in each case forgetting, or ignoring, that it belongs here,—I call it the Concord lynx.

Oct. 18. P. M. — To Merriam's white pine grove.

I often see amid or beside a pitch or white pine grove, though thirty years old, a few yet larger and older trees,

---

[1] But some English planters plant only an acorn to two or three rods, others four or five times as many.

Look through an oak wood, say twenty-five or thirty years old, north of the Sherman grove on the road. It appeared to me that there were fewer seedling oaks under this than under pines, and the roots of the other little ones that looked like seedlings were old and decaying, and the shoots slender, feeble, and more or less prostrate under the leaves. You will find seedling oaks under oaks, it is true, but I think that you will not find a great many of them. You will not find, as under pines, a great many of these little oaks one to eight or ten years old, with great fat, or fusiform, roots, all ready to spring up when the pines are cut.

If it were true that the little oaks under oaks steadily grew and came to trees there, then even that would be a reason why the soil would not be so well stocked with them when the wood was cut as when a pine wood is cut, for there would be only ten trees in the first case to one hundred in the last (according to our calculation before).

Most of the little oaks here were little or dwarfed, apparently because they were shoots from poor and diseased rootstocks, which were common in the ground.

But I think that neither pines nor oaks do well under older trees.

Methinks you do not see numerous oaks of all ages and sizes in an old oak wood, but commonly large trees of about the same age and little ones like huckleberry bushes under your feet; and so commonly with pine woods. In either case, if the woods are well grown and dense, all the trees in them appear to have been planted at the same time.

from which they came, rising above them, like patriarchs surrounded by their children.

Early cinquefoil again.

I find fair-looking white oak acorns, which abound on the trees near Beck Stow's, to be decayed on the tree. Wishing to see what proportion were decayed I pull down a bough, and pluck forty-one acorns, which I cut open successively with my knife. Every one is soft and spoiled, turned black or dark-brown within, though there is not a single worm in them. Indeed, abundant and beautiful as the crop is, they are all decayed on that and the neighboring trees, and I only find one sound one after long search. This is probably the reason why they hold on still so numerously, and beside the squirrels do not disturb them. I suspect that they were killed by the severe frost of about October 1st. Abundant as the crop is, perhaps half of them have already been destroyed thus. Those that were touched first and most severely are paler-brown on one or both sides. Here, or on *these* trees, is a whole crop destroyed before it fell, though remarkably abundant. How many thousand bushels there must be in this state in this town!

See how an acorn is planted by a squirrel, just under a loose covering of moist leaves where it is shaded and concealed, and lies on its side on the soil, ready to send down its radicle next year.

If there are not so many oak seedlings in a deciduous wood as in a pine one, it may be because both oaks (and acorns) and squirrels love warmth. The ground does not freeze nearly so hard under dense pines as in a deciduous wood.

For aught that I know, I would much rather have a young oak wood which has succeeded to pines than one that has succeeded to oaks, for they will make better trees, not only because the soil is new to them, but because they are all seedlings, while in the other case far the greater part are sprouts; just as I would prefer apple trees five or six years from the seed for my orchard to suckers from those which have come to maturity or decayed. Otherwise your young oaks will soon, when half grown, have the diseases of old trees, — warts and decay.

I find that Merriam's white pine grove is on the site of an oak wood, the old oak stumps being still very common. The pines appear to be some forty years old. The soil of pine leaves is an inch to an inch and a half thick. The oldest little oaks here are five years old and six inches high.

Am surprised to see that the pasture west of this, where the little pitch pines were cut down last year, is now even more generally green with pines than two years ago.

What shall we say to that management that halts between two courses, — does neither this nor that, but botches both? I see many a pasture on which the pitch or white pines are spreading, where the bush-whack is from time to time used with a show of vigor, and I despair of my trees, — I say mine, for the farmer evidently does not mean they shall be his, — and yet this questionable work is so poorly done that those very fields grow steadily greener and more forest-like from year to year in spite of cows and bush-whack, till at length the farmer gives up the contest from sheer weariness, and finds himself the owner of a wood-lot. Now whether wood-lots or pastures are most profitable for him I will not undertake to say, but I am certain that a wood-lot and pasture combined is not profitable.

I see spatter-dock pads and pontederia in that little pool at south end of Beck Stow's. How did they get there? There is no stream in this case? It was perhaps rather reptiles and birds than fishes, then. Indeed we might as well ask how they got anywhere, for all the pools and fields have been stocked thus, and we are not to suppose as many new creations as pools. This suggests to inquire how any plant came where it is, — how, for instance, the pools which were stocked with lilies before we were born or this town was settled, and ages ago, were so stocked, as well as those which we dug. I think that we are warranted only in supposing that the former was stocked in the same way as the latter, and that there was not a sudden new creation, — at least since the first; yet I have no doubt that peculiarities more or less considerable have thus been gradually produced in the lilies thus planted in various pools, in consequence of their various conditions, though they all came originally from one seed.

We find ourselves in a world that is already planted, but is also still being planted as at first. We say of some plants that they grow in wet places and of others that they grow in desert places. The truth is that their seeds are scattered almost everywhere, but here only do they succeed. Unless you can show me the pool where the lily was created, I shall believe that the oldest fossil

lilies which the geologist has detected (if this is found fossil) originated in that locality in a similar manner to these of Beck Stow's. We see thus how the fossil lilies which the geologist has detected are dispersed, as well as these which we carry in our hands to church.

The development theory implies a greater vital force in nature, because it is more flexible and accommodating, and equivalent to a sort of constant *new* creation.

Mr. Alcott tells me that the red squirrels which live in his elms go off to the woods (pitch pines behind his house) about June, and return in September, when the butternuts, etc., are ripe. Do they not go off for hazelnuts and pine seed? No doubt they are to be found where their food is.

Young oaks, especially white oaks, in open woodland hollows and on plains [are] almost annually killed down by frost, they are so tender. Large tracts in this town are bare for this reason. Hence it is very important that the little oaks, when they are tenderest, should have the shelter of pines and other trees as long as they can bear it, or perhaps till they get above the level of the frosts. I know of extensive open areas in the woods where it would be of no use to sow acorns or to set seedling oaks, for every one would be killed by the frost, as they have already been; but if you were to plant pines thinly there, or thickly at first and then thin them out, you could easily raise oaks, for often you have only got to protect them till they are five or six feet high, that they may be out of the way of ordinary frosts, whose surface is as level as that of a lake.

According to Loudon (*vide* Emerson on oaks), the

best authorities say plant some two hundred and fifty acorns to an acre (*i. e.* some from three hundred to five hundred, others from sixty to one hundred), or about one and one half acorns to a rod, or two hundred and forty to an acre.

In my walk in Walden Woods yesterday I found that the seedling oaks and chestnuts were most common under the fullest and densest white pines, as that of Brister Spring.

Oct. 19. P. M. — To Conantum.
Indian-summer-like and gossamer.
That white oak in Hubbard Grove which on the 7th was full of those glossy black acorns is still hanging full, to my surprise. Suspecting the cause, I proceed to cut them open, and find that they are all decayed or decaying. Even if not black within, they are already sour and softened. Yet Rice told me that he collected from this tree about a week ago some thousands of acorns and planted them in Sudbury. I can tell him that probably not more than half a dozen of them were alive, though they may then have looked well, as they do now externally. First, then, I was surprised at the abundance of the crop this year. Secondly, by the time I had got accustomed to that fact I was surprised at the vast proportion that were killed, apparently by frost. The squirrels are wiser than to gather these, but I see where they have gathered many black oak acorns, the ground beneath being strewn with their cups, which have each a piece bitten out in order to get out the acorn. I suspect that black and red oak acorns are not so easily injured

by frost. Indeed, I find this to be the case as far as I look.

Sophia tells me that the large swamp white oak acorns in their cups, which she gathered a fortnight ago, are now all mouldy about the cups, or base of the acorn.

It is a remarkable fact, and looks like a glaring imperfection in Nature, that the labor of the oaks for the year should be lost to this extent. The softening or freezing of cranberries, the rotting of potatoes, etc., etc., seem trifling in comparison. The pigeons, jays, squirrels, and woodlands are thus impoverished. It is hard to say what great purpose is served by this seeming waste.

I frequently see an old and tall pine wood standing in the midst of a younger but more extensive oak wood, it being merely a remnant of an extensive pine wood which once occupied the whole tract, but, having a different owner, or for some other reason, it has not been cut. Sometimes, also, I see these pines of the same age reappear at half a mile distant, the intermediate pines having been cut for thirty or forty years, and oaks having taken their place. Or the distant second growth of pines, especially if they stand on the land of another than he who owns the oaks, may, as we have seen, be a generation smaller and have sprung from the pines that stood where the oaks do. Two or three pines will run swiftly forward a quarter of a mile into a plain, which is their favorite field of battle, taking advantage of the least shelter, as a rock, or fence, that may be there, and intrench themselves behind it, and if you look sharp, you may see their plumes waving there. Or, as I have said, they will cross a broad river without a bridge, and as swiftly climb and permanently occupy a steep hill beyond.

At this season of the year, when each leaf acquires its peculiar color, Nature prints this history distinctly, as it were an illuminated edition. Every oak and hickory and birch and aspen sprinkled amid the pines tells its tale a mile off, and you have not to go laboriously through the wood examining the bark and leaves. These facts would be best illustrated by colors, — green, yellow, red, etc.

Pines take the first and longest strides. Oaks march deliberately in the rear.

The pines are the light infantry, *voltigeurs*, supplying the scouts and skirmishers; the oaks are the grenadiers, heavy-paced and strong, that form the solid phalanx.

It is evident to any who attend to the matter that pines are here the natural nurses of the oaks, and therefore they grow together. By the way, how nearly identical is the range of our pines with the range of our oaks? Perhaps oaks extend beyond them southward, where there is less danger of frost.

The *new* woodlands, *i. e.*, forests that spring up where there were no trees before, are pine (or birch or maple), and accordingly you may see spaces of bare pasture sod between the trees for many years. But oaks, in masses, are not seen springing up thus with old sod between them. They form a sprout-land, or stand amid the stumps of a recent pine lot.

It will be worth the while to compare seedling oaks with sprout-lands, to see which thrive best.

I see, on the side of Fair Haven Hill, pines which

have spread, apparently from the north, one hundred rods, and the hillside begins to wear the appearance of woodland, though there are many cows feeding amid the pines. The custom with us is to let the pines spread thus into the pasture, and at the same time to let the cattle wander there and contend with the former for the possession of the ground, from time to time coming to the aid of the cattle with a bush-whack. But when, after some fifteen or twenty years, the pines have fairly prevailed over us both, though they have suffered terribly and the ground is strewn with their dead, we then suddenly turn about, coming to the aid of the pines with a whip, and drive the cattle out. They shall no longer be allowed to scratch their heads on them, and we fence them in. This is the actual history of a great many of our wood-lots. While the English have taken great pains to learn how to create forests, this is peculiarly our mode. It is plain that we have thus both poor pastures and poor forests.

I examine that oak lot of Rice's next to the pine strip of the 16th. The oaks (at the southern end) are about a dozen [1] years old. As I expected, I find the stumps of the pines which stood there before quite fresh and distinct, not much decayed, and I find by their rings that they were about forty years old when cut, while the pines which sprang from [them] are now about twenty-five or thirty. But further, and unexpectedly, I find the stumps, in great numbers, now much decayed, of an oak wood which stood there more than sixty years ago. They are mostly shells, the sap-wood rotted off and the inside

[1] Oct. 31, count ten rings on one sprout.

turned to mould. Thus I distinguished four successions of trees.

Thus I can easily find in countless numbers in our forests, frequently in the third succession, the stumps of the oaks which were cut near the end of the last century. Perhaps I can recover thus generally the oak woods of the beginning of the last century, if the land has remained woodland. I have an advantage over the geologist, for I can not only detect the order of events but the time during which they elapsed, by counting the rings on the stumps. Thus you can unroll the rotten papyrus on which the history of the Concord forest is written.

It is easier far to recover the history of the trees which stood here a century or more ago than it is to recover the history of the men who walked beneath them. How much do we know — how little more can we know — of these two centuries of Concord life?

Go into a young oak wood, and commonly, if the oaks are not sprouts, then they were preceded by pines.

Of course, the gradual manner in which many wood-lots are cut — often only thinned out — must affect the truth of my statements in numerous instances. The regularity of the succession will be interfered with, and what is true of one end of a lot will not be true of the other.

If the ground chances to be broken or burned over or cleared the same year that a good crop of pine seed falls, then expect pines; not otherwise.

I examined the huckleberry bushes next the wall in that same dense pitch and white pine strip. I found

that the oldest bushes were about two feet high and some eight or ten years old, and digging with spade and hands, I found that their roots did not go deep, but that they spread by a vigorous shoot which forked several times, running just under the leaves or in the surface soil, so that they could be easily pulled up. One ran seven feet before it broke, and was probably ten feet or more in length. And three or four bushes stood on this shoot, and though these bushes after a few years did not grow more than an inch in a year, these subterranean shoots had grown six to twelve inches at the end, and there seemed to be all the vigor of the plant. The largest bushes preserved still a trace of their origin from a subterranean shoot, the limbs being one-sided and the brash aslant. It is very likely, then, if not certain, that these roots are as old as the pine wood which overshadows them; or it is so long since the seedling huckleberry came up there. The pines were thirty years old, but some of the separate huckleberry bushes were ten, and were sending up new vigorous shoots still. The same was the case with the *Vaccinium vacillans* and the *Pennsylvanicum*, the last one, of course, on a smaller scale. You could see the *V. vacillans* growing in rows for several feet above the subterranean shoots, indicating where it was. The shoot turns up to make a bush thus:

Thus the roots of huckleberries may survive till the woods are cut again. They certainly will here. A huckleberry bush is apparently in its prime at five to seven years, and the oldest are ten to twelve years. Plants of this order (*Ericaceæ*) are said to be among the earlier ones among fossil plants, and they are likely to be among the last.

The oldest oak, fairly speaking, in this wood was a black, thirteen years old. Its root, as usual, ran not straight down but with a half-turn or twist (as well as to one side), which would make it harder to pull up at any rate.

The white oak acorn has very little bitterness and is quite agreeable to eat. When chestnuts are away I am inclined to think them as good as they. At any rate it braces my thought more, and does me more good to eat them, than it does to eat chestnuts. I feel the stronger even before I have swallowed one. It gives me heart and back of oak.

I found that the squirrels, or *possibly* mice, which have their holes about those old oak stumps ran along in various directions through the roots, whose insides are rotted away, leaving a wall of thin bark which prevents the earth falling in. Such are their highways underground. The holes above led to them.

On the monuments of the old settlers of this town, if they can be found, are recorded their names and ages and the time of their death, and so much can be read on these monuments of the oaks, with some additional reliable information, as where they lived, and how healthily, and what trees succeeded them, etc., etc.

Looking at Sophia's large collection of acorns from Sleepy Hollow and elsewhere, I cannot find a sound white oak one (*i. e.* not decayed and blackened), but

the black and shrub oaks at least are sound. This suggests that the very fertile shrub oaks are more sure of succeeding and spreading, while the noblest oak of all may fail.

First, by examining the twigs (*vide* Coultas) you tell the age and the number of shoots and the leaves and the various accidents of the tree for half a dozen years past, — can read its history very minutely; and at length, when it is cut down, you read its ancient and general history on its stump.

If you would know the age of a young oak lot, look round for a sprout, — for there will commonly be some to be found even in a seedling wood, — cut, and count the rings. But if you have to count the rings of a seedling, begin about six inches from the ground, for it was probably so high when the previous wood was cut.

Oct. 20. E. Hosmer tells me to-day that while digging mud at the Pokelogan the other day he found several fresh acorns planted an inch or two deep under the grass just outside the oaks and bushes there. Almost every observant farmer finds one such deposit each year.

If that Merriam lot is fifteen rods square, then, instead of there being no oaks in it, there are some twenty-five hundred oaks in it, or far more oaks than pines, — say five times as many, for there are probably not nearly five hundred pines in the lot. This is only one of the thousand cases in which the proprietor and woodchopper tell you that there is not a single oak in the lot. So the tables were turned, and, so far as numbers were con-

cerned, it would have been truer to say that this was an exclusively oak wood and that there were no pines in it. Truly appearances are deceptive.

P. M. — To Walden Woods to examine old stumps.

In Trillium Wood the trees are chiefly pine, and I judge them to be forty to fifty years old, though there are not a few oaks, etc. Beneath them I find some old pitch pine stumps and one white pine. They would not be seen by a careless observer; they are indistinct mounds and preserve no form nor marks of the axe. This is low ground. Part of the cores, etc., of the stumps are, nevertheless, preserved by fat.

I then look at Farrar's [?] hill lot east of the Deep Cut. This is oak, cut, as I remember, some twenty-five years ago, the trees say five to eight inches [in] diameter. I find beneath the oaks innumerable pitch pine stumps, well preserved, or rather, distinct, some of them two feet and more in diameter, with bark nearly three inches thick at the ground, but generally fifteen inches in diameter. Though apparently thoroughly rotten and of a rough (crumbly) conical form and more or less covered with fine moss (hypnum), they were firm within on account of the fat in flakes on the whole core, and frequently showed the trace of the axe in the middle. I could get cartloads of fat pine there now, often lifting out with my hands the whole core, a clear mass of yellow fat. When the stump was almost a mere mound mossed over, breaking off an inch or two deep of the crust, with the moss, I could still trace on one side the straight edge made by the axe. There were also, especially on the lower, or northern, side, some large oak stumps, no doubt of the same age.

These were much better preserved than the pines, — at least the part above ground. The whole shape and almost every stroke of the axe apparent sometimes, as in a fresh stump. I counted from seventy to seventy-five rings on one. The present wood appears to be chiefly from the seed, with some sprouts. The latter two or more close together, with the old stump more or less overgrown. The sprouts, I think, were from small trees. (Methinks you do not see trees which have sprouted from old or large stumps two or three feet in diameter. I doubt if a very old wood, like E. Hubbard's, would send up sprouts from the stump.) I saw one large oak stump so much decayed that it may have belonged to a generation further back.

I next examined Ebby Hubbard's old oak and pine wood. The trees may be a hundred years old. The older or decaying trees have been cut out from time to time, neglecting these more recent stumps. The very oldest evidences of a tree were a hollow three or four feet across, in which you often slumped, — a hollow place in which squirrels have their holes covered with many layers of leaves, and perhaps with young oaks springing up in it, for the acorns rolled into it. But if you dug there, from under the moss (there was commonly a little green moss around it) and leaves and soil, in the midst of the virgin mould which the tree had turned to, you pulled up flakes and shoulder-blades of wood that might still be recognized for oak, portions preserved by some quality which they concentrated, like the fat leaves or veins of the pine, — the oak of oak. But for the most part it was but the mould and mildew of the grave, — the grave of a tree which was cut or died eighty or a hundred years ago there. It is with the graves of trees as with those of men, — at first an upright stump (for a monument), in course of time a mere mound, and finally, when the corpse has decayed and shrunk, a depression in the soil. In such a hollow it is better to plant a pine than an oak. The only other ancient traces of trees were perhaps the semiconical mounds which had been heaved up by trees which fell in some hurricane.

I saw where Ebby had tried a pitch pine with his axe, though there was not a green twig on it, and the wood-peckers had bored it from top to bottom, — effectually proved it, if he had not been blind.

Looked at that pitch and white pine wood just east of Close at Brister Spring, which I remember as pasture some thirty years ago. The pasture is still betrayed under the pines by the firmer, sward-like surface, there being fewer leaves and less of leafy mould formed, — less virgin soil, — and by the patches of green (*pine*) moss and white cladonia peeping out here and there.

Young chestnuts (I dig up three or four) have not the large roots that oaks have.

I see the acorn after the tree is five or six years old.

Brassica Napus, or rape, a second crop, is blooming now, especially where grain has been cut and the field laid down to grass and clover. It has there little slender plants; rough, or bristly, lower leaves.

1st. There is the primitive wood, woodland which was woodland when the township was settled, and which has not been cut at all. Of this I know of none in Con-

Vol. XIV

cord. Where is the nearest? There is, perhaps, a large tract in Winchendon.

2d. Second growth, the woodland which has been cut but once, — true second growth. This country has been so recently settled that a large part of the older States is covered now with this second growth, and the same name is occasionally still applied, though falsely, to those wood-lots which have been cut twice or many more times. Of this second growth I think that we have considerable left, and I remember much more. These are our forests which contain the largest and oldest trees, — shingle pines (very few indeed left) and oak timber.

3d. Primitive woodland, *i. e.*, which has always been woodland, never cultivated or converted into pasture or grain-field, nor burned over intentionally. Of two kinds, first, that which has only been thinned from time to time, and secondly, that which has been cut clean many times over. A larger *copsewood*.

4th. Woodland which has been cleared one or more times, enough to raise a crop of grain on it, burned over and perhaps harrowed or even plowed, and suffered to grow up again in a year or two. Call this "interrupted woodland" or "tamed."

5th. *New woods*, or which have sprung up *de novo* on land which has been cultivated or cleared long enough to kill all the roots in it. (The 3d, 4th, and 5th are a kind of copsewood.)

6th. Artificial woods, or those which have been set out or raised from the seed, artificially.

It happens that we have not begun to set out and plant till all the primitive wood is gone. All the *new woods* (or

5th kind) whose beginning I can (now) remember are pine or birch (maple, etc., I have not noticed enough). I suspect that the greater part (?) of our woodland is the 3d kind, or primitive woodland, never burned over intentionally nor plowed, though much of it is the 4th kind. Probably almost all the large wood cut ten or fifteen years ago (and since) here was second growth, and most that we had left was cut then.

Of the new woods I remember the beginning of E. Hubbard's east of Brister Spring; Bear Garden, pitch pine; Wheeler's pigeon-place, pitch pine; also his blackberry-field, pitch pine and a few white; West Fair Haven Spring woods, pitch pine and white; E. Hubbard's Close Mound, pitch pine; Conantum-top, pitch pine; Mason's pasture (?), white pine; behind Baker's (?), pitch pine; my field at Walden, pitch pine; Kettle Hill, pitch pine; Moore's corn-hill, pitch pine, cut say '59; behind Moore's house (??), pitch pine (was it new?); front of Sleepy Hollow, poplars, pitch pine; E. Wood's, front of Colburn place (??), pitch pine, not new wood; John Hosmer's, beyond house (?), pitch pine; Fair Haven Hill-side, white pine, just begun; Merriam's pasture, beyond Beck Stow's, just begun, pitch pine; old coast behind Heywood's, pitch pine; Conant's white pine crescent in front of W. Wheeler's; J. P. Brown pasture, white pine; at Hemlocks, pitch pine; northwest of Assabet stone bridge, pitch pine; Tarbell's pitch pines; Baker's, above beech, pitch pine; Henry Shattuck's, pitch pine; northwest of Farmer's, pitch pine; William Brown's, pitch pine; north of H. Shattuck's, pitch pine; white

and pitch pine south of Rice's lot; pitch pine northwest of old Corner schoolhouse, pitch pine southeast of new Corner schoolhouse; large pitch pine hill behind Hagar's in Lincoln.

In several of these new woods — pitch pine and birches — can see the old corn-hills still.

The woods within my recollection have gradually withdrawn further from the village, and woody capes which jutted from the forest toward the town are now cut off and separated by cleared land behind. The Irish have also made irruptions into our woods in several places, and cleared land.

Edmund Hosmer tells me of a gray squirrel which he kept in his old (Everett) house; that he would go off to the woods every summer, and in the winter come back and into his cage, where he whirled the wire cylinder. He would be surprised to see it take a whole and large ear of corn and run out a broken window and up over the roof of the corn-barn with it, and also up the elms.

We have a kitten a third grown which often carries its tail almost flat on its back like a squirrel.

Oct. 22. P. M. — To Walden Woods.

See in the yard many chip-birds, but methinks the chestnut crown is not so distinct as in the spring, — has a pale line in middle of it, — and many, maybe females or young, have no chestnut at all. I do not find them so described.

Are not maples inclined to die in a white pine wood? There was the one in Merriam's grove and the sickly ones in our grove in the yard.

I notice that the first shrubs and trees to spring up in the sand on railroad cuts in the woods are sweet-fern, birches, willows, and aspens, and pines, white and pitch; but all but the last two chiefly disappear in the thick wood that follows. The former are the pioneers. Such sandy places, the edges of meadows, and sprout-lands are almost the only localities of willows with us.

In the Deep Cut big wood (Stow's), pines and oaks, there are thousands of little white pines as well as many oaks. After a mixed wood like this you may have a mixed wood, but after dense pines, commonly oak chiefly, yet not always; for, to my surprise, I find that in the pretty dense pitch pine wood of Wheeler's blackberry-field, where there are only several white pines old enough to bear, and accordingly more than a thousand pitch pine seeds to one white pine one, yet there are countless white pines springing up under the pitch pines (as well as many oaks), and very few or scarcely any little pitch pines, and they sickly, or a thousand white pine seedlings to one pitch pine, — the same proportion reversed (in inverse proportion). It is the same in the pigeon-place lot east of this. So if you should cut these pitch pines you would have next a white pine wood with some oaks in it, the pines taking the lead. Indeed, these white pines bid fair to supplant the pitch pines at last, for they grow well and steadily. This reminds me that, though I often see little white pines under pines and under oaks, I rarely if ever (unless I am mistaken) see many young pitch pines there. How is it? Do the pitch pines require more light and air?

You may conveniently tell the age of a pine, especially

white pine, by cutting off the lowest branch that is still growing and counting its rings. Then estimate or count the rings of a pine growing near *in an opening*, of the same height as to that branch, and add the two sums together.

I found in the midst of this pitch pine wood a white oak some eight feet high and an inch and a half thick at ground, which had borne a great many — say sixty or a hundred — large oak-balls, and the ground beneath and near by was strewn with the fragments of fifty of them, which some creature, probably a squirrel, — for a bird could hardly have opened the hard nut-like kernel within, — had opened, no doubt for their living contents, and all the inside was gone. They looked like egg-shells strewn about. Opening one, I found within the hard kernel a humpbacked black fly nearly half an inch long, body and wings, with a very large or full shining black abdomen and two small black spots on each wing. The only two that I open have flies in them. Harris says that this fly is the *Cynips confluens*, and that the grub becomes a chrysalis in the autumn and not, commonly, a fly till spring, though he has known this gall-fly to come out in October. It must have been squirrels (or mice) that opened them, for birds could not break into the hard kernel.

Counted the rings of a white pine stump in Hubbard's owl wood by railroad. Ninety-four years. So this was probably second growth.

Swamps are, of course, least changed with us, — are nearest to their primitive state of any woodland. Commonly they have only been cut, not redeemed.

I see how meadows were primitively kept in the state of meadow by the aid of water, — and even fire and wind. For example, Heywood's meadow, though it may have been flowed a hundred years ago by the dam below, has been bare almost ever since in the midst of the wood. Trees have not grown over it. Maples, alders, birches, pitch and white pines are slow to spread into it. I have named them in the order of their slowness. The last are the foremost, — furthest into the meadow, — but they are sickly-looking. You may say that it takes a geological change to make a wood-lot there.

Looked at stumps in J. Hosmer's lot, hillside south of first Heywood meadow, cut eleven (?) years ago. One white pine perfect in shape, forty-one rings; two large oak stumps, each one hundred and nine rings; and a large pitch pine, probably same age. These stumps are all well preserved. The whole outline and the rings can for most part be counted; but they are successive ridges, and the bark is ready to fall off, and they are more or less mossed over with cockscomb moss. The main part of this lot north of this hole is apparently oak sprouts next railroad.

I next look through Emerson's lot (half-burned and cut last spring). The last year's growth (and present) chiefly oak, with a little pine. The stumps are chiefly oak and pitch pine, with apparently some hemlock (?) and chestnut and a little white pine. (So it seems the pitch pine and hemlock did not survive the old cutting; the pitch pine did not come up under itself.) The pitch pine stumps are all decayed but the core and the bark,

and hardly in any instance show a trace of the axe. They are low rounded mounds, yet the inmost parts are solid fat, and the bark edge is very plain. The oak stumps are very much better preserved, — have half or two thirds their form, and show that proportion of the cutting, — yet the sap-wood is often gone (with the bark), and as often the inmost heart. You can partially count rings even. Yet some of these are as decayed as the pines, and all flaky, and, turned up, look like stumps of old teeth with their prongs. They (the oaks) are all loose to the foot, yet you will see the white bark lying about a white oak stump when all the rest is about gone. Most of the old stumps, both oaks and pines, can easily be found now, but the rings of not one oak even can be wholly counted, or nearly. I could not be sure about the hemlock and chestnut, only that there was *some* of both. There was little moss on these stumps, either pine or oak; the latter too crumbly.

The southeast part of this lot, beyond the deep cove, is apparently an oak sprout-land and good part pine. I see what were sprouts from a scarlet oak stump eighteen or more inches in diameter and from white oaks one foot in diameter; yet in the other lot, though there were so many large oak stumps, I did not notice that trees had ever sprung from them. You find plenty of old oak stumps without their trees in the woods, which (if nothing else) shows that there is an end to this mode of propagation.

I could tell a white pine here when it was for the most part a mere rotten mound, by the regularity crosswise of the long knots a foot from the ground in the top of the rotten core, representing the peculiarly regular branches of the little white pine and the best preserved as the hardest and pitchiest part.

It is apparent that fires often hasten the destruction of these stumps. They are very apt to be charred.

I dug in the hollow where an oak had been, and though it was so completely decayed that I found not a particle that looked like decayed wood or even bark and my spade met with no resistance, yet there were perfectly open channels raying out from this hollow with the pellicle of the root for a wall still, which for a hundred years the earth had learned to respect. Indeed, these stumps, both of this age and more recent, are the very metropolis of the squirrels and mice. Such are their runways.

Yet what is the character of our gratitude to these squirrels, these planters of forests? We regard them as vermin, and annually shoot and destroy them in great numbers, because — if we have any excuse — they sometimes devour a little of our Indian corn, while, perhaps, they are planting the nobler oak-corn (acorn) in its place. In various parts of the country an army of grown-up boys assembles for a squirrel hunt. They choose sides, and the side that kills the greatest number of thousands enjoys a supper at the expense of the other side, and the whole neighborhood rejoices. Would it [not] be far more civilized and humane, not to say godlike, to recognize once in the year by some significant symbolical ceremony the part which the squirrel plays, the great service it performs, in the economy of the universe?

Vol. XIV

The Walden side of Emerson's main wood-lot is oak (except a few pines in the oaks at the northwest or railroad end), and the oaks are chiefly sprouts, some thirty years old. Yet, not to mention the pitch pine stumps, there are a great many oak stumps without sprouts, and yet not larger stumps than the others. How does this happen? They are all of the same age, *i. e.* cut at the same time.

Sometimes, evidently, when you see oak stumps from which no trees have sprung in the midst of a pine or birch wood, it may be because the land was cleared and burned over and cultivated after the oaks were cut.

Oct. 23. Anthony Wright tells me that he cut a pitch pine on Damon's land between the Peter Haynes road and his old farm, about '41, in which he counted two hundred and seventeen rings, which was therefore older than Concord, and one of the primitive forest. He tells me of a noted large and so-called primitive wood, Inches Wood, between the Harvard turnpike and Stow, sometimes called Stow Woods, in Boxboro and Stow. Also speaks of the wood north of Wetherbee's mill near Annursnack and belonging to W., as large and old, if not cut.

Melvin thinks that a fox would not on an average weigh more than ten pounds. Says that he saw a flock of brant yesterday by day. (Rarely seen by day or even by night here.) He says that Hildreth collects moss (probably cladonia) from the rocks for kindling.

There is no such mortality in nobler seeds — seeds of living creatures, as eggs of birds, for instance — as I

have noticed in white oak acorns. What if the eggs of any species of bird should be addled to this extent, so that it should be hard to find a sound one? In Egypt, where they hatch eggs artificially in an oven, they can afford to return one chicken for every two eggs they receive (and do so) and yet find it profitable. It is true one third of human infants are said to die before they are five years old, but even this is a far less mortality than that of the acorns. The oak is a scarce bearer, yet it lasts a good while.

More or less rain to-day and yesterday.

Oct. 24. P. M. — To Walden Woods.

See three little checkered adders lying in the sun by a stump on the sandy slope of the Deep Cut; yet sluggish. They are seven or eight inches long. The dark blotches or checkers are not so brown as in large ones. There is a transverse dark mark on the snout and a forked light space ⋁ on the back part [of] the head.

Examine again ⋁ Emerson's pond lot, to learn its age by the stumps cut last spring. I judge from them that they were some five (?) years cutting over the part next the water, for I count the rings of many stumps and they vary in number from twenty-four or five to thirty, though twenty-six, seven, and eight are commonest, as near as I can count. It is hard to distinguish the very first ring, and often one or more beside before you reach the circumference. But, these being almost all sprouts, I know that they were pretty large the first year. I repeatedly see beside the new

tree (cut last spring) the now well-rotted stump from which it sprang. But I do not see the stump from which the last sprang. I should like to know how long they may continue to spring from the stump. Here are shoots of this year which have sprung vigorously from stumps cut in the spring, which had sprung in like manner some twenty-eight or thirty years ago from a stump which is still very plain by their sides. I see that some of these thirty-year trees are sprouts from a white oak stump twenty inches in diameter, — four from one in one case. Sometimes, when a white pine stump is all crumbling beside, there is a broad shingle-like flake left from the centre to the circumference, the old ridge of the stump, only a quarter of an inch thick, and this betrays the axe in a straight inclined surface.

The southeast part of Emerson's lot, next the pond, is yet more exclusively oak sprouts, or oak from oak, with fewer pine stumps. I examine an oak seedling in this. There are two very slender shoots rising ten or more inches above the ground, which, traced downward, conduct to a little stub, which I mistook for a very old root or part of a larger tree, but, digging it up, I found it to be a true seedling. This seedling had died down to the ground six years ago, and then these two slender shoots, such as you commonly see in oak woods, had started. The root was a regular seedling root (fusiform if *straightened*), at least seven eighths of an inch thick, while the largest shoot was only one eighth of an inch thick, though six years old and ten inches high.

The root was probably ten years old when the seedling first died down, and is now some sixteen years old. Yet, as I say, the oak is only ten inches high. This shows how it endures and gradually pines and dies. As you look down on it, it has two turns, and three as you look from the side, so firmly is it rooted. Any one will be surprised on digging up some of these lusty oaken carrots.

Look at stumps in Heywood's lot, southeast side pond, from Emerson's to the swimming-place. They are white pine, oak, pitch pine, etc. I count rings of three white pine (from sixty to seventy). There are a few quite large white pine stumps; on one, ninety rings. One oak gives one hundred and sixteen rings. A pitch pine some fifteen or sixteen inches over gives about one hundred and thirty-five. All these are very easy, if not easier than ever, to count. The pores of the pines are distinct ridges, and the pitch is worn off. (Many white and pitch pines elsewhere cut this year cannot be counted, they are so covered with pitch.) I remember this as a particularly dense and good-sized wood, mixed pine and oak.

Mrs. Heywood's pitch pines by the shore, judging from some cut two or three years ago, are about eighty-five years old. As far as I have noticed, the pitch pine is the slowest-growing tree (of pines and oaks) and gives the most rings in the smallest diameter.

Then there are the countless downy seeds (thistle-like) of the goldenrods, so fine that we do not

notice them in the air. They cover our clothes like dust. No wonder they spread over all fields and far into the woods.

I see those narrow pointed yellow buds now laid bare so thickly along the slender twigs of the *Salix discolor*, which is almost bare of leaves.

Oct. 25. P. M. — To Eb. Hubbard's wood and Sleepy Hollow.

See a little reddish-brown snake (bright-red beneath) in the path; probably *Coluber amœnus*.

Cut one of the largest of the lilacs at the Nutting wall, eighteen inches from the ground. It there measures one and five sixteenths inches and has twenty distinct rings from centre, then about twelve very fine, not thicker than previous three; equals thirty-two in all. It evidently dies down many times, and yet lives and sends up fresh shoots from the root.

Jarvis's hill lot is oak, pitch pine, and some white, and quite old. There are a great many little white pines springing up under it, but I see no pitch. Yet the large pitch are much more common than the large white. Nevertheless the small white have come on much faster and more densely in the hollows just outside the large wood on the south.

E. Hubbard's mound of pitch pines contains not one seed-bearing white pine, yet there are under these pines many little white pines (whose seed must have blown some distance), but scarcely one pitch pine. The latter, however, are seen along its edge and in the larger openings. So at Moore's pitch pine promontory

south of the Foley house, cut off lately by Walcott. Where the large pines had stood are no little ones, but in the open pasture northward quite a little grove, which had spread from them. Yet from a hasty look at the south end of the Sleepy Hollow Cut pitch pines, it appeared that small pitch pines were abundant under them. *Vide* again.

I have seen an abundance of white oak acorns this year, and, as far as I looked, swamp white oak acorns were pretty numerous. Red oak acorns are also pretty common. Black and scarlet oak I find also, but not very abundant. I have seen but few shrub oak, comparatively. Of the above, only the white oak have decayed so remarkably. The others are generally sound, or a few wormy. The red oak, as far as I notice, are remarkably sound. The scarlet oak I cut this afternoon are *some* of them decaying, but not like the white oak. Only the white have sprouted at all, as far as I perceive.

I find some scarlet oak acorns on the back side northeast end of Sleepy Hollow which are rounder than usual, considerably like a filbert out of the shell. They are indistinctly marked with meridional lines and thus betray a relation to the black and black shrub oak.[1]

I see an immense quantity of asparagus seed in the mist of its dead branches, on Moore's great field of it, near Hawthorne's. There must be a great many bushels of the seed, and the sight suggested how extensively the birds must spread it. I saw, accordingly, on Hawthorne's hillside, a dozen rods north of it, many plants

[1] *Vide* swamp white oak, p. [180].

(with their own seed) two or three feet high. It is planted in the remotest swamps in the town.

Saw in E. Hubbard's clintonia swamp a large spider with a great golden-colored abdomen as big as a hazelnut, on the wet leaves. There was a figure in brown lines on the back, in the form of a pagoda with its stories successively smaller. The legs were pale or whitish, with dark or brown bars.

Find many of those pale-brown roughish fungi (it looks like Loudon's plate of *Scleroderma*, perhaps *verrucosum*), two to three inches in diameter. Those which are ripe are so softened at the top as to admit the rain through the skin (as well as after it opens), and the interior is shaking like a jelly, and if you open it you see what looks like a yellowish gum or jelly amid the dark fuscous dust, but it is this water colored by the dust; yet when they are half full of water they emit dust nevertheless. They are in various states, from a firm, hard and dry unopen[ed] to a half-empty and flabby moist cup.

See the yellow butterfly still and great devil's-needles

Dug up and brought home last night three English cherry trees from Heywood's Peak by Walden. There are a dozen or more there, and several are as handsome as any that you will find in a nursery. They remind me of some much larger which used to stand above the cliffs. This species too comes up in sprout-land, like the wild rum cherry. The amount of it is that such a tree, whose fruit is a favorite with birds, will spring up far and wide and wherever the earth is bared of trees, but since the forest overpowers and destroy them, and also cultivation, they are only found young in sprout-lands or grown up along fences. It looks as if this species preferred a hilltop. Whether the birds are more inclined to convey the seeds there or they find the light and exposure and the soil there which they prefer. These have each one great root, somewhat like a long straight horn, making a right angle with the stem and running far off one side close to the surface.

The thistles which I now see have their heads recurved, which at least saves their down from so great a soaking. But when I pull out the down, the seed is for the most part left in the receptacle (?), in regular order there, like the pricks in a thimble. A slightly convex surface. The seeds set like cartridges in a circular cartridge-box, in hollow cylinders which look like circles *crowded* into more or less of a diamond, pentagonal, or hexagonal form. The perfectly dry and bristly involucre which hedges them round, so repulsive externally, is very neat and attractive within, — as smooth and tender toward its charge as it is rough and prickly externally toward the foes that might do it injury. It is a hedge of imbricated thin and narrow leafets of a light-brown color, beautifully glossy like silk, a most fit receptacle for the delicate downy parachutes of the seed, a cradle lined with silk or satin. The latter are kept dry under this unsuspected silky or satiny ceiling, whose old and weather-worn and rough outside alone we see, like a mossy roof, little suspecting the delicate and glossy lining. I know of no object more unsightly to a careless glance than an empty thistle-head, yet, if you ex-

Vol. XIV

amine it closely, it may remind you of the silk-lined cradle in which a prince was rocked. Thus that which seemed a mere brown and worn-out relic of the summer, sinking into the earth by the roadside, turns out to be a precious casket.

I notice in the pitch pine wood behind Moore's the common pinweed (*Lechea major* or the next) growing on the top of a pitch pine stump which is yet quite in shape and firm, one foot from the ground, with its roots firmly set in it, reaching an inch or two deep. Probably the seed was blown there, perhaps over the snow when it was on a level with the stump.

Oct. 26. P. M. — To Baker's old chestnut lot near Flint's Pond.

As I go through what was formerly the dense pitch pine lot on Thrush Alley (G. Hubbard's), I observe that the present growth is scrub oak, birch, oaks of various kinds, white pines, pitch pines, willows, and poplars. Apparently, the birch, oaks, and pitch pines are the oldest of the *trees*. From the number of small white pines in the neighboring pitch pine wood, I should have expected to find larger and also more white pines here. It will finally become a mixed wood of oak and white and pitch pine. There is much cladonia in the lot.

Observed yesterday that the row of white pines set along the fence on the west side of Sleepy Hollow had grown very fast, apparently from about the time they were set out, or the last three years. Several had made about seven feet within the three years. Do they not

grow the fastest at just this age, or after they get to be about five feet high?

I see to-day sprouts from chestnut stumps which are two and a half feet in diameter (*i. e.* the stumps). One of these large stumps is cut quite low and hollowing, so as to hold water as well as leaves, and the leaves prevent the water from drying up. It is evident that in such a case the stump rots sooner than if high and roof-like.

I remember that there were a great many hickories with R. W. E.'s pitch pines when I lived there, but now there are but few comparatively, and they appear to have died down several times and come up again from the root. I suppose it is mainly on account of frosts, though perhaps the fires have done part of it. Are not hickories most commonly found on hills? There are a few hickories in the open land which I once cultivated there, and these may have been planted there by birds or squirrels. It must be more than thirty-five years since there was wood there.

I find little white pines under the pitch pines (of E.), near the pond end, and few or no little pitch pines, but between here and the road about as many of one as of the other, but the old pines are much less dense that way, or not dense at all.

This is the season of the fall when the leaves are whirled through the air like flocks of birds, the season of birch spangles, when you see afar a few clear-yellow leaves left on the tops of the birches.

It was a mistake for Britton to treat that Fox Hollow lot as he did. I remember a large old pine and chestnut

wood there some twenty years ago. He came and cut it off and burned it over, and ever since it has been good for nothing. I mean that acre at the bottom of the hollow. It is now one of those frosty hollows so common in Walden Woods, where little grows, sheep's fescue grass, sweet-fern, hazelnut bushes, and oak scrubs whose dead tops are two or three feet high, while the still living shoots are not more than half as high at their base. They have lingered so long and died down annually. At length I see a few birches and pines creeping into it, which at this rate in the course of a dozen years more will *suggest* a forest there. Was this wise?

Examined the stumps in the Baker chestnut lot which was cut when I surveyed it in the spring of '52. They were when cut commonly from fifty to sixty years old (some older, some younger). The sprouts from them are from three to six inches thick, and may average — the largest — four inches, and eighteen feet high. The wood is perhaps near half oak sprouts, and these are one and a half to four inches thick, or average two and a half, and not so high as the chestnut. Some of the largest chestnut stumps have sent up no sprout, yet others equally large and very much more decayed have sent up sprouts. Can this be owing to the different time when they were cut? The cutting was after April. The largest sprouts I chanced to notice were from a small stump in low ground. Some hemlock stumps there had a hundred rings.

Was overtaken by a sudden thunder-shower.

Cut a chestnut sprout two years old. It grew about

five and a half feet the first year and three and a half the next, and was an inch in diameter. The tops of these sprouts, the last few inches, had died in the winter, so that a side bud continued them, and this made a slight curve in the sprout, thus: There was on a cross-section, of course, but one ring of pores within the wood, just outside the large pith, the diameter of the first year's growth being just half an inch, radius a fourth of an inch. The thickness of the second year's growth was the same, or one fourth, but it was distinctly marked to the naked eye with about seven concentric lighter lines, which, I suppose, marked so many successive growths or waves of growth, or seasons in its year. These were not visible through a microscope of considerable power, but best to the naked eye. Probably you could tell a seedling chestnut from a vigorous sprout, however old or large, provided the heart were perfectly sound to the pith, by the much more rapid growth of the last the first half-dozen years of its existence.

There are scarcely any chestnuts this year near Britton's, but I find as many as usual east of Flint's Pond.

Oct. 27. Emerson planted his lot with acorns (chiefly white oak) pretty generally the other day. There were a few scarlet oak acorns planted there on the south side in spring of '59. There is on the Lee farm, west of hill, a small wood-lot of oak and hickory, the south end chiefly hickory.

I have come out this afternoon to get ten seedling oaks out of a purely oak wood, and as many out of a purely pine wood, and then compare them. I look for trees one foot or less in height, and convenient to dig up. I could not find one in the last-named wood. I then searched in the large Woodis Park, the most oaken parts of it, wood some twenty-five or thirty years old, but I found only three. There were many shrub oaks and others three or four feet high, but no more of the kind described. Two of these three had singularly old large and irregular roots, mere gnarled oblong knobs, as it were, with slender shoots, having died down many times. After searching here more than half an hour I went into the new pitch and white pine lot just southwest, toward the old Lee cellar, and there were thousands of the seedling oaks only a foot high and less, quite reddening the ground now in some places, and these had perfectly good roots, though not so large as those near the Corner Spring (next to Rice's wall).

Here is a new but quite open pitch and white pine wood (with birches on south) on cladonia ground. It is so open that many pitch pines are springing up.

E. Wood's dense pitch (and white) pine wood in front of Lee house site conforms to the rule of few or no little pitch pines within it, but many white pines (though not many far within), while the pitch pines are springing up with white pines on the edge and even further toward the road.

The white pine wood southeast of this and not far north of railroad, against Wood's open land, is a *new* wood

As I am coming out of this, looking for seedling oaks, I see a jay, which was screaming at me, fly to a white oak eight or ten rods from the wood in the pasture and directly alight on the ground, pick up an acorn, and fly back into the woods with it. This was one, perhaps the most effectual, way in which this wood was stocked with the numerous little oaks which I saw under that dense white pine grove. Where will you look for a jay sooner than in a dense pine thicket? It is there they commonly live, and build.

By looking to see what oaks grow in the open land near by or along the edge where the wood is extensively pine, I can tell surely what kinds of oaks I shall find under the pines.

What if the oaks are far off? Think how quickly a jay can come and go, and how many times in a day![1]

Swamp white oak acorns are pretty thick on the ground by the bridge, and all sound that I try. They have no more bitterness than the white oak acorns.

I have now examined many dense pine woods, both pitch and white, and several oak woods, in order to see how many and what kind of oak seedlings there were springing up in them, and I do not hesitate to say that seedlings under one foot high are *very* much more abundant under the pines than under the oaks. They prevail and are countless under the pines, while they are hard to find under the oaks, and what you do find have commonly — for whatever reason — very old and decayed roots and feeble shoots from them.

If you expect oaks to succeed a dense and purely oak

[1] *Vide* [p. 188].

wood you must depend almost entirely on sprouts, but they will succeed abundantly to pine where there is not an oak stump for them to sprout from. Notwithstanding that the acorns are produced only by oaks and not by pines, the fact is that there are comparatively few seedling oaks a foot or less in height under the oaks but thousands under the pines. I would not undertake to get a hundred oaks of this size suitable to transplant under a dense and pure oak wood, but I could easily get thousands from under pines. What are the reasons for this? First it is certain that, generally speaking, the soil under old oaks is more exhausted for oaks than under old pines. Second, seedling oaks under oaks would be less protected from frosts in the spring just after leafing, yet the sprouts prevail. Third, squirrels and jays resort to evergreens with their forage, and the oaks may not bear so many acorns but that the squirrels may carry off nearly all the sound ones. These are some of the reasons that occur to me.

To be more minute:—

I dug up three oak seedlings in the Woodis Park oaks, nine in the small open pitch and white pine and adjoining on southwest, and ten in the pitch and white pine of wood between road and railroad.

Woodis Park is oak and pine some twenty-five years old (the oak). I chose the oaken parts, but there was always a pine within a rod or two. I looked here till I was discouraged, finding only three in three quarters of an hour. One was like those in pine woods; the other two had singular gnarled and twisted great roots. You would think you had come upon a dead but buried stump. The largest, for instance, was perhaps a red oak nine inches high by one eighth inch at ground and apparently three years old, a slender shoot. The root broke off at about eighteen inches depth, where it was one eighth inch thick, and at three inches below the surface it was one and three eighths inches thick by one inch (being flattish). Two or three of the side or horizontal fibres had developed into stout roots which ran quite horizontally twenty inches and then broke off, and were apparently as long as the tap-root. One of these at three inches below surface was about half an inch thick and perfectly horizontal. It was thus fixed very firmly in the ground. I counted the dead bases or stubs of shoots (beside the present one) and several two or three times as large as this, which had formerly died down, being now perfectly decayed. If there was but one at a time and they decayed successively after living each three years only, — and they probably lived twice as long, — then the root would be thirty years old. But supposing there were one and a half shoots at a time, it would then be some twenty years old. I think that this root may be as old as the large oaks around, or some twenty-five years, more or less.

My next nine oaks, from the pines southwest, may be put with the ten from the E. Wood pines (leaving out one which was twice the required height). Their average age, i. e. of the present shoot, was four years, and average height seven inches. (This includes white oak, shrub oak, black, and apparently red oak.) The roots averaged about ten inches long by three eighths thick at thickest part. Quite a number were shrub oak,

Vol. XIV

which partly accounts for their slenderness. But the rest were not so thick as those near Rice's wall. Of all the above roots, or the whole twenty-two, none ran directly and perpendicularly downward, but they turned to one side (just under the acorn) and ran more or less horizontally or aslant one to five inches, or say three inches on an average.

Of the last nineteen, more than half had died down once at least, so that they were really considerably older than at first appeared. There are, in all cases, at the surface of the ground or head of the root, a ring of dormant buds, ready to shoot up when an injury happens to the original shoot. One shoot at least had been cut off, and so killed, by a rabbit.

See a very large flock of crows.

To speak from recollection of pines and oaks, I should say that our woods were chiefly pine and oak mixed, but we have also (to speak of the large growth, or trees) pure pine and pure oak woods. How are these three produced? Are not the pure pine woods commonly new woods, i. e. pioneers? After oaks have once got established, it must be hard to get them out without clearing the land. A pure oak wood may be obtained by cutting off at once and clean a pure and dense pine wood, and again sometimes by cutting the same oak wood. But pines are continually stealing into oaks, and oaks into pines, where respectively they are not too dense, as where they are burned or otherwise thinned, and so mixed woods may arise.

Oct. 28. In a pine wood are the little oak seedlings

which I have described, also, in the more open parts, little oaks three to six feet high, but unnoticed, and perhaps some other hardwood trees. The pines are cut, and the oaks, etc., soon fill the space, for there is nothing else ready to grow there.

Are not the most exclusively pine woods new woods, i. e., those which have recently sprung up in open land, where oaks do not begin a forest? It may be that where evergreens most prevail in *our* woods, there at the date of their springing up the earth was most bare.

P. M. — To Lincoln.

Do I not see tree sparrows?

I see little larches two to six feet high in the meadow on the north side the Turnpike, six to twelve rods from Everett's seed-bearing ones. The seed was evidently blown from these.

There is quite a dense birch wood in the field north of the Cut on the Turnpike hill.

See much cat-tail whose down has recently burst and shows white on the south side of the heads. The *Polygonum aviculare* is in bloom as freshly and abundantly in some places as ever I saw it. Those great tufts of sedge in the meadows are quite brown and withered. I suppose they have been so since the beginning of the month.

Smith's black walnuts are about half of them fallen.

Measure the chestnut stump near the brook northeast of the old Brooks Tavern on Asa White's land. Its height from the ground will average but twenty inches. Measured one way, its diameter is six feet nine inches, and at right angles with this, eight feet five inches. Its

average diameter seven feet seven inches. You might add three to four feet more for the whole stump above ground. Beginning at the outside, I count one hundred and two rings distinctly and am then fifteen inches from the apparent centre of the tree, for the middle is mostly rotted and gone. Measuring back fifteen inches and counting the rings, I get thirty-nine, which, added to one hundred and two, equals one hundred and forty-one for the probable age of the tree. This tree had grown very fast till the last fifty years of its existence, but since comparatively slowly. It had grown nine inches in the last forty-nine years, or one seventh [*sic*] of an inch in a year, but fifteen inches in the previous forty, or three eighths of an inch in a year. There may possibly have been two shoots or trees grown together, yet I think not. I measured this June 1st, 1852, and it had then been cut, as I remember, but a short time, — a winter, perhaps two winters, before. This would carry its origin back to about 1710. Probably chestnuts did not grow so large in the primitive woods, and this was a forest tree, which, as it stood near the edge of the meadow, was left standing. Another much smaller was cut apparently at the same time near by. Having light and air and room, it grew larger than it would have done if its neighbors had not been cut.

I also measured the stumps of the two great chestnuts which were cut on Weston's land south of the pond some five or six years ago.

They are cut low, some eight or nine inches above ground. The southeasternmost one measures four feet in diameter and has about eighty rings only (I estimate the first five or six, the heart or core being gone). The other is four and five twelfths feet in diameter and has seventy-three rings only. Or, putting both together, you have an average growth of about a third of an inch in a year. These were as large as any I know standing hereabouts except the Strawberry Hill one, and yet it seems they [were] only some eighty years old. Another, half a mile east of there, cut perhaps some dozen years ago, was twenty-three inches in diameter and had sixty-three rings, and I saw one which had grown faster than any of the above. Yet another stump near the last on the high woodland near the pond was but just two feet in diameter and had one hundred and one rings distinct to the very core, and so fine there I think it was a seedling. From this sprouts had grown some fifteen years ago and [had been] cut last winter on account of a fire, and fresh shoots several feet high had put out from the last. The one that had grown slowly was soundest at the core. None of the three largest stumps described had sprouts from them. Is not the very rapid growth and the hollow or rotten core one sign of a sprout? We make a great noise going through the fallen leaves in the woods and wood-paths now, so that we cannot hear other sounds, as of birds or other people. It reminds me of the tumult of the waves dashing against each other or your boat. This is the dash we hear as we sail the woods.

Cut a limb of a cedar (near the Irishman's shanty-site at Flint's Pond) some two inches thick and three and a half feet from the ground. It had about forty-one rings. Adding ten, you have say fifty years for the age of the tree. It was one foot in diameter at one foot

above ground and twenty or more feet high, standing in the young wood. A little cedar five feet high near it had some fifteen to seventeen rings. See a great many chestnut sprouts full six feet high and more and an inch or more thick the first year.

Aaron's-rod has minute chaffy seeds, now ripe, which by their very lightness could be blown along the highways.

Oct. 29. P. M. — To Eb. Hubbard's old black birch hill.

Henry Shattuck's is a *new* pitch pine wood, say thirty years old. The western, or greater, part contains not a single seed-bearing white pine. It is a remarkable proof of my theory, for it contains thousands of little white pines but scarcely one little pitch pine. It is also well stocked with minute oak seedlings. It is a dense wood, say a dozen rods wide by three or four times as long, running east and west, with an oak wood on the north, from which the squirrels brought the acorns. A strip of nearly the same width of the pitch pine was cut apparently within a year on the south (a part of the above), and has just been harrowed and sown with rye, and still it is all dotted over with the little oak seedlings between the [stumps], which are perhaps unnoticed by Shattuck, but if he would keep his plow and fire out he would still have a pretty green patch there by next fall. A thousand little red flags (changed oak leaves) already wave over the green rye amid the stumps. The farmer stumbles over these in his walk, and sweats while he endeavors to clear the land of them, and yet wonders

Vol. XIV

how oaks ever succeed to pines, as if he did not consider what *these* are. Where these pines are dense they are slender and tall. On the edge or in open land they are more stout and spreading.

Again, as day before yesterday, sitting on the edge of a pine wood, I see a jay fly to a white oak half a dozen rods off in the pasture, and, gathering an acorn from the ground, hammer away at it under its foot on a limb of the oak, with an awkward and rapid seesaw or teetering motion, it has to lift its head so high to acquire the requisite momentum. The jays scold about almost every white oak tree, since we hinder their coming to it.

At some of the white oaks visited on the 11th, where the acorns were so thick on the ground and trees, I now find them perhaps nearly half picked up, yet perhaps little more than two thirds spoiled. The good appear to be all sprouted now. There are certainly many more sound ones here than at Beck Stow's and Hubbard's Grove, and it looks as if the injury had been done by frost, but perhaps some of it was done by the very heavy rains of September alone.

Yesterday and to-day I have walked rapidly through extensive chestnut woods without seeing what I thought was a seedling chestnut, yet I can soon find them in our Concord pines a quarter or half a mile from the chestnut woods. Several have expressed their surprise to me that they cannot find a seedling chestnut to transplant. I think that [it] is with them precisely as with the oaks; not only a seedling is more difficult to distinguish in a chestnut wood, but it is really far more rare there than in the adjacent pine, mixed, and oak woods. After con-

siderable experience in searching for these and seedling oaks, I have learned to neglect the chestnut and oak woods and go only to the neighboring woods of a different species for them. Only that course will pay.

On the side of E. Hubbard's hill I see an old chestnut stump some two feet in diameter and nearly two feet high, and its outside and form well kept, yet all the inside gone; and from this shot up four sprouts in a square around it, which were cut down seven or eight years ago. Their rings number forty-six, and they are quite sound, so that the old stump was cut some fifty-three years ago. This is the oldest stump of whose age I am certain. Hence I have no doubt that there are many stumps left in this town which were cut in the last century. I am surprised to find on this hill (cut some seven or eight years ago) many remarkably old stumps wonderfully preserved, especially on the north side the hill, — walnuts, white oak and other oaks, and black birch. One white oak is eighteen and a half inches in diameter and has one hundred and forty-three rings. This is very one-sided in its growth, the centre being just four inches from the north side, or thirty-six rings to an inch. Of course I counted the other side. Another, close by, gave one hundred and forty-one rings, another white oak fifteen and a half inches in diameter had one hundred and fifty-five rings. It has so smooth (sawed off) and solid, almost a polished or marble-like, surface that I could not at first tell what kind of wood it was.[1] Another white oak the same as last in rings, *i. e.* one hundred and fifty-five, twenty-four inches [in]

[1] Was it not a walnut?

diameter. All these were sound to the very core, so that I could see the first circles, and I suspect that they were seedlings.

The smaller, but oldest ones had grown very slowly at first, and yet more slowly at last, but after some sixty-five years they had then grown much faster for about fifteen years, and then grew slower and slower to the last. The rings were exceedingly close together near the outside, yet not proportionably difficult to count. For aught that appeared, they might have continued to grow a century longer. The stumps are far apart, so that this formed an open grove, and that probably made the wood sounder and more durable. On the south slope many white pines had been cut about forty-six years ago, or when the chestnut was, amid the oaks. I suppose that these were seedlings, and perhaps the hill was cleared soon after the settlement of the town, and after a while pines sprang up in the open land, and seedling oaks under the pines, and, the latter being cut near the end of the seventeenth century, those oaks sprang up, with or without pines, but all but these were cut down when they were about sixty years old.

If these are seedlings, then seedlings make much the best timber. I should say that the pasture oaks *generally* must be seedlings on account of their age, being part of the primitive wood.

I suspect that sprouts, like the chestnut, for example, may grow very rapidly, and make large trees in comparatively few years, but they will be decaying [?] as fast at the core as they are growing at the circumference. The stumps of chestnuts, especially sprouts, are very

shaky. It is with men as with trees; you must grow slowly to last long. The oldest of these oaks began their existence about 1697.

I doubt if there were any as old trees in our primitive wood as stood in this town fifty years ago. The healthiest of the primitive wood, having at length more room, light, and air, probably grew larger than its ancestors.

Some of the black birch stumps gave about one hundred rings.

The pasture oak which Sted Buttrick cut some seven or eight years ago, northeast of this, was, as near as I could tell, — one third was calculation, — some one hundred years old only, though larger than any of these.

The fine chips which are left on the centre of a large stump preserve it moist there, and rapidly hasten its decay.

The site of the last-named pasture oak was easily discovered, by a very large open grass-sward where no sweet-fern, lambkill, huckleberry, and brakes grew, as they did almost everywhere else. This may be because of the cattle assembling under the oak, and so killing the bushes and at the same time manuring the ground for grass.

There is more chestnut in the northern part of the town than I was aware of. The first large wood north of Ponkawtasset is oak and chestnut. East of my house.

Oct. 30. P. M. — To Tarbell pitch pines, etc.

Quite a sultry, cloudy afternoon, — hot walking in woods and lowland where there is no air.

J. Hosmer cut off the northernmost part of his

pitch pine between roads, *i. e.* next the factory road, last winter. Here was a remarkable example of little white pines under pitch pines with scarcely any little pitch pines. He has accordingly cut off all the pitch pines — and they are some thirty-five years old — and left the white pines, now on an average five to eight feet high and forming already a pretty dense wood (E. Wood is doing the same thing now opposite the Colburn place), a valuable and salable woodland, while a great many little oaks, birches, black cherries, etc., are springing up in their midst; so that it may finally be a mixed wood, if the pines do not overshadow it too quickly. Yet there were only three or four seed-bearing white pines in the grove, — or as big as the pitch pines were. The white pines left are as thick as the pitch pines were under which they sprang up; quite dense enough to grow. I am more and more struck by the commonness of this phenomenon of seedling white pines under older pitch pines and the rareness with which pitch pines spring up under older pitch pines. Yet, going to the open land on east side of the wood, I find that it is mainly the little pitch pines that are spreading into the field there and extending the wood, some a dozen rods from its edge in the grass; and their relative proportion is reversed, *i. e.*, there are fifty to one hundred little pitch pines here to one white pine. He had also cut off some, a few, birches, and their sprouts had come up, as well as seedlings.

The oak seedlings between the young pitch pines were manifestly springing up with new vigor, though many may finally be choked by the white pines. Omit-

ting such as were of the character of sprouts, though not cut (*i. e.*, had shot up from old roots to three feet high merely on account of the influx of light and air), I measured this year's growth of the first four which were under a foot high, here where the pitch pines had been cut, and found it to average five and a half inches. The growth of [the] first four in the adjacent pitch pine wood not cut averaged seven and a half. As may be seen, this was not nearly fair enough to the partially cleared part, for I should have included the higher shoots.

The higher parts of this lot are cladonia land. I measured the diameter of several of the pitch pine stumps and counted the rings, with this result: —

Diameter (exclusive of bark)	Rings
7¼ inches	29
7½	33
6	40
6½	33
6	40
8½	35
7	30
7)48¾	7)240
7	34

That is, they averaged seven inches in diameter (or eight with bark) and were thirty-four years old. Had grown (68)7.0(.10) about one tenth of an inch a year from the centre.

White pines will find their way up between pitch pines if they are not very large and exceedingly dense, but pitch pines will not grow up under pitch pines.

I see nowadays in the pitch pine woods countless

white toadstools which have recently been devoured and broken in pieces and left on the ground and occasionally on the branches or forks of trees, no doubt by the squirrels. They appear to make a considerable part of their food at this season.

See a small copper butterfly.

In what I have called the Loring lot, next west of Hosmer's pitch pine on the back road, though far the greater part numerically is still shrub oak, there is now a considerable growth of young oaks rising above the shrub oaks. These oaks, as far as I observe, are almost, if not quite, all sprouts from small stumps which were unnoticed at first, and there are also a very few seedling white and other oaks no higher than the shrub oaks; i. e., though you may think his oak sprout-land all shrub oak, it probably is not, as will appear when the other kinds rise above the shrubs. Probably the shrub oaks can bear exposure when young better than the nobler oaks, and if the squirrels plant other acorns under them, — which may be doubted, — then it will turn out that they serve as nurses to the others.

I measure amid these young oaks a white pine stump.

Diameter (exclusive of bark)	Rings
13½ inches	35
Another 28	52
24	46
3)65½	133
22	44

Average growth one half inch a year at the level at which stumps are sawed.

This lot is now as exclusively oak as it was pines

before. You must search to find a few little white pines scattered in it. But why, if there are so many little white pines under the adjacent pitch pines, which are left when the pitch pines are cut, were there no more to be left under the pitch pine part (along the road) of this lot? I think of no reason, unless the pitch pines on this lot were too old and dense. Again, I notice that Hosmer's pitch pines have not spread west at all into this clearing, but only east into the grass ground.

Into this Loring lot years ago the squirrels brought acorns, and hence the oaks which now cover it. Also the wind blew its own seeds into an open strip across the road, and a dense pitch and white pine wood sprang up there. Already, the Loring lot having been cut seven or eight years, the squirrels are carrying the shrub oak acorns from it into that pine strip, and the pine seed from the most forward of that strip is blowing back into the shrub oak land.

Another advantage the shrub oak has over other oaks [is] that it gets to fruit so quickly — certainly in three or four years after the pines are cut — and then bears so profusely.

See a great flock of blackbirds, probably grackles.

Examine Tarbell's pitch pine grove. This is all of one age and very dense. The largest trees on the north side, as estimated by sawing a branch, are twenty-eight to thirty years old. Tarbell says this grove came up in 1826 on land which had been burnt over, — in fact open land. It is so dense that, though it has been thoroughly trimmed up and is only a dozen or fifteen rods wide, you cannot see through it in some directions.

Vol. XIV

About as dense a pitch pine grove as I know. It is twenty rods from the nearest wood on one side and five times as far from any other, and yet it is well planted with seedling oaks. Looking hastily to where they are most numerous, I counted ten within fifteen square feet, but only five pitch pines within any equal area; i. e. there were twice as many oaks as large pines there.

This wood also proves my theory of little white pines in large pitch pines. There is not a seed-bearing white pine, or one six feet high, in the wood, nor less than twenty rods from it, and yet there is a thriving little white pine some two feet high at every rod or two within this wood, and though not very numerous, they are conspicuously more numerous and thriving than the pitch pines, yet on the edge the little pitch pines were as much more numerous than the white.

Having seen this fall a great many pitch pine twigs which had been cut off and dropped under the trees by squirrels, I tried the other night while in bed to account for it. I began by referring it to their necessities, and, remembering my own experience, I said then it was done either for food, shelter, clothing, or fuel, but throwing out the last two, which they do not use, it was either for food or shelter. But I never see these twigs used in their nests. Hence I presume it was for food, and as all that I know them to eat on the pitch pine is its seeds, my swift conclusion was that they cut off these twigs in order to come at the cones and also to make them more portable. I am to-day convinced of this, — for I have been looking after it for a day or two. As usual, the ground under this grove is quite strewn

with the twigs, but here is one eleven inches long and nearly half an inch thick cut off close below two closed cones, one cone-stem also being partly cut. Also, three or four rods west from this grove, in open land, I see three twigs which have been dropped close together. One is just two feet long and cut off where half an inch thick and more than one foot below three cones (two on one branch and one on another), and the cones are left. Another is still larger, and the other smaller, but their cones are gone. The greater part of the twigs have been cut off above the cones, — mere plumes.

So even the squirrels carry and spread the pine seed far over the fields. I suspect that they bury these cones like nuts. I have seen the cones collected ready to be carried off, where they did not live. It is remarkable to consider how rudely they strip and spoil the trees. It is remarkable how they carried some of these great twigs with their burden of cones.[1]

The fact that the lower limbs of pines growing within a wood always die shows how much they depend on light and air. They are only a green spiring top.

Measure one of Tarbell's black birch stumps: 23 inches [in] diameter (exclusive of bark), 60 rings. A log from a different one: 21 inches, 71 (?) rings. A white oak stump near by: 15 inches, 90 rings (on brow of bank). A black (?) oak stump: 32 inches [in] diameter, 84 rings.

Examine a dozen white pines in a field, and conclude from these that they begin to grow faster the fifth or sixth year, counting by the whorls of branches.

[1] Vide Hosmer's gray squirrel.

J. Hosmer cut off his little pitch pine grove west of Clamshell, and left the single large old pine which seeded it to do him the same service again; and here now, where for the second time (since) he has sown winter-rye, I see the ineffectual oak sprouts uplifting a few colored leaves still and blushing for him.

The squirrels have no notion of starving in a hard winter, and therefore they are unceasingly employed in the fall in foraging. Every thick wood, especially evergreens, is their storehouse against necessity, and they pack it as thickly as they can with nuts and seeds of all kinds. The squirrel which you see at this season running so glibly along the fence with his tail waving over his head, with frequent pauses on a post or stone, which you watch, perhaps, for twenty or thirty rods, has probably a nut or two in his mouth which he is conveying to yonder thicket.

Evidently a great deal depends on the locality and other conditions of a stump to affect its durability. The oak stump at Clamshell cut some twenty years since barely shows a trace of the axe, while the chestnut stump on Hubbard's hill, cut more than fifty years ago, is much better preserved.

Oct. 31. P. M. — To Wheeler's artificial pine wood.
Exclusive and dense white pine woods are not nearly so common in this town as the same kind of pitch pine woods. They are more likely to have oaks in them. There is a dense birch wood in Witherell Vale.

Among old stumps I have not named those white pine ones used as fences with their roots. I think that some

of these must be older than any left in the ground. I remember some on the Corner road, which apparently have not changed for more than thirty years, and are said to be ninety years old. Lying thus high and dry, they are almost indestructible, and I can still easily count the rings of many of these. I count one hundred and twenty-six rings on one this afternoon, and who knows but it is a hundred years since it was cut? They decay much faster left upright in the ground than lying on their sides on the surface, supposing it open land in both cases.

Perhaps these great pine roots which grew in a swamp were provided with some peculiar quality by which to resist the influence of moisture and so endure the changes of the weather.

Yes, these dense and stretching oak forests, whose withered leaves now redden and rustle on the hills for many a New England mile, were all planted by the labor of animals. For after some weeks of close scrutiny I cannot avoid the conclusion that our modern oak woods sooner or later spring up from an acorn, not where it has fallen from its tree, for that is the exception, but where it has been dropped or placed by an animal. Consider what a vast work these forest-planters are doing!

I do not state the facts exactly in the order in which they were observed, but select out of very numerous observations extended over a series of years the most important ones, and describe them in their natural order.[1]

[1] [Evidently written for his lecture on the Succession of Forest Trees.]

So far as our noblest hardwood forests are concerned, the animals, especially squirrels and jays, are our greatest and almost only benefactors. It is to them that we owe this gift. It is not in vain that the squirrels live in or about every forest tree, or hollow log, and every wall and heap of stones.

Looked at the white pine grove set out by the father of Francis Wheeler some twenty-two or three years ago southwest of his house. They are in three or four irregular rows some eighteen rods long by four wide, — some one hundred trees, covering half an acre of sandy hillside. Probably not so many trees as Emerson's, but making more show. They are trimmed up. There are neither small white nor pitch pines beneath them, but I see that the seeds of the pitch pines which grow below them have been blown *through* this grove and come up thickly along its outer edge.

Look at a pure strip of old white pine wood on the hillside west of this. There are no little white pines coming up under them, but plenty of them in the open hollows around and under its edge. This I commonly notice. White pines, it is true, may come up in the more open parts of any wood, whether a pine or oak or mixed wood, in more open places caused by cutting, for instance; but the pitch pine requires much more of an opening.

I see by the road east of White Pond a large white pine wood with some oaks in it. There are no little white pines where it is dense, but one rod off across the road eastward there is a dense row concealing the lower rail (many quite under it) for many rods, — the only place where they are allowed to grow there.

Many a man's field has a dense border of pitch pines which strayed into it when the adjacent woods were of that species, though they are now hardwood.

Consider what a demand for arrowheads there must be, that the surface of the earth should be thus sprinkled with them, — the arrowhead and all the disposition it implies toward both man and brute. There they lie, pointed still, making part of the sands of almost every field.

I cut two shrub oaks (in different places) which have respectively ten and twenty rings. The last was a large and old one in a hedge.[1]

I first noticed the pitch pine twigs cut off by squirrels the 16th. Think how busy they were about that time in every pitch pine grove all over the State, cutting off the twigs and collecting the cones! While the farmer is digging his potatoes and gathering his corn he little thinks of this harvest of pine cones which the squirrel is gathering in the neighboring woods still more sedulously than himself.

I saw on the 28th, close by the stump of the easternmost big chestnut at Flint's Pond, the *Phallus impudicus*.

I hear the sound of the flail in M. Miles's barn, and gradually draw near to it from the woods, thinking many things. I find that the thresher is a Haynes of Sudbury, and he complains of the hard work and a lame back. Indeed, he cannot stand up straight. So all is not gold that glitters. This sound is not so musical after I have withdrawn. It was as well to have heard this music afar off. He complains also that the weather is not fit for his

[1] *Vide* [p. 208].

work, — that it is so muggy that he cannot dry the sheaves, and the grain will not fly out when struck. The floor, too, is uneven, and he pointed out one board more prominent on which he had broken two or three swingles.

He thought that there were larger trees in Sudbury, on what was John Hunt's land, now occupied by Thompson, near the old store, than in Inches Woods. Said there was a tree by the roadside on the farm of the late William Read in West Acton which nobody thereabouts knew the name of, but he had been South, and knew it to be a China-berry tree planted by a robin, for they are very fond of its fruit.

IV

NOVEMBER, 1860

(ÆT. 43)

Nov. 1. 2 P. M. — To Tommy Wheeler wood-lot.

A perfect Indian-summer day, and wonderfully warm. 72 + at 1 P. M. and probably warmer at two.

The butterflies are out again, — probably some new broods. I see the common yellow and two *Vanessa Antiopa*, and yellow-winged grasshoppers with blackish edges.

A striped snake basks in the sun amid dry leaves. Very much gossamer on the withered grass is shimmering in the fields, and flocks of it are sailing in the air.

Measure some pine stumps on Tommy Wheeler's land, about that now frosty hollow, cut as I judge from sprouts four years ago.

First the pitch pine: —

1 is 18½ inches [in] diameter and has 145 (?) rings						
2	18	"	"	"	137	"
3	20	"	"	"	128	"
4	21	"	"	"	148	"
5	21	"	"	"	140	"
6	22¾	"	"	"	160 + 4 (Counted the last 64 at home)	
7	20	"	"	"	167 or 168 (?)	

7)141¼   7)1026+4

Average 20   Average 147+1, or 148

That is, they all together averaged in growth from

first to last about a fifteenth of an inch in a year. But they grew very slowly indeed for the last fifty or more years. They did nearly half (?) their growing in the first third of their existence. For example, (I measure now on that side where I counted, *i. e.* the broadest, so that my figures are not absolutely but relatively true), —

No. 2 grew	5 inches	in first 32 years				
5	"	4½	"	"	50 and 3¾ in second 50
6	"	7¼	"	"	50 " 2½ " "
7	"	4½	"	"	50 " 2¾ " "
	21¼		182	3)8½	150

A little more than ⅑ inch a year.   Average ¹⁄₁₈ inch.

The 7th grew only something less than three inches (which was all of the sap) in the last sixty-seven or eight years, or one twenty-second of an inch a year only. Indeed, in one case, the 6th, the outside had grown only one and one fourth inches in sixty-four years, or about one fiftieth of an inch in a year, just one inch in the last fifty-three years, or one fifty-third of an inch a year, — equal to the finest scales. I should say that they averaged but one thirty-sixth part of an inch the third or last fifty years.

1st 50	2d 50	3d 50
⅑ inch	¹⁄₁₈	¹⁄₃₆

That is, their rate of growth the three successive periods of fifty years diminishes in geometrical progression, the quotient being two.

The seven pitch pine stumps measured on the 30th averaged thirty-four years and had grown a tenth of an inch in a year. This is a perfect and remarkable agreement, and quite unlooked for. They were a mile apart,

and I was not reminded of those previous measurements until I chanced to compare them afterward.

I may therefore take this to be [the] average growth of a pitch pine for the first fifty years. But I have not yet taken into the account the fact that, though the thickness of the layer is less, its superficies, or extent, is greater, as the diameter of the tree increases. Let us compare the three portions of wood. If the diameter at the end of the first fifty years is four, the second fifty, six, and the third fifty, seven, then the amount of wood added each term will be (to omit very minute fractions) twelve and a half, fifteen and a half, and ten respectively.[1] So that, though in the second fifty the rings are twice as near together, yet considerably more wood is produced than in the first, but in the third fifty the tree is evidently enfeebled, and it probably is not profitable (so far as bulk is concerned) to let it grow any more.

The very oldest trees whose rings I have counted (*i. e.* these pitch pines and the oaks on Eb. Hubbard's hill) grew thus slowly at last, which I think indicates that a tree has a definite age after which it grows more languidly or feebly, and thus gradually ceases to grow at all, — dies and decays. I should say that these pitch pines flourished till they were about a hundred years old, and that they then began to grow with less

[1] Or, actually averaging eight trees under Nov. 10th, it is 7, 10+, 10−.

vigor, though their old age (in this sense) might be a third or more of their whole life. Two or three more were dead or nearly dead when sawed four years ago, and I saw the rotted stumps of some others.

There were twenty or thirty of the pitch pines, — though I measured the largest of them, — and they were all but one or two perfectly sound to the core, and the inmost rings were the plainest. The sap was only from one and three quarters to three inches thick, and was the most decayed. (It was one and three quarters inches thick in No. 6.) The bark was generally from two to two and three quarters inches thick. This would have added four and three quarters to the average diameter of the trees, or made it twenty-four and three quarters. That is, where sawed off, which was rather low, or say eight to ten inches above ground.

There were also as many or more large white pines mixed with them. One of 24 inches diameter had 78 rings; second, 31 inches, 96 rings. Also one hemlock 21 inches, 81 rings. This had grown with remarkable equality throughout [1] and was very easy to count. An oak (probably black), 14 inches, 94 rings.

About a hundred and fifty years ago, then, there came up in and around this hollow in the woods a grove of pitch pines. Perhaps some came up twenty or thirty years earlier, which have now died and decayed. When the first had grown for about sixty years, many white pines sprang up amid and under them, as we see happen to-day

[1] And so it is generally.

Vol. XIV

PITCH PINE WOODS

Young, north of Loring's Pond.
Just beyond Concord bound on right hand, this side Wetherbee's, extensive and large. (Tarbell says that when he came to town in '26 these were just about as large as his now. Sixty to seventy years old, then.)
Heywood's small grove southeast of Peter's.
Large, southeast Copan.
Beyond Nathan Barrett's, both sides road, large.
Hill behind Abner Buttrick's.
Lane south of second Garfield house.
Southwest of Brooks's Pigeon-Place.
North G. M. Barrett's, by College Road.
Northeast of Sam Barrett's mill.
Northwest of Sam Barrett's mill, west of pond.

Nov. 2. P. M. — To D. Wetherbee's old oak lot.

As several days past, it has been cloudy and misty in the morning and fairer and warmer, if not Indian summer, in the afternoon; yet the mist lingers in drops on the cobwebs and grass until night.

HARDWOOD LOTS

Wetherbee's.
Blood's.
G. M. Barrett's hillside, behind house.
Walnuts (young) of Smith's Hill, Lincoln.
    "   "   " Annursnack, above orchard.
    "   " Fair Haven Hill slope.
        Also north side of path from Springs to bars.
    "   " site of Britton's shanty.
        South side of Bear Hill, Lincoln.

Saw off a very large and old-looking shrub oak on a pitch pine plain, twelve or more feet in height and three and one half inches in diameter (the wood) at one foot from the ground, where it has just twenty-seven

I occasionally (or frequently) see white pines springing up in a sprout-land when other trees have failed to fill it up for some years.

No. 6, having 164 rings and having been cut four years, sprang up at least one hundred and sixty-eight years ago, or about the year 1692, or fifty-seven years after the settlement, 1635.

In another case I counted fifteen rings (with a microscope) within the last quarter of an inch, which was at the rate of one sixtieth of an inch in a year, — equal, I think, to the finest scales ordinarily used.

WHITE PINE WOODS

The small dense grove of Clark's (?), north of Boze's [*sic*] Meadow.
Near road, southwest of Tarbell's.
Abel Hosmer's, north and northwest of house.
Mason's pasture (south of this, younger white pine with cedars intermixed).
The Holden Swamp woods as seen from north (except southwest part).
Northeast part of Baker Farm, quite young.
Behind Martial Miles's, southwest of cold pond-hole.
East side Second Division Brook, very extensive.

I have seen that a great many pitch pine cones have been cut off this fall, but it chances that I have not seen where they were eaten or stripped. I conclude, therefore, that they must be collected into some hole in a tree or in the earth, — there can hardly be a doubt of this, — and possibly some are buried as nuts are. What stores of them there must be collected in some places now!

rings. The first fourteen rings occupied one and a quarter inches from the centre, where the whole radius was but one and three quarters. It evidently began to grow more slowly when fifteen years old.

Wetherbee's oak lot may contain four or five acres.[1] The trees are white, red, scarlet, and swamp white oaks, maple, white pine, and ash. They are unusually large and old. Indeed, I doubt if there is another hereabouts of oaks as large. It is said that Wetherbee left them for the sake of mast for pigeons.

I measure a white oak at three feet from the ground, — eight feet four and one half inches in circumference. Another white oak at same height is six and three quarters in circumference; a red oak is six feet two inches in circumference; another, eight and a half; another, seven and four twelfths; and the scarlet oaks are of the same character, though the above were the largest, or among the largest. These oaks, though they form a wood, are some of them about as spreading as a pasture oak (*i. e.* one or two white ones near the outside), but generally they rise much higher before they branch. The white oaks have peculiarly smooth *tawny-white* boles for eight or ten feet up, the coarser flakes of the bark having scaled off so far. The red oaks, as well as scarlet, have a coarser and rougher, more deeply furrowed bark, and the trees rise higher before branching (commonly). One not very large had no limb for thirty feet or more, standing aslant. In the lowest part, on the brook, they were swamp white oaks and maples. The maples, being old, had a

[1] He says eight.

rough, dark, scaly bark. There were a few white pines straggling into this wood (only one large one).

Many of the oaks have been cut, and I counted about one hundred and ten rings on one small white oak, from which I should infer that the trees would average much more than that, perhaps between a hundred and fifty and two hundred years. Such a wood has got to be very rare in this neighborhood. Even the gray brushy tops of this attract your attention at a distance.

As you approach the wood, and even walk through it, the trees do not affect you as large, but as surely as you go quite up to one you are surprised. The very lichens and mosses which cover the rocks under these trees seem, and probably are in some respects, peculiar. Such a wood, at the same time that it suggests antiquity, imparts an unusual dignity to the earth.

It is pleasing to see under the trees great rocks covered with polypody, which has caught a great crop of shining brown oak leaves to contrast with its green. This oak wood is now bare and the leaves just fairly fallen.

This is probably one of those woods, like Ebby Hubbard's, which was never cut off but only cut out of.

I think it would be worth the while to introduce a school of children to such a grove, that they may get an idea of the primitive oaks before they are all gone, instead of hiring botanists to lecture to them when it is too late. Why, you do not now often meet with a respectable oak stump even, for they too have decayed.

I see a this year's sound red oak acorn tucked into a crevice in the bark of a white oak a foot or more from the ground.

Even in this old oak wood there is to be observed a resemblance to the primitive woods. The ground, never having been cleared nor cultivated, has a more primitive look; there are more ferns on it, and the rocks are far greener, with these and with lichens, never having been burned and bleached white by sun and fire.

Lee of the Corner speaks of an oak lot of his in Sudbury, which he bought in '31 and cut off (last and all of it last winter), but from the older stumps no sprouts have come up, but good ones from the younger.

You see the tufts of indigo now broken off and dropped exactly bottom up in the pastures, as if an industrious farmer had been collecting it by handfuls, which he had dropped thus.

It would be just as sensible for them to treat their young orchards or nurseries of apple trees in the same way, i. e., to burn them over and raise rye there a year or two, thinking to do them good.

As for the *Vaccinia*, I am disposed to agree with those who derive the name from *bacca*, a berry, for one species or another of this large family is the berry of berries in most northern parts of the world. They form an under-shrub, or sort of lower forest, even throughout our woodlands generally, to say nothing of open fields and hills. They form a humble and more or less dormant, but yet vivacious forest under a forest, which bides its time.

This wonderful activity of the squirrels in collecting and dispersing and planting nuts and acorns, etc., etc., every autumn is the more necessary since the trees on whose fruit they mainly live are not annual plants

Vol. XIV

like the wheat which supplies *our* staff of life. If the wheat crop fails this year, we have only to sow more the next year, and reap a speedy harvest, but if the forests were to be planted only at intervals equal to the age of the trees, there would be danger, what with fires and blight and insects, of a sudden failure and famine. It is important that there be countless trees in every stage of growth, — that there be an annual planting, as of wheat. Consider the amount of work they have to do, the area to be planted!

More or less rainy to-day.

I hear that geese went over to-day, alighted in Walden.

Nov. 4. P. M. — To Tommy Wheeler's lot.

As I go over John Hosmer's High Level, there being considerable wind, I notice for the first time that peculiar blueness of the river agitated by the wind and contrasting with the tawny fields, a fall phenomenon. Tarbell's white pine grove northwest of the Irishman's, in the swamp, and some thirty to forty years old, is so dense that there is no growth under it, only a tawny carpet of pine-needles.

In the Tommy Wheeler lot south of the old pitch pine hollow, I see the stumps of many white pines and oaks which were cut some four years ago, and no fire has been set there. These oak stumps have generally fifty-three or fifty-four rings, though some pitch pines and oaks are much older; but I scarcely see a stump of this age even which has sent up any shoots. I notice one. The sprouts are from a much younger growth. It is evident that all the larger stumps were too old and

effete, young as they were. In two or three cases I notice these stumps of oaks cut some four years ago and having fifty-three or four rings (from which no shoot has put forth), two together, half inclosing in a semicircle a very old and almost completely decayed stump, which, of course, was cut some fifty-eight years ago. These sprouts are rarely sound quite to the core. Perhaps the rest are sprouts whose stumps have quite disappeared, and this, i. e. the great age of the roots, may account for its sending up no more sprouts. I see, then, that the stumps of trees which were cut sixty years ago are still very common to be seen in our woods.

I have but little doubt that if Wetherbee's old oak lot should now be cut no sprouts would come up from the stumps. It is by seeds that oaks would have to be renewed there, if at all; but rather it is time for a different growth, i. e. for pines, and if he contemplates the removal of these oaks he should be considering how to favor the growth of pines there. They are already appearing thinly on various sides within that wood.

I frequently notice the seeds of small fruits and weeds left on stumps by birds and mice and even foxes (in their excrement).

There is *primitive wood* which has never been touched by the civilized man. We have none of this.

Then there is *primitive woodland*, i. e., which has never been cut clean off, and which in age now is mostly second growth.

Then there is *primitive copsewood*, i. e., which has been cut clean off but suffered to grow up again without further clearing or burning.

Then copsewood of other kinds.

Sophia brings me the drawer which held her acorns (almost all red oak). It is seventeen and a half inches by twelve and a half and two inches deep, and I count, crawling about on the bottom, one hundred and seventy-three great full-grown grubs with brown heads, which have come out of the acorns by a hole, oftenest at the edge of the cup on one side. And many of the grubs had been thrown away, and probably some had crawled away within a month, and no doubt more are still to come out. Also the bottom of this box is covered with four or five times as many minute pink grubs which may be the progeny of the former: here are at least eight hundred and sixty-five (or say one thousand) grubs to about four quarts of acorns *with their cups* (the box was hardly more than half full). I find that sixty red oak acorns with their cups make one pint. There were, therefore, about five hundred acorns to one hundred and seventy-three large grubs already out in the box, to say nothing of those that have been thrown and have crawled away, nor of the seven or eight hundred *young* grubs and probably more yet to be produced. Not quite half of the acorns, then, have grubs in them.[1] Now add the squirrels, jays, crows, and other birds and quadrupeds that feed on them, and the effect of the winter's cold and rain, and how many of the acorns of this year will be fit to plant next spring?

[1] Nov. 22, about a third as many more grubs have come out of these acorns, — both large and small grubs, — which will make nearly half as many large grubs as acorns ; and each of these large grubs has been the destruction of an acorn, so that already one half of these acorns have been destroyed by worms.

Vol. XIV

It appears that nearly half of these red oaks hav[e] already manifestly been destroyed by worms. It is ev[i]dent that there will be at least two grubs to one of thes[e] acorns, though of course the grubs will not always b[e] with the acorn. This is one of the nut weevils, and sinc[e] they come from eggs laid by a beetle, it would see[m] that many eggs must have been *recently* laid.

White birch seed has but recently begun to fall. I se[e] a quarter of an inch of many catkins bare. May hav[e] begun for a week. To-day also I see distinctly the tre[e] sparrows, and probably saw them, as supposed, som[e] days ago. Perhaps they feed on the birch seed as th[e] linarias do. Thus the birch begins to shed its seed abou[t] the time our winter birds arrive from the north.

Nov. 5. P. M. — To Blood's oak lot.

Measure the great white oak near the bars of th[e] bridle-road just beyond the northeast corner of th[e] Holden (?) farm. At the ground it is about ninetee[n] feet in circumference. At three feet from the ground [it] is eleven feet and seven inches in circumference, and th[e] same at five feet and apparently more above this. It [is] about sixteen feet to the lowest limb. The whole trun[k] standing aslant. It has a black and quite rough bar[k] not at all like that of the white oaks of Wetherbee's an[d] Blood's lots. There is a large open space amid th[e] huckleberry bushes beneath it, covered with a sho[rt] and peculiarly green sward, and this I see is the case wi[th] other oaks a quarter of a mile off.

There is a large chestnut in the lot east of this, and [I] observe that its top is composed of many small branch[es]

and twigs disposed very regularly and densely, brushwise, with a firm, distinct, more than semicircular edge against the horizon, very unlike the irregular, open, and more scraggy-twigged oak.

Blood's oak lot may contain about a dozen acres. It consists of red, black, white, and swamp white oaks, and a very little maple. The following are some of the largest that I saw. I measured one black oak which was, at three feet high, four feet eight inches in circumference; another, five feet six inches; and another the same. A red oak was six feet three inches; another, seven feet four inches; another, seven feet four inches; another, seven feet. One swamp white oak was six feet four inches. A white oak was seven feet seven inches, and another the same. The diameter of a third at one foot from ground (sawed off) was thirty-one and a half inches average.

This is quite a dense wood-lot, even without considering the size of the trees, and I was rather surprised to see how much spread there was to the tops of the trees in it, especially to the white oaks. The trees here rise far higher before branching, however, than in open land; some black oaks (if not others) were very straight and thirty to forty feet high without a limb. I think that there was not so much difference in color between the trunks of black and red oaks as commonly. The red oaks were oftener smooth, or smoothish, the largest of them. I saw very little decay. Considering their number and closeness, the trees were on the whole larger than I should have expected, though of course not nearly so large as the largest pasture oaks, — one to two and a half feet in diameter, or say generally (the sizable trees)

a foot and a half in diameter. This will probably do f[or] a specimen of a primitive oak forest hereabouts. Su[ch] probably was the size and aspect of the trees.

As for its age, I saw the stump of a white oak (n[ot] quite so large as those I measured) which had bee[n] sawed off at about one foot from the ground within fo[ur] or five years, perfectly level and sound to the core, a[nd] thirty-one and a half inches in diameter. The fir[st] thirty-three (?) rings were so close and indistinct as [to] be impossible to count exactly (occupying three quarte[rs] of an inch of the centre); the rest was perfectly distin[ct]. In all one hundred and forty-seven rings; or, by inch[es] from middle, thirty-nine, nine, six, seven, five, eleve[n], six, four, four, five, six, nine, ten, twelve, and then thre[e] quarters of an inch left. From which it appears that [it] grew much the fastest at about the age of eighty-ni[ne] years and very much the slowest for the first thirty-thr[ee] years.

I am struck by the fact that the more slowly tre[es] grow at first, the sounder they are at the core, and [I] think that the same is true of human beings. We do n[ot] wish to see children precocious, making great strid[es] in their early years like sprouts, producing a soft a[nd] perishable timber, but better if they expand slowly [at] first, as if contending with difficulties, and so are soli[di]fied and perfected. Such trees continue to expand wi[th] nearly equal rapidity to an extreme old age.

Another white oak stump, not so large but somewh[at] decayed, had one hundred and sixty and more ring[s]. So that you may say this wood is a hundred to a hundr[ed] and sixty years old.

I was struck by the orderly arrangement of the trees, as if each knew its own place; and it was just so at Wetherbee's lot. This being an oak wood, and like that, somewhat meadow [*sic*] in the midst, the swamp white oaks with a very few maples occupied that part, and I think it likely that a similar selection of the ground might have been detected often in the case of the other oaks, as the white compared with the red. As if in the natural state of things, when sufficient time is given, trees will be found occupying the places most suitable to each, but when they are interfered with, some are prompted to grow where they do not belong and a certain degree of confusion is produced. That is, our forest generally is in a transition state to a settled and normal condition.

Many young white pines — the largest twenty years old — are distributed through this wood, and I have no doubt that if let alone this would in a hundred years look more like a pine wood than an oak one.

Hence we see that the white pine may introduce itself into a primitive oak wood of average density.

The only sounds which I heard were the notes of the jays, evidently attracted by the acorns, and the only animal seen was a red squirrel, while there were the nests of several gray squirrels in the trees.

Last evening, the weather being cooler, there was an arch of northern lights in the north, with some redness. Thus our winter is heralded.

It is evident that the pasture oaks are commonly the survivors or relics of old oak woods, — not having been set out of course, nor springing up often in the

bare pasture, except sometimes along fences. I see that on the outskirts of Wetherbee's and Blood's lots are some larger, more spreading and straggling trees, which are not to be distinguished from those. Such trees are often found as stragglers beyond a fence in an adjacent lot. Or, as an old oak wood is very gradually thinned out, it becomes open, grassy, and park-like, and very many owners are inclined to respect a few larger trees on account of old associations, until at length they begin to value them for shade for their cattle. These are oftenest white oaks. I think that they grow the largest and are the hardiest. This final arrangement is in obedience to the demand of the cow. She says, looking at the oak woods: " Your tender twigs are good, but grass is better. Give me a few at intervals for shade and shelter in storms, and let the grass grow far and wide between them."

No doubt most of those white pines in pastures which branch close to the ground, their branches curving out and upward harpwise without one erect leading shoot, were broken down when young by cows. The cow does not value the pine, but rubs it out by scratching her head on it.

Nov. 6. Sawed off half of an old pitch pine stump at Tommy Wheeler's hollow. I found that, though the surface was entire and apparently sound except one or two small worm-holes, and the sap was evidently decaying, yet within, or just under the surface, it was extensively honeycombed by worms, which did not eat out to the surface. Those rings included in the outmost four or

Vol. XIV

five inches were the most decayed, — including the sapwood.

Nov. 7. To Cambridge and Boston.

Nov. 8. 2 P. M. — To Mt. Misery *via* sugar maples and Lee's Bridge.

The white oak near the English cress at three feet is nine feet and one twelfth in circumference and has a rough and dark bark. By its branching so low, it suggests that it may have stood in comparatively open ground most of its life, or such as the outmost oaks in Blood's wood toward his house.

I notice along the Corner road, beyond Abiel Wheeler's, quite a number of little white pines springing up against the south wall, whose seed must have been blown from Hubbard's Grove some fifty rods east. They extend along a quarter of a mile at least. Also a wet and brushy meadow some forty rods in front of Garfield's is being rapidly filled with white pines whose seeds must have been blown an equal distance.

We need not be surprised at these results when we consider how persevering Nature is, and how much time she has to work in, though she works slowly. A great pine wood may drop many millions of seeds in one year, and if only half a dozen are conveyed a quarter of a mile and lodge against some fence, and only one comes up and lives there, yet in the course of fifteen or twenty years there are fifteen or twenty young trees there, and they begin to make a show and betray their origin. It

does not imply any remarkable rapidity or success in Nature's operations.

In the wood north of the sugar maples a hickory but two feet in circumference has eighty-six rings. A white oak twenty-six inches [in] diameter has one hundred and twenty-eight rings.

The sugar maples occupy, together with oaks of the same size, about thirty rods, or say ten rods by three. The largest about five inches [in] diameter, but generally quite small. They have sprung from quite small stumps, commonly not bigger than themselves at most. They are peculiar among maples in retaining yet a part of their leaves, — a delicate fawn(?)-color, pale brown.

There is quite a pitch pine wood on the lane beyond the second Garfields, but though there are *very* few little white pines under it (no large ones), these are under the densest part, and there are no little pitch pines, though they are common in the more open parts. Seed-bearing pines are distant here. I observe on the trunk of one of the largest of these pitch pines (which may be forty years old), standing on the outside the wood, minute or short branches, commonly mere tufts of needles in rings around the trunk, — reminding you even of the branches of the horse-tail, they are in this case so regular, — perfectly horizontal and six to twelve inches apart. Some are two or three years old, but only three to six inches long. These seem to represent the old whorls of branches. Perhaps, the tree growing slowly at the top, the dormant buds here are stimulated. I afterward see in another wood an outside pitch pine, a tall one, on which some of these tufts had apparently developed into branches four or five feet long, in imperfect whorls, the top being partly dead.

A white oak stump, roadside west of Abel Minott house site, nineteen and one half inches [in] diameter (wood), sixty-five rings. A pitch pine standing on opposite side more westerly is five and nine twelfths feet in circumference at three feet.

I observe on the west side of Mt. Misery, cut off apparently last winter, mulleins, very tall, sprung up, — as well as fire-weed and goldenrods. I saw an abundance of mulleins in a young wood-lot with much bare ground, burnt over a year or so ago, behind Mason's on the bridle-road, on the 5th, so that the mullein too might be called a fire-weed. But I notice that those plants so called, as the epilobium and senecio, and which are supposed to owe their origin to the fire, generally spring up on a surface made bare by whatever cause. They are the first weeds after a clearing or cutting.

On this same Mt. Misery (cut last winter), an oak stump (apparently black) eleven and one half inches [in] diameter, sixty-one rings; a white oak, thirteen inches, fifty-eight rings. I count four or more of these stumps, — which are as plain as usual, — and make from fifty-four to sixty-one rings, say average fifty-eight years. Yet in several of these instances they were manifestly sprouts, and there was the old stump cut 58 + 1 years ago.[1] These stumps did not show any trace of the axe, but there was one which lay on its side, apparently of the same date, but from which no sprout had come, which

[1] Vide Nov. 13.

in woodland paths or in pastures, as if an industrious farmer or a simpler had been collecting it by handfuls and had dropped his parcels thus. The fact is that they grow up many stems close together, and their branches are so interlaced as not to be easily separated; so that the wind operates the more powerfully and breaks them all off together at the ground, and then, on account of their form, these parcels are deposited exactly bottom up commonly, and you see three or four to fifteen or more stems within a diameter of four or five inches, looking just as if somebody had plucked them and laid them together.[1] I also see the fly-away grass going over a wall or rock from time to time.

The *Salix sericea* has just blackened the ground with its leaves.

These are annual phenomena.

Dr. (?) Manasseh Cutler, in the first volume of the Boston Academy's Reports for 1785, speaks of whortleberries only in the half-converted or disparaging way in which the English do, — and have reason to, — saying that children love to eat them in milk. His eyes had not been opened to their significance; they were without honor in their native country. But I have no doubt that he ate them himself in secret.

Nov. 9.[2] 12 m. — To Inches' Woods in Boxboro.

This wood is some one and three quarters miles from West Acton, whither we went by railroad. It is in the east part of Boxboro, on both sides of the Harvard

[1] So these seeds and fly-away grass seed dispersed.
[2] Vide also Nov. 16.

was much better preserved and did show the traces of the axe plainly. These recent stumps, though only some sixty years old, had in no case sprouted again, and I think that this is because they are sprouts, and that the vitality of the stock was so nearly exhausted. These old stumps are frequently half inclosed in the recent stump. I think that I readily detected the sprout also by the greater breadth of the rings the first few years.

The stumps of trees which were cut in the last century — oaks at least — must be not uncommon in our woods.

Looking from this hill, I think that I see considerably more oak than pine wood.

Edward Hoar's pitch pine and white pine lot on the south side of this hill is evidently a new wood. You see the green moss, the cladonia, and birches (which I think do not spring up within an old wood), and even feel with your feet an old cow-path and see an old apple tree inclosed in the wood. Are not birches interspersed with pines a sign of a new wood?

When a pitch pine wood is cut, that fringe or edging of little pitch pines which commonly surrounds it may remain to grow up and in a measure represent it. Also, apparently, when for any reason, as from frost, land where the wood has been cut remains comparatively bare for several years and becomes only grassy, pitch pines (as well as white pines) may catch there thickly.

I constantly meet now with those tufts of indigo-weed (turned black) now broken off and dropped exactly bottom up, as it were dropped by a careful hand

turnpike. We walked mostly across lots from West Acton to a part of the wood about half a mile north of the turnpike, — and the woods appeared to reach as much further north. We then walked in the midst of the wood in a southwesterly by west direction, about three quarters of a mile, crossing the turnpike west of the maple swamp and the brook, and thence south by east nearly as much[1] more, — all the way in the woods, and chiefly old oak wood. The old oak wood, as we saw from the bare hill at the south end, extends a great deal further west and northwest, as well as north, than we went, and must be at least a mile and a half[1] from north to south by a mile to a mile and a quarter[1] *possibly* from east to west. Or there *may* be a thousand[2] acres[3] of old oak wood. The large wood is chiefly oak, and that white oak, though black, red, and scarlet oak are also common. White pine is in considerable quantity, and large pitch pine is scattered here and there, and saw some chestnut at the south end. Saw no hemlock or birch to speak of.

Beginning at the north end of our walk, the trees which I measured were (all at three feet from ground except when otherwise stated): a black oak, ten feet [in] circumference, trunk tall and of regular form; scarlet oak, seven feet three inches, by Guggins Brook; white oak, eight feet; white oak, ten feet, forks at ten feet; white oak, fifteen feet (at two and a half feet, bulging very much near ground; trunk of a pyramidal form;

[1] [Queried in pencil.]
[2] Four or five hundred.
[3] Vide [p. 227].

Old Chestnut Trees on a Hilltop in Boxboro

Hepatica and Bloodroot

rst branch at sixteen feet; this just north of turnpike nd near Guggins Brook); white oak, nine feet four ıches (divides to two at five feet); white oak, nine et six inches (divides to two at five feet); red oak, ght feet (south of road); white pine, nine feet; a arlet or red oak stump cut, twenty and a half inches n] diameter, one hundred and sixty rings.

I was pleased to find that the largest of the white oaks, rowing thus in a dense wood, often with a pine or other ee within two or three feet, were of pasture oak size and ven form, the largest commonly branching low. Very ıany divide to two trunks at four or five feet only from ıe ground. You see some white oaks and even some thers in the midst of the wood nearly as spreading as ı open land.

Looking from the high bare hill at the south end, the mits of the *old* oak wood (so far as we could overlook) were very distinct, its tops being a mass of gray rush, — contorted and intertwisted twigs and boughs, – while the younger oak wood around it, or bounding ., though still of respectable size, was still densely lothed with the reddish-brown leaves.

This famous oak lot — like Blood's and Wetherbee's – is a place of resort for those who hunt the gray squir- el. They have their leafy nests in the oak-tops.

It is an endless maze of gray oak trunks and boughs tretching far around. The great mass of individual runks which you stand near is very impressive.

Many sturdy trunks (they commonly stand a little slant) are remarkably straight and round, and have so ıuch regularity in their roughness as to suggest smooth-

ness. The older or largest white oaks were of a rougher and darker bark than Wetherbee's and Blood's, though often betraying the same tendency to smoothness, as if a rough layer had been stripped off near the ground.

I noticed that a great many trunks (the bark) had been gnawed near the ground, — different kinds of oak and chestnut, — perhaps by squirrels.

Nov. 10. Cheney gives me a little history of the Inches Woods. He says it was a grant to Jekil (John (?) Jekil) by the crown, and that it amounted to half of Boxboro as well as much of Stow and Acton. That Jekil had a summer house where Squire Hosmer's house stands in Stow, before the Revolution, but at that time withdrew into Boston. It was a great event when he used to come out to Stow in the summer. Boxboro was a part of Stow then. Mr. Hosmer had charge of the lands for Inches, and the kitchen of his house was partly the old summer house of Jekil, and he also remembered an old negro named York, who had been a slave of Jekil, and he, the negro, said that twenty of the thirty acres bought of Inches by Hosmer, behind his house, was once fenced in with a paling or picket fence ten or fifteen feet high, and formed a park in which Jekil kept deer. The neighbors used to come and peep through the paling at the deer. Henderson Inches, hearing of these lands about the time of the Revolution, went to the heirs of Jekil and purchased the whole tract quite cheap, and they had been a fortune to the family since. Many farms have been made of parts of the wood, and thou- sands of dollars' worth of wood have been sold at a time.

Vol. XIV

Iad realized maybe $150,000 from it. Cheney had eard that there were about four hundred acres of the nches lands left. Henderson Inches died two or three ears ago, and now his heirs wished to sell, but would ot divide it, but sell in one body. Ruggles, Nourse, and Iason wished to buy, but not the whole. Except what as been sold, or generally, Inches would not have it ut. He was sharp and stood out for his price, and also ked to keep it. Hence it is a primitive oak wood and aid to be the most of one in Massachusetts.

Collier tells me that his sunflower-head (now dried) ıeasures just twenty-one and a half inches [in] diame- er, — the solid part.

Most think that Inches Wood was worth more twenty r thirty years ago, — that the oaks are now decayed vithin. Some have suggested that it would be much for he benefit of Boxboro to have it cut off and made into ırms, but Boxboro people answer no, that they get a ood deal more in taxes from it now than they would hen.

How little there is on an ordinary map! How little, I ıean, that concerns the walker and the lover of nature. Setween those lines indicating roads is a plain blank pace in the form of a square or triangle or polygon or egment of a circle, and there is naught to distinguish his from another area of similar size and form. Yet the ne may be covered, in fact, with a primitive oak wood, ike that of Boxboro, waving and creaking in the wind, uch as may make the reputation of a county, while he other is a stretching plain with scarcely a tree on it. The waving woods, the dells and glades and green

banks and smiling fields, the huge boulders, etc., etc., are not on the map, nor to be inferred from the map.

That grand old oak wood is just the most remarkable and memorable thing in Boxboro, and yet if there is a history of this town written anywhere, the history or even mention of this is probably altogether omitted, while that of the first (and may be last) parish is enlarged on.

What sort of cultivation, or civilization and improve- ment, is ours to boast of, if it turns out that, as in this instance, unhandselled nature is worth more even by our modes of valuation than our improvements are, — if we leave the land poorer than we found it? Is it good economy, to try it by the lowest standards, to cut down all our forests, if a forest will pay into the town treasury a greater tax than the farms which may supplant it, — if the oaks by steadily growing according to their nature leave our improvements in the rear?

How little we insist on truly grand and beautiful natural features! How many have ever heard of the Boxboro oak woods? How many have ever explored them? I have lived so long in this neighborhood and but just heard of this noble forest, — probably as fine an oak wood as there is in New England, only eight miles west of me.

I noticed young white pines springing up in the more open places and dells. There were considerable tracts of large white pine wood and also pine and oak mixed, especially on the hills. So I see that the character of a primitive wood may gradually change, as from oak to pine, the oaks at last decaying and not being replaced by oaks.

Though a great many of those white oaks of the Inches Wood branch quite as low and are nearly as spreading as pasture oaks, yet generally they rise up in stately columns thirty or forty or fifty feet, diminishing very little. The black and red and scarlet oaks are especially columnar and tall, without branches for a long distance, and these trees are shaped more in their trunks like an elm than a pasture oak. They commonly stand aslant at various angles. When, in the midst of this great oak wood, you look around, you are struck by the great mass of gray-barked wood that fills the air. The leaves of these old oaks are now fairly fallen, and the ground is densely covered with their rustling reddish-brown scales.

A peculiarity of this, as compared with much younger woods, is that there is little or no underwood and you walk freely in every direction, though in the midst of a dense wood. You walk, in fact, *under* the wood.

The wood not having been cut to any extent, and the adjacent country being very little occupied, I did not notice a single cart-path where a wheel-track was visible, — at most a slight vista, and one footpath. I knew that I was near the southwest edge by the crowing of a cock.

This wood is said to have been a great resort for pigeons. We saw one large pigeon-place on the top of the hill where we first entered it. Now used.

Seeing this, I can realize how this country appeared when it was discovered. Such were the oak woods which the Indian threaded hereabouts.

Such a wood must have a peculiar fauna to some extent. Warblers must at least pass through it in the spring, which we do not see here.

We have but a faint conception of a full-grown oak forest stretching uninterrupted for miles, consisting of sturdy trees from one to three and even four feet in diameter, whose interlacing branches form a complete and uninterrupted canopy. Many trunks old and hollow, in which wild beasts den. Hawks nesting in the dense tops, and deer glancing between the trunks, and occasionally the Indian with a face the color of the faded oak leaf.

Grimes said that he could almost clasp the loins of my lynx as it hung up by the heels before it was skinned, it was so slender there that a man with a large hand could have done it.

Richardson in his "Fauna Boreali-Americana," which I consulted at Cambridge on the 7th, says that the French-Canadians call the Canada lynx indifferently *Le Chat* or *Le Peeshoo*, and Charlevoix falsely calls it *Carcajou*, which is the wolverene, and hence much confusion and error among naturalists. "Seven to nine thousand are annually procured by the Hudson's Bay Company. It is found on the Mackenzie River as far north as latitude 66°." Easily killed by a stroke with a small stick on the back! (?) Breeds once a year and has two young. Never attacks man. A poor runner, but a good swimmer. Audubon and Bachman repeat Richardson. According to Pennant, Lawson and Catesby repeat the falsehoods about its dropping from trees on deer, etc.

Vol. XIV

Observed in the dropping of a fox the other day, with fur, some quarter-shaped (or triangular segments) seeds, and roughish, which may have been seeds of rose hips. They were white. So are the sweet-briar hips, but the common wild rose hips are brownish. Were they prinos seeds? If rose hips, then the fox enjoys what Manasseh Cutler in 1785 called "the conserve of hepps of the London dispensatory" without the sugar.

Elijah Wood, senior, tells me that about 1814 (or before 1815, in which year he was married, and while he still lived at his father's on Carlisle road), as he was riding to town on horseback in the evening alone to singing to prepare for Thanksgiving, he stopped to let his horse drink at the brook beyond Winn's, when he heard a cry from some wild beast just across the river. It affected him so that he did not stop to let his horse drink much. When he returned later, — now with others, — they all heard it, as if answering to their shouts, somewhat further up the river. It was also heard by some teamsters, and also an animal supposed to be the same was said to have been seen by a woman crossing the road just west of where Wood now lives. It was thought to be a wolverene.

I have now measured in all eight pitch pine stumps at the Tommy Wheeler hollow, sawed off within a foot of the ground.

I measured the longest diameter, and then at right angles with that, and took the average, and then selected that side of the stump on which the radius was of average length and counted the number of rings in each inch, beginning at the centre, thus: —

Inch	1st tree	2	3	4	5 (diam 19¼)	6	7	8	Sum	Average
Rings, in all	158	164	176 (?); more correctly 168	148	171 *I have this*; more correctly 165	171	163	About 150		Av. age 162 or 163 years
Radius	9⅜	11⅝	10	9¼+	9½	9½+	7⅝	9¼	Av. R. about 9½	Av. Diam. 19.
12	in 5/8 inch 38									
11	33								33	33
10	in 3/8 inch 17	19	32	in 4/8+ inch 3	in 7/8 inch 25	in 4/8+ inch 16		in 1/4 inch 10	51	25+
9	26	13½	28	15	32	21		28	163½	23+
8	25	11	20	16	21	21	in 5/8 inch 24	19	133	19
7	26 (?)	9¼	16	18	17	23	42	14	165½	21—
6	16½ (?)	6½	21	19	23	19	29	14	148	18+
5	11½	5	15	24	11	18	22	11	117¼	15—
4	7+	5½	11	16	9	14	11	13	86¾	11—
3	9—	6	9	10	9	11	11	12	77	10—
2	12+	7+	11	12	12	13	11	13	91	11+
1st inch	9—	10+	13—	15	12	15	13	16	103	13—

Of these eight, average growth about one seventeenth of an inch per year.

Calling the smallest number of rings in an inch in each tree 1, the comparative slowness of growth of the inches is thus expressed, *viz.*: —

1	1.3	1.7	1.3	1.	1.6	2.3	3.7	3.6	3.7	3.8	6.6
2	2.	1.4	1.2	1.1	1.	1.3	1.9	2.1	2.7	3.8	
3	1.4	1.2	1.	1.2	1.7	2.3	1.6	2.2	3.1	3.4	
4	1.5	1.2	1.	1.6	2.4	1.9	1.8	1.6	1.5		
5	1.3	1.3	1.	1.	1.2	2.4	1.9	2.3	3.4		
6	1.4	1.2	1.	1.3	1.6	1.7	2.1	1.9	1.9	2.5	
7	1.2	1.	1.	1.	2.	2.6	3.8	3.6			
8	1.4	1.2	1.1	1.2	1.	1.3	1.3	1.7	2.5	3.6	

From the line x I calculate the average rate of growth in diameter (or radius) each successive ten years thus (in decimals of an inch): [1] —

1 to 10	10 to 20	20–30	30–40	40–50	50–60	60–70
(.77)	(.87)	(.96)	(.95)	(.78+)	(.66)	(.55+)

70–80	80–90	90–100	100–110	110–120	120–130
(.54–)	(.48–)	(.48+)	(.53–)	(.51)	(.43+)

130–140	140–150	150–160	160–170	170–180	180–190
(.43+)	(.403)	(.40)	(.36+)	(.30)	(.30)

Of course the error is great in proportion as the number of rings in an inch exceeds ten.

They grew in the first decade more than in any decade after their fiftieth year, and continued to grow with pretty regularly accelerated growth up to about the end of the third decade, or say about the twenty-ninth year, when they were increasing fastest in diameter, — 1.92 inches in ten years. They continued to

[1] It would have been much easier, as well as more correct if I had counted at first the number of rings to each inch.

grow at nearly the same rate through the fourth decade, and then their rate of growth very suddenly decreased, — *i. e.*, in fifth decade, or from the fortieth to the fiftieth years, when they grew only about the same as in the first decade. In the sixth and seventh decades the rate of growth steadily decreased as fast as it had increased in the first three decades, and it continued to decrease through the eighth, ninth, and tenth decades, though much more slowly. In the eleventh and twelfth decades, or from one hundred to one hundred and twenty years, the rate was accelerated, or they grew faster than from eighty to one hundred, but after the twelfth decade the rate of growth steadily decreased to the last, when it was less than one third what it was in the third decade.[1] When growing fastest, or between the twentieth and thirtieth year, the radius often was not increased one inch in ten years. But after they were one hundred and sixty years old they did not grow four tenths[2] of an inch in ten years — or one twenty-fifth[3] of an inch in one year.[4] On an average, by accurate observation these eight trees were gaining the most in diameter at about the thirtieth year, and least (with one exception) in the last ten years of their existence.

Many have inferred that it is most profitable to cut pitch pine when about thirty (or forty) years old, but they seem to forget that the most rapid increase in diameter when the tree is only ten or fifteen years old

[1] According to calculation, but *actually* still less.
[2] On an average, $\frac{28}{100}$.
[3] $\frac{1}{36}$
[4] And sometimes much less, as has been stated.

Vol. XIV

does not indicate so great bulk of wood added to the tree, as a much less increase in diameter when it is fifty or one hundred years old. Indeed these trees, slowly as they appeared to grow at last, increased in bulk far more rapidly in the last twenty years than in the first twenty, — or as thirty-six to ten.

The absolute area of the annual rings (which is in the same proportion as the bulk of wood formed) each ten years is (calculated from the measurement on the third page back): —

	1st tree	2	3	4	5*	6	7	8	(total)	Av.
1st 10 yrs. (inch)	3.9	3.1	2.4	2.1	2.6	2.1	2.4	2.	20.6	2.6—
2	7.9	17.3	6.7	5.	6.8	4.7	6.7	4.	59.1	7.4—
3	16.5	39.3	15.6	10.2	13.6	8.7	12.	7.8	123.7	15.5—
4	28.1	53.4	19.5	15.1	22.3	14.4	17.1	13.1	183.0	22.9—
5	23.2	43.2	19.2	13.8	25.4	15.7	17.1	16.5	174.1	21.7
6	21.6	44.8	18.4	12.4	18.2	15.7	12.8	22.2	166.1	20.8—
7	18.1	41.4	16.5	11.8	15.	15.7	12.7	25.2	156.4	19.5
8	15.7	33.	17.4	13.7	18.6	18.	11.9	25.2	153.5	19.2—
9	15.7	31.4	25.5	18.2	24.	18.2	11.9	29.2	174.1	21.8—
10	18.8	22.3	24.5	20.	23.	17.8	11.2	28.	165.6	20.7
11	18.8	20.	23.6	22.7	22.4	17.8	9.7	24.7	159.7	20.—
12	19.7	20.	21.3	26.7	19.	21.	9.7	20.2	157.6	19.9
13	20.5	16.	19.	29.5	16.7	22.4	9.7	19.1	152.9	19.1
14	20.5	12.	19.	35.6	16.7	24.2	9.9	19.1	157.0	19.6
15	14.	12.	18.8	29.7	17.2	25.4	11.8	14.9	143.8	18.
16		12.	18.7		18.1	23.4	11.8		84.0	16.8
17			18.7		18.1	21.3			58.1	19.4—

* By actually measuring the space covered by each successive ten rings for the fifth tree I got .9, .6, 1, 1.1, 1, .7, .5, .5, .56, .5, .5, .37, .25, .44, .25, .31, .25.

According to the above, most wood is made in the fourth decade, though there is but little decrease in amount afterward.

There is a loss of time if you cut at thirty or even forty years, for, supposing that a new pitch pine were at once to take the place of the old one, at the end of forty years more you would only have got $(2.6 + 7.4 + 15.5 + 22.9 =)$ 48.5 of wood more, instead of $(21.7 + 20.8 + 19.5 + 19.2 =)$ 81.2 more, which you would have had by this time if you had let the tree stand. Or if you had cut it at eighty years, you would only have 129.7 of wood after eighty years more, instead of the 155.9 that might have grown. Or even if you should cut every forty years, you would after one hundred and sixty years have got only 194 of wood to 285.6 that you might have had. From which I infer that the greater bulk of wood made in the third and fourth decade is so little more than that made in any succeeding ten years of the tree's age, and so much more than that made in the previous ten years, that if you want this kind of wood it is best to let the tree stand as long as it is sound and growing.

To be sure, the above calculation supposes the tree to increase in height in proportion to its age — which is hardly the case — and also that the same number of large trees can stand on the same area as of small ones. But even after these deductions, when we consider the proportionally greater value of large timber of this kind, it must be best to let it grow as long as it will.

The same is true until the last forty years makes less wood than the first forty. The first forty makes 48.5;

Vol. XIV

Near these apparently a black (?) oak, or maybe a chestnut (?), twenty inches [in] diameter and seventy-four rings, but the centre was within four inches of the westerly side.

A white oak standing by the fence west of Spanish Brook dam on Morse's lot, circumference six feet and two twelfths at three feet. Near by a hornbeam a foot and a half [in] circumference at three feet.

J. Baker's pitch pines south of upper wood-path north of his house abundantly confirm the rule of *young* white pines under pitch pines. That fine young white pine wood west of this is partly of these which were left when the pitch pines were cut.

Baker's hill between farm and Pleasant Meadow, oak (apparently a black), diameter twenty-six, seventy-one rings. The stumps here were cut some five or six years ago and have fifty to sixty rings. Commonly no sprouts from those of this age here.

On top of Mt. Misery, looked again at those old stumps (of the 8th). There are three or four quite plain, just showing themselves above the surface, with rounded, flaky, decaying and crumbling edge, close to the recent stump of the shoot or shoots which sprang from them and which were cut last winter. One of these recent stumps, counted to-night, gives sixty years, but the first two or three are uncertain. Hence this old stump is as old as the century.

There are several perfectly dry and exposed stumps on bare rocky shelves, or else lying on rocks on their sides, quite well preserved and showing the marks of the axe, which I have but little doubt are of the same

the last, 76.8. However, the time of cutting may depend partly on the number of trees that stand on a given area and also on whether they are wanted for fuel or for lumber, many small being about as good for the former use as a few large; *i. e.*, these trees made more wood any other forty years than the first. Why, then, employ them then only?

Nov. 10 *and* 11 were rainy, raising the river considerably on to the meadows.

Nov. 13. P. M. — To Mt. Misery.
A white birch (*Betula alba*) west edge of Trillium Wood, two feet seven inches [in] circumference at three feet.

On the Moore and Hosmer lot, cut in '52 (I think), west of railroad, south of Heywood's meadow, an oak stump fifteen and a half inches [in] diameter, ninety-three rings; another, white oak, fourteen and a half inches [in] diameter, ninety-four rings. In the first case there were two stumps of same age, evidently sprouts from an older stock, they curving around it, but I observed only a slight hollow where apparently the old stump had been. In the second case there was but one stump, but that rather concave on one side where there was a deep hollow in the earth. In both of these cases the tenacious mould, covered slightly with a fine greenish lichen, appeared heaved up about where the old stump had been. It was a good hundred years since that old stump was cut. The inmost rings of the recent stumps were coarse, as with sprouts.

age, preserved by being tipped out of the earth many years ago.[1]

Am surprised at the very slow growth of some hickory (stumps) along the wall on the top of this hill, — so fine I did not count quite accurately.

One was 10 inches in diameter with	104 rings
" " $6\frac{1}{2}$ [2] " "	*about* 115 "
" " $14\frac{1}{2}$ " "	" 84 "
" " $11\frac{3}{4}$ " "	121 "

I think that the oak stumps have lasted unusually long on this hill, on account of their having originally grown slowly here and since been so much exposed to the light and air over and amid the rocks.

Nov. 14. River two feet four inches above summer level (and at height) on account of rain of 10th and 11th and 12th.

The red maple on south edge of Trillium Wood is six feet three inches in circumference at three feet.

Yellow butterflies still.

Almost all holes in and about stumps have nutshells or nuts in them.

Nov. 16. This and yesterday Indian-summer days. P. M. — To Inches Woods.

Walked over these woods again, — first from Harvard turnpike at where Guggins Brook leaves it, which is the east edge of the old wood, due north along near the edge of the wood, and at last more northwest along edge to the cross-road, a strong mile.

[1] *Vide* account of pine stump, April 5, 1859.
[2] Have this. *Vide* Nov. 19th.

I observe that the black, red, and scarlet oaks are generally much more straight and perpendicular than the white, and not branched below. The white oak is much oftener branched below and is more irregular, — curved or knobby.

The first large erect black oak measured on the 9th was by the path at foot of hill southeast of pigeon-place. Another, more north, is (all at three feet when not otherwise stated) ten and a half [feet] in circumference.

There is not only a difference between most of the white oaks within Blood's wood and the pasture oaks without, — the former having a very finely divided and comparatively soft tawnyish bark, and the latter a very coarse rugged and dark-colored bark, — but there is here a similar difference within this wood; *i. e.*, some of the white oaks have a hard, rugged bark, in very regular oblong squares or checkers (an agreeably regular *roughness* like a coat of mail), while others have a comparatively finely divided and soft bark.

I see one white oak shaped like this: —

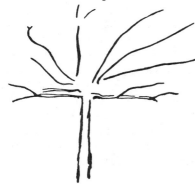

It happens oftenest here, I think, that the very largest white oaks have the most horizontal branches and branch nearest the ground, which would at first suggest that *these* trees were a different variety from the more upright and rather smaller ones, but it may be that these are older, and for that reason had more light and room and so temptation to spread when young.

Northwesterly from pigeon-place (near base of hill), —

A white oak $6\frac{3}{4}$ in circumference
"   "   " $8\frac{4}{12}$
"   "   " $6\frac{11}{12}$

The last one grows close against a rock (some three feet high), and it has grown over the top and sides of this rock to the breadth of twelve and eighteen inches in a thin, close-fitting, saddle-like manner, very remarkable and showing great vigor in the tree.

Here, too, coming to water, I see the swamp white oak rising out of it, elm-like in its bark and trunk. Red maples also appear here with them. It is interesting to see thus how surely the character of the ground determines the growth. It is evident that in a wood that has been let alone for the longest period the greatest regularity and harmony in the disposition of the trees will be observed, while in our ordinary woods man has often interfered and favored the growth of other kinds than are best fitted to grow there naturally. To some, which he does not want, he allows no place at all.

Hickories occasionally occur, — sometimes scaly-barked, if not shagbarks, — also black birch and a few little sugar maples.

Vol. XIV

Still going north, a white pine nine feet [in] circumference.

The wood at the extreme north end (along the road) is considerably smaller. After proceeding west along the road, we next went west by south through a maple and yellow birch swamp, in which a black oak eight feet and four twelfths [in] circumference, a red maple six feet and a half, a black birch seven feet, a black birch eight feet. And in the extreme northwesterly part of the wood, close to the road, are many large chestnuts, — one eleven and three quarters feet [in] circumference with many great knobs or excrescences, another twelve and seven twelfths.

We next walked across the open land by the road to the high hill northeast of Boxboro Centre. In this neighborhood are many very large chestnuts, of course related to the chestnut wood just named. 1st, along this road just over the north wall, beyond a new house, one $13\frac{11}{12}$ feet in circumference; 2d, 16, a few rods more west by the wall; then, perhaps fifty or sixty rods more west and maybe eight or ten rods north from the road, along a wall, the 3d, $15\frac{2}{12}$; and then, near the road, southwest from this, the 4th, $15\frac{4}{12}$; and some rods further north, toward hill and house of O. and J. Wetherbee, the 5th, $13\frac{7}{12}$; then northeast, in lower ground (?), the 6th, 16 feet, at ground $21\frac{2}{3}$; then, near base of hill, beyond house, the 7th, $16\frac{2}{12}$ at two feet from ground; next, some rods west of the hill, the 8th, $17\frac{8}{12}$ at three feet, at ground $23\frac{1}{2}$; and then, a considerable distance north and further down the hill, the 9th, $13\frac{4}{12}$. (There [were] also four other good-sized chestnuts

on this hillside, with the last three.) Or these nine trees averaged about $15\frac{1}{4}$ feet in circumference. The 3d tree had a limb four or five feet from the ground, which extended horizontally for a rod toward the south, declining a little toward the earth, and this was nine feet in circumference about eighteen inches from the tree. The 7th had a large limb broken off at one foot above the ground on the side, whose stump prevented measuring at the ordinary height. As I remember, the 8th was the finest tree.

These nine (or thirteen) trees are evidently the relics of one chestnut wood of which a part remains and makes the northwest part of Inches Wood, and the trees are all within about a quarter of a mile southeast and northwest, the first two being by themselves at the southeast.

The chestnut is remarkable for branching low, occasionally so low that you cannot pass under the lower limb. In several instances a large limb had fallen out on one side. Commonly, you see great rugged strips of bark, like straps or iron clamps made to bind the tree together, three or four inches wide and as many feet long, running more or less diagonally across the trunk and suggesting a very twisted grain, while the grain of the recent bark  beneath them may be perpendicular. Perhaps this may be owing to old portions of the bark which still adhere, being wrenched aside by the unequal growth of the wood. I think that all these old trunks show this.

Frank Brown tells me of a chestnut in his neighborhood nineteen feet and eight(?) inches in circumference at three feet.

White oaks within a wood commonly, at Wetherbee's and Blood's woods, have lost the outside rough and rugged bark near the base, like a jacket or vest cast off, revealing that peculiar smooth tawny-white inner garment or shirt. Probably the moisture and shade of a wood softens the bark and causes it to scale off. Apparently outside trees do not lose this outer bark, but it becomes far more rugged and dark exposed to the light and air, forming a strong coat of mail such as they need.

Most of the white oaks in Inches Wood are of a slight ashy tinge and have a rather loose, scaly bark, but the larger, losing this below, become tawny-white.

Having returned into Inches Wood, not far west of the meadow (which is west of the brook), at the angle made by the open land, a black oak stump recently cut, about one foot high and twenty-one inches in diameter, had only one hundred and six rings. A white oak only nine inches in diameter near by had eighty rings. I suspect that the smaller white oaks are much older comparatively (with the large) than their size would indicate, as well as sounder and harder wood. A white oak at three feet, six and one half in circumference. A black oak had been recently cut into at the west base of Pigeon Hill, and I counted about eighty-five rings in the outside three inches. The tree (wood only) was some twenty-three inches in diameter.

Looking at this wood from the Boxboro hill, the

white pines appeared to be confined chiefly to the higher land, forming a ridge from north to south. Young white pines have very generally come in (a good many being twenty feet high or more), though in some places much more abundantly than in others, all over this oak wood, though not high enough to be seen at a distance or from hills (except the first-named larger trees); but though there are very many large pitch pines in this wood, especially on the hills or moraines, young pitch pines are scarcely to be seen. I saw some only in a dell on the south side the turnpike. If these oaks were cut off with care, there would very soon be a dense white pine wood there. The white pines are not now densely planted, except in some more open places, but come up stragglingly every two or three rods. The natural succession is rapidly going on here, and as fast as an oak falls, its place is supplied by a pine or two. I have no doubt that, *if entirely let alone*, this which is now an oak wood would have become a white pine wood.

Measured on the map, this old woodland is fully a mile and a half long from north to south — one mile being north [of] the turnpike — and will average half a mile from east to west. Its extreme width, measuring due east and west, is from Guggins Brook on the turnpike to the first church. (It runs considerably further southeast, however, on to the high hill.) There is a considerable tract on the small road south [of] the turnpike covered with second growth. There is, therefore, some four hundred acres of this old wood.

There is a very little beech and hemlock and yellow birch in this wood. Many large black birches at the

---

Vol. XIV

northwest end. Chestnuts at the northwest and southeast ends.

The bark of the oaks is very frequently gnawed near the base by a squirrel or other animal.

Guggins Brook unites with Heather Meadow Brook, and then with Fort Pond Brook just this side of West Acton, and thus the water of this old oak wood comes into the Assabet and flows by our North Bridge. The seeds of whatever trees water will transport, provided they grow there, may thus be planted along our river.

I crossed the brook in the midst of the wood where there was no path, but four or five large stones had evidently been placed by man at convenient intervals for stepping-stones, and possibly this was an old Indian trail.

You occasionally see a massive old oak prostrate and decaying, rapidly sinking into the earth, and its place is evidently supplied by a pine rather than an oak.

There is now remarkably little life to be seen there. In my two walks I saw only one squirrel and a chickadee. Not a hawk or a jay. Yet at the base of very many oaks were acorn-shells left by the squirrels. In a perfectly round hole made by a woodpecker in a small dead oak five feet from the ground, were three good white oak acorns placed.

In the midst of the wood, west of the brook, is a natural meadow, — *i. e.* in a natural state, — a narrow strip without trees, yet not very wet. Evidently swamp white oaks and maples might grow there. The greater part of this wood is strewn with large rocks, more or less flat or table-like, very handsomely clothed with moss

and polypody. The surface of the ground is finely diversified, there being hills, dells, moraines, meadows, swamps, and a fine brook in the midst of all. Some parts are very thickly strewn with rocks (as at the northwest), others quite free from them. Nowhere any monotony.

It is very pleasant, as you walk in the shade below, to see the cheerful sunlight reflected from the maze of oak boughs above. They would be a fine sight after one of those sticking snows in the winter.

On the north end, also, the first evidence we had that we were coming out of the wood — approaching its border — was the crowing of a cock.

Nov. 17. P. M. — To Blood's woods.

Sawed off a branch of creeping juniper two inches [in] diameter with fifteen rings.

On one square of nine rods in Blood's wood, which seemed more dense than the average, are thirteen sizable trees. This would give about two hundred and thirty to an acre, but probably there are not more than one hundred and eighty to an acre, take the wood through. This is but little more than one to a square rod. Yet this is a quite dense wood. That very solid white oak stump recently sawed in this wood was evidently a seedling, the growth was so extremely slow at first. If I found the case to be the same with the other oaks here, I should feel sure that these were all seedlings and therefore had been preceded by pines or at least some dense evergreens, or possibly birches. When I find a dense oak wood, whether sprouts or edlings, I affirm that evergreens once stood [there] nd, if man does not prevent, will grow again. This I ust believe until I find a dense oak wood planted nder itself or in open land.

Minot Pratt's elm is sixteen and a quarter feet [in] rcumference at three feet.

These tawny-white oaks are thus by their color and aracter the lions among trees, or rather, not to com- are them with a foreign animal, they are the cougars r panthers — the American lions — among the trees, r nearly such is that of the cougar which walks eneath and amid or springs upon them. There is ainly this harmony between the color of our chief wild east of the cat kind and our chief tree.

How they do things in West Acton. As we were alking through West Acton the other afternoon, a w rods only west of the centre, on the main road, the arvard turnpike, we saw a rock larger than a man uld lift, lying in the road, exactly in the wheel-track, nd were puzzled to tell how it came there, but sup- osed it had slipped off a drag, — yet we noticed that it as peculiarly black. Returning the same way in the vilight, when we had got within four or five rods of this ery spot, looking up, we saw a man in the field, three r four rods on one side of that spot, running off as ust as he could. By the time he had got out of sight ver the hill it occurred to us that he was blasting rocks nd had just touched one off; so, at the eleventh hour, e turned about and ran the other way, and when we ad gone a few rods, off went two blasts, but fortunately one of the rocks struck us. Some time after we had

---

passed we saw the men returning. They looked out for themselves, but for nobody else. This is the way they do things in West Acton. We now understood that the big stone was blackened by powder.

Silas Hosmer tells me how —— and —— sold the Heywood lot between the railroad and Fair Haven. They lotted it off in this wise: i. e. in triangles, and, carry- ing plenty of liquor, they first treated all round, and then proceeded to sell at auction, but the purchasers, excited with liquor, were not aware when the stakes were pointed out that the lots were not as broad in the rear as in front, and the wood standing cost them as much as it should have done delivered at the door.

I frequently see the heads of teasel, called fuller's thistle, floating on our river, having come from factories above, and thus the factories which use it may distribute its seeds by means of the streams which turn their machinery, from one to another. The one who first cultivated the teasel extensively in this town is said to have obtained the seed when it was not to be pur- chased — the culture being monopolized — by sweep- ing a wagon which he had loaned to a teasel-raiser.

The growth of very old trees, as appears by calculating the bulk of wood formed, is feebler at last than when in middle age, or say in pitch pine at one hundred and sixty than at forty or fifty, especially when you consider the increased number of leaves, and this, together with the fact that old stumps send up no shoots, shows that trees are not indefinitely long-lived.

I have a section of a chestnut sprout — and not at

Vol. XIV

---

l a rank one — which has 6 rings in the first inch, or rings in five eighths of an inch, but a section of a estnut seedling has 10 rings in five eighths of an inch.

A section of a white oak sprout, far from rank, has rings in first five eighths of an inch; of a seedling itto, 16 or 17 in first five eighths of an inch; of a seed- ng ditto, 8 — in first five eighths of an inch; of a very ow-grown sprout, 6 — in first five eighths of an inch. r in the white oaks the proportion is as five to twelve.

The first seedling oak has the rough and tawny light- rown bark of an old tree, while the first sprout is quite nooth-barked.

A seedling white birch has 10 rings in first seven ghths of an inch.

A sprout white birch has 5 rings in first seven eighths f an inch. The first has the white bark of an old tree; e second, a smooth and reddish bark.

When a stump is sound to the pith I can commonly ll whether it was a seedling or a sprout by the rapidity f the growth at first. A seedling, it is true, may have ied down many times till it is fifteen or twenty years ld, and so at last send up a more vigorous shoot than at rst, but generally the difference is very marked.

Nov. 19. P. M. — To Mt. Misery.

Saw off a hickory stump which is scarcely six and a alf inches in diameter and has nearly a hundred rings. t is the one of November 13th, and then called about 15 (??). Counting it now in the evening, I make 92.) t is surprising how quickly this wood decays. This ee was cut last winter, and then evidently was per-

---

fectly sound, as appears from the surface, but on sawing it off three inches lower I find that it is rotted entirely through and is soft and no part sound, so that I cannot count it on the new face. In less than one year this stump is worthless, even for fuel!

I look again at the old oak stumps on this hill. One evidently, i. e. *surely*, a sprout (the older stump beside it), a white oak, grew nearly $1\frac{5}{8}$ inches in the first twelve years; another oak, a sprout (with older stump), $1\frac{5}{8}$ inches in the first eleven or twelve years; a white oak (without an older stump), $1\frac{5}{8}$ inches in the first twelve years; probably the last a sprout also, for, as seen on last page, a white oak seedling grows only $\frac{5}{8}$ of an inch in twelve years. There was also a hickory sprout stump of the same age with the others, though of course the old stump was long since gone. It was plainly seen to be a sprout by the very rapid growth at first and the concave form of one side.

My rule of small white pines under pitch pines is so true of E. Hoar's land that he very easily got a hundred white pines there to set by his house.

Mr. Bradshaw says that he got a little auk in Wayland last week, and heard of two more, one in Weston and the other in Natick. Thinks they came with the storm of the 10th and 11th.

He tells me of a small oak wood of old trees called More's, half a mile east of Wayland, behind the grave- yard.

Nov. 20. P. M. — To R. W. E.'s hill.

I see a pitch pine several years old on the west slope

of the railroad embankment, sixty rods by pacing from the nearest pitch pine, which was in Trillium Wood. I have seen several such. This tree would soon sow itself in our yards if they were neglected.

In the Moore and Hosmer lot which I surveyed in '49–'50, beyond Heywood meadow, a white oak stump ten inches [in] diameter with seventy rings (cut in winter of '49–'50), evidently a sprout, though the old stump appears to have been entirely overgrown and so concealed.

I see, on the southwest or railroad side, near top, of Emerson's hill, a great many oak stumps (which were sprouts) with the older stump still very plain.

One (probably black oak) with 35 rings cut some 2 years = 37.
2d, " " " " " " " " " " = 37.
3d, " " " " " " " " " " = 37.

(This last *old* stump being small and almost overgrown between the stumps of the sprouts and seen — a sliver of it — in a hole between them.) Also lower down-hill, toward railroad, old chestnut stumps with the stumps of sprouts of R. W. E.'s cutting twenty-five to thirty and odd years old, cut some dozen years ago; stumps, then, some forty years old.

Also, on the pond end of the hilltop, amid the piles of stones, where I suppose was a pasture once, I see oak stumps cut just thirty-eight years ago beside the stumps of their sprouts cut last winter, and here are many sprouts coming up the second time; but on the other end [of] the hill I notice no sprouts the second time. There were many oaks where these piles of stone are, some seventy or eighty years ago, then, at least, and I

think that if this ever was a pasture they must hav been preceded by pines. These oak stumps, cut abou thirty-eight years ago, are quite fresh, especially th white oak on the top of this rocky hill. So at M Misery. Such is evidently a favorable locality for thei preservation. Indeed, it is very common to see oa stumps forty years old in such places. They are th rule here.

Decidedly finger-cold to-night.

Nov. 21. If you cut a dense mixed wood of pine an oak in which no little pines have sown themselves, it evident that a wood exclusively of oak sprouts ma succeed, as I see is the case with part of R. W. E.'s hil side toward the pond.

I see a little pitch pine which bore a cone at twent two inches from the ground when it was only seven eight years old. It is now a dozen years old and ha borne two more since, and scattered the seed.

P. M. — To Fair Haven Hill.

On what was Stow's lot, southwest the Boilin Spring, adjacent to Wheeler's field, I count the ring of four oak stumps which are from eighteen to twent two inches in diameter. They are all about 120, an the oaks are evidently all from the seed. This wa both a pine and oak wood, and I suspect that abou one hundred and twenty years [ago] pines were c or burned or blown down or decayed there and thes oaks succeeded. These stumps are now in the ve best condition for counting, having been cut nine ten years ago. But not so with the pitch pine stump

(one is twenty-three inches in diameter) cut about a year later on what was R. Brown's, higher up. Their sap and more is covered with green and red cockspur lichens so thickly you cannot see the rings. On this lot (now open Wheeler lot) are not only these old pitch pine stumps (a few), but the stumps of oak sprouts forty-four years old, with the older stumps by their side, or half overgrown, yet quite plain, which last there were cut (44 + 9 =) 53 years ago. No sprouts from them.

In early times probably less wood was cut at once; commonly only the winter's wood for the owners' use. This Brown lot was variously treated apparently.

See young beeches near the upper edge of Stow's, about midway on Wheeler, near where some stones have been hauled into Stow's from Wheeler's land.

Another finger-cold evening, which I improve in pulling my turnips — the usual amusement of such weather — before they shall be frozen in. It is worth the while to see how green and lusty they are yet, still adding to their stock of nutriment for another year; and between the green and also withering leaves it does me good to see their great crimson round or scalloped tops, sometimes quite above ground, they are so bold. They remind you of rosy cheeks in cool weather, and indeed there is a relationship. All kinds of harvestry, even pulling turnips when the first cold weather numbs your fingers, are interesting, if you have been the sower, and have not sown too many.

Got a section to-day of a white cedar railroad sleeper which I am told came from the eastward and was

brought up from Charlestown. First count gives 25 rings; second, on opposite side, where the centre i less plain, 246 rings; average, 250. Its diameter i $16\frac{1}{4}$ inches, or nearly 31 rings to an inch. This is th oldest, as well as slowest-growing, tree that I hav counted the rings of. I see other sleepers nearly a old. Some smaller, or say $10\frac{1}{2}$ inches in diameter, ha 125 rings in the first three inches and then grew muc faster; as if they were at first part of a very dens thicket and grew very slowly, but afterward, prevailin over the rest, grew faster. This sleeper had, of course been cut a year at least. It may not have been the but end of the log, or at any rate it must have been severa years old before it reached the height at which it wa cut, so that it must have begun to exist before the set tlement of Jamestown. It was a flourishing youn cedar of at least some fifteen summers when the Pil grims came over. Thus the cars on our railroad, an all their passengers, roll over the trunks of trees *sleep ing* beneath them which were planted years before th first white man settled in New England.

Nov. 22. P. M. — To northwest part of Sudbury.

The *Linaria Canadensis* is still freshly blooming It is the freshest flower I notice now.

Considerable ice, lasting all day, on the river meadow and cold pools.

I measure the stump of that white pine which I use to see on the Marlborough road. It is thirty inches i diameter and has 85 rings.

There are two small clumps of laurel close to th

left side this road, by the woods, just this side the Sudbury line, going to Maynard's.

Here is a dense oak wood. I see many little white pines sprung up along its edge in the road, but scarcely one within the wood. They, too, want light and air, though not so much as the pitch pine.

All the sound white oak acorns that I see now have sprouted, and many have sent a root down into the earth. This is often four inches long. But I see no black nor scarlet nor red oak acorns sprouted, though I find sound ones. The white are evidently very much more sensitive and tender than they.

This is a very beautiful November day, — a cool but clear, crystalline air, through which even the white pines with their silvery sheen are an affecting sight. It is a day to behold and to ramble over the hard (stiffening) and withered surface of the tawny earth. Every plant's down glitters with a silvery light along the Marlborough road, — the sweet-fern, the lespedeza, and bare blueberry twigs, to say nothing of the weather-worn tufts of *Andropogon scoparius*. A thousand bare twigs gleam like cobwebs in the sun. I rejoice in the bare, bleak, hard, and barren-looking surface of the tawny pastures, the firm outline of the hills, so convenient to walk over, and the air so bracing and wholesome. Though you are finger-cold toward night, and you cast a stone on to your first ice, and see the unmelted crystals under every bank, it is glorious November weather, and only November fruits are out. On some hickories you see a thousand black nuts against the sky.

There is quite a white cedar swamp behind the old tavern south of Maynard's.

You walk fast and far, and every apple left out is grateful to your invigorated taste. You enjoy not only the bracing coolness, but all the heat and sunlight that there is, reflected back to you from the earth. The sandy road itself, lit by the November sun, is beautiful. Shrub oaks and young oaks generally, and hazel bushes and other hardy shrubs, now more or less bare, are your companions, as if it were an iron age, yet in simplicity, innocence, and strength a golden one.

(Day before yesterday the rustling of the withered oak leaves in the wind reminded me of the similar sound produced by snow falling on them.)

It is glorious to consider how independent man is of all enervating luxuries; and the poorer he is in respect to them, the richer he is. Summer is gone with all its infinite wealth, and still nature is genial to man. Though he no longer bathes in the stream, or reclines on the bank, or plucks berries on the hills, still he beholds the same inaccessible beauty around him. What though he has no juice of the grape stored up for him in cellars; the air itself is wine of an older vintage, and far more sanely exhilarating, than any cellar affords. It is ever some gouty senior and not a blithe child that drinks, or cares for, that so famous wine.

Though so many phenomena which we lately admired have now vanished, others are more remarkable and interesting than before. The smokes from distant chimneys, not only greater because more fire is required, but more distinct in the cooler atmosphere, are a very pleasing

sight, and conduct our thoughts quickly to the roof and hearth and family beneath, revealing the homes of men.

Maynard's yard and frontage, and all his barns and fences, are singularly neat and substantial, and the highroad is in effect converted into a private way through his grounds. It suggests unspeakable peace and happiness. Yet, strange to tell, I noticed that he had a tiger instead of a cock for a vane on his barn, and he himself looked overworked. He had allowed the surviving forest trees to grow into ancestral trees about his premises, and so attach themselves to him as if he had planted them. The dusty highway was so subdued that it seemed as if it were lost there. He had all but stretched a bar across it. Each traveller must have felt some misgivings, as if he were trespassing.

However, the farmer's life expresses only such content as an ox in his yard chewing the cud.

What though your hands are numb with cold, your sense of enjoyment is not benumbed. You cannot now find an apple but it is sweet to taste.

Simply to see to a distant horizon through a clear air, — the fine outline of a distant hill or a blue mountain-top through some new vista, — this is wealth enough for one afternoon.

We journeyed into the foreign land of Sudbury to see how the Sudbury men — the Hayneses, and the Puffers, and the Brighams — live. We traversed their pastures and their wood-lots, and were home again at night.

Nov. 23. George Minott tells me that sixty years ago wood was only two or three dollars a cord here — and

some of that hickory. Remembers when Peter Wheeler, sixty or more years ago, cut off all at once over a hundred acres of wood stretching from Flint's Pond to Goose Pond, — since cut again in part by Britton, and owned now partly by the Stows.

Most of us are still related to our native fields as the navigator to undiscovered islands in the sea. We can any autumn discover a new fruit there which will surprise us by its beauty or sweetness. So long as I saw one or two kinds of berries in my walks whose names I did not know, the proportion of the unknown seemed indefinitely if not infinitely great.

Famous fruits imported from the tropics and sold in our markets — as oranges, lemons, pineapples, and bananas — do not concern me so much as many an unnoticed wild berry whose beauty annually lends a new charm to some wild walk, or which I have found to be palatable to an outdoor taste.

The tropical fruits are for those who dwell within the tropics; their fairest and sweetest parts cannot be exported nor imported. Brought here, they chiefly concern those whose walks are through the market-place. It is not the orange of Cuba, but the checkerberry of the neighboring pasture, that most delights the eye and the palate of the New England child. What if the Concord Social Club, instead of eating oranges from Havana, should spend an hour in admiring the beauty of some wild berry from their own fields which they never attended to before? It is not the foreignness or size or nutritive qualities of a fruit that determine its absolute value.

It is not those far-fetched fruits which the speculator imports that concerns us chiefly, but rather those which you have fetched yourself in your basket from some far hill or swamp, journeying all the long afternoon in the hold of a basket, consigned to your friends at home, the first of the season.

We cultivate imported shrubs in our front yards for the beauty of their berries, when yet more beautiful berries grow unregarded by us in the surrounding fields.

As some beautiful or palatable fruit is perhaps the noblest gift of nature to man, so is a fruit with which a man has in some measure identified himself by cultivating or collecting it one of the most suitable presents to a friend. It was some compensation for Commodore Porter, who may have introduced some cannon-balls and bombshells into ports where they were not wanted, to have introduced the Valparaiso squash into the United States. I think that this eclipses his military glory.

As I sail the unexplored sea of Concord, many a dell and swamp and wooded hill is my Ceram and Amboyna.

At first, perchance, there would be an abundant crop of rank garden weeds and grasses in the cultivated land, — and rankest of all in the cellar-holes, — and of pinweed, hardhack, sumach, blackberry, thimble-berry, raspberry, etc., in the fields and pastures. Elm, ash, maples, etc., would grow vigorously along old garden limits and main streets. Garden weeds and grasses would soon disappear. Huckleberry and blueberry bushes, lambkill, hazel, sweet-fern, barberry, elder, also shad-bush, choke-berry, andromeda, and thorns,

Vol. XIV

etc., would rapidly prevail in the deserted pastures. At the same time the wild cherries, birch, poplar, willows, checkerberry would reëstablish themselves. Finally the pines, hemlock, spruce, larch, shrub oak, oaks, chestnut, beech, and walnuts would occupy the site of Concord once more. The apple and perhaps all exotic trees and shrubs and a great part of the indigenous ones named above would have disappeared, and the laurel and yew would to some extent be an underwood here, and perchance the red man once more thread his way through the mossy, swamp-like, primitive wood.

Nov. 24. P. M. — To Easterbrooks's.

Under the two white oaks by the second wall southeast of my house, on the east side the wall, I am surprised to find a great many sound acorns still, though every one is sprouted, — frequently more than a dozen on the short sward within a square foot, each with its radicle two inches long penetrated into the earth. But many have had their radicle broken or eaten off, and many have it now dead and withered. So far as my observation goes there, by far the greatest number of white oak acorns were destroyed by decaying (whether in consequence of frost or wet), both before and soon after falling. Not nearly so many have been carried off by squirrels and birds or consumed by grubs, though the number of acorns of all kinds lying under the trees is now comparatively small to what it was early in October.

It is true these two trees are exceptions and I do not find sound ones nearly as numerous under others.

Nevertheless, the sound white oak acorns are not so *generally* and *entirely* picked up as I supposed. However, there are a great many more shells or cups than acorns under the trees; even under these two trees, I think, there are not more than a third as many of any kind — sound or hollow — as there were, and generally those that remain are a very small fraction of what there were. It will be worth the while to see how many of these sprouted acorns are left and are sound in the spring. It is remarkable that all sound white oak acorns (and many which are not now sound) are sprouted, and that I have noticed no other kind sprouted, — though I have not seen the chestnut oak and little chinquapin at all. It remains to be seen how many of the above will be picked up by squirrels, etc., or destroyed by frost and grubs in the winter.

The first spitting of snow — a flurry or squall — from out a gray or slate-colored cloud that came up from the west. This consisted almost entirely of pellets an eighth of an inch or less in diameter. These drove along almost horizontally, or curving upward like the outline of a breaker, before the strong and chilling wind. The plowed fields were for a short time whitened with them. The green moss about the bases of trees was very prettily spotted white with them, and also the large beds of cladonia in the pastures. They come to contrast with the red cockspur lichens on the stumps, which you had not noticed before. Striking against the trunks of the trees on the west side they fell and accumulated in a white line at the base. Though a slight touch, this was the first wintry scene of the season. The air

was so filled with these snow pellets that we could not see a hill half a mile off for an hour. The hands seek the warmth of the pockets, and fingers are so benumbed that you cannot open your jack-knife. The rabbits in the swamps enjoy it, as well as you. Methinks the winter gives them more liberty, like a night. I see where a boy has set a box trap and baited it with half an apple, and, a mile off, come across a snare set for a rabbit or partridge in a cow-path in a pitch pine wood near where the rabbits have nibbled the apples which strew the wet ground. How pitiable that the most that many see of a rabbit should be the snare that some boy has set for one!

The bitter-sweet of a white oak acorn which you nibble in a bleak November walk over the tawny earth is more to me than a slice of imported pineapple. We do not think much of table-fruits. They are especially for aldermen and epicures. They do not feed the imagination. That would starve on them. These wild fruits, whether eaten or not, are a dessert for the imagination. The south may keep her pineapples, and we will be content with our strawberries.

Nov. 25. I count the rings in a spruce plank from the railroad bridge, which extend five and a half inches from the centre of the tree, and make them 146, — $\frac{1}{26}$ + to a ring. This is slower growth than I find in a black spruce to-day at —

Ministerial Swamp, P. M. — It is $10\frac{1}{2}$ feet high, $2\frac{1}{2}$ inches [in] diameter just above ground, and has 21 rings, $\frac{1}{17}$ inch to a ring. A larch near by is 21 feet high, $2\frac{13}{16}$ inches [in] diameter, and has 20 rings, which makes $\frac{1}{14}+$ to a ring. The larch has made nearly twice as much wood as the spruce in the same time.

The cones of the spruce which I see are still closed. A few sugar maple seeds still hang on.

Last night and to-day are very cold and blustering. Winter weather has come suddenly this year. The house was shaken by wind last night, and there was a general deficiency of bedclothes. This morning some windows were as handsomely covered with frost as ever in winter. I wear mittens or gloves and my greatcoat. There is much ice on the meadows now, the broken edges shining in the sun. Now for the phenomena of winter, — the red buds of the high blueberry and the purple berries of the smilax.

As I go up the meadow-side toward Clamshell, I see a very great collection of crows far and wide on the meadows, evidently gathered by this cold and blustering weather. Probably the moist meadows where they feed are frozen up against them. They flit before me in countless numbers, flying very low on account of the strong northwest wind that comes over the hill, and a cold gleam is reflected from the back and wings of each, as from a weather-stained shingle. Some perch within three or four rods of me, and seem weary. I see where they have been pecking the apples by the meadow-side. An immense cohort of cawing crows which sudden winter has driven near to the habitations of man. When I return after sunset I see them collecting and hovering over and settling in the dense pine woods west of E. Wood's, as if about to roost there. Yesterday I

saw one flying over the house, its wings so curved by the wind that I thought it a black hawk.

How is any scientific discovery made? Why, the discoverer takes it into his head first. He must all but see it.

I see several little white pines in Hosmer's meadow just beyond Lupine Hill, which must have sprung from seed which came some fifty rods, — probably blown so far in the fall. There are also a few in the road beyond Dennis's, which probably were blown from his swamp wood. So that there is nothing to prevent their springing up all over the village in a very few years — but our own plows and spades. They have also come up quite numerously in the young woodland north of J. P. B.'s Cold Pool (probably blown from the wood south of the pond), though they are evidently half a dozen years younger than the oaks there. I look at this large white pine wood by the pool to see if little ones come up under it. What was recently pasture comes up within a rod of this high wood on the north side, and, though the fence is gone, the different condition and history of the ground is very apparent by the different aspect of the little pines. There the old white pines are dense, and there are no little ones under them, but only a rod north they are very abundant, forming a dense thicket only two or three feet high bounded by a straight line on the south (or east and west), where the edge of the open land was within a rod of the great pines. Here they sprang up abundantly in the open land close by, but not at all under the pines. Yet within the great wood, wherever it is more open from any cause, I see a great many little pines springing up. Though they are thin and

feeble comparatively, yet most of them will evidently come to be trees. White pines will spring up in the more open parts of a white pine wood, even under pines, though they are thin and feeble just in proportion to the density of the larger pines, and, where the large trees are quite dense, they will not spring up at all.

How commonly you see pitch pines, white pines, and birches filling up a pasture, and, when they are a dozen or fifteen years old, shrub and other oaks beginning to show themselves, inclosing apple trees and walls and fences gradually and so changing the whole aspect of the region. These trees do not cover the whole surface equally at present, but are grouped very agreeably after natural laws which they obey. You remember, perhaps, that fifteen years ago there was not a single tree in this pasture, — not a germinating seed of one, — and now it is a pretty dense forest ten feet high. I confess that I love to be convinced of this inextinguishable vitality in Nature. I would rather that my body should be buried in a soil thus wide-awake than in a mere inert and dead earth. The cow-paths, the hollows where I slid in the winter, the rocks, are fast being enveloped and becoming rabbit-walks and hollows and rocks in the woods.

How often you make a man richer in spirit in proportion as you rob him of earthly luxuries and comforts!

I see much oak wood cut at thirty years of age, — sprout wood.

Many stumps which have only twenty-five or thirty rings send up no shoots, because they are the sprouts

from old stumps, which you may still see by their sides, and so are really old trees and exhausted. The chopper should foresee this when he cuts down a wood.

The bass by Dugan's cut a year ago. It is hard to count, so indistinct its rings, but I make 46 to 50 in a diameter of some twenty inches. The sprouts are quite peculiar, so light an ash-color with red tips and large blunt red buds.

The old pitch pines (vide back two or three weeks) one hundred and sixty years old, that stood on the south side of the Tommy Wheeler hollow, were twenty-three in number on a space about twelve rods by three (or thirty-six rods), with half a dozen white pines and as many oaks, the last two say twenty to fifty years younger than the pitch pines. Probably some of the pitch pines have died and left no trees, so that it may originally have been a pretty dense grove of pitch pines. There were as many more pitch pines (not to mention the oaks and white pines) on the other side of the hollow. These were on a slope toward the north. Now, four years after they were cut, this hillside is covered with hazel bushes, huckleberries, young oaks, red maples, Viburnum nudum, and a few little white pines, but the hollow below them has little beside grass (fine sedge) in it. It will be long before anything catches there. It is remarkable that no pitch pines grew there before, nor oaks, and very few white pines, which were the only trees there. Some pitch pines have shed their seeds.

Nov. 26. P. M. — To E. Hubbard's Wood.
I see in the open field east of Trillium Wood a few

pitch pines springing up, from seeds blown from the wood a dozen or fifteen rods off. Here is one just noticeable on the sod — though by most it would be mistaken for a single sprig of moss — which came from the seed this year. It is, as it were, a little green star with many rays, half an inch in diameter, lifted an inch and a half above the ground on a slender stem. What a feeble beginning for so long-lived a tree! By the next fall it will be a star of greater magnitude, and in a few years, if not disturbed, these seedlings will alter the face of nature here. How significant, how ominous, the presence of these green moss-like stars is to the grass, heralding its doom! Thus from pasture this portion of the earth's surface becomes forest. These which are now mistaken for mosses in the grass may become lofty trees which will endure two hundred years, under which no vestige of this grass will be left.

In Hubbard's Wood at north end I measure the stump of either a red or black oak: 21 inches [in] diameter and 141 rings.

I examine quite a number of oak stumps thereabouts and find them all seedlings. This, of course, must be the case with old forests generally, for in the beginning the trees were not cut.

A red oak about in middle of the wood 6½ feet circumference at 3 ft.
A canoe birch,   45 inches   "   " " "
Another "   "   45½ "   "   " " "
A white oak on the east
   side rather toward south,   7 feet   "   " " "

Some of the white oaks have a very loose scaly bark, commencing half a dozen feet from the ground. I see

pitch pine bark four to five inches thick at the ground. There are in this wood many little groves of white pines two to four feet high, quite dense and green, but these are in more open spaces, and are vigorous just in proportion to the openness. There are also seedling oaks and chestnuts ten to thirty years old, yet not nearly so numerous as the pines. The large wood is mixed oak and pine, — more oak at the north and more pine, especially pitch pine, at the south. The prospect is that in course of time the white pines will very greatly prevail over all other trees here. This is also the case with Inches', Blood's, and Wetherbee's woods.

If I am not mistaken, an evidence of more openness where the little pines are is to be found in the greater prevalence of pyrola and lycopodiums there. There are even some healthy *Juniperus repens* in the midst of these woods. Though the pitch pines are the prevailing trees at the south end, I see no young pitch pines under them.

Perhaps this is the way that a natural succession takes place. Perhaps oak seedlings do not so readily spring up and thrive within a mixed white pine and oak wood as pines do, — in the more open parts, — and thus, as the oaks decay, they are replaced by pines rather than by oaks.

But where did the pitch pines stand originally? Who cleared the land for its seedlings to spring up in? It is commonly referred to very poor and sandy land, yet I find it growing on the best land also. The expression "a pitch pine plain" is but another name for a poor and sandy level. It grows both on the sand and [in] the

swamp, and the fact that it grows on the sand chiefly is not so much evidence that it prefers it as that other trees have excluded it from better soil. If you cut down the pines on the pitch pine plain, oaks will come up there too. Who knows but the fires or clearings of the Indians may have to do with the presence of these trees there? They regularly cleared extensive tracts for cultivation, and these were always level tracts where the soil was light — such as they could turn over with their rude hoes. Such was the land which they are known to have cultivated extensively in this town, as the Great Fields and the rear of Mr. Dennis's, — sandy plains. It is in such places chiefly that you find their relics in any part of the county. They did not cultivate such soil as our maple swamps occupy, or such a succession of hills and dales as this oak wood covers. Other trees will grow where the pitch pine does, but the former will maintain its ground there the best. I know of no tree so likely to spread rapidly over such areas when abandoned by the aborigines as the pitch pines — and next birches and white pines.

While I am walking in the oak wood or counting the rings of a stump, I hear the faint note of a nuthatch like the creak of a limb, and detect [it] on the trunk of an oak much nearer than I suspected, and its mate or companion not far off. This is a constant phenomenon of the late fall or early winter; for we do not hear them in summer that I remember.[1] I heard one not long since in the street.

I see one of those common birch fungi on the side of

[1] In '61 hear one occasionally a month earlier than this.

a birch stake which has been used to bound a lot sold at auction, three feet or more from the ground, and its face is toward the earth as usual, though the birch is bottom up.

I saw that nuthatch to-day pick out from a crevice in the bark of an oak trunk, where it was perpendicular, something white once or twice and pretty large. May it not have been the meat of an acorn? Yet commonly they are steadily hopping about the trunks in search of insect food. Possibly some of those acorn-shells I see about the base of trees may have been dropped from the crevices in the bark above by birds — nuthatch or jay — as well as left by squirrels.

Mother says that Lidy Bay, an Indian woman (so considered), used to live in the house beyond Cæsar's and made baskets, which she brought to town to sell, with a ribbon about her hat. She had a husband.

The value of these wild fruits is not in the mere possession or eating of them, but in the sight or enjoyment of them. The very derivation of the word "fruit" would suggest this. It is from the Latin *fructus*, meaning that which is *used* or *enjoyed*. If it were not so, then going a-berrying and going to market would be nearly synonymous expressions. Of course it is the spirit in which you do a thing which makes it interesting, whether it is sweeping a room or pulling turnips. Peaches are unquestionably a very beautiful and palatable fruit, but the gathering of them for the market is not nearly so interesting as the gathering of huckleberries for your own use.

A man fits out a ship at a great expense and sends it to the West Indies with a crew of men and boys, and after six months or a year it comes back with a load of pineapples. Now, if no more gets accomplished than the speculator commonly aims at, — if it simply turns out what is called a successful venture, — I am less interested in this expedition than in some child's first excursion a-huckleberrying, in which it is introduced into a new world, experiences a new development, though it brings home only a gill of huckleberries in its basket. I know that the newspapers and the politicians declare otherwise, but they do not alter the fact. Then, I think that the fruit of the latter expedition was finer than that of the former. It was a more fruitful expedition. The value of any experience is measured, of course, not by the amount of money, but the amount of development we get out of it. If a New England boy's dealings with oranges and pineapples have had more to do with his development than picking huckleberries or pulling turnips have, then he rightly and naturally thinks more of the former; otherwise not.

Do not think that the fruits of New England are mean and insignificant, while those of some foreign land are noble and memorable. Our own, whatever they may be, are far more important to us than any others can be. They educate us, and fit us to live in New England. Better for us is the wild strawberry than the pineapple, the wild apple than the orange, the hazelnut or pignut than the cocoanut or almond, and not on account of their flavor merely, but the part they play in our education.

In the Massachusetts Historical Collections, First Series, volume x, Rev. John Gardner of Stow furnishes

a brief historical notice of that town in a letter dated 1767. He says, "The Indian names of this place were Pompociticut and Shabbukin, from two notable hills."

I anticipated the other day that if anybody should write the history of Boxboro, once a part of Stow, he would be pretty sure to omit to notice the most interesting thing in it — its forest — and lay all the stress on the history of its parish; and I find that I had conjectured rightly, for Mr. Gardner, after telling us who was his predecessor in the ministry and where he himself was settled, goes on to say: "As for any remarkables, I am of the mind there have been the fewest of any town of our standing in the Province. . . . I can't call to mind above one thing worthy of publick notice, and that is the grave of Mr. John Green," who, it appears, "was made . . . clerk of the exchequer" by Cromwell. "Whether he was excluded the Act of Oblivion or not I cannot tell," says Mr. Gardner. At any rate he tells us that he returned to New England, "lived and died, and lies buried in this place." I can assure Mr. Gardner that he was not excluded from the act of oblivion.

However, Boxboro was less peculiar for its woods a hundred years ago.

I have been surprised when a young man who had undertaken to write the history of a country town, — his native place, — the very name of which suggested a hundred things to me, referred to it, as the crowning fact of his story, that that town was the residence of General So-and-so and the family mansion was still standing.

Nov. 28. P. M. — To Annursnack.

Looking from the hilltop, I should say that there was more oak woodland than pine to be seen, especially in the north and northeast, but it is somewhat difficult to distinguish all in the gleaming sunlight of mid-afternoon. Most of the oak, however, is quite young. As for pines, I cannot say surely which kind is most prevalent, not being certain about the most distant woods. The white pine is much the most dispersed, and grows oftener in low ground than the pitch pine does. It oftenest forms mixed woods with oak, etc., growing in straight or meandering lines, occasionally swelling into a dense grove. The pitch pines commonly occupy a dry soil — a plain or brow of a hill, often the site of an old grain-field or pasture — and are much the most seclusive, for, being a new wood, oaks, etc., have had no opportunity to grow up there, if they could. I look down now on the top of a pitch pine wood southwest of Brooks's Pigeon-place, and its top, so nearly level, has a peculiarly rich and crispy look in the sun. Its limbs are short and its plumes stout as compared with the white pine and are of a yellowish green.

There are many handsome young walnuts ten or twelve feet high scattered over the southeast side of Annursnack, or above the orchard. How came they there? Were they planted before a wood was cut? It is remarkable how this tree loves a hillside.

Behind G. M. Barrett's barn a scarlet oak stump 18½ inches [in] diameter and about 94 rings, which has sent up a sprout two or three years since. On the plain just north of the east end of G. M. B.'s oaks,

many oaks were sawed off about a year ago. Those I look at are seedlings and very sound and rings very distinct and handsome. Generally no sprouts from them, though one white oak sprout had been killed by frost. One white oak, 17 inches [in] diameter, has 100 rings. A second,   16½ "   "   "   also 100 "

The last has two centres which coalesced at the thirtieth ring, which went round them both including old bark between them. This was an instance of natural grafting.

Many seem to be so constituted that they can respect only somebody who is dead or something which is distant.

The less you get, the happier and the richer you are. The rich man's son gets cocoanuts, and the poor man's, pignuts; but the worst of it is that the former never goes a-cocoanutting, and so he never gets the cream of the cocoanut as the latter does the cream of the pignut.

That on which commerce seizes is always the very coarsest part of a fruit, — the mere husk and rind, in fact, — for her hands are very clumsy. This is what fills the holds of ships, is exported and imported, pays duties, and is finally sold at the shops.

It is a grand fact that you cannot make the finer fruits or parts of fruits matter of commerce. You may buy a servant or slave, in short, but you cannot buy a friend. You can't buy the finer part of any fruit — *i. e.* the highest use and enjoyment of it. You cannot buy the pleasure which it yields to him who truly plucks it; you can't buy a good appetite even.

What are all the oranges imported into England to the hips and haws in her hedges? She could easily spare the one, but not the others. Ask Wordsworth, or any of her poets, which is the most to him.

The mass of men are very easily imposed on. They have their runways in which they always travel, and are sure to fall into any pit or box trap set therein. Whatever a great many grown-up boys are seriously engaged in is considered great and good, and, as such, is sure of the recognition of the churchman and statesman. What, for instance, are the blue juniper berries in the pasture, which the cowboy remembers so far as they are beautiful merely, to church or state? Mere trifles which deserve and get no protection. As an object of beauty, though significant to all who really live in the country, they do not receive the protection of any community. Anybody may grub up all that exist. But as an article of commerce they command the attention of the civilized world. I read that "several hundred tons of them are imported annually from the continent" into England to flavor g.n with; "but even this quantity," says my author, "is quite insufficient to meet the enormous consumption of the fiery liquid, and the deficiency is made up by spirits of turpentine." Go to the English Government, which, of course, is representative of the people, and ask, What is the use of juniper berries? The answer is, To flavor gin with. This is the gross abuse of juniper berries, with which an enlightened Government — if ever there shall be one — will have nothing to do.

Let us make distinctions, call things by the right names.

Vol. XIV

Nov. 29. Get up my boat, 7 A. M. Thin ice of the night is floating down the river. I hear that some boys went on to Goose Pond on the 26th and skated. It must have been thin.

P. M. — To Fair Haven Hill.

The pitch pine twigs have been so generally cut off by the squirrels for the sake of the cones that I easily detect the fertile trees, when going through a pitch pine wood, by seeing the green twigs strewn on the ground beneath. But few of the trees bear, and these are the ones.

The Bear Garden pitch pines are so generally open that young pitch pines of all sizes are intermixed with the others. There are many small white pines beside, but few if any seed-bearing ones.

I proceed through Potter's young wood south of this grove (toward Fair Haven Hill-side) and here I find by the stumps what I remember, — that a pitch pine wood was cut, some ten or twelve years ago, judging from the state of the stumps. It was for density, apparently, such a grove as now stands northward of this. It is a very poor soil. Shrub oaks chiefly appear to have succeeded to the pines, and now the growth consists of oaks, shrub and others (the latter four to six feet high), pitch pines two to ten feet high, and white birches. The soil is but poorly clad, owing to its barrenness and the prevalence of shrub oak at first. Probably the largest of these young pitch pines were such as stood in the open wood when it was cut — as they now do northward; but apparently the majority have been sown since, as others are still being sown by the large pitch

pines there are left here and there quite numerously, the ground is still so open and bare on account of the feeble growth of the oaks. The white birches have as yet done the best, the pines next. It will ere long be a mixed oak and pitch pine wood, the pines not standing so dense as in new woods, though pretty thick in spots. This shows how a mixed wood of this character may arise, owing first to the existence of young pitch pines under the old when cut, — the latter being so open as to admit of their growth, — and secondly to the barren soil and shrub oaks, which fail to cover it for a long time, so that even after six or eight years pitch pines may catch there from seed-bearing trees which are left.

I am pleased to find an evidence that the pitch pine wood cut down here a dozen years ago was just such a *new* wood as that now standing on [the] north. It is this. Along the southwest edge of this portion of the lot, where the almost abrupt descent begins, I see many stones which were cast over the edge of the bank in great heaps when it was cultivated.

The small pitch pine grove above the western Fair Haven spring fully proves my theory of white pines in pitch pine, though there is hardly a seed-bearing white pine there. Young white pines are rapidly spreading up Fair Haven Hill-side, though the nearest seed-bearing white pines are across the river, thirty to sixty rods off.

I remember when this hillside above the spring was clear of wood. In fact, I was here when this field was cleared and the brush burned, some thirty-five years ago. Yet I now see a good many hickories both within

and without the pines, five feet high, more or less. I feel about sure that these are not from stumps or old roots which have existed in the ground so long. How then did they come here? The[y] even keep in advance of the pines on some sides a rod or two further into the open land. I am constrained to believe that they were planted there by quadrupeds or birds. If so, the walnut differs from the oak in the mode of its spreading; for I do not see oaks anywhere thus springing up in groves in grass ground, in advance of pines. It will be worth the while to ascertain the age of these exactly.

It is remarkable that the walnut loves a hillside so. I saw such a grove yesterday on Annursnack. Here is another of still larger trees a little lower down the hill; and there is a much more extensive one on the similar slope of Smith's Hill. Are animals more likely to plant walnuts in open land than acorns? or is it that walnuts are more likely to live there when planted? What a lover of the hills is this tree! I may be mistaken about those on Smith's Hill, after all.

Fair Haven Pond is skimmed over, all but the channel.

Can that be the skeleton of a raccoon which I find (killed not long since) on the Cliff Hill? Measured by my book it — the body from shoulder to tail — is 15½ inches long; tail, 13½; hind leg, 14½. *Vide* skull and foot.

If a man has spent all his days about some business, by which he has merely got to be rich, as it is called, *i. e.*, has got much money, many houses and barns and wood-lots, then his life has been a failure, I think; but if he has been trying to better his condition in a higher sense than this, has been trying to invent something, to be somebody, — i. e., to invent and get a patent for himself, — so that all may see his originality, though he should never get above board, — and great inventors, you know, commonly die poor, — I shall think him comparatively successful.

From the Cliff I see more oak than pine.

Every interest, as the codfish and the mackerel, gets represented but the huckleberry interest. The first discoverers and explorers of the land make report of this fruit, but the last make comparatively little account of them.

You would say that some men had been tempted to live in this world at all only by the offer of a bounty by the general government — a bounty on living — to any one who will consent to be *out* at this era of the world, the object of the governors being to create a nursery for their navy. I told such a man the other day that I had got a Canada lynx here in Concord, and his instant question was, " Have you got the reward for him ? " What reward? Why, the ten dollars which the State offers. As long as I saw him he neither said nor thought anything about the lynx, but only about this reward. " Yes," said he, " this State offers ten dollars reward." You might have inferred that ten dollars was something rarer in his neighborhood than a lynx even, and he was anxious to see it on that account. I have thought that a lynx was a bright-eyed, four-legged, furry beast of the cat kind, very *current*, indeed, though its natural gait is by leaps. But he knew it to be a draught drawn

by the cashier of the wildcat bank on the State treasury, payable at sight. Then I reflected that the first money was of leather, or a whole creature (whence *pecunia*, from *pecus*, a herd), and, since leather was at first furry, I easily understood the connection between a lynx and ten dollars, and found that all money was traceable right back to the original wildcat bank. But the fact was that, instead of receiving ten dollars for the lynx which I had got, I had paid away some dollars in order to get him. So, you see, I was away back in a gray antiquity behind the institution of money, — further than history goes.

This reminded me that I once saw a cougar recently killed at the Adirondacks which had had its ears clipped. This was a ten-dollar cougar.

Yet, though money can buy no fine fruit whatever, and we are never made truly rich by the possession of it, the value of things generally is commonly estimated by the amount of money they will fetch. A thing is not valuable — e. g. a fine situation for a house — until it is convertible into so much money, that is, can cease to be what it is and become something else which you prefer. So you will see that all prosaic people who possess only the commonest sense, who believe strictly in this kind of wealth, are speculators in fancy stocks and continually cheat themselves, but poets and all discerning people, who have an object in life and know what they want, speculate in real values. The mean and low values of anything depend on it[s] convertibility into something else — i. e. have nothing to do with its intrinsic value.

Vol. XIV

This world and our life have practically a similar value only to most. The value of life is what anybody will give you for living. A man has his price at the South, is worth so many dollars, and so he has at the North. Many a man here sets out by saying, I will make so many dollars by such a time, or before I die, and that is his price, as much as if he were knocked off for it by a Southern auctioneer.

We hear a good deal said about moonshine by so-called practical people, and the next day, perchance, we hear of their failure, they having been dealing in fancy stocks; but there really never is any moonshine of this kind in the practice of poets and philosophers; there never are any hard times or failures with them, for they deal with permanent values.

V

DECEMBER, 1860

(ÆT. 43)

Dec. 1. P. M. — To Fair Haven Hill.

Yesterday, rain, raising river somewhat. Examined the young hickories on Fair Haven Hill slope to see how old they are. I sawed off three at two or three inches below the surface, and also higher up. These were about three feet high. The rings are very hard to discern, but I judge the smallest of them (which is about one inch in diameter and three feet high) to be seven years old. The other two are probably older, yet not nearly so old as the pines whose beginning I remember. It therefore must be that these hickories have sprung up from nuts within seven to twenty-five years past. They are most numerous in openings four or five rods over amid the pines, and are also found many rods from the pines in the open pasture, and also especially along walls, though yet very far from other trees of any kind. I infer, therefore, that animals plant them, and perhaps their growing along walls may be accounted for in part by the fact that the squirrels with nuts oftenest take that road. What is most remarkable is that they should be planted so often in open land, on a bare hillside, where oaks rarely are. I do not know of a grove of oaks springing up in this manner, — with broad intervals of bare sward between them, and away from pines.

How is this to be accounted for? Yet I did notice oak seedlings coming up in this manner in Potter's open field beyond Bear Garden.

It is wonderful how much these hickories have endured and prevailed over. Though I searched the whole hillside, not only for the smallest, but the most perpendicular and soundest, each of the three that I sawed off had died down once at least, years ago. Though it might not betray any scar above ground, on digging I found it an inch below the surface.

Most of these small ones consist of several stems from one root, and they are often of such fantastic forms and so diseased that they seem to be wholly dead at a little distance, and yet evidently many of them make erect, smooth, and sound trees at last, all defects smoothed over or obliterated. Some which have thus died down and sprung up again are in the form of rude harps and the like. These had great tap-roots considerably larger just beneath the surface than the stock above, and they were so firmly set in the ground that, though the tree was scarcely an inch in diameter and you had dug around it to the depth of three or four inches, it was impossible to pull one up; yet I did not notice any side roots, so high. They are iron trees, so rigid and so firm set are they. It may be that they are more persistent at the root than oaks, and so at last succeed in becoming trees in these localities where oaks fail. They may be more persevering. Perhaps, also, cattle do not browse them, but do oaks. It will be very suggestive to a novice just to go and dig up a dozen seedling oaks and hickories and see what they

Vol. XIV

have had to contend with. Theirs is like the early career of genius.

Measured a great red maple near the south end of E. Hubbard's swamp, dividing in two at the ground, the largest trunk 7 feet and 10 inches at three feet and draped for three or four feet up with the pulmonaria (?) lichen. This the largest I know. Another is $5\frac{1}{2}$ feet, a third $5\frac{1}{4}$, a fourth in open land just south of turnpike $6\frac{1}{8}$.

Dec. 2. P. M. — To Smith's Hickory Hill-side.

I come *via* Britton's to see if I can find a seedling hickory under half a dozen years old. After searching long amid the very numerous young hickories at Britton's shanty and Smith's Hill I fail to find one so recently planted. I find many at the last place only one or two feet, but they invariably have great roots, and old stubs which have died down are visible at or beneath the surface of the ground. It is very common — almost the rule — to find from one to three from one root each one inch in diameter and two or three feet high, while the common stock beneath the ground is two inches in diameter. Pulling at one at Britton's, which was two feet and a quarter in height, it came up easily, to my surprise, and I found that it had broken off at just one foot below the surface, being quite decayed there. It was three quarters of an inch in diameter at the surface, and increased regularly for five or six inches downward till it was one inch in diameter. There was the stub of an old shoot, and the root was suddenly enlarged to about one and a half inches in diameter and held about

the same to where it broke off, at a foot below the surface. There was another stub about three inches above the ground, and the more recent growth above this was the work of about four years. This last had died, and this year two shoots had put out at six and eight inches above the ground and had grown two and four inches respectively. Here were evident, then, at the very least, four efforts to rise to a tree.

The first stub was about the diameter of the
    whole tree at present (above ground). Call
    it, then,   **4 years**
The second was probably two years old when
    it died (at least)   **2**
The third (forming the present tree)   **4**
The fourth (growth of this year)   **1**
                                                    ———
                                                      11

This little hickory, two feet and a quarter high and three quarters of an inch in diameter, standing in open land, was then at least eleven years old. What more the root would have revealed if I had dug deeper, I do not know. The fact that the lowest observed stub was nearly six inches below the surface, showing plainly to the eye that the earth had been heaped up about, was significant and suggested that this root might have survived in the ground through clearing and burning and subsequent cultivation. I remember well when the field was cultivated, I should think within ten or twelve years. It must be seventeen or eighteen years since the woods were cut here; since which time a peach orchard (which I selected) has been

raised, a premium obtained for it, and the trees died and gone some years ago, also an apple orchard. The hickories are on the site and in the midst of these; and what makes it the more likely that these hickories may be from roots of young seedlings left in the ground is the fact that there are sprouts from several large chestnut stumps in the midst of the orchard, which, by their size, have probably been cut down once or twice since the tree was cut, and yet survived. What is true of these chestnut sprouts may be true of the hickories.

On Smith's Hill I selected a large and healthy-looking one (hickory), sawed it off, and found it nearly dead. It was four years old. It had been cut down before to a stub, which showed five years more. I did not look beneath the surface. The leading shoot was perfectly withered and dead. The same was very commonly the case, except when the tree had got above a certain height. I do not think that a single hickory has been planted in either of these places for some years at least. Indeed, why should squirrels bring the nuts to these particular localities where other hickories already stood? which they must do, supposing them to be planted still, and not to be all of one age.

They seem to be able to resist fire, cultivation, and frost. The last is apparently their great enemy at present. It is astonishing how many efforts they make, how persistent they are. Thus much is certain, at least.

In surrounding young wood they are common, and have got up three or four times as high. It may be that when pine and oaks and hickories, young and old, are cut off and the land cleared, the two former are exterminated but the hickories are tough and stubborn and do not give up the ground. I cannot as yet account for their existence in these two localities otherwise. Yet I still think that some must have been planted on Fair Haven Hill *without the pines* in a manner in which oaks are not, within a dozen years. Or perchance, if the oaks are *so* planted, they fail to come up?

In Stow's wood at Saw Mill Brook an old chestnut stump. Two sprouts from this were cut three years ago and have forty-two rings. From the stumps of the sprouts, other sprouts three years old have grown. The old stump was cut there forty-five years ago. The centre of the stumps of each of these sprouts is hollow for one and a half inches in diameter. See a chestnut stump, a seedling sawed off, with seventy-five rings and no sprout from it. Commonly the sprouts stand in a circle around the stump, — often a dozen or more of them.

Dec. 3.[1] P. M. — To Hill.

The hickory which was blown down by the wall has been cut up into lengths. The end of one some twelve feet from ground *apparently* is sixteen inches in diameter and has 112 rings distinct, the first 50 within five and three quarters inches. The bark is one inch thick.

Measured the three white oaks on the southeast side of hill.

[1] [Under date of March 22, 1861, Thoreau wrote to Daniel Ricketson: "I took a severe cold about the 3d of December, which at length resulted in a kind of bronchitis, so that I have been confined to the house ever since." — *Familiar Letters*, p. 376; Riv. 435.]

The northernmost   at three feet is 10 feet in circumference.
" southeasternmost "   "   " " 10¼ "   "
" southwesternmost "   "   " " 11½ "   "

I find no young hickories springing up on the *open* hillside. Yet, if they do so elsewhere, why should they not here, where nuts are abundant? But, under and about the hickory which stands near the white oak (under the north side of the hill), there are many small hickories two to four feet high amid the birches and pines, — the largest of which birches and pines have been lately cut off.

I am inclined to think now that both oaks and hickories are occasionally planted in open land a rod or two or more beyond the edge of a pine or other wood, but that the hickory roots are more persistent under these circumstances and hence oftener succeed there.

As for the planting of acorns, it is to be observed that they do not require to be buried but merely transported and dropped on the surface in a suitable place. All the sound white oak acorns that I can find have now sent down their radicle under these circumstances, though, no doubt, far the greatest part of them will be killed this winter.

Talking with Walcott and Staples to-day, they declared that John Brown did wrong. When I said that I thought he was right, they agreed in asserting that he did wrong because he threw his life away, and that no man had a right to undertake anything which he knew would cost him his life. I inquired if Christ did not foresee that he would be crucified if he preached such doctrines as he did, but they both, though as if

Vol. XIV

it was their only escape, asserted that they did not believe that he did. Upon which a third party threw in, "You do not think that he had so much foresight as Brown." Of course, they as good as said that, if Christ *had* foreseen that he would be crucified, he would have "backed out." Such are the principles and the logic of the mass of men.

It is to be remembered that by good deeds or words you encourage yourself, who always have need to witness or hear them.

Dec. 4. The first snow, four or five inches, this evening.

Talk about slavery! It is not the peculiar institution of the South. It exists wherever men are bought and sold, wherever a man allows himself to be made a mere thing or a tool, and surrenders his inalienable rights of reason and conscience. Indeed, this slavery is more complete than that which enslaves the body alone. It exists in the Northern States, and I am reminded by what I find in the newspapers that it exists in Canada. I never yet met with, or heard of, a judge who was not a slave of this kind, and so the finest and most unfailing weapon of injustice. He fetches a slightly higher price than the black man only because he is a more valuable slave.

It appears that a colored man killed his would-be kidnapper in Missouri and fled to Canada. The bloodhounds have tracked him to Toronto and now demand him of her judges. From all that I can learn, they are playing their parts like judges. They are servile,

while the poor fugitive in their jail is free in spirit at least.

This is what a Canadian writes to the *New York Tribune*: "Our judges may be compelled to render a judgment adverse to the prisoner. Depend upon it, they will not do it unless *compelled* [his italics].[1] And then the poor fellow will be taken back, and probably burned to death by the brutes of the South." Compelled! By whom? Does God compel them? or is it some other master whom they serve? Can't they hold out a little longer against the *tremendous pressure?* If they are fairly represented, I wouldn't trust their courage to defend a setting hen of mine against a weasel. Will this excuse avail them when the real day of judgment comes? They have not to fear the slightest bodily harm: no one stands over them with a stick or a knife even [?]. They have at the worst only to resign their places and not a mouse will squeak about it. And yet they are likely to assist in tying this victim to the stake! Would that his example might teach them to break their own fetters! They appear not to know what kind of justice that is which is to be done though the heavens fall. Better that the British Empire be destroyed than that it should help to reënslave this man!

This correspondent suggests that the "good people" of New York may rescue him as he is being carried back. There, then, is the only resort of justice, — not where the judges are, but where the mob is, where human hearts are beating, and hands move in obedience to their impulses. Perhaps his fellow-fugitives in Toronto

[1] [The brackets are Thoreau's.]

may not feel compelled to surrender him. Justice, departing from the Canadian soil, leaves her last traces among these.

What is called the religious world very generally deny virtue to all who have not received the Gospel. They accept no god as genuine but the one that bears a Hebrew name. The Greenlander's *Pirksoma* [?] (he that is above), or any the like, is always the name of a false god to them.

C. says that Walden was first frozen over on the 16th December.

Dec. 22. This evening and night, the second important snow, there having been sleighing since the 4th, and now, —

Dec. 23, — there is seven or eight inches of snow at least. Larks were about our house the middle of this month.

Dec. 26. Melvin sent to me yesterday a perfect *Strix asio*, or red owl of Wilson, — not at all gray. This is now generally made the same with the *nævia*, but, while some consider the red the old, others consider the red the young. This is, as Wilson says, a bright "nut brown" like a hazelnut or dried hazel bur (not *hazel*). It is twenty-three inches [in] alar extent by about eleven long. Feet extend one inch beyond tail. Cabot makes the old bird red; Audubon, the young. How well fitted these and other owls to withstand the winter! a mere core in the midst of such a muff of feathers! Then

the feet of this are feathered finely to the claws, looking like the feet of a furry quadruped. Accordingly owls are common here in winter; hawks, scarce.

It is no worse, I allow, than almost every other practice which custom has sanctioned, but that is the worst of it, for it shows how bad the rest are. To such a pass our civilization and division of labor has come that A, a professional huckleberry-picker, has hired B's field and, we will suppose, is now gathering the crop, perhaps with the aid of a patented machine; C, a professed cook, is superintending the cooking of a pudding made of some of the berries; while Professor D, for whom the pudding is intended, sits in his library writing a book, — a work on the Vacciniæ, of course. And now the result of this downward course will be seen in that book, which should be the ultimate fruit of the huckleberry-field and account for the existence of the two professors who come between D and A. It will be worthless. There will be none of the spirit of the huckleberry in it. The reading of it will be a weariness to the flesh. To use a homely illustration, this is to save at the spile but waste at the bung. I believe in a different kind of division of labor, and that Professor D should divide himself between the library and the huckleberry-field.

Dec. 30. Sunday. I saw the crows a week ago perched on the swamp white oaks over the road just beyond Wood's Bridge, and many acorns and bits of bark and moss, evidently dropped or knocked off by them, lay on the snow beneath. One sat within twenty feet over my head with what looked like a piece of acorn in his bill.

Vol. XIV

To-day I see that they have carried these same white oak acorns, cups and all, to the ash tree by the riverside, some thirty rods southeast, and dropped them there. Perhaps they find some grubs in the acorns, when they do not find meat. The crows now and of late frequent thus the large trees by the river, especially swamp white oak, and the snow beneath is strewn with bits of bark and moss and with acorns (commonly worthless). They are foraging. Under the first swamp white oak in Hubbard's great meadow (Cyanean) I see a little snap-turtle (shell some one and a quarter inches in diameter — on his second year, then) on its back on the ice — shell, legs, and tail perfect, but head pulled off, and most of the inwards with it by the same hole (where the neck was). What is left smells quite fresh, and this head must have been torn off to-day — or within a day or two. I see two crows on the next swamp white oak westward, and I can scarcely doubt that they did it. Probably one found the young turtle at an open and springy place in the meadow, or by the river, where they are constantly preying, and flew with it to this tree. Yet it is possible (?) that it was frozen to death when they found it.

I also saw under the oak where the crows were one of those large brown cocoons of the *Attacus Cecropia*, which no doubt they had torn off.

Eben Conant's sons tell me that there has been a turtle dove associating with their tame doves and feeding in the yard from time to time for a fortnight past. They saw it to-day.

The traveller Burton says that the word *Doab*, "which

means the land embraced by the bifurcation of two streams, has no English equivalent." ("Lake Regions of Central Africa," page 72.)

It is remarkable how universally, as it respects soil and exposure, the whortleberry family is distributed with us, one kind or another (of those of which I am speaking) flourishing in every soil and locality, — the Pennsylvania and Canada blueberries especially in elevated cool and airy places — on hills and mountains, and in openings in the woods and in sprout-lands; the high blueberry in swamps, and the second low blueberry in intermediate places, or almost anywhere but in swamps hereabouts; while we have two kinds confined to the Alpine tops of our highest mountains. The family thus ranges from the highest mountain-tops to the lowest swamps and forms the prevailing small shrubs of a great part of New England. Not only is this true of the family, but *hereabouts* of the genus *Gaylussacia*, or the huckleberries proper, alone. I do not know of a spot where any shrub grows in this neighborhood but one or another species or variety of the *Gaylussacia* may also grow there. It is stated in Loudon (page 1076) that all the plants of this order "require a peat soil, or a soil of a close cohesive nature," but this is not the case with the huckleberry. The huckleberry grows on the tops of our highest hills; no pasture is too rocky or barren for it; it grows in such deserts as we have, standing in pure sand; and, at the same time, it flourishes in the strongest and most fertile soil. One variety is peculiar to quaking bogs where there can hardly be said to be any soil beneath, not to mention another but

Blueberry Blossoms

Thoreau's Grave

unpalatable species, the hairy huckleberry, which is found in bogs. It extends through all our woods more or less thinly, and a distinct species, the dangle-berry, belongs especially to moist woods and the edges of swamps.

Such care has nature taken to furnish to birds and quadrupeds, and to men, a palatable berry of this kind, slightly modified by soil and climate, wherever the consumer may chance to be. Corn and potatoes, apples and pears, have comparatively a narrow range, but we can fill our basket with whortleberries on the summit of Mt. Washington, above almost all the shrubs with which we are familiar, — the same kind which they have in Greenland, — and again, when we get home, with another species in Beck Stow's Swamp.

I find that in Bomare's "Dictionnaire Raisonné" the *Vitis Idæa* (of many kinds) is called "raisin des bois." Our word "berry," according to lexicographers, is from the Saxon *beria*, a grape or cluster of grapes; but it must acquire a new significance here, if a new word is not substituted for it.

According to Father Rasles' Dictionary, the Abenaki word for bluets [1] was, fresh, *satar* (in another place *saté, tar*); dry, *sakisatar*.

First there is the early dwarf blueberry, the smallest of the whortleberry shrubs with us, and the first to ripen its fruit, not commonly an erect shrub, but more or less reclined and drooping, often covering the earth with a sort of dense matting. The twigs are green, the flowers commonly white. Both the shrub and its

[1] [See p. 300.]

fruit are the most tender and delicate of any that we have.

The *Vaccinium Canadense* may be considered a more northern form of the same.

Some ten days later comes the high blueberry, or swamp blueberry, the commonest stout shrub of our swamps, of which I have been obliged to cut down not a few when running lines as a surveyor through the low woods. They are a pretty sure indication of water, and, when I see their dense curving tops ahead, I prepare to wade, or for a wet foot. The flowers have an agreeable sweet and berry-promising fragrance, and a handful of them plucked and eaten have a subacid taste agreeable to some palates.

At the same time with the last the common low blueberry is ripe. This is an upright slender shrub with a few long wand-like branches, with green bark and pink-colored recent shoots and glaucous-green leaves. The flowers have a considerable rosy tinge, of a delicate tint.

The last two more densely flowered than the others.

The huckleberry, as you know, is an upright shrub, more or less stout depending on the exposure to the sun and air, with a spreading, bushy top, a dark-brown bark, and red recent shoots, with thick leaves. The flowers are much more red than those of the others.

As in old times they who dwelt on the heath remote from towns were backward to adopt the doctrines which prevailed there, and were therefore called heathen in a bad sense, so we dwellers in the huckleberry pastures, which are our heath lands, are slow to adopt the notions

Vol. XIV

of large towns and cities and may perchance be nicknamed huckleberry people. But the worst of it is that the emissaries of the towns care more for our berries than for our salvation.

In those days the very race had got a bad name, and *ethnicus* was only another name for heathen.

All our hills are or have been huckleberry hills, the three hills of Boston and, no doubt, Bunker Hill among the rest.

In May and June all our hills and fields are adorned with a profusion of the pretty little more or less bell-shaped flowers of this family, commonly turned toward the earth and more or less tinged with red or pink and resounding with the hum of insects, each one the fore-runner of a berry the most natural, wholesome, palatable that the soil can produce.

The early low blueberry, which I will call "bluet," adopting the name from the Canadians, is probably the prevailing kind of whortleberry in New England, for the high blueberry and huckleberry are unknown in many sections. In many New Hampshire towns a neighboring mountain-top is the common berry-field of many villages, and in the berry season such a summit will be swarming with pickers. A hundred at once will rush thither from all the surrounding villages, with pails and buckets of all descriptions, especially on a Sunday, which is their leisure day. When camping on such ground, thinking myself quite out of the world, I have had my solitude very unexpectedly interrupted by such an advent, and found that the week-days were the only Sabbath-days there.

For a mile or more on such a rocky mountain-top this will be the prevailing shrub, occupying every little shelf from several rods down to a few inches only in width, and then the berries droop in short wreaths over the rocks, sometimes the thickest and largest along a seam in a shelving rock, — either that light mealy-blue, or a shining black, or an intermediate blue, without bloom. When, at that season, I look from Concord toward the blue mountain-tops in the horizon, I am reminded that near at hand they are equally blue with berries.

The mountain-tops of New England, often lifted above the clouds, are thus covered with this beautiful blue fruit, in greater profusion than in any garden.

What though the woods be cut down, this emergency was long ago foreseen and provided for by Nature, and the interregnum is not allowed to be a barren one. She is full of resources: she not only begins instantly to heal that scar, but she consoles (compensates?) and refreshes us with fruits such as the forest did not produce. To console us she heaps our baskets with berries.

The timid or ill-shod confine themselves to the land side, where they get comparatively few berries and many scratches, but the more adventurous, making their way through the open swamp, which the bushes overhang, wading amid the water andromeda and sphagnum, where the surface quakes for a rod around, obtain access to those great drooping clusters of berries which no hand has disturbed. There is no wilder and richer sight than is afforded from such a point of view, of the edge of a blueberry swamp where various wild berries are intermixed.

As the sandalwood is said to diffuse its perfume around the woodman who cuts it, so in this case Nature rewards with unexpected fruits the hand that lays her waste.

VI

1861

(ÆT. 43–44)

Jan. 3. The third considerable snow-storm.

The berries which I celebrate appear to have a range — most of them — very nearly coterminous with what has been called the Algonquin Family of Indians, whose territories are now occupied by the Eastern, Middle, and Northwestern States and the Canadas, and completely surrounded those of the Iroquois, who occupied what is now the State of New York. These were the small fruits of the Algonquin and Iroquois families. The Algonquins appear to have described this kind of fruits generally by words ending in the syllables *meenar.*

It is true we have in the Northern States a few wild plums and inedible crab-apples, a few palatable grapes and nuts, but I think that our various species of berries are our *wild fruits* to be compared with the more celebrated ones of the tropics, and that, taking all things into consideration, New England will bear comparison with the West India Islands. I have not heard of any similar amusement there superior to huckleberrying here, the object not being merely to get a shipload of something which you can eat or sell.

Why should the Ornamental Tree Society confine its labors to the highway only? An Englishman laying out

his ground does not regard simply the avenues and walks. Does not the landscape deserve attention?

What are the natural features which make a township handsome? A river, with its waterfalls and meadows, a lake, a hill, a cliff or individual rocks, a forest, and ancient trees standing singly. Such things are beautiful; they have a high use which dollars and cents never represent. If the inhabitants of a town were wise, they would seek to preserve these things, though at a considerable expense; for such things educate far more than any hired teachers or preachers, or any at present recognized system of school education. I do not think him fit to be the founder of a state or even of a town who does not foresee the use of these things, but legislates chiefly for oxen, as it were.

Far the handsomest thing I saw in Boxboro was its noble oak wood. I doubt if there is a finer one in Massachusetts. Let her keep it a century longer, and men will make pilgrimages to it from all parts of the country; and yet it would be very like the rest of New England if Boxboro were ashamed of that woodland.

I have since heard, however, that she is contented to have that forest stand instead of the houses and farms that might supplant [it], because the land pays a much larger tax to the town now than it would then.

I said to myself, if the history of this town is written, the chief stress is probably laid on its parish and there is not a word about this forest in it.

It would be worth the while if in each town there were a committee appointed to see that the beauty of the town received no detriment. If we have the largest

boulder in the county, then it should not belong to an individual, nor be made into door-steps.

As in many countries precious metals belong to the crown, so here more precious natural objects of rare beauty should belong to the public.

Not only the channel but one or both banks of every river should be a public highway. The only use of a river is not to float on it.

Think of a mountain-top in the township — even to the minds of the Indians a sacred place — only accessible through private grounds! a temple, as it were, which you cannot enter except by trespassing and at the risk of letting out or letting in somebody's cattle! in fact the temple itself in this case private property and standing in a man's cow-yard, — for such is commonly the case!

New Hampshire courts have lately been deciding — as if it was for them to decide — whether the top of Mt. Washington belonged to A or to B; and, it being decided in favor of B, as I hear, he went up one winter with the proper officer and took formal possession of it. But I think that the top of Mt. Washington should not be private property; it should be left unappropriated for modesty and reverence's sake, or if only to suggest that earth has higher uses than we put her to. I know it is a mere figure of speech to talk about temples nowadays, when men recognize none, and, indeed, associate the word with heathenism.

It is true we as yet take liberties and go across lots, and steal, or "hook," a good many things, but we naturally take fewer and fewer liberties every year, as we meet with more resistance. In old countries, as England, going across lots is out of the question. You must walk in some beaten path or other, though it may [be] a narrow one. We are tending to the same state of things here, when practically a few will have grounds of their own, but most will have none to walk over but what the few allow them.

Thus we behave like oxen in a flower-garden. The true fruit of Nature can only be plucked with a delicate hand not bribed by any earthly reward, and a fluttering heart. No hired man can help us to gather this crop.

How few ever get beyond feeding, clothing, sheltering, and warming themselves in this world, and begin to treat themselves as human beings, — as intellectual and moral beings! Most seem not to see any further, — not to see over the ridge-pole of their barns, — or to be exhausted and accomplish nothing more than a full barn, though it may be accompanied by an empty head. They venture a little, run some risks, when it is a question of a larger crop of corn or potatoes; but they are commonly timid and count their coppers, when the question is whether their children shall be educated. He who has the reputation of being the thriftiest farmer and making the best bargains is really the most thriftless and makes the worst. It is safest to invest in knowledge, for the probability is that you can carry that with you wherever you go.

But most men, it seems to me, do not care for Nature and would sell their share in all her beauty, as long as they may live, for a stated sum — many for a glass of rum. Thank God, men cannot as yet fly, and lay waste

the sky as well as the earth! We are safe on that side for the present. It is for the very reason that some do not care for those things that we need to continue to protect all from the vandalism of a few.

We cut down the few old oaks which witnessed the transfer of the township from the Indian to the white man, and commence our museum with a cartridge-box taken from a British soldier in 1775!

He pauses at the end of his four or five thousand dollars, and then only fears that he has not got enough to carry him through, — that is, merely to pay for what he will eat and wear and burn and for his lodging for the rest of his life. But, pray, what does he stay here for? Suicide would be cheaper. Indeed, it would be nobler to found some good institution with the money and then cut your throat. If such is the whole upshot of their living, I think that it would be most profitable for all such to be carried or put through by being discharged from the mouth of a cannon as fast as they attained to years of such discretion.

As boys are sometimes required to show an excuse for being absent from school, so it seems to me that men should show some excuse for being here. Move along; you may come upon the town, sir.

I noticed a week or two ago that one of my white pines, some six feet high with a thick top, was bent under a great burden of very moist snow, almost to the point of breaking, so that an ounce more of weight would surely have broken it. As I was confined to the house by sickness, and the tree had already been four or five days in that position, I despaired of its ever recovering

Vol. XIV

itself; but, greatly to my surprise, when, a few days after, the snow had melted off, I saw the tree almost perfectly upright again.

It is evident that trees will bear to be bent by this cause and at this season much more than by the hand of man. Probably the less harm is done in the first place by the weight being so gradually applied, and perhaps the tree is better able to bear it at this season of the year.

Jan. 8. Trees, etc., covered with a dense hoar frost. It is not leaf-like, but composed of large spiculæ — spear-like — on the northeast sides of the twigs, the side from which the mist was blown. All trees are bristling with these spiculæ on that side, especially firs and arbor-vitæ.

They taught us not only the use of corn and how to plant it, but also of whortleberries and how to dry them for winter, and made us baskets to put them in. We should have hesitated long to eat some kinds, if they had not set us the example, knowing by old experience that they were not only harmless but salutary. I have added a few to my number of edible berries by walking behind an Indian in Maine, who ate such as I never thought of tasting before. Of course they made a much greater account of wild fruits than we do.

It appears from the above evidence[1] that the Indians used their dried berries commonly in the form of huckleberry cake, and also of huckleberry porridge or pudding.

What we call huckleberry cake, made of Indian meal

---
[1] [The "evidence" was omitted from the Journal.]

and huckleberries, was evidently the principal cake of the aborigines, and was generally known and used by them all over this part of North America, as much or more than plum-cake by us. They enjoyed it all alone ages before our ancestors heard of Indian meal or huckleberries.

We have no national cake so universal and well known as this was in all parts of the country where corn and huckleberries grew.

If you had travelled here a thousand years ago, it would probably have been offered you alike on the Connecticut, the Potomac, the Niagara, the Ottawa, and the Mississippi.

Botanists have long been inclined to associate this family in some way with Mt. Ida, and, according to Tournefort arrange [*sic*] whortleberries were what the ancients meant by the vine of Mt. Ida, and the common English raspberry is called *Rubus Idæus* from the old Greek name. The truth of it seems to be that blueberries and raspberries flourish best in cool and airy situations on hills and mountains, and I can easily believe that something like them, at least, grows on Mt. Ida. But Mt. Monadnock is as good as Mt. Ida, and probably better for blueberries, though it does not [*sic*] mean "bad rock," — but the worst rocks are the best for blueberries and for poets.

Jan. 11. Horace Mann brings me the contents of a crow's stomach in alcohol. It was killed in the village within a day or two. It is quite a mass of frozen-thawed apple, — pulp and skin, — with a good many pieces of skunk-cabbage berries one fourth inch or less in diameter, and commonly showing the pale-brown or blackish outside, interspersed, looking like bits of acorns, — never a whole or even half a berry, — and two little bones as of frogs (?) or mice (?) or *tadpoles;* also a street pebble a quarter of an inch in diameter, hard to be distinguished in appearance from the cabbage seeds.

I presume that every one of my audience knows what a huckleberry is, — has seen a huckleberry, gathered a huckleberry, and, finally, has tasted a huckleberry, — and, that being the case, I think that I need offer no apology if I make huckleberries my theme this evening.

What more encouraging sight at the end of a long ramble than the endless successive patches of green bushes, — perhaps in some rocky pasture, — fairly blackened with the profusion of fresh and glossy berries?

There are so many of these berries in their season that most do not perceive that birds and quadrupeds make any use of them, since they are not felt to rob us; yet they are more important to them than to us. We do not notice the robin when it plucks a berry, as when it visits our favorite cherry tree, and the fox pays his visits to the field when we are not there.

Jan. 14. Coldest morning yet; 20° (?).

Pliny says, "In minimis Natura praestat" (Nature excels in the least things). The *Wellingtonia gigantea,* the famous California tree, is a great thing; the seed from which it sprang, a little thing; and so are all seeds or origins of things.

that they come from seeds, *i. e.* are the result of causes still in operation, however slow and unobserved. It is a common saying that "little strokes fall great oaks," and it does not imply much wisdom in him who originated it. The sound of the axe invites our attention to such a catastrophe; we can easily count each stroke as it is given, and all the neighborhood is informed by a loud crash when the deed is consummated. But such, too, is the rise of the oak; little strokes of a different kind and often repeated raise great oaks, but scarcely a traveller hears these or turns aside to converse with Nature, who is dealing them the while.

Nature is slow but sure; she works no faster than need be; she is the tortoise that wins the race by her perseverance; she knows that seeds have many other uses than to reproduce their kind. In raising oaks and pines, she works with a leisureliness and security answering to the age and strength of the trees. If every acorn of this year's crop is destroyed, never fear! she has more years to come. It is not necessary that a pine or an oak should bear fruit every year, as it is that a pea-vine should. So, botanically, the greatest changes in the landscape are produced more gradually than we expected. If Nature has a pine or an oak wood to produce, she manifests no haste about it.

Thus we should say that oak forests are produced by a kind of accident, *i. e.* by the failure of animals to reap the fruit of their labors. Yet who shall say that they have not a fair knowledge of the value of their labors — that the squirrel when it plants an acorn,

Richard Porson said: "We all speak in metaphors. Those who appear not to do it, only use those which are worn out, and are overlooked as metaphors. The original fellow is therefore regarded as only witty; and the dull are consulted as the wise." He might have said that the former spoke a dead language.

John Horne Tooke is reported in "Recollections" by Samuel Rogers as having said: "Read few books well. We forget names and dates; and reproach our memory. They are of little consequence. We feel our limbs enlarge and strengthen; yet cannot tell the dinner or dish that caused the alteration. Our minds improve though we cannot name the author, and have forgotten the particulars." I think that the opposite would be the truer statement, books differ so immensely in their nutritive qualities, and good ones are so rare.

Gosse, in his "Letters from Alabama," says that he thinks he saw a large dragon-fly (*Æslona*), which was hawking over a brook, catch and devour some minnows about one inch long, and says it is known that "the larvæ of the greater water-beetles (*Dyticidæ*) devour fish."

It is the discovery of science that stupendous changes in the earth's surface, such as are referred to the Deluge, for instance, are the result of causes still in operation, which have been at work for an incalculable period. There has not been a sudden re-formation, or, as it were, new creation of the world, but a steady progress according to existing laws. The same is true in detail also. It is a vulgar prejudice that some plants are "spontaneously generated," but science knows

or the jay when it lets one slip from under its foot, has not a transient thought for its posterity?

Possibly here, a thousand years hence, every oak will know the human hand that planted it.

How many of the botanist's *arts* and inventions are thus but the rediscovery of a lost art, *i. e.* lost to him here or elsewhere!

Horace Mann told me some days ago that he found, near the shore in that muddy bay by the willows in the rear of Mrs. Ripley's, a great many of the *Sternothærus odoratus,* assembled, he supposed, at their breeding-time, or, rather, about to come out to lay their eggs. He waded in [and] collected — I think he said — about a hundred and fifty of them for Agassiz!

I see in the Boston *Journal* an account of robins in numbers on the savin trees in that neighborhood, feeding on their berries. This suggests that they may plant its berries as well as the crows.

Jan. 15. More snow last night, and still the first that fell remains on the ground. Rice thinks that it is two feet deep on a level now. We have had no thaw yet.

Rice tells me that he baits the "seedees" and the jays and crows to his door nowadays with corn. He thinks he has seen one of these jays stow away somewhere, without swallowing, as many as a dozen grains of corn, for, after picking it up, it will fly up into a tree near by and deposit so many successively in different crevices before it descends.

Speaking of Roman wormwood springing up abundantly when a field which has been in grass for twenty years or more is plowed, Rice says that, if you carefully examine such a field before it is plowed, you will find very short and stinted specimens of wormwood and pigweed there, — and remarkably full of seed too!

Feb. 5. Horace Mann brings me a screech owl, which was caught in Hastings's barn on the meeting-house avenue. It had killed a dove there. This is a decidedly gray owl, with none of the reddish or nut brown of the specimen of December 26, though it is about the same size, and answers exactly to Wilson's mottled owl.

Rice brings me an oak stick with a woodpecker's hole in it by which it reached a pupa.

The first slight rain and thaw of this winter was February 2d.

Feb. 8. Coldest day yet; −22° at least (all we can read), at 8 A. M., and, [so far] as I can learn, not above −6° all day.

Feb. 15. A little thunder and lightning late in the afternoon. I see two flashes and hear two claps.

A kitten is so flexible that she is almost double; the hind parts are equivalent to another kitten with which the fore part plays. She does not discover that her tail belongs to her till you tread upon it.

How eloquent she can be with her tail! Its sudden swellings and vibrations! She jumps into a chair and then stands on her hind legs to look out the window; looks steadily at objects far and near, first turning her

gaze to this side then to that, for she loves to look out a window as much as any gossip. Ever and anon she bends back her ears to hear what is going on within the room, and all the while her eloquent tail is reporting the progress and success of her survey by speaking gestures which betray her interest in what she sees.

Then what a delicate hint she can give with her tail! passing perhaps underneath, as you sit at table, and letting the tip of her tail just touch your legs, as much as to say, I am here and ready for that milk or meat, though she may not be so forward as to look round at you when she emerges.

Only skin-deep lies the feral nature of the cat, unchanged still. I just had the misfortune to rock on to our cat's leg, as she was lying playfully spread out under my chair. Imagine the sound that arose, and which was excusable; but what will you say to the fierce growls and flashing eyes with which she met me for a quarter of an hour thereafter? No tiger in its jungle could have been savager.

Feb. 21. I have just read a book called "Carolina Sports by Land and Water; including Incidents of Devil-Fishing, Wild-cat, Deer and Bear Hunting, Etc. By the Hon. Wm. Elliott."

The writer is evidently a regular sportsman, and describes his sporting with great zest. He was withal the inventor and institutor of devil-fishing, which consists in harpooning a monstrous salt-water fish, and represents himself in a plate harpooning him. His motive, however, was not profit or a subsistence, but sport.

However, I should have found nothing peculiar in the book, if it did not contain, near the end, so good an example of human inconsistency. I quote some sentences in the order in which they occur, only omitting the intermediate pages. After having described at length his own sporting exploits, using such words as these, for instance. Being in pursuit of a wildcat, he says (page 163): —

"It was at this moment that Dash, espying something in motion in the leafy top of a bay-tree, cracked off his Joe Manton with such good effect, that presently we heard a heavy body come tumbling through the limbs until it splashed into the water. Then came a stunning burst from the hounds — a clash from the whole orchestra in full chorus! — a growl from the assailed, with an occasional squeak on the part of the assailants, which showed that the game was not all on one side. We were compelled, all the while, to be delighted ear-witnesses only of the strife, which resulted in the victory of the hounds." This proved to be a raccoon, though they thought it the wildcat.

Again (page 168), being in pursuit of another cat, which had baffled them a long time with great cunning, he says: "The cat, with huge leaps, clambered up a tree; and now he had reached the very pinnacle, and as he gathered himself up to take a flying leap for a neighboring tree, I caught up my gun, and let slip at him in mid-flight. The arrowy posture in which he made his pitch, was suddenly changed, as the shot struck him to the heart; and doubling himself up, after one or two wild gyrations, into a heap, he fell dead, from a height of full fifty feet, into the very jaws of the dogs!"

Again (page 178), being [in] pursuit of a deer, which he had wounded, and his gun being discharged, he tried to run him down with his horse, but, as he tells us, "the noble animal refused to trample on his fellow quadruped," so he made up for it by kicking the deer in the side of the head with his spurred boot. The deer enters a thicket and he is compelled to pursue the panting animal on foot. "A large fallen oak lies across his path; he gathers himself up for the leap, and falls exhausted directly across it. Before he could recover his legs, and while he lay thus poised on the tree, I fling myself at full length upon the body of the struggling deer — my left hand clasps his neck, while my right detaches the knife; whose fatal blade, in another moment, is buried in his throat. There he lay in his blood, and I remained sole occupant of the field." Opposite is a plate which represents him in the act of stabbing the deer.

Page 267. — He tells us that his uncle once had a young wildcat, — a mere kitten, — but that, to prevent its worrying the poultry, "a cord was fastened round his neck, and a clog attached to the end." Still he would endeavor to catch the fowls.

"My uncle one day invited several of his friends, to witness this development of natural propensity in his savage pet. The kitten, with his clog attached, was let out of the box; and it was curious to observe with what stealthy pace he approached the spot where the poultry were feeding. They scarcely seemed to notice the diminutive thing that was creeping toward them; when, crouching low, and measuring exactly the distance which separated them, he sprang upon the back of the old rooster, and hung on by claw and teeth to the feathers, while the frightened bird dragged him, clog and all, over the yard. After several revolutions had been made, the cat let go his hold on the back of the fowl, and, with the quickness of lightning, *caught the head* in his mouth, clinched his teeth, shut his eyes, stiffened his legs, and hung on with the most desperate resolution, while the fowl, rolling over in agony, buffeted him with his wings. All in vain! In a few seconds more he was dead, and we looked with abhorrence on the savage animal, that had just taken his first degree in blood. In this case, there could have been no teaching — no imitation. It was the undoubted instinct of a cruel nature! We wondered that this young beast of prey should have known, from this instinct, *the vital part of its victim!* — and we wondered still more, that in the providence of God, he had seen fit to create an animal with an instinct so murderous. Philosophy is ready with her explanation, and our abhorrence may be misplaced, since from his very organization, he is compelled to destroy life *in order to live!* Yet, knowing this, our abhorrence still continues; whence we may draw the consolatory conclusion — that the instincts of a man naturally differ from those of a wild-cat."

A few pages further (page 282) in a chapter called "Random Thoughts on Hunting," which is altogether a eulogy on that pursuit, he praises it because it develops or cultivates among other qualities "the *observation*, that familiarizes itself with the nature and habits of the quarry — the *sagacity* that anticipates its projects of

escape — and the *promptitude* that defeats them! — the rapid glance, the steady aim, the quick perception, the ready execution; these are among the faculties and qualities continually called into pleasing exercise."

Physician, heal thyself!

This plucking and stripping a pine cone is a business which he and his family understand perfectly. That is their *forte*. I doubt if you could suggest any improvement. After ages of experiment their instinct has settled on the same method that our reason would finally, if we had to open a pine cone with our teeth; and they were thus accomplished before our race knew that a pine cone contained any seed.

He does not prick his fingers, nor pitch his whiskers, nor gnaw the solid core any more than is necessary. Having sheared off the twigs and needles that may be in his way, — for like a skillful woodchopper he first secures room and verge enough, — he neatly cuts off the stout stem of the cone with a few strokes of his chisels, and it is his. To be sure, he may let it fall to the ground and look down at it for a moment curiously, as if it were not his; but he is taking note where it lies and adding it to a heap of a hundred more like it in his mind, and it now is only so much the more his for his seeming carelessness. And, when the hour comes to open it, observe how he proceeds. He holds it in his hands, — a solid embossed cone, so hard it almost rings at the touch of his teeth. He pauses for a moment perhaps, — but not because he does not know how to begin, — he only listens to hear what is in the wind, not being in a hurry

He knows better than try to cut off the tip and work his way downward against a *chevaux-de-frise* of advanced scales and prickles, or to gnaw into the side for three quarters of an inch in the face of many armed shields. But he does not have to think of what he knows, having heard the latest æolian rumor. If there ever was an age of the world when the squirrels opened their cones wrong end foremost, it was not the golden age at any rate. He whirls the cone bottom upward in a twinkling, where the scales are smallest and the prickles slight or none and the short stem is cut so close as not to be in his way, and then he proceeds to cut through the thin and tender bases of the scales, and each stroke tells, laying bare at once a couple of seeds. And then he strips it as easily as if its scales were chaff, and so rapidly, twirling it as he advances, that you cannot tell how he does it till you drive him off and inspect his unfinished work.

Feb. 27. 2 p. m. — It is very pleasant and warm, and the ground half bare. As I am walking down the Boston road under the hill this side Clark's, it occurs to me that I have just heard the twitter of a bluebird. (C. heard one the 26th.) I stop and listen to hear it again, but cannot tell whether it comes from the buttonwoods high over my head or from the lower trees on the hilltop. It is not the complete bluebird warble, but the twitter only. And now it seems to come from Pratt's house, where the window is open, and I am not sure but it is a caged bird. I walk that way, and now think that I distinguish the minstrel in a black speck in the top of a great elm on the Common. Messer is shingling

Clark's barn; so, to make sure, I cross over and ask him if he has heard a bluebird to-day, and he says he ha several times. When I get to the elm near Minott' I hear one warble distinctly. Miss Minott and Mis Potter have both died within a fortnight past, and the cottage on the hillside seems strangely deserted; bu the first bluebird comes to warble there as usual.

Mother hears a robin to-day.

Buttonwood sap flows fast from wounds made las fall.

Feb. 28. P. M. — Down Boston road under the hill Air full of bluebirds as yesterday. The sidewal is bare and almost dry the whole distance under th hill.

Turn in at the gate this side of Moore's and sit o the yellow stones rolled down in the bay of a digging and examine the radical leaves, etc., etc.

Where the edges of grassy banks have caved I se the fine fibrous roots of the grass which have bee washed bare during the winter extending straigh downward two feet (and how much further within th earth I know not), — a pretty dense grayish mass.

The buttonwood seed has apparently scarcely begu to fall yet,[1] — only two balls under one tree, but the loose and broken.[2]

March 3. Sunday. Hear that there was a flock o

[1] Yes, many had been blown bare, for the balls do not fall often.
[2] Almost entirely fallen March 7th, leaving the dangling stems an bare receptacles.

geese in the river last night. See and hear song sparrows to-day; probably here for several days.

It is an exceedingly warm and pleasant day. The snow is suddenly all gone except heels, and — what is more remarkable — the frost is generally out of the ground, e. g. in our garden, for the reason that it has not been in it. The snow came December 4th, before the ground was frozen to any depth, has been unusually deep, and the ground has not been again exposed till now. Hence, though we have had a little very cold weather and a good deal of steady cold, the ground generally has not been frozen.

March 8. I just heard peculiar faint sounds made by the air escaping from a stick which I had just put into my stove. It sounded to my ear exactly like the peeping of the hylodes in a distant pool, a cool and breezy spring evening, — as if it were designed to remind me of that season.

Saw the *F. hyemalis* March 4th.

To continue subject of March 3d, —

It is remarkable that, though in ordinary winters, when the ground is alternately bare and covered with snow several times, or is not covered till after it is frozen, it may be frozen a foot or more in depth generally, yet, if it is kept covered with snow, though only a thin coating, from first to last, it will not be frozen at all.

For example, the ground was half bare on the 27th, the walk under the Boston road hills pretty fair on the

28th, and the 3d, after rain, the earth was bare, the ways were about settled, the melted snow and rain having been soaked up at once by the thirsty and open ground. There was probably no frost on level ground except where the earth had of late been partly exposed in the middle of the road. The recent rain and melting accordingly raised the river less than it otherwise would. There has been no breaking up of the frost on roads, — no bad travelling as usual, — but as soon as the snow is gone, the ways are settled.

In short, Nature uses all sorts of conveyances, from the rudest drag to a balloon, but she will get her seeds along in due season.

Is it not possible that Loudon is right as it respects the primitive distribution of the birch? Are not the dense patches always such as have sprung up in open land (commonly old fields cleared by man), as is the case with the pitch pine? It disappears at length from a dense oak or pine wood. Perhaps originally it formed dense woods only where a space had been cleared for it by a burning, as now at the eastward. Perhaps only the oaks and white pines could (originally) possess the soil here against all comers, maple succeeding because it does not mind a wet foot.

Suppose one were to take such a boxful of birch seed as I have described into the meeting-house belfry in the fall, and let some of it drop in every wind, but always more in proportion as the wind was stronger, and yet so husband it that there should be some left for every gale even till far into spring; so that this seed might be

blown toward every point of the compass and to various distances in each direction. Would not this represent a single birch tree on a hill? Of which trees (though only a part on hills) we have perhaps a million. And yet some feel compelled to suppose that the birch trees which spring up after a burning are spontaneously generated — for want of seed! It is true [it] does not come up in great quantities at the distance I have spoken of, but, if only one comes up there this year, you may have a million seeds matured there a few years hence.

It is true that the greater part of these seeds fall near the trees which bore them, and comparatively few germinate; yet, when the surface is in a favorable condition, they may spring up in very unexpected places.

A lady tells me that she met Deacon S. of Lincoln with a load of hay, and she, noticing that as he drove under the apple trees by the side of the road a considerable part of the hay was raked off by their boughs, informed him of it. But he answered, "It is not mine yet. I am going to the scales with it and intend to come back this way."

March 11. C. says that Walden is almost entirely open to-day, so that the lines on my map would not strike any ice, but that there is ice in the deep cove. It will be open then the 12th or 13th. This is earlier than I ever knew it to open. Fair Haven was solid ice two or three days ago, and probably is still, and Goose Pond is to-day all ice. Why, then, should Walden have

broken up thus early? for it froze over early and the winter was steadily cold up to February at least. I think it must have been because the ice was uncommonly covered with snow, just as the earth was, and so, as there was little or no frost in the earth, the ice also was thin, and it did not increase upward with snow ice as much as usual because there was no thaw or rain at all till February 2d, and then very little. According to all accounts there has been no skating on Walden the past winter on account of the snow. It was unusually covered with snow. This shows how many things are to be taken into account in judging of such a pond. I have not been able to go to the pond the past winter. I infer that, if it has broken up thus early, it must be because the ice was thin, and that it was thin not for want of cold generally, but because of the abundance of snow which lay on it.

The water is now high on the meadows and there is no ice there, owing to the recent heavy rains. Yet C. thinks it has been higher a few weeks since.

C. observes where mice (?) have gnawed the pitch pines the past winter. Is not this a phenomenon of a winter of deep snow only? as that when I lived at Walden, — a hard winter for them. I do not commonly observe it on a large scale.

My Aunt Sophia, now in her eightieth year, says that when she was a little girl my grandmother, who lived in Keene, N. H., eighty miles from Boston, went to Nova Scotia, and, in spite of all she could do, her dog Bob, a little black dog with his tail cut off, followed her to Boston, where she went aboard a vessel. Directly after, however, Bob returned to Keene. One day, Bob, lying as usual under his mistress's bed in Keene, the window being open, heard a dog bark in the street, and instantly, forgetting that he was in the second story, he sprang up and jumped out the chamber window. He came down squarely on all fours, but it surprised or shocked him so that he did not run an inch, — which greatly amused the children, — my mother and aunts.

The seed of the willow is exceedingly minute, — as I measure, from one twentieth to one twelfth of an inch in length by one fourth as much in width, — and is surrounded at base by a tuft of cotton-like hairs about one fourth of an inch long rising around and above it, forming a kind of parachute. These render it the most buoyant of the seeds of any of our trees, and it is borne the furthest horizontally with the least wind. It falls very slowly even in the still air of a chamber, and rapidly ascends over a stove. It floats the most like a mote of any, — in a meandering manner, — and, being enveloped in this tuft of cotton, the seed is hard to detect.

Each of the numerous little pods, more or less ovate and beaked, which form the fertile catkin is closely packed with down and seeds. At maturity these pods open their beaks, which curve back, and gradually discharge their burden like the milkweed. It would take a delicate gin indeed to separate these seeds from their cotton.

If you lay bare any spot in our woods, however

sandy, — as by a railroad cut, — no shrub or tree is surer to plant itself there sooner or later than a willow (commonly *S. humilis* or *tristis*) or poplar.

We have many kinds, but each is confined to its own habitat. I am not aware that the *S. nigra* has ever strayed from the river's brink. Though many of the *S. alba* have been set along our causeways, very few have sprung up and maintained their ground elsewhere.

The principal habitat of most of our species, such as love the water, is the river's bank and the adjacent river meadows, and when certain kinds spring up in an inland meadow where they were not known before, I feel pretty certain that they come from the river meadows. I have but little doubt that the seed of four of those that grow along the railroad causeway was blown from the river meadows, viz. *S. pedicellaris, lucida, Torreyana,* and *petiolaris.*

The barren and fertile flowers are usually on separate plants. I observe [?] that the greater part of the white willows set out on our causeways are sterile ones. You can easily distinguish the fertile ones at a distance when the pods are bursting. And it is said that no sterile weeping willows have been introduced into this country, so that it cannot be raised from the seed. Of two of the indigenous willows common along the brink of our river I have detected but one sex.

The seeds of the willow thus annually fill the air with their lint, being wafted to all parts of the country; and, though apparently not more than one in many millions gets to be a shrub, yet so lavish and persevering is Nature that her purpose is completely answered.

Vol. XIV

March 16. A severe, blocking-up snow-storm.

March 18. Tree sparrows have warbled faintly for a week.

When I pass by a twig of willow, though of the slenderest kind, rising above the sedge in some dry hollow early in December, or in midwinter above the snow, my spirits rise as if it were an oasis in the desert. The very name "sallow" (*salix*, from the Celtic *sal-lis*, near water) suggests that there is some natural sap or blood flowing there. It is a divining wand that has not failed, but stands with its root in the fountain.

The fertile willow catkins are those green caterpillar-like ones, commonly an inch or more in length, which develop themselves rapidly after the sterile yellow ones which we had so admired are fallen or effete. Arranged around the bare twigs, they often form green wands eight to eighteen inches long. A single catkin consists of from twenty-five to a hundred little pods, more or less ovate and beaked, each of which is closely packed with cotton, in which are numerous seeds so small that they are scarcely discernible by ordinary eyes.

I do not know what they mean who call this the emblem of despairing love! "The willow, worn by forlorn paramour!" It is rather the emblem of love and sympathy with all nature. It may droop, — it is so lithe, supple, and pliant, — but it never weeps. The willow of Babylon blooms not the less hopefully with us, though its other half is not in the New World at all, and never has been. It droops, not to represent David's tears, but rather to snatch the crown from Alexander's

head. (Nor were poplars ever the weeping sisters of Phaëton, for nothing rejoices them more than the sight of the Sun's chariot, and little reck they who drive it.)

Ah, willow! willow! Would that I always possessed thy good spirits.

No wonder its wood was anciently in demand for bucklers, for, take the whole tree, it is not only soft and pliant but tough and resilient (as Pliny says?), not splitting at the first blow, but closing its wounds at once and refusing to transmit its hurts.

I know of one foreign species which introduced itself into Concord as [a] withe used to tie up a bundle of trees. A gardener stuck it in the ground, and it lived and has its descendants.

Herodotus says that the Scythians divined by the help of willow rods. I do not know any better twigs for this purpose.

How various are the habits of men! Mother says that her father-in-law, Captain Minott, not only used to roast and eat a long row of little wild apples, reaching in a semicircle from jamb to jamb under the andirons on the reddened hearth (I used to buy many a pound of Spanish brown at the stores for mother to redden the jambs and hearth with), but he had a quart of new milk regularly placed at the head of his bed, which he drank at many draughts in the course of the night. It was so the night he died, and my grandmother discovered that he was dying, by his not turning over to reach his milk. I asked what he died of, and mother

nswered apoplexy! at which I did not wonder. Still
is habit may not have caused it.

I have a cousin, also, who regularly eats his bowl
f bread and milk just before going to bed, however
te. He is a very stirring man.

You can't read any genuine history — as that of
lerodotus or the Venerable Bede — without perceiving
at our interest depends not on the subject but on the
an, — on the manner in which he treats the subject
nd the importance he gives it. A feeble writer and
ithout genius must have what he thinks a great theme,
hich we are already interested in through the accounts
f others, but a genius — a Shakespeare, for instance —
ould make the history of his parish more interesting
an another's history of the world.

Wherever men have lived there is a story to be told,
nd it depends chiefly on the story-teller or historian
hether that is interesting or not. You are simply a
itness on the stand to tell what you know about your
eighbors and neighborhood. Your account of foreign
arts which you have never seen should by good rights
e less interesting.

March 22. A driving northeast snow-storm yesterday
nd last night, and to-day the drifts are high over the
nces and the trains stopped. The Boston train due at
.30 A. M. did not reach here till five this afternoon.
ne side of all the houses this morning was one color, —
. white with the moist snow plastered over them, —
that you could not tell whether they had blinds or not.
When we consider how soon some plants which

spread rapidly, by seeds or roots, would cover an area
equal to the surface of the globe, how soon some species
of trees, as the white willow, for instance, would equal
in mass the earth itself, if all their seeds became full-
grown trees, how soon some fishes would fill the ocean
if all their ova became full-grown fishes, we are tempted
to say that every organism, whether animal or vegetable, is contending for the possession of the planet, and,
if any one were sufficiently favored, supposing it still
possible to grow, as at first, it would at length convert
the entire mass of the globe into its own substance.[1]
Nature opposes to this many obstacles, as climate,
myriads of brute and also human foes, and of competitors which may preoccupy the ground. Each suggests an immense and wonderful greediness and tenacity of life (I speak of the species, not individual),
as if bent on taking entire possession of the globe
wherever the climate and soil will permit. And each
prevails as much as it does, because of the ample preparations it has made for the contest, — it has secured
a myriad chances, — because it never depends on spontaneous generation to save it.

A writer in the *Tribune* speaks of cherries as one of
the trees which come up numerously when the forest is
cut or burned, though not known there before. This
may be true because there was no one knowing in these
matters in that neighborhood. But I assert that it *was*
there before, nevertheless; just as the little oaks are in
the pine woods, but never grow up to trees till the pines
are cleared off. Scarcely any plant is more sure to come

[1] *Vide* Pliny on man's mission to keep down weeds.

Vol. XIV

p in a sprout-land here than the wild black cherry, and
t, though only a few inches high at the end of the first
ar after the cutting, it is commonly several years old,
aving maintained a feeble growth there so long. There
where the birds have dropped the stones, and it is
oubtful if those dropped in pastures and open land
re as likely to germinate. Yet the former rarely if
ver get to be trees.

Rice told me a month ago that when the earth be-
ame bare the jays, though they still came round the
ouse, no longer picked up the corn he had scattered
r them. I suggested that it was because they were
ow able to vary their diet.

Of course natural successions are taking place where
swamp is gradually filling up with sphagnum and
ushes and at length trees, *i. e.*, where the soil is chan-
ng.

Botanists talk about the possibility and impossibility
f plants being naturalized here or there. But what
lants have not been naturalized? Of course only those
hich grow to-day exactly where the original plant of
e species was created. It is true we do not know
hether one or many plants of a given kind were
riginally created, but I think it is the most reasonable
nd simple to suppose that only one was, — to sup-
ose as little departure as possible from the existing
rder of things. They commenced to spread them-
lves at once and by whatever means they possessed
far as they could, and they are still doing so. Many
ere common to Europe and America at the period
f the discovery of the latter country, and I have no

doubt that they had naturalized themselves in one or
the other country. This is more philosophical than to
suppose that they were independently created in each.

I suppose that most have seen — at any rate I can
show them — English cherry trees, so called, coming
up not uncommonly in our woods and under favorable circumstances becoming full-grown trees. Now
I think that they will not pretend that they came up
there in the same manner before this country was
discovered by the whites. But, if cherry trees come up
by spontaneous generation, why should they not have
sprung up there in that way a thousand years ago as
well as now?

If the pine seed is spontaneously generated, why
is it not so produced in the Old World as well as in
America? I have no doubt that it can be raised from
the seed in corresponding situations there, and that
it will seem to spring up just as mysteriously there as
it does here. Yet, if it will grow so *after* the seed has
been carried thither, why should it not before, if the
seed is unnecessary to its production?

The above-mentioned cherry trees come up, though
they are comparatively few, just like the red cherry,
and, no doubt, the same persons would consider them
as spontaneously generated. But why did Nature defer
raising that species here by spontaneous generation,
until we had raised it from the stones?

It is evident that Nature's designs would not be
accomplished if seeds, having been matured, were
simply dropped and so planted directly beneath their
parent stems, as many will always be in any case. The

next consideration with her, then, after determining to create a seed, must have been how to get it transported, though to never so little distance, — the width of the plant, or less, will often be sufficient, — even as the eagle drives her young at last from the neighborhood of her eyrie, — for their own good, since there is not food enough there for all, — without depending on botanists, patent offices, and seedsmen. It is not enough to have matured a seed which will reproduce its kind under favorable conditions, but she must also secure it those favorable conditions. Nature has left nothing to the mercy of man. She has taken care that a sufficient number of every kind of seeds, from a cocoanut to those which are invisible, shall be transported and planted in a suitable place.

A seed, which is a plant or tree in embryo, which has the principle of growth, of life, in it, is more important in my eyes, and in the economy of Nature, than the diamond of Kohinoor.

When we hear of an excellent fruit or a beautiful flower, the first question is if any man has got the seeds in his pocket; but men's pockets are only one of the means of conveyances which Nature has provided.

March 30. High water, — up to sixth slat (or gap) above Smith's second post. It is said to have been some nine inches higher about a month ago, when the snow first went off.

R. W. E. lately found a Norway pine cut down in Stow's wood by Saw Mill Brook.

According to Channing's account, Walden must have

Vol. XIV

fast falling. The white maple at the bridge not quite out. See a water-bug and a frog. Hylas are heard to-day.

I see where the meadow flood has gone down in a bay on the southeast side of the meadow, whither the foam had been driven. A delicate scum now left an inch high on the grass. It is a dirty white, yet silvery, and as thin as the thinnest foil, often unbroken and apparently air-tight for two or three inches across and almost as light as gossamer. What is the material? It is a kind of paper, but far more delicate than man makes.

Saw in a roadside gutter at Simon Brown's barn a bird like the solitary tattler, with a long bill, which at length flew off to the river. But it may have been a small species of snipe.

April 8. Examine the pitch pines, which have been much gnawed or barked this snowy winter. The marks on them show the fine teeth of the mouse, and they are also nicked as with a sharp knife. At the base of each, also, is a quantity of the mice droppings. It is probably the white-footed mouse.

April 9. Small reddish butterflies common; also, on snow banks, many of the small fuzzy gnats and cicindelæ and some large black dor-bug-like beetles. The two latter are easily detected from a distance on the snow.

The phœbe note of chickadee.

White frosts these mornings.

Worm-piles in grass at Clamshell.

April 10. Purple finch.

skimmed nearly, if not entirely, over again once sin the 11th or 12th, or after it had been some time con pletely clear. It seems, then, that in some years it ma thaw and freeze again.

April 2. A drifting snow-storm, perhaps a foot de on an average.

Pratt thought the cowslip was out the 4th.

April 6. Am surprised to find the river fallen son nine inches notwithstanding the melted snow. But read in Blodget that the equivalent in water is abo one tenth. Say one ninth in this case, and you have o and one third inches, and this falling on an unfroz surface, the river at the same time falling from a heigl shows why it was no more retarded (far from bei absolutely raised).

There is now scarcely a button-ball to be seen Moore's tree, where there were many a month ago more. The balls have not fallen entire, but been d composed and the seed dispersed gradually, leaving lon stringy stems and their cores dangling still. It is t storms of February and March that disperse them.

The (are they cinnamon?) sparrows are the fin singers I have heard yet, especially in Monroe's garde where I see no tree sparrows. Similar but more pr longed and remarkable and loud.

April 7. *Sunday*. Round the two-mile square.

I see where the common great tufted sedge (*Car stricta*) has started under the water on the meadows, n

April 11. Going to law. I hear that Judge Minc of Haverhill once told a client, by way of warning, th two millers who owned mills on the same stream we to law about a dam, and at the end of the lawsuit or lawyer owned one mill and the other the other.

April 16. Horace Mann says that he killed a bullfr in Walden Pond which had swallowed and contained common striped snake which measured one foot ar eight inches in length.

Says he saw two blue herons (?) go over a fortnig ago.

He brought me some days ago the contents of a stak driver's stomach or crop. It is apparently a perch (? some seven inches long originally, with three or fot pebble-shaped, compact masses of the fur of some ve small quadruped, as a meadow mouse, some one fourt inch thick by three fourths in diameter, also sever wing-cases of black beetles such as I see on the meado flood.

He brought me also some time ago the contents c a black duck's crop (killed at Goose Pond), — gree gobbets of fine grass (?) or weeds (?), apparently fror the bottom of the pond (just then begun to spring up but I have not yet examined these out of the bottle.

April 20. H. Mann brings me the hermit thrush.

April 21. Pratt collects very handsome tufts c *Hepatica triloba* in flower at Melrose, and the bloodroc out also there.

April 22. It was high water again about a week ago, - Mann thinks with[in] three or four inches as high as [a]t end of winter.

He obtained to-day the buffle-headed duck, diving [in] the river near the Nine-Acre Corner bridge. I iden[ti]fy it at sight as my bird seen on Walden.

I hear a chip-bird.

April 23. Think I hear bay-wings. Toads ring.

April 25. Horace Mann brings me apparently a [p]igeon hawk. The two middle tail-feathers are not [ti]pped with white and are pointed almost as a wood[p]ecker's.

May 1. Water in our neighbors' cellars quite gener[al]ly. May it not be partly owing to the fact that the [g]round was not frozen the last winter to any depth, and [so] the melted snow as well as rain has been chiefly [a]bsorbed by it?[1]

May 4. H. Mann brings me two small pewees, but not [y]ellowish about eye and bill, and bill is all black. Also [a] white-throat sparrow, Wilson's thrush, and myrtle-[b]ird.

May 5. Hear the seringo note.[2]

[1] Probably it was.
[2] [Pasted in at this point is a pencilled slip reading, "Strabo read far as 306th p.," with memoranda apparently referring to the [bo]ok.]

May 11. A boy brings me a salamander from S. Mason's. Sent it to Mann. What kind?

SET OUT FOR MINNESOTA *via* Worcester.[1]

May 12. Sunday. In Worcester.

Rode to east side of Quinsigamond Pond with Blake and Brown and a dry humorist, a gentleman who has been a sportsman and was well acquainted with dogs. He said that he once went by water to St. John, N. B., on a sporting excursion, taking his dog with him; but the latter had such a remarkable sense of decency that, seeing no suitable place aboard the vessel, he did not yield to the pressing demands of nature and, as the voyage lasted several days, swelled up very much. At length his master, by taking him aside and setting him the example, persuaded him to make water only. When at length he reached St. John, and was leading his dog by a rope up a long hill there which led to the town, he was compelled to stop repeatedly for his dog to empty himself and was the observed of all observers. This suggested that a dog could be educated to be far more cleanly in some respects than men are.

He also states that a fox does not regard all dogs, — or, rather, avoid them, — but only hunting dogs. He one day heard the voices of hounds in pursuit of a fox and soon after saw the fox come trotting along a path in which he himself was walking. Secreting himself behind a wall he watched the motions of the fox, wishing to get a shot at him, but at that moment his dog, a spaniel, leapt out into the path and advanced to meet

[1] [See *Familiar Letters*, pp. 380, 383–393; Riv. 439, 443–455.]

Vol. XIV

---

[t]he fox, which stood still without fear to receive him. [T]hey smelled of one another like dogs, and the sports[m]an was prevented from shooting the fox for fear of [h]itting his dog. So he suddenly showed himself in the [p]ath, hoping thus to separate them and get a shot. [T]he fox immediately cantered backward in the path, [b]ut his dog ran after him so directly in a line with [t]he fox that he was afraid to fire for fear of killing the [d]og.

May 13. Worcester to Albany.

The latter part of the day rainy. The hills come near [t]he railroad between Westfield and Chester Village. [T]hereafter in Massachusetts they may be as high or [h]igher, but are somewhat further off.

The leafing is decidedly more advanced in western [M]assachusetts than in eastern. Apple trees are greenish. [R]ed elder-berry is apparently just beginning to bloom.

Put up at the Delavan House. Not so good as costly.

May 14. Albany to Suspension Bridge.

Albany to Schenectady a level pitch pine plain with [a]lso white pine, white birch, and shad-bush in bloom, [w]ith *hills* at last. No houses; only two or three huts [o]n the edge of woods without any road. These were [t]he last pitch pines that I saw on my westward journey.

It is amusing to observe how a kitten regards the [a]ttic, kitchen, or shed where it was bred as its castle [to] resort to in time of danger. It loves best to sleep on

---

some elevated place, as a shelf or chair, and for many months does not venture far from the back door where it first saw the light. Two rods is a great range for it, but so far it is tempted, when the dew is off, by the motions of grasshoppers and crickets and other such small game, sufficiently novel and surprising to it. They frequently have a wheezing cough, which some refer to grasshoppers' wings across their windpipes. The kitten has been eating grasshoppers.

If some member of the household with whom they are familiar — their mistress or master — goes forth into the garden, they are then encouraged to take a wider range, and for a short season explore the more distant bean and cabbage rows, or, if several of the family go forth at once, — as it were a reconnaissance in force, — the kitten does a transient scout duty outside, but yet on the slightest alarm they are seen bounding back with great leaps over the grass toward the castle, where they stand panting on the door-step, with their small lower jaws fallen, until they fill up with courage again. A cat looks down with complacency on the strange dog from the corn-barn window.

The kitten when it is two or three months old is full of play. Ever and anon she takes up her plaything in her mouth and carries it to another place, — a distant corner of the room or some other nook, as under a rocker, — or perchance drops it at your feet, seeming to delight in the mere carriage of it, as if it were her prey — tiger-like. In proportion to her animal spirits are her quick motions and sudden whirlings about on the carpet or in the air. She may make a great show of scratching and biting, but let her have your hand and she will presently lick it instead.

They are so naturally stealthy, skulking and creeping about, affecting holes and darkness, that they will enter a shed rather by some hole under the door-sill than go over the sill through the open door.

Though able to bear cold, few creatures love warmth more or sooner find out where the fire is. The cat, whether she comes home wet or dry, directly squeezes herself under the cooking-stove, and stews her brain there, if permitted. If the cat is in the kitchen, she is most likely to be found under the stove.

This (October 5) is a rainy or drizzling day at last, and the robins and sparrows are more numerous in the yard and about the house than ever. They swarm on the ground where stood the heap of weeds which was burned yesterday, picking up the seeds which rattled from it. Why should these birds be so much more numerous about the house such a day as this? I think of no other reason than because it is darker and fewer people are moving about to frighten them. Our little mountain-ash is all alive with them. A dozen robins on it at once, busily reaching after and plucking the berries, actually make the whole tree shake. There are also some little birds (I think purple finches) with them. A robin will swallow half a dozen berries, at least, in rapid succession before it goes off, and apparently it soon comes back for more.

The reason why naturalists make so little account

of color is because it is so insignificant to them; the do not understand it. But the lover of flowers or anima makes very much of color. To a fancier of cats it is no indifferent whether one be black or gray, for the col expresses *character*.

Prescott is not inclined to go to the wars aga (October, '61), and so Concord has no company to repr sent her at present. Cyrus Warren thinks that Derb the first lieutenant (and butcher that was), would d for captain as well as Prescott, and adds, as his prir cipal qualification, "There is n't one in the compan can cut up a crittur like him."

Henry Mitchell of the Coast Survey (page 317)[1] ha invented a new kind of pile, to be made of some heav and strong wood and " so cut that the lower portio of it, for a space of six or eight feet, presents the a pearance of a number of inverted frustums of cone placed one above another." When this is swayed to an fro by the waves, instead of being loosened and washe out, it sinks deeper and deeper. This, as Professo Bache (in Coast Survey Report for 1859, page 30 says, " is a device borrowed from nature, he [Mitchel having observed that certain seed vessels, by virtue o their forms, bury themselves in the earth when agitate by wind or water." No seeds are named, but the must be similar to the seed of the porcupine grass of th West.

[1] [*Report of the Superintendent of the Coast Survey, showing th Progress of the Survey during the Year* 1859, Washington, 1860.]

Vol. XIV

Young Macey, who has been camping on Monadnock this summer, tells me that he found one of my spruce huts made last year in August, and that as many as eighteen, reshingling it, had camped in it while he was there.

See a large hornets' nest on a maple (September 29), the *half immersed* leaves turned scarlet.

Four little kittens just born; lay like stuffed skins o kittens in a heap, with pink feet; so flimsy and helpless they lie, yet blind, without any stiffness or ability to stand.

Edward Lord Herbert says in his autobiography, "It is well known to those that wait in my chamber, that the shirts, waistcoats, and other garments I wear next my body, are sweet, beyond what either easily can be believed, or hath been observed in any else, which sweetness also was found to be in my breath above others, before I used to take tobacco."

The kitten can already spit at a fortnight old, and it can mew from the first, though it often makes the motion of mewing without uttering any sound.

The cat about to bring forth seeks out some dark and secret place for the purpose, not frequented by other cats.

The kittens' ears are at first nearly concealed in the fur, and at a fortnight old they are mere broad-based triangles with a side foremost. But the old cat is ears for them at present, and comes running hastily to their

aid when she hears them mew and licks them into con tentment again. Even at three weeks the kitten can not fairly walk, but only creeps feebly with outsprea legs. But thenceforth its ears visibly though graduall lift and sharpen themselves.

At three weeks old the kitten begins to walk in staggering and creeping manner and even to play little with its mother, and, if you put your ear close you may hear it purr. It is remarkable that it will no wander far from the dark corner where the cat ha left it, but will instinctively find its way back to it, prob ably by the sense of touch, and will rest nowhere else Also it is careful not to venture too near the edge of precipice, and its claws are ever extended to save itsel in such places. It washes itself somewhat, and assume many of the attitudes of an old cat at this age. By th disproportionate size of its feet and head and leg now it reminds you [of] a lion.

I saw it scratch its ear to-day, probably for the firs time; yet it lifted one of its hind legs and scratched its ear as effectually as an old cat does. So this is in stinctive, and you may say that, when a kitten's ea first itches, Providence comes to the rescue and lifts its hind leg for it. You would say that this little creature was as perfectly protected by its instinct in its infancy as an old man can be by his wisdom. I observed when she first noticed the figures on the carpet, and also put up her paws to touch or play with surfaces a foot off. By the same instinct that they find the mother's teat before they can see they scratch their ears and guard against falling.

After a violent easterly storm in the night, which clears up at noon (November 3, 1861), I notice that the surface of the railroad causeway, composed of gravel, is singularly marked, as if stratified like some slate rocks, on their edges, so that I can tell within a small fraction of a degree from what quarter the rain came. These lines, as it were of stratification, are perfectly parallel, and straight as a ruler, diagonally across the flat surface of the causeway for its whole length. Behind each little pebble, as a protecting boulder, an eighth or a tenth of an inch in diameter, extends northwest a ridge of sand an inch or more, which it has protected from being washed away, while the heavy drops driven almost horizontally have washed out a furrow on each side, and on all sides are these ridges, half an inch apart and perfectly parallel.

All this is perfectly distinct to an observant eye, and yet could easily pass unnoticed by most. Thus each wind is self-registering.

NOTE TO MAP OF CONCORD

THE material used in this Map of Concord has been derived from a variety of sources. The town bounds, streets, and residences have been taken from a township map of Middlesex County made by H. F. Walling in 1856, reference also being had to a local map of Concord by the same engineer, dated 1852, on which credit for the surveys of White Pond and Walden Pond is given to "H. D. Thoreau, Civ. Engr." The course of the Concord River is drawn from an elaborate manuscript plan of Thoreau's, based on earlier surveys, showing the river from East Sudbury to Billerica Dam. This plan, on which Thoreau has entered the results of his investigation of the river in the summer of 1859, is now in the Concord Public Library. The outlines of Walden and White Ponds have also been taken from Thoreau's original surveys, now in the Concord Library. Loring's and Bateman's Ponds are according to surveys by Mr. Albert E. Wood of Concord, and Flint's Pond is from a survey for the Concord Water Works by Mr. William Wheeler, also of Concord.

All names of places are those used by Thoreau, no attention being given to other names perhaps more current either in his own time or at present. Only such names of residents are given as are mentioned in the Journal.

A few old wood roads, pasture lanes, etc. (Thoreau's preferred highways), are indicated, as to their general direction, by dotted lines.

The irregularity of the northeastern boundary of Concord arose from the fact that when Carlisle was set off from Concord in 1780, the farmers living on the border were given the option of remaining within the bounds of Concord or of being included in the new town. In 1903 the Massachusetts Legislature abolished this old division and continued the straight line forming the western half of the boundary directly to the river.

The identification of localities which were named by Thoreau apparently for his personal use alone has been accomplished, so far as it has proceeded, by a careful study of all the Journal references to each locality, an examination of a large number of Thoreau's manuscript surveys, and an extended personal investigation on the ground. Many of these localities are given more than one name in the Journal, and in a few cases the same name is given to different localities. Where doubt exists as to any particular location, the name is omitted from the map.

Hon. F. B. Sanborn, Judge John S. Keyes, Dr. Edward W. Emerson, the Misses Hosmer, and others among the older residents of Concord have been consulted in the preparation of the map, and have kindly supplied helpful information from their personal acquaintance with Thoreau.

H. W. GLEASON.

December, 1906.

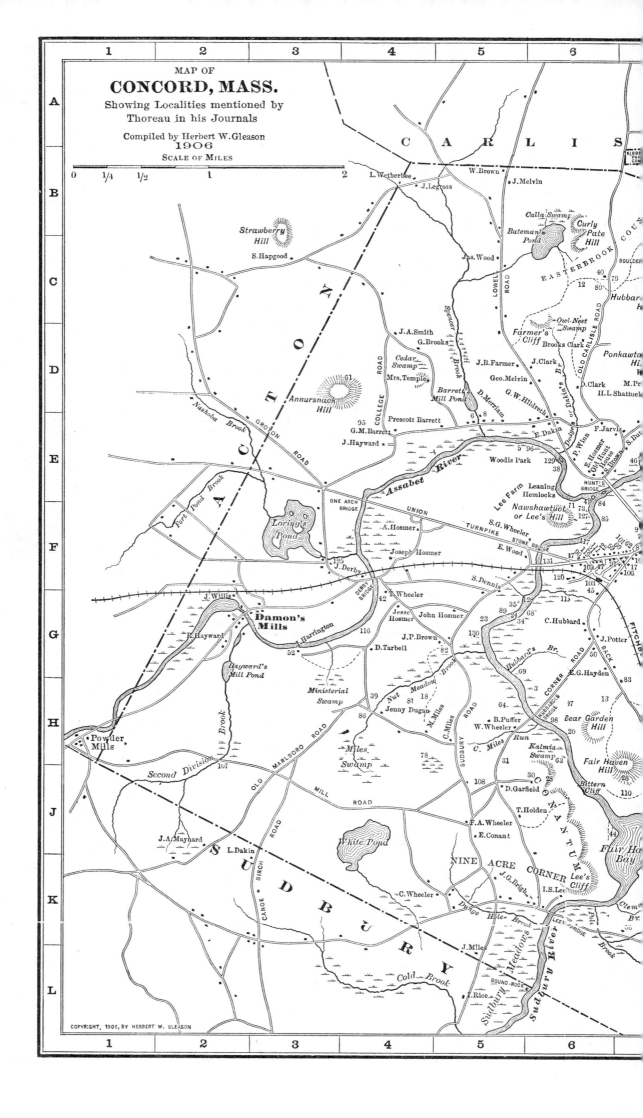

MAP OF
CONCORD, MASS.
Showing Localities mentioned by
Thoreau in his Journals

Compiled by Herbert W. Gleason
1906
SCALE OF MILES

0 1/4 1/2 1 2

FOR INDEX TO MAP SEE OVER

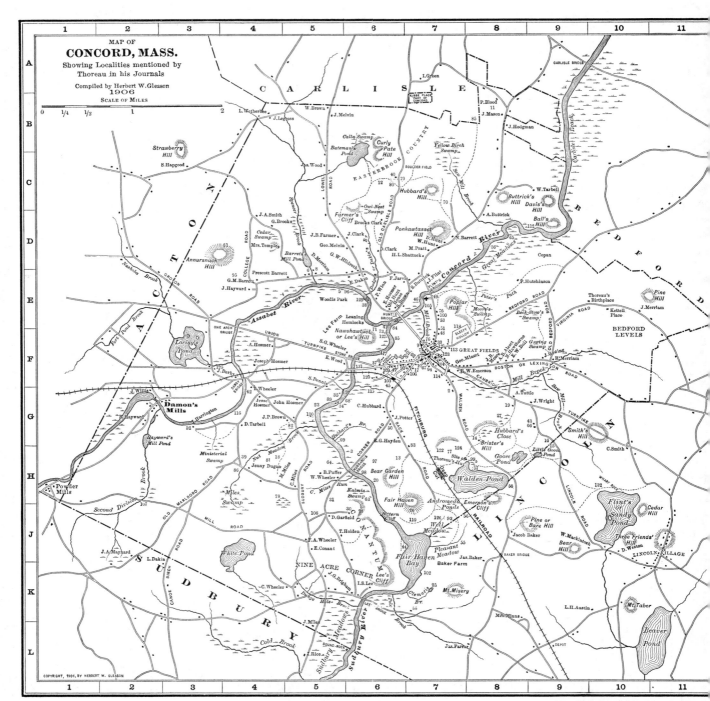

MAP OF
CONCORD, MASS.
Showing Localities mentioned by
Thoreau in his Journals
Compiled by Herbert W. Gleason
1906
SCALE OF MILES

FOR INDEX TO MAP SEE OVER

INDEX TO MAP OF CONCORD

Figures in parentheses correspond with figures on the map. A letter and figure combined indicate the space within which the locality may be found, this space being determined by the intersection of imaginary lines drawn from the corresponding letter and figure in the margin.

1 This name is spelled " Heywood " by Thoreau.

(66) Hosmer, Edmund (before 1853). G 9
Hosmer, Edmund (after 1853). E 6
Hosmer, Jesse. G 4
Hosmer, John. G 5
Hosmer, Joseph. F 4
Howard's Meadow. (See Heywood's Meadow.)
Hubbard, C. G 6
(67) Hubbard, Ebby. F 7
(68) Hubbard's Bath. G 6
Hubbard's Bridge. H 6
Hubbard's Brook. G 6
Hubbard's Close. G 8
(69) Hubbard's Grove. G 5
Hubbard's Hill. C 7
Hunt, D. D 7
Hunt, Wm. D 7
Hunt House, Old, or Winthrop House. E 6
Hunt's, or Red, Bridge. E 6
(70) Hunt's Pasture. C 7
Hutchinson, Peter. E 8
(71) Indian Field. E 6
(72) Inn kept by Thoreau's Aunts. F 7
(73) Island, the (at high water). F 6
(74) Jail. F 7
Jarvis, Francis. E 7
(75) Jones, Mrs. D 7
Kalmia glauca, or Holden Spruce, Swamp. H 6
Kettell Place. E 10
(76) Keyes, J. S. F 7
Kibbe Place. B 7
(77) Laurel Glen. H 7
Leaning Hemlocks. E 6
(78) Ledum Swamp. H 4
Lee Farm. E 5
Lee, I. S. K 6
Lee's, or Corner, Bridge. K 6
Lee's Cliff. K 6
Lee's Hill. (See Nawshawtuct.)
Legross, J. B 4
Lexington Road. (See Boston Road.)
Lily Bay.[2] (See Willow Bay.)
(79) Lime-kiln. C 6
(80) Lime Quarry. C 6
(81) Linnæa Hills. H 4
Little Goose Pond, or Ripple Lake. H 9
(82) Little Truro. G 5
(83) Lonely Graveyard. G 6
Loring's Pond. F 3
Lowell Road. C 5
Mackintosh, W. J 9
(84) Mantatuket Point or Rock. E 6
Marlborough Road, Old. H 3
Mason, J. B 8
Maynard's Place. J 2
Melvin, Geo. D 6
Melvin, J. B 5
Melvin Preserve. (See Easterbrook Country.)
Merriam, D. E 5
Merriam, J. E 10
Merriam, R. F 9
(85) Merrick's Pasture. F 6
Miles, Charles. H 5
Miles, J. L 5
Miles, Martial and Warren. H 4

(86) Miles's Mill, Warren. H 4
Miles's Run, Charles. H 5
Miles Swamp. H 4
Mill Brook. F 9
(87) Mill-dam. F 7
Mill Road. J 4
Ministerial Swamp. H 3
Minn's Place. K 8
(88) Minott, Abel. K 7
Minott, Geo. F 7
(89) Money-Diggers' Shore. G 5
(90) Monroe, Francis. F 6
(91) Monroe, Wm. F 6
Moore, J. B. F 8
Moore's Swamp. E 8
Mt. Misery. K 7
Mt. Tabor. K 10
Nashoba Brook. E 2
Nawshawtuct, or Lee's, Hill. F 6
Nightshade Pond. (See Clematis Pond.)
North Branch. (See Assabet River.)
(92) North Bridge, Site of Old. E 7 (Battle-Ground.)
North Bridge, Present. (See Flint's Bridge.)
Nut Meadow Brook. H 4
One-Arch, Eddy, or Assabet Stone, Bridge. E 4
(93) Orchis Swamp. J 7
(94) Orthodox Church. F 7
Owl-Nest, or Fox Castle, Swamp. C 6
(95) Painted-Cup Meadow. E 4
Peter's Path. E 8
Pine Hill (in Concord). E 10
Pine Hill (in Lincoln), or Bare Hill. J 9
(96) Pinxter Swamp. E 6
Pleasant Meadow. J 7
Pole, Creel, or Bidens, Brook. K 6
Ponkawtasset Hill. D 7
Poplar Hill. E 7
Potter, Jonas. G 6
(97) Potter's Field. H 6
(98) Potter's Swamp Meadow. H 6
(99) Pout's Nest, or Wyman Meadow. H 8
Pratt, Minot. D 7
(100) Prescott, G. L. E 7
(101) Prichard, M. F 7
Powder-Mills. H 1
Puffer, B. H 5
(102) Purple Utricularia Bay. K 7
(103) Railroad Depot (Concord). F 6
Railroad Depot (Lincoln). L 9
Red Bridge. (See Hunt's Bridge.)
Rice, Israel. L 5
Rice, Reuben. F 7
(104) Rice, Reuben. F 7
(105) Ripley, Mrs. ("Old Manse"). E 7
Ripley Hill. (See Poplar Hill.)
Ripple Lake. (See Little Goose Pond.)
Sandy Pond. (See Flint's Pond).
Saw Mill Brook (N. E.). C 7
Saw Mill Brook (S. E.).[3] G 9
(106) School where Thoreau taught. F 7
Second Division Brook. J 2
(107) Second Division Spring. H 2

(108) Seven-Star Lane. J 5
(109) Shattuck, D. F 6
Shattuck, H. L. D 7
(110) Shrub Oak Plain. J 7
Sleepy Hollow Cemetery. F 7
Smith, C. H 10
Smith, J. A. D 4
(111) Smith, J. M. F 6
Smith's Hill. G 10
South Bridge. (See Wood's Bridge.)
Spanish Brook. (See Well Meadow Brook.)
Spencer Brook. C 5
(112) Squam Harbor. D 9
(113) Staples, Sam. F 7
Stone Bridge. F 6
(114) Stow, Cyrus. F 7
Strawberry Hill. B 3
Sudbury Meadows. L 5
Sudbury Road. H 5
Sunset Reach. (See Clamshell Reach.)
(115) Swamp Bridge Brook. G 6
Tarbell, D. G 4
Tarbell, W. C 9
(116) Tarbell's Spring. G 4
Temple's Place. D 4
Thoreau's Birthplace. E 10
(117) Thoreau's Boat-Landing. F 6
(118) Thoreau's Grave. F 7
Thoreau's Hut, Site of. H 7
(119) Thoreau's Home in the Village. F 6
(120) Thoreau's "Texas" House. F 6
Three Friends', or Lincoln, Hill. J 10
(121) Town Hall. F 7
(122) Trillium Woods. H 7
Tupelo Cliff. (See Bittern Cliff.)
Tuttle, Aug. G 8
Union Turnpike. F 5
(123) Unitarian (First) Church. F 7
Virginia Road. E 9
Walden Pond. H 8
Walden Road. G 7
(124) Walden Woods. H 7
(125) Warner Pail Factory. F 3
Well Meadow. J 7
(126) Well Meadow, or Spanish, Brook. J 7
Weston, Daniel. J 10
Wetherbee, L. B 4
Wharf Rock. H 10
Wheeler, Cyrus. K 5
Wheeler, F. A. J 5
Wheeler, Samuel G. F 5
Wheeler, T. G 4
(127) Wheeler's Swamp. F 6
White Pond. J 4
Willis, J. G 2
(128) Willow Bay, or Lily Bay. G 5
(129) Willow Island. E 6
Winn, P. E 6
Winthrop House. (See Old Hunt House.)
(130) Witherell Vale or Glade. G 5
Wood, Elijah. F 5
Wood, Jas. C 5
(131) Wood's, or South, Bridge. F 6
Woodis Park. E 5
(132) Wood Thrush Path. H 10
Wright, J. G 9
Wyman Meadow. (See Pout's Nest.)
Yellow Birch Swamp. B 7

[2] This name was also given to a bay on the river in Sudbury.
[3] This is the "Saw Mill Brook" most frequently mentioned by Thoreau.

The Journal of Henry D. Thoreau

8, 354; brought out by warmth, **7**, 318; hibernating, **8**, 105, **10**, 328; first note of, in spring, **9**, 301; curious mortality among, 476; the study of, **10**, 375; sensitive to cold, 382, 388; water supply of the, **11**, 107, 108; in target-weed, 160; the breeding-note of the frog, **12**, 141; leaping, 217, 218; in a well, **13**, 183, 184; just developed from pollywogs, 411; of Mt. Monadnock, **14**, 35, 36. *See also* Bullfrog.

Frogs, unidentified, **4**, 34, **5**, 106, **8**, 286, **9**, 353, **10**, 401, 402, 488, 508.

Froissart's Chronicles, **2**, 429.

Frost, **3**, 15, **4**, 451, **6**, 62, 63, **7**, 279; on cistus, **4**, 428, **5**, 483, 484, **8**, 10, **11**, 316, 317; pellets of, **5**, 62; measurements of depth of, **6**, 138; 139; on windows, **7**, 172, **8**, 49, 99, **10**, 209; on trees, **7**, 179, **11**, 398–400, 403–407; feather, **7**, 185; on bare russet grass, 229; melting, 325; frozen fog, **8**, 74; effect on foliage, **9**, 14, 57, **11**, 164; the dying breath of water, **9**, 190, 191; coming out of the ground, 312; in July, 465; effect of one night of, **10**, 29; in August, **11**, 115; a bark-like formation of, 312; congealed breath of earth, 317, 318; a breeder of rain, **12**, 58, 59; foe to summer, 295, 296.

Frost, Rev. Barzillai, **3**, 171.

Frost, Charles C. (?), of Brattleboro, Vt., **7**, 103, **9**, 62, 64, 66, 67, 69, 70.

Frostweed. *See* Cistus.

Fruit, origin and meaning of the word, **14**, 273.

Fruits, forms of, in the snow, **1**, 183; as typical as flowers, **4**, 306, 307; fragrance of, 309; the season of small, **6**, 363, 364; eaten in the open air, **7**, 520, 526; elements composing, **10**, 49, 50; bloom on, 162; disappearance of wild, **11**, 79; status of different varieties in autumn, **12**, 380–383; native and tropical, **14**, 261, 262; native, 274; commerce and, 277, 278.

Fry, William Henry, **7**, 76.

Fuegians. *See* Tierra del Fuego.

Fuel, prices of, **2**, 201; gathering and buying compared, **5**, 444–446; a boat-load of, **7**, 459, 460; collecting, 462, 502, **8**, 12, **10**, 116; enjoyment gained from, 18, 29, 30.

Fugitive Slave Law, **2**, 176, 177, **6**, 362, 363.

Fuller, Margaret, **3**, 114; a search for the remains of, **2**, 43 note; and the *Sortes Virgilianae*, **3**, 134.

Fuller, Thomas, **1**, 238.

Fumitory, common, **4**, 97.

Funerals, customs of, **4**, 277.

Fungi, **4**, 352, 386, **8**, 306, 332, **14**, 173; their place in botany, **5**, 21; dissolving, 374, 375; decaying, smell of, 415; shelf-shaped, 503; scent of decaying, **7**, 30, **9**, 16; a melting fungus, **8**, 376; tints of, **9**, 50; an offensive fungus, 115–117; as hygrometers, 282; on trees, 334; a remarkable fungus, **10**, 6; like asbestos, 205; on aspens, 267; their interest as living things, **11**, 204; in dry weather, **12**, 294; a fungus in a wine-cellar, 377, 378; on goldenrod, **14**, 93. *See also* Puffballs *and* Toadstools.

Fungus, birch, **8**, 9, **10**, 248, **12**, 456; used by shoemakers, **4**, 172; growth of, **10**, 259, 260.

Fungus, election-cake, **5**, 343, **9**, 128.

Fungus, geiropodium, **6**, 150, **14**, 95.

Fungus, spunk, **6**, 218, **9**, 117.

Fungus, star. *See* Puffball, star-fingered.

Fungus, winkle (*Auricularia*), **6**, 136, 196, 197, 199, **9**, 341.

Fur trade, **12**, 121–124.

Furness, Mr., of Philadelphia, **7**, 74.

Furniture, old, **10**, 59.

Future, past and, **2**, 229, **13**, 17, 18.

Galapagos Archipelago, **2**, 262.

Galium Aparine, **9**, 388.

Galium circœzans, **10**, 12, 13.

Galium trifidum, **8**, 408.

Galium triflorum, **4**, 196, **8**, 404.

Gall, Castile-soap, **4**, 342, **6**, 477, 488, **7**, 10, **9**, 60, **14**, 63.

Gall, pincushion, **5**, 168, **6**, 279, 304, 305, 321; beautiful scarlet sins, **5**, 210.

Gall-flies, **14**, 163; eggs of, **6**, 483.

Galls, **3**, 432, **5**, 249, **7**, 33, 34, **8**, 116, **9**, 15, **13**, 359; on willows, **5**, 52; on goldenrod, 349, **8**, 450; on hickory leaves, **5**, 350; on shrub oak stems, 376; dome-shaped, **7**, 14. *See also* Oak-apples *and* Oak-balls.

Gambrel, origin of name, **7**, 479, 480.

Games, boys', **10**, 155.

Garden, a large and attractive, **2**, 38.

Gardener, the, **1**, 473.

Gardiner, Edmund, **7**, 92.

Gardiner, Capt. Edward W., **7**, 91–96.

Gardner, Rev. John, **14**, 274, 275.

Garfield, of Concord, **7**, 353, **11**, 302, **12**, 46; talks with, **7**, 25, 26, **10**, 195; house of, 349; his trapping, **12**, 43.

Garfield, Daniel, **7**, 283, **12**, 212.

Garfield, Edward, a talk with, **8**, 129, 170–173, 175.

Garfield, Isaac, a talk with, **8**, 169–173, 175.

Garfield, John, **2**, 63.

Garfields, one of the, talk with, **8**, 304.

Garlick, Theodatus, **10**, 379.

Garnets, **10**, 465.

Garrison, of Concord, **6**, 128.

Garrison, William Lloyd, **3**, 38, 225, **5**, 365.

Gay Head lighthouse, **8**, 393.

Gaylussacia, the genus, **14**, 297.

Gaylussacia dumosa var. *hirtella*. *See* Huckleberry, hairy.

Geiropodium, **6**, 150, **14**, 95.

Genealogist, an old, **7**, 95, 96.

Genealogy, Alcott's study of, **4**, 292–294.

Generation, spontaneous, **14**, 333.

Generosity, essential, **1**, 241.

Genii, **1**, 57.

Genista tinctoria, *or* broom, **9**, 6, **10**, 510, **11**, 76, **12**, 18, **14**, 91.

Genius, solitariness of, **1**, 93; various phenomena of, 124; *versus* learning, 147, 148; work of, 275; peculiarity of a work of, **3**, 236; the abundance of life or health, **4**, 218; born with a great head, 349; a common privilege, 422; above nature, **5**, 170; suggestions of one's, **9**, 36, 37; evanescent boundaries of, 265; likened to a paint-brush, **11**, 89; hermaphroditic, 204; wildness of, 450, 451.

Geniuses, maimed, **2**, 334, 335; a talk with Charles Dunbar on, **4**, 440; the country genius, **11**, 269, 270.

Gentian, closed (*Andrewsii*), **11**, 183.

Gentian, fringed, **7**, 45, **9**, 83, 85, 143, **11**, 158, 204; charm of, **4**, 390, 391; at night, 391; short career of, **5**, 500, 501; beauty of, **11**, 189.

Gentian, soapwort, **4**, 356, **5**, 416.

Gentleman, the, **2**, 329; tracks of, **7**, 196.

Gentlemen, **12**, 31.

Geology, **2**, 405.

George, the carpenter, **10**, 417.

Geranium, wild, **4**, 102, 115, 266; habitat of, 76; opening buds of, **5**, 192.

Geranium Robertianum, **10**, 453.

Gerard, John, **14**, 92, 119; his Herbal, **13**, 29, 30.

Gérard, Jules, the lion-killer, **8**, 403, 404, 421.

Gerardia, bushy, **4**, 329.

Gerardia flava, **5**, 361.

Gerardia pedicularia, **9**, 16.

Gerardia quercifolia, **5**, 361.

Gerardia tenuifolia, **10**, 17.

Gesner, Conrad, **3**, 118; quoted, **13**, 149–153; his point of view toward animals, 167, 168.

Geum radiatum, **11**, 23.

Ghost-horse, **4**, 316, 317, **11**, 184, **12**, 73.

Giant, a, **3**, 202, 203, 205, 206, **10**, 131, 132.

Gibbs, John, **7**, 97.

Giddings, Joshua R., **12**, 439.

Gifford's Union House, **7**, 432.

Gilpin, William, on copses, **3**, 366; on mist, and on the rising and setting sun, 369; his "Forest Scenery," 370, 373; on the hart-royal, 414, 415; on the flight of water-fowl, 416; on docking horses' tails, 419; on the "lawing" of dogs, 419; on the flight of birds, 420; on the black-cock, 427; on near distances, 444; style of, **4**, 283, 284; on tragedy, 335; on Loch Fyne, 338; on mountain distances, 339, 340; on woods in the Isle of Wight, 394; on drawing, **6**, 53; on the picturesque, 55–59; on the relations of beauty and morality, 58, 59; his æsthetics criticised, 103; on lichens, **11**, 297.

Gilson, the Littleton miller, **9**, 360, 361.

Gin, how flavored, **14**, 278.

Ginkgo, leaf of, **7**, 64.

Ginseng, **2**, 221, 232; sale of, **9**, 78.

Girard, Charles, **11**, 348.

Girard College, **7**, 74.

Giraud, J. P., quoted, **13**, 420, 421.

Girls, two bright Irish-American, **7**, 467, 468; a nature-loving girl, **9**, 335, 336.

Glade, meaning of the word, **10**, 53.

Gladness, righteousness of, **4**, 446.

Glass, beauty of, **4**, 186, 187; achromatic, **6**, 167.

Glass (telescope), use of, on mountains, **4**, 392. *See also* Telescopes.

Glaze. *See* Ice.

Gleason, Mr., **2**, 167.

Glen House, White Mountains, **11**, 14.

Gloucester, **11**, 187, 188.

Glow-worm, added to fireflies. **4**, 145, 259, 260, **10**, 3–5, 33, 34, 248, **11**, 338.

Glyceria fluitans, **11**, 289.

Gnaphalium. *See* Everlasting.

Gnats, **7**, 336, 340, **8**, 322; in their hibernaculum, **5**, 18; dancing swarms of, **9**, 123, 124, **10**, 307, **11**, 169, 299, **12**, 106, 206, **13**, 206; in a cobweb, **9**, 339; hum of, **11**, 229, **12**, 148; covering the ground in masses, **12**, 183.

Goat, hardness of head of, **8**, 25.

God, trust in, **1**, 180; in nature, 185, **2**, 472; the seals of His power, **1**, 188; the voice of, 227; love for, and love for man, 228; is mystery, 231; calmness of, 315; generous of happiness, 328; Hindoo and Hebrew ideas of, **2**, 3, 4; false conception of, **3**, 119; spelled with a little *g*, 179; liberties with the name of, 256; the universal appeal to, 335; design of, in universe, 368; abettor of Cadmus, **6**, 133; in man, **9**, 250; an artist, **10**, 159; maker of the dewdrop and snowflake, 239, 240; not glorified, 363, 364; patronized, **11**, 324; worship of, **12**, 23; as a stranger, 28; man's manner of glorifying, 170, 171.

Gods, the, favors of, **1**, 365; communications from, **8**, 269.

Goffstown (N. H.), **14**, 39.

Gold, the true value of, **3**, 291; the false and the true, **7**, 491, 492, 496; the value attached to, **14**, 117–119.

Gold-diggers, **3**, 329, 330, **7**, 491; the finder of the great Australian nugget, 500, 501.

Gold-diggings, the Australian, **7**, 491.

Golden-eye, *or* whistler, **6**, 183, **7**, 314–316, **12**, 71.

Goldenrod, **2**, 103, 104, **5**, 340, **7**, 48; preaches of the lapse of time, **4**, 225; list of, in order of blooming, **5**, 396, 397; fruit of the sun, 403, 404; unidentified species of, 420, 422; radical leaves of, in May, **6**, 258; status of various species, Sept. 24th, **9**, 89; status of various species, Oct. 8th, 106; tenderness of, **12**, 209; heads of, in winter, 442; of Mt. Monadnock, **14**, 31.